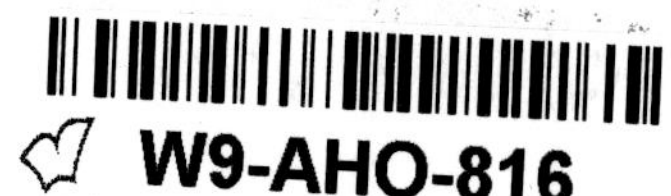

Religious Congregations & Membership in the United States 2000

An Enumeration by Region, State and County
Based on Data Reported for 149 Religious Bodies

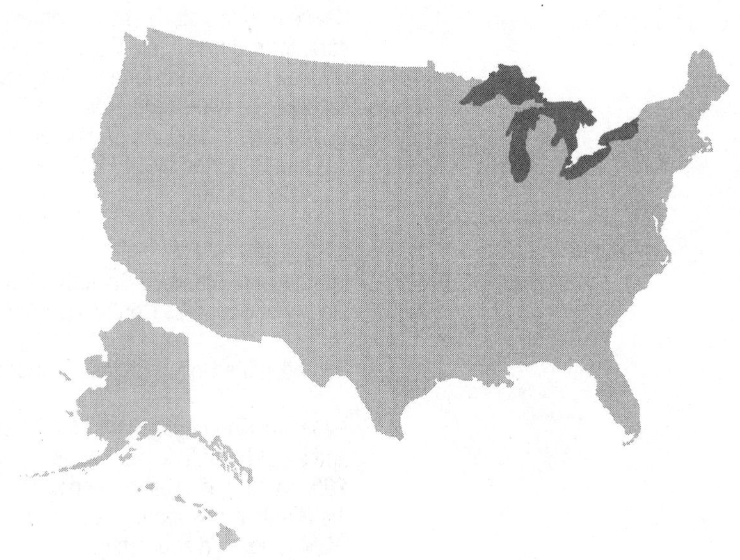

DALE E. JONES ▪ SHERRI DOTY ▪ CLIFFORD GRAMMICH
JAMES E. HORSCH ▪ RICHARD HOUSEAL ▪ MAC LYNN ▪ JOHN P. MARCUM
KENNETH M. SANCHAGRIN ▪ RICHARD H. TAYLOR

Glenmary Research Center / Nashville, Tennessee

Acknowledgments

The authors gratefully acknowledge the generous grant from **LILLY ENDOWMENT, INC.**, of Indianapolis, Indiana.

Additionally, the following denominations contributed varying amounts to enable this study to be made: American Baptist Churches in the USA; National Association of Free Will Baptists; Presbyterian Church (U.S.A.); United Church of Christ; and Wisconsin Evangelical Lutheran Synod. The generosity of these groups has made this study and its publication possible.

The Glenmary Home Missioners, based in Cincinnati, provided the funds for the collection and preparation of the Catholic data as well as for several smaller religious groups located largely in Appalachia.

Special thanks are due to the Church of the Nazarene International Headquarters in Kansas City, Missouri. Their Headquarters Operations Office and USA/Canada Missions/Evangelism Department made members of their staffs available for the project. These offices distributed the survey instruments, collected the data, and prepared the data for publication. This availability and interest allowed us to coordinate this task, and their continued support has been invaluable.

Credits

Published by Glenmary Research Center, 1312 Fifth Avenue North, Nashville, TN 37208. Phone: 615-256-1905. Fax: 615-251-1472. E-mail: grc@glenmary.org.

Citations to this study should contain all the following information in this or other form: Jones, Dale E., Sherri Doty, James E. Horsch, Richard Houseal, Mac Lynn, John P. Marcum, Kenneth M. Sanchagrin and Richard H. Taylor. 2002. Religious Congregations and Membership in the United States 2000: An Enumeration by Region, State and County Based on Data Reported by 149 Religious Bodies. Nashville, TN: Glenmary Research Center.

GRC A-130 / P-635
International Standard Book Number: 0-914422-26-x
Library of Congress Control Number: 2002111833

Printed in the United States of America.

Religious Congregations & Membership 2000 includes a fold-out wall map and a CD-ROM. The map, *Major Religious Families in the United States 2000* (A-131), is available separately and can be purchased for $17 from the Glenmary Research Center online at www.glenmary.org/grc. The CD-ROM is not sold separately.

License Agreement for CD-ROM Bound Into This Book

... ..E TO READ THIS LICENSE AGREEMENT BEFORE ACCESSING AND USING THE SOFTWARE AND DATA CONTAINED ON THE ACCOMPANYING CD-ROM.

You, the customer, and the Association of Statisticians of American Religious Bodies (hereinafter referred to as ASARB and/or Licensor), incur certain rights and obligations to each other when you open this package and use this product.

Single User Customer rights and obligations:
You enjoy a non-exclusive right to use the enclosed materials on no more than two computers, one at a central or main office and one at another office integral to the business of the customer. The software and data may be stored on a hard drive but not as part of an intranet or other multi-machine system.

You own the disk on which the program and data are recorded, but you acknowledge that you do not own the program or data recorded on the disk. One backup copy of the CD-ROM may be made for each legally obtained media copy you have received, provided that all ASARB and Third Party licensor information including copyright notices are maintained, and the copy is retained by you in a secure location.

You agree not to alter, remove or obscure any proprietary legend, copyright or trademark notice contained in or on the software or data and you, further agree:

- To place the following copyright notice on all documents, reports, publications or other presentations of data taken off this CD-ROM:
- [Descriptive title of the data or information used] In *Religious Congregations and Membership in the United States 2000.* © 2002 ASARB. Available: [CD-ROM]. Nashville, TN: Glenmary Research Center.
- And to use a standard citation format containing all the information in this recommended format for academic or other references in journal articles, books, et cetera:

  Jones, Dale E., Sherri Doty, James E. Horsch, Richard Houseal, Ma Lynn, John P. Marcum, Kenneth M. Sanchagrin and Richard H. Taylor. 2002. *Religious Congregations and Membership in the United States 2000: An Enumeration by Region, State, and County Based on Data Reported by 149 Religious Bodies.* Nashville, TN: Glenmary Research Center.

You acknowledge that the program and data are sold "AS IS" and that neither ASARB nor the publisher, Glenmary Research Center, will provide any technical support for use of these materials.

You agree not to sell, sub-license, rent, loan or otherwise network the software and/or data and that you will use reasonable efforts to protect the software and data from any unauthorized use, reproduction, distribution or publication.

You agree not to revise, translate, convert, disassemble, make other derivative works, or otherwise reverse engineer the program(s) or data on the CD-ROM.

If you do not accept the terms of this license agreement, you may obtain a refund of twenty percent (20%) of your original purchase price of the complete package if you return the unopened media package and proof of payment within seven (7) days to Glenmary Research Center.

Server Licenses:
The Single User license does not give you, the customer, the right to install the software or data on this CD-ROM on a Server nor to network or otherwise install the program or data on a multi-machine system.

You may apply to the publisher, Glenmary Research Center, for a license to load the software and data on one Server. License options are for either **Named Users** (either named individual users or single terminals / workstations used by individual users), **Concurrent Users** (i.e. a specified number of workstations—not individual persons—licensed to access the software / data at one time on the Server at any one time which access prohibits additional access at that time), or **Unlimited Internal (i.e. Intranet) Users**. In each case there will be a license fee in addition to the original package price. The term of the license and fee will be based on the number, or projected number, of users / workstations and the size and type of organization (i.e. nonprofit or for-profit) granted the license.

Limited External (i.e. Internet) User licenses may be granted. External User licenses will not include the right to allow or permit downloading of the software or data for public or general use. For further information contact the publisher, Glenmary Research Center.

Limited Warranty

ASARB through its agent, the Glenmary Research Center, warrants to the original customer that the optical media on which the Product is distributed is free of defects in materials and workmanship under normal use and service. ASARB and Glenmary Research Center's entire liability and your exclusive remedy as to defective media shall be at ASARB's option, either replacement of the defective media at no charge to you, or return of twenty percent (20%) of your original purchase price of the complete package, provided you return, in a traceable manner, the defective media with proof of purchase and date to Glenmary Research Center. 1312 Fifth Avenue North, Nashville, TN 37208.

If failure of the media has resulted from accident, abuse or misapplication, neither ASARB nor the Glenmary Research Center shall have any responsibility to replace the media.

Except as specifically provided herein, ASARB and the Glenmary Research Center make no warranty or representation, either expressed or implied, with respect to the product, including its quality, performance, merchantability, or fitness for any particular purpose. By way of example and not limitation, ASARB and the Glenmary Research Center make no representations or warranties, express or implied, with respect to the accuracy, reliability, or completeness of the data. By the way of further example and not limitation, ASARB and the Glenmary Research Center make no representations or agreements to provide any technical support or assistance with respect to accessing, using or otherwise manipulating the data contained on the CD-ROM. The entire risk as to the use of the software and data is assumed by the customer. Because the software is inherently complex and may not be completely free of errors, you are advised to use human judgment and validate your work. In no event will ASARB or the Glenmary Research Center be liable for direct, indirect, special, incidental, or consequential damages arising out of the use or inability to use this product.

License Agreement, continued

This warranty and the remedies set forth herein are exclusive and in lieu of all others, oral or written, expressed or implied. Some states do not allow the exclusion or limitation of implied warranties or limitation of liability for incidental or consequent damage, so that the above limitations or exclusions may not apply to you.

This license is the entire agreement between you, the customer, and ASARB and it shall be interpreted under the laws of the State of Pennsylvania, United States of America.

Contents

General Information

	Page
Preface	**vii**
Introduction	**ix**
Scope of the Study – Participating Religious Bodies – Participation in 1990 and 2000 Compared – Inclusiveness of the Study – Problems – Data Presentation – Methodology	
Abbreviations	**xix**

Tables

Table 1	Religious Congregations by Group for the United States: 2000	**1**
Table 2	Religious Congregations by Region and Group: 2000	**6**
Table 3	Religious Congregations by State and Group: 2000	**14**
Table 4	Religious Congregations by County and Group: 2000	**43**
Table 5	Religious Congregations by Metropolitan Size and Group: 2000	**517**

Appendices

A. Religious Groups: Definitions, Procedures, and Comments	**521**
B. Eastern Christian Groups	**534**
C. Eastern Religious Groups	**534**
D. Independent Churches Methodology	**535**
E. Jewish Estimate Methodology	**535**
F. Muslim Estimate Methodology	**536**
G. Instruments for Gathering the Data	**537**

Maps

Groups with 1,000,000 or More Adherents, or with Congregations Present in 50% of Counties	**541**
American Baptist Churches in the USA – Assemblies of God – Catholic Church – Christian Church (Disciples of Christ) – Christian Churches and Churches of Christ – Church of God (Cleveland, Tennessee) – Church of Jesus Christ of Latter-day Saints – Church of the Nazarene – Churches of Christ – Episcopal Church – Evangelical Lutheran Church in America – Jewish Estimate – Lutheran Church—Missouri Synod – Muslim Estimate – Presbyterian Church (U.S.A.) – Seventh-day Adventist Church – Southern Baptist Convention – United Church of Christ – United Methodist Church	
Participating Eastern Christian Groups	**560**
Participating Eastern Religious Groups	**561**
Largest Participating Religious Group	**562**
Largest Participating Protestant Religious Group	**563**
Percent of the Population Claimed by All Participating Religious Groups	**564**

Fold-out Map

Major Religious Families by Counties of the United States: 2000

Preface

This report contains statistics for 149 religious bodies, providing information on the number of their congregations within each region, state, and county of the United States. Where available, also included are actual membership figures (as defined by the religious body), total adherents, and average attendance.

The Association of Statisticians of American Religious Bodies (ASARB) sponsored the study on which this report is based. The permanent members of the Religious Congregations Membership Study Operations Committee, the secretary-treasurer of ASARB, and the director of the Glenmary Research Center served as authors of this book. Dale Jones, Church of the Nazarene, served as chairman of the Operations Committee. Richard Houseal, Church of the Nazarene, served as liaison for Data Collection. John Marcum, Presbyterian Church (U.S.A.), served as secretary-treasurer of ASARB during the length of the study. Other members of the committee were Sherri Doty, Assemblies of God; Clifford Grammich, Glenmary Research Center; James E. Horsch, Mennonite Church USA; Mac Lynn, Churches of Christ; Kenneth M. Sanchagrin, Glenmary Research Center; and Richard H. Taylor, United Church of Christ.

A generous grant from Lilly Endowment, Inc., covered major costs for the study. Additional funds came from proceeds of the sale of books and data tapes from *Churches and Church Membership in the United States 1990*. Five individual denominations contributed additional sums to make the study possible: American Baptist Churches in the USA; National Association of Free Will Baptists; Presbyterian Church (U.S.A.); United Church of Christ; and Wisconsin Evangelical Lutheran Synod.

The authors wish to thank the members of the study's advisory committee: Nancy Ammerman, Ihsan Bagby, Martin Bradley, Roger Finke, H. Allan Gleason, Kirk Hadaway, Peter Halvorson, Leland Harder, Ted Jelen, William McKinney, Dan Olson, Bernard Quinn, Jim Schwartz, Mark Shibley, Tom W. Smith, and Roger Stump.

Special thanks are also due those who served as denominational contact persons for furnishing the data: David L. Alderfer, David S. Allen, Sylvia Allen, Archbishop Antony, Nicholas Apostola, Lynette Augsburger, Beth A. Babbitt, Ihsan Bagby, Russell P. Baker, C. Ronald Beard, Paul A. Boeker, Rev. Fr. Boris, Julie Caulpetzer, Karen Ceplecha, Clifford R. Christensen, Metropolitan Christopher, Jean Clements, F. Donald Collins, Merry Cooper, Joseph Cunningham, Bishop David, Brian Davidson, Don Doezema, Sherri Doty, Marilee Duckworth, Donald J. Duff, Larry Elkington, David H. Engelhard, Metropolitan Ephraim, Michael Evans, Jeannette Flynn, Barbara Fox, Bishop Gabriel, Pathoorkudilil Geevarghese, Vasken Ghougassian, Clifford Grammich, Daria Greening, Glenn M. Gross, Philip J. Gross, Grove Harris, James Hodges, Warren L. Hoffman, James E. Horsch, C. Nelson Hostetter, Clyde M. Hughes, Joe Iaquinta, Nancy Irving, M. Johnson, Richard Johnson, Metropolitan Joseph, J. Julien, Eugene Kaplan, George Kassis, Ilia Katre, Thomas Kazich, Ronald D. Kelly, Sheila Kelly, Charles H. Klutz, Dale Koehn, Robert Koudratick, David Krogh, James Kunselman, Archbishop Kyrill, Roger Lamb, A. Bruce Lindgren, Arthur Liolin, Mac Lynn, Margaret L. Mahlman, William A. Meyer, Brian Miller, David I. Miller, David L. Miller, Mary C. Miller, Frank P. Miloro, Ronald R. Minor, Deborah Morris, Mike Naylor, Holley Ning, David Oancea, Donald P. Olsen, Julian B. Robinson, Jared Roth, Neil Routh, Robert D. Rush, Monte Sahlin, Marilyn Schaer, William R. Schlatter, Jim Schwartz, Stephen Scott, J. Ralph Shotwell, Diana E. Smith, James Solheim, Tome Stamatov, Nikki Stephanopoulos, Robert H. Stockman, Jack Stone, Donna Sullivan, Thomas L. Swank, L. Roy Taylor, Richard H. Taylor, Cliff Tharp, Lisa Theurer, Joyce Tucek, Kris Valerius, John Vaughan, Robert Vaughn, Paugratios Vironis, C. Vogelaar, Bert Waggoner, Frank Walker, Albert Wardin, Ronald W. Waters, David G. Weaver, Gene Weeke, Larry Wilson, and Melvin Worthington.

Several people provided special assistance in gathering data for this report. Jim Schwartz and Jeffrey Scheckner provided data on Jewish synagogues and adherents. Alexei Krindatch provided invaluable assistance in collecting the data for Orthodox groups. As in 1990, Albert Wardin was instrumental in locating data for several Baptist groups. John Vaughan replicated his 1990 study of large independent churches. Richard H. Taylor assisted in the collection and compilation process for several groups. We are especially grateful to Ihsan Bagby for providing basic Islamic data; this is the first such study to include information on this significant religious body. Grove Harris at the Pluralism Project of Harvard University providing location information for several religious groups outside the Judeo-Christian tradition.

Thanks go to Roger Finke, Chris Bader, and the American Religion Data Archive (ARDA) for providing reports and maps on the Web and CD.

The Glenmary Home Missioners, through the Glenmary Research Center, provided the funds for the collection and preparation of the Catholic data as well as for several smaller religious groups located largely in Appalachia. Glenmary staff deserving special recognition includes Karen Hurley, Communications Director of the Glenmary Home Missioners, and her staff, Jean Bach and Kay Tweddell, who assumed major responsibility to secure production of and publicity for the study. Wilfred Steinbacher, Associate Director of the Glenmary Research Center, handled over a thousand inquires by telephone and e-mail concerning the publication.

Persons who worked on the data at Nazarene Headquarters include Laura Lance, Casey Lane, Robert Mitchell, Connie Riddle, Serena Murphy, Michael Thomasson, and Lori Wright.

Statistics included in this study are also available electronically. A CD-ROM is included with the book itself, and several Websites have been established for retrieving quick reports. The links to such known sites can be found at the publisher's home page, www.glenmary.org/grc.

It is hoped that this report, despite its limitations, will stimulate ecumenical awareness at the judicatory and county levels, aid in denominational planning, and contribute to the study of long-range religious trends in the United States of America.

Introduction

SCOPE OF THE STUDY

This publication presents data reported for the 149 religious bodies that participated in a study sponsored by the Association of Statisticians of American Religious Bodies. Participants included 139 Christian denominations, associations, or communions (including Latter-day Saints and Unitarian/Universalist groups); two specially defined groups of independent Christian churches; Jewish and Islamic totals; and counts of temples for six Eastern religions.

The sponsors invited all religious bodies that could be identified as having congregations in the United States to participate. In addition, efforts were made to identify and gather data from large independent congregations. The 149 groups that furnished data reported 268,254 congregations with 141,371,963 adherents.[1]

The present study is related to four previous studies.[2] The first reported 1952 statistics and was sponsored and published by the National Council of Churches of Christ in the U.S.A. in 1956. The second reported 1971 statistics and was sponsored by the Office of Research, Evaluation and Planning of the National Council of Churches of Christ in the U.S.A., the Department of Research and Statistics of the Lutheran Church—Missouri Synod, and the Glenmary Research Center. It was published in 1974 by the Glenmary Research Center. The third reported 1979 statistics and was sponsored by the Department of Records and Research of the African Methodist Episcopal Zion Church, the Research Services Department of the Sunday School Board of the Southern Baptist Convention, the Office of Research, Evaluation and Planning of the National Council of the Churches of Christ in the U.S.A., the Lutheran Council in the U.S.A., and the Glenmary Research Center. The fourth, also published by Glenmary, reported 1990 statistics; it was sponsored by the Association of Statisticians of American Religious Bodies (ASARB).

PARTICIPATING RELIGIOUS BODIES

The 17 religious bodies with adherents of a million or more account for ninety-one percent of the reported adherents. The 31 groupings with adherents of 100,000 to 999,999 account for an additional seven percent. The 87 other groupings reporting adherents account for two percent. There are 14 additional groupings that were able to report congregations by county but were unable to estimate adherents.

The following bodies are included in this 2000 study. The number of counties in which the bodies report congregations or adherents will provide a general idea of their geographic extension. (At the time of the study, there were 3,141 counties or county-equivalents in the United States.)

Groups with 1,000,000 or More Adherents	Counties with a Presence
American Baptist Churches in the USA	1,111
Assemblies of God	2,616
Catholic Church	2,987
Christian Church (Disciples of Christ)	1,290
Christian Churches and Churches of Christ	1,600
Church of Jesus Christ of Latter-day Saints, The	1,802
Churches of Christ	2,429
Episcopal Church	2,118
Evangelical Lutheran Church in America	1,756
Independent, Non-Charismatic Churches	458
Jewish Estimate	672
Lutheran Church—Missouri Synod	1,801
Muslim Estimate	424
Presbyterian Church (U.S.A.)	2,377
Southern Baptist Convention	2,670
United Church of Christ	1,229
United Methodist Church, The	3,003

Groups with 100,000 to 999,999 Adherents	Counties with a Presence
American Baptist Association, The	594
Baha'i	2,407
Baptist General Conference	346
Baptist Missionary Association of America	358
Christian and Missionary Alliance, The	709
Christian Reformed Church in North America	236
Church of God (Anderson, Indiana)	990
Church of God (Cleveland, Tennessee)	1,595
Church of the Brethren	432
Church of the Nazarene	1,858
Conservative Baptist Association of America	418
Evangelical Covenant Church, The	312
Evangelical Free Church of America, The	720
Friends (Quakers)	573

1: For purposes of this study, adherents were defined as "all members, including full members, their children and the estimated number of other regular participants who are not considered as communicant, confirmed or full members; for example, the 'baptized,' 'not confirmed,' 'those not eligible for communion,' and the like." See "Defining Membership," below.

2: Lauris B. Whitman and Glen W. Trimble. 1956-1958. *Churches and Church Membership in the United States: An Enumeration and Analysis by Counties, States, and Regions* (80 bulletins). New York, New York: National Council of the Church of Christ in the U.S.A.; Douglas Johnson, Paul R. Picard and Bernard Quinn. 1974. *Churches and Church Membership in the United States 1971: An Enumeration by Region, State, and County.* Washington, D.C.: Glenmary Research Center; Bernard Quinn, Herman Anderson, Martin Bradley, Paul Goetting and Peggy Shriver. 1982. *Churches and Church Membership in the United States 1980: An Enumeration by Region, State, and County Based on Data Reported by 111 Religious Bodies.* Atlanta, Georgia: Glenmary Research Center; Martin B. Bradley, Norman M. Green, Jr., Dale E. Jones, Mac Lynn and Lou McNeil. 1992. *Churches and Church Membership in the United States 1990: An Enumeration by Region, State and County Based on Data Reported for 133 Church Groupings.* Atlanta, Georgia: Glenmary Research Center.

General Association of Regular Baptist Churches 642
Greek Orthodox Archdiocese of America 336
Independent, Charismatic Churches 305
International Church of the Foursquare Gospel 726
International Pentecostal Holiness Church 627
Mennonite Church USA 400
National Association of Free Will Baptists 710
New Testament Association of Independent Baptist Churches and other Fundamental Baptists 314
Pentecostal Church of God 574
Presbyterian Church in America 631
Reformed Church in America 237
Salvation Army, The 818
Seventh-day Adventist Church 1,747
Unitarian Universalist Association of Congregations 593
Vineyard USA 339
Wesleyan Church, The 766
Wisconsin Evangelical Lutheran Synod 535

Groups with Less Than 100,000 Adherents — **Counties with a Presence**

Albanian Orthodox Diocese of America 2
Allegheny Wesleyan Methodist Connection 61
American Carpatho-Russian Orthodox Greek Catholic Church 52
Amish; Other Groups 56
Antiochian Orthodox Christian Archdiocese of North America, The 160
Apostolic Catholic Assyrian Church of the East, North American Dioceses 14
Apostolic Christian Church of America, Inc. 73
Apostolic Christian Churches (Nazarean) 38
Armenian Apostolic Church / Catholicossate of Cilicia 33
Armenian Apostolic Church / Catholicossate of Etchmiadzin 70
Associate Reformed Presbyterian Church, The General Synod of the 115
Association of Free Lutheran Congregations, The 146
Beachy Amish Mennonite Churches 78
Brethren Church, The (Ashland, Ohio) 73
Brethren In Christ Church 88
Bruderhof Communities, Inc. 4
Bulgarian Orthodox Diocese of the USA 9
Christian Union 59
Church of God General Conference 69
Church of God in Christ, Mennonite 82
Church of God of Prophecy 932
Churches of God, General Conference 125
Community of Christ 615
Congregational Christian Churches, Additional (not part of any national CCC body) 79
Conservative Congregational Christian Conference 169
Conservative Mennonite Conference 59
Cumberland Presbyterian Church 269
Duck River and Kindred Baptists Associations 25
Eastern Pennsylvania Mennonite Church 34
Enterprise Baptists Association 26
Evangelical Mennonite Church 23
Evangelical Presbyterian Church 121
Fellowship of Evangelical Bible Churches 15
Free Methodist Church of North America 480
Fundamental Methodist Church, Inc. 7
General Six Principle Baptists 1
Greek Orthodox Archdiocese of Vasiloupulis 30
Holy Orthodox Church in North America 26
Hutterian Brethren 60
Independent Free Will Baptists Associations 53
International Churches of Christ 99
International Council of Community Churches 118
International Pentecostal Church of Christ 49
Interstate & Foreign Landmark Missionary Baptists Association 30
Jasper Baptist and Pleasant Valley Baptist Associations 5
Landmark Missionary Baptists, Independent Associations and Unaffiliated Churches 31
Macedonian Orthodox Church: American Diocese 17
Malankara Archdiocese of the Syrian Orthodox Church in North America 18
Malankara Orthodox Syrian Church, American Diocese of the 35
Mennonite Brethren Churches, U.S. Conference of 82
Mennonite; Other Groups 237
Midwest Congregational Christian Fellowship 8
Missionary Church, The 136
Moravian Church in America—Alaska Province 3
Moravian Church in America—Northern Province 44
Moravian Church in America—Southern Province 19
National Association of Congregational Christian Churches 232
National Primitive Baptist Convention, USA 147
Netherlands Reformed Congregations 13
New Hope Baptist Association 6
North American Baptist Conference 167
"Old" Missionary Baptists Associations 85
Old Order Amish Church 238
Old Order Mennonite 51
Old Order River Brethren 3
Original Free Will Baptists 38
Orthodox Church in America: Albanian Orthodox Archdiocese 9
Orthodox Church in America: Bulgarian Diocese 15
Orthodox Church in America: Romanian Orthodox Episcopate of America 45
Orthodox Church in America: Territorial Dioceses 226
Orthodox Presbyterian Church, The 217
Primitive Baptists, Eastern District Association of 15
Primitive Methodist Church in the USA 35
Progressive Primitive Baptists 71

Protestant Reformed Churches in America 15
Reformed Church in the United States 35
Reformed Mennonite Church 9
Romanian Orthodox Archdiocese in America and Canada 12
Separate Baptists in Christ 35
Serbian Orthodox Church in the USA 61
Strict Baptists 3
Syrian Orthodox Church of Antioch 19
Two-Seed-in-the-Spirit Predestinarian Baptists 4
Ukrainian Orthodox Church of the USA 77
United Reformed Churches in North America 34
Universal Fellowship of Metropolitan Community Churches 179
Wayne Trail Missionary Baptist Association 9

Groups Not Reporting Total Adherents	Counties with a Presence
Buddhists	359
Calvary Chapel Fellowship Churches	380
Coptic Orthodox Church	39
Hindus	206
Jains	71
Patriarchal Parishes of the Russian Orthodox Church in the USA	29
Primitive Baptist Churches—Old Line	713
Reformed Baptist Churches	167
Russian Orthodox Church Outside of Russia	101
Serbian Orthodox Church in the USA (New Gracanica Metropolitanate)	32
Sikhs	118
Southwide Baptist Fellowship	327
Taoists	24
Zoroastrians	26

PARTICIPATION IN 1990 AND 2000 COMPARED

There are 95 bodies that participated in both studies, 54 bodies that participated in 2000 but not 1990, and 37 that participated in 1990 but not 2000.

95 Participants in Both Studies:

Albanian Orthodox Diocese of America
Allegheny Wesleyan Methodist Connection
American Baptist Churches in the USA
American Carpatho-Russian Orthodox Greek Catholic Church
Apostolic Catholic Assyrian Church of the East, North American Dioceses
Apostolic Christian Church of America, Inc.
Apostolic Christian Churches (Nazarean)
Armenian Apostolic Church / Catholicossate of Cilicia
Assemblies of God
Associate Reformed Presbyterian Church, The General Synod of the
Association of Free Lutheran Congregations, The
Baptist General Conference
Baptist Missionary Association of America
Beachy Amish Mennonite Churches
Brethren Church, The (Ashland, Ohio)
Brethren In Christ Church
Catholic Church
Christian and Missionary Alliance, The
Christian Church (Disciples of Christ)
Christian Churches and Churches of Christ
Christian Reformed Church in North America
Church of God (Anderson, Indiana)
Church of God (Cleveland, Tennessee)
Church of God General Conference
Church of God in Christ, Mennonite
Church of God of Prophecy
Church of Jesus Christ of Latter-day Saints, The
Church of the Brethren
Church of the Nazarene
Churches of Christ
Churches of God, General Conference
Congregational Christian Churches, Additional (not part of any national CCC body)
Conservative Baptist Association of America
Conservative Congregational Christian Conference
Cumberland Presbyterian Church
Duck River and Kindred Baptists Associations
Eastern Pennsylvania Mennonite Church
Enterprise Baptists Association
Episcopal Church
Evangelical Free Church of America, The
Evangelical Lutheran Church in America
Evangelical Mennonite Church
Evangelical Presbyterian Church
Fellowship of Evangelical Bible Churches
Free Methodist Church of North America
Friends (Quakers)
Fundamental Methodist Church, Inc.
General Six Principle Baptists
Greek Orthodox Archdiocese of America
Hutterian Brethren
Independent, Charismatic Churches
Independent, Non-Charismatic Churches
International Church of the Foursquare Gospel
International Pentecostal Church of Christ
International Pentecostal Holiness Church
Interstate & Foreign Landmark Missionary Baptists Association
Jasper Baptist and Pleasant Valley Baptist Associations
Jewish Estimate
Lutheran Church—Missouri Synod
Mennonite Brethren Churches, U.S. Conference of
Mennonite Church USA (a merger of 1990 participants Mennonite

Church and Mennonite Church, The General Conference)
Midwest Congregational Christian Fellowship
Missionary Church, The
Moravian Church in America—Alaska Province
Moravian Church in America—Northern Province
Moravian Church in America—Southern Province
National Association of Congregational Christian Churches
National Association of Free Will Baptists
Netherlands Reformed Congregations
New Hope Baptist Association
North American Baptist Conference
"Old" Missionary Baptists Associations
Old Order Amish Church
Old Order River Brethren
Orthodox Church in America: Albanian Orthodox Archdiocese
Orthodox Church in America: Romanian Orthodox Episcopate of America
Orthodox Church in America: Territorial Dioceses
Pentecostal Church of God
Presbyterian Church (U.S.A.)
Presbyterian Church in America
Primitive Methodist Church in the USA
Reformed Church in America
Reformed Church in the United States
Salvation Army, The
Seventh-day Adventist Church
Southern Baptist Convention
Syrian Orthodox Church of Antioch
Two-Seed-in-the-Spirit Predestinarian Baptists
Ukrainian Orthodox Church of the USA
Unitarian Universalist Association of Congregations
United Church of Christ
United Methodist Church, The
Wayne Trail Missionary Baptist Association
Wesleyan Church, The
Wisconsin Evangelical Lutheran Synod

The 95 bodies that took part in both studies reported 126,721,485 adherents in 1990 and 137,814,924 in 2000. This represents an increase of 8.8% for these combined groups.

54 New Participants in 2000:

American Baptist Association, The
Amish; Other Groups
Antiochian Orthodox Christian Archdiocese of North America, The
Armenian Apostolic Church / Catholicossate of Etchmiadzin
Baha'í
Bruderhof Communities, Inc.
Buddhists
Bulgarian Orthodox Diocese of the USA
Calvary Chapel Fellowship Churches
Christian Union
Community of Christ
Conservative Mennonite Conference
Coptic Orthodox Church
Evangelical Covenant Church, The
General Association of Regular Baptist Churches
Greek Orthodox Archdiocese of Vasiloupulis
Hindus
Holy Orthodox Church in North America
Independent Free Will Baptists Associations
International Churches of Christ
International Council of Community Churches
Jains
Landmark Missionary Baptists, Independent Associations and Unaffiliated Churches
Macedonian Orthodox Church: American Diocese
Malankara Archdiocese of the Syrian Orthodox Church in North America
Malankara Orthodox Syrian Church, American Diocese of the
Mennonite; Other Groups
Muslim Estimate
National Primitive Baptist Convention, USA
New Testament Association of Independent Baptist Churches and other Fundamental Baptists
Old Order Mennonite
Original Free Will Baptists
Orthodox Church in America: Bulgarian Diocese
Orthodox Presbyterian Church, The
Patriarchal Parishes of the Russian Orthodox Church in the USA
Primitive Baptist Churches--Old Line
Primitive Baptists, Eastern District Association of
Progressive Primitive Baptists
Protestant Reformed Churches in America
Reformed Baptist Churches
Reformed Mennonite Church
Romanian Orthodox Archdiocese in America and Canada
Russian Orthodox Church Outside of Russia
Separate Baptists in Christ
Serbian Orthodox Church in the USA
Serbian Orthodox Church in the USA (New Gracanica Metropolitanate)
Sikhs
Southwide Baptist Fellowship
Strict Baptists
Taoists
United Reformed Churches in North America
Universal Fellowship of Metropolitan Community Churches
Vineyard USA
Zoroastrians

The 54 newly participating groups had a combined adherent total of 3,557,039 in 2000.

37 Groups Participating in 1990 but not 2000:

Advent Christian Church
African Methodist Episcopal Zion Church
American Association of Lutheran Churches
Apostolic Lutheran Church of America
Barren River Missionary Baptists
Berean Fundamental Church
Bible Church of Christ, Inc.
Black Baptists Estimate
Byelorussion Council Of Orthodox Churches In North America
Central Baptist Association Ministries
Christ Catholic Church
Christian Brethren
Church of Christ, Scientist
Church of God (Seventh Day)
Church of God, Mountain Assembly, Inc.
Church of the Lutheran Brethren of America
Church of the Lutheran Confession
Church of the United Brethren in Christ
Estonian Evangelical Lutheran Church
Evangelical Congregational Church, The
Evangelical Lutheran Synod
Evangelical Methodist Church
Fire Baptized Holiness Church, (Wesleyan), The
Independent Fundamental Churches of America
Latvian Evangelical Lutheran Church in America
Old Regular Baptists
Open Bible Standard Churches, Inc.
Primitive Advent Christian Church
Primitive Baptists Associations
Reformed Episcopal Church
Regular Baptists
Schwenkfelder Church
Seventh Day Baptist General Conference, USA and Canada
The Protestant Conference (Lutheran)
Truevine Baptists Association
United Baptists
United Christian Church

The 37 bodies that participated in 1990 but not in 2000 reported a combined adherent figure of 10,343,024 in 1990. Two groups account for over 95% of these adherents: the Black Baptist Estimate and the African Methodist Episcopal Zion Church. (See below for comments on African American participation.)

INCLUSIVENESS OF THE STUDY

The study identified by county over 140 million adherents in 149 groups. It is not known what percent of total religious adherents in America this represents. The difficulty is in obtaining an agreed-upon basis for determining the total adherent figure for the United States.

National polls regularly report that at least 80% of American adults claim a religious preference. For instance, the City University of New York (CUNY) in its *American Religious Identification Survey 2001*[3] indicates that 81% of Americans identify themselves with a religious group. The figures in this book, however, reflect actual participation in religious congregations rather than self-identification. For instance, the CUNY study reports that 24.5% of adults claim to be Catholics, while the dioceses themselves claim only 22% of the population, a difference of nearly seven million people. Likewise, self-identified Lutherans (based on the CUNY study) outnumber those claimed by the known Lutheran groups, as reported in the *Yearbook of American and Canadian Churches 2000*[4], by nearly five million; more than a 50% difference.

Independent Congregations: There are independent and community churches, religious movements, and associations whose memberships are not reported to the *Yearbook* or other compilers. As a result, the total membership of these groups is unknown, and there is no way to determine what proportion of their membership has been included in this study.

Adherent figures for large (300 or more in attendance) independent churches were obtained directly from 1,705 such churches throughout the United States by John Vaughan of the Megachurch Research Center (a ministry of Church Growth Today). These churches and adherents were identified by county, and are included in the study under two headings: Independent, Charismatic Churches and Independent, Non-charismatic Churches (see Appendix D for methodology).

Jewish Estimate: Jim Schwartz and Jeffrey Scheckner provided city estimates of the Jewish population for this study, based upon their article published in the *American Jewish Year Book 2001*. Separately, Schwartz and Scheckner provided a count of synagogues by county throughout the United States. The adherent estimates were allocated to counties based on synagogue location and are included in the study. Together, the reports indicate 6,141,325 Jewish adherents in 3,727 synagogues. Due to the differing reporting procedures, some counties report adherents with no synagogues.

African American Bodies: Major efforts to enlist the participation of historically African American denominations were made. Generally, membership records are not kept nationally, at least not in a form conducive to participation in a study such as this. The omission of these bodies must be considered when studying religious adherence within areas of the country with significant African American population.

It should not be assumed that no African Americans are included in the reporting denominations. In 89 counties throughout the South, the reported adherents exceed the non-African American population, yet are reasonable ratios of the entire population. Many large cities in the South appear to have significant numbers of African Americans reported in this book: Atlanta, Baltimore, Washington, New Orleans, Richmond, and Jackson,

3: Barry A. Kosmin, Egon Mayer, and Ariela Keysar. 2001. *American Religious Identification Survey 2001*. New York, New York: The Graduate Center, The City University of New York.

4: Eileen W. Lindner. 2000. *Yearbook of American and Canadian Churches 2000*. Nashville, Tennessee: Abingdon Press.

Mississippi; as well as smaller cities such as Lafayette, Louisiana, and Selma, Alabama. Even so, the authors advise caution in assuming that the African American community is well-represented in this study.

Eastern Christian Bodies: Twenty-one Eastern Christian bodies, primarily but not exclusively Orthodox, participated in the study, accounting for combined adherents of 996,490. Four other groups were able to provide lists of churches that were identified by county only. Alexei Krindatch served as coordinator of the study's work with these Eastern Christian bodies.

Other Groups: Strong efforts were made to include figures from other faith traditions in this study. The major hindrance is a lack of Western European-style record keeping by these bodies. Dale Jones, Rich Houseal, and Clifford Grammich estimated adherent figures for Islamic bodies, based largely upon the work of Ihsan Bagby. While Buddhist groups do not have a theology of membership, a list of temples was obtained and the number in each county has been included. Similar location data was available for Hindu, Jain, Sikh, Tao, and Zoroastrian groups. The Baha'i group was able to provide information on the location of adherents as well as congregations.

Non-participating Groups: There are 14 non-participating religious bodies that reported more than 100,000 members to the *Yearbook of American and Canadian Churches: 2000.* These groups reported a combined membership of 31,040,360 in the *Yearbook.*

The following groups were specifically invited to participate, but for various reasons were unable to do so (groups reporting over 100,000 in the Yearbook are listed in italics): Advent Christian Church; *African Methodist Episcopal Church*; *African Methodist Episcopal Zion Church*; Alliance of Reformed Churches; Amana Church Society; American Association of Lutheran Churches; American Catholic Church; American Evangelical Christian Churches; American Presbyterian Church; American Reformed Church; American Rescue Workers; Anglican Orthodox Church; Apostolic Episcopal Church; Apostolic Faith Mission Church of God; Apostolic Faith Mission of Portland, Oregon; Apostolic Lutheran Church of America; Apostolic Orthodox Catholic Church; Apostolic Overcoming Holy Church of God, Inc.; Assemblies of God International Fellowship; Association of Covenant Charismatic Churches; Association of Unity Churches; Baptist Bible Fellowship; Berean Fundamental Church; Bible Church of Christ, Inc.; Bible Fellowship Church; Bible Holiness Church; Bible Presbyterian Church; Bible Presbyterian Church (Collingswood Synod); Bible Way Church of Our Lord Jesus Christ World Wide, Inc.; Central Baptist Association Ministries; Christ Catholic Church; Christ Community Church; Christadelphians; Christian Brethren; Christian Church of North America, General Council; Christian Congregation, Inc.; *Christian Methodist Episcopal Church*; Christian Presbyterian Church (Korean); Church of Christ; Church of Christ, Scientist; Church of God (Seventh Day); Church of God by Faith, Inc.; *Church of God In Christ*; *Church of God in Christ, International*; Church of God, Mountain Assembly, Inc.; Church of Illumination; Church of Jesus Christ (Bickertonites); Church of Our Lord Jesus Christ of the Apostolic Faith, Inc.; Church of the Living God; Church of the Lutheran Brethren of America; Church of the Lutheran Confession; Church of the United Brethren in Christ; Churches of Christ in Christian Union; Congregational Holiness Church; Conservative Lutheran Association; Convention of Original Free Will Baptists; Council of the Church of Christ; Covenanted Reformed Presbyterian Church (Stellite); Cumberland Presbyterian Church in America; Elim Fellowship; Estonian Evangelical Lutheran Church; Evangelical Association of Congregational Christian and Reformed Churches; Evangelical Church Alliance; Evangelical Church; Evangelical Congregational Church; Evangelical Friends Internationa–North America Region; Evangelical Lutheran Synod; Evangelical Methodist Church; Federation of Reformed Churches; Fellowship of Fundamental Bible Churches; Free Christian Zion Church of Christ; Free Church of Scotland; Free Presbyterian Church of North America; Free Reformed Churches of North America; Full Gospel Assemblies International; Full Gospel Fellowship of Churches and Ministers International; General Assembly of the Korean Presbyterian Church in America; General Association of General Baptists; General Church of the New Jerusalem; Grace Brethren Churches, Fellowship of; Grace Gospel Fellowship; House of God, Which is the Church of the Living God, the Pillar and Ground of the Truth, Inc.; Hungarian Reformed Church in America; Independent Fundamental Churches of America; *Jehovah's Witnesses*; Korean American Presbyterian Church; Latvian Evangelical Lutheran Church in America; Liberal Catholic Church-Province of the United States of America; Malankara Mar Thoma Church; Metropolitan Church Association, Inc.; Nation of Islam; *National Baptist Convention of America, Inc.*; *National Baptist Convention, USA, Inc.*; *National Missionary Baptist Convention of America*; National Organization of the New Apostolic Church of North America; National Primitive Baptist Convention, Inc.; National Spiritualist Association of Churches; North American Old Roman Catholic Church; Old German Baptist Brethren; Open Bible Standard Churches, Inc.; Orthodox Christian Reformed Churches in North America; *Pentecostal Assemblies of the World, Inc.*; Pentecostal Fire-Baptized Holiness Church; Pentecostal Free Will Baptist Church, Inc.; Pillar of Fire; Polish National Catholic Church of America; Presbyterian Reformed Church; Primitive Advent Christian Church; Primitive Baptists; *Progressive National Baptist Convention, Inc.*; Puritan Evangelical Church of America; Reformed Congregational Fellowship; Reformed Episcopal Church; Reformed Methodist Union Episcopal Church; Reformed Presbyterian Church; Reformed Presbyterian Church (Hanover Presbytery); Reformed Presbyterian Church General Assembly; Reformed Presbyterian Church in America; Reformed Presbyterian Church of North America; Reformed Zion Union Apostolic Church; Schwenkfelder Church; Seventh Day Baptist General Conference, USA and Canada; Southern Methodist Church; Sovereign Grace Baptist Churches; Sovereign Grace Believers; Swedenborgian Church; Triumph the Church and Kingdom of God in Christ Inc.; United American Free Will Baptist Denomination, Inc.; United Christian Church; United Holy Church of America, Inc.; United House of Prayer; *United Pentecostal Church International*; United Pentecostal Churches of Christ; United Zion Church; Unity of the Brethren; Upper Cumberland Presbyterian Church.

PROBLEMS

Defining Membership: The most critical methodological problem was that of defining membership. Since there is no generally acceptable statistical definition of membership, it was felt that the designation of members rested finally with the religious bodies themselves.

In an effort to achieve comparability of data, however, two major categories were established:

MEMBERS: all individuals with full membership status; and

TOTAL ADHERENTS: all members, including full members, their children and the estimated number of other participants who are not considered members; for example, the "baptized," "those not confirmed," "those not eligible for communion," "those regularly attending services," and the like.

Of the 149 reporting groups, 49 reported members and adherents; 19 reported adherents only; 67 reported members only; and 14 reported only church locations. For purposes of this report, the staff estimated the total adherents for the 67 groups that reported members only, usually according to a formula discussed below.

Estimating Total Adherents: The total adherent figure is used to compute the percent of membership to total population. For those 67 groups that reported members but neither reported adherents nor suggested a different method for computing them, total adherents were estimated according to the following formula: The total county population was divided by the total county population less children 13 years and under, and the resulting figure was multiplied by the number of members. The 2000 U.S. Census SF1 files were used to determine for each county the total population and the population 13 years and under. An asterisk after a figure in the tables indicates that total adherents were estimated through use of this procedure, rather than reported directly by the groups.

The 67 groups whose total adherents were estimated in this way were asked to comment on the procedure. The comments submitted are reproduced in Appendix A.

Locating Members by County: Membership statistics are generally reported for the county in which the congregation itself is located, rather than for the county in which the member resides. It is assumed the county of residence will correspond to the county where the church is located in the large majority of cases, although modern mobility patterns suggest caution in accepting this assumption in every case. Especially in the case of large urban areas, combining counties into standard metropolitan areas might be wiser when citing membership proportions. The accompanying CD and Websites accessible through www.glenmary.org/grc can aid in such compilations.

Membership or Adherents without Congregations: In nearly all cases, members and adherents were reported for congregations. Exceptions include Southern Baptist, Baha'i, Catholic, and Jewish groups. Because the Southern Baptist Convention counts as members some individuals whose congregations have not met the criteria for official recognition as SBC congregations, there are 65 counties with Southern Baptist membership or adherent (or, in one case, attendance) figures that have no reported SBC congregation. For the Baha'i, Catholic, and Jewish groups, there are independent records for the location of at least some adherents. Nearly 1,954 counties have such adherents reported, 1,906 of them by the Baha'i.

Average Attendance: Each group that provided average attendance figures was asked to provide a definition of the average attendance figure they were reporting. Those explanations are reproduced in Appendix A.

County Listings: *Religious Congregations and Membership in the United States 2000* uses the same 3,141 counties or county-equivalents as the 2000 U.S. Census. Since *Churches and Church Membership in the United States 1990* was published, several changes to county boundaries and names have taken place: Miami-Dade County replaced Dade County, Florida; Yellowstone Park County, Montana, was apportioned into neighboring counties and eliminated; South Boston independent city was merged into Halifax county, Virginia; the incorporated section of Takoma Park in Prince Georges County was transferred to Montgomery County, Maryland; and Alaska saw the creation of two new county equivalents (Denali Borough and Yakutat Borough) and changed boundaries for four others (Juneau Borough, Skagway-Hoonah-Angoon Census Area, Southeast Fairbanks Census Area, and Yukon-Koyukuk Census Area). These changes have been incorporated into the 2000 study. Comparisons of data with previous studies should take into account these boundary changes.

In Virginia, there are independent cities that are legally separate from the counties of that state. In prior publications, the congregational data for these cities was included with that of neighboring counties. However, now that electronic census data is readily available that reports these cities separately, many denominations prefer to keep the congregational data separate as well. Therefore, each such city is now treated as a separate county equivalent. The same is true for the independent cities in Maryland (Baltimore), Missouri (St. Louis), and Nevada (Carson City).

Louisiana's parishes are treated as county equivalents. The District of Columbia is treated as a county equivalent. The census areas and boroughs of Alaska are treated as county equivalents as well. As noted above, several Alaska areas have undergone boundary changes.

Reporting Date: The study was designed to gather statistics comparable to the April 1, 2000, U.S. Census. Accordingly, the request to the religious groups asked for data for their reporting year ending within calendar year 2000.

Accuracy of Reporting Procedures: Most large Protestant denominations maintain national offices that receive statistical reports from their individual congregations; these reports were used to provide county membership figures for this study. On the other hand, many smaller groups, as well as those in which local congregations have a great deal of autonomy, only request and do not require such reports. This means that data for several groups is not as complete and current as might be desired.

During the course of the study, groups furnishing data were asked to comment on the accuracy of their own reporting procedures and to furnish copies of the forms they used to collect the data. Those forms that were received are filed in the data collection office at the denominational headquarters of the Church of the Nazarene. Comments are reproduced in Appendix A.

Dual Affiliation: In the 2000 study, some attempt was made to assess the extent of the practice whereby a local congregation affiliates with more than one denomination. The groups were asked: "Do any local congregations of your denomination maintain affiliation with another denomination as well?" The comments are reported in Appendix A.

Membership Greater Than Population: There are 39 counties (or equivalents) in this study reporting more adherents than total population: KENTUCKY: Caldwell, Washington; MINNESOTA: Big Stone, Lac qui Parle; MONTANA: Chouteau, Daniels; NEBRASKA: Greeley; NORTH DAKOTA: Benson, Bowman, Burke, Hettinger, McIntosh, Rolette, Steele; OKLAHOMA: Dewey, Grant, Harmon; SOUTH DAKOTA: Douglas, Hutchinson, Potter; TENNESSEE: Potter; TEXAS: Baylor, Briscoe, Cottle, Dimmit, Fisher, Hardeman, Haskell, Jim Hogg, Knox, La Salle, Sherman, Terrell, Throckmorton, Yoakum; VIRGINIA: Campbell county, Fairfax city, Falls Church city, Fredericksburg city.

Reasons for the discrepancy will no doubt differ from county to county, but the most reasonable explanations would include U.S. Census undercount, church membership overcount, and county of residence differing from county of membership. This is especially likely in Virginia, where many cities have been separated from their adjoining counties.

DATA PRESENTATION

This report consists of five tables, twenty-four color maps included in the book, a fold-out map insert, and a CD-ROM with the database in several user-friendly formats.

In all the tables, group names are abbreviated. A list of abbreviations will be found on the pages immediately preceding Table 1.

Table 1: The first table, "Religious Congregations by Group for the United States: 2000," presents for each group the number of congregations; the number of communicant, confirmed, or full members; the average attendance (if any) reported by the group; and the total adherents the group has throughout the entire United States. It also indicates what percent of the U.S. population and what percent of the total reported adherents each group comprises. Population figures used for these calculations are from the 2000 U.S. Census.

Table 2: The second table, "Religious Congregations by Region and Group: 2000," presents group totals for each of the nine census regions of the United States: the total of congregations; communicant, confirmed, or full members; average attendance; and adherents. Also shown are the percent of regional population and of total regional adherents that each group has. Regions are arranged geographically, as in U.S. Census publications.

A map showing the nine census regions will be found on the page immediately preceding Table 2.

Table 3: The third table, "Religious Congregations by State and Group: 2000," presents group totals for each state (and the District of Columbia): the total of congregations; communicant, confirmed, or full members; average attendance; and adherents. Also shown are the percent of state population and of total state adherents that each group has. States are arranged alphabetically within the table.

Table 4: The fourth table, "Religious Congregations by County and Group: 2000," provides the detailed data on which the totals in Tables 1-3 and 5 are based.

For each county or county equivalent of the United States, the numbers of congregations, members, and attendees for each participating religious group are shown. Both communicant, confirmed, or full members and the total adherents are given, as well as the percent of the county population and of total county adherents that each group has.

Table 5: The fifth table, "Religious Congregations by Metropolitan Size and Group: 2000," presents for each group the proportion of its adherents in different-sized metropolitan areas. Also shown is the proportion of congregations within each group located outside metropolitan areas. For comparison, the proportion of the total U.S. population in each metropolitan category is shown on the first line of the table; and the proportion of total adherents within each category is shown on the second line.

Sizes are based on the four standard categories of the U.S. Census Bureau, with a fifth category of "Non-metropolitan" included for comparison. The Metropolitan Statistical Area definitions are those of the Office of Management and the Budget as of April 1, 2000, with population figures from the 2000 census. All PMSA's were included in the largest size category, inasmuch as each is part of a consolidated area of at least one million people. For New England, the New England County Metropolitan Areas were used, with the New Haven-Bridgeport-Stamford-Waterbury-Danbury CT NECMA included in the New York-Northern New Jersey-Long Island, NY-NJ-CT-PA CMSA.

Maps Included in the Book: The color map section begins with the 19 groups reporting at least one million adherents *or* with congregations present in at least 50% of U.S. counties. These maps show the proportion of the population of each county that is claimed by the group. The same scale is used on each map to make comparisons easier. Similarly, map 20 shows the proportion of each counties' population claimed by the Eastern Christian groups.

Map 21 shows the ratio of Eastern religion temples to county population. Map 22 illustrates the largest single religious group in each county. Similarly, map 23 shows the largest Protestant denomination in each county. Finally, map 24 shows the proportion of the population claimed by all participating religious groups.

Fold-out Map: Accompanying this report is a color map, 28" x 41", entitled "Major Religious Families by Counties of the United States: 2000." By means of a color code, this map indicates, for each county of the United States, the participating group that predominates. Based primarily upon family groupings found in the *Yearbook*, the various Adventist, Baptist, Brethren, Christian, Churches of God, Congregational, Eastern Christians,

Latter-day Saints, Lutheran, Mennonite, Methodist, Moravian, Pentecostal, Presbyterian, and Reformed church bodies were grouped into families[5]. Other groups, such as the Catholics and Episcopalians, were not grouped into families but were treated as separate units.

The number of counties in which the above-mentioned families predominate is as follows:

Baptist	1,287
Catholic	1,118
Lutheran	243
Methodist	190
Latter-day Saints	75
Christian	56
Reformed	8
Mennonite	6
United Church of Christ	6
Pentecostal	5
Episcopal	4
Eastern Christians	4
Presbyterian	4
Adventist	1
Brethren	1
Christian and Missionary Alliance	1
Friends	1
Muslim	1
Salvation Army	1

A solid color on the map indicates that a group has 50 percent or more of the total adherents in that county, as reported in the present study. When no group has 50 percent, striped shading indicates the largest group with 25 to 49 percent of adherents in a county. The 129 counties where no group has 25 percent are left blank. The percentages on which the map is based can be found in Table 4, column 8 of this report.

METHODOLOGY

The actual data collection was carried out in the offices of the Church of the Nazarene, Kansas City, Missouri. Richard Houseal, Media Center Coordinator for USA/Canada Mission/Evangelism, oversaw the data collection.

In 1999, an invitation to participate in the study was sent to every U.S. religious body listed in the *Yearbook of American and Canadian Churches.* Additional contacts were suggested by the Advisory Committee and by members of the Operations Committee. The initial written invitation was followed by two additional general mailings, and where needed by special letters, personal contacts, and phone calls. As a result of these efforts, which extended over a two-year period, 285 groups were invited, 149 actually participated, 22 expressed the intention to participate but were unable to do so, 12 declined to participate, and 102 did not respond.

Groups agreeing to participate were asked to appoint a contact person. Two forms were then sent to the contact person: instructions for reporting data; and a transmittal sheet to be signed and sent with the data collected. A state-county form for listing the statistics themselves was made available by request. The contact persons were given the option of submitting the data via their own computer printout, sending the data electronically, or using the state-county listing provided by the Church of the Nazarene Research Center staff.

The process put the major burden of work on the offices of the various religious groups, since they were asked to compile data by county for all their congregations. In some cases, however, groups were able to furnish information only in the form of yearbooks or other sources. Transferring yearbook information into county data then became the responsibility of the Church of the Nazarene Research Center staff. In a few cases the groups instructed the staff to estimate congregational membership according to some formula, and approved the result. In all instances, the contact person was asked to review the statistics.

5: The family groups are as follows: ADVENTIST: Church of God General Conference; Seventh-day Adventist Church; BAPTIST: American Baptist Association; American Baptist Churches in the USA; Baptist General Conference; Baptist Missionary Association of America; Conservative Baptist Association of America; Duck River and Kindred Baptists Associations; Enterprise Baptists Association; General Association of Regular Baptist Churches; General Six Principle Baptists; Independent Free Will Baptists Associations; Interstate & Foreign Landmark Missionary Baptists Association; Jasper Baptist and Pleasant Valley Baptist Associations; Landmark Missionary Baptists, Independent Associations and Unaffiliated Churches; National Association of Free Will Baptists; National Primitive Baptist Convention, USA; New Hope Baptist Association; New Testament Association of Independent Baptist Churches and other Fundamental Baptist Associations/Fellowships; North American Baptist Conference; "Old" Missionary Baptists Associations; Original Free Will Baptists; Primitive Baptists, Eastern District Association of; Progressive Primitive Baptists; Separate Baptists in Christ; Southern Baptist Convention; Strict Baptists; Two-Seed-in-the-Spirit Predestinarian Baptists; Wayne Trail Missionary Baptist Association; BRETHREN: Brethren Church (Ashland, Ohio); Church of the Brethren; Old Order River Brethren; CHRISTIAN: Christian Church (Disciples of Christ); Christian Churches and Churches of Christ; Churches of Christ; International Churches of Christ; CHURCHES OF GOD: Church of God (Anderson, Indiana); Churches of God, General Conference; CONGREGATIONAL: Congregational Christian Churches, Additional (not part of any national CCC body); Midwest Congregational Christian Fellowship; National Association of Congregational Christian Churches; Conservative Congregational Christian Conference; EASTERN CHRISTIANS: Albanian Orthodox Diocese of America; American Carpatho-Russian Orthodox Greek Catholic Church; Antiochian Orthodox Christian Archdiocese of North America; Apostolic Catholic Assyrian Church of the East, North American Dioceses; Armenian Apostolic Church / Catholicossate of Cilicia; Armenian Apostolic Church / Catholicossate of Etchmiadzin; Bulgarian Orthodox Diocese of the USA; Greek Orthodox Archdiocese of America; Greek Orthodox Archdiocese of Vasiloupulis; Holy Orthodox Church in North America; Macedonian Orthodox Church: American Diocese; Malankara Archdiocese of the Syrian Orthodox Church in North America; Malankara Orthodox Syrian Church, American Diocese of the; Orthodox Church in America: Albanian Orthodox Archdiocese; Orthodox Church in America: Bulgarian Diocese; Orthodox Church in America: Romanian Orthodox Episcopate of America; Orthodox Church in America: Territorial Dioceses; Romanian Orthodox Archdiocese in America and Canada; Serbian Orthodox Church in the USA; Syrian Orthodox Church of Antioch; Ukrainian Orthodox Church of the USA; LATTER-DAY SAINTS: Church of Jesus Christ of Latter-day Saints; Community of Christ; LUTHERAN: Association of Free Lutheran Congregations; Evangelical Lutheran Church in America; Lutheran Church--Missouri Synod; Wisconsin Evangelical Lutheran Synod; MENNONITE: Amish (Other Groups); Beachy Amish Mennonite Churches; Brethren In Christ Church; Bruderhof Communities, Inc.; Church of God in Christ, Mennonite; Conservative Mennonite Conference; Eastern Pennsylvania Mennonite Church; Evangelical Mennonite Church; Fellowship of Evangelical Bible Churches; Hutterian Brethren; Mennonite Brethren Churches, U.S. Conference of; Mennonite Church USA; Mennonite (Other Groups); Old Order Amish Church; Old Order Mennonite; Reformed Mennonite Church; METHODIST: Allegheny Wesleyan Methodist Connection; Free Methodist Church of North America; Fundamental Methodist Conference, Inc.; Primitive Methodist Church in the USA; United Methodist Church; Wesleyan Church; MORAVIAN: Moravian Church in America—Alaska Province, Northern Province, Southern Province; PENTECOSTAL: Assemblies of God; Church of God (Cleveland, Tennessee); Church of God of Prophecy; Independent, Charismatic Churches; International Church of the Foursquare Gospel; International Pentecostal Church of Christ; International Pentecostal Holiness Church; Pentecostal Church of God; Vineyard USA; PRESBYTERIAN: Associate Reformed Presbyterian Church; Cumberland Presbyterian Church; Evangelical Presbyterian Church; Orthodox Presbyterian Church; Presbyterian Church (U.S.A.); Presbyterian Church in America; REFORMED: Christian Reformed Church in North America; Netherlands Reformed Congregations; Protestant Reformed Churches in America; Reformed Church in America; Reformed Church in the United States; United Reformed Churches in North America.

The Research Center staff employed standard procedures for checking the accuracy of data submitted. The state and national totals were checked against the county data and discrepancies adjusted. (Any adjustments were noted and sent to the contact person for review.) When appropriate, the estimating procedure for adherents was applied. A printout was made of the data, comparing 1990 figures to 2000 figures for each county and state. A series of four maps was also created, comparing 1990 and 2000 presence by county, location of congregations, ratio of adherents to each county's population, and number of adherents by county. These materials were reviewed by the staff and then sent to the contact person. Only after all problems raised by both the staff and the contact person were resolved were the statistics considered ready for publication.

The final step was to run a series of computer edit tests to check for errors. Finding incorrect county codes and locating records with no data were the most common corrections at that step. Finally, the Church of the Nazarene staff produced the printouts of tables and maps for this document.

Abbreviations

Code	Abbreviation	Full Group Name
007	OCA: Alban Dioc	Orthodox Church in America: Albanian Orthodox Archdiocese
009	Alban Orth Dio	Albanian Orthodox Diocese of America
011	A.W.M.C.	Allegheny Wesleyan Methodist Connection
017	Amer Bapt Assn	American Baptist Association, The
019	Amer Bapt USA	American Baptist Churches in the USA
022	Carp Rus Orth	American Carpatho-Russian Orthodox Greek Catholic Church
032	Amish; other	Amish; Other Groups
034	Ant Orth of NA	Antiochian Orthodox Christian Archdiocese of North America, The
039	Ap Chr Ch(Naz)	Apostolic Christian Churches (Nazarean)
040	Ap Chr Ch-Amer	Apostolic Christian Church of America, Inc.
049	Armen Ap Cilic	Armenian Apostolic Church / Catholicossate of Cilicia
050	Armen Ap Etchm	Armenian Apostolic Church / Catholicossate of Etchmiadzin
053	Assemb of God	Assemblies of God
055	As Ref Pres Ch	Associate Reformed Presbyterian Church
056	Baha'i	Baha'i
057	Bapt Gen Conf	Baptist General Conference
059	Bapt Miss Assn	Baptist Missionary Association of America
061	Beachy Amish	Beachy Amish Mennonite Churches
070	Bruderhof Comm	Bruderhof Communities, Inc.
071	Brethren (Ash)	Brethren Church, The (Ashland, Ohio)
075	Brethren in Cr	Brethren In Christ Church
076	Buddhism	Buddhists
078	Bulgar Orth USA	Bulgarian Orthodox Diocese of the USA
081	Catholic	Catholic Church
084	Calvary Chapel	Calvary Chapel Fellowship Churches
089	Chr & Miss Al	Christian and Missionary Alliance, The
093	Chr Ch (Disc)	Christian Church (Disciples of Christ)
097	Chr Chs&Chs Cr	Christian Churches and Churches of Christ
105	Christian Ref	Christian Reformed Church in North America
107	Christian Un	Christian Union
121	Ch God (Abr)	Church of God General Conference
123	Ch God (Ander)	Church of God (Anderson, Indiana)
127	Ch God (Cleve)	Church of God (Cleveland, Tennessee)
143	CG in Cr(Menn)	Church of God in Christ, Mennonite
145	Ch God Prophcy	Church of God of Prophecy
151	L-D Saints	Church of Jesus Christ of Latter-day Saints, The
157	Ch of Brethren	Church of the Brethren
165	Ch of Nazarene	Church of the Nazarene
167	Chs of Christ	Churches of Christ
171	Ch God-Gen Con	Churches of God, General Conference

Abbreviations

Code	Abbreviation	Full Group Name
173	Comm of Christ	Community of Christ
175	Congr Chr Chs	National Association of Congregational Christian Churches
176	Congr Ad Afl	Congregational Christian Churches, Additional (not part of any national CCC body)
179	Consrv Bapt	Conservative Baptist Association of America
181	Consrv Congr	Conservative Congregational Christian Conference
183	Cons Menn Conf	Conservative Mennonite Conference
185	Cumber Presb	Cumberland Presbyterian Church
186	Coptic Orth Ch	Coptic Orthodox Church
189	Duck Rivr Bapt	Duck River and Kindred Baptists Associations
191	Entrpr Bpt Asc	Enterprise Baptists Association
193	Episcopal	Episcopal Church
201	Evan Cov Ch	Evangelical Covenant Church, The
203	Evan Free Ch	Evangelical Free Church of America, The
207	E.L.C.A.	Evangelical Lutheran Church in America
211	Fel Evg Bib Ch	Fellowship of Evangelical Bible Churches
213	Evan Menn Inc	Evangelical Mennonite Church
216	Evan Presby Ch	Evangelical Presbyterian Church
220	Free Lutheran	Association of Free Lutheran Congregations, The
221	Free Methodist	Free Methodist Church of North America
223	Free Will Bapt	National Association of Free Will Baptists
226	Friends-USA	Friends (Quakers)
230	Fund Methodist	Fundamental Methodist Conference, Inc.
237	Menn Br US Conf	Mennonite Brethren Churches, U.S. Conference of
241	Gen Six Pr Bpt	General Six Principle Baptists
245	Greek Orth Vslp	Greek Orthodox Archdiocese of Vasiloupulis
246	Greek Orthodox	Greek Orthodox Archdiocese of America
249	Assyr Apost Ch	Apostolic Catholic Assyrian Church of the East, North American Dioceses
251	Holy Orth in NA	Holy Orthodox Church in North America
252	Hindu	Hindus
257	Hutterian Br	Hutterian Brethren
258	IndFreeWillBapt	Independent Free Will Baptists Associations
262	Int Cou Comm Ch	International Council of Community Churches
263	Int Foursq Gos	International Church of the Foursquare Gospel
264	Int Chs of Crst	International Churches of Christ
265	Int Pent C Chr	International Pentecostal Church of Christ
266	Intrstat & Asc	Interstate & Foreign Landmark Missionary Baptists Association
267	Muslim Est	Muslim Estimate
268	Jain	Jains
269	Jasper&PVB Asc	Jasper Baptist and Pleasant Valley Baptist Associations
273	LandmrkBapt,I&U	Landmark Missionary Baptists, Independent Associations and Unaffiliated Churches

Code	Abbreviation	Full Group Name
283	Luth—MO Synod	Lutheran Church—Missouri Synod
286	E.PA Mennonite	Eastern Pennsylvania Mennonite Church
288	Mennonite USA	Mennonite Church USA
289	New Hope B Asc	New Hope Baptist Association
290	Metro Comm Ch	Universal Fellowship of Metropolitan Community Churches
291	Missionary Ch	Missionary Church, The
292	Morav Ch-AK	Moravian Church in America—Alaska Province
293	Morav Ch-North	Moravian Church in America—Northern Province
295	Morav Ch-South	Moravian Church in America—Southern Province
296	Midw Congr Fel	Midwest Congregational Christian Fellowship
297	Mennonite;Other	Mennonite; Other Groups
304	NatPrimBapt USA	National Primitive Baptist Convention, USA
306	NT IndBapt&Rltd	New Testament Association of Independent Baptist Churches and other Fundamental Baptist Associations/Fellowships
307	Neth Ref Congr	Netherlands Reformed Congregations
313	N Am Bapt Conf	North American Baptist Conference
320	"Old" MB Ascs	"Old" Missionary Baptists Associations
322	Old Ord Menn Ch	Old Order Mennonite
323	Old Ord Amish	Old Order Amish Church
324	Old Ord Rvr Br	Old Order River Brethren
330	Macedonian Orth	Macedonian Orthodox Church: American Diocese
331	OCA: Ter Diocs	Orthodox Church in America: Territorial Dioceses
332	OCA: Bulg Dioc	Orthodox Church in America: Bulgarian Diocese
333	Malan Dioc Am	Malankara Orthodox Syrian Church, American Diocese of the
334	Malan Syr Orth	Malankara Archdiocese of the Syrian Orthodox Church in North America
335	Orth Pres Ch	Orthodox Presbyterian Church, The
336	OrigFreeWillBpt	Original Free Will Baptists
339	Pent Ch of God	Pentecostal Church of God
349	Pent Holiness	International Pentecostal Holiness Church
355	Presb Ch (USA)	Presbyterian Church (U.S.A.)
356	Presb Ch Amer	Presbyterian Church in America
360	Prim Bapt Chrch	Primitive Baptist Churches—Old Line
362	Prim Bapt E Dst	Primitive Baptists, Eastern District Association of
363	Primitive Meth	Primitive Methodist Church in the USA
365	Prog Prim Bapt	Progressive Primitive Baptists
369	Prot Ref Chs	Protestant Reformed Churches in America
370	Ref Baptist Chs	Reformed Baptist Churches
371	Ref Ch in Am	Reformed Church in America
373	Ref Ch in U.S.	Reformed Church in the United States
379	Ref Mennonite	Reformed Mennonite Church

Abbreviations

Code	Abbreviation	Full Group Name
388	Reg Bapt Gen As	General Association of Regular Baptist Churches
395	Romania Orth Ar	Romanian Orthodox Archdiocese in America and Canada
397	OCA: Roman Dioc	Orthodox Church in America: Romanian Orthodox Episcopate of America
400	Rus Orth Moscow	Patriarchal Parishes of the Russian Orthodox Church in the USA
401	Rus Orth Abroad	Russian Orthodox Church Outside of Russia
403	Salvation Army	Salvation Army, The
409	Separate Bapt	Separate Baptists in Christ
410	Serb Orth USA	Serbian Orthodox Church in the USA
411	Serb Orth: Grac	Serbian Orthodox Church in the USA (New Gracanica Metropolitanate)
413	S.D.A.	Seventh-day Adventist Church
416	Sikh	Sikhs
418	Southw Bapt Fel	Southwide Baptist Fellowship
419	So Bapt Conv	Southern Baptist Convention
420	Strict Baptists	Strict Baptists
423	Syrian Orth Ch	Syrian Orthodox Church of Antioch
425	Tao	Taoists
426	2Seed Sprt Bpt	Two-Seed-in-the-Spirit Predestinarian Baptists
431	Ukrainian Orth	Ukrainian Orthodox Church of the USA
435	Unitarian-Univ	Unitarian Universalist Association of Congregations
443	Un C of Christ	United Church of Christ
449	Un Methodist	United Methodist Church, The
455	Un Ref Chs N.A.	United Reformed Churches in North America
463	Vineyard	Vineyard USA
466	Wayn Tr MB Asc	Wayne Trail Missionary Baptist Association
467	Wesleyan	Wesleyan Church, The
469	WELS	Wisconsin Evangelical Lutheran Synod
490	Zoroastrian	Zoroastrians
496	Jewish Est	Jewish Estimate
498	Indep.Charis.	Independent, Charismatic Churches
499	Indep.Non-Char	Independent, Non-Charismatic Churches

Table 1: Religious Congregations by Group for the United States: 2000

Religious Group		Number of Churches, Synagogues, Mosques, or Temples	Number of Communicant, Confirmed, Full Members	Number of Attendees	Total Adherents		
					Number of Adherents	% of Total Population	% of Total Adherents
THE NATION		**268,254**	**48,881,291**	**24,493,448**	**141,371,963 ***	**50.2**	**100.0**
007	OCA: Alban Dioc	12	NR	NR	5,775	-	-
009	Alban Orth Dio	2	350	NR	395	-	-
011	A.W.M.C.	115	1,734	5,721	1,864	-	-
017	Amer Bapt Assn	1,867	225,479	NR	280,973 *	.1	.2
019	Amer Bapt USA	5,555	1,417,543	661,225	1,767,462 *	.6	1.3
022	Carp Rus Orth	75	11,753	NR	20,000	-	-
032	Amish; other	90	5,263	NR	6,671 *	-	-
034	Ant Orth of NA	210	41,187	NR	82,374	-	.1
039	Ap Chr Ch(Naz)	50	2,756	4,367	4,393 *	-	-
040	Ap Chr Ch-Amer	84	12,720	23,980	23,980 *	-	-
049	Armen Ap Cilic	38	9,871	NR	46,354	-	-
050	Armen Ap Etchm	89	8,529	NR	91,513	-	.1
053	Assemb of God	11,880	1,489,281	1,623,889	2,561,998	.9	1.8
055	As Ref Pres Ch	242	34,678	NR	40,397	-	-
056	Baha'i	1,198	146,756	NR	146,756	.1	.1
057	Bapt Gen Conf	866	140,925	200,651	238,920 *	.1	.2
059	Bapt Miss Assn	1,322	235,345	91,334	295,239 *	.1	.2
061	Beachy Amish	102	7,532	NR	9,422 *	-	-
070	Bruderhof Comm	7	924	NR	924	-	-
071	Brethren (Ash)	119	13,096	12,367	16,266 *	-	-
075	Brethren in Cr	216	20,587	23,961	25,512	-	-
076	Buddhism	1,656	NR	NR	NR	-	-
078	Bulgar Orth USA	9	NR	NR	5,340	-	-
081	Catholic	21,791	NR	NR	62,035,042	22.0	43.9
084	Calvary Chapel	728	NR	NR	NR	-	-
089	Chr & Miss Al	1,878	163,875	NR	331,106	.1	.2
093	Chr Ch (Disc)	3,339	817,902	265,282	1,017,784 *	.4	.7
097	Chr Chs&Chs Cr	5,471	1,156,699	NR	1,439,253 *	.5	1.0
105	Christian Ref	740	196,555	149,378	248,938 *	.1	.2
107	Christian Un	114	5,634	5,381	7,319 *	-	-
121	Ch God (Abr)	89	3,487	3,900	4,925 *	-	-
123	Ch God (Ander)	2,286	NR	238,609	238,609	.1	.2
127	Ch God (Cleve)	5,612	767,188	473,753	974,198 *	.3	.7
143	CG in Cr(Menn)	100	12,103	NR	15,337 *	-	-
145	Ch God Prophcy	1,858	73,261	NR	91,106 *	-	.1
151	L-D Saints	11,515	NR	NR	4,224,026	1.5	3.0

NR–Not Reported   *Total adherents estimated from known number of communicant, confirmed, full members.   - Represents a percentage less than 0.1.   Percentages may not total 100 due to rounding.

Table 1: Religious Congregations by Group for the United States: 2000

	Religious Group	Number of Churches, Synagogues, Mosques, or Temples	Number of Communicant, Confirmed, Full Members	Number of Attendees	Total Adherents		
					Number of Adherents	% of Total Population	% of Total Adherents
157	Ch of Brethren	1,074	137,959	71,518	171,281 *	.1	.1
165	Ch of Nazarene	5,209	633,231	502,094	907,331	.3	.6
167	Chs of Christ	13,027	1,264,808	1,256,845	1,645,584	.6	1.2
171	Ch God-Gen Con	336	32,208	27,459	42,204 *	-	-
173	Comm of Christ	892	98,874	NR	98,874	-	.1
175	Congr Chr Chs	426	67,709	37,724	84,380 *	-	.1
176	Congr Ad Afl	104	14,416	NR	17,821 *	-	-
179	Consrv Bapt	1,191	NR	224,306	224,306	.1	.2
181	Consrv Congr	250	40,783	30,210	50,940 *	-	-
183	Cons Menn Conf	104	10,223	12,483	14,865	-	-
185	Cumber Presb	706	46,674	NR	77,686	-	.1
186	Coptic Orth Ch	55	NR	NR	NR	-	-
189	Duck Rivr Bapt	99	10,188	NR	12,542 *	-	-
191	Entrpr Bpt Asc	65	4,310	NR	5,289 *	-	-
193	Episcopal	7,314	NR	836,143	2,314,756	.8	1.6
201	Evan Cov Ch	671	102,342	124,533	153,116 *	.1	.1
203	Evan Free Ch	1,365	145,190	283,549	285,699	.1	.2
207	E.L.C.A.	10,739	3,798,370	1,560,712	5,113,418	1.8	3.6
211	Fel Evg Bib Ch	17	1,962	1,360	1,811	-	-
213	Evan Menn Inc	34	5,278	10,347	6,625 *	-	-
216	Evan Presby Ch	179	63,783	NR	80,207 *	-	.1
220	Free Lutheran	234	24,350	16,066	32,098	-	-
221	Free Methodist	950	60,185	90,777	96,237	-	.1
223	Free Will Bapt	2,466	205,617	NR	254,170 *	.1	.2
226	Friends-USA	1,302	90,791	NR	113,086 *	-	.1
230	Fund Methodist	13	814	NR	1,009 *	-	-
237	Menn Br US Conf	171	22,092	NR	28,142 *	-	-
241	Gen Six Pr Bpt	1	20	NR	25 *	-	-
245	Greek Orth Vslp	38	14,926	NR	30,148	-	-
246	Greek Orthodox	518	NR	NR	427,659	.2	.3
249	Assyr Apost Ch	18	NR	NR	35,118	-	-
251	Holy Orth in NA	30	NR	NR	1,889	-	-
252	Hindu	629	NR	NR	NR	-	-
257	Hutterian Br	123	8,118	NR	12,300	-	-
258	IndFreeWillBapt	264	19,946	NR	24,107 *	-	-
262	Int Cou Comm Ch	192	51,626	NR	64,186 *	-	-
263	Int Foursq Gos	1,844	218,981	325,456	347,367 *	.1	.2
264	Int Chs of Crst	99	56,952	96,747	79,161	-	.1

NR–Not Reported   *Total adherents estimated from known number of communicant, confirmed, full members.   - Represents a percentage less than 0.1.   Percentages may not total 100 due to rounding.

Table 1: Religious Congregations by Group for the United States: 2000

	Religious Group	Number of Churches, Synagogues, Mosques, or Temples	Number of Communicant, Confirmed, Full Members	Number of Attendees	Total Adherents		
					Number of Adherents	% of Total Population	% of Total Adherents
265	Int Pent C Chr	67	2,184	2,321	5,453	-	-
266	Intrstat & Asc	121	12,737	NR	16,127 *	-	-
267	Muslim Est	1,209	NR	353,738	1,559,294	.6	1.1
268	Jain	92	NR	NR	NR	-	-
269	Jasper&PVB Asc	31	5,659	NR	7,078 *	-	-
273	LandmrkBapt,I&U	59	4,556	NR	5,682 *	-	-
283	Luth--MO Synod	6,077	1,922,763	968,073	2,521,062	.9	1.8
286	E.PA Mennonite	49	3,540	NR	4,384 *	-	-
288	Mennonite USA	1,066	121,050	106,386	156,345 *	.1	.1
289	New Hope B Asc	20	2,131	NR	2,772 *	-	-
290	Metro Comm Ch	206	19,413	18,317	23,440 *	-	-
291	Missionary Ch	284	29,101	48,475	49,528	-	-
292	Morav Ch-AK	24	1,765	NR	2,562 *	-	-
293	Morav Ch-North	93	20,281	NR	25,872	-	-
295	Morav Ch-South	59	15,893	NR	19,764	-	-
296	Midw Congr Fel	29	1,367	1,451	1,705 *	-	-
297	Mennonite;Other	412	27,789	NR	34,617 *	-	-
304	NatPrimBapt USA	547	53,630	NR	66,452 *	-	-
306	NT IndBapt&Rltd	649	106,130	NR	132,684 *	-	-
307	Neth Ref Congr	15	2,291	NR	4,442	-	.1
313	N Am Bapt Conf	290	47,112	49,762	59,545 *	-	-
320	"Old" MB Ascs	302	40,200	NR	49,870 *	-	-
322	Old Ord Menn Ch	132	16,906	NR	21,116 *	-	-
323	Old Ord Amish	1,290	76,649	NR	96,986 *	-	-
324	Old Ord Rvr Br	5	331	485	540	-	.1
330	Macedonian Orth	17	NR	NR	16,640	-	-
331	OCA: Ter Diocs	370	34,133	NR	77,110	-	-
332	OCA: Bulg Dioc	18	2,198	NR	8,791	-	.1
333	Malan Dioc Am	59	NR	NR	13,225	-	-
334	Malan Syr Orth	24	878	NR	4,336	-	-
335	Orth Pres Ch	278	17,782	21,728	26,346	-	-
336	OrigFreeWillBpt	237	37,198	NR	46,211 *	-	-
339	Pent Ch of God	1,173	44,976	NR	101,921	-	.1
349	Pent Holiness	1,843	194,688	147,569	241,828 *	.1	.2
355	Presb Ch (USA)	11,106	2,516,816	1,303,216	3,141,566 *	1.1	2.2
356	Presb Ch Amer	1,441	243,298	220,168	315,293	.1	.2
360	Prim Bapt Chrch	1,381	NR	NR	NR	-	-
362	Prim Bapt E Dst	67	6,468	NR	7,840 *	-	-

NR–Not Reported *Total adherents estimated from known number of communicant, confirmed, full members. - Represents a percentage less than 0.1. Percentages may not total 100 due to rounding.

Table 1: Religious Congregations by Group for the United States: 2000

	Religious Group	Number of Churches, Synagogues, Mosques, or Temples	Number of Communicant, Confirmed, Full Members	Number of Attendees	Total Adherents		
					Number of Adherents	% of Total Population	% of Total Adherents
363	Primitive Meth	79	4,502	NR	4,796	-	-
365	Prog Prim Bapt	121	7,739	NR	9,615 *	-	-
369	Prot Ref Chs	26	3,366	NR	5,875	-	-
370	Ref Baptist Chs	197	NR	NR	NR	-	-
371	Ref Ch in Am	896	177,058	164,349	335,677	.1	.2
373	Ref Ch in U.S.	38	3,206	NR	4,236	-	-
379	Ref Mennonite	9	278	NR	347 *	-	-
388	Reg Bapt Gen As	1,422	188,274	205,631	245,636 *	.1	.2
395	Romania Orth Ar	14	NR	NR	7,543	-	-
397	OCA: Roman Dioc	56	NR	NR	17,201	-	-
400	Rus Orth Moscow	32	NR	NR	NR	-	-
401	Rus Orth Abroad	129	NR	NR	NR	-	-
403	Salvation Army	1,332	139,620	96,171	415,060	.1	.3
409	Separate Bapt	94	8,716	NR	10,674 *	-	-
410	Serb Orth USA	75	NR	NR	55,807	-	-
411	Serb Orth: Grac	38	NR	NR	NR	-	-
413	S.D.A.	4,507	775,625	NR	923,046	.3	.7
416	Sikh	211	NR	NR	NR	-	-
418	Southw Bapt Fel	501	NR	NR	NR	-	-
419	So Bapt Conv	41,514	15,922,039	5,535,891	19,881,467 *	7.1	14.1
420	Strict Baptists	3	26	NR	33 *	-	-
423	Syrian Orth Ch	23	NR	NR	13,845	-	-
425	Tao	38	NR	NR	NR	-	-
426	2Seed Sprt Bpt	4	53	NR	65 *	-	-
431	Ukrainian Orth	104	NR	NR	35,586	-	-
435	Unitarian-Univ	999	147,771	NR	182,698 *	.1	.1
443	Un C of Christ	5,863	1,371,593	568,552	1,698,918 *	.6	1.2
449	Un Methodist	35,721	8,326,616	3,487,039	10,350,629 *	3.7	7.3
455	Un Ref Chs N.A.	49	7,529	NR	11,449	-	-
463	Vineyard	529	122,081	99,954	155,170 *	.1	.1
466	Wayn Tr MB Asc	13	2,192	NR	2,756 *	-	-
467	Wesleyan	1,657	108,430	169,152	381,459	.1	.3
469	WELS	1,277	314,941	179,837	405,078	.1	.3
490	Zoroastrian	35	NR	NR	NR	-	-
496	Jewish Est	3,727	NR	NR	6,141,325	2.2	4.3
498	Indep.Charis.	621	588,530	598,434	935,168	.3	.7
499	Indep.Non-Char	1,084	753,454	854,622	1,116,769	.4	.8

NR–Not Reported *Total adherents estimated from known number of communicant, confirmed, full members. - Represents a percentage less than 0.1. Percentages may not total 100 due to rounding.

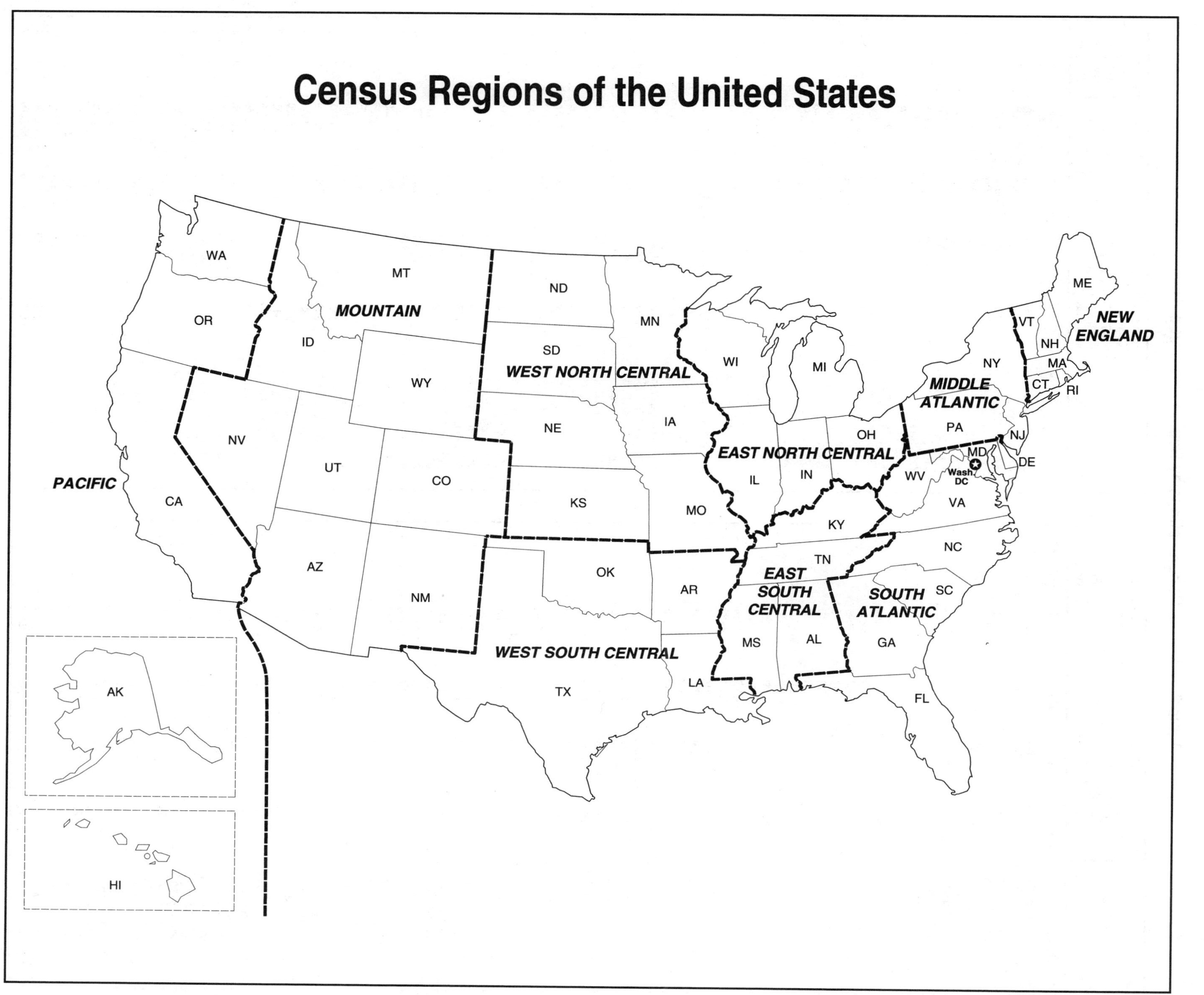
Census Regions of the United States
PACIFIC
MOUNTAIN
WEST NORTH CENTRAL
WEST SOUTH CENTRAL
EAST NORTH CENTRAL
EAST SOUTH CENTRAL
MIDDLE ATLANTIC
SOUTH ATLANTIC
NEW ENGLAND
WA
OR
CA
NV
ID
MT
WY
UT
CO
AZ
NM
ND
SD
NE
KS
OK
TX
MN
IA
MO
AR
LA
WI
MI
IL
IN
OH
KY
TN
MS
AL
NY
PA
NJ
DE
MD
Wash. DC
WV
VA
NC
SC
GA
FL
VT
NH
ME
MA
CT
RI
AK
HI

Table 2: Religious Congregations by Region and Group: 2000

Religious Group	Number of Churches, Synagogues, Mosques, or Temples	Number of Communicant, Confirmed, or Full Members	Number of Attendees	Total Adherents		
				Number of Adherents	% of Total Pop.	% of Total Adh.
NEW ENGLAND	**9,010**	**936,509**	**562,272**	**7,996,692 ***	**57.4**	**100.0**
007 OCA: Alban Dioc	6	NR	NR	3,775	-	-
009 Alban Orth Dio	1	100	NR	125	-	-
011 A.W.M.C.	1	0	18	0	-	-
017 Amer Bapt Assn	7	160	NR	195 *	-	-
019 Amer Bapt USA	746	138,200	60,110	169,908 *	1.2	2.1
022 Carp Rus Orth	4	1,123	NR	1,913	-	-
034 Ant Orth of NA	12	5,117	NR	10,234	.1	.1
039 Ap Chr Ch(Naz)	1	20	35	35 *	-	-
040 Ap Chr Ch-Amer	1	345	575	575 *	-	-
049 Armen Ap Cilic	7	1,787	NR	5,544	-	.1
050 Armen Ap Etchm	13	3,092	NR	18,490	.1	.2
053 Assemb of God	355	35,167	41,082	56,492	.4	.7
056 Baha'i	61	5,609	NR	5,609	-	.1
057 Bapt Gen Conf	51	7,031	7,506	10,095 *	.1	.1
059 Bapt Miss Assn	1	16	17	19 *	-	-
061 Beachy Amish	1	8	NR	10 *	-	-
076 Buddhism	101	NR	NR	NR	-	-
081 Catholic	1,831	NR	NR	5,869,303	42.2	73.4
084 Calvary Chapel	15	NR	NR	NR	-	-
089 Chr & Miss Al	81	4,978	NR	12,034	.1	.2
093 Chr Ch (Disc)	7	721	160	900 *	-	-
097 Chr Chs&Chs Cr	21	1,973	NR	2,464 *	-	-
105 Christian Ref	8	1,994	1,301	2,482 *	-	-
123 Ch God (Ander)	10	NR	4,547	4,547	-	.1
127 Ch God (Cleve)	149	12,304	8,231	15,748 *	.1	.2
145 Ch God Prophcy	28	2,111	NR	2,604 *	-	-
151 L-D Saints	149	NR	NR	44,803	.3	.6
157 Ch of Brethren	4	144	201	208 *	-	-
165 Ch of Nazarene	156	13,270	12,334	21,576	.2	.3
167 Chs of Christ	104	5,749	6,467	8,306	.1	.1
171 Ch God-Gen Con	1	0	65	65 *	-	-
173 Comm of Christ	21	1,628	NR	1,628	-	-
175 Congr Chr Chs	116	13,019	7,698	15,958 *	.1	.2
176 Congr Ad Afl	47	6,546	NR	8,051 *	.1	.1
179 Consrv Bapt	131	NR	19,125	19,125	.1	.2
181 Consrv Congr	62	7,421	7,372	9,139 *	.1	.1
185 Cumber Presb	1	20	NR	20	-	-
193 Episcopal	669	NR	75,005	240,374	1.7	3.0
201 Evan Cov Ch	45	7,208	6,965	9,581 *	.1	.1
203 Evan Free Ch	45	3,677	7,151	7,151	.1	.1
207 E.L.C.A.	194	55,419	21,942	76,145	.5	1.0
221 Free Methodist	18	795	1,210	1,317	-	-
223 Free Will Bapt	3	210	NR	256 *	-	-
226 Friends-USA	104	4,604	NR	5,620 *	-	.1
245 Greek Orth Vslp	6	1,562	NR	3,045	-	-
246 Greek Orthodox	72	NR	NR	66,969	.5	.8
249 Assyr Apost Ch	1	NR	NR	516	-	-
251 Holy Orth in NA	8	NR	NR	970	-	-
252 Hindu	26	NR	NR	NR	-	-
262 Int Cou Comm Ch	11	2,986	NR	3,693 *	-	-
263 Int Foursq Gos	51	3,175	7,279	7,393 *	.1	.1
264 Int Chs of Crst	6	4,853	8,384	6,949	-	.1
265 Int Pent C Chr	2	60	50	85	-	-
267 Muslim Est	53	NR	17,209	77,662	.6	1.0
268 Jain	6	NR	NR	NR	-	-
283 Luth—MO Synod	73	18,431	9,338	24,890	.2	.3
286 E.PA Mennonite	2	49	NR	61 *	-	-
288 Mennonite USA	11	591	573	768 *	-	-
290 Metro Comm Ch	5	202	165	205 *	-	-
297 Mennonite;Other	2	92	NR	112 *	-	-
313 N Am Bapt Conf	1	10	8	12 *	-	-
322 Old Ord Menn Ch	1	19	NR	23 *	-	-
331 OCA: Ter Diocs	27	2,667	NR	4,140	-	.1
333 Malan Dioc Am	1	NR	NR	175	-	-
335 Orth Pres Ch	15	1,115	1,331	1,581	-	-
339 Pent Ch of God	2	110	NR	125	-	-
349 Pent Holiness	2	24	28	29 *	-	-
355 Presb Ch (USA)	90	16,780	10,769	21,100 *	.2	.3
356 Presb Ch Amer	23	1,180	1,500	1,747	-	-
363 Primitive Meth	12	684	NR	728	-	-
370 Ref Baptist Chs	11	NR	NR	NR	-	-
371 Ref Ch in Am	1	56	57	104	-	-
388 Reg Bapt Gen As	20	1,516	1,951	2,104 *	-	-

Religious Group	Number of Churches, Synagogues, Mosques, or Temples	Number of Communicant, Confirmed, or Full Members	Number of Attendees	Total Adherents		
				Number of Adherents	% of Total Pop.	% of Total Adh.
395 Romania Orth Ar	3	NR	NR	1,750	-	-
397 OCA: Roman Dioc	3	NR	NR	429	-	-
400 Rus Orth Moscow	1	NR	NR	NR	-	-
401 Rus Orth Abroad	10	NR	NR	NR	-	-
403 Salvation Army	89	7,122	4,973	18,571	.1	.2
410 Serb Orth USA	1	NR	NR	300	-	-
413 S.D.A.	168	21,914	NR	26,082	.2	.3
416 Sikh	8	NR	NR	NR	-	-
418 Southw Bapt Fel	2	NR	NR	NR	-	-
419 So Bapt Conv	157	20,569	13,017	25,234 *	.2	.3
423 Syrian Orth Ch	3	NR	NR	850	-	-
425 Tao	2	NR	NR	NR	-	-
431 Ukrainian Orth	7	NR	NR	3,423	-	-
435 Unitarian-Univ	240	33,001	NR	40,496 *	.3	.5
443 Un C of Christ	1,167	276,351	115,597	340,476 *	2.4	4.3
449 Un Methodist	796	157,225	56,175	193,419 *	1.4	2.4
455 Un Ref Chs N.A.	1	119	NR	199	-	-
463 Vineyard	15	3,092	2,834	3,846 *	-	-
467 Wesleyan	19	626	1,826	4,349	-	.1
469 WELS	7	571	378	778	-	-
490 Zoroastrian	1	NR	NR	NR	-	-
496 Jewish Est	342	NR	NR	423,500	3.0	5.3
498 Indep.Charis.	12	6,881	7,043	8,845	.1	.1
499 Indep.Non-Char	26	11,310	12,670	16,535	.1	.2
MIDDLE ATLANTIC	**28,637**	**3,826,274**	**2,101,563**	**23,436,865 ***	**59.1**	**100.0**
007 OCA: Alban Dioc	4	NR	NR	1,350	-	-
011 A.W.M.C.	57	1,004	3,109	1,090	-	-
017 Amer Bapt Assn	22	1,020	NR	1,248 *	-	-
019 Amer Bapt USA	1,238	343,507	157,473	424,676 *	1.1	1.8
022 Carp Rus Orth	50	8,069	NR	13,738	-	.1
032 Amish; other	9	592	NR	734 *	-	-
034 Ant Orth of NA	36	8,029	NR	16,058	-	.1
039 Ap Chr Ch(Naz)	5	236	331	334 *	-	-
040 Ap Chr Ch-Amer	2	77	199	199 *	-	-
049 Armen Ap Cilic	7	1,579	NR	5,810	-	-
050 Armen Ap Etchm	18	3,070	NR	26,602	.1	.1
053 Assemb of God	1,118	146,127	153,730	234,427	.6	1.0
055 As Ref Pres Ch	7	375	NR	459	-	-
056 Baha'i	56	7,614	NR	7,614	-	-
057 Bapt Gen Conf	35	5,090	5,640	7,363 *	-	-
059 Bapt Miss Assn	5	308	284	387 *	-	-
061 Beachy Amish	18	1,815	NR	2,249 *	-	-
070 Bruderhof Comm	7	924	NR	924	-	-
071 Brethren (Ash)	19	1,237	1,194	1,491 *	-	-
075 Brethren in Cr	104	13,491	15,810	16,681	-	.1
076 Buddhism	172	NR	NR	NR	-	-
078 Bulgar Orth USA	3	NR	NR	980	-	-
081 Catholic	4,182	NR	NR	14,756,035	37.2	63.0
084 Calvary Chapel	49	NR	NR	NR	-	-
089 Chr & Miss Al	485	39,404	NR	84,586	.2	.4
093 Chr Ch (Disc)	113	20,066	6,083	24,467 *	.1	.1
097 Chr Chs&Chs Cr	204	26,815	NR	32,589 *	.1	.1
105 Christian Ref	33	7,233	5,699	9,014 *	-	-
123 Ch God (Ander)	150	NR	18,200	18,200	-	.1
127 Ch God (Cleve)	342	36,557	29,824	47,865 *	.1	.2
143 CG in Cr(Menn)	5	407	NR	496 *	-	-
145 Ch God Prophcy	104	5,822	NR	7,248 *	-	-
151 L-D Saints	323	NR	NR	95,874	.2	.4
157 Ch of Brethren	239	43,143	23,230	53,223 *	.1	.2
165 Ch of Nazarene	364	35,248	30,420	52,360	.1	.2
167 Chs of Christ	271	18,574	19,259	24,549	.1	.1
171 Ch God-Gen Con	158	17,721	14,698	22,763 *	.1	.1
173 Comm of Christ	26	2,208	NR	2,208	-	-
175 Congr Chr Chs	33	2,881	1,984	3,568 *	-	-
176 Congr Ad Afl	14	1,571	NR	1,927 *	-	-
179 Consrv Bapt	219	NR	31,853	31,853	.1	.1
181 Consrv Congr	42	5,068	3,848	6,249 *	-	-
183 Cons Menn Conf	10	1,700	2,076	2,472	-	-
185 Cumber Presb	1	122	NR	122	-	-
193 Episcopal	1,393	NR	140,539	410,272	1.0	1.8
201 Evan Cov Ch	32	4,169	3,177	5,349 *	-	-
203 Evan Free Ch	119	12,689	24,338	24,494	.1	.1
207 E.L.C.A.	1,970	624,061	218,086	860,506	2.2	3.7

NR–Not Reported *Total adherents estimated from known number of communicant, confirmed, full members. - Represents a percentage less than 0.1. Percentages may not total 100 due to rounding.

Table 2: Religious Congregations by Region and Group: 2000

Religious Group	Number of Churches, Synagogues, Mosques, or Temples	Number of Communicant, Confirmed, or Full Members	Number of Attendees	Total Adherents: Number of Adherents	Total Adherents: % of Total Pop.	Total Adherents: % of Total Adh.
216 Evan Presby Ch	7	1,650	NR	2,032 *	-	-
220 Free Lutheran	3	967	712	1,389	-	-
221 Free Methodist	190	10,571	16,365	17,294	-	.1
223 Free Will Bapt	6	297	NR	363 *	-	-
226 Friends-USA	184	15,538	NR	19,240 *	-	.1
237 Menn Br US Conf	1	20	NR	24 *	-	-
241 Gen Six Pr Bpt	1	20	NR	25 *	-	-
245 Greek Orth Vslp	9	5,060	NR	9,373	-	-
246 Greek Orthodox	125	NR	NR	111,423	.3	.5
249 Assyr Apost Ch	1	NR	NR	760	-	-
251 Holy Orth in NA	4	NR	NR	221	-	-
252 Hindu	153	NR	NR	NR	-	-
262 Int Cou Comm Ch	23	7,228	NR	8,990 *	-	-
263 Int Foursq Gos	45	3,379	4,455	5,506 *	-	-
264 Int Chs of Crst	7	7,442	13,898	9,933	-	-
265 Int Pent C Chr	2	70	27	114	-	-
267 Muslim Est	269	NR	96,908	415,882	1.0	1.8
268 Jain	24	NR	NR	NR	-	-
283 Luth—MO Synod	355	91,441	40,502	125,039	.3	.5
286 E.PA Mennonite	34	2,741	NR	3,391 *	-	-
288 Mennonite USA	371	40,166	39,146	51,989 *	.1	.2
290 Metro Comm Ch	9	835	818	985 *	-	-
291 Missionary Ch	15	915	1,116	1,230	-	-
293 Morav Ch-North	41	11,047	NR	14,336	-	.1
297 Mennonite;Other	112	7,348	NR	9,086 *	-	-
304 NatPrimBapt USA	10	1,361	NR	1,699 *	-	-
306 NT IndBapt&Rltd	2	273	NR	343 *	-	-
307 Neth Ref Congr	2	446	NR	813	-	-
313 N Am Bapt Conf	26	3,622	3,627	4,509 *	-	-
322 Old Ord Menn Ch	68	11,047	NR	13,758 *	-	.1
323 Old Ord Amish	347	22,680	NR	28,092 *	.1	.1
324 Old Ord Rvr Br	4	298	430	477	-	-
330 Macedonian Orth	6	NR	NR	6,000	-	-
331 OCA: Ter Diocs	132	12,641	NR	21,324	.1	.1
333 Malan Dioc Am	30	NR	NR	6,900	-	-
334 Malan Syr Orth	11	464	NR	2,320	-	-
335 Orth Pres Ch	66	4,732	5,767	6,984	-	-
339 Pent Ch of God	8	718	NR	1,101	-	-
349 Pent Holiness	26	2,238	1,661	2,728 *	-	-
355 Presb Ch (USA)	2,173	492,180	230,942	606,676 *	1.5	2.6
356 Presb Ch Amer	146	21,327	22,234	28,504	.1	.1
360 Prim Bapt Chrch	4	NR	NR	NR	-	-
363 Primitive Meth	46	2,621	NR	2,791	-	-
369 Prot Ref Chs	1	18	NR	27	-	-
370 Ref Baptist Chs	43	NR	NR	NR	-	-
371 Ref Ch in Am	393	46,661	35,790	104,156	.3	.4
373 Ref Ch in U.S.	1	30	NR	53	-	-
379 Ref Mennonite	3	127	NR	158 *	-	-
388 Reg Bapt Gen As	238	25,338	29,156	33,486 *	.1	.1
395 Romania Orth Ar	3	NR	NR	1,925	-	-
397 OCA: Roman Dioc	11	NR	NR	1,917	-	-
400 Rus Orth Moscow	18	NR	NR	NR	-	-
401 Rus Orth Abroad	44	NR	NR	NR	-	-
403 Salvation Army	224	19,179	14,033	61,474	.2	.3
410 Serb Orth USA	14	NR	NR	11,842	-	.1
411 Serb Orth: Grac	6	NR	NR	NR	-	-
413 S.D.A.	477	81,915	NR	97,489	.2	.4
416 Sikh	30	NR	NR	NR	-	-
418 Southw Bapt Fel	26	NR	NR	NR	-	-
419 So Bapt Conv	521	70,097	45,681	86,831 *	.2	.4
423 Syrian Orth Ch	6	NR	NR	3,600	-	-
425 Tao	5	NR	NR	NR	-	-
431 Ukrainian Orth	55	NR	NR	20,658	.1	.1
435 Unitarian-Univ	121	19,834	NR	24,376 *	.1	.1
443 Un C of Christ	1,083	256,914	97,385	315,086 *	.8	1.3
449 Un Methodist	4,424	980,268	371,338	1,202,845 *	3.0	5.1
455 Un Ref Chs N.A.	4	655	NR	1,092	-	-
463 Vineyard	21	2,884	2,623	3,625 *	-	-
467 Wesleyan	235	10,458	26,478	65,778	.2	.3
469 WELS	12	1,032	755	1,320	-	-
490 Zoroastrian	5	NR	NR	NR	-	-
496 Jewish Est	1,523	NR	NR	2,404,870	6.1	10.3
498 Indep.Charis.	41	38,211	34,855	45,728	.1	.2
499 Indep.Non-Char	78	39,647	53,777	62,182	.2	.3

Religious Group	Number of Churches, Synagogues, Mosques, or Temples	Number of Communicant, Confirmed, or Full Members	Number of Attendees	Total Adherents: Number of Adherents	Total Adherents: % of Total Pop.	Total Adherents: % of Total Adh.
EAST NORTH CENTRAL	**41,507**	**7,349,149**	**3,940,683**	**21,978,569 ***	**48.7**	**100.0**
007 OCA: Alban Dioc	2	NR	NR	650	-	-
009 Alban Orth Dio	1	250	NR	270	-	-
011 A.W.M.C.	28	455	1,519	482	-	-
017 Amer Bapt Assn	75	4,110	NR	5,135 *	-	-
019 Amer Bapt USA	1,211	318,441	137,958	397,005 *	.9	1.8
022 Carp Rus Orth	11	1,341	NR	2,279	-	-
032 Amish; other	47	2,714	NR	3,509 *	-	-
034 Ant Orth of NA	33	7,363	NR	14,726	-	.1
039 Ap Chr Ch(Naz)	19	1,507	2,389	2,403 *	-	-
040 Ap Chr Ch-Amer	42	9,553	17,498	17,498 *	-	.1
049 Armen Ap Cilic	6	831	NR	3,486	-	-
050 Armen Ap Etchm	13	1,521	NR	10,123	-	-
053 Assemb of God	1,334	169,724	208,570	346,194	.8	1.6
055 As Ref Pres Ch	2	17	NR	17	-	-
056 Baha'i	127	13,484	NR	13,484	-	.1
057 Bapt Gen Conf	224	30,579	36,712	46,124 *	.1	.2
059 Bapt Miss Assn	35	3,798	2,572	4,846 *	-	-
061 Beachy Amish	39	2,779	NR	3,562 *	-	-
071 Brethren (Ash)	61	9,274	8,592	11,619 *	-	.1
075 Brethren in Cr	29	1,511	1,556	1,761	-	-
076 Buddhism	152	NR	NR	NR	-	-
078 Bulgar Orth USA	5	NR	NR	3,920	-	-
081 Catholic	4,354	NR	NR	10,658,360	23.6	48.5
084 Calvary Chapel	58	NR	NR	NR	-	-
089 Chr & Miss Al	276	26,421	NR	56,677	.1	.3
093 Chr Ch (Disc)	582	177,988	51,533	220,945 *	.5	1.0
097 Chr Chs&Chs Cr	1,726	412,130	NR	512,636 *	1.1	2.3
105 Christian Ref	324	114,357	82,742	145,437 *	.3	.7
107 Christian Un	70	3,231	3,376	4,253 *	-	-
121 Ch God (Abr)	37	1,466	1,840	2,149 *	-	-
123 Ch God (Ander)	617	NR	77,629	77,629	.2	.4
127 Ch God (Cleve)	574	87,888	53,245	113,360 *	.3	.5
143 CG in Cr(Menn)	9	1,080	NR	1,335 *	-	-
145 Ch God Prophcy	133	4,589	NR	5,716 *	-	-
151 L-D Saints	482	NR	NR	149,855	.3	.7
157 Ch of Brethren	274	33,606	18,021	42,155 *	.1	.2
165 Ch of Nazarene	1,194	148,739	125,387	225,821	.5	1.0
167 Chs of Christ	1,329	110,936	111,534	146,161	.3	.7
171 Ch God-Gen Con	91	10,097	8,733	13,453 *	-	.1
173 Comm of Christ	212	24,120	NR	24,120	.1	.1
175 Congr Chr Chs	156	29,109	15,135	36,359 *	.1	.2
176 Congr Ad Afl	17	3,026	NR	3,783 *	-	-
179 Consrv Bapt	82	NR	18,209	18,209	-	.1
181 Consrv Congr	65	9,557	5,970	11,947 *	-	.1
183 Cons Menn Conf	48	5,230	6,386	7,605	-	-
185 Cumber Presb	50	1,970	NR	4,142	-	-
191 Entrpr Bpt Asc	29	1,651	NR	2,048 *	-	-
193 Episcopal	851	NR	78,948	212,082	.5	1.0
201 Evan Cov Ch	149	24,523	22,570	32,428 *	.1	.1
203 Evan Free Ch	301	33,298	64,796	65,118	.1	.3
207 E.L.C.A.	2,491	949,000	376,305	1,278,513	2.8	5.8
211 Fel Evg Bib Ch	1	119	25	25	-	-
213 Evan Menn Inc	30	4,897	9,760	6,156 *	-	-
216 Evan Presby Ch	34	13,734	NR	17,375 *	-	.1
220 Free Lutheran	41	4,548	3,003	6,015	-	-
221 Free Methodist	295	21,538	31,369	33,338	.1	.2
223 Free Will Bapt	279	16,966	NR	21,111 *	-	.1
226 Friends-USA	315	21,119	NR	26,261 *	.1	.1
237 Menn Br US Conf	1	11	NR	14 *	-	-
245 Greek Orth Vslp	3	980	NR	2,680	-	-
246 Greek Orthodox	91	NR	NR	90,768	.2	.4
249 Assyr Apost Ch	6	NR	NR	24,110	.1	.1
251 Holy Orth in NA	1	NR	NR	18	-	-
252 Hindu	70	NR	NR	NR	-	-
258 IndFreeWillBapt	12	932	NR	1,149 *	-	-
262 Int Cou Comm Ch	60	18,833	NR	23,631 *	.1	.1
263 Int Foursq Gos	184	19,374	21,083	28,134 *	.1	.1
264 Int Chs of Crst	13	6,087	10,033	8,779	-	-
265 Int Pent C Chr	27	1,179	1,202	2,482	-	-
267 Muslim Est	205	NR	58,118	265,797	.6	1.2
268 Jain	15	NR	NR	NR	-	-
283 Luth—MO Synod	1,781	724,805	352,026	955,043	2.1	4.3
286 E.PA Mennonite	4	290	NR	355 *	-	-

NR–Not Reported   *Total adherents estimated from known number of communicant, confirmed, full members.   - Represents a percentage less than 0.1.   Percentages may not total 100 due to rounding.

Table 2: Religious Congregations by Region and Group: 2000

Religious Group	Number of Churches, Synagogues, Mosques, or Temples	Number of Communicant, Confirmed, or Full Members	Number of Attendees	Total Adherents: Number of Adherents	Total Adherents: % of Total Pop.	Total Adherents: % of Total Adh.
288 Mennonite USA	242	33,610	28,552	43,833 *	.1	.2
290 Metro Comm Ch	20	1,089	1,006	1,265 *	-	-
291 Missionary Ch	182	16,107	31,017	31,366	.1	.1
293 Morav Ch-North	34	6,628	NR	8,128	-	-
296 Midw Congr Fel	29	1,367	1,451	1,705 *	-	-
297 Mennonite;Other	97	6,297	NR	7,961 *	-	-
304 NatPrimBapt USA	18	1,615	NR	2,027 *	-	-
306 NT IndBapt&Rltd	386	74,013	NR	92,399 *	.2	.4
307 Neth Ref Congr	6	716	NR	1,440	-	-
313 N Am Bapt Conf	55	11,029	10,964	14,123 *	-	.1
320 "Old" MB Ascs	17	1,772	NR	2,219 *	-	-
322 Old Ord Menn Ch	27	2,612	NR	3,311 *	-	-
323 Old Ord Amish	758	44,210	NR	56,739 *	.1	.3
330 Macedonian Orth	9	NR	NR	9,440	-	-
331 OCA: Ter Diocs	51	5,591	NR	11,553	-	.1
332 OCA: Bulg Dioc	9	1,495	NR	4,062	-	-
333 Malan Dioc Am	5	NR	NR	1,375	-	-
334 Malan Syr Orth	3	90	NR	450	-	-
335 Orth Pres Ch	42	3,295	4,090	5,101	-	-
339 Pent Ch of God	161	6,571	NR	16,657	-	.1
349 Pent Holiness	40	2,395	1,858	2,975 *	-	-
355 Presb Ch (USA)	1,739	408,033	195,275	511,562 *	1.1	2.3
356 Presb Ch Amer	93	12,741	12,220	15,985	-	.1
360 Prim Bapt Chrch	113	NR	NR	NR	-	-
362 Prim Bapt E Dst	4	393	NR	483 *	-	-
363 Primitive Meth	15	855	NR	912	-	-
365 Prog Prim Bapt	6	187	NR	234 *	-	-
369 Prot Ref Chs	18	2,542	NR	4,592	-	-
370 Ref Baptist Chs	22	NR	NR	NR	-	-
371 Ref Ch in Am	249	73,810	67,286	120,512	.3	.5
373 Ref Ch in U.S.	2	341	NR	414	-	-
379 Ref Mennonite	5	143	NR	179 *	-	-
388 Reg Bapt Gen As	607	104,957	109,613	135,795 *	.3	.6
395 Romania Orth Ar	5	NR	NR	2,538	-	-
397 OCA: Roman Dioc	18	NR	NR	6,744	-	-
400 Rus Orth Moscow	7	NR	NR	NR	-	-
401 Rus Orth Abroad	17	NR	NR	NR	-	-
403 Salvation Army	247	26,404	21,631	94,041	.2	.4
409 Separate Bapt	29	2,778	NR	3,433 *	-	-
410 Serb Orth USA	20	NR	NR	25,466	.1	.1
411 Serb Orth: Grac	17	NR	NR	NR	-	-
413 S.D.A.	589	88,549	NR	105,372	.2	.5
416 Sikh	22	NR	NR	NR	-	-
418 Southw Bapt Fel	55	NR	NR	NR	-	-
419 So Bapt Conv	2,168	554,039	204,499	687,850 *	1.5	3.1
420 Strict Baptists	2	20	NR	25 *	-	-
423 Syrian Orth Ch	2	NR	NR	870	-	-
425 Tao	1	NR	NR	NR	-	-
426 2Seed Sprt Bpt	1	16	NR	20 *	-	-
431 Ukrainian Orth	21	NR	NR	6,777	-	-
435 Unitarian-Univ	137	20,927	NR	26,056 *	.1	.1
443 Un C of Christ	1,393	413,868	160,865	516,940 *	1.1	2.4
449 Un Methodist	6,165	1,261,411	622,800	1,571,059 *	3.5	7.1
455 Un Ref Chs N.A.	19	3,376	NR	5,103	-	-
463 Vineyard	86	32,063	24,422	40,914 *	.1	.2
466 Wayn Tr MB Asc	13	2,192	NR	2,756 *	-	-
467 Wesleyan	519	35,945	58,803	128,871	.3	.6
469 WELS	623	212,754	115,734	271,839	.6	1.2
490 Zoroastrian	5	NR	NR	NR	-	-
496 Jewish Est	409	NR	NR	568,485	1.3	2.6
498 Indep.Charis.	76	54,367	70,773	85,345	.2	.4
499 Indep.Non-Char	232	167,260	171,480	244,638	.5	1.1
WEST NORTH CENTRAL	**27,260**	**5,060,743**	**2,398,537**	**10,956,188 ***	**57.0**	**100.0**
017 Amer Bapt Assn	50	2,740	NR	3,430 *	-	-
019 Amer Bapt USA	513	109,219	47,350	136,128 *	.7	1.2
032 Amish; other	7	720	NR	894 *	-	-
034 Ant Orth of NA	13	2,288	NR	4,576	-	-
039 Ap Chr Ch(Naz)	2	2	5	5 *	-	-
040 Ap Chr Ch-Amer	21	2,065	4,391	4,391 *	-	-
049 Armen Ap Cilic	2	0	NR	160	-	-
050 Armen Ap Etchm	2	20	NR	805	-	-
053 Assemb of God	1,211	124,959	151,111	243,733	1.3	2.2
055 As Ref Pres Ch	3	155	NR	158	-	-

Religious Group	Number of Churches, Synagogues, Mosques, or Temples	Number of Communicant, Confirmed, or Full Members	Number of Attendees	Total Adherents: Number of Adherents	Total Adherents: % of Total Pop.	Total Adherents: % of Total Adh.
056 Baha'i	73	7,649	NR	7,649	-	.1
057 Bapt Gen Conf	239	37,499	52,307	60,735 *	.3	.6
059 Bapt Miss Assn	100	9,550	4,784	11,992 *	.1	.1
061 Beachy Amish	8	608	NR	742 *	-	-
071 Brethren (Ash)	5	271	258	336 *	-	-
075 Brethren in Cr	5	406	504	554	-	-
076 Buddhism	55	NR	NR	NR	-	-
081 Catholic	3,010	NR	NR	3,815,134	19.8	34.8
084 Calvary Chapel	23	NR	NR	NR	-	-
089 Chr & Miss Al	163	17,530	NR	36,714	.2	.3
093 Chr Ch (Disc)	664	188,630	54,387	234,028 *	1.2	2.1
097 Chr Chs&Chs Cr	833	149,306	NR	186,075 *	1.0	1.7
105 Christian Ref	109	29,570	22,440	36,792 *	.2	.3
107 Christian Un	29	1,983	1,547	2,516 *	-	-
121 Ch God (Abr)	20	612	560	823 *	-	-
123 Ch God (Ander)	182	NR	16,204	16,204	.1	.1
127 Ch God (Cleve)	154	13,062	9,028	16,961 *	.1	.2
143 CG in Cr(Menn)	36	4,824	NR	6,064 *	-	.1
145 Ch God Prophcy	72	2,037	NR	2,524 *	-	-
151 L-D Saints	428	NR	NR	121,394	.6	1.1
157 Ch of Brethren	88	7,142	3,533	9,090 *	-	.1
165 Ch of Nazarene	509	58,335	45,942	84,280	.4	.8
167 Chs of Christ	826	57,997	60,146	75,865	.4	.7
171 Ch God-Gen Con	24	1,512	1,252	1,988 *	-	-
173 Comm of Christ	247	32,685	NR	32,685	.2	.3
175 Congr Chr Chs	33	8,869	4,052	10,983 *	.1	.1
176 Congr Ad Afl	8	721	NR	890 *	-	-
179 Consrv Bapt	55	NR	8,210	8,210	-	.1
181 Consrv Congr	41	8,143	4,724	10,098 *	.1	.1
183 Cons Menn Conf	8	693	846	1,007	-	-
185 Cumber Presb	31	763	NR	1,447	-	-
193 Episcopal	556	NR	38,730	111,989	.6	1.0
201 Evan Cov Ch	181	25,206	30,040	36,087 *	.2	.3
203 Evan Free Ch	375	35,214	70,543	70,676	.4	.6
207 E.L.C.A.	2,885	1,211,900	471,724	1,617,468	8.4	14.8
211 Fel Evg Bib Ch	10	1,170	1,118	1,390	-	-
213 Evan Menn Inc	4	381	587	469 *	-	-
216 Evan Presby Ch	13	4,223	NR	5,232 *	-	-
220 Free Lutheran	150	16,208	10,018	21,216	.1	.2
221 Free Methodist	74	2,918	3,931	4,205	-	-
223 Free Will Bapt	198	16,034	NR	19,944 *	.1	.2
226 Friends-USA	151	8,413	NR	10,452 *	.1	.1
230 Fund Methodist	13	814	NR	1,009 *	-	-
237 Menn Br US Conf	40	6,043	NR	7,552 *	-	.1
245 Greek Orth Vslp	4	3,185	NR	6,385	-	.1
246 Greek Orthodox	20	NR	NR	11,424	.1	.1
251 Holy Orth in NA	3	NR	NR	58	-	-
252 Hindu	17	NR	NR	NR	-	-
257 Hutterian Br	69	4,554	NR	6,900	-	.1
258 IndFreeWillBapt	11	499	NR	617 *	-	-
262 Int Cou Comm Ch	9	2,027	NR	2,492 *	-	-
263 Int Foursq Gos	114	10,146	13,648	16,063 *	.1	.1
264 Int Chs of Crst	10	1,570	2,773	2,339	-	-
267 Muslim Est	54	NR	10,007	43,918	.2	.4
268 Jain	6	NR	NR	NR	-	-
283 Luth—MO Synod	1,704	543,764	255,449	699,628	3.6	6.4
286 E.PA Mennonite	2	100	NR	123 *	-	-
288 Mennonite USA	129	21,194	14,697	26,456 *	.1	.2
290 Metro Comm Ch	15	1,250	1,271	1,564 *	-	-
291 Missionary Ch	18	944	1,485	1,543	-	-
293 Morav Ch-North	11	1,455	NR	1,846	-	-
297 Mennonite;Other	41	3,176	NR	3,990 *	-	-
304 NatPrimBapt USA	4	270	NR	338 *	-	-
306 NT IndBapt&Rltd	76	8,009	NR	10,050 *	.1	.1
307 Neth Ref Congr	4	964	NR	1,853	-	-
313 N Am Bapt Conf	94	12,235	10,684	15,047 *	.1	.1
320 "Old" MB Ascs	79	6,420	NR	7,886 *	-	.1
322 Old Ord Menn Ch	15	1,441	NR	1,800 *	-	-
323 Old Ord Amish	106	5,756	NR	7,151 *	-	.1
324 Old Ord Rvr Br	1	33	55	63	-	-
331 OCA: Ter Diocs	10	1,373	NR	2,233	-	-
333 Malan Dioc Am	1	NR	NR	75	-	-
335 Orth Pres Ch	13	595	678	881	-	-
339 Pent Ch of God	94	3,127	NR	8,992	-	.1

NR–Not Reported *Total adherents estimated from known number of communicant, confirmed, full members. - Represents a percentage less than 0.1. Percentages may not total 100 due to rounding.

Table 2: Religious Congregations by Region and Group: 2000

Religious Group	Number of Churches, Synagogues, Mosques, or Temples	Number of Communicant, Confirmed, or Full Members	Number of Attendees	Total Adherents		
				Number of Adherents	% of Total Pop.	% of Total Adh.
349 Pent Holiness	54	4,723	4,049	5,914 *	-	.1
355 Presb Ch (USA)	1,283	242,883	114,931	302,559 *	1.6	2.8
356 Presb Ch Amer	60	8,687	8,679	11,573	.1	.1
360 Prim Bapt Chrch	53	NR	NR	NR	-	-
363 Primitive Meth	2	114	NR	121	-	-
365 Prog Prim Bapt	2	232	NR	282 *	-	-
369 Prot Ref Chs	4	454	NR	856	-	-
370 Ref Baptist Chs	6	NR	NR	NR	-	-
371 Ref Ch in Am	145	34,004	32,731	56,018	.3	.5
373 Ref Ch in U.S.	21	2,088	NR	2,675	-	-
388 Reg Bapt Gen As	184	17,734	18,352	22,849 *	.1	.2
395 Romania Orth Ar	1	NR	NR	262	-	-
397 OCA: Roman Dioc	2	NR	NR	475	-	-
401 Rus Orth Abroad	6	NR	NR	NR	-	-
403 Salvation Army	111	13,263	9,866	45,800	.2	.4
410 Serb Orth USA	8	NR	NR	2,659	-	-
411 Serb Orth: Grac	4	NR	NR	NR	-	-
413 S.D.A.	366	36,927	NR	43,956	.2	.4
416 Sikh	10	NR	NR	NR	-	-
418 Southw Bapt Fel	8	NR	NR	NR	-	-
419 So Bapt Conv	2,381	758,947	244,695	945,075 *	4.9	8.6
431 Ukrainian Orth	5	NR	NR	1,275	-	-
435 Unitarian-Univ	60	9,039	NR	11,189 *	.1	.1
443 Un C of Christ	832	164,887	66,921	204,356 *	1.1	1.9
449 Un Methodist	3,651	784,922	333,806	973,682 *	5.1	8.9
455 Un Ref Chs N.A.	6	685	NR	1,111	-	-
463 Vineyard	36	6,686	6,197	8,776 *	-	.1
467 Wesleyan	158	10,561	14,910	33,281	.2	.3
469 WELS	289	59,133	32,577	74,803	.4	.7
490 Zoroastrian	2	NR	NR	NR	-	-
496 Jewish Est	96	NR	NR	133,395	.7	1.2
498 Indep.Charis.	50	27,418	34,794	41,630	.2	.4
499 Indep.Non-Char	78	32,180	45,010	54,152	.3	.5
SOUTH ATLANTIC	**52,385**	**11,609,349**	**5,438,774**	**22,423,937 ***	**43.3**	**100.0**
011 A.W.M.C.	20	173	678	181	-	-
017 Amer Bapt Assn	194	22,116	NR	27,184 *	.1	.1
019 Amer Bapt USA	810	266,596	106,811	325,443 *	.6	1.5
022 Carp Rus Orth	10	1,220	NR	2,070	-	-
032 Amish; other	6	232	NR	277 *	-	-
034 Ant Orth of NA	32	4,550	NR	9,100	-	-
039 Ap Chr Ch(Naz)	6	128	196	196 *	-	-
040 Ap Chr Ch-Amer	5	136	224	224 *	-	-
049 Armen Ap Cilic	5	474	NR	1,894	-	-
050 Armen Ap Etchm	10	521	NR	5,470	-	-
053 Assemb of God	1,650	229,568	245,889	382,536	.7	1.7
055 As Ref Pres Ch	183	30,605	NR	35,903	.1	.2
056 Baha'i	248	43,926	NR	43,926	.1	.2
057 Bapt Gen Conf	36	8,280	7,755	10,901 *	-	-
059 Bapt Miss Assn	14	1,150	456	1,419 *	-	-
061 Beachy Amish	17	1,312	NR	1,611 *	-	-
071 Brethren (Ash)	22	1,838	1,641	2,224 *	-	-
075 Brethren in Cr	42	2,816	3,475	3,573	-	-
076 Buddhism	188	NR	NR	NR	-	-
078 Bulgar Orth USA	1	NR	NR	440	-	-
081 Catholic	1,783	NR	NR	5,398,257	10.4	24.1
084 Calvary Chapel	83	NR	NR	NR	-	-
089 Chr & Miss Al	320	24,469	NR	41,544	.1	.2
093 Chr Ch (Disc)	573	120,758	41,320	148,414 *	.3	.7
097 Chr Chs&Chs Cr	884	174,335	NR	214,244 *	.4	1.0
105 Christian Ref	30	3,435	2,734	4,194 *	-	-
121 Ch God (Abr)	15	857	904	1,128 *	-	-
123 Ch God (Ander)	435	NR	37,570	37,570	.1	.2
127 Ch God (Cleve)	2,324	373,426	227,399	468,230 *	.9	2.1
143 CG in Cr(Menn)	5	627	NR	784 *	-	-
145 Ch God Prophcy	727	29,119	NR	35,898 *	.1	.2
151 L-D Saints	765	NR	NR	273,371	.5	1.2
157 Ch of Brethren	355	45,102	23,131	55,371 *	.1	.2
165 Ch of Nazarene	743	94,326	72,039	127,690	.2	.6
167 Chs of Christ	1,740	157,503	155,515	205,938	.4	.9
171 Ch God-Gen Con	28	1,535	1,419	2,025 *	-	-
173 Comm of Christ	71	5,875	NR	5,875	-	-
175 Congr Chr Chs	20	2,755	1,980	3,308 *	-	-
176 Congr Ad Afl	6	918	NR	1,135 *	-	-
179 Consrv Bapt	18	NR	1,995	1,995	-	-
181 Consrv Congr	5	1,114	490	1,393 *	-	-
183 Cons Menn Conf	19	1,788	2,185	2,600	-	-
185 Cumber Presb	15	564	NR	1,008	-	-
186 Coptic Orth Ch	12	NR	NR	NR	-	-
189 Duck Rivr Bapt	1	73	NR	90 *	-	-
193 Episcopal	1,614	NR	233,307	609,000	1.2	2.7
201 Evan Cov Ch	41	3,917	3,765	5,274 *	-	-
203 Evan Free Ch	64	5,977	11,543	11,679	-	.1
207 E.L.C.A.	1,195	357,856	171,450	471,985	.9	2.1
216 Evan Presby Ch	54	15,842	NR	19,577 *	-	.1
220 Free Lutheran	2	46	56	62	-	-
221 Free Methodist	82	4,520	6,253	6,725	-	-
223 Free Will Bapt	788	59,542	NR	73,389 *	.1	.3
226 Friends-USA	208	19,339	NR	23,792 *	-	.1
237 Menn Br US Conf	6	209	NR	252 *	-	-
245 Greek Orth Vslp	5	1,432	NR	4,207	-	-
246 Greek Orthodox	88	NR	NR	70,557	.1	.3
251 Holy Orth in NA	6	NR	NR	180	-	-
252 Hindu	115	NR	NR	NR	-	-
258 IndFreeWillBapt	87	5,197	NR	6,212 *	-	-
262 Int Cou Comm Ch	26	7,685	NR	9,362 *	-	-
263 Int Foursq Gos	175	15,642	21,766	23,121 *	-	.1
264 Int Chs of Crst	21	11,922	20,589	16,995	-	.1
265 Int Pent C Chr	28	435	680	1,516	-	-
266 Intrstat & Asc	1	117	NR	143 *	-	-
267 Muslim Est	201	NR	57,676	266,027	.5	1.2
268 Jain	19	NR	NR	NR	-	-
269 Jasper&PVB Asc	31	5,659	NR	7,078 *	-	-
283 Luth—MO Synod	408	118,705	69,268	155,847	.3	.7
286 E.PA Mennonite	6	309	NR	389 *	-	-
288 Mennonite USA	141	14,604	13,379	18,902 *	-	.1
289 New Hope B Asc	20	2,131	NR	2,772 *	-	-
290 Metro Comm Ch	59	6,391	6,160	7,579 *	-	-
291 Missionary Ch	8	323	659	665	-	-
293 Morav Ch-North	4	829	NR	1,117	-	-
295 Morav Ch-South	59	15,893	NR	19,764	-	.1
297 Mennonite;Other	75	5,494	NR	6,620 *	-	-
304 NatPrimBapt USA	220	24,511	NR	30,026 *	.1	.1
306 NT IndBapt&Rltd	1	45	NR	56 *	-	-
313 N Am Bapt Conf	4	745	677	910 *	-	-
320 "Old" MB Ascs	81	13,573	NR	17,120 *	-	.1
322 Old Ord Menn Ch	7	1,005	NR	1,248 *	-	-
323 Old Ord Amish	21	1,046	NR	1,314 *	-	-
330 Macedonian Orth	1	NR	NR	600	-	-
331 OCA: Ter Diocs	38	2,283	NR	5,691	-	-
332 OCA: Bulg Dioc	1	130	NR	354	-	-
333 Malan Dioc Am	8	NR	NR	1,175	-	-
334 Malan Syr Orth	5	116	NR	526	-	-
335 Orth Pres Ch	43	2,685	3,296	3,969	-	-
336 OrigFreeWillBpt	237	37,198	NR	46,211 *	.1	.2
339 Pent Ch of God	76	2,256	NR	4,559	-	-
349 Pent Holiness	1,091	127,953	92,974	157,875 *	.3	.7
355 Presb Ch (USA)	2,651	648,166	336,220	802,353 *	1.5	3.6
356 Presb Ch Amer	579	113,934	103,331	147,211	.3	.7
360 Prim Bapt Chrch	539	NR	NR	NR	-	-
362 Prim Bapt E Dst	24	1,556	NR	1,868 *	-	-
363 Primitive Meth	4	228	NR	244	-	-
365 Prog Prim Bapt	96	6,300	NR	7,839 *	-	-
370 Ref Baptist Chs	40	NR	NR	NR	-	-
371 Ref Ch in Am	19	1,707	2,020	3,597	-	-
373 Ref Ch in U.S.	1	12	NR	19	-	-
388 Reg Bapt Gen As	93	11,181	11,968	13,961 *	-	.1
397 OCA: Roman Dioc	7	NR	NR	2,946	-	-
400 Rus Orth Moscow	2	NR	NR	NR	-	-
401 Rus Orth Abroad	12	NR	NR	NR	-	-
403 Salvation Army	191	23,888	12,236	44,805	.1	.2
409 Separate Bapt	9	368	NR	437 *	-	-
410 Serb Orth USA	9	NR	NR	4,305	-	-
411 Serb Orth: Grac	3	NR	NR	NR	-	-
413 S.D.A.	864	167,655	NR	199,508	.4	.9
416 Sikh	32	NR	NR	NR	-	-
418 Southw Bapt Fel	299	NR	NR	NR	-	-
419 So Bapt Conv	13,180	5,209,337	1,958,142	6,457,786 *	12.5	28.8

NR–Not Reported *Total adherents estimated from known number of communicant, confirmed, full members. - Represents a percentage less than 0.1. Percentages may not total 100 due to rounding.

Table 2: Religious Congregations by Region and Group: 2000

Religious Group	Number of Churches, Synagogues, Mosques, or Temples	Number of Communicant, Confirmed, or Full Members	Number of Attendees	Total Adherents: Number of Adherents	Total Adherents: % of Total Pop.	Total Adherents: % of Total Adh.
423 Syrian Orth Ch	3	NR	NR	780	-	-
425 Tao	2	NR	NR	NR	-	-
431 Ukrainian Orth	9	NR	NR	1,794	-	-
435 Unitarian-Univ	149	24,567	NR	30,060 *	.1	.1
443 Un C of Christ	560	115,631	57,218	141,861 *	.3	.6
449 Un Methodist	9,533	2,398,520	985,957	2,964,489 *	5.7	13.2
455 Un Ref Chs N.A.	2	171	NR	241	-	-
463 Vineyard	75	14,087	12,527	17,349 *	-	.1
467 Wesleyan	465	32,594	41,121	92,288	.2	.4
469 WELS	72	7,958	6,215	10,687	-	-
490 Zoroastrian	2	NR	NR	NR	-	-
496 Jewish Est	553	NR	NR	1,092,070	2.1	4.9
498 Indep.Charis.	141	121,794	108,040	163,647	.3	.7
499 Indep.Non-Char	218	161,913	154,475	222,736	.4	1.0
EAST SOUTH CENTRAL	**30,625**	**6,312,548**	**2,609,331**	**9,055,016 ***	**53.2**	**100.0**
011 A.W.M.C.	3	8	82	12	-	-
017 Amer Bapt Assn	119	17,020	NR	21,117 *	.1	.2
019 Amer Bapt USA	20	12,950	5,091	16,232 *	.1	.2
032 Amish; other	14	662	NR	828 *	-	-
034 Ant Orth of NA	8	1,598	NR	3,196	-	-
040 Ap Chr Ch-Amer	3	63	135	135 *	-	-
050 Armen Ap Etchm	2	58	NR	230	-	-
053 Assemb of God	902	111,539	104,467	149,987	.9	1.7
055 As Ref Pres Ch	28	2,820	NR	3,080	-	-
056 Baha'i	32	4,283	NR	4,283	-	-
059 Bapt Miss Assn	214	35,333	15,593	44,603 *	.3	.5
061 Beachy Amish	14	796	NR	984 *	-	-
071 Brethren (Ash)	2	56	84	68 *	-	-
075 Brethren in Cr	9	500	472	562	-	-
076 Buddhism	31	NR	NR	NR	-	-
081 Catholic	806	NR	NR	855,589	5.0	9.4
084 Calvary Chapel	20	NR	NR	NR	-	-
089 Chr & Miss Al	50	2,163	NR	4,219	-	-
093 Chr Ch (Disc)	389	89,368	30,828	111,249 *	.7	1.2
097 Chr Chs&Chs Cr	637	125,231	NR	154,298 *	.9	1.7
105 Christian Ref	1	145	95	176 *	-	-
107 Christian Un	2	28	50	50 *	-	-
121 Ch God (Abr)	1	20	25	25 *	-	-
123 Ch God (Ander)	331	NR	24,277	24,277	.1	.3
127 Ch God (Cleve)	1,141	152,239	88,197	191,315 *	1.1	2.1
143 CG in Cr(Menn)	12	1,526	NR	1,963 *	-	-
145 Ch God Prophcy	370	15,860	NR	19,623 *	.1	.2
151 L-D Saints	251	NR	NR	75,430	.4	.8
157 Ch of Brethren	30	1,711	595	2,088 *	-	-
165 Ch of Nazarene	480	50,108	35,872	67,296	.4	.7
167 Chs of Christ	3,360	338,023	345,231	437,695	2.6	4.8
171 Ch God-Gen Con	2	81	76	103 *	-	-
173 Comm of Christ	37	4,687	NR	4,687	-	.1
175 Congr Chr Chs	6	250	305	308 *	-	-
176 Congr Ad Afl	1	49	NR	61 *	-	-
179 Consrv Bapt	2	NR	215	215	-	-
183 Cons Menn Conf	7	221	269	322	-	-
185 Cumber Presb	464	32,372	NR	53,322	.3	.6
186 Coptic Orth Ch	6	NR	NR	NR	-	-
189 Duck Rivr Bapt	98	10,115	NR	12,452 *	.1	.1
191 Entrpr Bpt Asc	36	2,659	NR	3,241 *	-	-
193 Episcopal	392	NR	45,285	120,545	.7	1.3
201 Evan Cov Ch	6	374	412	519 *	-	-
203 Evan Free Ch	24	1,699	4,378	4,398	-	-
207 E.L.C.A.	127	25,806	12,896	33,350	.2	.4
216 Evan Presby Ch	26	13,069	NR	16,423 *	.1	.2
220 Free Lutheran	1	57	47	60	-	-
221 Free Methodist	30	1,082	1,755	1,812	-	-
223 Free Will Bapt	581	61,702	NR	75,670 *	.4	.8
226 Friends-USA	17	1,069	NR	1,311 *	-	-
246 Greek Orthodox	13	NR	NR	6,501	-	.1
252 Hindu	18	NR	NR	NR	-	-
258 IndFreeWillBapt	152	13,184	NR	15,960 *	.1	.2
262 Int Cou Comm Ch	15	3,600	NR	4,412 *	-	-
263 Int Foursq Gos	38	3,243	5,254	5,705 *	-	.1
264 Int Chs of Crst	6	1,324	2,225	1,852	-	-
265 Int Pent C Chr	7	440	362	1,241	-	-
266 Intrstat & Asc	85	9,104	NR	11,550 *	.1	.1
267 Muslim Est	60	NR	8,325	34,749	.2	.4
268 Jain	2	NR	NR	NR	-	-
273 LandmrkBapt,I&U	14	2,286	NR	2,881 *	-	-
283 Luth—MO Synod	175	29,637	17,710	38,242	.2	.4
288 Mennonite USA	18	634	661	850 *	-	-
290 Metro Comm Ch	16	856	926	956 *	-	-
291 Missionary Ch	3	27	140	140	-	-
297 Mennonite;Other	33	1,430	NR	1,775 *	-	-
304 NatPrimBapt USA	229	21,478	NR	26,795 *	.2	.3
320 "Old" MB Ascs	124	18,429	NR	22,638 *	.1	.3
322 Old Ord Menn Ch	14	782	NR	976 *	-	-
323 Old Ord Amish	44	2,430	NR	3,029 *	-	-
331 OCA: Ter Diocs	5	147	NR	406	-	-
335 Orth Pres Ch	9	273	397	420	-	-
339 Pent Ch of God	51	2,325	NR	4,043	-	-
349 Pent Holiness	101	7,964	5,841	9,878 *	.1	.1
355 Presb Ch (USA)	784	126,035	64,845	156,890 *	.9	1.7
356 Presb Ch Amer	303	57,691	44,087	72,473	.4	.8
360 Prim Bapt Chrch	414	NR	NR	NR	-	-
362 Prim Bapt E Dst	39	4,519	NR	5,489 *	-	.1
365 Prog Prim Bapt	13	797	NR	983 *	-	-
370 Ref Baptist Chs	13	NR	NR	NR	-	-
371 Ref Ch in Am	4	208	246	376	-	-
379 Ref Mennonite	1	8	NR	10 *	-	-
388 Reg Bapt Gen As	4	200	250	250 *	-	-
400 Rus Orth Moscow	1	NR	NR	NR	-	-
401 Rus Orth Abroad	2	NR	NR	NR	-	-
403 Salvation Army	64	7,176	3,832	12,109	.1	.1
409 Separate Bapt	56	5,570	NR	6,804 *	-	.1
413 S.D.A.	307	47,504	NR	56,532	.3	.6
416 Sikh	4	NR	NR	NR	-	-
418 Southw Bapt Fel	80	NR	NR	NR	-	-
419 So Bapt Conv	10,581	3,780,525	1,268,853	4,690,754 *	27.6	51.8
426 2Seed Sprt Bpt	2	13	NR	16 *	-	-
435 Unitarian-Univ	36	3,852	NR	4,757 *	-	.1
443 Un C of Christ	71	11,664	5,382	14,430 *	.1	.2
449 Un Methodist	5,181	943,161	397,571	1,171,024 *	6.9	12.9
463 Vineyard	27	4,280	3,704	5,484 *	-	.1
467 Wesleyan	79	3,788	4,246	8,251	-	.1
469 WELS	15	1,169	940	1,590	-	-
496 Jewish Est	62	NR	NR	40,100	.2	.4
498 Indep.Charis.	34	15,140	16,425	20,805	.1	.2
499 Indep.Non-Char	71	60,255	40,377	71,481	.4	.8
WEST SOUTH CENTRAL	**34,280**	**8,582,972**	**3,627,934**	**17,824,012 ***	**56.7**	**100.0**
011 A.W.M.C.	1	0	12	0	-	-
017 Amer Bapt Assn	1,155	164,254	NR	204,647 *	.7	1.1
019 Amer Bapt USA	38	11,804	2,980	14,916 *	-	.1
032 Amish; other	4	281	NR	352 *	-	-
034 Ant Orth of NA	21	3,438	NR	6,876	-	-
040 Ap Chr Ch-Amer	2	15	27	27 *	-	-
049 Armen Ap Cilic	3	0	NR	260	-	-
050 Armen Ap Etchm	6	247	NR	1,475	-	-
053 Assemb of God	2,458	290,060	285,723	432,627	1.4	2.4
055 As Ref Pres Ch	8	285	NR	324	-	-
056 Baha'i	97	14,880	NR	14,880	-	.1
057 Bapt Gen Conf	5	241	228	340 *	-	-
059 Bapt Miss Assn	915	182,797	66,010	228,750 *	.7	1.3
061 Beachy Amish	5	214	NR	264 *	-	-
075 Brethren in Cr	3	248	199	261	-	-
076 Buddhism	116	NR	NR	NR	-	-
081 Catholic	2,243	NR	NR	6,036,164	19.2	33.9
084 Calvary Chapel	30	NR	NR	NR	-	-
089 Chr & Miss Al	58	2,711	NR	5,190	-	-
093 Chr Ch (Disc)	630	144,202	50,633	181,761 *	.6	1.0
097 Chr Chs&Chs Cr	431	78,406	NR	98,524 *	.3	.6
105 Christian Ref	10	1,506	1,416	1,936 *	-	-
107 Christian Un	13	392	408	500 *	-	-
121 Ch God (Abr)	9	390	324	499 *	-	-
123 Ch God (Ander)	234	NR	17,967	17,967	.1	.1
127 Ch God (Cleve)	443	49,055	28,716	63,928 *	.2	.4
143 CG in Cr(Menn)	16	1,674	NR	2,126 *	-	-
145 Ch God Prophcy	179	4,981	NR	6,314 *	-	-
151 L-D Saints	631	NR	NR	211,011	.7	1.2

NR–Not Reported *Total adherents estimated from known number of communicant, confirmed, full members. - Represents a percentage less than 0.1. Percentages may not total 100 due to rounding.

Table 2: Religious Congregations by Region and Group: 2000

Religious Group	Number of Churches, Synagogues, Mosques, or Temples	Number of Communicant, Confirmed, or Full Members	Number of Attendees	Total Adherents		
				Number of Adherents	% of Total Pop.	% of Total Adh.
157 Ch of Brethren	15	851	300	1,055 *	-	-
165 Ch of Nazarene	699	79,935	54,200	108,463	.3	.6
167 Chs of Christ	3,774	442,832	424,019	572,552	1.8	3.2
171 Ch God-Gen Con	21	852	740	1,110 *	-	-
173 Comm of Christ	98	7,456	NR	7,456	-	-
175 Congr Chr Chs	5	574	309	753 *	-	-
181 Consrv Congr	1	20	20	25 *	-	-
183 Cons Menn Conf	5	320	391	464	-	-
185 Cumber Presb	136	8,984	NR	13,870	-	.1
186 Coptic Orth Ch	13	NR	NR	NR	-	-
193 Episcopal	657	NR	90,970	244,854	.8	1.4
201 Evan Cov Ch	17	2,656	5,389	5,874 *	-	-
203 Evan Free Ch	57	5,850	11,215	11,273	-	.1
207 E.L.C.A.	489	137,803	66,530	177,820	.6	1.0
211 Fel Evg Bib Ch	2	62	0	62	-	-
216 Evan Presby Ch	12	1,550	NR	1,980 *	-	-
220 Free Lutheran	10	575	415	668	-	-
221 Free Methodist	41	1,339	1,555	1,921	-	-
223 Free Will Bapt	511	46,660	NR	58,007 *	.2	.3
226 Friends-USA	50	2,071	NR	2,587 *	-	-
237 Menn Br US Conf	26	2,839	NR	3,563 *	-	-
245 Greek Orth Vslp	1	105	NR	135	-	-
246 Greek Orthodox	26	NR	NR	12,162	-	.1
251 Holy Orth in NA	1	NR	NR	6	-	-
252 Hindu	42	NR	NR	NR	-	-
258 IndFreeWillBapt	2	134	NR	169 *	-	-
262 Int Cou Comm Ch	7	1,411	NR	1,791 *	-	-
263 Int Foursq Gos	130	11,311	13,529	17,247 *	.1	.1
264 Int Chs of Crst	13	3,544	5,514	4,816	-	-
266 Intrstat & Asc	35	3,516	NR	4,434 *	-	-
267 Muslim Est	130	NR	33,588	136,238	.4	.8
268 Jain	9	NR	NR	NR	-	-
273 LandmrkBapt,I&U	13	901	NR	1,087 *	-	-
283 Luth—MO Synod	542	149,256	82,705	193,184	.6	1.1
286 E.PA Mennonite	1	51	NR	65 *	-	-
288 Mennonite USA	43	2,464	2,132	3,220 *	-	-
290 Metro Comm Ch	25	4,701	4,249	5,923 *	-	-
291 Missionary Ch	4	219	403	403	-	-
297 Mennonite;Other	13	1,515	NR	2,008 *	-	-
304 NatPrimBapt USA	62	3,540	NR	4,463 *	-	-
306 NT IndBapt&Rltd	1	40	NR	47 *	-	-
313 N Am Bapt Conf	19	1,626	1,491	2,066 *	-	-
320 "Old" MB Ascs	1	6	NR	7 *	-	-
323 Old Ord Amish	9	310	NR	389 *	-	-
331 OCA: Ter Diocs	9	381	NR	2,160	-	-
333 Malan Dioc Am	11	NR	NR	2,925	-	-
334 Malan Syr Orth	4	190	NR	950	-	-
335 Orth Pres Ch	18	653	790	982	-	-
339 Pent Ch of God	361	15,105	NR	29,232	.1	.2
349 Pent Holiness	314	34,206	25,018	43,030 *	.1	.2
355 Presb Ch (USA)	937	206,263	98,497	262,013 *	.8	1.5
356 Presb Ch Amer	96	13,633	11,622	18,270	.1	.1
360 Prim Bapt Chrch	210	NR	NR	NR	-	-
365 Prog Prim Bapt	4	223	NR	277 *	-	-
370 Ref Baptist Chs	17	NR	NR	NR	-	-
371 Ref Ch in Am	7	1,511	1,265	3,192	-	-
388 Reg Bapt Gen As	18	1,014	1,084	1,236 *	-	-
397 OCA: Roman Dioc	2	NR	NR	413	-	-
401 Rus Orth Abroad	6	NR	NR	NR	-	-
403 Salvation Army	100	11,700	7,873	41,667	.1	.2
410 Serb Orth USA	3	NR	NR	1,110	-	-
411 Serb Orth: Grac	2	NR	NR	NR	-	-
413 S.D.A.	479	59,852	NR	71,233	.2	.4
416 Sikh	15	NR	NR	NR	-	-
418 Southw Bapt Fel	20	NR	NR	NR	-	-
419 So Bapt Conv	9,358	4,690,527	1,441,960	5,920,576 *	18.8	33.2
423 Syrian Orth Ch	1	NR	NR	60	-	-
425 Tao	3	NR	NR	NR	-	-
426 2Seed Sprt Bpt	1	24	NR	29 *	-	-
431 Ukrainian Orth	1	NR	NR	180	-	-
435 Unitarian-Univ	69	8,461	NR	10,729 *	-	.1
443 Un C of Christ	106	17,454	7,729	22,124 *	.1	.1
449 Un Methodist	4,040	1,332,612	478,001	1,684,672 *	5.4	9.5
463 Vineyard	55	12,314	9,680	16,054 *	.1	.1
467 Wesleyan	30	1,686	3,067	6,769	-	-
469 WELS	52	5,470	4,063	7,585	-	-
490 Zoroastrian	3	NR	NR	NR	-	-
496 Jewish Est	129	NR	NR	151,150	.5	.8
498 Indep.Charis.	113	163,842	152,903	226,618	.7	1.3
499 Indep.Non-Char	154	125,891	130,075	162,640	.5	.9
MOUNTAIN	**18,030**	**1,684,192**	**1,113,359**	**8,418,559 ***	**46.3**	**100.0**
011 A.W.M.C.	4	70	183	71	-	-
017 Amer Bapt Assn	68	3,155	NR	4,018 *	-	-
019 Amer Bapt USA	237	51,502	26,442	64,738 *	.4	.8
032 Amish; other	3	62	NR	77 *	-	-
034 Ant Orth of NA	17	1,888	NR	3,776	-	-
039 Ap Chr Ch(Naz)	5	379	671	671 *	-	-
040 Ap Chr Ch-Amer	4	239	433	433 *	-	-
050 Armen Ap Etchm	5	0	NR	2,723	-	-
053 Assemb of God	894	113,057	120,408	217,039	1.2	2.6
055 As Ref Pres Ch	1	29	NR	32	-	-
056 Baha'i	116	14,088	NR	14,088	.1	.2
057 Bapt Gen Conf	53	8,685	11,447	13,301 *	.1	.2
059 Bapt Miss Assn	13	562	511	829 *	-	-
071 Brethren (Ash)	6	326	412	405 *	-	-
075 Brethren in Cr	4	102	109	133	-	-
076 Buddhism	155	NR	NR	NR	-	-
081 Catholic	1,543	NR	NR	3,207,346	17.6	38.1
084 Calvary Chapel	105	NR	NR	NR	-	-
089 Chr & Miss Al	114	5,837	NR	13,959	.1	.2
093 Chr Ch (Disc)	119	28,706	12,018	35,850 *	.2	.4
097 Chr Chs&Chs Cr	262	69,960	NR	88,370 *	.5	1.0
105 Christian Ref	63	10,022	8,321	12,737 *	.1	.2
121 Ch God (Abr)	2	91	82	115 *	-	-
123 Ch God (Ander)	85	NR	9,934	9,934	.1	.1
127 Ch God (Cleve)	175	14,489	9,369	19,073 *	.1	.2
143 CG in Cr(Menn)	11	953	NR	1,215 *	-	-
145 Ch God Prophcy	74	2,128	NR	2,689 *	-	-
151 L-D Saints	6,245	NR	NR	2,378,624	13.1	28.3
157 Ch of Brethren	24	1,767	919	2,330 *	-	-
165 Ch of Nazarene	353	47,293	39,421	64,119	.4	.8
167 Chs of Christ	626	46,877	47,924	61,484	.3	.7
171 Ch God-Gen Con	3	26	142	142 *	-	-
173 Comm of Christ	70	6,742	NR	6,742	-	.1
175 Congr Chr Chs	11	1,943	1,287	2,446 *	-	-
176 Congr Ad Afl	1	838	NR	1,039 *	-	-
179 Consrv Bapt	210	NR	35,583	35,583	.2	.4
181 Consrv Congr	16	2,583	1,638	3,270 *	-	-
183 Cons Menn Conf	7	271	330	395	-	-
185 Cumber Presb	3	1,060	NR	2,602	-	-
186 Coptic Orth Ch	3	NR	NR	NR	-	-
193 Episcopal	413	NR	42,190	113,008	.6	1.3
201 Evan Cov Ch	26	4,601	7,509	8,095 *	-	.1
203 Evan Free Ch	141	12,599	27,117	27,253	.1	.3
207 E.L.C.A.	483	173,470	87,927	237,840	1.3	2.8
211 Fel Evg Bib Ch	2	136	37	154	-	-
216 Evan Presby Ch	24	11,817	NR	15,225 *	.1	.2
220 Free Lutheran	11	592	637	867	-	-
221 Free Methodist	42	2,249	4,424	4,584	-	.1
223 Free Will Bapt	31	827	NR	1,049 *	-	-
226 Friends-USA	88	4,278	NR	5,410 *	-	.1
237 Menn Br US Conf	10	689	NR	852 *	-	-
246 Greek Orthodox	30	NR	NR	15,336	.1	.2
249 Assyr Apost Ch	1	NR	NR	1,568	-	-
251 Holy Orth in NA	2	NR	NR	45	-	-
252 Hindu	24	NR	NR	NR	-	-
257 Hutterian Br	48	3,168	NR	4,800	-	.1
262 Int Cou Comm Ch	10	2,423	NR	2,996 *	-	-
263 Int Foursq Gos	226	19,760	32,318	34,455 *	.2	.4
264 Int Chs of Crst	12	3,238	5,718	4,807	-	.1
265 Int Pent C Chr	1	0	0	15	-	-
267 Muslim Est	45	NR	8,899	36,492	.2	.4
268 Jain	2	NR	NR	NR	-	-
283 Luth—MO Synod	410	97,351	55,257	129,903	.7	1.5
288 Mennonite USA	47	3,477	2,970	4,574 *	-	.1
290 Metro Comm Ch	18	1,138	1,041	1,416 *	-	-
291 Missionary Ch	6	1,573	2,085	2,093	-	-

NR–Not Reported *Total adherents estimated from known number of communicant, confirmed, full members. - Represents a percentage less than 0.1. Percentages may not total 100 due to rounding.

Table 2: Religious Congregations by Region and Group: 2000

Religious Group	Number of Churches, Synagogues, Mosques, or Temples	Number of Communicant, Confirmed, or Full Members	Number of Attendees	Total Adherents		
				Number of Adherents	% of Total Pop.	% of Total Adh.
293 Morav Ch-North	1	61	NR	100	-	-
297 Mennonite;Other	18	589	NR	748 *	-	-
306 NT IndBapt&Rltd	87	8,895	NR	11,069 *	.1	.1
313 N Am Bapt Conf	10	849	883	1,076 *	-	-
323 Old Ord Amish	4	190	NR	238 *	-	-
331 OCA: Ter Diocs	17	744	NR	2,220	-	-
333 Malan Dioc Am	1	NR	NR	75	-	-
335 Orth Pres Ch	15	924	1,109	1,334	-	-
339 Pent Ch of God	108	3,934	NR	7,397	-	.1
349 Pent Holiness	50	2,326	2,305	2,916 *	-	-
355 Presb Ch (USA)	465	105,028	63,659	132,132 *	.7	1.6
356 Presb Ch Amer	42	4,555	5,505	6,547	-	.1
360 Prim Bapt Chrch	17	NR	NR	NR	-	-
369 Prot Ref Chs	1	144	NR	24	-	-
370 Ref Baptist Chs	11	NR	NR	NR	-	-
371 Ref Ch in Am	24	4,004	4,566	7,805	-	.1
373 Ref Ch in U.S.	3	100	NR	144	-	-
388 Reg Bapt Gen As	68	5,145	6,101	6,753 *	-	.1
395 Romania Orth Ar	1	NR	NR	630	-	-
397 OCA: Roman Dioc	3	NR	NR	878	-	-
401 Rus Orth Abroad	6	NR	NR	NR	-	-
403 Salvation Army	84	8,012	4,906	21,894	.1	.3
410 Serb Orth USA	6	NR	NR	2,220	-	-
411 Serb Orth: Grac	1	NR	NR	NR	-	-
413 S.D.A.	352	43,285	NR	51,511	.3	.6
416 Sikh	20	NR	NR	NR	-	-
418 Southw Bapt Fel	4	NR	NR	NR	-	-
419 So Bapt Conv	1,289	361,694	141,372	457,640 *	2.5	5.4
420 Strict Baptists	1	6	NR	8 *	-	-
423 Syrian Orth Ch	1	NR	NR	60	-	-
425 Tao	4	NR	NR	NR	-	-
431 Ukrainian Orth	1	NR	NR	66	-	-
435 Unitarian-Univ	60	8,029	NR	10,018 *	.1	.1
443 Un C of Christ	177	38,300	18,093	48,049 *	.3	.6
449 Un Methodist	729	188,022	96,926	236,446 *	1.3	2.8
455 Un Ref Chs N.A.	3	399	NR	630	-	-
463 Vineyard	68	17,491	14,615	22,006 *	.1	.3
467 Wesleyan	60	3,719	6,325	13,257	.1	.2
469 WELS	113	15,054	10,843	20,778	.1	.2
490 Zoroastrian	4	NR	NR	NR	-	-
496 Jewish Est	128	NR	NR	248,105	1.4	2.9
498 Indep.Charis.	44	37,455	55,548	93,920	.5	1.1
499 Indep.Non-Char	66	46,122	74,890	84,630	.5	1.0
PACIFIC	**26,520**	**3,519,555**	**2,700,995**	**19,282,125 ***	**42.8**	**100.0**
011 A.W.M.C.	1	24	120	28	-	-
017 Amer Bapt Assn	177	10,904	NR	13,999 *	-	.1
019 Amer Bapt USA	742	165,324	117,010	218,416 *	.5	1.1
034 Ant Orth of NA	38	6,916	NR	13,832	-	.1
039 Ap Chr Ch(Naz)	12	484	740	749 *	-	-
040 Ap Chr Ch-Amer	4	227	498	498 *	-	-
049 Armen Ap Cilic	8	5,200	NR	29,200	.1	.2
050 Armen Ap Etchm	20	0	NR	25,595	.1	.1
053 Assemb of God	1,958	269,080	312,909	498,963	1.1	2.6
055 As Ref Pres Ch	10	392	NR	424	-	-
056 Baha'i	388	35,223	NR	35,223	.1	.2
057 Bapt Gen Conf	223	43,520	79,056	90,061 *	.2	.5
059 Bapt Miss Assn	25	1,831	1,107	2,394 *	-	-
071 Brethren (Ash)	4	94	186	123 *	-	-
075 Brethren in Cr	20	1,513	1,836	1,987	-	-
076 Buddhism	686	NR	NR	NR	-	-
081 Catholic	2,039	NR	NR	11,438,854	25.4	59.3
084 Calvary Chapel	345	NR	NR	NR	-	-
089 Chr & Miss Al	331	40,362	NR	76,183	.2	.4
093 Chr Ch (Disc)	262	47,463	18,320	60,170 *	.1	.3
097 Chr Chs&Chs Cr	473	118,543	NR	150,053 *	.3	.8
105 Christian Ref	162	28,293	24,630	36,170 *	.1	.2
121 Ch God (Abr)	5	51	165	186 *	-	-
123 Ch God (Ander)	242	NR	32,281	32,281	.1	.2
127 Ch God (Cleve)	310	28,168	19,744	37,718 *	.1	.2
143 CG in Cr(Menn)	6	1,012	NR	1,354 *	-	-
145 Ch God Prophcy	171	6,614	NR	8,490 *	-	-
151 L-D Saints	2,241	NR	NR	873,664	1.9	4.5
157 Ch of Brethren	45	4,493	1,588	5,761 *	-	-
165 Ch of Nazarene	711	105,977	86,479	155,726	.3	.8
167 Chs of Christ	997	86,317	86,750	113,034	.3	.6
171 Ch God-Gen Con	8	384	334	555 *	-	-
173 Comm of Christ	110	13,473	NR	13,473	-	.1
175 Congr Chr Chs	46	8,309	4,974	10,697 *	-	.1
176 Congr Ad Afl	10	747	NR	935 *	-	-
179 Consrv Bapt	474	NR	109,116	109,116	.2	.6
181 Consrv Congr	18	6,877	6,148	8,819 *	-	-
185 Cumber Presb	5	819	NR	1,153	-	-
186 Coptic Orth Ch	21	NR	NR	NR	-	-
193 Episcopal	769	NR	91,169	252,632	.6	1.3
201 Evan Cov Ch	174	29,688	44,706	49,909 *	.1	.3
203 Evan Free Ch	239	34,187	62,468	63,657	.1	.3
207 E.L.C.A.	905	263,055	133,852	359,791	.8	1.9
211 Fel Evg Bib Ch	2	475	180	180	-	-
216 Evan Presby Ch	9	1,898	NR	2,363 *	-	-
220 Free Lutheran	16	1,357	1,178	1,821	-	-
221 Free Methodist	178	15,173	23,915	25,041	.1	.1
223 Free Will Bapt	69	3,379	NR	4,381 *	-	-
226 Friends-USA	185	14,360	NR	18,413 *	-	.1
237 Menn Br US Conf	87	12,281	NR	15,885 *	-	.1
245 Greek Orth Vslp	10	2,602	NR	4,323	-	-
246 Greek Orthodox	53	NR	NR	42,519	.1	.2
249 Assyr Apost Ch	9	NR	NR	8,164	-	-
251 Holy Orth in NA	5	NR	NR	391	-	-
252 Hindu	164	NR	NR	NR	-	-
257 Hutterian Br	6	396	NR	600	-	-
262 Int Cou Comm Ch	31	5,433	NR	6,819 *	-	-
263 Int Foursq Gos	881	132,951	206,124	209,743 *	.5	1.1
264 Int Chs of Crst	11	16,972	27,613	22,691	.1	.1
267 Muslim Est	192	NR	63,008	282,529	.6	1.5
268 Jain	9	NR	NR	NR	-	-
273 LandmrkBapt,I&U	32	1,369	NR	1,714 *	-	-
283 Luth—MO Synod	629	149,373	85,818	199,286	.4	1.0
288 Mennonite USA	64	4,310	4,276	5,753 *	-	-
290 Metro Comm Ch	39	2,951	2,681	3,547 *	-	-
291 Missionary Ch	48	8,993	11,570	12,088	-	.1
292 Morav Ch-AK	24	1,765	NR	2,562 *	-	-
293 Morav Ch-North	2	261	NR	345	-	-
297 Mennonite;Other	21	1,848	NR	2,317 *	-	-
304 NatPrimBapt USA	4	855	NR	1,104 *	-	-
306 NT IndBapt&Rltd	96	14,855	NR	18,720 *	-	.1
307 Neth Ref Congr	3	165	NR	336	-	-
313 N Am Bapt Conf	81	16,996	21,428	21,802 *	-	.1
323 Old Ord Amish	1	27	NR	34 *	-	-
330 Macedonian Orth	1	NR	NR	600	-	-
331 OCA: Ter Diocs	81	8,306	NR	27,383	.1	.1
332 OCA: Bulg Dioc	8	573	NR	4,375	-	-
333 Malan Dioc Am	2	NR	NR	525	-	-
334 Malan Syr Orth	1	18	NR	90	-	-
335 Orth Pres Ch	57	3,510	4,270	5,094	-	-
339 Pent Ch of God	312	10,830	NR	29,815	.1	.2
349 Pent Holiness	165	12,859	13,835	16,483 *	-	.1
355 Presb Ch (USA)	984	271,448	188,078	346,281 *	.8	1.8
356 Presb Ch Amer	99	9,550	10,990	12,983	-	.1
360 Prim Bapt Chrch	31	NR	NR	NR	-	-
369 Prot Ref Chs	2	208	NR	376	-	-
370 Ref Baptist Chs	34	NR	NR	NR	-	-
371 Ref Ch in Am	54	15,097	20,388	39,917	.1	.2
373 Ref Ch in U.S.	10	635	NR	931	-	-
388 Reg Bapt Gen As	190	21,189	27,156	29,202 *	.1	.2
395 Romania Orth Ar	1	NR	NR	438	-	-
397 OCA: Roman Dioc	10	NR	NR	3,399	-	-
400 Rus Orth Moscow	3	NR	NR	NR	-	-
401 Rus Orth Abroad	26	NR	NR	NR	-	-
403 Salvation Army	222	22,876	16,821	74,699	.2	.4
410 Serb Orth USA	14	NR	NR	7,905	-	-
411 Serb Orth: Grac	5	NR	NR	NR	-	-
413 S.D.A.	905	228,024	NR	271,363	.6	1.4
416 Sikh	70	NR	NR	NR	-	-
418 Southw Bapt Fel	7	NR	NR	NR	-	-
419 So Bapt Conv	1,879	476,304	217,672	609,721 *	1.4	3.2
423 Syrian Orth Ch	7	NR	NR	7,625	-	-
425 Tao	21	NR	NR	NR	-	-

NR–Not Reported   *Total adherents estimated from known number of communicant, confirmed, full members.   - Represents a percentage less than 0.1.   Percentages may not total 100 due to rounding.

Table 2: Religious Congregations by Region and Group: 2000

	Religious Group	Number of Churches, Synagogues, Mosques, or Temples	Number of Communicant, Confirmed, or Full Members	Number of Attendees	Total Adherents		
					Number of Adherents	% of Total Pop.	% of Total Adh.
431	Ukrainian Orth	5	NR	NR	1,413	-	-
435	Unitarian-Univ	127	20,061	NR	25,017 *	.1	.1
443	Un C of Christ	474	76,524	39,362	95,596 *	.2	.5
449	Un Methodist	1,202	280,475	144,465	352,993 *	.8	1.8
455	Un Ref Chs N.A.	14	2,124	NR	3,073	-	-
463	Vineyard	146	29,184	23,352	37,116 *	.1	.2
467	Wesleyan	92	9,053	12,376	28,615	.1	.1
469	WELS	94	11,800	8,332	15,698	-	.1
490	Zoroastrian	13	NR	NR	NR	-	-
496	Jewish Est	485	NR	NR	1,079,650	2.4	5.6
498	Indep.Charis.	110	123,422	118,053	248,630	.6	1.3
499	Indep.Non-Char	161	108,876	171,868	197,775	.4	1.0

Religious Group	Number of Churches, Synagogues, Mosques, or Temples	Number of Communicant, Confirmed, or Full Members	Number of Attendees	Total Adherents		
				Number of Adherents	% of Total Pop.	% of Total Adh.

NR–Not Reported *Total adherents estimated from known number of communicant, confirmed, full members. - Represents a percentage less than 0.1. Percentages may not total 100 due to rounding.

Table 3: Religious Congregations by State and Group: 2000

Religious Group	Number of Churches, Synagogues, Mosques, or Temples	Number of Communicant, Confirmed, or Full Members	Number of Attendees	Total Adherents: Number of Adherents	Total Adherents: % of Total Pop.	Total Adherents: % of Total Adh.
ALABAMA	**8,343**	**1,758,393**	**760,721**	**2,435,373 ***	**54.8**	**100.0**
017 Amer Bapt Assn	36	5,038	NR	6,286 *	.1	.3
019 Amer Bapt USA	3	6,622	2,774	8,304 *	.2	.3
034 Ant Orth of NA	1	0	NR	0	-	-
040 Ap Chr Ch-Amer	1	45	90	90 *	-	-
053 Assemb of God	367	43,599	42,053	59,970	1.3	2.5
055 As Ref Pres Ch	8	360	NR	388	-	-
056 Baha'i	9	1,423	NR	1,423	-	.1
059 Bapt Miss Assn	17	1,676	934	2,106 *	-	.1
061 Beachy Amish	2	52	NR	66 *	-	-
076 Buddhism	7	NR	NR	NR	-	-
081 Catholic	168	NR	NR	150,647	3.4	6.2
084 Calvary Chapel	2	NR	NR	NR	-	-
089 Chr & Miss Al	19	768	NR	1,150	-	-
093 Chr Ch (Disc)	56	7,653	3,213	9,572 *	.2	.4
097 Chr Chs&Chs Cr	30	3,172	NR	3,972 *	.1	.2
107 Christian Un	2	28	50	50 *	-	-
123 Ch God (Ander)	68	NR	4,082	4,082	.1	.2
127 Ch God (Cleve)	386	55,226	31,652	68,766 *	1.5	2.8
143 CG in Cr(Menn)	2	316	NR	405 *	-	-
145 Ch God Prophcy	88	3,154	NR	3,908 *	.1	.2
151 L-D Saints	69	NR	NR	20,397	.5	.8
157 Ch of Brethren	5	240	50	305 *	-	-
165 Ch of Nazarene	123	11,222	7,420	13,635	.3	.6
167 Chs of Christ	895	92,243	94,188	119,049	2.7	4.9
173 Comm of Christ	17	2,083	NR	2,083	-	.1
175 Congr Chr Chs	5	185	249	230 *	-	-
176 Congr Ad Afl	1	49	NR	61 *	-	-
179 Consrv Bapt	1	NR	15	15	-	-
185 Cumber Presb	61	4,436	NR	6,590	.1	.3
186 Coptic Orth Ch	2	NR	NR	NR	-	-
189 Duck Rivr Bapt	26	3,151	NR	3,896 *	.1	.2
193 Episcopal	118	NR	15,858	45,041	1.0	1.8
201 Evan Cov Ch	3	207	235	273 *	-	-
203 Evan Free Ch	3	233	525	525	-	-
207 E.L.C.A.	24	4,026	2,319	5,346	.1	.2
216 Evan Presby Ch	2	174	NR	218 *	-	-
220 Free Lutheran	1	57	47	60	-	-
221 Free Methodist	5	141	139	166	-	-
223 Free Will Bapt	165	19,252	NR	23,716 *	.5	1.0
226 Friends-USA	2	128	NR	159 *	-	-
246 Greek Orthodox	4	NR	NR	2,796	.1	.1
252 Hindu	3	NR	NR	NR	-	-
258 IndFreeWillBapt	3	127	NR	154 *	-	-
262 Int Cou Comm Ch	10	1,970	NR	2,442 *	.1	.1
263 Int Foursq Gos	6	750	1,069	1,200 *	-	-
264 Int Chs of Crst	1	107	216	169	-	-
266 Intrstat & Asc	7	926	NR	1,175 *	-	-
267 Muslim Est	20	NR	2,207	7,670	.2	.3
283 Luth—MO Synod	63	9,242	5,506	11,488	.3	.5
288 Mennonite USA	1	45	40	55 *	-	-
290 Metro Comm Ch	6	352	454	444 *	-	-
297 Mennonite;Other	14	474	NR	587 *	-	-
304 NatPrimBapt USA	113	13,552	NR	16,984 *	.4	.7
320 "Old" MB Ascs	29	3,503	NR	4,324 *	.1	.2
331 OCA: Ter Diocs	3	61	NR	204	-	-
335 Orth Pres Ch	2	37	60	61	-	-
339 Pent Ch of God	5	160	NR	285	-	-
349 Pent Holiness	42	3,706	2,372	4,601 *	.1	.2
355 Presb Ch (USA)	158	27,110	14,533	34,551 *	.8	1.4
356 Presb Ch Amer	108	19,265	13,996	24,020	.5	1.0
360 Prim Bapt Chrch	147	NR	NR	NR	-	-
365 Prog Prim Bapt	6	426	NR	530 *	-	-
370 Ref Baptist Chs	3	NR	NR	NR	-	-
400 Rus Orth Moscow	1	NR	NR	NR	-	-
401 Rus Orth Abroad	1	NR	NR	NR	-	-
403 Salvation Army	15	1,390	661	2,468	.1	.1
413 S.D.A.	80	14,108	NR	16,792	.4	.7
416 Sikh	1	NR	NR	NR	-	-
418 Southw Bapt Fel	20	NR	NR	NR	-	-
419 So Bapt Conv	3,148	1,112,560	382,473	1,380,121 *	31.0	56.7
426 2Seed Sprt Bpt	1	3	NR	4 *	-	-
435 Unitarian-Univ	9	710	NR	879 *	-	-
443 Un C of Christ	23	2,761	1,282	3,412 *	.1	.1
449 Un Methodist	1,416	263,880	116,939	327,734 *	7.4	13.5
463 Vineyard	13	1,515	1,343	1,902 *	-	.1
467 Wesleyan	12	1,519	1,662	2,312	.1	.1
469 WELS	3	165	130	210	-	-
496 Jewish Est	18	NR	NR	9,100	.2	.4
498 Indep.Charis.	14	4,935	4,875	6,430	.1	.3
499 Indep.Non-Char	14	6,075	5,010	7,319	.2	.3
ALASKA	**856**	**82,963**	**50,988**	**215,223 ***	**34.3**	**100.0**
019 Amer Bapt USA	12	1,802	858	2,343 *	.4	1.1
034 Ant Orth of NA	3	383	NR	766	.1	.4
053 Assemb of God	81	5,585	7,118	11,638	1.9	5.4
057 Bapt Gen Conf	4	260	292	347 *	.1	.2
076 Buddhism	11	NR	NR	NR	-	-
081 Catholic	102	NR	NR	54,359	8.7	25.3
084 Calvary Chapel	2	NR	NR	NR	-	-
089 Chr & Miss Al	15	658	NR	1,433	.2	.7
093 Chr Ch (Disc)	1	197	95	255 *	-	.1
097 Chr Chs&Chs Cr	12	2,682	NR	3,473 *	.6	1.6
105 Christian Ref	4	298	320	387 *	.1	.2
123 Ch God (Ander)	7	NR	538	538	.1	.2
127 Ch God (Cleve)	21	2,140	1,174	2,833 *	.5	1.3
145 Ch God Prophcy	4	121	NR	158 *	-	.1
151 L-D Saints	64	NR	NR	19,019	3.0	8.8
165 Ch of Nazarene	25	2,034	1,786	3,670	.6	1.7
167 Chs of Christ	24	1,668	1,824	2,283	.4	1.1
173 Comm of Christ	2	392	NR	392	.1	.2
175 Congr Chr Chs	5	520	280	673 *	.1	.3
179 Consrv Bapt	5	NR	920	920	.1	.4
193 Episcopal	44	NR	2,205	6,693	1.1	3.1
201 Evan Cov Ch	18	1,060	1,718	1,990 *	.3	.9
203 Evan Free Ch	2	129	235	235	-	.1
207 E.L.C.A.	30	7,349	3,281	11,343	1.8	5.3
221 Free Methodist	2	91	137	137	-	.1
223 Free Will Bapt	1	0	NR	0 *	-	-
226 Friends-USA	14	1,246	NR	1,803 *	.3	.8
246 Greek Orthodox	1	NR	NR	450	.1	.2
252 Hindu	1	NR	NR	NR	-	-
262 Int Cou Comm Ch	1	13	NR	17 *	-	-
263 Int Foursq Gos	7	213	367	368 *	.1	.2
264 Int Chs of Crst	1	156	244	219	-	.1
267 Muslim Est	3	NR	367	1,381	.2	.6
283 Luth—MO Synod	12	2,835	1,823	4,128	.7	1.9
288 Mennonite USA	1	18	30	30 *	-	-
290 Metro Comm Ch	1	11	23	23 *	-	-
292 Morav Ch-AK	24	1,765	NR	2,562 *	.4	1.2
331 OCA: Ter Diocs	46	6,705	NR	20,000	3.2	9.3
335 Orth Pres Ch	2	71	128	128	-	.1
339 Pent Ch of God	5	121	NR	268	-	.1
349 Pent Holiness	8	137	177	185 *	-	.1
355 Presb Ch (USA)	37	4,784	3,932	6,311 *	1.0	2.9
370 Ref Baptist Chs	1	NR	NR	NR	-	-
388 Reg Bapt Gen As	7	506	727	691 *	.1	.3
403 Salvation Army	22	1,599	861	2,919	.5	1.4
410 Serb Orth USA	1	NR	NR	40	-	-
413 S.D.A.	32	3,228	NR	3,841	.6	1.8
416 Sikh	2	NR	NR	NR	-	-
419 So Bapt Conv	68	17,705	7,223	22,959 *	3.7	10.7
435 Unitarian-Univ	5	355	NR	457 *	.1	.2
449 Un Methodist	28	3,972	2,532	5,133 *	.8	2.4
463 Vineyard	1	400	336	518 *	.1	.2
467 Wesleyan	3	19	47	92	-	-
469 WELS	9	883	640	1,290	.2	.6
496 Jewish Est	5	NR	NR	3,525	.6	1.6
498 Indep.Charis.	3	1,752	1,850	2,400	.4	1.1
499 Indep.Non-Char	4	7,100	6,900	7,600	1.2	3.5
ARIZONA	**3,307**	**471,913**	**337,369**	**2,048,023 ***	**39.9**	**100.0**
011 A.W.M.C.	1	0	33	0	-	-
017 Amer Bapt Assn	24	980	NR	1,252 *	-	.1
019 Amer Bapt USA	44	9,535	5,086	12,129 *	.2	.6
034 Ant Orth of NA	3	788	NR	1,576	-	.1
039 Ap Chr Ch(Naz)	2	218	370	370 *	-	-

NR–Not Reported *Total adherents estimated from known number of communicant, confirmed, full members. - Represents a percentage less than 0.1. Percentages may not total 100 due to rounding.

Table 3: Religious Congregations by State and Group: 2000

Religious Group	Number of Churches, Synagogues, Mosques, or Temples	Number of Communicant, Confirmed, or Full Members	Number of Attendees	Total Adherents		
				Number of Adherents	% of Total Pop.	% of Total Adh.
040 Ap Chr Ch-Amer	3	199	343	343 *	-	-
050 Armen Ap Etchm	1	0	NR	1,232	-	.1
053 Assemb of God	243	42,122	36,471	82,802	1.6	4.0
056 Baha'i	30	5,690	NR	5,690	.1	.3
057 Bapt Gen Conf	11	2,012	3,228	3,452 *	.1	.2
059 Bapt Miss Assn	4	122	95	170 *	-	-
071 Brethren (Ash)	4	268	337	333 *	-	-
076 Buddhism	25	NR	NR	NR	-	-
081 Catholic	267	NR	NR	974,883	19.0	47.6
084 Calvary Chapel	28	NR	NR	NR	-	-
089 Chr & Miss Al	21	893	NR	1,736	-	.1
093 Chr Ch (Disc)	19	4,233	2,086	5,338 *	.1	.3
097 Chr Chs&Chs Cr	72	26,226	NR	33,162 *	.6	1.6
105 Christian Ref	12	1,333	956	1,731 *	-	.1
121 Ch God (Abr)	1	86	77	109 *	-	-
123 Ch God (Ander)	22	NR	4,518	4,518	.1	.2
127 Ch God (Cleve)	62	5,876	3,787	7,719 *	.2	.4
143 CG in Cr(Menn)	3	174	NR	221 *	-	-
145 Ch God Prophcy	15	526	NR	675 *	-	-
151 L-D Saints	643	NR	NR	251,974	4.9	12.3
157 Ch of Brethren	4	296	208	375 *	-	-
165 Ch of Nazarene	102	12,922	10,282	18,143	.4	.9
167 Chs of Christ	138	11,376	11,395	14,471	.3	.7
171 Ch God-Gen Con	1	13	80	80 *	-	-
173 Comm of Christ	11	1,993	NR	1,993	-	.1
175 Congr Chr Chs	3	512	485	651 *	-	-
179 Consrv Bapt	104	NR	17,362	17,362	.3	.8
183 Cons Menn Conf	4	151	184	220	-	-
185 Cumber Presb	1	36	NR	36	-	-
186 Coptic Orth Ch	2	NR	NR	NR	-	-
193 Episcopal	70	NR	10,927	31,104	.6	1.5
201 Evan Cov Ch	6	748	1,027	1,075 *	-	.1
203 Evan Free Ch	27	2,353	5,016	5,026	.1	.2
207 E.L.C.A.	96	51,000	31,875	69,393	1.4	3.4
216 Evan Presby Ch	4	398	NR	507 *	-	-
220 Free Lutheran	4	150	150	210	-	-
221 Free Methodist	15	816	1,127	1,283	-	.1
223 Free Will Bapt	9	306	NR	388 *	-	-
226 Friends-USA	9	542	NR	695 *	-	-
237 Menn Br US Conf	3	57	NR	73 *	-	-
246 Greek Orthodox	5	NR	NR	4,230	.1	.2
249 Assyr Apost Ch	1	NR	NR	1,568	-	.1
251 Holy Orth in NA	1	NR	NR	30	-	-
252 Hindu	9	NR	NR	NR	-	-
262 Int Cou Comm Ch	6	1,525	NR	1,926 *	-	.1
263 Int Foursq Gos	45	2,492	4,597	4,609 *	.1	.2
264 Int Chs of Crst	2	1,192	2,223	1,812	-	.1
265 Int Pent C Chr	1	0	0	15	-	-
267 Muslim Est	12	NR	3,494	11,857	.2	.6
268 Jain	1	NR	NR	NR	-	-
283 Luth—MO Synod	64	19,672	13,578	24,977	.5	1.2
288 Mennonite USA	10	897	769	1,206 *	-	.1
290 Metro Comm Ch	3	180	101	226 *	-	-
291 Missionary Ch	4	1,529	1,827	1,827	-	.1
293 Morav Ch-North	1	61	NR	100	-	-
297 Mennonite;Other	5	63	NR	84 *	-	-
306 NT IndBapt&Rltd	1	0	NR	0 *	-	-
331 OCA: Ter Diocs	3	89	NR	781	-	-
335 Orth Pres Ch	2	140	139	177	-	-
339 Pent Ch of God	46	1,771	NR	3,091	.1	.2
349 Pent Holiness	11	625	648	798 *	-	-
355 Presb Ch (USA)	97	26,563	17,581	33,554 *	.7	1.6
356 Presb Ch Amer	10	1,075	1,402	1,445	-	.1
360 Prim Bapt Chrch	5	NR	NR	NR	-	-
370 Ref Baptist Chs	5	NR	NR	NR	-	-
371 Ref Ch in Am	9	1,256	1,470	2,206	-	.1
388 Reg Bapt Gen As	14	921	1,135	1,262 *	-	.1
397 OCA: Roman Dioc	2	NR	NR	850	-	-
401 Rus Orth Abroad	2	NR	NR	NR	-	-
403 Salvation Army	29	3,034	1,775	10,226	.2	.5
410 Serb Orth USA	2	NR	NR	750	-	-
411 Serb Orth: Grac	1	NR	NR	NR	-	-
413 S.D.A.	58	9,674	NR	11,513	.2	.6
416 Sikh	6	NR	NR	NR	-	-
419 So Bapt Conv	323	109,636	40,864	138,516 *	2.7	6.8
423 Syrian Orth Ch	1	NR	NR	60	-	-
425 Tao	1	NR	NR	NR	-	-
431 Ukrainian Orth	1	NR	NR	66	-	-
435 Unitarian-Univ	12	1,792	NR	2,249 *	-	.1
443 Un C of Christ	30	9,297	4,835	11,751 *	.2	.6
449 Un Methodist	114	42,184	26,942	53,232 *	1.0	2.6
455 Un Ref Chs N.A.	1	85	NR	120	-	-
463 Vineyard	17	4,404	3,805	5,560 *	.1	.3
467 Wesleyan	16	1,192	1,652	2,600	.1	.1
469 WELS	50	9,078	6,342	12,689	.2	.6
490 Zoroastrian	3	NR	NR	NR	-	-
496 Jewish Est	38	NR	NR	81,675	1.6	4.0
498 Indep.Charis.	20	13,965	21,405	29,755	.6	1.5
499 Indep.Non-Char	34	22,571	33,280	34,130	.7	1.7
ARKANSAS	**5,802**	**1,079,272**	**426,516**	**1,526,959 ***	**57.1**	**100.0**
017 Amer Bapt Assn	570	93,560	NR	115,916 *	4.3	7.6
019 Amer Bapt USA	1	128	70	162 *	-	-
032 Amish; other	3	228	NR	284 *	-	-
034 Ant Orth of NA	1	39	NR	78	-	-
053 Assemb of God	440	38,583	43,737	67,187	2.5	4.4
055 As Ref Pres Ch	6	257	NR	296	-	-
056 Baha'i	6	1,137	NR	1,137	-	.1
059 Bapt Miss Assn	359	70,123	26,121	87,244 *	3.3	5.7
061 Beachy Amish	2	67	NR	81 *	-	-
076 Buddhism	11	NR	NR	NR	-	-
081 Catholic	130	NR	NR	115,967	4.3	7.6
084 Calvary Chapel	3	NR	NR	NR	-	-
089 Chr & Miss Al	5	115	NR	270	-	-
093 Chr Ch (Disc)	52	9,240	4,058	11,475 *	.4	.8
097 Chr Chs&Chs Cr	63	7,538	NR	9,367 *	.4	.6
107 Christian Un	4	47	73	73 *	-	-
121 Ch God (Abr)	5	160	124	206 *	-	-
123 Ch God (Ander)	29	NR	1,439	1,439	.1	.1
127 Ch God (Cleve)	85	7,365	3,761	9,339 *	.3	.6
143 CG in Cr(Menn)	2	273	NR	346 *	-	-
145 Ch God Prophcy	33	957	NR	1,201 *	-	.1
151 L-D Saints	52	NR	NR	14,916	.6	1.0
157 Ch of Brethren	2	43	28	55 *	-	-
165 Ch of Nazarene	117	12,408	8,381	17,110	.6	1.1
167 Chs of Christ	754	67,216	68,394	86,342	3.2	5.7
171 Ch God-Gen Con	8	337	282	422 *	-	-
173 Comm of Christ	18	1,192	NR	1,192	-	.1
183 Cons Menn Conf	1	31	38	45	-	-
185 Cumber Presb	64	2,287	NR	3,998	.1	.3
193 Episcopal	56	NR	5,352	13,956	.5	.9
203 Evan Free Ch	5	369	650	650	-	-
207 E.L.C.A.	21	4,895	2,809	5,902	.2	.4
221 Free Methodist	1	17	35	35	-	-
223 Free Will Bapt	209	21,178	NR	26,268 *	1.0	1.7
226 Friends-USA	3	45	NR	57 *	-	-
237 Menn Br US Conf	2	71	NR	87 *	-	-
246 Greek Orthodox	2	NR	NR	483	-	-
262 Int Cou Comm Ch	1	40	NR	51 *	-	-
263 Int Foursq Gos	10	821	809	1,280 *	-	.1
264 Int Chs of Crst	2	124	200	178	-	-
266 Intrstat & Asc	2	36	NR	44 *	-	-
267 Muslim Est	6	NR	768	2,044	.1	.1
273 LandmrkBapt,I&U	2	102	NR	123 *	-	-
283 Luth—MO Synod	61	11,569	6,866	14,088	.5	.9
288 Mennonite USA	3	76	92	100 *	-	-
290 Metro Comm Ch	4	103	91	118 *	-	-
297 Mennonite;Other	3	88	NR	106 *	-	-
306 NT IndBapt&Rltd	1	40	NR	47 *	-	-
320 "Old" MB Ascs	1	6	NR	7 *	-	-
323 Old Ord Amish	1	15	NR	19 *	-	-
331 OCA: Ter Diocs	1	24	NR	45	-	-
335 Orth Pres Ch	1	8	22	22	-	-
339 Pent Ch of God	124	4,653	NR	10,285	.4	.7
349 Pent Holiness	15	619	609	777 *	-	.1
355 Presb Ch (USA)	127	20,413	10,397	25,345 *	.9	1.7
356 Presb Ch Amer	8	658	491	805	-	.1
360 Prim Bapt Chrch	46	NR	NR	NR	-	-

NR–Not Reported *Total adherents estimated from known number of communicant, confirmed, full members. - Represents a percentage less than 0.1. Percentages may not total 100 due to rounding.

Table 3: Religious Congregations by State and Group: 2000

Religious Group	Number of Churches, Synagogues, Mosques, or Temples	Number of Communicant, Confirmed, or Full Members	Number of Attendees	Total Adherents		
				Number of Adherents	% of Total Pop.	% of Total Adh.
370 Ref Baptist Chs	1	NR	NR	NR	-	-
388 Reg Bapt Gen As	9	440	305	465 *	-	-
401 Rus Orth Abroad	1	NR	NR	NR	-	-
403 Salvation Army	15	1,060	861	2,153	.1	.1
411 Serb Orth: Grac	1	NR	NR	NR	-	-
413 S.D.A.	61	5,605	NR	6,669	.2	.4
418 Southw Bapt Fel	3	NR	NR	NR	-	-
419 So Bapt Conv	1,372	534,534	163,772	665,307 *	24.9	43.6
425 Tao	1	NR	NR	NR	-	-
435 Unitarian-Univ	6	459	NR	566 *	-	-
443 Un C of Christ	3	117	66	147 *	-	-
449 Un Methodist	747	144,342	59,548	179,383 *	6.7	11.7
463 Vineyard	4	520	480	644 *	-	-
467 Wesleyan	3	154	138	256	-	-
469 WELS	6	436	334	575	-	-
496 Jewish Est	10	NR	NR	1,600	.1	.1
498 Indep.Charis.	7	8,374	11,450	15,374	.6	1.0
499 Indep.Non-Char	8	3,930	3,865	4,750	.2	.3
CALIFORNIA	**16,921**	**2,358,618**	**1,809,259**	**15,614,071 ***	**46.1**	**100.0**
011 A.W.M.C.	1	24	120	28	-	-
017 Amer Bapt Assn	131	8,985	NR	11,612 *	-	.1
019 Amer Bapt USA	556	126,983	97,821	170,932 *	.5	1.1
034 Ant Orth of NA	28	5,782	NR	11,564	-	.1
039 Ap Chr Ch(Naz)	10	343	560	564 *	-	-
040 Ap Chr Ch-Amer	2	77	132	132 *	-	-
049 Armen Ap Cilic	8	5,200	NR	29,200	.1	.2
050 Armen Ap Etchm	18	0	NR	24,055	.1	.2
053 Assemb of God	1,222	173,137	201,349	310,522	.9	2.0
055 As Ref Pres Ch	9	379	NR	405	-	-
056 Baha'i	259	24,849	NR	24,849	.1	.2
057 Bapt Gen Conf	155	31,025	61,626	69,649 *	.2	.4
059 Bapt Miss Assn	15	1,280	687	1,697 *	-	-
071 Brethren (Ash)	4	94	186	123 *	-	-
075 Brethren in Cr	18	1,411	1,683	1,834	-	-
076 Buddhism	489	NR	NR	NR	-	-
081 Catholic	1,315	NR	NR	10,079,310	29.8	64.6
084 Calvary Chapel	252	NR	NR	NR	-	-
089 Chr & Miss Al	201	27,583	NR	44,068	.1	.3
093 Chr Ch (Disc)	160	27,136	10,371	34,750 *	.1	.2
097 Chr Chs&Chs Cr	226	65,426	NR	84,169 *	.2	.5
105 Christian Ref	107	18,033	16,320	23,359 *	.1	.1
121 Ch God (Abr)	2	39	46	67 *	-	-
123 Ch God (Ander)	141	NR	18,215	18,215	.1	.1
127 Ch God (Cleve)	193	17,242	12,430	23,558 *	.1	.2
143 CG in Cr(Menn)	3	797	NR	1,075 *	-	-
145 Ch God Prophcy	124	5,176	NR	6,672 *	-	-
151 L-D Saints	1,316	NR	NR	529,575	1.6	3.4
157 Ch of Brethren	29	3,063	1,242	3,983 *	-	-
165 Ch of Nazarene	411	58,852	47,738	89,522	.3	.6
167 Chs of Christ	707	64,464	62,969	83,392	.2	.5
171 Ch God-Gen Con	8	384	334	555 *	-	-
173 Comm of Christ	55	6,137	NR	6,137	-	-
175 Congr Chr Chs	33	6,943	4,050	8,965 *	-	.1
176 Congr Ad Afl	1	131	NR	167 *	-	-
179 Consrv Bapt	215	NR	55,435	55,435	.2	.4
181 Consrv Congr	12	6,661	5,888	8,555 *	-	.1
185 Cumber Presb	5	819	NR	1,153	-	-
186 Coptic Orth Ch	20	NR	NR	NR	-	-
193 Episcopal	449	NR	61,263	168,895	.5	1.1
201 Evan Cov Ch	95	19,402	30,725	33,994 *	.1	.2
203 Evan Free Ch	175	29,302	53,263	54,227	.2	.3
207 E.L.C.A.	464	124,874	68,521	171,110	.5	1.1
216 Evan Presby Ch	7	1,233	NR	1,557 *	-	-
220 Free Lutheran	5	430	392	560	-	-
221 Free Methodist	94	7,334	10,649	11,749	-	.1
223 Free Will Bapt	62	2,985	NR	3,891 *	-	-
226 Friends-USA	75	7,066	NR	9,061 *	-	.1
237 Menn Br US Conf	62	8,895	NR	11,698 *	-	.1
245 Greek Orth Vslp	10	2,602	NR	4,323	-	-
246 Greek Orthodox	41	NR	NR	35,010	.1	.2
249 Assyr Apost Ch	8	NR	NR	7,884	-	.1
251 Holy Orth in NA	2	NR	NR	165	-	-
252 Hindu	131	NR	NR	NR	-	-
262 Int Cou Comm Ch	24	4,425	NR	5,572 *	-	-
263 Int Foursq Gos	578	77,759	114,067	116,039 *	.3	.7
264 Int Chs of Crst	5	15,090	24,601	20,167	.1	.1
267 Muslim Est	163	NR	57,511	259,762	.8	1.7
268 Jain	7	NR	NR	NR	-	-
273 LandmrkBapt,I&U	12	469	NR	614 *	-	-
283 Luth—MO Synod	401	97,955	56,481	130,336	.4	.8
288 Mennonite USA	36	1,936	1,906	2,607 *	-	-
290 Metro Comm Ch	25	2,275	2,131	2,799 *	-	-
291 Missionary Ch	26	7,432	8,814	9,327	-	.1
293 Morav Ch-North	2	261	NR	345	-	-
297 Mennonite;Other	3	64	NR	80 *	-	-
304 NatPrimBapt USA	4	855	NR	1,104 *	-	-
306 NT IndBapt&Rltd	96	14,855	NR	18,720 *	.1	.1
307 Neth Ref Congr	1	13	NR	15	-	-
313 N Am Bapt Conf	45	13,049	17,233	16,772 *	-	.1
330 Macedonian Orth	1	NR	NR	600	-	-
331 OCA: Ter Diocs	25	1,139	NR	6,075	-	-
332 OCA: Bulg Dioc	8	573	NR	4,375	-	-
333 Malan Dioc Am	2	NR	NR	525	-	-
334 Malan Syr Orth	1	18	NR	90	-	-
335 Orth Pres Ch	41	2,608	3,081	3,756	-	-
339 Pent Ch of God	246	9,142	NR	25,574	.1	.2
349 Pent Holiness	111	9,760	10,181	12,517 *	-	.1
355 Presb Ch (USA)	584	180,795	119,558	229,918 *	.7	1.5
356 Presb Ch Amer	76	7,572	8,133	9,955	-	.1
360 Prim Bapt Chrch	25	NR	NR	NR	-	-
369 Prot Ref Chs	1	140	NR	245	-	-
370 Ref Baptist Chs	18	NR	NR	NR	-	-
371 Ref Ch in Am	44	13,022	18,356	36,358	.1	.2
373 Ref Ch in U.S.	10	635	NR	931	-	-
388 Reg Bapt Gen As	102	11,598	14,293	15,130 *	-	.1
395 Romania Orth Ar	1	NR	NR	438	-	-
397 OCA: Roman Dioc	7	NR	NR	2,813	-	-
400 Rus Orth Moscow	2	NR	NR	NR	-	-
401 Rus Orth Abroad	22	NR	NR	NR	-	-
403 Salvation Army	135	14,572	12,167	49,330	.1	.3
410 Serb Orth USA	11	NR	NR	7,265	-	-
411 Serb Orth: Grac	5	NR	NR	NR	-	-
413 S.D.A.	516	157,183	NR	187,058	.6	1.2
416 Sikh	58	NR	NR	NR	-	-
418 Southw Bapt Fel	5	NR	NR	NR	-	-
419 So Bapt Conv	1,392	365,675	171,448	471,119 *	1.4	3.0
423 Syrian Orth Ch	6	NR	NR	7,500	-	-
425 Tao	19	NR	NR	NR	-	-
431 Ukrainian Orth	4	NR	NR	1,308	-	-
435 Unitarian-Univ	73	12,073	NR	15,173 *	-	.1
443 Un C of Christ	244	39,941	19,994	50,493 *	.1	.3
449 Un Methodist	710	180,858	96,402	228,844 *	.7	1.5
455 Un Ref Chs N.A.	11	1,727	NR	2,474	-	-
463 Vineyard	107	23,042	18,029	29,388 *	.1	.2
467 Wesleyan	67	8,646	10,864	23,858	.1	.2
469 WELS	46	6,851	4,856	8,950	-	.1
490 Zoroastrian	11	NR	NR	NR	-	-
496 Jewish Est	425	NR	NR	994,000	2.9	6.4
498 Indep.Charis.	68	100,019	77,625	195,425	.6	1.3
499 Indep.Non-Char	112	82,013	117,513	134,355	.4	.9
COLORADO	**3,228**	**512,435**	**343,323**	**1,697,259 ***	**39.5**	**100.0**
017 Amer Bapt Assn	11	404	NR	509 *	-	-
019 Amer Bapt USA	77	21,887	10,662	27,153 *	.6	1.6
032 Amish; other	1	30	NR	37 *	-	-
034 Ant Orth of NA	6	398	NR	796	-	-
039 Ap Chr Ch(Naz)	2	157	281	281 *	-	-
040 Ap Chr Ch-Amer	1	40	90	90 *	-	-
053 Assemb of God	180	23,912	26,483	41,123	1.0	2.4
055 As Ref Pres Ch	1	29	NR	32	-	-
056 Baha'i	30	2,420	NR	2,420	.1	.1
057 Bapt Gen Conf	31	5,640	6,703	8,113 *	.2	.5
059 Bapt Miss Assn	3	168	285	310 *	-	-
071 Brethren (Ash)	1	0	0	0 *	-	-
075 Brethren in Cr	1	2	24	24	-	-
076 Buddhism	72	NR	NR	NR	-	-
081 Catholic	298	NR	NR	752,505	17.5	44.3

NR–Not Reported   *Total adherents estimated from known number of communicant, confirmed, full members.   - Represents a percentage less than 0.1.   Percentages may not total 100 due to rounding.

Table 3: Religious Congregations by State and Group: 2000

Religious Group	Number of Churches, Synagogues, Mosques, or Temples	Number of Communicant, Confirmed, or Full Members	Number of Attendees	Total Adherents		
				Number of Adherents	% of Total Pop.	% of Total Adh.
084 Calvary Chapel	21	NR	NR	NR	-	-
089 Chr & Miss Al	18	1,686	NR	2,898	.1	.2
093 Chr Ch (Disc)	39	12,099	4,846	14,973 *	.3	.9
097 Chr Chs&Chs Cr	80	19,932	NR	25,105 *	.6	1.5
105 Christian Ref	19	4,579	3,815	5,698 *	.1	.3
121 Ch God (Abr)	1	5	5	6 *	-	-
123 Ch God (Ander)	25	NR	1,688	1,688	-	.1
127 Ch God (Cleve)	26	3,748	2,199	4,823 *	.1	.3
143 CG in Cr(Menn)	2	136	NR	172 *	-	-
145 Ch God Prophcy	13	284	NR	353 *	-	-
151 L-D Saints	243	NR	NR	92,326	2.1	5.4
157 Ch of Brethren	10	622	360	847 *	-	-
165 Ch of Nazarene	90	14,325	10,770	16,814	.4	1.0
167 Chs of Christ	149	12,404	13,244	16,356	.4	1.0
173 Comm of Christ	20	2,153	NR	2,153	.1	.1
175 Congr Chr Chs	3	122	131	147 *	-	-
176 Congr Ad Afl	1	838	NR	1,039 *	-	.1
179 Consrv Bapt	51	NR	10,488	10,488	.2	.6
181 Consrv Congr	8	1,310	838	1,669 *	-	.1
193 Episcopal	102	NR	14,316	34,942	.8	2.1
201 Evan Cov Ch	18	3,723	6,293	6,773 *	.2	.4
203 Evan Free Ch	65	7,117	14,891	14,996	.3	.9
207 E.L.C.A.	120	49,157	23,167	66,877	1.6	3.9
216 Evan Presby Ch	20	11,419	NR	14,718 *	.3	.9
220 Free Lutheran	3	143	157	230	-	-
221 Free Methodist	13	508	1,129	1,130	-	.1
223 Free Will Bapt	7	210	NR	263 *	-	-
226 Friends-USA	31	1,276	NR	1,574 *	-	.1
237 Menn Br US Conf	4	482	NR	588 *	-	-
246 Greek Orthodox	7	NR	NR	4,413	.1	.3
252 Hindu	7	NR	NR	NR	-	-
262 Int Cou Comm Ch	2	648	NR	763 *	-	-
263 Int Foursq Gos	57	6,322	8,923	9,880 *	.2	.6
264 Int Chs of Crst	2	1,109	1,872	1,624	-	.1
267 Muslim Est	12	NR	2,907	14,855	.3	.9
268 Jain	1	NR	NR	NR	-	-
283 Luth—MO Synod	121	35,835	19,885	47,283	1.1	2.8
288 Mennonite USA	20	1,555	1,312	1,982 *	-	.1
290 Metro Comm Ch	5	477	485	587 *	-	-
291 Missionary Ch	1	1	223	223	-	-
297 Mennonite;Other	3	117	NR	143 *	-	-
306 NT IndBapt&Rltd	57	6,270	NR	7,810 *	.2	.5
313 N Am Bapt Conf	5	332	320	424 *	-	-
331 OCA: Ter Diocs	7	310	NR	662	-	-
333 Malan Dioc Am	1	NR	NR	75	-	-
335 Orth Pres Ch	4	186	249	282	-	-
339 Pent Ch of God	8	156	NR	339	-	-
349 Pent Holiness	20	1,055	1,059	1,301 *	-	.1
355 Presb Ch (USA)	124	37,331	21,945	46,454 *	1.1	2.7
356 Presb Ch Amer	15	2,385	2,737	3,460	.1	.2
360 Prim Bapt Chrch	4	NR	NR	NR	-	-
369 Prot Ref Chs	1	144	NR	24	-	-
370 Ref Baptist Chs	1	NR	NR	NR	-	-
371 Ref Ch in Am	8	1,490	1,671	3,026	.1	.2
373 Ref Ch in U.S.	2	74	NR	109	-	-
388 Reg Bapt Gen As	14	1,378	1,384	1,606 *	-	.1
401 Rus Orth Abroad	1	NR	NR	NR	-	-
403 Salvation Army	17	1,652	997	4,493	.1	.3
410 Serb Orth USA	1	NR	NR	250	-	-
413 S.D.A.	88	13,981	NR	16,634	.4	1.0
416 Sikh	5	NR	NR	NR	-	-
418 Southw Bapt Fel	1	NR	NR	NR	-	-
419 So Bapt Conv	243	68,064	31,240	85,083 *	2.0	5.0
425 Tao	3	NR	NR	NR	-	-
435 Unitarian-Univ	18	2,890	NR	3,559 *	.1	.2
443 Un C of Christ	63	16,698	7,312	20,919 *	.5	1.2
449 Un Methodist	222	61,940	30,821	77,286 *	1.8	4.6
455 Un Ref Chs N.A.	1	91	NR	143	-	-
463 Vineyard	21	7,029	5,357	8,699 *	.2	.5
467 Wesleyan	17	1,279	2,105	4,489	.1	.3
469 WELS	27	2,770	2,069	3,740	.1	.2
490 Zoroastrian	1	NR	NR	NR	-	-
496 Jewish Est	41	NR	NR	72,000	1.7	4.2
498 Indep.Charis.	13	21,100	26,975	54,575	1.3	3.2

Religious Group	Number of Churches, Synagogues, Mosques, or Temples	Number of Communicant, Confirmed, or Full Members	Number of Attendees	Total Adherents		
				Number of Adherents	% of Total Pop.	% of Total Adh.
499 Indep.Non-Char	19	14,401	18,610	25,025	.6	1.5
CONNECTICUT	**1,955**	**278,823**	**151,206**	**1,971,102 ***	**57.9**	**100.0**
007 OCA: Alban Dioc	1	NR	NR	225	-	-
017 Amer Bapt Assn	1	20	NR	25 *	-	-
019 Amer Bapt USA	116	36,390	12,015	45,225 *	1.3	2.3
022 Carp Rus Orth	4	1,123	NR	1,913	.1	.1
034 Ant Orth of NA	2	628	NR	1,256	-	.1
039 Ap Chr Ch(Naz)	1	20	35	35 *	-	-
040 Ap Chr Ch-Amer	1	345	575	575 *	-	-
049 Armen Ap Cilic	1	94	NR	420	-	-
050 Armen Ap Etchm	3	310	NR	1,240	-	.1
053 Assemb of God	84	8,927	10,375	14,632	.4	.7
056 Baha'i	13	997	NR	997	-	.1
057 Bapt Gen Conf	13	2,410	2,596	3,671 *	.1	.2
076 Buddhism	12	NR	NR	NR	-	-
081 Catholic	411	NR	NR	1,372,562	40.3	69.6
084 Calvary Chapel	3	NR	NR	NR	-	-
089 Chr & Miss Al	19	897	NR	1,773	.1	.1
093 Chr Ch (Disc)	4	473	50	595 *	-	-
097 Chr Chs&Chs Cr	7	344	NR	428 *	-	-
105 Christian Ref	2	465	260	576 *	-	-
123 Ch God (Ander)	2	NR	180	180	-	-
127 Ch God (Cleve)	45	5,378	3,171	6,829 *	.2	.3
145 Ch God Prophcy	7	543	NR	678 *	-	-
151 L-D Saints	34	NR	NR	9,593	.3	.5
165 Ch of Nazarene	20	1,173	1,240	1,964	.1	.1
167 Chs of Christ	25	1,668	1,795	2,410	.1	.1
173 Comm of Christ	4	266	NR	266	-	-
175 Congr Chr Chs	30	3,538	1,703	4,370 *	.1	.2
176 Congr Ad Afl	6	1,298	NR	1,607 *	-	.1
179 Consrv Bapt	14	NR	1,487	1,487	-	.1
181 Consrv Congr	6	567	370	699 *	-	-
193 Episcopal	186	NR	23,123	73,550	2.2	3.7
201 Evan Cov Ch	15	2,674	2,688	3,509 *	.1	.2
203 Evan Free Ch	16	1,754	3,353	3,353	.1	.2
207 E.L.C.A.	74	23,773	8,603	31,960	.9	1.6
221 Free Methodist	2	374	440	508	-	-
226 Friends-USA	10	451	NR	558 *	-	-
246 Greek Orthodox	14	NR	NR	10,635	.3	.5
249 Assyr Apost Ch	1	NR	NR	516	-	-
252 Hindu	5	NR	NR	NR	-	-
262 Int Cou Comm Ch	1	32	NR	40 *	-	-
263 Int Foursq Gos	5	153	339	339 *	-	-
264 Int Chs of Crst	3	463	950	678	-	-
265 Int Pent C Chr	1	60	50	75	-	-
267 Muslim Est	20	NR	6,693	29,647	.9	1.5
268 Jain	4	NR	NR	NR	-	-
283 Luth—MO Synod	37	10,210	4,477	13,317	.4	.7
288 Mennonite USA	3	169	135	231 *	-	-
290 Metro Comm Ch	2	129	101	118 *	-	-
313 N Am Bapt Conf	1	10	8	12 *	-	-
331 OCA: Ter Diocs	15	1,950	NR	2,549	.1	.1
335 Orth Pres Ch	2	128	168	219	-	-
339 Pent Ch of God	1	70	NR	80	-	-
355 Presb Ch (USA)	20	7,143	3,677	8,952 *	.3	.5
356 Presb Ch Amer	6	317	394	458	-	-
370 Ref Baptist Chs	2	NR	NR	NR	-	-
388 Reg Bapt Gen As	5	525	816	820 *	-	-
397 OCA: Roman Dioc	1	NR	NR	312	-	-
401 Rus Orth Abroad	4	NR	NR	NR	-	-
403 Salvation Army	23	1,735	1,300	3,890	.1	.2
413 S.D.A.	36	4,985	NR	5,934	.2	.3
416 Sikh	3	NR	NR	NR	-	-
418 Southw Bapt Fel	2	NR	NR	NR	-	-
419 So Bapt Conv	32	4,582	2,183	5,681 *	.2	.3
431 Ukrainian Orth	5	NR	NR	2,049	.1	.1
435 Unitarian-Univ	19	3,235	NR	4,022 *	.1	.2
443 Un C of Christ	253	100,676	37,063	124,770 *	3.7	6.3
449 Un Methodist	133	41,192	13,373	51,183 *	1.5	2.6
463 Vineyard	3	310	261	384 *	-	-
467 Wesleyan	2	0	179	420	-	-
469 WELS	2	209	140	282	-	-
496 Jewish Est	87	NR	NR	108,280	3.2	5.5

NR–Not Reported *Total adherents estimated from known number of communicant, confirmed, full members. - Represents a percentage less than 0.1. Percentages may not total 100 due to rounding.

Table 3: Religious Congregations by State and Group: 2000

Religious Group	Number of Churches, Synagogues, Mosques, or Temples	Number of Communicant, Confirmed, or Full Members	Number of Attendees	Total Adherents		
				Number of Adherents	% of Total Pop.	% of Total Adh.
498 Indep.Charis.	1	1,800	1,700	1,800	.1	.1
499 Indep.Non-Char	7	1,840	3,140	3,740	.1	.2
DELAWARE	**571**	**98,788**	**52,276**	**318,122 ***	**40.6**	**100.0**
017 Amer Bapt Assn	2	60	NR	76 *	-	-
019 Amer Bapt USA	14	4,385	2,314	5,477 *	.7	1.7
034 Ant Orth of NA	1	49	NR	98	-	-
039 Ap Chr Ch(Naz)	1	0	0	0 *	-	-
053 Assemb of God	13	1,734	2,267	3,808	.5	1.2
056 Baha'i	7	251	NR	251	-	.1
057 Bapt Gen Conf	2	764	659	950 *	.1	.3
071 Brethren (Ash)	1	26	26	31 *	-	-
076 Buddhism	1	NR	NR	NR	-	-
081 Catholic	46	NR	NR	151,740	19.4	47.7
089 Chr & Miss Al	6	430	NR	884	.1	.3
093 Chr Ch (Disc)	1	25	0	30 *	-	-
097 Chr Chs&Chs Cr	8	990	NR	1,214 *	.2	.4
123 Ch God (Ander)	6	NR	337	337	-	.1
127 Ch God (Cleve)	20	3,143	2,092	3,934 *	.5	1.2
145 Ch God Prophcy	9	417	NR	516 *	.1	.2
151 L-D Saints	7	NR	NR	2,760	.4	.9
157 Ch of Brethren	3	260	176	320 *	-	.1
165 Ch of Nazarene	13	1,178	1,044	1,762	.2	.6
167 Chs of Christ	10	900	808	1,156	.1	.4
173 Comm of Christ	2	188	NR	188	-	.1
179 Consrv Bapt	1	NR	100	100	-	-
183 Cons Menn Conf	5	607	741	883	.1	.3
193 Episcopal	35	NR	4,238	12,993	1.7	4.1
203 Evan Free Ch	4	534	630	715	.1	.2
207 E.L.C.A.	14	5,004	1,912	6,631	.8	2.1
223 Free Will Bapt	2	197	NR	245 *	-	.1
226 Friends-USA	6	630	NR	785 *	.1	.2
246 Greek Orthodox	1	NR	NR	2,076	.3	.7
252 Hindu	2	NR	NR	NR	-	-
263 Int Foursq Gos	1	12	29	29 *	-	-
264 Int Chs of Crst	1	11	30	11	-	-
267 Muslim Est	3	NR	1,174	3,691	.5	1.2
283 Luth—MO Synod	7	1,681	742	2,281	.3	.7
286 E.PA Mennonite	2	137	NR	172 *	-	.1
288 Mennonite USA	2	154	123	187 *	-	.1
290 Metro Comm Ch	1	56	70	70 *	-	-
297 Mennonite;Other	1	25	NR	30 *	-	-
323 Old Ord Amish	8	480	NR	608 *	.1	.2
331 OCA: Ter Diocs	1	100	NR	456	.1	.1
335 Orth Pres Ch	2	211	218	305	-	.1
339 Pent Ch of God	2	23	NR	24	-	-
349 Pent Holiness	1	112	81	139 *	-	-
355 Presb Ch (USA)	37	10,931	6,252	14,880 *	1.9	4.7
356 Presb Ch Amer	11	2,647	3,361	3,937	.5	1.2
360 Prim Bapt Chrch	2	NR	NR	NR	-	-
370 Ref Baptist Chs	1	NR	NR	NR	-	-
388 Reg Bapt Gen As	5	610	648	696 *	.1	.2
403 Salvation Army	4	363	233	509	.1	.2
413 S.D.A.	15	2,095	NR	2,492	.3	.8
416 Sikh	1	NR	NR	NR	-	-
418 Southw Bapt Fel	4	NR	NR	NR	-	-
419 So Bapt Conv	19	5,078	2,476	6,310 *	.8	2.0
431 Ukrainian Orth	1	NR	NR	450	.1	.1
435 Unitarian-Univ	4	1,292	NR	1,602 *	.2	.5
443 Un C of Christ	3	598	279	753 *	.1	.2
449 Un Methodist	162	48,140	16,758	59,471 *	7.6	18.7
467 Wesleyan	17	201	1,657	2,928	.4	.9
469 WELS	1	159	126	231	-	.1
496 Jewish Est	7	NR	NR	13,500	1.7	4.2
498 Indep.Charis.	1	400	250	400	.1	.1
499 Indep.Non-Char	1	1,500	425	2,000	.3	.6
DISTRICT OF COLUMBIA	**390**	**120,092**	**63,535**	**418,543 ***	**73.2**	**100.0**
019 Amer Bapt USA	62	43,457	16,243	51,836 *	9.1	12.4
032 Amish; other	1	18	NR	21 *	-	-
034 Ant Orth of NA	2	357	NR	714	.1	.2
040 Ap Chr Ch-Amer	1	6	19	19 *	-	-
050 Armen Ap Etchm	1	255	NR	1,000	.2	.2

Religious Group	Number of Churches, Synagogues, Mosques, or Temples	Number of Communicant, Confirmed, or Full Members	Number of Attendees	Total Adherents		
				Number of Adherents	% of Total Pop.	% of Total Adh.
053 Assemb of God	7	1,230	1,134	1,526	.3	.4
056 Baha'i	1	357	NR	357	.1	.1
071 Brethren (Ash)	1	106	105	126 *	-	-
076 Buddhism	15	NR	NR	NR	-	-
078 Bulgar Orth USA	1	NR	NR	440	.1	.1
081 Catholic	42	NR	NR	160,048	28.0	38.2
089 Chr & Miss Al	1	62	NR	90	-	-
093 Chr Ch (Disc)	4	1,298	679	1,548 *	.3	.4
105 Christian Ref	1	147	110	175 *	-	-
123 Ch God (Ander)	6	NR	498	498	.1	.1
127 Ch God (Cleve)	2	92	85	110 *	-	-
145 Ch God Prophcy	5	234	NR	277 *	-	.1
151 L-D Saints	3	NR	NR	609	.1	.1
157 Ch of Brethren	2	178	56	213 *	-	.1
165 Ch of Nazarene	2	514	320	550	.1	.1
167 Chs of Christ	4	491	473	630	.1	.2
173 Comm of Christ	1	214	NR	214	-	.1
179 Consrv Bapt	1	NR	65	65	-	-
193 Episcopal	34	NR	8,428	19,698	3.4	4.7
207 E.L.C.A.	13	3,101	1,375	4,048	.7	1.0
226 Friends-USA	2	210	NR	250 *	-	.1
246 Greek Orthodox	2	NR	NR	4,317	.8	1.0
252 Hindu	3	NR	NR	NR	-	-
262 Int Cou Comm Ch	2	378	NR	451 *	.1	.1
264 Int Chs of Crst	1	1,899	3,322	2,492	.4	.6
267 Muslim Est	16	NR	9,448	60,479	10.6	14.4
283 Luth—MO Synod	3	595	311	739	.1	.2
288 Mennonite USA	4	79	481	481 *	.1	.1
290 Metro Comm Ch	1	493	458	588 *	.1	.1
293 Morav Ch-North	1	157	NR	235	-	.1
331 OCA: Ter Diocs	1	300	NR	405	.1	.1
355 Presb Ch (USA)	17	6,936	3,281	8,273 *	1.4	2.0
401 Rus Orth Abroad	1	NR	NR	NR	-	-
403 Salvation Army	3	504	129	1,588	.3	.4
410 Serb Orth USA	1	NR	NR	555	.1	.1
411 Serb Orth: Grac	1	NR	NR	NR	-	-
413 S.D.A.	9	6,309	NR	7,508	1.3	1.8
416 Sikh	3	NR	NR	NR	-	-
419 So Bapt Conv	49	32,572	9,758	38,852 *	6.8	9.3
425 Tao	1	NR	NR	NR	-	-
435 Unitarian-Univ	2	599	NR	714 *	.1	.2
443 Un C of Christ	8	4,064	1,710	4,848 *	.8	1.2
449 Un Methodist	33	12,840	4,912	15,313 *	2.7	3.7
463 Vineyard	1	40	40	48 *	-	-
467 Wesleyan	1	0	95	95	-	-
496 Jewish Est	11	NR	NR	25,500	4.5	6.1
FLORIDA	**10,078**	**2,416,540**	**1,287,696**	**6,576,205 ***	**41.1**	**100.0**
011 A.W.M.C.	1	0	20	0	-	-
017 Amer Bapt Assn	123	15,626	NR	19,012 *	.1	.3
019 Amer Bapt USA	26	4,007	1,286	4,908 *	-	.1
022 Carp Rus Orth	3	366	NR	621	-	-
032 Amish; other	2	68	NR	77 *	-	-
034 Ant Orth of NA	13	1,537	NR	3,074	-	-
039 Ap Chr Ch(Naz)	3	76	114	114 *	-	-
040 Ap Chr Ch-Amer	3	119	178	178 *	-	-
049 Armen Ap Cilic	2	117	NR	490	-	-
050 Armen Ap Etchm	6	186	NR	3,350	-	.1
053 Assemb of God	645	113,668	115,345	189,387	1.2	2.9
055 As Ref Pres Ch	20	4,631	NR	5,459	-	.1
056 Baha'i	67	7,735	NR	7,735	-	.1
057 Bapt Gen Conf	25	2,364	2,789	3,302 *	-	.1
059 Bapt Miss Assn	12	973	406	1,201 *	-	-
061 Beachy Amish	2	171	NR	196 *	-	-
071 Brethren (Ash)	3	233	203	269 *	-	-
075 Brethren in Cr	26	1,958	2,399	2,458	-	-
076 Buddhism	43	NR	NR	NR	-	-
081 Catholic	527	NR	NR	2,596,148	16.2	39.5
084 Calvary Chapel	36	NR	NR	NR	-	-
089 Chr & Miss Al	144	10,011	NR	16,989	.1	.3
093 Chr Ch (Disc)	81	18,533	8,764	22,545 *	.1	.3
097 Chr Chs&Chs Cr	192	48,604	NR	58,690 *	.4	.9
105 Christian Ref	19	2,411	1,787	2,932 *	-	-
123 Ch God (Ander)	114	NR	14,107	14,107	.1	.2

NR–Not Reported   *Total adherents estimated from known number of communicant, confirmed, full members.   - Represents a percentage less than 0.1.   Percentages may not total 100 due to rounding.

Table 3: Religious Congregations by State and Group: 2000

Religious Group	Number of Churches, Synagogues, Mosques, or Temples	Number of Communicant, Confirmed, or Full Members	Number of Attendees	Total Adherents: Number of Adherents	Total Adherents: % of Total Pop.	Total Adherents: % of Total Adh.
127 Ch God (Cleve)	567	81,580	52,665	101,188 *	.6	1.5
143 CG in Cr(Menn)	1	194	NR	237 *	-	-
145 Ch God Prophcy	132	5,320	NR	6,472 *	-	.1
151 L-D Saints	201	NR	NR	75,620	.5	1.1
157 Ch of Brethren	16	1,730	1,047	2,148 *	-	-
165 Ch of Nazarene	244	35,225	27,152	44,208	.3	.7
167 Chs of Christ	509	55,744	53,024	72,540	.5	1.1
173 Comm of Christ	34	2,738	NR	2,738	-	-
175 Congr Chr Chs	11	2,300	1,567	2,745 *	-	-
179 Consrv Bapt	9	NR	835	835	-	-
183 Cons Menn Conf	8	784	958	1,140	-	-
185 Cumber Presb	6	237	NR	503	-	-
186 Coptic Orth Ch	11	NR	NR	NR	-	-
193 Episcopal	339	NR	64,764	152,526	1.0	2.3
201 Evan Cov Ch	28	2,589	2,589	3,540 *	-	.1
203 Evan Free Ch	30	2,542	4,917	4,947	-	.1
207 E.L.C.A.	215	70,554	39,635	90,594	.6	1.4
216 Evan Presby Ch	8	1,822	NR	2,229 *	-	-
220 Free Lutheran	1	23	18	24	-	-
221 Free Methodist	38	2,526	3,483	3,688	-	.1
223 Free Will Bapt	74	6,096	NR	7,462 *	-	.1
226 Friends-USA	24	949	NR	1,138 *	-	-
245 Greek Orth Vslp	2	227	NR	502	-	-
246 Greek Orthodox	33	NR	NR	24,798	.2	.4
251 Holy Orth in NA	1	NR	NR	15	-	-
252 Hindu	42	NR	NR	NR	-	-
262 Int Cou Comm Ch	13	4,388	NR	5,255 *	-	.1
263 Int Foursq Gos	49	2,973	4,035	4,302 *	-	.1
264 Int Chs of Crst	7	3,768	6,061	5,303	-	.1
265 Int Pent C Chr	2	0	0	30	-	-
266 Intrstat & Asc	1	117	NR	143 *	-	-
267 Muslim Est	37	NR	8,512	31,661	.2	.5
268 Jain	10	NR	NR	NR	-	-
283 Luth—MO Synod	167	56,116	34,486	71,970	.5	1.1
286 E.PA Mennonite	1	20	NR	24 *	-	-
288 Mennonite USA	26	2,610	2,813	3,394 *	-	.1
290 Metro Comm Ch	22	3,094	3,212	3,839 *	-	.1
291 Missionary Ch	3	209	315	315	-	-
295 Morav Ch-South	5	714	NR	1,096	-	-
297 Mennonite;Other	7	214	NR	255 *	-	-
304 NatPrimBapt USA	174	17,895	NR	21,780 *	.1	.3
313 N Am Bapt Conf	3	675	575	822 *	-	-
330 Macedonian Orth	1	NR	NR	600	-	-
331 OCA: Ter Diocs	17	833	NR	2,561	-	-
333 Malan Dioc Am	4	NR	NR	525	-	-
334 Malan Syr Orth	1	24	NR	120	-	-
335 Orth Pres Ch	11	457	531	670	-	-
339 Pent Ch of God	26	785	NR	1,453	-	-
349 Pent Holiness	161	22,895	19,172	27,907 *	.2	.4
355 Presb Ch (USA)	362	130,382	76,640	157,751 *	1.0	2.4
356 Presb Ch Amer	135	35,598	32,112	43,745	.3	.7
360 Prim Bapt Chrch	74	NR	NR	NR	-	-
363 Primitive Meth	4	228	NR	244	-	-
365 Prog Prim Bapt	10	449	NR	556 *	-	-
370 Ref Baptist Chs	11	NR	NR	NR	-	-
371 Ref Ch in Am	16	1,358	1,551	2,811	-	-
388 Reg Bapt Gen As	47	5,626	7,066	7,476 *	-	.1
397 OCA: Roman Dioc	4	NR	NR	2,460	-	-
400 Rus Orth Moscow	1	NR	NR	NR	-	-
401 Rus Orth Abroad	3	NR	NR	NR	-	-
403 Salvation Army	49	6,689	2,978	11,248	.1	.2
409 Separate Bapt	1	20	NR	25 *	-	-
410 Serb Orth USA	4	NR	NR	2,150	-	-
411 Serb Orth: Grac	2	NR	NR	NR	-	-
413 S.D.A.	292	61,024	NR	72,619	.5	1.1
416 Sikh	9	NR	NR	NR	-	-
418 Southw Bapt Fel	52	NR	NR	NR	-	-
419 So Bapt Conv	2,054	1,057,240	414,835	1,292,097 *	8.1	19.6
423 Syrian Orth Ch	2	NR	NR	500	-	-
425 Tao	1	NR	NR	NR	-	-
431 Ukrainian Orth	3	NR	NR	432	-	-
435 Unitarian-Univ	43	4,966	NR	5,960 *	-	.1
443 Un C of Christ	103	32,854	19,241	39,326 *	.2	.6
449 Un Methodist	844	378,522	177,545	458,623 *	2.9	7.0
455 Un Ref Chs N.A.	1	58	NR	72	-	-
463 Vineyard	29	5,083	4,481	6,180 *	-	.1
467 Wesleyan	45	2,275	3,597	7,174	-	.1
469 WELS	37	4,305	3,361	5,599	-	.1
490 Zoroastrian	1	NR	NR	NR	-	-
496 Jewish Est	263	NR	NR	628,485	3.9	9.6
498 Indep.Charis.	46	21,647	24,065	34,325	.2	.5
499 Indep.Non-Char	60	43,855	40,460	57,243	.4	.9
GEORGIA	**8,962**	**2,389,923**	**1,016,770**	**3,665,550 ***	**44.8**	**100.0**
017 Amer Bapt Assn	31	2,128	NR	2,712 *	-	.1
019 Amer Bapt USA	18	9,060	2,220	11,301 *	.1	.3
022 Carp Rus Orth	1	122	NR	207	-	-
034 Ant Orth of NA	2	438	NR	876	-	-
040 Ap Chr Ch-Amer	1	11	27	27 *	-	-
049 Armen Ap Cilic	1	0	NR	320	-	-
050 Armen Ap Etchm	1	0	NR	300	-	-
053 Assemb of God	231	27,192	28,610	44,469	.5	1.2
055 As Ref Pres Ch	17	1,457	NR	1,668	-	-
056 Baha'i	46	6,233	NR	6,233	.1	.2
057 Bapt Gen Conf	1	18	12	23 *	-	-
061 Beachy Amish	3	315	NR	399 *	-	-
075 Brethren in Cr	2	88	99	99	-	-
076 Buddhism	16	NR	NR	NR	-	-
081 Catholic	179	NR	NR	374,185	4.6	10.2
084 Calvary Chapel	13	NR	NR	NR	-	-
089 Chr & Miss Al	48	4,500	NR	6,783	.1	.2
093 Chr Ch (Disc)	68	17,653	5,501	22,172 *	.3	.6
097 Chr Chs&Chs Cr	151	35,228	NR	44,571 *	.5	1.2
105 Christian Ref	4	193	202	240 *	-	-
121 Ch God (Abr)	4	142	218	222 *	-	-
123 Ch God (Ander)	52	NR	3,388	3,388	-	.1
127 Ch God (Cleve)	493	108,714	59,421	138,123 *	1.7	3.8
143 CG in Cr(Menn)	3	335	NR	427 *	-	-
145 Ch God Prophcy	126	5,220	NR	6,588 *	.1	.2
151 L-D Saints	121	NR	NR	43,910	.5	1.2
165 Ch of Nazarene	95	10,329	7,558	13,002	.2	.4
167 Chs of Christ	403	36,117	36,131	48,015	.6	1.3
173 Comm of Christ	7	561	NR	561	-	-
175 Congr Chr Chs	5	235	250	299 *	-	-
176 Congr Ad Afl	1	113	NR	145 *	-	-
183 Cons Menn Conf	2	37	46	54	-	-
185 Cumber Presb	9	327	NR	505	-	-
186 Coptic Orth Ch	1	NR	NR	NR	-	-
189 Duck Rivr Bapt	1	73	NR	90 *	-	-
193 Episcopal	157	NR	25,647	71,950	.9	2.0
201 Evan Cov Ch	3	194	183	241 *	-	-
203 Evan Free Ch	4	457	620	620	-	-
207 E.L.C.A.	90	28,190	13,620	37,096	.5	1.0
216 Evan Presby Ch	3	1,147	NR	1,418 *	-	-
221 Free Methodist	5	273	455	487	-	-
223 Free Will Bapt	120	9,619	NR	12,126 *	.1	.3
226 Friends-USA	6	264	NR	324 *	-	-
246 Greek Orthodox	8	NR	NR	4,302	.1	.1
251 Holy Orth in NA	1	NR	NR	15	-	-
252 Hindu	15	NR	NR	NR	-	-
262 Int Cou Comm Ch	3	570	NR	710 *	-	-
263 Int Foursq Gos	19	1,110	1,692	1,845 *	-	.1
264 Int Chs of Crst	1	3,399	6,031	5,069	.1	.1
265 Int Pent C Chr	2	0	13	55	-	-
267 Muslim Est	39	NR	8,636	38,882	.5	1.1
268 Jain	3	NR	NR	NR	-	-
269 Jasper&PVB Asc	31	5,659	NR	7,078 *	.1	.2
283 Luth—MO Synod	37	7,292	5,023	9,887	.1	.3
286 E.PA Mennonite	1	38	NR	48 *	-	-
288 Mennonite USA	4	100	155	155 *	-	-
289 New Hope B Asc	20	2,131	NR	2,772 *	-	.1
290 Metro Comm Ch	8	673	655	852 *	-	-
291 Missionary Ch	3	93	312	318	-	-
295 Morav Ch-South	1	139	NR	180	-	-
297 Mennonite;Other	10	407	NR	515 *	-	-
304 NatPrimBapt USA	22	1,391	NR	1,749 *	-	-
320 "Old" MB Ascs	78	13,498	NR	17,028 *	.2	.5
331 OCA: Ter Diocs	3	78	NR	257	-	-

NR–Not Reported *Total adherents estimated from known number of communicant, confirmed, full members. - Represents a percentage less than 0.1. Percentages may not total 100 due to rounding.

Table 3: Religious Congregations by State and Group: 2000

Religious Group	Number of Churches, Synagogues, Mosques, or Temples	Number of Communicant, Confirmed, or Full Members	Number of Attendees	Total Adherents		
				Number of Adherents	% of Total Pop.	% of Total Adh.
333 Malan Dioc Am	1	NR	NR	125	-	-
334 Malan Syr Orth	2	45	NR	225	-	-
335 Orth Pres Ch	3	197	270	318	-	-
339 Pent Ch of God	8	320	NR	631	-	-
349 Pent Holiness	89	8,297	5,582	10,317 *	.1	.3
355 Presb Ch (USA)	307	84,237	39,539	105,774 *	1.3	2.9
356 Presb Ch Amer	107	18,652	17,485	24,092	.3	.7
360 Prim Bapt Chrch	216	NR	NR	NR	-	-
365 Prog Prim Bapt	85	5,806	NR	7,227 *	.1	.2
370 Ref Baptist Chs	9	NR	NR	NR	-	-
371 Ref Ch in Am	1	118	205	245	-	-
388 Reg Bapt Gen As	2	600	250	758 *	-	-
397 OCA: Roman Dioc	1	NR	NR	86	-	-
401 Rus Orth Abroad	2	NR	NR	NR	-	-
403 Salvation Army	29	3,160	2,422	7,074	.1	.2
410 Serb Orth USA	2	NR	NR	1,100	-	-
413 S.D.A.	121	27,105	NR	32,256	.4	.9
416 Sikh	5	NR	NR	NR	-	-
418 Southw Bapt Fel	72	NR	NR	NR	-	-
419 So Bapt Conv	3,233	1,362,799	493,967	1,719,484 *	21.0	46.9
431 Ukrainian Orth	1	NR	NR	60	-	-
435 Unitarian-Univ	18	2,075	NR	2,573 *	-	.1
443 Un C of Christ	18	2,209	1,055	2,771 *	-	.1
449 Un Methodist	1,614	452,715	185,269	570,674 *	7.0	15.6
463 Vineyard	15	3,143	2,761	3,956 *	-	.1
467 Wesleyan	24	1,253	2,513	5,369	.1	.1
469 WELS	7	1,122	847	1,509	-	-
496 Jewish Est	52	NR	NR	93,500	1.1	2.6
498 Indep.Charis.	30	38,855	32,100	47,530	.6	1.3
499 Indep.Non-Char	34	33,654	25,780	40,003	.5	1.1
HAWAII	**939**	**98,147**	**73,062**	**438,694 ***	**36.2**	**100.0**
017 Amer Bapt Assn	5	139	NR	171 *	-	-
019 Amer Bapt USA	3	488	437	600 *	-	.1
053 Assemb of God	80	15,007	13,328	21,754	1.8	5.0
057 Bapt Gen Conf	4	190	243	278 *	-	.1
076 Buddhism	73	NR	NR	NR	-	-
081 Catholic	95	NR	NR	240,813	19.9	54.9
084 Calvary Chapel	16	NR	NR	NR	-	-
089 Chr & Miss Al	10	764	NR	1,699	.1	.4
093 Chr Ch (Disc)	4	243	70	299 *	-	.1
097 Chr Chs&Chs Cr	12	1,445	NR	1,779 *	.1	.4
105 Christian Ref	3	60	160	74 *	-	-
123 Ch God (Ander)	1	NR	10	10	-	-
127 Ch God (Cleve)	24	2,044	968	2,545 *	.2	.6
145 Ch God Prophcy	5	223	NR	276 *	-	.1
151 L-D Saints	112	NR	NR	42,758	3.5	9.7
165 Ch of Nazarene	21	2,115	1,301	2,742	.2	.6
167 Chs of Christ	13	765	895	1,012	.1	.2
173 Comm of Christ	6	886	NR	886	.1	.2
175 Congr Chr Chs	1	30	50	38 *	-	-
176 Congr Ad Afl	9	616	NR	768 *	.1	.2
179 Consrv Bapt	1	NR	150	150	-	-
181 Consrv Congr	2	108	175	134 *	-	-
186 Coptic Orth Ch	1	NR	NR	NR	-	-
193 Episcopal	40	NR	3,575	11,084	.9	2.5
201 Evan Cov Ch	1	0	0	0 *	-	-
203 Evan Free Ch	6	960	1,425	1,649	.1	.4
207 E.L.C.A.	11	2,049	1,638	2,677	.2	.6
223 Free Will Bapt	1	49	NR	60 *	-	-
226 Friends-USA	3	96	NR	119 *	-	-
246 Greek Orthodox	1	NR	NR	282	-	.1
252 Hindu	8	NR	NR	NR	-	-
263 Int Foursq Gos	39	11,382	15,022	15,076 *	1.2	3.4
264 Int Chs of Crst	3	973	1,357	1,287	.1	.3
267 Muslim Est	1	NR	156	609	.1	.1
283 Luth—MO Synod	10	1,335	1,170	1,775	.1	.4
288 Mennonite USA	2	78	62	96 *	-	-
290 Metro Comm Ch	2	18	21	21 *	-	-
291 Missionary Ch	12	974	1,865	1,865	.2	.4
339 Pent Ch of God	1	24	NR	80	-	-
349 Pent Holiness	7	1,252	961	1,559 *	.1	.4
355 Presb Ch (USA)	6	1,410	1,129	1,755 *	.1	.4
356 Presb Ch Amer	4	141	328	328	-	.1

Religious Group	Number of Churches, Synagogues, Mosques, or Temples	Number of Communicant, Confirmed, or Full Members	Number of Attendees	Total Adherents		
				Number of Adherents	% of Total Pop.	% of Total Adh.
370 Ref Baptist Chs	2	NR	NR	NR	-	-
388 Reg Bapt Gen As	2	0	0	0 *	-	-
401 Rus Orth Abroad	1	NR	NR	NR	-	-
403 Salvation Army	14	1,940	858	8,742	.7	2.0
413 S.D.A.	28	5,305	NR	6,313	.5	1.4
416 Sikh	1	NR	NR	NR	-	-
419 So Bapt Conv	71	16,951	7,496	20,901 *	1.7	4.8
435 Unitarian-Univ	1	158	NR	194 *	-	-
443 Un C of Christ	113	18,507	9,696	22,856 *	1.9	5.2
449 Un Methodist	31	6,708	4,080	8,267 *	.7	1.9
463 Vineyard	3	390	360	482 *	-	.1
467 Wesleyan	1	0	0	0	-	-
469 WELS	1	84	101	156	-	-
496 Jewish Est	4	NR	NR	7,000	.6	1.6
498 Indep.Charis.	5	1,075	2,350	2,975	.2	.7
499 Indep.Non-Char	2	1,165	1,625	1,700	.1	.4
IDAHO	**1,855**	**119,911**	**81,036**	**627,262 ***	**48.5**	**100.0**
017 Amer Bapt Assn	8	212	NR	275 *	-	-
019 Amer Bapt USA	37	5,738	3,328	7,373 *	.6	1.2
034 Ant Orth of NA	3	173	NR	346	-	.1
053 Assemb of God	88	8,023	10,810	18,745	1.4	3.0
056 Baha'i	10	690	NR	690	.1	.1
057 Bapt Gen Conf	1	165	180	208 *	-	-
076 Buddhism	1	NR	NR	NR	-	-
081 Catholic	102	NR	NR	130,847	10.1	20.9
084 Calvary Chapel	14	NR	NR	NR	-	-
089 Chr & Miss Al	7	354	NR	745	.1	.1
093 Chr Ch (Disc)	16	3,099	1,031	4,009 *	.3	.6
097 Chr Chs&Chs Cr	25	6,192	NR	7,880 *	.6	1.3
105 Christian Ref	1	65	35	79 *	-	-
123 Ch God (Ander)	9	NR	829	829	.1	.1
127 Ch God (Cleve)	12	694	551	896 *	.1	.1
143 CG in Cr(Menn)	6	643	NR	822 *	.1	.1
145 Ch God Prophcy	9	236	NR	303 *	-	-
151 L-D Saints	846	NR	NR	311,425	24.1	49.6
157 Ch of Brethren	7	708	296	922 *	.1	.1
165 Ch of Nazarene	51	11,305	10,700	15,320	1.2	2.4
167 Chs of Christ	43	2,353	2,692	3,399	.3	.5
173 Comm of Christ	10	777	NR	777	.1	.1
179 Consrv Bapt	12	NR	1,596	1,596	.1	.3
181 Consrv Congr	4	600	422	745 *	.1	.1
193 Episcopal	38	NR	2,449	7,244	.6	1.2
201 Evan Cov Ch	1	44	0	58 *	-	-
203 Evan Free Ch	8	279	839	845	.1	.1
207 E.L.C.A.	43	9,420	4,713	13,187	1.0	2.1
221 Free Methodist	8	920	2,039	2,042	.2	.3
223 Free Will Bapt	6	251	NR	322 *	-	.1
226 Friends-USA	22	1,724	NR	2,217 *	.2	.4
246 Greek Orthodox	2	NR	NR	459	-	.1
252 Hindu	1	NR	NR	NR	-	-
263 Int Foursq Gos	29	1,569	2,623	2,718 *	.2	.4
264 Int Chs of Crst	1	146	228	196	-	-
267 Muslim Est	2	NR	115	363	-	.1
283 Luth—MO Synod	43	9,814	4,465	13,289	1.0	2.1
288 Mennonite USA	5	488	407	675 *	.1	.1
290 Metro Comm Ch	1	31	21	39 *	-	-
291 Missionary Ch	1	43	35	43	-	-
297 Mennonite;Other	3	128	NR	163 *	-	-
313 N Am Bapt Conf	2	251	305	329 *	-	.1
323 Old Ord Amish	1	60	NR	76 *	-	-
335 Orth Pres Ch	2	47	62	91	-	-
339 Pent Ch of God	9	234	NR	824	.1	.1
349 Pent Holiness	6	111	143	144 *	-	-
355 Presb Ch (USA)	51	7,624	4,275	9,720 *	.8	1.5
356 Presb Ch Amer	2	26	117	117	-	-
370 Ref Baptist Chs	1	NR	NR	NR	-	-
371 Ref Ch in Am	3	964	1,200	1,895	.1	.3
388 Reg Bapt Gen As	13	1,227	1,383	1,693 *	.1	.3
401 Rus Orth Abroad	1	NR	NR	NR	-	-
403 Salvation Army	7	514	359	1,165	.1	.2
413 S.D.A.	50	6,714	NR	7,985	.6	1.3
419 So Bapt Conv	66	12,135	4,960	15,456 *	1.2	2.5
435 Unitarian-Univ	6	523	NR	653 *	.1	.1

NR–Not Reported *Total adherents estimated from known number of communicant, confirmed, full members. - Represents a percentage less than 0.1. Percentages may not total 100 due to rounding.

Table 3: Religious Congregations by State and Group: 2000

Religious Group	Number of Churches, Synagogues, Mosques, or Temples	Number of Communicant, Confirmed, or Full Members	Number of Attendees	Total Adherents		
				Number of Adherents	% of Total Pop.	% of Total Adh.
443 Un C of Christ	13	1,476	1,195	1,876 *	.1	.3
449 Un Methodist	63	13,878	6,198	17,683 *	1.4	2.8
455 Un Ref Chs N.A.	1	223	NR	367	-	.1
463 Vineyard	6	2,307	1,933	2,949 *	.2	.5
467 Wesleyan	3	0	150	763	.1	.1
469 WELS	4	313	302	435	-	.1
496 Jewish Est	2	NR	NR	1,050	.1	.2
498 Indep.Charis.	3	600	3,050	3,800	.3	.6
499 Indep.Non-Char	4	3,800	5,000	6,100	.5	1.0
ILLINOIS	**10,140**	**1,806,932**	**925,592**	**6,867,625 ***	**55.3**	**100.0**
009 Alban Orth Dio	1	250	NR	270	-	-
011 A.W.M.C.	1	17	19	18	-	-
017 Amer Bapt Assn	19	920	NR	1,146 *	-	-
019 Amer Bapt USA	296	70,916	28,244	87,962 *	.7	1.3
022 Carp Rus Orth	2	244	NR	414	-	-
032 Amish; other	5	351	NR	431 *	-	-
034 Ant Orth of NA	5	945	NR	1,890	-	-
039 Ap Chr Ch(Naz)	4	321	555	558 *	-	-
040 Ap Chr Ch-Amer	19	5,506	9,812	9,812 *	.1	.1
049 Armen Ap Cilic	3	244	NR	1,421	-	-
050 Armen Ap Etchm	5	342	NR	4,296	-	.1
053 Assemb of God	337	43,611	54,893	96,893	.8	1.4
056 Baha'i	45	5,327	NR	5,327	-	.1
057 Bapt Gen Conf	78	13,652	14,060	19,217 *	.2	.3
059 Bapt Miss Assn	14	952	627	1,201 *	-	-
061 Beachy Amish	4	296	NR	367 *	-	-
071 Brethren (Ash)	3	427	287	521 *	-	-
075 Brethren in Cr	1	62	63	63	-	-
076 Buddhism	63	NR	NR	NR	-	-
078 Bulgar Orth USA	2	NR	NR	1,260	-	-
081 Catholic	1,125	NR	NR	3,874,933	31.2	56.4
084 Calvary Chapel	9	NR	NR	NR	-	-
089 Chr & Miss Al	54	3,806	NR	6,222	.1	.1
093 Chr Ch (Disc)	170	46,163	11,580	56,638 *	.5	.8
097 Chr Chs&Chs Cr	519	109,301	NR	134,325 *	1.1	2.0
105 Christian Ref	48	14,978	10,585	18,866 *	.2	.3
121 Ch God (Abr)	13	461	671	792 *	-	-
123 Ch God (Ander)	105	NR	10,028	10,028	.1	.1
127 Ch God (Cleve)	123	14,498	8,144	18,246 *	.1	.3
143 CG in Cr(Menn)	1	24	NR	30 *	-	-
145 Ch God Prophcy	21	888	NR	1,118 *	-	-
151 L-D Saints	116	NR	NR	35,859	.3	.5
157 Ch of Brethren	45	4,979	2,063	6,206 *	-	.1
165 Ch of Nazarene	247	24,883	20,137	38,050	.3	.6
167 Chs of Christ	293	22,146	21,671	29,295	.2	.4
171 Ch God-Gen Con	27	3,419	2,429	4,413 *	-	.1
173 Comm of Christ	54	4,395	NR	4,395	-	.1
175 Congr Chr Chs	29	3,972	2,204	4,979 *	-	.1
179 Consrv Bapt	33	NR	7,575	7,575	.1	.1
181 Consrv Congr	10	1,690	733	2,146 *	-	-
183 Cons Menn Conf	2	258	315	375	-	-
185 Cumber Presb	40	1,552	NR	2,959	-	-
193 Episcopal	200	NR	21,099	52,578	.4	.8
201 Evan Cov Ch	69	13,616	10,939	17,759 *	.1	.3
203 Evan Free Ch	127	16,209	29,317	29,402	.2	.4
207 E.L.C.A.	553	206,846	84,617	279,724	2.3	4.1
213 Evan Menn Inc	12	1,974	4,642	2,442 *	-	-
216 Evan Presby Ch	4	559	NR	694 *	-	-
220 Free Lutheran	15	2,990	1,817	3,959	-	.1
221 Free Methodist	69	4,349	5,377	5,818	-	.1
223 Free Will Bapt	41	3,521	NR	4,351 *	-	.1
226 Friends-USA	26	1,900	NR	2,358 *	-	-
237 Menn Br US Conf	1	11	NR	14 *	-	-
245 Greek Orth Vslp	1	700	NR	1,200	-	-
246 Greek Orthodox	35	NR	NR	36,801	.3	.5
249 Assyr Apost Ch	4	NR	NR	22,785	.2	.3
251 Holy Orth in NA	1	NR	NR	18	-	-
252 Hindu	30	NR	NR	NR	-	-
262 Int Cou Comm Ch	17	6,696	NR	8,424 *	.1	.1
263 Int Foursq Gos	56	8,200	6,138	10,785 *	.1	.2
264 Int Chs of Crst	4	3,545	5,421	5,108	-	.1
267 Muslim Est	79	NR	25,199	125,203	1.0	1.8
268 Jain	2	NR	NR	NR	-	-

Religious Group	Number of Churches, Synagogues, Mosques, or Temples	Number of Communicant, Confirmed, or Full Members	Number of Attendees	Total Adherents		
				Number of Adherents	% of Total Pop.	% of Total Adh.
283 Luth—MO Synod	521	208,788	97,486	278,008	2.2	4.0
286 E.PA Mennonite	3	236	NR	286 *	-	-
288 Mennonite USA	52	6,698	5,708	8,589 *	.1	.1
290 Metro Comm Ch	6	299	278	359 *	-	-
291 Missionary Ch	13	1,621	3,183	3,183	-	-
293 Morav Ch-North	1	242	NR	298	-	-
297 Mennonite;Other	3	150	NR	186 *	-	-
304 NatPrimBapt USA	5	532	NR	669 *	-	-
306 NT IndBapt&Rltd	89	20,002	NR	24,871 *	.2	.4
307 Neth Ref Congr	1	18	NR	31	-	-
313 N Am Bapt Conf	11	1,594	1,213	2,012 *	-	-
322 Old Ord Menn Ch	1	29	NR	35 *	-	-
323 Old Ord Amish	34	1,870	NR	2,306 *	-	-
330 Macedonian Orth	2	NR	NR	1,800	-	-
331 OCA: Ter Diocs	11	1,193	NR	3,428	-	-
332 OCA: Bulg Dioc	2	540	NR	1,986	-	-
333 Malan Dioc Am	3	NR	NR	1,000	-	-
334 Malan Syr Orth	2	60	NR	300	-	-
335 Orth Pres Ch	8	497	662	808	-	-
339 Pent Ch of God	25	1,282	NR	2,460	-	-
349 Pent Holiness	6	174	178	223 *	-	-
355 Presb Ch (USA)	453	105,582	52,369	133,977 *	1.1	2.0
356 Presb Ch Amer	44	7,316	6,614	8,570	.1	.1
360 Prim Bapt Chrch	33	NR	NR	NR	-	-
363 Primitive Meth	1	57	NR	61	-	-
365 Prog Prim Bapt	2	56	NR	68 *	-	-
369 Prot Ref Chs	3	383	NR	654	-	-
370 Ref Baptist Chs	3	NR	NR	NR	-	-
371 Ref Ch in Am	53	11,103	10,420	17,936	.1	.3
379 Ref Mennonite	1	43	NR	53 *	-	-
388 Reg Bapt Gen As	69	7,631	6,975	9,552 *	.1	.1
395 Romania Orth Ar	1	NR	NR	525	-	-
397 OCA: Roman Dioc	2	NR	NR	3,000	-	-
400 Rus Orth Moscow	1	NR	NR	NR	-	-
401 Rus Orth Abroad	2	NR	NR	NR	-	-
403 Salvation Army	56	6,263	8,222	22,765	.2	.3
409 Separate Bapt	8	480	NR	567 *	-	-
410 Serb Orth USA	5	NR	NR	8,430	.1	.1
411 Serb Orth: Grac	5	NR	NR	NR	-	-
413 S.D.A.	134	21,051	NR	25,046	.2	.4
416 Sikh	3	NR	NR	NR	-	-
418 Southw Bapt Fel	7	NR	NR	NR	-	-
419 So Bapt Conv	981	247,810	86,615	305,838 *	2.5	4.5
423 Syrian Orth Ch	1	NR	NR	270	-	-
425 Tao	1	NR	NR	NR	-	-
431 Ukrainian Orth	4	NR	NR	1,728	-	-
435 Unitarian-Univ	36	5,761	NR	7,244 *	.1	.1
443 Un C of Christ	390	132,644	51,748	166,772 *	1.3	2.4
449 Un Methodist	1,388	293,861	129,287	365,182 *	2.9	5.3
455 Un Ref Chs N.A.	4	627	NR	860	-	-
463 Vineyard	24	5,422	4,640	7,282 *	.1	.1
467 Wesleyan	28	2,085	3,302	6,961	.1	.1
469 WELS	33	7,225	4,266	9,563	.1	.1
490 Zoroastrian	3	NR	NR	NR	-	-
496 Jewish Est	161	NR	NR	270,000	2.2	3.9
498 Indep.Charis.	17	8,208	9,785	11,398	.1	.2
499 Indep.Non-Char	47	24,587	41,380	50,545	.4	.7
INDIANA	**7,492**	**1,247,145**	**652,481**	**2,608,882 ***	**42.9**	**100.0**
011 A.W.M.C.	2	11	50	11	-	-
017 Amer Bapt Assn	23	1,520	NR	1,899 *	-	.1
019 Amer Bapt USA	362	92,325	36,024	115,101 *	1.9	4.4
022 Carp Rus Orth	4	487	NR	830	-	-
032 Amish; other	4	229	NR	288 *	-	-
034 Ant Orth of NA	6	1,018	NR	2,036	-	.1
040 Ap Chr Ch-Amer	11	2,324	3,955	3,955 *	.1	.2
053 Assemb of God	251	30,114	35,450	56,948	.9	2.2
056 Baha'i	10	1,213	NR	1,213	-	-
057 Bapt Gen Conf	4	268	232	348 *	-	-
059 Bapt Miss Assn	4	373	249	451 *	-	-
061 Beachy Amish	14	990	NR	1,279 *	-	-
071 Brethren (Ash)	34	3,654	3,555	4,632 *	.1	.2
075 Brethren in Cr	5	234	275	318	-	-
076 Buddhism	4	NR	NR	NR	-	-

NR–Not Reported *Total adherents estimated from known number of communicant, confirmed, full members. - Represents a percentage less than 0.1. Percentages may not total 100 due to rounding.

Table 3: Religious Congregations by State and Group: 2000

Religious Group	Number of Churches, Synagogues, Mosques, or Temples	Number of Communicant, Confirmed, or Full Members	Number of Attendees	Total Adherents		
				Number of Adherents	% of Total Pop.	% of Total Adh.
078 Bulgar Orth USA	1	NR	NR	500	-	-
081 Catholic	462	NR	NR	836,009	13.7	32.0
084 Calvary Chapel	17	NR	NR	NR	-	-
089 Chr & Miss Al	25	1,468	NR	3,794	.1	.1
093 Chr Ch (Disc)	185	67,380	18,987	84,079 *	1.4	3.2
097 Chr Chs&Chs Cr	585	164,056	NR	205,408 *	3.4	7.9
105 Christian Ref	17	4,989	3,257	6,269 *	.1	.2
107 Christian Un	8	659	404	840 *	-	-
121 Ch God (Abr)	7	240	240	305 *	-	-
123 Ch God (Ander)	157	NR	21,786	21,786	.4	.8
127 Ch God (Cleve)	86	10,672	6,209	13,564 *	.2	.5
143 CG in Cr(Menn)	1	52	NR	65 *	-	-
145 Ch God Prophcy	32	1,149	NR	1,423 *	-	.1
151 L-D Saints	91	NR	NR	28,309	.5	1.1
157 Ch of Brethren	99	11,975	7,060	15,204 *	.3	.6
165 Ch of Nazarene	301	39,314	31,055	60,097	1.0	2.3
167 Chs of Christ	345	27,426	28,282	35,927	.6	1.4
171 Ch God-Gen Con	23	3,147	2,925	4,201 *	.1	.2
173 Comm of Christ	13	1,203	NR	1,203	-	-
175 Congr Chr Chs	9	934	569	1,162 *	-	-
176 Congr Ad Afl	11	978	NR	1,219 *	-	-
179 Consrv Bapt	6	NR	750	750	-	-
181 Consrv Congr	2	477	185	601 *	-	-
183 Cons Menn Conf	10	1,309	1,598	1,904	-	.1
185 Cumber Presb	7	361	NR	954	-	-
191 Entrpr Bpt Asc	1	39	NR	49 *	-	-
193 Episcopal	86	NR	7,917	18,396	.3	.7
201 Evan Cov Ch	7	1,145	1,426	1,745 *	-	.1
203 Evan Free Ch	21	2,966	6,415	6,459	.1	.2
207 E.L.C.A.	198	54,631	23,595	72,772	1.2	2.8
213 Evan Menn Inc	8	1,344	2,470	1,710 *	-	.1
216 Evan Presby Ch	2	312	NR	396 *	-	-
220 Free Lutheran	2	148	67	183	-	-
221 Free Methodist	41	4,111	4,621	5,542	.1	.2
223 Free Will Bapt	26	59	NR	79 *	-	-
226 Friends-USA	138	8,870	NR	11,069 *	.2	.4
246 Greek Orthodox	7	NR	NR	8,169	.1	.3
258 IndFreeWillBapt	11	912	NR	1,124 *	-	-
262 Int Cou Comm Ch	4	1,898	NR	2,373 *	-	.1
263 Int Foursq Gos	31	3,977	4,434	5,539 *	.1	.2
264 Int Chs of Crst	2	517	969	831	-	-
265 Int Pent C Chr	1	75	39	75	-	-
267 Muslim Est	20	NR	3,043	11,002	.2	.4
283 Luth—MO Synod	225	83,386	43,798	111,522	1.8	4.3
288 Mennonite USA	69	12,096	10,202	15,884 *	.3	.6
290 Metro Comm Ch	1	150	189	189 *	-	-
291 Missionary Ch	69	8,433	16,282	16,583	.3	.6
293 Morav Ch-North	3	432	NR	524	-	-
296 Midw Congr Fel	18	797	1,008	986 *	-	-
297 Mennonite;Other	30	1,721	NR	2,218 *	-	.1
304 NatPrimBapt USA	4	61	NR	77 *	-	-
306 NT IndBapt&Rltd	126	25,200	NR	31,579 *	.5	1.2
313 N Am Bapt Conf	1	60	30	75 *	-	-
320 "Old" MB Ascs	12	1,321	NR	1,664 *	-	.1
322 Old Ord Menn Ch	8	741	NR	958 *	-	-
323 Old Ord Amish	244	14,680	NR	19,177 *	.3	.7
330 Macedonian Orth	1	NR	NR	2,000	-	.1
331 OCA: Ter Diocs	4	223	NR	455	-	-
332 OCA: Bulg Dioc	1	200	NR	285	-	-
335 Orth Pres Ch	2	52	72	81	-	-
339 Pent Ch of God	28	1,037	NR	2,243	-	.1
349 Pent Holiness	5	129	181	166 *	-	-
355 Presb Ch (USA)	256	56,882	29,743	71,414 *	1.2	2.7
356 Presb Ch Amer	18	1,614	1,654	2,179	-	.1
360 Prim Bapt Chrch	37	NR	NR	NR	-	-
363 Primitive Meth	1	57	NR	61	-	-
365 Prog Prim Bapt	4	131	NR	166 *	-	-
369 Prot Ref Chs	1	77	NR	122	-	-
370 Ref Baptist Chs	7	NR	NR	NR	-	-
371 Ref Ch in Am	10	2,231	1,851	3,437	.1	.1
388 Reg Bapt Gen As	121	27,585	29,563	36,701 *	.6	1.4
395 Romania Orth Ar	1	NR	NR	88	-	-
397 OCA: Roman Dioc	2	NR	NR	163	-	-
401 Rus Orth Abroad	3	NR	NR	NR	-	-
403 Salvation Army	36	3,662	2,254	12,818	.2	.5
409 Separate Bapt	20	2,219	NR	2,767 *	-	.1
410 Serb Orth USA	3	NR	NR	2,212	-	.1
411 Serb Orth: Grac	3	NR	NR	NR	-	-
413 S.D.A.	86	9,782	NR	11,641	.2	.4
416 Sikh	2	NR	NR	NR	-	-
418 Southw Bapt Fel	18	NR	NR	NR	-	-
419 So Bapt Conv	345	100,140	34,265	124,452 *	2.0	4.8
426 2Seed Sprt Bpt	1	16	NR	20 *	-	-
431 Ukrainian Orth	4	NR	NR	570	-	-
435 Unitarian-Univ	16	2,373	NR	2,936 *	-	.1
443 Un C of Christ	165	41,042	16,169	51,177 *	.8	2.0
449 Un Methodist	1,286	230,262	138,134	288,308 *	4.7	11.1
455 Un Ref Chs N.A.	2	307	NR	558	-	-
463 Vineyard	16	3,960	3,181	4,975 *	.1	.2
467 Wesleyan	227	14,151	18,016	38,774	.6	1.5
469 WELS	10	1,287	913	1,696	-	.1
496 Jewish Est	27	NR	NR	18,000	.3	.7
498 Indep.Charis.	14	3,627	8,503	12,966	.2	.5
499 Indep.Non-Char	55	41,468	38,380	51,620	.8	2.0
IOWA	**4,584**	**838,132**	**403,602**	**1,711,426 ***	**58.5**	**100.0**
017 Amer Bapt Assn	1	30	NR	37 *	-	-
019 Amer Bapt USA	113	20,787	8,345	25,646 *	.9	1.5
034 Ant Orth of NA	2	496	NR	992	-	.1
040 Ap Chr Ch-Amer	8	948	2,116	2,116 *	.1	.1
049 Armen Ap Cilic	1	0	NR	80	-	-
053 Assemb of God	137	11,996	15,663	28,026	1.0	1.6
056 Baha'i	9	1,012	NR	1,012	-	.1
057 Bapt Gen Conf	31	5,014	4,909	6,433 *	.2	.4
061 Beachy Amish	2	174	NR	208 *	-	-
071 Brethren (Ash)	1	81	48	98 *	-	-
075 Brethren in Cr	1	29	20	29	-	-
076 Buddhism	7	NR	NR	NR	-	-
081 Catholic	508	NR	NR	558,092	19.1	32.6
084 Calvary Chapel	2	NR	NR	NR	-	-
089 Chr & Miss Al	24	1,913	NR	4,694	.2	.3
093 Chr Ch (Disc)	146	44,605	11,965	55,157 *	1.9	3.2
097 Chr Chs&Chs Cr	128	20,606	NR	25,391 *	.9	1.5
105 Christian Ref	57	17,465	13,404	21,725 *	.7	1.3
107 Christian Un	8	355	290	453 *	-	-
121 Ch God (Abr)	4	65	81	121 *	-	-
123 Ch God (Ander)	10	NR	333	333	-	-
127 Ch God (Cleve)	18	944	814	1,217 *	-	.1
143 CG in Cr(Menn)	3	162	NR	203 *	-	-
145 Ch God Prophcy	10	341	NR	421 *	-	-
151 L-D Saints	62	NR	NR	15,236	.5	.9
157 Ch of Brethren	27	2,601	1,348	3,423 *	.1	.2
165 Ch of Nazarene	70	6,382	5,742	11,011	.4	.6
167 Chs of Christ	71	3,124	3,377	4,229	.1	.2
171 Ch God-Gen Con	7	352	278	451 *	-	-
173 Comm of Christ	61	6,137	NR	6,137	.2	.4
175 Congr Chr Chs	12	1,771	782	2,177 *	.1	.1
176 Congr Ad Afl	5	458	NR	563 *	-	-
179 Consrv Bapt	12	NR	2,615	2,615	.1	.2
181 Consrv Congr	5	734	550	899 *	-	.1
183 Cons Menn Conf	5	471	575	684	-	-
185 Cumber Presb	1	26	NR	134	-	-
193 Episcopal	64	NR	4,200	12,730	.4	.7
201 Evan Cov Ch	18	2,041	1,844	2,622 *	.1	.2
203 Evan Free Ch	79	6,815	13,087	13,087	.4	.8
207 E.L.C.A.	510	204,974	79,940	268,543	9.2	15.7
216 Evan Presby Ch	1	340	NR	426 *	-	-
220 Free Lutheran	7	602	342	721	-	-
221 Free Methodist	18	568	638	719	-	-
223 Free Will Bapt	2	0	NR	0 *	-	-
226 Friends-USA	61	3,765	NR	4,637 *	.2	.3
245 Greek Orth Vslp	1	35	NR	35	-	-
246 Greek Orthodox	6	NR	NR	1,758	.1	.1
252 Hindu	3	NR	NR	NR	-	-
262 Int Cou Comm Ch	3	1,104	NR	1,351 *	-	.1
263 Int Foursq Gos	28	2,908	3,767	4,654 *	.2	.3
264 Int Chs of Crst	1	100	156	142	-	-
267 Muslim Est	9	NR	1,134	4,717	.2	.3

NR–Not Reported *Total adherents estimated from known number of communicant, confirmed, full members. - Represents a percentage less than 0.1. Percentages may not total 100 due to rounding.

Table 3: Religious Congregations by State and Group: 2000

Religious Group	Number of Churches, Synagogues, Mosques, or Temples	Number of Communicant, Confirmed, or Full Members	Number of Attendees	Total Adherents: Number of Adherents	Total Adherents: % of Total Pop.	Total Adherents: % of Total Adh.
283 Luth—MO Synod	294	91,862	41,432	120,075	4.1	7.0
288 Mennonite USA	22	3,156	2,531	3,926 *	.1	.2
290 Metro Comm Ch	2	113	117	142 *	-	-
291 Missionary Ch	4	165	389	392	-	-
297 Mennonite;Other	4	105	NR	131 *	-	-
306 NT IndBapt&Rltd	3	110	NR	134 *	-	-
307 Neth Ref Congr	2	842	NR	1,585	.1	.1
313 N Am Bapt Conf	14	1,874	1,561	2,304 *	.1	.1
322 Old Ord Menn Ch	3	160	NR	199 *	-	-
323 Old Ord Amish	38	2,085	NR	2,601 *	.1	.2
324 Old Ord Rvr Br	1	33	55	63	-	-
335 Orth Pres Ch	3	100	107	146	-	-
339 Pent Ch of God	6	294	NR	714	-	-
349 Pent Holiness	3	88	194	110 *	-	-
355 Presb Ch (USA)	306	56,613	25,633	69,974 *	2.4	4.1
356 Presb Ch Amer	8	826	661	1,143	-	.1
360 Prim Bapt Chrch	6	NR	NR	NR	-	-
363 Primitive Meth	2	114	NR	121	-	-
369 Prot Ref Chs	3	412	NR	788	-	-
370 Ref Baptist Chs	1	NR	NR	NR	-	-
371 Ref Ch in Am	78	22,615	22,012	36,709	1.3	2.1
373 Ref Ch in U.S.	1	125	NR	157	-	-
388 Reg Bapt Gen As	101	11,048	11,860	14,390 *	.5	.8
403 Salvation Army	19	2,513	2,593	9,230	.3	.5
413 S.D.A.	47	3,759	NR	4,476	.2	.3
416 Sikh	2	NR	NR	NR	-	-
419 So Bapt Conv	75	10,836	6,070	13,322 *	.5	.8
435 Unitarian-Univ	11	1,484	NR	1,816 *	.1	.1
443 Un C of Christ	195	39,912	15,320	49,205 *	1.7	2.9
449 Un Methodist	862	201,204	75,988	248,211 *	8.5	14.5
455 Un Ref Chs N.A.	4	563	NR	874	-	.1
463 Vineyard	9	1,380	1,793	2,085 *	.1	.1
467 Wesleyan	28	3,079	2,851	5,952	.2	.3
469 WELS	12	1,311	837	1,756	.1	.1
496 Jewish Est	16	NR	NR	6,400	.2	.4
498 Indep.Charis.	6	2,750	4,510	5,000	.2	.3
499 Indep.Non-Char	13	4,270	8,725	11,110	.4	.6
KANSAS	**3,959**	**655,970**	**319,323**	**1,327,235 ***	**49.4**	**100.0**
017 Amer Bapt Assn	18	848	NR	1,076 *	-	.1
019 Amer Bapt USA	224	51,372	21,228	64,312 *	2.4	4.8
032 Amish; other	2	110	NR	134 *	-	-
034 Ant Orth of NA	6	1,086	NR	2,172	.1	.2
040 Ap Chr Ch-Amer	6	506	1,017	1,017 *	-	.1
053 Assemb of God	163	15,412	19,175	27,860	1.0	2.1
056 Baha'i	9	1,255	NR	1,255	-	.1
059 Bapt Miss Assn	10	1,129	443	1,407 *	.1	.1
061 Beachy Amish	3	320	NR	392 *	-	-
071 Brethren (Ash)	3	115	161	146 *	-	-
075 Brethren in Cr	4	377	484	525	-	-
076 Buddhism	10	NR	NR	NR	-	-
081 Catholic	354	NR	NR	405,844	15.1	30.6
084 Calvary Chapel	7	NR	NR	NR	-	-
089 Chr & Miss Al	3	1,023	NR	1,071	-	.1
093 Chr Ch (Disc)	137	45,492	13,604	56,908 *	2.1	4.3
097 Chr Chs&Chs Cr	216	45,163	NR	56,793 *	2.1	4.3
105 Christian Ref	2	379	260	460 *	-	-
123 Ch God (Ander)	53	NR	7,341	7,341	.3	.6
127 Ch God (Cleve)	27	1,925	1,013	2,432 *	.1	.2
143 CG in Cr(Menn)	22	3,628	NR	4,587 *	.2	.3
145 Ch God Prophcy	12	322	NR	400 *	-	-
151 L-D Saints	71	NR	NR	20,356	.8	1.5
157 Ch of Brethren	30	2,943	1,405	3,690 *	.1	.3
165 Ch of Nazarene	139	23,097	18,538	31,902	1.2	2.4
167 Chs of Christ	178	14,391	14,365	18,969	.7	1.4
171 Ch God-Gen Con	3	344	303	417 *	-	-
173 Comm of Christ	39	4,169	NR	4,169	.2	.3
175 Congr Chr Chs	5	1,052	587	1,323 *	-	.1
181 Consrv Congr	3	690	626	874 *	-	.1
183 Cons Menn Conf	2	195	238	284	-	-
193 Episcopal	84	NR	6,905	16,687	.6	1.3
201 Evan Cov Ch	22	3,760	4,894	5,338 *	.2	.4
203 Evan Free Ch	19	2,007	4,175	4,175	.2	.3
207 E.L.C.A.	135	32,240	13,963	42,491	1.6	3.2
211 Fel Evg Bib Ch	1	138	141	141	-	-
213 Evan Menn Inc	3	381	587	469 *	-	-
216 Evan Presby Ch	3	706	NR	869 *	-	.1
221 Free Methodist	22	1,395	1,909	2,003	.1	.2
223 Free Will Bapt	10	311	NR	397 *	-	-
226 Friends-USA	62	3,228	NR	4,056 *	.2	.3
237 Menn Br US Conf	17	3,740	NR	4,691 *	.2	.4
246 Greek Orthodox	2	NR	NR	0	-	-
252 Hindu	1	NR	NR	NR	-	-
263 Int Foursq Gos	27	3,035	3,614	4,222 *	.2	.3
264 Int Chs of Crst	4	709	1,316	1,053	-	.1
267 Muslim Est	9	NR	991	3,470	.1	.3
268 Jain	2	NR	NR	NR	-	-
283 Luth—MO Synod	166	48,060	24,733	62,712	2.3	4.7
288 Mennonite USA	53	11,529	7,281	14,297 *	.5	1.1
290 Metro Comm Ch	3	179	162	188 *	-	-
291 Missionary Ch	5	473	566	612	-	-
297 Mennonite;Other	9	1,259	NR	1,609 *	.1	.1
304 NatPrimBapt USA	1	25	NR	31 *	-	-
306 NT IndBapt&Rltd	1	100	NR	133 *	-	-
313 N Am Bapt Conf	10	1,091	875	1,337 *	-	.1
323 Old Ord Amish	6	330	NR	406 *	-	-
331 OCA: Ter Diocs	1	113	NR	162	-	-
335 Orth Pres Ch	2	139	214	231	-	-
339 Pent Ch of God	7	163	NR	388	-	-
349 Pent Holiness	25	3,198	2,375	4,015 *	.1	.3
355 Presb Ch (USA)	193	40,495	19,176	50,806 *	1.9	3.8
356 Presb Ch Amer	6	640	1,010	1,059	-	.1
360 Prim Bapt Chrch	2	NR	NR	NR	-	-
370 Ref Baptist Chs	2	NR	NR	NR	-	-
371 Ref Ch in Am	3	278	287	583	-	-
388 Reg Bapt Gen As	27	1,865	1,613	2,418 *	.1	.2
403 Salvation Army	17	1,688	1,762	6,705	.2	.5
410 Serb Orth USA	1	NR	NR	387	-	-
411 Serb Orth: Grac	1	NR	NR	NR	-	-
413 S.D.A.	63	6,221	NR	7,408	.3	.6
416 Sikh	2	NR	NR	NR	-	-
418 Southw Bapt Fel	2	NR	NR	NR	-	-
419 So Bapt Conv	254	80,320	28,753	101,696 *	3.8	7.7
435 Unitarian-Univ	7	681	NR	845 *	-	.1
443 Un C of Christ	75	10,963	4,728	13,568 *	.5	1.0
449 Un Methodist	735	165,166	69,218	206,187 *	7.7	15.5
463 Vineyard	6	1,473	1,270	1,889 *	.1	.1
467 Wesleyan	44	3,236	5,224	11,973	.4	.9
469 WELS	9	710	505	944	-	.1
490 Zoroastrian	1	NR	NR	NR	-	-
496 Jewish Est	10	NR	NR	14,500	.5	1.1
498 Indep.Charis.	10	877	2,973	3,468	.1	.3
499 Indep.Non-Char	16	5,705	7,315	8,500	.3	.6
KENTUCKY	**7,143**	**1,353,901**	**490,206**	**2,159,541 ***	**53.4**	**100.0**
011 A.W.M.C.	1	8	42	12	-	-
017 Amer Bapt Assn	21	5,250	NR	6,373 *	.2	.3
019 Amer Bapt USA	5	2,428	912	2,993 *	.1	.1
032 Amish; other	8	449	NR	565 *	-	-
034 Ant Orth of NA	2	794	NR	1,588	-	.1
040 Ap Chr Ch-Amer	1	9	27	27 *	-	-
053 Assemb of God	167	24,309	20,443	30,103	.7	1.4
055 As Ref Pres Ch	1	66	NR	72	-	-
056 Baha'i	4	635	NR	635	-	-
059 Bapt Miss Assn	1	97	71	118 *	-	-
061 Beachy Amish	8	493	NR	613 *	-	-
071 Brethren (Ash)	2	56	84	68 *	-	-
075 Brethren in Cr	5	240	279	294	-	-
076 Buddhism	7	NR	NR	NR	-	-
081 Catholic	323	NR	NR	406,021	10.0	18.8
084 Calvary Chapel	5	NR	NR	NR	-	-
089 Chr & Miss Al	20	863	NR	2,151	.1	.1
093 Chr Ch (Disc)	231	54,720	17,442	67,611 *	1.7	3.1
097 Chr Chs&Chs Cr	405	86,169	NR	106,638 *	2.6	4.9
123 Ch God (Ander)	133	NR	11,507	11,507	.3	.5
127 Ch God (Cleve)	236	27,181	13,004	33,572 *	.8	1.6
143 CG in Cr(Menn)	2	193	NR	238 *	-	-
145 Ch God Prophcy	81	3,972	NR	4,901 *	.1	.2

NR–Not Reported   *Total adherents estimated from known number of communicant, confirmed, full members.   - Represents a percentage less than 0.1.   Percentages may not total 100 due to rounding.

Table 3: Religious Congregations by State and Group: 2000

Religious Group	Number of Churches, Synagogues, Mosques, or Temples	Number of Communicant, Confirmed, or Full Members	Number of Attendees	Total Adherents		
				Number of Adherents	% of Total Pop.	% of Total Adh.
151 L-D Saints	63	NR	NR	17,966	.4	.8
157 Ch of Brethren	4	262	88	327 *	-	-
165 Ch of Nazarene	136	13,685	9,768	19,667	.5	.9
167 Chs of Christ	621	45,571	46,733	58,602	1.4	2.7
173 Comm of Christ	5	383	NR	383	-	-
179 Consrv Bapt	1	NR	200	200	-	-
183 Cons Menn Conf	7	221	269	322	-	-
185 Cumber Presb	104	6,156	NR	10,859	.3	.5
189 Duck Rivr Bapt	1	32	NR	39 *	-	-
191 Entrpr Bpt Asc	36	2,659	NR	3,241 *	.1	.2
193 Episcopal	76	NR	7,530	19,343	.5	.9
201 Evan Cov Ch	1	32	76	76 *	-	-
203 Evan Free Ch	11	483	943	963	-	-
207 E.L.C.A.	40	7,281	3,681	9,485	.2	.4
216 Evan Presby Ch	2	72	NR	90 *	-	-
221 Free Methodist	13	612	1,037	1,065	-	-
223 Free Will Bapt	133	16,711	NR	20,441 *	.5	.9
226 Friends-USA	3	180	NR	219 *	-	-
246 Greek Orthodox	2	NR	NR	522	-	-
252 Hindu	3	NR	NR	NR	-	-
258 IndFreeWillBapt	39	3,277	NR	3,989 *	.1	.2
263 Int Foursq Gos	9	331	838	856 *	-	-
264 Int Chs of Crst	1	302	472	422	-	-
265 Int Pent C Chr	7	440	362	1,241	-	.1
267 Muslim Est	10	NR	1,162	4,696	.1	.2
283 Luth—MO Synod	29	4,868	2,872	6,499	.2	.3
288 Mennonite USA	4	78	98	105 *	-	-
290 Metro Comm Ch	4	191	211	244 *	-	-
291 Missionary Ch	3	27	140	140	-	-
297 Mennonite;Other	9	403	NR	495 *	-	-
304 NatPrimBapt USA	13	672	NR	826 *	-	-
320 "Old" MB Ascs	42	7,941	NR	9,735 *	.2	.5
322 Old Ord Menn Ch	10	643	NR	805 *	-	-
323 Old Ord Amish	32	1,825	NR	2,272 *	.1	.1
335 Orth Pres Ch	2	24	72	72	-	-
339 Pent Ch of God	19	1,036	NR	1,746	-	.1
349 Pent Holiness	9	420	347	515 *	-	-
355 Presb Ch (USA)	196	30,013	15,501	36,940 *	.9	1.7
356 Presb Ch Amer	9	650	699	831	-	-
360 Prim Bapt Chrch	65	NR	NR	NR	-	-
362 Prim Bapt E Dst	9	871	NR	1,069 *	-	-
370 Ref Baptist Chs	3	NR	NR	NR	-	-
371 Ref Ch in Am	3	180	172	297	-	-
388 Reg Bapt Gen As	2	0	0	0 *	-	-
403 Salvation Army	19	2,075	1,206	3,432	.1	.2
409 Separate Bapt	54	5,540	NR	6,767 *	.2	.3
413 S.D.A.	57	4,959	NR	5,900	.1	.3
418 Southw Bapt Fel	12	NR	NR	NR	-	-
419 So Bapt Conv	2,424	794,040	245,922	979,994 *	24.2	45.4
435 Unitarian-Univ	9	880	NR	1,081 *	-	.1
443 Un C of Christ	32	7,071	2,980	8,763 *	.2	.4
449 Un Methodist	991	169,622	69,953	208,720 *	5.2	9.7
463 Vineyard	5	1,212	1,132	1,603 *	-	.1
467 Wesleyan	45	1,517	1,747	4,112	.1	.2
469 WELS	4	220	204	305	-	-
496 Jewish Est	11	NR	NR	11,350	.3	.5
498 Indep.Charis.	6	1,575	3,190	3,450	.1	.2
499 Indep.Non-Char	14	8,726	6,790	10,359	.3	.5
LOUISIANA	**4,158**	**900,511**	**358,469**	**2,627,028 ***	**58.8**	**100.0**
011 A.W.M.C.	1	0	12	0	-	-
017 Amer Bapt Assn	91	10,405	NR	13,084 *	.3	.5
019 Amer Bapt USA	7	2,134	675	2,672 *	.1	.1
034 Ant Orth of NA	4	261	NR	522	-	-
049 Armen Ap Cilic	1	0	NR	100	-	-
050 Armen Ap Etchm	1	0	NR	200	-	-
053 Assemb of God	237	35,042	31,340	49,041	1.1	1.9
056 Baha'i	10	1,251	NR	1,251	-	-
059 Bapt Miss Assn	35	7,131	2,448	8,943 *	.2	.3
076 Buddhism	9	NR	NR	NR	-	-
081 Catholic	625	NR	NR	1,382,603	30.9	52.6
084 Calvary Chapel	3	NR	NR	NR	-	-
089 Chr & Miss Al	5	150	NR	345	-	-
093 Chr Ch (Disc)	23	4,178	1,443	5,269 *	.1	.2
097 Chr Chs&Chs Cr	26	2,248	NR	2,847 *	.1	.1
121 Ch God (Abr)	3	187	163	238 *	-	-
123 Ch God (Ander)	56	NR	3,907	3,907	.1	.1
127 Ch God (Cleve)	54	6,716	3,161	8,572 *	.2	.3
143 CG in Cr(Menn)	2	298	NR	380 *	-	-
145 Ch God Prophcy	24	654	NR	832 *	-	-
151 L-D Saints	62	NR	NR	16,080	.4	.6
157 Ch of Brethren	2	171	56	218 *	-	-
165 Ch of Nazarene	46	3,324	2,318	4,355	.1	.2
167 Chs of Christ	229	19,303	18,309	25,899	.6	1.0
171 Ch God-Gen Con	1	6	12	12 *	-	-
173 Comm of Christ	5	512	NR	512	-	-
185 Cumber Presb	4	145	NR	241	-	-
186 Coptic Orth Ch	3	NR	NR	NR	-	-
193 Episcopal	102	NR	11,691	33,653	.8	1.3
203 Evan Free Ch	2	149	375	375	-	-
207 E.L.C.A.	19	4,299	2,120	5,794	.1	.2
216 Evan Presby Ch	4	419	NR	531 *	-	-
221 Free Methodist	11	401	362	504	-	-
223 Free Will Bapt	4	68	NR	84 *	-	-
226 Friends-USA	2	30	NR	38 *	-	-
246 Greek Orthodox	4	NR	NR	1,422	-	.1
252 Hindu	6	NR	NR	NR	-	-
262 Int Cou Comm Ch	1	100	NR	126 *	-	-
263 Int Foursq Gos	7	469	499	675 *	-	-
264 Int Chs of Crst	1	173	285	232	-	-
266 Intrstat & Asc	32	3,408	NR	4,297 *	.1	.2
267 Muslim Est	23	NR	3,792	13,050	.3	.5
268 Jain	1	NR	NR	NR	-	-
283 Luth—MO Synod	57	12,205	6,076	14,791	.3	.6
288 Mennonite USA	4	153	144	216 *	-	-
290 Metro Comm Ch	2	103	98	129 *	-	-
313 N Am Bapt Conf	1	99	80	127 *	-	-
333 Malan Dioc Am	1	NR	NR	125	-	-
335 Orth Pres Ch	3	101	109	177	-	-
339 Pent Ch of God	5	113	NR	191	-	-
349 Pent Holiness	13	3,035	3,125	3,796 *	.1	.1
355 Presb Ch (USA)	114	16,780	8,746	21,142 *	.5	.8
356 Presb Ch Amer	20	2,012	1,808	2,548	.1	.1
360 Prim Bapt Chrch	21	NR	NR	NR	-	-
365 Prog Prim Bapt	1	64	NR	80 *	-	-
370 Ref Baptist Chs	1	NR	NR	NR	-	-
388 Reg Bapt Gen As	1	20	15	25 *	-	-
403 Salvation Army	8	1,096	528	2,902	.1	.1
413 S.D.A.	51	8,564	NR	10,193	.2	.4
416 Sikh	1	NR	NR	NR	-	-
418 Southw Bapt Fel	3	NR	NR	NR	-	-
419 So Bapt Conv	1,435	609,259	182,455	768,587 *	17.2	29.3
425 Tao	1	NR	NR	NR	-	-
435 Unitarian-Univ	7	786	NR	990 *	-	-
443 Un C of Christ	17	2,174	918	2,734 *	.1	.1
449 Un Methodist	547	127,060	48,455	160,153 *	3.6	6.1
463 Vineyard	12	2,284	2,025	2,864 *	.1	.1
467 Wesleyan	5	149	364	770	-	-
469 WELS	4	311	195	388	-	-
496 Jewish Est	17	NR	NR	16,500	.4	.6
498 Indep.Charis.	9	8,065	16,225	23,625	.5	.9
499 Indep.Non-Char	9	2,446	4,135	5,071	.1	.2
MAINE	**1,301**	**109,033**	**68,142**	**463,541 ***	**36.4**	**100.0**
011 A.W.M.C.	1	0	18	0	-	-
017 Amer Bapt Assn	2	60	NR	73 *	-	-
019 Amer Bapt USA	164	21,620	10,837	26,259 *	2.1	5.7
053 Assemb of God	52	3,674	4,849	6,253	.5	1.3
056 Baha'i	8	739	NR	739	.1	.2
057 Bapt Gen Conf	2	208	127	249 *	-	.1
059 Bapt Miss Assn	1	16	17	19 *	-	-
061 Beachy Amish	1	8	NR	10 *	-	-
076 Buddhism	6	NR	NR	NR	-	-
081 Catholic	186	NR	NR	283,024	22.2	61.1
084 Calvary Chapel	2	NR	NR	NR	-	-
089 Chr & Miss Al	12	361	NR	876	.1	.2
093 Chr Ch (Disc)	1	120	65	145 *	-	-
097 Chr Chs&Chs Cr	2	26	NR	31 *	-	-

NR–Not Reported *Total adherents estimated from known number of communicant, confirmed, full members. - Represents a percentage less than 0.1. Percentages may not total 100 due to rounding.

Table 3: Religious Congregations by State and Group: 2000

Religious Group	Number of Churches, Synagogues, Mosques, or Temples	Number of Communicant, Confirmed, or Full Members	Number of Attendees	Total Adherents: Number of Adherents	Total Adherents: % of Total Pop.	Total Adherents: % of Total Adh.
127 Ch God (Cleve)	25	1,997	1,500	2,599 *	.2	.6
145 Ch God Prophcy	2	164	NR	201 *	-	-
151 L-D Saints	28	NR	NR	7,119	.6	1.5
157 Ch of Brethren	3	92	135	142 *	-	-
165 Ch of Nazarene	50	3,719	2,852	5,185	.4	1.1
167 Chs of Christ	22	741	831	1,064	.1	.2
173 Comm of Christ	10	778	NR	778	.1	.2
175 Congr Chr Chs	34	3,067	1,921	3,720 *	.3	.8
176 Congr Ad Afl	11	1,081	NR	1,318 *	.1	.3
179 Consrv Bapt	36	NR	5,562	5,562	.4	1.2
181 Consrv Congr	6	236	223	286 *	-	.1
193 Episcopal	66	NR	5,493	15,794	1.2	3.4
201 Evan Cov Ch	3	248	186	301 *	-	.1
203 Evan Free Ch	7	457	986	986	.1	.2
207 E.L.C.A.	17	3,243	1,635	4,531	.4	1.0
221 Free Methodist	2	57	84	84	-	-
223 Free Will Bapt	1	70	NR	84 *	-	-
226 Friends-USA	26	1,118	NR	1,360 *	.1	.3
246 Greek Orthodox	4	NR	NR	2,532	.2	.5
262 Int Cou Comm Ch	3	280	NR	338 *	-	.1
263 Int Foursq Gos	5	437	445	549 *	-	.1
264 Int Chs of Crst	1	36	59	46	-	-
267 Muslim Est	2	NR	201	809	.1	.2
283 Luth—MO Synod	2	301	167	435	-	.1
288 Mennonite USA	1	31	50	50 *	-	-
290 Metro Comm Ch	2	25	23	30 *	-	-
322 Old Ord Menn Ch	1	19	NR	23 *	-	-
335 Orth Pres Ch	5	452	465	603	-	.1
349 Pent Holiness	2	24	28	29 *	-	-
355 Presb Ch (USA)	10	649	408	797 *	.1	.2
356 Presb Ch Amer	1	0	0	0	-	-
370 Ref Baptist Chs	2	NR	NR	NR	-	-
388 Reg Bapt Gen As	6	434	504	556 *	-	.1
401 Rus Orth Abroad	2	NR	NR	NR	-	-
403 Salvation Army	12	1,186	721	2,366	.2	.5
410 Serb Orth USA	1	NR	NR	300	-	.1
413 S.D.A.	22	2,233	NR	2,657	.2	.6
419 So Bapt Conv	13	1,945	1,030	2,373 *	.2	.5
435 Unitarian-Univ	29	2,658	NR	3,234 *	.3	.7
443 Un C of Christ	176	23,928	11,849	29,122 *	2.3	6.3
449 Un Methodist	178	26,097	9,962	31,689 *	2.5	6.8
463 Vineyard	4	806	676	986 *	.1	.2
467 Wesleyan	11	626	1,424	3,403	.3	.7
469 WELS	1	36	16	37	-	-
496 Jewish Est	10	NR	NR	8,290	.7	1.8
498 Indep.Charis.	2	1,050	1,123	1,225	.1	.3
499 Indep.Non-Char	4	1,880	1,670	2,270	.2	.5
MARYLAND	**3,855**	**709,239**	**365,589**	**2,291,896 ***	**43.3**	**100.0**
011 A.W.M.C.	1	0	50	0	-	-
017 Amer Bapt Assn	14	1,960	NR	2,484 *	-	.1
019 Amer Bapt USA	85	35,904	16,075	44,959 *	.8	2.0
022 Carp Rus Orth	2	244	NR	414	-	-
032 Amish; other	1	40	NR	49 *	-	-
034 Ant Orth of NA	3	821	NR	1,642	-	.1
039 Ap Chr Ch(Naz)	1	22	34	34 *	-	-
049 Armen Ap Cilic	1	357	NR	924	-	-
053 Assemb of God	116	13,986	17,251	25,214	.5	1.1
055 As Ref Pres Ch	7	745	NR	918	-	-
056 Baha'i	30	2,346	NR	2,346	-	.1
057 Bapt Gen Conf	5	4,805	3,860	6,129 *	.1	.3
061 Beachy Amish	1	55	NR	65 *	-	-
071 Brethren (Ash)	4	452	376	556 *	-	-
075 Brethren in Cr	5	253	457	462	-	-
076 Buddhism	32	NR	NR	NR	-	-
081 Catholic	309	NR	NR	952,389	18.0	41.6
084 Calvary Chapel	5	NR	NR	NR	-	-
089 Chr & Miss Al	19	1,622	NR	3,147	.1	.1
093 Chr Ch (Disc)	35	6,436	2,026	8,002 *	.2	.3
097 Chr Chs&Chs Cr	31	6,227	NR	7,765 *	.1	.3
105 Christian Ref	1	152	159	190 *	-	-
123 Ch God (Ander)	22	NR	2,811	2,811	.1	.1
127 Ch God (Cleve)	108	25,285	12,875	31,715 *	.6	1.4
145 Ch God Prophcy	25	1,136	NR	1,405 *	-	.1
151 L-D Saints	81	NR	NR	25,882	.5	1.1
157 Ch of Brethren	61	8,809	4,707	11,031 *	.2	.5
165 Ch of Nazarene	49	5,606	5,006	8,576	.2	.4
167 Chs of Christ	51	6,640	6,389	8,466	.2	.4
171 Ch God-Gen Con	18	903	966	1,221 *	-	.1
173 Comm of Christ	5	419	NR	419	-	-
175 Congr Chr Chs	1	100	83	118 *	-	-
179 Consrv Bapt	3	NR	480	480	-	-
181 Consrv Congr	1	30	22	37 *	-	-
183 Cons Menn Conf	1	265	324	385	-	-
193 Episcopal	217	NR	26,746	81,061	1.5	3.5
201 Evan Cov Ch	1	81	100	103 *	-	-
203 Evan Free Ch	8	652	1,745	1,755	-	.1
207 E.L.C.A.	210	72,224	28,576	103,644	2.0	4.5
216 Evan Presby Ch	2	2,816	NR	3,513 *	.1	.2
220 Free Lutheran	1	23	38	38	-	-
221 Free Methodist	12	579	754	866	-	-
223 Free Will Bapt	4	395	NR	502 *	-	-
226 Friends-USA	17	1,775	NR	2,211 *	-	.1
245 Greek Orth Vslp	2	505	NR	2,305	-	.1
246 Greek Orthodox	8	NR	NR	14,112	.3	.6
251 Holy Orth in NA	1	NR	NR	90	-	-
252 Hindu	26	NR	NR	NR	-	-
262 Int Cou Comm Ch	7	1,489	NR	1,864 *	-	.1
263 Int Foursq Gos	13	1,037	2,006	2,042 *	-	.1
265 Int Pent C Chr	2	25	38	85	-	-
267 Muslim Est	31	NR	11,801	52,867	1.0	2.3
268 Jain	2	NR	NR	NR	-	-
283 Luth—MO Synod	70	20,095	9,967	27,544	.5	1.2
286 E.PA Mennonite	2	114	NR	145 *	-	-
288 Mennonite USA	25	1,477	1,513	1,961 *	-	.1
290 Metro Comm Ch	5	347	320	433 *	-	-
291 Missionary Ch	1	13	24	24	-	-
293 Morav Ch-North	3	672	NR	882	-	-
297 Mennonite;Other	18	1,504	NR	1,837 *	-	.1
322 Old Ord Menn Ch	1	170	NR	218 *	-	-
323 Old Ord Amish	6	330	NR	420 *	-	-
331 OCA: Ter Diocs	4	507	NR	857	-	-
332 OCA: Bulg Dioc	1	130	NR	354	-	-
333 Malan Dioc Am	3	NR	NR	525	-	-
334 Malan Syr Orth	2	47	NR	181	-	-
335 Orth Pres Ch	8	919	1,179	1,354	-	.1
339 Pent Ch of God	5	182	NR	351	-	-
349 Pent Holiness	15	1,903	1,362	2,357 *	-	.1
355 Presb Ch (USA)	144	34,191	19,567	44,243 *	.8	1.9
356 Presb Ch Amer	52	9,846	9,058	13,539	.3	.6
360 Prim Bapt Chrch	7	NR	NR	NR	-	-
370 Ref Baptist Chs	1	NR	NR	NR	-	-
371 Ref Ch in Am	1	109	158	292	-	-
373 Ref Ch in U.S.	1	12	NR	19	-	-
388 Reg Bapt Gen As	13	1,522	1,517	1,914 *	-	.1
400 Rus Orth Moscow	1	NR	NR	NR	-	-
401 Rus Orth Abroad	1	NR	NR	NR	-	-
403 Salvation Army	13	1,327	443	3,854	.1	.2
413 S.D.A.	102	25,554	NR	30,411	.6	1.3
416 Sikh	6	NR	NR	NR	-	-
418 Southw Bapt Fel	17	NR	NR	NR	-	-
419 So Bapt Conv	405	113,662	45,612	142,401 *	2.7	6.2
423 Syrian Orth Ch	1	NR	NR	280	-	-
431 Ukrainian Orth	3	NR	NR	552	-	-
435 Unitarian-Univ	22	4,843	NR	6,068 *	.1	.3
443 Un C of Christ	75	15,384	6,489	19,210 *	.4	.8
449 Un Methodist	927	239,093	91,057	297,729 *	5.6	13.0
463 Vineyard	2	487	451	609 *	-	-
467 Wesleyan	43	762	3,338	15,755	.3	.7
469 WELS	4	419	334	637	-	-
496 Jewish Est	107	NR	NR	216,000	4.1	9.4
498 Indep.Charis.	14	13,792	9,620	15,552	.3	.7
499 Indep.Non-Char	26	12,605	17,825	26,095	.5	1.1
MASSACHUSETTS	**3,535**	**358,619**	**229,953**	**4,069,606 ***	**64.1**	**100.0**
007 OCA: Alban Dioc	5	NR	NR	3,550	.1	.1
009 Alban Orth Dio	1	100	NR	125	-	-
019 Amer Bapt USA	244	43,015	22,279	52,716 *	.8	1.3

NR–Not Reported *Total adherents estimated from known number of communicant, confirmed, full members. - Represents a percentage less than 0.1. Percentages may not total 100 due to rounding.

Table 3: Religious Congregations by State and Group: 2000

Religious Group	Number of Churches, Synagogues, Mosques, or Temples	Number of Communicant, Confirmed, or Full Members	Number of Attendees	Total Adherents: Number of Adherents	Total Adherents: % of Total Pop.	Total Adherents: % of Total Adh.
034 Ant Orth of NA	9	4,489	NR	8,978	.1	.2
049 Armen Ap Cilic	5	1,183	NR	3,724	.1	.1
050 Armen Ap Etchm	9	2,304	NR	14,850	.2	.4
053 Assemb of God	135	16,224	17,913	24,802	.4	.6
056 Baha'i	26	2,577	NR	2,577	-	.1
057 Bapt Gen Conf	33	4,123	4,323	5,645 *	.1	.1
076 Buddhism	57	NR	NR	NR	-	-
081 Catholic	782	NR	NR	3,092,296	48.7	76.0
084 Calvary Chapel	5	NR	NR	NR	-	-
089 Chr & Miss Al	28	2,103	NR	4,450	.1	.1
093 Chr Ch (Disc)	2	128	45	160 *	-	-
097 Chr Chs&Chs Cr	3	280	NR	344 *	-	-
105 Christian Ref	4	1,262	830	1,576 *	-	-
123 Ch God (Ander)	3	NR	3,975	3,975	.1	.1
127 Ch God (Cleve)	49	3,318	2,493	4,230 *	.1	.1
145 Ch God Prophcy	11	809	NR	993 *	-	-
151 L-D Saints	47	NR	NR	16,396	.3	.4
165 Ch of Nazarene	58	6,489	5,940	10,706	.2	.3
167 Chs of Christ	27	1,761	2,003	2,507	-	.1
171 Ch God-Gen Con	1	0	65	65 *	-	-
173 Comm of Christ	5	458	NR	458	-	-
175 Congr Chr Chs	33	4,821	2,770	5,897 *	.1	.1
176 Congr Ad Afl	10	2,239	NR	2,761 *	-	.1
179 Consrv Bapt	43	NR	6,852	6,852	.1	.2
181 Consrv Congr	39	5,495	5,782	6,759 *	.1	.2
185 Cumber Presb	1	20	NR	20	-	-
193 Episcopal	254	NR	30,408	98,963	1.6	2.4
201 Evan Cov Ch	17	2,997	2,612	3,908 *	.1	.1
203 Evan Free Ch	12	819	1,587	1,587	-	-
207 E.L.C.A.	71	20,635	8,014	28,360	.4	.7
221 Free Methodist	12	343	632	667	-	-
226 Friends-USA	32	1,376	NR	1,678 *	-	-
245 Greek Orth Vslp	3	350	NR	650	-	-
246 Greek Orthodox	38	NR	NR	42,945	.7	1.1
251 Holy Orth in NA	7	NR	NR	934	-	-
252 Hindu	20	NR	NR	NR	-	-
262 Int Cou Comm Ch	6	2,484	NR	3,085 *	-	.1
263 Int Foursq Gos	25	1,950	4,660	4,670 *	.1	.1
264 Int Chs of Crst	1	4,308	7,304	6,162	.1	.2
265 Int Pent C Chr	1	0	0	10	-	-
267 Muslim Est	25	NR	8,983	41,497	.7	1.0
268 Jain	2	NR	NR	NR	-	-
283 Luth—MO Synod	21	5,327	3,103	7,456	.1	.2
286 E.PA Mennonite	1	28	NR	35 *	-	-
288 Mennonite USA	5	303	274	367 *	-	-
290 Metro Comm Ch	1	48	41	57 *	-	-
297 Mennonite;Other	1	11	NR	14 *	-	-
331 OCA: Ter Diocs	7	507	NR	1,232	-	-
333 Malan Dioc Am	1	NR	NR	175	-	-
335 Orth Pres Ch	5	406	521	562	-	-
355 Presb Ch (USA)	32	4,224	3,731	5,453 *	.1	.1
356 Presb Ch Amer	8	445	662	695	-	-
363 Primitive Meth	7	399	NR	424	-	-
370 Ref Baptist Chs	4	NR	NR	NR	-	-
371 Ref Ch in Am	1	56	57	104	-	-
388 Reg Bapt Gen As	6	413	431	528 *	-	-
395 Romania Orth Ar	3	NR	NR	1,750	-	-
401 Rus Orth Abroad	4	NR	NR	NR	-	-
403 Salvation Army	35	2,814	2,061	8,109	.1	.2
413 S.D.A.	79	12,558	NR	14,946	.2	.4
416 Sikh	5	NR	NR	NR	-	-
419 So Bapt Conv	73	8,941	6,814	10,867 *	.2	.3
423 Syrian Orth Ch	2	NR	NR	600	-	-
425 Tao	1	NR	NR	NR	-	-
431 Ukrainian Orth	1	NR	NR	900	-	-
435 Unitarian-Univ	141	21,108	NR	25,834 *	.4	.6
443 Un C of Christ	423	99,041	43,615	121,826 *	1.9	3.0
449 Un Methodist	237	52,106	18,062	64,028 *	1.0	1.6
463 Vineyard	7	1,846	1,777	2,316 *	-	.1
467 Wesleyan	2	0	102	171	-	-
469 WELS	2	207	122	284	-	-
490 Zoroastrian	1	NR	NR	NR	-	-
496 Jewish Est	201	NR	NR	275,000	4.3	6.8
498 Indep.Charis.	6	3,131	2,995	4,595	.1	.1

Religious Group	Number of Churches, Synagogues, Mosques, or Temples	Number of Communicant, Confirmed, or Full Members	Number of Attendees	Total Adherents: Number of Adherents	Total Adherents: % of Total Pop.	Total Adherents: % of Total Adh.
499 Indep.Non-Char	11	6,240	6,115	8,750	.1	.2
MICHIGAN	**7,527**	**1,295,337**	**842,244**	**4,158,134 ***	**41.8**	**100.0**
007 OCA: Alban Dioc	1	NR	NR	450	-	-
011 A.W.M.C.	2	9	60	10	-	-
017 Amer Bapt Assn	17	850	NR	1,067 *	-	-
019 Amer Bapt USA	159	47,486	24,370	59,935 *	.6	1.4
032 Amish; other	1	45	NR	53 *	-	-
034 Ant Orth of NA	10	2,675	NR	5,350	.1	.1
039 Ap Chr Ch(Naz)	2	82	116	116 *	-	-
040 Ap Chr Ch-Amer	3	342	832	832 *	-	-
049 Armen Ap Cilic	1	472	NR	1,680	-	-
050 Armen Ap Etchm	3	720	NR	3,482	-	.1
053 Assemb of God	289	39,348	49,987	83,610	.8	2.0
055 As Ref Pres Ch	1	0	NR	0	-	-
056 Baha'i	30	2,829	NR	2,829	-	.1
057 Bapt Gen Conf	59	6,576	7,232	9,062 *	.1	.2
059 Bapt Miss Assn	16	2,323	1,636	3,005 *	-	.1
061 Beachy Amish	1	51	NR	65 *	-	-
071 Brethren (Ash)	1	5	20	6 *	-	-
075 Brethren in Cr	6	261	320	336	-	-
076 Buddhism	21	NR	NR	NR	-	-
078 Bulgar Orth USA	1	NR	NR	1,600	-	-
081 Catholic	888	NR	NR	2,019,926	20.3	48.6
084 Calvary Chapel	13	NR	NR	NR	-	-
089 Chr & Miss Al	29	2,504	NR	4,167	-	.1
093 Chr Ch (Disc)	39	7,738	3,156	9,755 *	.1	.2
097 Chr Chs&Chs Cr	113	18,990	NR	23,739 *	.2	.6
105 Christian Ref	232	88,264	64,347	112,711 *	1.1	2.7
121 Ch God (Abr)	7	322	412	457 *	-	-
123 Ch God (Ander)	120	NR	14,347	14,347	.1	.3
127 Ch God (Cleve)	119	19,451	11,011	25,040 *	.3	.6
143 CG in Cr(Menn)	2	365	NR	450 *	-	-
145 Ch God Prophcy	22	788	NR	986 *	-	-
151 L-D Saints	100	NR	NR	30,020	.3	.7
157 Ch of Brethren	25	1,468	788	1,812 *	-	-
165 Ch of Nazarene	186	22,560	21,792	35,703	.4	.9
167 Chs of Christ	195	21,948	21,701	28,527	.3	.7
171 Ch God-Gen Con	8	341	421	521 *	-	-
173 Comm of Christ	94	13,649	NR	13,649	.1	.3
175 Congr Chr Chs	63	11,370	5,937	14,219 *	.1	.3
176 Congr Ad Afl	5	1,990	NR	2,492 *	-	.1
179 Consrv Bapt	20	NR	5,710	5,710	.1	.1
181 Consrv Congr	21	2,412	2,042	3,026 *	-	.1
183 Cons Menn Conf	10	715	873	1,039	-	-
185 Cumber Presb	3	57	NR	229	-	-
193 Episcopal	245	NR	20,103	58,482	.6	1.4
201 Evan Cov Ch	39	6,250	6,746	8,251 *	.1	.2
203 Evan Free Ch	36	3,206	6,278	6,471	.1	.2
207 E.L.C.A.	356	118,476	48,344	160,836	1.6	3.9
211 Fel Evg Bib Ch	1	119	25	25	-	-
213 Evan Menn Inc	4	220	694	278 *	-	-
216 Evan Presby Ch	23	11,783	NR	14,958 *	.2	.4
220 Free Lutheran	7	512	423	672	-	-
221 Free Methodist	130	9,536	16,055	16,402	.2	.4
223 Free Will Bapt	44	3,141	NR	3,952 *	-	.1
226 Friends-USA	23	1,423	NR	1,750 *	-	-
246 Greek Orthodox	20	NR	NR	17,598	.2	.4
249 Assyr Apost Ch	2	NR	NR	1,325	-	-
252 Hindu	18	NR	NR	NR	-	-
262 Int Cou Comm Ch	20	4,866	NR	6,165 *	.1	.1
263 Int Foursq Gos	22	862	1,434	1,498 *	-	-
264 Int Chs of Crst	2	600	1,055	786	-	-
265 Int Pent C Chr	5	137	93	175	-	-
267 Muslim Est	51	NR	18,616	80,515	.8	1.9
268 Jain	3	NR	NR	NR	-	-
283 Luth—MO Synod	411	184,331	91,787	244,231	2.5	5.9
288 Mennonite USA	33	1,877	1,713	2,419 *	-	.1
290 Metro Comm Ch	7	305	257	298 *	-	-
291 Missionary Ch	66	4,132	8,041	8,043	.1	.2
293 Morav Ch-North	3	460	NR	561	-	-
297 Mennonite;Other	13	465	NR	576 *	-	-
304 NatPrimBapt USA	4	250	NR	318 *	-	-
306 NT IndBapt&Rltd	59	16,052	NR	20,180 *	.2	.5

NR–Not Reported   *Total adherents estimated from known number of communicant, confirmed, full members.   - Represents a percentage less than 0.1.   Percentages may not total 100 due to rounding.

Table 3: Religious Congregations by State and Group: 2000

Religious Group	Number of Churches, Synagogues, Mosques, or Temples	Number of Communicant, Confirmed, or Full Members	Number of Attendees	Total Adherents: Number of Adherents	Total Adherents: % of Total Pop.	Total Adherents: % of Total Adh.
307 Neth Ref Congr	3	574	NR	1,124	-	-
313 N Am Bapt Conf	22	4,686	4,680	5,861 *	.1	.1
320 "Old" MB Ascs	2	302	NR	372 *	-	-
322 Old Ord Menn Ch	2	135	NR	169 *	-	-
323 Old Ord Amish	70	3,840	NR	4,771 *	-	.1
330 Macedonian Orth	2	NR	NR	3,000	-	.1
331 OCA: Ter Diocs	6	702	NR	1,869	-	-
332 OCA: Bulg Dioc	2	310	NR	951	-	-
333 Malan Dioc Am	2	NR	NR	375	-	-
334 Malan Syr Orth	1	30	NR	150	-	-
335 Orth Pres Ch	16	1,109	1,606	1,816	-	-
339 Pent Ch of God	59	2,155	NR	6,469	.1	.2
349 Pent Holiness	8	285	256	361 *	-	-
355 Presb Ch (USA)	268	83,268	37,411	104,471 *	1.1	2.5
356 Presb Ch Amer	5	1,003	912	1,335	-	-
360 Prim Bapt Chrch	8	NR	NR	NR	-	-
369 Prot Ref Chs	13	1,982	NR	3,646	-	.1
370 Ref Baptist Chs	5	NR	NR	NR	-	-
371 Ref Ch in Am	153	51,246	47,681	84,265	.8	2.0
379 Ref Mennonite	1	30	NR	38 *	-	-
388 Reg Bapt Gen As	199	34,077	38,174	45,689 *	.5	1.1
395 Romania Orth Ar	2	NR	NR	1,225	-	-
397 OCA: Roman Dioc	7	NR	NR	1,670	-	-
400 Rus Orth Moscow	5	NR	NR	NR	-	-
401 Rus Orth Abroad	5	NR	NR	NR	-	-
403 Salvation Army	58	7,279	5,645	23,960	.2	.6
410 Serb Orth USA	3	NR	NR	5,600	.1	.1
411 Serb Orth: Grac	2	NR	NR	NR	-	-
413 S.D.A.	185	31,689	NR	37,712	.4	.9
416 Sikh	6	NR	NR	NR	-	-
418 Southw Bapt Fel	4	NR	NR	NR	-	-
419 So Bapt Conv	264	44,656	18,430	56,004 *	.6	1.3
420 Strict Baptists	1	14	NR	18 *	-	-
423 Syrian Orth Ch	1	NR	NR	600	-	-
431 Ukrainian Orth	3	NR	NR	594	-	-
435 Unitarian-Univ	23	3,758	NR	4,667 *	-	.1
443 Un C of Christ	172	46,362	18,586	58,043 *	.6	1.4
449 Un Methodist	897	177,930	101,049	222,269 *	2.2	5.3
455 Un Ref Chs N.A.	12	2,394	NR	3,609	-	.1
463 Vineyard	12	2,634	2,377	3,604 *	-	.1
466 Wayn Tr MB Asc	2	294	NR	371 *	-	-
467 Wesleyan	143	11,617	26,586	53,934	.5	1.3
469 WELS	140	34,279	18,242	44,476	.4	1.1
490 Zoroastrian	2	NR	NR	NR	-	-
496 Jewish Est	71	NR	NR	110,000	1.1	2.6
498 Indep.Charis.	16	20,285	23,480	30,200	.3	.7
499 Indep.Non-Char	59	38,403	38,355	54,068	.5	1.3
MINNESOTA	**5,115**	**1,213,184**	**612,978**	**3,035,510 ***	**61.7**	**100.0**
019 Amer Bapt USA	35	9,427	3,837	11,643 *	.2	.4
034 Ant Orth of NA	1	256	NR	512	-	-
039 Ap Chr Ch(Naz)	1	2	5	5 *	-	-
040 Ap Chr Ch-Amer	3	389	795	795 *	-	-
050 Armen Ap Etchm	1	0	NR	560	-	-
053 Assemb of God	212	26,248	30,657	56,028	1.1	1.8
056 Baha'i	19	1,710	NR	1,710	-	.1
057 Bapt Gen Conf	150	26,629	41,060	46,577 *	.9	1.5
061 Beachy Amish	1	82	NR	102 *	-	-
076 Buddhism	17	NR	NR	NR	-	-
081 Catholic	730	NR	NR	1,260,660	25.6	41.5
084 Calvary Chapel	2	NR	NR	NR	-	-
089 Chr & Miss Al	88	10,368	NR	18,946	.4	.6
093 Chr Ch (Disc)	11	2,056	661	2,537 *	.1	.1
097 Chr Chs&Chs Cr	56	6,015	NR	7,523 *	.2	.2
105 Christian Ref	31	7,791	5,728	9,675 *	.2	.3
121 Ch God (Abr)	6	247	216	312 *	-	-
123 Ch God (Ander)	6	NR	434	434	-	-
127 Ch God (Cleve)	16	1,324	1,237	1,754 *	-	.1
143 CG in Cr(Menn)	1	41	NR	50 *	-	-
145 Ch God Prophcy	4	137	NR	174 *	-	-
151 L-D Saints	68	NR	NR	20,122	.4	.7
157 Ch of Brethren	4	242	133	299 *	-	-
165 Ch of Nazarene	43	2,970	2,415	4,442	.1	.1
167 Chs of Christ	42	2,075	2,333	2,975	.1	.1
173 Comm of Christ	9	595	NR	595	-	-
175 Congr Chr Chs	9	5,314	2,236	6,575 *	.1	.2
176 Congr Ad Afl	1	206	NR	256 *	-	-
179 Consrv Bapt	38	NR	5,090	5,090	.1	.2
181 Consrv Congr	16	4,271	1,959	5,296 *	.1	.2
183 Cons Menn Conf	1	27	33	39	-	-
193 Episcopal	121	NR	9,424	30,547	.6	1.0
201 Evan Cov Ch	101	15,469	19,229	22,515 *	.5	.7
203 Evan Free Ch	136	15,083	28,745	28,873	.6	1.0
207 E.L.C.A.	1,183	630,262	240,904	853,448	17.3	28.1
211 Fel Evg Bib Ch	2	272	0	272	-	-
213 Evan Menn Inc	1	0	0	0 *	-	-
220 Free Lutheran	84	9,462	5,956	12,542	.3	.4
221 Free Methodist	10	284	440	440	-	-
226 Friends-USA	10	454	NR	558 *	-	-
237 Menn Br US Conf	4	481	NR	613 *	-	-
246 Greek Orthodox	4	NR	NR	4,029	.1	.1
251 Holy Orth in NA	1	NR	NR	36	-	-
252 Hindu	4	NR	NR	NR	-	-
257 Hutterian Br	9	594	NR	900	-	-
262 Int Cou Comm Ch	2	228	NR	275 *	-	-
263 Int Foursq Gos	12	485	855	860 *	-	-
264 Int Chs of Crst	1	333	547	478	-	-
267 Muslim Est	11	NR	2,741	12,305	.3	.4
268 Jain	1	NR	NR	NR	-	-
283 Luth—MO Synod	453	156,861	69,328	203,863	4.1	6.7
288 Mennonite USA	16	1,065	868	1,402 *	-	-
290 Metro Comm Ch	2	330	281	407 *	-	-
293 Morav Ch-North	7	1,037	NR	1,350	-	-
297 Mennonite;Other	6	322	NR	398 *	-	-
306 NT IndBapt&Rltd	67	7,524	NR	9,446 *	.2	.3
313 N Am Bapt Conf	11	1,098	933	1,393 *	-	-
322 Old Ord Menn Ch	1	24	NR	30 *	-	-
323 Old Ord Amish	13	685	NR	844 *	-	-
331 OCA: Ter Diocs	4	1,094	NR	1,662	-	.1
339 Pent Ch of God	7	165	NR	307	-	-
349 Pent Holiness	2	78	108	95 *	-	-
355 Presb Ch (USA)	190	45,589	20,806	56,579 *	1.2	1.9
356 Presb Ch Amer	5	399	411	533	-	-
369 Prot Ref Chs	1	42	NR	68	-	-
370 Ref Baptist Chs	1	NR	NR	NR	-	-
371 Ref Ch in Am	24	4,847	4,363	7,836	.2	.3
373 Ref Ch in U.S.	2	299	NR	382	-	-
388 Reg Bapt Gen As	26	2,453	2,476	3,127 *	.1	.1
395 Romania Orth Ar	1	NR	NR	262	-	-
397 OCA: Roman Dioc	1	NR	NR	175	-	-
401 Rus Orth Abroad	3	NR	NR	NR	-	-
403 Salvation Army	23	2,947	1,509	8,141	.2	.3
410 Serb Orth USA	4	NR	NR	1,672	-	.1
411 Serb Orth: Grac	2	NR	NR	NR	-	-
413 S.D.A.	69	5,788	NR	6,894	.1	.2
416 Sikh	2	NR	NR	NR	-	-
418 Southw Bapt Fel	1	NR	NR	NR	-	-
419 So Bapt Conv	45	4,380	2,780	5,458 *	.1	.2
431 Ukrainian Orth	3	NR	NR	1,191	-	-
435 Unitarian-Univ	23	3,993	NR	4,956 *	.1	.2
443 Un C of Christ	146	35,647	14,519	44,175 *	.9	1.5
449 Un Methodist	414	94,798	44,433	117,990 *	2.4	3.9
455 Un Ref Chs N.A.	1	66	NR	127	-	-
463 Vineyard	7	1,306	1,039	1,616 *	-	.1
467 Wesleyan	15	649	932	1,682	-	.1
469 WELS	153	42,794	23,467	53,867	1.1	1.8
496 Jewish Est	25	NR	NR	42,000	.9	1.4
498 Indep.Charis.	10	11,116	9,805	12,980	.3	.4
499 Indep.Non-Char	10	3,959	7,250	8,225	.2	.3
MISSISSIPPI	**5,505**	**1,100,306**	**438,476**	**1,554,483 ***	**54.6**	**100.0**
017 Amer Bapt Assn	41	4,360	NR	5,472 *	.2	.4
019 Amer Bapt USA	3	350	60	457 *	-	-
034 Ant Orth of NA	2	296	NR	592	-	-
053 Assemb of God	177	13,377	15,113	19,484	.7	1.3
055 As Ref Pres Ch	9	738	NR	786	-	.1
056 Baha'i	4	811	NR	811	-	.1
059 Bapt Miss Assn	186	32,106	13,794	40,558 *	1.4	2.6

NR–Not Reported *Total adherents estimated from known number of communicant, confirmed, full members. - Represents a percentage less than 0.1. Percentages may not total 100 due to rounding.

Table 3: Religious Congregations by State and Group: 2000

Religious Group	Number of Churches, Synagogues, Mosques, or Temples	Number of Communicant, Confirmed, or Full Members	Number of Attendees	Total Adherents		
				Number of Adherents	% of Total Pop.	% of Total Adh.
076 Buddhism	5	NR	NR	NR	-	-
081 Catholic	163	NR	NR	115,760	4.1	7.4
084 Calvary Chapel	2	NR	NR	NR	-	-
089 Chr & Miss Al	1	27	NR	32	-	-
093 Chr Ch (Disc)	46	4,693	1,572	5,958 *	.2	.4
097 Chr Chs&Chs Cr	30	3,216	NR	4,045 *	.1	.3
123 Ch God (Ander)	60	NR	3,397	3,397	.1	.2
127 Ch God (Cleve)	157	16,344	11,138	22,841 *	.8	1.5
143 CG in Cr(Menn)	6	907	NR	1,186 *	-	.1
145 Ch God Prophcy	69	2,038	NR	2,589 *	.1	.2
151 L-D Saints	42	NR	NR	12,992	.5	.8
165 Ch of Nazarene	48	4,467	2,720	5,456	.2	.4
167 Chs of Christ	378	32,898	31,020	43,396	1.5	2.8
171 Ch God-Gen Con	2	81	76	103 *	-	-
173 Comm of Christ	7	1,174	NR	1,174	-	.1
185 Cumber Presb	19	1,125	NR	1,458	.1	.1
193 Episcopal	86	NR	8,227	21,124	.7	1.4
201 Evan Cov Ch	1	94	75	121 *	-	-
207 E.L.C.A.	14	1,706	992	2,280	.1	.1
216 Evan Presby Ch	9	1,602	NR	2,020 *	.1	.1
221 Free Methodist	1	1	0	2	-	-
223 Free Will Bapt	56	3,648	NR	4,578 *	.2	.3
246 Greek Orthodox	2	NR	NR	525	-	-
252 Hindu	5	NR	NR	NR	-	-
263 Int Foursq Gos	4	314	329	418 *	-	-
266 Intrstat & Asc	78	8,178	NR	10,375 *	.4	.7
267 Muslim Est	14	NR	1,145	3,919	.1	.3
273 LandmrkBapt,I&U	14	2,286	NR	2,881 *	.1	.2
283 Luth—MO Synod	26	2,615	1,566	3,372	.1	.2
288 Mennonite USA	8	352	384	498 *	-	-
290 Metro Comm Ch	1	13	5	5 *	-	-
297 Mennonite;Other	6	330	NR	424 *	-	-
304 NatPrimBapt USA	16	939	NR	1,174 *	-	.1
323 Old Ord Amish	1	40	NR	51 *	-	-
331 OCA: Ter Diocs	1	50	NR	96	-	-
335 Orth Pres Ch	1	47	62	67	-	-
339 Pent Ch of God	14	501	NR	1,000	-	.1
349 Pent Holiness	21	1,264	1,138	1,596 *	.1	.1
355 Presb Ch (USA)	125	13,946	6,863	17,599 *	.6	1.1
356 Presb Ch Amer	122	15,913	10,995	18,776	.7	1.2
360 Prim Bapt Chrch	87	NR	NR	NR	-	-
370 Ref Baptist Chs	3	NR	NR	NR	-	-
403 Salvation Army	13	1,512	525	2,663	.1	.2
413 S.D.A.	45	5,306	NR	6,315	.2	.4
416 Sikh	1	NR	NR	NR	-	-
418 Southw Bapt Fel	5	NR	NR	NR	-	-
419 So Bapt Conv	2,037	725,313	245,994	916,440 *	32.2	59.0
435 Unitarian-Univ	5	184	NR	228 *	-	-
443 Un C of Christ	1	37	16	48 *	-	-
449 Un Methodist	1,197	190,395	76,666	240,576 *	8.5	15.5
463 Vineyard	3	263	229	352 *	-	-
467 Wesleyan	1	69	79	100	-	-
469 WELS	1	30	21	38	-	-
496 Jewish Est	14	NR	NR	1,400	-	.1
498 Indep.Charis.	3	550	1,075	1,075	-	.1
499 Indep.Non-Char	6	3,800	3,200	3,800	.1	.2
MISSOURI	**7,771**	**1,465,017**	**622,821**	**2,893,159 ***	**51.7**	**100.0**
017 Amer Bapt Assn	26	1,744	NR	2,171 *	-	.1
019 Amer Bapt USA	29	10,715	4,968	13,373 *	.2	.5
032 Amish; other	5	610	NR	760 *	-	-
039 Ap Chr Ch(Naz)	1	0	0	0 *	-	-
040 Ap Chr Ch-Amer	4	222	463	463 *	-	-
049 Armen Ap Cilic	1	0	NR	80	-	-
050 Armen Ap Etchm	1	20	NR	245	-	-
053 Assemb of God	483	52,943	63,201	95,429	1.7	3.3
055 As Ref Pres Ch	3	155	NR	158	-	-
056 Baha'i	17	1,635	NR	1,635	-	.1
057 Bapt Gen Conf	6	595	785	822 *	-	-
059 Bapt Miss Assn	90	8,421	4,341	10,585 *	.2	.4
061 Beachy Amish	2	32	NR	40 *	-	-
076 Buddhism	14	NR	NR	NR	-	-
081 Catholic	537	NR	NR	856,964	15.3	29.6
084 Calvary Chapel	9	NR	NR	NR	-	-
089 Chr & Miss Al	5	346	NR	483	-	-
093 Chr Ch (Disc)	317	85,317	24,764	105,583 *	1.9	3.6
097 Chr Chs&Chs Cr	334	63,001	NR	78,235 *	1.4	2.7
105 Christian Ref	1	123	80	152 *	-	-
107 Christian Un	21	1,628	1,257	2,063 *	-	.1
121 Ch God (Abr)	9	212	194	279 *	-	-
123 Ch God (Ander)	86	NR	6,548	6,548	.1	.2
127 Ch God (Cleve)	61	7,229	4,597	9,327 *	.2	.3
143 CG in Cr(Menn)	5	529	NR	654 *	-	-
145 Ch God Prophcy	34	909	NR	1,120 *	-	-
151 L-D Saints	124	NR	NR	41,014	.7	1.4
157 Ch of Brethren	20	841	376	1,045 *	-	-
165 Ch of Nazarene	179	20,767	14,454	29,348	.5	1.0
167 Chs of Christ	454	33,847	34,980	43,423	.8	1.5
171 Ch God-Gen Con	14	816	671	1,120 *	-	-
173 Comm of Christ	117	20,053	NR	20,053	.4	.7
175 Congr Chr Chs	3	290	185	362 *	-	-
181 Consrv Congr	1	22	20	28 *	-	-
185 Cumber Presb	30	737	NR	1,313	-	-
193 Episcopal	109	NR	10,282	26,846	.5	.9
201 Evan Cov Ch	7	548	767	950 *	-	-
203 Evan Free Ch	30	2,929	6,018	6,018	.1	.2
207 E.L.C.A.	79	21,332	10,274	27,991	.5	1.0
216 Evan Presby Ch	9	3,177	NR	3,937 *	.1	.1
220 Free Lutheran	1	75	38	90	-	-
221 Free Methodist	13	411	489	588	-	-
223 Free Will Bapt	185	15,723	NR	19,547 *	.3	.7
226 Friends-USA	9	429	NR	533 *	-	-
230 Fund Methodist	13	814	NR	1,009 *	-	-
237 Menn Br US Conf	1	17	NR	21 *	-	-
246 Greek Orthodox	3	NR	NR	4,524	.1	.2
251 Holy Orth in NA	1	NR	NR	12	-	-
252 Hindu	8	NR	NR	NR	-	-
258 IndFreeWillBapt	11	499	NR	617 *	-	-
262 Int Cou Comm Ch	4	695	NR	866 *	-	-
263 Int Foursq Gos	26	1,883	2,343	2,719 *	-	.1
264 Int Chs of Crst	2	326	558	508	-	-
267 Muslim Est	15	NR	3,975	19,359	.3	.7
268 Jain	3	NR	NR	NR	-	-
283 Luth—MO Synod	311	113,595	54,144	140,315	2.5	4.8
286 E.PA Mennonite	2	100	NR	123 *	-	-
288 Mennonite USA	12	962	1,034	1,310 *	-	-
290 Metro Comm Ch	5	498	597	663 *	-	-
291 Missionary Ch	1	6	45	45	-	-
297 Mennonite;Other	13	747	NR	935 *	-	-
304 NatPrimBapt USA	2	95	NR	118 *	-	-
313 N Am Bapt Conf	1	114	120	143 *	-	-
320 "Old" MB Ascs	79	6,420	NR	7,886 *	.1	.3
322 Old Ord Menn Ch	11	1,257	NR	1,571 *	-	.1
323 Old Ord Amish	49	2,656	NR	3,300 *	.1	.1
331 OCA: Ter Diocs	4	137	NR	361	-	-
333 Malan Dioc Am	1	NR	NR	75	-	-
339 Pent Ch of God	65	2,383	NR	7,328	.1	.3
349 Pent Holiness	23	1,284	1,337	1,602 *	-	.1
355 Presb Ch (USA)	297	51,477	26,311	64,277 *	1.1	2.2
356 Presb Ch Amer	25	5,225	5,069	6,702	.1	.2
360 Prim Bapt Chrch	43	NR	NR	NR	-	-
365 Prog Prim Bapt	2	232	NR	282 *	-	-
370 Ref Baptist Chs	1	NR	NR	NR	-	-
371 Ref Ch in Am	1	139	164	320	-	-
373 Ref Ch in U.S.	1	49	NR	81	-	-
388 Reg Bapt Gen As	13	1,259	1,262	1,484 *	-	.1
397 OCA: Roman Dioc	1	NR	NR	300	-	-
401 Rus Orth Abroad	2	NR	NR	NR	-	-
403 Salvation Army	28	3,254	2,503	10,508	.2	.4
410 Serb Orth USA	2	NR	NR	200	-	-
411 Serb Orth: Grac	1	NR	NR	NR	-	-
413 S.D.A.	77	10,556	NR	12,559	.2	.4
416 Sikh	4	NR	NR	NR	-	-
418 Southw Bapt Fel	4	NR	NR	NR	-	-
419 So Bapt Conv	1,884	642,093	195,093	797,732 *	14.3	27.6
435 Unitarian-Univ	9	1,972	NR	2,445 *	-	.1
443 Un C of Christ	165	41,251	16,804	51,490 *	.9	1.8
449 Un Methodist	933	182,725	83,093	226,578 *	4.0	7.8

NR–Not Reported *Total adherents estimated from known number of communicant, confirmed, full members. - Represents a percentage less than 0.1. Percentages may not total 100 due to rounding.

Table 3: Religious Congregations by State and Group: 2000

Religious Group	Number of Churches, Synagogues, Mosques, or Temples	Number of Communicant, Confirmed, or Full Members	Number of Attendees	Total Adherents		
				Number of Adherents	% of Total Pop.	% of Total Adh.
455 Un Ref Chs N.A.	1	56	NR	110	-	-
463 Vineyard	11	2,052	1,675	2,593 *	-	.1
467 Wesleyan	15	661	801	2,695	-	.1
469 WELS	10	884	491	1,181	-	-
490 Zoroastrian	1	NR	NR	NR	-	-
496 Jewish Est	33	NR	NR	62,315	1.1	2.2
498 Indep.Charis.	22	12,375	16,940	19,315	.3	.7
499 Indep.Non-Char	34	15,886	18,710	23,207	.4	.8
MONTANA	**1,543**	**134,676**	**81,628**	**403,492 ***	**44.7**	**100.0**
011 A.W.M.C.	2	61	150	62	-	-
017 Amer Bapt Assn	9	156	NR	192 *	-	-
019 Amer Bapt USA	26	2,472	1,665	3,105 *	.3	.8
032 Amish; other	1	18	NR	23 *	-	-
053 Assemb of God	79	8,079	10,703	16,365	1.8	4.1
056 Baha'i	7	645	NR	645	.1	.2
057 Bapt Gen Conf	4	216	316	352 *	-	.1
076 Buddhism	5	NR	NR	NR	-	-
081 Catholic	215	NR	NR	169,250	18.8	41.9
084 Calvary Chapel	9	NR	NR	NR	-	-
089 Chr & Miss Al	40	1,849	NR	5,050	.6	1.3
093 Chr Ch (Disc)	17	2,377	978	2,933 *	.3	.7
097 Chr Chs&Chs Cr	24	2,838	NR	3,522 *	.4	.9
105 Christian Ref	6	1,656	1,411	1,997 *	.2	.5
123 Ch God (Ander)	11	NR	596	596	.1	.1
127 Ch God (Cleve)	9	246	344	454 *	.1	.1
145 Ch God Prophcy	6	143	NR	173 *	-	-
151 L-D Saints	117	NR	NR	32,726	3.6	8.1
157 Ch of Brethren	1	30	26	41 *	-	-
165 Ch of Nazarene	21	1,733	1,478	2,416	.3	.6
167 Chs of Christ	52	2,001	2,280	2,719	.3	.7
173 Comm of Christ	10	418	NR	418	-	.1
175 Congr Chr Chs	2	167	156	205 *	-	.1
179 Consrv Bapt	6	NR	758	758	.1	.2
181 Consrv Congr	4	673	378	856 *	.1	.2
183 Cons Menn Conf	1	24	29	35	-	-
193 Episcopal	47	NR	2,319	6,509	.7	1.6
201 Evan Cov Ch	1	86	189	189 *	-	-
203 Evan Free Ch	13	709	1,670	1,670	.2	.4
207 E.L.C.A.	148	36,379	14,511	50,287	5.6	12.5
211 Fel Evg Bib Ch	2	136	37	154	-	-
220 Free Lutheran	4	299	330	427	-	.1
221 Free Methodist	1	0	64	64	-	-
223 Free Will Bapt	2	16	NR	20 *	-	-
226 Friends-USA	6	132	NR	160 *	-	-
237 Menn Br US Conf	2	150	NR	191 *	-	-
246 Greek Orthodox	2	NR	NR	324	-	.1
257 Hutterian Br	48	3,168	NR	4,800	.5	1.2
263 Int Foursq Gos	24	3,107	7,581	7,637 *	.8	1.9
264 Int Chs of Crst	1	102	175	147	-	-
267 Muslim Est	3	NR	211	614	.1	.2
283 Luth—MO Synod	63	11,448	5,612	15,441	1.7	3.8
288 Mennonite USA	9	437	345	561 *	.1	.1
290 Metro Comm Ch	1	33	20	41 *	-	-
297 Mennonite;Other	3	122	NR	150 *	-	-
306 NT IndBapt&Rltd	22	1,845	NR	2,278 *	.3	.6
313 N Am Bapt Conf	3	266	258	323 *	-	.1
323 Old Ord Amish	3	130	NR	162 *	-	-
331 OCA: Ter Diocs	2	76	NR	103	-	-
335 Orth Pres Ch	3	437	492	604	.1	.1
339 Pent Ch of God	11	294	NR	662	.1	.2
349 Pent Holiness	2	125	122	154 *	-	-
355 Presb Ch (USA)	53	7,497	4,107	9,372 *	1.0	2.3
356 Presb Ch Amer	1	60	80	80	-	-
370 Ref Baptist Chs	1	NR	NR	NR	-	-
371 Ref Ch in Am	1	49	32	104	-	-
388 Reg Bapt Gen As	13	992	1,279	1,274 *	.1	.3
403 Salvation Army	8	642	374	1,414	.2	.4
410 Serb Orth USA	1	NR	NR	300	-	.1
413 S.D.A.	46	3,591	NR	4,275	.5	1.1
416 Sikh	1	NR	NR	NR	-	-
419 So Bapt Conv	105	12,377	6,159	15,318 *	1.7	3.8
420 Strict Baptists	1	6	NR	8 *	-	-
435 Unitarian-Univ	5	217	NR	266 *	-	.1

Religious Group	Number of Churches, Synagogues, Mosques, or Temples	Number of Communicant, Confirmed, or Full Members	Number of Attendees	Total Adherents		
				Number of Adherents	% of Total Pop.	% of Total Adh.
443 Un C of Christ	36	5,423	2,272	6,713 *	.7	1.7
449 Un Methodist	118	14,561	7,405	17,993 *	2.0	4.5
463 Vineyard	8	1,008	993	1,275 *	.1	.3
467 Wesleyan	14	347	871	1,514	.2	.4
469 WELS	11	757	499	996	.1	.2
496 Jewish Est	6	NR	NR	850	.1	.2
498 Indep.Charis.	1	0	428	800	.1	.2
499 Indep.Non-Char	3	1,850	1,925	2,375	.3	.6
NEBRASKA	**2,612**	**446,871**	**221,845**	**1,006,860 ***	**58.8**	**100.0**
017 Amer Bapt Assn	2	58	NR	72 *	-	-
019 Amer Bapt USA	61	10,185	4,985	12,634 *	.7	1.3
034 Ant Orth of NA	3	442	NR	884	.1	.1
053 Assemb of God	98	9,875	11,488	18,958	1.1	1.9
056 Baha'i	7	660	NR	660	-	.1
057 Bapt Gen Conf	32	2,122	2,359	2,857 *	.2	.3
071 Brethren (Ash)	1	75	49	92 *	-	-
076 Buddhism	7	NR	NR	NR	-	-
081 Catholic	368	NR	NR	372,791	21.8	37.0
084 Calvary Chapel	1	NR	NR	NR	-	-
089 Chr & Miss Al	26	3,346	NR	10,090	.6	1.0
093 Chr Ch (Disc)	51	10,596	3,181	13,135 *	.8	1.3
097 Chr Chs&Chs Cr	82	12,820	NR	16,021 *	.9	1.6
105 Christian Ref	3	274	296	344 *	-	-
121 Ch God (Abr)	1	88	69	111 *	-	-
123 Ch God (Ander)	18	NR	818	818	-	.1
127 Ch God (Cleve)	10	610	276	766 *	-	.1
143 CG in Cr(Menn)	2	210	NR	259 *	-	-
145 Ch God Prophcy	4	137	NR	173 *	-	-
151 L-D Saints	57	NR	NR	15,003	.9	1.5
157 Ch of Brethren	4	365	201	445 *	-	-
165 Ch of Nazarene	37	2,608	2,542	3,894	.2	.4
167 Chs of Christ	51	3,252	3,546	4,409	.3	.4
173 Comm of Christ	16	1,507	NR	1,507	.1	.1
175 Congr Chr Chs	4	442	262	546 *	-	.1
179 Consrv Bapt	2	NR	96	96	-	-
181 Consrv Congr	7	1,701	878	2,118 *	.1	.2
193 Episcopal	69	NR	4,175	11,005	.6	1.1
201 Evan Cov Ch	19	2,488	2,145	3,250 *	.2	.3
203 Evan Free Ch	67	5,489	12,270	12,270	.7	1.2
207 E.L.C.A.	266	99,367	42,432	128,570	7.5	12.8
211 Fel Evg Bib Ch	6	690	927	927	.1	.1
220 Free Lutheran	4	574	307	667	-	.1
221 Free Methodist	6	168	315	315	-	-
226 Friends-USA	7	447	NR	558 *	-	.1
237 Menn Br US Conf	6	498	NR	621 *	-	.1
245 Greek Orth Vslp	3	3,150	NR	6,350	.4	.6
246 Greek Orthodox	4	NR	NR	891	.1	.1
252 Hindu	1	NR	NR	NR	-	-
263 Int Foursq Gos	16	1,299	1,277	1,763 *	.1	.2
264 Int Chs of Crst	1	88	170	131	-	-
267 Muslim Est	5	NR	819	3,115	.2	.3
283 Luth—MO Synod	270	90,141	45,718	117,419	6.9	11.7
288 Mennonite USA	12	2,585	1,622	3,175 *	.2	.3
290 Metro Comm Ch	1	71	75	90 *	-	-
291 Missionary Ch	5	214	398	400	-	-
297 Mennonite;Other	1	56	NR	68 *	-	-
304 NatPrimBapt USA	1	150	NR	189 *	-	-
313 N Am Bapt Conf	3	141	90	178 *	-	-
335 Orth Pres Ch	1	49	35	63	-	-
339 Pent Ch of God	5	34	NR	90	-	-
349 Pent Holiness	1	75	35	92 *	-	-
355 Presb Ch (USA)	146	31,515	14,474	39,420 *	2.3	3.9
356 Presb Ch Amer	7	570	750	858	.1	.1
360 Prim Bapt Chrch	2	NR	NR	NR	-	-
371 Ref Ch in Am	7	1,193	1,251	1,987	.1	.2
373 Ref Ch in U.S.	3	497	NR	667	-	.1
388 Reg Bapt Gen As	13	1,013	1,009	1,292 *	.1	.1
403 Salvation Army	11	1,623	853	6,947	.4	.7
410 Serb Orth USA	1	NR	NR	400	-	-
413 S.D.A.	48	6,345	NR	7,550	.4	.7
419 So Bapt Conv	49	13,547	8,343	17,109 *	1.0	1.7
431 Ukrainian Orth	1	NR	NR	24	-	-
435 Unitarian-Univ	4	690	NR	857 *	.1	.1

NR–Not Reported *Total adherents estimated from known number of communicant, confirmed, full members. - Represents a percentage less than 0.1. Percentages may not total 100 due to rounding.

Table 3: Religious Congregations by State and Group: 2000

Religious Group	Number of Churches, Synagogues, Mosques, or Temples	Number of Communicant, Confirmed, or Full Members	Number of Attendees	Total Adherents		
				Number of Adherents	% of Total Pop.	% of Total Adh.
443 Un C of Christ	103	18,749	7,536	23,234 *	1.4	2.3
449 Un Methodist	415	94,388	36,886	117,277 *	6.9	11.6
463 Vineyard	2	345	300	430 *	-	-
467 Wesleyan	18	583	827	1,722	.1	.2
469 WELS	35	4,566	2,774	5,829	.3	.6
496 Jewish Est	7	NR	NR	7,100	.4	.7
498 Indep.Charis.	1	0	326	517	-	.1
499 Indep.Non-Char	4	2,100	2,660	2,760	.2	.3
NEVADA	**938**	**104,143**	**66,629**	**685,119 ***	**34.3**	**100.0**
017 Amer Bapt Assn	4	636	NR	802 *	-	.1
019 Amer Bapt USA	21	6,216	2,486	7,863 *	.4	1.1
034 Ant Orth of NA	1	165	NR	330	-	-
050 Armen Ap Etchm	2	0	NR	847	-	.1
053 Assemb of God	56	10,810	11,645	22,691	1.1	3.3
056 Baha'i	11	1,124	NR	1,124	.1	.2
059 Bapt Miss Assn	1	68	25	86 *	-	-
076 Buddhism	12	NR	NR	NR	-	-
081 Catholic	67	NR	NR	331,844	16.6	48.4
084 Calvary Chapel	10	NR	NR	NR	-	-
089 Chr & Miss Al	5	100	NR	247	-	-
093 Chr Ch (Disc)	2	528	275	665 *	-	.1
097 Chr Chs&Chs Cr	7	7,297	NR	9,164 *	.5	1.3
105 Christian Ref	3	293	300	369 *	-	.1
123 Ch God (Ander)	6	NR	262	262	-	-
127 Ch God (Cleve)	9	762	537	960 *	-	.1
145 Ch God Prophcy	4	140	NR	175 *	-	-
151 L-D Saints	282	NR	NR	116,925	5.9	17.1
165 Ch of Nazarene	19	1,574	1,788	2,502	.1	.4
167 Chs of Christ	26	1,707	1,749	2,326	.1	.3
173 Comm of Christ	2	518	NR	518	-	.1
179 Consrv Bapt	8	NR	1,140	1,140	.1	.2
193 Episcopal	34	NR	2,390	5,469	.3	.8
203 Evan Free Ch	5	416	957	957	-	.1
207 E.L.C.A.	17	7,782	4,437	10,663	.5	1.6
221 Free Methodist	3	5	45	45	-	-
226 Friends-USA	2	64	NR	80 *	-	-
246 Greek Orthodox	4	NR	NR	1,392	.1	.2
252 Hindu	1	NR	NR	NR	-	-
263 Int Foursq Gos	27	2,365	3,310	3,311 *	.2	.5
264 Int Chs of Crst	2	331	610	494	-	.1
267 Muslim Est	3	NR	612	2,291	.1	.3
283 Luth—MO Synod	23	4,588	3,328	7,654	.4	1.1
290 Metro Comm Ch	2	205	178	258 *	-	-
331 OCA: Ter Diocs	2	211	NR	498	-	.1
335 Orth Pres Ch	1	13	20	20	-	-
339 Pent Ch of God	4	87	NR	220	-	-
349 Pent Holiness	3	158	127	198 *	-	-
355 Presb Ch (USA)	19	5,723	3,719	7,202 *	.4	1.1
356 Presb Ch Amer	2	114	200	200	-	-
370 Ref Baptist Chs	1	NR	NR	NR	-	-
388 Reg Bapt Gen As	3	185	320	272 *	-	-
395 Romania Orth Ar	1	NR	NR	630	-	.1
397 OCA: Roman Dioc	1	NR	NR	28	-	-
403 Salvation Army	7	594	550	1,239	.1	.2
410 Serb Orth USA	1	NR	NR	800	-	.1
413 S.D.A.	16	2,344	NR	2,789	.1	.4
416 Sikh	3	NR	NR	NR	-	-
419 So Bapt Conv	111	31,952	13,888	40,233 *	2.0	5.9
435 Unitarian-Univ	2	231	NR	289 *	-	-
443 Un C of Christ	4	550	279	688 *	-	.1
449 Un Methodist	31	8,334	4,788	10,452 *	.5	1.5
463 Vineyard	7	978	777	1,219 *	.1	.2
467 Wesleyan	3	228	315	514	-	.1
469 WELS	7	1,207	857	1,634	.1	.2
496 Jewish Est	23	NR	NR	77,100	3.9	11.3
498 Indep.Charis.	2	690	1,090	1,090	.1	.2
499 Indep.Non-Char	3	2,850	3,625	4,350	.2	.6
NEW HAMPSHIRE	**872**	**84,506**	**51,192**	**589,022 ***	**47.7**	**100.0**
017 Amer Bapt Assn	1	20	NR	24 *	-	-
019 Amer Bapt USA	90	13,236	5,986	16,359 *	1.3	2.8
053 Assemb of God	37	2,520	3,269	4,393	.4	.7
056 Baha'i	8	694	NR	694	.1	.1
076 Buddhism	5	NR	NR	NR	-	-
081 Catholic	154	NR	NR	431,259	34.9	73.2
084 Calvary Chapel	2	NR	NR	NR	-	-
089 Chr & Miss Al	6	234	NR	578	-	.1
097 Chr Chs&Chs Cr	5	1,193	NR	1,503 *	.1	.3
105 Christian Ref	1	58	46	73 *	-	-
123 Ch God (Ander)	1	NR	40	40	-	-
127 Ch God (Cleve)	5	458	193	595 *	-	.1
145 Ch God Prophcy	2	164	NR	204 *	-	-
151 L-D Saints	21	NR	NR	6,354	.5	1.1
165 Ch of Nazarene	12	1,005	1,031	1,939	.2	.3
167 Chs of Christ	14	795	932	1,202	.1	.2
175 Congr Chr Chs	14	1,286	1,054	1,598 *	.1	.3
176 Congr Ad Afl	8	704	NR	872 *	.1	.1
179 Consrv Bapt	26	NR	3,614	3,614	.3	.6
181 Consrv Congr	7	804	786	1,004 *	.1	.2
193 Episcopal	50	NR	5,203	16,148	1.3	2.7
201 Evan Cov Ch	5	707	734	951 *	.1	.2
203 Evan Free Ch	5	347	640	640	.1	.1
207 E.L.C.A.	13	2,780	1,420	4,062	.3	.7
223 Free Will Bapt	2	140	NR	172 *	-	-
226 Friends-USA	13	559	NR	683 *	.1	.1
246 Greek Orthodox	11	NR	NR	7,071	.6	1.2
251 Holy Orth in NA	1	NR	NR	36	-	-
263 Int Foursq Gos	9	405	1,203	1,203 *	.1	.2
267 Muslim Est	2	NR	824	3,782	.3	.6
283 Luth—MO Synod	7	1,391	883	2,015	.2	.3
331 OCA: Ter Diocs	2	72	NR	85	-	-
335 Orth Pres Ch	2	77	110	115	-	-
339 Pent Ch of God	1	40	NR	45	-	-
355 Presb Ch (USA)	10	2,097	1,290	2,638 *	.2	.4
356 Presb Ch Amer	6	301	384	426	-	.1
370 Ref Baptist Chs	1	NR	NR	NR	-	-
388 Reg Bapt Gen As	2	98	130	130 *	-	-
397 OCA: Roman Dioc	1	NR	NR	36	-	-
400 Rus Orth Moscow	1	NR	NR	NR	-	-
403 Salvation Army	11	891	531	2,651	.2	.5
413 S.D.A.	13	969	NR	1,153	.1	.2
419 So Bapt Conv	14	2,718	1,654	3,402 *	.3	.6
435 Unitarian-Univ	21	3,183	NR	3,968 *	.3	.7
443 Un C of Christ	138	27,787	11,672	34,299 *	2.8	5.8
449 Un Methodist	94	15,342	5,716	18,927 *	1.5	3.2
467 Wesleyan	1	0	29	161	-	-
469 WELS	1	81	73	123	-	-
496 Jewish Est	12	NR	NR	10,020	.8	1.7
498 Indep.Charis.	1	300	300	300	-	.1
499 Indep.Non-Char	3	1,050	1,445	1,475	.1	.3
NEW JERSEY	**4,531**	**507,739**	**327,936**	**4,858,756 ***	**57.7**	**100.0**
017 Amer Bapt Assn	2	40	NR	50 *	-	-
019 Amer Bapt USA	262	70,955	26,952	88,521 *	1.1	1.8
022 Carp Rus Orth	7	1,161	NR	1,974	-	-
034 Ant Orth of NA	4	1,120	NR	2,240	-	-
039 Ap Chr Ch(Naz)	1	76	101	101 *	-	-
049 Armen Ap Cilic	1	500	NR	2,100	-	-
050 Armen Ap Etchm	5	1,058	NR	9,980	.1	.2
053 Assemb of God	238	30,087	33,193	52,065	.6	1.1
056 Baha'i	14	1,531	NR	1,531	-	-
057 Bapt Gen Conf	2	262	242	349 *	-	-
059 Bapt Miss Assn	2	172	180	219 *	-	-
071 Brethren (Ash)	1	5	21	6 *	-	-
076 Buddhism	21	NR	NR	NR	-	-
081 Catholic	774	NR	NR	3,403,020	40.4	70.0
084 Calvary Chapel	14	NR	NR	NR	-	-
089 Chr & Miss Al	70	6,410	NR	14,518	.2	.3
093 Chr Ch (Disc)	6	1,266	5	1,594 *	-	-
097 Chr Chs&Chs Cr	12	1,635	NR	2,044 *	-	-
105 Christian Ref	20	4,820	3,971	5,976 *	.1	.1
123 Ch God (Ander)	19	NR	1,003	1,003	-	-
127 Ch God (Cleve)	68	5,801	5,071	7,699 *	.1	.2
145 Ch God Prophcy	19	901	NR	1,129 *	-	-
151 L-D Saints	61	NR	NR	19,855	.2	.4
157 Ch of Brethren	1	124	0	156 *	-	-

NR–Not Reported *Total adherents estimated from known number of communicant, confirmed, full members. - Represents a percentage less than 0.1. Percentages may not total 100 due to rounding.

Table 3: Religious Congregations by State and Group: 2000

Religious Group	Number of Churches, Synagogues, Mosques, or Temples	Number of Communicant, Confirmed, or Full Members	Number of Attendees	Total Adherents: Number of Adherents	Total Adherents: % of Total Pop.	Total Adherents: % of Total Adh.
165 Ch of Nazarene	50	4,746	4,177	7,435	.1	.2
167 Chs of Christ	38	3,730	3,800	4,703	.1	.1
173 Comm of Christ	3	306	NR	306	-	-
175 Congr Chr Chs	5	643	417	810 *	-	-
179 Consrv Bapt	53	NR	8,626	8,626	.1	.2
193 Episcopal	287	NR	29,834	91,964	1.1	1.9
201 Evan Cov Ch	4	395	222	490 *	-	-
203 Evan Free Ch	28	2,943	5,130	5,187	.1	.1
207 E.L.C.A.	200	54,752	21,511	79,264	.9	1.6
216 Evan Presby Ch	1	304	NR	383 *	-	-
221 Free Methodist	9	555	904	1,071	-	-
223 Free Will Bapt	3	0	NR	0 *	-	-
226 Friends-USA	35	3,125	NR	3,894 *	-	.1
246 Greek Orthodox	24	NR	NR	25,770	.3	.5
252 Hindu	52	NR	NR	NR	-	-
262 Int Cou Comm Ch	8	2,854	NR	3,565 *	-	.1
263 Int Foursq Gos	6	625	1,270	1,390 *	-	-
265 Int Pent C Chr	2	70	27	114	-	-
267 Muslim Est	68	NR	27,943	120,724	1.4	2.5
268 Jain	5	NR	NR	NR	-	-
283 Luth—MO Synod	72	16,880	7,392	22,319	.3	.5
286 E.PA Mennonite	1	41	NR	51 *	-	-
288 Mennonite USA	14	534	905	1,006 *	-	-
290 Metro Comm Ch	1	19	27	27 *	-	-
291 Missionary Ch	1	38	51	51	-	-
293 Morav Ch-North	4	654	NR	808	-	-
297 Mennonite;Other	1	48	NR	60 *	-	-
304 NatPrimBapt USA	9	1,132	NR	1,413 *	-	-
306 NT IndBapt&Rltd	1	23	NR	29 *	-	-
307 Neth Ref Congr	2	446	NR	813	-	-
313 N Am Bapt Conf	3	155	200	191 *	-	-
330 Macedonian Orth	2	NR	NR	3,000	-	.1
331 OCA: Ter Diocs	23	2,364	NR	3,471	-	.1
333 Malan Dioc Am	4	NR	NR	650	-	-
334 Malan Syr Orth	1	40	NR	200	-	-
335 Orth Pres Ch	20	1,443	1,605	2,056	-	-
339 Pent Ch of God	1	162	NR	207	-	-
349 Pent Holiness	4	492	410	609 *	-	-
355 Presb Ch (USA)	373	95,976	42,911	119,735 *	1.4	2.5
356 Presb Ch Amer	26	1,673	2,015	2,503	-	.1
369 Prot Ref Chs	1	18	NR	27	-	-
370 Ref Baptist Chs	10	NR	NR	NR	-	-
371 Ref Ch in Am	133	16,182	11,542	32,691	.4	.7
388 Reg Bapt Gen As	29	4,325	5,892	6,866 *	.1	.1
400 Rus Orth Moscow	6	NR	NR	NR	-	-
401 Rus Orth Abroad	14	NR	NR	NR	-	-
403 Salvation Army	28	2,421	1,830	7,256	.1	.1
410 Serb Orth USA	2	NR	NR	1,400	-	-
411 Serb Orth: Grac	1	NR	NR	NR	-	-
413 S.D.A.	111	11,533	NR	13,725	.2	.3
416 Sikh	3	NR	NR	NR	-	-
418 Southw Bapt Fel	8	NR	NR	NR	-	-
419 So Bapt Conv	76	14,446	9,969	18,035 *	.2	.4
423 Syrian Orth Ch	4	NR	NR	3,250	-	.1
431 Ukrainian Orth	11	NR	NR	5,082	.1	.1
435 Unitarian-Univ	23	4,103	NR	5,109 *	.1	.1
443 Un C of Christ	57	11,461	4,804	14,293 *	.2	.3
449 Un Methodist	578	112,484	55,761	140,133 *	1.7	2.9
455 Un Ref Chs N.A.	3	554	NR	922	-	-
463 Vineyard	1	265	223	324 *	-	-
467 Wesleyan	19	119	1,221	2,873	-	.1
469 WELS	2	191	138	255	-	-
496 Jewish Est	331	NR	NR	468,000	5.6	9.6
498 Indep.Charis.	4	2,400	1,750	2,550	-	.1
499 Indep.Non-Char	8	2,145	4,690	4,940	.1	.1
NEW MEXICO	**2,026**	**230,984**	**130,959**	**1,057,828 ***	**58.2**	**100.0**
011 A.W.M.C.	1	9	0	9	-	-
017 Amer Bapt Assn	6	627	NR	807 *	-	.1
019 Amer Bapt USA	3	1,168	520	1,449 *	.1	.1
032 Amish; other	1	14	NR	17 *	-	-
034 Ant Orth of NA	2	79	NR	158	-	-
050 Armen Ap Etchm	1	0	NR	182	-	-
053 Assemb of God	164	13,679	15,773	22,070	1.2	2.1

Religious Group	Number of Churches, Synagogues, Mosques, or Temples	Number of Communicant, Confirmed, or Full Members	Number of Attendees	Total Adherents: Number of Adherents	Total Adherents: % of Total Pop.	Total Adherents: % of Total Adh.
056 Baha'i	20	2,665	NR	2,665	.1	.3
059 Bapt Miss Assn	5	204	106	263 *	-	-
075 Brethren in Cr	3	100	85	109	-	-
076 Buddhism	25	NR	NR	NR	-	-
081 Catholic	450	NR	NR	670,511	36.9	63.4
084 Calvary Chapel	15	NR	NR	NR	-	-
089 Chr & Miss Al	2	97	NR	288	-	-
093 Chr Ch (Disc)	19	4,171	1,841	5,214 *	.3	.5
097 Chr Chs&Chs Cr	33	5,133	NR	6,565 *	.4	.6
105 Christian Ref	16	1,681	1,499	2,314 *	.1	.2
123 Ch God (Ander)	7	NR	505	505	-	-
127 Ch God (Cleve)	47	2,553	1,514	3,422 *	.2	.3
145 Ch God Prophcy	13	455	NR	585 *	-	.1
151 L-D Saints	120	NR	NR	42,261	2.3	4.0
157 Ch of Brethren	2	111	29	145 *	-	-
165 Ch of Nazarene	48	4,008	3,081	5,548	.3	.5
167 Chs of Christ	169	14,673	13,881	18,985	1.0	1.8
171 Ch God-Gen Con	2	13	62	62 *	-	-
173 Comm of Christ	8	411	NR	411	-	-
179 Consrv Bapt	5	NR	670	670	-	.1
183 Cons Menn Conf	2	96	117	140	-	-
185 Cumber Presb	2	1,024	NR	2,566	.1	.2
186 Coptic Orth Ch	1	NR	NR	NR	-	-
193 Episcopal	49	NR	4,991	12,219	.7	1.2
203 Evan Free Ch	5	519	1,080	1,080	.1	.1
207 E.L.C.A.	22	7,947	3,898	10,969	.6	1.0
221 Free Methodist	2	0	20	20	-	-
223 Free Will Bapt	4	44	NR	56 *	-	-
226 Friends-USA	12	360	NR	450 *	-	-
246 Greek Orthodox	2	NR	NR	717	-	.1
252 Hindu	4	NR	NR	NR	-	-
262 Int Cou Comm Ch	2	250	NR	307 *	-	-
263 Int Foursq Gos	19	2,330	2,818	3,773 *	.2	.4
264 Int Chs of Crst	2	235	366	342	-	-
267 Muslim Est	7	NR	734	2,604	.1	.2
283 Luth—MO Synod	34	4,386	2,846	5,584	.3	.5
288 Mennonite USA	3	100	137	150 *	-	-
290 Metro Comm Ch	2	141	156	175 *	-	-
297 Mennonite;Other	2	105	NR	139 *	-	-
306 NT IndBapt&Rltd	2	350	NR	450 *	-	-
331 OCA: Ter Diocs	2	51	NR	156	-	-
335 Orth Pres Ch	2	74	79	92	-	-
339 Pent Ch of God	24	1,168	NR	1,676	.1	.2
349 Pent Holiness	5	187	136	237 *	-	-
355 Presb Ch (USA)	67	10,442	6,435	13,224 *	.7	1.3
356 Presb Ch Amer	5	638	519	792	-	.1
360 Prim Bapt Chrch	8	NR	NR	NR	-	-
370 Ref Baptist Chs	1	NR	NR	NR	-	-
371 Ref Ch in Am	3	245	193	574	-	.1
388 Reg Bapt Gen As	5	261	400	397 *	-	-
401 Rus Orth Abroad	2	NR	NR	NR	-	-
403 Salvation Army	9	844	465	2,123	.1	.2
413 S.D.A.	54	4,677	NR	5,570	.3	.5
416 Sikh	3	NR	NR	NR	-	-
419 So Bapt Conv	301	103,847	34,972	132,675 *	7.3	12.5
435 Unitarian-Univ	9	1,350	NR	1,684 *	.1	.2
443 Un C of Christ	10	1,974	918	2,445 *	.1	.2
449 Un Methodist	120	32,700	14,716	41,597 *	2.3	3.9
463 Vineyard	3	510	480	656 *	-	.1
467 Wesleyan	3	70	107	137	-	-
469 WELS	8	458	360	587	-	.1
496 Jewish Est	10	NR	NR	10,500	.6	1.0
498 Indep.Charis.	4	1,100	2,000	3,100	.2	.3
499 Indep.Non-Char	3	650	12,450	12,650	.7	1.2
NEW YORK	**11,001**	**1,231,358**	**721,476**	**11,461,411 ***	**60.4**	**100.0**
007 OCA: Alban Dioc	2	NR	NR	600	-	-
011 A.W.M.C.	2	25	53	25	-	-
017 Amer Bapt Assn	4	80	NR	98 *	-	-
019 Amer Bapt USA	541	164,420	68,105	203,297 *	1.1	1.8
022 Carp Rus Orth	8	1,830	NR	3,112	-	-
032 Amish; other	1	42	NR	52 *	-	-
034 Ant Orth of NA	12	2,440	NR	4,880	-	-
039 Ap Chr Ch(Naz)	2	110	150	150 *	-	-

NR–Not Reported *Total adherents estimated from known number of communicant, confirmed, full members. - Represents a percentage less than 0.1. Percentages may not total 100 due to rounding.

Table 3: Religious Congregations by State and Group: 2000

Religious Group	Number of Churches, Synagogues, Mosques, or Temples	Number of Communicant, Confirmed, or Full Members	Number of Attendees	Total Adherents: Number of Adherents	Total Adherents: % of Total Pop.	Total Adherents: % of Total Adh.
040 Ap Chr Ch-Amer	1	44	125	125 *	-	-
049 Armen Ap Cilic	5	519	NR	2,660	-	-
050 Armen Ap Etchm	10	1,337	NR	11,362	.1	.1
053 Assemb of God	506	71,096	66,071	98,209	.5	.9
055 As Ref Pres Ch	5	257	NR	311	-	-
056 Baha'i	32	4,499	NR	4,499	-	-
057 Bapt Gen Conf	17	2,563	2,468	3,607 *	-	-
059 Bapt Miss Assn	3	136	104	168 *	-	-
061 Beachy Amish	3	128	NR	159 *	-	-
070 Bruderhof Comm	5	660	NR	660	-	-
075 Brethren in Cr	2	62	60	63	-	-
076 Buddhism	121	NR	NR	NR	-	-
078 Bulgar Orth USA	2	NR	NR	760	-	-
081 Catholic	1,784	NR	NR	7,550,491	39.8	65.9
084 Calvary Chapel	23	NR	NR	NR	-	-
089 Chr & Miss Al	161	13,037	NR	24,142	.1	.2
093 Chr Ch (Disc)	45	5,705	1,817	7,040 *	-	.1
097 Chr Chs&Chs Cr	64	5,313	NR	6,607 *	-	.1
105 Christian Ref	11	2,197	1,488	2,770 *	-	-
123 Ch God (Ander)	35	NR	2,772	2,772	-	-
127 Ch God (Cleve)	162	17,183	15,054	23,248 *	.1	.2
143 CG in Cr(Menn)	1	20	NR	25 *	-	-
145 Ch God Prophcy	44	3,240	NR	4,062 *	-	-
151 L-D Saints	160	NR	NR	44,987	.2	.4
157 Ch of Brethren	2	302	0	383 *	-	-
165 Ch of Nazarene	158	13,411	11,928	17,433	.1	.2
167 Chs of Christ	96	7,340	7,565	9,749	.1	.1
171 Ch God-Gen Con	2	56	46	71 *	-	-
173 Comm of Christ	7	466	NR	466	-	-
175 Congr Chr Chs	13	1,448	895	1,803 *	-	-
176 Congr Ad Afl	7	694	NR	867 *	-	-
179 Consrv Bapt	109	NR	13,971	13,971	.1	.1
181 Consrv Congr	27	2,596	2,617	3,215 *	-	-
183 Cons Menn Conf	5	997	1,218	1,450	-	-
193 Episcopal	693	NR	68,501	201,797	1.1	1.8
201 Evan Cov Ch	15	2,852	2,083	3,710 *	-	-
203 Evan Free Ch	33	2,443	4,015	4,034	-	-
207 E.L.C.A.	427	118,398	43,184	169,329	.9	1.5
216 Evan Presby Ch	2	467	NR	586 *	-	-
220 Free Lutheran	1	20	15	28	-	-
221 Free Methodist	82	5,554	9,068	9,482	-	.1
226 Friends-USA	57	2,843	NR	3,502 *	-	-
237 Menn Br US Conf	1	20	NR	24 *	-	-
245 Greek Orth Vslp	6	4,185	NR	8,260	-	.1
246 Greek Orthodox	64	NR	NR	61,407	.3	.5
249 Assyr Apost Ch	1	NR	NR	760	-	-
251 Holy Orth in NA	2	NR	NR	39	-	-
252 Hindu	83	NR	NR	NR	-	-
262 Int Cou Comm Ch	11	3,665	NR	4,552 *	-	-
263 Int Foursq Gos	15	646	964	1,072 *	-	-
264 Int Chs of Crst	4	6,202	11,958	8,287	-	.1
267 Muslim Est	144	NR	51,617	223,968	1.2	2.0
268 Jain	12	NR	NR	NR	-	-
283 Luth—MO Synod	195	58,200	25,229	81,705	.4	.7
286 E.PA Mennonite	2	135	NR	168 *	-	-
288 Mennonite USA	38	2,050	2,184	2,768 *	-	-
290 Metro Comm Ch	3	459	413	538 *	-	-
291 Missionary Ch	5	462	429	519	-	-
293 Morav Ch-North	11	2,344	NR	3,435	-	-
297 Mennonite;Other	6	248	NR	308 *	-	-
306 NT IndBapt&Rltd	1	250	NR	314 *	-	-
313 N Am Bapt Conf	10	1,309	1,545	1,618 *	-	-
322 Old Ord Menn Ch	7	1,207	NR	1,512 *	-	-
323 Old Ord Amish	41	2,235	NR	2,752 *	-	-
330 Macedonian Orth	3	NR	NR	2,800	-	-
331 OCA: Ter Diocs	31	2,929	NR	5,471	-	-
333 Malan Dioc Am	22	NR	NR	5,350	-	-
334 Malan Syr Orth	8	264	NR	1,320	-	-
335 Orth Pres Ch	11	643	845	1,009	-	-
339 Pent Ch of God	5	513	NR	819	-	-
349 Pent Holiness	6	400	391	495 *	-	-
355 Presb Ch (USA)	717	131,046	62,649	162,227 *	.9	1.4
356 Presb Ch Amer	26	3,287	4,052	4,651	-	-
363 Primitive Meth	2	114	NR	122	-	-
370 Ref Baptist Chs	17	NR	NR	NR	-	-
371 Ref Ch in Am	249	28,869	22,983	68,261	.4	.6
388 Reg Bapt Gen As	145	13,081	14,356	16,300 *	.1	.1
395 Romania Orth Ar	2	NR	NR	1,575	-	-
397 OCA: Roman Dioc	4	NR	NR	1,080	-	-
400 Rus Orth Moscow	4	NR	NR	NR	-	-
401 Rus Orth Abroad	19	NR	NR	NR	-	-
403 Salvation Army	97	8,044	6,132	24,065	.1	.2
410 Serb Orth USA	2	NR	NR	4,800	-	-
411 Serb Orth: Grac	1	NR	NR	NR	-	-
413 S.D.A.	249	56,292	NR	66,998	.4	.6
416 Sikh	21	NR	NR	NR	-	-
418 Southw Bapt Fel	4	NR	NR	NR	-	-
419 So Bapt Conv	219	19,644	13,579	24,364 *	.1	.2
423 Syrian Orth Ch	2	NR	NR	350	-	-
425 Tao	4	NR	NR	NR	-	-
431 Ukrainian Orth	19	NR	NR	4,884	-	-
435 Unitarian-Univ	62	10,228	NR	12,489 *	.1	.1
443 Un C of Christ	291	47,957	20,902	58,949 *	.3	.5
449 Un Methodist	1,404	326,537	105,444	403,362 *	2.1	3.5
455 Un Ref Chs N.A.	1	101	NR	170	-	-
463 Vineyard	15	2,312	2,023	2,875 *	-	-
467 Wesleyan	124	5,543	16,777	41,898	.2	.4
469 WELS	6	391	350	534	-	-
490 Zoroastrian	3	NR	NR	NR	-	-
496 Jewish Est	995	NR	NR	1,653,870	8.7	14.4
498 Indep.Charis.	20	24,314	21,495	29,250	.2	.3
499 Indep.Non-Char	19	8,402	11,786	14,250	.1	.1
NORTH CAROLINA	**11,132**	**2,529,714**	**1,124,710**	**3,651,416 ***	**45.4**	**100.0**
017 Amer Bapt Assn	1	100	NR	120 *	-	-
019 Amer Bapt USA	40	31,146	13,657	38,740 *	.5	1.1
022 Carp Rus Orth	1	122	NR	207	-	-
032 Amish; other	2	106	NR	130 *	-	-
034 Ant Orth of NA	2	214	NR	428	-	-
049 Armen Ap Cilic	1	0	NR	160	-	-
050 Armen Ap Etchm	1	0	NR	420	-	-
053 Assemb of God	218	27,046	29,020	41,036	.5	1.1
055 As Ref Pres Ch	59	9,414	NR	11,101	.1	.3
056 Baha'i	24	5,162	NR	5,162	.1	.1
057 Bapt Gen Conf	1	39	110	110 *	-	-
059 Bapt Miss Assn	1	0	0	0 *	-	-
076 Buddhism	46	NR	NR	NR	-	-
081 Catholic	180	NR	NR	315,606	3.9	8.6
084 Calvary Chapel	10	NR	NR	NR	-	-
089 Chr & Miss Al	49	4,666	NR	7,287	.1	.2
093 Chr Ch (Disc)	136	29,131	11,284	36,098 *	.4	1.0
097 Chr Chs&Chs Cr	161	27,650	NR	34,035 *	.4	.9
105 Christian Ref	3	257	240	314 *	-	-
121 Ch God (Abr)	2	109	92	133 *	-	-
123 Ch God (Ander)	52	NR	4,042	4,042	.1	.1
127 Ch God (Cleve)	465	64,321	45,043	81,037 *	1.0	2.2
143 CG in Cr(Menn)	1	98	NR	120 *	-	-
145 Ch God Prophcy	152	6,345	NR	7,863 *	.1	.2
151 L-D Saints	112	NR	NR	40,936	.5	1.1
157 Ch of Brethren	16	1,477	1,015	1,805 *	-	-
165 Ch of Nazarene	72	7,934	6,318	10,731	.1	.3
167 Chs of Christ	189	16,212	16,082	21,522	.3	.6
173 Comm of Christ	5	383	NR	383	-	-
175 Congr Chr Chs	2	85	60	103 *	-	-
176 Congr Ad Afl	2	553	NR	691 *	-	-
181 Consrv Congr	2	571	264	703 *	-	-
193 Episcopal	253	NR	30,424	80,068	1.0	2.2
201 Evan Cov Ch	7	921	769	1,207 *	-	-
203 Evan Free Ch	5	786	1,480	1,480	-	-
207 E.L.C.A.	237	70,330	35,401	88,830	1.1	2.4
216 Evan Presby Ch	21	6,045	NR	7,417 *	.1	.2
221 Free Methodist	2	41	66	66	-	-
223 Free Will Bapt	202	21,085	NR	26,045 *	.3	.7
226 Friends-USA	110	11,481	NR	14,165 *	.2	.4
237 Menn Br US Conf	6	209	NR	252 *	-	-
246 Greek Orthodox	11	NR	NR	7,161	.1	.2
252 Hindu	10	NR	NR	NR	-	-
258 IndFreeWillBapt	40	2,490	NR	2,978 *	-	.1

NR–Not Reported *Total adherents estimated from known number of communicant, confirmed, full members. - Represents a percentage less than 0.1. Percentages may not total 100 due to rounding.

Table 3: Religious Congregations by State and Group: 2000

Religious Group	Number of Churches, Synagogues, Mosques, or Temples	Number of Communicant, Confirmed, or Full Members	Number of Attendees	Total Adherents: Number of Adherents	Total Adherents: % of Total Pop.	Total Adherents: % of Total Adh.
263 Int Foursq Gos	54	6,817	8,737	9,294 *	.1	.3
264 Int Chs of Crst	3	1,634	2,986	2,363	-	.1
265 Int Pent C Chr	5	32	40	291	-	-
267 Muslim Est	29	NR	6,461	20,137	.3	.6
268 Jain	3	NR	NR	NR	-	-
283 Luth—MO Synod	56	15,623	9,255	20,651	.3	.6
288 Mennonite USA	11	632	555	781 *	-	-
290 Metro Comm Ch	12	845	841	1,026 *	-	-
291 Missionary Ch	1	8	8	8	-	-
295 Morav Ch-South	50	14,807	NR	18,180	.2	.5
297 Mennonite;Other	5	232	NR	282 *	-	-
304 NatPrimBapt USA	20	4,873	NR	6,072 *	.1	.2
313 N Am Bapt Conf	1	70	102	88 *	-	-
331 OCA: Ter Diocs	4	68	NR	384	-	-
335 Orth Pres Ch	7	294	349	408	-	-
336 OrigFreeWillBpt	234	37,039	NR	46,020 *	.6	1.3
339 Pent Ch of God	2	91	NR	156	-	-
349 Pent Holiness	328	40,290	28,957	50,265 *	.6	1.4
355 Presb Ch (USA)	738	163,988	81,927	203,647 *	2.5	5.6
356 Presb Ch Amer	93	14,197	13,584	19,630	.2	.5
360 Prim Bapt Chrch	94	NR	NR	NR	-	-
370 Ref Baptist Chs	7	NR	NR	NR	-	-
371 Ref Ch in Am	1	122	106	249	-	-
388 Reg Bapt Gen As	1	98	120	122 *	-	-
401 Rus Orth Abroad	2	NR	NR	NR	-	-
403 Salvation Army	36	4,161	2,760	7,719	.1	.2
409 Separate Bapt	4	199	NR	234 *	-	-
410 Serb Orth USA	2	NR	NR	500	-	-
413 S.D.A.	118	19,973	NR	23,769	.3	.7
416 Sikh	2	NR	NR	NR	-	-
418 Southw Bapt Fel	73	NR	NR	NR	-	-
419 So Bapt Conv	3,717	1,225,077	486,244	1,512,058 *	18.8	41.4
435 Unitarian-Univ	22	4,244	NR	5,181 *	.1	.1
443 Un C of Christ	234	40,516	19,226	50,088 *	.6	1.4
449 Un Methodist	1,964	516,299	205,538	638,785 *	7.9	17.5
455 Un Ref Chs N.A.	1	113	NR	169	-	-
463 Vineyard	12	2,335	2,094	2,837 *	-	.1
467 Wesleyan	174	18,582	17,101	32,475	.4	.9
469 WELS	9	613	477	821	-	-
496 Jewish Est	34	NR	NR	25,545	.3	.7
498 Indep.Charis.	20	16,494	11,035	17,930	.2	.5
499 Indep.Non-Char	37	32,819	30,840	42,559	.5	1.2
NORTH DAKOTA	**1,507**	**211,256**	**95,361**	**470,112 ***	**73.2**	**100.0**
019 Amer Bapt USA	16	1,698	914	2,103 *	.3	.4
034 Ant Orth of NA	1	8	NR	16	-	-
053 Assemb of God	67	5,038	6,604	9,994	1.6	2.1
056 Baha'i	3	345	NR	345	.1	.1
057 Bapt Gen Conf	5	299	351	412 *	.1	.1
081 Catholic	261	NR	NR	179,349	27.9	38.2
089 Chr & Miss Al	5	147	NR	337	.1	.1
097 Chr Chs&Chs Cr	1	50	NR	63 *	-	-
105 Christian Ref	1	114	0	139 *	-	-
123 Ch God (Ander)	2	NR	125	125	-	-
127 Ch God (Cleve)	11	555	594	766 *	.1	.2
143 CG in Cr(Menn)	1	98	NR	120 *	-	-
145 Ch God Prophcy	5	119	NR	146 *	-	-
151 L-D Saints	15	NR	NR	3,665	.6	.8
157 Ch of Brethren	3	150	70	188 *	-	-
165 Ch of Nazarene	24	1,742	1,635	2,675	.4	.6
167 Chs of Christ	6	365	410	532	.1	.1
173 Comm of Christ	4	185	NR	185	-	-
176 Congr Ad Afl	1	31	NR	38 *	-	-
179 Consrv Bapt	3	NR	409	409	.1	.1
181 Consrv Congr	9	725	691	883 *	.1	.2
193 Episcopal	24	NR	852	2,983	.5	.6
201 Evan Cov Ch	3	259	480	517 *	.1	.1
203 Evan Free Ch	29	1,973	4,268	4,273	.7	.9
207 E.L.C.A.	453	132,236	46,275	174,554	27.2	37.1
220 Free Lutheran	35	3,567	1,938	4,661	.7	1.0
221 Free Methodist	2	14	39	39	-	-
226 Friends-USA	2	90	NR	110 *	-	-
237 Menn Br US Conf	3	202	NR	243 *	-	.1
257 Hutterian Br	6	396	NR	600	.1	.1

Religious Group	Number of Churches, Synagogues, Mosques, or Temples	Number of Communicant, Confirmed, or Full Members	Number of Attendees	Total Adherents: Number of Adherents	Total Adherents: % of Total Pop.	Total Adherents: % of Total Adh.
263 Int Foursq Gos	2	120	327	327 *	.1	.1
267 Muslim Est	4	NR	312	902	.1	.2
283 Luth—MO Synod	94	18,583	7,943	23,720	3.7	5.0
288 Mennonite USA	4	143	141	183 *	-	-
293 Morav Ch-North	4	418	NR	496	.1	.1
297 Mennonite;Other	3	114	NR	143 *	-	-
313 N Am Bapt Conf	32	4,443	3,803	5,386 *	.8	1.1
331 OCA: Ter Diocs	1	29	NR	48	-	-
335 Orth Pres Ch	2	45	68	79	-	-
339 Pent Ch of God	2	57	NR	100	-	-
355 Presb Ch (USA)	66	7,093	3,009	8,740 *	1.4	1.9
356 Presb Ch Amer	1	53	40	61	-	-
371 Ref Ch in Am	6	505	597	1,067	.2	.2
373 Ref Ch in U.S.	3	119	NR	144	-	-
403 Salvation Army	6	488	218	1,465	.2	.3
413 S.D.A.	38	2,495	NR	2,971	.5	.6
419 So Bapt Conv	27	2,520	1,455	3,150 *	.5	.7
431 Ukrainian Orth	1	NR	NR	60	-	-
435 Unitarian-Univ	3	129	NR	158 *	-	-
443 Un C of Christ	57	5,485	2,300	6,697 *	1.0	1.4
449 Un Methodist	128	16,542	8,228	20,159 *	3.1	4.3
467 Wesleyan	7	273	674	1,392	.2	.3
469 WELS	13	1,196	591	1,464	.2	.3
496 Jewish Est	2	NR	NR	730	.1	.2
OHIO	**11,167**	**1,918,844**	**983,633**	**5,102,269 ***	**44.9**	**100.0**
007 OCA: Alban Dioc	1	NR	NR	200	-	-
011 A.W.M.C.	23	418	1,390	443	-	-
017 Amer Bapt Assn	13	650	NR	813 *	-	-
019 Amer Bapt USA	323	94,696	42,359	117,757 *	1.0	2.3
022 Carp Rus Orth	5	610	NR	1,035	-	-
032 Amish; other	34	1,881	NR	2,479 *	-	-
034 Ant Orth of NA	9	2,506	NR	5,012	-	.1
039 Ap Chr Ch(Naz)	13	1,104	1,718	1,729 *	-	-
040 Ap Chr Ch-Amer	9	1,381	2,899	2,899 *	-	.1
049 Armen Ap Cilic	1	32	NR	105	-	-
050 Armen Ap Etchm	2	97	NR	665	-	-
053 Assemb of God	284	36,793	42,412	67,738	.6	1.3
055 As Ref Pres Ch	1	17	NR	17	-	-
056 Baha'i	21	2,004	NR	2,004	-	-
057 Bapt Gen Conf	15	2,801	3,172	4,001 *	-	.1
059 Bapt Miss Assn	1	150	60	189 *	-	-
061 Beachy Amish	20	1,442	NR	1,851 *	-	-
071 Brethren (Ash)	23	5,188	4,730	6,460 *	.1	.1
075 Brethren in Cr	15	876	760	906	-	-
076 Buddhism	34	NR	NR	NR	-	-
078 Bulgar Orth USA	1	NR	NR	560	-	-
081 Catholic	1,000	NR	NR	2,231,832	19.7	43.7
084 Calvary Chapel	10	NR	NR	NR		
089 Chr & Miss Al	116	12,110	NR	29,067	.3	.6
093 Chr Ch (Disc)	185	56,390	17,696	70,075 *	.6	1.4
097 Chr Chs&Chs Cr	477	114,483	NR	142,571 *	1.3	2.8
105 Christian Ref	6	833	798	1,044 *	-	-
107 Christian Un	62	2,572	2,972	3,413 *	-	.1
121 Ch God (Abr)	9	426	485	563 *	-	-
123 Ch God (Ander)	222	NR	30,700	30,700	.3	.6
127 Ch God (Cleve)	228	42,108	27,086	55,022 *	.5	1.1
143 CG in Cr(Menn)	2	284	NR	355 *	-	-
145 Ch God Prophcy	51	1,470	NR	1,824 *	-	-
151 L-D Saints	117	NR	NR	38,824	.3	.8
157 Ch of Brethren	103	15,106	8,054	18,836 *	.2	.4
165 Ch of Nazarene	410	59,450	50,590	87,767	.8	1.7
167 Chs of Christ	428	35,974	35,969	47,472	.4	.9
171 Ch God-Gen Con	33	3,190	2,958	4,318 *	-	.1
173 Comm of Christ	40	4,036	NR	4,036	-	.1
175 Congr Chr Chs	19	4,971	2,485	6,170 *	.1	.1
176 Congr Ad Afl	1	58	NR	72 *	-	-
179 Consrv Bapt	12	NR	2,357	2,357	-	-
181 Consrv Congr	20	3,582	2,025	4,440 *	-	.1
183 Cons Menn Conf	26	2,948	3,600	4,287	-	.1
191 Entrpr Bpt Asc	28	1,612	NR	1,999 *	-	-
193 Episcopal	191	NR	20,534	58,684	.5	1.2
201 Evan Cov Ch	10	1,522	1,213	1,904 *	-	-
203 Evan Free Ch	23	2,431	5,311	5,311	-	.1

NR–Not Reported *Total adherents estimated from known number of communicant, confirmed, full members. - Represents a percentage less than 0.1. Percentages may not total 100 due to rounding.

Table 3: Religious Congregations by State and Group: 2000

Religious Group	Number of Churches, Synagogues, Mosques, or Temples	Number of Communicant, Confirmed, or Full Members	Number of Attendees	Total Adherents		
				Number of Adherents	% of Total Pop.	% of Total Adh.
207 E.L.C.A.	640	223,668	92,747	301,749	2.7	5.9
213 Evan Menn Inc	6	1,359	1,954	1,726 *	-	-
216 Evan Presby Ch	4	980	NR	1,202 *	-	-
220 Free Lutheran	2	30	25	30	-	-
221 Free Methodist	43	2,819	4,476	4,630	-	.1
223 Free Will Bapt	167	10,210	NR	12,687 *	.1	.2
226 Friends-USA	115	8,303	NR	10,319 *	.1	.2
246 Greek Orthodox	22	NR	NR	22,428	.2	.4
252 Hindu	19	NR	NR	NR	-	-
258 IndFreeWillBapt	1	20	NR	25 *	-	-
262 Int Cou Comm Ch	14	3,678	NR	4,545 *	-	.1
263 Int Foursq Gos	54	4,620	7,055	7,925 *	.1	.2
264 Int Chs of Crst	3	1,010	1,733	1,463	-	-
265 Int Pent C Chr	21	967	1,070	2,232	-	-
267 Muslim Est	41	NR	8,412	41,281	.4	.8
268 Jain	7	NR	NR	NR	-	-
283 Luth—MO Synod	189	59,978	30,527	79,976	.7	1.6
288 Mennonite USA	83	12,736	10,700	16,673 *	.1	.3
290 Metro Comm Ch	4	258	207	322 *	-	-
291 Missionary Ch	33	1,822	3,260	3,306	-	.1
293 Morav Ch-North	7	1,662	NR	2,067	-	-
296 Midw Congr Fel	11	570	443	719 *	-	-
297 Mennonite;Other	36	3,323	NR	4,190 *	-	.1
304 NatPrimBapt USA	5	772	NR	963 *	-	-
313 N Am Bapt Conf	7	1,767	2,150	2,521 *	-	-
320 "Old" MB Ascs	3	149	NR	183 *	-	-
322 Old Ord Menn Ch	10	1,078	NR	1,342 *	-	-
323 Old Ord Amish	324	19,110	NR	24,613 *	.2	.5
330 Macedonian Orth	4	NR	NR	2,640	-	.1
331 OCA: Ter Diocs	21	3,107	NR	4,957	-	.1
332 OCA: Bulg Dioc	4	445	NR	840	-	-
335 Orth Pres Ch	5	328	481	550	-	-
339 Pent Ch of God	40	1,648	NR	4,461	-	.1
349 Pent Holiness	19	1,788	1,224	2,201 *	-	-
355 Presb Ch (USA)	597	129,276	60,591	160,800 *	1.4	3.2
356 Presb Ch Amer	16	2,175	2,243	2,982	-	.1
360 Prim Bapt Chrch	35	NR	NR	NR	-	-
362 Prim Bapt E Dst	4	393	NR	483 *	-	-
363 Primitive Meth	3	171	NR	183	-	-
370 Ref Baptist Chs	5	NR	NR	NR	-	-
371 Ref Ch in Am	7	1,207	1,112	2,280	-	-
373 Ref Ch in U.S.	1	76	NR	104	-	-
379 Ref Mennonite	3	70	NR	88 *	-	-
388 Reg Bapt Gen As	180	32,172	30,258	38,758 *	.3	.8
395 Romania Orth Ar	1	NR	NR	700	-	-
397 OCA: Roman Dioc	7	NR	NR	1,911	-	-
400 Rus Orth Moscow	1	NR	NR	NR	-	-
401 Rus Orth Abroad	5	NR	NR	NR	-	-
403 Salvation Army	77	6,835	4,062	21,547	.2	.4
409 Separate Bapt	1	79	NR	99 *	-	-
410 Serb Orth USA	7	NR	NR	4,924	-	.1
411 Serb Orth: Grac	5	NR	NR	NR	-	-
413 S.D.A.	112	19,289	NR	22,956	.2	.4
416 Sikh	9	NR	NR	NR	-	-
418 Southw Bapt Fel	25	NR	NR	NR	-	-
419 So Bapt Conv	514	150,034	60,977	187,227 *	1.6	3.7
431 Ukrainian Orth	7	NR	NR	3,714	-	.1
435 Unitarian-Univ	36	4,918	NR	6,116 *	.1	.1
443 Un C of Christ	424	126,224	47,383	157,180 *	1.4	3.1
449 Un Methodist	2,094	454,994	207,449	566,084 *	5.0	11.1
463 Vineyard	28	19,590	13,809	24,480 *	.2	.5
466 Wayn Tr MB Asc	11	1,898	NR	2,385 *	-	-
467 Wesleyan	93	5,833	7,546	19,507	.2	.4
469 WELS	21	3,284	2,211	4,473	-	.1
496 Jewish Est	114	NR	NR	142,255	1.3	2.8
498 Indep.Charis.	28	18,447	21,005	22,781	.2	.4
499 Indep.Non-Char	55	55,472	44,190	73,680	.6	1.4
OKLAHOMA	**5,854**	**1,465,067**	**539,046**	**2,096,476 ***	**60.8**	**100.0**
017 Amer Bapt Assn	114	11,521	NR	14,375 *	.4	.7
019 Amer Bapt USA	14	4,024	1,398	5,025 *	.1	.2
034 Ant Orth of NA	2	817	NR	1,634	-	.1
049 Armen Ap Cilic	1	0	NR	80	-	-
053 Assemb of God	490	54,090	58,018	88,301	2.6	4.2
056 Baha'i	11	1,715	NR	1,715	-	.1
059 Bapt Miss Assn	48	7,528	2,810	9,365 *	.3	.4
061 Beachy Amish	1	46	NR	56 *	-	-
075 Brethren in Cr	3	248	199	261	-	-
076 Buddhism	8	NR	NR	NR	-	-
081 Catholic	195	NR	NR	168,625	4.9	8.0
084 Calvary Chapel	5	NR	NR	NR	-	-
089 Chr & Miss Al	6	484	NR	717	-	-
093 Chr Ch (Disc)	177	43,267	16,151	53,729 *	1.6	2.6
097 Chr Chs&Chs Cr	193	34,431	NR	42,708 *	1.2	2.0
107 Christian Un	9	345	335	427 *	-	-
123 Ch God (Ander)	62	NR	7,952	7,952	.2	.4
127 Ch God (Cleve)	74	6,162	4,539	7,758 *	.2	.4
143 CG in Cr(Menn)	4	449	NR	551 *	-	-
145 Ch God Prophcy	38	1,102	NR	1,375 *	-	.1
151 L-D Saints	76	NR	NR	24,564	.7	1.2
157 Ch of Brethren	6	412	196	498 *	-	-
165 Ch of Nazarene	213	28,677	18,880	36,470	1.1	1.7
167 Chs of Christ	603	63,838	63,391	83,047	2.4	4.0
171 Ch God-Gen Con	12	509	446	676 *	-	-
173 Comm of Christ	30	2,935	NR	2,935	.1	.1
175 Congr Chr Chs	1	30	25	37 *	-	-
183 Cons Menn Conf	1	157	192	228	-	-
185 Cumber Presb	19	755	NR	1,209	-	.1
186 Coptic Orth Ch	2	NR	NR	NR	-	-
193 Episcopal	72	NR	7,414	19,335	.6	.9
201 Evan Cov Ch	7	1,919	4,608	4,852 *	.1	.2
203 Evan Free Ch	5	352	515	528	-	-
207 E.L.C.A.	37	8,319	4,294	11,105	.3	.5
211 Fel Evg Bib Ch	2	62	0	62	-	-
220 Free Lutheran	3	270	181	300	-	-
221 Free Methodist	11	405	468	508	-	-
223 Free Will Bapt	245	23,173	NR	28,833 *	.8	1.4
226 Friends-USA	20	1,151	NR	1,418 *	-	.1
237 Menn Br US Conf	13	2,465	NR	3,051 *	.1	.1
246 Greek Orthodox	2	NR	NR	813	-	-
251 Holy Orth in NA	1	NR	NR	6	-	-
252 Hindu	2	NR	NR	NR	-	-
258 IndFreeWillBapt	2	134	NR	169 *	-	-
262 Int Cou Comm Ch	1	370	NR	462 *	-	-
263 Int Foursq Gos	19	1,551	2,562	2,791 *	.1	.1
264 Int Chs of Crst	2	252	371	365	-	-
267 Muslim Est	10	NR	1,891	6,145	.2	.3
268 Jain	2	NR	NR	NR	-	-
283 Luth—MO Synod	78	18,315	9,954	24,199	.7	1.2
288 Mennonite USA	16	1,359	1,010	1,689 *	-	.1
290 Metro Comm Ch	2	84	87	106 *	-	-
297 Mennonite;Other	5	201	NR	247 *	-	-
313 N Am Bapt Conf	5	303	219	370 *	-	-
323 Old Ord Amish	5	275	NR	346 *	-	-
331 OCA: Ter Diocs	1	11	NR	19	-	-
333 Malan Dioc Am	1	NR	NR	125	-	-
334 Malan Syr Orth	1	25	NR	125	-	-
335 Orth Pres Ch	3	102	96	139	-	-
339 Pent Ch of God	96	4,015	NR	7,164	.2	.3
349 Pent Holiness	167	22,603	13,364	28,192 *	.8	1.3
355 Presb Ch (USA)	147	28,240	13,367	35,211 *	1.0	1.7
356 Presb Ch Amer	5	717	558	971	-	-
360 Prim Bapt Chrch	25	NR	NR	NR	-	-
370 Ref Baptist Chs	5	NR	NR	NR	-	-
371 Ref Ch in Am	3	565	459	1,152	-	.1
388 Reg Bapt Gen As	1	50	35	62 *	-	-
401 Rus Orth Abroad	1	NR	NR	NR	-	-
403 Salvation Army	21	2,143	1,133	11,542	.3	.6
413 S.D.A.	85	6,808	NR	8,103	.2	.4
416 Sikh	1	NR	NR	NR	-	-
418 Southw Bapt Fel	1	NR	NR	NR	-	-
419 So Bapt Conv	1,578	776,847	207,276	967,223 *	28.0	46.1
431 Ukrainian Orth	1	NR	NR	180	-	-
435 Unitarian-Univ	11	1,837	NR	2,301 *	.1	.1
443 Un C of Christ	16	2,136	1,209	2,656 *	.1	.1
449 Un Methodist	636	259,258	66,030	322,794 *	9.4	15.4
463 Vineyard	7	730	683	909 *	-	-
467 Wesleyan	14	1,123	1,450	4,203	.1	.2

NR–Not Reported   *Total adherents estimated from known number of communicant, confirmed, full members.   - Represents a percentage less than 0.1.   Percentages may not total 100 due to rounding.

Table 3: Religious Congregations by State and Group: 2000

Religious Group	Number of Churches, Synagogues, Mosques, or Temples	Number of Communicant, Confirmed, or Full Members	Number of Attendees	Total Adherents: Number of Adherents	Total Adherents: % of Total Pop.	Total Adherents: % of Total Adh.
469 WELS	3	430	322	597	-	-
496 Jewish Est	10	NR	NR	5,050	.1	.2
498 Indep.Charis.	18	26,765	18,713	28,170	.8	1.3
499 Indep.Non-Char	11	6,160	6,245	7,570	.2	.4
OREGON	**3,155**	**354,298**	**289,255**	**1,071,287 ***	**31.3**	**100.0**
017 Amer Bapt Assn	19	856	NR	1,057 *	-	.1
019 Amer Bapt USA	50	10,966	5,695	13,454 *	.4	1.3
034 Ant Orth of NA	2	161	NR	322	-	-
039 Ap Chr Ch(Naz)	1	95	110	115 *	-	-
040 Ap Chr Ch-Amer	2	150	366	366 *	-	-
050 Armen Ap Etchm	1	0	NR	616	-	.1
053 Assemb of God	228	24,544	30,859	49,357	1.4	4.6
056 Baha'i	43	4,557	NR	4,557	.1	.4
057 Bapt Gen Conf	14	1,634	1,533	2,236 *	.1	.2
059 Bapt Miss Assn	4	196	220	242 *	-	-
075 Brethren in Cr	2	102	153	153	-	-
076 Buddhism	33	NR	NR	NR	-	-
081 Catholic	215	NR	NR	348,239	10.2	32.5
084 Calvary Chapel	31	NR	NR	NR	-	-
089 Chr & Miss Al	31	3,022	NR	9,178	.3	.9
093 Chr Ch (Disc)	37	9,997	4,060	12,459 *	.4	1.2
097 Chr Chs&Chs Cr	160	31,582	NR	39,011 *	1.1	3.6
105 Christian Ref	8	1,057	912	1,317 *	-	.1
123 Ch God (Ander)	46	NR	5,791	5,791	.2	.5
127 Ch God (Cleve)	32	2,360	1,576	3,013 *	.1	.3
143 CG in Cr(Menn)	1	109	NR	136 *	-	-
145 Ch God Prophcy	14	367	NR	457 *	-	-
151 L-D Saints	278	NR	NR	104,312	3.0	9.7
157 Ch of Brethren	4	260	97	323 *	-	-
165 Ch of Nazarene	113	18,435	15,413	22,707	.7	2.1
167 Chs of Christ	120	8,634	9,296	11,544	.3	1.1
173 Comm of Christ	16	2,194	NR	2,194	.1	.2
175 Congr Chr Chs	2	165	132	207 *	-	-
179 Consrv Bapt	183	NR	36,017	36,017	1.1	3.4
181 Consrv Congr	1	9	18	11 *	-	-
193 Episcopal	100	NR	8,895	24,229	.7	2.3
201 Evan Cov Ch	18	2,369	3,786	4,124 *	.1	.4
203 Evan Free Ch	10	862	1,898	1,898	.1	.2
207 E.L.C.A.	121	35,168	17,173	46,807	1.4	4.4
211 Fel Evg Bib Ch	2	475	180	180	-	-
220 Free Lutheran	2	155	136	196	-	-
221 Free Methodist	31	2,302	3,468	3,478	.1	.3
223 Free Will Bapt	3	207	NR	257 *	-	-
226 Friends-USA	48	3,474	NR	4,324 *	.1	.4
237 Menn Br US Conf	13	1,544	NR	1,895 *	.1	.2
246 Greek Orthodox	3	NR	NR	2,880	.1	.3
251 Holy Orth in NA	1	NR	NR	42	-	-
252 Hindu	7	NR	NR	NR	-	-
263 Int Foursq Gos	107	26,052	43,386	44,826 *	1.3	4.2
264 Int Chs of Crst	1	294	560	417	-	-
267 Muslim Est	7	NR	1,366	5,224	.2	.5
268 Jain	2	NR	NR	NR	-	-
273 LandmrkBapt,I&U	20	900	NR	1,100 *	-	.1
283 Luth—MO Synod	89	17,490	10,157	22,429	.7	2.1
288 Mennonite USA	19	1,814	1,904	2,427 *	.1	.2
290 Metro Comm Ch	4	332	245	390 *	-	-
291 Missionary Ch	4	270	498	498	-	-
297 Mennonite;Other	14	1,673	NR	2,092 *	.1	.2
313 N Am Bapt Conf	13	1,516	1,438	1,974 *	.1	.2
331 OCA: Ter Diocs	5	232	NR	496	-	-
335 Orth Pres Ch	6	436	497	612	-	.1
339 Pent Ch of God	35	915	NR	2,349	.1	.2
349 Pent Holiness	9	385	572	482 *	-	-
355 Presb Ch (USA)	133	27,179	18,240	33,909 *	1.0	3.2
356 Presb Ch Amer	4	188	320	320	-	-
360 Prim Bapt Chrch	4	NR	NR	NR	-	-
370 Ref Baptist Chs	6	NR	NR	NR	-	-
388 Reg Bapt Gen As	13	1,438	1,658	1,882 *	.1	.2
397 OCA: Roman Dioc	2	NR	NR	509	-	-
400 Rus Orth Moscow	1	NR	NR	NR	-	-
401 Rus Orth Abroad	2	NR	NR	NR	-	-
403 Salvation Army	23	1,708	1,158	6,103	.2	.6
410 Serb Orth USA	1	NR	NR	200	-	-
413 S.D.A.	140	25,990	NR	30,929	.9	2.9
416 Sikh	5	NR	NR	NR	-	-
419 So Bapt Conv	128	26,258	10,222	32,433 *	.9	3.0
423 Syrian Orth Ch	1	NR	NR	125	-	-
425 Tao	1	NR	NR	NR	-	-
431 Ukrainian Orth	1	NR	NR	105	-	-
435 Unitarian-Univ	19	2,748	NR	3,365 *	.1	.3
443 Un C of Christ	34	6,343	3,181	7,817 *	.2	.7
449 Un Methodist	175	27,576	14,169	34,101 *	1.0	3.2
455 Un Ref Chs N.A.	1	105	NR	165	-	-
463 Vineyard	13	2,285	2,081	2,854 *	.1	.3
467 Wesleyan	12	353	955	3,154	.1	.3
469 WELS	11	897	604	1,224	-	.1
490 Zoroastrian	1	NR	NR	NR	-	-
496 Jewish Est	15	NR	NR	31,625	.9	3.0
498 Indep.Charis.	11	7,188	13,650	14,400	.4	1.3
499 Indep.Non-Char	13	3,725	14,610	21,050	.6	2.0
PENNSYLVANIA	**13,105**	**2,087,177**	**1,052,151**	**7,116,698 ***	**57.9**	**100.0**
007 OCA: Alban Dioc	2	NR	NR	750	-	-
011 A.W.M.C.	55	979	3,056	1,065	-	-
017 Amer Bapt Assn	16	900	NR	1,100 *	-	-
019 Amer Bapt USA	435	108,132	62,416	132,858 *	1.1	1.9
022 Carp Rus Orth	35	5,078	NR	8,652	.1	.1
032 Amish; other	8	550	NR	682 *	-	-
034 Ant Orth of NA	20	4,469	NR	8,938	.1	.1
039 Ap Chr Ch(Naz)	2	50	80	83 *	-	-
040 Ap Chr Ch-Amer	1	33	74	74 *	-	-
049 Armen Ap Cilic	1	560	NR	1,050	-	-
050 Armen Ap Etchm	3	675	NR	5,260	-	.1
053 Assemb of God	374	44,944	54,466	84,153	.7	1.2
055 As Ref Pres Ch	2	118	NR	148	-	-
056 Baha'i	10	1,584	NR	1,584	-	-
057 Bapt Gen Conf	16	2,265	2,930	3,407 *	-	-
061 Beachy Amish	15	1,687	NR	2,090 *	-	-
070 Bruderhof Comm	2	264	NR	264	-	-
071 Brethren (Ash)	18	1,232	1,173	1,485 *	-	-
075 Brethren in Cr	102	13,429	15,750	16,618	.1	.2
076 Buddhism	30	NR	NR	NR	-	-
078 Bulgar Orth USA	1	NR	NR	220	-	-
081 Catholic	1,624	NR	NR	3,802,524	31.0	53.4
084 Calvary Chapel	12	NR	NR	NR	-	-
089 Chr & Miss Al	254	19,957	NR	45,926	.4	.6
093 Chr Ch (Disc)	62	13,095	4,261	15,833 *	.1	.2
097 Chr Chs&Chs Cr	128	19,867	NR	23,938 *	.2	.3
105 Christian Ref	2	216	240	268 *	-	-
123 Ch God (Ander)	96	NR	14,425	14,425	.1	.2
127 Ch God (Cleve)	112	13,573	9,699	16,918 *	.1	.2
143 CG in Cr(Menn)	4	387	NR	471 *	-	-
145 Ch God Prophcy	41	1,681	NR	2,057 *	-	-
151 L-D Saints	102	NR	NR	31,032	.3	.4
157 Ch of Brethren	236	42,717	23,230	52,684 *	.4	.7
165 Ch of Nazarene	156	17,091	14,315	27,492	.2	.4
167 Chs of Christ	137	7,504	7,894	10,097	.1	.1
171 Ch God-Gen Con	156	17,665	14,652	22,692 *	.2	.3
173 Comm of Christ	16	1,436	NR	1,436	-	-
175 Congr Chr Chs	15	790	672	955 *	-	-
176 Congr Ad Afl	7	877	NR	1,060 *	-	-
179 Consrv Bapt	57	NR	9,256	9,256	.1	.1
181 Consrv Congr	15	2,472	1,231	3,034 *	-	-
183 Cons Menn Conf	5	703	858	1,022	-	-
185 Cumber Presb	1	122	NR	122	-	-
193 Episcopal	413	NR	42,204	116,511	.9	1.6
201 Evan Cov Ch	13	922	872	1,149 *	-	-
203 Evan Free Ch	58	7,303	15,193	15,273	.1	.2
207 E.L.C.A.	1,343	450,911	153,391	611,913	5.0	8.6
216 Evan Presby Ch	4	879	NR	1,063 *	-	-
220 Free Lutheran	2	947	697	1,361	-	-
221 Free Methodist	99	4,462	6,393	6,741	.1	.1
223 Free Will Bapt	3	297	NR	363 *	-	-
226 Friends-USA	92	9,570	NR	11,844 *	.1	.2
241 Gen Six Pr Bpt	1	20	NR	25 *	-	-
245 Greek Orth Vslp	3	875	NR	1,113	-	-
246 Greek Orthodox	37	NR	NR	24,246	.2	.3

NR–Not Reported *Total adherents estimated from known number of communicant, confirmed, full members. - Represents a percentage less than 0.1. Percentages may not total 100 due to rounding.

Table 3: Religious Congregations by State and Group: 2000

Religious Group	Number of Churches, Synagogues, Mosques, or Temples	Number of Communicant, Confirmed, or Full Members	Number of Attendees	Total Adherents		
				Number of Adherents	% of Total Pop.	% of Total Adh.
251 Holy Orth in NA	2	NR	NR	182	-	-
252 Hindu	18	NR	NR	NR	-	-
262 Int Cou Comm Ch	4	709	NR	873 *	-	-
263 Int Foursq Gos	24	2,108	2,221	3,044 *	-	-
264 Int Chs of Crst	3	1,240	1,940	1,646	-	-
267 Muslim Est	57	NR	17,348	71,190	.6	1.0
268 Jain	7	NR	NR	NR	-	-
283 Luth—MO Synod	88	16,361	7,881	21,015	.2	.3
286 E.PA Mennonite	31	2,565	NR	3,172 *	-	-
288 Mennonite USA	319	37,582	36,057	48,215 *	.4	.7
290 Metro Comm Ch	5	357	378	420 *	-	-
291 Missionary Ch	9	415	636	660	-	-
293 Morav Ch-North	26	8,049	NR	10,093	.1	.1
297 Mennonite;Other	105	7,052	NR	8,718 *	.1	.1
304 NatPrimBapt USA	1	229	NR	286 *	-	-
313 N Am Bapt Conf	13	2,158	1,882	2,700 *	-	-
322 Old Ord Menn Ch	61	9,840	NR	12,246 *	.1	.2
323 Old Ord Amish	306	20,445	NR	25,340 *	.2	.4
324 Old Ord Rvr Br	4	298	430	477	-	-
330 Macedonian Orth	1	NR	NR	200	-	-
331 OCA: Ter Diocs	78	7,348	NR	12,382	.1	.2
333 Malan Dioc Am	4	NR	NR	900	-	-
334 Malan Syr Orth	2	160	NR	800	-	-
335 Orth Pres Ch	35	2,646	3,317	3,919	-	.1
339 Pent Ch of God	2	43	NR	75	-	-
349 Pent Holiness	16	1,346	860	1,624 *	-	-
355 Presb Ch (USA)	1,083	265,158	125,382	324,714 *	2.6	4.6
356 Presb Ch Amer	94	16,367	16,167	21,350	.2	.3
360 Prim Bapt Chrch	4	NR	NR	NR	-	-
363 Primitive Meth	44	2,507	NR	2,669	-	-
370 Ref Baptist Chs	16	NR	NR	NR	-	-
371 Ref Ch in Am	11	1,610	1,265	3,204	-	-
373 Ref Ch in U.S.	1	30	NR	53	-	-
379 Ref Mennonite	3	127	NR	158 *	-	-
388 Reg Bapt Gen As	64	7,932	8,908	10,320 *	.1	.1
395 Romania Orth Ar	1	NR	NR	350	-	-
397 OCA: Roman Dioc	7	NR	NR	837	-	-
400 Rus Orth Moscow	8	NR	NR	NR	-	-
401 Rus Orth Abroad	11	NR	NR	NR	-	-
403 Salvation Army	99	8,714	6,071	30,153	.2	.4
410 Serb Orth USA	10	NR	NR	5,642	-	.1
411 Serb Orth: Grac	4	NR	NR	NR	-	-
413 S.D.A.	117	14,090	NR	16,766	.1	.2
416 Sikh	6	NR	NR	NR	-	-
418 Southw Bapt Fel	14	NR	NR	NR	-	-
419 So Bapt Conv	226	36,007	22,133	44,432 *	.4	.6
425 Tao	1	NR	NR	NR	-	-
431 Ukrainian Orth	25	NR	NR	10,692	.1	.2
435 Unitarian-Univ	36	5,503	NR	6,778 *	.1	.1
443 Un C of Christ	735	197,496	71,679	241,844 *	2.0	3.4
449 Un Methodist	2,442	541,247	210,133	659,350 *	5.4	9.3
463 Vineyard	5	307	377	426 *	-	-
467 Wesleyan	92	4,796	8,480	21,007	.2	.3
469 WELS	4	450	267	531	-	-
490 Zoroastrian	2	NR	NR	NR	-	-
496 Jewish Est	197	NR	NR	283,000	2.3	4.0
498 Indep.Charis.	17	11,497	11,610	13,928	.1	.2
499 Indep.Non-Char	51	29,100	37,301	42,992	.4	.6
RHODE ISLAND	**572**	**51,815**	**32,957**	**665,170 ***	**63.5**	**100.0**
017 Amer Bapt Assn	1	20	NR	25 *	-	-
019 Amer Bapt USA	73	17,104	6,337	20,997 *	2.0	3.2
034 Ant Orth of NA	1	0	NR	0	-	-
049 Armen Ap Cilic	1	510	NR	1,400	.1	.2
050 Armen Ap Etchm	1	478	NR	2,400	.2	.4
053 Assemb of God	23	2,270	2,835	3,564	.3	.5
056 Baha'i	3	261	NR	261	-	-
057 Bapt Gen Conf	2	140	120	190 *	-	-
076 Buddhism	5	NR	NR	NR	-	-
081 Catholic	165	NR	NR	542,244	51.7	81.5
084 Calvary Chapel	1	NR	NR	NR	-	-
089 Chr & Miss Al	3	553	NR	780	.1	.1
097 Chr Chs&Chs Cr	1	0	NR	0 *	-	-
123 Ch God (Ander)	3	NR	332	332	-	-
127 Ch God (Cleve)	22	1,063	717	1,314 *	.1	.2
145 Ch God Prophcy	4	267	NR	328 *	-	-
151 L-D Saints	7	NR	NR	2,295	.2	.3
165 Ch of Nazarene	6	367	557	660	.1	.1
167 Chs of Christ	6	257	307	382	-	.1
173 Comm of Christ	2	126	NR	126	-	-
175 Congr Chr Chs	2	128	65	156 *	-	-
176 Congr Ad Afl	2	807	NR	981 *	.1	.1
179 Consrv Bapt	8	NR	1,350	1,350	.1	.2
181 Consrv Congr	1	157	110	193 *	-	-
193 Episcopal	64	NR	7,615	26,756	2.6	4.0
201 Evan Cov Ch	4	486	603	770 *	.1	.1
207 E.L.C.A.	12	4,036	1,836	5,914	.6	.9
221 Free Methodist	1	2	35	35	-	-
226 Friends-USA	9	491	NR	599 *	.1	.1
245 Greek Orth Vslp	1	175	NR	675	.1	.1
246 Greek Orthodox	3	NR	NR	3,438	.3	.5
252 Hindu	1	NR	NR	NR	-	-
263 Int Foursq Gos	3	119	336	336 *	-	.1
267 Muslim Est	3	NR	468	1,827	.2	.3
283 Luth—MO Synod	3	742	448	1,017	.1	.2
331 OCA: Ter Diocs	1	64	NR	178	-	-
355 Presb Ch (USA)	9	1,977	1,261	2,417 *	.2	.4
356 Presb Ch Amer	1	80	0	108	-	-
363 Primitive Meth	5	285	NR	304	-	-
370 Ref Baptist Chs	1	NR	NR	NR	-	-
388 Reg Bapt Gen As	1	46	70	70 *	-	-
397 OCA: Roman Dioc	1	NR	NR	81	-	-
403 Salvation Army	3	237	188	1,000	.1	.2
413 S.D.A.	7	674	NR	802	.1	.1
419 So Bapt Conv	8	1,559	609	1,903 *	.2	.3
423 Syrian Orth Ch	1	NR	NR	250	-	-
431 Ukrainian Orth	1	NR	NR	474	-	.1
435 Unitarian-Univ	9	1,060	NR	1,299 *	.1	.2
443 Un C of Christ	28	7,224	3,143	8,862 *	.8	1.3
449 Un Methodist	26	7,020	2,270	8,592 *	.8	1.3
463 Vineyard	1	130	120	160 *	-	-
496 Jewish Est	19	NR	NR	16,100	1.5	2.4
498 Indep.Charis.	2	600	925	925	.1	.1
499 Indep.Non-Char	1	300	300	300	-	-
SOUTH CAROLINA	**5,522**	**1,338,172**	**583,451**	**1,908,638 ***	**47.6**	**100.0**
017 Amer Bapt Assn	9	672	NR	832 *	-	-
019 Amer Bapt USA	4	2,360	1,675	2,902 *	.1	.2
034 Ant Orth of NA	5	148	NR	296	-	-
053 Assemb of God	112	11,641	12,920	18,219	.5	1.0
055 As Ref Pres Ch	69	12,469	NR	14,659	.4	.8
056 Baha'i	33	17,586	NR	17,586	.4	.9
061 Beachy Amish	3	216	NR	270 *	-	-
076 Buddhism	4	NR	NR	NR	-	-
081 Catholic	118	NR	NR	136,719	3.4	7.2
084 Calvary Chapel	8	NR	NR	NR	-	-
089 Chr & Miss Al	12	891	NR	1,362	-	.1
093 Chr Ch (Disc)	40	5,273	848	6,613 *	.2	.3
097 Chr Chs&Chs Cr	31	3,664	NR	4,567 *	.1	.2
121 Ch God (Abr)	5	496	482	636 *	-	-
123 Ch God (Ander)	45	NR	2,856	2,856	.1	.1
127 Ch God (Cleve)	297	45,152	26,573	56,612 *	1.4	3.0
145 Ch God Prophcy	130	4,635	NR	5,763 *	.1	.3
151 L-D Saints	54	NR	NR	20,424	.5	1.1
157 Ch of Brethren	2	186	91	231 *	-	-
165 Ch of Nazarene	64	9,214	6,475	12,824	.3	.7
167 Chs of Christ	118	10,022	9,810	13,091	.3	.7
173 Comm of Christ	3	258	NR	258	-	-
179 Consrv Bapt	1	NR	100	100	-	-
183 Cons Menn Conf	1	21	26	31	-	-
193 Episcopal	138	NR	21,155	52,486	1.3	2.7
203 Evan Free Ch	1	59	100	100	-	-
207 E.L.C.A.	167	48,831	23,183	61,380	1.5	3.2
216 Evan Presby Ch	5	628	NR	783 *	-	-
221 Free Methodist	1	0	51	51	-	-
223 Free Will Bapt	123	6,103	NR	7,583 *	.2	.4
226 Friends-USA	3	135	NR	166 *	-	-
246 Greek Orthodox	7	NR	NR	3,867	.1	.2

NR–Not Reported *Total adherents estimated from known number of communicant, confirmed, full members. - Represents a percentage less than 0.1. Percentages may not total 100 due to rounding.

Table 3: Religious Congregations by State and Group: 2000

Religious Group	Number of Churches, Synagogues, Mosques, or Temples	Number of Communicant, Confirmed, or Full Members	Number of Attendees	Total Adherents: Number of Adherents	Total Adherents: % of Total Pop.	Total Adherents: % of Total Adh.
252 Hindu	3	NR	NR	NR	-	-
258 IndFreeWillBapt	1	18	NR	22 *	-	-
262 Int Cou Comm Ch	1	860	NR	1,082 *	-	.1
263 Int Foursq Gos	11	813	1,104	1,136 *	-	.1
264 Int Chs of Crst	3	652	1,103	967	-	.1
267 Muslim Est	15	NR	1,575	5,761	.1	.3
283 Luth—MO Synod	16	2,636	1,750	3,440	.1	.2
288 Mennonite USA	2	58	47	71 *	-	-
290 Metro Comm Ch	3	353	206	206 *	-	-
297 Mennonite;Other	6	411	NR	510 *	-	-
306 NT IndBapt&Rltd	1	45	NR	56 *	-	-
331 OCA: Ter Diocs	2	69	NR	179	-	-
335 Orth Pres Ch	1	22	35	35	-	-
336 OrigFreeWillBpt	3	159	NR	191 *	-	-
349 Pent Holiness	249	27,170	20,059	33,820 *	.8	1.8
355 Presb Ch (USA)	325	83,701	41,636	103,883 *	2.6	5.4
356 Presb Ch Amer	98	18,576	13,128	23,313	.6	1.2
360 Prim Bapt Chrch	10	NR	NR	NR	-	-
370 Ref Baptist Chs	2	NR	NR	NR	-	-
401 Rus Orth Abroad	1	NR	NR	NR	-	-
403 Salvation Army	18	1,720	1,452	2,930	.1	.2
413 S.D.A.	57	7,720	NR	9,187	.2	.5
418 Southw Bapt Fel	27	NR	NR	NR	-	-
419 So Bapt Conv	1,878	747,092	272,515	928,341 *	23.1	48.6
435 Unitarian-Univ	9	1,235	NR	1,519 *	-	.1
443 Un C of Christ	2	405	181	497 *	-	-
449 Un Methodist	1,047	242,891	100,588	302,528 *	7.5	15.9
463 Vineyard	4	526	470	645 *	-	-
467 Wesleyan	67	4,332	3,900	9,081	.2	.5
469 WELS	4	239	212	336	-	-
496 Jewish Est	15	NR	NR	11,000	.3	.6
498 Indep.Charis.	12	6,225	9,200	13,200	.3	.7
499 Indep.Non-Char	16	9,584	7,945	11,435	.3	.6
SOUTH DAKOTA	**1,712**	**230,313**	**122,607**	**511,886 ***	**67.8**	**100.0**
017 Amer Bapt Assn	3	60	NR	74 *	-	-
019 Amer Bapt USA	35	5,035	3,073	6,417 *	.9	1.3
053 Assemb of God	51	3,447	4,323	7,438	1.0	1.5
056 Baha'i	9	1,032	NR	1,032	.1	.2
057 Bapt Gen Conf	15	2,840	2,843	3,634 *	.5	.7
081 Catholic	252	NR	NR	181,434	24.0	35.4
084 Calvary Chapel	2	NR	NR	NR	-	-
089 Chr & Miss Al	12	387	NR	1,093	.1	.2
093 Chr Ch (Disc)	2	564	212	708 *	.1	.1
097 Chr Chs&Chs Cr	16	1,651	NR	2,049 *	.3	.4
105 Christian Ref	14	3,424	2,672	4,297 *	.6	.8
123 Ch God (Ander)	7	NR	605	605	.1	.1
127 Ch God (Cleve)	11	475	497	699 *	.1	.1
143 CG in Cr(Menn)	2	156	NR	191 *	-	-
145 Ch God Prophcy	3	72	NR	90 *	-	-
151 L-D Saints	31	NR	NR	5,998	.8	1.2
165 Ch of Nazarene	17	769	616	1,008	.1	.2
167 Chs of Christ	24	943	1,135	1,328	.2	.3
173 Comm of Christ	1	39	NR	39	-	-
176 Congr Ad Afl	1	26	NR	33 *	-	-
193 Episcopal	85	NR	2,892	11,191	1.5	2.2
201 Evan Cov Ch	11	641	681	895 *	.1	.2
203 Evan Free Ch	15	918	1,980	1,980	.3	.4
207 E.L.C.A.	259	91,489	37,936	121,871	16.1	23.8
211 Fel Evg Bib Ch	1	70	50	50	-	-
220 Free Lutheran	19	1,928	1,437	2,535	.3	.5
221 Free Methodist	3	78	101	101	-	-
223 Free Will Bapt	1	0	NR	0 *	-	-
237 Menn Br US Conf	9	1,105	NR	1,363 *	.2	.3
246 Greek Orthodox	1	NR	NR	222	-	-
251 Holy Orth in NA	1	NR	NR	10	-	-
257 Hutterian Br	54	3,564	NR	5,400	.7	1.1
263 Int Foursq Gos	3	416	1,465	1,518 *	.2	.3
264 Int Chs of Crst	1	14	26	27	-	-
267 Muslim Est	1	NR	35	50	-	-
283 Luth—MO Synod	116	24,662	12,151	31,524	4.2	6.2
288 Mennonite USA	10	1,754	1,220	2,163 *	.3	.4
290 Metro Comm Ch	2	59	39	74 *	-	-
291 Missionary Ch	3	86	87	94	-	-

Religious Group	Number of Churches, Synagogues, Mosques, or Temples	Number of Communicant, Confirmed, or Full Members	Number of Attendees	Total Adherents: Number of Adherents	Total Adherents: % of Total Pop.	Total Adherents: % of Total Adh.
297 Mennonite;Other	5	573	NR	706 *	.1	.1
306 NT IndBapt&Rltd	5	275	NR	337 *	-	.1
307 Neth Ref Congr	2	122	NR	268	-	.1
313 N Am Bapt Conf	23	3,474	3,302	4,306 *	.6	.8
335 Orth Pres Ch	5	262	254	362	-	.1
339 Pent Ch of God	2	31	NR	65	-	-
355 Presb Ch (USA)	85	10,101	5,522	12,763 *	1.7	2.5
356 Presb Ch Amer	8	974	738	1,217	.2	.2
370 Ref Baptist Chs	1	NR	NR	NR	-	-
371 Ref Ch in Am	26	4,427	4,057	7,516	1.0	1.5
373 Ref Ch in U.S.	11	999	NR	1,244	.2	.2
388 Reg Bapt Gen As	4	96	132	138 *	-	-
401 Rus Orth Abroad	1	NR	NR	NR	-	-
403 Salvation Army	7	750	428	2,804	.4	.5
413 S.D.A.	24	1,763	NR	2,098	.3	.4
418 Southw Bapt Fel	1	NR	NR	NR	-	-
419 So Bapt Conv	47	5,251	2,201	6,608 *	.9	1.3
435 Unitarian-Univ	3	90	NR	112 *	-	-
443 Un C of Christ	91	12,880	5,714	15,987 *	2.1	3.1
449 Un Methodist	164	30,099	15,960	37,280 *	4.9	7.3
463 Vineyard	1	130	120	163 *	-	-
467 Wesleyan	31	2,080	3,601	7,865	1.0	1.5
469 WELS	57	7,672	3,912	9,762	1.3	1.9
496 Jewish Est	3	NR	NR	350	-	.1
498 Indep.Charis.	1	300	240	350	-	.1
499 Indep.Non-Char	1	260	350	350	-	.1
TENNESSEE	**9,634**	**2,099,948**	**919,928**	**2,905,619 ***	**51.1**	**100.0**
011 A.W.M.C.	2	0	40	0	-	-
017 Amer Bapt Assn	21	2,372	NR	2,986 *	.1	.1
019 Amer Bapt USA	9	3,550	1,345	4,478 *	.1	.2
032 Amish; other	6	213	NR	263 *	-	-
034 Ant Orth of NA	3	508	NR	1,016	-	-
040 Ap Chr Ch-Amer	1	9	18	18 *	-	-
050 Armen Ap Etchm	2	58	NR	230	-	-
053 Assemb of God	191	30,254	26,858	40,430	.7	1.4
055 As Ref Pres Ch	10	1,656	NR	1,834	-	.1
056 Baha'i	15	1,414	NR	1,414	-	-
059 Bapt Miss Assn	10	1,454	794	1,821 *	-	.1
061 Beachy Amish	4	251	NR	305 *	-	-
075 Brethren in Cr	4	260	193	268	-	-
076 Buddhism	12	NR	NR	NR	-	-
081 Catholic	152	NR	NR	183,161	3.2	6.3
084 Calvary Chapel	11	NR	NR	NR	-	-
089 Chr & Miss Al	10	505	NR	886	-	-
093 Chr Ch (Disc)	56	22,302	8,601	28,108 *	.5	1.0
097 Chr Chs&Chs Cr	172	32,674	NR	39,643 *	.7	1.4
105 Christian Ref	1	145	95	176 *	-	-
121 Ch God (Abr)	1	20	25	25 *	-	-
123 Ch God (Ander)	70	NR	5,291	5,291	.1	.2
127 Ch God (Cleve)	362	53,488	32,403	66,136 *	1.2	2.3
143 CG in Cr(Menn)	2	110	NR	134 *	-	-
145 Ch God Prophcy	132	6,696	NR	8,225 *	.1	.3
151 L-D Saints	77	NR	NR	24,075	.4	.8
157 Ch of Brethren	21	1,209	457	1,456 *	-	.1
165 Ch of Nazarene	173	20,734	15,964	28,538	.5	1.0
167 Chs of Christ	1,466	167,311	173,290	216,648	3.8	7.5
173 Comm of Christ	8	1,047	NR	1,047	-	-
175 Congr Chr Chs	1	65	56	78 *	-	-
185 Cumber Presb	280	20,655	NR	34,415	.6	1.2
186 Coptic Orth Ch	4	NR	NR	NR	-	-
189 Duck Rivr Bapt	71	6,932	NR	8,517 *	.1	.3
193 Episcopal	112	NR	13,670	35,037	.6	1.2
201 Evan Cov Ch	1	41	26	49 *	-	-
203 Evan Free Ch	10	983	2,910	2,910	.1	.1
207 E.L.C.A.	49	12,793	5,904	16,239	.3	.6
216 Evan Presby Ch	13	11,221	NR	14,095 *	.2	.5
221 Free Methodist	11	328	579	579	-	-
223 Free Will Bapt	227	22,091	NR	26,935 *	.5	.9
226 Friends-USA	12	761	NR	933 *	-	-
246 Greek Orthodox	5	NR	NR	2,658	-	.1
252 Hindu	7	NR	NR	NR	-	-
258 IndFreeWillBapt	110	9,780	NR	11,817 *	.2	.4
262 Int Cou Comm Ch	5	1,630	NR	1,970 *	-	.1

NR–Not Reported   *Total adherents estimated from known number of communicant, confirmed, full members.   - Represents a percentage less than 0.1.   Percentages may not total 100 due to rounding.

Table 3: Religious Congregations by State and Group: 2000

Religious Group	Number of Churches, Synagogues, Mosques, or Temples	Number of Communicant, Confirmed, or Full Members	Number of Attendees	Total Adherents		
				Number of Adherents	% of Total Pop.	% of Total Adh.
263 Int Foursq Gos	19	1,848	3,018	3,231 *	.1	.1
264 Int Chs of Crst	4	915	1,537	1,261	-	-
267 Muslim Est	16	NR	3,811	18,464	.3	.6
268 Jain	2	NR	NR	NR	-	-
283 Luth—MO Synod	57	12,912	7,766	16,883	.3	.6
288 Mennonite USA	5	159	139	192 *	-	-
290 Metro Comm Ch	5	300	256	263 *	-	-
297 Mennonite;Other	4	223	NR	269 *	-	-
304 NatPrimBapt USA	87	6,315	NR	7,811 *	.1	.3
320 "Old" MB Ascs	53	6,985	NR	8,579 *	.2	.3
322 Old Ord Menn Ch	4	139	NR	171 *	-	-
323 Old Ord Amish	11	565	NR	706 *	-	-
331 OCA: Ter Diocs	1	36	NR	106	-	-
335 Orth Pres Ch	4	165	203	220	-	-
339 Pent Ch of God	13	628	NR	1,012	-	-
349 Pent Holiness	29	2,574	1,984	3,166 *	.1	.1
355 Presb Ch (USA)	305	54,966	27,948	67,800 *	1.2	2.3
356 Presb Ch Amer	64	21,863	18,397	28,846	.5	1.0
360 Prim Bapt Chrch	115	NR	NR	NR	-	-
362 Prim Bapt E Dst	30	3,648	NR	4,420 *	.1	.2
365 Prog Prim Bapt	7	371	NR	453 *	-	-
370 Ref Baptist Chs	4	NR	NR	NR	-	-
371 Ref Ch in Am	1	28	74	79	-	-
379 Ref Mennonite	1	8	NR	10 *	-	-
388 Reg Bapt Gen As	2	200	250	250 *	-	-
401 Rus Orth Abroad	1	NR	NR	NR	-	-
403 Salvation Army	17	2,199	1,440	3,546	.1	.1
409 Separate Bapt	2	30	NR	37 *	-	-
413 S.D.A.	125	23,131	NR	27,525	.5	.9
416 Sikh	2	NR	NR	NR	-	-
418 Southw Bapt Fel	43	NR	NR	NR	-	-
419 So Bapt Conv	2,972	1,148,612	394,464	1,414,199 *	24.9	48.7
426 2Seed Sprt Bpt	1	10	NR	12 *	-	-
435 Unitarian-Univ	13	2,078	NR	2,569 *	-	.1
443 Un C of Christ	15	1,795	1,104	2,207 *	-	.1
449 Un Methodist	1,577	319,264	134,013	393,994 *	6.9	13.6
463 Vineyard	6	1,290	1,000	1,627 *	-	.1
467 Wesleyan	21	683	758	1,727	-	.1
469 WELS	7	754	585	1,037	-	-
496 Jewish Est	19	NR	NR	18,250	.3	.6
498 Indep.Charis.	11	8,080	7,285	9,850	.2	.3
499 Indep.Non-Char	37	41,654	25,377	50,003	.9	1.7
TEXAS	**18,466**	**5,138,122**	**2,303,903**	**11,573,549 ***	**55.5**	**100.0**
017 Amer Bapt Assn	380	48,768	NR	61,272 *	.3	.5
019 Amer Bapt USA	16	5,518	837	7,057 *	-	.1
032 Amish; other	1	53	NR	68 *	-	-
034 Ant Orth of NA	14	2,321	NR	4,642	-	-
040 Ap Chr Ch-Amer	2	15	27	27 *	-	-
049 Armen Ap Cilic	1	0	NR	80	-	-
050 Armen Ap Etchm	5	247	NR	1,275	-	-
053 Assemb of God	1,291	162,345	152,628	228,098	1.1	2.0
055 As Ref Pres Ch	2	28	NR	28	-	-
056 Baha'i	70	10,777	NR	10,777	.1	.1
057 Bapt Gen Conf	5	241	228	340 *	-	-
059 Bapt Miss Assn	473	98,015	34,631	123,198 *	.6	1.1
061 Beachy Amish	2	101	NR	127 *	-	-
076 Buddhism	88	NR	NR	NR	-	-
081 Catholic	1,293	NR	NR	4,368,969	21.0	37.7
084 Calvary Chapel	19	NR	NR	NR	-	-
089 Chr & Miss Al	42	1,962	NR	3,858	-	-
093 Chr Ch (Disc)	378	87,517	28,981	111,288 *	.5	1.0
097 Chr Chs&Chs Cr	149	34,189	NR	43,602 *	.2	.4
105 Christian Ref	10	1,506	1,416	1,936 *	-	-
121 Ch God (Abr)	1	43	37	55 *	-	-
123 Ch God (Ander)	87	NR	4,669	4,669	-	-
127 Ch God (Cleve)	230	28,812	17,255	38,259 *	.2	.3
143 CG in Cr(Menn)	8	654	NR	849 *	-	-
145 Ch God Prophcy	84	2,268	NR	2,906 *	-	-
151 L-D Saints	441	NR	NR	155,451	.7	1.3
157 Ch of Brethren	5	225	20	284 *	-	-
165 Ch of Nazarene	323	35,526	24,621	50,528	.2	.4
167 Chs of Christ	2,188	292,475	273,925	377,264	1.8	3.3
173 Comm of Christ	45	2,817	NR	2,817	-	-
175 Congr Chr Chs	4	544	284	716 *	-	-
181 Consrv Congr	1	20	20	25 *	-	-
183 Cons Menn Conf	3	132	161	191	-	-
185 Cumber Presb	49	5,797	NR	8,422	-	.1
186 Coptic Orth Ch	8	NR	NR	NR	-	-
193 Episcopal	427	NR	66,513	177,910	.9	1.5
201 Evan Cov Ch	10	737	781	1,022 *	-	-
203 Evan Free Ch	45	4,980	9,675	9,720	-	.1
207 E.L.C.A.	412	120,290	57,307	155,019	.7	1.3
216 Evan Presby Ch	8	1,131	NR	1,449 *	-	-
220 Free Lutheran	7	305	234	368	-	-
221 Free Methodist	18	516	690	874	-	-
223 Free Will Bapt	53	2,241	NR	2,822 *	-	-
226 Friends-USA	25	845	NR	1,074 *	-	-
237 Menn Br US Conf	11	303	NR	425 *	-	-
245 Greek Orth Vslp	1	105	NR	135	-	-
246 Greek Orthodox	18	NR	NR	9,444	-	.1
252 Hindu	34	NR	NR	NR	-	-
262 Int Cou Comm Ch	4	901	NR	1,152 *	-	-
263 Int Foursq Gos	94	8,470	9,659	12,501 *	.1	.1
264 Int Chs of Crst	8	2,995	4,658	4,041	-	-
266 Intrstat & Asc	1	72	NR	93 *	-	-
267 Muslim Est	91	NR	27,137	114,999	.6	1.0
268 Jain	6	NR	NR	NR	-	-
273 LandmrkBapt,I&U	11	799	NR	964 *	-	-
283 Luth—MO Synod	346	107,167	59,809	140,106	.7	1.2
286 E.PA Mennonite	1	51	NR	65 *	-	-
288 Mennonite USA	20	876	886	1,215 *	-	-
290 Metro Comm Ch	17	4,411	3,973	5,570 *	-	-
291 Missionary Ch	4	219	403	403	-	-
297 Mennonite;Other	5	1,226	NR	1,655 *	-	-
304 NatPrimBapt USA	62	3,540	NR	4,463 *	-	-
313 N Am Bapt Conf	13	1,224	1,192	1,569 *	-	-
323 Old Ord Amish	3	20	NR	24 *	-	-
331 OCA: Ter Diocs	7	346	NR	2,096	-	-
333 Malan Dioc Am	9	NR	NR	2,675	-	-
334 Malan Syr Orth	3	165	NR	825	-	-
335 Orth Pres Ch	11	442	563	644	-	-
339 Pent Ch of God	136	6,324	NR	11,592	.1	.1
349 Pent Holiness	119	7,949	7,920	10,265 *	-	.1
355 Presb Ch (USA)	549	140,830	65,987	180,315 *	.9	1.6
356 Presb Ch Amer	63	10,246	8,765	13,946	.1	.1
360 Prim Bapt Chrch	118	NR	NR	NR	-	-
365 Prog Prim Bapt	3	159	NR	197 *	-	-
370 Ref Baptist Chs	10	NR	NR	NR	-	-
371 Ref Ch in Am	4	946	806	2,040	-	-
388 Reg Bapt Gen As	7	504	729	684 *	-	-
397 OCA: Roman Dioc	2	NR	NR	413	-	-
401 Rus Orth Abroad	4	NR	NR	NR	-	-
403 Salvation Army	56	7,401	5,351	25,070	.1	.2
410 Serb Orth USA	3	NR	NR	1,110	-	-
411 Serb Orth: Grac	1	NR	NR	NR	-	-
413 S.D.A.	282	38,875	NR	46,268	.2	.4
416 Sikh	13	NR	NR	NR	-	-
418 Southw Bapt Fel	13	NR	NR	NR	-	-
419 So Bapt Conv	4,973	2,769,887	888,457	3,519,459 *	16.9	30.4
423 Syrian Orth Ch	1	NR	NR	60	-	-
425 Tao	1	NR	NR	NR	-	-
426 2Seed Sprt Bpt	1	24	NR	29 *	-	-
435 Unitarian-Univ	45	5,379	NR	6,872 *	-	.1
443 Un C of Christ	70	13,027	5,536	16,587 *	.1	.1
449 Un Methodist	2,110	801,952	303,968	1,022,342 *	4.9	8.8
463 Vineyard	32	8,780	6,492	11,637 *	.1	.1
467 Wesleyan	8	260	1,115	1,540	-	-
469 WELS	39	4,293	3,212	6,025	-	.1
490 Zoroastrian	3	NR	NR	NR	-	-
496 Jewish Est	92	NR	NR	128,000	.6	1.1
498 Indep.Charis.	79	120,638	106,515	159,449	.8	1.4
499 Indep.Non-Char	126	113,355	115,830	145,249	.7	1.3
UTAH	**4,343**	**45,170**	**34,243**	**1,668,851 ***	**74.7**	**100.0**
017 Amer Bapt Assn	3	70	NR	93 *	-	-
019 Amer Bapt USA	9	1,582	1,203	2,084 *	.1	.1
034 Ant Orth of NA	1	235	NR	470	-	-

NR–Not Reported *Total adherents estimated from known number of communicant, confirmed, full members. - Represents a percentage less than 0.1. Percentages may not total 100 due to rounding.

Table 3: Religious Congregations by State and Group: 2000

Religious Group	Number of Churches, Synagogues, Mosques, or Temples	Number of Communicant, Confirmed, or Full Members	Number of Attendees	Total Adherents: Number of Adherents	Total Adherents: % of Total Pop.	Total Adherents: % of Total Adh.
039 Ap Chr Ch(Naz)	1	4	20	20 *	-	-
050 Armen Ap Etchm	1	0	NR	462	-	-
053 Assemb of God	38	3,824	5,357	8,176	.4	.5
056 Baha'i	6	621	NR	621	-	-
076 Buddhism	15	NR	NR	NR	-	-
081 Catholic	71	NR	NR	97,085	4.3	5.8
084 Calvary Chapel	6	NR	NR	NR	-	-
089 Chr & Miss Al	7	291	NR	946	-	.1
093 Chr Ch (Disc)	3	367	199	478 *	-	-
097 Chr Chs&Chs Cr	4	935	NR	1,228 *	.1	.1
105 Christian Ref	6	415	305	549 *	-	-
127 Ch God (Cleve)	7	456	322	605 *	-	-
145 Ch God Prophcy	4	105	NR	137 *	-	-
151 L-D Saints	3,851	NR	NR	1,483,858	66.4	88.9
165 Ch of Nazarene	4	316	334	1,609	.1	.1
167 Chs of Christ	17	709	824	1,022	-	.1
173 Comm of Christ	3	213	NR	213	-	-
175 Congr Chr Chs	1	327	150	428 *	-	-
179 Consrv Bapt	11	NR	1,660	1,660	.1	.1
193 Episcopal	24	NR	1,980	6,853	.3	.4
203 Evan Free Ch	10	744	1,602	1,617	.1	.1
207 E.L.C.A.	16	4,591	2,437	6,426	.3	.4
223 Free Will Bapt	2	0	NR	0 *	-	-
226 Friends-USA	5	150	NR	196 *	-	-
237 Menn Br US Conf	1	0	NR	0 *	-	-
246 Greek Orthodox	4	NR	NR	3,801	.2	.2
251 Holy Orth in NA	1	NR	NR	15	-	-
252 Hindu	2	NR	NR	NR	-	-
263 Int Foursq Gos	11	1,005	1,338	1,395 *	.1	.1
264 Int Chs of Crst	1	85	166	129	-	-
267 Muslim Est	4	NR	736	3,645	.2	.2
283 Luth—MO Synod	18	3,249	1,732	4,562	.2	.3
290 Metro Comm Ch	3	57	75	85 *	-	-
297 Mennonite;Other	1	20	NR	27 *	-	-
331 OCA: Ter Diocs	1	7	NR	20	-	-
335 Orth Pres Ch	1	27	68	68	-	-
339 Pent Ch of God	4	74	NR	191	-	-
349 Pent Holiness	1	35	40	46 *	-	-
355 Presb Ch (USA)	23	4,524	2,945	6,006 *	.3	.4
356 Presb Ch Amer	4	124	270	271	-	-
388 Reg Bapt Gen As	5	181	200	249 *	-	-
403 Salvation Army	3	368	243	469	-	-
410 Serb Orth USA	1	NR	NR	120	-	-
413 S.D.A.	16	1,013	NR	1,207	.1	.1
416 Sikh	2	NR	NR	NR	-	-
418 Southw Bapt Fel	1	NR	NR	NR	-	-
419 So Bapt Conv	62	9,989	5,120	13,258 *	.6	.8
435 Unitarian-Univ	4	754	NR	988 *	-	.1
443 Un C of Christ	10	1,143	664	1,518 *	.1	.1
449 Un Methodist	19	5,168	2,252	6,772 *	.3	.4
463 Vineyard	5	1,160	1,210	1,525 *	.1	.1
469 WELS	2	232	191	348	-	-
496 Jewish Est	6	NR	NR	4,500	.2	.3
498 Indep.Charis.	1	0	600	800	-	-
VERMONT	**775**	**53,713**	**28,822**	**238,251 ***	**39.1**	**100.0**
017 Amer Bapt Assn	2	40	NR	48 *	-	-
019 Amer Bapt USA	59	6,835	2,656	8,352 *	1.4	3.5
053 Assemb of God	24	1,552	1,841	2,848	.5	1.2
056 Baha'i	3	341	NR	341	.1	.1
057 Bapt Gen Conf	1	150	340	340 *	.1	.1
076 Buddhism	16	NR	NR	NR	-	-
081 Catholic	133	NR	NR	147,918	24.3	62.1
084 Calvary Chapel	2	NR	NR	NR	-	-
089 Chr & Miss Al	13	830	NR	3,577	.6	1.5
097 Chr Chs&Chs Cr	3	130	NR	158 *	-	.1
105 Christian Ref	1	209	165	257 *	-	.1
123 Ch God (Ander)	1	NR	20	20	-	-
127 Ch God (Cleve)	3	90	157	181 *	-	.1
145 Ch God Prophcy	2	164	NR	200 *	-	.1
151 L-D Saints	12	NR	NR	3,046	.5	1.3
157 Ch of Brethren	1	52	66	66 *	-	-
165 Ch of Nazarene	10	517	714	1,122	.2	.5
167 Chs of Christ	10	527	599	741	.1	.3
175 Congr Chr Chs	3	179	185	217 *	-	.1
176 Congr Ad Afl	10	417	NR	512 *	.1	.2
179 Consrv Bapt	4	NR	260	260	-	.1
181 Consrv Congr	3	162	101	198 *	-	.1
193 Episcopal	49	NR	3,163	9,163	1.5	3.8
201 Evan Cov Ch	1	96	142	142 *	-	.1
203 Evan Free Ch	5	300	585	585	.1	.2
207 E.L.C.A.	7	952	434	1,318	.2	.6
221 Free Methodist	1	19	19	23	-	-
226 Friends-USA	14	609	NR	742 *	.1	.3
245 Greek Orth Vslp	2	1,037	NR	1,720	.3	.7
246 Greek Orthodox	2	NR	NR	348	.1	.1
262 Int Cou Comm Ch	1	190	NR	230 *	-	.1
263 Int Foursq Gos	4	111	296	296 *	-	.1
264 Int Chs of Crst	1	46	71	63	-	-
267 Muslim Est	1	NR	40	100	-	-
283 Luth—MO Synod	3	460	260	650	.1	.3
286 E.PA Mennonite	1	21	NR	26 *	-	-
288 Mennonite USA	2	88	114	120 *	-	.1
297 Mennonite;Other	1	81	NR	98 *	-	-
331 OCA: Ter Diocs	2	74	NR	96	-	-
335 Orth Pres Ch	1	52	67	82	-	-
355 Presb Ch (USA)	9	690	402	843 *	.1	.4
356 Presb Ch Amer	1	37	60	60	-	-
370 Ref Baptist Chs	1	NR	NR	NR	-	-
403 Salvation Army	5	259	172	555	.1	.2
413 S.D.A.	11	495	NR	590	.1	.2
419 So Bapt Conv	17	824	727	1,008 *	.2	.4
425 Tao	1	NR	NR	NR	-	-
435 Unitarian-Univ	21	1,757	NR	2,139 *	.4	.9
443 Un C of Christ	149	17,695	8,255	21,597 *	3.5	9.1
449 Un Methodist	128	15,468	6,792	19,000 *	3.1	8.0
455 Un Ref Chs N.A.	1	119	NR	199	-	.1
467 Wesleyan	3	0	92	194	-	.1
469 WELS	1	38	27	52	-	-
496 Jewish Est	13	NR	NR	5,810	1.0	2.4
VIRGINIA	**7,736**	**1,595,757**	**739,896**	**2,943,551 ***	**41.6**	**100.0**
011 A.W.M.C.	3	14	97	18	-	-
017 Amer Bapt Assn	7	550	NR	684 *	-	-
019 Amer Bapt USA	98	46,414	18,057	57,233 *	.8	1.9
022 Carp Rus Orth	1	122	NR	207	-	-
034 Ant Orth of NA	1	28	NR	56	-	-
039 Ap Chr Ch(Naz)	1	30	48	48 *	-	-
050 Armen Ap Etchm	1	80	NR	400	-	-
053 Assemb of God	196	25,505	30,477	45,035	.6	1.5
055 As Ref Pres Ch	9	1,668	NR	1,870	-	.1
056 Baha'i	37	3,778	NR	3,778	.1	.1
057 Bapt Gen Conf	2	290	325	387 *	-	-
059 Bapt Miss Assn	1	177	50	218 *	-	-
061 Beachy Amish	8	555	NR	681 *	-	-
071 Brethren (Ash)	8	793	763	966 *	-	-
075 Brethren in Cr	8	392	400	429	-	-
076 Buddhism	29	NR	NR	NR	-	-
081 Catholic	233	NR	NR	606,059	8.6	20.6
084 Calvary Chapel	10	NR	NR	NR	-	-
089 Chr & Miss Al	30	1,623	NR	3,050	-	.1
093 Chr Ch (Disc)	170	32,916	9,976	40,030 *	.6	1.4
097 Chr Chs&Chs Cr	220	40,476	NR	49,566 *	.7	1.7
105 Christian Ref	2	275	236	343 *	-	-
121 Ch God (Abr)	4	110	112	137 *	-	-
123 Ch God (Ander)	57	NR	4,297	4,297	.1	.1
127 Ch God (Cleve)	177	27,241	18,212	33,854 *	.5	1.2
145 Ch God Prophcy	118	4,855	NR	5,870 *	.1	.2
151 L-D Saints	150	NR	NR	53,308	.8	1.8
157 Ch of Brethren	175	25,756	13,098	31,421 *	.4	1.1
165 Ch of Nazarene	81	9,787	8,501	14,648	.2	.5
167 Chs of Christ	162	12,471	13,372	16,375	.2	.6
173 Comm of Christ	4	562	NR	562	-	-
176 Congr Ad Afl	3	252	NR	299 *	-	-
179 Consrv Bapt	1	NR	130	130	-	-
181 Consrv Congr	2	513	204	653 *	-	-
183 Cons Menn Conf	2	74	90	107	-	-
193 Episcopal	359	NR	47,643	126,874	1.8	4.3

NR–Not Reported *Total adherents estimated from known number of communicant, confirmed, full members. - Represents a percentage less than 0.1. Percentages may not total 100 due to rounding.

Table 3: Religious Congregations by State and Group: 2000

Religious Group	Number of Churches, Synagogues, Mosques, or Temples	Number of Communicant, Confirmed, or Full Members	Number of Attendees	Total Adherents: Number of Adherents	Total Adherents: % of Total Pop.	Total Adherents: % of Total Adh.
201 Evan Cov Ch	2	132	124	183 *	-	-
203 Evan Free Ch	10	846	1,876	1,887	-	.1
207 E.L.C.A.	196	49,092	23,899	65,798	.9	2.2
216 Evan Presby Ch	13	2,673	NR	3,368 *	-	.1
221 Free Methodist	3	182	233	234	-	-
223 Free Will Bapt	84	7,000	NR	8,543 *	.1	.3
226 Friends-USA	38	3,796	NR	4,636 *	.1	.2
245 Greek Orth Vslp	1	700	NR	1,400	-	-
246 Greek Orthodox	12	NR	NR	7,944	.1	.3
251 Holy Orth in NA	3	NR	NR	60	-	-
252 Hindu	10	NR	NR	NR	-	-
258 IndFreeWillBapt	46	2,689	NR	3,212 *	-	.1
263 Int Foursq Gos	21	2,458	3,255	3,565 *	.1	.1
264 Int Chs of Crst	4	497	954	702	-	-
265 Int Pent C Chr	8	163	251	590	-	-
267 Muslim Est	27	NR	9,647	51,021	.7	1.7
283 Luth—MO Synod	49	14,216	7,444	18,751	.3	.6
288 Mennonite USA	59	9,207	7,458	11,517 *	.2	.4
290 Metro Comm Ch	6	496	364	524 *	-	-
295 Morav Ch-South	3	233	NR	308	-	-
297 Mennonite;Other	23	2,524	NR	2,978 *	-	.1
304 NatPrimBapt USA	4	352	NR	425 *	-	-
320 "Old" MB Ascs	1	29	NR	35 *	-	-
322 Old Ord Menn Ch	6	835	NR	1,030 *	-	-
323 Old Ord Amish	5	204	NR	247 *	-	-
331 OCA: Ter Diocs	4	184	NR	441	-	-
335 Orth Pres Ch	10	523	642	777	-	-
339 Pent Ch of God	10	292	NR	784	-	-
349 Pent Holiness	201	23,397	15,467	28,412 *	.4	1.0
355 Presb Ch (USA)	519	110,150	55,830	135,435 *	1.9	4.6
356 Presb Ch Amer	71	13,553	13,913	17,933	.3	.6
360 Prim Bapt Chrch	100	NR	NR	NR	-	-
362 Prim Bapt E Dst	24	1,556	NR	1,868 *	-	.1
365 Prog Prim Bapt	1	45	NR	56 *	-	-
370 Ref Baptist Chs	8	NR	NR	NR	-	-
388 Reg Bapt Gen As	8	922	925	1,084 *	-	-
397 OCA: Roman Dioc	2	NR	NR	400	-	-
401 Rus Orth Abroad	2	NR	NR	NR	-	-
403 Salvation Army	25	4,441	1,310	7,231	.1	.2
409 Separate Bapt	3	89	NR	105 *	-	-
413 S.D.A.	110	15,084	NR	17,946	.3	.6
416 Sikh	6	NR	NR	NR	-	-
418 Southw Bapt Fel	40	NR	NR	NR	-	-
419 So Bapt Conv	1,660	629,586	219,421	774,637 *	10.9	26.3
431 Ukrainian Orth	1	NR	NR	300	-	-
435 Unitarian-Univ	24	5,083	NR	6,170 *	.1	.2
443 Un C of Christ	110	18,706	8,657	23,284 *	.3	.8
449 Un Methodist	1,601	382,684	143,479	470,381 *	6.6	16.0
463 Vineyard	9	1,655	1,483	2,097 *	-	.1
467 Wesleyan	64	4,504	7,868	16,830	.2	.6
469 WELS	10	1,101	858	1,554	-	.1
490 Zoroastrian	1	NR	NR	NR	-	-
496 Jewish Est	53	NR	NR	76,140	1.1	2.6
498 Indep.Charis.	17	22,881	20,770	33,210	.5	1.1
499 Indep.Non-Char	38	23,690	27,680	37,925	.5	1.3
WASHINGTON	**4,649**	**625,529**	**478,431**	**1,942,850 ***	**33.0**	**100.0**
017 Amer Bapt Assn	22	924	NR	1,159 *	-	.1
019 Amer Bapt USA	121	25,085	12,199	31,087 *	.5	1.6
034 Ant Orth of NA	5	590	NR	1,180	-	.1
039 Ap Chr Ch(Naz)	1	46	70	70 *	-	-
050 Armen Ap Etchm	1	0	NR	924	-	-
053 Assemb of God	347	50,807	60,255	105,692	1.8	5.4
055 As Ref Pres Ch	1	13	NR	19	-	-
056 Baha'i	86	5,817	NR	5,817	.1	.3
057 Bapt Gen Conf	46	10,411	15,362	17,551 *	.3	.9
059 Bapt Miss Assn	6	355	200	455 *	-	-
076 Buddhism	80	NR	NR	NR	-	-
081 Catholic	312	NR	NR	716,133	12.1	36.9
084 Calvary Chapel	44	NR	NR	NR	-	-
089 Chr & Miss Al	74	8,335	NR	19,805	.3	1.0
093 Chr Ch (Disc)	60	9,890	3,724	12,407 *	.2	.6
097 Chr Chs&Chs Cr	63	17,408	NR	21,621 *	.4	1.1
105 Christian Ref	40	8,845	6,918	11,033 *	.2	.6
121 Ch God (Abr)	3	12	119	119 *	-	-
123 Ch God (Ander)	47	NR	7,727	7,727	.1	.4
127 Ch God (Cleve)	40	4,382	3,596	5,769 *	.1	.3
143 CG in Cr(Menn)	2	106	NR	143 *	-	-
145 Ch God Prophcy	24	727	NR	927 *	-	-
151 L-D Saints	471	NR	NR	178,000	3.0	9.2
157 Ch of Brethren	12	1,170	249	1,455 *	-	.1
165 Ch of Nazarene	141	24,541	20,241	37,085	.6	1.9
167 Chs of Christ	133	10,786	11,766	14,803	.3	.8
173 Comm of Christ	31	3,864	NR	3,864	.1	.2
175 Congr Chr Chs	5	651	462	814 *	-	-
179 Consrv Bapt	70	NR	16,594	16,594	.3	.9
181 Consrv Congr	3	99	67	119 *	-	-
193 Episcopal	136	NR	15,231	41,731	.7	2.1
201 Evan Cov Ch	42	6,857	8,477	9,801 *	.2	.5
203 Evan Free Ch	46	2,934	5,647	5,648	.1	.3
207 E.L.C.A.	279	93,615	43,239	127,854	2.2	6.6
216 Evan Presby Ch	2	665	NR	806 *	-	-
220 Free Lutheran	9	772	650	1,065	-	.1
221 Free Methodist	51	5,446	9,661	9,677	.2	.5
223 Free Will Bapt	2	138	NR	173 *	-	-
226 Friends-USA	45	2,478	NR	3,106 *	.1	.2
237 Menn Br US Conf	12	1,842	NR	2,292 *	-	.1
246 Greek Orthodox	7	NR	NR	3,897	.1	.2
249 Assyr Apost Ch	1	NR	NR	280	-	-
251 Holy Orth in NA	2	NR	NR	184	-	-
252 Hindu	17	NR	NR	NR	-	-
257 Hutterian Br	6	396	NR	600	-	-
262 Int Cou Comm Ch	6	995	NR	1,230 *	-	.1
263 Int Foursq Gos	150	17,545	33,282	33,434 *	.6	1.7
264 Int Chs of Crst	1	459	851	601	-	-
267 Muslim Est	18	NR	3,608	15,553	.3	.8
283 Luth—MO Synod	117	29,758	16,187	40,618	.7	2.1
288 Mennonite USA	6	464	374	593 *	-	-
290 Metro Comm Ch	7	315	261	314 *	-	-
291 Missionary Ch	6	317	393	398	-	-
297 Mennonite;Other	4	111	NR	145 *	-	-
307 Neth Ref Congr	2	152	NR	321	-	-
313 N Am Bapt Conf	23	2,431	2,757	3,056 *	.1	.2
323 Old Ord Amish	1	27	NR	34 *	-	-
331 OCA: Ter Diocs	5	230	NR	812	-	-
335 Orth Pres Ch	8	395	564	598	-	-
339 Pent Ch of God	25	628	NR	1,544	-	.1
349 Pent Holiness	30	1,325	1,944	1,740 *	-	.1
355 Presb Ch (USA)	224	57,280	45,219	74,388 *	1.3	3.8
356 Presb Ch Amer	15	1,649	2,209	2,380	-	.1
360 Prim Bapt Chrch	2	NR	NR	NR	-	-
369 Prot Ref Chs	1	68	NR	131	-	-
370 Ref Baptist Chs	7	NR	NR	NR	-	-
371 Ref Ch in Am	10	2,075	2,032	3,559	.1	.2
388 Reg Bapt Gen As	66	7,647	10,478	11,499 *	.2	.6
397 OCA: Roman Dioc	1	NR	NR	77	-	-
401 Rus Orth Abroad	1	NR	NR	NR	-	-
403 Salvation Army	28	3,057	1,777	7,605	.1	.4
410 Serb Orth USA	1	NR	NR	400	-	-
413 S.D.A.	189	36,318	NR	43,222	.7	2.2
416 Sikh	4	NR	NR	NR	-	-
418 Southw Bapt Fel	2	NR	NR	NR	-	-
419 So Bapt Conv	220	49,715	21,283	62,309 *	1.1	3.2
425 Tao	1	NR	NR	NR	-	-
435 Unitarian-Univ	29	4,727	NR	5,828 *	.1	.3
443 Un C of Christ	83	11,733	6,491	14,430 *	.2	.7
449 Un Methodist	258	61,361	27,282	76,648 *	1.3	3.9
455 Un Ref Chs N.A.	2	292	NR	434	-	-
463 Vineyard	22	3,067	2,546	3,874 *	.1	.2
467 Wesleyan	9	35	510	1,511	-	.1
469 WELS	27	3,085	2,131	4,078	.1	.2
490 Zoroastrian	1	NR	NR	NR	-	-
496 Jewish Est	36	NR	NR	43,500	.7	2.2
498 Indep.Charis.	23	13,388	22,578	33,430	.6	1.7
499 Indep.Non-Char	30	14,873	31,220	33,070	.6	1.7
WEST VIRGINIA	**4,139**	**411,124**	**204,851**	**650,016 ***	**35.9**	**100.0**
011 A.W.M.C.	15	159	511	163	-	-

NR–Not Reported   *Total adherents estimated from known number of communicant, confirmed, full members.   - Represents a percentage less than 0.1.   Percentages may not total 100 due to rounding.

Table 3: Religious Congregations by State and Group: 2000

Religious Group	Number of Churches, Synagogues, Mosques, or Temples	Number of Communicant, Confirmed, or Full Members	Number of Attendees	Total Adherents: Number of Adherents	Total Adherents: % of Total Pop.	Total Adherents: % of Total Adh.
017 Amer Bapt Assn	7	1,020	NR	1,264 *	.1	.2
019 Amer Bapt USA	463	89,863	35,284	108,087 *	6.0	16.6
022 Carp Rus Orth	2	244	NR	414	-	.1
034 Ant Orth of NA	3	958	NR	1,916	.1	.3
053 Assemb of God	112	7,566	8,865	13,842	.8	2.1
055 As Ref Pres Ch	2	221	NR	228	-	-
056 Baha'i	3	478	NR	478	-	.1
071 Brethren (Ash)	5	228	168	276 *	-	-
075 Brethren in Cr	1	125	120	125	-	-
076 Buddhism	2	NR	NR	NR	-	-
081 Catholic	149	NR	NR	105,363	5.8	16.2
084 Calvary Chapel	1	NR	NR	NR	-	-
089 Chr & Miss Al	11	664	NR	1,952	.1	.3
093 Chr Ch (Disc)	38	9,493	2,242	11,376 *	.6	1.8
097 Chr Chs&Chs Cr	90	11,496	NR	13,836 *	.8	2.1
123 Ch God (Ander)	81	NR	5,234	5,234	.3	.8
127 Ch God (Cleve)	195	17,898	10,433	21,657 *	1.2	3.3
145 Ch God Prophcy	30	957	NR	1,144 *	.1	.2
151 L-D Saints	36	NR	NR	9,922	.5	1.5
157 Ch of Brethren	80	6,706	2,941	8,202 *	.5	1.3
165 Ch of Nazarene	123	14,539	9,665	21,389	1.2	3.3
167 Chs of Christ	294	18,906	19,426	24,143	1.3	3.7
171 Ch God-Gen Con	10	632	453	804 *	-	.1
173 Comm of Christ	10	552	NR	552	-	.1
175 Congr Chr Chs	1	35	20	43 *	-	-
179 Consrv Bapt	2	NR	285	285	-	-
193 Episcopal	82	NR	4,262	11,344	.6	1.7
203 Evan Free Ch	2	101	175	175	-	-
207 E.L.C.A.	53	10,530	3,849	13,964	.8	2.1
216 Evan Presby Ch	2	711	NR	849 *	-	.1
221 Free Methodist	21	919	1,211	1,333	.1	.2
223 Free Will Bapt	179	9,047	NR	10,883 *	.6	1.7
226 Friends-USA	2	99	NR	117 *	-	-
246 Greek Orthodox	6	NR	NR	1,980	.1	.3
252 Hindu	4	NR	NR	NR	-	-
263 Int Foursq Gos	7	422	908	908 *	.1	.1
264 Int Chs of Crst	1	62	102	88	-	-
265 Int Pent C Chr	9	215	338	465	-	.1
267 Muslim Est	4	NR	422	1,528	.1	.2
268 Jain	1	NR	NR	NR	-	-
283 Luth—MO Synod	3	451	290	584	-	.1
288 Mennonite USA	8	287	234	355 *	-	.1
290 Metro Comm Ch	1	34	34	41 *	-	-
297 Mennonite;Other	5	177	NR	213 *	-	-
320 "Old" MB Ascs	2	46	NR	57 *	-	-
323 Old Ord Amish	2	32	NR	39 *	-	-
331 OCA: Ter Diocs	2	144	NR	151	-	-
335 Orth Pres Ch	1	62	72	102	-	-
339 Pent Ch of God	23	563	NR	1,160	.1	.2
349 Pent Holiness	47	3,889	2,294	4,658 *	.3	.7
355 Presb Ch (USA)	202	23,650	11,548	28,467 *	1.6	4.4
356 Presb Ch Amer	12	865	690	1,022	.1	.2
360 Prim Bapt Chrch	36	NR	NR	NR	-	-
370 Ref Baptist Chs	1	NR	NR	NR	-	-
388 Reg Bapt Gen As	17	1,803	1,442	1,911 *	.1	.3
403 Salvation Army	14	1,523	509	2,652	.1	.4
409 Separate Bapt	1	60	NR	73 *	-	-
413 S.D.A.	40	2,791	NR	3,320	.2	.5
418 Southw Bapt Fel	14	NR	NR	NR	-	-
419 So Bapt Conv	165	36,231	13,314	43,606 *	2.4	6.7
435 Unitarian-Univ	5	230	NR	273 *	-	-
443 Un C of Christ	7	895	380	1,084 *	.1	.2
449 Un Methodist	1,341	125,336	60,811	150,985 *	8.3	23.2
463 Vineyard	3	818	747	977 *	.1	.2
467 Wesleyan	30	685	1,052	2,581	.1	.4
496 Jewish Est	11	NR	NR	2,400	.1	.4
498 Indep.Charis.	1	1,500	1,000	1,500	.1	.2
499 Indep.Non-Char	6	4,206	3,520	5,476	.3	.8
WISCONSIN	**5,181**	**1,080,891**	**536,733**	**3,241,659 ***	**60.4**	**100.0**
017 Amer Bapt Assn	3	170	NR	210 *	-	-
019 Amer Bapt USA	71	13,018	6,961	16,250 *	.3	.5
032 Amish; other	3	208	NR	258 *	-	-
034 Ant Orth of NA	3	219	NR	438	-	-

Religious Group	Number of Churches, Synagogues, Mosques, or Temples	Number of Communicant, Confirmed, or Full Members	Number of Attendees	Total Adherents: Number of Adherents	Total Adherents: % of Total Pop.	Total Adherents: % of Total Adh.
049 Armen Ap Cilic	1	83	NR	280	-	-
050 Armen Ap Etchm	3	362	NR	1,680	-	.1
053 Assemb of God	173	19,858	25,828	41,005	.8	1.3
056 Baha'i	21	2,111	NR	2,111	-	.1
057 Bapt Gen Conf	68	7,282	12,016	13,496 *	.3	.4
075 Brethren in Cr	2	78	138	138	-	-
076 Buddhism	30	NR	NR	NR	-	-
081 Catholic	879	NR	NR	1,695,660	31.6	52.3
084 Calvary Chapel	9	NR	NR	NR	-	-
089 Chr & Miss Al	52	6,533	NR	13,427	.3	.4
093 Chr Ch (Disc)	3	317	114	398 *	-	-
097 Chr Chs&Chs Cr	32	5,300	NR	6,593 *	.1	.2
105 Christian Ref	21	5,293	3,755	6,547 *	.1	.2
121 Ch God (Abr)	1	17	32	32 *	-	-
123 Ch God (Ander)	13	NR	768	768	-	-
127 Ch God (Cleve)	18	1,159	795	1,488 *	-	-
143 CG in Cr(Menn)	3	355	NR	435 *	-	-
145 Ch God Prophcy	7	294	NR	365 *	-	-
151 L-D Saints	58	NR	NR	16,843	.3	.5
157 Ch of Brethren	2	78	56	97 *	-	-
165 Ch of Nazarene	50	2,532	1,813	4,204	.1	.1
167 Chs of Christ	68	3,442	3,911	4,940	.1	.2
173 Comm of Christ	11	837	NR	837	-	-
175 Congr Chr Chs	36	7,862	3,940	9,829 *	.2	.3
179 Consrv Bapt	11	NR	1,817	1,817	-	.1
181 Consrv Congr	12	1,396	985	1,734 *	-	.1
193 Episcopal	129	NR	9,295	23,942	.4	.7
201 Evan Cov Ch	24	1,990	2,246	2,769 *	.1	.1
203 Evan Free Ch	94	8,486	17,475	17,475	.3	.5
207 E.L.C.A.	744	345,379	127,002	463,432	8.6	14.3
216 Evan Presby Ch	1	100	NR	125 *	-	-
220 Free Lutheran	15	868	671	1,171	-	-
221 Free Methodist	12	723	840	946	-	-
223 Free Will Bapt	1	35	NR	42 *	-	-
226 Friends-USA	13	623	NR	765 *	-	-
245 Greek Orth Vslp	2	280	NR	1,480	-	-
246 Greek Orthodox	7	NR	NR	5,772	.1	.2
252 Hindu	3	NR	NR	NR	-	-
262 Int Cou Comm Ch	5	1,695	NR	2,124 *	-	.1
263 Int Foursq Gos	21	1,715	2,022	2,387 *	-	.1
264 Int Chs of Crst	2	415	855	591	-	-
267 Muslim Est	14	NR	2,848	7,796	.1	.2
268 Jain	3	NR	NR	NR	-	-
283 Luth—MO Synod	435	188,322	88,428	241,306	4.5	7.4
286 E.PA Mennonite	1	54	NR	69 *	-	-
288 Mennonite USA	5	203	229	268 *	-	-
290 Metro Comm Ch	2	77	75	97 *	-	-
291 Missionary Ch	1	99	251	251	-	-
293 Morav Ch-North	20	3,832	NR	4,678	.1	.1
297 Mennonite;Other	15	638	NR	791 *	-	-
306 NT IndBapt&Rltd	112	12,759	NR	15,769 *	.3	.5
307 Neth Ref Congr	2	124	NR	285	-	-
313 N Am Bapt Conf	14	2,922	2,891	3,654 *	.1	.1
322 Old Ord Menn Ch	6	629	NR	807 *	-	-
323 Old Ord Amish	86	4,710	NR	5,872 *	.1	.2
331 OCA: Ter Diocs	9	366	NR	844	-	-
335 Orth Pres Ch	11	1,309	1,269	1,846	-	.1
339 Pent Ch of God	9	449	NR	1,024	-	-
349 Pent Holiness	2	19	19	24 *	-	-
355 Presb Ch (USA)	165	33,025	15,161	40,900 *	.8	1.3
356 Presb Ch Amer	10	633	797	919	-	-
363 Primitive Meth	10	570	NR	607	-	-
369 Prot Ref Chs	1	100	NR	170	-	-
370 Ref Baptist Chs	2	NR	NR	NR	-	-
371 Ref Ch in Am	26	8,023	6,222	12,594	.2	.4
373 Ref Ch in U.S.	1	265	NR	310	-	-
388 Reg Bapt Gen As	38	3,492	4,643	5,095 *	.1	.2
401 Rus Orth Abroad	2	NR	NR	NR	-	-
403 Salvation Army	20	2,365	1,448	12,951	.2	.4
410 Serb Orth USA	2	NR	NR	4,300	.1	.1
411 Serb Orth: Grac	2	NR	NR	NR	-	-
413 S.D.A.	72	6,738	NR	8,017	.1	.2
416 Sikh	2	NR	NR	NR	-	-
418 Southw Bapt Fel	1	NR	NR	NR	-	-

NR–Not Reported *Total adherents estimated from known number of communicant, confirmed, full members. - Represents a percentage less than 0.1. Percentages may not total 100 due to rounding.

Table 3: Religious Congregations by State and Group: 2000

Religious Group	Number of Churches, Synagogues, Mosques, or Temples	Number of Communicant, Confirmed, or Full Members	Number of Attendees	Total Adherents		
				Number of Adherents	% of Total Pop.	% of Total Adh.
419 So Bapt Conv	64	11,399	4,212	14,329 *	.3	.4
420 Strict Baptists	1	6	NR	7 *	-	-
431 Ukrainian Orth	3	NR	NR	171	-	-
435 Unitarian-Univ	26	4,117	NR	5,093 *	.1	.2
443 Un C of Christ	242	67,596	26,979	83,768 *	1.6	2.6
449 Un Methodist	500	104,364	46,881	129,216 *	2.4	4.0
455 Un Ref Chs N.A.	1	48	NR	76	-	-
463 Vineyard	6	457	415	573 *	-	-
467 Wesleyan	28	2,259	3,353	9,695	.2	.3
469 WELS	419	166,679	90,102	211,631	3.9	6.5
496 Jewish Est	36	NR	NR	28,230	.5	.9
498 Indep.Charis.	1	3,800	8,000	8,000	.1	.2
499 Indep.Non-Char	16	7,330	9,175	14,725	.3	.5
WYOMING	**790**	**64,960**	**38,172**	**230,725 ***	**46.7**	**100.0**
017 Amer Bapt Assn	3	70	NR	88 *	-	-
019 Amer Bapt USA	20	2,904	1,492	3,582 *	.7	1.6
034 Ant Orth of NA	1	50	NR	100	-	-
053 Assemb of God	46	2,608	3,166	5,067	1.0	2.2
056 Baha'i	2	233	NR	233	-	.1
057 Bapt Gen Conf	6	652	1,020	1,176 *	.2	.5
071 Brethren (Ash)	1	58	75	72 *	-	-
081 Catholic	73	NR	NR	80,421	16.3	34.9
084 Calvary Chapel	2	NR	NR	NR	-	-
089 Chr & Miss Al	14	567	NR	2,049	.4	.9
093 Chr Ch (Disc)	4	1,832	762	2,240 *	.5	1.0
097 Chr Chs&Chs Cr	17	1,407	NR	1,744 *	.4	.8
123 Ch God (Ander)	5	NR	1,536	1,536	.3	.7
127 Ch God (Cleve)	3	154	115	194 *	-	.1
145 Ch God Prophcy	10	239	NR	288 *	.1	.1
151 L-D Saints	143	NR	NR	47,129	9.5	20.4
165 Ch of Nazarene	18	1,110	988	1,767	.4	.8
167 Chs of Christ	32	1,654	1,859	2,206	.4	1.0
173 Comm of Christ	6	259	NR	259	.1	.1
175 Congr Chr Chs	2	815	365	1,015 *	.2	.4
179 Consrv Bapt	13	NR	1,909	1,909	.4	.8
193 Episcopal	49	NR	2,818	8,668	1.8	3.8
203 Evan Free Ch	8	462	1,062	1,062	.2	.5
207 E.L.C.A.	21	7,194	2,889	10,038	2.0	4.4
223 Free Will Bapt	1	0	NR	0 *	-	-
226 Friends-USA	1	30	NR	38 *	-	-
246 Greek Orthodox	4	NR	NR	0	-	-
263 Int Foursq Gos	14	570	1,128	1,132 *	.2	.5
264 Int Chs of Crst	1	38	78	63	-	-
267 Muslim Est	2	NR	90	263	.1	.1
283 Luth—MO Synod	44	8,359	3,811	11,113	2.3	4.8
290 Metro Comm Ch	1	14	5	5 *	-	-
297 Mennonite;Other	1	34	NR	42 *	-	-
306 NT IndBapt&Rltd	5	430	NR	531 *	.1	.2
339 Pent Ch of God	2	150	NR	394	.1	.2
349 Pent Holiness	2	30	30	38 *	-	-
355 Presb Ch (USA)	31	5,324	2,652	6,600 *	1.3	2.9
356 Presb Ch Amer	3	133	180	182	-	.1
370 Ref Baptist Chs	1	NR	NR	NR	-	-
373 Ref Ch in U.S.	1	26	NR	35	-	-
388 Reg Bapt Gen As	1	0	0	0 *	-	-
403 Salvation Army	4	364	143	765	.2	.3
413 S.D.A.	24	1,291	NR	1,538	.3	.7
418 Southw Bapt Fel	2	NR	NR	NR	-	-
419 So Bapt Conv	78	13,694	4,169	17,101 *	3.5	7.4
435 Unitarian-Univ	4	272	NR	330 *	.1	.1
443 Un C of Christ	11	1,739	618	2,139 *	.4	.9
449 Un Methodist	42	9,257	3,804	11,431 *	2.3	5.0
463 Vineyard	1	95	60	123 *	-	.1
467 Wesleyan	4	603	1,125	3,240	.7	1.4
469 WELS	4	239	223	349	.1	.2
496 Jewish Est	2	NR	NR	430	.1	.2

NR–Not Reported   *Total adherents estimated from known number of communicant, confirmed, full members.   - Represents a percentage less than 0.1.   Percentages may not total 100 due to rounding.

Table 4: Religious Congregations by County and Group: 2000

Religious Group	Number of Churches, Synagogues, Mosques, or Temples	Number of Communicant, Confirmed, or Full Members	Number of Attendees	Total Adherents: Number of Adherents	% of Total Pop.	% of Total Adh.
ALABAMA						
The State.....	8,343	1,758,393	760,721	2,435,373 *	54.8	100.0
AUTAUGA	**73**	**17,055**	**7,761**	**24,505 ***	**56.1**	**100.0**
017 Amer Bapt Assn	2	185	NR	237 *	.5	1.0
053 Assemb of God	5	556	652	880	2.0	3.6
056 Baha'i	0	32	NR	32	.1	.1
081 Catholic	1	NR	NR	1,490	3.4	6.1
089 Chr & Miss Al	1	156	NR	263	.6	1.1
097 Chr Chs&Chs Cr	1	65	NR	83 *	.2	.3
123 Ch God (Ander)	1	NR	35	35	.1	.1
127 Ch God (Cleve)	4	425	230	546 *	1.3	2.2
151 L-D Saints	1	NR	NR	433	1.0	1.8
167 Chs of Christ	7	576	683	778	1.8	3.2
193 Episcopal	1	NR	136	352	.8	1.4
223 Free Will Bapt	1	117	NR	150 *	.3	.6
283 Luth—MO Synod	1	70	33	88	.2	.4
304 NatPrimBapt USA	1	35	NR	45 *	.1	.2
349 Pent Holiness	1	200	90	257 *	.6	1.0
356 Presb Ch Amer	1	406	215	456	1.0	1.9
360 Prim Bapt Chrch	2	NR	NR	NR	-	-
413 S.D.A.	1	61	NR	73	.2	.3
419 So Bapt Conv	29	11,469	4,374	14,727 *	33.7	60.1
449 Un Methodist	11	2,575	1,185	3,305 *	7.6	13.5
467 Wesleyan	1	127	128	275	.6	1.1
BALDWIN	**201**	**41,656**	**22,090**	**66,336 ***	**47.2**	**100.0**
017 Amer Bapt Assn	1	45	NR	55 *	-	.1
053 Assemb of God	16	1,581	1,886	3,022	2.2	4.6
056 Baha'i	1	32	NR	32	-	-
076 Buddhism	1	NR	NR	NR	-	-
081 Catholic	13	NR	NR	10,482	7.5	15.8
084 Calvary Chapel	1	NR	NR	NR	-	-
089 Chr & Miss Al	3	137	NR	196	.1	.3
093 Chr Ch (Disc)	2	405	189	498 *	.4	.8
097 Chr Chs&Chs Cr	1	91	NR	112 *	.1	.2
123 Ch God (Ander)	2	NR	144	144	.1	.2
127 Ch God (Cleve)	11	1,574	1,054	1,959 *	1.4	3.0
145 Ch God Prophcy	2	72	NR	88 *	.1	.1
151 L-D Saints	1	NR	NR	689	.5	1.0
165 Ch of Nazarene	3	122	78	199	.1	.3
167 Chs of Christ	11	978	1,180	1,184	.8	1.8
173 Comm of Christ	2	298	NR	298	.2	.4
193 Episcopal	8	NR	1,242	2,898	2.1	4.4
201 Evan Cov Ch	3	207	235	273 *	.2	.4
207 E.L.C.A.	1	23	150	150	.1	.2
220 Free Lutheran	1	57	47	60	-	.1
221 Free Methodist	1	16	24	24	-	-
223 Free Will Bapt	1	117	NR	143 *	.1	.2
246 Greek Orthodox	1	NR	NR	0	-	-
283 Luth—MO Synod	8	1,260	910	1,324	.9	2.0
349 Pent Holiness	4	375	309	461 *	.3	.7
355 Presb Ch (USA)	8	2,408	1,388	2,960 *	2.1	4.5
356 Presb Ch Amer	5	510	526	690	.5	1.0
360 Prim Bapt Chrch	1	NR	NR	NR	-	-
413 S.D.A.	1	20	NR	24	-	-
419 So Bapt Conv	59	22,602	8,062	27,789 *	19.8	41.9
435 Unitarian-Univ	1	52	NR	64 *	-	.1
449 Un Methodist	25	8,049	4,246	9,893 *	7.0	14.9
467 Wesleyan	1	225	120	225	.2	.3
499 Indep.Non-Char	1	400	300	400	.3	.6
BARBOUR	**66**	**8,978**	**4,716**	**11,955 ***	**41.2**	**100.0**
053 Assemb of God	9	616	688	734	2.5	6.1
081 Catholic	1	NR	NR	265	.9	2.2
123 Ch God (Ander)	1	NR	86	86	.3	.7
127 Ch God (Cleve)	1	41	49	51 *	.2	.4
151 L-D Saints	1	NR	NR	263	.9	2.2
167 Chs of Christ	2	107	120	147	.5	1.2
193 Episcopal	1	NR	117	278	1.0	2.3
223 Free Will Bapt	1	117	NR	144 *	.5	1.2
355 Presb Ch (USA)	1	282	82	349 *	1.2	2.9
356 Presb Ch Amer	4	155	80	165	.6	1.4
360 Prim Bapt Chrch	2	NR	NR	NR	-	-
413 S.D.A.	1	27	NR	32	.1	.3
419 So Bapt Conv	26	6,125	2,779	7,576 *	26.1	63.4
443 Un C of Christ	1	44	30	54 *	.2	.5
449 Un Methodist	14	1,464	685	1,811 *	6.2	15.1
BIBB	**67**	**7,799**	**3,398**	**9,656 ***	**46.4**	**100.0**
053 Assemb of God	2	225	128	215	1.0	2.2
056 Baha'i	0	2	NR	2	-	-
127 Ch God (Cleve)	2	98	34	123 *	.6	1.3
145 Ch God Prophcy	3	107	NR	135 *	.6	1.4
165 Ch of Nazarene	2	143	98	168	.8	1.7
167 Chs of Christ	3	100	120	134	.6	1.4
223 Free Will Bapt	1	117	NR	146 *	.7	1.5
355 Presb Ch (USA)	1	16	11	20 *	.1	.2
356 Presb Ch Amer	2	158	126	164	.8	1.7
360 Prim Bapt Chrch	1	NR	NR	NR	-	-
413 S.D.A.	1	10	NR	12	.1	.1
419 So Bapt Conv	41	6,429	2,671	8,044 *	38.6	83.3
449 Un Methodist	8	394	210	493 *	2.4	5.1
BLOUNT	**138**	**20,387**	**8,621**	**25,916 ***	**50.8**	**100.0**
053 Assemb of God	2	523	470	505	1.0	1.9
081 Catholic	1	NR	NR	376	.7	1.5
089 Chr & Miss Al	1	49	NR	73	.1	.3
127 Ch God (Cleve)	11	1,025	671	1,306 *	2.6	5.0
145 Ch God Prophcy	2	72	NR	90 *	.2	.3
151 L-D Saints	1	NR	NR	176	.3	.7
157 Ch of Brethren	2	51	0	64 *	.1	.2
165 Ch of Nazarene	5	388	259	453	.9	1.7
167 Chs of Christ	8	318	375	417	.8	1.6
185 Cumber Presb	4	136	NR	233	.5	.9
223 Free Will Bapt	1	117	NR	145 *	.3	.6
297 Mennonite;Other	1	49	NR	61 *	.1	.2
349 Pent Holiness	1	158	109	197 *	.4	.8
360 Prim Bapt Chrch	6	NR	NR	NR	-	-
413 S.D.A.	1	25	NR	30	.1	.1
419 So Bapt Conv	65	14,563	5,402	18,158 *	35.6	70.1
449 Un Methodist	26	2,913	1,335	3,632 *	7.1	14.0
BULLOCK	**21**	**1,932**	**822**	**2,465 ***	**21.0**	**100.0**
053 Assemb of God	2	57	70	80	.7	3.2
056 Baha'i	0	54	NR	54	.5	2.2
081 Catholic	1	NR	NR	35	.3	1.4
167 Chs of Christ	1	30	38	60	.5	2.4
193 Episcopal	1	NR	4	10	.1	.4
355 Presb Ch (USA)	1	43	23	54 *	.5	2.2
356 Presb Ch Amer	1	17	17	17	.1	.7
413 S.D.A.	1	16	NR	19	.2	.8
419 So Bapt Conv	7	1,378	491	1,716 *	14.6	69.6
449 Un Methodist	6	337	179	420 *	3.6	17.0
BUTLER	**86**	**8,189**	**3,906**	**10,701 ***	**50.0**	**100.0**
053 Assemb of God	1	98	137	150	.7	1.4
056 Baha'i	0	1	NR	1	-	-
081 Catholic	1	NR	NR	151	.7	1.4
093 Chr Ch (Disc)	2	283	125	353 *	1.6	3.3
097 Chr Chs&Chs Cr	1	50	NR	62 *	.3	.6
127 Ch God (Cleve)	4	97	122	146 *	.7	1.4
151 L-D Saints	1	NR	NR	85	.4	.8
167 Chs of Christ	13	735	705	906	4.2	8.5
173 Comm of Christ	1	3	NR	3	-	-
193 Episcopal	1	NR	68	214	1.0	2.0
349 Pent Holiness	5	203	209	253 *	1.2	2.4
356 Presb Ch Amer	1	154	94	190	.9	1.8
360 Prim Bapt Chrch	4	NR	NR	NR	-	-
419 So Bapt Conv	31	5,523	1,967	6,889 *	32.2	64.4
449 Un Methodist	20	1,042	479	1,298 *	6.1	12.1

NR–Not Reported   *Total adherents estimated from known number of communicant, confirmed, full members.   - Represents a percentage less than 0.1.   Percentages may not total 100 due to rounding.

Table 4: Religious Congregations by County and Group: 2000

Religious Group	Number of Churches, Synagogues, Mosques, or Temples	Number of Communicant, Confirmed, or Full Members	Number of Attendees	Total Adherents: Number of Adherents	Total Adherents: % of Total Pop.	Total Adherents: % of Total Adh.
CALHOUN	**211**	**56,563**	**22,885**	**72,169 ***	**64.3**	**100.0**
053 Assemb of God	7	819	692	1,087	1.0	1.5
056 Baha'i	0	19	NR	19	-	-
081 Catholic	4	NR	NR	816	.7	1.1
093 Chr Ch (Disc)	1	114	0	139 *	.1	.2
097 Chr Chs&Chs Cr	4	246	NR	300 *	.3	.4
123 Ch God (Ander)	1	NR	45	45	-	.1
127 Ch God (Cleve)	14	3,172	1,721	3,875 *	3.5	5.4
145 Ch God Prophcy	1	36	NR	44 *	-	.1
151 L-D Saints	2	NR	NR	605	.5	.8
165 Ch of Nazarene	2	136	80	136	.1	.2
167 Chs of Christ	18	2,144	2,131	2,783	2.5	3.9
185 Cumber Presb	1	92	NR	152	.1	.2
193 Episcopal	3	NR	330	857	.8	1.2
207 E.L.C.A.	3	215	110	322	.3	.4
263 Int Foursq Gos	1	473	506	577 *	.5	.8
267 Muslim Est	1	NR	101	288	.3	.4
349 Pent Holiness	1	261	110	318 *	.3	.4
355 Presb Ch (USA)	7	769	408	939 *	.8	1.3
356 Presb Ch Amer	1	199	160	236	.2	.3
360 Prim Bapt Chrch	2	NR	NR	NR	-	-
403 Salvation Army	1	162	56	264	.2	.4
413 S.D.A.	2	127	NR	151	.1	.2
418 Southw Bapt Fel	2	NR	NR	NR	-	-
419 So Bapt Conv	99	41,638	13,777	50,799 *	45.3	70.4
449 Un Methodist	30	5,843	2,534	7,129 *	6.4	9.9
463 Vineyard	1	60	70	73 *	.1	.1
467 Wesleyan	1	38	54	125	.1	.2
496 Jewish Est	1	NR	NR	90	.1	.1
CHAMBERS	**107**	**15,698**	**6,160**	**19,843 ***	**54.2**	**100.0**
053 Assemb of God	3	345	318	418	1.1	2.1
056 Baha'i	0	1	NR	1	-	-
081 Catholic	1	NR	NR	276	.8	1.4
093 Chr Ch (Disc)	2	210	59	260 *	.7	1.3
097 Chr Chs&Chs Cr	2	430	NR	532 *	1.5	2.7
123 Ch God (Ander)	3	NR	129	129	.4	.7
127 Ch God (Cleve)	1	124	73	153 *	.4	.8
151 L-D Saints	1	NR	NR	136	.4	.7
165 Ch of Nazarene	5	720	406	740	2.0	3.7
167 Chs of Christ	4	242	268	334	.9	1.7
175 Congr Chr Chs	2	88	64	109 *	.3	.5
339 Pent Ch of God	1	60	NR	87	.2	.4
355 Presb Ch (USA)	1	11	12	14 *	-	.1
360 Prim Bapt Chrch	5	NR	NR	NR	-	-
413 S.D.A.	1	16	NR	19	.1	.1
419 So Bapt Conv	39	9,857	3,099	12,191 *	33.3	61.4
443 Un C of Christ	4	363	164	449 *	1.2	2.3
449 Un Methodist	31	3,166	1,518	3,915 *	10.7	19.7
463 Vineyard	1	65	50	80 *	.2	.4
CHEROKEE	**80**	**10,324**	**4,503**	**12,614 ***	**52.6**	**100.0**
127 Ch God (Cleve)	2	157	163	197 *	.8	1.6
145 Ch God Prophcy	1	36	NR	43 *	.2	.3
151 L-D Saints	1	NR	NR	113	.5	.9
167 Chs of Christ	4	170	173	216	.9	1.7
355 Presb Ch (USA)	1	24	20	29 *	.1	.2
419 So Bapt Conv	49	8,257	3,406	9,983 *	41.6	79.1
449 Un Methodist	22	1,680	741	2,033 *	8.5	16.1
CHILTON	**97**	**19,526**	**8,190**	**24,829 ***	**62.7**	**100.0**
053 Assemb of God	8	935	835	1,097	2.8	4.4
056 Baha'i	0	2	NR	2	-	-
081 Catholic	1	NR	NR	321	.8	1.3
123 Ch God (Ander)	1	NR	25	25	.1	.1
127 Ch God (Cleve)	8	1,021	577	1,275 *	3.2	5.1
145 Ch God Prophcy	1	36	NR	45 *	.1	.2
151 L-D Saints	1	NR	NR	129	.3	.5
165 Ch of Nazarene	1	32	26	32	.1	.1
167 Chs of Christ	7	247	276	347	.9	1.4
175 Congr Chr Chs	1	7	75	9 *	-	-
356 Presb Ch Amer	1	54	70	70	.2	.3
360 Prim Bapt Chrch	2	NR	NR	NR	-	-
413 S.D.A.	1	108	NR	129	.3	.5
419 So Bapt Conv	52	15,846	5,609	19,802 *	50.0	79.8
449 Un Methodist	12	1,238	697	1,546 *	3.9	6.2
CHOCTAW	**70**	**6,154**	**3,021**	**8,221 ***	**51.6**	**100.0**
017 Amer Bapt Assn	1	50	NR	62 *	.4	.8
053 Assemb of God	10	444	608	865	5.4	10.5
081 Catholic	1	NR	NR	105	.7	1.3
123 Ch God (Ander)	1	NR	5	5	-	.1
127 Ch God (Cleve)	3	265	223	334 *	2.1	4.1
151 L-D Saints	1	NR	NR	126	.8	1.5
167 Chs of Christ	2	81	85	115	.7	1.4
304 NatPrimBapt USA	1	0	NR	0 *	-	-
349 Pent Holiness	1	20	15	25 *	.2	.3
355 Presb Ch (USA)	1	14	12	17 *	.1	.2
413 S.D.A.	1	53	NR	63	.4	.8
419 So Bapt Conv	29	4,327	1,705	5,385 *	33.8	65.5
449 Un Methodist	18	900	368	1,119 *	7.0	13.6
CLARKE	**86**	**12,085**	**5,285**	**16,013 ***	**57.5**	**100.0**
053 Assemb of God	5	627	513	964	3.5	6.0
081 Catholic	3	NR	NR	229	.8	1.4
127 Ch God (Cleve)	2	144	86	184 *	.7	1.1
145 Ch God Prophcy	1	36	NR	46 *	.2	.3
151 L-D Saints	1	NR	NR	115	.4	.7
165 Ch of Nazarene	1	21	10	23	.1	.1
167 Chs of Christ	7	243	237	338	1.2	2.1
193 Episcopal	1	NR	25	52	.2	.3
283 Luth—MO Synod	1	19	20	37	.1	.2
355 Presb Ch (USA)	1	71	40	91 *	.3	.6
360 Prim Bapt Chrch	1	NR	NR	NR	-	-
413 S.D.A.	2	83	NR	99	.4	.6
418 Southw Bapt Fel	1	NR	NR	NR	-	-
419 So Bapt Conv	44	9,284	3,723	11,848 *	42.5	74.0
449 Un Methodist	15	1,557	631	1,987 *	7.1	12.4
CLAY	**81**	**8,528**	**3,588**	**10,548 ***	**74.0**	**100.0**
053 Assemb of God	2	147	151	193	1.4	1.8
056 Baha'i	0	1	NR	1	-	-
081 Catholic	1	NR	NR	70	.5	.7
127 Ch God (Cleve)	2	103	68	125 *	.9	1.2
151 L-D Saints	1	NR	NR	61	.4	.6
167 Chs of Christ	7	303	291	368	2.6	3.5
349 Pent Holiness	1	15	15	18 *	.1	.2
360 Prim Bapt Chrch	5	NR	NR	NR	-	-
419 So Bapt Conv	44	6,583	2,464	8,034 *	56.4	76.2
449 Un Methodist	18	1,376	599	1,678 *	11.8	15.9
CLEBURNE	**58**	**7,935**	**3,067**	**9,796 ***	**69.4**	**100.0**
053 Assemb of God	1	38	49	69	.5	.7
056 Baha'i	0	1	NR	1	-	-
127 Ch God (Cleve)	4	321	231	396 *	2.8	4.0
167 Chs of Christ	2	112	120	146	1.0	1.5
360 Prim Bapt Chrch	2	NR	NR	NR	-	-
419 So Bapt Conv	34	6,684	2,225	8,225 *	58.2	84.0
449 Un Methodist	15	779	442	959 *	6.8	9.8
COFFEE	**99**	**22,809**	**9,455**	**30,349 ***	**69.6**	**100.0**
053 Assemb of God	17	1,004	1,156	1,552	3.6	5.1
056 Baha'i	0	3	NR	3	-	-
081 Catholic	1	NR	NR	1,242	2.8	4.1
127 Ch God (Cleve)	3	403	412	497 *	1.1	1.6
145 Ch God Prophcy	1	36	NR	44 *	.1	.1
151 L-D Saints	2	NR	NR	519	1.2	1.7
167 Chs of Christ	7	809	669	1,024	2.3	3.4
193 Episcopal	1	NR	59	148	.3	.5
223 Free Will Bapt	1	117	NR	144 *	.3	.5
283 Luth—MO Synod	1	4	87	5	-	-
349 Pent Holiness	1	35	29	43 *	.1	.1
355 Presb Ch (USA)	1	131	75	161 *	.4	.5
356 Presb Ch Amer	1	121	98	165	.4	.5

NR–Not Reported   *Total adherents estimated from known number of communicant, confirmed, full members.   - Represents a percentage less than 0.1.   Percentages may not total 100 due to rounding.

Table 4: Religious Congregations by County and Group: 2000

Religious Group	Number of Churches, Synagogues, Mosques, or Temples	Number of Communicant, Confirmed, or Full Members	Number of Attendees	Total Adherents		
				Number of Adherents	% of Total Pop.	% of Total Adh.
360 Prim Bapt Chrch	1	NR	NR	NR	-	-
419 So Bapt Conv	45	17,239	5,623	21,225 *	48.7	69.9
449 Un Methodist	16	2,907	1,247	3,577 *	8.2	11.8
COLBERT	**127**	**28,293**	**13,273**	**36,744 ***	**66.8**	**100.0**
017 Amer Bapt Assn	3	294	NR	360 *	.7	1.0
053 Assemb of God	2	144	158	158	.3	.4
055 As Ref Pres Ch	1	23	NR	23	-	.1
056 Baha'i	0	9	NR	9	-	-
081 Catholic	1	NR	NR	1,085	2.0	3.0
123 Ch God (Ander)	1	NR	25	25	-	.1
127 Ch God (Cleve)	4	353	241	432 *	.8	1.2
145 Ch God Prophcy	1	36	NR	44 *	.1	.1
151 L-D Saints	1	NR	NR	578	1.1	1.6
165 Ch of Nazarene	3	343	206	349	.6	.9
167 Chs of Christ	35	4,134	4,265	5,307	9.7	14.4
185 Cumber Presb	6	204	NR	327	.6	.9
193 Episcopal	1	NR	83	209	.4	.6
223 Free Will Bapt	3	350	NR	428 *	.8	1.2
263 Int Foursq Gos	1	34	44	44 *	.1	.1
283 Luth—MO Synod	1	123	79	144	.3	.4
304 NatPrimBapt USA	2	76	NR	93 *	.2	.3
320 "Old" MB Ascs	2	350	NR	428 *	.8	1.2
355 Presb Ch (USA)	2	232	105	284 *	.5	.8
356 Presb Ch Amer	1	294	180	354	.6	1.0
413 S.D.A.	1	117	NR	139	.3	.4
419 So Bapt Conv	41	18,327	6,583	22,436 *	40.8	61.1
449 Un Methodist	14	2,850	1,304	3,488 *	6.3	9.5
CONECUH	**60**	**4,825**	**1,890**	**5,927 ***	**42.1**	**100.0**
053 Assemb of God	4	317	173	289	2.1	4.9
127 Ch God (Cleve)	1	48	19	60 *	.4	1.0
167 Chs of Christ	4	252	265	385	2.7	6.5
173 Comm of Christ	2	196	NR	196	1.4	3.3
223 Free Will Bapt	3	350	NR	436 *	3.1	7.4
349 Pent Holiness	2	49	47	61 *	.4	1.0
355 Presb Ch (USA)	1	9	5	11 *	.1	.2
360 Prim Bapt Chrch	3	NR	NR	NR	-	-
419 So Bapt Conv	22	2,606	776	3,247 *	23.0	54.8
449 Un Methodist	18	998	605	1,242 *	8.8	21.0
COOSA	**33**	**2,779**	**1,216**	**3,393 ***	**27.8**	**100.0**
056 Baha'i	0	3	NR	3	-	.1
059 Bapt Miss Assn	1	15	12	18 *	.1	.5
127 Ch God (Cleve)	2	105	53	128 *	1.0	3.8
145 Ch God Prophcy	1	36	NR	44 *	.4	1.3
167 Chs of Christ	2	50	50	58	.5	1.7
355 Presb Ch (USA)	2	98	57	120 *	1.0	3.5
360 Prim Bapt Chrch	2	NR	NR	NR	-	-
419 So Bapt Conv	11	1,622	612	1,984 *	16.3	58.5
449 Un Methodist	12	850	432	1,038 *	8.5	30.6
COVINGTON	**119**	**21,035**	**7,912**	**26,315 ***	**69.9**	**100.0**
053 Assemb of God	14	650	688	891	2.4	3.4
055 As Ref Pres Ch	1	85	NR	97	.3	.4
056 Baha'i	0	3	NR	3	-	-
081 Catholic	1	NR	NR	326	.9	1.2
127 Ch God (Cleve)	5	390	246	476 *	1.3	1.8
151 L-D Saints	1	NR	NR	165	.4	.6
165 Ch of Nazarene	1	25	26	28	.1	.1
167 Chs of Christ	11	777	730	993	2.6	3.8
193 Episcopal	1	NR	59	100	.3	.4
223 Free Will Bapt	1	117	NR	142 *	.4	.5
266 Intrstat & Asc	1	22	NR	27 *	.1	.1
283 Luth—MO Synod	2	81	63	89	.2	.3
349 Pent Holiness	2	121	62	147 *	.4	.6
355 Presb Ch (USA)	1	187	75	228 *	.6	.9
356 Presb Ch Amer	1	82	55	82	.2	.3
360 Prim Bapt Chrch	3	NR	NR	NR	-	-
413 S.D.A.	1	54	NR	64	.2	.2
419 So Bapt Conv	59	16,651	5,116	20,277 *	53.9	77.1
449 Un Methodist	13	1,790	792	2,180 *	5.8	8.3
CRENSHAW	**67**	**6,195**	**3,098**	**7,993 ***	**58.5**	**100.0**
053 Assemb of God	5	135	152	211	1.5	2.6
056 Baha'i	0	2	NR	2	-	-
127 Ch God (Cleve)	1	0	65	65 *	.5	.8
145 Ch God Prophcy	1	36	NR	44 *	.3	.6
151 L-D Saints	1	NR	NR	196	1.4	2.5
167 Chs of Christ	12	532	625	718	5.3	9.0
360 Prim Bapt Chrch	1	NR	NR	NR	-	-
419 So Bapt Conv	32	4,567	1,779	5,621 *	41.1	70.3
443 Un C of Christ	1	26	11	32 *	.2	.4
449 Un Methodist	13	897	466	1,104 *	8.1	13.8
CULLMAN	**220**	**42,899**	**18,680**	**55,136 ***	**71.2**	**100.0**
053 Assemb of God	4	276	265	305	.4	.6
056 Baha'i	0	4	NR	4	-	-
081 Catholic	2	NR	NR	1,865	2.4	3.4
093 Chr Ch (Disc)	1	85	34	104 *	.1	.2
097 Chr Chs&Chs Cr	1	30	NR	37 *	-	.1
123 Ch God (Ander)	1	NR	142	142	.2	.3
127 Ch God (Cleve)	11	1,448	1,032	1,777 *	2.3	3.2
165 Ch of Nazarene	6	542	399	682	.9	1.2
167 Chs of Christ	30	2,235	2,628	2,977	3.8	5.4
185 Cumber Presb	6	319	NR	512	.7	.9
193 Episcopal	1	NR	123	311	.4	.6
223 Free Will Bapt	3	350	NR	430 *	.6	.8
283 Luth—MO Synod	2	906	354	1,211	1.6	2.2
355 Presb Ch (USA)	1	121	77	149 *	.2	.3
356 Presb Ch Amer	1	176	180	215	.3	.4
360 Prim Bapt Chrch	5	NR	NR	NR	-	-
413 S.D.A.	1	82	NR	98	.1	.2
418 Southw Bapt Fel	1	NR	NR	NR	-	-
419 So Bapt Conv	111	30,135	10,569	36,992 *	47.7	67.1
443 Un C of Christ	3	1,300	543	1,596 *	2.1	2.9
449 Un Methodist	27	3,550	1,684	4,359 *	5.6	7.9
463 Vineyard	1	130	120	160 *	.2	.3
499 Indep.Non-Char	1	1,210	530	1,210	1.6	2.2
DALE	**97**	**17,957**	**6,766**	**23,887 ***	**48.6**	**100.0**
053 Assemb of God	11	824	729	1,085	2.2	4.5
056 Baha'i	0	6	NR	6	-	-
081 Catholic	1	NR	NR	768	1.6	3.2
127 Ch God (Cleve)	4	117	177	177 *	.4	.7
151 L-D Saints	1	NR	NR	387	.8	1.6
165 Ch of Nazarene	1	63	21	63	.1	.3
167 Chs of Christ	5	442	420	524	1.1	2.2
193 Episcopal	1	NR	24	63	.1	.3
223 Free Will Bapt	7	817	NR	1,030 *	2.1	4.3
263 Int Foursq Gos	2	82	46	103 *	.2	.4
283 Luth—MO Synod	1	122	120	172	.4	.7
355 Presb Ch (USA)	1	8	4	10 *	-	-
356 Presb Ch Amer	1	72	50	82	.2	.3
360 Prim Bapt Chrch	2	NR	NR	NR	-	-
365 Prog Prim Bapt	1	41	NR	52 *	.1	.2
413 S.D.A.	1	134	NR	159	.3	.7
419 So Bapt Conv	33	11,595	3,425	14,627 *	29.8	61.2
449 Un Methodist	23	3,234	1,300	4,079 *	8.3	17.1
498 Indep.Charis.	1	400	450	500	1.0	2.1
DALLAS	**95**	**14,776**	**5,256**	**20,219 ***	**43.6**	**100.0**
053 Assemb of God	1	74	80	97	.2	.5
055 As Ref Pres Ch	1	32	NR	32	.1	.2
056 Baha'i	0	32	NR	32	.1	.2
061 Beachy Amish	1	21	NR	27 *	.1	.1
081 Catholic	1	NR	NR	502	1.1	2.5
093 Chr Ch (Disc)	2	114	70	146 *	.3	.7
097 Chr Chs&Chs Cr	3	277	NR	354 *	.8	1.8
123 Ch God (Ander)	1	NR	40	40	.1	.2
127 Ch God (Cleve)	4	368	207	469 *	1.0	2.3
145 Ch God Prophcy	1	36	NR	46 *	.1	.2
151 L-D Saints	1	NR	NR	201	.4	1.0
165 Ch of Nazarene	2	280	147	280	.6	1.4
167 Chs of Christ	8	545	469	743	1.6	3.7

NR–Not Reported   *Total adherents estimated from known number of communicant, confirmed, full members.   - Represents a percentage less than 0.1.   Percentages may not total 100 due to rounding.

Table 4: Religious Congregations by County and Group: 2000

Religious Group	Number of Churches, Synagogues, Mosques, or Temples	Number of Communicant, Confirmed, or Full Members	Number of Attendees	Total Adherents		
				Number of Adherents	% of Total Pop.	% of Total Adh.
193 Episcopal	2	NR	206	551	1.2	2.7
223 Free Will Bapt	1	117	NR	149 *	.3	.7
262 Int Cou Comm Ch	1	190	NR	243 *	.5	1.2
267 Muslim Est	1	NR	20	60	.1	.3
283 Luth—MO Synod	2	220	130	290	.6	1.4
304 NatPrimBapt USA	8	307	NR	392 *	.8	1.9
355 Presb Ch (USA)	8	670	352	855 *	1.8	4.2
356 Presb Ch Amer	3	214	170	248	.5	1.2
403 Salvation Army	1	93	33	104	.2	.5
413 S.D.A.	1	55	NR	65	.1	.3
419 So Bapt Conv	28	9,879	2,761	12,610 *	27.2	62.4
449 Un Methodist	12	1,252	571	1,598 *	3.4	7.9
496 Jewish Est	1	NR	NR	85	.2	.4
DE KALB	**195**	**30,687**	**11,960**	**38,658 ***	**60.0**	**100.0**
053 Assemb of God	2	58	79	79	.1	.2
056 Baha'i	0	3	NR	3	-	-
081 Catholic	1	NR	NR	284	.4	.7
097 Chr Chs&Chs Cr	1	50	NR	62 *	.1	.2
127 Ch God (Cleve)	18	1,774	1,275	2,208 *	3.4	5.7
145 Ch God Prophcy	5	179	NR	220 *	.3	.6
165 Ch of Nazarene	2	87	65	141	.2	.4
167 Chs of Christ	10	427	493	567	.9	1.5
189 Duck Rivr Bapt	22	2,683	NR	3,323 *	5.2	8.6
193 Episcopal	2	NR	107	277	.4	.7
283 Luth—MO Synod	1	16	10	19	-	-
355 Presb Ch (USA)	3	115	60	143 *	.2	.4
356 Presb Ch Amer	1	137	120	137	.2	.4
360 Prim Bapt Chrch	2	NR	NR	NR	-	-
365 Prog Prim Bapt	2	195	NR	242 *	.4	.6
413 S.D.A.	3	176	NR	209	.3	.5
419 So Bapt Conv	83	21,335	8,054	26,427 *	41.0	68.4
449 Un Methodist	35	3,351	1,571	4,149 *	6.4	10.7
467 Wesleyan	2	101	126	168	.3	.4
ELMORE	**105**	**23,239**	**9,934**	**30,644 ***	**46.5**	**100.0**
017 Amer Bapt Assn	1	775	NR	968 *	1.5	3.2
053 Assemb of God	5	492	625	728	1.1	2.4
056 Baha'i	0	12	NR	12	-	-
059 Bapt Miss Assn	1	125	56	156 *	.2	.5
081 Catholic	3	NR	NR	825	1.3	2.7
093 Chr Ch (Disc)	1	91	0	114 *	.2	.4
123 Ch God (Ander)	1	NR	20	20	-	.1
127 Ch God (Cleve)	5	766	365	961 *	1.5	3.1
151 L-D Saints	1	NR	NR	318	.5	1.0
165 Ch of Nazarene	1	115	146	193	.3	.6
167 Chs of Christ	10	708	755	907	1.4	3.0
175 Congr Chr Chs	1	40	80	50 *	.1	.2
185 Cumber Presb	1	0	NR	0	-	-
193 Episcopal	2	NR	128	266	.4	.9
207 E.L.C.A.	1	100	72	128	.2	.4
355 Presb Ch (USA)	1	221	110	276 *	.4	.9
356 Presb Ch Amer	1	246	150	296	.4	1.0
360 Prim Bapt Chrch	4	NR	NR	NR	-	-
365 Prog Prim Bapt	1	110	NR	137 *	.2	.4
418 Southw Bapt Fel	2	NR	NR	NR	-	-
419 So Bapt Conv	44	15,522	5,673	19,397 *	29.4	63.3
449 Un Methodist	18	3,916	1,754	4,892 *	7.4	16.0
ESCAMBIA	**104**	**15,547**	**5,873**	**20,396 ***	**53.1**	**100.0**
017 Amer Bapt Assn	1	50	NR	61 *	.2	.3
053 Assemb of God	8	995	1,127	1,271	3.3	6.2
056 Baha'i	0	9	NR	9	-	-
081 Catholic	2	NR	NR	363	.9	1.8
127 Ch God (Cleve)	3	124	91	153 *	.4	.8
145 Ch God Prophcy	1	36	NR	44 *	.1	.2
151 L-D Saints	2	NR	NR	537	1.4	2.6
165 Ch of Nazarene	2	147	128	245	.6	1.2
167 Chs of Christ	8	390	405	487	1.3	2.4
173 Comm of Christ	4	393	NR	393	1.0	1.9
193 Episcopal	3	NR	168	416	1.1	2.0
223 Free Will Bapt	2	233	NR	286 *	.7	1.4
283 Luth—MO Synod	1	100	20	170	.4	.8

Religious Group	Number of Churches, Synagogues, Mosques, or Temples	Number of Communicant, Confirmed, or Full Members	Number of Attendees	Total Adherents		
				Number of Adherents	% of Total Pop.	% of Total Adh.
288 Mennonite USA	1	45	40	55 *	.1	.3
297 Mennonite;Other	5	253	NR	311 *	.8	1.5
304 NatPrimBapt USA	1	200	NR	245 *	.6	1.2
349 Pent Holiness	7	606	368	743 *	1.9	3.6
356 Presb Ch Amer	2	366	210	378	1.0	1.9
360 Prim Bapt Chrch	4	NR	NR	NR	-	-
413 S.D.A.	1	55	NR	65	.2	.3
419 So Bapt Conv	33	9,751	2,517	11,962 *	31.1	58.6
449 Un Methodist	13	1,794	799	2,202 *	5.7	10.8
ETOWAH	**214**	**54,281**	**20,594**	**70,675 ***	**68.3**	**100.0**
053 Assemb of God	8	725	679	853	.8	1.2
056 Baha'i	0	6	NR	6	-	-
081 Catholic	1	NR	NR	2,056	2.0	2.9
089 Chr & Miss Al	1	69	NR	95	.1	.1
093 Chr Ch (Disc)	1	20	12	24 *	-	-
123 Ch God (Ander)	1	NR	52	52	.1	.1
127 Ch God (Cleve)	15	2,813	1,553	3,439 *	3.3	4.9
145 Ch God Prophcy	2	72	NR	88 *	.1	.1
151 L-D Saints	1	NR	NR	556	.5	.8
165 Ch of Nazarene	2	220	189	390	.4	.6
167 Chs of Christ	15	1,595	1,591	2,042	2.0	2.9
185 Cumber Presb	4	330	NR	523	.5	.7
189 Duck Rivr Bapt	1	108	NR	132 *	.1	.2
193 Episcopal	2	NR	231	581	.6	.8
267 Muslim Est	1	NR	101	288	.3	.4
283 Luth—MO Synod	3	239	156	285	.3	.4
290 Metro Comm Ch	1	10	16	16 *	-	-
349 Pent Holiness	1	87	63	106 *	.1	.1
355 Presb Ch (USA)	1	101	54	123 *	.1	.2
356 Presb Ch Amer	3	538	332	561	.5	.8
360 Prim Bapt Chrch	2	NR	NR	NR	-	-
403 Salvation Army	1	87	26	188	.2	.3
413 S.D.A.	2	68	NR	81	.1	.1
418 Southw Bapt Fel	1	NR	NR	NR	-	-
419 So Bapt Conv	101	39,844	12,025	48,700 *	47.1	68.9
449 Un Methodist	39	6,869	2,854	8,396 *	8.1	11.9
463 Vineyard	1	130	120	159 *	.2	.2
496 Jewish Est	1	NR	NR	85	.1	.1
498 Indep.Charis.	1	350	250	500	.5	.7
499 Indep.Non-Char	1	0	290	350	.3	.5
FAYETTE	**86**	**8,031**	**4,314**	**10,143 ***	**54.8**	**100.0**
053 Assemb of God	1	90	75	125	.7	1.2
059 Bapt Miss Assn	1	67	30	82 *	.4	.8
081 Catholic	1	NR	NR	121	.7	1.2
127 Ch God (Cleve)	5	437	306	532 *	2.9	5.2
145 Ch God Prophcy	1	36	NR	44 *	.2	.4
165 Ch of Nazarene	4	149	162	219	1.2	2.2
167 Chs of Christ	21	1,342	1,342	1,731	9.4	17.1
193 Episcopal	1	NR	42	93	.5	.9
223 Free Will Bapt	4	467	NR	568 *	3.1	5.6
266 Intrstat & Asc	1	19	NR	23 *	.1	.2
360 Prim Bapt Chrch	1	NR	NR	NR	-	-
419 So Bapt Conv	34	4,557	2,008	5,550 *	30.0	54.7
449 Un Methodist	11	867	349	1,055 *	5.7	10.4
FRANKLIN	**108**	**15,940**	**9,614**	**20,168 ***	**64.6**	**100.0**
017 Amer Bapt Assn	6	945	NR	1,164 *	3.7	5.8
053 Assemb of God	1	66	70	128	.4	.6
081 Catholic	1	NR	NR	201	.6	1.0
127 Ch God (Cleve)	3	517	283	638 *	2.0	3.2
145 Ch God Prophcy	4	143	NR	176 *	.6	.9
151 L-D Saints	1	NR	NR	166	.5	.8
165 Ch of Nazarene	2	175	167	207	.7	1.0
167 Chs of Christ	27	1,824	1,912	2,346	7.5	11.6
185 Cumber Presb	1	5	NR	20	.1	.1
223 Free Will Bapt	5	583	NR	719 *	2.3	3.6
320 "Old" MB Ascs	13	1,856	NR	2,288 *	7.3	11.3
355 Presb Ch (USA)	1	13	16	16 *	.1	.1
356 Presb Ch Amer	1	40	50	50	.2	.2
413 S.D.A.	1	20	NR	24	.1	.1
419 So Bapt Conv	31	8,409	6,433	10,368 *	33.2	51.4

NR–Not Reported *Total adherents estimated from known number of communicant, confirmed, full members. - Represents a percentage less than 0.1. Percentages may not total 100 due to rounding.

Table 4: Religious Congregations by County and Group: 2000

Religious Group	Number of Churches, Synagogues, Mosques, or Temples	Number of Communicant, Confirmed, or Full Members	Number of Attendees	Total Adherents: Number of Adherents	Total Adherents: % of Total Pop.	Total Adherents: % of Total Adh.
449 Un Methodist	10	1,344	683	1,657 *	5.3	8.2
GENEVA	**97**	**13,594**	**5,725**	**16,943 ***	**65.8**	**100.0**
053 Assemb of God	18	811	990	1,275	4.9	7.5
056 Baha'i	0	3	NR	3	-	-
081 Catholic	1	NR	NR	39	.2	.2
127 Ch God (Cleve)	3	115	107	151 *	.6	.9
167 Chs of Christ	9	421	453	542	2.1	3.2
223 Free Will Bapt	4	467	NR	569 *	2.2	3.4
355 Presb Ch (USA)	1	12	8	15 *	.1	.1
360 Prim Bapt Chrch	1	NR	NR	NR	-	-
419 So Bapt Conv	40	9,795	3,206	11,948 *	46.4	70.5
449 Un Methodist	20	1,970	961	2,401 *	9.3	14.2
GREENE	**27**	**1,408**	**710**	**1,891 ***	**19.0**	**100.0**
056 Baha'i	0	23	NR	23	.2	1.2
081 Catholic	1	NR	NR	41	.4	2.2
093 Chr Ch (Disc)	1	40	25	51 *	.5	2.7
167 Chs of Christ	1	20	20	20	.2	1.1
185 Cumber Presb	1	32	NR	48	.5	2.5
193 Episcopal	3	NR	53	90	.9	4.8
304 NatPrimBapt USA	1	38	NR	49 *	.5	2.6
356 Presb Ch Amer	3	162	75	168	1.7	8.9
413 S.D.A.	1	34	NR	40	.4	2.1
419 So Bapt Conv	5	495	174	636 *	6.4	33.6
449 Un Methodist	10	564	363	725 *	7.3	38.3
HALE	**44**	**4,972**	**2,095**	**6,792 ***	**39.5**	**100.0**
056 Baha'i	0	6	NR	6	-	.1
081 Catholic	1	NR	NR	53	.3	.8
123 Ch God (Ander)	1	NR	50	50	.3	.7
151 L-D Saints	1	NR	NR	137	.8	2.0
165 Ch of Nazarene	2	154	106	211	1.2	3.1
167 Chs of Christ	2	87	105	106	.6	1.6
193 Episcopal	1	NR	44	111	.6	1.6
304 NatPrimBapt USA	2	90	NR	117 *	.7	1.7
355 Presb Ch (USA)	1	9	9	12 *	.1	.2
356 Presb Ch Amer	3	135	93	161	.9	2.4
360 Prim Bapt Chrch	1	NR	NR	NR	-	-
419 So Bapt Conv	16	3,318	1,100	4,306 *	25.1	63.4
449 Un Methodist	13	1,173	588	1,522 *	8.9	22.4
HENRY	**46**	**7,933**	**2,777**	**9,884 ***	**60.6**	**100.0**
053 Assemb of God	4	80	98	143	.9	1.4
167 Chs of Christ	2	60	65	78	.5	.8
223 Free Will Bapt	5	583	NR	711 *	4.4	7.2
267 Muslim Est	1	NR	55	163	1.0	1.6
360 Prim Bapt Chrch	3	NR	NR	NR	-	-
419 So Bapt Conv	25	6,267	2,145	7,640 *	46.8	77.3
449 Un Methodist	6	943	414	1,149 *	7.0	11.6
HOUSTON	**135**	**44,016**	**17,068**	**60,219 ***	**67.8**	**100.0**
017 Amer Bapt Assn	1	72	NR	90 *	.1	.1
034 Ant Orth of NA	1	0	NR	0	-	-
053 Assemb of God	16	1,434	1,605	2,379	2.7	4.0
056 Baha'i	0	4	NR	4	-	-
081 Catholic	2	NR	NR	3,025	3.4	5.0
093 Chr Ch (Disc)	1	134	57	167 *	.2	.3
127 Ch God (Cleve)	2	141	94	191 *	.2	.3
145 Ch God Prophcy	1	36	NR	45 *	.1	.1
151 L-D Saints	2	NR	NR	643	.7	1.1
165 Ch of Nazarene	2	200	139	247	.3	.4
167 Chs of Christ	7	928	857	1,208	1.4	2.0
193 Episcopal	1	NR	225	608	.7	1.0
207 E.L.C.A.	1	73	58	98	.1	.2
223 Free Will Bapt	10	1,167	NR	1,456 *	1.6	2.4
262 Int Cou Comm Ch	1	190	NR	237 *	.3	.4
267 Muslim Est	1	NR	101	288	.3	.5
283 Luth—MO Synod	1	168	115	209	.2	.3
355 Presb Ch (USA)	2	292	147	368 *	.4	.6
356 Presb Ch Amer	2	886	455	1,077	1.2	1.8
360 Prim Bapt Chrch	2	NR	NR	NR	-	-
370 Ref Baptist Chs	1	NR	NR	NR	-	-
403 Salvation Army	1	103	32	124	.1	.2
413 S.D.A.	3	343	NR	409	.5	.7
418 Southw Bapt Fel	1	NR	NR	NR	-	-
419 So Bapt Conv	49	31,652	10,451	39,515 *	44.5	65.6
449 Un Methodist	22	6,063	2,627	7,569 *	8.5	12.6
463 Vineyard	1	130	105	162 *	.2	.3
496 Jewish Est	1	NR	NR	100	.1	.2
JACKSON	**147**	**20,065**	**8,136**	**25,659 ***	**47.6**	**100.0**
053 Assemb of God	1	51	71	71	.1	.3
056 Baha'i	0	5	NR	5	-	-
081 Catholic	1	NR	NR	463	.9	1.8
127 Ch God (Cleve)	17	1,622	994	1,989 *	3.7	7.8
151 L-D Saints	1	NR	NR	222	.4	.9
165 Ch of Nazarene	1	58	41	64	.1	.2
167 Chs of Christ	21	1,125	1,164	1,475	2.7	5.7
185 Cumber Presb	5	402	NR	594	1.1	2.3
189 Duck Rivr Bapt	3	360	NR	441 *	.8	1.7
193 Episcopal	1	NR	87	177	.3	.7
283 Luth—MO Synod	1	30	28	35	.1	.1
304 NatPrimBapt USA	2	66	NR	81 *	.2	.3
355 Presb Ch (USA)	1	5	10	10 *	-	-
360 Prim Bapt Chrch	5	NR	NR	NR	-	-
413 S.D.A.	2	230	NR	274	.5	1.1
418 Southw Bapt Fel	1	NR	NR	NR	-	-
419 So Bapt Conv	60	14,157	4,760	17,361 *	32.2	67.7
449 Un Methodist	24	1,954	981	2,397 *	4.4	9.3
JEFFERSON	**794**	**264,322**	**102,715**	**398,071 ***	**60.1**	**100.0**
017 Amer Bapt Assn	1	100	NR	124 *	-	-
053 Assemb of God	18	7,513	5,143	8,430	1.3	2.1
055 As Ref Pres Ch	2	51	NR	51	-	-
056 Baha'i	2	299	NR	299	-	.1
059 Bapt Miss Assn	1	82	60	101 *	-	-
076 Buddhism	1	NR	NR	NR	-	-
081 Catholic	30	NR	NR	44,044	6.7	11.1
089 Chr & Miss Al	8	280	NR	387	.1	.1
093 Chr Ch (Disc)	6	636	191	787 *	.1	.2
097 Chr Chs&Chs Cr	2	262	NR	324 *	-	.1
107 Christian Un	1	18	35	35 *	-	-
123 Ch God (Ander)	16	NR	982	982	.1	.2
127 Ch God (Cleve)	44	10,098	5,724	12,488 *	1.9	3.1
145 Ch God Prophcy	11	394	NR	484 *	.1	.1
151 L-D Saints	7	NR	NR	2,219	.3	.6
157 Ch of Brethren	1	15	0	19 *	-	-
165 Ch of Nazarene	12	1,581	774	1,643	.2	.4
167 Chs of Christ	73	9,873	9,276	12,691	1.9	3.2
173 Comm of Christ	1	119	NR	119	-	-
185 Cumber Presb	6	673	NR	1,092	.2	.3
186 Coptic Orth Ch	1	NR	NR	NR	-	-
193 Episcopal	19	NR	4,636	14,785	2.2	3.7
203 Evan Free Ch	1	79	200	200	-	.1
207 E.L.C.A.	5	895	426	1,066	.2	.3
221 Free Methodist	2	87	77	100	-	-
223 Free Will Bapt	14	1,633	NR	2,020 *	.3	.5
226 Friends-USA	1	64	NR	79 *	-	-
246 Greek Orthodox	1	NR	NR	1,644	.2	.4
252 Hindu	2	NR	NR	NR	-	-
262 Int Cou Comm Ch	7	1,390	NR	1,719 *	.3	.4
264 Int Chs of Crst	1	107	216	169	-	-
267 Muslim Est	3	NR	468	1,827	.3	.5
283 Luth—MO Synod	11	1,586	796	2,087	.3	.5
290 Metro Comm Ch	1	172	164	213 *	-	.1
297 Mennonite;Other	5	109	NR	135 *	-	-
304 NatPrimBapt USA	10	1,231	NR	1,523 *	.2	.4
331 OCA: Ter Diocs	2	55	NR	177	-	-
335 Orth Pres Ch	1	30	48	48	-	-
349 Pent Holiness	6	525	284	649 *	.1	.2
355 Presb Ch (USA)	29	8,062	3,265	9,975 *	1.5	2.5
356 Presb Ch Amer	11	6,466	4,460	8,132	1.2	2.0
360 Prim Bapt Chrch	8	NR	NR	NR	-	-
370 Ref Baptist Chs	1	NR	NR	NR	-	-

NR–Not Reported *Total adherents estimated from known number of communicant, confirmed, full members. - Represents a percentage less than 0.1. Percentages may not total 100 due to rounding.

Table 4: Religious Congregations by County and Group: 2000

Religious Group	Number of Churches, Synagogues, Mosques, or Temples	Number of Communicant, Confirmed, or Full Members	Number of Attendees	Total Adherents		
				Number of Adherents	% of Total Pop.	% of Total Adh.
400 Rus Orth Moscow	1	NR	NR	NR	-	-
403 Salvation Army	2	144	135	450	.1	.1
413 S.D.A.	10	3,589	NR	4,272	.6	1.1
416 Sikh	1	NR	NR	NR	-	-
418 Southw Bapt Fel	1	NR	NR	NR	-	-
419 So Bapt Conv	263	159,021	46,261	196,690 *	29.7	49.4
435 Unitarian-Univ	1	184	NR	228 *	-	.1
443 Un C of Christ	2	273	153	338 *	.1	.1
449 Un Methodist	110	43,000	15,462	53,181 *	8.0	13.4
463 Vineyard	3	341	348	443 *	.1	.1
467 Wesleyan	1	91	104	263	-	.1
469 WELS	1	52	32	60	-	-
496 Jewish Est	5	NR	NR	5,300	.8	1.3
498 Indep.Charis.	3	820	795	1,320	.2	.3
499 Indep.Non-Char	5	2,322	2,200	2,659	.4	.7
LAMAR	**94**	**9,186**	**3,667**	**11,315 ***	**71.1**	**100.0**
017 Amer Bapt Assn	1	108	NR	131 *	.8	1.2
053 Assemb of God	2	147	210	246	1.5	2.2
059 Bapt Miss Assn	1	95	85	116 *	.7	1.0
127 Ch God (Cleve)	7	336	147	408 *	2.6	3.6
165 Ch of Nazarene	2	104	27	104	.7	.9
167 Chs of Christ	13	979	991	1,289	8.1	11.4
223 Free Will Bapt	17	1,983	NR	2,412 *	15.2	21.3
419 So Bapt Conv	27	3,892	1,464	4,733 *	29.8	41.8
449 Un Methodist	24	1,542	743	1,876 *	11.8	16.6
LAUDERDALE	**178**	**37,891**	**22,632**	**49,818 ***	**56.6**	**100.0**
017 Amer Bapt Assn	2	273	NR	331 *	.4	.7
053 Assemb of God	1	303	375	375	.4	.8
056 Baha'i	1	20	NR	20	-	-
081 Catholic	2	NR	NR	2,089	2.4	4.2
093 Chr Ch (Disc)	1	335	123	407 *	.5	.8
123 Ch God (Ander)	2	NR	79	79	.1	.2
127 Ch God (Cleve)	3	249	134	303 *	.3	.6
165 Ch of Nazarene	3	300	222	344	.4	.7
167 Chs of Christ	63	10,244	10,801	13,296	15.1	26.7
185 Cumber Presb	6	591	NR	856	1.0	1.7
193 Episcopal	2	NR	238	615	.7	1.2
207 E.L.C.A.	1	113	77	145	.2	.3
223 Free Will Bapt	6	700	NR	850 *	1.0	1.7
258 IndFreeWillBapt	3	127	NR	154 *	.2	.3
262 Int Cou Comm Ch	1	200	NR	243 *	.3	.5
283 Luth—MO Synod	1	128	78	145	.2	.3
304 NatPrimBapt USA	3	276	NR	335 *	.4	.7
355 Presb Ch (USA)	3	605	301	735 *	.8	1.5
356 Presb Ch Amer	1	21	90	90	.1	.2
360 Prim Bapt Chrch	3	NR	NR	NR	-	-
403 Salvation Army	1	111	38	177	.2	.4
413 S.D.A.	1	49	NR	58	.1	.1
419 So Bapt Conv	34	15,473	6,158	18,787 *	21.4	37.7
435 Unitarian-Univ	1	21	NR	25 *	-	.1
449 Un Methodist	31	6,802	3,143	8,259 *	9.4	16.6
498 Indep.Charis.	1	700	550	800	.9	1.6
499 Indep.Non-Char	1	250	225	300	.3	.6
LAWRENCE	**81**	**14,479**	**5,841**	**18,102 ***	**52.0**	**100.0**
053 Assemb of God	2	299	278	313	.9	1.7
081 Catholic	1	NR	NR	60	.2	.3
127 Ch God (Cleve)	1	195	58	243 *	.7	1.3
145 Ch God Prophcy	2	72	NR	90 *	.3	.5
167 Chs of Christ	17	1,342	1,440	1,751	5.0	9.7
185 Cumber Presb	1	15	NR	26	.1	.1
223 Free Will Bapt	1	117	NR	145 *	.4	.8
304 NatPrimBapt USA	1	70	NR	87 *	.2	.5
320 "Old" MB Ascs	9	968	NR	1,205 *	3.5	6.7
355 Presb Ch (USA)	1	53	48	66 *	.2	.4
356 Presb Ch Amer	1	34	18	37	.1	.2
413 S.D.A.	1	15	NR	18	.1	.1
419 So Bapt Conv	28	10,073	3,351	12,535 *	36.0	69.2
449 Un Methodist	15	1,226	648	1,526 *	4.4	8.4

Religious Group	Number of Churches, Synagogues, Mosques, or Temples	Number of Communicant, Confirmed, or Full Members	Number of Attendees	Total Adherents		
				Number of Adherents	% of Total Pop.	% of Total Adh.
LEE	**97**	**29,554**	**13,123**	**39,807 ***	**34.6**	**100.0**
053 Assemb of God	8	1,162	1,231	1,416	1.2	3.6
056 Baha'i	0	25	NR	25	-	.1
076 Buddhism	1	NR	NR	NR	-	-
081 Catholic	2	NR	NR	2,115	1.8	5.3
089 Chr & Miss Al	1	7	NR	44	-	.1
093 Chr Ch (Disc)	2	191	68	233 *	.2	.6
123 Ch God (Ander)	2	NR	35	35	-	.1
127 Ch God (Cleve)	1	164	69	200 *	.2	.5
151 L-D Saints	1	NR	NR	482	.4	1.2
165 Ch of Nazarene	1	47	32	47	-	.1
167 Chs of Christ	8	960	1,100	1,238	1.1	3.1
193 Episcopal	2	NR	266	724	.6	1.8
223 Free Will Bapt	1	117	NR	143 *	.1	.4
267 Muslim Est	1	NR	101	288	.3	.7
283 Luth—MO Synod	1	253	193	296	.3	.7
331 OCA: Ter Diocs	1	6	NR	27	-	.1
355 Presb Ch (USA)	2	589	261	720 *	.6	1.8
356 Presb Ch Amer	2	476	480	542	.5	1.4
360 Prim Bapt Chrch	2	NR	NR	NR	-	-
365 Prog Prim Bapt	1	45	NR	55 *	-	.1
403 Salvation Army	1	5	16	5	-	-
413 S.D.A.	1	71	NR	84	.1	.2
419 So Bapt Conv	32	18,384	5,842	22,470 *	19.5	56.4
435 Unitarian-Univ	1	96	NR	117 *	.1	.3
449 Un Methodist	22	6,956	3,429	8,501 *	7.4	21.4
LIMESTONE	**143**	**26,518**	**15,442**	**34,804 ***	**53.0**	**100.0**
040 Ap Chr Ch-Amer	1	45	90	90 *	.1	.3
053 Assemb of God	2	96	122	435	.7	1.2
081 Catholic	1	NR	NR	669	1.0	1.9
093 Chr Ch (Disc)	1	150	75	186 *	.3	.5
123 Ch God (Ander)	1	NR	100	100	.2	.3
127 Ch God (Cleve)	1	67	7	83 *	.1	.2
145 Ch God Prophcy	1	36	NR	44 *	.1	.1
151 L-D Saints	1	NR	NR	325	.5	.9
167 Chs of Christ	54	5,980	6,556	7,773	11.8	22.3
185 Cumber Presb	1	104	NR	144	.2	.4
193 Episcopal	1	NR	52	101	.2	.3
223 Free Will Bapt	1	117	NR	145 *	.2	.4
283 Luth—MO Synod	1	83	52	104	.2	.3
304 NatPrimBapt USA	6	481	NR	597 *	.9	1.7
320 "Old" MB Ascs	1	28	NR	35 *	.1	.1
355 Presb Ch (USA)	4	468	273	582 *	.9	1.7
360 Prim Bapt Chrch	2	NR	NR	NR	-	-
413 S.D.A.	2	115	NR	137	.2	.4
419 So Bapt Conv	37	15,382	6,720	19,079 *	29.1	54.8
426 2Seed Sprt Bpt	1	3	NR	4 *	-	-
443 Un C of Christ	1	32	14	40 *	.1	.1
449 Un Methodist	22	3,331	1,381	4,131 *	6.3	11.9
LOWNDES	**41**	**2,937**	**1,838**	**3,897 ***	**28.9**	**100.0**
017 Amer Bapt Assn	1	50	NR	65 *	.5	1.7
053 Assemb of God	1	31	35	40	.3	1.0
056 Baha'i	0	1	NR	1	-	-
093 Chr Ch (Disc)	10	995	674	1,286 *	9.5	33.0
097 Chr Chs&Chs Cr	1	97	NR	125 *	.9	3.2
167 Chs of Christ	6	223	216	298	2.2	7.6
193 Episcopal	1	NR	62	83	.6	2.1
304 NatPrimBapt USA	3	226	NR	292 *	2.2	7.5
356 Presb Ch Amer	3	94	100	130	1.0	3.3
419 So Bapt Conv	8	876	429	1,132 *	8.4	29.0
449 Un Methodist	7	344	322	445 *	3.3	11.4
MACON	**37**	**3,152**	**1,631**	**4,648 ***	**19.3**	**100.0**
053 Assemb of God	2	71	54	74	.3	1.6
056 Baha'i	0	80	NR	80	.3	1.7
081 Catholic	1	NR	NR	250	1.0	5.4
093 Chr Ch (Disc)	2	335	154	417 *	1.7	9.0
151 L-D Saints	1	NR	NR	161	.7	3.5
167 Chs of Christ	3	199	153	259	1.1	5.6
193 Episcopal	1	NR	70	132	.5	2.8

NR–Not Reported *Total adherents estimated from known number of communicant, confirmed, full members. - Represents a percentage less than 0.1. Percentages may not total 100 due to rounding.

Table 4: Religious Congregations by County and Group: 2000

Religious Group	Number of Churches, Synagogues, Mosques, or Temples	Number of Communicant, Confirmed, or Full Members	Number of Attendees	Total Adherents: Number of Adherents	Total Adherents: % of Total Pop.	Total Adherents: % of Total Adh.
207 E.L.C.A.	1	48	25	52	.2	1.1
267 Muslim Est	2	NR	115	223	.9	4.8
355 Presb Ch (USA)	3	175	95	217 *	.9	4.7
356 Presb Ch Amer	2	27	19	27	.1	.6
419 So Bapt Conv	8	1,349	465	1,678 *	7.0	36.1
449 Un Methodist	11	868	481	1,078 *	4.5	23.2
MADISON	**343**	**101,958**	**45,779**	**152,804 ***	**55.2**	**100.0**
017 Amer Bapt Assn	1	49	NR	61 *	-	-
019 Amer Bapt USA	1	1,672	924	2,090 *	.8	1.4
053 Assemb of God	5	574	634	949	.3	.6
055 As Ref Pres Ch	1	46	NR	46	-	-
056 Baha'i	2	134	NR	134	-	.1
076 Buddhism	2	NR	NR	NR	-	-
081 Catholic	6	NR	NR	15,905	5.7	10.4
084 Calvary Chapel	1	NR	NR	NR	-	-
089 Chr & Miss Al	1	23	NR	39	-	-
093 Chr Ch (Disc)	2	893	408	1,116 *	.4	.7
097 Chr Chs&Chs Cr	2	122	NR	152 *	.1	.1
123 Ch God (Ander)	2	NR	241	241	.1	.2
127 Ch God (Cleve)	7	1,639	1,091	2,062 *	.7	1.3
145 Ch God Prophcy	4	143	NR	180 *	.1	.1
151 L-D Saints	6	NR	NR	2,225	.8	1.5
165 Ch of Nazarene	7	708	509	890	.3	.6
167 Chs of Christ	42	8,376	8,116	10,782	3.9	7.1
173 Comm of Christ	1	107	NR	107	-	.1
179 Consrv Bapt	1	NR	15	15	-	-
185 Cumber Presb	8	561	NR	713	.3	.5
193 Episcopal	5	NR	1,067	2,931	1.1	1.9
203 Evan Free Ch	1	85	200	200	.1	.1
207 E.L.C.A.	5	1,480	721	1,871	.7	1.2
221 Free Methodist	1	34	30	34	-	-
223 Free Will Bapt	2	233	NR	292 *	.1	.2
226 Friends-USA	1	64	NR	80 *	-	.1
246 Greek Orthodox	1	NR	NR	213	.1	.1
263 Int Foursq Gos	1	123	429	429 *	.2	.3
267 Muslim Est	2	NR	312	1,218	.4	.8
283 Luth—MO Synod	3	798	496	980	.4	.6
290 Metro Comm Ch	1	13	110	16 *	-	-
304 NatPrimBapt USA	43	6,863	NR	8,577 *	3.1	5.6
335 Orth Pres Ch	1	7	12	13	-	-
349 Pent Holiness	3	319	214	399 *	.1	.3
355 Presb Ch (USA)	12	2,862	2,601	4,459 *	1.6	2.9
356 Presb Ch Amer	5	1,044	995	1,471	.5	1.0
360 Prim Bapt Chrch	5	NR	NR	NR	-	-
365 Prog Prim Bapt	1	35	NR	44 *	-	-
370 Ref Baptist Chs	1	NR	NR	NR	-	-
403 Salvation Army	1	100	60	205	.1	.1
413 S.D.A.	8	4,771	NR	5,678	2.1	3.7
418 Southw Bapt Fel	2	NR	NR	NR	-	-
419 So Bapt Conv	82	49,606	16,469	61,995 *	22.4	40.6
435 Unitarian-Univ	1	143	NR	179 *	.1	.1
443 Un C of Christ	1	169	75	211 *	.1	.1
449 Un Methodist	43	16,953	8,404	21,184 *	7.7	13.9
463 Vineyard	1	44	51	55 *	-	-
469 WELS	1	57	55	73	-	-
496 Jewish Est	2	NR	NR	750	.3	.5
498 Indep.Charis.	3	515	840	840	.3	.5
499 Indep.Non-Char	2	593	700	700	.3	.5
MARENGO	**65**	**8,585**	**3,484**	**11,519 ***	**51.1**	**100.0**
053 Assemb of God	1	181	145	175	.8	1.5
056 Baha'i	0	8	NR	8	-	.1
081 Catholic	1	NR	NR	248	1.1	2.2
097 Chr Chs&Chs Cr	1	65	NR	83 *	.4	.7
127 Ch God (Cleve)	1	29	12	37 *	.2	.3
143 CG in Cr(Menn)	1	173	NR	221 *	1.0	1.9
151 L-D Saints	1	NR	NR	76	.3	.7
165 Ch of Nazarene	1	22	19	22	.1	.2
167 Chs of Christ	3	167	140	217	1.0	1.9
193 Episcopal	2	NR	115	288	1.3	2.5
304 NatPrimBapt USA	4	0	NR	0 *	-	-
356 Presb Ch Amer	5	285	206	353	1.6	3.1

Religious Group	Number of Churches, Synagogues, Mosques, or Temples	Number of Communicant, Confirmed, or Full Members	Number of Attendees	Total Adherents: Number of Adherents	Total Adherents: % of Total Pop.	Total Adherents: % of Total Adh.
419 So Bapt Conv	29	6,162	2,127	7,881 *	35.0	68.4
449 Un Methodist	15	1,493	720	1,910 *	8.5	16.6
MARION	**113**	**15,002**	**6,659**	**18,594 ***	**59.6**	**100.0**
017 Amer Bapt Assn	2	196	NR	237 *	.8	1.3
053 Assemb of God	3	377	293	442	1.4	2.4
059 Bapt Miss Assn	1	63	37	76 *	.2	.4
081 Catholic	1	NR	NR	227	.7	1.2
089 Chr & Miss Al	1	36	NR	41	.1	.2
127 Ch God (Cleve)	8	618	284	746 *	2.4	4.0
145 Ch God Prophcy	3	107	NR	129 *	.4	.7
167 Chs of Christ	27	2,011	2,164	2,641	8.5	14.2
223 Free Will Bapt	23	2,683	NR	3,246 *	10.4	17.5
339 Pent Ch of God	1	20	NR	53	.2	.3
360 Prim Bapt Chrch	1	NR	NR	NR	-	-
419 So Bapt Conv	29	7,244	3,124	8,764 *	28.1	47.1
449 Un Methodist	13	1,647	757	1,992 *	6.4	10.7
MARSHALL	**208**	**41,633**	**17,439**	**53,670 ***	**65.3**	**100.0**
053 Assemb of God	7	690	839	856	1.0	1.6
056 Baha'i	0	3	NR	3	-	-
081 Catholic	1	NR	NR	999	1.2	1.9
123 Ch God (Ander)	2	NR	85	85	.1	.2
127 Ch God (Cleve)	13	1,489	1,075	1,860 *	2.3	3.5
145 Ch God Prophcy	4	143	NR	176 *	.2	.3
151 L-D Saints	1	NR	NR	409	.5	.8
165 Ch of Nazarene	4	200	161	240	.3	.4
167 Chs of Christ	22	2,079	2,153	2,405	2.9	4.5
193 Episcopal	2	NR	268	763	.9	1.4
221 Free Methodist	1	4	8	8	-	-
283 Luth—MO Synod	1	76	54	96	.1	.2
304 NatPrimBapt USA	1	80	NR	99 *	.1	.2
355 Presb Ch (USA)	2	302	127	373 *	.5	.7
356 Presb Ch Amer	1	70	120	120	.1	.2
360 Prim Bapt Chrch	8	NR	NR	NR	-	-
413 S.D.A.	2	119	NR	142	.2	.3
418 Southw Bapt Fel	1	NR	NR	NR	-	-
419 So Bapt Conv	99	30,513	9,856	37,776 *	45.9	70.4
449 Un Methodist	35	5,785	2,613	7,161 *	8.7	13.3
463 Vineyard	1	80	80	99 *	.1	.2
MOBILE	**382**	**129,533**	**47,280**	**212,931 ***	**53.3**	**100.0**
017 Amer Bapt Assn	7	1,566	NR	1,990 *	.5	.9
019 Amer Bapt USA	1	850	350	1,080 *	.3	.5
053 Assemb of God	34	5,200	5,139	6,910	1.7	3.2
056 Baha'i	1	76	NR	76	-	-
059 Bapt Miss Assn	9	1,008	519	1,281 *	.3	.6
076 Buddhism	2	NR	NR	NR	-	-
081 Catholic	36	NR	NR	36,021	9.0	16.9
093 Chr Ch (Disc)	3	785	106	997 *	.2	.5
097 Chr Chs&Chs Cr	3	657	NR	835 *	.2	.4
123 Ch God (Ander)	4	NR	174	174	-	.1
127 Ch God (Cleve)	25	7,645	3,392	9,712 *	2.4	4.6
145 Ch God Prophcy	4	143	NR	184 *	-	.1
151 L-D Saints	3	NR	NR	1,429	.4	.7
157 Ch of Brethren	1	115	50	146 *	-	.1
165 Ch of Nazarene	6	570	340	799	.2	.4
167 Chs of Christ	19	2,522	2,587	3,297	.8	1.5
173 Comm of Christ	3	746	NR	746	.2	.4
186 Coptic Orth Ch	1	NR	NR	NR	-	-
193 Episcopal	15	NR	2,139	6,394	1.6	3.0
207 E.L.C.A.	3	283	180	455	.1	.2
246 Greek Orthodox	1	NR	NR	939	.2	.4
266 Intrstat & Asc	4	832	NR	1,057 *	.3	.5
267 Muslim Est	3	NR	468	1,827	.5	.9
283 Luth—MO Synod	6	1,328	751	1,743	.4	.8
290 Metro Comm Ch	1	61	61	78 *	-	-
297 Mennonite;Other	2	28	NR	36 *	-	-
304 NatPrimBapt USA	9	2,630	NR	3,342 *	.8	1.6
349 Pent Holiness	4	528	270	671 *	.2	.3
355 Presb Ch (USA)	13	2,734	1,480	3,473 *	.9	1.6
356 Presb Ch Amer	2	141	120	205	.1	.1
360 Prim Bapt Chrch	2	NR	NR	NR	-	-

NR–Not Reported   *Total adherents estimated from known number of communicant, confirmed, full members.   - Represents a percentage less than 0.1.   Percentages may not total 100 due to rounding.

Table 4: Religious Congregations by County and Group: 2000

Religious Group	Number of Churches, Synagogues, Mosques, or Temples	Number of Communicant, Confirmed, or Full Members	Number of Attendees	Total Adherents: Number of Adherents	Total Adherents: % of Total Pop.	Total Adherents: % of Total Adh.
401 Rus Orth Abroad	1	NR	NR	NR	-	-
403 Salvation Army	2	214	83	329	.1	.2
413 S.D.A.	5	272	NR	323	.1	.2
418 Southw Bapt Fel	1	NR	NR	NR	-	-
419 So Bapt Conv	92	77,571	20,772	98,565 *	24.7	46.3
435 Unitarian-Univ	1	33	NR	42 *	-	-
449 Un Methodist	45	19,465	6,873	24,734 *	6.2	11.6
463 Vineyard	1	35	28	44 *	-	-
467 Wesleyan	1	89	115	200	.1	.1
469 WELS	1	56	43	77	-	-
496 Jewish Est	2	NR	NR	1,100	.3	.5
498 Indep.Charis.	3	1,350	1,240	1,620	.4	.8
MONROE	**67**	**9,483**	**8,917**	**12,730 ***	**52.3**	**100.0**
053 Assemb of God	7	424	491	723	3.0	5.7
056 Baha'i	0	2	NR	2	-	-
081 Catholic	3	NR	NR	277	1.1	2.2
127 Ch God (Cleve)	1	48	61	61 *	.3	.5
165 Ch of Nazarene	2	240	143	289	1.2	2.3
167 Chs of Christ	1	140	130	170	.7	1.3
193 Episcopal	1	NR	88	209	.9	1.6
223 Free Will Bapt	1	117	NR	149 *	.6	1.2
283 Luth—MO Synod	1	37	33	50	.2	.4
356 Presb Ch Amer	1	141	57	160	.7	1.3
360 Prim Bapt Chrch	5	NR	NR	NR	-	-
418 Southw Bapt Fel	1	NR	NR	NR	-	-
419 So Bapt Conv	28	7,053	7,225	9,005 *	37.0	70.7
449 Un Methodist	15	1,281	689	1,635 *	6.7	12.8
MONTGOMERY	**208**	**78,785**	**35,230**	**113,045 ***	**50.6**	**100.0**
017 Amer Bapt Assn	1	50	NR	63 *	-	.1
019 Amer Bapt USA	1	4,100	1,500	5,134 *	2.3	4.5
053 Assemb of God	6	2,328	1,723	2,759	1.2	2.4
056 Baha'i	1	299	NR	299	.1	.3
059 Bapt Miss Assn	2	221	135	276 *	.1	.2
081 Catholic	8	NR	NR	7,600	3.4	6.7
093 Chr Ch (Disc)	4	301	125	377 *	.2	.3
097 Chr Chs&Chs Cr	1	100	NR	125 *	.1	.1
123 Ch God (Ander)	2	NR	153	153	.1	.1
127 Ch God (Cleve)	2	561	230	703 *	.3	.6
145 Ch God Prophcy	1	36	NR	45 *	-	-
151 L-D Saints	2	NR	NR	1,054	.5	.9
165 Ch of Nazarene	2	104	71	123	.1	.1
167 Chs of Christ	39	7,295	6,915	9,184	4.1	8.1
173 Comm of Christ	1	147	NR	147	.1	.1
193 Episcopal	7	NR	1,279	4,070	1.8	3.6
207 E.L.C.A.	2	286	170	358	.2	.3
216 Evan Presby Ch	1	112	NR	140 *	.1	.1
223 Free Will Bapt	2	233	NR	292 *	.1	.3
267 Muslim Est	1	NR	156	609	.3	.5
283 Luth—MO Synod	4	455	278	509	.2	.5
290 Metro Comm Ch	1	60	77	77 *	-	.1
304 NatPrimBapt USA	2	320	NR	401 *	.2	.4
355 Presb Ch (USA)	6	1,194	792	1,498 *	.7	1.3
356 Presb Ch Amer	8	2,299	1,449	2,838	1.3	2.5
360 Prim Bapt Chrch	3	NR	NR	NR	-	-
403 Salvation Army	1	105	58	284	.1	.3
413 S.D.A.	4	1,901	NR	2,263	1.0	2.0
418 Southw Bapt Fel	2	NR	NR	NR	-	-
419 So Bapt Conv	53	37,742	10,860	47,256 *	21.1	41.8
435 Unitarian-Univ	1	87	NR	109 *	-	.1
443 Un C of Christ	2	338	189	423 *	.2	.4
449 Un Methodist	32	18,111	9,070	22,676 *	10.1	20.1
496 Jewish Est	3	NR	NR	1,200	.5	1.1
MORGAN	**195**	**48,076**	**23,167**	**65,145 ***	**58.7**	**100.0**
053 Assemb of God	3	1,059	1,448	2,010	1.8	3.1
056 Baha'i	0	26	NR	26	-	-
061 Beachy Amish	1	31	NR	39 *	-	.1
081 Catholic	2	NR	NR	2,789	2.5	4.3
093 Chr Ch (Disc)	4	483	236	601 *	.5	.9
097 Chr Chs&Chs Cr	3	344	NR	428 *	.4	.7
123 Ch God (Ander)	6	NR	602	602	.5	.9

Religious Group	Number of Churches, Synagogues, Mosques, or Temples	Number of Communicant, Confirmed, or Full Members	Number of Attendees	Total Adherents: Number of Adherents	Total Adherents: % of Total Pop.	Total Adherents: % of Total Adh.
127 Ch God (Cleve)	8	953	482	1,185 *	1.1	1.8
145 Ch God Prophcy	3	107	NR	135 *	.1	.2
151 L-D Saints	1	NR	NR	477	.4	.7
165 Ch of Nazarene	5	398	247	493	.4	.8
167 Chs of Christ	22	3,509	3,635	4,459	4.0	6.8
173 Comm of Christ	1	61	NR	61	.1	.1
193 Episcopal	2	NR	255	812	.7	1.2
223 Free Will Bapt	3	350	NR	436 *	.4	.7
283 Luth—MO Synod	2	588	324	745	.7	1.1
304 NatPrimBapt USA	4	323	NR	402 *	.4	.6
349 Pent Holiness	1	155	109	193 *	.2	.3
355 Presb Ch (USA)	4	970	463	1,207 *	1.1	1.9
356 Presb Ch Amer	2	224	211	304	.3	.5
360 Prim Bapt Chrch	2	NR	NR	NR	-	-
403 Salvation Army	1	140	49	143	.1	.2
413 S.D.A.	3	198	NR	236	.2	.4
418 Southw Bapt Fel	1	NR	NR	NR	-	-
419 So Bapt Conv	73	29,548	10,851	36,772 *	33.1	56.4
449 Un Methodist	37	8,109	3,755	10,090 *	9.1	15.5
498 Indep.Charis.	1	500	500	500	.5	.8
PERRY	**31**	**2,714**	**1,025**	**3,567 ***	**30.1**	**100.0**
053 Assemb of God	1	44	46	78	.7	2.2
056 Baha'i	0	4	NR	4	-	.1
127 Ch God (Cleve)	3	102	51	132 *	1.1	3.7
193 Episcopal	1	NR	40	66	.6	1.9
223 Free Will Bapt	1	117	NR	151 *	1.3	4.2
304 NatPrimBapt USA	4	150	NR	194 *	1.6	5.4
356 Presb Ch Amer	2	80	44	80	.7	2.2
419 So Bapt Conv	8	1,284	414	1,658 *	14.0	46.5
443 Un C of Christ	1	16	12	21 *	.2	.6
449 Un Methodist	10	917	418	1,183 *	10.0	33.2
PICKENS	**87**	**9,724**	**3,621**	**12,437 ***	**59.4**	**100.0**
053 Assemb of God	2	67	68	85	.4	.7
056 Baha'i	0	4	NR	4	-	-
081 Catholic	1	NR	NR	80	.4	.6
127 Ch God (Cleve)	3	148	111	186 *	.9	1.5
145 Ch God Prophcy	4	143	NR	180 *	.9	1.4
151 L-D Saints	1	NR	NR	105	.5	.8
167 Chs of Christ	5	148	163	189	.9	1.5
185 Cumber Presb	1	19	NR	24	.1	.2
223 Free Will Bapt	9	1,050	NR	1,321 *	6.3	10.6
267 Muslim Est	1	NR	7	15	.1	.1
339 Pent Ch of God	2	55	NR	110	.5	.9
355 Presb Ch (USA)	2	49	25	61 *	.3	.5
356 Presb Ch Amer	2	248	125	271	1.3	2.2
419 So Bapt Conv	34	5,970	2,247	7,512 *	35.9	60.4
449 Un Methodist	20	1,823	875	2,294 *	11.0	18.4
PIKE	**80**	**11,251**	**5,372**	**14,709 ***	**49.7**	**100.0**
053 Assemb of God	5	289	374	563	1.9	3.8
056 Baha'i	0	5	NR	5	-	-
081 Catholic	1	NR	NR	297	1.0	2.0
127 Ch God (Cleve)	3	91	64	114 *	.4	.8
151 L-D Saints	1	NR	NR	158	.5	1.1
167 Chs of Christ	7	528	607	719	2.4	4.9
173 Comm of Christ	1	13	NR	13	-	.1
193 Episcopal	1	NR	75	176	.6	1.2
355 Presb Ch (USA)	1	13	7	16 *	.1	.1
356 Presb Ch Amer	1	132	80	132	.4	.9
360 Prim Bapt Chrch	1	NR	NR	NR	-	-
413 S.D.A.	2	55	NR	66	.2	.4
419 So Bapt Conv	38	8,198	3,186	10,080 *	34.0	68.5
449 Un Methodist	17	1,797	859	2,210 *	7.5	15.0
463 Vineyard	1	130	120	160 *	.5	1.1
RANDOLPH	**102**	**8,738**	**4,622**	**11,162 ***	**49.9**	**100.0**
053 Assemb of God	1	100	53	84	.4	.8
056 Baha'i	0	1	NR	1	-	-
081 Catholic	1	NR	NR	126	.6	1.1
097 Chr Chs&Chs Cr	2	156	NR	194 *	.9	1.7

NR–Not Reported *Total adherents estimated from known number of communicant, confirmed, full members. - Represents a percentage less than 0.1. Percentages may not total 100 due to rounding.

Table 4: Religious Congregations by County and Group: 2000

Religious Group	Number of Churches, Synagogues, Mosques, or Temples	Number of Communicant, Confirmed, or Full Members	Number of Attendees	Total Adherents: Number of Adherents	Total Adherents: % of Total Pop.	Total Adherents: % of Total Adh.
123 Ch God (Ander)	1	NR	57	57	.3	.5
127 Ch God (Cleve)	7	569	301	708 *	3.2	6.3
165 Ch of Nazarene	2	134	139	209	.9	1.9
167 Chs of Christ	11	535	588	683	3.1	6.1
175 Congr Chr Chs	1	50	30	62 *	.3	.6
176 Congr Ad Afl	1	49	NR	61 *	.3	.5
193 Episcopal	1	NR	30	93	.4	.8
360 Prim Bapt Chrch	3	NR	NR	NR	-	-
419 So Bapt Conv	37	4,797	2,277	5,965 *	26.7	53.4
443 Un C of Christ	2	73	32	91 *	.4	.8
449 Un Methodist	32	2,274	1,115	2,828 *	12.6	25.3
RUSSELL	**75**	**17,168**	**6,495**	**23,302 ***	**46.8**	**100.0**
053 Assemb of God	9	883	1,010	1,315	2.6	5.6
056 Baha'i	0	16	NR	16	-	.1
081 Catholic	3	NR	NR	941	1.9	4.0
093 Chr Ch (Disc)	1	50	0	63 *	.1	.3
123 Ch God (Ander)	1	NR	11	11	-	-
127 Ch God (Cleve)	2	246	204	309 *	.6	1.3
151 L-D Saints	1	NR	NR	380	.8	1.6
165 Ch of Nazarene	1	168	140	204	.4	.9
167 Chs of Christ	6	510	396	658	1.3	2.8
193 Episcopal	2	NR	99	165	.3	.7
223 Free Will Bapt	2	233	NR	294 *	.6	1.3
355 Presb Ch (USA)	1	35	26	44 *	.1	.2
413 S.D.A.	4	330	NR	393	.8	1.7
419 So Bapt Conv	30	12,503	3,665	15,746 *	31.6	67.6
443 Un C of Christ	1	28	12	35 *	.1	.2
449 Un Methodist	11	2,166	932	2,728 *	5.5	11.7
ST. CLAIR	**125**	**24,672**	**9,835**	**32,407 ***	**50.1**	**100.0**
017 Amer Bapt Assn	1	50	NR	62 *	.1	.2
053 Assemb of God	2	168	195	215	.3	.7
056 Baha'i	0	8	NR	8	-	-
081 Catholic	1	NR	NR	724	1.1	2.2
127 Ch God (Cleve)	8	694	500	877 *	1.4	2.7
145 Ch God Prophcy	2	72	NR	90 *	.1	.3
151 L-D Saints	1	NR	NR	289	.4	.9
165 Ch of Nazarene	1	52	24	52	.1	.2
167 Chs of Christ	8	308	346	396	.6	1.2
185 Cumber Presb	3	96	NR	114	.2	.4
193 Episcopal	1	NR	162	606	.9	1.9
223 Free Will Bapt	6	700	NR	871 *	1.3	2.7
297 Mennonite;Other	1	35	NR	44 *	.1	.1
355 Presb Ch (USA)	2	92	57	115 *	.2	.4
356 Presb Ch Amer	2	330	339	495	.8	1.5
360 Prim Bapt Chrch	2	NR	NR	NR	-	-
413 S.D.A.	1	107	NR	127	.2	.4
418 Southw Bapt Fel	1	NR	NR	NR	-	-
419 So Bapt Conv	63	19,014	7,001	23,656 *	36.5	73.0
449 Un Methodist	19	2,946	1,211	3,666 *	5.7	11.3
SHELBY	**162**	**48,634**	**27,180**	**65,373 ***	**45.6**	**100.0**
017 Amer Bapt Assn	2	130	NR	164 *	.1	.3
053 Assemb of God	13	3,146	2,845	4,340	3.0	6.6
056 Baha'i	0	13	NR	13	-	-
081 Catholic	1	NR	NR	1,462	1.0	2.2
093 Chr Ch (Disc)	2	528	296	666 *	.5	1.0
097 Chr Chs&Chs Cr	1	130	NR	164 *	.1	.3
123 Ch God (Ander)	3	NR	395	395	.3	.6
127 Ch God (Cleve)	9	1,053	687	1,337 *	.9	2.0
145 Ch God Prophcy	5	179	NR	225 *	.2	.3
151 L-D Saints	3	NR	NR	924	.6	1.4
165 Ch of Nazarene	2	312	241	485	.3	.7
167 Chs of Christ	15	1,218	1,472	1,661	1.2	2.5
185 Cumber Presb	4	726	NR	975	.7	1.5
193 Episcopal	2	NR	174	323	.2	.5
203 Evan Free Ch	1	69	125	125	.1	.2
207 E.L.C.A.	1	510	330	701	.5	1.1
216 Evan Presby Ch	1	62	NR	78 *	.1	.1
223 Free Will Bapt	3	350	NR	441 *	.3	.7
252 Hindu	1	NR	NR	NR	-	-
355 Presb Ch (USA)	2	116	60	146 *	.1	.2
356 Presb Ch Amer	3	1,246	1,152	1,757	1.2	2.7
360 Prim Bapt Chrch	1	NR	NR	NR	-	-
403 Salvation Army	1	27	33	27	-	-
419 So Bapt Conv	60	29,221	14,448	36,857 *	25.7	56.4
449 Un Methodist	25	9,228	4,671	11,640 *	8.1	17.8
463 Vineyard	1	370	251	467 *	.3	.7
SUMTER	**45**	**2,921**	**1,410**	**4,013 ***	**27.1**	**100.0**
081 Catholic	1	NR	NR	70	.5	1.7
123 Ch God (Ander)	1	NR	0	0	-	-
127 Ch God (Cleve)	1	33	32	43 *	.3	1.1
143 CG in Cr(Menn)	1	143	NR	184 *	1.2	4.6
151 L-D Saints	1	NR	NR	97	.7	2.4
167 Chs of Christ	3	160	170	210	1.4	5.2
193 Episcopal	2	NR	32	83	.6	2.1
304 NatPrimBapt USA	2	50	NR	64 *	.4	1.6
355 Presb Ch (USA)	4	156	100	201 *	1.4	5.0
356 Presb Ch Amer	6	69	70	86	.6	2.1
419 So Bapt Conv	12	1,686	671	2,172 *	14.7	54.1
449 Un Methodist	11	624	335	803 *	5.4	20.0
TALLADEGA	**165**	**31,282**	**11,887**	**40,245 ***	**50.1**	**100.0**
053 Assemb of God	7	472	429	762	.9	1.9
056 Baha'i	0	8	NR	8	-	-
081 Catholic	3	NR	NR	593	.7	1.5
089 Chr & Miss Al	1	0	NR	0	-	-
123 Ch God (Ander)	2	NR	80	80	.1	.2
127 Ch God (Cleve)	10	1,631	576	2,013 *	2.5	5.0
145 Ch God Prophcy	3	107	NR	132 *	.2	.3
151 L-D Saints	2	NR	NR	316	.4	.8
165 Ch of Nazarene	3	301	158	319	.4	.8
167 Chs of Christ	10	1,015	1,010	1,295	1.6	3.2
193 Episcopal	4	NR	207	480	.6	1.2
223 Free Will Bapt	3	350	NR	432 *	.5	1.1
263 Int Foursq Gos	1	38	44	47 *	.1	.1
355 Presb Ch (USA)	3	373	236	460 *	.6	1.1
356 Presb Ch Amer	3	145	140	168	.2	.4
360 Prim Bapt Chrch	5	NR	NR	NR	-	-
413 S.D.A.	3	238	NR	283	.4	.7
419 So Bapt Conv	69	22,011	7,081	27,188 *	33.8	67.6
443 Un C of Christ	2	58	26	72 *	.1	.2
449 Un Methodist	29	4,519	1,888	5,581 *	6.9	13.9
467 Wesleyan	2	16	12	16	-	-
TALLAPOOSA	**120**	**18,965**	**8,449**	**24,075 ***	**58.0**	**100.0**
053 Assemb of God	3	206	238	238	.6	1.0
056 Baha'i	0	4	NR	4	-	-
081 Catholic	1	NR	NR	451	1.1	1.9
093 Chr Ch (Disc)	1	26	15	32 *	.1	.1
123 Ch God (Ander)	1	NR	15	15	-	.1
127 Ch God (Cleve)	2	169	92	208 *	.5	.9
145 Ch God Prophcy	1	36	NR	44 *	.1	.2
165 Ch of Nazarene	1	77	78	155	.4	.6
167 Chs of Christ	7	587	508	747	1.8	3.1
193 Episcopal	1	NR	112	295	.7	1.2
349 Pent Holiness	1	49	69	60 *	.1	.2
355 Presb Ch (USA)	5	445	252	548 *	1.3	2.3
360 Prim Bapt Chrch	10	NR	NR	NR	-	-
419 So Bapt Conv	54	12,846	4,937	15,805 *	38.1	65.6
435 Unitarian-Univ	1	9	NR	11 *	-	-
443 Un C of Christ	2	41	21	50 *	.1	.2
449 Un Methodist	27	3,870	1,772	4,762 *	11.5	19.8
498 Indep.Charis.	1	300	250	350	.8	1.5
499 Indep.Non-Char	1	300	90	300	.7	1.2
TUSCALOOSA	**221**	**61,388**	**25,611**	**83,805 ***	**50.8**	**100.0**
017 Amer Bapt Assn	1	50	NR	61 *	-	.1
053 Assemb of God	7	1,162	1,104	2,292	1.4	2.7
056 Baha'i	1	100	NR	100	.1	.1
081 Catholic	3	NR	NR	3,550	2.2	4.2
093 Chr Ch (Disc)	2	357	123	436 *	.3	.5
123 Ch God (Ander)	4	NR	168	168	.1	.2

NR–Not Reported *Total adherents estimated from known number of communicant, confirmed, full members. - Represents a percentage less than 0.1. Percentages may not total 100 due to rounding.

Table 4: Religious Congregations by County and Group: 2000

Religious Group	Number of Churches, Synagogues, Mosques, or Temples	Number of Communicant, Confirmed, or Full Members	Number of Attendees	Total Adherents: Number of Adherents	Total Adherents: % of Total Pop.	Total Adherents: % of Total Adh.
127 Ch God (Cleve)	7	1,195	726	1,470 *	.9	1.8
145 Ch God Prophcy	2	72	NR	88 *	.1	.1
151 L-D Saints	2	NR	NR	818	.5	1.0
165 Ch of Nazarene	7	800	520	990	.6	1.2
167 Chs of Christ	7	1,898	1,894	2,472	1.5	2.9
185 Cumber Presb	2	131	NR	237	.1	.3
193 Episcopal	3	NR	780	2,059	1.2	2.5
223 Free Will Bapt	8	933	NR	1,141 *	.7	1.4
267 Muslim Est	2	NR	202	576	.3	.7
283 Luth—MO Synod	3	304	202	351	.2	.4
290 Metro Comm Ch	1	36	26	44 *	-	.1
355 Presb Ch (USA)	6	1,787	823	2,185 *	1.3	2.6
356 Presb Ch Amer	2	357	80	412	.2	.5
360 Prim Bapt Chrch	3	NR	NR	NR	-	-
403 Salvation Army	1	99	42	168	.1	.2
413 S.D.A.	2	364	NR	434	.3	.5
419 So Bapt Conv	103	41,037	13,808	50,165 *	30.4	59.9
435 Unitarian-Univ	1	85	NR	104 *	.1	.1
449 Un Methodist	35	8,789	3,435	10,744 *	6.5	12.8
467 Wesleyan	3	832	1,003	1,040	.6	1.2
496 Jewish Est	1	NR	NR	300	.2	.4
499 Indep.Non-Char	2	1,000	675	1,400	.8	1.7
WALKER	**222**	**34,077**	**15,775**	**43,639 ***	**61.7**	**100.0**
053 Assemb of God	8	645	663	815	1.2	1.9
056 Baha'i	0	9	NR	9	-	-
081 Catholic	1	NR	NR	983	1.4	2.3
089 Chr & Miss Al	1	11	NR	12	-	-
093 Chr Ch (Disc)	1	92	48	112 *	.2	.3
107 Christian Un	1	10	15	15 *	-	-
123 Ch God (Ander)	2	NR	107	107	.2	.2
127 Ch God (Cleve)	23	4,182	2,017	5,112 *	7.2	11.7
145 Ch God Prophcy	7	251	NR	308 *	.4	.7
151 L-D Saints	1	NR	NR	367	.5	.8
165 Ch of Nazarene	8	856	576	1,002	1.4	2.3
167 Chs of Christ	47	3,365	3,492	4,479	6.3	10.3
193 Episcopal	1	NR	51	126	.2	.3
223 Free Will Bapt	8	933	NR	1,139 *	1.6	2.6
304 NatPrimBapt USA	1	40	NR	49 *	.1	.1
320 "Old" MB Ascs	1	41	NR	50 *	.1	.1
355 Presb Ch (USA)	1	44	24	54 *	.1	.1
356 Presb Ch Amer	1	99	80	122	.2	.3
360 Prim Bapt Chrch	5	NR	NR	NR	-	-
418 Southw Bapt Fel	1	NR	NR	NR	-	-
419 So Bapt Conv	75	20,681	7,344	25,245 *	35.7	57.8
449 Un Methodist	27	2,818	1,358	3,443 *	4.9	7.9
496 Jewish Est	1	NR	NR	90	.1	.2
WASHINGTON	**74**	**6,697**	**3,269**	**8,807 ***	**48.7**	**100.0**
053 Assemb of God	10	411	531	694	3.8	7.9
081 Catholic	2	NR	NR	60	.3	.7
127 Ch God (Cleve)	4	199	125	256 *	1.4	2.9
157 Ch of Brethren	1	59	0	76 *	.4	.9
165 Ch of Nazarene	2	90	70	105	.6	1.2
266 Intrstat & Asc	1	53	NR	68 *	.4	.8
419 So Bapt Conv	36	4,590	1,924	5,886 *	32.5	66.8
449 Un Methodist	18	1,295	619	1,662 *	9.2	18.9
WILCOX	**45**	**3,399**	**1,619**	**4,499 ***	**34.1**	**100.0**
055 As Ref Pres Ch	2	123	NR	139	1.1	3.1
081 Catholic	2	NR	NR	51	.4	1.1
127 Ch God (Cleve)	2	105	125	149 *	1.1	3.3
151 L-D Saints	1	NR	NR	65	.5	1.4
167 Chs of Christ	4	141	150	181	1.4	4.0
283 Luth—MO Synod	3	248	124	304	2.3	6.8
304 NatPrimBapt USA	2	0	NR	0 *	-	-
355 Presb Ch (USA)	2	124	57	162 *	1.2	3.6
356 Presb Ch Amer	2	115	55	126	1.0	2.8
419 So Bapt Conv	16	2,089	823	2,729 *	20.7	60.7
449 Un Methodist	9	454	285	593 *	4.5	13.2

Religious Group	Number of Churches, Synagogues, Mosques, or Temples	Number of Communicant, Confirmed, or Full Members	Number of Attendees	Total Adherents: Number of Adherents	Total Adherents: % of Total Pop.	Total Adherents: % of Total Adh.
WINSTON	**76**	**11,579**	**5,348**	**14,831 ***	**59.7**	**100.0**
053 Assemb of God	2	314	320	417	1.7	2.8
081 Catholic	1	NR	NR	91	.4	.6
127 Ch God (Cleve)	5	610	453	748 *	3.0	5.0
145 Ch God Prophcy	1	36	NR	44 *	.2	.3
151 L-D Saints	2	NR	NR	465	1.9	3.1
165 Ch of Nazarene	1	38	30	50	.2	.3
167 Chs of Christ	10	842	934	1,098	4.4	7.4
320 "Old" MB Ascs	3	260	NR	318 *	1.3	2.1
339 Pent Ch of God	1	25	NR	35	.1	.2
360 Prim Bapt Chrch	1	NR	NR	NR	-	-
419 So Bapt Conv	40	8,456	3,129	10,344 *	41.6	69.7
449 Un Methodist	9	998	482	1,221 *	4.9	8.2

ALASKA

Religious Group	Number of Churches, Synagogues, Mosques, or Temples	Number of Communicant, Confirmed, or Full Members	Number of Attendees	Total Adherents: Number of Adherents	Total Adherents: % of Total Pop.	Total Adherents: % of Total Adh.
The State.....	856	82,963	50,988	215,223 *	34.3	100.0
ALEUTIANS EAST	**4**	**203**	**167**	**298 ***	**11.0**	**100.0**
053 Assemb of God	1	6	7	7	.3	2.3
057 Bapt Gen Conf	1	69	80	80 *	3.0	26.8
331 OCA: Ter Diocs	1	50	NR	122	4.5	40.9
419 So Bapt Conv	1	78	80	89 *	3.3	29.9
ALEUTIANS WEST	**7**	**435**	**43**	**907 ***	**16.6**	**100.0**
081 Catholic	1	NR	NR	272	5.0	30.0
151 L-D Saints	1	NR	NR	46	.8	5.1
331 OCA: Ter Diocs	4	385	NR	532	9.7	58.7
449 Un Methodist	1	50	43	57 *	1.0	6.3
ANCHORAGE	**216**	**39,587**	**24,487**	**96,871 ***	**37.2**	**100.0**
019 Amer Bapt USA	4	1,240	410	1,605 *	.6	1.7
034 Ant Orth of NA	1	298	NR	596	.2	.6
053 Assemb of God	12	1,892	2,679	4,620	1.8	4.8
057 Bapt Gen Conf	3	191	212	267 *	.1	.3
076 Buddhism	9	NR	NR	NR	-	-
081 Catholic	11	NR	NR	23,017	8.8	23.8
084 Calvary Chapel	1	NR	NR	NR	-	-
089 Chr & Miss Al	2	118	NR	302	.1	.3
093 Chr Ch (Disc)	1	197	95	255 *	.1	.3
097 Chr Chs&Chs Cr	5	1,788	NR	2,314 *	.9	2.4
105 Christian Ref	3	280	300	362 *	.1	.4
123 Ch God (Ander)	2	NR	153	153	.1	.2
127 Ch God (Cleve)	9	1,081	387	1,399 *	.5	1.4
145 Ch God Prophcy	2	61	NR	78 *	-	.1
151 L-D Saints	19	NR	NR	8,203	3.2	8.5
165 Ch of Nazarene	6	674	575	938	.4	1.0
167 Chs of Christ	6	754	823	1,070	.4	1.1
173 Comm of Christ	1	317	NR	317	.1	.3
175 Congr Chr Chs	4	495	260	641 *	.2	.7
179 Consrv Bapt	1	NR	25	25	-	-
193 Episcopal	5	NR	489	1,556	.6	1.6
201 Evan Cov Ch	4	399	809	809 *	.3	.8
203 Evan Free Ch	2	129	235	235	.1	.2
207 E.L.C.A.	9	3,133	1,289	4,678	1.8	4.8
221 Free Methodist	2	91	137	137	.1	.1
226 Friends-USA	1	41	NR	53 *	-	.1
246 Greek Orthodox	1	NR	NR	450	.2	.5
252 Hindu	1	NR	NR	NR	-	-
263 Int Foursq Gos	1	115	150	150 *	.1	.2
264 Int Chs of Crst	1	156	244	219	.1	.2
267 Muslim Est	2	NR	312	1,218	.5	1.3
283 Luth—MO Synod	5	1,419	1,010	2,107	.8	2.2
288 Mennonite USA	1	18	30	30 *	-	-
290 Metro Comm Ch	1	11	23	23 *	-	-
292 Morav Ch-AK	1	15	NR	19 *	-	-
331 OCA: Ter Diocs	3	2,650	NR	9,631	3.7	9.9
335 Orth Pres Ch	1	45	73	73	-	.1
349 Pent Holiness	1	20	32	26 *	-	-
355 Presb Ch (USA)	6	1,555	1,227	2,012 *	.8	2.1
388 Reg Bapt Gen As	2	216	215	284 *	.1	.3

NR–Not Reported *Total adherents estimated from known number of communicant, confirmed, full members. - Represents a percentage less than 0.1. Percentages may not total 100 due to rounding.

Table 4: Religious Congregations by County and Group: 2000

Religious Group	Number of Churches, Synagogues, Mosques, or Temples	Number of Communicant, Confirmed, or Full Members	Number of Attendees	Total Adherents: Number of Adherents	Total Adherents: % of Total Pop.	Total Adherents: % of Total Adh.
403 Salvation Army	4	415	205	492	.2	.5
410 Serb Orth USA	1	NR	NR	40	-	-
413 S.D.A.	8	1,190	NR	1,416	.5	1.5
416 Sikh	2	NR	NR	NR	-	-
419 So Bapt Conv	26	9,325	3,751	12,069 *	4.6	12.5
435 Unitarian-Univ	1	194	NR	251 *	.1	.3
449 Un Methodist	9	1,772	1,187	2,294 *	.9	2.4
463 Vineyard	1	400	336	518 *	.2	.5
467 Wesleyan	2	6	15	60	-	.1
469 WELS	3	434	299	659	.3	.7
496 Jewish Est	3	NR	NR	2,300	.9	2.4
498 Indep.Charis.	2	452	900	900	.3	.9
499 Indep.Non-Char	2	6,000	5,600	6,000	2.3	6.2
BETHEL	**43**	**2,773**	**290**	**7,666 ***	**47.9**	**100.0**
053 Assemb of God	2	43	56	71	.4	.9
081 Catholic	8	NR	NR	3,541	22.1	46.2
151 L-D Saints	1	NR	NR	120	.7	1.6
201 Evan Cov Ch	2	105	194	195 *	1.2	2.5
292 Morav Ch-AK	18	1,465	NR	2,135 *	13.3	27.9
331 OCA: Ter Diocs	9	1,110	NR	1,539	9.6	20.1
349 Pent Holiness	2	19	40	28 *	.2	.4
413 S.D.A.	1	31	NR	37	.2	.5
BRISTOL BAY	**5**	**129**	**15**	**270 ***	**21.5**	**100.0**
081 Catholic	1	NR	NR	66	5.2	24.4
151 L-D Saints	1	NR	NR	32	2.5	11.9
331 OCA: Ter Diocs	2	100	NR	134	10.7	49.6
419 So Bapt Conv	1	29	15	38 *	3.0	14.1
DENALI	**6**	**123**	**134**	**366 ***	**19.3**	**100.0**
053 Assemb of God	2	41	47	62	3.3	16.9
081 Catholic	1	NR	NR	130	6.9	35.5
151 L-D Saints	1	NR	NR	74	3.9	20.2
419 So Bapt Conv	2	82	87	100 *	5.3	27.3
DILLINGHAM	**15**	**1,008**	**153**	**1,702 ***	**34.6**	**100.0**
053 Assemb of God	3	125	106	171	3.5	10.0
081 Catholic	1	NR	NR	233	4.7	13.7
151 L-D Saints	1	NR	NR	47	1.0	2.8
207 E.L.C.A.	1	53	47	118	2.4	6.9
292 Morav Ch-AK	5	285	NR	408 *	8.3	24.0
331 OCA: Ter Diocs	2	325	NR	457	9.3	26.9
413 S.D.A.	2	195	NR	232	4.7	13.6
419 So Bapt Conv	0	25	0	36 *	.7	2.1
FAIRBANKS NORTH STAR	**77**	**11,267**	**7,401**	**28,433 ***	**34.3**	**100.0**
019 Amer Bapt USA	3	241	183	315 *	.4	1.1
053 Assemb of God	6	557	752	1,324	1.6	4.7
076 Buddhism	1	NR	NR	NR	-	-
081 Catholic	5	NR	NR	5,284	6.4	18.6
097 Chr Chs&Chs Cr	1	150	NR	196 *	.2	.7
123 Ch God (Ander)	1	NR	200	200	.2	.7
127 Ch God (Cleve)	2	180	100	235 *	.3	.8
145 Ch God Prophcy	1	30	NR	40 *	-	.1
151 L-D Saints	7	NR	NR	2,783	3.4	9.8
165 Ch of Nazarene	4	210	168	251	.3	.9
167 Chs of Christ	3	233	255	275	.3	1.0
173 Comm of Christ	1	75	NR	75	.1	.3
179 Consrv Bapt	2	NR	635	635	.8	2.2
193 Episcopal	2	NR	362	1,318	1.6	4.6
201 Evan Cov Ch	1	62	191	191 *	.2	.7
207 E.L.C.A.	3	898	432	1,348	1.6	4.7
223 Free Will Bapt	1	0	NR	0 *	-	-
226 Friends-USA	1	41	NR	54 *	.1	.2
267 Muslim Est	1	NR	55	163	.2	.6
283 Luth—MO Synod	1	459	321	652	.8	2.3
331 OCA: Ter Diocs	1	50	NR	2,272	2.7	8.0
339 Pent Ch of God	1	8	NR	20	-	.1
349 Pent Holiness	1	20	25	26 *	-	.1
355 Presb Ch (USA)	5	742	578	970 *	1.2	3.4
403 Salvation Army	1	60	34	222	.3	.8
413 S.D.A.	2	396	NR	471	.6	1.7
419 So Bapt Conv	11	4,085	1,242	5,336 *	6.4	18.8
435 Unitarian-Univ	1	58	NR	76 *	.1	.3
449 Un Methodist	3	729	359	952 *	1.1	3.3
469 WELS	1	83	59	109	.1	.4
496 Jewish Est	1	NR	NR	540	.7	1.9
498 Indep.Charis.	1	1,300	950	1,500	1.8	5.3
499 Indep.Non-Char	1	600	500	600	.7	2.1
HAINES	**9**	**259**	**310**	**909 ***	**38.0**	**100.0**
053 Assemb of God	2	62	94	124	5.2	13.6
081 Catholic	1	NR	NR	275	11.5	30.3
151 L-D Saints	1	NR	NR	66	2.8	7.3
165 Ch of Nazarene	1	17	0	17	.7	1.9
193 Episcopal	1	NR	24	81	3.4	8.9
263 Int Foursq Gos	1	33	43	43 *	1.8	4.7
355 Presb Ch (USA)	1	72	120	120 *	5.0	13.2
403 Salvation Army	1	66	20	172	7.2	18.9
419 So Bapt Conv	0	9	9	11 *	.5	1.2
JUNEAU	**37**	**3,531**	**2,512**	**9,227 ***	**30.0**	**100.0**
053 Assemb of God	3	362	495	507	1.7	5.5
076 Buddhism	1	NR	NR	NR	-	-
081 Catholic	2	NR	NR	2,199	7.2	23.8
084 Calvary Chapel	1	NR	NR	NR	-	-
123 Ch God (Ander)	1	NR	70	70	.2	.8
127 Ch God (Cleve)	2	125	130	166 *	.5	1.8
151 L-D Saints	4	NR	NR	1,018	3.3	11.0
165 Ch of Nazarene	1	164	110	214	.7	2.3
167 Chs of Christ	1	141	132	180	.6	2.0
193 Episcopal	2	NR	171	227	.7	2.5
207 E.L.C.A.	2	460	181	641	2.1	6.9
226 Friends-USA	1	41	NR	52 *	.2	.6
263 Int Foursq Gos	1	13	17	17 *	.1	.2
283 Luth—MO Synod	1	41	25	51	.2	.6
331 OCA: Ter Diocs	1	150	NR	974	3.2	10.6
355 Presb Ch (USA)	2	664	534	837 *	2.7	9.1
403 Salvation Army	1	129	69	203	.7	2.2
413 S.D.A.	1	130	NR	155	.5	1.7
419 So Bapt Conv	3	593	263	747 *	2.4	8.1
435 Unitarian-Univ	1	27	NR	34 *	.1	.4
449 Un Methodist	3	353	209	445 *	1.4	4.8
469 WELS	1	138	106	205	.7	2.2
496 Jewish Est	1	NR	NR	285	.9	3.1
KENAI PENINSULA	**79**	**4,969**	**3,301**	**13,725 ***	**27.6**	**100.0**
034 Ant Orth of NA	1	40	NR	80	.2	.6
053 Assemb of God	9	566	741	1,378	2.8	10.0
081 Catholic	7	NR	NR	2,168	4.4	15.8
097 Chr Chs&Chs Cr	4	475	NR	610 *	1.2	4.4
127 Ch God (Cleve)	2	171	240	267 *	.5	1.9
151 L-D Saints	5	NR	NR	1,972	4.0	14.4
165 Ch of Nazarene	5	433	387	1,234	2.5	9.0
167 Chs of Christ	7	252	295	348	.7	2.5
179 Consrv Bapt	1	NR	60	60	.1	.4
193 Episcopal	3	NR	41	74	.1	.5
207 E.L.C.A.	2	300	168	461	.9	3.4
226 Friends-USA	1	41	NR	53 *	.1	.4
263 Int Foursq Gos	1	28	37	37 *	.1	.3
283 Luth—MO Synod	3	318	225	462	.9	3.4
331 OCA: Ter Diocs	5	695	NR	2,028	4.1	14.8
339 Pent Ch of God	1	50	NR	75	.2	.5
370 Ref Baptist Chs	1	NR	NR	NR	-	-
388 Reg Bapt Gen As	1	15	45	45 *	.1	.3
403 Salvation Army	3	148	130	311	.6	2.3
413 S.D.A.	2	150	NR	178	.4	1.3
419 So Bapt Conv	5	548	400	704 *	1.4	5.1
435 Unitarian-Univ	1	33	NR	42 *	.1	.3
449 Un Methodist	7	605	413	777 *	1.6	5.7
467 Wesleyan	1	13	32	32	.1	.2
469 WELS	1	88	87	129	.3	.9
496 Jewish Est	0	NR	NR	200	.4	1.5

NR–Not Reported *Total adherents estimated from known number of communicant, confirmed, full members. - Represents a percentage less than 0.1. Percentages may not total 100 due to rounding.

Table 4: Religious Congregations by County and Group: 2000

Religious Group	Number of Churches, Synagogues, Mosques, or Temples	Number of Communicant, Confirmed, or Full Members	Number of Attendees	Total Adherents: Number of Adherents	Total Adherents: % of Total Pop.	Total Adherents: % of Total Adh.
KETCHIKAN GATEWAY	**26**	**1,532**	**1,014**	**4,844 ***	**34.4**	**100.0**
053 Assemb of God	2	165	208	340	2.4	7.0
081 Catholic	2	NR	NR	1,374	9.8	28.4
089 Chr & Miss Al	7	301	NR	588	4.2	12.1
127 Ch God (Cleve)	1	205	73	262 *	1.9	5.4
151 L-D Saints	1	NR	NR	383	2.7	7.9
165 Ch of Nazarene	1	56	73	162	1.2	3.3
167 Chs of Christ	1	70	75	105	.7	2.2
193 Episcopal	1	NR	75	201	1.4	4.1
207 E.L.C.A.	1	246	156	446	3.2	9.2
263 Int Foursq Gos	1	4	94	94 *	.7	1.9
339 Pent Ch of God	1	15	NR	35	.2	.7
355 Presb Ch (USA)	1	58	48	74 *	.5	1.5
403 Salvation Army	2	164	83	269	1.9	5.6
413 S.D.A.	1	70	NR	83	.6	1.7
419 So Bapt Conv	2	90	74	115 *	.8	2.4
449 Un Methodist	1	88	55	113 *	.8	2.3
496 Jewish Est	0	NR	NR	200	1.4	4.1
KODIAK ISLAND	**20**	**1,233**	**870**	**3,563 ***	**25.6**	**100.0**
019 Amer Bapt USA	2	130	123	175 *	1.3	4.9
053 Assemb of God	2	190	262	262	1.9	7.4
081 Catholic	1	NR	NR	1,140	8.2	32.0
089 Chr & Miss Al	1	119	NR	253	1.8	7.1
151 L-D Saints	1	NR	NR	252	1.8	7.1
165 Ch of Nazarene	1	60	55	60	.4	1.7
167 Chs of Christ	1	35	40	45	.3	1.3
193 Episcopal	1	NR	48	121	.9	3.4
207 E.L.C.A.	1	278	84	383	2.8	10.7
331 OCA: Ter Diocs	4	200	NR	573	4.1	16.1
388 Reg Bapt Gen As	1	59	155	80 *	.6	2.2
403 Salvation Army	1	49	21	74	.5	2.1
413 S.D.A.	1	69	NR	82	.6	2.3
419 So Bapt Conv	1	30	65	40 *	.3	1.1
469 WELS	1	14	17	23	.2	.6
LAKE AND PENINSULA	**6**	**300**	**NR**	**349**	**19.1**	**100.0**
331 OCA: Ter Diocs	6	300	NR	349	19.1	100.0
MATANUSKA-SUSITNA	**65**	**6,471**	**4,333**	**16,453 ***	**27.7**	**100.0**
019 Amer Bapt USA	2	102	57	134 *	.2	.8
034 Ant Orth of NA	1	45	NR	90	.2	.5
053 Assemb of God	4	318	437	697	1.2	4.2
081 Catholic	6	NR	NR	3,767	6.4	22.9
089 Chr & Miss Al	3	77	NR	212	.4	1.3
097 Chr Chs&Chs Cr	2	269	NR	353 *	.6	2.1
123 Ch God (Ander)	2	NR	85	85	.1	.5
127 Ch God (Cleve)	2	194	144	254 *	.4	1.5
145 Ch God Prophcy	1	30	NR	40 *	.1	.2
151 L-D Saints	6	NR	NR	2,692	4.5	16.4
165 Ch of Nazarene	2	305	257	461	.8	2.8
167 Chs of Christ	1	97	125	149	.3	.9
193 Episcopal	3	NR	143	376	.6	2.3
201 Evan Cov Ch	1	82	145	145 *	.2	.9
207 E.L.C.A.	2	490	242	709	1.2	4.3
226 Friends-USA	1	41	NR	54 *	.1	.3
262 Int Cou Comm Ch	1	13	NR	17 *	-	.1
283 Luth—MO Synod	2	598	242	856	1.4	5.2
335 Orth Pres Ch	1	26	55	55	.1	.3
339 Pent Ch of God	1	22	NR	38	.1	.2
355 Presb Ch (USA)	2	367	278	482 *	.8	2.9
388 Reg Bapt Gen As	3	216	312	282 *	.5	1.7
403 Salvation Army	1	68	53	134	.2	.8
413 S.D.A.	3	479	NR	570	1.0	3.5
419 So Bapt Conv	8	1,825	730	2,394 *	4.0	14.6
449 Un Methodist	2	201	166	264 *	.4	1.6
469 WELS	1	106	62	143	.2	.9
499 Indep.Non-Char	1	500	800	1,000	1.7	6.1
NOME	**32**	**1,786**	**1,022**	**4,467 ***	**48.6**	**100.0**
053 Assemb of God	5	206	156	302	3.3	6.8
081 Catholic	6	NR	NR	1,422	15.5	31.8
151 L-D Saints	1	NR	NR	69	.8	1.5
165 Ch of Nazarene	1	20	16	64	.7	1.4
201 Evan Cov Ch	7	277	306	437 *	4.8	9.8
207 E.L.C.A.	5	808	360	1,539	16.7	34.5
355 Presb Ch (USA)	3	206	154	289 *	3.1	6.5
413 S.D.A.	3	150	NR	178	1.9	4.0
419 So Bapt Conv	0	43	0	60 *	.7	1.3
449 Un Methodist	1	76	30	107 *	1.2	2.4
NORTH SLOPE	**14**	**719**	**734**	**1,704 ***	**23.1**	**100.0**
053 Assemb of God	4	139	193	283	3.8	16.6
081 Catholic	1	NR	NR	235	3.2	13.8
105 Christian Ref	1	18	20	25 *	.3	1.5
151 L-D Saints	1	NR	NR	96	1.3	5.6
193 Episcopal	2	NR	60	270	3.7	15.8
355 Presb Ch (USA)	5	562	461	795 *	10.8	46.7
NORTHWEST ARCTIC	**16**	**1,129**	**221**	**2,821 ***	**39.1**	**100.0**
053 Assemb of God	1	15	23	36	.5	1.3
081 Catholic	1	NR	NR	700	9.7	24.8
127 Ch God (Cleve)	1	67	44	99 *	1.4	3.5
151 L-D Saints	1	NR	NR	43	.6	1.5
167 Chs of Christ	1	6	6	8	.1	.3
193 Episcopal	2	NR	63	390	5.4	13.8
226 Friends-USA	8	1,000	NR	1,484 *	20.6	52.6
419 So Bapt Conv	1	41	85	61 *	.8	2.2
PRINCE OF WALES-OUTER KETCHIKAN	**22**	**485**	**368**	**1,338 ***	**21.8**	**100.0**
053 Assemb of God	2	51	80	93	1.5	7.0
081 Catholic	7	NR	NR	577	9.4	43.1
089 Chr & Miss Al	2	43	NR	78	1.3	5.8
127 Ch God (Cleve)	2	117	56	151 *	2.5	11.3
151 L-D Saints	1	NR	NR	94	1.5	7.0
175 Congr Chr Chs	1	25	20	32 *	.5	2.4
355 Presb Ch (USA)	3	113	130	154 *	2.5	11.5
403 Salvation Army	2	43	57	45	.7	3.4
413 S.D.A.	1	55	NR	65	1.1	4.9
419 So Bapt Conv	1	38	25	49 *	.8	3.7
SITKA	**17**	**1,532**	**907**	**3,428 ***	**38.8**	**100.0**
053 Assemb of God	1	109	145	250	2.8	7.3
081 Catholic	1	NR	NR	550	6.2	16.0
151 L-D Saints	1	NR	NR	180	2.0	5.3
165 Ch of Nazarene	1	61	80	122	1.4	3.6
167 Chs of Christ	1	65	55	78	.9	2.3
179 Consrv Bapt	1	NR	200	200	2.3	5.8
193 Episcopal	1	NR	84	185	2.1	5.4
207 E.L.C.A.	1	294	70	402	4.6	11.7
331 OCA: Ter Diocs	2	200	NR	437	4.9	12.7
355 Presb Ch (USA)	1	123	101	155 *	1.8	4.5
403 Salvation Army	1	60	42	97	1.1	2.8
413 S.D.A.	1	94	NR	112	1.3	3.3
419 So Bapt Conv	1	365	50	460 *	5.2	13.4
435 Unitarian-Univ	1	43	NR	54 *	.6	1.6
449 Un Methodist	1	98	70	124 *	1.4	3.6
469 WELS	1	20	10	22	.2	.6
SKAGWAY-HOONAH-ANGOON	**16**	**307**	**247**	**861 ***	**25.1**	**100.0**
053 Assemb of God	2	52	63	107	3.1	12.4
081 Catholic	7	NR	NR	166	4.8	19.3
151 L-D Saints	2	NR	NR	81	2.4	9.4
355 Presb Ch (USA)	3	136	144	183 *	5.3	21.3
403 Salvation Army	2	119	40	324	9.4	37.6
SOUTHEAST FAIRBANKS	**14**	**531**	**355**	**1,325 ***	**21.5**	**100.0**
053 Assemb of God	3	133	141	188	3.0	14.2
081 Catholic	2	NR	NR	275	4.5	20.8
151 L-D Saints	2	NR	NR	188	3.0	14.2
193 Episcopal	1	NR	39	93	1.5	7.0
263 Int Foursq Gos	1	9	11	12 *	.2	.9
339 Pent Ch of God	1	26	NR	100	1.6	7.5

NR–Not Reported *Total adherents estimated from known number of communicant, confirmed, full members. - Represents a percentage less than 0.1. Percentages may not total 100 due to rounding.

Table 4: Religious Congregations by County and Group: 2000

Religious Group	Number of Churches, Synagogues, Mosques, or Temples	Number of Communicant, Confirmed, or Full Members	Number of Attendees	Total Adherents: Number of Adherents	Total Adherents: % of Total Pop.	Total Adherents: % of Total Adh.
355 Presb Ch (USA)	1	33	30	44 *	.7	3.3
413 S.D.A.	2	91	NR	109	1.8	8.2
419 So Bapt Conv	1	239	134	316 *	5.1	23.8
VALDEZ-CORDOVA	**22**	**659**	**511**	**2,297 ***	**22.5**	**100.0**
019 Amer Bapt USA	1	89	85	114 *	1.1	5.0
053 Assemb of God	3	107	101	148	1.5	6.4
081 Catholic	3	NR	NR	665	6.5	29.0
151 L-D Saints	3	NR	NR	347	3.4	15.1
165 Ch of Nazarene	2	34	65	147	1.4	6.4
167 Chs of Christ	1	10	10	15	.1	.7
193 Episcopal	1	NR	27	41	.4	1.8
207 E.L.C.A.	1	117	72	192	1.9	8.4
331 OCA: Ter Diocs	2	100	NR	373	3.7	16.2
413 S.D.A.	2	52	NR	62	.6	2.7
419 So Bapt Conv	3	150	151	193 *	1.9	8.4
WADE HAMPTON	**23**	**710**	**126**	**5,409 ***	**77.0**	**100.0**
053 Assemb of God	4	185	53	244	3.5	4.5
081 Catholic	12	NR	NR	4,373	62.2	80.8
201 Evan Cov Ch	3	135	73	213 *	3.0	3.9
331 OCA: Ter Diocs	4	390	NR	579	8.2	10.7
WRANGELL-PETERSBURG	**24**	**1,071**	**709**	**2,568 ***	**38.4**	**100.0**
053 Assemb of God	3	148	177	220	3.3	8.6
081 Catholic	3	NR	NR	577	8.6	22.5
123 Ch God (Ander)	1	NR	30	30	.4	1.2
151 L-D Saints	2	NR	NR	178	2.7	6.9
193 Episcopal	2	NR	29	88	1.3	3.4
207 E.L.C.A.	2	272	180	426	6.4	16.6
226 Friends-USA	1	41	NR	53 *	.8	2.1
263 Int Foursq Gos	1	11	15	15 *	.2	.6
355 Presb Ch (USA)	3	135	109	173 *	2.6	6.7
403 Salvation Army	3	278	107	576	8.6	22.4
413 S.D.A.	2	76	NR	91	1.4	3.5
419 So Bapt Conv	1	110	62	141 *	2.1	5.5
YAKUTAT	**4**	**51**	**63**	**230 ***	**28.5**	**100.0**
053 Assemb of God	1	33	45	70	8.7	30.4
081 Catholic	1	NR	NR	82	10.1	35.7
151 L-D Saints	1	NR	NR	55	6.8	23.9
355 Presb Ch (USA)	1	18	18	23 *	2.8	10.0
YUKON-KOYUKUK	**37**	**163**	**695**	**3,192 ***	**48.7**	**100.0**
053 Assemb of God	4	80	57	134	2.0	4.2
081 Catholic	11	NR	NR	1,271	19.4	39.8
167 Chs of Christ	1	5	8	10	.2	.3
193 Episcopal	17	NR	550	1,672	25.5	52.4
349 Pent Holiness	4	78	80	105 *	1.6	3.3
ARIZONA						
The State.....	3,307	471,913	337,369	2,048,023 *	39.9	100.0
APACHE	**115**	**3,217**	**2,601**	**34,620 ***	**49.9**	**100.0**
017 Amer Bapt Assn	2	90	NR	128 *	.2	.4
019 Amer Bapt USA	1	17	25	25 *	-	.1
053 Assemb of God	10	666	721	980	1.4	2.8
056 Baha'i	2	215	NR	215	.3	.6
081 Catholic	18	NR	NR	19,965	28.8	57.7
097 Chr Chs&Chs Cr	1	12	NR	17 *	-	-
105 Christian Ref	3	265	216	376 *	.5	1.1
123 Ch God (Ander)	1	NR	65	65	.1	.2
127 Ch God (Cleve)	5	69	94	111 *	.2	.3
151 L-D Saints	24	NR	NR	8,947	12.9	25.8
165 Ch of Nazarene	5	146	95	182	.3	.5
167 Chs of Christ	4	137	118	198	.3	.6
171 Ch God-Gen Con	1	13	80	80 *	.1	.2
193 Episcopal	6	NR	153	1,053	1.5	3.0
207 E.L.C.A.	1	94	50	159	.2	.5

Religious Group	Number of Churches, Synagogues, Mosques, or Temples	Number of Communicant, Confirmed, or Full Members	Number of Attendees	Total Adherents: Number of Adherents	Total Adherents: % of Total Pop.	Total Adherents: % of Total Adh.
226 Friends-USA	2	88	NR	125 *	.2	.4
263 Int Foursq Gos	1	30	50	50 *	.1	.1
288 Mennonite USA	2	17	13	24 *	-	.1
297 Mennonite;Other	1	4	NR	6 *	-	-
339 Pent Ch of God	1	50	NR	70	.1	.2
349 Pent Holiness	1	31	33	44 *	.1	.1
355 Presb Ch (USA)	5	348	245	496 *	.7	1.4
413 S.D.A.	2	90	NR	107	.2	.3
419 So Bapt Conv	14	773	598	1,098 *	1.6	3.2
449 Un Methodist	1	36	45	51 *	.1	.1
469 WELS	1	26	0	48	.1	.1
COCHISE	**149**	**10,944**	**7,448**	**48,007 ***	**40.8**	**100.0**
019 Amer Bapt USA	1	30	25	38 *	-	.1
053 Assemb of God	17	838	984	2,185	1.9	4.6
056 Baha'i	1	132	NR	132	.1	.3
081 Catholic	17	NR	NR	25,837	21.9	53.8
084 Calvary Chapel	1	NR	NR	NR	-	-
097 Chr Chs&Chs Cr	2	330	NR	413 *	.4	.9
123 Ch God (Ander)	1	NR	45	45	-	.1
127 Ch God (Cleve)	3	131	39	164 *	.1	.3
143 CG in Cr(Menn)	1	56	NR	70 *	.1	.1
151 L-D Saints	16	NR	NR	5,232	4.4	10.9
165 Ch of Nazarene	5	436	353	534	.5	1.1
167 Chs of Christ	9	446	506	628	.5	1.3
173 Comm of Christ	1	42	NR	42	-	.1
175 Congr Chr Chs	1	55	65	69 *	.1	.1
179 Consrv Bapt	5	NR	523	523	.4	1.1
193 Episcopal	6	NR	195	358	.3	.7
203 Evan Free Ch	2	117	255	255	.2	.5
207 E.L.C.A.	2	502	328	617	.5	1.3
223 Free Will Bapt	1	34	NR	43 *	-	.1
263 Int Foursq Gos	2	83	151	151 *	.1	.3
283 Luth—MO Synod	3	233	191	286	.2	.6
339 Pent Ch of God	1	20	NR	31	-	.1
355 Presb Ch (USA)	4	564	357	705 *	.6	1.5
356 Presb Ch Amer	1	0	0	0	-	-
403 Salvation Army	1	50	23	93	.1	.2
410 Serb Orth USA	1	NR	NR	150	.1	.3
413 S.D.A.	6	279	NR	332	.3	.7
419 So Bapt Conv	19	4,792	1,957	5,999 *	5.1	12.5
435 Unitarian-Univ	1	60	NR	75 *	.1	.2
443 Un C of Christ	2	341	212	427 *	.4	.9
449 Un Methodist	10	1,174	749	1,469 *	1.2	3.1
469 WELS	4	199	140	229	.2	.5
496 Jewish Est	1	NR	NR	350	.3	.7
498 Indep.Charis.	1	0	350	525	.4	1.1
COCONINO	**141**	**11,362**	**7,771**	**35,932 ***	**30.9**	**100.0**
019 Amer Bapt USA	1	86	78	110 *	.1	.3
053 Assemb of God	12	720	812	1,405	1.2	3.9
056 Baha'i	4	300	NR	300	.3	.8
076 Buddhism	1	NR	NR	NR	-	-
081 Catholic	9	NR	NR	8,117	7.0	22.6
084 Calvary Chapel	2	NR	NR	NR	-	-
089 Chr & Miss Al	1	10	NR	30	-	.1
097 Chr Chs&Chs Cr	2	1,030	NR	1,320 *	1.1	3.7
105 Christian Ref	1	69	85	88 *	.1	.2
127 Ch God (Cleve)	1	85	71	109 *	.1	.3
151 L-D Saints	31	NR	NR	10,985	9.4	30.6
165 Ch of Nazarene	10	655	461	720	.6	2.0
167 Chs of Christ	6	199	208	252	.2	.7
173 Comm of Christ	1	38	NR	38	-	.1
179 Consrv Bapt	10	NR	1,026	1,026	.9	2.9
193 Episcopal	3	NR	267	429	.4	1.2
203 Evan Free Ch	1	55	180	180	.2	.5
207 E.L.C.A.	3	870	584	1,123	1.0	3.1
226 Friends-USA	1	30	NR	38 *	-	.1
263 Int Foursq Gos	3	291	379	379 *	.3	1.1
267 Muslim Est	1	NR	101	288	.2	.8
283 Luth—MO Synod	2	297	195	154	.1	.4
290 Metro Comm Ch	1	8	7	7 *	-	-
339 Pent Ch of God	4	162	NR	232	.2	.6

NR–Not Reported *Total adherents estimated from known number of communicant, confirmed, full members. - Represents a percentage less than 0.1. Percentages may not total 100 due to rounding.

Table 4: Religious Congregations by County and Group: 2000

Religious Group	Number of Churches, Synagogues, Mosques, or Temples	Number of Communicant, Confirmed, or Full Members	Number of Attendees	Total Adherents		
				Number of Adherents	% of Total Pop.	% of Total Adh.
355 Presb Ch (USA)	3	247	129	316 *	.3	.9
403 Salvation Army	1	111	56	165	.1	.5
413 S.D.A.	2	191	NR	227	.2	.6
416 Sikh	1	NR	NR	NR	-	-
419 So Bapt Conv	10	1,903	794	2,440 *	2.1	6.8
435 Unitarian-Univ	1	128	NR	164 *	.1	.5
443 Un C of Christ	2	700	339	897 *	.8	2.5
449 Un Methodist	5	1,043	611	1,337 *	1.1	3.7
463 Vineyard	1	130	120	167 *	.1	.5
467 Wesleyan	1	115	186	330	.3	.9
469 WELS	1	189	132	259	.2	.7
496 Jewish Est	1	NR	NR	500	.4	1.4
499 Indep.Non-Char	1	1,700	950	1,800	1.5	5.0
GILA	**74**	**7,189**	**4,402**	**22,587 ***	**44.0**	**100.0**
019 Amer Bapt USA	1	30	17	37 *	.1	.2
053 Assemb of God	7	645	893	1,322	2.6	5.9
056 Baha'i	0	35	NR	35	.1	.2
081 Catholic	7	NR	NR	7,525	14.7	33.3
093 Chr Ch (Disc)	1	81	76	100 *	.2	.4
097 Chr Chs&Chs Cr	2	198	NR	244 *	.5	1.1
127 Ch God (Cleve)	1	60	39	74 *	.1	.3
151 L-D Saints	12	NR	NR	4,197	8.2	18.6
165 Ch of Nazarene	2	281	177	281	.5	1.2
167 Chs of Christ	5	220	245	273	.5	1.2
179 Consrv Bapt	4	NR	287	287	.6	1.3
193 Episcopal	2	NR	81	258	.5	1.1
203 Evan Free Ch	1	138	350	350	.7	1.5
207 E.L.C.A.	2	337	262	478	.9	2.1
263 Int Foursq Gos	1	49	64	64 *	.1	.3
283 Luth—MO Synod	1	131	88	147	.3	.7
339 Pent Ch of God	1	65	NR	130	.3	.6
355 Presb Ch (USA)	3	240	182	297 *	.6	1.3
403 Salvation Army	1	80	56	155	.3	.7
413 S.D.A.	2	149	NR	177	.3	.8
419 So Bapt Conv	11	3,369	781	4,166 *	8.1	18.4
449 Un Methodist	3	544	343	673 *	1.3	3.0
469 WELS	4	537	461	1,317	2.6	5.8
GRAHAM	**54**	**2,088**	**1,190**	**22,465 ***	**67.1**	**100.0**
053 Assemb of God	3	149	183	453	1.4	2.0
056 Baha'i	0	13	NR	13	-	.1
059 Bapt Miss Assn	1	32	20	42 *	.1	.2
081 Catholic	7	NR	NR	10,665	31.8	47.5
097 Chr Chs&Chs Cr	1	40	NR	52 *	.2	.2
127 Ch God (Cleve)	1	53	21	69 *	.2	.3
151 L-D Saints	25	NR	NR	8,614	25.7	38.3
165 Ch of Nazarene	1	28	34	34	.1	.2
167 Chs of Christ	1	100	95	150	.4	.7
179 Consrv Bapt	1	NR	70	70	.2	.3
193 Episcopal	1	NR	25	47	.1	.2
207 E.L.C.A.	2	183	136	253	.8	1.1
355 Presb Ch (USA)	1	69	64	90 *	.3	.4
413 S.D.A.	1	101	NR	120	.4	.5
419 So Bapt Conv	4	665	181	864 *	2.6	3.8
449 Un Methodist	2	397	170	516 *	1.5	2.3
469 WELS	2	258	191	413	1.2	1.8
GREENLEE	**19**	**1,181**	**503**	**7,844 ***	**91.8**	**100.0**
019 Amer Bapt USA	1	227	50	298 *	3.5	3.8
053 Assemb of God	1	75	81	110	1.3	1.4
056 Baha'i	0	12	NR	12	.1	.2
081 Catholic	3	NR	NR	4,956	58.0	63.2
151 L-D Saints	3	NR	NR	1,179	13.8	15.0
165 Ch of Nazarene	1	23	0	48	.6	.6
167 Chs of Christ	2	117	130	158	1.8	2.0
179 Consrv Bapt	2	NR	95	95	1.1	1.2
193 Episcopal	1	NR	13	31	.4	.4
355 Presb Ch (USA)	1	59	50	78 *	.9	1.0
419 So Bapt Conv	3	649	69	853 *	10.0	10.9
469 WELS	1	19	15	26	.3	.3

Religious Group	Number of Churches, Synagogues, Mosques, or Temples	Number of Communicant, Confirmed, or Full Members	Number of Attendees	Total Adherents		
				Number of Adherents	% of Total Pop.	% of Total Adh.
LA PAZ	**27**	**1,597**	**689**	**4,829 ***	**24.5**	**100.0**
019 Amer Bapt USA	1	40	40	47 *	.2	1.0
053 Assemb of God	4	174	166	231	1.2	4.8
056 Baha'i	0	16	NR	16	.1	.3
081 Catholic	4	NR	NR	1,498	7.6	31.0
089 Chr & Miss Al	1	65	NR	215	1.1	4.5
097 Chr Chs&Chs Cr	1	170	NR	202 *	1.0	4.2
151 L-D Saints	3	NR	NR	822	4.2	17.0
165 Ch of Nazarene	2	70	37	98	.5	2.0
167 Chs of Christ	1	35	20	40	.2	.8
179 Consrv Bapt	3	NR	196	196	1.0	4.1
283 Luth—MO Synod	1	105	97	149	.8	3.1
339 Pent Ch of God	2	100	NR	140	.7	2.9
413 S.D.A.	1	57	NR	68	.3	1.4
419 So Bapt Conv	1	634	83	752 *	3.8	15.6
449 Un Methodist	1	131	50	155 *	.8	3.2
496 Jewish Est	1	NR	NR	200	1.0	4.1
MARICOPA	**1,552**	**297,002**	**209,635**	**1,220,609 ***	**39.7**	**100.0**
017 Amer Bapt Assn	11	470	NR	600 *	-	-
019 Amer Bapt USA	28	8,451	4,280	10,760 *	.4	.9
034 Ant Orth of NA	2	619	NR	1,238	-	.1
039 Ap Chr Ch(Naz)	2	218	370	370 *	-	-
040 Ap Chr Ch-Amer	1	160	270	270 *	-	-
050 Armen Ap Etchm	1	0	NR	1,232	-	.1
053 Assemb of God	88	29,483	21,647	57,633	1.9	4.7
056 Baha'i	11	3,289	NR	3,289	.1	.3
057 Bapt Gen Conf	9	1,503	2,523	2,652 *	.1	.2
059 Bapt Miss Assn	2	70	37	90 *	-	-
071 Brethren (Ash)	1	44	85	56 *	-	-
076 Buddhism	14	NR	NR	NR	-	-
081 Catholic	91	NR	NR	530,135	17.3	43.4
084 Calvary Chapel	11	NR	NR	NR	-	-
089 Chr & Miss Al	8	444	NR	694	-	.1
093 Chr Ch (Disc)	9	2,850	1,344	3,629 *	.1	.3
097 Chr Chs&Chs Cr	35	17,418	NR	22,177 *	.7	1.8
105 Christian Ref	6	837	655	1,066 *	-	.1
121 Ch God (Abr)	1	86	77	109 *	-	-
123 Ch God (Ander)	11	NR	3,857	3,857	.1	.3
127 Ch God (Cleve)	27	3,327	2,569	4,468 *	.1	.4
143 CG in Cr(Menn)	1	80	NR	102 *	-	-
145 Ch God Prophcy	10	351	NR	450 *	-	-
151 L-D Saints	375	NR	NR	153,980	5.0	12.6
157 Ch of Brethren	3	247	168	314 *	-	-
165 Ch of Nazarene	38	7,355	6,097	11,321	.4	.9
167 Chs of Christ	45	6,144	5,904	7,704	.3	.6
173 Comm of Christ	4	1,488	NR	1,488	-	.1
175 Congr Chr Chs	2	457	420	582 *	-	-
179 Consrv Bapt	37	NR	8,664	8,664	.3	.7
183 Cons Menn Conf	4	151	184	220	-	-
186 Coptic Orth Ch	1	NR	NR	NR	-	-
193 Episcopal	26	NR	5,775	16,844	.5	1.4
201 Evan Cov Ch	4	507	771	777 *	-	.1
203 Evan Free Ch	14	1,133	2,710	2,710	.1	.2
207 E.L.C.A.	57	37,238	22,584	50,995	1.7	4.2
216 Evan Presby Ch	4	398	NR	507 *	-	-
220 Free Lutheran	1	52	47	52	-	-
221 Free Methodist	10	564	895	975	-	.1
223 Free Will Bapt	7	238	NR	303 *	-	-
226 Friends-USA	3	212	NR	270 *	-	-
237 Menn Br US Conf	3	57	NR	73 *	-	-
246 Greek Orthodox	4	NR	NR	3,417	.1	.3
249 Assyr Apost Ch	1	NR	NR	1,568	.1	.1
252 Hindu	6	NR	NR	NR	-	-
262 Int Cou Comm Ch	5	1,335	NR	1,700 *	.1	.1
263 Int Foursq Gos	21	1,488	3,020	3,020 *	.1	.2
264 Int Chs of Crst	1	950	1,776	1,455	-	.1
265 Int Pent C Chr	1	0	0	15	-	-
267 Muslim Est	9	NR	2,765	10,028	.3	.8
268 Jain	1	NR	NR	NR	-	-
283 Luth—MO Synod	30	12,922	8,668	16,880	.5	1.4
288 Mennonite USA	7	827	656	1,082 *	-	.1
290 Metro Comm Ch	1	98	0	125 *	-	-

NR–Not Reported *Total adherents estimated from known number of communicant, confirmed, full members. - Represents a percentage less than 0.1. Percentages may not total 100 due to rounding.

Table 4: Religious Congregations by County and Group: 2000

Religious Group	Number of Churches, Synagogues, Mosques, or Temples	Number of Communicant, Confirmed, or Full Members	Number of Attendees	Total Adherents		
				Number of Adherents	% of Total Pop.	% of Total Adh.
291 Missionary Ch	4	1,529	1,827	1,827	.1	.1
293 Morav Ch-North	1	61	NR	100	-	-
297 Mennonite;Other	1	34	NR	43 *	-	-
306 NT IndBapt&Rltd	1	0	NR	0 *	-	-
331 OCA: Ter Diocs	2	71	NR	735	-	.1
335 Orth Pres Ch	1	83	80	108	-	-
339 Pent Ch of God	22	771	NR	1,375	-	.1
349 Pent Holiness	7	383	348	488 *	-	-
355 Presb Ch (USA)	41	14,388	9,438	18,328 *	.6	1.5
356 Presb Ch Amer	6	276	327	348	-	-
360 Prim Bapt Chrch	4	NR	NR	NR	-	-
370 Ref Baptist Chs	4	NR	NR	NR	-	-
371 Ref Ch in Am	6	960	1,166	1,698	.1	.1
388 Reg Bapt Gen As	5	484	538	616 *	-	.1
397 OCA: Roman Dioc	2	NR	NR	850	-	.1
401 Rus Orth Abroad	1	NR	NR	NR	-	-
403 Salvation Army	14	1,863	1,041	7,305	.2	.6
410 Serb Orth USA	1	NR	NR	600	-	-
411 Serb Orth: Grac	1	NR	NR	NR	-	-
413 S.D.A.	21	5,036	NR	5,993	.2	.5
416 Sikh	4	NR	NR	NR	-	-
419 So Bapt Conv	126	60,058	19,138	76,468 *	2.5	6.3
423 Syrian Orth Ch	1	NR	NR	60	-	-
425 Tao	1	NR	NR	NR	-	-
431 Ukrainian Orth	1	NR	NR	66	-	-
435 Unitarian-Univ	4	880	NR	1,120 *	-	.1
443 Un C of Christ	16	6,016	3,022	7,660 *	.2	.6
449 Un Methodist	50	25,771	15,650	32,811 *	1.1	2.7
455 Un Ref Chs N.A.	1	85	NR	120	-	-
463 Vineyard	9	3,505	2,979	4,464 *	.1	.4
467 Wesleyan	7	647	845	1,078	-	.1
469 WELS	16	4,204	2,883	5,592	.2	.5
490 Zoroastrian	2	NR	NR	NR	-	-
496 Jewish Est	20	NR	NR	60,000	2.0	4.9
498 Indep.Charis.	16	12,465	17,805	25,080	.8	2.1
499 Indep.Non-Char	28	13,871	23,730	23,730	.8	1.9
MOHAVE	**92**	**10,856**	**7,637**	**43,405 ***	**28.0**	**100.0**
053 Assemb of God	9	810	993	1,560	1.0	3.6
056 Baha'i	0	56	NR	56	-	.1
057 Bapt Gen Conf	1	328	305	400 *	.3	.9
081 Catholic	4	NR	NR	22,239	14.3	51.2
084 Calvary Chapel	3	NR	NR	NR	-	-
089 Chr & Miss Al	2	86	NR	197	.1	.5
097 Chr Chs&Chs Cr	4	475	NR	579 *	.4	1.3
127 Ch God (Cleve)	1	44	53	54 *	-	.1
151 L-D Saints	12	NR	NR	5,011	3.2	11.5
165 Ch of Nazarene	3	258	199	281	.2	.6
167 Chs of Christ	6	326	377	409	.3	.9
179 Consrv Bapt	3	NR	435	435	.3	1.0
193 Episcopal	3	NR	210	463	.3	1.1
207 E.L.C.A.	3	1,555	1,034	1,970	1.3	4.5
221 Free Methodist	1	73	98	98	.1	.2
263 Int Foursq Gos	5	227	449	449 *	.3	1.0
267 Muslim Est	1	NR	228	841	.5	1.9
283 Luth—MO Synod	3	381	245	416	.3	1.0
331 OCA: Ter Diocs	1	18	NR	46	-	.1
339 Pent Ch of God	2	50	NR	116	.1	.3
355 Presb Ch (USA)	2	502	303	612 *	.4	1.4
388 Reg Bapt Gen As	1	47	60	60 *	-	.1
403 Salvation Army	3	105	87	180	.1	.4
413 S.D.A.	1	95	NR	113	.1	.3
419 So Bapt Conv	13	4,056	1,678	4,946 *	3.2	11.4
449 Un Methodist	3	1,244	795	1,517 *	1.0	3.5
469 WELS	1	120	88	157	.1	.4
496 Jewish Est	1	NR	NR	200	.1	.5
NAVAJO	**168**	**7,503**	**5,010**	**38,249 ***	**39.2**	**100.0**
019 Amer Bapt USA	4	76	81	104 *	.1	.3
053 Assemb of God	13	843	883	1,338	1.4	3.5
056 Baha'i	3	224	NR	224	.2	.6
081 Catholic	12	NR	NR	7,651	7.8	20.0
084 Calvary Chapel	2	NR	NR	NR	-	-

Religious Group	Number of Churches, Synagogues, Mosques, or Temples	Number of Communicant, Confirmed, or Full Members	Number of Attendees	Total Adherents		
				Number of Adherents	% of Total Pop.	% of Total Adh.
089 Chr & Miss Al	3	8	NR	48	-	.1
097 Chr Chs&Chs Cr	2	103	NR	141 *	.1	.4
127 Ch God (Cleve)	1	46	12	63 *	.1	.2
151 L-D Saints	53	NR	NR	19,481	20.0	50.9
165 Ch of Nazarene	8	481	291	534	.5	1.4
167 Chs of Christ	9	248	273	320	.3	.8
173 Comm of Christ	1	31	NR	31	-	.1
179 Consrv Bapt	3	NR	325	325	.3	.8
193 Episcopal	3	NR	145	288	.3	.8
207 E.L.C.A.	1	33	31	47	-	.1
263 Int Foursq Gos	1	18	29	29 *	-	.1
283 Luth—MO Synod	2	128	140	195	.2	.5
297 Mennonite;Other	3	25	NR	35 *	-	.1
339 Pent Ch of God	5	219	NR	325	.3	.8
355 Presb Ch (USA)	4	357	214	490 *	.5	1.3
388 Reg Bapt Gen As	3	106	117	145 *	.1	.4
413 S.D.A.	1	357	NR	425	.4	1.1
419 So Bapt Conv	15	2,555	1,423	3,508 *	3.6	9.2
449 Un Methodist	4	525	347	722 *	.7	1.9
467 Wesleyan	4	0	0	0	-	-
469 WELS	8	1,120	699	1,780	1.8	4.7
PIMA	**448**	**78,296**	**60,558**	**378,651 ***	**44.9**	**100.0**
017 Amer Bapt Assn	2	70	NR	87 *	-	-
019 Amer Bapt USA	3	458	375	567 *	.1	.1
034 Ant Orth of NA	1	169	NR	338	-	.1
040 Ap Chr Ch-Amer	1	22	39	39 *	-	-
053 Assemb of God	28	3,941	4,677	7,319	.9	1.9
056 Baha'i	5	699	NR	699	.1	.2
057 Bapt Gen Conf	1	181	400	400 *	-	.1
059 Bapt Miss Assn	1	20	38	38 *	-	-
071 Brethren (Ash)	3	224	252	277 *	-	.1
076 Buddhism	8	NR	NR	NR	-	-
081 Catholic	45	NR	NR	225,425	26.7	59.5
084 Calvary Chapel	2	NR	NR	NR	-	-
089 Chr & Miss Al	4	231	NR	435	.1	.1
093 Chr Ch (Disc)	8	1,249	622	1,546 *	.2	.4
097 Chr Chs&Chs Cr	10	2,664	NR	3,298 *	.4	.9
105 Christian Ref	2	162	0	201 *	-	.1
123 Ch God (Ander)	4	NR	347	347	-	.1
127 Ch God (Cleve)	11	1,319	567	1,652 *	.2	.4
145 Ch God Prophcy	1	35	NR	43 *	-	-
151 L-D Saints	44	NR	NR	17,077	2.0	4.5
157 Ch of Brethren	1	49	40	61 *	-	-
165 Ch of Nazarene	14	1,546	1,191	2,029	.2	.5
167 Chs of Christ	19	1,688	1,771	2,182	.3	.6
173 Comm of Christ	2	278	NR	278	-	.1
179 Consrv Bapt	16	NR	2,457	2,457	.3	.6
185 Cumber Presb	1	36	NR	36	-	-
186 Coptic Orth Ch	1	NR	NR	NR	-	-
193 Episcopal	11	NR	3,200	8,725	1.0	2.3
201 Evan Cov Ch	2	241	256	298 *	-	.1
203 Evan Free Ch	6	686	1,221	1,221	.1	.3
207 E.L.C.A.	18	8,005	4,893	10,906	1.3	2.9
220 Free Lutheran	2	48	78	83	-	-
221 Free Methodist	3	81	57	107	-	-
223 Free Will Bapt	1	34	NR	42 *	-	-
226 Friends-USA	3	212	NR	262 *	-	.1
246 Greek Orthodox	1	NR	NR	813	.1	.2
251 Holy Orth in NA	1	NR	NR	30	-	-
252 Hindu	2	NR	NR	NR	-	-
263 Int Foursq Gos	4	112	182	182 *	-	-
264 Int Chs of Crst	1	242	447	357	-	.1
267 Muslim Est	1	NR	400	700	.1	.2
283 Luth—MO Synod	9	3,461	2,277	4,281	.5	1.1
288 Mennonite USA	1	53	100	100 *	-	-
290 Metro Comm Ch	1	74	94	94 *	-	-
339 Pent Ch of God	3	116	NR	175	-	-
349 Pent Holiness	1	83	120	103 *	-	-
355 Presb Ch (USA)	15	7,291	4,732	9,036 *	1.1	2.4
356 Presb Ch Amer	3	799	1,075	1,097	.1	.3
360 Prim Bapt Chrch	1	NR	NR	NR	-	-
371 Ref Ch in Am	2	163	155	253	-	.1
388 Reg Bapt Gen As	3	216	300	300 *	-	.1

NR–Not Reported *Total adherents estimated from known number of communicant, confirmed, full members. - Represents a percentage less than 0.1. Percentages may not total 100 due to rounding.

Table 4: Religious Congregations by County and Group: 2000

Religious Group	Number of Churches, Synagogues, Mosques, or Temples	Number of Communicant, Confirmed, or Full Members	Number of Attendees	Total Adherents: Number of Adherents	Total Adherents: % of Total Pop.	Total Adherents: % of Total Adh.
401 Rus Orth Abroad	1	NR	NR	NR	-	-
403 Salvation Army	3	427	247	1,433	.2	.4
413 S.D.A.	8	1,658	NR	1,973	.2	.5
416 Sikh	1	NR	NR	NR	-	-
419 So Bapt Conv	48	18,480	10,248	22,875 *	2.7	6.0
435 Unitarian-Univ	3	559	NR	692 *	.1	.2
443 Un C of Christ	6	1,765	952	2,185 *	.3	.6
449 Un Methodist	15	7,683	4,743	9,510 *	1.1	2.5
463 Vineyard	3	264	259	327 *	-	.1
467 Wesleyan	3	430	621	1,192	.1	.3
469 WELS	5	1,572	1,025	1,868	.2	.5
490 Zoroastrian	1	NR	NR	NR	-	-
496 Jewish Est	12	NR	NR	20,000	2.4	5.3
498 Indep.Charis.	1	1,500	1,500	2,000	.2	.5
499 Indep.Non-Char	5	7,000	8,600	8,600	1.0	2.3
PINAL	**158**	**14,298**	**8,721**	**57,855 ***	**32.2**	**100.0**
017 Amer Bapt Assn	2	90	NR	112 *	.1	.2
053 Assemb of God	23	1,393	1,530	2,721	1.5	4.7
056 Baha'i	1	299	NR	299	.2	.5
081 Catholic	22	NR	NR	32,078	17.8	55.4
084 Calvary Chapel	1	NR	NR	NR	-	-
089 Chr & Miss Al	1	0	NR	25	-	-
097 Chr Chs&Chs Cr	4	1,428	NR	1,774 *	1.0	3.1
127 Ch God (Cleve)	5	156	153	217 *	.1	.4
145 Ch God Prophcy	1	35	NR	44 *	-	.1
151 L-D Saints	15	NR	NR	6,043	3.4	10.4
165 Ch of Nazarene	2	386	313	391	.2	.7
167 Chs of Christ	11	606	612	772	.4	1.3
179 Consrv Bapt	6	NR	455	455	.3	.8
193 Episcopal	3	NR	114	367	.2	.6
207 E.L.C.A.	2	659	555	837	.5	1.4
263 Int Foursq Gos	1	10	14	14 *	-	-
283 Luth—MO Synod	3	565	667	662	.4	1.1
339 Pent Ch of God	1	104	NR	260	.1	.4
349 Pent Holiness	1	68	52	85 *	-	.1
355 Presb Ch (USA)	9	1,204	985	1,521 *	.8	2.6
370 Ref Baptist Chs	1	NR	NR	NR	-	-
388 Reg Bapt Gen As	1	0	60	60 *	-	.1
403 Salvation Army	2	105	115	215	.1	.4
413 S.D.A.	4	255	NR	304	.2	.5
419 So Bapt Conv	27	5,842	1,755	7,261 *	4.0	12.6
449 Un Methodist	6	892	1,139	1,109 *	.6	1.9
467 Wesleyan	1	0	0	0	-	-
469 WELS	2	201	202	229	.1	.4
SANTA CRUZ	**31**	**1,402**	**1,211**	**25,355 ***	**66.1**	**100.0**
053 Assemb of God	3	295	317	422	1.1	1.7
056 Baha'i	0	64	NR	64	.2	.3
081 Catholic	7	NR	NR	22,464	58.5	88.6
127 Ch God (Cleve)	1	70	0	95 *	.2	.4
145 Ch God Prophcy	1	35	NR	48 *	.1	.2
151 L-D Saints	2	NR	NR	493	1.3	1.9
167 Chs of Christ	1	26	28	34	.1	.1
179 Consrv Bapt	3	NR	280	280	.7	1.1
193 Episcopal	1	NR	91	230	.6	.9
203 Evan Free Ch	1	69	125	125	.3	.5
220 Free Lutheran	1	50	25	75	.2	.3
263 Int Foursq Gos	1	29	51	51 *	.1	.2
283 Luth—MO Synod	1	9	11	9	-	-
413 S.D.A.	3	357	NR	425	1.1	1.7
419 So Bapt Conv	2	152	98	206 *	.5	.8
443 Un C of Christ	1	100	30	136 *	.4	.5
449 Un Methodist	2	146	155	198 *	.5	.8
YAVAPAI	**179**	**15,618**	**12,915**	**49,809 ***	**29.7**	**100.0**
011 A.W.M.C.	1	0	33	0	-	-
017 Amer Bapt Assn	3	120	NR	143 *	.1	.3
019 Amer Bapt USA	3	120	115	143 *	.1	.3
040 Ap Chr Ch-Amer	1	17	34	34 *	-	.1
053 Assemb of God	15	1,282	1,654	2,364	1.4	4.7
056 Baha'i	2	172	NR	172	.1	.3
076 Buddhism	1	NR	NR	NR	-	-
081 Catholic	14	NR	NR	18,584	11.1	37.3
084 Calvary Chapel	5	NR	NR	NR	-	-
089 Chr & Miss Al	1	49	NR	92	.1	.2
093 Chr Ch (Disc)	1	53	44	63 *	-	.1
097 Chr Chs&Chs Cr	6	1,038	NR	1,235 *	.7	2.5
123 Ch God (Ander)	3	NR	105	105	.1	.2
127 Ch God (Cleve)	3	243	113	289 *	.2	.6
151 L-D Saints	17	NR	NR	6,376	3.8	12.8
165 Ch of Nazarene	5	825	689	1,149	.7	2.3
167 Chs of Christ	12	633	638	746	.4	1.5
173 Comm of Christ	1	83	NR	83	-	.2
179 Consrv Bapt	6	NR	1,952	1,952	1.2	3.9
193 Episcopal	3	NR	435	768	.5	1.5
203 Evan Free Ch	2	155	175	185	.1	.4
207 E.L.C.A.	3	1,194	970	1,442	.9	2.9
221 Free Methodist	1	98	77	103	.1	.2
262 Int Cou Comm Ch	1	190	NR	226 *	.1	.5
263 Int Foursq Gos	4	144	159	171 *	.1	.3
283 Luth—MO Synod	7	834	596	940	.6	1.9
335 Orth Pres Ch	1	57	59	69	-	.1
339 Pent Ch of God	2	82	NR	172	.1	.3
355 Presb Ch (USA)	4	898	559	1,068 *	.6	2.1
371 Ref Ch in Am	1	133	149	255	.2	.5
388 Reg Bapt Gen As	1	68	60	81 *	-	.2
403 Salvation Army	2	104	62	317	.2	.6
413 S.D.A.	4	579	NR	689	.4	1.4
419 So Bapt Conv	21	2,964	333	3,525 *	2.1	7.1
435 Unitarian-Univ	2	156	NR	186 *	.1	.4
443 Un C of Christ	3	375	280	446 *	.3	.9
449 Un Methodist	7	1,900	1,347	2,260 *	1.3	4.5
463 Vineyard	4	505	447	602 *	.4	1.2
469 WELS	4	547	430	674	.4	1.4
496 Jewish Est	1	NR	NR	300	.2	.6
498 Indep.Charis.	1	0	1,400	1,800	1.1	3.6
YUMA	**100**	**9,360**	**7,078**	**57,806 ***	**36.1**	**100.0**
017 Amer Bapt Assn	4	140	NR	182 *	.1	.3
053 Assemb of God	10	808	930	2,759	1.7	4.8
056 Baha'i	1	164	NR	164	.1	.3
076 Buddhism	1	NR	NR	NR	-	-
081 Catholic	7	NR	NR	37,744	23.6	65.3
084 Calvary Chapel	1	NR	NR	NR	-	-
097 Chr Chs&Chs Cr	2	1,320	NR	1,710 *	1.1	3.0
123 Ch God (Ander)	2	NR	99	99	.1	.2
127 Ch God (Cleve)	2	273	56	354 *	.2	.6
143 CG in Cr(Menn)	1	38	NR	49 *	-	.1
145 Ch God Prophcy	2	70	NR	90 *	.1	.2
151 L-D Saints	11	NR	NR	3,537	2.2	6.1
165 Ch of Nazarene	6	432	345	541	.3	.9
167 Chs of Christ	7	451	470	605	.4	1.0
173 Comm of Christ	1	33	NR	33	-	.1
179 Consrv Bapt	5	NR	597	597	.4	1.0
193 Episcopal	1	NR	223	1,243	.8	2.2
207 E.L.C.A.	2	330	448	566	.4	1.0
252 Hindu	1	NR	NR	NR	-	-
263 Int Foursq Gos	1	11	49	49 *	-	.1
283 Luth—MO Synod	2	606	403	858	.5	1.5
339 Pent Ch of God	2	32	NR	65	-	.1
349 Pent Holiness	1	60	95	78 *	-	.1
355 Presb Ch (USA)	5	396	323	517 *	.3	.9
403 Salvation Army	2	189	88	363	.2	.6
413 S.D.A.	2	470	NR	560	.3	1.0
419 So Bapt Conv	9	2,744	1,728	3,555 *	2.2	6.1
435 Unitarian-Univ	1	9	NR	12 *	-	-
449 Un Methodist	5	698	798	904 *	.6	1.6
469 WELS	1	86	76	97	.1	.2
496 Jewish Est	1	NR	NR	125	.1	.2
498 Indep.Charis.	1	0	350	350	.2	.6

NR–Not Reported   *Total adherents estimated from known number of communicant, confirmed, full members.   - Represents a percentage less than 0.1.   Percentages may not total 100 due to rounding.

Table 4: Religious Congregations by County and Group: 2000

Religious Group	Number of Churches, Synagogues, Mosques, or Temples	Number of Communicant, Confirmed, or Full Members	Number of Attendees	Total Adherents		
				Number of Adherents	% of Total Pop.	% of Total Adh.
ARKANSAS						
The State.....	5,802	1,079,272	426,516	1,526,959 *	57.1	100.0
ARKANSAS	**65**	**11,277**	**3,438**	**14,501 ***	**69.9**	**100.0**
017 Amer Bapt Assn	12	1,750	NR	2,165 *	10.4	14.9
053 Assemb of God	4	272	312	355	1.7	2.4
056 Baha'i	0	37	NR	37	.2	.3
059 Bapt Miss Assn	7	940	363	1,164 *	5.6	8.0
081 Catholic	1	NR	NR	642	3.1	4.4
093 Chr Ch (Disc)	1	393	97	486 *	2.3	3.4
097 Chr Chs&Chs Cr	2	238	NR	295 *	1.4	2.0
165 Ch of Nazarene	2	62	28	75	.4	.5
167 Chs of Christ	3	173	183	239	1.2	1.6
193 Episcopal	1	NR	31	87	.4	.6
207 E.L.C.A.	1	185	82	239	1.2	1.6
283 Luth—MO Synod	3	829	420	783	3.8	5.4
339 Pent Ch of God	2	30	NR	50	.2	.3
355 Presb Ch (USA)	1	25	23	31 *	.1	.2
419 So Bapt Conv	11	4,123	1,054	5,103 *	24.6	35.2
449 Un Methodist	14	2,220	845	2,750 *	13.3	19.0
ASHLEY	**79**	**14,535**	**4,080**	**19,343 ***	**79.9**	**100.0**
017 Amer Bapt Assn	10	2,298	NR	2,890 *	11.9	14.9
053 Assemb of God	5	299	364	494	2.0	2.6
056 Baha'i	0	6	NR	6	-	-
059 Bapt Miss Assn	2	345	142	434 *	1.8	2.2
081 Catholic	2	NR	NR	682	2.8	3.5
123 Ch God (Ander)	1	NR	95	95	.4	.5
127 Ch God (Cleve)	1	39	0	49 *	.2	.3
151 L-D Saints	1	NR	NR	86	.4	.4
165 Ch of Nazarene	1	0	0	0	-	-
167 Chs of Christ	6	530	400	661	2.7	3.4
173 Comm of Christ	1	46	NR	46	.2	.2
193 Episcopal	1	NR	32	84	.3	.4
223 Free Will Bapt	5	507	NR	638 *	2.6	3.3
283 Luth—MO Synod	1	20	15	22	.1	.1
339 Pent Ch of God	1	8	NR	25	.1	.1
355 Presb Ch (USA)	1	110	57	138 *	.6	.7
419 So Bapt Conv	30	9,060	2,472	11,398 *	47.1	58.9
449 Un Methodist	10	1,267	503	1,595 *	6.6	8.2
BAXTER	**70**	**12,503**	**7,090**	**19,743 ***	**51.4**	**100.0**
017 Amer Bapt Assn	4	98	NR	114 *	.3	.6
053 Assemb of God	5	526	506	742	1.9	3.8
056 Baha'i	0	10	NR	10	-	.1
059 Bapt Miss Assn	1	35	28	41 *	.1	.2
081 Catholic	1	NR	NR	3,905	10.2	19.8
093 Chr Ch (Disc)	1	407	224	473 *	1.2	2.4
097 Chr Chs&Chs Cr	1	130	NR	151 *	.4	.8
127 Ch God (Cleve)	2	45	28	53 *	.1	.3
165 Ch of Nazarene	2	185	148	200	.5	1.0
167 Chs of Christ	17	1,217	1,324	1,403	3.7	7.1
173 Comm of Christ	1	57	NR	57	.1	.3
185 Cumber Presb	2	154	NR	312	.8	1.6
193 Episcopal	1	NR	105	195	.5	1.0
207 E.L.C.A.	1	334	158	383	1.0	1.9
223 Free Will Bapt	2	203	NR	236 *	.6	1.2
283 Luth—MO Synod	1	1,138	587	1,298	3.4	6.6
288 Mennonite USA	1	15	12	17 *	-	.1
306 NT IndBapt&Rltd	1	40	NR	47 *	.1	.2
355 Presb Ch (USA)	2	373	223	434 *	1.1	2.2
403 Salvation Army	1	59	38	154	.4	.8
413 S.D.A.	1	96	NR	114	.3	.6
419 So Bapt Conv	16	5,840	2,318	6,794 *	17.7	34.4
435 Unitarian-Univ	1	21	NR	24 *	.1	.1
449 Un Methodist	3	1,414	520	1,645 *	4.3	8.3
469 WELS	1	106	71	141	.4	.7
499 Indep.Non-Char	1	0	800	800	2.1	4.1
BENTON	**231**	**49,983**	**29,480**	**82,501 ***	**53.8**	**100.0**
017 Amer Bapt Assn	6	695	NR	878 *	.6	1.1
019 Amer Bapt USA	1	128	70	162 *	.1	.2
053 Assemb of God	20	2,005	2,795	3,268	2.1	4.0
056 Baha'i	1	60	NR	60	-	.1
059 Bapt Miss Assn	21	2,877	1,370	3,665 *	2.4	4.4
081 Catholic	4	NR	NR	9,014	5.9	10.9
084 Calvary Chapel	1	NR	NR	NR	-	-
093 Chr Ch (Disc)	3	1,081	589	1,367 *	.9	1.7
097 Chr Chs&Chs Cr	10	1,862	NR	2,355 *	1.5	2.9
123 Ch God (Ander)	1	NR	20	20	-	-
127 Ch God (Cleve)	1	141	65	178 *	.1	.2
143 CG in Cr(Menn)	1	168	NR	212 *	.1	.3
145 Ch God Prophcy	1	29	NR	37 *	-	-
151 L-D Saints	5	NR	NR	2,133	1.4	2.6
157 Ch of Brethren	1	26	20	33 *	-	-
165 Ch of Nazarene	8	893	725	1,255	.8	1.5
167 Chs of Christ	17	2,127	2,175	2,601	1.7	3.2
193 Episcopal	3	NR	455	958	.6	1.2
203 Evan Free Ch	3	151	285	285	.2	.3
207 E.L.C.A.	3	1,647	912	1,960	1.3	2.4
221 Free Methodist	1	17	35	35	-	-
223 Free Will Bapt	7	709	NR	897 *	.6	1.1
237 Menn Br US Conf	1	19	NR	24 *	-	-
283 Luth—MO Synod	4	960	675	1,151	.8	1.4
288 Mennonite USA	1	21	35	35 *	-	-
335 Orth Pres Ch	1	8	22	22	-	-
339 Pent Ch of God	5	218	NR	485	.3	.6
349 Pent Holiness	7	293	327	370 *	.2	.4
355 Presb Ch (USA)	7	1,520	807	1,926 *	1.3	2.3
360 Prim Bapt Chrch	3	NR	NR	NR	-	-
388 Reg Bapt Gen As	2	149	89	117 *	.1	.1
403 Salvation Army	1	32	32	42	-	.1
413 S.D.A.	7	1,536	NR	1,828	1.2	2.2
419 So Bapt Conv	39	23,358	7,718	29,531 *	19.3	35.8
449 Un Methodist	27	6,337	3,021	8,011 *	5.2	9.7
463 Vineyard	1	130	120	164 *	.1	.2
467 Wesleyan	2	111	92	156	.1	.2
469 WELS	2	195	161	266	.2	.3
498 Indep.Charis.	1	0	6,500	6,500	4.2	7.9
499 Indep.Non-Char	1	480	365	500	.3	.6
BOONE	**80**	**12,790**	**6,453**	**18,578 ***	**54.7**	**100.0**
017 Amer Bapt Assn	3	309	NR	377 *	1.1	2.0
053 Assemb of God	8	1,046	1,118	2,445	7.2	13.2
056 Baha'i	0	3	NR	3	-	-
059 Bapt Miss Assn	1	124	125	152 *	.4	.8
061 Beachy Amish	1	26	NR	32 *	.1	.2
081 Catholic	1	NR	NR	988	2.9	5.3
093 Chr Ch (Disc)	1	459	266	561 *	1.7	3.0
097 Chr Chs&Chs Cr	1	83	NR	101 *	.3	.5
123 Ch God (Ander)	1	NR	92	92	.3	.5
127 Ch God (Cleve)	1	68	0	83 *	.2	.4
151 L-D Saints	1	NR	NR	350	1.0	1.9
165 Ch of Nazarene	1	71	78	99	.3	.5
167 Chs of Christ	14	1,019	1,197	1,258	3.7	6.8
193 Episcopal	1	NR	91	230	.7	1.2
207 E.L.C.A.	1	34	33	44	.1	.2
223 Free Will Bapt	1	101	NR	124 *	.4	.7
283 Luth—MO Synod	1	257	128	322	.9	1.7
339 Pent Ch of God	1	34	NR	80	.2	.4
355 Presb Ch (USA)	2	358	172	437 *	1.3	2.4
360 Prim Bapt Chrch	1	NR	NR	NR	-	-
413 S.D.A.	1	155	NR	184	.5	1.0
419 So Bapt Conv	26	7,562	2,582	9,246 *	27.2	49.8
449 Un Methodist	10	1,038	525	1,270 *	3.7	6.8
467 Wesleyan	1	43	46	100	.3	.5
BRADLEY	**49**	**6,916**	**2,195**	**8,796 ***	**69.8**	**100.0**
017 Amer Bapt Assn	1	169	NR	206 *	1.6	2.3
053 Assemb of God	2	200	200	280	2.2	3.2
055 As Ref Pres Ch	1	28	NR	28	.2	.3
059 Bapt Miss Assn	7	1,138	403	1,385 *	11.0	15.7
081 Catholic	1	NR	NR	309	2.5	3.5
127 Ch God (Cleve)	1	61	22	74 *	.6	.8

NR–Not Reported   *Total adherents estimated from known number of communicant, confirmed, full members.   - Represents a percentage less than 0.1.   Percentages may not total 100 due to rounding.

Table 4: Religious Congregations by County and Group: 2000

Religious Group	Number of Churches, Synagogues, Mosques, or Temples	Number of Communicant, Confirmed, or Full Members	Number of Attendees	Total Adherents: Number of Adherents	Total Adherents: % of Total Pop.	Total Adherents: % of Total Adh.
167 Chs of Christ	3	125	125	160	1.3	1.8
223 Free Will Bapt	7	709	NR	864 *	6.9	9.8
339 Pent Ch of God	1	35	NR	70	.6	.8
355 Presb Ch (USA)	2	166	90	202 *	1.6	2.3
360 Prim Bapt Chrch	1	NR	NR	NR	-	-
419 So Bapt Conv	14	3,468	1,043	4,222 *	33.5	48.0
449 Un Methodist	8	817	312	996 *	7.9	11.3
CALHOUN	**32**	**2,706**	**1,230**	**3,412 ***	**59.4**	**100.0**
017 Amer Bapt Assn	2	126	NR	154 *	2.7	4.5
053 Assemb of God	4	171	220	250	4.4	7.3
059 Bapt Miss Assn	8	832	374	1,018 *	17.7	29.8
167 Chs of Christ	3	177	191	231	4.0	6.8
185 Cumber Presb	1	80	NR	144	2.5	4.2
360 Prim Bapt Chrch	2	NR	NR	NR	-	-
419 So Bapt Conv	7	1,062	312	1,299 *	22.6	38.1
449 Un Methodist	5	258	133	316 *	5.5	9.3
CARROLL	**54**	**7,010**	**3,447**	**11,068 ***	**43.6**	**100.0**
017 Amer Bapt Assn	1	50	NR	61 *	.2	.6
032 Amish; other	1	70	NR	86 *	.3	.8
053 Assemb of God	5	706	991	1,713	6.8	15.5
056 Baha'i	0	8	NR	8	-	.1
059 Bapt Miss Assn	1	25	20	31 *	.1	.3
076 Buddhism	1	NR	NR	NR	-	-
081 Catholic	2	NR	NR	1,235	4.9	11.2
093 Chr Ch (Disc)	1	194	66	238 *	.9	2.2
097 Chr Chs&Chs Cr	2	186	NR	228 *	.9	2.1
151 L-D Saints	1	NR	NR	198	.8	1.8
165 Ch of Nazarene	2	46	47	109	.4	1.0
167 Chs of Christ	5	260	345	335	1.3	3.0
173 Comm of Christ	1	53	NR	53	.2	.5
193 Episcopal	1	NR	71	154	.6	1.4
223 Free Will Bapt	5	507	NR	620 *	2.4	5.6
283 Luth—MO Synod	2	101	260	118	.5	1.1
290 Metro Comm Ch	1	21	14	26 *	.1	.2
355 Presb Ch (USA)	2	99	63	122 *	.5	1.1
413 S.D.A.	1	31	NR	37	.1	.3
419 So Bapt Conv	13	3,751	1,180	4,592 *	18.1	41.5
425 Tao	1	NR	NR	NR	-	-
435 Unitarian-Univ	1	35	NR	43 *	.2	.4
449 Un Methodist	4	867	390	1,061 *	4.2	9.6
CHICOT	**32**	**4,540**	**1,363**	**6,430 ***	**45.5**	**100.0**
017 Amer Bapt Assn	2	128	NR	161 *	1.1	2.5
053 Assemb of God	3	55	66	135	1.0	2.1
056 Baha'i	0	1	NR	1	-	-
081 Catholic	2	NR	NR	609	4.3	9.5
167 Chs of Christ	3	93	126	121	.9	1.9
193 Episcopal	1	NR	15	32	.2	.5
223 Free Will Bapt	2	203	NR	255 *	1.8	4.0
355 Presb Ch (USA)	3	92	60	115 *	.8	1.8
419 So Bapt Conv	13	3,509	912	4,422 *	31.3	68.8
449 Un Methodist	3	459	184	579 *	4.1	9.0
CLARK	**82**	**12,676**	**4,603**	**16,110 ***	**68.4**	**100.0**
017 Amer Bapt Assn	9	915	NR	1,096 *	4.7	6.8
053 Assemb of God	5	225	270	444	1.9	2.8
056 Baha'i	0	16	NR	16	.1	.1
059 Bapt Miss Assn	5	745	205	894 *	3.8	5.5
081 Catholic	1	NR	NR	371	1.6	2.3
093 Chr Ch (Disc)	2	14	9	17 *	.1	.1
123 Ch God (Ander)	2	NR	87	87	.4	.5
127 Ch God (Cleve)	1	39	20	47 *	.2	.3
151 L-D Saints	1	NR	NR	187	.8	1.2
165 Ch of Nazarene	1	46	55	80	.3	.5
167 Chs of Christ	4	211	218	276	1.2	1.7
223 Free Will Bapt	1	101	NR	122 *	.5	.8
273 LandmrkBapt,I&U	1	66	NR	79 *	.3	.5
339 Pent Ch of God	1	30	NR	70	.3	.4
355 Presb Ch (USA)	4	258	148	309 *	1.3	1.9
360 Prim Bapt Chrch	2	NR	NR	NR	-	-

Religious Group	Number of Churches, Synagogues, Mosques, or Temples	Number of Communicant, Confirmed, or Full Members	Number of Attendees	Total Adherents: Number of Adherents	Total Adherents: % of Total Pop.	Total Adherents: % of Total Adh.
413 S.D.A.	1	47	NR	56	.2	.3
419 So Bapt Conv	29	8,411	2,884	10,096 *	42.9	62.7
449 Un Methodist	12	1,552	707	1,863 *	7.9	11.6
CLAY	**71**	**7,701**	**3,388**	**9,670 ***	**54.9**	**100.0**
017 Amer Bapt Assn	11	542	NR	660 *	3.7	6.8
053 Assemb of God	3	83	119	135	.8	1.4
059 Bapt Miss Assn	5	616	247	751 *	4.3	7.8
081 Catholic	2	NR	NR	83	.5	.9
097 Chr Chs&Chs Cr	2	170	NR	207 *	1.2	2.1
123 Ch God (Ander)	1	NR	35	35	.2	.4
165 Ch of Nazarene	1	24	35	64	.4	.7
167 Chs of Christ	15	1,130	1,152	1,445	8.2	14.9
223 Free Will Bapt	1	101	NR	123 *	.7	1.3
283 Luth—MO Synod	1	80	35	102	.6	1.1
339 Pent Ch of God	1	45	NR	85	.5	.9
355 Presb Ch (USA)	1	30	24	37 *	.2	.4
360 Prim Bapt Chrch	1	NR	NR	NR	-	-
419 So Bapt Conv	18	3,948	1,376	4,808 *	27.3	49.7
449 Un Methodist	8	932	365	1,135 *	6.4	11.7
CLEBURNE	**56**	**8,272**	**3,975**	**10,614 ***	**44.1**	**100.0**
017 Amer Bapt Assn	2	70	NR	84 *	.3	.8
053 Assemb of God	2	271	370	480	2.0	4.5
055 As Ref Pres Ch	1	0	NR	0	-	-
056 Baha'i	0	3	NR	3	-	-
059 Bapt Miss Assn	5	666	187	794 *	3.3	7.5
081 Catholic	1	NR	NR	468	1.9	4.4
097 Chr Chs&Chs Cr	2	185	NR	221 *	.9	2.1
127 Ch God (Cleve)	2	106	64	126 *	.5	1.2
165 Ch of Nazarene	3	106	97	122	.5	1.1
167 Chs of Christ	6	413	458	499	2.1	4.7
193 Episcopal	1	NR	63	131	.5	1.2
207 E.L.C.A.	2	249	161	284	1.2	2.7
223 Free Will Bapt	2	203	NR	242 *	1.0	2.3
283 Luth—MO Synod	1	43	30	45	.2	.4
339 Pent Ch of God	1	26	NR	46	.2	.4
355 Presb Ch (USA)	1	122	81	145 *	.6	1.4
360 Prim Bapt Chrch	1	NR	NR	NR	-	-
418 Southw Bapt Fel	1	NR	NR	NR	-	-
419 So Bapt Conv	18	4,364	1,775	5,202 *	21.6	49.0
449 Un Methodist	4	1,445	689	1,722 *	7.2	16.2
CLEVELAND	**37**	**4,234**	**1,290**	**5,281 ***	**61.6**	**100.0**
017 Amer Bapt Assn	10	1,644	NR	2,041 *	23.8	38.6
053 Assemb of God	2	170	144	181	2.1	3.4
059 Bapt Miss Assn	8	965	421	1,199 *	14.0	22.7
123 Ch God (Ander)	1	NR	55	55	.6	1.0
127 Ch God (Cleve)	1	8	18	18 *	.2	.3
167 Chs of Christ	1	80	70	90	1.1	1.7
223 Free Will Bapt	2	203	NR	252 *	2.9	4.8
419 So Bapt Conv	3	524	220	651 *	7.6	12.3
449 Un Methodist	9	640	362	794 *	9.3	15.0
COLUMBIA	**78**	**12,899**	**4,701**	**16,426 ***	**64.2**	**100.0**
017 Amer Bapt Assn	10	1,195	NR	1,470 *	5.7	8.9
053 Assemb of God	3	144	167	216	.8	1.3
059 Bapt Miss Assn	23	5,025	2,109	6,180 *	24.1	37.6
081 Catholic	1	NR	NR	173	.7	1.1
123 Ch God (Ander)	1	NR	20	20	.1	.1
151 L-D Saints	1	NR	NR	147	.6	.9
165 Ch of Nazarene	1	0	0	0	-	-
167 Chs of Christ	7	667	611	909	3.6	5.5
185 Cumber Presb	2	18	NR	51	.2	.3
193 Episcopal	1	NR	29	70	.3	.4
283 Luth—MO Synod	1	22	14	22	.1	.1
355 Presb Ch (USA)	1	216	81	266 *	1.0	1.6
413 S.D.A.	1	8	NR	10	-	.1
419 So Bapt Conv	7	3,551	860	4,367 *	17.1	26.6
449 Un Methodist	18	2,053	810	2,525 *	9.9	15.4

NR–Not Reported *Total adherents estimated from known number of communicant, confirmed, full members. - Represents a percentage less than 0.1. Percentages may not total 100 due to rounding.

Table 4: Religious Congregations by County and Group: 2000

Religious Group	Number of Churches, Synagogues, Mosques, or Temples	Number of Communicant, Confirmed, or Full Members	Number of Attendees	Total Adherents: Number of Adherents	Total Adherents: % of Total Pop.	Total Adherents: % of Total Adh.
CONWAY	**69**	**7,062**	**3,271**	**11,580 ***	**56.9**	**100.0**
017 Amer Bapt Assn	9	1,089	NR	1,347 *	6.6	11.6
053 Assemb of God	4	322	385	682	3.4	5.9
056 Baha'i	0	2	NR	2	-	-
059 Bapt Miss Assn	10	1,518	613	1,881 *	9.2	16.2
081 Catholic	4	NR	NR	2,228	11.0	19.2
121 Ch God (Abr)	1	20	11	25 *	.1	.2
145 Ch God Prophcy	1	29	NR	36 *	.2	.3
151 L-D Saints	1	NR	NR	210	1.0	1.8
165 Ch of Nazarene	1	98	71	125	.6	1.1
167 Chs of Christ	15	1,152	1,180	1,476	7.3	12.7
185 Cumber Presb	1	26	NR	65	.3	.6
223 Free Will Bapt	2	203	NR	251 *	1.2	2.2
320 "Old" MB Ascs	1	6	NR	7 *	-	.1
339 Pent Ch of God	2	71	NR	120	.6	1.0
355 Presb Ch (USA)	2	167	90	207 *	1.0	1.8
419 So Bapt Conv	7	1,448	509	1,792 *	8.8	15.5
449 Un Methodist	8	911	412	1,126 *	5.5	9.7
CRAIGHEAD	**152**	**38,921**	**15,873**	**53,113 ***	**64.7**	**100.0**
017 Amer Bapt Assn	2	352	NR	434 *	.5	.8
053 Assemb of God	11	909	901	1,474	1.8	2.8
056 Baha'i	0	5	NR	5	-	-
059 Bapt Miss Assn	24	6,036	2,138	7,447 *	9.1	14.0
081 Catholic	2	NR	NR	3,466	4.2	6.5
093 Chr Ch (Disc)	2	215	95	265 *	.3	.5
097 Chr Chs&Chs Cr	5	480	NR	592 *	.7	1.1
127 Ch God (Cleve)	2	239	101	295 *	.4	.6
145 Ch God Prophcy	2	58	NR	72 *	.1	.1
151 L-D Saints	1	NR	NR	478	.6	.9
165 Ch of Nazarene	3	535	451	983	1.2	1.9
167 Chs of Christ	20	3,531	3,759	4,320	5.3	8.1
173 Comm of Christ	3	273	NR	273	.3	.5
193 Episcopal	1	NR	135	445	.5	.8
207 E.L.C.A.	1	74	52	88	.1	.2
223 Free Will Bapt	3	304	NR	375 *	.5	.7
267 Muslim Est	1	NR	55	163	.2	.3
283 Luth—MO Synod	1	110	73	146	.2	.3
339 Pent Ch of God	2	45	NR	120	.1	.2
349 Pent Holiness	1	10	12	12 *	-	-
355 Presb Ch (USA)	1	417	212	515 *	.6	1.0
360 Prim Bapt Chrch	1	NR	NR	NR	-	-
388 Reg Bapt Gen As	1	49	34	60 *	.1	.1
403 Salvation Army	1	96	49	124	.2	.2
413 S.D.A.	1	54	NR	64	.1	.1
419 So Bapt Conv	37	20,088	5,510	24,786 *	30.2	46.7
435 Unitarian-Univ	1	22	NR	27 *	-	.1
449 Un Methodist	20	4,419	1,896	5,454 *	6.6	10.3
496 Jewish Est	1	NR	NR	30	-	.1
498 Indep.Charis.	1	600	400	600	.7	1.1
CRAWFORD	**108**	**18,613**	**8,273**	**28,185 ***	**52.9**	**100.0**
017 Amer Bapt Assn	9	1,093	NR	1,398 *	2.6	5.0
053 Assemb of God	17	2,787	2,743	5,539	10.4	19.7
056 Baha'i	0	6	NR	6	-	-
081 Catholic	1	NR	NR	1,359	2.6	4.8
089 Chr & Miss Al	1	37	NR	70	.1	.2
093 Chr Ch (Disc)	1	86	41	110 *	.2	.4
123 Ch God (Ander)	1	NR	100	100	.2	.4
151 L-D Saints	1	NR	NR	436	.8	1.5
165 Ch of Nazarene	2	266	193	331	.6	1.2
167 Chs of Christ	10	726	756	960	1.8	3.4
171 Ch God-Gen Con	1	20	20	26 *	-	.1
193 Episcopal	1	NR	93	157	.3	.6
223 Free Will Bapt	17	1,723	NR	2,204 *	4.1	7.8
262 Int Cou Comm Ch	1	40	NR	51 *	.1	.2
283 Luth—MO Synod	1	51	18	60	.1	.2
339 Pent Ch of God	9	380	NR	797	1.5	2.8
355 Presb Ch (USA)	3	550	290	703 *	1.3	2.5
419 So Bapt Conv	21	9,116	3,271	11,662 *	21.9	41.4
449 Un Methodist	11	1,732	748	2,216 *	4.2	7.9

Religious Group	Number of Churches, Synagogues, Mosques, or Temples	Number of Communicant, Confirmed, or Full Members	Number of Attendees	Total Adherents: Number of Adherents	Total Adherents: % of Total Pop.	Total Adherents: % of Total Adh.
CRITTENDEN	**51**	**15,191**	**5,130**	**21,197 ***	**41.7**	**100.0**
017 Amer Bapt Assn	2	350	NR	462 *	.9	2.2
053 Assemb of God	4	769	549	1,193	2.3	5.6
056 Baha'i	0	6	NR	6	-	-
059 Bapt Miss Assn	1	347	20	458 *	.9	2.2
081 Catholic	3	NR	NR	562	1.1	2.7
093 Chr Ch (Disc)	1	86	55	114 *	.2	.5
127 Ch God (Cleve)	4	455	223	602 *	1.2	2.8
145 Ch God Prophcy	1	29	NR	38 *	.1	.2
151 L-D Saints	1	NR	NR	254	.5	1.2
165 Ch of Nazarene	2	110	76	154	.3	.7
167 Chs of Christ	8	1,289	1,042	1,625	3.2	7.7
193 Episcopal	1	NR	98	194	.4	.9
283 Luth—MO Synod	1	51	24	60	.1	.3
339 Pent Ch of God	2	46	NR	90	.2	.4
355 Presb Ch (USA)	1	263	140	347 *	.7	1.6
413 S.D.A.	1	87	NR	104	.2	.5
419 So Bapt Conv	13	9,365	2,239	12,373 *	24.3	58.4
449 Un Methodist	5	1,938	664	2,561 *	5.0	12.1
CROSS	**53**	**11,799**	**3,590**	**15,822 ***	**81.0**	**100.0**
017 Amer Bapt Assn	2	120	NR	152 *	.8	1.0
053 Assemb of God	10	732	654	1,064	5.4	6.7
056 Baha'i	0	1	NR	1	-	-
059 Bapt Miss Assn	3	543	169	687 *	3.5	4.3
081 Catholic	1	NR	NR	711	3.6	4.5
127 Ch God (Cleve)	4	322	148	408 *	2.1	2.6
157 Ch of Brethren	1	17	8	22 *	.1	.1
165 Ch of Nazarene	1	0	0	0	-	-
167 Chs of Christ	4	387	460	497	2.5	3.1
193 Episcopal	1	NR	6	14	.1	.1
223 Free Will Bapt	1	101	NR	128 *	.7	.8
339 Pent Ch of God	1	8	NR	20	.1	.1
355 Presb Ch (USA)	1	147	50	186 *	1.0	1.2
419 So Bapt Conv	14	8,139	1,621	10,308 *	52.8	65.1
449 Un Methodist	9	1,282	474	1,624 *	8.3	10.3
DALLAS	**44**	**6,083**	**1,638**	**7,856 ***	**85.3**	**100.0**
017 Amer Bapt Assn	4	2,094	NR	2,592 *	28.1	33.0
053 Assemb of God	4	243	265	396	4.3	5.0
059 Bapt Miss Assn	4	914	322	1,131 *	12.3	14.4
081 Catholic	1	NR	NR	163	1.8	2.1
151 L-D Saints	1	NR	NR	64	.7	.8
167 Chs of Christ	3	84	88	107	1.2	1.4
223 Free Will Bapt	1	101	NR	125 *	1.4	1.6
355 Presb Ch (USA)	3	75	38	93 *	1.0	1.2
360 Prim Bapt Chrch	1	NR	NR	NR	-	-
419 So Bapt Conv	11	2,032	610	2,515 *	27.3	32.0
449 Un Methodist	11	540	315	670 *	7.3	8.5
DESHA	**46**	**6,906**	**2,132**	**9,546 ***	**62.2**	**100.0**
017 Amer Bapt Assn	3	441	NR	563 *	3.7	5.9
053 Assemb of God	7	287	343	541	3.5	5.7
056 Baha'i	0	34	NR	34	.2	.4
059 Bapt Miss Assn	2	301	98	383 *	2.5	4.0
081 Catholic	2	NR	NR	304	2.0	3.2
097 Chr Chs&Chs Cr	1	115	NR	147 *	1.0	1.5
143 CG in Cr(Menn)	1	105	NR	134 *	.9	1.4
145 Ch God Prophcy	1	29	NR	37 *	.2	.4
165 Ch of Nazarene	1	128	72	317	2.1	3.3
167 Chs of Christ	2	166	178	216	1.4	2.3
171 Ch God-Gen Con	1	7	5	9 *	.1	.1
193 Episcopal	1	NR	14	20	.1	.2
223 Free Will Bapt	1	101	NR	129 *	.8	1.4
339 Pent Ch of God	2	49	NR	117	.8	1.2
355 Presb Ch (USA)	1	112	66	143 *	.9	1.5
419 So Bapt Conv	14	4,120	1,034	5,254 *	34.2	55.0
449 Un Methodist	5	911	322	1,163 *	7.6	12.2
496 Jewish Est	1	NR	NR	35	.2	.4
DREW	**51**	**9,141**	**3,039**	**12,101 ***	**64.6**	**100.0**
017 Amer Bapt Assn	6	1,244	NR	1,546 *	8.3	12.8

NR–Not Reported *Total adherents estimated from known number of communicant, confirmed, full members. - Represents a percentage less than 0.1. Percentages may not total 100 due to rounding.

Table 4: Religious Congregations by County and Group: 2000

Religious Group	Number of Churches, Synagogues, Mosques, or Temples	Number of Communicant, Confirmed, or Full Members	Number of Attendees	Total Adherents: Number of Adherents	Total Adherents: % of Total Pop.	Total Adherents: % of Total Adh.
053 Assemb of God	3	273	316	575	3.1	4.8
055 As Ref Pres Ch	1	37	NR	41	.2	.3
056 Baha'i	0	3	NR	3	-	-
059 Bapt Miss Assn	2	388	54	482 *	2.6	4.0
081 Catholic	1	NR	NR	247	1.3	2.0
151 L-D Saints	1	NR	NR	124	.7	1.0
167 Chs of Christ	2	239	238	358	1.9	3.0
173 Comm of Christ	1	12	NR	12	.1	.1
185 Cumber Presb	1	49	NR	122	.7	1.0
193 Episcopal	1	NR	12	18	.1	.1
223 Free Will Bapt	3	304	NR	378 *	2.0	3.1
339 Pent Ch of God	1	68	NR	91	.5	.8
355 Presb Ch (USA)	2	395	215	491 *	2.6	4.1
419 So Bapt Conv	16	5,041	1,573	6,263 *	33.5	51.8
449 Un Methodist	10	1,088	631	1,350 *	7.2	11.2
FAULKNER	**121**	**31,000**	**14,586**	**48,624 ***	**56.5**	**100.0**
017 Amer Bapt Assn	5	775	NR	967 *	1.1	2.0
053 Assemb of God	5	844	987	1,408	1.6	2.9
056 Baha'i	0	21	NR	21	-	-
059 Bapt Miss Assn	18	5,652	2,744	7,052 *	8.2	14.5
081 Catholic	1	NR	NR	7,928	9.2	16.3
093 Chr Ch (Disc)	1	85	35	106 *	.1	.2
121 Ch God (Abr)	1	76	59	95 *	.1	.2
127 Ch God (Cleve)	1	89	84	111 *	.1	.2
151 L-D Saints	3	NR	NR	874	1.0	1.8
165 Ch of Nazarene	6	1,106	687	1,339	1.6	2.8
167 Chs of Christ	18	2,011	2,213	2,846	3.3	5.9
193 Episcopal	1	NR	187	536	.6	1.1
207 E.L.C.A.	1	112	92	152	.2	.3
223 Free Will Bapt	6	608	NR	759 *	.9	1.6
263 Int Foursq Gos	1	20	13	25 *	-	.1
283 Luth—MO Synod	2	250	193	324	.4	.7
339 Pent Ch of God	2	40	NR	101	.1	.2
355 Presb Ch (USA)	1	490	277	611 *	.7	1.3
360 Prim Bapt Chrch	2	NR	NR	NR	-	-
403 Salvation Army	1	21	29	25	-	.1
413 S.D.A.	1	49	NR	58	.1	.1
419 So Bapt Conv	30	14,292	4,771	17,833 *	20.7	36.7
449 Un Methodist	13	4,009	1,765	5,003 *	5.8	10.3
499 Indep.Non-Char	1	450	450	450	.5	.9
FRANKLIN	**51**	**5,941**	**1,916**	**8,630 ***	**48.6**	**100.0**
017 Amer Bapt Assn	6	784	NR	968 *	5.4	11.2
053 Assemb of God	7	257	312	395	2.2	4.6
081 Catholic	2	NR	NR	1,114	6.3	12.9
093 Chr Ch (Disc)	1	75	40	93 *	.5	1.1
165 Ch of Nazarene	2	131	64	145	.8	1.7
167 Chs of Christ	5	249	327	340	1.9	3.9
185 Cumber Presb	1	21	NR	21	.1	.2
223 Free Will Bapt	6	608	NR	751 *	4.2	8.7
339 Pent Ch of God	2	124	NR	245	1.4	2.8
355 Presb Ch (USA)	1	53	35	65 *	.4	.8
360 Prim Bapt Chrch	1	NR	NR	NR	-	-
413 S.D.A.	1	38	NR	45	.3	.5
419 So Bapt Conv	7	2,651	717	3,274 *	18.4	37.9
449 Un Methodist	9	950	421	1,174 *	6.6	13.6
FULTON	**47**	**4,253**	**2,356**	**5,365 ***	**46.1**	**100.0**
017 Amer Bapt Assn	1	40	NR	48 *	.4	.9
053 Assemb of God	3	214	299	369	3.2	6.9
059 Bapt Miss Assn	1	50	28	60 *	.5	1.1
093 Chr Ch (Disc)	1	56	30	67 *	.6	1.2
167 Chs of Christ	17	844	1,055	1,098	9.4	20.5
185 Cumber Presb	3	25	NR	59	.5	1.1
339 Pent Ch of God	1	30	NR	70	.6	1.3
355 Presb Ch (USA)	1	6	3	7 *	.1	.1
388 Reg Bapt Gen As	1	14	8	8 *	.1	.1
413 S.D.A.	1	23	NR	27	.2	.5
419 So Bapt Conv	13	2,701	800	3,251 *	27.9	60.6
449 Un Methodist	4	250	133	301 *	2.6	5.6

Religious Group	Number of Churches, Synagogues, Mosques, or Temples	Number of Communicant, Confirmed, or Full Members	Number of Attendees	Total Adherents: Number of Adherents	Total Adherents: % of Total Pop.	Total Adherents: % of Total Adh.
GARLAND	**143**	**37,829**	**14,114**	**52,580 ***	**59.7**	**100.0**
017 Amer Bapt Assn	27	4,388	NR	5,235 *	5.9	10.0
053 Assemb of God	7	605	737	1,026	1.2	2.0
056 Baha'i	1	35	NR	35	-	.1
059 Bapt Miss Assn	1	56	38	67 *	.1	.1
076 Buddhism	1	NR	NR	NR	-	-
081 Catholic	3	NR	NR	5,541	6.3	10.5
093 Chr Ch (Disc)	2	360	168	429 *	.5	.8
097 Chr Chs&Chs Cr	2	118	NR	140 *	.2	.3
123 Ch God (Ander)	2	NR	225	225	.3	.4
127 Ch God (Cleve)	1	102	82	122 *	.1	.2
145 Ch God Prophcy	1	29	NR	35 *	-	.1
165 Ch of Nazarene	3	620	391	754	.9	1.4
167 Chs of Christ	8	842	833	1,006	1.1	1.9
173 Comm of Christ	1	164	NR	164	.2	.3
185 Cumber Presb	1	33	NR	38	-	.1
193 Episcopal	2	NR	381	821	.9	1.6
203 Evan Free Ch	1	190	320	320	.4	.6
207 E.L.C.A.	3	892	526	1,034	1.2	2.0
223 Free Will Bapt	2	203	NR	242 *	.3	.5
246 Greek Orthodox	1	NR	NR	66	.1	.1
283 Luth—MO Synod	2	605	412	737	.8	1.4
339 Pent Ch of God	1	40	NR	125	.1	.2
355 Presb Ch (USA)	5	2,036	951	2,429 *	2.8	4.6
356 Presb Ch Amer	1	0	0	0	-	-
360 Prim Bapt Chrch	3	NR	NR	NR	-	-
388 Reg Bapt Gen As	1	21	24	25 *	-	-
403 Salvation Army	1	127	46	301	.3	.6
411 Serb Orth: Grac	1	NR	NR	NR	-	-
413 S.D.A.	3	405	NR	482	.5	.9
419 So Bapt Conv	36	19,091	5,626	22,769 *	25.9	43.3
435 Unitarian-Univ	1	31	NR	37 *	-	.1
449 Un Methodist	14	6,313	2,704	7,527 *	8.5	14.3
463 Vineyard	1	130	120	155 *	.2	.3
469 WELS	1	43	30	43	-	.1
496 Jewish Est	1	NR	NR	150	.2	.3
498 Indep.Charis.	1	350	500	500	.6	1.0
GRANT	**50**	**10,118**	**1,670**	**12,978 ***	**78.8**	**100.0**
017 Amer Bapt Assn	25	6,302	NR	7,868 *	47.8	60.6
053 Assemb of God	4	286	300	499	3.0	3.8
056 Baha'i	0	2	NR	2	-	-
059 Bapt Miss Assn	1	757	275	945 *	5.7	7.3
081 Catholic	1	NR	NR	86	.5	.7
093 Chr Ch (Disc)	1	37	20	46 *	.3	.4
165 Ch of Nazarene	1	11	21	21	.1	.2
167 Chs of Christ	2	139	131	199	1.2	1.5
185 Cumber Presb	1	84	NR	96	.6	.7
339 Pent Ch of God	1	30	NR	133	.8	1.0
419 So Bapt Conv	6	1,749	588	2,183 *	13.3	16.8
449 Un Methodist	7	721	335	900 *	5.5	6.9
GREENE	**94**	**17,627**	**8,527**	**22,947 ***	**61.5**	**100.0**
017 Amer Bapt Assn	4	285	NR	354 *	.9	1.5
053 Assemb of God	3	185	211	284	.8	1.2
056 Baha'i	0	1	NR	1	-	-
059 Bapt Miss Assn	3	411	145	511 *	1.4	2.2
081 Catholic	1	NR	NR	618	1.7	2.7
097 Chr Chs&Chs Cr	1	50	NR	62 *	.2	.3
123 Ch God (Ander)	1	NR	51	51	.1	.2
127 Ch God (Cleve)	2	189	42	235 *	.6	1.0
145 Ch God Prophcy	1	29	NR	36 *	.1	.2
165 Ch of Nazarene	3	138	76	149	.4	.6
167 Chs of Christ	21	2,409	2,673	3,339	8.9	14.6
193 Episcopal	1	NR	15	21	.1	.1
223 Free Will Bapt	3	304	NR	378 *	1.0	1.6
283 Luth—MO Synod	2	332	185	368	1.0	1.6
339 Pent Ch of God	1	11	NR	25	.1	.1
355 Presb Ch (USA)	1	22	19	27 *	.1	.1
419 So Bapt Conv	35	11,305	4,246	14,054 *	37.6	61.2
449 Un Methodist	11	1,956	864	2,434 *	6.5	10.6

NR–Not Reported *Total adherents estimated from known number of communicant, confirmed, full members. - Represents a percentage less than 0.1. Percentages may not total 100 due to rounding.

Table 4: Religious Congregations by County and Group: 2000

Religious Group	Number of Churches, Synagogues, Mosques, or Temples	Number of Communicant, Confirmed, or Full Members	Number of Attendees	Total Adherents		
				Number of Adherents	% of Total Pop.	% of Total Adh.
HEMPSTEAD	**64**	**8,996**	**3,665**	**11,980 ***	**50.8**	**100.0**
017 Amer Bapt Assn	2	81	NR	102 *	.4	.9
053 Assemb of God	1	120	140	200	.8	1.7
059 Bapt Miss Assn	16	3,526	1,226	4,458 *	18.9	37.2
081 Catholic	1	NR	NR	355	1.5	3.0
097 Chr Chs&Chs Cr	1	108	NR	137 *	.6	1.1
123 Ch God (Ander)	1	NR	25	25	.1	.2
145 Ch God Prophcy	1	29	NR	37 *	.2	.3
151 L-D Saints	1	NR	NR	97	.4	.8
165 Ch of Nazarene	2	106	75	141	.6	1.2
167 Chs of Christ	8	573	563	718	3.0	6.0
193 Episcopal	1	NR	26	75	.3	.6
226 Friends-USA	1	15	NR	19 *	.1	.2
339 Pent Ch of God	1	13	NR	20	.1	.2
355 Presb Ch (USA)	2	87	46	110 *	.5	.9
413 S.D.A.	1	26	NR	31	.1	.3
419 So Bapt Conv	9	2,973	1,038	3,760 *	15.9	31.4
449 Un Methodist	15	1,339	526	1,695 *	7.2	14.1
HOT SPRING	**90**	**13,701**	**2,850**	**17,750 ***	**58.5**	**100.0**
017 Amer Bapt Assn	37	7,459	NR	9,232 *	30.4	52.0
053 Assemb of God	11	778	858	1,007	3.3	5.7
056 Baha'i	0	2	NR	2	-	-
059 Bapt Miss Assn	2	499	150	617 *	2.0	3.5
081 Catholic	1	NR	NR	309	1.0	1.7
121 Ch God (Abr)	1	35	27	43 *	.1	.2
127 Ch God (Cleve)	1	45	34	56 *	.2	.3
145 Ch God Prophcy	1	29	NR	36 *	.1	.2
151 L-D Saints	1	NR	NR	436	1.4	2.5
165 Ch of Nazarene	1	9	23	26	.1	.1
167 Chs of Christ	4	189	192	232	.8	1.3
223 Free Will Bapt	1	101	NR	125 *	.4	.7
283 Luth—MO Synod	1	71	50	84	.3	.5
339 Pent Ch of God	1	8	NR	20	.1	.1
355 Presb Ch (USA)	1	170	95	210 *	.7	1.2
360 Prim Bapt Chrch	2	NR	NR	NR	-	-
413 S.D.A.	2	263	NR	313	1.0	1.8
419 So Bapt Conv	11	2,503	793	3,097 *	10.2	17.4
449 Un Methodist	11	1,540	628	1,905 *	6.3	10.7
HOWARD	**57**	**7,097**	**3,095**	**9,427 ***	**65.9**	**100.0**
017 Amer Bapt Assn	7	765	NR	963 *	6.7	10.2
032 Amish; other	1	105	NR	132 *	.9	1.4
053 Assemb of God	2	142	170	482	3.4	5.1
059 Bapt Miss Assn	12	1,753	605	2,205 *	15.4	23.4
081 Catholic	1	NR	NR	124	.9	1.3
097 Chr Chs&Chs Cr	1	65	NR	82 *	.6	.9
123 Ch God (Ander)	2	NR	130	130	.9	1.4
167 Chs of Christ	14	1,247	1,136	1,514	10.6	16.1
173 Comm of Christ	1	12	NR	12	.1	.1
413 S.D.A.	1	15	NR	18	.1	.2
419 So Bapt Conv	6	2,260	737	2,843 *	19.9	30.2
449 Un Methodist	9	733	317	922 *	6.4	9.8
INDEPENDENCE	**112**	**16,863**	**6,879**	**22,033 ***	**64.4**	**100.0**
017 Amer Bapt Assn	16	1,648	NR	2,019 *	5.9	9.2
053 Assemb of God	6	445	592	810	2.4	3.7
056 Baha'i	0	6	NR	6	-	-
059 Bapt Miss Assn	7	1,096	359	1,345 *	3.9	6.1
081 Catholic	1	NR	NR	614	1.8	2.8
084 Calvary Chapel	1	NR	NR	NR	-	-
127 Ch God (Cleve)	3	170	105	208 *	.6	.9
145 Ch God Prophcy	1	29	NR	36 *	.1	.2
151 L-D Saints	1	NR	NR	203	.6	.9
165 Ch of Nazarene	1	151	108	223	.7	1.0
167 Chs of Christ	19	1,550	1,565	1,934	5.6	8.8
185 Cumber Presb	2	97	NR	159	.5	.7
193 Episcopal	1	NR	111	224	.7	1.0
223 Free Will Bapt	7	709	NR	869 *	2.5	3.9
283 Luth—MO Synod	1	127	97	165	.5	.7
339 Pent Ch of God	1	21	NR	40	.1	.2
355 Presb Ch (USA)	1	289	116	354 *	1.0	1.6
413 S.D.A.	1	72	NR	86	.3	.4
419 So Bapt Conv	23	7,789	2,633	9,542 *	27.9	43.3
449 Un Methodist	18	2,364	943	2,896 *	8.5	13.1
499 Indep.Non-Char	1	300	250	300	.9	1.4
IZARD	**61**	**5,784**	**2,678**	**7,349 ***	**55.5**	**100.0**
017 Amer Bapt Assn	8	356	NR	424 *	3.2	5.8
053 Assemb of God	5	159	212	279	2.1	3.8
056 Baha'i	0	9	NR	9	.1	.1
059 Bapt Miss Assn	1	62	45	74 *	.6	1.0
081 Catholic	1	NR	NR	263	2.0	3.6
165 Ch of Nazarene	1	41	24	41	.3	.6
167 Chs of Christ	9	304	408	424	3.2	5.8
185 Cumber Presb	6	296	NR	397	3.0	5.4
193 Episcopal	1	NR	23	34	.3	.5
223 Free Will Bapt	2	203	NR	241 *	1.8	3.3
283 Luth—MO Synod	1	145	106	155	1.2	2.1
288 Mennonite USA	1	40	45	48 *	.4	.7
355 Presb Ch (USA)	1	74	61	88 *	.7	1.2
419 So Bapt Conv	16	3,473	1,405	4,132 *	31.2	56.2
449 Un Methodist	8	622	349	740 *	5.6	10.1
JACKSON	**70**	**8,203**	**3,537**	**10,434 ***	**56.7**	**100.0**
017 Amer Bapt Assn	7	630	NR	758 *	4.1	7.3
053 Assemb of God	5	209	256	357	1.9	3.4
059 Bapt Miss Assn	3	430	163	517 *	2.8	5.0
081 Catholic	1	NR	NR	124	.7	1.2
093 Chr Ch (Disc)	1	73	31	88 *	.5	.8
127 Ch God (Cleve)	1	110	0	132 *	.7	1.3
165 Ch of Nazarene	1	41	13	41	.2	.4
167 Chs of Christ	22	1,547	1,615	1,931	10.5	18.5
193 Episcopal	1	NR	57	138	.7	1.3
223 Free Will Bapt	4	405	NR	488 *	2.6	4.7
339 Pent Ch of God	3	129	NR	290	1.6	2.8
355 Presb Ch (USA)	1	122	80	147 *	.8	1.4
419 So Bapt Conv	13	3,831	1,037	4,610 *	25.0	44.2
449 Un Methodist	7	676	285	813 *	4.4	7.8
JEFFERSON	**116**	**29,400**	**9,097**	**40,290 ***	**47.8**	**100.0**
017 Amer Bapt Assn	14	5,042	NR	6,311 *	7.5	15.7
053 Assemb of God	6	809	918	1,553	1.8	3.9
056 Baha'i	0	30	NR	30	-	.1
059 Bapt Miss Assn	8	839	357	1,049 *	1.2	2.6
081 Catholic	4	NR	NR	2,011	2.4	5.0
093 Chr Ch (Disc)	2	213	95	267 *	.3	.7
097 Chr Chs&Chs Cr	1	50	NR	63 *	.1	.2
123 Ch God (Ander)	1	NR	10	10	-	-
127 Ch God (Cleve)	3	338	86	423 *	.5	1.0
151 L-D Saints	1	NR	NR	329	.4	.8
165 Ch of Nazarene	1	94	38	94	.1	.2
167 Chs of Christ	10	819	816	1,089	1.3	2.7
185 Cumber Presb	2	62	NR	169	.2	.4
193 Episcopal	2	NR	175	390	.5	1.0
223 Free Will Bapt	1	101	NR	127 *	.2	.3
283 Luth—MO Synod	1	211	100	247	.3	.6
339 Pent Ch of God	3	54	NR	118	.1	.3
355 Presb Ch (USA)	4	959	463	1,200 *	1.4	3.0
360 Prim Bapt Chrch	1	NR	NR	NR	-	-
403 Salvation Army	1	57	22	112	.1	.3
413 S.D.A.	3	260	NR	310	.4	.8
419 So Bapt Conv	31	15,577	4,512	19,494 *	23.1	48.4
449 Un Methodist	15	3,885	1,505	4,864 *	5.8	12.1
496 Jewish Est	1	NR	NR	30	-	.1
JOHNSON	**51**	**7,869**	**2,969**	**10,925 ***	**48.0**	**100.0**
017 Amer Bapt Assn	2	616	NR	763 *	3.3	7.0
053 Assemb of God	10	516	624	847	3.7	7.8
056 Baha'i	0	6	NR	6	-	.1
059 Bapt Miss Assn	1	120	75	149 *	.7	1.4
081 Catholic	1	NR	NR	803	3.5	7.4
097 Chr Chs&Chs Cr	1	23	NR	28 *	.1	.3
165 Ch of Nazarene	1	53	42	118	.5	1.1

NR–Not Reported *Total adherents estimated from known number of communicant, confirmed, full members. - Represents a percentage less than 0.1. Percentages may not total 100 due to rounding.

Table 4: Religious Congregations by County and Group: 2000

Religious Group	Number of Churches, Synagogues, Mosques, or Temples	Number of Communicant, Confirmed, or Full Members	Number of Attendees	Total Adherents: Number of Adherents	Total Adherents: % of Total Pop.	Total Adherents: % of Total Adh.
167 Chs of Christ	7	535	414	628	2.8	5.7
223 Free Will Bapt	2	203	NR	251 *	1.1	2.3
283 Luth—MO Synod	1	112	55	155	.7	1.4
339 Pent Ch of God	1	91	NR	251	1.1	2.3
355 Presb Ch (USA)	3	322	153	399 *	1.8	3.7
413 S.D.A.	1	59	NR	70	.3	.6
419 So Bapt Conv	14	4,242	1,258	5,255 *	23.1	48.1
449 Un Methodist	6	971	348	1,202 *	5.3	11.0
LAFAYETTE	**32**	**3,766**	**1,317**	**4,681 ***	**54.7**	**100.0**
017 Amer Bapt Assn	2	196	NR	242 *	2.8	5.2
053 Assemb of God	2	64	67	81	.9	1.7
056 Baha'i	0	2	NR	2	-	-
059 Bapt Miss Assn	8	878	270	1,084 *	12.7	23.2
165 Ch of Nazarene	1	45	21	56	.7	1.2
167 Chs of Christ	6	292	293	384	4.5	8.2
356 Presb Ch Amer	1	15	20	23	.3	.5
419 So Bapt Conv	6	1,691	417	2,088 *	24.4	44.6
449 Un Methodist	6	583	229	721 *	8.4	15.4
LAWRENCE	**74**	**8,391**	**3,455**	**10,800 ***	**60.8**	**100.0**
017 Amer Bapt Assn	10	954	NR	1,166 *	6.6	10.8
053 Assemb of God	6	221	251	384	2.2	3.6
056 Baha'i	0	1	NR	1	-	-
059 Bapt Miss Assn	2	897	305	1,095 *	6.2	10.1
081 Catholic	1	NR	NR	99	.6	.9
167 Chs of Christ	16	1,000	1,491	1,440	8.1	13.3
223 Free Will Bapt	8	811	NR	990 *	5.6	9.2
297 Mennonite;Other	1	42	NR	51 *	.3	.5
339 Pent Ch of God	2	46	NR	178	1.0	1.6
355 Presb Ch (USA)	1	77	55	94 *	.5	.9
419 So Bapt Conv	15	3,371	842	4,116 *	23.2	38.1
449 Un Methodist	12	971	511	1,186 *	6.7	11.0
LEE	**27**	**3,393**	**784**	**4,331 ***	**34.4**	**100.0**
017 Amer Bapt Assn	5	821	NR	1,018 *	8.1	23.5
053 Assemb of God	1	34	45	45	.4	1.0
056 Baha'i	0	1	NR	1	-	-
059 Bapt Miss Assn	2	248	93	307 *	2.4	7.1
081 Catholic	1	NR	NR	49	.4	1.1
097 Chr Chs&Chs Cr	1	125	NR	155 *	1.2	3.6
127 Ch God (Cleve)	1	64	26	79 *	.6	1.8
145 Ch God Prophcy	1	29	NR	36 *	.3	.8
167 Chs of Christ	5	140	159	184	1.5	4.2
193 Episcopal	1	NR	17	63	.5	1.5
355 Presb Ch (USA)	1	44	20	55 *	.4	1.3
419 So Bapt Conv	4	1,469	289	1,821 *	14.5	42.0
449 Un Methodist	4	418	135	518 *	4.1	12.0
LINCOLN	**38**	**4,598**	**1,010**	**5,741 ***	**39.6**	**100.0**
017 Amer Bapt Assn	10	1,835	NR	2,208 *	15.2	38.5
053 Assemb of God	2	159	185	256	1.8	4.5
056 Baha'i	0	6	NR	6	-	.1
059 Bapt Miss Assn	1	45	25	54 *	.4	.9
081 Catholic	2	NR	NR	130	.9	2.3
097 Chr Chs&Chs Cr	2	129	NR	155 *	1.1	2.7
167 Chs of Christ	3	126	135	164	1.1	2.9
185 Cumber Presb	1	6	NR	7	-	.1
223 Free Will Bapt	3	304	NR	366 *	2.5	6.4
355 Presb Ch (USA)	2	12	14	16 *	.1	.3
419 So Bapt Conv	8	1,628	469	1,960 *	13.5	34.1
449 Un Methodist	4	348	182	419 *	2.9	7.3
LITTLE RIVER	**36**	**5,534**	**2,250**	**7,257 ***	**53.3**	**100.0**
017 Amer Bapt Assn	3	314	NR	390 *	2.9	5.4
053 Assemb of God	2	149	186	263	1.9	3.6
059 Bapt Miss Assn	2	698	285	866 *	6.4	11.9
081 Catholic	2	NR	NR	183	1.3	2.5
165 Ch of Nazarene	1	76	91	109	.8	1.5
167 Chs of Christ	4	370	376	472	3.5	6.5
173 Comm of Christ	1	45	NR	45	.3	.6
185 Cumber Presb	2	54	NR	104	.8	1.4
193 Episcopal	1	NR	27	67	.5	.9
339 Pent Ch of God	1	15	NR	28	.2	.4
355 Presb Ch (USA)	1	29	23	36 *	.3	.5
419 So Bapt Conv	9	3,081	955	3,823 *	28.1	52.7
449 Un Methodist	7	703	307	871 *	6.4	12.0
LOGAN	**88**	**10,010**	**3,908**	**16,680 ***	**74.2**	**100.0**
017 Amer Bapt Assn	4	618	NR	769 *	3.4	4.6
053 Assemb of God	13	798	1,000	1,425	6.3	8.5
056 Baha'i	0	4	NR	4	-	-
059 Bapt Miss Assn	1	109	28	135 *	.6	.8
081 Catholic	8	NR	NR	3,021	13.4	18.1
093 Chr Ch (Disc)	1	151	60	188 *	.8	1.1
121 Ch God (Abr)	1	10	19	19 *	.1	.1
127 Ch God (Cleve)	1	103	21	128 *	.6	.8
151 L-D Saints	1	NR	NR	317	1.4	1.9
167 Chs of Christ	6	354	377	457	2.0	2.7
171 Ch God-Gen Con	1	20	32	32 *	.1	.2
185 Cumber Presb	7	258	NR	510	2.3	3.1
207 E.L.C.A.	1	45	35	67	.3	.4
223 Free Will Bapt	4	405	NR	504 *	2.2	3.0
339 Pent Ch of God	4	168	NR	445	2.0	2.7
349 Pent Holiness	2	163	118	203 *	.9	1.2
355 Presb Ch (USA)	1	7	8	9 *	-	.1
360 Prim Bapt Chrch	4	NR	NR	NR	-	-
413 S.D.A.	1	18	NR	21	.1	.1
419 So Bapt Conv	18	5,713	1,770	7,101 *	31.6	42.6
449 Un Methodist	9	1,066	440	1,325 *	5.9	7.9
LONOKE	**95**	**22,733**	**8,028**	**30,149 ***	**57.1**	**100.0**
017 Amer Bapt Assn	13	2,548	NR	3,264 *	6.2	10.8
053 Assemb of God	4	441	623	756	1.4	2.5
056 Baha'i	0	63	NR	63	.1	.2
059 Bapt Miss Assn	6	1,532	497	1,964 *	3.7	6.5
081 Catholic	2	NR	NR	252	.5	.8
127 Ch God (Cleve)	1	70	26	90 *	.2	.3
145 Ch God Prophcy	1	29	NR	37 *	.1	.1
151 L-D Saints	1	NR	NR	301	.6	1.0
165 Ch of Nazarene	1	103	92	200	.4	.7
167 Chs of Christ	9	1,028	866	1,382	2.6	4.6
263 Int Foursq Gos	1	185	41	237 *	.4	.8
339 Pent Ch of God	6	180	NR	395	.7	1.3
355 Presb Ch (USA)	3	264	157	338 *	.6	1.1
418 Southw Bapt Fel	1	NR	NR	NR	-	-
419 So Bapt Conv	28	13,086	4,320	16,765 *	31.7	55.6
449 Un Methodist	18	3,204	1,406	4,105 *	7.8	13.6
MADISON	**39**	**3,650**	**1,940**	**4,983 ***	**35.0**	**100.0**
017 Amer Bapt Assn	1	70	NR	88 *	.6	1.8
053 Assemb of God	3	265	366	501	3.5	10.1
056 Baha'i	0	3	NR	3	-	.1
059 Bapt Miss Assn	1	88	19	110 *	.8	2.2
076 Buddhism	1	NR	NR	NR	-	-
081 Catholic	1	NR	NR	53	.4	1.1
107 Christian Un	1	5	8	8 *	.1	.2
151 L-D Saints	1	NR	NR	158	1.1	3.2
167 Chs of Christ	16	714	725	932	6.5	18.7
223 Free Will Bapt	4	405	NR	507 *	3.6	10.2
355 Presb Ch (USA)	1	109	55	136 *	1.0	2.7
413 S.D.A.	1	72	NR	86	.6	1.7
419 So Bapt Conv	6	1,745	688	2,184 *	15.3	43.8
449 Un Methodist	2	174	79	217 *	1.5	4.4
MARION	**35**	**4,269**	**2,039**	**5,820 ***	**36.1**	**100.0**
017 Amer Bapt Assn	1	43	NR	51 *	.3	.9
053 Assemb of God	2	98	120	173	1.1	3.0
081 Catholic	1	NR	NR	185	1.1	3.2
097 Chr Chs&Chs Cr	2	280	NR	336 *	2.1	5.8
127 Ch God (Cleve)	1	83	45	99 *	.6	1.7
151 L-D Saints	1	NR	NR	456	2.8	7.8
167 Chs of Christ	7	316	319	378	2.3	6.5
207 E.L.C.A.	1	206	117	226	1.4	3.9

NR–Not Reported *Total adherents estimated from known number of communicant, confirmed, full members. - Represents a percentage less than 0.1. Percentages may not total 100 due to rounding.

Table 4: Religious Congregations by County and Group: 2000

Religious Group	Number of Churches, Synagogues, Mosques, or Temples	Number of Communicant, Confirmed, or Full Members	Number of Attendees	Total Adherents: Number of Adherents	Total Adherents: % of Total Pop.	Total Adherents: % of Total Adh.
339 Pent Ch of God	1	20	NR	60	.4	1.0
355 Presb Ch (USA)	2	239	188	286 *	1.8	4.9
413 S.D.A.	1	23	NR	27	.2	.5
419 So Bapt Conv	10	2,257	982	2,701 *	16.7	46.4
449 Un Methodist	5	704	268	842 *	5.2	14.5
MILLER	**76**	**18,955**	**6,982**	**25,918 ***	**64.1**	**100.0**
017 Amer Bapt Assn	5	1,466	NR	1,847 *	4.6	7.1
053 Assemb of God	6	619	610	689	1.7	2.7
056 Baha'i	0	5	NR	5	-	-
059 Bapt Miss Assn	2	547	173	689 *	1.7	2.7
081 Catholic	1	NR	NR	2,048	5.1	7.9
093 Chr Ch (Disc)	1	372	159	468 *	1.2	1.8
123 Ch God (Ander)	1	NR	18	18	-	.1
145 Ch God Prophcy	1	29	NR	37 *	.1	.1
165 Ch of Nazarene	1	277	116	443	1.1	1.7
167 Chs of Christ	12	784	759	886	2.2	3.4
339 Pent Ch of God	3	99	NR	205	.5	.8
355 Presb Ch (USA)	1	264	110	332 *	.8	1.3
360 Prim Bapt Chrch	1	NR	NR	NR	-	-
370 Ref Baptist Chs	1	NR	NR	NR	-	-
419 So Bapt Conv	27	11,994	3,902	15,104 *	37.3	58.3
449 Un Methodist	13	2,499	1,135	3,147 *	7.8	12.1
MISSISSIPPI	**122**	**24,371**	**7,391**	**32,928 ***	**63.3**	**100.0**
053 Assemb of God	8	312	351	527	1.0	1.6
056 Baha'i	0	7	NR	7	-	-
059 Bapt Miss Assn	7	1,287	480	1,672 *	3.2	5.1
081 Catholic	2	NR	NR	679	1.3	2.1
093 Chr Ch (Disc)	2	291	195	378 *	.7	1.1
097 Chr Chs&Chs Cr	1	108	NR	140 *	.3	.4
127 Ch God (Cleve)	9	1,218	666	1,582 *	3.0	4.8
145 Ch God Prophcy	1	29	NR	38 *	.1	.1
151 L-D Saints	1	NR	NR	234	.5	.7
165 Ch of Nazarene	2	106	57	158	.3	.5
167 Chs of Christ	17	1,009	966	1,173	2.3	3.6
193 Episcopal	2	NR	47	78	.2	.2
223 Free Will Bapt	1	101	NR	132 *	.3	.4
283 Luth—MO Synod	1	110	61	143	.3	.4
339 Pent Ch of God	5	250	NR	588	1.1	1.8
349 Pent Holiness	1	40	43	52 *	.1	.2
355 Presb Ch (USA)	1	265	160	344 *	.7	1.0
356 Presb Ch Amer	2	125	61	153	.3	.5
419 So Bapt Conv	46	16,914	3,565	21,961 *	42.2	66.7
449 Un Methodist	12	2,199	739	2,854 *	5.5	8.7
496 Jewish Est	1	NR	NR	35	.1	.1
MONROE	**33**	**4,294**	**1,382**	**5,740 ***	**56.0**	**100.0**
017 Amer Bapt Assn	5	717	NR	907 *	8.8	15.8
053 Assemb of God	2	99	129	281	2.7	4.9
059 Bapt Miss Assn	3	145	92	183 *	1.8	3.2
081 Catholic	1	NR	NR	119	1.2	2.1
127 Ch God (Cleve)	1	16	6	20 *	.2	.3
145 Ch God Prophcy	1	29	NR	37 *	.4	.6
167 Chs of Christ	4	241	205	339	3.3	5.9
193 Episcopal	1	NR	10	16	.2	.3
283 Luth—MO Synod	1	84	25	100	1.0	1.7
355 Presb Ch (USA)	2	78	64	98 *	1.0	1.7
356 Presb Ch Amer	1	49	35	54	.5	.9
413 S.D.A.	1	15	NR	18	.2	.3
419 So Bapt Conv	5	2,242	590	2,836 *	27.7	49.4
449 Un Methodist	5	579	226	732 *	7.1	12.8
MONTGOMERY	**44**	**3,790**	**2,006**	**4,887 ***	**52.9**	**100.0**
017 Amer Bapt Assn	5	261	NR	318 *	3.4	6.5
053 Assemb of God	2	86	116	143	1.5	2.9
081 Catholic	1	NR	NR	67	.7	1.4
165 Ch of Nazarene	2	241	217	422	4.6	8.6
167 Chs of Christ	3	120	150	160	1.7	3.3
171 Ch God-Gen Con	3	243	172	296 *	3.2	6.1
266 Intrstat & Asc	1	18	NR	22 *	.2	.5
339 Pent Ch of God	1	17	NR	40	.4	.8

Religious Group	Number of Churches, Synagogues, Mosques, or Temples	Number of Communicant, Confirmed, or Full Members	Number of Attendees	Total Adherents: Number of Adherents	Total Adherents: % of Total Pop.	Total Adherents: % of Total Adh.
355 Presb Ch (USA)	2	39	32	47 *	.5	1.0
360 Prim Bapt Chrch	3	NR	NR	NR	-	-
419 So Bapt Conv	17	2,361	1,087	2,880 *	31.2	58.9
449 Un Methodist	4	404	232	492 *	5.3	10.1
NEVADA	**41**	**4,899**	**2,043**	**6,010 ***	**60.4**	**100.0**
017 Amer Bapt Assn	4	437	NR	540 *	5.4	9.0
053 Assemb of God	1	45	53	60	.6	1.0
059 Bapt Miss Assn	15	2,487	944	3,074 *	30.9	51.1
123 Ch God (Ander)	1	NR	15	15	.2	.2
165 Ch of Nazarene	3	177	82	177	1.8	2.9
167 Chs of Christ	6	426	364	504	5.1	8.4
355 Presb Ch (USA)	1	42	30	52 *	.5	.9
419 So Bapt Conv	3	749	269	926 *	9.3	15.4
449 Un Methodist	7	536	286	662 *	6.6	11.0
NEWTON	**22**	**1,568**	**1,090**	**2,067 ***	**24.0**	**100.0**
017 Amer Bapt Assn	1	39	NR	48 *	.6	2.3
053 Assemb of God	4	262	323	437	5.1	21.1
056 Baha'i	0	1	NR	1	-	-
107 Christian Un	1	10	20	20 *	.2	1.0
167 Chs of Christ	6	227	253	304	3.5	14.7
223 Free Will Bapt	1	101	NR	124 *	1.4	6.0
419 So Bapt Conv	8	823	441	1,005 *	11.7	48.6
449 Un Methodist	1	105	53	128 *	1.5	6.2
OUACHITA	**81**	**14,301**	**5,145**	**18,035 ***	**62.6**	**100.0**
017 Amer Bapt Assn	7	583	NR	723 *	2.5	4.0
053 Assemb of God	10	1,235	976	1,367	4.7	7.6
056 Baha'i	0	2	NR	2	-	-
059 Bapt Miss Assn	4	1,146	305	1,422 *	4.9	7.9
081 Catholic	1	NR	NR	235	.8	1.3
093 Chr Ch (Disc)	1	60	12	74 *	.3	.4
123 Ch God (Ander)	1	NR	0	0	-	-
151 L-D Saints	1	NR	NR	77	.3	.4
165 Ch of Nazarene	1	54	43	75	.3	.4
167 Chs of Christ	8	758	667	982	3.4	5.4
185 Cumber Presb	5	185	NR	268	.9	1.5
193 Episcopal	1	NR	37	55	.2	.3
283 Luth—MO Synod	1	0	5	3	-	-
355 Presb Ch (USA)	2	279	114	347 *	1.2	1.9
360 Prim Bapt Chrch	1	NR	NR	NR	-	-
413 S.D.A.	1	10	NR	12	-	.1
419 So Bapt Conv	20	7,697	2,157	9,550 *	33.2	53.0
449 Un Methodist	16	2,292	829	2,843 *	9.9	15.8
PERRY	**34**	**3,863**	**1,531**	**5,171 ***	**50.7**	**100.0**
017 Amer Bapt Assn	4	317	NR	393 *	3.8	7.6
053 Assemb of God	4	196	214	330	3.2	6.4
081 Catholic	1	NR	NR	241	2.4	4.7
165 Ch of Nazarene	1	25	20	74	.7	1.4
167 Chs of Christ	5	175	185	222	2.2	4.3
223 Free Will Bapt	1	101	NR	126 *	1.2	2.4
419 So Bapt Conv	13	2,709	901	3,363 *	32.9	65.0
449 Un Methodist	5	340	211	422 *	4.1	8.2
PHILLIPS	**47**	**7,989**	**2,377**	**11,465 ***	**43.4**	**100.0**
017 Amer Bapt Assn	2	273	NR	362 *	1.4	3.2
053 Assemb of God	2	77	92	156	.6	1.4
056 Baha'i	0	1	NR	1	-	-
059 Bapt Miss Assn	6	1,033	242	1,371 *	5.2	12.0
081 Catholic	1	NR	NR	469	1.8	4.1
097 Chr Chs&Chs Cr	1	59	NR	78 *	.3	.7
127 Ch God (Cleve)	2	191	73	253 *	1.0	2.2
145 Ch God Prophcy	2	58	NR	78 *	.3	.7
165 Ch of Nazarene	1	43	38	45	.2	.4
167 Chs of Christ	5	455	431	640	2.4	5.6
193 Episcopal	1	NR	93	292	1.1	2.5
355 Presb Ch (USA)	2	127	55	169 *	.6	1.5
360 Prim Bapt Chrch	1	NR	NR	NR	-	-
413 S.D.A.	2	105	NR	125	.5	1.1
419 So Bapt Conv	12	4,562	1,029	6,057 *	22.9	52.8

NR–Not Reported *Total adherents estimated from known number of communicant, confirmed, full members. - Represents a percentage less than 0.1. Percentages may not total 100 due to rounding.

Table 4: Religious Congregations by County and Group: 2000

Religious Group	Number of Churches, Synagogues, Mosques, or Temples	Number of Communicant, Confirmed, or Full Members	Number of Attendees	Total Adherents		
				Number of Adherents	% of Total Pop.	% of Total Adh.
443 Un C of Christ	1	22	14	29 *	.1	.3
449 Un Methodist	5	983	310	1,305 *	4.9	11.4
496 Jewish Est	1	NR	NR	35	.1	.3
PIKE	**57**	**5,153**	**1,978**	**6,756 ***	**59.8**	**100.0**
017 Amer Bapt Assn	12	1,165	NR	1,437 *	12.7	21.3
053 Assemb of God	5	331	365	518	4.6	7.7
059 Bapt Miss Assn	1	37	25	46 *	.4	.7
081 Catholic	1	NR	NR	93	.8	1.4
097 Chr Chs&Chs Cr	1	300	NR	370 *	3.3	5.5
151 L-D Saints	1	NR	NR	144	1.3	2.1
167 Chs of Christ	13	861	826	1,102	9.7	16.3
223 Free Will Bapt	5	507	NR	626 *	5.5	9.3
273 LandmrkBapt,I&U	1	36	NR	44 *	.4	.7
339 Pent Ch of God	2	24	NR	41	.4	.6
360 Prim Bapt Chrch	1	NR	NR	NR	-	-
413 S.D.A.	1	25	NR	30	.3	.4
419 So Bapt Conv	5	1,331	486	1,643 *	14.5	24.3
449 Un Methodist	8	536	276	662 *	5.9	9.8
POINSETT	**86**	**13,640**	**4,731**	**17,476 ***	**68.2**	**100.0**
017 Amer Bapt Assn	2	146	NR	182 *	.7	1.0
053 Assemb of God	6	289	349	406	1.6	2.3
059 Bapt Miss Assn	4	605	217	754 *	2.9	4.3
081 Catholic	2	NR	NR	235	.9	1.3
093 Chr Ch (Disc)	2	186	69	232 *	.9	1.3
097 Chr Chs&Chs Cr	1	165	NR	206 *	.8	1.2
127 Ch God (Cleve)	4	381	197	476 *	1.9	2.7
145 Ch God Prophcy	4	116	NR	144 *	.6	.8
167 Chs of Christ	13	836	765	1,133	4.4	6.5
173 Comm of Christ	1	42	NR	42	.2	.2
283 Luth—MO Synod	1	147	92	171	.7	1.0
339 Pent Ch of God	2	135	NR	270	1.1	1.5
419 So Bapt Conv	33	9,266	2,616	11,567 *	45.2	66.2
449 Un Methodist	11	1,326	426	1,658 *	6.5	9.5
POLK	**65**	**8,457**	**2,994**	**11,934 ***	**59.0**	**100.0**
017 Amer Bapt Assn	3	61	NR	76 *	.4	.6
032 Amish; other	1	53	NR	66 *	.3	.6
053 Assemb of God	3	219	212	374	1.8	3.1
056 Baha'i	0	4	NR	4	-	-
059 Bapt Miss Assn	2	417	145	517 *	2.6	4.3
081 Catholic	1	NR	NR	768	3.8	6.4
097 Chr Chs&Chs Cr	4	417	NR	518 *	2.6	4.3
127 Ch God (Cleve)	1	163	113	202 *	1.0	1.7
145 Ch God Prophcy	1	29	NR	36 *	.2	.3
151 L-D Saints	1	NR	NR	239	1.2	2.0
165 Ch of Nazarene	3	379	288	551	2.7	4.6
167 Chs of Christ	8	357	381	444	2.2	3.7
173 Comm of Christ	1	31	NR	31	.2	.3
193 Episcopal	1	NR	39	39	.2	.3
223 Free Will Bapt	1	101	NR	126 *	.6	1.1
266 Intrstat & Asc	1	18	NR	22 *	.1	.2
283 Luth—MO Synod	1	62	36	74	.4	.6
339 Pent Ch of God	3	149	NR	407	2.0	3.4
355 Presb Ch (USA)	1	75	38	93 *	.5	.8
360 Prim Bapt Chrch	1	NR	NR	NR	-	-
413 S.D.A.	2	107	NR	128	.6	1.1
419 So Bapt Conv	19	4,932	1,338	6,123 *	30.3	51.3
449 Un Methodist	6	883	404	1,096 *	5.4	9.2
POPE	**127**	**18,397**	**9,242**	**27,635 ***	**50.7**	**100.0**
017 Amer Bapt Assn	8	1,006	NR	1,252 *	2.3	4.5
053 Assemb of God	25	2,319	2,720	3,862	7.1	14.0
055 As Ref Pres Ch	1	92	NR	110	.2	.4
056 Baha'i	0	14	NR	14	-	.1
059 Bapt Miss Assn	1	348	140	433 *	.8	1.6
081 Catholic	3	NR	NR	2,070	3.8	7.5
089 Chr & Miss Al	1	3	NR	49	.1	.2
093 Chr Ch (Disc)	2	150	76	187 *	.3	.7
097 Chr Chs&Chs Cr	1	50	NR	62 *	.1	.2
127 Ch God (Cleve)	1	120	71	149 *	.3	.5

Religious Group	Number of Churches, Synagogues, Mosques, or Temples	Number of Communicant, Confirmed, or Full Members	Number of Attendees	Total Adherents		
				Number of Adherents	% of Total Pop.	% of Total Adh.
145 Ch God Prophcy	1	29	NR	36 *	.1	.1
151 L-D Saints	2	NR	NR	594	1.1	2.1
165 Ch of Nazarene	1	69	41	69	.1	.2
167 Chs of Christ	14	1,277	1,188	1,650	3.0	6.0
185 Cumber Presb	6	306	NR	496	.9	1.8
193 Episcopal	1	NR	138	396	.7	1.4
223 Free Will Bapt	17	1,723	NR	2,143 *	3.9	7.8
263 Int Foursq Gos	1	30	50	50 *	.1	.2
283 Luth—MO Synod	2	460	217	595	1.1	2.2
339 Pent Ch of God	5	160	NR	352	.6	1.3
349 Pent Holiness	1	50	37	62 *	.1	.2
355 Presb Ch (USA)	2	520	197	646 *	1.2	2.3
360 Prim Bapt Chrch	1	NR	NR	NR	-	-
403 Salvation Army	1	43	39	43	.1	.2
413 S.D.A.	1	78	NR	93	.2	.3
419 So Bapt Conv	17	7,084	2,430	8,809 *	16.2	31.9
449 Un Methodist	9	2,409	1,513	2,995 *	5.5	10.8
469 WELS	1	57	35	68	.1	.2
498 Indep.Charis.	1	0	350	350	.6	1.3
PRAIRIE	**32**	**4,873**	**1,279**	**6,422 ***	**67.3**	**100.0**
017 Amer Bapt Assn	8	2,003	NR	2,434 *	25.5	37.9
053 Assemb of God	2	104	115	170	1.8	2.6
059 Bapt Miss Assn	1	13	6	16 *	.2	.2
081 Catholic	1	NR	NR	222	2.3	3.5
145 Ch God Prophcy	1	29	NR	35 *	.4	.5
165 Ch of Nazarene	1	37	27	74	.8	1.2
167 Chs of Christ	4	151	161	197	2.1	3.1
193 Episcopal	1	NR	44	174	1.8	2.7
283 Luth—MO Synod	1	243	90	291	3.1	4.5
339 Pent Ch of God	1	10	NR	35	.4	.5
355 Presb Ch (USA)	1	22	14	27 *	.3	.4
419 So Bapt Conv	5	1,601	521	1,945 *	20.4	30.3
449 Un Methodist	5	660	301	802 *	8.4	12.5
PULASKI	**400**	**140,781**	**55,297**	**213,782 ***	**59.1**	**100.0**
017 Amer Bapt Assn	24	7,028	NR	8,749 *	2.4	4.1
034 Ant Orth of NA	1	39	NR	78	-	-
053 Assemb of God	25	4,188	4,371	6,695	1.9	3.1
055 As Ref Pres Ch	1	78	NR	95	-	-
056 Baha'i	3	517	NR	517	.1	.2
059 Bapt Miss Assn	16	5,740	1,881	7,147 *	2.0	3.3
076 Buddhism	2	NR	NR	NR	-	-
081 Catholic	16	NR	NR	29,444	8.1	13.8
089 Chr & Miss Al	1	29	NR	54	-	-
093 Chr Ch (Disc)	10	2,020	814	2,515 *	.7	1.2
097 Chr Chs&Chs Cr	4	383	NR	477 *	.1	.2
121 Ch God (Abr)	1	19	8	24 *	-	-
123 Ch God (Ander)	3	NR	144	144	-	.1
127 Ch God (Cleve)	2	289	160	360 *	.1	.2
145 Ch God Prophcy	3	87	NR	108 *	-	.1
151 L-D Saints	6	NR	NR	2,217	.6	1.0
165 Ch of Nazarene	14	2,861	1,662	3,338	.9	1.6
167 Chs of Christ	36	7,387	6,849	9,478	2.6	4.4
173 Comm of Christ	1	79	NR	79	-	-
185 Cumber Presb	2	121	NR	252	.1	.1
193 Episcopal	8	NR	1,562	4,614	1.3	2.2
207 E.L.C.A.	2	313	137	386	.1	.2
223 Free Will Bapt	7	709	NR	883 *	.2	.4
226 Friends-USA	1	15	NR	19 *	-	-
246 Greek Orthodox	1	NR	NR	417	.1	.2
263 Int Foursq Gos	1	71	38	88 *	-	-
264 Int Chs of Crst	1	84	136	110	-	.1
267 Muslim Est	3	NR	456	984	.3	.5
283 Luth—MO Synod	8	2,314	1,273	3,019	.8	1.4
290 Metro Comm Ch	2	67	68	83 *	-	-
339 Pent Ch of God	7	431	NR	825	.2	.4
349 Pent Holiness	1	10	10	12 *	-	-
355 Presb Ch (USA)	11	3,403	1,625	4,236 *	1.2	2.0
356 Presb Ch Amer	2	316	235	372	.1	.2
360 Prim Bapt Chrch	3	NR	NR	NR	-	-
388 Reg Bapt Gen As	1	49	34	61 *	-	-
403 Salvation Army	3	212	311	327	.1	.2

NR–Not Reported *Total adherents estimated from known number of communicant, confirmed, full members. - Represents a percentage less than 0.1. Percentages may not total 100 due to rounding.

Table 4: Religious Congregations by County and Group: 2000

Religious Group	Number of Churches, Synagogues, Mosques, or Temples	Number of Communicant, Confirmed, or Full Members	Number of Attendees	Total Adherents		
				Number of Adherents	% of Total Pop.	% of Total Adh.
413 S.D.A.	4	827	NR	983	.3	.5
419 So Bapt Conv	104	64,361	18,336	80,134 *	22.2	37.5
435 Unitarian-Univ	1	192	NR	239 *	.1	.1
443 Un C of Christ	2	95	52	118 *	-	.1
449 Un Methodist	46	26,508	9,528	33,008 *	9.1	15.4
463 Vineyard	1	130	120	162 *	-	.1
469 WELS	1	35	37	57	-	-
496 Jewish Est	2	NR	NR	1,100	.3	.5
498 Indep.Charis.	2	7,074	3,450	7,074	2.0	3.3
499 Indep.Non-Char	4	2,700	2,000	2,700	.7	1.3
RANDOLPH	**56**	**6,821**	**2,438**	**10,510 ***	**57.8**	**100.0**
017 Amer Bapt Assn	1	23	NR	28 *	.2	.3
053 Assemb of God	2	90	112	196	1.1	1.9
059 Bapt Miss Assn	2	281	130	345 *	1.9	3.3
081 Catholic	2	NR	NR	1,674	9.2	15.9
145 Ch God Prophcy	1	29	NR	36 *	.2	.3
151 L-D Saints	1	NR	NR	179	1.0	1.7
167 Chs of Christ	21	1,344	1,506	1,790	9.8	17.0
223 Free Will Bapt	9	912	NR	1,120 *	6.2	10.7
283 Luth—MO Synod	1	38	30	46	.3	.4
339 Pent Ch of God	1	51	NR	120	.7	1.1
355 Presb Ch (USA)	1	55	23	68 *	.4	.6
413 S.D.A.	1	38	NR	45	.2	.4
419 So Bapt Conv	10	3,555	492	4,366 *	24.0	41.5
449 Un Methodist	3	405	145	497 *	2.7	4.7
ST. FRANCIS	**57**	**10,065**	**3,281**	**13,221 ***	**45.1**	**100.0**
017 Amer Bapt Assn	3	810	NR	1,031 *	3.5	7.8
053 Assemb of God	2	75	94	146	.5	1.1
059 Bapt Miss Assn	3	643	221	818 *	2.8	6.2
081 Catholic	1	NR	NR	188	.6	1.4
093 Chr Ch (Disc)	2	49	23	62 *	.2	.5
127 Ch God (Cleve)	3	484	362	616 *	2.1	4.7
165 Ch of Nazarene	1	35	46	72	.2	.5
167 Chs of Christ	6	354	310	449	1.5	3.4
185 Cumber Presb	1	105	NR	134	.5	1.0
193 Episcopal	2	NR	51	139	.5	1.1
283 Luth—MO Synod	1	52	32	75	.3	.6
355 Presb Ch (USA)	1	178	103	227 *	.8	1.7
413 S.D.A.	2	32	NR	38	.1	.3
419 So Bapt Conv	19	6,156	1,637	7,836 *	26.7	59.3
449 Un Methodist	10	1,092	402	1,390 *	4.7	10.5
SALINE	**117**	**31,547**	**9,328**	**41,612 ***	**49.8**	**100.0**
017 Amer Bapt Assn	37	11,164	NR	13,850 *	16.6	33.3
053 Assemb of God	7	469	599	759	.9	1.8
056 Baha'i	0	1	NR	1	-	-
059 Bapt Miss Assn	2	511	95	633 *	.8	1.5
081 Catholic	1	NR	NR	1,729	2.1	4.2
084 Calvary Chapel	1	NR	NR	NR	-	-
093 Chr Ch (Disc)	2	145	65	180 *	.2	.4
123 Ch God (Ander)	3	NR	138	138	.2	.3
127 Ch God (Cleve)	3	206	64	256 *	.3	.6
165 Ch of Nazarene	3	433	300	655	.8	1.6
167 Chs of Christ	12	1,265	1,246	1,662	2.0	4.0
193 Episcopal	1	NR	60	90	.1	.2
223 Free Will Bapt	1	101	NR	126 *	.2	.3
263 Int Foursq Gos	1	303	163	376 *	.5	.9
283 Luth—MO Synod	3	546	365	722	.9	1.7
339 Pent Ch of God	2	37	NR	124	.1	.3
355 Presb Ch (USA)	1	208	85	258 *	.3	.6
403 Salvation Army	1	16	23	34	-	.1
413 S.D.A.	1	86	NR	102	.1	.2
419 So Bapt Conv	25	11,972	4,619	14,851 *	17.8	35.7
449 Un Methodist	10	4,084	1,506	5,066 *	6.1	12.2
SCOTT	**55**	**4,541**	**1,627**	**6,313 ***	**57.4**	**100.0**
017 Amer Bapt Assn	3	81	NR	103 *	.9	1.6
053 Assemb of God	5	250	326	484	4.4	7.7
081 Catholic	1	NR	NR	124	1.1	2.0
089 Chr & Miss Al	1	12	NR	33	.3	.5
165 Ch of Nazarene	1	176	188	362	3.3	5.7
167 Chs of Christ	3	172	163	224	2.0	3.5
185 Cumber Presb	2	18	NR	24	.2	.4
223 Free Will Bapt	6	608	NR	767 *	7.0	12.1
339 Pent Ch of God	4	114	NR	268	2.4	4.2
360 Prim Bapt Chrch	2	NR	NR	NR	-	-
419 So Bapt Conv	21	2,803	800	3,536 *	32.2	56.0
449 Un Methodist	6	307	150	388 *	3.5	6.1
SEARCY	**31**	**2,364**	**1,192**	**2,946 ***	**35.7**	**100.0**
017 Amer Bapt Assn	3	143	NR	172 *	2.1	5.8
053 Assemb of God	4	204	283	297	3.6	10.1
097 Chr Chs&Chs Cr	1	86	NR	103 *	1.2	3.5
127 Ch God (Cleve)	1	19	33	33 *	.4	1.1
165 Ch of Nazarene	1	31	21	31	.4	1.1
167 Chs of Christ	6	271	295	372	4.5	12.6
223 Free Will Bapt	1	101	NR	122 *	1.5	4.1
237 Menn Br US Conf	1	52	NR	63 *	.8	2.1
419 So Bapt Conv	10	1,254	460	1,508 *	18.3	51.2
449 Un Methodist	3	203	100	245 *	3.0	8.3
SEBASTIAN	**181**	**50,519**	**18,460**	**79,223 ***	**68.8**	**100.0**
017 Amer Bapt Assn	7	1,954	NR	2,447 *	2.1	3.1
053 Assemb of God	16	1,595	2,126	5,120	4.4	6.5
056 Baha'i	0	30	NR	30	-	-
059 Bapt Miss Assn	4	244	160	306 *	.3	.4
076 Buddhism	3	NR	NR	NR	-	-
081 Catholic	6	NR	NR	9,950	8.6	12.6
093 Chr Ch (Disc)	1	565	275	707 *	.6	.9
097 Chr Chs&Chs Cr	3	562	NR	703 *	.6	.9
123 Ch God (Ander)	1	NR	34	34	-	-
127 Ch God (Cleve)	1	24	24	30 *	-	-
151 L-D Saints	3	NR	NR	1,263	1.1	1.6
165 Ch of Nazarene	5	783	455	1,127	1.0	1.4
167 Chs of Christ	21	2,325	1,935	2,963	2.6	3.7
171 Ch God-Gen Con	1	30	33	38 *	-	-
173 Comm of Christ	1	86	NR	86	.1	.1
185 Cumber Presb	1	77	NR	192	.2	.2
193 Episcopal	3	NR	271	741	.6	.9
207 E.L.C.A.	1	240	141	335	.3	.4
223 Free Will Bapt	10	1,014	NR	1,269 *	1.1	1.6
263 Int Foursq Gos	1	63	152	152 *	.1	.2
267 Muslim Est	1	NR	101	288	.3	.4
283 Luth—MO Synod	4	930	495	1,184	1.0	1.5
331 OCA: Ter Diocs	1	24	NR	45	-	.1
339 Pent Ch of God	7	307	NR	534	.5	.7
349 Pent Holiness	1	34	24	43 *	-	.1
355 Presb Ch (USA)	4	1,492	625	1,868 *	1.6	2.4
360 Prim Bapt Chrch	2	NR	NR	NR	-	-
403 Salvation Army	1	169	94	310	.3	.4
413 S.D.A.	3	304	NR	362	.3	.5
419 So Bapt Conv	46	29,350	8,274	36,737 *	31.9	46.4
449 Un Methodist	19	7,837	2,871	9,811 *	8.5	12.4
463 Vineyard	1	130	120	163 *	.1	.2
496 Jewish Est	1	NR	NR	35	-	-
498 Indep.Charis.	1	350	250	350	.3	.4
SEVIER	**53**	**7,102**	**2,404**	**10,336 ***	**65.6**	**100.0**
017 Amer Bapt Assn	8	1,128	NR	1,445 *	9.2	14.0
053 Assemb of God	2	238	331	364	2.3	3.5
056 Baha'i	0	1	NR	1	-	-
059 Bapt Miss Assn	2	210	75	269 *	1.7	2.6
081 Catholic	1	NR	NR	1,112	7.1	10.8
097 Chr Chs&Chs Cr	1	60	NR	77 *	.5	.7
165 Ch of Nazarene	2	61	31	120	.8	1.2
167 Chs of Christ	5	475	460	556	3.5	5.4
185 Cumber Presb	5	70	NR	127	.8	1.2
207 E.L.C.A.	1	26	20	32	.2	.3
339 Pent Ch of God	1	68	NR	160	1.0	1.5
355 Presb Ch (USA)	1	32	16	41 *	.3	.4
401 Rus Orth Abroad	1	NR	NR	NR	-	-
413 S.D.A.	2	260	NR	309	2.0	3.0
419 So Bapt Conv	10	3,637	1,070	4,653 *	29.5	45.0

NR–Not Reported *Total adherents estimated from known number of communicant, confirmed, full members. - Represents a percentage less than 0.1. Percentages may not total 100 due to rounding.

Table 4: Religious Congregations by County and Group: 2000

Religious Group	Number of Churches, Synagogues, Mosques, or Temples	Number of Communicant, Confirmed, or Full Members	Number of Attendees	Total Adherents		
				Number of Adherents	% of Total Pop.	% of Total Adh.
449 Un Methodist	11	836	401	1,070 *	6.8	10.4
SHARP	**73**	**8,117**	**3,703**	**11,076 ***	**64.7**	**100.0**
017 Amer Bapt Assn	9	1,594	NR	1,910 *	11.2	17.2
053 Assemb of God	5	319	404	527	3.1	4.8
056 Baha'i	0	1	NR	1	-	-
059 Bapt Miss Assn	5	400	190	480 *	2.8	4.3
081 Catholic	1	NR	NR	938	5.5	8.5
093 Chr Ch (Disc)	1	42	20	50 *	.3	.5
127 Ch God (Cleve)	4	229	86	275 *	1.6	2.5
151 L-D Saints	1	NR	NR	144	.8	1.3
167 Chs of Christ	14	854	947	1,135	6.6	10.2
173 Comm of Christ	1	47	NR	47	.3	.4
185 Cumber Presb	2	22	NR	36	.2	.3
193 Episcopal	1	NR	33	44	.3	.4
203 Evan Free Ch	1	28	45	45	.3	.4
207 E.L.C.A.	1	82	78	87	.5	.8
223 Free Will Bapt	2	203	NR	243 *	1.4	2.2
283 Luth—MO Synod	1	242	145	258	1.5	2.3
355 Presb Ch (USA)	1	114	96	137 *	.8	1.2
388 Reg Bapt Gen As	1	60	48	72 *	.4	.7
413 S.D.A.	1	21	NR	25	.1	.2
419 So Bapt Conv	12	2,912	1,102	3,488 *	20.4	31.5
449 Un Methodist	9	947	509	1,134 *	6.6	10.2
STONE	**38**	**4,583**	**1,622**	**5,837 ***	**50.8**	**100.0**
017 Amer Bapt Assn	10	1,519	NR	1,828 *	15.9	31.3
053 Assemb of God	4	199	264	319	2.8	5.5
056 Baha'i	0	4	NR	4	-	.1
061 Beachy Amish	1	41	NR	49 *	.4	.8
081 Catholic	1	NR	NR	86	.7	1.5
097 Chr Chs&Chs Cr	1	35	NR	42 *	.4	.7
145 Ch God Prophcy	1	29	NR	35 *	.3	.6
151 L-D Saints	1	NR	NR	86	.7	1.5
165 Ch of Nazarene	1	39	41	84	.7	1.4
167 Chs of Christ	5	431	420	554	4.8	9.5
297 Mennonite;Other	2	46	NR	55 *	.5	.9
413 S.D.A.	1	64	NR	76	.7	1.3
419 So Bapt Conv	8	1,809	723	2,177 *	18.9	37.3
449 Un Methodist	2	367	174	442 *	3.8	7.6
UNION	**124**	**23,381**	**8,246**	**30,774 ***	**67.4**	**100.0**
017 Amer Bapt Assn	13	523	NR	647 *	1.4	2.1
053 Assemb of God	10	896	706	1,188	2.6	3.9
056 Baha'i	0	2	NR	2	-	-
059 Bapt Miss Assn	12	2,133	780	2,651 *	5.8	8.6
081 Catholic	1	NR	NR	627	1.4	2.0
093 Chr Ch (Disc)	1	154	74	192 *	.4	.6
123 Ch God (Ander)	2	NR	110	110	.2	.4
127 Ch God (Cleve)	1	80	0	100 *	.2	.3
151 L-D Saints	1	NR	NR	186	.4	.6
165 Ch of Nazarene	1	100	32	100	.2	.3
167 Chs of Christ	14	924	895	1,099	2.4	3.6
173 Comm of Christ	1	23	NR	23	.1	.1
183 Cons Menn Conf	1	31	38	45	.1	.1
185 Cumber Presb	1	13	NR	13	-	-
193 Episcopal	1	NR	178	509	1.1	1.7
283 Luth—MO Synod	1	77	70	102	.2	.3
339 Pent Ch of God	2	34	NR	52	.1	.2
355 Presb Ch (USA)	4	542	253	674 *	1.5	2.2
360 Prim Bapt Chrch	1	NR	NR	NR	-	-
403 Salvation Army	1	65	27	334	.7	1.1
419 So Bapt Conv	35	14,560	3,845	18,110 *	39.7	58.8
449 Un Methodist	20	3,224	1,238	4,010 *	8.8	13.0
VAN BUREN	**55**	**6,770**	**3,421**	**8,803 ***	**54.4**	**100.0**
017 Amer Bapt Assn	4	182	NR	217 *	1.3	2.5
053 Assemb of God	3	330	255	469	2.9	5.3
056 Baha'i	0	1	NR	1	-	-
059 Bapt Miss Assn	3	570	188	679 *	4.2	7.7
081 Catholic	2	NR	NR	388	2.4	4.4
151 L-D Saints	1	NR	NR	90	.6	1.0

Religious Group	Number of Churches, Synagogues, Mosques, or Temples	Number of Communicant, Confirmed, or Full Members	Number of Attendees	Total Adherents		
				Number of Adherents	% of Total Pop.	% of Total Adh.
165 Ch of Nazarene	1	34	39	98	.6	1.1
167 Chs of Christ	10	578	593	733	4.5	8.3
263 Int Foursq Gos	3	109	223	223 *	1.4	2.5
283 Luth—MO Synod	1	105	79	106	.7	1.2
355 Presb Ch (USA)	1	184	109	220 *	1.4	2.5
360 Prim Bapt Chrch	1	NR	NR	NR	-	-
413 S.D.A.	1	69	NR	82	.5	.9
419 So Bapt Conv	19	3,695	1,547	4,409 *	27.2	50.1
449 Un Methodist	5	913	388	1,088 *	6.7	12.4
WASHINGTON	**211**	**51,712**	**22,661**	**79,058 ***	**50.1**	**100.0**
017 Amer Bapt Assn	5	711	NR	883 *	.6	1.1
053 Assemb of God	15	1,443	1,754	2,164	1.4	2.7
056 Baha'i	1	98	NR	98	.1	.1
059 Bapt Miss Assn	12	2,671	921	3,319 *	2.1	4.2
076 Buddhism	3	NR	NR	NR	-	-
081 Catholic	5	NR	NR	9,895	6.3	12.5
093 Chr Ch (Disc)	2	1,064	305	1,322 *	.8	1.7
097 Chr Chs&Chs Cr	4	795	NR	987 *	.6	1.2
107 Christian Un	2	32	45	45 *	-	.1
127 Ch God (Cleve)	6	406	193	563 *	.4	.7
151 L-D Saints	3	NR	NR	981	.6	1.2
165 Ch of Nazarene	7	577	458	833	.5	1.1
167 Chs of Christ	27	3,143	3,211	4,279	2.7	5.4
173 Comm of Christ	1	128	NR	128	.1	.2
185 Cumber Presb	2	55	NR	90	.1	.1
193 Episcopal	2	NR	454	1,496	.9	1.9
207 E.L.C.A.	1	456	265	585	.4	.7
223 Free Will Bapt	14	1,419	NR	1,764 *	1.1	2.2
226 Friends-USA	1	15	NR	19 *	-	-
263 Int Foursq Gos	1	40	129	129 *	.1	.2
264 Int Chs of Crst	1	40	64	68	-	.1
267 Muslim Est	1	NR	156	609	.4	.8
283 Luth—MO Synod	3	450	267	593	.4	.8
290 Metro Comm Ch	1	15	9	9 *	-	-
323 Old Ord Amish	1	15	NR	19 *	-	-
339 Pent Ch of God	8	480	NR	1,053	.7	1.3
355 Presb Ch (USA)	9	1,319	722	1,664 *	1.1	2.1
356 Presb Ch Amer	1	153	140	203	.1	.3
360 Prim Bapt Chrch	1	NR	NR	NR	-	-
388 Reg Bapt Gen As	2	98	68	122 *	.1	.2
403 Salvation Army	2	163	151	347	.2	.4
413 S.D.A.	3	172	NR	205	.1	.3
418 Southw Bapt Fel	1	NR	NR	NR	-	-
419 So Bapt Conv	40	27,410	10,364	34,066 *	21.6	43.1
435 Unitarian-Univ	1	158	NR	196 *	.1	.2
449 Un Methodist	21	8,186	2,985	10,174 *	6.5	12.9
496 Jewish Est	1	NR	NR	150	.1	.2
WHITE	**194**	**31,837**	**16,251**	**41,989 ***	**62.5**	**100.0**
017 Amer Bapt Assn	37	3,988	NR	4,913 *	7.3	11.7
053 Assemb of God	11	1,283	1,673	2,415	3.6	5.8
056 Baha'i	0	14	NR	14	-	-
059 Bapt Miss Assn	14	4,389	1,532	5,405 *	8.0	12.9
081 Catholic	2	NR	NR	713	1.1	1.7
093 Chr Ch (Disc)	2	157	50	193 *	.3	.5
097 Chr Chs&Chs Cr	2	121	NR	149 *	.2	.4
127 Ch God (Cleve)	8	573	415	708 *	1.1	1.7
145 Ch God Prophcy	2	58	NR	72 *	.1	.2
151 L-D Saints	2	NR	NR	644	1.0	1.5
165 Ch of Nazarene	4	383	235	569	.8	1.4
167 Chs of Christ	36	5,649	6,334	7,170	10.7	17.1
173 Comm of Christ	1	94	NR	94	.1	.2
185 Cumber Presb	3	32	NR	82	.1	.2
193 Episcopal	1	NR	66	115	.2	.3
223 Free Will Bapt	6	608	NR	749 *	1.1	1.8
283 Luth—MO Synod	1	194	107	242	.4	.6
339 Pent Ch of God	4	118	NR	285	.4	.7
349 Pent Holiness	1	19	38	23 *	-	.1
355 Presb Ch (USA)	2	160	118	197 *	.3	.5
413 S.D.A.	1	27	NR	32	-	.1
419 So Bapt Conv	31	10,468	3,647	12,891 *	19.2	30.7
449 Un Methodist	23	3,502	2,036	4,314 *	6.4	10.3

NR–Not Reported *Total adherents estimated from known number of communicant, confirmed, full members. - Represents a percentage less than 0.1. Percentages may not total 100 due to rounding.

Table 4: Religious Congregations by County and Group: 2000

Religious Group	Number of Churches, Synagogues, Mosques, or Temples	Number of Communicant, Confirmed, or Full Members	Number of Attendees	Total Adherents: Number of Adherents	Total Adherents: % of Total Pop.	Total Adherents: % of Total Adh.
WOODRUFF	**32**	**4,017**	**1,317**	**5,160 ***	**59.0**	**100.0**
017 Amer Bapt Assn	4	224	NR	280 *	3.2	5.4
053 Assemb of God	1	53	63	76	.9	1.5
056 Baha'i	0	40	NR	40	.5	.8
081 Catholic	1	NR	NR	101	1.2	2.0
127 Ch God (Cleve)	2	80	58	100 *	1.1	1.9
145 Ch God Prophcy	1	29	NR	36 *	.4	.7
165 Ch of Nazarene	1	126	69	196	2.2	3.8
167 Chs of Christ	4	337	297	426	4.9	8.3
419 So Bapt Conv	10	2,535	623	3,165 *	36.2	61.3
449 Un Methodist	8	593	207	740 *	8.5	14.3
YELL	**77**	**7,782**	**2,748**	**10,248 ***	**48.5**	**100.0**
017 Amer Bapt Assn	6	672	NR	835 *	4.0	8.1
053 Assemb of God	7	465	494	646	3.1	6.3
055 As Ref Pres Ch	1	22	NR	22	.1	.2
056 Baha'i	0	1	NR	1	-	-
059 Bapt Miss Assn	1	140	39	174 *	.8	1.7
081 Catholic	2	NR	NR	371	1.8	3.6
089 Chr & Miss Al	1	34	NR	64	.3	.6
123 Ch God (Ander)	1	NR	35	35	.2	.3
165 Ch of Nazarene	1	66	33	66	.3	.6
167 Chs of Christ	12	636	674	838	4.0	8.2
171 Ch God-Gen Con	1	17	20	21 *	.1	.2
185 Cumber Presb	1	20	NR	30	.1	.3
223 Free Will Bapt	11	1,115	NR	1,387 *	6.6	13.5
339 Pent Ch of God	2	56	NR	116	.5	1.1
355 Presb Ch (USA)	1	109	59	136 *	.6	1.3
360 Prim Bapt Chrch	1	NR	NR	NR	-	-
413 S.D.A.	1	28	NR	33	.2	.3
419 So Bapt Conv	11	3,434	935	4,271 *	20.2	41.7
449 Un Methodist	16	967	459	1,202 *	5.7	11.7
CALIFORNIA						
The State.....	16,921	2,358,618	1,809,259	15,614,071 *	46.1	100.0
ALAMEDA	**742**	**84,375**	**63,977**	**504,563 ***	**34.9**	**100.0**
017 Amer Bapt Assn	4	182	NR	226 *	-	-
019 Amer Bapt USA	30	6,113	7,025	7,594 *	.5	1.5
050 Armen Ap Etchm	1	0	NR	924	.1	.2
053 Assemb of God	38	4,459	4,883	8,444	.6	1.7
056 Baha'i	12	863	NR	863	.1	.2
057 Bapt Gen Conf	10	1,722	2,376	2,740 *	.2	.5
059 Bapt Miss Assn	2	281	60	349 *	-	.1
076 Buddhism	47	NR	NR	NR	-	-
081 Catholic	69	NR	NR	306,437	21.2	60.7
084 Calvary Chapel	3	NR	NR	NR	-	-
089 Chr & Miss Al	13	1,029	NR	1,692	.1	.3
093 Chr Ch (Disc)	9	715	150	888 *	.1	.2
097 Chr Chs&Chs Cr	7	826	NR	1,025 *	.1	.2
105 Christian Ref	3	396	460	492 *	-	.1
123 Ch God (Ander)	4	NR	282	282	-	.1
127 Ch God (Cleve)	7	506	263	648 *	-	.1
145 Ch God Prophcy	2	74	NR	92 *	-	-
151 L-D Saints	40	NR	NR	16,697	1.2	3.3
157 Ch of Brethren	1	26	0	32 *	-	-
165 Ch of Nazarene	10	1,278	637	1,423	.1	.3
167 Chs of Christ	24	1,940	1,708	2,572	.2	.5
173 Comm of Christ	3	206	NR	206	-	-
175 Congr Chr Chs	1	35	30	43 *	-	-
179 Consrv Bapt	11	NR	1,190	1,190	.1	.2
193 Episcopal	21	NR	2,369	5,432	.4	1.1
201 Evan Cov Ch	9	1,765	1,602	2,273 *	.2	.5
203 Evan Free Ch	6	748	1,811	1,811	.1	.4
207 E.L.C.A.	25	5,617	2,441	7,734	.5	1.5
221 Free Methodist	2	75	120	121	-	-
223 Free Will Bapt	1	48	NR	60 *	-	-
226 Friends-USA	3	216	NR	268 *	-	.1
237 Menn Br US Conf	3	104	NR	129 *	-	-
246 Greek Orthodox	2	NR	NR	4,272	.3	.8
251 Holy Orth in NA	1	NR	NR	30	-	-

Religious Group	Number of Churches, Synagogues, Mosques, or Temples	Number of Communicant, Confirmed, or Full Members	Number of Attendees	Total Adherents: Number of Adherents	Total Adherents: % of Total Pop.	Total Adherents: % of Total Adh.
252 Hindu	14	NR	NR	NR	-	-
262 Int Cou Comm Ch	3	464	NR	576 *	-	.1
263 Int Foursq Gos	10	1,249	1,665	1,665 *	.1	.3
267 Muslim Est	17	NR	5,481	22,760	1.6	4.5
283 Luth—MO Synod	16	3,408	2,035	4,616	.3	.9
290 Metro Comm Ch	3	163	155	200 *	-	-
306 NT IndBapt&Rltd	8	1,015	NR	1,261 *	.1	.2
313 N Am Bapt Conf	1	90	160	112 *	-	-
331 OCA: Ter Diocs	2	100	NR	399	-	.1
332 OCA: Bulg Dioc	1	80	NR	451	-	.1
335 Orth Pres Ch	2	24	34	34	-	-
339 Pent Ch of God	3	124	NR	509	-	.1
349 Pent Holiness	4	463	388	575 *	-	.1
355 Presb Ch (USA)	32	8,058	5,822	10,017 *	.7	2.0
356 Presb Ch Amer	6	98	480	480	-	.1
360 Prim Bapt Chrch	3	NR	NR	NR	-	-
370 Ref Baptist Chs	1	NR	NR	NR	-	-
371 Ref Ch in Am	2	171	172	328	-	.1
388 Reg Bapt Gen As	5	346	445	433 *	-	.1
397 OCA: Roman Dioc	1	NR	NR	300	-	.1
403 Salvation Army	8	603	450	1,514	.1	.3
411 Serb Orth: Grac	1	NR	NR	NR	-	-
413 S.D.A.	12	4,048	NR	4,816	.3	1.0
416 Sikh	4	NR	NR	NR	-	-
419 So Bapt Conv	78	18,132	8,160	22,524 *	1.6	4.5
425 Tao	3	NR	NR	NR	-	-
435 Unitarian-Univ	6	1,288	NR	1,600 *	.1	.3
443 Un C of Christ	21	2,766	1,378	3,436 *	.2	.7
449 Un Methodist	31	7,674	3,699	9,535 *	.7	1.9
463 Vineyard	2	200	170	248 *	-	-
469 WELS	2	180	156	235	-	-
496 Jewish Est	8	NR	NR	32,500	2.3	6.4
498 Indep.Charis.	2	600	1,750	1,750	.1	.3
499 Indep.Non-Char	6	3,807	3,970	4,700	.3	.9
ALPINE	**2**	**NR**	**NR**	**651**	**53.9**	**100.0**
151 L-D Saints	1	NR	NR	601	49.8	92.3
496 Jewish Est	1	NR	NR	50	4.1	7.7
AMADOR	**36**	**2,384**	**2,191**	**8,557 ***	**24.4**	**100.0**
053 Assemb of God	4	292	403	448	1.3	5.2
056 Baha'i	0	2	NR	2	-	-
081 Catholic	6	NR	NR	3,616	10.3	42.3
084 Calvary Chapel	1	NR	NR	NR	-	-
151 L-D Saints	2	NR	NR	1,002	2.9	11.7
165 Ch of Nazarene	1	148	226	311	.9	3.6
167 Chs of Christ	2	35	40	45	.1	.5
179 Consrv Bapt	2	NR	205	205	.6	2.4
193 Episcopal	1	NR	196	292	.8	3.4
203 Evan Free Ch	1	285	260	285	.8	3.3
207 E.L.C.A.	1	236	101	288	.8	3.4
223 Free Will Bapt	1	48	NR	56 *	.2	.7
263 Int Foursq Gos	2	189	308	308 *	.9	3.6
339 Pent Ch of God	1	18	NR	73	.2	.9
410 Serb Orth USA	1	NR	NR	250	.7	2.9
411 Serb Orth: Grac	1	NR	NR	NR	-	-
413 S.D.A.	1	157	NR	187	.5	2.2
419 So Bapt Conv	4	466	262	545 *	1.6	6.4
449 Un Methodist	3	508	190	594 *	1.7	6.9
496 Jewish Est	1	NR	NR	50	.1	.6
BUTTE	**152**	**17,676**	**11,524**	**55,651 ***	**27.4**	**100.0**
017 Amer Bapt Assn	1	41	NR	50 *	-	.1
019 Amer Bapt USA	3	759	431	927 *	.5	1.7
053 Assemb of God	14	1,079	1,450	1,717	.8	3.1
056 Baha'i	2	169	NR	169	.1	.3
076 Buddhism	1	NR	NR	NR	-	-
081 Catholic	6	NR	NR	19,483	9.6	35.0
084 Calvary Chapel	4	NR	NR	NR	-	-
089 Chr & Miss Al	7	1,614	NR	4,287	2.1	7.7
093 Chr Ch (Disc)	2	679	198	829 *	.4	1.5
097 Chr Chs&Chs Cr	4	390	NR	476 *	.2	.9
123 Ch God (Ander)	1	NR	55	55	-	.1

NR–Not Reported *Total adherents estimated from known number of communicant, confirmed, full members. - Represents a percentage less than 0.1. Percentages may not total 100 due to rounding.

Table 4: Religious Congregations by County and Group: 2000

Religious Group	Number of Churches, Synagogues, Mosques, or Temples	Number of Communicant, Confirmed, or Full Members	Number of Attendees	Total Adherents: Number of Adherents	Total Adherents: % of Total Pop.	Total Adherents: % of Total Adh.
127 Ch God (Cleve)	3	224	679	680 *	.3	1.2
145 Ch God Prophcy	1	37	NR	45 *	-	.1
151 L-D Saints	16	NR	NR	7,172	3.5	12.9
157 Ch of Brethren	1	41	32	50 *	-	.1
165 Ch of Nazarene	4	722	784	1,099	.5	2.0
167 Chs of Christ	6	427	423	499	.2	.9
173 Comm of Christ	1	93	NR	93	-	.2
175 Congr Chr Chs	1	350	225	427 *	.2	.8
179 Consrv Bapt	1	NR	150	150	.1	.3
193 Episcopal	4	NR	373	1,105	.5	2.0
203 Evan Free Ch	5	735	1,535	1,575	.8	2.8
207 E.L.C.A.	2	832	469	1,078	.5	1.9
221 Free Methodist	1	143	214	214	.1	.4
226 Friends-USA	1	32	NR	39 *	-	.1
263 Int Foursq Gos	3	269	541	541 *	.3	1.0
267 Muslim Est	1	NR	101	288	.1	.5
283 Luth—MO Synod	4	817	493	1,191	.6	2.1
306 NT IndBapt&Rltd	3	435	NR	531 *	.3	1.0
331 OCA: Ter Diocs	1	9	NR	50	-	.1
339 Pent Ch of God	6	200	NR	643	.3	1.2
349 Pent Holiness	1	40	75	49 *	-	.1
355 Presb Ch (USA)	3	1,011	769	1,234 *	.6	2.2
356 Presb Ch Amer	1	40	80	80	-	.1
373 Ref Ch in U.S.	1	15	NR	19	-	-
388 Reg Bapt Gen As	4	162	202	202 *	.1	.4
403 Salvation Army	3	230	296	355	.2	.6
413 S.D.A.	6	2,522	NR	3,001	1.5	5.4
419 So Bapt Conv	10	1,623	914	1,982 *	1.0	3.6
423 Syrian Orth Ch	1	NR	NR	150	.1	.3
435 Unitarian-Univ	1	58	NR	71 *	-	.1
443 Un C of Christ	2	174	92	213 *	.1	.4
449 Un Methodist	7	1,474	750	1,801 *	.9	3.2
463 Vineyard	1	230	193	281 *	.1	.5
496 Jewish Est	1	NR	NR	750	.4	1.3
CALAVERAS	**42**	**2,273**	**2,089**	**7,494 ***	**18.5**	**100.0**
017 Amer Bapt Assn	1	63	NR	76 *	.2	1.0
019 Amer Bapt USA	1	55	100	100 *	.2	1.3
053 Assemb of God	3	144	195	200	.5	2.7
056 Baha'i	0	16	NR	16	-	.2
081 Catholic	7	NR	NR	3,506	8.6	46.8
084 Calvary Chapel	1	NR	NR	NR	-	-
151 L-D Saints	2	NR	NR	783	1.9	10.4
165 Ch of Nazarene	1	16	47	47	.1	.6
167 Chs of Christ	4	113	120	139	.3	1.9
193 Episcopal	2	NR	115	299	.7	4.0
201 Evan Cov Ch	5	1,010	931	1,211 *	3.0	16.2
203 Evan Free Ch	1	25	70	70	.2	.9
207 E.L.C.A.	1	96	60	133	.3	1.8
263 Int Foursq Gos	2	33	53	53 *	.1	.7
283 Luth—MO Synod	1	30	25	30	.1	.4
339 Pent Ch of God	1	24	NR	40	.1	.5
410 Serb Orth USA	1	NR	NR	15	-	.2
413 S.D.A.	1	99	NR	118	.3	1.6
419 So Bapt Conv	5	282	214	338 *	.8	4.5
443 Un C of Christ	2	267	159	320 *	.8	4.3
COLUSA	**30**	**1,362**	**782**	**5,496 ***	**29.2**	**100.0**
019 Amer Bapt USA	1	17	15	22 *	.1	.4
053 Assemb of God	5	223	289	379	2.0	6.9
056 Baha'i	0	3	NR	3	-	.1
081 Catholic	7	NR	NR	3,255	17.3	59.2
093 Chr Ch (Disc)	1	63	20	83 *	.4	1.5
123 Ch God (Ander)	1	NR	0	0	-	-
151 L-D Saints	1	NR	NR	270	1.4	4.9
193 Episcopal	1	NR	40	93	.5	1.7
283 Luth—MO Synod	1	54	22	66	.4	1.2
306 NT IndBapt&Rltd	1	145	NR	190 *	1.0	3.5
339 Pent Ch of God	1	8	NR	20	.1	.4
355 Presb Ch (USA)	1	174	148	229 *	1.2	4.2
360 Prim Bapt Chrch	1	NR	NR	NR	-	-
388 Reg Bapt Gen As	1	32	45	45 *	.2	.8
413 S.D.A.	1	22	NR	26	.1	.5

Religious Group	Number of Churches, Synagogues, Mosques, or Temples	Number of Communicant, Confirmed, or Full Members	Number of Attendees	Total Adherents: Number of Adherents	Total Adherents: % of Total Pop.	Total Adherents: % of Total Adh.
419 So Bapt Conv	2	304	55	399 *	2.1	7.3
449 Un Methodist	4	317	148	416 *	2.2	7.6
CONTRA COSTA	**477**	**61,777**	**68,442**	**368,979 ***	**38.9**	**100.0**
017 Amer Bapt Assn	6	654	NR	825 *	.1	.2
019 Amer Bapt USA	19	3,210	2,696	4,052 *	.4	1.1
034 Ant Orth of NA	2	265	NR	530	.1	.1
053 Assemb of God	22	4,043	5,614	8,036	.8	2.2
056 Baha'i	15	653	NR	653	.1	.2
057 Bapt Gen Conf	5	1,277	24,711	24,803 *	2.6	6.7
076 Buddhism	7	NR	NR	NR	-	-
081 Catholic	34	NR	NR	204,070	21.5	55.3
084 Calvary Chapel	2	NR	NR	NR	-	-
089 Chr & Miss Al	7	741	NR	1,468	.2	.4
093 Chr Ch (Disc)	4	799	353	1,008 *	.1	.3
097 Chr Chs&Chs Cr	4	613	NR	775 *	.1	.2
105 Christian Ref	2	247	201	312 *	-	.1
123 Ch God (Ander)	3	NR	155	155	-	-
127 Ch God (Cleve)	6	565	498	713 *	.1	.2
145 Ch God Prophcy	4	157	NR	200 *	-	.1
151 L-D Saints	46	NR	NR	18,562	2.0	5.0
165 Ch of Nazarene	7	1,155	696	1,852	.2	.5
167 Chs of Christ	21	2,148	1,824	2,806	.3	.8
173 Comm of Christ	1	181	NR	181	-	-
175 Congr Chr Chs	1	36	30	45 *	-	-
179 Consrv Bapt	7	NR	1,250	1,250	.1	.3
193 Episcopal	17	NR	2,232	6,505	.7	1.8
201 Evan Cov Ch	7	1,345	2,107	2,302 *	.2	.6
203 Evan Free Ch	5	731	1,349	1,349	.1	.4
207 E.L.C.A.	15	4,817	2,436	6,652	.7	1.8
216 Evan Presby Ch	2	708	NR	894 *	.1	.2
221 Free Methodist	3	234	176	272	-	.1
223 Free Will Bapt	4	193	NR	243 *	-	.1
226 Friends-USA	1	152	NR	192 *	-	.1
245 Greek Orth Vslp	1	87	NR	117	-	-
246 Greek Orthodox	2	NR	NR	453	-	.1
252 Hindu	7	NR	NR	NR	-	-
263 Int Foursq Gos	9	1,747	2,235	2,235 *	.2	.6
267 Muslim Est	6	NR	1,646	6,503	.7	1.8
283 Luth—MO Synod	14	2,414	1,245	3,374	.4	.9
290 Metro Comm Ch	1	10	10	13 *	-	-
306 NT IndBapt&Rltd	8	1,410	NR	1,780 *	.2	.5
331 OCA: Ter Diocs	1	40	NR	237	-	.1
332 OCA: Bulg Dioc	2	105	NR	348	-	.1
335 Orth Pres Ch	1	122	150	177	-	-
339 Pent Ch of God	9	443	NR	2,447	.3	.7
349 Pent Holiness	5	325	311	410 *	-	.1
355 Presb Ch (USA)	15	9,348	5,747	11,799 *	1.2	3.2
356 Presb Ch Amer	2	195	340	340	-	.1
388 Reg Bapt Gen As	8	1,148	1,425	1,458 *	.2	.4
403 Salvation Army	3	255	242	475	.1	.1
410 Serb Orth USA	1	NR	NR	350	-	.1
413 S.D.A.	7	2,306	NR	2,743	.3	.7
416 Sikh	2	NR	NR	NR	-	-
419 So Bapt Conv	40	6,163	2,811	7,779 *	.8	2.1
435 Unitarian-Univ	1	375	NR	473 *	-	.1
443 Un C of Christ	9	1,981	774	2,500 *	.3	.7
449 Un Methodist	21	5,916	3,026	7,468 *	.8	2.0
455 Un Ref Chs N.A.	1	81	NR	108	-	-
463 Vineyard	2	407	305	514 *	.1	.1
467 Wesleyan	2	90	157	250	-	.1
469 WELS	1	54	40	92	-	-
496 Jewish Est	15	NR	NR	22,000	2.3	6.0
499 Indep.Non-Char	2	1,831	1,650	1,831	.2	.5
DEL NORTE	**28**	**2,356**	**1,894**	**9,796 ***	**35.6**	**100.0**
053 Assemb of God	2	134	177	180	.7	1.8
056 Baha'i	1	24	NR	24	.1	.2
081 Catholic	2	NR	NR	5,600	20.4	57.2
084 Calvary Chapel	1	NR	NR	NR	-	-
097 Chr Chs&Chs Cr	1	85	NR	104 *	.4	1.1
127 Ch God (Cleve)	1	19	0	23 *	.1	.2
145 Ch God Prophcy	1	37	NR	45 *	.2	.5

NR–Not Reported *Total adherents estimated from known number of communicant, confirmed, full members. - Represents a percentage less than 0.1. Percentages may not total 100 due to rounding.

Table 4: Religious Congregations by County and Group: 2000

Religious Group	Number of Churches, Synagogues, Mosques, or Temples	Number of Communicant, Confirmed, or Full Members	Number of Attendees	Total Adherents		
				Number of Adherents	% of Total Pop.	% of Total Adh.
151 L-D Saints	2	NR	NR	685	2.5	7.0
165 Ch of Nazarene	1	91	66	139	.5	1.4
167 Chs of Christ	1	12	15	14	.1	.1
193 Episcopal	1	NR	46	101	.4	1.0
203 Evan Free Ch	1	61	150	150	.5	1.5
263 Int Foursq Gos	3	268	585	585 *	2.1	6.0
283 Luth—MO Synod	1	378	182	510	1.9	5.2
339 Pent Ch of God	1	38	NR	75	.3	.8
388 Reg Bapt Gen As	1	120	237	237 *	.9	2.4
413 S.D.A.	1	306	NR	364	1.3	3.7
419 So Bapt Conv	3	407	190	499 *	1.8	5.1
449 Un Methodist	3	376	246	461 *	1.7	4.7
EL DORADO	**89**	**9,451**	**8,850**	**42,172 ***	**27.0**	**100.0**
017 Amer Bapt Assn	2	65	NR	81 *	.1	.2
019 Amer Bapt USA	1	191	209	238 *	.2	.6
053 Assemb of God	4	1,604	1,682	2,144	1.4	5.1
056 Baha'i	2	134	NR	134	.1	.3
081 Catholic	5	NR	NR	22,080	14.1	52.4
084 Calvary Chapel	4	NR	NR	NR	-	-
089 Chr & Miss Al	1	244	NR	350	.2	.8
097 Chr Chs&Chs Cr	1	70	NR	87 *	.1	.2
145 Ch God Prophcy	1	37	NR	46 *	-	.1
151 L-D Saints	13	NR	NR	4,964	3.2	11.8
165 Ch of Nazarene	1	138	117	234	.1	.6
167 Chs of Christ	5	347	365	428	.3	1.0
173 Comm of Christ	1	47	NR	47	-	.1
175 Congr Chr Chs	1	72	50	90 *	.1	.2
179 Consrv Bapt	4	NR	1,540	1,540	1.0	3.7
193 Episcopal	2	NR	313	725	.5	1.7
201 Evan Cov Ch	2	134	353	353 *	.2	.8
203 Evan Free Ch	2	212	695	695	.4	1.6
207 E.L.C.A.	2	410	281	511	.3	1.2
221 Free Methodist	1	14	25	25	-	.1
252 Hindu	1	NR	NR	NR	-	-
263 Int Foursq Gos	4	224	376	376 *	.2	.9
283 Luth—MO Synod	3	814	501	969	.6	2.3
306 NT IndBapt&Rltd	1	125	NR	156 *	.1	.4
313 N Am Bapt Conf	1	151	260	188 *	.1	.4
339 Pent Ch of God	4	331	NR	533	.3	1.3
355 Presb Ch (USA)	2	818	640	1,019 *	.7	2.4
401 Rus Orth Abroad	1	NR	NR	NR	-	-
413 S.D.A.	5	1,145	NR	1,363	.9	3.2
419 So Bapt Conv	6	696	508	867 *	.6	2.1
435 Unitarian-Univ	1	24	NR	30 *	-	.1
443 Un C of Christ	1	22	20	27 *	-	.1
449 Un Methodist	3	1,382	915	1,722 *	1.1	4.1
467 Wesleyan	1	0	0	0	-	-
496 Jewish Est	0	NR	NR	150	.1	.4
FRESNO	**515**	**79,096**	**53,711**	**380,156 ***	**47.6**	**100.0**
017 Amer Bapt Assn	7	843	NR	1,125 *	.1	.3
019 Amer Bapt USA	20	4,859	2,876	6,482 *	.8	1.7
039 Ap Chr Ch(Naz)	1	14	25	25 *	-	-
049 Armen Ap Cilic	1	600	NR	1,400	.2	.4
050 Armen Ap Etchm	3	0	NR	2,834	.4	.7
053 Assemb of God	53	8,654	10,960	24,084	3.0	6.3
056 Baha'i	3	417	NR	417	.1	.1
057 Bapt Gen Conf	7	2,842	3,979	4,328 *	.5	1.1
076 Buddhism	8	NR	NR	NR	-	-
081 Catholic	40	NR	NR	232,565	29.1	61.2
084 Calvary Chapel	2	NR	NR	NR	-	-
089 Chr & Miss Al	4	1,373	NR	1,429	.2	.4
093 Chr Ch (Disc)	2	277	144	370 *	-	.1
097 Chr Chs&Chs Cr	4	2,030	NR	2,708 *	.3	.7
105 Christian Ref	3	280	243	374 *	-	.1
123 Ch God (Ander)	7	NR	781	781	.1	.2
127 Ch God (Cleve)	8	1,114	691	1,520 *	.2	.4
145 Ch God Prophcy	9	361	NR	480 *	.1	.1
151 L-D Saints	34	NR	NR	14,527	1.8	3.8
157 Ch of Brethren	3	630	99	840 *	.1	.2
165 Ch of Nazarene	13	1,861	1,321	2,692	.3	.7
167 Chs of Christ	30	3,109	3,445	4,018	.5	1.1

Religious Group	Number of Churches, Synagogues, Mosques, or Temples	Number of Communicant, Confirmed, or Full Members	Number of Attendees	Total Adherents		
				Number of Adherents	% of Total Pop.	% of Total Adh.
173 Comm of Christ	1	191	NR	191	-	.1
175 Congr Chr Chs	1	500	230	667 *	.1	.2
179 Consrv Bapt	3	NR	909	909	.1	.2
181 Consrv Congr	1	349	110	466 *	.1	.1
193 Episcopal	9	NR	1,100	2,230	.3	.6
201 Evan Cov Ch	5	727	698	969 *	.1	.3
203 Evan Free Ch	6	1,451	2,330	2,375	.3	.6
207 E.L.C.A.	17	4,722	2,513	6,630	.8	1.7
221 Free Methodist	2	81	106	106	-	-
223 Free Will Bapt	6	289	NR	386 *	-	.1
226 Friends-USA	1	152	NR	203 *	-	.1
237 Menn Br US Conf	17	3,192	NR	4,258 *	.5	1.1
246 Greek Orthodox	1	NR	NR	624	.1	.2
252 Hindu	1	NR	NR	NR	-	-
263 Int Foursq Gos	14	3,287	4,851	4,851 *	.6	1.3
264 Int Chs of Crst	1	102	156	144	-	-
267 Muslim Est	3	NR	662	2,218	.3	.6
283 Luth—MO Synod	5	794	376	913	.1	.2
288 Mennonite USA	5	439	348	585 *	.1	.2
306 NT IndBapt&Rltd	5	685	NR	914 *	.1	.2
339 Pent Ch of God	15	619	NR	1,590	.2	.4
349 Pent Holiness	12	541	864	722 *	.1	.2
355 Presb Ch (USA)	16	3,826	2,703	5,103 *	.6	1.3
356 Presb Ch Amer	1	38	60	77	-	-
360 Prim Bapt Chrch	1	NR	NR	NR	-	-
388 Reg Bapt Gen As	4	512	541	702 *	.1	.2
401 Rus Orth Abroad	1	NR	NR	NR	-	-
403 Salvation Army	4	260	239	568	.1	.1
410 Serb Orth USA	1	NR	NR	300	-	.1
413 S.D.A.	13	4,066	NR	4,838	.6	1.3
416 Sikh	4	NR	NR	NR	-	-
418 Southw Bapt Fel	1	NR	NR	NR	-	-
419 So Bapt Conv	42	16,816	6,554	22,432 *	2.8	5.9
435 Unitarian-Univ	1	279	NR	372 *	-	.1
443 Un C of Christ	4	1,033	564	1,378 *	.2	.4
449 Un Methodist	20	4,035	2,007	5,380 *	.7	1.4
455 Un Ref Chs N.A.	1	20	NR	68	-	-
463 Vineyard	2	194	180	258 *	-	.1
469 WELS	1	132	96	180	-	-
496 Jewish Est	3	NR	NR	2,300	.3	.6
498 Indep.Charis.	1	500	500	800	.1	.2
499 Indep.Non-Char	1	0	450	450	.1	.1
GLENN	**37**	**3,080**	**1,265**	**11,724 ***	**44.3**	**100.0**
019 Amer Bapt USA	3	408	191	533 *	2.0	4.5
053 Assemb of God	3	109	154	307	1.2	2.6
056 Baha'i	0	7	NR	7	-	.1
081 Catholic	3	NR	NR	6,718	25.4	57.3
089 Chr & Miss Al	1	129	NR	134	.5	1.1
097 Chr Chs&Chs Cr	2	200	NR	261 *	1.0	2.2
143 CG in Cr(Menn)	1	239	NR	312 *	1.2	2.7
151 L-D Saints	2	NR	NR	581	2.2	5.0
165 Ch of Nazarene	1	34	27	52	.2	.4
167 Chs of Christ	2	32	28	61	.2	.5
193 Episcopal	2	NR	115	171	.6	1.5
203 Evan Free Ch	2	169	241	241	.9	2.1
207 E.L.C.A.	1	171	86	262	1.0	2.2
226 Friends-USA	1	152	NR	198 *	.7	1.7
237 Menn Br US Conf	1	52	NR	68 *	.3	.6
263 Int Foursq Gos	1	30	50	50 *	.2	.4
283 Luth—MO Synod	2	167	77	227	.9	1.9
339 Pent Ch of God	1	23	NR	26	.1	.2
355 Presb Ch (USA)	1	68	45	89 *	.3	.8
373 Ref Ch in U.S.	1	34	NR	58	.2	.5
413 S.D.A.	2	94	NR	112	.4	1.0
419 So Bapt Conv	2	597	77	779 *	2.9	6.6
449 Un Methodist	2	365	174	477 *	1.8	4.1
HUMBOLDT	**152**	**12,321**	**8,529**	**46,951 ***	**37.1**	**100.0**
017 Amer Bapt Assn	4	167	NR	202 *	.2	.4
019 Amer Bapt USA	3	385	539	539 *	.4	1.1
053 Assemb of God	16	1,103	1,309	1,633	1.3	3.5
056 Baha'i	2	136	NR	136	.1	.3

NR–Not Reported *Total adherents estimated from known number of communicant, confirmed, full members. - Represents a percentage less than 0.1. Percentages may not total 100 due to rounding.

Table 4: Religious Congregations by County and Group: 2000

Religious Group	Number of Churches, Synagogues, Mosques, or Temples	Number of Communicant, Confirmed, or Full Members	Number of Attendees	Total Adherents: Number of Adherents	Total Adherents: % of Total Pop.	Total Adherents: % of Total Adh.
081 Catholic	15	NR	NR	25,520	20.2	54.4
084 Calvary Chapel	3	NR	NR	NR	-	-
093 Chr Ch (Disc)	1	87	32	105 *	.1	.2
097 Chr Chs&Chs Cr	3	300	NR	362 *	.3	.8
127 Ch God (Cleve)	3	96	122	126 *	.1	.3
151 L-D Saints	7	NR	NR	2,647	2.1	5.6
165 Ch of Nazarene	5	640	527	1,027	.8	2.2
167 Chs of Christ	4	166	155	222	.2	.5
173 Comm of Christ	1	22	NR	22	-	-
179 Consrv Bapt	1	NR	130	130	.1	.3
193 Episcopal	5	NR	312	1,225	1.0	2.6
201 Evan Cov Ch	1	136	216	216 *	.2	.5
203 Evan Free Ch	3	275	396	396	.3	.8
207 E.L.C.A.	7	1,018	402	1,448	1.1	3.1
226 Friends-USA	2	64	NR	77 *	.1	.2
263 Int Foursq Gos	6	602	822	822 *	.6	1.8
283 Luth—MO Synod	4	296	199	394	.3	.8
297 Mennonite;Other	1	23	NR	28 *	-	.1
331 OCA: Ter Diocs	1	12	NR	38	-	.1
335 Orth Pres Ch	1	32	46	46	-	.1
339 Pent Ch of God	5	125	NR	317	.3	.7
355 Presb Ch (USA)	14	1,802	1,511	2,214 *	1.7	4.7
388 Reg Bapt Gen As	3	155	308	308 *	.2	.7
403 Salvation Army	1	97	70	144	.1	.3
413 S.D.A.	6	1,319	NR	1,568	1.2	3.3
419 So Bapt Conv	15	2,192	864	2,652 *	2.1	5.6
435 Unitarian-Univ	1	178	NR	215 *	.2	.5
443 Un C of Christ	1	77	65	93 *	.1	.2
449 Un Methodist	3	618	317	748 *	.6	1.6
463 Vineyard	2	150	135	181 *	.1	.4
467 Wesleyan	1	48	52	150	.1	.3
496 Jewish Est	1	NR	NR	1,000	.8	2.1
IMPERIAL	**104**	**9,145**	**4,942**	**89,057 ***	**62.6**	**100.0**
017 Amer Bapt Assn	1	100	NR	132 *	.1	.1
019 Amer Bapt USA	4	646	355	851 *	.6	1.0
053 Assemb of God	14	1,589	2,012	3,022	2.1	3.4
056 Baha'i	0	120	NR	120	.1	.1
081 Catholic	17	NR	NR	73,475	51.6	82.5
084 Calvary Chapel	2	NR	NR	NR	-	-
097 Chr Chs&Chs Cr	4	772	NR	1,016 *	.7	1.1
145 Ch God Prophcy	3	130	NR	171 *	.1	.2
151 L-D Saints	4	NR	NR	1,618	1.1	1.8
165 Ch of Nazarene	5	258	221	576	.4	.6
167 Chs of Christ	8	251	291	321	.2	.4
193 Episcopal	2	NR	91	357	.3	.4
226 Friends-USA	3	456	NR	600 *	.4	.7
252 Hindu	1	NR	NR	NR	-	-
263 Int Foursq Gos	3	104	169	169 *	.1	.2
267 Muslim Est	1	NR	55	163	.1	.2
283 Luth—MO Synod	3	416	217	578	.4	.6
313 N Am Bapt Conf	1	120	100	158 *	.1	.2
339 Pent Ch of God	1	12	NR	60	-	.1
355 Presb Ch (USA)	2	229	151	302 *	.2	.3
360 Prim Bapt Chrch	1	NR	NR	NR	-	-
388 Reg Bapt Gen As	2	25	255	255 *	.2	.3
403 Salvation Army	1	102	70	153	.1	.2
413 S.D.A.	5	884	NR	1,051	.7	1.2
416 Sikh	1	NR	NR	NR	-	-
419 So Bapt Conv	10	2,426	710	3,195 *	2.2	3.6
449 Un Methodist	4	505	245	664 *	.5	.7
496 Jewish Est	1	NR	NR	50	-	.1
INYO	**31**	**1,475**	**1,399**	**10,690 ***	**59.6**	**100.0**
053 Assemb of God	2	133	185	385	2.1	3.6
056 Baha'i	0	9	NR	9	.1	.1
081 Catholic	4	NR	NR	7,702	42.9	72.0
084 Calvary Chapel	1	NR	NR	NR	-	-
151 L-D Saints	2	NR	NR	524	2.9	4.9
165 Ch of Nazarene	2	131	124	193	1.1	1.8
167 Chs of Christ	1	40	40	48	.3	.4
179 Consrv Bapt	2	NR	168	168	.9	1.6
193 Episcopal	2	NR	82	143	.8	1.3
203 Evan Free Ch	1	69	125	125	.7	1.2
263 Int Foursq Gos	1	30	50	50 *	.3	.5
283 Luth—MO Synod	1	230	120	326	1.8	3.0
355 Presb Ch (USA)	2	169	188	210 *	1.2	2.0
370 Ref Baptist Chs	2	NR	NR	NR	-	-
413 S.D.A.	2	123	NR	147	.8	1.4
419 So Bapt Conv	3	117	105	143 *	.8	1.3
449 Un Methodist	3	424	212	517 *	2.9	4.8
KERN	**481**	**67,994**	**49,393**	**288,811 ***	**43.7**	**100.0**
017 Amer Bapt Assn	12	738	NR	985 *	.1	.3
019 Amer Bapt USA	14	3,360	2,103	4,477 *	.7	1.6
034 Ant Orth of NA	1	2	NR	4	-	-
053 Assemb of God	43	5,575	6,942	10,515	1.6	3.6
056 Baha'i	1	144	NR	144	-	-
057 Bapt Gen Conf	2	132	130	188 *	-	.1
059 Bapt Miss Assn	1	50	25	67 *	-	-
076 Buddhism	3	NR	NR	NR	-	-
081 Catholic	30	NR	NR	168,455	25.5	58.3
084 Calvary Chapel	6	NR	NR	NR	-	-
089 Chr & Miss Al	2	429	NR	1,006	.2	.3
093 Chr Ch (Disc)	2	456	200	608 *	.1	.2
097 Chr Chs&Chs Cr	7	790	NR	1,054 *	.2	.4
123 Ch God (Ander)	1	NR	139	139	-	-
127 Ch God (Cleve)	11	1,126	638	1,500 *	.2	.5
145 Ch God Prophcy	8	343	NR	457 *	.1	.2
151 L-D Saints	35	NR	NR	13,821	2.1	4.8
157 Ch of Brethren	2	167	90	223 *	-	.1
165 Ch of Nazarene	15	2,751	2,208	3,853	.6	1.3
167 Chs of Christ	37	3,538	3,449	4,687	.7	1.6
171 Ch God-Gen Con	1	84	33	112 *	-	-
173 Comm of Christ	2	132	NR	132	-	-
179 Consrv Bapt	3	NR	280	280	-	.1
181 Consrv Congr	1	5	14	7 *	-	-
186 Coptic Orth Ch	1	NR	NR	NR	-	-
193 Episcopal	9	NR	779	2,225	.3	.8
203 Evan Free Ch	3	146	315	315	-	.1
207 E.L.C.A.	6	1,689	664	2,312	.3	.8
223 Free Will Bapt	6	289	NR	385 *	.1	.1
226 Friends-USA	1	265	NR	353 *	.1	.1
237 Menn Br US Conf	8	1,613	NR	2,151 *	.3	.7
246 Greek Orthodox	1	NR	NR	282	-	.1
252 Hindu	1	NR	NR	NR	-	-
263 Int Foursq Gos	19	3,653	8,620	8,620 *	1.3	3.0
267 Muslim Est	3	NR	468	1,827	.3	.6
273 LandmrkBapt,I&U	1	23	NR	31 *	-	-
283 Luth—MO Synod	13	2,420	1,411	3,623	.5	1.3
290 Metro Comm Ch	1	25	11	33 *	-	-
291 Missionary Ch	1	62	138	138	-	-
297 Mennonite;Other	1	15	NR	20 *	-	-
306 NT IndBapt&Rltd	2	245	NR	326 *	-	.1
339 Pent Ch of God	20	1,191	NR	3,559	.5	1.2
349 Pent Holiness	11	431	503	574 *	.1	.2
355 Presb Ch (USA)	6	1,717	1,219	2,288 *	.3	.8
356 Presb Ch Amer	1	29	32	41	-	-
373 Ref Ch in U.S.	2	229	NR	291	-	.1
403 Salvation Army	3	257	253	240	-	.1
413 S.D.A.	17	3,226	NR	3,840	.6	1.3
416 Sikh	1	NR	NR	NR	-	-
419 So Bapt Conv	64	21,645	11,707	28,843 *	4.4	10.0
435 Unitarian-Univ	1	56	NR	75 *	-	-
443 Un C of Christ	5	593	342	790 *	.1	.3
449 Un Methodist	18	3,190	1,654	4,251 *	.6	1.5
463 Vineyard	2	230	205	306 *	-	.1
467 Wesleyan	4	358	221	396	.1	.1
469 WELS	1	11	15	15	-	-
496 Jewish Est	2	NR	NR	1,600	.2	.6
498 Indep.Charis.	2	650	440	680	.1	.2
499 Indep.Non-Char	4	3,914	4,145	5,667	.9	2.0
KINGS	**90**	**8,516**	**6,095**	**51,639 ***	**39.9**	**100.0**
017 Amer Bapt Assn	3	306	NR	397 *	.3	.8
019 Amer Bapt USA	4	939	944	1,217 *	.9	2.4

NR–Not Reported *Total adherents estimated from known number of communicant, confirmed, full members. - Represents a percentage less than 0.1. Percentages may not total 100 due to rounding.

Table 4: Religious Congregations by County and Group: 2000

Religious Group	Number of Churches, Synagogues, Mosques, or Temples	Number of Communicant, Confirmed, or Full Members	Number of Attendees	Total Adherents: Number of Adherents	Total Adherents: % of Total Pop.	Total Adherents: % of Total Adh.
053 Assemb of God	11	1,083	1,208	1,739	1.3	3.4
056 Baha'i	0	20	NR	20	-	-
076 Buddhism	1	NR	NR	NR	-	-
081 Catholic	8	NR	NR	37,542	29.0	72.7
084 Calvary Chapel	1	NR	NR	NR	-	-
089 Chr & Miss Al	1	146	NR	146	.1	.3
093 Chr Ch (Disc)	1	311	147	403 *	.3	.8
105 Christian Ref	1	595	560	771 *	.6	1.5
123 Ch God (Ander)	2	NR	115	115	.1	.2
127 Ch God (Cleve)	1	92	21	119 *	.1	.2
151 L-D Saints	4	NR	NR	1,613	1.2	3.1
165 Ch of Nazarene	4	374	368	541	.4	1.0
167 Chs of Christ	8	544	592	754	.6	1.5
179 Consrv Bapt	1	NR	135	135	.1	.3
193 Episcopal	3	NR	171	293	.2	.6
203 Evan Free Ch	1	95	210	210	.2	.4
207 E.L.C.A.	1	142	83	217	.2	.4
223 Free Will Bapt	2	96	NR	125 *	.1	.2
263 Int Foursq Gos	1	56	110	110 *	.1	.2
283 Luth—MO Synod	1	133	48	164	.1	.3
306 NT IndBapt&Rltd	1	145	NR	188 *	.1	.4
335 Orth Pres Ch	1	102	136	176	.1	.3
339 Pent Ch of God	6	147	NR	395	.3	.8
349 Pent Holiness	2	113	64	146 *	.1	.3
355 Presb Ch (USA)	4	688	476	891 *	.7	1.7
403 Salvation Army	1	82	111	312	.2	.6
413 S.D.A.	4	840	NR	1,000	.8	1.9
419 So Bapt Conv	5	926	343	1,200 *	.9	2.3
425 Tao	1	NR	NR	NR	-	-
449 Un Methodist	5	541	253	700 *	.5	1.4
LAKE	**61**	**4,767**	**3,179**	**18,880 ***	**32.4**	**100.0**
019 Amer Bapt USA	2	265	174	324 *	.6	1.7
053 Assemb of God	4	697	740	1,005	1.7	5.3
056 Baha'i	1	54	NR	54	.1	.3
076 Buddhism	1	NR	NR	NR	-	-
081 Catholic	6	NR	NR	11,140	19.1	59.0
084 Calvary Chapel	1	NR	NR	NR	-	-
093 Chr Ch (Disc)	1	146	115	178 *	.3	.9
097 Chr Chs&Chs Cr	1	25	NR	31 *	.1	.2
127 Ch God (Cleve)	1	43	29	53 *	.1	.3
151 L-D Saints	4	NR	NR	1,569	2.7	8.3
165 Ch of Nazarene	1	87	77	112	.2	.6
167 Chs of Christ	3	150	130	175	.3	.9
193 Episcopal	1	NR	34	90	.2	.5
203 Evan Free Ch	2	190	380	380	.7	2.0
207 E.L.C.A.	1	93	60	126	.2	.7
263 Int Foursq Gos	1	19	18	23 *	-	.1
283 Luth—MO Synod	2	136	98	63	.1	.3
306 NT IndBapt&Rltd	1	70	NR	85 *	.1	.5
332 OCA: Bulg Dioc	1	3	NR	18	-	.1
339 Pent Ch of God	1	15	NR	50	.1	.3
349 Pent Holiness	1	40	45	49 *	.1	.3
355 Presb Ch (USA)	2	207	195	282 *	.5	1.5
388 Reg Bapt Gen As	1	90	110	110 *	.2	.6
413 S.D.A.	4	505	NR	602	1.0	3.2
419 So Bapt Conv	7	953	338	1,165 *	2.0	6.2
435 Unitarian-Univ	1	31	NR	38 *	.1	.2
449 Un Methodist	7	688	396	840 *	1.4	4.4
463 Vineyard	2	260	240	318 *	.5	1.7
LASSEN	**32**	**1,826**	**1,624**	**5,375 ***	**15.9**	**100.0**
017 Amer Bapt Assn	1	30	NR	36 *	.1	.7
053 Assemb of God	4	537	767	913	2.7	17.0
056 Baha'i	0	17	NR	17	.1	.3
081 Catholic	3	NR	NR	1,655	4.9	30.8
084 Calvary Chapel	2	NR	NR	NR	-	-
093 Chr Ch (Disc)	1	163	0	195 *	.6	3.6
151 L-D Saints	4	NR	NR	980	2.9	18.2
165 Ch of Nazarene	1	70	87	145	.4	2.7
167 Chs of Christ	1	45	60	50	.1	.9
193 Episcopal	1	NR	34	73	.2	1.4
203 Evan Free Ch	1	92	150	150	.4	2.8
263 Int Foursq Gos	1	45	86	86 *	.3	1.6
283 Luth—MO Synod	1	100	76	100	.3	1.9
306 NT IndBapt&Rltd	1	145	NR	174 *	.5	3.2
339 Pent Ch of God	2	55	NR	108	.3	2.0
403 Salvation Army	1	29	75	97	.3	1.8
413 S.D.A.	2	15	NR	18	.1	.3
419 So Bapt Conv	4	289	130	346 *	1.0	6.4
449 Un Methodist	1	194	159	232 *	.7	4.3
LOS ANGELES	**4,044**	**620,220**	**439,286**	**5,528,814 ***	**58.1**	**100.0**
017 Amer Bapt Assn	16	1,081	NR	1,392 *	-	-
019 Amer Bapt USA	211	56,866	31,932	73,217 *	.8	1.3
034 Ant Orth of NA	6	1,894	NR	3,788	-	.1
039 Ap Chr Ch(Naz)	4	175	277	277 *	-	-
040 Ap Chr Ch-Amer	1	48	80	80 *	-	-
049 Armen Ap Cilic	5	3,700	NR	23,600	.2	.4
050 Armen Ap Etchm	6	0	NR	13,182	.1	.2
053 Assemb of God	260	42,130	41,648	64,327	.7	1.2
055 As Ref Pres Ch	7	311	NR	335	-	-
056 Baha'i	44	6,346	NR	6,346	.1	.1
057 Bapt Gen Conf	32	7,586	10,857	13,490 *	.1	.2
059 Bapt Miss Assn	2	363	115	468 *	-	-
071 Brethren (Ash)	1	15	28	19 *	-	-
075 Brethren in Cr	3	141	210	210	-	-
076 Buddhism	145	NR	NR	NR	-	-
081 Catholic	278	NR	NR	3,806,377	40.0	68.8
084 Calvary Chapel	37	NR	NR	NR	-	-
089 Chr & Miss Al	48	5,349	NR	7,174	.1	.1
093 Chr Ch (Disc)	63	9,729	3,771	12,526 *	.1	.2
097 Chr Chs&Chs Cr	62	18,475	NR	23,789 *	.2	.4
105 Christian Ref	40	4,916	4,272	6,330 *	.1	.1
121 Ch God (Abr)	1	26	12	33 *	-	-
123 Ch God (Ander)	40	NR	5,928	5,928	.1	.1
127 Ch God (Cleve)	36	2,981	1,388	3,998 *	-	.1
145 Ch God Prophcy	22	974	NR	1,255 *	-	-
151 L-D Saints	239	NR	NR	97,347	1.0	1.8
157 Ch of Brethren	12	1,220	525	1,570 *	-	-
165 Ch of Nazarene	105	14,590	10,150	19,347	.2	.3
167 Chs of Christ	109	15,332	12,887	19,507	.2	.4
173 Comm of Christ	11	1,285	NR	1,285	-	-
175 Congr Chr Chs	13	3,174	1,630	4,087 *	-	.1
179 Consrv Bapt	53	NR	12,347	12,347	.1	.2
181 Consrv Congr	4	4,928	4,355	6,345 *	.1	.1
186 Coptic Orth Ch	8	NR	NR	NR	-	-
193 Episcopal	84	NR	13,884	46,304	.5	.8
201 Evan Cov Ch	14	3,560	5,892	6,161 *	.1	.1
203 Evan Free Ch	30	4,176	7,747	7,828	.1	.1
207 E.L.C.A.	116	23,762	14,336	32,408	.3	.6
216 Evan Presby Ch	1	24	NR	31 *	-	-
220 Free Lutheran	1	14	18	20	-	-
221 Free Methodist	33	2,488	3,607	4,028	-	.1
223 Free Will Bapt	6	289	NR	372 *	-	-
226 Friends-USA	22	2,497	NR	3,215 *	-	.1
237 Menn Br US Conf	14	342	NR	440 *	-	-
245 Greek Orth Vslp	1	245	NR	315	-	-
246 Greek Orthodox	8	NR	NR	7,845	.1	.1
249 Assyr Apost Ch	1	NR	NR	2,288	-	-
251 Holy Orth in NA	1	NR	NR	135	-	-
252 Hindu	37	NR	NR	NR	-	-
262 Int Cou Comm Ch	10	1,685	NR	2,173 *	-	-
263 Int Foursq Gos	225	40,668	50,839	52,362 *	.6	.9
264 Int Chs of Crst	1	9,404	15,458	12,429	.1	.2
267 Muslim Est	48	NR	20,393	92,919	1.0	1.7
273 LandmrkBapt,I&U	4	121	NR	156 *	-	-
283 Luth—MO Synod	96	19,731	11,211	25,116	.3	.5
288 Mennonite USA	18	1,016	1,047	1,309 *	-	-
290 Metro Comm Ch	7	639	601	777 *	-	-
291 Missionary Ch	9	943	1,165	1,352	-	-
293 Morav Ch-North	1	180	NR	228	-	-
304 NatPrimBapt USA	3	800	NR	1,030 *	-	-
306 NT IndBapt&Rltd	5	725	NR	933 *	-	-
307 Neth Ref Congr	1	13	NR	15	-	-
313 N Am Bapt Conf	3	87	90	112 *	-	-
330 Macedonian Orth	1	NR	NR	600	-	-

NR–Not Reported   *Total adherents estimated from known number of communicant, confirmed, full members.   - Represents a percentage less than 0.1.   Percentages may not total 100 due to rounding.

Table 4: Religious Congregations by County and Group: 2000

Religious Group	Number of Churches, Synagogues, Mosques, or Temples	Number of Communicant, Confirmed, or Full Members	Number of Attendees	Total Adherents		
				Number of Adherents	% of Total Pop.	% of Total Adh.
331 OCA: Ter Diocs	3	261	NR	1,731	-	-
332 OCA: Bulg Dioc	3	345	NR	2,788	-	.1
333 Malan Dioc Am	1	NR	NR	375	-	-
334 Malan Syr Orth	1	18	NR	90	-	-
335 Orth Pres Ch	7	396	487	546	-	-
339 Pent Ch of God	25	751	NR	1,175	-	-
349 Pent Holiness	18	2,592	2,190	3,337 *	-	.1
355 Presb Ch (USA)	167	40,339	27,152	52,125 *	.5	.9
356 Presb Ch Amer	23	804	715	1,066	-	-
360 Prim Bapt Chrch	4	NR	NR	NR	-	-
370 Ref Baptist Chs	3	NR	NR	NR	-	-
371 Ref Ch in Am	12	3,249	3,607	6,591	.1	.1
373 Ref Ch in U.S.	1	38	NR	63	-	-
388 Reg Bapt Gen As	19	2,094	2,547	2,729 *	-	-
395 Romania Orth Ar	1	NR	NR	438	-	-
397 OCA: Roman Dioc	2	NR	NR	1,070	-	-
401 Rus Orth Abroad	3	NR	NR	NR	-	-
403 Salvation Army	33	4,329	3,820	8,790	.1	.2
410 Serb Orth USA	2	NR	NR	4,800	.1	.1
411 Serb Orth: Grac	1	NR	NR	NR	-	-
413 S.D.A.	121	40,751	NR	48,495	.5	.9
416 Sikh	14	NR	NR	NR	-	-
418 Southw Bapt Fel	3	NR	NR	NR	-	-
419 So Bapt Conv	312	86,703	33,728	111,634 *	1.2	2.0
423 Syrian Orth Ch	2	NR	NR	6,500	.1	.1
425 Tao	4	NR	NR	NR	-	-
431 Ukrainian Orth	2	NR	NR	840	-	-
435 Unitarian-Univ	13	2,136	NR	2,750 *	-	-
443 Un C of Christ	51	9,073	4,510	11,682 *	.1	.2
449 Un Methodist	177	42,471	24,171	54,676 *	.6	1.0
455 Un Ref Chs N.A.	1	29	NR	34	-	-
463 Vineyard	20	3,294	3,119	4,295 *	-	.1
467 Wesleyan	31	3,315	2,889	4,540	-	.1
469 WELS	8	1,038	616	1,257	-	-
490 Zoroastrian	2	NR	NR	NR	-	-
496 Jewish Est	202	NR	NR	564,700	5.9	10.2
498 Indep.Charis.	11	33,830	19,060	71,500	.8	1.3
499 Indep.Non-Char	16	25,320	21,975	25,320	.3	.5
MADERA	**88**	**8,329**	**6,331**	**38,932 ***	**31.6**	**100.0**
017 Amer Bapt Assn	2	124	NR	161 *	.1	.4
019 Amer Bapt USA	3	697	333	903 *	.7	2.3
039 Ap Chr Ch(Naz)	2	29	58	58 *	-	.1
053 Assemb of God	11	1,080	1,282	1,905	1.5	4.9
056 Baha'i	2	54	NR	54	-	.1
057 Bapt Gen Conf	3	204	172	265 *	.2	.7
081 Catholic	5	NR	NR	23,935	19.4	61.5
084 Calvary Chapel	1	NR	NR	NR	-	-
097 Chr Chs&Chs Cr	1	139	NR	180 *	.1	.5
123 Ch God (Ander)	3	NR	707	707	.6	1.8
127 Ch God (Cleve)	2	96	82	125 *	.1	.3
145 Ch God Prophcy	2	83	NR	108 *	.1	.3
151 L-D Saints	6	NR	NR	2,345	1.9	6.0
165 Ch of Nazarene	3	230	193	275	.2	.7
167 Chs of Christ	4	483	425	552	.4	1.4
193 Episcopal	2	NR	116	217	.2	.6
203 Evan Free Ch	2	123	244	244	.2	.6
207 E.L.C.A.	3	559	280	787	.6	2.0
223 Free Will Bapt	2	96	NR	125 *	.1	.3
237 Menn Br US Conf	2	135	NR	175 *	.1	.4
263 Int Foursq Gos	2	105	152	152 *	.1	.4
267 Muslim Est	1	NR	55	300	.2	.8
339 Pent Ch of God	2	65	NR	182	.1	.5
349 Pent Holiness	1	20	25	26 *	-	.1
355 Presb Ch (USA)	2	614	738	797 *	.6	2.0
360 Prim Bapt Chrch	1	NR	NR	NR	-	-
371 Ref Ch in Am	1	158	170	259	.2	.7
388 Reg Bapt Gen As	1	63	48	82 *	.1	.2
413 S.D.A.	5	1,120	NR	1,332	1.1	3.4
419 So Bapt Conv	7	1,238	507	1,604 *	1.3	4.1
443 Un C of Christ	1	51	45	66 *	.1	.2
449 Un Methodist	2	433	249	561 *	.5	1.4
499 Indep.Non-Char	1	330	450	450	.4	1.2

Religious Group	Number of Churches, Synagogues, Mosques, or Temples	Number of Communicant, Confirmed, or Full Members	Number of Attendees	Total Adherents		
				Number of Adherents	% of Total Pop.	% of Total Adh.
MARIN	**128**	**10,716**	**8,311**	**80,448 ***	**32.5**	**100.0**
019 Amer Bapt USA	7	1,120	658	1,332 *	.5	1.7
053 Assemb of God	5	698	859	1,179	.5	1.5
056 Baha'i	4	244	NR	244	.1	.3
076 Buddhism	12	NR	NR	NR	-	-
081 Catholic	14	NR	NR	42,163	17.1	52.4
084 Calvary Chapel	1	NR	NR	NR	-	-
097 Chr Chs&Chs Cr	1	100	NR	119 *	-	.1
123 Ch God (Ander)	1	NR	75	75	-	.1
127 Ch God (Cleve)	1	45	0	54 *	-	.1
151 L-D Saints	3	NR	NR	1,496	.6	1.9
165 Ch of Nazarene	1	87	42	170	.1	.2
167 Chs of Christ	3	111	134	149	.1	.2
173 Comm of Christ	1	22	NR	22	-	-
179 Consrv Bapt	1	NR	150	150	.1	.2
193 Episcopal	11	NR	1,189	3,570	1.4	4.4
201 Evan Cov Ch	1	317	406	406 *	.2	.5
207 E.L.C.A.	6	1,108	600	1,514	.6	1.9
226 Friends-USA	1	32	NR	38 *	-	-
246 Greek Orthodox	1	NR	NR	783	.3	1.0
252 Hindu	1	NR	NR	NR	-	-
267 Muslim Est	1	NR	95	200	.1	.2
283 Luth—MO Synod	3	617	326	757	.3	.9
306 NT IndBapt&Rltd	1	75	NR	89 *	-	.1
331 OCA: Ter Diocs	1	53	NR	103	-	.1
335 Orth Pres Ch	1	37	30	44	-	.1
355 Presb Ch (USA)	16	2,937	1,888	3,505 *	1.4	4.4
403 Salvation Army	1	50	30	144	.1	.2
413 S.D.A.	1	141	NR	168	.1	.2
419 So Bapt Conv	12	1,579	1,157	1,878 *	.8	2.3
435 Unitarian-Univ	1	193	NR	229 *	.1	.3
443 Un C of Christ	4	440	248	523 *	.2	.7
449 Un Methodist	4	614	328	730 *	.3	.9
463 Vineyard	1	96	96	114 *	-	.1
496 Jewish Est	5	NR	NR	18,500	7.5	23.0
MARIPOSA	**20**	**1,239**	**751**	**8,965 ***	**52.3**	**100.0**
053 Assemb of God	1	58	75	120	.7	1.3
056 Baha'i	1	33	NR	33	.2	.4
081 Catholic	4	NR	NR	6,936	40.5	77.4
123 Ch God (Ander)	1	NR	200	200	1.2	2.2
151 L-D Saints	1	NR	NR	239	1.4	2.7
167 Chs of Christ	3	85	76	97	.6	1.1
193 Episcopal	1	NR	25	39	.2	.4
207 E.L.C.A.	1	246	97	324	1.9	3.6
263 Int Foursq Gos	1	43	57	57 *	.3	.6
306 NT IndBapt&Rltd	2	290	NR	345 *	2.0	3.8
413 S.D.A.	1	64	NR	76	.4	.8
419 So Bapt Conv	1	95	72	113 *	.7	1.3
449 Un Methodist	2	325	149	386 *	2.3	4.3
MENDOCINO	**89**	**6,222**	**3,587**	**28,648 ***	**33.2**	**100.0**
019 Amer Bapt USA	3	582	400	719 *	.8	2.5
053 Assemb of God	8	457	603	794	.9	2.8
056 Baha'i	1	80	NR	80	.1	.3
076 Buddhism	4	NR	NR	NR	-	-
081 Catholic	10	NR	NR	17,564	20.4	61.3
084 Calvary Chapel	2	NR	NR	NR	-	-
093 Chr Ch (Disc)	1	55	25	68 *	.1	.2
145 Ch God Prophcy	1	37	NR	46 *	.1	.2
151 L-D Saints	6	NR	NR	1,962	2.3	6.8
165 Ch of Nazarene	2	98	52	106	.1	.4
167 Chs of Christ	4	149	166	184	.2	.6
179 Consrv Bapt	2	NR	235	235	.3	.8
193 Episcopal	3	NR	165	317	.4	1.1
203 Evan Free Ch	1	132	175	175	.2	.6
207 E.L.C.A.	2	450	180	594	.7	2.1
252 Hindu	1	NR	NR	NR	-	-
263 Int Foursq Gos	2	88	161	161 *	.2	.6
283 Luth—MO Synod	3	253	162	308	.4	1.1
306 NT IndBapt&Rltd	1	145	NR	179 *	.2	.6
339 Pent Ch of God	2	83	NR	130	.2	.5
355 Presb Ch (USA)	5	754	486	932 *	1.1	3.3

NR–Not Reported *Total adherents estimated from known number of communicant, confirmed, full members. - Represents a percentage less than 0.1. Percentages may not total 100 due to rounding.

Table 4: Religious Congregations by County and Group: 2000

Religious Group	Number of Churches, Synagogues, Mosques, or Temples	Number of Communicant, Confirmed, or Full Members	Number of Attendees	Total Adherents		
				Number of Adherents	% of Total Pop.	% of Total Adh.
388 Reg Bapt Gen As	1	40	65	65 *	.1	.2
401 Rus Orth Abroad	1	NR	NR	NR	-	-
413 S.D.A.	4	1,201	NR	1,430	1.7	5.0
419 So Bapt Conv	9	900	373	1,112 *	1.3	3.9
435 Unitarian-Univ	1	19	NR	23 *	-	.1
449 Un Methodist	8	699	339	864 *	1.0	3.0
496 Jewish Est	1	NR	NR	600	.7	2.1
MERCED	**139**	**14,938**	**9,537**	**106,068 ***	**50.4**	**100.0**
017 Amer Bapt Assn	1	19	NR	26 *	-	-
019 Amer Bapt USA	4	322	222	440 *	.2	.4
053 Assemb of God	15	1,468	1,772	2,267	1.1	2.1
056 Baha'i	2	255	NR	255	.1	.2
081 Catholic	16	NR	NR	80,043	38.0	75.5
084 Calvary Chapel	1	NR	NR	NR	-	-
089 Chr & Miss Al	1	569	NR	577	.3	.5
093 Chr Ch (Disc)	2	93	11	127 *	.1	.1
097 Chr Chs&Chs Cr	1	120	NR	164 *	.1	.2
105 Christian Ref	1	250	222	342 *	.2	.3
123 Ch God (Ander)	2	NR	188	188	.1	.2
127 Ch God (Cleve)	1	16	10	22 *	-	-
143 CG in Cr(Menn)	2	558	NR	763 *	.4	.7
145 Ch God Prophcy	1	37	NR	50 *	-	-
151 L-D Saints	10	NR	NR	3,032	1.4	2.9
165 Ch of Nazarene	3	403	378	450	.2	.4
167 Chs of Christ	10	647	702	808	.4	.8
173 Comm of Christ	1	95	NR	95	-	.1
179 Consrv Bapt	2	NR	190	190	.1	.2
193 Episcopal	3	NR	202	332	.2	.3
201 Evan Cov Ch	1	371	274	507 *	.2	.5
203 Evan Free Ch	2	174	295	295	.1	.3
207 E.L.C.A.	4	535	380	749	.4	.7
263 Int Foursq Gos	2	370	571	571 *	.3	.5
267 Muslim Est	1	NR	101	288	.1	.3
283 Luth—MO Synod	2	491	276	706	.3	.7
306 NT IndBapt&Rltd	1	145	NR	198 *	.1	.2
331 OCA: Ter Diocs	1	20	NR	62	-	.1
339 Pent Ch of God	7	238	NR	571	.3	.5
355 Presb Ch (USA)	4	794	564	1,086 *	.5	1.0
360 Prim Bapt Chrch	1	NR	NR	NR	-	-
403 Salvation Army	1	52	31	124	.1	.1
413 S.D.A.	4	572	NR	681	.3	.6
416 Sikh	2	NR	NR	NR	-	-
419 So Bapt Conv	18	4,583	1,229	6,263 *	3.0	5.9
449 Un Methodist	6	1,541	869	2,106 *	1.0	2.0
496 Jewish Est	1	NR	NR	190	.1	.2
498 Indep.Charis.	1	200	200	300	.1	.3
499 Indep.Non-Char	1	0	850	1,200	.6	1.1
MODOC	**20**	**535**	**410**	**1,845 ***	**19.5**	**100.0**
053 Assemb of God	2	112	160	225	2.4	12.2
056 Baha'i	1	28	NR	28	.3	1.5
081 Catholic	2	NR	NR	708	7.5	38.4
151 L-D Saints	2	NR	NR	280	3.0	15.2
167 Chs of Christ	2	46	48	48	.5	2.6
179 Consrv Bapt	2	NR	85	85	.9	4.6
193 Episcopal	1	NR	25	44	.5	2.4
297 Mennonite;Other	1	26	NR	32 *	.3	1.7
413 S.D.A.	2	81	NR	97	1.0	5.3
419 So Bapt Conv	2	103	31	127 *	1.3	6.9
443 Un C of Christ	3	139	61	171 *	1.8	9.3
MONO	**15**	**455**	**417**	**2,419 ***	**18.8**	**100.0**
056 Baha'i	0	3	NR	3	-	.1
081 Catholic	3	NR	NR	1,593	12.4	65.9
084 Calvary Chapel	2	NR	NR	NR	-	-
151 L-D Saints	2	NR	NR	233	1.8	9.6
193 Episcopal	1	NR	20	23	.2	1.0
203 Evan Free Ch	1	50	70	70	.5	2.9
283 Luth—MO Synod	1	75	75	100	.8	4.1
355 Presb Ch (USA)	1	20	13	24 *	.2	1.0
419 So Bapt Conv	3	265	213	322 *	2.5	13.3
449 Un Methodist	1	42	26	51 *	.4	2.1

Religious Group	Number of Churches, Synagogues, Mosques, or Temples	Number of Communicant, Confirmed, or Full Members	Number of Attendees	Total Adherents		
				Number of Adherents	% of Total Pop.	% of Total Adh.
MONTEREY	**216**	**20,051**	**13,448**	**180,593 ***	**45.0**	**100.0**
017 Amer Bapt Assn	1	50	NR	64 *	-	-
019 Amer Bapt USA	4	485	408	625 *	.2	.3
053 Assemb of God	19	1,629	2,293	3,148	.8	1.7
056 Baha'i	4	1,474	NR	1,474	.4	.8
076 Buddhism	13	NR	NR	NR	-	-
081 Catholic	23	NR	NR	139,105	34.6	77.0
084 Calvary Chapel	3	NR	NR	NR	-	-
089 Chr & Miss Al	1	130	NR	159	-	.1
093 Chr Ch (Disc)	1	93	55	120 *	-	.1
097 Chr Chs&Chs Cr	1	114	NR	147 *	-	.1
123 Ch God (Ander)	1	NR	55	55	-	-
127 Ch God (Cleve)	4	237	72	305 *	.1	.2
145 Ch God Prophcy	2	83	NR	108 *	-	.1
151 L-D Saints	8	NR	NR	2,974	.7	1.6
165 Ch of Nazarene	2	329	319	537	.1	.3
167 Chs of Christ	10	566	761	831	.2	.5
173 Comm of Christ	1	44	NR	44	-	-
175 Congr Chr Chs	1	67	46	86 *	-	-
179 Consrv Bapt	7	NR	1,120	1,120	.3	.6
193 Episcopal	14	NR	1,422	3,681	.9	2.0
201 Evan Cov Ch	1	20	57	57 *	-	-
203 Evan Free Ch	1	69	125	125	-	.1
207 E.L.C.A.	6	1,170	657	1,577	.4	.9
223 Free Will Bapt	3	145	NR	186 *	-	.1
226 Friends-USA	1	32	NR	41 *	-	-
246 Greek Orthodox	1	NR	NR	381	.1	.2
262 Int Cou Comm Ch	1	190	NR	245 *	.1	.1
263 Int Foursq Gos	4	125	334	334 *	.1	.2
267 Muslim Est	3	NR	228	1,019	.3	.6
283 Luth—MO Synod	3	466	302	707	.2	.4
306 NT IndBapt&Rltd	2	370	NR	477 *	.1	.3
335 Orth Pres Ch	1	45	44	63	-	-
339 Pent Ch of God	10	655	NR	2,500	.6	1.4
349 Pent Holiness	1	20	22	26 *	-	-
355 Presb Ch (USA)	9	3,474	2,126	4,483 *	1.1	2.5
356 Presb Ch Amer	1	42	45	50	-	-
370 Ref Baptist Chs	1	NR	NR	NR	-	-
401 Rus Orth Abroad	1	NR	NR	NR	-	-
403 Salvation Army	3	266	175	674	.2	.4
413 S.D.A.	5	874	NR	1,041	.3	.6
416 Sikh	1	NR	NR	NR	-	-
419 So Bapt Conv	19	4,153	1,630	5,350 *	1.3	3.0
435 Unitarian-Univ	1	250	NR	322 *	.1	.2
443 Un C of Christ	3	141	62	182 *	-	.1
449 Un Methodist	9	1,656	688	2,134 *	.5	1.2
463 Vineyard	1	300	252	386 *	.1	.2
496 Jewish Est	3	NR	NR	3,300	.8	1.8
498 Indep.Charis.	1	287	150	350	.1	.2
NAPA	**76**	**12,443**	**4,443**	**47,021 ***	**37.8**	**100.0**
017 Amer Bapt Assn	1	100	NR	123 *	.1	.3
019 Amer Bapt USA	2	314	200	385 *	.3	.8
053 Assemb of God	5	666	694	2,923	2.4	6.2
056 Baha'i	1	42	NR	42	-	.1
057 Bapt Gen Conf	1	450	372	552 *	.4	1.2
076 Buddhism	1	NR	NR	NR	-	-
081 Catholic	8	NR	NR	25,400	20.4	54.0
084 Calvary Chapel	2	NR	NR	NR	-	-
089 Chr & Miss Al	1	63	NR	122	.1	.3
097 Chr Chs&Chs Cr	3	1,100	NR	1,350 *	1.1	2.9
105 Christian Ref	1	117	84	144 *	.1	.3
123 Ch God (Ander)	1	NR	27	27	-	.1
151 L-D Saints	4	NR	NR	1,742	1.4	3.7
165 Ch of Nazarene	1	186	180	352	.3	.7
167 Chs of Christ	2	65	70	84	.1	.2
193 Episcopal	3	NR	485	894	.7	1.9
203 Evan Free Ch	1	108	215	215	.2	.5
207 E.L.C.A.	2	377	157	504	.4	1.1
226 Friends-USA	1	32	NR	39 *	-	.1
252 Hindu	2	NR	NR	NR	-	-
263 Int Foursq Gos	1	65	85	85 *	.1	.2
283 Luth—MO Synod	2	745	395	1,011	.8	2.2

NR–Not Reported   *Total adherents estimated from known number of communicant, confirmed, full members.   - Represents a percentage less than 0.1.   Percentages may not total 100 due to rounding.

Table 4: Religious Congregations by County and Group: 2000

Religious Group	Number of Churches, Synagogues, Mosques, or Temples	Number of Communicant, Confirmed, or Full Members	Number of Attendees	Total Adherents		
				Number of Adherents	% of Total Pop.	% of Total Adh.
306 NT IndBapt&Rltd	2	290	NR	356 *	.3	.8
339 Pent Ch of God	1	5	NR	10	-	-
355 Presb Ch (USA)	4	976	543	1,198 *	1.0	2.5
356 Presb Ch Amer	1	0	0	0	-	-
401 Rus Orth Abroad	1	NR	NR	NR	-	-
403 Salvation Army	1	45	31	178	.1	.4
413 S.D.A.	9	5,086	NR	6,053	4.9	12.9
419 So Bapt Conv	6	722	209	886 *	.7	1.9
435 Unitarian-Univ	1	48	NR	59 *	-	.1
449 Un Methodist	2	641	326	787 *	.6	1.7
496 Jewish Est	1	NR	NR	1,000	.8	2.1
499 Indep.Non-Char	1	200	370	500	.4	1.1
NEVADA	**67**	**8,297**	**8,391**	**28,479 ***	**30.9**	**100.0**
017 Amer Bapt Assn	1	32	NR	39 *	-	.1
019 Amer Bapt USA	1	68	60	82 *	.1	.3
053 Assemb of God	3	337	431	1,303	1.4	4.6
056 Baha'i	2	113	NR	113	.1	.4
076 Buddhism	2	NR	NR	NR	-	-
081 Catholic	4	NR	NR	12,458	13.5	43.7
084 Calvary Chapel	4	NR	NR	NR	-	-
089 Chr & Miss Al	1	137	NR	397	.4	1.4
097 Chr Chs&Chs Cr	1	56	NR	67 *	.1	.2
123 Ch God (Ander)	1	NR	0	0	-	-
151 L-D Saints	5	NR	NR	1,809	2.0	6.4
165 Ch of Nazarene	1	38	41	63	.1	.2
167 Chs of Christ	7	280	289	370	.4	1.3
179 Consrv Bapt	1	NR	150	150	.2	.5
193 Episcopal	2	NR	316	712	.8	2.5
201 Evan Cov Ch	1	43	88	88 *	.1	.3
207 E.L.C.A.	2	499	254	624	.7	2.2
226 Friends-USA	1	32	NR	39 *	-	.1
252 Hindu	2	NR	NR	NR	-	-
263 Int Foursq Gos	2	237	334	334 *	.4	1.2
283 Luth—MO Synod	1	202	135	226	.2	.8
355 Presb Ch (USA)	1	606	533	729 *	.8	2.6
388 Reg Bapt Gen As	1	15	70	70 *	.1	.2
403 Salvation Army	1	50	40	50	.1	.2
413 S.D.A.	3	673	NR	802	.9	2.8
419 So Bapt Conv	5	2,495	1,563	3,003 *	3.3	10.5
435 Unitarian-Univ	1	86	NR	103 *	.1	.4
449 Un Methodist	5	1,060	665	1,275 *	1.4	4.5
467 Wesleyan	1	38	22	68	.1	.2
496 Jewish Est	2	NR	NR	105	.1	.4
499 Indep.Non-Char	2	1,200	3,400	3,400	3.7	11.9
ORANGE	**1,085**	**197,573**	**178,651**	**1,274,591 ***	**44.8**	**100.0**
017 Amer Bapt Assn	2	117	NR	149 *	-	-
019 Amer Bapt USA	20	4,734	3,693	6,034 *	.2	.5
034 Ant Orth of NA	4	983	NR	1,966	.1	.2
049 Armen Ap Cilic	1	400	NR	1,400	-	.1
050 Armen Ap Etchm	1	0	NR	1,848	.1	.1
053 Assemb of God	71	13,493	15,538	21,198	.7	1.7
055 As Ref Pres Ch	1	0	NR	0	-	-
056 Baha'i	27	2,137	NR	2,137	.1	.2
057 Bapt Gen Conf	9	963	1,121	1,369 *	-	.1
059 Bapt Miss Assn	2	94	62	120 *	-	-
076 Buddhism	40	NR	NR	NR	-	-
081 Catholic	61	NR	NR	779,647	27.4	61.2
084 Calvary Chapel	35	NR	NR	NR	-	-
089 Chr & Miss Al	19	2,054	NR	2,588	.1	.2
093 Chr Ch (Disc)	10	2,036	812	2,595 *	.1	.2
097 Chr Chs&Chs Cr	22	11,748	NR	14,973 *	.5	1.2
105 Christian Ref	19	2,463	2,841	3,140 *	.1	.2
123 Ch God (Ander)	7	NR	778	778	-	.1
127 Ch God (Cleve)	11	2,518	1,663	3,244 *	.1	.3
145 Ch God Prophcy	5	223	NR	283 *	-	-
151 L-D Saints	115	NR	NR	48,776	1.7	3.8
157 Ch of Brethren	1	46	63	63 *	-	-
165 Ch of Nazarene	22	2,694	2,358	7,544	.3	.6
167 Chs of Christ	41	4,053	4,272	5,162	.2	.4
173 Comm of Christ	4	510	NR	510	-	-
175 Congr Chr Chs	2	239	180	305 *	-	-
176 Congr Ad Afl	1	131	NR	167 *	-	-
179 Consrv Bapt	10	NR	4,836	4,836	.2	.4
186 Coptic Orth Ch	3	NR	NR	NR	-	-
193 Episcopal	22	NR	4,564	12,652	.4	1.0
201 Evan Cov Ch	5	1,195	2,197	2,212 *	.1	.2
203 Evan Free Ch	16	6,847	8,583	9,116	.3	.7
207 E.L.C.A.	37	15,972	9,588	22,140	.8	1.7
221 Free Methodist	8	731	1,040	1,074	-	.1
223 Free Will Bapt	2	96	NR	123 *	-	-
226 Friends-USA	9	1,128	NR	1,438 *	.1	.1
237 Menn Br US Conf	1	530	NR	676 *	-	.1
246 Greek Orthodox	2	NR	NR	2,253	.1	.2
249 Assyr Apost Ch	1	NR	NR	392	-	-
252 Hindu	13	NR	NR	NR	-	-
263 Int Foursq Gos	28	2,113	3,758	3,758 *	.1	.3
267 Muslim Est	16	NR	8,506	39,583	1.4	3.1
268 Jain	2	NR	NR	NR	-	-
283 Luth—MO Synod	30	13,405	7,605	19,073	.7	1.5
288 Mennonite USA	1	0	100	100 *	-	-
290 Metro Comm Ch	2	75	56	96 *	-	-
291 Missionary Ch	1	150	200	200	-	-
313 N Am Bapt Conf	12	1,764	1,807	2,249 *	.1	.2
332 OCA: Bulg Dioc	1	40	NR	770	-	.1
335 Orth Pres Ch	6	353	312	494	-	-
339 Pent Ch of God	3	90	NR	184	-	-
349 Pent Holiness	2	111	96	141 *	-	-
355 Presb Ch (USA)	38	20,073	12,818	25,740 *	.9	2.0
356 Presb Ch Amer	7	3,343	3,130	3,678	.1	.3
371 Ref Ch in Am	5	3,374	6,578	14,911	.5	1.2
388 Reg Bapt Gen As	3	157	240	240 *	-	-
397 OCA: Roman Dioc	1	NR	NR	1,200	-	.1
403 Salvation Army	5	1,283	937	4,885	.2	.4
410 Serb Orth USA	1	NR	NR	400	-	-
413 S.D.A.	16	5,995	NR	7,134	.3	.6
416 Sikh	2	NR	NR	NR	-	-
419 So Bapt Conv	77	25,616	20,063	32,652 *	1.1	2.6
423 Syrian Orth Ch	1	NR	NR	400	-	-
435 Unitarian-Univ	7	564	NR	719 *	-	.1
443 Un C of Christ	13	1,933	1,115	2,464 *	.1	.2
449 Un Methodist	43	12,361	6,771	15,757 *	.6	1.2
455 Un Ref Chs N.A.	2	252	NR	411	-	-
463 Vineyard	16	6,031	3,283	7,699 *	.3	.6
467 Wesleyan	2	60	74	345	-	-
469 WELS	3	638	393	810	-	.1
490 Zoroastrian	4	NR	NR	NR	-	-
496 Jewish Est	28	NR	NR	60,000	2.1	4.7
498 Indep.Charis.	13	4,257	18,565	43,100	1.5	3.4
499 Indep.Non-Char	12	15,400	18,055	22,490	.8	1.8
PLACER	**165**	**24,493**	**25,013**	**92,441 ***	**37.2**	**100.0**
017 Amer Bapt Assn	1	60	NR	75 *	-	.1
053 Assemb of God	11	2,381	3,248	4,377	1.8	4.7
056 Baha'i	3	163	NR	163	.1	.2
076 Buddhism	1	NR	NR	NR	-	-
081 Catholic	10	NR	NR	39,286	15.8	42.5
084 Calvary Chapel	3	NR	NR	NR	-	-
089 Chr & Miss Al	2	74	NR	170	.1	.2
093 Chr Ch (Disc)	1	115	47	144 *	.1	.2
097 Chr Chs&Chs Cr	3	2,342	NR	2,940 *	1.2	3.2
105 Christian Ref	1	164	225	206 *	.1	.2
123 Ch God (Ander)	2	NR	10	10	-	-
127 Ch God (Cleve)	1	44	25	55 *	-	.1
145 Ch God Prophcy	1	37	NR	46 *	-	-
151 L-D Saints	24	NR	NR	10,203	4.1	11.0
165 Ch of Nazarene	4	718	831	1,416	.6	1.5
167 Chs of Christ	7	444	529	606	.2	.7
179 Consrv Bapt	2	NR	440	440	.2	.5
193 Episcopal	4	NR	513	1,491	.6	1.6
201 Evan Cov Ch	2	1,787	4,359	4,452 *	1.8	4.8
203 Evan Free Ch	2	304	625	675	.3	.7
207 E.L.C.A.	7	2,185	1,111	2,786	1.1	3.0
246 Greek Orthodox	1	NR	NR	3	-	-
263 Int Foursq Gos	7	684	993	993 *	.4	1.1
268 Jain	1	NR	NR	NR	-	-

NR–Not Reported *Total adherents estimated from known number of communicant, confirmed, full members. - Represents a percentage less than 0.1. Percentages may not total 100 due to rounding.

Table 4: Religious Congregations by County and Group: 2000

Religious Group	Number of Churches, Synagogues, Mosques, or Temples	Number of Communicant, Confirmed, or Full Members	Number of Attendees	Total Adherents		
				Number of Adherents	% of Total Pop.	% of Total Adh.
283 Luth—MO Synod	3	529	355	681	.3	.7
306 NT IndBapt&Rltd	1	145	NR	182 *	.1	.2
313 N Am Bapt Conf	4	730	1,138	916 *	.4	1.0
335 Orth Pres Ch	1	47	84	84	-	.1
339 Pent Ch of God	4	90	NR	216	.1	.2
355 Presb Ch (USA)	3	1,305	1,127	1,638 *	.7	1.8
356 Presb Ch Amer	1	336	500	500	.2	.5
388 Reg Bapt Gen As	2	187	240	235 *	.1	.3
403 Salvation Army	2	107	100	212	.1	.2
413 S.D.A.	6	1,632	NR	1,942	.8	2.1
419 So Bapt Conv	13	3,791	2,596	4,758 *	1.9	5.1
435 Unitarian-Univ	1	89	NR	112 *	-	.1
443 Un C of Christ	4	496	284	623 *	.3	.7
449 Un Methodist	10	1,807	877	2,268 *	.9	2.5
463 Vineyard	3	330	270	415 *	.2	.4
467 Wesleyan	3	206	444	758	.3	.8
469 WELS	1	164	142	214	.1	.2
496 Jewish Est	1	NR	NR	2,250	.9	2.4
499 Indep.Non-Char	1	1,000	3,900	3,900	1.6	4.2
PLUMAS	**33**	**1,894**	**1,462**	**6,147 ***	**29.5**	**100.0**
053 Assemb of God	4	208	263	312	1.5	5.1
056 Baha'i	0	6	NR	6	-	.1
081 Catholic	4	NR	NR	2,998	14.4	48.8
151 L-D Saints	4	NR	NR	747	3.6	12.2
167 Chs of Christ	2	100	110	115	.6	1.9
193 Episcopal	2	NR	25	55	.3	.9
207 E.L.C.A.	1	98	50	113	.5	1.8
283 Luth—MO Synod	3	109	70	117	.6	1.9
388 Reg Bapt Gen As	1	25	42	42 *	.2	.7
413 S.D.A.	1	38	NR	45	.2	.7
419 So Bapt Conv	4	468	440	560 *	2.7	9.1
449 Un Methodist	5	721	344	861 *	4.1	14.0
463 Vineyard	1	100	85	120 *	.6	2.0
467 Wesleyan	1	21	33	56	.3	.9
RIVERSIDE	**711**	**104,486**	**80,836**	**664,803 ***	**43.0**	**100.0**
017 Amer Bapt Assn	2	86	NR	113 *	-	-
019 Amer Bapt USA	15	3,015	2,493	3,961 *	.3	.6
034 Ant Orth of NA	2	140	NR	280	-	-
050 Armen Ap Etchm	1	0	NR	123	-	-
053 Assemb of God	51	7,115	8,629	11,702	.8	1.8
056 Baha'i	11	677	NR	677	-	.1
057 Bapt Gen Conf	11	954	1,056	1,337 *	.1	.2
075 Brethren in Cr	3	208	254	257	-	-
076 Buddhism	9	NR	NR	NR	-	-
081 Catholic	53	NR	NR	436,440	28.2	65.6
084 Calvary Chapel	22	NR	NR	NR	-	-
089 Chr & Miss Al	7	1,692	NR	4,799	.3	.7
093 Chr Ch (Disc)	4	739	276	971 *	.1	.1
097 Chr Chs&Chs Cr	11	6,701	NR	8,805 *	.6	1.3
105 Christian Ref	3	500	405	657 *	-	.1
123 Ch God (Ander)	5	NR	729	729	-	.1
127 Ch God (Cleve)	10	991	729	1,340 *	.1	.2
145 Ch God Prophcy	6	269	NR	353 *	-	.1
151 L-D Saints	82	NR	NR	34,314	2.2	5.2
165 Ch of Nazarene	16	2,625	2,273	3,521	.2	.5
167 Chs of Christ	34	2,932	2,981	3,792	.2	.6
173 Comm of Christ	2	265	NR	265	-	-
179 Consrv Bapt	10	NR	1,667	1,667	.1	.3
181 Consrv Congr	1	34	46	45 *	-	-
186 Coptic Orth Ch	4	NR	NR	NR	-	-
193 Episcopal	16	NR	2,134	5,756	.4	.9
203 Evan Free Ch	7	1,535	5,009	5,009	.3	.8
207 E.L.C.A.	16	5,566	3,067	7,750	.5	1.2
216 Evan Presby Ch	1	58	NR	76 *	-	-
221 Free Methodist	7	467	867	946	.1	.1
223 Free Will Bapt	1	48	NR	63 *	-	-
226 Friends-USA	1	152	NR	200 *	-	-
246 Greek Orthodox	2	NR	NR	642	-	.1
252 Hindu	1	NR	NR	NR	-	-
263 Int Foursq Gos	31	2,742	5,168	5,168 *	.3	.8
267 Muslim Est	5	NR	1,848	7,864	.5	1.2

Religious Group	Number of Churches, Synagogues, Mosques, or Temples	Number of Communicant, Confirmed, or Full Members	Number of Attendees	Total Adherents		
				Number of Adherents	% of Total Pop.	% of Total Adh.
273 LandmrkBapt,I&U	2	44	NR	58 *	-	-
283 Luth—MO Synod	19	5,888	3,505	6,932	.4	1.0
290 Metro Comm Ch	2	84	146	147 *	-	-
291 Missionary Ch	5	678	834	969	.1	.1
293 Morav Ch-North	1	81	NR	117	-	-
306 NT IndBapt&Rltd	1	145	NR	190 *	-	-
313 N Am Bapt Conf	1	75	98	99 *	-	-
335 Orth Pres Ch	2	68	115	127	-	-
339 Pent Ch of God	7	325	NR	817	.1	.1
349 Pent Holiness	7	487	679	640 *	-	.1
355 Presb Ch (USA)	14	3,878	2,637	5,097 *	.3	.8
360 Prim Bapt Chrch	2	NR	NR	NR	-	-
370 Ref Baptist Chs	1	NR	NR	NR	-	-
371 Ref Ch in Am	7	2,247	3,555	6,442	.4	1.0
388 Reg Bapt Gen As	3	1,393	990	952 *	.1	.1
397 OCA: Roman Dioc	1	NR	NR	21	-	-
403 Salvation Army	5	453	343	1,000	.1	.2
413 S.D.A.	31	12,117	NR	14,423	.9	2.2
416 Sikh	2	NR	NR	NR	-	-
419 So Bapt Conv	64	16,635	7,589	21,857 *	1.4	3.3
435 Unitarian-Univ	3	233	NR	306 *	-	-
443 Un C of Christ	8	1,397	806	1,836 *	.1	.3
449 Un Methodist	23	5,256	3,183	6,906 *	.4	1.0
463 Vineyard	7	3,077	2,277	4,043 *	.3	.6
467 Wesleyan	1	104	173	240	-	-
469 WELS	3	285	215	407	-	.1
496 Jewish Est	11	NR	NR	19,750	1.3	3.0
498 Indep.Charis.	5	5,900	4,725	11,700	.8	1.8
499 Indep.Non-Char	10	4,125	9,335	10,105	.7	1.5
SACRAMENTO	**583**	**111,152**	**80,834**	**451,919 ***	**36.9**	**100.0**
011 A.W.M.C.	1	24	120	28	-	-
017 Amer Bapt Assn	6	491	NR	627 *	.1	.1
019 Amer Bapt USA	18	3,392	2,255	4,328 *	.4	1.0
034 Ant Orth of NA	1	73	NR	146	-	-
050 Armen Ap Etchm	1	0	NR	616	.1	.1
053 Assemb of God	40	11,318	13,076	27,227	2.2	6.0
056 Baha'i	9	1,266	NR	1,266	.1	.3
057 Bapt Gen Conf	6	374	513	588 *	-	.1
076 Buddhism	8	NR	NR	NR	-	-
081 Catholic	41	NR	NR	224,265	18.3	49.6
084 Calvary Chapel	5	NR	NR	NR	-	-
089 Chr & Miss Al	7	2,138	NR	2,532	.2	.6
093 Chr Ch (Disc)	5	708	243	903 *	.1	.2
097 Chr Chs&Chs Cr	5	1,210	NR	1,546 *	.1	.3
105 Christian Ref	4	193	125	246 *	-	.1
123 Ch God (Ander)	8	NR	1,862	1,862	.2	.4
127 Ch God (Cleve)	6	806	454	1,028 *	.1	.2
145 Ch God Prophcy	3	111	NR	141 *	-	-
151 L-D Saints	66	NR	NR	30,936	2.5	6.8
157 Ch of Brethren	1	62	30	79 *	-	-
165 Ch of Nazarene	15	2,428	2,081	3,650	.3	.8
167 Chs of Christ	21	2,295	2,443	3,044	.2	.7
173 Comm of Christ	2	278	NR	278	-	.1
179 Consrv Bapt	9	NR	4,376	4,376	.4	1.0
193 Episcopal	12	NR	1,972	4,878	.4	1.1
201 Evan Cov Ch	4	1,139	2,908	2,908 *	.2	.6
203 Evan Free Ch	4	469	843	843	.1	.2
207 E.L.C.A.	20	6,228	3,284	8,705	.7	1.9
216 Evan Presby Ch	1	44	NR	56 *	-	-
221 Free Methodist	5	317	387	457	-	.1
223 Free Will Bapt	1	48	NR	61 *	-	-
226 Friends-USA	4	488	NR	623 *	.1	.1
237 Menn Br US Conf	2	347	NR	443 *	-	.1
245 Greek Orth Vslp	1	1,050	NR	1,750	.1	.4
246 Greek Orthodox	2	NR	NR	2,994	.2	.7
249 Assyr Apost Ch	1	NR	NR	108	-	-
252 Hindu	4	NR	NR	NR	-	-
262 Int Cou Comm Ch	1	26	NR	33 *	-	-
263 Int Foursq Gos	11	2,521	4,639	4,639 *	.4	1.0
264 Int Chs of Crst	1	282	510	433	-	.1
267 Muslim Est	9	NR	2,071	6,637	.5	1.5
273 LandmrkBapt,I&U	1	31	NR	40 *	-	-
283 Luth—MO Synod	12	2,445	1,586	3,510	.3	.8

NR–Not Reported *Total adherents estimated from known number of communicant, confirmed, full members. - Represents a percentage less than 0.1. Percentages may not total 100 due to rounding.

Table 4: Religious Congregations by County and Group: 2000

Religious Group	Number of Churches, Synagogues, Mosques, or Temples	Number of Communicant, Confirmed, or Full Members	Number of Attendees	Total Adherents: Number of Adherents	Total Adherents: % of Total Pop.	Total Adherents: % of Total Adh.
290 Metro Comm Ch	1	134	113	171 *	-	-
306 NT IndBapt&Rltd	5	610	NR	779 *	.1	.2
313 N Am Bapt Conf	8	5,685	9,111	7,254 *	.6	1.6
331 OCA: Ter Diocs	1	51	NR	301	-	.1
339 Pent Ch of God	6	146	NR	356	-	.1
349 Pent Holiness	7	540	543	689 *	.1	.2
355 Presb Ch (USA)	17	8,495	5,485	10,869 *	.9	2.4
356 Presb Ch Amer	5	293	170	357	-	.1
360 Prim Bapt Chrch	1	NR	NR	NR	-	-
370 Ref Baptist Chs	2	NR	NR	NR	-	-
371 Ref Ch in Am	3	840	902	1,804	.1	.4
373 Ref Ch in U.S.	1	115	NR	205	-	-
388 Reg Bapt Gen As	2	45	52	58 *	-	-
397 OCA: Roman Dioc	1	NR	NR	52	-	-
401 Rus Orth Abroad	1	NR	NR	NR	-	-
403 Salvation Army	4	481	311	1,594	.1	.4
410 Serb Orth USA	1	NR	NR	450	-	.1
413 S.D.A.	17	5,410	NR	6,438	.5	1.4
416 Sikh	1	NR	NR	NR	-	-
419 So Bapt Conv	56	16,027	5,067	20,451 *	1.7	4.5
435 Unitarian-Univ	2	501	NR	639 *	.1	.1
443 Un C of Christ	6	593	298	757 *	.1	.2
449 Un Methodist	25	5,814	3,157	7,419 *	.6	1.6
463 Vineyard	2	240	200	306 *	-	.1
467 Wesleyan	6	518	943	1,247	.1	.3
469 WELS	2	726	479	898	.1	.2
496 Jewish Est	7	NR	NR	16,800	1.4	3.7
498 Indep.Charis.	5	20,595	6,175	20,595	1.7	4.6
499 Indep.Non-Char	4	691	2,050	2,600	.2	.6
SAN BENITO	**26**	**1,605**	**1,460**	**36,824 ***	**69.2**	**100.0**
053 Assemb of God	2	137	175	194	.4	.5
056 Baha'i	1	45	NR	45	.1	.1
057 Bapt Gen Conf	1	67	200	200 *	.4	.5
081 Catholic	3	NR	NR	33,105	62.2	89.9
127 Ch God (Cleve)	1	37	27	50 *	.1	.1
145 Ch God Prophcy	1	46	NR	62 *	.1	.2
151 L-D Saints	3	NR	NR	1,028	1.9	2.8
167 Chs of Christ	2	29	32	37	.1	.1
193 Episcopal	1	NR	49	102	.2	.3
207 E.L.C.A.	1	158	128	259	.5	.7
263 Int Foursq Gos	1	77	310	310 *	.6	.8
306 NT IndBapt&Rltd	1	150	NR	202 *	.4	.5
339 Pent Ch of God	1	6	NR	15	-	-
355 Presb Ch (USA)	1	347	289	466 *	.9	1.3
403 Salvation Army	1	63	72	174	.3	.5
413 S.D.A.	1	125	NR	149	.3	.4
419 So Bapt Conv	1	30	20	40 *	.1	.1
449 Un Methodist	1	202	103	271 *	.5	.7
463 Vineyard	1	86	55	115 *	.2	.3
490 Zoroastrian	1	NR	NR	NR	-	-
SAN BERNARDINO	**875**	**151,287**	**102,012**	**717,905 ***	**42.0**	**100.0**
017 Amer Bapt Assn	8	482	NR	647 *	-	.1
019 Amer Bapt USA	33	8,643	11,233	11,595 *	.7	1.6
034 Ant Orth of NA	1	315	NR	630	-	.1
053 Assemb of God	68	6,875	8,489	11,179	.7	1.6
056 Baha'i	10	588	NR	588	-	.1
057 Bapt Gen Conf	8	2,269	2,146	3,319 *	.2	.5
059 Bapt Miss Assn	4	317	255	425 *	-	.1
075 Brethren in Cr	11	1,035	1,190	1,338	.1	.2
076 Buddhism	11	NR	NR	NR	-	-
081 Catholic	65	NR	NR	445,655	26.1	62.1
084 Calvary Chapel	22	NR	NR	NR	-	-
089 Chr & Miss Al	12	880	NR	1,524	.1	.2
093 Chr Ch (Disc)	7	1,531	407	2,054 *	.1	.3
097 Chr Chs&Chs Cr	13	3,320	NR	4,454 *	.3	.6
105 Christian Ref	5	1,788	1,620	2,399 *	.1	.3
123 Ch God (Ander)	7	NR	849	849	-	.1
127 Ch God (Cleve)	11	845	776	1,221 *	.1	.2
145 Ch God Prophcy	8	353	NR	470 *	-	.1
151 L-D Saints	99	NR	NR	36,936	2.2	5.1
165 Ch of Nazarene	29	5,315	4,010	8,029	.5	1.1
167 Chs of Christ	40	2,950	3,096	3,886	.2	.5
173 Comm of Christ	3	514	NR	514	-	.1
175 Congr Chr Chs	3	1,434	840	1,924 *	.1	.3
179 Consrv Bapt	12	NR	5,794	5,794	.3	.8
185 Cumber Presb	1	18	NR	114	-	-
186 Coptic Orth Ch	1	NR	NR	NR	-	-
193 Episcopal	17	NR	1,319	3,853	.2	.5
203 Evan Free Ch	8	1,290	2,100	2,140	.1	.3
207 E.L.C.A.	16	3,791	1,929	4,888	.3	.7
221 Free Methodist	12	1,297	2,061	2,313	.1	.3
223 Free Will Bapt	1	48	NR	65 *	-	-
226 Friends-USA	1	32	NR	43 *	-	-
246 Greek Orthodox	2	NR	NR	906	.1	.1
252 Hindu	1	NR	NR	NR	-	-
262 Int Cou Comm Ch	2	285	NR	382 *	-	.1
263 Int Foursq Gos	38	1,896	3,104	3,104 *	.2	.4
267 Muslim Est	7	NR	2,884	13,237	.8	1.8
273 LandmrkBapt,I&U	1	52	NR	70 *	-	-
283 Luth—MO Synod	23	4,867	2,903	6,582	.4	.9
288 Mennonite USA	6	215	175	288 *	-	-
291 Missionary Ch	1	90	99	99	-	-
304 NatPrimBapt USA	1	55	NR	74 *	-	-
306 NT IndBapt&Rltd	3	435	NR	584 *	-	.1
313 N Am Bapt Conf	3	513	524	688 *	-	.1
331 OCA: Ter Diocs	1	31	NR	84	-	-
339 Pent Ch of God	10	320	NR	782	-	.1
349 Pent Holiness	7	726	908	974 *	.1	.1
355 Presb Ch (USA)	20	4,911	3,043	6,587 *	.4	.9
356 Presb Ch Amer	2	0	0	0	-	-
360 Prim Bapt Chrch	1	NR	NR	NR	-	-
369 Prot Ref Chs	1	140	NR	245	-	-
370 Ref Baptist Chs	1	NR	NR	NR	-	-
371 Ref Ch in Am	3	693	683	1,168	.1	.2
388 Reg Bapt Gen As	1	114	140	153 *	-	-
403 Salvation Army	4	643	414	1,036	.1	.1
413 S.D.A.	45	21,977	NR	26,152	1.5	3.6
416 Sikh	1	NR	NR	NR	-	-
418 Southw Bapt Fel	1	NR	NR	NR	-	-
419 So Bapt Conv	66	38,575	20,702	51,748 *	3.0	7.2
435 Unitarian-Univ	1	170	NR	228 *	-	-
443 Un C of Christ	15	1,586	797	2,128 *	.1	.3
449 Un Methodist	27	5,019	2,980	6,731 *	.4	.9
455 Un Ref Chs N.A.	3	660	NR	916	.1	.1
463 Vineyard	4	535	460	717 *	-	.1
467 Wesleyan	1	33	55	110	-	-
469 WELS	3	235	167	286	-	-
496 Jewish Est	7	NR	NR	3,000	.2	.4
498 Indep.Charis.	8	19,400	4,885	19,400	1.1	2.7
499 Indep.Non-Char	7	1,181	8,975	10,600	.6	1.5
SAN DIEGO	**1,179**	**173,530**	**142,009**	**1,230,063 ***	**43.7**	**100.0**
017 Amer Bapt Assn	5	270	NR	340 *	-	-
019 Amer Bapt USA	25	3,501	2,141	4,397 *	.2	.4
034 Ant Orth of NA	2	280	NR	560	-	-
039 Ap Chr Ch(Naz)	2	110	184	184 *	-	-
040 Ap Chr Ch-Amer	1	29	52	52 *	-	-
050 Armen Ap Etchm	1	0	NR	924	-	.1
053 Assemb of God	72	10,054	12,055	16,770	.6	1.4
055 As Ref Pres Ch	1	68	NR	70	-	-
056 Baha'i	18	2,446	NR	2,446	.1	.2
057 Bapt Gen Conf	21	5,929	6,953	7,660 *	.3	.6
059 Bapt Miss Assn	1	24	60	60 *	-	-
071 Brethren (Ash)	1	0	60	0 *	-	-
076 Buddhism	25	NR	NR	NR	-	-
081 Catholic	105	NR	NR	829,933	29.5	67.5
084 Calvary Chapel	34	NR	NR	NR	-	-
089 Chr & Miss Al	17	1,399	NR	1,958	.1	.2
093 Chr Ch (Disc)	10	4,067	1,703	5,108 *	.2	.4
097 Chr Chs&Chs Cr	10	2,860	NR	3,592 *	.1	.3
105 Christian Ref	3	552	600	693 *	-	.1
123 Ch God (Ander)	9	NR	1,720	1,720	.1	.1
127 Ch God (Cleve)	5	442	224	556 *	-	-
145 Ch God Prophcy	7	277	NR	346 *	-	-
151 L-D Saints	117	NR	NR	46,268	1.6	3.8

NR–Not Reported   *Total adherents estimated from known number of communicant, confirmed, full members.   - Represents a percentage less than 0.1.   Percentages may not total 100 due to rounding.

Table 4: Religious Congregations by County and Group: 2000

Religious Group	Number of Churches, Synagogues, Mosques, or Temples	Number of Communicant, Confirmed, or Full Members	Number of Attendees	Total Adherents		
				Number of Adherents	% of Total Pop.	% of Total Adh.
157 Ch of Brethren	2	201	0	252 *	-	-
165 Ch of Nazarene	26	4,485	3,045	5,181	.2	.4
167 Chs of Christ	51	5,614	5,666	7,501	.3	.6
171 Ch God-Gen Con	2	66	130	130 *	-	-
173 Comm of Christ	5	1,035	NR	1,035	-	.1
175 Congr Chr Chs	6	702	472	882 *	-	.1
179 Consrv Bapt	14	NR	2,175	2,175	.1	.2
181 Consrv Congr	3	1,221	1,213	1,534 *	.1	.1
186 Coptic Orth Ch	1	NR	NR	NR	-	-
193 Episcopal	38	NR	6,977	16,284	.6	1.3
201 Evan Cov Ch	6	794	1,451	1,506 *	.1	.1
203 Evan Free Ch	13	2,814	6,330	6,330	.2	.5
207 E.L.C.A.	39	13,090	8,087	17,873	.6	1.5
216 Evan Presby Ch	1	301	NR	378 *	-	-
220 Free Lutheran	2	187	178	248	-	-
221 Free Methodist	4	194	498	498	-	-
223 Free Will Bapt	1	48	NR	61 *	-	-
226 Friends-USA	4	368	NR	462 *	-	-
237 Menn Br US Conf	1	10	NR	13 *	-	-
245 Greek Orth Vslp	1	95	NR	211	-	-
246 Greek Orthodox	3	NR	NR	3,198	.1	.3
252 Hindu	14	NR	NR	NR	-	-
262 Int Cou Comm Ch	2	380	NR	478 *	-	-
263 Int Foursq Gos	24	1,463	2,469	2,469 *	.1	.2
264 Int Chs of Crst	1	2,429	4,423	3,505	.1	.3
267 Muslim Est	6	NR	1,740	7,878	.3	.6
268 Jain	1	NR	NR	NR	-	-
283 Luth—MO Synod	38	10,418	6,597	13,271	.5	1.1
288 Mennonite USA	2	37	51	53 *	-	-
290 Metro Comm Ch	1	324	370	407 *	-	-
291 Missionary Ch	2	680	954	1,066	-	.1
306 NT IndBapt&Rltd	2	290	NR	364 *	-	-
331 OCA: Ter Diocs	2	140	NR	736	-	.1
335 Orth Pres Ch	6	752	764	999	-	.1
339 Pent Ch of God	4	122	NR	353	-	-
349 Pent Holiness	4	224	208	281 *	-	-
355 Presb Ch (USA)	31	19,076	10,877	24,008 *	.9	2.0
356 Presb Ch Amer	10	1,552	1,399	1,950	.1	.2
360 Prim Bapt Chrch	1	NR	NR	NR	-	-
370 Ref Baptist Chs	3	NR	NR	NR	-	-
371 Ref Ch in Am	2	249	278	506	-	-
388 Reg Bapt Gen As	6	655	960	966 *	-	.1
400 Rus Orth Moscow	1	NR	NR	NR	-	-
401 Rus Orth Abroad	1	NR	NR	NR	-	-
403 Salvation Army	9	1,151	950	4,517	.2	.4
410 Serb Orth USA	2	NR	NR	650	-	.1
413 S.D.A.	32	9,814	NR	11,679	.4	.9
416 Sikh	2	NR	NR	NR	-	-
419 So Bapt Conv	104	21,679	9,559	27,228 *	1.0	2.2
423 Syrian Orth Ch	1	NR	NR	300	-	-
425 Tao	2	NR	NR	NR	-	-
431 Ukrainian Orth	1	NR	NR	150	-	-
435 Unitarian-Univ	6	1,435	NR	1,802 *	.1	.1
443 Un C of Christ	23	5,244	2,700	6,586 *	.2	.5
449 Un Methodist	43	16,563	9,710	20,799 *	.7	1.7
455 Un Ref Chs N.A.	2	500	NR	687	-	.1
463 Vineyard	7	1,124	896	1,412 *	.1	.1
467 Wesleyan	10	3,686	5,577	15,440	.5	1.3
469 WELS	7	1,120	923	1,504	.1	.1
490 Zoroastrian	1	NR	NR	NR	-	-
496 Jewish Est	29	NR	NR	70,000	2.5	5.7
498 Indep.Charis.	3	250	3,050	3,050	.1	.2
499 Indep.Non-Char	16	8,640	15,580	15,580	.6	1.3
SAN FRANCISCO	**408**	**44,991**	**31,515**	**324,882 ***	**41.8**	**100.0**
019 Amer Bapt USA	14	4,492	1,470	5,066 *	.7	1.6
034 Ant Orth of NA	1	607	NR	1,214	.2	.4
049 Armen Ap Cilic	1	500	NR	2,800	.4	.9
050 Armen Ap Etchm	1	0	NR	924	.1	.3
053 Assemb of God	19	2,416	2,676	3,311	.4	1.0
056 Baha'i	1	703	NR	703	.1	.2
057 Bapt Gen Conf	3	123	130	153 *	-	-
076 Buddhism	55	NR	NR	NR	-	-
081 Catholic	49	NR	NR	180,798	23.3	55.7
084 Calvary Chapel	1	NR	NR	NR	-	-
089 Chr & Miss Al	2	535	NR	901	.1	.3
093 Chr Ch (Disc)	1	124	0	140 *	-	-
097 Chr Chs&Chs Cr	1	30	NR	34 *	-	-
105 Christian Ref	1	369	315	416 *	.1	.1
123 Ch God (Ander)	1	NR	29	29	-	-
127 Ch God (Cleve)	4	322	444	498 *	.1	.2
145 Ch God Prophcy	2	83	NR	94 *	-	-
151 L-D Saints	2	NR	NR	1,210	.2	.4
157 Ch of Brethren	1	50	0	56 *	-	-
165 Ch of Nazarene	10	679	566	2,008	.3	.6
167 Chs of Christ	8	825	608	899	.1	.3
173 Comm of Christ	1	62	NR	62	-	-
185 Cumber Presb	2	750	NR	974	.1	.3
193 Episcopal	19	NR	2,698	6,295	.8	1.9
201 Evan Cov Ch	3	406	341	479 *	.1	.1
203 Evan Free Ch	2	422	575	575	.1	.2
207 E.L.C.A.	10	1,287	750	1,634	.2	.5
221 Free Methodist	1	15	20	20	-	-
226 Friends-USA	1	32	NR	36 *	-	-
246 Greek Orthodox	2	NR	NR	2,787	.4	.9
249 Assyr Apost Ch	1	NR	NR	288	-	.1
252 Hindu	8	NR	NR	NR	-	-
262 Int Cou Comm Ch	1	700	NR	789 *	.1	.2
263 Int Foursq Gos	3	161	469	469 *	.1	.1
264 Int Chs of Crst	1	2,873	4,054	3,656	.5	1.1
267 Muslim Est	6	NR	2,085	22,664	2.9	7.0
283 Luth—MO Synod	7	1,711	1,074	2,187	.3	.7
288 Mennonite USA	2	98	110	113 *	-	-
290 Metro Comm Ch	2	598	477	675 *	.1	.2
306 NT IndBapt&Rltd	4	845	NR	953 *	.1	.3
313 N Am Bapt Conf	1	249	660	281 *	-	.1
331 OCA: Ter Diocs	3	131	NR	1,181	.2	.4
335 Orth Pres Ch	1	78	80	100	-	-
349 Pent Holiness	3	77	82	87 *	-	-
355 Presb Ch (USA)	18	3,526	2,220	3,976 *	.5	1.2
356 Presb Ch Amer	1	54	220	220	-	.1
371 Ref Ch in Am	1	40	40	62	-	-
400 Rus Orth Moscow	1	NR	NR	NR	-	-
401 Rus Orth Abroad	4	NR	NR	NR	-	-
403 Salvation Army	7	779	775	2,316	.3	.7
411 Serb Orth: Grac	1	NR	NR	NR	-	-
413 S.D.A.	8	970	NR	1,156	.1	.4
416 Sikh	1	NR	NR	NR	-	-
419 So Bapt Conv	30	2,911	2,081	3,283 *	.4	1.0
425 Tao	7	NR	NR	NR	-	-
431 Ukrainian Orth	1	NR	NR	318	-	.1
435 Unitarian-Univ	1	503	NR	567 *	.1	.2
443 Un C of Christ	8	1,317	638	1,485 *	.2	.5
449 Un Methodist	16	11,989	4,950	13,522 *	1.7	4.2
463 Vineyard	2	149	128	168 *	-	.1
490 Zoroastrian	1	NR	NR	NR	-	-
496 Jewish Est	36	NR	NR	49,500	6.4	15.2
499 Indep.Non-Char	2	400	750	750	.1	.2
SAN JOAQUIN	**312**	**43,086**	**31,676**	**215,084 ***	**38.2**	**100.0**
017 Amer Bapt Assn	6	432	NR	570 *	.1	.3
019 Amer Bapt USA	4	1,291	1,431	1,700 *	.3	.8
053 Assemb of God	25	4,135	5,668	7,098	1.3	3.3
056 Baha'i	3	366	NR	366	.1	.2
057 Bapt Gen Conf	2	198	216	264 *	-	.1
059 Bapt Miss Assn	1	81	20	107 *	-	-
071 Brethren (Ash)	2	79	98	104 *	-	-
076 Buddhism	6	NR	NR	NR	-	-
081 Catholic	19	NR	NR	138,485	24.6	64.4
084 Calvary Chapel	1	NR	NR	NR	-	-
089 Chr & Miss Al	7	1,339	NR	1,414	.3	.7
093 Chr Ch (Disc)	3	572	277	753 *	.1	.4
097 Chr Chs&Chs Cr	3	300	NR	396 *	.1	.2
105 Christian Ref	6	2,235	1,740	2,943 *	.5	1.4
123 Ch God (Ander)	4	NR	241	241	-	.1
127 Ch God (Cleve)	4	209	269	318 *	.1	.1
145 Ch God Prophcy	2	83	NR	110 *	-	.1
151 L-D Saints	26	NR	NR	10,299	1.8	4.8

NR–Not Reported *Total adherents estimated from known number of communicant, confirmed, full members. - Represents a percentage less than 0.1. Percentages may not total 100 due to rounding.

Table 4: Religious Congregations by County and Group: 2000

Religious Group	Number of Churches, Synagogues, Mosques, or Temples	Number of Communicant, Confirmed, or Full Members	Number of Attendees	Total Adherents		
				Number of Adherents	% of Total Pop.	% of Total Adh.
165 Ch of Nazarene	10	990	858	1,295	.2	.6
167 Chs of Christ	21	1,610	1,801	2,139	.4	1.0
171 Ch God-Gen Con	1	52	26	68 *	-	-
173 Comm of Christ	1	126	NR	126	-	.1
179 Consrv Bapt	4	NR	1,290	1,290	.2	.6
181 Consrv Congr	1	50	50	66 *	-	-
193 Episcopal	7	NR	672	1,530	.3	.7
201 Evan Cov Ch	4	564	604	768 *	.1	.4
203 Evan Free Ch	5	166	462	462	.1	.2
207 E.L.C.A.	5	2,282	1,021	2,907	.5	1.4
221 Free Methodist	2	98	127	141	-	.1
223 Free Will Bapt	4	193	NR	254 *	-	.1
226 Friends-USA	1	32	NR	42 *	-	-
237 Menn Br US Conf	1	285	NR	375 *	.1	.2
246 Greek Orthodox	1	NR	NR	903	.2	.4
263 Int Foursq Gos	6	920	1,719	1,719 *	.3	.8
267 Muslim Est	4	NR	632	2,068	.4	1.0
283 Luth—MO Synod	6	2,760	1,610	3,715	.7	1.7
290 Metro Comm Ch	1	43	49	57 *	-	-
306 NT IndBapt&Rltd	2	270	NR	356 *	.1	.2
313 N Am Bapt Conf	6	3,373	2,986	4,441 *	.8	2.1
339 Pent Ch of God	13	408	NR	985	.2	.5
349 Pent Holiness	2	104	120	137 *	-	.1
355 Presb Ch (USA)	9	1,849	1,109	2,436 *	.4	1.1
356 Presb Ch Amer	1	120	70	120	-	.1
371 Ref Ch in Am	1	612	604	1,389	.2	.6
373 Ref Ch in U.S.	1	58	NR	81	-	-
388 Reg Bapt Gen As	1	42	50	55 *	-	-
403 Salvation Army	3	253	192	382	.1	.2
413 S.D.A.	12	3,408	NR	4,056	.7	1.9
416 Sikh	1	NR	NR	NR	-	-
419 So Bapt Conv	28	5,803	3,123	7,641 *	1.4	3.6
435 Unitarian-Univ	1	189	NR	249 *	-	.1
443 Un C of Christ	3	516	263	679 *	.1	.3
449 Un Methodist	14	3,961	1,661	5,216 *	.9	2.4
455 Un Ref Chs N.A.	1	185	NR	250	-	.1
467 Wesleyan	1	94	110	110	-	.1
469 WELS	1	111	72	123	-	.1
496 Jewish Est	1	NR	NR	850	.2	.4
499 Indep.Non-Char	1	239	435	435	.1	.2
SAN LUIS OBISPO	**182**	**21,172**	**20,899**	**107,121 ***	**43.4**	**100.0**
017 Amer Bapt Assn	2	142	NR	170 *	.1	.2
019 Amer Bapt USA	4	520	587	621 *	.3	.6
053 Assemb of God	13	1,088	1,486	1,834	.7	1.7
056 Baha'i	4	215	NR	215	.1	.2
057 Bapt Gen Conf	3	538	848	848 *	.3	.8
076 Buddhism	2	NR	NR	NR	-	-
081 Catholic	16	NR	NR	68,264	27.7	63.7
084 Calvary Chapel	7	NR	NR	NR	-	-
089 Chr & Miss Al	1	0	NR	181	.1	.2
093 Chr Ch (Disc)	1	72	48	86 *	-	.1
097 Chr Chs&Chs Cr	5	586	NR	701 *	.3	.7
123 Ch God (Ander)	1	NR	62	62	-	.1
127 Ch God (Cleve)	1	50	21	60 *	-	.1
145 Ch God Prophcy	3	120	NR	144 *	.1	.1
151 L-D Saints	12	NR	NR	5,418	2.2	5.1
165 Ch of Nazarene	5	2,082	2,953	3,229	1.3	3.0
167 Chs of Christ	10	551	594	721	.3	.7
173 Comm of Christ	1	58	NR	58	-	.1
193 Episcopal	7	NR	679	1,673	.7	1.6
203 Evan Free Ch	5	764	1,640	1,640	.7	1.5
207 E.L.C.A.	5	1,319	790	1,670	.7	1.6
226 Friends-USA	2	64	NR	76 *	-	.1
246 Greek Orthodox	1	NR	NR	0	-	-
263 Int Foursq Gos	9	937	1,525	1,525 *	.6	1.4
267 Muslim Est	1	NR	20	50	-	-
283 Luth—MO Synod	4	1,016	661	1,433	.6	1.3
288 Mennonite USA	1	116	55	139 *	.1	.1
306 NT IndBapt&Rltd	1	145	NR	173 *	.1	.2
335 Orth Pres Ch	1	0	69	69	-	.1
339 Pent Ch of God	2	59	NR	317	.1	.3
355 Presb Ch (USA)	7	1,507	1,077	1,800 *	.7	1.7
356 Presb Ch Amer	2	169	250	301	.1	.3

Religious Group	Number of Churches, Synagogues, Mosques, or Temples	Number of Communicant, Confirmed, or Full Members	Number of Attendees	Total Adherents		
				Number of Adherents	% of Total Pop.	% of Total Adh.
388 Reg Bapt Gen As	3	260	340	340 *	.1	.3
403 Salvation Army	1	32	20	80	-	.1
413 S.D.A.	4	812	NR	966	.4	.9
419 So Bapt Conv	10	1,382	809	1,651 *	.7	1.5
435 Unitarian-Univ	1	175	NR	209 *	.1	.2
443 Un C of Christ	3	692	327	827 *	.3	.8
449 Un Methodist	9	1,834	1,035	2,191 *	.9	2.0
463 Vineyard	5	1,867	1,628	2,229 *	.9	2.1
496 Jewish Est	2	NR	NR	1,700	.7	1.6
498 Indep.Charis.	2	0	1,075	1,150	.5	1.1
499 Indep.Non-Char	3	2,000	2,300	2,300	.9	2.1
SAN MATEO	**310**	**32,365**	**26,847**	**295,968 ***	**41.9**	**100.0**
019 Amer Bapt USA	13	1,967	1,101	2,402 *	.3	.8
053 Assemb of God	24	2,221	2,502	2,937	.4	1.0
056 Baha'i	10	542	NR	542	.1	.2
057 Bapt Gen Conf	4	147	146	199 *	-	.1
076 Buddhism	10	NR	NR	NR	-	-
081 Catholic	34	NR	NR	205,991	29.1	69.6
084 Calvary Chapel	1	NR	NR	NR	-	-
089 Chr & Miss Al	3	263	NR	329	-	.1
093 Chr Ch (Disc)	2	120	65	147 *	-	-
097 Chr Chs&Chs Cr	2	210	NR	257 *	-	.1
123 Ch God (Ander)	3	NR	724	724	.1	.2
127 Ch God (Cleve)	6	381	476	519 *	.1	.2
151 L-D Saints	23	NR	NR	9,423	1.3	3.2
165 Ch of Nazarene	3	304	218	524	.1	.2
167 Chs of Christ	9	742	698	926	.1	.3
173 Comm of Christ	1	28	NR	28	-	-
179 Consrv Bapt	7	NR	955	955	.1	.3
193 Episcopal	15	NR	2,181	5,942	.8	2.0
201 Evan Cov Ch	3	776	766	947 *	.1	.3
203 Evan Free Ch	4	219	407	407	.1	.1
207 E.L.C.A.	10	2,218	996	2,924	.4	1.0
221 Free Methodist	4	181	232	286	-	.1
226 Friends-USA	1	32	NR	39 *	-	-
245 Greek Orth Vslp	1	245	NR	545	.1	.2
246 Greek Orthodox	1	NR	NR	2,166	.3	.7
252 Hindu	1	NR	NR	NR	-	-
263 Int Foursq Gos	4	265	362	362 *	.1	.1
267 Muslim Est	3	NR	849	3,832	.5	1.3
283 Luth—MO Synod	7	1,856	971	2,514	.4	.8
291 Missionary Ch	1	13	15	15	-	-
306 NT IndBapt&Rltd	4	580	NR	708 *	.1	.2
331 OCA: Ter Diocs	1	43	NR	191	-	.1
333 Malan Dioc Am	1	NR	NR	150	-	.1
335 Orth Pres Ch	1	57	72	73	-	-
355 Presb Ch (USA)	10	8,489	6,016	10,365 *	1.5	3.5
371 Ref Ch in Am	1	182	170	224	-	.1
401 Rus Orth Abroad	2	NR	NR	NR	-	-
403 Salvation Army	3	326	208	367	.1	.1
413 S.D.A.	7	996	NR	1,184	.2	.4
416 Sikh	1	NR	NR	NR	-	-
419 So Bapt Conv	27	2,265	1,747	2,766 *	.4	.9
435 Unitarian-Univ	2	377	NR	460 *	.1	.2
443 Un C of Christ	13	2,301	1,038	2,810 *	.4	.9
449 Un Methodist	17	3,295	1,717	4,024 *	.6	1.4
463 Vineyard	1	150	200	200 *	-	.1
469 WELS	1	74	65	114	-	-
496 Jewish Est	7	NR	NR	24,500	3.5	8.3
499 Indep.Non-Char	1	500	1,950	1,950	.3	.7
SANTA BARBARA	**229**	**27,800**	**25,369**	**222,819 ***	**55.8**	**100.0**
017 Amer Bapt Assn	2	52	NR	65 *	-	-
019 Amer Bapt USA	8	556	447	691 *	.2	.3
034 Ant Orth of NA	2	331	NR	662	.2	.3
053 Assemb of God	12	2,164	2,545	3,267	.8	1.5
056 Baha'i	5	305	NR	305	.1	.1
057 Bapt Gen Conf	5	1,907	1,886	2,723 *	.7	1.2
076 Buddhism	9	NR	NR	NR	-	-
081 Catholic	18	NR	NR	164,882	41.3	74.0
084 Calvary Chapel	5	NR	NR	NR	-	-
089 Chr & Miss Al	2	148	NR	148	-	.1

NR–Not Reported *Total adherents estimated from known number of communicant, confirmed, full members. - Represents a percentage less than 0.1. Percentages may not total 100 due to rounding.

Table 4: Religious Congregations by County and Group: 2000

Religious Group	Number of Churches, Synagogues, Mosques, or Temples	Number of Communicant, Confirmed, or Full Members	Number of Attendees	Total Adherents: Number of Adherents	Total Adherents: % of Total Pop.	Total Adherents: % of Total Adh.
093 Chr Ch (Disc)	2	198	117	246 *	.1	.1
097 Chr Chs&Chs Cr	1	59	NR	73 *	-	-
123 Ch God (Ander)	1	NR	68	68	-	-
127 Ch God (Cleve)	1	217	91	270 *	.1	.1
145 Ch God Prophcy	6	269	NR	336 *	.1	.2
151 L-D Saints	15	NR	NR	5,607	1.4	2.5
165 Ch of Nazarene	4	982	1,007	1,087	.3	.5
167 Chs of Christ	10	713	710	949	.2	.4
173 Comm of Christ	1	38	NR	38	-	-
179 Consrv Bapt	3	NR	485	485	.1	.2
181 Consrv Congr	1	74	100	92 *	-	-
193 Episcopal	7	NR	1,548	3,752	.9	1.7
201 Evan Cov Ch	3	379	1,373	1,414 *	.4	.6
203 Evan Free Ch	4	246	470	470	.1	.2
207 E.L.C.A.	7	1,737	881	2,217	.6	1.0
216 Evan Presby Ch	1	98	NR	122 *	-	.1
221 Free Methodist	1	396	409	409	.1	.2
226 Friends-USA	1	32	NR	40 *	-	-
246 Greek Orthodox	1	NR	NR	573	.1	.3
252 Hindu	1	NR	NR	NR	-	-
263 Int Foursq Gos	12	2,359	3,605	3,605 *	.9	1.6
267 Muslim Est	1	NR	156	609	.2	.3
283 Luth—MO Synod	7	1,922	1,170	2,429	.6	1.1
291 Missionary Ch	2	286	327	327	.1	.1
306 NT IndBapt&Rltd	2	545	NR	678 *	.2	.3
331 OCA: Ter Diocs	3	46	NR	129	-	.1
335 Orth Pres Ch	2	82	108	117	-	.1
339 Pent Ch of God	1	28	NR	80	-	-
355 Presb Ch (USA)	11	3,790	2,567	4,723 *	1.2	2.1
356 Presb Ch Amer	1	57	101	101	-	-
388 Reg Bapt Gen As	2	215	220	285 *	.1	.1
401 Rus Orth Abroad	1	NR	NR	NR	-	-
403 Salvation Army	2	74	89	327	.1	.1
413 S.D.A.	4	1,115	NR	1,327	.3	.6
419 So Bapt Conv	12	1,592	920	1,979 *	.5	.9
435 Unitarian-Univ	2	572	NR	711 *	.2	.3
443 Un C of Christ	3	403	192	501 *	.1	.2
449 Un Methodist	8	2,178	1,110	2,708 *	.7	1.2
463 Vineyard	4	665	590	828 *	.2	.4
469 WELS	2	230	201	289	.1	.1
496 Jewish Est	4	NR	NR	7,700	1.9	3.5
498 Indep.Charis.	2	490	450	600	.2	.3
499 Indep.Non-Char	2	250	1,426	1,775	.4	.8
SANTA CLARA	**687**	**97,431**	**79,584**	**727,752 ***	**43.3**	**100.0**
017 Amer Bapt Assn	3	232	NR	289 *	-	-
019 Amer Bapt USA	13	1,555	1,419	1,935 *	.1	.3
034 Ant Orth of NA	2	451	NR	902	.1	.1
050 Armen Ap Etchm	1	0	NR	1,540	.1	.2
053 Assemb of God	54	6,439	7,381	12,113	.7	1.7
056 Baha'i	14	1,160	NR	1,160	.1	.2
057 Bapt Gen Conf	7	737	987	1,134 *	.1	.2
076 Buddhism	32	NR	NR	NR	-	-
081 Catholic	55	NR	NR	483,079	28.7	66.4
084 Calvary Chapel	1	NR	NR	NR	-	-
089 Chr & Miss Al	12	2,510	NR	2,695	.2	.4
093 Chr Ch (Disc)	4	626	112	779 *	-	.1
097 Chr Chs&Chs Cr	12	2,604	NR	3,243 *	.2	.4
105 Christian Ref	5	566	557	704 *	-	.1
123 Ch God (Ander)	2	NR	214	214	-	-
127 Ch God (Cleve)	7	389	332	484 *	-	.1
145 Ch God Prophcy	2	83	NR	104 *	-	-
151 L-D Saints	55	NR	NR	20,172	1.2	2.8
165 Ch of Nazarene	14	1,352	825	1,908	.1	.3
167 Chs of Christ	15	1,742	1,715	2,416	.1	.3
173 Comm of Christ	1	191	NR	191	-	-
175 Congr Chr Chs	1	25	18	31 *	-	-
179 Consrv Bapt	15	NR	5,244	5,244	.3	.7
185 Cumber Presb	2	51	NR	65	-	-
193 Episcopal	22	NR	3,952	10,102	.6	1.4
201 Evan Cov Ch	5	433	479	616 *	-	.1
203 Evan Free Ch	2	516	705	705	-	.1
207 E.L.C.A.	27	7,187	3,759	10,254	.6	1.4
221 Free Methodist	1	81	113	113	-	-
223 Free Will Bapt	1	48	NR	60 *	-	-
226 Friends-USA	1	32	NR	40 *	-	-
237 Menn Br US Conf	6	1,089	NR	1,355 *	.1	.2
246 Greek Orthodox	2	NR	NR	1,860	.1	.3
249 Assyr Apost Ch	1	NR	NR	1,516	.1	.2
252 Hindu	15	NR	NR	NR	-	-
262 Int Cou Comm Ch	1	190	NR	236 *	-	-
263 Int Foursq Gos	10	978	1,578	1,578 *	.1	.2
267 Muslim Est	10	NR	5,607	19,206	1.1	2.6
268 Jain	3	NR	NR	NR	-	-
283 Luth—MO Synod	13	3,744	2,035	4,972	.3	.7
288 Mennonite USA	1	15	20	20 *	-	-
290 Metro Comm Ch	1	64	50	80 *	-	-
306 NT IndBapt&Rltd	2	245	NR	305 *	-	-
313 N Am Bapt Conf	1	50	70	62 *	-	-
331 OCA: Ter Diocs	1	53	NR	401	-	.1
335 Orth Pres Ch	2	208	270	286	-	-
339 Pent Ch of God	7	298	NR	678	-	.1
349 Pent Holiness	9	2,206	2,137	2,745 *	.2	.4
355 Presb Ch (USA)	26	7,408	5,088	9,218 *	.5	1.3
356 Presb Ch Amer	9	290	300	353	-	-
360 Prim Bapt Chrch	1	NR	NR	NR	-	-
370 Ref Baptist Chs	2	NR	NR	NR	-	-
371 Ref Ch in Am	1	590	775	1,350	.1	.2
388 Reg Bapt Gen As	4	416	424	487 *	-	.1
397 OCA: Roman Dioc	1	NR	NR	170	-	-
401 Rus Orth Abroad	1	NR	NR	NR	-	-
403 Salvation Army	4	408	352	1,040	.1	.1
410 Serb Orth USA	1	NR	NR	50	-	-
411 Serb Orth: Grac	1	NR	NR	NR	-	-
413 S.D.A.	19	4,869	NR	5,794	.3	.8
416 Sikh	6	NR	NR	NR	-	-
419 So Bapt Conv	54	13,512	7,058	16,814 *	1.0	2.3
423 Syrian Orth Ch	1	NR	NR	150	-	-
435 Unitarian-Univ	4	962	NR	1,197 *	.1	.2
443 Un C of Christ	11	2,434	1,108	3,029 *	.2	.4
449 Un Methodist	30	11,607	5,982	14,444 *	.9	2.0
463 Vineyard	5	1,101	1,087	1,380 *	.1	.2
469 WELS	3	824	581	1,164	.1	.2
490 Zoroastrian	2	NR	NR	NR	-	-
496 Jewish Est	17	NR	NR	54,000	3.2	7.4
498 Indep.Charis.	5	11,100	11,600	13,200	.8	1.8
499 Indep.Non-Char	6	3,760	5,650	6,320	.4	.9
SANTA CRUZ	**150**	**11,247**	**12,557**	**88,117 ***	**34.5**	**100.0**
017 Amer Bapt Assn	3	165	NR	202 *	.1	.2
019 Amer Bapt USA	2	164	82	201 *	.1	.2
034 Ant Orth of NA	1	178	NR	356	.1	.4
053 Assemb of God	12	1,191	1,526	2,065	.8	2.3
056 Baha'i	8	725	NR	725	.3	.8
076 Buddhism	12	NR	NR	NR	-	-
081 Catholic	14	NR	NR	55,350	21.7	62.8
084 Calvary Chapel	3	NR	NR	NR	-	-
089 Chr & Miss Al	1	46	NR	71	-	.1
093 Chr Ch (Disc)	2	159	78	195 *	.1	.2
123 Ch God (Ander)	1	NR	45	45	-	.1
127 Ch God (Cleve)	3	150	92	184 *	.1	.2
151 L-D Saints	6	NR	NR	2,687	1.1	3.0
165 Ch of Nazarene	3	362	184	548	.2	.6
167 Chs of Christ	2	145	175	180	.1	.2
175 Congr Chr Chs	1	264	234	323 *	.1	.4
179 Consrv Bapt	5	NR	4,525	4,525	1.8	5.1
193 Episcopal	5	NR	522	1,575	.6	1.8
201 Evan Cov Ch	1	126	229	229 *	.1	.3
203 Evan Free Ch	2	269	325	325	.1	.4
207 E.L.C.A.	5	785	397	1,129	.4	1.3
221 Free Methodist	2	112	227	227	.1	.3
226 Friends-USA	1	32	NR	39 *	-	-
237 Menn Br US Conf	1	46	NR	56 *	-	.1
246 Greek Orthodox	1	NR	NR	345	.1	.4
252 Hindu	2	NR	NR	NR	-	-
263 Int Foursq Gos	5	496	967	967 *	.4	1.1
267 Muslim Est	1	NR	412	1,891	.7	2.1
283 Luth—MO Synod	3	428	247	572	.2	.6

NR–Not Reported *Total adherents estimated from known number of communicant, confirmed, full members. - Represents a percentage less than 0.1. Percentages may not total 100 due to rounding.

CALIFORNIA

Table 4: Religious Congregations by County and Group: 2000

Religious Group	Number of Churches, Synagogues, Mosques, or Temples	Number of Communicant, Confirmed, or Full Members	Number of Attendees	Total Adherents		
				Number of Adherents	% of Total Pop.	% of Total Adh.
290 Metro Comm Ch	1	25	17	31 *	-	-
335 Orth Pres Ch	1	21	18	24	-	-
339 Pent Ch of God	2	50	NR	240	.1	.3
349 Pent Holiness	2	90	100	110 *	-	.1
355 Presb Ch (USA)	7	1,074	637	1,327 *	.5	1.5
403 Salvation Army	3	286	219	696	.3	.8
413 S.D.A.	5	1,304	NR	1,551	.6	1.8
419 So Bapt Conv	4	607	315	743 *	.3	.8
425 Tao	2	NR	NR	NR	-	-
435 Unitarian-Univ	1	146	NR	179 *	.1	.2
443 Un C of Christ	3	592	257	725 *	.3	.8
449 Un Methodist	6	909	427	1,112 *	.4	1.3
463 Vineyard	1	300	300	367 *	.1	.4
496 Jewish Est	4	NR	NR	6,000	2.3	6.8
SHASTA	**127**	**13,753**	**9,968**	**39,059 ***	**23.9**	**100.0**
017 Amer Bapt Assn	2	145	NR	180 *	.1	.5
019 Amer Bapt USA	2	310	243	385 *	.2	1.0
053 Assemb of God	9	1,171	1,361	1,645	1.0	4.2
056 Baha'i	2	75	NR	75	-	.2
081 Catholic	8	NR	NR	11,989	7.3	30.7
084 Calvary Chapel	4	NR	NR	NR	-	-
089 Chr & Miss Al	4	760	NR	2,728	1.7	7.0
093 Chr Ch (Disc)	1	96	0	119 *	.1	.3
097 Chr Chs&Chs Cr	1	20	NR	25 *	-	.1
123 Ch God (Ander)	1	NR	48	48	-	.1
127 Ch God (Cleve)	2	116	292	302 *	.2	.8
145 Ch God Prophcy	1	37	NR	46 *	-	.1
151 L-D Saints	12	NR	NR	4,838	3.0	12.4
165 Ch of Nazarene	4	603	732	1,235	.8	3.2
167 Chs of Christ	9	657	703	843	.5	2.2
173 Comm of Christ	2	131	NR	131	.1	.3
179 Consrv Bapt	4	NR	400	400	.2	1.0
193 Episcopal	2	NR	257	597	.4	1.5
203 Evan Free Ch	2	70	185	185	.1	.5
207 E.L.C.A.	1	480	266	621	.4	1.6
221 Free Methodist	1	24	28	28	-	.1
223 Free Will Bapt	1	48	NR	60 *	-	.2
226 Friends-USA	1	32	NR	40 *	-	.1
246 Greek Orthodox	1	NR	NR	123	.1	.3
262 Int Cou Comm Ch	1	15	NR	19 *	-	-
263 Int Foursq Gos	6	352	550	550 *	.3	1.4
283 Luth—MO Synod	2	418	251	477	.3	1.2
306 NT IndBapt&Rltd	2	1,145	NR	1,420 *	.9	3.6
339 Pent Ch of God	5	201	NR	603	.4	1.5
355 Presb Ch (USA)	2	274	200	340 *	.2	.9
373 Ref Ch in U.S.	1	32	NR	40	-	.1
388 Reg Bapt Gen As	2	349	365	434 *	.3	1.1
401 Rus Orth Abroad	1	NR	NR	NR	-	-
403 Salvation Army	1	72	25	199	.1	.5
413 S.D.A.	5	1,322	NR	1,574	1.0	4.0
419 So Bapt Conv	9	1,430	589	1,775 *	1.1	4.5
435 Unitarian-Univ	1	10	NR	12 *	-	-
443 Un C of Christ	1	335	140	416 *	.3	1.1
449 Un Methodist	4	973	542	1,208 *	.7	3.1
463 Vineyard	1	190	140	236 *	.1	.6
469 WELS	2	460	301	613	.4	1.6
496 Jewish Est	1	NR	NR	150	.1	.4
499 Indep.Non-Char	3	1,400	2,350	2,350	1.4	6.0
SIERRA	**10**	**315**	**271**	**1,419 ***	**39.9**	**100.0**
019 Amer Bapt USA	1	157	105	188 *	5.3	13.2
053 Assemb of God	2	106	131	177	5.0	12.5
056 Baha'i	0	3	NR	3	.1	.2
081 Catholic	3	NR	NR	428	12.0	30.2
151 L-D Saints	2	NR	NR	564	15.9	39.7
449 Un Methodist	2	49	35	59 *	1.7	4.2
SISKIYOU	**75**	**4,815**	**2,439**	**14,343 ***	**32.4**	**100.0**
019 Amer Bapt USA	3	150	110	181 *	.4	1.3
053 Assemb of God	8	358	458	644	1.5	4.5
056 Baha'i	1	42	NR	42	.1	.3
076 Buddhism	1	NR	NR	NR	-	-
081 Catholic	12	NR	NR	6,186	14.0	43.1
084 Calvary Chapel	2	NR	NR	NR	-	-
089 Chr & Miss Al	1	66	NR	160	.4	1.1
097 Chr Chs&Chs Cr	3	131	NR	159 *	.4	1.1
105 Christian Ref	1	26	80	31 *	.1	.2
151 L-D Saints	5	NR	NR	1,201	2.7	8.4
165 Ch of Nazarene	3	153	168	303	.7	2.1
167 Chs of Christ	4	92	95	141	.3	1.0
193 Episcopal	2	NR	83	210	.5	1.5
203 Evan Free Ch	1	120	260	260	.6	1.8
207 E.L.C.A.	2	170	93	219	.5	1.5
245 Greek Orth Vslp	4	635	NR	1,040	2.3	7.3
252 Hindu	1	NR	NR	NR	-	-
263 Int Foursq Gos	1	28	78	78 *	.2	.5
283 Luth—MO Synod	1	83	63	92	.2	.6
339 Pent Ch of God	1	33	NR	103	.2	.7
355 Presb Ch (USA)	3	213	163	258 *	.6	1.8
413 S.D.A.	3	357	NR	425	1.0	3.0
419 So Bapt Conv	6	1,475	394	1,784 *	4.0	12.4
449 Un Methodist	6	683	394	826 *	1.9	5.8
SOLANO	**213**	**30,010**	**31,501**	**147,716 ***	**37.4**	**100.0**
017 Amer Bapt Assn	1	50	NR	64 *	-	-
019 Amer Bapt USA	13	4,039	13,072	13,072 *	3.3	8.8
034 Ant Orth of NA	1	155	NR	310	.1	.2
053 Assemb of God	21	2,681	3,231	4,412	1.1	3.0
056 Baha'i	5	213	NR	213	.1	.1
057 Bapt Gen Conf	4	545	493	699 *	.2	.5
059 Bapt Miss Assn	1	50	75	75 *	-	.1
076 Buddhism	1	NR	NR	NR	-	-
081 Catholic	11	NR	NR	83,685	21.2	56.7
084 Calvary Chapel	2	NR	NR	NR	-	-
089 Chr & Miss Al	2	80	NR	168	-	.1
093 Chr Ch (Disc)	2	303	126	389 *	.1	.3
097 Chr Chs&Chs Cr	3	669	NR	859 *	.2	.6
105 Christian Ref	1	195	140	250 *	.1	.2
123 Ch God (Ander)	1	NR	35	35	-	-
127 Ch God (Cleve)	4	294	268	443 *	.1	.3
145 Ch God Prophcy	4	157	NR	201 *	.1	.1
151 L-D Saints	21	NR	NR	8,486	2.2	5.7
165 Ch of Nazarene	7	866	1,033	2,382	.6	1.6
167 Chs of Christ	8	912	995	1,152	.3	.8
171 Ch God-Gen Con	1	5	7	7 *	-	-
173 Comm of Christ	1	58	NR	58	-	-
179 Consrv Bapt	3	NR	420	420	.1	.3
193 Episcopal	4	NR	595	2,008	.5	1.4
203 Evan Free Ch	1	471	1,300	1,300	.3	.9
207 E.L.C.A.	4	954	455	1,230	.3	.8
223 Free Will Bapt	2	96	NR	124 *	-	.1
246 Greek Orthodox	1	NR	NR	402	.1	.3
263 Int Foursq Gos	4	186	443	443 *	.1	.3
267 Muslim Est	2	NR	135	600	.2	.4
283 Luth—MO Synod	4	1,406	729	2,063	.5	1.4
306 NT IndBapt&Rltd	8	1,020	NR	1,309 *	.3	.9
313 N Am Bapt Conf	1	54	75	69 *	-	-
339 Pent Ch of God	3	152	NR	650	.2	.4
349 Pent Holiness	1	22	60	28 *	-	-
355 Presb Ch (USA)	7	1,992	1,227	2,556 *	.6	1.7
360 Prim Bapt Chrch	2	NR	NR	NR	-	-
388 Reg Bapt Gen As	3	367	485	491 *	.1	.3
403 Salvation Army	3	202	160	349	.1	.2
413 S.D.A.	5	792	NR	943	.2	.6
416 Sikh	1	NR	NR	NR	-	-
419 So Bapt Conv	20	7,973	3,746	10,231 *	2.6	6.9
443 Un C of Christ	4	394	222	506 *	.1	.3
449 Un Methodist	6	1,558	748	1,999 *	.5	1.4
463 Vineyard	1	124	181	181 *	-	.1
469 WELS	2	175	113	222	.1	.2
496 Jewish Est	3	NR	NR	1,700	.4	1.2
499 Indep.Non-Char	3	800	932	932	.2	.6
SONOMA	**238**	**24,971**	**18,679**	**147,452 ***	**32.2**	**100.0**
017 Amer Bapt Assn	1	33	NR	41 *	-	-

NR–Not Reported *Total adherents estimated from known number of communicant, confirmed, full members. - Represents a percentage less than 0.1. Percentages may not total 100 due to rounding.

Table 4: Religious Congregations by County and Group: 2000

Religious Group	Number of Churches, Synagogues, Mosques, or Temples	Number of Communicant, Confirmed, or Full Members	Number of Attendees	Total Adherents		
				Number of Adherents	% of Total Pop.	% of Total Adh.
019 Amer Bapt USA	1	117	145	145 *	-	.1
034 Ant Orth of NA	1	31	NR	62	-	-
053 Assemb of God	17	1,486	1,804	2,439	.5	1.7
056 Baha'i	7	324	NR	324	.1	.2
057 Bapt Gen Conf	1	260	300	320 *	.1	.2
076 Buddhism	10	NR	NR	NR	-	-
081 Catholic	21	NR	NR	90,020	19.6	61.1
084 Calvary Chapel	3	NR	NR	NR	-	-
089 Chr & Miss Al	6	454	NR	1,354	.3	.9
093 Chr Ch (Disc)	1	45	0	55 *	-	-
097 Chr Chs&Chs Cr	3	755	NR	928 *	.2	.6
105 Christian Ref	1	49	65	60 *	-	-
123 Ch God (Ander)	3	NR	27	27	-	-
127 Ch God (Cleve)	1	130	0	160 *	-	.1
145 Ch God Prophcy	3	120	NR	147 *	-	.1
151 L-D Saints	20	NR	NR	7,518	1.6	5.1
165 Ch of Nazarene	3	496	355	693	.2	.5
167 Chs of Christ	12	667	653	837	.2	.6
173 Comm of Christ	1	56	NR	56	-	-
175 Congr Chr Chs	1	45	65	55 *	-	-
179 Consrv Bapt	3	NR	770	770	.2	.5
193 Episcopal	9	NR	1,068	2,630	.6	1.8
201 Evan Cov Ch	2	383	848	895 *	.2	.6
203 Evan Free Ch	2	139	280	280	.1	.2
207 E.L.C.A.	5	1,751	970	2,753	.6	1.9
221 Free Methodist	1	29	37	37	-	-
223 Free Will Bapt	1	48	NR	59 *	-	-
226 Friends-USA	2	64	NR	79 *	-	.1
263 Int Foursq Gos	6	536	849	849 *	.2	.6
267 Muslim Est	1	NR	412	1,891	.4	1.3
283 Luth—MO Synod	8	2,396	1,489	3,469	.8	2.4
290 Metro Comm Ch	2	91	76	112 *	-	.1
306 NT IndBapt&Rltd	4	535	NR	658 *	.1	.4
331 OCA: Ter Diocs	1	81	NR	174	-	.1
339 Pent Ch of God	4	132	NR	287	.1	.2
355 Presb Ch (USA)	9	2,493	1,812	3,100 *	.7	2.1
356 Presb Ch Amer	1	112	241	241	.1	.2
371 Ref Ch in Am	1	29	32	71	-	-
388 Reg Bapt Gen As	4	641	1,153	1,153 *	.3	.8
401 Rus Orth Abroad	2	NR	NR	NR	-	-
403 Salvation Army	2	280	147	472	.1	.3
413 S.D.A.	7	1,664	NR	1,981	.4	1.3
419 So Bapt Conv	16	3,815	1,853	4,693 *	1.0	3.2
435 Unitarian-Univ	1	262	NR	322 *	.1	.2
443 Un C of Christ	8	1,273	641	1,566 *	.3	1.1
449 Un Methodist	9	2,392	1,427	2,943 *	.6	2.0
463 Vineyard	1	130	120	160 *	-	.1
469 WELS	1	52	40	66	-	-
496 Jewish Est	7	NR	NR	9,000	2.0	6.1
499 Indep.Non-Char	1	575	1,000	1,500	.3	1.0
STANISLAUS	**278**	**39,293**	**26,582**	**195,446 ***	**43.7**	**100.0**
017 Amer Bapt Assn	8	584	NR	771 *	.2	.4
019 Amer Bapt USA	7	879	659	1,160 *	.3	.6
050 Armen Ap Etchm	1	0	NR	370	.1	.2
053 Assemb of God	33	5,625	6,958	11,538	2.6	5.9
056 Baha'i	3	276	NR	276	.1	.1
057 Bapt Gen Conf	1	228	221	301 *	.1	.2
059 Bapt Miss Assn	1	20	15	26 *	-	-
081 Catholic	14	NR	NR	105,628	23.6	54.0
084 Calvary Chapel	1	NR	NR	NR	-	-
089 Chr & Miss Al	2	78	NR	149	-	.1
093 Chr Ch (Disc)	4	518	276	684 *	.2	.3
097 Chr Chs&Chs Cr	3	1,000	NR	1,320 *	.3	.7
105 Christian Ref	2	902	580	1,190 *	.3	.6
123 Ch God (Ander)	1	NR	315	315	.1	.2
127 Ch God (Cleve)	5	432	219	570 *	.1	.3
145 Ch God Prophcy	2	74	NR	98 *	-	.1
151 L-D Saints	21	NR	NR	10,444	2.3	5.3
157 Ch of Brethren	3	455	266	601 *	.1	.3
165 Ch of Nazarene	8	1,157	1,174	1,859	.4	1.0
167 Chs of Christ	19	1,784	1,821	2,359	.5	1.2
173 Comm of Christ	1	106	NR	106	-	.1
179 Consrv Bapt	4	NR	339	339	.1	.2
193 Episcopal	6	NR	753	1,810	.4	.9
201 Evan Cov Ch	6	1,160	1,125	1,589 *	.4	.8
203 Evan Free Ch	3	792	1,167	1,167	.3	.6
207 E.L.C.A.	3	856	433	1,091	.2	.6
221 Free Methodist	3	357	355	434	.1	.2
223 Free Will Bapt	4	193	NR	254 *	.1	.1
226 Friends-USA	1	152	NR	201 *	-	.1
246 Greek Orthodox	1	NR	NR	840	.2	.4
249 Assyr Apost Ch	3	NR	NR	3,292	.7	1.7
263 Int Foursq Gos	6	1,218	1,163	1,607 *	.4	.8
267 Muslim Est	1	NR	100	300	.1	.2
273 LandmrkBapt,I&U	1	55	NR	73 *	-	-
283 Luth—MO Synod	5	1,474	727	2,025	.5	1.0
291 Missionary Ch	1	251	172	251	.1	.1
313 N Am Bapt Conf	2	108	154	143 *	-	.1
335 Orth Pres Ch	2	99	172	194	-	.1
339 Pent Ch of God	13	400	NR	884	.2	.5
349 Pent Holiness	2	172	194	227 *	.1	.1
355 Presb Ch (USA)	9	1,790	1,158	2,363 *	.5	1.2
360 Prim Bapt Chrch	3	NR	NR	NR	-	-
371 Ref Ch in Am	2	183	294	439	.1	.2
373 Ref Ch in U.S.	1	63	NR	106	-	.1
388 Reg Bapt Gen As	2	397	345	524 *	.1	.3
403 Salvation Army	3	263	178	14,717	3.3	7.5
413 S.D.A.	8	2,518	NR	2,996	.7	1.5
416 Sikh	2	NR	NR	NR	-	-
419 So Bapt Conv	25	7,930	2,293	10,465 *	2.3	5.4
435 Unitarian-Univ	1	113	NR	149 *	-	.1
443 Un C of Christ	2	319	200	421 *	.1	.2
449 Un Methodist	9	3,110	1,377	4,104 *	.9	2.1
463 Vineyard	1	130	120	172 *	-	.1
469 WELS	1	222	159	304	.1	.2
496 Jewish Est	1	NR	NR	500	.1	.3
499 Indep.Non-Char	1	850	1,100	1,700	.4	.9
SUTTER	**70**	**8,957**	**7,058**	**24,214 ***	**30.7**	**100.0**
053 Assemb of God	5	997	1,430	1,435	1.8	5.9
056 Baha'i	0	5	NR	5	-	-
076 Buddhism	1	NR	NR	NR	-	-
081 Catholic	2	NR	NR	9,410	11.9	38.9
084 Calvary Chapel	1	NR	NR	NR	-	-
089 Chr & Miss Al	1	999	NR	999	1.3	4.1
093 Chr Ch (Disc)	1	173	57	223 *	.3	.9
097 Chr Chs&Chs Cr	2	145	NR	187 *	.2	.8
123 Ch God (Ander)	3	NR	537	537	.7	2.2
151 L-D Saints	5	NR	NR	2,033	2.6	8.4
157 Ch of Brethren	1	95	63	122 *	.2	.5
165 Ch of Nazarene	2	424	422	549	.7	2.3
167 Chs of Christ	4	370	378	458	.6	1.9
173 Comm of Christ	1	125	NR	125	.2	.5
179 Consrv Bapt	1	NR	30	30	-	.1
193 Episcopal	1	NR	21	20	-	.1
203 Evan Free Ch	2	290	494	494	.6	2.0
223 Free Will Bapt	1	48	NR	62 *	.1	.3
252 Hindu	1	NR	NR	NR	-	-
263 Int Foursq Gos	2	106	326	326 *	.4	1.3
267 Muslim Est	2	NR	202	576	.7	2.4
273 LandmrkBapt,I&U	1	112	NR	144 *	.2	.6
283 Luth—MO Synod	1	445	215	575	.7	2.4
306 NT IndBapt&Rltd	1	150	NR	193 *	.2	.8
339 Pent Ch of God	2	52	NR	217	.3	.9
349 Pent Holiness	1	128	181	165 *	.2	.7
355 Presb Ch (USA)	1	606	385	781 *	1.0	3.2
373 Ref Ch in U.S.	1	51	NR	68	.1	.3
388 Reg Bapt Gen As	1	275	285	354 *	.4	1.5
413 S.D.A.	1	375	NR	446	.6	1.8
416 Sikh	8	NR	NR	NR	-	-
419 So Bapt Conv	7	1,017	628	1,310 *	1.7	5.4
449 Un Methodist	5	869	454	1,120 *	1.4	4.6
498 Indep.Charis.	1	1,100	950	1,250	1.6	5.2
TEHAMA	**57**	**4,352**	**3,183**	**15,886 ***	**28.3**	**100.0**
017 Amer Bapt Assn	1	28	NR	35 *	.1	.2

NR–Not Reported *Total adherents estimated from known number of communicant, confirmed, full members. - Represents a percentage less than 0.1. Percentages may not total 100 due to rounding.

Table 4: Religious Congregations by County and Group: 2000

Religious Group	Number of Churches, Synagogues, Mosques, or Temples	Number of Communicant, Confirmed, or Full Members	Number of Attendees	Total Adherents: Number of Adherents	Total Adherents: % of Total Pop.	Total Adherents: % of Total Adh.
019 Amer Bapt USA	2	254	200	320 *	.6	2.0
053 Assemb of God	4	460	635	815	1.5	5.1
056 Baha'i	2	61	NR	61	.1	.4
081 Catholic	3	NR	NR	7,778	13.9	49.0
084 Calvary Chapel	1	NR	NR	NR	-	-
093 Chr Ch (Disc)	1	40	24	50 *	.1	.3
123 Ch God (Ander)	2	NR	205	205	.4	1.3
127 Ch God (Cleve)	2	94	191	205 *	.4	1.3
151 L-D Saints	3	NR	NR	1,476	2.6	9.3
165 Ch of Nazarene	2	161	129	161	.3	1.0
167 Chs of Christ	4	265	250	295	.5	1.9
179 Consrv Bapt	1	NR	40	40	.1	.3
193 Episcopal	2	NR	81	213	.4	1.3
203 Evan Free Ch	1	69	125	125	.2	.8
245 Greek Orth Vslp	1	245	NR	345	.6	2.2
263 Int Foursq Gos	2	75	142	142 *	.3	.9
283 Luth—MO Synod	2	220	122	280	.5	1.8
306 NT IndBapt&Rltd	1	145	NR	183 *	.3	1.2
339 Pent Ch of God	4	79	NR	350	.6	2.2
349 Pent Holiness	1	20	42	25 *	-	.2
355 Presb Ch (USA)	2	289	197	365 *	.7	2.3
388 Reg Bapt Gen As	1	145	225	225 *	.4	1.4
403 Salvation Army	1	53	37	133	.2	.8
413 S.D.A.	2	289	NR	344	.6	2.2
419 So Bapt Conv	3	589	152	743 *	1.3	4.7
449 Un Methodist	5	521	206	657 *	1.2	4.1
463 Vineyard	1	250	180	315 *	.6	2.0
TRINITY	**19**	**823**	**709**	**2,730 ***	**21.0**	**100.0**
053 Assemb of God	3	216	285	332	2.5	12.2
056 Baha'i	0	6	NR	6	-	.2
076 Buddhism	1	NR	NR	NR	-	-
081 Catholic	3	NR	NR	1,145	8.8	41.9
151 L-D Saints	2	NR	NR	274	2.1	10.0
165 Ch of Nazarene	1	108	118	332	2.5	12.2
167 Chs of Christ	2	60	60	76	.6	2.8
193 Episcopal	1	NR	13	16	.1	.6
207 E.L.C.A.	1	70	46	85	.7	3.1
388 Reg Bapt Gen As	1	105	156	156 *	1.2	5.7
413 S.D.A.	3	187	NR	223	1.7	8.2
443 Un C of Christ	1	71	31	85 *	.7	3.1
TULARE	**326**	**41,604**	**28,000**	**190,624 ***	**51.8**	**100.0**
017 Amer Bapt Assn	5	411	NR	557 *	.2	.3
019 Amer Bapt USA	9	4,150	2,035	5,626 *	1.5	3.0
039 Ap Chr Ch(Naz)	1	15	16	20 *	-	-
050 Armen Ap Etchm	1	0	NR	770	.2	.4
053 Assemb of God	36	4,976	6,136	10,497	2.9	5.5
056 Baha'i	0	269	NR	269	.1	.1
057 Bapt Gen Conf	4	604	588	823 *	.2	.4
075 Brethren in Cr	1	27	29	29	-	-
076 Buddhism	3	NR	NR	NR	-	-
081 Catholic	25	NR	NR	119,080	32.4	62.5
084 Calvary Chapel	2	NR	NR	NR	-	-
089 Chr & Miss Al	2	100	NR	172	-	.1
093 Chr Ch (Disc)	2	522	247	708 *	.2	.4
097 Chr Chs&Chs Cr	5	1,841	NR	2,496 *	.7	1.3
105 Christian Ref	2	1,110	845	1,505 *	.4	.8
123 Ch God (Ander)	5	NR	728	728	.2	.4
127 Ch God (Cleve)	13	829	632	1,123 *	.3	.6
145 Ch God Prophcy	6	250	NR	339 *	.1	.2
151 L-D Saints	14	NR	NR	5,001	1.4	2.6
157 Ch of Brethren	1	70	74	95 *	-	-
165 Ch of Nazarene	15	2,770	2,317	4,547	1.2	2.4
167 Chs of Christ	24	1,739	1,813	2,309	.6	1.2
171 Ch God-Gen Con	2	87	68	119 *	-	.1
173 Comm of Christ	1	119	NR	119	-	.1
186 Coptic Orth Ch	1	NR	NR	NR	-	-
193 Episcopal	5	NR	452	1,320	.4	.7
201 Evan Cov Ch	2	121	165	169 *	-	.1
203 Evan Free Ch	4	406	960	960	.3	.5
207 E.L.C.A.	3	996	653	1,305	.4	.7
223 Free Will Bapt	7	337	NR	457 *	.1	.2

Religious Group	Number of Churches, Synagogues, Mosques, or Temples	Number of Communicant, Confirmed, or Full Members	Number of Attendees	Total Adherents: Number of Adherents	Total Adherents: % of Total Pop.	Total Adherents: % of Total Adh.
226 Friends-USA	1	32	NR	43 *	-	-
237 Menn Br US Conf	5	1,150	NR	1,559 *	.4	.8
263 Int Foursq Gos	9	553	1,316	1,316 *	.4	.7
273 LandmrkBapt,I&U	1	31	NR	42 *	-	-
283 Luth—MO Synod	5	1,228	642	1,582	.4	.8
306 NT IndBapt&Rltd	4	580	NR	786 *	.2	.4
339 Pent Ch of God	19	590	NR	1,451	.4	.8
349 Pent Holiness	4	120	170	163 *	-	.1
355 Presb Ch (USA)	10	1,773	1,054	2,404 *	.7	1.3
360 Prim Bapt Chrch	1	NR	NR	NR	-	-
371 Ref Ch in Am	2	405	496	814	.2	.4
388 Reg Bapt Gen As	4	455	514	560 *	.2	.3
403 Salvation Army	3	443	437	586	.2	.3
413 S.D.A.	13	2,525	NR	3,004	.8	1.6
419 So Bapt Conv	25	6,363	2,210	8,627 *	2.3	4.5
435 Unitarian-Univ	2	49	NR	66 *	-	-
443 Un C of Christ	2	389	156	527 *	.1	.3
449 Un Methodist	10	2,519	1,447	3,415 *	.9	1.8
463 Vineyard	1	100	100	136 *	-	.1
496 Jewish Est	1	NR	NR	350	.1	.2
498 Indep.Charis.	2	0	850	1,200	.3	.6
499 Indep.Non-Char	1	550	850	850	.2	.4
TUOLUMNE	**53**	**5,563**	**4,197**	**14,732 ***	**27.0**	**100.0**
017 Amer Bapt Assn	1	100	NR	118 *	.2	.8
019 Amer Bapt USA	1	133	113	157 *	.3	1.1
053 Assemb of God	4	532	763	1,441	2.6	9.8
056 Baha'i	1	40	NR	40	.1	.3
076 Buddhism	1	NR	NR	NR	-	-
081 Catholic	7	NR	NR	5,416	9.9	36.8
084 Calvary Chapel	1	NR	NR	NR	-	-
123 Ch God (Ander)	1	NR	120	120	.2	.8
151 L-D Saints	3	NR	NR	1,096	2.0	7.4
165 Ch of Nazarene	1	70	102	105	.2	.7
167 Chs of Christ	4	184	190	234	.4	1.6
193 Episcopal	2	NR	145	282	.5	1.9
203 Evan Free Ch	2	223	350	350	.6	2.4
207 E.L.C.A.	1	211	121	268	.5	1.8
263 Int Foursq Gos	2	46	128	128 *	.2	.9
283 Luth—MO Synod	1	282	165	313	.6	2.1
306 NT IndBapt&Rltd	1	125	NR	148 *	.3	1.0
335 Orth Pres Ch	1	50	54	59	.1	.4
339 Pent Ch of God	2	43	NR	99	.2	.7
355 Presb Ch (USA)	1	210	154	248 *	.5	1.7
413 S.D.A.	2	721	NR	858	1.6	5.8
419 So Bapt Conv	4	696	300	820 *	1.5	5.6
435 Unitarian-Univ	1	47	NR	55 *	.1	.4
449 Un Methodist	4	482	189	568 *	1.0	3.9
463 Vineyard	1	8	3	9 *	-	.1
496 Jewish Est	1	NR	NR	50	.1	.3
498 Indep.Charis.	1	160	550	550	1.0	3.7
499 Indep.Non-Char	1	1,200	750	1,200	2.2	8.1
VENTURA	**364**	**54,025**	**40,870**	**335,672 ***	**44.6**	**100.0**
017 Amer Bapt Assn	7	369	NR	473 *	.1	.1
019 Amer Bapt USA	6	1,203	785	1,548 *	.2	.5
053 Assemb of God	19	1,923	2,346	3,409	.5	1.0
056 Baha'i	10	525	NR	525	.1	.2
057 Bapt Gen Conf	4	943	1,185	1,306 *	.2	.4
076 Buddhism	3	NR	NR	NR	-	-
081 Catholic	16	NR	NR	220,762	29.3	65.8
084 Calvary Chapel	6	NR	NR	NR	-	-
089 Chr & Miss Al	2	15	NR	24	-	-
093 Chr Ch (Disc)	3	252	135	324 *	-	.1
097 Chr Chs&Chs Cr	9	2,590	NR	3,334 *	.4	1.0
105 Christian Ref	2	120	140	154 *	-	-
121 Ch God (Abr)	1	13	34	34 *	-	-
123 Ch God (Ander)	2	NR	32	32	-	-
127 Ch God (Cleve)	6	555	520	750 *	.1	.2
145 Ch God Prophcy	3	120	NR	154 *	-	-
151 L-D Saints	42	NR	NR	15,907	2.1	4.7
165 Ch of Nazarene	10	1,031	773	1,172	.2	.3
167 Chs of Christ	20	1,701	1,676	2,067	.3	.6

NR–Not Reported *Total adherents estimated from known number of communicant, confirmed, full members. - Represents a percentage less than 0.1. Percentages may not total 100 due to rounding.

Table 4: Religious Congregations by County and Group: 2000

Religious Group	Number of Churches, Synagogues, Mosques, or Temples	Number of Communicant, Confirmed, or Full Members	Number of Attendees	Total Adherents: Number of Adherents	Total Adherents: % of Total Pop.	Total Adherents: % of Total Adh.
173 Comm of Christ	2	119	NR	119	-	-
179 Consrv Bapt	3	NR	165	165	-	-
186 Coptic Orth Ch	1	NR	NR	NR	-	-
193 Episcopal	9	NR	1,243	4,859	.6	1.4
201 Evan Cov Ch	1	433	546	557 *	.1	.2
203 Evan Free Ch	5	745	1,180	1,330	.2	.4
207 E.L.C.A.	12	5,912	2,667	8,503	1.1	2.5
220 Free Lutheran	2	229	196	292	-	.1
223 Free Will Bapt	3	145	NR	186 *	-	.1
226 Friends-USA	3	216	NR	278 *	-	.1
246 Greek Orthodox	1	NR	NR	375	-	.1
252 Hindu	1	NR	NR	NR	-	-
262 Int Cou Comm Ch	1	190	NR	245 *	-	.1
263 Int Foursq Gos	28	3,456	5,095	5,095 *	.7	1.5
267 Muslim Est	1	NR	412	1,891	.3	.6
283 Luth—MO Synod	11	3,232	1,469	4,827	.6	1.4
291 Missionary Ch	3	4,279	4,910	4,910	.7	1.5
306 NT IndBapt&Rltd	1	145	NR	186 *	-	.1
331 OCA: Ter Diocs	1	31	NR	188	-	.1
335 Orth Pres Ch	1	35	36	44	-	-
339 Pent Ch of God	4	120	NR	246	-	.1
349 Pent Holiness	2	130	145	167 *	-	-
355 Presb Ch (USA)	13	5,189	3,583	6,679 *	.9	2.0
360 Prim Bapt Chrch	1	NR	NR	NR	-	-
370 Ref Baptist Chs	2	NR	NR	NR	-	-
388 Reg Bapt Gen As	3	120	153	171 *	-	.1
401 Rus Orth Abroad	1	NR	NR	NR	-	-
403 Salvation Army	3	154	216	261	-	.1
413 S.D.A.	10	3,003	NR	3,575	.5	1.1
419 So Bapt Conv	19	4,705	1,653	6,056 *	.8	1.8
435 Unitarian-Univ	3	368	NR	474 *	.1	.1
443 Un C of Christ	4	519	245	668 *	.1	.2
449 Un Methodist	17	5,451	2,788	7,016 *	.9	2.1
463 Vineyard	6	994	831	1,279 *	.2	.4
467 Wesleyan	2	75	114	148	-	-
469 WELS	1	120	82	157	-	-
496 Jewish Est	6	NR	NR	15,000	2.0	4.5
498 Indep.Charis.	3	700	2,650	4,250	.6	1.3
499 Indep.Non-Char	3	1,850	2,865	3,500	.5	1.0
YOLO	**98**	**8,457**	**7,693**	**53,898 ***	**32.0**	**100.0**
019 Amer Bapt USA	1	40	81	81 *	-	.2
034 Ant Orth of NA	1	77	NR	154	.1	.3
053 Assemb of God	6	686	935	1,605	1.0	3.0
056 Baha'i	3	152	NR	152	.1	.3
057 Bapt Gen Conf	1	26	40	40 *	-	.1
076 Buddhism	2	NR	NR	NR	-	-
081 Catholic	10	NR	NR	33,691	20.0	62.5
084 Calvary Chapel	1	NR	NR	NR	-	-
089 Chr & Miss Al	1	0	NR	63	-	.1
093 Chr Ch (Disc)	1	400	100	498 *	.3	.9
123 Ch God (Ander)	2	NR	130	130	.1	.2
127 Ch God (Cleve)	3	175	162	218 *	.1	.4
145 Ch God Prophcy	1	37	NR	46 *	-	.1
151 L-D Saints	9	NR	NR	2,943	1.7	5.5
165 Ch of Nazarene	2	113	126	158	.1	.3
167 Chs of Christ	6	232	247	334	.2	.6
179 Consrv Bapt	2	NR	1,250	1,250	.7	2.3
193 Episcopal	2	NR	334	946	.6	1.8
201 Evan Cov Ch	1	278	710	710 *	.4	1.3
207 E.L.C.A.	4	881	380	1,107	.7	2.1
226 Friends-USA	1	32	NR	40 *	-	.1
263 Int Foursq Gos	4	85	239	239 *	.1	.4
267 Muslim Est	2	NR	155	500	.3	.9
283 Luth—MO Synod	2	444	184	567	.3	1.1
306 NT IndBapt&Rltd	1	145	NR	181 *	.1	.3
331 OCA: Ter Diocs	1	37	NR	70	-	.1
339 Pent Ch of God	3	137	NR	355	.2	.7
355 Presb Ch (USA)	5	1,385	842	1,723 *	1.0	3.2
388 Reg Bapt Gen As	2	433	616	553 *	.3	1.0
413 S.D.A.	2	345	NR	411	.2	.8
416 Sikh	1	NR	NR	NR	-	-
419 So Bapt Conv	7	904	511	1,125 *	.7	2.1
435 Unitarian-Univ	1	287	NR	357 *	.2	.7

Religious Group	Number of Churches, Synagogues, Mosques, or Temples	Number of Communicant, Confirmed, or Full Members	Number of Attendees	Total Adherents: Number of Adherents	Total Adherents: % of Total Pop.	Total Adherents: % of Total Adh.
443 Un C of Christ	2	380	216	473 *	.3	.9
449 Un Methodist	4	746	435	928 *	.6	1.7
496 Jewish Est	1	NR	NR	2,250	1.3	4.2
YUBA	**55**	**4,249**	**2,587**	**15,570 ***	**25.9**	**100.0**
017 Amer Bapt Assn	1	141	NR	186 *	.3	1.2
019 Amer Bapt USA	1	60	50	79 *	.1	.5
053 Assemb of God	6	592	832	1,207	2.0	7.8
056 Baha'i	0	54	NR	54	.1	.3
076 Buddhism	1	NR	NR	NR	-	-
081 Catholic	4	NR	NR	6,813	11.3	43.8
084 Calvary Chapel	1	NR	NR	NR	-	-
093 Chr Ch (Disc)	1	54	0	71 *	.1	.5
097 Chr Chs&Chs Cr	1	100	NR	132 *	.2	.8
127 Ch God (Cleve)	1	56	30	74 *	.1	.5
145 Ch God Prophcy	1	37	NR	49 *	.1	.3
151 L-D Saints	3	NR	NR	1,695	2.8	10.9
165 Ch of Nazarene	2	169	192	490	.8	3.1
167 Chs of Christ	7	395	415	445	.7	2.9
171 Ch God-Gen Con	1	90	70	119 *	.2	.8
193 Episcopal	2	NR	162	552	.9	3.5
207 E.L.C.A.	1	141	62	207	.3	1.3
223 Free Will Bapt	1	48	NR	64 *	.1	.4
262 Int Cou Comm Ch	1	300	NR	396 *	.7	2.5
283 Luth—MO Synod	1	42	29	3	-	-
339 Pent Ch of God	2	91	NR	293	.5	1.9
349 Pent Holiness	1	18	29	24 *	-	.2
355 Presb Ch (USA)	1	224	136	295 *	.5	1.9
403 Salvation Army	1	59	52	169	.3	1.1
413 S.D.A.	3	263	NR	313	.5	2.0
419 So Bapt Conv	7	1,015	376	1,339 *	2.2	8.6
449 Un Methodist	1	300	152	396 *	.7	2.5
496 Jewish Est	2	NR	NR	105	.2	.7
COLORADO						
The State.....	3,228	512,435	343,323	1,697,259 *	39.5	100.0
ADAMS	**173**	**28,704**	**16,346**	**110,429 ***	**30.3**	**100.0**
017 Amer Bapt Assn	1	40	NR	52 *	-	-
019 Amer Bapt USA	3	1,458	935	1,887 *	.5	1.7
053 Assemb of God	11	1,352	1,702	1,812	.5	1.6
056 Baha'i	2	227	NR	227	.1	.2
057 Bapt Gen Conf	3	744	536	963 *	.3	.9
076 Buddhism	2	NR	NR	NR	-	-
081 Catholic	9	NR	NR	60,429	16.6	54.7
084 Calvary Chapel	1	NR	NR	NR	-	-
089 Chr & Miss Al	2	660	NR	691	.2	.6
093 Chr Ch (Disc)	3	292	178	378 *	.1	.3
097 Chr Chs&Chs Cr	6	2,218	NR	2,870 *	.8	2.6
123 Ch God (Ander)	1	NR	29	29	-	-
127 Ch God (Cleve)	1	291	187	377 *	.1	.3
145 Ch God Prophcy	2	43	NR	56 *	-	.1
151 L-D Saints	15	NR	NR	6,808	1.9	6.2
165 Ch of Nazarene	5	924	811	1,055	.3	1.0
167 Chs of Christ	4	261	280	345	.1	.3
173 Comm of Christ	3	308	NR	308	.1	.3
179 Consrv Bapt	2	NR	135	135	-	.1
181 Consrv Congr	1	153	103	198 *	.1	.2
193 Episcopal	3	NR	243	545	.1	.5
203 Evan Free Ch	2	160	320	320	.1	.3
207 E.L.C.A.	9	2,913	1,305	3,992	1.1	3.6
221 Free Methodist	1	48	63	63	-	.1
223 Free Will Bapt	2	60	NR	77 *	-	.1
226 Friends-USA	1	44	NR	57 *	-	.1
263 Int Foursq Gos	5	591	1,049	1,049 *	.3	.9
283 Luth—MO Synod	7	2,966	1,488	4,063	1.1	3.7
306 NT IndBapt&Rltd	10	1,054	NR	1,363 *	.4	1.2
313 N Am Bapt Conf	1	0	0	0 *	-	-
335 Orth Pres Ch	2	105	137	153	-	.1
349 Pent Holiness	1	121	88	157 *	-	.1
355 Presb Ch (USA)	9	1,787	1,146	2,312 *	.6	2.1

NR–Not Reported   *Total adherents estimated from known number of communicant, confirmed, full members.   - Represents a percentage less than 0.1.   Percentages may not total 100 due to rounding.

Table 4: Religious Congregations by County and Group: 2000

Religious Group	Number of Churches, Synagogues, Mosques, or Temples	Number of Communicant, Confirmed, or Full Members	Number of Attendees	Total Adherents		
				Number of Adherents	% of Total Pop.	% of Total Adh.
356 Presb Ch Amer	1	12	55	55	-	-
371 Ref Ch in Am	1	80	86	186	.1	.2
388 Reg Bapt Gen As	5	621	689	804 *	.2	.7
403 Salvation Army	2	198	118	843	.2	.8
413 S.D.A.	3	842	NR	1,002	.3	.9
419 So Bapt Conv	13	2,847	1,255	3,684 *	1.0	3.3
443 Un C of Christ	4	389	186	503 *	.1	.5
449 Un Methodist	8	2,437	1,212	3,153 *	.9	2.9
467 Wesleyan	1	34	56	115	-	.1
469 WELS	1	224	204	313	.1	.3
496 Jewish Est	2	NR	NR	4,400	1.2	4.0
498 Indep.Charis.	2	2,200	1,750	2,600	.7	2.4
ALAMOSA	**21**	**1,856**	**1,279**	**9,662 ***	**64.6**	**100.0**
053 Assemb of God	2	235	330	334	2.2	3.5
056 Baha'i	0	24	NR	24	.2	.2
057 Bapt Gen Conf	1	53	50	67 *	.4	.7
081 Catholic	1	NR	NR	5,716	38.2	59.2
093 Chr Ch (Disc)	1	143	45	181 *	1.2	1.9
097 Chr Chs&Chs Cr	1	100	NR	126 *	.8	1.3
105 Christian Ref	1	168	120	212 *	1.4	2.2
127 Ch God (Cleve)	1	50	100	100 *	.7	1.0
151 L-D Saints	3	NR	NR	1,155	7.7	12.0
165 Ch of Nazarene	1	54	68	93	.6	1.0
167 Chs of Christ	1	75	74	109	.7	1.1
179 Consrv Bapt	1	NR	100	100	.7	1.0
193 Episcopal	1	NR	65	260	1.7	2.7
283 Luth—MO Synod	1	161	65	193	1.3	2.0
355 Presb Ch (USA)	1	153	61	193 *	1.3	2.0
413 S.D.A.	1	123	NR	146	1.0	1.5
419 So Bapt Conv	1	218	87	275 *	1.8	2.8
449 Un Methodist	2	299	114	378 *	2.5	3.9
ARAPAHOE	**202**	**73,298**	**43,626**	**176,076 ***	**36.1**	**100.0**
019 Amer Bapt USA	4	636	371	801 *	.2	.5
040 Ap Chr Ch-Amer	1	40	90	90 *	-	.1
053 Assemb of God	11	5,763	3,690	5,697	1.2	3.2
056 Baha'i	3	96	NR	96	-	.1
057 Bapt Gen Conf	4	1,788	2,660	2,789 *	.6	1.6
076 Buddhism	3	NR	NR	NR	-	-
081 Catholic	11	NR	NR	63,755	13.1	36.2
084 Calvary Chapel	1	NR	NR	NR	-	-
089 Chr & Miss Al	1	168	NR	368	.1	.2
097 Chr Chs&Chs Cr	2	575	NR	724 *	.1	.4
105 Christian Ref	1	792	740	998 *	.2	.6
127 Ch God (Cleve)	3	610	375	805 *	.2	.5
151 L-D Saints	28	NR	NR	10,295	2.1	5.8
157 Ch of Brethren	1	169	72	213 *	-	.1
165 Ch of Nazarene	4	3,384	2,312	3,462	.7	2.0
167 Chs of Christ	8	1,326	1,491	1,820	.4	1.0
173 Comm of Christ	1	239	NR	239	-	.1
179 Consrv Bapt	3	NR	285	285	.1	.2
193 Episcopal	6	NR	1,336	3,109	.6	1.8
201 Evan Cov Ch	1	249	436	436 *	.1	.2
203 Evan Free Ch	4	693	1,663	1,663	.3	.9
207 E.L.C.A.	11	7,395	2,954	9,832	2.0	5.6
216 Evan Presby Ch	8	3,526	NR	4,441 *	.9	2.5
220 Free Lutheran	1	0	0	0	-	-
221 Free Methodist	2	154	360	360	.1	.2
246 Greek Orthodox	1	NR	NR	780	.2	.4
263 Int Foursq Gos	3	629	1,017	1,017 *	.2	.6
283 Luth—MO Synod	7	5,185	2,899	7,242	1.5	4.1
288 Mennonite USA	1	111	105	140 *	-	.1
306 NT IndBapt&Rltd	3	317	NR	400 *	.1	.2
313 N Am Bapt Conf	1	88	95	111 *	-	.1
331 OCA: Ter Diocs	1	48	NR	150	-	.1
349 Pent Holiness	4	177	166	223 *	-	.1
355 Presb Ch (USA)	8	3,046	1,705	3,837 *	.8	2.2
371 Ref Ch in Am	1	197	194	340	.1	.2
388 Reg Bapt Gen As	1	75	70	94 *	-	.1
403 Salvation Army	1	164	62	285	.1	.2
413 S.D.A.	4	770	NR	916	.2	.5
419 So Bapt Conv	14	7,465	3,164	9,402 *	1.9	5.3
443 Un C of Christ	5	2,837	1,132	3,573 *	.7	2.0
449 Un Methodist	9	5,926	2,565	7,464 *	1.5	4.2
463 Vineyard	3	1,490	1,212	1,877 *	.4	1.1
467 Wesleyan	2	90	160	485	.1	.3
469 WELS	1	230	190	307	.1	.2
496 Jewish Est	3	NR	NR	6,600	1.4	3.7
498 Indep.Charis.	2	16,000	7,500	16,000	3.3	9.1
499 Indep.Non-Char	4	850	2,555	2,555	.5	1.5
ARCHULETA	**16**	**1,182**	**892**	**5,971 ***	**60.3**	**100.0**
053 Assemb of God	1	134	202	265	2.7	4.4
056 Baha'i	0	15	NR	15	.2	.3
076 Buddhism	1	NR	NR	NR	-	-
081 Catholic	3	NR	NR	3,951	39.9	66.2
151 L-D Saints	1	NR	NR	312	3.2	5.2
167 Chs of Christ	2	50	66	68	.7	1.1
193 Episcopal	1	NR	74	143	1.4	2.4
283 Luth—MO Synod	1	129	97	173	1.7	2.9
413 S.D.A.	1	36	NR	43	.4	.7
419 So Bapt Conv	3	477	315	584 *	5.9	9.8
435 Unitarian-Univ	1	35	NR	43 *	.4	.7
449 Un Methodist	1	306	138	374 *	3.8	6.3
BACA	**21**	**1,109**	**636**	**1,819 ***	**40.3**	**100.0**
053 Assemb of God	1	55	87	104	2.3	5.7
056 Baha'i	0	3	NR	3	.1	.2
081 Catholic	1	NR	NR	200	4.4	11.0
123 Ch God (Ander)	2	NR	70	70	1.5	3.8
167 Chs of Christ	4	93	100	130	2.9	7.1
226 Friends-USA	4	200	NR	242 *	5.4	13.3
306 NT IndBapt&Rltd	1	102	NR	124 *	2.7	6.8
349 Pent Holiness	1	47	39	57 *	1.3	3.1
413 S.D.A.	1	13	NR	15	.3	.8
419 So Bapt Conv	1	211	68	256 *	5.7	14.1
449 Un Methodist	3	342	198	415 *	9.2	22.8
467 Wesleyan	2	43	74	203	4.5	11.2
BENT	**12**	**616**	**410**	**2,076 ***	**34.6**	**100.0**
056 Baha'i	0	3	NR	3	.1	.1
081 Catholic	1	NR	NR	1,138	19.0	54.8
165 Ch of Nazarene	1	43	69	100	1.7	4.8
167 Chs of Christ	2	34	42	52	.9	2.5
179 Consrv Bapt	1	NR	94	94	1.6	4.5
226 Friends-USA	2	88	NR	107 *	1.8	5.2
355 Presb Ch (USA)	1	83	48	101 *	1.7	4.9
419 So Bapt Conv	1	70	30	85 *	1.4	4.1
449 Un Methodist	2	254	99	308 *	5.1	14.8
469 WELS	1	41	28	48	.8	2.3
496 Jewish Est	0	NR	NR	40	.7	1.9
BOULDER	**204**	**35,510**	**26,063**	**137,473 ***	**47.2**	**100.0**
019 Amer Bapt USA	3	542	235	659 *	.2	.5
034 Ant Orth of NA	2	166	NR	332	.1	.2
053 Assemb of God	8	534	685	926	.3	.7
056 Baha'i	5	219	NR	219	.1	.2
057 Bapt Gen Conf	2	141	317	317 *	.1	.2
076 Buddhism	26	NR	NR	NR	-	-
081 Catholic	10	NR	NR	58,746	20.2	42.7
084 Calvary Chapel	2	NR	NR	NR	-	-
089 Chr & Miss Al	1	209	NR	209	.1	.2
093 Chr Ch (Disc)	1	303	117	369 *	.1	.3
097 Chr Chs&Chs Cr	4	2,815	NR	3,423 *	1.2	2.5
105 Christian Ref	3	258	270	314 *	.1	.2
123 Ch God (Ander)	1	NR	30	30	-	-
151 L-D Saints	12	NR	NR	4,750	1.6	3.5
157 Ch of Brethren	1	4	68	68 *	-	-
165 Ch of Nazarene	4	490	308	568	.2	.4
167 Chs of Christ	5	609	690	795	.3	.6
173 Comm of Christ	1	74	NR	74	-	.1
175 Congr Chr Chs	1	62	46	75 *	-	.1
179 Consrv Bapt	4	NR	1,400	1,400	.5	1.0
181 Consrv Congr	1	80	41	97 *	-	.1

NR–Not Reported   *Total adherents estimated from known number of communicant, confirmed, full members.   - Represents a percentage less than 0.1.   Percentages may not total 100 due to rounding.

Table 4: Religious Congregations by County and Group: 2000

Religious Group	Number of Churches, Synagogues, Mosques, or Temples	Number of Communicant, Confirmed, or Full Members	Number of Attendees	Total Adherents		
				Number of Adherents	% of Total Pop.	% of Total Adh.
193 Episcopal	6	NR	1,319	3,196	1.1	2.3
201 Evan Cov Ch	2	348	567	580 *	.2	.4
203 Evan Free Ch	6	1,625	2,588	2,688	.9	2.0
207 E.L.C.A.	12	6,389	3,082	8,773	3.0	6.4
221 Free Methodist	1	37	43	44	-	-
226 Friends-USA	1	30	NR	36 *	-	-
246 Greek Orthodox	1	NR	NR	543	.2	.4
252 Hindu	1	NR	NR	NR	-	-
263 Int Foursq Gos	2	390	619	619 *	.2	.5
267 Muslim Est	1	NR	500	4,000	1.4	2.9
283 Luth—MO Synod	9	1,935	1,029	2,629	.9	1.9
288 Mennonite USA	1	68	75	83 *	-	.1
290 Metro Comm Ch	1	13	16	16 *	-	-
306 NT IndBapt&Rltd	1	102	NR	124 *	-	.1
349 Pent Holiness	3	225	245	274 *	.1	.2
355 Presb Ch (USA)	9	4,236	2,743	5,153 *	1.8	3.7
356 Presb Ch Amer	1	46	80	80	-	.1
388 Reg Bapt Gen As	1	105	145	145 *	-	.1
403 Salvation Army	1	32	38	53	-	-
413 S.D.A.	5	1,058	NR	1,259	.4	.9
416 Sikh	3	NR	NR	NR	-	-
419 So Bapt Conv	8	2,263	1,010	2,753 *	.9	2.0
435 Unitarian-Univ	2	469	NR	571 *	.2	.4
443 Un C of Christ	4	1,622	588	1,973 *	.7	1.4
449 Un Methodist	13	4,320	2,415	5,253 *	1.8	3.8
463 Vineyard	1	130	120	158 *	.1	.1
469 WELS	2	211	134	274	.1	.2
496 Jewish Est	6	NR	NR	13,200	4.5	9.6
498 Indep.Charis.	1	0	800	2,000	.7	1.5
499 Indep.Non-Char	2	3,350	3,700	7,625	2.6	5.5
CHAFFEE	**26**	**3,226**	**2,007**	**8,620 ***	**53.1**	**100.0**
053 Assemb of God	2	106	152	229	1.4	2.7
056 Baha'i	0	6	NR	6	-	.1
081 Catholic	2	NR	NR	3,801	23.4	44.1
093 Chr Ch (Disc)	1	114	35	133 *	.8	1.5
127 Ch God (Cleve)	1	118	42	138 *	.8	1.6
151 L-D Saints	1	NR	NR	212	1.3	2.5
165 Ch of Nazarene	1	67	64	67	.4	.8
167 Chs of Christ	4	156	168	221	1.4	2.6
179 Consrv Bapt	2	NR	300	300	1.8	3.5
193 Episcopal	2	NR	155	391	2.4	4.5
216 Evan Presby Ch	1	250	NR	292 *	1.8	3.4
283 Luth—MO Synod	2	290	154	351	2.2	4.1
355 Presb Ch (USA)	1	175	174	205 *	1.3	2.4
413 S.D.A.	1	14	NR	17	.1	.2
419 So Bapt Conv	2	1,225	281	1,433 *	8.8	16.6
443 Un C of Christ	1	258	144	302 *	1.9	3.5
449 Un Methodist	1	197	73	230 *	1.4	2.7
463 Vineyard	1	250	265	292 *	1.8	3.4
CHEYENNE	**10**	**460**	**216**	**1,207 ***	**54.1**	**100.0**
081 Catholic	2	NR	NR	624	28.0	51.7
097 Chr Chs&Chs Cr	1	110	NR	138 *	6.2	11.4
167 Chs of Christ	1	17	18	22	1.0	1.8
207 E.L.C.A.	1	14	10	14	.6	1.2
283 Luth—MO Synod	2	145	70	191	8.6	15.8
419 So Bapt Conv	1	33	29	41 *	1.8	3.4
449 Un Methodist	2	141	89	177 *	7.9	14.7
CLEAR CREEK	**9**	**343**	**195**	**1,437 ***	**15.4**	**100.0**
056 Baha'i	0	6	NR	6	.1	.4
057 Bapt Gen Conf	1	34	40	41 *	.4	2.9
081 Catholic	2	NR	NR	781	8.4	54.3
151 L-D Saints	1	NR	NR	198	2.1	13.8
193 Episcopal	1	NR	15	12	.1	.8
207 E.L.C.A.	1	109	48	166	1.8	11.6
355 Presb Ch (USA)	2	126	74	152 *	1.6	10.6
419 So Bapt Conv	0	17	18	20 *	.2	1.4
449 Un Methodist	1	51	0	61 *	.7	4.2

Religious Group	Number of Churches, Synagogues, Mosques, or Temples	Number of Communicant, Confirmed, or Full Members	Number of Attendees	Total Adherents		
				Number of Adherents	% of Total Pop.	% of Total Adh.
CONEJOS	**24**	**213**	**267**	**5,641 ***	**67.2**	**100.0**
053 Assemb of God	2	73	77	96	1.1	1.7
056 Baha'i	0	15	NR	15	.2	.3
081 Catholic	10	NR	NR	3,013	35.9	53.4
151 L-D Saints	8	NR	NR	2,298	27.4	40.7
203 Evan Free Ch	1	69	125	125	1.5	2.2
288 Mennonite USA	1	7	30	30 *	.4	.5
355 Presb Ch (USA)	2	49	35	64 *	.8	1.1
COSTILLA	**10**	**57**	**21**	**3,190 ***	**87.1**	**100.0**
056 Baha'i	0	19	NR	19	.5	.6
081 Catholic	9	NR	NR	3,124	85.3	97.9
355 Presb Ch (USA)	1	16	14	20 *	.5	.6
419 So Bapt Conv	0	22	7	27 *	.7	.8
CROWLEY	**10**	**401**	**168**	**1,383 ***	**25.1**	**100.0**
053 Assemb of God	1	30	40	80	1.4	5.8
056 Baha'i	0	2	NR	2	-	.1
081 Catholic	1	NR	NR	875	15.9	63.3
093 Chr Ch (Disc)	1	0	0	0 *	-	-
207 E.L.C.A.	1	26	20	31	.6	2.2
283 Luth—MO Synod	1	22	13	23	.4	1.7
306 NT IndBapt&Rltd	1	102	NR	119 *	2.2	8.6
360 Prim Bapt Chrch	1	NR	NR	NR	-	-
449 Un Methodist	2	211	91	245 *	4.4	17.7
469 WELS	1	8	4	8	.1	.6
CUSTER	**8**	**529**	**238**	**1,142 ***	**32.6**	**100.0**
056 Baha'i	0	2	NR	2	.1	.2
081 Catholic	1	NR	NR	378	10.8	33.1
151 L-D Saints	1	NR	NR	80	2.3	7.0
193 Episcopal	1	NR	29	59	1.7	5.2
283 Luth—MO Synod	1	197	87	228	6.5	20.0
297 Mennonite;Other	1	36	NR	43 *	1.2	3.8
419 So Bapt Conv	1	152	40	182 *	5.2	15.9
425 Tao	1	NR	NR	NR	-	-
449 Un Methodist	1	142	82	170 *	4.9	14.9
DELTA	**54**	**4,345**	**2,280**	**10,025 ***	**36.0**	**100.0**
019 Amer Bapt USA	3	427	205	520 *	1.9	5.2
032 Amish; other	1	30	NR	37 *	.1	.4
053 Assemb of God	4	557	680	1,048	3.8	10.5
056 Baha'i	0	12	NR	12	-	.1
081 Catholic	4	NR	NR	2,758	9.9	27.5
084 Calvary Chapel	1	NR	NR	NR	-	-
097 Chr Chs&Chs Cr	2	338	NR	412 *	1.5	4.1
123 Ch God (Ander)	2	NR	72	72	.3	.7
151 L-D Saints	3	NR	NR	1,311	4.7	13.1
165 Ch of Nazarene	3	123	117	196	.7	2.0
167 Chs of Christ	3	136	145	181	.7	1.8
173 Comm of Christ	1	37	NR	37	.1	.4
193 Episcopal	2	NR	75	133	.5	1.3
203 Evan Free Ch	1	69	125	125	.4	1.2
207 E.L.C.A.	1	90	47	101	.4	1.0
226 Friends-USA	2	88	NR	107 *	.4	1.1
283 Luth—MO Synod	2	224	128	262	.9	2.6
306 NT IndBapt&Rltd	2	205	NR	250 *	.9	2.5
331 OCA: Ter Diocs	1	38	NR	44	.2	.4
339 Pent Ch of God	1	21	NR	50	.2	.5
349 Pent Holiness	1	10	20	12 *	-	.1
355 Presb Ch (USA)	2	220	126	268 *	1.0	2.7
413 S.D.A.	3	261	NR	311	1.1	3.1
419 So Bapt Conv	3	659	218	803 *	2.9	8.0
449 Un Methodist	5	773	295	942 *	3.4	9.4
463 Vineyard	1	27	27	33 *	.1	.3
DENVER	**356**	**58,603**	**38,371**	**293,989 ***	**53.0**	**100.0**
017 Amer Bapt Assn	3	90	NR	110 *	-	-
019 Amer Bapt USA	17	8,910	5,138	10,810 *	1.9	3.7
034 Ant Orth of NA	3	209	NR	418	.1	.1
039 Ap Chr Ch(Naz)	1	116	190	190 *	-	.1

NR–Not Reported   *Total adherents estimated from known number of communicant, confirmed, full members.   - Represents a percentage less than 0.1.   Percentages may not total 100 due to rounding.

Table 4: Religious Congregations by County and Group: 2000

Religious Group	Number of Churches, Synagogues, Mosques, or Temples	Number of Communicant, Confirmed, or Full Members	Number of Attendees	Total Adherents: Number of Adherents	Total Adherents: % of Total Pop.	Total Adherents: % of Total Adh.
053 Assemb of God	15	2,114	1,930	3,371	.6	1.1
055 As Ref Pres Ch	1	29	NR	32	-	-
056 Baha'i	1	387	NR	387	.1	.1
057 Bapt Gen Conf	6	403	492	567 *	.1	.2
076 Buddhism	23	NR	NR	NR	-	-
081 Catholic	41	NR	NR	159,196	28.7	54.2
089 Chr & Miss Al	2	9	NR	29	-	-
093 Chr Ch (Disc)	8	3,506	1,816	4,254 *	.8	1.4
097 Chr Chs&Chs Cr	3	553	NR	671 *	.1	.2
105 Christian Ref	9	2,032	1,500	2,465 *	.4	.8
123 Ch God (Ander)	3	NR	263	263	-	.1
127 Ch God (Cleve)	2	463	205	577 *	.1	.2
145 Ch God Prophcy	2	43	NR	52 *	-	-
151 L-D Saints	7	NR	NR	3,340	.6	1.1
157 Ch of Brethren	1	14	7	17 *	-	-
165 Ch of Nazarene	5	426	353	715	.1	.2
167 Chs of Christ	9	1,752	1,780	2,348	.4	.8
173 Comm of Christ	1	153	NR	153	-	.1
179 Consrv Bapt	7	NR	1,089	1,089	.2	.4
193 Episcopal	14	NR	3,395	8,810	1.6	3.0
201 Evan Cov Ch	1	110	49	133 *	-	-
203 Evan Free Ch	6	297	790	790	.1	.3
207 E.L.C.A.	12	3,594	1,618	4,812	.9	1.6
216 Evan Presby Ch	3	819	NR	993 *	.2	.3
226 Friends-USA	2	74	NR	90 *	-	-
237 Menn Br US Conf	3	364	NR	442 *	.1	.2
246 Greek Orthodox	1	NR	NR	1,845	.3	.6
252 Hindu	3	NR	NR	NR	-	-
263 Int Foursq Gos	4	503	309	610 *	.1	.2
264 Int Chs of Crst	1	923	1,562	1,348	.2	.5
267 Muslim Est	6	NR	1,270	6,132	1.1	2.1
283 Luth—MO Synod	10	2,714	1,439	3,447	.6	1.2
288 Mennonite USA	1	265	203	322 *	.1	.1
290 Metro Comm Ch	1	294	309	357 *	.1	.1
306 NT IndBapt&Rltd	4	809	NR	981 *	.2	.3
331 OCA: Ter Diocs	1	64	NR	170	-	.1
335 Orth Pres Ch	1	38	40	45	-	-
339 Pent Ch of God	2	68	NR	118	-	-
349 Pent Holiness	2	123	150	149 *	-	.1
355 Presb Ch (USA)	16	5,081	2,863	6,160 *	1.1	2.1
356 Presb Ch Amer	1	0	0	0	-	-
371 Ref Ch in Am	4	622	582	1,067	.2	.4
401 Rus Orth Abroad	1	NR	NR	NR	-	-
403 Salvation Army	6	510	396	910	.2	.3
413 S.D.A.	7	3,695	NR	4,397	.8	1.5
419 So Bapt Conv	10	5,847	2,926	7,094 *	1.3	2.4
425 Tao	1	NR	NR	NR	-	-
435 Unitarian-Univ	2	840	NR	1,019 *	.2	.3
443 Un C of Christ	10	1,587	836	1,925 *	.3	.7
449 Un Methodist	26	7,088	3,508	8,600 *	1.6	2.9
463 Vineyard	2	310	257	376 *	.1	.1
467 Wesleyan	1	70	94	200	-	.1
469 WELS	1	385	262	393	.1	.1
490 Zoroastrian	1	NR	NR	NR	-	-
496 Jewish Est	17	NR	NR	38,100	6.9	13.0
498 Indep.Charis.	2	300	750	1,100	.2	.4
DOLORES	**8**	**388**	**154**	**538 ***	**29.2**	**100.0**
053 Assemb of God	1	18	25	38	2.1	7.1
056 Baha'i	0	1	NR	1	.1	.2
081 Catholic	2	NR	NR	55	3.0	10.2
167 Chs of Christ	1	7	13	13	.7	2.4
413 S.D.A.	1	33	NR	39	2.1	7.2
419 So Bapt Conv	2	281	90	335 *	18.2	62.3
449 Un Methodist	1	48	26	57 *	3.1	10.6
DOUGLAS	**79**	**16,924**	**9,409**	**49,642 ***	**28.2**	**100.0**
053 Assemb of God	1	62	83	128	.1	.3
056 Baha'i	1	99	NR	99	.1	.2
057 Bapt Gen Conf	2	335	465	465 *	.3	.9
071 Brethren (Ash)	1	0	0	0 *	-	-
081 Catholic	3	NR	NR	16,874	9.6	34.0
084 Calvary Chapel	1	NR	NR	NR	-	-
097 Chr Chs&Chs Cr	3	1,172	NR	1,581 *	.9	3.2
105 Christian Ref	1	472	450	637 *	.4	1.3
123 Ch God (Ander)	1	NR	260	260	.1	.5
151 L-D Saints	16	NR	NR	6,892	3.9	13.9
165 Ch of Nazarene	2	193	186	327	.2	.7
167 Chs of Christ	2	145	205	199	.1	.4
179 Consrv Bapt	2	NR	292	292	.2	.6
193 Episcopal	4	NR	589	1,407	.8	2.8
201 Evan Cov Ch	1	0	102	102 *	.1	.2
203 Evan Free Ch	3	187	410	410	.2	.8
207 E.L.C.A.	3	2,224	1,168	3,388	1.9	6.8
216 Evan Presby Ch	2	4,950	NR	6,677 *	3.8	13.5
220 Free Lutheran	1	71	113	139	.1	.3
263 Int Foursq Gos	3	113	143	152 *	.1	.3
283 Luth—MO Synod	4	879	627	1,229	.7	2.5
355 Presb Ch (USA)	1	379	380	511 *	.3	1.0
356 Presb Ch Amer	3	99	170	170	.1	.3
410 Serb Orth USA	1	NR	NR	250	.1	.5
413 S.D.A.	1	131	NR	156	.1	.3
419 So Bapt Conv	8	1,734	1,031	2,339 *	1.3	4.7
435 Unitarian-Univ	1	65	NR	88 *	.1	.2
443 Un C of Christ	1	126	96	170 *	.1	.3
449 Un Methodist	3	2,383	1,294	3,215 *	1.8	6.5
463 Vineyard	1	54	14	73 *	-	.1
469 WELS	1	151	131	212	.1	.4
499 Indep.Non-Char	1	900	1,200	1,200	.7	2.4
EAGLE	**30**	**1,990**	**1,399**	**14,059 ***	**33.7**	**100.0**
053 Assemb of God	1	92	141	216	.5	1.5
056 Baha'i	0	10	NR	10	-	.1
081 Catholic	7	NR	NR	9,854	23.7	70.1
084 Calvary Chapel	1	NR	NR	NR	-	-
151 L-D Saints	2	NR	NR	480	1.2	3.4
167 Chs of Christ	2	34	60	58	.1	.4
193 Episcopal	2	NR	158	312	.7	2.2
203 Evan Free Ch	1	15	90	90	.2	.6
207 E.L.C.A.	2	481	309	684	1.6	4.9
216 Evan Presby Ch	1	30	NR	37 *	.1	.3
283 Luth—MO Synod	1	247	134	325	.8	2.3
306 NT IndBapt&Rltd	1	102	NR	125 *	.3	.9
355 Presb Ch (USA)	1	108	80	133 *	.3	.9
419 So Bapt Conv	3	537	296	662 *	1.6	4.7
449 Un Methodist	3	292	95	360 *	.9	2.6
469 WELS	1	42	36	63	.2	.4
496 Jewish Est	1	NR	NR	650	1.6	4.6
ELBERT	**13**	**840**	**889**	**1,840 ***	**9.3**	**100.0**
019 Amer Bapt USA	2	75	63	97 *	.5	5.3
056 Baha'i	0	6	NR	6	-	.3
059 Bapt Miss Assn	1	113	240	240 *	1.2	13.0
081 Catholic	1	NR	NR	0	-	-
097 Chr Chs&Chs Cr	2	121	NR	157 *	.8	8.5
151 L-D Saints	1	NR	NR	585	2.9	31.8
165 Ch of Nazarene	1	10	20	27	.1	1.5
179 Consrv Bapt	1	NR	50	50	.3	2.7
283 Luth—MO Synod	1	46	45	70	.4	3.8
355 Presb Ch (USA)	1	218	240	282 *	1.4	15.3
419 So Bapt Conv	1	185	191	240 *	1.2	13.0
449 Un Methodist	1	66	40	86 *	.4	4.7
EL PASO	**294**	**72,915**	**52,928**	**191,791 ***	**37.1**	**100.0**
017 Amer Bapt Assn	1	40	NR	51 *	-	-
019 Amer Bapt USA	6	3,048	628	3,887 *	.8	2.0
039 Ap Chr Ch(Naz)	1	41	91	91 *	-	-
053 Assemb of God	17	2,790	3,424	4,157	.8	2.2
056 Baha'i	3	291	NR	291	.1	.2
057 Bapt Gen Conf	1	154	178	196 *	-	.1
075 Brethren in Cr	1	2	24	24	-	-
076 Buddhism	1	NR	NR	NR	-	-
081 Catholic	21	NR	NR	58,155	11.3	30.3
084 Calvary Chapel	3	NR	NR	NR	-	-
089 Chr & Miss Al	5	432	NR	965	.2	.5
093 Chr Ch (Disc)	3	890	367	1,135 *	.2	.6

NR–Not Reported *Total adherents estimated from known number of communicant, confirmed, full members. - Represents a percentage less than 0.1. Percentages may not total 100 due to rounding.

Table 4: Religious Congregations by County and Group: 2000

Religious Group	Number of Churches, Synagogues, Mosques, or Temples	Number of Communicant, Confirmed, or Full Members	Number of Attendees	Total Adherents		
				Number of Adherents	% of Total Pop.	% of Total Adh.
097 Chr Chs&Chs Cr	8	2,361	NR	3,012 *	.6	1.6
105 Christian Ref	1	321	260	409 *	.1	.2
123 Ch God (Ander)	1	NR	140	140	-	.1
127 Ch God (Cleve)	3	325	248	423 *	.1	.2
145 Ch God Prophcy	1	22	NR	28 *	-	-
151 L-D Saints	26	NR	NR	11,489	2.2	6.0
165 Ch of Nazarene	19	3,726	2,713	4,198	.8	2.2
167 Chs of Christ	9	1,492	1,509	1,767	.3	.9
173 Comm of Christ	1	309	NR	309	.1	.2
179 Consrv Bapt	3	NR	1,725	1,725	.3	.9
193 Episcopal	8	NR	1,944	4,363	.8	2.3
201 Evan Cov Ch	2	258	224	329 *	.1	.2
203 Evan Free Ch	6	590	1,155	1,155	.2	.6
207 E.L.C.A.	14	6,443	3,172	8,385	1.6	4.4
221 Free Methodist	2	24	91	91	-	-
223 Free Will Bapt	1	30	NR	38 *	-	-
226 Friends-USA	2	74	NR	94 *	-	-
246 Greek Orthodox	1	NR	NR	543	.1	.3
263 Int Foursq Gos	3	468	760	760 *	.1	.4
264 Int Chs of Crst	1	186	310	276	.1	.1
267 Muslim Est	1	NR	156	609	.1	.3
283 Luth—MO Synod	8	3,772	2,072	4,811	.9	2.5
288 Mennonite USA	3	317	288	404 *	.1	.2
290 Metro Comm Ch	1	116	116	148 *	-	.1
331 OCA: Ter Diocs	2	125	NR	231	-	.1
339 Pent Ch of God	1	12	NR	50	-	-
355 Presb Ch (USA)	8	6,751	3,483	8,610 *	1.7	4.5
356 Presb Ch Amer	4	1,801	1,817	2,392	.5	1.2
360 Prim Bapt Chrch	1	NR	NR	NR	-	-
371 Ref Ch in Am	1	354	558	857	.2	.4
373 Ref Ch in U.S.	1	35	NR	45	-	-
388 Reg Bapt Gen As	1	122	140	156 *	-	.1
403 Salvation Army	2	250	119	1,066	.2	.6
413 S.D.A.	6	1,347	NR	1,602	.3	.8
418 Southw Bapt Fel	1	NR	NR	NR	-	-
419 So Bapt Conv	31	16,221	5,419	20,687 *	4.0	10.8
435 Unitarian-Univ	2	304	NR	388 *	.1	.2
443 Un C of Christ	8	2,942	1,303	3,752 *	.7	2.0
449 Un Methodist	19	8,051	5,150	10,266 *	2.0	5.4
463 Vineyard	3	970	899	1,238 *	.2	.6
467 Wesleyan	4	348	351	665	.1	.3
469 WELS	2	270	194	428	.1	.2
496 Jewish Est	4	NR	NR	1,500	.3	.8
498 Indep.Charis.	1	0	5,500	17,000	3.3	8.9
499 Indep.Non-Char	4	4,490	6,400	6,400	1.2	3.3
FREMONT	**47**	**6,113**	**3,255**	**16,618 ***	**36.0**	**100.0**
019 Amer Bapt USA	2	338	76	400 *	.9	2.4
053 Assemb of God	2	395	221	370	.8	2.2
056 Baha'i	0	35	NR	35	.1	.2
081 Catholic	3	NR	NR	7,527	16.3	45.3
093 Chr Ch (Disc)	1	370	170	438 *	.9	2.6
097 Chr Chs&Chs Cr	3	450	NR	533 *	1.2	3.2
123 Ch God (Ander)	1	NR	41	41	.1	.2
127 Ch God (Cleve)	1	44	19	52 *	.1	.3
145 Ch God Prophcy	1	22	NR	26 *	.1	.2
151 L-D Saints	2	NR	NR	948	2.1	5.7
165 Ch of Nazarene	3	214	194	257	.6	1.5
167 Chs of Christ	3	183	185	225	.5	1.4
193 Episcopal	1	NR	105	263	.6	1.6
203 Evan Free Ch	1	240	550	550	1.2	3.3
207 E.L.C.A.	1	358	188	479	1.0	2.9
221 Free Methodist	1	0	45	45	.1	.3
226 Friends-USA	1	44	NR	52 *	.1	.3
263 Int Foursq Gos	2	72	128	128 *	.3	.8
283 Luth—MO Synod	1	113	88	127	.3	.8
306 NT IndBapt&Rltd	1	102	NR	121 *	.3	.7
349 Pent Holiness	1	87	57	103 *	.2	.6
355 Presb Ch (USA)	3	407	190	482 *	1.0	2.9
413 S.D.A.	1	306	NR	364	.8	2.2
419 So Bapt Conv	6	1,705	481	2,020 *	4.4	12.2
449 Un Methodist	2	443	275	525 *	1.1	3.2
463 Vineyard	1	128	108	152 *	.3	.9
467 Wesleyan	2	57	134	355	.8	2.1

Religious Group	Number of Churches, Synagogues, Mosques, or Temples	Number of Communicant, Confirmed, or Full Members	Number of Attendees	Total Adherents		
				Number of Adherents	% of Total Pop.	% of Total Adh.
GARFIELD	**49**	**4,045**	**2,461**	**12,198 ***	**27.9**	**100.0**
019 Amer Bapt USA	2	128	150	162 *	.4	1.3
053 Assemb of God	4	339	365	573	1.3	4.7
056 Baha'i	0	29	NR	29	.1	.2
057 Bapt Gen Conf	1	215	300	300 *	.7	2.5
081 Catholic	5	NR	NR	5,379	12.3	44.1
097 Chr Chs&Chs Cr	2	250	NR	315 *	.7	2.6
145 Ch God Prophcy	1	22	NR	27 *	.1	.2
151 L-D Saints	3	NR	NR	1,201	2.7	9.8
165 Ch of Nazarene	1	62	39	62	.1	.5
167 Chs of Christ	3	216	290	324	.7	2.7
173 Comm of Christ	1	15	NR	15	-	.1
193 Episcopal	2	NR	90	200	.5	1.6
207 E.L.C.A.	1	293	96	410	.9	3.4
226 Friends-USA	1	30	NR	38 *	.1	.3
263 Int Foursq Gos	1	101	100	128 *	.3	1.0
283 Luth—MO Synod	2	335	238	513	1.2	4.2
288 Mennonite USA	1	49	36	62 *	.1	.5
306 NT IndBapt&Rltd	4	410	NR	518 *	1.2	4.2
355 Presb Ch (USA)	1	170	100	215 *	.5	1.8
413 S.D.A.	4	229	NR	272	.6	2.2
419 So Bapt Conv	4	421	326	532 *	1.2	4.4
443 Un C of Christ	1	25	11	32 *	.1	.3
449 Un Methodist	4	706	320	891 *	2.0	7.3
GILPIN	**3**	**121**	**80**	**284 ***	**6.0**	**100.0**
056 Baha'i	0	2	NR	2	-	.7
081 Catholic	1	NR	NR	120	2.5	42.3
193 Episcopal	1	NR	15	20	.4	7.0
449 Un Methodist	1	119	65	142 *	3.0	50.0
GRAND	**17**	**708**	**641**	**2,642 ***	**21.2**	**100.0**
053 Assemb of God	1	56	80	86	.7	3.3
056 Baha'i	0	5	NR	5	-	.2
081 Catholic	4	NR	NR	1,398	11.2	52.9
151 L-D Saints	1	NR	NR	163	1.3	6.2
167 Chs of Christ	2	26	26	30	.2	1.1
193 Episcopal	2	NR	84	196	1.6	7.4
207 E.L.C.A.	1	81	68	118	.9	4.5
355 Presb Ch (USA)	2	299	247	358 *	2.9	13.6
413 S.D.A.	1	27	NR	32	.3	1.2
419 So Bapt Conv	3	214	136	256 *	2.1	9.7
GUNNISON	**15**	**1,501**	**746**	**5,353 ***	**38.4**	**100.0**
053 Assemb of God	1	39	58	61	.4	1.1
056 Baha'i	0	7	NR	7	.1	.1
057 Bapt Gen Conf	1	97	195	195 *	1.4	3.6
081 Catholic	2	NR	NR	3,200	22.9	59.8
151 L-D Saints	1	NR	NR	175	1.3	3.3
167 Chs of Christ	1	22	65	41	.3	.8
193 Episcopal	1	NR	59	121	.9	2.3
262 Int Cou Comm Ch	1	526	NR	609 *	4.4	11.4
283 Luth—MO Synod	1	78	48	95	.7	1.8
306 NT IndBapt&Rltd	1	102	NR	118 *	.8	2.2
413 S.D.A.	1	35	NR	42	.3	.8
419 So Bapt Conv	3	399	186	462 *	3.3	8.6
443 Un C of Christ	1	196	135	227 *	1.6	4.2
HINSDALE	**4**	**149**	**266**	**261 ***	**33.0**	**100.0**
081 Catholic	1	NR	NR	45	5.7	17.2
193 Episcopal	1	NR	31	41	5.2	15.7
355 Presb Ch (USA)	1	81	85	95 *	12.0	36.4
419 So Bapt Conv	1	68	150	80 *	10.1	30.7
HUERFANO	**18**	**628**	**427**	**4,263 ***	**54.2**	**100.0**
019 Amer Bapt USA	1	23	15	27 *	.3	.6
053 Assemb of God	1	23	30	31	.4	.7
056 Baha'i	0	3	NR	3	-	.1
076 Buddhism	1	NR	NR	NR	-	-
081 Catholic	5	NR	NR	3,447	43.8	80.9
167 Chs of Christ	1	40	50	60	.8	1.4

NR–Not Reported *Total adherents estimated from known number of communicant, confirmed, full members. - Represents a percentage less than 0.1. Percentages may not total 100 due to rounding.

Table 4: Religious Congregations by County and Group: 2000

Religious Group	Number of Churches, Synagogues, Mosques, or Temples	Number of Communicant, Confirmed, or Full Members	Number of Attendees	Total Adherents		
				Number of Adherents	% of Total Pop.	% of Total Adh.
221 Free Methodist	1	0	12	12	.2	.3
283 Luth—MO Synod	1	19	12	29	.4	.7
288 Mennonite USA	1	11	12	13 *	.2	.3
413 S.D.A.	1	25	NR	30	.4	.7
419 So Bapt Conv	2	212	82	250 *	3.2	5.9
449 Un Methodist	2	142	94	168 *	2.1	3.9
463 Vineyard	1	130	120	153 *	1.9	3.6
496 Jewish Est	0	NR	NR	40	.5	.9
JACKSON	**5**	**204**	**90**	**333 ***	**21.1**	**100.0**
053 Assemb of God	1	11	15	15	1.0	4.5
081 Catholic	1	NR	NR	78	4.9	23.4
167 Chs of Christ	1	20	25	28	1.8	8.4
306 NT IndBapt&Rltd	1	102	NR	125 *	7.9	37.5
449 Un Methodist	1	71	50	87 *	5.5	26.1
JEFFERSON	**264**	**49,647**	**45,057**	**187,287 ***	**35.5**	**100.0**
019 Amer Bapt USA	4	253	166	314 *	.1	.2
053 Assemb of God	8	923	1,238	1,801	.3	1.0
056 Baha'i	5	209	NR	209	-	.1
057 Bapt Gen Conf	5	679	765	949 *	.2	.5
076 Buddhism	8	NR	NR	NR	-	-
081 Catholic	15	NR	NR	84,960	16.1	45.4
084 Calvary Chapel	3	NR	NR	NR	-	-
089 Chr & Miss Al	1	32	NR	121	-	.1
093 Chr Ch (Disc)	3	752	375	932 *	.2	.5
097 Chr Chs&Chs Cr	6	728	NR	902 *	.2	.5
123 Ch God (Ander)	2	NR	136	136	-	.1
127 Ch God (Cleve)	3	578	107	717 *	.1	.4
151 L-D Saints	31	NR	NR	10,982	2.1	5.9
165 Ch of Nazarene	5	1,041	691	1,136	.2	.6
167 Chs of Christ	9	1,433	1,623	2,013	.4	1.1
173 Comm of Christ	1	219	NR	219	-	.1
176 Congr Ad Afl	1	838	NR	1,039 *	.2	.6
179 Consrv Bapt	10	NR	3,240	3,240	.6	1.7
193 Episcopal	10	NR	1,599	3,279	.6	1.8
201 Evan Cov Ch	6	1,852	2,680	2,950 *	.6	1.6
203 Evan Free Ch	9	968	1,968	1,968	.4	1.1
207 E.L.C.A.	15	7,411	3,833	10,422	2.0	5.6
216 Evan Presby Ch	3	1,325	NR	1,643 *	.3	.9
221 Free Methodist	1	164	333	333	.1	.2
226 Friends-USA	3	132	NR	164 *	-	.1
237 Menn Br US Conf	1	118	NR	146 *	-	.1
252 Hindu	1	NR	NR	NR	-	-
263 Int Foursq Gos	7	472	434	585 *	.1	.3
267 Muslim Est	1	NR	290	1,313	.2	.7
268 Jain	1	NR	NR	NR	-	-
283 Luth—MO Synod	10	4,794	3,100	6,318	1.2	3.4
288 Mennonite USA	3	173	178	215 *	-	.1
306 NT IndBapt&Rltd	8	819	NR	1,016 *	.2	.5
333 Malan Dioc Am	1	NR	NR	75	-	-
355 Presb Ch (USA)	8	3,147	1,764	3,900 *	.7	2.1
356 Presb Ch Amer	2	279	505	534	.1	.3
360 Prim Bapt Chrch	1	NR	NR	NR	-	-
370 Ref Baptist Chs	1	NR	NR	NR	-	-
371 Ref Ch in Am	1	237	251	576	.1	.3
388 Reg Bapt Gen As	1	98	99	99 *	-	.1
403 Salvation Army	1	37	74	130	-	.1
413 S.D.A.	4	546	NR	650	.1	.3
416 Sikh	1	NR	NR	NR	-	-
419 So Bapt Conv	15	8,152	5,844	10,104 *	1.9	5.4
425 Tao	1	NR	NR	NR	-	-
435 Unitarian-Univ	2	546	NR	677 *	.1	.4
443 Un C of Christ	6	1,382	825	1,713 *	.3	.9
449 Un Methodist	11	5,742	2,697	7,116 *	1.4	3.8
469 WELS	2	348	242	516	.1	.3
496 Jewish Est	2	NR	NR	4,400	.8	2.3
498 Indep.Charis.	2	0	7,000	12,000	2.3	6.4
499 Indep.Non-Char	3	3,220	3,000	4,775	.9	2.5
KIOWA	**7**	**550**	**199**	**666 ***	**41.1**	**100.0**
053 Assemb of God	1	42	44	44	2.7	6.6
056 Baha'i	0	1	NR	1	.1	.2

Religious Group	Number of Churches, Synagogues, Mosques, or Temples	Number of Communicant, Confirmed, or Full Members	Number of Attendees	Total Adherents		
				Number of Adherents	% of Total Pop.	% of Total Adh.
097 Chr Chs&Chs Cr	1	100	NR	122 *	7.5	18.3
226 Friends-USA	2	88	NR	108 *	6.7	16.2
419 So Bapt Conv	1	187	75	229 *	14.1	34.4
449 Un Methodist	2	132	80	162 *	10.0	24.3
KIT CARSON	**29**	**2,767**	**1,442**	**5,652 ***	**70.6**	**100.0**
019 Amer Bapt USA	1	223	59	278 *	3.5	4.9
053 Assemb of God	1	109	130	130	1.6	2.3
081 Catholic	3	NR	NR	2,003	25.0	35.4
093 Chr Ch (Disc)	1	296	85	369 *	4.6	6.5
097 Chr Chs&Chs Cr	2	220	NR	274 *	3.4	4.8
123 Ch God (Ander)	1	NR	50	50	.6	.9
165 Ch of Nazarene	1	2	0	2	-	-
167 Chs of Christ	2	80	102	116	1.4	2.1
173 Comm of Christ	1	73	NR	73	.9	1.3
179 Consrv Bapt	1	NR	50	50	.6	.9
181 Consrv Congr	2	217	202	271 *	3.4	4.8
203 Evan Free Ch	2	63	150	150	1.9	2.7
207 E.L.C.A.	2	337	184	459	5.7	8.1
283 Luth—MO Synod	2	363	139	451	5.6	8.0
288 Mennonite USA	1	16	13	20 *	.2	.4
413 S.D.A.	1	12	NR	14	.2	.2
419 So Bapt Conv	3	321	130	400 *	5.0	7.1
449 Un Methodist	2	435	148	542 *	6.8	9.6
LAKE	**11**	**455**	**323**	**5,894 ***	**75.4**	**100.0**
053 Assemb of God	1	33	36	36	.5	.6
056 Baha'i	0	9	NR	9	.1	.2
081 Catholic	1	NR	NR	5,144	65.8	87.3
151 L-D Saints	1	NR	NR	84	1.1	1.4
167 Chs of Christ	1	2	2	2	-	-
193 Episcopal	1	NR	15	46	.6	.8
203 Evan Free Ch	1	35	110	110	1.4	1.9
283 Luth—MO Synod	1	57	30	64	.8	1.1
306 NT IndBapt&Rltd	1	102	NR	129 *	1.7	2.2
355 Presb Ch (USA)	1	133	90	169 *	2.2	2.9
413 S.D.A.	1	65	NR	77	1.0	1.3
419 So Bapt Conv	1	19	40	24 *	.3	.4
LA PLATA	**49**	**3,948**	**3,299**	**15,531 ***	**35.3**	**100.0**
053 Assemb of God	3	100	115	191	.4	1.2
056 Baha'i	2	80	NR	80	.2	.5
081 Catholic	5	NR	NR	8,329	19.0	53.6
084 Calvary Chapel	1	NR	NR	NR	-	-
089 Chr & Miss Al	1	0	NR	40	.1	.3
097 Chr Chs&Chs Cr	2	95	NR	114 *	.3	.7
151 L-D Saints	4	NR	NR	1,516	3.5	9.8
165 Ch of Nazarene	1	113	90	186	.4	1.2
167 Chs of Christ	7	307	413	399	.9	2.6
173 Comm of Christ	1	55	NR	55	.1	.4
179 Consrv Bapt	1	NR	150	150	.3	1.0
193 Episcopal	1	NR	141	308	.7	2.0
207 E.L.C.A.	1	426	250	553	1.3	3.6
221 Free Methodist	1	35	43	43	.1	.3
226 Friends-USA	1	30	NR	36 *	.1	.2
263 Int Foursq Gos	2	524	919	919 *	2.1	5.9
283 Luth—MO Synod	1	130	100	151	.3	1.0
355 Presb Ch (USA)	4	613	453	735 *	1.7	4.7
413 S.D.A.	1	175	NR	208	.5	1.3
419 So Bapt Conv	6	656	293	787 *	1.8	5.1
435 Unitarian-Univ	1	28	NR	34 *	.1	.2
449 Un Methodist	2	581	332	697 *	1.6	4.5
LARIMER	**173**	**36,512**	**28,700**	**98,728 ***	**39.3**	**100.0**
017 Amer Bapt Assn	1	40	NR	49 *	-	-
019 Amer Bapt USA	2	437	216	535 *	.2	.5
034 Ant Orth of NA	1	23	NR	46	-	-
053 Assemb of God	8	2,309	3,285	7,977	3.2	8.1
056 Baha'i	3	201	NR	201	.1	.2
057 Bapt Gen Conf	2	478	284	585 *	.2	.6
076 Buddhism	1	NR	NR	NR	-	-
081 Catholic	8	NR	NR	32,259	12.8	32.7

NR–Not Reported *Total adherents estimated from known number of communicant, confirmed, full members. - Represents a percentage less than 0.1. Percentages may not total 100 due to rounding.

Table 4: Religious Congregations by County and Group: 2000

Religious Group	Number of Churches, Synagogues, Mosques, or Temples	Number of Communicant, Confirmed, or Full Members	Number of Attendees	Total Adherents: Number of Adherents	Total Adherents: % of Total Pop.	Total Adherents: % of Total Adh.
084 Calvary Chapel	1	NR	NR	NR	-	-
093 Chr Ch (Disc)	2	1,644	478	2,011 *	.8	2.0
097 Chr Chs&Chs Cr	4	530	NR	649 *	.3	.7
105 Christian Ref	1	295	200	361 *	.1	.4
123 Ch God (Ander)	2	NR	245	245	.1	.2
127 Ch God (Cleve)	1	29	8	35 *	-	-
145 Ch God Prophcy	1	22	NR	27 *	-	-
151 L-D Saints	15	NR	NR	6,330	2.5	6.4
165 Ch of Nazarene	4	282	233	450	.2	.5
167 Chs of Christ	8	870	925	1,043	.4	1.1
173 Comm of Christ	2	187	NR	187	.1	.2
179 Consrv Bapt	2	NR	500	500	.2	.5
193 Episcopal	5	NR	878	2,435	1.0	2.5
201 Evan Cov Ch	3	876	1,984	1,984 *	.8	2.0
203 Evan Free Ch	7	877	2,665	2,665	1.1	2.7
207 E.L.C.A.	8	4,032	2,058	5,369	2.1	5.4
216 Evan Presby Ch	2	519	NR	635 *	.3	.6
220 Free Lutheran	1	72	44	91	-	.1
221 Free Methodist	1	0	42	42	-	-
223 Free Will Bapt	2	60	NR	73 *	-	.1
226 Friends-USA	2	74	NR	91 *	-	.1
252 Hindu	1	NR	NR	NR	-	-
263 Int Foursq Gos	6	307	568	568 *	.2	.6
267 Muslim Est	1	NR	300	1,200	.5	1.2
283 Luth—MO Synod	7	3,263	1,809	4,345	1.7	4.4
288 Mennonite USA	1	28	55	55 *	-	.1
290 Metro Comm Ch	1	32	28	39 *	-	-
291 Missionary Ch	1	1	223	223	.1	.2
306 NT IndBapt&Rltd	1	102	NR	124 *	-	.1
335 Orth Pres Ch	1	43	72	84	-	.1
349 Pent Holiness	1	63	70	77 *	-	.1
355 Presb Ch (USA)	10	3,663	2,022	4,481 *	1.8	4.5
356 Presb Ch Amer	1	52	110	110	-	.1
369 Prot Ref Chs	1	144	NR	24	-	-
403 Salvation Army	1	92	33	251	.1	.3
413 S.D.A.	7	1,218	NR	1,450	.6	1.5
419 So Bapt Conv	9	1,800	678	2,202 *	.9	2.2
435 Unitarian-Univ	2	392	NR	480 *	.2	.5
443 Un C of Christ	2	836	317	1,023 *	.4	1.0
449 Un Methodist	6	4,302	1,939	5,263 *	2.1	5.3
455 Un Ref Chs N.A.	1	91	NR	143	.1	.1
463 Vineyard	3	2,930	1,850	3,584 *	1.4	3.6
467 Wesleyan	2	29	103	200	.1	.2
469 WELS	2	282	238	382	.2	.4
496 Jewish Est	1	NR	NR	1,000	.4	1.0
498 Indep.Charis.	2	2,300	3,475	3,575	1.4	3.6
499 Indep.Non-Char	2	685	765	970	.4	1.0
LAS ANIMAS	**22**	**1,149**	**472**	**12,060 ***	**79.3**	**100.0**
019 Amer Bapt USA	1	27	25	33 *	.2	.3
053 Assemb of God	2	48	62	63	.4	.5
056 Baha'i	0	11	NR	11	.1	.1
081 Catholic	6	NR	NR	10,130	66.6	84.0
151 L-D Saints	1	NR	NR	289	1.9	2.4
165 Ch of Nazarene	1	32	30	82	.5	.7
167 Chs of Christ	2	48	51	58	.4	.5
193 Episcopal	1	NR	12	75	.5	.6
207 E.L.C.A.	1	88	38	126	.8	1.0
263 Int Foursq Gos	1	53	25	65 *	.4	.5
355 Presb Ch (USA)	2	57	32	70 *	.5	.6
413 S.D.A.	1	55	NR	65	.4	.5
419 So Bapt Conv	2	541	97	662 *	4.4	5.5
449 Un Methodist	1	189	100	231 *	1.5	1.9
496 Jewish Est	0	NR	NR	100	.7	.8
LINCOLN	**21**	**1,102**	**749**	**2,104 ***	**34.6**	**100.0**
019 Amer Bapt USA	1	117	109	141 *	2.3	6.7
081 Catholic	2	NR	NR	703	11.5	33.4
157 Ch of Brethren	1	19	20	23 *	.4	1.1
165 Ch of Nazarene	1	19	34	34	.6	1.6
167 Chs of Christ	1	50	70	75	1.2	3.6
173 Comm of Christ	1	37	NR	37	.6	1.8
181 Consrv Congr	1	45	25	54 *	.9	2.6
193 Episcopal	1	NR	12	25	.4	1.2
207 E.L.C.A.	1	80	43	117	1.9	5.6
283 Luth—MO Synod	3	93	52	103	1.7	4.9
373 Ref Ch in U.S.	1	39	NR	64	1.1	3.0
413 S.D.A.	1	17	NR	20	.3	1.0
419 So Bapt Conv	2	189	160	228 *	3.7	10.8
449 Un Methodist	4	397	224	480 *	7.9	22.8
LOGAN	**32**	**4,275**	**2,636**	**9,090 ***	**44.3**	**100.0**
019 Amer Bapt USA	1	463	167	569 *	2.8	6.3
053 Assemb of God	3	122	152	217	1.1	2.4
056 Baha'i	0	4	NR	4	-	-
081 Catholic	4	NR	NR	3,072	15.0	33.8
093 Chr Ch (Disc)	1	270	118	332 *	1.6	3.7
123 Ch God (Ander)	1	NR	30	30	.1	.3
151 L-D Saints	1	NR	NR	371	1.8	4.1
165 Ch of Nazarene	1	184	231	315	1.5	3.5
167 Chs of Christ	1	40	45	50	.2	.6
193 Episcopal	1	NR	41	107	.5	1.2
203 Evan Free Ch	1	80	75	80	.4	.9
207 E.L.C.A.	1	287	77	353	1.7	3.9
263 Int Foursq Gos	1	129	275	275 *	1.3	3.0
283 Luth—MO Synod	3	594	330	732	3.6	8.1
355 Presb Ch (USA)	1	558	219	686 *	3.3	7.5
413 S.D.A.	1	36	NR	43	.2	.5
419 So Bapt Conv	2	480	401	590 *	2.9	6.5
443 Un C of Christ	1	115	56	141 *	.7	1.6
449 Un Methodist	7	913	419	1,123 *	5.5	12.4
MESA	**112**	**15,065**	**8,575**	**33,221 ***	**28.6**	**100.0**
019 Amer Bapt USA	4	865	446	1,067 *	.9	3.2
053 Assemb of God	9	1,088	1,428	2,292	2.0	6.9
056 Baha'i	2	88	NR	88	.1	.3
081 Catholic	4	NR	NR	5,326	4.6	16.0
084 Calvary Chapel	2	NR	NR	NR	-	-
089 Chr & Miss Al	1	52	NR	152	.1	.5
093 Chr Ch (Disc)	1	290	163	358 *	.3	1.1
097 Chr Chs&Chs Cr	6	1,379	NR	1,700 *	1.5	5.1
105 Christian Ref	1	139	190	171 *	.1	.5
123 Ch God (Ander)	1	NR	37	37	-	.1
127 Ch God (Cleve)	2	386	177	475 *	.4	1.4
145 Ch God Prophcy	1	22	NR	27 *	-	.1
151 L-D Saints	15	NR	NR	5,890	5.1	17.7
157 Ch of Brethren	1	118	48	145 *	.1	.4
165 Ch of Nazarene	2	391	312	565	.5	1.7
167 Chs of Christ	3	517	364	598	.5	1.8
173 Comm of Christ	1	80	NR	80	.1	.2
179 Consrv Bapt	2	NR	70	70	.1	.2
193 Episcopal	2	NR	292	892	.8	2.7
203 Evan Free Ch	2	108	197	197	.2	.6
207 E.L.C.A.	2	729	348	945	.8	2.8
223 Free Will Bapt	1	30	NR	37 *	-	.1
226 Friends-USA	2	74	NR	91 *	.1	.3
246 Greek Orthodox	1	NR	NR	315	.3	.9
263 Int Foursq Gos	3	487	572	600 *	.5	1.8
283 Luth—MO Synod	1	897	466	1,152	1.0	3.5
297 Mennonite;Other	1	40	NR	49 *	-	.1
306 NT IndBapt&Rltd	3	307	NR	378 *	.3	1.1
339 Pent Ch of God	1	4	NR	12	-	-
349 Pent Holiness	2	81	74	100 *	.1	.3
355 Presb Ch (USA)	2	721	490	889 *	.8	2.7
403 Salvation Army	1	149	96	435	.4	1.3
413 S.D.A.	3	646	NR	768	.7	2.3
416 Sikh	1	NR	NR	NR	-	-
419 So Bapt Conv	10	2,209	869	2,724 *	2.3	8.2
435 Unitarian-Univ	1	74	NR	91 *	.1	.3
443 Un C of Christ	2	390	223	481 *	.4	1.4
449 Un Methodist	7	2,302	1,018	2,839 *	2.4	8.5
463 Vineyard	1	130	120	160 *	.1	.5
469 WELS	2	122	85	155	.1	.5
496 Jewish Est	1	NR	NR	320	.3	1.0
499 Indep.Non-Char	2	150	490	550	.5	1.7

NR–Not Reported   *Total adherents estimated from known number of communicant, confirmed, full members.   - Represents a percentage less than 0.1.   Percentages may not total 100 due to rounding.

Table 4: Religious Congregations by County and Group: 2000

Religious Group	Number of Churches, Synagogues, Mosques, or Temples	Number of Communicant, Confirmed, or Full Members	Number of Attendees	Total Adherents		
				Number of Adherents	% of Total Pop.	% of Total Adh.
MINERAL	**5**	**224**	**176**	**319 ***	**38.4**	**100.0**
081 Catholic	1	NR	NR	40	4.8	12.5
167 Chs of Christ	1	4	33	8	1.0	2.5
193 Episcopal	1	NR	12	8	1.0	2.5
419 So Bapt Conv	1	172	63	206 *	24.8	64.6
443 Un C of Christ	1	48	68	57 *	6.9	17.9
MOFFAT	**22**	**2,075**	**675**	**5,203 ***	**39.5**	**100.0**
053 Assemb of God	2	83	137	210	1.6	4.0
081 Catholic	1	NR	NR	1,170	8.9	22.5
097 Chr Chs&Chs Cr	1	250	NR	317 *	2.4	6.1
127 Ch God (Cleve)	1	116	33	147 *	1.1	2.8
151 L-D Saints	3	NR	NR	1,068	8.1	20.5
165 Ch of Nazarene	1	31	0	31	.2	.6
167 Chs of Christ	2	106	100	148	1.1	2.8
193 Episcopal	1	NR	22	62	.5	1.2
207 E.L.C.A.	1	79	30	103	.8	2.0
246 Greek Orthodox	1	NR	NR	153	1.2	2.9
283 Luth—MO Synod	1	150	61	200	1.5	3.8
306 NT IndBapt&Rltd	1	102	NR	129 *	1.0	2.5
413 S.D.A.	1	40	NR	48	.4	.9
419 So Bapt Conv	2	855	180	1,083 *	8.2	20.8
443 Un C of Christ	2	201	80	255 *	1.9	4.9
449 Un Methodist	1	62	32	79 *	.6	1.5
MONTEZUMA	**40**	**3,119**	**1,712**	**7,340 ***	**30.8**	**100.0**
017 Amer Bapt Assn	2	74	NR	94 *	.4	1.3
019 Amer Bapt USA	2	328	181	415 *	1.7	5.7
053 Assemb of God	5	332	449	825	3.5	11.2
056 Baha'i	1	40	NR	40	.2	.5
059 Bapt Miss Assn	2	55	45	70 *	.3	1.0
081 Catholic	3	NR	NR	1,015	4.3	13.8
097 Chr Chs&Chs Cr	1	125	NR	158 *	.7	2.2
151 L-D Saints	5	NR	NR	1,729	7.3	23.6
165 Ch of Nazarene	1	91	58	91	.4	1.2
167 Chs of Christ	4	246	245	304	1.3	4.1
193 Episcopal	1	NR	84	289	1.2	3.9
226 Friends-USA	1	30	NR	38 *	.2	.5
263 Int Foursq Gos	1	18	24	24 *	.1	.3
283 Luth—MO Synod	1	319	172	416	1.7	5.7
355 Presb Ch (USA)	1	154	75	195 *	.8	2.7
360 Prim Bapt Chrch	1	NR	NR	NR	-	-
413 S.D.A.	1	201	NR	239	1.0	3.3
419 So Bapt Conv	4	647	148	818 *	3.4	11.1
449 Un Methodist	3	459	231	580 *	2.4	7.9
MONTROSE	**47**	**5,072**	**3,071**	**9,918 ***	**29.7**	**100.0**
019 Amer Bapt USA	2	404	130	506 *	1.5	5.1
053 Assemb of God	4	272	380	439	1.3	4.4
056 Baha'i	0	16	NR	16	-	.2
081 Catholic	3	NR	NR	2,000	6.0	20.2
084 Calvary Chapel	1	NR	NR	NR	-	-
097 Chr Chs&Chs Cr	2	770	NR	965 *	2.9	9.7
127 Ch God (Cleve)	1	220	81	276 *	.8	2.8
143 CG in Cr(Menn)	1	62	NR	78 *	.2	.8
145 Ch God Prophcy	1	22	NR	27 *	.1	.3
151 L-D Saints	3	NR	NR	770	2.3	7.8
165 Ch of Nazarene	1	99	72	99	.3	1.0
167 Chs of Christ	3	179	245	281	.8	2.8
179 Consrv Bapt	1	NR	112	112	.3	1.1
193 Episcopal	1	NR	85	127	.4	1.3
207 E.L.C.A.	1	432	130	538	1.6	5.4
263 Int Foursq Gos	2	72	481	481 *	1.4	4.8
283 Luth—MO Synod	1	84	55	103	.3	1.0
297 Mennonite;Other	1	41	NR	51 *	.2	.5
306 NT IndBapt&Rltd	2	205	NR	256 *	.8	2.6
339 Pent Ch of God	2	27	NR	60	.2	.6
355 Presb Ch (USA)	1	423	501	530 *	1.6	5.3
356 Presb Ch Amer	1	96	0	119	.4	1.2
413 S.D.A.	3	283	NR	337	1.0	3.4
419 So Bapt Conv	3	580	331	727 *	2.2	7.3
443 Un C of Christ	2	128	82	160 *	.5	1.6
449 Un Methodist	2	606	363	759 *	2.3	7.7
469 WELS	2	51	23	101	.3	1.0
MORGAN	**41**	**6,211**	**2,891**	**15,976 ***	**58.8**	**100.0**
019 Amer Bapt USA	1	370	78	483 *	1.8	3.0
053 Assemb of God	3	312	403	575	2.1	3.6
056 Baha'i	0	19	NR	19	.1	.1
081 Catholic	3	NR	NR	7,162	26.4	44.8
093 Chr Ch (Disc)	1	331	131	432 *	1.6	2.7
145 Ch God Prophcy	1	22	NR	28 *	.1	.2
151 L-D Saints	1	NR	NR	419	1.5	2.6
165 Ch of Nazarene	2	243	228	257	.9	1.6
167 Chs of Christ	2	124	130	168	.6	1.1
173 Comm of Christ	1	57	NR	57	.2	.4
179 Consrv Bapt	1	NR	50	50	.2	.3
181 Consrv Congr	1	165	90	216 *	.8	1.4
193 Episcopal	1	NR	29	98	.4	.6
207 E.L.C.A.	3	589	256	800	2.9	5.0
263 Int Foursq Gos	2	173	235	235 *	.9	1.5
283 Luth—MO Synod	1	576	206	776	2.9	4.9
306 NT IndBapt&Rltd	1	102	NR	133 *	.5	.8
355 Presb Ch (USA)	3	491	208	642 *	2.4	4.0
413 S.D.A.	1	38	NR	45	.2	.3
419 So Bapt Conv	3	1,038	186	1,356 *	5.0	8.5
443 Un C of Christ	3	791	276	1,033 *	3.8	6.5
449 Un Methodist	4	676	335	883 *	3.2	5.5
469 WELS	2	94	50	109	.4	.7
OTERO	**52**	**4,436**	**2,329**	**15,714 ***	**77.4**	**100.0**
019 Amer Bapt USA	3	328	193	410 *	2.0	2.6
053 Assemb of God	3	129	187	291	1.4	1.9
056 Baha'i	0	9	NR	9	-	.1
081 Catholic	4	NR	NR	9,441	46.5	60.1
093 Chr Ch (Disc)	4	552	134	690 *	3.4	4.4
097 Chr Chs&Chs Cr	1	60	NR	75 *	.4	.5
123 Ch God (Ander)	2	NR	80	80	.4	.5
127 Ch God (Cleve)	1	15	12	19 *	.1	.1
151 L-D Saints	1	NR	NR	372	1.8	2.4
157 Ch of Brethren	1	39	25	49 *	.2	.3
165 Ch of Nazarene	4	230	223	296	1.5	1.9
167 Chs of Christ	3	154	166	196	1.0	1.2
193 Episcopal	1	NR	41	114	.6	.7
207 E.L.C.A.	2	204	102	251	1.2	1.6
283 Luth—MO Synod	2	139	68	154	.8	1.0
288 Mennonite USA	3	304	176	381 *	1.9	2.4
306 NT IndBapt&Rltd	1	102	NR	127 *	.6	.8
355 Presb Ch (USA)	2	374	183	468 *	2.3	3.0
388 Reg Bapt Gen As	2	138	106	173 *	.9	1.1
413 S.D.A.	1	118	NR	140	.7	.9
419 So Bapt Conv	5	631	231	789 *	3.9	5.0
449 Un Methodist	6	910	402	1,139 *	5.6	7.2
496 Jewish Est	0	NR	NR	50	.2	.3
OURAY	**8**	**287**	**336**	**1,295 ***	**34.6**	**100.0**
053 Assemb of God	1	32	42	42	1.1	3.2
076 Buddhism	1	NR	NR	NR	-	-
081 Catholic	1	NR	NR	358	9.6	27.6
151 L-D Saints	1	NR	NR	486	13.0	37.5
167 Chs of Christ	1	5	10	7	.2	.5
193 Episcopal	1	NR	49	100	2.7	7.7
355 Presb Ch (USA)	1	154	165	186 *	5.0	14.4
419 So Bapt Conv	1	96	70	116 *	3.1	9.0
PARK	**15**	**591**	**433**	**1,724 ***	**11.9**	**100.0**
053 Assemb of God	1	12	12	16	.1	.9
056 Baha'i	0	11	NR	11	.1	.6
057 Bapt Gen Conf	1	122	170	170 *	1.2	9.9
081 Catholic	2	NR	NR	639	4.4	37.1
097 Chr Chs&Chs Cr	1	60	NR	73 *	.5	4.2
151 L-D Saints	2	NR	NR	538	3.7	31.2
167 Chs of Christ	1	4	4	4	-	.2
283 Luth—MO Synod	1	160	90	0	-	-

NR–Not Reported *Total adherents estimated from known number of communicant, confirmed, full members. - Represents a percentage less than 0.1. Percentages may not total 100 due to rounding.

Table 4: Religious Congregations by County and Group: 2000

Religious Group	Number of Churches, Synagogues, Mosques, or Temples	Number of Communicant, Confirmed, or Full Members	Number of Attendees	Total Adherents		
				Number of Adherents	% of Total Pop.	% of Total Adh.
331 OCA: Ter Diocs	1	4	NR	7	-	.4
355 Presb Ch (USA)	1	51	47	62 *	.4	3.6
413 S.D.A.	1	29	NR	35	.2	2.0
419 So Bapt Conv	2	30	33	37 *	.3	2.1
449 Un Methodist	1	108	77	132 *	.9	7.7
PHILLIPS	**16**	**1,573**	**834**	**2,734 ***	**61.0**	**100.0**
053 Assemb of God	1	28	35	35	.8	1.3
081 Catholic	2	NR	NR	663	14.8	24.3
097 Chr Chs&Chs Cr	1	150	NR	188 *	4.2	6.9
157 Ch of Brethren	1	74	37	93 *	2.1	3.4
165 Ch of Nazarene	1	31	0	31	.7	1.1
167 Chs of Christ	2	72	81	99	2.2	3.6
179 Consrv Bapt	1	NR	75	75	1.7	2.7
201 Evan Cov Ch	1	30	30	38 *	.8	1.4
283 Luth—MO Synod	3	568	289	734	16.4	26.8
413 S.D.A.	1	13	NR	15	.3	.5
419 So Bapt Conv	0	61	78	77 *	1.7	2.8
449 Un Methodist	2	546	209	686 *	15.3	25.1
PITKIN	**11**	**183**	**278**	**2,764 ***	**18.6**	**100.0**
056 Baha'i	0	7	NR	7	-	.3
081 Catholic	2	NR	NR	1,144	7.7	41.4
151 L-D Saints	1	NR	NR	157	1.1	5.7
179 Consrv Bapt	1	NR	50	50	.3	1.8
193 Episcopal	1	NR	123	442	3.0	16.0
283 Luth—MO Synod	1	40	39	58	.4	2.1
435 Unitarian-Univ	1	10	NR	11 *	.1	.4
449 Un Methodist	2	126	66	145 *	1.0	5.2
496 Jewish Est	2	NR	NR	750	5.0	27.1
PROWERS	**38**	**3,126**	**1,452**	**8,086 ***	**55.8**	**100.0**
017 Amer Bapt Assn	1	40	NR	52 *	.4	.6
019 Amer Bapt USA	2	471	221	611 *	4.2	7.6
053 Assemb of God	2	75	98	139	1.0	1.7
056 Baha'i	0	4	NR	4	-	-
081 Catholic	3	NR	NR	3,513	24.3	43.4
097 Chr Chs&Chs Cr	2	601	NR	779 *	5.4	9.6
123 Ch God (Ander)	2	NR	105	105	.7	1.3
151 L-D Saints	1	NR	NR	187	1.3	2.3
157 Ch of Brethren	1	110	50	143 *	1.0	1.8
165 Ch of Nazarene	3	125	119	161	1.1	2.0
167 Chs of Christ	5	163	160	245	1.7	3.0
193 Episcopal	1	NR	32	93	.6	1.2
203 Evan Free Ch	1	15	25	25	.2	.3
226 Friends-USA	2	88	NR	114 *	.8	1.4
263 Int Foursq Gos	1	113	147	147 *	1.0	1.8
283 Luth—MO Synod	1	105	49	150	1.0	1.9
306 NT IndBapt&Rltd	1	102	NR	132 *	.9	1.6
355 Presb Ch (USA)	2	125	86	162 *	1.1	2.0
413 S.D.A.	1	71	NR	84	.6	1.0
419 So Bapt Conv	1	196	54	254 *	1.8	3.1
449 Un Methodist	5	722	306	936 *	6.5	11.6
496 Jewish Est	0	NR	NR	50	.3	.6
PUEBLO	**124**	**16,188**	**9,534**	**79,927 ***	**56.5**	**100.0**
017 Amer Bapt Assn	1	40	NR	50 *	-	.1
019 Amer Bapt USA	4	1,415	500	1,763 *	1.2	2.2
053 Assemb of God	6	1,313	1,915	2,854	2.0	3.6
056 Baha'i	1	96	NR	96	.1	.1
081 Catholic	21	NR	NR	54,408	38.5	68.1
084 Calvary Chapel	1	NR	NR	NR	-	-
089 Chr & Miss Al	1	82	NR	135	.1	.2
093 Chr Ch (Disc)	2	1,158	307	1,443 *	1.0	1.8
097 Chr Chs&Chs Cr	3	275	NR	343 *	.2	.4
121 Ch God (Abr)	1	5	5	6 *	-	-
123 Ch God (Ander)	1	NR	80	80	.1	.1
127 Ch God (Cleve)	3	459	578	626 *	.4	.8
145 Ch God Prophcy	1	22	NR	27 *	-	-
151 L-D Saints	5	NR	NR	2,347	1.7	2.9
157 Ch of Brethren	1	9	0	11 *	-	-
165 Ch of Nazarene	4	727	361	741	.5	.9

Religious Group	Number of Churches, Synagogues, Mosques, or Temples	Number of Communicant, Confirmed, or Full Members	Number of Attendees	Total Adherents		
				Number of Adherents	% of Total Pop.	% of Total Adh.
167 Chs of Christ	5	621	504	812	.6	1.0
173 Comm of Christ	1	189	NR	189	.1	.2
179 Consrv Bapt	1	NR	30	30	-	-
193 Episcopal	2	NR	309	735	.5	.9
203 Evan Free Ch	2	117	205	205	.1	.3
207 E.L.C.A.	2	719	344	957	.7	1.2
221 Free Methodist	1	30	55	55	-	.1
226 Friends-USA	1	44	NR	55 *	-	.1
246 Greek Orthodox	1	NR	NR	234	.2	.3
263 Int Foursq Gos	2	111	186	186 *	.1	.2
267 Muslim Est	1	NR	101	288	.2	.4
283 Luth—MO Synod	3	600	279	785	.6	1.0
288 Mennonite USA	1	50	30	62 *	-	.1
290 Metro Comm Ch	1	22	16	27 *	-	-
306 NT IndBapt&Rltd	1	102	NR	127 *	.1	.2
331 OCA: Ter Diocs	1	31	NR	60	-	.1
349 Pent Holiness	1	20	20	25 *	-	-
355 Presb Ch (USA)	3	1,209	556	1,507 *	1.1	1.9
388 Reg Bapt Gen As	2	189	85	85 *	.1	.1
403 Salvation Army	1	97	21	120	.1	.2
413 S.D.A.	2	502	NR	598	.4	.7
419 So Bapt Conv	13	2,165	1,119	2,697 *	1.9	3.4
435 Unitarian-Univ	1	42	NR	52 *	-	.1
443 Un C of Christ	2	229	106	285 *	.2	.4
449 Un Methodist	10	2,243	955	2,795 *	2.0	3.5
463 Vineyard	2	350	245	436 *	.3	.5
467 Wesleyan	1	19	28	42	-	.1
469 WELS	2	130	94	173	.1	.2
496 Jewish Est	1	NR	NR	425	.3	.5
499 Indep.Non-Char	1	756	500	950	.7	1.2
RIO BLANCO	**19**	**478**	**359**	**2,231 ***	**37.3**	**100.0**
019 Amer Bapt USA	1	44	70	70 *	1.2	3.1
053 Assemb of God	2	32	43	77	1.3	3.5
056 Baha'i	0	2	NR	2	-	.1
081 Catholic	2	NR	NR	584	9.8	26.2
097 Chr Chs&Chs Cr	2	160	NR	198 *	3.3	8.9
151 L-D Saints	3	NR	NR	835	13.9	37.4
167 Chs of Christ	2	29	31	35	.6	1.6
193 Episcopal	2	NR	62	172	2.9	7.7
283 Luth—MO Synod	1	23	10	26	.4	1.2
413 S.D.A.	1	11	NR	13	.2	.6
419 So Bapt Conv	2	46	77	57 *	1.0	2.6
449 Un Methodist	1	131	66	162 *	2.7	7.3
RIO GRANDE	**26**	**2,117**	**1,253**	**7,161 ***	**57.7**	**100.0**
019 Amer Bapt USA	1	66	45	84 *	.7	1.2
053 Assemb of God	3	191	259	371	3.0	5.2
056 Baha'i	0	1	NR	1	-	-
081 Catholic	3	NR	NR	3,913	31.5	54.6
089 Chr & Miss Al	1	10	NR	73	.6	1.0
093 Chr Ch (Disc)	1	36	15	46 *	.4	.6
151 L-D Saints	2	NR	NR	444	3.6	6.2
165 Ch of Nazarene	1	250	243	250	2.0	3.5
167 Chs of Christ	2	81	100	105	.8	1.5
262 Int Cou Comm Ch	1	122	NR	154 *	1.2	2.2
283 Luth—MO Synod	1	121	75	151	1.2	2.1
355 Presb Ch (USA)	2	199	127	252 *	2.0	3.5
413 S.D.A.	1	34	NR	40	.3	.6
419 So Bapt Conv	3	635	231	804 *	6.5	11.2
449 Un Methodist	3	355	143	449 *	3.6	6.3
469 WELS	1	16	15	24	.2	.3
ROUTT	**20**	**1,424**	**1,043**	**6,013 ***	**30.5**	**100.0**
053 Assemb of God	1	65	86	112	.6	1.9
056 Baha'i	0	7	NR	7	-	.1
081 Catholic	2	NR	NR	3,068	15.6	51.0
151 L-D Saints	1	NR	NR	222	1.1	3.7
167 Chs of Christ	2	48	53	69	.4	1.1
193 Episcopal	1	NR	155	572	2.9	9.5
203 Evan Free Ch	1	48	90	90	.5	1.5
283 Luth—MO Synod	1	352	250	535	2.7	8.9
306 NT IndBapt&Rltd	2	205	NR	247 *	1.3	4.1

NR–Not Reported *Total adherents estimated from known number of communicant, confirmed, full members. - Represents a percentage less than 0.1. Percentages may not total 100 due to rounding.

Table 4: Religious Congregations by County and Group: 2000

Religious Group	Number of Churches, Synagogues, Mosques, or Temples	Number of Communicant, Confirmed, or Full Members	Number of Attendees	Total Adherents		
				Number of Adherents	% of Total Pop.	% of Total Adh.
413 S.D.A.	1	21	NR	25	.1	.4
419 So Bapt Conv	3	140	145	169 *	.9	2.8
443 Un C of Christ	1	106	56	128 *	.7	2.1
449 Un Methodist	2	415	193	500 *	2.5	8.3
469 WELS	1	17	15	19	.1	.3
496 Jewish Est	1	NR	NR	250	1.3	4.2
SAGUACHE	**22**	**660**	**335**	**2,915 ***	**49.3**	**100.0**
019 Amer Bapt USA	1	75	30	95 *	1.6	3.3
053 Assemb of God	1	29	35	56	.9	1.9
056 Baha'i	0	13	NR	13	.2	.4
076 Buddhism	3	NR	NR	NR	-	-
081 Catholic	3	NR	NR	1,856	31.4	63.7
089 Chr & Miss Al	1	0	NR	45	.8	1.5
127 Ch God (Cleve)	1	16	0	20 *	.3	.7
143 CG in Cr(Menn)	1	74	NR	94 *	1.6	3.2
151 L-D Saints	1	NR	NR	163	2.8	5.6
167 Chs of Christ	2	28	28	33	.6	1.1
252 Hindu	1	NR	NR	NR	-	-
313 N Am Bapt Conf	1	0	0	0 *	-	-
419 So Bapt Conv	4	224	166	284 *	4.8	9.7
449 Un Methodist	2	201	76	256 *	4.3	8.8
SAN JUAN	**4**	**45**	**32**	**188 ***	**33.7**	**100.0**
056 Baha'i	0	2	NR	2	.4	1.1
081 Catholic	1	NR	NR	112	20.1	59.6
151 L-D Saints	1	NR	NR	22	3.9	11.7
167 Chs of Christ	1	10	10	13	2.3	6.9
419 So Bapt Conv	0	4	8	5 *	.9	2.7
443 Un C of Christ	1	29	14	34 *	6.1	18.1
SAN MIGUEL	**9**	**384**	**288**	**2,131 ***	**32.3**	**100.0**
056 Baha'i	0	2	NR	2	-	.1
081 Catholic	1	NR	NR	1,253	19.0	58.8
097 Chr Chs&Chs Cr	1	50	NR	58 *	.9	2.7
151 L-D Saints	1	NR	NR	273	4.1	12.8
175 Congr Chr Chs	1	35	60	40 *	.6	1.9
193 Episcopal	1	NR	15	36	.5	1.7
349 Pent Holiness	1	43	50	50 *	.8	2.3
355 Presb Ch (USA)	1	94	52	109 *	1.7	5.1
419 So Bapt Conv	2	160	111	185 *	2.8	8.7
496 Jewish Est	0	NR	NR	125	1.9	5.9
SEDGWICK	**11**	**840**	**386**	**1,479 ***	**53.8**	**100.0**
053 Assemb of God	1	30	35	55	2.0	3.7
081 Catholic	2	NR	NR	394	14.3	26.6
097 Chr Chs&Chs Cr	1	150	NR	181 *	6.6	12.2
179 Consrv Bapt	1	NR	75	75	2.7	5.1
283 Luth—MO Synod	1	172	80	187	6.8	12.6
288 Mennonite USA	1	65	41	78 *	2.8	5.3
355 Presb Ch (USA)	1	38	30	46 *	1.7	3.1
413 S.D.A.	1	19	NR	23	.8	1.6
449 Un Methodist	2	366	125	440 *	16.0	29.7
SUMMIT	**17**	**1,001**	**1,108**	**4,074 ***	**17.3**	**100.0**
053 Assemb of God	1	64	78	92	.4	2.3
056 Baha'i	0	4	NR	4	-	.1
081 Catholic	4	NR	NR	2,334	9.9	57.3
151 L-D Saints	1	NR	NR	297	1.3	7.3
167 Chs of Christ	1	45	65	65	.3	1.6
193 Episcopal	1	NR	119	171	.7	4.2
207 E.L.C.A.	1	396	239	544	2.3	13.4
283 Luth—MO Synod	1	45	41	48	.2	1.2
413 S.D.A.	1	0	NR	0	-	-
419 So Bapt Conv	4	109	396	127 *	.5	3.1
435 Unitarian-Univ	1	27	NR	31 *	.1	.8
449 Un Methodist	1	311	170	361 *	1.5	8.9
TELLER	**21**	**1,978**	**1,009**	**4,991 ***	**24.3**	**100.0**
019 Amer Bapt USA	1	78	0	96 *	.5	1.9
053 Assemb of God	1	22	30	38	.2	.8
056 Baha'i	0	12	NR	12	.1	.2
081 Catholic	3	NR	NR	1,901	9.2	38.1
084 Calvary Chapel	1	NR	NR	NR	-	-
097 Chr Chs&Chs Cr	1	206	NR	255 *	1.2	5.1
151 L-D Saints	1	NR	NR	416	2.0	8.3
165 Ch of Nazarene	1	67	72	134	.7	2.7
167 Chs of Christ	1	75	95	90	.4	1.8
193 Episcopal	2	NR	76	131	.6	2.6
226 Friends-USA	1	44	NR	54 *	.3	1.1
283 Luth—MO Synod	1	425	255	576	2.8	11.5
306 NT IndBapt&Rltd	1	102	NR	126 *	.6	2.5
413 S.D.A.	2	171	NR	203	1.0	4.1
419 So Bapt Conv	3	424	254	524 *	2.5	10.5
449 Un Methodist	1	352	227	435 *	2.1	8.7
WASHINGTON	**17**	**1,401**	**880**	**2,579 ***	**52.4**	**100.0**
053 Assemb of God	2	30	36	52	1.1	2.0
081 Catholic	1	NR	NR	708	14.4	27.5
167 Chs of Christ	2	53	48	65	1.3	2.5
207 E.L.C.A.	3	333	154	462	9.4	17.9
263 Int Foursq Gos	1	203	316	316 *	6.4	12.3
283 Luth—MO Synod	1	74	40	100	2.0	3.9
306 NT IndBapt&Rltd	1	102	NR	126 *	2.6	4.9
355 Presb Ch (USA)	2	289	121	358 *	7.3	13.9
413 S.D.A.	1	22	NR	26	.5	1.0
419 So Bapt Conv	1	69	72	86 *	1.7	3.3
449 Un Methodist	2	226	93	280 *	5.7	10.9
WELD	**157**	**23,424**	**14,322**	**66,592 ***	**36.8**	**100.0**
017 Amer Bapt Assn	1	40	NR	51 *	-	.1
019 Amer Bapt USA	2	338	210	433 *	.2	.7
053 Assemb of God	14	1,262	1,666	2,385	1.3	3.6
056 Baha'i	1	47	NR	47	-	.1
057 Bapt Gen Conf	1	397	251	509 *	.3	.8
076 Buddhism	2	NR	NR	NR	-	-
081 Catholic	16	NR	NR	26,623	14.7	40.0
084 Calvary Chapel	1	NR	NR	NR	-	-
089 Chr & Miss Al	1	32	NR	70	-	.1
093 Chr Ch (Disc)	3	802	242	1,028 *	.6	1.5
097 Chr Chs&Chs Cr	4	2,895	NR	3,710 *	2.1	5.6
105 Christian Ref	1	102	85	131 *	.1	.2
123 Ch God (Ander)	1	NR	20	20	-	-
127 Ch God (Cleve)	1	28	27	36 *	-	.1
145 Ch God Prophcy	1	22	NR	28 *	-	-
151 L-D Saints	9	NR	NR	3,427	1.9	5.1
157 Ch of Brethren	1	66	33	85 *	-	.1
165 Ch of Nazarene	2	454	328	539	.3	.8
167 Chs of Christ	3	265	205	348	.2	.5
173 Comm of Christ	1	37	NR	37	-	.1
175 Congr Chr Chs	1	25	25	32 *	-	-
179 Consrv Bapt	3	NR	616	616	.3	.9
181 Consrv Congr	2	650	377	833 *	.5	1.3
193 Episcopal	3	NR	332	1,044	.6	1.6
201 Evan Cov Ch	1	0	221	221 *	.1	.3
203 Evan Free Ch	8	861	1,590	1,590	.9	2.4
207 E.L.C.A.	6	2,605	996	3,693	2.0	5.5
221 Free Methodist	1	16	42	42	-	.1
223 Free Will Bapt	1	30	NR	38 *	-	.1
263 Int Foursq Gos	4	773	613	991 *	.5	1.5
267 Muslim Est	1	NR	290	1,313	.7	2.0
283 Luth—MO Synod	7	1,567	780	2,095	1.2	3.1
288 Mennonite USA	1	91	70	117 *	.1	.2
306 NT IndBapt&Rltd	2	205	NR	263 *	.1	.4
313 N Am Bapt Conf	2	244	225	313 *	.2	.5
339 Pent Ch of God	1	24	NR	49	-	.1
349 Pent Holiness	2	58	80	74 *	-	.1
355 Presb Ch (USA)	4	1,134	754	1,452 *	.8	2.2
356 Presb Ch Amer	1	0	0	0	-	-
388 Reg Bapt Gen As	1	30	50	50 *	-	.1
403 Salvation Army	1	123	40	400	.2	.6
413 S.D.A.	4	644	NR	766	.4	1.2
419 So Bapt Conv	10	1,348	642	1,727 *	1.0	2.6
435 Unitarian-Univ	1	58	NR	74 *	-	.1

NR–Not Reported *Total adherents estimated from known number of communicant, confirmed, full members. - Represents a percentage less than 0.1. Percentages may not total 100 due to rounding.

Table 4: Religious Congregations by County and Group: 2000

Religious Group	Number of Churches, Synagogues, Mosques, or Temples	Number of Communicant, Confirmed, or Full Members	Number of Attendees	Total Adherents: Number of Adherents	Total Adherents: % of Total Pop.	Total Adherents: % of Total Adh.
443 Un C of Christ	4	2,355	731	3,018 *	1.7	4.5
449 Un Methodist	13	2,629	1,232	3,368 *	1.9	5.1
463 Vineyard	1	130	120	167 *	.1	.3
467 Wesleyan	2	589	1,105	2,224	1.2	3.3
469 WELS	2	148	124	215	.1	.3
498 Indep.Charis.	1	300	200	300	.2	.5
YUMA	**28**	**3,150**	**1,375**	**5,710 ***	**58.0**	**100.0**
053 Assemb of God	2	47	50	71	.7	1.2
056 Baha'i	0	1	NR	1	-	-
081 Catholic	2	NR	NR	1,663	16.9	29.1
093 Chr Ch (Disc)	1	350	70	444 *	4.5	7.8
097 Chr Chs&Chs Cr	1	65	NR	82 *	.8	1.4
165 Ch of Nazarene	3	197	191	287	2.9	5.0
167 Chs of Christ	2	51	54	71	.7	1.2
173 Comm of Christ	1	84	NR	84	.9	1.5
263 Int Foursq Gos	1	20	3	25 *	.3	.4
283 Luth—MO Synod	2	667	287	872	8.9	15.3
306 NT IndBapt&Rltd	1	102	NR	129 *	1.3	2.3
355 Presb Ch (USA)	2	319	176	404 *	4.1	7.1
413 S.D.A.	2	49	NR	59	.6	1.0
419 So Bapt Conv	3	397	222	503 *	5.1	8.8
443 Un C of Christ	1	106	47	134 *	1.4	2.3
449 Un Methodist	4	695	275	881 *	9.0	15.4

CONNECTICUT

Religious Group	Number of Churches, Synagogues, Mosques, or Temples	Number of Communicant, Confirmed, or Full Members	Number of Attendees	Total Adherents: Number of Adherents	Total Adherents: % of Total Pop.	Total Adherents: % of Total Adh.
The State.....	1,955	278,823	151,206	1,971,102 *	57.9	100.0
FAIRFIELD	**475**	**72,974**	**40,293**	**619,007 ***	**70.1**	**100.0**
007 OCA: Alban Dioc	1	NR	NR	225	-	-
019 Amer Bapt USA	23	9,955	3,169	12,538 *	1.4	2.0
022 Carp Rus Orth	4	1,123	NR	1,913	.2	.3
034 Ant Orth of NA	2	628	NR	1,256	.1	.2
050 Armen Ap Etchm	1	96	NR	600	.1	.1
053 Assemb of God	21	2,852	3,222	4,560	.5	.7
056 Baha'i	4	241	NR	241	-	-
057 Bapt Gen Conf	2	678	85	854 *	.1	.1
076 Buddhism	1	NR	NR	NR	-	-
081 Catholic	94	NR	NR	433,832	49.2	70.1
084 Calvary Chapel	1	NR	NR	NR	-	-
089 Chr & Miss Al	5	257	NR	425	-	.1
093 Chr Ch (Disc)	3	428	50	539 *	.1	.1
097 Chr Chs&Chs Cr	1	56	NR	71 *	-	-
127 Ch God (Cleve)	21	2,345	1,465	3,054 *	.3	.5
145 Ch God Prophcy	3	246	NR	309 *	-	-
151 L-D Saints	13	NR	NR	2,759	.3	.4
165 Ch of Nazarene	7	294	351	544	.1	.1
167 Chs of Christ	3	346	355	495	.1	.1
173 Comm of Christ	1	87	NR	87	-	-
175 Congr Chr Chs	1	40	30	50 *	-	-
176 Congr Ad Afl	1	477	NR	601 *	.1	.1
179 Consrv Bapt	3	NR	231	231	-	-
193 Episcopal	47	NR	7,352	27,173	3.1	4.4
201 Evan Cov Ch	2	282	316	355 *	-	.1
203 Evan Free Ch	5	786	1,705	1,705	.2	.3
207 E.L.C.A.	16	5,185	1,861	6,823	.8	1.1
221 Free Methodist	2	374	440	508	.1	.1
226 Friends-USA	2	100	NR	126 *	-	-
246 Greek Orthodox	4	NR	NR	4,380	.5	.7
252 Hindu	1	NR	NR	NR	-	-
263 Int Foursq Gos	1	30	50	50 *	-	-
264 Int Chs of Crst	1	137	229	184	-	-
265 Int Pent C Chr	1	60	50	75	-	-
267 Muslim Est	9	NR	3,284	14,737	1.7	2.4
268 Jain	2	NR	NR	NR	-	-
283 Luth—MO Synod	10	3,274	1,324	4,246	.5	.7
288 Mennonite USA	2	89	71	132 *	-	-
331 OCA: Ter Diocs	3	398	NR	560	.1	.1
335 Orth Pres Ch	1	52	68	108	-	-
355 Presb Ch (USA)	9	5,115	2,167	6,443 *	.7	1.0
356 Presb Ch Amer	2	0	0	0	-	-
388 Reg Bapt Gen As	1	105	163	163 *	-	-
397 OCA: Roman Dioc	1	NR	NR	312	-	.1
403 Salvation Army	4	275	195	642	.1	.1
413 S.D.A.	10	1,540	NR	1,833	.2	.3
416 Sikh	1	NR	NR	NR	-	-
419 So Bapt Conv	8	1,510	590	1,902 *	.2	.3
431 Ukrainian Orth	2	NR	NR	351	-	.1
435 Unitarian-Univ	4	911	NR	1,147 *	.1	.2
443 Un C of Christ	45	20,379	7,532	25,667 *	2.9	4.1
449 Un Methodist	34	12,135	3,876	15,284 *	1.7	2.5
469 WELS	1	88	62	117	-	-
496 Jewish Est	28	NR	NR	38,800	4.4	6.3
HARTFORD	**473**	**82,244**	**41,219**	**492,316 ***	**57.4**	**100.0**
019 Amer Bapt USA	29	10,744	3,136	13,304 *	1.6	2.7
049 Armen Ap Cilic	1	94	NR	420	-	.1
050 Armen Ap Etchm	2	214	NR	640	.1	.1
053 Assemb of God	16	2,196	2,424	3,694	.4	.8
056 Baha'i	6	299	NR	299	-	.1
057 Bapt Gen Conf	6	1,281	2,053	2,242 *	.3	.5
076 Buddhism	3	NR	NR	NR	-	-
081 Catholic	97	NR	NR	329,076	38.4	66.8
084 Calvary Chapel	1	NR	NR	NR	-	-
089 Chr & Miss Al	4	175	NR	437	.1	.1
093 Chr Ch (Disc)	1	45	0	56 *	-	-
097 Chr Chs&Chs Cr	1	100	NR	124 *	-	-
105 Christian Ref	2	465	260	576 *	.1	.1
123 Ch God (Ander)	1	NR	80	80	-	-
127 Ch God (Cleve)	11	1,718	1,102	2,147 *	.3	.4
145 Ch God Prophcy	1	82	NR	102 *	-	-
151 L-D Saints	7	NR	NR	2,194	.3	.4
165 Ch of Nazarene	6	536	418	696	.1	.1
167 Chs of Christ	7	517	583	683	.1	.1
173 Comm of Christ	1	68	NR	68	-	-
175 Congr Chr Chs	4	1,157	317	1,433 *	.2	.3
176 Congr Ad Afl	1	93	NR	115 *	-	-
179 Consrv Bapt	1	NR	85	85	-	-
181 Consrv Congr	1	276	135	342 *	-	.1
193 Episcopal	39	NR	4,814	15,382	1.8	3.1
201 Evan Cov Ch	5	1,253	1,219	1,595 *	.2	.3
203 Evan Free Ch	3	280	355	355	-	.1
207 E.L.C.A.	24	9,235	3,136	12,696	1.5	2.6
226 Friends-USA	1	43	NR	53 *	-	-
246 Greek Orthodox	4	NR	NR	3,096	.4	.6
249 Assyr Apost Ch	1	NR	NR	516	.1	.1
252 Hindu	2	NR	NR	NR	-	-
262 Int Cou Comm Ch	1	32	NR	40 *	-	-
264 Int Chs of Crst	1	205	489	301	-	.1
267 Muslim Est	4	NR	912	3,364	.4	.7
283 Luth—MO Synod	8	2,952	1,245	3,750	.4	.8
290 Metro Comm Ch	1	30	20	37 *	-	-
331 OCA: Ter Diocs	2	405	NR	562	.1	.1
339 Pent Ch of God	1	70	NR	80	-	-
355 Presb Ch (USA)	5	1,065	720	1,318 *	.2	.3
356 Presb Ch Amer	1	72	84	94	-	-
370 Ref Baptist Chs	1	NR	NR	NR	-	-
388 Reg Bapt Gen As	2	170	215	219 *	-	-
401 Rus Orth Abroad	2	NR	NR	NR	-	-
403 Salvation Army	9	683	588	1,352	.2	.3
413 S.D.A.	9	1,866	NR	2,221	.3	.5
416 Sikh	1	NR	NR	NR	-	-
418 Southw Bapt Fel	1	NR	NR	NR	-	-
419 So Bapt Conv	9	853	405	1,056 *	.1	.2
431 Ukrainian Orth	2	NR	NR	1,521	.2	.3
435 Unitarian-Univ	5	1,366	NR	1,691 *	.2	.3
443 Un C of Christ	55	29,274	10,608	36,249 *	4.2	7.4
449 Un Methodist	32	10,979	3,669	13,595 *	1.6	2.8
463 Vineyard	1	40	50	50 *	-	-
467 Wesleyan	1	0	79	205	-	-
469 WELS	1	121	78	165	-	-
496 Jewish Est	25	NR	NR	30,000	3.5	6.1
499 Indep.Non-Char	4	1,190	1,940	1,940	.2	.4

NR–Not Reported *Total adherents estimated from known number of communicant, confirmed, full members. - Represents a percentage less than 0.1. Percentages may not total 100 due to rounding.

Table 4: Religious Congregations by County and Group: 2000

Religious Group	Number of Churches, Synagogues, Mosques, or Temples	Number of Communicant, Confirmed, or Full Members	Number of Attendees	Total Adherents		
				Number of Adherents	% of Total Pop.	% of Total Adh.
LITCHFIELD	**145**	**19,992**	**10,512**	**97,389 ***	**53.5**	**100.0**
019 Amer Bapt USA	5	1,083	541	1,337 *	.7	1.4
053 Assemb of God	3	304	303	680	.4	.7
056 Baha'i	0	77	NR	77	-	.1
081 Catholic	28	NR	NR	63,630	34.9	65.3
089 Chr & Miss Al	1	57	NR	132	.1	.1
097 Chr Chs&Chs Cr	1	30	NR	37 *	-	-
151 L-D Saints	1	NR	NR	329	.2	.3
167 Chs of Christ	1	72	65	102	.1	.1
175 Congr Chr Chs	4	310	160	383 *	.2	.4
193 Episcopal	22	NR	2,075	5,928	3.3	6.1
201 Evan Cov Ch	3	401	352	524 *	.3	.5
207 E.L.C.A.	5	1,631	566	2,124	1.2	2.2
226 Friends-USA	3	136	NR	168 *	.1	.2
263 Int Foursq Gos	1	23	43	43 *	-	-
283 Luth—MO Synod	4	833	418	1,116	.6	1.1
331 OCA: Ter Diocs	3	209	NR	242	.1	.2
388 Reg Bapt Gen As	2	250	438	438 *	.2	.4
403 Salvation Army	1	36	35	73	-	.1
413 S.D.A.	2	66	NR	78	-	.1
419 So Bapt Conv	2	403	299	497 *	.3	.5
435 Unitarian-Univ	2	105	NR	130 *	.1	.1
443 Un C of Christ	35	10,065	3,863	12,425 *	6.8	12.8
449 Un Methodist	13	3,901	1,354	4,816 *	2.6	4.9
496 Jewish Est	3	NR	NR	2,080	1.1	2.1
MIDDLESEX	**95**	**13,846**	**6,512**	**84,241 ***	**54.3**	**100.0**
019 Amer Bapt USA	6	898	190	1,097 *	.7	1.3
053 Assemb of God	5	206	209	338	.2	.4
056 Baha'i	0	19	NR	19	-	-
076 Buddhism	1	NR	NR	NR	-	-
081 Catholic	18	NR	NR	59,633	38.5	70.8
127 Ch God (Cleve)	1	46	45	56 *	-	.1
151 L-D Saints	1	NR	NR	395	.3	.5
167 Chs of Christ	1	35	45	50	-	.1
175 Congr Chr Chs	2	318	100	388 *	.3	.5
176 Congr Ad Afl	1	598	NR	730 *	.5	.9
193 Episcopal	12	NR	1,094	3,959	2.6	4.7
201 Evan Cov Ch	2	277	174	338 *	.2	.4
203 Evan Free Ch	1	153	263	263	.2	.3
207 E.L.C.A.	6	1,760	688	2,442	1.6	2.9
226 Friends-USA	1	43	NR	53 *	-	.1
252 Hindu	2	NR	NR	NR	-	-
283 Luth—MO Synod	1	269	108	358	.2	.4
331 OCA: Ter Diocs	1	40	NR	68	-	.1
403 Salvation Army	1	65	27	228	.1	.3
413 S.D.A.	1	29	NR	35	-	-
419 So Bapt Conv	2	96	0	117 *	.1	.1
443 Un C of Christ	19	6,686	2,505	8,165 *	5.3	9.7
449 Un Methodist	8	1,808	764	2,209 *	1.4	2.6
496 Jewish Est	1	NR	NR	2,800	1.8	3.3
499 Indep.Non-Char	1	500	300	500	.3	.6
NEW HAVEN	**423**	**51,027**	**30,096**	**442,847 ***	**53.7**	**100.0**
017 Amer Bapt Assn	1	20	NR	25 *	-	-
019 Amer Bapt USA	20	6,902	2,443	8,540 *	1.0	1.9
039 Ap Chr Ch(Naz)	1	20	35	35 *	-	-
053 Assemb of God	25	2,166	2,644	3,466	.4	.8
056 Baha'i	2	179	NR	179	-	-
057 Bapt Gen Conf	5	451	458	575 *	.1	.1
076 Buddhism	7	NR	NR	NR	-	-
081 Catholic	103	NR	NR	319,399	38.8	72.1
089 Chr & Miss Al	7	237	NR	529	.1	.1
097 Chr Chs&Chs Cr	4	158	NR	196 *	-	-
123 Ch God (Ander)	1	NR	100	100	-	-
127 Ch God (Cleve)	8	802	366	995 *	.1	.2
145 Ch God Prophcy	3	215	NR	267 *	-	.1
151 L-D Saints	7	NR	NR	1,896	.2	.4
165 Ch of Nazarene	3	52	61	93	-	-
167 Chs of Christ	8	537	552	860	.1	.2
173 Comm of Christ	1	60	NR	60	-	-
175 Congr Chr Chs	2	237	137	293 *	-	.1
179 Consrv Bapt	1	NR	150	150	-	-
193 Episcopal	43	NR	5,090	13,200	1.6	3.0
201 Evan Cov Ch	2	143	107	177 *	-	-
203 Evan Free Ch	5	433	825	825	.1	.2
207 E.L.C.A.	14	3,597	1,355	4,706	.6	1.1
226 Friends-USA	1	43	NR	53 *	-	-
246 Greek Orthodox	3	NR	NR	2,346	.3	.5
263 Int Foursq Gos	1	68	123	123 *	-	-
267 Muslim Est	7	NR	2,497	11,546	1.4	2.6
268 Jain	1	NR	NR	NR	-	-
283 Luth—MO Synod	7	1,730	821	2,306	.3	.5
288 Mennonite USA	1	80	64	99 *	-	-
290 Metro Comm Ch	1	99	81	81 *	-	-
313 N Am Bapt Conf	1	10	8	12 *	-	-
331 OCA: Ter Diocs	4	791	NR	942	.1	.2
335 Orth Pres Ch	1	76	100	111	-	-
355 Presb Ch (USA)	4	632	550	782 *	.1	.2
356 Presb Ch Amer	1	75	75	112	-	-
370 Ref Baptist Chs	1	NR	NR	NR	-	-
401 Rus Orth Abroad	1	NR	NR	NR	-	-
403 Salvation Army	5	400	307	924	.1	.2
413 S.D.A.	8	1,055	NR	1,256	.2	.3
416 Sikh	1	NR	NR	NR	-	-
419 So Bapt Conv	5	235	319	291 *	-	.1
431 Ukrainian Orth	1	NR	NR	177	-	-
435 Unitarian-Univ	4	601	NR	744 *	.1	.2
443 Un C of Christ	45	18,783	6,391	23,241 *	2.8	5.2
449 Un Methodist	23	7,920	2,226	9,801 *	1.2	2.2
463 Vineyard	2	270	211	334 *	-	.1
496 Jewish Est	19	NR	NR	28,900	3.5	6.5
498 Indep.Charis.	1	1,800	1,700	1,800	.2	.4
499 Indep.Non-Char	1	150	300	300	-	.1
NEW LONDON	**169**	**19,293**	**11,552**	**117,654 ***	**45.4**	**100.0**
019 Amer Bapt USA	19	5,261	1,850	6,502 *	2.5	5.5
053 Assemb of God	9	765	991	1,142	.4	1.0
056 Baha'i	1	85	NR	85	-	.1
081 Catholic	33	NR	NR	80,563	31.1	68.5
084 Calvary Chapel	1	NR	NR	NR	-	-
089 Chr & Miss Al	1	143	NR	201	.1	.2
127 Ch God (Cleve)	2	356	94	440 *	.2	.4
151 L-D Saints	3	NR	NR	1,236	.5	1.1
165 Ch of Nazarene	1	54	57	57	-	-
167 Chs of Christ	2	81	112	117	-	.1
173 Comm of Christ	1	51	NR	51	-	-
175 Congr Chr Chs	12	1,230	751	1,520 *	.6	1.3
176 Congr Ad Afl	1	41	NR	51 *	-	-
179 Consrv Bapt	5	NR	634	634	.2	.5
193 Episcopal	11	NR	1,567	4,915	1.9	4.2
203 Evan Free Ch	1	41	115	115	-	.1
207 E.L.C.A.	2	858	392	1,089	.4	.9
226 Friends-USA	1	43	NR	53 *	-	-
246 Greek Orthodox	1	NR	NR	537	.2	.5
263 Int Foursq Gos	1	28	111	111 *	-	.1
264 Int Chs of Crst	1	121	232	193	.1	.2
283 Luth—MO Synod	4	791	363	1,022	.4	.9
331 OCA: Ter Diocs	1	90	NR	138	.1	.1
355 Presb Ch (USA)	2	331	240	409 *	.2	.3
356 Presb Ch Amer	1	29	25	42	-	-
401 Rus Orth Abroad	1	NR	NR	NR	-	-
403 Salvation Army	2	192	109	586	.2	.5
413 S.D.A.	3	224	NR	267	.1	.2
418 Southw Bapt Fel	1	NR	NR	NR	-	-
419 So Bapt Conv	3	408	133	504 *	.2	.4
435 Unitarian-Univ	2	184	NR	227 *	.1	.2
443 Un C of Christ	20	5,509	2,420	6,809 *	2.6	5.8
449 Un Methodist	12	2,377	756	2,938 *	1.1	2.5
496 Jewish Est	7	NR	NR	4,100	1.6	3.5
499 Indep.Non-Char	1	0	600	1,000	.4	.8
TOLLAND	**80**	**12,308**	**6,572**	**64,021 ***	**46.9**	**100.0**
019 Amer Bapt USA	3	372	180	453 *	.3	.7
040 Ap Chr Ch-Amer	1	345	575	575 *	.4	.9
053 Assemb of God	2	82	109	137	.1	.2

NR–Not Reported *Total adherents estimated from known number of communicant, confirmed, full members. - Represents a percentage less than 0.1. Percentages may not total 100 due to rounding.

Table 4: Religious Congregations by County and Group: 2000

Religious Group	Number of Churches, Synagogues, Mosques, or Temples	Number of Communicant, Confirmed, or Full Members	Number of Attendees	Total Adherents: Number of Adherents	Total Adherents: % of Total Pop.	Total Adherents: % of Total Adh.
056 Baha'i	0	68	NR	68	-	.1
081 Catholic	15	NR	NR	45,002	33.0	70.3
151 L-D Saints	1	NR	NR	449	.3	.7
165 Ch of Nazarene	1	88	196	341	.3	.5
167 Chs of Christ	2	39	43	48	-	.1
175 Congr Chr Chs	1	38	45	46 *	-	.1
179 Consrv Bapt	3	NR	212	212	.2	.3
181 Consrv Congr	2	190	120	232 *	.2	.4
193 Episcopal	5	NR	591	1,698	1.2	2.7
207 E.L.C.A.	4	927	412	1,240	.9	1.9
226 Friends-USA	1	43	NR	52 *	-	.1
246 Greek Orthodox	1	NR	NR	0	-	-
263 Int Foursq Gos	1	4	12	12 *	-	-
268 Jain	1	NR	NR	NR	-	-
283 Luth—MO Synod	3	361	198	519	.4	.8
356 Presb Ch Amer	1	141	210	210	.2	.3
413 S.D.A.	1	66	NR	79	.1	.1
419 So Bapt Conv	2	997	437	1,215 *	.9	1.9
435 Unitarian-Univ	1	50	NR	61 *	-	.1
443 Un C of Christ	19	7,293	2,669	8,890 *	6.5	13.9
449 Un Methodist	6	1,204	463	1,467 *	1.1	2.3
467 Wesleyan	1	0	100	215	.2	.3
496 Jewish Est	2	NR	NR	800	.6	1.2
WINDHAM	**95**	**7,139**	**4,450**	**53,627 ***	**49.2**	**100.0**
019 Amer Bapt USA	11	1,175	506	1,454 *	1.3	2.7
053 Assemb of God	3	356	473	615	.6	1.1
056 Baha'i	0	29	NR	29	-	.1
081 Catholic	23	NR	NR	41,427	38.0	77.3
089 Chr & Miss Al	1	28	NR	49	-	.1
127 Ch God (Cleve)	2	111	99	137 *	.1	.3
151 L-D Saints	1	NR	NR	335	.3	.6
165 Ch of Nazarene	2	149	157	233	.2	.4
167 Chs of Christ	1	41	40	55	.1	.1
175 Congr Chr Chs	4	208	163	257 *	.2	.5
176 Congr Ad Afl	2	89	NR	110 *	.1	.2
179 Consrv Bapt	1	NR	175	175	.2	.3
181 Consrv Congr	3	101	115	125 *	.1	.2
193 Episcopal	7	NR	540	1,295	1.2	2.4
201 Evan Cov Ch	1	318	520	520 *	.5	1.0
203 Evan Free Ch	1	61	90	90	.1	.2
207 E.L.C.A.	3	580	193	840	.8	1.6
246 Greek Orthodox	1	NR	NR	276	.3	.5
331 OCA: Ter Diocs	1	17	NR	37	-	.1
403 Salvation Army	1	84	39	85	.1	.2
413 S.D.A.	2	139	NR	165	.2	.3
419 So Bapt Conv	1	80	0	99 *	.1	.2
435 Unitarian-Univ	1	18	NR	22 *	-	-
443 Un C of Christ	15	2,687	1,075	3,324 *	3.0	6.2
449 Un Methodist	5	868	265	1,073 *	1.0	2.0
496 Jewish Est	2	NR	NR	800	.7	1.5
DELAWARE						
The State.....	571	98,788	52,276	318,122 *	40.6	100.0
KENT	**109**	**15,844**	**9,535**	**40,681 ***	**32.1**	**100.0**
017 Amer Bapt Assn	2	60	NR	76 *	.1	.2
019 Amer Bapt USA	3	1,060	315	1,345 *	1.1	3.3
053 Assemb of God	2	675	957	1,586	1.3	3.9
056 Baha'i	2	77	NR	77	.1	.2
081 Catholic	4	NR	NR	12,964	10.2	31.9
089 Chr & Miss Al	1	0	NR	62	-	.2
097 Chr Chs&Chs Cr	2	280	NR	356 *	.3	.9
123 Ch God (Ander)	2	NR	110	110	.1	.3
127 Ch God (Cleve)	2	127	95	161 *	.1	.4
145 Ch God Prophcy	2	91	NR	116 *	.1	.3
151 L-D Saints	1	NR	NR	628	.5	1.5
157 Ch of Brethren	1	31	22	39 *	-	.1
165 Ch of Nazarene	6	607	527	914	.7	2.2
167 Chs of Christ	1	70	60	100	.1	.2
173 Comm of Christ	1	23	NR	23	-	.1
183 Cons Menn Conf	2	153	187	222	.2	.5
193 Episcopal	5	NR	453	1,712	1.4	4.2
203 Evan Free Ch	1	17	60	60	-	.1
207 E.L.C.A.	1	398	173	545	.4	1.3
226 Friends-USA	1	105	NR	133 *	.1	.3
283 Luth—MO Synod	2	496	186	631	.5	1.6
286 E.PA Mennonite	1	72	NR	91 *	.1	.2
323 Old Ord Amish	8	480	NR	608 *	.5	1.5
339 Pent Ch of God	2	23	NR	24	-	.1
355 Presb Ch (USA)	2	498	1,880	1,955 *	1.5	4.8
356 Presb Ch Amer	2	334	385	449	.4	1.1
360 Prim Bapt Chrch	1	NR	NR	NR	-	-
370 Ref Baptist Chs	1	NR	NR	NR	-	-
388 Reg Bapt Gen As	1	56	80	80 *	.1	.2
403 Salvation Army	1	81	51	135	.1	.3
413 S.D.A.	5	547	NR	650	.5	1.6
419 So Bapt Conv	5	786	450	998 *	.8	2.5
443 Un C of Christ	1	371	163	471 *	.4	1.2
449 Un Methodist	29	8,326	2,664	10,567 *	8.3	26.0
467 Wesleyan	5	0	717	1,193	.9	2.9
496 Jewish Est	1	NR	NR	1,600	1.3	3.9
NEW CASTLE	**278**	**56,058**	**28,207**	**228,405 ***	**45.7**	**100.0**
019 Amer Bapt USA	11	3,325	1,999	4,132 *	.8	1.8
034 Ant Orth of NA	1	49	NR	98	-	-
039 Ap Chr Ch(Naz)	1	0	0	0 *	-	-
053 Assemb of God	8	826	1,005	1,797	.4	.8
056 Baha'i	4	112	NR	112	-	-
057 Bapt Gen Conf	2	764	659	950 *	.2	.4
076 Buddhism	1	NR	NR	NR	-	-
081 Catholic	36	NR	NR	126,612	25.3	55.4
089 Chr & Miss Al	2	172	NR	322	.1	.1
123 Ch God (Ander)	4	NR	227	227	-	.1
127 Ch God (Cleve)	4	424	280	547 *	.1	.2
145 Ch God Prophcy	4	183	NR	228 *	-	.1
151 L-D Saints	5	NR	NR	1,823	.4	.8
157 Ch of Brethren	1	129	72	160 *	-	.1
165 Ch of Nazarene	4	353	251	386	.1	.2
167 Chs of Christ	6	645	573	796	.2	.3
173 Comm of Christ	1	165	NR	165	-	.1
179 Consrv Bapt	1	NR	100	100	-	-
193 Episcopal	19	NR	2,875	9,162	1.8	4.0
203 Evan Free Ch	2	448	445	530	.1	.2
207 E.L.C.A.	11	4,005	1,499	5,384	1.1	2.4
223 Free Will Bapt	2	197	NR	245 *	-	.1
226 Friends-USA	5	525	NR	652 *	.1	.3
246 Greek Orthodox	1	NR	NR	2,076	.4	.9
252 Hindu	2	NR	NR	NR	-	-
263 Int Foursq Gos	1	12	29	29 *	-	-
264 Int Chs of Crst	1	11	30	11	-	-
267 Muslim Est	3	NR	1,174	3,691	.7	1.6
283 Luth—MO Synod	3	674	279	1,033	.2	.5
286 E.PA Mennonite	1	65	NR	81 *	-	-
288 Mennonite USA	1	24	19	30 *	-	-
331 OCA: Ter Diocs	1	100	NR	456	.1	.2
335 Orth Pres Ch	2	211	218	305	.1	.1
349 Pent Holiness	1	112	81	139 *	-	.1
355 Presb Ch (USA)	26	9,131	3,653	11,350 *	2.3	5.0
356 Presb Ch Amer	7	2,151	2,730	3,241	.6	1.4
360 Prim Bapt Chrch	1	NR	NR	NR	-	-
388 Reg Bapt Gen As	1	120	80	80 *	-	-
403 Salvation Army	2	271	158	340	.1	.1
413 S.D.A.	5	1,229	NR	1,462	.3	.6
416 Sikh	1	NR	NR	NR	-	-
418 Southw Bapt Fel	2	NR	NR	NR	-	-
419 So Bapt Conv	11	3,643	1,673	4,527 *	.9	2.0
431 Ukrainian Orth	1	NR	NR	450	.1	.2
435 Unitarian-Univ	3	1,196	NR	1,486 *	.3	.7
443 Un C of Christ	1	224	115	278 *	.1	.1
449 Un Methodist	54	22,903	7,315	28,460 *	5.7	12.5
467 Wesleyan	3	0	117	321	.1	.1
469 WELS	1	159	126	231	-	.1
496 Jewish Est	6	NR	NR	11,900	2.4	5.2
499 Indep.Non-Char	1	1,500	425	2,000	.4	.9

NR–Not Reported   *Total adherents estimated from known number of communicant, confirmed, full members.   - Represents a percentage less than 0.1.   Percentages may not total 100 due to rounding.

Table 4: Religious Congregations by County and Group: 2000

Religious Group	Number of Churches, Synagogues, Mosques, or Temples	Number of Communicant, Confirmed, or Full Members	Number of Attendees	Total Adherents: Number of Adherents	Total Adherents: % of Total Pop.	Total Adherents: % of Total Adh.
SUSSEX	**184**	**26,886**	**14,534**	**49,036 ***	**31.3**	**100.0**
053 Assemb of God	3	233	305	425	.3	.9
056 Baha'i	1	62	NR	62	-	.1
071 Brethren (Ash)	1	26	26	31 *	-	.1
081 Catholic	6	NR	NR	12,164	7.8	24.8
089 Chr & Miss Al	3	258	NR	500	.3	1.0
093 Chr Ch (Disc)	1	25	0	30 *	-	.1
097 Chr Chs&Chs Cr	6	710	NR	858 *	.5	1.7
127 Ch God (Cleve)	14	2,592	1,717	3,226 *	2.1	6.6
145 Ch God Prophcy	3	143	NR	172 *	.1	.4
151 L-D Saints	1	NR	NR	309	.2	.6
157 Ch of Brethren	1	100	82	121 *	.1	.2
165 Ch of Nazarene	3	218	266	462	.3	.9
167 Chs of Christ	3	185	175	260	.2	.5
183 Cons Menn Conf	3	454	554	661	.4	1.3
193 Episcopal	11	NR	910	2,119	1.4	4.3
203 Evan Free Ch	1	69	125	125	.1	.3
207 E.L.C.A.	2	601	240	702	.4	1.4
283 Luth—MO Synod	2	511	277	617	.4	1.3
288 Mennonite USA	1	130	104	157 *	.1	.3
290 Metro Comm Ch	1	56	70	70 *	-	.1
297 Mennonite;Other	1	25	NR	30 *	-	.1
355 Presb Ch (USA)	9	1,302	719	1,575 *	1.0	3.2
356 Presb Ch Amer	2	162	246	247	.2	.5
388 Reg Bapt Gen As	3	434	488	536 *	.3	1.1
403 Salvation Army	1	11	24	34	-	.1
413 S.D.A.	5	319	NR	380	.2	.8
418 Southw Bapt Fel	2	NR	NR	NR	-	-
419 So Bapt Conv	3	649	353	785 *	.5	1.6
435 Unitarian-Univ	1	96	NR	116 *	.1	.2
443 Un C of Christ	1	3	1	4 *	-	-
449 Un Methodist	79	16,911	6,779	20,444 *	13.1	41.7
467 Wesleyan	9	201	823	1,414	.9	2.9
498 Indep.Charis.	1	400	250	400	.3	.8

DISTRICT OF COLUMBIA

Religious Group	Number of Churches, Synagogues, Mosques, or Temples	Number of Communicant, Confirmed, or Full Members	Number of Attendees	Total Adherents: Number of Adherents	Total Adherents: % of Total Pop.	Total Adherents: % of Total Adh.
The State.....	390	120,092	63,535	418,543 *	73.2	100.0
DISTRICT OF COLUMBIA	**390**	**120,092**	**63,535**	**418,543 ***	**73.2**	**100.0**
019 Amer Bapt USA	62	43,457	16,243	51,836 *	9.1	12.4
032 Amish; other	1	18	NR	21 *	-	-
034 Ant Orth of NA	2	357	NR	714	.1	.2
040 Ap Chr Ch-Amer	1	6	19	19 *	-	-
050 Armen Ap Etchm	1	255	NR	1,000	.2	.2
053 Assemb of God	7	1,230	1,134	1,526	.3	.4
056 Baha'i	1	357	NR	357	.1	.1
071 Brethren (Ash)	1	106	105	126 *	-	-
076 Buddhism	15	NR	NR	NR	-	-
078 Bulgar Orth USA	1	NR	NR	440	.1	.1
081 Catholic	42	NR	NR	160,048	28.0	38.2
089 Chr & Miss Al	1	62	NR	90	-	-
093 Chr Ch (Disc)	4	1,298	679	1,548 *	.3	.4
105 Christian Ref	1	147	110	175 *	-	-
123 Ch God (Ander)	6	NR	498	498	.1	.1
127 Ch God (Cleve)	2	92	85	110 *	-	-
145 Ch God Prophcy	5	234	NR	277 *	-	.1
151 L-D Saints	3	NR	NR	609	.1	.1
157 Ch of Brethren	2	178	56	213 *	-	.1
165 Ch of Nazarene	2	514	320	550	.1	.1
167 Chs of Christ	4	491	473	630	.1	.2
173 Comm of Christ	1	214	NR	214	-	.1
179 Consrv Bapt	1	NR	65	65	-	-
193 Episcopal	34	NR	8,428	19,698	3.4	4.7
207 E.L.C.A.	13	3,101	1,375	4,048	.7	1.0
226 Friends-USA	2	210	NR	250 *	-	.1
246 Greek Orthodox	2	NR	NR	4,317	.8	1.0
252 Hindu	3	NR	NR	NR	-	-
262 Int Cou Comm Ch	2	378	NR	451 *	.1	.1
264 Int Chs of Crst	1	1,899	3,322	2,492	.4	.6
267 Muslim Est	16	NR	9,448	60,479	10.6	14.4
283 Luth—MO Synod	3	595	311	739	.1	.2
288 Mennonite USA	4	79	481	481 *	.1	.1
290 Metro Comm Ch	1	493	458	588 *	.1	.1
293 Morav Ch-North	1	157	NR	235	-	.1
331 OCA: Ter Diocs	1	300	NR	405	.1	.1
355 Presb Ch (USA)	17	6,936	3,281	8,273 *	1.4	2.0
401 Rus Orth Abroad	1	NR	NR	NR	-	-
403 Salvation Army	3	504	129	1,588	.3	.4
410 Serb Orth USA	1	NR	NR	555	.1	.1
411 Serb Orth: Grac	1	NR	NR	NR	-	-
413 S.D.A.	9	6,309	NR	7,508	1.3	1.8
416 Sikh	3	NR	NR	NR	-	-
419 So Bapt Conv	49	32,572	9,758	38,852 *	6.8	9.3
425 Tao	1	NR	NR	NR	-	-
435 Unitarian-Univ	2	599	NR	714 *	.1	.2
443 Un C of Christ	8	4,064	1,710	4,848 *	.8	1.2
449 Un Methodist	33	12,840	4,912	15,313 *	2.7	3.7
463 Vineyard	1	40	40	48 *	-	-
467 Wesleyan	1	0	95	95	-	-
496 Jewish Est	11	NR	NR	25,500	4.5	6.1

FLORIDA

Religious Group	Number of Churches, Synagogues, Mosques, or Temples	Number of Communicant, Confirmed, or Full Members	Number of Attendees	Total Adherents: Number of Adherents	Total Adherents: % of Total Pop.	Total Adherents: % of Total Adh.
The State.....	10,078	2,416,540	1,287,696	6,576,205 *	41.1	100.0
ALACHUA	**194**	**41,780**	**21,741**	**73,237 ***	**33.6**	**100.0**
017 Amer Bapt Assn	2	120	NR	142 *	.1	.2
053 Assemb of God	6	597	703	935	.4	1.3
056 Baha'i	2	306	NR	306	.1	.4
076 Buddhism	2	NR	NR	NR	-	-
081 Catholic	6	NR	NR	15,984	7.3	21.8
084 Calvary Chapel	1	NR	NR	NR	-	-
089 Chr & Miss Al	1	19	NR	23	-	-
093 Chr Ch (Disc)	1	116	80	137 *	.1	.2
097 Chr Chs&Chs Cr	1	100	NR	118 *	.1	.2
127 Ch God (Cleve)	7	939	566	1,118 *	.5	1.5
145 Ch God Prophcy	1	41	NR	48 *	-	.1
151 L-D Saints	4	NR	NR	1,504	.7	2.1
165 Ch of Nazarene	5	584	342	688	.3	.9
167 Chs of Christ	13	1,474	1,617	2,016	.9	2.8
173 Comm of Christ	1	25	NR	25	-	-
186 Coptic Orth Ch	1	NR	NR	NR	-	-
193 Episcopal	7	NR	884	2,389	1.1	3.3
203 Evan Free Ch	1	282	570	570	.3	.8
207 E.L.C.A.	2	704	252	916	.4	1.3
226 Friends-USA	1	24	NR	28 *	-	-
246 Greek Orthodox	1	NR	NR	201	.1	.3
252 Hindu	2	NR	NR	NR	-	-
263 Int Foursq Gos	1	30	50	50 *	-	.1
264 Int Chs of Crst	1	107	173	127	.1	.2
267 Muslim Est	1	NR	300	450	.2	.6
283 Luth—MO Synod	2	858	519	1,074	.5	1.5
288 Mennonite USA	1	37	33	44 *	-	.1
290 Metro Comm Ch	1	57	52	67 *	-	.1
304 NatPrimBapt USA	2	60	NR	71 *	-	.1
349 Pent Holiness	3	275	233	325 *	.1	.4
355 Presb Ch (USA)	9	1,985	1,138	2,349 *	1.1	3.2
356 Presb Ch Amer	2	271	352	424	.2	.6
360 Prim Bapt Chrch	2	NR	NR	NR	-	-
388 Reg Bapt Gen As	1	29	30	34 *	-	-
403 Salvation Army	1	85	44	251	.1	.3
413 S.D.A.	4	749	NR	892	.4	1.2
419 So Bapt Conv	50	20,606	8,208	24,366 *	11.2	33.3
435 Unitarian-Univ	1	296	NR	350 *	.2	.5
443 Un C of Christ	1	547	350	647 *	.3	.9
449 Un Methodist	38	10,018	4,882	11,844 *	5.4	16.2
463 Vineyard	1	340	300	402 *	.2	.5
469 WELS	1	99	63	122	.1	.2
496 Jewish Est	3	NR	NR	2,200	1.0	3.0
BAKER	**29**	**4,202**	**2,516**	**6,670 ***	**30.0**	**100.0**
053 Assemb of God	5	560	583	796	3.6	11.9
056 Baha'i	0	1	NR	1	-	-

NR–Not Reported *Total adherents estimated from known number of communicant, confirmed, full members. - Represents a percentage less than 0.1. Percentages may not total 100 due to rounding.

Table 4: Religious Congregations by County and Group: 2000

Religious Group	Number of Churches, Synagogues, Mosques, or Temples	Number of Communicant, Confirmed, or Full Members	Number of Attendees	Total Adherents		
				Number of Adherents	% of Total Pop.	% of Total Adh.
081 Catholic	1	NR	NR	247	1.1	3.7
097 Chr Chs&Chs Cr	1	175	NR	221 *	1.0	3.3
127 Ch God (Cleve)	4	394	338	497 *	2.2	7.5
151 L-D Saints	1	NR	NR	503	2.3	7.5
165 Ch of Nazarene	1	51	45	68	.3	1.0
167 Chs of Christ	2	115	145	201	.9	3.0
193 Episcopal	1	NR	39	66	.3	1.0
360 Prim Bapt Chrch	5	NR	NR	NR	-	-
418 Southw Bapt Fel	1	NR	NR	NR	-	-
419 So Bapt Conv	5	2,507	870	3,166 *	14.2	47.5
449 Un Methodist	1	399	121	504 *	2.3	7.6
498 Indep.Charis.	1	0	375	400	1.8	6.0
BAY	**147**	**40,100**	**19,280**	**61,468 ***	**41.5**	**100.0**
017 Amer Bapt Assn	1	86	NR	105 *	.1	.2
053 Assemb of God	19	2,086	2,606	3,808	2.6	6.2
056 Baha'i	0	41	NR	41	-	.1
081 Catholic	7	NR	NR	7,025	4.7	11.4
089 Chr & Miss Al	3	142	NR	217	.1	.4
097 Chr Chs&Chs Cr	3	233	NR	286 *	.2	.5
123 Ch God (Ander)	1	NR	35	35	-	.1
127 Ch God (Cleve)	5	383	223	493 *	.3	.8
145 Ch God Prophcy	2	82	NR	100 *	.1	.2
151 L-D Saints	5	NR	NR	1,445	1.0	2.4
165 Ch of Nazarene	2	160	114	164	.1	.3
167 Chs of Christ	9	1,081	1,145	1,349	.9	2.2
173 Comm of Christ	1	63	NR	63	-	.1
193 Episcopal	5	NR	800	1,426	1.0	2.3
207 E.L.C.A.	1	286	185	359	.2	.6
223 Free Will Bapt	1	82	NR	101 *	.1	.2
246 Greek Orthodox	1	NR	NR	123	.1	.2
267 Muslim Est	1	NR	101	288	.2	.5
283 Luth—MO Synod	4	888	513	1,511	1.0	2.5
304 NatPrimBapt USA	1	54	NR	66 *	-	.1
339 Pent Ch of God	1	18	NR	30	-	-
349 Pent Holiness	3	152	162	186 *	.1	.3
355 Presb Ch (USA)	5	1,028	721	1,260 *	.9	2.0
356 Presb Ch Amer	4	683	580	792	.5	1.3
360 Prim Bapt Chrch	1	NR	NR	NR	-	-
403 Salvation Army	1	117	46	150	.1	.2
413 S.D.A.	3	436	NR	519	.4	.8
418 Southw Bapt Fel	1	NR	NR	NR	-	-
419 So Bapt Conv	32	22,786	7,389	27,934 *	18.8	45.4
435 Unitarian-Univ	1	11	NR	13 *	-	-
449 Un Methodist	15	7,879	3,227	9,658 *	6.5	15.7
463 Vineyard	1	130	120	159 *	.1	.3
467 Wesleyan	1	7	25	50	-	.1
469 WELS	1	66	63	82	.1	.1
496 Jewish Est	1	NR	NR	15	-	-
498 Indep.Charis.	2	750	900	1,150	.8	1.9
499 Indep.Non-Char	2	370	325	465	.3	.8
BRADFORD	**38**	**9,453**	**3,756**	**12,028 ***	**46.1**	**100.0**
056 Baha'i	0	1	NR	1	-	-
081 Catholic	1	NR	NR	195	.7	1.6
097 Chr Chs&Chs Cr	1	150	NR	180 *	.7	1.5
127 Ch God (Cleve)	4	536	400	662 *	2.5	5.5
145 Ch God Prophcy	2	82	NR	98 *	.4	.8
151 L-D Saints	1	NR	NR	364	1.4	3.0
167 Chs of Christ	4	133	149	167	.6	1.4
193 Episcopal	1	NR	53	120	.5	1.0
355 Presb Ch (USA)	2	287	186	344 *	1.3	2.9
360 Prim Bapt Chrch	1	NR	NR	NR	-	-
413 S.D.A.	1	33	NR	39	.1	.3
419 So Bapt Conv	16	7,357	2,616	8,812 *	33.8	73.3
449 Un Methodist	4	874	352	1,046 *	4.0	8.7
BREVARD	**284**	**71,785**	**41,120**	**186,516 ***	**39.2**	**100.0**
017 Amer Bapt Assn	4	374	NR	449 *	.1	.2
019 Amer Bapt USA	1	80	50	96 *	-	.1
022 Carp Rus Orth	1	122	NR	207	-	.1
053 Assemb of God	12	988	1,077	1,484	.3	.8
055 As Ref Pres Ch	2	576	NR	706	.1	.4
056 Baha'i	2	170	NR	170	-	.1
076 Buddhism	1	NR	NR	NR	-	-
081 Catholic	14	NR	NR	79,847	16.8	42.8
084 Calvary Chapel	2	NR	NR	NR	-	-
089 Chr & Miss Al	4	65	NR	161	-	.1
093 Chr Ch (Disc)	2	632	395	759 *	.2	.4
097 Chr Chs&Chs Cr	8	1,924	NR	2,312 *	.5	1.2
105 Christian Ref	1	28	0	34 *	-	-
123 Ch God (Ander)	2	NR	77	77	-	-
127 Ch God (Cleve)	18	2,245	1,226	2,713 *	.6	1.5
145 Ch God Prophcy	4	163	NR	196 *	-	.1
151 L-D Saints	7	NR	NR	3,302	.7	1.8
165 Ch of Nazarene	9	1,231	788	1,255	.3	.7
167 Chs of Christ	13	1,900	1,925	2,411	.5	1.3
173 Comm of Christ	1	83	NR	83	-	-
186 Coptic Orth Ch	1	NR	NR	NR	-	-
193 Episcopal	11	NR	2,160	5,267	1.1	2.8
203 Evan Free Ch	2	119	205	205	-	.1
207 E.L.C.A.	13	3,025	1,806	3,743	.8	2.0
220 Free Lutheran	1	23	18	24	-	-
223 Free Will Bapt	5	412	NR	496 *	.1	.3
226 Friends-USA	1	24	NR	29 *	-	-
245 Greek Orth Vslp	1	52	NR	127	-	.1
246 Greek Orthodox	2	NR	NR	2,337	.5	1.3
252 Hindu	3	NR	NR	NR	-	-
262 Int Cou Comm Ch	1	190	NR	228 *	-	.1
283 Luth—MO Synod	7	2,185	1,426	2,636	.6	1.4
290 Metro Comm Ch	1	51	30	61 *	-	-
304 NatPrimBapt USA	5	325	NR	391 *	.1	.2
331 OCA: Ter Diocs	1	46	NR	133	-	.1
349 Pent Holiness	1	187	110	225 *	-	.1
355 Presb Ch (USA)	12	4,701	3,028	5,648 *	1.2	3.0
356 Presb Ch Amer	4	1,052	1,240	1,267	.3	.7
360 Prim Bapt Chrch	1	NR	NR	NR	-	-
403 Salvation Army	2	316	125	470	.1	.3
413 S.D.A.	7	981	NR	1,169	.2	.6
419 So Bapt Conv	47	25,504	9,978	30,647 *	6.4	16.4
435 Unitarian-Univ	3	159	NR	191 *	-	.1
443 Un C of Christ	4	715	510	859 *	.2	.5
449 Un Methodist	22	15,986	7,544	19,211 *	4.0	10.3
463 Vineyard	2	170	146	204 *	-	.1
467 Wesleyan	3	36	80	160	-	.1
469 WELS	2	220	176	276	.1	.1
496 Jewish Est	2	NR	NR	5,000	1.0	2.7
498 Indep.Charis.	5	1,750	5,100	6,275	1.3	3.4
499 Indep.Non-Char	4	2,975	1,900	2,975	.6	1.6
BROWARD	**583**	**129,068**	**79,580**	**744,145 ***	**45.8**	**100.0**
017 Amer Bapt Assn	4	238	NR	292 *	-	-
019 Amer Bapt USA	2	750	0	921 *	.1	.1
022 Carp Rus Orth	1	122	NR	207	-	-
034 Ant Orth of NA	1	199	NR	398	-	.1
039 Ap Chr Ch(Naz)	2	49	60	60 *	-	-
040 Ap Chr Ch-Amer	1	45	70	70 *	-	-
049 Armen Ap Cilic	1	80	NR	280	-	-
050 Armen Ap Etchm	1	55	NR	420	-	.1
053 Assemb of God	38	6,849	7,294	12,260	.8	1.6
055 As Ref Pres Ch	1	171	NR	254	-	-
056 Baha'i	12	1,052	NR	1,052	.1	.1
057 Bapt Gen Conf	2	79	92	106 *	-	-
075 Brethren in Cr	3	670	848	848	.1	.1
076 Buddhism	4	NR	NR	NR	-	-
081 Catholic	50	NR	NR	341,773	21.1	45.9
084 Calvary Chapel	2	NR	NR	NR	-	-
089 Chr & Miss Al	12	692	NR	946	.1	.1
093 Chr Ch (Disc)	6	1,994	977	2,449 *	.2	.3
097 Chr Chs&Chs Cr	9	1,855	NR	2,278 *	.1	.3
105 Christian Ref	2	267	195	328 *	-	-
123 Ch God (Ander)	10	NR	1,136	1,136	.1	.2
127 Ch God (Cleve)	36	5,110	4,785	6,486 *	.4	.9
145 Ch God Prophcy	11	449	NR	550 *	-	.1
151 L-D Saints	13	NR	NR	4,744	.3	.6
165 Ch of Nazarene	10	1,488	1,068	1,808	.1	.2
167 Chs of Christ	18	5,090	3,134	6,110	.4	.8

NR–Not Reported *Total adherents estimated from known number of communicant, confirmed, full members. - Represents a percentage less than 0.1. Percentages may not total 100 due to rounding.

Table 4: Religious Congregations by County and Group: 2000

Religious Group		Number of Churches, Synagogues, Mosques, or Temples	Number of Communicant, Confirmed, or Full Members	Number of Attendees	Total Adherents: Number of Adherents	% of Total Pop.	% of Total Adh.
173	Comm of Christ	1	45	NR	45	-	-
179	Consrv Bapt	1	NR	100	100	-	-
186	Coptic Orth Ch	1	NR	NR	NR	-	-
193	Episcopal	16	NR	3,106	6,928	.4	.9
201	Evan Cov Ch	1	96	84	118 *	-	-
203	Evan Free Ch	1	100	160	160	-	-
207	E.L.C.A.	14	3,660	1,748	5,420	.3	.7
216	Evan Presby Ch	1	716	NR	879 *	.1	.1
221	Free Methodist	2	250	230	265	-	-
223	Free Will Bapt	2	165	NR	203 *	-	-
226	Friends-USA	1	24	NR	29 *	-	-
246	Greek Orthodox	2	NR	NR	1,845	.1	.2
252	Hindu	7	NR	NR	NR	-	-
263	Int Foursq Gos	1	33	50	50 *	-	-
265	Int Pent C Chr	1	0	0	15	-	-
267	Muslim Est	5	NR	1,530	6,689	.4	.9
268	Jain	1	NR	NR	NR	-	-
283	Luth—MO Synod	13	4,012	2,145	5,245	.3	.7
290	Metro Comm Ch	1	361	505	505 *	-	.1
304	NatPrimBapt USA	4	235	NR	289 *	-	-
313	N Am Bapt Conf	1	425	275	522 *	-	.1
330	Macedonian Orth	1	NR	NR	600	-	.1
331	OCA: Ter Diocs	1	75	NR	373	-	.1
333	Malan Dioc Am	2	NR	NR	300	-	-
349	Pent Holiness	8	1,842	1,498	2,262 *	.1	.3
355	Presb Ch (USA)	15	5,306	3,238	6,514 *	.4	.9
356	Presb Ch Amer	12	11,383	7,474	12,471	.8	1.7
365	Prog Prim Bapt	1	50	NR	61 *	-	-
370	Ref Baptist Chs	3	NR	NR	NR	-	-
371	Ref Ch in Am	3	239	300	514	-	.1
388	Reg Bapt Gen As	2	94	165	165 *	-	-
397	OCA: Roman Dioc	2	NR	NR	2,300	.1	.3
401	Rus Orth Abroad	1	NR	NR	NR	-	-
403	Salvation Army	1	311	109	449	-	.1
413	S.D.A.	28	6,685	NR	7,954	.5	1.1
416	Sikh	2	NR	NR	NR	-	-
418	Southw Bapt Fel	1	NR	NR	NR	-	-
419	So Bapt Conv	67	47,210	27,620	57,974 *	3.6	7.8
431	Ukrainian Orth	1	NR	NR	270	-	-
435	Unitarian-Univ	3	263	NR	323 *	-	-
443	Un C of Christ	4	597	352	733 *	-	.1
449	Un Methodist	25	15,196	6,339	18,660 *	1.1	2.5
463	Vineyard	1	130	120	160 *	-	-
467	Wesleyan	4	149	276	510	-	.1
469	WELS	1	77	47	84	-	-
496	Jewish Est	59	NR	NR	213,000	13.1	28.6
498	Indep.Charis.	4	1,735	1,250	1,885	.1	.3
499	Indep.Non-Char	2	300	1,200	1,500	.1	.2
CALHOUN		**29**	**3,246**	**1,693**	**4,335 ***	**33.3**	**100.0**
017	Amer Bapt Assn	1	22	NR	27 *	.2	.6
053	Assemb of God	2	103	126	203	1.6	4.7
081	Catholic	1	NR	NR	162	1.2	3.7
127	Ch God (Cleve)	3	165	316	321 *	2.5	7.4
165	Ch of Nazarene	1	21	36	42	.3	1.0
167	Chs of Christ	1	9	10	12	.1	.3
183	Cons Menn Conf	1	102	125	148	1.1	3.4
223	Free Will Bapt	2	165	NR	200 *	1.5	4.6
288	Mennonite USA	1	18	20	22 *	.2	.5
297	Mennonite;Other	1	42	NR	51 *	.4	1.2
349	Pent Holiness	4	284	305	344 *	2.6	7.9
355	Presb Ch (USA)	1	9	8	11 *	.1	.3
419	So Bapt Conv	8	1,876	571	2,271 *	17.4	52.4
449	Un Methodist	2	430	176	521 *	4.0	12.0
CHARLOTTE		**78**	**16,328**	**10,161**	**50,717 ***	**35.8**	**100.0**
053	Assemb of God	4	885	1,131	1,516	1.1	3.0
056	Baha'i	0	15	NR	15	-	-
081	Catholic	5	NR	NR	25,994	18.4	51.3
084	Calvary Chapel	1	NR	NR	NR	-	-
089	Chr & Miss Al	3	307	NR	664	.5	1.3
097	Chr Chs&Chs Cr	4	971	NR	1,101 *	.8	2.2
123	Ch God (Ander)	1	NR	30	30	-	.1
127	Ch God (Cleve)	4	601	399	686 *	.5	1.4
145	Ch God Prophcy	1	41	NR	46 *	-	.1
151	L-D Saints	1	NR	NR	476	.3	.9
165	Ch of Nazarene	2	136	140	391	.3	.8
167	Chs of Christ	3	140	196	185	.1	.4
193	Episcopal	2	NR	616	1,295	.9	2.6
207	E.L.C.A.	5	1,503	1,013	1,761	1.2	3.5
245	Greek Orth Vslp	1	175	NR	375	.3	.7
246	Greek Orthodox	1	NR	NR	231	.2	.5
267	Muslim Est	1	NR	50	250	.2	.5
283	Luth—MO Synod	3	854	657	912	.6	1.8
304	NatPrimBapt USA	1	150	NR	170 *	.1	.3
355	Presb Ch (USA)	4	1,791	1,075	2,031 *	1.4	4.0
388	Reg Bapt Gen As	1	207	188	235 *	.2	.5
403	Salvation Army	1	66	39	72	.1	.1
413	S.D.A.	4	791	NR	941	.7	1.9
418	Southw Bapt Fel	1	NR	NR	NR	-	-
419	So Bapt Conv	10	3,013	1,578	3,418 *	2.4	6.7
435	Unitarian-Univ	1	75	NR	85 *	.1	.2
443	Un C of Christ	2	752	451	853 *	.6	1.7
449	Un Methodist	8	3,737	2,502	4,240 *	3.0	8.4
469	WELS	1	118	96	144	.1	.3
496	Jewish Est	2	NR	NR	2,600	1.8	5.1
CITRUS		**96**	**19,219**	**11,801**	**42,730 ***	**36.2**	**100.0**
017	Amer Bapt Assn	2	399	NR	457 *	.4	1.1
053	Assemb of God	6	902	597	1,384	1.2	3.2
056	Baha'i	1	23	NR	23	-	.1
057	Bapt Gen Conf	1	112	66	128 *	.1	.3
081	Catholic	6	NR	NR	17,145	14.5	40.1
089	Chr & Miss Al	1	10	NR	10	-	-
097	Chr Chs&Chs Cr	5	509	NR	584 *	.5	1.4
123	Ch God (Ander)	2	NR	155	155	.1	.4
127	Ch God (Cleve)	7	1,649	989	1,911 *	1.6	4.5
151	L-D Saints	2	NR	NR	577	.5	1.4
165	Ch of Nazarene	1	279	293	492	.4	1.2
167	Chs of Christ	9	482	585	635	.5	1.5
175	Congr Chr Chs	1	140	125	161 *	.1	.4
193	Episcopal	3	NR	507	1,215	1.0	2.8
207	E.L.C.A.	3	1,326	751	1,514	1.3	3.5
246	Greek Orthodox	1	NR	NR	468	.4	1.1
263	Int Foursq Gos	2	51	106	106 *	.1	.2
283	Luth—MO Synod	2	377	243	497	.4	1.2
355	Presb Ch (USA)	2	1,170	759	1,342 *	1.1	3.1
356	Presb Ch Amer	3	1,106	1,178	1,586	1.3	3.7
370	Ref Baptist Chs	1	NR	NR	NR	-	-
388	Reg Bapt Gen As	2	135	105	116 *	.1	.3
403	Salvation Army	1	51	24	83	.1	.2
413	S.D.A.	3	314	NR	374	.3	.9
418	Southw Bapt Fel	2	NR	NR	NR	-	-
419	So Bapt Conv	16	5,810	2,795	6,662 *	5.6	15.6
435	Unitarian-Univ	1	47	NR	54 *	-	.1
449	Un Methodist	6	3,620	2,011	4,151 *	3.5	9.7
463	Vineyard	1	165	167	189 *	.2	.4
469	WELS	1	142	120	196	.2	.5
496	Jewish Est	1	NR	NR	115	.1	.3
499	Indep.Non-Char	1	400	225	400	.3	.9
CLAY		**105**	**31,651**	**15,367**	**57,615 ***	**40.9**	**100.0**
053	Assemb of God	6	834	808	1,133	.8	2.0
056	Baha'i	1	52	NR	52	-	.1
081	Catholic	4	NR	NR	13,609	9.7	23.6
084	Calvary Chapel	1	NR	NR	NR	-	-
089	Chr & Miss Al	2	187	NR	336	.2	.6
097	Chr Chs&Chs Cr	2	255	NR	324 *	.2	.6
123	Ch God (Ander)	1	NR	81	81	.1	.1
127	Ch God (Cleve)	6	384	293	499 *	.4	.9
145	Ch God Prophcy	1	41	NR	52 *	-	.1
151	L-D Saints	3	NR	NR	1,127	.8	2.0
157	Ch of Brethren	1	139	75	176 *	.1	.3
165	Ch of Nazarene	1	87	77	130	.1	.2
167	Chs of Christ	6	560	568	726	.5	1.3
173	Comm of Christ	1	30	NR	30	-	.1

NR–Not Reported *Total adherents estimated from known number of communicant, confirmed, full members. - Represents a percentage less than 0.1. Percentages may not total 100 due to rounding.

Table 4: Religious Congregations by County and Group: 2000

Religious Group	Number of Churches, Synagogues, Mosques, or Temples	Number of Communicant, Confirmed, or Full Members	Number of Attendees	Total Adherents: Number of Adherents	Total Adherents: % of Total Pop.	Total Adherents: % of Total Adh.
193 Episcopal	5	NR	985	2,221	1.6	3.9
203 Evan Free Ch	1	17	50	50	-	.1
207 E.L.C.A.	2	867	468	1,229	.9	2.1
223 Free Will Bapt	1	82	NR	105 *	.1	.2
252 Hindu	1	NR	NR	NR	-	-
268 Jain	1	NR	NR	NR	-	-
283 Luth—MO Synod	1	110	91	148	.1	.3
349 Pent Holiness	3	203	217	257 *	.2	.4
355 Presb Ch (USA)	4	1,316	589	1,669 *	1.2	2.9
356 Presb Ch Amer	1	778	715	1,077	.8	1.9
403 Salvation Army	1	69	17	101	.1	.2
413 S.D.A.	1	100	NR	119	.1	.2
418 Southw Bapt Fel	3	NR	NR	NR	-	-
419 So Bapt Conv	32	19,985	7,730	25,349 *	18.0	44.0
435 Unitarian-Univ	1	78	NR	99 *	.1	.2
449 Un Methodist	7	4,987	2,177	6,324 *	4.5	11.0
463 Vineyard	2	317	302	402 *	.3	.7
467 Wesleyan	1	109	76	109	.1	.2
469 WELS	1	64	48	81	.1	.1
COLLIER	**111**	**29,120**	**20,576**	**92,607 ***	**36.8**	**100.0**
034 Ant Orth of NA	1	40	NR	80	-	.1
053 Assemb of God	8	1,640	1,907	2,391	1.0	2.6
056 Baha'i	1	121	NR	121	-	.1
081 Catholic	9	NR	NR	48,590	19.3	52.5
089 Chr & Miss Al	4	357	NR	436	.2	.5
093 Chr Ch (Disc)	1	306	156	362 *	.1	.4
097 Chr Chs&Chs Cr	4	545	NR	645 *	.3	.7
127 Ch God (Cleve)	6	815	379	970 *	.4	1.0
151 L-D Saints	2	NR	NR	421	.2	.5
165 Ch of Nazarene	5	742	618	1,188	.5	1.3
167 Chs of Christ	3	263	295	317	.1	.3
193 Episcopal	6	NR	1,542	3,034	1.2	3.3
203 Evan Free Ch	1	33	59	59	-	.1
207 E.L.C.A.	3	1,219	1,120	1,580	.6	1.7
221 Free Methodist	2	140	346	346	.1	.4
246 Greek Orthodox	1	NR	NR	255	.1	.3
264 Int Chs of Crst	1	20	45	26	-	-
283 Luth—MO Synod	4	1,436	1,166	1,726	.7	1.9
288 Mennonite USA	1	30	50	50 *	-	.1
331 OCA: Ter Diocs	1	41	NR	87	-	.1
339 Pent Ch of God	1	14	NR	32	-	-
349 Pent Holiness	2	165	135	195 *	.1	.2
355 Presb Ch (USA)	4	3,597	2,374	4,257 *	1.7	4.6
356 Presb Ch Amer	3	589	796	796	.3	.9
403 Salvation Army	2	220	93	157	.1	.2
413 S.D.A.	4	560	NR	666	.3	.7
419 So Bapt Conv	14	8,158	4,468	9,652 *	3.8	10.4
435 Unitarian-Univ	1	216	NR	256 *	.1	.3
443 Un C of Christ	4	2,866	1,482	3,391 *	1.3	3.7
449 Un Methodist	7	4,416	2,670	5,225 *	2.1	5.6
463 Vineyard	1	120	120	142 *	.1	.2
467 Wesleyan	1	51	55	154	.1	.2
496 Jewish Est	2	NR	NR	4,200	1.7	4.5
499 Indep.Non-Char	1	400	700	800	.3	.9
COLUMBIA	**67**	**12,382**	**5,013**	**19,092 ***	**33.8**	**100.0**
053 Assemb of God	3	145	183	236	.4	1.2
056 Baha'i	0	6	NR	6	-	-
081 Catholic	1	NR	NR	2,400	4.2	12.6
097 Chr Chs&Chs Cr	2	172	NR	213 *	.4	1.1
127 Ch God (Cleve)	5	728	250	901 *	1.6	4.7
151 L-D Saints	3	NR	NR	1,102	1.9	5.8
165 Ch of Nazarene	2	182	110	196	.3	1.0
167 Chs of Christ	6	357	358	524	.9	2.7
193 Episcopal	1	NR	122	189	.3	1.0
207 E.L.C.A.	2	165	115	198	.4	1.0
283 Luth—MO Synod	1	142	72	156	.3	.8
339 Pent Ch of God	1	15	NR	23	-	.1
349 Pent Holiness	2	110	125	136 *	.2	.7
355 Presb Ch (USA)	2	460	280	569 *	1.0	3.0
388 Reg Bapt Gen As	1	30	30	37 *	.1	.2
413 S.D.A.	2	123	NR	146	.3	.8

Religious Group	Number of Churches, Synagogues, Mosques, or Temples	Number of Communicant, Confirmed, or Full Members	Number of Attendees	Total Adherents: Number of Adherents	Total Adherents: % of Total Pop.	Total Adherents: % of Total Adh.
419 So Bapt Conv	21	7,909	2,545	9,786 *	17.3	51.3
449 Un Methodist	12	1,838	823	2,274 *	4.0	11.9
DE SOTO	**42**	**7,220**	**3,147**	**10,092 ***	**31.3**	**100.0**
017 Amer Bapt Assn	1	92	NR	111 *	.3	1.1
053 Assemb of God	2	178	190	435	1.4	4.3
056 Baha'i	0	9	NR	9	-	.1
081 Catholic	1	NR	NR	851	2.6	8.4
097 Chr Chs&Chs Cr	1	135	NR	163 *	.5	1.6
127 Ch God (Cleve)	6	377	328	482 *	1.5	4.8
145 Ch God Prophcy	1	41	NR	49 *	.2	.5
151 L-D Saints	1	NR	NR	93	.3	.9
157 Ch of Brethren	1	22	24	27 *	.1	.3
165 Ch of Nazarene	1	132	81	193	.6	1.9
167 Chs of Christ	3	167	168	216	.7	2.1
193 Episcopal	1	NR	51	79	.2	.8
263 Int Foursq Gos	1	33	105	105 *	.3	1.0
283 Luth—MO Synod	1	89	68	104	.3	1.0
286 E.PA Mennonite	1	20	NR	24 *	.1	.2
288 Mennonite USA	1	29	53	53 *	.2	.5
355 Presb Ch (USA)	1	344	140	414 *	1.3	4.1
356 Presb Ch Amer	1	77	90	90	.3	.9
413 S.D.A.	1	80	NR	95	.3	.9
419 So Bapt Conv	11	4,003	1,270	4,822 *	15.0	47.8
449 Un Methodist	5	1,392	579	1,677 *	5.2	16.6
DIXIE	**31**	**4,792**	**1,867**	**6,120 ***	**44.3**	**100.0**
053 Assemb of God	2	157	180	190	1.4	3.1
056 Baha'i	0	2	NR	2	-	-
081 Catholic	1	NR	NR	180	1.3	2.9
127 Ch God (Cleve)	2	236	149	283 *	2.0	4.6
151 L-D Saints	1	NR	NR	195	1.4	3.2
167 Chs of Christ	2	87	80	111	.8	1.8
349 Pent Holiness	4	257	121	308 *	2.2	5.0
413 S.D.A.	1	75	NR	89	.6	1.5
419 So Bapt Conv	14	3,553	1,121	4,253 *	30.8	69.5
449 Un Methodist	4	425	216	509 *	3.7	8.3
DUVAL	**542**	**199,044**	**82,477**	**344,215 ***	**44.2**	**100.0**
017 Amer Bapt Assn	6	540	NR	681 *	.1	.2
019 Amer Bapt USA	4	901	70	1,136 *	.1	.3
034 Ant Orth of NA	1	181	NR	362	-	.1
050 Armen Ap Etchm	1	0	NR	200	-	.1
053 Assemb of God	30	8,527	5,437	11,416	1.5	3.3
056 Baha'i	2	335	NR	335	-	.1
059 Bapt Miss Assn	2	350	85	441 *	.1	.1
076 Buddhism	3	NR	NR	NR	-	-
081 Catholic	27	NR	NR	64,888	8.3	18.9
084 Calvary Chapel	1	NR	NR	NR	-	-
089 Chr & Miss Al	4	584	NR	618	.1	.2
093 Chr Ch (Disc)	10	2,508	901	3,161 *	.4	.9
097 Chr Chs&Chs Cr	7	4,408	NR	5,556 *	.7	1.6
105 Christian Ref	2	144	130	181 *	-	.1
123 Ch God (Ander)	8	NR	868	868	.1	.3
127 Ch God (Cleve)	30	4,074	2,012	5,175 *	.7	1.5
145 Ch God Prophcy	10	408	NR	510 *	.1	.1
151 L-D Saints	10	NR	NR	5,096	.7	1.5
157 Ch of Brethren	1	37	28	47 *	-	-
165 Ch of Nazarene	14	1,996	1,362	2,447	.3	.7
167 Chs of Christ	27	5,735	4,130	7,339	.9	2.1
173 Comm of Christ	1	90	NR	90	-	-
186 Coptic Orth Ch	1	NR	NR	NR	-	-
193 Episcopal	22	NR	4,929	13,177	1.7	3.8
203 Evan Free Ch	2	194	385	385	-	.1
207 E.L.C.A.	10	2,972	1,459	3,904	.5	1.1
223 Free Will Bapt	4	330	NR	416 *	.1	.1
226 Friends-USA	1	24	NR	30 *	-	-
246 Greek Orthodox	1	NR	NR	1,449	.2	.4
263 Int Foursq Gos	3	447	399	563 *	.1	.2
264 Int Chs of Crst	1	274	478	444	.1	.1
267 Muslim Est	3	NR	526	2,182	.3	.6
283 Luth—MO Synod	7	1,996	1,263	2,611	.3	.8
290 Metro Comm Ch	1	150	130	189 *	-	.1

NR–Not Reported *Total adherents estimated from known number of communicant, confirmed, full members. - Represents a percentage less than 0.1. Percentages may not total 100 due to rounding.

Table 4: Religious Congregations by County and Group: 2000

Religious Group	Number of Churches, Synagogues, Mosques, or Temples	Number of Communicant, Confirmed, or Full Members	Number of Attendees	Total Adherents		
				Number of Adherents	% of Total Pop.	% of Total Adh.
304 NatPrimBapt USA	6	355	NR	447 *	.1	.1
331 OCA: Ter Diocs	2	98	NR	241	-	.1
349 Pent Holiness	6	708	345	892 *	.1	.3
355 Presb Ch (USA)	25	10,623	5,510	13,389 *	1.7	3.9
356 Presb Ch Amer	7	657	652	835	.1	.2
360 Prim Bapt Chrch	3	NR	NR	NR	-	-
365 Prog Prim Bapt	2	160	NR	202 *	-	.1
388 Reg Bapt Gen As	2	139	185	186 *	-	.1
397 OCA: Roman Dioc	1	NR	NR	160	-	-
403 Salvation Army	1	243	72	253	-	.1
409 Separate Bapt	1	20	NR	25 *	-	-
410 Serb Orth USA	1	NR	NR	250	-	.1
413 S.D.A.	6	1,826	NR	2,173	.3	.6
418 Southw Bapt Fel	7	NR	NR	NR	-	-
419 So Bapt Conv	149	113,927	36,527	143,587 *	18.4	41.7
423 Syrian Orth Ch	1	NR	NR	200	-	.1
435 Unitarian-Univ	1	184	NR	232 *	-	.1
443 Un C of Christ	1	316	192	398 *	.1	.1
449 Un Methodist	45	22,705	9,445	28,615 *	3.7	8.3
463 Vineyard	2	625	505	788 *	.1	.2
469 WELS	2	241	177	333	-	.1
496 Jewish Est	5	NR	NR	6,100	.8	1.8
498 Indep.Charis.	3	922	550	922	.1	.3
499 Indep.Non-Char	6	8,090	3,725	8,090	1.0	2.4
ESCAMBIA	**249**	**83,512**	**34,653**	**139,690 ***	**47.4**	**100.0**
017 Amer Bapt Assn	7	1,068	NR	1,305 *	.4	.9
019 Amer Bapt USA	1	44	20	54 *	-	-
053 Assemb of God	20	4,523	5,011	9,567	3.2	6.8
056 Baha'i	0	53	NR	53	-	-
059 Bapt Miss Assn	3	203	75	248 *	.1	.2
076 Buddhism	1	NR	NR	NR	-	-
081 Catholic	18	NR	NR	25,026	8.5	17.9
084 Calvary Chapel	1	NR	NR	NR	-	-
089 Chr & Miss Al	1	0	NR	0	-	-
093 Chr Ch (Disc)	3	503	271	615 *	.2	.4
097 Chr Chs&Chs Cr	2	190	NR	232 *	.1	.2
123 Ch God (Ander)	1	NR	24	24	-	-
127 Ch God (Cleve)	5	653	262	798 *	.3	.6
143 CG in Cr(Menn)	1	194	NR	237 *	.1	.2
145 Ch God Prophcy	1	41	NR	50 *	-	-
151 L-D Saints	4	NR	NR	1,389	.5	1.0
165 Ch of Nazarene	2	605	377	611	.2	.4
167 Chs of Christ	17	2,505	2,413	3,193	1.1	2.3
173 Comm of Christ	4	451	NR	451	.2	.3
175 Congr Chr Chs	1	8	9	10 *	-	-
193 Episcopal	7	NR	1,539	4,909	1.7	3.5
203 Evan Free Ch	1	50	120	120	-	.1
207 E.L.C.A.	2	520	305	650	.2	.5
223 Free Will Bapt	5	412	NR	504 *	.2	.4
246 Greek Orthodox	1	NR	NR	918	.3	.7
266 Intrstat & Asc	1	117	NR	143 *	-	.1
267 Muslim Est	1	NR	156	609	.2	.4
283 Luth—MO Synod	7	2,072	1,065	2,775	.9	2.0
290 Metro Comm Ch	1	113	101	138 *	-	.1
297 Mennonite;Other	2	37	NR	45 *	-	-
304 NatPrimBapt USA	8	2,928	NR	3,578 *	1.2	2.6
335 Orth Pres Ch	1	13	13	13	-	-
349 Pent Holiness	5	501	229	612 *	.2	.4
355 Presb Ch (USA)	4	2,135	1,031	2,608 *	.9	1.9
356 Presb Ch Amer	5	1,100	793	1,355	.5	1.0
360 Prim Bapt Chrch	2	NR	NR	NR	-	-
388 Reg Bapt Gen As	1	30	30	37 *	-	-
403 Salvation Army	1	157	92	160	.1	.1
413 S.D.A.	2	537	NR	639	.2	.5
418 Southw Bapt Fel	2	NR	NR	NR	-	-
419 So Bapt Conv	64	48,908	14,855	59,768 *	20.3	42.8
435 Unitarian-Univ	1	94	NR	115 *	-	.1
449 Un Methodist	28	12,022	4,933	14,691 *	5.0	10.5
467 Wesleyan	1	25	29	40	-	-
496 Jewish Est	1	NR	NR	500	.2	.4
498 Indep.Charis.	2	700	900	900	.3	.6

Religious Group	Number of Churches, Synagogues, Mosques, or Temples	Number of Communicant, Confirmed, or Full Members	Number of Attendees	Total Adherents		
				Number of Adherents	% of Total Pop.	% of Total Adh.
FLAGLER	**31**	**5,120**	**3,444**	**17,626 ***	**35.4**	**100.0**
053 Assemb of God	2	285	355	365	.7	2.1
056 Baha'i	0	5	NR	5	-	-
081 Catholic	4	NR	NR	10,513	21.1	59.6
084 Calvary Chapel	1	NR	NR	NR	-	-
089 Chr & Miss Al	1	86	NR	207	.4	1.2
127 Ch God (Cleve)	1	34	20	39 *	.1	.2
151 L-D Saints	1	NR	NR	429	.9	2.4
165 Ch of Nazarene	1	20	8	20	-	.1
167 Chs of Christ	1	25	31	36	.1	.2
193 Episcopal	1	NR	301	597	1.2	3.4
207 E.L.C.A.	1	502	313	575	1.2	3.3
251 Holy Orth in NA	1	NR	NR	15	-	.1
283 Luth—MO Synod	1	211	158	238	.5	1.4
331 OCA: Ter Diocs	1	18	NR	27	.1	.2
349 Pent Holiness	1	35	47	40 *	.1	.2
356 Presb Ch Amer	1	48	70	70	.1	.4
413 S.D.A.	1	73	NR	87	.2	.5
419 So Bapt Conv	8	2,320	1,345	2,679 *	5.4	15.2
449 Un Methodist	3	1,458	796	1,684 *	3.4	9.6
FRANKLIN	**24**	**1,978**	**1,412**	**2,994 ***	**27.1**	**100.0**
053 Assemb of God	4	191	199	522	4.7	17.4
081 Catholic	2	NR	NR	194	1.8	6.5
127 Ch God (Cleve)	3	381	387	442 *	4.0	14.8
193 Episcopal	2	NR	154	207	1.9	6.9
304 NatPrimBapt USA	2	7	NR	8 *	.1	.3
349 Pent Holiness	2	200	169	232 *	2.1	7.7
419 So Bapt Conv	5	662	235	767 *	6.9	25.6
449 Un Methodist	4	537	268	622 *	5.6	20.8
GADSDEN	**73**	**9,946**	**2,762**	**13,191 ***	**29.3**	**100.0**
053 Assemb of God	7	215	260	294	.7	2.2
056 Baha'i	2	139	NR	139	.3	1.1
081 Catholic	2	NR	NR	417	.9	3.2
145 Ch God Prophcy	3	122	NR	153 *	.3	1.2
151 L-D Saints	1	NR	NR	154	.3	1.2
167 Chs of Christ	2	110	115	140	.3	1.1
193 Episcopal	2	NR	66	170	.4	1.3
223 Free Will Bapt	1	82	NR	103 *	.2	.8
304 NatPrimBapt USA	17	1,388	NR	1,738 *	3.9	13.2
349 Pent Holiness	2	259	110	324 *	.7	2.5
355 Presb Ch (USA)	4	613	260	767 *	1.7	5.8
356 Presb Ch Amer	2	98	83	128	.3	1.0
413 S.D.A.	1	45	NR	54	.1	.4
418 Southw Bapt Fel	1	NR	NR	NR	-	-
419 So Bapt Conv	18	5,401	1,357	6,764 *	15.0	51.3
449 Un Methodist	8	1,474	511	1,846 *	4.1	14.0
GILCHRIST	**25**	**4,708**	**1,621**	**5,999 ***	**41.6**	**100.0**
017 Amer Bapt Assn	2	125	NR	153 *	1.1	2.6
053 Assemb of God	1	41	45	102	.7	1.7
056 Baha'i	0	3	NR	3	-	.1
123 Ch God (Ander)	1	NR	123	123	.9	2.1
127 Ch God (Cleve)	2	154	39	189 *	1.3	3.2
165 Ch of Nazarene	1	88	83	127	.9	2.1
167 Chs of Christ	6	290	352	397	2.7	6.6
360 Prim Bapt Chrch	2	NR	NR	NR	-	-
413 S.D.A.	1	34	NR	40	.3	.7
419 So Bapt Conv	8	3,774	904	4,621 *	32.0	77.0
449 Un Methodist	1	199	75	244 *	1.7	4.1
GLADES	**11**	**1,454**	**604**	**3,450 ***	**32.6**	**100.0**
056 Baha'i	0	49	NR	49	.5	1.4
081 Catholic	2	NR	NR	1,708	16.1	49.5
097 Chr Chs&Chs Cr	1	60	NR	72 *	.7	2.1
127 Ch God (Cleve)	1	76	37	92 *	.9	2.7
145 Ch God Prophcy	1	41	NR	49 *	.5	1.4
349 Pent Holiness	1	26	69	31 *	.3	.9
419 So Bapt Conv	4	1,019	431	1,228 *	11.6	35.6
449 Un Methodist	1	183	67	221 *	2.1	6.4

NR–Not Reported   *Total adherents estimated from known number of communicant, confirmed, full members.   - Represents a percentage less than 0.1.   Percentages may not total 100 due to rounding.

Table 4: Religious Congregations by County and Group: 2000

Religious Group	Number of Churches, Synagogues, Mosques, or Temples	Number of Communicant, Confirmed, or Full Members	Number of Attendees	Total Adherents		
				Number of Adherents	% of Total Pop.	% of Total Adh.
GULF	**32**	**4,885**	**2,377**	**6,492 ***	**48.7**	**100.0**
053 Assemb of God	3	378	488	596	4.5	9.2
056 Baha'i	0	2	NR	2	-	-
081 Catholic	2	NR	NR	275	2.1	4.2
127 Ch God (Cleve)	2	69	65	86 *	.6	1.3
165 Ch of Nazarene	1	25	37	50	.4	.8
167 Chs of Christ	2	41	52	62	.5	1.0
193 Episcopal	2	NR	97	190	1.4	2.9
304 NatPrimBapt USA	1	150	NR	180 *	1.4	2.8
349 Pent Holiness	2	265	129	317 *	2.4	4.9
355 Presb Ch (USA)	2	57	41	68 *	.5	1.0
419 So Bapt Conv	10	3,001	1,030	3,592 *	26.9	55.3
449 Un Methodist	4	767	318	918 *	6.9	14.1
463 Vineyard	1	130	120	156 *	1.2	2.4
HAMILTON	**29**	**3,091**	**1,284**	**3,897 ***	**29.2**	**100.0**
053 Assemb of God	2	66	82	108	.8	2.8
056 Baha'i	0	1	NR	1	-	-
081 Catholic	1	NR	NR	90	.7	2.3
097 Chr Chs&Chs Cr	1	175	NR	213 *	1.6	5.5
127 Ch God (Cleve)	5	360	253	438 *	3.3	11.2
165 Ch of Nazarene	1	50	53	67	.5	1.7
167 Chs of Christ	2	83	103	117	.9	3.0
304 NatPrimBapt USA	1	30	NR	36 *	.3	.9
355 Presb Ch (USA)	2	108	74	132 *	1.0	3.4
360 Prim Bapt Chrch	1	NR	NR	NR	-	-
365 Prog Prim Bapt	1	64	NR	78 *	.6	2.0
419 So Bapt Conv	9	1,792	569	2,177 *	16.3	55.9
449 Un Methodist	3	362	150	440 *	3.3	11.3
HARDEE	**50**	**10,589**	**3,502**	**18,661 ***	**69.3**	**100.0**
017 Amer Bapt Assn	1	228	NR	289 *	1.1	1.5
053 Assemb of God	2	301	355	550	2.0	2.9
056 Baha'i	0	32	NR	32	.1	.2
081 Catholic	3	NR	NR	4,966	18.4	26.6
097 Chr Chs&Chs Cr	2	547	NR	694 *	2.6	3.7
127 Ch God (Cleve)	5	668	283	848 *	3.1	4.5
165 Ch of Nazarene	1	41	34	41	.2	.2
167 Chs of Christ	2	117	90	141	.5	.8
193 Episcopal	1	NR	34	76	.3	.4
263 Int Foursq Gos	1	166	287	287 *	1.1	1.5
283 Luth—MO Synod	1	35	50	45	.2	.2
291 Missionary Ch	1	49	65	65	.2	.3
304 NatPrimBapt USA	1	30	NR	38 *	.1	.2
356 Presb Ch Amer	1	106	70	123	.5	.7
360 Prim Bapt Chrch	3	NR	NR	NR	-	-
363 Primitive Meth	1	57	NR	61	.2	.3
413 S.D.A.	2	189	NR	224	.8	1.2
419 So Bapt Conv	18	7,257	1,831	9,209 *	34.2	49.3
449 Un Methodist	4	766	403	972 *	3.6	5.2
HENDRY	**40**	**4,730**	**2,760**	**8,311 ***	**23.0**	**100.0**
017 Amer Bapt Assn	1	52	NR	67 *	.2	.8
053 Assemb of God	4	382	481	913	2.5	11.0
056 Baha'i	0	112	NR	112	.3	1.3
081 Catholic	2	NR	NR	1,318	3.6	15.9
093 Chr Ch (Disc)	1	53	35	69 *	.2	.8
097 Chr Chs&Chs Cr	1	90	NR	117 *	.3	1.4
123 Ch God (Ander)	1	NR	50	50	.1	.6
127 Ch God (Cleve)	5	623	366	816 *	2.3	9.8
167 Chs of Christ	3	95	145	115	.3	1.4
193 Episcopal	2	NR	123	315	.9	3.8
283 Luth—MO Synod	2	59	75	76	.2	.9
339 Pent Ch of God	1	36	NR	156	.4	1.9
349 Pent Holiness	1	18	37	23 *	.1	.3
355 Presb Ch (USA)	1	68	60	88 *	.2	1.1
360 Prim Bapt Chrch	1	NR	NR	NR	-	-
388 Reg Bapt Gen As	1	45	60	60 *	.2	.7
419 So Bapt Conv	11	2,281	971	2,958 *	8.2	35.6
449 Un Methodist	2	816	357	1,058 *	2.9	12.7

Religious Group	Number of Churches, Synagogues, Mosques, or Temples	Number of Communicant, Confirmed, or Full Members	Number of Attendees	Total Adherents		
				Number of Adherents	% of Total Pop.	% of Total Adh.
HERNANDO	**87**	**16,475**	**10,914**	**57,762 ***	**44.2**	**100.0**
017 Amer Bapt Assn	1	100	NR	117 *	.1	.2
022 Carp Rus Orth	1	122	NR	207	.2	.4
053 Assemb of God	6	1,308	1,574	2,276	1.7	3.9
056 Baha'i	1	34	NR	34	-	.1
081 Catholic	6	NR	NR	34,894	26.7	60.4
089 Chr & Miss Al	1	30	NR	66	.1	.1
097 Chr Chs&Chs Cr	3	503	NR	588 *	.4	1.0
123 Ch God (Ander)	2	NR	49	49	-	.1
127 Ch God (Cleve)	3	231	240	339 *	.3	.6
145 Ch God Prophcy	1	41	NR	48 *	-	.1
151 L-D Saints	1	NR	NR	461	.4	.8
165 Ch of Nazarene	3	297	304	566	.4	1.0
167 Chs of Christ	6	302	375	389	.3	.7
173 Comm of Christ	1	41	NR	41	-	.1
193 Episcopal	2	NR	632	1,121	.9	1.9
203 Evan Free Ch	1	32	65	65	-	.1
207 E.L.C.A.	3	1,282	762	1,528	1.2	2.6
216 Evan Presby Ch	1	292	NR	341 *	.3	.6
246 Greek Orthodox	1	NR	NR	0	-	-
283 Luth—MO Synod	3	1,000	712	1,149	.9	2.0
339 Pent Ch of God	1	25	NR	30	-	.1
355 Presb Ch (USA)	2	878	495	1,025 *	.8	1.8
356 Presb Ch Amer	1	141	120	141	.1	.2
388 Reg Bapt Gen As	2	330	600	600 *	.5	1.0
403 Salvation Army	1	63	32	80	.1	.1
413 S.D.A.	3	266	NR	317	.2	.5
419 So Bapt Conv	17	5,019	2,343	5,862 *	4.5	10.1
435 Unitarian-Univ	1	28	NR	33 *	-	.1
443 Un C of Christ	2	296	256	346 *	.3	.6
449 Un Methodist	6	3,438	1,909	4,014 *	3.1	6.9
467 Wesleyan	2	254	348	875	.7	1.5
469 WELS	1	122	98	145	.1	.3
496 Jewish Est	1	NR	NR	15	-	-
HIGHLANDS	**96**	**20,952**	**10,828**	**31,233 ***	**35.7**	**100.0**
017 Amer Bapt Assn	1	56	NR	66 *	.1	.2
053 Assemb of God	5	550	680	1,048	1.2	3.4
055 As Ref Pres Ch	3	1,141	NR	1,201	1.4	3.8
056 Baha'i	0	7	NR	7	-	-
081 Catholic	4	NR	NR	4,639	5.3	14.9
089 Chr & Miss Al	1	47	NR	85	.1	.3
093 Chr Ch (Disc)	2	311	162	364 *	.4	1.2
097 Chr Chs&Chs Cr	4	697	NR	816 *	.9	2.6
123 Ch God (Ander)	2	NR	222	222	.3	.7
127 Ch God (Cleve)	8	931	726	1,184 *	1.4	3.8
145 Ch God Prophcy	1	41	NR	48 *	.1	.2
151 L-D Saints	1	NR	NR	309	.4	1.0
157 Ch of Brethren	2	420	331	492 *	.6	1.6
165 Ch of Nazarene	3	365	375	553	.6	1.8
167 Chs of Christ	5	382	410	496	.6	1.6
193 Episcopal	3	NR	359	634	.7	2.0
207 E.L.C.A.	2	299	238	332	.4	1.1
283 Luth—MO Synod	3	548	450	620	.7	2.0
291 Missionary Ch	1	75	120	120	.1	.4
349 Pent Holiness	1	70	70	82 *	.1	.3
355 Presb Ch (USA)	1	136	80	159 *	.2	.5
356 Presb Ch Amer	1	155	198	198	.2	.6
370 Ref Baptist Chs	1	NR	NR	NR	-	-
388 Reg Bapt Gen As	4	669	819	839 *	1.0	2.7
403 Salvation Army	1	79	27	333	.4	1.1
413 S.D.A.	6	1,445	NR	1,718	2.0	5.5
419 So Bapt Conv	20	8,295	3,111	9,706 *	11.1	31.1
443 Un C of Christ	2	760	497	889 *	1.0	2.8
449 Un Methodist	7	3,473	1,953	4,063 *	4.7	13.0
496 Jewish Est	1	NR	NR	10	-	-
HILLSBOROUGH	**632**	**168,256**	**85,202**	**417,425 ***	**41.8**	**100.0**
017 Amer Bapt Assn	7	1,173	NR	1,464 *	.1	.4
019 Amer Bapt USA	2	183	163	228 *	-	.1
053 Assemb of God	50	6,197	6,828	8,891	.9	2.1
055 As Ref Pres Ch	2	196	NR	237	-	.1
056 Baha'i	3	295	NR	295	-	.1

NR–Not Reported *Total adherents estimated from known number of communicant, confirmed, full members. - Represents a percentage less than 0.1. Percentages may not total 100 due to rounding.

Table 4: Religious Congregations by County and Group: 2000

Religious Group	Number of Churches, Synagogues, Mosques, or Temples	Number of Communicant, Confirmed, or Full Members	Number of Attendees	Total Adherents		
				Number of Adherents	% of Total Pop.	% of Total Adh.
057 Bapt Gen Conf	4	399	350	511 *	.1	.1
076 Buddhism	3	NR	NR	NR	-	-
081 Catholic	25	NR	NR	166,122	16.6	39.8
084 Calvary Chapel	2	NR	NR	NR	-	-
089 Chr & Miss Al	6	212	NR	355	-	.1
093 Chr Ch (Disc)	4	923	487	1,152 *	.1	.3
097 Chr Chs&Chs Cr	11	2,846	NR	3,552 *	.4	.9
123 Ch God (Ander)	9	NR	1,144	1,144	.1	.3
127 Ch God (Cleve)	41	7,172	4,091	8,958 *	.9	2.1
145 Ch God Prophcy	6	237	NR	296 *	-	.1
151 L-D Saints	10	NR	NR	3,837	.4	.9
157 Ch of Brethren	1	69	44	86 *	-	-
165 Ch of Nazarene	15	1,875	1,466	2,349	.2	.6
167 Chs of Christ	51	5,100	5,399	6,730	.7	1.6
173 Comm of Christ	1	124	NR	124	-	-
179 Consrv Bapt	1	NR	60	60	-	-
185 Cumber Presb	6	237	NR	503	.1	.1
186 Coptic Orth Ch	1	NR	NR	NR	-	-
193 Episcopal	16	NR	3,085	7,854	.8	1.9
203 Evan Free Ch	2	134	240	270	-	.1
207 E.L.C.A.	13	5,475	2,744	6,722	.7	1.6
216 Evan Presby Ch	2	470	NR	587 *	.1	.1
221 Free Methodist	2	199	246	304	-	.1
223 Free Will Bapt	3	247	NR	309 *	-	.1
226 Friends-USA	1	24	NR	30 *	-	-
246 Greek Orthodox	1	NR	NR	672	.1	.2
252 Hindu	4	NR	NR	NR	-	-
262 Int Cou Comm Ch	3	570	NR	711 *	.1	.2
263 Int Foursq Gos	7	291	543	543 *	.1	.1
264 Int Chs of Crst	1	283	531	408	-	.1
267 Muslim Est	3	NR	1,280	4,826	.5	1.2
283 Luth—MO Synod	9	2,783	1,263	3,794	.4	.9
288 Mennonite USA	2	97	25	121 *	-	-
290 Metro Comm Ch	1	258	235	322 *	-	.1
304 NatPrimBapt USA	8	1,624	NR	2,028 *	.2	.5
333 Malan Dioc Am	1	NR	NR	150	-	-
334 Malan Syr Orth	1	24	NR	120	-	-
339 Pent Ch of God	7	212	NR	379	-	.1
349 Pent Holiness	7	1,003	1,048	1,252 *	.1	.3
355 Presb Ch (USA)	20	7,701	4,287	9,614 *	1.0	2.3
356 Presb Ch Amer	6	841	1,048	1,237	.1	.3
360 Prim Bapt Chrch	6	NR	NR	NR	-	-
365 Prog Prim Bapt	3	80	NR	100 *	-	-
370 Ref Baptist Chs	2	NR	NR	NR	-	-
371 Ref Ch in Am	1	154	150	285	-	.1
388 Reg Bapt Gen As	1	77	110	96 *	-	-
400 Rus Orth Moscow	1	NR	NR	NR	-	-
403 Salvation Army	1	445	116	789	.1	.2
413 S.D.A.	18	3,363	NR	4,002	.4	1.0
418 Southw Bapt Fel	3	NR	NR	NR	-	-
419 So Bapt Conv	136	82,698	31,563	103,254 *	10.3	24.7
431 Ukrainian Orth	1	NR	NR	87	-	-
435 Unitarian-Univ	3	228	NR	285 *	-	.1
443 Un C of Christ	4	1,350	718	1,686 *	.2	.4
449 Un Methodist	46	26,430	12,330	32,999 *	3.3	7.9
463 Vineyard	1	130	120	162 *	-	-
467 Wesleyan	2	16	240	622	.1	.1
469 WELS	2	186	138	236	-	.1
496 Jewish Est	10	NR	NR	20,000	2.0	4.8
498 Indep.Charis.	4	1,550	1,240	1,600	.2	.4
499 Indep.Non-Char	6	2,075	1,870	2,075	.2	.5
HOLMES	**72**	**8,059**	**3,996**	**10,350 ***	**55.8**	**100.0**
053 Assemb of God	18	1,407	1,510	1,832	9.9	17.7
056 Baha'i	0	3	NR	3	-	-
081 Catholic	1	NR	NR	203	1.1	2.0
127 Ch God (Cleve)	2	99	68	119 *	.6	1.1
145 Ch God Prophcy	2	82	NR	98 *	.5	.9
151 L-D Saints	1	NR	NR	250	1.3	2.4
165 Ch of Nazarene	1	20	27	27	.1	.3
167 Chs of Christ	4	150	160	194	1.0	1.9
223 Free Will Bapt	1	82	NR	100 *	.5	1.0
283 Luth—MO Synod	1	41	26	48	.3	.5
339 Pent Ch of God	1	24	NR	49	.3	.5
355 Presb Ch (USA)	1	9	7	11 *	.1	.1
360 Prim Bapt Chrch	1	NR	NR	NR	-	-
413 S.D.A.	1	33	NR	39	.2	.4
419 So Bapt Conv	28	5,437	1,908	6,567 *	35.4	63.4
449 Un Methodist	9	672	290	810 *	4.4	7.8
INDIAN RIVER	**81**	**18,227**	**12,195**	**57,379 ***	**50.8**	**100.0**
053 Assemb of God	3	759	965	1,235	1.1	2.2
055 As Ref Pres Ch	1	69	NR	130	.1	.2
056 Baha'i	1	59	NR	59	.1	.1
081 Catholic	4	NR	NR	30,138	26.7	52.5
084 Calvary Chapel	1	NR	NR	NR	-	-
089 Chr & Miss Al	2	47	NR	197	.2	.3
093 Chr Ch (Disc)	1	56	83	66 *	.1	.1
097 Chr Chs&Chs Cr	3	480	NR	562 *	.5	1.0
123 Ch God (Ander)	2	NR	1,441	1,441	1.3	2.5
127 Ch God (Cleve)	7	991	555	1,160 *	1.0	2.0
151 L-D Saints	1	NR	NR	408	.4	.7
165 Ch of Nazarene	2	487	327	605	.5	1.1
167 Chs of Christ	3	277	313	392	.3	.7
179 Consrv Bapt	1	NR	70	70	.1	.1
193 Episcopal	3	NR	1,123	2,706	2.4	4.7
201 Evan Cov Ch	1	94	84	110 *	.1	.2
207 E.L.C.A.	3	1,064	637	1,347	1.2	2.3
223 Free Will Bapt	1	82	NR	96 *	.1	.2
252 Hindu	1	NR	NR	NR	-	-
283 Luth—MO Synod	1	197	137	216	.2	.4
304 NatPrimBapt USA	2	0	NR	0 *	-	-
355 Presb Ch (USA)	3	1,244	764	1,456 *	1.3	2.5
356 Presb Ch Amer	1	0	0	0	-	-
360 Prim Bapt Chrch	1	NR	NR	NR	-	-
388 Reg Bapt Gen As	1	44	35	51 *	-	.1
403 Salvation Army	1	58	20	66	.1	.1
413 S.D.A.	1	85	NR	101	.1	.2
418 Southw Bapt Fel	1	NR	NR	NR	-	-
419 So Bapt Conv	15	5,791	1,886	6,776 *	6.0	11.8
435 Unitarian-Univ	1	122	NR	143 *	.1	.2
443 Un C of Christ	2	2,328	1,651	2,724 *	2.4	4.7
449 Un Methodist	6	3,576	1,729	4,185 *	3.7	7.3
467 Wesleyan	1	17	25	39	-	.1
496 Jewish Est	2	NR	NR	400	.4	.7
498 Indep.Charis.	1	300	350	500	.4	.9
JACKSON	**114**	**15,041**	**6,039**	**19,415 ***	**41.5**	**100.0**
017 Amer Bapt Assn	1	69	NR	83 *	.2	.4
053 Assemb of God	17	1,657	1,407	2,330	5.0	12.0
056 Baha'i	0	7	NR	7	-	-
081 Catholic	1	NR	NR	238	.5	1.2
089 Chr & Miss Al	1	36	NR	76	.2	.4
127 Ch God (Cleve)	4	245	103	294 *	.6	1.5
145 Ch God Prophcy	1	41	NR	49 *	.1	.3
151 L-D Saints	1	NR	NR	500	1.1	2.6
165 Ch of Nazarene	1	39	24	39	.1	.2
167 Chs of Christ	2	140	150	181	.4	.9
193 Episcopal	1	NR	103	169	.4	.9
223 Free Will Bapt	10	825	NR	989 *	2.1	5.1
283 Luth—MO Synod	1	50	29	54	.1	.3
339 Pent Ch of God	1	15	NR	28	.1	.1
349 Pent Holiness	6	313	305	375 *	.8	1.9
355 Presb Ch (USA)	1	217	100	260 *	.6	1.3
360 Prim Bapt Chrch	1	NR	NR	NR	-	-
413 S.D.A.	3	110	NR	131	.3	.7
419 So Bapt Conv	39	8,948	2,942	10,729 *	22.9	55.3
449 Un Methodist	21	2,262	825	2,713 *	5.8	14.0
467 Wesleyan	1	67	51	170	.4	.9
JEFFERSON	**27**	**3,376**	**1,602**	**4,498 ***	**34.9**	**100.0**
053 Assemb of God	1	30	38	51	.4	1.1
056 Baha'i	0	35	NR	35	.3	.8
081 Catholic	1	NR	NR	153	1.2	3.4
127 Ch God (Cleve)	1	35	40	42 *	.3	.9
145 Ch God Prophcy	1	41	NR	49 *	.4	1.1
165 Ch of Nazarene	1	73	55	77	.6	1.7

NR–Not Reported *Total adherents estimated from known number of communicant, confirmed, full members. - Represents a percentage less than 0.1. Percentages may not total 100 due to rounding.

Table 4: Religious Congregations by County and Group: 2000

Religious Group	Number of Churches, Synagogues, Mosques, or Temples	Number of Communicant, Confirmed, or Full Members	Number of Attendees	Total Adherents		
				Number of Adherents	% of Total Pop.	% of Total Adh.
167 Chs of Christ	2	56	72	72	.6	1.6
193 Episcopal	1	NR	104	277	2.1	6.2
304 NatPrimBapt USA	2	106	NR	128 *	1.0	2.8
349 Pent Holiness	2	270	191	325 *	2.5	7.2
355 Presb Ch (USA)	1	72	42	87 *	.7	1.9
360 Prim Bapt Chrch	1	NR	NR	NR	-	-
419 So Bapt Conv	7	1,904	668	2,293 *	17.8	51.0
449 Un Methodist	6	754	392	909 *	7.0	20.2
LAFAYETTE	**20**	**2,925**	**1,319**	**3,600 ***	**51.3**	**100.0**
053 Assemb of God	1	68	85	118	1.7	3.3
127 Ch God (Cleve)	1	152	152	182 *	2.6	5.1
167 Chs of Christ	2	50	70	75	1.1	2.1
193 Episcopal	2	NR	18	49	.7	1.4
419 So Bapt Conv	12	2,420	922	2,895 *	41.2	80.4
449 Un Methodist	2	235	72	281 *	4.0	7.8
LAKE	**194**	**49,209**	**25,297**	**83,522 ***	**39.7**	**100.0**
011 A.W.M.C.	1	0	20	0	-	-
017 Amer Bapt Assn	7	1,081	NR	1,285 *	.6	1.5
034 Ant Orth of NA	1	84	NR	168	.1	.2
053 Assemb of God	8	1,032	1,243	1,685	.8	2.0
056 Baha'i	0	48	NR	48	-	.1
081 Catholic	4	NR	NR	19,248	9.1	23.0
089 Chr & Miss Al	2	181	NR	345	.2	.4
093 Chr Ch (Disc)	1	149	58	177 *	.1	.2
097 Chr Chs&Chs Cr	7	1,723	NR	2,048 *	1.0	2.5
123 Ch God (Ander)	4	NR	270	270	.1	.3
127 Ch God (Cleve)	21	2,033	1,365	2,441 *	1.2	2.9
145 Ch God Prophcy	3	122	NR	144 *	.1	.2
151 L-D Saints	4	NR	NR	2,016	1.0	2.4
165 Ch of Nazarene	4	546	454	766	.4	.9
167 Chs of Christ	12	1,170	1,300	1,553	.7	1.9
173 Comm of Christ	2	141	NR	141	.1	.2
175 Congr Chr Chs	1	156	75	185 *	.1	.2
183 Cons Menn Conf	1	46	56	67	-	.1
193 Episcopal	5	NR	1,009	2,422	1.2	2.9
201 Evan Cov Ch	2	97	88	116 *	.1	.1
203 Evan Free Ch	3	374	590	590	.3	.7
207 E.L.C.A.	4	1,168	769	1,425	.7	1.7
221 Free Methodist	2	36	33	51	-	.1
262 Int Cou Comm Ch	1	210	NR	249 *	.1	.3
283 Luth—MO Synod	4	1,817	1,303	2,128	1.0	2.5
304 NatPrimBapt USA	1	0	NR	0 *	-	-
349 Pent Holiness	6	333	278	396 *	.2	.5
355 Presb Ch (USA)	10	4,492	3,059	5,337 *	2.5	6.4
356 Presb Ch Amer	2	175	195	221	.1	.3
360 Prim Bapt Chrch	1	NR	NR	NR	-	-
370 Ref Baptist Chs	1	NR	NR	NR	-	-
388 Reg Bapt Gen As	1	98	85	85 *	-	.1
403 Salvation Army	1	32	32	33	-	-
413 S.D.A.	5	623	NR	741	.4	.9
418 Southw Bapt Fel	2	NR	NR	NR	-	-
419 So Bapt Conv	34	21,541	7,533	25,592 *	12.2	30.6
435 Unitarian-Univ	1	33	NR	39 *	-	-
443 Un C of Christ	2	419	325	498 *	.2	.6
449 Un Methodist	16	8,328	4,451	9,894 *	4.7	11.8
463 Vineyard	1	136	90	162 *	.1	.2
467 Wesleyan	2	90	133	218	.1	.3
469 WELS	1	70	83	83	-	.1
496 Jewish Est	2	NR	NR	30	-	-
498 Indep.Charis.	1	625	400	625	.3	.7
LEE	**250**	**57,470**	**41,043**	**168,506 ***	**38.2**	**100.0**
017 Amer Bapt Assn	1	77	NR	91 *	-	.1
040 Ap Chr Ch-Amer	1	17	33	33 *	-	-
053 Assemb of God	15	4,112	5,419	13,639	3.1	8.1
056 Baha'i	2	105	NR	105	-	.1
057 Bapt Gen Conf	1	76	97	97 *	-	.1
059 Bapt Miss Assn	2	93	65	110 *	-	.1
076 Buddhism	1	NR	NR	NR	-	-
081 Catholic	18	NR	NR	75,329	17.1	44.7
084 Calvary Chapel	1	NR	NR	NR	-	-
089 Chr & Miss Al	6	838	NR	1,599	.4	.9
093 Chr Ch (Disc)	3	434	298	512 *	.1	.3
097 Chr Chs&Chs Cr	7	2,028	NR	2,394 *	.5	1.4
123 Ch God (Ander)	2	NR	108	108	-	.1
127 Ch God (Cleve)	10	2,259	1,520	2,869 *	.7	1.7
145 Ch God Prophcy	5	196	NR	231 *	.1	.1
151 L-D Saints	4	NR	NR	1,686	.4	1.0
157 Ch of Brethren	2	163	110	202 *	-	.1
165 Ch of Nazarene	5	844	737	1,201	.3	.7
167 Chs of Christ	8	895	908	1,510	.3	.9
173 Comm of Christ	1	106	NR	106	-	.1
175 Congr Chr Chs	2	232	221	274 *	.1	.2
179 Consrv Bapt	1	NR	120	120	-	.1
193 Episcopal	11	NR	2,058	3,746	.8	2.2
203 Evan Free Ch	1	112	200	200	-	.1
207 E.L.C.A.	10	3,675	2,441	5,104	1.2	3.0
221 Free Methodist	4	256	341	343	.1	.2
226 Friends-USA	2	119	NR	140 *	-	.1
246 Greek Orthodox	1	NR	NR	342	.1	.2
263 Int Foursq Gos	1	30	50	50 *	-	-
267 Muslim Est	2	NR	236	909	.2	.5
268 Jain	1	NR	NR	NR	-	-
283 Luth—MO Synod	7	2,303	1,776	2,768	.6	1.6
288 Mennonite USA	3	363	570	630 *	.1	.4
290 Metro Comm Ch	1	124	129	146 *	-	.1
331 OCA: Ter Diocs	1	39	NR	120	-	.1
349 Pent Holiness	3	452	420	534 *	.1	.3
355 Presb Ch (USA)	10	5,891	3,895	6,956 *	1.6	4.1
356 Presb Ch Amer	2	546	537	696	.2	.4
360 Prim Bapt Chrch	1	NR	NR	NR	-	-
388 Reg Bapt Gen As	2	401	373	481 *	.1	.3
403 Salvation Army	1	167	102	306	.1	.2
413 S.D.A.	6	1,026	NR	1,222	.3	.7
418 Southw Bapt Fel	2	NR	NR	NR	-	-
419 So Bapt Conv	38	15,387	8,258	18,165 *	4.1	10.8
435 Unitarian-Univ	1	348	NR	411 *	.1	.2
443 Un C of Christ	4	1,542	1,128	1,820 *	.4	1.1
449 Un Methodist	21	10,962	6,928	12,939 *	2.9	7.7
455 Un Ref Chs N.A.	1	58	NR	72	-	-
463 Vineyard	2	440	320	519 *	.1	.3
467 Wesleyan	4	180	376	751	.2	.4
469 WELS	3	414	319	570	.1	.3
496 Jewish Est	4	NR	NR	5,400	1.2	3.2
499 Indep.Non-Char	2	160	950	950	.2	.6
LEON	**195**	**54,542**	**24,919**	**89,959 ***	**37.6**	**100.0**
017 Amer Bapt Assn	2	539	NR	645 *	.3	.7
053 Assemb of God	10	1,343	1,681	2,391	1.0	2.7
056 Baha'i	2	101	NR	101	-	.1
076 Buddhism	2	NR	NR	NR	-	-
081 Catholic	5	NR	NR	13,678	5.7	15.2
084 Calvary Chapel	1	NR	NR	NR	-	-
089 Chr & Miss Al	1	135	NR	225	.1	.3
097 Chr Chs&Chs Cr	4	520	NR	623 *	.3	.7
123 Ch God (Ander)	2	NR	50	50	-	.1
127 Ch God (Cleve)	5	600	243	718 *	.3	.8
145 Ch God Prophcy	4	163	NR	196 *	.1	.2
151 L-D Saints	5	NR	NR	1,974	.8	2.2
165 Ch of Nazarene	2	188	149	246	.1	.3
167 Chs of Christ	6	1,164	1,115	1,481	.6	1.6
173 Comm of Christ	1	39	NR	39	-	-
183 Cons Menn Conf	1	64	78	93	-	.1
186 Coptic Orth Ch	1	NR	NR	NR	-	-
193 Episcopal	7	NR	1,782	4,771	2.0	5.3
203 Evan Free Ch	1	101	350	350	.1	.4
207 E.L.C.A.	2	733	376	901	.4	1.0
226 Friends-USA	1	24	NR	29 *	-	-
246 Greek Orthodox	1	NR	NR	393	.2	.4
252 Hindu	2	NR	NR	NR	-	-
263 Int Foursq Gos	1	64	69	77 *	-	.1
264 Int Chs of Crst	1	321	522	434	.2	.5
267 Muslim Est	2	NR	181	664	.3	.7
283 Luth—MO Synod	2	661	483	786	.3	.9
290 Metro Comm Ch	1	36	32	43 *	-	-

NR–Not Reported *Total adherents estimated from known number of communicant, confirmed, full members. - Represents a percentage less than 0.1. Percentages may not total 100 due to rounding.

Table 4: Religious Congregations by County and Group: 2000

Religious Group	Number of Churches, Synagogues, Mosques, or Temples	Number of Communicant, Confirmed, or Full Members	Number of Attendees	Total Adherents		
				Number of Adherents	% of Total Pop.	% of Total Adh.
304 NatPrimBapt USA	36	4,355	NR	5,213 *	2.2	5.8
335 Orth Pres Ch	1	92	116	116	-	.1
349 Pent Holiness	9	2,244	976	2,686 *	1.1	3.0
355 Presb Ch (USA)	8	3,089	1,351	3,698 *	1.5	4.1
356 Presb Ch Amer	3	682	681	746	.3	.8
388 Reg Bapt Gen As	1	12	25	25 *	-	-
403 Salvation Army	1	77	32	110	-	.1
413 S.D.A.	2	393	NR	467	.2	.5
418 Southw Bapt Fel	2	NR	NR	NR	-	-
419 So Bapt Conv	33	24,907	9,819	29,814 *	12.5	33.1
435 Unitarian-Univ	1	158	NR	189 *	.1	.2
443 Un C of Christ	1	111	125	133 *	.1	.1
449 Un Methodist	14	9,383	3,372	11,231 *	4.7	12.5
463 Vineyard	1	135	100	162 *	.1	.2
469 WELS	1	41	36	61	-	.1
496 Jewish Est	3	NR	NR	2,200	.9	2.4
498 Indep.Charis.	1	1,800	775	1,800	.8	2.0
499 Indep.Non-Char	2	267	400	400	.2	.4
LEVY	**50**	**8,473**	**4,041**	**11,655 ***	**33.8**	**100.0**
053 Assemb of God	3	205	300	334	1.0	2.9
056 Baha'i	0	17	NR	17	-	.1
081 Catholic	3	NR	NR	680	2.0	5.8
097 Chr Chs&Chs Cr	1	38	NR	46 *	.1	.4
127 Ch God (Cleve)	5	523	398	642 *	1.9	5.5
151 L-D Saints	1	NR	NR	270	.8	2.3
167 Chs of Christ	9	442	489	621	1.8	5.3
193 Episcopal	3	NR	147	222	.6	1.9
203 Evan Free Ch	1	13	35	35	.1	.3
283 Luth—MO Synod	1	66	41	71	.2	.6
355 Presb Ch (USA)	2	123	86	149 *	.4	1.3
419 So Bapt Conv	13	5,956	1,992	7,244 *	21.0	62.2
449 Un Methodist	8	1,090	553	1,324 *	3.8	11.4
LIBERTY	**18**	**2,077**	**863**	**3,286 ***	**46.8**	**100.0**
053 Assemb of God	4	186	171	241	3.4	7.3
097 Chr Chs&Chs Cr	1	90	NR	107 *	1.5	3.3
127 Ch God (Cleve)	1	197	103	235 *	3.3	7.2
145 Ch God Prophcy	1	41	NR	49 *	.7	1.5
151 L-D Saints	3	NR	NR	790	11.3	24.0
349 Pent Holiness	1	80	55	95 *	1.4	2.9
419 So Bapt Conv	5	1,356	462	1,617 *	23.0	49.2
449 Un Methodist	2	127	72	152 *	2.2	4.6
MADISON	**50**	**6,488**	**2,584**	**8,358 ***	**44.6**	**100.0**
017 Amer Bapt Assn	2	125	NR	153 *	.8	1.8
053 Assemb of God	1	17	27	27	.1	.3
056 Baha'i	0	3	NR	3	-	-
081 Catholic	1	NR	NR	156	.8	1.9
127 Ch God (Cleve)	3	157	114	193 *	1.0	2.3
151 L-D Saints	1	NR	NR	131	.7	1.6
165 Ch of Nazarene	1	14	19	25	.1	.3
167 Chs of Christ	2	31	49	48	.3	.6
193 Episcopal	1	NR	47	105	.6	1.3
304 NatPrimBapt USA	4	243	NR	298 *	1.6	3.6
355 Presb Ch (USA)	1	16	9	20 *	.1	.2
356 Presb Ch Amer	1	133	82	154	.8	1.8
360 Prim Bapt Chrch	2	NR	NR	NR	-	-
413 S.D.A.	1	43	NR	51	.3	.6
419 So Bapt Conv	21	4,498	1,647	5,513 *	29.4	66.0
449 Un Methodist	8	1,208	590	1,481 *	7.9	17.7
MANATEE	**158**	**41,864**	**21,595**	**94,601 ***	**35.8**	**100.0**
019 Amer Bapt USA	1	77	45	92 *	-	.1
053 Assemb of God	6	664	883	1,012	.4	1.1
055 As Ref Pres Ch	1	236	NR	326	.1	.3
056 Baha'i	1	60	NR	60	-	.1
057 Bapt Gen Conf	1	530	574	633 *	.2	.7
071 Brethren (Ash)	1	46	43	55 *	-	.1
075 Brethren in Cr	1	0	0	0	-	-
081 Catholic	8	NR	NR	35,048	13.3	37.0
089 Chr & Miss Al	3	47	NR	183	.1	.2
093 Chr Ch (Disc)	1	106	65	127 *	-	.1
097 Chr Chs&Chs Cr	5	1,175	NR	1,404 *	.5	1.5
105 Christian Ref	1	651	0	777 *	.3	.8
123 Ch God (Ander)	2	NR	493	493	.2	.5
127 Ch God (Cleve)	10	903	495	1,086 *	.4	1.1
145 Ch God Prophcy	1	41	NR	49 *	-	.1
151 L-D Saints	2	NR	NR	954	.4	1.0
157 Ch of Brethren	1	323	0	386 *	.1	.4
165 Ch of Nazarene	3	1,019	896	1,277	.5	1.3
167 Chs of Christ	10	874	985	1,100	.4	1.2
173 Comm of Christ	1	189	NR	189	.1	.2
193 Episcopal	4	NR	1,127	2,394	.9	2.5
201 Evan Cov Ch	2	331	281	396 *	.1	.4
203 Evan Free Ch	1	79	180	180	.1	.2
207 E.L.C.A.	4	1,411	982	1,660	.6	1.8
221 Free Methodist	1	55	107	107	-	.1
246 Greek Orthodox	1	NR	NR	507	.2	.5
262 Int Cou Comm Ch	3	1,280	NR	1,528 *	.6	1.6
283 Luth—MO Synod	2	1,206	739	1,291	.5	1.4
290 Metro Comm Ch	1	133	169	169 *	.1	.2
304 NatPrimBapt USA	3	225	NR	269 *	.1	.3
331 OCA: Ter Diocs	1	50	NR	98	-	.1
339 Pent Ch of God	1	33	NR	70	-	.1
349 Pent Holiness	2	528	405	631 *	.2	.7
355 Presb Ch (USA)	6	2,736	1,560	3,267 *	1.2	3.5
356 Presb Ch Amer	2	110	130	148	.1	.2
360 Prim Bapt Chrch	1	NR	NR	NR	-	-
371 Ref Ch in Am	1	155	166	356	.1	.4
403 Salvation Army	2	206	94	380	.1	.4
413 S.D.A.	3	431	NR	513	.2	.5
418 Southw Bapt Fel	1	NR	NR	NR	-	-
419 So Bapt Conv	31	17,613	5,525	21,035 *	8.0	22.2
435 Unitarian-Univ	1	100	NR	119 *	-	.1
443 Un C of Christ	2	645	405	770 *	.3	.8
449 Un Methodist	17	6,874	4,279	8,211 *	3.1	8.7
467 Wesleyan	1	99	115	248	.1	.3
469 WELS	1	223	152	303	.1	.3
496 Jewish Est	2	NR	NR	4,000	1.5	4.2
499 Indep.Non-Char	1	400	700	700	.3	.7
MARION	**222**	**45,644**	**25,385**	**89,092 ***	**34.4**	**100.0**
017 Amer Bapt Assn	2	261	NR	312 *	.1	.4
034 Ant Orth of NA	1	27	NR	54	-	.1
049 Armen Ap Cilic	1	37	NR	210	.1	.2
050 Armen Ap Etchm	1	0	NR	50	-	.1
053 Assemb of God	9	1,215	1,530	1,665	.6	1.9
056 Baha'i	1	66	NR	66	-	.1
057 Bapt Gen Conf	1	30	41	41 *	-	-
081 Catholic	10	NR	NR	29,725	11.5	33.4
089 Chr & Miss Al	2	92	NR	176	.1	.2
093 Chr Ch (Disc)	2	619	24	740 *	.3	.8
097 Chr Chs&Chs Cr	4	1,308	NR	1,564 *	.6	1.8
123 Ch God (Ander)	2	NR	273	273	.1	.3
127 Ch God (Cleve)	14	2,858	1,893	3,430 *	1.3	3.8
145 Ch God Prophcy	2	82	NR	98 *	-	.1
151 L-D Saints	4	NR	NR	1,305	.5	1.5
165 Ch of Nazarene	4	351	298	421	.2	.5
167 Chs of Christ	12	1,089	1,165	1,420	.5	1.6
173 Comm of Christ	1	37	NR	37	-	-
193 Episcopal	6	NR	1,214	1,977	.8	2.2
207 E.L.C.A.	6	1,335	986	1,532	.6	1.7
221 Free Methodist	2	65	124	124	-	.1
223 Free Will Bapt	2	165	NR	197 *	.1	.2
263 Int Foursq Gos	2	154	152	184 *	.1	.2
283 Luth—MO Synod	5	1,167	902	1,324	.5	1.5
304 NatPrimBapt USA	5	35	NR	42 *	-	-
335 Orth Pres Ch	1	17	36	36	-	-
349 Pent Holiness	5	337	294	403 *	.2	.5
355 Presb Ch (USA)	10	2,935	1,524	3,508 *	1.4	3.9
356 Presb Ch Amer	4	761	815	977	.4	1.1
360 Prim Bapt Chrch	1	NR	NR	NR	-	-
363 Primitive Meth	1	57	NR	61	-	.1
388 Reg Bapt Gen As	2	120	210	210 *	.1	.2
403 Salvation Army	1	142	71	138	.1	.2

NR–Not Reported *Total adherents estimated from known number of communicant, confirmed, full members. - Represents a percentage less than 0.1. Percentages may not total 100 due to rounding.

Table 4: Religious Congregations by County and Group: 2000

Religious Group	Number of Churches, Synagogues, Mosques, or Temples	Number of Communicant, Confirmed, or Full Members	Number of Attendees	Total Adherents: Number of Adherents	Total Adherents: % of Total Pop.	Total Adherents: % of Total Adh.
413 S.D.A.	6	845	NR	1,005	.4	1.1
418 Southw Bapt Fel	2	NR	NR	NR	-	-
419 So Bapt Conv	52	20,236	9,440	24,183 *	9.3	27.1
435 Unitarian-Univ	1	48	NR	57 *	-	.1
443 Un C of Christ	2	382	168	457 *	.2	.5
449 Un Methodist	30	8,635	4,089	10,317 *	4.0	11.6
467 Wesleyan	1	43	54	127	-	.1
469 WELS	1	93	82	146	.1	.2
496 Jewish Est	1	NR	NR	500	.2	.6
MARTIN	**77**	**15,091**	**10,899**	**59,692 ***	**47.1**	**100.0**
017 Amer Bapt Assn	2	353	NR	412 *	.3	.7
053 Assemb of God	4	401	540	577	.5	1.0
056 Baha'i	0	39	NR	39	-	.1
081 Catholic	6	NR	NR	35,428	28.0	59.4
089 Chr & Miss Al	1	37	NR	87	.1	.1
097 Chr Chs&Chs Cr	2	105	NR	123 *	.1	.2
127 Ch God (Cleve)	9	825	752	993 *	.8	1.7
145 Ch God Prophcy	1	41	NR	48 *	-	.1
151 L-D Saints	1	NR	NR	412	.3	.7
165 Ch of Nazarene	3	600	421	600	.5	1.0
167 Chs of Christ	4	380	295	460	.4	.8
193 Episcopal	6	NR	1,257	3,681	2.9	6.2
207 E.L.C.A.	2	1,043	624	1,331	1.1	2.2
283 Luth—MO Synod	2	848	556	1,099	.9	1.8
304 NatPrimBapt USA	1	0	NR	0 *	-	-
355 Presb Ch (USA)	4	1,590	1,156	1,857 *	1.5	3.1
356 Presb Ch Amer	2	133	150	172	.1	.3
403 Salvation Army	1	45	46	67	.1	.1
413 S.D.A.	2	154	NR	183	.1	.3
419 So Bapt Conv	13	3,454	2,526	4,034 *	3.2	6.8
435 Unitarian-Univ	1	61	NR	71 *	.1	.1
443 Un C of Christ	3	844	563	986 *	.8	1.7
449 Un Methodist	5	4,138	2,013	4,832 *	3.8	8.1
496 Jewish Est	2	NR	NR	2,200	1.7	3.7
MIAMI-DADE	**861**	**154,200**	**93,807**	**892,934 ***	**39.6**	**100.0**
017 Amer Bapt Assn	2	83	NR	103 *	-	-
034 Ant Orth of NA	3	475	NR	950	-	.1
053 Assemb of God	52	8,045	8,681	12,637	.6	1.4
056 Baha'i	4	684	NR	684	-	.1
057 Bapt Gen Conf	5	606	613	765 *	-	.1
075 Brethren in Cr	16	1,061	1,194	1,253	.1	.1
076 Buddhism	8	NR	NR	NR	-	-
081 Catholic	69	NR	NR	542,984	24.1	60.8
084 Calvary Chapel	4	NR	NR	NR	-	-
089 Chr & Miss Al	14	894	NR	1,125	-	.1
093 Chr Ch (Disc)	6	551	321	682 *	-	.1
097 Chr Chs&Chs Cr	4	465	NR	576 *	-	.1
105 Christian Ref	4	565	512	699 *	-	.1
123 Ch God (Ander)	7	NR	1,028	1,028	-	.1
127 Ch God (Cleve)	31	5,026	4,016	6,402 *	.3	.7
145 Ch God Prophcy	14	556	NR	682 *	-	.1
151 L-D Saints	20	NR	NR	7,385	.3	.8
157 Ch of Brethren	2	205	264	305 *	-	-
165 Ch of Nazarene	26	4,803	3,316	6,134	.3	.7
167 Chs of Christ	27	3,200	2,968	4,300	.2	.5
179 Consrv Bapt	1	NR	70	70	-	-
183 Cons Menn Conf	1	10	12	15	-	-
193 Episcopal	29	NR	5,515	13,065	.6	1.5
201 Evan Cov Ch	7	592	781	1,006 *	-	.1
203 Evan Free Ch	1	69	125	125	-	-
207 E.L.C.A.	22	4,915	2,293	7,121	.3	.8
216 Evan Presby Ch	1	126	NR	156 *	-	-
221 Free Methodist	5	363	528	599	-	.1
223 Free Will Bapt	6	495	NR	612 *	-	.1
226 Friends-USA	2	137	NR	170 *	-	-
246 Greek Orthodox	4	NR	NR	2,130	.1	.2
252 Hindu	8	NR	NR	NR	-	-
262 Int Cou Comm Ch	1	190	NR	235 *	-	-
263 Int Foursq Gos	11	630	823	823 *	-	.1
264 Int Chs of Crst	1	1,759	2,671	2,391	.1	.3
267 Muslim Est	6	NR	1,670	6,239	.3	.7
268 Jain	1	NR	NR	NR	-	-
283 Luth—MO Synod	11	1,493	1,032	2,304	.1	.3
288 Mennonite USA	8	565	676	699 *	-	.1
290 Metro Comm Ch	3	168	132	222 *	-	-
295 Morav Ch-South	3	516	NR	848	-	.1
304 NatPrimBapt USA	5	540	NR	668 *	-	.1
331 OCA: Ter Diocs	2	76	NR	490	-	.1
335 Orth Pres Ch	2	32	27	57	-	-
349 Pent Holiness	8	328	316	406 *	-	-
355 Presb Ch (USA)	20	3,928	2,802	4,870 *	.2	.5
356 Presb Ch Amer	15	3,298	2,847	4,377	.2	.5
370 Ref Baptist Chs	1	NR	NR	NR	-	-
371 Ref Ch in Am	2	113	119	191	-	-
388 Reg Bapt Gen As	1	98	125	125 *	-	-
401 Rus Orth Abroad	1	NR	NR	NR	-	-
403 Salvation Army	4	830	372	834	-	.1
413 S.D.A.	50	14,757	NR	17,564	.8	2.0
418 Southw Bapt Fel	2	NR	NR	NR	-	-
419 So Bapt Conv	153	65,845	35,419	81,495 *	3.6	9.1
435 Unitarian-Univ	1	196	NR	243 *	-	-
443 Un C of Christ	13	4,371	2,001	5,410 *	.2	.6
449 Un Methodist	47	13,709	5,367	16,963 *	.8	1.9
463 Vineyard	3	814	714	1,008 *	-	.1
467 Wesleyan	1	117	103	160	-	-
469 WELS	2	101	79	121	-	-
496 Jewish Est	70	NR	NR	124,000	5.5	13.9
498 Indep.Charis.	5	2,800	2,725	3,428	.2	.4
499 Indep.Non-Char	3	3,000	1,550	3,000	.1	.3
MONROE	**72**	**7,154**	**4,282**	**23,422 ***	**29.4**	**100.0**
053 Assemb of God	3	171	135	180	.2	.8
056 Baha'i	1	101	NR	101	.1	.4
081 Catholic	5	NR	NR	13,028	16.4	55.6
127 Ch God (Cleve)	4	295	288	376 *	.5	1.6
145 Ch God Prophcy	1	41	NR	47 *	.1	.2
151 L-D Saints	2	NR	NR	269	.3	1.1
165 Ch of Nazarene	1	34	47	47	.1	.2
167 Chs of Christ	3	69	108	105	.1	.4
193 Episcopal	6	NR	552	1,021	1.3	4.4
201 Evan Cov Ch	1	67	31	77 *	.1	.3
207 E.L.C.A.	2	137	144	167	.2	.7
226 Friends-USA	1	24	NR	28 *	-	.1
246 Greek Orthodox	1	NR	NR	0	-	-
283 Luth—MO Synod	3	342	212	411	.5	1.8
290 Metro Comm Ch	1	127	108	146 *	.2	.6
335 Orth Pres Ch	1	28	35	39	-	.2
355 Presb Ch (USA)	3	216	191	248 *	.3	1.1
403 Salvation Army	1	50	22	110	.1	.5
413 S.D.A.	5	770	NR	916	1.2	3.9
419 So Bapt Conv	11	2,759	1,092	3,177 *	4.0	13.6
435 Unitarian-Univ	1	48	NR	55 *	.1	.2
443 Un C of Christ	2	113	102	130 *	.2	.6
449 Un Methodist	7	1,449	856	1,668 *	2.1	7.1
463 Vineyard	3	300	312	348 *	.4	1.5
467 Wesleyan	1	13	47	78	.1	.3
496 Jewish Est	2	NR	NR	650	.8	2.8
NASSAU	**61**	**18,886**	**8,380**	**27,977 ***	**48.5**	**100.0**
053 Assemb of God	4	460	557	780	1.4	2.8
056 Baha'i	0	11	NR	11	-	-
081 Catholic	1	NR	NR	3,000	5.2	10.7
089 Chr & Miss Al	2	44	NR	134	.2	.5
123 Ch God (Ander)	1	NR	120	120	.2	.4
127 Ch God (Cleve)	8	967	631	1,197 *	2.1	4.3
145 Ch God Prophcy	1	41	NR	50 *	.1	.2
151 L-D Saints	2	NR	NR	568	1.0	2.0
165 Ch of Nazarene	1	124	116	127	.2	.5
167 Chs of Christ	3	190	215	225	.4	.8
193 Episcopal	2	NR	323	627	1.1	2.2
207 E.L.C.A.	1	322	152	422	.7	1.5
221 Free Methodist	1	32	48	48	.1	.2
263 Int Foursq Gos	1	79	80	98 *	.2	.4
349 Pent Holiness	1	26	69	32 *	.1	.1

NR–Not Reported *Total adherents estimated from known number of communicant, confirmed, full members. - Represents a percentage less than 0.1. Percentages may not total 100 due to rounding.

Table 4: Religious Congregations by County and Group: 2000

Religious Group	Number of Churches, Synagogues, Mosques, or Temples	Number of Communicant, Confirmed, or Full Members	Number of Attendees	Total Adherents: Number of Adherents	Total Adherents: % of Total Pop.	Total Adherents: % of Total Adh.
355 Presb Ch (USA)	1	781	348	965 *	1.7	3.4
356 Presb Ch Amer	1	22	40	40	.1	.1
360 Prim Bapt Chrch	1	NR	NR	NR	-	-
419 So Bapt Conv	20	13,610	4,520	16,818 *	29.2	60.1
449 Un Methodist	6	1,749	665	2,160 *	3.7	7.7
467 Wesleyan	1	28	26	85	.1	.3
499 Indep.Non-Char	2	400	470	470	.8	1.7
OKALOOSA	**155**	**45,961**	**22,181**	**74,631 ***	**43.8**	**100.0**
053 Assemb of God	21	2,489	2,857	3,811	2.2	5.1
056 Baha'i	1	42	NR	42	-	.1
059 Bapt Miss Assn	1	40	21	49 *	-	.1
076 Buddhism	1	NR	NR	NR	-	-
081 Catholic	6	NR	NR	11,389	6.7	15.3
084 Calvary Chapel	1	NR	NR	NR	-	-
093 Chr Ch (Disc)	1	131	82	162 *	.1	.2
097 Chr Chs&Chs Cr	1	16	NR	20 *	-	-
127 Ch God (Cleve)	4	372	227	459 *	.3	.6
145 Ch God Prophcy	2	82	NR	100 *	.1	.1
151 L-D Saints	6	NR	NR	2,072	1.2	2.8
165 Ch of Nazarene	2	180	141	211	.1	.3
167 Chs of Christ	14	1,189	1,379	1,757	1.0	2.4
173 Comm of Christ	3	254	NR	254	.1	.3
186 Coptic Orth Ch	1	NR	NR	NR	-	-
193 Episcopal	4	NR	1,074	2,153	1.3	2.9
207 E.L.C.A.	3	1,089	603	1,531	.9	2.1
223 Free Will Bapt	1	82	NR	102 *	.1	.1
246 Greek Orthodox	1	NR	NR	219	.1	.3
267 Muslim Est	1	NR	20	25	-	-
283 Luth—MO Synod	3	992	733	1,353	.8	1.8
297 Mennonite;Other	1	10	NR	12 *	-	-
335 Orth Pres Ch	1	22	25	38	-	.1
349 Pent Holiness	1	6	9	7 *	-	-
355 Presb Ch (USA)	6	804	494	992 *	.6	1.3
356 Presb Ch Amer	5	566	522	708	.4	.9
360 Prim Bapt Chrch	1	NR	NR	NR	-	-
403 Salvation Army	1	63	38	56	-	.1
413 S.D.A.	2	184	NR	219	.1	.3
418 Southw Bapt Fel	1	NR	NR	NR	-	-
419 So Bapt Conv	45	27,947	9,097	34,477 *	20.2	46.2
435 Unitarian-Univ	1	106	NR	131 *	.1	.2
449 Un Methodist	10	9,295	4,259	11,467 *	6.7	15.4
496 Jewish Est	1	NR	NR	15	-	-
498 Indep.Charis.	1	0	600	800	.5	1.1
OKEECHOBEE	**34**	**7,330**	**3,156**	**12,650 ***	**35.2**	**100.0**
017 Amer Bapt Assn	1	173	NR	213 *	.6	1.7
053 Assemb of God	3	218	272	437	1.2	3.5
056 Baha'i	0	10	NR	10	-	.1
081 Catholic	1	NR	NR	2,776	7.7	21.9
097 Chr Chs&Chs Cr	3	332	NR	409 *	1.1	3.2
127 Ch God (Cleve)	4	494	485	609 *	1.7	4.8
145 Ch God Prophcy	1	41	NR	50 *	.1	.4
151 L-D Saints	1	NR	NR	199	.6	1.6
165 Ch of Nazarene	1	92	74	144	.4	1.1
167 Chs of Christ	3	88	118	120	.3	.9
193 Episcopal	1	NR	204	413	1.2	3.3
223 Free Will Bapt	1	82	NR	102 *	.3	.8
283 Luth—MO Synod	1	340	217	449	1.3	3.5
349 Pent Holiness	1	24	12	30 *	.1	.2
355 Presb Ch (USA)	1	100	122	123 *	.3	1.0
356 Presb Ch Amer	1	27	22	34	.1	.3
360 Prim Bapt Chrch	1	NR	NR	NR	-	-
413 S.D.A.	1	135	NR	161	.4	1.3
419 So Bapt Conv	7	4,634	1,346	5,706 *	15.9	45.1
449 Un Methodist	1	540	284	665 *	1.9	5.3
ORANGE	**504**	**161,480**	**86,193**	**360,812 ***	**40.3**	**100.0**
017 Amer Bapt Assn	11	1,127	NR	1,407 *	.2	.4
019 Amer Bapt USA	7	681	521	850 *	.1	.2
034 Ant Orth of NA	1	160	NR	320	-	.1
050 Armen Ap Etchm	1	0	NR	280	-	.1
053 Assemb of God	30	10,296	10,258	22,332	2.5	6.2

Religious Group	Number of Churches, Synagogues, Mosques, or Temples	Number of Communicant, Confirmed, or Full Members	Number of Attendees	Total Adherents: Number of Adherents	Total Adherents: % of Total Pop.	Total Adherents: % of Total Adh.
055 As Ref Pres Ch	1	69	NR	69	-	-
056 Baha'i	3	364	NR	364	-	.1
057 Bapt Gen Conf	5	253	369	412 *	-	.1
075 Brethren in Cr	2	40	105	105	-	-
076 Buddhism	3	NR	NR	NR	-	-
081 Catholic	19	NR	NR	118,737	13.2	32.9
084 Calvary Chapel	1	NR	NR	NR	-	-
089 Chr & Miss Al	14	731	NR	1,401	.2	.4
093 Chr Ch (Disc)	7	1,701	614	2,122 *	.2	.6
097 Chr Chs&Chs Cr	12	2,760	NR	3,442 *	.4	1.0
105 Christian Ref	1	144	147	180 *	-	-
123 Ch God (Ander)	5	NR	913	913	.1	.3
127 Ch God (Cleve)	24	4,745	2,638	6,201 *	.7	1.7
145 Ch God Prophcy	11	425	NR	531 *	.1	.1
151 L-D Saints	12	NR	NR	5,491	.6	1.5
157 Ch of Brethren	3	203	65	253 *	-	.1
165 Ch of Nazarene	25	4,920	3,182	5,146	.6	1.4
167 Chs of Christ	19	2,529	2,587	3,317	.4	.9
173 Comm of Christ	1	188	NR	188	-	.1
179 Consrv Bapt	1	NR	100	100	-	-
193 Episcopal	15	NR	4,013	8,905	1.0	2.5
201 Evan Cov Ch	2	252	195	314 *	-	.1
203 Evan Free Ch	1	69	125	125	-	-
207 E.L.C.A.	9	3,474	1,754	4,945	.6	1.4
221 Free Methodist	2	84	112	112	-	-
223 Free Will Bapt	4	330	NR	412 *	-	.1
226 Friends-USA	1	24	NR	30 *	-	-
246 Greek Orthodox	1	NR	NR	1,185	.1	.3
252 Hindu	6	NR	NR	NR	-	-
262 Int Cou Comm Ch	1	200	NR	250 *	-	.1
263 Int Foursq Gos	5	383	528	528 *	.1	.1
264 Int Chs of Crst	1	1,004	1,641	1,473	.2	.4
267 Muslim Est	3	NR	853	2,191	.2	.6
268 Jain	3	NR	NR	NR	-	-
283 Luth—MO Synod	8	3,424	1,824	4,650	.5	1.3
288 Mennonite USA	1	100	155	155 *	-	-
290 Metro Comm Ch	1	461	387	575 *	.1	.2
304 NatPrimBapt USA	2	450	NR	561 *	.1	.2
333 Malan Dioc Am	1	NR	NR	75	-	-
335 Orth Pres Ch	1	167	152	234	-	.1
339 Pent Ch of God	1	15	NR	28	-	-
349 Pent Holiness	8	4,725	5,546	5,895 *	.7	1.6
355 Presb Ch (USA)	20	11,839	5,566	14,768 *	1.6	4.1
356 Presb Ch Amer	8	2,558	2,666	3,517	.4	1.0
360 Prim Bapt Chrch	2	NR	NR	NR	-	-
371 Ref Ch in Am	2	260	208	337	-	.1
403 Salvation Army	3	463	191	860	.1	.2
413 S.D.A.	29	10,183	NR	12,119	1.4	3.4
418 Southw Bapt Fel	1	NR	NR	NR	-	-
419 So Bapt Conv	68	59,214	24,415	73,874 *	8.2	20.5
435 Unitarian-Univ	2	356	NR	444 *	-	.1
443 Un C of Christ	5	1,570	830	1,959 *	.2	.5
449 Un Methodist	43	23,925	9,365	29,850 *	3.3	8.3
463 Vineyard	1	300	285	374 *	-	.1
467 Wesleyan	2	49	87	165	-	-
469 WELS	3	440	351	616	.1	.2
496 Jewish Est	9	NR	NR	11,000	1.2	3.0
498 Indep.Charis.	5	2,840	2,200	2,840	.3	.8
499 Indep.Non-Char	5	985	1,245	1,285	.1	.4
OSCEOLA	**94**	**20,574**	**12,285**	**50,136 ***	**29.1**	**100.0**
017 Amer Bapt Assn	6	1,044	NR	1,317 *	.8	2.6
053 Assemb of God	11	1,471	1,583	2,082	1.2	4.2
055 As Ref Pres Ch	1	95	NR	105	.1	.2
056 Baha'i	0	31	NR	31	-	.1
076 Buddhism	2	NR	NR	NR	-	-
081 Catholic	4	NR	NR	19,031	11.0	38.0
089 Chr & Miss Al	2	189	NR	393	.2	.8
093 Chr Ch (Disc)	1	500	650	631 *	.4	1.3
097 Chr Chs&Chs Cr	3	2,080	NR	2,624 *	1.5	5.2
123 Ch God (Ander)	1	NR	120	120	.1	.2
127 Ch God (Cleve)	12	838	720	1,065 *	.6	2.1
151 L-D Saints	4	NR	NR	1,651	1.0	3.3
165 Ch of Nazarene	4	443	473	602	.3	1.2

NR–Not Reported *Total adherents estimated from known number of communicant, confirmed, full members. - Represents a percentage less than 0.1. Percentages may not total 100 due to rounding.

Table 4: Religious Congregations by County and Group: 2000

Religious Group	Number of Churches, Synagogues, Mosques, or Temples	Number of Communicant, Confirmed, or Full Members	Number of Attendees	Total Adherents		
				Number of Adherents	% of Total Pop.	% of Total Adh.
167 Chs of Christ	3	275	305	349	.2	.7
179 Consrv Bapt	2	NR	215	215	.1	.4
193 Episcopal	2	NR	460	919	.5	1.8
207 E.L.C.A.	1	766	514	1,007	.6	2.0
221 Free Methodist	1	39	50	54	-	.1
223 Free Will Bapt	2	165	NR	208 *	.1	.4
263 Int Foursq Gos	1	30	50	50 *	-	.1
267 Muslim Est	1	NR	250	500	.3	1.0
283 Luth—MO Synod	1	205	132	202	.1	.4
335 Orth Pres Ch	1	30	37	46	-	.1
355 Presb Ch (USA)	3	682	430	861 *	.5	1.7
388 Reg Bapt Gen As	1	100	140	140 *	.1	.3
403 Salvation Army	1	69	53	31	-	.1
413 S.D.A.	5	502	NR	598	.3	1.2
416 Sikh	1	NR	NR	NR	-	-
419 So Bapt Conv	11	7,283	3,708	9,189 *	5.3	18.3
449 Un Methodist	3	2,893	1,160	3,650 *	2.1	7.3
467 Wesleyan	1	44	35	65	-	.1
496 Jewish Est	1	NR	NR	1,200	.7	2.4
499 Indep.Non-Char	1	800	1,200	1,200	.7	2.4
PALM BEACH	**477**	**121,007**	**74,673**	**632,544 ***	**55.9**	**100.0**
017 Amer Bapt Assn	4	301	NR	361 *	-	.1
019 Amer Bapt USA	1	50	0	60 *	-	-
034 Ant Orth of NA	1	193	NR	386	-	.1
050 Armen Ap Etchm	1	131	NR	1,700	.2	.3
053 Assemb of God	16	5,882	5,574	8,259	.7	1.3
056 Baha'i	10	1,851	NR	1,851	.2	.3
057 Bapt Gen Conf	1	60	50	72 *	-	-
075 Brethren in Cr	3	112	177	177	-	-
076 Buddhism	1	NR	NR	NR	-	-
081 Catholic	36	NR	NR	300,456	26.6	47.5
084 Calvary Chapel	5	NR	NR	NR	-	-
089 Chr & Miss Al	17	1,458	NR	1,851	.2	.3
093 Chr Ch (Disc)	3	799	287	958 *	.1	.2
097 Chr Chs&Chs Cr	7	1,199	NR	1,439 *	.1	.2
105 Christian Ref	3	398	520	477 *	-	.1
123 Ch God (Ander)	6	NR	952	952	.1	.2
127 Ch God (Cleve)	36	4,758	3,743	5,888 *	.5	.9
145 Ch God Prophcy	13	522	NR	628 *	.1	.1
151 L-D Saints	8	NR	NR	3,160	.3	.5
165 Ch of Nazarene	15	1,740	1,727	2,448	.2	.4
167 Chs of Christ	11	1,812	1,484	2,420	.2	.4
173 Comm of Christ	1	28	NR	28	-	-
175 Congr Chr Chs	2	1,498	946	1,797 *	.2	.3
179 Consrv Bapt	1	NR	100	100	-	-
193 Episcopal	22	NR	4,087	11,124	1.0	1.8
201 Evan Cov Ch	3	99	232	281 *	-	-
203 Evan Free Ch	1	69	125	125	-	-
207 E.L.C.A.	11	5,192	2,461	7,121	.6	1.1
221 Free Methodist	4	91	113	130	-	-
223 Free Will Bapt	1	82	NR	99 *	-	-
226 Friends-USA	1	24	NR	29 *	-	-
246 Greek Orthodox	1	NR	NR	1,341	.1	.2
252 Hindu	4	NR	NR	NR	-	-
265 Int Pent C Chr	1	0	0	15	-	-
267 Muslim Est	1	NR	228	841	.1	.1
268 Jain	1	NR	NR	NR	-	-
283 Luth—MO Synod	9	3,644	2,272	5,027	.4	.8
290 Metro Comm Ch	2	176	194	195 *	-	-
295 Morav Ch-South	1	65	NR	102	-	-
304 NatPrimBapt USA	7	20	NR	24 *	-	-
313 N Am Bapt Conf	2	250	300	300 *	-	-
331 OCA: Ter Diocs	1	31	NR	239	-	-
335 Orth Pres Ch	1	32	58	58	-	-
349 Pent Holiness	9	2,425	1,902	2,909 *	.3	.5
355 Presb Ch (USA)	14	5,930	3,584	7,120 *	.6	1.1
356 Presb Ch Amer	7	3,224	2,825	3,430	.3	.5
360 Prim Bapt Chrch	1	NR	NR	NR	-	-
365 Prog Prim Bapt	1	50	NR	60 *	-	-
371 Ref Ch in Am	1	63	80	158	-	-
388 Reg Bapt Gen As	2	210	400	400 *	-	.1
403 Salvation Army	3	345	148	506	-	.1
413 S.D.A.	17	2,578	NR	3,069	.3	.5

Religious Group	Number of Churches, Synagogues, Mosques, or Temples	Number of Communicant, Confirmed, or Full Members	Number of Attendees	Total Adherents		
				Number of Adherents	% of Total Pop.	% of Total Adh.
418 Southw Bapt Fel	1	NR	NR	NR	-	-
419 So Bapt Conv	53	35,095	16,403	42,099 *	3.7	6.7
435 Unitarian-Univ	2	426	NR	511 *	-	.1
443 Un C of Christ	7	3,326	1,720	3,990 *	.4	.6
449 Un Methodist	22	15,518	7,208	18,616 *	1.6	2.9
467 Wesleyan	2	67	49	118	-	-
469 WELS	2	118	114	149	-	-
490 Zoroastrian	1	NR	NR	NR	-	-
496 Jewish Est	45	NR	NR	167,000	14.8	26.4
498 Indep.Charis.	4	4,075	2,400	4,900	.4	.8
499 Indep.Non-Char	7	14,990	12,210	14,990	1.3	2.4
PASCO	**190**	**36,646**	**23,886**	**107,631 ***	**31.2**	**100.0**
017 Amer Bapt Assn	5	390	NR	463 *	.1	.4
053 Assemb of God	12	2,161	2,625	4,371	1.3	4.1
056 Baha'i	1	61	NR	61	-	.1
061 Beachy Amish	1	18	NR	21 *	-	-
081 Catholic	12	NR	NR	55,527	16.1	51.6
089 Chr & Miss Al	3	169	NR	377	.1	.4
093 Chr Ch (Disc)	1	315	145	374 *	.1	.3
097 Chr Chs&Chs Cr	5	1,031	NR	1,224 *	.4	1.1
123 Ch God (Ander)	2	NR	191	191	.1	.2
127 Ch God (Cleve)	13	2,565	1,290	3,044 *	.9	2.8
145 Ch God Prophcy	1	41	NR	48 *	-	-
151 L-D Saints	4	NR	NR	1,552	.5	1.4
165 Ch of Nazarene	7	676	485	794	.2	.7
167 Chs of Christ	7	523	690	652	.2	.6
173 Comm of Christ	1	46	NR	46	-	-
193 Episcopal	5	NR	956	1,824	.5	1.7
203 Evan Free Ch	1	135	300	300	.1	.3
207 E.L.C.A.	8	2,038	1,401	2,361	.7	2.2
221 Free Methodist	2	132	200	200	.1	.2
246 Greek Orthodox	1	NR	NR	1,083	.3	1.0
263 Int Foursq Gos	1	29	38	38 *	-	-
283 Luth—MO Synod	4	1,407	925	1,626	.5	1.5
290 Metro Comm Ch	1	162	183	192 *	.1	.2
331 OCA: Ter Diocs	1	80	NR	143	-	.1
339 Pent Ch of God	3	78	NR	105	-	.1
355 Presb Ch (USA)	6	2,088	1,672	2,499 *	.7	2.3
356 Presb Ch Amer	1	200	266	285	.1	.3
360 Prim Bapt Chrch	2	NR	NR	NR	-	-
363 Primitive Meth	1	57	NR	61	-	.1
371 Ref Ch in Am	2	146	202	263	.1	.2
388 Reg Bapt Gen As	3	380	576	576 *	.2	.5
403 Salvation Army	1	113	53	156	-	.1
413 S.D.A.	2	728	NR	866	.3	.8
418 Southw Bapt Fel	3	NR	NR	NR	-	-
419 So Bapt Conv	40	12,801	5,723	15,188 *	4.4	14.1
443 Un C of Christ	3	528	460	626 *	.2	.6
449 Un Methodist	15	6,365	4,300	7,552 *	2.2	7.0
463 Vineyard	1	60	40	71 *	-	.1
467 Wesleyan	3	139	269	550	.2	.5
469 WELS	2	211	146	248	.1	.2
496 Jewish Est	1	NR	NR	1,000	.3	.9
498 Indep.Charis.	1	300	150	400	.1	.4
499 Indep.Non-Char	1	473	600	673	.2	.6
PINELLAS	**436**	**132,100**	**64,876**	**324,314 ***	**35.2**	**100.0**
017 Amer Bapt Assn	4	815	NR	958 *	.1	.3
019 Amer Bapt USA	3	581	164	683 *	.1	.2
034 Ant Orth of NA	2	88	NR	176	-	.1
050 Armen Ap Etchm	1	0	NR	700	.1	.2
053 Assemb of God	17	5,870	4,949	8,574	.9	2.6
056 Baha'i	4	530	NR	530	.1	.2
057 Bapt Gen Conf	2	88	227	227 *	-	.1
076 Buddhism	8	NR	NR	NR	-	-
081 Catholic	31	NR	NR	112,037	12.2	34.5
084 Calvary Chapel	3	NR	NR	NR	-	-
089 Chr & Miss Al	7	502	NR	851	.1	.3
093 Chr Ch (Disc)	4	1,176	392	1,382 *	.1	.4
097 Chr Chs&Chs Cr	9	9,801	NR	11,518 *	1.2	3.6
105 Christian Ref	3	90	133	106 *	-	-
123 Ch God (Ander)	4	NR	675	675	.1	.2

NR–Not Reported   *Total adherents estimated from known number of communicant, confirmed, full members.   - Represents a percentage less than 0.1.   Percentages may not total 100 due to rounding.

Table 4: Religious Congregations by County and Group: 2000

Religious Group	Number of Churches, Synagogues, Mosques, or Temples	Number of Communicant, Confirmed, or Full Members	Number of Attendees	Total Adherents: Number of Adherents	Total Adherents: % of Total Pop.	Total Adherents: % of Total Adh.
127 Ch God (Cleve)	13	4,869	2,209	5,762 *	.6	1.8
145 Ch God Prophcy	2	82	NR	96 *	-	-
151 L-D Saints	5	NR	NR	2,241	.2	.7
157 Ch of Brethren	1	119	81	140 *	-	-
165 Ch of Nazarene	14	1,367	992	1,902	.2	.6
167 Chs of Christ	24	3,679	3,091	4,611	.5	1.4
173 Comm of Christ	3	221	NR	221	-	.1
175 Congr Chr Chs	1	85	45	100 *	-	-
186 Coptic Orth Ch	1	NR	NR	NR	-	-
193 Episcopal	21	NR	4,241	9,657	1.0	3.0
201 Evan Cov Ch	3	424	325	498 *	.1	.2
203 Evan Free Ch	1	71	141	141	-	-
207 E.L.C.A.	18	6,793	3,790	8,330	.9	2.6
221 Free Methodist	3	490	575	575	.1	.2
223 Free Will Bapt	1	82	NR	97 *	-	-
226 Friends-USA	2	48	NR	56 *	-	-
246 Greek Orthodox	3	NR	NR	7,275	.8	2.2
252 Hindu	1	NR	NR	NR	-	-
262 Int Cou Comm Ch	3	1,748	NR	2,054 *	.2	.6
263 Int Foursq Gos	3	239	251	281 *	-	.1
267 Muslim Est	4	NR	930	4,239	.5	1.3
268 Jain	1	NR	NR	NR	-	-
283 Luth—MO Synod	8	4,842	2,669	6,175	.7	1.9
288 Mennonite USA	1	20	40	40 *	-	-
290 Metro Comm Ch	1	332	478	478 *	.1	.1
304 NatPrimBapt USA	4	1,517	NR	1,783 *	.2	.5
331 OCA: Ter Diocs	2	36	NR	205	-	.1
339 Pent Ch of God	1	100	NR	200	-	.1
349 Pent Holiness	5	266	233	313 *	-	.1
355 Presb Ch (USA)	33	10,362	6,218	12,273 *	1.3	3.8
356 Presb Ch Amer	4	175	240	243	-	.1
360 Prim Bapt Chrch	1	NR	NR	NR	-	-
370 Ref Baptist Chs	1	NR	NR	NR	-	-
371 Ref Ch in Am	2	112	169	225	-	.1
388 Reg Bapt Gen As	1	40	20	47 *	-	-
401 Rus Orth Abroad	1	NR	NR	NR	-	-
403 Salvation Army	3	789	429	2,243	.2	.7
410 Serb Orth USA	2	NR	NR	1,600	.2	.5
411 Serb Orth: Grac	1	NR	NR	NR	-	-
413 S.D.A.	7	1,631	NR	1,940	.2	.6
418 Southw Bapt Fel	1	NR	NR	NR	-	-
419 So Bapt Conv	44	30,734	12,129	36,121 *	3.9	11.1
423 Syrian Orth Ch	1	NR	NR	300	-	.1
425 Tao	1	NR	NR	NR	-	-
431 Ukrainian Orth	1	NR	NR	75	-	-
435 Unitarian-Univ	4	523	NR	615 *	.1	.2
443 Un C of Christ	9	2,768	1,602	3,253 *	.4	1.0
449 Un Methodist	41	34,334	14,314	40,350 *	4.4	12.4
463 Vineyard	1	256	220	301 *	-	.1
467 Wesleyan	4	522	824	1,315	.1	.4
469 WELS	3	613	415	756	.1	.2
496 Jewish Est	12	NR	NR	24,200	2.6	7.5
499 Indep.Non-Char	6	2,270	1,665	2,570	.3	.8
POLK	**470**	**119,498**	**61,693**	**202,576 ***	**41.9**	**100.0**
017 Amer Bapt Assn	14	2,854	NR	3,519 *	.7	1.7
019 Amer Bapt USA	1	98	73	121 *	-	.1
053 Assemb of God	43	8,659	8,951	13,786	2.8	6.8
055 As Ref Pres Ch	6	1,927	NR	2,275	.5	1.1
056 Baha'i	2	157	NR	157	-	.1
057 Bapt Gen Conf	1	36	190	190 *	-	.1
059 Bapt Miss Assn	2	181	88	223 *	-	.1
081 Catholic	11	NR	NR	37,589	7.8	18.6
084 Calvary Chapel	1	NR	NR	NR	-	-
089 Chr & Miss Al	4	264	NR	415	.1	.2
093 Chr Ch (Disc)	5	1,099	443	1,355 *	.3	.7
097 Chr Chs&Chs Cr	9	1,824	NR	2,250 *	.5.	1.1
123 Ch God (Ander)	11	NR	1,268	1,268	.3	.6
127 Ch God (Cleve)	31	6,004	3,885	7,679 *	1.6	3.8
145 Ch God Prophcy	3	122	NR	150 *	-	.1
151 L-D Saints	10	NR	NR	2,722	.6	1.3
165 Ch of Nazarene	14	3,190	2,593	3,957	.8	2.0
167 Chs of Christ	27	2,761	2,770	3,725	.8	1.8
173 Comm of Christ	1	114	NR	114	-	.1
193 Episcopal	12	NR	1,774	4,400	.9	2.2
203 Evan Free Ch	1	78	112	112	-	.1
207 E.L.C.A.	5	1,520	1,046	1,774	.4	.9
221 Free Methodist	3	249	340	340	.1	.2
223 Free Will Bapt	11	907	NR	1,119 *	.2	.6
226 Friends-USA	1	24	NR	30 *	-	-
246 Greek Orthodox	1	NR	NR	87	-	-
263 Int Foursq Gos	3	112	252	252 *	.1	.1
283 Luth—MO Synod	5	3,602	2,102	4,771	1.0	2.4
290 Metro Comm Ch	1	73	76	90 *	-	-
291 Missionary Ch	1	85	130	130	-	.1
304 NatPrimBapt USA	10	1,215	NR	1,498 *	.3	.7
339 Pent Ch of God	2	74	NR	103	-	.1
349 Pent Holiness	2	463	370	571 *	.1	.3
355 Presb Ch (USA)	14	5,430	3,265	6,703 *	1.4	3.3
356 Presb Ch Amer	5	709	754	820	.2	.4
360 Prim Bapt Chrch	8	NR	NR	NR	-	-
363 Primitive Meth	1	57	NR	61	-	-
365 Prog Prim Bapt	1	30	NR	37 *	-	-
388 Reg Bapt Gen As	6	1,532	1,870	1,916 *	.4	.9
403 Salvation Army	2	383	135	438	.1	.2
413 S.D.A.	11	1,092	NR	1,299	.3	.6
418 Southw Bapt Fel	5	NR	NR	NR	-	-
419 So Bapt Conv	119	54,980	17,988	67,799 *	14.0	33.5
435 Unitarian-Univ	1	124	NR	153 *	-	.1
443 Un C of Christ	1	164	72	202 *	-	.1
449 Un Methodist	33	15,286	7,036	18,850 *	3.9	9.3
463 Vineyard	1	175	180	216 *	-	.1
467 Wesleyan	1	44	105	210	-	.1
496 Jewish Est	2	NR	NR	1,300	.3	.6
498 Indep.Charis.	3	400	2,900	4,400	.9	2.2
499 Indep.Non-Char	2	1,400	925	1,400	.3	.7
PUTNAM	**91**	**18,559**	**7,499**	**26,870 ***	**38.2**	**100.0**
053 Assemb of God	3	536	693	698	1.0	2.6
056 Baha'i	0	9	NR	9	-	-
059 Bapt Miss Assn	1	34	25	42 *	.1	.2
081 Catholic	3	NR	NR	2,230	3.2	8.3
089 Chr & Miss Al	1	35	NR	35	-	.1
097 Chr Chs&Chs Cr	1	50	NR	62 *	.1	.2
123 Ch God (Ander)	2	NR	92	92	.1	.3
127 Ch God (Cleve)	7	311	237	384 *	.5	1.4
145 Ch God Prophcy	2	82	NR	100 *	.1	.4
151 L-D Saints	3	NR	NR	1,033	1.5	3.8
165 Ch of Nazarene	2	100	86	211	.3	.8
167 Chs of Christ	4	347	335	446	.6	1.7
175 Congr Chr Chs	1	57	46	70 *	.1	.3
193 Episcopal	6	NR	355	519	.7	1.9
207 E.L.C.A.	2	202	91	236	.3	.9
304 NatPrimBapt USA	3	320	NR	395 *	.6	1.5
349 Pent Holiness	4	1,006	420	1,241 *	1.8	4.6
355 Presb Ch (USA)	3	621	373	766 *	1.1	2.9
360 Prim Bapt Chrch	1	NR	NR	NR	-	-
413 S.D.A.	3	297	NR	353	.5	1.3
416 Sikh	1	NR	NR	NR	-	-
419 So Bapt Conv	28	12,485	3,807	15,398 *	21.9	57.3
443 Un C of Christ	1	68	65	84 *	.1	.3
449 Un Methodist	9	1,999	874	2,466 *	3.5	9.2
ST. JOHNS	**74**	**15,782**	**9,696**	**47,495 ***	**38.6**	**100.0**
053 Assemb of God	3	175	222	256	.2	.5
056 Baha'i	1	32	NR	32	-	.1
081 Catholic	7	NR	NR	20,094	16.3	42.3
089 Chr & Miss Al	1	0	NR	16	-	-
097 Chr Chs&Chs Cr	2	240	NR	291 *	.2	.6
123 Ch God (Ander)	1	NR	6	6	-	-
127 Ch God (Cleve)	3	144	75	175 *	.1	.4
151 L-D Saints	2	NR	NR	943	.8	2.0
165 Ch of Nazarene	1	127	70	178	.1	.4
167 Chs of Christ	2	165	205	185	.2	.4
193 Episcopal	5	NR	1,753	5,519	4.5	11.6
207 E.L.C.A.	2	604	295	730	.6	1.5
246 Greek Orthodox	1	NR	NR	192	.2	.4

NR–Not Reported *Total adherents estimated from known number of communicant, confirmed, full members. - Represents a percentage less than 0.1. Percentages may not total 100 due to rounding.

Table 4: Religious Congregations by County and Group: 2000

Religious Group	Number of Churches, Synagogues, Mosques, or Temples	Number of Communicant, Confirmed, or Full Members	Number of Attendees	Total Adherents: Number of Adherents	Total Adherents: % of Total Pop.	Total Adherents: % of Total Adh.
252 Hindu	1	NR	NR	NR	-	-
283 Luth—MO Synod	1	79	56	104	.1	.2
290 Metro Comm Ch	1	93	47	47 *	-	.1
304 NatPrimBapt USA	1	30	NR	36 *	-	.1
349 Pent Holiness	4	1,035	545	1,256 *	1.0	2.6
355 Presb Ch (USA)	2	1,005	627	1,220 *	1.0	2.6
356 Presb Ch Amer	3	1,034	1,195	1,650	1.3	3.5
403 Salvation Army	1	38	19	40	-	.1
413 S.D.A.	2	179	NR	213	.2	.4
418 Southw Bapt Fel	1	NR	NR	NR	-	-
419 So Bapt Conv	16	8,833	3,774	10,722 *	8.7	22.6
435 Unitarian-Univ	1	60	NR	73 *	.1	.2
443 Un C of Christ	1	46	31	56 *	-	.1
449 Un Methodist	7	1,863	776	2,261 *	1.8	4.8
496 Jewish Est	1	NR	NR	1,200	1.0	2.5
ST. LUCIE	**108**	**19,020**	**10,707**	**74,385 ***	**38.6**	**100.0**
017 Amer Bapt Assn	3	215	NR	261 *	.1	.4
053 Assemb of God	3	532	667	689	.4	.9
056 Baha'i	0	43	NR	43	-	.1
081 Catholic	8	NR	NR	45,126	23.4	60.7
084 Calvary Chapel	1	NR	NR	NR	-	-
089 Chr & Miss Al	2	93	NR	121	.1	.2
093 Chr Ch (Disc)	2	158	75	192 *	.1	.3
097 Chr Chs&Chs Cr	3	477	NR	578 *	.3	.8
105 Christian Ref	1	124	150	150 *	.1	.2
123 Ch God (Ander)	2	NR	192	192	.1	.3
127 Ch God (Cleve)	7	885	633	1,157 *	.6	1.6
151 L-D Saints	1	NR	NR	581	.3	.8
165 Ch of Nazarene	4	645	523	684	.4	.9
167 Chs of Christ	5	506	465	599	.3	.8
193 Episcopal	2	NR	377	1,187	.6	1.6
203 Evan Free Ch	1	75	130	130	.1	.2
207 E.L.C.A.	3	884	556	1,061	.6	1.4
216 Evan Presby Ch	1	64	NR	78 *	-	.1
226 Friends-USA	3	214	NR	259 *	.1	.3
246 Greek Orthodox	1	NR	NR	762	.4	1.0
263 Int Foursq Gos	1	30	50	50 *	-	.1
267 Muslim Est	1	NR	45	150	.1	.2
283 Luth—MO Synod	2	470	320	621	.3	.8
304 NatPrimBapt USA	3	0	NR	0 *	-	-
331 OCA: Ter Diocs	1	46	NR	81	-	.1
335 Orth Pres Ch	1	24	32	33	-	-
339 Pent Ch of God	2	95	NR	155	.1	.2
349 Pent Holiness	1	220	400	267 *	.1	.4
355 Presb Ch (USA)	4	1,099	719	1,333 *	.7	1.8
356 Presb Ch Amer	1	41	40	41	-	.1
360 Prim Bapt Chrch	1	NR	NR	NR	-	-
388 Reg Bapt Gen As	1	62	110	75 *	-	.1
403 Salvation Army	1	106	40	145	.1	.2
413 S.D.A.	4	751	NR	894	.5	1.2
418 Southw Bapt Fel	1	NR	NR	NR	-	-
419 So Bapt Conv	17	6,844	2,878	8,297 *	4.3	11.2
443 Un C of Christ	3	963	622	1,167 *	.6	1.6
449 Un Methodist	6	3,144	1,483	3,811 *	2.0	5.1
463 Vineyard	2	210	200	255 *	.1	.3
496 Jewish Est	2	NR	NR	3,160	1.6	4.2
SANTA ROSA	**132**	**33,957**	**14,954**	**48,891 ***	**41.5**	**100.0**
017 Amer Bapt Assn	7	299	NR	374 *	.3	.8
053 Assemb of God	20	7,028	3,227	6,753	5.7	13.8
056 Baha'i	1	25	NR	25	-	.1
076 Buddhism	1	NR	NR	NR	-	-
081 Catholic	4	NR	NR	6,230	5.3	12.7
084 Calvary Chapel	1	NR	NR	NR	-	-
089 Chr & Miss Al	1	20	NR	20	-	-
123 Ch God (Ander)	1	NR	19	19	-	-
127 Ch God (Cleve)	1	51	43	64 *	.1	.1
145 Ch God Prophcy	1	41	NR	51 *	-	.1
151 L-D Saints	3	NR	NR	1,081	.9	2.2
165 Ch of Nazarene	1	68	46	79	.1	.2
167 Chs of Christ	8	729	766	948	.8	1.9
173 Comm of Christ	4	331	NR	331	.3	.7

Religious Group	Number of Churches, Synagogues, Mosques, or Temples	Number of Communicant, Confirmed, or Full Members	Number of Attendees	Total Adherents: Number of Adherents	Total Adherents: % of Total Pop.	Total Adherents: % of Total Adh.
193 Episcopal	3	NR	350	613	.5	1.3
283 Luth—MO Synod	2	510	297	761	.6	1.6
297 Mennonite;Other	1	30	NR	38 *	-	.1
304 NatPrimBapt USA	2	275	NR	344 *	.3	.7
349 Pent Holiness	2	60	60	75 *	.1	.2
355 Presb Ch (USA)	4	773	392	969 *	.8	2.0
356 Presb Ch Amer	3	219	176	227	.2	.5
360 Prim Bapt Chrch	2	NR	NR	NR	-	-
413 S.D.A.	1	70	NR	83	.1	.2
418 Southw Bapt Fel	1	NR	NR	NR	-	-
419 So Bapt Conv	37	15,665	5,339	19,613 *	16.7	40.1
443 Un C of Christ	1	244	141	305 *	.3	.6
449 Un Methodist	17	7,468	4,045	9,350 *	7.9	19.1
469 WELS	1	51	53	63	.1	.1
496 Jewish Est	1	NR	NR	475	.4	1.0
SARASOTA	**202**	**54,325**	**36,455**	**152,587 ***	**46.8**	**100.0**
032 Amish; other	2	68	NR	77 *	-	.1
039 Ap Chr Ch(Naz)	1	27	54	54 *	-	-
040 Ap Chr Ch-Amer	1	57	75	75 *	-	-
053 Assemb of God	6	942	1,361	1,876	.6	1.2
056 Baha'i	1	114	NR	114	-	.1
061 Beachy Amish	1	153	NR	175 *	.1	.1
071 Brethren (Ash)	2	187	160	214 *	.1	.1
075 Brethren in Cr	1	75	75	75	-	-
076 Buddhism	1	NR	NR	NR	-	-
081 Catholic	10	NR	NR	64,957	19.9	42.6
084 Calvary Chapel	2	NR	NR	NR	-	-
089 Chr & Miss Al	2	172	NR	501	.2	.3
093 Chr Ch (Disc)	3	887	402	1,013 *	.3	.7
097 Chr Chs&Chs Cr	7	1,138	NR	1,301 *	.4	.9
123 Ch God (Ander)	5	NR	475	475	.1	.3
127 Ch God (Cleve)	6	1,186	563	1,369 *	.4	.9
151 L-D Saints	2	NR	NR	817	.3	.5
157 Ch of Brethren	1	30	25	34 *	-	-
165 Ch of Nazarene	5	833	999	1,011	.3	.7
167 Chs of Christ	9	727	808	962	.3	.6
175 Congr Chr Chs	1	68	62	78 *	-	.1
183 Cons Menn Conf	4	562	687	817	.3	.5
186 Coptic Orth Ch	1	NR	NR	NR	-	-
193 Episcopal	11	NR	2,824	5,803	1.8	3.8
201 Evan Cov Ch	4	496	464	568 *	.2	.4
203 Evan Free Ch	3	255	500	500	.2	.3
207 E.L.C.A.	8	3,934	2,242	4,854	1.5	3.2
226 Friends-USA	2	119	NR	136 *	-	.1
263 Int Foursq Gos	1	29	30	33 *	-	-
283 Luth—MO Synod	4	1,972	1,101	2,309	.7	1.5
288 Mennonite USA	7	1,351	1,191	1,580 *	.5	1.0
290 Metro Comm Ch	1	139	144	159 *	-	.1
297 Mennonite;Other	2	95	NR	109 *	-	.1
304 NatPrimBapt USA	2	275	NR	314 *	.1	.2
331 OCA: Ter Diocs	1	90	NR	150	-	.1
355 Presb Ch (USA)	12	8,562	5,238	9,774 *	3.0	6.4
356 Presb Ch Amer	4	803	1,163	1,187	.4	.8
360 Prim Bapt Chrch	3	NR	NR	NR	-	-
371 Ref Ch in Am	2	116	157	482	.1	.3
388 Reg Bapt Gen As	3	277	370	370 *	.1	.2
403 Salvation Army	2	220	116	768	.2	.5
411 Serb Orth: Grac	1	NR	NR	NR	-	-
413 S.D.A.	4	322	NR	383	.1	.3
419 So Bapt Conv	20	13,847	5,395	15,811 *	4.9	10.4
435 Unitarian-Univ	2	349	NR	399 *	.1	.3
443 Un C of Christ	5	1,817	973	2,075 *	.6	1.4
449 Un Methodist	12	9,843	5,630	11,238 *	3.4	7.4
469 WELS	2	288	221	390	.1	.3
496 Jewish Est	5	NR	NR	13,500	4.1	8.8
498 Indep.Charis.	2	600	1,000	1,000	.3	.7
499 Indep.Non-Char	3	1,300	1,950	2,700	.8	1.8
SEMINOLE	**177**	**47,214**	**29,843**	**134,295 ***	**36.8**	**100.0**
017 Amer Bapt Assn	2	159	NR	198 *	.1	.1
019 Amer Bapt USA	1	27	30	34 *	-	-
053 Assemb of God	12	2,139	2,184	2,858	.8	2.1

NR–Not Reported   *Total adherents estimated from known number of communicant, confirmed, full members.   - Represents a percentage less than 0.1.   Percentages may not total 100 due to rounding.

Table 4: Religious Congregations by County and Group: 2000

Religious Group	Number of Churches, Synagogues, Mosques, or Temples	Number of Communicant, Confirmed, or Full Members	Number of Attendees	Total Adherents: Number of Adherents	Total Adherents: % of Total Pop.	Total Adherents: % of Total Adh.
055 As Ref Pres Ch	1	90	NR	95	-	.1
056 Baha'i	2	116	NR	116	-	.1
057 Bapt Gen Conf	1	95	120	120 *	-	.1
076 Buddhism	1	NR	NR	NR	-	-
081 Catholic	7	NR	NR	60,191	16.5	44.8
084 Calvary Chapel	1	NR	NR	NR	-	-
089 Chr & Miss Al	4	216	NR	440	.1	.3
093 Chr Ch (Disc)	2	329	305	409 *	.1	.3
097 Chr Chs&Chs Cr	5	750	NR	932 *	.3	.7
105 Christian Ref	1	0	0	0 *	-	-
123 Ch God (Ander)	2	NR	315	315	.1	.2
127 Ch God (Cleve)	6	1,188	507	1,484 *	.4	1.1
145 Ch God Prophcy	5	196	NR	245 *	.1	.2
151 L-D Saints	5	NR	NR	1,771	.5	1.3
165 Ch of Nazarene	5	490	474	690	.2	.5
167 Chs of Christ	9	1,051	1,020	1,357	.4	1.0
173 Comm of Christ	1	40	NR	40	-	-
175 Congr Chr Chs	1	56	38	70 *	-	.1
186 Coptic Orth Ch	1	NR	NR	NR	-	-
193 Episcopal	5	NR	1,014	2,433	.7	1.8
201 Evan Cov Ch	2	41	24	56 *	-	-
207 E.L.C.A.	5	1,742	852	2,010	.6	1.5
216 Evan Presby Ch	1	82	NR	102 *	-	.1
223 Free Will Bapt	1	82	NR	102 *	-	.1
252 Hindu	1	NR	NR	NR	-	-
283 Luth—MO Synod	4	3,627	1,947	4,744	1.3	3.5
295 Morav Ch-South	1	133	NR	146	-	.1
304 NatPrimBapt USA	4	310	NR	385 *	.1	.3
331 OCA: Ter Diocs	1	107	NR	174	-	.1
339 Pent Ch of God	1	20	NR	40	-	-
349 Pent Holiness	2	49	43	61 *	-	-
355 Presb Ch (USA)	10	3,541	2,040	4,398 *	1.2	3.3
356 Presb Ch Amer	2	490	766	766	.2	.6
360 Prim Bapt Chrch	1	NR	NR	NR	-	-
370 Ref Baptist Chs	1	NR	NR	NR	-	-
388 Reg Bapt Gen As	1	120	150	150 *	-	.1
397 OCA: Roman Dioc	1	NR	NR	0	-	-
403 Salvation Army	1	119	43	221	.1	.2
410 Serb Orth USA	1	NR	NR	300	.1	.2
413 S.D.A.	8	2,983	NR	3,550	1.0	2.6
416 Sikh	5	NR	NR	NR	-	-
418 Southw Bapt Fel	1	NR	NR	NR	-	-
419 So Bapt Conv	23	15,577	7,434	19,354 *	5.3	14.4
443 Un C of Christ	2	548	351	681 *	.2	.5
449 Un Methodist	11	7,672	4,071	9,532 *	2.6	7.1
467 Wesleyan	1	29	65	125	-	.1
496 Jewish Est	3	NR	NR	3,600	1.0	2.7
498 Indep.Charis.	1	500	250	500	.1	.4
499 Indep.Non-Char	1	2,500	5,800	9,500	2.6	7.1
SUMTER	**64**	**11,842**	**4,844**	**15,606 ***	**29.3**	**100.0**
017 Amer Bapt Assn	2	833	NR	948 *	1.8	6.1
053 Assemb of God	6	481	614	1,118	2.1	7.2
055 As Ref Pres Ch	1	61	NR	61	.1	.4
056 Baha'i	0	6	NR	6	-	-
081 Catholic	2	NR	NR	1,097	2.1	7.0
123 Ch God (Ander)	1	NR	65	65	.1	.4
127 Ch God (Cleve)	9	1,322	761	1,587 *	3.0	10.2
165 Ch of Nazarene	1	28	38	183	.3	1.2
167 Chs of Christ	5	202	231	256	.5	1.6
193 Episcopal	1	NR	35	135	.3	.9
223 Free Will Bapt	1	82	NR	94 *	.2	.6
304 NatPrimBapt USA	1	110	NR	125 *	.2	.8
349 Pent Holiness	1	225	200	256 *	.5	1.6
355 Presb Ch (USA)	3	125	103	143 *	.3	.9
360 Prim Bapt Chrch	1	NR	NR	NR	-	-
413 S.D.A.	1	98	NR	117	.2	.7
419 So Bapt Conv	18	6,978	2,030	7,946 *	14.9	50.9
449 Un Methodist	10	1,291	767	1,469 *	2.8	9.4
SUWANNEE	**73**	**12,693**	**5,422**	**17,554 ***	**50.4**	**100.0**
017 Amer Bapt Assn	1	29	NR	35 *	.1	.2
053 Assemb of God	2	161	225	245	.7	1.4

Religious Group	Number of Churches, Synagogues, Mosques, or Temples	Number of Communicant, Confirmed, or Full Members	Number of Attendees	Total Adherents: Number of Adherents	Total Adherents: % of Total Pop.	Total Adherents: % of Total Adh.
056 Baha'i	0	6	NR	6	-	-
059 Bapt Miss Assn	1	72	47	88 *	.3	.5
081 Catholic	2	NR	NR	1,075	3.1	6.1
097 Chr Chs&Chs Cr	2	155	NR	189 *	.5	1.1
123 Ch God (Ander)	2	NR	92	92	.3	.5
127 Ch God (Cleve)	6	750	448	915 *	2.6	5.2
151 L-D Saints	1	NR	NR	511	1.5	2.9
165 Ch of Nazarene	1	52	36	59	.2	.3
167 Chs of Christ	5	365	331	435	1.2	2.5
193 Episcopal	1	NR	190	363	1.0	2.1
223 Free Will Bapt	1	82	NR	101 *	.3	.6
252 Hindu	1	NR	NR	NR	-	-
304 NatPrimBapt USA	1	0	NR	0 *	-	-
355 Presb Ch (USA)	2	102	58	124 *	.4	.7
356 Presb Ch Amer	1	220	120	262	.8	1.5
360 Prim Bapt Chrch	4	NR	NR	NR	-	-
413 S.D.A.	1	32	NR	38	.1	.2
419 So Bapt Conv	33	9,806	3,542	11,965 *	34.3	68.2
449 Un Methodist	5	861	333	1,051 *	3.0	6.0
TAYLOR	**44**	**6,914**	**3,008**	**9,075 ***	**47.1**	**100.0**
053 Assemb of God	1	145	180	200	1.0	2.2
056 Baha'i	0	3	NR	3	-	-
081 Catholic	1	NR	NR	371	1.9	4.1
123 Ch God (Ander)	1	NR	100	100	.5	1.1
127 Ch God (Cleve)	4	250	185	307 *	1.6	3.4
145 Ch God Prophcy	2	82	NR	100 *	.5	1.1
167 Chs of Christ	4	274	285	345	1.8	3.8
193 Episcopal	1	NR	39	62	.3	.7
304 NatPrimBapt USA	2	58	NR	71 *	.4	.8
349 Pent Holiness	1	10	30	12 *	.1	.1
355 Presb Ch (USA)	1	179	135	220 *	1.1	2.4
360 Prim Bapt Chrch	2	NR	NR	NR	-	-
413 S.D.A.	1	53	NR	63	.3	.7
419 So Bapt Conv	17	5,332	1,745	6,553 *	34.0	72.2
449 Un Methodist	5	511	295	628 *	3.3	6.9
467 Wesleyan	1	17	14	40	.2	.4
UNION	**18**	**3,195**	**879**	**4,158 ***	**30.9**	**100.0**
056 Baha'i	0	1	NR	1	-	-
097 Chr Chs&Chs Cr	1	175	NR	209 *	1.6	5.0
127 Ch God (Cleve)	1	69	71	83 *	.6	2.0
151 L-D Saints	1	NR	NR	373	2.8	9.0
167 Chs of Christ	2	136	183	185	1.4	4.4
223 Free Will Bapt	2	165	NR	197 *	1.5	4.7
360 Prim Bapt Chrch	2	NR	NR	NR	-	-
419 So Bapt Conv	6	2,196	527	2,627 *	19.5	63.2
449 Un Methodist	2	153	48	183 *	1.4	4.4
499 Indep.Non-Char	1	300	50	300	2.2	7.2
VOLUSIA	**293**	**64,639**	**36,883**	**166,028 ***	**37.4**	**100.0**
017 Amer Bapt Assn	3	126	NR	149 *	-	.1
019 Amer Bapt USA	2	535	150	633 *	.1	.4
034 Ant Orth of NA	1	90	NR	180	-	.1
053 Assemb of God	10	2,609	3,265	5,115	1.2	3.1
056 Baha'i	2	120	NR	120	-	.1
081 Catholic	16	NR	NR	67,442	15.2	40.6
084 Calvary Chapel	1	NR	NR	NR	-	-
089 Chr & Miss Al	8	1,073	NR	2,297	.5	1.4
093 Chr Ch (Disc)	8	2,177	1,056	2,575 *	.6	1.6
097 Chr Chs&Chs Cr	10	2,069	NR	2,448 *	.6	1.5
123 Ch God (Ander)	5	NR	855	855	.2	.5
127 Ch God (Cleve)	15	2,288	1,596	2,744 *	.6	1.7
145 Ch God Prophcy	5	204	NR	240 *	.1	.1
151 L-D Saints	5	NR	NR	2,086	.5	1.3
165 Ch of Nazarene	5	677	516	871	.2	.5
167 Chs of Christ	13	1,216	1,255	1,555	.4	.9
173 Comm of Christ	1	52	NR	52	-	-
186 Coptic Orth Ch	1	NR	NR	NR	-	-
193 Episcopal	12	NR	2,225	5,517	1.2	3.3
203 Evan Free Ch	1	81	150	150	-	.1
207 E.L.C.A.	8	2,708	1,347	3,193	.7	1.9
221 Free Methodist	2	45	90	90	-	.1

NR–Not Reported *Total adherents estimated from known number of communicant, confirmed, full members. - Represents a percentage less than 0.1. Percentages may not total 100 due to rounding.

Table 4: Religious Congregations by County and Group: 2000

Religious Group	Number of Churches, Synagogues, Mosques, or Temples	Number of Communicant, Confirmed, or Full Members	Number of Attendees	Total Adherents: Number of Adherents	Total Adherents: % of Total Pop.	Total Adherents: % of Total Adh.
223 Free Will Bapt	1	82	NR	98 *	-	.1
226 Friends-USA	3	72	NR	85 *	-	.1
246 Greek Orthodox	2	NR	NR	783	.2	.5
263 Int Foursq Gos	2	113	122	134 *	-	.1
267 Muslim Est	1	NR	156	609	.1	.4
268 Jain	1	NR	NR	NR	-	-
283 Luth—MO Synod	3	1,070	679	1,255	.3	.8
290 Metro Comm Ch	1	80	80	95 *	-	.1
304 NatPrimBapt USA	5	0	NR	0 *	-	-
339 Pent Ch of God	1	11	NR	25	-	-
349 Pent Holiness	13	671	675	794 *	.2	.5
355 Presb Ch (USA)	15	4,995	3,032	5,908 *	1.3	3.6
356 Presb Ch Amer	3	387	421	454	.1	.3
360 Prim Bapt Chrch	1	NR	NR	NR	-	-
365 Prog Prim Bapt	1	15	NR	18 *	-	-
388 Reg Bapt Gen As	3	347	255	420 *	.1	.3
403 Salvation Army	2	152	86	392	.1	.2
413 S.D.A.	7	1,124	NR	1,337	.3	.8
418 Southw Bapt Fel	1	NR	NR	NR	-	-
419 So Bapt Conv	47	25,318	10,433	29,946 *	6.8	18.0
435 Unitarian-Univ	3	229	NR	271 *	.1	.2
443 Un C of Christ	10	1,858	1,098	2,198 *	.5	1.3
449 Un Methodist	24	11,675	6,167	13,810 *	3.1	8.3
467 Wesleyan	2	63	90	190	-	.1
469 WELS	2	307	284	394	.1	.2
496 Jewish Est	4	NR	NR	7,700	1.7	4.6
499 Indep.Non-Char	1	0	800	800	.2	.5
WAKULLA	**37**	**3,966**	**1,797**	**5,312 ***	**23.2**	**100.0**
053 Assemb of God	2	177	225	276	1.2	5.2
056 Baha'i	0	6	NR	6	-	.1
151 L-D Saints	2	NR	NR	350	1.5	6.6
167 Chs of Christ	3	44	44	52	.2	1.0
193 Episcopal	1	NR	8	9	-	.2
283 Luth—MO Synod	1	86	40	106	.5	2.0
304 NatPrimBapt USA	10	435	NR	538 *	2.4	10.1
349 Pent Holiness	4	200	232	247 *	1.1	4.6
413 S.D.A.	1	71	NR	84	.4	1.6
419 So Bapt Conv	9	2,239	867	2,768 *	12.1	52.1
449 Un Methodist	4	708	381	876 *	3.8	16.5
WALTON	**79**	**9,753**	**4,276**	**13,451 ***	**33.1**	**100.0**
053 Assemb of God	10	357	454	625	1.5	4.6
081 Catholic	3	NR	NR	1,027	2.5	7.6
097 Chr Chs&Chs Cr	1	35	NR	42 *	.1	.3
127 Ch God (Cleve)	3	172	92	206 *	.5	1.5
151 L-D Saints	1	NR	NR	290	.7	2.2
167 Chs of Christ	5	202	200	260	.6	1.9
193 Episcopal	2	NR	195	216	.5	1.6
216 Evan Presby Ch	1	72	NR	86 *	.2	.6
304 NatPrimBapt USA	1	40	NR	48 *	.1	.4
355 Presb Ch (USA)	5	399	243	496 *	1.2	3.7
413 S.D.A.	1	36	NR	43	.1	.3
419 So Bapt Conv	33	6,852	2,270	8,209 *	20.2	61.0
449 Un Methodist	13	1,588	822	1,903 *	4.7	14.1
WASHINGTON	**49**	**6,273**	**2,786**	**8,640 ***	**41.2**	**100.0**
053 Assemb of God	6	680	607	873	4.2	10.1
056 Baha'i	0	3	NR	3	-	-
081 Catholic	2	NR	NR	678	3.2	7.8
127 Ch God (Cleve)	2	166	99	201 *	1.0	2.3
145 Ch God Prophcy	1	41	NR	50 *	.2	.6
151 L-D Saints	1	NR	NR	250	1.2	2.9
167 Chs of Christ	2	104	120	132	.6	1.5
193 Episcopal	1	NR	27	44	.2	.5
223 Free Will Bapt	3	247	NR	300 *	1.4	3.5
349 Pent Holiness	2	39	27	47 *	.2	.5
355 Presb Ch (USA)	1	94	61	114 *	.5	1.3
360 Prim Bapt Chrch	1	NR	NR	NR	-	-
418 Southw Bapt Fel	1	NR	NR	NR	-	-
419 So Bapt Conv	18	4,287	1,595	5,204 *	24.8	60.2
449 Un Methodist	8	612	250	744 *	3.5	8.6

Religious Group	Number of Churches, Synagogues, Mosques, or Temples	Number of Communicant, Confirmed, or Full Members	Number of Attendees	Total Adherents: Number of Adherents	Total Adherents: % of Total Pop.	Total Adherents: % of Total Adh.
GEORGIA						
The State.....	8,962	2,389,923	1,016,770	3,665,550 *	44.8	100.0
APPLING	**55**	**10,793**	**4,416**	**13,695 ***	**78.6**	**100.0**
053 Assemb of God	6	738	834	992	5.7	7.2
056 Baha'i	0	2	NR	2	-	-
081 Catholic	1	NR	NR	34	.2	.2
127 Ch God (Cleve)	6	1,496	763	1,877 *	10.8	13.7
145 Ch God Prophcy	2	83	NR	104 *	.6	.8
167 Chs of Christ	1	13	15	17	.1	.1
193 Episcopal	1	NR	24	57	.3	.4
223 Free Will Bapt	5	401	NR	503 *	2.9	3.7
365 Prog Prim Bapt	1	99	NR	124 *	.7	.9
413 S.D.A.	1	102	NR	121	.7	.9
419 So Bapt Conv	21	6,351	2,081	7,971 *	45.8	58.2
449 Un Methodist	10	1,508	699	1,893 *	10.9	13.8
ATKINSON	**27**	**2,284**	**749**	**3,533 ***	**46.4**	**100.0**
053 Assemb of God	1	107	150	150	2.0	4.2
081 Catholic	1	NR	NR	114	1.5	3.2
127 Ch God (Cleve)	2	159	38	210 *	2.8	5.9
145 Ch God Prophcy	2	83	NR	110 *	1.4	3.1
151 L-D Saints	1	NR	NR	394	5.2	11.2
223 Free Will Bapt	2	160	NR	212 *	2.8	6.0
320 "Old" MB Ascs	4	179	NR	236 *	3.1	6.7
360 Prim Bapt Chrch	1	NR	NR	NR	-	-
419 So Bapt Conv	6	1,214	373	1,603 *	21.1	45.4
449 Un Methodist	7	382	188	504 *	6.6	14.3
BACON	**29**	**3,718**	**1,422**	**4,808 ***	**47.6**	**100.0**
081 Catholic	1	NR	NR	31	.3	.6
127 Ch God (Cleve)	4	752	523	941 *	9.3	19.6
145 Ch God Prophcy	1	42	NR	52 *	.5	1.1
151 L-D Saints	1	NR	NR	115	1.1	2.4
167 Chs of Christ	1	14	15	18	.2	.4
223 Free Will Bapt	3	241	NR	301 *	3.0	6.3
360 Prim Bapt Chrch	1	NR	NR	NR	-	-
413 S.D.A.	1	0	NR	0	-	-
419 So Bapt Conv	11	2,247	666	2,814 *	27.9	58.5
449 Un Methodist	4	408	200	511 *	5.1	10.6
467 Wesleyan	1	14	18	25	.2	.5
BAKER	**15**	**904**	**271**	**1,216 ***	**29.8**	**100.0**
053 Assemb of God	1	26	30	50	1.2	4.1
056 Baha'i	0	10	NR	10	.2	.8
081 Catholic	0	NR	NR	11	.3	.9
167 Chs of Christ	1	5	5	6	.1	.5
223 Free Will Bapt	2	160	NR	204 *	5.0	16.8
339 Pent Ch of God	1	28	NR	75	1.8	6.2
355 Presb Ch (USA)	1	21	10	27 *	.7	2.2
419 So Bapt Conv	7	577	204	735 *	18.0	60.4
449 Un Methodist	2	77	22	98 *	2.4	8.1
BALDWIN	**45**	**9,340**	**3,351**	**12,890 ***	**28.8**	**100.0**
053 Assemb of God	1	19	25	25	.1	.2
056 Baha'i	2	64	NR	64	.1	.5
081 Catholic	1	NR	NR	897	2.0	7.0
097 Chr Chs&Chs Cr	2	585	NR	696 *	1.6	5.4
127 Ch God (Cleve)	2	182	145	216 *	.5	1.7
151 L-D Saints	1	NR	NR	408	.9	3.2
165 Ch of Nazarene	1	27	40	40	.1	.3
167 Chs of Christ	2	80	67	88	.2	.7
193 Episcopal	1	NR	146	457	1.0	3.5
263 Int Foursq Gos	1	33	59	59 *	.1	.5
283 Luth—MO Synod	1	43	32	55	.1	.4
349 Pent Holiness	1	39	29	46 *	.1	.4
355 Presb Ch (USA)	1	291	146	346 *	.8	2.7
356 Presb Ch Amer	1	108	118	142	.3	1.1
360 Prim Bapt Chrch	1	NR	NR	NR	-	-
365 Prog Prim Bapt	1	45	NR	54 *	.1	.4

NR–Not Reported *Total adherents estimated from known number of communicant, confirmed, full members. - Represents a percentage less than 0.1. Percentages may not total 100 due to rounding.

Table 4: Religious Congregations by County and Group: 2000

Religious Group	Number of Churches, Synagogues, Mosques, or Temples	Number of Communicant, Confirmed, or Full Members	Number of Attendees	Total Adherents: Number of Adherents	Total Adherents: % of Total Pop.	Total Adherents: % of Total Adh.
403 Salvation Army	1	64	75	64	.1	.5
413 S.D.A.	2	103	NR	123	.3	1.0
419 So Bapt Conv	16	5,967	1,920	7,099 *	15.9	55.1
449 Un Methodist	6	1,690	549	2,011 *	4.5	15.6
BANKS	**31**	**5,320**	**2,069**	**6,712 ***	**46.5**	**100.0**
056 Baha'i	0	6	NR	6	-	.1
089 Chr & Miss Al	1	0	NR	24	.2	.4
097 Chr Chs&Chs Cr	3	419	NR	527 *	3.7	7.9
127 Ch God (Cleve)	2	431	382	542 *	3.8	8.1
221 Free Methodist	1	13	13	18	.1	.3
355 Presb Ch (USA)	1	49	23	62 *	.4	.9
419 So Bapt Conv	17	4,074	1,436	5,120 *	35.5	76.3
449 Un Methodist	6	328	215	413 *	2.9	6.2
BARROW	**48**	**11,127**	**3,655**	**15,570 ***	**33.7**	**100.0**
017 Amer Bapt Assn	1	103	NR	133 *	.3	.9
053 Assemb of God	1	70	25	65	.1	.4
056 Baha'i	0	9	NR	9	-	.1
081 Catholic	1	NR	NR	702	1.5	4.5
093 Chr Ch (Disc)	3	708	90	918 *	2.0	5.9
097 Chr Chs&Chs Cr	4	816	NR	1,058 *	2.3	6.8
127 Ch God (Cleve)	2	193	58	250 *	.5	1.6
145 Ch God Prophcy	1	42	NR	54 *	.1	.3
151 L-D Saints	1	NR	NR	370	.8	2.4
167 Chs of Christ	1	97	135	149	.3	1.0
193 Episcopal	1	NR	80	130	.3	.8
355 Presb Ch (USA)	2	156	140	203 *	.4	1.3
356 Presb Ch Amer	1	60	46	78	.2	.5
413 S.D.A.	1	31	NR	37	.1	.2
418 Southw Bapt Fel	1	NR	NR	NR	-	-
419 So Bapt Conv	14	5,961	1,908	7,726 *	16.7	49.6
449 Un Methodist	12	2,691	1,053	3,488 *	7.6	22.4
467 Wesleyan	1	190	120	200	.4	1.3
BARTOW	**84**	**23,788**	**10,162**	**32,796 ***	**43.1**	**100.0**
053 Assemb of God	1	37	37	83	.1	.3
056 Baha'i	0	37	NR	37	-	.1
081 Catholic	1	NR	NR	1,311	1.7	4.0
097 Chr Chs&Chs Cr	2	375	NR	482 *	.6	1.5
127 Ch God (Cleve)	4	3,187	1,183	4,099 *	5.4	12.5
145 Ch God Prophcy	1	42	NR	54 *	.1	.2
151 L-D Saints	1	NR	NR	565	.7	1.7
165 Ch of Nazarene	1	90	63	90	.1	.3
167 Chs of Christ	4	278	295	402	.5	1.2
185 Cumber Presb	1	85	NR	117	.2	.4
193 Episcopal	1	NR	123	246	.3	.8
263 Int Foursq Gos	2	100	189	189 *	.2	.6
265 Int Pent C Chr	1	0	13	15	-	-
283 Luth—MO Synod	1	2	143	13	-	-
320 "Old" MB Ascs	1	189	NR	243 *	.3	.7
355 Presb Ch (USA)	2	646	335	831 *	1.1	2.5
360 Prim Bapt Chrch	1	NR	NR	NR	-	-
403 Salvation Army	1	27	24	29	-	.1
419 So Bapt Conv	39	14,060	5,637	18,084 *	23.8	55.1
449 Un Methodist	17	4,183	1,695	5,381 *	7.1	16.4
463 Vineyard	1	175	175	225 *	.3	.7
498 Indep.Charis.	1	275	250	300	.4	.9
BEN HILL	**33**	**7,469**	**2,529**	**10,303 ***	**58.9**	**100.0**
053 Assemb of God	1	36	40	47	.3	.5
056 Baha'i	0	2	NR	2	-	-
081 Catholic	1	NR	NR	171	1.0	1.7
127 Ch God (Cleve)	1	531	240	673 *	3.8	6.5
165 Ch of Nazarene	1	253	112	253	1.4	2.5
167 Chs of Christ	3	209	171	287	1.6	2.8
193 Episcopal	1	NR	21	60	.3	.6
355 Presb Ch (USA)	1	70	39	89 *	.5	.9
360 Prim Bapt Chrch	1	NR	NR	NR	-	-
365 Prog Prim Bapt	2	84	NR	106 *	.6	1.0
410 Serb Orth USA	1	NR	NR	660	3.8	6.4
413 S.D.A.	1	77	NR	92	.5	.9
419 So Bapt Conv	16	5,111	1,566	6,474 *	37.0	62.8
449 Un Methodist	3	1,096	340	1,389 *	7.9	13.5
BERRIEN	**30**	**5,082**	**1,432**	**6,796 ***	**41.9**	**100.0**
081 Catholic	2	NR	NR	117	.7	1.7
127 Ch God (Cleve)	4	243	159	307 *	1.9	4.5
151 L-D Saints	1	NR	NR	185	1.1	2.7
165 Ch of Nazarene	1	79	87	172	1.1	2.5
167 Chs of Christ	1	25	24	30	.2	.4
320 "Old" MB Ascs	7	830	NR	1,049 *	6.5	15.4
360 Prim Bapt Chrch	1	NR	NR	NR	-	-
419 So Bapt Conv	6	2,884	767	3,645 *	22.5	53.6
449 Un Methodist	7	1,021	395	1,291 *	8.0	19.0
BIBB	**155**	**49,625**	**21,564**	**72,797 ***	**47.3**	**100.0**
053 Assemb of God	4	423	520	931	.6	1.3
056 Baha'i	1	52	NR	52	-	.1
081 Catholic	3	NR	NR	5,715	3.7	7.9
093 Chr Ch (Disc)	2	490	93	620 *	.4	.9
097 Chr Chs&Chs Cr	3	328	NR	415 *	.3	.6
123 Ch God (Ander)	2	NR	315	315	.2	.4
127 Ch God (Cleve)	6	1,013	574	1,562 *	1.0	2.1
145 Ch God Prophcy	2	83	NR	106 *	.1	.1
151 L-D Saints	2	NR	NR	825	.5	1.1
165 Ch of Nazarene	2	316	215	361	.2	.5
167 Chs of Christ	8	674	711	841	.5	1.2
193 Episcopal	4	NR	563	1,285	.8	1.8
207 E.L.C.A.	1	403	131	554	.4	.8
221 Free Methodist	1	37	17	37	-	.1
223 Free Will Bapt	1	80	NR	101 *	.1	.1
246 Greek Orthodox	1	NR	NR	153	.1	.2
263 Int Foursq Gos	1	43	56	56 *	-	.1
267 Muslim Est	1	NR	156	609	.4	.8
283 Luth—MO Synod	1	81	58	111	.1	.2
290 Metro Comm Ch	1	8	15	15 *	-	-
304 NatPrimBapt USA	1	89	NR	113 *	.1	.2
331 OCA: Ter Diocs	1	17	NR	45	-	.1
349 Pent Holiness	3	304	119	385 *	.3	.5
355 Presb Ch (USA)	5	575	294	727 *	.5	1.0
356 Presb Ch Amer	4	1,458	995	1,747	1.1	2.4
360 Prim Bapt Chrch	4	NR	NR	NR	-	-
365 Prog Prim Bapt	1	80	NR	101 *	.1	.1
403 Salvation Army	1	156	95	350	.2	.5
413 S.D.A.	2	729	NR	868	.6	1.2
418 Southw Bapt Fel	4	NR	NR	NR	-	-
419 So Bapt Conv	45	26,382	10,337	33,372 *	21.7	45.8
435 Unitarian-Univ	1	114	NR	144 *	.1	.2
449 Un Methodist	28	13,163	4,531	16,649 *	10.8	22.9
467 Wesleyan	1	42	59	147	.1	.2
496 Jewish Est	2	NR	NR	1,000	.6	1.4
499 Indep.Non-Char	5	2,485	1,710	2,485	1.6	3.4
BLECKLEY	**27**	**5,188**	**1,948**	**7,028 ***	**60.2**	**100.0**
053 Assemb of God	2	63	75	82	.7	1.2
056 Baha'i	0	15	NR	15	.1	.2
081 Catholic	0	NR	NR	29	.2	.4
127 Ch God (Cleve)	1	154	41	192 *	1.6	2.7
145 Ch God Prophcy	1	42	NR	52 *	.4	.7
151 L-D Saints	1	NR	NR	463	4.0	6.6
165 Ch of Nazarene	1	93	60	101	.9	1.4
167 Chs of Christ	1	25	30	35	.3	.5
193 Episcopal	1	NR	36	72	.6	1.0
223 Free Will Bapt	2	160	NR	200 *	1.7	2.8
360 Prim Bapt Chrch	3	NR	NR	NR	-	-
419 So Bapt Conv	12	4,183	1,567	5,222 *	44.8	74.3
449 Un Methodist	2	453	139	565 *	4.8	8.0
BRANTLEY	**30**	**6,207**	**2,447**	**8,136 ***	**55.6**	**100.0**
056 Baha'i	0	1	NR	1	-	-
127 Ch God (Cleve)	6	411	176	528 *	3.6	6.5
145 Ch God Prophcy	3	125	NR	159 *	1.1	2.0
419 So Bapt Conv	15	5,344	2,032	6,830 *	46.7	83.9

NR–Not Reported *Total adherents estimated from known number of communicant, confirmed, full members. - Represents a percentage less than 0.1. Percentages may not total 100 due to rounding.

Table 4: Religious Congregations by County and Group: 2000

Religious Group	Number of Churches, Synagogues, Mosques, or Temples	Number of Communicant, Confirmed, or Full Members	Number of Attendees	Total Adherents: Number of Adherents	% of Total Pop.	% of Total Adh.
449 Un Methodist	3	186	117	238 *	1.6	2.9
467 Wesleyan	3	140	122	380	2.6	4.7
BROOKS	**43**	**5,602**	**2,090**	**7,109 ***	**43.2**	**100.0**
053 Assemb of God	1	57	65	90	.5	1.3
056 Baha'i	0	4	NR	4	-	.1
093 Chr Ch (Disc)	1	140	0	176 *	1.1	2.5
127 Ch God (Cleve)	2	67	55	85 *	.5	1.2
165 Ch of Nazarene	1	34	25	48	.3	.7
167 Chs of Christ	5	460	385	573	3.5	8.1
193 Episcopal	1	NR	33	59	.4	.8
355 Presb Ch (USA)	1	74	38	93 *	.6	1.3
360 Prim Bapt Chrch	1	NR	NR	NR	-	-
365 Prog Prim Bapt	2	20	NR	25 *	.2	.4
413 S.D.A.	1	55	NR	65	.4	.9
419 So Bapt Conv	18	3,894	1,182	4,891 *	29.7	68.8
449 Un Methodist	9	797	307	1,000 *	6.1	14.1
BRYAN	**23**	**6,461**	**2,839**	**9,619 ***	**41.1**	**100.0**
053 Assemb of God	1	64	53	70	.3	.7
056 Baha'i	0	3	NR	3	-	-
081 Catholic	2	NR	NR	639	2.7	6.6
093 Chr Ch (Disc)	1	197	95	258 *	1.1	2.7
127 Ch God (Cleve)	2	292	124	382 *	1.6	4.0
151 L-D Saints	1	NR	NR	362	1.5	3.8
167 Chs of Christ	2	100	118	127	.5	1.3
193 Episcopal	1	NR	103	184	.8	1.9
355 Presb Ch (USA)	1	140	120	183 *	.8	1.9
419 So Bapt Conv	9	4,154	1,587	5,434 *	23.2	56.5
449 Un Methodist	3	1,511	639	1,977 *	8.4	20.6
BULLOCH	**72**	**14,670**	**5,775**	**19,492 ***	**34.8**	**100.0**
053 Assemb of God	1	37	42	52	.1	.3
056 Baha'i	0	18	NR	18	-	.1
081 Catholic	1	NR	NR	977	1.7	5.0
123 Ch God (Ander)	3	NR	204	204	.4	1.0
127 Ch God (Cleve)	4	859	500	1,035 *	1.8	5.3
151 L-D Saints	1	NR	NR	389	.7	2.0
167 Chs of Christ	1	68	63	88	.2	.5
193 Episcopal	1	NR	106	164	.3	.8
223 Free Will Bapt	1	80	NR	97 *	.2	.5
283 Luth—MO Synod	1	60	40	80	.1	.4
304 NatPrimBapt USA	2	125	NR	151 *	.3	.8
349 Pent Holiness	1	97	75	117 *	.2	.6
355 Presb Ch (USA)	1	343	155	414 *	.7	2.1
356 Presb Ch Amer	1	201	250	291	.5	1.5
360 Prim Bapt Chrch	10	NR	NR	NR	-	-
365 Prog Prim Bapt	7	1,044	NR	1,259 *	2.2	6.5
413 S.D.A.	1	85	NR	101	.2	.5
419 So Bapt Conv	23	8,184	3,031	9,870 *	17.6	50.6
435 Unitarian-Univ	1	43	NR	52 *	.1	.3
449 Un Methodist	11	3,426	1,309	4,133 *	7.4	21.2
BURKE	**38**	**6,100**	**2,170**	**8,514 ***	**38.3**	**100.0**
056 Baha'i	0	100	NR	100	.4	1.2
081 Catholic	1	NR	NR	343	1.5	4.0
089 Chr & Miss Al	1	11	NR	14	.1	.2
093 Chr Ch (Disc)	1	194	75	255 *	1.1	3.0
123 Ch God (Ander)	1	NR	35	35	.2	.4
127 Ch God (Cleve)	1	137	123	180 *	.8	2.1
145 Ch God Prophcy	1	42	NR	55 *	.2	.6
167 Chs of Christ	1	36	28	64	.3	.8
193 Episcopal	1	NR	57	153	.7	1.8
223 Free Will Bapt	1	80	NR	105 *	.5	1.2
297 Mennonite;Other	1	45	NR	59 *	.3	.7
355 Presb Ch (USA)	2	56	29	74 *	.3	.9
356 Presb Ch Amer	1	142	80	165	.7	1.9
419 So Bapt Conv	13	3,885	1,204	5,108 *	23.0	60.0
449 Un Methodist	12	1,372	539	1,804 *	8.1	21.2
BUTTS	**26**	**5,185**	**2,120**	**6,832 ***	**35.0**	**100.0**
017 Amer Bapt Assn	1	50	NR	61 *	.3	.9

Religious Group	Number of Churches, Synagogues, Mosques, or Temples	Number of Communicant, Confirmed, or Full Members	Number of Attendees	Total Adherents: Number of Adherents	% of Total Pop.	% of Total Adh.
053 Assemb of God	1	110	150	234	1.2	3.4
056 Baha'i	0	6	NR	6	-	.1
081 Catholic	1	NR	NR	383	2.0	5.6
097 Chr Chs&Chs Cr	1	77	NR	95 *	.5	1.4
165 Ch of Nazarene	1	92	72	92	.5	1.3
167 Chs of Christ	1	25	30	30	.2	.4
355 Presb Ch (USA)	2	116	80	142 *	.7	2.1
360 Prim Bapt Chrch	2	NR	NR	NR	-	-
419 So Bapt Conv	11	3,811	1,403	4,686 *	24.0	68.6
449 Un Methodist	5	898	385	1,103 *	5.7	16.1
CALHOUN	**15**	**1,773**	**574**	**2,194 ***	**34.7**	**100.0**
056 Baha'i	0	28	NR	28	.4	1.3
081 Catholic	0	NR	NR	42	.7	1.9
127 Ch God (Cleve)	1	30	22	36 *	.6	1.6
167 Chs of Christ	1	13	30	30	.5	1.4
223 Free Will Bapt	1	80	NR	97 *	1.5	4.4
360 Prim Bapt Chrch	2	NR	NR	NR	-	-
418 Southw Bapt Fel	1	NR	NR	NR	-	-
419 So Bapt Conv	5	1,202	335	1,453 *	23.0	66.2
449 Un Methodist	4	420	187	508 *	8.0	23.2
CAMDEN	**46**	**9,501**	**4,121**	**13,443 ***	**30.8**	**100.0**
017 Amer Bapt Assn	1	14	NR	19 *	-	.1
053 Assemb of God	2	89	120	159	.4	1.2
056 Baha'i	0	3	NR	3	-	-
081 Catholic	1	NR	NR	395	.9	2.9
127 Ch God (Cleve)	6	1,029	588	1,374 *	3.1	10.2
145 Ch God Prophcy	1	42	NR	56 *	.1	.4
165 Ch of Nazarene	1	39	0	39	.1	.3
167 Chs of Christ	2	128	135	163	.4	1.2
193 Episcopal	2	NR	127	205	.5	1.5
207 E.L.C.A.	1	0	80	114	.3	.8
223 Free Will Bapt	1	80	NR	107 *	.2	.8
283 Luth—MO Synod	1	118	94	182	.4	1.4
355 Presb Ch (USA)	1	171	135	228 *	.5	1.7
370 Ref Baptist Chs	1	NR	NR	NR	-	-
413 S.D.A.	1	36	NR	43	.1	.3
418 Southw Bapt Fel	1	NR	NR	NR	-	-
419 So Bapt Conv	10	4,948	1,473	6,610 *	15.1	49.2
449 Un Methodist	13	2,804	1,369	3,746 *	8.6	27.9
CANDLER	**25**	**3,225**	**1,247**	**4,159 ***	**43.4**	**100.0**
056 Baha'i	0	1	NR	1	-	-
081 Catholic	1	NR	NR	75	.8	1.8
127 Ch God (Cleve)	2	261	174	330 *	3.4	7.9
167 Chs of Christ	2	29	35	39	.4	.9
223 Free Will Bapt	1	80	NR	102 *	1.1	2.5
286 E.PA Mennonite	1	38	NR	48 *	.5	1.2
304 NatPrimBapt USA	1	75	NR	95 *	1.0	2.3
355 Presb Ch (USA)	1	39	18	49 *	.5	1.2
360 Prim Bapt Chrch	1	NR	NR	NR	-	-
365 Prog Prim Bapt	4	308	NR	390 *	4.1	9.4
419 So Bapt Conv	9	1,987	865	2,515 *	26.3	60.5
449 Un Methodist	2	407	155	515 *	5.4	12.4
CARROLL	**123**	**29,144**	**12,556**	**40,253 ***	**46.1**	**100.0**
053 Assemb of God	1	16	17	28	-	.1
056 Baha'i	0	40	NR	40	-	.1
081 Catholic	1	NR	NR	1,578	1.8	3.9
097 Chr Chs&Chs Cr	9	1,450	NR	1,820 *	2.1	4.5
127 Ch God (Cleve)	10	1,135	555	1,441 *	1.7	3.6
145 Ch God Prophcy	3	125	NR	156 *	.2	.4
151 L-D Saints	1	NR	NR	284	.3	.7
167 Chs of Christ	6	364	333	437	.5	1.1
193 Episcopal	1	NR	180	617	.7	1.5
207 E.L.C.A.	1	129	79	155	.2	.4
226 Friends-USA	1	64	NR	80 *	.1	.2
267 Muslim Est	1	NR	290	1,313	1.5	3.3
289 New Hope B Asc	2	86	NR	108 *	.1	.3
339 Pent Ch of God	1	15	NR	27	-	.1
349 Pent Holiness	1	82	47	103 *	.1	.3

NR–Not Reported *Total adherents estimated from known number of communicant, confirmed, full members. - Represents a percentage less than 0.1. Percentages may not total 100 due to rounding.

Table 4: Religious Congregations by County and Group: 2000

Religious Group	Number of Churches, Synagogues, Mosques, or Temples	Number of Communicant, Confirmed, or Full Members	Number of Attendees	Total Adherents		
				Number of Adherents	% of Total Pop.	% of Total Adh.
355 Presb Ch (USA)	2	324	151	406 *	.5	1.0
356 Presb Ch Amer	2	186	240	278	.3	.7
360 Prim Bapt Chrch	8	NR	NR	NR	-	-
413 S.D.A.	1	85	NR	101	.1	.3
419 So Bapt Conv	44	19,238	7,653	24,130 *	27.7	59.9
449 Un Methodist	25	5,080	2,511	6,371 *	7.3	15.8
498 Indep.Charis.	2	725	500	780	.9	1.9
CATOOSA	**53**	**15,317**	**6,678**	**20,426 ***	**38.3**	**100.0**
053 Assemb of God	1	17	20	20	-	.1
056 Baha'i	0	8	NR	8	-	-
081 Catholic	1	NR	NR	787	1.5	3.9
127 Ch God (Cleve)	3	388	212	487 *	.9	2.4
145 Ch God Prophcy	2	83	NR	104 *	.2	.5
151 L-D Saints	1	NR	NR	382	.7	1.9
165 Ch of Nazarene	1	579	386	579	1.1	2.8
167 Chs of Christ	2	286	320	367	.7	1.8
193 Episcopal	1	NR	75	165	.3	.8
355 Presb Ch (USA)	2	91	60	114 *	.2	.6
356 Presb Ch Amer	1	59	90	90	.2	.4
360 Prim Bapt Chrch	2	NR	NR	NR	-	-
413 S.D.A.	1	102	NR	121	.2	.6
418 Southw Bapt Fel	1	NR	NR	NR	-	-
419 So Bapt Conv	26	11,386	4,398	14,292 *	26.8	70.0
449 Un Methodist	7	2,188	997	2,747 *	5.2	13.4
463 Vineyard	1	130	120	163 *	.3	.8
CHARLTON	**24**	**3,750**	**1,481**	**4,825 ***	**46.9**	**100.0**
017 Amer Bapt Assn	1	17	NR	22 *	.2	.5
053 Assemb of God	1	33	35	63	.6	1.3
081 Catholic	1	NR	NR	57	.6	1.2
127 Ch God (Cleve)	3	171	155	217 *	2.1	4.5
145 Ch God Prophcy	1	42	NR	53 *	.5	1.1
167 Chs of Christ	1	17	15	24	.2	.5
223 Free Will Bapt	1	80	NR	101 *	1.0	2.1
419 So Bapt Conv	9	2,760	987	3,491 *	34.0	72.4
449 Un Methodist	6	630	289	797 *	7.8	16.5
CHATHAM	**203**	**58,667**	**22,315**	**104,597 ***	**45.1**	**100.0**
017 Amer Bapt Assn	3	149	NR	185 *	.1	.2
019 Amer Bapt USA	1	213	75	265 *	.1	.3
053 Assemb of God	7	705	867	981	.4	.9
056 Baha'i	1	111	NR	111	-	.1
081 Catholic	13	NR	NR	20,861	9.0	19.9
084 Calvary Chapel	1	NR	NR	NR	-	-
089 Chr & Miss Al	5	380	NR	597	.3	.6
093 Chr Ch (Disc)	1	394	107	490 *	.2	.5
097 Chr Chs&Chs Cr	6	2,374	NR	2,952 *	1.3	2.8
123 Ch God (Ander)	2	NR	165	165	.1	.2
127 Ch God (Cleve)	7	1,983	1,246	2,467 *	1.1	2.4
145 Ch God Prophcy	1	42	NR	52 *	-	-
151 L-D Saints	2	NR	NR	780	.3	.7
165 Ch of Nazarene	3	188	154	244	.1	.2
167 Chs of Christ	10	1,126	895	1,449	.6	1.4
193 Episcopal	12	NR	1,973	5,125	2.2	4.9
207 E.L.C.A.	9	2,728	1,161	3,442	1.5	3.3
223 Free Will Bapt	1	80	NR	100 *	-	.1
226 Friends-USA	1	24	NR	30 *	-	-
246 Greek Orthodox	1	NR	NR	738	.3	.7
263 Int Foursq Gos	2	298	275	371 *	.2	.4
267 Muslim Est	1	NR	156	609	.3	.6
283 Luth—MO Synod	1	405	255	519	.2	.5
304 NatPrimBapt USA	1	15	NR	19 *	-	-
331 OCA:Ter Diocs	1	27	NR	70	-	.1
349 Pent Holiness	5	948	779	1,180 *	.5	1.1
355 Presb Ch (USA)	6	2,579	1,137	3,208 *	1.4	3.1
356 Presb Ch Amer	5	513	463	656	.3	.6
360 Prim Bapt Chrch	2	NR	NR	NR	-	-
365 Prog Prim Bapt	4	370	NR	460 *	.2	.4
403 Salvation Army	1	142	100	266	.1	.3
413 S.D.A.	3	2,317	NR	2,757	1.2	2.6
418 Southw Bapt Fel	1	NR	NR	NR	-	-
419 So Bapt Conv	48	27,782	7,853	34,568 *	14.9	33.0
435 Unitarian-Univ	1	101	NR	126 *	.1	.1
443 Un C of Christ	1	82	55	102 *	-	.1
449 Un Methodist	29	12,520	4,529	15,581 *	6.7	14.9
469 WELS	1	71	70	71	-	.1
496 Jewish Est	3	NR	NR	3,000	1.3	2.9
CHATTAHOOCHEE	**4**	**595**	**185**	**781 ***	**5.2**	**100.0**
056 Baha'i	0	3	NR	3	-	.4
167 Chs of Christ	1	25	25	32	.2	4.1
419 So Bapt Conv	1	483	110	636 *	4.3	81.4
449 Un Methodist	2	84	50	110 *	.7	14.1
CHATTOOGA	**74**	**10,376**	**4,437**	**12,739 ***	**50.0**	**100.0**
056 Baha'i	0	1	NR	1	-	-
089 Chr & Miss Al	1	93	NR	126	.5	1.0
127 Ch God (Cleve)	3	553	191	672 *	2.6	5.3
145 Ch God Prophcy	2	75	NR	91 *	.4	.7
165 Ch of Nazarene	1	21	5	21	.1	.2
167 Chs of Christ	13	812	730	1,067	4.2	8.4
193 Episcopal	1	NR	34	60	.2	.5
216 Evan Presby Ch	1	50	NR	61 *	.2	.5
355 Presb Ch (USA)	4	270	139	328 *	1.3	2.6
356 Presb Ch Amer	1	95	50	95	.4	.7
418 Southw Bapt Fel	1	NR	NR	NR	-	-
419 So Bapt Conv	36	7,482	2,862	9,094 *	35.7	71.4
449 Un Methodist	10	924	426	1,123 *	4.4	8.8
CHEROKEE	**95**	**35,507**	**15,032**	**53,061 ***	**37.4**	**100.0**
022 Carp Rus Orth	1	122	NR	207	.1	.4
053 Assemb of God	1	127	140	216	.2	.4
056 Baha'i	1	56	NR	56	-	.1
081 Catholic	2	NR	NR	5,803	4.1	10.9
084 Calvary Chapel	1	NR	NR	NR	-	-
097 Chr Chs&Chs Cr	3	728	NR	943 *	.7	1.8
127 Ch God (Cleve)	7	1,131	422	1,465 *	1.0	2.8
145 Ch God Prophcy	2	83	NR	108 *	.1	.2
151 L-D Saints	1	NR	NR	398	.3	.8
167 Chs of Christ	3	350	322	475	.3	.9
193 Episcopal	1	NR	105	262	.2	.5
207 E.L.C.A.	1	697	462	1,076	.8	2.0
269 Jasper&PVB Asc	10	1,616	NR	2,094 *	1.5	3.9
283 Luth—MO Synod	1	390	234	544	.4	1.0
355 Presb Ch (USA)	4	925	398	1,198 *	.8	2.3
356 Presb Ch Amer	1	172	130	204	.1	.4
360 Prim Bapt Chrch	2	NR	NR	NR	-	-
413 S.D.A.	1	45	NR	54	-	.1
419 So Bapt Conv	32	23,254	9,548	30,130 *	21.2	56.8
449 Un Methodist	19	5,811	3,086	7,528 *	5.3	14.2
499 Indep.Non-Char	1	0	185	300	.2	.6
CLARKE	**68**	**23,901**	**11,020**	**36,401 ***	**35.9**	**100.0**
053 Assemb of God	1	167	236	400	.4	1.1
056 Baha'i	1	76	NR	76	.1	.2
081 Catholic	2	NR	NR	4,926	4.9	13.5
084 Calvary Chapel	1	NR	NR	NR	-	-
089 Chr & Miss Al	1	0	NR	71	.1	.2
093 Chr Ch (Disc)	2	431	202	501 *	.5	1.4
097 Chr Chs&Chs Cr	1	200	NR	233 *	.2	.6
127 Ch God (Cleve)	2	457	330	532 *	.5	1.5
151 L-D Saints	2	NR	NR	479	.5	1.3
167 Chs of Christ	3	449	485	645	.6	1.8
193 Episcopal	2	NR	548	1,692	1.7	4.6
207 E.L.C.A.	1	371	151	439	.4	1.2
226 Friends-USA	1	64	NR	74 *	.1	.2
246 Greek Orthodox	1	NR	NR	0	-	-
267 Muslim Est	1	NR	101	288	.3	.8
283 Luth—MO Synod	2	372	234	454	.4	1.2
290 Metro Comm Ch	1	31	48	48 *	-	.1
349 Pent Holiness	2	403	190	469 *	.5	1.3
355 Presb Ch (USA)	3	2,161	846	2,514 *	2.5	6.9
356 Presb Ch Amer	1	225	300	300	.3	.8
360 Prim Bapt Chrch	1	NR	NR	NR	-	-

NR–Not Reported   *Total adherents estimated from known number of communicant, confirmed, full members.   - Represents a percentage less than 0.1.   Percentages may not total 100 due to rounding.

Table 4: Religious Congregations by County and Group: 2000

Religious Group	Number of Churches, Synagogues, Mosques, or Temples	Number of Communicant, Confirmed, or Full Members	Number of Attendees	Total Adherents		
				Number of Adherents	% of Total Pop.	% of Total Adh.
403 Salvation Army	1	108	67	340	.3	.9
413 S.D.A.	2	307	NR	366	.4	1.0
418 Southw Bapt Fel	2	NR	NR	NR	-	-
419 So Bapt Conv	16	11,137	4,088	12,957 *	12.8	35.6
435 Unitarian-Univ	1	201	NR	234 *	.2	.6
449 Un Methodist	11	6,131	2,639	7,133 *	7.0	19.6
463 Vineyard	1	60	80	80 *	.1	.2
496 Jewish Est	1	NR	NR	400	.4	1.1
498 Indep.Charis.	1	550	475	750	.7	2.1
CLAY	**15**	**1,258**	**447**	**1,638 ***	**48.8**	**100.0**
056 Baha'i	0	4	NR	4	.1	.2
355 Presb Ch (USA)	1	29	32	36 *	1.1	2.2
419 So Bapt Conv	7	874	249	1,087 *	32.4	66.4
449 Un Methodist	5	351	166	436 *	13.0	26.6
496 Jewish Est	2	NR	NR	75	2.2	4.6
CLAYTON	**108**	**42,302**	**15,097**	**67,081 ***	**28.4**	**100.0**
019 Amer Bapt USA	1	0	0	0 *	-	-
053 Assemb of God	4	344	373	686	.3	1.0
056 Baha'i	1	70	NR	70	-	.1
081 Catholic	2	NR	NR	9,073	3.8	13.5
089 Chr & Miss Al	1	140	NR	143	.1	.2
093 Chr Ch (Disc)	1	117	125	154 *	.1	.2
097 Chr Chs&Chs Cr	4	887	NR	1,165 *	.5	1.7
121 Ch God (Abr)	2	60	75	79 *	-	.1
123 Ch God (Ander)	2	NR	107	107	-	.2
127 Ch God (Cleve)	3	1,128	448	1,481 *	.6	2.2
145 Ch God Prophcy	1	42	NR	55 *	-	.1
165 Ch of Nazarene	2	363	236	371	.2	.6
167 Chs of Christ	7	797	780	1,017	.4	1.5
193 Episcopal	1	NR	109	277	.1	.4
207 E.L.C.A.	3	891	394	1,073	.5	1.6
252 Hindu	2	NR	NR	NR	-	-
267 Muslim Est	2	NR	440	2,513	1.1	3.7
283 Luth—MO Synod	2	321	219	420	.2	.6
339 Pent Ch of God	1	103	NR	182	.1	.3
349 Pent Holiness	1	71	61	93 *	-	.1
355 Presb Ch (USA)	5	1,015	549	1,333 *	.6	2.0
356 Presb Ch Amer	1	176	30	176	.1	.3
360 Prim Bapt Chrch	1	NR	NR	NR	-	-
403 Salvation Army	1	46	66	95	-	.1
413 S.D.A.	1	170	NR	202	.1	.3
418 Southw Bapt Fel	4	NR	NR	NR	-	-
419 So Bapt Conv	33	28,386	7,804	37,267 *	15.8	55.6
443 Un C of Christ	1	65	29	85 *	-	.1
449 Un Methodist	12	5,475	1,788	7,189 *	3.0	10.7
467 Wesleyan	1	57	19	57	-	.1
498 Indep.Charis.	1	260	260	300	.1	.4
499 Indep.Non-Char	4	1,318	1,185	1,418	.6	2.1
CLINCH	**16**	**1,899**	**949**	**2,417 ***	**35.1**	**100.0**
053 Assemb of God	1	64	85	85	1.2	3.5
127 Ch God (Cleve)	3	659	379	837 *	12.2	34.6
145 Ch God Prophcy	1	42	NR	53 *	.8	2.2
167 Chs of Christ	1	18	22	22	.3	.9
223 Free Will Bapt	1	80	NR	102 *	1.5	4.2
320 "Old" MB Ascs	1	24	NR	31 *	.5	1.3
355 Presb Ch (USA)	1	88	80	112 *	1.6	4.6
360 Prim Bapt Chrch	1	NR	NR	NR	-	-
419 So Bapt Conv	3	701	258	891 *	13.0	36.9
449 Un Methodist	3	223	125	284 *	4.1	11.8
COBB	**322**	**156,303**	**68,906**	**278,056 ***	**45.8**	**100.0**
017 Amer Bapt Assn	1	200	NR	252 *	-	.1
019 Amer Bapt USA	1	0	0	0 *	-	-
053 Assemb of God	12	1,134	1,147	1,360	.2	.5
055 As Ref Pres Ch	1	48	NR	53	-	-
056 Baha'i	10	574	NR	574	.1	.2
081 Catholic	7	NR	NR	59,408	9.8	21.4
084 Calvary Chapel	1	NR	NR	NR	-	-
089 Chr & Miss Al	1	161	NR	315	.1	.1

Religious Group	Number of Churches, Synagogues, Mosques, or Temples	Number of Communicant, Confirmed, or Full Members	Number of Attendees	Total Adherents		
				Number of Adherents	% of Total Pop.	% of Total Adh.
093 Chr Ch (Disc)	4	549	202	690 *	.1	.2
097 Chr Chs&Chs Cr	9	1,212	NR	1,524 *	.3	.5
123 Ch God (Ander)	3	NR	385	385	.1	.1
127 Ch God (Cleve)	13	8,963	5,667	11,313 *	1.9	4.1
145 Ch God Prophcy	6	242	NR	302 *	-	.1
151 L-D Saints	9	NR	NR	3,954	.7	1.4
165 Ch of Nazarene	5	506	352	676	.1	.2
167 Chs of Christ	12	2,367	2,418	2,983	.5	1.1
185 Cumber Presb	1	0	NR	0	-	-
193 Episcopal	7	NR	2,301	6,271	1.0	2.3
203 Evan Free Ch	1	60	60	60	-	-
207 E.L.C.A.	7	3,346	1,496	4,407	.7	1.6
223 Free Will Bapt	1	80	NR	101 *	-	-
246 Greek Orthodox	1	NR	NR	384	.1	.1
252 Hindu	2	NR	NR	NR	-	-
262 Int Cou Comm Ch	1	190	NR	239 *	-	.1
263 Int Foursq Gos	2	45	116	116 *	-	-
267 Muslim Est	1	NR	350	400	.1	.1
269 Jasper&PVB Asc	2	382	NR	480 *	.1	.2
283 Luth—MO Synod	2	653	487	958	.2	.3
289 New Hope B Asc	1	119	NR	150 *	-	.1
335 Orth Pres Ch	1	44	82	82	-	-
349 Pent Holiness	1	14	15	18 *	-	-
355 Presb Ch (USA)	15	7,075	3,641	8,947 *	1.5	3.2
356 Presb Ch Amer	9	1,679	1,629	2,269	.4	.8
360 Prim Bapt Chrch	2	NR	NR	NR	-	-
365 Prog Prim Bapt	1	27	NR	34 *	-	-
403 Salvation Army	1	63	45	669	.1	.2
413 S.D.A.	5	1,291	NR	1,537	.3	.6
418 Southw Bapt Fel	2	NR	NR	NR	-	-
419 So Bapt Conv	108	89,340	33,697	112,360 *	18.5	40.4
435 Unitarian-Univ	2	163	NR	205 *	-	.1
443 Un C of Christ	1	204	90	257 *	-	.1
449 Un Methodist	38	32,736	12,210	41,170 *	6.8	14.8
463 Vineyard	3	500	472	629 *	.1	.2
469 WELS	1	286	194	374	.1	.1
496 Jewish Est	4	NR	NR	10,000	1.6	3.6
498 Indep.Charis.	2	650	750	750	.1	.3
499 Indep.Non-Char	2	1,400	1,100	1,400	.2	.5
COFFEE	**67**	**11,650**	**5,035**	**16,605 ***	**44.4**	**100.0**
053 Assemb of God	2	240	335	335	.9	2.0
056 Baha'i	0	3	NR	3	-	-
081 Catholic	1	NR	NR	626	1.7	3.8
123 Ch God (Ander)	1	NR	19	19	.1	.1
127 Ch God (Cleve)	10	2,082	1,093	2,673 *	7.1	16.1
145 Ch God Prophcy	4	167	NR	216 *	.6	1.3
151 L-D Saints	2	NR	NR	805	2.2	4.8
165 Ch of Nazarene	1	8	15	26	.1	.2
167 Chs of Christ	2	90	88	118	.3	.7
193 Episcopal	1	NR	70	154	.4	.9
320 "Old" MB Ascs	7	491	NR	630 *	1.7	3.8
355 Presb Ch (USA)	1	93	49	119 *	.3	.7
365 Prog Prim Bapt	2	180	NR	231 *	.6	1.4
419 So Bapt Conv	24	7,066	2,933	9,070 *	24.2	54.6
449 Un Methodist	9	1,230	433	1,580 *	4.2	9.5
COLQUITT	**83**	**17,522**	**6,278**	**23,047 ***	**54.8**	**100.0**
017 Amer Bapt Assn	1	6	NR	8 *	-	-
053 Assemb of God	4	453	612	733	1.7	3.2
056 Baha'i	0	17	NR	17	-	.1
081 Catholic	1	NR	NR	457	1.1	2.0
089 Chr & Miss Al	1	92	NR	211	.5	.9
127 Ch God (Cleve)	3	274	136	347 *	.8	1.5
145 Ch God Prophcy	1	42	NR	53 *	.1	.2
165 Ch of Nazarene	1	218	148	230	.5	1.0
167 Chs of Christ	1	50	55	78	.2	.3
193 Episcopal	2	NR	73	160	.4	.7
223 Free Will Bapt	6	481	NR	610 *	1.5	2.6
355 Presb Ch (USA)	1	517	189	656 *	1.6	2.8
360 Prim Bapt Chrch	7	NR	NR	NR	-	-
413 S.D.A.	1	103	NR	123	.3	.5
419 So Bapt Conv	42	13,604	4,355	17,253 *	41.0	74.9

NR–Not Reported   *Total adherents estimated from known number of communicant, confirmed, full members.   - Represents a percentage less than 0.1.   Percentages may not total 100 due to rounding.

Table 4: Religious Congregations by County and Group: 2000

Religious Group	Number of Churches, Synagogues, Mosques, or Temples	Number of Communicant, Confirmed, or Full Members	Number of Attendees	Total Adherents: Number of Adherents	Total Adherents: % of Total Pop.	Total Adherents: % of Total Adh.
449 Un Methodist	11	1,665	710	2,111 *	5.0	9.2
COLUMBIA	**54**	**17,545**	**9,846**	**24,658 ***	**27.6**	**100.0**
056 Baha'i	1	61	NR	61	.1	.2
081 Catholic	0	NR	NR	29	-	.1
127 Ch God (Cleve)	2	948	1,015	1,224 *	1.4	5.0
151 L-D Saints	2	NR	NR	1,207	1.4	4.9
165 Ch of Nazarene	1	57	57	57	.1	.2
167 Chs of Christ	3	437	480	559	.6	2.3
193 Episcopal	2	NR	245	551	.6	2.2
252 Hindu	1	NR	NR	NR	-	-
355 Presb Ch (USA)	2	144	69	186 *	.2	.8
356 Presb Ch Amer	3	75	80	89	.1	.4
360 Prim Bapt Chrch	1	NR	NR	NR	-	-
416 Sikh	1	NR	NR	NR	-	-
419 So Bapt Conv	24	11,703	5,345	15,112 *	16.9	61.3
449 Un Methodist	9	3,820	2,015	4,933 *	5.5	20.0
498 Indep.Charis.	1	300	190	300	.3	1.2
499 Indep.Non-Char	1	0	350	350	.4	1.4
COOK	**31**	**5,823**	**2,284**	**7,543 ***	**47.8**	**100.0**
053 Assemb of God	1	147	170	205	1.3	2.7
081 Catholic	1	NR	NR	40	.3	.5
127 Ch God (Cleve)	2	355	171	456 *	2.9	6.0
165 Ch of Nazarene	1	21	10	21	.1	.3
167 Chs of Christ	2	136	124	188	1.2	2.5
223 Free Will Bapt	1	80	NR	103 *	.7	1.4
355 Presb Ch (USA)	1	10	10	13 *	.1	.2
360 Prim Bapt Chrch	4	NR	NR	NR	-	-
419 So Bapt Conv	14	4,138	1,465	5,315 *	33.7	70.5
449 Un Methodist	4	936	334	1,202 *	7.6	15.9
COWETA	**95**	**23,724**	**11,966**	**35,510 ***	**39.8**	**100.0**
053 Assemb of God	3	239	248	248	.3	.7
055 As Ref Pres Ch	1	212	NR	257	.3	.7
056 Baha'i	0	90	NR	90	.1	.3
081 Catholic	1	NR	NR	3,334	3.7	9.4
093 Chr Ch (Disc)	1	32	0	42 *	-	.1
097 Chr Chs&Chs Cr	3	875	NR	1,136 *	1.3	3.2
127 Ch God (Cleve)	4	984	637	1,278 *	1.4	3.6
145 Ch God Prophcy	2	83	NR	108 *	.1	.3
151 L-D Saints	2	NR	NR	921	1.0	2.6
165 Ch of Nazarene	1	56	77	86	.1	.2
167 Chs of Christ	5	583	526	788	.9	2.2
173 Comm of Christ	1	24	NR	24	-	.1
193 Episcopal	1	NR	162	403	.5	1.1
207 E.L.C.A.	2	215	175	347	.4	1.0
283 Luth—MO Synod	1	78	46	90	.1	.3
339 Pent Ch of God	1	25	NR	35	-	.1
349 Pent Holiness	1	178	125	231 *	.3	.7
355 Presb Ch (USA)	1	583	207	757 *	.8	2.1
356 Presb Ch Amer	1	0	100	100	.1	.3
370 Ref Baptist Chs	1	NR	NR	NR	-	-
413 S.D.A.	2	382	NR	455	.5	1.3
418 Southw Bapt Fel	1	NR	NR	NR	-	-
419 So Bapt Conv	36	14,687	7,502	19,066 *	21.4	53.7
449 Un Methodist	22	4,352	2,112	5,649 *	6.3	15.9
469 WELS	1	46	49	65	.1	.2
CRAWFORD	**11**	**1,309**	**562**	**1,651 ***	**13.2**	**100.0**
056 Baha'i	0	37	NR	37	.3	2.2
175 Congr Chr Chs	1	30	30	38 *	.3	2.3
360 Prim Bapt Chrch	1	NR	NR	NR	-	-
419 So Bapt Conv	4	822	350	1,043 *	8.3	63.2
449 Un Methodist	5	420	182	533 *	4.3	32.3
CRISP	**47**	**7,518**	**2,780**	**10,034 ***	**45.6**	**100.0**
053 Assemb of God	1	56	59	75	.3	.7
056 Baha'i	0	26	NR	26	.1	.3
081 Catholic	1	NR	NR	175	.8	1.7
127 Ch God (Cleve)	1	95	28	122 *	.6	1.2
145 Ch God Prophcy	2	83	NR	108 *	.5	1.1
151 L-D Saints	1	NR	NR	140	.6	1.4
167 Chs of Christ	3	128	150	150	.7	1.5
193 Episcopal	1	NR	23	51	.2	.5
223 Free Will Bapt	2	160	NR	207 *	.9	2.1
349 Pent Holiness	1	30	45	39 *	.2	.4
355 Presb Ch (USA)	2	87	66	112 *	.5	1.1
360 Prim Bapt Chrch	3	NR	NR	NR	-	-
365 Prog Prim Bapt	1	29	NR	37 *	.2	.4
419 So Bapt Conv	22	5,378	1,962	6,928 *	31.5	69.0
449 Un Methodist	6	1,446	447	1,864 *	8.5	18.6
DADE	**31**	**3,864**	**1,802**	**5,204 ***	**34.3**	**100.0**
056 Baha'i	0	1	NR	1	-	-
081 Catholic	1	NR	NR	470	3.1	9.0
127 Ch God (Cleve)	5	296	179	362 *	2.4	7.0
167 Chs of Christ	4	226	225	293	1.9	5.6
413 S.D.A.	2	197	NR	235	1.6	4.5
418 Southw Bapt Fel	2	NR	NR	NR	-	-
419 So Bapt Conv	9	2,274	923	2,780 *	18.3	53.4
449 Un Methodist	8	870	475	1,063 *	7.0	20.4
DAWSON	**22**	**4,041**	**1,351**	**5,210 ***	**32.6**	**100.0**
056 Baha'i	0	3	NR	3	-	.1
081 Catholic	1	NR	NR	166	1.0	3.2
127 Ch God (Cleve)	1	422	280	528 *	3.3	10.1
145 Ch God Prophcy	1	42	NR	52 *	.3	1.0
167 Chs of Christ	1	37	30	40	.3	.8
419 So Bapt Conv	14	3,049	776	3,811 *	23.8	73.1
449 Un Methodist	4	488	265	610 *	3.8	11.7
DECATUR	**58**	**10,095**	**3,890**	**13,522 ***	**47.9**	**100.0**
053 Assemb of God	3	265	302	359	1.3	2.7
056 Baha'i	0	23	NR	23	.1	.2
081 Catholic	1	NR	NR	145	.5	1.1
097 Chr Chs&Chs Cr	1	120	NR	154 *	.5	1.1
123 Ch God (Ander)	1	NR	39	39	.1	.3
127 Ch God (Cleve)	3	485	206	624 *	2.2	4.6
145 Ch God Prophcy	1	42	NR	54 *	.2	.4
151 L-D Saints	1	NR	NR	181	.6	1.3
165 Ch of Nazarene	1	100	105	105	.4	.8
167 Chs of Christ	3	158	158	193	.7	1.4
193 Episcopal	1	NR	64	135	.5	1.0
223 Free Will Bapt	4	321	NR	412 *	1.5	3.0
304 NatPrimBapt USA	2	210	NR	270 *	1.0	2.0
355 Presb Ch (USA)	1	267	92	343 *	1.2	2.5
360 Prim Bapt Chrch	1	NR	NR	NR	-	-
413 S.D.A.	1	73	NR	87	.3	.6
419 So Bapt Conv	21	6,296	2,161	8,089 *	28.6	59.8
449 Un Methodist	10	1,485	513	1,909 *	6.8	14.1
496 Jewish Est	1	NR	NR	100	.4	.7
499 Indep.Non-Char	1	250	250	300	1.1	2.2
DE KALB	**326**	**144,438**	**62,202**	**234,299 ***	**35.2**	**100.0**
019 Amer Bapt USA	1	478	250	594 *	.1	.3
034 Ant Orth of NA	1	363	NR	726	.1	.3
049 Armen Ap Cilic	1	0	NR	320	-	.1
053 Assemb of God	7	1,946	2,247	4,124	.6	1.8
055 As Ref Pres Ch	2	148	NR	198	-	.1
056 Baha'i	6	651	NR	651	.1	.3
075 Brethren in Cr	1	54	54	54	-	-
076 Buddhism	10	NR	NR	NR	-	-
081 Catholic	10	NR	NR	36,223	5.4	15.5
089 Chr & Miss Al	7	1,205	NR	1,459	.2	.6
093 Chr Ch (Disc)	6	6,233	1,418	7,746 *	1.2	3.3
097 Chr Chs&Chs Cr	6	4,153	NR	5,162 *	.8	2.2
105 Christian Ref	4	193	202	240 *	-	.1
123 Ch God (Ander)	2	NR	131	131	-	.1
127 Ch God (Cleve)	6	2,507	901	3,145 *	.5	1.3
145 Ch God Prophcy	5	200	NR	249 *	-	.1
151 L-D Saints	2	NR	NR	1,083	.2	.5
165 Ch of Nazarene	4	755	328	990	.1	.4
167 Chs of Christ	9	3,237	3,129	4,532	.7	1.9

NR–Not Reported   *Total adherents estimated from known number of communicant, confirmed, full members.   - Represents a percentage less than 0.1.   Percentages may not total 100 due to rounding.

Table 4: Religious Congregations by County and Group: 2000

Religious Group	Number of Churches, Synagogues, Mosques, or Temples	Number of Communicant, Confirmed, or Full Members	Number of Attendees	Total Adherents		
				Number of Adherents	% of Total Pop.	% of Total Adh.
185 Cumber Presb	1	0	NR	0	-	-
193 Episcopal	9	NR	2,868	8,483	1.3	3.6
201 Evan Cov Ch	2	128	118	159 *	-	.1
207 E.L.C.A.	7	1,265	653	1,587	.2	.7
223 Free Will Bapt	1	80	NR	100 *	-	-
226 Friends-USA	1	64	NR	80 *	-	-
246 Greek Orthodox	1	NR	NR	2,625	.4	1.1
252 Hindu	3	NR	NR	NR	-	-
265 Int Pent C Chr	1	0	0	40	-	-
267 Muslim Est	4	NR	1,120	4,439	.7	1.9
268 Jain	1	NR	NR	NR	-	-
283 Luth—MO Synod	2	247	173	335	.1	.1
288 Mennonite USA	2	51	85	85 *	-	-
290 Metro Comm Ch	2	484	443	601 *	.1	.3
295 Morav Ch-South	1	139	NR	180	-	.1
320 "Old" MB Ascs	7	1,605	NR	1,995 *	.3	.9
333 Malan Dioc Am	1	NR	NR	125	-	.1
334 Malan Syr Orth	1	15	NR	75	-	-
335 Orth Pres Ch	1	110	132	158	-	.1
349 Pent Holiness	3	926	774	1,151 *	.2	.5
355 Presb Ch (USA)	26	8,490	4,903	10,571 *	1.6	4.5
356 Presb Ch Amer	8	1,482	1,661	2,017	.3	.9
360 Prim Bapt Chrch	4	NR	NR	NR	-	-
403 Salvation Army	4	715	689	1,459	.2	.6
413 S.D.A.	11	2,933	NR	3,490	.5	1.5
416 Sikh	1	NR	NR	NR	-	-
418 Southw Bapt Fel	1	NR	NR	NR	-	-
419 So Bapt Conv	72	63,553	22,894	78,981 *	11.9	33.7
435 Unitarian-Univ	1	667	NR	829 *	.1	.4
443 Un C of Christ	3	746	355	927 *	.1	.4
449 Un Methodist	47	27,395	9,527	34,050 *	5.1	14.5
467 Wesleyan	1	99	57	150	-	.1
469 WELS	1	121	90	180	-	.1
498 Indep.Charis.	2	1,800	1,200	1,800	.3	.8
499 Indep.Non-Char	3	9,200	5,800	10,000	1.5	4.3
DODGE	**69**	**10,283**	**4,344**	**12,800 ***	**66.8**	**100.0**
053 Assemb of God	1	51	45	64	.3	.5
056 Baha'i	0	8	NR	8	-	.1
081 Catholic	1	NR	NR	93	.5	.7
093 Chr Ch (Disc)	2	90	40	111 *	.6	.9
127 Ch God (Cleve)	5	366	292	452 *	2.4	3.5
165 Ch of Nazarene	1	86	80	126	.7	1.0
167 Chs of Christ	1	45	48	58	.3	.5
223 Free Will Bapt	5	401	NR	495 *	2.6	3.9
349 Pent Holiness	1	191	204	236 *	1.2	1.8
355 Presb Ch (USA)	2	129	64	159 *	.8	1.2
360 Prim Bapt Chrch	2	NR	NR	NR	-	-
419 So Bapt Conv	40	8,301	3,318	10,239 *	53.4	80.0
449 Un Methodist	8	615	253	759 *	4.0	5.9
DOOLY	**33**	**4,562**	**1,451**	**5,641 ***	**48.9**	**100.0**
017 Amer Bapt Assn	1	43	NR	53 *	.5	.9
056 Baha'i	0	103	NR	103	.9	1.8
127 Ch God (Cleve)	1	191	98	237 *	2.1	4.2
167 Chs of Christ	1	3	10	4	-	.1
223 Free Will Bapt	2	160	NR	199 *	1.7	3.5
419 So Bapt Conv	20	3,195	927	3,968 *	34.4	70.3
449 Un Methodist	8	867	416	1,077 *	9.3	19.1
DOUGHERTY	**84**	**28,502**	**11,774**	**42,359 ***	**44.1**	**100.0**
053 Assemb of God	3	870	856	1,104	1.1	2.6
056 Baha'i	1	86	NR	86	.1	.2
081 Catholic	1	NR	NR	4,272	4.4	10.1
089 Chr & Miss Al	1	17	NR	30	-	.1
093 Chr Ch (Disc)	1	246	75	313 *	.3	.7
097 Chr Chs&Chs Cr	1	225	NR	287 *	.3	.7
127 Ch God (Cleve)	5	945	455	1,204 *	1.3	2.8
145 Ch God Prophcy	1	42	NR	53 *	.1	.1
151 L-D Saints	1	NR	NR	354	.4	.8
165 Ch of Nazarene	3	344	217	386	.4	.9
167 Chs of Christ	8	1,297	936	1,416	1.5	3.3
193 Episcopal	3	NR	360	1,128	1.2	2.7
207 E.L.C.A.	1	222	74	290	.3	.7
223 Free Will Bapt	3	241	NR	306 *	.3	.7
267 Muslim Est	3	NR	217	601	.6	1.4
283 Luth—MO Synod	1	70	66	99	.1	.2
349 Pent Holiness	1	48	30	61 *	.1	.1
355 Presb Ch (USA)	4	641	281	815 *	.8	1.9
356 Presb Ch Amer	1	41	55	57	.1	.1
360 Prim Bapt Chrch	1	NR	NR	NR	-	-
403 Salvation Army	1	150	52	349	.4	.8
413 S.D.A.	2	387	NR	460	.5	1.1
418 Southw Bapt Fel	3	NR	NR	NR	-	-
419 So Bapt Conv	22	14,117	4,960	17,976 *	18.7	42.4
449 Un Methodist	9	7,313	2,440	9,312 *	9.7	22.0
496 Jewish Est	1	NR	NR	200	.2	.5
498 Indep.Charis.	2	1,200	700	1,200	1.2	2.8
DOUGLAS	**65**	**26,733**	**9,687**	**40,046 ***	**43.4**	**100.0**
017 Amer Bapt Assn	1	50	NR	64 *	.1	.2
053 Assemb of God	3	660	415	825	.9	2.1
056 Baha'i	1	61	NR	61	.1	.2
081 Catholic	1	NR	NR	4,779	5.2	11.9
089 Chr & Miss Al	1	0	NR	0	-	-
097 Chr Chs&Chs Cr	3	485	NR	618 *	.7	1.5
123 Ch God (Ander)	1	NR	25	25	-	.1
127 Ch God (Cleve)	5	2,187	757	2,787 *	3.0	7.0
145 Ch God Prophcy	1	42	NR	53 *	.1	.1
151 L-D Saints	2	NR	NR	680	.7	1.7
165 Ch of Nazarene	1	126	112	187	.2	.5
167 Chs of Christ	5	342	384	448	.5	1.1
193 Episcopal	2	NR	230	516	.6	1.3
207 E.L.C.A.	1	218	147	291	.3	.7
283 Luth—MO Synod	1	143	98	192	.2	.5
355 Presb Ch (USA)	1	837	450	1,067 *	1.2	2.7
356 Presb Ch Amer	2	128	132	150	.2	.4
360 Prim Bapt Chrch	3	NR	NR	NR	-	-
413 S.D.A.	1	390	NR	464	.5	1.2
418 Southw Bapt Fel	1	NR	NR	NR	-	-
419 So Bapt Conv	20	16,345	4,902	20,827 *	22.6	52.0
449 Un Methodist	7	4,614	1,945	5,878 *	6.4	14.7
463 Vineyard	1	105	90	134 *	.1	.3
EARLY	**32**	**4,195**	**1,485**	**5,452 ***	**44.1**	**100.0**
053 Assemb of God	3	82	81	134	1.1	2.5
056 Baha'i	0	7	NR	7	.1	.1
081 Catholic	1	NR	NR	57	.5	1.0
123 Ch God (Ander)	1	NR	6	6	-	.1
127 Ch God (Cleve)	1	74	34	94 *	.8	1.7
167 Chs of Christ	3	95	103	126	1.0	2.3
193 Episcopal	1	NR	11	19	.2	.3
223 Free Will Bapt	4	321	NR	409 *	3.3	7.5
355 Presb Ch (USA)	1	43	20	55 *	.4	1.0
413 S.D.A.	1	99	NR	118	1.0	2.2
419 So Bapt Conv	10	2,608	954	3,323 *	26.9	61.0
449 Un Methodist	6	866	276	1,104 *	8.9	20.2
ECHOLS	**6**	**572**	**325**	**737 ***	**19.6**	**100.0**
127 Ch God (Cleve)	1	101	37	129 *	3.4	17.5
167 Chs of Christ	1	65	85	90	2.4	12.2
419 So Bapt Conv	2	278	108	354 *	9.4	48.0
449 Un Methodist	2	128	95	164 *	4.4	22.3
EFFINGHAM	**52**	**11,486**	**4,976**	**15,367 ***	**40.9**	**100.0**
053 Assemb of God	2	116	139	165	.4	1.1
056 Baha'i	0	2	NR	2	-	-
081 Catholic	1	NR	NR	211	.6	1.4
093 Chr Ch (Disc)	1	157	84	204 *	.5	1.3
097 Chr Chs&Chs Cr	3	229	NR	298 *	.8	1.9
123 Ch God (Ander)	1	NR	15	15	-	.1
127 Ch God (Cleve)	1	358	185	465 *	1.2	3.0
145 Ch God Prophcy	1	42	NR	54 *	.1	.4
151 L-D Saints	1	NR	NR	274	.7	1.8
167 Chs of Christ	2	101	116	136	.4	.9

NR–Not Reported   *Total adherents estimated from known number of communicant, confirmed, full members.   - Represents a percentage less than 0.1.   Percentages may not total 100 due to rounding.

Table 4: Religious Congregations by County and Group: 2000

Religious Group	Number of Churches, Synagogues, Mosques, or Temples	Number of Communicant, Confirmed, or Full Members	Number of Attendees	Total Adherents		
				Number of Adherents	% of Total Pop.	% of Total Adh.
207 E.L.C.A.	6	1,024	468	1,272	3.4	8.3
349 Pent Holiness	1	25	30	32 *	.1	.2
355 Presb Ch (USA)	1	42	20	55 *	.1	.4
365 Prog Prim Bapt	1	323	NR	419 *	1.1	2.7
418 Southw Bapt Fel	1	NR	NR	NR	-	-
419 So Bapt Conv	18	6,664	2,783	8,648 *	23.0	56.3
449 Un Methodist	11	2,403	1,136	3,117 *	8.3	20.3
ELBERT	**53**	**9,759**	**3,944**	**12,256 ***	**59.8**	**100.0**
053 Assemb of God	1	36	40	40	.2	.3
056 Baha'i	0	1	NR	1	-	-
081 Catholic	1	NR	NR	93	.5	.8
097 Chr Chs&Chs Cr	1	275	NR	342 *	1.7	2.8
127 Ch God (Cleve)	2	350	247	435 *	2.1	3.5
145 Ch God Prophcy	1	42	NR	52 *	.3	.4
167 Chs of Christ	2	60	61	63	.3	.5
175 Congr Chr Chs	1	40	35	50 *	.2	.4
193 Episcopal	1	NR	33	62	.3	.5
207 E.L.C.A.	1	72	28	79	.4	.6
349 Pent Holiness	4	504	235	626 *	3.1	5.1
355 Presb Ch (USA)	3	236	150	293 *	1.4	2.4
419 So Bapt Conv	21	6,228	2,350	7,737 *	37.7	63.1
449 Un Methodist	13	1,886	739	2,343 *	11.4	19.1
467 Wesleyan	1	29	26	40	.2	.3
EMANUEL	**66**	**6,632**	**2,411**	**8,702 ***	**39.8**	**100.0**
053 Assemb of God	1	31	35	35	.2	.4
081 Catholic	1	NR	NR	229	1.0	2.6
127 Ch God (Cleve)	5	370	256	502 *	2.3	5.8
151 L-D Saints	1	NR	NR	119	.5	1.4
165 Ch of Nazarene	2	53	54	83	.4	1.0
167 Chs of Christ	1	3	3	4	-	-
223 Free Will Bapt	2	160	NR	201 *	.9	2.3
349 Pent Holiness	2	45	35	56 *	.3	.6
355 Presb Ch (USA)	1	24	11	30 *	.1	.3
360 Prim Bapt Chrch	7	NR	NR	NR	-	-
365 Prog Prim Bapt	7	404	NR	506 *	2.3	5.8
418 Southw Bapt Fel	1	NR	NR	NR	-	-
419 So Bapt Conv	22	3,956	1,302	4,951 *	22.7	56.9
449 Un Methodist	13	1,586	715	1,986 *	9.1	22.8
EVANS	**24**	**3,324**	**1,191**	**4,532 ***	**43.2**	**100.0**
053 Assemb of God	1	24	32	40	.4	.9
056 Baha'i	0	1	NR	1	-	-
081 Catholic	2	NR	NR	286	2.7	6.3
123 Ch God (Ander)	1	NR	5	5	-	.1
127 Ch God (Cleve)	1	83	65	105 *	1.0	2.3
145 Ch God Prophcy	1	42	NR	53 *	.5	1.2
165 Ch of Nazarene	1	45	36	90	.9	2.0
167 Chs of Christ	1	30	30	36	.3	.8
365 Prog Prim Bapt	2	200	NR	253 *	2.4	5.6
418 Southw Bapt Fel	1	NR	NR	NR	-	-
419 So Bapt Conv	6	1,617	615	2,043 *	19.5	45.1
449 Un Methodist	7	1,282	408	1,620 *	15.4	35.7
FANNIN	**53**	**11,253**	**3,326**	**13,749 ***	**69.4**	**100.0**
017 Amer Bapt Assn	1	50	NR	59 *	.3	.4
056 Baha'i	0	4	NR	4	-	-
081 Catholic	1	NR	NR	318	1.6	2.3
089 Chr & Miss Al	1	23	NR	29	.1	.2
127 Ch God (Cleve)	2	510	250	606 *	3.1	4.4
145 Ch God Prophcy	1	42	NR	50 *	.3	.4
167 Chs of Christ	4	326	330	442	2.2	3.2
207 E.L.C.A.	1	116	84	141	.7	1.0
413 S.D.A.	1	53	NR	63	.3	.5
419 So Bapt Conv	35	9,384	2,252	11,152 *	56.3	81.1
449 Un Methodist	6	745	410	885 *	4.5	6.4
FAYETTE	**78**	**38,074**	**16,862**	**65,455 ***	**71.7**	**100.0**
053 Assemb of God	3	254	240	335	.4	.5
056 Baha'i	1	43	NR	43	-	.1
081 Catholic	3	NR	NR	12,327	13.5	18.8
093 Chr Ch (Disc)	2	220	62	280 *	.3	.4
097 Chr Chs&Chs Cr	7	2,455	NR	3,128 *	3.4	4.8
121 Ch God (Abr)	1	20	30	30 *	-	-
127 Ch God (Cleve)	1	190	99	242 *	.3	.4
145 Ch God Prophcy	1	42	NR	53 *	.1	.1
151 L-D Saints	3	NR	NR	1,042	1.1	1.6
167 Chs of Christ	3	507	511	708	.8	1.1
193 Episcopal	2	NR	267	849	.9	1.3
207 E.L.C.A.	2	2,179	1,083	2,844	3.1	4.3
221 Free Methodist	1	100	180	180	.2	.3
283 Luth—MO Synod	1	160	147	239	.3	.4
355 Presb Ch (USA)	2	1,186	700	1,511 *	1.7	2.3
356 Presb Ch Amer	3	727	749	956	1.0	1.5
360 Prim Bapt Chrch	1	NR	NR	NR	-	-
370 Ref Baptist Chs	1	NR	NR	NR	-	-
418 Southw Bapt Fel	1	NR	NR	NR	-	-
419 So Bapt Conv	24	22,257	8,907	28,361 *	31.1	43.3
449 Un Methodist	13	7,084	3,487	9,027 *	9.9	13.8
496 Jewish Est	1	NR	NR	2,500	2.7	3.8
499 Indep.Non-Char	1	650	400	800	.9	1.2
FLOYD	**140**	**44,447**	**15,542**	**59,264 ***	**65.4**	**100.0**
053 Assemb of God	2	175	190	222	.2	.4
056 Baha'i	0	13	NR	13	-	-
081 Catholic	1	NR	NR	2,229	2.5	3.8
089 Chr & Miss Al	1	14	NR	24	-	-
093 Chr Ch (Disc)	1	78	35	97 *	.1	.2
097 Chr Chs&Chs Cr	2	165	NR	204 *	.2	.3
127 Ch God (Cleve)	8	2,056	1,282	2,572 *	2.8	4.3
145 Ch God Prophcy	2	83	NR	104 *	.1	.2
151 L-D Saints	1	NR	NR	407	.4	.7
165 Ch of Nazarene	1	37	43	59	.1	.1
167 Chs of Christ	6	748	817	1,056	1.2	1.8
193 Episcopal	2	NR	247	821	.9	1.4
216 Evan Presby Ch	1	994	NR	1,231 *	1.4	2.1
263 Int Foursq Gos	1	58	76	76 *	.1	.1
269 Jasper&PVB Asc	1	60	NR	74 *	.1	.1
283 Luth—MO Synod	1	187	87	215	.2	.4
289 New Hope B Asc	1	40	NR	50 *	.1	.1
355 Presb Ch (USA)	2	505	229	625 *	.7	1.1
360 Prim Bapt Chrch	4	NR	NR	NR	-	-
403 Salvation Army	1	87	24	251	.3	.4
413 S.D.A.	1	47	NR	56	.1	.1
418 Southw Bapt Fel	1	NR	NR	NR	-	-
419 So Bapt Conv	68	33,803	9,650	41,849 *	46.2	70.6
449 Un Methodist	29	5,072	2,212	6,279 *	6.9	10.6
496 Jewish Est	1	NR	NR	100	.1	.2
499 Indep.Non-Char	1	225	650	650	.7	1.1
FORSYTH	**79**	**25,981**	**11,945**	**40,106 ***	**40.8**	**100.0**
053 Assemb of God	1	200	120	173	.2	.4
056 Baha'i	1	20	NR	20	-	-
081 Catholic	1	NR	NR	5,096	5.2	12.7
097 Chr Chs&Chs Cr	2	974	NR	1,269 *	1.3	3.2
127 Ch God (Cleve)	2	618	398	805 *	.8	2.0
145 Ch God Prophcy	1	42	NR	54 *	.1	.1
151 L-D Saints	1	NR	NR	422	.4	1.1
167 Chs of Christ	3	171	228	256	.3	.6
193 Episcopal	1	NR	150	601	.6	1.5
207 E.L.C.A.	1	354	249	488	.5	1.2
246 Greek Orthodox	1	NR	NR	0	-	-
251 Holy Orth in NA	1	NR	NR	15	-	-
349 Pent Holiness	1	48	48	63 *	.1	.2
355 Presb Ch (USA)	2	566	359	737 *	.7	1.8
356 Presb Ch Amer	1	66	110	113	.1	.3
401 Rus Orth Abroad	1	NR	NR	NR	-	-
418 Southw Bapt Fel	1	NR	NR	NR	-	-
419 So Bapt Conv	45	18,773	8,094	24,457 *	24.9	61.0
449 Un Methodist	11	4,149	2,171	5,406 *	5.5	13.5
467 Wesleyan	1	0	18	131	.1	.3
FRANKLIN	**56**	**10,904**	**4,454**	**13,392 ***	**66.0**	**100.0**
056 Baha'i	0	1	NR	1	-	-

NR–Not Reported   *Total adherents estimated from known number of communicant, confirmed, full members.   - Represents a percentage less than 0.1.   Percentages may not total 100 due to rounding.

Table 4: Religious Congregations by County and Group: 2000

Religious Group	Number of Churches, Synagogues, Mosques, or Temples	Number of Communicant, Confirmed, or Full Members	Number of Attendees	Total Adherents		
				Number of Adherents	% of Total Pop.	% of Total Adh.
097 Chr Chs&Chs Cr	1	200	NR	246 *	1.2	1.8
127 Ch God (Cleve)	7	1,186	706	1,457 *	7.2	10.9
167 Chs of Christ	1	17	18	22	.1	.2
216 Evan Presby Ch	1	103	NR	126 *	.6	.9
349 Pent Holiness	7	776	525	953 *	4.7	7.1
355 Presb Ch (USA)	4	109	73	133 *	.7	1.0
419 So Bapt Conv	24	7,064	2,442	8,676 *	42.8	64.8
435 Unitarian-Univ	1	10	NR	12 *	.1	.1
449 Un Methodist	10	1,438	690	1,766 *	8.7	13.2
FULTON	**471**	**236,453**	**117,297**	**479,185 ***	**58.7**	**100.0**
019 Amer Bapt USA	10	6,649	1,270	8,258 *	1.0	1.7
040 Ap Chr Ch-Amer	1	11	27	27 *	-	-
053 Assemb of God	5	596	509	4,180	.5	.9
056 Baha'i	8	768	NR	768	.1	.2
076 Buddhism	4	NR	NR	NR	-	-
081 Catholic	19	NR	NR	72,148	8.8	15.1
084 Calvary Chapel	2	NR	NR	NR	-	-
089 Chr & Miss Al	1	50	NR	106	-	-
093 Chr Ch (Disc)	4	2,357	981	2,927 *	.4	.6
097 Chr Chs&Chs Cr	16	4,185	NR	5,197 *	.6	1.1
123 Ch God (Ander)	3	NR	793	793	.1	.2
127 Ch God (Cleve)	14	11,891	7,087	14,921 *	1.8	3.1
145 Ch God Prophcy	1	42	NR	52 *	-	-
151 L-D Saints	6	NR	NR	2,673	.3	.6
165 Ch of Nazarene	3	270	291	379	-	.1
167 Chs of Christ	21	2,451	2,507	3,359	.4	.7
173 Comm of Christ	1	191	NR	191	-	-
186 Coptic Orth Ch	1	NR	NR	NR	-	-
193 Episcopal	16	NR	5,474	18,769	2.3	3.9
201 Evan Cov Ch	1	66	65	82 *	-	-
203 Evan Free Ch	1	268	325	325	-	.1
207 E.L.C.A.	14	5,013	2,391	6,513	.8	1.4
252 Hindu	1	NR	NR	NR	-	-
262 Int Cou Comm Ch	1	190	NR	236 *	-	-
264 Int Chs of Crst	1	3,399	6,031	5,069	.6	1.1
267 Muslim Est	13	NR	3,910	21,791	2.7	4.5
283 Luth—MO Synod	5	1,357	986	1,933	.2	.4
288 Mennonite USA	1	19	30	30 *	-	-
290 Metro Comm Ch	1	74	71	92 *	-	-
297 Mennonite;Other	1	45	NR	56 *	-	-
320 "Old" MB Ascs	1	160	NR	199 *	-	-
339 Pent Ch of God	1	50	NR	50	-	-
349 Pent Holiness	1	66	18	82 *	-	-
355 Presb Ch (USA)	30	24,493	8,412	30,452 *	3.7	6.4
356 Presb Ch Amer	5	796	747	1,047	.1	.2
360 Prim Bapt Chrch	9	NR	NR	NR	-	-
365 Prog Prim Bapt	1	63	NR	78 *	-	-
371 Ref Ch in Am	1	118	205	245	-	.1
388 Reg Bapt Gen As	1	300	125	373 *	-	.1
403 Salvation Army	2	261	193	239	-	-
413 S.D.A.	12	8,796	NR	10,467	1.3	2.2
416 Sikh	2	NR	NR	NR	-	-
419 So Bapt Conv	103	65,353	23,117	81,163 *	9.9	16.9
435 Unitarian-Univ	3	332	NR	412 *	.1	.1
443 Un C of Christ	5	661	290	821 *	.1	.2
449 Un Methodist	82	60,700	23,822	75,388 *	9.2	15.7
463 Vineyard	1	1,000	788	1,242 *	.2	.3
469 WELS	1	112	92	152	-	-
496 Jewish Est	26	NR	NR	65,900	8.1	13.8
498 Indep.Charis.	4	24,300	20,200	31,000	3.8	6.5
499 Indep.Non-Char	4	9,000	6,540	9,000	1.1	1.9
GILMER	**38**	**6,725**	**2,600**	**8,644 ***	**36.9**	**100.0**
056 Baha'i	0	4	NR	4	-	-
081 Catholic	1	NR	NR	257	1.1	3.0
089 Chr & Miss Al	1	27	NR	37	.2	.4
093 Chr Ch (Disc)	1	138	122	170 *	.7	2.0
127 Ch God (Cleve)	2	212	49	262 *	1.1	3.0
145 Ch God Prophcy	1	42	NR	52 *	.2	.6
167 Chs of Christ	3	252	302	378	1.6	4.4
207 E.L.C.A.	1	59	52	91	.4	1.1
320 "Old" MB Ascs	4	1,088	NR	1,344 *	5.7	15.5

Religious Group	Number of Churches, Synagogues, Mosques, or Temples	Number of Communicant, Confirmed, or Full Members	Number of Attendees	Total Adherents		
				Number of Adherents	% of Total Pop.	% of Total Adh.
349 Pent Holiness	1	200	60	247 *	1.1	2.9
360 Prim Bapt Chrch	2	NR	NR	NR	-	-
413 S.D.A.	1	180	NR	214	.9	2.5
419 So Bapt Conv	13	3,623	1,673	4,475 *	19.1	51.8
435 Unitarian-Univ	1	36	NR	44 *	.2	.5
449 Un Methodist	6	864	342	1,069 *	4.6	12.4
GLASCOCK	**14**	**1,258**	**508**	**1,585 ***	**62.0**	**100.0**
081 Catholic	0	NR	NR	3	.1	.2
123 Ch God (Ander)	1	NR	20	20	.8	1.3
127 Ch God (Cleve)	2	155	129	214 *	8.4	13.5
365 Prog Prim Bapt	1	33	NR	40 *	1.6	2.5
419 So Bapt Conv	6	851	202	1,040 *	40.7	65.6
449 Un Methodist	4	219	157	268 *	10.5	16.9
GLYNN	**87**	**20,204**	**10,192**	**31,294 ***	**46.3**	**100.0**
053 Assemb of God	3	90	91	123	.2	.4
056 Baha'i	1	47	NR	47	.1	.2
081 Catholic	2	NR	NR	3,772	5.6	12.1
097 Chr Chs&Chs Cr	1	100	NR	124 *	.2	.4
123 Ch God (Ander)	1	NR	10	10	-	-
127 Ch God (Cleve)	5	2,358	1,284	2,924 *	4.3	9.3
145 Ch God Prophcy	2	83	NR	104 *	.2	.3
151 L-D Saints	2	NR	NR	687	1.0	2.2
165 Ch of Nazarene	3	232	134	250	.4	.8
167 Chs of Christ	3	136	138	174	.3	.6
193 Episcopal	6	NR	931	1,684	2.5	5.4
207 E.L.C.A.	2	389	248	452	.7	1.4
223 Free Will Bapt	1	80	NR	99 *	.1	.3
246 Greek Orthodox	1	NR	NR	0	-	-
349 Pent Holiness	2	324	152	402 *	.6	1.3
355 Presb Ch (USA)	6	1,425	645	1,767 *	2.6	5.6
356 Presb Ch Amer	2	140	135	193	.3	.6
360 Prim Bapt Chrch	1	NR	NR	NR	-	-
365 Prog Prim Bapt	1	87	NR	108 *	.2	.3
403 Salvation Army	1	43	42	130	.2	.4
413 S.D.A.	3	293	NR	348	.5	1.1
418 Southw Bapt Fel	1	NR	NR	NR	-	-
419 So Bapt Conv	18	8,722	3,640	10,816 *	16.0	34.6
435 Unitarian-Univ	1	34	NR	42 *	.1	.1
449 Un Methodist	14	5,131	2,221	6,362 *	9.4	20.3
463 Vineyard	1	40	40	50 *	.1	.2
467 Wesleyan	1	50	31	76	.1	.2
496 Jewish Est	1	NR	NR	100	.1	.3
499 Indep.Non-Char	1	400	450	450	.7	1.4
GORDON	**87**	**19,225**	**7,110**	**24,928 ***	**56.5**	**100.0**
053 Assemb of God	2	101	125	134	.3	.5
056 Baha'i	0	1	NR	1	-	-
081 Catholic	1	NR	NR	570	1.3	2.3
127 Ch God (Cleve)	10	2,235	1,098	2,804 *	6.4	11.2
145 Ch God Prophcy	3	117	NR	145 *	.3	.6
151 L-D Saints	1	NR	NR	141	.3	.6
165 Ch of Nazarene	1	11	12	33	.1	.1
167 Chs of Christ	3	388	345	488	1.1	2.0
185 Cumber Presb	1	10	NR	29	.1	.1
193 Episcopal	1	NR	80	126	.3	.5
269 Jasper&PVB Asc	2	389	NR	488 *	1.1	2.0
320 "Old" MB Ascs	6	936	NR	1,174 *	2.7	4.7
355 Presb Ch (USA)	1	245	145	307 *	.7	1.2
360 Prim Bapt Chrch	1	NR	NR	NR	-	-
413 S.D.A.	2	1,114	NR	1,326	3.0	5.3
419 So Bapt Conv	38	12,199	4,683	15,306 *	34.7	61.4
449 Un Methodist	14	1,479	622	1,856 *	4.2	7.4
GRADY	**58**	**10,052**	**3,462**	**12,872 ***	**54.4**	**100.0**
053 Assemb of God	1	37	49	70	.3	.5
056 Baha'i	0	1	NR	1	-	-
081 Catholic	1	NR	NR	57	.2	.4
097 Chr Chs&Chs Cr	2	374	NR	471 *	2.0	3.7
127 Ch God (Cleve)	2	567	268	715 *	3.0	5.6
145 Ch God Prophcy	1	42	NR	53 *	.2	.4

NR–Not Reported *Total adherents estimated from known number of communicant, confirmed, full members. - Represents a percentage less than 0.1. Percentages may not total 100 due to rounding.

Table 4: Religious Congregations by County and Group: 2000

Religious Group	Number of Churches, Synagogues, Mosques, or Temples	Number of Communicant, Confirmed, or Full Members	Number of Attendees	Total Adherents: Number of Adherents	Total Adherents: % of Total Pop.	Total Adherents: % of Total Adh.
151 L-D Saints	1	NR	NR	103	.4	.8
165 Ch of Nazarene	1	72	57	118	.5	.9
167 Chs of Christ	2	57	57	69	.3	.5
223 Free Will Bapt	1	80	NR	101 *	.4	.8
304 NatPrimBapt USA	3	310	NR	390 *	1.6	3.0
349 Pent Holiness	2	189	146	238 *	1.0	1.8
355 Presb Ch (USA)	1	67	40	84 *	.4	.7
360 Prim Bapt Chrch	5	NR	NR	NR	-	-
419 So Bapt Conv	23	6,894	2,270	8,684 *	36.7	67.5
443 Un C of Christ	1	73	60	92 *	.4	.7
449 Un Methodist	11	1,289	515	1,626 *	6.9	12.6
GREENE	**33**	**4,421**	**1,778**	**6,349 ***	**44.1**	**100.0**
056 Baha'i	0	6	NR	6	-	.1
081 Catholic	1	NR	NR	683	4.7	10.8
093 Chr Ch (Disc)	1	57	0	70 *	.5	1.1
127 Ch God (Cleve)	1	105	39	130 *	.9	2.0
167 Chs of Christ	1	25	25	35	.2	.6
193 Episcopal	1	NR	49	103	.7	1.6
262 Int Cou Comm Ch	1	190	NR	235 *	1.6	3.7
355 Presb Ch (USA)	3	133	81	164 *	1.1	2.6
356 Presb Ch Amer	2	24	60	60	.4	.9
419 So Bapt Conv	14	2,694	956	3,328 *	23.1	52.4
449 Un Methodist	7	1,142	526	1,410 *	9.8	22.2
467 Wesleyan	1	45	42	125	.9	2.0
GWINNETT	**305**	**142,058**	**66,218**	**249,329 ***	**42.4**	**100.0**
017 Amer Bapt Assn	1	27	NR	35 *	-	-
050 Armen Ap Etchm	1	0	NR	300	.1	.1
053 Assemb of God	10	2,050	1,828	2,449	.4	1.0
055 As Ref Pres Ch	5	535	NR	571	.1	.2
056 Baha'i	3	378	NR	378	.1	.2
057 Bapt Gen Conf	1	18	12	23 *	-	-
075 Brethren in Cr	1	34	45	45	-	-
076 Buddhism	1	NR	NR	NR	-	-
081 Catholic	9	NR	NR	47,177	8.0	18.9
084 Calvary Chapel	3	NR	NR	NR	-	-
089 Chr & Miss Al	8	1,038	NR	1,624	.3	.7
093 Chr Ch (Disc)	5	1,367	524	1,758 *	.3	.7
097 Chr Chs&Chs Cr	10	2,853	NR	3,669 *	.6	1.5
123 Ch God (Ander)	2	NR	137	137	-	.1
127 Ch God (Cleve)	15	5,150	2,670	6,657 *	1.1	2.7
145 Ch God Prophcy	1	42	NR	54 *	-	-
151 L-D Saints	16	NR	NR	6,010	1.0	2.4
165 Ch of Nazarene	2	329	405	415	.1	.2
167 Chs of Christ	9	2,536	2,565	3,426	.6	1.4
173 Comm of Christ	2	228	NR	228	-	.1
176 Congr Ad Afl	1	113	NR	145 *	-	.1
185 Cumber Presb	4	126	NR	162	-	.1
193 Episcopal	4	NR	1,121	3,250	.6	1.3
203 Evan Free Ch	1	60	110	110	-	-
207 E.L.C.A.	9	4,315	1,995	5,932	1.0	2.4
252 Hindu	2	NR	NR	NR	-	-
267 Muslim Est	1	NR	450	700	.1	.3
283 Luth—MO Synod	2	457	300	648	.1	.3
291 Missionary Ch	2	77	302	302	.1	.1
320 "Old" MB Ascs	11	1,751	NR	2,252 *	.4	.9
331 OCA: Ter Diocs	1	34	NR	142	-	.1
349 Pent Holiness	3	196	193	252 *	-	.1
355 Presb Ch (USA)	12	5,811	3,354	7,474 *	1.3	3.0
356 Presb Ch Amer	14	4,120	4,095	5,228	.9	2.1
360 Prim Bapt Chrch	3	NR	NR	NR	-	-
370 Ref Baptist Chs	2	NR	NR	NR	-	-
397 OCA: Roman Dioc	1	NR	NR	86	-	-
401 Rus Orth Abroad	1	NR	NR	NR	-	-
403 Salvation Army	1	76	110	160	-	.1
410 Serb Orth USA	1	NR	NR	440	.1	.2
413 S.D.A.	3	397	NR	473	.1	.2
418 Southw Bapt Fel	2	NR	NR	NR	-	-
419 So Bapt Conv	68	71,411	27,200	91,854 *	15.6	36.8
431 Ukrainian Orth	1	NR	NR	60	-	-
435 Unitarian-Univ	1	100	NR	129 *	-	.1
449 Un Methodist	38	31,582	13,653	40,623 *	6.9	16.3

Religious Group	Number of Churches, Synagogues, Mosques, or Temples	Number of Communicant, Confirmed, or Full Members	Number of Attendees	Total Adherents: Number of Adherents	Total Adherents: % of Total Pop.	Total Adherents: % of Total Adh.
463 Vineyard	1	180	138	232 *	-	.1
467 Wesleyan	3	312	1,629	3,090	.5	1.2
469 WELS	1	355	257	479	.1	.2
496 Jewish Est	2	NR	NR	5,000	.8	2.0
498 Indep.Charis.	3	3,200	2,625	3,650	.6	1.5
499 Indep.Non-Char	1	800	500	1,500	.3	.6
HABERSHAM	**62**	**14,242**	**5,730**	**18,863 ***	**52.5**	**100.0**
053 Assemb of God	1	50	41	47	.1	.2
056 Baha'i	0	7	NR	7	-	-
081 Catholic	1	NR	NR	656	1.8	3.5
089 Chr & Miss Al	2	0	NR	42	.1	.2
097 Chr Chs&Chs Cr	2	374	NR	456 *	1.3	2.4
127 Ch God (Cleve)	5	583	348	723 *	2.0	3.8
151 L-D Saints	1	NR	NR	397	1.1	2.1
167 Chs of Christ	1	42	62	60	.2	.3
175 Congr Chr Chs	1	30	35	37 *	.1	.2
193 Episcopal	1	NR	169	371	1.0	2.0
263 Int Foursq Gos	2	57	107	107 *	.3	.6
349 Pent Holiness	1	65	70	79 *	.2	.4
355 Presb Ch (USA)	2	497	277	605 *	1.7	3.2
418 Southw Bapt Fel	1	NR	NR	NR	-	-
419 So Bapt Conv	31	10,829	3,872	13,195 *	36.8	70.0
443 Un C of Christ	1	23	35	28 *	.1	.1
449 Un Methodist	9	1,685	714	2,053 *	5.7	10.9
HALL	**122**	**45,353**	**19,692**	**65,295 ***	**46.9**	**100.0**
053 Assemb of God	5	730	726	962	.7	1.5
056 Baha'i	1	49	NR	49	-	.1
081 Catholic	1	NR	NR	5,843	4.2	8.9
084 Calvary Chapel	1	NR	NR	NR	-	-
097 Chr Chs&Chs Cr	1	155	NR	197 *	.1	.3
127 Ch God (Cleve)	4	346	217	441 *	.3	.7
145 Ch God Prophcy	2	83	NR	106 *	.1	.2
151 L-D Saints	1	NR	NR	583	.4	.9
165 Ch of Nazarene	2	319	236	323	.2	.5
167 Chs of Christ	3	147	171	200	.1	.3
193 Episcopal	1	NR	341	1,003	.7	1.5
207 E.L.C.A.	1	308	175	445	.3	.7
221 Free Methodist	1	43	38	45	-	.1
223 Free Will Bapt	1	80	NR	102 *	.1	.2
267 Muslim Est	1	NR	55	163	.1	.2
283 Luth—MO Synod	1	161	106	264	.2	.4
320 "Old" MB Ascs	4	1,108	NR	1,408 *	1.0	2.2
355 Presb Ch (USA)	2	1,219	584	1,550 *	1.1	2.4
356 Presb Ch Amer	3	872	759	1,085	.8	1.7
403 Salvation Army	2	199	177	299	.2	.5
413 S.D.A.	2	315	NR	375	.3	.6
418 Southw Bapt Fel	3	NR	NR	NR	-	-
419 So Bapt Conv	54	32,372	13,050	41,149 *	29.5	63.0
449 Un Methodist	24	6,747	2,957	8,576 *	6.2	13.1
463 Vineyard	1	100	100	127 *	.1	.2
HANCOCK	**24**	**1,427**	**491**	**1,760 ***	**17.5**	**100.0**
056 Baha'i	0	7	NR	7	.1	.4
127 Ch God (Cleve)	1	45	16	55 *	.5	3.1
167 Chs of Christ	2	71	36	89	.9	5.1
356 Presb Ch Amer	1	10	25	25	.2	1.4
419 So Bapt Conv	12	950	241	1,163 *	11.5	66.1
449 Un Methodist	8	344	173	421 *	4.2	23.9
HARALSON	**55**	**10,343**	**4,177**	**13,225 ***	**51.5**	**100.0**
053 Assemb of God	1	112	101	220	.9	1.7
097 Chr Chs&Chs Cr	3	197	NR	248 *	1.0	1.9
127 Ch God (Cleve)	3	437	208	548 *	2.1	4.1
151 L-D Saints	1	NR	NR	230	.9	1.7
167 Chs of Christ	3	440	370	491	1.9	3.7
289 New Hope B Asc	5	489	NR	613 *	2.4	4.6
349 Pent Holiness	1	38	25	48 *	.2	.4
355 Presb Ch (USA)	2	61	53	76 *	.3	.6
360 Prim Bapt Chrch	2	NR	NR	NR	-	-
419 So Bapt Conv	26	7,343	2,847	9,212 *	35.9	69.7

NR–Not Reported *Total adherents estimated from known number of communicant, confirmed, full members. - Represents a percentage less than 0.1. Percentages may not total 100 due to rounding.

Table 4: Religious Congregations by County and Group: 2000

Religious Group	Number of Churches, Synagogues, Mosques, or Temples	Number of Communicant, Confirmed, or Full Members	Number of Attendees	Total Adherents		
				Number of Adherents	% of Total Pop.	% of Total Adh.
449 Un Methodist	8	1,226	573	1,539 *	6.0	11.6
HARRIS	**37**	**5,816**	**2,688**	**7,582 ***	**32.0**	**100.0**
017 Amer Bapt Assn	1	66	NR	82 *	.3	1.1
053 Assemb of God	1	40	25	36	.2	.5
056 Baha'i	0	2	NR	2	-	-
081 Catholic	1	NR	NR	143	.6	1.9
127 Ch God (Cleve)	1	162	69	201 *	.8	2.7
151 L-D Saints	1	NR	NR	228	1.0	3.0
167 Chs of Christ	2	57	60	74	.3	1.0
339 Pent Ch of God	1	15	NR	27	.1	.4
413 S.D.A.	1	96	NR	114	.5	1.5
419 So Bapt Conv	19	4,289	1,930	5,324 *	22.5	70.2
449 Un Methodist	9	1,089	604	1,351 *	5.7	17.8
HART	**47**	**9,507**	**3,692**	**12,512 ***	**54.4**	**100.0**
056 Baha'i	0	2	NR	2	-	-
081 Catholic	1	NR	NR	549	2.4	4.4
089 Chr & Miss Al	1	35	NR	80	.3	.6
097 Chr Chs&Chs Cr	1	30	NR	37 *	.2	.3
127 Ch God (Cleve)	3	310	215	380 *	1.7	3.0
143 CG in Cr(Menn)	1	35	NR	43 *	.2	.3
145 Ch God Prophcy	1	42	NR	51 *	.2	.4
151 L-D Saints	1	NR	NR	171	.7	1.4
167 Chs of Christ	1	35	45	43	.2	.3
193 Episcopal	1	NR	57	120	.5	1.0
207 E.L.C.A.	1	94	42	100	.4	.8
297 Mennonite;Other	1	44	NR	54 *	.2	.4
349 Pent Holiness	1	21	12	26 *	.1	.2
355 Presb Ch (USA)	2	120	98	147 *	.6	1.2
419 So Bapt Conv	21	7,217	2,562	8,845 *	38.5	70.7
449 Un Methodist	10	1,522	661	1,864 *	8.1	14.9
HEARD	**34**	**4,036**	**2,050**	**5,235 ***	**47.5**	**100.0**
056 Baha'i	0	4	NR	4	-	.1
093 Chr Ch (Disc)	2	26	0	34 *	.3	.6
127 Ch God (Cleve)	3	323	195	419 *	3.8	8.0
167 Chs of Christ	2	30	27	36	.3	.7
360 Prim Bapt Chrch	1	NR	NR	NR	-	-
419 So Bapt Conv	12	2,166	896	2,812 *	25.5	53.7
449 Un Methodist	14	1,487	932	1,930 *	17.5	36.9
HENRY	**96**	**32,436**	**16,920**	**48,019 ***	**40.2**	**100.0**
017 Amer Bapt Assn	1	20	NR	26 *	-	.1
053 Assemb of God	5	572	618	831	.7	1.7
056 Baha'i	0	50	NR	50	-	.1
081 Catholic	1	NR	NR	3,206	2.7	6.7
097 Chr Chs&Chs Cr	4	2,045	NR	2,665 *	2.2	5.5
121 Ch God (Abr)	1	62	113	113 *	.1	.2
127 Ch God (Cleve)	6	1,719	631	2,240 *	1.9	4.7
145 Ch God Prophcy	2	83	NR	108 *	.1	.2
151 L-D Saints	3	NR	NR	1,443	1.2	3.0
167 Chs of Christ	2	315	300	433	.4	.9
175 Congr Chr Chs	1	70	90	91 *	.1	.2
193 Episcopal	1	NR	165	597	.5	1.2
207 E.L.C.A.	1	49	37	60	.1	.1
223 Free Will Bapt	1	80	NR	105 *	.1	.2
263 Int Foursq Gos	1	122	370	370 *	.3	.8
355 Presb Ch (USA)	5	1,245	807	1,623 *	1.4	3.4
356 Presb Ch Amer	3	82	63	112	.1	.2
360 Prim Bapt Chrch	5	NR	NR	NR	-	-
413 S.D.A.	1	139	NR	165	.1	.3
418 Southw Bapt Fel	2	NR	NR	NR	-	-
419 So Bapt Conv	30	16,295	8,346	21,238 *	17.8	44.2
449 Un Methodist	19	5,788	2,480	7,543 *	6.3	15.7
499 Indep.Non-Char	1	3,700	2,900	5,000	4.2	10.4
HOUSTON	**103**	**40,373**	**17,854**	**58,407 ***	**52.7**	**100.0**
053 Assemb of God	6	796	1,194	1,209	1.1	2.1
056 Baha'i	0	141	NR	141	.1	.2
081 Catholic	2	NR	NR	3,229	2.9	5.5
084 Calvary Chapel	1	NR	NR	NR	-	-
089 Chr & Miss Al	1	46	NR	87	.1	.1
093 Chr Ch (Disc)	1	186	57	238 *	.2	.4
097 Chr Chs&Chs Cr	2	335	NR	429 *	.4	.7
127 Ch God (Cleve)	9	2,524	1,153	3,227 *	2.9	5.5
145 Ch God Prophcy	1	42	NR	53 *	-	.1
151 L-D Saints	3	NR	NR	1,053	1.0	1.8
165 Ch of Nazarene	1	193	149	277	.3	.5
167 Chs of Christ	5	453	504	596	.5	1.0
173 Comm of Christ	1	58	NR	58	.1	.1
193 Episcopal	2	NR	291	603	.5	1.0
207 E.L.C.A.	1	205	90	279	.3	.5
223 Free Will Bapt	2	160	NR	205 *	.2	.4
263 Int Foursq Gos	1	71	92	92 *	.1	.2
267 Muslim Est	1	NR	156	609	.5	1.0
283 Luth—MO Synod	1	498	325	686	.6	1.2
349 Pent Holiness	1	63	42	81 *	.1	.1
355 Presb Ch (USA)	3	325	194	416 *	.4	.7
356 Presb Ch Amer	2	373	275	465	.4	.8
360 Prim Bapt Chrch	5	NR	NR	NR	-	-
403 Salvation Army	1	87	68	174	.2	.3
413 S.D.A.	2	227	NR	270	.2	.5
418 Southw Bapt Fel	2	NR	NR	NR	-	-
419 So Bapt Conv	33	27,103	9,591	34,639 *	31.3	59.3
449 Un Methodist	12	6,487	2,673	8,291 *	7.5	14.2
499 Indep.Non-Char	1	0	1,000	1,000	.9	1.7
IRWIN	**23**	**3,433**	**1,050**	**4,300 ***	**43.3**	**100.0**
017 Amer Bapt Assn	2	76	NR	96 *	1.0	2.2
056 Baha'i	0	1	NR	1	-	-
127 Ch God (Cleve)	1	360	155	451 *	4.5	10.5
167 Chs of Christ	1	8	10	10	.1	.2
360 Prim Bapt Chrch	1	NR	NR	NR	-	-
365 Prog Prim Bapt	5	373	NR	467 *	4.7	10.9
419 So Bapt Conv	11	2,303	776	2,884 *	29.0	67.1
449 Un Methodist	2	312	109	391 *	3.9	9.1
JACKSON	**63**	**11,450**	**3,960**	**15,069 ***	**36.2**	**100.0**
053 Assemb of God	1	39	45	49	.1	.3
056 Baha'i	0	8	NR	8	-	.1
081 Catholic	1	NR	NR	275	.7	1.8
089 Chr & Miss Al	1	274	NR	284	.7	1.9
097 Chr Chs&Chs Cr	4	984	NR	1,246 *	3.0	8.3
127 Ch God (Cleve)	2	235	85	298 *	.7	2.0
145 Ch God Prophcy	2	83	NR	106 *	.3	.7
151 L-D Saints	1	NR	NR	356	.9	2.4
167 Chs of Christ	1	55	56	75	.2	.5
349 Pent Holiness	1	5	6	6 *	-	-
355 Presb Ch (USA)	4	353	222	447 *	1.1	3.0
370 Ref Baptist Chs	1	NR	NR	NR	-	-
418 Southw Bapt Fel	2	NR	NR	NR	-	-
419 So Bapt Conv	28	7,182	2,453	9,093 *	21.9	60.3
449 Un Methodist	14	2,232	1,093	2,826 *	6.8	18.8
JASPER	**20**	**2,845**	**1,369**	**3,606 ***	**31.6**	**100.0**
056 Baha'i	0	8	NR	8	.1	.2
167 Chs of Christ	1	16	13	19	.2	.5
297 Mennonite;Other	1	8	NR	10 *	.1	.3
355 Presb Ch (USA)	1	207	127	263 *	2.3	7.3
360 Prim Bapt Chrch	3	NR	NR	NR	-	-
419 So Bapt Conv	9	2,123	1,029	2,693 *	23.6	74.7
449 Un Methodist	5	483	200	613 *	5.4	17.0
JEFF DAVIS	**35**	**7,085**	**2,431**	**9,079 ***	**71.6**	**100.0**
081 Catholic	1	NR	NR	103	.8	1.1
089 Chr & Miss Al	1	0	NR	0	-	-
127 Ch God (Cleve)	6	1,074	599	1,360 *	10.7	15.0
145 Ch God Prophcy	1	42	NR	53 *	.4	.6
167 Chs of Christ	2	53	52	72	.6	.8
223 Free Will Bapt	1	80	NR	102 *	.8	1.1
360 Prim Bapt Chrch	1	NR	NR	NR	-	-
365 Prog Prim Bapt	1	9	NR	11 *	.1	.1
413 S.D.A.	1	12	NR	14	.1	.2

NR–Not Reported *Total adherents estimated from known number of communicant, confirmed, full members. - Represents a percentage less than 0.1. Percentages may not total 100 due to rounding.

Table 4: Religious Congregations by County and Group: 2000

Religious Group	Number of Churches, Synagogues, Mosques, or Temples	Number of Communicant, Confirmed, or Full Members	Number of Attendees	Total Adherents: Number of Adherents	% of Total Pop.	% of Total Adh.
418 Southw Bapt Fel	1	NR	NR	NR	-	-
419 So Bapt Conv	16	5,236	1,571	6,631 *	52.3	73.0
449 Un Methodist	3	579	209	733 *	5.8	8.1
JEFFERSON	**51**	**5,763**	**2,359**	**7,552 ***	**43.7**	**100.0**
053 Assemb of God	1	4	5	12	.1	.2
055 As Ref Pres Ch	4	163	NR	177	1.0	2.3
056 Baha'i	0	4	NR	4	-	.1
081 Catholic	1	NR	NR	63	.4	.8
123 Ch God (Ander)	1	NR	55	55	.3	.7
127 Ch God (Cleve)	3	296	211	378 *	2.2	5.0
143 CG in Cr(Menn)	2	300	NR	384 *	2.2	5.1
165 Ch of Nazarene	2	86	50	95	.6	1.3
167 Chs of Christ	1	15	18	18	.1	.2
193 Episcopal	2	NR	69	126	.7	1.7
297 Mennonite;Other	1	24	NR	31 *	.2	.4
304 NatPrimBapt USA	1	30	NR	38 *	.2	.5
365 Prog Prim Bapt	1	22	NR	28 *	.2	.4
413 S.D.A.	1	227	NR	270	1.6	3.6
419 So Bapt Conv	18	3,163	1,311	4,045 *	23.4	53.6
449 Un Methodist	12	1,429	640	1,828 *	10.6	24.2
JENKINS	**19**	**3,455**	**1,067**	**4,505 ***	**52.5**	**100.0**
056 Baha'i	0	3	NR	3	-	.1
081 Catholic	1	NR	NR	51	.6	1.1
123 Ch God (Ander)	1	NR	34	34	.4	.8
127 Ch God (Cleve)	1	95	35	122 *	1.4	2.7
360 Prim Bapt Chrch	1	NR	NR	NR	-	-
419 So Bapt Conv	10	2,845	774	3,640 *	42.4	80.8
449 Un Methodist	5	512	224	655 *	7.6	14.5
JOHNSON	**40**	**3,557**	**1,731**	**4,668 ***	**54.5**	**100.0**
053 Assemb of God	3	155	154	198	2.3	4.2
081 Catholic	0	NR	NR	24	.3	.5
097 Chr Chs&Chs Cr	2	319	NR	398 *	4.6	8.5
127 Ch God (Cleve)	2	252	115	313 *	3.7	6.7
165 Ch of Nazarene	2	392	309	701	8.2	15.0
304 NatPrimBapt USA	1	5	NR	6 *	.1	.1
349 Pent Holiness	1	5	7	6 *	.1	.1
360 Prim Bapt Chrch	1	NR	NR	NR	-	-
365 Prog Prim Bapt	3	147	NR	183 *	2.1	3.9
419 So Bapt Conv	14	1,707	795	2,125 *	24.8	45.5
449 Un Methodist	11	575	351	714 *	8.3	15.3
JONES	**19**	**4,851**	**2,058**	**6,114 ***	**25.9**	**100.0**
056 Baha'i	0	13	NR	13	.1	.2
127 Ch God (Cleve)	1	172	59	217 *	.9	3.5
167 Chs of Christ	1	25	25	32	.1	.5
355 Presb Ch (USA)	1	54	26	68 *	.3	1.1
419 So Bapt Conv	10	3,577	1,462	4,511 *	19.1	73.8
449 Un Methodist	5	1,001	475	1,262 *	5.3	20.6
467 Wesleyan	1	9	11	11	-	.2
LAMAR	**33**	**4,949**	**1,991**	**6,332 ***	**39.8**	**100.0**
053 Assemb of God	1	38	50	50	.3	.8
056 Baha'i	0	17	NR	17	.1	.3
081 Catholic	1	NR	NR	209	1.3	3.3
127 Ch God (Cleve)	1	32	24	40 *	.3	.6
165 Ch of Nazarene	1	150	121	174	1.1	2.7
167 Chs of Christ	1	65	32	72	.5	1.1
349 Pent Holiness	2	49	39	61 *	.4	1.0
355 Presb Ch (USA)	1	48	23	60 *	.4	.9
360 Prim Bapt Chrch	3	NR	NR	NR	-	-
365 Prog Prim Bapt	1	108	NR	134 *	.8	2.1
419 So Bapt Conv	10	3,514	1,280	4,361 *	27.4	68.9
449 Un Methodist	11	928	422	1,154 *	7.3	18.2
LANIER	**17**	**2,267**	**517**	**3,278 ***	**45.3**	**100.0**
081 Catholic	1	NR	NR	57	.8	1.7
127 Ch God (Cleve)	2	191	6	241 *	3.3	7.4
145 Ch God Prophcy	1	42	NR	53 *	.7	1.6

Religious Group	Number of Churches, Synagogues, Mosques, or Temples	Number of Communicant, Confirmed, or Full Members	Number of Attendees	Total Adherents: Number of Adherents	% of Total Pop.	% of Total Adh.
151 L-D Saints	1	NR	NR	342	4.7	10.4
167 Chs of Christ	2	100	90	150	2.1	4.6
320 "Old" MB Ascs	1	99	NR	125 *	1.7	3.8
360 Prim Bapt Chrch	1	NR	NR	NR	-	-
413 S.D.A.	2	166	NR	198	2.7	6.0
419 So Bapt Conv	3	1,113	249	1,408 *	19.4	43.0
449 Un Methodist	3	556	172	704 *	9.7	21.5
LAURENS	**96**	**17,981**	**7,266**	**24,093 ***	**53.7**	**100.0**
053 Assemb of God	5	252	267	479	1.1	2.0
056 Baha'i	0	7	NR	7	-	-
081 Catholic	1	NR	NR	629	1.4	2.6
093 Chr Ch (Disc)	2	121	48	153 *	.3	.6
123 Ch God (Ander)	2	NR	113	113	.3	.5
127 Ch God (Cleve)	3	293	177	369 *	.8	1.5
145 Ch God Prophcy	2	83	NR	106 *	.2	.4
151 L-D Saints	1	NR	NR	323	.7	1.3
165 Ch of Nazarene	3	535	403	715	1.6	3.0
167 Chs of Christ	4	145	160	182	.4	.8
193 Episcopal	1	NR	61	174	.4	.7
223 Free Will Bapt	1	80	NR	101 *	.2	.4
297 Mennonite;Other	1	48	NR	61 *	.1	.3
349 Pent Holiness	1	37	33	47 *	.1	.2
355 Presb Ch (USA)	2	178	85	225 *	.5	.9
360 Prim Bapt Chrch	4	NR	NR	NR	-	-
365 Prog Prim Bapt	1	7	NR	9 *	-	-
413 S.D.A.	2	224	NR	266	.6	1.1
419 So Bapt Conv	42	12,897	4,539	16,258 *	36.2	67.5
449 Un Methodist	18	3,074	1,380	3,876 *	8.6	16.1
LEE	**17**	**3,939**	**2,015**	**6,132 ***	**24.8**	**100.0**
056 Baha'i	0	23	NR	23	.1	.4
081 Catholic	0	NR	NR	557	2.2	9.1
127 Ch God (Cleve)	1	210	160	273 *	1.1	4.5
151 L-D Saints	1	NR	NR	336	1.4	5.5
167 Chs of Christ	2	67	85	114	.5	1.9
193 Episcopal	1	NR	36	67	.3	1.1
263 Int Foursq Gos	1	80	136	136 *	.5	2.2
355 Presb Ch (USA)	1	12	6	16 *	.1	.3
360 Prim Bapt Chrch	1	NR	NR	NR	-	-
370 Ref Baptist Chs	1	NR	NR	NR	-	-
419 So Bapt Conv	6	2,771	1,340	3,602 *	14.5	58.7
449 Un Methodist	2	776	252	1,008 *	4.1	16.4
LIBERTY	**39**	**8,738**	**4,144**	**13,277 ***	**21.6**	**100.0**
017 Amer Bapt Assn	1	50	NR	68 *	.1	.5
053 Assemb of God	2	93	118	205	.3	1.5
056 Baha'i	0	13	NR	13	-	.1
081 Catholic	1	NR	NR	862	1.4	6.5
123 Ch God (Ander)	1	NR	45	45	.1	.3
127 Ch God (Cleve)	4	1,700	1,095	2,318 *	3.8	17.5
151 L-D Saints	1	NR	NR	491	.8	3.7
165 Ch of Nazarene	1	66	41	66	.1	.5
167 Chs of Christ	2	198	229	247	.4	1.9
193 Episcopal	2	NR	85	120	.2	.9
355 Presb Ch (USA)	7	492	348	667 *	1.1	5.0
419 So Bapt Conv	10	4,356	1,306	5,902 *	9.6	44.5
443 Un C of Christ	1	116	51	157 *	.3	1.2
449 Un Methodist	5	1,304	626	1,766 *	2.9	13.3
498 Indep.Charis.	1	350	200	350	.6	2.6
LINCOLN	**21**	**2,975**	**1,398**	**3,699 ***	**44.3**	**100.0**
053 Assemb of God	1	192	225	300	3.6	8.1
056 Baha'i	0	3	NR	3	-	.1
127 Ch God (Cleve)	1	43	10	53 *	.6	1.4
355 Presb Ch (USA)	1	16	18	20 *	.2	.5
419 So Bapt Conv	11	1,987	788	2,426 *	29.1	65.6
449 Un Methodist	7	734	357	897 *	10.7	24.2
LONG	**9**	**2,367**	**880**	**3,219 ***	**31.2**	**100.0**
017 Amer Bapt Assn	1	194	NR	264 *	2.6	8.2
056 Baha'i	0	1	NR	1	-	-

NR–Not Reported *Total adherents estimated from known number of communicant, confirmed, full members. - Represents a percentage less than 0.1. Percentages may not total 100 due to rounding.

Table 4: Religious Congregations by County and Group: 2000

Religious Group	Number of Churches, Synagogues, Mosques, or Temples	Number of Communicant, Confirmed, or Full Members	Number of Attendees	Total Adherents: Number of Adherents	Total Adherents: % of Total Pop.	Total Adherents: % of Total Adh.
127 Ch God (Cleve)	1	237	150	322 *	3.1	10.0
419 So Bapt Conv	5	1,776	652	2,416 *	23.4	75.1
449 Un Methodist	2	159	78	216 *	2.1	6.7
LOWNDES	**114**	**28,018**	**14,172**	**40,703 ***	**44.2**	**100.0**
017 Amer Bapt Assn	1	90	NR	113 *	.1	.3
053 Assemb of God	3	399	390	536	.6	1.3
056 Baha'i	1	35	NR	35	-	.1
081 Catholic	1	NR	NR	4,115	4.5	10.1
093 Chr Ch (Disc)	3	480	190	604 *	.7	1.5
123 Ch God (Ander)	1	NR	22	22	-	.1
127 Ch God (Cleve)	10	1,448	1,068	1,833 *	2.0	4.5
145 Ch God Prophcy	2	83	NR	106 *	.1	.3
151 L-D Saints	1	NR	NR	287	.3	.7
165 Ch of Nazarene	2	230	153	278	.3	.7
167 Chs of Christ	19	2,521	2,524	3,307	3.6	8.1
193 Episcopal	3	NR	487	905	1.0	2.2
207 E.L.C.A.	1	91	50	139	.2	.3
223 Free Will Bapt	2	160	NR	202 *	.2	.5
283 Luth—MO Synod	1	179	95	194	.2	.5
290 Metro Comm Ch	1	16	14	20 *	-	-
349 Pent Holiness	1	29	22	37 *	-	.1
355 Presb Ch (USA)	4	721	356	907 *	1.0	2.2
356 Presb Ch Amer	1	211	133	247	.3	.6
360 Prim Bapt Chrch	4	NR	NR	NR	-	-
365 Prog Prim Bapt	1	50	NR	63 *	.1	.2
403 Salvation Army	1	108	57	192	.2	.5
413 S.D.A.	2	193	NR	229	.2	.6
418 Southw Bapt Fel	1	NR	NR	NR	-	-
419 So Bapt Conv	30	13,800	5,571	17,371 *	18.9	42.7
435 Unitarian-Univ	1	34	NR	43 *	-	.1
449 Un Methodist	13	6,090	2,130	7,668 *	8.3	18.8
496 Jewish Est	1	NR	NR	100	.1	.2
498 Indep.Charis.	1	550	550	650	.7	1.6
499 Indep.Non-Char	1	500	360	500	.5	1.2
LUMPKIN	**26**	**4,448**	**1,033**	**5,970 ***	**28.4**	**100.0**
053 Assemb of God	1	34	40	57	.3	1.0
056 Baha'i	0	1	NR	1	-	-
081 Catholic	1	NR	NR	360	1.7	6.0
127 Ch God (Cleve)	1	155	45	191 *	.9	3.2
145 Ch God Prophcy	1	42	NR	51 *	.2	.9
167 Chs of Christ	2	31	43	45	.2	.8
193 Episcopal	1	NR	63	120	.6	2.0
320 "Old" MB Ascs	9	1,923	NR	2,364 *	11.2	39.6
355 Presb Ch (USA)	1	90	36	111 *	.5	1.9
419 So Bapt Conv	4	1,275	347	1,567 *	7.5	26.2
435 Unitarian-Univ	1	60	NR	74 *	.4	1.2
449 Un Methodist	4	837	459	1,029 *	4.9	17.2
MCDUFFIE	**28**	**7,283**	**2,815**	**9,889 ***	**46.6**	**100.0**
053 Assemb of God	1	68	80	115	.5	1.2
055 As Ref Pres Ch	1	276	NR	326	1.5	3.3
056 Baha'i	0	30	NR	30	.1	.3
081 Catholic	1	NR	NR	595	2.8	6.0
127 Ch God (Cleve)	2	121	74	154 *	.7	1.6
167 Chs of Christ	2	113	80	135	.6	1.4
193 Episcopal	1	NR	23	66	.3	.7
419 So Bapt Conv	14	5,304	1,972	6,728 *	31.7	68.0
449 Un Methodist	6	1,371	586	1,740 *	8.2	17.6
MCINTOSH	**21**	**2,525**	**1,245**	**3,678 ***	**33.9**	**100.0**
053 Assemb of God	1	30	42	54	.5	1.5
056 Baha'i	0	3	NR	3	-	.1
081 Catholic	1	NR	NR	63	.6	1.7
127 Ch God (Cleve)	2	404	373	512 *	4.7	13.9
145 Ch God Prophcy	2	83	NR	106 *	1.0	2.9
151 L-D Saints	1	NR	NR	177	1.6	4.8
167 Chs of Christ	1	25	25	33	.3	.9
193 Episcopal	2	NR	103	220	2.0	6.0
226 Friends-USA	1	24	NR	30 *	.3	.8
355 Presb Ch (USA)	2	135	60	171 *	1.6	4.6
419 So Bapt Conv	6	1,528	517	1,937 *	17.9	52.7
449 Un Methodist	2	293	125	372 *	3.4	10.1
MACON	**31**	**4,029**	**1,106**	**5,113 ***	**36.3**	**100.0**
017 Amer Bapt Assn	1	50	NR	63 *	.4	1.2
056 Baha'i	0	228	NR	228	1.6	4.5
061 Beachy Amish	2	268	NR	340 *	2.4	6.6
081 Catholic	1	NR	NR	38	.3	.7
145 Ch God Prophcy	1	42	NR	53 *	.4	1.0
167 Chs of Christ	2	53	58	58	.4	1.1
193 Episcopal	1	NR	15	46	.3	.9
207 E.L.C.A.	1	134	56	163	1.2	3.2
223 Free Will Bapt	1	80	NR	102 *	.7	2.0
297 Mennonite;Other	1	80	NR	101 *	.7	2.0
360 Prim Bapt Chrch	1	NR	NR	NR	-	-
413 S.D.A.	1	52	NR	62	.4	1.2
419 So Bapt Conv	12	2,409	702	3,056 *	21.7	59.8
449 Un Methodist	6	633	275	803 *	5.7	15.7
MADISON	**35**	**7,827**	**2,666**	**9,866 ***	**38.3**	**100.0**
056 Baha'i	0	2	NR	2	-	-
167 Chs of Christ	1	15	22	24	.1	.2
349 Pent Holiness	2	183	155	231 *	.9	2.3
355 Presb Ch (USA)	2	114	43	144 *	.6	1.5
419 So Bapt Conv	24	6,413	2,027	8,079 *	31.4	81.9
449 Un Methodist	6	1,100	419	1,386 *	5.4	14.0
MARION	**22**	**1,660**	**596**	**2,151 ***	**30.1**	**100.0**
053 Assemb of God	1	11	0	14	.2	.7
056 Baha'i	0	17	NR	17	.2	.8
081 Catholic	1	NR	NR	23	.3	1.1
167 Chs of Christ	1	24	22	35	.5	1.6
223 Free Will Bapt	1	80	NR	103 *	1.4	4.8
360 Prim Bapt Chrch	2	NR	NR	NR	-	-
365 Prog Prim Bapt	1	1	NR	1 *	-	-
413 S.D.A.	1	18	NR	21	.3	1.0
419 So Bapt Conv	9	1,065	384	1,367 *	19.1	63.6
449 Un Methodist	5	444	190	570 *	8.0	26.5
MERIWETHER	**53**	**8,039**	**3,002**	**10,200 ***	**45.3**	**100.0**
053 Assemb of God	1	124	140	140	.6	1.4
056 Baha'i	0	45	NR	45	.2	.4
081 Catholic	1	NR	NR	154	.7	1.5
127 Ch God (Cleve)	1	45	50	57 *	.3	.6
145 Ch God Prophcy	1	42	NR	52 *	.2	.5
165 Ch of Nazarene	2	168	114	168	.7	1.6
167 Chs of Christ	2	135	125	180	.8	1.8
355 Presb Ch (USA)	2	89	42	112 *	.5	1.1
365 Prog Prim Bapt	2	34	NR	43 *	.2	.4
413 S.D.A.	1	41	NR	49	.2	.5
418 Southw Bapt Fel	1	NR	NR	NR	-	-
419 So Bapt Conv	20	5,281	1,591	6,641 *	29.5	65.1
443 Un C of Christ	1	125	37	157 *	.7	1.5
449 Un Methodist	18	1,910	903	2,402 *	10.7	23.5
MILLER	**22**	**2,648**	**589**	**3,303 ***	**51.7**	**100.0**
053 Assemb of God	1	23	14	20	.3	.6
056 Baha'i	0	3	NR	3	-	.1
127 Ch God (Cleve)	4	87	71	117 *	1.8	3.5
167 Chs of Christ	2	66	66	84	1.3	2.5
223 Free Will Bapt	7	562	NR	700 *	11.0	21.2
297 Mennonite;Other	1	8	NR	10 *	.2	.3
360 Prim Bapt Chrch	1	NR	NR	NR	-	-
419 So Bapt Conv	4	1,376	185	1,716 *	26.9	52.0
449 Un Methodist	2	523	253	653 *	10.2	19.8
MITCHELL	**43**	**7,962**	**2,577**	**10,374 ***	**43.3**	**100.0**
053 Assemb of God	2	193	185	442	1.8	4.3
056 Baha'i	0	4	NR	4	-	-
081 Catholic	1	NR	NR	67	.3	.6
097 Chr Chs&Chs Cr	1	38	NR	48 *	.2	.5

NR–Not Reported *Total adherents estimated from known number of communicant, confirmed, full members. - Represents a percentage less than 0.1. Percentages may not total 100 due to rounding.

Table 4: Religious Congregations by County and Group: 2000

Religious Group	Number of Churches, Synagogues, Mosques, or Temples	Number of Communicant, Confirmed, or Full Members	Number of Attendees	Total Adherents		
				Number of Adherents	% of Total Pop.	% of Total Adh.
127 Ch God (Cleve)	2	81	69	103 *	.4	1.0
167 Chs of Christ	2	45	43	60	.3	.6
193 Episcopal	1	NR	23	50	.2	.5
223 Free Will Bapt	4	321	NR	405 *	1.7	3.9
304 NatPrimBapt USA	1	50	NR	63 *	.3	.6
349 Pent Holiness	1	15	25	19 *	.1	.2
355 Presb Ch (USA)	2	59	19	75 *	.3	.7
360 Prim Bapt Chrch	1	NR	NR	NR	-	-
419 So Bapt Conv	19	6,081	1,831	7,681 *	32.1	74.0
449 Un Methodist	6	1,075	382	1,357 *	5.7	13.1
MONROE	**38**	**5,917**	**2,340**	**7,456 ***	**34.3**	**100.0**
053 Assemb of God	1	26	27	29	.1	.4
056 Baha'i	0	16	NR	16	.1	.2
081 Catholic	1	NR	NR	54	.2	.7
127 Ch God (Cleve)	1	195	55	244 *	1.1	3.3
145 Ch God Prophcy	1	42	NR	52 *	.2	.7
167 Chs of Christ	1	75	45	90	.4	1.2
355 Presb Ch (USA)	1	84	45	105 *	.5	1.4
356 Presb Ch Amer	1	67	80	99	.5	1.3
360 Prim Bapt Chrch	2	NR	NR	NR	-	-
365 Prog Prim Bapt	2	104	NR	130 *	.6	1.7
419 So Bapt Conv	17	4,194	1,560	5,245 *	24.1	70.3
449 Un Methodist	10	1,114	528	1,392 *	6.4	18.7
MONTGOMERY	**27**	**2,789**	**1,066**	**3,451 ***	**41.7**	**100.0**
127 Ch God (Cleve)	3	362	189	447 *	5.4	13.0
145 Ch God Prophcy	1	42	NR	52 *	.6	1.5
355 Presb Ch (USA)	2	56	35	69 *	.8	2.0
360 Prim Bapt Chrch	1	NR	NR	NR	-	-
419 So Bapt Conv	12	1,831	603	2,266 *	27.4	65.7
449 Un Methodist	8	498	239	617 *	7.5	17.9
MORGAN	**28**	**4,394**	**2,064**	**6,176 ***	**40.0**	**100.0**
056 Baha'i	0	6	NR	6	-	.1
081 Catholic	1	NR	NR	225	1.5	3.6
093 Chr Ch (Disc)	1	71	0	90 *	.6	1.5
127 Ch God (Cleve)	1	180	150	227 *	1.5	3.7
167 Chs of Christ	1	100	90	168	1.1	2.7
193 Episcopal	1	NR	82	359	2.3	5.8
355 Presb Ch (USA)	1	330	195	417 *	2.7	6.8
360 Prim Bapt Chrch	1	NR	NR	NR	-	-
413 S.D.A.	1	23	NR	27	.2	.4
419 So Bapt Conv	10	2,639	1,070	3,335 *	21.6	54.0
449 Un Methodist	10	1,045	477	1,322 *	8.6	21.4
MURRAY	**37**	**8,715**	**2,960**	**11,273 ***	**30.9**	**100.0**
127 Ch God (Cleve)	5	517	172	665 *	1.8	5.9
145 Ch God Prophcy	1	42	NR	54 *	.1	.5
167 Chs of Christ	1	55	70	80	.2	.7
185 Cumber Presb	1	106	NR	197	.5	1.7
320 "Old" MB Ascs	3	858	NR	1,103 *	3.0	9.8
360 Prim Bapt Chrch	1	NR	NR	NR	-	-
413 S.D.A.	1	10	NR	12	-	.1
418 Southw Bapt Fel	1	NR	NR	NR	-	-
419 So Bapt Conv	16	6,377	2,346	8,197 *	22.5	72.7
449 Un Methodist	7	750	372	965 *	2.6	8.6
MUSCOGEE	**163**	**62,573**	**26,144**	**92,915 ***	**49.9**	**100.0**
053 Assemb of God	15	3,201	3,186	4,830	2.6	5.2
056 Baha'i	1	41	NR	41	-	-
081 Catholic	4	NR	NR	6,781	3.6	7.3
093 Chr Ch (Disc)	1	265	105	335 *	.2	.4
097 Chr Chs&Chs Cr	1	96	NR	121 *	.1	.1
123 Ch God (Ander)	1	NR	24	24	-	-
127 Ch God (Cleve)	5	947	543	1,203 *	.6	1.3
145 Ch God Prophcy	3	125	NR	159 *	.1	.2
151 L-D Saints	4	NR	NR	1,115	.6	1.2
165 Ch of Nazarene	3	428	247	449	.2	.5
167 Chs of Christ	10	806	997	1,341	.7	1.4
193 Episcopal	3	NR	506	1,488	.8	1.6
207 E.L.C.A.	1	329	212	387	.2	.4
221 Free Methodist	1	80	207	207	.1	.2
223 Free Will Bapt	3	241	NR	304 *	.2	.3
263 Int Foursq Gos	1	90	57	114 *	.1	.1
267 Muslim Est	3	NR	468	1,827	1.0	2.0
283 Luth—MO Synod	2	332	195	460	.2	.5
290 Metro Comm Ch	1	12	13	15 *	-	-
339 Pent Ch of God	2	84	NR	235	.1	.3
355 Presb Ch (USA)	9	2,087	896	2,639 *	1.4	2.8
356 Presb Ch Amer	2	147	223	223	.1	.2
360 Prim Bapt Chrch	3	NR	NR	NR	-	-
365 Prog Prim Bapt	1	23	NR	29 *	-	-
403 Salvation Army	1	181	70	578	.3	.6
413 S.D.A.	3	934	NR	1,112	.6	1.2
418 Southw Bapt Fel	2	NR	NR	NR	-	-
419 So Bapt Conv	49	37,960	12,728	47,978 *	25.8	51.6
435 Unitarian-Univ	1	32	NR	40 *	-	-
443 Un C of Christ	1	7	3	9 *	-	-
449 Un Methodist	23	13,825	5,264	17,471 *	9.4	18.8
496 Jewish Est	2	NR	NR	1,100	.6	1.2
499 Indep.Non-Char	1	300	200	300	.2	.3
NEWTON	**73**	**18,867**	**8,395**	**25,688 ***	**41.4**	**100.0**
053 Assemb of God	2	116	131	156	.3	.6
055 As Ref Pres Ch	1	27	NR	32	.1	.1
056 Baha'i	0	102	NR	102	.2	.4
081 Catholic	1	NR	NR	683	1.1	2.7
089 Chr & Miss Al	1	74	NR	74	.1	.3
097 Chr Chs&Chs Cr	2	785	NR	1,008 *	1.6	3.9
151 L-D Saints	3	NR	NR	1,005	1.6	3.9
165 Ch of Nazarene	1	130	152	255	.4	1.0
167 Chs of Christ	3	156	165	198	.3	.8
193 Episcopal	1	NR	101	228	.4	.9
355 Presb Ch (USA)	6	690	428	887 *	1.4	3.5
356 Presb Ch Amer	1	89	115	120	.2	.5
360 Prim Bapt Chrch	1	NR	NR	NR	-	-
388 Reg Bapt Gen As	1	300	125	385 *	.6	1.5
413 S.D.A.	1	133	NR	158	.3	.6
418 Southw Bapt Fel	1	NR	NR	NR	-	-
419 So Bapt Conv	20	8,428	3,105	10,819 *	17.4	42.1
449 Un Methodist	25	6,137	3,073	7,878 *	12.7	30.7
499 Indep.Non-Char	2	1,700	1,000	1,700	2.7	6.6
OCONEE	**31**	**6,746**	**2,806**	**9,192 ***	**35.1**	**100.0**
056 Baha'i	0	10	NR	10	-	.1
093 Chr Ch (Disc)	4	922	176	1,201 *	4.6	13.1
127 Ch God (Cleve)	1	302	190	393 *	1.5	4.3
151 L-D Saints	1	NR	NR	401	1.5	4.4
167 Chs of Christ	1	52	54	68	.3	.7
223 Free Will Bapt	1	80	NR	104 *	.4	1.1
349 Pent Holiness	2	71	72	92 *	.4	1.0
355 Presb Ch (USA)	1	178	88	232 *	.9	2.5
356 Presb Ch Amer	2	385	300	510	1.9	5.5
419 So Bapt Conv	10	3,739	1,476	4,870 *	18.6	53.0
449 Un Methodist	8	1,007	450	1,311 *	5.0	14.3
OGLETHORPE	**25**	**2,912**	**1,020**	**3,640 ***	**28.8**	**100.0**
056 Baha'i	0	32	NR	32	.3	.9
097 Chr Chs&Chs Cr	1	174	NR	218 *	1.7	6.0
127 Ch God (Cleve)	1	16	22	22 *	.2	.6
167 Chs of Christ	1	20	20	25	.2	.7
355 Presb Ch (USA)	1	17	10	21 *	.2	.6
419 So Bapt Conv	14	2,224	799	2,786 *	22.0	76.5
449 Un Methodist	7	429	169	536 *	4.2	14.7
PAULDING	**70**	**16,705**	**6,202**	**24,006 ***	**29.4**	**100.0**
017 Amer Bapt Assn	1	50	NR	67 *	.1	.3
034 Ant Orth of NA	1	75	NR	150	.2	.6
053 Assemb of God	1	110	129	129	.2	.5
056 Baha'i	0	24	NR	24	-	.1
081 Catholic	1	NR	NR	991	1.2	4.1
097 Chr Chs&Chs Cr	2	396	NR	530 *	.6	2.2
127 Ch God (Cleve)	2	487	159	651 *	.8	2.7

NR–Not Reported   *Total adherents estimated from known number of communicant, confirmed, full members.   - Represents a percentage less than 0.1.   Percentages may not total 100 due to rounding.

Table 4: Religious Congregations by County and Group: 2000

Religious Group	Number of Churches, Synagogues, Mosques, or Temples	Number of Communicant, Confirmed, or Full Members	Number of Attendees	Total Adherents		
				Number of Adherents	% of Total Pop.	% of Total Adh.
151 L-D Saints	1	NR	NR	651	.8	2.7
167 Chs of Christ	4	126	165	177	.2	.7
207 E.L.C.A.	1	49	36	64	.1	.3
283 Luth—MO Synod	1	104	76	134	.2	.6
289 New Hope B Asc	9	1,198	NR	1,602 *	2.0	6.7
360 Prim Bapt Chrch	4	NR	NR	NR	-	-
413 S.D.A.	1	28	NR	33	-	.1
419 So Bapt Conv	29	11,866	4,602	15,871 *	19.4	66.1
449 Un Methodist	12	2,192	1,035	2,932 *	3.6	12.2
PEACH	**25**	**3,947**	**1,533**	**5,391 ***	**22.8**	**100.0**
053 Assemb of God	1	56	65	75	.3	1.4
056 Baha'i	2	152	NR	152	.6	2.8
081 Catholic	1	NR	NR	223	.9	4.1
089 Chr & Miss Al	1	0	NR	90	.4	1.7
127 Ch God (Cleve)	1	29	35	36 *	.2	.7
165 Ch of Nazarene	1	36	16	36	.2	.7
167 Chs of Christ	2	106	101	128	.5	2.4
193 Episcopal	2	NR	95	204	.9	3.8
355 Presb Ch (USA)	1	66	45	82 *	.3	1.5
360 Prim Bapt Chrch	4	NR	NR	NR	-	-
413 S.D.A.	1	29	NR	35	.1	.6
419 So Bapt Conv	5	2,309	697	2,879 *	12.2	53.4
449 Un Methodist	3	1,164	479	1,451 *	6.1	26.9
PICKENS	**39**	**7,311**	**1,788**	**9,930 ***	**43.2**	**100.0**
053 Assemb of God	1	24	16	23	.1	.2
056 Baha'i	0	9	NR	9	-	.1
081 Catholic	1	NR	NR	549	2.4	5.5
089 Chr & Miss Al	1	57	NR	57	.2	.6
097 Chr Chs&Chs Cr	1	115	NR	141 *	.6	1.4
127 Ch God (Cleve)	1	152	82	187 *	.8	1.9
151 L-D Saints	1	NR	NR	294	1.3	3.0
167 Chs of Christ	4	150	172	196	.9	2.0
193 Episcopal	1	NR	103	125	.5	1.3
269 Jasper&PVB Asc	16	3,212	NR	3,942 *	17.2	39.7
355 Presb Ch (USA)	1	255	151	313 *	1.4	3.2
413 S.D.A.	1	47	NR	56	.2	.6
419 So Bapt Conv	7	2,471	871	3,033 *	13.2	30.5
449 Un Methodist	3	819	393	1,005 *	4.4	10.1
PIERCE	**36**	**7,398**	**3,331**	**9,785 ***	**62.6**	**100.0**
053 Assemb of God	1	53	58	95	.6	1.0
127 Ch God (Cleve)	4	545	287	683 *	4.4	7.0
145 Ch God Prophcy	1	42	NR	52 *	.3	.5
151 L-D Saints	1	NR	NR	483	3.1	4.9
167 Chs of Christ	1	14	25	21	.1	.2
223 Free Will Bapt	2	160	NR	201 *	1.3	2.1
355 Presb Ch (USA)	1	135	63	169 *	1.1	1.7
360 Prim Bapt Chrch	1	NR	NR	NR	-	-
419 So Bapt Conv	17	5,771	2,568	7,231 *	46.2	73.9
449 Un Methodist	7	678	330	850 *	5.4	8.7
PIKE	**31**	**5,118**	**2,312**	**7,159 ***	**52.3**	**100.0**
053 Assemb of God	1	63	85	151	1.1	2.1
056 Baha'i	0	28	NR	28	.2	.4
093 Chr Ch (Disc)	1	22	0	28 *	.2	.4
151 L-D Saints	1	NR	NR	590	4.3	8.2
165 Ch of Nazarene	2	178	143	211	1.5	2.9
349 Pent Holiness	1	32	31	41 *	.3	.6
355 Presb Ch (USA)	1	42	7	54 *	.4	.8
365 Prog Prim Bapt	1	7	NR	9 *	.1	.1
419 So Bapt Conv	15	4,194	1,733	5,345 *	39.0	74.7
449 Un Methodist	8	552	313	702 *	5.1	9.8
POLK	**63**	**16,566**	**5,339**	**21,322 ***	**55.9**	**100.0**
053 Assemb of God	1	0	0	0	-	-
056 Baha'i	0	7	NR	7	-	-
081 Catholic	1	NR	NR	445	1.2	2.1
127 Ch God (Cleve)	3	448	203	560 *	1.5	2.6
145 Ch God Prophcy	1	42	NR	52 *	.1	.2
151 L-D Saints	1	NR	NR	119	.3	.6
167 Chs of Christ	3	286	255	377	1.0	1.8
193 Episcopal	1	NR	33	52	.1	.2
289 New Hope B Asc	2	199	NR	249 *	.7	1.2
349 Pent Holiness	1	81	40	101 *	.3	.5
355 Presb Ch (USA)	2	248	127	310 *	.8	1.5
356 Presb Ch Amer	1	25	30	30	.1	.1
360 Prim Bapt Chrch	1	NR	NR	NR	-	-
413 S.D.A.	1	17	NR	20	.1	.1
419 So Bapt Conv	35	13,481	3,975	16,837 *	44.2	79.0
449 Un Methodist	9	1,732	676	2,163 *	5.7	10.1
PULASKI	**17**	**4,760**	**1,258**	**5,866 ***	**61.2**	**100.0**
056 Baha'i	0	62	NR	62	.6	1.1
081 Catholic	0	NR	NR	17	.2	.3
127 Ch God (Cleve)	1	27	17	33 *	.3	.6
193 Episcopal	1	NR	30	69	.7	1.2
349 Pent Holiness	1	40	30	49 *	.5	.8
360 Prim Bapt Chrch	1	NR	NR	NR	-	-
419 So Bapt Conv	12	4,156	1,003	5,058 *	52.8	86.2
449 Un Methodist	1	475	178	578 *	6.0	9.9
PUTNAM	**28**	**3,797**	**1,627**	**4,671 ***	**24.8**	**100.0**
056 Baha'i	0	17	NR	17	.1	.4
123 Ch God (Ander)	1	NR	30	30	.2	.6
127 Ch God (Cleve)	1	115	33	140 *	.7	3.0
145 Ch God Prophcy	1	42	NR	51 *	.3	1.1
167 Chs of Christ	1	20	25	27	.1	.6
263 Int Foursq Gos	1	21	28	28 *	.1	.6
349 Pent Holiness	2	183	72	222 *	1.2	4.8
355 Presb Ch (USA)	1	112	67	136 *	.7	2.9
356 Presb Ch Amer	1	73	120	120	.6	2.6
360 Prim Bapt Chrch	1	NR	NR	NR	-	-
418 Southw Bapt Fel	1	NR	NR	NR	-	-
419 So Bapt Conv	8	2,074	785	2,517 *	13.4	53.9
449 Un Methodist	9	1,140	467	1,383 *	7.4	29.6
QUITMAN	**5**	**648**	**247**	**814 ***	**31.3**	**100.0**
056 Baha'i	0	1	NR	1	-	.1
081 Catholic	0	NR	NR	15	.6	1.8
167 Chs of Christ	1	83	97	106	4.1	13.0
419 So Bapt Conv	2	463	125	568 *	21.9	69.8
449 Un Methodist	2	101	25	124 *	4.8	15.2
RABUN	**42**	**5,555**	**2,499**	**7,190 ***	**47.8**	**100.0**
053 Assemb of God	1	61	68	70	.5	1.0
081 Catholic	1	NR	NR	422	2.8	5.9
097 Chr Chs&Chs Cr	1	65	NR	78 *	.5	1.1
127 Ch God (Cleve)	5	398	264	476 *	3.2	6.6
167 Chs of Christ	1	20	25	30	.2	.4
193 Episcopal	1	NR	85	124	.8	1.7
252 Hindu	1	NR	NR	NR	-	-
355 Presb Ch (USA)	6	272	155	324 *	2.2	4.5
418 Southw Bapt Fel	1	NR	NR	NR	-	-
419 So Bapt Conv	17	3,924	1,529	4,692 *	31.2	65.3
449 Un Methodist	7	815	373	974 *	6.5	13.5
RANDOLPH	**24**	**2,767**	**890**	**3,501 ***	**44.9**	**100.0**
053 Assemb of God	1	24	26	30	.4	.9
056 Baha'i	0	67	NR	67	.9	1.9
081 Catholic	0	NR	NR	25	.3	.7
127 Ch God (Cleve)	1	20	15	25 *	.3	.7
183 Cons Menn Conf	2	37	46	54	.7	1.5
355 Presb Ch (USA)	1	58	27	73 *	.9	2.1
419 So Bapt Conv	14	2,161	625	2,723 *	35.0	77.8
449 Un Methodist	5	400	151	504 *	6.5	14.4
RICHMOND	**170**	**55,902**	**23,859**	**91,294 ***	**45.7**	**100.0**
019 Amer Bapt USA	2	595	375	752 *	.4	.8
053 Assemb of God	6	781	484	1,263	.6	1.4
055 As Ref Pres Ch	1	31	NR	37	-	-
056 Baha'i	1	101	NR	101	.1	.1

NR–Not Reported *Total adherents estimated from known number of communicant, confirmed, full members. - Represents a percentage less than 0.1. Percentages may not total 100 due to rounding.

Table 4: Religious Congregations by County and Group: 2000

Religious Group	Number of Churches, Synagogues, Mosques, or Temples	Number of Communicant, Confirmed, or Full Members	Number of Attendees	Total Adherents: Number of Adherents	Total Adherents: % of Total Pop.	Total Adherents: % of Total Adh.
076 Buddhism	1	NR	NR	NR	-	-
081 Catholic	5	NR	NR	11,493	5.8	12.6
084 Calvary Chapel	1	NR	NR	NR	-	-
089 Chr & Miss Al	1	35	NR	66	-	.1
093 Chr Ch (Disc)	2	475	214	601 *	.3	.7
097 Chr Chs&Chs Cr	3	355	NR	449 *	.2	.5
123 Ch God (Ander)	2	NR	66	66	-	.1
127 Ch God (Cleve)	3	890	705	1,125 *	.6	1.2
145 Ch God Prophcy	1	42	NR	53 *	-	.1
151 L-D Saints	2	NR	NR	738	.4	.8
165 Ch of Nazarene	2	129	169	188	.1	.2
167 Chs of Christ	3	486	345	661	.3	.7
173 Comm of Christ	1	46	NR	46	-	.1
193 Episcopal	6	NR	1,301	3,936	2.0	4.3
207 E.L.C.A.	4	1,722	723	2,335	1.2	2.6
223 Free Will Bapt	2	160	NR	203 *	.1	.2
226 Friends-USA	1	24	NR	30 *	-	-
246 Greek Orthodox	1	NR	NR	402	.2	.4
252 Hindu	3	NR	NR	NR	-	-
263 Int Foursq Gos	1	26	34	34 *	-	-
267 Muslim Est	2	NR	312	1,218	.6	1.3
268 Jain	2	NR	NR	NR	-	-
283 Luth—MO Synod	1	495	295	633	.3	.7
290 Metro Comm Ch	1	48	51	61 *	-	.1
291 Missionary Ch	1	16	10	16	-	-
297 Mennonite;Other	1	59	NR	75 *	-	.1
334 Malan Syr Orth	1	30	NR	150	.1	.2
349 Pent Holiness	6	602	207	761 *	.4	.8
355 Presb Ch (USA)	8	1,955	917	2,472 *	1.2	2.7
356 Presb Ch Amer	4	2,557	1,898	3,227	1.6	3.5
365 Prog Prim Bapt	2	238	NR	301 *	.2	.3
403 Salvation Army	1	244	138	333	.2	.4
413 S.D.A.	2	777	NR	924	.5	1.0
416 Sikh	1	NR	NR	NR	-	-
418 Southw Bapt Fel	1	NR	NR	NR	-	-
419 So Bapt Conv	45	28,903	7,870	36,544 *	18.3	40.0
435 Unitarian-Univ	1	148	NR	187 *	.1	.2
449 Un Methodist	22	8,858	3,430	11,201 *	5.6	12.3
463 Vineyard	3	723	638	914 *	.5	1.0
467 Wesleyan	1	44	132	210	.1	.2
469 WELS	1	131	95	188	.1	.2
496 Jewish Est	2	NR	NR	1,300	.7	1.4
498 Indep.Charis.	4	3,000	2,550	3,800	1.9	4.2
499 Indep.Non-Char	2	1,176	900	2,200	1.1	2.4
ROCKDALE	**51**	**19,165**	**8,459**	**33,049 ***	**47.1**	**100.0**
053 Assemb of God	2	78	96	133	.2	.4
056 Baha'i	0	37	NR	37	.1	.1
081 Catholic	2	NR	NR	5,561	7.9	16.8
089 Chr & Miss Al	1	76	NR	213	.3	.6
097 Chr Chs&Chs Cr	2	600	NR	757 *	1.1	2.3
127 Ch God (Cleve)	3	1,247	338	1,574 *	2.2	4.8
151 L-D Saints	1	NR	NR	434	.6	1.3
167 Chs of Christ	2	146	230	239	.3	.7
193 Episcopal	1	NR	178	332	.5	1.0
207 E.L.C.A.	1	469	240	573	.8	1.7
320 "Old" MB Ascs	2	388	NR	490 *	.7	1.5
349 Pent Holiness	1	52	62	66 *	.1	.2
355 Presb Ch (USA)	3	1,527	659	1,927 *	2.7	5.8
356 Presb Ch Amer	1	40	80	80	.1	.2
360 Prim Bapt Chrch	1	NR	NR	NR	-	-
413 S.D.A.	1	226	NR	269	.4	.8
419 So Bapt Conv	17	8,928	3,992	11,265 *	16.1	34.1
449 Un Methodist	6	4,318	1,765	5,449 *	7.8	16.5
467 Wesleyan	1	33	19	150	.2	.5
496 Jewish Est	1	NR	NR	2,500	3.6	7.6
498 Indep.Charis.	2	1,000	800	1,000	1.4	3.0
SCHLEY	**7**	**1,347**	**298**	**1,743 ***	**46.3**	**100.0**
056 Baha'i	0	24	NR	24	.6	1.4
419 So Bapt Conv	2	791	110	1,028 *	27.3	59.0
449 Un Methodist	5	532	188	691 *	18.3	39.6

Religious Group	Number of Churches, Synagogues, Mosques, or Temples	Number of Communicant, Confirmed, or Full Members	Number of Attendees	Total Adherents: Number of Adherents	Total Adherents: % of Total Pop.	Total Adherents: % of Total Adh.
SCREVEN	**53**	**6,198**	**2,069**	**8,075 ***	**52.5**	**100.0**
055 As Ref Pres Ch	1	17	NR	17	.1	.2
056 Baha'i	0	1	NR	1	-	-
081 Catholic	1	NR	NR	154	1.0	1.9
093 Chr Ch (Disc)	2	42	30	53 *	.3	.7
097 Chr Chs&Chs Cr	2	82	NR	105 *	.7	1.3
123 Ch God (Ander)	2	NR	35	35	.2	.4
167 Chs of Christ	1	25	25	32	.2	.4
263 Int Foursq Gos	1	36	47	47 *	.3	.6
356 Presb Ch Amer	1	20	19	22	.1	.3
418 Southw Bapt Fel	1	NR	NR	NR	-	-
419 So Bapt Conv	21	3,857	1,076	4,912 *	32.0	60.8
449 Un Methodist	20	2,118	837	2,697 *	17.5	33.4
SEMINOLE	**25**	**3,385**	**1,314**	**4,351 ***	**46.4**	**100.0**
053 Assemb of God	1	22	25	33	.4	.8
056 Baha'i	0	1	NR	1	-	-
081 Catholic	1	NR	NR	35	.4	.8
127 Ch God (Cleve)	4	399	332	499 *	5.3	11.5
165 Ch of Nazarene	1	70	77	160	1.7	3.7
167 Chs of Christ	2	53	60	68	.7	1.6
223 Free Will Bapt	5	401	NR	502 *	5.4	11.5
349 Pent Holiness	1	60	45	75 *	.8	1.7
355 Presb Ch (USA)	1	172	81	215 *	2.3	4.9
360 Prim Bapt Chrch	1	NR	NR	NR	-	-
419 So Bapt Conv	4	1,522	470	1,905 *	20.3	43.8
449 Un Methodist	4	685	224	858 *	9.2	19.7
SPALDING	**74**	**24,330**	**11,292**	**35,070 ***	**60.0**	**100.0**
019 Amer Bapt USA	2	1,125	250	1,432 *	2.5	4.1
053 Assemb of God	4	2,073	2,416	3,725	6.4	10.6
056 Baha'i	0	359	NR	359	.6	1.0
081 Catholic	1	NR	NR	838	1.4	2.4
089 Chr & Miss Al	1	14	NR	31	.1	.1
093 Chr Ch (Disc)	2	186	59	237 *	.4	.7
127 Ch God (Cleve)	3	1,426	410	1,816 *	3.1	5.2
145 Ch God Prophcy	1	42	NR	53 *	.1	.2
165 Ch of Nazarene	1	126	100	180	.3	.5
167 Chs of Christ	3	182	185	242	.4	.7
193 Episcopal	1	NR	187	679	1.2	1.9
207 E.L.C.A.	1	237	137	334	.6	1.0
267 Muslim Est	1	NR	290	1,313	2.2	3.7
349 Pent Holiness	1	15	12	19 *	-	.1
355 Presb Ch (USA)	1	417	178	531 *	.9	1.5
360 Prim Bapt Chrch	1	NR	NR	NR	-	-
370 Ref Baptist Chs	1	NR	NR	NR	-	-
403 Salvation Army	1	102	80	377	.6	1.1
413 S.D.A.	1	169	NR	201	.3	.6
418 Southw Bapt Fel	1	NR	NR	NR	-	-
419 So Bapt Conv	27	13,779	5,201	17,545 *	30.0	50.0
449 Un Methodist	17	3,514	1,472	4,473 *	7.7	12.8
467 Wesleyan	1	14	15	35	.1	.1
499 Indep.Non-Char	1	550	300	650	1.1	1.9
STEPHENS	**54**	**13,855**	**6,043**	**18,082 ***	**71.1**	**100.0**
017 Amer Bapt Assn	1	15	NR	18 *	.1	.1
053 Assemb of God	3	410	528	604	2.4	3.3
056 Baha'i	0	2	NR	2	-	-
081 Catholic	1	NR	NR	520	2.0	2.9
089 Chr & Miss Al	3	638	NR	949	3.7	5.2
097 Chr Chs&Chs Cr	1	55	NR	67 *	.3	.4
123 Ch God (Ander)	1	NR	25	25	.1	.1
127 Ch God (Cleve)	5	847	550	1,039 *	4.1	5.7
167 Chs of Christ	1	50	50	65	.3	.4
193 Episcopal	1	NR	121	236	.9	1.3
203 Evan Free Ch	1	69	125	125	.5	.7
283 Luth—MO Synod	1	121	84	144	.6	.8
349 Pent Holiness	1	143	83	175 *	.7	1.0
355 Presb Ch (USA)	1	183	107	225 *	.9	1.2
360 Prim Bapt Chrch	1	NR	NR	NR	-	-
403 Salvation Army	1	65	69	76	.3	.4
413 S.D.A.	1	72	NR	86	.3	.5

NR–Not Reported *Total adherents estimated from known number of communicant, confirmed, full members. - Represents a percentage less than 0.1. Percentages may not total 100 due to rounding.

Table 4: Religious Congregations by County and Group: 2000

Religious Group	Number of Churches, Synagogues, Mosques, or Temples	Number of Communicant, Confirmed, or Full Members	Number of Attendees	Total Adherents: Number of Adherents	Total Adherents: % of Total Pop.	Total Adherents: % of Total Adh.
419 So Bapt Conv	22	9,828	3,693	12,060 *	47.4	66.7
449 Un Methodist	7	1,227	488	1,506 *	5.9	8.3
463 Vineyard	1	130	120	160 *	.6	.9
STEWART	**15**	**1,323**	**433**	**1,628 ***	**31.0**	**100.0**
053 Assemb of God	1	17	28	34	.6	2.1
056 Baha'i	0	89	NR	89	1.7	5.5
419 So Bapt Conv	8	774	279	958 *	18.2	58.8
449 Un Methodist	6	443	126	547 *	10.4	33.6
SUMTER	**49**	**9,833**	**4,315**	**13,672 ***	**41.2**	**100.0**
053 Assemb of God	1	65	70	125	.4	.9
056 Baha'i	0	79	NR	79	.2	.6
081 Catholic	1	NR	NR	485	1.5	3.5
093 Chr Ch (Disc)	1	25	16	32 *	.1	.2
127 Ch God (Cleve)	1	81	124	124 *	.4	.9
145 Ch God Prophcy	2	83	NR	106 *	.3	.8
151 L-D Saints	1	NR	NR	218	.7	1.6
167 Chs of Christ	3	205	201	277	.8	2.0
193 Episcopal	1	NR	127	258	.8	1.9
207 E.L.C.A.	1	67	40	92	.3	.7
288 Mennonite USA	1	30	40	40 *	.1	.3
355 Presb Ch (USA)	1	288	135	369 *	1.1	2.7
356 Presb Ch Amer	1	53	59	74	.2	.5
413 S.D.A.	2	290	NR	346	1.0	2.5
418 Southw Bapt Fel	1	NR	NR	NR	-	-
419 So Bapt Conv	20	5,823	2,569	7,459 *	22.5	54.6
449 Un Methodist	10	2,699	891	3,458 *	10.4	25.3
467 Wesleyan	1	45	43	130	.4	1.0
TALBOT	**22**	**1,458**	**464**	**1,801 ***	**27.7**	**100.0**
056 Baha'i	0	2	NR	2	-	.1
127 Ch God (Cleve)	2	117	38	144 *	2.2	8.0
167 Chs of Christ	1	40	43	52	.8	2.9
223 Free Will Bapt	3	241	NR	297 *	4.6	16.5
355 Presb Ch (USA)	1	11	5	14 *	.2	.8
360 Prim Bapt Chrch	1	NR	NR	NR	-	-
419 So Bapt Conv	6	768	225	947 *	14.6	52.6
449 Un Methodist	8	279	153	345 *	5.3	19.2
TALIAFERRO	**14**	**614**	**296**	**761 ***	**36.6**	**100.0**
081 Catholic	1	NR	NR	6	.3	.8
356 Presb Ch Amer	2	30	30	45	2.2	5.9
419 So Bapt Conv	7	483	187	587 *	28.3	77.1
449 Un Methodist	4	101	79	123 *	5.9	16.2
TATTNALL	**52**	**7,004**	**2,759**	**8,817 ***	**39.5**	**100.0**
017 Amer Bapt Assn	1	42	NR	51 *	.2	.6
053 Assemb of God	1	28	35	51	.2	.6
056 Baha'i	0	1	NR	1	-	-
081 Catholic	2	NR	NR	87	.4	1.0
093 Chr Ch (Disc)	1	263	119	319 *	1.4	3.6
123 Ch God (Ander)	2	NR	205	205	.9	2.3
127 Ch God (Cleve)	3	156	176	212 *	1.0	2.4
145 Ch God Prophcy	1	42	NR	51 *	.2	.6
223 Free Will Bapt	3	241	NR	292 *	1.3	3.3
304 NatPrimBapt USA	1	40	NR	48 *	.2	.5
349 Pent Holiness	3	212	190	257 *	1.2	2.9
360 Prim Bapt Chrch	3	NR	NR	NR	-	-
365 Prog Prim Bapt	6	448	NR	543 *	2.4	6.2
419 So Bapt Conv	16	4,330	1,452	5,245 *	23.5	59.5
449 Un Methodist	9	1,201	582	1,455 *	6.5	16.5
TAYLOR	**30**	**2,862**	**1,053**	**3,595 ***	**40.8**	**100.0**
056 Baha'i	0	30	NR	30	.3	.8
127 Ch God (Cleve)	2	216	89	272 *	3.1	7.6
145 Ch God Prophcy	1	42	NR	53 *	.6	1.5
223 Free Will Bapt	4	321	NR	404 *	4.6	11.2
360 Prim Bapt Chrch	5	NR	NR	NR	-	-
419 So Bapt Conv	9	1,609	595	2,025 *	23.0	56.3
449 Un Methodist	9	644	369	811 *	9.2	22.6

Religious Group	Number of Churches, Synagogues, Mosques, or Temples	Number of Communicant, Confirmed, or Full Members	Number of Attendees	Total Adherents: Number of Adherents	Total Adherents: % of Total Pop.	Total Adherents: % of Total Adh.
TELFAIR	**44**	**3,912**	**1,831**	**5,107 ***	**43.3**	**100.0**
056 Baha'i	0	5	NR	5	-	.1
081 Catholic	1	NR	NR	103	.9	2.0
123 Ch God (Ander)	1	NR	15	15	.1	.3
127 Ch God (Cleve)	6	401	289	487 *	4.1	9.5
145 Ch God Prophcy	1	42	NR	50 *	.4	1.0
151 L-D Saints	1	NR	NR	274	2.3	5.4
167 Chs of Christ	1	17	18	25	.2	.5
355 Presb Ch (USA)	1	66	25	79 *	.7	1.5
365 Prog Prim Bapt	1	7	NR	8 *	.1	.2
419 So Bapt Conv	17	2,239	977	2,695 *	22.9	52.8
449 Un Methodist	14	1,135	507	1,366 *	11.6	26.7
TERRELL	**22**	**2,454**	**948**	**3,231 ***	**29.5**	**100.0**
053 Assemb of God	1	101	63	160	1.5	5.0
056 Baha'i	0	251	NR	251	2.3	7.8
081 Catholic	0	NR	NR	64	.6	2.0
167 Chs of Christ	2	71	71	117	1.1	3.6
193 Episcopal	1	NR	20	31	.3	1.0
355 Presb Ch (USA)	1	44	22	56 *	.5	1.7
360 Prim Bapt Chrch	1	NR	NR	NR	-	-
365 Prog Prim Bapt	1	23	NR	30 *	.3	.9
419 So Bapt Conv	10	1,386	547	1,779 *	16.2	55.1
449 Un Methodist	5	578	225	743 *	6.8	23.0
THOMAS	**98**	**16,933**	**6,647**	**22,850 ***	**53.5**	**100.0**
053 Assemb of God	4	306	330	373	.9	1.6
056 Baha'i	0	12	NR	12	-	.1
081 Catholic	1	NR	NR	109	.3	.5
084 Calvary Chapel	1	NR	NR	NR	-	-
093 Chr Ch (Disc)	1	35	0	44 *	.1	.2
097 Chr Chs&Chs Cr	1	60	NR	76 *	.2	.3
127 Ch God (Cleve)	9	760	592	957 *	2.2	4.2
151 L-D Saints	2	NR	NR	563	1.3	2.5
165 Ch of Nazarene	1	110	76	110	.3	.5
167 Chs of Christ	5	360	413	529	1.2	2.3
193 Episcopal	3	NR	268	682	1.6	3.0
223 Free Will Bapt	1	80	NR	101 *	.2	.4
297 Mennonite;Other	1	46	NR	58 *	.1	.3
304 NatPrimBapt USA	8	442	NR	556 *	1.3	2.4
349 Pent Holiness	1	78	26	98 *	.2	.4
355 Presb Ch (USA)	5	834	389	1,050 *	2.5	4.6
356 Presb Ch Amer	1	119	100	141	.3	.6
360 Prim Bapt Chrch	2	NR	NR	NR	-	-
365 Prog Prim Bapt	2	42	NR	53 *	.1	.2
403 Salvation Army	1	72	84	199	.5	.9
413 S.D.A.	3	303	NR	360	.8	1.6
418 Southw Bapt Fel	2	NR	NR	NR	-	-
419 So Bapt Conv	28	10,710	3,173	13,484 *	31.6	59.0
443 Un C of Christ	1	25	20	31 *	.1	.1
449 Un Methodist	12	2,194	676	2,764 *	6.5	12.1
498 Indep.Charis.	2	345	500	500	1.2	2.2
TIFT	**68**	**15,737**	**5,727**	**21,360 ***	**55.6**	**100.0**
017 Amer Bapt Assn	3	516	NR	657 *	1.7	3.1
053 Assemb of God	1	154	185	225	.6	1.1
081 Catholic	1	NR	NR	420	1.1	2.0
127 Ch God (Cleve)	7	1,629	630	2,073 *	5.4	9.7
145 Ch God Prophcy	2	83	NR	106 *	.3	.5
151 L-D Saints	1	NR	NR	335	.9	1.6
165 Ch of Nazarene	1	163	75	163	.4	.8
167 Chs of Christ	2	175	155	245	.6	1.1
173 Comm of Christ	1	14	NR	14	-	.1
193 Episcopal	1	NR	174	584	1.5	2.7
223 Free Will Bapt	2	160	NR	204 *	.5	1.0
283 Luth—MO Synod	1	140	75	160	.4	.7
355 Presb Ch (USA)	1	163	85	207 *	.5	1.0
356 Presb Ch Amer	1	56	85	85	.2	.4
360 Prim Bapt Chrch	3	NR	NR	NR	-	-
365 Prog Prim Bapt	4	180	NR	229 *	.6	1.1
413 S.D.A.	1	33	NR	39	.1	.2
418 Southw Bapt Fel	3	NR	NR	NR	-	-

NR–Not Reported *Total adherents estimated from known number of communicant, confirmed, full members. - Represents a percentage less than 0.1. Percentages may not total 100 due to rounding.

Table 4: Religious Congregations by County and Group: 2000

Religious Group	Number of Churches, Synagogues, Mosques, or Temples	Number of Communicant, Confirmed, or Full Members	Number of Attendees	Total Adherents: Number of Adherents	% of Total Pop.	% of Total Adh.
419 So Bapt Conv	22	9,617	3,467	12,237 *	31.9	57.3
449 Un Methodist	10	2,654	796	3,377 *	8.8	15.8
TOOMBS	**56**	**9,838**	**4,028**	**13,942 ***	**53.5**	**100.0**
053 Assemb of God	2	136	172	327	1.3	2.3
056 Baha'i	0	4	NR	4	-	-
081 Catholic	1	NR	NR	675	2.6	4.8
127 Ch God (Cleve)	7	821	569	1,052 *	4.0	7.5
145 Ch God Prophcy	2	83	NR	106 *	.4	.8
151 L-D Saints	1	NR	NR	277	1.1	2.0
165 Ch of Nazarene	1	55	46	95	.4	.7
167 Chs of Christ	2	41	46	57	.2	.4
193 Episcopal	1	NR	80	201	.8	1.4
223 Free Will Bapt	3	241	NR	308 *	1.2	2.2
355 Presb Ch (USA)	3	285	160	366 *	1.4	2.6
360 Prim Bapt Chrch	4	NR	NR	NR	-	-
365 Prog Prim Bapt	1	35	NR	45 *	.2	.3
419 So Bapt Conv	17	5,947	2,180	7,622 *	29.2	54.7
449 Un Methodist	11	2,190	775	2,807 *	10.8	20.1
TOWNS	**23**	**4,031**	**1,946**	**4,853 ***	**52.1**	**100.0**
056 Baha'i	0	1	NR	1	-	-
127 Ch God (Cleve)	2	345	319	397 *	4.3	8.2
151 L-D Saints	1	NR	NR	246	2.6	5.1
167 Chs of Christ	2	17	18	21	.2	.4
355 Presb Ch (USA)	1	105	101	120 *	1.3	2.5
419 So Bapt Conv	14	2,956	1,143	3,375 *	36.2	69.5
449 Un Methodist	3	607	365	693 *	7.4	14.3
TREUTLEN	**17**	**2,098**	**793**	**2,709 ***	**39.5**	**100.0**
053 Assemb of God	1	78	85	125	1.8	4.6
081 Catholic	0	NR	NR	6	.1	.2
127 Ch God (Cleve)	1	155	80	194 *	2.8	7.2
165 Ch of Nazarene	1	14	20	67	1.0	2.5
167 Chs of Christ	1	10	11	13	.2	.5
349 Pent Holiness	1	20	45	25 *	.4	.9
360 Prim Bapt Chrch	1	NR	NR	NR	-	-
419 So Bapt Conv	8	1,430	436	1,790 *	26.1	66.1
449 Un Methodist	3	391	116	489 *	7.1	18.1
TROUP	**112**	**22,271**	**8,556**	**30,803 ***	**52.4**	**100.0**
053 Assemb of God	2	194	205	327	.6	1.1
056 Baha'i	0	5	NR	5	-	-
081 Catholic	1	NR	NR	1,246	2.1	4.0
097 Chr Chs&Chs Cr	1	110	NR	140 *	.2	.5
123 Ch God (Ander)	1	NR	71	71	.1	.2
127 Ch God (Cleve)	4	620	307	792 *	1.3	2.6
151 L-D Saints	1	NR	NR	186	.3	.6
165 Ch of Nazarene	1	34	10	34	.1	.1
167 Chs of Christ	8	525	621	718	1.2	2.3
175 Congr Chr Chs	1	65	60	83 *	.1	.3
193 Episcopal	2	NR	186	437	.7	1.4
207 E.L.C.A.	1	185	57	238	.4	.8
267 Muslim Est	2	NR	110	326	.6	1.1
335 Orth Pres Ch	1	43	56	78	.1	.3
349 Pent Holiness	1	38	30	48 *	.1	.2
355 Presb Ch (USA)	6	1,040	534	1,328 *	2.3	4.3
360 Prim Bapt Chrch	3	NR	NR	NR	-	-
403 Salvation Army	1	23	21	56	.1	.2
413 S.D.A.	1	34	NR	40	.1	.1
418 Southw Bapt Fel	1	NR	NR	NR	-	-
419 So Bapt Conv	37	13,949	3,659	17,802 *	30.3	57.8
443 Un C of Christ	1	82	30	105 *	.2	.3
449 Un Methodist	34	4,974	2,249	6,343 *	10.8	20.6
498 Indep.Charis.	1	350	350	400	.7	1.3
TURNER	**26**	**4,368**	**1,570**	**5,655 ***	**59.5**	**100.0**
127 Ch God (Cleve)	1	171	101	222 *	2.3	3.9
145 Ch God Prophcy	1	42	NR	54 *	.6	1.0
165 Ch of Nazarene	1	20	9	20	.2	.4
167 Chs of Christ	1	35	32	45	.5	.8
223 Free Will Bapt	1	80	NR	104 *	1.1	1.8
360 Prim Bapt Chrch	2	NR	NR	NR	-	-
419 So Bapt Conv	14	3,365	1,189	4,362 *	45.9	77.1
449 Un Methodist	5	655	239	848 *	8.9	15.0
TWIGGS	**18**	**2,580**	**865**	**3,266 ***	**30.8**	**100.0**
017 Amer Bapt Assn	1	50	NR	63 *	.6	1.9
053 Assemb of God	1	19	25	25	.2	.8
056 Baha'i	0	9	NR	9	.1	.3
081 Catholic	0	NR	NR	16	.2	.5
127 Ch God (Cleve)	1	170	130	214 *	2.0	6.6
360 Prim Bapt Chrch	2	NR	NR	NR	-	-
419 So Bapt Conv	8	2,016	664	2,541 *	24.0	77.8
449 Un Methodist	5	316	46	398 *	3.8	12.2
UNION	**40**	**7,292**	**3,260**	**9,680 ***	**56.0**	**100.0**
053 Assemb of God	1	35	40	60	.3	.6
081 Catholic	1	NR	NR	955	5.5	9.9
127 Ch God (Cleve)	3	248	82	292 *	1.7	3.0
165 Ch of Nazarene	1	58	44	85	.5	.9
167 Chs of Christ	1	75	80	97	.6	1.0
193 Episcopal	1	NR	69	97	.6	1.0
283 Luth—MO Synod	1	118	73	125	.7	1.3
356 Presb Ch Amer	1	67	75	75	.4	.8
419 So Bapt Conv	24	5,729	2,243	6,758 *	39.1	69.8
449 Un Methodist	6	962	554	1,136 *	6.6	11.7
UPSON	**53**	**13,168**	**4,885**	**16,627 ***	**60.2**	**100.0**
053 Assemb of God	1	760	538	850	3.1	5.1
056 Baha'i	0	67	NR	67	.2	.4
081 Catholic	1	NR	NR	216	.8	1.3
127 Ch God (Cleve)	1	474	172	590 *	2.1	3.5
151 L-D Saints	1	NR	NR	129	.5	.8
167 Chs of Christ	3	92	105	125	.5	.8
223 Free Will Bapt	2	160	NR	200 *	.7	1.2
349 Pent Holiness	1	101	60	126 *	.5	.8
355 Presb Ch (USA)	1	282	112	351 *	1.3	2.1
360 Prim Bapt Chrch	3	NR	NR	NR	-	-
365 Prog Prim Bapt	4	160	NR	199 *	.7	1.2
413 S.D.A.	2	131	NR	156	.6	.9
418 Southw Bapt Fel	1	NR	NR	NR	-	-
419 So Bapt Conv	25	9,478	3,456	11,797 *	42.7	71.0
449 Un Methodist	7	1,463	442	1,821 *	6.6	11.0
WALKER	**119**	**23,876**	**11,137**	**30,296 ***	**49.6**	**100.0**
053 Assemb of God	3	307	373	378	.6	1.2
056 Baha'i	0	3	NR	3	-	-
123 Ch God (Ander)	3	NR	122	122	.2	.4
127 Ch God (Cleve)	12	1,859	913	2,297 *	3.8	7.6
145 Ch God Prophcy	5	209	NR	260 *	.4	.9
151 L-D Saints	1	NR	NR	256	.4	.8
165 Ch of Nazarene	5	489	392	675	1.1	2.2
167 Chs of Christ	12	1,059	1,108	1,406	2.3	4.6
189 Duck Rivr Bapt	1	73	NR	90 *	.1	.3
355 Presb Ch (USA)	2	116	75	144 *	.2	.5
356 Presb Ch Amer	4	361	407	464	.8	1.5
413 S.D.A.	2	175	NR	209	.3	.7
418 Southw Bapt Fel	1	NR	NR	NR	-	-
419 So Bapt Conv	49	16,812	6,581	20,786 *	34.0	68.6
449 Un Methodist	17	2,323	1,050	2,871 *	4.7	9.5
467 Wesleyan	2	90	116	335	.5	1.1
WALTON	**58**	**14,036**	**6,427**	**19,257 ***	**31.7**	**100.0**
017 Amer Bapt Assn	1	96	NR	124 *	.2	.6
053 Assemb of God	2	191	204	204	.3	1.1
056 Baha'i	0	18	NR	18	-	.1
081 Catholic	1	NR	NR	751	1.2	3.9
097 Chr Chs&Chs Cr	1	265	NR	343 *	.6	1.8
127 Ch God (Cleve)	2	632	186	817 *	1.3	4.2
167 Chs of Christ	3	60	68	69	.1	.4
193 Episcopal	1	NR	151	420	.7	2.2
320 "Old" MB Ascs	4	642	NR	830 *	1.4	4.3
349 Pent Holiness	2	41	41	53 *	.1	.3

NR–Not Reported   *Total adherents estimated from known number of communicant, confirmed, full members.   - Represents a percentage less than 0.1.   Percentages may not total 100 due to rounding.

Table 4: Religious Congregations by County and Group: 2000

Religious Group	Number of Churches, Synagogues, Mosques, or Temples	Number of Communicant, Confirmed, or Full Members	Number of Attendees	Total Adherents: Number of Adherents	Total Adherents: % of Total Pop.	Total Adherents: % of Total Adh.
355 Presb Ch (USA)	1	174	118	225 *	.4	1.2
360 Prim Bapt Chrch	3	NR	NR	NR	-	-
418 Southw Bapt Fel	3	NR	NR	NR	-	-
419 So Bapt Conv	23	9,593	4,608	12,400 *	20.4	64.4
449 Un Methodist	11	2,324	1,051	3,003 *	4.9	15.6
WARE	**73**	**14,678**	**5,507**	**19,668 ***	**55.4**	**100.0**
053 Assemb of God	1	170	190	241	.7	1.2
056 Baha'i	0	3	NR	3	-	-
081 Catholic	1	NR	NR	686	1.9	3.5
093 Chr Ch (Disc)	1	125	70	154 *	.4	.8
127 Ch God (Cleve)	8	922	564	1,141 *	3.2	5.8
145 Ch God Prophcy	6	250	NR	312 *	.9	1.6
151 L-D Saints	1	NR	NR	366	1.0	1.9
165 Ch of Nazarene	1	91	68	134	.4	.7
167 Chs of Christ	3	135	152	172	.5	.9
193 Episcopal	1	NR	109	292	.8	1.5
223 Free Will Bapt	4	321	NR	396 *	1.1	2.0
263 Int Foursq Gos	1	30	50	50 *	.1	.3
320 "Old" MB Ascs	1	22	NR	27 *	.1	.1
349 Pent Holiness	4	314	165	388 *	1.1	2.0
355 Presb Ch (USA)	1	285	149	352 *	1.0	1.8
365 Prog Prim Bapt	1	85	NR	105 *	.3	.5
403 Salvation Army	1	71	31	213	.6	1.1
413 S.D.A.	2	182	NR	217	.6	1.1
419 So Bapt Conv	23	8,723	3,002	10,777 *	30.4	54.8
449 Un Methodist	12	2,949	957	3,642 *	10.3	18.5
WARREN	**17**	**1,960**	**948**	**2,446 ***	**38.6**	**100.0**
167 Chs of Christ	1	54	52	60	.9	2.5
413 S.D.A.	1	12	NR	14	.2	.6
419 So Bapt Conv	8	1,232	530	1,543 *	24.4	63.1
449 Un Methodist	7	662	366	829 *	13.1	33.9
WASHINGTON	**53**	**6,820**	**2,551**	**8,643 ***	**40.8**	**100.0**
056 Baha'i	0	5	NR	5	-	.1
081 Catholic	1	NR	NR	70	.3	.8
093 Chr Ch (Disc)	2	214	87	269 *	1.3	3.1
097 Chr Chs&Chs Cr	3	200	NR	252 *	1.2	2.9
123 Ch God (Ander)	1	NR	15	15	.1	.2
127 Ch God (Cleve)	5	410	238	516 *	2.4	6.0
165 Ch of Nazarene	2	403	265	450	2.1	5.2
167 Chs of Christ	3	60	53	79	.4	.9
193 Episcopal	1	NR	26	44	.2	.5
356 Presb Ch Amer	1	20	14	20	.1	.2
360 Prim Bapt Chrch	2	NR	NR	NR	-	-
413 S.D.A.	1	31	NR	37	.2	.4
419 So Bapt Conv	22	4,008	1,230	5,039 *	23.8	58.3
449 Un Methodist	9	1,469	623	1,847 *	8.7	21.4
WAYNE	**61**	**11,876**	**4,862**	**16,790 ***	**63.2**	**100.0**
017 Amer Bapt Assn	2	104	NR	129 *	.5	.8
053 Assemb of God	1	101	135	135	.5	.8
056 Baha'i	0	1	NR	1	-	-
061 Beachy Amish	1	47	NR	59 *	.2	.4
081 Catholic	1	NR	NR	915	3.4	5.4
097 Chr Chs&Chs Cr	1	50	NR	62 *	.2	.4
123 Ch God (Ander)	1	NR	30	30	.1	.2
127 Ch God (Cleve)	12	2,379	1,498	2,969 *	11.2	17.7
145 Ch God Prophcy	1	42	NR	52 *	.2	.3
151 L-D Saints	2	NR	NR	872	3.3	5.2
167 Chs of Christ	1	20	20	25	.1	.1
193 Episcopal	1	NR	60	142	.5	.8
223 Free Will Bapt	3	241	NR	300 *	1.1	1.8
355 Presb Ch (USA)	2	75	55	94 *	.4	.6
360 Prim Bapt Chrch	1	NR	NR	NR	-	-
365 Prog Prim Bapt	2	237	NR	296 *	1.1	1.8
370 Ref Baptist Chs	1	NR	NR	NR	-	-
419 So Bapt Conv	21	7,230	2,477	9,019 *	34.0	53.7
449 Un Methodist	6	1,331	568	1,660 *	6.2	9.9
467 Wesleyan	1	18	19	30	.1	.2
WEBSTER	**9**	**1,083**	**342**	**1,348 ***	**56.4**	**100.0**
056 Baha'i	0	4	NR	4	.2	.3
167 Chs of Christ	1	32	29	54	2.3	4.0
360 Prim Bapt Chrch	1	NR	NR	NR	-	-
419 So Bapt Conv	5	885	264	1,090 *	45.6	80.9
449 Un Methodist	2	162	49	200 *	8.4	14.8
WHEELER	**23**	**2,343**	**1,021**	**2,937 ***	**47.5**	**100.0**
056 Baha'i	0	2	NR	2	-	.1
081 Catholic	0	NR	NR	44	.7	1.5
123 Ch God (Ander)	2	NR	70	70	1.1	2.4
127 Ch God (Cleve)	4	302	173	364 *	5.9	12.4
365 Prog Prim Bapt	1	44	NR	53 *	.9	1.8
419 So Bapt Conv	10	1,516	600	1,827 *	29.6	62.2
449 Un Methodist	6	479	178	577 *	9.3	19.6
WHITE	**31**	**5,393**	**2,543**	**7,648 ***	**38.3**	**100.0**
053 Assemb of God	1	53	47	71	.4	.9
056 Baha'i	0	2	NR	2	-	-
081 Catholic	1	NR	NR	625	3.1	8.2
127 Ch God (Cleve)	1	130	347	347 *	1.7	4.5
167 Chs of Christ	1	23	40	35	.2	.5
193 Episcopal	1	NR	136	206	1.0	2.7
207 E.L.C.A.	1	89	67	115	.6	1.5
320 "Old" MB Ascs	1	158	NR	193 *	1.0	2.5
355 Presb Ch (USA)	3	394	195	482 *	2.4	6.3
413 S.D.A.	1	89	NR	106	.5	1.4
419 So Bapt Conv	11	3,032	1,042	3,706 *	18.6	48.5
449 Un Methodist	8	1,401	652	1,713 *	8.6	22.4
467 Wesleyan	1	22	17	47	.2	.6
WHITFIELD	**98**	**30,242**	**12,690**	**44,450 ***	**53.2**	**100.0**
053 Assemb of God	3	172	192	349	.4	.8
056 Baha'i	0	10	NR	10	-	-
081 Catholic	1	NR	NR	4,651	5.6	10.5
097 Chr Chs&Chs Cr	1	174	NR	222 *	.3	.5
127 Ch God (Cleve)	9	3,157	1,301	4,036 *	4.8	9.1
145 Ch God Prophcy	3	117	NR	148 *	.2	.3
151 L-D Saints	1	NR	NR	339	.4	.8
165 Ch of Nazarene	2	156	85	165	.2	.4
167 Chs of Christ	8	892	856	1,078	1.3	2.4
193 Episcopal	1	NR	187	635	.8	1.4
207 E.L.C.A.	1	156	57	185	.2	.4
267 Muslim Est	1	NR	55	163	.2	.4
320 "Old" MB Ascs	4	1,047	NR	1,335 *	1.6	3.0
355 Presb Ch (USA)	2	1,045	395	1,332 *	1.6	3.0
356 Presb Ch Amer	1	322	250	322	.4	.7
403 Salvation Army	1	70	45	176	.2	.4
413 S.D.A.	3	625	NR	744	.9	1.7
418 Southw Bapt Fel	2	NR	NR	NR	-	-
419 So Bapt Conv	36	17,707	7,486	22,579 *	27.0	50.8
449 Un Methodist	17	4,592	1,781	5,856 *	7.0	13.2
496 Jewish Est	1	NR	NR	125	.1	.3
WILCOX	**33**	**3,818**	**1,433**	**4,671 ***	**54.5**	**100.0**
056 Baha'i	0	2	NR	2	-	-
081 Catholic	0	NR	NR	46	.5	1.0
127 Ch God (Cleve)	1	197	86	239 *	2.8	5.1
223 Free Will Bapt	1	80	NR	97 *	1.1	2.1
360 Prim Bapt Chrch	3	NR	NR	NR	-	-
419 So Bapt Conv	22	3,178	1,182	3,849 *	44.9	82.4
449 Un Methodist	6	361	165	438 *	5.1	9.4
WILKES	**30**	**3,639**	**1,486**	**4,692 ***	**43.9**	**100.0**
056 Baha'i	0	16	NR	16	.1	.3
081 Catholic	1	NR	NR	165	1.5	3.5
127 Ch God (Cleve)	1	55	37	67 *	.6	1.4
167 Chs of Christ	1	29	28	38	.4	.8
193 Episcopal	1	NR	42	95	.9	2.0
355 Presb Ch (USA)	2	94	49	114 *	1.1	2.4
413 S.D.A.	1	46	NR	55	.5	1.2

NR–Not Reported *Total adherents estimated from known number of communicant, confirmed, full members. - Represents a percentage less than 0.1. Percentages may not total 100 due to rounding.

Table 4: Religious Congregations by County and Group: 2000

Religious Group	Number of Churches, Synagogues, Mosques, or Temples	Number of Communicant, Confirmed, or Full Members	Number of Attendees	Total Adherents: Number of Adherents	Total Adherents: % of Total Pop.	Total Adherents: % of Total Adh.
418 Southw Bapt Fel	1	NR	NR	NR	-	-
419 So Bapt Conv	15	2,770	1,011	3,375 *	31.6	71.9
449 Un Methodist	7	629	319	767 *	7.2	16.3
WILKINSON	**32**	**3,032**	**1,240**	**3,852 ***	**37.7**	**100.0**
056 Baha'i	0	10	NR	10	.1	.3
081 Catholic	0	NR	NR	21	.2	.5
097 Chr Chs&Chs Cr	1	50	NR	63 *	.6	1.6
145 Ch God Prophcy	1	42	NR	53 *	.5	1.4
167 Chs of Christ	2	48	90	75	.7	1.9
360 Prim Bapt Chrch	4	NR	NR	NR	-	-
419 So Bapt Conv	15	2,173	796	2,736 *	26.8	71.0
449 Un Methodist	9	709	354	894 *	8.7	23.2
WORTH	**43**	**7,044**	**2,789**	**9,093 ***	**41.4**	**100.0**
053 Assemb of God	1	50	39	46	.2	.5
056 Baha'i	0	1	NR	1	-	-
081 Catholic	0	NR	NR	120	.5	1.3
127 Ch God (Cleve)	1	77	42	98 *	.4	1.1
145 Ch God Prophcy	1	42	NR	53 *	.2	.6
167 Chs of Christ	1	39	46	52	.2	.6
223 Free Will Bapt	3	241	NR	307 *	1.4	3.4
355 Presb Ch (USA)	1	30	16	38 *	.2	.4
360 Prim Bapt Chrch	1	NR	NR	NR	-	-
365 Prog Prim Bapt	1	26	NR	33 *	.2	.4
419 So Bapt Conv	25	5,665	2,266	7,231 *	32.9	79.5
449 Un Methodist	8	873	380	1,114 *	5.1	12.3
HAWAII						
The State.....	939	98,147	73,062	438,694 *	36.2	100.0
HAWAII	**168**	**14,070**	**10,884**	**59,129 ***	**39.8**	**100.0**
017 Amer Bapt Assn	1	6	NR	7 *	-	-
053 Assemb of God	19	2,519	2,438	3,116	2.1	5.3
057 Bapt Gen Conf	1	30	50	50 *	-	.1
076 Buddhism	6	NR	NR	NR	-	-
081 Catholic	24	NR	NR	32,851	22.1	55.6
084 Calvary Chapel	2	NR	NR	NR	-	-
089 Chr & Miss Al	1	0	NR	83	.1	.1
127 Ch God (Cleve)	3	254	119	317 *	.2	.5
145 Ch God Prophcy	1	45	NR	56 *	-	.1
151 L-D Saints	15	NR	NR	6,825	4.6	11.5
165 Ch of Nazarene	3	191	167	291	.2	.5
167 Chs of Christ	4	69	120	117	.1	.2
173 Comm of Christ	2	206	NR	206	.1	.3
176 Congr Ad Afl	6	428	NR	534 *	.4	.9
193 Episcopal	7	NR	343	1,009	.7	1.7
203 Evan Free Ch	1	67	140	140	.1	.2
207 E.L.C.A.	1	138	130	192	.1	.3
226 Friends-USA	1	32	NR	40 *	-	.1
263 Int Foursq Gos	8	1,745	2,310	2,310 *	1.6	3.9
264 Int Chs of Crst	1	43	84	57	-	.1
283 Luth—MO Synod	2	135	129	167	.1	.3
291 Missionary Ch	2	141	240	240	.2	.4
339 Pent Ch of God	1	24	NR	80	.1	.1
349 Pent Holiness	3	1,000	800	1,247 *	.8	2.1
355 Presb Ch (USA)	4	1,265	1,013	1,577 *	1.1	2.7
388 Reg Bapt Gen As	2	0	0	0 *	-	-
403 Salvation Army	4	433	167	771	.5	1.3
413 S.D.A.	5	743	NR	884	.6	1.5
419 So Bapt Conv	12	1,818	978	2,267 *	1.5	3.8
443 Un C of Christ	22	2,373	1,368	2,959 *	2.0	5.0
449 Un Methodist	4	365	288	456 *	.3	.8
496 Jewish Est	0	NR	NR	280	.2	.5
HONOLULU	**565**	**66,596**	**49,122**	**291,933 ***	**33.3**	**100.0**
017 Amer Bapt Assn	4	133	NR	164 *	-	.1
019 Amer Bapt USA	3	488	437	600 *	.1	.2
053 Assemb of God	51	6,402	7,302	10,565	1.2	3.6
057 Bapt Gen Conf	3	160	193	228 *	-	.1

Religious Group	Number of Churches, Synagogues, Mosques, or Temples	Number of Communicant, Confirmed, or Full Members	Number of Attendees	Total Adherents: Number of Adherents	Total Adherents: % of Total Pop.	Total Adherents: % of Total Adh.
076 Buddhism	60	NR	NR	NR	-	-
081 Catholic	38	NR	NR	153,755	17.5	52.7
084 Calvary Chapel	8	NR	NR	NR	-	-
089 Chr & Miss Al	9	764	NR	1,616	.2	.6
093 Chr Ch (Disc)	4	243	70	299 *	-	.1
097 Chr Chs&Chs Cr	9	1,328	NR	1,633 *	.2	.6
105 Christian Ref	3	60	160	74 *	-	-
123 Ch God (Ander)	1	NR	10	10	-	-
127 Ch God (Cleve)	13	1,300	623	1,604 *	.2	.5
145 Ch God Prophcy	4	178	NR	220 *	-	.1
151 L-D Saints	80	NR	NR	28,802	3.3	9.9
165 Ch of Nazarene	13	1,663	851	1,817	.2	.6
167 Chs of Christ	7	618	640	774	.1	.3
173 Comm of Christ	4	680	NR	680	.1	.2
179 Consrv Bapt	1	NR	150	150	-	.1
186 Coptic Orth Ch	1	NR	NR	NR	-	-
193 Episcopal	23	NR	2,330	7,499	.9	2.6
201 Evan Cov Ch	1	0	0	0 *	-	-
203 Evan Free Ch	3	824	1,100	1,324	.2	.5
207 E.L.C.A.	8	1,678	1,253	2,178	.2	.7
223 Free Will Bapt	1	49	NR	60 *	-	-
226 Friends-USA	1	32	NR	39 *	-	-
246 Greek Orthodox	1	NR	NR	282	-	.1
252 Hindu	3	NR	NR	NR	-	-
263 Int Foursq Gos	26	9,288	12,320	12,320 *	1.4	4.2
264 Int Chs of Crst	1	853	1,148	1,121	.1	.4
267 Muslim Est	1	NR	156	609	.1	.2
283 Luth—MO Synod	6	1,022	907	1,343	.2	.5
288 Mennonite USA	2	78	62	96 *	-	-
290 Metro Comm Ch	1	8	14	14 *	-	-
291 Missionary Ch	6	555	985	985	.1	.3
349 Pent Holiness	3	177	101	218 *	-	.1
355 Presb Ch (USA)	2	145	116	178 *	-	.1
356 Presb Ch Amer	4	141	328	328	-	.1
370 Ref Baptist Chs	1	NR	NR	NR	-	-
401 Rus Orth Abroad	1	NR	NR	NR	-	-
403 Salvation Army	4	707	449	6,627	.8	2.3
413 S.D.A.	16	3,817	NR	4,543	.5	1.6
416 Sikh	1	NR	NR	NR	-	-
419 So Bapt Conv	46	13,651	5,205	16,788 *	1.9	5.8
435 Unitarian-Univ	1	158	NR	194 *	-	.1
443 Un C of Christ	52	12,486	6,380	15,355 *	1.8	5.3
449 Un Methodist	22	5,676	3,216	6,980 *	.8	2.4
463 Vineyard	2	260	240	320 *	-	.1
467 Wesleyan	1	0	0	0	-	-
469 WELS	1	84	101	156	-	.1
496 Jewish Est	3	NR	NR	6,410	.7	2.2
498 Indep.Charis.	4	725	1,850	2,475	.3	.8
499 Indep.Non-Char	1	165	425	500	.1	.2
KALAWAO	**1**	**19**	**12**	**19 ***	**12.9**	**100.0**
443 Un C of Christ	1	19	12	19 *	12.9	100.0
KAUAI	**77**	**4,136**	**3,767**	**30,587 ***	**52.3**	**100.0**
053 Assemb of God	4	481	603	736	1.3	2.4
076 Buddhism	3	NR	NR	NR	-	-
081 Catholic	10	NR	NR	20,875	35.7	68.2
084 Calvary Chapel	2	NR	NR	NR	-	-
097 Chr Chs&Chs Cr	2	37	NR	47 *	.1	.2
127 Ch God (Cleve)	2	91	70	114 *	.2	.4
151 L-D Saints	6	NR	NR	2,646	4.5	8.7
165 Ch of Nazarene	2	72	56	126	.2	.4
167 Chs of Christ	1	48	75	71	.1	.2
175 Congr Chr Chs	1	30	50	38 *	.1	.1
181 Consrv Congr	1	20	15	25 *	-	.1
193 Episcopal	5	NR	389	1,154	2.0	3.8
203 Evan Free Ch	1	0	60	60	.1	.2
207 E.L.C.A.	1	145	160	188	.3	.6
252 Hindu	4	NR	NR	NR	-	-
263 Int Foursq Gos	4	203	264	264 *	.5	.9
291 Missionary Ch	4	278	640	640	1.1	2.1
349 Pent Holiness	1	75	60	94 *	.2	.3
370 Ref Baptist Chs	1	NR	NR	NR	-	-

NR–Not Reported *Total adherents estimated from known number of communicant, confirmed, full members. - Represents a percentage less than 0.1. Percentages may not total 100 due to rounding.

Table 4: Religious Congregations by County and Group: 2000

Religious Group	Number of Churches, Synagogues, Mosques, or Temples	Number of Communicant, Confirmed, or Full Members	Number of Attendees	Total Adherents		
				Number of Adherents	% of Total Pop.	% of Total Adh.
403 Salvation Army	3	336	109	528	.9	1.7
413 S.D.A.	2	363	NR	432	.7	1.4
419 So Bapt Conv	4	450	282	563 *	1.0	1.8
443 Un C of Christ	11	1,301	802	1,628 *	2.8	5.3
449 Un Methodist	2	206	132	258 *	.4	.8
496 Jewish Est	0	NR	NR	100	.2	.3
MAUI	**128**	**13,326**	**9,277**	**57,026 ***	**44.5**	**100.0**
053 Assemb of God	6	5,605	2,985	7,337	5.7	12.9
076 Buddhism	4	NR	NR	NR	-	-
081 Catholic	23	NR	NR	33,332	26.0	58.5
084 Calvary Chapel	4	NR	NR	NR	-	-
097 Chr Chs&Chs Cr	1	80	NR	99 *	.1	.2
127 Ch God (Cleve)	6	399	156	510 *	.4	.9
151 L-D Saints	11	NR	NR	4,485	3.5	7.9
165 Ch of Nazarene	3	189	227	508	.4	.9
167 Chs of Christ	1	30	60	50	-	.1
176 Congr Ad Afl	3	188	NR	234 *	.2	.4
181 Consrv Congr	1	88	160	109 *	.1	.2
193 Episcopal	5	NR	513	1,422	1.1	2.5
203 Evan Free Ch	1	69	125	125	.1	.2
207 E.L.C.A.	1	88	95	119	.1	.2
226 Friends-USA	1	32	NR	40 *	-	.1
252 Hindu	1	NR	NR	NR	-	-
263 Int Foursq Gos	1	146	128	182 *	.1	.3
264 Int Chs of Crst	1	77	125	109	.1	.2
283 Luth—MO Synod	2	178	134	265	.2	.5
290 Metro Comm Ch	1	10	7	7 *	-	-
403 Salvation Army	3	464	133	816	.6	1.4
413 S.D.A.	5	382	NR	454	.4	.8
419 So Bapt Conv	9	1,032	1,031	1,283 *	1.0	2.2
443 Un C of Christ	27	2,328	1,134	2,895 *	2.3	5.1
449 Un Methodist	3	461	444	573 *	.4	1.0
463 Vineyard	1	130	120	162 *	.1	.3
496 Jewish Est	1	NR	NR	210	.2	.4
498 Indep.Charis.	1	350	500	500	.4	.9
499 Indep.Non-Char	1	1,000	1,200	1,200	.9	2.1

IDAHO

Religious Group	Number of Churches, Synagogues, Mosques, or Temples	Number of Communicant, Confirmed, or Full Members	Number of Attendees	Total Adherents		
				Number of Adherents	% of Total Pop.	% of Total Adh.
The State.....	1,855	119,911	81,036	627,262 *	48.5	100.0
ADA	**261**	**31,873**	**23,930**	**133,823 ***	**44.5**	**100.0**
017 Amer Bapt Assn	2	43	NR	58 *	-	-
019 Amer Bapt USA	6	1,522	1,333	1,932 *	.6	1.4
034 Ant Orth of NA	1	25	NR	50	-	-
053 Assemb of God	9	1,529	1,915	4,312	1.4	3.2
056 Baha'i	1	149	NR	149	-	.1
076 Buddhism	1	NR	NR	NR	-	-
081 Catholic	7	NR	NR	36,989	12.3	27.6
084 Calvary Chapel	3	NR	NR	NR	-	-
093 Chr Ch (Disc)	3	735	393	933 *	.3	.7
097 Chr Chs&Chs Cr	7	2,393	NR	3,039 *	1.0	2.3
123 Ch God (Ander)	1	NR	356	356	.1	.3
127 Ch God (Cleve)	1	50	70	70 *	-	.1
145 Ch God Prophcy	2	53	NR	66 *	-	-
151 L-D Saints	111	NR	NR	45,593	15.2	34.1
157 Ch of Brethren	2	196	133	249 *	.1	.2
165 Ch of Nazarene	8	2,246	1,959	2,593	.9	1.9
167 Chs of Christ	5	384	410	560	.2	.4
173 Comm of Christ	1	192	NR	192	.1	.1
179 Consrv Bapt	1	NR	225	225	.1	.2
193 Episcopal	4	NR	736	2,459	.8	1.8
203 Evan Free Ch	1	35	75	75	-	.1
207 E.L.C.A.	5	2,064	1,289	3,059	1.0	2.3
221 Free Methodist	1	171	481	481	.2	.4
223 Free Will Bapt	1	42	NR	53 *	-	-
226 Friends-USA	10	778	NR	988 *	.3	.7
246 Greek Orthodox	1	NR	NR	162	.1	.1
252 Hindu	1	NR	NR	NR	-	-
263 Int Foursq Gos	5	387	508	508 *	.2	.4
264 Int Chs of Crst	1	146	228	196	.1	.1
267 Muslim Est	1	NR	60	200	.1	.1
283 Luth—MO Synod	4	1,199	623	1,696	.6	1.3
288 Mennonite USA	2	60	95	106 *	-	.1
290 Metro Comm Ch	1	31	21	39 *	-	-
335 Orth Pres Ch	1	47	62	91	-	.1
339 Pent Ch of God	1	10	NR	30	-	-
355 Presb Ch (USA)	4	1,565	669	1,988 *	.7	1.5
356 Presb Ch Amer	1	0	70	70	-	.1
371 Ref Ch in Am	1	84	150	216	.1	.2
388 Reg Bapt Gen As	4	531	444	674 *	.2	.5
401 Rus Orth Abroad	1	NR	NR	NR	-	-
403 Salvation Army	1	135	125	233	.1	.2
413 S.D.A.	6	1,337	NR	1,591	.5	1.2
419 So Bapt Conv	9	2,323	907	2,950 *	1.0	2.2
435 Unitarian-Univ	1	179	NR	227 *	.1	.2
443 Un C of Christ	2	516	346	655 *	.2	.5
449 Un Methodist	8	4,668	2,150	5,926 *	2.0	4.4
455 Un Ref Chs N.A.	1	223	NR	367	.1	.3
463 Vineyard	2	1,882	1,524	2,390 *	.8	1.8
469 WELS	3	143	173	227	.1	.2
496 Jewish Est	1	NR	NR	800	.3	.6
498 Indep.Charis.	1	0	2,000	2,500	.8	1.9
499 Indep.Non-Char	3	3,800	4,400	5,500	1.8	4.1
ADAMS	**8**	**244**	**189**	**1,058 ***	**30.4**	**100.0**
034 Ant Orth of NA	1	62	NR	124	3.6	11.7
053 Assemb of God	2	75	80	93	2.7	8.8
056 Baha'i	0	2	NR	2	.1	.2
081 Catholic	1	NR	NR	280	8.1	26.5
151 L-D Saints	2	NR	NR	353	10.2	33.4
165 Ch of Nazarene	1	41	74	129	3.7	12.2
449 Un Methodist	1	64	35	77 *	2.2	7.3
BANNOCK	**132**	**4,797**	**2,018**	**47,282 ***	**62.6**	**100.0**
019 Amer Bapt USA	1	162	5	207 *	.3	.4
053 Assemb of God	2	186	268	488	.6	1.0
056 Baha'i	1	42	NR	42	.1	.1
081 Catholic	5	NR	NR	4,281	5.7	9.1
084 Calvary Chapel	1	NR	NR	NR	-	-
089 Chr & Miss Al	1	69	NR	217	.3	.5
093 Chr Ch (Disc)	1	373	104	476 *	.6	1.0
097 Chr Chs&Chs Cr	1	165	NR	210 *	.3	.4
127 Ch God (Cleve)	1	78	35	99 *	.1	.2
145 Ch God Prophcy	1	26	NR	33 *	-	.1
151 L-D Saints	98	NR	NR	35,659	47.2	75.4
165 Ch of Nazarene	1	155	165	205	.3	.4
167 Chs of Christ	1	94	105	135	.2	.3
173 Comm of Christ	1	62	NR	62	.1	.1
193 Episcopal	1	NR	112	348	.5	.7
207 E.L.C.A.	1	285	69	389	.5	.8
246 Greek Orthodox	1	NR	NR	297	.4	.6
263 Int Foursq Gos	1	24	31	31 *	-	.1
283 Luth—MO Synod	2	1,010	480	1,435	1.9	3.0
355 Presb Ch (USA)	1	242	109	309 *	.4	.7
403 Salvation Army	1	45	30	100	.1	.2
413 S.D.A.	1	133	NR	158	.2	.3
419 So Bapt Conv	2	798	103	1,018 *	1.3	2.2
435 Unitarian-Univ	1	53	NR	68 *	.1	.1
443 Un C of Christ	1	76	37	97 *	.1	.2
449 Un Methodist	2	589	245	752 *	1.0	1.6
463 Vineyard	1	130	120	166 *	.2	.4
BEAR LAKE	**20**	**54**	**39**	**5,412 ***	**84.4**	**100.0**
056 Baha'i	0	5	NR	5	.1	.1
081 Catholic	1	NR	NR	70	1.1	1.3
151 L-D Saints	17	NR	NR	5,273	82.2	97.4
263 Int Foursq Gos	1	18	24	24 *	.4	.4
355 Presb Ch (USA)	1	31	15	40 *	.6	.7
BENEWAH	**15**	**1,142**	**773**	**3,315 ***	**36.1**	**100.0**
053 Assemb of God	2	95	116	155	1.7	4.7
056 Baha'i	0	6	NR	6	.1	.2

NR–Not Reported *Total adherents estimated from known number of communicant, confirmed, full members. - Represents a percentage less than 0.1. Percentages may not total 100 due to rounding.

Table 4: Religious Congregations by County and Group: 2000

Religious Group	Number of Churches, Synagogues, Mosques, or Temples	Number of Communicant, Confirmed, or Full Members	Number of Attendees	Total Adherents		
				Number of Adherents	% of Total Pop.	% of Total Adh.
081 Catholic	4	NR	NR	1,330	14.5	40.1
151 L-D Saints	1	NR	NR	260	2.8	7.8
165 Ch of Nazarene	1	174	197	380	4.1	11.5
167 Chs of Christ	1	12	12	16	.2	.5
179 Consrv Bapt	1	NR	75	75	.8	2.3
207 E.L.C.A.	1	142	57	208	2.3	6.3
221 Free Methodist	1	21	20	23	.3	.7
263 Int Foursq Gos	1	150	112	188 *	2.0	5.7
355 Presb Ch (USA)	1	169	90	212 *	2.3	6.4
413 S.D.A.	1	93	NR	111	1.2	3.3
419 So Bapt Conv	0	280	94	351 *	3.8	10.6
BINGHAM	**84**	**1,419**	**870**	**29,282 ***	**70.2**	**100.0**
019 Amer Bapt USA	1	260	176	351 *	.8	1.2
053 Assemb of God	3	86	107	161	.4	.5
056 Baha'i	1	60	NR	60	.1	.2
081 Catholic	5	NR	NR	3,156	7.6	10.8
151 L-D Saints	61	NR	NR	23,938	57.4	81.7
167 Chs of Christ	1	30	32	39	.1	.1
193 Episcopal	2	NR	56	286	.7	1.0
207 E.L.C.A.	2	182	116	216	.5	.7
263 Int Foursq Gos	1	49	64	66 *	.2	.2
283 Luth—MO Synod	1	90	22	114	.3	.4
288 Mennonite USA	1	241	112	326 *	.8	1.1
419 So Bapt Conv	2	127	35	172 *	.4	.6
449 Un Methodist	3	294	150	397 *	1.0	1.4
BLAINE	**16**	**389**	**477**	**4,885 ***	**25.7**	**100.0**
019 Amer Bapt USA	1	28	15	34 *	.2	.7
053 Assemb of God	1	56	65	120	.6	2.5
056 Baha'i	0	3	NR	3	-	.1
081 Catholic	2	NR	NR	1,890	10.0	38.7
151 L-D Saints	5	NR	NR	1,760	9.3	36.0
193 Episcopal	2	NR	165	699	3.7	14.3
207 E.L.C.A.	1	0	0	0	-	-
263 Int Foursq Gos	1	13	17	17 *	.1	.3
283 Luth—MO Synod	1	29	25	45	.2	.9
355 Presb Ch (USA)	1	202	190	248 *	1.3	5.1
413 S.D.A.	1	58	NR	69	.4	1.4
BOISE	**10**	**186**	**218**	**893 ***	**13.4**	**100.0**
053 Assemb of God	2	85	111	137	2.1	15.3
056 Baha'i	0	1	NR	1	-	.1
081 Catholic	3	NR	NR	224	3.4	25.1
151 L-D Saints	2	NR	NR	350	5.2	39.2
207 E.L.C.A.	2	100	107	181	2.7	20.3
419 So Bapt Conv	1	0	0	0 *	-	-
BONNER	**43**	**3,084**	**1,733**	**8,550 ***	**23.2**	**100.0**
017 Amer Bapt Assn	1	21	NR	26 *	.1	.3
053 Assemb of God	2	176	237	288	.8	3.4
056 Baha'i	0	7	NR	7	-	.1
081 Catholic	4	NR	NR	2,359	6.4	27.6
084 Calvary Chapel	1	NR	NR	NR	-	-
097 Chr Chs&Chs Cr	1	550	NR	677 *	1.8	7.9
123 Ch God (Ander)	1	NR	30	30	.1	.4
127 Ch God (Cleve)	1	12	18	18 *	-	.2
151 L-D Saints	5	NR	NR	1,776	4.8	20.8
165 Ch of Nazarene	1	65	72	110	.3	1.3
167 Chs of Christ	3	44	74	76	.2	.9
173 Comm of Christ	1	58	NR	58	.2	.7
179 Consrv Bapt	2	NR	290	290	.8	3.4
181 Consrv Congr	1	104	150	128 *	.3	1.5
193 Episcopal	1	NR	48	69	.2	.8
203 Evan Free Ch	1	13	30	30	.1	.4
207 E.L.C.A.	3	554	238	796	2.2	9.3
221 Free Methodist	1	17	27	27	.1	.3
226 Friends-USA	1	22	NR	27 *	.1	.3
283 Luth—MO Synod	1	116	82	141	.4	1.6
355 Presb Ch (USA)	1	176	109	217 *	.6	2.5
388 Reg Bapt Gen As	2	75	105	105 *	.3	1.2
413 S.D.A.	3	628	NR	746	2.0	8.7
419 So Bapt Conv	3	155	102	191 *	.5	2.2
449 Un Methodist	2	291	121	358 *	1.0	4.2
BONNEVILLE	**147**	**6,056**	**2,912**	**63,004 ***	**76.3**	**100.0**
019 Amer Bapt USA	1	461	105	609 *	.7	1.0
053 Assemb of God	3	182	220	276	.3	.4
056 Baha'i	1	43	NR	43	.1	.1
081 Catholic	2	NR	NR	9,380	11.4	14.9
084 Calvary Chapel	1	NR	NR	NR	-	-
089 Chr & Miss Al	1	115	NR	171	.2	.3
093 Chr Ch (Disc)	1	95	60	125 *	.2	.2
097 Chr Chs&Chs Cr	1	21	NR	28 *	-	-
151 L-D Saints	114	NR	NR	44,671	54.1	70.9
165 Ch of Nazarene	1	225	148	225	.3	.4
167 Chs of Christ	1	132	145	202	.2	.3
193 Episcopal	2	NR	179	454	.6	.7
207 E.L.C.A.	1	382	263	723	.9	1.1
263 Int Foursq Gos	2	149	319	319 *	.4	.5
283 Luth—MO Synod	2	854	358	1,116	1.4	1.8
313 N Am Bapt Conf	1	43	155	57 *	.1	.1
335 Orth Pres Ch	1	0	0	0	-	-
355 Presb Ch (USA)	2	750	203	990 *	1.2	1.6
403 Salvation Army	1	40	34	245	.3	.4
413 S.D.A.	1	113	NR	134	.2	.2
419 So Bapt Conv	2	1,273	201	1,681 *	2.0	2.7
435 Unitarian-Univ	1	50	NR	66 *	.1	.1
443 Un C of Christ	1	63	28	83 *	.1	.1
449 Un Methodist	2	935	374	1,234 *	1.5	2.0
463 Vineyard	1	130	120	172 *	.2	.3
BOUNDARY	**16**	**1,820**	**919**	**3,535 ***	**35.8**	**100.0**
053 Assemb of God	1	107	182	182	1.8	5.1
056 Baha'i	0	5	NR	5	.1	.1
081 Catholic	1	NR	NR	420	4.3	11.9
143 CG in Cr(Menn)	1	284	NR	362 *	3.7	10.2
151 L-D Saints	2	NR	NR	588	6.0	16.6
165 Ch of Nazarene	1	35	61	108	1.1	3.1
167 Chs of Christ	1	55	85	75	.8	2.1
173 Comm of Christ	1	26	NR	26	.3	.7
193 Episcopal	1	NR	12	19	.2	.5
207 E.L.C.A.	1	329	169	466	4.7	13.2
221 Free Methodist	1	49	112	112	1.1	3.2
297 Mennonite;Other	1	75	NR	95 *	1.0	2.7
323 Old Ord Amish	1	60	NR	76 *	.8	2.1
413 S.D.A.	1	133	NR	158	1.6	4.5
419 So Bapt Conv	1	428	195	545 *	5.5	15.4
449 Un Methodist	1	234	103	298 *	3.0	8.4
BUTTE	**8**	**62**	**53**	**1,656 ***	**57.1**	**100.0**
019 Amer Bapt USA	1	61	45	78 *	2.7	4.7
056 Baha'i	0	1	NR	1	-	.1
081 Catholic	1	NR	NR	56	1.9	3.4
151 L-D Saints	5	NR	NR	1,507	52.0	91.0
193 Episcopal	1	NR	8	14	.5	.8
CAMAS	**1**	**4**	**0**	**18**	**1.8**	**100.0**
056 Baha'i	0	4	NR	4	.4	22.2
081 Catholic	1	NR	NR	14	1.4	77.8
CANYON	**143**	**15,120**	**11,036**	**54,480 ***	**41.4**	**100.0**
019 Amer Bapt USA	4	407	237	539 *	.4	1.0
053 Assemb of God	10	790	1,116	1,513	1.2	2.8
056 Baha'i	1	53	NR	53	-	.1
081 Catholic	4	NR	NR	14,108	10.7	25.9
084 Calvary Chapel	3	NR	NR	NR	-	-
093 Chr Ch (Disc)	2	1,031	237	1,366 *	1.0	2.5
097 Chr Chs&Chs Cr	1	400	NR	530 *	.4	1.0
123 Ch God (Ander)	1	NR	167	167	.1	.3
127 Ch God (Cleve)	2	78	72	103 *	.1	.2
145 Ch God Prophcy	4	105	NR	140 *	.1	.3
151 L-D Saints	42	NR	NR	18,536	14.1	34.0
157 Ch of Brethren	2	316	148	418 *	.3	.8

NR–Not Reported *Total adherents estimated from known number of communicant, confirmed, full members. - Represents a percentage less than 0.1. Percentages may not total 100 due to rounding.

Table 4: Religious Congregations by County and Group: 2000

Religious Group	Number of Churches, Synagogues, Mosques, or Temples	Number of Communicant, Confirmed, or Full Members	Number of Attendees	Total Adherents: Number of Adherents	Total Adherents: % of Total Pop.	Total Adherents: % of Total Adh.
165 Ch of Nazarene	11	4,403	3,903	5,883	4.5	10.8
167 Chs of Christ	5	338	380	456	.3	.8
173 Comm of Christ	1	56	NR	56	-	.1
179 Consrv Bapt	2	NR	451	451	.3	.8
193 Episcopal	2	NR	129	277	.2	.5
207 E.L.C.A.	2	448	195	630	.5	1.2
221 Free Methodist	2	517	1,060	1,060	.8	1.9
223 Free Will Bapt	1	42	NR	55 *	-	.1
226 Friends-USA	5	420	NR	556 *	.4	1.0
263 Int Foursq Gos	1	49	97	97 *	.1	.2
283 Luth—MO Synod	2	835	376	1,099	.8	2.0
288 Mennonite USA	1	106	140	140 *	.1	.3
339 Pent Ch of God	1	30	NR	40	-	.1
349 Pent Holiness	3	29	23	38 *	-	.1
355 Presb Ch (USA)	4	1,011	579	1,339 *	1.0	2.5
388 Reg Bapt Gen As	4	323	443	500 *	.4	.9
403 Salvation Army	2	178	111	288	.2	.5
413 S.D.A.	6	894	NR	1,065	.8	2.0
419 So Bapt Conv	4	845	302	1,119 *	.9	2.1
443 Un C of Christ	1	125	68	166 *	.1	.3
449 Un Methodist	5	991	553	1,312 *	1.0	2.4
463 Vineyard	1	130	120	172 *	.1	.3
469 WELS	1	170	129	208	.2	.4
CARIBOU	**20**	**251**	**174**	**5,802 ***	**79.4**	**100.0**
053 Assemb of God	1	13	16	23	.3	.4
081 Catholic	1	NR	NR	420	5.8	7.2
151 L-D Saints	14	NR	NR	5,004	68.5	86.2
263 Int Foursq Gos	1	30	50	50 *	.7	.9
283 Luth—MO Synod	1	82	30	141	1.9	2.4
355 Presb Ch (USA)	1	87	43	113 *	1.5	1.9
419 So Bapt Conv	1	39	35	51 *	.7	.9
CASSIA	**47**	**1,714**	**1,011**	**16,530 ***	**77.2**	**100.0**
053 Assemb of God	3	171	232	469	2.2	2.8
056 Baha'i	0	3	NR	3	-	-
081 Catholic	1	NR	NR	2,800	13.1	16.9
093 Chr Ch (Disc)	1	226	55	304 *	1.4	1.8
151 L-D Saints	33	NR	NR	10,920	51.0	66.1
167 Chs of Christ	1	18	19	23	.1	.1
179 Consrv Bapt	1	NR	125	125	.6	.8
193 Episcopal	1	NR	29	71	.3	.4
263 Int Foursq Gos	1	32	61	61 *	.3	.4
283 Luth—MO Synod	1	260	60	402	1.9	2.4
355 Presb Ch (USA)	1	164	100	221 *	1.0	1.3
419 So Bapt Conv	2	560	165	754 *	3.5	4.6
449 Un Methodist	1	280	165	377 *	1.8	2.3
CLARK	**3**	**50**	**19**	**351 ***	**34.3**	**100.0**
019 Amer Bapt USA	1	50	19	68 *	6.7	19.4
081 Catholic	1	NR	NR	14	1.4	4.0
151 L-D Saints	1	NR	NR	269	26.3	76.6
CLEARWATER	**23**	**1,227**	**493**	**3,114 ***	**34.9**	**100.0**
053 Assemb of God	1	34	40	50	.6	1.6
056 Baha'i	0	1	NR	1	-	-
081 Catholic	2	NR	NR	469	5.3	15.1
089 Chr & Miss Al	1	22	NR	53	.6	1.7
093 Chr Ch (Disc)	1	0	0	0 *	-	-
123 Ch God (Ander)	1	NR	80	80	.9	2.6
145 Ch God Prophcy	1	26	NR	31 *	.3	1.0
151 L-D Saints	2	NR	NR	422	4.7	13.6
165 Ch of Nazarene	1	50	34	50	.6	1.6
207 E.L.C.A.	2	123	74	222	2.5	7.1
263 Int Foursq Gos	1	10	13	13 *	.1	.4
339 Pent Ch of God	1	33	NR	67	.8	2.2
355 Presb Ch (USA)	1	7	4	8 *	.1	.3
413 S.D.A.	2	156	NR	185	2.1	5.9
419 So Bapt Conv	3	514	112	617 *	6.9	19.8
449 Un Methodist	2	251	52	301 *	3.4	9.7
467 Wesleyan	1	0	84	545	6.1	17.5
CUSTER	**10**	**76**	**61**	**1,204 ***	**27.7**	**100.0**
053 Assemb of God	1	36	34	48	1.1	4.0
056 Baha'i	0	2	NR	2	-	.2
081 Catholic	2	NR	NR	70	1.6	5.8
151 L-D Saints	4	NR	NR	872	20.1	72.4
193 Episcopal	1	NR	10	16	.4	1.3
443 Un C of Christ	1	38	17	46 *	1.1	3.8
496 Jewish Est	1	NR	NR	150	3.5	12.5
ELMORE	**31**	**2,964**	**1,702**	**10,014 ***	**34.4**	**100.0**
019 Amer Bapt USA	1	88	62	113 *	.4	1.1
053 Assemb of God	2	176	250	380	1.3	3.8
056 Baha'i	0	6	NR	6	-	.1
081 Catholic	3	NR	NR	3,431	11.8	34.3
093 Chr Ch (Disc)	1	63	17	81 *	.3	.8
097 Chr Chs&Chs Cr	1	80	NR	103 *	.4	1.0
127 Ch God (Cleve)	1	193	98	248 *	.9	2.5
151 L-D Saints	5	NR	NR	2,016	6.9	20.1
165 Ch of Nazarene	1	275	362	649	2.2	6.5
167 Chs of Christ	1	50	65	80	.3	.8
193 Episcopal	2	NR	79	246	.8	2.5
203 Evan Free Ch	1	25	19	25	.1	.2
207 E.L.C.A.	1	176	82	259	.9	2.6
283 Luth—MO Synod	1	241	94	314	1.1	3.1
297 Mennonite;Other	1	20	NR	26 *	.1	.3
339 Pent Ch of God	1	21	NR	50	.2	.5
349 Pent Holiness	1	35	45	45 *	.2	.4
355 Presb Ch (USA)	1	16	16	21 *	.1	.2
413 S.D.A.	1	69	NR	82	.3	.8
419 So Bapt Conv	3	1,126	378	1,448 *	5.0	14.5
443 Un C of Christ	1	222	111	286 *	1.0	2.9
449 Un Methodist	1	82	24	105 *	.4	1.0
FRANKLIN	**30**	**29**	**20**	**10,484 ***	**92.5**	**100.0**
081 Catholic	1	NR	NR	70	.6	.7
151 L-D Saints	28	NR	NR	10,374	91.6	99.0
355 Presb Ch (USA)	1	29	20	40 *	.4	.4
FREMONT	**32**	**538**	**276**	**10,105 ***	**85.5**	**100.0**
056 Baha'i	0	3	NR	3	-	-
081 Catholic	2	NR	NR	1,302	11.0	12.9
151 L-D Saints	25	NR	NR	8,090	68.4	80.1
167 Chs of Christ	1	30	30	39	.3	.4
263 Int Foursq Gos	1	10	14	14 *	.1	.1
283 Luth—MO Synod	1	257	95	344	2.9	3.4
355 Presb Ch (USA)	1	73	35	96 *	.8	1.0
419 So Bapt Conv	0	60	70	79 *	.7	.8
449 Un Methodist	1	105	32	138 *	1.2	1.4
GEM	**23**	**1,606**	**1,041**	**5,343 ***	**35.2**	**100.0**
019 Amer Bapt USA	1	179	90	227 *	1.5	4.2
053 Assemb of God	1	62	61	82	.5	1.5
056 Baha'i	0	7	NR	7	-	.1
081 Catholic	1	NR	NR	574	3.8	10.7
097 Chr Chs&Chs Cr	1	240	NR	305 *	2.0	5.7
127 Ch God (Cleve)	1	105	72	133 *	.9	2.5
145 Ch God Prophcy	1	26	NR	33 *	.2	.6
151 L-D Saints	6	NR	NR	2,461	16.2	46.1
165 Ch of Nazarene	1	196	139	196	1.3	3.7
167 Chs of Christ	1	40	43	52	.3	1.0
179 Consrv Bapt	1	NR	85	85	.6	1.6
193 Episcopal	1	NR	58	124	.8	2.3
263 Int Foursq Gos	1	133	255	255 *	1.7	4.8
283 Luth—MO Synod	1	220	105	307	2.0	5.7
355 Presb Ch (USA)	1	68	38	86 *	.6	1.6
413 S.D.A.	1	50	NR	60	.4	1.1
419 So Bapt Conv	1	140	20	178 *	1.2	3.3
449 Un Methodist	2	140	75	178 *	1.2	3.3
GOODING	**31**	**1,476**	**919**	**6,014 ***	**42.5**	**100.0**
019 Amer Bapt USA	1	50	30	64 *	.5	1.1

NR–Not Reported   *Total adherents estimated from known number of communicant, confirmed, full members.   - Represents a percentage less than 0.1.   Percentages may not total 100 due to rounding.

Table 4: Religious Congregations by County and Group: 2000

Religious Group	Number of Churches, Synagogues, Mosques, or Temples	Number of Communicant, Confirmed, or Full Members	Number of Attendees	Total Adherents: Number of Adherents	Total Adherents: % of Total Pop.	Total Adherents: % of Total Adh.
053 Assemb of God	1	23	31	40	.3	.7
056 Baha'i	0	4	NR	4	-	.1
081 Catholic	3	NR	NR	966	6.8	16.1
097 Chr Chs&Chs Cr	1	250	NR	321 *	2.3	5.3
151 L-D Saints	10	NR	NR	2,877	20.3	47.8
165 Ch of Nazarene	1	41	69	118	.8	2.0
167 Chs of Christ	2	68	88	100	.7	1.7
173 Comm of Christ	1	81	NR	81	.6	1.3
193 Episcopal	1	NR	15	51	.4	.8
283 Luth—MO Synod	2	71	50	92	.6	1.5
355 Presb Ch (USA)	1	165	178	212 *	1.5	3.5
371 Ref Ch in Am	1	148	210	350	2.5	5.8
419 So Bapt Conv	3	170	77	218 *	1.5	3.6
449 Un Methodist	3	405	171	520 *	3.7	8.6
IDAHO	**34**	**1,493**	**1,068**	**5,981 ***	**38.6**	**100.0**
053 Assemb of God	2	147	189	316	2.0	5.3
056 Baha'i	0	3	NR	3	-	.1
081 Catholic	6	NR	NR	2,790	18.0	46.6
089 Chr & Miss Al	1	26	NR	32	.2	.5
097 Chr Chs&Chs Cr	1	200	NR	244 *	1.6	4.1
105 Christian Ref	1	65	35	79 *	.5	1.3
127 Ch God (Cleve)	2	103	122	130 *	.8	2.2
151 L-D Saints	4	NR	NR	1,136	7.3	19.0
165 Ch of Nazarene	2	229	253	344	2.2	5.8
193 Episcopal	1	NR	20	27	.2	.5
203 Evan Free Ch	1	15	30	30	.2	.5
283 Luth—MO Synod	1	107	46	124	.8	2.1
355 Presb Ch (USA)	2	54	42	65 *	.4	1.1
413 S.D.A.	1	33	NR	39	.3	.7
419 So Bapt Conv	7	326	262	397 *	2.6	6.6
449 Un Methodist	2	185	69	225 *	1.5	3.8
JEFFERSON	**45**	**234**	**203**	**14,854 ***	**77.5**	**100.0**
019 Amer Bapt USA	1	72	45	99 *	.5	.7
056 Baha'i	0	7	NR	7	-	-
081 Catholic	2	NR	NR	154	.8	1.0
151 L-D Saints	39	NR	NR	14,375	75.0	96.8
263 Int Foursq Gos	1	50	65	69 *	.4	.5
283 Luth—MO Synod	1	57	61	84	.4	.6
355 Presb Ch (USA)	1	48	32	66 *	.3	.4
JEROME	**29**	**1,653**	**1,024**	**9,812 ***	**53.5**	**100.0**
017 Amer Bapt Assn	1	30	NR	39 *	.2	.4
019 Amer Bapt USA	1	175	104	230 *	1.3	2.3
053 Assemb of God	2	131	192	224	1.2	2.3
056 Baha'i	0	9	NR	9	-	.1
081 Catholic	1	NR	NR	3,500	19.1	35.7
093 Chr Ch (Disc)	1	100	22	131 *	.7	1.3
123 Ch God (Ander)	1	NR	69	69	.4	.7
143 CG in Cr(Menn)	1	35	NR	46 *	.3	.5
151 L-D Saints	9	NR	NR	3,887	21.2	39.6
167 Chs of Christ	2	72	84	117	.6	1.2
193 Episcopal	1	NR	13	46	.3	.5
203 Evan Free Ch	1	51	130	130	.7	1.3
223 Free Will Bapt	1	42	NR	55 *	.3	.6
283 Luth—MO Synod	2	554	185	738	4.0	7.5
355 Presb Ch (USA)	2	301	160	395 *	2.2	4.0
413 S.D.A.	2	40	NR	48	.3	.5
449 Un Methodist	1	113	65	148 *	.8	1.5
KOOTENAI	**76**	**10,467**	**8,136**	**34,786 ***	**32.0**	**100.0**
017 Amer Bapt Assn	1	28	NR	35 *	-	.1
019 Amer Bapt USA	2	154	90	194 *	.2	.6
034 Ant Orth of NA	1	86	NR	172	.2	.5
053 Assemb of God	4	1,844	2,979	4,877	4.5	14.0
056 Baha'i	1	62	NR	62	.1	.2
057 Bapt Gen Conf	1	165	180	208 *	.2	.6
081 Catholic	1	NR	NR	12,573	11.6	36.1
084 Calvary Chapel	2	NR	NR	NR	-	-
093 Chr Ch (Disc)	1	117	0	148 *	.1	.4
123 Ch God (Ander)	1	NR	37	37	-	.1
127 Ch God (Cleve)	1	27	35	35 *	-	.1
151 L-D Saints	12	NR	NR	4,808	4.4	13.8
165 Ch of Nazarene	2	354	411	419	.4	1.2
167 Chs of Christ	2	257	355	509	.5	1.5
173 Comm of Christ	1	65	NR	65	.1	.2
193 Episcopal	1	NR	191	453	.4	1.3
203 Evan Free Ch	1	100	465	465	.4	1.3
207 E.L.C.A.	4	1,473	646	1,919	1.8	5.5
221 Free Methodist	1	20	30	30	-	.1
226 Friends-USA	4	336	NR	424 *	.4	1.2
263 Int Foursq Gos	2	145	189	189 *	.2	.5
283 Luth—MO Synod	4	1,523	575	2,277	2.1	6.5
297 Mennonite;Other	1	33	NR	42 *	-	.1
339 Pent Ch of God	1	13	NR	50	-	.1
355 Presb Ch (USA)	4	660	506	832 *	.8	2.4
356 Presb Ch Amer	1	26	47	47	-	.1
413 S.D.A.	5	927	NR	1,103	1.0	3.2
419 So Bapt Conv	7	970	845	1,224 *	1.1	3.5
435 Unitarian-Univ	1	50	NR	63 *	.1	.2
449 Un Methodist	3	997	440	1,259 *	1.2	3.6
463 Vineyard	1	35	49	49 *	-	.1
467 Wesleyan	2	0	66	218	.2	.6
LATAH	**46**	**3,984**	**2,658**	**10,942 ***	**31.3**	**100.0**
019 Amer Bapt USA	1	78	62	92 *	.3	.8
053 Assemb of God	2	125	158	168	.5	1.5
056 Baha'i	1	49	NR	49	.1	.4
081 Catholic	2	NR	NR	2,730	7.8	24.9
093 Chr Ch (Disc)	1	123	55	146 *	.4	1.3
123 Ch God (Ander)	1	NR	14	14	-	.1
151 L-D Saints	10	NR	NR	2,612	7.5	23.9
165 Ch of Nazarene	4	684	892	1,183	3.4	10.8
167 Chs of Christ	1	15	18	25	.1	.2
193 Episcopal	1	NR	72	168	.5	1.5
207 E.L.C.A.	7	970	503	1,230	3.5	11.2
263 Int Foursq Gos	1	30	50	50 *	.1	.5
267 Muslim Est	1	NR	55	163	.5	1.5
355 Presb Ch (USA)	3	453	273	536 *	1.5	4.9
388 Reg Bapt Gen As	1	80	85	95 *	.3	.9
413 S.D.A.	4	372	NR	442	1.3	4.0
419 So Bapt Conv	1	388	190	459 *	1.3	4.2
435 Unitarian-Univ	1	153	NR	181 *	.5	1.7
449 Un Methodist	3	464	231	549 *	1.6	5.0
496 Jewish Est	0	NR	NR	50	.1	.5
LEMHI	**17**	**841**	**674**	**3,470 ***	**44.5**	**100.0**
053 Assemb of God	1	34	42	42	.5	1.2
056 Baha'i	0	2	NR	2	-	.1
081 Catholic	2	NR	NR	577	7.4	16.6
151 L-D Saints	5	NR	NR	1,615	20.7	46.5
167 Chs of Christ	1	27	38	35	.4	1.0
193 Episcopal	1	NR	36	82	1.1	2.4
263 Int Foursq Gos	1	80	226	226 *	2.9	6.5
283 Luth—MO Synod	1	156	90	228	2.9	6.6
355 Presb Ch (USA)	1	30	20	37 *	.5	1.1
413 S.D.A.	1	96	NR	114	1.5	3.3
419 So Bapt Conv	1	264	155	325 *	4.2	9.4
449 Un Methodist	2	152	67	187 *	2.4	5.4
LEWIS	**19**	**886**	**422**	**1,909 ***	**50.9**	**100.0**
053 Assemb of God	2	83	94	167	4.5	8.7
056 Baha'i	0	2	NR	2	.1	.1
081 Catholic	2	NR	NR	592	15.8	31.0
093 Chr Ch (Disc)	1	52	25	64 *	1.7	3.4
097 Chr Chs&Chs Cr	1	75	NR	92 *	2.5	4.8
157 Ch of Brethren	1	8	0	10 *	.3	.5
167 Chs of Christ	1	20	22	25	.7	1.3
207 E.L.C.A.	2	176	66	199	5.3	10.4
339 Pent Ch of God	1	52	NR	247	6.6	12.9
355 Presb Ch (USA)	5	191	137	235 *	6.3	12.3
413 S.D.A.	1	85	NR	101	2.7	5.3
419 So Bapt Conv	1	104	65	128 *	3.4	6.7
449 Un Methodist	1	38	13	47 *	1.3	2.5

NR–Not Reported *Total adherents estimated from known number of communicant, confirmed, full members. - Represents a percentage less than 0.1. Percentages may not total 100 due to rounding.

Table 4: Religious Congregations by County and Group: 2000

Religious Group	Number of Churches, Synagogues, Mosques, or Temples	Number of Communicant, Confirmed, or Full Members	Number of Attendees	Total Adherents		
				Number of Adherents	% of Total Pop.	% of Total Adh.
LINCOLN	**10**	**233**	**164**	**1,687 ***	**41.7**	**100.0**
019 Amer Bapt USA	1	90	30	117 *	2.9	6.9
053 Assemb of God	2	58	82	104	2.6	6.2
056 Baha'i	0	1	NR	1	-	.1
081 Catholic	1	NR	NR	210	5.2	12.4
151 L-D Saints	3	NR	NR	1,107	27.4	65.6
193 Episcopal	1	NR	17	39	1.0	2.3
449 Un Methodist	2	84	35	109 *	2.7	6.5
MADISON	**80**	**73**	**64**	**22,021 ***	**80.2**	**100.0**
053 Assemb of God	1	7	10	10	-	-
056 Baha'i	0	2	NR	2	-	-
081 Catholic	1	NR	NR	154	.6	.7
151 L-D Saints	76	NR	NR	21,775	79.3	98.9
263 Int Foursq Gos	1	22	28	28 *	.1	.1
355 Presb Ch (USA)	1	42	26	52 *	.2	.2
MINIDOKA	**36**	**2,155**	**890**	**14,129 ***	**70.0**	**100.0**
053 Assemb of God	2	72	90	172	.9	1.2
056 Baha'i	0	3	NR	3	-	-
081 Catholic	1	NR	NR	4,200	20.8	29.7
097 Chr Chs&Chs Cr	2	677	NR	887 *	4.4	6.3
127 Ch God (Cleve)	1	15	0	20 *	.1	.1
151 L-D Saints	19	NR	NR	6,983	34.6	49.4
165 Ch of Nazarene	1	24	21	37	.2	.3
167 Chs of Christ	1	75	80	97	.5	.7
181 Consrv Congr	1	146	160	191 *	.9	1.4
193 Episcopal	1	NR	28	86	.4	.6
223 Free Will Bapt	1	42	NR	54 *	.3	.4
283 Luth—MO Synod	1	305	150	376	1.9	2.7
313 N Am Bapt Conf	1	208	150	272 *	1.3	1.9
413 S.D.A.	1	150	NR	178	.9	1.3
419 So Bapt Conv	1	20	25	26 *	.1	.2
449 Un Methodist	2	418	186	547 *	2.7	3.9
NEZ PERCE	**45**	**4,560**	**4,059**	**14,610 ***	**39.1**	**100.0**
017 Amer Bapt Assn	1	30	NR	37 *	.1	.3
019 Amer Bapt USA	1	71	65	87 *	.2	.6
053 Assemb of God	3	399	438	1,439	3.8	9.8
056 Baha'i	3	91	NR	91	.2	.6
081 Catholic	4	NR	NR	4,656	12.4	31.9
084 Calvary Chapel	1	NR	NR	NR	-	-
089 Chr & Miss Al	1	110	NR	252	.7	1.7
097 Chr Chs&Chs Cr	1	117	NR	143 *	.4	1.0
123 Ch God (Ander)	1	NR	16	16	-	.1
151 L-D Saints	4	NR	NR	1,714	4.6	11.7
165 Ch of Nazarene	2	556	494	708	1.9	4.8
167 Chs of Christ	1	130	126	145	.4	1.0
193 Episcopal	1	NR	52	332	.9	2.3
207 E.L.C.A.	4	944	391	1,184	3.2	8.1
263 Int Foursq Gos	1	15	19	19 *	.1	.1
283 Luth—MO Synod	1	72	40	84	.2	.6
355 Presb Ch (USA)	3	467	372	569 *	1.5	3.9
370 Ref Baptist Chs	1	NR	NR	NR	-	-
388 Reg Bapt Gen As	1	124	200	200 *	.5	1.4
403 Salvation Army	1	54	29	108	.3	.7
413 S.D.A.	1	260	NR	309	.8	2.1
419 So Bapt Conv	2	437	233	533 *	1.4	3.6
443 Un C of Christ	1	59	339	72 *	.2	.5
449 Un Methodist	3	624	195	762 *	2.0	5.2
496 Jewish Est	0	NR	NR	50	.1	.3
498 Indep.Charis.	1	0	450	500	1.3	3.4
499 Indep.Non-Char	1	0	600	600	1.6	4.1
ONEIDA	**11**	**57**	**32**	**3,256 ***	**78.9**	**100.0**
081 Catholic	1	NR	NR	14	.3	.4
151 L-D Saints	9	NR	NR	3,168	76.8	97.3
355 Presb Ch (USA)	1	16	15	21 *	.5	.6
419 So Bapt Conv	0	41	17	53 *	1.3	1.6

Religious Group	Number of Churches, Synagogues, Mosques, or Temples	Number of Communicant, Confirmed, or Full Members	Number of Attendees	Total Adherents		
				Number of Adherents	% of Total Pop.	% of Total Adh.
OWYHEE	**26**	**754**	**517**	**3,204 ***	**30.1**	**100.0**
017 Amer Bapt Assn	2	60	NR	80 *	.8	2.5
053 Assemb of God	2	71	82	90	.8	2.8
056 Baha'i	0	1	NR	1	-	-
081 Catholic	6	NR	NR	791	7.4	24.7
093 Chr Ch (Disc)	1	51	24	67 *	.6	2.1
123 Ch God (Ander)	1	NR	60	60	.6	1.9
143 CG in Cr(Menn)	1	44	NR	58 *	.5	1.8
151 L-D Saints	4	NR	NR	1,340	12.6	41.8
165 Ch of Nazarene	2	195	182	264	2.5	8.2
167 Chs of Christ	1	20	30	30	.3	.9
203 Evan Free Ch	1	25	55	55	.5	1.7
226 Friends-USA	2	168	NR	222 *	2.1	6.9
283 Luth—MO Synod	1	43	30	45	.4	1.4
355 Presb Ch (USA)	1	61	43	81 *	.8	2.5
419 So Bapt Conv	1	15	11	20 *	.2	.6
PAYETTE	**35**	**2,524**	**1,631**	**8,562 ***	**41.6**	**100.0**
019 Amer Bapt USA	2	505	215	658 *	3.2	7.7
053 Assemb of God	3	299	370	487	2.4	5.7
056 Baha'i	0	4	NR	4	-	-
081 Catholic	2	NR	NR	2,100	10.2	24.5
097 Chr Chs&Chs Cr	1	140	NR	182 *	.9	2.1
143 CG in Cr(Menn)	1	51	NR	66 *	.3	.8
151 L-D Saints	7	NR	NR	2,797	13.6	32.7
157 Ch of Brethren	1	170	0	222 *	1.1	2.6
165 Ch of Nazarene	2	198	189	340	1.7	4.0
167 Chs of Christ	2	95	105	121	.6	1.4
173 Comm of Christ	1	79	NR	79	.4	.9
179 Consrv Bapt	1	NR	80	80	.4	.9
193 Episcopal	1	NR	27	58	.3	.7
221 Free Methodist	1	125	309	309	1.5	3.6
263 Int Foursq Gos	1	39	51	51 *	.2	.6
283 Luth—MO Synod	1	77	50	84	.4	1.0
413 S.D.A.	3	374	NR	445	2.2	5.2
419 So Bapt Conv	1	47	42	61 *	.3	.7
443 Un C of Christ	2	93	74	121 *	.6	1.4
449 Un Methodist	2	228	119	297 *	1.4	3.5
POWER	**16**	**771**	**520**	**5,081 ***	**67.4**	**100.0**
053 Assemb of God	2	131	157	336	4.5	6.6
056 Baha'i	0	13	NR	13	.2	.3
081 Catholic	1	NR	NR	1,470	19.5	28.9
151 L-D Saints	6	NR	NR	2,394	31.8	47.1
181 Consrv Congr	1	24	25	32 *	.4	.6
193 Episcopal	1	NR	11	7	.1	.1
207 E.L.C.A.	1	407	161	567	7.5	11.2
349 Pent Holiness	1	15	35	20 *	.3	.4
419 So Bapt Conv	1	57	32	76 *	1.0	1.5
443 Un C of Christ	1	67	56	90 *	1.2	1.8
449 Un Methodist	1	57	43	76 *	1.0	1.5
SHOSHONE	**26**	**1,572**	**838**	**4,656 ***	**33.8**	**100.0**
019 Amer Bapt USA	1	46	35	56 *	.4	1.2
053 Assemb of God	3	81	105	164	1.2	3.5
056 Baha'i	0	1	NR	1	-	-
081 Catholic	3	NR	NR	1,739	12.6	37.3
127 Ch God (Cleve)	1	33	29	40 *	.3	.9
151 L-D Saints	3	NR	NR	668	4.9	14.3
165 Ch of Nazarene	1	45	37	58	.4	1.2
167 Chs of Christ	1	60	48	70	.5	1.5
181 Consrv Congr	1	326	87	394 *	2.9	8.5
193 Episcopal	2	NR	52	55	.4	1.2
203 Evan Free Ch	1	15	35	35	.3	.8
207 E.L.C.A.	2	440	169	646	4.7	13.9
283 Luth—MO Synod	2	115	73	0	-	-
339 Pent Ch of God	1	63	NR	313	2.3	6.7
413 S.D.A.	1	85	NR	101	.7	2.2
419 So Bapt Conv	1	145	108	175 *	1.3	3.8
443 Un C of Christ	1	84	35	101 *	.7	2.2
449 Un Methodist	1	33	25	40 *	.3	.9

NR–Not Reported *Total adherents estimated from known number of communicant, confirmed, full members. - Represents a percentage less than 0.1. Percentages may not total 100 due to rounding.

Table 4: Religious Congregations by County and Group: 2000

Religious Group	Number of Churches, Synagogues, Mosques, or Temples	Number of Communicant, Confirmed, or Full Members	Number of Attendees	Total Adherents: Number of Adherents	Total Adherents: % of Total Pop.	Total Adherents: % of Total Adh.
TETON	**11**	**46**	**119**	**3,092 ***	**51.5**	**100.0**
056 Baha'i	0	1	NR	1	-	-
081 Catholic	1	NR	NR	84	1.4	2.7
151 L-D Saints	7	NR	NR	2,858	47.6	92.4
193 Episcopal	1	NR	80	52	.9	1.7
201 Evan Cov Ch	1	44	0	58 *	1.0	1.9
263 Int Foursq Gos	1	1	39	39 *	.7	1.3
TWIN FALLS	**98**	**9,557**	**5,662**	**31,998 ***	**49.8**	**100.0**
019 Amer Bapt USA	5	977	442	1,237 *	1.9	3.9
053 Assemb of God	6	425	514	1,015	1.6	3.2
056 Baha'i	0	22	NR	22	-	.1
081 Catholic	3	NR	NR	5,740	8.9	17.9
084 Calvary Chapel	1	NR	NR	NR	-	-
089 Chr & Miss Al	2	12	NR	20	-	.1
093 Chr Ch (Disc)	1	133	39	168 *	.3	.5
097 Chr Chs&Chs Cr	4	709	NR	898 *	1.4	2.8
143 CG in Cr(Menn)	2	229	NR	290 *	.5	.9
151 L-D Saints	30	NR	NR	12,603	19.6	39.4
157 Ch of Brethren	1	18	15	23 *	-	.1
165 Ch of Nazarene	4	888	801	983	1.5	3.1
167 Chs of Christ	3	202	203	255	.4	.8
173 Comm of Christ	2	158	NR	158	.2	.5
179 Consrv Bapt	1	NR	90	90	.1	.3
193 Episcopal	1	NR	148	523	.8	1.6
207 E.L.C.A.	1	225	118	293	.5	.9
223 Free Will Bapt	2	83	NR	105 *	.2	.3
263 Int Foursq Gos	1	130	152	165 *	.3	.5
283 Luth—MO Synod	5	1,388	634	1,871	2.9	5.8
288 Mennonite USA	1	81	60	103 *	.2	.3
291 Missionary Ch	1	43	35	43	.1	.1
339 Pent Ch of God	1	10	NR	17	-	.1
349 Pent Holiness	1	32	40	41 *	.1	.1
355 Presb Ch (USA)	3	472	196	598 *	.9	1.9
371 Ref Ch in Am	1	732	840	1,329	2.1	4.2
388 Reg Bapt Gen As	1	94	106	119 *	.2	.4
403 Salvation Army	1	62	30	191	.3	.6
413 S.D.A.	2	278	NR	330	.5	1.0
419 So Bapt Conv	3	360	139	456 *	.7	1.4
435 Unitarian-Univ	1	38	NR	48 *	.1	.2
449 Un Methodist	6	1,156	460	1,464 *	2.3	4.6
498 Indep.Charis.	1	600	600	800	1.2	2.5
VALLEY	**16**	**670**	**608**	**2,108 ***	**27.6**	**100.0**
053 Assemb of God	2	135	105	150	2.0	7.1
056 Baha'i	0	9	NR	9	.1	.4
081 Catholic	2	NR	NR	420	5.5	19.9
084 Calvary Chapel	1	NR	NR	NR	-	-
151 L-D Saints	2	NR	NR	713	9.3	33.8
165 Ch of Nazarene	1	105	116	135	1.8	6.4
167 Chs of Christ	1	20	20	37	.5	1.8
179 Consrv Bapt	1	NR	100	100	1.3	4.7
193 Episcopal	1	NR	31	114	1.5	5.4
283 Luth—MO Synod	2	124	112	100	1.3	4.7
413 S.D.A.	1	81	NR	96	1.3	4.6
419 So Bapt Conv	1	63	40	75 *	1.0	3.6
443 Un C of Christ	1	133	84	159 *	2.1	7.5
WASHINGTON	**25**	**1,200**	**864**	**4,950 ***	**49.6**	**100.0**
019 Amer Bapt USA	3	302	123	381 *	3.8	7.7
053 Assemb of God	2	99	122	167	1.7	3.4
056 Baha'i	0	1	NR	1	-	-
081 Catholic	2	NR	NR	1,680	16.8	33.9
097 Chr Chs&Chs Cr	1	175	NR	221 *	2.2	4.5
151 L-D Saints	4	NR	NR	1,303	13.1	26.3
165 Ch of Nazarene	1	121	121	203	2.0	4.1
167 Chs of Christ	2	65	75	80	.8	1.6
179 Consrv Bapt	1	NR	75	75	.8	1.5
193 Episcopal	1	NR	35	69	.7	1.4
263 Int Foursq Gos	1	3	239	239 *	2.4	4.8
283 Luth—MO Synod	1	29	19	32	.3	.6
339 Pent Ch of God	1	2	NR	10	.1	.2

Religious Group	Number of Churches, Synagogues, Mosques, or Temples	Number of Communicant, Confirmed, or Full Members	Number of Attendees	Total Adherents: Number of Adherents	Total Adherents: % of Total Pop.	Total Adherents: % of Total Adh.
355 Presb Ch (USA)	1	74	55	93 *	.9	1.9
413 S.D.A.	3	269	NR	320	3.2	6.5
419 So Bapt Conv	1	60	0	76 *	.8	1.5

ILLINOIS

Religious Group	Number of Churches, Synagogues, Mosques, or Temples	Number of Communicant, Confirmed, or Full Members	Number of Attendees	Total Adherents: Number of Adherents	Total Adherents: % of Total Pop.	Total Adherents: % of Total Adh.
The State.....	10,140	1,806,932	925,592	6,867,625 *	55.3	100.0
ADAMS	**95**	**18,149**	**7,541**	**40,667 ***	**59.6**	**100.0**
019 Amer Bapt USA	5	1,087	632	1,341 *	2.0	3.3
053 Assemb of God	3	534	668	805	1.2	2.0
056 Baha'i	0	27	NR	27	-	.1
057 Bapt Gen Conf	1	35	35	43 *	.1	.1
061 Beachy Amish	1	82	NR	101 *	.1	.2
081 Catholic	11	NR	NR	15,933	23.3	39.2
093 Chr Ch (Disc)	3	967	179	1,193 *	1.7	2.9
097 Chr Chs&Chs Cr	10	2,683	NR	3,313 *	4.9	8.1
151 L-D Saints	1	NR	NR	509	.7	1.3
157 Ch of Brethren	1	50	0	62 *	.1	.2
165 Ch of Nazarene	1	75	47	125	.2	.3
167 Chs of Christ	2	99	97	136	.2	.3
173 Comm of Christ	1	31	NR	31	-	.1
175 Congr Chr Chs	1	300	95	370 *	.5	.9
193 Episcopal	1	NR	86	219	.3	.5
203 Evan Free Ch	1	50	50	50	.1	.1
207 E.L.C.A.	8	1,865	865	2,424	3.6	6.0
283 Luth—MO Synod	5	2,151	1,112	2,912	4.3	7.2
355 Presb Ch (USA)	4	566	339	698 *	1.0	1.7
388 Reg Bapt Gen As	3	668	485	786 *	1.2	1.9
403 Salvation Army	1	253	162	1,385	2.0	3.4
413 S.D.A.	1	74	NR	88	.1	.2
419 So Bapt Conv	3	567	165	700 *	1.0	1.7
435 Unitarian-Univ	1	82	NR	101 *	.1	.2
443 Un C of Christ	7	2,599	917	3,208 *	4.7	7.9
449 Un Methodist	16	3,004	1,507	3,707 *	5.4	9.1
496 Jewish Est	2	NR	NR	100	.1	.2
498 Indep.Charis.	1	300	100	300	.4	.7
ALEXANDER	**25**	**2,549**	**825**	**3,561 ***	**37.1**	**100.0**
019 Amer Bapt USA	1	275	170	342 *	3.6	9.6
053 Assemb of God	2	73	84	145	1.5	4.1
056 Baha'i	0	39	NR	39	.4	1.1
081 Catholic	1	NR	NR	324	3.4	9.1
093 Chr Ch (Disc)	1	38	0	47 *	.5	1.3
097 Chr Chs&Chs Cr	1	87	NR	108 *	1.1	3.0
167 Chs of Christ	1	23	23	30	.3	.8
193 Episcopal	1	NR	12	20	.2	.6
207 E.L.C.A.	1	37	30	50	.5	1.4
223 Free Will Bapt	1	86	NR	107 *	1.1	3.0
355 Presb Ch (USA)	1	33	20	41 *	.4	1.2
413 S.D.A.	1	12	NR	14	.1	.4
419 So Bapt Conv	9	1,654	326	2,055 *	21.4	57.7
449 Un Methodist	4	192	160	239 *	2.5	6.7
BOND	**48**	**5,277**	**2,178**	**7,999 ***	**45.4**	**100.0**
019 Amer Bapt USA	1	252	112	302 *	1.7	3.8
053 Assemb of God	3	108	141	206	1.2	2.6
056 Baha'i	0	5	NR	5	-	.1
081 Catholic	3	NR	NR	1,453	8.2	18.2
097 Chr Chs&Chs Cr	5	1,561	NR	1,871 *	10.6	23.4
157 Ch of Brethren	1	14	15	17 *	.1	.2
167 Chs of Christ	1	88	80	95	.5	1.2
185 Cumber Presb	2	35	NR	58	.3	.7
193 Episcopal	1	NR	4	10	.1	.1
221 Free Methodist	3	414	627	627	3.6	7.8
283 Luth—MO Synod	1	150	90	176	1.0	2.2
339 Pent Ch of God	1	4	NR	9	.1	.1
355 Presb Ch (USA)	3	280	139	335 *	1.9	4.2
360 Prim Bapt Chrch	1	NR	NR	NR	-	-
413 S.D.A.	1	12	NR	14	.1	.2
419 So Bapt Conv	12	1,473	497	1,765 *	10.0	22.1
443 Un C of Christ	2	124	51	149 *	.8	1.9

NR–Not Reported   *Total adherents estimated from known number of communicant, confirmed, full members.   - Represents a percentage less than 0.1.   Percentages may not total 100 due to rounding.

Table 4: Religious Congregations by County and Group: 2000

Religious Group	Number of Churches, Synagogues, Mosques, or Temples	Number of Communicant, Confirmed, or Full Members	Number of Attendees	Total Adherents: Number of Adherents	Total Adherents: % of Total Pop.	Total Adherents: % of Total Adh.
449 Un Methodist	7	757	422	907 *	5.1	11.3
BOONE	**28**	**6,816**	**3,271**	**17,598 ***	**42.1**	**100.0**
019 Amer Bapt USA	1	314	117	409 *	1.0	2.3
040 Ap Chr Ch-Amer	1	29	78	78 *	.2	.4
053 Assemb of God	1	125	110	120	.3	.7
056 Baha'i	0	6	NR	6	-	-
076 Buddhism	1	NR	NR	NR	-	-
081 Catholic	1	NR	NR	7,970	19.1	45.3
165 Ch of Nazarene	1	0	0	0	-	-
167 Chs of Christ	1	145	150	200	.5	1.1
175 Congr Chr Chs	1	50	40	65 *	.2	.4
193 Episcopal	1	NR	67	257	.6	1.5
201 Evan Cov Ch	1	141	158	184 *	.4	1.0
203 Evan Free Ch	1	69	125	125	.3	.7
207 E.L.C.A.	2	782	302	1,119	2.7	6.4
283 Luth—MO Synod	1	1,669	783	2,515	6.0	14.3
306 NT IndBapt&Rltd	1	225	NR	293 *	.7	1.7
355 Presb Ch (USA)	2	761	308	991 *	2.4	5.6
403 Salvation Army	1	59	42	85	.2	.5
419 So Bapt Conv	2	153	145	199 *	.5	1.1
443 Un C of Christ	2	541	238	705 *	1.7	4.0
449 Un Methodist	5	1,661	559	2,163 *	5.2	12.3
469 WELS	1	86	49	114	.3	.6
BROWN	**13**	**1,543**	**395**	**2,615 ***	**37.6**	**100.0**
019 Amer Bapt USA	2	544	188	626 *	9.0	23.9
056 Baha'i	0	4	NR	4	.1	.2
081 Catholic	1	NR	NR	830	11.9	31.7
093 Chr Ch (Disc)	2	259	0	298 *	4.3	11.4
097 Chr Chs&Chs Cr	3	300	NR	346 *	5.0	13.2
165 Ch of Nazarene	1	66	30	75	1.1	2.9
283 Luth—MO Synod	1	60	27	79	1.1	3.0
355 Presb Ch (USA)	1	59	40	68 *	1.0	2.6
360 Prim Bapt Chrch	1	NR	NR	NR	-	-
449 Un Methodist	1	251	110	289 *	4.2	11.1
BUREAU	**70**	**8,665**	**3,804**	**19,019 ***	**53.6**	**100.0**
019 Amer Bapt USA	5	737	421	903 *	2.5	4.7
034 Ant Orth of NA	1	84	NR	168	.5	.9
053 Assemb of God	2	89	83	96	.3	.5
056 Baha'i	0	2	NR	2	-	-
078 Bulgar Orth USA	1	NR	NR	360	1.0	1.9
081 Catholic	15	NR	NR	7,443	21.0	39.1
089 Chr & Miss Al	1	0	NR	85	.2	.4
093 Chr Ch (Disc)	3	636	226	779 *	2.2	4.1
165 Ch of Nazarene	1	55	69	73	.2	.4
167 Chs of Christ	1	18	20	24	.1	.1
171 Ch God-Gen Con	1	233	140	285 *	.8	1.5
175 Congr Chr Chs	2	97	105	119 *	.3	.6
193 Episcopal	1	NR	25	52	.1	.3
201 Evan Cov Ch	1	338	271	414 *	1.2	2.2
207 E.L.C.A.	6	2,267	792	2,986	8.4	15.7
263 Int Foursq Gos	1	55	72	72 *	.2	.4
283 Luth—MO Synod	1	114	60	136	.4	.7
288 Mennonite USA	2	107	127	136 *	.4	.7
291 Missionary Ch	1	58	85	85	.2	.4
355 Presb Ch (USA)	2	190	102	233 *	.7	1.2
413 S.D.A.	1	14	NR	17	-	.1
419 So Bapt Conv	1	159	45	195 *	.5	1.0
443 Un C of Christ	6	853	301	1,045 *	2.9	5.5
449 Un Methodist	13	2,487	796	3,046 *	8.6	16.0
467 Wesleyan	1	72	64	265	.7	1.4
CALHOUN	**23**	**969**	**438**	**3,296 ***	**64.8**	**100.0**
059 Bapt Miss Assn	1	2	11	11 *	.2	.3
081 Catholic	7	NR	NR	2,083	41.0	63.2
165 Ch of Nazarene	1	31	15	57	1.1	1.7
167 Chs of Christ	4	143	158	182	3.6	5.5
207 E.L.C.A.	1	53	10	59	1.2	1.8
283 Luth—MO Synod	3	306	136	383	7.5	11.6
306 NT IndBapt&Rltd	1	225	NR	271 *	5.3	8.2
355 Presb Ch (USA)	2	153	76	184 *	3.6	5.6
419 So Bapt Conv	1	32	16	38 *	.7	1.2
449 Un Methodist	2	24	16	28 *	.6	.8
CARROLL	**41**	**6,085**	**2,495**	**9,944 ***	**59.6**	**100.0**
019 Amer Bapt USA	2	172	81	210 *	1.3	2.1
053 Assemb of God	1	21	25	25	.1	.3
056 Baha'i	0	5	NR	5	-	.1
071 Brethren (Ash)	2	361	237	440 *	2.6	4.4
081 Catholic	3	NR	NR	2,465	14.8	24.8
157 Ch of Brethren	3	452	241	552 *	3.3	5.6
171 Ch God-Gen Con	3	415	301	506 *	3.0	5.1
175 Congr Chr Chs	1	99	49	121 *	.7	1.2
193 Episcopal	1	NR	5	14	.1	.1
203 Evan Free Ch	1	45	47	47	.3	.5
207 E.L.C.A.	4	1,089	333	1,383	8.3	13.9
306 NT IndBapt&Rltd	1	225	NR	274 *	1.6	2.8
355 Presb Ch (USA)	2	224	114	273 *	1.6	2.7
360 Prim Bapt Chrch	1	NR	NR	NR	-	-
371 Ref Ch in Am	1	40	35	62	.4	.6
413 S.D.A.	1	28	NR	33	.2	.3
419 So Bapt Conv	1	39	40	48 *	.3	.5
443 Un C of Christ	1	237	57	289 *	1.7	2.9
449 Un Methodist	10	2,357	786	2,873 *	17.2	28.9
469 WELS	2	276	144	324	1.9	3.3
CASS	**37**	**5,476**	**1,792**	**10,858 ***	**79.3**	**100.0**
019 Amer Bapt USA	1	263	85	325 *	2.4	3.0
053 Assemb of God	1	52	59	156	1.1	1.4
056 Baha'i	0	1	NR	1	-	-
081 Catholic	4	NR	NR	3,784	27.6	34.8
093 Chr Ch (Disc)	2	116	47	143 *	1.0	1.3
097 Chr Chs&Chs Cr	3	565	NR	699 *	5.1	6.4
123 Ch God (Ander)	1	NR	20	20	.1	.2
165 Ch of Nazarene	2	213	226	301	2.2	2.8
173 Comm of Christ	1	122	NR	122	.9	1.1
185 Cumber Presb	1	41	NR	107	.8	1.0
207 E.L.C.A.	4	952	284	1,186	8.7	10.9
283 Luth—MO Synod	4	950	368	1,291	9.4	11.9
306 NT IndBapt&Rltd	1	225	NR	278 *	2.0	2.6
355 Presb Ch (USA)	2	159	95	196 *	1.4	1.8
419 So Bapt Conv	3	552	131	683 *	5.0	6.3
443 Un C of Christ	1	70	25	87 *	.6	.8
449 Un Methodist	6	1,195	452	1,479 *	10.8	13.6
CHAMPAIGN	**173**	**38,042**	**21,373**	**75,149 ***	**41.8**	**100.0**
019 Amer Bapt USA	5	1,367	706	1,636 *	.9	2.2
034 Ant Orth of NA	1	23	NR	46	-	.1
040 Ap Chr Ch-Amer	1	58	130	130 *	.1	.2
053 Assemb of God	5	933	1,268	4,075	2.3	5.4
056 Baha'i	2	144	NR	144	.1	.2
081 Catholic	18	NR	NR	19,503	10.9	26.0
084 Calvary Chapel	1	NR	NR	NR	-	-
089 Chr & Miss Al	1	48	NR	110	.1	.1
093 Chr Ch (Disc)	4	1,091	86	1,305 *	.7	1.7
097 Chr Chs&Chs Cr	11	3,173	NR	3,795 *	2.1	5.0
105 Christian Ref	1	101	60	121 *	.1	.2
123 Ch God (Ander)	1	NR	18	18	-	-
127 Ch God (Cleve)	1	379	143	454 *	.3	.6
151 L-D Saints	4	NR	NR	978	.5	1.3
157 Ch of Brethren	1	62	24	74 *	-	.1
165 Ch of Nazarene	6	503	467	892	.5	1.2
167 Chs of Christ	5	342	387	477	.3	.6
179 Consrv Bapt	1	NR	650	650	.4	.9
193 Episcopal	3	NR	539	970	.5	1.3
203 Evan Free Ch	2	80	270	270	.2	.4
207 E.L.C.A.	11	6,075	2,540	7,906	4.4	10.5
213 Evan Menn Inc	1	84	97	101 *	.1	.1
221 Free Methodist	2	192	209	251	.1	.3
226 Friends-USA	1	55	NR	66 *	-	.1
246 Greek Orthodox	1	NR	NR	282	.2	.4
252 Hindu	1	NR	NR	NR	-	-
263 Int Foursq Gos	2	192	370	370 *	.2	.5

NR–Not Reported   *Total adherents estimated from known number of communicant, confirmed, full members.   - Represents a percentage less than 0.1.   Percentages may not total 100 due to rounding.

Table 4: Religious Congregations by County and Group: 2000

Religious Group	Number of Churches, Synagogues, Mosques, or Temples	Number of Communicant, Confirmed, or Full Members	Number of Attendees	Total Adherents: Number of Adherents	Total Adherents: % of Total Pop.	Total Adherents: % of Total Adh.
264 Int Chs of Crst	1	195	221	274	.2	.4
267 Muslim Est	2	NR	116	338	.2	.4
283 Luth—MO Synod	8	2,581	1,586	3,383	1.9	4.5
288 Mennonite USA	2	420	289	503 *	.3	.7
306 NT IndBapt&Rltd	3	674	NR	806 *	.4	1.1
355 Presb Ch (USA)	9	2,830	1,643	3,510 *	2.0	4.7
356 Presb Ch Amer	1	580	550	630	.4	.8
360 Prim Bapt Chrch	1	NR	NR	NR	-	-
388 Reg Bapt Gen As	1	60	85	85 *	-	.1
403 Salvation Army	1	191	297	316	.2	.4
413 S.D.A.	2	138	NR	165	.1	.2
419 So Bapt Conv	6	1,230	564	1,472 *	.8	2.0
425 Tao	1	NR	NR	NR	-	-
435 Unitarian-Univ	1	250	NR	299 *	.2	.4
443 Un C of Christ	3	1,030	351	1,232 *	.7	1.6
449 Un Methodist	31	7,351	3,645	8,796 *	4.9	11.7
463 Vineyard	1	2,300	1,100	2,752 *	1.5	3.7
467 Wesleyan	1	69	83	232	.1	.3
469 WELS	1	43	29	52	-	.1
496 Jewish Est	1	NR	NR	1,400	.8	1.9
498 Indep.Charis.	1	2,000	1,400	2,000	1.1	2.7
499 Indep.Non-Char	2	1,198	1,450	2,280	1.3	3.0
CHRISTIAN	**66**	**10,709**	**4,022**	**19,048 ***	**53.9**	**100.0**
019 Amer Bapt USA	4	825	218	1,012 *	2.9	5.3
053 Assemb of God	3	226	202	306	.9	1.6
056 Baha'i	0	4	NR	4	-	-
081 Catholic	6	NR	NR	5,850	16.5	30.7
093 Chr Ch (Disc)	2	777	147	953 *	2.7	5.0
097 Chr Chs&Chs Cr	6	1,445	NR	1,771 *	5.0	9.3
127 Ch God (Cleve)	1	222	76	272 *	.8	1.4
165 Ch of Nazarene	4	324	291	473	1.3	2.5
167 Chs of Christ	2	68	66	87	.2	.5
171 Ch God-Gen Con	1	133	93	163 *	.5	.9
173 Comm of Christ	2	142	NR	142	.4	.7
203 Evan Free Ch	1	110	160	160	.5	.8
221 Free Methodist	2	64	78	78	.2	.4
283 Luth—MO Synod	4	1,105	400	1,452	4.1	7.6
306 NT IndBapt&Rltd	2	449	NR	551 *	1.6	2.9
355 Presb Ch (USA)	5	627	279	769 *	2.2	4.0
388 Reg Bapt Gen As	1	386	233	473 *	1.3	2.5
418 Southw Bapt Fel	1	NR	NR	NR	-	-
419 So Bapt Conv	4	441	125	541 *	1.5	2.8
443 Un C of Christ	1	176	84	216 *	.6	1.1
449 Un Methodist	13	2,610	1,045	3,200 *	9.0	16.8
499 Indep.Non-Char	1	575	525	575	1.6	3.0
CLARK	**57**	**7,459**	**3,151**	**10,432 ***	**61.3**	**100.0**
053 Assemb of God	1	62	80	120	.7	1.2
081 Catholic	2	NR	NR	669	3.9	6.4
093 Chr Ch (Disc)	1	342	155	422 *	2.5	4.0
097 Chr Chs&Chs Cr	5	867	NR	1,070 *	6.3	10.3
121 Ch God (Abr)	1	3	3	4 *	-	-
165 Ch of Nazarene	3	301	361	754	4.4	7.2
167 Chs of Christ	4	250	255	324	1.9	3.1
171 Ch God-Gen Con	4	481	304	602 *	3.5	5.8
173 Comm of Christ	1	49	NR	49	.3	.5
185 Cumber Presb	3	88	NR	203	1.2	1.9
283 Luth—MO Synod	1	80	45	80	.5	.8
306 NT IndBapt&Rltd	1	225	NR	278 *	1.6	2.7
360 Prim Bapt Chrch	1	NR	NR	NR	-	-
419 So Bapt Conv	12	2,733	834	3,374 *	19.8	32.3
443 Un C of Christ	1	141	62	174 *	1.0	1.7
449 Un Methodist	15	1,808	1,012	2,233 *	13.1	21.4
467 Wesleyan	1	29	40	76	.4	.7
CLAY	**50**	**6,742**	**1,811**	**9,956 ***	**68.4**	**100.0**
019 Amer Bapt USA	1	276	75	337 *	2.3	3.4
053 Assemb of God	1	53	70	70	.5	.7
081 Catholic	2	NR	NR	1,522	10.5	15.3
097 Chr Chs&Chs Cr	14	2,456	NR	3,003 *	20.6	30.2
123 Ch God (Ander)	1	NR	85	85	.6	.9
127 Ch God (Cleve)	1	66	44	81 *	.6	.8
145 Ch God Prophcy	1	42	NR	52 *	.4	.5
165 Ch of Nazarene	1	172	193	348	2.4	3.5
167 Chs of Christ	2	65	65	85	.6	.9
173 Comm of Christ	2	300	NR	300	2.1	3.0
283 Luth—MO Synod	1	224	89	297	2.0	3.0
355 Presb Ch (USA)	1	16	8	20 *	.1	.2
360 Prim Bapt Chrch	1	NR	NR	NR	-	-
419 So Bapt Conv	11	1,927	562	2,356 *	16.2	23.7
443 Un C of Christ	1	43	25	53 *	.4	.5
449 Un Methodist	9	1,102	595	1,347 *	9.3	13.5
CLINTON	**43**	**5,313**	**2,050**	**26,774 ***	**75.3**	**100.0**
053 Assemb of God	1	27	33	47	.1	.2
056 Baha'i	0	6	NR	6	-	-
081 Catholic	14	NR	NR	19,915	56.0	74.4
097 Chr Chs&Chs Cr	2	187	NR	230 *	.6	.9
127 Ch God (Cleve)	1	30	13	37 *	.1	.1
151 L-D Saints	1	NR	NR	292	.8	1.1
165 Ch of Nazarene	1	78	52	87	.2	.3
283 Luth—MO Synod	4	1,153	518	1,435	4.0	5.4
306 NT IndBapt&Rltd	1	225	NR	277 *	.8	1.0
313 N Am Bapt Conf	1	136	150	168 *	.5	.6
419 So Bapt Conv	5	1,427	424	1,759 *	5.0	6.6
443 Un C of Christ	4	1,024	345	1,262 *	3.6	4.7
449 Un Methodist	8	1,020	515	1,259 *	3.5	4.7
COLES	**70**	**13,350**	**4,761**	**20,554 ***	**38.6**	**100.0**
019 Amer Bapt USA	3	1,452	566	1,707 *	3.2	8.3
053 Assemb of God	2	135	180	267	.5	1.3
056 Baha'i	0	5	NR	5	-	-
081 Catholic	2	NR	NR	3,331	6.3	16.2
089 Chr & Miss Al	2	48	NR	77	.1	.4
093 Chr Ch (Disc)	2	317	166	373 *	.7	1.8
097 Chr Chs&Chs Cr	6	2,656	NR	3,123 *	5.9	15.2
123 Ch God (Ander)	1	NR	181	181	.3	.9
151 L-D Saints	2	NR	NR	502	.9	2.4
165 Ch of Nazarene	3	340	235	379	.7	1.8
167 Chs of Christ	3	157	144	194	.4	.9
171 Ch God-Gen Con	3	591	221	759 *	1.4	3.7
185 Cumber Presb	1	113	NR	146	.3	.7
193 Episcopal	1	NR	40	77	.1	.4
207 E.L.C.A.	1	218	92	275	.5	1.3
221 Free Methodist	1	26	25	30	.1	.1
267 Muslim Est	1	NR	4	40	.1	.2
283 Luth—MO Synod	3	1,497	765	2,028	3.8	9.9
306 NT IndBapt&Rltd	1	225	NR	264 *	.5	1.3
323 Old Ord Amish	1	55	NR	65 *	.1	.3
355 Presb Ch (USA)	4	971	466	1,141 *	2.1	5.6
360 Prim Bapt Chrch	1	NR	NR	NR	-	-
388 Reg Bapt Gen As	1	46	50	54 *	.1	.3
403 Salvation Army	1	91	52	225	.4	1.1
409 Separate Bapt	6	438	NR	515 *	1.0	2.5
413 S.D.A.	1	21	NR	25	-	.1
419 So Bapt Conv	6	1,696	495	1,993 *	3.7	9.7
435 Unitarian-Univ	1	11	NR	13 *	-	.1
449 Un Methodist	9	2,241	1,079	2,635 *	5.0	12.8
496 Jewish Est	1	NR	NR	130	.2	.6
COOK	**2,346**	**388,992**	**234,042**	**3,098,473 ***	**57.6**	**100.0**
009 Alban Orth Dio	1	250	NR	270	-	-
017 Amer Bapt Assn	1	50	NR	63 *	-	-
019 Amer Bapt USA	57	17,353	6,163	21,825 *	.4	.7
022 Carp Rus Orth	1	122	NR	207	-	-
034 Ant Orth of NA	2	714	NR	1,428	-	-
040 Ap Chr Ch-Amer	1	115	175	175 *	-	-
049 Armen Ap Cilic	1	165	NR	980	-	-
050 Armen Ap Etchm	3	307	NR	3,688	.1	.1
053 Assemb of God	66	8,379	10,081	14,013	.3	.5
056 Baha'i	20	2,505	NR	2,505	-	.1
057 Bapt Gen Conf	43	6,796	7,092	9,353 *	.2	.3
059 Bapt Miss Assn	2	67	45	84 *	-	-
076 Buddhism	47	NR	NR	NR	-	-
078 Bulgar Orth USA	1	NR	NR	900	-	-

NR–Not Reported *Total adherents estimated from known number of communicant, confirmed, full members. - Represents a percentage less than 0.1. Percentages may not total 100 due to rounding.

Table 4: Religious Congregations by County and Group: 2000

Religious Group	Number of Churches, Synagogues, Mosques, or Temples	Number of Communicant, Confirmed, or Full Members	Number of Attendees	Total Adherents		
				Number of Adherents	% of Total Pop.	% of Total Adh.
081 Catholic	370	NR	NR	2,146,961	39.9	69.3
084 Calvary Chapel	3	NR	NR	NR	-	-
089 Chr & Miss Al	22	2,050	NR	2,884	.1	.1
093 Chr Ch (Disc)	15	2,501	399	3,146 *	.1	.1
097 Chr Chs&Chs Cr	21	4,191	NR	5,272 *	.1	.2
105 Christian Ref	28	9,741	6,899	12,251 *	.2	.4
123 Ch God (Ander)	19	NR	3,408	3,408	.1	.1
127 Ch God (Cleve)	34	3,868	2,361	4,995 *	.1	.2
145 Ch God Prophcy	4	169	NR	212 *	-	-
151 L-D Saints	22	NR	NR	8,862	.2	.3
157 Ch of Brethren	5	506	95	637 *	-	-
165 Ch of Nazarene	38	3,124	2,382	3,861	.1	.1
167 Chs of Christ	51	5,789	4,865	7,614	.1	.2
173 Comm of Christ	3	329	NR	329	-	-
175 Congr Chr Chs	6	830	440	1,044 *	-	-
179 Consrv Bapt	16	NR	3,220	3,220	.1	.1
181 Consrv Congr	1	188	55	236 *	-	-
185 Cumber Presb	2	41	NR	53	-	-
193 Episcopal	74	NR	8,794	22,255	.4	.7
201 Evan Cov Ch	38	7,415	5,918	9,841 *	.2	.3
203 Evan Free Ch	40	4,112	8,653	8,678	.2	.3
207 E.L.C.A.	160	47,489	19,526	63,421	1.2	2.0
213 Evan Menn Inc	2	41	64	52 *	-	-
220 Free Lutheran	1	55	20	55	-	-
221 Free Methodist	4	131	193	226	-	-
223 Free Will Bapt	2	172	NR	216 *	-	-
226 Friends-USA	7	479	NR	602 *	-	-
237 Menn Br US Conf	1	11	NR	14 *	-	-
246 Greek Orthodox	19	NR	NR	29,049	.5	.9
249 Assyr Apost Ch	3	NR	NR	19,650	.4	.6
252 Hindu	13	NR	NR	NR	-	-
262 Int Cou Comm Ch	16	6,516	NR	8,196 *	.2	.3
263 Int Foursq Gos	5	1,128	773	1,419 *	-	-
264 Int Chs of Crst	1	3,179	4,926	4,582	.1	.1
267 Muslim Est	46	NR	18,207	95,623	1.8	3.1
268 Jain	1	NR	NR	NR	-	-
283 Luth—MO Synod	135	48,302	21,415	63,814	1.2	2.1
288 Mennonite USA	17	2,281	2,271	2,974 *	.1	.1
290 Metro Comm Ch	3	153	157	174 *	-	-
291 Missionary Ch	1	170	297	297	-	-
304 NatPrimBapt USA	5	532	NR	669 *	-	-
306 NT IndBapt&Rltd	9	2,022	NR	2,543 *	-	.1
307 Neth Ref Congr	1	18	NR	31	-	-
313 N Am Bapt Conf	5	694	455	873 *	-	-
330 Macedonian Orth	1	NR	NR	800	-	-
331 OCA: Ter Diocs	6	553	NR	2,244	-	.1
332 OCA: Bulg Dioc	1	450	NR	1,830	-	.1
333 Malan Dioc Am	3	NR	NR	1,000	-	-
334 Malan Syr Orth	2	60	NR	300	-	-
335 Orth Pres Ch	3	236	284	374	-	-
339 Pent Ch of God	1	47	NR	80	-	-
349 Pent Holiness	2	68	78	86 *	-	-
355 Presb Ch (USA)	101	29,336	15,028	36,966 *	.7	1.2
356 Presb Ch Amer	13	1,072	1,098	1,403	-	-
360 Prim Bapt Chrch	2	NR	NR	NR	-	-
369 Prot Ref Chs	2	332	NR	564	-	-
371 Ref Ch in Am	22	5,538	5,220	8,818	.2	.3
388 Reg Bapt Gen As	4	675	596	849 *	-	-
395 Romania Orth Ar	1	NR	NR	525	-	-
397 OCA: Roman Dioc	2	NR	NR	3,000	.1	.1
401 Rus Orth Abroad	1	NR	NR	NR	-	-
403 Salvation Army	19	1,983	2,383	6,128	.1	.2
410 Serb Orth USA	2	NR	NR	7,500	.1	.2
411 Serb Orth: Grac	4	NR	NR	NR	-	-
413 S.D.A.	58	13,046	NR	15,521	.3	.5
416 Sikh	2	NR	NR	NR	-	-
418 Southw Bapt Fel	1	NR	NR	NR	-	-
419 So Bapt Conv	150	50,158	22,337	63,084 *	1.2	2.0
431 Ukrainian Orth	3	NR	NR	1,356	-	-
435 Unitarian-Univ	12	2,124	NR	2,671 *	-	.1
443 Un C of Christ	110	41,939	19,501	52,747 *	1.0	1.7
449 Un Methodist	144	33,957	14,611	42,712 *	.8	1.4
455 Un Ref Chs N.A.	3	572	NR	775	-	-
463 Vineyard	6	968	1,160	1,434 *	-	-

Religious Group	Number of Churches, Synagogues, Mosques, or Temples	Number of Communicant, Confirmed, or Full Members	Number of Attendees	Total Adherents		
				Number of Adherents	% of Total Pop.	% of Total Adh.
467 Wesleyan	4	316	355	948	-	-
469 WELS	5	1,399	705	1,826	-	.1
496 Jewish Est	117	NR	NR	234,400	4.4	7.6
498 Indep.Charis.	7	3,900	4,775	4,775	.1	.2
499 Indep.Non-Char	17	5,213	6,562	8,027	.1	.3
CRAWFORD	**63**	**7,855**	**2,857**	**10,585 ***	**51.8**	**100.0**
011 A.W.M.C.	1	17	19	18	.1	.2
019 Amer Bapt USA	2	547	180	659 *	3.2	6.2
032 Amish; other	1	34	NR	41 *	.2	.4
053 Assemb of God	2	143	186	299	1.5	2.8
056 Baha'i	0	1	NR	1	-	-
081 Catholic	2	NR	NR	850	4.2	8.0
093 Chr Ch (Disc)	2	1,170	207	1,409 *	6.9	13.3
097 Chr Chs&Chs Cr	9	1,749	NR	2,107 *	10.3	19.9
127 Ch God (Cleve)	1	47	33	57 *	.3	.5
157 Ch of Brethren	1	26	0	31 *	.2	.3
165 Ch of Nazarene	1	44	29	44	.2	.4
167 Chs of Christ	3	142	160	185	.9	1.7
185 Cumber Presb	1	25	NR	51	.2	.5
193 Episcopal	1	NR	16	27	.1	.3
203 Evan Free Ch	1	69	125	125	.6	1.2
221 Free Methodist	2	38	58	58	.3	.5
226 Friends-USA	1	102	NR	123 *	.6	1.2
283 Luth—MO Synod	1	60	40	90	.4	.9
355 Presb Ch (USA)	2	209	112	252 *	1.2	2.4
365 Prog Prim Bapt	1	12	NR	14 *	.1	.1
419 So Bapt Conv	7	1,510	535	1,819 *	8.9	17.2
443 Un C of Christ	1	45	38	54 *	.3	.5
449 Un Methodist	18	1,791	1,056	2,155 *	10.5	20.4
467 Wesleyan	2	74	63	116	.6	1.1
CUMBERLAND	**36**	**2,777**	**1,123**	**4,507 ***	**40.1**	**100.0**
081 Catholic	3	NR	NR	931	8.3	20.7
097 Chr Chs&Chs Cr	3	770	NR	960 *	8.5	21.3
167 Chs of Christ	2	70	75	91	.8	2.0
171 Ch God-Gen Con	3	183	87	229 *	2.0	5.1
221 Free Methodist	2	93	122	122	1.1	2.7
226 Friends-USA	1	102	NR	127 *	1.1	2.8
355 Presb Ch (USA)	2	174	74	217 *	1.9	4.8
409 Separate Bapt	2	42	NR	52 *	.5	1.2
419 So Bapt Conv	6	670	331	835 *	7.4	18.5
449 Un Methodist	10	625	373	779 *	6.9	17.3
467 Wesleyan	2	48	61	164	1.5	3.6
DE KALB	**90**	**18,391**	**8,990**	**43,217 ***	**48.6**	**100.0**
019 Amer Bapt USA	3	806	500	983 *	1.1	2.3
053 Assemb of God	3	409	602	1,029	1.2	2.4
056 Baha'i	1	43	NR	43	-	.1
057 Bapt Gen Conf	1	67	69	82 *	.1	.2
059 Bapt Miss Assn	1	332	215	405 *	.5	.9
081 Catholic	7	NR	NR	17,079	19.2	39.5
097 Chr Chs&Chs Cr	1	80	NR	98 *	.1	.2
127 Ch God (Cleve)	1	91	103	111 *	.1	.3
151 L-D Saints	2	NR	NR	588	.7	1.4
165 Ch of Nazarene	2	130	141	279	.3	.6
167 Chs of Christ	3	186	220	241	.3	.6
173 Comm of Christ	1	81	NR	81	.1	.2
179 Consrv Bapt	1	NR	350	350	.4	.8
193 Episcopal	2	NR	135	411	.5	1.0
201 Evan Cov Ch	1	172	136	210 *	.2	.5
203 Evan Free Ch	1	150	270	270	.3	.6
207 E.L.C.A.	9	4,299	1,919	5,750	6.5	13.3
220 Free Lutheran	1	80	60	125	.1	.3
226 Friends-USA	1	55	NR	67 *	.1	.2
246 Greek Orthodox	1	NR	NR	171	.2	.4
263 Int Foursq Gos	2	381	330	465 *	.5	1.1
267 Muslim Est	1	NR	60	200	.2	.5
283 Luth—MO Synod	4	2,245	829	2,959	3.3	6.8
306 NT IndBapt&Rltd	3	674	NR	822 *	.9	1.9
355 Presb Ch (USA)	4	614	462	749 *	.8	1.7
403 Salvation Army	1	80	77	273	.3	.6
413 S.D.A.	1	80	NR	95	.1	.2

NR–Not Reported   *Total adherents estimated from known number of communicant, confirmed, full members.   - Represents a percentage less than 0.1.   Percentages may not total 100 due to rounding.

Table 4: Religious Congregations by County and Group: 2000

Religious Group	Number of Churches, Synagogues, Mosques, or Temples	Number of Communicant, Confirmed, or Full Members	Number of Attendees	Total Adherents: Number of Adherents	Total Adherents: % of Total Pop.	Total Adherents: % of Total Adh.
419 So Bapt Conv	3	461	154	562 *	.6	1.3
435 Unitarian-Univ	2	79	NR	96 *	.1	.2
443 Un C of Christ	8	2,520	613	3,074 *	3.5	7.1
449 Un Methodist	14	4,085	1,466	4,982 *	5.6	11.5
463 Vineyard	1	106	85	129 *	.1	.3
467 Wesleyan	2	85	194	258	.3	.6
496 Jewish Est	1	NR	NR	180	.2	.4
DE WITT	**30**	**5,266**	**1,349**	**8,342 ***	**49.7**	**100.0**
053 Assemb of God	1	207	255	345	2.1	4.1
056 Baha'i	0	3	NR	3	-	-
081 Catholic	3	NR	NR	1,717	10.2	20.6
097 Chr Chs&Chs Cr	7	2,691	NR	3,310 *	19.7	39.7
123 Ch God (Ander)	1	NR	16	16	.1	.2
127 Ch God (Cleve)	2	104	43	128 *	.8	1.5
165 Ch of Nazarene	1	237	141	266	1.6	3.2
167 Chs of Christ	1	35	48	52	.3	.6
185 Cumber Presb	1	40	NR	58	.3	.7
203 Evan Free Ch	1	26	90	90	.5	1.1
283 Luth—MO Synod	1	106	55	121	.7	1.5
306 NT IndBapt&Rltd	1	225	NR	277 *	1.6	3.3
355 Presb Ch (USA)	1	205	80	252 *	1.5	3.0
419 So Bapt Conv	2	137	60	169 *	1.0	2.0
449 Un Methodist	7	1,250	561	1,538 *	9.2	18.4
DOUGLAS	**70**	**8,159**	**2,706**	**12,813 ***	**64.3**	**100.0**
019 Amer Bapt USA	6	763	462	957 *	4.8	7.5
053 Assemb of God	1	81	54	100	.5	.8
056 Baha'i	0	3	NR	3	-	-
061 Beachy Amish	1	135	NR	169 *	.8	1.3
081 Catholic	3	NR	NR	2,260	11.3	17.6
093 Chr Ch (Disc)	3	845	211	1,060 *	5.3	8.3
097 Chr Chs&Chs Cr	6	1,286	NR	1,613 *	8.1	12.6
123 Ch God (Ander)	2	NR	72	72	.4	.6
143 CG in Cr(Menn)	1	24	NR	30 *	.2	.2
151 L-D Saints	1	NR	NR	98	.5	.8
165 Ch of Nazarene	3	120	92	229	1.1	1.8
167 Chs of Christ	1	96	79	136	.7	1.1
183 Cons Menn Conf	2	258	315	375	1.9	2.9
221 Free Methodist	1	18	27	27	.1	.2
283 Luth—MO Synod	1	327	133	411	2.1	3.2
288 Mennonite USA	1	261	225	327 *	1.6	2.6
306 NT IndBapt&Rltd	2	449	NR	563 *	2.8	4.4
323 Old Ord Amish	21	1,155	NR	1,449 *	7.3	11.3
355 Presb Ch (USA)	2	62	41	78 *	.4	.6
360 Prim Bapt Chrch	1	NR	NR	NR	-	-
419 So Bapt Conv	1	10	7	13 *	.1	.1
443 Un C of Christ	2	298	113	374 *	1.9	2.9
449 Un Methodist	8	1,968	875	2,469 *	12.4	19.3
DU PAGE	**392**	**107,735**	**63,490**	**532,409 ***	**58.9**	**100.0**
017 Amer Bapt Assn	1	50	NR	63 *	-	-
019 Amer Bapt USA	6	486	225	615 *	.1	.1
034 Ant Orth of NA	1	124	NR	248	-	-
053 Assemb of God	11	3,689	5,792	10,457	1.2	2.0
056 Baha'i	6	372	NR	372	-	.1
057 Bapt Gen Conf	6	543	441	791 *	.1	.1
076 Buddhism	7	NR	NR	NR	-	-
081 Catholic	50	NR	NR	349,415	38.6	65.6
089 Chr & Miss Al	13	877	NR	1,679	.2	.3
093 Chr Ch (Disc)	3	478	290	605 *	.1	.1
097 Chr Chs&Chs Cr	4	2,610	NR	3,301 *	.4	.6
105 Christian Ref	9	3,671	2,499	4,643 *	.5	.9
121 Ch God (Abr)	1	25	22	32 *	-	-
123 Ch God (Ander)	1	NR	62	62	-	-
127 Ch God (Cleve)	2	245	120	310 *	-	.1
151 L-D Saints	7	NR	NR	2,805	.3	.5
157 Ch of Brethren	2	424	161	536 *	.1	.1
165 Ch of Nazarene	3	619	622	947	.1	.2
167 Chs of Christ	6	658	680	796	.1	.1
173 Comm of Christ	1	124	NR	124	-	-
175 Congr Chr Chs	2	186	143	235 *	-	-
179 Consrv Bapt	3	NR	638	638	.1	.1

Religious Group	Number of Churches, Synagogues, Mosques, or Temples	Number of Communicant, Confirmed, or Full Members	Number of Attendees	Total Adherents: Number of Adherents	Total Adherents: % of Total Pop.	Total Adherents: % of Total Adh.
193 Episcopal	11	NR	2,923	6,651	.7	1.2
201 Evan Cov Ch	7	1,384	1,369	1,795 *	.2	.3
203 Evan Free Ch	10	1,589	2,762	2,762	.3	.5
207 E.L.C.A.	30	18,724	8,261	26,865	3.0	5.0
216 Evan Presby Ch	1	302	NR	382 *	-	.1
221 Free Methodist	1	44	25	44	-	-
223 Free Will Bapt	1	86	NR	108 *	-	-
226 Friends-USA	1	55	NR	70 *	-	-
246 Greek Orthodox	2	NR	NR	2,082	.2	.4
249 Assyr Apost Ch	1	NR	NR	3,135	.3	.6
252 Hindu	13	NR	NR	NR	-	-
267 Muslim Est	5	NR	3,312	14,991	1.7	2.8
283 Luth—MO Synod	25	19,676	10,068	27,470	3.0	5.2
288 Mennonite USA	1	146	119	185 *	-	-
290 Metro Comm Ch	1	62	51	78 *	-	-
291 Missionary Ch	1	7	70	70	-	-
306 NT IndBapt&Rltd	3	674	NR	852 *	.1	.2
313 N Am Bapt Conf	2	360	330	455 *	.1	.1
330 Macedonian Orth	1	NR	NR	1,000	.1	.2
331 OCA: Ter Diocs	2	417	NR	708	.1	.1
335 Orth Pres Ch	1	124	144	183	-	-
355 Presb Ch (USA)	18	7,955	3,499	10,062 *	1.1	1.9
356 Presb Ch Amer	5	1,043	1,258	1,273	.1	.2
369 Prot Ref Chs	1	51	NR	90	-	-
371 Ref Ch in Am	4	413	424	699	.1	.1
388 Reg Bapt Gen As	5	501	632	706 *	.1	.1
403 Salvation Army	1	102	61	889	.1	.2
413 S.D.A.	9	2,499	NR	2,974	.3	.6
419 So Bapt Conv	11	1,694	926	2,142 *	.2	.4
423 Syrian Orth Ch	1	NR	NR	270	-	.1
431 Ukrainian Orth	1	NR	NR	372	-	.1
435 Unitarian-Univ	3	608	NR	769 *	.1	.1
443 Un C of Christ	22	11,211	3,948	14,179 *	1.6	2.7
449 Un Methodist	30	15,891	6,471	20,098 *	2.2	3.8
463 Vineyard	2	260	240	328 *	-	.1
467 Wesleyan	2	210	187	416	-	.1
469 WELS	2	497	369	713	.1	.1
490 Zoroastrian	3	NR	NR	NR	-	-
496 Jewish Est	1	NR	NR	1,900	.2	.4
499 Indep.Non-Char	6	5,969	4,346	5,969	.7	1.1
EDGAR	**54**	**7,458**	**2,247**	**10,642 ***	**54.0**	**100.0**
019 Amer Bapt USA	2	383	156	467 *	2.4	4.4
053 Assemb of God	2	70	67	116	.6	1.1
056 Baha'i	0	4	NR	4	-	-
081 Catholic	3	NR	NR	1,412	7.2	13.3
093 Chr Ch (Disc)	1	704	241	858 *	4.4	8.1
097 Chr Chs&Chs Cr	12	2,430	NR	2,960 *	15.0	27.8
127 Ch God (Cleve)	1	105	66	128 *	.6	1.2
165 Ch of Nazarene	2	241	164	469	2.4	4.4
167 Chs of Christ	3	112	120	145	.7	1.4
193 Episcopal	1	NR	7	27	.1	.3
226 Friends-USA	1	102	NR	124 *	.6	1.2
283 Luth—MO Synod	1	375	173	430	2.2	4.0
306 NT IndBapt&Rltd	2	449	NR	547 *	2.8	5.1
339 Pent Ch of God	1	10	NR	10	.1	.1
355 Presb Ch (USA)	3	286	164	348 *	1.8	3.3
413 S.D.A.	1	44	NR	52	.3	.5
419 So Bapt Conv	1	72	32	88 *	.4	.8
449 Un Methodist	16	1,771	837	2,157 *	10.9	20.3
499 Indep.Non-Char	1	300	220	300	1.5	2.8
EDWARDS	**31**	**4,315**	**1,348**	**5,158 ***	**74.0**	**100.0**
093 Chr Ch (Disc)	1	256	63	310 *	4.4	6.0
097 Chr Chs&Chs Cr	7	1,341	NR	1,624 *	23.3	31.5
175 Congr Chr Chs	1	60	30	73 *	1.0	1.4
193 Episcopal	1	NR	20	40	.6	.8
221 Free Methodist	2	61	101	102	1.5	2.0
293 Morav Ch-North	1	242	NR	298	4.3	5.8
355 Presb Ch (USA)	1	35	20	42 *	.6	.8
360 Prim Bapt Chrch	2	NR	NR	NR	-	-
419 So Bapt Conv	3	830	245	1,006 *	14.4	19.5
449 Un Methodist	10	815	469	988 *	14.2	19.2

NR–Not Reported   *Total adherents estimated from known number of communicant, confirmed, full members.   - Represents a percentage less than 0.1.   Percentages may not total 100 due to rounding.

Table 4: Religious Congregations by County and Group: 2000

Religious Group	Number of Churches, Synagogues, Mosques, or Temples	Number of Communicant, Confirmed, or Full Members	Number of Attendees	Total Adherents		
				Number of Adherents	% of Total Pop.	% of Total Adh.
499 Indep.Non-Char	2	675	400	675	9.7	13.1
EFFINGHAM	**63**	**9,366**	**4,440**	**25,173 ***	**73.5**	**100.0**
053 Assemb of God	1	190	253	253	.7	1.0
056 Baha'i	0	1	NR	1	-	-
081 Catholic	10	NR	NR	12,695	37.1	50.4
097 Chr Chs&Chs Cr	9	1,076	NR	1,376 *	4.0	5.5
123 Ch God (Ander)	1	NR	216	216	.6	.9
151 L-D Saints	1	NR	NR	125	.4	.5
165 Ch of Nazarene	2	109	61	231	.7	.9
167 Chs of Christ	1	68	73	88	.3	.3
173 Comm of Christ	1	45	NR	45	.1	.2
193 Episcopal	1	NR	10	13	-	.1
207 E.L.C.A.	2	321	170	400	1.2	1.6
223 Free Will Bapt	1	86	NR	110 *	.3	.4
283 Luth—MO Synod	10	2,930	1,912	3,816	11.1	15.2
355 Presb Ch (USA)	1	278	140	355 *	1.0	1.4
419 So Bapt Conv	7	2,494	673	3,188 *	9.3	12.7
449 Un Methodist	15	1,768	932	2,261 *	6.6	9.0
FAYETTE	**68**	**8,355**	**3,001**	**11,366 ***	**52.1**	**100.0**
053 Assemb of God	2	105	128	296	1.4	2.6
056 Baha'i	0	2	NR	2	-	-
081 Catholic	3	NR	NR	846	3.9	7.4
093 Chr Ch (Disc)	1	90	60	110 *	.5	1.0
097 Chr Chs&Chs Cr	10	871	NR	1,059 *	4.9	9.3
123 Ch God (Ander)	3	NR	113	113	.5	1.0
157 Ch of Brethren	1	84	0	102 *	.5	.9
167 Chs of Christ	3	97	91	130	.6	1.1
185 Cumber Presb	1	11	NR	14	.1	.1
207 E.L.C.A.	2	350	130	458	2.1	4.0
221 Free Methodist	3	170	152	196	.9	1.7
283 Luth—MO Synod	4	1,384	507	1,715	7.9	15.1
322 Old Ord Menn Ch	1	29	NR	35 *	.2	.3
355 Presb Ch (USA)	1	84	40	102 *	.5	.9
360 Prim Bapt Chrch	1	NR	NR	NR	-	-
413 S.D.A.	1	45	NR	54	.2	.5
419 So Bapt Conv	16	3,483	1,023	4,245 *	19.5	37.3
443 Un C of Christ	1	195	73	238 *	1.1	2.1
449 Un Methodist	14	1,355	684	1,651 *	7.6	14.5
FORD	**38**	**5,778**	**2,001**	**9,004 ***	**63.2**	**100.0**
053 Assemb of God	1	43	40	55	.4	.6
056 Baha'i	0	1	NR	1	-	-
081 Catholic	6	NR	NR	1,585	11.1	17.6
093 Chr Ch (Disc)	1	315	79	391 *	2.7	4.3
097 Chr Chs&Chs Cr	1	330	NR	410 *	2.9	4.6
165 Ch of Nazarene	2	79	86	163	1.1	1.8
167 Chs of Christ	1	57	55	65	.5	.7
175 Congr Chr Chs	1	35	27	43 *	.3	.5
201 Evan Cov Ch	1	195	88	242 *	1.7	2.7
203 Evan Free Ch	1	69	125	125	.9	1.4
207 E.L.C.A.	6	1,346	420	1,816	12.8	20.2
306 NT IndBapt&Rltd	2	449	NR	558 *	3.9	6.2
355 Presb Ch (USA)	3	284	151	353 *	2.5	3.9
356 Presb Ch Amer	1	52	60	61	.4	.7
419 So Bapt Conv	2	412	104	512 *	3.6	5.7
443 Un C of Christ	1	44	48	55 *	.4	.6
449 Un Methodist	8	2,067	718	2,569 *	18.0	28.5
FRANKLIN	**119**	**17,404**	**5,699**	**23,618 ***	**60.5**	**100.0**
019 Amer Bapt USA	5	986	262	1,195 *	3.1	5.1
053 Assemb of God	2	86	86	151	.4	.6
056 Baha'i	0	2	NR	2	-	-
081 Catholic	6	NR	NR	1,521	3.9	6.4
093 Chr Ch (Disc)	1	480	107	582 *	1.5	2.5
097 Chr Chs&Chs Cr	11	1,898	NR	2,299 *	5.9	9.7
123 Ch God (Ander)	3	NR	180	180	.5	.8
127 Ch God (Cleve)	7	1,175	613	1,423 *	3.6	6.0
151 L-D Saints	1	NR	NR	342	.9	1.4
165 Ch of Nazarene	3	258	231	476	1.2	2.0
167 Chs of Christ	7	308	325	400	1.0	1.7
173 Comm of Christ	1	20	NR	20	.1	.1
193 Episcopal	1	NR	43	101	.3	.4
223 Free Will Bapt	6	515	NR	624 *	1.6	2.6
283 Luth—MO Synod	1	170	125	220	.6	.9
286 E.PA Mennonite	1	80	NR	97 *	.2	.4
331 OCA: Ter Diocs	1	74	NR	87	.2	.4
355 Presb Ch (USA)	1	59	29	71 *	.2	.3
356 Presb Ch Amer	1	40	40	41	.1	.2
360 Prim Bapt Chrch	1	NR	NR	NR	-	-
403 Salvation Army	1	32	19	158	.4	.7
413 S.D.A.	2	137	NR	163	.4	.7
419 So Bapt Conv	42	9,925	3,021	12,025 *	30.8	50.9
449 Un Methodist	13	1,148	597	1,390 *	3.6	5.9
467 Wesleyan	1	11	21	50	.1	.2
FULTON	**85**	**10,006**	**4,243**	**14,964 ***	**39.1**	**100.0**
019 Amer Bapt USA	2	629	285	755 *	2.0	5.0
053 Assemb of God	4	146	185	320	.8	2.1
056 Baha'i	0	3	NR	3	-	-
081 Catholic	4	NR	NR	1,980	5.2	13.2
093 Chr Ch (Disc)	5	1,399	232	1,679 *	4.4	11.2
097 Chr Chs&Chs Cr	6	928	NR	1,114 *	2.9	7.4
123 Ch God (Ander)	1	NR	0	0	-	-
145 Ch God Prophcy	1	42	NR	51 *	.1	.3
151 L-D Saints	1	NR	NR	140	.4	.9
157 Ch of Brethren	3	356	198	427 *	1.1	2.9
165 Ch of Nazarene	10	517	464	878	2.3	5.9
167 Chs of Christ	2	79	85	103	.3	.7
173 Comm of Christ	1	21	NR	21	.1	.1
193 Episcopal	2	NR	51	165	.4	1.1
203 Evan Free Ch	1	98	160	160	.4	1.1
207 E.L.C.A.	2	370	148	470	1.2	3.1
221 Free Methodist	2	89	75	98	.3	.7
283 Luth—MO Synod	1	91	58	123	.3	.8
306 NT IndBapt&Rltd	1	225	NR	270 *	.7	1.8
355 Presb Ch (USA)	4	678	269	814 *	2.1	5.4
371 Ref Ch in Am	1	147	108	220	.6	1.5
403 Salvation Army	1	149	229	325	.8	2.2
413 S.D.A.	1	53	NR	63	.2	.4
419 So Bapt Conv	1	150	70	180 *	.5	1.2
435 Unitarian-Univ	1	13	NR	16 *	-	.1
443 Un C of Christ	3	587	176	705 *	1.8	4.7
449 Un Methodist	24	3,236	1,450	3,884 *	10.2	26.0
GALLATIN	**22**	**1,243**	**456**	**2,838 ***	**44.0**	**100.0**
056 Baha'i	0	1	NR	1	-	-
081 Catholic	4	NR	NR	1,139	17.7	40.1
097 Chr Chs&Chs Cr	1	50	NR	60 *	.9	2.1
127 Ch God (Cleve)	3	70	67	83 *	1.3	2.9
151 L-D Saints	1	NR	NR	199	3.1	7.0
165 Ch of Nazarene	1	45	22	46	.7	1.6
185 Cumber Presb	1	10	NR	29	.4	1.0
355 Presb Ch (USA)	4	115	55	137 *	2.1	4.8
419 So Bapt Conv	3	755	177	908 *	14.1	32.0
449 Un Methodist	4	197	135	236 *	3.7	8.3
GREENE	**42**	**5,896**	**1,904**	**9,418 ***	**63.8**	**100.0**
019 Amer Bapt USA	10	2,106	687	2,603 *	17.6	27.6
053 Assemb of God	2	69	88	151	1.0	1.6
056 Baha'i	0	1	NR	1	-	-
081 Catholic	3	NR	NR	2,025	13.7	21.5
093 Chr Ch (Disc)	1	163	74	201 *	1.4	2.1
167 Chs of Christ	3	16	26	29	.2	.3
283 Luth—MO Synod	1	181	84	255	1.7	2.7
355 Presb Ch (USA)	2	97	44	120 *	.8	1.3
388 Reg Bapt Gen As	1	61	50	75 *	.5	.8
419 So Bapt Conv	13	2,482	560	3,068 *	20.8	32.6
449 Un Methodist	6	720	291	890 *	6.0	9.4
GRUNDY	**29**	**6,621**	**2,229**	**18,646 ***	**49.7**	**100.0**
019 Amer Bapt USA	1	136	121	170 *	.5	.9
053 Assemb of God	1	60	80	80	.2	.4

NR–Not Reported   *Total adherents estimated from known number of communicant, confirmed, full members.   - Represents a percentage less than 0.1.   Percentages may not total 100 due to rounding.

Table 4: Religious Congregations by County and Group: 2000

Religious Group	Number of Churches, Synagogues, Mosques, or Temples	Number of Communicant, Confirmed, or Full Members	Number of Attendees	Total Adherents: Number of Adherents	Total Adherents: % of Total Pop.	Total Adherents: % of Total Adh.
056 Baha'i	0	5	NR	5	-	-
081 Catholic	5	NR	NR	9,987	26.6	53.6
097 Chr Chs&Chs Cr	1	1,252	NR	1,568 *	4.2	8.4
165 Ch of Nazarene	1	90	0	90	.2	.5
167 Chs of Christ	1	40	50	45	.1	.2
193 Episcopal	1	NR	38	90	.2	.5
207 E.L.C.A.	2	1,096	431	1,568	4.2	8.4
220 Free Lutheran	1	517	245	751	2.0	4.0
283 Luth—MO Synod	1	63	39	84	.2	.5
355 Presb Ch (USA)	3	732	259	916 *	2.4	4.9
388 Reg Bapt Gen As	1	60	66	75 *	.2	.4
419 So Bapt Conv	2	322	127	403 *	1.1	2.2
443 Un C of Christ	1	283	94	354 *	.9	1.9
449 Un Methodist	7	1,965	679	2,460 *	6.6	13.2
HAMILTON	**44**	**3,249**	**1,360**	**5,027 ***	**58.3**	**100.0**
053 Assemb of God	1	28	44	44	.5	.9
056 Baha'i	0	1	NR	1	-	-
081 Catholic	3	NR	NR	1,019	11.8	20.3
097 Chr Chs&Chs Cr	3	264	NR	322 *	3.7	6.4
127 Ch God (Cleve)	1	94	45	114 *	1.3	2.3
167 Chs of Christ	2	76	78	100	1.2	2.0
185 Cumber Presb	2	26	NR	39	.5	.8
193 Episcopal	1	NR	22	34	.4	.7
283 Luth—MO Synod	1	17	14	18	.2	.4
355 Presb Ch (USA)	1	35	33	43 *	.5	.9
360 Prim Bapt Chrch	2	NR	NR	NR	-	-
419 So Bapt Conv	18	2,359	873	2,868 *	33.3	57.1
449 Un Methodist	9	349	251	425 *	4.9	8.5
HANCOCK	**68**	**6,586**	**2,590**	**11,622 ***	**57.8**	**100.0**
019 Amer Bapt USA	2	206	115	252 *	1.3	2.2
053 Assemb of God	5	236	229	622	3.1	5.4
056 Baha'i	0	2	NR	2	-	-
081 Catholic	5	NR	NR	2,605	12.9	22.4
093 Chr Ch (Disc)	3	547	202	669 *	3.3	5.8
097 Chr Chs&Chs Cr	8	1,048	NR	1,282 *	6.4	11.0
151 L-D Saints	2	NR	NR	437	2.2	3.8
165 Ch of Nazarene	1	16	0	16	.1	.1
173 Comm of Christ	2	75	NR	75	.4	.6
175 Congr Chr Chs	1	189	192	231 *	1.1	2.0
193 Episcopal	1	NR	31	47	.2	.4
207 E.L.C.A.	4	873	392	1,155	5.7	9.9
263 Int Foursq Gos	1	79	103	103 *	.5	.9
283 Luth—MO Synod	2	216	95	273	1.4	2.3
306 NT IndBapt&Rltd	1	225	NR	275 *	1.4	2.4
323 Old Ord Amish	1	55	NR	67 *	.3	.6
339 Pent Ch of God	1	50	NR	125	.6	1.1
355 Presb Ch (USA)	7	564	332	690 *	3.4	5.9
360 Prim Bapt Chrch	2	NR	NR	NR	-	-
413 S.D.A.	1	16	NR	19	.1	.2
419 So Bapt Conv	1	161	45	197 *	1.0	1.7
443 Un C of Christ	2	394	174	482 *	2.4	4.1
449 Un Methodist	15	1,634	680	1,998 *	9.9	17.2
HARDIN	**12**	**1,036**	**350**	**1,369 ***	**28.5**	**100.0**
056 Baha'i	0	1	NR	1	-	.1
081 Catholic	1	NR	NR	157	3.3	11.5
097 Chr Chs&Chs Cr	2	180	NR	211 *	4.4	15.4
167 Chs of Christ	2	122	102	141	2.9	10.3
419 So Bapt Conv	4	626	169	734 *	15.3	53.6
449 Un Methodist	3	107	79	125 *	2.6	9.1
HENDERSON	**17**	**1,882**	**654**	**2,834 ***	**34.5**	**100.0**
019 Amer Bapt USA	1	186	37	224 *	2.7	7.9
053 Assemb of God	1	20	18	100	1.2	3.5
056 Baha'i	0	1	NR	1	-	-
081 Catholic	2	NR	NR	358	4.4	12.6
093 Chr Ch (Disc)	1	180	54	217 *	2.6	7.7
097 Chr Chs&Chs Cr	1	250	NR	302 *	3.7	10.7
165 Ch of Nazarene	1	39	43	162	2.0	5.7
207 E.L.C.A.	1	137	50	179	2.2	6.3
355 Presb Ch (USA)	3	272	123	329 *	4.0	11.6
371 Ref Ch in Am	1	36	41	43	.5	1.5
449 Un Methodist	5	761	288	919 *	11.2	32.4
HENRY	**82**	**15,887**	**6,391**	**30,267 ***	**59.3**	**100.0**
017 Amer Bapt Assn	1	50	NR	62 *	.1	.2
019 Amer Bapt USA	5	1,611	458	1,987 *	3.9	6.6
053 Assemb of God	4	214	261	530	1.0	1.8
056 Baha'i	0	17	NR	17	-	.1
057 Bapt Gen Conf	1	64	45	79 *	.2	.3
081 Catholic	10	NR	NR	9,802	19.2	32.4
097 Chr Chs&Chs Cr	3	550	NR	678 *	1.3	2.2
127 Ch God (Cleve)	3	118	80	146 *	.3	.5
151 L-D Saints	1	NR	NR	82	.2	.3
165 Ch of Nazarene	2	150	137	219	.4	.7
167 Chs of Christ	3	122	125	164	.3	.5
193 Episcopal	2	NR	55	98	.2	.3
203 Evan Free Ch	2	194	391	391	.8	1.3
207 E.L.C.A.	10	4,139	1,356	5,273	10.3	17.4
221 Free Methodist	1	25	29	29	.1	.1
223 Free Will Bapt	1	86	NR	106 *	.2	.4
283 Luth—MO Synod	4	1,186	304	1,517	3.0	5.0
355 Presb Ch (USA)	4	882	396	1,088 *	2.1	3.6
388 Reg Bapt Gen As	1	55	75	75 *	.1	.2
419 So Bapt Conv	2	622	160	767 *	1.5	2.5
443 Un C of Christ	6	1,186	401	1,463 *	2.9	4.8
449 Un Methodist	16	4,616	2,118	5,694 *	11.2	18.8
IROQUOIS	**70**	**10,632**	**4,363**	**17,783 ***	**56.8**	**100.0**
040 Ap Chr Ch-Amer	1	230	370	370 *	1.2	2.1
053 Assemb of God	1	171	34	228	.7	1.3
056 Baha'i	0	1	NR	1	-	-
081 Catholic	9	NR	NR	4,055	12.9	22.8
093 Chr Ch (Disc)	2	301	95	372 *	1.2	2.1
097 Chr Chs&Chs Cr	8	1,271	NR	1,569 *	5.0	8.8
123 Ch God (Ander)	1	NR	17	17	.1	.1
165 Ch of Nazarene	4	151	141	305	1.0	1.7
175 Congr Chr Chs	1	50	20	62 *	.2	.3
193 Episcopal	1	NR	15	37	.1	.2
203 Evan Free Ch	1	110	220	220	.7	1.2
207 E.L.C.A.	5	1,659	622	2,189	7.0	12.3
220 Free Lutheran	1	237	155	295	.9	1.7
283 Luth—MO Synod	10	2,848	1,303	3,567	11.4	20.1
306 NT IndBapt&Rltd	1	225	NR	278 *	.9	1.6
355 Presb Ch (USA)	1	103	25	127 *	.4	.7
371 Ref Ch in Am	1	98	88	132	.4	.7
419 So Bapt Conv	2	72	50	89 *	.3	.5
443 Un C of Christ	3	558	184	689 *	2.2	3.9
449 Un Methodist	16	2,475	972	3,055 *	9.7	17.2
467 Wesleyan	1	72	52	126	.4	.7
JACKSON	**88**	**16,256**	**6,718**	**24,038 ***	**40.3**	**100.0**
019 Amer Bapt USA	9	1,944	540	2,272 *	3.8	9.5
032 Amish; other	1	52	NR	61 *	.1	.3
053 Assemb of God	4	428	440	553	.9	2.3
056 Baha'i	0	52	NR	52	.1	.2
059 Bapt Miss Assn	1	64	35	75 *	.1	.3
081 Catholic	4	NR	NR	2,783	4.7	11.6
093 Chr Ch (Disc)	1	279	102	326 *	.5	1.4
097 Chr Chs&Chs Cr	5	1,079	NR	1,260 *	2.1	5.2
123 Ch God (Ander)	2	NR	50	50	.1	.2
127 Ch God (Cleve)	1	121	47	141 *	.2	.6
151 L-D Saints	2	NR	NR	550	.9	2.3
165 Ch of Nazarene	1	107	74	112	.2	.5
167 Chs of Christ	3	273	200	359	.6	1.5
173 Comm of Christ	1	35	NR	35	.1	.1
193 Episcopal	1	NR	84	188	.3	.8
207 E.L.C.A.	5	1,045	407	1,304	2.2	5.4
226 Friends-USA	1	55	NR	64 *	.1	.3
267 Muslim Est	2	NR	275	1,050	1.8	4.4
283 Luth—MO Synod	5	1,612	814	2,177	3.7	9.1
323 Old Ord Amish	1	55	NR	64 *	.1	.3
355 Presb Ch (USA)	4	425	224	497 *	.8	2.1

NR–Not Reported   *Total adherents estimated from known number of communicant, confirmed, full members.   - Represents a percentage less than 0.1.   Percentages may not total 100 due to rounding.

Table 4: Religious Congregations by County and Group: 2000

Religious Group	Number of Churches, Synagogues, Mosques, or Temples	Number of Communicant, Confirmed, or Full Members	Number of Attendees	Total Adherents: Number of Adherents	Total Adherents: % of Total Pop.	Total Adherents: % of Total Adh.
356 Presb Ch Amer	1	74	100	100	.2	.4
419 So Bapt Conv	17	5,580	1,568	6,521 *	10.9	27.1
435 Unitarian-Univ	1	128	NR	150 *	.3	.6
443 Un C of Christ	2	243	93	284 *	.5	1.2
449 Un Methodist	11	1,994	1,079	2,331 *	3.9	9.7
463 Vineyard	1	303	261	354 *	.6	1.5
498 Indep.Charis.	1	308	325	325	.5	1.4
JASPER	**32**	**2,761**	**971**	**5,739 ***	**56.7**	**100.0**
019 Amer Bapt USA	1	403	167	496 *	4.9	8.6
053 Assemb of God	1	30	40	53	.5	.9
056 Baha'i	0	1	NR	1	-	-
081 Catholic	3	NR	NR	2,244	22.2	39.1
097 Chr Chs&Chs Cr	6	833	NR	1,025 *	10.1	17.9
167 Chs of Christ	4	140	168	186	1.8	3.2
185 Cumber Presb	1	33	NR	80	.8	1.4
207 E.L.C.A.	1	43	14	51	.5	.9
221 Free Methodist	1	35	58	58	.6	1.0
283 Luth—MO Synod	1	82	38	118	1.2	2.1
355 Presb Ch (USA)	1	67	30	82 *	.8	1.4
419 So Bapt Conv	3	417	98	513 *	5.1	8.9
449 Un Methodist	9	677	358	832 *	8.2	14.5
JEFFERSON	**94**	**15,083**	**4,393**	**21,841 ***	**54.5**	**100.0**
019 Amer Bapt USA	2	204	95	250 *	.6	1.1
053 Assemb of God	1	47	56	79	.2	.4
081 Catholic	2	NR	NR	2,414	6.0	11.1
097 Chr Chs&Chs Cr	14	2,461	NR	3,016 *	7.5	13.8
123 Ch God (Ander)	3	NR	177	177	.4	.8
127 Ch God (Cleve)	2	277	138	340 *	.8	1.6
151 L-D Saints	1	NR	NR	235	.6	1.1
165 Ch of Nazarene	1	73	42	158	.4	.7
167 Chs of Christ	2	195	200	235	.6	1.1
173 Comm of Christ	1	80	NR	80	.2	.4
193 Episcopal	1	NR	71	248	.6	1.1
207 E.L.C.A.	1	220	93	282	.7	1.3
223 Free Will Bapt	7	600	NR	736 *	1.8	3.4
283 Luth—MO Synod	1	269	120	350	.9	1.6
323 Old Ord Amish	3	165	NR	201 *	.5	.9
339 Pent Ch of God	1	100	NR	270	.7	1.2
355 Presb Ch (USA)	1	222	110	272 *	.7	1.2
413 S.D.A.	1	38	NR	45	.1	.2
419 So Bapt Conv	33	8,445	2,396	10,356 *	25.9	47.4
435 Unitarian-Univ	1	28	NR	34 *	.1	.2
449 Un Methodist	14	1,659	874	2,033 *	5.1	9.3
467 Wesleyan	1	0	21	30	.1	.1
JERSEY	**30**	**5,301**	**2,419**	**11,525 ***	**53.2**	**100.0**
019 Amer Bapt USA	2	1,206	368	1,482 *	6.8	12.9
053 Assemb of God	3	375	342	1,070	4.9	9.3
056 Baha'i	0	8	NR	8	-	.1
081 Catholic	5	NR	NR	4,348	20.1	37.7
093 Chr Ch (Disc)	1	418	86	514 *	2.4	4.5
097 Chr Chs&Chs Cr	1	30	NR	37 *	.2	.3
165 Ch of Nazarene	1	77	60	123	.6	1.1
167 Chs of Christ	1	101	108	131	.6	1.1
283 Luth—MO Synod	1	272	120	353	1.6	3.1
355 Presb Ch (USA)	1	232	115	285 *	1.3	2.5
388 Reg Bapt Gen As	2	273	175	336 *	1.6	2.9
419 So Bapt Conv	5	1,096	381	1,347 *	6.2	11.7
443 Un C of Christ	2	563	190	692 *	3.2	6.0
449 Un Methodist	5	650	474	799 *	3.7	6.9
JO DAVIESS	**41**	**4,799**	**2,210**	**17,487 ***	**78.5**	**100.0**
053 Assemb of God	2	65	75	103	.5	.6
056 Baha'i	0	8	NR	8	-	-
081 Catholic	10	NR	NR	11,152	50.0	63.8
165 Ch of Nazarene	1	41	23	42	.2	.2
193 Episcopal	1	NR	42	108	.5	.6
203 Evan Free Ch	1	93	230	230	1.0	1.3
207 E.L.C.A.	8	1,736	781	2,351	10.5	13.4
283 Luth—MO Synod	1	230	95	296	1.3	1.7

Religious Group	Number of Churches, Synagogues, Mosques, or Temples	Number of Communicant, Confirmed, or Full Members	Number of Attendees	Total Adherents: Number of Adherents	Total Adherents: % of Total Pop.	Total Adherents: % of Total Adh.
355 Presb Ch (USA)	6	499	270	605 *	2.7	3.5
435 Unitarian-Univ	1	106	NR	128 *	.6	.7
449 Un Methodist	9	1,943	627	2,355 *	10.6	13.5
469 WELS	1	78	67	109	.5	.6
JOHNSON	**33**	**3,504**	**1,292**	**4,323 ***	**33.6**	**100.0**
019 Amer Bapt USA	1	78	45	90 *	.7	2.1
053 Assemb of God	2	48	55	81	.6	1.9
056 Baha'i	0	3	NR	3	-	.1
081 Catholic	1	NR	NR	189	1.5	4.4
097 Chr Chs&Chs Cr	1	80	NR	93 *	.7	2.2
167 Chs of Christ	3	110	129	130	1.0	3.0
173 Comm of Christ	1	86	NR	86	.7	2.0
185 Cumber Presb	1	76	NR	147	1.1	3.4
323 Old Ord Amish	1	55	NR	64 *	.5	1.5
419 So Bapt Conv	14	2,388	770	2,768 *	21.5	64.0
449 Un Methodist	8	580	293	672 *	5.2	15.5
KANE	**236**	**56,420**	**31,268**	**226,258 ***	**56.0**	**100.0**
019 Amer Bapt USA	7	3,616	1,547	4,747 *	1.2	2.1
039 Ap Chr Ch(Naz)	1	11	12	14 *	-	-
040 Ap Chr Ch-Amer	1	200	380	380 *	.1	.2
053 Assemb of God	7	1,392	1,599	2,296	.6	1.0
056 Baha'i	2	181	NR	181	-	.1
057 Bapt Gen Conf	3	652	1,345	1,368 *	.3	.6
059 Bapt Miss Assn	1	45	70	70 *	-	-
076 Buddhism	2	NR	NR	NR	-	-
081 Catholic	26	NR	NR	138,972	34.4	61.4
084 Calvary Chapel	1	NR	NR	NR	-	-
089 Chr & Miss Al	2	286	NR	286	.1	.1
097 Chr Chs&Chs Cr	4	1,275	NR	1,674 *	.4	.7
123 Ch God (Ander)	1	NR	70	70	-	-
127 Ch God (Cleve)	4	664	320	872 *	.2	.4
145 Ch God Prophcy	3	127	NR	168 *	-	.1
151 L-D Saints	4	NR	NR	1,410	.3	.6
157 Ch of Brethren	3	463	237	608 *	.2	.3
165 Ch of Nazarene	1	119	35	119	-	.1
167 Chs of Christ	4	281	335	377	.1	.2
173 Comm of Christ	1	178	NR	178	-	.1
179 Consrv Bapt	1	NR	270	270	.1	.1
181 Consrv Congr	1	280	135	368 *	.1	.2
193 Episcopal	8	NR	1,082	2,525	.6	1.1
201 Evan Cov Ch	3	498	388	653 *	.2	.3
203 Evan Free Ch	4	334	657	657	.2	.3
207 E.L.C.A.	19	10,279	3,947	14,330	3.5	6.3
221 Free Methodist	3	141	251	268	.1	.1
223 Free Will Bapt	1	86	NR	113 *	-	-
246 Greek Orthodox	1	NR	NR	687	.2	.3
252 Hindu	3	NR	NR	NR	-	-
263 Int Foursq Gos	4	228	157	299 *	.1	.1
267 Muslim Est	1	NR	100	500	.1	.2
283 Luth—MO Synod	19	11,431	5,346	14,871	3.7	6.6
306 NT IndBapt&Rltd	1	225	NR	295 *	.1	.1
313 N Am Bapt Conf	1	69	50	91 *	-	-
335 Orth Pres Ch	1	25	50	57	-	-
339 Pent Ch of God	1	100	NR	100	-	-
349 Pent Holiness	1	25	40	33 *	-	-
355 Presb Ch (USA)	6	2,479	1,428	3,255 *	.8	1.4
356 Presb Ch Amer	2	251	258	333	.1	.1
388 Reg Bapt Gen As	3	239	300	300 *	.1	.1
403 Salvation Army	3	274	250	2,818	.7	1.2
413 S.D.A.	8	922	NR	1,097	.3	.5
419 So Bapt Conv	15	1,844	1,426	2,421 *	.6	1.1
435 Unitarian-Univ	2	419	NR	550 *	.1	.2
443 Un C of Christ	13	5,742	2,136	7,539 *	1.9	3.3
449 Un Methodist	24	10,189	3,805	13,378 *	3.3	5.9
463 Vineyard	3	332	400	506 *	.1	.2
467 Wesleyan	1	196	109	211	.1	.1
469 WELS	2	322	233	443	.1	.2
496 Jewish Est	2	NR	NR	1,000	.2	.4
499 Indep.Non-Char	1	0	2,500	2,500	.6	1.1

NR–Not Reported *Total adherents estimated from known number of communicant, confirmed, full members. - Represents a percentage less than 0.1. Percentages may not total 100 due to rounding.

Table 4: Religious Congregations by County and Group: 2000

Religious Group	Number of Churches, Synagogues, Mosques, or Temples	Number of Communicant, Confirmed, or Full Members	Number of Attendees	Total Adherents: Number of Adherents	% of Total Pop.	% of Total Adh.
KANKAKEE	**105**	**18,169**	**10,693**	**49,364 ***	**47.5**	**100.0**
019 Amer Bapt USA	2	425	201	538 *	.5	1.1
053 Assemb of God	2	78	92	100	.1	.2
056 Baha'i	0	7	NR	7	-	-
081 Catholic	14	NR	NR	22,213	21.4	45.0
093 Chr Ch (Disc)	2	398	127	504 *	.5	1.0
097 Chr Chs&Chs Cr	3	348	NR	440 *	.4	.9
105 Christian Ref	1	146	60	185 *	.2	.4
123 Ch God (Ander)	2	NR	57	57	.1	.1
127 Ch God (Cleve)	2	272	349	349 *	.3	.7
151 L-D Saints	1	NR	NR	364	.4	.7
165 Ch of Nazarene	10	2,708	3,082	5,415	5.2	11.0
167 Chs of Christ	4	229	208	301	.3	.6
173 Comm of Christ	1	38	NR	38	-	.1
179 Consrv Bapt	1	NR	57	57	.1	.1
193 Episcopal	2	NR	119	305	.3	.6
203 Evan Free Ch	1	136	275	275	.3	.6
207 E.L.C.A.	3	895	329	1,112	1.1	2.3
223 Free Will Bapt	1	86	NR	109 *	.1	.2
246 Greek Orthodox	1	NR	NR	156	.2	.3
262 Int Cou Comm Ch	1	180	NR	228 *	.2	.5
263 Int Foursq Gos	1	77	44	97 *	.1	.2
283 Luth—MO Synod	8	3,588	1,336	4,692	4.5	9.5
288 Mennonite USA	2	39	46	49 *	-	.1
306 NT IndBapt&Rltd	1	225	NR	285 *	.3	.6
313 N Am Bapt Conf	1	295	200	373 *	.4	.8
355 Presb Ch (USA)	3	635	252	804 *	.8	1.6
371 Ref Ch in Am	4	552	532	953	.9	1.9
388 Reg Bapt Gen As	1	14	15	18 *	-	-
403 Salvation Army	1	109	466	625	.6	1.3
413 S.D.A.	2	153	NR	182	.2	.4
419 So Bapt Conv	3	1,119	280	1,416 *	1.4	2.9
443 Un C of Christ	3	918	335	1,162 *	1.1	2.4
449 Un Methodist	17	3,799	1,758	4,809 *	4.6	9.7
469 WELS	2	200	123	246	.2	.5
496 Jewish Est	1	NR	NR	100	.1	.2
499 Indep.Non-Char	1	500	350	800	.8	1.6
KENDALL	**50**	**10,184**	**4,981**	**23,837 ***	**43.7**	**100.0**
019 Amer Bapt USA	2	444	125	577 *	1.1	2.4
053 Assemb of God	2	94	135	265	.5	1.1
056 Baha'i	0	5	NR	5	-	-
057 Bapt Gen Conf	1	100	95	130 *	.2	.5
059 Bapt Miss Assn	1	55	46	72 *	.1	.3
081 Catholic	3	NR	NR	9,761	17.9	40.9
097 Chr Chs&Chs Cr	2	352	NR	458 *	.8	1.9
105 Christian Ref	1	12	30	16 *	-	.1
127 Ch God (Cleve)	2	277	54	361 *	.7	1.5
151 L-D Saints	1	NR	NR	343	.6	1.4
157 Ch of Brethren	1	122	65	159 *	.3	.7
167 Chs of Christ	1	75	80	97	.2	.4
173 Comm of Christ	1	146	NR	146	.3	.6
207 E.L.C.A.	4	884	700	1,228	2.3	5.2
220 Free Lutheran	5	1,339	781	1,630	3.0	6.8
245 Greek Orth Vslp	1	700	NR	1,200	2.2	5.0
283 Luth—MO Synod	3	1,364	946	1,940	3.6	8.1
306 NT IndBapt&Rltd	1	225	NR	293 *	.5	1.2
349 Pent Holiness	1	34	20	44 *	.1	.2
355 Presb Ch (USA)	2	762	369	991 *	1.8	4.2
388 Reg Bapt Gen As	1	240	345	345 *	.6	1.4
413 S.D.A.	1	0	NR	0	-	-
419 So Bapt Conv	3	186	97	242 *	.4	1.0
443 Un C of Christ	1	665	293	865 *	1.6	3.6
449 Un Methodist	8	1,803	600	2,344 *	4.3	9.8
499 Indep.Non-Char	1	300	200	325	.6	1.4
KNOX	**74**	**13,007**	**6,173**	**22,798 ***	**40.8**	**100.0**
019 Amer Bapt USA	1	319	139	384 *	.7	1.7
053 Assemb of God	2	268	352	520	.9	2.3
056 Baha'i	0	21	NR	21	-	.1
057 Bapt Gen Conf	1	852	622	1,024 *	1.8	4.5
081 Catholic	7	NR	NR	5,781	10.4	25.4
093 Chr Ch (Disc)	3	1,410	410	1,695 *	3.0	7.4
097 Chr Chs&Chs Cr	1	165	NR	198 *	.4	.9
123 Ch God (Ander)	1	NR	188	188	.3	.8
127 Ch God (Cleve)	1	72	59	87 *	.2	.4
145 Ch God Prophcy	1	42	NR	51 *	.1	.2
151 L-D Saints	1	NR	NR	349	.6	1.5
165 Ch of Nazarene	3	340	268	425	.8	1.9
167 Chs of Christ	2	59	60	79	.1	.3
173 Comm of Christ	1	83	NR	83	.1	.4
175 Congr Chr Chs	3	393	205	473 *	.8	2.1
193 Episcopal	1	NR	52	231	.4	1.0
201 Evan Cov Ch	1	315	178	379 *	.7	1.7
207 E.L.C.A.	6	2,505	854	3,154	5.6	13.8
226 Friends-USA	1	55	NR	66 *	.1	.3
263 Int Foursq Gos	1	99	68	119 *	.2	.5
283 Luth—MO Synod	1	305	130	376	.7	1.6
306 NT IndBapt&Rltd	1	225	NR	271 *	.5	1.2
355 Presb Ch (USA)	5	1,172	384	1,408 *	2.5	6.2
388 Reg Bapt Gen As	2	222	202	266 *	.5	1.2
403 Salvation Army	1	133	189	173	.3	.8
413 S.D.A.	1	123	NR	146	.3	.6
418 Southw Bapt Fel	1	NR	NR	NR	-	-
419 So Bapt Conv	5	265	164	319 *	.6	1.4
443 Un C of Christ	2	278	130	334 *	.6	1.5
449 Un Methodist	15	3,245	1,454	3,903 *	7.0	17.1
467 Wesleyan	1	41	65	165	.3	.7
496 Jewish Est	1	NR	NR	130	.2	.6
LAKE	**288**	**52,164**	**50,048**	**381,334 ***	**59.2**	**100.0**
017 Amer Bapt Assn	1	50	NR	65 *	-	-
019 Amer Bapt USA	5	798	346	1,042 *	.2	.3
049 Armen Ap Cilic	1	24	NR	105	-	-
050 Armen Ap Etchm	1	35	NR	300	-	.1
053 Assemb of God	13	1,415	1,919	2,608	.4	.7
056 Baha'i	4	311	NR	311	-	.1
057 Bapt Gen Conf	8	1,650	2,076	2,342 *	.4	.6
059 Bapt Miss Assn	1	82	40	107 *	-	-
076 Buddhism	3	NR	NR	NR	-	-
081 Catholic	32	NR	NR	253,000	39.3	66.3
084 Calvary Chapel	1	NR	NR	NR	-	-
089 Chr & Miss Al	1	0	NR	0	-	-
093 Chr Ch (Disc)	2	558	102	728 *	.1	.2
097 Chr Chs&Chs Cr	6	955	NR	1,247 *	.2	.3
123 Ch God (Ander)	1	NR	20	20	-	-
127 Ch God (Cleve)	5	695	300	907 *	.1	.2
145 Ch God Prophcy	2	85	NR	110 *	-	-
151 L-D Saints	9	NR	NR	2,307	.4	.6
165 Ch of Nazarene	4	278	214	375	.1	.1
167 Chs of Christ	7	403	493	572	.1	.1
173 Comm of Christ	1	119	NR	119	-	-
175 Congr Chr Chs	1	550	350	718 *	.1	.2
181 Consrv Congr	1	147	61	192 *	-	.1
193 Episcopal	11	NR	1,671	5,523	.9	1.4
201 Evan Cov Ch	2	316	277	412 *	.1	.1
203 Evan Free Ch	19	2,383	4,371	4,381	.7	1.1
207 E.L.C.A.	21	11,287	5,045	16,259	2.5	4.3
221 Free Methodist	1	298	300	300	-	.1
226 Friends-USA	1	55	NR	72 *	-	-
246 Greek Orthodox	2	NR	NR	603	.1	.2
263 Int Foursq Gos	4	166	271	271 *	-	.1
267 Muslim Est	4	NR	534	2,727	.4	.7
283 Luth—MO Synod	10	3,865	1,648	5,204	.8	1.4
288 Mennonite USA	1	24	50	50 *	-	-
290 Metro Comm Ch	1	35	16	46 *	-	-
291 Missionary Ch	2	721	1,741	1,741	.3	.5
306 NT IndBapt&Rltd	3	674	NR	880 *	.1	.2
313 N Am Bapt Conf	1	40	28	52 *	-	-
335 Orth Pres Ch	1	22	43	44	-	-
339 Pent Ch of God	1	54	NR	84	-	-
355 Presb Ch (USA)	9	7,960	2,730	10,392 *	1.6	2.7
356 Presb Ch Amer	2	239	160	291	-	.1
388 Reg Bapt Gen As	1	186	140	243 *	-	.1
403 Salvation Army	1	54	33	158	-	-
410 Serb Orth USA	1	NR	NR	500	.1	.1
413 S.D.A.	3	499	NR	594	.1	.2

NR–Not Reported *Total adherents estimated from known number of communicant, confirmed, full members. - Represents a percentage less than 0.1. Percentages may not total 100 due to rounding.

Table 4: Religious Congregations by County and Group: 2000

Religious Group	Number of Churches, Synagogues, Mosques, or Temples	Number of Communicant, Confirmed, or Full Members	Number of Attendees	Total Adherents: Number of Adherents	Total Adherents: % of Total Pop.	Total Adherents: % of Total Adh.
416 Sikh	1	NR	NR	NR	-	-
418 Southw Bapt Fel	1	NR	NR	NR	-	-
419 So Bapt Conv	17	2,182	1,249	2,849 *	.4	.7
435 Unitarian-Univ	1	392	NR	512 *	.1	.1
443 Un C of Christ	12	3,392	1,381	4,428 *	.7	1.2
449 Un Methodist	19	6,816	2,397	8,897 *	1.4	2.3
463 Vineyard	1	140	475	475 *	.1	.1
469 WELS	7	2,059	1,217	2,771	.4	.7
496 Jewish Est	15	NR	NR	25,000	3.9	6.6
498 Indep.Charis.	1	150	350	400	.1	.1
499 Indep.Non-Char	1	0	18,000	18,000	2.8	4.7
LA SALLE	**136**	**17,912**	**8,397**	**69,685 ***	**62.5**	**100.0**
019 Amer Bapt USA	3	273	170	337 *	.3	.5
053 Assemb of God	5	443	399	667	.6	1.0
056 Baha'i	0	8	NR	8	-	-
081 Catholic	30	NR	NR	44,736	40.1	64.2
097 Chr Chs&Chs Cr	4	1,111	NR	1,373 *	1.2	2.0
123 Ch God (Ander)	1	NR	55	55	-	.1
127 Ch God (Cleve)	1	46	37	57 *	.1	.1
151 L-D Saints	1	NR	NR	330	.3	.5
165 Ch of Nazarene	7	823	715	1,469	1.3	2.1
167 Chs of Christ	2	101	115	150	.1	.2
173 Comm of Christ	2	148	NR	148	.1	.2
179 Consrv Bapt	1	NR	122	122	.1	.2
193 Episcopal	3	NR	128	320	.3	.5
203 Evan Free Ch	1	35	62	62	.1	.1
207 E.L.C.A.	11	4,134	1,718	5,552	5.0	8.0
220 Free Lutheran	4	595	376	887	.8	1.3
263 Int Foursq Gos	2	139	353	353 *	.3	.5
283 Luth—MO Synod	4	933	465	1,337	1.2	1.9
339 Pent Ch of God	1	100	NR	300	.3	.4
355 Presb Ch (USA)	6	1,278	662	1,579 *	1.4	2.3
363 Primitive Meth	1	57	NR	61	.1	.1
388 Reg Bapt Gen As	2	132	120	163 *	.1	.2
403 Salvation Army	2	158	241	350	.3	.5
413 S.D.A.	3	206	NR	245	.2	.4
419 So Bapt Conv	7	572	220	707 *	.6	1.0
443 Un C of Christ	6	1,090	434	1,347 *	1.2	1.9
449 Un Methodist	25	5,530	2,005	6,830 *	6.1	9.8
496 Jewish Est	1	NR	NR	140	.1	.2
LAWRENCE	**56**	**5,361**	**2,252**	**7,617 ***	**49.3**	**100.0**
053 Assemb of God	1	93	112	145	.9	1.9
081 Catholic	3	NR	NR	804	5.2	10.6
093 Chr Ch (Disc)	1	311	80	375 *	2.4	4.9
097 Chr Chs&Chs Cr	10	1,313	NR	1,582 *	10.2	20.8
123 Ch God (Ander)	1	NR	25	25	.2	.3
127 Ch God (Cleve)	2	166	83	200 *	1.3	2.6
145 Ch God Prophcy	1	42	NR	51 *	.3	.7
157 Ch of Brethren	1	70	44	84 *	.5	1.1
165 Ch of Nazarene	1	51	17	52	.3	.7
167 Chs of Christ	2	29	35	39	.3	.5
175 Congr Chr Chs	1	70	65	84 *	.5	1.1
221 Free Methodist	6	233	269	303	2.0	4.0
283 Luth—MO Synod	1	40	15	65	.4	.9
355 Presb Ch (USA)	4	234	121	282 *	1.8	3.7
419 So Bapt Conv	2	658	160	793 *	5.1	10.4
449 Un Methodist	17	1,952	1,123	2,353 *	15.2	30.9
467 Wesleyan	2	99	103	380	2.5	5.0
LEE	**56**	**8,382**	**3,399**	**23,122 ***	**64.1**	**100.0**
019 Amer Bapt USA	3	439	188	538 *	1.5	2.3
053 Assemb of God	1	80	105	255	.7	1.1
056 Baha'i	0	3	NR	3	-	-
081 Catholic	9	NR	NR	11,995	33.3	51.9
089 Chr & Miss Al	3	83	NR	223	.6	1.0
093 Chr Ch (Disc)	1	124	45	152 *	.4	.7
097 Chr Chs&Chs Cr	1	85	NR	104 *	.3	.4
121 Ch God (Abr)	1	14	16	17 *	-	.1
123 Ch God (Ander)	1	NR	54	54	.1	.2
157 Ch of Brethren	2	408	175	500 *	1.4	2.2
165 Ch of Nazarene	1	25	35	38	.1	.2

Religious Group	Number of Churches, Synagogues, Mosques, or Temples	Number of Communicant, Confirmed, or Full Members	Number of Attendees	Total Adherents: Number of Adherents	Total Adherents: % of Total Pop.	Total Adherents: % of Total Adh.
167 Chs of Christ	1	26	28	34	.1	.1
193 Episcopal	1	NR	58	149	.4	.6
203 Evan Free Ch	1	36	95	95	.3	.4
207 E.L.C.A.	8	2,834	1,004	3,751	10.4	16.2
263 Int Foursq Gos	1	87	125	125 *	.3	.5
283 Luth—MO Synod	1	153	83	211	.6	.9
306 NT IndBapt&Rltd	2	449	NR	550 *	1.5	2.4
355 Presb Ch (USA)	3	410	171	502 *	1.4	2.2
419 So Bapt Conv	2	498	190	610 *	1.7	2.6
443 Un C of Christ	2	121	66	148 *	.4	.6
449 Un Methodist	11	2,507	961	3,068 *	8.5	13.3
LIVINGSTON	**75**	**12,663**	**6,583**	**24,241 ***	**61.1**	**100.0**
019 Amer Bapt USA	6	1,273	514	1,566 *	3.9	6.5
040 Ap Chr Ch-Amer	2	665	1,396	1,396 *	3.5	5.8
053 Assemb of God	3	180	212	310	.8	1.3
056 Baha'i	0	4	NR	4	-	-
081 Catholic	10	NR	NR	7,035	17.7	29.0
093 Chr Ch (Disc)	3	310	89	381 *	1.0	1.6
097 Chr Chs&Chs Cr	2	171	NR	211 *	.5	.9
127 Ch God (Cleve)	1	70	44	86 *	.2	.4
151 L-D Saints	1	NR	NR	138	.3	.6
165 Ch of Nazarene	3	92	79	194	.5	.8
167 Chs of Christ	3	108	145	154	.4	.6
193 Episcopal	1	NR	35	248	.6	1.0
207 E.L.C.A.	11	3,790	1,459	5,025	12.7	20.7
283 Luth—MO Synod	2	661	223	945	2.4	3.9
288 Mennonite USA	2	165	112	203 *	.5	.8
306 NT IndBapt&Rltd	1	225	NR	277 *	.7	1.1
355 Presb Ch (USA)	2	558	237	687 *	1.7	2.8
388 Reg Bapt Gen As	2	91	123	123 *	.3	.5
419 So Bapt Conv	0	28	14	34 *	.1	.1
443 Un C of Christ	3	415	189	511 *	1.3	2.1
449 Un Methodist	16	3,577	1,400	4,401 *	11.1	18.2
499 Indep.Non-Char	1	280	312	312	.8	1.3
LOGAN	**52**	**11,094**	**3,393**	**17,871 ***	**57.3**	**100.0**
019 Amer Bapt USA	1	375	115	449 *	1.4	2.5
053 Assemb of God	1	52	63	100	.3	.6
056 Baha'i	0	6	NR	6	-	-
081 Catholic	5	NR	NR	3,869	12.4	21.6
097 Chr Chs&Chs Cr	11	4,017	NR	4,815 *	15.4	26.9
127 Ch God (Cleve)	1	63	34	75 *	.2	.4
165 Ch of Nazarene	1	81	41	119	.4	.7
167 Chs of Christ	1	42	55	53	.2	.3
185 Cumber Presb	1	63	NR	153	.5	.9
193 Episcopal	1	NR	62	105	.3	.6
207 E.L.C.A.	4	1,463	503	1,916	6.1	10.7
220 Free Lutheran	1	121	110	146	.5	.8
221 Free Methodist	1	20	30	30	.1	.2
283 Luth—MO Synod	5	1,613	1,186	2,228	7.1	12.5
306 NT IndBapt&Rltd	1	225	NR	270 *	.9	1.5
355 Presb Ch (USA)	2	296	151	354 *	1.1	2.0
419 So Bapt Conv	1	193	45	231 *	.7	1.3
443 Un C of Christ	1	487	214	584 *	1.9	3.3
449 Un Methodist	13	1,977	784	2,368 *	7.6	13.3
MCDONOUGH	**56**	**6,961**	**3,511**	**11,634 ***	**35.3**	**100.0**
019 Amer Bapt USA	3	509	176	588 *	1.8	5.1
053 Assemb of God	3	342	480	925	2.8	8.0
056 Baha'i	0	11	NR	11	-	.1
059 Bapt Miss Assn	1	13	13	15 *	-	.1
081 Catholic	3	NR	NR	2,232	6.8	19.2
093 Chr Ch (Disc)	2	470	149	543 *	1.6	4.7
097 Chr Chs&Chs Cr	6	1,040	NR	1,200 *	3.6	10.3
121 Ch God (Abr)	1	68	55	78 *	.2	.7
151 L-D Saints	1	NR	NR	293	.9	2.5
165 Ch of Nazarene	2	121	96	155	.5	1.3
167 Chs of Christ	1	73	75	90	.3	.8
179 Consrv Bapt	1	NR	55	55	.2	.5
193 Episcopal	1	NR	43	116	.4	1.0
207 E.L.C.A.	1	158	85	194	.6	1.7
263 Int Foursq Gos	1	44	61	61 *	.2	.5

NR–Not Reported *Total adherents estimated from known number of communicant, confirmed, full members. - Represents a percentage less than 0.1. Percentages may not total 100 due to rounding.

Table 4: Religious Congregations by County and Group: 2000

Religious Group	Number of Churches, Synagogues, Mosques, or Temples	Number of Communicant, Confirmed, or Full Members	Number of Attendees	Total Adherents: Number of Adherents	Total Adherents: % of Total Pop.	Total Adherents: % of Total Adh.
267 Muslim Est	1	NR	50	150	.5	1.3
283 Luth—MO Synod	1	222	162	294	.9	2.5
323 Old Ord Amish	2	110	NR	126 *	.4	1.1
355 Presb Ch (USA)	5	1,087	435	1,255 *	3.8	10.8
356 Presb Ch Amer	1	41	48	56	.2	.5
403 Salvation Army	1	87	222	238	.7	2.0
419 So Bapt Conv	1	136	97	157 *	.5	1.3
435 Unitarian-Univ	1	48	NR	55 *	.2	.5
449 Un Methodist	15	2,221	1,109	2,562 *	7.8	22.0
463 Vineyard	1	160	100	185 *	.6	1.6
MCHENRY	**126**	**31,840**	**16,454**	**124,301 ***	**47.8**	**100.0**
019 Amer Bapt USA	2	253	231	332 *	.1	.3
053 Assemb of God	6	666	885	1,027	.4	.8
056 Baha'i	1	63	NR	63	-	.1
057 Bapt Gen Conf	3	239	565	586 *	.2	.5
081 Catholic	17	NR	NR	76,437	29.4	61.5
084 Calvary Chapel	1	NR	NR	NR	-	-
089 Chr & Miss Al	2	118	NR	274	.1	.2
097 Chr Chs&Chs Cr	2	200	NR	263 *	.1	.2
105 Christian Ref	1	79	72	104 *	-	.1
151 L-D Saints	5	NR	NR	1,414	.5	1.1
165 Ch of Nazarene	1	73	40	88	-	.1
167 Chs of Christ	2	108	135	141	.1	.1
173 Comm of Christ	1	17	NR	17	-	-
193 Episcopal	5	NR	625	1,608	.6	1.3
201 Evan Cov Ch	1	161	197	211 *	.1	.2
203 Evan Free Ch	4	595	1,157	1,157	.4	.9
207 E.L.C.A.	12	8,751	3,578	12,820	4.9	10.3
221 Free Methodist	1	146	125	161	.1	.1
226 Friends-USA	1	55	NR	72 *	-	.1
263 Int Foursq Gos	2	351	166	461 *	.2	.4
283 Luth—MO Synod	13	7,651	3,399	10,490	4.0	8.4
339 Pent Ch of God	2	80	NR	100	-	.1
355 Presb Ch (USA)	5	1,434	713	1,883 *	.7	1.5
388 Reg Bapt Gen As	1	40	75	75 *	-	.1
403 Salvation Army	1	71	163	247	.1	.2
419 So Bapt Conv	6	708	501	930 *	.4	.7
435 Unitarian-Univ	1	184	NR	242 *	.1	.2
443 Un C of Christ	8	4,182	1,474	5,493 *	2.1	4.4
449 Un Methodist	15	5,211	2,077	6,845 *	2.6	5.5
463 Vineyard	1	130	120	171 *	.1	.1
469 WELS	1	274	156	339	.1	.3
496 Jewish Est	2	NR	NR	250	.1	.2
MCLEAN	**139**	**35,462**	**16,795**	**66,474 ***	**44.2**	**100.0**
019 Amer Bapt USA	6	981	492	1,203 *	.8	1.8
040 Ap Chr Ch-Amer	2	642	1,058	1,058 *	.7	1.6
053 Assemb of God	4	714	1,062	1,476	1.0	2.2
056 Baha'i	1	73	NR	73	-	.1
081 Catholic	10	NR	NR	19,032	12.7	28.6
089 Chr & Miss Al	1	26	NR	51	-	.1
093 Chr Ch (Disc)	12	3,038	815	3,725 *	2.5	5.6
097 Chr Chs&Chs Cr	9	4,560	NR	5,591 *	3.7	8.4
123 Ch God (Ander)	3	NR	291	291	.2	.4
127 Ch God (Cleve)	1	95	52	116 *	.1	.2
151 L-D Saints	2	NR	NR	838	.6	1.3
165 Ch of Nazarene	2	320	201	353	.2	.5
167 Chs of Christ	5	395	421	515	.3	.8
173 Comm of Christ	1	21	NR	21	-	-
193 Episcopal	2	NR	224	470	.3	.7
203 Evan Free Ch	1	140	278	278	.2	.4
207 E.L.C.A.	7	3,239	1,489	4,404	2.9	6.6
213 Evan Menn Inc	2	178	290	218 *	.1	.3
221 Free Methodist	1	55	72	72	-	.1
263 Int Foursq Gos	1	167	84	205 *	.1	.3
264 Int Chs of Crst	1	123	181	174	.1	.3
283 Luth—MO Synod	8	4,130	2,036	5,600	3.7	8.4
288 Mennonite USA	4	659	406	809 *	.5	1.2
306 NT IndBapt&Rltd	3	674	NR	826 *	.5	1.2
355 Presb Ch (USA)	10	3,184	1,461	3,929 *	2.6	5.9
356 Presb Ch Amer	1	131	270	270	.2	.4
403 Salvation Army	1	203	322	316	.2	.5
413 S.D.A.	1	61	NR	73	-	.1
419 So Bapt Conv	5	1,406	639	1,724 *	1.1	2.6
435 Unitarian-Univ	1	247	NR	303 *	.2	.5
443 Un C of Christ	3	415	267	509 *	.3	.8
449 Un Methodist	24	7,990	3,383	9,794 *	6.5	14.7
463 Vineyard	1	118	95	145 *	.1	.2
469 WELS	1	77	56	112	.1	.2
496 Jewish Est	1	NR	NR	500	.3	.8
499 Indep.Non-Char	1	1,400	850	1,400	.9	2.1
MACON	**139**	**34,325**	**17,264**	**57,146 ***	**49.8**	**100.0**
019 Amer Bapt USA	1	545	190	673 *	.6	1.2
053 Assemb of God	5	1,783	1,702	3,668	3.2	6.4
056 Baha'i	1	42	NR	42	-	.1
081 Catholic	8	NR	NR	10,623	9.3	18.6
093 Chr Ch (Disc)	9	3,913	1,298	4,831 *	4.2	8.5
097 Chr Chs&Chs Cr	5	1,094	NR	1,350 *	1.2	2.4
123 Ch God (Ander)	5	NR	464	464	.4	.8
127 Ch God (Cleve)	1	140	35	173 *	.2	.3
151 L-D Saints	2	NR	NR	660	.6	1.2
157 Ch of Brethren	2	136	27	168 *	.1	.3
165 Ch of Nazarene	5	1,388	920	1,717	1.5	3.0
167 Chs of Christ	4	677	485	766	.7	1.3
171 Ch God-Gen Con	7	1,023	772	1,263 *	1.1	2.2
173 Comm of Christ	1	107	NR	107	.1	.2
193 Episcopal	1	NR	165	327	.3	.6
203 Evan Free Ch	1	32	60	60	.1	.1
207 E.L.C.A.	2	782	328	1,009	.9	1.8
221 Free Methodist	1	346	364	364	.3	.6
223 Free Will Bapt	1	86	NR	106 *	.1	.2
226 Friends-USA	1	55	NR	68 *	.1	.1
246 Greek Orthodox	1	NR	NR	123	.1	.2
263 Int Foursq Gos	3	1,068	695	1,319 *	1.1	2.3
267 Muslim Est	1	NR	101	288	.3	.5
283 Luth—MO Synod	8	5,120	2,441	6,562	5.7	11.5
306 NT IndBapt&Rltd	3	674	NR	832 *	.7	1.5
355 Presb Ch (USA)	7	2,035	964	2,512 *	2.2	4.4
360 Prim Bapt Chrch	1	NR	NR	NR	-	-
388 Reg Bapt Gen As	4	501	326	618 *	.5	1.1
403 Salvation Army	1	205	494	1,030	.9	1.8
413 S.D.A.	2	130	NR	155	.1	.3
419 So Bapt Conv	14	4,489	1,934	5,543 *	4.8	9.7
435 Unitarian-Univ	1	60	NR	74 *	.1	.1
443 Un C of Christ	2	546	202	674 *	.6	1.2
449 Un Methodist	24	6,329	2,881	7,814 *	6.8	13.7
463 Vineyard	1	15	6	19 *	-	-
467 Wesleyan	1	4	10	14	-	-
496 Jewish Est	1	NR	NR	130	.1	.2
499 Indep.Non-Char	1	1,000	400	1,000	.9	1.7
MACOUPIN	**108**	**14,315**	**5,404**	**25,166 ***	**51.3**	**100.0**
019 Amer Bapt USA	5	565	247	691 *	1.4	2.7
053 Assemb of God	6	546	646	987	2.0	3.9
056 Baha'i	0	8	NR	8	-	-
081 Catholic	15	NR	NR	7,068	14.4	28.1
093 Chr Ch (Disc)	3	703	232	860 *	1.8	3.4
097 Chr Chs&Chs Cr	8	864	NR	1,057 *	2.2	4.2
157 Ch of Brethren	2	252	100	309 *	.6	1.2
165 Ch of Nazarene	2	141	87	175	.4	.7
167 Chs of Christ	3	46	44	58	.1	.2
173 Comm of Christ	1	64	NR	64	.1	.3
193 Episcopal	2	NR	58	146	.3	.6
207 E.L.C.A.	4	762	320	988	2.0	3.9
283 Luth—MO Synod	6	2,484	854	3,138	6.4	12.5
339 Pent Ch of God	1	100	NR	100	.2	.4
355 Presb Ch (USA)	4	272	177	333 *	.7	1.3
360 Prim Bapt Chrch	1	NR	NR	NR	-	-
365 Prog Prim Bapt	1	44	NR	54 *	.1	.2
388 Reg Bapt Gen As	2	228	155	279 *	.6	1.1
400 Rus Orth Moscow	1	NR	NR	NR	-	-
419 So Bapt Conv	20	3,735	1,106	4,569 *	9.3	18.2
443 Un C of Christ	3	1,016	310	1,243 *	2.5	4.9
449 Un Methodist	18	2,485	1,068	3,039 *	6.2	12.1

NR–Not Reported   *Total adherents estimated from known number of communicant, confirmed, full members.   - Represents a percentage less than 0.1.   Percentages may not total 100 due to rounding.

Table 4: Religious Congregations by County and Group: 2000

Religious Group	Number of Churches, Synagogues, Mosques, or Temples	Number of Communicant, Confirmed, or Full Members	Number of Attendees	Total Adherents		
				Number of Adherents	% of Total Pop.	% of Total Adh.
MADISON	**290**	**63,206**	**29,153**	**129,959 ***	**50.2**	**100.0**
017 Amer Bapt Assn	3	120	NR	149 *	.1	.1
019 Amer Bapt USA	16	2,871	1,028	3,545 *	1.4	2.7
039 Ap Chr Ch(Naz)	1	2	2	2 *	-	-
049 Armen Ap Cilic	1	55	NR	336	.1	.3
053 Assemb of God	24	2,275	2,920	4,095	1.6	3.2
056 Baha'i	1	141	NR	141	.1	.1
081 Catholic	24	NR	NR	42,557	16.4	32.7
084 Calvary Chapel	1	NR	NR	NR	-	-
093 Chr Ch (Disc)	3	561	160	693 *	.3	.5
097 Chr Chs&Chs Cr	10	1,798	NR	2,221 *	.9	1.7
123 Ch God (Ander)	5	NR	320	320	.1	.2
127 Ch God (Cleve)	4	1,087	570	1,343 *	.5	1.0
145 Ch God Prophcy	2	85	NR	104 *	-	.1
151 L-D Saints	6	NR	NR	1,452	.6	1.1
165 Ch of Nazarene	7	841	530	1,161	.4	.9
167 Chs of Christ	15	1,241	1,407	1,648	.6	1.3
173 Comm of Christ	2	175	NR	175	.1	.1
175 Congr Chr Chs	1	50	42	62 *	-	-
179 Consrv Bapt	1	NR	285	285	.1	.2
181 Consrv Congr	1	236	125	291 *	.1	.2
193 Episcopal	5	NR	390	758	.3	.6
203 Evan Free Ch	1	16	30	30	-	-
207 E.L.C.A.	4	1,025	503	1,398	.5	1.1
216 Evan Presby Ch	1	37	NR	46 *	-	-
221 Free Methodist	3	131	327	327	.1	.3
223 Free Will Bapt	2	172	NR	212 *	.1	.2
263 Int Foursq Gos	3	365	489	489 *	.2	.4
267 Muslim Est	2	NR	580	2,626	1.0	2.0
283 Luth—MO Synod	22	10,660	4,801	13,792	5.3	10.6
331 OCA: Ter Diocs	1	84	NR	168	.1	.1
332 OCA: Bulg Dioc	1	90	NR	156	.1	.1
339 Pent Ch of God	4	102	NR	306	.1	.2
355 Presb Ch (USA)	13	3,323	1,311	4,103 *	1.6	3.2
356 Presb Ch Amer	3	282	368	405	.2	.3
360 Prim Bapt Chrch	1	NR	NR	NR	-	-
388 Reg Bapt Gen As	7	697	606	765 *	.3	.6
403 Salvation Army	2	276	144	1,122	.4	.9
413 S.D.A.	1	92	NR	109	-	.1
419 So Bapt Conv	41	17,750	5,584	21,915 *	8.5	16.9
435 Unitarian-Univ	1	60	NR	74 *	-	.1
443 Un C of Christ	17	8,997	3,101	11,108 *	4.3	8.5
449 Un Methodist	26	7,509	3,530	9,270 *	3.6	7.1
496 Jewish Est	1	NR	NR	200	.1	.2
MARION	**99**	**17,650**	**6,199**	**26,073 ***	**62.5**	**100.0**
019 Amer Bapt USA	1	302	120	374 *	.9	1.4
053 Assemb of God	3	287	345	415	1.0	1.6
056 Baha'i	0	4	NR	4	-	-
059 Bapt Miss Assn	1	10	7	12 *	-	-
081 Catholic	4	NR	NR	3,554	8.5	13.6
093 Chr Ch (Disc)	3	572	171	709 *	1.7	2.7
097 Chr Chs&Chs Cr	17	3,671	NR	4,553 *	10.9	17.5
123 Ch God (Ander)	2	NR	75	75	.2	.3
127 Ch God (Cleve)	2	221	61	274 *	.7	1.1
157 Ch of Brethren	1	28	0	35 *	.1	.1
165 Ch of Nazarene	1	163	244	589	1.4	2.3
167 Chs of Christ	4	285	310	366	.9	1.4
173 Comm of Christ	2	174	NR	174	.4	.7
193 Episcopal	2	NR	55	100	.2	.4
207 E.L.C.A.	1	86	45	111	.3	.4
221 Free Methodist	2	136	150	150	.4	.6
223 Free Will Bapt	2	172	NR	213 *	.5	.8
267 Muslim Est	1	NR	25	50	.1	.2
283 Luth—MO Synod	3	1,769	874	2,196	5.3	8.4
355 Presb Ch (USA)	4	383	199	475 *	1.1	1.8
360 Prim Bapt Chrch	1	NR	NR	NR	-	-
403 Salvation Army	1	75	71	130	.3	.5
419 So Bapt Conv	20	5,785	1,662	7,171 *	17.2	27.5
443 Un C of Christ	2	396	132	491 *	1.2	1.9
449 Un Methodist	17	2,181	1,228	2,702 *	6.5	10.4
496 Jewish Est	1	NR	NR	200	.5	.8
499 Indep.Non-Char	1	950	425	950	2.3	3.6

Religious Group	Number of Churches, Synagogues, Mosques, or Temples	Number of Communicant, Confirmed, or Full Members	Number of Attendees	Total Adherents		
				Number of Adherents	% of Total Pop.	% of Total Adh.
MARSHALL	**32**	**3,722**	**1,482**	**8,166 ***	**62.0**	**100.0**
019 Amer Bapt USA	1	97	80	118 *	.9	1.4
053 Assemb of God	1	25	34	40	.3	.5
056 Baha'i	0	1	NR	1	-	-
081 Catholic	6	NR	NR	3,523	26.7	43.1
093 Chr Ch (Disc)	2	535	139	652 *	4.9	8.0
097 Chr Chs&Chs Cr	2	363	NR	443 *	3.4	5.4
165 Ch of Nazarene	1	32	26	37	.3	.5
193 Episcopal	1	NR	22	28	.2	.3
207 E.L.C.A.	4	709	308	928	7.0	11.4
283 Luth—MO Synod	3	408	174	511	3.9	6.3
288 Mennonite USA	1	79	63	96 *	.7	1.2
355 Presb Ch (USA)	4	417	213	508 *	3.9	6.2
388 Reg Bapt Gen As	1	10	5	5 *	-	.1
443 Un C of Christ	1	296	130	361 *	2.7	4.4
449 Un Methodist	4	750	288	915 *	6.9	11.2
MASON	**36**	**5,726**	**2,079**	**8,722 ***	**54.4**	**100.0**
019 Amer Bapt USA	2	618	122	758 *	4.7	8.7
053 Assemb of God	2	175	169	432	2.7	5.0
056 Baha'i	0	2	NR	2	-	-
081 Catholic	3	NR	NR	1,061	6.6	12.2
093 Chr Ch (Disc)	1	305	67	374 *	2.3	4.3
097 Chr Chs&Chs Cr	2	540	NR	663 *	4.1	7.6
151 L-D Saints	1	NR	NR	72	.4	.8
165 Ch of Nazarene	2	106	68	221	1.4	2.5
193 Episcopal	1	NR	29	103	.6	1.2
283 Luth—MO Synod	7	1,672	733	2,227	13.9	25.5
291 Missionary Ch	2	131	139	139	.9	1.6
306 NT IndBapt&Rltd	1	225	NR	276 *	1.7	3.2
355 Presb Ch (USA)	1	182	90	223 *	1.4	2.6
388 Reg Bapt Gen As	1	54	53	66 *	.4	.8
419 So Bapt Conv	4	525	102	644 *	4.0	7.4
449 Un Methodist	6	1,191	507	1,461 *	9.1	16.8
MASSAC	**41**	**7,970**	**3,120**	**10,108 ***	**66.7**	**100.0**
053 Assemb of God	1	112	132	132	.9	1.3
056 Baha'i	0	7	NR	7	-	.1
081 Catholic	1	NR	NR	345	2.3	3.4
093 Chr Ch (Disc)	1	201	105	244 *	1.6	2.4
097 Chr Chs&Chs Cr	2	200	NR	243 *	1.6	2.4
123 Ch God (Ander)	1	NR	55	55	.4	.5
127 Ch God (Cleve)	1	182	108	221 *	1.5	2.2
165 Ch of Nazarene	1	59	44	66	.4	.7
167 Chs of Christ	6	413	343	545	3.6	5.4
173 Comm of Christ	1	119	NR	119	.8	1.2
185 Cumber Presb	1	145	NR	167	1.1	1.7
207 E.L.C.A.	4	635	358	788	5.2	7.8
220 Free Lutheran	1	46	70	70	.5	.7
355 Presb Ch (USA)	1	68	57	83 *	.5	.8
419 So Bapt Conv	12	4,732	1,354	5,747 *	37.9	56.9
443 Un C of Christ	2	316	147	384 *	2.5	3.8
449 Un Methodist	5	735	347	892 *	5.9	8.8
MENARD	**29**	**4,571**	**1,191**	**7,154 ***	**57.3**	**100.0**
017 Amer Bapt Assn	1	50	NR	62 *	.5	.9
053 Assemb of God	1	75	64	100	.8	1.4
056 Baha'i	0	9	NR	9	.1	.1
081 Catholic	2	NR	NR	1,428	11.4	20.0
093 Chr Ch (Disc)	2	221	45	276 *	2.2	3.9
097 Chr Chs&Chs Cr	4	1,075	NR	1,341 *	10.7	18.7
185 Cumber Presb	1	9	NR	9	.1	.1
223 Free Will Bapt	1	86	NR	107 *	.9	1.5
263 Int Foursq Gos	1	80	73	100 *	.8	1.4
283 Luth—MO Synod	2	506	159	651	5.2	9.1
355 Presb Ch (USA)	4	624	228	779 *	6.2	10.9
360 Prim Bapt Chrch	2	NR	NR	NR	-	-
419 So Bapt Conv	4	844	193	1,053 *	8.4	14.7
443 Un C of Christ	1	375	165	468 *	3.7	6.5
449 Un Methodist	3	617	264	771 *	6.2	10.8

NR–Not Reported *Total adherents estimated from known number of communicant, confirmed, full members. - Represents a percentage less than 0.1. Percentages may not total 100 due to rounding.

Table 4: Religious Congregations by County and Group: 2000

Religious Group	Number of Churches, Synagogues, Mosques, or Temples	Number of Communicant, Confirmed, or Full Members	Number of Attendees	Total Adherents: Number of Adherents	Total Adherents: % of Total Pop.	Total Adherents: % of Total Adh.
MERCER	**33**	**4,716**	**1,887**	**8,575 ***	**50.6**	**100.0**
019 Amer Bapt USA	1	477	216	584 *	3.4	6.8
053 Assemb of God	2	73	57	153	.9	1.8
056 Baha'i	0	3	NR	3	-	-
057 Bapt Gen Conf	1	96	68	118 *	.7	1.4
081 Catholic	5	NR	NR	2,586	15.3	30.2
093 Chr Ch (Disc)	1	330	0	404 *	2.4	4.7
165 Ch of Nazarene	1	47	21	47	.3	.5
193 Episcopal	1	NR	13	16	.1	.2
203 Evan Free Ch	1	72	100	100	.6	1.2
207 E.L.C.A.	4	1,062	297	1,420	8.4	16.6
355 Presb Ch (USA)	7	960	483	1,175 *	6.9	13.7
356 Presb Ch Amer	1	65	95	95	.6	1.1
419 So Bapt Conv	1	205	100	251 *	1.5	2.9
449 Un Methodist	7	1,326	437	1,623 *	9.6	18.9
MONROE	**30**	**7,800**	**3,139**	**19,696 ***	**71.3**	**100.0**
053 Assemb of God	2	36	45	75	.3	.4
056 Baha'i	0	2	NR	2	-	-
081 Catholic	7	NR	NR	9,779	35.4	49.6
097 Chr Chs&Chs Cr	1	125	NR	156 *	.6	.8
127 Ch God (Cleve)	1	25	9	31 *	.1	.2
165 Ch of Nazarene	1	25	40	40	.1	.2
167 Chs of Christ	1	33	40	35	.1	.2
207 E.L.C.A.	1	129	91	169	.6	.9
283 Luth—MO Synod	4	1,757	750	2,316	8.4	11.8
356 Presb Ch Amer	1	92	125	125	.5	.6
419 So Bapt Conv	3	1,374	704	1,717 *	6.2	8.7
443 Un C of Christ	7	4,054	1,200	5,066 *	18.3	25.7
449 Un Methodist	1	148	135	185 *	.7	.9
MONTGOMERY	**76**	**9,975**	**4,206**	**16,129 ***	**52.6**	**100.0**
019 Amer Bapt USA	2	436	179	531 *	1.7	3.3
053 Assemb of God	4	186	230	337	1.1	2.1
056 Baha'i	0	5	NR	5	-	-
081 Catholic	8	NR	NR	3,344	10.9	20.7
093 Chr Ch (Disc)	5	658	68	802 *	2.6	5.0
097 Chr Chs&Chs Cr	5	562	NR	685 *	2.2	4.2
151 L-D Saints	1	NR	NR	302	1.0	1.9
167 Chs of Christ	1	25	25	25	.1	.2
207 E.L.C.A.	9	1,055	460	1,335	4.4	8.3
221 Free Methodist	2	160	238	238	.8	1.5
283 Luth—MO Synod	5	1,606	1,183	2,087	6.8	12.9
306 NT IndBapt&Rltd	1	225	NR	274 *	.9	1.7
355 Presb Ch (USA)	7	586	302	714 *	2.3	4.4
419 So Bapt Conv	16	3,174	882	3,869 *	12.6	24.0
443 Un C of Christ	1	31	14	38 *	.1	.2
449 Un Methodist	9	1,266	625	1,543 *	5.0	9.6
MORGAN	**67**	**11,559**	**4,071**	**18,868 ***	**51.5**	**100.0**
017 Amer Bapt Assn	1	50	NR	60 *	.2	.3
019 Amer Bapt USA	3	1,219	330	1,465 *	4.0	7.8
053 Assemb of God	1	173	186	240	.7	1.3
056 Baha'i	0	120	NR	120	.3	.6
081 Catholic	5	NR	NR	4,119	11.2	21.8
093 Chr Ch (Disc)	5	1,917	224	2,304 *	6.3	12.2
097 Chr Chs&Chs Cr	5	916	NR	1,100 *	3.0	5.8
123 Ch God (Ander)	1	NR	12	12	-	.1
151 L-D Saints	1	NR	NR	345	.9	1.8
167 Chs of Christ	2	106	115	130	.4	.7
173 Comm of Christ	1	38	NR	38	.1	.2
193 Episcopal	1	NR	85	187	.5	1.0
207 E.L.C.A.	3	382	184	539	1.5	2.9
263 Int Foursq Gos	1	10	14	14 *	-	.1
283 Luth—MO Synod	5	1,494	717	1,927	5.3	10.2
355 Presb Ch (USA)	3	565	266	684 *	1.9	3.6
403 Salvation Army	1	50	29	255	.7	1.4
413 S.D.A.	1	18	NR	21	.1	.1
419 So Bapt Conv	10	1,658	546	1,993 *	5.4	10.6
443 Un C of Christ	2	130	61	156 *	.4	.8
449 Un Methodist	14	2,213	912	2,659 *	7.3	14.1
499 Indep.Non-Char	1	500	390	500	1.4	2.6

Religious Group	Number of Churches, Synagogues, Mosques, or Temples	Number of Communicant, Confirmed, or Full Members	Number of Attendees	Total Adherents: Number of Adherents	Total Adherents: % of Total Pop.	Total Adherents: % of Total Adh.
MOULTRIE	**34**	**4,265**	**1,523**	**6,323 ***	**44.3**	**100.0**
019 Amer Bapt USA	1	165	75	204 *	1.4	3.2
053 Assemb of God	1	63	39	55	.4	.9
056 Baha'i	0	3	NR	3	-	-
061 Beachy Amish	1	41	NR	51 *	.4	.8
081 Catholic	2	NR	NR	605	4.2	9.6
093 Chr Ch (Disc)	3	1,156	263	1,431 *	10.0	22.6
097 Chr Chs&Chs Cr	3	310	NR	384 *	2.7	6.1
123 Ch God (Ander)	3	NR	256	256	1.8	4.0
167 Chs of Christ	3	102	106	126	.9	2.0
171 Ch God-Gen Con	1	44	27	54 *	.4	.9
185 Cumber Presb	1	96	NR	297	2.1	4.7
221 Free Methodist	1	37	41	41	.3	.6
283 Luth—MO Synod	1	336	150	449	3.1	7.1
306 NT IndBapt&Rltd	1	225	NR	279 *	2.0	4.4
323 Old Ord Amish	2	110	NR	136 *	1.0	2.2
355 Presb Ch (USA)	1	29	20	36 *	.3	.6
419 So Bapt Conv	4	692	220	857 *	6.0	13.6
449 Un Methodist	5	856	326	1,059 *	7.4	16.7
OGLE	**73**	**13,715**	**6,527**	**27,395 ***	**53.7**	**100.0**
053 Assemb of God	4	352	441	712	1.4	2.6
056 Baha'i	0	3	NR	3	-	-
057 Bapt Gen Conf	2	293	202	370 *	.7	1.4
081 Catholic	4	NR	NR	8,354	16.4	30.5
093 Chr Ch (Disc)	1	103	0	130 *	.3	.5
097 Chr Chs&Chs Cr	3	312	NR	394 *	.8	1.4
121 Ch God (Abr)	3	214	229	271 *	.5	1.0
123 Ch God (Ander)	1	NR	412	412	.8	1.5
127 Ch God (Cleve)	1	119	34	150 *	.3	.5
157 Ch of Brethren	3	645	221	815 *	1.6	3.0
165 Ch of Nazarene	2	52	19	116	.2	.4
167 Chs of Christ	1	75	80	97	.2	.4
175 Congr Chr Chs	1	663	150	837 *	1.6	3.1
179 Consrv Bapt	1	NR	70	70	.1	.3
181 Consrv Congr	1	36	31	45 *	.1	.2
193 Episcopal	2	NR	90	211	.4	.8
201 Evan Cov Ch	1	141	133	178 *	.3	.6
203 Evan Free Ch	1	115	175	175	.3	.6
207 E.L.C.A.	9	2,954	1,173	3,978	7.8	14.5
263 Int Foursq Gos	1	17	25	25 *	-	.1
283 Luth—MO Synod	2	854	392	1,320	2.6	4.8
306 NT IndBapt&Rltd	3	674	NR	851 *	1.7	3.1
355 Presb Ch (USA)	6	1,279	670	1,615 *	3.2	5.9
356 Presb Ch Amer	1	259	156	259	.5	.9
371 Ref Ch in Am	4	609	477	1,024	2.0	3.7
413 S.D.A.	1	14	NR	17	-	.1
419 So Bapt Conv	1	223	10	282 *	.6	1.0
443 Un C of Christ	1	663	292	837 *	1.6	3.1
449 Un Methodist	12	3,046	1,045	3,847 *	7.5	14.0
PEORIA	**180**	**36,435**	**22,738**	**89,445 ***	**48.8**	**100.0**
017 Amer Bapt Assn	2	100	NR	124 *	.1	.1
019 Amer Bapt USA	3	880	409	1,094 *	.6	1.2
039 Ap Chr Ch(Naz)	1	58	71	72 *	-	.1
040 Ap Chr Ch-Amer	1	626	1,042	1,042 *	.6	1.2
053 Assemb of God	8	498	659	932	.5	1.0
056 Baha'i	1	85	NR	85	-	.1
059 Bapt Miss Assn	1	12	10	15 *	-	-
081 Catholic	19	NR	NR	35,462	19.3	39.6
093 Chr Ch (Disc)	5	2,004	497	2,491 *	1.4	2.8
097 Chr Chs&Chs Cr	3	480	NR	597 *	.3	.7
123 Ch God (Ander)	3	NR	240	240	.1	.3
127 Ch God (Cleve)	2	68	97	104 *	.1	.1
151 L-D Saints	3	NR	NR	855	.5	1.0
157 Ch of Brethren	1	160	108	199 *	.1	.2
165 Ch of Nazarene	5	390	306	547	.3	.6
167 Chs of Christ	5	398	468	605	.3	.7
179 Consrv Bapt	1	NR	800	800	.4	.9
193 Episcopal	4	NR	430	1,009	.6	1.1
201 Evan Cov Ch	1	79	105	105 *	.1	.1
203 Evan Free Ch	3	205	357	357	.2	.4
207 E.L.C.A.	10	4,916	1,821	6,404	3.5	7.2

NR–Not Reported *Total adherents estimated from known number of communicant, confirmed, full members. - Represents a percentage less than 0.1. Percentages may not total 100 due to rounding.

Table 4: Religious Congregations by County and Group: 2000

Religious Group	Number of Churches, Synagogues, Mosques, or Temples	Number of Communicant, Confirmed, or Full Members	Number of Attendees	Total Adherents: Number of Adherents	Total Adherents: % of Total Pop.	Total Adherents: % of Total Adh.
213 Evan Menn Inc	1	588	2,638	731 *	.4	.8
221 Free Methodist	2	111	126	133	.1	.1
223 Free Will Bapt	1	86	NR	107 *	.1	.1
246 Greek Orthodox	1	NR	NR	555	.3	.6
263 Int Foursq Gos	1	29	38	38 *	-	-
267 Muslim Est	5	NR	793	3,027	1.7	3.4
283 Luth—MO Synod	9	4,367	2,350	5,716	3.1	6.4
288 Mennonite USA	3	140	115	174 *	.1	.2
291 Missionary Ch	4	234	509	509	.3	.6
306 NT IndBapt&Rltd	5	1,124	NR	1,397 *	.8	1.6
355 Presb Ch (USA)	10	2,891	1,539	3,593 *	2.0	4.0
356 Presb Ch Amer	3	2,452	1,574	2,480	1.4	2.8
388 Reg Bapt Gen As	1	57	40	71 *	-	.1
403 Salvation Army	1	199	433	601	.3	.7
413 S.D.A.	3	491	NR	585	.3	.7
419 So Bapt Conv	10	2,900	828	3,604 *	2.0	4.0
435 Unitarian-Univ	1	233	NR	290 *	.2	.3
443 Un C of Christ	6	1,404	700	1,745 *	1.0	2.0
449 Un Methodist	26	7,995	3,471	9,938 *	5.4	11.1
463 Vineyard	1	130	120	162 *	.1	.2
469 WELS	1	45	44	50	-	.1
496 Jewish Est	3	NR	NR	800	.4	.9
PERRY	**45**	**8,227**	**2,892**	**13,291 ***	**57.6**	**100.0**
019 Amer Bapt USA	3	192	95	230 *	1.0	1.7
053 Assemb of God	2	129	157	183	.8	1.4
081 Catholic	5	NR	NR	3,399	14.7	25.6
093 Chr Ch (Disc)	1	479	95	575 *	2.5	4.3
097 Chr Chs&Chs Cr	3	309	NR	371 *	1.6	2.8
165 Ch of Nazarene	1	68	28	68	.3	.5
167 Chs of Christ	1	21	16	22	.1	.2
283 Luth—MO Synod	3	254	184	312	1.4	2.3
355 Presb Ch (USA)	2	195	85	234 *	1.0	1.8
356 Presb Ch Amer	1	106	60	129	.6	1.0
413 S.D.A.	1	13	NR	15	.1	.1
419 So Bapt Conv	17	5,038	1,596	6,045 *	26.2	45.5
443 Un C of Christ	2	596	216	715 *	3.1	5.4
449 Un Methodist	3	827	360	993 *	4.3	7.5
PIATT	**35**	**5,979**	**2,155**	**8,725 ***	**53.3**	**100.0**
053 Assemb of God	1	15	15	15	.1	.2
056 Baha'i	0	3	NR	3	-	-
071 Brethren (Ash)	1	66	50	81 *	.5	.9
081 Catholic	2	NR	NR	943	5.8	10.8
093 Chr Ch (Disc)	1	0	0	0 *	-	-
097 Chr Chs&Chs Cr	2	775	NR	957 *	5.8	11.0
151 L-D Saints	1	NR	NR	162	1.0	1.9
157 Ch of Brethren	2	241	135	298 *	1.8	3.4
165 Ch of Nazarene	2	121	78	223	1.4	2.6
167 Chs of Christ	2	86	89	123	.8	1.4
171 Ch God-Gen Con	1	92	133	133 *	.8	1.5
207 E.L.C.A.	1	355	161	512	3.1	5.9
263 Int Foursq Gos	1	26	92	92 *	.6	1.1
306 NT IndBapt&Rltd	1	225	NR	278 *	1.7	3.2
355 Presb Ch (USA)	2	364	168	449 *	2.7	5.1
419 So Bapt Conv	5	801	307	988 *	6.0	11.3
443 Un C of Christ	2	529	150	653 *	4.0	7.5
449 Un Methodist	8	2,280	777	2,815 *	17.2	32.3
PIKE	**58**	**6,366**	**2,609**	**8,789 ***	**50.6**	**100.0**
019 Amer Bapt USA	2	158	115	193 *	1.1	2.2
053 Assemb of God	2	291	376	605	3.5	6.9
081 Catholic	2	NR	NR	525	3.0	6.0
093 Chr Ch (Disc)	2	760	192	928 *	5.3	10.6
097 Chr Chs&Chs Cr	11	1,302	NR	1,591 *	9.2	18.1
151 L-D Saints	1	NR	NR	48	.3	.5
165 Ch of Nazarene	4	386	373	592	3.4	6.7
167 Chs of Christ	6	307	323	404	2.3	4.6
173 Comm of Christ	2	46	NR	46	.3	.5
193 Episcopal	1	NR	19	55	.3	.6
283 Luth—MO Synod	1	133	58	150	.9	1.7
323 Old Ord Amish	2	110	NR	134 *	.8	1.5
339 Pent Ch of God	1	6	NR	16	.1	.2

Religious Group	Number of Churches, Synagogues, Mosques, or Temples	Number of Communicant, Confirmed, or Full Members	Number of Attendees	Total Adherents: Number of Adherents	Total Adherents: % of Total Pop.	Total Adherents: % of Total Adh.
355 Presb Ch (USA)	1	19	20	23 *	.1	.3
388 Reg Bapt Gen As	2	167	126	204 *	1.2	2.3
419 So Bapt Conv	4	1,005	280	1,227 *	7.1	14.0
449 Un Methodist	14	1,676	727	2,048 *	11.8	23.3
POPE	**18**	**1,688**	**740**	**1,983 ***	**44.9**	**100.0**
056 Baha'i	0	2	NR	2	-	.1
127 Ch God (Cleve)	1	98	82	115 *	2.6	5.8
167 Chs of Christ	1	19	20	24	.5	1.2
283 Luth—MO Synod	1	98	50	118	2.7	6.0
355 Presb Ch (USA)	1	33	20	39 *	.9	2.0
419 So Bapt Conv	11	1,269	467	1,487 *	33.7	75.0
449 Un Methodist	3	169	101	198 *	4.5	10.0
PULASKI	**28**	**2,827**	**957**	**4,165 ***	**56.7**	**100.0**
053 Assemb of God	1	28	36	40	.5	1.0
056 Baha'i	0	50	NR	50	.7	1.2
081 Catholic	3	NR	NR	619	8.4	14.9
097 Chr Chs&Chs Cr	1	80	NR	101 *	1.4	2.4
167 Chs of Christ	3	160	171	209	2.8	5.0
181 Consrv Congr	2	176	57	221 *	3.0	5.3
283 Luth—MO Synod	1	94	35	112	1.5	2.7
419 So Bapt Conv	8	1,783	358	2,241 *	30.5	53.8
443 Un C of Christ	1	56	25	70 *	1.0	1.7
449 Un Methodist	8	400	275	502 *	6.8	12.1
PUTNAM	**11**	**903**	**371**	**2,766 ***	**45.4**	**100.0**
081 Catholic	3	NR	NR	1,650	27.1	59.7
097 Chr Chs&Chs Cr	1	30	NR	37 *	.6	1.3
207 E.L.C.A.	2	227	67	282	4.6	10.2
226 Friends-USA	1	55	NR	68 *	1.1	2.5
443 Un C of Christ	1	332	146	409 *	6.7	14.8
449 Un Methodist	3	259	158	320 *	5.3	11.6
RANDOLPH	**67**	**12,172**	**4,616**	**21,465 ***	**63.3**	**100.0**
019 Amer Bapt USA	1	90	30	108 *	.3	.5
053 Assemb of God	3	114	148	299	.9	1.4
056 Baha'i	0	6	NR	6	-	-
059 Bapt Miss Assn	1	67	55	80 *	.2	.4
081 Catholic	10	NR	NR	6,369	18.8	29.7
097 Chr Chs&Chs Cr	2	110	NR	132 *	.4	.6
165 Ch of Nazarene	2	33	46	78	.2	.4
167 Chs of Christ	3	44	48	67	.2	.3
173 Comm of Christ	1	52	NR	52	.2	.2
193 Episcopal	1	NR	10	12	-	.1
207 E.L.C.A.	5	1,495	530	1,856	5.5	8.6
216 Evan Presby Ch	1	10	NR	12 *	-	.1
283 Luth—MO Synod	9	5,027	1,741	6,274	18.5	29.2
355 Presb Ch (USA)	6	933	463	1,119 *	3.3	5.2
356 Presb Ch Amer	2	235	174	258	.8	1.2
419 So Bapt Conv	9	2,231	671	2,675 *	7.9	12.5
443 Un C of Christ	2	563	133	675 *	2.0	3.1
449 Un Methodist	9	1,162	567	1,393 *	4.1	6.5
RICHLAND	**45**	**5,808**	**2,435**	**10,394 ***	**64.4**	**100.0**
019 Amer Bapt USA	1	353	125	432 *	2.7	4.2
053 Assemb of God	1	188	210	250	1.5	2.4
081 Catholic	2	NR	NR	2,397	14.8	23.1
093 Chr Ch (Disc)	1	103	0	126 *	.8	1.2
097 Chr Chs&Chs Cr	9	1,792	NR	2,193 *	13.6	21.1
127 Ch God (Cleve)	1	38	26	46 *	.3	.4
151 L-D Saints	2	NR	NR	290	1.8	2.8
157 Ch of Brethren	1	29	23	35 *	.2	.3
165 Ch of Nazarene	1	118	97	276	1.7	2.7
167 Chs of Christ	5	241	287	328	2.0	3.2
193 Episcopal	1	NR	16	39	.2	.4
207 E.L.C.A.	1	495	156	631	3.9	6.1
221 Free Methodist	1	173	115	242	1.5	2.3
355 Presb Ch (USA)	1	171	85	209 *	1.3	2.0
413 S.D.A.	1	49	NR	58	.4	.6
419 So Bapt Conv	3	618	258	756 *	4.7	7.3
443 Un C of Christ	2	100	51	122 *	.8	1.2

NR–Not Reported *Total adherents estimated from known number of communicant, confirmed, full members. - Represents a percentage less than 0.1. Percentages may not total 100 due to rounding.

Table 4: Religious Congregations by County and Group: 2000

Religious Group	Number of Churches, Synagogues, Mosques, or Temples	Number of Communicant, Confirmed, or Full Members	Number of Attendees	Total Adherents		
				Number of Adherents	% of Total Pop.	% of Total Adh.
449 Un Methodist	10	1,340	701	1,639 *	10.1	15.8
499 Indep.Non-Char	1	0	285	325	2.0	3.1
ROCK ISLAND	**143**	**31,665**	**15,966**	**74,429 ***	**49.8**	**100.0**
017 Amer Bapt Assn	2	100	NR	122 *	.1	.2
019 Amer Bapt USA	5	1,427	489	1,745 *	1.2	2.3
053 Assemb of God	6	620	745	1,436	1.0	1.9
056 Baha'i	0	107	NR	107	.1	.1
057 Bapt Gen Conf	1	300	0	367 *	.2	.5
076 Buddhism	2	NR	NR	NR	-	-
081 Catholic	15	NR	NR	27,891	18.7	37.5
089 Chr & Miss Al	1	56	NR	72	-	.1
093 Chr Ch (Disc)	4	2,272	435	2,778 *	1.9	3.7
097 Chr Chs&Chs Cr	3	305	NR	372 *	.2	.5
123 Ch God (Ander)	1	NR	50	50	-	.1
127 Ch God (Cleve)	2	207	71	253 *	.2	.3
151 L-D Saints	1	NR	NR	391	.3	.5
157 Ch of Brethren	1	42	27	51 *	-	.1
165 Ch of Nazarene	6	458	317	687	.5	.9
167 Chs of Christ	2	180	188	220	.1	.3
173 Comm of Christ	1	155	NR	155	.1	.2
175 Congr Chr Chs	1	28	26	34 *	-	-
179 Consrv Bapt	1	NR	400	400	.3	.5
193 Episcopal	3	NR	382	760	.5	1.0
201 Evan Cov Ch	2	518	320	634 *	.4	.9
203 Evan Free Ch	4	910	1,228	1,228	.8	1.6
207 E.L.C.A.	11	5,178	1,853	6,766	4.5	9.1
223 Free Will Bapt	2	172	NR	210 *	.1	.3
246 Greek Orthodox	2	NR	NR	939	.6	1.3
263 Int Foursq Gos	4	2,903	1,143	3,549 *	2.4	4.8
267 Muslim Est	1	NR	40	320	.2	.4
283 Luth—MO Synod	7	3,777	1,391	5,238	3.5	7.0
288 Mennonite USA	1	0	50	50 *	-	.1
355 Presb Ch (USA)	10	2,843	1,276	3,477 *	2.3	4.7
370 Ref Baptist Chs	1	NR	NR	NR	-	-
388 Reg Bapt Gen As	4	615	452	752 *	.5	1.0
403 Salvation Army	1	124	303	296	.2	.4
413 S.D.A.	1	131	NR	156	.1	.2
419 So Bapt Conv	7	726	243	888 *	.6	1.2
443 Un C of Christ	4	2,008	682	2,455 *	1.6	3.3
449 Un Methodist	20	4,754	2,073	5,810 *	3.9	7.8
467 Wesleyan	1	589	1,681	3,018	2.0	4.1
469 WELS	1	160	101	202	.1	.3
496 Jewish Est	1	NR	NR	550	.4	.7
ST. CLAIR	**214**	**42,830**	**19,952**	**112,569 ***	**44.0**	**100.0**
017 Amer Bapt Assn	2	100	NR	126 *	-	.1
019 Amer Bapt USA	5	1,300	663	1,650 *	.6	1.5
050 Armen Ap Etchm	1	0	NR	308	.1	.3
053 Assemb of God	10	841	956	1,444	.6	1.3
056 Baha'i	0	147	NR	147	.1	.1
059 Bapt Miss Assn	1	157	45	199 *	.1	.2
081 Catholic	32	NR	NR	52,674	20.6	46.8
089 Chr & Miss Al	1	24	NR	35	-	-
093 Chr Ch (Disc)	3	270	114	343 *	.1	.3
097 Chr Chs&Chs Cr	5	1,306	NR	1,657 *	.6	1.5
123 Ch God (Ander)	6	NR	475	475	.2	.4
127 Ch God (Cleve)	2	314	69	399 *	.2	.4
151 L-D Saints	4	NR	NR	1,300	.5	1.2
165 Ch of Nazarene	7	552	476	836	.3	.7
167 Chs of Christ	6	1,214	1,035	1,851	.7	1.6
173 Comm of Christ	2	271	NR	271	.1	.2
193 Episcopal	3	NR	311	683	.3	.6
203 Evan Free Ch	1	26	55	55	-	-
207 E.L.C.A.	5	1,165	705	1,531	.6	1.4
223 Free Will Bapt	1	86	NR	109 *	-	.1
246 Greek Orthodox	1	NR	NR	312	.1	.3
263 Int Foursq Gos	2	25	68	68 *	-	.1
267 Muslim Est	1	NR	290	1,313	.5	1.2
283 Luth—MO Synod	14	3,922	1,867	4,979	1.9	4.4
339 Pent Ch of God	2	134	NR	248	.1	.2
355 Presb Ch (USA)	2	1,000	370	1,270 *	.5	1.1
356 Presb Ch Amer	1	227	100	241	.1	.2

Religious Group	Number of Churches, Synagogues, Mosques, or Temples	Number of Communicant, Confirmed, or Full Members	Number of Attendees	Total Adherents		
				Number of Adherents	% of Total Pop.	% of Total Adh.
360 Prim Bapt Chrch	1	NR	NR	NR	-	-
388 Reg Bapt Gen As	1	111	101	141 *	.1	.1
403 Salvation Army	2	194	113	454	.2	.4
413 S.D.A.	2	427	NR	508	.2	.5
419 So Bapt Conv	45	13,384	4,724	16,989 *	6.6	15.1
443 Un C of Christ	24	8,722	2,809	11,071 *	4.3	9.8
449 Un Methodist	17	5,461	3,456	6,932 *	2.7	6.2
498 Indep.Charis.	1	150	600	600	.2	.5
499 Indep.Non-Char	1	1,300	550	1,350	.5	1.2
SALINE	**74**	**11,669**	**3,785**	**15,744 ***	**58.9**	**100.0**
019 Amer Bapt USA	1	48	48	58 *	.2	.4
053 Assemb of God	1	30	39	39	.1	.2
061 Beachy Amish	1	38	NR	46 *	.2	.3
081 Catholic	2	NR	NR	1,162	4.3	7.4
097 Chr Chs&Chs Cr	2	315	NR	380 *	1.4	2.4
121 Ch God (Abr)	1	37	19	45 *	.2	.3
123 Ch God (Ander)	3	NR	212	212	.8	1.3
127 Ch God (Cleve)	4	349	237	422 *	1.6	2.7
165 Ch of Nazarene	1	118	77	138	.5	.9
167 Chs of Christ	2	89	90	113	.4	.7
173 Comm of Christ	2	49	NR	49	.2	.3
185 Cumber Presb	5	110	NR	354	1.3	2.2
193 Episcopal	1	NR	17	30	.1	.2
207 E.L.C.A.	1	121	20	159	.6	1.0
339 Pent Ch of God	1	10	NR	30	.1	.2
355 Presb Ch (USA)	2	256	142	309 *	1.2	2.0
360 Prim Bapt Chrch	2	NR	NR	NR	-	-
413 S.D.A.	1	34	NR	40	.1	.3
419 So Bapt Conv	33	9,104	2,383	10,996 *	41.1	69.8
449 Un Methodist	8	961	501	1,162 *	4.3	7.4
SANGAMON	**181**	**43,386**	**24,810**	**107,494 ***	**56.9**	**100.0**
017 Amer Bapt Assn	1	50	NR	62 *	-	.1
019 Amer Bapt USA	10	2,386	1,219	2,950 *	1.6	2.7
053 Assemb of God	5	4,378	5,690	15,010	7.9	14.0
056 Baha'i	1	118	NR	118	.1	.1
057 Bapt Gen Conf	1	14	14	17 *	-	-
081 Catholic	20	NR	NR	36,769	19.5	34.2
084 Calvary Chapel	1	NR	NR	NR	-	-
093 Chr Ch (Disc)	4	1,429	272	1,767 *	.9	1.6
097 Chr Chs&Chs Cr	17	5,975	NR	7,385 *	3.9	6.9
123 Ch God (Ander)	4	NR	306	306	.2	.3
127 Ch God (Cleve)	2	271	123	335 *	.2	.3
151 L-D Saints	2	NR	NR	863	.5	.8
157 Ch of Brethren	1	101	66	125 *	.1	.1
165 Ch of Nazarene	5	678	499	1,049	.6	1.0
167 Chs of Christ	4	365	380	493	.3	.5
173 Comm of Christ	1	77	NR	77	-	.1
193 Episcopal	3	NR	457	1,365	.7	1.3
203 Evan Free Ch	1	288	625	625	.3	.6
207 E.L.C.A.	5	2,504	913	3,447	1.8	3.2
221 Free Methodist	1	97	105	105	.1	.1
223 Free Will Bapt	1	86	NR	106 *	.1	.1
226 Friends-USA	1	55	NR	68 *	-	.1
246 Greek Orthodox	1	NR	NR	171	.1	.2
263 Int Foursq Gos	2	121	116	150 *	.1	.1
264 Int Chs of Crst	1	48	93	78	-	.1
267 Muslim Est	1	NR	101	288	.2	.3
283 Luth—MO Synod	12	6,146	3,067	8,177	4.3	7.6
290 Metro Comm Ch	1	49	54	61 *	-	.1
306 NT IndBapt&Rltd	2	449	NR	555 *	.3	.5
335 Orth Pres Ch	1	24	35	40	-	-
355 Presb Ch (USA)	12	3,297	3,718	5,858 *	3.1	5.4
356 Presb Ch Amer	1	27	40	40	-	-
388 Reg Bapt Gen As	1	185	175	229 *	.1	.2
403 Salvation Army	1	135	110	375	.2	.3
413 S.D.A.	2	145	NR	172	.1	.2
419 So Bapt Conv	14	4,008	1,550	4,955 *	2.6	4.6
435 Unitarian-Univ	1	162	NR	200 *	.1	.2
443 Un C of Christ	2	325	130	402 *	.2	.4
449 Un Methodist	32	9,243	4,802	11,426 *	6.0	10.6
463 Vineyard	1	150	150	185 *	.1	.2

NR–Not Reported *Total adherents estimated from known number of communicant, confirmed, full members. - Represents a percentage less than 0.1. Percentages may not total 100 due to rounding.

Table 4: Religious Congregations by County and Group: 2000

Religious Group	Number of Churches, Synagogues, Mosques, or Temples	Number of Communicant, Confirmed, or Full Members	Number of Attendees	Total Adherents		
				Number of Adherents	% of Total Pop.	% of Total Adh.
496 Jewish Est	2	NR	NR	1,090	.6	1.0
SCHUYLER	**27**	**2,746**	**1,280**	**3,687 ***	**51.3**	**100.0**
053 Assemb of God	1	31	40	68	.9	1.8
056 Baha'i	0	4	NR	4	.1	.1
081 Catholic	1	NR	NR	295	4.1	8.0
093 Chr Ch (Disc)	2	390	120	471 *	6.6	12.8
097 Chr Chs&Chs Cr	4	531	NR	641 *	8.9	17.4
121 Ch God (Abr)	1	27	26	33 *	.5	.9
165 Ch of Nazarene	1	30	22	36	.5	1.0
167 Chs of Christ	1	17	18	22	.3	.6
221 Free Methodist	1	135	181	181	2.5	4.9
283 Luth—MO Synod	1	114	49	155	2.2	4.2
355 Presb Ch (USA)	1	121	68	146 *	2.0	4.0
388 Reg Bapt Gen As	1	50	70	70 *	1.0	1.9
419 So Bapt Conv	1	347	93	419 *	5.8	11.4
449 Un Methodist	11	949	593	1,146 *	15.9	31.1
SCOTT	**23**	**2,726**	**1,029**	**3,888 ***	**70.2**	**100.0**
019 Amer Bapt USA	3	805	228	992 *	17.9	25.5
053 Assemb of God	1	30	25	40	.7	1.0
056 Baha'i	0	2	NR	2	-	.1
081 Catholic	2	NR	NR	480	8.7	12.3
093 Chr Ch (Disc)	1	232	67	286 *	5.2	7.4
207 E.L.C.A.	1	127	20	163	2.9	4.2
283 Luth—MO Synod	2	395	151	526	9.5	13.5
360 Prim Bapt Chrch	1	NR	NR	NR	-	-
419 So Bapt Conv	7	771	302	951 *	17.2	24.5
449 Un Methodist	5	364	236	448 *	8.1	11.5
SHELBY	**71**	**9,000**	**3,308**	**12,919 ***	**56.4**	**100.0**
019 Amer Bapt USA	1	358	145	441 *	1.9	3.4
032 Amish; other	1	35	NR	43 *	.2	.3
053 Assemb of God	1	65	88	160	.7	1.2
056 Baha'i	0	1	NR	1	-	-
081 Catholic	4	NR	NR	1,733	7.6	13.4
093 Chr Ch (Disc)	1	374	0	461 *	2.0	3.6
097 Chr Chs&Chs Cr	10	2,476	NR	3,052 *	13.3	23.6
127 Ch God (Cleve)	1	20	25	25 *	.1	.2
165 Ch of Nazarene	1	221	100	296	1.3	2.3
167 Chs of Christ	9	254	245	309	1.3	2.4
171 Ch God-Gen Con	1	51	25	63 *	.3	.5
207 E.L.C.A.	2	201	105	256	1.1	2.0
221 Free Methodist	3	123	159	161	.7	1.2
283 Luth—MO Synod	5	1,441	740	1,754	7.7	13.6
355 Presb Ch (USA)	1	116	65	143 *	.6	1.1
388 Reg Bapt Gen As	2	231	206	285 *	1.2	2.2
413 S.D.A.	1	46	NR	55	.2	.4
418 Southw Bapt Fel	1	NR	NR	NR	-	-
419 So Bapt Conv	7	728	318	897 *	3.9	6.9
443 Un C of Christ	1	77	34	95 *	.4	.7
449 Un Methodist	18	2,182	1,053	2,689 *	11.7	20.8
STARK	**20**	**2,173**	**1,727**	**4,061 ***	**64.1**	**100.0**
017 Amer Bapt Assn	1	50	NR	62 *	1.0	1.5
019 Amer Bapt USA	1	180	70	222 *	3.5	5.5
040 Ap Chr Ch-Amer	2	475	923	923 *	14.6	22.7
056 Baha'i	0	3	NR	3	-	.1
081 Catholic	3	NR	NR	860	13.6	21.2
165 Ch of Nazarene	1	67	65	187	3.0	4.6
175 Congr Chr Chs	1	100	65	123 *	1.9	3.0
179 Consrv Bapt	1	NR	72	72	1.1	1.8
207 E.L.C.A.	1	96	60	126	2.0	3.1
306 NT IndBapt&Rltd	1	225	NR	278 *	4.4	6.8
355 Presb Ch (USA)	1	66	41	81 *	1.3	2.0
443 Un C of Christ	2	178	78	220 *	3.5	5.4
449 Un Methodist	5	733	353	904 *	14.3	22.3
STEPHENSON	**73**	**14,654**	**8,391**	**28,525 ***	**58.2**	**100.0**
053 Assemb of God	1	687	926	1,475	3.0	5.2
056 Baha'i	0	6	NR	6	-	-
081 Catholic	4	NR	NR	8,362	17.1	29.3
105 Christian Ref	1	101	75	125 *	.3	.4
123 Ch God (Ander)	1	NR	75	75	.2	.3
151 L-D Saints	1	NR	NR	296	.6	1.0
157 Ch of Brethren	3	175	89	216 *	.4	.8
165 Ch of Nazarene	1	179	112	304	.6	1.1
167 Chs of Christ	1	116	130	170	.3	.6
171 Ch God-Gen Con	1	106	101	131 *	.3	.5
181 Consrv Congr	1	157	90	194 *	.4	.7
193 Episcopal	1	NR	134	329	.7	1.2
203 Evan Free Ch	5	823	1,329	1,334	2.7	4.7
207 E.L.C.A.	6	2,007	846	2,562	5.2	9.0
221 Free Methodist	3	120	182	192	.4	.7
283 Luth—MO Synod	3	1,517	884	1,963	4.0	6.9
288 Mennonite USA	1	163	139	201 *	.4	.7
297 Mennonite;Other	1	8	NR	10 *	-	-
306 NT IndBapt&Rltd	1	225	NR	278 *	.6	1.0
355 Presb Ch (USA)	3	452	198	558 *	1.1	2.0
371 Ref Ch in Am	2	282	215	434	.9	1.5
401 Rus Orth Abroad	1	NR	NR	NR	-	-
403 Salvation Army	1	82	97	298	.6	1.0
413 S.D.A.	1	43	NR	51	.1	.2
443 Un C of Christ	6	1,873	706	2,313 *	4.7	8.1
449 Un Methodist	21	4,597	1,614	5,674 *	11.6	19.9
469 WELS	1	109	74	148	.3	.5
499 Indep.Non-Char	1	826	375	826	1.7	2.9
TAZEWELL	**134**	**31,805**	**17,788**	**57,847 ***	**45.0**	**100.0**
019 Amer Bapt USA	3	785	253	964 *	.8	1.7
039 Ap Chr Ch(Naz)	1	250	470	470 *	.4	.8
040 Ap Chr Ch-Amer	3	1,033	1,678	1,678 *	1.3	2.9
053 Assemb of God	5	1,224	1,643	1,928	1.5	3.3
056 Baha'i	0	39	NR	39	-	.1
059 Bapt Miss Assn	1	46	35	56 *	-	.1
081 Catholic	7	NR	NR	14,130	11.0	24.4
093 Chr Ch (Disc)	4	1,687	532	2,072 *	1.6	3.6
097 Chr Chs&Chs Cr	8	2,294	NR	2,818 *	2.2	4.9
121 Ch God (Abr)	1	37	34	45 *	-	.1
123 Ch God (Ander)	3	NR	570	570	.4	1.0
127 Ch God (Cleve)	1	91	119	119 *	.1	.2
145 Ch God Prophcy	1	42	NR	52 *	-	.1
151 L-D Saints	2	NR	NR	744	.6	1.3
165 Ch of Nazarene	6	903	676	1,240	1.0	2.1
167 Chs of Christ	4	484	459	648	.5	1.1
173 Comm of Christ	1	59	NR	59	-	.1
179 Consrv Bapt	1	NR	490	490	.4	.8
193 Episcopal	2	NR	119	250	.2	.4
203 Evan Free Ch	1	35	70	70	.1	.1
207 E.L.C.A.	4	2,084	820	2,678	2.1	4.6
213 Evan Menn Inc	3	730	940	896 *	.7	1.5
221 Free Methodist	2	160	162	173	.1	.3
263 Int Foursq Gos	1	12	27	27 *	-	-
283 Luth—MO Synod	9	4,759	2,126	6,642	5.2	11.5
288 Mennonite USA	9	1,404	1,000	1,723 *	1.3	3.0
291 Missionary Ch	2	300	342	342	.3	.6
306 NT IndBapt&Rltd	2	449	NR	551 *	.4	1.0
339 Pent Ch of God	3	125	NR	242	.2	.4
355 Presb Ch (USA)	6	772	397	947 *	.7	1.6
371 Ref Ch in Am	2	225	180	434	.3	.8
403 Salvation Army	1	124	250	329	.3	.6
419 So Bapt Conv	13	3,190	994	3,918 *	3.0	6.8
443 Un C of Christ	6	2,212	677	2,717 *	2.1	4.7
449 Un Methodist	14	6,098	2,587	7,489 *	5.8	12.9
463 Vineyard	1	120	89	147 *	.1	.3
467 Wesleyan	1	32	49	150	.1	.3
UNION	**50**	**8,993**	**2,866**	**12,460 ***	**68.1**	**100.0**
019 Amer Bapt USA	2	116	38	140 *	.8	1.1
056 Baha'i	0	4	NR	4	-	-
081 Catholic	2	NR	NR	1,407	7.7	11.3
097 Chr Chs&Chs Cr	1	300	NR	363 *	2.0	2.9
123 Ch God (Ander)	1	NR	20	20	.1	.2
127 Ch God (Cleve)	2	122	24	147 *	.8	1.2
165 Ch of Nazarene	1	164	142	249	1.4	2.0

NR–Not Reported   *Total adherents estimated from known number of communicant, confirmed, full members.   - Represents a percentage less than 0.1.   Percentages may not total 100 due to rounding.

Table 4: Religious Congregations by County and Group: 2000

Religious Group	Number of Churches, Synagogues, Mosques, or Temples	Number of Communicant, Confirmed, or Full Members	Number of Attendees	Total Adherents		
				Number of Adherents	% of Total Pop.	% of Total Adh.
167 Chs of Christ	2	120	145	173	.9	1.4
185 Cumber Presb	4	51	NR	85	.5	.7
207 E.L.C.A.	4	726	385	929	5.1	7.5
216 Evan Presby Ch	1	210	NR	254 *	1.4	2.0
283 Luth—MO Synod	1	115	64	137	.7	1.1
286 E.PA Mennonite	1	68	NR	82 *	.4	.7
355 Presb Ch (USA)	1	78	48	94 *	.5	.8
419 So Bapt Conv	22	6,621	1,784	8,016 *	43.8	64.3
449 Un Methodist	5	298	216	360 *	2.0	2.9
VERMILION	**133**	**20,545**	**7,658**	**33,455 ***	**39.9**	**100.0**
019 Amer Bapt USA	4	1,375	451	1,703 *	2.0	5.1
053 Assemb of God	3	412	412	698	.8	2.1
056 Baha'i	0	23	NR	23	-	.1
081 Catholic	6	NR	NR	5,881	7.0	17.6
089 Chr & Miss Al	1	66	NR	231	.3	.7
093 Chr Ch (Disc)	2	668	202	827 *	1.0	2.5
097 Chr Chs&Chs Cr	27	5,136	NR	6,363 *	7.6	19.0
123 Ch God (Ander)	3	NR	304	304	.4	.9
127 Ch God (Cleve)	2	215	99	266 *	.3	.8
165 Ch of Nazarene	14	1,726	1,107	2,231	2.7	6.7
167 Chs of Christ	3	208	230	287	.3	.9
173 Comm of Christ	1	83	NR	83	.1	.2
175 Congr Chr Chs	1	12	20	15 *	-	-
185 Cumber Presb	1	46	NR	79	.1	.2
193 Episcopal	1	NR	75	150	.2	.4
207 E.L.C.A.	2	310	123	396	.5	1.2
221 Free Methodist	1	88	87	98	.1	.3
226 Friends-USA	5	510	NR	632 *	.8	1.9
263 Int Foursq Gos	2	47	39	58 *	.1	.2
283 Luth—MO Synod	3	1,616	679	2,176	2.6	6.5
306 NT IndBapt&Rltd	6	1,348	NR	1,670 *	2.0	5.0
339 Pent Ch of God	1	75	NR	75	.1	.2
355 Presb Ch (USA)	4	570	244	707 *	.8	2.1
403 Salvation Army	1	143	160	329	.4	1.0
413 S.D.A.	2	97	NR	115	.1	.3
419 So Bapt Conv	1	317	75	393 *	.5	1.2
443 Un C of Christ	3	589	239	730 *	.9	2.2
449 Un Methodist	28	4,165	1,897	5,157 *	6.1	15.4
496 Jewish Est	1	NR	NR	100	.1	.3
498 Indep.Charis.	2	0	690	898	1.1	2.7
499 Indep.Non-Char	2	700	525	780	.9	2.3
WABASH	**32**	**4,297**	**1,858**	**7,099 ***	**54.9**	**100.0**
081 Catholic	2	NR	NR	1,643	12.7	23.1
093 Chr Ch (Disc)	2	554	148	675 *	5.2	9.5
097 Chr Chs&Chs Cr	6	1,015	NR	1,238 *	9.6	17.4
123 Ch God (Ander)	1	NR	112	112	.9	1.6
165 Ch of Nazarene	1	108	68	108	.8	1.5
167 Chs of Christ	1	350	380	500	3.9	7.0
193 Episcopal	1	NR	28	36	.3	.5
207 E.L.C.A.	1	152	57	201	1.6	2.8
221 Free Methodist	2	135	158	172	1.3	2.4
283 Luth—MO Synod	1	76	35	91	.7	1.3
306 NT IndBapt&Rltd	1	225	NR	274 *	2.1	3.9
355 Presb Ch (USA)	2	132	91	161 *	1.2	2.3
419 So Bapt Conv	1	454	202	553 *	4.3	7.8
443 Un C of Christ	1	39	17	48 *	.4	.7
449 Un Methodist	9	1,057	562	1,287 *	9.9	18.1
WARREN	**35**	**5,418**	**2,042**	**8,766 ***	**46.8**	**100.0**
019 Amer Bapt USA	3	332	131	401 *	2.1	4.6
053 Assemb of God	1	39	52	52	.3	.6
056 Baha'i	0	6	NR	6	-	.1
057 Bapt Gen Conf	1	108	110	131 *	.7	1.5
081 Catholic	2	NR	NR	2,061	11.0	23.5
093 Chr Ch (Disc)	3	716	167	865 *	4.6	9.9
097 Chr Chs&Chs Cr	3	796	NR	962 *	5.1	11.0
151 L-D Saints	1	NR	NR	129	.7	1.5
165 Ch of Nazarene	2	87	62	113	.6	1.3
193 Episcopal	1	NR	19	10	.1	.1
207 E.L.C.A.	1	511	147	612	3.3	7.0
263 Int Foursq Gos	1	133	175	175 *	.9	2.0
355 Presb Ch (USA)	7	1,111	531	1,342 *	7.2	15.3
419 So Bapt Conv	1	82	18	99 *	.5	1.1
449 Un Methodist	8	1,497	630	1,808 *	9.7	20.6
WASHINGTON	**42**	**5,865**	**2,748**	**11,805 ***	**77.9**	**100.0**
053 Assemb of God	1	35	48	56	.4	.5
056 Baha'i	0	1	NR	1	-	-
081 Catholic	6	NR	NR	4,540	30.0	38.5
097 Chr Chs&Chs Cr	1	40	NR	49 *	.3	.4
165 Ch of Nazarene	1	9	12	19	.1	.2
263 Int Foursq Gos	1	33	59	59 *	.4	.5
283 Luth—MO Synod	7	2,233	1,189	2,768	18.3	23.4
355 Presb Ch (USA)	2	164	91	201 *	1.3	1.7
418 Southw Bapt Fel	1	NR	NR	NR	-	-
419 So Bapt Conv	6	836	224	1,026 *	6.8	8.7
443 Un C of Christ	11	1,908	808	2,342 *	15.5	19.8
449 Un Methodist	5	606	317	744 *	4.9	6.3
WAYNE	**63**	**7,909**	**2,120**	**10,126 ***	**59.0**	**100.0**
053 Assemb of God	1	182	260	260	1.5	2.6
056 Baha'i	0	1	NR	1	-	-
081 Catholic	1	NR	NR	214	1.2	2.1
097 Chr Chs&Chs Cr	9	1,773	NR	2,159 *	12.6	21.3
127 Ch God (Cleve)	2	168	143	239 *	1.4	2.4
151 L-D Saints	1	NR	NR	92	.5	.9
157 Ch of Brethren	1	29	0	35 *	.2	.3
165 Ch of Nazarene	2	101	61	123	.7	1.2
167 Chs of Christ	1	75	80	97	.6	1.0
173 Comm of Christ	2	234	NR	234	1.4	2.3
185 Cumber Presb	5	411	NR	621	3.6	6.1
223 Free Will Bapt	3	257	NR	314 *	1.8	3.1
283 Luth—MO Synod	1	23	18	28	.2	.3
286 E.PA Mennonite	1	88	NR	107 *	.6	1.1
297 Mennonite;Other	1	58	NR	71 *	.4	.7
360 Prim Bapt Chrch	1	NR	NR	NR	-	-
419 So Bapt Conv	17	3,304	889	4,027 *	23.5	39.8
449 Un Methodist	13	1,182	625	1,443 *	8.4	14.3
467 Wesleyan	1	23	44	61	.4	.6
WHITE	**60**	**6,810**	**2,590**	**9,134 ***	**59.4**	**100.0**
053 Assemb of God	2	126	173	218	1.4	2.4
081 Catholic	2	NR	NR	837	5.4	9.2
097 Chr Chs&Chs Cr	8	1,682	NR	1,996 *	13.0	21.9
123 Ch God (Ander)	1	NR	12	12	.1	.1
127 Ch God (Cleve)	3	269	108	319 *	2.1	3.5
165 Ch of Nazarene	1	69	70	193	1.3	2.1
167 Chs of Christ	3	116	117	148	1.0	1.6
173 Comm of Christ	1	76	NR	76	.5	.8
185 Cumber Presb	4	82	NR	209	1.4	2.3
283 Luth—MO Synod	1	38	28	44	.3	.5
355 Presb Ch (USA)	3	232	126	276 *	1.8	3.0
360 Prim Bapt Chrch	4	NR	NR	NR	-	-
419 So Bapt Conv	12	2,289	785	2,717 *	17.7	29.7
449 Un Methodist	14	1,381	746	1,639 *	10.7	17.9
498 Indep.Charis.	1	450	425	450	2.9	4.9
WHITESIDE	**99**	**19,747**	**9,437**	**40,435 ***	**66.7**	**100.0**
019 Amer Bapt USA	4	610	245	754 *	1.2	1.9
032 Amish; other	1	155	NR	192 *	.3	.5
053 Assemb of God	3	215	293	310	.5	.8
056 Baha'i	0	30	NR	30	-	.1
075 Brethren in Cr	1	62	63	63	.1	.2
081 Catholic	9	NR	NR	13,794	22.7	34.1
093 Chr Ch (Disc)	2	416	60	514 *	.8	1.3
097 Chr Chs&Chs Cr	6	750	NR	928 *	1.5	2.3
105 Christian Ref	3	762	495	942 *	1.6	2.3
123 Ch God (Ander)	1	NR	48	48	.1	.1
151 L-D Saints	2	NR	NR	642	1.1	1.6
165 Ch of Nazarene	3	505	545	670	1.1	1.7
167 Chs of Christ	1	190	185	242	.4	.6
173 Comm of Christ	1	96	NR	96	.2	.2
179 Consrv Bapt	1	NR	16	16	-	-

NR–Not Reported   *Total adherents estimated from known number of communicant, confirmed, full members.   - Represents a percentage less than 0.1.   Percentages may not total 100 due to rounding.

Table 4: Religious Congregations by County and Group: 2000

Religious Group	Number of Churches, Synagogues, Mosques, or Temples	Number of Communicant, Confirmed, or Full Members	Number of Attendees	Total Adherents		
				Number of Adherents	% of Total Pop.	% of Total Adh.
193 Episcopal	2	NR	157	317	.5	.8
203 Evan Free Ch	1	58	100	100	.2	.2
207 E.L.C.A.	7	3,194	1,211	4,029	6.6	10.0
263 Int Foursq Gos	1	89	16	110 *	.2	.3
267 Muslim Est	1	NR	55	163	.3	.4
283 Luth—MO Synod	4	1,405	583	1,933	3.2	4.8
288 Mennonite USA	1	146	100	181 *	.3	.4
306 NT IndBapt&Rltd	2	449	NR	555 *	.9	1.4
355 Presb Ch (USA)	4	808	334	999 *	1.6	2.5
370 Ref Baptist Chs	1	NR	NR	NR	-	-
371 Ref Ch in Am	8	2,103	1,675	3,406	5.6	8.4
379 Ref Mennonite	1	43	NR	53 *	.1	.1
388 Reg Bapt Gen As	1	14	31	31 *	.1	.1
403 Salvation Army	1	119	247	257	.4	.6
413 S.D.A.	1	49	NR	58	.1	.1
419 So Bapt Conv	5	1,118	181	1,383 *	2.3	3.4
443 Un C of Christ	3	657	231	813 *	1.3	2.0
449 Un Methodist	14	4,104	1,501	5,076 *	8.4	12.6
496 Jewish Est	1	NR	NR	130	.2	.3
499 Indep.Non-Char	2	1,600	1,065	1,600	2.6	4.0
WILL	**250**	**48,519**	**27,121**	**270,571 ***	**53.9**	**100.0**
019 Amer Bapt USA	6	1,267	809	1,663 *	.3	.6
053 Assemb of God	8	1,408	2,136	4,740	.9	1.8
056 Baha'i	2	164	NR	164	-	.1
057 Bapt Gen Conf	3	1,344	881	1,787 *	.4	.7
081 Catholic	41	NR	NR	195,271	38.9	72.2
089 Chr & Miss Al	3	124	NR	215	-	.1
097 Chr Chs&Chs Cr	9	1,785	NR	2,343 *	.5	.9
105 Christian Ref	3	365	395	479 *	.1	.2
123 Ch God (Ander)	2	NR	253	253	.1	.1
127 Ch God (Cleve)	1	46	68	68 *	-	-
145 Ch God Prophcy	2	85	NR	112 *	-	-
151 L-D Saints	5	NR	NR	1,706	.3	.6
165 Ch of Nazarene	4	521	348	682	.1	.3
167 Chs of Christ	5	362	395	483	.1	.2
171 Ch God-Gen Con	1	67	225	225 *	-	.1
175 Congr Chr Chs	1	110	80	144 *	-	.1
181 Consrv Congr	1	125	69	164 *	-	.1
193 Episcopal	5	NR	438	1,007	.2	.4
201 Evan Cov Ch	2	232	251	305 *	.1	.1
203 Evan Free Ch	3	192	650	655	.1	.2
207 E.L.C.A.	18	7,708	3,957	11,615	2.3	4.3
221 Free Methodist	1	38	62	62	-	-
223 Free Will Bapt	1	86	NR	113 *	-	-
246 Greek Orthodox	1	NR	NR	1,125	.2	.4
251 Holy Orth in NA	1	NR	NR	18	-	-
263 Int Foursq Gos	1	14	19	19 *	-	-
267 Muslim Est	2	NR	400	900	.2	.3
268 Jain	1	NR	NR	NR	-	-
283 Luth—MO Synod	17	6,894	3,029	9,686	1.9	3.6
306 NT IndBapt&Rltd	3	674	NR	885 *	.2	.3
331 OCA: Ter Diocs	1	65	NR	221	-	.1
335 Orth Pres Ch	1	66	106	110	-	-
349 Pent Holiness	1	12	10	16 *	-	-
355 Presb Ch (USA)	11	2,222	972	2,918 *	.6	1.1
356 Presb Ch Amer	2	48	80	80	-	-
371 Ref Ch in Am	2	963	1,336	1,563	.3	.6
388 Reg Bapt Gen As	6	567	649	745 *	.1	.3
403 Salvation Army	1	60	147	208	-	.1
410 Serb Orth USA	1	NR	NR	350	.1	.1
411 Serb Orth: Grac	1	NR	NR	NR	-	-
413 S.D.A.	5	453	NR	539	.1	.2
418 Southw Bapt Fel	1	NR	NR	NR	-	-
419 So Bapt Conv	19	4,322	1,978	5,674 *	1.1	2.1
435 Unitarian-Univ	1	65	NR	85 *	-	-
443 Un C of Christ	13	4,808	1,635	6,312 *	1.3	2.3
449 Un Methodist	22	7,737	3,306	10,159 *	2.0	3.8
455 Un Ref Chs N.A.	1	55	NR	85	-	-
463 Vineyard	2	190	239	290 *	.1	.1
467 Wesleyan	1	50	45	138	-	.1
469 WELS	2	1,274	653	1,668	.3	.6
496 Jewish Est	1	NR	NR	270	.1	.1
498 Indep.Charis.	1	650	600	950	.2	.4
499 Indep.Non-Char	1	1,301	900	1,301	.3	.5
WILLIAMSON	**106**	**21,827**	**8,247**	**31,922 ***	**52.1**	**100.0**
019 Amer Bapt USA	9	1,266	676	1,537 *	2.5	4.8
053 Assemb of God	3	160	204	285	.5	.9
056 Baha'i	0	13	NR	13	-	-
081 Catholic	5	NR	NR	4,676	7.6	14.6
093 Chr Ch (Disc)	1	211	70	256 *	.4	.8
097 Chr Chs&Chs Cr	8	1,480	NR	1,797 *	2.9	5.6
123 Ch God (Ander)	2	NR	302	302	.5	.9
127 Ch God (Cleve)	3	949	604	1,152 *	1.9	3.6
145 Ch God Prophcy	2	85	NR	102 *	.2	.3
165 Ch of Nazarene	2	125	64	136	.2	.4
167 Chs of Christ	2	195	195	258	.4	.8
173 Comm of Christ	1	133	NR	133	.2	.4
193 Episcopal	1	NR	26	36	.1	.1
207 E.L.C.A.	1	264	131	330	.5	1.0
221 Free Methodist	2	36	49	54	.1	.2
223 Free Will Bapt	4	343	NR	417 *	.7	1.3
283 Luth—MO Synod	2	306	190	397	.6	1.2
339 Pent Ch of God	1	125	NR	240	.4	.8
355 Presb Ch (USA)	4	345	192	418 *	.7	1.3
388 Reg Bapt Gen As	1	35	43	43 *	.1	.1
403 Salvation Army	1	39	41	63	.1	.2
413 S.D.A.	2	173	NR	206	.3	.6
419 So Bapt Conv	31	12,313	3,754	14,948 *	24.4	46.8
443 Un C of Christ	1	556	177	675 *	1.1	2.1
449 Un Methodist	16	2,675	1,529	3,248 *	5.3	10.2
496 Jewish Est	1	NR	NR	200	.3	.6
WINNEBAGO	**196**	**50,673**	**26,874**	**139,181 ***	**50.0**	**100.0**
017 Amer Bapt Assn	2	100	NR	126 *	-	.1
019 Amer Bapt USA	4	1,679	650	2,115 *	.8	1.5
022 Carp Rus Orth	1	122	NR	207	.1	.1
053 Assemb of God	7	2,058	2,582	6,579	2.4	4.7
056 Baha'i	2	164	NR	164	.1	.1
057 Bapt Gen Conf	1	499	400	629 *	.2	.5
076 Buddhism	1	NR	NR	NR	-	-
081 Catholic	15	NR	NR	61,827	22.2	44.4
093 Chr Ch (Disc)	3	655	328	825 *	.3	.6
097 Chr Chs&Chs Cr	3	1,367	NR	1,722 *	.6	1.2
121 Ch God (Abr)	3	36	267	267 *	.1	.2
123 Ch God (Ander)	3	NR	80	80	-	.1
127 Ch God (Cleve)	2	67	108	115 *	-	.1
145 Ch God Prophcy	1	42	NR	53 *	-	-
151 L-D Saints	3	NR	NR	980	.4	.7
157 Ch of Brethren	1	92	0	116 *	-	.1
165 Ch of Nazarene	5	585	397	786	.3	.6
167 Chs of Christ	9	1,213	1,230	1,574	.6	1.1
173 Comm of Christ	1	97	NR	97	-	.1
175 Congr Chr Chs	1	100	60	126 *	-	.1
179 Consrv Bapt	1	NR	80	80	-	.1
181 Consrv Congr	1	345	110	435 *	.2	.3
193 Episcopal	3	NR	291	748	.3	.5
201 Evan Cov Ch	7	1,711	1,150	2,196 *	.8	1.6
203 Evan Free Ch	7	2,866	3,865	3,905	1.4	2.8
207 E.L.C.A.	23	15,226	5,447	19,797	7.1	14.2
221 Free Methodist	1	30	45	45	-	-
223 Free Will Bapt	1	86	NR	108 *	-	.1
226 Friends-USA	1	55	NR	69 *	-	-
246 Greek Orthodox	1	NR	NR	546	.2	.4
263 Int Foursq Gos	2	35	73	73 *	-	.1
267 Muslim Est	1	NR	156	609	.2	.4
283 Luth—MO Synod	9	3,543	1,950	5,447	2.0	3.9
306 NT IndBapt&Rltd	4	899	NR	1,132 *	.4	.8
339 Pent Ch of God	1	60	NR	125	-	.1
349 Pent Holiness	1	35	30	44 *	-	-
355 Presb Ch (USA)	7	2,608	1,138	3,285 *	1.2	2.4
370 Ref Baptist Chs	1	NR	NR	NR	-	-
371 Ref Ch in Am	1	97	89	148	.1	.1
403 Salvation Army	2	409	375	2,309	.8	1.7
410 Serb Orth USA	1	NR	NR	80	-	.1
413 S.D.A.	4	425	NR	507	.2	.4

NR–Not Reported *Total adherents estimated from known number of communicant, confirmed, full members. - Represents a percentage less than 0.1. Percentages may not total 100 due to rounding.

Table 4: Religious Congregations by County and Group: 2000

Religious Group	Number of Churches, Synagogues, Mosques, or Temples	Number of Communicant, Confirmed, or Full Members	Number of Attendees	Total Adherents		
				Number of Adherents	% of Total Pop.	% of Total Adh.
419 So Bapt Conv	9	1,695	596	2,135 *	.8	1.5
435 Unitarian-Univ	1	462	NR	582 *	.2	.4
443 Un C of Christ	7	2,472	917	3,114 *	1.1	2.2
449 Un Methodist	23	8,047	2,889	10,135 *	3.6	7.3
467 Wesleyan	1	65	55	143	.1	.1
469 WELS	3	326	246	446	.2	.3
496 Jewish Est	2	NR	NR	1,100	.4	.8
498 Indep.Charis.	1	300	520	700	.3	.5
499 Indep.Non-Char	1	0	750	750	.3	.5
WOODFORD	**63**	**10,399**	**7,547**	**19,971 ***	**56.3**	**100.0**
019 Amer Bapt USA	3	712	287	894 *	2.5	4.5
032 Amish; other	1	75	NR	94 *	.3	.5
040 Ap Chr Ch-Amer	4	1,433	2,582	2,582 *	7.3	12.9
053 Assemb of God	2	52	61	70	.2	.4
056 Baha'i	0	15	NR	15	-	.1
081 Catholic	8	NR	NR	5,645	15.9	28.3
093 Chr Ch (Disc)	1	480	184	603 *	1.7	3.0
097 Chr Chs&Chs Cr	2	96	NR	120 *	.3	.6
157 Ch of Brethren	1	12	12	15 *	-	.1
165 Ch of Nazarene	2	251	226	532	1.5	2.7
167 Chs of Christ	2	100	100	127	.4	.6
193 Episcopal	1	NR	29	107	.3	.5
203 Evan Free Ch	1	48	100	100	.3	.5
207 E.L.C.A.	3	799	336	1,114	3.1	5.6
213 Evan Menn Inc	3	353	613	444 *	1.3	2.2
283 Luth—MO Synod	5	1,191	505	1,412	4.0	7.1
288 Mennonite USA	4	664	596	928 *	2.6	4.6
297 Mennonite;Other	1	84	NR	105 *	.3	.5
306 NT IndBapt&Rltd	1	225	NR	282 *	.8	1.4
355 Presb Ch (USA)	3	198	99	249 *	.7	1.2
388 Reg Bapt Gen As	1	160	170	201 *	.6	1.0
419 So Bapt Conv	1	161	17	202 *	.6	1.0
443 Un C of Christ	4	1,211	412	1,520 *	4.3	7.6
449 Un Methodist	9	2,079	1,218	2,610 *	7.4	13.1
INDIANA						
The State.....	7,492	1,247,145	652,481	2,608,882 *	42.9	100.0
ADAMS	**83**	**11,745**	**6,936**	**21,061 ***	**62.6**	**100.0**
019 Amer Bapt USA	2	231	99	304 *	.9	1.4
053 Assemb of God	2	74	100	146	.4	.7
061 Beachy Amish	1	32	NR	42 *	.1	.2
081 Catholic	2	NR	NR	4,810	14.3	22.8
097 Chr Chs&Chs Cr	2	160	NR	211 *	.6	1.0
123 Ch God (Ander)	1	NR	458	458	1.4	2.2
157 Ch of Brethren	1	306	237	403 *	1.2	1.9
165 Ch of Nazarene	4	400	345	779	2.3	3.7
193 Episcopal	1	NR	21	21	.1	.1
213 Evan Menn Inc	1	158	215	208 *	.6	1.0
283 Luth—MO Synod	7	2,934	1,611	3,909	11.6	18.6
288 Mennonite USA	1	1,085	660	1,428 *	4.2	6.8
291 Missionary Ch	4	812	1,014	1,020	3.0	4.8
323 Old Ord Amish	34	2,040	NR	2,686 *	8.0	12.8
349 Pent Holiness	2	63	122	83 *	.2	.4
355 Presb Ch (USA)	1	133	85	175 *	.5	.8
388 Reg Bapt Gen As	1	65	95	95 *	.3	.5
418 Southw Bapt Fel	1	NR	NR	NR	-	-
443 Un C of Christ	4	1,145	553	1,507 *	4.5	7.2
449 Un Methodist	10	2,048	1,273	2,696 *	8.0	12.8
467 Wesleyan	1	59	48	80	.2	.4
ALLEN	**291**	**72,857**	**48,906**	**166,540 ***	**50.2**	**100.0**
019 Amer Bapt USA	7	3,284	2,216	4,195 *	1.3	2.5
034 Ant Orth of NA	1	98	NR	196	.1	.1
040 Ap Chr Ch-Amer	1	133	240	240 *	.1	.1
053 Assemb of God	8	1,386	1,665	3,619	1.1	2.2
056 Baha'i	1	72	NR	72	-	-
061 Beachy Amish	2	53	NR	68 *	-	-
071 Brethren (Ash)	1	42	37	54 *	-	-
081 Catholic	24	NR	NR	57,680	17.4	34.6
084 Calvary Chapel	2	NR	NR	NR	-	-
089 Chr & Miss Al	2	190	NR	495	.1	.3
093 Chr Ch (Disc)	3	1,076	282	1,375 *	.4	.8
097 Chr Chs&Chs Cr	10	3,796	NR	4,850 *	1.5	2.9
105 Christian Ref	1	113	86	144 *	-	.1
107 Christian Un	1	36	41	46 *	-	-
123 Ch God (Ander)	9	NR	1,048	1,048	.3	.6
127 Ch God (Cleve)	2	364	123	465 *	.1	.3
145 Ch God Prophcy	1	36	NR	46 *	-	-
151 L-D Saints	2	NR	NR	883	.3	.5
157 Ch of Brethren	3	653	386	835 *	.3	.5
165 Ch of Nazarene	10	1,375	1,046	2,011	.6	1.2
167 Chs of Christ	6	560	695	855	.3	.5
171 Ch God-Gen Con	5	611	430	802 *	.2	.5
173 Comm of Christ	1	95	NR	95	-	.1
183 Cons Menn Conf	1	100	122	145	-	.1
193 Episcopal	3	NR	531	1,405	.4	.8
207 E.L.C.A.	19	9,544	2,977	12,491	3.8	7.5
213 Evan Menn Inc	5	890	1,325	1,137 *	.3	.7
221 Free Methodist	1	66	100	100	-	.1
223 Free Will Bapt	2	5	NR	6 *	-	-
226 Friends-USA	3	163	NR	208 *	.1	.1
246 Greek Orthodox	1	NR	NR	366	.1	.2
263 Int Foursq Gos	1	47	61	61 *	-	-
264 Int Chs of Crst	1	32	64	51	-	-
267 Muslim Est	1	NR	156	609	.2	.4
283 Luth—MO Synod	33	19,027	10,880	25,425	7.7	15.3
288 Mennonite USA	6	840	808	1,080 *	.3	.6
291 Missionary Ch	12	2,119	4,276	4,294	1.3	2.6
297 Mennonite;Other	2	148	NR	189 *	.1	.1
306 NT IndBapt&Rltd	1	200	NR	255 *	.1	.2
323 Old Ord Amish	9	540	NR	693 *	.2	.4
332 OCA: Bulg Dioc	1	200	NR	285	.1	.2
349 Pent Holiness	1	25	22	32 *	-	-
355 Presb Ch (USA)	5	2,650	963	3,385 *	1.0	2.0
356 Presb Ch Amer	1	24	60	60	-	-
360 Prim Bapt Chrch	1	NR	NR	NR	-	-
371 Ref Ch in Am	1	124	119	221	.1	.1
388 Reg Bapt Gen As	5	2,281	2,250	3,030 *	.9	1.8
401 Rus Orth Abroad	1	NR	NR	NR	-	-
403 Salvation Army	1	163	73	260	.1	.2
413 S.D.A.	3	404	NR	481	.1	.3
419 So Bapt Conv	9	2,757	960	3,522 *	1.1	2.1
431 Ukrainian Orth	1	NR	NR	30	-	-
435 Unitarian-Univ	1	178	NR	227 *	.1	.1
443 Un C of Christ	6	2,147	643	2,743 *	.8	1.6
449 Un Methodist	36	11,762	7,612	15,026 *	4.5	9.0
463 Vineyard	1	130	120	166 *	.1	.1
467 Wesleyan	5	426	532	899	.3	.5
469 WELS	2	308	207	384	.1	.2
496 Jewish Est	2	NR	NR	950	.3	.6
498 Indep.Charis.	2	100	2,150	2,650	.8	1.6
499 Indep.Non-Char	2	1,484	3,600	3,600	1.1	2.2
BARTHOLOMEW	**85**	**23,089**	**8,485**	**36,596 ***	**51.2**	**100.0**
017 Amer Bapt Assn	1	200	NR	253 *	.4	.7
019 Amer Bapt USA	5	3,197	913	4,046 *	5.7	11.1
053 Assemb of God	4	370	457	595	.8	1.6
056 Baha'i	0	18	NR	18	-	-
081 Catholic	1	NR	NR	5,492	7.7	15.0
089 Chr & Miss Al	1	42	NR	106	.1	.3
093 Chr Ch (Disc)	1	658	193	833 *	1.2	2.3
097 Chr Chs&Chs Cr	9	4,856	NR	6,147 *	8.6	16.8
107 Christian Un	1	11	22	22 *	-	.1
123 Ch God (Ander)	1	NR	111	111	.2	.3
127 Ch God (Cleve)	1	204	57	258 *	.4	.7
151 L-D Saints	2	NR	NR	730	1.0	2.0
165 Ch of Nazarene	4	499	375	644	.9	1.8
167 Chs of Christ	3	261	275	333	.5	.9
193 Episcopal	1	NR	89	291	.4	.8
207 E.L.C.A.	1	347	239	493	.7	1.3
221 Free Methodist	1	192	305	305	.4	.8
226 Friends-USA	1	102	NR	129 *	.2	.4
283 Luth—MO Synod	7	4,786	2,571	6,006	8.4	16.4

NR–Not Reported *Total adherents estimated from known number of communicant, confirmed, full members. - Represents a percentage less than 0.1. Percentages may not total 100 due to rounding.

Table 4: Religious Congregations by County and Group: 2000

Religious Group	Number of Churches, Synagogues, Mosques, or Temples	Number of Communicant, Confirmed, or Full Members	Number of Attendees	Total Adherents: Number of Adherents	Total Adherents: % of Total Pop.	Total Adherents: % of Total Adh.
293 Morav Ch-North	1	363	NR	442	.6	1.2
306 NT IndBapt&Rltd	1	200	NR	253 *	.4	.7
320 "Old" MB Ascs	1	122	NR	154 *	.2	.4
355 Presb Ch (USA)	3	691	365	874 *	1.2	2.4
403 Salvation Army	1	33	23	127	.2	.3
409 Separate Bapt	3	134	NR	170 *	.2	.5
413 S.D.A.	1	115	NR	137	.2	.4
419 So Bapt Conv	4	1,058	267	1,339 *	1.9	3.7
435 Unitarian-Univ	1	61	NR	77 *	.1	.2
443 Un C of Christ	1	62	65	78 *	.1	.2
449 Un Methodist	16	4,338	1,907	5,490 *	7.7	15.0
467 Wesleyan	6	169	251	523	.7	1.4
496 Jewish Est	1	NR	NR	120	.2	.3
BENTON	**25**	**2,346**	**813**	**6,298 ***	**66.9**	**100.0**
081 Catholic	4	NR	NR	3,264	34.6	51.8
093 Chr Ch (Disc)	1	80	46	101 *	1.1	1.6
097 Chr Chs&Chs Cr	5	790	NR	1,001 *	10.6	15.9
207 E.L.C.A.	1	203	40	274	2.9	4.4
221 Free Methodist	1	19	40	40	.4	.6
355 Presb Ch (USA)	3	200	118	254 *	2.7	4.0
419 So Bapt Conv	2	207	93	262 *	2.8	4.2
449 Un Methodist	7	830	448	1,052 *	11.2	16.7
467 Wesleyan	1	17	28	50	.5	.8
BLACKFORD	**27**	**2,654**	**1,425**	**4,468 ***	**31.8**	**100.0**
019 Amer Bapt USA	1	227	97	280 *	2.0	6.3
053 Assemb of God	2	67	85	85	.6	1.9
056 Baha'i	0	6	NR	6	-	.1
081 Catholic	2	NR	NR	829	5.9	18.6
093 Chr Ch (Disc)	1	352	74	435 *	3.1	9.7
097 Chr Chs&Chs Cr	2	179	NR	221 *	1.6	4.9
123 Ch God (Ander)	1	NR	15	15	.1	.3
157 Ch of Brethren	1	35	0	43 *	.3	1.0
165 Ch of Nazarene	3	289	186	484	3.4	10.8
207 E.L.C.A.	1	259	119	371	2.6	8.3
283 Luth—MO Synod	1	26	23	39	.3	.9
355 Presb Ch (USA)	1	120	72	148 *	1.1	3.3
413 S.D.A.	1	26	NR	31	.2	.7
449 Un Methodist	9	969	591	1,196 *	8.5	26.8
467 Wesleyan	1	99	163	285	2.0	6.4
BOONE	**58**	**11,399**	**5,237**	**21,716 ***	**47.1**	**100.0**
019 Amer Bapt USA	2	442	297	567 *	1.2	2.6
053 Assemb of God	1	41	48	115	.2	.5
056 Baha'i	0	8	NR	8	-	-
081 Catholic	2	NR	NR	4,631	10.0	21.3
089 Chr & Miss Al	1	135	NR	735	1.6	3.4
093 Chr Ch (Disc)	3	1,804	370	2,314 *	5.0	10.7
097 Chr Chs&Chs Cr	6	1,710	NR	2,193 *	4.8	10.1
123 Ch God (Ander)	1	NR	37	37	.1	.2
145 Ch God Prophcy	2	71	NR	92 *	.2	.4
151 L-D Saints	2	NR	NR	671	1.5	3.1
165 Ch of Nazarene	1	137	175	342	.7	1.6
167 Chs of Christ	4	232	250	280	.6	1.3
176 Congr Ad Afl	1	89	NR	114 *	.2	.5
193 Episcopal	2	NR	214	607	1.3	2.8
207 E.L.C.A.	2	434	301	616	1.3	2.8
220 Free Lutheran	1	50	21	62	.1	.3
226 Friends-USA	1	102	NR	131 *	.3	.6
283 Luth—MO Synod	1	294	338	507	1.1	2.3
306 NT IndBapt&Rltd	4	800	NR	1,026 *	2.2	4.7
339 Pent Ch of God	2	58	NR	140	.3	.6
355 Presb Ch (USA)	3	2,121	1,576	2,720 *	5.9	12.5
365 Prog Prim Bapt	1	61	NR	78 *	.2	.4
388 Reg Bapt Gen As	1	175	130	224 *	.5	1.0
419 So Bapt Conv	2	200	67	256 *	.6	1.2
443 Un C of Christ	1	18	8	23 *	-	.1
449 Un Methodist	9	2,311	1,284	2,965 *	6.4	13.7
467 Wesleyan	2	106	121	262	.6	1.2
BROWN	**25**	**2,486**	**1,197**	**4,275 ***	**28.6**	**100.0**
019 Amer Bapt USA	2	635	309	769 *	5.1	18.0
056 Baha'i	0	7	NR	7	-	.2
081 Catholic	1	NR	NR	1,056	7.1	24.7
097 Chr Chs&Chs Cr	4	740	NR	896 *	6.0	21.0
123 Ch God (Ander)	1	NR	50	50	.3	1.2
165 Ch of Nazarene	1	222	196	248	1.7	5.8
167 Chs of Christ	2	75	77	100	.7	2.3
193 Episcopal	1	NR	61	75	.5	1.8
283 Luth—MO Synod	1	119	66	176	1.2	4.1
288 Mennonite USA	1	53	42	64 *	.4	1.5
409 Separate Bapt	1	47	NR	57 *	.4	1.3
419 So Bapt Conv	3	83	63	100 *	.7	2.3
449 Un Methodist	5	473	288	572 *	3.8	13.4
467 Wesleyan	2	32	45	105	.7	2.5
CARROLL	**39**	**5,265**	**2,532**	**7,828 ***	**38.8**	**100.0**
019 Amer Bapt USA	3	354	90	444 *	2.2	5.7
053 Assemb of God	2	331	376	714	3.5	9.1
056 Baha'i	0	1	NR	1	-	-
071 Brethren (Ash)	2	168	118	211 *	1.0	2.7
081 Catholic	1	NR	NR	810	4.0	10.3
093 Chr Ch (Disc)	1	381	141	478 *	2.4	6.1
097 Chr Chs&Chs Cr	4	737	NR	924 *	4.6	11.8
127 Ch God (Cleve)	1	23	16	29 *	.1	.4
157 Ch of Brethren	3	454	155	570 *	2.8	7.3
167 Chs of Christ	1	15	20	30	.1	.4
207 E.L.C.A.	3	338	152	464	2.3	5.9
355 Presb Ch (USA)	6	775	352	972 *	4.8	12.4
388 Reg Bapt Gen As	1	49	90	90 *	.4	1.1
419 So Bapt Conv	1	189	84	237 *	1.2	3.0
443 Un C of Christ	1	216	62	271 *	1.3	3.5
449 Un Methodist	8	1,204	843	1,511 *	7.5	19.3
467 Wesleyan	1	30	33	72	.4	.9
CASS	**57**	**8,480**	**4,219**	**15,734 ***	**38.4**	**100.0**
019 Amer Bapt USA	4	1,120	403	1,393 *	3.4	8.9
053 Assemb of God	1	255	316	545	1.3	3.5
056 Baha'i	0	8	NR	8	-	.1
071 Brethren (Ash)	1	125	94	155 *	.4	1.0
081 Catholic	2	NR	NR	4,144	10.1	26.3
089 Chr & Miss Al	1	110	NR	212	.5	1.3
093 Chr Ch (Disc)	1	359	137	446 *	1.1	2.8
097 Chr Chs&Chs Cr	5	821	NR	1,021 *	2.5	6.5
123 Ch God (Ander)	1	NR	90	90	.2	.6
127 Ch God (Cleve)	1	342	220	425 *	1.0	2.7
151 L-D Saints	1	NR	NR	331	.8	2.1
157 Ch of Brethren	1	95	110	118 *	.3	.7
165 Ch of Nazarene	1	226	154	226	.6	1.4
167 Chs of Christ	3	113	118	168	.4	1.1
176 Congr Ad Afl	2	179	NR	223 *	.5	1.4
193 Episcopal	1	NR	60	178	.4	1.1
207 E.L.C.A.	2	361	116	414	1.0	2.6
263 Int Foursq Gos	1	115	101	143 *	.3	.9
283 Luth—MO Synod	1	275	90	367	.9	2.3
306 NT IndBapt&Rltd	1	200	NR	249 *	.6	1.6
355 Presb Ch (USA)	3	661	275	822 *	2.0	5.2
403 Salvation Army	1	104	47	303	.7	1.9
413 S.D.A.	1	57	NR	68	.2	.4
443 Un C of Christ	2	423	186	526 *	1.3	3.3
449 Un Methodist	17	2,400	1,570	2,984 *	7.3	19.0
463 Vineyard	1	100	100	124 *	.3	.8
467 Wesleyan	1	31	32	51	.1	.3
CLARK	**117**	**19,685**	**8,282**	**38,570 ***	**40.0**	**100.0**
017 Amer Bapt Assn	1	50	NR	62 *	.1	.2
019 Amer Bapt USA	7	1,538	453	1,896 *	2.0	4.9
053 Assemb of God	3	296	288	313	.3	.8
056 Baha'i	0	15	NR	15	-	-
081 Catholic	8	NR	NR	12,258	12.7	31.8
093 Chr Ch (Disc)	6	1,703	394	2,099 *	2.2	5.4
097 Chr Chs&Chs Cr	15	2,184	NR	2,690 *	2.8	7.0

NR–Not Reported *Total adherents estimated from known number of communicant, confirmed, full members. - Represents a percentage less than 0.1. Percentages may not total 100 due to rounding.

Table 4: Religious Congregations by County and Group: 2000

Religious Group	Number of Churches, Synagogues, Mosques, or Temples	Number of Communicant, Confirmed, or Full Members	Number of Attendees	Total Adherents		
				Number of Adherents	% of Total Pop.	% of Total Adh.
123 Ch God (Ander)	4	NR	442	442	.5	1.1
127 Ch God (Cleve)	1	12	20	20 *	-	.1
151 L-D Saints	2	NR	NR	570	.6	1.5
165 Ch of Nazarene	5	268	223	453	.5	1.2
167 Chs of Christ	12	1,404	1,198	1,871	1.9	4.9
193 Episcopal	1	NR	104	144	.1	.4
207 E.L.C.A.	1	288	110	401	.4	1.0
221 Free Methodist	1	6	34	34	-	.1
262 Int Cou Comm Ch	1	600	NR	740 *	.8	1.9
306 NT IndBapt&Rltd	1	200	NR	247 *	.3	.6
320 "Old" MB Ascs	1	41	NR	51 *	.1	.1
355 Presb Ch (USA)	7	715	366	882 *	.9	2.3
388 Reg Bapt Gen As	1	98	90	90 *	.1	.2
413 S.D.A.	2	105	NR	125	.1	.3
419 So Bapt Conv	13	6,547	1,881	8,071 *	8.4	20.9
443 Un C of Christ	1	405	97	499 *	.5	1.3
449 Un Methodist	22	3,210	1,942	3,957 *	4.1	10.3
499 Indep.Non-Char	1	0	640	640	.7	1.7
CLAY	**54**	**6,358**	**3,622**	**9,165 ***	**34.5**	**100.0**
019 Amer Bapt USA	4	873	543	1,087 *	4.1	11.9
053 Assemb of God	2	65	75	135	.5	1.5
056 Baha'i	0	5	NR	5	-	.1
081 Catholic	1	NR	NR	938	3.5	10.2
097 Chr Chs&Chs Cr	4	1,160	NR	1,445 *	5.4	15.8
127 Ch God (Cleve)	2	126	102	157 *	.6	1.7
151 L-D Saints	1	NR	NR	150	.6	1.6
165 Ch of Nazarene	4	552	436	728	2.7	7.9
167 Chs of Christ	6	261	262	341	1.3	3.7
221 Free Methodist	2	55	69	74	.3	.8
263 Int Foursq Gos	1	65	85	85 *	.3	.9
355 Presb Ch (USA)	2	351	225	438 *	1.6	4.8
388 Reg Bapt Gen As	1	228	244	284 *	1.1	3.1
419 So Bapt Conv	2	217	179	270 *	1.0	2.9
443 Un C of Christ	3	656	269	817 *	3.1	8.9
449 Un Methodist	18	1,714	1,098	2,136 *	8.0	23.3
467 Wesleyan	1	30	35	75	.3	.8
CLINTON	**59**	**8,797**	**4,331**	**13,211 ***	**39.0**	**100.0**
019 Amer Bapt USA	4	718	283	908 *	2.7	6.9
053 Assemb of God	3	174	217	301	.9	2.3
056 Baha'i	0	6	NR	6	-	-
081 Catholic	1	NR	NR	1,431	4.2	10.8
093 Chr Ch (Disc)	1	519	254	656 *	1.9	5.0
097 Chr Chs&Chs Cr	7	1,748	NR	2,211 *	6.5	16.7
121 Ch God (Abr)	1	32	26	40 *	.1	.3
123 Ch God (Ander)	2	NR	82	82	.2	.6
151 L-D Saints	1	NR	NR	150	.4	1.1
157 Ch of Brethren	1	177	169	224 *	.7	1.7
165 Ch of Nazarene	1	342	279	474	1.4	3.6
167 Chs of Christ	2	95	125	155	.5	1.2
176 Congr Ad Afl	1	69	NR	87 *	.3	.7
181 Consrv Congr	1	326	110	412 *	1.2	3.1
207 E.L.C.A.	2	188	87	225	.7	1.7
306 NT IndBapt&Rltd	1	200	NR	253 *	.7	1.9
355 Presb Ch (USA)	5	828	453	1,046 *	3.1	7.9
388 Reg Bapt Gen As	1	135	125	171 *	.5	1.3
413 S.D.A.	1	33	NR	39	.1	.3
419 So Bapt Conv	3	803	633	1,015 *	3.0	7.7
443 Un C of Christ	2	180	85	228 *	.7	1.7
449 Un Methodist	13	1,968	1,125	2,487 *	7.3	18.8
467 Wesleyan	5	256	278	610	1.8	4.6
CRAWFORD	**29**	**2,703**	**1,030**	**4,101 ***	**38.2**	**100.0**
019 Amer Bapt USA	2	81	26	101 *	.9	2.5
056 Baha'i	0	1	NR	1	-	-
075 Brethren in Cr	1	27	29	29	.3	.7
081 Catholic	1	NR	NR	158	1.5	3.9
097 Chr Chs&Chs Cr	9	1,334	NR	1,663 *	15.5	40.6
151 L-D Saints	1	NR	NR	262	2.4	6.4
165 Ch of Nazarene	1	14	0	14	.1	.3
173 Comm of Christ	1	28	NR	28	.3	.7
221 Free Methodist	1	29	40	40	.4	1.0

Religious Group	Number of Churches, Synagogues, Mosques, or Temples	Number of Communicant, Confirmed, or Full Members	Number of Attendees	Total Adherents		
				Number of Adherents	% of Total Pop.	% of Total Adh.
355 Presb Ch (USA)	1	114	40	142 *	1.3	3.5
388 Reg Bapt Gen As	1	228	244	284 *	2.6	6.9
449 Un Methodist	7	607	439	756 *	7.0	18.4
467 Wesleyan	3	240	212	623	5.8	15.2
DAVIESS	**79**	**9,721**	**3,515**	**17,253 ***	**57.9**	**100.0**
019 Amer Bapt USA	4	1,180	362	1,518 *	5.1	8.8
053 Assemb of God	1	62	90	206	.7	1.2
061 Beachy Amish	1	140	NR	180 *	.6	1.0
081 Catholic	4	NR	NR	4,182	14.0	24.2
093 Chr Ch (Disc)	1	287	0	369 *	1.2	2.1
097 Chr Chs&Chs Cr	8	2,272	NR	2,923 *	9.8	16.9
123 Ch God (Ander)	1	NR	45	45	.2	.3
127 Ch God (Cleve)	1	27	27	35 *	.1	.2
165 Ch of Nazarene	2	114	141	335	1.1	1.9
167 Chs of Christ	3	265	275	341	1.1	2.0
171 Ch God-Gen Con	1	95	57	122 *	.4	.7
173 Comm of Christ	1	56	NR	56	.2	.3
185 Cumber Presb	1	20	NR	37	.1	.2
193 Episcopal	1	NR	31	45	.2	.3
207 E.L.C.A.	1	126	72	166	.6	1.0
221 Free Methodist	1	182	180	263	.9	1.5
288 Mennonite USA	3	696	516	896 *	3.0	5.2
297 Mennonite;Other	4	179	NR	231 *	.8	1.3
320 "Old" MB Ascs	1	42	NR	54 *	.2	.3
323 Old Ord Amish	15	900	NR	1,155 *	3.9	6.7
355 Presb Ch (USA)	1	120	60	154 *	.5	.9
388 Reg Bapt Gen As	1	74	79	95 *	.3	.6
413 S.D.A.	1	4	NR	5	-	-
419 So Bapt Conv	3	280	54	360 *	1.2	2.1
449 Un Methodist	14	1,992	1,030	2,561 *	8.6	14.8
467 Wesleyan	3	108	96	319	1.1	1.8
499 Indep.Non-Char	1	500	400	600	2.0	3.5
DEARBORN	**62**	**8,678**	**4,199**	**20,085 ***	**43.6**	**100.0**
019 Amer Bapt USA	9	1,559	768	1,974 *	4.3	9.8
053 Assemb of God	1	66	43	58	.1	.3
056 Baha'i	0	1	NR	1	-	-
081 Catholic	7	NR	NR	8,628	18.7	43.0
089 Chr & Miss Al	1	79	NR	150	.3	.7
097 Chr Chs&Chs Cr	7	1,270	NR	1,608 *	3.5	8.0
107 Christian Un	1	73	41	92 *	.2	.5
123 Ch God (Ander)	1	NR	40	40	.1	.2
151 L-D Saints	1	NR	NR	202	.4	1.0
165 Ch of Nazarene	1	44	45	45	.1	.2
167 Chs of Christ	1	17	30	30	.1	.1
193 Episcopal	1	NR	38	63	.1	.3
207 E.L.C.A.	4	792	302	1,080	2.3	5.4
223 Free Will Bapt	1	2	NR	3 *	-	-
283 Luth—MO Synod	4	1,013	453	1,447	3.1	7.2
306 NT IndBapt&Rltd	2	400	NR	507 *	1.1	2.5
355 Presb Ch (USA)	4	375	205	474 *	1.0	2.4
419 So Bapt Conv	1	36	0	46 *	.1	.2
443 Un C of Christ	2	116	80	147 *	.3	.7
449 Un Methodist	10	1,671	891	2,115 *	4.6	10.5
467 Wesleyan	2	64	63	175	.4	.9
499 Indep.Non-Char	1	1,100	1,200	1,200	2.6	6.0
DECATUR	**55**	**7,207**	**2,727**	**15,002 ***	**61.1**	**100.0**
019 Amer Bapt USA	12	3,141	938	3,952 *	16.1	26.3
053 Assemb of God	1	31	38	53	.2	.4
056 Baha'i	0	2	NR	2	-	-
081 Catholic	4	NR	NR	5,441	22.2	36.3
093 Chr Ch (Disc)	2	525	199	661 *	2.7	4.4
097 Chr Chs&Chs Cr	5	809	NR	1,019 *	4.1	6.8
123 Ch God (Ander)	1	NR	135	135	.5	.9
165 Ch of Nazarene	1	72	77	97	.4	.6
167 Chs of Christ	1	20	20	20	.1	.1
207 E.L.C.A.	2	141	83	185	.8	1.2
221 Free Methodist	1	41	30	41	.2	.3
258 IndFreeWillBapt	1	52	NR	65 *	.3	.4
283 Luth—MO Synod	1	131	65	194	.8	1.3
323 Old Ord Amish	1	60	NR	75 *	.3	.5

NR–Not Reported   *Total adherents estimated from known number of communicant, confirmed, full members.   - Represents a percentage less than 0.1.   Percentages may not total 100 due to rounding.

Table 4: Religious Congregations by County and Group: 2000

Religious Group	Number of Churches, Synagogues, Mosques, or Temples	Number of Communicant, Confirmed, or Full Members	Number of Attendees	Total Adherents: Number of Adherents	Total Adherents: % of Total Pop.	Total Adherents: % of Total Adh.
355 Presb Ch (USA)	3	354	180	445 *	1.8	3.0
409 Separate Bapt	1	62	NR	78 *	.3	.5
419 So Bapt Conv	4	369	195	464 *	1.9	3.1
449 Un Methodist	11	1,280	576	1,610 *	6.6	10.7
467 Wesleyan	3	117	191	465	1.9	3.1
DE KALB	**67**	**8,455**	**4,334**	**15,306 ***	**38.0**	**100.0**
019 Amer Bapt USA	1	336	106	430 *	1.1	2.8
053 Assemb of God	4	196	251	385	1.0	2.5
075 Brethren in Cr	1	42	33	42	.1	.3
081 Catholic	3	NR	NR	3,332	8.3	21.8
089 Chr & Miss Al	1	66	NR	181	.4	1.2
093 Chr Ch (Disc)	1	280	0	359 *	.9	2.3
097 Chr Chs&Chs Cr	8	1,728	NR	2,212 *	5.5	14.5
123 Ch God (Ander)	3	NR	114	114	.3	.7
157 Ch of Brethren	3	314	209	402 *	1.0	2.6
165 Ch of Nazarene	4	464	350	757	1.9	4.9
167 Chs of Christ	1	40	65	75	.2	.5
171 Ch God-Gen Con	1	89	93	114 *	.3	.7
207 E.L.C.A.	5	754	315	1,019	2.5	6.7
216 Evan Presby Ch	1	190	NR	243 *	.6	1.6
265 Int Pent C Chr	1	75	39	75	.2	.5
283 Luth—MO Synod	3	772	377	1,011	2.5	6.6
291 Missionary Ch	1	0	431	431	1.1	2.8
297 Mennonite;Other	1	12	NR	15 *	-	.1
323 Old Ord Amish	4	240	NR	308 *	.8	2.0
355 Presb Ch (USA)	2	424	217	543 *	1.3	3.5
388 Reg Bapt Gen As	1	200	400	400 *	1.0	2.6
419 So Bapt Conv	1	167	76	214 *	.5	1.4
443 Un C of Christ	1	37	25	47 *	.1	.3
449 Un Methodist	15	2,029	1,233	2,597 *	6.4	17.0
DELAWARE	**133**	**18,264**	**12,950**	**32,418 ***	**27.3**	**100.0**
019 Amer Bapt USA	3	1,121	462	1,351 *	1.1	4.2
053 Assemb of God	3	396	499	709	.6	2.2
056 Baha'i	1	43	NR	43	-	.1
071 Brethren (Ash)	3	252	239	304 *	.3	.9
081 Catholic	3	NR	NR	7,081	6.0	21.8
089 Chr & Miss Al	1	28	NR	278	.2	.9
093 Chr Ch (Disc)	4	1,240	449	1,495 *	1.3	4.6
097 Chr Chs&Chs Cr	3	502	NR	605 *	.5	1.9
123 Ch God (Ander)	9	NR	1,027	1,027	.9	3.2
127 Ch God (Cleve)	1	22	27	27 *	-	.1
145 Ch God Prophcy	1	36	NR	43 *	-	.1
151 L-D Saints	1	NR	NR	377	.3	1.2
157 Ch of Brethren	2	89	35	124 *	.1	.4
165 Ch of Nazarene	15	1,921	1,254	2,913	2.5	9.0
167 Chs of Christ	7	487	630	675	.6	2.1
193 Episcopal	1	NR	92	231	.2	.7
207 E.L.C.A.	3	610	271	771	.6	2.4
226 Friends-USA	3	141	NR	170 *	.1	.5
258 IndFreeWillBapt	3	207	NR	249 *	.2	.8
263 Int Foursq Gos	2	337	449	449 *	.4	1.4
267 Muslim Est	1	NR	40	100	.1	.3
283 Luth—MO Synod	1	321	198	399	.3	1.2
288 Mennonite USA	1	24	40	40 *	-	.1
296 Midw Congr Fel	3	112	152	135 *	.1	.4
306 NT IndBapt&Rltd	2	400	NR	482 *	.4	1.5
355 Presb Ch (USA)	2	921	497	1,110 *	.9	3.4
356 Presb Ch Amer	2	575	548	747	.6	2.3
360 Prim Bapt Chrch	1	NR	NR	NR	-	-
388 Reg Bapt Gen As	1	52	70	70 *	.1	.2
409 Separate Bapt	1	50	NR	60 *	.1	.2
413 S.D.A.	2	86	NR	102	.1	.3
419 So Bapt Conv	8	1,653	416	1,992 *	1.7	6.1
435 Unitarian-Univ	1	236	NR	284 *	.2	.9
443 Un C of Christ	4	519	311	626 *	.5	1.9
449 Un Methodist	30	5,789	5,113	6,978 *	5.9	21.5
467 Wesleyan	3	94	131	251	.2	.8
496 Jewish Est	1	NR	NR	120	.1	.4
DUBOIS	**54**	**6,837**	**3,525**	**32,263 ***	**81.3**	**100.0**
053 Assemb of God	2	124	162	272	.7	.8
056 Baha'i	0	5	NR	5	-	-
081 Catholic	11	NR	NR	23,044	58.1	71.4
097 Chr Chs&Chs Cr	7	955	NR	1,207 *	3.0	3.7
151 L-D Saints	1	NR	NR	167	.4	.5
165 Ch of Nazarene	2	168	173	398	1.0	1.2
167 Chs of Christ	2	92	122	142	.4	.4
203 Evan Free Ch	1	69	125	125	.3	.4
207 E.L.C.A.	7	2,064	860	2,544	6.4	7.9
263 Int Foursq Gos	2	195	352	352 *	.9	1.1
283 Luth—MO Synod	1	36	22	54	.1	.2
355 Presb Ch (USA)	1	91	37	115 *	.3	.4
360 Prim Bapt Chrch	1	NR	NR	NR	-	-
388 Reg Bapt Gen As	2	100	97	128 *	.3	.4
413 S.D.A.	2	34	NR	41	.1	.1
419 So Bapt Conv	2	379	326	479 *	1.2	1.5
443 Un C of Christ	6	1,621	571	2,049 *	5.2	6.4
449 Un Methodist	3	896	678	1,133 *	2.9	3.5
467 Wesleyan	1	8	0	8	-	-
ELKHART	**281**	**40,604**	**30,708**	**70,199 ***	**38.4**	**100.0**
017 Amer Bapt Assn	1	4	NR	5 *	-	-
032 Amish; other	1	34	NR	44 *	-	.1
034 Ant Orth of NA	1	36	NR	72	-	.1
053 Assemb of God	7	951	1,220	1,740	1.0	2.5
056 Baha'i	0	25	NR	25	-	-
061 Beachy Amish	4	365	NR	473 *	.3	.7
071 Brethren (Ash)	6	1,366	1,382	1,771 *	1.0	2.5
075 Brethren in Cr	2	165	132	166	.1	.2
081 Catholic	4	NR	NR	11,373	6.2	16.2
093 Chr Ch (Disc)	2	604	140	782 *	.4	1.1
097 Chr Chs&Chs Cr	2	360	NR	467 *	.3	.7
105 Christian Ref	1	203	132	263 *	.1	.4
123 Ch God (Ander)	7	NR	941	941	.5	1.3
127 Ch God (Cleve)	3	592	372	780 *	.4	1.1
145 Ch God Prophcy	1	36	NR	46 *	-	.1
151 L-D Saints	2	NR	NR	822	.4	1.2
157 Ch of Brethren	18	2,930	2,047	3,830 *	2.1	5.5
165 Ch of Nazarene	6	1,014	726	1,389	.8	2.0
167 Chs of Christ	3	350	370	380	.2	.5
183 Cons Menn Conf	6	872	1,064	1,269	.7	1.8
193 Episcopal	4	NR	367	1,006	.6	1.4
203 Evan Free Ch	1	200	850	850	.5	1.2
207 E.L.C.A.	10	2,642	1,249	3,458	1.9	4.9
221 Free Methodist	1	57	39	58	-	.1
223 Free Will Bapt	1	2	NR	3 *	-	-
283 Luth—MO Synod	3	996	726	1,283	.7	1.8
288 Mennonite USA	34	6,697	5,568	8,765 *	4.8	12.5
291 Missionary Ch	18	2,690	5,415	5,450	3.0	7.8
297 Mennonite;Other	11	810	NR	1,047 *	.6	1.5
306 NT IndBapt&Rltd	4	800	NR	1,036 *	.6	1.5
322 Old Ord Menn Ch	6	660	NR	855 *	.5	1.2
323 Old Ord Amish	61	3,660	NR	4,758 *	2.6	6.8
339 Pent Ch of God	2	64	NR	153	.1	.2
355 Presb Ch (USA)	3	1,136	537	1,471 *	.8	2.1
360 Prim Bapt Chrch	2	NR	NR	NR	-	-
388 Reg Bapt Gen As	4	1,385	1,105	1,105 *	.6	1.6
401 Rus Orth Abroad	1	NR	NR	NR	-	-
403 Salvation Army	2	175	123	680	.4	1.0
413 S.D.A.	3	227	NR	270	.1	.4
419 So Bapt Conv	3	194	122	251 *	.1	.4
431 Ukrainian Orth	1	NR	NR	108	.1	.2
435 Unitarian-Univ	1	121	NR	157 *	.1	.2
443 Un C of Christ	4	1,022	355	1,324 *	.7	1.9
449 Un Methodist	20	6,350	4,623	8,225 *	4.5	11.7
467 Wesleyan	1	32	28	83	-	.1
499 Indep.Non-Char	3	777	1,075	1,165	.6	1.7
FAYETTE	**43**	**6,440**	**2,878**	**11,247 ***	**44.0**	**100.0**
019 Amer Bapt USA	1	668	215	822 *	3.2	7.3
053 Assemb of God	1	90	120	120	.5	1.1
081 Catholic	1	NR	NR	2,854	11.2	25.4
093 Chr Ch (Disc)	2	464	147	571 *	2.2	5.1
097 Chr Chs&Chs Cr	3	731	NR	900 *	3.5	8.0

NR–Not Reported　　*Total adherents estimated from known number of communicant, confirmed, full members.　　- Represents a percentage less than 0.1.　　Percentages may not total 100 due to rounding.

Table 4: Religious Congregations by County and Group: 2000

Religious Group	Number of Churches, Synagogues, Mosques, or Temples	Number of Communicant, Confirmed, or Full Members	Number of Attendees	Total Adherents: Number of Adherents	Total Adherents: % of Total Pop.	Total Adherents: % of Total Adh.
123 Ch God (Ander)	1	NR	100	100	.4	.9
127 Ch God (Cleve)	1	100	85	123 *	.5	1.1
145 Ch God Prophcy	1	36	NR	44 *	.2	.4
151 L-D Saints	1	NR	NR	269	1.1	2.4
165 Ch of Nazarene	2	180	109	402	1.6	3.6
167 Chs of Christ	3	100	100	127	.5	1.1
193 Episcopal	1	NR	33	49	.2	.4
207 E.L.C.A.	2	224	100	260	1.0	2.3
283 Luth—MO Synod	1	32	25	43	.2	.4
306 NT IndBapt&Rltd	2	400	NR	492 *	1.9	4.4
355 Presb Ch (USA)	1	189	99	233 *	.9	2.1
360 Prim Bapt Chrch	3	NR	NR	NR	-	-
388 Reg Bapt Gen As	1	228	244	281 *	1.1	2.5
403 Salvation Army	1	82	32	170	.7	1.5
413 S.D.A.	1	23	NR	27	.1	.2
418 Southw Bapt Fel	1	NR	NR	NR	-	-
419 So Bapt Conv	2	758	204	933 *	3.6	8.3
449 Un Methodist	8	1,270	553	1,562 *	6.1	13.9
467 Wesleyan	1	15	12	15	.1	.1
499 Indep.Non-Char	1	850	700	850	3.3	7.6
FLOYD	**70**	**21,964**	**8,202**	**44,232 ***	**62.5**	**100.0**
019 Amer Bapt USA	3	1,039	353	1,296 *	1.8	2.9
053 Assemb of God	3	231	223	240	.3	.5
056 Baha'i	0	9	NR	9	-	-
081 Catholic	5	NR	NR	14,782	20.9	33.4
093 Chr Ch (Disc)	4	1,202	275	1,500 *	2.1	3.4
097 Chr Chs&Chs Cr	5	2,946	NR	3,676 *	5.2	8.3
123 Ch God (Ander)	2	NR	376	376	.5	.9
127 Ch God (Cleve)	1	50	8	62 *	.1	.1
145 Ch God Prophcy	1	36	NR	44 *	.1	.1
165 Ch of Nazarene	3	588	463	933	1.3	2.1
167 Chs of Christ	3	390	441	472	.7	1.1
173 Comm of Christ	2	144	NR	144	.2	.3
193 Episcopal	1	NR	70	386	.5	.9
267 Muslim Est	1	NR	228	841	1.2	1.9
283 Luth—MO Synod	2	1,063	509	1,387	2.0	3.1
355 Presb Ch (USA)	2	482	243	601 *	.8	1.4
403 Salvation Army	1	71	30	339	.5	.8
413 S.D.A.	1	149	NR	177	.2	.4
419 So Bapt Conv	11	8,813	2,434	10,997 *	15.5	24.9
443 Un C of Christ	1	807	285	1,007 *	1.4	2.3
449 Un Methodist	15	3,918	2,241	4,889 *	6.9	11.1
467 Wesleyan	3	26	23	74	.1	.2
FOUNTAIN	**44**	**4,843**	**2,062**	**7,527 ***	**41.9**	**100.0**
053 Assemb of God	2	204	169	348	1.9	4.6
081 Catholic	2	NR	NR	888	4.9	11.8
093 Chr Ch (Disc)	3	293	42	367 *	2.0	4.9
097 Chr Chs&Chs Cr	9	1,303	NR	1,629 *	9.1	21.6
123 Ch God (Ander)	1	NR	95	95	.5	1.3
127 Ch God (Cleve)	1	75	36	94 *	.5	1.2
165 Ch of Nazarene	3	329	273	507	2.8	6.7
167 Chs of Christ	1	48	63	69	.4	.9
176 Congr Ad Afl	3	313	NR	392 *	2.2	5.2
207 E.L.C.A.	2	145	53	182	1.0	2.4
221 Free Methodist	1	65	107	107	.6	1.4
306 NT IndBapt&Rltd	3	600	NR	751 *	4.2	10.0
355 Presb Ch (USA)	1	84	53	105 *	.6	1.4
388 Reg Bapt Gen As	1	25	31	31 *	.2	.4
419 So Bapt Conv	1	20	0	25 *	.1	.3
443 Un C of Christ	1	78	85	98 *	.5	1.3
449 Un Methodist	8	1,111	605	1,389 *	7.7	18.5
499 Indep.Non-Char	1	150	450	450	2.5	6.0
FRANKLIN	**39**	**4,541**	**1,269**	**11,225 ***	**50.7**	**100.0**
056 Baha'i	0	5	NR	5	-	-
071 Brethren (Ash)	1	43	48	55 *	.2	.5
081 Catholic	7	NR	NR	5,409	24.4	48.2
097 Chr Chs&Chs Cr	8	1,590	NR	2,035 *	9.2	18.1
165 Ch of Nazarene	1	28	25	62	.3	.6
207 E.L.C.A.	2	391	125	482	2.2	4.3
355 Presb Ch (USA)	1	27	20	35 *	.2	.3
419 So Bapt Conv	8	1,662	575	2,126 *	9.6	18.9
443 Un C of Christ	1	65	45	83 *	.4	.7
449 Un Methodist	10	730	431	933 *	4.2	8.3
FULTON	**40**	**4,285**	**3,038**	**7,039 ***	**34.3**	**100.0**
019 Amer Bapt USA	2	519	225	647 *	3.2	9.2
053 Assemb of God	1	77	90	140	.7	2.0
056 Baha'i	0	1	NR	1	-	-
081 Catholic	2	NR	NR	1,067	5.2	15.2
093 Chr Ch (Disc)	1	389	120	485 *	2.4	6.9
097 Chr Chs&Chs Cr	1	60	NR	75 *	.4	1.1
123 Ch God (Ander)	3	NR	343	343	1.7	4.9
127 Ch God (Cleve)	1	61	97	97 *	.5	1.4
157 Ch of Brethren	1	60	0	75 *	.4	1.1
165 Ch of Nazarene	1	108	107	155	.8	2.2
167 Chs of Christ	1	95	110	140	.7	2.0
263 Int Foursq Gos	1	120	315	315 *	1.5	4.5
283 Luth—MO Synod	1	281	99	355	1.7	5.0
291 Missionary Ch	1	54	83	83	.4	1.2
306 NT IndBapt&Rltd	2	400	NR	499 *	2.4	7.1
323 Old Ord Amish	1	60	NR	75 *	.4	1.1
355 Presb Ch (USA)	1	118	75	147 *	.7	2.1
388 Reg Bapt Gen As	2	288	304	359 *	1.8	5.1
413 S.D.A.	1	31	NR	37	.2	.5
449 Un Methodist	14	1,543	1,052	1,924 *	9.4	27.3
467 Wesleyan	2	20	18	20	.1	.3
GIBSON	**58**	**5,698**	**3,649**	**14,329 ***	**44.1**	**100.0**
053 Assemb of God	3	409	497	833	2.6	5.8
056 Baha'i	0	1	NR	1	-	-
081 Catholic	6	NR	NR	6,068	18.7	42.3
093 Chr Ch (Disc)	2	302	106	372 *	1.1	2.6
097 Chr Chs&Chs Cr	2	350	NR	432 *	1.3	3.0
123 Ch God (Ander)	2	NR	168	168	.5	1.2
151 L-D Saints	1	NR	NR	108	.3	.8
165 Ch of Nazarene	6	634	557	1,019	3.1	7.1
167 Chs of Christ	2	48	62	62	.2	.4
207 E.L.C.A.	1	139	42	165	.5	1.2
355 Presb Ch (USA)	6	491	287	605 *	1.9	4.2
388 Reg Bapt Gen As	1	330	300	407 *	1.3	2.8
403 Salvation Army	1	75	56	149	.5	1.0
419 So Bapt Conv	3	264	57	326 *	1.0	2.3
443 Un C of Christ	5	528	227	651 *	2.0	4.5
449 Un Methodist	14	1,999	1,081	2,466 *	7.6	17.2
467 Wesleyan	3	128	209	497	1.5	3.5
GRANT	**125**	**17,827**	**11,696**	**30,334 ***	**41.3**	**100.0**
017 Amer Bapt Assn	2	89	NR	109 *	.1	.4
019 Amer Bapt USA	4	732	203	896 *	1.2	3.0
053 Assemb of God	4	471	633	710	1.0	2.3
056 Baha'i	0	15	NR	15	-	-
081 Catholic	2	NR	NR	4,197	5.7	13.8
089 Chr & Miss Al	1	57	NR	96	.1	.3
093 Chr Ch (Disc)	6	1,915	467	2,344 *	3.2	7.7
097 Chr Chs&Chs Cr	2	428	NR	523 *	.7	1.7
123 Ch God (Ander)	4	NR	241	241	.3	.8
127 Ch God (Cleve)	1	101	127	127 *	.2	.4
145 Ch God Prophcy	1	36	NR	44 *	.1	.1
151 L-D Saints	1	NR	NR	368	.5	1.2
157 Ch of Brethren	1	51	60	62 *	.1	.2
165 Ch of Nazarene	7	480	339	788	1.1	2.6
167 Chs of Christ	4	310	373	361	.5	1.2
176 Congr Ad Afl	1	104	NR	127 *	.2	.4
193 Episcopal	2	NR	141	204	.3	.7
207 E.L.C.A.	2	208	89	256	.3	.8
213 Evan Menn Inc	1	196	369	240 *	.3	.8
223 Free Will Bapt	2	5	NR	6 *	-	-
226 Friends-USA	14	658	NR	805 *	1.1	2.7
258 IndFreeWillBapt	1	18	NR	22 *	-	.1
283 Luth—MO Synod	1	385	220	563	.8	1.9
306 NT IndBapt&Rltd	3	600	NR	734 *	1.0	2.4
339 Pent Ch of God	1	19	NR	45	.1	.1
355 Presb Ch (USA)	2	497	217	608 *	.8	2.0

NR–Not Reported *Total adherents estimated from known number of communicant, confirmed, full members. - Represents a percentage less than 0.1. Percentages may not total 100 due to rounding.

Table 4: Religious Congregations by County and Group: 2000

Religious Group	Number of Churches, Synagogues, Mosques, or Temples	Number of Communicant, Confirmed, or Full Members	Number of Attendees	Total Adherents		
				Number of Adherents	% of Total Pop.	% of Total Adh.
360 Prim Bapt Chrch	1	NR	NR	NR	-	-
388 Reg Bapt Gen As	1	160	184	196 *	.3	.6
403 Salvation Army	1	102	112	109	.1	.4
413 S.D.A.	2	227	NR	270	.4	.9
419 So Bapt Conv	4	3,886	1,540	4,757 *	6.5	15.7
443 Un C of Christ	1	124	54	152 *	.2	.5
449 Un Methodist	26	3,220	2,973	3,940 *	5.4	13.0
467 Wesleyan	18	2,733	3,354	6,289	8.6	20.7
496 Jewish Est	1	NR	NR	130	.2	.4
GREENE	**88**	**9,350**	**3,906**	**13,153 ***	**39.7**	**100.0**
017 Amer Bapt Assn	1	40	NR	49 *	.1	.4
019 Amer Bapt USA	7	1,673	559	2,066 *	6.2	15.7
032 Amish; other	1	65	NR	80 *	.2	.6
053 Assemb of God	5	453	561	796	2.4	6.1
056 Baha'i	0	1	NR	1	-	-
061 Beachy Amish	1	45	NR	56 *	.2	.4
081 Catholic	3	NR	NR	820	2.5	6.2
093 Chr Ch (Disc)	2	574	155	709 *	2.1	5.4
097 Chr Chs&Chs Cr	12	2,109	NR	2,605 *	7.9	19.8
123 Ch God (Ander)	1	NR	40	40	.1	.3
127 Ch God (Cleve)	4	367	182	453 *	1.4	3.4
145 Ch God Prophcy	1	36	NR	44 *	.1	.3
151 L-D Saints	1	NR	NR	302	.9	2.3
165 Ch of Nazarene	3	141	39	180	.5	1.4
167 Chs of Christ	10	661	644	836	2.5	6.4
171 Ch God-Gen Con	3	124	112	155 *	.5	1.2
207 E.L.C.A.	1	154	59	188	.6	1.4
306 NT IndBapt&Rltd	1	200	NR	247 *	.7	1.9
339 Pent Ch of God	2	40	NR	66	.2	.5
355 Presb Ch (USA)	2	123	68	152 *	.5	1.2
388 Reg Bapt Gen As	1	228	244	282 *	.9	2.1
413 S.D.A.	1	56	NR	67	.2	.5
418 Southw Bapt Fel	1	NR	NR	NR	-	-
419 So Bapt Conv	1	97	43	120 *	.4	.9
443 Un C of Christ	1	381	150	470 *	1.4	3.6
449 Un Methodist	18	1,686	910	2,081 *	6.3	15.8
467 Wesleyan	4	96	140	288	.9	2.2
HAMILTON	**117**	**26,430**	**15,590**	**78,410 ***	**42.9**	**100.0**
017 Amer Bapt Assn	1	50	NR	67 *	-	.1
019 Amer Bapt USA	1	164	57	218 *	.1	.3
053 Assemb of God	4	1,276	1,733	1,782	1.0	2.3
056 Baha'i	0	22	NR	22	-	-
057 Bapt Gen Conf	1	40	40	53 *	-	.1
075 Brethren in Cr	1	0	81	81	-	.1
081 Catholic	7	NR	NR	36,787	20.1	46.9
089 Chr & Miss Al	3	285	NR	566	.3	.7
093 Chr Ch (Disc)	5	2,121	575	2,824 *	1.5	3.6
097 Chr Chs&Chs Cr	13	5,328	NR	7,092 *	3.9	9.0
123 Ch God (Ander)	4	NR	524	524	.3	.7
127 Ch God (Cleve)	1	163	104	217 *	.1	.3
145 Ch God Prophcy	1	36	NR	47 *	-	.1
151 L-D Saints	3	NR	NR	1,112	.6	1.4
157 Ch of Brethren	1	88	91	117 *	.1	.1
165 Ch of Nazarene	1	311	326	378	.2	.5
167 Chs of Christ	3	381	379	441	.2	.6
193 Episcopal	3	NR	572	1,380	.8	1.8
203 Evan Free Ch	1	450	950	950	.5	1.2
207 E.L.C.A.	4	2,485	1,348	3,855	2.1	4.9
226 Friends-USA	6	557	NR	742 *	.4	.9
283 Luth—MO Synod	5	1,933	1,210	2,812	1.5	3.6
291 Missionary Ch	1	50	118	118	.1	.2
306 NT IndBapt&Rltd	2	400	NR	532 *	.3	.7
355 Presb Ch (USA)	2	670	615	892 *	.5	1.1
356 Presb Ch Amer	2	151	270	300	.2	.4
370 Ref Baptist Chs	1	NR	NR	NR	-	-
371 Ref Ch in Am	1	80	129	167	.1	.2
388 Reg Bapt Gen As	4	684	1,207	1,387 *	.8	1.8
413 S.D.A.	2	499	NR	594	.3	.8
416 Sikh	1	NR	NR	NR	-	-
419 So Bapt Conv	6	628	343	836 *	.5	1.1
443 Un C of Christ	1	317	174	422 *	.2	.5

Religious Group	Number of Churches, Synagogues, Mosques, or Temples	Number of Communicant, Confirmed, or Full Members	Number of Attendees	Total Adherents		
				Number of Adherents	% of Total Pop.	% of Total Adh.
449 Un Methodist	16	6,749	3,452	8,984 *	4.9	11.5
467 Wesleyan	7	426	520	1,290	.7	1.6
469 WELS	1	86	72	121	.1	.2
499 Indep.Non-Char	1	0	700	700	.4	.9
HANCOCK	**69**	**11,497**	**5,469**	**19,562 ***	**35.3**	**100.0**
053 Assemb of God	1	51	78	100	.2	.5
056 Baha'i	1	27	NR	27	-	.1
081 Catholic	2	NR	NR	4,039	7.3	20.6
097 Chr Chs&Chs Cr	7	2,368	NR	2,973 *	5.4	15.2
123 Ch God (Ander)	2	NR	262	262	.5	1.3
127 Ch God (Cleve)	1	150	35	188 *	.3	1.0
145 Ch God Prophcy	1	36	NR	45 *	.1	.2
165 Ch of Nazarene	6	635	488	1,266	2.3	6.5
167 Chs of Christ	2	108	114	135	.2	.7
207 E.L.C.A.	2	382	212	492	.9	2.5
226 Friends-USA	5	235	NR	295 *	.5	1.5
258 IndFreeWillBapt	1	18	NR	23 *	-	.1
283 Luth—MO Synod	2	808	485	1,083	2.0	5.5
306 NT IndBapt&Rltd	3	600	NR	753 *	1.4	3.8
355 Presb Ch (USA)	1	109	67	137 *	.2	.7
360 Prim Bapt Chrch	1	NR	NR	NR	-	-
388 Reg Bapt Gen As	1	228	244	286 *	.5	1.5
413 S.D.A.	1	34	NR	40	.1	.2
418 Southw Bapt Fel	1	NR	NR	NR	-	-
419 So Bapt Conv	3	945	285	1,186 *	2.1	6.1
443 Un C of Christ	1	133	59	167 *	.3	.9
449 Un Methodist	20	4,016	2,408	5,042 *	9.1	25.8
463 Vineyard	1	160	160	201 *	.4	1.0
467 Wesleyan	2	134	222	472	.9	2.4
499 Indep.Non-Char	1	320	350	350	.6	1.8
HARRISON	**78**	**9,388**	**4,795**	**18,027 ***	**52.5**	**100.0**
053 Assemb of God	4	814	505	746	2.2	4.1
081 Catholic	6	NR	NR	6,360	18.5	35.3
093 Chr Ch (Disc)	4	1,330	352	1,651 *	4.8	9.2
097 Chr Chs&Chs Cr	4	782	NR	970 *	2.8	5.4
145 Ch God Prophcy	1	36	NR	44 *	.1	.2
151 L-D Saints	1	NR	NR	112	.3	.6
165 Ch of Nazarene	1	163	120	190	.6	1.1
167 Chs of Christ	4	330	313	454	1.3	2.5
207 E.L.C.A.	2	288	109	401	1.2	2.2
283 Luth—MO Synod	2	701	313	941	2.7	5.2
355 Presb Ch (USA)	5	415	205	515 *	1.5	2.9
418 Southw Bapt Fel	1	NR	NR	NR	-	-
419 So Bapt Conv	8	1,127	562	1,399 *	4.1	7.8
443 Un C of Christ	1	45	20	56 *	.2	.3
449 Un Methodist	33	3,345	2,263	4,155 *	12.1	23.0
467 Wesleyan	1	12	33	33	.1	.2
HENDRICKS	**103**	**25,146**	**9,436**	**45,733 ***	**43.9**	**100.0**
019 Amer Bapt USA	7	1,712	494	2,186 *	2.1	4.8
053 Assemb of God	4	943	514	1,209	1.2	2.6
056 Baha'i	0	10	NR	10	-	-
081 Catholic	3	NR	NR	12,342	11.9	27.0
084 Calvary Chapel	1	NR	NR	NR	-	-
093 Chr Ch (Disc)	6	1,701	722	2,172 *	2.1	4.7
097 Chr Chs&Chs Cr	13	7,668	NR	9,792 *	9.4	21.4
123 Ch God (Ander)	2	NR	32	32	-	.1
145 Ch God Prophcy	1	36	NR	46 *	-	.1
151 L-D Saints	2	NR	NR	872	.8	1.9
165 Ch of Nazarene	4	494	407	779	.7	1.7
167 Chs of Christ	8	652	786	832	.8	1.8
173 Comm of Christ	1	70	NR	70	.1	.2
193 Episcopal	3	NR	240	356	.3	.8
207 E.L.C.A.	1	478	257	671	.6	1.5
221 Free Methodist	1	130	181	181	.2	.4
226 Friends-USA	5	510	NR	651 *	.6	1.4
267 Muslim Est	1	NR	50	100	.1	.2
283 Luth—MO Synod	2	191	133	76	.1	.2
306 NT IndBapt&Rltd	9	1,800	NR	2,298 *	2.2	5.0
320 "Old" MB Ascs	1	64	NR	82 *	.1	.2
355 Presb Ch (USA)	3	326	233	417 *	.4	.9

NR–Not Reported *Total adherents estimated from known number of communicant, confirmed, full members. - Represents a percentage less than 0.1. Percentages may not total 100 due to rounding.

Table 4: Religious Congregations by County and Group: 2000

Religious Group	Number of Churches, Synagogues, Mosques, or Temples	Number of Communicant, Confirmed, or Full Members	Number of Attendees	Total Adherents: Number of Adherents	Total Adherents: % of Total Pop.	Total Adherents: % of Total Adh.
360 Prim Bapt Chrch	1	NR	NR	NR	-	-
388 Reg Bapt Gen As	5	3,016	2,859	3,857 *	3.7	8.4
413 S.D.A.	1	59	NR	70	.1	.2
419 So Bapt Conv	4	793	383	1,013 *	1.0	2.2
435 Unitarian-Univ	1	65	NR	83 *	.1	.2
449 Un Methodist	11	3,750	1,887	4,790 *	4.6	10.5
467 Wesleyan	1	78	78	146	.1	.3
499 Indep.Non-Char	1	600	180	600	.6	1.3
HENRY	**100**	**13,771**	**6,788**	**19,936 ***	**41.1**	**100.0**
011 A.W.M.C.	1	0	0	0	-	-
019 Amer Bapt USA	1	947	420	1,163 *	2.4	5.8
053 Assemb of God	1	242	278	278	.6	1.4
056 Baha'i	0	3	NR	3	-	-
081 Catholic	2	NR	NR	998	2.1	5.0
089 Chr & Miss Al	1	40	NR	46	.1	.2
093 Chr Ch (Disc)	4	1,684	383	2,068 *	4.3	10.4
097 Chr Chs&Chs Cr	11	1,725	NR	2,118 *	4.4	10.6
123 Ch God (Ander)	2	NR	309	309	.6	1.5
127 Ch God (Cleve)	1	108	48	133 *	.3	.7
151 L-D Saints	1	NR	NR	205	.4	1.0
157 Ch of Brethren	3	152	62	186 *	.4	.9
165 Ch of Nazarene	8	1,367	1,279	2,253	4.6	11.3
167 Chs of Christ	7	294	315	391	.8	2.0
193 Episcopal	1	NR	36	102	.2	.5
203 Evan Free Ch	1	69	125	125	.3	.6
207 E.L.C.A.	1	302	136	395	.8	2.0
221 Free Methodist	1	54	49	57	.1	.3
223 Free Will Bapt	1	2	NR	3 *	-	-
226 Friends-USA	12	564	NR	693 *	1.4	3.5
263 Int Foursq Gos	1	855	628	1,050 *	2.2	5.3
296 Midw Congr Fel	1	30	40	37 *	.1	.2
306 NT IndBapt&Rltd	3	600	NR	737 *	1.5	3.7
355 Presb Ch (USA)	4	564	287	692 *	1.4	3.5
360 Prim Bapt Chrch	1	NR	NR	NR	-	-
403 Salvation Army	1	45	31	247	.5	1.2
413 S.D.A.	1	22	NR	26	.1	.1
419 So Bapt Conv	8	1,853	773	2,276 *	4.7	11.4
443 Un C of Christ	1	206	114	253 *	.5	1.3
449 Un Methodist	14	1,737	1,009	2,133 *	4.4	10.7
467 Wesleyan	5	306	466	959	2.0	4.8
HOWARD	**104**	**20,321**	**12,024**	**40,463 ***	**47.6**	**100.0**
017 Amer Bapt Assn	2	211	NR	263 *	.3	.6
019 Amer Bapt USA	3	858	502	1,070 *	1.3	2.6
053 Assemb of God	5	671	802	1,370	1.6	3.4
056 Baha'i	1	51	NR	51	.1	.1
061 Beachy Amish	1	102	NR	127 *	.1	.3
081 Catholic	2	NR	NR	9,597	11.3	23.7
089 Chr & Miss Al	1	48	NR	107	.1	.3
093 Chr Ch (Disc)	3	1,523	385	1,899 *	2.2	4.7
097 Chr Chs&Chs Cr	8	2,560	NR	3,191 *	3.8	7.9
121 Ch God (Abr)	1	30	42	42 *	-	.1
123 Ch God (Ander)	1	NR	255	255	.3	.6
127 Ch God (Cleve)	2	418	176	521 *	.6	1.3
145 Ch God Prophcy	1	36	NR	44 *	.1	.1
151 L-D Saints	1	NR	NR	405	.5	1.0
157 Ch of Brethren	1	198	110	247 *	.3	.6
165 Ch of Nazarene	3	1,083	871	1,528	1.8	3.8
167 Chs of Christ	2	401	430	512	.6	1.3
193 Episcopal	1	NR	207	348	.4	.9
203 Evan Free Ch	1	69	125	125	.1	.3
207 E.L.C.A.	1	256	181	324	.4	.8
221 Free Methodist	2	180	212	233	.3	.6
226 Friends-USA	7	659	NR	822 *	1.0	2.0
263 Int Foursq Gos	3	740	507	923 *	1.1	2.3
283 Luth—MO Synod	3	1,158	597	1,554	1.8	3.8
288 Mennonite USA	1	76	68	95 *	.1	.2
297 Mennonite;Other	1	40	NR	50 *	.1	.1
320 "Old" MB Ascs	1	106	NR	132 *	.2	.3
323 Old Ord Amish	2	120	NR	150 *	.2	.4
331 OCA: Ter Diocs	1	33	NR	60	.1	.1
339 Pent Ch of God	1	25	NR	50	.1	.1
349 Pent Holiness	1	34	30	42 *	-	.1
355 Presb Ch (USA)	2	1,049	568	1,308 *	1.5	3.2
388 Reg Bapt Gen As	3	672	600	755 *	.9	1.9
403 Salvation Army	1	201	137	643	.8	1.6
409 Separate Bapt	3	1,100	NR	1,371 *	1.6	3.4
413 S.D.A.	1	125	NR	149	.2	.4
419 So Bapt Conv	4	1,115	208	1,390 *	1.6	3.4
435 Unitarian-Univ	1	19	NR	24 *	-	.1
443 Un C of Christ	1	340	150	424 *	.5	1.0
449 Un Methodist	15	3,276	2,201	4,085 *	4.8	10.1
467 Wesleyan	4	361	332	787	.9	1.9
469 WELS	1	77	53	110	.1	.3
496 Jewish Est	1	NR	NR	130	.2	.3
498 Indep.Charis.	1	0	625	1,500	1.8	3.7
499 Indep.Non-Char	2	300	1,650	1,650	1.9	4.1
HUNTINGTON	**69**	**9,310**	**4,421**	**19,423 ***	**51.0**	**100.0**
019 Amer Bapt USA	2	305	177	381 *	1.0	2.0
053 Assemb of God	1	61	85	104	.3	.5
056 Baha'i	0	4	NR	4	-	-
071 Brethren (Ash)	2	116	103	145 *	.4	.7
081 Catholic	3	NR	NR	5,059	13.3	26.0
089 Chr & Miss Al	2	54	NR	143	.4	.7
093 Chr Ch (Disc)	2	805	206	1,005 *	2.6	5.2
097 Chr Chs&Chs Cr	3	1,169	NR	1,460 *	3.8	7.5
123 Ch God (Ander)	1	NR	170	170	.4	.9
127 Ch God (Cleve)	1	13	11	16 *	-	.1
145 Ch God Prophcy	1	36	NR	45 *	.1	.2
157 Ch of Brethren	5	415	210	518 *	1.4	2.7
165 Ch of Nazarene	4	783	604	957	2.5	4.9
167 Chs of Christ	3	120	154	210	.6	1.1
193 Episcopal	1	NR	64	216	.6	1.1
223 Free Will Bapt	2	5	NR	6 *	-	-
283 Luth—MO Synod	2	592	196	807	2.1	4.2
306 NT IndBapt&Rltd	2	400	NR	500 *	1.3	2.6
355 Presb Ch (USA)	1	208	80	260 *	.7	1.3
360 Prim Bapt Chrch	1	NR	NR	NR	-	-
388 Reg Bapt Gen As	1	45	65	65 *	.2	.3
403 Salvation Army	1	184	59	1,827	4.8	9.4
413 S.D.A.	1	24	NR	29	.1	.1
419 So Bapt Conv	1	125	87	156 *	.4	.8
443 Un C of Christ	5	1,250	423	1,561 *	4.1	8.0
449 Un Methodist	16	2,373	1,417	2,964 *	7.8	15.3
467 Wesleyan	5	223	310	815	2.1	4.2
JACKSON	**80**	**17,085**	**6,924**	**23,632 ***	**57.2**	**100.0**
017 Amer Bapt Assn	1	50	NR	62 *	.1	.3
019 Amer Bapt USA	8	1,797	745	2,242 *	5.4	9.5
053 Assemb of God	2	51	63	63	.2	.3
056 Baha'i	0	4	NR	4	-	-
081 Catholic	2	NR	NR	1,463	3.5	6.2
089 Chr & Miss Al	1	21	NR	31	.1	.1
093 Chr Ch (Disc)	1	895	289	1,116 *	2.7	4.7
097 Chr Chs&Chs Cr	16	3,236	NR	4,035 *	9.8	17.1
123 Ch God (Ander)	1	NR	43	43	.1	.2
127 Ch God (Cleve)	2	207	132	258 *	.6	1.1
151 L-D Saints	1	NR	NR	212	.5	.9
157 Ch of Brethren	1	23	0	29 *	.1	.1
165 Ch of Nazarene	6	1,602	1,013	2,165	5.2	9.2
167 Chs of Christ	2	101	95	131	.3	.6
193 Episcopal	1	NR	21	36	.1	.2
207 E.L.C.A.	1	398	206	506	1.2	2.1
221 Free Methodist	1	51	41	51	.1	.2
263 Int Foursq Gos	1	35	57	57 *	.1	.2
283 Luth—MO Synod	9	5,622	2,947	7,253	17.5	30.7
323 Old Ord Amish	1	60	NR	75 *	.2	.3
355 Presb Ch (USA)	2	307	193	382 *	.9	1.6
419 So Bapt Conv	3	992	140	1,237 *	3.0	5.2
443 Un C of Christ	2	135	71	168 *	.4	.7
449 Un Methodist	13	1,463	797	1,826 *	4.4	7.7
467 Wesleyan	2	35	71	187	.5	.8

NR–Not Reported *Total adherents estimated from known number of communicant, confirmed, full members. - Represents a percentage less than 0.1. Percentages may not total 100 due to rounding.

Table 4: Religious Congregations by County and Group: 2000

Religious Group	Number of Churches, Synagogues, Mosques, or Temples	Number of Communicant, Confirmed, or Full Members	Number of Attendees	Total Adherents		
				Number of Adherents	% of Total Pop.	% of Total Adh.
JASPER	**48**	**6,883**	**3,969**	**13,485 ***	**44.9**	**100.0**
019 Amer Bapt USA	2	315	80	398 *	1.3	3.0
040 Ap Chr Ch-Amer	1	105	204	204 *	.7	1.5
053 Assemb of God	3	253	328	483	1.6	3.6
056 Baha'i	0	1	NR	1	-	-
081 Catholic	4	NR	NR	4,111	13.7	30.5
093 Chr Ch (Disc)	1	312	120	394 *	1.3	2.9
097 Chr Chs&Chs Cr	3	505	NR	638 *	2.1	4.7
105 Christian Ref	3	1,147	415	1,450 *	4.8	10.8
123 Ch God (Ander)	1	NR	21	21	.1	.2
151 L-D Saints	1	NR	NR	61	.2	.5
165 Ch of Nazarene	2	112	95	112	.4	.8
167 Chs of Christ	2	77	90	111	.4	.8
193 Episcopal	1	NR	13	17	.1	.1
203 Evan Free Ch	1	35	60	60	.2	.4
283 Luth—MO Synod	4	625	376	866	2.9	6.4
288 Mennonite USA	1	64	80	81 *	.3	.6
339 Pent Ch of God	2	111	NR	244	.8	1.8
355 Presb Ch (USA)	2	193	82	244 *	.8	1.8
360 Prim Bapt Chrch	1	NR	NR	NR	-	-
371 Ref Ch in Am	2	1,087	863	1,574	5.2	11.7
418 Southw Bapt Fel	1	NR	NR	NR	-	-
419 So Bapt Conv	2	191	107	241 *	.8	1.8
449 Un Methodist	6	1,281	715	1,619 *	5.4	12.0
455 Un Ref Chs N.A.	1	94	NR	180	.6	1.3
499 Indep.Non-Char	1	375	320	375	1.2	2.8
JAY	**63**	**5,295**	**2,814**	**9,408 ***	**43.1**	**100.0**
019 Amer Bapt USA	1	35	23	44 *	.2	.5
053 Assemb of God	1	44	58	75	.3	.8
056 Baha'i	0	4	NR	4	-	-
081 Catholic	3	NR	NR	2,052	9.4	21.8
097 Chr Chs&Chs Cr	5	613	NR	779 *	3.6	8.3
123 Ch God (Ander)	1	NR	20	20	.1	.2
145 Ch God Prophcy	1	36	NR	45 *	.2	.5
151 L-D Saints	1	NR	NR	80	.4	.9
157 Ch of Brethren	2	85	0	108 *	.5	1.1
165 Ch of Nazarene	6	623	547	1,157	5.3	12.3
167 Chs of Christ	1	58	50	61	.3	.6
207 E.L.C.A.	3	516	185	738	3.4	7.8
226 Friends-USA	4	188	NR	239 *	1.1	2.5
258 IndFreeWillBapt	1	82	NR	104 *	.5	1.1
296 Midw Congr Fel	3	67	117	85 *	.4	.9
306 NT IndBapt&Rltd	3	600	NR	762 *	3.5	8.1
323 Old Ord Amish	3	180	NR	228 *	1.0	2.4
355 Presb Ch (USA)	1	235	104	299 *	1.4	3.2
388 Reg Bapt Gen As	1	224	225	285 *	1.3	3.0
419 So Bapt Conv	1	59	37	75 *	.3	.8
443 Un C of Christ	2	68	35	86 *	.4	.9
449 Un Methodist	17	1,382	1,162	1,757 *	8.1	18.7
463 Vineyard	1	130	120	165 *	.8	1.8
467 Wesleyan	1	66	131	160	.7	1.7
JEFFERSON	**67**	**10,334**	**3,331**	**16,438 ***	**51.8**	**100.0**
019 Amer Bapt USA	17	3,135	1,016	3,858 *	12.2	23.5
053 Assemb of God	1	429	491	513	1.6	3.1
056 Baha'i	0	9	NR	9	-	.1
081 Catholic	1	NR	NR	2,885	9.1	17.6
089 Chr & Miss Al	1	37	NR	112	.4	.7
093 Chr Ch (Disc)	1	242	130	298 *	.9	1.8
097 Chr Chs&Chs Cr	7	1,246	NR	1,533 *	4.8	9.3
123 Ch God (Ander)	1	NR	5	5	-	-
151 L-D Saints	2	NR	NR	459	1.4	2.8
165 Ch of Nazarene	1	80	70	137	.4	.8
167 Chs of Christ	1	82	88	107	.3	.7
193 Episcopal	1	NR	72	152	.5	.9
207 E.L.C.A.	1	120	62	159	.5	1.0
283 Luth—MO Synod	1	107	70	137	.4	.8
297 Mennonite;Other	1	11	NR	14 *	-	.1
306 NT IndBapt&Rltd	3	600	NR	738 *	2.3	4.5
355 Presb Ch (USA)	4	392	233	482 *	1.5	2.9
403 Salvation Army	1	78	48	184	.6	1.1
413 S.D.A.	1	32	NR	38	.1	.2
418 Southw Bapt Fel	1	NR	NR	NR	-	-
419 So Bapt Conv	3	2,130	209	2,621 *	8.3	15.9
443 Un C of Christ	1	107	40	132 *	.4	.8
449 Un Methodist	14	1,435	730	1,769 *	5.6	10.8
467 Wesleyan	2	62	67	96	.3	.6
JENNINGS	**55**	**6,088**	**2,722**	**11,051 ***	**40.1**	**100.0**
017 Amer Bapt Assn	1	50	NR	64 *	.2	.6
019 Amer Bapt USA	13	2,814	1,117	3,599 *	13.1	32.6
053 Assemb of God	1	69	87	110	.4	1.0
081 Catholic	4	NR	NR	2,600	9.4	23.5
097 Chr Chs&Chs Cr	4	771	NR	986 *	3.6	8.9
107 Christian Un	1	30	40	40 *	.1	.4
123 Ch God (Ander)	4	NR	195	195	.7	1.8
127 Ch God (Cleve)	1	132	28	169 *	.6	1.5
151 L-D Saints	1	NR	NR	386	1.4	3.5
165 Ch of Nazarene	1	265	196	352	1.3	3.2
167 Chs of Christ	2	80	92	104	.4	.9
283 Luth—MO Synod	1	114	63	144	.5	1.3
297 Mennonite;Other	1	69	NR	88 *	.3	.8
306 NT IndBapt&Rltd	1	200	NR	256 *	.9	2.3
355 Presb Ch (USA)	4	202	123	257 *	.9	2.3
413 S.D.A.	1	79	NR	94	.3	.9
419 So Bapt Conv	2	292	150	373 *	1.4	3.4
449 Un Methodist	11	887	564	1,134 *	4.1	10.3
467 Wesleyan	1	34	67	100	.4	.9
JOHNSON	**95**	**29,684**	**13,656**	**48,009 ***	**41.7**	**100.0**
017 Amer Bapt Assn	3	140	NR	177 *	.2	.4
019 Amer Bapt USA	5	1,468	566	1,862 *	1.6	3.9
053 Assemb of God	5	450	577	854	.7	1.8
056 Baha'i	0	6	NR	6	-	-
057 Bapt Gen Conf	1	25	40	40 *	-	.1
081 Catholic	4	NR	NR	9,816	8.5	20.4
093 Chr Ch (Disc)	6	2,049	644	2,599 *	2.3	5.4
097 Chr Chs&Chs Cr	13	6,512	NR	8,260 *	7.2	17.2
127 Ch God (Cleve)	1	411	410	521 *	.5	1.1
151 L-D Saints	2	NR	NR	846	.7	1.8
157 Ch of Brethren	1	93	0	118 *	.1	.2
165 Ch of Nazarene	2	252	230	350	.3	.7
167 Chs of Christ	3	507	570	715	.6	1.5
175 Congr Chr Chs	1	317	125	402 *	.3	.8
193 Episcopal	1	NR	95	176	.2	.4
207 E.L.C.A.	2	246	186	314	.3	.7
283 Luth—MO Synod	3	916	491	1,246	1.1	2.6
306 NT IndBapt&Rltd	3	600	NR	761 *	.7	1.6
320 "Old" MB Ascs	2	170	NR	216 *	.2	.4
355 Presb Ch (USA)	5	1,201	640	1,525 *	1.3	3.2
356 Presb Ch Amer	1	30	35	35	-	.1
365 Prog Prim Bapt	1	25	NR	32 *	-	.1
388 Reg Bapt Gen As	3	2,101	2,165	2,675 *	2.3	5.6
409 Separate Bapt	3	180	NR	228 *	.2	.5
413 S.D.A.	1	42	NR	50	-	.1
419 So Bapt Conv	4	1,533	502	1,945 *	1.7	4.1
443 Un C of Christ	2	132	61	167 *	.1	.3
449 Un Methodist	9	2,712	1,549	3,439 *	3.0	7.2
463 Vineyard	1	1,542	1,067	1,956 *	1.7	4.1
467 Wesleyan	5	124	203	778	.7	1.6
499 Indep.Non-Char	2	5,900	3,500	5,900	5.1	12.3
KNOX	**78**	**10,465**	**5,507**	**19,476 ***	**49.6**	**100.0**
019 Amer Bapt USA	4	1,636	772	1,970 *	5.0	10.1
053 Assemb of God	2	29	36	81	.2	.4
056 Baha'i	0	13	NR	13	-	.1
081 Catholic	6	NR	NR	5,682	14.5	29.2
093 Chr Ch (Disc)	3	663	159	798 *	2.0	4.1
097 Chr Chs&Chs Cr	8	1,158	NR	1,394 *	3.6	7.2
123 Ch God (Ander)	2	NR	630	630	1.6	3.2
127 Ch God (Cleve)	1	21	21	25 *	.1	.1
145 Ch God Prophcy	1	36	NR	43 *	.1	.2
165 Ch of Nazarene	3	357	275	578	1.5	3.0
167 Chs of Christ	4	185	165	218	.6	1.1
179 Consrv Bapt	1	NR	8	8	-	-

NR–Not Reported   *Total adherents estimated from known number of communicant, confirmed, full members.   - Represents a percentage less than 0.1.   Percentages may not total 100 due to rounding.

Table 4: Religious Congregations by County and Group: 2000

Religious Group		Number of Churches, Synagogues, Mosques, or Temples	Number of Communicant, Confirmed, or Full Members	Number of Attendees	Total Adherents		
					Number of Adherents	% of Total Pop.	% of Total Adh.
185	Cumber Presb	1	22	NR	22	.1	.1
193	Episcopal	1	NR	50	122	.3	.6
207	E.L.C.A.	1	179	85	265	.7	1.4
221	Free Methodist	1	180	167	221	.6	1.1
263	Int Foursq Gos	1	255	202	307 *	.8	1.6
283	Luth—MO Synod	2	628	244	796	2.0	4.1
306	NT IndBapt&Rltd	1	200	NR	241 *	.6	1.2
355	Presb Ch (USA)	7	438	281	527 *	1.3	2.7
356	Presb Ch Amer	1	33	40	55	.1	.3
403	Salvation Army	1	62	35	238	.6	1.2
413	S.D.A.	1	37	NR	44	.1	.2
419	So Bapt Conv	2	756	222	910 *	2.3	4.7
443	Un C of Christ	3	1,262	539	1,519 *	3.9	7.8
449	Un Methodist	17	1,959	1,260	2,359 *	6.0	12.1
467	Wesleyan	2	56	66	110	.3	.6
499	Indep.Non-Char	1	300	250	300	.8	1.5
KOSCIUSKO		**100**	**15,128**	**11,380**	**27,958 ***	**37.8**	**100.0**
019	Amer Bapt USA	1	65	40	83 *	.1	.3
040	Ap Chr Ch-Amer	1	106	175	175 *	.2	.6
053	Assemb of God	2	183	207	272	.4	1.0
056	Baha'i	0	20	NR	20	-	.1
061	Beachy Amish	1	74	NR	94 *	.1	.3
071	Brethren (Ash)	3	293	246	373 *	.5	1.3
081	Catholic	4	NR	NR	4,758	6.4	17.0
097	Chr Chs&Chs Cr	3	2,582	NR	3,285 *	4.4	11.7
123	Ch God (Ander)	2	NR	737	737	1.0	2.6
127	Ch God (Cleve)	1	10	7	13 *	-	-
151	L-D Saints	1	NR	NR	266	.4	1.0
157	Ch of Brethren	8	740	404	943 *	1.3	3.4
165	Ch of Nazarene	2	334	219	437	.6	1.6
167	Chs of Christ	2	95	110	120	.2	.4
171	Ch God-Gen Con	3	488	282	621 *	.8	2.2
193	Episcopal	2	NR	312	611	.8	2.2
203	Evan Free Ch	1	25	50	50	.1	.2
207	E.L.C.A.	1	138	76	179	.2	.6
221	Free Methodist	1	224	247	300	.4	1.1
223	Free Will Bapt	3	7	NR	9 *	-	-
226	Friends-USA	2	94	NR	120 *	.2	.4
263	Int Foursq Gos	1	20	48	48 *	.1	.2
283	Luth—MO Synod	2	420	229	594	.8	2.1
288	Mennonite USA	3	308	354	444 *	.6	1.6
291	Missionary Ch	1	61	110	110	.1	.4
297	Mennonite;Other	1	59	NR	75 *	.1	.3
306	NT IndBapt&Rltd	1	200	NR	254 *	.3	.9
322	Old Ord Menn Ch	1	40	NR	51 *	.1	.2
323	Old Ord Amish	6	360	NR	456 *	.6	1.6
339	Pent Ch of God	1	120	NR	140	.2	.5
355	Presb Ch (USA)	3	892	690	1,135 *	1.5	4.1
360	Prim Bapt Chrch	1	NR	NR	NR	-	-
370	Ref Baptist Chs	1	NR	NR	NR	-	-
388	Reg Bapt Gen As	4	816	882	1,038 *	1.4	3.7
403	Salvation Army	1	124	45	164	.2	.6
413	S.D.A.	1	30	NR	36	-	.1
419	So Bapt Conv	0	139	71	177 *	.2	.6
449	Un Methodist	23	4,138	2,698	5,266 *	7.1	18.8
463	Vineyard	1	160	134	204 *	.3	.7
467	Wesleyan	2	476	607	1,900	2.6	6.8
499	Indep.Non-Char	2	1,287	2,400	2,400	3.2	8.6
LAGRANGE		**129**	**10,181**	**3,639**	**14,834 ***	**42.5**	**100.0**
019	Amer Bapt USA	2	215	107	292 *	.8	2.0
061	Beachy Amish	2	132	NR	179 *	.5	1.2
071	Brethren (Ash)	1	163	186	221 *	.6	1.5
081	Catholic	2	NR	NR	715	2.0	4.8
084	Calvary Chapel	2	NR	NR	NR	-	-
097	Chr Chs&Chs Cr	2	600	NR	814 *	2.3	5.5
123	Ch God (Ander)	2	NR	280	280	.8	1.9
157	Ch of Brethren	1	52	0	71 *	.2	.5
165	Ch of Nazarene	2	152	128	213	.6	1.4
167	Chs of Christ	1	98	137	143	.4	1.0
183	Cons Menn Conf	1	89	109	129	.4	.9
193	Episcopal	1	NR	35	64	.2	.4
207	E.L.C.A.	1	438	121	562	1.6	3.8
223	Free Will Bapt	2	5	NR	7 *	-	-
283	Luth—MO Synod	2	318	148	406	1.2	2.7
288	Mennonite USA	7	1,194	945	1,621 *	4.6	10.9
291	Missionary Ch	3	132	205	205	.6	1.4
297	Mennonite;Other	1	152	NR	206 *	.6	1.4
306	NT IndBapt&Rltd	1	200	NR	271 *	.8	1.8
323	Old Ord Amish	74	4,440	NR	5,994 *	17.2	40.4
355	Presb Ch (USA)	2	175	117	238 *	.7	1.6
413	S.D.A.	1	19	NR	23	.1	.2
418	Southw Bapt Fel	1	NR	NR	NR	-	-
419	So Bapt Conv	1	35	45	47 *	.1	.3
449	Un Methodist	14	1,572	1,076	2,133 *	6.1	14.4
LAKE		**346**	**55,587**	**28,028**	**217,068 ***	**44.8**	**100.0**
019	Amer Bapt USA	9	3,139	1,525	3,956 *	.8	1.8
022	Carp Rus Orth	2	243	NR	416	.1	.2
034	Ant Orth of NA	1	62	NR	124	-	.1
053	Assemb of God	18	2,046	2,266	3,651	.8	1.7
056	Baha'i	0	64	NR	64	-	-
057	Bapt Gen Conf	1	153	102	193 *	-	.1
059	Bapt Miss Assn	1	45	14	57 *	-	-
081	Catholic	59	NR	NR	128,404	26.5	59.2
093	Chr Ch (Disc)	4	426	166	537 *	.1	.2
097	Chr Chs&Chs Cr	19	4,911	NR	6,191 *	1.3	2.9
105	Christian Ref	8	2,630	2,079	3,315 *	.7	1.5
123	Ch God (Ander)	7	NR	728	728	.2	.3
127	Ch God (Cleve)	5	720	459	924 *	.2	.4
145	Ch God Prophcy	1	36	NR	45 *	-	-
151	L-D Saints	2	NR	NR	874	.2	.4
165	Ch of Nazarene	12	1,735	1,170	1,993	.4	.9
167	Chs of Christ	10	748	814	950	.2	.4
173	Comm of Christ	1	83	NR	83	-	-
175	Congr Chr Chs	2	65	37	82 *	-	-
179	Consrv Bapt	1	NR	0	0	-	-
191	Entrpr Bpt Asc	1	39	NR	49 *	-	-
193	Episcopal	7	NR	409	1,049	.2	.5
201	Evan Cov Ch	2	155	110	195 *	-	.1
203	Evan Free Ch	2	159	325	325	.1	.1
207	E.L.C.A.	12	3,322	1,568	4,334	.9	2.0
221	Free Methodist	3	124	131	158	-	.1
246	Greek Orthodox	3	NR	NR	4,437	.9	2.0
262	Int Cou Comm Ch	1	865	NR	1,090 *	.2	.5
267	Muslim Est	3	NR	365	2,441	.5	1.1
283	Luth—MO Synod	21	7,230	3,037	9,349	1.9	4.3
306	NT IndBapt&Rltd	4	800	NR	1,008 *	.2	.5
330	Macedonian Orth	1	NR	NR	2,000	.4	.9
331	OCA: Ter Diocs	2	157	NR	314	.1	.1
339	Pent Ch of God	3	94	NR	152	-	.1
349	Pent Holiness	1	7	7	9 *	-	-
355	Presb Ch (USA)	13	3,200	1,504	4,034 *	.8	1.9
356	Presb Ch Amer	2	362	220	391	.1	.2
360	Prim Bapt Chrch	2	NR	NR	NR	-	-
369	Prot Ref Chs	1	77	NR	122	-	.1
371	Ref Ch in Am	3	477	297	724	.1	.3
388	Reg Bapt Gen As	10	1,749	2,402	3,064 *	.6	1.4
397	OCA: Roman Dioc	1	NR	NR	100	-	-
403	Salvation Army	3	234	325	621	.1	.3
410	Serb Orth USA	2	NR	NR	1,830	.4	.8
411	Serb Orth: Grac	2	NR	NR	NR	-	-
413	S.D.A.	6	1,465	NR	1,743	.4	.8
416	Sikh	1	NR	NR	NR	-	-
419	So Bapt Conv	30	8,599	3,333	10,837 *	2.2	5.0
431	Ukrainian Orth	1	NR	NR	300	.1	.1
435	Unitarian-Univ	1	82	NR	103 *	-	-
443	Un C of Christ	8	1,985	659	2,502 *	.5	1.2
449	Un Methodist	22	6,159	3,241	7,763 *	1.6	3.6
455	Un Ref Chs N.A.	1	213	NR	378	.1	.2
467	Wesleyan	1	28	35	130	-	.1
469	WELS	1	124	75	124	-	.1
496	Jewish Est	3	NR	NR	2,000	.4	.9
498	Indep.Charis.	2	500	325	500	.1	.2
499	Indep.Non-Char	1	275	300	305	.1	.1

NR–Not Reported   *Total adherents estimated from known number of communicant, confirmed, full members.   - Represents a percentage less than 0.1.   Percentages may not total 100 due to rounding.

Table 4: Religious Congregations by County and Group: 2000

Religious Group	Number of Churches, Synagogues, Mosques, or Temples	Number of Communicant, Confirmed, or Full Members	Number of Attendees	Total Adherents		
				Number of Adherents	% of Total Pop.	% of Total Adh.
LA PORTE	**109**	**16,684**	**7,638**	**49,389 ***	**44.9**	**100.0**
017 Amer Bapt Assn	1	43	NR	53 *	-	.1
019 Amer Bapt USA	3	698	210	860 *	.8	1.7
040 Ap Chr Ch-Amer	1	78	145	145 *	.1	.3
053 Assemb of God	5	474	593	1,060	1.0	2.1
056 Baha'i	0	13	NR	13	-	-
059 Bapt Miss Assn	2	178	125	220 *	.2	.4
081 Catholic	12	NR	NR	25,296	23.0	51.2
093 Chr Ch (Disc)	1	575	70	709 *	.6	1.4
097 Chr Chs&Chs Cr	8	2,111	NR	2,601 *	2.4	5.3
123 Ch God (Ander)	1	NR	258	258	.2	.5
127 Ch God (Cleve)	2	193	90	238 *	.2	.5
151 L-D Saints	1	NR	NR	269	.2	.5
157 Ch of Brethren	2	119	69	147 *	.1	.3
165 Ch of Nazarene	1	91	75	185	.2	.4
167 Chs of Christ	3	149	159	205	.2	.4
173 Comm of Christ	1	56	NR	56	.1	.1
175 Congr Chr Chs	1	40	30	49 *	-	.1
193 Episcopal	3	NR	237	489	.4	1.0
207 E.L.C.A.	5	2,212	997	3,064	2.8	6.2
221 Free Methodist	2	196	177	233	.2	.5
223 Free Will Bapt	1	2	NR	3 *	-	-
267 Muslim Est	1	NR	55	163	.1	.3
283 Luth—MO Synod	9	2,658	1,068	3,780	3.4	7.7
288 Mennonite USA	1	38	33	47 *	-	.1
291 Missionary Ch	1	84	174	174	.2	.4
306 NT IndBapt&Rltd	1	200	NR	246 *	.2	.5
339 Pent Ch of God	2	200	NR	250	.2	.5
355 Presb Ch (USA)	3	1,186	547	1,462 *	1.3	3.0
356 Presb Ch Amer	1	26	47	47	-	.1
388 Reg Bapt Gen As	3	271	217	334 *	.3	.7
401 Rus Orth Abroad	1	NR	NR	NR	-	-
403 Salvation Army	2	195	139	563	.5	1.1
413 S.D.A.	3	201	NR	239	.2	.5
419 So Bapt Conv	3	393	142	484 *	.4	1.0
431 Ukrainian Orth	1	NR	NR	132	.1	.3
443 Un C of Christ	3	1,241	366	1,529 *	1.4	3.1
449 Un Methodist	13	2,480	1,380	3,056 *	2.8	6.2
463 Vineyard	1	200	160	246 *	.2	.5
467 Wesleyan	1	51	41	150	.1	.3
469 WELS	1	32	34	34	-	.1
496 Jewish Est	2	NR	NR	300	.3	.6
LAWRENCE	**88**	**12,518**	**5,767**	**21,501 ***	**46.8**	**100.0**
017 Amer Bapt Assn	2	100	NR	124 *	.3	.6
019 Amer Bapt USA	9	3,007	1,234	3,709 *	8.1	17.3
053 Assemb of God	1	477	660	1,254	2.7	5.8
056 Baha'i	0	5	NR	5	-	-
081 Catholic	2	NR	NR	2,541	5.5	11.8
093 Chr Ch (Disc)	2	967	163	1,193 *	2.6	5.5
097 Chr Chs&Chs Cr	14	3,248	NR	4,005 *	8.7	18.6
123 Ch God (Ander)	4	NR	571	571	1.2	2.7
127 Ch God (Cleve)	2	259	94	320 *	.7	1.5
145 Ch God Prophcy	1	36	NR	44 *	.1	.2
151 L-D Saints	3	NR	NR	1,275	2.8	5.9
165 Ch of Nazarene	4	598	399	977	2.1	4.5
167 Chs of Christ	16	1,131	1,108	1,399	3.0	6.5
193 Episcopal	1	NR	68	212	.5	1.0
221 Free Methodist	1	547	426	728	1.6	3.4
283 Luth—MO Synod	2	295	120	413	.9	1.9
339 Pent Ch of God	1	42	NR	150	.3	.7
355 Presb Ch (USA)	2	274	147	338 *	.7	1.6
360 Prim Bapt Chrch	1	NR	NR	NR	-	-
403 Salvation Army	1	97	17	255	.6	1.2
413 S.D.A.	1	104	NR	124	.3	.6
418 Southw Bapt Fel	2	NR	NR	NR	-	-
419 So Bapt Conv	1	44	34	54 *	.1	.3
449 Un Methodist	13	1,099	664	1,355 *	3.0	6.3
467 Wesleyan	2	188	62	455	1.0	2.1
MADISON	**154**	**23,768**	**18,070**	**49,275 ***	**36.9**	**100.0**
017 Amer Bapt Assn	1	120	NR	147 *	.1	.3
019 Amer Bapt USA	11	3,319	1,234	4,071 *	3.1	8.3
053 Assemb of God	3	547	731	1,112	.8	2.3
056 Baha'i	0	11	NR	11	-	-
081 Catholic	4	NR	NR	8,133	6.1	16.5
089 Chr & Miss Al	1	66	NR	145	.1	.3
093 Chr Ch (Disc)	10	2,923	1,096	3,586 *	2.7	7.3
097 Chr Chs&Chs Cr	7	2,327	NR	2,854 *	2.1	5.8
123 Ch God (Ander)	15	NR	5,547	5,547	4.2	11.3
127 Ch God (Cleve)	3	379	203	466 *	.3	.9
145 Ch God Prophcy	1	36	NR	44 *	-	.1
151 L-D Saints	3	NR	NR	887	.7	1.8
157 Ch of Brethren	2	362	218	444 *	.3	.9
165 Ch of Nazarene	9	1,806	1,338	2,703	2.0	5.5
167 Chs of Christ	7	808	878	1,159	.9	2.4
193 Episcopal	2	NR	145	402	.3	.8
207 E.L.C.A.	4	770	331	1,081	.8	2.2
221 Free Methodist	2	145	239	247	.2	.5
223 Free Will Bapt	1	2	NR	3 *	-	-
226 Friends-USA	5	301	NR	369 *	.3	.7
258 IndFreeWillBapt	2	458	NR	562 *	.4	1.1
263 Int Foursq Gos	2	88	80	108 *	.1	.2
283 Luth—MO Synod	1	371	171	482	.4	1.0
296 Midw Congr Fel	1	47	30	58 *	-	.1
306 NT IndBapt&Rltd	2	400	NR	491 *	.4	1.0
355 Presb Ch (USA)	2	530	261	650 *	.5	1.3
370 Ref Baptist Chs	1	NR	NR	NR	-	-
403 Salvation Army	1	171	60	907	.7	1.8
409 Separate Bapt	1	30	NR	37 *	-	.1
413 S.D.A.	2	253	NR	301	.2	.6
419 So Bapt Conv	5	733	388	899 *	.7	1.8
443 Un C of Christ	1	191	104	234 *	.2	.5
449 Un Methodist	26	4,855	2,703	5,955 *	4.5	12.1
467 Wesleyan	13	919	983	2,450	1.8	5.0
499 Indep.Non-Char	3	800	1,330	2,730	2.0	5.5
MARION	**577**	**164,253**	**86,041**	**346,702 ***	**40.3**	**100.0**
017 Amer Bapt Assn	1	198	NR	249 *	-	.1
019 Amer Bapt USA	25	7,362	3,215	9,249 *	1.1	2.7
034 Ant Orth of NA	1	472	NR	944	.1	.3
040 Ap Chr Ch-Amer	1	113	223	223 *	-	.1
053 Assemb of God	18	3,850	4,862	10,005	1.2	2.9
056 Baha'i	1	242	NR	242	-	.1
076 Buddhism	3	NR	NR	NR	-	-
078 Bulgar Orth USA	1	NR	NR	500	.1	.1
081 Catholic	40	NR	NR	109,137	12.7	31.5
084 Calvary Chapel	4	NR	NR	NR	-	-
089 Chr & Miss Al	1	0	NR	0	-	-
093 Chr Ch (Disc)	29	13,847	4,005	17,396 *	2.0	5.0
097 Chr Chs&Chs Cr	34	19,786	NR	24,857 *	2.9	7.2
105 Christian Ref	1	40	35	50 *	-	-
123 Ch God (Ander)	13	NR	2,578	2,578	.3	.7
127 Ch God (Cleve)	6	1,394	796	1,763 *	.2	.5
145 Ch God Prophcy	2	71	NR	90 *	-	-
151 L-D Saints	8	NR	NR	2,813	.3	.8
157 Ch of Brethren	1	80	72	101 *	-	-
165 Ch of Nazarene	22	4,191	3,422	6,644	.8	1.9
167 Chs of Christ	35	4,841	4,615	6,349	.7	1.8
173 Comm of Christ	1	223	NR	223	-	.1
179 Consrv Bapt	2	NR	272	272	-	.1
185 Cumber Presb	1	30	NR	61	-	-
193 Episcopal	9	NR	1,308	3,112	.4	.9
201 Evan Cov Ch	1	92	152	152 *	-	-
203 Evan Free Ch	3	501	863	863	.1	.2
207 E.L.C.A.	18	4,877	2,509	6,304	.7	1.8
220 Free Lutheran	1	98	46	121	-	-
221 Free Methodist	6	876	1,017	1,158	.1	.3
223 Free Will Bapt	1	2	NR	3 *	-	-
226 Friends-USA	9	874	NR	1,098 *	.1	.3
246 Greek Orthodox	1	NR	NR	2,154	.3	.6
258 IndFreeWillBapt	1	14	NR	18 *	-	-
262 Int Cou Comm Ch	1	233	NR	293 *	-	.1
263 Int Foursq Gos	3	220	263	276 *	-	.1
264 Int Chs of Crst	1	485	905	780	.1	.2
267 Muslim Est	2	NR	750	2,200	.3	.6
283 Luth—MO Synod	15	5,750	3,356	7,880	.9	2.3

NR–Not Reported *Total adherents estimated from known number of communicant, confirmed, full members. - Represents a percentage less than 0.1. Percentages may not total 100 due to rounding.

Table 4: Religious Congregations by County and Group: 2000

Religious Group	Number of Churches, Synagogues, Mosques, or Temples	Number of Communicant, Confirmed, or Full Members	Number of Attendees	Total Adherents: Number of Adherents	Total Adherents: % of Total Pop.	Total Adherents: % of Total Adh.
288 Mennonite USA	2	208	251	290 *	-	.1
290 Metro Comm Ch	1	150	189	189 *	-	.1
293 Morav Ch-North	2	69	NR	82	-	-
304 NatPrimBapt USA	4	61	NR	77 *	-	-
306 NT IndBapt&Rltd	22	4,400	NR	5,528 *	.6	1.6
313 N Am Bapt Conf	1	60	30	75 *	-	-
320 "Old" MB Ascs	5	776	NR	975 *	.1	.3
339 Pent Ch of God	3	118	NR	318	-	.1
355 Presb Ch (USA)	19	12,501	6,024	15,704 *	1.8	4.5
356 Presb Ch Amer	4	105	148	161	-	-
360 Prim Bapt Chrch	1	NR	NR	NR	-	-
371 Ref Ch in Am	1	137	130	202	-	.1
388 Reg Bapt Gen As	10	3,579	4,383	5,414 *	.6	1.6
395 Romania Orth Ar	1	NR	NR	88	-	-
397 OCA: Roman Dioc	1	NR	NR	63	-	-
403 Salvation Army	4	454	448	2,780	.3	.8
409 Separate Bapt	1	52	NR	65 *	-	-
411 Serb Orth: Grac	1	NR	NR	NR	-	-
413 S.D.A.	10	2,651	NR	3,154	.4	.9
418 Southw Bapt Fel	1	NR	NR	NR	-	-
419 So Bapt Conv	37	11,529	4,477	14,484 *	1.7	4.2
435 Unitarian-Univ	4	919	NR	1,155 *	.1	.3
443 Un C of Christ	14	4,566	1,940	5,736 *	.7	1.7
449 Un Methodist	59	24,999	13,924	31,408 *	3.7	9.1
463 Vineyard	3	635	555	797 *	.1	.2
467 Wesleyan	13	1,008	1,267	2,344	.3	.7
469 WELS	2	322	248	465	.1	.1
496 Jewish Est	6	NR	NR	10,000	1.2	2.9
498 Indep.Charis.	5	1,642	1,858	2,440	.3	.7
499 Indep.Non-Char	17	22,550	14,905	22,550	2.6	6.5
MARSHALL	**82**	**9,742**	**6,643**	**18,421 ***	**40.8**	**100.0**
053 Assemb of God	3	94	106	167	.4	.9
056 Baha'i	0	10	NR	10	-	.1
061 Beachy Amish	1	47	NR	60 *	.1	.3
071 Brethren (Ash)	1	15	18	19 *	-	.1
081 Catholic	3	NR	NR	4,647	10.3	25.2
097 Chr Chs&Chs Cr	1	85	NR	108 *	.2	.6
121 Ch God (Abr)	3	64	42	81 *	.2	.4
123 Ch God (Ander)	2	NR	155	155	.3	.8
157 Ch of Brethren	6	900	400	1,146 *	2.5	6.2
165 Ch of Nazarene	1	109	40	109	.2	.6
167 Chs of Christ	2	38	45	57	.1	.3
183 Cons Menn Conf	1	200	244	291	.6	1.6
193 Episcopal	2	NR	118	229	.5	1.2
201 Evan Cov Ch	1	96	66	122 *	.3	.7
203 Evan Free Ch	1	69	125	125	.3	.7
207 E.L.C.A.	2	222	89	279	.6	1.5
283 Luth—MO Synod	3	920	455	1,261	2.8	6.8
291 Missionary Ch	2	199	252	252	.6	1.4
297 Mennonite;Other	1	70	NR	89 *	.2	.5
306 NT IndBapt&Rltd	3	600	NR	764 *	1.7	4.1
322 Old Ord Menn Ch	1	41	NR	52 *	.1	.3
323 Old Ord Amish	8	480	NR	608 *	1.3	3.3
355 Presb Ch (USA)	1	138	65	176 *	.4	1.0
360 Prim Bapt Chrch	1	NR	NR	NR	-	-
370 Ref Baptist Chs	1	NR	NR	NR	-	-
388 Reg Bapt Gen As	4	449	495	563 *	1.2	3.1
413 S.D.A.	1	37	NR	44	.1	.2
419 So Bapt Conv	2	230	216	293 *	.6	1.6
443 Un C of Christ	4	1,114	404	1,418 *	3.1	7.7
449 Un Methodist	15	2,544	1,636	3,239 *	7.2	17.6
467 Wesleyan	3	521	972	1,357	3.0	7.4
499 Indep.Non-Char	2	450	700	700	1.6	3.8
MARTIN	**34**	**2,802**	**1,135**	**6,157 ***	**59.4**	**100.0**
053 Assemb of God	3	82	102	109	1.1	1.8
081 Catholic	4	NR	NR	2,632	25.4	42.7
097 Chr Chs&Chs Cr	3	825	NR	1,017 *	9.8	16.5
165 Ch of Nazarene	1	45	34	59	.6	1.0
167 Chs of Christ	5	206	208	272	2.6	4.4
207 E.L.C.A.	1	270	74	368	3.5	6.0
297 Mennonite;Other	1	12	NR	15 *	.1	.2
323 Old Ord Amish	4	240	NR	296 *	2.9	4.8
419 So Bapt Conv	1	63	34	78 *	.8	1.3
449 Un Methodist	8	926	589	1,139 *	11.0	18.5
467 Wesleyan	3	133	94	172	1.7	2.8
MIAMI	**62**	**9,630**	**4,803**	**15,540 ***	**43.1**	**100.0**
019 Amer Bapt USA	8	2,126	671	2,653 *	7.4	17.1
053 Assemb of God	2	273	306	557	1.5	3.6
056 Baha'i	0	10	NR	10	-	.1
071 Brethren (Ash)	5	211	311	263 *	.7	1.7
081 Catholic	1	NR	NR	2,435	6.7	15.7
093 Chr Ch (Disc)	1	955	199	1,192 *	3.3	7.7
097 Chr Chs&Chs Cr	5	1,453	NR	1,812 *	5.0	11.7
123 Ch God (Ander)	1	NR	25	25	.1	.2
127 Ch God (Cleve)	1	51	48	64 *	.2	.4
151 L-D Saints	1	NR	NR	467	1.3	3.0
157 Ch of Brethren	3	647	397	807 *	2.2	5.2
165 Ch of Nazarene	1	196	121	196	.5	1.3
167 Chs of Christ	1	47	50	61	.2	.4
223 Free Will Bapt	1	2	NR	3 *	-	-
226 Friends-USA	2	94	NR	117 *	.3	.8
263 Int Foursq Gos	1	194	176	242 *	.7	1.6
283 Luth—MO Synod	1	839	322	1,195	3.3	7.7
288 Mennonite USA	1	279	234	348 *	1.0	2.2
291 Missionary Ch	1	58	26	58	.2	.4
355 Presb Ch (USA)	1	273	137	341 *	.9	2.2
388 Reg Bapt Gen As	1	150	180	187 *	.5	1.2
403 Salvation Army	1	46	12	280	.8	1.8
419 So Bapt Conv	1	0	0	0 *	-	-
449 Un Methodist	20	1,703	1,556	2,124 *	5.9	13.7
467 Wesleyan	1	23	32	103	.3	.7
MONROE	**104**	**19,532**	**9,675**	**40,169 ***	**33.3**	**100.0**
017 Amer Bapt Assn	1	50	NR	58 *	-	.1
019 Amer Bapt USA	5	2,026	578	2,355 *	2.0	5.9
034 Ant Orth of NA	1	105	NR	210	.2	.5
053 Assemb of God	8	704	854	1,159	1.0	2.9
056 Baha'i	1	85	NR	85	.1	.2
059 Bapt Miss Assn	1	150	110	174 *	.1	.4
081 Catholic	3	NR	NR	12,600	10.5	31.4
084 Calvary Chapel	1	NR	NR	NR	-	-
093 Chr Ch (Disc)	3	1,161	347	1,349 *	1.1	3.4
097 Chr Chs&Chs Cr	9	4,210	NR	4,892 *	4.1	12.2
123 Ch God (Ander)	2	NR	120	120	.1	.3
127 Ch God (Cleve)	1	97	66	113 *	.1	.3
145 Ch God Prophcy	1	36	NR	41 *	-	.1
151 L-D Saints	3	NR	NR	951	.8	2.4
165 Ch of Nazarene	4	762	423	866	.7	2.2
167 Chs of Christ	20	1,536	1,512	2,054	1.7	5.1
193 Episcopal	1	NR	232	766	.6	1.9
203 Evan Free Ch	1	58	175	175	.1	.4
207 E.L.C.A.	1	309	234	385	.3	1.0
221 Free Methodist	1	344	270	381	.3	.9
226 Friends-USA	1	102	NR	119 *	.1	.3
267 Muslim Est	1	NR	200	400	.3	1.0
283 Luth—MO Synod	2	571	349	749	.6	1.9
288 Mennonite USA	1	7	6	8 *	-	-
355 Presb Ch (USA)	2	479	255	557 *	.5	1.4
360 Prim Bapt Chrch	2	NR	NR	NR	-	-
388 Reg Bapt Gen As	2	487	320	572 *	.5	1.4
403 Salvation Army	1	108	42	486	.4	1.2
419 So Bapt Conv	2	555	162	645 *	.5	1.6
435 Unitarian-Univ	1	304	NR	353 *	.3	.9
443 Un C of Christ	1	392	150	456 *	.4	1.1
449 Un Methodist	12	3,855	2,041	4,482 *	3.7	11.2
463 Vineyard	1	140	120	163 *	.1	.4
467 Wesleyan	3	74	89	195	.2	.5
496 Jewish Est	1	NR	NR	1,000	.8	2.5
499 Indep.Non-Char	3	825	1,020	1,250	1.0	3.1
MONTGOMERY	**71**	**11,477**	**4,082**	**17,222 ***	**45.8**	**100.0**
019 Amer Bapt USA	5	1,309	716	1,641 *	4.4	9.5
022 Carp Rus Orth	1	122	NR	207	.6	1.2

NR–Not Reported *Total adherents estimated from known number of communicant, confirmed, full members. - Represents a percentage less than 0.1. Percentages may not total 100 due to rounding.

Table 4: Religious Congregations by County and Group: 2000

Religious Group	Number of Churches, Synagogues, Mosques, or Temples	Number of Communicant, Confirmed, or Full Members	Number of Attendees	Total Adherents: Number of Adherents	Total Adherents: % of Total Pop.	Total Adherents: % of Total Adh.
053 Assemb of God	1	134	182	304	.8	1.8
056 Baha'i	0	13	NR	13	-	.1
081 Catholic	1	NR	NR	1,981	5.3	11.5
084 Calvary Chapel	1	NR	NR	NR	-	-
093 Chr Ch (Disc)	3	1,090	216	1,366 *	3.6	7.9
097 Chr Chs&Chs Cr	18	3,507	NR	4,394 *	11.7	25.5
107 Christian Un	1	70	27	88 *	.2	.5
123 Ch God (Ander)	1	NR	60	60	.2	.3
127 Ch God (Cleve)	1	86	22	108 *	.3	.6
151 L-D Saints	1	NR	NR	313	.8	1.8
165 Ch of Nazarene	2	251	171	279	.7	1.6
167 Chs of Christ	3	169	188	218	.6	1.3
181 Consrv Congr	1	151	75	189 *	.5	1.1
193 Episcopal	1	NR	105	197	.5	1.1
207 E.L.C.A.	1	326	114	493	1.3	2.9
226 Friends-USA	1	102	NR	128 *	.3	.7
263 Int Foursq Gos	1	13	29	29 *	.1	.2
283 Luth—MO Synod	1	120	61	125	.3	.7
306 NT IndBapt&Rltd	1	200	NR	251 *	.7	1.5
355 Presb Ch (USA)	4	400	194	501 *	1.3	2.9
370 Ref Baptist Chs	1	NR	NR	NR	-	-
388 Reg Bapt Gen As	2	320	435	561 *	1.5	3.3
418 Southw Bapt Fel	1	NR	NR	NR	-	-
419 So Bapt Conv	2	444	126	557 *	1.5	3.2
443 Un C of Christ	1	52	48	65 *	.2	.4
449 Un Methodist	12	2,056	935	2,577 *	6.8	15.0
467 Wesleyan	1	17	18	52	.1	.3
499 Indep.Non-Char	1	525	360	525	1.4	3.0
MORGAN	**87**	**15,813**	**6,903**	**25,374 ***	**38.0**	**100.0**
019 Amer Bapt USA	7	2,154	510	2,725 *	4.1	10.7
053 Assemb of God	4	442	535	718	1.1	2.8
056 Baha'i	0	6	NR	6	-	-
081 Catholic	2	NR	NR	3,191	4.8	12.6
093 Chr Ch (Disc)	4	1,913	438	2,420 *	3.6	9.5
097 Chr Chs&Chs Cr	11	2,913	NR	3,686 *	5.5	14.5
123 Ch God (Ander)	3	NR	340	340	.5	1.3
127 Ch God (Cleve)	1	44	50	56 *	.1	.2
151 L-D Saints	1	NR	NR	415	.6	1.6
165 Ch of Nazarene	6	684	532	1,319	2.0	5.2
167 Chs of Christ	6	436	411	545	.8	2.1
173 Comm of Christ	1	151	NR	151	.2	.6
193 Episcopal	1	NR	30	53	.1	.2
221 Free Methodist	1	45	65	65	.1	.3
226 Friends-USA	3	306	NR	387 *	.6	1.5
283 Luth—MO Synod	2	251	164	345	.5	1.4
291 Missionary Ch	2	243	531	531	.8	2.1
297 Mennonite;Other	1	10	NR	13 *	-	.1
306 NT IndBapt&Rltd	3	600	NR	759 *	1.1	3.0
355 Presb Ch (USA)	1	243	117	307 *	.5	1.2
409 Separate Bapt	2	107	NR	135 *	.2	.5
413 S.D.A.	1	60	NR	71	.1	.3
419 So Bapt Conv	8	2,576	865	3,259 *	4.9	12.8
449 Un Methodist	9	1,735	952	2,194 *	3.3	8.6
467 Wesleyan	4	94	133	453	.7	1.8
499 Indep.Non-Char	3	800	1,230	1,230	1.8	4.8
NEWTON	**23**	**2,751**	**1,259**	**4,796 ***	**32.9**	**100.0**
019 Amer Bapt USA	2	443	160	552 *	3.8	11.5
053 Assemb of God	1	64	80	80	.5	1.7
056 Baha'i	0	3	NR	3	-	.1
057 Bapt Gen Conf	1	50	50	62 *	.4	1.3
081 Catholic	3	NR	NR	1,320	9.1	27.5
093 Chr Ch (Disc)	2	450	155	560 *	3.8	11.7
097 Chr Chs&Chs Cr	1	271	NR	338 *	2.3	7.0
283 Luth—MO Synod	1	84	51	116	.8	2.4
339 Pent Ch of God	1	8	NR	48	.3	1.0
355 Presb Ch (USA)	2	136	123	169 *	1.2	3.5
419 So Bapt Conv	2	365	186	455 *	3.1	9.5
449 Un Methodist	7	877	454	1,093 *	7.5	22.8
NOBLE	**59**	**6,921**	**4,043**	**13,712 ***	**29.6**	**100.0**
019 Amer Bapt USA	2	39	20	50 *	.1	.4
053 Assemb of God	3	346	441	649	1.4	4.7
056 Baha'i	0	2	NR	2	-	-
081 Catholic	6	NR	NR	3,591	7.8	26.2
097 Chr Chs&Chs Cr	2	95	NR	122 *	.3	.9
123 Ch God (Ander)	1	NR	61	61	.1	.4
151 L-D Saints	1	NR	NR	279	.6	2.0
157 Ch of Brethren	1	52	30	67 *	.1	.5
165 Ch of Nazarene	3	186	138	357	.8	2.6
167 Chs of Christ	2	45	50	51	.1	.4
207 E.L.C.A.	4	410	201	532	1.1	3.9
283 Luth—MO Synod	3	1,771	684	2,585	5.6	18.9
291 Missionary Ch	1	17	26	26	.1	.2
306 NT IndBapt&Rltd	1	200	NR	258 *	.6	1.9
323 Old Ord Amish	2	120	NR	154 *	.3	1.1
355 Presb Ch (USA)	4	395	184	509 *	1.1	3.7
388 Reg Bapt Gen As	1	27	40	40 *	.1	.3
413 S.D.A.	1	22	NR	26	.1	.2
419 So Bapt Conv	0	26	25	34 *	.1	.2
443 Un C of Christ	1	103	55	133 *	.3	1.0
449 Un Methodist	16	2,755	1,680	3,551 *	7.7	25.9
463 Vineyard	1	100	80	129 *	.3	.9
467 Wesleyan	3	210	328	506	1.1	3.7
OHIO	**13**	**1,628**	**602**	**2,040 ***	**36.3**	**100.0**
019 Amer Bapt USA	3	347	135	427 *	7.6	20.9
056 Baha'i	0	2	NR	2	-	.1
097 Chr Chs&Chs Cr	1	500	NR	615 *	10.9	30.1
165 Ch of Nazarene	1	55	80	80	1.4	3.9
207 E.L.C.A.	2	189	99	234	4.2	11.5
419 So Bapt Conv	1	116	60	143 *	2.5	7.0
443 Un C of Christ	1	151	35	186 *	3.3	9.1
449 Un Methodist	3	259	159	319 *	5.7	15.6
467 Wesleyan	1	9	34	34	.6	1.7
ORANGE	**56**	**6,417**	**2,351**	**9,080 ***	**47.0**	**100.0**
019 Amer Bapt USA	5	1,305	437	1,629 *	8.4	17.9
053 Assemb of God	2	53	70	131	.7	1.4
081 Catholic	2	NR	NR	587	3.0	6.5
093 Chr Ch (Disc)	1	148	0	185 *	1.0	2.0
097 Chr Chs&Chs Cr	8	1,959	NR	2,446 *	12.7	26.9
127 Ch God (Cleve)	1	144	35	180 *	.9	2.0
165 Ch of Nazarene	3	189	153	305	1.6	3.4
167 Chs of Christ	6	286	303	363	1.9	4.0
226 Friends-USA	2	204	NR	255 *	1.3	2.8
288 Mennonite USA	1	78	115	115 *	.6	1.3
306 NT IndBapt&Rltd	1	200	NR	250 *	1.3	2.8
323 Old Ord Amish	4	220	NR	274 *	1.4	3.0
355 Presb Ch (USA)	1	64	44	80 *	.4	.9
360 Prim Bapt Chrch	2	NR	NR	NR	-	-
413 S.D.A.	1	35	NR	42	.2	.5
419 So Bapt Conv	1	214	170	267 *	1.4	2.9
449 Un Methodist	11	1,114	654	1,390 *	7.2	15.3
467 Wesleyan	4	204	370	581	3.0	6.4
OWEN	**45**	**4,116**	**1,777**	**5,681 ***	**26.1**	**100.0**
019 Amer Bapt USA	7	970	291	1,214 *	5.6	21.4
053 Assemb of God	2	54	71	84	.4	1.5
056 Baha'i	0	2	NR	2	-	-
081 Catholic	1	NR	NR	305	1.4	5.4
097 Chr Chs&Chs Cr	4	825	NR	1,033 *	4.7	18.2
127 Ch God (Cleve)	1	18	21	23 *	.1	.4
145 Ch God Prophcy	1	36	NR	45 *	.2	.8
151 L-D Saints	1	NR	NR	170	.8	3.0
165 Ch of Nazarene	5	285	260	477	2.2	8.4
167 Chs of Christ	5	271	279	357	1.6	6.3
355 Presb Ch (USA)	2	146	95	183 *	.8	3.2
360 Prim Bapt Chrch	1	NR	NR	NR	-	-
409 Separate Bapt	2	147	NR	184 *	.8	3.2
413 S.D.A.	1	102	NR	121	.6	2.1
419 So Bapt Conv	0	16	17	20 *	.1	.4
443 Un C of Christ	1	42	18	53 *	.2	.9
449 Un Methodist	9	688	395	863 *	4.0	15.2
467 Wesleyan	1	14	30	47	.2	.8

NR–Not Reported *Total adherents estimated from known number of communicant, confirmed, full members. - Represents a percentage less than 0.1. Percentages may not total 100 due to rounding.

Table 4: Religious Congregations by County and Group: 2000

Religious Group	Number of Churches, Synagogues, Mosques, or Temples	Number of Communicant, Confirmed, or Full Members	Number of Attendees	Total Adherents: Number of Adherents	Total Adherents: % of Total Pop.	Total Adherents: % of Total Adh.
499 Indep.Non-Char	1	500	300	500	2.3	8.8
PARKE	**41**	**4,518**	**1,357**	**5,912 ***	**34.3**	**100.0**
019 Amer Bapt USA	4	259	175	316 *	1.8	5.3
053 Assemb of God	1	113	125	125	.7	2.1
056 Baha'i	0	2	NR	2	-	-
081 Catholic	2	NR	NR	320	1.9	5.4
093 Chr Ch (Disc)	1	335	160	408 *	2.4	6.9
097 Chr Chs&Chs Cr	7	1,649	NR	2,011 *	11.7	34.0
151 L-D Saints	1	NR	NR	91	.5	1.5
165 Ch of Nazarene	2	107	83	126	.7	2.1
167 Chs of Christ	3	188	150	237	1.4	4.0
226 Friends-USA	4	408	NR	497 *	2.9	8.4
323 Old Ord Amish	3	225	NR	273 *	1.6	4.6
339 Pent Ch of God	1	10	NR	16	.1	.3
355 Presb Ch (USA)	2	146	75	178 *	1.0	3.0
418 Southw Bapt Fel	1	NR	NR	NR	-	-
419 So Bapt Conv	2	377	260	460 *	2.7	7.8
449 Un Methodist	7	699	329	852 *	4.9	14.4
PERRY	**31**	**3,103**	**1,504**	**10,146 ***	**53.7**	**100.0**
019 Amer Bapt USA	3	597	258	719 *	3.8	7.1
056 Baha'i	0	2	NR	2	-	-
081 Catholic	8	NR	NR	6,250	33.1	61.6
097 Chr Chs&Chs Cr	1	150	NR	181 *	1.0	1.8
151 L-D Saints	1	NR	NR	142	.8	1.4
165 Ch of Nazarene	1	114	76	114	.6	1.1
167 Chs of Christ	2	360	250	395	2.1	3.9
173 Comm of Christ	1	38	NR	38	.2	.4
193 Episcopal	1	NR	28	41	.2	.4
283 Luth—MO Synod	1	257	71	355	1.9	3.5
360 Prim Bapt Chrch	1	NR	NR	NR	-	-
388 Reg Bapt Gen As	1	228	244	275 *	1.5	2.7
413 S.D.A.	1	51	NR	61	.3	.6
419 So Bapt Conv	0	28	30	34 *	.2	.3
443 Un C of Christ	2	765	278	922 *	4.9	9.1
449 Un Methodist	7	513	269	617 *	3.3	6.1
PIKE	**38**	**2,359**	**1,789**	**3,583 ***	**27.9**	**100.0**
019 Amer Bapt USA	1	264	200	324 *	2.5	9.0
053 Assemb of God	2	49	65	101	.8	2.8
081 Catholic	1	NR	NR	324	2.5	9.0
093 Chr Ch (Disc)	1	52	18	64 *	.5	1.8
097 Chr Chs&Chs Cr	2	235	NR	288 *	2.2	8.0
123 Ch God (Ander)	3	NR	207	207	1.6	5.8
165 Ch of Nazarene	2	118	164	267	2.1	7.5
167 Chs of Christ	5	120	127	161	1.3	4.5
185 Cumber Presb	1	50	NR	50	.4	1.4
207 E.L.C.A.	1	179	119	220	1.7	6.1
221 Free Methodist	2	113	120	132	1.0	3.7
355 Presb Ch (USA)	1	110	49	135 *	1.1	3.8
360 Prim Bapt Chrch	1	NR	NR	NR	-	-
365 Prog Prim Bapt	1	20	NR	25 *	.2	.7
419 So Bapt Conv	1	70	35	86 *	.7	2.4
449 Un Methodist	11	917	630	1,126 *	8.8	31.4
467 Wesleyan	2	62	55	73	.6	2.0
PORTER	**109**	**21,226**	**13,420**	**61,398 ***	**41.8**	**100.0**
040 Ap Chr Ch-Amer	1	48	100	100 *	.1	.2
053 Assemb of God	5	302	415	578	.4	.9
056 Baha'i	0	12	NR	12	-	-
081 Catholic	9	NR	NR	30,531	20.8	49.7
093 Chr Ch (Disc)	2	730	279	906 *	.6	1.5
097 Chr Chs&Chs Cr	7	1,441	NR	1,788 *	1.2	2.9
123 Ch God (Ander)	1	NR	140	140	.1	.2
127 Ch God (Cleve)	2	425	246	527 *	.4	.9
145 Ch God Prophcy	2	71	NR	88 *	.1	.1
151 L-D Saints	3	NR	NR	903	.6	1.5
165 Ch of Nazarene	6	1,664	1,900	2,544	1.7	4.1
167 Chs of Christ	4	388	411	465	.3	.8
193 Episcopal	2	NR	197	510	.3	.8
201 Evan Cov Ch	1	176	98	218 *	.1	.4
203 Evan Free Ch	3	705	1,717	1,717	1.2	2.8
207 E.L.C.A.	5	2,391	1,042	3,329	2.3	5.4
226 Friends-USA	1	55	NR	68 *	-	.1
246 Greek Orthodox	1	NR	NR	438	.3	.7
263 Int Foursq Gos	1	42	55	55 *	-	.1
267 Muslim Est	1	NR	70	520	.4	.8
283 Luth—MO Synod	9	3,970	1,713	4,941	3.4	8.0
288 Mennonite USA	2	250	235	312 *	.2	.5
291 Missionary Ch	1	23	56	56	-	.1
297 Mennonite;Other	1	78	NR	97 *	.1	.2
306 NT IndBapt&Rltd	1	200	NR	248 *	.2	.4
331 OCA: Ter Diocs	1	33	NR	81	.1	.1
355 Presb Ch (USA)	6	1,489	638	1,849 *	1.3	3.0
356 Presb Ch Amer	2	77	70	105	.1	.2
363 Primitive Meth	1	57	NR	61	-	.1
388 Reg Bapt Gen As	9	1,072	1,046	1,179 *	.8	1.9
403 Salvation Army	1	50	25	70	-	.1
419 So Bapt Conv	6	1,183	414	1,468 *	1.0	2.4
443 Un C of Christ	2	441	173	547 *	.4	.9
449 Un Methodist	7	3,031	1,554	3,763 *	2.6	6.1
463 Vineyard	1	350	300	434 *	.3	.7
467 Wesleyan	1	172	231	450	.3	.7
498 Indep.Charis.	1	300	295	300	.2	.5
POSEY	**44**	**5,668**	**2,500**	**13,374 ***	**49.4**	**100.0**
053 Assemb of God	2	366	474	770	2.8	5.8
056 Baha'i	0	2	NR	2	-	-
081 Catholic	5	NR	NR	5,642	20.8	42.2
093 Chr Ch (Disc)	2	385	127	485 *	1.8	3.6
097 Chr Chs&Chs Cr	4	482	NR	606 *	2.2	4.5
165 Ch of Nazarene	3	264	182	413	1.5	3.1
167 Chs of Christ	1	28	35	35	.1	.3
193 Episcopal	2	NR	110	211	.8	1.6
226 Friends-USA	1	102	NR	128 *	.5	1.0
355 Presb Ch (USA)	2	117	57	147 *	.5	1.1
413 S.D.A.	1	5	NR	6	-	-
418 Southw Bapt Fel	1	NR	NR	NR	-	-
419 So Bapt Conv	2	716	110	901 *	3.3	6.7
443 Un C of Christ	6	1,483	607	1,866 *	6.9	14.0
449 Un Methodist	12	1,718	798	2,162 *	8.0	16.2
PULASKI	**35**	**3,439**	**1,740**	**6,937 ***	**50.4**	**100.0**
040 Ap Chr Ch-Amer	1	280	460	460 *	3.3	6.6
053 Assemb of God	2	42	67	115	.8	1.7
081 Catholic	5	NR	NR	2,461	17.9	35.5
093 Chr Ch (Disc)	2	470	89	589 *	4.3	8.5
097 Chr Chs&Chs Cr	3	600	NR	752 *	5.5	10.8
165 Ch of Nazarene	1	249	200	267	1.9	3.8
167 Chs of Christ	1	15	20	25	.2	.4
176 Congr Ad Afl	1	46	NR	58 *	.4	.8
223 Free Will Bapt	1	2	NR	3 *	-	-
283 Luth—MO Synod	3	363	185	477	3.5	6.9
306 NT IndBapt&Rltd	1	200	NR	251 *	1.8	3.6
355 Presb Ch (USA)	2	126	59	158 *	1.1	2.3
388 Reg Bapt Gen As	3	189	225	250 *	1.8	3.6
413 S.D.A.	1	51	NR	61	.4	.9
419 So Bapt Conv	1	8	0	10 *	.1	.1
443 Un C of Christ	2	185	82	232 *	1.7	3.3
449 Un Methodist	5	613	353	768 *	5.6	11.1
PUTNAM	**60**	**9,544**	**3,952**	**13,575 ***	**37.7**	**100.0**
019 Amer Bapt USA	5	1,218	466	1,486 *	4.1	10.9
053 Assemb of God	2	350	441	481	1.3	3.5
056 Baha'i	0	20	NR	20	.1	.1
081 Catholic	1	NR	NR	1,030	2.9	7.6
093 Chr Ch (Disc)	4	1,680	274	2,050 *	5.7	15.1
097 Chr Chs&Chs Cr	5	1,580	NR	1,929 *	5.4	14.2
123 Ch God (Ander)	1	NR	20	20	.1	.1
127 Ch God (Cleve)	1	78	16	95 *	.3	.7
151 L-D Saints	1	NR	NR	148	.4	1.1
165 Ch of Nazarene	3	160	135	225	.6	1.7
167 Chs of Christ	5	410	303	511	1.4	3.8
175 Congr Chr Chs	1	50	50	61 *	.2	.4

NR–Not Reported *Total adherents estimated from known number of communicant, confirmed, full members. - Represents a percentage less than 0.1. Percentages may not total 100 due to rounding.

Table 4: Religious Congregations by County and Group: 2000

Religious Group	Number of Churches, Synagogues, Mosques, or Temples	Number of Communicant, Confirmed, or Full Members	Number of Attendees	Total Adherents: Number of Adherents	Total Adherents: % of Total Pop.	Total Adherents: % of Total Adh.
179 Consrv Bapt	1	NR	330	330	.9	2.4
193 Episcopal	1	NR	60	156	.4	1.1
203 Evan Free Ch	1	0	65	65	.2	.5
263 Int Foursq Gos	1	19	44	44 *	.1	.3
283 Luth—MO Synod	2	256	172	382	1.1	2.8
306 NT IndBapt&Rltd	4	800	NR	976 *	2.7	7.2
355 Presb Ch (USA)	3	254	119	310 *	.9	2.3
360 Prim Bapt Chrch	1	NR	NR	NR	-	-
370 Ref Baptist Chs	1	NR	NR	NR	-	-
388 Reg Bapt Gen As	1	75	80	92 *	.3	.7
413 S.D.A.	1	33	NR	39	.1	.3
419 So Bapt Conv	3	842	504	1,027 *	2.9	7.6
426 2Seed Sprt Bpt	1	16	NR	20 *	.1	.1
443 Un C of Christ	1	435	191	531 *	1.5	3.9
449 Un Methodist	9	1,268	682	1,547 *	4.3	11.4
RANDOLPH	**78**	**6,302**	**3,279**	**9,803 ***	**35.8**	**100.0**
053 Assemb of God	2	308	369	790	2.9	8.1
056 Baha'i	0	2	NR	2	-	-
081 Catholic	2	NR	NR	1,033	3.8	10.5
093 Chr Ch (Disc)	3	1,039	286	1,289 *	4.7	13.1
097 Chr Chs&Chs Cr	4	665	NR	825 *	3.0	8.4
123 Ch God (Ander)	2	NR	117	117	.4	1.2
151 L-D Saints	1	NR	NR	115	.4	1.2
165 Ch of Nazarene	7	745	417	943	3.4	9.6
167 Chs of Christ	2	87	100	121	.4	1.2
207 E.L.C.A.	2	376	143	473	1.7	4.8
226 Friends-USA	17	799	NR	992 *	3.6	10.1
296 Midw Congr Fel	10	541	669	671 *	2.4	6.8
355 Presb Ch (USA)	2	111	54	137 *	.5	1.4
388 Reg Bapt Gen As	1	30	35	37 *	.1	.4
409 Separate Bapt	1	60	NR	74 *	.3	.8
419 So Bapt Conv	2	160	55	199 *	.7	2.0
449 Un Methodist	18	1,331	952	1,650 *	6.0	16.8
467 Wesleyan	2	48	82	335	1.2	3.4
RIPLEY	**63**	**8,546**	**3,113**	**20,747 ***	**78.2**	**100.0**
019 Amer Bapt USA	11	2,447	801	3,132 *	11.8	15.1
053 Assemb of God	2	209	244	296	1.1	1.4
056 Baha'i	0	3	NR	3	-	-
081 Catholic	8	NR	NR	9,198	34.7	44.3
097 Chr Chs&Chs Cr	7	1,011	NR	1,295 *	4.9	6.2
151 L-D Saints	1	NR	NR	301	1.1	1.5
165 Ch of Nazarene	1	16	14	67	.3	.3
167 Chs of Christ	1	48	52	63	.2	.3
193 Episcopal	1	NR	21	34	.1	.2
207 E.L.C.A.	6	1,794	636	2,225	8.4	10.7
258 IndFreeWillBapt	1	63	NR	81 *	.3	.4
283 Luth—MO Synod	1	154	65	191	.7	.9
360 Prim Bapt Chrch	1	NR	NR	NR	-	-
419 So Bapt Conv	3	408	120	522 *	2.0	2.5
443 Un C of Christ	4	996	381	1,275 *	4.8	6.1
449 Un Methodist	11	1,311	660	1,678 *	6.3	8.1
467 Wesleyan	4	86	119	386	1.5	1.9
RUSH	**42**	**5,480**	**2,087**	**9,172 ***	**50.2**	**100.0**
019 Amer Bapt USA	1	315	160	398 *	2.2	4.3
053 Assemb of God	1	14	20	20	.1	.2
056 Baha'i	0	2	NR	2	-	-
081 Catholic	1	NR	NR	1,784	9.8	19.5
093 Chr Ch (Disc)	5	1,159	349	1,464 *	8.0	16.0
097 Chr Chs&Chs Cr	9	1,400	NR	1,768 *	9.7	19.3
107 Christian Un	1	110	60	139 *	.8	1.5
123 Ch God (Ander)	1	NR	120	120	.7	1.3
165 Ch of Nazarene	2	144	107	229	1.3	2.5
167 Chs of Christ	2	85	80	105	.6	1.1
193 Episcopal	1	NR	10	25	.1	.3
226 Friends-USA	1	47	NR	59 *	.3	.6
323 Old Ord Amish	3	180	NR	228 *	1.2	2.5
355 Presb Ch (USA)	2	251	463	582 *	3.2	6.3
419 So Bapt Conv	3	748	214	945 *	5.2	10.3
449 Un Methodist	6	953	451	1,203 *	6.6	13.1
467 Wesleyan	3	72	53	101	.6	1.1

Religious Group	Number of Churches, Synagogues, Mosques, or Temples	Number of Communicant, Confirmed, or Full Members	Number of Attendees	Total Adherents: Number of Adherents	Total Adherents: % of Total Pop.	Total Adherents: % of Total Adh.
ST. JOSEPH	**219**	**31,641**	**21,857**	**116,150 ***	**43.7**	**100.0**
017 Amer Bapt Assn	3	125	NR	157 *	.1	.1
019 Amer Bapt USA	2	245	157	306 *	.1	.3
040 Ap Chr Ch-Amer	1	23	46	46 *	-	-
053 Assemb of God	8	1,162	1,089	2,946	1.1	2.5
056 Baha'i	3	106	NR	106	-	.1
071 Brethren (Ash)	4	366	299	457 *	.2	.4
081 Catholic	30	NR	NR	63,209	23.8	54.4
084 Calvary Chapel	1	NR	NR	NR	-	-
093 Chr Ch (Disc)	3	1,156	333	1,445 *	.5	1.2
097 Chr Chs&Chs Cr	8	1,955	NR	2,444 *	.9	2.1
105 Christian Ref	1	419	250	524 *	.2	.5
121 Ch God (Abr)	1	84	100	105 *	-	.1
123 Ch God (Ander)	2	NR	215	215	.1	.2
127 Ch God (Cleve)	3	378	278	473 *	.2	.4
145 Ch God Prophcy	1	36	NR	45 *	-	-
151 L-D Saints	3	NR	NR	1,106	.4	1.0
157 Ch of Brethren	7	670	386	839 *	.3	.7
165 Ch of Nazarene	4	526	526	906	.3	.8
167 Chs of Christ	4	489	500	624	.2	.5
173 Comm of Christ	1	165	NR	165	.1	.1
175 Congr Chr Chs	1	174	100	218 *	.1	.2
193 Episcopal	4	NR	552	1,049	.4	.9
201 Evan Cov Ch	1	112	82	140 *	.1	.1
203 Evan Free Ch	2	378	725	725	.3	.6
207 E.L.C.A.	8	3,003	1,089	4,308	1.6	3.7
221 Free Methodist	1	23	75	75	-	.1
246 Greek Orthodox	1	NR	NR	774	.3	.7
262 Int Cou Comm Ch	1	200	NR	250 *	.1	.2
263 Int Foursq Gos	1	16	61	61 *	-	.1
267 Muslim Est	3	NR	447	1,568	.6	1.3
283 Luth—MO Synod	6	1,468	736	2,321	.9	2.0
288 Mennonite USA	2	188	237	237 *	.1	.2
291 Missionary Ch	13	1,100	1,792	2,002	.8	1.7
297 Mennonite;Other	1	38	NR	48 *	-	-
306 NT IndBapt&Rltd	4	800	NR	1,000 *	.4	.9
335 Orth Pres Ch	1	28	36	36	-	-
339 Pent Ch of God	1	19	NR	54	-	-
355 Presb Ch (USA)	8	2,381	1,158	2,984 *	1.1	2.6
356 Presb Ch Amer	1	45	50	50	-	-
388 Reg Bapt Gen As	5	961	949	1,396 *	.5	1.2
403 Salvation Army	2	227	84	314	.1	.3
410 Serb Orth USA	1	NR	NR	382	.1	.3
413 S.D.A.	6	1,007	NR	1,199	.5	1.0
419 So Bapt Conv	3	922	767	1,153 *	.4	1.0
435 Unitarian-Univ	1	108	NR	135 *	.1	.1
443 Un C of Christ	7	1,306	492	1,633 *	.6	1.4
449 Un Methodist	31	8,141	5,525	10,183 *	3.8	8.8
463 Vineyard	2	270	235	338 *	.1	.3
467 Wesleyan	4	179	256	555	.2	.5
469 WELS	1	292	190	394	.1	.3
496 Jewish Est	3	NR	NR	1,850	.7	1.6
498 Indep.Charis.	1	0	1,500	2,000	.8	1.7
499 Indep.Non-Char	2	350	540	600	.2	.5
SCOTT	**45**	**7,588**	**1,996**	**10,324 ***	**45.0**	**100.0**
019 Amer Bapt USA	8	2,415	766	3,032 *	13.2	29.4
053 Assemb of God	1	6	6	8	-	.1
056 Baha'i	0	1	NR	1	-	-
081 Catholic	1	NR	NR	665	2.9	6.4
097 Chr Chs&Chs Cr	6	3,293	NR	4,135 *	18.0	40.1
123 Ch God (Ander)	1	NR	87	87	.4	.8
127 Ch God (Cleve)	5	572	372	721 *	3.1	7.0
145 Ch God Prophcy	1	36	NR	45 *	.2	.4
165 Ch of Nazarene	1	54	25	54	.2	.5
167 Chs of Christ	2	122	123	148	.6	1.4
183 Cons Menn Conf	1	48	59	70	.3	.7
283 Luth—MO Synod	1	43	26	55	.2	.5
355 Presb Ch (USA)	2	168	107	211 *	.9	2.0
413 S.D.A.	1	37	NR	44	.2	.4
418 Southw Bapt Fel	1	NR	NR	NR	-	-
419 So Bapt Conv	3	202	70	254 *	1.1	2.5
449 Un Methodist	8	547	337	687 *	3.0	6.7

NR–Not Reported *Total adherents estimated from known number of communicant, confirmed, full members. - Represents a percentage less than 0.1. Percentages may not total 100 due to rounding.

Table 4: Religious Congregations by County and Group: 2000

Religious Group	Number of Churches, Synagogues, Mosques, or Temples	Number of Communicant, Confirmed, or Full Members	Number of Attendees	Total Adherents		
				Number of Adherents	% of Total Pop.	% of Total Adh.
467 Wesleyan	2	44	18	107	.5	1.0
SHELBY	**65**	**9,346**	**3,753**	**16,707 ***	**38.5**	**100.0**
019 Amer Bapt USA	9	2,697	1,024	3,388 *	7.8	20.3
053 Assemb of God	1	28	31	47	.1	.3
056 Baha'i	0	2	NR	2	-	-
081 Catholic	2	NR	NR	3,941	9.1	23.6
093 Chr Ch (Disc)	1	534	251	671 *	1.5	4.0
097 Chr Chs&Chs Cr	6	1,148	NR	1,442 *	3.3	8.6
107 Christian Un	2	329	173	413 *	1.0	2.5
123 Ch God (Ander)	1	NR	48	48	.1	.3
127 Ch God (Cleve)	1	88	52	111 *	.3	.7
151 L-D Saints	1	NR	NR	293	.7	1.8
165 Ch of Nazarene	3	324	224	635	1.5	3.8
167 Chs of Christ	1	17	18	22	.1	.1
193 Episcopal	1	NR	50	88	.2	.5
207 E.L.C.A.	1	187	80	233	.5	1.4
226 Friends-USA	2	94	NR	118 *	.3	.7
283 Luth—MO Synod	1	81	37	117	.3	.7
306 NT IndBapt&Rltd	1	200	NR	251 *	.6	1.5
355 Presb Ch (USA)	2	402	201	505 *	1.2	3.0
388 Reg Bapt Gen As	1	48	90	90 *	.2	.5
403 Salvation Army	1	75	39	162	.4	1.0
413 S.D.A.	1	72	NR	86	.2	.5
419 So Bapt Conv	3	221	153	278 *	.6	1.7
443 Un C of Christ	2	468	166	588 *	1.4	3.5
449 Un Methodist	18	2,214	997	2,780 *	6.4	16.6
467 Wesleyan	3	117	119	398	.9	2.4
SPENCER	**49**	**4,748**	**2,152**	**10,519 ***	**51.6**	**100.0**
019 Amer Bapt USA	5	767	270	960 *	4.7	9.1
081 Catholic	8	NR	NR	4,549	22.3	43.2
097 Chr Chs&Chs Cr	3	563	NR	704 *	3.5	6.7
165 Ch of Nazarene	3	172	101	225	1.1	2.1
167 Chs of Christ	1	25	30	35	.2	.3
207 E.L.C.A.	1	119	60	157	.8	1.5
283 Luth—MO Synod	1	318	146	405	2.0	3.9
355 Presb Ch (USA)	1	78	51	98 *	.5	.9
360 Prim Bapt Chrch	1	NR	NR	NR	-	-
370 Ref Baptist Chs	1	NR	NR	NR	-	-
419 So Bapt Conv	4	635	272	794 *	3.9	7.5
443 Un C of Christ	4	391	171	489 *	2.4	4.6
449 Un Methodist	16	1,680	1,051	2,103 *	10.3	20.0
STARKE	**26**	**2,447**	**1,248**	**5,047 ***	**21.4**	**100.0**
053 Assemb of God	2	95	109	273	1.2	5.4
056 Baha'i	0	7	NR	7	-	.1
081 Catholic	6	NR	NR	1,560	6.6	30.9
097 Chr Chs&Chs Cr	1	100	NR	126 *	.5	2.5
127 Ch God (Cleve)	1	21	0	26 *	.1	.5
165 Ch of Nazarene	1	69	65	116	.5	2.3
223 Free Will Bapt	2	5	NR	6 *	-	.1
283 Luth—MO Synod	3	1,003	547	1,349	5.7	26.7
297 Mennonite;Other	1	15	NR	19 *	.1	.4
306 NT IndBapt&Rltd	1	200	NR	251 *	1.1	5.0
388 Reg Bapt Gen As	1	75	50	94 *	.4	1.9
419 So Bapt Conv	1	176	0	221 *	.9	4.4
443 Un C of Christ	1	154	64	193 *	.8	3.8
449 Un Methodist	4	470	337	591 *	2.5	11.7
467 Wesleyan	1	57	76	215	.9	4.3
STEUBEN	**47**	**5,208**	**3,943**	**9,503 ***	**28.6**	**100.0**
019 Amer Bapt USA	1	31	35	39 *	.1	.4
053 Assemb of God	1	211	296	400	1.2	4.2
056 Baha'i	0	6	NR	6	-	.1
081 Catholic	2	NR	NR	1,683	5.1	17.7
097 Chr Chs&Chs Cr	4	740	NR	922 *	2.8	9.7
123 Ch God (Ander)	1	NR	41	41	.1	.4
151 L-D Saints	1	NR	NR	151	.5	1.6
165 Ch of Nazarene	2	143	118	304	.9	3.2
167 Chs of Christ	2	110	121	130	.4	1.4
176 Congr Ad Afl	1	78	NR	97 *	.3	1.0

Religious Group	Number of Churches, Synagogues, Mosques, or Temples	Number of Communicant, Confirmed, or Full Members	Number of Attendees	Total Adherents		
				Number of Adherents	% of Total Pop.	% of Total Adh.
193 Episcopal	1	NR	27	51	.2	.5
207 E.L.C.A.	1	512	193	641	1.9	6.7
213 Evan Menn Inc	1	100	561	125 *	.4	1.3
267 Muslim Est	1	NR	55	163	.5	1.7
283 Luth—MO Synod	3	577	422	716	2.2	7.5
291 Missionary Ch	3	361	922	922	2.8	9.7
306 NT IndBapt&Rltd	1	200	NR	249 *	.7	2.6
323 Old Ord Amish	2	120	NR	150 *	.5	1.6
339 Pent Ch of God	1	22	NR	52	.2	.5
355 Presb Ch (USA)	2	219	175	273 *	.8	2.9
413 S.D.A.	1	51	NR	61	.2	.6
419 So Bapt Conv	1	4	0	5 *	-	.1
443 Un C of Christ	1	316	75	394 *	1.2	4.1
449 Un Methodist	12	1,349	804	1,683 *	5.1	17.7
467 Wesleyan	1	58	98	245	.7	2.6
SULLIVAN	**59**	**5,994**	**2,785**	**7,951 ***	**36.6**	**100.0**
019 Amer Bapt USA	4	1,256	468	1,513 *	7.0	19.0
053 Assemb of God	3	125	152	218	1.0	2.7
081 Catholic	1	NR	NR	421	1.9	5.3
093 Chr Ch (Disc)	1	141	61	170 *	.8	2.1
097 Chr Chs&Chs Cr	4	1,460	NR	1,758 *	8.1	22.1
127 Ch God (Cleve)	3	171	171	225 *	1.0	2.8
145 Ch God Prophcy	1	36	NR	43 *	.2	.5
165 Ch of Nazarene	1	62	55	95	.4	1.2
167 Chs of Christ	12	613	627	824	3.8	10.4
171 Ch God-Gen Con	1	128	250	250 *	1.1	3.1
306 NT IndBapt&Rltd	1	200	NR	241 *	1.1	3.0
355 Presb Ch (USA)	2	169	86	203 *	.9	2.6
418 Southw Bapt Fel	1	NR	NR	NR	-	-
419 So Bapt Conv	4	399	167	480 *	2.2	6.0
443 Un C of Christ	1	0	0	0 *	-	-
449 Un Methodist	17	1,209	703	1,456 *	6.7	18.3
467 Wesleyan	2	25	45	54	.2	.7
SWITZERLAND	**26**	**1,857**	**562**	**2,561 ***	**28.3**	**100.0**
019 Amer Bapt USA	9	976	315	1,219 *	13.4	47.6
081 Catholic	1	NR	NR	147	1.6	5.7
097 Chr Chs&Chs Cr	3	373	NR	466 *	5.1	18.2
165 Ch of Nazarene	2	10	20	49	.5	1.9
323 Old Ord Amish	2	120	NR	150 *	1.7	5.9
355 Presb Ch (USA)	1	37	19	46 *	.5	1.8
419 So Bapt Conv	1	88	56	110 *	1.2	4.3
449 Un Methodist	6	244	127	304 *	3.4	11.9
467 Wesleyan	1	9	25	70	.8	2.7
TIPPECANOE	**114**	**23,721**	**15,396**	**55,093 ***	**37.0**	**100.0**
019 Amer Bapt USA	2	880	329	1,053 *	.7	1.9
022 Carp Rus Orth	1	122	NR	207	.1	.4
053 Assemb of God	4	1,117	1,386	1,652	1.1	3.0
056 Baha'i	1	40	NR	40	-	.1
076 Buddhism	1	NR	NR	NR	-	-
081 Catholic	6	NR	NR	19,578	13.1	35.5
084 Calvary Chapel	2	NR	NR	NR	-	-
089 Chr & Miss Al	2	58	NR	97	.1	.2
093 Chr Ch (Disc)	2	1,237	429	1,481 *	1.0	2.7
097 Chr Chs&Chs Cr	7	1,485	NR	1,777 *	1.2	3.2
105 Christian Ref	2	437	260	523 *	.4	.9
123 Ch God (Ander)	2	NR	103	103	.1	.2
127 Ch God (Cleve)	1	28	0	34 *	-	.1
151 L-D Saints	3	NR	NR	1,230	.8	2.2
157 Ch of Brethren	1	50	51	60 *	-	.1
165 Ch of Nazarene	1	233	241	519	.3	.9
167 Chs of Christ	3	399	465	571	.4	1.0
193 Episcopal	2	NR	222	485	.3	.9
201 Evan Cov Ch	1	514	918	918 *	.6	1.7
207 E.L.C.A.	3	920	466	1,203	.8	2.2
221 Free Methodist	1	20	36	36	-	.1
226 Friends-USA	2	160	NR	192 *	.1	.3
263 Int Foursq Gos	1	67	67	80 *	.1	.1
267 Muslim Est	1	NR	300	700	.5	1.3
283 Luth—MO Synod	4	1,867	1,113	2,720	1.8	4.9
288 Mennonite USA	1	11	10	13 *	-	-

NR–Not Reported   *Total adherents estimated from known number of communicant, confirmed, full members.   - Represents a percentage less than 0.1.   Percentages may not total 100 due to rounding.

Table 4: Religious Congregations by County and Group: 2000

Religious Group	Number of Churches, Synagogues, Mosques, or Temples	Number of Communicant, Confirmed, or Full Members	Number of Attendees	Total Adherents		
				Number of Adherents	% of Total Pop.	% of Total Adh.
306 NT IndBapt&Rltd	1	200	NR	239 *	.2	.4
339 Pent Ch of God	3	79	NR	337	.2	.6
355 Presb Ch (USA)	8	3,580	1,809	4,315 *	2.9	7.8
371 Ref Ch in Am	2	326	313	549	.4	1.0
388 Reg Bapt Gen As	3	1,541	1,794	1,946 *	1.3	3.5
403 Salvation Army	1	76	48	207	.1	.4
413 S.D.A.	1	159	NR	189	.1	.3
418 Southw Bapt Fel	1	NR	NR	NR	-	-
419 So Bapt Conv	10	1,462	788	1,750 *	1.2	3.2
435 Unitarian-Univ	1	162	NR	194 *	.1	.4
443 Un C of Christ	2	796	268	953 *	.6	1.7
449 Un Methodist	19	5,036	3,378	6,030 *	4.0	10.9
467 Wesleyan	2	159	202	562	.4	1.0
496 Jewish Est	2	NR	NR	550	.4	1.0
498 Indep.Charis.	1	500	400	2,000	1.3	3.6
TIPTON	**29**	**4,511**	**1,557**	**7,440 ***	**44.9**	**100.0**
019 Amer Bapt USA	1	225	75	277 *	1.7	3.7
053 Assemb of God	1	49	55	87	.5	1.2
056 Baha'i	0	1	NR	1	-	-
081 Catholic	1	NR	NR	1,528	9.2	20.5
093 Chr Ch (Disc)	2	928	211	1,143 *	6.9	15.4
097 Chr Chs&Chs Cr	6	1,185	NR	1,459 *	8.8	19.6
127 Ch God (Cleve)	1	37	39	46 *	.3	.6
157 Ch of Brethren	1	43	37	53 *	.3	.7
165 Ch of Nazarene	1	72	47	72	.4	1.0
167 Chs of Christ	2	137	145	172	1.0	2.3
283 Luth—MO Synod	1	434	235	547	3.3	7.4
306 NT IndBapt&Rltd	1	200	NR	246 *	1.5	3.3
355 Presb Ch (USA)	1	88	41	108 *	.7	1.5
409 Separate Bapt	1	250	NR	308 *	1.9	4.1
449 Un Methodist	5	654	319	806 *	4.9	10.8
467 Wesleyan	4	208	353	587	3.5	7.9
UNION	**15**	**1,748**	**457**	**2,876 ***	**39.1**	**100.0**
032 Amish; other	1	65	NR	82 *	1.1	2.9
081 Catholic	1	NR	NR	610	8.3	21.2
097 Chr Chs&Chs Cr	1	367	NR	464 *	6.3	16.1
157 Ch of Brethren	1	33	0	42 *	.6	1.5
165 Ch of Nazarene	2	109	100	194	2.6	6.7
226 Friends-USA	1	47	NR	59 *	.8	2.1
306 NT IndBapt&Rltd	1	200	NR	253 *	3.4	8.8
355 Presb Ch (USA)	1	72	38	91 *	1.2	3.2
360 Prim Bapt Chrch	1	NR	NR	NR	-	-
419 So Bapt Conv	1	180	0	228 *	3.1	7.9
449 Un Methodist	4	675	319	853 *	11.6	29.7
VANDERBURGH	**161**	**41,972**	**16,656**	**86,941 ***	**50.6**	**100.0**
019 Amer Bapt USA	4	1,116	461	1,358 *	.8	1.6
053 Assemb of God	8	956	1,240	1,437	.8	1.7
056 Baha'i	0	24	NR	24	-	-
081 Catholic	20	NR	NR	31,497	18.3	36.2
084 Calvary Chapel	2	NR	NR	NR	-	-
093 Chr Ch (Disc)	3	948	173	1,154 *	.7	1.3
097 Chr Chs&Chs Cr	2	2,600	NR	3,164 *	1.8	3.6
123 Ch God (Ander)	1	NR	135	135	.1	.2
127 Ch God (Cleve)	2	137	191	229 *	.1	.3
145 Ch God Prophcy	1	36	NR	43 *	-	-
151 L-D Saints	3	NR	NR	1,017	.6	1.2
165 Ch of Nazarene	4	502	320	694	.4	.8
167 Chs of Christ	6	887	872	1,149	.7	1.3
173 Comm of Christ	1	94	NR	94	.1	.1
179 Consrv Bapt	1	NR	140	140	.1	.2
185 Cumber Presb	2	109	NR	440	.3	.5
193 Episcopal	1	NR	176	354	.2	.4
203 Evan Free Ch	1	179	135	179	.1	.2
207 E.L.C.A.	6	899	512	1,258	.7	1.4
221 Free Methodist	1	77	93	93	.1	.1
263 Int Foursq Gos	2	103	292	292 *	.2	.3
267 Muslim Est	2	NR	226	909	.5	1.0
283 Luth—MO Synod	8	2,545	1,446	3,337	1.9	3.8
297 Mennonite;Other	1	18	NR	22 *	-	-
306 NT IndBapt&Rltd	1	200	NR	243 *	.1	.3
335 Orth Pres Ch	1	24	36	45	-	.1
355 Presb Ch (USA)	8	1,228	764	1,494 *	.9	1.7
360 Prim Bapt Chrch	1	NR	NR	NR	-	-
388 Reg Bapt Gen As	2	381	286	437 *	.3	.5
413 S.D.A.	3	346	NR	411	.2	.5
418 Southw Bapt Fel	1	NR	NR	NR	-	-
419 So Bapt Conv	24	15,809	3,329	19,243 *	11.2	22.1
435 Unitarian-Univ	1	72	NR	88 *	.1	.1
443 Un C of Christ	14	6,041	2,419	7,353 *	4.3	8.5
449 Un Methodist	18	5,882	3,201	7,160 *	4.2	8.2
463 Vineyard	1	43	30	52 *	-	.1
467 Wesleyan	3	716	179	996	.6	1.1
496 Jewish Est	1	NR	NR	400	.2	.5
VERMILLION	**33**	**3,516**	**1,274**	**5,873 ***	**35.0**	**100.0**
019 Amer Bapt USA	2	679	91	831 *	4.9	14.1
053 Assemb of God	3	134	154	229	1.4	3.9
081 Catholic	2	NR	NR	1,143	6.8	19.5
093 Chr Ch (Disc)	1	182	82	223 *	1.3	3.8
097 Chr Chs&Chs Cr	1	550	NR	673 *	4.0	11.5
127 Ch God (Cleve)	1	60	33	73 *	.4	1.2
151 L-D Saints	1	NR	NR	347	2.1	5.9
165 Ch of Nazarene	4	198	162	270	1.6	4.6
167 Chs of Christ	1	40	53	52	.3	.9
226 Friends-USA	2	149	NR	182 *	1.1	3.1
306 NT IndBapt&Rltd	1	200	NR	245 *	1.5	4.2
355 Presb Ch (USA)	2	182	96	223 *	1.3	3.8
419 So Bapt Conv	1	150	96	184 *	1.1	3.1
449 Un Methodist	10	923	507	1,129 *	6.7	19.2
467 Wesleyan	1	69	0	69	.4	1.2
VIGO	**124**	**18,793**	**10,752**	**36,145 ***	**34.1**	**100.0**
019 Amer Bapt USA	8	2,086	885	2,531 *	2.4	7.0
034 Ant Orth of NA	1	245	NR	490	.5	1.4
053 Assemb of God	8	1,030	1,285	1,835	1.7	5.1
056 Baha'i	0	41	NR	41	-	.1
081 Catholic	9	NR	NR	9,277	8.8	25.7
084 Calvary Chapel	1	NR	NR	NR	-	-
089 Chr & Miss Al	1	21	NR	33	-	.1
093 Chr Ch (Disc)	1	453	112	550 *	.5	1.5
097 Chr Chs&Chs Cr	7	2,417	NR	2,933 *	2.8	8.1
123 Ch God (Ander)	2	NR	40	40	-	.1
127 Ch God (Cleve)	2	115	200	200 *	.2	.6
145 Ch God Prophcy	1	36	NR	43 *	-	.1
151 L-D Saints	2	NR	NR	643	.6	1.8
165 Ch of Nazarene	3	440	371	527	.5	1.5
167 Chs of Christ	8	791	714	906	.9	2.5
175 Congr Chr Chs	2	185	121	224 *	.2	.6
176 Congr Ad Afl	1	100	NR	121 *	.1	.3
193 Episcopal	2	NR	163	379	.4	1.0
207 E.L.C.A.	3	435	221	582	.5	1.6
221 Free Methodist	1	47	96	96	.1	.3
226 Friends-USA	1	47	NR	57 *	.1	.2
263 Int Foursq Gos	2	398	495	495 *	.5	1.4
267 Muslim Est	1	NR	101	288	.3	.8
283 Luth—MO Synod	1	333	164	420	.4	1.2
306 NT IndBapt&Rltd	5	1,000	NR	1,213 *	1.1	3.4
355 Presb Ch (USA)	2	629	290	763 *	.7	2.1
388 Reg Bapt Gen As	2	598	439	726 *	.7	2.0
403 Salvation Army	1	85	66	411	.4	1.1
413 S.D.A.	3	222	NR	264	.2	.7
419 So Bapt Conv	6	1,237	490	1,501 *	1.4	4.2
435 Unitarian-Univ	1	46	NR	56 *	.1	.2
443 Un C of Christ	2	489	198	593 *	.6	1.6
449 Un Methodist	22	4,293	2,413	5,209 *	4.9	14.4
467 Wesleyan	9	343	504	858	.8	2.4
469 WELS	1	46	34	64	.1	.2
496 Jewish Est	1	NR	NR	200	.2	.6
498 Indep.Charis.	1	585	1,350	1,576	1.5	4.4
WABASH	**77**	**10,992**	**5,413**	**17,270 ***	**49.4**	**100.0**
019 Amer Bapt USA	1	50	20	61 *	.2	.4
053 Assemb of God	3	276	325	489	1.4	2.8

NR–Not Reported *Total adherents estimated from known number of communicant, confirmed, full members. - Represents a percentage less than 0.1. Percentages may not total 100 due to rounding.

Table 4: Religious Congregations by County and Group: 2000

Religious Group	Number of Churches, Synagogues, Mosques, or Temples	Number of Communicant, Confirmed, or Full Members	Number of Attendees	Total Adherents: Number of Adherents	Total Adherents: % of Total Pop.	Total Adherents: % of Total Adh.
056 Baha'i	0	1	NR	1	-	-
071 Brethren (Ash)	4	494	474	604 *	1.7	3.5
081 Catholic	2	NR	NR	2,537	7.3	14.7
089 Chr & Miss Al	1	114	NR	212	.6	1.2
093 Chr Ch (Disc)	1	597	137	731 *	2.1	4.2
097 Chr Chs&Chs Cr	10	2,403	NR	2,940 *	8.4	17.0
123 Ch God (Ander)	1	NR	95	95	.3	.6
127 Ch God (Cleve)	1	86	27	105 *	.3	.6
151 L-D Saints	1	NR	NR	471	1.3	2.7
157 Ch of Brethren	5	1,267	621	1,550 *	4.4	9.0
165 Ch of Nazarene	2	148	118	426	1.2	2.5
167 Chs of Christ	2	75	95	107	.3	.6
171 Ch God-Gen Con	1	272	444	444 *	1.3	2.6
175 Congr Chr Chs	1	103	106	126 *	.4	.7
207 E.L.C.A.	2	695	268	882	2.5	5.1
223 Free Will Bapt	3	7	NR	9 *	-	.1
226 Friends-USA	2	94	NR	115 *	.3	.7
283 Luth—MO Synod	1	135	99	189	.5	1.1
291 Missionary Ch	1	142	167	167	.5	1.0
306 NT IndBapt&Rltd	1	200	NR	245 *	.7	1.4
355 Presb Ch (USA)	2	334	126	409 *	1.2	2.4
388 Reg Bapt Gen As	3	408	429	499 *	1.4	2.9
443 Un C of Christ	3	363	186	444 *	1.3	2.6
449 Un Methodist	19	2,660	1,582	3,256 *	9.3	18.9
467 Wesleyan	4	68	94	156	.4	.9
WARREN	**19**	**2,701**	**857**	**3,676 ***	**43.7**	**100.0**
053 Assemb of God	1	23	30	34	.4	.9
081 Catholic	0	NR	NR	233	2.8	6.3
097 Chr Chs&Chs Cr	5	1,318	NR	1,645 *	19.5	44.7
121 Ch God (Abr)	1	30	30	37 *	.4	1.0
151 L-D Saints	1	NR	NR	124	1.5	3.4
165 Ch of Nazarene	1	106	107	187	2.2	5.1
355 Presb Ch (USA)	2	125	72	156 *	1.9	4.2
449 Un Methodist	7	649	338	810 *	9.6	22.0
499 Indep.Non-Char	1	450	280	450	5.3	12.2
WARRICK	**52**	**9,483**	**4,164**	**19,535 ***	**37.3**	**100.0**
019 Amer Bapt USA	2	629	207	790 *	1.5	4.0
053 Assemb of God	2	202	172	274	.5	1.4
081 Catholic	3	NR	NR	6,907	13.2	35.4
097 Chr Chs&Chs Cr	2	759	NR	954 *	1.8	4.9
165 Ch of Nazarene	4	350	373	642	1.2	3.3
167 Chs of Christ	2	215	280	349	.7	1.8
185 Cumber Presb	1	130	NR	344	.7	1.8
207 E.L.C.A.	1	176	93	249	.5	1.3
221 Free Methodist	1	23	35	35	.1	.2
223 Free Will Bapt	1	2	NR	3 *	-	-
283 Luth—MO Synod	1	152	71	235	.4	1.2
355 Presb Ch (USA)	2	364	163	457 *	.9	2.3
365 Prog Prim Bapt	1	25	NR	31 *	.1	.2
388 Reg Bapt Gen As	1	228	244	286 *	.5	1.5
403 Salvation Army	1	183	60	183	.3	.9
413 S.D.A.	1	50	NR	60	.1	.3
419 So Bapt Conv	4	2,035	508	2,557 *	4.9	13.1
443 Un C of Christ	5	1,309	497	1,645 *	3.1	8.4
449 Un Methodist	15	2,610	1,418	3,278 *	6.3	16.8
467 Wesleyan	1	41	43	136	.3	.7
496 Jewish Est	1	NR	NR	120	.2	.6
WASHINGTON	**78**	**9,212**	**3,736**	**12,989 ***	**47.7**	**100.0**
019 Amer Bapt USA	8	1,613	614	2,026 *	7.4	15.6
032 Amish; other	1	65	NR	82 *	.3	.6
053 Assemb of God	2	175	145	275	1.0	2.1
056 Baha'i	0	5	NR	5	-	-
081 Catholic	1	NR	NR	572	2.1	4.4
093 Chr Ch (Disc)	1	829	178	1,041 *	3.8	8.0
097 Chr Chs&Chs Cr	14	2,993	NR	3,760 *	13.8	28.9
123 Ch God (Ander)	1	NR	65	65	.2	.5
127 Ch God (Cleve)	1	9	18	18 *	.1	.1
143 CG in Cr(Menn)	1	52	NR	65 *	.2	.5
145 Ch God Prophcy	1	36	NR	45 *	.2	.3
151 L-D Saints	1	NR	NR	294	1.1	2.3
165 Ch of Nazarene	3	160	137	430	1.6	3.3
167 Chs of Christ	15	1,208	1,455	1,619	5.9	12.5
226 Friends-USA	1	102	NR	128 *	.5	1.0
283 Luth—MO Synod	1	35	35	43	.2	.3
323 Old Ord Amish	2	120	NR	150 *	.6	1.2
355 Presb Ch (USA)	2	183	95	229 *	.8	1.8
360 Prim Bapt Chrch	4	NR	NR	NR	-	-
388 Reg Bapt Gen As	1	42	50	53 *	.2	.4
419 So Bapt Conv	4	610	350	766 *	2.8	5.9
449 Un Methodist	11	910	509	1,143 *	4.2	8.8
467 Wesleyan	2	65	85	180	.7	1.4
WAYNE	**117**	**17,403**	**7,305**	**29,229 ***	**41.1**	**100.0**
011 A.W.M.C.	1	11	50	11	-	-
019 Amer Bapt USA	3	1,494	584	1,835 *	2.6	6.3
053 Assemb of God	4	523	536	747	1.1	2.6
056 Baha'i	0	26	NR	26	-	.1
081 Catholic	4	NR	NR	5,497	7.7	18.8
089 Chr & Miss Al	1	17	NR	49	.1	.2
093 Chr Ch (Disc)	2	897	257	1,102 *	1.5	3.8
097 Chr Chs&Chs Cr	11	2,492	NR	3,060 *	4.3	10.5
123 Ch God (Ander)	2	NR	56	56	.1	.2
127 Ch God (Cleve)	1	815	150	1,001 *	1.4	3.4
151 L-D Saints	1	NR	NR	475	.7	1.6
157 Ch of Brethren	3	221	182	273 *	.4	.9
165 Ch of Nazarene	8	803	510	1,230	1.7	4.2
167 Chs of Christ	5	203	218	268	.4	.9
193 Episcopal	1	NR	69	204	.3	.7
207 E.L.C.A.	6	1,811	834	2,341	3.3	8.0
226 Friends-USA	16	763	NR	937 *	1.3	3.2
263 Int Foursq Gos	1	33	67	67 *	.1	.2
306 NT IndBapt&Rltd	2	400	NR	491 *	.7	1.7
323 Old Ord Amish	2	135	NR	166 *	.2	.6
355 Presb Ch (USA)	4	619	321	760 *	1.1	2.6
356 Presb Ch Amer	1	186	166	228	.3	.8
360 Prim Bapt Chrch	1	NR	NR	NR	-	-
388 Reg Bapt Gen As	1	90	80	80 *	.1	.3
403 Salvation Army	1	162	38	139	.2	.5
413 S.D.A.	1	147	NR	175	.2	.6
419 So Bapt Conv	12	2,119	778	2,603 *	3.7	8.9
443 Un C of Christ	1	131	65	161 *	.2	.6
449 Un Methodist	18	3,008	1,467	3,694 *	5.2	12.6
467 Wesleyan	2	297	877	1,423	2.0	4.9
496 Jewish Est	1	NR	NR	130	.2	.4
WELLS	**45**	**7,695**	**6,332**	**16,635 ***	**60.3**	**100.0**
019 Amer Bapt USA	3	400	167	504 *	1.8	3.0
040 Ap Chr Ch-Amer	2	1,340	2,175	2,175 *	7.9	13.1
056 Baha'i	0	4	NR	4	-	-
081 Catholic	3	NR	NR	4,899	17.8	29.4
097 Chr Chs&Chs Cr	2	600	NR	756 *	2.7	4.5
127 Ch God (Cleve)	1	130	37	164 *	.6	1.0
151 L-D Saints	1	NR	NR	189	.7	1.1
165 Ch of Nazarene	2	416	445	697	2.5	4.2
167 Chs of Christ	1	30	40	65	.2	.4
207 E.L.C.A.	3	635	222	918	3.3	5.5
226 Friends-USA	1	47	NR	59 *	.2	.4
283 Luth—MO Synod	2	540	322	728	2.6	4.4
291 Missionary Ch	2	254	644	644	2.3	3.9
355 Presb Ch (USA)	2	555	277	700 *	2.5	4.2
443 Un C of Christ	2	591	235	745 *	2.7	4.5
449 Un Methodist	16	1,920	1,356	2,418 *	8.8	14.5
467 Wesleyan	2	233	412	970	3.5	5.8
WHITE	**45**	**6,178**	**3,114**	**9,599 ***	**38.0**	**100.0**
019 Amer Bapt USA	7	1,033	446	1,283 *	5.1	13.4
040 Ap Chr Ch-Amer	1	98	187	187 *	.7	1.9
053 Assemb of God	2	192	255	383	1.5	4.0
056 Baha'i	0	6	NR	6	-	.1
081 Catholic	2	NR	NR	1,606	6.4	16.7
093 Chr Ch (Disc)	3	841	370	1,045 *	4.1	10.9
097 Chr Chs&Chs Cr	3	490	NR	609 *	2.4	6.3
157 Ch of Brethren	4	181	33	225 *	.9	2.3

NR–Not Reported *Total adherents estimated from known number of communicant, confirmed, full members. - Represents a percentage less than 0.1. Percentages may not total 100 due to rounding.

Table 4: Religious Congregations by County and Group: 2000

Religious Group	Number of Churches, Synagogues, Mosques, or Temples	Number of Communicant, Confirmed, or Full Members	Number of Attendees	Total Adherents: Number of Adherents	Total Adherents: % of Total Pop.	Total Adherents: % of Total Adh.
167 Chs of Christ	2	78	100	118	.5	1.2
171 Ch God-Gen Con	2	255	204	317 *	1.3	3.3
193 Episcopal	1	NR	11	15	.1	.2
207 E.L.C.A.	1	272	134	344	1.4	3.6
283 Luth—MO Synod	2	482	166	630	2.5	6.6
306 NT IndBapt&Rltd	1	200	NR	248 *	1.0	2.6
355 Presb Ch (USA)	3	463	278	576 *	2.3	6.0
413 S.D.A.	1	42	NR	50	.2	.5
419 So Bapt Conv	1	90	65	112 *	.4	1.2
449 Un Methodist	8	1,422	807	1,768 *	7.0	18.4
467 Wesleyan	1	33	58	77	.3	.8
WHITLEY	**54**	**6,983**	**5,476**	**13,025 ***	**42.4**	**100.0**
019 Amer Bapt USA	1	255	78	321 *	1.0	2.5
053 Assemb of God	1	31	40	80	.3	.6
056 Baha'i	0	1	NR	1	-	-
081 Catholic	3	NR	NR	2,646	8.6	20.3
097 Chr Chs&Chs Cr	1	75	NR	94 *	.3	.7
123 Ch God (Ander)	2	NR	373	373	1.2	2.9
127 Ch God (Cleve)	1	38	24	48 *	.2	.4
151 L-D Saints	1	NR	NR	178	.6	1.4
157 Ch of Brethren	4	340	279	427 *	1.4	3.3
165 Ch of Nazarene	2	431	395	846	2.8	6.5
167 Chs of Christ	1	39	65	62	.2	.5
171 Ch God-Gen Con	6	1,085	1,053	1,376 *	4.5	10.6
207 E.L.C.A.	3	742	342	969	3.2	7.4
216 Evan Presby Ch	1	122	NR	153 *	.5	1.2
223 Free Will Bapt	1	2	NR	3 *	-	-
283 Luth—MO Synod	3	889	414	1,204	3.9	9.2
291 Missionary Ch	1	34	40	40	.1	.3
323 Old Ord Amish	1	60	NR	75 *	.2	.6
339 Pent Ch of God	1	8	NR	28	.1	.2
355 Presb Ch (USA)	2	270	162	340 *	1.1	2.6
388 Reg Bapt Gen As	3	472	477	556 *	1.8	4.3
419 So Bapt Conv	0	6	6	8 *	-	.1
449 Un Methodist	12	1,915	1,400	2,407 *	7.8	18.5
467 Wesleyan	3	168	328	790	2.6	6.1

IOWA

Religious Group	Number of Churches, Synagogues, Mosques, or Temples	Number of Communicant, Confirmed, or Full Members	Number of Attendees	Total Adherents: Number of Adherents	Total Adherents: % of Total Pop.	Total Adherents: % of Total Adh.
The State.....	4,584	838,132	403,602	1,711,426 *	58.5	100.0
ADAIR	**19**	**3,162**	**1,181**	**5,597 ***	**67.9**	**100.0**
081 Catholic	2	NR	NR	1,003	12.2	17.9
203 Evan Free Ch	1	69	125	125	1.5	2.2
207 E.L.C.A.	2	728	210	978	11.9	17.5
226 Friends-USA	1	64	NR	78 *	.9	1.4
283 Luth—MO Synod	2	531	237	1,268	15.4	22.7
355 Presb Ch (USA)	2	166	89	201 *	2.4	3.6
449 Un Methodist	9	1,604	520	1,944 *	23.6	34.7
ADAMS	**16**	**1,193**	**476**	**1,999 ***	**44.6**	**100.0**
053 Assemb of God	1	34	47	112	2.5	5.6
056 Baha'i	0	2	NR	2	-	.1
081 Catholic	1	NR	NR	444	9.9	22.2
093 Chr Ch (Disc)	2	63	0	77 *	1.7	3.9
157 Ch of Brethren	1	21	21	26 *	.6	1.3
207 E.L.C.A.	1	98	30	130	2.9	6.5
283 Luth—MO Synod	1	146	60	194	4.3	9.7
355 Presb Ch (USA)	1	234	90	285 *	6.4	14.3
388 Reg Bapt Gen As	1	25	35	35 *	.8	1.8
449 Un Methodist	7	570	193	694 *	15.5	34.7
ALLAMAKEE	**40**	**5,507**	**2,235**	**13,916 ***	**94.8**	**100.0**
053 Assemb of God	1	107	157	212	1.4	1.5
056 Baha'i	0	4	NR	4	-	-
057 Bapt Gen Conf	1	84	25	104 *	.7	.7
076 Buddhism	1	NR	NR	NR	-	-
081 Catholic	10	NR	NR	6,711	45.7	48.2
151 L-D Saints	1	NR	NR	150	1.0	1.1
203 Evan Free Ch	1	69	125	125	.9	.9
207 E.L.C.A.	7	2,860	886	3,522	24.0	25.3
323 Old Ord Amish	1	55	NR	68 *	.5	.5
355 Presb Ch (USA)	7	975	461	1,202 *	8.2	8.6
413 S.D.A.	1	46	NR	55	.4	.4
443 Un C of Christ	4	826	326	1,019 *	6.9	7.3
449 Un Methodist	4	481	255	594 *	4.0	4.3
496 Jewish Est	1	NR	NR	150	1.0	1.1
APPANOOSE	**31**	**3,101**	**1,362**	**5,490 ***	**40.0**	**100.0**
019 Amer Bapt USA	1	295	177	359 *	2.6	6.5
053 Assemb of God	1	40	29	48	.3	.9
056 Baha'i	0	1	NR	1	-	-
081 Catholic	1	NR	NR	1,509	11.0	27.5
093 Chr Ch (Disc)	2	818	180	995 *	7.3	18.1
097 Chr Chs&Chs Cr	5	260	NR	317 *	2.3	5.8
123 Ch God (Ander)	1	NR	25	25	.2	.5
127 Ch God (Cleve)	1	123	104	150 *	1.1	2.7
151 L-D Saints	1	NR	NR	66	.5	1.2
157 Ch of Brethren	1	47	0	57 *	.4	1.0
165 Ch of Nazarene	2	170	276	326	2.4	5.9
173 Comm of Christ	1	22	NR	22	.2	.4
193 Episcopal	1	NR	5	3	-	.1
201 Evan Cov Ch	1	42	31	51 *	.4	.9
207 E.L.C.A.	1	110	51	134	1.0	2.4
355 Presb Ch (USA)	1	102	53	124 *	.9	2.3
388 Reg Bapt Gen As	1	35	40	43 *	.3	.8
413 S.D.A.	1	40	NR	48	.3	.9
419 So Bapt Conv	1	38	12	46 *	.3	.8
449 Un Methodist	7	958	379	1,166 *	8.5	21.2
AUDUBON	**23**	**3,851**	**1,445**	**5,665 ***	**82.9**	**100.0**
053 Assemb of God	1	30	40	59	.9	1.0
081 Catholic	2	NR	NR	815	11.9	14.4
093 Chr Ch (Disc)	1	262	65	324 *	4.7	5.7
097 Chr Chs&Chs Cr	1	100	NR	124 *	1.8	2.2
203 Evan Free Ch	1	69	125	125	1.8	2.2
207 E.L.C.A.	7	1,934	629	2,442	35.8	43.1
283 Luth—MO Synod	2	355	137	445	6.5	7.9
355 Presb Ch (USA)	1	214	104	265 *	3.9	4.7
388 Reg Bapt Gen As	1	100	95	95 *	1.4	1.7
413 S.D.A.	2	41	NR	49	.7	.9
443 Un C of Christ	1	55	24	68 *	1.0	1.2
449 Un Methodist	3	691	226	854 *	12.5	15.1
BENTON	**46**	**7,498**	**3,508**	**14,654 ***	**57.9**	**100.0**
019 Amer Bapt USA	2	141	75	178 *	.7	1.2
053 Assemb of God	1	36	49	83	.3	.6
056 Baha'i	0	3	NR	3	-	-
081 Catholic	8	NR	NR	4,785	18.9	32.7
093 Chr Ch (Disc)	2	416	166	526 *	2.1	3.6
121 Ch God (Abr)	2	50	55	93 *	.4	.6
151 L-D Saints	1	NR	NR	105	.4	.7
203 Evan Free Ch	1	69	125	125	.5	.9
207 E.L.C.A.	2	521	283	734	2.9	5.0
263 Int Foursq Gos	1	50	65	65 *	.3	.4
283 Luth—MO Synod	10	3,544	1,526	4,584	18.1	31.3
355 Presb Ch (USA)	5	1,001	439	1,265 *	5.0	8.6
443 Un C of Christ	1	102	55	129 *	.5	.9
449 Un Methodist	10	1,565	670	1,979 *	7.8	13.5
BLACK HAWK	**135**	**35,482**	**19,041**	**75,812 ***	**59.2**	**100.0**
019 Amer Bapt USA	3	1,015	347	1,232 *	1.0	1.6
053 Assemb of God	5	456	634	920	.7	1.2
056 Baha'i	1	46	NR	46	-	.1
057 Bapt Gen Conf	2	851	628	1,033 *	.8	1.4
071 Brethren (Ash)	1	81	48	98 *	.1	.1
081 Catholic	15	NR	NR	25,505	19.9	33.6
093 Chr Ch (Disc)	2	848	301	1,029 *	.8	1.4
097 Chr Chs&Chs Cr	3	309	NR	375 *	.3	.5
105 Christian Ref	1	68	35	83 *	.1	.1
121 Ch God (Abr)	1	15	16	18 *	-	-
151 L-D Saints	2	NR	NR	779	.6	1.0

NR–Not Reported   *Total adherents estimated from known number of communicant, confirmed, full members.   - Represents a percentage less than 0.1.   Percentages may not total 100 due to rounding.

Table 4: Religious Congregations by County and Group: 2000

Religious Group	Number of Churches, Synagogues, Mosques, or Temples	Number of Communicant, Confirmed, or Full Members	Number of Attendees	Total Adherents: Number of Adherents	Total Adherents: % of Total Pop.	Total Adherents: % of Total Adh.
157 Ch of Brethren	2	416	180	505 *	.4	.7
165 Ch of Nazarene	2	177	141	404	.3	.5
167 Chs of Christ	2	112	112	158	.1	.2
173 Comm of Christ	1	79	NR	79	.1	.1
193 Episcopal	2	NR	199	519	.4	.7
203 Evan Free Ch	1	55	95	95	.1	.1
207 E.L.C.A.	17	10,720	4,639	14,442	11.3	19.0
221 Free Methodist	1	33	23	34	-	-
246 Greek Orthodox	1	NR	NR	132	.1	.2
262 Int Cou Comm Ch	1	896	NR	1,087 *	.8	1.4
263 Int Foursq Gos	2	69	107	107 *	.1	.1
267 Muslim Est	1	NR	101	288	.2	.4
283 Luth—MO Synod	8	2,714	1,112	4,539	3.5	6.0
288 Mennonite USA	1	35	40	42 *	-	.1
313 N Am Bapt Conf	1	33	48	40 *	-	.1
335 Orth Pres Ch	1	18	16	22	-	-
355 Presb Ch (USA)	10	2,751	1,197	3,337 *	2.6	4.4
371 Ref Ch in Am	3	1,059	1,209	2,086	1.6	2.8
388 Reg Bapt Gen As	5	1,510	1,164	1,834 *	1.4	2.4
403 Salvation Army	1	277	341	560	.4	.7
413 S.D.A.	1	127	NR	151	.1	.2
419 So Bapt Conv	5	446	238	541 *	.4	.7
435 Unitarian-Univ	1	118	NR	143 *	.1	.2
443 Un C of Christ	3	767	280	931 *	.7	1.2
449 Un Methodist	16	5,553	2,203	6,739 *	5.3	8.9
463 Vineyard	1	350	749	749 *	.6	1.0
467 Wesleyan	6	2,138	1,668	3,560	2.8	4.7
496 Jewish Est	1	NR	NR	170	.1	.2
499 Indep.Non-Char	2	1,340	1,170	1,400	1.1	1.8
BOONE	**44**	**8,545**	**3,477**	**14,325 ***	**54.6**	**100.0**
019 Amer Bapt USA	2	513	142	631 *	2.4	4.4
053 Assemb of God	1	32	41	48	.2	.3
056 Baha'i	0	14	NR	14	.1	.1
081 Catholic	3	NR	NR	3,172	12.1	22.1
089 Chr & Miss Al	2	200	NR	427	1.6	3.0
093 Chr Ch (Disc)	2	856	130	1,052 *	4.0	7.3
123 Ch God (Ander)	1	NR	15	15	.1	.1
145 Ch God Prophcy	1	34	NR	42 *	.2	.3
151 L-D Saints	1	NR	NR	248	.9	1.7
157 Ch of Brethren	1	30	10	37 *	.1	.3
165 Ch of Nazarene	1	30	13	39	.1	.3
167 Chs of Christ	1	55	80	90	.3	.6
193 Episcopal	1	NR	31	96	.4	.7
203 Evan Free Ch	3	389	604	604	2.3	4.2
207 E.L.C.A.	4	2,065	763	2,575	9.8	18.0
283 Luth—MO Synod	3	1,371	643	1,709	6.5	11.9
306 NT IndBapt&Rltd	1	35	NR	43 *	.2	.3
355 Presb Ch (USA)	1	303	118	373 *	1.4	2.6
363 Primitive Meth	2	114	NR	121	.5	.8
403 Salvation Army	1	115	49	53	.2	.4
413 S.D.A.	1	30	NR	36	.1	.3
443 Un C of Christ	2	331	145	407 *	1.6	2.8
449 Un Methodist	9	2,028	693	2,493 *	9.5	17.4
BREMER	**45**	**12,380**	**5,353**	**19,215 ***	**82.4**	**100.0**
019 Amer Bapt USA	1	163	64	198 *	.8	1.0
053 Assemb of God	1	22	10	21	.1	.1
056 Baha'i	0	11	NR	11	-	.1
057 Bapt Gen Conf	2	195	246	246 *	1.1	1.3
081 Catholic	3	NR	NR	3,512	15.1	18.3
151 L-D Saints	1	NR	NR	101	.4	.5
165 Ch of Nazarene	1	51	42	107	.5	.6
193 Episcopal	1	NR	11	24	.1	.1
207 E.L.C.A.	12	6,349	2,447	8,135	34.9	42.3
283 Luth—MO Synod	7	1,824	822	2,221	9.5	11.6
313 N Am Bapt Conf	1	80	30	97 *	.4	.5
388 Reg Bapt Gen As	2	151	202	244 *	1.0	1.3
443 Un C of Christ	5	1,246	503	1,515 *	6.5	7.9
449 Un Methodist	7	2,248	936	2,734 *	11.7	14.2
463 Vineyard	1	40	40	49 *	.2	.3

Religious Group	Number of Churches, Synagogues, Mosques, or Temples	Number of Communicant, Confirmed, or Full Members	Number of Attendees	Total Adherents: Number of Adherents	Total Adherents: % of Total Pop.	Total Adherents: % of Total Adh.
BUCHANAN	**46**	**5,872**	**2,217**	**14,847 ***	**70.4**	**100.0**
019 Amer Bapt USA	3	202	73	257 *	1.2	1.7
056 Baha'i	0	3	NR	3	-	-
081 Catholic	8	NR	NR	7,173	34.0	48.3
097 Chr Chs&Chs Cr	1	40	NR	51 *	.2	.3
193 Episcopal	1	NR	13	17	.1	.1
207 E.L.C.A.	3	1,473	519	1,929	9.1	13.0
220 Free Lutheran	1	115	60	127	.6	.9
262 Int Cou Comm Ch	1	190	NR	241 *	1.1	1.6
263 Int Foursq Gos	1	163	140	207 *	1.0	1.4
283 Luth—MO Synod	3	513	189	634	3.0	4.3
323 Old Ord Amish	6	330	NR	420 *	2.0	2.8
335 Orth Pres Ch	1	34	36	37	.2	.2
355 Presb Ch (USA)	5	633	279	804 *	3.8	5.4
419 So Bapt Conv	1	43	41	55 *	.3	.4
443 Un C of Christ	1	162	71	206 *	1.0	1.4
449 Un Methodist	9	1,863	680	2,369 *	11.2	16.0
467 Wesleyan	1	108	116	317	1.5	2.1
BUENA VISTA	**43**	**8,803**	**3,848**	**13,655 ***	**66.9**	**100.0**
019 Amer Bapt USA	1	145	49	179 *	.9	1.3
053 Assemb of God	1	38	53	82	.4	.6
056 Baha'i	0	12	NR	12	.1	.1
081 Catholic	2	NR	NR	2,518	12.3	18.4
097 Chr Chs&Chs Cr	2	315	NR	390 *	1.9	2.9
193 Episcopal	1	NR	31	71	.3	.5
201 Evan Cov Ch	1	146	117	180 *	.9	1.3
203 Evan Free Ch	3	200	430	430	2.1	3.1
207 E.L.C.A.	10	2,598	814	3,158	15.5	23.1
283 Luth—MO Synod	7	2,134	1,016	2,665	13.1	19.5
349 Pent Holiness	1	38	82	47 *	.2	.3
355 Presb Ch (USA)	3	1,007	344	1,244 *	6.1	9.1
419 So Bapt Conv	1	78	65	96 *	.5	.7
443 Un C of Christ	4	344	163	425 *	2.1	3.1
449 Un Methodist	6	1,748	684	2,158 *	10.6	15.8
BUTLER	**46**	**8,280**	**3,983**	**11,900 ***	**77.8**	**100.0**
081 Catholic	3	NR	NR	1,030	6.7	8.7
097 Chr Chs&Chs Cr	2	130	NR	158 *	1.0	1.3
105 Christian Ref	2	362	243	442 *	2.9	3.7
151 L-D Saints	1	NR	NR	132	.9	1.1
157 Ch of Brethren	1	40	21	49 *	.3	.4
181 Consrv Congr	1	314	213	383 *	2.5	3.2
207 E.L.C.A.	7	3,068	1,150	3,864	25.2	32.5
283 Luth—MO Synod	1	112	22	134	.9	1.1
313 N Am Bapt Conf	2	329	191	401 *	2.6	3.4
355 Presb Ch (USA)	4	497	312	607 *	4.0	5.1
371 Ref Ch in Am	6	1,012	774	1,714	11.2	14.4
388 Reg Bapt Gen As	3	103	110	135 *	.9	1.1
443 Un C of Christ	4	953	373	1,162 *	7.6	9.8
449 Un Methodist	8	1,336	537	1,629 *	10.6	13.7
467 Wesleyan	1	24	37	60	.4	.5
CALHOUN	**36**	**6,167**	**2,302**	**9,381 ***	**84.4**	**100.0**
019 Amer Bapt USA	1	140	31	168 *	1.5	1.8
081 Catholic	5	NR	NR	1,828	16.4	19.5
093 Chr Ch (Disc)	2	567	120	680 *	6.1	7.2
097 Chr Chs&Chs Cr	1	150	NR	180 *	1.6	1.9
201 Evan Cov Ch	1	190	115	228 *	2.1	2.4
203 Evan Free Ch	1	0	60	60	.5	.6
207 E.L.C.A.	4	1,869	627	2,302	20.7	24.5
283 Luth—MO Synod	5	1,174	546	1,444	13.0	15.4
288 Mennonite USA	1	131	96	157 *	1.4	1.7
355 Presb Ch (USA)	2	254	95	305 *	2.7	3.3
413 S.D.A.	1	28	NR	33	.3	.4
443 Un C of Christ	3	267	118	320 *	2.9	3.4
449 Un Methodist	9	1,397	494	1,676 *	15.1	17.9
CARROLL	**42**	**5,175**	**2,225**	**18,381 ***	**85.8**	**100.0**
053 Assemb of God	1	74	113	116	.5	.6
056 Baha'i	0	1	NR	1	-	-
081 Catholic	15	NR	NR	11,722	54.7	63.8

NR–Not Reported *Total adherents estimated from known number of communicant, confirmed, full members. - Represents a percentage less than 0.1. Percentages may not total 100 due to rounding.

Table 4: Religious Congregations by County and Group: 2000

Religious Group	Number of Churches, Synagogues, Mosques, or Temples	Number of Communicant, Confirmed, or Full Members	Number of Attendees	Total Adherents		
				Number of Adherents	% of Total Pop.	% of Total Adh.
093 Chr Ch (Disc)	1	259	60	322 *	1.5	1.8
097 Chr Chs&Chs Cr	1	113	NR	141 *	.7	.8
151 L-D Saints	2	NR	NR	103	.5	.6
193 Episcopal	1	NR	10	13	.1	.1
207 E.L.C.A.	2	389	201	513	2.4	2.8
226 Friends-USA	2	128	NR	159 *	.7	.9
283 Luth—MO Synod	5	2,073	972	2,613	12.2	14.2
355 Presb Ch (USA)	5	539	203	672 *	3.1	3.7
388 Reg Bapt Gen As	2	110	145	153 *	.7	.8
449 Un Methodist	5	1,489	521	1,853 *	8.7	10.1
CASS	**41**	**6,991**	**2,479**	**10,743 ***	**73.2**	**100.0**
019 Amer Bapt USA	1	105	27	127 *	.9	1.2
053 Assemb of God	1	102	134	179	1.2	1.7
081 Catholic	5	NR	NR	1,853	12.6	17.2
093 Chr Ch (Disc)	1	633	156	768 *	5.2	7.1
097 Chr Chs&Chs Cr	4	655	NR	794 *	5.4	7.4
145 Ch God Prophcy	1	34	NR	42 *	.3	.4
151 L-D Saints	1	NR	NR	162	1.1	1.5
165 Ch of Nazarene	1	34	18	34	.2	.3
167 Chs of Christ	1	20	18	30	.2	.3
203 Evan Free Ch	1	70	200	200	1.4	1.9
207 E.L.C.A.	2	860	366	1,066	7.3	9.9
283 Luth—MO Synod	3	1,204	330	1,519	10.3	14.1
355 Presb Ch (USA)	1	316	143	383 *	2.6	3.6
388 Reg Bapt Gen As	1	35	40	42 *	.3	.4
413 S.D.A.	1	51	NR	61	.4	.6
443 Un C of Christ	5	813	315	986 *	6.7	9.2
449 Un Methodist	11	2,059	732	2,497 *	17.0	23.2
CEDAR	**32**	**5,640**	**1,946**	**9,370 ***	**51.5**	**100.0**
019 Amer Bapt USA	1	51	20	63 *	.3	.7
056 Baha'i	0	4	NR	4	-	-
081 Catholic	3	NR	NR	2,019	11.1	21.5
193 Episcopal	1	NR	54	173	1.0	1.8
207 E.L.C.A.	3	1,054	359	1,529	8.4	16.3
226 Friends-USA	4	226	NR	278 *	1.5	3.0
263 Int Foursq Gos	1	37	74	74 *	.4	.8
283 Luth—MO Synod	3	679	300	807	4.4	8.6
355 Presb Ch (USA)	3	203	95	251 *	1.4	2.7
388 Reg Bapt Gen As	1	68	40	84 *	.5	.9
443 Un C of Christ	4	1,648	519	2,030 *	11.2	21.7
449 Un Methodist	8	1,670	485	2,058 *	11.3	22.0
CERRO GORDO	**58**	**16,401**	**6,760**	**31,204 ***	**67.2**	**100.0**
019 Amer Bapt USA	1	190	135	232 *	.5	.7
053 Assemb of God	1	147	185	450	1.0	1.4
056 Baha'i	0	11	NR	11	-	-
081 Catholic	6	NR	NR	8,893	19.1	28.5
089 Chr & Miss Al	1	35	NR	65	.1	.2
093 Chr Ch (Disc)	2	444	80	541 *	1.2	1.7
097 Chr Chs&Chs Cr	2	227	NR	276 *	.6	.9
105 Christian Ref	1	197	155	240 *	.5	.8
165 Ch of Nazarene	1	79	71	103	.2	.3
167 Chs of Christ	1	34	27	45	.1	.1
173 Comm of Christ	1	39	NR	39	.1	.1
175 Congr Chr Chs	1	272	80	331 *	.7	1.1
176 Congr Ad Afl	1	100	NR	122 *	.3	.4
193 Episcopal	1	NR	114	332	.7	1.1
201 Evan Cov Ch	1	238	243	290 *	.6	.9
203 Evan Free Ch	2	340	538	538	1.2	1.7
207 E.L.C.A.	8	7,090	2,355	9,378	20.2	30.1
221 Free Methodist	1	18	21	21	-	.1
226 Friends-USA	1	64	NR	78 *	.2	.2
246 Greek Orthodox	1	NR	NR	465	1.0	1.5
283 Luth—MO Synod	3	933	430	1,223	2.6	3.9
355 Presb Ch (USA)	1	423	150	515 *	1.1	1.7
371 Ref Ch in Am	1	166	150	313	.7	1.0
388 Reg Bapt Gen As	2	313	325	383 *	.8	1.2
403 Salvation Army	1	130	53	341	.7	1.1
413 S.D.A.	1	103	NR	123	.3	.4
419 So Bapt Conv	1	34	33	41 *	.1	.1
435 Unitarian-Univ	1	12	NR	15 *	-	-
443 Un C of Christ	1	307	123	374 *	.8	1.2
449 Un Methodist	11	4,346	1,457	5,297 *	11.4	17.0
469 WELS	1	109	35	129	.3	.4
CHEROKEE	**34**	**5,756**	**2,415**	**9,972 ***	**76.5**	**100.0**
019 Amer Bapt USA	2	75	39	91 *	.7	.9
056 Baha'i	0	2	NR	2	-	-
081 Catholic	4	NR	NR	2,762	21.2	27.7
084 Calvary Chapel	1	NR	NR	NR	-	-
093 Chr Ch (Disc)	1	1	0	1 *	-	-
097 Chr Chs&Chs Cr	1	400	NR	487 *	3.7	4.9
173 Comm of Christ	1	59	NR	59	.5	.6
181 Consrv Congr	1	90	60	110 *	.8	1.1
203 Evan Free Ch	2	235	360	360	2.8	3.6
207 E.L.C.A.	2	882	344	1,132	8.7	11.4
283 Luth—MO Synod	5	1,509	683	1,919	14.7	19.2
306 NT IndBapt&Rltd	1	25	NR	30 *	.2	.3
355 Presb Ch (USA)	3	528	252	643 *	4.9	6.4
413 S.D.A.	1	15	NR	18	.1	.2
419 So Bapt Conv	1	59	35	72 *	.6	.7
443 Un C of Christ	1	72	32	88 *	.7	.9
449 Un Methodist	7	1,804	610	2,198 *	16.9	22.0
CHICKASAW	**28**	**4,525**	**1,604**	**12,005 ***	**91.7**	**100.0**
019 Amer Bapt USA	2	349	169	432 *	3.3	3.6
081 Catholic	9	NR	NR	6,461	49.3	53.8
157 Ch of Brethren	1	237	70	293 *	2.2	2.4
176 Congr Ad Afl	1	101	NR	125 *	1.0	1.0
207 E.L.C.A.	5	2,195	712	2,654	20.3	22.1
283 Luth—MO Synod	1	193	103	245	1.9	2.0
443 Un C of Christ	4	540	227	669 *	5.1	5.6
449 Un Methodist	5	910	323	1,126 *	8.6	9.4
CLARKE	**18**	**2,339**	**898**	**3,736 ***	**40.9**	**100.0**
053 Assemb of God	1	141	169	317	3.5	8.5
056 Baha'i	0	1	NR	1	-	-
081 Catholic	1	NR	NR	450	4.9	12.0
093 Chr Ch (Disc)	2	715	186	890 *	9.7	23.8
097 Chr Chs&Chs Cr	1	350	NR	435 *	4.8	11.6
107 Christian Un	1	25	20	31 *	.3	.8
167 Chs of Christ	1	62	70	86	.9	2.3
173 Comm of Christ	1	78	NR	78	.9	2.1
203 Evan Free Ch	1	27	73	73	.8	2.0
283 Luth—MO Synod	1	3	105	200	2.2	5.4
388 Reg Bapt Gen As	1	23	40	40 *	.4	1.1
413 S.D.A.	1	39	NR	46	.5	1.2
419 So Bapt Conv	1	55	15	68 *	.7	1.8
449 Un Methodist	5	820	220	1,021 *	11.2	27.3
CLAY	**37**	**6,955**	**3,263**	**11,794 ***	**67.9**	**100.0**
019 Amer Bapt USA	1	50	35	61 *	.4	.5
053 Assemb of God	1	71	85	165	.9	1.4
056 Baha'i	0	21	NR	21	.1	.2
081 Catholic	3	NR	NR	2,370	13.6	20.1
093 Chr Ch (Disc)	1	314	129	385 *	2.2	3.3
151 L-D Saints	1	NR	NR	142	.8	1.2
165 Ch of Nazarene	1	32	32	35	.2	.3
167 Chs of Christ	1	28	30	36	.2	.3
171 Ch God-Gen Con	1	23	45	45 *	.3	.4
175 Congr Chr Chs	3	539	231	661 *	3.8	5.6
203 Evan Free Ch	1	69	125	125	.7	1.1
207 E.L.C.A.	4	1,865	773	2,422	13.9	20.5
283 Luth—MO Synod	3	1,165	356	1,540	8.9	13.1
371 Ref Ch in Am	2	478	322	816	4.7	6.9
413 S.D.A.	1	73	NR	87	.5	.7
419 So Bapt Conv	1	87	34	107 *	.6	.9
443 Un C of Christ	1	49	25	60 *	.3	.5
449 Un Methodist	10	1,928	741	2,366 *	13.6	20.1
499 Indep.Non-Char	1	163	300	350	2.0	3.0
CLAYTON	**45**	**7,440**	**2,818**	**15,282 ***	**81.8**	**100.0**
081 Catholic	9	NR	NR	6,029	32.3	39.5

NR–Not Reported *Total adherents estimated from known number of communicant, confirmed, full members. - Represents a percentage less than 0.1. Percentages may not total 100 due to rounding.

Table 4: Religious Congregations by County and Group: 2000

Religious Group	Number of Churches, Synagogues, Mosques, or Temples	Number of Communicant, Confirmed, or Full Members	Number of Attendees	Total Adherents: Number of Adherents	Total Adherents: % of Total Pop.	Total Adherents: % of Total Adh.
175 Congr Chr Chs	3	143	95	176 *	.9	1.2
203 Evan Free Ch	1	69	118	118	.6	.8
207 E.L.C.A.	20	4,925	1,732	6,123	32.8	40.1
283 Luth—MO Synod	2	287	130	352	1.9	2.3
323 Old Ord Amish	1	55	NR	68 *	.4	.4
388 Reg Bapt Gen As	1	30	40	40 *	.2	.3
443 Un C of Christ	2	641	224	789 *	4.2	5.2
449 Un Methodist	6	1,290	479	1,587 *	8.5	10.4
CLINTON	**68**	**11,754**	**5,768**	**26,894 ***	**53.6**	**100.0**
019 Amer Bapt USA	2	263	208	326 *	.7	1.2
053 Assemb of God	2	73	103	191	.4	.7
056 Baha'i	0	16	NR	16	-	.1
081 Catholic	9	NR	NR	10,581	21.1	39.3
097 Chr Chs&Chs Cr	2	296	NR	367 *	.7	1.4
123 Ch God (Ander)	1	NR	14	14	-	.1
151 L-D Saints	1	NR	NR	247	.5	.9
165 Ch of Nazarene	1	31	10	94	.2	.3
167 Chs of Christ	1	55	48	62	.1	.2
173 Comm of Christ	1	64	NR	64	.1	.2
193 Episcopal	2	NR	99	503	1.0	1.9
203 Evan Free Ch	2	173	380	380	.8	1.4
207 E.L.C.A.	11	2,995	1,046	4,054	8.1	15.1
220 Free Lutheran	1	166	124	213	.4	.8
263 Int Foursq Gos	1	560	661	695 *	1.4	2.6
267 Muslim Est	1	NR	15	60	.1	.2
283 Luth—MO Synod	5	2,500	1,185	3,317	6.6	12.3
355 Presb Ch (USA)	3	422	178	524 *	1.0	1.9
371 Ref Ch in Am	1	111	92	201	.4	.7
403 Salvation Army	1	122	144	141	.3	.5
413 S.D.A.	1	63	NR	75	.1	.3
419 So Bapt Conv	3	354	146	439 *	.9	1.6
435 Unitarian-Univ	1	19	NR	24 *	-	.1
443 Un C of Christ	5	1,379	432	1,711 *	3.4	6.4
449 Un Methodist	10	2,092	883	2,595 *	5.2	9.6
CRAWFORD	**40**	**7,394**	**3,054**	**12,308 ***	**72.6**	**100.0**
019 Amer Bapt USA	1	118	85	146 *	.9	1.2
053 Assemb of God	1	17	26	29	.2	.2
057 Bapt Gen Conf	2	283	222	351 *	2.1	2.9
081 Catholic	6	NR	NR	3,029	17.9	24.6
167 Chs of Christ	1	4	4	4	-	-
173 Comm of Christ	2	136	NR	136	.8	1.1
193 Episcopal	1	NR	7	19	.1	.2
207 E.L.C.A.	1	145	53	177	1.0	1.4
283 Luth—MO Synod	12	4,649	1,789	5,793	34.2	47.1
355 Presb Ch (USA)	4	637	266	790 *	4.7	6.4
419 So Bapt Conv	1	86	80	107 *	.6	.9
443 Un C of Christ	2	455	152	565 *	3.3	4.6
449 Un Methodist	4	842	270	1,045 *	6.2	8.5
467 Wesleyan	2	22	100	117	.7	1.0
DALLAS	**65**	**9,104**	**4,062**	**17,473 ***	**42.9**	**100.0**
053 Assemb of God	4	112	138	166	.4	1.0
056 Baha'i	0	7	NR	7	-	-
081 Catholic	5	NR	NR	5,172	12.7	29.6
093 Chr Ch (Disc)	6	1,855	452	2,379 *	5.8	13.6
097 Chr Chs&Chs Cr	1	66	NR	85 *	.2	.5
107 Christian Un	1	18	22	23 *	.1	.1
151 L-D Saints	2	NR	NR	238	.6	1.4
157 Ch of Brethren	2	296	202	379 *	.9	2.2
167 Chs of Christ	1	40	60	75	.2	.4
173 Comm of Christ	1	69	NR	69	.2	.4
193 Episcopal	1	NR	31	65	.2	.4
203 Evan Free Ch	1	69	125	125	.3	.7
207 E.L.C.A.	6	1,393	594	1,827	4.5	10.5
263 Int Foursq Gos	1	32	48	48 *	.1	.3
283 Luth—MO Synod	4	939	413	1,273	3.1	7.3
324 Old Ord Rvr Br	1	33	55	63	.2	.4
355 Presb Ch (USA)	4	401	155	513 *	1.3	2.9
371 Ref Ch in Am	1	118	188	262	.6	1.5
388 Reg Bapt Gen As	3	221	270	298 *	.7	1.7
419 So Bapt Conv	4	173	63	222 *	.5	1.3

Religious Group	Number of Churches, Synagogues, Mosques, or Temples	Number of Communicant, Confirmed, or Full Members	Number of Attendees	Total Adherents: Number of Adherents	Total Adherents: % of Total Pop.	Total Adherents: % of Total Adh.
449 Un Methodist	16	3,262	1,246	4,184 *	10.3	23.9
DAVIS	**24**	**2,733**	**973**	**3,556 ***	**41.6**	**100.0**
040 Ap Chr Ch-Amer	1	51	115	115 *	1.3	3.2
081 Catholic	1	NR	NR	68	.8	1.9
093 Chr Ch (Disc)	2	794	190	998 *	11.7	28.1
097 Chr Chs&Chs Cr	1	140	NR	176 *	2.1	4.9
143 CG in Cr(Menn)	1	35	NR	44 *	.5	1.2
165 Ch of Nazarene	1	35	50	61	.7	1.7
207 E.L.C.A.	1	70	38	113	1.3	3.2
288 Mennonite USA	1	124	98	156 *	1.8	4.4
323 Old Ord Amish	7	385	NR	483 *	5.7	13.6
339 Pent Ch of God	1	50	NR	70	.8	2.0
388 Reg Bapt Gen As	2	222	185	232 *	2.7	6.5
449 Un Methodist	5	827	297	1,040 *	12.2	29.2
DECATUR	**34**	**2,438**	**666**	**3,345 ***	**38.5**	**100.0**
040 Ap Chr Ch-Amer	1	12	33	33 *	.4	1.0
053 Assemb of God	4	108	118	176	2.0	5.3
061 Beachy Amish	1	68	NR	82 *	.9	2.5
081 Catholic	2	NR	NR	267	3.1	8.0
097 Chr Chs&Chs Cr	1	104	NR	126 *	1.5	3.8
151 L-D Saints	1	NR	NR	252	2.9	7.5
167 Chs of Christ	4	89	83	108	1.2	3.2
173 Comm of Christ	5	979	NR	979	11.3	29.3
183 Cons Menn Conf	1	19	23	28	.3	.8
283 Luth—MO Synod	1	60	17	86	1.0	2.6
323 Old Ord Amish	1	50	NR	60 *	.7	1.8
355 Presb Ch (USA)	2	86	46	104 *	1.2	3.1
419 So Bapt Conv	2	332	106	401 *	4.6	12.0
449 Un Methodist	8	531	240	643 *	7.4	19.2
DELAWARE	**37**	**4,205**	**1,999**	**16,249 ***	**88.3**	**100.0**
053 Assemb of God	1	9	12	28	.2	.2
056 Baha'i	0	1	NR	1	-	-
081 Catholic	12	NR	NR	10,525	57.2	64.8
151 L-D Saints	1	NR	NR	69	.4	.4
179 Consrv Bapt	1	NR	187	187	1.0	1.2
203 Evan Free Ch	1	69	125	125	.7	.8
207 E.L.C.A.	6	1,230	493	1,620	8.8	10.0
283 Luth—MO Synod	2	462	207	604	3.3	3.7
355 Presb Ch (USA)	2	442	189	561 *	3.0	3.5
443 Un C of Christ	3	320	150	406 *	2.2	2.5
449 Un Methodist	8	1,672	636	2,123 *	11.5	13.1
DES MOINES	**63**	**10,215**	**5,984**	**19,474 ***	**46.0**	**100.0**
019 Amer Bapt USA	3	513	229	629 *	1.5	3.2
040 Ap Chr Ch-Amer	1	65	160	160 *	.4	.8
053 Assemb of God	1	207	273	420	1.0	2.2
056 Baha'i	0	17	NR	17	-	.1
057 Bapt Gen Conf	1	98	75	120 *	.3	.6
081 Catholic	2	NR	NR	5,294	12.5	27.2
093 Chr Ch (Disc)	1	655	268	803 *	1.9	4.1
097 Chr Chs&Chs Cr	1	330	NR	405 *	1.0	2.1
127 Ch God (Cleve)	1	18	40	40 *	.1	.2
165 Ch of Nazarene	2	305	295	558	1.3	2.9
167 Chs of Christ	1	73	80	82	.2	.4
173 Comm of Christ	1	71	NR	71	.2	.4
175 Congr Chr Chs	1	223	92	274 *	.6	1.4
185 Cumber Presb	1	26	NR	134	.3	.7
193 Episcopal	1	NR	104	235	.6	1.2
203 Evan Free Ch	1	20	45	45	.1	.2
207 E.L.C.A.	6	1,839	617	2,319	5.5	11.9
221 Free Methodist	1	15	11	19	-	.1
263 Int Foursq Gos	1	42	127	127 *	.3	.7
283 Luth—MO Synod	1	75	42	116	.3	.6
288 Mennonite USA	1	19	26	26 *	.1	.1
313 N Am Bapt Conf	1	394	407	483 *	1.1	2.5
355 Presb Ch (USA)	4	680	335	835 *	2.0	4.3
388 Reg Bapt Gen As	2	230	262	282 *	.7	1.4
403 Salvation Army	1	77	178	183	.4	.9
413 S.D.A.	1	123	NR	146	.3	.7

NR–Not Reported *Total adherents estimated from known number of communicant, confirmed, full members. - Represents a percentage less than 0.1. Percentages may not total 100 due to rounding.

Table 4: Religious Congregations by County and Group: 2000

Religious Group	Number of Churches, Synagogues, Mosques, or Temples	Number of Communicant, Confirmed, or Full Members	Number of Attendees	Total Adherents: Number of Adherents	Total Adherents: % of Total Pop.	Total Adherents: % of Total Adh.
419 So Bapt Conv	2	81	73	99 *	.2	.5
435 Unitarian-Univ	1	77	NR	94 *	.2	.5
443 Un C of Christ	7	991	350	1,216 *	2.9	6.2
449 Un Methodist	11	2,587	1,038	3,172 *	7.5	16.3
469 WELS	1	64	57	90	.2	.5
496 Jewish Est	2	NR	NR	180	.4	.9
499 Indep.Non-Char	1	300	800	800	1.9	4.1
DICKINSON	**26**	**6,219**	**3,058**	**12,343 ***	**75.2**	**100.0**
019 Amer Bapt USA	1	30	25	36 *	.2	.3
056 Baha'i	0	7	NR	7	-	.1
057 Bapt Gen Conf	1	101	132	132 *	.8	1.1
081 Catholic	2	NR	NR	4,160	25.3	33.7
173 Comm of Christ	1	36	NR	36	.2	.3
193 Episcopal	1	NR	74	221	1.3	1.8
203 Evan Free Ch	1	81	205	205	1.2	1.7
207 E.L.C.A.	3	1,646	774	2,157	13.1	17.5
226 Friends-USA	2	128	NR	153 *	.9	1.2
283 Luth—MO Synod	3	1,033	467	1,230	7.5	10.0
355 Presb Ch (USA)	2	559	255	668 *	4.1	5.4
371 Ref Ch in Am	1	324	399	618	3.8	5.0
443 Un C of Christ	1	213	67	255 *	1.6	2.1
449 Un Methodist	7	2,061	660	2,465 *	15.0	20.0
DUBUQUE	**72**	**8,117**	**4,258**	**69,794 ***	**78.3**	**100.0**
019 Amer Bapt USA	1	57	55	71 *	.1	.1
053 Assemb of God	1	61	86	100	.1	.1
056 Baha'i	0	10	NR	10	-	-
081 Catholic	30	NR	NR	57,829	64.9	82.9
127 Ch God (Cleve)	1	39	63	63 *	.1	.1
151 L-D Saints	1	NR	NR	444	.5	.6
165 Ch of Nazarene	1	34	44	79	.1	.1
167 Chs of Christ	1	22	30	33	-	-
193 Episcopal	1	NR	120	286	.3	.4
203 Evan Free Ch	2	100	201	201	.2	.3
207 E.L.C.A.	7	2,649	1,091	3,521	3.9	5.0
246 Greek Orthodox	1	NR	NR	81	.1	.1
283 Luth—MO Synod	3	1,109	498	1,531	1.7	2.2
355 Presb Ch (USA)	4	1,063	590	1,322 *	1.5	1.9
403 Salvation Army	1	64	156	517	.6	.7
413 S.D.A.	1	40	NR	48	.1	.1
419 So Bapt Conv	2	167	75	208 *	.2	.3
435 Unitarian-Univ	1	27	NR	34 *	-	-
443 Un C of Christ	5	990	501	1,231 *	1.4	1.8
449 Un Methodist	7	1,685	748	2,095 *	2.4	3.0
496 Jewish Est	1	NR	NR	90	.1	.1
EMMET	**25**	**5,660**	**2,052**	**8,572 ***	**77.7**	**100.0**
056 Baha'i	0	2	NR	2	-	-
057 Bapt Gen Conf	1	185	95	223 *	2.0	2.6
081 Catholic	2	NR	NR	1,575	14.3	18.4
093 Chr Ch (Disc)	1	400	120	483 *	4.4	5.6
165 Ch of Nazarene	1	22	13	84	.8	1.0
167 Chs of Christ	1	40	45	50	.5	.6
207 E.L.C.A.	8	2,935	1,002	3,638	33.0	42.4
221 Free Methodist	1	32	53	53	.5	.6
283 Luth—MO Synod	1	301	132	362	3.3	4.2
349 Pent Holiness	1	10	10	12 *	.1	.1
355 Presb Ch (USA)	4	663	240	800 *	7.3	9.3
449 Un Methodist	4	1,070	342	1,290 *	11.7	15.0
FAYETTE	**56**	**8,580**	**3,310**	**16,678 ***	**75.8**	**100.0**
019 Amer Bapt USA	2	341	100	419 *	1.9	2.5
040 Ap Chr Ch-Amer	1	36	94	94 *	.4	.6
053 Assemb of God	1	22	25	29	.1	.2
056 Baha'i	0	4	NR	4	-	-
081 Catholic	7	NR	NR	5,693	25.9	34.1
097 Chr Chs&Chs Cr	2	167	NR	205 *	.9	1.2
167 Chs of Christ	1	19	20	34	.2	.2
173 Comm of Christ	1	34	NR	34	.2	.2
193 Episcopal	1	NR	7	6	-	-
203 Evan Free Ch	1	31	67	67	.3	.4

Religious Group	Number of Churches, Synagogues, Mosques, or Temples	Number of Communicant, Confirmed, or Full Members	Number of Attendees	Total Adherents: Number of Adherents	Total Adherents: % of Total Pop.	Total Adherents: % of Total Adh.
207 E.L.C.A.	11	4,185	1,418	5,411	24.6	32.4
263 Int Foursq Gos	1	42	107	107 *	.5	.6
283 Luth—MO Synod	4	697	302	838	3.8	5.0
313 N Am Bapt Conf	1	175	108	215 *	1.0	1.3
355 Presb Ch (USA)	4	741	249	911 *	4.1	5.5
388 Reg Bapt Gen As	1	46	50	56 *	.3	.3
413 S.D.A.	1	44	NR	52	.2	.3
449 Un Methodist	14	1,916	673	2,353 *	10.7	14.1
467 Wesleyan	2	80	90	150	.7	.9
FLOYD	**34**	**5,252**	**2,179**	**11,337 ***	**67.1**	**100.0**
019 Amer Bapt USA	1	207	85	255 *	1.5	2.2
053 Assemb of God	1	36	60	80	.5	.7
056 Baha'i	0	3	NR	3	-	-
081 Catholic	4	NR	NR	4,042	23.9	35.7
089 Chr & Miss Al	1	85	NR	231	1.4	2.0
093 Chr Ch (Disc)	2	240	56	296 *	1.8	2.6
151 L-D Saints	1	NR	NR	256	1.5	2.3
193 Episcopal	1	NR	9	22	.1	.2
203 Evan Free Ch	1	15	70	70	.4	.6
207 E.L.C.A.	5	1,932	881	2,488	14.7	21.9
322 Old Ord Menn Ch	1	65	NR	80 *	.5	.7
355 Presb Ch (USA)	1	154	85	190 *	1.1	1.7
388 Reg Bapt Gen As	1	45	65	65 *	.4	.6
413 S.D.A.	1	10	NR	12	.1	.1
443 Un C of Christ	2	345	106	425 *	2.5	3.7
449 Un Methodist	7	1,933	598	2,383 *	14.1	21.0
467 Wesleyan	3	131	164	382	2.3	3.4
469 WELS	1	51	0	57	.3	.5
FRANKLIN	**31**	**5,553**	**2,426**	**8,204 ***	**76.6**	**100.0**
019 Amer Bapt USA	1	184	75	224 *	2.1	2.7
053 Assemb of God	1	55	57	73	.7	.9
057 Bapt Gen Conf	1	107	219	219 *	2.0	2.7
081 Catholic	2	NR	NR	1,172	10.9	14.3
093 Chr Ch (Disc)	1	227	0	276 *	2.6	3.4
097 Chr Chs&Chs Cr	1	170	NR	207 *	1.9	2.5
207 E.L.C.A.	4	1,236	485	1,585	14.8	19.3
283 Luth—MO Synod	2	782	401	852	8.0	10.4
313 N Am Bapt Conf	1	44	24	53 *	.5	.6
371 Ref Ch in Am	2	281	238	542	5.1	6.6
413 S.D.A.	1	24	NR	29	.3	.4
443 Un C of Christ	3	790	368	960 *	9.0	11.7
449 Un Methodist	11	1,653	559	2,012 *	18.8	24.5
FREMONT	**26**	**2,357**	**715**	**3,687 ***	**46.0**	**100.0**
019 Amer Bapt USA	1	120	45	148 *	1.8	4.0
053 Assemb of God	1	17	23	36	.4	1.0
056 Baha'i	0	1	NR	1	-	-
081 Catholic	2	NR	NR	722	9.0	19.6
097 Chr Chs&Chs Cr	2	358	NR	441 *	5.5	12.0
165 Ch of Nazarene	1	84	69	132	1.6	3.6
176 Congr Ad Afl	1	75	NR	92 *	1.1	2.5
221 Free Methodist	1	17	23	23	.3	.6
283 Luth—MO Synod	1	68	0	102	1.3	2.8
355 Presb Ch (USA)	3	217	99	266 *	3.3	7.2
443 Un C of Christ	4	252	105	310 *	3.9	8.4
449 Un Methodist	9	1,148	351	1,414 *	17.7	38.4
GREENE	**27**	**4,491**	**1,633**	**7,501 ***	**72.4**	**100.0**
019 Amer Bapt USA	2	446	108	550 *	5.3	7.3
053 Assemb of God	1	282	305	500	4.8	6.7
081 Catholic	4	NR	NR	1,741	16.8	23.2
093 Chr Ch (Disc)	1	600	140	740 *	7.1	9.9
097 Chr Chs&Chs Cr	1	136	NR	168 *	1.6	2.2
167 Chs of Christ	1	40	50	65	.6	.9
173 Comm of Christ	1	32	NR	32	.3	.4
207 E.L.C.A.	1	76	46	93	.9	1.2
226 Friends-USA	1	64	NR	79 *	.8	1.1
283 Luth—MO Synod	2	600	220	802	7.7	10.7
355 Presb Ch (USA)	3	326	201	402 *	3.9	5.4
449 Un Methodist	9	1,889	563	2,329 *	22.5	31.0

NR–Not Reported *Total adherents estimated from known number of communicant, confirmed, full members. - Represents a percentage less than 0.1. Percentages may not total 100 due to rounding.

Table 4: Religious Congregations by County and Group: 2000

Religious Group	Number of Churches, Synagogues, Mosques, or Temples	Number of Communicant, Confirmed, or Full Members	Number of Attendees	Total Adherents: Number of Adherents	Total Adherents: % of Total Pop.	Total Adherents: % of Total Adh.
GRUNDY	**36**	**6,616**	**3,329**	**9,234 ***	**74.7**	**100.0**
053 Assemb of God	2	116	139	261	2.1	2.8
081 Catholic	3	NR	NR	812	6.6	8.8
105 Christian Ref	3	505	340	620 *	5.0	6.7
157 Ch of Brethren	1	170	98	209 *	1.7	2.3
171 Ch God-Gen Con	1	78	46	96 *	.8	1.0
207 E.L.C.A.	3	1,074	399	1,355	11.0	14.7
283 Luth—MO Synod	2	358	171	452	3.7	4.9
355 Presb Ch (USA)	5	958	486	1,176 *	9.5	12.7
356 Presb Ch Amer	1	282	148	374	3.0	4.1
371 Ref Ch in Am	3	513	420	728	5.9	7.9
388 Reg Bapt Gen As	3	263	235	330 *	2.7	3.6
443 Un C of Christ	2	632	236	776 *	6.3	8.4
449 Un Methodist	6	1,610	611	1,978 *	16.0	21.4
455 Un Ref Chs N.A.	1	57	NR	67	.5	.7
GUTHRIE	**34**	**3,694**	**1,405**	**5,885 ***	**51.8**	**100.0**
053 Assemb of God	1	20	35	70	.6	1.2
056 Baha'i	0	4	NR	4	-	.1
081 Catholic	5	NR	NR	1,259	11.1	21.4
093 Chr Ch (Disc)	2	540	137	655 *	5.8	11.1
097 Chr Chs&Chs Cr	4	237	NR	287 *	2.5	4.9
157 Ch of Brethren	1	312	198	378 *	3.3	6.4
167 Chs of Christ	1	14	15	18	.2	.3
226 Friends-USA	1	64	NR	78 *	.7	1.3
283 Luth—MO Synod	4	656	239	877	7.7	14.9
355 Presb Ch (USA)	1	105	78	127 *	1.1	2.2
388 Reg Bapt Gen As	1	47	80	80 *	.7	1.4
413 S.D.A.	1	30	NR	36	.3	.6
419 So Bapt Conv	0	26	40	32 *	.3	.5
449 Un Methodist	11	1,622	568	1,967 *	17.3	33.4
467 Wesleyan	1	17	15	17	.1	.3
HAMILTON	**37**	**7,179**	**2,760**	**11,636 ***	**70.8**	**100.0**
019 Amer Bapt USA	1	330	96	409 *	2.5	3.5
053 Assemb of God	1	31	45	63	.4	.5
056 Baha'i	0	2	NR	2	-	-
057 Bapt Gen Conf	1	80	96	99 *	.6	.9
081 Catholic	3	NR	NR	2,081	12.7	17.9
089 Chr & Miss Al	1	120	NR	285	1.7	2.4
093 Chr Ch (Disc)	1	200	65	248 *	1.5	2.1
097 Chr Chs&Chs Cr	2	490	NR	606 *	3.7	5.2
151 L-D Saints	1	NR	NR	348	2.1	3.0
193 Episcopal	1	NR	25	66	.4	.6
201 Evan Cov Ch	1	6	0	7 *	-	.1
207 E.L.C.A.	7	2,571	1,097	3,297	20.1	28.3
220 Free Lutheran	1	85	50	108	.7	.9
252 Hindu	1	NR	NR	NR	-	-
283 Luth—MO Synod	1	455	172	602	3.7	5.2
355 Presb Ch (USA)	1	101	64	125 *	.8	1.1
388 Reg Bapt Gen As	1	112	75	75 *	.5	.6
443 Un C of Christ	3	749	262	928 *	5.6	8.0
449 Un Methodist	9	1,847	713	2,287 *	13.9	19.7
HANCOCK	**36**	**5,711**	**2,675**	**9,431 ***	**77.9**	**100.0**
056 Baha'i	0	1	NR	1	-	-
081 Catholic	5	NR	NR	2,159	17.8	22.9
105 Christian Ref	4	491	250	610 *	5.0	6.5
165 Ch of Nazarene	1	104	77	104	.9	1.1
203 Evan Free Ch	2	187	315	315	2.6	3.3
207 E.L.C.A.	7	1,285	580	1,658	13.7	17.6
283 Luth—MO Synod	2	830	365	1,087	9.0	11.5
355 Presb Ch (USA)	2	195	112	242 *	2.0	2.6
373 Ref Ch in U.S.	1	125	NR	157	1.3	1.7
388 Reg Bapt Gen As	2	89	97	113 *	.9	1.2
443 Un C of Christ	3	620	227	770 *	6.4	8.2
449 Un Methodist	7	1,784	652	2,215 *	18.3	23.5
HARDIN	**53**	**9,677**	**4,395**	**13,307 ***	**70.7**	**100.0**
019 Amer Bapt USA	1	65	56	79 *	.4	.6
053 Assemb of God	1	17	18	58	.3	.4
056 Baha'i	0	3	NR	3	-	-
081 Catholic	2	NR	NR	1,217	6.5	9.1
093 Chr Ch (Disc)	2	542	92	655 *	3.5	4.9
097 Chr Chs&Chs Cr	1	60	NR	73 *	.4	.5
123 Ch God (Ander)	1	NR	24	24	.1	.2
165 Ch of Nazarene	1	39	43	76	.4	.6
193 Episcopal	1	NR	22	38	.2	.3
203 Evan Free Ch	2	159	305	305	1.6	2.3
207 E.L.C.A.	4	1,019	488	1,249	6.6	9.4
220 Free Lutheran	2	181	58	208	1.1	1.6
226 Friends-USA	4	256	NR	309 *	1.6	2.3
245 Greek Orth Vslp	1	35	NR	35	.2	.3
283 Luth—MO Synod	5	1,775	802	2,185	11.6	16.4
313 N Am Bapt Conf	1	284	170	343 *	1.8	2.6
355 Presb Ch (USA)	3	402	272	486 *	2.6	3.7
356 Presb Ch Amer	2	247	170	301	1.6	2.3
371 Ref Ch in Am	1	119	150	239	1.3	1.8
388 Reg Bapt Gen As	3	224	230	288 *	1.5	2.2
443 Un C of Christ	6	1,793	612	2,167 *	11.5	16.3
449 Un Methodist	9	2,457	883	2,969 *	15.8	22.3
HARRISON	**42**	**4,316**	**1,227**	**8,065 ***	**51.5**	**100.0**
017 Amer Bapt Assn	1	30	NR	37 *	.2	.5
019 Amer Bapt USA	1	44	28	55 *	.4	.7
053 Assemb of God	1	36	46	46	.3	.6
056 Baha'i	0	4	NR	4	-	-
081 Catholic	5	NR	NR	2,279	14.5	28.3
089 Chr & Miss Al	1	0	NR	80	.5	1.0
093 Chr Ch (Disc)	1	288	83	358 *	2.3	4.4
097 Chr Chs&Chs Cr	5	765	NR	951 *	6.1	11.8
151 L-D Saints	1	NR	NR	269	1.7	3.3
165 Ch of Nazarene	1	52	34	117	.7	1.5
173 Comm of Christ	5	506	NR	506	3.2	6.3
179 Consrv Bapt	1	NR	22	22	.1	.3
207 E.L.C.A.	3	523	177	761	4.9	9.4
283 Luth—MO Synod	4	705	330	884	5.6	11.0
355 Presb Ch (USA)	2	145	69	181 *	1.2	2.2
449 Un Methodist	10	1,218	438	1,515 *	9.7	18.8
HENRY	**38**	**6,292**	**3,269**	**9,834 ***	**48.4**	**100.0**
019 Amer Bapt USA	2	245	128	301 *	1.5	3.1
053 Assemb of God	1	32	50	50	.2	.5
056 Baha'i	0	8	NR	8	-	.1
081 Catholic	1	NR	NR	1,363	6.7	13.9
097 Chr Chs&Chs Cr	2	263	NR	323 *	1.6	3.3
151 L-D Saints	1	NR	NR	408	2.0	4.1
165 Ch of Nazarene	1	11	24	24	.1	.2
171 Ch God-Gen Con	2	93	60	114 *	.6	1.2
173 Comm of Christ	1	70	NR	70	.3	.7
175 Congr Chr Chs	1	58	23	71 *	.3	.7
193 Episcopal	1	NR	43	157	.8	1.6
203 Evan Free Ch	1	46	57	57	.3	.6
207 E.L.C.A.	1	442	168	561	2.8	5.7
226 Friends-USA	2	128	NR	157 *	.8	1.6
283 Luth—MO Synod	1	302	151	462	2.3	4.7
288 Mennonite USA	3	669	408	821 *	4.0	8.3
291 Missionary Ch	1	31	28	31	.2	.3
355 Presb Ch (USA)	3	708	281	870 *	4.3	8.8
388 Reg Bapt Gen As	1	220	325	325 *	1.6	3.3
419 So Bapt Conv	1	30	27	37 *	.2	.4
443 Un C of Christ	1	127	56	156 *	.8	1.6
449 Un Methodist	9	2,009	740	2,468 *	12.1	25.1
498 Indep.Charis.	1	800	700	1,000	4.9	10.2
HOWARD	**32**	**3,203**	**1,238**	**9,199 ***	**92.6**	**100.0**
019 Amer Bapt USA	1	47	35	59 *	.6	.6
053 Assemb of God	1	28	33	36	.4	.4
056 Baha'i	0	2	NR	2	-	-
081 Catholic	6	NR	NR	5,109	51.4	55.5
143 CG in Cr(Menn)	1	68	NR	85 *	.9	.9
181 Consrv Congr	1	51	85	64 *	.6	.7
207 E.L.C.A.	6	1,599	636	2,096	21.1	22.8
221 Free Methodist	1	5	0	5	.1	.1
283 Luth—MO Synod	1	132	60	157	1.6	1.7

NR–Not Reported   *Total adherents estimated from known number of communicant, confirmed, full members.   - Represents a percentage less than 0.1.   Percentages may not total 100 due to rounding.

Table 4: Religious Congregations by County and Group: 2000

Religious Group	Number of Churches, Synagogues, Mosques, or Temples	Number of Communicant, Confirmed, or Full Members	Number of Attendees	Total Adherents		
				Number of Adherents	% of Total Pop.	% of Total Adh.
322 Old Ord Menn Ch	1	55	NR	69 *	.7	.8
323 Old Ord Amish	4	220	NR	276 *	2.8	3.0
388 Reg Bapt Gen As	1	22	24	27 *	.3	.3
443 Un C of Christ	2	59	34	73 *	.7	.8
449 Un Methodist	6	915	331	1,141 *	11.5	12.4
HUMBOLDT	**18**	**5,724**	**2,275**	**8,844 ***	**85.2**	**100.0**
019 Amer Bapt USA	1	83	38	101 *	1.0	1.1
057 Bapt Gen Conf	1	295	198	359 *	3.5	4.1
081 Catholic	2	NR	NR	1,655	15.9	18.7
207 E.L.C.A.	8	2,357	884	3,044	29.3	34.4
283 Luth—MO Synod	2	799	372	1,022	9.8	11.6
443 Un C of Christ	1	283	90	344 *	3.3	3.9
449 Un Methodist	3	1,907	693	2,319 *	22.3	26.2
IDA	**15**	**4,041**	**1,605**	**6,006 ***	**76.6**	**100.0**
081 Catholic	2	NR	NR	1,095	14.0	18.2
203 Evan Free Ch	1	116	161	161	2.1	2.7
207 E.L.C.A.	1	805	308	955	12.2	15.9
283 Luth—MO Synod	3	1,508	530	1,820	23.2	30.3
355 Presb Ch (USA)	2	473	197	579 *	7.4	9.6
419 So Bapt Conv	1	30	21	37 *	.5	.6
449 Un Methodist	5	1,109	388	1,359 *	17.3	22.6
IOWA	**31**	**5,435**	**2,572**	**8,678 ***	**55.4**	**100.0**
056 Baha'i	0	2	NR	2	-	-
081 Catholic	5	NR	NR	2,265	14.5	26.1
093 Chr Ch (Disc)	1	193	45	243 *	1.6	2.8
165 Ch of Nazarene	1	35	32	40	.3	.5
207 E.L.C.A.	1	238	75	290	1.9	3.3
283 Luth—MO Synod	8	2,706	1,345	2,995	19.1	34.5
288 Mennonite USA	1	305	210	384 *	2.5	4.4
313 N Am Bapt Conf	1	82	144	103 *	.7	1.2
355 Presb Ch (USA)	2	558	260	701 *	4.5	8.1
443 Un C of Christ	1	174	47	219 *	1.4	2.5
449 Un Methodist	10	1,142	414	1,436 *	9.2	16.5
JACKSON	**34**	**4,773**	**1,653**	**14,895 ***	**73.4**	**100.0**
019 Amer Bapt USA	1	185	48	230 *	1.1	1.5
053 Assemb of God	1	12	20	25	.1	.2
056 Baha'i	0	2	NR	2	-	-
081 Catholic	10	NR	NR	8,719	43.0	58.5
173 Comm of Christ	1	35	NR	35	.2	.2
193 Episcopal	1	NR	25	80	.4	.5
207 E.L.C.A.	8	3,064	1,039	3,973	19.6	26.7
226 Friends-USA	1	45	NR	56 *	.3	.4
323 Old Ord Amish	1	55	NR	68 *	.3	.5
355 Presb Ch (USA)	3	302	103	375 *	1.8	2.5
443 Un C of Christ	2	329	130	408 *	2.0	2.7
449 Un Methodist	5	744	288	924 *	4.6	6.2
JASPER	**64**	**11,799**	**5,855**	**18,991 ***	**51.0**	**100.0**
019 Amer Bapt USA	1	267	112	329 *	.9	1.7
053 Assemb of God	2	208	248	381	1.0	2.0
056 Baha'i	0	5	NR	5	-	-
081 Catholic	2	NR	NR	2,791	7.5	14.7
089 Chr & Miss Al	1	340	NR	1,117	3.0	5.9
093 Chr Ch (Disc)	5	1,385	232	1,706 *	4.6	9.0
105 Christian Ref	3	1,192	1,045	1,468 *	3.9	7.7
127 Ch God (Cleve)	2	95	70	117 *	.3	.6
151 L-D Saints	1	NR	NR	195	.5	1.0
157 Ch of Brethren	1	183	0	225 *	.6	1.2
165 Ch of Nazarene	1	120	88	165	.4	.9
167 Chs of Christ	3	50	54	59	.2	.3
173 Comm of Christ	2	122	NR	122	.3	.6
179 Consrv Bapt	1	NR	167	167	.4	.9
181 Consrv Congr	1	165	72	203 *	.5	1.1
193 Episcopal	1	NR	64	161	.4	.8
203 Evan Free Ch	1	50	80	80	.2	.4
207 E.L.C.A.	4	847	386	1,005	2.7	5.3
226 Friends-USA	3	192	NR	236 *	.6	1.2
263 Int Foursq Gos	1	262	226	323 *	.9	1.7

Religious Group	Number of Churches, Synagogues, Mosques, or Temples	Number of Communicant, Confirmed, or Full Members	Number of Attendees	Total Adherents		
				Number of Adherents	% of Total Pop.	% of Total Adh.
283 Luth—MO Synod	1	266	121	308	.8	1.6
355 Presb Ch (USA)	4	856	373	1,054 *	2.8	5.5
371 Ref Ch in Am	3	794	793	1,276	3.4	6.7
388 Reg Bapt Gen As	3	420	311	517 *	1.4	2.7
403 Salvation Army	1	94	23	195	.5	1.0
413 S.D.A.	1	25	NR	30	.1	.2
419 So Bapt Conv	1	28	21	34 *	.1	.2
443 Un C of Christ	3	952	283	1,172 *	3.1	6.2
449 Un Methodist	11	2,881	1,086	3,550 *	9.5	18.7
JEFFERSON	**27**	**4,407**	**1,680**	**6,794 ***	**42.0**	**100.0**
019 Amer Bapt USA	3	534	173	649 *	4.0	9.6
053 Assemb of God	1	22	30	45	.3	.7
056 Baha'i	1	35	NR	35	.2	.5
081 Catholic	1	NR	NR	1,165	7.2	17.1
093 Chr Ch (Disc)	2	810	208	984 *	6.1	14.5
097 Chr Chs&Chs Cr	1	137	NR	166 *	1.0	2.4
151 L-D Saints	1	NR	NR	205	1.3	3.0
157 Ch of Brethren	1	57	18	69 *	.4	1.0
165 Ch of Nazarene	1	86	47	86	.5	1.3
207 E.L.C.A.	2	605	219	787	4.9	11.6
221 Free Methodist	1	77	47	77	.5	1.1
226 Friends-USA	2	128	NR	156 *	1.0	2.3
263 Int Foursq Gos	1	219	217	266 *	1.6	3.9
283 Luth—MO Synod	1	159	91	230	1.4	3.4
355 Presb Ch (USA)	1	349	100	424 *	2.6	6.2
388 Reg Bapt Gen As	1	46	62	62 *	.4	.9
413 S.D.A.	1	16	NR	19	.1	.3
419 So Bapt Conv	1	90	40	109 *	.7	1.6
449 Un Methodist	4	1,037	428	1,260 *	7.8	18.5
JOHNSON	**76**	**16,074**	**8,072**	**41,291 ***	**37.2**	**100.0**
019 Amer Bapt USA	1	130	30	154 *	.1	.4
040 Ap Chr Ch-Amer	1	21	53	53 *	-	.1
053 Assemb of God	2	70	95	172	.2	.4
056 Baha'i	1	83	NR	83	.1	.2
057 Bapt Gen Conf	1	132	142	157 *	.1	.4
061 Beachy Amish	1	106	NR	126 *	.1	.3
076 Buddhism	3	NR	NR	NR	-	-
081 Catholic	7	NR	NR	17,206	15.5	41.7
093 Chr Ch (Disc)	1	275	0	327 *	.3	.8
097 Chr Chs&Chs Cr	2	316	NR	376 *	.3	.9
105 Christian Ref	1	60	0	71 *	.1	.2
151 L-D Saints	3	NR	NR	1,051	.9	2.5
165 Ch of Nazarene	1	125	104	210	.2	.5
167 Chs of Christ	1	50	50	75	.1	.2
173 Comm of Christ	1	91	NR	91	.1	.2
193 Episcopal	2	NR	286	649	.6	1.6
203 Evan Free Ch	1	350	900	900	.8	2.2
207 E.L.C.A.	3	3,177	960	4,265	3.8	10.3
221 Free Methodist	1	26	52	52	-	.1
226 Friends-USA	1	49	NR	58 *	.1	.1
263 Int Foursq Gos	1	25	35	35 *	-	.1
267 Muslim Est	1	NR	101	288	.3	.7
283 Luth—MO Synod	4	1,178	563	1,647	1.5	4.0
288 Mennonite USA	3	753	701	894 *	.8	2.2
355 Presb Ch (USA)	4	2,058	768	2,444 *	2.2	5.9
356 Presb Ch Amer	1	8	46	46	-	.1
371 Ref Ch in Am	1	109	142	281	.3	.7
388 Reg Bapt Gen As	1	93	150	150 *	.1	.4
403 Salvation Army	1	40	92	66	.1	.2
413 S.D.A.	1	57	NR	68	.1	.2
419 So Bapt Conv	3	623	315	740 *	.7	1.8
435 Unitarian-Univ	1	251	NR	298 *	.3	.7
443 Un C of Christ	3	457	194	543 *	.5	1.3
449 Un Methodist	13	5,331	2,208	6,330 *	5.7	15.3
463 Vineyard	1	30	85	85 *	.1	.2
496 Jewish Est	2	NR	NR	1,300	1.2	3.1
JONES	**39**	**5,983**	**2,187**	**14,044 ***	**69.5**	**100.0**
019 Amer Bapt USA	1	48	32	59 *	.3	.4
053 Assemb of God	1	14	8	37	.2	.3
056 Baha'i	0	6	NR	6	-	-

NR–Not Reported *Total adherents estimated from known number of communicant, confirmed, full members. - Represents a percentage less than 0.1. Percentages may not total 100 due to rounding.

Table 4: Religious Congregations by County and Group: 2000

Religious Group	Number of Churches, Synagogues, Mosques, or Temples	Number of Communicant, Confirmed, or Full Members	Number of Attendees	Total Adherents: Number of Adherents	Total Adherents: % of Total Pop.	Total Adherents: % of Total Adh.
081 Catholic	7	NR	NR	6,219	30.8	44.3
097 Chr Chs&Chs Cr	1	237	NR	289 *	1.4	2.1
165 Ch of Nazarene	1	50	54	99	.5	.7
193 Episcopal	1	NR	6	14	.1	.1
207 E.L.C.A.	7	2,544	855	3,493	17.3	24.9
263 Int Foursq Gos	1	26	92	92 *	.5	.7
283 Luth—MO Synod	1	327	107	382	1.9	2.7
355 Presb Ch (USA)	4	385	155	471 *	2.3	3.4
388 Reg Bapt Gen As	1	40	70	70 *	.3	.5
419 So Bapt Conv	1	138	30	168 *	.8	1.2
443 Un C of Christ	3	993	352	1,212 *	6.0	8.6
449 Un Methodist	9	1,175	426	1,433 *	7.1	10.2
KEOKUK	**37**	**3,223**	**1,284**	**6,236 ***	**54.7**	**100.0**
019 Amer Bapt USA	2	101	63	125 *	1.1	2.0
056 Baha'i	0	2	NR	2	-	-
081 Catholic	4	NR	NR	2,291	20.1	36.7
093 Chr Ch (Disc)	6	667	162	826 *	7.2	13.2
107 Christian Un	1	55	58	68 *	.6	1.1
157 Ch of Brethren	1	97	47	120 *	1.1	1.9
207 E.L.C.A.	1	28	14	37	.3	.6
226 Friends-USA	4	256	NR	317 *	2.8	5.1
283 Luth—MO Synod	1	122	55	102	.9	1.6
297 Mennonite;Other	1	16	NR	20 *	.2	.3
355 Presb Ch (USA)	4	377	156	467 *	4.1	7.5
419 So Bapt Conv	0	21	21	26 *	.2	.4
449 Un Methodist	12	1,481	708	1,835 *	16.1	29.4
KOSSUTH	**42**	**6,569**	**3,411**	**14,127 ***	**82.3**	**100.0**
019 Amer Bapt USA	1	38	35	47 *	.3	.3
053 Assemb of God	1	98	110	125	.7	.9
056 Baha'i	0	1	NR	1	-	-
057 Bapt Gen Conf	1	107	90	131 *	.8	.9
081 Catholic	7	NR	NR	5,898	34.4	41.7
193 Episcopal	1	NR	25	59	.3	.4
203 Evan Free Ch	2	57	112	112	.7	.8
207 E.L.C.A.	4	1,459	574	1,816	10.6	12.9
283 Luth—MO Synod	7	2,030	1,018	2,509	14.6	17.8
355 Presb Ch (USA)	5	573	299	703 *	4.1	5.0
356 Presb Ch Amer	1	212	127	252	1.5	1.8
371 Ref Ch in Am	1	159	100	244	1.4	1.7
388 Reg Bapt Gen As	1	82	80	80 *	.5	.6
443 Un C of Christ	1	166	70	204 *	1.2	1.4
449 Un Methodist	9	1,587	771	1,946 *	11.3	13.8
LEE	**61**	**10,123**	**4,187**	**21,067 ***	**55.4**	**100.0**
019 Amer Bapt USA	2	1,165	237	1,425 *	3.7	6.8
053 Assemb of God	3	198	257	354	.9	1.7
056 Baha'i	0	8	NR	8	-	-
081 Catholic	7	NR	NR	7,420	19.5	35.2
093 Chr Ch (Disc)	2	1,523	394	1,863 *	4.9	8.8
097 Chr Chs&Chs Cr	2	775	NR	948 *	2.5	4.5
151 L-D Saints	2	NR	NR	311	.8	1.5
165 Ch of Nazarene	3	222	211	329	.9	1.6
167 Chs of Christ	2	37	64	73	.2	.3
173 Comm of Christ	2	106	NR	106	.3	.5
183 Cons Menn Conf	1	20	24	29	.1	.1
193 Episcopal	2	NR	94	227	.6	1.1
203 Evan Free Ch	1	125	165	165	.4	.8
207 E.L.C.A.	2	554	203	692	1.8	3.3
263 Int Foursq Gos	2	139	615	615 *	1.6	2.9
283 Luth—MO Synod	2	178	86	215	.6	1.0
288 Mennonite USA	1	128	65	157 *	.4	.7
355 Presb Ch (USA)	6	554	279	677 *	1.8	3.2
403 Salvation Army	1	111	77	221	.6	1.0
413 S.D.A.	1	93	NR	111	.3	.5
419 So Bapt Conv	3	955	253	1,168 *	3.1	5.5
443 Un C of Christ	5	1,440	495	1,761 *	4.6	8.4
449 Un Methodist	9	1,792	668	2,192 *	5.8	10.4
LINN	**169**	**41,783**	**23,614**	**109,373 ***	**57.1**	**100.0**
019 Amer Bapt USA	4	1,174	414	1,464 *	.8	1.3
034 Ant Orth of NA	1	285	NR	570	.3	.5
053 Assemb of God	4	1,217	1,594	2,899	1.5	2.7
056 Baha'i	1	107	NR	107	.1	.1
057 Bapt Gen Conf	2	270	225	337 *	.2	.3
076 Buddhism	1	NR	NR	NR	-	-
081 Catholic	19	NR	NR	44,642	23.3	40.8
089 Chr & Miss Al	1	28	NR	93	-	.1
093 Chr Ch (Disc)	7	2,551	966	3,181 *	1.7	2.9
097 Chr Chs&Chs Cr	4	560	NR	698 *	.4	.6
105 Christian Ref	1	250	160	312 *	.2	.3
123 Ch God (Ander)	1	NR	51	51	-	-
127 Ch God (Cleve)	1	44	14	55 *	-	.1
145 Ch God Prophcy	1	34	NR	43 *	-	-
151 L-D Saints	3	NR	NR	1,242	.6	1.1
157 Ch of Brethren	2	77	248	295 *	.2	.3
165 Ch of Nazarene	2	622	416	678	.4	.6
167 Chs of Christ	4	367	387	513	.3	.5
173 Comm of Christ	1	158	NR	158	.1	.1
179 Consrv Bapt	3	NR	695	695	.4	.6
193 Episcopal	3	NR	489	1,296	.7	1.2
203 Evan Free Ch	1	152	320	320	.2	.3
207 E.L.C.A.	13	7,963	3,584	10,875	5.7	9.9
221 Free Methodist	2	81	104	104	.1	.1
226 Friends-USA	1	49	NR	61 *	-	.1
246 Greek Orthodox	1	NR	NR	267	.1	.2
252 Hindu	1	NR	NR	NR	-	-
263 Int Foursq Gos	1	240	167	299 *	.2	.3
267 Muslim Est	2	NR	500	2,300	1.2	2.1
283 Luth—MO Synod	9	4,708	2,205	6,148	3.2	5.6
313 N Am Bapt Conf	1	63	54	79 *	-	.1
355 Presb Ch (USA)	15	4,406	1,970	5,491 *	2.9	5.0
356 Presb Ch Amer	2	55	100	100	.1	.1
360 Prim Bapt Chrch	1	NR	NR	NR	-	-
371 Ref Ch in Am	2	243	332	480	.3	.4
388 Reg Bapt Gen As	1	84	100	105 *	.1	.1
403 Salvation Army	1	136	205	1,247	.7	1.1
413 S.D.A.	2	432	NR	514	.3	.5
419 So Bapt Conv	3	956	295	1,192 *	.6	1.1
435 Unitarian-Univ	1	211	NR	263 *	.1	.2
443 Un C of Christ	4	1,387	460	1,729 *	.9	1.6
449 Un Methodist	30	11,456	4,512	14,284 *	7.5	13.1
463 Vineyard	1	166	100	207 *	.1	.2
467 Wesleyan	3	366	401	829	.4	.8
469 WELS	1	235	146	330	.2	.3
496 Jewish Est	1	NR	NR	420	.2	.4
498 Indep.Charis.	1	0	800	800	.4	.7
499 Indep.Non-Char	2	650	1,600	1,600	.8	1.5
LOUISA	**20**	**2,979**	**1,376**	**4,879 ***	**40.0**	**100.0**
040 Ap Chr Ch-Amer	1	260	437	437 *	3.6	9.0
053 Assemb of God	1	16	20	45	.4	.9
081 Catholic	2	NR	NR	914	7.5	18.7
165 Ch of Nazarene	1	45	47	106	.9	2.2
171 Ch God-Gen Con	1	28	15	36 *	.3	.7
221 Free Methodist	1	15	13	15	.1	.3
283 Luth—MO Synod	1	103	48	126	1.0	2.6
355 Presb Ch (USA)	5	628	216	800 *	6.6	16.4
419 So Bapt Conv	0	95	95	121 *	1.0	2.5
449 Un Methodist	7	1,789	485	2,279 *	18.7	46.7
LUCAS	**24**	**2,739**	**1,070**	**4,165 ***	**44.2**	**100.0**
019 Amer Bapt USA	1	450	175	558 *	5.9	13.4
053 Assemb of God	3	60	84	116	1.2	2.8
056 Baha'i	0	1	NR	1	-	-
081 Catholic	1	NR	NR	650	6.9	15.6
093 Chr Ch (Disc)	1	318	0	395 *	4.2	9.5
107 Christian Un	1	23	29	29 *	.3	.7
127 Ch God (Cleve)	1	12	0	15 *	.2	.4
165 Ch of Nazarene	1	193	168	314	3.3	7.5
167 Chs of Christ	1	20	14	25	.3	.6
173 Comm of Christ	1	120	NR	120	1.3	2.9
193 Episcopal	1	NR	10	19	.2	.5
207 E.L.C.A.	1	328	123	401	4.3	9.6

NR–Not Reported *Total adherents estimated from known number of communicant, confirmed, full members. - Represents a percentage less than 0.1. Percentages may not total 100 due to rounding.

Table 4: Religious Congregations by County and Group: 2000

Religious Group	Number of Churches, Synagogues, Mosques, or Temples	Number of Communicant, Confirmed, or Full Members	Number of Attendees	Total Adherents		
				Number of Adherents	% of Total Pop.	% of Total Adh.
283 Luth—MO Synod	1	52	36	80	.8	1.9
323 Old Ord Amish	2	110	NR	136 *	1.4	3.3
355 Presb Ch (USA)	2	140	77	174 *	1.8	4.2
388 Reg Bapt Gen As	1	60	50	74 *	.8	1.8
449 Un Methodist	5	852	304	1,058 *	11.2	25.4
LYON	**37**	**6,225**	**4,392**	**10,301 ***	**87.6**	**100.0**
040 Ap Chr Ch-Amer	1	304	714	714 *	6.1	6.9
053 Assemb of God	1	49	59	82	.7	.8
056 Baha'i	0	1	NR	1	-	-
081 Catholic	3	NR	NR	1,525	13.0	14.8
093 Chr Ch (Disc)	1	60	0	76 *	.6	.7
105 Christian Ref	2	744	585	944 *	8.0	9.2
176 Congr Ad Afl	1	56	NR	71 *	.6	.7
201 Evan Cov Ch	1	52	59	66 *	.6	.6
207 E.L.C.A.	5	1,380	575	1,730	14.7	16.8
283 Luth—MO Synod	2	465	173	545	4.6	5.3
313 N Am Bapt Conf	3	306	320	388 *	3.3	3.8
355 Presb Ch (USA)	4	686	418	871 *	7.4	8.5
369 Prot Ref Chs	1	151	NR	249	2.1	2.4
371 Ref Ch in Am	6	1,220	1,165	2,028	17.2	19.7
443 Un C of Christ	2	258	116	328 *	2.8	3.2
449 Un Methodist	3	391	208	496 *	4.2	4.8
455 Un Ref Chs N.A.	1	102	NR	187	1.6	1.8
MADISON	**32**	**4,088**	**1,920**	**6,499 ***	**46.4**	**100.0**
056 Baha'i	0	2	NR	2	-	-
081 Catholic	2	NR	NR	931	6.6	14.3
093 Chr Ch (Disc)	3	899	240	1,132 *	8.1	17.4
097 Chr Chs&Chs Cr	1	138	NR	174 *	1.2	2.7
107 Christian Un	1	10	20	20 *	.1	.3
165 Ch of Nazarene	1	73	80	189	1.3	2.9
193 Episcopal	1	NR	6	12	.1	.2
203 Evan Free Ch	2	69	190	190	1.4	2.9
207 E.L.C.A.	1	298	140	499	3.6	7.7
226 Friends-USA	2	128	NR	161 *	1.1	2.5
263 Int Foursq Gos	1	73	170	170 *	1.2	2.6
283 Luth—MO Synod	1	219	120	277	2.0	4.3
355 Presb Ch (USA)	2	251	119	316 *	2.3	4.9
360 Prim Bapt Chrch	1	NR	NR	NR	-	-
388 Reg Bapt Gen As	1	105	107	132 *	.9	2.0
413 S.D.A.	1	35	NR	42	.3	.6
419 So Bapt Conv	1	297	200	374 *	2.7	5.8
443 Un C of Christ	1	97	41	122 *	.9	1.9
449 Un Methodist	9	1,394	487	1,756 *	12.5	27.0
MAHASKA	**40**	**6,963**	**4,351**	**10,728 ***	**48.0**	**100.0**
019 Amer Bapt USA	2	90	67	112 *	.5	1.0
053 Assemb of God	2	332	407	678	3.0	6.3
056 Baha'i	0	6	NR	6	-	.1
081 Catholic	1	NR	NR	1,273	5.7	11.9
089 Chr & Miss Al	1	25	NR	43	.2	.4
093 Chr Ch (Disc)	1	865	270	1,074 *	4.8	10.0
097 Chr Chs&Chs Cr	1	90	NR	112 *	.5	1.0
105 Christian Ref	5	1,160	949	1,440 *	6.4	13.4
127 Ch God (Cleve)	1	41	44	51 *	.2	.5
151 L-D Saints	1	NR	NR	147	.7	1.4
165 Ch of Nazarene	2	636	600	922	4.1	8.6
167 Chs of Christ	1	29	30	39	.2	.4
173 Comm of Christ	1	36	NR	36	.2	.3
193 Episcopal	1	NR	35	68	.3	.6
221 Free Methodist	1	32	15	33	.1	.3
226 Friends-USA	3	192	NR	238 *	1.1	2.2
283 Luth—MO Synod	1	262	109	363	1.6	3.4
355 Presb Ch (USA)	2	200	97	249 *	1.1	2.3
371 Ref Ch in Am	2	622	538	891	4.0	8.3
388 Reg Bapt Gen As	1	160	200	200 *	.9	1.9
443 Un C of Christ	1	236	104	293 *	1.3	2.7
449 Un Methodist	7	1,824	772	2,266 *	10.1	21.1
467 Wesleyan	1	0	0	0	-	-
469 WELS	1	125	114	194	.9	1.8
MARION	**63**	**11,896**	**7,852**	**18,178 ***	**56.7**	**100.0**
019 Amer Bapt USA	2	835	294	1,034 *	3.2	5.7
053 Assemb of God	4	127	150	201	.6	1.1
056 Baha'i	0	7	NR	7	-	-
057 Bapt Gen Conf	1	65	85	85 *	.3	.5
081 Catholic	3	NR	NR	1,923	6.0	10.6
093 Chr Ch (Disc)	3	619	223	767 *	2.4	4.2
097 Chr Chs&Chs Cr	4	626	NR	776 *	2.4	4.3
105 Christian Ref	7	2,567	1,730	3,180 *	9.9	17.5
127 Ch God (Cleve)	1	58	25	72 *	.2	.4
151 L-D Saints	1	NR	NR	148	.5	.8
165 Ch of Nazarene	2	189	166	340	1.1	1.9
167 Chs of Christ	1	36	40	54	.2	.3
173 Comm of Christ	1	103	NR	103	.3	.6
203 Evan Free Ch	1	94	200	200	.6	1.1
207 E.L.C.A.	2	637	346	861	2.7	4.7
221 Free Methodist	1	20	30	30	.1	.2
263 Int Foursq Gos	1	60	119	119 *	.4	.7
283 Luth—MO Synod	3	482	258	645	2.0	3.5
355 Presb Ch (USA)	1	165	75	204 *	.6	1.1
369 Prot Ref Chs	1	25	NR	44	.1	.2
371 Ref Ch in Am	6	2,716	2,896	4,292	13.4	23.6
388 Reg Bapt Gen As	2	236	295	337 *	1.1	1.9
413 S.D.A.	1	86	NR	102	.3	.6
419 So Bapt Conv	1	51	44	63 *	.2	.3
449 Un Methodist	13	2,092	876	2,591 *	8.1	14.3
MARSHALL	**66**	**12,175**	**5,199**	**22,372 ***	**56.9**	**100.0**
019 Amer Bapt USA	2	947	564	1,170 *	3.0	5.2
053 Assemb of God	1	84	92	120	.3	.5
056 Baha'i	0	27	NR	27	.1	.1
081 Catholic	5	NR	NR	6,337	16.1	28.3
093 Chr Ch (Disc)	3	1,139	272	1,407 *	3.6	6.3
097 Chr Chs&Chs Cr	3	830	NR	1,026 *	2.6	4.6
123 Ch God (Ander)	1	NR	22	22	.1	.1
151 L-D Saints	1	NR	NR	231	.6	1.0
157 Ch of Brethren	1	107	60	132 *	.3	.6
165 Ch of Nazarene	1	120	146	374	1.0	1.7
167 Chs of Christ	2	79	102	123	.3	.5
173 Comm of Christ	1	43	NR	43	.1	.2
175 Congr Chr Chs	2	450	205	556 *	1.4	2.5
193 Episcopal	1	NR	56	160	.4	.7
203 Evan Free Ch	1	32	60	60	.2	.3
207 E.L.C.A.	4	1,779	722	2,249	5.7	10.1
226 Friends-USA	4	256	NR	316 *	.8	1.4
283 Luth—MO Synod	4	1,145	577	1,459	3.7	6.5
339 Pent Ch of God	1	19	NR	45	.1	.2
355 Presb Ch (USA)	3	663	285	819 *	2.1	3.7
388 Reg Bapt Gen As	1	300	280	371 *	.9	1.7
403 Salvation Army	1	203	68	445	1.1	2.0
413 S.D.A.	1	75	NR	89	.2	.4
419 So Bapt Conv	1	61	22	75 *	.2	.3
443 Un C of Christ	6	520	227	642 *	1.6	2.9
449 Un Methodist	13	3,166	1,303	3,913 *	10.0	17.5
463 Vineyard	1	130	136	161 *	.4	.7
467 Wesleyan	1	0	0	0	-	-
MILLS	**25**	**3,924**	**1,237**	**6,670 ***	**45.9**	**100.0**
019 Amer Bapt USA	2	565	113	708 *	4.9	10.6
081 Catholic	1	NR	NR	1,400	9.6	21.0
093 Chr Ch (Disc)	1	400	126	501 *	3.4	7.5
097 Chr Chs&Chs Cr	1	150	NR	188 *	1.3	2.8
151 L-D Saints	1	NR	NR	304	2.1	4.6
165 Ch of Nazarene	1	33	25	50	.3	.7
193 Episcopal	1	NR	13	19	.1	.3
203 Evan Free Ch	1	60	103	103	.7	1.5
207 E.L.C.A.	1	466	145	594	4.1	8.9
283 Luth—MO Synod	2	442	159	537	3.7	8.1
355 Presb Ch (USA)	1	31	10	39 *	.3	.6
419 So Bapt Conv	1	67	18	84 *	.6	1.3
443 Un C of Christ	1	253	75	317 *	2.2	4.8
449 Un Methodist	10	1,457	450	1,826 *	12.6	27.4

NR–Not Reported   *Total adherents estimated from known number of communicant, confirmed, full members.   - Represents a percentage less than 0.1.   Percentages may not total 100 due to rounding.

Table 4: Religious Congregations by County and Group: 2000

Religious Group	Number of Churches, Synagogues, Mosques, or Temples	Number of Communicant, Confirmed, or Full Members	Number of Attendees	Total Adherents: Number of Adherents	Total Adherents: % of Total Pop.	Total Adherents: % of Total Adh.
MITCHELL	**28**	**4,865**	**1,962**	**9,988 ***	**91.9**	**100.0**
019 Amer Bapt USA	2	175	60	219 *	2.0	2.2
056 Baha'i	0	6	NR	6	.1	.1
081 Catholic	5	NR	NR	3,665	33.7	36.7
089 Chr & Miss Al	1	107	NR	237	2.2	2.4
143 CG in Cr(Menn)	1	59	NR	74 *	.7	.7
207 E.L.C.A.	7	2,473	1,057	3,161	29.1	31.6
283 Luth—MO Synod	4	1,033	476	1,360	12.5	13.6
322 Old Ord Menn Ch	1	40	NR	50 *	.5	.5
388 Reg Bapt Gen As	1	42	30	53 *	.5	.5
443 Un C of Christ	2	244	135	305 *	2.8	3.1
449 Un Methodist	4	686	204	858 *	7.9	8.6
MONONA	**27**	**3,930**	**1,167**	**5,881 ***	**58.7**	**100.0**
081 Catholic	3	NR	NR	1,030	10.3	17.5
093 Chr Ch (Disc)	1	240	66	290 *	2.9	4.9
097 Chr Chs&Chs Cr	3	640	NR	774 *	7.7	13.2
173 Comm of Christ	1	50	NR	50	.5	.9
203 Evan Free Ch	1	35	52	52	.5	.9
207 E.L.C.A.	3	840	263	1,088	10.9	18.5
283 Luth—MO Synod	2	856	323	1,062	10.6	18.1
413 S.D.A.	2	27	NR	32	.3	.5
419 So Bapt Conv	0	9	20	11 *	.1	.2
443 Un C of Christ	6	566	226	685 *	6.8	11.6
449 Un Methodist	5	667	217	807 *	8.1	13.7
MONROE	**16**	**1,903**	**635**	**4,342 ***	**54.2**	**100.0**
019 Amer Bapt USA	2	111	46	138 *	1.7	3.2
081 Catholic	3	NR	NR	1,948	24.3	44.9
093 Chr Ch (Disc)	1	433	109	537 *	6.7	12.4
097 Chr Chs&Chs Cr	1	137	NR	170 *	2.1	3.9
157 Ch of Brethren	1	17	0	21 *	.3	.5
173 Comm of Christ	1	41	NR	41	.5	.9
193 Episcopal	1	NR	17	34	.4	.8
207 E.L.C.A.	1	150	82	199	2.5	4.6
413 S.D.A.	1	54	NR	64	.8	1.5
419 So Bapt Conv	1	121	52	150 *	1.9	3.5
449 Un Methodist	3	839	329	1,040 *	13.0	24.0
MONTGOMERY	**31**	**4,638**	**1,703**	**7,122 ***	**60.5**	**100.0**
019 Amer Bapt USA	1	157	62	193 *	1.6	2.7
053 Assemb of God	1	38	45	72	.6	1.0
081 Catholic	2	NR	NR	811	6.9	11.4
089 Chr & Miss Al	1	88	NR	364	3.1	5.1
093 Chr Ch (Disc)	1	419	88	516 *	4.4	7.2
097 Chr Chs&Chs Cr	2	128	NR	157 *	1.3	2.2
151 L-D Saints	1	NR	NR	318	2.7	4.5
165 Ch of Nazarene	1	67	53	77	.7	1.1
193 Episcopal	1	NR	13	13	.1	.2
201 Evan Cov Ch	2	274	161	337 *	2.9	4.7
207 E.L.C.A.	3	1,251	417	1,550	13.2	21.8
283 Luth—MO Synod	2	204	116	259	2.2	3.6
355 Presb Ch (USA)	3	417	180	513 *	4.4	7.2
443 Un C of Christ	1	66	28	81 *	.7	1.1
449 Un Methodist	8	1,291	429	1,588 *	13.5	22.3
469 WELS	1	238	111	273	2.3	3.8
MUSCATINE	**66**	**10,518**	**5,500**	**20,796 ***	**49.8**	**100.0**
019 Amer Bapt USA	1	643	170	810 *	1.9	3.9
053 Assemb of God	4	174	175	200	.5	1.0
056 Baha'i	0	9	NR	9	-	-
057 Bapt Gen Conf	1	88	92	111 *	.3	.5
081 Catholic	5	NR	NR	5,215	12.5	25.1
093 Chr Ch (Disc)	3	940	239	1,184 *	2.8	5.7
097 Chr Chs&Chs Cr	1	40	NR	50 *	.1	.2
127 Ch God (Cleve)	1	40	19	50 *	.1	.2
151 L-D Saints	1	NR	NR	437	1.0	2.1
165 Ch of Nazarene	1	61	28	91	.2	.4
167 Chs of Christ	1	110	110	150	.4	.7
173 Comm of Christ	1	148	NR	148	.4	.7
179 Consrv Bapt	2	NR	987	987	2.4	4.7
193 Episcopal	1	NR	88	196	.5	.9

Religious Group	Number of Churches, Synagogues, Mosques, or Temples	Number of Communicant, Confirmed, or Full Members	Number of Attendees	Total Adherents: Number of Adherents	Total Adherents: % of Total Pop.	Total Adherents: % of Total Adh.
203 Evan Free Ch	1	184	229	229	.5	1.1
207 E.L.C.A.	6	1,839	742	2,501	6.0	12.0
226 Friends-USA	3	192	NR	242 *	.6	1.2
263 Int Foursq Gos	1	110	77	139 *	.3	.7
283 Luth—MO Synod	2	826	354	1,297	3.1	6.2
288 Mennonite USA	1	0	50	50 *	.1	.2
355 Presb Ch (USA)	4	784	318	989 *	2.4	4.8
388 Reg Bapt Gen As	2	189	220	241 *	.6	1.2
403 Salvation Army	1	78	99	365	.9	1.8
413 S.D.A.	1	205	NR	244	.6	1.2
419 So Bapt Conv	1	65	25	82 *	.2	.4
443 Un C of Christ	4	659	291	830 *	2.0	4.0
449 Un Methodist	15	2,970	1,052	3,742 *	9.0	18.0
463 Vineyard	1	164	135	207 *	.5	1.0
O'BRIEN	**41**	**9,039**	**5,183**	**13,492 ***	**89.3**	**100.0**
053 Assemb of God	1	73	90	150	1.0	1.1
081 Catholic	5	NR	NR	1,734	11.5	12.9
097 Chr Chs&Chs Cr	2	200	NR	245 *	1.6	1.8
105 Christian Ref	3	1,187	952	1,451 *	9.6	10.8
151 L-D Saints	1	NR	NR	59	.4	.4
157 Ch of Brethren	1	59	30	72 *	.5	.5
203 Evan Free Ch	1	0	45	45	.3	.3
207 E.L.C.A.	3	886	353	1,118	7.4	8.3
226 Friends-USA	1	49	NR	60 *	.4	.4
283 Luth—MO Synod	5	1,804	887	2,241	14.8	16.6
306 NT IndBapt&Rltd	1	50	NR	61 *	.4	.5
355 Presb Ch (USA)	2	362	164	443 *	2.9	3.3
371 Ref Ch in Am	5	1,536	1,587	2,269	15.0	16.8
443 Un C of Christ	3	733	289	896 *	5.9	6.6
449 Un Methodist	6	1,899	786	2,322 *	15.4	17.2
455 Un Ref Chs N.A.	1	201	NR	326	2.2	2.4
OSCEOLA	**21**	**3,438**	**2,138**	**5,539 ***	**79.1**	**100.0**
081 Catholic	2	NR	NR	1,066	15.2	19.2
089 Chr & Miss Al	1	66	NR	86	1.2	1.6
105 Christian Ref	2	454	365	564 *	8.1	10.2
179 Consrv Bapt	1	NR	165	165	2.4	3.0
207 E.L.C.A.	2	791	335	851	12.2	15.4
283 Luth—MO Synod	4	578	296	712	10.2	12.9
355 Presb Ch (USA)	2	387	249	481 *	6.9	8.7
371 Ref Ch in Am	2	523	415	820	11.7	14.8
443 Un C of Christ	1	77	34	96 *	1.4	1.7
449 Un Methodist	4	562	279	698 *	10.0	12.6
PAGE	**47**	**7,295**	**3,336**	**9,933 ***	**58.5**	**100.0**
019 Amer Bapt USA	2	296	110	356 *	2.1	3.6
053 Assemb of God	2	208	282	282	1.7	2.8
056 Baha'i	0	1	NR	1	-	-
081 Catholic	2	NR	NR	810	4.8	8.2
093 Chr Ch (Disc)	3	732	225	879 *	5.2	8.8
097 Chr Chs&Chs Cr	1	53	NR	64 *	.4	.6
127 Ch God (Cleve)	1	87	61	105 *	.6	1.1
145 Ch God Prophcy	1	34	NR	41 *	.2	.4
165 Ch of Nazarene	2	52	63	89	.5	.9
171 Ch God-Gen Con	1	54	22	65 *	.4	.7
173 Comm of Christ	1	104	NR	104	.6	1.0
193 Episcopal	1	NR	18	40	.2	.4
201 Evan Cov Ch	1	89	66	107 *	.6	1.1
207 E.L.C.A.	5	1,011	354	1,254	7.4	12.6
221 Free Methodist	1	24	30	30	.2	.3
283 Luth—MO Synod	4	1,269	547	1,632	9.6	16.4
291 Missionary Ch	2	104	260	260	1.5	2.6
355 Presb Ch (USA)	5	849	455	1,020 *	6.0	10.3
419 So Bapt Conv	2	370	127	444 *	2.6	4.5
443 Un C of Christ	1	183	63	220 *	1.3	2.2
449 Un Methodist	8	1,758	641	2,111 *	12.4	21.3
469 WELS	1	17	12	19	.1	.2
PALO ALTO	**26**	**4,331**	**2,183**	**9,431 ***	**92.9**	**100.0**
040 Ap Chr Ch-Amer	1	199	510	510 *	5.0	5.4
053 Assemb of God	1	45	48	130	1.3	1.4

NR–Not Reported *Total adherents estimated from known number of communicant, confirmed, full members. - Represents a percentage less than 0.1. Percentages may not total 100 due to rounding.

Table 4: Religious Congregations by County and Group: 2000

Religious Group	Number of Churches, Synagogues, Mosques, or Temples	Number of Communicant, Confirmed, or Full Members	Number of Attendees	Total Adherents: Number of Adherents	Total Adherents: % of Total Pop.	Total Adherents: % of Total Adh.
056 Baha'i	0	1	NR	1	-	-
081 Catholic	6	NR	NR	3,667	36.1	38.9
193 Episcopal	1	NR	14	28	.3	.3
207 E.L.C.A.	5	1,332	554	1,689	16.6	17.9
283 Luth—MO Synod	5	971	460	1,242	12.2	13.2
388 Reg Bapt Gen As	1	55	80	80 *	.8	.8
449 Un Methodist	6	1,728	517	2,084 *	20.5	22.1
PLYMOUTH	**49**	**7,437**	**3,505**	**18,487 ***	**74.4**	**100.0**
019 Amer Bapt USA	2	196	100	248 *	1.0	1.3
053 Assemb of God	1	31	40	56	.2	.3
056 Baha'i	0	9	NR	9	-	-
081 Catholic	10	NR	NR	8,807	35.4	47.6
097 Chr Chs&Chs Cr	2	146	NR	184 *	.7	1.0
105 Christian Ref	1	285	175	360 *	1.4	1.9
151 L-D Saints	1	NR	NR	280	1.1	1.5
157 Ch of Brethren	1	21	45	45 *	.2	.2
165 Ch of Nazarene	1	38	34	42	.2	.2
167 Chs of Christ	1	33	36	41	.2	.2
193 Episcopal	1	NR	18	23	.1	.1
207 E.L.C.A.	9	2,772	1,193	3,435	13.8	18.6
283 Luth—MO Synod	4	1,579	664	2,013	8.1	10.9
355 Presb Ch (USA)	3	426	196	539 *	2.2	2.9
419 So Bapt Conv	0	35	25	44 *	.2	.2
443 Un C of Christ	3	200	284	253 *	1.0	1.4
449 Un Methodist	9	1,666	695	2,108 *	8.5	11.4
POCAHONTAS	**27**	**3,356**	**1,186**	**7,054 ***	**81.4**	**100.0**
081 Catholic	7	NR	NR	2,796	32.3	39.6
093 Chr Ch (Disc)	1	174	65	212 *	2.4	3.0
097 Chr Chs&Chs Cr	1	36	NR	44 *	.5	.6
151 L-D Saints	1	NR	NR	138	1.6	2.0
207 E.L.C.A.	7	1,716	535	2,111	24.4	29.9
283 Luth—MO Synod	1	32	0	42	.5	.6
355 Presb Ch (USA)	3	215	85	263 *	3.0	3.7
388 Reg Bapt Gen As	1	18	25	25 *	.3	.4
443 Un C of Christ	1	49	28	60 *	.7	.9
449 Un Methodist	4	1,116	448	1,363 *	15.7	19.3
POLK	**288**	**76,154**	**47,330**	**180,521 ***	**48.2**	**100.0**
019 Amer Bapt USA	7	1,003	648	1,258 *	.3	.7
053 Assemb of God	14	3,171	4,609	9,975	2.7	5.5
056 Baha'i	2	123	NR	123	-	.1
057 Bapt Gen Conf	3	463	421	598 *	.2	.3
075 Brethren in Cr	1	29	20	29	-	-
076 Buddhism	2	NR	NR	NR	-	-
081 Catholic	19	NR	NR	58,127	15.5	32.2
084 Calvary Chapel	1	NR	NR	NR	-	-
089 Chr & Miss Al	2	249	NR	304	.1	.2
093 Chr Ch (Disc)	17	7,983	2,475	10,011 *	2.7	5.5
097 Chr Chs&Chs Cr	9	1,735	NR	2,176 *	.6	1.2
105 Christian Ref	1	293	171	367 *	.1	.2
123 Ch God (Ander)	1	NR	35	35	-	-
127 Ch God (Cleve)	2	103	125	133 *	-	.1
145 Ch God Prophcy	2	69	NR	86 *	-	-
151 L-D Saints	5	NR	NR	1,766	.5	1.0
157 Ch of Brethren	2	166	25	208 *	.1	.1
165 Ch of Nazarene	6	771	710	1,270	.3	.7
167 Chs of Christ	9	540	601	704	.2	.4
173 Comm of Christ	4	525	NR	525	.1	.3
175 Congr Chr Chs	1	86	56	108 *	-	.1
179 Consrv Bapt	1	NR	187	187	-	.1
193 Episcopal	6	NR	871	2,833	.8	1.6
201 Evan Cov Ch	3	426	587	593 *	.2	.3
203 Evan Free Ch	8	1,189	2,103	2,103	.6	1.2
207 E.L.C.A.	27	17,300	8,707	23,622	6.3	13.1
216 Evan Presby Ch	1	340	NR	426 *	.1	.2
221 Free Methodist	1	70	74	74	-	-
226 Friends-USA	1	49	NR	61 *	-	-
246 Greek Orthodox	1	NR	NR	531	.1	.3
262 Int Cou Comm Ch	1	18	NR	23 *	-	-
263 Int Foursq Gos	1	248	125	311 *	.1	.2
264 Int Chs of Crst	1	100	156	142	-	.1
267 Muslim Est	2	NR	312	1,218	.3	.7
283 Luth—MO Synod	11	5,677	3,175	7,947	2.1	4.4
288 Mennonite USA	1	66	67	83 *	-	-
290 Metro Comm Ch	1	48	50	60 *	-	-
335 Orth Pres Ch	1	48	55	87	-	-
339 Pent Ch of God	1	20	NR	25	-	-
355 Presb Ch (USA)	17	5,612	2,514	7,037 *	1.9	3.9
356 Presb Ch Amer	1	22	70	70	-	-
371 Ref Ch in Am	4	1,787	1,491	2,880	.8	1.6
388 Reg Bapt Gen As	14	1,770	2,671	3,001 *	.8	1.7
403 Salvation Army	2	292	146	2,317	.6	1.3
413 S.D.A.	3	814	NR	969	.3	.5
416 Sikh	2	NR	NR	NR	-	-
419 So Bapt Conv	7	650	427	815 *	.2	.5
435 Unitarian-Univ	1	251	NR	315 *	.1	.2
443 Un C of Christ	5	4,114	1,404	5,159 *	1.4	2.9
449 Un Methodist	39	15,893	6,706	19,931 *	5.3	11.0
463 Vineyard	1	120	128	150 *	-	.1
467 Wesleyan	3	137	175	384	.1	.2
469 WELS	2	184	173	274	.1	.2
496 Jewish Est	3	NR	NR	2,100	.6	1.2
498 Indep.Charis.	1	600	1,700	1,700	.5	.9
499 Indep.Non-Char	4	1,000	3,360	5,290	1.4	2.9
POTTAWATTAMIE	**100**	**20,353**	**7,570**	**38,701 ***	**44.1**	**100.0**
019 Amer Bapt USA	2	568	227	708 *	.8	1.8
053 Assemb of God	4	162	155	202	.2	.5
056 Baha'i	0	15	NR	15	-	-
081 Catholic	9	NR	NR	10,811	12.3	27.9
089 Chr & Miss Al	2	102	NR	248	.3	.6
093 Chr Ch (Disc)	2	648	238	808 *	.9	2.1
097 Chr Chs&Chs Cr	5	2,078	NR	2,592 *	3.0	6.7
127 Ch God (Cleve)	2	185	184	242 *	.3	.6
145 Ch God Prophcy	1	34	NR	43 *	-	.1
151 L-D Saints	2	NR	NR	941	1.1	2.4
157 Ch of Brethren	1	70	47	87 *	.1	.2
165 Ch of Nazarene	2	405	497	1,221	1.4	3.2
167 Chs of Christ	1	225	250	290	.3	.7
173 Comm of Christ	5	1,117	NR	1,117	1.3	2.9
193 Episcopal	1	NR	65	115	.1	.3
203 Evan Free Ch	1	67	120	120	.1	.3
207 E.L.C.A.	8	4,495	1,426	6,036	6.9	15.6
252 Hindu	1	NR	NR	NR	-	-
283 Luth—MO Synod	6	1,902	853	2,470	2.8	6.4
339 Pent Ch of God	2	114	NR	445	.5	1.1
355 Presb Ch (USA)	12	1,649	756	2,058 *	2.3	5.3
360 Prim Bapt Chrch	1	NR	NR	NR	-	-
388 Reg Bapt Gen As	2	201	130	130 *	.1	.3
403 Salvation Army	1	158	42	296	.3	.8
413 S.D.A.	1	90	NR	107	.1	.3
419 So Bapt Conv	2	315	192	393 *	.4	1.0
443 Un C of Christ	7	1,390	594	1,733 *	2.0	4.5
449 Un Methodist	14	3,769	1,370	4,700 *	5.4	12.1
469 WELS	1	44	29	53	.1	.1
496 Jewish Est	0	NR	NR	150	.2	.4
499 Indep.Non-Char	2	550	395	570	.6	1.5
POWESHIEK	**41**	**6,022**	**2,305**	**9,792 ***	**52.0**	**100.0**
019 Amer Bapt USA	1	226	80	272 *	1.4	2.8
053 Assemb of God	1	87	115	156	.8	1.6
056 Baha'i	0	9	NR	9	-	.1
081 Catholic	2	NR	NR	2,239	11.9	22.9
089 Chr & Miss Al	1	57	NR	148	.8	1.5
093 Chr Ch (Disc)	1	50	0	60 *	.3	.6
097 Chr Chs&Chs Cr	3	1,097	NR	1,322 *	7.0	13.5
157 Ch of Brethren	1	15	13	18 *	.1	.2
165 Ch of Nazarene	2	27	42	74	.4	.8
167 Chs of Christ	4	84	85	99	.5	1.0
193 Episcopal	1	NR	43	74	.4	.8
207 E.L.C.A.	2	653	255	839	4.5	8.6
226 Friends-USA	3	192	NR	231 *	1.2	2.4
283 Luth—MO Synod	2	350	139	425	2.3	4.3
355 Presb Ch (USA)	6	650	327	784 *	4.2	8.0

NR–Not Reported *Total adherents estimated from known number of communicant, confirmed, full members. - Represents a percentage less than 0.1. Percentages may not total 100 due to rounding.

Table 4: Religious Congregations by County and Group: 2000

Religious Group	Number of Churches, Synagogues, Mosques, or Temples	Number of Communicant, Confirmed, or Full Members	Number of Attendees	Total Adherents: Number of Adherents	Total Adherents: % of Total Pop.	Total Adherents: % of Total Adh.
360 Prim Bapt Chrch	1	NR	NR	NR	-	-
388 Reg Bapt Gen As	2	229	257	276 *	1.5	2.8
443 Un C of Christ	1	343	151	413 *	2.2	4.2
449 Un Methodist	7	1,953	798	2,353 *	12.5	24.0
RINGGOLD	**26**	**2,126**	**847**	**2,767 ***	**50.6**	**100.0**
019 Amer Bapt USA	1	194	40	234 *	4.3	8.5
053 Assemb of God	2	54	64	94	1.7	3.4
081 Catholic	2	NR	NR	185	3.4	6.7
093 Chr Ch (Disc)	4	630	232	760 *	13.9	27.5
173 Comm of Christ	1	62	NR	62	1.1	2.2
221 Free Methodist	1	24	19	26	.5	.9
283 Luth—MO Synod	1	84	24	103	1.9	3.7
323 Old Ord Amish	1	55	NR	66 *	1.2	2.4
355 Presb Ch (USA)	3	137	57	166 *	3.0	6.0
388 Reg Bapt Gen As	1	54	50	65 *	1.2	2.3
449 Un Methodist	9	832	361	1,006 *	18.4	36.4
SAC	**35**	**5,589**	**2,096**	**9,489 ***	**82.3**	**100.0**
019 Amer Bapt USA	1	28	25	34 *	.3	.4
056 Baha'i	0	1	NR	1	-	-
081 Catholic	5	NR	NR	2,609	22.6	27.5
093 Chr Ch (Disc)	1	356	81	433 *	3.8	4.6
167 Chs of Christ	1	9	10	12	.1	.1
207 E.L.C.A.	2	638	229	824	7.1	8.7
283 Luth—MO Synod	8	2,082	770	2,565	22.2	27.0
355 Presb Ch (USA)	8	743	352	903 *	7.8	9.5
388 Reg Bapt Gen As	1	46	31	56 *	.5	.6
443 Un C of Christ	2	239	105	291 *	2.5	3.1
449 Un Methodist	6	1,447	493	1,761 *	15.3	18.6
SCOTT	**115**	**29,393**	**13,921**	**76,796 ***	**48.4**	**100.0**
019 Amer Bapt USA	2	399	226	501 *	.3	.7
049 Armen Ap Cilic	1	0	NR	80	.1	.1
053 Assemb of God	5	586	761	1,388	.9	1.8
056 Baha'i	1	162	NR	162	.1	.2
057 Bapt Gen Conf	4	968	1,041	1,218 *	.8	1.6
081 Catholic	13	NR	NR	33,162	20.9	43.2
089 Chr & Miss Al	1	0	NR	39	-	.1
093 Chr Ch (Disc)	3	1,315	231	1,650 *	1.0	2.1
097 Chr Chs&Chs Cr	3	920	NR	1,153 *	.7	1.5
127 Ch God (Cleve)	2	71	50	89 *	.1	.1
151 L-D Saints	4	NR	NR	858	.5	1.1
165 Ch of Nazarene	2	183	151	277	.2	.4
167 Chs of Christ	2	252	225	344	.2	.4
173 Comm of Christ	3	201	NR	201	.1	.3
193 Episcopal	3	NR	390	1,794	1.1	2.3
203 Evan Free Ch	2	154	243	243	.2	.3
207 E.L.C.A.	13	9,682	3,326	13,594	8.6	17.7
223 Free Will Bapt	2	0	NR	0 *	-	-
226 Friends-USA	1	64	NR	80 *	.1	.1
263 Int Foursq Gos	1	118	91	148 *	.1	.2
267 Muslim Est	1	NR	50	400	.3	.5
283 Luth—MO Synod	6	3,889	1,857	5,446	3.4	7.1
290 Metro Comm Ch	1	65	67	82 *	.1	.1
355 Presb Ch (USA)	10	3,105	1,345	3,894 *	2.5	5.1
360 Prim Bapt Chrch	1	NR	NR	NR	-	-
371 Ref Ch in Am	1	283	248	504	.3	.7
388 Reg Bapt Gen As	2	325	340	408 *	.3	.5
403 Salvation Army	1	146	213	268	.2	.3
413 S.D.A.	2	267	NR	318	.2	.4
419 So Bapt Conv	4	733	334	920 *	.6	1.2
435 Unitarian-Univ	1	195	NR	245 *	.2	.3
443 Un C of Christ	2	577	213	724 *	.5	.9
449 Un Methodist	11	4,233	2,012	5,310 *	3.3	6.9
463 Vineyard	2	380	420	477 *	.3	.6
469 WELS	1	120	87	169	.1	.2
496 Jewish Est	1	NR	NR	650	.4	.8
SHELBY	**35**	**4,582**	**1,938**	**10,234 ***	**77.7**	**100.0**
019 Amer Bapt USA	2	458	238	569 *	4.3	5.6
053 Assemb of God	1	61	75	120	.9	1.2

Religious Group	Number of Churches, Synagogues, Mosques, or Temples	Number of Communicant, Confirmed, or Full Members	Number of Attendees	Total Adherents: Number of Adherents	Total Adherents: % of Total Pop.	Total Adherents: % of Total Adh.
056 Baha'i	0	2	NR	2	-	-
081 Catholic	6	NR	NR	4,297	32.6	42.0
097 Chr Chs&Chs Cr	3	220	NR	273 *	2.1	2.7
167 Chs of Christ	2	101	110	132	1.0	1.3
173 Comm of Christ	1	21	NR	21	.2	.2
179 Consrv Bapt	1	NR	95	95	.7	.9
193 Episcopal	1	NR	19	21	.2	.2
207 E.L.C.A.	5	1,947	725	2,502	19.0	24.4
283 Luth—MO Synod	1	59	34	77	.6	.8
355 Presb Ch (USA)	1	74	31	92 *	.7	.9
388 Reg Bapt Gen As	2	159	152	197 *	1.5	1.9
413 S.D.A.	1	12	NR	14	.1	.1
443 Un C of Christ	1	179	38	222 *	1.7	2.2
449 Un Methodist	7	1,289	421	1,600 *	12.1	15.6
SIOUX	**67**	**19,860**	**15,489**	**30,472 ***	**96.5**	**100.0**
019 Amer Bapt USA	1	222	88	279 *	.9	.9
053 Assemb of God	1	29	40	40	.1	.1
056 Baha'i	0	1	NR	1	-	-
081 Catholic	5	NR	NR	2,461	7.8	8.1
089 Chr & Miss Al	1	170	NR	424	1.3	1.4
105 Christian Ref	16	7,285	5,925	9,140 *	28.9	30.0
203 Evan Free Ch	2	67	175	175	.6	.6
207 E.L.C.A.	6	1,261	628	1,663	5.3	5.5
283 Luth—MO Synod	4	1,092	463	1,366	4.3	4.5
307 Neth Ref Congr	2	842	NR	1,585	5.0	5.2
355 Presb Ch (USA)	4	434	371	545 *	1.7	1.8
369 Prot Ref Chs	1	236	NR	495	1.6	1.6
371 Ref Ch in Am	19	7,443	7,517	11,282	35.7	37.0
419 So Bapt Conv	0	27	20	34 *	.1	.1
443 Un C of Christ	1	80	35	100 *	.3	.3
449 Un Methodist	3	468	227	588 *	1.9	1.9
455 Un Ref Chs N.A.	1	203	NR	294	.9	1.0
STORY	**92**	**22,468**	**12,408**	**40,765 ***	**51.0**	**100.0**
019 Amer Bapt USA	1	171	65	200 *	.3	.5
053 Assemb of God	3	276	379	681	.9	1.7
056 Baha'i	1	48	NR	48	.1	.1
081 Catholic	6	NR	NR	9,280	11.6	22.8
093 Chr Ch (Disc)	5	1,089	208	1,274 *	1.6	3.1
097 Chr Chs&Chs Cr	2	375	NR	438 *	.5	1.1
105 Christian Ref	2	309	268	362 *	.5	.9
145 Ch God Prophcy	1	34	NR	40 *	.1	.1
151 L-D Saints	3	NR	NR	631	.8	1.5
157 Ch of Brethren	1	17	15	20 *	-	-
165 Ch of Nazarene	1	115	98	160	.2	.4
167 Chs of Christ	2	48	60	70	.1	.2
173 Comm of Christ	1	152	NR	152	.2	.4
193 Episcopal	1	NR	176	412	.5	1.0
203 Evan Free Ch	5	589	1,316	1,316	1.6	3.2
207 E.L.C.A.	16	8,622	3,021	11,358	14.2	27.9
226 Friends-USA	1	49	NR	57 *	.1	.1
263 Int Foursq Gos	1	3	10	10 *	-	-
267 Muslim Est	1	NR	55	163	.2	.4
283 Luth—MO Synod	2	1,212	634	1,620	2.0	4.0
288 Mennonite USA	1	8	8	9 *	-	-
297 Mennonite;Other	1	8	NR	9 *	-	-
355 Presb Ch (USA)	5	1,274	523	1,492 *	1.9	3.7
388 Reg Bapt Gen As	4	688	760	835 *	1.0	2.0
413 S.D.A.	2	178	NR	212	.3	.5
419 So Bapt Conv	4	843	1,462	986 *	1.2	2.4
435 Unitarian-Univ	1	262	NR	307 *	.4	.8
443 Un C of Christ	1	376	153	440 *	.6	1.1
449 Un Methodist	15	5,455	2,097	6,383 *	8.0	15.7
496 Jewish Est	1	NR	NR	700	.9	1.7
499 Indep.Non-Char	1	267	1,100	1,100	1.4	2.7
TAMA	**39**	**4,968**	**1,961**	**9,428 ***	**52.1**	**100.0**
053 Assemb of God	3	120	97	144	.8	1.5
056 Baha'i	0	10	NR	10	.1	.1
081 Catholic	8	NR	NR	3,091	17.1	32.8
089 Chr & Miss Al	2	72	NR	123	.7	1.3
093 Chr Ch (Disc)	1	72	13	90 *	.5	1.0

NR–Not Reported   *Total adherents estimated from known number of communicant, confirmed, full members.   - Represents a percentage less than 0.1.   Percentages may not total 100 due to rounding.

Table 4: Religious Congregations by County and Group: 2000

Religious Group	Number of Churches, Synagogues, Mosques, or Temples	Number of Communicant, Confirmed, or Full Members	Number of Attendees	Total Adherents: Number of Adherents	% of Total Pop.	% of Total Adh.
121 Ch God (Abr)	1	0	10	10 *	.1	.1
173 Comm of Christ	1	27	NR	27	.1	.3
207 E.L.C.A.	3	956	329	1,287	7.1	13.7
283 Luth—MO Synod	1	104	37	133	.7	1.4
355 Presb Ch (USA)	3	366	246	458 *	2.5	4.9
370 Ref Baptist Chs	1	NR	NR	NR	-	-
388 Reg Bapt Gen As	1	58	70	73 *	.4	.8
443 Un C of Christ	4	799	301	1,000 *	5.5	10.6
449 Un Methodist	9	2,384	858	2,982 *	16.5	31.6
467 Wesleyan	1	0	0	0	-	-
TAYLOR	**28**	**3,039**	**1,028**	**4,065 ***	**58.4**	**100.0**
019 Amer Bapt USA	1	589	130	715 *	10.3	17.6
081 Catholic	2	NR	NR	296	4.3	7.3
093 Chr Ch (Disc)	3	470	172	570 *	8.2	14.0
097 Chr Chs&Chs Cr	4	340	NR	412 *	5.9	10.1
157 Ch of Brethren	1	18	0	22 *	.3	.5
165 Ch of Nazarene	1	17	11	41	.6	1.0
167 Chs of Christ	2	31	30	39	.6	1.0
283 Luth—MO Synod	1	28	25	30	.4	.7
291 Missionary Ch	1	30	101	101	1.5	2.5
355 Presb Ch (USA)	3	253	152	307 *	4.4	7.6
413 S.D.A.	1	45	NR	54	.8	1.3
419 So Bapt Conv	1	55	8	67 *	1.0	1.6
443 Un C of Christ	1	23	10	28 *	.4	.7
449 Un Methodist	6	1,140	389	1,383 *	19.9	34.0
UNION	**28**	**4,498**	**1,700**	**7,182 ***	**58.3**	**100.0**
019 Amer Bapt USA	1	45	22	54 *	.4	.8
053 Assemb of God	2	108	131	205	1.7	2.9
081 Catholic	2	NR	NR	1,480	12.0	20.6
093 Chr Ch (Disc)	1	1,070	178	1,296 *	10.5	18.0
097 Chr Chs&Chs Cr	1	31	NR	38 *	.3	.5
123 Ch God (Ander)	1	NR	28	28	.2	.4
151 L-D Saints	1	NR	NR	108	.9	1.5
165 Ch of Nazarene	1	8	0	8	.1	.1
173 Comm of Christ	1	89	NR	89	.7	1.2
193 Episcopal	1	NR	10	13	.1	.2
207 E.L.C.A.	1	358	120	443	3.6	6.2
283 Luth—MO Synod	1	248	140	343	2.8	4.8
355 Presb Ch (USA)	2	324	144	393 *	3.2	5.5
388 Reg Bapt Gen As	1	493	297	597 *	4.9	8.3
413 S.D.A.	1	11	NR	13	.1	.2
419 So Bapt Conv	1	129	103	156 *	1.3	2.2
443 Un C of Christ	3	517	198	626 *	5.1	8.7
449 Un Methodist	6	1,067	329	1,292 *	10.5	18.0
VAN BUREN	**28**	**2,221**	**795**	**3,041 ***	**38.9**	**100.0**
019 Amer Bapt USA	1	26	6	32 *	.4	1.1
053 Assemb of God	1	26	35	55	.7	1.8
081 Catholic	1	NR	NR	281	3.6	9.2
097 Chr Chs&Chs Cr	3	335	NR	411 *	5.3	13.5
165 Ch of Nazarene	1	34	14	56	.7	1.8
173 Comm of Christ	1	23	NR	23	.3	.8
283 Luth—MO Synod	1	30	15	41	.5	1.3
323 Old Ord Amish	3	165	NR	201 *	2.6	6.6
355 Presb Ch (USA)	3	240	102	294 *	3.8	9.7
388 Reg Bapt Gen As	1	109	117	134 *	1.7	4.4
443 Un C of Christ	1	51	24	63 *	.8	2.1
449 Un Methodist	11	1,182	482	1,450 *	18.6	47.7
WAPELLO	**62**	**8,619**	**3,482**	**15,235 ***	**42.3**	**100.0**
019 Amer Bapt USA	2	403	141	491 *	1.4	3.2
053 Assemb of God	4	426	508	854	2.4	5.6
056 Baha'i	0	11	NR	11	-	.1
081 Catholic	2	NR	NR	3,172	8.8	20.8
089 Chr & Miss Al	1	96	NR	252	.7	1.7
093 Chr Ch (Disc)	6	1,702	412	2,073 *	5.8	13.6
097 Chr Chs&Chs Cr	3	335	NR	409 *	1.1	2.7
123 Ch God (Ander)	2	NR	119	119	.3	.8
145 Ch God Prophcy	1	34	NR	42 *	.1	.3
151 L-D Saints	1	NR	NR	273	.8	1.8

Religious Group	Number of Churches, Synagogues, Mosques, or Temples	Number of Communicant, Confirmed, or Full Members	Number of Attendees	Total Adherents: Number of Adherents	% of Total Pop.	% of Total Adh.
157 Ch of Brethren	1	128	0	156 *	.4	1.0
165 Ch of Nazarene	2	262	159	387	1.1	2.5
167 Chs of Christ	2	82	100	113	.3	.7
193 Episcopal	1	NR	43	102	.3	.7
203 Evan Free Ch	1	20	40	40	.1	.3
207 E.L.C.A.	3	688	283	885	2.5	5.8
221 Free Methodist	1	70	109	109	.3	.7
263 Int Foursq Gos	2	255	108	311 *	.9	2.0
283 Luth—MO Synod	1	246	110	344	1.0	2.3
339 Pent Ch of God	1	91	NR	129	.4	.8
355 Presb Ch (USA)	3	554	211	675 *	1.9	4.4
360 Prim Bapt Chrch	1	NR	NR	NR	-	-
371 Ref Ch in Am	1	24	32	69	.2	.5
388 Reg Bapt Gen As	1	87	70	70 *	.2	.5
403 Salvation Army	1	149	80	454	1.3	3.0
413 S.D.A.	1	81	NR	96	.3	.6
419 So Bapt Conv	1	604	85	736 *	2.0	4.8
443 Un C of Christ	3	139	79	169 *	.5	1.1
449 Un Methodist	11	2,129	781	2,592 *	7.2	17.0
467 Wesleyan	1	3	12	12	-	.1
496 Jewish Est	1	NR	NR	90	.2	.6
WARREN	**66**	**9,328**	**4,422**	**16,964 ***	**41.7**	**100.0**
019 Amer Bapt USA	1	165	86	208 *	.5	1.2
053 Assemb of God	1	129	172	314	.8	1.9
056 Baha'i	0	7	NR	7	-	-
081 Catholic	6	NR	NR	3,914	9.6	23.1
093 Chr Ch (Disc)	4	830	255	1,045 *	2.6	6.2
097 Chr Chs&Chs Cr	1	150	NR	189 *	.5	1.1
107 Christian Un	3	224	141	282 *	.7	1.7
151 L-D Saints	2	NR	NR	520	1.3	3.1
165 Ch of Nazarene	2	131	71	215	.5	1.3
167 Chs of Christ	2	58	70	76	.2	.4
173 Comm of Christ	1	76	NR	76	.2	.4
203 Evan Free Ch	5	314	720	720	1.8	4.2
207 E.L.C.A.	3	1,011	432	1,475	3.6	8.7
226 Friends-USA	8	512	NR	645 *	1.6	3.8
263 Int Foursq Gos	1	16	22	22 *	.1	.1
283 Luth—MO Synod	3	580	297	795	2.0	4.7
355 Presb Ch (USA)	3	752	281	947 *	2.3	5.6
388 Reg Bapt Gen As	4	294	330	379 *	.9	2.2
413 S.D.A.	1	10	NR	12	-	.1
419 So Bapt Conv	2	229	115	288 *	.7	1.7
443 Un C of Christ	1	36	32	45 *	.1	.3
449 Un Methodist	12	3,804	1,398	4,790 *	11.8	28.2
WASHINGTON	**53**	**6,715**	**3,410**	**11,609 ***	**56.2**	**100.0**
019 Amer Bapt USA	3	543	171	679 *	3.3	5.8
053 Assemb of God	1	45	51	65	.3	.6
056 Baha'i	0	10	NR	10	-	.1
057 Bapt Gen Conf	1	119	156	156 *	.8	1.3
081 Catholic	3	NR	NR	2,914	14.1	25.1
093 Chr Ch (Disc)	3	376	106	470 *	2.3	4.0
127 Ch God (Cleve)	1	28	15	35 *	.2	.3
151 L-D Saints	1	NR	NR	108	.5	.9
165 Ch of Nazarene	1	37	101	101	.5	.9
167 Chs of Christ	1	12	10	12	.1	.1
171 Ch God-Gen Con	1	76	90	95 *	.5	.8
183 Cons Menn Conf	3	432	528	627	3.0	5.4
207 E.L.C.A.	1	441	175	590	2.9	5.1
226 Friends-USA	1	64	NR	80 *	.4	.7
283 Luth—MO Synod	1	29	22	33	.2	.3
288 Mennonite USA	6	868	719	1,086 *	5.3	9.4
297 Mennonite;Other	2	81	NR	102 *	.5	.9
323 Old Ord Amish	9	495	NR	621 *	3.0	5.3
355 Presb Ch (USA)	5	978	442	1,223 *	5.9	10.5
388 Reg Bapt Gen As	1	95	110	119 *	.6	1.0
449 Un Methodist	8	1,986	714	2,483 *	12.0	21.4
WAYNE	**28**	**2,572**	**1,056**	**3,317 ***	**49.3**	**100.0**
019 Amer Bapt USA	2	336	189	406 *	6.0	12.2
053 Assemb of God	3	135	176	265	3.9	8.0
056 Baha'i	0	1	NR	1	-	-

NR–Not Reported *Total adherents estimated from known number of communicant, confirmed, full members. - Represents a percentage less than 0.1. Percentages may not total 100 due to rounding.

Table 4: Religious Congregations by County and Group: 2000

Religious Group	Number of Churches, Synagogues, Mosques, or Temples	Number of Communicant, Confirmed, or Full Members	Number of Attendees	Total Adherents		
				Number of Adherents	% of Total Pop.	% of Total Adh.
081 Catholic	1	NR	NR	110	1.6	3.3
093 Chr Ch (Disc)	3	355	133	429 *	6.4	12.9
097 Chr Chs&Chs Cr	1	100	NR	121 *	1.8	3.6
145 Ch God Prophcy	1	34	NR	42 *	.6	1.3
167 Chs of Christ	2	42	45	53	.8	1.6
173 Comm of Christ	1	35	NR	35	.5	1.1
323 Old Ord Amish	2	110	NR	134 *	2.0	4.0
355 Presb Ch (USA)	1	83	40	100 *	1.5	3.0
419 So Bapt Conv	1	239	57	289 *	4.3	8.7
449 Un Methodist	10	1,102	416	1,332 *	19.8	40.2
WEBSTER	**63**	**13,576**	**6,094**	**24,574 ***	**61.1**	**100.0**
019 Amer Bapt USA	2	460	131	565 *	1.4	2.3
053 Assemb of God	1	58	62	97	.2	.4
056 Baha'i	0	5	NR	5	-	-
057 Bapt Gen Conf	1	55	35	68 *	.2	.3
081 Catholic	8	NR	NR	7,184	17.9	29.2
093 Chr Ch (Disc)	1	75	35	92 *	.2	.4
097 Chr Chs&Chs Cr	1	95	NR	117 *	.3	.5
165 Ch of Nazarene	1	62	40	154	.4	.6
167 Chs of Christ	1	50	45	63	.2	.3
173 Comm of Christ	1	100	NR	100	.2	.4
193 Episcopal	1	NR	51	125	.3	.5
201 Evan Cov Ch	3	334	249	411 *	1.0	1.7
203 Evan Free Ch	1	134	212	212	.5	.9
207 E.L.C.A.	13	3,852	1,582	5,030	12.5	20.5
283 Luth—MO Synod	6	2,769	1,154	3,568	8.9	14.5
288 Mennonite USA	1	50	43	61 *	.2	.2
355 Presb Ch (USA)	2	873	426	1,072 *	2.7	4.4
388 Reg Bapt Gen As	1	86	60	60 *	.1	.2
403 Salvation Army	1	111	32	301	.7	1.2
413 S.D.A.	1	42	NR	50	.1	.2
419 So Bapt Conv	1	120	50	147 *	.4	.6
443 Un C of Christ	2	343	127	421 *	1.0	1.7
449 Un Methodist	11	3,152	1,050	3,871 *	9.6	15.8
498 Indep.Charis.	2	750	710	800	2.0	3.3
WINNEBAGO	**26**	**6,959**	**3,055**	**10,076 ***	**86.0**	**100.0**
056 Baha'i	0	1	NR	1	-	-
057 Bapt Gen Conf	1	289	385	385 *	3.3	3.8
081 Catholic	3	NR	NR	1,165	9.9	11.6
176 Congr Ad Afl	1	126	NR	153 *	1.3	1.5
181 Consrv Congr	1	114	120	139 *	1.2	1.4
207 E.L.C.A.	11	4,799	1,771	6,146	52.4	61.0
220 Free Lutheran	1	22	20	22	.2	.2
263 Int Foursq Gos	1	58	72	72 *	.6	.7
313 N Am Bapt Conf	1	84	65	102 *	.9	1.0
371 Ref Ch in Am	1	211	130	391	3.3	3.9
388 Reg Bapt Gen As	1	100	96	96 *	.8	1.0
449 Un Methodist	4	1,155	396	1,404 *	12.0	13.9
WINNESHIEK	**43**	**8,289**	**3,482**	**19,782 ***	**92.8**	**100.0**
053 Assemb of God	1	56	70	93	.4	.5
056 Baha'i	0	4	NR	4	-	-
057 Bapt Gen Conf	1	69	155	155 *	.7	.8
081 Catholic	9	NR	NR	8,473	39.8	42.8
167 Chs of Christ	1	11	17	17	.1	.1
193 Episcopal	1	NR	25	50	.2	.3
201 Evan Cov Ch	1	32	83	83 *	.4	.4
207 E.L.C.A.	20	7,032	2,790	9,602	45.1	48.5
226 Friends-USA	3	177	NR	213 *	1.0	1.1
355 Presb Ch (USA)	1	59	70	71 *	.3	.4
419 So Bapt Conv	0	20	15	24 *	.1	.1
443 Un C of Christ	1	88	39	106 *	.5	.5
449 Un Methodist	4	741	218	891 *	4.2	4.5
WOODBURY	**123**	**25,995**	**13,316**	**60,310 ***	**58.1**	**100.0**
019 Amer Bapt USA	2	200	110	254 *	.2	.4
034 Ant Orth of NA	1	211	NR	422	.4	.7
053 Assemb of God	5	703	912	1,752	1.7	2.9
056 Baha'i	1	49	NR	49	-	.1
057 Bapt Gen Conf	1	110	146	146 *	.1	.2
081 Catholic	13	NR	NR	21,563	20.8	35.8
089 Chr & Miss Al	2	73	NR	128	.1	.2
093 Chr Ch (Disc)	3	405	90	515 *	.5	.9
097 Chr Chs&Chs Cr	3	405	NR	515 *	.5	.9
105 Christian Ref	2	56	56	71 *	.1	.1
151 L-D Saints	2	NR	NR	446	.4	.7
165 Ch of Nazarene	3	244	196	334	.3	.6
167 Chs of Christ	2	61	60	77	.1	.1
173 Comm of Christ	1	278	NR	278	.3	.5
179 Consrv Bapt	1	NR	110	110	.1	.2
193 Episcopal	3	NR	221	1,227	1.2	2.0
201 Evan Cov Ch	2	212	133	269 *	.3	.4
203 Evan Free Ch	2	185	355	355	.3	.6
207 E.L.C.A.	14	7,035	3,084	9,298	9.0	15.4
221 Free Methodist	1	9	14	14	-	-
246 Greek Orthodox	1	NR	NR	282	.3	.5
263 Int Foursq Gos	1	33	106	106 *	.1	.2
283 Luth—MO Synod	12	4,044	1,810	5,398	5.2	9.0
349 Pent Holiness	1	40	102	51 *	-	.1
355 Presb Ch (USA)	7	1,850	797	2,352 *	2.3	3.9
371 Ref Ch in Am	1	606	544	1,238	1.2	2.1
403 Salvation Army	1	210	595	1,260	1.2	2.1
413 S.D.A.	1	177	NR	211	.2	.3
419 So Bapt Conv	2	657	460	835 *	.8	1.4
435 Unitarian-Univ	1	61	NR	78 *	.1	.1
443 Un C of Christ	4	739	289	939 *	.9	1.6
449 Un Methodist	21	6,565	2,380	8,345 *	8.0	13.8
467 Wesleyan	2	53	73	124	.1	.2
469 WELS	1	124	73	168	.2	.3
496 Jewish Est	2	NR	NR	400	.4	.7
498 Indep.Charis.	1	600	600	700	.7	1.2
WORTH	**16**	**4,470**	**1,448**	**5,911 ***	**74.7**	**100.0**
081 Catholic	1	NR	NR	371	4.7	6.3
097 Chr Chs&Chs Cr	1	200	NR	244 *	3.1	4.1
207 E.L.C.A.	10	3,410	1,129	4,249	53.7	71.9
419 So Bapt Conv	1	114	35	139 *	1.8	2.4
449 Un Methodist	3	746	284	908 *	11.5	15.4
WRIGHT	**42**	**6,840**	**2,888**	**11,243 ***	**78.4**	**100.0**
019 Amer Bapt USA	1	117	38	143 *	1.0	1.3
053 Assemb of God	2	79	59	132	.9	1.2
056 Baha'i	0	4	NR	4	-	-
081 Catholic	3	NR	NR	2,326	16.2	20.7
097 Chr Chs&Chs Cr	2	320	NR	392 *	2.7	3.5
165 Ch of Nazarene	1	29	38	135	.9	1.2
203 Evan Free Ch	2	92	188	188	1.3	1.7
207 E.L.C.A.	9	2,707	918	3,435	24.0	30.6
220 Free Lutheran	1	33	30	43	.3	.4
263 Int Foursq Gos	1	28	186	186 *	1.3	1.7
283 Luth—MO Synod	3	182	95	234	1.6	2.1
355 Presb Ch (USA)	3	357	168	436 *	3.0	3.9
371 Ref Ch in Am	2	158	140	245	1.7	2.2
388 Reg Bapt Gen As	1	80	85	98 *	.7	.9
443 Un C of Christ	4	719	285	879 *	6.1	7.8
449 Un Methodist	7	1,935	658	2,367 *	16.5	21.1
KANSAS						
The State.....	3,959	655,970	319,323	1,327,235 *	49.4	100.0
ALLEN	**40**	**5,840**	**2,247**	**8,978 ***	**62.4**	**100.0**
019 Amer Bapt USA	2	953	243	1,168 *	8.1	13.0
053 Assemb of God	4	385	503	796	5.5	8.9
056 Baha'i	0	2	NR	2	-	-
081 Catholic	2	NR	NR	1,437	10.0	16.0
093 Chr Ch (Disc)	1	381	98	467 *	3.2	5.2
097 Chr Chs&Chs Cr	4	619	NR	759 *	5.3	8.5
165 Ch of Nazarene	2	178	90	196	1.4	2.2
167 Chs of Christ	1	35	40	60	.4	.7
173 Comm of Christ	1	55	NR	55	.4	.6
193 Episcopal	1	NR	13	23	.2	.3

NR–Not Reported *Total adherents estimated from known number of communicant, confirmed, full members. - Represents a percentage less than 0.1. Percentages may not total 100 due to rounding.

Table 4: Religious Congregations by County and Group: 2000

Religious Group	Number of Churches, Synagogues, Mosques, or Temples	Number of Communicant, Confirmed, or Full Members	Number of Attendees	Total Adherents: Number of Adherents	Total Adherents: % of Total Pop.	Total Adherents: % of Total Adh.
201 Evan Cov Ch	1	76	64	93 *	.6	1.0
207 E.L.C.A.	1	125	55	157	1.1	1.7
226 Friends-USA	1	50	NR	61 *	.4	.7
283 Luth—MO Synod	2	536	231	709	4.9	7.9
355 Presb Ch (USA)	3	277	130	340 *	2.4	3.8
388 Reg Bapt Gen As	1	45	45	55 *	.4	.6
413 S.D.A.	1	88	NR	105	.7	1.2
419 So Bapt Conv	2	597	223	732 *	5.1	8.2
449 Un Methodist	10	1,438	512	1,763 *	12.3	19.6
ANDERSON	**24**	**2,151**	**701**	**4,742 ***	**58.5**	**100.0**
019 Amer Bapt USA	2	543	156	676 *	8.3	14.3
053 Assemb of God	1	53	45	50	.6	1.1
081 Catholic	5	NR	NR	1,955	24.1	41.2
097 Chr Chs&Chs Cr	3	595	NR	742 *	9.1	15.6
157 Ch of Brethren	1	38	38	47 *	.6	1.0
165 Ch of Nazarene	1	101	152	221	2.7	4.7
167 Chs of Christ	1	37	50	60	.7	1.3
283 Luth—MO Synod	1	49	31	75	.9	1.6
323 Old Ord Amish	2	110	NR	138 *	1.7	2.9
355 Presb Ch (USA)	1	50	22	62 *	.8	1.3
449 Un Methodist	6	575	207	716 *	8.8	15.1
ATCHISON	**30**	**4,821**	**1,727**	**10,486 ***	**62.5**	**100.0**
019 Amer Bapt USA	1	594	160	737 *	4.4	7.0
053 Assemb of God	1	72	100	190	1.1	1.8
056 Baha'i	0	2	NR	2	-	-
081 Catholic	6	NR	NR	4,070	24.3	38.8
093 Chr Ch (Disc)	2	1,101	266	1,366 *	8.1	13.0
097 Chr Chs&Chs Cr	4	290	NR	360 *	2.1	3.4
165 Ch of Nazarene	1	30	42	75	.4	.7
167 Chs of Christ	1	15	15	29	.2	.3
173 Comm of Christ	1	80	NR	80	.5	.8
193 Episcopal	1	NR	92	174	1.0	1.7
207 E.L.C.A.	2	417	122	529	3.2	5.0
283 Luth—MO Synod	1	1,003	485	1,344	8.0	12.8
339 Pent Ch of God	1	12	NR	38	.2	.4
355 Presb Ch (USA)	2	448	142	556 *	3.3	5.3
413 S.D.A.	1	55	NR	65	.4	.6
449 Un Methodist	5	702	303	871 *	5.2	8.3
BARBER	**23**	**2,346**	**795**	**3,938 ***	**74.2**	**100.0**
019 Amer Bapt USA	1	50	25	61 *	1.1	1.5
040 Ap Chr Ch-Amer	1	35	76	76 *	1.4	1.9
053 Assemb of God	1	32	38	48	.9	1.2
056 Baha'i	0	2	NR	2	-	.1
081 Catholic	3	NR	NR	1,012	19.1	25.7
097 Chr Chs&Chs Cr	4	759	NR	926 *	17.4	23.5
167 Chs of Christ	2	37	50	46	.9	1.2
193 Episcopal	1	NR	6	10	.2	.3
283 Luth—MO Synod	1	111	40	147	2.8	3.7
355 Presb Ch (USA)	1	26	12	32 *	.6	.8
419 So Bapt Conv	1	157	110	191 *	3.6	4.9
443 Un C of Christ	2	195	80	238 *	4.5	6.0
449 Un Methodist	5	942	358	1,149 *	21.7	29.2
BARTON	**56**	**8,629**	**4,044**	**21,277 ***	**75.4**	**100.0**
017 Amer Bapt Assn	1	24	NR	30 *	.1	.1
019 Amer Bapt USA	1	436	82	540 *	1.9	2.5
053 Assemb of God	2	365	424	598	2.1	2.8
056 Baha'i	0	3	NR	3	-	-
081 Catholic	7	NR	NR	9,579	34.0	45.0
093 Chr Ch (Disc)	2	650	282	806 *	2.9	3.8
097 Chr Chs&Chs Cr	2	320	NR	397 *	1.4	1.9
123 Ch God (Ander)	1	NR	66	66	.2	.3
151 L-D Saints	1	NR	NR	263	.9	1.2
165 Ch of Nazarene	2	270	212	347	1.2	1.6
167 Chs of Christ	2	160	140	203	.7	1.0
173 Comm of Christ	1	31	NR	31	.1	.1
193 Episcopal	1	NR	28	63	.2	.3
203 Evan Free Ch	2	138	250	250	.9	1.2
207 E.L.C.A.	4	1,189	520	1,745	6.2	8.2

Religious Group	Number of Churches, Synagogues, Mosques, or Temples	Number of Communicant, Confirmed, or Full Members	Number of Attendees	Total Adherents: Number of Adherents	Total Adherents: % of Total Pop.	Total Adherents: % of Total Adh.
226 Friends-USA	1	50	NR	62 *	.2	.3
263 Int Foursq Gos	2	64	138	138 *	.5	.6
283 Luth—MO Synod	4	757	361	961	3.4	4.5
288 Mennonite USA	1	79	45	98 *	.3	.5
313 N Am Bapt Conf	1	240	157	298 *	1.1	1.4
355 Presb Ch (USA)	1	264	86	327 *	1.2	1.5
413 S.D.A.	1	82	NR	98	.3	.5
419 So Bapt Conv	5	1,154	406	1,431 *	5.1	6.7
443 Un C of Christ	2	425	153	527 *	1.9	2.5
449 Un Methodist	9	1,928	694	2,391 *	8.5	11.2
496 Jewish Est	0	NR	NR	25	.1	.1
BOURBON	**37**	**5,129**	**2,353**	**7,952 ***	**51.7**	**100.0**
019 Amer Bapt USA	3	1,020	317	1,263 *	8.2	15.9
040 Ap Chr Ch-Amer	1	36	75	75 *	.5	.9
053 Assemb of God	1	43	51	103	.7	1.3
059 Bapt Miss Assn	1	123	32	152 *	1.0	1.9
071 Brethren (Ash)	1	25	38	31 *	.2	.4
081 Catholic	1	NR	NR	1,500	9.8	18.9
093 Chr Ch (Disc)	1	259	178	321 *	2.1	4.0
097 Chr Chs&Chs Cr	2	279	NR	346 *	2.2	4.4
151 L-D Saints	1	NR	NR	97	.6	1.2
157 Ch of Brethren	1	25	32	32 *	.2	.4
165 Ch of Nazarene	2	326	270	447	2.9	5.6
167 Chs of Christ	2	67	90	83	.5	1.0
171 Ch God-Gen Con	1	158	148	196 *	1.3	2.5
173 Comm of Christ	2	271	NR	271	1.8	3.4
193 Episcopal	1	NR	15	29	.2	.4
283 Luth—MO Synod	1	136	108	180	1.2	2.3
355 Presb Ch (USA)	1	339	125	420 *	2.7	5.3
413 S.D.A.	1	47	NR	56	.4	.7
419 So Bapt Conv	1	228	106	282 *	1.8	3.5
449 Un Methodist	11	1,347	538	1,668 *	10.8	21.0
499 Indep.Non-Char	1	400	230	400	2.6	5.0
BROWN	**34**	**3,962**	**1,550**	**6,408 ***	**59.8**	**100.0**
017 Amer Bapt Assn	1	23	NR	28 *	.3	.4
019 Amer Bapt USA	4	765	304	946 *	8.8	14.8
053 Assemb of God	1	38	48	100	.9	1.6
056 Baha'i	0	13	NR	13	.1	.2
081 Catholic	3	NR	NR	1,400	13.1	21.8
093 Chr Ch (Disc)	3	370	143	458 *	4.3	7.1
097 Chr Chs&Chs Cr	2	189	NR	233 *	2.2	3.6
167 Chs of Christ	1	15	15	19	.2	.3
173 Comm of Christ	1	73	NR	73	.7	1.1
207 E.L.C.A.	2	249	112	354	3.3	5.5
283 Luth—MO Synod	4	469	217	603	5.6	9.4
339 Pent Ch of God	1	6	NR	15	.1	.2
355 Presb Ch (USA)	1	82	40	101 *	.9	1.6
443 Un C of Christ	2	241	90	298 *	2.8	4.7
449 Un Methodist	8	1,429	581	1,767 *	16.5	27.6
BUTLER	**81**	**16,270**	**7,722**	**29,041 ***	**48.8**	**100.0**
017 Amer Bapt Assn	1	50	NR	64 *	.1	.2
019 Amer Bapt USA	8	3,304	1,379	4,222 *	7.1	14.5
053 Assemb of God	4	319	412	666	1.1	2.3
056 Baha'i	0	23	NR	23	-	.1
059 Bapt Miss Assn	1	4	7	7 *	-	-
081 Catholic	3	NR	NR	6,585	11.1	22.7
093 Chr Ch (Disc)	5	2,028	591	2,592 *	4.4	8.9
097 Chr Chs&Chs Cr	5	640	NR	819 *	1.4	2.8
123 Ch God (Ander)	2	NR	931	931	1.6	3.2
143 CG in Cr(Menn)	1	191	NR	244 *	.4	.8
145 Ch God Prophcy	1	27	NR	34 *	.1	.1
151 L-D Saints	1	NR	NR	389	.7	1.3
165 Ch of Nazarene	3	210	114	210	.4	.7
167 Chs of Christ	5	334	391	413	.7	1.4
173 Comm of Christ	1	78	NR	78	.1	.3
193 Episcopal	1	NR	108	206	.3	.7
226 Friends-USA	1	50	NR	64 *	.1	.2
263 Int Foursq Gos	1	246	76	314 *	.5	1.1
283 Luth—MO Synod	3	597	295	699	1.2	2.4
288 Mennonite USA	1	145	109	185 *	.3	.6

NR–Not Reported *Total adherents estimated from known number of communicant, confirmed, full members. - Represents a percentage less than 0.1. Percentages may not total 100 due to rounding.

Table 4: Religious Congregations by County and Group: 2000

Religious Group	Number of Churches, Synagogues, Mosques, or Temples	Number of Communicant, Confirmed, or Full Members	Number of Attendees	Total Adherents: Number of Adherents	Total Adherents: % of Total Pop.	Total Adherents: % of Total Adh.
297 Mennonite;Other	2	496	NR	634 *	1.1	2.2
355 Presb Ch (USA)	2	370	170	473 *	.8	1.6
403 Salvation Army	1	40	32	178	.3	.6
413 S.D.A.	1	40	NR	48	.1	.2
419 So Bapt Conv	10	3,184	1,011	4,069 *	6.8	14.0
443 Un C of Christ	2	142	83	181 *	.3	.6
449 Un Methodist	14	3,452	1,713	4,413 *	7.4	15.2
498 Indep.Charis.	1	300	300	300	.5	1.0
CHASE	**12**	**980**	**336**	**1,582 ***	**52.2**	**100.0**
056 Baha'i	0	1	NR	1	-	.1
081 Catholic	1	NR	NR	400	13.2	25.3
097 Chr Chs&Chs Cr	2	55	NR	67 *	2.2	4.2
226 Friends-USA	1	50	NR	61 *	2.0	3.9
283 Luth—MO Synod	1	56	30	54	1.8	3.4
355 Presb Ch (USA)	1	105	54	128 *	4.2	8.1
419 So Bapt Conv	1	262	60	320 *	10.6	20.2
449 Un Methodist	5	451	192	551 *	18.2	34.8
CHAUTAUQUA	**22**	**1,678**	**701**	**2,213 ***	**50.8**	**100.0**
019 Amer Bapt USA	2	660	202	794 *	18.2	35.9
053 Assemb of God	2	58	78	93	2.1	4.2
081 Catholic	1	NR	NR	40	.9	1.8
093 Chr Ch (Disc)	1	158	0	190 *	4.4	8.6
097 Chr Chs&Chs Cr	1	25	NR	30 *	.7	1.4
127 Ch God (Cleve)	1	10	2	12 *	.3	.5
167 Chs of Christ	3	88	109	117	2.7	5.3
193 Episcopal	2	NR	54	96	2.2	4.3
339 Pent Ch of God	1	21	NR	50	1.1	2.3
413 S.D.A.	1	39	NR	46	1.1	2.1
419 So Bapt Conv	1	325	75	391 *	9.0	17.7
449 Un Methodist	6	294	181	354 *	8.1	16.0
CHEROKEE	**52**	**7,320**	**2,590**	**13,384 ***	**59.2**	**100.0**
019 Amer Bapt USA	1	150	47	188 *	.8	1.4
053 Assemb of God	4	620	874	1,223	5.4	9.1
059 Bapt Miss Assn	1	426	145	533 *	2.4	4.0
081 Catholic	4	NR	NR	3,724	16.5	27.8
093 Chr Ch (Disc)	2	1,014	321	1,269 *	5.6	9.5
097 Chr Chs&Chs Cr	6	662	NR	827 *	3.7	6.2
145 Ch God Prophcy	1	27	NR	33 *	.1	.2
165 Ch of Nazarene	3	126	145	179	.8	1.3
167 Chs of Christ	2	65	68	83	.4	.6
173 Comm of Christ	1	77	NR	77	.3	.6
193 Episcopal	2	NR	42	53	.2	.4
226 Friends-USA	5	250	NR	313 *	1.4	2.3
355 Presb Ch (USA)	4	214	102	268 *	1.2	2.0
413 S.D.A.	1	54	NR	64	.3	.5
419 So Bapt Conv	8	2,958	551	3,702 *	16.4	27.7
449 Un Methodist	7	677	295	848 *	3.8	6.3
CHEYENNE	**13**	**1,420**	**701**	**2,149 ***	**67.9**	**100.0**
053 Assemb of God	1	24	30	37	1.2	1.7
081 Catholic	2	NR	NR	325	10.3	15.1
093 Chr Ch (Disc)	1	0	0	0 *	-	-
167 Chs of Christ	1	42	45	55	1.7	2.6
207 E.L.C.A.	3	565	258	736	23.3	34.2
413 S.D.A.	1	54	NR	64	2.0	3.0
419 So Bapt Conv	1	72	80	87 *	2.7	4.0
449 Un Methodist	2	626	241	756 *	23.9	35.2
467 Wesleyan	1	37	47	89	2.8	4.1
CLARK	**11**	**931**	**366**	**1,568 ***	**65.6**	**100.0**
019 Amer Bapt USA	1	44	10	55 *	2.3	3.5
081 Catholic	1	NR	NR	353	14.8	22.5
097 Chr Chs&Chs Cr	4	239	NR	297 *	12.4	18.9
123 Ch God (Ander)	1	NR	55	55	2.3	3.5
167 Chs of Christ	1	18	22	25	1.0	1.6
355 Presb Ch (USA)	1	102	27	127 *	5.3	8.1
449 Un Methodist	2	528	252	656 *	27.4	41.8
CLAY	**27**	**3,573**	**1,919**	**5,352 ***	**60.7**	**100.0**
019 Amer Bapt USA	1	368	177	451 *	5.1	8.4
053 Assemb of God	1	45	67	100	1.1	1.9
056 Baha'i	0	1	NR	1	-	-
081 Catholic	2	NR	NR	502	5.7	9.4
097 Chr Chs&Chs Cr	2	125	NR	153 *	1.7	2.9
127 Ch God (Cleve)	1	32	21	39 *	.4	.7
193 Episcopal	2	NR	60	110	1.2	2.1
201 Evan Cov Ch	1	170	316	316 *	3.6	5.9
207 E.L.C.A.	1	84	27	101	1.1	1.9
283 Luth—MO Synod	1	557	222	703	8.0	13.1
355 Presb Ch (USA)	3	536	229	657 *	7.4	12.3
419 So Bapt Conv	1	36	26	44 *	.5	.8
449 Un Methodist	10	1,486	661	1,821 *	20.6	34.0
467 Wesleyan	1	133	113	354	4.0	6.6
CLOUD	**26**	**3,237**	**1,477**	**6,324 ***	**61.6**	**100.0**
019 Amer Bapt USA	1	731	208	872 *	8.5	13.8
053 Assemb of God	1	34	54	84	.8	1.3
056 Baha'i	0	1	NR	1	-	-
081 Catholic	4	NR	NR	2,019	19.7	31.9
097 Chr Chs&Chs Cr	4	310	NR	370 *	3.6	5.9
193 Episcopal	1	NR	26	57	.6	.9
201 Evan Cov Ch	1	147	88	175 *	1.7	2.8
207 E.L.C.A.	2	368	146	490	4.8	7.7
263 Int Foursq Gos	1	30	50	50 *	.5	.8
355 Presb Ch (USA)	2	147	87	176 *	1.7	2.8
449 Un Methodist	7	1,180	430	1,407 *	13.7	22.2
467 Wesleyan	2	289	388	623	6.1	9.9
COFFEY	**26**	**3,639**	**1,360**	**5,383 ***	**60.7**	**100.0**
019 Amer Bapt USA	2	380	134	470 *	5.3	8.7
053 Assemb of God	2	109	146	255	2.9	4.7
056 Baha'i	0	4	NR	4	-	.1
081 Catholic	2	NR	NR	665	7.5	12.4
097 Chr Chs&Chs Cr	4	682	NR	845 *	9.5	15.7
151 L-D Saints	1	NR	NR	136	1.5	2.5
157 Ch of Brethren	1	5	7	7 *	.1	.1
165 Ch of Nazarene	1	12	17	17	.2	.3
167 Chs of Christ	3	114	135	159	1.8	3.0
283 Luth—MO Synod	2	322	183	407	4.6	7.6
419 So Bapt Conv	1	331	94	410 *	4.6	7.6
449 Un Methodist	6	1,380	484	1,708 *	19.3	31.7
499 Indep.Non-Char	1	300	160	300	3.4	5.6
COMANCHE	**13**	**1,160**	**448**	**1,461 ***	**74.3**	**100.0**
019 Amer Bapt USA	1	141	78	170 *	8.6	11.6
053 Assemb of God	1	59	60	75	3.8	5.1
081 Catholic	1	NR	NR	59	3.0	4.0
093 Chr Ch (Disc)	2	0	0	0 *	-	-
097 Chr Chs&Chs Cr	2	327	NR	394 *	20.0	27.0
288 Mennonite USA	1	122	98	147 *	7.5	10.1
355 Presb Ch (USA)	1	55	20	66 *	3.4	4.5
419 So Bapt Conv	1	14	11	17 *	.9	1.2
449 Un Methodist	3	442	181	533 *	27.1	36.5
COWLEY	**67**	**12,536**	**5,600**	**18,838 ***	**51.9**	**100.0**
019 Amer Bapt USA	4	2,081	588	2,591 *	7.1	13.8
053 Assemb of God	3	415	337	563	1.6	3.0
056 Baha'i	0	39	NR	39	.1	.2
081 Catholic	2	NR	NR	2,264	6.2	12.0
084 Calvary Chapel	1	NR	NR	NR	-	-
093 Chr Ch (Disc)	3	1,020	410	1,270 *	3.5	6.7
097 Chr Chs&Chs Cr	4	290	NR	361 *	1.0	1.9
123 Ch God (Ander)	1	NR	0	0	-	-
127 Ch God (Cleve)	2	192	90	239 *	.7	1.3
151 L-D Saints	1	NR	NR	324	.9	1.7
165 Ch of Nazarene	3	400	289	506	1.4	2.7
167 Chs of Christ	4	365	328	412	1.1	2.2
173 Comm of Christ	1	60	NR	60	.2	.3
193 Episcopal	2	NR	120	291	.8	1.5
203 Evan Free Ch	1	120	240	240	.7	1.3

NR–Not Reported *Total adherents estimated from known number of communicant, confirmed, full members. - Represents a percentage less than 0.1. Percentages may not total 100 due to rounding.

Table 4: Religious Congregations by County and Group: 2000

Religious Group	Number of Churches, Synagogues, Mosques, or Temples	Number of Communicant, Confirmed, or Full Members	Number of Attendees	Total Adherents		
				Number of Adherents	% of Total Pop.	% of Total Adh.
221 Free Methodist	1	15	12	16	-	.1
226 Friends-USA	3	150	NR	187 *	.5	1.0
263 Int Foursq Gos	2	222	315	315 *	.9	1.7
283 Luth—MO Synod	2	785	508	1,143	3.1	6.1
349 Pent Holiness	1	50	50	62 *	.2	.3
355 Presb Ch (USA)	3	672	300	837 *	2.3	4.4
403 Salvation Army	1	84	98	179	.5	1.0
413 S.D.A.	2	22	NR	26	.1	.1
419 So Bapt Conv	7	2,417	548	3,009 *	8.3	16.0
449 Un Methodist	13	3,137	1,367	3,904 *	10.8	20.7
CRAWFORD	**56**	**8,685**	**3,362**	**17,215 ***	**45.0**	**100.0**
019 Amer Bapt USA	3	551	252	667 *	1.7	3.9
053 Assemb of God	2	80	64	155	.4	.9
056 Baha'i	0	23	NR	23	.1	.1
059 Bapt Miss Assn	2	239	127	289 *	.8	1.7
081 Catholic	4	NR	NR	5,686	14.9	33.0
093 Chr Ch (Disc)	2	1,558	354	1,885 *	4.9	10.9
097 Chr Chs&Chs Cr	4	721	NR	872 *	2.3	5.1
127 Ch God (Cleve)	1	73	45	88 *	.2	.5
145 Ch God Prophcy	1	27	NR	32 *	.1	.2
151 L-D Saints	1	NR	NR	397	1.0	2.3
157 Ch of Brethren	1	133	70	161 *	.4	.9
165 Ch of Nazarene	3	371	402	754	2.0	4.4
167 Chs of Christ	2	170	178	227	.6	1.3
173 Comm of Christ	1	215	NR	215	.6	1.2
193 Episcopal	1	NR	60	132	.3	.8
207 E.L.C.A.	1	333	113	426	1.1	2.5
283 Luth—MO Synod	3	594	352	767	2.0	4.5
355 Presb Ch (USA)	4	502	251	608 *	1.6	3.5
403 Salvation Army	1	87	105	186	.5	1.1
413 S.D.A.	1	24	NR	29	.1	.2
419 So Bapt Conv	4	696	171	842 *	2.2	4.9
449 Un Methodist	13	2,219	767	2,684 *	7.0	15.6
469 WELS	1	69	51	90	.2	.5
DECATUR	**21**	**1,553**	**778**	**2,741 ***	**78.9**	**100.0**
019 Amer Bapt USA	1	120	52	144 *	4.1	5.3
053 Assemb of God	1	50	75	75	2.2	2.7
081 Catholic	3	NR	NR	730	21.0	26.6
093 Chr Ch (Disc)	1	115	55	138 *	4.0	5.0
167 Chs of Christ	1	20	30	35	1.0	1.3
201 Evan Cov Ch	2	79	128	137 *	3.9	5.0
207 E.L.C.A.	2	149	53	197	5.7	7.2
283 Luth—MO Synod	1	245	126	356	10.3	13.0
355 Presb Ch (USA)	1	20	9	24 *	.7	.9
413 S.D.A.	1	15	NR	18	.5	.7
419 So Bapt Conv	1	7	15	8 *	.2	.3
449 Un Methodist	6	733	235	879 *	25.3	32.1
DICKINSON	**56**	**6,363**	**3,191**	**10,112 ***	**52.3**	**100.0**
019 Amer Bapt USA	3	443	178	546 *	2.8	5.4
053 Assemb of God	1	36	50	50	.3	.5
056 Baha'i	0	5	NR	5	-	-
075 Brethren in Cr	3	290	256	297	1.5	2.9
081 Catholic	5	NR	NR	2,054	10.6	20.3
093 Chr Ch (Disc)	1	175	59	216 *	1.1	2.1
097 Chr Chs&Chs Cr	3	445	NR	549 *	2.8	5.4
123 Ch God (Ander)	1	NR	12	12	.1	.1
127 Ch God (Cleve)	1	12	21	21 *	.1	.2
157 Ch of Brethren	2	66	38	82 *	.4	.8
165 Ch of Nazarene	1	32	28	47	.2	.5
167 Chs of Christ	1	15	17	18	.1	.2
193 Episcopal	1	NR	30	76	.4	.8
207 E.L.C.A.	3	614	313	867	4.5	8.6
263 Int Foursq Gos	1	41	23	51 *	.3	.5
283 Luth—MO Synod	4	687	351	844	4.4	8.3
313 N Am Bapt Conf	2	118	62	146 *	.8	1.4
355 Presb Ch (USA)	5	394	244	487 *	2.5	4.8
419 So Bapt Conv	1	150	45	185 *	1.0	1.8
443 Un C of Christ	3	239	101	295 *	1.5	2.9
449 Un Methodist	13	2,560	1,323	3,157 *	16.3	31.2
467 Wesleyan	1	41	40	107	.6	1.1

Religious Group	Number of Churches, Synagogues, Mosques, or Temples	Number of Communicant, Confirmed, or Full Members	Number of Attendees	Total Adherents		
				Number of Adherents	% of Total Pop.	% of Total Adh.
DONIPHAN	**22**	**2,682**	**909**	**4,064 ***	**49.3**	**100.0**
019 Amer Bapt USA	2	638	237	789 *	9.6	19.4
053 Assemb of God	1	43	48	129	1.6	3.2
056 Baha'i	0	2	NR	2	-	-
081 Catholic	4	NR	NR	716	8.7	17.6
093 Chr Ch (Disc)	1	286	93	354 *	4.3	8.7
097 Chr Chs&Chs Cr	1	250	NR	309 *	3.7	7.6
127 Ch God (Cleve)	1	16	15	20 *	.2	.5
173 Comm of Christ	1	324	NR	324	3.9	8.0
207 E.L.C.A.	1	204	60	263	3.2	6.5
283 Luth—MO Synod	1	174	85	236	2.9	5.8
355 Presb Ch (USA)	1	56	27	69 *	.8	1.7
419 So Bapt Conv	1	67	45	83 *	1.0	2.0
443 Un C of Christ	1	82	45	101 *	1.2	2.5
449 Un Methodist	6	540	254	669 *	8.1	16.5
DOUGLAS	**84**	**13,537**	**7,892**	**29,075 ***	**29.1**	**100.0**
019 Amer Bapt USA	1	617	249	733 *	.7	2.5
053 Assemb of God	4	336	429	765	.8	2.6
056 Baha'i	1	70	NR	70	.1	.2
076 Buddhism	1	NR	NR	NR	-	-
081 Catholic	5	NR	NR	7,364	7.4	25.3
084 Calvary Chapel	1	NR	NR	NR	-	-
093 Chr Ch (Disc)	1	471	262	560 *	.6	1.9
097 Chr Chs&Chs Cr	2	230	NR	273 *	.3	.9
123 Ch God (Ander)	1	NR	69	69	.1	.2
151 L-D Saints	4	NR	NR	1,231	1.2	4.2
157 Ch of Brethren	2	116	65	138 *	.1	.5
165 Ch of Nazarene	2	294	242	325	.3	1.1
167 Chs of Christ	9	403	436	525	.5	1.8
173 Comm of Christ	2	170	NR	170	.2	.6
193 Episcopal	3	NR	589	944	.9	3.2
203 Evan Free Ch	1	47	110	110	.1	.4
207 E.L.C.A.	2	1,341	426	1,921	1.9	6.6
216 Evan Presby Ch	1	352	NR	418 *	.4	1.4
221 Free Methodist	1	143	330	330	.3	1.1
226 Friends-USA	2	100	NR	119 *	.1	.4
264 Int Chs of Crst	1	60	113	82	.1	.3
267 Muslim Est	2	NR	110	326	.3	1.1
283 Luth—MO Synod	2	774	371	1,052	1.1	3.6
288 Mennonite USA	1	66	80	80 *	.1	.3
355 Presb Ch (USA)	4	1,051	526	1,259 *	1.3	4.3
388 Reg Bapt Gen As	1	20	27	27 *	-	.1
403 Salvation Army	1	66	47	1,113	1.1	3.8
413 S.D.A.	1	49	NR	58	.1	.2
419 So Bapt Conv	5	1,495	549	1,777 *	1.8	6.1
435 Unitarian-Univ	1	113	NR	134 *	.1	.5
443 Un C of Christ	3	1,401	610	1,665 *	1.7	5.7
449 Un Methodist	13	3,649	1,590	4,337 *	4.3	14.9
467 Wesleyan	1	103	212	500	.5	1.7
496 Jewish Est	1	NR	NR	150	.2	.5
498 Indep.Charis.	1	0	450	450	.5	1.5
EDWARDS	**16**	**910**	**435**	**2,296 ***	**66.6**	**100.0**
019 Amer Bapt USA	1	36	26	44 *	1.3	1.9
053 Assemb of God	1	16	23	49	1.4	2.1
056 Baha'i	0	2	NR	2	.1	.1
081 Catholic	3	NR	NR	1,118	32.4	48.7
093 Chr Ch (Disc)	2	168	61	205 *	5.9	8.9
165 Ch of Nazarene	1	17	20	48	1.4	2.1
193 Episcopal	1	NR	8	18	.5	.8
283 Luth—MO Synod	1	124	64	145	4.2	6.3
443 Un C of Christ	1	78	32	95 *	2.8	4.1
449 Un Methodist	5	469	201	572 *	16.6	24.9
ELK	**15**	**930**	**381**	**1,220 ***	**37.4**	**100.0**
019 Amer Bapt USA	3	196	113	234 *	7.2	19.2
053 Assemb of God	1	40	34	106	3.3	8.7
056 Baha'i	0	1	NR	1	-	.1
081 Catholic	1	NR	NR	50	1.5	4.1
084 Calvary Chapel	1	NR	NR	NR	-	-
097 Chr Chs&Chs Cr	3	202	NR	241 *	7.4	19.8

NR–Not Reported *Total adherents estimated from known number of communicant, confirmed, full members. - Represents a percentage less than 0.1. Percentages may not total 100 due to rounding.

Table 4: Religious Congregations by County and Group: 2000

Religious Group	Number of Churches, Synagogues, Mosques, or Temples	Number of Communicant, Confirmed, or Full Members	Number of Attendees	Total Adherents: Number of Adherents	Total Adherents: % of Total Pop.	Total Adherents: % of Total Adh.
167 Chs of Christ	1	28	30	36	1.1	3.0
449 Un Methodist	5	463	204	552 *	16.9	45.2
ELLIS	**24**	**3,487**	**1,838**	**13,503 ***	**49.1**	**100.0**
019 Amer Bapt USA	1	79	60	94 *	.3	.7
053 Assemb of God	1	48	65	74	.3	.5
056 Baha'i	0	19	NR	19	.1	.1
081 Catholic	4	NR	NR	9,075	33.0	67.2
093 Chr Ch (Disc)	1	215	225	257 *	.9	1.9
097 Chr Chs&Chs Cr	1	60	NR	72 *	.3	.5
151 L-D Saints	1	NR	NR	274	1.0	2.0
165 Ch of Nazarene	1	137	70	156	.6	1.2
167 Chs of Christ	1	45	50	50	.2	.4
193 Episcopal	2	NR	82	163	.6	1.2
207 E.L.C.A.	3	813	341	1,055	3.8	7.8
237 Menn Br US Conf	1	90	NR	108 *	.4	.8
283 Luth—MO Synod	1	219	150	39	.1	.3
355 Presb Ch (USA)	1	244	105	292 *	1.1	2.2
388 Reg Bapt Gen As	1	125	85	85 *	.3	.6
419 So Bapt Conv	2	170	141	203 *	.7	1.5
449 Un Methodist	2	1,223	464	1,462 *	5.3	10.8
496 Jewish Est	0	NR	NR	25	.1	.2
ELLSWORTH	**21**	**2,593**	**1,312**	**4,134 ***	**63.4**	**100.0**
053 Assemb of God	1	44	59	59	.9	1.4
081 Catholic	4	NR	NR	923	14.1	22.3
193 Episcopal	1	NR	20	53	.8	1.3
203 Evan Free Ch	1	33	85	85	1.3	2.1
207 E.L.C.A.	2	216	110	281	4.3	6.8
283 Luth—MO Synod	3	863	414	1,047	16.0	25.3
313 N Am Bapt Conf	1	139	76	163 *	2.5	3.9
355 Presb Ch (USA)	2	457	177	536 *	8.2	13.0
388 Reg Bapt Gen As	1	56	55	66 *	1.0	1.6
443 Un C of Christ	1	191	84	224 *	3.4	5.4
449 Un Methodist	4	594	232	697 *	10.7	16.9
FINNEY	**34**	**7,205**	**3,558**	**21,162 ***	**52.2**	**100.0**
019 Amer Bapt USA	1	118	67	162 *	.4	.8
053 Assemb of God	2	248	310	395	1.0	1.9
056 Baha'i	0	36	NR	36	.1	.2
076 Buddhism	1	NR	NR	NR	-	-
081 Catholic	2	NR	NR	10,001	24.7	47.3
093 Chr Ch (Disc)	1	852	255	1,172 *	2.9	5.5
097 Chr Chs&Chs Cr	1	500	NR	688 *	1.7	3.3
151 L-D Saints	2	NR	NR	436	1.1	2.1
157 Ch of Brethren	1	225	85	309 *	.8	1.5
165 Ch of Nazarene	2	364	345	629	1.6	3.0
167 Chs of Christ	1	117	125	152	.4	.7
193 Episcopal	1	NR	62	214	.5	1.0
207 E.L.C.A.	1	147	80	177	.4	.8
237 Menn Br US Conf	1	289	NR	397 *	1.0	1.9
283 Luth—MO Synod	1	513	290	802	2.0	3.8
349 Pent Holiness	1	30	35	41 *	.1	.2
355 Presb Ch (USA)	2	370	134	509 *	1.3	2.4
403 Salvation Army	1	71	83	73	.2	.3
413 S.D.A.	2	224	NR	267	.7	1.3
419 So Bapt Conv	3	1,235	557	1,698 *	4.2	8.0
443 Un C of Christ	1	150	75	206 *	.5	1.0
449 Un Methodist	4	1,711	645	2,353 *	5.8	11.1
467 Wesleyan	1	5	60	95	.2	.4
498 Indep.Charis.	1	0	350	350	.9	1.7
FORD	**31**	**6,249**	**2,558**	**15,486 ***	**47.7**	**100.0**
019 Amer Bapt USA	1	150	85	199 *	.6	1.3
053 Assemb of God	2	207	218	383	1.2	2.5
056 Baha'i	0	18	NR	18	.1	.1
081 Catholic	3	NR	NR	6,958	21.4	44.9
097 Chr Chs&Chs Cr	4	1,886	NR	2,503 *	7.7	16.2
123 Ch God (Ander)	1	NR	68	68	.2	.4
151 L-D Saints	1	NR	NR	285	.9	1.8
165 Ch of Nazarene	1	364	326	538	1.7	3.5
167 Chs of Christ	1	217	174	296	.9	1.9
193 Episcopal	1	NR	80	168	.5	1.1
207 E.L.C.A.	1	226	143	292	.9	1.9
221 Free Methodist	1	6	16	16	-	.1
283 Luth—MO Synod	2	592	263	146	.4	.9
291 Missionary Ch	1	215	176	215	.7	1.4
355 Presb Ch (USA)	3	325	178	432 *	1.3	2.8
403 Salvation Army	1	50	55	300	.9	1.9
413 S.D.A.	1	14	NR	17	.1	.1
419 So Bapt Conv	2	514	182	682 *	2.1	4.4
443 Un C of Christ	1	20	5	27 *	.1	.2
449 Un Methodist	3	1,445	589	1,918 *	5.9	12.4
496 Jewish Est	0	NR	NR	25	.1	.2
FRANKLIN	**40**	**5,627**	**3,197**	**8,887 ***	**35.9**	**100.0**
019 Amer Bapt USA	8	1,549	903	1,957 *	7.9	22.0
053 Assemb of God	3	213	288	377	1.5	4.2
056 Baha'i	0	6	NR	6	-	.1
059 Bapt Miss Assn	1	62	32	78 *	.3	.9
081 Catholic	2	NR	NR	1,380	5.6	15.5
093 Chr Ch (Disc)	1	337	112	426 *	1.7	4.8
097 Chr Chs&Chs Cr	2	85	NR	108 *	.4	1.2
157 Ch of Brethren	1	67	55	85 *	.3	1.0
165 Ch of Nazarene	1	120	109	148	.6	1.7
167 Chs of Christ	2	137	160	223	.9	2.5
173 Comm of Christ	1	57	NR	57	.2	.6
193 Episcopal	1	NR	34	55	.2	.6
263 Int Foursq Gos	1	122	94	154 *	.6	1.7
283 Luth—MO Synod	1	334	175	465	1.9	5.2
355 Presb Ch (USA)	2	528	296	667 *	2.7	7.5
413 S.D.A.	1	67	NR	80	.3	.9
419 So Bapt Conv	1	40	40	51 *	.2	.6
449 Un Methodist	10	1,817	789	2,295 *	9.3	25.8
467 Wesleyan	1	86	110	275	1.1	3.1
GEARY	**30**	**5,154**	**2,543**	**8,563 ***	**30.6**	**100.0**
019 Amer Bapt USA	2	1,231	389	1,616 *	5.8	18.9
053 Assemb of God	2	122	75	156	.6	1.8
056 Baha'i	0	17	NR	17	.1	.2
081 Catholic	1	NR	NR	971	3.5	11.3
097 Chr Chs&Chs Cr	1	448	NR	588 *	2.1	6.9
123 Ch God (Ander)	1	NR	157	157	.6	1.8
127 Ch God (Cleve)	1	40	50	53 *	.2	.6
165 Ch of Nazarene	2	329	398	586	2.1	6.8
167 Chs of Christ	2	90	116	142	.5	1.7
181 Consrv Congr	1	40	35	53 *	.2	.6
193 Episcopal	1	NR	76	203	.7	2.4
207 E.L.C.A.	1	79	57	92	.3	1.1
263 Int Foursq Gos	1	50	103	103 *	.4	1.2
267 Muslim Est	1	NR	55	163	.6	1.9
283 Luth—MO Synod	2	359	131	521	1.9	6.1
313 N Am Bapt Conf	1	35	82	46 *	.2	.5
349 Pent Holiness	1	22	22	29 *	.1	.3
355 Presb Ch (USA)	1	411	143	539 *	1.9	6.3
413 S.D.A.	1	25	NR	30	.1	.4
419 So Bapt Conv	2	985	212	1,293 *	4.6	15.1
443 Un C of Christ	1	123	64	161 *	.6	1.9
449 Un Methodist	3	700	315	919 *	3.3	10.7
467 Wesleyan	1	48	63	125	.4	1.5
GOVE	**8**	**734**	**328**	**1,959 ***	**63.9**	**100.0**
081 Catholic	3	NR	NR	1,048	34.2	53.5
157 Ch of Brethren	1	248	137	308 *	10.0	15.7
449 Un Methodist	4	486	191	603 *	19.7	30.8
GRAHAM	**15**	**861**	**386**	**1,572 ***	**53.4**	**100.0**
053 Assemb of God	2	48	58	81	2.7	5.2
056 Baha'i	0	1	NR	1	-	.1
081 Catholic	2	NR	NR	489	16.6	31.1
097 Chr Chs&Chs Cr	1	200	NR	237 *	8.0	15.1
123 Ch God (Ander)	1	NR	40	40	1.4	2.5
127 Ch God (Cleve)	1	52	18	62 *	2.1	3.9
283 Luth—MO Synod	1	66	26	76	2.6	4.8

NR–Not Reported   *Total adherents estimated from known number of communicant, confirmed, full members.   - Represents a percentage less than 0.1.   Percentages may not total 100 due to rounding.

Table 4: Religious Congregations by County and Group: 2000

Religious Group	Number of Churches, Synagogues, Mosques, or Temples	Number of Communicant, Confirmed, or Full Members	Number of Attendees	Total Adherents: Number of Adherents	% of Total Pop.	% of Total Adh.
355 Presb Ch (USA)	1	73	35	87 *	3.0	5.5
419 So Bapt Conv	2	53	45	63 *	2.1	4.0
449 Un Methodist	4	368	164	436 *	14.8	27.7
GRANT	**20**	**2,781**	**1,100**	**5,840 ***	**73.8**	**100.0**
019 Amer Bapt USA	1	165	100	220 *	2.8	3.8
053 Assemb of God	2	84	105	124	1.6	2.1
081 Catholic	1	NR	NR	1,765	22.3	30.2
093 Chr Ch (Disc)	1	335	120	447 *	5.7	7.7
123 Ch God (Ander)	1	NR	78	78	1.0	1.3
127 Ch God (Cleve)	1	174	114	232 *	2.9	4.0
143 CG in Cr(Menn)	1	197	NR	263 *	3.3	4.5
151 L-D Saints	1	NR	NR	155	2.0	2.7
165 Ch of Nazarene	1	34	30	82	1.0	1.4
167 Chs of Christ	1	159	150	220	2.8	3.8
193 Episcopal	1	NR	36	77	1.0	1.3
223 Free Will Bapt	1	31	NR	42 *	.5	.7
237 Menn Br US Conf	1	114	NR	152 *	1.9	2.6
283 Luth—MO Synod	1	133	56	177	2.2	3.0
306 NT IndBapt&Rltd	1	100	NR	133 *	1.7	2.3
349 Pent Holiness	1	25	30	33 *	.4	.6
419 So Bapt Conv	2	519	66	692 *	8.7	11.8
449 Un Methodist	1	711	215	948 *	12.0	16.2
GRAY	**19**	**2,439**	**628**	**3,892 ***	**65.9**	**100.0**
056 Baha'i	0	1	NR	1	-	-
081 Catholic	1	NR	NR	701	11.9	18.0
093 Chr Ch (Disc)	1	237	40	311 *	5.3	8.0
097 Chr Chs&Chs Cr	1	60	NR	79 *	1.3	2.0
143 CG in Cr(Menn)	5	867	NR	1,138 *	19.3	29.2
165 Ch of Nazarene	1	230	180	273	4.6	7.0
237 Menn Br US Conf	1	110	NR	144 *	2.4	3.7
288 Mennonite USA	2	32	50	62 *	1.1	1.6
297 Mennonite;Other	1	33	NR	43 *	.7	1.1
349 Pent Holiness	1	66	50	87 *	1.5	2.2
419 So Bapt Conv	1	91	58	119 *	2.0	3.1
449 Un Methodist	4	712	250	934 *	15.8	24.0
GREELEY	**6**	**674**	**230**	**1,195 ***	**77.9**	**100.0**
019 Amer Bapt USA	1	252	60	319 *	20.8	26.7
053 Assemb of God	1	43	57	75	4.9	6.3
081 Catholic	1	NR	NR	341	22.2	28.5
173 Comm of Christ	1	77	NR	77	5.0	6.4
355 Presb Ch (USA)	1	52	25	66 *	4.3	5.5
449 Un Methodist	1	250	88	317 *	20.7	26.5
GREENWOOD	**33**	**3,257**	**1,156**	**4,774 ***	**62.2**	**100.0**
040 Ap Chr Ch-Amer	1	45	85	85 *	1.1	1.8
053 Assemb of God	1	33	42	75	1.0	1.6
056 Baha'i	0	2	NR	2	-	-
081 Catholic	3	NR	NR	400	5.2	8.4
093 Chr Ch (Disc)	2	636	67	767 *	10.0	16.1
097 Chr Chs&Chs Cr	2	185	NR	223 *	2.9	4.7
123 Ch God (Ander)	1	NR	12	12	.2	.3
151 L-D Saints	1	NR	NR	88	1.1	1.8
165 Ch of Nazarene	1	62	47	87	1.1	1.8
167 Chs of Christ	1	20	30	26	.3	.5
203 Evan Free Ch	1	35	70	70	.9	1.5
207 E.L.C.A.	1	269	84	349	4.5	7.3
349 Pent Holiness	1	80	50	96 *	1.3	2.0
355 Presb Ch (USA)	1	31	15	37 *	.5	.8
413 S.D.A.	1	67	NR	80	1.0	1.7
419 So Bapt Conv	4	607	250	732 *	9.5	15.3
443 Un C of Christ	1	250	110	301 *	3.9	6.3
449 Un Methodist	9	906	215	1,094 *	14.3	22.9
467 Wesleyan	1	29	79	250	3.3	5.2
HAMILTON	**10**	**887**	**407**	**1,966 ***	**73.6**	**100.0**
081 Catholic	1	NR	NR	529	19.8	26.9
097 Chr Chs&Chs Cr	2	136	NR	173 *	6.5	8.8
151 L-D Saints	1	NR	NR	107	4.0	5.4
165 Ch of Nazarene	1	27	18	58	2.2	3.0

Religious Group	Number of Churches, Synagogues, Mosques, or Temples	Number of Communicant, Confirmed, or Full Members	Number of Attendees	Total Adherents: Number of Adherents	% of Total Pop.	% of Total Adh.
355 Presb Ch (USA)	1	149	71	189 *	7.1	9.6
419 So Bapt Conv	1	85	35	108 *	4.0	5.5
449 Un Methodist	2	393	131	498 *	18.7	25.3
467 Wesleyan	1	97	152	304	11.4	15.5
HARPER	**28**	**2,517**	**975**	**4,330 ***	**66.2**	**100.0**
019 Amer Bapt USA	2	272	78	330 *	5.0	7.6
053 Assemb of God	3	128	145	178	2.7	4.1
081 Catholic	1	NR	NR	1,148	17.6	26.5
097 Chr Chs&Chs Cr	3	670	NR	813 *	12.4	18.8
165 Ch of Nazarene	1	45	42	113	1.7	2.6
167 Chs of Christ	4	143	154	202	3.1	4.7
193 Episcopal	1	NR	14	22	.3	.5
288 Mennonite USA	2	205	130	248 *	3.8	5.7
355 Presb Ch (USA)	3	127	72	153 *	2.3	3.5
413 S.D.A.	1	24	NR	29	.4	.7
443 Un C of Christ	2	119	36	144 *	2.2	3.3
449 Un Methodist	5	784	304	950 *	14.5	21.9
HARVEY	**64**	**12,618**	**6,818**	**20,003 ***	**60.9**	**100.0**
017 Amer Bapt Assn	1	38	NR	47 *	.1	.2
019 Amer Bapt USA	2	825	269	1,025 *	3.1	5.1
053 Assemb of God	1	41	61	61	.2	.3
056 Baha'i	0	85	NR	85	.3	.4
081 Catholic	3	NR	NR	3,087	9.4	15.4
093 Chr Ch (Disc)	1	405	116	503 *	1.5	2.5
097 Chr Chs&Chs Cr	3	440	NR	546 *	1.7	2.7
123 Ch God (Ander)	2	NR	125	125	.4	.6
127 Ch God (Cleve)	1	15	15	19 *	.1	.1
143 CG in Cr(Menn)	3	566	NR	703 *	2.1	3.5
151 L-D Saints	1	NR	NR	233	.7	1.2
157 Ch of Brethren	1	39	26	48 *	.1	.2
165 Ch of Nazarene	2	545	402	1,191	3.6	6.0
167 Chs of Christ	3	168	193	232	.7	1.2
193 Episcopal	1	NR	103	274	.8	1.4
207 E.L.C.A.	1	133	40	178	.5	.9
213 Evan Menn Inc	1	204	384	253 *	.8	1.3
221 Free Methodist	1	49	58	61	.2	.3
237 Menn Br US Conf	2	278	NR	345 *	1.0	1.7
263 Int Foursq Gos	1	167	97	207 *	.6	1.0
283 Luth—MO Synod	1	390	220	479	1.5	2.4
288 Mennonite USA	11	3,675	2,397	4,584 *	13.9	22.9
291 Missionary Ch	1	74	130	130	.4	.6
297 Mennonite;Other	1	133	NR	165 *	.5	.8
355 Presb Ch (USA)	3	526	425	678 *	2.1	3.4
388 Reg Bapt Gen As	1	230	175	286 *	.9	1.4
413 S.D.A.	1	22	NR	26	.1	.1
419 So Bapt Conv	2	378	198	469 *	1.4	2.3
443 Un C of Christ	3	334	165	415 *	1.3	2.1
449 Un Methodist	9	2,858	1,219	3,548 *	10.8	17.7
HASKELL	**11**	**1,663**	**632**	**2,565 ***	**59.6**	**100.0**
056 Baha'i	0	1	NR	1	-	-
081 Catholic	1	NR	NR	235	5.5	9.2
097 Chr Chs&Chs Cr	1	350	NR	468 *	10.9	18.2
123 Ch God (Ander)	1	NR	89	89	2.1	3.5
165 Ch of Nazarene	1	97	72	148	3.4	5.8
167 Chs of Christ	2	44	47	57	1.3	2.2
297 Mennonite;Other	1	78	NR	104 *	2.4	4.1
419 So Bapt Conv	2	524	238	701 *	16.3	27.3
449 Un Methodist	2	569	186	762 *	17.7	29.7
HODGEMAN	**11**	**726**	**423**	**1,311 ***	**62.9**	**100.0**
019 Amer Bapt USA	2	135	55	170 *	8.2	13.0
081 Catholic	2	NR	NR	353	16.9	26.9
167 Chs of Christ	1	16	35	30	1.4	2.3
283 Luth—MO Synod	1	0	17	35	1.7	2.7
288 Mennonite USA	1	22	20	28 *	1.3	2.1
355 Presb Ch (USA)	1	106	50	133 *	6.4	10.1
419 So Bapt Conv	1	80	18	101 *	4.8	7.7
449 Un Methodist	2	367	228	461 *	22.1	35.2

NR–Not Reported *Total adherents estimated from known number of communicant, confirmed, full members. - Represents a percentage less than 0.1. Percentages may not total 100 due to rounding.

Table 4: Religious Congregations by County and Group: 2000

Religious Group	Number of Churches, Synagogues, Mosques, or Temples	Number of Communicant, Confirmed, or Full Members	Number of Attendees	Total Adherents: Number of Adherents	Total Adherents: % of Total Pop.	Total Adherents: % of Total Adh.
JACKSON	**27**	**3,298**	**1,059**	**4,994 ***	**39.5**	**100.0**
019 Amer Bapt USA	4	535	307	678 *	5.4	13.6
056 Baha'i	0	2	NR	2	-	-
081 Catholic	2	NR	NR	1,000	7.9	20.0
093 Chr Ch (Disc)	2	216	0	274 *	2.2	5.5
097 Chr Chs&Chs Cr	3	395	NR	501 *	4.0	10.0
165 Ch of Nazarene	1	59	45	68	.5	1.4
173 Comm of Christ	1	25	NR	25	.2	.5
283 Luth—MO Synod	2	323	150	239	1.9	4.8
355 Presb Ch (USA)	2	113	65	143 *	1.1	2.9
449 Un Methodist	10	1,630	492	2,064 *	16.3	41.3
JEFFERSON	**32**	**3,810**	**1,517**	**7,257 ***	**39.4**	**100.0**
017 Amer Bapt Assn	1	67	NR	84 *	.5	1.2
019 Amer Bapt USA	1	311	128	390 *	2.1	5.4
053 Assemb of God	1	68	91	91	.5	1.3
056 Baha'i	0	4	NR	4	-	.1
081 Catholic	5	NR	NR	2,366	12.8	32.6
097 Chr Chs&Chs Cr	5	585	NR	734 *	4.0	10.1
165 Ch of Nazarene	1	129	121	202	1.1	2.8
167 Chs of Christ	1	16	22	24	.1	.3
203 Evan Free Ch	1	69	125	125	.7	1.7
207 E.L.C.A.	1	68	25	89	.5	1.2
226 Friends-USA	1	50	NR	63 *	.3	.9
283 Luth—MO Synod	1	239	139	317	1.7	4.4
355 Presb Ch (USA)	1	63	26	79 *	.4	1.1
388 Reg Bapt Gen As	1	69	60	87 *	.5	1.2
419 So Bapt Conv	1	140	35	176 *	1.0	2.4
449 Un Methodist	10	1,932	745	2,426 *	13.2	33.4
JEWELL	**21**	**1,316**	**542**	**1,978 ***	**52.2**	**100.0**
053 Assemb of God	1	15	18	18	.5	.9
081 Catholic	2	NR	NR	234	6.2	11.8
097 Chr Chs&Chs Cr	2	135	NR	160 *	4.2	8.1
165 Ch of Nazarene	1	40	46	121	3.2	6.1
167 Chs of Christ	1	14	9	18	.5	.9
203 Evan Free Ch	1	0	60	60	1.6	3.0
207 E.L.C.A.	1	177	73	257	6.8	13.0
226 Friends-USA	1	50	NR	59 *	1.6	3.0
419 So Bapt Conv	1	40	33	48 *	1.3	2.4
449 Un Methodist	10	845	303	1,003 *	26.5	50.7
JOHNSON	**237**	**82,651**	**52,286**	**229,211 ***	**50.8**	**100.0**
017 Amer Bapt Assn	1	50	NR	63 *	-	-
019 Amer Bapt USA	12	4,244	2,097	5,382 *	1.2	2.3
053 Assemb of God	9	2,071	2,830	3,562	.8	1.6
056 Baha'i	2	104	NR	104	-	-
081 Catholic	18	NR	NR	96,095	21.3	41.9
084 Calvary Chapel	1	NR	NR	NR	-	-
093 Chr Ch (Disc)	12	4,976	2,100	6,311 *	1.4	2.8
097 Chr Chs&Chs Cr	5	2,469	NR	3,131 *	.7	1.4
123 Ch God (Ander)	2	NR	973	973	.2	.4
127 Ch God (Cleve)	1	11	6	14 *	-	-
145 Ch God Prophcy	2	53	NR	68 *	-	-
151 L-D Saints	10	NR	NR	3,474	.8	1.5
157 Ch of Brethren	2	63	34	80 *	-	-
165 Ch of Nazarene	12	6,311	5,776	8,786	1.9	3.8
167 Chs of Christ	6	1,443	1,263	1,890	.4	.8
173 Comm of Christ	3	772	NR	772	.2	.3
193 Episcopal	6	NR	2,079	4,844	1.1	2.1
201 Evan Cov Ch	4	1,412	1,846	1,997 *	.4	.9
203 Evan Free Ch	2	335	750	750	.2	.3
207 E.L.C.A.	12	6,249	2,973	8,199	1.8	3.6
216 Evan Presby Ch	1	258	NR	327 *	.1	.1
221 Free Methodist	2	45	114	114	-	-
223 Free Will Bapt	1	31	NR	40 *	-	-
226 Friends-USA	2	100	NR	127 *	-	.1
237 Menn Br US Conf	1	126	NR	160 *	-	.1
246 Greek Orthodox	1	NR	NR	0	-	-
252 Hindu	1	NR	NR	NR	-	-
263 Int Foursq Gos	1	30	50	50 *	-	-
264 Int Chs of Crst	1	429	817	649	.1	.3
268 Jain	2	NR	NR	NR	-	-
283 Luth—MO Synod	8	6,931	3,817	9,456	2.1	4.1
290 Metro Comm Ch	1	18	12	23 *	-	-
335 Orth Pres Ch	1	89	171	171	-	.1
355 Presb Ch (USA)	14	12,354	5,375	15,669 *	3.5	6.8
356 Presb Ch Amer	4	436	615	646	.1	.3
371 Ref Ch in Am	1	102	75	236	.1	.1
388 Reg Bapt Gen As	2	262	225	332 *	.1	.1
403 Salvation Army	1	75	199	63	-	-
413 S.D.A.	3	832	NR	990	.2	.4
416 Sikh	1	NR	NR	NR	-	-
419 So Bapt Conv	22	10,928	5,800	13,859 *	3.1	6.0
435 Unitarian-Univ	2	194	NR	246 *	.1	.1
443 Un C of Christ	1	860	298	1,091 *	.2	.5
449 Un Methodist	20	15,979	7,714	20,263 *	4.5	8.8
463 Vineyard	1	130	120	165 *	-	.1
467 Wesleyan	5	376	616	1,833	.4	.8
469 WELS	1	273	186	356	.1	.2
490 Zoroastrian	1	NR	NR	NR	-	-
496 Jewish Est	6	NR	NR	12,000	2.7	5.2
498 Indep.Charis.	4	400	1,305	1,800	.4	.8
499 Indep.Non-Char	3	830	2,050	2,050	.5	.9
KEARNY	**13**	**1,295**	**586**	**2,942 ***	**64.9**	**100.0**
019 Amer Bapt USA	1	32	20	44 *	1.0	1.5
053 Assemb of God	1	22	24	32	.7	1.1
081 Catholic	2	NR	NR	998	22.0	33.9
093 Chr Ch (Disc)	1	62	22	84 *	1.9	2.9
143 CG in Cr(Menn)	1	92	NR	125 *	2.8	4.2
167 Chs of Christ	1	52	56	63	1.4	2.1
283 Luth—MO Synod	1	172	97	246	5.4	8.4
355 Presb Ch (USA)	1	104	49	141 *	3.1	4.8
419 So Bapt Conv	1	63	20	86 *	1.9	2.9
449 Un Methodist	2	635	185	863 *	19.0	29.3
467 Wesleyan	1	61	113	260	5.7	8.8
KINGMAN	**28**	**2,715**	**1,023**	**6,000 ***	**69.2**	**100.0**
019 Amer Bapt USA	2	433	147	543 *	6.3	9.1
053 Assemb of God	1	25	30	40	.5	.7
081 Catholic	5	NR	NR	2,199	25.4	36.7
093 Chr Ch (Disc)	1	388	0	486 *	5.6	8.1
097 Chr Chs&Chs Cr	2	245	NR	307 *	3.5	5.1
151 L-D Saints	1	NR	NR	341	3.9	5.7
165 Ch of Nazarene	1	46	24	52	.6	.9
167 Chs of Christ	3	120	147	174	2.0	2.9
193 Episcopal	1	NR	18	20	.2	.3
283 Luth—MO Synod	1	103	49	139	1.6	2.3
288 Mennonite USA	1	181	90	227 *	2.6	3.8
355 Presb Ch (USA)	1	77	44	96 *	1.1	1.6
388 Reg Bapt Gen As	1	69	60	86 *	1.0	1.4
419 So Bapt Conv	1	15	8	19 *	.2	.3
449 Un Methodist	6	1,013	406	1,271 *	14.7	21.2
KIOWA	**14**	**1,713**	**577**	**2,260 ***	**68.9**	**100.0**
019 Amer Bapt USA	1	89	46	108 *	3.3	4.8
053 Assemb of God	1	23	30	30	.9	1.3
056 Baha'i	0	1	NR	1	-	-
081 Catholic	1	NR	NR	176	5.4	7.8
093 Chr Ch (Disc)	1	475	0	576 *	17.6	25.5
143 CG in Cr(Menn)	1	110	NR	133 *	4.1	5.9
167 Chs of Christ	1	45	65	60	1.8	2.7
226 Friends-USA	2	100	NR	121 *	3.7	5.4
283 Luth—MO Synod	1	47	30	58	1.8	2.6
288 Mennonite USA	1	88	77	107 *	3.3	4.7
449 Un Methodist	4	735	329	890 *	27.2	39.4
LABETTE	**55**	**8,258**	**3,229**	**11,852 ***	**51.9**	**100.0**
019 Amer Bapt USA	3	1,573	347	1,950 *	8.5	16.5
053 Assemb of God	4	271	344	395	1.7	3.3
056 Baha'i	0	3	NR	3	-	-
081 Catholic	3	NR	NR	1,069	4.7	9.0
093 Chr Ch (Disc)	1	710	215	880 *	3.9	7.4

NR–Not Reported *Total adherents estimated from known number of communicant, confirmed, full members. - Represents a percentage less than 0.1. Percentages may not total 100 due to rounding.

Table 4: Religious Congregations by County and Group: 2000

Religious Group	Number of Churches, Synagogues, Mosques, or Temples	Number of Communicant, Confirmed, or Full Members	Number of Attendees	Total Adherents		
				Number of Adherents	% of Total Pop.	% of Total Adh.
097 Chr Chs&Chs Cr	7	783	NR	972 *	4.3	8.2
127 Ch God (Cleve)	2	141	69	175 *	.8	1.5
151 L-D Saints	1	NR	NR	161	.7	1.4
157 Ch of Brethren	1	50	54	62 *	.3	.5
165 Ch of Nazarene	2	287	247	429	1.9	3.6
167 Chs of Christ	1	69	65	89	.4	.8
193 Episcopal	1	NR	53	266	1.2	2.2
263 Int Foursq Gos	1	388	390	481 *	2.1	4.1
283 Luth—MO Synod	2	223	116	259	1.1	2.2
355 Presb Ch (USA)	2	225	123	279 *	1.2	2.4
388 Reg Bapt Gen As	1	150	100	186 *	.8	1.6
413 S.D.A.	2	33	NR	39	.2	.3
419 So Bapt Conv	5	1,267	268	1,571 *	6.9	13.3
449 Un Methodist	15	1,955	718	2,425 *	10.6	20.5
463 Vineyard	1	130	120	161 *	.7	1.4
LANE	**6**	**1,116**	**348**	**1,699 ***	**78.8**	**100.0**
081 Catholic	1	NR	NR	335	15.5	19.7
093 Chr Ch (Disc)	1	449	81	550 *	25.5	32.4
283 Luth—MO Synod	1	39	10	44	2.0	2.6
419 So Bapt Conv	1	76	58	93 *	4.3	5.5
449 Un Methodist	2	552	199	677 *	31.4	39.8
LEAVENWORTH	**60**	**9,002**	**4,117**	**21,832 ***	**31.8**	**100.0**
017 Amer Bapt Assn	1	45	NR	57 *	.1	.3
019 Amer Bapt USA	4	1,025	625	1,290 *	1.9	5.9
053 Assemb of God	3	200	224	315	.5	1.4
056 Baha'i	0	9	NR	9	-	-
059 Bapt Miss Assn	1	14	10	18 *	-	.1
081 Catholic	10	NR	NR	8,601	12.5	39.4
093 Chr Ch (Disc)	1	637	183	802 *	1.2	3.7
097 Chr Chs&Chs Cr	2	668	NR	841 *	1.2	3.9
123 Ch God (Ander)	1	NR	0	0	-	-
151 L-D Saints	3	NR	NR	682	1.0	3.1
165 Ch of Nazarene	2	171	141	270	.4	1.2
167 Chs of Christ	2	220	225	270	.4	1.2
173 Comm of Christ	2	178	NR	178	.3	.8
193 Episcopal	1	NR	135	431	.6	2.0
226 Friends-USA	3	150	NR	189 *	.3	.9
283 Luth—MO Synod	4	1,499	718	2,332	3.4	10.7
355 Presb Ch (USA)	1	235	112	296 *	.4	1.4
403 Salvation Army	1	81	63	385	.6	1.8
413 S.D.A.	2	97	NR	116	.2	.5
419 So Bapt Conv	3	1,497	590	1,885 *	2.7	8.6
443 Un C of Christ	2	246	100	310 *	.5	1.4
449 Un Methodist	10	1,900	871	2,391 *	3.5	11.0
463 Vineyard	1	130	120	164 *	.2	.8
LINCOLN	**14**	**1,330**	**547**	**1,938 ***	**54.2**	**100.0**
019 Amer Bapt USA	1	52	25	62 *	1.7	3.2
056 Baha'i	0	3	NR	3	.1	.2
081 Catholic	1	NR	NR	245	6.8	12.6
097 Chr Chs&Chs Cr	1	100	NR	120 *	3.4	6.2
207 E.L.C.A.	1	34	33	46	1.3	2.4
283 Luth—MO Synod	3	710	303	941	26.3	48.6
355 Presb Ch (USA)	2	98	59	117 *	3.3	6.0
449 Un Methodist	4	315	110	379 *	10.6	19.6
467 Wesleyan	1	18	17	25	.7	1.3
LINN	**26**	**2,481**	**914**	**3,622 ***	**37.8**	**100.0**
019 Amer Bapt USA	3	449	298	552 *	5.8	15.2
053 Assemb of God	1	34	47	117	1.2	3.2
059 Bapt Miss Assn	1	98	31	120 *	1.3	3.3
081 Catholic	2	NR	NR	380	4.0	10.5
097 Chr Chs&Chs Cr	4	695	NR	854 *	8.9	23.6
145 Ch God Prophcy	1	27	NR	33 *	.3	.9
151 L-D Saints	1	NR	NR	119	1.2	3.3
165 Ch of Nazarene	1	69	54	93	1.0	2.6
173 Comm of Christ	1	36	NR	36	.4	1.0
263 Int Foursq Gos	1	10	13	13 *	.1	.4
349 Pent Holiness	1	32	16	39 *	.4	1.1
355 Presb Ch (USA)	1	75	58	92 *	1.0	2.5

Religious Group	Number of Churches, Synagogues, Mosques, or Temples	Number of Communicant, Confirmed, or Full Members	Number of Attendees	Total Adherents		
				Number of Adherents	% of Total Pop.	% of Total Adh.
419 So Bapt Conv	1	105	67	129 *	1.3	3.6
443 Un C of Christ	1	107	47	131 *	1.4	3.6
449 Un Methodist	6	744	283	914 *	9.6	25.2
LOGAN	**10**	**972**	**270**	**2,196 ***	**72.1**	**100.0**
081 Catholic	1	NR	NR	784	25.7	35.7
097 Chr Chs&Chs Cr	1	325	NR	400 *	13.1	18.2
151 L-D Saints	1	NR	NR	87	2.9	4.0
167 Chs of Christ	1	35	38	46	1.5	2.1
193 Episcopal	1	NR	15	30	1.0	1.4
207 E.L.C.A.	1	38	19	57	1.9	2.6
283 Luth—MO Synod	1	125	60	165	5.4	7.5
449 Un Methodist	2	419	109	516 *	16.9	23.5
467 Wesleyan	1	30	29	111	3.6	5.1
LYON	**60**	**9,181**	**4,176**	**16,530 ***	**46.0**	**100.0**
019 Amer Bapt USA	2	290	192	361 *	1.0	2.2
053 Assemb of God	2	218	305	456	1.3	2.8
056 Baha'i	1	23	NR	23	.1	.1
081 Catholic	4	NR	NR	4,136	11.5	25.0
093 Chr Ch (Disc)	1	546	170	679 *	1.9	4.1
097 Chr Chs&Chs Cr	2	455	NR	566 *	1.6	3.4
123 Ch God (Ander)	1	NR	8	8	-	-
145 Ch God Prophcy	1	27	NR	33 *	.1	.2
151 L-D Saints	1	NR	NR	376	1.0	2.3
157 Ch of Brethren	1	16	7	20 *	.1	.1
165 Ch of Nazarene	1	261	146	261	.7	1.6
167 Chs of Christ	1	125	100	125	.3	.8
173 Comm of Christ	1	49	NR	49	.1	.3
175 Congr Chr Chs	1	250	130	311 *	.9	1.9
181 Consrv Congr	1	245	130	305 *	.8	1.8
193 Episcopal	1	NR	117	176	.5	1.1
207 E.L.C.A.	1	414	137	528	1.5	3.2
221 Free Methodist	1	29	76	76	.2	.5
223 Free Will Bapt	1	31	NR	39 *	.1	.2
226 Friends-USA	6	300	NR	373 *	1.0	2.3
263 Int Foursq Gos	1	171	192	213 *	.6	1.3
283 Luth—MO Synod	2	877	399	1,202	3.3	7.3
355 Presb Ch (USA)	4	409	225	509 *	1.4	3.1
403 Salvation Army	1	88	57	392	1.1	2.4
413 S.D.A.	1	19	NR	23	.1	.1
419 So Bapt Conv	6	629	435	782 *	2.2	4.7
449 Un Methodist	12	3,182	900	3,958 *	11.0	23.9
498 Indep.Charis.	1	177	200	200	.6	1.2
499 Indep.Non-Char	1	350	250	350	1.0	2.1
MCPHERSON	**64**	**14,185**	**7,168**	**18,807 ***	**63.6**	**100.0**
019 Amer Bapt USA	3	789	404	970 *	3.3	5.2
053 Assemb of God	1	71	91	133	.5	.7
056 Baha'i	0	9	NR	9	-	-
081 Catholic	2	NR	NR	900	3.0	4.8
093 Chr Ch (Disc)	3	1,117	310	1,373 *	4.6	7.3
097 Chr Chs&Chs Cr	2	250	NR	307 *	1.0	1.6
127 Ch God (Cleve)	1	32	13	39 *	.1	.2
143 CG in Cr(Menn)	4	1,058	NR	1,300 *	4.4	6.9
151 L-D Saints	1	NR	NR	109	.4	.6
157 Ch of Brethren	2	514	285	632 *	2.1	3.4
165 Ch of Nazarene	1	56	42	67	.2	.4
167 Chs of Christ	2	155	163	175	.6	.9
193 Episcopal	1	NR	42	156	.5	.8
201 Evan Cov Ch	4	783	1,088	1,128 *	3.8	6.0
207 E.L.C.A.	7	2,531	1,009	3,124	10.6	16.6
221 Free Methodist	2	597	611	677	2.3	3.6
237 Menn Br US Conf	1	239	NR	294 *	1.0	1.6
263 Int Foursq Gos	1	143	198	198 *	.7	1.1
283 Luth—MO Synod	3	270	237	371	1.3	2.0
288 Mennonite USA	9	2,380	1,297	2,925 *	9.9	15.6
355 Presb Ch (USA)	2	324	200	398 *	1.3	2.1
413 S.D.A.	1	42	NR	50	.2	.3
419 So Bapt Conv	1	307	200	377 *	1.3	2.0
443 Un C of Christ	2	353	163	434 *	1.5	2.3
449 Un Methodist	8	2,165	815	2,661 *	9.0	14.1

NR–Not Reported *Total adherents estimated from known number of communicant, confirmed, full members. - Represents a percentage less than 0.1. Percentages may not total 100 due to rounding.

Table 4: Religious Congregations by County and Group: 2000

Religious Group	Number of Churches, Synagogues, Mosques, or Temples	Number of Communicant, Confirmed, or Full Members	Number of Attendees	Total Adherents: Number of Adherents	Total Adherents: % of Total Pop.	Total Adherents: % of Total Adh.
MARION	**43**	**6,381**	**2,547**	**8,607 ***	**64.4**	**100.0**
019 Amer Bapt USA	1	135	33	165 *	1.2	1.9
056 Baha'i	0	4	NR	4	-	-
081 Catholic	1	NR	NR	160	1.2	1.9
093 Chr Ch (Disc)	1	0	0	0 *	-	-
097 Chr Chs&Chs Cr	2	291	NR	356 *	2.7	4.1
143 CG in Cr(Menn)	2	168	NR	206 *	1.5	2.4
151 L-D Saints	1	NR	NR	645	4.8	7.5
167 Chs of Christ	1	10	10	10	.1	.1
207 E.L.C.A.	1	43	32	54	.4	.6
237 Menn Br US Conf	4	1,196	NR	1,464 *	11.0	17.0
283 Luth—MO Synod	5	606	355	735	5.5	8.5
288 Mennonite USA	6	1,697	903	2,078 *	15.6	24.1
297 Mennonite;Other	1	87	NR	106 *	.8	1.2
313 N Am Bapt Conf	3	323	295	395 *	3.0	4.6
355 Presb Ch (USA)	2	136	74	166 *	1.2	1.9
419 So Bapt Conv	2	129	20	158 *	1.2	1.8
449 Un Methodist	10	1,556	825	1,905 *	14.3	22.1
MARSHALL	**43**	**4,066**	**2,133**	**8,315 ***	**75.8**	**100.0**
019 Amer Bapt USA	1	91	40	110 *	1.0	1.3
053 Assemb of God	1	62	86	102	.9	1.2
056 Baha'i	0	1	NR	1	-	-
081 Catholic	8	NR	NR	3,287	30.0	39.5
093 Chr Ch (Disc)	1	209	70	254 *	2.3	3.1
097 Chr Chs&Chs Cr	1	80	NR	97 *	.9	1.2
167 Chs of Christ	1	45	50	60	.5	.7
193 Episcopal	2	NR	51	88	.8	1.1
201 Evan Cov Ch	1	20	16	24 *	.2	.3
207 E.L.C.A.	3	348	140	397	3.6	4.8
283 Luth—MO Synod	5	941	582	1,134	10.3	13.6
355 Presb Ch (USA)	4	353	165	428 *	3.9	5.1
388 Reg Bapt Gen As	3	113	120	147 *	1.3	1.8
413 S.D.A.	1	2	NR	2	-	-
443 Un C of Christ	2	448	188	543 *	5.0	6.5
449 Un Methodist	8	1,253	537	1,520 *	13.9	18.3
463 Vineyard	1	100	88	121 *	1.1	1.5
MEADE	**22**	**2,448**	**782**	**4,097 ***	**88.5**	**100.0**
019 Amer Bapt USA	2	399	96	517 *	11.2	12.6
081 Catholic	3	NR	NR	952	20.6	23.2
097 Chr Chs&Chs Cr	2	140	NR	181 *	3.9	4.4
143 CG in Cr(Menn)	1	59	NR	76 *	1.6	1.9
165 Ch of Nazarene	1	142	118	149	3.2	3.6
167 Chs of Christ	1	42	56	64	1.4	1.6
193 Episcopal	1	NR	11	13	.3	.3
211 Fel Evg Bib Ch	1	138	141	141	3.0	3.4
226 Friends-USA	3	150	NR	194 *	4.2	4.7
283 Luth—MO Synod	1	305	99	420	9.1	10.3
297 Mennonite;Other	2	405	NR	524 *	11.3	12.8
349 Pent Holiness	1	50	40	65 *	1.4	1.6
449 Un Methodist	3	618	221	801 *	17.3	19.6
MIAMI	**44**	**6,614**	**2,809**	**14,241 ***	**50.2**	**100.0**
019 Amer Bapt USA	5	952	516	1,206 *	4.3	8.5
053 Assemb of God	3	284	408	439	1.5	3.1
056 Baha'i	0	2	NR	2	-	-
081 Catholic	4	NR	NR	5,448	19.2	38.3
093 Chr Ch (Disc)	2	362	161	459 *	1.6	3.2
097 Chr Chs&Chs Cr	2	280	NR	355 *	1.3	2.5
151 L-D Saints	1	NR	NR	292	1.0	2.1
165 Ch of Nazarene	1	143	59	143	.5	1.0
167 Chs of Christ	3	50	62	77	.3	.5
173 Comm of Christ	1	51	NR	51	.2	.4
226 Friends-USA	2	100	NR	127 *	.4	.9
283 Luth—MO Synod	2	1,018	406	1,379	4.9	9.7
355 Presb Ch (USA)	4	648	341	820 *	2.9	5.8
413 S.D.A.	1	29	NR	35	.1	.2
418 Southw Bapt Fel	1	NR	NR	NR	-	-
419 So Bapt Conv	2	733	219	928 *	3.3	6.5
449 Un Methodist	8	1,330	460	1,685 *	5.9	11.8
467 Wesleyan	1	32	27	45	.2	.3
499 Indep.Non-Char	1	600	150	750	2.6	5.3
MITCHELL	**25**	**2,502**	**1,009**	**5,519 ***	**79.6**	**100.0**
019 Amer Bapt USA	3	208	92	252 *	3.6	4.6
053 Assemb of God	1	69	76	115	1.7	2.1
056 Baha'i	0	1	NR	1	-	-
081 Catholic	3	NR	NR	2,258	32.6	40.9
093 Chr Ch (Disc)	1	0	0	0 *	-	-
097 Chr Chs&Chs Cr	1	148	NR	179 *	2.6	3.2
105 Christian Ref	1	187	120	226 *	3.3	4.1
151 L-D Saints	1	NR	NR	108	1.6	2.0
167 Chs of Christ	2	111	100	149	2.1	2.7
207 E.L.C.A.	1	359	118	518	7.5	9.4
226 Friends-USA	2	100	NR	121 *	1.7	2.2
283 Luth—MO Synod	1	114	39	134	1.9	2.4
313 N Am Bapt Conf	1	93	60	112 *	1.6	2.0
355 Presb Ch (USA)	1	123	73	149 *	2.1	2.7
419 So Bapt Conv	0	8	25	10 *	.1	.2
449 Un Methodist	6	981	306	1,187 *	17.1	21.5
MONTGOMERY	**85**	**13,801**	**4,935**	**20,988 ***	**57.9**	**100.0**
019 Amer Bapt USA	4	1,824	741	2,243 *	6.2	10.7
053 Assemb of God	4	247	297	510	1.4	2.4
056 Baha'i	0	24	NR	24	.1	.1
081 Catholic	4	NR	NR	2,914	8.0	13.9
093 Chr Ch (Disc)	2	955	168	1,175 *	3.2	5.6
097 Chr Chs&Chs Cr	7	1,860	NR	2,288 *	6.3	10.9
123 Ch God (Ander)	1	NR	98	98	.3	.5
127 Ch God (Cleve)	2	251	83	309 *	.9	1.5
157 Ch of Brethren	1	66	45	81 *	.2	.4
165 Ch of Nazarene	6	752	499	1,047	2.9	5.0
167 Chs of Christ	5	358	346	475	1.3	2.3
173 Comm of Christ	1	34	NR	34	.1	.2
193 Episcopal	2	NR	119	295	.8	1.4
226 Friends-USA	3	150	NR	184 *	.5	.9
263 Int Foursq Gos	1	14	17	17 *	-	.1
283 Luth—MO Synod	3	930	450	1,194	3.3	5.7
335 Orth Pres Ch	1	50	43	60	.2	.3
349 Pent Holiness	2	266	80	327 *	.9	1.6
355 Presb Ch (USA)	3	582	238	716 *	2.0	3.4
403 Salvation Army	1	90	53	402	1.1	1.9
413 S.D.A.	4	194	NR	232	.6	1.1
419 So Bapt Conv	12	2,663	633	3,275 *	9.0	15.6
443 Un C of Christ	1	35	15	43 *	.1	.2
449 Un Methodist	14	2,437	989	2,997 *	8.3	14.3
467 Wesleyan	1	19	21	48	.1	.2
MORRIS	**18**	**2,027**	**716**	**3,230 ***	**52.9**	**100.0**
019 Amer Bapt USA	1	134	100	165 *	2.7	5.1
081 Catholic	1	NR	NR	900	14.7	27.9
093 Chr Ch (Disc)	1	0	0	0 *	-	-
097 Chr Chs&Chs Cr	3	510	NR	626 *	10.3	19.4
207 E.L.C.A.	2	148	83	198	3.2	6.1
283 Luth—MO Synod	2	230	79	106	1.7	3.3
355 Presb Ch (USA)	1	46	25	57 *	.9	1.8
443 Un C of Christ	1	121	37	149 *	2.4	4.6
449 Un Methodist	6	838	392	1,029 *	16.9	31.9
MORTON	**17**	**1,217**	**652**	**2,215 ***	**63.4**	**100.0**
019 Amer Bapt USA	1	114	8	147 *	4.2	6.6
053 Assemb of God	2	36	46	48	1.4	2.2
081 Catholic	1	NR	NR	382	10.9	17.2
097 Chr Chs&Chs Cr	1	100	NR	129 *	3.7	5.8
123 Ch God (Ander)	1	NR	138	138	3.9	6.2
151 L-D Saints	1	NR	NR	105	3.0	4.7
165 Ch of Nazarene	2	139	124	218	6.2	9.8
167 Chs of Christ	1	19	20	24	.7	1.1
173 Comm of Christ	1	50	NR	50	1.4	2.3
283 Luth—MO Synod	1	61	12	76	2.2	3.4
349 Pent Holiness	1	30	35	39 *	1.1	1.8
419 So Bapt Conv	1	268	75	345 *	9.9	15.6
449 Un Methodist	3	400	194	514 *	14.7	23.2

NR–Not Reported *Total adherents estimated from known number of communicant, confirmed, full members. - Represents a percentage less than 0.1. Percentages may not total 100 due to rounding.

Table 4: Religious Congregations by County and Group: 2000

Religious Group	Number of Churches, Synagogues, Mosques, or Temples	Number of Communicant, Confirmed, or Full Members	Number of Attendees	Total Adherents		
				Number of Adherents	% of Total Pop.	% of Total Adh.
NEMAHA	**27**	**2,568**	**2,017**	**9,551 ***	**89.1**	**100.0**
019 Amer Bapt USA	1	68	34	87 *	.8	.9
040 Ap Chr Ch-Amer	2	352	719	719 *	6.7	7.5
056 Baha'i	0	1	NR	1	-	-
081 Catholic	7	NR	NR	5,733	53.5	60.0
151 L-D Saints	1	NR	NR	202	1.9	2.1
157 Ch of Brethren	1	30	28	38 *	.4	.4
167 Chs of Christ	1	42	50	70	.7	.7
181 Consrv Congr	1	405	461	516 *	4.8	5.4
283 Luth—MO Synod	1	235	114	321	3.0	3.4
419 So Bapt Conv	1	23	25	29 *	.3	.3
443 Un C of Christ	2	358	126	456 *	4.3	4.8
449 Un Methodist	8	1,012	408	1,289 *	12.0	13.5
467 Wesleyan	1	42	52	90	.8	.9
NEOSHO	**36**	**5,449**	**2,399**	**9,929 ***	**58.4**	**100.0**
019 Amer Bapt USA	3	988	385	1,218 *	7.2	12.3
053 Assemb of God	1	210	250	525	3.1	5.3
056 Baha'i	0	3	NR	3	-	-
081 Catholic	3	NR	NR	2,459	14.5	24.8
093 Chr Ch (Disc)	2	867	279	1,068 *	6.3	10.8
097 Chr Chs&Chs Cr	3	461	NR	568 *	3.3	5.7
123 Ch God (Ander)	1	NR	21	21	.1	.2
127 Ch God (Cleve)	1	139	85	171 *	1.0	1.7
151 L-D Saints	1	NR	NR	325	1.9	3.3
165 Ch of Nazarene	2	235	154	235	1.4	2.4
167 Chs of Christ	2	73	94	103	.6	1.0
173 Comm of Christ	1	38	NR	38	.2	.4
193 Episcopal	1	NR	35	164	1.0	1.7
226 Friends-USA	1	50	NR	62 *	.4	.6
283 Luth—MO Synod	2	455	229	522	3.1	5.3
355 Presb Ch (USA)	2	172	73	212 *	1.2	2.1
419 So Bapt Conv	1	257	90	317 *	1.9	3.2
449 Un Methodist	8	1,463	646	1,803 *	10.6	18.2
467 Wesleyan	1	38	58	115	.7	1.2
NESS	**19**	**1,686**	**599**	**3,280 ***	**95.0**	**100.0**
019 Amer Bapt USA	2	331	100	394 *	11.4	12.0
053 Assemb of God	1	8	8	10	.3	.3
081 Catholic	2	NR	NR	1,270	36.8	38.7
093 Chr Ch (Disc)	1	109	31	130 *	3.8	4.0
167 Chs of Christ	2	48	60	65	1.9	2.0
207 E.L.C.A.	1	71	27	81	2.3	2.5
283 Luth—MO Synod	1	93	54	109	3.2	3.3
288 Mennonite USA	1	100	40	119 *	3.4	3.6
413 S.D.A.	1	40	NR	48	1.4	1.5
449 Un Methodist	7	886	279	1,054 *	30.5	32.1
NORTON	**18**	**2,066**	**673**	**3,530 ***	**59.3**	**100.0**
019 Amer Bapt USA	1	63	36	75 *	1.3	2.1
056 Baha'i	0	4	NR	4	.1	.1
081 Catholic	2	NR	NR	878	14.7	24.9
097 Chr Chs&Chs Cr	1	986	NR	1,173 *	19.7	33.2
123 Ch God (Ander)	2	NR	133	133	2.2	3.8
157 Ch of Brethren	1	50	29	59 *	1.0	1.7
167 Chs of Christ	1	28	30	36	.6	1.0
193 Episcopal	1	NR	30	53	.9	1.5
283 Luth—MO Synod	1	108	73	136	2.3	3.9
413 S.D.A.	1	17	NR	20	.3	.6
419 So Bapt Conv	0	8	0	10 *	.2	.3
443 Un C of Christ	1	121	35	144 *	2.4	4.1
449 Un Methodist	5	628	257	747 *	12.5	21.2
469 WELS	1	53	50	62	1.0	1.8
OSAGE	**27**	**3,167**	**1,665**	**5,999 ***	**35.9**	**100.0**
019 Amer Bapt USA	1	650	120	816 *	4.9	13.6
053 Assemb of God	2	51	66	72	.4	1.2
056 Baha'i	0	3	NR	3	-	.1
081 Catholic	2	NR	NR	1,653	9.9	27.6
097 Chr Chs&Chs Cr	1	15	NR	19 *	.1	.3
123 Ch God (Ander)	1	NR	40	40	.2	.7
167 Chs of Christ	2	82	83	101	.6	1.7
201 Evan Cov Ch	2	156	202	207 *	1.2	3.5
207 E.L.C.A.	1	201	93	278	1.7	4.6
221 Free Methodist	1	4	55	55	.3	.9
263 Int Foursq Gos	1	58	141	141 *	.8	2.4
283 Luth—MO Synod	1	296	125	440	2.6	7.3
355 Presb Ch (USA)	1	74	35	93 *	.6	1.6
388 Reg Bapt Gen As	1	13	33	33 *	.2	.6
419 So Bapt Conv	1	10	6	13 *	.1	.2
443 Un C of Christ	1	100	46	126 *	.8	2.1
449 Un Methodist	7	1,401	528	1,759 *	10.5	29.3
467 Wesleyan	1	53	92	150	.9	2.5
OSBORNE	**24**	**1,967**	**997**	**3,271 ***	**73.5**	**100.0**
019 Amer Bapt USA	1	145	85	175 *	3.9	5.4
053 Assemb of God	1	63	73	203	4.6	6.2
081 Catholic	2	NR	NR	691	15.5	21.1
093 Chr Ch (Disc)	1	148	0	179 *	4.0	5.5
097 Chr Chs&Chs Cr	1	100	NR	121 *	2.7	3.7
165 Ch of Nazarene	1	28	19	29	.7	.9
207 E.L.C.A.	1	88	36	121	2.7	3.7
221 Free Methodist	1	21	38	38	.9	1.2
226 Friends-USA	1	50	NR	60 *	1.3	1.8
283 Luth—MO Synod	2	340	195	430	9.7	13.1
355 Presb Ch (USA)	1	8	45	45 *	1.0	1.4
413 S.D.A.	1	30	NR	36	.8	1.1
443 Un C of Christ	2	140	103	169 *	3.8	5.2
449 Un Methodist	8	806	403	974 *	21.9	29.8
OTTAWA	**21**	**1,408**	**802**	**2,350 ***	**38.1**	**100.0**
019 Amer Bapt USA	2	169	81	207 *	3.4	8.8
081 Catholic	2	NR	NR	473	7.7	20.1
165 Ch of Nazarene	1	46	59	117	1.9	5.0
193 Episcopal	1	NR	11	44	.7	1.9
207 E.L.C.A.	1	85	55	132	2.1	5.6
221 Free Methodist	1	21	29	29	.5	1.2
349 Pent Holiness	1	10	20	12 *	.2	.5
355 Presb Ch (USA)	4	317	140	388 *	6.3	16.5
449 Un Methodist	7	695	340	851 *	13.8	36.2
467 Wesleyan	1	65	67	97	1.6	4.1
PAWNEE	**18**	**2,413**	**982**	**4,296 ***	**59.4**	**100.0**
019 Amer Bapt USA	2	114	63	137 *	1.9	3.2
053 Assemb of God	1	55	55	85	1.2	2.0
056 Baha'i	0	4	NR	4	.1	.1
081 Catholic	1	NR	NR	1,234	17.1	28.7
093 Chr Ch (Disc)	1	501	134	604 *	8.4	14.1
165 Ch of Nazarene	1	65	71	143	2.0	3.3
167 Chs of Christ	1	50	55	80	1.1	1.9
193 Episcopal	1	NR	15	23	.3	.5
207 E.L.C.A.	1	32	16	45	.6	1.0
283 Luth—MO Synod	1	214	60	281	3.9	6.5
355 Presb Ch (USA)	1	142	64	171 *	2.4	4.0
413 S.D.A.	1	37	NR	44	.6	1.0
419 So Bapt Conv	1	237	79	286 *	4.0	6.7
449 Un Methodist	5	962	370	1,159 *	16.0	27.0
PHILLIPS	**29**	**2,637**	**1,305**	**4,521 ***	**75.3**	**100.0**
019 Amer Bapt USA	1	120	15	146 *	2.4	3.2
053 Assemb of God	2	98	133	194	3.2	4.3
081 Catholic	2	NR	NR	616	10.3	13.6
093 Chr Ch (Disc)	1	394	0	481 *	8.0	10.6
097 Chr Chs&Chs Cr	1	130	NR	159 *	2.6	3.5
105 Christian Ref	1	192	140	234 *	3.9	5.2
123 Ch God (Ander)	1	NR	49	49	.8	1.1
151 L-D Saints	1	NR	NR	248	4.1	5.5
165 Ch of Nazarene	2	37	10	39	.6	.9
167 Chs of Christ	2	45	48	58	1.0	1.3
193 Episcopal	1	NR	18	24	.4	.5
207 E.L.C.A.	2	391	188	482	8.0	10.7
283 Luth—MO Synod	1	162	80	257	4.3	5.7
355 Presb Ch (USA)	1	111	70	135 *	2.2	3.0
371 Ref Ch in Am	1	93	65	156	2.6	3.5

NR–Not Reported   *Total adherents estimated from known number of communicant, confirmed, full members.   - Represents a percentage less than 0.1.   Percentages may not total 100 due to rounding.

Table 4: Religious Congregations by County and Group: 2000

Religious Group	Number of Churches, Synagogues, Mosques, or Temples	Number of Communicant, Confirmed, or Full Members	Number of Attendees	Total Adherents: Number of Adherents	% of Total Pop.	% of Total Adh.
388 Reg Bapt Gen As	1	29	45	45 *	.7	1.0
449 Un Methodist	6	755	300	922 *	15.4	20.4
467 Wesleyan	2	80	144	276	4.6	6.1
POTTAWATOMIE	**34**	**3,336**	**1,695**	**7,340 ***	**40.3**	**100.0**
019 Amer Bapt USA	3	204	84	262 *	1.4	3.6
053 Assemb of God	1	27	40	127	.7	1.7
056 Baha'i	0	1	NR	1	-	-
081 Catholic	6	NR	NR	2,547	14.0	34.7
097 Chr Chs&Chs Cr	2	230	NR	295 *	1.6	4.0
127 Ch God (Cleve)	1	15	10	19 *	.1	.3
193 Episcopal	1	NR	22	90	.5	1.2
207 E.L.C.A.	2	231	127	303	1.7	4.1
283 Luth—MO Synod	3	452	368	899	4.9	12.2
355 Presb Ch (USA)	1	148	94	190 *	1.0	2.6
388 Reg Bapt Gen As	1	28	25	36 *	.2	.5
419 So Bapt Conv	3	400	350	514 *	2.8	7.0
443 Un C of Christ	2	183	49	235 *	1.3	3.2
449 Un Methodist	8	1,417	526	1,822 *	10.0	24.8
PRATT	**26**	**3,481**	**1,590**	**6,308 ***	**65.4**	**100.0**
019 Amer Bapt USA	1	186	90	226 *	2.3	3.6
053 Assemb of God	1	181	263	347	3.6	5.5
056 Baha'i	0	1	NR	1	-	-
081 Catholic	1	NR	NR	1,759	18.2	27.9
093 Chr Ch (Disc)	2	586	25	713 *	7.4	11.3
123 Ch God (Ander)	1	NR	115	115	1.2	1.8
165 Ch of Nazarene	1	77	43	77	.8	1.2
167 Chs of Christ	1	100	80	120	1.2	1.9
193 Episcopal	1	NR	22	50	.5	.8
221 Free Methodist	1	49	55	55	.6	.9
226 Friends-USA	2	100	NR	122 *	1.3	1.9
283 Luth—MO Synod	2	416	196	551	5.7	8.7
349 Pent Holiness	1	23	6	28 *	.3	.4
355 Presb Ch (USA)	1	192	91	234 *	2.4	3.7
413 S.D.A.	2	21	NR	25	.3	.4
419 So Bapt Conv	1	414	165	504 *	5.2	8.0
449 Un Methodist	7	1,135	439	1,381 *	14.3	21.9
RAWLINS	**8**	**836**	**473**	**1,728 ***	**58.3**	**100.0**
081 Catholic	2	NR	NR	733	24.7	42.4
093 Chr Ch (Disc)	1	114	60	137 *	4.6	7.9
165 Ch of Nazarene	1	10	3	15	.5	.9
201 Evan Cov Ch	1	80	75	96 *	3.2	5.6
283 Luth—MO Synod	1	341	185	399	13.5	23.1
443 Un C of Christ	1	41	25	49 *	1.7	2.8
449 Un Methodist	1	250	125	299 *	10.1	17.3
RENO	**93**	**20,420**	**9,729**	**33,286 ***	**51.4**	**100.0**
019 Amer Bapt USA	3	989	470	1,213 *	1.9	3.6
032 Amish; other	2	110	NR	134 *	.2	.4
053 Assemb of God	2	132	157	213	.3	.6
056 Baha'i	1	44	NR	44	.1	.1
061 Beachy Amish	3	320	NR	392 *	.6	1.2
081 Catholic	3	NR	NR	6,482	10.0	19.5
084 Calvary Chapel	1	NR	NR	NR	-	-
093 Chr Ch (Disc)	2	2,022	330	2,479 *	3.8	7.4
097 Chr Chs&Chs Cr	3	648	NR	794 *	1.2	2.4
123 Ch God (Ander)	2	NR	155	155	.2	.5
151 L-D Saints	1	NR	NR	372	.6	1.1
157 Ch of Brethren	2	261	137	320 *	.5	1.0
165 Ch of Nazarene	5	1,300	974	1,559	2.4	4.7
167 Chs of Christ	5	687	630	952	1.5	2.9
173 Comm of Christ	1	56	NR	56	.1	.2
175 Congr Chr Chs	1	195	95	239 *	.4	.7
183 Cons Menn Conf	2	195	238	284	.4	.9
193 Episcopal	1	NR	131	435	.7	1.3
203 Evan Free Ch	1	63	120	120	.2	.4
207 E.L.C.A.	2	559	292	828	1.3	2.5
213 Evan Menn Inc	1	0	0	0 *	-	-
223 Free Will Bapt	1	31	NR	38 *	.1	.1
226 Friends-USA	2	100	NR	123 *	.2	.4
237 Menn Br US Conf	1	436	NR	535 *	.8	1.6
263 Int Foursq Gos	1	30	50	50 *	.1	.2
283 Luth—MO Synod	3	1,127	529	1,451	2.2	4.4
288 Mennonite USA	6	1,687	1,102	2,068 *	3.2	6.2
297 Mennonite;Other	1	27	NR	33 *	.1	.1
323 Old Ord Amish	4	220	NR	268 *	.4	.8
349 Pent Holiness	3	1,299	802	1,593 *	2.5	4.8
355 Presb Ch (USA)	4	1,184	435	1,452 *	2.2	4.4
403 Salvation Army	1	144	117	366	.6	1.1
413 S.D.A.	1	158	NR	188	.3	.6
419 So Bapt Conv	3	1,372	538	1,682 *	2.6	5.1
443 Un C of Christ	2	183	102	224 *	.3	.7
449 Un Methodist	14	4,644	1,968	5,694 *	8.8	17.1
467 Wesleyan	1	47	57	150	.2	.5
499 Indep.Non-Char	1	150	300	300	.5	.9
REPUBLIC	**23**	**2,628**	**947**	**3,990 ***	**68.4**	**100.0**
019 Amer Bapt USA	1	98	35	116 *	2.0	2.9
053 Assemb of God	1	31	35	35	.6	.9
081 Catholic	3	NR	NR	602	10.3	15.1
097 Chr Chs&Chs Cr	1	239	NR	283 *	4.9	7.1
201 Evan Cov Ch	1	48	42	57 *	1.0	1.4
207 E.L.C.A.	4	626	193	841	14.4	21.1
263 Int Foursq Gos	1	12	32	32 *	.5	.8
355 Presb Ch (USA)	3	317	106	375 *	6.4	9.4
449 Un Methodist	7	1,084	356	1,284 *	22.0	32.2
467 Wesleyan	1	173	148	365	6.3	9.1
RICE	**32**	**4,136**	**1,960**	**6,308 ***	**58.6**	**100.0**
019 Amer Bapt USA	4	576	216	704 *	6.5	11.2
053 Assemb of God	2	41	45	75	.7	1.2
056 Baha'i	0	5	NR	5	-	.1
081 Catholic	4	NR	NR	1,109	10.3	17.6
093 Chr Ch (Disc)	1	429	128	524 *	4.9	8.3
097 Chr Chs&Chs Cr	1	50	NR	61 *	.6	1.0
165 Ch of Nazarene	1	54	55	106	1.0	1.7
167 Chs of Christ	1	65	75	80	.7	1.3
193 Episcopal	1	NR	30	67	.6	1.1
213 Evan Menn Inc	1	177	203	216 *	2.0	3.4
283 Luth—MO Synod	1	129	75	171	1.6	2.7
355 Presb Ch (USA)	3	371	239	454 *	4.2	7.2
418 Southw Bapt Fel	1	NR	NR	NR	-	-
419 So Bapt Conv	1	49	17	60 *	.6	1.0
443 Un C of Christ	2	274	137	335 *	3.1	5.3
449 Un Methodist	8	1,916	740	2,341 *	21.8	37.1
RILEY	**60**	**10,857**	**6,177**	**21,903 ***	**34.9**	**100.0**
019 Amer Bapt USA	2	363	183	426 *	.7	1.9
034 Ant Orth of NA	1	0	NR	0	-	-
053 Assemb of God	1	305	475	500	.8	2.3
056 Baha'i	0	24	NR	24	-	.1
076 Buddhism	1	NR	NR	NR	-	-
081 Catholic	3	NR	NR	4,933	7.8	22.5
093 Chr Ch (Disc)	1	785	170	921 *	1.5	4.2
097 Chr Chs&Chs Cr	3	520	NR	610 *	1.0	2.8
123 Ch God (Ander)	1	NR	60	60	.1	.3
151 L-D Saints	3	NR	NR	930	1.5	4.2
165 Ch of Nazarene	1	140	109	154	.2	.7
167 Chs of Christ	2	238	210	310	.5	1.4
173 Comm of Christ	1	73	NR	73	.1	.3
193 Episcopal	2	NR	154	276	.4	1.3
201 Evan Cov Ch	1	60	87	87 *	.1	.4
203 Evan Free Ch	1	101	260	260	.4	1.2
207 E.L.C.A.	3	1,420	545	1,796	2.9	8.2
221 Free Methodist	1	19	38	38	.1	.2
237 Menn Br US Conf	1	73	NR	86 *	.1	.4
264 Int Chs of Crst	1	55	87	78	.1	.4
267 Muslim Est	1	NR	55	163	.3	.7
283 Luth—MO Synod	2	760	385	1,069	1.7	4.9
288 Mennonite USA	1	78	66	92 *	.1	.4
355 Presb Ch (USA)	4	1,164	442	1,367 *	2.2	6.2
403 Salvation Army	1	22	72	22	-	.1
413 S.D.A.	1	86	NR	102	.2	.5

NR–Not Reported *Total adherents estimated from known number of communicant, confirmed, full members. - Represents a percentage less than 0.1. Percentages may not total 100 due to rounding.

Table 4: Religious Congregations by County and Group: 2000

Religious Group	Number of Churches, Synagogues, Mosques, or Temples	Number of Communicant, Confirmed, or Full Members	Number of Attendees	Total Adherents		
				Number of Adherents	% of Total Pop.	% of Total Adh.
419 So Bapt Conv	4	905	399	1,062 *	1.7	4.8
435 Unitarian-Univ	1	85	NR	100 *	.2	.5
443 Un C of Christ	1	212	127	249 *	.4	1.1
449 Un Methodist	10	2,960	1,188	3,475 *	5.5	15.9
463 Vineyard	1	83	122	122 *	.2	.6
467 Wesleyan	1	298	943	2,045	3.3	9.3
469 WELS	1	28	0	48	.1	.2
496 Jewish Est	1	NR	NR	425	.7	1.9
ROOKS	**19**	**2,150**	**713**	**4,320 ***	**76.0**	**100.0**
019 Amer Bapt USA	1	71	42	87 *	1.5	2.0
053 Assemb of God	2	72	93	132	2.3	3.1
056 Baha'i	0	1	NR	1	-	-
081 Catholic	4	NR	NR	1,507	26.5	34.9
097 Chr Chs&Chs Cr	2	555	NR	683 *	12.0	15.8
123 Ch God (Ander)	1	NR	67	67	1.2	1.6
165 Ch of Nazarene	2	93	76	172	3.0	4.0
283 Luth—MO Synod	1	96	43	119	2.1	2.8
419 So Bapt Conv	1	309	50	380 *	6.7	8.8
443 Un C of Christ	1	67	29	82 *	1.4	1.9
449 Un Methodist	4	886	313	1,090 *	19.2	25.2
RUSH	**14**	**1,335**	**420**	**2,553 ***	**71.9**	**100.0**
081 Catholic	3	NR	NR	913	25.7	35.8
097 Chr Chs&Chs Cr	1	110	NR	131 *	3.7	5.1
207 E.L.C.A.	4	506	213	651	18.3	25.5
413 S.D.A.	1	82	NR	98	2.8	3.8
449 Un Methodist	5	637	207	760 *	21.4	29.8
RUSSELL	**28**	**2,974**	**1,372**	**4,802 ***	**65.2**	**100.0**
019 Amer Bapt USA	2	62	26	74 *	1.0	1.5
053 Assemb of God	1	31	35	40	.5	.8
081 Catholic	3	NR	NR	1,096	14.9	22.8
097 Chr Chs&Chs Cr	1	70	NR	84 *	1.1	1.7
165 Ch of Nazarene	1	19	8	23	.3	.5
167 Chs of Christ	1	51	55	67	.9	1.4
193 Episcopal	1	NR	12	22	.3	.5
207 E.L.C.A.	5	1,216	542	1,530	20.8	31.9
388 Reg Bapt Gen As	1	45	80	80 *	1.1	1.7
419 So Bapt Conv	1	150	67	179 *	2.4	3.7
443 Un C of Christ	2	126	69	150 *	2.0	3.1
449 Un Methodist	8	1,172	461	1,399 *	19.0	29.1
469 WELS	1	32	17	33	.4	.7
496 Jewish Est	0	NR	NR	25	.3	.5
SALINE	**68**	**14,686**	**8,188**	**30,270 ***	**56.5**	**100.0**
019 Amer Bapt USA	2	589	230	737 *	1.4	2.4
034 Ant Orth of NA	1	94	NR	188	.4	.6
053 Assemb of God	2	145	198	280	.5	.9
056 Baha'i	0	14	NR	14	-	-
075 Brethren in Cr	1	87	228	228	.4	.8
081 Catholic	13	NR	NR	9,769	18.2	32.3
093 Chr Ch (Disc)	2	642	292	803 *	1.5	2.7
097 Chr Chs&Chs Cr	1	211	NR	264 *	.5	.9
123 Ch God (Ander)	1	NR	20	20	-	.1
127 Ch God (Cleve)	1	54	27	68 *	.1	.2
151 L-D Saints	1	NR	NR	381	.7	1.3
165 Ch of Nazarene	2	682	418	801	1.5	2.6
167 Chs of Christ	1	197	200	294	.5	1.0
173 Comm of Christ	1	37	NR	37	.1	.1
193 Episcopal	2	NR	147	481	.9	1.6
201 Evan Cov Ch	1	504	738	738 *	1.4	2.4
207 E.L.C.A.	7	2,230	804	3,100	5.8	10.2
221 Free Methodist	1	24	25	25	-	.1
223 Free Will Bapt	1	31	NR	39 *	.1	.1
263 Int Foursq Gos	3	871	1,160	1,160 *	2.2	3.8
283 Luth—MO Synod	2	1,304	624	1,736	3.2	5.7
288 Mennonite USA	1	62	60	78 *	.1	.3
355 Presb Ch (USA)	2	1,152	472	1,440 *	2.7	4.8
403 Salvation Army	1	121	80	338	.6	1.1
413 S.D.A.	1	146	NR	174	.3	.6
419 So Bapt Conv	3	1,592	505	1,991 *	3.7	6.6
435 Unitarian-Univ	1	30	NR	38 *	.1	.1
443 Un C of Christ	1	32	12	40 *	.1	.1
449 Un Methodist	9	3,518	1,558	4,398 *	8.2	14.5
467 Wesleyan	1	51	68	201	.4	.7
469 WELS	1	66	47	84	.2	.3
496 Jewish Est	0	NR	NR	25	-	.1
499 Indep.Non-Char	1	200	275	300	.6	1.0
SCOTT	**13**	**3,047**	**878**	**4,622 ***	**90.3**	**100.0**
019 Amer Bapt USA	1	658	210	823 *	16.1	17.8
053 Assemb of God	1	23	28	36	.7	.8
081 Catholic	1	NR	NR	765	14.9	16.6
093 Chr Ch (Disc)	1	731	115	914 *	17.9	19.8
097 Chr Chs&Chs Cr	1	135	NR	169 *	3.3	3.7
143 CG in Cr(Menn)	1	151	NR	189 *	3.7	4.1
157 Ch of Brethren	1	103	54	129 *	2.5	2.8
165 Ch of Nazarene	1	86	59	86	1.7	1.9
167 Chs of Christ	1	35	36	40	.8	.9
193 Episcopal	1	NR	21	47	.9	1.0
283 Luth—MO Synod	1	227	95	301	5.9	6.5
419 So Bapt Conv	1	178	78	223 *	4.4	4.8
449 Un Methodist	1	720	182	900 *	17.6	19.5
SEDGWICK	**392**	**102,946**	**50,782**	**211,369 ***	**46.7**	**100.0**
017 Amer Bapt Assn	5	359	NR	461 *	.1	.2
019 Amer Bapt USA	17	3,650	1,706	4,687 *	1.0	2.2
034 Ant Orth of NA	3	916	NR	1,832	.4	.9
040 Ap Chr Ch-Amer	1	38	62	62 *	-	-
053 Assemb of God	18	3,087	3,727	5,484	1.2	2.6
056 Baha'i	1	379	NR	379	.1	.2
059 Bapt Miss Assn	1	59	34	76 *	-	-
071 Brethren (Ash)	1	47	78	60 *	-	-
076 Buddhism	6	NR	NR	NR	-	-
081 Catholic	32	NR	NR	62,630	13.8	29.6
084 Calvary Chapel	1	NR	NR	NR	-	-
093 Chr Ch (Disc)	17	4,374	1,653	5,617 *	1.2	2.7
097 Chr Chs&Chs Cr	17	11,875	NR	15,249 *	3.4	7.2
123 Ch God (Ander)	8	NR	2,650	2,650	.6	1.3
127 Ch God (Cleve)	5	579	268	744 *	.2	.4
145 Ch God Prophcy	1	27	NR	34 *	-	-
151 L-D Saints	11	NR	NR	3,424	.8	1.6
157 Ch of Brethren	1	520	0	668 *	.1	.3
165 Ch of Nazarene	16	3,646	2,299	4,015	.9	1.9
167 Chs of Christ	22	3,332	3,312	4,347	1.0	2.1
173 Comm of Christ	3	382	NR	382	.1	.2
175 Congr Chr Chs	2	480	282	616 *	.1	.3
193 Episcopal	8	NR	1,019	2,674	.6	1.3
201 Evan Cov Ch	1	43	57	57 *	-	-
203 Evan Free Ch	5	942	1,865	1,865	.4	.9
207 E.L.C.A.	9	2,309	1,293	3,140	.7	1.5
221 Free Methodist	2	100	138	138	-	.1
223 Free Will Bapt	2	63	NR	80 *	-	-
226 Friends-USA	8	528	NR	678 *	.1	.3
237 Menn Br US Conf	2	640	NR	821 *	.2	.4
246 Greek Orthodox	1	NR	NR	0	-	-
263 Int Foursq Gos	2	274	292	352 *	.1	.2
264 Int Chs of Crst	1	165	299	244	.1	.1
267 Muslim Est	3	NR	468	1,827	.4	.9
283 Luth—MO Synod	11	5,664	3,145	7,571	1.7	3.6
288 Mennonite USA	3	551	374	707 *	.2	.3
290 Metro Comm Ch	1	76	83	98 *	-	-
291 Missionary Ch	3	184	260	267	.1	.1
339 Pent Ch of God	3	113	NR	260	.1	.1
349 Pent Holiness	4	571	328	733 *	.2	.3
355 Presb Ch (USA)	17	5,625	2,964	7,224 *	1.6	3.4
356 Presb Ch Amer	2	204	395	413	.1	.2
371 Ref Ch in Am	1	83	147	191	-	.1
388 Reg Bapt Gen As	1	25	35	35 *	-	-
403 Salvation Army	2	413	495	1,847	.4	.9
413 S.D.A.	6	1,369	NR	1,629	.4	.8
419 So Bapt Conv	40	24,773	7,455	31,812 *	7.0	15.1
435 Unitarian-Univ	1	135	NR	173 *	-	.1
443 Un C of Christ	5	721	331	926 *	.2	.4

NR–Not Reported *Total adherents estimated from known number of communicant, confirmed, full members. - Represents a percentage less than 0.1. Percentages may not total 100 due to rounding.

Table 4: Religious Congregations by County and Group: 2000

Religious Group	Number of Churches, Synagogues, Mosques, or Temples	Number of Communicant, Confirmed, or Full Members	Number of Attendees	Total Adherents: Number of Adherents	Total Adherents: % of Total Pop.	Total Adherents: % of Total Adh.
449 Un Methodist	48	21,133	10,382	27,137 *	6.0	12.8
463 Vineyard	1	900	700	1,156 *	.3	.5
467 Wesleyan	4	224	327	698	.2	.3
469 WELS	1	93	91	131	-	.1
496 Jewish Est	1	NR	NR	1,300	.3	.6
498 Indep.Charis.	2	0	368	368	.1	.2
499 Indep.Non-Char	2	1,275	1,400	1,400	.3	.7
SEWARD	**26**	**4,348**	**2,091**	**8,929 ***	**39.7**	**100.0**
053 Assemb of God	2	114	146	245	1.1	2.7
056 Baha'i	0	9	NR	9	-	.1
081 Catholic	1	NR	NR	2,559	11.4	28.7
093 Chr Ch (Disc)	1	222	103	297 *	1.3	3.3
097 Chr Chs&Chs Cr	1	350	NR	468 *	2.1	5.2
123 Ch God (Ander)	2	NR	122	122	.5	1.4
151 L-D Saints	1	NR	NR	212	.9	2.4
165 Ch of Nazarene	1	119	57	119	.5	1.3
167 Chs of Christ	2	302	310	410	1.8	4.6
173 Comm of Christ	1	11	NR	11	-	.1
193 Episcopal	1	NR	70	170	.8	1.9
207 E.L.C.A.	1	135	50	177	.8	2.0
226 Friends-USA	2	100	NR	134 *	.6	1.5
283 Luth—MO Synod	1	170	78	254	1.1	2.8
288 Mennonite USA	1	52	60	70 *	.3	.8
355 Presb Ch (USA)	1	118	75	158 *	.7	1.8
413 S.D.A.	1	33	NR	39	.2	.4
419 So Bapt Conv	2	1,359	462	1,817 *	8.1	20.3
449 Un Methodist	3	904	283	1,208 *	5.4	13.5
496 Jewish Est	0	NR	NR	25	.1	.3
499 Indep.Non-Char	1	350	275	425	1.9	4.8
SHAWNEE	**169**	**35,476**	**19,796**	**78,404 ***	**46.2**	**100.0**
017 Amer Bapt Assn	1	22	NR	27 *	-	-
019 Amer Bapt USA	11	2,753	1,345	3,414 *	2.0	4.4
034 Ant Orth of NA	1	76	NR	152	.1	.2
053 Assemb of God	5	779	1,040	1,630	1.0	2.1
056 Baha'i	2	67	NR	67	-	.1
081 Catholic	9	NR	NR	26,615	15.7	33.9
093 Chr Ch (Disc)	5	2,992	563	3,710 *	2.2	4.7
097 Chr Chs&Chs Cr	7	1,161	NR	1,440 *	.8	1.8
123 Ch God (Ander)	3	NR	91	91	.1	.1
127 Ch God (Cleve)	1	40	46	50 *	-	.1
145 Ch God Prophcy	1	27	NR	33 *	-	-
151 L-D Saints	5	NR	NR	1,849	1.1	2.4
157 Ch of Brethren	1	144	67	179 *	.1	.2
165 Ch of Nazarene	6	1,510	1,381	2,402	1.4	3.1
167 Chs of Christ	8	978	1,025	1,265	.7	1.6
173 Comm of Christ	1	245	NR	245	.1	.3
193 Episcopal	3	NR	544	1,653	1.0	2.1
201 Evan Cov Ch	1	182	147	226 *	.1	.3
203 Evan Free Ch	1	55	110	110	.1	.1
207 E.L.C.A.	3	1,322	588	1,730	1.0	2.2
221 Free Methodist	1	62	70	75	-	.1
223 Free Will Bapt	1	31	NR	39 *	-	-
237 Menn Br US Conf	1	149	NR	185 *	.1	.2
263 Int Foursq Gos	2	82	145	145 *	.1	.2
267 Muslim Est	1	NR	75	150	.1	.2
283 Luth—MO Synod	7	3,788	1,991	4,919	2.9	6.3
288 Mennonite USA	1	91	116	116 *	.1	.1
290 Metro Comm Ch	1	85	67	67 *	-	.1
304 NatPrimBapt USA	1	25	NR	31 *	-	-
339 Pent Ch of God	1	11	NR	25	-	-
355 Presb Ch (USA)	12	2,568	1,311	3,184 *	1.9	4.1
370 Ref Baptist Chs	2	NR	NR	NR	-	-
388 Reg Bapt Gen As	2	42	80	80 *	-	.1
403 Salvation Army	1	116	93	440	.3	.6
413 S.D.A.	2	471	NR	561	.3	.7
416 Sikh	1	NR	NR	NR	-	-
419 So Bapt Conv	19	3,940	2,071	4,886 *	2.9	6.2
435 Unitarian-Univ	1	124	NR	154 *	.1	.2
443 Un C of Christ	4	991	384	1,229 *	.7	1.6
449 Un Methodist	24	8,921	3,651	11,063 *	6.5	14.1
467 Wesleyan	3	284	512	1,407	.8	1.8

Religious Group	Number of Churches, Synagogues, Mosques, or Temples	Number of Communicant, Confirmed, or Full Members	Number of Attendees	Total Adherents: Number of Adherents	Total Adherents: % of Total Pop.	Total Adherents: % of Total Adh.
469 WELS	1	92	58	135	.1	.2
496 Jewish Est	1	NR	NR	400	.2	.5
499 Indep.Non-Char	4	1,250	2,225	2,225	1.3	2.8
SHERIDAN	**13**	**992**	**479**	**2,404 ***	**85.5**	**100.0**
019 Amer Bapt USA	1	286	155	351 *	12.5	14.6
056 Baha'i	0	1	NR	1	-	-
081 Catholic	4	NR	NR	1,193	42.4	49.6
093 Chr Ch (Disc)	1	195	80	239 *	8.5	9.9
167 Chs of Christ	1	23	25	30	1.1	1.2
283 Luth—MO Synod	1	122	65	143	5.1	5.9
355 Presb Ch (USA)	1	129	56	158 *	5.6	6.6
449 Un Methodist	4	236	98	289 *	10.3	12.0
SHERMAN	**15**	**1,604**	**664**	**3,003 ***	**44.4**	**100.0**
019 Amer Bapt USA	1	86	80	105 *	1.6	3.5
081 Catholic	1	NR	NR	735	10.9	24.5
089 Chr & Miss Al	1	22	NR	31	.5	1.0
093 Chr Ch (Disc)	1	295	98	361 *	5.3	12.0
097 Chr Chs&Chs Cr	1	55	NR	67 *	1.0	2.2
151 L-D Saints	1	NR	NR	164	2.4	5.5
165 Ch of Nazarene	1	35	44	59	.9	2.0
167 Chs of Christ	1	23	25	35	.5	1.2
193 Episcopal	1	NR	34	84	1.2	2.8
207 E.L.C.A.	1	349	138	433	6.4	14.4
263 Int Foursq Gos	1	10	38	38 *	.6	1.3
413 S.D.A.	1	23	NR	27	.4	.9
419 So Bapt Conv	1	2	0	2 *	-	.1
449 Un Methodist	2	704	207	862 *	12.8	28.7
SMITH	**26**	**2,698**	**1,486**	**3,538 ***	**78.0**	**100.0**
053 Assemb of God	1	38	50	50	1.1	1.4
081 Catholic	2	NR	NR	220	4.9	6.2
093 Chr Ch (Disc)	3	461	311	546 *	12.0	15.4
097 Chr Chs&Chs Cr	3	161	NR	191 *	4.2	5.4
165 Ch of Nazarene	2	113	112	186	4.1	5.3
203 Evan Free Ch	1	69	130	130	2.9	3.7
207 E.L.C.A.	3	872	339	1,054	23.2	29.8
283 Luth—MO Synod	1	148	94	173	3.8	4.9
355 Presb Ch (USA)	1	70	45	83 *	1.8	2.3
388 Reg Bapt Gen As	1	45	40	53 *	1.2	1.5
443 Un C of Christ	2	111	78	131 *	2.9	3.7
449 Un Methodist	6	610	287	721 *	15.9	20.4
STAFFORD	**23**	**2,059**	**1,032**	**3,058 ***	**63.9**	**100.0**
017 Amer Bapt Assn	1	32	NR	40 *	.8	1.3
019 Amer Bapt USA	2	230	79	285 *	6.0	9.3
056 Baha'i	0	1	NR	1	-	-
081 Catholic	2	NR	NR	488	10.2	16.0
093 Chr Ch (Disc)	2	255	56	316 *	6.6	10.3
157 Ch of Brethren	1	69	50	85 *	1.8	2.8
165 Ch of Nazarene	1	75	61	93	1.9	3.0
167 Chs of Christ	2	170	160	218	4.6	7.1
221 Free Methodist	1	37	59	59	1.2	1.9
313 N Am Bapt Conf	1	143	143	177 *	3.7	5.8
355 Presb Ch (USA)	1	61	66	75 *	1.6	2.5
419 So Bapt Conv	1	62	28	77 *	1.6	2.5
443 Un C of Christ	2	223	89	276 *	5.8	9.0
449 Un Methodist	6	701	241	868 *	18.1	28.4
STANTON	**7**	**649**	**391**	**1,673 ***	**69.5**	**100.0**
081 Catholic	1	NR	NR	471	19.6	28.2
165 Ch of Nazarene	1	56	49	79	3.3	4.7
167 Chs of Christ	1	10	11	13	.5	.8
349 Pent Holiness	1	7	14	9 *	.4	.5
449 Un Methodist	2	503	164	655 *	27.2	39.2
467 Wesleyan	1	73	153	446	18.5	26.7
STEVENS	**18**	**2,032**	**857**	**3,372 ***	**61.7**	**100.0**
019 Amer Bapt USA	1	54	45	70 *	1.3	2.1
053 Assemb of God	1	102	143	153	2.8	4.5

NR–Not Reported *Total adherents estimated from known number of communicant, confirmed, full members. - Represents a percentage less than 0.1. Percentages may not total 100 due to rounding.

Table 4: Religious Congregations by County and Group: 2000

Religious Group	Number of Churches, Synagogues, Mosques, or Temples	Number of Communicant, Confirmed, or Full Members	Number of Attendees	Total Adherents: Number of Adherents	Total Adherents: % of Total Pop.	Total Adherents: % of Total Adh.
081 Catholic	1	NR	NR	529	9.7	15.7
097 Chr Chs&Chs Cr	1	525	NR	685 *	12.5	20.3
123 Ch God (Ander)	1	NR	83	83	1.5	2.5
165 Ch of Nazarene	1	45	40	101	1.8	3.0
167 Chs of Christ	1	90	100	120	2.2	3.6
193 Episcopal	1	NR	18	37	.7	1.1
226 Friends-USA	4	200	NR	261 *	4.8	7.7
283 Luth—MO Synod	1	38	0	57	1.0	1.7
349 Pent Holiness	1	150	177	196 *	3.6	5.8
419 So Bapt Conv	2	308	74	402 *	7.4	11.9
449 Un Methodist	2	520	177	678 *	12.4	20.1
SUMNER	**67**	**9,248**	**4,005**	**16,960 ***	**65.4**	**100.0**
017 Amer Bapt Assn	1	16	NR	20 *	.1	.1
019 Amer Bapt USA	6	1,098	327	1,395 *	5.4	8.2
053 Assemb of God	3	246	307	418	1.6	2.5
056 Baha'i	0	19	NR	19	.1	.1
071 Brethren (Ash)	1	43	45	55 *	.2	.3
081 Catholic	6	NR	NR	4,513	17.4	26.6
084 Calvary Chapel	1	NR	NR	NR	-	-
093 Chr Ch (Disc)	4	1,255	570	1,594 *	6.1	9.4
097 Chr Chs&Chs Cr	1	320	NR	406 *	1.6	2.4
123 Ch God (Ander)	1	NR	18	18	.1	.1
151 L-D Saints	1	NR	NR	294	1.1	1.7
165 Ch of Nazarene	1	96	80	178	.7	1.0
167 Chs of Christ	8	539	524	690	2.7	4.1
193 Episcopal	1	NR	9	13	.1	.1
207 E.L.C.A.	1	55	32	90	.3	.5
223 Free Will Bapt	1	31	NR	40 *	.2	.2
226 Friends-USA	2	100	NR	127 *	.5	.7
283 Luth—MO Synod	2	236	112	327	1.3	1.9
355 Presb Ch (USA)	5	379	182	482 *	1.9	2.8
360 Prim Bapt Chrch	1	NR	NR	NR	-	-
413 S.D.A.	1	40	NR	48	.2	.3
419 So Bapt Conv	6	1,796	477	2,281 *	8.8	13.4
449 Un Methodist	12	2,918	1,240	3,707 *	14.3	21.9
467 Wesleyan	1	61	82	245	.9	1.4
THOMAS	**15**	**1,910**	**934**	**3,945 ***	**48.2**	**100.0**
019 Amer Bapt USA	1	83	40	104 *	1.3	2.6
053 Assemb of God	1	71	85	135	1.7	3.4
056 Baha'i	0	1	NR	1	-	-
081 Catholic	1	NR	NR	1,311	16.0	33.2
093 Chr Ch (Disc)	1	218	56	272 *	3.3	6.9
097 Chr Chs&Chs Cr	1	20	NR	25 *	.3	.6
167 Chs of Christ	1	40	39	64	.8	1.6
193 Episcopal	1	NR	15	40	.5	1.0
207 E.L.C.A.	1	57	23	76	.9	1.9
283 Luth—MO Synod	1	255	119	341	4.2	8.6
355 Presb Ch (USA)	1	142	70	177 *	2.2	4.5
419 So Bapt Conv	1	111	35	138 *	1.7	3.5
449 Un Methodist	3	790	303	986 *	12.1	25.0
467 Wesleyan	1	122	149	275	3.4	7.0
TREGO	**11**	**1,006**	**468**	**2,169 ***	**65.4**	**100.0**
053 Assemb of God	1	19	22	29	.9	1.3
056 Baha'i	0	2	NR	2	.1	.1
081 Catholic	2	NR	NR	849	25.6	39.1
097 Chr Chs&Chs Cr	1	126	NR	150 *	4.5	6.9
123 Ch God (Ander)	1	NR	95	95	2.9	4.4
207 E.L.C.A.	4	519	211	639	19.3	29.5
355 Presb Ch (USA)	1	83	32	99 *	3.0	4.6
449 Un Methodist	1	257	108	306 *	9.2	14.1
WABAUNSEE	**23**	**2,143**	**974**	**3,252 ***	**47.2**	**100.0**
019 Amer Bapt USA	1	25	15	31 *	.5	1.0
081 Catholic	3	NR	NR	582	8.5	17.9
097 Chr Chs&Chs Cr	1	80	NR	99 *	1.4	3.0
167 Chs of Christ	3	79	78	104	1.5	3.2
175 Congr Chr Chs	1	127	80	157 *	2.3	4.8
283 Luth—MO Synod	3	813	352	1,018	14.8	31.3
355 Presb Ch (USA)	1	33	40	41 *	.6	1.3
419 So Bapt Conv	1	65	40	80 *	1.2	2.5
443 Un C of Christ	3	335	147	414 *	6.0	12.7
449 Un Methodist	6	586	222	726 *	10.5	22.3
WALLACE	**12**	**662**	**376**	**1,093 ***	**62.5**	**100.0**
019 Amer Bapt USA	2	82	73	103 *	5.9	9.4
053 Assemb of God	1	20	20	42	2.4	3.8
081 Catholic	2	NR	NR	236	13.5	21.6
089 Chr & Miss Al	1	27	NR	66	3.8	6.0
143 CG in Cr(Menn)	1	46	NR	58 *	3.3	5.3
207 E.L.C.A.	2	82	40	107	6.1	9.8
449 Un Methodist	2	294	133	370 *	21.2	33.9
467 Wesleyan	1	111	110	111	6.3	10.2
WASHINGTON	**34**	**3,288**	**1,425**	**5,220 ***	**80.5**	**100.0**
056 Baha'i	0	1	NR	1	-	-
081 Catholic	5	NR	NR	1,198	18.5	23.0
097 Chr Chs&Chs Cr	3	435	NR	528 *	8.1	10.1
145 Ch God Prophcy	1	27	NR	32 *	.5	.6
157 Ch of Brethren	1	17	20	21 *	.3	.4
207 E.L.C.A.	8	701	309	865	13.3	16.6
283 Luth—MO Synod	6	1,268	789	1,556	24.0	29.8
355 Presb Ch (USA)	3	271	95	329 *	5.1	6.3
419 So Bapt Conv	1	75	33	91 *	1.4	1.7
449 Un Methodist	5	489	174	594 *	9.2	11.4
469 WELS	1	4	5	5	.1	.1
WICHITA	**11**	**838**	**408**	**1,862 ***	**73.6**	**100.0**
019 Amer Bapt USA	1	177	80	228 *	9.0	12.2
053 Assemb of God	1	62	85	85	3.4	4.6
081 Catholic	2	NR	NR	654	25.8	35.1
151 L-D Saints	1	NR	NR	143	5.6	7.7
216 Evan Presby Ch	1	96	NR	124 *	4.9	6.7
221 Free Methodist	1	74	61	76	3.0	4.1
355 Presb Ch (USA)	2	77	65	99 *	3.9	5.3
449 Un Methodist	2	352	117	453 *	17.9	24.3
WILSON	**37**	**3,065**	**1,265**	**4,856 ***	**47.0**	**100.0**
017 Amer Bapt Assn	1	22	NR	27 *	.3	.6
019 Amer Bapt USA	1	82	32	101 *	1.0	2.1
053 Assemb of God	1	91	109	204	2.0	4.2
081 Catholic	2	NR	NR	830	8.0	17.1
093 Chr Ch (Disc)	2	597	225	739 *	7.2	15.2
097 Chr Chs&Chs Cr	5	456	NR	565 *	5.5	11.6
123 Ch God (Ander)	1	NR	26	26	.3	.5
127 Ch God (Cleve)	1	47	15	58 *	.6	1.2
143 CG in Cr(Menn)	1	123	NR	152 *	1.5	3.1
157 Ch of Brethren	1	25	10	31 *	.3	.6
165 Ch of Nazarene	3	221	98	270	2.6	5.6
167 Chs of Christ	1	28	30	36	.3	.7
171 Ch God-Gen Con	1	35	30	43 *	.4	.9
193 Episcopal	1	NR	11	55	.5	1.1
207 E.L.C.A.	1	8	10	10	.1	.2
349 Pent Holiness	1	35	35	43 *	.4	.9
355 Presb Ch (USA)	2	49	26	61 *	.6	1.3
388 Reg Bapt Gen As	1	69	60	85 *	.8	1.8
413 S.D.A.	1	30	NR	36	.3	.7
419 So Bapt Conv	2	207	125	256 *	2.5	5.3
449 Un Methodist	6	830	306	1,028 *	9.9	21.2
467 Wesleyan	1	110	117	200	1.9	4.1
WOODSON	**17**	**1,548**	**523**	**2,281 ***	**60.2**	**100.0**
053 Assemb of God	1	34	35	35	.9	1.5
081 Catholic	2	NR	NR	420	11.1	18.4
093 Chr Ch (Disc)	1	340	62	401 *	10.6	17.6
097 Chr Chs&Chs Cr	1	75	NR	89 *	2.3	3.9
165 Ch of Nazarene	1	29	5	29	.8	1.3
171 Ch God-Gen Con	1	151	125	178 *	4.7	7.8
193 Episcopal	1	NR	18	45	1.2	2.0
355 Presb Ch (USA)	2	66	44	77 *	2.0	3.4
419 So Bapt Conv	2	337	58	398 *	10.5	17.4
449 Un Methodist	5	516	176	609 *	16.1	26.7

NR–Not Reported *Total adherents estimated from known number of communicant, confirmed, full members. - Represents a percentage less than 0.1. Percentages may not total 100 due to rounding.

Table 4: Religious Congregations by County and Group: 2000

Religious Group	Number of Churches, Synagogues, Mosques, or Temples	Number of Communicant, Confirmed, or Full Members	Number of Attendees	Total Adherents		
				Number of Adherents	% of Total Pop.	% of Total Adh.
WYANDOTTE	**173**	**24,078**	**10,170**	**56,419 ***	**35.7**	**100.0**
017 Amer Bapt Assn	2	100	NR	128 *	.1	.2
019 Amer Bapt USA	20	3,046	1,201	3,927 *	2.5	7.0
053 Assemb of God	7	1,029	1,032	1,725	1.1	3.1
056 Baha'i	1	100	NR	100	.1	.2
059 Bapt Miss Assn	1	104	25	134 *	.1	.2
076 Buddhism	1	NR	NR	NR	-	-
081 Catholic	13	NR	NR	21,759	13.8	38.6
089 Chr & Miss Al	1	974	NR	974	.6	1.7
093 Chr Ch (Disc)	12	3,087	675	3,980 *	2.5	7.1
097 Chr Chs&Chs Cr	5	1,276	NR	1,645 *	1.0	2.9
123 Ch God (Ander)	4	NR	677	677	.4	1.2
145 Ch God Prophcy	2	53	NR	68 *	-	.1
151 L-D Saints	2	NR	NR	898	.6	1.6
157 Ch of Brethren	1	53	32	68 *	-	.1
165 Ch of Nazarene	10	954	750	1,528	1.0	2.7
167 Chs of Christ	8	923	800	1,233	.8	2.2
173 Comm of Christ	4	564	NR	564	.4	1.0
193 Episcopal	3	NR	121	310	.2	.5
207 E.L.C.A.	2	245	97	305	.2	.5
221 Free Methodist	2	100	124	125	.1	.2
223 Free Will Bapt	1	31	NR	40 *	-	.1
226 Friends-USA	1	50	NR	64 *	-	.1
267 Muslim Est	1	NR	228	841	.5	1.5
283 Luth—MO Synod	7	1,595	609	2,002	1.3	3.5
288 Mennonite USA	2	216	167	278 *	.2	.5
331 OCA: Ter Diocs	1	113	NR	162	.1	.3
349 Pent Holiness	2	452	585	583 *	.4	1.0
355 Presb Ch (USA)	5	398	218	513 *	.3	.9
360 Prim Bapt Chrch	1	NR	NR	NR	-	-
388 Reg Bapt Gen As	5	430	263	614 *	.4	1.1
403 Salvation Army	1	140	113	421	.3	.7
410 Serb Orth USA	1	NR	NR	387	.2	.7
411 Serb Orth: Grac	1	NR	NR	NR	-	-
413 S.D.A.	5	1,378	NR	1,640	1.0	2.9
419 So Bapt Conv	17	3,082	874	3,973 *	2.5	7.0
443 Un C of Christ	5	585	258	754 *	.5	1.3
449 Un Methodist	15	3,000	1,263	3,866 *	2.4	6.9
467 Wesleyan	1	0	58	58	-	.1
496 Jewish Est	0	NR	NR	75	-	.1
KENTUCKY						
The State.....	7,143	1,353,901	490,206	2,159,541 *	53.4	100.0
ADAIR	**69**	**6,623**	**2,552**	**8,265 ***	**47.9**	**100.0**
053 Assemb of God	1	43	52	100	.6	1.2
056 Baha'i	0	2	NR	2	-	-
075 Brethren in Cr	4	202	243	256	1.5	3.1
081 Catholic	1	NR	NR	125	.7	1.5
097 Chr Chs&Chs Cr	8	1,126	NR	1,371 *	8.0	16.6
123 Ch God (Ander)	1	NR	32	32	.2	.4
127 Ch God (Cleve)	1	114	70	139 *	.8	1.7
145 Ch God Prophcy	2	99	NR	120 *	.7	1.5
165 Ch of Nazarene	3	291	278	350	2.0	4.2
167 Chs of Christ	3	250	240	281	1.6	3.4
185 Cumber Presb	1	5	NR	18	.1	.2
323 Old Ord Amish	2	110	NR	134 *	.8	1.6
355 Presb Ch (USA)	1	81	2	99 *	.6	1.2
409 Separate Bapt	8	509	NR	620 *	3.6	7.5
413 S.D.A.	1	85	NR	101	.6	1.2
419 So Bapt Conv	13	1,609	542	1,960 *	11.4	23.7
449 Un Methodist	19	2,097	1,093	2,557 *	14.8	30.9
ALLEN	**41**	**4,750**	**1,823**	**5,986 ***	**33.6**	**100.0**
056 Baha'i	0	2	NR	2	-	-
081 Catholic	1	NR	NR	83	.5	1.4
145 Ch God Prophcy	2	99	NR	122 *	.7	2.0
165 Ch of Nazarene	1	79	55	97	.5	1.6
167 Chs of Christ	2	203	183	253	1.4	4.2
221 Free Methodist	1	49	50	50	.3	.8
320 "Old" MB Ascs	5	850	NR	1,059 *	5.9	17.7
322 Old Ord Menn Ch	3	244	NR	303 *	1.7	5.1
419 So Bapt Conv	15	2,037	902	2,537 *	14.3	42.4
449 Un Methodist	11	1,187	633	1,480 *	8.3	24.7
ANDERSON	**40**	**8,974**	**3,224**	**12,112 ***	**63.4**	**100.0**
053 Assemb of God	1	115	92	107	.6	.9
056 Baha'i	0	2	NR	2	-	-
081 Catholic	1	NR	NR	636	3.3	5.3
093 Chr Ch (Disc)	3	1,202	365	1,526 *	8.0	12.6
097 Chr Chs&Chs Cr	8	1,726	NR	2,192 *	11.5	18.1
127 Ch God (Cleve)	1	97	50	123 *	.6	1.0
167 Chs of Christ	3	200	233	254	1.3	2.1
193 Episcopal	1	NR	11	8	-	.1
339 Pent Ch of God	1	65	NR	200	1.0	1.7
355 Presb Ch (USA)	1	82	45	104 *	.5	.9
413 S.D.A.	1	57	NR	68	.4	.6
419 So Bapt Conv	16	4,819	2,158	6,119 *	32.0	50.5
449 Un Methodist	3	609	270	773 *	4.0	6.4
BALLARD	**31**	**5,567**	**2,104**	**7,034 ***	**84.9**	**100.0**
081 Catholic	1	NR	NR	230	2.8	3.3
093 Chr Ch (Disc)	3	355	218	431 *	5.2	6.1
167 Chs of Christ	1	13	13	13	.2	.2
185 Cumber Presb	2	187	NR	275	3.3	3.9
419 So Bapt Conv	17	4,298	1,591	5,218 *	63.0	74.2
449 Un Methodist	7	714	282	867 *	10.5	12.3
BARREN	**83**	**14,456**	**5,859**	**18,660 ***	**49.1**	**100.0**
053 Assemb of God	1	115	140	190	.5	1.0
056 Baha'i	0	1	NR	1	-	-
081 Catholic	1	NR	NR	278	.7	1.5
093 Chr Ch (Disc)	1	458	200	564 *	1.5	3.0
097 Chr Chs&Chs Cr	3	530	NR	652 *	1.7	3.5
123 Ch God (Ander)	1	NR	18	18	-	.1
127 Ch God (Cleve)	2	252	94	311 *	.8	1.7
151 L-D Saints	1	NR	NR	217	.6	1.2
165 Ch of Nazarene	2	253	131	329	.9	1.8
167 Chs of Christ	12	1,316	1,467	1,673	4.4	9.0
185 Cumber Presb	3	293	NR	413	1.1	2.2
193 Episcopal	1	NR	33	45	.1	.2
223 Free Will Bapt	2	251	NR	309 *	.8	1.7
320 "Old" MB Ascs	2	359	NR	442 *	1.2	2.4
323 Old Ord Amish	4	210	NR	260 *	.7	1.4
355 Presb Ch (USA)	1	156	72	192 *	.5	1.0
360 Prim Bapt Chrch	1	NR	NR	NR	-	-
409 Separate Bapt	1	12	NR	15 *	-	.1
413 S.D.A.	1	67	NR	80	.2	.4
419 So Bapt Conv	25	8,306	2,666	10,220 *	26.9	54.8
449 Un Methodist	17	1,814	928	2,231 *	5.9	12.0
467 Wesleyan	1	63	110	220	.6	1.2
BATH	**34**	**2,393**	**1,258**	**3,688 ***	**33.3**	**100.0**
081 Catholic	1	NR	NR	37	.3	1.0
093 Chr Ch (Disc)	4	558	135	687 *	6.2	18.6
097 Chr Chs&Chs Cr	6	819	NR	1,009 *	9.1	27.4
123 Ch God (Ander)	9	NR	608	608	5.5	16.5
127 Ch God (Cleve)	1	120	85	148 *	1.3	4.0
151 L-D Saints	1	NR	NR	90	.8	2.4
167 Chs of Christ	3	117	116	151	1.4	4.1
223 Free Will Bapt	1	126	NR	155 *	1.4	4.2
355 Presb Ch (USA)	3	97	82	119 *	1.1	3.2
419 So Bapt Conv	2	196	102	241 *	2.2	6.5
449 Un Methodist	3	360	130	443 *	4.0	12.0
BELL	**96**	**16,026**	**4,756**	**20,478 ***	**68.1**	**100.0**
019 Amer Bapt USA	1	940	250	1,154 *	3.8	5.6
053 Assemb of God	1	58	75	85	.3	.4
056 Baha'i	0	2	NR	2	-	-
081 Catholic	2	NR	NR	559	1.9	2.7
093 Chr Ch (Disc)	2	321	150	394 *	1.3	1.9
127 Ch God (Cleve)	3	280	75	343 *	1.1	1.7
145 Ch God Prophcy	3	148	NR	180 *	.6	.9

NR–Not Reported *Total adherents estimated from known number of communicant, confirmed, full members. - Represents a percentage less than 0.1. Percentages may not total 100 due to rounding.

Table 4: Religious Congregations by County and Group: 2000

Religious Group	Number of Churches, Synagogues, Mosques, or Temples	Number of Communicant, Confirmed, or Full Members	Number of Attendees	Total Adherents		
				Number of Adherents	% of Total Pop.	% of Total Adh.
165 Ch of Nazarene	2	102	90	283	.9	1.4
167 Chs of Christ	1	74	85	105	.3	.5
193 Episcopal	1	NR	57	81	.3	.4
320 "Old" MB Ascs	4	1,083	NR	1,329 *	4.4	6.5
355 Presb Ch (USA)	2	127	78	156 *	.5	.8
360 Prim Bapt Chrch	5	NR	NR	NR	-	-
403 Salvation Army	1	82	36	46	.2	.2
413 S.D.A.	1	33	NR	39	.1	.2
419 So Bapt Conv	61	11,869	3,283	14,566 *	48.5	71.1
449 Un Methodist	5	657	277	806 *	2.7	3.9
498 Indep.Charis.	1	250	300	350	1.2	1.7
BOONE	**65**	**20,942**	**9,719**	**46,671 ***	**54.3**	**100.0**
053 Assemb of God	1	477	550	1,275	1.5	2.7
056 Baha'i	0	13	NR	13	-	-
081 Catholic	5	NR	NR	17,508	20.4	37.5
084 Calvary Chapel	1	NR	NR	NR	-	-
089 Chr & Miss Al	1	28	NR	77	.1	.2
093 Chr Ch (Disc)	6	1,705	191	2,203 *	2.6	4.7
097 Chr Chs&Chs Cr	4	1,766	NR	2,282 *	2.7	4.9
123 Ch God (Ander)	1	NR	85	85	.1	.2
127 Ch God (Cleve)	3	389	266	503 *	.6	1.1
151 L-D Saints	1	NR	NR	672	.8	1.4
157 Ch of Brethren	1	72	30	93 *	.1	.2
165 Ch of Nazarene	2	84	68	100	.1	.2
167 Chs of Christ	4	258	315	381	.4	.8
193 Episcopal	1	NR	139	332	.4	.7
207 E.L.C.A.	2	1,059	532	1,501	1.7	3.2
283 Luth—MO Synod	1	121	98	161	.2	.3
355 Presb Ch (USA)	2	336	263	434 *	.5	.9
419 So Bapt Conv	19	10,529	3,637	13,604 *	15.8	29.1
443 Un C of Christ	1	27	16	35 *	-	.1
449 Un Methodist	4	1,740	785	2,248 *	2.6	4.8
463 Vineyard	1	850	730	1,098 *	1.3	2.4
467 Wesleyan	1	11	18	39	-	.1
469 WELS	1	53	46	77	.1	.2
498 Indep.Charis.	1	600	1,100	1,100	1.3	2.4
499 Indep.Non-Char	1	824	850	850	1.0	1.8
BOURBON	**44**	**7,369**	**2,541**	**10,912 ***	**56.4**	**100.0**
053 Assemb of God	1	113	150	187	1.0	1.7
056 Baha'i	0	2	NR	2	-	-
081 Catholic	1	NR	NR	863	4.5	7.9
093 Chr Ch (Disc)	8	1,586	407	1,967 *	10.2	18.0
097 Chr Chs&Chs Cr	4	811	NR	1,006 *	5.2	9.2
123 Ch God (Ander)	2	NR	292	292	1.5	2.7
127 Ch God (Cleve)	2	39	51	51 *	.3	.5
151 L-D Saints	1	NR	NR	312	1.6	2.9
165 Ch of Nazarene	3	210	113	215	1.1	2.0
167 Chs of Christ	2	139	157	190	1.0	1.7
193 Episcopal	1	NR	107	273	1.4	2.5
355 Presb Ch (USA)	3	242	116	300 *	1.5	2.7
360 Prim Bapt Chrch	1	NR	NR	NR	-	-
419 So Bapt Conv	6	3,013	698	3,736 *	19.3	34.2
449 Un Methodist	8	1,175	438	1,458 *	7.5	13.4
467 Wesleyan	1	39	12	60	.3	.5
BOYD	**98**	**23,660**	**7,176**	**31,624 ***	**63.6**	**100.0**
053 Assemb of God	2	108	137	184	.4	.6
056 Baha'i	0	3	NR	3	-	-
081 Catholic	1	NR	NR	1,975	4.0	6.2
093 Chr Ch (Disc)	1	715	230	855 *	1.7	2.7
097 Chr Chs&Chs Cr	5	906	NR	1,084 *	2.2	3.4
123 Ch God (Ander)	4	NR	538	538	1.1	1.7
127 Ch God (Cleve)	4	577	214	693 *	1.4	2.2
165 Ch of Nazarene	9	1,409	865	1,841	3.7	5.8
167 Chs of Christ	4	93	109	118	.2	.4
193 Episcopal	1	NR	73	370	.7	1.2
223 Free Will Bapt	16	2,010	NR	2,405 *	4.8	7.6
265 Int Pent C Chr	2	66	52	134	.3	.4
283 Luth—MO Synod	1	190	80	240	.5	.8
355 Presb Ch (USA)	4	539	270	644 *	1.3	2.0
403 Salvation Army	1	153	49	143	.3	.5
413 S.D.A.	1	84	NR	100	.2	.3
418 Southw Bapt Fel	1	NR	NR	NR	-	-
419 So Bapt Conv	25	12,010	3,007	14,366 *	28.9	45.4
449 Un Methodist	14	4,717	1,486	5,642 *	11.3	17.8
467 Wesleyan	2	80	66	289	.6	.9
BOYLE	**55**	**15,611**	**5,302**	**21,343 ***	**77.1**	**100.0**
053 Assemb of God	1	120	150	201	.7	.9
056 Baha'i	0	15	NR	15	.1	.1
081 Catholic	2	NR	NR	1,367	4.9	6.4
093 Chr Ch (Disc)	2	952	394	1,154 *	4.2	5.4
097 Chr Chs&Chs Cr	2	600	NR	727 *	2.6	3.4
123 Ch God (Ander)	2	NR	305	305	1.1	1.4
127 Ch God (Cleve)	4	649	317	786 *	2.8	3.7
151 L-D Saints	1	NR	NR	292	1.1	1.4
165 Ch of Nazarene	1	56	58	149	.5	.7
167 Chs of Christ	5	417	371	524	1.9	2.5
193 Episcopal	1	NR	95	226	.8	1.1
283 Luth—MO Synod	1	78	44	94	.3	.4
304 NatPrimBapt USA	1	18	NR	22 *	.1	.1
339 Pent Ch of God	1	20	NR	35	.1	.2
355 Presb Ch (USA)	2	611	264	741 *	2.7	3.5
356 Presb Ch Amer	1	42	60	60	.2	.3
403 Salvation Army	1	93	70	164	.6	.8
418 Southw Bapt Fel	1	NR	NR	NR	-	-
419 So Bapt Conv	21	10,776	2,616	13,065 *	47.2	61.2
449 Un Methodist	4	1,146	532	1,390 *	5.0	6.5
467 Wesleyan	1	18	26	26	.1	.1
BRACKEN	**32**	**2,954**	**632**	**4,507 ***	**54.4**	**100.0**
053 Assemb of God	1	20	26	36	.4	.8
081 Catholic	2	NR	NR	750	9.1	16.6
097 Chr Chs&Chs Cr	10	1,230	NR	1,534 *	18.5	34.0
165 Ch of Nazarene	1	101	84	171	2.1	3.8
207 E.L.C.A.	1	102	41	134	1.6	3.0
355 Presb Ch (USA)	2	144	74	179 *	2.2	4.0
419 So Bapt Conv	7	893	190	1,113 *	13.4	24.7
449 Un Methodist	7	450	188	561 *	6.8	12.4
467 Wesleyan	1	14	29	29	.4	.6
BREATHITT	**24**	**1,739**	**1,151**	**2,533 ***	**15.7**	**100.0**
053 Assemb of God	1	73	55	75	.5	3.0
056 Baha'i	0	3	NR	3	-	.1
071 Brethren (Ash)	1	18	43	22 *	.1	.9
081 Catholic	1	NR	NR	53	.3	2.1
123 Ch God (Ander)	1	NR	100	100	.6	3.9
127 Ch God (Cleve)	1	119	79	146 *	.9	5.8
151 L-D Saints	1	NR	NR	191	1.2	7.5
167 Chs of Christ	1	20	17	25	.2	1.0
183 Cons Menn Conf	2	83	101	121	.8	4.8
203 Evan Free Ch	1	40	60	60	.4	2.4
221 Free Methodist	2	41	90	90	.6	3.6
355 Presb Ch (USA)	1	50	26	61 *	.4	2.4
360 Prim Bapt Chrch	1	NR	NR	NR	-	-
413 S.D.A.	2	27	NR	32	.2	1.3
419 So Bapt Conv	4	889	246	1,092 *	6.8	43.1
449 Un Methodist	4	376	334	462 *	2.9	18.2
BRECKINRIDGE	**68**	**7,476**	**3,075**	**12,188 ***	**65.4**	**100.0**
053 Assemb of God	1	29	42	42	.2	.3
056 Baha'i	0	2	NR	2	-	-
081 Catholic	5	NR	NR	2,611	14.0	21.4
097 Chr Chs&Chs Cr	1	50	NR	61 *	.3	.5
123 Ch God (Ander)	1	NR	32	32	.2	.3
167 Chs of Christ	2	66	70	84	.5	.7
185 Cumber Presb	6	195	NR	389	2.1	3.2
291 Missionary Ch	1	0	69	69	.4	.6
297 Mennonite;Other	1	57	NR	70 *	.4	.6
323 Old Ord Amish	1	55	NR	68 *	.4	.6
419 So Bapt Conv	24	4,829	1,663	5,939 *	31.8	48.7
449 Un Methodist	23	2,138	1,109	2,630 *	14.1	21.6
467 Wesleyan	2	55	90	191	1.0	1.6

NR–Not Reported *Total adherents estimated from known number of communicant, confirmed, full members. - Represents a percentage less than 0.1. Percentages may not total 100 due to rounding.

Table 4: Religious Congregations by County and Group: 2000

Religious Group	Number of Churches, Synagogues, Mosques, or Temples	Number of Communicant, Confirmed, or Full Members	Number of Attendees	Total Adherents		
				Number of Adherents	% of Total Pop.	% of Total Adh.
BULLITT	**64**	**18,498**	**6,162**	**27,090 ***	**44.2**	**100.0**
053 Assemb of God	5	466	377	886	1.4	3.3
056 Baha'i	0	2	NR	2	-	-
081 Catholic	3	NR	NR	3,169	5.2	11.7
093 Chr Ch (Disc)	1	204	74	259 *	.4	1.0
097 Chr Chs&Chs Cr	3	618	NR	783 *	1.3	2.9
127 Ch God (Cleve)	3	327	182	414 *	.7	1.5
145 Ch God Prophcy	4	197	NR	248 *	.4	.9
165 Ch of Nazarene	2	92	78	133	.2	.5
167 Chs of Christ	5	275	330	361	.6	1.3
263 Int Foursq Gos	1	11	32	32 *	.1	.1
283 Luth—MO Synod	1	89	90	130	.2	.5
355 Presb Ch (USA)	1	111	68	141 *	.2	.5
409 Separate Bapt	1	145	NR	184 *	.3	.7
419 So Bapt Conv	27	14,853	4,518	18,829 *	30.7	69.5
449 Un Methodist	6	1,093	396	1,385 *	2.3	5.1
467 Wesleyan	1	15	17	134	.2	.5
BUTLER	**52**	**6,388**	**2,569**	**7,993 ***	**61.4**	**100.0**
053 Assemb of God	1	13	18	37	.3	.5
081 Catholic	1	NR	NR	81	.6	1.0
127 Ch God (Cleve)	1	42	29	52 *	.4	.7
165 Ch of Nazarene	1	55	51	55	.4	.7
167 Chs of Christ	11	433	466	549	4.2	6.9
185 Cumber Presb	3	37	NR	43	.3	.5
288 Mennonite USA	1	10	8	12 *	.1	.2
419 So Bapt Conv	27	5,342	1,792	6,600 *	50.7	82.6
449 Un Methodist	6	456	205	564 *	4.3	7.1
CALDWELL	**43**	**10,911**	**3,491**	**13,431 ***	**102.8**	**100.0**
053 Assemb of God	1	72	58	96	.7	.7
081 Catholic	1	NR	NR	201	1.5	1.5
093 Chr Ch (Disc)	2	242	90	291 *	2.2	2.2
097 Chr Chs&Chs Cr	1	90	NR	108 *	.8	.8
167 Chs of Christ	1	100	100	110	.8	.8
185 Cumber Presb	3	143	NR	266	2.0	2.0
355 Presb Ch (USA)	1	84	55	101 *	.8	.8
419 So Bapt Conv	27	9,245	2,844	11,133 *	85.2	82.9
449 Un Methodist	6	935	344	1,125 *	8.6	8.4
CALLOWAY	**80**	**16,234**	**7,432**	**20,589 ***	**60.2**	**100.0**
053 Assemb of God	1	388	263	423	1.2	2.1
056 Baha'i	0	11	NR	11	-	.1
081 Catholic	1	NR	NR	793	2.3	3.9
093 Chr Ch (Disc)	1	420	141	490 *	1.4	2.4
151 L-D Saints	1	NR	NR	257	.8	1.2
165 Ch of Nazarene	1	64	26	64	.2	.3
167 Chs of Christ	17	2,448	2,282	3,213	9.4	15.6
185 Cumber Presb	3	169	NR	254	.7	1.2
193 Episcopal	1	NR	79	163	.5	.8
283 Luth—MO Synod	1	136	68	172	.5	.8
339 Pent Ch of God	3	114	NR	179	.5	.9
355 Presb Ch (USA)	1	190	120	222 *	.6	1.1
360 Prim Bapt Chrch	1	NR	NR	NR	-	-
413 S.D.A.	1	36	NR	43	.1	.2
418 Southw Bapt Fel	1	NR	NR	NR	-	-
419 So Bapt Conv	28	9,327	3,130	10,883 *	31.8	52.9
449 Un Methodist	18	2,931	1,323	3,422 *	10.0	16.6
CAMPBELL	**82**	**16,076**	**6,984**	**46,826 ***	**52.8**	**100.0**
053 Assemb of God	4	611	328	578	.7	1.2
056 Baha'i	0	3	NR	3	-	-
081 Catholic	13	NR	NR	24,874	28.1	53.1
093 Chr Ch (Disc)	2	287	138	358 *	.4	.8
097 Chr Chs&Chs Cr	5	580	NR	724 *	.8	1.5
123 Ch God (Ander)	2	NR	72	72	.1	.2
127 Ch God (Cleve)	4	558	312	698 *	.8	1.5
151 L-D Saints	1	NR	NR	391	.4	.8
165 Ch of Nazarene	4	425	271	901	1.0	1.9
167 Chs of Christ	1	120	145	159	.2	.3
193 Episcopal	2	NR	253	720	.8	1.5
207 E.L.C.A.	4	433	206	537	.6	1.1
223 Free Will Bapt	1	126	NR	157 *	.2	.3
355 Presb Ch (USA)	2	335	173	417 *	.5	.9
403 Salvation Army	1	55	30	96	.1	.2
419 So Bapt Conv	20	8,489	3,477	10,586 *	11.9	22.6
443 Un C of Christ	6	1,856	679	2,314 *	2.6	4.9
449 Un Methodist	10	2,198	900	2,741 *	3.1	5.9
496 Jewish Est	0	NR	NR	500	.6	1.1
CARLISLE	**21**	**3,050**	**1,225**	**3,943 ***	**73.7**	**100.0**
053 Assemb of God	1	20	23	26	.5	.7
081 Catholic	1	NR	NR	231	4.3	5.9
093 Chr Ch (Disc)	2	105	60	127 *	2.4	3.2
167 Chs of Christ	2	118	135	152	2.8	3.9
419 So Bapt Conv	11	2,436	825	2,956 *	55.2	75.0
449 Un Methodist	4	371	182	451 *	8.4	11.4
CARROLL	**21**	**3,581**	**882**	**4,997 ***	**49.2**	**100.0**
053 Assemb of God	1	17	23	24	.2	.5
056 Baha'i	0	2	NR	2	-	-
081 Catholic	1	NR	NR	505	5.0	10.1
093 Chr Ch (Disc)	2	375	0	466 *	4.6	9.3
097 Chr Chs&Chs Cr	2	180	NR	223 *	2.2	4.5
167 Chs of Christ	1	26	30	39	.4	.8
207 E.L.C.A.	1	48	42	64	.6	1.3
419 So Bapt Conv	9	2,305	612	2,862 *	28.2	57.3
449 Un Methodist	3	496	103	616 *	6.1	12.3
467 Wesleyan	1	132	72	196	1.9	3.9
CARTER	**53**	**6,100**	**1,503**	**8,308 ***	**30.9**	**100.0**
053 Assemb of God	1	62	73	150	.6	1.8
056 Baha'i	0	2	NR	2	-	-
081 Catholic	1	NR	NR	105	.4	1.3
097 Chr Chs&Chs Cr	11	1,704	NR	2,105 *	7.8	25.3
127 Ch God (Cleve)	2	74	34	91 *	.3	1.1
145 Ch God Prophcy	1	49	NR	61 *	.2	.7
165 Ch of Nazarene	3	181	183	450	1.7	5.4
167 Chs of Christ	2	57	78	74	.3	.9
223 Free Will Bapt	8	1,005	NR	1,241 *	4.6	14.9
355 Presb Ch (USA)	1	38	20	47 *	.2	.6
360 Prim Bapt Chrch	1	NR	NR	NR	-	-
419 So Bapt Conv	10	2,093	574	2,583 *	9.6	31.1
449 Un Methodist	6	646	300	798 *	3.0	9.6
467 Wesleyan	6	189	241	601	2.2	7.2
CASEY	**66**	**6,924**	**1,948**	**8,996 ***	**58.2**	**100.0**
053 Assemb of God	1	19	30	57	.4	.6
056 Baha'i	0	1	NR	1	-	-
061 Beachy Amish	1	53	NR	65 *	.4	.7
081 Catholic	2	NR	NR	311	2.0	3.5
093 Chr Ch (Disc)	1	225	0	277 *	1.8	3.1
097 Chr Chs&Chs Cr	10	1,067	NR	1,313 *	8.5	14.6
123 Ch God (Ander)	3	NR	134	134	.9	1.5
127 Ch God (Cleve)	1	112	72	138 *	.9	1.5
165 Ch of Nazarene	1	42	38	42	.3	.5
167 Chs of Christ	9	288	307	362	2.3	4.0
322 Old Ord Menn Ch	1	92	NR	113 *	.7	1.3
323 Old Ord Amish	2	110	NR	136 *	.9	1.5
360 Prim Bapt Chrch	1	NR	NR	NR	-	-
409 Separate Bapt	8	821	NR	1,010 *	6.5	11.2
419 So Bapt Conv	13	2,614	780	3,216 *	20.8	35.7
449 Un Methodist	12	1,480	587	1,821 *	11.8	20.2
CHRISTIAN	**108**	**23,043**	**8,519**	**32,715 ***	**45.3**	**100.0**
032 Amish; other	1	68	NR	89 *	.1	.3
053 Assemb of God	4	282	315	315	.4	1.0
056 Baha'i	0	13	NR	13	-	-
081 Catholic	2	NR	NR	1,770	2.4	5.4
093 Chr Ch (Disc)	9	1,324	553	1,732 *	2.4	5.3
127 Ch God (Cleve)	2	167	111	227 *	.3	.7
145 Ch God Prophcy	1	49	NR	64 *	.1	.2
151 L-D Saints	1	NR	NR	355	.5	1.1
165 Ch of Nazarene	1	65	51	138	.2	.4

NR–Not Reported *Total adherents estimated from known number of communicant, confirmed, full members. - Represents a percentage less than 0.1. Percentages may not total 100 due to rounding.

Table 4: Religious Congregations by County and Group: 2000

Religious Group	Number of Churches, Synagogues, Mosques, or Temples	Number of Communicant, Confirmed, or Full Members	Number of Attendees	Total Adherents: Number of Adherents	% of Total Pop.	% of Total Adh.
167 Chs of Christ	9	780	855	1,009	1.4	3.1
185 Cumber Presb	3	198	NR	408	.6	1.2
193 Episcopal	1	NR	73	315	.4	1.0
223 Free Will Bapt	1	126	NR	164 *	.2	.5
263 Int Foursq Gos	1	19	37	37 *	.1	.1
283 Luth—MO Synod	1	111	64	136	.2	.4
322 Old Ord Menn Ch	2	150	NR	196 *	.3	.6
323 Old Ord Amish	3	225	NR	294 *	.4	.9
355 Presb Ch (USA)	3	377	201	494 *	.7	1.5
403 Salvation Army	1	146	77	201	.3	.6
413 S.D.A.	3	159	NR	190	.3	.6
419 So Bapt Conv	43	15,989	5,018	20,913 *	28.9	63.9
435 Unitarian-Univ	1	25	NR	33 *	-	.1
449 Un Methodist	15	2,770	1,164	3,622 *	5.0	11.1
CLARK	**55**	**12,501**	**4,246**	**18,169 ***	**54.8**	**100.0**
053 Assemb of God	1	45	51	51	.2	.3
056 Baha'i	0	17	NR	17	.1	.1
081 Catholic	1	NR	NR	1,000	3.0	5.5
093 Chr Ch (Disc)	2	543	161	671 *	2.0	3.7
097 Chr Chs&Chs Cr	7	1,868	NR	2,307 *	7.0	12.7
123 Ch God (Ander)	2	NR	448	448	1.4	2.5
127 Ch God (Cleve)	3	1,258	219	1,555 *	4.7	8.6
145 Ch God Prophcy	1	49	NR	61 *	.2	.3
151 L-D Saints	2	NR	NR	615	1.9	3.4
165 Ch of Nazarene	1	37	69	91	.3	.5
167 Chs of Christ	4	285	335	385	1.2	2.1
193 Episcopal	2	NR	216	414	1.2	2.3
263 Int Foursq Gos	1	34	44	44 *	.1	.2
283 Luth—MO Synod	1	109	50	151	.5	.8
355 Presb Ch (USA)	2	309	166	382 *	1.2	2.1
360 Prim Bapt Chrch	1	NR	NR	NR	-	-
413 S.D.A.	1	101	NR	120	.4	.7
419 So Bapt Conv	15	5,589	1,545	6,907 *	20.8	38.0
449 Un Methodist	6	1,990	612	2,458 *	7.4	13.5
467 Wesleyan	1	42	40	42	.1	.2
498 Indep.Charis.	1	225	290	450	1.4	2.5
CLAY	**47**	**6,569**	**2,254**	**8,174 ***	**33.3**	**100.0**
081 Catholic	1	NR	NR	83	.3	1.0
089 Chr & Miss Al	1	27	NR	31	.1	.4
097 Chr Chs&Chs Cr	4	406	NR	500 *	2.0	6.1
127 Ch God (Cleve)	3	609	233	750 *	3.1	9.2
157 Ch of Brethren	1	168	47	207 *	.8	2.5
167 Chs of Christ	2	70	60	90	.4	1.1
183 Cons Menn Conf	1	28	34	41	.2	.5
263 Int Foursq Gos	1	50	44	62 *	.3	.8
297 Mennonite;Other	2	53	NR	65 *	.3	.8
355 Presb Ch (USA)	3	123	78	151 *	.6	1.8
360 Prim Bapt Chrch	1	NR	NR	NR	-	-
413 S.D.A.	1	118	NR	140	.6	1.7
419 So Bapt Conv	22	4,675	1,654	5,756 *	23.4	70.4
449 Un Methodist	4	242	104	298 *	1.2	3.6
CLINTON	**33**	**4,336**	**1,745**	**5,476 ***	**56.8**	**100.0**
053 Assemb of God	1	20	26	26	.3	.5
081 Catholic	1	NR	NR	91	.9	1.7
093 Chr Ch (Disc)	1	55	20	67 *	.7	1.2
097 Chr Chs&Chs Cr	1	81	NR	98 *	1.0	1.8
165 Ch of Nazarene	3	281	244	471	4.9	8.6
167 Chs of Christ	1	35	38	46	.5	.8
223 Free Will Bapt	2	251	NR	304 *	3.2	5.6
409 Separate Bapt	1	124	NR	150 *	1.6	2.7
419 So Bapt Conv	7	1,826	536	2,210 *	22.9	40.4
449 Un Methodist	15	1,663	881	2,013 *	20.9	36.8
CRITTENDEN	**36**	**4,029**	**1,428**	**5,290 ***	**56.4**	**100.0**
081 Catholic	1	NR	NR	167	1.8	3.2
093 Chr Ch (Disc)	1	47	24	57 *	.6	1.1
123 Ch God (Ander)	1	NR	0	0	-	-
167 Chs of Christ	1	30	50	60	.6	1.1
185 Cumber Presb	3	202	NR	462	4.9	8.7

Religious Group	Number of Churches, Synagogues, Mosques, or Temples	Number of Communicant, Confirmed, or Full Members	Number of Attendees	Total Adherents: Number of Adherents	% of Total Pop.	% of Total Adh.
189 Duck Rivr Bapt	1	32	NR	39 *	.4	.7
323 Old Ord Amish	4	220	NR	268 *	2.9	5.1
355 Presb Ch (USA)	3	83	52	100 *	1.1	1.9
370 Ref Baptist Chs	1	NR	NR	NR	-	-
419 So Bapt Conv	16	2,957	1,131	3,583 *	38.2	67.7
449 Un Methodist	4	458	171	554 *	5.9	10.5
CUMBERLAND	**42**	**2,814**	**1,578**	**3,591 ***	**50.2**	**100.0**
032 Amish; other	1	32	NR	39 *	.5	1.1
053 Assemb of God	1	91	112	140	2.0	3.9
081 Catholic	1	NR	NR	125	1.7	3.5
093 Chr Ch (Disc)	1	153	75	186 *	2.6	5.2
097 Chr Chs&Chs Cr	1	45	NR	55 *	.8	1.5
165 Ch of Nazarene	1	58	42	58	.8	1.6
167 Chs of Christ	11	484	517	621	8.7	17.3
185 Cumber Presb	1	20	NR	22	.3	.6
320 "Old" MB Ascs	1	72	NR	87 *	1.2	2.4
413 S.D.A.	1	18	NR	21	.3	.6
419 So Bapt Conv	4	600	201	729 *	10.2	20.3
449 Un Methodist	18	1,241	631	1,508 *	21.1	42.0
DAVIESS	**132**	**36,300**	**11,194**	**66,122 ***	**72.2**	**100.0**
053 Assemb of God	3	401	445	698	.8	1.1
056 Baha'i	0	1	NR	1	-	-
081 Catholic	17	NR	NR	19,487	21.3	29.5
093 Chr Ch (Disc)	3	1,029	353	1,280 *	1.4	1.9
097 Chr Chs&Chs Cr	2	2,360	NR	2,935 *	3.2	4.4
123 Ch God (Ander)	2	NR	82	82	.1	.1
127 Ch God (Cleve)	2	168	75	209 *	.2	.3
145 Ch God Prophcy	3	148	NR	183 *	.2	.3
151 L-D Saints	1	NR	NR	248	.3	.4
165 Ch of Nazarene	2	271	168	406	.4	.6
167 Chs of Christ	6	513	573	680	.7	1.0
185 Cumber Presb	4	213	NR	358	.4	.5
193 Episcopal	1	NR	134	316	.3	.5
207 E.L.C.A.	1	115	71	141	.2	.2
223 Free Will Bapt	1	126	NR	156 *	.2	.2
263 Int Foursq Gos	1	52	68	68 *	.1	.1
283 Luth—MO Synod	1	104	56	130	.1	.2
355 Presb Ch (USA)	3	695	225	865 *	.9	1.3
356 Presb Ch Amer	1	41	51	53	.1	.1
370 Ref Baptist Chs	1	NR	NR	NR	-	-
403 Salvation Army	1	208	130	407	.4	.6
413 S.D.A.	2	155	NR	185	.2	.3
419 So Bapt Conv	53	25,076	6,868	31,187 *	34.1	47.2
435 Unitarian-Univ	1	36	NR	45 *	-	.1
443 Un C of Christ	1	246	98	306 *	.3	.5
449 Un Methodist	16	4,243	1,607	5,277 *	5.8	8.0
467 Wesleyan	2	99	190	369	.4	.6
496 Jewish Est	1	NR	NR	50	.1	.1
EDMONSON	**26**	**3,629**	**406**	**4,555 ***	**39.1**	**100.0**
081 Catholic	1	NR	NR	138	1.2	3.0
167 Chs of Christ	3	251	200	316	2.7	6.9
185 Cumber Presb	1	79	NR	87	.7	1.9
320 "Old" MB Ascs	11	2,724	NR	3,314 *	28.5	72.8
355 Presb Ch (USA)	1	180	98	219 *	1.9	4.8
419 So Bapt Conv	8	349	87	425 *	3.6	9.3
449 Un Methodist	1	46	21	56 *	.5	1.2
ELLIOTT	**11**	**983**	**198**	**1,217 ***	**18.0**	**100.0**
191 Entrpr Bpt Asc	7	482	NR	597 *	8.8	49.1
360 Prim Bapt Chrch	1	NR	NR	NR	-	-
419 So Bapt Conv	1	210	68	260 *	3.9	21.4
449 Un Methodist	2	291	130	360 *	5.3	29.6
ESTILL	**46**	**5,088**	**2,445**	**7,005 ***	**45.8**	**100.0**
056 Baha'i	0	3	NR	3	-	-
081 Catholic	1	NR	NR	90	.6	1.3
093 Chr Ch (Disc)	2	418	140	512 *	3.3	7.3
097 Chr Chs&Chs Cr	3	602	NR	737 *	4.8	10.5
123 Ch God (Ander)	5	NR	494	494	3.2	7.1

NR–Not Reported   *Total adherents estimated from known number of communicant, confirmed, full members.   - Represents a percentage less than 0.1.   Percentages may not total 100 due to rounding.

Table 4: Religious Congregations by County and Group: 2000

Religious Group	Number of Churches, Synagogues, Mosques, or Temples	Number of Communicant, Confirmed, or Full Members	Number of Attendees	Total Adherents: Number of Adherents	Total Adherents: % of Total Pop.	Total Adherents: % of Total Adh.
127 Ch God (Cleve)	1	342	163	419 *	2.7	6.0
145 Ch God Prophcy	1	49	NR	60 *	.4	.9
151 L-D Saints	1	NR	NR	104	.7	1.5
165 Ch of Nazarene	3	251	272	348	2.3	5.0
167 Chs of Christ	4	103	124	146	1.0	2.1
193 Episcopal	1	NR	11	10	.1	.1
221 Free Methodist	1	35	58	58	.4	.8
360 Prim Bapt Chrch	1	NR	NR	NR	-	-
419 So Bapt Conv	18	2,852	1,005	3,494 *	22.8	49.9
449 Un Methodist	4	433	178	530 *	3.5	7.6
FAYETTE	**196**	**71,334**	**26,081**	**123,244 ***	**47.3**	**100.0**
017 Amer Bapt Assn	3	750	NR	903 *	.3	.7
034 Ant Orth of NA	1	90	NR	180	.1	.1
040 Ap Chr Ch-Amer	1	9	27	27 *	-	-
053 Assemb of God	8	750	916	1,603	.6	1.3
056 Baha'i	1	80	NR	80	-	.1
076 Buddhism	3	NR	NR	NR	-	-
081 Catholic	8	NR	NR	26,146	10.0	21.2
084 Calvary Chapel	1	NR	NR	NR	-	-
089 Chr & Miss Al	3	234	NR	959	.4	.8
093 Chr Ch (Disc)	15	5,836	1,845	7,017 *	2.7	5.7
097 Chr Chs&Chs Cr	14	8,823	NR	10,608 *	4.1	8.6
123 Ch God (Ander)	2	NR	545	545	.2	.4
127 Ch God (Cleve)	6	1,542	574	1,854 *	.7	1.5
151 L-D Saints	5	NR	NR	1,813	.7	1.5
165 Ch of Nazarene	5	813	468	1,166	.4	.9
167 Chs of Christ	8	1,168	1,275	1,513	.6	1.2
173 Comm of Christ	1	49	NR	49	-	-
183 Cons Menn Conf	1	19	23	28	-	-
185 Cumber Presb	1	32	NR	32	-	-
193 Episcopal	7	NR	1,367	3,477	1.3	2.8
201 Evan Cov Ch	1	32	76	76 *	-	.1
207 E.L.C.A.	3	965	506	1,220	.5	1.0
221 Free Methodist	1	44	38	50	-	-
223 Free Will Bapt	2	251	NR	302 *	.1	.2
226 Friends-USA	1	58	NR	70 *	-	.1
246 Greek Orthodox	1	NR	NR	270	.1	.2
267 Muslim Est	2	NR	270	1,109	.4	.9
283 Luth—MO Synod	3	632	388	808	.3	.7
290 Metro Comm Ch	1	14	24	24 *	-	-
291 Missionary Ch	1	1	18	18	-	-
339 Pent Ch of God	1	13	NR	60	-	-
349 Pent Holiness	2	69	51	83 *	-	.1
355 Presb Ch (USA)	12	3,874	1,802	4,657 *	1.8	3.8
356 Presb Ch Amer	2	331	380	434	.2	.4
360 Prim Bapt Chrch	1	NR	NR	NR	-	-
403 Salvation Army	1	161	125	237	.1	.2
413 S.D.A.	3	433	NR	515	.2	.4
418 Southw Bapt Fel	2	NR	NR	NR	-	-
419 So Bapt Conv	42	30,537	10,412	36,717 *	14.1	29.8
435 Unitarian-Univ	1	260	NR	313 *	.1	.3
443 Un C of Christ	1	60	26	72 *	-	.1
449 Un Methodist	12	13,209	4,762	15,881 *	6.1	12.9
467 Wesleyan	2	167	132	285	.1	.2
469 WELS	1	28	31	43	-	-
496 Jewish Est	3	NR	NR	2,000	.8	1.6
FLEMING	**50**	**5,014**	**1,590**	**6,691 ***	**48.5**	**100.0**
053 Assemb of God	3	110	140	203	1.5	3.0
081 Catholic	1	NR	NR	160	1.2	2.4
093 Chr Ch (Disc)	2	578	187	718 *	5.2	10.7
097 Chr Chs&Chs Cr	12	1,470	NR	1,827 *	13.2	27.3
123 Ch God (Ander)	3	NR	141	141	1.0	2.1
127 Ch God (Cleve)	1	128	44	159 *	1.2	2.4
165 Ch of Nazarene	1	102	157	157	1.1	2.3
191 Entrpr Bpt Asc	1	32	NR	40 *	.3	.6
193 Episcopal	1	NR	18	39	.3	.6
297 Mennonite;Other	1	99	NR	123 *	.9	1.8
323 Old Ord Amish	1	55	NR	68 *	.5	1.0
349 Pent Holiness	1	86	50	107 *	.8	1.6
355 Presb Ch (USA)	1	25	13	31 *	.2	.5
419 So Bapt Conv	4	759	260	943 *	6.8	14.1
449 Un Methodist	16	1,551	559	1,929 *	14.0	28.8
467 Wesleyan	1	19	21	46	.3	.7
FLOYD	**84**	**9,961**	**4,005**	**13,102 ***	**30.9**	**100.0**
053 Assemb of God	3	397	320	376	.9	2.9
081 Catholic	1	NR	NR	310	.7	2.4
097 Chr Chs&Chs Cr	3	350	NR	425 *	1.0	3.2
123 Ch God (Ander)	1	NR	50	50	.1	.4
127 Ch God (Cleve)	3	152	73	184 *	.4	1.4
145 Ch God Prophcy	5	246	NR	300 *	.7	2.3
151 L-D Saints	2	NR	NR	455	1.1	3.5
167 Chs of Christ	11	833	790	1,020	2.4	7.8
193 Episcopal	1	NR	38	80	.2	.6
203 Evan Free Ch	1	69	125	125	.3	1.0
221 Free Methodist	1	0	7	7	-	.1
223 Free Will Bapt	18	2,262	NR	2,746 *	6.5	21.0
258 IndFreeWillBapt	1	114	NR	138 *	.3	1.1
267 Muslim Est	1	NR	55	163	.4	1.2
349 Pent Holiness	1	26	18	32 *	.1	.2
355 Presb Ch (USA)	2	134	81	163 *	.4	1.2
413 S.D.A.	1	28	NR	33	.1	.3
419 So Bapt Conv	15	3,175	1,555	3,855 *	9.1	29.4
449 Un Methodist	13	2,175	893	2,640 *	6.2	20.1
FRANKLIN	**66**	**21,382**	**7,115**	**29,990 ***	**62.9**	**100.0**
053 Assemb of God	1	224	278	425	.9	1.4
056 Baha'i	1	43	NR	43	.1	.1
081 Catholic	1	NR	NR	2,963	6.2	9.9
089 Chr & Miss Al	1	21	NR	58	.1	.2
093 Chr Ch (Disc)	5	2,790	719	3,379 *	7.1	11.3
097 Chr Chs&Chs Cr	4	1,213	NR	1,469 *	3.1	4.9
123 Ch God (Ander)	1	NR	140	140	.3	.5
127 Ch God (Cleve)	2	349	132	423 *	.9	1.4
165 Ch of Nazarene	2	336	162	547	1.1	1.8
167 Chs of Christ	4	371	373	474	1.0	1.6
193 Episcopal	1	NR	186	667	1.4	2.2
207 E.L.C.A.	1	230	90	293	.6	1.0
339 Pent Ch of God	2	331	NR	450	.9	1.5
349 Pent Holiness	1	75	59	91 *	.2	.3
355 Presb Ch (USA)	2	559	244	677 *	1.4	2.3
403 Salvation Army	1	60	36	145	.3	.5
413 S.D.A.	2	35	NR	42	.1	.1
419 So Bapt Conv	28	11,791	3,680	14,280 *	29.9	47.6
449 Un Methodist	4	2,087	584	2,528 *	5.3	8.4
467 Wesleyan	1	17	32	46	.1	.2
499 Indep.Non-Char	1	850	400	850	1.8	2.8
FULTON	**33**	**5,285**	**1,757**	**6,928 ***	**89.4**	**100.0**
053 Assemb of God	2	65	59	83	1.1	1.2
081 Catholic	2	NR	NR	302	3.9	4.4
093 Chr Ch (Disc)	1	55	0	68 *	.9	1.0
097 Chr Chs&Chs Cr	1	80	NR	99 *	1.3	1.4
123 Ch God (Ander)	1	NR	41	41	.5	.6
165 Ch of Nazarene	1	77	62	98	1.3	1.4
167 Chs of Christ	2	262	212	302	3.9	4.4
193 Episcopal	2	NR	32	77	1.0	1.1
360 Prim Bapt Chrch	1	NR	NR	NR	-	-
419 So Bapt Conv	12	3,621	958	4,468 *	57.6	64.5
449 Un Methodist	8	1,125	393	1,390 *	17.9	20.1
GALLATIN	**16**	**2,638**	**615**	**3,747 ***	**47.6**	**100.0**
081 Catholic	1	NR	NR	327	4.2	8.7
093 Chr Ch (Disc)	2	278	87	360 *	4.6	9.6
097 Chr Chs&Chs Cr	1	50	NR	65 *	.8	1.7
127 Ch God (Cleve)	1	49	29	64 *	.8	1.7
167 Chs of Christ	1	17	18	21	.3	.6
419 So Bapt Conv	8	2,027	431	2,629 *	33.4	70.2
449 Un Methodist	2	217	50	281 *	3.6	7.5
GARRARD	**32**	**5,791**	**1,902**	**7,334 ***	**49.6**	**100.0**
053 Assemb of God	1	116	140	210	1.4	2.9
056 Baha'i	0	17	NR	17	.1	.2

NR–Not Reported   *Total adherents estimated from known number of communicant, confirmed, full members.   - Represents a percentage less than 0.1.   Percentages may not total 100 due to rounding.

Table 4: Religious Congregations by County and Group: 2000

Religious Group	Number of Churches, Synagogues, Mosques, or Temples	Number of Communicant, Confirmed, or Full Members	Number of Attendees	Total Adherents: Number of Adherents	Total Adherents: % of Total Pop.	Total Adherents: % of Total Adh.
081 Catholic	1	NR	NR	153	1.0	2.1
093 Chr Ch (Disc)	2	280	103	345 *	2.3	4.7
097 Chr Chs&Chs Cr	3	506	NR	623 *	4.2	8.5
127 Ch God (Cleve)	2	317	105	390 *	2.6	5.3
165 Ch of Nazarene	1	240	162	305	2.1	4.2
167 Chs of Christ	2	99	80	102	.7	1.4
304 NatPrimBapt USA	1	66	NR	81 *	.5	1.1
355 Presb Ch (USA)	2	114	59	140 *	.9	1.9
419 So Bapt Conv	12	3,484	983	4,289 *	29.0	58.5
449 Un Methodist	5	552	270	679 *	4.6	9.3
GRANT	**40**	**7,880**	**1,792**	**10,745 ***	**48.0**	**100.0**
053 Assemb of God	2	85	110	110	.5	1.0
081 Catholic	1	NR	NR	556	2.5	5.2
093 Chr Ch (Disc)	2	332	163	429 *	1.9	4.0
097 Chr Chs&Chs Cr	10	1,504	NR	1,945 *	8.7	18.1
127 Ch God (Cleve)	2	190	42	245 *	1.1	2.3
283 Luth—MO Synod	1	43	32	59	.3	.5
355 Presb Ch (USA)	1	35	18	45 *	.2	.4
360 Prim Bapt Chrch	1	NR	NR	NR	-	-
419 So Bapt Conv	18	5,458	1,344	7,055 *	31.5	65.7
449 Un Methodist	2	233	83	301 *	1.3	2.8
GRAVES	**105**	**20,825**	**9,395**	**28,171 ***	**76.1**	**100.0**
053 Assemb of God	2	1,158	556	1,040	2.8	3.7
061 Beachy Amish	1	102	NR	126 *	.3	.4
081 Catholic	2	NR	NR	2,642	7.1	9.4
093 Chr Ch (Disc)	2	603	224	743 *	2.0	2.6
127 Ch God (Cleve)	2	96	10	119 *	.3	.4
143 CG in Cr(Menn)	1	171	NR	211 *	.6	.7
145 Ch God Prophcy	1	49	NR	61 *	.2	.2
151 L-D Saints	1	NR	NR	132	.4	.5
165 Ch of Nazarene	1	112	83	116	.3	.4
167 Chs of Christ	21	2,263	2,259	2,843	7.7	10.1
173 Comm of Christ	1	90	NR	90	.2	.3
185 Cumber Presb	3	142	NR	265	.7	.9
193 Episcopal	1	NR	16	28	.1	.1
349 Pent Holiness	2	115	125	142 *	.4	.5
355 Presb Ch (USA)	1	162	115	200 *	.5	.7
413 S.D.A.	1	21	NR	25	.1	.1
419 So Bapt Conv	44	13,768	5,115	16,958 *	45.8	60.2
449 Un Methodist	18	1,973	892	2,430 *	6.6	8.6
GRAYSON	**57**	**5,613**	**1,205**	**8,521 ***	**35.4**	**100.0**
053 Assemb of God	1	59	69	69	.3	.8
056 Baha'i	0	2	NR	2	-	-
061 Beachy Amish	1	39	NR	48 *	.2	.6
081 Catholic	6	NR	NR	1,510	6.3	17.7
097 Chr Chs&Chs Cr	2	300	NR	369 *	1.5	4.3
127 Ch God (Cleve)	1	183	92	225 *	.9	2.6
145 Ch God Prophcy	2	99	NR	122 *	.5	1.4
167 Chs of Christ	12	589	597	752	3.1	8.8
185 Cumber Presb	4	111	NR	223	.9	2.6
283 Luth—MO Synod	1	30	20	35	.1	.4
320 "Old" MB Ascs	2	196	NR	241 *	1.0	2.8
413 S.D.A.	1	47	NR	56	.2	.7
419 So Bapt Conv	16	3,144	25	3,868 *	16.1	45.4
449 Un Methodist	8	814	402	1,001 *	4.2	11.7
GREEN	**46**	**7,003**	**2,573**	**8,731 ***	**75.8**	**100.0**
061 Beachy Amish	1	24	NR	29 *	.3	.3
081 Catholic	1	NR	NR	82	.7	.9
097 Chr Chs&Chs Cr	1	50	NR	60 *	.5	.7
165 Ch of Nazarene	2	149	164	240	2.1	2.7
167 Chs of Christ	2	25	30	34	.3	.4
185 Cumber Presb	3	253	NR	443	3.8	5.1
355 Presb Ch (USA)	2	166	105	200 *	1.7	2.3
409 Separate Bapt	3	262	NR	316 *	2.7	3.6
419 So Bapt Conv	21	5,096	1,746	6,147 *	53.4	70.4
449 Un Methodist	10	978	528	1,180 *	10.2	13.5

Religious Group	Number of Churches, Synagogues, Mosques, or Temples	Number of Communicant, Confirmed, or Full Members	Number of Attendees	Total Adherents: Number of Adherents	Total Adherents: % of Total Pop.	Total Adherents: % of Total Adh.
GREENUP	**73**	**10,924**	**3,784**	**14,764 ***	**40.0**	**100.0**
053 Assemb of God	1	209	285	450	1.2	3.0
056 Baha'i	0	5	NR	5	-	-
081 Catholic	1	NR	NR	50	.1	.3
097 Chr Chs&Chs Cr	9	2,574	NR	3,133 *	8.5	21.2
123 Ch God (Ander)	3	NR	323	323	.9	2.2
127 Ch God (Cleve)	6	445	326	542 *	1.5	3.7
145 Ch God Prophcy	1	49	NR	60 *	.2	.4
151 L-D Saints	1	NR	NR	630	1.7	4.3
165 Ch of Nazarene	7	735	543	1,142	3.1	7.7
167 Chs of Christ	3	202	200	238	.6	1.6
191 Entrpr Bpt Asc	5	217	NR	264 *	.7	1.8
207 E.L.C.A.	1	79	25	102	.3	.7
223 Free Will Bapt	5	628	NR	765 *	2.1	5.2
265 Int Pent C Chr	1	30	49	49	.1	.3
339 Pent Ch of God	1	50	NR	70	.2	.5
355 Presb Ch (USA)	1	36	19	44 *	.1	.3
419 So Bapt Conv	12	3,487	1,130	4,246 *	11.5	28.8
449 Un Methodist	14	2,164	866	2,633 *	7.1	17.8
467 Wesleyan	1	14	18	18	-	.1
HANCOCK	**24**	**4,654**	**1,782**	**6,532 ***	**77.8**	**100.0**
081 Catholic	2	NR	NR	630	7.5	9.6
097 Chr Chs&Chs Cr	1	50	NR	63 *	.8	1.0
185 Cumber Presb	1	20	NR	36	.4	.6
419 So Bapt Conv	13	3,615	1,392	4,576 *	54.5	70.1
449 Un Methodist	6	969	390	1,227 *	14.6	18.8
467 Wesleyan	1	0	0	0	-	-
HARDIN	**128**	**29,798**	**11,490**	**47,909 ***	**50.9**	**100.0**
053 Assemb of God	8	915	1,057	1,468	1.6	3.1
056 Baha'i	0	22	NR	22	-	-
081 Catholic	8	NR	NR	9,332	9.9	19.5
089 Chr & Miss Al	1	69	NR	77	.1	.2
093 Chr Ch (Disc)	1	80	35	101 *	.1	.2
097 Chr Chs&Chs Cr	9	2,042	NR	2,585 *	2.7	5.4
123 Ch God (Ander)	1	NR	30	30	-	.1
127 Ch God (Cleve)	6	293	205	376 *	.4	.8
145 Ch God Prophcy	3	148	NR	186 *	.2	.4
165 Ch of Nazarene	2	126	114	196	.2	.4
167 Chs of Christ	6	681	581	762	.8	1.6
185 Cumber Presb	3	69	NR	77	.1	.2
193 Episcopal	2	NR	166	355	.4	.7
207 E.L.C.A.	1	135	76	168	.2	.4
223 Free Will Bapt	1	126	NR	159 *	.2	.3
267 Muslim Est	1	NR	55	163	.2	.3
283 Luth—MO Synod	1	200	155	271	.3	.6
290 Metro Comm Ch	1	40	29	51 *	.1	.1
323 Old Ord Amish	2	105	NR	133 *	.1	.3
355 Presb Ch (USA)	1	303	156	384 *	.4	.8
413 S.D.A.	1	48	NR	57	.1	.1
419 So Bapt Conv	45	20,626	7,031	26,111 *	27.7	54.5
449 Un Methodist	19	3,602	1,599	4,558 *	4.8	9.5
463 Vineyard	1	47	47	59 *	.1	.1
467 Wesleyan	3	79	102	160	.2	.3
469 WELS	1	42	52	68	.1	.1
HARLAN	**103**	**12,854**	**3,663**	**16,415 ***	**49.4**	**100.0**
053 Assemb of God	3	90	98	221	.7	1.3
056 Baha'i	0	1	NR	1	-	-
081 Catholic	3	NR	NR	280	.8	1.7
093 Chr Ch (Disc)	1	150	84	185 *	.6	1.1
097 Chr Chs&Chs Cr	6	581	NR	715 *	2.2	4.4
123 Ch God (Ander)	1	NR	40	40	.1	.2
127 Ch God (Cleve)	13	1,484	648	1,834 *	5.5	11.2
145 Ch God Prophcy	3	148	NR	183 *	.6	1.1
151 L-D Saints	1	NR	NR	109	.3	.7
165 Ch of Nazarene	2	59	60	102	.3	.6
167 Chs of Christ	7	241	255	300	.9	1.8
258 IndFreeWillBapt	1	51	NR	63 *	.2	.4
288 Mennonite USA	1	16	25	25 *	.1	.2
355 Presb Ch (USA)	3	122	71	151 *	.5	.9

NR–Not Reported   *Total adherents estimated from known number of communicant, confirmed, full members.   - Represents a percentage less than 0.1.   Percentages may not total 100 due to rounding.

Table 4: Religious Congregations by County and Group: 2000

Religious Group	Number of Churches, Synagogues, Mosques, or Temples	Number of Communicant, Confirmed, or Full Members	Number of Attendees	Total Adherents		
				Number of Adherents	% of Total Pop.	% of Total Adh.
362 Prim Bapt E Dst	2	273	NR	336 *	1.0	2.0
413 S.D.A.	1	26	NR	31	.1	.2
419 So Bapt Conv	45	8,302	2,000	10,225 *	30.8	62.3
449 Un Methodist	10	1,310	382	1,614 *	4.9	9.8
HARRISON	**50**	**7,705**	**2,161**	**10,401 ***	**57.8**	**100.0**
053 Assemb of God	1	49	59	90	.5	.9
081 Catholic	1	NR	NR	677	3.8	6.5
093 Chr Ch (Disc)	4	843	319	1,043 *	5.8	10.0
097 Chr Chs&Chs Cr	11	2,259	NR	2,796 *	15.5	26.9
123 Ch God (Ander)	1	NR	132	132	.7	1.3
127 Ch God (Cleve)	1	61	36	75 *	.4	.7
165 Ch of Nazarene	1	41	18	41	.2	.4
167 Chs of Christ	1	93	100	113	.6	1.1
193 Episcopal	1	NR	26	63	.4	.6
339 Pent Ch of God	1	49	NR	55	.3	.5
355 Presb Ch (USA)	1	184	95	228 *	1.3	2.2
356 Presb Ch Amer	1	107	70	117	.7	1.1
360 Prim Bapt Chrch	1	NR	NR	NR	-	-
419 So Bapt Conv	9	1,963	634	2,428 *	13.5	23.3
449 Un Methodist	15	2,056	672	2,543 *	14.1	24.4
HART	**62**	**7,032**	**2,082**	**9,003 ***	**51.6**	**100.0**
081 Catholic	1	NR	NR	127	.7	1.4
097 Chr Chs&Chs Cr	1	85	NR	106 *	.6	1.2
127 Ch God (Cleve)	1	38	29	47 *	.3	.5
145 Ch God Prophcy	2	99	NR	122 *	.7	1.4
167 Chs of Christ	7	256	297	343	2.0	3.8
185 Cumber Presb	3	80	NR	197	1.1	2.2
323 Old Ord Amish	6	330	NR	408 *	2.3	4.5
355 Presb Ch (USA)	1	15	8	19 *	.1	.2
409 Separate Bapt	2	83	NR	103 *	.6	1.1
419 So Bapt Conv	27	5,181	1,329	6,453 *	37.0	71.7
449 Un Methodist	11	865	419	1,078 *	6.2	12.0
HENDERSON	**63**	**19,537**	**6,480**	**29,481 ***	**65.8**	**100.0**
017 Amer Bapt Assn	1	250	NR	307 *	.7	1.0
053 Assemb of God	2	266	333	548	1.2	1.9
056 Baha'i	0	3	NR	3	-	-
081 Catholic	2	NR	NR	4,511	10.1	15.3
093 Chr Ch (Disc)	2	458	198	563 *	1.3	1.9
097 Chr Chs&Chs Cr	3	336	NR	413 *	.9	1.4
127 Ch God (Cleve)	1	34	20	42 *	.1	.1
145 Ch God Prophcy	2	99	NR	122 *	.3	.4
151 L-D Saints	1	NR	NR	177	.4	.6
165 Ch of Nazarene	1	177	118	268	.6	.9
167 Chs of Christ	2	291	342	427	1.0	1.4
193 Episcopal	1	NR	96	320	.7	1.1
283 Luth—MO Synod	1	96	67	155	.3	.5
355 Presb Ch (USA)	1	274	120	337 *	.8	1.1
403 Salvation Army	1	88	48	135	.3	.5
413 S.D.A.	1	63	NR	75	.2	.3
419 So Bapt Conv	28	13,740	3,887	16,892 *	37.7	57.3
443 Un C of Christ	1	183	77	225 *	.5	.8
449 Un Methodist	11	3,170	1,162	3,898 *	8.7	13.2
467 Wesleyan	1	9	12	63	.1	.2
HENRY	**40**	**6,502**	**1,822**	**8,242 ***	**54.7**	**100.0**
081 Catholic	1	NR	NR	151	1.0	1.8
093 Chr Ch (Disc)	10	1,282	322	1,595 *	10.6	19.4
097 Chr Chs&Chs Cr	1	200	NR	249 *	1.7	3.0
127 Ch God (Cleve)	1	86	0	107 *	.7	1.3
355 Presb Ch (USA)	1	50	35	62 *	.4	.8
419 So Bapt Conv	17	4,000	1,163	4,978 *	33.1	60.4
449 Un Methodist	9	884	302	1,100 *	7.3	13.3
HICKMAN	**29**	**3,339**	**1,491**	**4,390 ***	**83.4**	**100.0**
053 Assemb of God	1	136	185	223	4.2	5.1
081 Catholic	2	NR	NR	305	5.8	6.9
093 Chr Ch (Disc)	1	29	12	35 *	.7	.8
167 Chs of Christ	1	56	60	73	1.4	1.7
360 Prim Bapt Chrch	1	NR	NR	NR	-	-

Religious Group	Number of Churches, Synagogues, Mosques, or Temples	Number of Communicant, Confirmed, or Full Members	Number of Attendees	Total Adherents		
				Number of Adherents	% of Total Pop.	% of Total Adh.
419 So Bapt Conv	13	2,270	921	2,733 *	51.9	62.3
449 Un Methodist	10	848	313	1,021 *	19.4	23.3
HOPKINS	**95**	**19,811**	**6,991**	**26,626 ***	**57.2**	**100.0**
053 Assemb of God	4	646	511	681	1.5	2.6
081 Catholic	3	NR	NR	1,263	2.7	4.7
093 Chr Ch (Disc)	5	1,066	419	1,309 *	2.8	4.9
097 Chr Chs&Chs Cr	4	555	NR	682 *	1.5	2.6
123 Ch God (Ander)	1	NR	111	111	.2	.4
127 Ch God (Cleve)	2	143	68	175 *	.4	.7
145 Ch God Prophcy	1	49	NR	60 *	.1	.2
151 L-D Saints	1	NR	NR	378	.8	1.4
165 Ch of Nazarene	1	69	85	120	.3	.5
167 Chs of Christ	4	365	369	511	1.1	1.9
185 Cumber Presb	4	208	NR	410	.9	1.5
193 Episcopal	1	NR	76	181	.4	.7
203 Evan Free Ch	1	0	50	50	.1	.2
207 E.L.C.A.	1	66	51	89	.2	.3
339 Pent Ch of God	1	67	NR	242	.5	.9
349 Pent Holiness	1	14	14	17 *	-	.1
355 Presb Ch (USA)	1	331	132	407 *	.9	1.5
360 Prim Bapt Chrch	3	NR	NR	NR	-	-
403 Salvation Army	1	106	71	171	.4	.6
413 S.D.A.	1	41	NR	49	.1	.2
418 Southw Bapt Fel	1	NR	NR	NR	-	-
419 So Bapt Conv	38	13,392	4,006	16,447 *	35.4	61.8
449 Un Methodist	14	2,543	928	3,123 *	6.7	11.7
498 Indep.Charis.	1	150	100	150	.3	.6
JACKSON	**28**	**2,417**	**988**	**3,133 ***	**23.2**	**100.0**
081 Catholic	1	NR	NR	50	.4	1.6
127 Ch God (Cleve)	1	62	8	77 *	.6	2.5
167 Chs of Christ	2	49	54	61	.5	1.9
360 Prim Bapt Chrch	1	NR	NR	NR	-	-
371 Ref Ch in Am	3	180	172	297	2.2	9.5
419 So Bapt Conv	19	2,099	739	2,614 *	19.4	83.4
449 Un Methodist	1	27	15	34 *	.3	1.1
JEFFERSON	**594**	**163,595**	**57,804**	**378,742 ***	**54.6**	**100.0**
011 A.W.M.C.	1	8	42	12	-	-
019 Amer Bapt USA	3	1,471	650	1,817 *	.3	.5
034 Ant Orth of NA	1	704	NR	1,408	.2	.4
053 Assemb of God	15	9,285	5,830	8,396	1.2	2.2
055 As Ref Pres Ch	1	66	NR	72	-	-
056 Baha'i	2	210	NR	210	-	.1
076 Buddhism	3	NR	NR	NR	-	-
081 Catholic	71	NR	NR	156,949	22.6	41.4
084 Calvary Chapel	1	NR	NR	NR	-	-
089 Chr & Miss Al	3	165	NR	279	-	.1
093 Chr Ch (Disc)	16	7,215	2,232	8,911 *	1.3	2.4
097 Chr Chs&Chs Cr	19	6,694	NR	8,267 *	1.2	2.2
123 Ch God (Ander)	7	NR	429	429	.1	.1
127 Ch God (Cleve)	17	3,009	1,567	3,716 *	.5	1.0
145 Ch God Prophcy	5	246	NR	305 *	-	.1
151 L-D Saints	7	NR	NR	2,446	.4	.6
165 Ch of Nazarene	9	1,170	648	1,384	.2	.4
167 Chs of Christ	46	5,017	5,152	6,453	.9	1.7
173 Comm of Christ	3	244	NR	244	-	.1
183 Cons Menn Conf	1	38	46	55	-	-
185 Cumber Presb	2	269	NR	512	.1	.1
193 Episcopal	19	NR	2,462	6,612	1.0	1.7
203 Evan Free Ch	1	89	165	165	-	-
207 E.L.C.A.	14	2,740	1,288	3,559	.5	.9
221 Free Methodist	1	8	12	12	-	-
223 Free Will Bapt	3	377	NR	466 *	.1	.1
226 Friends-USA	1	58	NR	72 *	-	-
246 Greek Orthodox	1	NR	NR	252	-	.1
252 Hindu	3	NR	NR	NR	-	-
263 Int Foursq Gos	1	98	204	204 *	-	.1
264 Int Chs of Crst	1	302	472	422	.1	.1
267 Muslim Est	4	NR	398	1,811	.3	.5
283 Luth—MO Synod	6	1,627	798	2,174	.3	.6
290 Metro Comm Ch	1	113	138	140 *	-	-

NR–Not Reported *Total adherents estimated from known number of communicant, confirmed, full members. - Represents a percentage less than 0.1. Percentages may not total 100 due to rounding.

Table 4: Religious Congregations by County and Group: 2000

Religious Group	Number of Churches, Synagogues, Mosques, or Temples	Number of Communicant, Confirmed, or Full Members	Number of Attendees	Total Adherents: Number of Adherents	Total Adherents: % of Total Pop.	Total Adherents: % of Total Adh.
304 NatPrimBapt USA	8	491	NR	606 *	.1	.2
320 "Old" MB Ascs	3	451	NR	557 *	.1	.1
339 Pent Ch of God	1	28	NR	44	-	-
355 Presb Ch (USA)	31	8,647	4,359	10,687 *	1.5	2.8
356 Presb Ch Amer	2	84	94	116	-	-
360 Prim Bapt Chrch	1	NR	NR	NR	-	-
370 Ref Baptist Chs	1	NR	NR	NR	-	-
403 Salvation Army	4	489	283	944	.1	.2
409 Separate Bapt	5	501	NR	619 *	.1	.2
413 S.D.A.	6	1,628	NR	1,937	.3	.5
418 Southw Bapt Fel	3	NR	NR	NR	-	-
419 So Bapt Conv	164	87,730	20,188	108,354 *	15.6	28.6
435 Unitarian-Univ	3	464	NR	573 *	.1	.2
443 Un C of Christ	18	4,274	1,872	5,279 *	.8	1.4
449 Un Methodist	41	16,090	6,554	19,870 *	2.9	5.2
463 Vineyard	1	60	130	130 *	-	-
467 Wesleyan	3	113	96	303	-	.1
469 WELS	1	97	75	117	-	-
496 Jewish Est	5	NR	NR	8,700	1.3	2.3
499 Indep.Non-Char	4	1,225	1,620	2,152	.3	.6
JESSAMINE	**46**	**15,047**	**5,030**	**21,795 ***	**55.8**	**100.0**
053 Assemb of God	1	53	62	64	.2	.3
056 Baha'i	0	3	NR	3	-	-
081 Catholic	1	NR	NR	800	2.0	3.7
089 Chr & Miss Al	2	70	NR	80	.2	.4
093 Chr Ch (Disc)	2	585	230	739 *	1.9	3.4
097 Chr Chs&Chs Cr	4	7,545	NR	9,529 *	24.4	43.7
123 Ch God (Ander)	1	NR	30	30	.1	.1
127 Ch God (Cleve)	1	145	22	183 *	.5	.8
151 L-D Saints	2	NR	NR	357	.9	1.6
165 Ch of Nazarene	2	90	74	101	.3	.5
167 Chs of Christ	2	117	152	180	.5	.8
193 Episcopal	1	NR	135	256	.7	1.2
203 Evan Free Ch	1	40	65	65	.2	.3
221 Free Methodist	2	329	647	647	1.7	3.0
263 Int Foursq Gos	1	15	47	47 *	.1	.2
291 Missionary Ch	1	26	53	53	.1	.2
355 Presb Ch (USA)	3	279	165	353 *	.9	1.6
356 Presb Ch Amer	1	0	0	0	-	-
388 Reg Bapt Gen As	1	0	0	0 *	-	-
419 So Bapt Conv	7	3,574	985	4,513 *	11.6	20.7
449 Un Methodist	7	1,846	993	2,331 *	6.0	10.7
463 Vineyard	1	130	120	164 *	.4	.8
498 Indep.Charis.	1	0	900	900	2.3	4.1
499 Indep.Non-Char	1	200	350	400	1.0	1.8
JOHNSON	**62**	**6,523**	**1,898**	**9,604 ***	**41.0**	**100.0**
056 Baha'i	0	2	NR	2	-	-
081 Catholic	1	NR	NR	279	1.2	2.9
097 Chr Chs&Chs Cr	3	471	NR	573 *	2.4	6.0
123 Ch God (Ander)	6	NR	520	520	2.2	5.4
127 Ch God (Cleve)	2	69	48	84 *	.4	.9
151 L-D Saints	1	NR	NR	179	.8	1.9
165 Ch of Nazarene	1	38	35	49	.2	.5
167 Chs of Christ	8	425	421	518	2.2	5.4
191 Entrpr Bpt Asc	9	809	NR	987 *	4.2	10.3
223 Free Will Bapt	21	2,638	NR	3,218 *	13.7	33.5
265 Int Pent C Chr	2	194	186	905	3.9	9.4
297 Mennonite;Other	1	48	NR	59 *	.3	.6
360 Prim Bapt Chrch	1	NR	NR	NR	-	-
419 So Bapt Conv	3	1,107	343	1,350 *	5.8	14.1
449 Un Methodist	3	722	345	881 *	3.8	9.2
KENTON	**113**	**28,325**	**10,530**	**80,024 ***	**52.8**	**100.0**
053 Assemb of God	2	393	442	560	.4	.7
056 Baha'i	0	13	NR	13	-	-
081 Catholic	20	NR	NR	41,538	27.4	51.9
093 Chr Ch (Disc)	10	2,188	583	2,758 *	1.8	3.4
097 Chr Chs&Chs Cr	8	3,000	NR	3,781 *	2.5	4.7
123 Ch God (Ander)	2	NR	226	226	.1	.3
127 Ch God (Cleve)	3	306	196	386 *	.3	.5
151 L-D Saints	1	NR	NR	477	.3	.6
165 Ch of Nazarene	4	625	510	889	.6	1.1
167 Chs of Christ	2	175	175	228	.2	.3
193 Episcopal	2	NR	238	653	.4	.8
203 Evan Free Ch	1	50	140	140	.1	.2
207 E.L.C.A.	1	503	258	661	.4	.8
216 Evan Presby Ch	1	66	NR	83 *	.1	.1
223 Free Will Bapt	2	251	NR	317 *	.2	.4
267 Muslim Est	1	NR	228	841	.6	1.1
283 Luth—MO Synod	1	61	54	80	.1	.1
355 Presb Ch (USA)	2	866	422	1,092 *	.7	1.4
403 Salvation Army	1	80	35	276	.2	.3
413 S.D.A.	1	199	NR	237	.2	.3
419 So Bapt Conv	28	13,804	4,045	17,400 *	11.5	21.7
435 Unitarian-Univ	1	26	NR	33 *	-	-
443 Un C of Christ	2	348	153	439 *	.3	.5
449 Un Methodist	15	4,028	1,478	5,076 *	3.4	6.3
467 Wesleyan	1	43	47	90	.1	.1
499 Indep.Non-Char	1	1,300	1,300	1,750	1.2	2.2
KNOTT	**17**	**3,079**	**1,260**	**3,772 ***	**21.4**	**100.0**
056 Baha'i	0	1	NR	1	-	-
127 Ch God (Cleve)	1	79	18	96 *	.5	2.5
167 Chs of Christ	3	26	39	37	.2	1.0
203 Evan Free Ch	2	87	90	110	.6	2.9
288 Mennonite USA	1	37	50	50 *	.3	1.3
297 Mennonite;Other	1	47	NR	57 *	.3	1.5
349 Pent Holiness	1	35	30	43 *	.2	1.1
419 So Bapt Conv	7	2,584	953	3,155 *	17.9	83.6
449 Un Methodist	1	183	80	223 *	1.3	5.9
KNOX	**72**	**14,246**	**3,561**	**18,550 ***	**58.3**	**100.0**
053 Assemb of God	2	238	71	184	.6	1.0
081 Catholic	2	NR	NR	704	2.2	3.8
093 Chr Ch (Disc)	1	100	40	125 *	.4	.7
097 Chr Chs&Chs Cr	3	278	NR	348 *	1.1	1.9
127 Ch God (Cleve)	2	287	140	360 *	1.1	1.9
165 Ch of Nazarene	1	95	77	168	.5	.9
193 Episcopal	1	NR	32	58	.2	.3
419 So Bapt Conv	57	12,655	3,105	15,860 *	49.9	85.5
449 Un Methodist	3	593	96	743 *	2.3	4.0
LARUE	**38**	**7,581**	**2,567**	**10,516 ***	**78.6**	**100.0**
053 Assemb of God	1	65	70	77	.6	.7
081 Catholic	1	NR	NR	886	6.6	8.4
093 Chr Ch (Disc)	1	82	43	101 *	.8	1.0
097 Chr Chs&Chs Cr	2	396	NR	488 *	3.6	4.6
127 Ch God (Cleve)	1	176	56	217 *	1.6	2.1
145 Ch God Prophcy	1	49	NR	61 *	.5	.6
151 L-D Saints	1	NR	NR	188	1.4	1.8
165 Ch of Nazarene	1	61	76	126	.9	1.2
167 Chs of Christ	2	72	75	93	.7	.9
185 Cumber Presb	1	142	NR	226	1.7	2.1
409 Separate Bapt	4	791	NR	974 *	7.3	9.3
419 So Bapt Conv	18	5,238	1,962	6,452 *	48.2	61.4
449 Un Methodist	4	509	285	627 *	4.7	6.0
LAUREL	**80**	**16,753**	**5,945**	**22,222 ***	**42.2**	**100.0**
053 Assemb of God	2	350	439	690	1.3	3.1
056 Baha'i	0	1	NR	1	-	-
081 Catholic	1	NR	NR	612	1.2	2.8
093 Chr Ch (Disc)	1	461	201	574 *	1.1	2.6
097 Chr Chs&Chs Cr	5	547	NR	681 *	1.3	3.1
123 Ch God (Ander)	1	NR	49	49	.1	.2
127 Ch God (Cleve)	5	480	244	597 *	1.1	2.7
151 L-D Saints	1	NR	NR	341	.6	1.5
165 Ch of Nazarene	1	76	84	178	.3	.8
167 Chs of Christ	7	535	571	692	1.3	3.1
335 Orth Pres Ch	1	24	44	44	.1	.2
339 Pent Ch of God	1	50	NR	50	.1	.2
355 Presb Ch (USA)	1	240	120	299 *	.6	1.3
413 S.D.A.	1	78	NR	93	.2	.4
419 So Bapt Conv	44	13,055	3,904	16,255 *	30.8	73.1

NR–Not Reported   *Total adherents estimated from known number of communicant, confirmed, full members.   - Represents a percentage less than 0.1.   Percentages may not total 100 due to rounding.

Table 4: Religious Congregations by County and Group: 2000

Religious Group	Number of Churches, Synagogues, Mosques, or Temples	Number of Communicant, Confirmed, or Full Members	Number of Attendees	Total Adherents: Number of Adherents	Total Adherents: % of Total Pop.	Total Adherents: % of Total Adh.
449 Un Methodist	8	856	289	1,066 *	2.0	4.8
LAWRENCE	**42**	**5,218**	**937**	**6,527 ***	**41.9**	**100.0**
056 Baha'i	0	1	NR	1	-	-
081 Catholic	1	NR	NR	95	.6	1.5
097 Chr Chs&Chs Cr	2	248	NR	305 *	2.0	4.7
127 Ch God (Cleve)	1	212	88	261 *	1.7	4.0
167 Chs of Christ	1	11	25	15	.1	.2
191 Entrpr Bpt Asc	4	330	NR	407 *	2.6	6.2
223 Free Will Bapt	16	2,010	NR	2,478 *	15.9	38.0
362 Prim Bapt E Dst	2	392	NR	483 *	3.1	7.4
419 So Bapt Conv	5	1,028	447	1,267 *	8.1	19.4
449 Un Methodist	10	986	377	1,215 *	7.8	18.6
LEE	**29**	**1,838**	**1,057**	**2,679 ***	**33.8**	**100.0**
053 Assemb of God	1	44	61	61	.8	2.3
056 Baha'i	0	1	NR	1	-	-
081 Catholic	1	NR	NR	91	1.1	3.4
097 Chr Chs&Chs Cr	3	373	NR	448 *	5.7	16.7
123 Ch God (Ander)	5	NR	312	312	3.9	11.6
127 Ch God (Cleve)	1	79	41	95 *	1.2	3.5
145 Ch God Prophcy	1	49	NR	59 *	.7	2.2
165 Ch of Nazarene	1	94	79	115	1.5	4.3
167 Chs of Christ	7	296	258	371	4.7	13.8
193 Episcopal	1	NR	22	43	.5	1.6
355 Presb Ch (USA)	2	51	33	61 *	.8	2.3
419 So Bapt Conv	5	774	231	930 *	11.7	34.7
449 Un Methodist	1	77	20	92 *	1.2	3.4
LESLIE	**29**	**2,375**	**1,297**	**2,989 ***	**24.1**	**100.0**
089 Chr & Miss Al	1	0	NR	50	.4	1.7
127 Ch God (Cleve)	5	529	276	647 *	5.2	21.6
167 Chs of Christ	7	329	355	436	3.5	14.6
355 Presb Ch (USA)	3	170	94	208 *	1.7	7.0
419 So Bapt Conv	6	947	355	1,159 *	9.3	38.8
449 Un Methodist	7	400	217	489 *	3.9	16.4
LETCHER	**63**	**5,897**	**2,173**	**7,441 ***	**29.4**	**100.0**
053 Assemb of God	1	24	25	42	.2	.6
081 Catholic	2	NR	NR	69	.3	.9
089 Chr & Miss Al	1	9	NR	30	.1	.4
123 Ch God (Ander)	1	NR	103	103	.4	1.4
127 Ch God (Cleve)	2	134	74	162 *	.6	2.2
145 Ch God Prophcy	1	49	NR	60 *	.2	.8
165 Ch of Nazarene	1	27	31	45	.2	.6
167 Chs of Christ	10	321	347	400	1.6	5.4
258 IndFreeWillBapt	10	640	NR	776 *	3.1	10.4
263 Int Foursq Gos	1	14	56	56 *	.2	.8
335 Orth Pres Ch	1	0	28	28	.1	.4
355 Presb Ch (USA)	4	276	209	334 *	1.3	4.5
360 Prim Bapt Chrch	3	NR	NR	NR	-	-
362 Prim Bapt E Dst	5	206	NR	250 *	1.0	3.4
418 Southw Bapt Fel	1	NR	NR	NR	-	-
419 So Bapt Conv	13	3,541	1,061	4,292 *	17.0	57.7
449 Un Methodist	6	656	239	794 *	3.1	10.7
LEWIS	**41**	**3,928**	**737**	**4,950 ***	**35.1**	**100.0**
053 Assemb of God	1	14	19	40	.3	.8
081 Catholic	1	NR	NR	46	.3	.9
097 Chr Chs&Chs Cr	16	1,683	NR	2,085 *	14.8	42.1
123 Ch God (Ander)	1	NR	35	35	.2	.7
127 Ch God (Cleve)	2	234	79	289 *	2.1	5.8
165 Ch of Nazarene	1	49	33	49	.3	1.0
167 Chs of Christ	1	30	30	30	.2	.6
223 Free Will Bapt	1	126	NR	156 *	1.1	3.2
355 Presb Ch (USA)	1	3	2	4 *	-	.1
419 So Bapt Conv	6	1,040	233	1,288 *	9.1	26.0
449 Un Methodist	10	749	306	928 *	6.6	18.7
LINCOLN	**78**	**12,323**	**4,192**	**15,558 ***	**66.6**	**100.0**
053 Assemb of God	1	394	172	320	1.4	2.1
056 Baha'i	0	5	NR	5	-	-
081 Catholic	1	NR	NR	124	.5	.8
093 Chr Ch (Disc)	2	343	95	428 *	1.8	2.8
097 Chr Chs&Chs Cr	6	648	NR	808 *	3.5	5.2
123 Ch God (Ander)	5	NR	270	270	1.2	1.7
127 Ch God (Cleve)	4	268	147	335 *	1.4	2.2
145 Ch God Prophcy	1	49	NR	61 *	.3	.4
165 Ch of Nazarene	2	110	17	110	.5	.7
167 Chs of Christ	10	343	364	422	1.8	2.7
283 Luth—MO Synod	1	14	10	14	.1	.1
297 Mennonite;Other	1	13	NR	16 *	.1	.1
323 Old Ord Amish	2	110	NR	138 *	.6	.9
355 Presb Ch (USA)	1	122	63	152 *	.7	1.0
413 S.D.A.	1	47	NR	56	.2	.4
419 So Bapt Conv	31	9,039	2,751	11,280 *	48.3	72.5
449 Un Methodist	9	818	303	1,019 *	4.4	6.5
LIVINGSTON	**46**	**5,659**	**2,193**	**6,927 ***	**70.7**	**100.0**
056 Baha'i	0	2	NR	2	-	-
081 Catholic	1	NR	NR	75	.8	1.1
093 Chr Ch (Disc)	1	15	0	18 *	.2	.3
167 Chs of Christ	3	99	105	126	1.3	1.8
185 Cumber Presb	2	114	NR	158	1.6	2.3
323 Old Ord Amish	1	55	NR	66 *	.7	1.0
419 So Bapt Conv	26	4,465	1,583	5,386 *	54.9	77.8
449 Un Methodist	12	909	505	1,096 *	11.2	15.8
LOGAN	**78**	**14,329**	**6,235**	**18,563 ***	**69.9**	**100.0**
053 Assemb of God	1	21	16	23	.1	.1
061 Beachy Amish	1	54	NR	67 *	.3	.4
081 Catholic	1	NR	NR	460	1.7	2.5
093 Chr Ch (Disc)	3	326	152	406 *	1.5	2.2
127 Ch God (Cleve)	1	11	15	15 *	.1	.1
145 Ch God Prophcy	1	49	NR	61 *	.2	.3
151 L-D Saints	1	NR	NR	141	.5	.8
167 Chs of Christ	10	673	799	926	3.5	5.0
185 Cumber Presb	5	258	NR	361	1.4	1.9
193 Episcopal	1	NR	31	53	.2	.3
323 Old Ord Amish	1	55	NR	69 *	.3	.4
355 Presb Ch (USA)	2	148	97	185 *	.7	1.0
419 So Bapt Conv	33	10,842	4,020	13,510 *	50.8	72.8
449 Un Methodist	16	1,592	825	1,986 *	7.5	10.7
499 Indep.Non-Char	1	300	280	300	1.1	1.6
LYON	**24**	**3,998**	**1,684**	**4,929 ***	**61.0**	**100.0**
053 Assemb of God	1	30	27	40	.5	.8
081 Catholic	1	NR	NR	189	2.3	3.8
151 L-D Saints	1	NR	NR	168	2.1	3.4
167 Chs of Christ	2	117	125	151	1.9	3.1
419 So Bapt Conv	13	3,122	1,176	3,551 *	43.9	72.0
449 Un Methodist	6	729	356	830 *	10.3	16.8
MCCRACKEN	**92**	**30,137**	**11,779**	**44,000 ***	**67.2**	**100.0**
053 Assemb of God	2	267	193	267	.4	.6
056 Baha'i	0	10	NR	10	-	-
081 Catholic	4	NR	NR	4,981	7.6	11.3
093 Chr Ch (Disc)	3	705	233	860 *	1.3	2.0
097 Chr Chs&Chs Cr	1	142	NR	173 *	.3	.4
123 Ch God (Ander)	3	NR	328	328	.5	.7
127 Ch God (Cleve)	2	145	89	177 *	.3	.4
151 L-D Saints	1	NR	NR	399	.6	.9
165 Ch of Nazarene	1	111	102	203	.3	.5
167 Chs of Christ	11	2,141	1,978	2,881	4.4	6.5
185 Cumber Presb	5	933	NR	1,781	2.7	4.0
193 Episcopal	1	NR	183	571	.9	1.3
207 E.L.C.A.	1	187	118	225	.3	.5
223 Free Will Bapt	1	126	NR	153 *	.2	.3
283 Luth—MO Synod	1	479	270	661	1.0	1.5
290 Metro Comm Ch	1	24	20	29 *	-	.1
355 Presb Ch (USA)	3	581	275	708 *	1.1	1.6
403 Salvation Army	1	100	57	151	.2	.3
413 S.D.A.	1	149	NR	177	.3	.4

NR–Not Reported *Total adherents estimated from known number of communicant, confirmed, full members. - Represents a percentage less than 0.1. Percentages may not total 100 due to rounding.

Table 4: Religious Congregations by County and Group: 2000

Religious Group	Number of Churches, Synagogues, Mosques, or Temples	Number of Communicant, Confirmed, or Full Members	Number of Attendees	Total Adherents		
				Number of Adherents	% of Total Pop.	% of Total Adh.
418 Southw Bapt Fel	1	NR	NR	NR	-	-
419 So Bapt Conv	31	18,964	5,779	23,125 *	35.3	52.6
443 Un C of Christ	1	66	54	80 *	.1	.2
449 Un Methodist	14	4,575	1,900	5,578 *	8.5	12.7
496 Jewish Est	1	NR	NR	50	.1	.1
499 Indep.Non-Char	1	432	200	432	.7	1.0
MCCREARY	**18**	**3,105**	**856**	**4,068 ***	**23.8**	**100.0**
056 Baha'i	0	1	NR	1	-	-
081 Catholic	1	NR	NR	55	.3	1.4
093 Chr Ch (Disc)	1	28	0	35 *	.2	.9
097 Chr Chs&Chs Cr	1	40	NR	51 *	.3	1.3
151 L-D Saints	1	NR	NR	99	.6	2.4
167 Chs of Christ	1	30	20	35	.2	.9
413 S.D.A.	1	79	NR	94	.6	2.3
419 So Bapt Conv	9	2,666	716	3,368 *	19.7	82.8
449 Un Methodist	3	261	120	330 *	1.9	8.1
MCLEAN	**34**	**4,847**	**1,690**	**6,325 ***	**63.6**	**100.0**
081 Catholic	2	NR	NR	203	2.0	3.2
093 Chr Ch (Disc)	1	68	55	83 *	.8	1.3
097 Chr Chs&Chs Cr	1	170	NR	209 *	2.1	3.3
145 Ch God Prophcy	2	99	NR	120 *	1.2	1.9
167 Chs of Christ	1	51	55	76	.8	1.2
185 Cumber Presb	3	178	NR	370	3.7	5.8
221 Free Methodist	1	10	18	18	.2	.3
360 Prim Bapt Chrch	1	NR	NR	NR	-	-
419 So Bapt Conv	11	2,972	1,053	3,647 *	36.7	57.7
449 Un Methodist	10	1,283	495	1,574 *	15.8	24.9
467 Wesleyan	1	16	14	25	.3	.4
MADISON	**103**	**21,251**	**8,343**	**29,250 ***	**41.3**	**100.0**
053 Assemb of God	3	116	136	184	.3	.6
056 Baha'i	0	54	NR	54	.1	.2
081 Catholic	2	NR	NR	2,305	3.3	7.9
089 Chr & Miss Al	1	124	NR	261	.4	.9
093 Chr Ch (Disc)	6	2,000	516	2,420 *	3.4	8.3
097 Chr Chs&Chs Cr	10	1,385	NR	1,677 *	2.4	5.7
123 Ch God (Ander)	1	NR	112	112	.2	.4
127 Ch God (Cleve)	7	986	690	1,193 *	1.7	4.1
165 Ch of Nazarene	3	240	185	338	.5	1.2
167 Chs of Christ	4	389	373	453	.6	1.5
193 Episcopal	1	NR	48	84	.1	.3
207 E.L.C.A.	1	97	65	125	.2	.4
226 Friends-USA	1	64	NR	77 *	.1	.3
263 Int Foursq Gos	1	38	306	306 *	.4	1.0
267 Muslim Est	1	NR	156	609	.9	2.1
304 NatPrimBapt USA	3	97	NR	117 *	.2	.4
355 Presb Ch (USA)	2	453	244	548 *	.8	1.9
356 Presb Ch Amer	1	45	44	51	.1	.2
360 Prim Bapt Chrch	1	NR	NR	NR	-	-
403 Salvation Army	1	76	60	80	.1	.3
413 S.D.A.	1	53	NR	63	.1	.2
419 So Bapt Conv	42	13,309	4,608	16,105 *	22.7	55.1
435 Unitarian-Univ	1	22	NR	27 *	-	.1
449 Un Methodist	9	1,703	800	2,061 *	2.9	7.0
MAGOFFIN	**21**	**2,319**	**773**	**2,930 ***	**22.0**	**100.0**
053 Assemb of God	1	135	85	118	.9	4.0
081 Catholic	1	NR	NR	65	.5	2.2
097 Chr Chs&Chs Cr	1	83	NR	104 *	.8	3.5
123 Ch God (Ander)	1	NR	35	35	.3	1.2
167 Chs of Christ	2	90	105	123	.9	4.2
223 Free Will Bapt	4	503	NR	628 *	4.7	21.4
265 Int Pent C Chr	2	150	75	153	1.1	5.2
339 Pent Ch of God	1	50	NR	70	.5	2.4
360 Prim Bapt Chrch	2	NR	NR	NR	-	-
419 So Bapt Conv	5	1,034	393	1,292 *	9.7	44.1
449 Un Methodist	1	274	80	342 *	2.6	11.7
MARION	**35**	**5,189**	**1,667**	**15,650 ***	**85.9**	**100.0**
053 Assemb of God	1	59	73	102	.6	.7
081 Catholic	7	NR	NR	8,964	49.2	57.3
093 Chr Ch (Disc)	1	85	45	106 *	.6	.7
097 Chr Chs&Chs Cr	4	486	NR	604 *	3.3	3.9
151 L-D Saints	1	NR	NR	202	1.1	1.3
167 Chs of Christ	2	100	100	127	.7	.8
355 Presb Ch (USA)	2	138	72	172 *	.9	1.1
419 So Bapt Conv	11	3,654	1,054	4,544 *	25.0	29.0
449 Un Methodist	6	667	323	829 *	4.6	5.3
MARSHALL	**73**	**16,095**	**8,361**	**19,903 ***	**66.1**	**100.0**
017 Amer Bapt Assn	1	250	NR	299 *	1.0	1.5
053 Assemb of God	1	27	36	36	.1	.2
056 Baha'i	0	3	NR	3	-	-
081 Catholic	2	NR	NR	606	2.0	3.0
093 Chr Ch (Disc)	1	165	85	197 *	.7	1.0
097 Chr Chs&Chs Cr	1	55	NR	66 *	.2	.3
165 Ch of Nazarene	1	75	59	93	.3	.5
167 Chs of Christ	12	2,065	2,028	2,604	8.6	13.1
185 Cumber Presb	4	305	NR	392	1.3	2.0
193 Episcopal	1	NR	31	57	.2	.3
207 E.L.C.A.	1	155	90	198	.7	1.0
355 Presb Ch (USA)	1	80	55	96 *	.3	.5
360 Prim Bapt Chrch	4	NR	NR	NR	-	-
413 S.D.A.	1	22	NR	26	.1	.1
419 So Bapt Conv	27	9,724	4,086	11,635 *	38.6	58.5
449 Un Methodist	14	2,169	1,191	2,595 *	8.6	13.0
499 Indep.Non-Char	1	1,000	700	1,000	3.3	5.0
MARTIN	**26**	**2,639**	**837**	**3,356 ***	**26.7**	**100.0**
081 Catholic	1	NR	NR	28	.2	.8
127 Ch God (Cleve)	4	323	50	410 *	3.3	12.2
157 Ch of Brethren	1	13	5	16 *	.1	.5
165 Ch of Nazarene	3	262	215	332	2.6	9.9
167 Chs of Christ	6	299	311	365	2.9	10.9
223 Free Will Bapt	7	879	NR	1,113 *	8.8	33.2
419 So Bapt Conv	2	665	199	842 *	6.7	25.1
449 Un Methodist	2	198	57	250 *	2.0	7.4
MASON	**55**	**7,919**	**2,541**	**11,577 ***	**68.9**	**100.0**
053 Assemb of God	2	148	137	195	1.2	1.7
056 Baha'i	0	3	NR	3	-	-
081 Catholic	3	NR	NR	1,166	6.9	10.1
093 Chr Ch (Disc)	5	999	346	1,227 *	7.3	10.6
097 Chr Chs&Chs Cr	6	899	NR	1,103 *	6.6	9.5
127 Ch God (Cleve)	1	46	34	56 *	.3	.5
151 L-D Saints	1	NR	NR	350	2.1	3.0
165 Ch of Nazarene	1	327	258	397	2.4	3.4
167 Chs of Christ	1	20	18	25	.1	.2
193 Episcopal	1	NR	47	163	1.0	1.4
283 Luth—MO Synod	1	65	27	85	.5	.7
355 Presb Ch (USA)	3	183	76	224 *	1.3	1.9
419 So Bapt Conv	11	2,296	731	2,819 *	16.8	24.4
449 Un Methodist	18	2,902	842	3,564 *	21.2	30.8
467 Wesleyan	1	31	25	200	1.2	1.7
MEADE	**35**	**6,559**	**2,039**	**13,818 ***	**52.4**	**100.0**
053 Assemb of God	1	205	250	310	1.2	2.2
081 Catholic	4	NR	NR	4,739	18.0	34.3
097 Chr Chs&Chs Cr	2	145	NR	189 *	.7	1.4
127 Ch God (Cleve)	1	84	56	109 *	.4	.8
145 Ch God Prophcy	1	49	NR	64 *	.2	.5
151 L-D Saints	1	NR	NR	447	1.7	3.2
165 Ch of Nazarene	1	58	35	60	.2	.4
167 Chs of Christ	2	63	85	92	.3	.7
193 Episcopal	1	NR	26	47	.2	.3
355 Presb Ch (USA)	1	52	45	68 *	.3	.5
419 So Bapt Conv	15	5,119	1,202	6,670 *	25.3	48.3
449 Un Methodist	5	784	340	1,023 *	3.9	7.4
MENIFEE	**13**	**367**	**724**	**840 ***	**12.8**	**100.0**
053 Assemb of God	1	24	30	31	.5	3.7
097 Chr Chs&Chs Cr	1	25	NR	30 *	.5	3.6

NR–Not Reported   *Total adherents estimated from known number of communicant, confirmed, full members.   - Represents a percentage less than 0.1.   Percentages may not total 100 due to rounding.

Table 4: Religious Congregations by County and Group: 2000

Religious Group	Number of Churches, Synagogues, Mosques, or Temples	Number of Communicant, Confirmed, or Full Members	Number of Attendees	Total Adherents		
				Number of Adherents	% of Total Pop.	% of Total Adh.
123 Ch God (Ander)	1	NR	130	130	2.0	15.5
127 Ch God (Cleve)	1	70	130	130 *	2.0	15.5
167 Chs of Christ	2	60	80	90	1.4	10.7
179 Consrv Bapt	1	NR	200	200	3.1	23.8
216 Evan Presby Ch	1	6	NR	7 *	.1	.8
355 Presb Ch (USA)	1	28	29	34 *	.5	4.0
360 Prim Bapt Chrch	1	NR	NR	NR	-	-
418 Southw Bapt Fel	1	NR	NR	NR	-	-
419 So Bapt Conv	2	154	125	188 *	2.9	22.4
MERCER	**50**	**12,108**	**3,754**	**15,797 ***	**75.9**	**100.0**
053 Assemb of God	1	19	25	37	.2	.2
081 Catholic	1	NR	NR	582	2.8	3.7
093 Chr Ch (Disc)	3	874	312	1,081 *	5.2	6.8
097 Chr Chs&Chs Cr	5	1,017	NR	1,258 *	6.0	8.0
127 Ch God (Cleve)	3	259	170	321 *	1.5	2.0
167 Chs of Christ	4	289	308	363	1.7	2.3
185 Cumber Presb	2	90	NR	251	1.2	1.6
193 Episcopal	1	NR	36	65	.3	.4
297 Mennonite;Other	1	28	NR	35 *	.2	.2
339 Pent Ch of God	1	13	NR	25	.1	.2
355 Presb Ch (USA)	3	259	126	321 *	1.5	2.0
419 So Bapt Conv	18	8,527	2,411	10,551 *	50.7	66.8
449 Un Methodist	7	733	366	907 *	4.4	5.7
METCALFE	**40**	**3,668**	**1,453**	**5,107 ***	**50.9**	**100.0**
081 Catholic	1	NR	NR	227	2.3	4.4
097 Chr Chs&Chs Cr	1	107	NR	132 *	1.3	2.6
127 Ch God (Cleve)	1	29	17	36 *	.4	.7
151 L-D Saints	1	NR	NR	251	2.5	4.9
167 Chs of Christ	8	477	530	645	6.4	12.6
185 Cumber Presb	6	175	NR	251	2.5	4.9
320 "Old" MB Ascs	2	352	NR	436 *	4.3	8.5
409 Separate Bapt	1	44	NR	54 *	.5	1.1
419 So Bapt Conv	11	1,867	614	2,311 *	23.0	45.3
449 Un Methodist	8	617	292	764 *	7.6	15.0
MONROE	**51**	**4,737**	**2,565**	**6,520 ***	**55.5**	**100.0**
032 Amish; other	1	70	NR	85 *	.7	1.3
081 Catholic	1	NR	NR	159	1.4	2.4
143 CG in Cr(Menn)	1	22	NR	27 *	.2	.4
151 L-D Saints	1	NR	NR	269	2.3	4.1
167 Chs of Christ	29	1,404	1,776	2,023	17.2	31.0
320 "Old" MB Ascs	3	191	NR	233 *	2.0	3.6
322 Old Ord Menn Ch	1	75	NR	92 *	.8	1.4
419 So Bapt Conv	10	2,604	617	3,180 *	27.1	48.8
449 Un Methodist	4	371	172	452 *	3.8	6.9
MONTGOMERY	**40**	**6,227**	**3,466**	**9,207 ***	**40.8**	**100.0**
053 Assemb of God	2	241	265	265	1.2	2.9
056 Baha'i	0	1	NR	1	-	-
081 Catholic	1	NR	NR	403	1.8	4.4
093 Chr Ch (Disc)	4	1,149	398	1,424 *	6.3	15.5
097 Chr Chs&Chs Cr	2	550	NR	682 *	3.0	7.4
123 Ch God (Ander)	6	NR	995	995	4.4	10.8
127 Ch God (Cleve)	2	266	64	330 *	1.5	3.6
145 Ch God Prophcy	1	49	NR	61 *	.3	.7
165 Ch of Nazarene	1	183	85	183	.8	2.0
167 Chs of Christ	8	541	525	709	3.1	7.7
193 Episcopal	1	NR	62	129	.6	1.4
223 Free Will Bapt	1	126	NR	156 *	.7	1.7
355 Presb Ch (USA)	1	185	75	229 *	1.0	2.5
419 So Bapt Conv	7	2,300	705	2,851 *	12.6	31.0
449 Un Methodist	3	636	292	789 *	3.5	8.6
MORGAN	**30**	**2,243**	**814**	**2,991 ***	**21.4**	**100.0**
056 Baha'i	0	1	NR	1	-	-
081 Catholic	1	NR	NR	70	.5	2.3
093 Chr Ch (Disc)	2	91	48	109 *	.8	3.6
097 Chr Chs&Chs Cr	1	250	NR	300 *	2.2	10.0
123 Ch God (Ander)	4	NR	202	202	1.4	6.8
127 Ch God (Cleve)	1	106	64	127 *	.9	4.2

Religious Group	Number of Churches, Synagogues, Mosques, or Temples	Number of Communicant, Confirmed, or Full Members	Number of Attendees	Total Adherents		
				Number of Adherents	% of Total Pop.	% of Total Adh.
167 Chs of Christ	4	140	167	198	1.4	6.6
191 Entrpr Bpt Asc	9	754	NR	904 *	6.5	30.2
288 Mennonite USA	1	15	15	18 *	.1	.6
297 Mennonite;Other	1	58	NR	70 *	.5	2.3
355 Presb Ch (USA)	1	60	50	72 *	.5	2.4
360 Prim Bapt Chrch	1	NR	NR	NR	-	-
419 So Bapt Conv	3	596	218	714 *	5.1	23.9
449 Un Methodist	1	172	50	206 *	1.5	6.9
MUHLENBERG	**93**	**17,377**	**5,778**	**21,757 ***	**68.3**	**100.0**
053 Assemb of God	2	95	132	134	.4	.6
081 Catholic	1	NR	NR	240	.8	1.1
093 Chr Ch (Disc)	2	213	92	257 *	.8	1.2
097 Chr Chs&Chs Cr	2	205	NR	247 *	.8	1.1
127 Ch God (Cleve)	3	243	136	293 *	.9	1.3
145 Ch God Prophcy	1	49	NR	59 *	.2	.3
151 L-D Saints	2	NR	NR	406	1.3	1.9
165 Ch of Nazarene	1	60	17	66	.2	.3
167 Chs of Christ	11	622	649	810	2.5	3.7
185 Cumber Presb	3	137	NR	241	.8	1.1
355 Presb Ch (USA)	5	184	117	221 *	.7	1.0
413 S.D.A.	1	38	NR	45	.1	.2
419 So Bapt Conv	46	14,203	4,031	17,136 *	53.8	78.8
449 Un Methodist	13	1,328	604	1,602 *	5.0	7.4
NELSON	**57**	**8,262**	**3,326**	**24,080 ***	**64.3**	**100.0**
019 Amer Bapt USA	1	17	12	22 *	.1	.1
053 Assemb of God	2	113	113	147	.4	.6
081 Catholic	9	NR	NR	12,516	33.4	52.0
093 Chr Ch (Disc)	5	910	344	1,158 *	3.1	4.8
097 Chr Chs&Chs Cr	4	545	NR	693 *	1.8	2.9
127 Ch God (Cleve)	2	346	141	440 *	1.2	1.8
145 Ch God Prophcy	1	49	NR	63 *	.2	.3
151 L-D Saints	2	NR	NR	917	2.4	3.8
167 Chs of Christ	4	239	252	311	.8	1.3
193 Episcopal	1	NR	44	130	.3	.5
283 Luth—MO Synod	1	23	15	25	.1	.1
355 Presb Ch (USA)	2	116	63	147 *	.4	.6
419 So Bapt Conv	17	4,965	1,943	6,316 *	16.9	26.2
449 Un Methodist	6	939	399	1,195 *	3.2	5.0
NICHOLAS	**21**	**2,748**	**707**	**3,453 ***	**50.7**	**100.0**
053 Assemb of God	1	98	115	150	2.2	4.3
081 Catholic	1	NR	NR	70	1.0	2.0
093 Chr Ch (Disc)	3	191	49	233 *	3.4	6.7
097 Chr Chs&Chs Cr	4	843	NR	1,028 *	15.1	29.8
167 Chs of Christ	1	28	30	36	.5	1.0
355 Presb Ch (USA)	1	54	35	66 *	1.0	1.9
419 So Bapt Conv	3	703	188	857 *	12.6	24.8
449 Un Methodist	7	831	290	1,013 *	14.9	29.3
OHIO	**86**	**12,081**	**4,722**	**15,244 ***	**66.5**	**100.0**
053 Assemb of God	1	51	70	100	.4	.7
081 Catholic	2	NR	NR	251	1.1	1.6
097 Chr Chs&Chs Cr	2	501	NR	617 *	2.7	4.0
127 Ch God (Cleve)	4	411	267	506 *	2.2	3.3
145 Ch God Prophcy	4	197	NR	244 *	1.1	1.6
151 L-D Saints	1	NR	NR	90	.4	.6
167 Chs of Christ	7	500	417	577	2.5	3.8
185 Cumber Presb	2	61	NR	108	.5	.7
355 Presb Ch (USA)	1	9	8	11 *	-	.1
413 S.D.A.	1	65	NR	77	.3	.5
419 So Bapt Conv	44	9,048	3,471	11,137 *	48.6	73.1
449 Un Methodist	17	1,238	489	1,526 *	6.7	10.0
OLDHAM	**44**	**12,045**	**4,668**	**25,776 ***	**55.8**	**100.0**
053 Assemb of God	2	309	181	380	.8	1.5
056 Baha'i	0	8	NR	8	-	-
081 Catholic	3	NR	NR	9,897	21.4	38.4
084 Calvary Chapel	1	NR	NR	NR	-	-
093 Chr Ch (Disc)	2	488	202	618 *	1.3	2.4
097 Chr Chs&Chs Cr	3	215	NR	272 *	.6	1.1

NR–Not Reported *Total adherents estimated from known number of communicant, confirmed, full members. - Represents a percentage less than 0.1. Percentages may not total 100 due to rounding.

Table 4: Religious Congregations by County and Group: 2000

Religious Group	Number of Churches, Synagogues, Mosques, or Temples	Number of Communicant, Confirmed, or Full Members	Number of Attendees	Total Adherents: Number of Adherents	Total Adherents: % of Total Pop.	Total Adherents: % of Total Adh.
127 Ch God (Cleve)	1	100	18	127 *	.3	.5
151 L-D Saints	2	NR	NR	519	1.1	2.0
165 Ch of Nazarene	1	32	34	50	.1	.2
167 Chs of Christ	3	97	115	128	.3	.5
193 Episcopal	1	NR	51	92	.2	.4
207 E.L.C.A.	1	87	69	120	.3	.5
283 Luth—MO Synod	1	130	71	195	.4	.8
355 Presb Ch (USA)	2	606	306	767 *	1.7	3.0
413 S.D.A.	1	227	NR	270	.6	1.0
419 So Bapt Conv	14	6,193	2,254	7,837 *	17.0	30.4
449 Un Methodist	6	3,553	1,367	4,496 *	9.7	17.4
OWEN	**39**	**6,589**	**2,317**	**8,403 ***	**79.7**	**100.0**
053 Assemb of God	2	116	145	155	1.5	1.8
081 Catholic	2	NR	NR	228	2.2	2.7
093 Chr Ch (Disc)	3	210	74	260 *	2.5	3.1
097 Chr Chs&Chs Cr	1	160	NR	198 *	1.9	2.4
167 Chs of Christ	1	20	25	28	.3	.3
339 Pent Ch of God	1	50	NR	55	.5	.7
413 S.D.A.	1	73	NR	87	.8	1.0
419 So Bapt Conv	25	5,748	1,987	7,129 *	67.6	84.8
449 Un Methodist	3	212	86	263 *	2.5	3.1
OWSLEY	**19**	**1,088**	**475**	**1,347 ***	**27.7**	**100.0**
053 Assemb of God	2	39	36	59	1.2	4.4
081 Catholic	1	NR	NR	30	.6	2.2
123 Ch God (Ander)	1	NR	0	0	-	-
127 Ch God (Cleve)	1	62	28	75 *	1.5	5.6
167 Chs of Christ	1	100	25	105	2.2	7.8
355 Presb Ch (USA)	2	195	101	237 *	4.9	17.6
360 Prim Bapt Chrch	2	NR	NR	NR	-	-
419 So Bapt Conv	6	502	149	611 *	12.6	45.4
449 Un Methodist	3	190	136	230 *	4.7	17.1
PENDLETON	**44**	**7,229**	**1,979**	**9,812 ***	**68.2**	**100.0**
053 Assemb of God	1	58	60	60	.4	.6
081 Catholic	2	NR	NR	561	3.9	5.7
093 Chr Ch (Disc)	5	663	113	849 *	5.9	8.7
097 Chr Chs&Chs Cr	8	1,400	NR	1,794 *	12.5	18.3
127 Ch God (Cleve)	1	86	33	110 *	.8	1.1
165 Ch of Nazarene	1	17	14	35	.2	.4
355 Presb Ch (USA)	1	80	40	102 *	.7	1.0
419 So Bapt Conv	19	4,177	1,488	5,351 *	37.2	54.5
449 Un Methodist	5	721	204	923 *	6.4	9.4
467 Wesleyan	1	27	27	27	.2	.3
PERRY	**76**	**8,459**	**2,996**	**10,825 ***	**36.8**	**100.0**
053 Assemb of God	1	24	24	31	.1	.3
071 Brethren (Ash)	1	38	41	46 *	.2	.4
081 Catholic	1	NR	NR	220	.7	2.0
093 Chr Ch (Disc)	1	30	9	37 *	.1	.3
097 Chr Chs&Chs Cr	2	296	NR	362 *	1.2	3.3
123 Ch God (Ander)	1	NR	95	95	.3	.9
127 Ch God (Cleve)	13	1,115	396	1,362 *	4.6	12.6
145 Ch God Prophcy	2	99	NR	120 *	.4	1.1
165 Ch of Nazarene	1	6	25	56	.2	.5
167 Chs of Christ	14	488	522	633	2.2	5.8
183 Cons Menn Conf	2	53	65	77	.3	.7
193 Episcopal	1	NR	13	25	.1	.2
203 Evan Free Ch	2	68	133	133	.5	1.2
258 IndFreeWillBapt	2	118	NR	144 *	.5	1.3
355 Presb Ch (USA)	5	397	226	485 *	1.7	4.5
360 Prim Bapt Chrch	3	NR	NR	NR	-	-
388 Reg Bapt Gen As	1	0	0	0 *	-	-
419 So Bapt Conv	20	5,448	1,340	6,658 *	22.7	61.5
449 Un Methodist	3	279	107	341 *	1.2	3.2
PIKE	**155**	**19,189**	**5,925**	**24,373 ***	**35.5**	**100.0**
053 Assemb of God	2	222	231	261	.4	1.1
056 Baha'i	0	2	NR	2	-	-
081 Catholic	3	NR	NR	384	.6	1.6
089 Chr & Miss Al	3	81	NR	159	.2	.7

Religious Group	Number of Churches, Synagogues, Mosques, or Temples	Number of Communicant, Confirmed, or Full Members	Number of Attendees	Total Adherents: Number of Adherents	Total Adherents: % of Total Pop.	Total Adherents: % of Total Adh.
093 Chr Ch (Disc)	1	285	120	347 *	.5	1.4
097 Chr Chs&Chs Cr	13	2,003	NR	2,440 *	3.5	10.0
123 Ch God (Ander)	5	NR	219	219	.3	.9
127 Ch God (Cleve)	9	626	340	764 *	1.1	3.1
145 Ch God Prophcy	1	49	NR	60 *	.1	.2
157 Ch of Brethren	1	9	6	11 *	-	-
167 Chs of Christ	25	1,402	1,544	1,789	2.6	7.3
193 Episcopal	1	NR	14	21	-	.1
223 Free Will Bapt	13	1,633	NR	1,990 *	2.9	8.2
258 IndFreeWillBapt	25	2,354	NR	2,868 *	4.2	11.8
355 Presb Ch (USA)	6	559	316	681 *	1.0	2.8
360 Prim Bapt Chrch	13	NR	NR	NR	-	-
413 S.D.A.	1	31	NR	37	.1	.2
419 So Bapt Conv	21	8,197	2,368	9,986 *	14.5	41.0
449 Un Methodist	10	1,676	695	2,042 *	3.0	8.4
467 Wesleyan	2	60	72	312	.5	1.3
POWELL	**27**	**2,317**	**1,441**	**3,569 ***	**27.0**	**100.0**
053 Assemb of God	1	23	28	33	.2	.9
076 Buddhism	1	NR	NR	NR	-	-
081 Catholic	1	NR	NR	88	.7	2.5
097 Chr Chs&Chs Cr	2	343	NR	430 *	3.2	12.0
123 Ch God (Ander)	7	NR	591	591	4.5	16.6
127 Ch God (Cleve)	1	199	98	250 *	1.9	7.0
145 Ch God Prophcy	1	49	NR	62 *	.5	1.7
167 Chs of Christ	4	244	256	284	2.1	8.0
355 Presb Ch (USA)	1	201	104	252 *	1.9	7.1
419 So Bapt Conv	4	935	215	1,173 *	8.9	32.9
449 Un Methodist	4	323	149	406 *	3.1	11.4
PULASKI	**155**	**30,919**	**10,025**	**39,005 ***	**69.4**	**100.0**
017 Amer Bapt Assn	16	4,000	NR	4,864 *	8.7	12.5
053 Assemb of God	3	144	158	193	.3	.5
056 Baha'i	0	2	NR	2	-	-
081 Catholic	1	NR	NR	1,026	1.8	2.6
093 Chr Ch (Disc)	2	699	0	850 *	1.5	2.2
097 Chr Chs&Chs Cr	3	335	NR	407 *	.7	1.0
123 Ch God (Ander)	5	NR	233	233	.4	.6
127 Ch God (Cleve)	7	734	406	900 *	1.6	2.3
145 Ch God Prophcy	5	246	NR	300 *	.5	.8
151 L-D Saints	1	NR	NR	167	.3	.4
165 Ch of Nazarene	7	796	538	963	1.7	2.5
167 Chs of Christ	16	686	735	969	1.7	2.5
193 Episcopal	1	NR	80	260	.5	.7
207 E.L.C.A.	1	77	49	89	.2	.2
355 Presb Ch (USA)	2	259	229	315 *	.6	.8
409 Separate Bapt	1	75	NR	91 *	.2	.2
413 S.D.A.	1	79	NR	94	.2	.2
419 So Bapt Conv	65	18,808	5,934	22,878 *	40.7	58.7
443 Un C of Christ	1	11	5	13 *	-	-
449 Un Methodist	15	1,948	936	2,369 *	4.2	6.1
467 Wesleyan	1	20	22	22	-	.1
499 Indep.Non-Char	1	2,000	700	2,000	3.6	5.1
ROBERTSON	**7**	**656**	**157**	**811 ***	**35.8**	**100.0**
053 Assemb of God	1	24	35	35	1.5	4.3
097 Chr Chs&Chs Cr	2	245	NR	301 *	13.3	37.1
419 So Bapt Conv	1	173	45	212 *	9.4	26.1
449 Un Methodist	3	214	77	263 *	11.6	32.4
ROCKCASTLE	**42**	**6,877**	**2,084**	**8,598 ***	**51.9**	**100.0**
053 Assemb of God	2	101	120	229	1.4	2.7
081 Catholic	1	NR	NR	24	.1	.3
097 Chr Chs&Chs Cr	6	875	NR	1,075 *	6.5	12.5
127 Ch God (Cleve)	3	211	82	259 *	1.6	3.0
165 Ch of Nazarene	1	24	32	63	.4	.7
167 Chs of Christ	7	321	293	391	2.4	4.5
419 So Bapt Conv	22	5,345	1,557	6,557 *	39.5	76.3
ROWAN	**31**	**2,554**	**1,694**	**4,949 ***	**22.4**	**100.0**
053 Assemb of God	1	7	7	7	-	.1
056 Baha'i	0	3	NR	3	-	.1

NR–Not Reported   *Total adherents estimated from known number of communicant, confirmed, full members.   - Represents a percentage less than 0.1.   Percentages may not total 100 due to rounding.

Table 4: Religious Congregations by County and Group: 2000

Religious Group	Number of Churches, Synagogues, Mosques, or Temples	Number of Communicant, Confirmed, or Full Members	Number of Attendees	Total Adherents: Number of Adherents	Total Adherents: % of Total Pop.	Total Adherents: % of Total Adh.
081 Catholic	1	NR	NR	440	2.0	8.9
093 Chr Ch (Disc)	1	215	85	255 *	1.2	5.2
097 Chr Chs&Chs Cr	2	145	NR	172 *	.8	3.5
123 Ch God (Ander)	6	NR	904	904	4.1	18.3
127 Ch God (Cleve)	1	75	45	89 *	.4	1.8
151 L-D Saints	1	NR	NR	556	2.5	11.2
165 Ch of Nazarene	1	69	50	69	.3	1.4
167 Chs of Christ	1	42	46	50	.2	1.0
191 Entrpr Bpt Asc	1	35	NR	42 *	.2	.8
193 Episcopal	1	NR	25	31	.1	.6
223 Free Will Bapt	4	503	NR	597 *	2.7	12.1
355 Presb Ch (USA)	1	49	40	58 *	.3	1.2
360 Prim Bapt Chrch	4	NR	NR	NR	-	-
413 S.D.A.	1	48	NR	57	.3	1.2
419 So Bapt Conv	3	730	285	867 *	3.9	17.5
449 Un Methodist	1	633	207	752 *	3.4	15.2
RUSSELL	**64**	**8,046**	**2,787**	**10,172 ***	**62.3**	**100.0**
081 Catholic	1	NR	NR	142	.9	1.4
097 Chr Chs&Chs Cr	4	845	NR	1,020 *	6.3	10.0
127 Ch God (Cleve)	6	562	409	678 *	4.2	6.7
145 Ch God Prophcy	3	148	NR	177 *	1.1	1.7
151 L-D Saints	1	NR	NR	102	.6	1.0
165 Ch of Nazarene	3	198	203	446	2.7	4.4
167 Chs of Christ	4	122	137	157	1.0	1.5
207 E.L.C.A.	1	59	35	73	.4	.7
409 Separate Bapt	13	1,612	NR	1,945 *	11.9	19.1
413 S.D.A.	1	40	NR	48	.3	.5
419 So Bapt Conv	15	3,198	1,348	3,859 *	23.7	37.9
449 Un Methodist	10	1,238	626	1,496 *	9.2	14.7
467 Wesleyan	2	24	29	29	.2	.3
SCOTT	**53**	**9,334**	**3,736**	**13,691 ***	**41.4**	**100.0**
053 Assemb of God	1	498	325	550	1.7	4.0
056 Baha'i	0	2	NR	2	-	-
081 Catholic	2	NR	NR	1,352	4.1	9.9
093 Chr Ch (Disc)	4	1,174	363	1,484 *	4.5	10.8
097 Chr Chs&Chs Cr	6	1,163	NR	1,469 *	4.4	10.7
123 Ch God (Ander)	3	NR	204	204	.6	1.5
127 Ch God (Cleve)	2	186	132	235 *	.7	1.7
151 L-D Saints	1	NR	NR	171	.5	1.2
165 Ch of Nazarene	1	489	231	598	1.8	4.4
167 Chs of Christ	4	119	133	156	.5	1.1
193 Episcopal	1	NR	96	196	.6	1.4
203 Evan Free Ch	1	40	115	115	.3	.8
339 Pent Ch of God	2	95	NR	120	.4	.9
355 Presb Ch (USA)	3	259	141	327 *	1.0	2.4
403 Salvation Army	1	27	17	34	.1	.2
419 So Bapt Conv	15	4,138	1,456	5,232 *	15.8	38.2
449 Un Methodist	6	1,144	523	1,446 *	4.4	10.6
SHELBY	**54**	**13,982**	**4,386**	**18,997 ***	**57.0**	**100.0**
053 Assemb of God	2	110	126	140	.4	.7
056 Baha'i	0	4	NR	4	-	-
081 Catholic	1	NR	NR	1,331	4.0	7.0
093 Chr Ch (Disc)	3	822	280	1,019 *	3.1	5.4
097 Chr Chs&Chs Cr	2	1,065	NR	1,319 *	4.0	6.9
127 Ch God (Cleve)	1	60	38	74 *	.2	.4
145 Ch God Prophcy	1	33	NR	41 *	.1	.2
165 Ch of Nazarene	1	22	13	88	.3	.5
167 Chs of Christ	2	127	128	190	.6	1.0
193 Episcopal	1	NR	47	75	.2	.4
283 Luth—MO Synod	1	118	81	168	.5	.9
355 Presb Ch (USA)	1	330	170	409 *	1.2	2.2
413 S.D.A.	2	65	NR	77	.2	.4
419 So Bapt Conv	27	9,253	2,292	11,465 *	34.4	60.4
449 Un Methodist	7	1,552	618	1,922 *	5.8	10.1
467 Wesleyan	1	71	93	175	.5	.9
498 Indep.Charis.	1	350	500	500	1.5	2.6
SIMPSON	**39**	**7,517**	**3,069**	**9,727 ***	**59.3**	**100.0**
053 Assemb of God	1	36	47	50	.3	.5
056 Baha'i	0	5	NR	5	-	.1
061 Beachy Amish	2	190	NR	240 *	1.5	2.5
081 Catholic	1	NR	NR	238	1.5	2.4
145 Ch God Prophcy	1	49	NR	62 *	.4	.6
165 Ch of Nazarene	1	54	43	99	.6	1.0
167 Chs of Christ	8	909	773	1,106	6.7	11.4
207 E.L.C.A.	1	101	44	137	.8	1.4
320 "Old" MB Ascs	2	136	NR	172 *	1.0	1.8
355 Presb Ch (USA)	2	185	109	233 *	1.4	2.4
413 S.D.A.	1	48	NR	57	.3	.6
419 So Bapt Conv	13	4,867	1,671	6,145 *	37.5	63.2
449 Un Methodist	6	937	382	1,183 *	7.2	12.2
SPENCER	**20**	**3,576**	**1,167**	**5,100 ***	**43.3**	**100.0**
053 Assemb of God	1	100	85	146	1.2	2.9
056 Baha'i	0	1	NR	1	-	-
081 Catholic	1	NR	NR	545	4.6	10.7
093 Chr Ch (Disc)	1	111	49	141 *	1.2	2.8
097 Chr Chs&Chs Cr	4	582	NR	738 *	6.3	14.5
145 Ch God Prophcy	1	49	NR	63 *	.5	1.2
167 Chs of Christ	1	51	55	62	.5	1.2
419 So Bapt Conv	10	2,582	913	3,277 *	27.9	64.3
449 Un Methodist	1	100	65	127 *	1.1	2.5
TAYLOR	**67**	**12,589**	**4,738**	**16,957 ***	**74.0**	**100.0**
053 Assemb of God	1	13	18	23	.1	.1
056 Baha'i	0	3	NR	3	-	-
075 Brethren in Cr	1	38	36	38	.2	.2
081 Catholic	2	NR	NR	1,168	5.1	6.9
097 Chr Chs&Chs Cr	4	865	NR	1,052 *	4.6	6.2
123 Ch God (Ander)	3	NR	323	323	1.4	1.9
165 Ch of Nazarene	1	40	44	44	.2	.3
167 Chs of Christ	3	160	180	227	1.0	1.3
185 Cumber Presb	4	296	NR	493	2.2	2.9
207 E.L.C.A.	1	0	0	0	-	-
322 Old Ord Menn Ch	1	37	NR	45 *	.2	.3
323 Old Ord Amish	1	55	NR	67 *	.3	.4
355 Presb Ch (USA)	1	166	72	202 *	.9	1.2
360 Prim Bapt Chrch	1	NR	NR	NR	-	-
409 Separate Bapt	4	367	NR	446 *	1.9	2.6
413 S.D.A.	1	11	NR	13	.1	.1
419 So Bapt Conv	24	7,998	2,857	9,724 *	42.4	57.3
449 Un Methodist	13	2,415	1,103	2,937 *	12.8	17.3
463 Vineyard	1	125	105	152 *	.7	.9
TODD	**49**	**5,982**	**2,556**	**7,981 ***	**66.7**	**100.0**
032 Amish; other	4	216	NR	274 *	2.3	3.4
053 Assemb of God	1	70	85	85	.7	1.1
081 Catholic	2	NR	NR	152	1.3	1.9
093 Chr Ch (Disc)	2	187	72	236 *	2.0	3.0
127 Ch God (Cleve)	1	50	5	63 *	.5	.8
151 L-D Saints	1	NR	NR	170	1.4	2.1
165 Ch of Nazarene	1	61	41	163	1.4	2.0
167 Chs of Christ	7	358	380	465	3.9	5.8
185 Cumber Presb	2	24	NR	40	.3	.5
322 Old Ord Menn Ch	1	24	NR	30 *	.3	.4
323 Old Ord Amish	1	75	NR	95 *	.8	1.2
355 Presb Ch (USA)	1	29	15	37 *	.3	.5
419 So Bapt Conv	14	3,874	1,391	4,892 *	40.9	61.3
449 Un Methodist	11	1,014	567	1,279 *	10.7	16.0
TRIGG	**40**	**7,129**	**2,765**	**9,033 ***	**71.7**	**100.0**
081 Catholic	1	NR	NR	338	2.7	3.7
093 Chr Ch (Disc)	2	398	170	485 *	3.9	5.4
097 Chr Chs&Chs Cr	2	273	NR	332 *	2.6	3.7
167 Chs of Christ	2	144	154	187	1.5	2.1
322 Old Ord Menn Ch	1	21	NR	26 *	.2	.3
419 So Bapt Conv	22	5,384	1,977	6,557 *	52.1	72.6
449 Un Methodist	10	909	464	1,108 *	8.8	12.3
TRIMBLE	**21**	**2,926**	**984**	**3,754 ***	**46.2**	**100.0**
053 Assemb of God	1	24	26	33	.4	.9

NR–Not Reported *Total adherents estimated from known number of communicant, confirmed, full members. - Represents a percentage less than 0.1. Percentages may not total 100 due to rounding.

Table 4: Religious Congregations by County and Group: 2000

Religious Group	Number of Churches, Synagogues, Mosques, or Temples	Number of Communicant, Confirmed, or Full Members	Number of Attendees	Total Adherents: Number of Adherents	Total Adherents: % of Total Pop.	Total Adherents: % of Total Adh.
081 Catholic	1	NR	NR	20	.2	.5
093 Chr Ch (Disc)	1	158	56	199 *	2.4	5.3
097 Chr Chs&Chs Cr	2	358	NR	450 *	5.5	12.0
419 So Bapt Conv	8	1,661	526	2,088 *	25.7	55.6
449 Un Methodist	6	675	282	849 *	10.4	22.6
467 Wesleyan	2	50	94	115	1.4	3.1
UNION	**44**	**5,685**	**1,762**	**10,662 ***	**68.2**	**100.0**
053 Assemb of God	1	83	112	150	1.0	1.4
056 Baha'i	0	1	NR	1	-	-
081 Catholic	6	NR	NR	3,593	23.0	33.7
093 Chr Ch (Disc)	1	99	78	120 *	.8	1.1
097 Chr Chs&Chs Cr	3	447	NR	544 *	3.5	5.1
145 Ch God Prophcy	2	99	NR	120 *	.8	1.1
167 Chs of Christ	5	196	205	242	1.5	2.3
185 Cumber Presb	2	153	NR	264	1.7	2.5
193 Episcopal	1	NR	10	25	.2	.2
355 Presb Ch (USA)	2	58	45	71 *	.5	.7
419 So Bapt Conv	16	4,031	1,105	4,902 *	31.3	46.0
449 Un Methodist	5	518	207	630 *	4.0	5.9
WARREN	**144**	**35,118**	**18,516**	**48,223 ***	**52.1**	**100.0**
053 Assemb of God	3	264	431	381	.4	.8
056 Baha'i	0	13	NR	13	-	-
059 Bapt Miss Assn	1	97	71	118 *	.1	.2
081 Catholic	2	NR	NR	3,603	3.9	7.5
084 Calvary Chapel	1	NR	NR	NR	-	-
089 Chr & Miss Al	2	35	NR	90	.1	.2
093 Chr Ch (Disc)	3	800	299	973 *	1.1	2.0
097 Chr Chs&Chs Cr	5	409	NR	498 *	.5	1.0
123 Ch God (Ander)	1	NR	20	20	-	-
127 Ch God (Cleve)	2	154	90	187 *	.2	.4
145 Ch God Prophcy	1	49	NR	60 *	.1	.1
151 L-D Saints	2	NR	NR	702	.8	1.5
165 Ch of Nazarene	3	390	217	444	.5	.9
167 Chs of Christ	24	3,240	3,092	4,032	4.4	8.4
185 Cumber Presb	2	228	NR	500	.5	1.0
193 Episcopal	1	NR	296	666	.7	1.4
207 E.L.C.A.	1	43	25	49	.1	.1
221 Free Methodist	3	96	117	133	.1	.3
223 Free Will Bapt	2	251	NR	306 *	.3	.6
283 Luth—MO Synod	1	412	334	555	.6	1.2
320 "Old" MB Ascs	6	1,327	NR	1,615 *	1.7	3.3
355 Presb Ch (USA)	6	964	451	1,173 *	1.3	2.4
403 Salvation Army	1	151	82	202	.2	.4
413 S.D.A.	3	264	NR	314	.3	.7
419 So Bapt Conv	46	21,213	10,860	25,812 *	27.9	53.5
435 Unitarian-Univ	1	47	NR	57 *	.1	.1
449 Un Methodist	19	4,471	1,931	5,440 *	5.9	11.3
496 Jewish Est	1	NR	NR	50	.1	.1
499 Indep.Non-Char	1	200	200	230	.2	.5
WASHINGTON	**36**	**5,030**	**1,549**	**11,414 ***	**104.6**	**100.0**
081 Catholic	5	NR	NR	5,226	47.9	45.8
097 Chr Chs&Chs Cr	4	745	NR	916 *	8.4	8.0
127 Ch God (Cleve)	2	145	84	178 *	1.6	1.6
145 Ch God Prophcy	1	49	NR	61 *	.6	.5
167 Chs of Christ	3	131	136	163	1.5	1.4
323 Old Ord Amish	1	55	NR	68 *	.6	.6
355 Presb Ch (USA)	2	103	76	126 *	1.2	1.1
419 So Bapt Conv	14	3,541	1,094	4,355 *	39.9	38.2
449 Un Methodist	4	261	159	321 *	2.9	2.8
WAYNE	**49**	**9,861**	**2,770**	**12,492 ***	**62.7**	**100.0**
032 Amish; other	1	63	NR	78 *	.4	.6
053 Assemb of God	1	130	85	120	.6	1.0
056 Baha'i	0	2	NR	2	-	-
081 Catholic	1	NR	NR	100	.5	.8
097 Chr Chs&Chs Cr	2	375	NR	465 *	2.3	3.7
123 Ch God (Ander)	1	NR	110	110	.6	.9
127 Ch God (Cleve)	1	189	12	234 *	1.2	1.9
151 L-D Saints	1	NR	NR	54	.3	.4
165 Ch of Nazarene	1	188	142	280	1.4	2.2
167 Chs of Christ	5	228	243	293	1.5	2.3
409 Separate Bapt	2	194	NR	240 *	1.2	1.9
419 So Bapt Conv	24	7,512	1,828	9,302 *	46.7	74.5
449 Un Methodist	9	980	350	1,214 *	6.1	9.7
WEBSTER	**44**	**6,545**	**2,328**	**8,257 ***	**58.5**	**100.0**
053 Assemb of God	1	59	78	78	.6	.9
061 Beachy Amish	1	31	NR	38 *	.3	.5
081 Catholic	2	NR	NR	173	1.2	2.1
093 Chr Ch (Disc)	3	266	115	325 *	2.3	3.9
145 Ch God Prophcy	2	99	NR	120 *	.8	1.5
167 Chs of Christ	4	330	342	410	2.9	5.0
185 Cumber Presb	4	137	NR	233	1.7	2.8
360 Prim Bapt Chrch	3	NR	NR	NR	-	-
419 So Bapt Conv	17	4,392	1,205	5,374 *	38.1	65.1
449 Un Methodist	7	1,231	588	1,506 *	10.7	18.2
WHITLEY	**87**	**19,624**	**5,764**	**24,516 ***	**68.4**	**100.0**
053 Assemb of God	1	20	24	24	.1	.1
081 Catholic	1	NR	NR	130	.4	.5
093 Chr Ch (Disc)	2	466	102	581 *	1.6	2.4
097 Chr Chs&Chs Cr	6	1,026	NR	1,281 *	3.6	5.2
127 Ch God (Cleve)	6	1,184	639	1,476 *	4.1	6.0
145 Ch God Prophcy	1	49	NR	61 *	.2	.2
167 Chs of Christ	3	283	310	358	1.0	1.5
320 "Old" MB Ascs	1	200	NR	250 *	.7	1.0
355 Presb Ch (USA)	1	142	83	177 *	.5	.7
413 S.D.A.	1	33	NR	39	.1	.2
419 So Bapt Conv	56	15,038	4,013	18,761 *	52.3	76.5
449 Un Methodist	7	788	403	983 *	2.7	4.0
499 Indep.Non-Char	1	395	190	395	1.1	1.6
WOLFE	**10**	**693**	**562**	**1,123 ***	**15.9**	**100.0**
056 Baha'i	0	2	NR	2	-	.2
081 Catholic	1	NR	NR	23	.3	2.0
093 Chr Ch (Disc)	1	84	34	104 *	1.5	9.3
123 Ch God (Ander)	3	NR	239	239	3.4	21.3
127 Ch God (Cleve)	1	59	10	73 *	1.0	6.5
167 Chs of Christ	1	45	48	58	.8	5.2
419 So Bapt Conv	1	291	125	361 *	5.1	32.1
449 Un Methodist	2	212	106	263 *	3.7	23.4
WOODFORD	**40**	**8,857**	**3,566**	**13,725 ***	**59.1**	**100.0**
053 Assemb of God	3	273	355	518	2.2	3.8
081 Catholic	1	NR	NR	1,619	7.0	11.8
093 Chr Ch (Disc)	4	833	286	1,034 *	4.5	7.5
097 Chr Chs&Chs Cr	2	475	NR	589 *	2.5	4.3
127 Ch God (Cleve)	1	107	48	133 *	.6	1.0
145 Ch God Prophcy	1	49	NR	61 *	.3	.4
151 L-D Saints	1	NR	NR	360	1.6	2.6
165 Ch of Nazarene	2	105	90	193	.8	1.4
167 Chs of Christ	3	151	163	185	.8	1.3
193 Episcopal	1	NR	199	471	2.0	3.4
339 Pent Ch of God	1	41	NR	91	.4	.7
355 Presb Ch (USA)	4	873	522	1,083 *	4.7	7.9
419 So Bapt Conv	11	4,461	1,446	5,539 *	23.9	40.4
449 Un Methodist	5	1,489	457	1,849 *	8.0	13.5

LOUISIANA

Religious Group	Number of Churches, Synagogues, Mosques, or Temples	Number of Communicant, Confirmed, or Full Members	Number of Attendees	Total Adherents: Number of Adherents	Total Adherents: % of Total Pop.	Total Adherents: % of Total Adh.
The State.....	4,158	900,511	358,469	2,627,028 *	58.8	100.0
ACADIA	**55**	**5,469**	**2,812**	**47,698 ***	**81.0**	**100.0**
053 Assemb of God	3	932	1,042	1,523	2.6	3.2
056 Baha'i	0	3	NR	3	-	-
081 Catholic	21	NR	NR	40,026	68.0	83.9
093 Chr Ch (Disc)	1	27	14	35 *	.1	.1
097 Chr Chs&Chs Cr	2	185	NR	240 *	.4	.5
127 Ch God (Cleve)	1	39	30	51 *	.1	.1
151 L-D Saints	1	NR	NR	123	.2	.3

NR–Not Reported *Total adherents estimated from known number of communicant, confirmed, full members. - Represents a percentage less than 0.1. Percentages may not total 100 due to rounding.

Table 4: Religious Congregations by County and Group: 2000

Religious Group	Number of Churches, Synagogues, Mosques, or Temples	Number of Communicant, Confirmed, or Full Members	Number of Attendees	Total Adherents: Number of Adherents	% of Total Pop.	% of Total Adh.
165 Ch of Nazarene	3	254	194	337	.6	.7
167 Chs of Christ	2	138	99	179	.3	.4
193 Episcopal	1	NR	60	133	.2	.3
283 Luth—MO Synod	2	151	68	177	.3	.4
355 Presb Ch (USA)	1	81	55	105 *	.2	.2
419 So Bapt Conv	10	2,987	965	3,874 *	6.6	8.1
449 Un Methodist	7	672	285	872 *	1.5	1.8
496 Jewish Est	0	NR	NR	20	-	-
ALLEN	**41**	**6,629**	**2,065**	**12,662 ***	**49.8**	**100.0**
017 Amer Bapt Assn	1	50	NR	62 *	.2	.5
053 Assemb of God	5	176	167	228	.9	1.8
081 Catholic	7	NR	NR	4,339	17.1	34.3
151 L-D Saints	1	NR	NR	57	.2	.5
167 Chs of Christ	3	166	172	236	.9	1.9
193 Episcopal	1	NR	9	9	-	.1
349 Pent Holiness	1	200	200	247 *	1.0	2.0
419 So Bapt Conv	17	5,610	1,364	6,936 *	27.3	54.8
449 Un Methodist	5	427	153	528 *	2.1	4.2
496 Jewish Est	0	NR	NR	20	.1	.2
ASCENSION	**46**	**6,029**	**3,608**	**40,759 ***	**53.2**	**100.0**
053 Assemb of God	2	115	95	128	.2	.3
056 Baha'i	0	11	NR	11	-	-
081 Catholic	14	NR	NR	31,478	41.1	77.2
151 L-D Saints	1	NR	NR	523	.7	1.3
167 Chs of Christ	2	120	85	147	.2	.4
193 Episcopal	1	NR	29	68	.1	.2
263 Int Foursq Gos	1	34	45	45 *	.1	.1
283 Luth—MO Synod	1	109	53	149	.2	.4
339 Pent Ch of God	1	45	NR	84	.1	.2
355 Presb Ch (USA)	1	55	38	72 *	.1	.2
413 S.D.A.	1	85	NR	101	.1	.2
419 So Bapt Conv	12	4,148	1,801	5,405 *	7.1	13.3
449 Un Methodist	8	1,307	637	1,703 *	2.2	4.2
496 Jewish Est	0	NR	NR	20	-	-
498 Indep.Charis.	1	0	825	825	1.1	2.0
ASSUMPTION	**17**	**680**	**401**	**19,188 ***	**82.0**	**100.0**
053 Assemb of God	1	116	147	155	.7	.8
081 Catholic	9	NR	NR	18,312	78.3	95.4
145 Ch God Prophcy	1	27	NR	35 *	.1	.2
419 So Bapt Conv	3	275	113	351 *	1.5	1.8
449 Un Methodist	3	262	141	335 *	1.4	1.7
AVOYELLES	**49**	**3,888**	**1,322**	**24,226 ***	**58.4**	**100.0**
017 Amer Bapt Assn	1	50	NR	63 *	.2	.3
056 Baha'i	0	3	NR	3	-	-
081 Catholic	22	NR	NR	19,280	46.5	79.6
165 Ch of Nazarene	1	106	92	130	.3	.5
167 Chs of Christ	1	51	55	67	.2	.3
193 Episcopal	1	NR	27	75	.2	.3
283 Luth—MO Synod	1	30	20	35	.1	.1
419 So Bapt Conv	14	3,107	920	3,894 *	9.4	16.1
449 Un Methodist	8	541	208	679 *	1.6	2.8
BEAUREGARD	**60**	**12,039**	**4,165**	**17,869 ***	**54.2**	**100.0**
017 Amer Bapt Assn	1	59	NR	75 *	.2	.4
053 Assemb of God	2	47	29	100	.3	.6
081 Catholic	4	NR	NR	2,224	6.7	12.4
143 CG in Cr(Menn)	1	238	NR	302 *	.9	1.7
151 L-D Saints	1	NR	NR	135	.4	.8
165 Ch of Nazarene	1	71	51	90	.3	.5
167 Chs of Christ	9	499	419	680	2.1	3.8
193 Episcopal	1	NR	46	161	.5	.9
283 Luth—MO Synod	1	101	38	115	.3	.6
355 Presb Ch (USA)	1	47	25	60 *	.2	.3
356 Presb Ch Amer	1	15	30	30	.1	.2
360 Prim Bapt Chrch	1	NR	NR	NR	-	-
413 S.D.A.	1	53	NR	63	.2	.4
419 So Bapt Conv	30	9,876	3,089	12,524 *	38.0	70.1
449 Un Methodist	5	1,033	438	1,310 *	4.0	7.3

Religious Group	Number of Churches, Synagogues, Mosques, or Temples	Number of Communicant, Confirmed, or Full Members	Number of Attendees	Total Adherents: Number of Adherents	% of Total Pop.	% of Total Adh.
BIENVILLE	**46**	**6,523**	**2,102**	**8,251 ***	**52.4**	**100.0**
017 Amer Bapt Assn	3	188	NR	236 *	1.5	2.9
053 Assemb of God	4	200	162	238	1.5	2.9
056 Baha'i	0	2	NR	2	-	-
059 Bapt Miss Assn	2	366	77	459 *	2.9	5.6
081 Catholic	1	NR	NR	88	.6	1.1
167 Chs of Christ	2	73	78	95	.6	1.2
360 Prim Bapt Chrch	1	NR	NR	NR	-	-
365 Prog Prim Bapt	1	64	NR	80 *	.5	1.0
419 So Bapt Conv	25	4,990	1,486	6,253 *	39.7	75.8
449 Un Methodist	7	640	299	800 *	5.1	9.7
BOSSIER	**89**	**31,627**	**11,742**	**49,553 ***	**50.4**	**100.0**
017 Amer Bapt Assn	6	627	NR	801 *	.8	1.6
019 Amer Bapt USA	1	0	0	0 *	-	-
053 Assemb of God	14	957	970	1,832	1.9	3.7
056 Baha'i	0	32	NR	32	-	.1
059 Bapt Miss Assn	2	246	75	314 *	.3	.6
081 Catholic	4	NR	NR	6,941	7.1	14.0
093 Chr Ch (Disc)	1	68	0	87 *	.1	.2
097 Chr Chs&Chs Cr	1	140	NR	179 *	.2	.4
123 Ch God (Ander)	1	NR	80	80	.1	.2
127 Ch God (Cleve)	1	27	18	34 *	-	.1
151 L-D Saints	1	NR	NR	563	.6	1.1
165 Ch of Nazarene	2	80	67	124	.1	.3
167 Chs of Christ	6	877	891	1,200	1.2	2.4
193 Episcopal	1	NR	83	182	.2	.4
263 Int Foursq Gos	1	17	81	81 *	.1	.2
267 Muslim Est	1	NR	156	609	.6	1.2
283 Luth—MO Synod	1	286	190	389	.4	.8
355 Presb Ch (USA)	7	476	333	609 *	.6	1.2
360 Prim Bapt Chrch	1	NR	NR	NR	-	-
370 Ref Baptist Chs	1	NR	NR	NR	-	-
419 So Bapt Conv	25	23,239	7,086	29,645 *	30.2	59.8
449 Un Methodist	10	4,487	1,657	5,725 *	5.8	11.6
467 Wesleyan	1	68	55	126	.1	.3
CADDO	**214**	**91,799**	**34,846**	**142,192 ***	**56.4**	**100.0**
017 Amer Bapt Assn	6	730	NR	916 *	.4	.6
019 Amer Bapt USA	1	0	0	0 *	-	-
034 Ant Orth of NA	1	47	NR	94	-	.1
053 Assemb of God	12	3,735	2,990	6,970	2.8	4.9
056 Baha'i	1	98	NR	98	-	.1
059 Bapt Miss Assn	2	749	325	941 *	.4	.7
081 Catholic	11	NR	NR	15,608	6.2	11.0
093 Chr Ch (Disc)	3	1,110	484	1,394 *	.6	1.0
097 Chr Chs&Chs Cr	4	414	NR	519 *	.2	.4
123 Ch God (Ander)	4	NR	520	520	.2	.4
127 Ch God (Cleve)	1	185	67	232 *	.1	.2
145 Ch God Prophcy	2	54	NR	68 *	-	-
151 L-D Saints	3	NR	NR	1,148	.5	.8
165 Ch of Nazarene	6	757	455	916	.4	.6
167 Chs of Christ	19	2,267	1,991	2,971	1.2	2.1
186 Coptic Orth Ch	1	NR	NR	NR	-	-
193 Episcopal	5	NR	1,726	3,950	1.6	2.8
207 E.L.C.A.	3	559	279	763	.3	.5
221 Free Methodist	1	0	45	45	-	-
223 Free Will Bapt	1	17	NR	21 *	-	-
246 Greek Orthodox	1	NR	NR	516	.2	.4
263 Int Foursq Gos	1	219	104	275 *	.1	.2
267 Muslim Est	2	NR	312	1,218	.5	.9
283 Luth—MO Synod	4	599	309	745	.3	.5
355 Presb Ch (USA)	7	1,763	910	2,214 *	.9	1.6
356 Presb Ch Amer	1	69	53	82	-	.1
360 Prim Bapt Chrch	2	NR	NR	NR	-	-
403 Salvation Army	1	259	66	1,236	.5	.9
413 S.D.A.	4	738	NR	878	.3	.6
418 Southw Bapt Fel	1	NR	NR	NR	-	-
419 So Bapt Conv	65	59,331	17,066	74,497 *	29.5	52.4
435 Unitarian-Univ	1	167	NR	210 *	.1	.1
449 Un Methodist	34	14,792	5,026	18,571 *	7.4	13.1
463 Vineyard	1	140	118	176 *	.1	.1
496 Jewish Est	1	NR	NR	400	.2	.3

NR–Not Reported *Total adherents estimated from known number of communicant, confirmed, full members. - Represents a percentage less than 0.1. Percentages may not total 100 due to rounding.

Table 4: Religious Congregations by County and Group: 2000

Religious Group	Number of Churches, Synagogues, Mosques, or Temples	Number of Communicant, Confirmed, or Full Members	Number of Attendees	Total Adherents		
				Number of Adherents	% of Total Pop.	% of Total Adh.
498 Indep.Charis.	1	3,000	2,000	4,000	1.6	2.8
CALCASIEU	**157**	**43,584**	**18,003**	**119,734 ***	**65.2**	**100.0**
017 Amer Bapt Assn	1	50	NR	63 *	-	.1
019 Amer Bapt USA	1	0	0	0 *	-	-
034 Ant Orth of NA	1	30	NR	60	-	.1
053 Assemb of God	9	2,183	2,642	3,593	2.0	3.0
056 Baha'i	0	59	NR	59	-	-
081 Catholic	27	NR	NR	59,826	32.6	50.0
089 Chr & Miss Al	1	0	NR	130	.1	.1
093 Chr Ch (Disc)	2	524	161	662 *	.4	.6
097 Chr Chs&Chs Cr	2	300	NR	379 *	.2	.3
123 Ch God (Ander)	5	NR	599	599	.3	.5
127 Ch God (Cleve)	2	106	6	134 *	.1	.1
151 L-D Saints	3	NR	NR	827	.5	.7
157 Ch of Brethren	1	90	0	114 *	.1	.1
165 Ch of Nazarene	4	260	157	335	.2	.3
167 Chs of Christ	9	1,206	1,040	1,634	.9	1.4
173 Comm of Christ	1	71	NR	71	-	.1
193 Episcopal	6	NR	770	1,758	1.0	1.5
207 E.L.C.A.	1	143	50	176	.1	.1
267 Muslim Est	1	NR	101	288	.2	.2
283 Luth—MO Synod	3	465	253	567	.3	.5
349 Pent Holiness	1	100	100	126 *	.1	.1
355 Presb Ch (USA)	3	576	256	728 *	.4	.6
356 Presb Ch Amer	1	116	100	146	.1	.1
388 Reg Bapt Gen As	1	20	15	25 *	-	-
403 Salvation Army	1	145	42	331	.2	.3
413 S.D.A.	2	295	NR	351	.2	.3
419 So Bapt Conv	48	29,392	8,570	37,125 *	20.2	31.0
443 Un C of Christ	1	62	27	78 *	-	.1
449 Un Methodist	16	6,796	2,619	8,585 *	4.7	7.2
463 Vineyard	1	130	120	164 *	.1	.1
496 Jewish Est	1	NR	NR	200	.1	.2
498 Indep.Charis.	1	465	375	600	.3	.5
CALDWELL	**27**	**3,849**	**1,336**	**4,905 ***	**46.4**	**100.0**
053 Assemb of God	2	32	38	38	.4	.8
081 Catholic	1	NR	NR	71	.7	1.4
123 Ch God (Ander)	2	NR	75	75	.7	1.5
127 Ch God (Cleve)	2	152	92	188 *	1.8	3.8
167 Chs of Christ	1	42	45	55	.5	1.1
360 Prim Bapt Chrch	1	NR	NR	NR	-	-
419 So Bapt Conv	15	3,301	951	4,080 *	38.6	83.2
449 Un Methodist	3	322	135	398 *	3.8	8.1
CAMERON	**18**	**1,636**	**330**	**6,878 ***	**68.8**	**100.0**
056 Baha'i	0	1	NR	1	-	-
081 Catholic	10	NR	NR	4,803	48.1	69.8
419 So Bapt Conv	5	1,454	278	1,844 *	18.5	26.8
449 Un Methodist	3	181	52	230 *	2.3	3.3
CATAHOULA	**31**	**3,961**	**1,320**	**5,048 ***	**46.2**	**100.0**
053 Assemb of God	1	10	10	11	.1	.2
081 Catholic	1	NR	NR	130	1.2	2.6
123 Ch God (Ander)	1	NR	43	43	.4	.9
167 Chs of Christ	1	10	10	10	.1	.2
221 Free Methodist	1	56	41	56	.5	1.1
355 Presb Ch (USA)	1	101	53	125 *	1.1	2.5
419 So Bapt Conv	22	3,541	1,080	4,373 *	40.0	86.6
449 Un Methodist	3	243	83	300 *	2.7	5.9
CLAIBORNE	**44**	**5,820**	**2,449**	**7,351 ***	**43.6**	**100.0**
017 Amer Bapt Assn	2	180	NR	223 *	1.3	3.0
053 Assemb of God	2	91	96	104	.6	1.4
056 Baha'i	0	2	NR	2	-	-
081 Catholic	1	NR	NR	80	.5	1.1
123 Ch God (Ander)	1	NR	36	36	.2	.5
167 Chs of Christ	7	299	309	400	2.4	5.4
355 Presb Ch (USA)	3	212	112	263 *	1.6	3.6
360 Prim Bapt Chrch	2	NR	NR	NR	-	-
419 So Bapt Conv	16	3,819	1,400	4,734 *	28.1	64.4
449 Un Methodist	10	1,217	496	1,509 *	9.0	20.5
CONCORDIA	**41**	**7,400**	**2,246**	**10,019 ***	**49.5**	**100.0**
017 Amer Bapt Assn	1	50	NR	63 *	.3	.6
053 Assemb of God	4	171	179	215	1.1	2.1
056 Baha'i	0	1	NR	1	-	-
059 Bapt Miss Assn	1	346	157	439 *	2.2	4.4
081 Catholic	2	NR	NR	413	2.0	4.1
093 Chr Ch (Disc)	2	71	14	90 *	.4	.9
097 Chr Chs&Chs Cr	1	125	NR	158 *	.8	1.6
123 Ch God (Ander)	4	NR	142	142	.7	1.4
127 Ch God (Cleve)	1	70	53	89 *	.4	.9
167 Chs of Christ	2	128	138	180	.9	1.8
193 Episcopal	1	NR	28	66	.3	.7
355 Presb Ch (USA)	2	198	86	251 *	1.2	2.5
419 So Bapt Conv	17	5,770	1,337	7,316 *	36.1	73.0
449 Un Methodist	3	470	112	596 *	2.9	5.9
DE SOTO	**65**	**9,716**	**3,234**	**13,775 ***	**54.0**	**100.0**
017 Amer Bapt Assn	3	250	NR	318 *	1.2	2.3
053 Assemb of God	3	131	119	146	.6	1.1
056 Baha'i	0	26	NR	26	.1	.2
081 Catholic	2	NR	NR	1,250	4.9	9.1
093 Chr Ch (Disc)	1	4	3	5 *	-	-
167 Chs of Christ	5	211	208	283	1.1	2.1
193 Episcopal	1	NR	85	162	.6	1.2
355 Presb Ch (USA)	5	144	108	201 *	.8	1.5
360 Prim Bapt Chrch	2	NR	NR	NR	-	-
413 S.D.A.	1	116	NR	138	.5	1.0
419 So Bapt Conv	28	7,582	2,164	9,652 *	37.9	70.1
449 Un Methodist	14	1,252	547	1,594 *	6.3	11.6
EAST BATON ROUGE	**218**	**80,812**	**39,157**	**217,470 ***	**52.7**	**100.0**
017 Amer Bapt Assn	4	433	NR	543 *	.1	.2
019 Amer Bapt USA	3	1,784	500	2,231 *	.5	1.0
050 Armen Ap Etchm	1	0	NR	200	-	.1
053 Assemb of God	8	667	662	1,370	.3	.6
056 Baha'i	2	133	NR	133	-	.1
059 Bapt Miss Assn	2	912	148	1,141 *	.3	.5
076 Buddhism	3	NR	NR	NR	-	-
081 Catholic	25	NR	NR	95,878	23.2	44.1
093 Chr Ch (Disc)	1	801	184	1,002 *	.2	.5
097 Chr Chs&Chs Cr	3	155	NR	195 *	-	.1
121 Ch God (Abr)	1	17	12	21 *	-	-
123 Ch God (Ander)	3	NR	372	372	.1	.2
127 Ch God (Cleve)	2	890	232	1,113 *	.3	.5
145 Ch God Prophcy	2	54	NR	68 *	-	-
151 L-D Saints	6	NR	NR	1,738	.4	.8
165 Ch of Nazarene	2	274	170	288	.1	.1
167 Chs of Christ	12	1,508	1,451	1,979	.5	.9
173 Comm of Christ	1	89	NR	89	-	-
193 Episcopal	9	NR	1,857	5,477	1.3	2.5
207 E.L.C.A.	2	621	295	803	.2	.4
246 Greek Orthodox	1	NR	NR	0	-	-
252 Hindu	3	NR	NR	NR	-	-
266 Intrstat & Asc	2	151	NR	189 *	-	.1
267 Muslim Est	2	NR	456	1,609	.4	.7
283 Luth—MO Synod	3	1,084	629	1,420	.3	.7
290 Metro Comm Ch	1	60	58	75 *	-	-
349 Pent Holiness	1	140	140	175 *	-	.1
355 Presb Ch (USA)	9	3,346	1,694	4,186 *	1.0	1.9
356 Presb Ch Amer	4	806	570	953	.2	.4
360 Prim Bapt Chrch	2	NR	NR	NR	-	-
403 Salvation Army	1	201	184	230	.1	.1
413 S.D.A.	4	1,016	NR	1,209	.3	.6
419 So Bapt Conv	57	45,106	14,124	56,415 *	13.7	25.9
435 Unitarian-Univ	1	290	NR	363 *	.1	.2
449 Un Methodist	26	18,849	6,193	23,573 *	5.7	10.8
463 Vineyard	2	265	237	332 *	.1	.2
469 WELS	1	60	39	75	-	-
496 Jewish Est	1	NR	NR	800	.2	.4
498 Indep.Charis.	1	0	8,000	10,000	2.4	4.6
499 Indep.Non-Char	4	1,100	950	1,225	.3	.6

NR–Not Reported *Total adherents estimated from known number of communicant, confirmed, full members. - Represents a percentage less than 0.1. Percentages may not total 100 due to rounding.

Table 4: Religious Congregations by County and Group: 2000

Religious Group	Number of Churches, Synagogues, Mosques, or Temples	Number of Communicant, Confirmed, or Full Members	Number of Attendees	Total Adherents		
				Number of Adherents	% of Total Pop.	% of Total Adh.
EAST CARROLL	**19**	**2,863**	**719**	**3,996 ***	**42.4**	**100.0**
053 Assemb of God	1	33	37	66	.7	1.7
081 Catholic	1	NR	NR	170	1.8	4.3
127 Ch God (Cleve)	1	21	21	27 *	.3	.7
143 CG in Cr(Menn)	1	60	NR	78 *	.8	2.0
167 Chs of Christ	1	75	75	100	1.1	2.5
193 Episcopal	1	NR	26	65	.7	1.6
355 Presb Ch (USA)	1	46	24	60 *	.6	1.5
419 So Bapt Conv	10	2,407	443	3,141 *	33.3	78.6
449 Un Methodist	2	221	93	289 *	3.1	7.2
EAST FELICIANA	**32**	**5,660**	**2,062**	**7,426 ***	**34.8**	**100.0**
056 Baha'i	0	2	NR	2	-	-
081 Catholic	1	NR	NR	300	1.4	4.0
167 Chs of Christ	1	45	50	60	.3	.8
193 Episcopal	1	NR	25	133	.6	1.8
283 Luth—MO Synod	1	180	61	210	1.0	2.8
355 Presb Ch (USA)	3	59	46	73 *	.3	1.0
356 Presb Ch Amer	1	66	49	85	.4	1.1
419 So Bapt Conv	11	3,824	1,047	4,728 *	22.1	63.7
449 Un Methodist	13	1,484	784	1,835 *	8.6	24.7
EVANGELINE	**39**	**4,407**	**1,933**	**25,995 ***	**73.4**	**100.0**
053 Assemb of God	2	252	295	305	.9	1.2
056 Baha'i	0	2	NR	2	-	-
081 Catholic	13	NR	NR	20,317	57.3	78.2
097 Chr Chs&Chs Cr	2	93	NR	120 *	.3	.5
167 Chs of Christ	3	221	230	282	.8	1.1
349 Pent Holiness	2	85	85	110 *	.3	.4
419 So Bapt Conv	14	3,708	1,298	4,800 *	13.5	18.5
449 Un Methodist	3	46	25	59 *	.2	.2
FRANKLIN	**52**	**10,918**	**3,017**	**14,177 ***	**66.7**	**100.0**
053 Assemb of God	3	122	135	158	.7	1.1
081 Catholic	1	NR	NR	297	1.4	2.1
097 Chr Chs&Chs Cr	1	78	NR	99 *	.5	.7
165 Ch of Nazarene	1	42	22	61	.3	.4
167 Chs of Christ	2	117	120	154	.7	1.1
193 Episcopal	1	NR	16	24	.1	.2
221 Free Methodist	1	18	13	18	.1	.1
355 Presb Ch (USA)	3	54	43	77 *	.4	.5
419 So Bapt Conv	33	9,804	2,417	12,424 *	58.4	87.6
449 Un Methodist	6	683	251	865 *	4.1	6.1
GRANT	**46**	**7,476**	**2,565**	**10,159 ***	**54.3**	**100.0**
053 Assemb of God	2	64	68	72	.4	.7
081 Catholic	3	NR	NR	486	2.6	4.8
127 Ch God (Cleve)	1	30	5	38 *	.2	.4
167 Chs of Christ	4	186	173	250	1.3	2.5
360 Prim Bapt Chrch	1	NR	NR	NR	-	-
419 So Bapt Conv	27	6,666	2,044	8,532 *	45.6	84.0
449 Un Methodist	7	449	185	574 *	3.1	5.7
467 Wesleyan	1	81	90	187	1.0	1.8
496 Jewish Est	0	NR	NR	20	.1	.2
IBERIA	**39**	**8,214**	**3,808**	**52,025 ***	**71.0**	**100.0**
053 Assemb of God	2	1,377	982	1,453	2.0	2.8
056 Baha'i	0	4	NR	4	-	-
081 Catholic	13	NR	NR	41,130	56.1	79.1
165 Ch of Nazarene	1	61	52	74	.1	.1
167 Chs of Christ	2	201	165	251	.3	.5
193 Episcopal	1	NR	121	469	.6	.9
355 Presb Ch (USA)	1	62	35	81 *	.1	.2
413 S.D.A.	1	32	NR	38	.1	.1
419 So Bapt Conv	6	3,936	961	5,113 *	7.0	9.8
443 Un C of Christ	3	188	102	244 *	.3	.5
449 Un Methodist	7	1,553	490	2,018 *	2.8	3.9
496 Jewish Est	1	NR	NR	250	.3	.5
498 Indep.Charis.	1	800	900	900	1.2	1.7
IBERVILLE	**32**	**2,143**	**908**	**14,109 ***	**42.3**	**100.0**
053 Assemb of God	2	66	66	81	.2	.6
056 Baha'i	0	13	NR	13	-	.1
081 Catholic	9	NR	NR	11,055	33.2	78.4
123 Ch God (Ander)	1	NR	30	30	.1	.2
145 Ch God Prophcy	1	27	NR	34 *	.1	.2
151 L-D Saints	1	NR	NR	148	.4	1.0
167 Chs of Christ	1	12	19	25	.1	.2
193 Episcopal	2	NR	49	174	.5	1.2
419 So Bapt Conv	7	1,400	432	1,748 *	5.2	12.4
449 Un Methodist	8	625	312	781 *	2.3	5.5
496 Jewish Est	0	NR	NR	20	.1	.1
JACKSON	**51**	**7,297**	**2,700**	**9,578 ***	**62.2**	**100.0**
017 Amer Bapt Assn	1	88	NR	108 *	.7	1.1
053 Assemb of God	2	319	316	470	3.1	4.9
081 Catholic	1	NR	NR	250	1.6	2.6
123 Ch God (Ander)	3	NR	158	158	1.0	1.6
151 L-D Saints	1	NR	NR	88	.6	.9
165 Ch of Nazarene	1	7	18	41	.3	.4
167 Chs of Christ	1	80	95	115	.7	1.2
173 Comm of Christ	1	139	NR	139	.9	1.5
185 Cumber Presb	1	50	NR	64	.4	.7
349 Pent Holiness	2	155	145	191 *	1.2	2.0
360 Prim Bapt Chrch	1	NR	NR	NR	-	-
413 S.D.A.	1	12	NR	14	.1	.1
419 So Bapt Conv	26	5,658	1,574	6,968 *	45.3	72.8
449 Un Methodist	9	789	394	972 *	6.3	10.1
JEFFERSON	**181**	**43,648**	**22,591**	**259,013 ***	**56.9**	**100.0**
017 Amer Bapt Assn	1	100	NR	124 *	-	-
034 Ant Orth of NA	1	133	NR	266	.1	.1
053 Assemb of God	15	4,950	4,137	7,471	1.6	2.9
056 Baha'i	1	107	NR	107	-	-
059 Bapt Miss Assn	1	125	60	155 *	-	.1
076 Buddhism	2	NR	NR	NR	-	-
081 Catholic	41	NR	NR	188,862	41.5	72.9
084 Calvary Chapel	1	NR	NR	NR	-	-
093 Chr Ch (Disc)	1	258	150	320 *	.1	.1
123 Ch God (Ander)	1	NR	48	48	-	-
127 Ch God (Cleve)	4	537	293	665 *	.1	.3
145 Ch God Prophcy	3	87	NR	109 *	-	-
151 L-D Saints	9	NR	NR	1,775	.4	.7
165 Ch of Nazarene	1	78	37	78	-	-
167 Chs of Christ	6	699	564	908	.2	.4
185 Cumber Presb	1	56	NR	107	-	-
193 Episcopal	6	NR	906	2,827	.6	1.1
207 E.L.C.A.	4	790	391	1,092	.2	.4
252 Hindu	2	NR	NR	NR	-	-
267 Muslim Est	4	NR	934	2,923	.6	1.1
268 Jain	1	NR	NR	NR	-	-
283 Luth—MO Synod	6	2,238	991	2,151	.5	.8
288 Mennonite USA	2	15	32	32 *	-	-
355 Presb Ch (USA)	7	1,466	710	1,817 *	.4	.7
356 Presb Ch Amer	1	142	175	223	-	.1
403 Salvation Army	1	165	65	368	.1	.1
413 S.D.A.	4	570	NR	679	.1	.3
419 So Bapt Conv	30	25,070	7,894	31,077 *	6.8	12.0
425 Tao	1	NR	NR	NR	-	-
443 Un C of Christ	4	649	244	805 *	.2	.3
449 Un Methodist	13	4,513	1,514	5,596 *	1.2	2.2
463 Vineyard	1	900	800	1,116 *	.2	.4
467 Wesleyan	1	0	46	112	-	-
496 Jewish Est	2	NR	NR	2,800	.6	1.1
498 Indep.Charis.	1	0	1,700	3,500	.8	1.4
499 Indep.Non-Char	1	0	900	900	.2	.3
JEFFERSON DAVIS	**40**	**5,330**	**1,617**	**21,900 ***	**69.7**	**100.0**
017 Amer Bapt Assn	1	23	NR	30 *	.1	.1
053 Assemb of God	2	169	149	192	.6	.9
056 Baha'i	0	1	NR	1	-	-
081 Catholic	13	NR	NR	15,027	47.8	68.6

NR–Not Reported   *Total adherents estimated from known number of communicant, confirmed, full members.   - Represents a percentage less than 0.1.   Percentages may not total 100 due to rounding.

Table 4: Religious Congregations by County and Group: 2000

Religious Group	Number of Churches, Synagogues, Mosques, or Temples	Number of Communicant, Confirmed, or Full Members	Number of Attendees	Total Adherents: Number of Adherents	Total Adherents: % of Total Pop.	Total Adherents: % of Total Adh.
097 Chr Chs&Chs Cr	1	175	NR	225 *	.7	1.0
157 Ch of Brethren	1	81	56	104 *	.3	.5
193 Episcopal	1	NR	19	33	.1	.2
283 Luth—MO Synod	1	75	0	99	.3	.5
355 Presb Ch (USA)	2	109	54	140 *	.4	.6
413 S.D.A.	1	25	NR	30	.1	.1
419 So Bapt Conv	9	3,560	958	4,586 *	14.6	20.9
449 Un Methodist	8	1,112	381	1,433 *	4.6	6.5
LAFAYETTE	**81**	**19,902**	**9,098**	**150,877 ***	**79.2**	**100.0**
034 Ant Orth of NA	1	51	NR	102	.1	.1
053 Assemb of God	5	1,685	1,658	2,038	1.1	1.4
056 Baha'i	1	77	NR	77	-	.1
081 Catholic	30	NR	NR	122,385	64.2	81.1
093 Chr Ch (Disc)	1	100	80	127 *	.1	.1
097 Chr Chs&Chs Cr	1	90	NR	114 *	.1	.1
123 Ch God (Ander)	1	NR	9	9	-	-
127 Ch God (Cleve)	1	145	60	184 *	.1	.1
151 L-D Saints	1	NR	NR	631	.3	.4
165 Ch of Nazarene	1	45	38	48	-	-
167 Chs of Christ	3	529	465	728	.4	.5
186 Coptic Orth Ch	1	NR	NR	NR	-	-
193 Episcopal	3	NR	589	1,714	.9	1.1
207 E.L.C.A.	1	328	199	529	.3	.4
267 Muslim Est	1	NR	156	609	.3	.4
283 Luth—MO Synod	2	226	123	314	.2	.2
349 Pent Holiness	1	1,100	1,100	1,392 *	.7	.9
355 Presb Ch (USA)	3	703	354	890 *	.5	.6
356 Presb Ch Amer	1	31	30	32	-	-
403 Salvation Army	1	49	35	280	.1	.2
413 S.D.A.	2	96	NR	114	.1	.1
419 So Bapt Conv	12	9,763	2,490	12,358 *	6.5	8.2
435 Unitarian-Univ	1	12	NR	15 *	-	-
449 Un Methodist	5	4,722	1,562	5,977 *	3.1	4.0
463 Vineyard	1	150	150	190 *	.1	.1
496 Jewish Est	0	NR	NR	20	-	-
LAFOURCHE	**52**	**6,146**	**2,812**	**75,595 ***	**84.0**	**100.0**
053 Assemb of God	4	578	728	875	1.0	1.2
056 Baha'i	0	144	NR	144	.2	.2
081 Catholic	19	NR	NR	67,301	74.8	89.0
151 L-D Saints	1	NR	NR	60	.1	.1
167 Chs of Christ	3	91	90	90	.1	.1
193 Episcopal	2	NR	149	391	.4	.5
263 Int Foursq Gos	1	31	34	39 *	-	.1
355 Presb Ch (USA)	4	338	193	426 *	.5	.6
413 S.D.A.	1	100	NR	119	.1	.2
419 So Bapt Conv	10	3,296	832	4,157 *	4.6	5.5
449 Un Methodist	6	1,168	501	1,473 *	1.6	1.9
496 Jewish Est	0	NR	NR	20	-	-
499 Indep.Non-Char	1	400	285	500	.6	.7
LA SALLE	**53**	**10,086**	**3,529**	**12,553 ***	**87.9**	**100.0**
053 Assemb of God	3	344	360	492	3.4	3.9
081 Catholic	2	NR	NR	92	.6	.7
127 Ch God (Cleve)	1	33	18	41 *	.3	.3
165 Ch of Nazarene	2	81	55	91	.6	.7
167 Chs of Christ	2	101	108	131	.9	1.0
221 Free Methodist	4	89	76	121	.8	1.0
419 So Bapt Conv	33	8,770	2,726	10,764 *	75.4	85.7
449 Un Methodist	6	668	186	821 *	5.7	6.5
LINCOLN	**56**	**16,816**	**6,669**	**21,733 ***	**51.1**	**100.0**
017 Amer Bapt Assn	2	176	NR	212 *	.5	1.0
053 Assemb of God	3	212	219	271	.6	1.2
056 Baha'i	0	6	NR	6	-	-
081 Catholic	2	NR	NR	922	2.2	4.2
123 Ch God (Ander)	1	NR	30	30	.1	.1
151 L-D Saints	1	NR	NR	209	.5	1.0
165 Ch of Nazarene	1	27	16	27	.1	.1
167 Chs of Christ	4	265	299	344	.8	1.6
193 Episcopal	2	NR	135	262	.6	1.2
267 Muslim Est	1	NR	45	100	.2	.5
283 Luth—MO Synod	1	18	13	18	-	.1
349 Pent Holiness	1	550	550	660 *	1.6	3.0
355 Presb Ch (USA)	2	393	199	472 *	1.1	2.2
356 Presb Ch Amer	2	83	80	87	.2	.4
419 So Bapt Conv	23	12,152	3,940	14,590 *	34.3	67.1
449 Un Methodist	10	2,934	1,143	3,523 *	8.3	16.2
LIVINGSTON	**102**	**31,735**	**12,170**	**54,243 ***	**59.1**	**100.0**
017 Amer Bapt Assn	2	100	NR	128 *	.1	.2
053 Assemb of God	4	314	294	334	.4	.6
056 Baha'i	0	5	NR	5	-	-
059 Bapt Miss Assn	2	342	89	441 *	.5	.8
081 Catholic	9	NR	NR	13,315	14.5	24.5
121 Ch God (Abr)	1	76	73	98 *	.1	.2
145 Ch God Prophcy	1	27	NR	35 *	-	.1
151 L-D Saints	2	NR	NR	605	.7	1.1
165 Ch of Nazarene	1	26	32	76	.1	.1
167 Chs of Christ	4	181	199	245	.3	.5
193 Episcopal	1	NR	93	181	.2	.3
226 Friends-USA	1	15	NR	19 *	-	-
339 Pent Ch of God	2	25	NR	55	.1	.1
349 Pent Holiness	2	130	130	168 *	.2	.3
355 Presb Ch (USA)	3	114	67	147 *	.2	.3
413 S.D.A.	1	146	NR	174	.2	.3
419 So Bapt Conv	51	24,079	8,039	31,057 *	33.8	57.3
449 Un Methodist	13	3,055	1,304	3,940 *	4.3	7.3
496 Jewish Est	0	NR	NR	20	-	-
498 Indep.Charis.	1	2,500	1,500	2,500	2.7	4.6
499 Indep.Non-Char	1	600	350	700	.8	1.3
MADISON	**14**	**3,705**	**811**	**4,981 ***	**36.3**	**100.0**
017 Amer Bapt Assn	1	88	NR	114 *	.8	2.3
081 Catholic	1	NR	NR	120	.9	2.4
167 Chs of Christ	1	32	30	42	.3	.8
193 Episcopal	1	NR	36	60	.4	1.2
355 Presb Ch (USA)	1	50	26	65 *	.5	1.3
413 S.D.A.	1	41	NR	49	.4	1.0
419 So Bapt Conv	7	3,168	627	4,108 *	29.9	82.5
449 Un Methodist	1	326	92	423 *	3.1	8.5
MOREHOUSE	**71**	**11,262**	**4,660**	**15,564 ***	**50.2**	**100.0**
017 Amer Bapt Assn	5	208	NR	263 *	.8	1.7
053 Assemb of God	6	586	680	1,011	3.3	6.5
056 Baha'i	0	1	NR	1	-	-
059 Bapt Miss Assn	1	158	35	200 *	.6	1.3
081 Catholic	1	NR	NR	365	1.2	2.3
123 Ch God (Ander)	4	NR	217	217	.7	1.4
127 Ch God (Cleve)	3	183	100	231 *	.7	1.5
145 Ch God Prophcy	1	27	NR	34 *	.1	.2
151 L-D Saints	1	NR	NR	146	.5	.9
167 Chs of Christ	3	447	335	554	1.8	3.6
193 Episcopal	3	NR	154	342	1.1	2.2
223 Free Will Bapt	1	17	NR	21 *	.1	.1
339 Pent Ch of God	1	3	NR	12	-	.1
355 Presb Ch (USA)	1	130	85	164 *	.5	1.1
360 Prim Bapt Chrch	1	NR	NR	NR	-	-
419 So Bapt Conv	28	8,481	2,525	10,713 *	34.5	68.8
449 Un Methodist	11	1,021	529	1,290 *	4.2	8.3
NATCHITOCHES	**83**	**11,984**	**3,660**	**20,421 ***	**52.3**	**100.0**
017 Amer Bapt Assn	2	116	NR	144 *	.4	.7
053 Assemb of God	5	432	497	560	1.4	2.7
056 Baha'i	0	11	NR	11	-	.1
059 Bapt Miss Assn	1	156	45	195 *	.5	1.0
081 Catholic	14	NR	NR	4,902	12.5	24.0
151 L-D Saints	1	NR	NR	229	.6	1.1
165 Ch of Nazarene	1	62	67	110	.3	.5
167 Chs of Christ	2	205	150	274	.7	1.3
185 Cumber Presb	1	8	NR	25	.1	.1
193 Episcopal	1	NR	73	107	.3	.5
221 Free Methodist	1	10	16	16	-	.1

NR–Not Reported *Total adherents estimated from known number of communicant, confirmed, full members. - Represents a percentage less than 0.1. Percentages may not total 100 due to rounding.

Table 4: Religious Congregations by County and Group: 2000

Religious Group	Number of Churches, Synagogues, Mosques, or Temples	Number of Communicant, Confirmed, or Full Members	Number of Attendees	Total Adherents: Number of Adherents	Total Adherents: % of Total Pop.	Total Adherents: % of Total Adh.
267 Muslim Est	1	NR	55	163	.4	.8
283 Luth—MO Synod	1	66	53	76	.2	.4
335 Orth Pres Ch	1	0	0	0	-	-
355 Presb Ch (USA)	1	72	60	90 *	.2	.4
413 S.D.A.	2	94	NR	112	.3	.5
419 So Bapt Conv	34	9,010	1,905	11,235 *	28.7	55.0
449 Un Methodist	14	1,742	739	2,172 *	5.6	10.6
ORLEANS	**253**	**45,483**	**22,566**	**213,895 ***	**44.1**	**100.0**
019 Amer Bapt USA	1	350	175	441 *	.1	.2
053 Assemb of God	8	925	638	1,143	.2	.5
056 Baha'i	1	98	NR	98	-	-
076 Buddhism	4	NR	NR	NR	-	-
081 Catholic	69	NR	NR	136,377	28.1	63.8
089 Chr & Miss Al	2	99	NR	104	-	-
093 Chr Ch (Disc)	4	187	67	236 *	-	.1
123 Ch God (Ander)	1	NR	70	70	-	-
127 Ch God (Cleve)	3	132	107	166 *	-	.1
151 L-D Saints	2	NR	NR	327	.1	.2
165 Ch of Nazarene	2	63	48	78	-	-
167 Chs of Christ	6	986	1,002	1,296	.3	.6
186 Coptic Orth Ch	1	NR	NR	NR	-	-
193 Episcopal	12	NR	1,762	6,138	1.3	2.9
203 Evan Free Ch	1	69	125	125	-	.1
207 E.L.C.A.	3	659	296	864	.2	.4
226 Friends-USA	1	15	NR	19 *	-	-
246 Greek Orthodox	1	NR	NR	795	.2	.4
252 Hindu	1	NR	NR	NR	-	-
262 Int Cou Comm Ch	1	100	NR	126 *	-	.1
264 Int Chs of Crst	1	173	285	232	-	.1
267 Muslim Est	6	NR	1,107	4,014	.8	1.9
283 Luth—MO Synod	16	3,182	1,534	3,981	.8	1.9
290 Metro Comm Ch	1	43	40	54 *	-	-
333 Malan Dioc Am	1	NR	NR	125	-	.1
335 Orth Pres Ch	1	10	42	42	-	-
349 Pent Holiness	1	500	600	630 *	.1	.3
355 Presb Ch (USA)	12	2,538	1,334	3,196 *	.7	1.5
356 Presb Ch Amer	2	0	80	80	-	-
360 Prim Bapt Chrch	1	NR	NR	NR	-	-
413 S.D.A.	6	2,820	NR	3,356	.7	1.6
416 Sikh	1	NR	NR	NR	-	-
419 So Bapt Conv	29	22,069	9,149	27,793 *	5.7	13.0
435 Unitarian-Univ	2	215	NR	271 *	.1	.1
443 Un C of Christ	6	1,015	421	1,278 *	.3	.6
449 Un Methodist	34	8,888	3,390	11,193 *	2.3	5.2
463 Vineyard	2	260	240	328 *	.1	.2
469 WELS	1	87	54	119	-	.1
496 Jewish Est	6	NR	NR	8,800	1.8	4.1
OUACHITA	**162**	**56,296**	**21,324**	**83,976 ***	**57.0**	**100.0**
017 Amer Bapt Assn	6	490	NR	624 *	.4	.7
053 Assemb of God	19	2,502	1,747	2,755	1.9	3.3
056 Baha'i	1	32	NR	32	-	-
059 Bapt Miss Assn	2	266	68	339 *	.2	.4
081 Catholic	8	NR	NR	7,846	5.3	9.3
093 Chr Ch (Disc)	1	446	105	567 *	.4	.7
123 Ch God (Ander)	5	NR	361	361	.2	.4
127 Ch God (Cleve)	3	2,120	930	2,697 *	1.8	3.2
151 L-D Saints	2	NR	NR	867	.6	1.0
165 Ch of Nazarene	3	212	131	276	.2	.3
167 Chs of Christ	14	2,120	1,953	3,055	2.1	3.6
173 Comm of Christ	1	188	NR	188	.1	.2
193 Episcopal	4	NR	554	2,212	1.5	2.6
207 E.L.C.A.	1	73	48	91	.1	.1
223 Free Will Bapt	1	17	NR	21 *	-	-
246 Greek Orthodox	1	NR	NR	111	.1	.1
267 Muslim Est	2	NR	202	576	.4	.7
283 Luth—MO Synod	1	215	120	298	.2	.4
355 Presb Ch (USA)	4	949	461	1,207 *	.8	1.4
356 Presb Ch Amer	1	199	250	250	.2	.3
360 Prim Bapt Chrch	1	NR	NR	NR	-	-
403 Salvation Army	1	124	55	167	.1	.2
413 S.D.A.	3	452	NR	538	.4	.6

Religious Group	Number of Churches, Synagogues, Mosques, or Temples	Number of Communicant, Confirmed, or Full Members	Number of Attendees	Total Adherents: Number of Adherents	Total Adherents: % of Total Pop.	Total Adherents: % of Total Adh.
419 So Bapt Conv	54	38,686	11,697	49,215 *	33.4	58.6
449 Un Methodist	21	7,205	2,595	9,163 *	6.2	10.9
467 Wesleyan	1	0	47	120	.1	.1
496 Jewish Est	1	NR	NR	400	.3	.5
PLAQUEMINES	**25**	**2,303**	**856**	**15,066 ***	**56.3**	**100.0**
053 Assemb of God	2	122	129	144	.5	1.0
056 Baha'i	0	21	NR	21	.1	.1
081 Catholic	9	NR	NR	12,078	45.1	80.2
151 L-D Saints	1	NR	NR	51	.2	.3
165 Ch of Nazarene	1	46	24	46	.2	.3
167 Chs of Christ	2	65	85	90	.3	.6
288 Mennonite USA	1	17	27	27 *	.1	.2
413 S.D.A.	1	50	NR	60	.2	.4
419 So Bapt Conv	5	1,650	388	2,122 *	7.9	14.1
449 Un Methodist	3	332	203	427 *	1.6	2.8
POINTE COUPEE	**25**	**1,648**	**706**	**13,902 ***	**61.1**	**100.0**
056 Baha'i	0	1	NR	1	-	-
081 Catholic	8	NR	NR	11,108	48.8	79.9
151 L-D Saints	1	NR	NR	424	1.9	3.0
193 Episcopal	3	NR	112	285	1.3	2.1
419 So Bapt Conv	7	1,438	479	1,802 *	7.9	13.0
449 Un Methodist	6	209	115	262 *	1.2	1.9
496 Jewish Est	0	NR	NR	20	.1	.1
RAPIDES	**190**	**44,603**	**15,869**	**79,537 ***	**63.0**	**100.0**
011 A.W.M.C.	1	0	12	0	-	-
017 Amer Bapt Assn	3	544	NR	685 *	.5	.9
053 Assemb of God	7	817	685	834	.7	1.0
056 Baha'i	0	10	NR	10	-	-
081 Catholic	20	NR	NR	21,089	16.7	26.5
093 Chr Ch (Disc)	1	55	29	69 *	.1	.1
097 Chr Chs&Chs Cr	3	245	NR	308 *	.2	.4
123 Ch God (Ander)	4	NR	188	188	.1	.2
127 Ch God (Cleve)	1	72	34	91 *	.1	.1
145 Ch God Prophcy	1	27	NR	34 *	-	-
151 L-D Saints	2	NR	NR	688	.5	.9
165 Ch of Nazarene	2	133	78	165	.1	.2
167 Chs of Christ	6	514	559	824	.7	1.0
173 Comm of Christ	1	25	NR	25	-	-
193 Episcopal	6	NR	432	1,232	1.0	1.5
216 Evan Presby Ch	1	237	NR	298 *	.2	.4
221 Free Methodist	3	228	171	248	.2	.3
283 Luth—MO Synod	3	372	75	461	.4	.6
335 Orth Pres Ch	1	91	67	135	.1	.2
355 Presb Ch (USA)	3	204	153	257 *	.2	.3
360 Prim Bapt Chrch	2	NR	NR	NR	-	-
403 Salvation Army	1	78	34	124	.1	.2
413 S.D.A.	2	594	NR	707	.6	.9
419 So Bapt Conv	86	34,862	10,733	43,866 *	34.7	55.2
435 Unitarian-Univ	1	10	NR	13 *	-	-
449 Un Methodist	23	4,297	1,733	5,408 *	4.3	6.8
467 Wesleyan	1	0	126	225	.2	.3
469 WELS	1	42	35	57	-	.1
496 Jewish Est	2	NR	NR	350	.3	.4
498 Indep.Charis.	1	800	475	800	.6	1.0
499 Indep.Non-Char	1	346	250	346	.3	.4
RED RIVER	**23**	**3,496**	**1,107**	**4,801 ***	**49.9**	**100.0**
017 Amer Bapt Assn	1	50	NR	64 *	.7	1.3
053 Assemb of God	1	52	20	41	.4	.9
056 Baha'i	0	3	NR	3	-	.1
059 Bapt Miss Assn	1	195	40	250 *	2.6	5.2
081 Catholic	1	NR	NR	210	2.2	4.4
151 L-D Saints	1	NR	NR	142	1.5	3.0
167 Chs of Christ	1	12	13	16	.2	.3
413 S.D.A.	1	92	NR	109	1.1	2.3
418 Southw Bapt Fel	1	NR	NR	NR	-	-
419 So Bapt Conv	11	2,758	882	3,538 *	36.8	73.7
449 Un Methodist	4	334	152	428 *	4.4	8.9

NR–Not Reported   *Total adherents estimated from known number of communicant, confirmed, full members.   - Represents a percentage less than 0.1.   Percentages may not total 100 due to rounding.

Table 4: Religious Congregations by County and Group: 2000

Religious Group	Number of Churches, Synagogues, Mosques, or Temples	Number of Communicant, Confirmed, or Full Members	Number of Attendees	Total Adherents: Number of Adherents	% of Total Pop.	% of Total Adh.
RICHLAND	**58**	**10,253**	**3,734**	**13,436 ***	**64.0**	**100.0**
017 Amer Bapt Assn	1	88	NR	111 *	.5	.8
053 Assemb of God	6	242	254	298	1.4	2.2
081 Catholic	2	NR	NR	305	1.5	2.3
127 Ch God (Cleve)	4	118	85	150 *	.7	1.1
151 L-D Saints	1	NR	NR	96	.5	.7
167 Chs of Christ	5	370	403	499	2.4	3.7
193 Episcopal	1	NR	36	72	.3	.5
355 Presb Ch (USA)	2	26	18	33 *	.2	.2
356 Presb Ch Amer	1	279	235	326	1.6	2.4
419 So Bapt Conv	28	8,217	2,358	10,391 *	49.5	77.3
449 Un Methodist	7	913	345	1,155 *	5.5	8.6
SABINE	**78**	**10,298**	**3,736**	**16,630 ***	**70.9**	**100.0**
053 Assemb of God	2	131	148	200	.9	1.2
056 Baha'i	0	2	NR	2	-	-
081 Catholic	5	NR	NR	3,397	14.5	20.4
123 Ch God (Ander)	1	NR	7	7	-	-
145 Ch God Prophcy	1	27	NR	34 *	.1	.2
151 L-D Saints	1	NR	NR	310	1.3	1.9
165 Ch of Nazarene	4	234	234	333	1.4	2.0
167 Chs of Christ	3	105	96	139	.6	.8
185 Cumber Presb	1	31	NR	45	.2	.3
419 So Bapt Conv	52	9,125	2,953	11,363 *	48.4	68.3
449 Un Methodist	8	643	298	800 *	3.4	4.8
ST. BERNARD	**31**	**3,411**	**1,838**	**38,388 ***	**57.1**	**100.0**
017 Amer Bapt Assn	1	50	NR	62 *	.1	.2
053 Assemb of God	4	460	627	756	1.1	2.0
056 Baha'i	0	2	NR	2	-	-
059 Bapt Miss Assn	1	40	10	49 *	.1	.1
081 Catholic	8	NR	NR	33,407	49.7	87.0
084 Calvary Chapel	1	NR	NR	NR	-	-
127 Ch God (Cleve)	2	139	80	172 *	.3	.4
151 L-D Saints	1	NR	NR	308	.5	.8
167 Chs of Christ	2	77	83	101	.2	.3
193 Episcopal	1	NR	48	136	.2	.4
207 E.L.C.A.	1	505	213	652	1.0	1.7
267 Muslim Est	1	NR	40	100	.1	.3
283 Luth—MO Synod	1	410	141	507	.8	1.3
355 Presb Ch (USA)	2	94	57	116 *	.2	.3
413 S.D.A.	1	50	NR	60	.1	.2
419 So Bapt Conv	3	1,265	439	1,565 *	2.3	4.1
449 Un Methodist	1	319	100	395 *	.6	1.0
ST. CHARLES	**28**	**6,311**	**1,845**	**30,060 ***	**62.5**	**100.0**
017 Amer Bapt Assn	1	39	NR	50 *	.1	.2
049 Armen Ap Cilic	1	0	NR	100	.2	.3
053 Assemb of God	3	297	310	580	1.2	1.9
056 Baha'i	0	17	NR	17	-	.1
081 Catholic	8	NR	NR	21,519	44.8	71.6
167 Chs of Christ	1	93	100	121	.3	.4
193 Episcopal	1	NR	13	83	.2	.3
288 Mennonite USA	1	121	85	157 *	.3	.5
355 Presb Ch (USA)	1	223	98	289 *	.6	1.0
419 So Bapt Conv	7	4,752	907	6,149 *	12.8	20.5
449 Un Methodist	4	769	332	995 *	2.1	3.3
ST. HELENA	**24**	**3,790**	**1,100**	**5,077 ***	**48.2**	**100.0**
056 Baha'i	0	6	NR	6	.1	.1
081 Catholic	2	NR	NR	220	2.1	4.3
419 So Bapt Conv	13	3,097	770	3,971 *	37.7	78.2
449 Un Methodist	9	687	330	880 *	8.4	17.3
ST. JAMES	**14**	**545**	**370**	**14,708 ***	**69.3**	**100.0**
053 Assemb of God	1	115	115	115	.5	.8
056 Baha'i	0	1	NR	1	-	-
081 Catholic	7	NR	NR	14,041	66.2	95.5
419 So Bapt Conv	2	281	120	360 *	1.7	2.4
449 Un Methodist	4	148	135	191 *	.9	1.3
SAINT JOHN THE BAPTIST	**16**	**1,963**	**817**	**24,473 ***	**56.9**	**100.0**
053 Assemb of God	1	69	90	165	.4	.7
056 Baha'i	1	20	NR	20	-	.1
081 Catholic	6	NR	NR	21,543	50.0	88.0
151 L-D Saints	1	NR	NR	237	.6	1.0
167 Chs of Christ	1	50	70	65	.2	.3
193 Episcopal	1	NR	32	53	.1	.2
207 E.L.C.A.	1	131	63	168	.4	.7
355 Presb Ch (USA)	1	20	16	26 *	.1	.1
419 So Bapt Conv	2	1,409	440	1,849 *	4.3	7.6
449 Un Methodist	1	264	106	347 *	.8	1.4
ST. LANDRY	**77**	**6,904**	**2,675**	**67,871 ***	**77.4**	**100.0**
017 Amer Bapt Assn	1	30	NR	39 *	-	.1
053 Assemb of God	1	136	140	140	.2	.2
081 Catholic	35	NR	NR	58,700	66.9	86.5
123 Ch God (Ander)	1	NR	75	75	.1	.1
151 L-D Saints	1	NR	NR	109	.1	.2
167 Chs of Christ	3	118	96	156	.2	.2
193 Episcopal	2	NR	74	120	.1	.2
216 Evan Presby Ch	1	57	NR	73 *	.1	.1
313 N Am Bapt Conf	1	99	80	127 *	.1	.2
349 Pent Holiness	1	75	75	97 *	.1	.1
356 Presb Ch Amer	2	130	81	138	.2	.2
419 So Bapt Conv	19	4,976	1,622	6,405 *	7.3	9.4
449 Un Methodist	9	1,283	432	1,652 *	1.9	2.4
496 Jewish Est	0	NR	NR	40	-	.1
ST. MARTIN	**20**	**1,069**	**311**	**42,374 ***	**87.2**	**100.0**
053 Assemb of God	1	71	81	85	.2	.2
056 Baha'i	0	20	NR	20	-	-
081 Catholic	14	NR	NR	41,007	84.4	96.8
167 Chs of Christ	1	25	15	34	.1	.1
266 Intrstat & Asc	1	111	NR	143 *	.3	.3
419 So Bapt Conv	2	735	165	947 *	1.9	2.2
449 Un Methodist	1	107	50	138 *	.3	.3
ST. MARY	**53**	**7,380**	**2,527**	**34,605 ***	**64.7**	**100.0**
053 Assemb of God	3	474	473	600	1.1	1.7
056 Baha'i	0	2	NR	2	-	-
081 Catholic	16	NR	NR	24,564	45.9	71.0
089 Chr & Miss Al	1	31	NR	91	.2	.3
145 Ch God Prophcy	3	81	NR	105 *	.2	.3
151 L-D Saints	1	NR	NR	149	.3	.4
167 Chs of Christ	3	120	110	164	.3	.5
193 Episcopal	2	NR	91	291	.5	.8
355 Presb Ch (USA)	2	90	54	116 *	.2	.3
419 So Bapt Conv	11	5,105	1,174	6,593 *	12.3	19.1
449 Un Methodist	10	1,347	505	1,742 *	3.3	5.0
463 Vineyard	1	130	120	168 *	.3	.5
496 Jewish Est	0	NR	NR	20	-	.1
ST. TAMMANY	**133**	**35,546**	**16,077**	**107,794 ***	**56.4**	**100.0**
017 Amer Bapt Assn	4	1,048	NR	1,339 *	.7	1.2
053 Assemb of God	7	2,594	1,454	2,474	1.3	2.3
056 Baha'i	2	72	NR	72	-	.1
059 Bapt Miss Assn	2	267	222	341 *	.2	.3
081 Catholic	15	NR	NR	57,336	30.0	53.2
093 Chr Ch (Disc)	2	310	94	396 *	.2	.4
097 Chr Chs&Chs Cr	2	75	NR	96 *	.1	.1
123 Ch God (Ander)	2	NR	129	129	.1	.1
127 Ch God (Cleve)	6	1,000	367	1,277 *	.7	1.2
145 Ch God Prophcy	3	81	NR	105 *	.1	.1
151 L-D Saints	2	NR	NR	1,000	.5	.9
165 Ch of Nazarene	2	216	158	349	.2	.3
167 Chs of Christ	3	500	530	660	.3	.6
193 Episcopal	3	NR	738	2,296	1.2	2.1
203 Evan Free Ch	1	80	250	250	.1	.2
207 E.L.C.A.	2	490	286	656	.3	.6
216 Evan Presby Ch	1	60	NR	77 *	-	.1
266 Intrstat & Asc	7	538	NR	687 *	.4	.6
267 Muslim Est	1	NR	228	841	.4	.8

NR–Not Reported *Total adherents estimated from known number of communicant, confirmed, full members. - Represents a percentage less than 0.1. Percentages may not total 100 due to rounding.

Table 4: Religious Congregations by County and Group: 2000

Religious Group	Number of Churches, Synagogues, Mosques, or Temples	Number of Communicant, Confirmed, or Full Members	Number of Attendees	Total Adherents		
				Number of Adherents	% of Total Pop.	% of Total Adh.
283 Luth—MO Synod	4	1,847	1,125	2,365	1.2	2.2
355 Presb Ch (USA)	5	903	446	1,154 *	.6	1.1
356 Presb Ch Amer	2	76	75	116	.1	.1
413 S.D.A.	4	325	NR	386	.2	.4
419 So Bapt Conv	33	17,238	6,608	22,016 *	11.5	20.4
435 Unitarian-Univ	1	92	NR	118 *	.1	.1
449 Un Methodist	13	7,422	3,140	9,478 *	5.0	8.8
463 Vineyard	2	190	160	243 *	.1	.2
469 WELS	1	122	67	137	.1	.1
496 Jewish Est	1	NR	NR	1,400	.7	1.3
TANGIPAHOA	**120**	**24,260**	**9,470**	**46,726 ***	**46.5**	**100.0**
017 Amer Bapt Assn	5	442	NR	560 *	.6	1.2
053 Assemb of God	4	1,328	1,045	1,657	1.6	3.5
056 Baha'i	0	27	NR	27	-	.1
059 Bapt Miss Assn	3	89	58	113 *	.1	.2
081 Catholic	6	NR	NR	14,543	14.5	31.1
084 Calvary Chapel	1	NR	NR	NR	-	-
093 Chr Ch (Disc)	1	138	58	175 *	.2	.4
121 Ch God (Abr)	1	94	78	119 *	.1	.3
123 Ch God (Ander)	2	NR	105	105	.1	.2
127 Ch God (Cleve)	5	304	222	385 *	.4	.8
145 Ch God Prophcy	2	54	NR	68 *	.1	.1
151 L-D Saints	3	NR	NR	820	.8	1.8
167 Chs of Christ	10	486	464	645	.6	1.4
171 Ch God-Gen Con	1	6	12	12 *	-	-
193 Episcopal	3	NR	151	551	.5	1.2
266 Intrstat & Asc	4	372	NR	472 *	.5	1.0
283 Luth—MO Synod	1	218	88	285	.3	.6
339 Pent Ch of God	1	40	NR	40	-	.1
355 Presb Ch (USA)	3	557	245	706 *	.7	1.5
413 S.D.A.	2	532	NR	634	.6	1.4
419 So Bapt Conv	51	17,603	6,128	22,312 *	22.2	47.8
449 Un Methodist	11	1,970	816	2,497 *	2.5	5.3
TENSAS	**21**	**2,328**	**613**	**3,123 ***	**47.2**	**100.0**
053 Assemb of God	1	28	30	30	.5	1.0
081 Catholic	2	NR	NR	134	2.0	4.3
123 Ch God (Ander)	1	NR	15	15	.2	.5
145 Ch God Prophcy	1	27	NR	34 *	.5	1.1
167 Chs of Christ	2	55	71	80	1.2	2.6
193 Episcopal	2	NR	31	76	1.1	2.4
355 Presb Ch (USA)	2	73	38	91 *	1.4	2.9
419 So Bapt Conv	7	1,901	340	2,360 *	35.7	75.6
449 Un Methodist	3	244	88	303 *	4.6	9.7
TERREBONNE	**58**	**10,144**	**4,526**	**70,484 ***	**67.4**	**100.0**
053 Assemb of God	4	426	479	479	.5	.7
056 Baha'i	0	9	NR	9	-	-
081 Catholic	18	NR	NR	55,177	52.8	78.3
127 Ch God (Cleve)	2	115	92	148 *	.1	.2
145 Ch God Prophcy	1	27	NR	35 *	-	-
151 L-D Saints	2	NR	NR	475	.5	.7
165 Ch of Nazarene	1	31	28	93	.1	.1
167 Chs of Christ	3	318	228	455	.4	.6
193 Episcopal	1	NR	123	280	.3	.4
216 Evan Presby Ch	1	65	NR	83 *	.1	.1
263 Int Foursq Gos	3	168	235	235 *	.2	.3
283 Luth—MO Synod	1	172	87	219	.2	.3
403 Salvation Army	1	75	47	166	.2	.2
413 S.D.A.	2	104	NR	124	.1	.2
419 So Bapt Conv	12	7,462	1,428	9,581 *	9.2	13.6
449 Un Methodist	5	1,172	379	1,505 *	1.4	2.1
496 Jewish Est	0	NR	NR	20	-	-
499 Indep.Non-Char	1	0	1,400	1,400	1.3	2.0
UNION	**77**	**12,502**	**5,448**	**15,957 ***	**70.0**	**100.0**
017 Amer Bapt Assn	1	100	NR	124 *	.5	.8
053 Assemb of God	4	960	894	1,130	5.0	7.1
056 Baha'i	0	3	NR	3	-	-
059 Bapt Miss Assn	5	1,020	380	1,269 *	5.6	8.0
081 Catholic	1	NR	NR	270	1.2	1.7

Religious Group	Number of Churches, Synagogues, Mosques, or Temples	Number of Communicant, Confirmed, or Full Members	Number of Attendees	Total Adherents		
				Number of Adherents	% of Total Pop.	% of Total Adh.
151 L-D Saints	1	NR	NR	176	.8	1.1
167 Chs of Christ	15	862	850	1,097	4.8	6.9
419 So Bapt Conv	41	8,820	2,984	10,972 *	48.1	68.8
449 Un Methodist	9	737	340	916 *	4.0	5.7
VERMILION	**40**	**3,168**	**1,429**	**51,938 ***	**96.5**	**100.0**
053 Assemb of God	1	99	133	185	.3	.4
056 Baha'i	0	4	NR	4	-	-
081 Catholic	17	NR	NR	47,859	88.9	92.1
097 Chr Chs&Chs Cr	1	30	NR	38 *	.1	.1
127 Ch God (Cleve)	1	30	44	44 *	.1	.1
167 Chs of Christ	2	71	94	110	.2	.2
193 Episcopal	1	NR	43	95	.2	.2
355 Presb Ch (USA)	1	36	33	46 *	.1	.1
419 So Bapt Conv	6	1,260	237	1,596 *	3.0	3.1
443 Un C of Christ	3	260	124	329 *	.6	.6
449 Un Methodist	6	878	271	1,112 *	2.1	2.1
496 Jewish Est	0	NR	NR	20	-	-
498 Indep.Charis.	1	500	450	500	.9	1.0
VERNON	**78**	**16,070**	**5,121**	**22,450 ***	**42.7**	**100.0**
017 Amer Bapt Assn	1	50	NR	66 *	.1	.3
053 Assemb of God	5	351	388	477	.9	2.1
056 Baha'i	0	12	NR	12	-	.1
081 Catholic	1	NR	NR	814	1.5	3.6
093 Chr Ch (Disc)	1	79	0	104 *	.2	.5
123 Ch God (Ander)	2	NR	87	87	.2	.4
127 Ch God (Cleve)	1	90	15	118 *	.2	.5
151 L-D Saints	1	NR	NR	388	.7	1.7
165 Ch of Nazarene	1	107	63	117	.2	.5
167 Chs of Christ	4	258	285	353	.7	1.6
193 Episcopal	1	NR	30	50	.1	.2
283 Luth—MO Synod	1	89	62	131	.2	.6
360 Prim Bapt Chrch	1	NR	NR	NR	-	-
419 So Bapt Conv	53	14,498	3,928	19,010 *	36.2	84.7
449 Un Methodist	5	536	263	703 *	1.3	3.1
496 Jewish Est	0	NR	NR	20	-	.1
WASHINGTON	**85**	**20,655**	**5,088**	**27,728 ***	**63.1**	**100.0**
017 Amer Bapt Assn	7	2,339	NR	2,935 *	6.7	10.6
053 Assemb of God	3	135	145	165	.4	.6
056 Baha'i	0	136	NR	136	.3	.5
059 Bapt Miss Assn	1	304	175	381 *	.9	1.4
081 Catholic	2	NR	NR	1,564	3.6	5.6
127 Ch God (Cleve)	1	0	60	60 *	.1	.2
145 Ch God Prophcy	1	27	NR	34 *	.1	.1
151 L-D Saints	1	NR	NR	162	.4	.6
167 Chs of Christ	2	56	65	72	.2	.3
193 Episcopal	1	NR	34	73	.2	.3
266 Intrstat & Asc	18	2,236	NR	2,806 *	6.4	10.1
283 Luth—MO Synod	1	72	43	79	.2	.3
355 Presb Ch (USA)	1	193	85	242 *	.6	.9
419 So Bapt Conv	34	13,480	3,459	16,914 *	38.5	61.0
449 Un Methodist	12	1,677	1,022	2,105 *	4.8	7.6
WEBSTER	**85**	**19,744**	**5,735**	**26,061 ***	**62.3**	**100.0**
017 Amer Bapt Assn	12	1,476	NR	1,827 *	4.4	7.0
053 Assemb of God	7	664	566	893	2.1	3.4
056 Baha'i	0	2	NR	2	-	-
059 Bapt Miss Assn	6	1,550	484	1,916 *	4.6	7.4
081 Catholic	3	NR	NR	1,122	2.7	4.3
097 Chr Chs&Chs Cr	2	143	NR	177 *	.4	.7
127 Ch God (Cleve)	1	34	0	42 *	.1	.2
151 L-D Saints	1	NR	NR	141	.3	.5
167 Chs of Christ	8	500	585	613	1.5	2.4
193 Episcopal	1	NR	92	323	.8	1.2
355 Presb Ch (USA)	1	160	80	198 *	.5	.8
413 S.D.A.	2	126	NR	150	.4	.6
418 Southw Bapt Fel	1	NR	NR	NR	-	-
419 So Bapt Conv	26	12,562	2,848	15,534 *	37.1	59.6
449 Un Methodist	13	2,408	1,000	2,976 *	7.1	11.4
463 Vineyard	1	119	80	147 *	.4	.6

NR–Not Reported *Total adherents estimated from known number of communicant, confirmed, full members. - Represents a percentage less than 0.1. Percentages may not total 100 due to rounding.

Table 4: Religious Congregations by County and Group: 2000

Religious Group	Number of Churches, Synagogues, Mosques, or Temples	Number of Communicant, Confirmed, or Full Members	Number of Attendees	Total Adherents: Number of Adherents	Total Adherents: % of Total Pop.	Total Adherents: % of Total Adh.
WEST BATON ROUGE	**13**	**2,048**	**665**	**10,426 ***	**48.3**	**100.0**
053 Assemb of God	1	75	45	70	.3	.7
056 Baha'i	0	4	NR	4	-	-
081 Catholic	2	NR	NR	7,053	32.7	67.6
089 Chr & Miss Al	1	20	NR	20	.1	.2
167 Chs of Christ	1	84	60	114	.5	1.1
355 Presb Ch (USA)	1	76	40	96 *	.4	.9
419 So Bapt Conv	4	1,610	410	2,042 *	9.5	19.6
449 Un Methodist	2	179	110	227 *	1.1	2.2
496 Jewish Est	1	NR	NR	800	3.7	7.7
WEST CARROLL	**41**	**7,001**	**2,640**	**9,214 ***	**74.8**	**100.0**
053 Assemb of God	3	473	373	544	4.4	5.9
081 Catholic	1	NR	NR	105	.9	1.1
123 Ch God (Ander)	5	NR	511	511	4.1	5.5
127 Ch God (Cleve)	3	144	130	195 *	1.6	2.1
167 Chs of Christ	3	160	126	186	1.5	2.0
223 Free Will Bapt	1	17	NR	21 *	.2	.2
360 Prim Bapt Chrch	1	NR	NR	NR	-	-
419 So Bapt Conv	18	5,728	1,302	7,061 *	57.3	76.6
449 Un Methodist	6	479	198	591 *	4.8	6.4
WEST FELICIANA	**11**	**1,621**	**784**	**3,264 ***	**21.6**	**100.0**
017 Amer Bapt Assn	1	30	NR	35 *	.2	1.1
056 Baha'i	0	1	NR	1	-	-
081 Catholic	2	NR	NR	950	6.3	29.1
193 Episcopal	1	NR	169	408	2.7	12.5
419 So Bapt Conv	3	1,086	365	1,278 *	8.5	39.2
449 Un Methodist	4	504	250	592 *	3.9	18.1
WINN	**58**	**8,618**	**3,025**	**11,141 ***	**65.9**	**100.0**
017 Amer Bapt Assn	2	63	NR	77 *	.5	.7
053 Assemb of God	5	430	362	581	3.4	5.2
056 Baha'i	0	2	NR	2	-	-
081 Catholic	1	NR	NR	222	1.3	2.0
151 L-D Saints	1	NR	NR	205	1.2	1.8
165 Ch of Nazarene	1	51	31	72	.4	.6
167 Chs of Christ	4	216	208	285	1.7	2.6
193 Episcopal	1	NR	15	56	.3	.5
355 Presb Ch (USA)	1	43	22	53 *	.3	.5
419 So Bapt Conv	36	7,306	2,196	8,965 *	53.1	80.5
449 Un Methodist	6	507	191	623 *	3.7	5.6
MAINE						
The State.....	1,301	109,033	68,142	463,541 *	36.4	100.0
ANDROSCOGGIN	**75**	**7,404**	**5,509**	**51,674 ***	**49.8**	**100.0**
019 Amer Bapt USA	7	1,619	580	1,980 *	1.9	3.8
053 Assemb of God	2	291	402	446	.4	.9
056 Baha'i	2	42	NR	42	-	.1
081 Catholic	12	NR	NR	39,058	37.6	75.6
127 Ch God (Cleve)	1	89	28	109 *	.1	.2
151 L-D Saints	2	NR	NR	584	.6	1.1
157 Ch of Brethren	2	69	89	96 *	.1	.2
165 Ch of Nazarene	6	380	327	595	.6	1.2
176 Congr Ad Afl	1	4	NR	5 *	-	-
179 Consrv Bapt	5	NR	1,087	1,087	1.0	2.1
193 Episcopal	3	NR	255	471	.5	.9
207 E.L.C.A.	1	193	74	221	.2	.4
226 Friends-USA	4	172	NR	210 *	.2	.4
246 Greek Orthodox	1	NR	NR	366	.4	.7
263 Int Foursq Gos	1	12	16	16 *	-	-
355 Presb Ch (USA)	3	255	142	312 *	.3	.6
388 Reg Bapt Gen As	1	72	84	88 *	.1	.2
403 Salvation Army	1	141	95	410	.4	.8
419 So Bapt Conv	1	343	60	420 *	.4	.8
435 Unitarian-Univ	1	154	NR	188 *	.2	.4
443 Un C of Christ	6	713	297	872 *	.8	1.7
449 Un Methodist	6	1,384	432	1,693 *	1.6	3.3
463 Vineyard	2	641	521	785 *	.8	1.5
496 Jewish Est	1	NR	NR	500	.5	1.0
498 Indep.Charis.	1	500	500	600	.6	1.2
499 Indep.Non-Char	2	330	520	520	.5	1.0
AROOSTOOK	**106**	**8,106**	**5,243**	**44,987 ***	**60.8**	**100.0**
019 Amer Bapt USA	16	3,267	1,702	3,916 *	5.3	8.7
053 Assemb of God	6	439	592	732	1.0	1.6
056 Baha'i	0	11	NR	11	-	-
057 Bapt Gen Conf	2	208	127	249 *	.3	.6
081 Catholic	27	NR	NR	31,816	43.0	70.7
089 Chr & Miss Al	1	27	NR	53	.1	.1
151 L-D Saints	4	NR	NR	483	.7	1.1
167 Chs of Christ	2	57	85	90	.1	.2
175 Congr Chr Chs	1	5	20	6 *	-	-
179 Consrv Bapt	1	NR	150	150	.2	.3
193 Episcopal	6	NR	181	460	.6	1.0
201 Evan Cov Ch	1	69	48	83 *	.1	.2
207 E.L.C.A.	3	434	139	582	.8	1.3
223 Free Will Bapt	1	70	NR	84 *	.1	.2
322 Old Ord Menn Ch	1	19	NR	23 *	-	.1
403 Salvation Army	1	54	51	144	.2	.3
413 S.D.A.	2	142	NR	169	.2	.4
419 So Bapt Conv	1	19	16	23 *	-	.1
435 Unitarian-Univ	2	71	NR	85 *	.1	.2
443 Un C of Christ	10	610	309	731 *	1.0	1.6
449 Un Methodist	12	2,158	744	2,587 *	3.5	5.8
467 Wesleyan	6	446	1,079	2,510	3.4	5.6
CUMBERLAND	**208**	**24,613**	**15,264**	**107,296 ***	**40.4**	**100.0**
019 Amer Bapt USA	15	2,005	1,204	2,446 *	.9	2.3
053 Assemb of God	6	637	767	1,063	.4	1.0
056 Baha'i	2	196	NR	196	.1	.2
076 Buddhism	2	NR	NR	NR	-	-
081 Catholic	31	NR	NR	61,495	23.2	57.3
084 Calvary Chapel	1	NR	NR	NR	-	-
089 Chr & Miss Al	4	173	NR	282	.1	.3
097 Chr Chs&Chs Cr	1	6	NR	7 *	-	-
127 Ch God (Cleve)	3	602	345	778 *	.3	.7
145 Ch God Prophcy	1	82	NR	100 *	-	.1
151 L-D Saints	3	NR	NR	891	.3	.8
157 Ch of Brethren	1	23	46	46 *	-	-
165 Ch of Nazarene	9	858	770	1,275	.5	1.2
167 Chs of Christ	3	110	120	159	.1	.1
173 Comm of Christ	1	0	NR	0	-	-
175 Congr Chr Chs	4	499	256	609 *	.2	.6
176 Congr Ad Afl	1	510	NR	622 *	.2	.6
179 Consrv Bapt	6	NR	1,509	1,509	.6	1.4
193 Episcopal	11	NR	1,368	4,577	1.7	4.3
201 Evan Cov Ch	1	94	82	115 *	-	.1
203 Evan Free Ch	2	154	286	286	.1	.3
207 E.L.C.A.	6	1,162	653	1,716	.6	1.6
221 Free Methodist	1	17	31	31	-	-
226 Friends-USA	2	86	NR	105 *	-	.1
246 Greek Orthodox	1	NR	NR	666	.3	.6
264 Int Chs of Crst	1	36	59	46	-	-
267 Muslim Est	1	NR	156	609	.2	.6
283 Luth—MO Synod	1	197	95	304	.1	.3
290 Metro Comm Ch	1	11	10	13 *	-	-
335 Orth Pres Ch	1	154	140	209	.1	.2
356 Presb Ch Amer	1	0	0	0	-	-
401 Rus Orth Abroad	1	NR	NR	NR	-	-
403 Salvation Army	2	183	70	395	.1	.4
410 Serb Orth USA	1	NR	NR	300	.1	.3
413 S.D.A.	3	702	NR	835	.3	.8
419 So Bapt Conv	4	977	405	1,192 *	.4	1.1
435 Unitarian-Univ	5	939	NR	1,145 *	.4	1.1
443 Un C of Christ	33	8,330	3,832	10,160 *	3.8	9.5
449 Un Methodist	26	4,584	1,774	5,590 *	2.1	5.2
463 Vineyard	1	130	120	159 *	.1	.1
467 Wesleyan	1	20	77	153	.1	.1
469 WELS	1	36	16	37	-	-
496 Jewish Est	4	NR	NR	6,000	2.3	5.6
498 Indep.Charis.	1	550	623	625	.2	.6

NR–Not Reported   *Total adherents estimated from known number of communicant, confirmed, full members.   - Represents a percentage less than 0.1.   Percentages may not total 100 due to rounding.

Table 4: Religious Congregations by County and Group: 2000

Religious Group	Number of Churches, Synagogues, Mosques, or Temples	Number of Communicant, Confirmed, or Full Members	Number of Attendees	Total Adherents: Number of Adherents	Total Adherents: % of Total Pop.	Total Adherents: % of Total Adh.
499 Indep.Non-Char	1	550	450	550	.2	.5
FRANKLIN	**43**	**2,219**	**1,561**	**9,824 ***	**33.3**	**100.0**
019 Amer Bapt USA	4	183	175	222 *	.8	2.3
053 Assemb of God	2	89	125	142	.5	1.4
056 Baha'i	0	6	NR	6	-	.1
081 Catholic	6	NR	NR	6,173	20.9	62.8
151 L-D Saints	1	NR	NR	354	1.2	3.6
165 Ch of Nazarene	2	131	72	156	.5	1.6
167 Chs of Christ	2	34	50	57	.2	.6
179 Consrv Bapt	1	NR	125	125	.4	1.3
181 Consrv Congr	1	18	25	22 *	.1	.2
193 Episcopal	2	NR	183	419	1.4	4.3
226 Friends-USA	1	43	NR	52 *	.2	.5
355 Presb Ch (USA)	2	122	84	148 *	.5	1.5
388 Reg Bapt Gen As	1	25	50	50 *	.2	.5
413 S.D.A.	2	68	NR	81	.3	.8
419 So Bapt Conv	1	107	83	130 *	.4	1.3
443 Un C of Christ	7	646	290	782 *	2.7	8.0
449 Un Methodist	8	747	299	905 *	3.1	9.2
HANCOCK	**97**	**5,533**	**3,362**	**14,427 ***	**27.9**	**100.0**
019 Amer Bapt USA	17	1,481	764	1,774 *	3.4	12.3
053 Assemb of God	3	98	137	230	.4	1.6
056 Baha'i	0	35	NR	35	.1	.2
076 Buddhism	2	NR	NR	NR	-	-
081 Catholic	10	NR	NR	6,292	12.1	43.6
127 Ch God (Cleve)	4	246	251	321 *	.6	2.2
151 L-D Saints	1	NR	NR	202	.4	1.4
165 Ch of Nazarene	2	67	110	135	.3	.9
167 Chs of Christ	1	5	5	5	-	-
173 Comm of Christ	3	261	NR	261	.5	1.8
176 Congr Ad Afl	1	132	NR	158 *	.3	1.1
179 Consrv Bapt	1	NR	50	50	.1	.3
181 Consrv Congr	1	101	50	121 *	.2	.8
193 Episcopal	8	NR	635	1,122	2.2	7.8
207 E.L.C.A.	1	231	120	274	.5	1.9
226 Friends-USA	4	172	NR	206 *	.4	1.4
435 Unitarian-Univ	2	175	NR	210 *	.4	1.5
443 Un C of Christ	19	1,634	837	1,957 *	3.8	13.6
449 Un Methodist	17	895	403	1,074 *	2.1	7.4
KENNEBEC	**112**	**10,013**	**6,336**	**42,439 ***	**36.2**	**100.0**
019 Amer Bapt USA	23	2,398	1,367	2,917 *	2.5	6.9
053 Assemb of God	2	180	220	305	.3	.7
056 Baha'i	1	53	NR	53	-	.1
081 Catholic	15	NR	NR	25,291	21.6	59.6
089 Chr & Miss Al	1	29	NR	56	-	.1
127 Ch God (Cleve)	3	226	197	298 *	.3	.7
151 L-D Saints	2	NR	NR	1,003	.9	2.4
165 Ch of Nazarene	4	430	320	662	.6	1.6
167 Chs of Christ	2	61	63	88	.1	.2
176 Congr Ad Afl	1	18	NR	22 *	-	.1
179 Consrv Bapt	3	NR	608	608	.5	1.4
181 Consrv Congr	1	42	36	51 *	-	.1
193 Episcopal	6	NR	525	2,305	2.0	5.4
203 Evan Free Ch	1	73	275	275	.2	.6
207 E.L.C.A.	1	456	140	697	.6	1.6
221 Free Methodist	1	40	53	53	-	.1
226 Friends-USA	4	172	NR	209 *	.2	.5
262 Int Cou Comm Ch	2	90	NR	109 *	.1	.3
263 Int Foursq Gos	1	222	191	270 *	.2	.6
283 Luth—MO Synod	1	104	72	131	.1	.3
288 Mennonite USA	1	31	50	50 *	-	.1
290 Metro Comm Ch	1	14	13	17 *	-	-
349 Pent Holiness	1	10	10	12 *	-	-
388 Reg Bapt Gen As	1	64	65	78 *	.1	.2
403 Salvation Army	2	126	64	247	.2	.6
413 S.D.A.	1	112	NR	133	.1	.3
419 So Bapt Conv	1	146	146	178 *	.2	.4
435 Unitarian-Univ	3	342	NR	416 *	.4	1.0
443 Un C of Christ	9	1,309	622	1,592 *	1.4	3.8
449 Un Methodist	16	3,265	1,299	3,973 *	3.4	9.4

Religious Group	Number of Churches, Synagogues, Mosques, or Temples	Number of Communicant, Confirmed, or Full Members	Number of Attendees	Total Adherents: Number of Adherents	Total Adherents: % of Total Pop.	Total Adherents: % of Total Adh.
496 Jewish Est	1	NR	NR	340	.3	.8
KNOX	**49**	**4,199**	**2,671**	**10,824 ***	**27.3**	**100.0**
019 Amer Bapt USA	11	1,240	574	1,490 *	3.8	13.8
053 Assemb of God	1	94	130	130	.3	1.2
056 Baha'i	0	14	NR	14	-	.1
059 Bapt Miss Assn	1	16	17	19 *	-	.2
076 Buddhism	1	NR	NR	NR	-	-
081 Catholic	5	NR	NR	4,274	10.8	39.5
127 Ch God (Cleve)	1	28	64	64 *	.2	.6
151 L-D Saints	1	NR	NR	170	.4	1.6
165 Ch of Nazarene	2	140	52	143	.4	1.3
173 Comm of Christ	1	35	NR	35	.1	.3
175 Congr Chr Chs	2	390	190	468 *	1.2	4.3
176 Congr Ad Afl	1	17	NR	20 *	.1	.2
179 Consrv Bapt	1	NR	123	123	.3	1.1
193 Episcopal	3	NR	430	836	2.1	7.7
207 E.L.C.A.	1	180	82	222	.6	2.1
226 Friends-USA	1	43	NR	52 *	.1	.5
335 Orth Pres Ch	1	96	102	124	.3	1.1
403 Salvation Army	1	60	29	121	.3	1.1
413 S.D.A.	1	78	NR	93	.2	.9
419 So Bapt Conv	1	70	100	84 *	.2	.8
435 Unitarian-Univ	1	162	NR	195 *	.5	1.8
443 Un C of Christ	3	590	324	709 *	1.8	6.6
449 Un Methodist	7	946	454	1,138 *	2.9	10.5
496 Jewish Est	1	NR	NR	300	.8	2.8
LINCOLN	**42**	**3,055**	**2,202**	**7,731 ***	**23.0**	**100.0**
019 Amer Bapt USA	7	644	361	775 *	2.3	10.0
053 Assemb of God	1	35	50	65	.2	.8
056 Baha'i	0	12	NR	12	-	.2
081 Catholic	3	NR	NR	2,730	8.1	35.3
151 L-D Saints	1	NR	NR	136	.4	1.8
165 Ch of Nazarene	2	127	88	163	.5	2.1
175 Congr Chr Chs	1	26	29	31 *	.1	.4
179 Consrv Bapt	2	NR	200	200	.6	2.6
193 Episcopal	4	NR	366	952	2.8	12.3
207 E.L.C.A.	1	80	66	101	.3	1.3
226 Friends-USA	1	43	NR	52 *	.2	.7
388 Reg Bapt Gen As	1	150	150	181 *	.5	2.3
435 Unitarian-Univ	1	72	NR	87 *	.3	1.1
443 Un C of Christ	8	917	458	1,104 *	3.3	14.3
449 Un Methodist	8	914	399	1,100 *	3.3	14.2
463 Vineyard	1	35	35	42 *	.1	.5
OXFORD	**74**	**3,765**	**2,092**	**11,274 ***	**20.6**	**100.0**
019 Amer Bapt USA	9	496	265	604 *	1.1	5.4
053 Assemb of God	3	141	191	279	.5	2.5
056 Baha'i	0	32	NR	32	.1	.3
081 Catholic	8	NR	NR	5,698	10.4	50.5
089 Chr & Miss Al	2	64	NR	236	.4	2.1
097 Chr Chs&Chs Cr	1	20	NR	24 *	-	.2
127 Ch God (Cleve)	1	21	38	38 *	.1	.3
151 L-D Saints	2	NR	NR	384	.7	3.4
165 Ch of Nazarene	3	148	129	203	.4	1.8
167 Chs of Christ	2	89	110	120	.2	1.1
175 Congr Chr Chs	4	337	200	410 *	.7	3.6
176 Congr Ad Afl	1	28	NR	34 *	.1	.3
179 Consrv Bapt	1	NR	75	75	.1	.7
181 Consrv Congr	1	19	17	23 *	-	.2
193 Episcopal	2	NR	111	239	.4	2.1
207 E.L.C.A.	1	116	64	140	.3	1.2
355 Presb Ch (USA)	1	63	47	77 *	.1	.7
413 S.D.A.	3	370	NR	440	.8	3.9
435 Unitarian-Univ	5	90	NR	110 *	.2	1.0
443 Un C of Christ	19	1,292	686	1,573 *	2.9	14.0
449 Un Methodist	5	439	159	535 *	1.0	4.7
PENOBSCOT	**132**	**12,628**	**7,513**	**48,809 ***	**33.7**	**100.0**
019 Amer Bapt USA	14	1,870	887	2,257 *	1.6	4.6
053 Assemb of God	5	385	474	750	.5	1.5

NR–Not Reported *Total adherents estimated from known number of communicant, confirmed, full members. - Represents a percentage less than 0.1. Percentages may not total 100 due to rounding.

Table 4: Religious Congregations by County and Group: 2000

Religious Group	Number of Churches, Synagogues, Mosques, or Temples	Number of Communicant, Confirmed, or Full Members	Number of Attendees	Total Adherents		
				Number of Adherents	% of Total Pop.	% of Total Adh.
056 Baha'i	0	37	NR	37	-	.1
061 Beachy Amish	1	8	NR	10 *	-	-
081 Catholic	18	NR	NR	28,136	19.4	57.6
084 Calvary Chapel	1	NR	NR	NR	-	-
089 Chr & Miss Al	2	39	NR	187	.1	.4
127 Ch God (Cleve)	8	475	282	587 *	.4	1.2
151 L-D Saints	3	NR	NR	789	.5	1.6
165 Ch of Nazarene	4	477	294	493	.3	1.0
167 Chs of Christ	3	78	90	109	.1	.2
173 Comm of Christ	1	41	NR	41	-	.1
175 Congr Chr Chs	6	869	472	1,049 *	.7	2.1
176 Congr Ad Afl	1	20	NR	24 *	-	-
179 Consrv Bapt	5	NR	741	741	.5	1.5
193 Episcopal	6	NR	470	1,227	.8	2.5
201 Evan Cov Ch	1	85	56	103 *	.1	.2
207 E.L.C.A.	1	183	118	248	.2	.5
226 Friends-USA	1	43	NR	52 *	-	.1
246 Greek Orthodox	1	NR	NR	543	.4	1.1
262 Int Cou Comm Ch	1	190	NR	229 *	.2	.5
263 Int Foursq Gos	1	71	85	86 *	.1	.2
267 Muslim Est	1	NR	45	200	.1	.4
335 Orth Pres Ch	1	134	149	185	.1	.4
403 Salvation Army	1	145	79	265	.2	.5
413 S.D.A.	3	203	NR	242	.2	.5
419 So Bapt Conv	1	12	35	14 *	-	-
435 Unitarian-Univ	2	181	NR	218 *	.2	.4
443 Un C of Christ	14	2,036	974	2,458 *	1.7	5.0
449 Un Methodist	19	3,991	1,386	4,819 *	3.3	9.9
467 Wesleyan	2	55	176	510	.4	1.0
496 Jewish Est	3	NR	NR	1,000	.7	2.0
499 Indep.Non-Char	1	1,000	700	1,200	.8	2.5
PISCATAQUIS	**29**	**2,596**	**1,221**	**5,797 ***	**33.6**	**100.0**
017 Amer Bapt Assn	1	30	NR	36 *	.2	.6
019 Amer Bapt USA	2	602	190	722 *	4.2	12.5
053 Assemb of God	3	119	164	184	1.1	3.2
056 Baha'i	0	2	NR	2	-	-
081 Catholic	5	NR	NR	2,137	12.4	36.9
151 L-D Saints	1	NR	NR	239	1.4	4.1
165 Ch of Nazarene	1	73	82	190	1.1	3.3
193 Episcopal	2	NR	35	92	.5	1.6
203 Evan Free Ch	2	114	210	210	1.2	3.6
435 Unitarian-Univ	1	55	NR	66 *	.4	1.1
443 Un C of Christ	4	473	243	567 *	3.3	9.8
449 Un Methodist	7	1,128	297	1,352 *	7.8	23.3
SAGADAHOC	**35**	**2,389**	**1,544**	**6,659 ***	**18.9**	**100.0**
019 Amer Bapt USA	7	795	395	989 *	2.8	14.9
053 Assemb of God	1	85	100	130	.4	2.0
056 Baha'i	0	24	NR	24	.1	.4
081 Catholic	3	NR	NR	2,612	7.4	39.2
089 Chr & Miss Al	1	10	NR	18	.1	.3
151 L-D Saints	1	NR	NR	433	1.2	6.5
165 Ch of Nazarene	5	150	155	183	.5	2.7
179 Consrv Bapt	1	NR	60	60	.2	.9
193 Episcopal	1	NR	110	367	1.0	5.5
226 Friends-USA	1	43	NR	54 *	.2	.8
263 Int Foursq Gos	1	45	71	71 *	.2	1.1
335 Orth Pres Ch	1	47	48	54	.2	.8
355 Presb Ch (USA)	1	169	97	210 *	.6	3.2
370 Ref Baptist Chs	1	NR	NR	NR	-	-
401 Rus Orth Abroad	1	NR	NR	NR	-	-
403 Salvation Army	1	96	39	234	.7	3.5
413 S.D.A.	2	126	NR	150	.4	2.3
443 Un C of Christ	3	373	211	464 *	1.3	7.0
449 Un Methodist	3	426	258	531 *	1.5	8.0
496 Jewish Est	0	NR	NR	75	.2	1.1
SOMERSET	**64**	**4,101**	**2,793**	**15,194 ***	**29.9**	**100.0**
017 Amer Bapt Assn	1	30	NR	37 *	.1	.2
019 Amer Bapt USA	6	877	598	1,072 *	2.1	7.1
053 Assemb of God	4	269	333	498	1.0	3.3
056 Baha'i	0	28	NR	28	.1	.2
081 Catholic	8	NR	NR	9,022	17.7	59.4
089 Chr & Miss Al	1	19	NR	44	.1	.3
127 Ch God (Cleve)	1	19	48	48 *	.1	.3
151 L-D Saints	1	NR	NR	320	.6	2.1
165 Ch of Nazarene	5	430	249	667	1.3	4.4
167 Chs of Christ	1	40	45	62	.1	.4
175 Congr Chr Chs	6	463	365	566 *	1.1	3.7
179 Consrv Bapt	3	NR	156	156	.3	1.0
193 Episcopal	2	NR	93	251	.5	1.7
203 Evan Free Ch	2	116	215	215	.4	1.4
226 Friends-USA	2	86	NR	105 *	.2	.7
263 Int Foursq Gos	1	87	82	106 *	.2	.7
335 Orth Pres Ch	1	21	26	31	.1	.2
349 Pent Holiness	1	14	18	17 *	-	.1
355 Presb Ch (USA)	3	40	38	50 *	.1	.3
413 S.D.A.	2	322	NR	383	.8	2.5
435 Unitarian-Univ	1	30	NR	37 *	.1	.2
443 Un C of Christ	4	283	133	346 *	.7	2.3
449 Un Methodist	8	927	394	1,133 *	2.2	7.5
WALDO	**38**	**2,440**	**1,689**	**4,841 ***	**13.3**	**100.0**
019 Amer Bapt USA	5	579	323	710 *	2.0	14.7
056 Baha'i	0	14	NR	14	-	.3
076 Buddhism	1	NR	NR	NR	-	-
081 Catholic	2	NR	NR	1,187	3.3	24.5
127 Ch God (Cleve)	1	220	192	270 *	.7	5.6
145 Ch God Prophcy	1	82	NR	101 *	.3	2.1
151 L-D Saints	1	NR	NR	229	.6	4.7
165 Ch of Nazarene	1	97	55	99	.3	2.0
167 Chs of Christ	2	68	60	90	.2	1.9
175 Congr Chr Chs	2	177	111	217 *	.6	4.5
176 Congr Ad Afl	1	56	NR	69 *	.2	1.4
179 Consrv Bapt	2	NR	225	225	.6	4.6
193 Episcopal	1	NR	92	228	.6	4.7
226 Friends-USA	1	43	NR	53 *	.1	1.1
403 Salvation Army	1	14	15	14	-	.3
419 So Bapt Conv	1	49	55	60 *	.2	1.2
435 Unitarian-Univ	1	53	NR	65 *	.2	1.3
443 Un C of Christ	8	426	298	522 *	1.4	10.8
449 Un Methodist	6	562	263	688 *	1.9	14.2
WASHINGTON	**75**	**3,274**	**1,687**	**8,778 ***	**25.9**	**100.0**
011 A.W.M.C.	1	0	18	0	-	-
019 Amer Bapt USA	4	373	204	449 *	1.3	5.1
053 Assemb of God	5	72	99	107	.3	1.2
056 Baha'i	0	25	NR	25	.1	.3
081 Catholic	12	NR	NR	4,155	12.2	47.3
093 Chr Ch (Disc)	1	120	65	145 *	.4	1.7
127 Ch God (Cleve)	2	71	55	86 *	.3	1.0
151 L-D Saints	1	NR	NR	86	.3	1.0
167 Chs of Christ	2	58	73	93	.3	1.1
173 Comm of Christ	4	441	NR	441	1.3	5.0
175 Congr Chr Chs	7	231	228	278 *	.8	3.2
176 Congr Ad Afl	1	42	NR	51 *	.2	.6
179 Consrv Bapt	1	NR	100	100	.3	1.1
193 Episcopal	3	NR	109	441	1.3	5.0
226 Friends-USA	2	86	NR	104 *	.3	1.2
413 S.D.A.	1	20	NR	24	.1	.3
419 So Bapt Conv	1	62	30	75 *	.2	.9
435 Unitarian-Univ	1	8	NR	10 *	-	.1
443 Un C of Christ	9	479	255	577 *	1.7	6.6
449 Un Methodist	15	1,081	359	1,301 *	3.8	14.8
467 Wesleyan	2	105	92	230	.7	2.6
YORK	**122**	**12,698**	**7,455**	**72,987 ***	**39.1**	**100.0**
019 Amer Bapt USA	17	3,191	1,248	3,936 *	2.1	5.4
053 Assemb of God	8	740	1,065	1,192	.6	1.6
056 Baha'i	3	208	NR	208	.1	.3
081 Catholic	21	NR	NR	52,948	28.4	72.5
151 L-D Saints	3	NR	NR	816	.4	1.1
165 Ch of Nazarene	4	211	149	221	.1	.3
167 Chs of Christ	2	141	130	191	.1	.3
175 Congr Chr Chs	1	70	50	86 *	-	.1

NR–Not Reported   *Total adherents estimated from known number of communicant, confirmed, full members.   - Represents a percentage less than 0.1.   Percentages may not total 100 due to rounding.

Table 4: Religious Congregations by County and Group: 2000

Religious Group	Number of Churches, Synagogues, Mosques, or Temples	Number of Communicant, Confirmed, or Full Members	Number of Attendees	Total Adherents: Number of Adherents	Total Adherents: % of Total Pop.	Total Adherents: % of Total Adh.
176 Congr Ad Afl	2	254	NR	313 *	.2	.4
179 Consrv Bapt	3	NR	353	353	.2	.5
181 Consrv Congr	2	56	95	69 *	-	.1
193 Episcopal	6	NR	530	1,807	1.0	2.5
207 E.L.C.A.	1	208	179	330	.2	.5
226 Friends-USA	2	86	NR	106 *	.1	.1
246 Greek Orthodox	1	NR	NR	957	.5	1.3
370 Ref Baptist Chs	1	NR	NR	NR	-	-
388 Reg Bapt Gen As	2	123	155	159 *	.1	.2
403 Salvation Army	2	367	279	536	.3	.7
413 S.D.A.	2	90	NR	107	.1	.1
419 So Bapt Conv	1	160	100	197 *	.1	.3
435 Unitarian-Univ	3	326	NR	402 *	.2	.6
443 Un C of Christ	20	3,817	2,080	4,708 *	2.5	6.5
449 Un Methodist	15	2,650	1,042	3,270 *	1.8	4.5
496 Jewish Est	0	NR	NR	75	-	.1

MARYLAND

Religious Group	Number of Churches, Synagogues, Mosques, or Temples	Number of Communicant, Confirmed, or Full Members	Number of Attendees	Total Adherents: Number of Adherents	Total Adherents: % of Total Pop.	Total Adherents: % of Total Adh.
The State.....	3,855	709,239	365,589	2,291,896 *	43.3	100.0
ALLEGANY	**136**	**20,241**	**9,241**	**42,256 ***	**56.4**	**100.0**
053 Assemb of God	11	1,312	1,650	3,593	4.8	8.5
056 Baha'i	0	10	NR	10	-	-
081 Catholic	10	NR	NR	13,217	17.6	31.3
093 Chr Ch (Disc)	1	100	30	118 *	.2	.3
097 Chr Chs&Chs Cr	1	250	NR	296 *	.4	.7
123 Ch God (Ander)	1	NR	60	60	.1	.1
127 Ch God (Cleve)	1	461	174	545 *	.7	1.3
145 Ch God Prophcy	1	32	NR	38 *	.1	.1
151 L-D Saints	1	NR	NR	753	1.0	1.8
157 Ch of Brethren	6	631	287	746 *	1.0	1.8
165 Ch of Nazarene	4	451	306	628	.8	1.5
167 Chs of Christ	1	86	75	114	.2	.3
175 Congr Chr Chs	1	100	83	118 *	.2	.3
193 Episcopal	5	NR	366	1,050	1.4	2.5
207 E.L.C.A.	6	2,350	748	3,086	4.1	7.3
226 Friends-USA	1	105	NR	124 *	.2	.3
252 Hindu	1	NR	NR	NR	-	-
267 Muslim Est	1	NR	101	288	.4	.7
283 Luth—MO Synod	1	170	68	205	.3	.5
288 Mennonite USA	1	157	113	186 *	.2	.4
297 Mennonite;Other	1	50	NR	59 *	.1	.1
349 Pent Holiness	2	199	240	235 *	.3	.6
355 Presb Ch (USA)	6	826	415	976 *	1.3	2.3
356 Presb Ch Amer	1	70	91	91	.1	.2
388 Reg Bapt Gen As	2	312	297	369 *	.5	.9
413 S.D.A.	2	264	NR	314	.4	.7
419 So Bapt Conv	12	2,341	857	2,768 *	3.7	6.6
435 Unitarian-Univ	1	35	NR	41 *	.1	.1
443 Un C of Christ	6	370	173	438 *	.6	1.0
449 Un Methodist	45	9,559	3,017	11,305 *	15.1	26.8
467 Wesleyan	2	0	90	210	.3	.5
496 Jewish Est	1	NR	NR	275	.4	.7
ANNE ARUNDEL	**259**	**61,241**	**32,003**	**203,375 ***	**41.5**	**100.0**
017 Amer Bapt Assn	1	50	NR	62 *	-	-
034 Ant Orth of NA	1	116	NR	232	-	.1
053 Assemb of God	11	1,095	1,255	1,784	.4	.9
056 Baha'i	3	94	NR	94	-	-
057 Bapt Gen Conf	1	45	85	85 *	-	-
081 Catholic	20	NR	NR	107,463	21.9	52.8
097 Chr Chs&Chs Cr	2	600	NR	748 *	.2	.4
123 Ch God (Ander)	2	NR	133	133	-	.1
127 Ch God (Cleve)	11	2,659	2,070	3,319 *	.7	1.6
145 Ch God Prophcy	1	46	NR	57 *	-	-
151 L-D Saints	9	NR	NR	2,588	.5	1.3
157 Ch of Brethren	1	192	80	239 *	-	.1
165 Ch of Nazarene	4	504	482	666	.1	.3
167 Chs of Christ	5	390	420	495	.1	.2
193 Episcopal	15	NR	2,569	7,822	1.6	3.8
203 Evan Free Ch	1	25	60	60	-	-
207 E.L.C.A.	12	5,843	2,326	9,053	1.8	4.5
221 Free Methodist	1	36	36	38	-	-
223 Free Will Bapt	1	99	NR	123 *	-	.1
226 Friends-USA	1	105	NR	131 *	-	.1
246 Greek Orthodox	1	NR	NR	1,269	.3	.6
252 Hindu	1	NR	NR	NR	-	-
265 Int Pent C Chr	1	0	0	45	-	-
283 Luth—MO Synod	6	2,489	1,304	4,095	.8	2.0
290 Metro Comm Ch	1	24	17	30 *	-	-
349 Pent Holiness	1	48	38	60 *	-	-
355 Presb Ch (USA)	7	4,232	2,068	5,275 *	1.1	2.6
356 Presb Ch Amer	8	2,490	1,859	3,739	.8	1.8
388 Reg Bapt Gen As	3	389	399	517 *	.1	.3
403 Salvation Army	2	96	44	619	.1	.3
413 S.D.A.	9	839	NR	1,000	.2	.5
416 Sikh	1	NR	NR	NR	-	-
418 Southw Bapt Fel	2	NR	NR	NR	-	-
419 So Bapt Conv	30	10,239	4,564	12,763 *	2.6	6.3
435 Unitarian-Univ	1	390	NR	486 *	.1	.2
443 Un C of Christ	1	57	25	71 *	-	-
449 Un Methodist	71	26,662	11,081	33,235 *	6.8	16.3
463 Vineyard	1	457	421	570 *	.1	.3
467 Wesleyan	4	0	117	419	.1	.2
496 Jewish Est	3	NR	NR	3,000	.6	1.5
498 Indep.Charis.	2	930	550	990	.2	.5
BALTIMORE	**386**	**75,858**	**45,127**	**347,901 ***	**46.1**	**100.0**
019 Amer Bapt USA	3	1,213	500	1,485 *	.2	.4
034 Ant Orth of NA	1	118	NR	236	-	.1
053 Assemb of God	5	1,335	1,617	2,345	.3	.7
056 Baha'i	4	392	NR	392	.1	.1
075 Brethren in Cr	1	29	30	30	-	-
076 Buddhism	3	NR	NR	NR	-	-
081 Catholic	37	NR	NR	181,212	24.0	52.1
084 Calvary Chapel	2	NR	NR	NR	-	-
089 Chr & Miss Al	2	368	NR	454	.1	.1
093 Chr Ch (Disc)	4	529	218	648 *	.1	.2
097 Chr Chs&Chs Cr	3	764	NR	935 *	.1	.3
123 Ch God (Ander)	3	NR	183	183	-	.1
127 Ch God (Cleve)	10	2,857	2,060	3,558 *	.5	1.0
145 Ch God Prophcy	1	46	NR	56 *	-	-
151 L-D Saints	6	NR	NR	1,320	.2	.4
157 Ch of Brethren	4	376	193	461 *	.1	.1
165 Ch of Nazarene	2	197	207	494	.1	.1
167 Chs of Christ	5	597	588	720	.1	.2
173 Comm of Christ	2	258	NR	258	-	.1
193 Episcopal	23	NR	3,228	10,492	1.4	3.0
207 E.L.C.A.	27	11,033	3,978	16,697	2.2	4.8
216 Evan Presby Ch	1	237	NR	290 *	-	.1
221 Free Methodist	2	135	207	242	-	.1
226 Friends-USA	1	105	NR	129 *	-	-
246 Greek Orthodox	1	NR	NR	1,521	.2	.4
252 Hindu	2	NR	NR	NR	-	-
267 Muslim Est	4	NR	2,084	7,007	.9	2.0
283 Luth—MO Synod	14	4,041	2,059	5,336	.7	1.5
288 Mennonite USA	2	87	97	106 *	-	-
349 Pent Holiness	2	822	375	1,006 *	.1	.3
355 Presb Ch (USA)	10	1,434	747	1,756 *	.2	.5
356 Presb Ch Amer	12	2,726	2,257	3,485	.5	1.0
360 Prim Bapt Chrch	2	NR	NR	NR	-	-
370 Ref Baptist Chs	1	NR	NR	NR	-	-
403 Salvation Army	4	405	136	1,544	.2	.4
413 S.D.A.	4	774	NR	921	.1	.3
416 Sikh	2	NR	NR	NR	-	-
419 So Bapt Conv	47	14,287	4,991	17,488 *	2.3	5.0
435 Unitarian-Univ	1	355	NR	435 *	.1	.1
443 Un C of Christ	7	1,753	858	2,146 *	.3	.6
449 Un Methodist	95	27,787	9,885	34,013 *	4.5	9.8
469 WELS	1	98	79	150	-	-
496 Jewish Est	19	NR	NR	38,000	5.0	10.9
499 Indep.Non-Char	4	700	8,550	10,350	1.4	3.0

NR–Not Reported *Total adherents estimated from known number of communicant, confirmed, full members. - Represents a percentage less than 0.1. Percentages may not total 100 due to rounding.

Table 4: Religious Congregations by County and Group: 2000

Religious Group	Number of Churches, Synagogues, Mosques, or Temples	Number of Communicant, Confirmed, or Full Members	Number of Attendees	Total Adherents: Number of Adherents	Total Adherents: % of Total Pop.	Total Adherents: % of Total Adh.
BALTIMORE CITY	**401**	**65,644**	**36,583**	**254,661 ***	**39.1**	**100.0**
019 Amer Bapt USA	18	11,807	4,755	14,658 *	2.3	5.8
053 Assemb of God	15	1,551	1,849	2,661	.4	1.0
076 Buddhism	5	NR	NR	NR	-	-
081 Catholic	53	NR	NR	81,058	12.4	31.8
093 Chr Ch (Disc)	4	563	81	699 *	.1	.3
097 Chr Chs&Chs Cr	4	391	NR	484 *	.1	.2
123 Ch God (Ander)	3	NR	337	337	.1	.1
127 Ch God (Cleve)	9	781	558	989 *	.2	.4
145 Ch God Prophcy	1	51	NR	64 *	-	-
151 L-D Saints	4	NR	NR	913	.1	.4
157 Ch of Brethren	1	79	0	98 *	-	-
165 Ch of Nazarene	1	62	64	78	-	-
167 Chs of Christ	3	1,954	1,371	2,195	.3	.9
173 Comm of Christ	1	58	NR	58	-	-
181 Consrv Congr	1	30	22	37 *	-	-
193 Episcopal	30	NR	3,535	11,651	1.8	4.6
203 Evan Free Ch	1	100	90	100	-	-
207 E.L.C.A.	31	8,453	3,708	11,840	1.8	4.6
221 Free Methodist	1	55	42	65	-	-
226 Friends-USA	3	305	NR	379 *	.1	.1
245 Greek Orth Vslp	1	260	NR	1,260	.2	.5
246 Greek Orthodox	2	NR	NR	7,887	1.2	3.1
262 Int Cou Comm Ch	1	654	NR	812 *	.1	.3
265 Int Pent C Chr	1	25	38	40	-	-
267 Muslim Est	7	NR	2,480	10,555	1.6	4.1
283 Luth—MO Synod	11	2,759	1,154	4,173	.6	1.6
288 Mennonite USA	1	55	100	100 *	-	-
290 Metro Comm Ch	1	117	105	145 *	-	.1
331 OCA: Ter Diocs	1	165	NR	285	-	.1
335 Orth Pres Ch	1	26	22	26	-	-
355 Presb Ch (USA)	27	8,103	4,197	10,059 *	1.5	3.9
356 Presb Ch Amer	6	649	729	883	.1	.3
388 Reg Bapt Gen As	1	23	25	29 *	-	-
400 Rus Orth Moscow	1	NR	NR	NR	-	-
401 Rus Orth Abroad	1	NR	NR	NR	-	-
413 S.D.A.	9	2,640	NR	3,141	.5	1.2
419 So Bapt Conv	29	4,259	1,988	5,287 *	.8	2.1
431 Ukrainian Orth	1	NR	NR	123	-	-
435 Unitarian-Univ	1	205	NR	255 *	-	.1
443 Un C of Christ	10	2,044	935	2,538 *	.4	1.0
449 Un Methodist	64	14,270	5,461	17,714 *	2.7	7.0
467 Wesleyan	1	0	42	210	-	.1
496 Jewish Est	27	NR	NR	56,500	8.7	22.2
498 Indep.Charis.	6	3,150	2,595	3,975	.6	1.6
499 Indep.Non-Char	1	0	300	300	-	.1
CALVERT	**50**	**8,779**	**4,819**	**31,629 ***	**42.4**	**100.0**
053 Assemb of God	2	131	172	214	.3	.7
056 Baha'i	0	12	NR	12	-	-
081 Catholic	6	NR	NR	18,062	24.2	57.1
145 Ch God Prophcy	1	46	NR	59 *	.1	.2
151 L-D Saints	1	NR	NR	427	.6	1.4
165 Ch of Nazarene	1	25	0	25	-	.1
167 Chs of Christ	1	90	120	150	.2	.5
179 Consrv Bapt	1	NR	100	100	.1	.3
193 Episcopal	4	NR	596	1,564	2.1	4.9
207 E.L.C.A.	1	246	157	371	.5	1.2
226 Friends-USA	1	105	NR	136 *	.2	.4
283 Luth—MO Synod	1	412	244	421	.6	1.3
356 Presb Ch Amer	1	47	69	78	.1	.2
413 S.D.A.	2	199	NR	237	.3	.7
418 Southw Bapt Fel	1	NR	NR	NR	-	-
419 So Bapt Conv	4	1,627	959	2,106 *	2.8	6.7
449 Un Methodist	20	5,794	2,319	7,501 *	10.1	23.7
467 Wesleyan	1	0	27	100	.1	.3
469 WELS	1	45	56	66	.1	.2
CAROLINE	**55**	**5,792**	**2,830**	**13,117 ***	**44.1**	**100.0**
056 Baha'i	0	18	NR	18	.1	.1
081 Catholic	3	NR	NR	4,203	14.1	32.0
097 Chr Chs&Chs Cr	1	40	NR	50 *	.2	.4
123 Ch God (Ander)	1	NR	85	85	.3	.6
127 Ch God (Cleve)	1	255	64	321 *	1.1	2.4
145 Ch God Prophcy	1	46	NR	57 *	.2	.4
151 L-D Saints	1	NR	NR	344	1.2	2.6
157 Ch of Brethren	2	154	104	194 *	.7	1.5
165 Ch of Nazarene	2	262	283	488	1.6	3.7
167 Chs of Christ	1	19	20	24	.1	.2
193 Episcopal	2	NR	59	185	.6	1.4
283 Luth—MO Synod	1	288	115	377	1.3	2.9
339 Pent Ch of God	1	25	NR	125	.4	1.0
413 S.D.A.	1	38	NR	45	.2	.3
419 So Bapt Conv	4	733	457	922 *	3.1	7.0
449 Un Methodist	26	3,828	1,273	4,814 *	16.2	36.7
467 Wesleyan	7	86	370	865	2.9	6.6
CARROLL	**140**	**33,200**	**14,154**	**74,222 ***	**49.2**	**100.0**
053 Assemb of God	2	455	560	576	.4	.8
055 As Ref Pres Ch	3	284	NR	325	.2	.4
056 Baha'i	1	55	NR	55	-	.1
071 Brethren (Ash)	1	70	62	89 *	.1	.1
076 Buddhism	1	NR	NR	NR	-	-
081 Catholic	4	NR	NR	28,694	19.0	38.7
097 Chr Chs&Chs Cr	1	141	NR	180 *	.1	.2
127 Ch God (Cleve)	3	438	420	562 *	.4	.8
145 Ch God Prophcy	1	46	NR	58 *	-	.1
151 L-D Saints	2	NR	NR	743	.5	1.0
157 Ch of Brethren	7	1,184	662	1,508 *	1.0	2.0
165 Ch of Nazarene	2	145	181	198	.1	.3
167 Chs of Christ	3	183	217	272	.2	.4
171 Ch God-Gen Con	4	113	197	200 *	.1	.3
193 Episcopal	3	NR	422	1,166	.8	1.6
207 E.L.C.A.	22	6,979	2,652	10,488	7.0	14.1
221 Free Methodist	1	23	31	31	-	-
226 Friends-USA	1	105	NR	134 *	.1	.2
263 Int Foursq Gos	1	125	123	159 *	.1	.2
283 Luth—MO Synod	1	214	174	279	.2	.4
286 E.PA Mennonite	1	60	NR	76 *	.1	.1
288 Mennonite USA	1	27	22	34 *	-	-
355 Presb Ch (USA)	3	566	303	721 *	.5	1.0
356 Presb Ch Amer	1	1,529	1,400	1,853	1.2	2.5
403 Salvation Army	1	16	18	16	-	-
413 S.D.A.	1	215	NR	256	.2	.3
419 So Bapt Conv	9	3,128	1,472	3,984 *	2.6	5.4
435 Unitarian-Univ	1	103	NR	131 *	.1	.2
443 Un C of Christ	11	2,357	901	3,002 *	2.0	4.0
449 Un Methodist	42	11,489	4,037	14,632 *	9.7	19.7
467 Wesleyan	2	0	0	0	-	-
496 Jewish Est	1	NR	NR	500	.3	.7
499 Indep.Non-Char	2	3,150	300	3,300	2.2	4.4
CECIL	**82**	**11,896**	**5,831**	**26,333 ***	**30.6**	**100.0**
017 Amer Bapt Assn	1	50	NR	64 *	.1	.2
053 Assemb of God	1	235	328	437	.5	1.7
056 Baha'i	0	6	NR	6	-	-
081 Catholic	8	NR	NR	9,269	10.8	35.2
127 Ch God (Cleve)	3	276	132	352 *	.4	1.3
145 Ch God Prophcy	1	46	NR	58 *	.1	.2
151 L-D Saints	1	NR	NR	262	.3	1.0
165 Ch of Nazarene	3	313	262	474	.6	1.8
167 Chs of Christ	4	106	121	142	.2	.5
193 Episcopal	5	NR	465	1,440	1.7	5.5
207 E.L.C.A.	1	120	60	164	.2	.6
297 Mennonite;Other	1	12	NR	15 *	-	.1
323 Old Ord Amish	1	55	NR	70 *	.1	.3
355 Presb Ch (USA)	6	856	419	1,093 *	1.3	4.2
356 Presb Ch Amer	1	95	153	197	.2	.7
360 Prim Bapt Chrch	1	NR	NR	NR	-	-
413 S.D.A.	3	359	NR	427	.5	1.6
419 So Bapt Conv	9	3,484	1,419	4,449 *	5.2	16.9
449 Un Methodist	31	5,533	2,272	7,064 *	8.2	26.8
499 Indep.Non-Char	1	350	200	350	.4	1.3
CHARLES	**76**	**13,676**	**7,137**	**48,138 ***	**39.9**	**100.0**
019 Amer Bapt USA	2	99	94	127 *	.1	.3

NR–Not Reported *Total adherents estimated from known number of communicant, confirmed, full members. - Represents a percentage less than 0.1. Percentages may not total 100 due to rounding.

Table 4: Religious Congregations by County and Group: 2000

Religious Group	Number of Churches, Synagogues, Mosques, or Temples	Number of Communicant, Confirmed, or Full Members	Number of Attendees	Total Adherents: Number of Adherents	Total Adherents: % of Total Pop.	Total Adherents: % of Total Adh.
022 Carp Rus Orth	1	122	NR	207	.2	.4
053 Assemb of God	2	93	115	157	.1	.3
056 Baha'i	0	11	NR	11	-	-
081 Catholic	12	NR	NR	24,506	20.3	50.9
084 Calvary Chapel	1	NR	NR	NR	-	-
123 Ch God (Ander)	1	NR	54	54	-	.1
127 Ch God (Cleve)	1	669	302	860 *	.7	1.8
151 L-D Saints	2	NR	NR	758	.6	1.6
165 Ch of Nazarene	2	251	238	475	.4	1.0
167 Chs of Christ	2	166	191	237	.2	.5
193 Episcopal	6	NR	552	1,719	1.4	3.6
207 E.L.C.A.	1	303	170	435	.4	.9
223 Free Will Bapt	1	99	NR	127 *	.1	.3
267 Muslim Est	1	NR	412	1,891	1.6	3.9
283 Luth—MO Synod	2	656	357	896	.7	1.9
355 Presb Ch (USA)	1	281	188	361 *	.3	.7
356 Presb Ch Amer	1	62	79	94	.1	.2
388 Reg Bapt Gen As	1	117	117	150 *	.1	.3
413 S.D.A.	2	421	NR	501	.4	1.0
418 Southw Bapt Fel	1	NR	NR	NR	-	-
419 So Bapt Conv	17	6,227	2,336	8,004 *	6.6	16.6
449 Un Methodist	14	4,069	1,607	5,229 *	4.3	10.9
463 Vineyard	1	30	30	39 *	-	.1
467 Wesleyan	1	0	295	1,300	1.1	2.7
DORCHESTER	**85**	**8,410**	**3,281**	**12,735 ***	**41.5**	**100.0**
053 Assemb of God	1	12	9	16	.1	.1
056 Baha'i	0	35	NR	35	.1	.3
081 Catholic	4	NR	NR	1,450	4.7	11.4
089 Chr & Miss Al	2	119	NR	301	1.0	2.4
097 Chr Chs&Chs Cr	1	110	NR	134 *	.4	1.1
127 Ch God (Cleve)	3	481	417	608 *	2.0	4.8
145 Ch God Prophcy	3	137	NR	165 *	.5	1.3
165 Ch of Nazarene	1	59	32	59	.2	.5
167 Chs of Christ	1	65	60	100	.3	.8
193 Episcopal	6	NR	210	637	2.1	5.0
283 Luth—MO Synod	1	67	34	86	.3	.7
356 Presb Ch Amer	1	17	37	37	.1	.3
388 Reg Bapt Gen As	1	117	117	142 *	.5	1.1
403 Salvation Army	1	120	18	108	.4	.8
413 S.D.A.	2	94	NR	112	.4	.9
418 Southw Bapt Fel	1	NR	NR	NR	-	-
419 So Bapt Conv	3	982	274	1,192 *	3.9	9.4
443 Un C of Christ	1	168	76	204 *	.7	1.6
449 Un Methodist	48	5,716	1,836	6,937 *	22.6	54.5
467 Wesleyan	4	111	161	412	1.3	3.2
FREDERICK	**205**	**38,070**	**17,230**	**93,067 ***	**47.7**	**100.0**
017 Amer Bapt Assn	5	500	NR	639 *	.3	.7
019 Amer Bapt USA	1	63	28	80 *	-	.1
053 Assemb of God	5	569	722	1,137	.6	1.2
055 As Ref Pres Ch	1	21	NR	27	-	-
056 Baha'i	1	74	NR	74	-	.1
075 Brethren in Cr	1	58	107	107	.1	.1
076 Buddhism	1	NR	NR	NR	-	-
081 Catholic	12	NR	NR	35,153	18.0	37.8
089 Chr & Miss Al	3	151	NR	353	.2	.4
097 Chr Chs&Chs Cr	1	125	NR	159 *	.1	.2
127 Ch God (Cleve)	4	1,251	674	1,595 *	.8	1.7
145 Ch God Prophcy	2	91	NR	116 *	.1	.1
151 L-D Saints	5	NR	NR	1,586	.8	1.7
157 Ch of Brethren	10	2,858	1,300	3,647 *	1.9	3.9
165 Ch of Nazarene	3	288	275	440	.2	.5
167 Chs of Christ	2	182	210	218	.1	.2
171 Ch God-Gen Con	7	340	272	449 *	.2	.5
173 Comm of Christ	1	32	NR	32	-	-
193 Episcopal	8	NR	897	2,060	1.1	2.2
203 Evan Free Ch	1	69	125	125	.1	.1
207 E.L.C.A.	30	9,637	3,091	14,239	7.3	15.3
226 Friends-USA	1	105	NR	134 *	.1	.1
245 Greek Orth Vslp	1	245	NR	1,045	.5	1.1
246 Greek Orthodox	1	NR	NR	288	.1	.3
263 Int Foursq Gos	1	151	475	475 *	.2	.5
283 Luth—MO Synod	1	169	111	213	.1	.2
288 Mennonite USA	1	25	20	32 *	-	-
293 Morav Ch-North	1	336	NR	413	.2	.4
335 Orth Pres Ch	1	127	166	181	.1	.2
339 Pent Ch of God	1	58	NR	78	-	.1
355 Presb Ch (USA)	4	591	310	753 *	.4	.8
356 Presb Ch Amer	2	179	215	246	.1	.3
360 Prim Bapt Chrch	1	NR	NR	NR	-	-
371 Ref Ch in Am	1	109	158	292	.1	.3
373 Ref Ch in U.S.	1	12	NR	19	-	-
403 Salvation Army	1	144	31	452	.2	.5
413 S.D.A.	3	850	NR	1,011	.5	1.1
418 Southw Bapt Fel	3	NR	NR	NR	-	-
419 So Bapt Conv	9	3,365	1,175	4,292 *	2.2	4.6
435 Unitarian-Univ	1	196	NR	250 *	.1	.3
443 Un C of Christ	14	2,891	1,128	3,688 *	1.9	4.0
449 Un Methodist	49	12,008	5,300	15,319 *	7.8	16.5
467 Wesleyan	1	0	40	50	-	.1
496 Jewish Est	1	NR	NR	1,200	.6	1.3
499 Indep.Non-Char	1	200	400	400	.2	.4
GARRETT	**88**	**7,546**	**5,002**	**11,807 ***	**39.6**	**100.0**
032 Amish; other	1	40	NR	49 *	.2	.4
053 Assemb of God	9	506	590	1,003	3.4	8.5
056 Baha'i	0	1	NR	1	-	-
081 Catholic	3	NR	NR	1,366	4.6	11.6
093 Chr Ch (Disc)	1	0	0	0 *	-	-
097 Chr Chs&Chs Cr	1	50	NR	62 *	.2	.5
123 Ch God (Ander)	1	NR	51	51	.2	.4
127 Ch God (Cleve)	3	336	305	414 *	1.4	3.5
145 Ch God Prophcy	1	46	NR	56 *	.2	.5
157 Ch of Brethren	11	963	664	1,199 *	4.0	10.2
165 Ch of Nazarene	1	64	83	109	.4	.9
167 Chs of Christ	1	40	43	52	.2	.4
171 Ch God-Gen Con	1	46	48	57 *	.2	.5
183 Cons Menn Conf	1	265	324	385	1.3	3.3
193 Episcopal	2	NR	71	308	1.0	2.6
203 Evan Free Ch	1	129	230	230	.8	1.9
207 E.L.C.A.	10	1,624	633	2,225	7.5	18.8
283 Luth—MO Synod	2	431	243	528	1.8	4.5
288 Mennonite USA	5	314	300	398 *	1.3	3.4
297 Mennonite;Other	2	144	NR	178 *	.6	1.5
413 S.D.A.	1	79	NR	94	.3	.8
418 Southw Bapt Fel	1	NR	NR	NR	-	-
419 So Bapt Conv	5	343	316	423 *	1.4	3.6
443 Un C of Christ	2	252	115	311 *	1.0	2.6
449 Un Methodist	22	1,873	986	2,308 *	7.7	19.5
HARFORD	**138**	**29,237**	**14,140**	**109,164 ***	**49.9**	**100.0**
053 Assemb of God	7	807	1,028	1,428	.7	1.3
056 Baha'i	1	43	NR	43	-	-
081 Catholic	13	NR	NR	65,201	29.8	59.7
089 Chr & Miss Al	1	40	NR	80	-	.1
097 Chr Chs&Chs Cr	4	1,890	NR	2,418 *	1.1	2.2
127 Ch God (Cleve)	7	734	504	940 *	.4	.9
145 Ch God Prophcy	1	46	NR	58 *	-	.1
151 L-D Saints	4	NR	NR	1,073	.5	1.0
165 Ch of Nazarene	2	541	444	541	.2	.5
167 Chs of Christ	2	159	195	247	.1	.2
193 Episcopal	9	NR	970	2,516	1.2	2.3
207 E.L.C.A.	7	4,154	1,753	6,452	3.0	5.9
223 Free Will Bapt	2	197	NR	252 *	.1	.2
226 Friends-USA	2	210	NR	269 *	.1	.2
283 Luth—MO Synod	2	1,102	532	1,625	.7	1.5
349 Pent Holiness	2	70	64	90 *	-	.1
355 Presb Ch (USA)	11	3,024	1,495	3,867 *	1.8	3.5
356 Presb Ch Amer	2	246	230	413	.2	.4
360 Prim Bapt Chrch	2	NR	NR	NR	-	-
403 Salvation Army	1	70	23	120	.1	.1
413 S.D.A.	3	301	NR	358	.2	.3
418 Southw Bapt Fel	1	NR	NR	NR	-	-
419 So Bapt Conv	15	5,110	2,349	6,536 *	3.0	6.0
435 Unitarian-Univ	1	162	NR	207 *	.1	.2

NR–Not Reported *Total adherents estimated from known number of communicant, confirmed, full members. - Represents a percentage less than 0.1. Percentages may not total 100 due to rounding.

Table 4: Religious Congregations by County and Group: 2000

Religious Group	Number of Churches, Synagogues, Mosques, or Temples	Number of Communicant, Confirmed, or Full Members	Number of Attendees	Total Adherents: Number of Adherents	% of Total Pop.	% of Total Adh.
443 Un C of Christ	1	165	70	211 *	.1	.2
449 Un Methodist	33	9,866	4,183	12,619 *	5.8	11.6
496 Jewish Est	1	NR	NR	1,200	.5	1.1
499 Indep.Non-Char	1	300	300	400	.2	.4
HOWARD	**133**	**25,905**	**15,872**	**122,290 ***	**49.3**	**100.0**
019 Amer Bapt USA	1	360	0	463 *	.2	.4
053 Assemb of God	5	461	611	863	.3	.7
056 Baha'i	1	232	NR	232	.1	.2
081 Catholic	9	NR	NR	66,119	26.7	54.1
093 Chr Ch (Disc)	1	75	0	96 *	-	.1
123 Ch God (Ander)	5	NR	1,552	1,552	.6	1.3
127 Ch God (Cleve)	2	122	51	157 *	.1	.1
145 Ch God Prophcy	1	46	NR	59 *	-	-
151 L-D Saints	5	NR	NR	2,147	.9	1.8
157 Ch of Brethren	1	86	75	111 *	-	.1
165 Ch of Nazarene	1	340	305	698	.3	.6
167 Chs of Christ	1	117	130	163	.1	.1
193 Episcopal	8	NR	1,559	5,211	2.1	4.3
207 E.L.C.A.	9	4,393	2,099	6,050	2.4	4.9
262 Int Cou Comm Ch	1	190	NR	244 *	.1	.2
263 Int Foursq Gos	1	30	39	39 *	-	-
267 Muslim Est	1	NR	412	1,891	.8	1.5
283 Luth—MO Synod	2	230	144	256	.1	.2
288 Mennonite USA	2	47	59	66 *	-	.1
331 OCA: Ter Diocs	1	113	NR	159	.1	.1
333 Malan Dioc Am	1	NR	NR	150	.1	.1
334 Malan Syr Orth	1	20	NR	100	-	.1
335 Orth Pres Ch	1	376	538	579	.2	.5
355 Presb Ch (USA)	4	1,807	904	2,323 *	.9	1.9
356 Presb Ch Amer	1	120	0	120	-	.1
413 S.D.A.	4	984	NR	1,171	.5	1.0
418 Southw Bapt Fel	1	NR	NR	NR	-	-
419 So Bapt Conv	22	5,763	2,804	7,409 *	3.0	6.1
435 Unitarian-Univ	2	392	NR	504 *	.2	.4
443 Un C of Christ	1	53	23	68 *	-	.1
449 Un Methodist	30	9,470	3,707	12,174 *	4.9	10.0
469 WELS	1	78	60	116	-	.1
496 Jewish Est	5	NR	NR	10,000	4.0	8.2
499 Indep.Non-Char	1	0	800	1,000	.4	.8
KENT	**45**	**4,654**	**1,991**	**8,870 ***	**46.2**	**100.0**
053 Assemb of God	1	35	45	45	.2	.5
056 Baha'i	0	1	NR	1	-	-
061 Beachy Amish	1	55	NR	65 *	.3	.7
081 Catholic	4	NR	NR	2,248	11.7	25.3
127 Ch God (Cleve)	1	23	44	44 *	.2	.5
193 Episcopal	5	NR	401	1,069	5.6	12.1
226 Friends-USA	1	105	NR	125 *	.7	1.4
283 Luth—MO Synod	1	264	82	324	1.7	3.7
355 Presb Ch (USA)	1	194	131	230 *	1.2	2.6
413 S.D.A.	2	223	NR	265	1.4	3.0
419 So Bapt Conv	1	133	114	158 *	.8	1.8
435 Unitarian-Univ	1	30	NR	36 *	.2	.4
449 Un Methodist	25	3,591	1,174	4,260 *	22.2	48.0
467 Wesleyan	1	0	0	0	-	-
MONTGOMERY	**546**	**115,663**	**55,855**	**459,923 ***	**52.7**	**100.0**
017 Amer Bapt Assn	2	80	NR	99 *	-	-
019 Amer Bapt USA	30	11,938	6,849	14,919 *	1.7	3.2
022 Carp Rus Orth	1	122	NR	207	-	-
034 Ant Orth of NA	1	587	NR	1,174	.1	.3
049 Armen Ap Cilic	1	357	NR	924	.1	.2
053 Assemb of God	10	1,059	1,264	1,615	.2	.4
055 As Ref Pres Ch	3	440	NR	566	.1	.1
056 Baha'i	11	756	NR	756	.1	.2
076 Buddhism	20	NR	NR	NR	-	-
081 Catholic	37	NR	NR	185,136	21.2	40.3
089 Chr & Miss Al	7	779	NR	1,486	.2	.3
093 Chr Ch (Disc)	8	1,251	520	1,563 *	.2	.3
097 Chr Chs&Chs Cr	1	340	NR	425 *	-	.1
105 Christian Ref	1	152	159	190 *	-	-
123 Ch God (Ander)	1	NR	85	85	-	-

Religious Group	Number of Churches, Synagogues, Mosques, or Temples	Number of Communicant, Confirmed, or Full Members	Number of Attendees	Total Adherents: Number of Adherents	% of Total Pop.	% of Total Adh.
127 Ch God (Cleve)	12	931	799	1,199 *	.1	.3
145 Ch God Prophcy	1	46	NR	57 *	-	-
151 L-D Saints	22	NR	NR	6,744	.8	1.5
157 Ch of Brethren	2	88	40	110 *	-	-
165 Ch of Nazarene	4	478	466	612	.1	.1
167 Chs of Christ	5	569	585	766	.1	.2
193 Episcopal	25	NR	4,741	14,714	1.7	3.2
203 Evan Free Ch	3	164	760	760	.1	.2
207 E.L.C.A.	15	6,989	3,059	9,232	1.1	2.0
216 Evan Presby Ch	1	2,579	NR	3,223 *	.4	.7
221 Free Methodist	5	226	350	371	-	.1
226 Friends-USA	3	315	NR	394 *	-	.1
246 Greek Orthodox	1	NR	NR	2,160	.2	.5
252 Hindu	17	NR	NR	NR	-	-
262 Int Cou Comm Ch	3	405	NR	505 *	.1	.1
263 Int Foursq Gos	4	462	844	844 *	.1	.2
267 Muslim Est	8	NR	3,482	18,426	2.1	4.0
268 Jain	2	NR	NR	NR	-	-
283 Luth—MO Synod	7	2,605	1,056	3,347	.4	.7
288 Mennonite USA	1	41	50	51 *	-	-
290 Metro Comm Ch	1	128	104	160 *	-	-
331 OCA: Ter Diocs	1	182	NR	342	-	.1
332 OCA: Bulg Dioc	1	130	NR	354	-	.1
333 Malan Dioc Am	2	NR	NR	375	-	.1
334 Malan Syr Orth	1	27	NR	81	-	-
335 Orth Pres Ch	4	331	373	487	.1	.1
339 Pent Ch of God	1	45	NR	54	-	-
349 Pent Holiness	3	162	158	202 *	-	-
355 Presb Ch (USA)	27	6,644	5,143	9,815 *	1.1	2.1
356 Presb Ch Amer	6	404	459	572	.1	.1
360 Prim Bapt Chrch	1	NR	NR	NR	-	-
403 Salvation Army	1	99	42	156	-	-
413 S.D.A.	30	10,259	NR	12,210	1.4	2.7
416 Sikh	3	NR	NR	NR	-	-
418 Southw Bapt Fel	1	NR	NR	NR	-	-
419 So Bapt Conv	64	23,468	6,944	29,328 *	3.4	6.4
423 Syrian Orth Ch	1	NR	NR	280	-	.1
431 Ukrainian Orth	1	NR	NR	369	-	.1
435 Unitarian-Univ	5	2,271	NR	2,838 *	.3	.6
443 Un C of Christ	6	2,156	849	2,694 *	.3	.6
449 Un Methodist	61	26,511	9,254	33,129 *	3.8	7.2
467 Wesleyan	5	0	195	205	-	-
496 Jewish Est	36	NR	NR	83,800	9.6	18.2
498 Indep.Charis.	3	6,287	4,500	6,287	.7	1.4
499 Indep.Non-Char	6	2,800	2,725	3,525	.4	.8
PRINCE GEORGE'S	**442**	**93,992**	**47,528**	**245,782 ***	**30.7**	**100.0**
017 Amer Bapt Assn	4	1,180	NR	1,498 *	.2	.6
019 Amer Bapt USA	29	10,224	3,709	12,983 *	1.6	5.3
039 Ap Chr Ch(Naz)	1	22	34	34 *	-	-
053 Assemb of God	13	2,059	2,474	3,427	.4	1.4
056 Baha'i	6	255	NR	255	-	.1
057 Bapt Gen Conf	4	4,760	3,775	6,044 *	.8	2.5
076 Buddhism	2	NR	NR	NR	-	-
081 Catholic	36	NR	NR	78,954	9.9	32.1
084 Calvary Chapel	1	NR	NR	NR	-	-
089 Chr & Miss Al	2	51	NR	94	-	-
093 Chr Ch (Disc)	8	1,943	475	2,467 *	.3	1.0
097 Chr Chs&Chs Cr	2	143	NR	182 *	-	.1
123 Ch God (Ander)	2	NR	105	105	-	-
127 Ch God (Cleve)	14	7,871	1,100	9,994 *	1.2	4.1
145 Ch God Prophcy	3	137	NR	174 *	-	.1
151 L-D Saints	8	NR	NR	3,186	.4	1.3
157 Ch of Brethren	1	107	48	136 *	-	.1
165 Ch of Nazarene	6	424	349	594	.1	.2
167 Chs of Christ	9	1,519	1,625	2,026	.3	.8
173 Comm of Christ	1	71	NR	71	-	-
179 Consrv Bapt	2	NR	380	380	-	.2
193 Episcopal	24	NR	2,451	6,721	.8	2.7
201 Evan Cov Ch	1	81	100	103 *	-	-
207 E.L.C.A.	12	2,557	1,076	3,377	.4	1.4
220 Free Lutheran	1	23	38	38	-	-
221 Free Methodist	2	104	88	119	-	-
246 Greek Orthodox	1	NR	NR	285	-	.1

NR–Not Reported *Total adherents estimated from known number of communicant, confirmed, full members. - Represents a percentage less than 0.1. Percentages may not total 100 due to rounding.

Table 4: Religious Congregations by County and Group: 2000

Religious Group	Number of Churches, Synagogues, Mosques, or Temples	Number of Communicant, Confirmed, or Full Members	Number of Attendees	Total Adherents		
				Number of Adherents	% of Total Pop.	% of Total Adh.
251 Holy Orth in NA	1	NR	NR	90	-	-
252 Hindu	4	NR	NR	NR	-	-
262 Int Cou Comm Ch	1	220	NR	279 *	-	.1
263 Int Foursq Gos	4	222	439	439 *	.1	.2
267 Muslim Est	7	NR	2,697	12,346	1.5	5.0
283 Luth—MO Synod	10	2,689	1,423	3,482	.4	1.4
288 Mennonite USA	3	318	345	450 *	.1	.2
290 Metro Comm Ch	1	23	25	29 *	-	-
293 Morav Ch-North	2	336	NR	469	.1	.2
335 Orth Pres Ch	1	59	80	81	-	-
339 Pent Ch of God	1	22	NR	34	-	-
349 Pent Holiness	5	602	487	764 *	.1	.3
355 Presb Ch (USA)	21	3,067	1,834	3,895 *	.5	1.6
356 Presb Ch Amer	4	637	647	854	.1	.3
388 Reg Bapt Gen As	4	339	362	432 *	.1	.2
403 Salvation Army	1	219	99	581	.1	.2
413 S.D.A.	14	5,130	NR	6,104	.8	2.5
418 Southw Bapt Fel	3	NR	NR	NR	-	-
419 So Bapt Conv	87	18,366	8,241	23,321 *	2.9	9.5
435 Unitarian-Univ	3	447	NR	568 *	.1	.2
443 Un C of Christ	4	602	280	764 *	.1	.3
449 Un Methodist	42	20,185	7,599	25,633 *	3.2	10.4
467 Wesleyan	5	0	249	1,945	.2	.8
469 WELS	1	198	139	305	-	.1
496 Jewish Est	9	NR	NR	20,700	2.6	8.4
498 Indep.Charis.	3	3,425	1,975	4,300	.5	1.7
499 Indep.Non-Char	6	3,355	2,780	4,670	.6	1.9
QUEEN ANNE'S	**46**	**5,972**	**2,758**	**15,491 ***	**38.2**	**100.0**
053 Assemb of God	2	56	56	103	.3	.7
056 Baha'i	0	10	NR	10	-	.1
081 Catholic	3	NR	NR	6,676	16.5	43.1
089 Chr & Miss Al	1	114	NR	306	.8	2.0
127 Ch God (Cleve)	4	415	197	517 *	1.3	3.3
151 L-D Saints	1	NR	NR	138	.3	.9
165 Ch of Nazarene	1	73	74	77	.2	.5
167 Chs of Christ	1	47	50	60	.1	.4
193 Episcopal	3	NR	397	1,027	2.5	6.6
207 E.L.C.A.	1	0	0	0	-	-
263 Int Foursq Gos	1	20	51	51 *	.1	.3
283 Luth—MO Synod	1	101	62	142	.4	.9
356 Presb Ch Amer	1	151	180	180	.4	1.2
413 S.D.A.	1	173	NR	206	.5	1.3
419 So Bapt Conv	1	155	99	193 *	.5	1.2
449 Un Methodist	24	4,657	1,592	5,805 *	14.3	37.5
SAINT MARY'S	**61**	**6,906**	**4,521**	**24,332 ***	**28.2**	**100.0**
053 Assemb of God	2	300	331	472	.5	1.9
056 Baha'i	0	22	NR	22	-	.1
081 Catholic	15	NR	NR	12,972	15.0	53.3
093 Chr Ch (Disc)	1	36	24	46 *	.1	.2
127 Ch God (Cleve)	1	258	118	330 *	.4	1.4
151 L-D Saints	2	NR	NR	663	.8	2.7
165 Ch of Nazarene	2	278	179	282	.3	1.2
167 Chs of Christ	1	120	141	181	.2	.7
193 Episcopal	7	NR	730	1,823	2.1	7.5
207 E.L.C.A.	1	137	145	186	.2	.8
263 Int Foursq Gos	1	27	35	35 *	-	.1
283 Luth—MO Synod	2	513	296	622	.7	2.6
286 E.PA Mennonite	1	54	NR	69 *	.1	.3
322 Old Ord Menn Ch	1	170	NR	218 *	.3	.9
323 Old Ord Amish	5	275	NR	350 *	.4	1.4
355 Presb Ch (USA)	1	320	183	410 *	.5	1.7
356 Presb Ch Amer	1	179	219	255	.3	1.0
413 S.D.A.	1	59	NR	70	.1	.3
418 Southw Bapt Fel	1	NR	NR	NR	-	-
419 So Bapt Conv	3	1,798	808	2,303 *	2.7	9.5
435 Unitarian-Univ	1	71	NR	91 *	.1	.4
449 Un Methodist	11	2,289	1,312	2,932 *	3.4	12.0
SOMERSET	**58**	**5,910**	**2,934**	**7,330 ***	**29.6**	**100.0**
053 Assemb of God	1	132	160	160	.6	2.2
056 Baha'i	0	51	NR	51	.2	.7
081 Catholic	1	NR	NR	80	.3	1.1
093 Chr Ch (Disc)	1	46	15	54 *	.2	.7
127 Ch God (Cleve)	2	686	353	801 *	3.2	10.9
145 Ch God Prophcy	1	46	NR	53 *	.2	.7
157 Ch of Brethren	1	84	52	98 *	.4	1.3
193 Episcopal	3	NR	99	208	.8	2.8
288 Mennonite USA	1	152	120	177 *	.7	2.4
355 Presb Ch (USA)	2	164	70	192 *	.8	2.6
419 So Bapt Conv	5	793	310	925 *	3.7	12.6
449 Un Methodist	39	3,756	1,694	4,381 *	17.7	59.8
467 Wesleyan	1	0	61	150	.6	2.0
TALBOT	**46**	**6,583**	**4,045**	**16,033 ***	**47.4**	**100.0**
053 Assemb of God	1	12	7	10	-	.1
056 Baha'i	0	6	NR	6	-	-
081 Catholic	3	NR	NR	5,300	15.7	33.1
127 Ch God (Cleve)	1	648	302	777 *	2.3	4.8
157 Ch of Brethren	2	333	184	399 *	1.2	2.5
165 Ch of Nazarene	1	127	118	206	.6	1.3
193 Episcopal	7	NR	778	2,417	7.1	15.1
207 E.L.C.A.	2	387	179	535	1.6	3.3
226 Friends-USA	1	105	NR	126 *	.4	.8
262 Int Cou Comm Ch	1	20	NR	24 *	.1	.1
283 Luth—MO Synod	1	305	184	395	1.2	2.5
355 Presb Ch (USA)	1	337	160	404 *	1.2	2.5
419 So Bapt Conv	4	677	525	811 *	2.4	5.1
435 Unitarian-Univ	1	88	NR	105 *	.3	.7
449 Un Methodist	18	3,369	1,320	4,038 *	11.9	25.2
467 Wesleyan	2	169	288	480	1.4	3.0
WASHINGTON	**187**	**34,494**	**17,336**	**59,027 ***	**44.7**	**100.0**
011 A.W.M.C.	1	0	50	0	-	-
017 Amer Bapt Assn	1	100	NR	122 *	.1	.2
019 Amer Bapt USA	1	200	140	244 *	.2	.4
053 Assemb of God	6	1,353	1,830	2,491	1.9	4.2
056 Baha'i	0	13	NR	13	-	-
071 Brethren (Ash)	3	382	314	467 *	.4	.8
075 Brethren in Cr	3	166	320	325	.2	.6
081 Catholic	9	NR	NR	10,675	8.1	18.1
089 Chr & Miss Al	1	0	NR	73	.1	.1
093 Chr Ch (Disc)	5	1,815	623	2,218 *	1.7	3.8
097 Chr Chs&Chs Cr	3	875	NR	1,069 *	.8	1.8
127 Ch God (Cleve)	9	1,937	1,526	2,369 *	1.8	4.0
151 L-D Saints	5	NR	NR	1,484	1.1	2.5
157 Ch of Brethren	11	1,654	983	2,050 *	1.6	3.5
165 Ch of Nazarene	3	193	238	415	.3	.7
167 Chs of Christ	1	150	140	200	.2	.3
171 Ch God-Gen Con	6	404	449	515 *	.4	.9
193 Episcopal	7	NR	576	1,930	1.5	3.3
203 Evan Free Ch	1	165	480	480	.4	.8
207 E.L.C.A.	20	6,506	2,322	8,558	6.5	14.5
267 Muslim Est	1	NR	78	300	.2	.5
283 Luth—MO Synod	2	276	179	349	.3	.6
288 Mennonite USA	6	221	227	301 *	.2	.5
290 Metro Comm Ch	1	55	69	69 *	.1	.1
291 Missionary Ch	1	13	24	24	-	-
297 Mennonite;Other	12	1,220	NR	1,491 *	1.1	2.5
331 OCA: Ter Diocs	1	47	NR	71	.1	.1
339 Pent Ch of God	1	32	NR	60	-	.1
355 Presb Ch (USA)	5	782	486	955 *	.7	1.6
356 Presb Ch Amer	2	103	149	157	.1	.3
388 Reg Bapt Gen As	1	225	200	275 *	.2	.5
403 Salvation Army	1	158	32	258	.2	.4
413 S.D.A.	4	1,287	NR	1,532	1.2	2.6
418 Southw Bapt Fel	1	NR	NR	NR	-	-
419 So Bapt Conv	10	1,659	681	2,027 *	1.5	3.4
435 Unitarian-Univ	1	52	NR	64 *	-	.1
443 Un C of Christ	11	2,516	1,056	3,075 *	2.3	5.2
449 Un Methodist	26	8,785	3,164	10,736 *	8.1	18.2
467 Wesleyan	1	0	30	60	-	.1
496 Jewish Est	1	NR	NR	325	.2	.6
499 Indep.Non-Char	2	1,150	970	1,200	.9	2.0

NR–Not Reported   *Total adherents estimated from known number of communicant, confirmed, full members.   - Represents a percentage less than 0.1.   Percentages may not total 100 due to rounding.

Table 4: Religious Congregations by County and Group: 2000

Religious Group	Number of Churches, Synagogues, Mosques, or Temples	Number of Communicant, Confirmed, or Full Members	Number of Attendees	Total Adherents		
				Number of Adherents	% of Total Pop.	% of Total Adh.
WICOMICO	**107**	**18,471**	**9,733**	**40,580 ***	**47.9**	**100.0**
053 Assemb of God	2	51	60	85	.1	.2
056 Baha'i	2	184	NR	184	.2	.5
081 Catholic	2	NR	NR	5,675	6.7	14.0
084 Calvary Chapel	1	NR	NR	NR	-	-
097 Chr Chs&Chs Cr	4	450	NR	555 *	.7	1.4
123 Ch God (Ander)	2	NR	166	166	.2	.4
127 Ch God (Cleve)	3	918	571	1,134 *	1.3	2.8
145 Ch God Prophcy	2	91	NR	112 *	.1	.3
151 L-D Saints	2	NR	NR	753	.9	1.9
157 Ch of Brethren	1	20	35	35 *	-	.1
165 Ch of Nazarene	2	503	394	962	1.1	2.4
167 Chs of Christ	2	81	87	104	.1	.3
193 Episcopal	5	NR	467	1,449	1.7	3.6
207 E.L.C.A.	1	109	58	141	.2	.3
226 Friends-USA	1	105	NR	130 *	.2	.3
252 Hindu	1	NR	NR	NR	-	-
267 Muslim Est	1	NR	55	163	.2	.4
283 Luth—MO Synod	1	314	146	393	.5	1.0
297 Mennonite;Other	1	34	NR	42 *	-	.1
355 Presb Ch (USA)	1	353	171	436 *	.5	1.1
356 Presb Ch Amer	1	142	285	285	.3	.7
413 S.D.A.	2	289	NR	344	.4	.8
419 So Bapt Conv	7	2,189	905	2,703 *	3.2	6.7
435 Unitarian-Univ	1	46	NR	57 *	.1	.1
449 Un Methodist	52	11,596	4,460	14,323 *	16.9	35.3
467 Wesleyan	5	396	1,373	9,349	11.0	23.0
496 Jewish Est	1	NR	NR	400	.5	1.0
499 Indep.Non-Char	1	600	500	600	.7	1.5
WORCESTER	**83**	**11,099**	**5,638**	**23,833 ***	**51.2**	**100.0**
053 Assemb of God	2	367	518	592	1.3	2.5
056 Baha'i	0	65	NR	65	.1	.3
081 Catholic	5	NR	NR	7,700	16.5	32.3
093 Chr Ch (Disc)	1	78	40	93 *	.2	.4
097 Chr Chs&Chs Cr	2	58	NR	68 *	.1	.3
127 Ch God (Cleve)	3	278	134	330 *	.7	1.4
145 Ch God Prophcy	2	91	NR	108 *	.2	.5
165 Ch of Nazarene	1	28	26	55	.1	.2
193 Episcopal	5	NR	607	1,882	4.0	7.9
207 E.L.C.A.	1	404	362	515	1.1	2.2
246 Greek Orthodox	1	NR	NR	702	1.5	2.9
288 Mennonite USA	1	33	60	60 *	.1	.3
297 Mennonite;Other	1	44	NR	52 *	.1	.2
355 Presb Ch (USA)	6	610	343	722 *	1.6	3.0
413 S.D.A.	2	77	NR	92	.2	.4
419 So Bapt Conv	8	2,536	1,024	3,009 *	6.5	12.6
431 Ukrainian Orth	1	NR	NR	60	.1	.3
449 Un Methodist	39	6,430	2,524	7,628 *	16.4	32.0
496 Jewish Est	2	NR	NR	100	.2	.4
MASSACHUSETTS						
The State.....	3,535	358,619	229,953	4,069,606 *	64.1	100.0
BARNSTABLE	**133**	**14,956**	**10,180**	**95,326 ***	**42.9**	**100.0**
019 Amer Bapt USA	9	1,019	950	1,209 *	.5	1.3
034 Ant Orth of NA	1	30	NR	60	-	.1
050 Armen Ap Etchm	1	0	NR	280	.1	.3
053 Assemb of God	5	375	500	600	.3	.6
056 Baha'i	1	110	NR	110	-	.1
057 Bapt Gen Conf	1	93	100	110 *	-	.1
076 Buddhism	1	NR	NR	NR	-	-
081 Catholic	29	NR	NR	63,729	28.7	66.9
084 Calvary Chapel	1	NR	NR	NR	-	-
089 Chr & Miss Al	2	169	NR	375	.2	.4
151 L-D Saints	1	NR	NR	258	.1	.3
165 Ch of Nazarene	2	152	195	273	.1	.3
167 Chs of Christ	1	64	85	96	-	.1
175 Congr Chr Chs	1	445	225	528 *	.2	.6
179 Consrv Bapt	5	NR	745	745	.3	.8
193 Episcopal	11	NR	2,219	7,093	3.2	7.4
201 Evan Cov Ch	1	229	195	272 *	.1	.3
203 Evan Free Ch	1	69	125	125	.1	.1
207 E.L.C.A.	3	1,263	511	1,564	.7	1.6
226 Friends-USA	5	215	NR	255 *	.1	.3
246 Greek Orthodox	1	NR	NR	1,533	.7	1.6
263 Int Foursq Gos	1	26	84	84 *	-	.1
283 Luth—MO Synod	1	44	34	69	-	.1
335 Orth Pres Ch	1	42	36	42	-	-
403 Salvation Army	1	108	64	207	.1	.2
413 S.D.A.	1	132	NR	157	.1	.2
419 So Bapt Conv	1	115	156	136 *	.1	.1
435 Unitarian-Univ	7	1,504	NR	1,784 *	.8	1.9
443 Un C of Christ	17	5,176	2,282	6,141 *	2.8	6.4
449 Un Methodist	15	3,576	1,674	4,241 *	1.9	4.4
496 Jewish Est	5	NR	NR	3,250	1.5	3.4
BERKSHIRE	**131**	**9,924**	**5,491**	**90,604 ***	**67.1**	**100.0**
019 Amer Bapt USA	10	1,904	654	2,286 *	1.7	2.5
053 Assemb of God	3	427	526	758	.6	.8
056 Baha'i	0	38	NR	38	-	-
076 Buddhism	1	NR	NR	NR	-	-
081 Catholic	37	NR	NR	69,757	51.7	77.0
151 L-D Saints	1	NR	NR	369	.3	.4
165 Ch of Nazarene	1	125	155	155	.1	.2
167 Chs of Christ	1	100	75	160	.1	.2
175 Congr Chr Chs	8	458	358	550 *	.4	.6
176 Congr Ad Afl	2	200	NR	240 *	.2	.3
181 Consrv Congr	1	36	47	43 *	-	-
193 Episcopal	15	NR	1,187	3,708	2.7	4.1
203 Evan Free Ch	1	60	100	100	.1	.1
207 E.L.C.A.	2	648	236	863	.6	1.0
246 Greek Orthodox	1	NR	NR	354	.3	.4
331 OCA: Ter Diocs	1	13	NR	38	-	-
370 Ref Baptist Chs	1	NR	NR	NR	-	-
388 Reg Bapt Gen As	1	20	35	35 *	-	-
403 Salvation Army	2	147	123	351	.3	.4
413 S.D.A.	1	123	NR	146	.1	.2
419 So Bapt Conv	1	92	112	110 *	.1	.1
435 Unitarian-Univ	2	180	NR	216 *	.2	.2
443 Un C of Christ	21	3,083	1,239	3,702 *	2.7	4.1
449 Un Methodist	10	2,182	606	2,620 *	1.9	2.9
469 WELS	1	88	38	105	.1	.1
496 Jewish Est	6	NR	NR	3,900	2.9	4.3
BRISTOL	**274**	**21,858**	**15,717**	**320,781 ***	**60.0**	**100.0**
019 Amer Bapt USA	19	3,259	1,390	4,035 *	.8	1.3
053 Assemb of God	12	1,479	1,865	2,456	.5	.8
056 Baha'i	0	77	NR	77	-	-
057 Bapt Gen Conf	3	791	510	1,043 *	.2	.3
081 Catholic	85	NR	NR	268,434	50.2	83.7
089 Chr & Miss Al	4	240	NR	375	.1	.1
127 Ch God (Cleve)	6	145	128	197 *	-	.1
145 Ch God Prophcy	1	82	NR	102 *	-	-
151 L-D Saints	3	NR	NR	913	.2	.3
165 Ch of Nazarene	3	1,015	650	1,050	.2	.3
167 Chs of Christ	3	285	302	382	.1	.1
173 Comm of Christ	2	74	NR	74	-	-
175 Congr Chr Chs	5	930	335	1,151 *	.2	.4
179 Consrv Bapt	5	NR	569	569	.1	.2
181 Consrv Congr	4	377	317	467 *	.1	.1
193 Episcopal	18	NR	1,698	5,100	1.0	1.6
201 Evan Cov Ch	2	611	497	756 *	.1	.2
207 E.L.C.A.	3	954	355	1,435	.3	.4
221 Free Methodist	1	27	33	33	-	-
226 Friends-USA	7	301	NR	373 *	.1	.1
246 Greek Orthodox	3	NR	NR	1,386	.3	.4
252 Hindu	1	NR	NR	NR	-	-
263 Int Foursq Gos	2	197	412	412 *	.1	.1
267 Muslim Est	1	NR	412	1,891	.4	.6
268 Jain	1	NR	NR	NR	-	-
283 Luth—MO Synod	1	153	99	213	-	.1
335 Orth Pres Ch	1	8	10	10	-	-
355 Presb Ch (USA)	3	174	156	215 *	-	.1

NR–Not Reported   *Total adherents estimated from known number of communicant, confirmed, full members.   - Represents a percentage less than 0.1.   Percentages may not total 100 due to rounding.

Table 4: Religious Congregations by County and Group: 2000

Religious Group	Number of Churches, Synagogues, Mosques, or Temples	Number of Communicant, Confirmed, or Full Members	Number of Attendees	Total Adherents		
				Number of Adherents	% of Total Pop.	% of Total Adh.
363 Primitive Meth	3	171	NR	182	-	.1
370 Ref Baptist Chs	1	NR	NR	NR	-	-
403 Salvation Army	3	304	150	716	.1	.2
413 S.D.A.	12	1,123	NR	1,338	.3	.4
419 So Bapt Conv	2	55	38	68 *	-	-
435 Unitarian-Univ	7	870	NR	1,077 *	.2	.3
443 Un C of Christ	19	4,627	1,991	5,728 *	1.1	1.8
449 Un Methodist	17	2,895	1,121	3,583 *	.7	1.1
463 Vineyard	1	130	120	161 *	-	.1
469 WELS	1	119	84	179	-	.1
496 Jewish Est	5	NR	NR	11,600	2.2	3.6
498 Indep.Charis.	1	0	800	1,000	.2	.3
499 Indep.Non-Char	3	385	1,675	2,000	.4	.6
DUKES	**24**	**1,607**	**1,262**	**12,883 ***	**86.0**	**100.0**
019 Amer Bapt USA	3	382	205	461 *	3.1	3.6
053 Assemb of God	2	130	174	174	1.2	1.4
056 Baha'i	0	5	NR	5	-	-
057 Bapt Gen Conf	1	51	81	81 *	.5	.6
081 Catholic	3	NR	NR	9,951	66.4	77.2
151 L-D Saints	1	NR	NR	49	.3	.4
176 Congr Ad Afl	1	244	NR	295 *	2.0	2.3
193 Episcopal	3	NR	336	608	4.1	4.7
226 Friends-USA	1	43	NR	52 *	.3	.4
388 Reg Bapt Gen As	1	69	72	83 *	.6	.6
435 Unitarian-Univ	1	69	NR	83 *	.6	.6
443 Un C of Christ	1	180	121	217 *	1.4	1.7
449 Un Methodist	5	434	273	524 *	3.5	4.1
496 Jewish Est	1	NR	NR	300	2.0	2.3
ESSEX	**378**	**37,600**	**23,445**	**466,354 ***	**64.5**	**100.0**
019 Amer Bapt USA	24	4,242	2,635	5,291 *	.7	1.1
034 Ant Orth of NA	1	346	NR	692	.1	.1
049 Armen Ap Cilic	1	84	NR	420	.1	.1
050 Armen Ap Etchm	2	209	NR	1,360	.2	.3
053 Assemb of God	16	1,791	1,766	3,110	.4	.7
056 Baha'i	2	211	NR	211	-	-
057 Bapt Gen Conf	1	178	402	402 *	.1	.1
076 Buddhism	3	NR	NR	NR	-	-
081 Catholic	70	NR	NR	362,900	50.2	77.8
089 Chr & Miss Al	3	300	NR	650	.1	.1
093 Chr Ch (Disc)	1	39	0	49 *	-	-
127 Ch God (Cleve)	4	231	281	367 *	.1	.1
145 Ch God Prophcy	1	51	NR	64 *	-	-
151 L-D Saints	5	NR	NR	1,430	.2	.3
165 Ch of Nazarene	7	541	520	2,844	.4	.6
167 Chs of Christ	3	128	125	213	-	-
175 Congr Chr Chs	2	160	87	200 *	-	-
176 Congr Ad Afl	1	520	NR	649 *	.1	.1
179 Consrv Bapt	3	NR	400	400	.1	.1
181 Consrv Congr	9	1,594	1,452	1,988 *	.3	.4
193 Episcopal	28	NR	3,641	14,064	1.9	3.0
201 Evan Cov Ch	1	184	138	229 *	-	-
207 E.L.C.A.	6	1,492	614	2,228	.3	.5
221 Free Methodist	9	278	524	546	.1	.1
226 Friends-USA	3	129	NR	161 *	-	-
246 Greek Orthodox	6	NR	NR	10,272	1.4	2.2
251 Holy Orth in NA	1	NR	NR	99	-	-
252 Hindu	1	NR	NR	NR	-	-
262 Int Cou Comm Ch	2	404	NR	504 *	.1	.1
263 Int Foursq Gos	1	25	32	32 *	-	-
267 Muslim Est	1	NR	412	1,891	.3	.4
283 Luth—MO Synod	2	341	219	543	.1	.1
331 OCA: Ter Diocs	1	128	NR	261	-	.1
335 Orth Pres Ch	2	337	448	483	.1	.1
355 Presb Ch (USA)	3	371	326	463 *	.1	.1
363 Primitive Meth	2	114	NR	121	-	-
370 Ref Baptist Chs	1	NR	NR	NR	-	-
388 Reg Bapt Gen As	1	52	70	70 *	-	-
401 Rus Orth Abroad	2	NR	NR	NR	-	-
403 Salvation Army	6	382	275	1,103	.2	.2
413 S.D.A.	8	570	NR	678	.1	.1
419 So Bapt Conv	7	457	462	570 *	.1	.1

Religious Group	Number of Churches, Synagogues, Mosques, or Temples	Number of Communicant, Confirmed, or Full Members	Number of Attendees	Total Adherents		
				Number of Adherents	% of Total Pop.	% of Total Adh.
435 Unitarian-Univ	15	2,185	NR	2,725 *	.4	.6
443 Un C of Christ	49	12,314	6,048	15,358 *	2.1	3.3
449 Un Methodist	31	6,987	2,318	8,713 *	1.2	1.9
496 Jewish Est	29	NR	NR	21,700	3.0	4.7
499 Indep.Non-Char	1	225	250	300	-	.1
FRANKLIN	**89**	**5,948**	**2,867**	**51,527 ***	**72.0**	**100.0**
019 Amer Bapt USA	6	844	317	1,022 *	1.4	2.0
053 Assemb of God	3	193	175	280	.4	.5
056 Baha'i	2	101	NR	101	.1	.2
057 Bapt Gen Conf	2	117	75	165 *	.2	.3
076 Buddhism	3	NR	NR	NR	-	-
081 Catholic	17	NR	NR	41,847	58.5	81.2
089 Chr & Miss Al	1	214	NR	587	.8	1.1
151 L-D Saints	1	NR	NR	257	.4	.5
165 Ch of Nazarene	1	56	53	56	.1	.1
167 Chs of Christ	1	11	15	15	-	-
181 Consrv Congr	2	195	165	236 *	.3	.5
193 Episcopal	4	NR	218	682	1.0	1.3
201 Evan Cov Ch	1	31	39	39 *	.1	.1
207 E.L.C.A.	2	346	158	456	.6	.9
226 Friends-USA	1	43	NR	52 *	.1	.1
263 Int Foursq Gos	1	40	38	48 *	.1	.1
403 Salvation Army	1	77	37	128	.2	.2
413 S.D.A.	1	79	NR	94	.1	.2
416 Sikh	1	NR	NR	NR	-	-
435 Unitarian-Univ	6	226	NR	274 *	.4	.5
443 Un C of Christ	26	2,752	1,369	3,334 *	4.7	6.5
449 Un Methodist	5	623	208	754 *	1.1	1.5
496 Jewish Est	1	NR	NR	1,100	1.5	2.1
HAMPDEN	**247**	**27,492**	**15,707**	**295,436 ***	**64.8**	**100.0**
019 Amer Bapt USA	19	4,435	1,719	5,551 *	1.2	1.9
049 Armen Ap Cilic	1	145	NR	280	.1	.1
050 Armen Ap Etchm	1	112	NR	400	.1	.1
053 Assemb of God	13	2,200	2,659	2,935	.6	1.0
056 Baha'i	3	268	NR	268	.1	.1
081 Catholic	75	NR	NR	239,076	52.4	80.9
084 Calvary Chapel	1	NR	NR	NR	-	-
089 Chr & Miss Al	2	82	NR	115	-	-
123 Ch God (Ander)	1	NR	0	0	-	-
127 Ch God (Cleve)	5	558	381	699 *	.2	.2
145 Ch God Prophcy	1	82	NR	103 *	-	-
151 L-D Saints	2	NR	NR	1,075	.2	.4
165 Ch of Nazarene	2	238	157	249	.1	.1
167 Chs of Christ	2	194	220	245	.1	.1
175 Congr Chr Chs	2	145	150	181 *	-	.1
179 Consrv Bapt	1	NR	350	350	.1	.1
181 Consrv Congr	1	43	57	54 *	-	-
193 Episcopal	14	NR	1,676	4,539	1.0	1.5
201 Evan Cov Ch	2	454	772	772 *	.2	.3
203 Evan Free Ch	1	100	260	260	.1	.1
207 E.L.C.A.	5	1,694	654	2,311	.5	.8
246 Greek Orthodox	4	NR	NR	2,934	.6	1.0
262 Int Cou Comm Ch	1	250	NR	313 *	.1	.1
267 Muslim Est	2	NR	312	1,218	.3	.4
283 Luth—MO Synod	4	1,651	963	2,053	.4	.7
297 Mennonite;Other	1	11	NR	14 *	-	-
331 OCA: Ter Diocs	1	144	NR	228	-	.1
355 Presb Ch (USA)	3	316	311	428 *	.1	.1
356 Presb Ch Amer	1	94	127	150	-	.1
370 Ref Baptist Chs	1	NR	NR	NR	-	-
388 Reg Bapt Gen As	1	69	72	86 *	-	-
401 Rus Orth Abroad	1	NR	NR	NR	-	-
403 Salvation Army	2	296	166	479	.1	.2
413 S.D.A.	4	781	NR	930	.2	.3
419 So Bapt Conv	4	307	79	384 *	.1	.1
435 Unitarian-Univ	3	310	NR	388 *	.1	.1
443 Un C of Christ	32	9,016	3,431	11,284 *	2.5	3.8
449 Un Methodist	17	3,497	1,153	4,377 *	1.0	1.5
467 Wesleyan	1	0	38	107	-	-
496 Jewish Est	10	NR	NR	10,600	2.3	3.6

NR–Not Reported *Total adherents estimated from known number of communicant, confirmed, full members. - Represents a percentage less than 0.1. Percentages may not total 100 due to rounding.

Table 4: Religious Congregations by County and Group: 2000

Religious Group	Number of Churches, Synagogues, Mosques, or Temples	Number of Communicant, Confirmed, or Full Members	Number of Attendees	Total Adherents		
				Number of Adherents	% of Total Pop.	% of Total Adh.
HAMPSHIRE	**95**	**8,866**	**5,140**	**51,409 ***	**33.8**	**100.0**
019 Amer Bapt USA	3	474	435	556 *	.4	1.1
053 Assemb of God	4	232	259	331	.2	.6
056 Baha'i	3	243	NR	243	.2	.5
076 Buddhism	6	NR	NR	NR	-	-
081 Catholic	21	NR	NR	35,273	23.2	68.6
089 Chr & Miss Al	1	39	NR	100	.1	.2
127 Ch God (Cleve)	1	13	0	15 *	-	-
151 L-D Saints	1	NR	NR	431	.3	.8
175 Congr Chr Chs	2	313	195	367 *	.2	.7
193 Episcopal	5	NR	622	1,729	1.1	3.4
203 Evan Free Ch	1	75	120	120	.1	.2
207 E.L.C.A.	3	643	278	816	.5	1.6
226 Friends-USA	3	129	NR	151 *	.1	.3
267 Muslim Est	1	NR	156	609	.4	1.2
283 Luth—MO Synod	1	202	79	245	.2	.5
413 S.D.A.	2	43	NR	51	-	.1
419 So Bapt Conv	0	5	10	6 *	-	-
435 Unitarian-Univ	2	678	NR	795 *	.5	1.5
443 Un C of Christ	26	4,384	1,945	5,140 *	3.4	10.0
449 Un Methodist	5	1,093	391	1,281 *	.8	2.5
496 Jewish Est	3	NR	NR	2,500	1.6	4.9
499 Indep.Non-Char	1	300	650	650	.4	1.3
MIDDLESEX	**737**	**83,149**	**47,077**	**1,078,903 ***	**73.6**	**100.0**
007 OCA: Alban Dioc	1	NR	NR	200	-	-
019 Amer Bapt USA	56	8,887	4,501	10,811 *	.7	1.0
034 Ant Orth of NA	2	489	NR	978	.1	.1
049 Armen Ap Cilic	1	730	NR	2,100	.1	.2
050 Armen Ap Etchm	4	1,547	NR	10,710	.7	1.0
053 Assemb of God	23	3,767	3,292	4,670	.3	.4
056 Baha'i	11	793	NR	793	.1	.1
057 Bapt Gen Conf	3	108	126	142 *	-	-
076 Buddhism	24	NR	NR	NR	-	-
081 Catholic	136	NR	NR	793,922	54.2	73.6
084 Calvary Chapel	1	NR	NR	NR	-	-
089 Chr & Miss Al	3	93	NR	237	-	-
097 Chr Chs&Chs Cr	2	190	NR	231 *	-	-
105 Christian Ref	1	72	0	88 *	-	-
127 Ch God (Cleve)	11	750	443	914 *	.1	.1
151 L-D Saints	16	NR	NR	6,418	.4	.6
165 Ch of Nazarene	17	1,546	1,249	1,945	.1	.2
167 Chs of Christ	5	327	431	497	-	-
171 Ch God-Gen Con	1	0	65	65 *	-	-
173 Comm of Christ	1	174	NR	174	-	-
176 Congr Ad Afl	3	544	NR	662 *	-	.1
179 Consrv Bapt	8	NR	865	865	.1	.1
181 Consrv Congr	5	551	483	670 *	-	.1
185 Cumber Presb	1	20	NR	20	-	-
193 Episcopal	54	NR	5,874	21,262	1.5	2.0
201 Evan Cov Ch	4	398	320	485 *	-	-
203 Evan Free Ch	5	346	670	670	-	.1
207 E.L.C.A.	15	4,036	1,641	5,622	.4	.5
226 Friends-USA	4	172	NR	209 *	-	-
245 Greek Orth Vslp	1	140	NR	340	-	-
246 Greek Orthodox	12	NR	NR	14,553	1.0	1.3
252 Hindu	8	NR	NR	NR	-	-
262 Int Cou Comm Ch	2	630	NR	766 *	.1	.1
263 Int Foursq Gos	2	51	175	175 *	-	-
265 Int Pent C Chr	1	0	0	10	-	-
267 Muslim Est	7	NR	2,672	12,846	.9	1.2
283 Luth—MO Synod	2	775	584	1,118	.1	.1
288 Mennonite USA	2	111	87	135 *	-	-
331 OCA: Ter Diocs	1	67	NR	336	-	-
333 Malan Dioc Am	1	NR	NR	175	-	-
355 Presb Ch (USA)	8	1,401	886	1,704 *	.1	.2
356 Presb Ch Amer	5	321	510	510	-	-
363 Primitive Meth	2	114	NR	121	-	-
371 Ref Ch in Am	1	56	57	104	-	-
395 Romania Orth Ar	1	NR	NR	612	-	.1
403 Salvation Army	5	384	329	1,834	.1	.2
413 S.D.A.	14	1,807	NR	2,150	.1	.2
419 So Bapt Conv	19	2,774	2,404	3,375 *	.2	.3
425 Tao	1	NR	NR	NR	-	-
435 Unitarian-Univ	33	7,636	NR	9,289 *	.6	.9
443 Un C of Christ	79	20,100	9,185	24,451 *	1.7	2.3
449 Un Methodist	49	14,920	4,667	18,152 *	1.2	1.7
463 Vineyard	5	1,191	1,216	1,492 *	.1	.1
490 Zoroastrian	1	NR	NR	NR	-	-
496 Jewish Est	51	NR	NR	113,700	7.8	10.5
498 Indep.Charis.	4	1,131	1,595	1,595	.1	.1
499 Indep.Non-Char	2	4,000	2,750	4,000	.3	.4
NANTUCKET	**8**	**616**	**481**	**3,649 ***	**38.3**	**100.0**
019 Amer Bapt USA	1	80	100	100 *	1.1	2.7
056 Baha'i	0	9	NR	9	.1	.2
081 Catholic	1	NR	NR	2,000	21.0	54.8
175 Congr Chr Chs	1	326	150	384 *	4.0	10.5
193 Episcopal	1	NR	201	669	7.0	18.3
226 Friends-USA	1	43	NR	51 *	.5	1.4
435 Unitarian-Univ	1	124	NR	146 *	1.5	4.0
449 Un Methodist	1	34	30	40 *	.4	1.1
496 Jewish Est	1	NR	NR	250	2.6	6.9
NORFOLK	**315**	**30,698**	**20,244**	**484,380 ***	**74.5**	**100.0**
019 Amer Bapt USA	14	2,275	1,148	2,792 *	.4	.6
034 Ant Orth of NA	2	1,222	NR	2,444	.4	.5
053 Assemb of God	6	646	859	1,598	.2	.3
056 Baha'i	2	180	NR	180	-	-
057 Bapt Gen Conf	7	741	882	973 *	.1	.2
076 Buddhism	4	NR	NR	NR	-	-
081 Catholic	63	NR	NR	380,930	58.6	78.6
089 Chr & Miss Al	1	112	NR	350	.1	.1
105 Christian Ref	1	46	180	56 *	-	-
127 Ch God (Cleve)	1	19	12	23 *	-	-
151 L-D Saints	4	NR	NR	1,438	.2	.3
165 Ch of Nazarene	4	791	858	1,031	.2	.2
167 Chs of Christ	2	70	60	87	-	-
173 Comm of Christ	1	119	NR	119	-	-
175 Congr Chr Chs	4	1,042	486	1,279 *	.2	.3
176 Congr Ad Afl	1	222	NR	272 *	-	.1
179 Consrv Bapt	4	NR	910	910	.1	.2
181 Consrv Congr	2	609	635	747 *	.1	.2
193 Episcopal	31	NR	3,536	12,778	2.0	2.6
201 Evan Cov Ch	1	76	46	93 *	-	-
203 Evan Free Ch	1	55	102	102	-	-
207 E.L.C.A.	5	1,290	571	1,626	.3	.3
226 Friends-USA	2	86	NR	106 *	-	-
246 Greek Orthodox	3	NR	NR	5,040	.8	1.0
251 Holy Orth in NA	2	NR	NR	59	-	-
252 Hindu	6	NR	NR	NR	-	-
263 Int Foursq Gos	5	369	919	919 *	.1	.2
267 Muslim Est	2	NR	824	3,782	.6	.8
268 Jain	1	NR	NR	NR	-	-
283 Luth—MO Synod	3	720	321	967	.1	.2
288 Mennonite USA	1	35	45	45 *	-	-
355 Presb Ch (USA)	7	1,097	1,294	1,558 *	.2	.3
403 Salvation Army	1	134	73	720	.1	.1
413 S.D.A.	5	308	NR	367	.1	.1
416 Sikh	2	NR	NR	NR	-	-
419 So Bapt Conv	5	187	184	230 *	-	-
435 Unitarian-Univ	17	2,154	NR	2,644 *	.4	.5
443 Un C of Christ	36	12,262	4,941	15,050 *	2.3	3.1
449 Un Methodist	14	3,831	1,294	4,701 *	.7	1.0
467 Wesleyan	1	0	64	64	-	-
496 Jewish Est	41	NR	NR	38,300	5.9	7.9
PLYMOUTH	**229**	**25,283**	**15,158**	**273,068 ***	**57.8**	**100.0**
019 Amer Bapt USA	16	2,252	879	2,846 *	.6	1.0
034 Ant Orth of NA	1	25	NR	50	-	-
053 Assemb of God	9	948	1,320	1,925	.4	.7
056 Baha'i	0	64	NR	64	-	-
057 Bapt Gen Conf	4	562	562	734 *	.2	.3
076 Buddhism	1	NR	NR	NR	-	-
081 Catholic	40	NR	NR	205,060	43.4	75.1
084 Calvary Chapel	1	NR	NR	NR	-	-

NR–Not Reported   *Total adherents estimated from known number of communicant, confirmed, full members.   - Represents a percentage less than 0.1.   Percentages may not total 100 due to rounding.

Table 4: Religious Congregations by County and Group: 2000

Religious Group	Number of Churches, Synagogues, Mosques, or Temples	Number of Communicant, Confirmed, or Full Members	Number of Attendees	Total Adherents: Number of Adherents	Total Adherents: % of Total Pop.	Total Adherents: % of Total Adh.
089 Chr & Miss Al	3	130	NR	762	.2	.3
127 Ch God (Cleve)	4	86	47	108 *	-	-
145 Ch God Prophcy	1	82	NR	104 *	-	-
151 L-D Saints	3	NR	NR	1,202	.3	.4
165 Ch of Nazarene	8	998	858	1,265	.3	.5
167 Chs of Christ	1	15	15	15	-	-
173 Comm of Christ	1	91	NR	91	-	-
175 Congr Chr Chs	7	877	709	1,108 *	.2	.4
176 Congr Ad Afl	2	509	NR	643 *	.1	.2
179 Consrv Bapt	4	NR	763	763	.2	.3
181 Consrv Congr	3	354	357	447 *	.1	.2
193 Episcopal	15	NR	1,890	6,834	1.4	2.5
201 Evan Cov Ch	1	183	161	231 *	-	.1
203 Evan Free Ch	1	69	125	125	-	-
207 E.L.C.A.	6	2,006	616	2,685	.6	1.0
226 Friends-USA	3	129	NR	163 *	-	.1
246 Greek Orthodox	1	NR	NR	1,146	.2	.4
251 Holy Orth in NA	1	NR	NR	21	-	-
263 Int Foursq Gos	5	640	994	994 *	.2	.4
283 Luth—MO Synod	2	363	201	586	.1	.2
331 OCA: Ter Diocs	1	25	NR	112	-	-
403 Salvation Army	2	133	120	557	.1	.2
413 S.D.A.	6	716	NR	852	.2	.3
419 So Bapt Conv	4	330	292	417 *	.1	.2
435 Unitarian-Univ	14	1,748	NR	2,209 *	.5	.8
443 Un C of Christ	25	7,510	3,274	9,491 *	2.0	3.5
449 Un Methodist	23	3,913	1,334	4,945 *	1.0	1.8
463 Vineyard	1	525	441	663 *	.1	.2
496 Jewish Est	8	NR	NR	23,600	5.0	8.6
499 Indep.Non-Char	1	0	200	250	.1	.1
SUFFOLK	**343**	**35,147**	**35,380**	**413,990 ***	**60.0**	**100.0**
007 OCA: Alban Dioc	2	NR	NR	2,750	.4	.7
009 Alban Orth Dio	1	100	NR	125	-	-
019 Amer Bapt USA	35	7,656	4,359	9,115 *	1.3	2.2
034 Ant Orth of NA	1	1,234	NR	2,468	.4	.6
053 Assemb of God	14	1,315	1,290	1,610	.2	.4
056 Baha'i	1	288	NR	288	-	.1
057 Bapt Gen Conf	2	214	340	346 *	.1	.1
076 Buddhism	9	NR	NR	NR	-	-
081 Catholic	73	NR	NR	310,150	45.0	74.9
089 Chr & Miss Al	5	440	NR	582	.1	.1
123 Ch God (Ander)	2	NR	3,975	3,975	.6	1.0
127 Ch God (Cleve)	8	1,172	873	1,438 *	.2	.3
145 Ch God Prophcy	5	379	NR	453 *	.1	.1
151 L-D Saints	3	NR	NR	500	.1	.1
165 Ch of Nazarene	7	548	660	775	.1	.2
167 Chs of Christ	3	311	370	434	.1	.1
175 Congr Chr Chs	1	125	75	149 *	-	-
179 Consrv Bapt	5	NR	950	950	.1	.2
181 Consrv Congr	3	1,079	1,704	1,285 *	.2	.3
193 Episcopal	25	NR	3,884	9,405	1.4	2.3
201 Evan Cov Ch	1	157	98	187 *	-	-
203 Evan Free Ch	1	45	85	85	-	-
207 E.L.C.A.	6	537	349	747	.1	.2
221 Free Methodist	2	38	75	88	-	-
226 Friends-USA	1	43	NR	51 *	-	-
245 Greek Orth Vslp	2	210	NR	310	-	.1
246 Greek Orthodox	2	NR	NR	975	.1	.2
251 Holy Orth in NA	2	NR	NR	605	.1	.1
252 Hindu	4	NR	NR	NR	-	-
263 Int Foursq Gos	1	57	136	136 *	-	-
264 Int Chs of Crst	1	4,308	7,304	6,162	.9	1.5
267 Muslim Est	8	NR	2,959	13,587	2.0	3.3
283 Luth—MO Synod	2	378	168	642	.1	.2
288 Mennonite USA	2	157	142	187 *	-	-
290 Metro Comm Ch	1	48	41	57 *	-	-
331 OCA: Ter Diocs	2	130	NR	257	-	.1
335 Orth Pres Ch	1	19	27	27	-	-
355 Presb Ch (USA)	5	396	411	498 *	.1	.1
401 Rus Orth Abroad	1	NR	NR	NR	-	-
403 Salvation Army	7	436	466	1,206	.2	.3
413 S.D.A.	9	3,029	NR	3,605	.5	.9
419 So Bapt Conv	16	3,425	2,183	4,077 *	.6	1.0
423 Syrian Orth Ch	1	NR	NR	300	-	.1
431 Ukrainian Orth	1	NR	NR	900	.1	.2
435 Unitarian-Univ	8	1,343	NR	1,599 *	.2	.4
443 Un C of Christ	18	2,387	1,195	2,842 *	.4	.7
449 Un Methodist	10	1,143	661	1,362 *	.2	.3
496 Jewish Est	22	NR	NR	24,700	3.6	6.0
498 Indep.Charis.	1	2,000	600	2,000	.3	.5
WORCESTER	**532**	**55,475**	**31,804**	**431,296 ***	**57.4**	**100.0**
007 OCA: Alban Dioc	2	NR	NR	600	.1	.1
019 Amer Bapt USA	29	5,306	2,987	6,641 *	.9	1.5
034 Ant Orth of NA	1	1,143	NR	2,286	.3	.5
049 Armen Ap Cilic	2	224	NR	924	.1	.2
050 Armen Ap Etchm	1	436	NR	2,100	.3	.5
053 Assemb of God	25	2,721	3,228	4,355	.6	1.0
056 Baha'i	1	190	NR	190	-	-
057 Bapt Gen Conf	9	1,268	1,245	1,649 *	.2	.4
076 Buddhism	5	NR	NR	NR	-	-
081 Catholic	132	NR	NR	309,267	41.2	71.7
084 Calvary Chapel	1	NR	NR	NR	-	-
089 Chr & Miss Al	3	284	NR	317	-	.1
093 Chr Ch (Disc)	1	89	45	111 *	-	-
097 Chr Chs&Chs Cr	1	90	NR	113 *	-	-
105 Christian Ref	2	1,144	650	1,432 *	.2	.3
127 Ch God (Cleve)	9	344	328	469 *	.1	.1
145 Ch God Prophcy	2	133	NR	167 *	-	-
151 L-D Saints	6	NR	NR	2,056	.3	.5
165 Ch of Nazarene	6	479	585	1,063	.1	.2
167 Chs of Christ	5	256	305	363	-	.1
179 Consrv Bapt	8	NR	1,300	1,300	.2	.3
181 Consrv Congr	9	657	565	822 *	.1	.2
193 Episcopal	30	NR	3,426	10,492	1.4	2.4
201 Evan Cov Ch	3	674	346	844 *	.1	.2
207 E.L.C.A.	15	5,726	2,031	8,007	1.1	1.9
226 Friends-USA	1	43	NR	54 *	-	-
246 Greek Orthodox	5	NR	NR	4,752	.6	1.1
251 Holy Orth in NA	1	NR	NR	150	-	-
262 Int Cou Comm Ch	1	1,200	NR	1,502 *	.2	.3
263 Int Foursq Gos	7	545	1,870	1,870 *	.2	.4
267 Muslim Est	3	NR	1,236	5,673	.8	1.3
283 Luth—MO Synod	3	700	435	1,020	.1	.2
286 E.PA Mennonite	1	28	NR	35 *	-	-
355 Presb Ch (USA)	3	469	347	587 *	.1	.1
356 Presb Ch Amer	2	30	25	35	-	-
388 Reg Bapt Gen As	2	203	182	254 *	-	.1
395 Romania Orth Ar	2	NR	NR	1,138	.2	.3
403 Salvation Army	5	413	258	808	.1	.2
413 S.D.A.	16	3,847	NR	4,578	.6	1.1
416 Sikh	2	NR	NR	NR	-	-
419 So Bapt Conv	14	1,194	894	1,494 *	.2	.3
423 Syrian Orth Ch	1	NR	NR	300	-	.1
435 Unitarian-Univ	25	2,081	NR	2,605 *	.3	.6
443 Un C of Christ	74	15,250	6,594	19,088 *	2.5	4.4
449 Un Methodist	35	6,978	2,332	8,735 *	1.2	2.0
496 Jewish Est	18	NR	NR	19,500	2.6	4.5
499 Indep.Non-Char	3	1,330	590	1,550	.2	.4

MICHIGAN

Religious Group	Number of Churches, Synagogues, Mosques, or Temples	Number of Communicant, Confirmed, or Full Members	Number of Attendees	Total Adherents: Number of Adherents	Total Adherents: % of Total Pop.	Total Adherents: % of Total Adh.
The State.....	7,527	1,295,337	842,244	4,158,134 *	41.8	100.0
ALCONA	**20**	**1,238**	**701**	**2,535 ***	**21.6**	**100.0**
019 Amer Bapt USA	1	171	80	199 *	1.7	7.9
056 Baha'i	0	1	NR	1	-	-
081 Catholic	3	NR	NR	1,061	9.1	41.9
127 Ch God (Cleve)	1	43	44	50 *	.4	2.0
173 Comm of Christ	1	127	NR	127	1.1	5.0
193 Episcopal	1	NR	17	29	.2	1.1
207 E.L.C.A.	3	198	109	250	2.1	9.9
283 Luth—MO Synod	2	59	56	90	.8	3.6
355 Presb Ch (USA)	2	202	135	235 *	2.0	9.3
413 S.D.A.	1	16	NR	19	.2	.7

NR–Not Reported   *Total adherents estimated from known number of communicant, confirmed, full members.   - Represents a percentage less than 0.1.   Percentages may not total 100 due to rounding.

Table 4: Religious Congregations by County and Group: 2000

Religious Group	Number of Churches, Synagogues, Mosques, or Temples	Number of Communicant, Confirmed, or Full Members	Number of Attendees	Total Adherents		
				Number of Adherents	% of Total Pop.	% of Total Adh.
449 Un Methodist	4	325	206	378 *	3.2	14.9
469 WELS	1	96	54	96	.8	3.8
ALGER	**21**	**1,626**	**893**	**5,530 ***	**56.1**	**100.0**
053 Assemb of God	1	30	42	52	.5	.9
056 Baha'i	0	3	NR	3	-	.1
081 Catholic	4	NR	NR	3,150	31.9	57.0
193 Episcopal	1	NR	20	59	.6	1.1
207 E.L.C.A.	4	602	218	839	8.5	15.2
220 Free Lutheran	1	160	80	180	1.8	3.3
283 Luth—MO Synod	2	413	125	543	5.5	9.8
288 Mennonite USA	1	8	25	25 *	.3	.5
355 Presb Ch (USA)	1	76	41	89 *	.9	1.6
388 Reg Bapt Gen As	1	89	130	130 *	1.3	2.4
413 S.D.A.	1	63	NR	75	.8	1.4
449 Un Methodist	3	182	121	214 *	2.2	3.9
467 Wesleyan	1	0	91	171	1.7	3.1
ALLEGAN	**119**	**18,836**	**15,298**	**40,221 ***	**38.1**	**100.0**
019 Amer Bapt USA	1	100	60	128 *	.1	.3
053 Assemb of God	4	247	320	491	.5	1.2
056 Baha'i	0	11	NR	11	-	-
081 Catholic	9	NR	NR	11,992	11.3	29.8
093 Chr Ch (Disc)	1	209	150	268 *	.3	.7
105 Christian Ref	26	7,966	5,236	10,233 *	9.7	25.4
123 Ch God (Ander)	2	NR	356	356	.3	.9
127 Ch God (Cleve)	2	128	76	165 *	.2	.4
151 L-D Saints	1	NR	NR	144	.1	.4
165 Ch of Nazarene	1	12	14	16	-	-
167 Chs of Christ	1	90	80	100	.1	.2
173 Comm of Christ	1	96	NR	96	.1	.2
175 Congr Chr Chs	4	515	377	662 *	.6	1.6
179 Consrv Bapt	2	NR	283	283	.3	.7
193 Episcopal	4	NR	262	668	.6	1.7
201 Evan Cov Ch	1	326	266	419 *	.4	1.0
203 Evan Free Ch	1	35	70	70	.1	.2
207 E.L.C.A.	2	554	212	779	.7	1.9
252 Hindu	1	NR	NR	NR	-	-
262 Int Cou Comm Ch	1	40	NR	51 *	-	.1
283 Luth—MO Synod	1	158	142	232	.2	.6
306 NT IndBapt&Rltd	1	45	NR	58 *	.1	.1
349 Pent Holiness	1	12	12	15 *	-	-
355 Presb Ch (USA)	2	174	126	224 *	.2	.6
371 Ref Ch in Am	11	2,617	2,869	4,439	4.2	11.0
388 Reg Bapt Gen As	4	639	730	839 *	.8	2.1
413 S.D.A.	3	186	NR	222	.2	.6
443 Un C of Christ	2	258	235	331 *	.3	.8
449 Un Methodist	19	2,566	1,829	3,294 *	3.1	8.2
467 Wesleyan	4	415	614	1,265	1.2	3.1
469 WELS	5	837	579	1,170	1.1	2.9
499 Indep.Non-Char	1	600	400	1,200	1.1	3.0
ALPENA	**44**	**7,207**	**3,809**	**24,389 ***	**77.9**	**100.0**
019 Amer Bapt USA	2	181	165	219 *	.7	.9
053 Assemb of God	1	95	100	205	.7	.8
056 Baha'i	0	42	NR	42	.1	.2
081 Catholic	6	NR	NR	13,650	43.6	56.0
097 Chr Chs&Chs Cr	1	153	NR	185 *	.6	.8
123 Ch God (Ander)	1	NR	86	86	.3	.4
145 Ch God Prophcy	1	36	NR	43 *	.1	.2
151 L-D Saints	1	NR	NR	88	.3	.4
165 Ch of Nazarene	1	24	30	40	.1	.2
167 Chs of Christ	1	33	20	40	.1	.2
173 Comm of Christ	2	274	NR	274	.9	1.1
175 Congr Chr Chs	1	117	99	142 *	.5	.6
193 Episcopal	2	NR	180	444	1.4	1.8
207 E.L.C.A.	5	2,465	872	3,460	11.0	14.2
221 Free Methodist	1	110	124	124	.4	.5
246 Greek Orthodox	1	NR	NR	225	.7	.9
283 Luth—MO Synod	3	1,781	775	2,544	8.1	10.4
313 N Am Bapt Conf	1	213	332	258 *	.8	1.1
323 Old Ord Amish	1	55	NR	67 *	.2	.3
355 Presb Ch (USA)	1	128	76	155 *	.5	.6

Religious Group	Number of Churches, Synagogues, Mosques, or Temples	Number of Communicant, Confirmed, or Full Members	Number of Attendees	Total Adherents		
				Number of Adherents	% of Total Pop.	% of Total Adh.
388 Reg Bapt Gen As	1	171	192	207 *	.7	.8
403 Salvation Army	1	111	65	282	.9	1.2
413 S.D.A.	1	102	NR	121	.4	.5
419 So Bapt Conv	2	195	176	236 *	.8	1.0
443 Un C of Christ	1	268	108	325 *	1.0	1.3
449 Un Methodist	4	653	409	792 *	2.5	3.2
496 Jewish Est	1	NR	NR	135	.4	.6
ANTRIM	**39**	**3,430**	**2,753**	**6,322 ***	**27.4**	**100.0**
056 Baha'i	0	4	NR	4	-	.1
081 Catholic	3	NR	NR	1,309	5.7	20.7
097 Chr Chs&Chs Cr	1	190	NR	233 *	1.0	3.7
105 Christian Ref	3	487	391	597 *	2.6	9.4
165 Ch of Nazarene	1	19	23	36	.2	.6
175 Congr Chr Chs	1	170	85	208 *	.9	3.3
193 Episcopal	1	NR	89	233	1.0	3.7
207 E.L.C.A.	1	123	64	146	.6	2.3
221 Free Methodist	1	30	63	63	.3	1.0
283 Luth—MO Synod	3	289	156	368	1.6	5.8
288 Mennonite USA	1	59	47	72 *	.3	1.1
291 Missionary Ch	1	93	186	186	.8	2.9
335 Orth Pres Ch	1	10	34	34	.1	.5
339 Pent Ch of God	2	34	NR	101	.4	1.6
349 Pent Holiness	1	25	20	31 *	.1	.5
355 Presb Ch (USA)	2	609	428	747 *	3.2	11.8
371 Ref Ch in Am	1	167	105	262	1.1	4.1
388 Reg Bapt Gen As	2	301	287	305 *	1.3	4.8
413 S.D.A.	2	42	NR	50	.2	.8
419 So Bapt Conv	1	75	72	92 *	.4	1.5
449 Un Methodist	8	703	492	862 *	3.7	13.6
467 Wesleyan	2	0	211	383	1.7	6.1
ARENAC	**30**	**1,971**	**1,321**	**6,171 ***	**35.7**	**100.0**
053 Assemb of God	1	32	50	65	.4	1.1
056 Baha'i	0	2	NR	2	-	-
081 Catholic	5	NR	NR	3,104	18.0	50.3
173 Comm of Christ	1	81	NR	81	.5	1.3
183 Cons Menn Conf	2	152	186	221	1.3	3.6
193 Episcopal	1	NR	26	67	.4	1.1
207 E.L.C.A.	1	197	82	260	1.5	4.2
221 Free Methodist	2	33	73	73	.4	1.2
283 Luth—MO Synod	2	478	217	661	3.8	10.7
339 Pent Ch of God	1	42	NR	175	1.0	2.8
355 Presb Ch (USA)	1	42	30	51 *	.3	.8
388 Reg Bapt Gen As	1	81	50	98 *	.6	1.6
419 So Bapt Conv	2	69	39	83 *	.5	1.3
449 Un Methodist	6	676	405	818 *	4.7	13.3
467 Wesleyan	2	0	106	298	1.7	4.8
469 WELS	2	86	57	114	.7	1.8
BARAGA	**14**	**1,716**	**720**	**4,906 ***	**56.1**	**100.0**
056 Baha'i	0	1	NR	1	-	-
081 Catholic	3	NR	NR	2,477	28.3	50.5
151 L-D Saints	1	NR	NR	131	1.5	2.7
207 E.L.C.A.	5	1,184	420	1,664	19.0	33.9
283 Luth—MO Synod	1	237	73	277	3.2	5.6
388 Reg Bapt Gen As	1	75	130	91 *	1.0	1.9
413 S.D.A.	1	18	NR	21	.2	.4
449 Un Methodist	2	201	97	244 *	2.8	5.0
BARRY	**46**	**5,893**	**4,459**	**12,374 ***	**21.8**	**100.0**
053 Assemb of God	2	109	149	256	.5	2.1
056 Baha'i	0	5	NR	5	-	-
081 Catholic	4	NR	NR	3,830	6.7	31.0
093 Chr Ch (Disc)	1	117	72	147 *	.3	1.2
097 Chr Chs&Chs Cr	1	25	NR	32 *	.1	.3
105 Christian Ref	1	119	0	150 *	.3	1.2
127 Ch God (Cleve)	1	17	24	24 *	-	.2
157 Ch of Brethren	2	214	70	270 *	.5	2.2
165 Ch of Nazarene	2	215	218	430	.8	3.5
167 Chs of Christ	1	25	28	26	-	.2
173 Comm of Christ	1	65	NR	65	.1	.5

NR–Not Reported *Total adherents estimated from known number of communicant, confirmed, full members. - Represents a percentage less than 0.1. Percentages may not total 100 due to rounding.

Table 4: Religious Congregations by County and Group: 2000

Religious Group	Number of Churches, Synagogues, Mosques, or Temples	Number of Communicant, Confirmed, or Full Members	Number of Attendees	Total Adherents		
				Number of Adherents	% of Total Pop.	% of Total Adh.
193 Episcopal	1	NR	70	252	.4	2.0
207 E.L.C.A.	2	502	250	676	1.2	5.5
221 Free Methodist	1	67	135	135	.2	1.1
283 Luth—MO Synod	1	100	67	121	.2	1.0
306 NT IndBapt&Rltd	1	135	NR	170 *	.3	1.4
355 Presb Ch (USA)	1	527	260	664 *	1.2	5.4
371 Ref Ch in Am	1	425	542	849	1.5	6.9
388 Reg Bapt Gen As	2	750	767	945 *	1.7	7.6
413 S.D.A.	2	161	NR	191	.3	1.5
419 So Bapt Conv	1	150	86	189 *	.3	1.5
449 Un Methodist	14	1,954	1,485	2,464 *	4.3	19.9
467 Wesleyan	3	211	236	483	.9	3.9
BAY	**89**	**18,538**	**9,726**	**65,783 ***	**59.7**	**100.0**
019 Amer Bapt USA	2	397	231	488 *	.4	.7
040 Ap Chr Ch-Amer	1	160	400	400 *	.4	.6
053 Assemb of God	2	34	42	42	-	.1
056 Baha'i	0	16	NR	16	-	-
081 Catholic	22	NR	NR	39,915	36.2	60.7
084 Calvary Chapel	1	NR	NR	NR	-	-
089 Chr & Miss Al	2	60	NR	100	.1	.2
123 Ch God (Ander)	2	NR	232	232	.2	.4
151 L-D Saints	1	NR	NR	239	.2	.4
165 Ch of Nazarene	2	144	143	237	.2	.4
167 Chs of Christ	2	79	88	106	.1	.2
173 Comm of Christ	2	387	NR	387	.4	.6
193 Episcopal	2	NR	266	755	.7	1.1
203 Evan Free Ch	1	90	111	111	.1	.2
207 E.L.C.A.	1	466	191	579	.5	.9
221 Free Methodist	1	52	72	74	.1	.1
262 Int Cou Comm Ch	1	249	NR	306 *	.3	.5
283 Luth—MO Synod	11	9,288	4,021	12,357	11.2	18.8
291 Missionary Ch	1	107	114	114	.1	.2
313 N Am Bapt Conf	1	132	89	162 *	.1	.2
339 Pent Ch of God	1	5	NR	40	-	.1
355 Presb Ch (USA)	4	1,382	546	1,699 *	1.5	2.6
388 Reg Bapt Gen As	3	428	402	473 *	.4	.7
403 Salvation Army	1	102	43	219	.2	.3
413 S.D.A.	1	70	NR	83	.1	.1
419 So Bapt Conv	2	250	60	307 *	.3	.5
443 Un C of Christ	2	193	94	237 *	.2	.4
449 Un Methodist	9	1,850	934	2,275 *	2.1	3.5
467 Wesleyan	2	0	149	310	.3	.5
469 WELS	5	2,597	1,498	3,370	3.1	5.1
496 Jewish Est	1	NR	NR	150	.1	.2
BENZIE	**29**	**2,814**	**1,994**	**4,728 ***	**29.6**	**100.0**
053 Assemb of God	1	140	128	186	1.2	3.9
081 Catholic	2	NR	NR	667	4.2	14.1
093 Chr Ch (Disc)	1	27	0	33 *	.2	.7
097 Chr Chs&Chs Cr	1	150	NR	183 *	1.1	3.9
127 Ch God (Cleve)	1	8	15	15 *	.1	.3
151 L-D Saints	1	NR	NR	290	1.8	6.1
165 Ch of Nazarene	1	42	50	70	.4	1.5
167 Chs of Christ	1	40	40	50	.3	1.1
175 Congr Chr Chs	1	100	70	122 *	.8	2.6
181 Consrv Congr	2	156	144	190 *	1.2	4.0
193 Episcopal	1	NR	71	86	.5	1.8
207 E.L.C.A.	1	529	170	629	3.9	13.3
283 Luth—MO Synod	1	163	116	228	1.4	4.8
355 Presb Ch (USA)	1	165	142	201 *	1.3	4.3
388 Reg Bapt Gen As	2	114	118	139 *	.9	2.9
413 S.D.A.	1	26	NR	31	.2	.7
419 So Bapt Conv	1	57	45	70 *	.4	1.5
443 Un C of Christ	1	395	149	482 *	3.0	10.2
449 Un Methodist	5	702	628	856 *	5.4	18.1
467 Wesleyan	3	0	108	200	1.3	4.2
BERRIEN	**186**	**36,432**	**17,710**	**76,180 ***	**46.9**	**100.0**
017 Amer Bapt Assn	3	150	NR	186 *	.1	.2
019 Amer Bapt USA	3	571	280	714 *	.4	.9
053 Assemb of God	5	872	1,108	1,842	1.1	2.4
056 Baha'i	1	65	NR	65	-	.1

Religious Group	Number of Churches, Synagogues, Mosques, or Temples	Number of Communicant, Confirmed, or Full Members	Number of Attendees	Total Adherents		
				Number of Adherents	% of Total Pop.	% of Total Adh.
057 Bapt Gen Conf	2	180	340	340 *	.2	.4
059 Bapt Miss Assn	1	25	13	31 *	-	-
081 Catholic	12	NR	NR	25,366	15.6	33.3
093 Chr Ch (Disc)	1	142	84	177 *	.1	.2
097 Chr Chs&Chs Cr	5	832	NR	1,038 *	.6	1.4
105 Christian Ref	1	394	219	492 *	.3	.6
123 Ch God (Ander)	7	NR	1,521	1,521	.9	2.0
127 Ch God (Cleve)	5	536	273	669 *	.4	.9
145 Ch God Prophcy	2	71	NR	90 *	.1	.1
151 L-D Saints	2	NR	NR	557	.3	.7
165 Ch of Nazarene	3	210	242	351	.2	.5
167 Chs of Christ	4	399	430	549	.3	.7
173 Comm of Christ	2	143	NR	143	.1	.2
175 Congr Chr Chs	3	213	135	266 *	.2	.3
181 Consrv Congr	1	165	122	206 *	.1	.3
193 Episcopal	4	NR	302	667	.4	.9
201 Evan Cov Ch	1	190	182	237 *	.1	.3
203 Evan Free Ch	2	297	204	397	.2	.5
207 E.L.C.A.	5	1,370	597	1,736	1.1	2.3
221 Free Methodist	3	191	305	305	.2	.4
223 Free Will Bapt	1	71	NR	89 *	.1	.1
246 Greek Orthodox	1	NR	NR	120	.1	.2
263 Int Foursq Gos	1	54	56	67 *	-	.1
283 Luth—MO Synod	10	6,659	2,939	8,960	5.5	11.8
291 Missionary Ch	3	204	360	360	.2	.5
306 NT IndBapt&Rltd	1	95	NR	119 *	.1	.2
313 N Am Bapt Conf	5	1,144	943	1,430 *	.9	1.9
339 Pent Ch of God	3	75	NR	250	.2	.3
355 Presb Ch (USA)	5	1,202	516	1,503 *	.9	2.0
371 Ref Ch in Am	1	82	105	154	.1	.2
388 Reg Bapt Gen As	4	642	677	831 *	.5	1.1
401 Rus Orth Abroad	1	NR	NR	NR	-	-
403 Salvation Army	2	237	120	676	.4	.9
413 S.D.A.	17	7,510	NR	8,937	5.5	11.7
419 So Bapt Conv	7	1,110	275	1,387 *	.9	1.8
435 Unitarian-Univ	1	34	NR	42 *	-	.1
443 Un C of Christ	13	2,496	1,113	3,119 *	1.9	4.1
449 Un Methodist	24	4,142	2,352	5,175 *	3.2	6.8
469 WELS	6	3,309	1,697	4,176	2.6	5.5
496 Jewish Est	1	NR	NR	240	.1	.3
498 Indep.Charis.	1	350	200	600	.4	.8
BRANCH	**50**	**4,892**	**3,617**	**13,687 ***	**29.9**	**100.0**
019 Amer Bapt USA	2	678	561	841 *	1.8	6.1
053 Assemb of God	2	124	157	250	.5	1.8
056 Baha'i	0	3	NR	3	-	-
071 Brethren (Ash)	1	5	20	6 *	-	-
081 Catholic	3	NR	NR	6,440	14.1	47.1
097 Chr Chs&Chs Cr	2	198	NR	245 *	.5	1.8
165 Ch of Nazarene	1	103	126	223	.5	1.6
167 Chs of Christ	1	38	42	50	.1	.4
173 Comm of Christ	1	165	NR	165	.4	1.2
193 Episcopal	1	NR	151	270	.6	2.0
203 Evan Free Ch	1	30	80	80	.2	.6
207 E.L.C.A.	1	105	53	160	.3	1.2
221 Free Methodist	2	168	355	355	.8	2.6
283 Luth—MO Synod	3	530	454	776	1.7	5.7
291 Missionary Ch	2	120	222	222	.5	1.6
306 NT IndBapt&Rltd	1	170	NR	211 *	.5	1.5
323 Old Ord Amish	10	550	NR	680 *	1.5	5.0
355 Presb Ch (USA)	2	454	275	563 *	1.2	4.1
388 Reg Bapt Gen As	2	100	135	124 *	.3	.9
413 S.D.A.	1	119	NR	142	.3	1.0
419 So Bapt Conv	1	0	0	0 *	-	-
443 Un C of Christ	2	151	107	187 *	.4	1.4
449 Un Methodist	6	939	660	1,164 *	2.5	8.5
467 Wesleyan	2	142	219	530	1.2	3.9
CALHOUN	**128**	**17,832**	**12,286**	**45,533 ***	**33.0**	**100.0**
019 Amer Bapt USA	7	861	532	1,076 *	.8	2.4
053 Assemb of God	5	629	812	1,224	.9	2.7
056 Baha'i	0	21	NR	21	-	-
059 Bapt Miss Assn	2	94	58	117 *	.1	.3

NR–Not Reported *Total adherents estimated from known number of communicant, confirmed, full members. - Represents a percentage less than 0.1. Percentages may not total 100 due to rounding.

Table 4: Religious Congregations by County and Group: 2000

Religious Group	Number of Churches, Synagogues, Mosques, or Temples	Number of Communicant, Confirmed, or Full Members	Number of Attendees	Total Adherents		
				Number of Adherents	% of Total Pop.	% of Total Adh.
076 Buddhism	1	NR	NR	NR	-	-
081 Catholic	5	NR	NR	12,456	9.0	27.4
093 Chr Ch (Disc)	1	35	25	44 *	-	.1
097 Chr Chs&Chs Cr	2	310	NR	387 *	.3	.8
105 Christian Ref	1	273	200	341 *	.2	.7
123 Ch God (Ander)	4	NR	532	532	.4	1.2
127 Ch God (Cleve)	3	698	1,037	1,190 *	.9	2.6
145 Ch God Prophcy	1	36	NR	45 *	-	.1
151 L-D Saints	3	NR	NR	912	.7	2.0
157 Ch of Brethren	1	37	20	46 *	-	.1
165 Ch of Nazarene	4	495	340	777	.6	1.7
167 Chs of Christ	6	447	420	533	.4	1.2
171 Ch God-Gen Con	1	26	16	32 *	-	.1
173 Comm of Christ	1	21	NR	21	-	-
176 Congr Ad Afl	1	40	NR	50 *	-	.1
179 Consrv Bapt	1	NR	97	97	.1	.2
193 Episcopal	4	NR	449	1,043	.8	2.3
207 E.L.C.A.	2	487	213	615	.4	1.4
221 Free Methodist	2	109	192	198	.1	.4
223 Free Will Bapt	1	71	NR	89 *	.1	.2
226 Friends-USA	1	95	NR	119 *	.1	.3
263 Int Foursq Gos	1	10	29	29 *	-	.1
283 Luth—MO Synod	6	1,959	1,032	3,582	2.6	7.9
288 Mennonite USA	1	45	36	56 *	-	.1
290 Metro Comm Ch	1	15	16	19 *	-	-
291 Missionary Ch	2	108	198	198	.1	.4
323 Old Ord Amish	1	55	NR	69 *	.1	.2
331 OCA: Ter Diocs	1	27	NR	73	.1	.2
339 Pent Ch of God	1	113	NR	713	.5	1.6
355 Presb Ch (USA)	6	2,029	812	2,535 *	1.8	5.6
371 Ref Ch in Am	1	79	90	137	.1	.3
388 Reg Bapt Gen As	3	548	540	703 *	.5	1.5
400 Rus Orth Moscow	1	NR	NR	NR	-	-
403 Salvation Army	1	219	122	497	.4	1.1
413 S.D.A.	5	1,522	NR	1,812	1.3	4.0
419 So Bapt Conv	9	836	349	1,044 *	.8	2.3
443 Un C of Christ	4	1,346	441	1,682 *	1.2	3.7
449 Un Methodist	18	3,417	1,840	4,268 *	3.1	9.4
467 Wesleyan	5	610	1,775	6,012	4.4	13.2
469 WELS	1	109	63	139	.1	.3
CASS	**46**	**4,134**	**2,318**	**13,528 ***	**26.5**	**100.0**
019 Amer Bapt USA	2	288	130	357 *	.7	2.6
053 Assemb of God	1	22	29	29	.1	.2
056 Baha'i	0	4	NR	4	-	-
059 Bapt Miss Assn	1	55	30	68 *	.1	.5
075 Brethren in Cr	1	10	28	28	.1	.2
081 Catholic	5	NR	NR	7,974	15.6	58.9
093 Chr Ch (Disc)	1	140	79	173 *	.3	1.3
097 Chr Chs&Chs Cr	2	306	NR	380 *	.7	2.8
123 Ch God (Ander)	3	NR	110	110	.2	.8
165 Ch of Nazarene	1	130	134	250	.5	1.8
167 Chs of Christ	1	60	60	70	.1	.5
183 Cons Menn Conf	1	35	43	51	.1	.4
193 Episcopal	1	NR	50	125	.2	.9
203 Evan Free Ch	1	30	32	32	.1	.2
223 Free Will Bapt	1	71	NR	89 *	.2	.7
226 Friends-USA	2	94	NR	116 *	.2	.9
283 Luth—MO Synod	1	99	70	127	.2	.9
291 Missionary Ch	3	126	193	193	.4	1.4
339 Pent Ch of God	1	200	NR	250	.5	1.8
355 Presb Ch (USA)	2	204	128	253 *	.5	1.9
413 S.D.A.	3	351	NR	417	.8	3.1
419 So Bapt Conv	1	136	45	169 *	.3	1.2
443 Un C of Christ	1	138	122	171 *	.3	1.3
449 Un Methodist	9	1,260	874	1,561 *	3.1	11.5
469 WELS	1	375	161	531	1.0	3.9
CHARLEVOIX	**42**	**3,600**	**2,710**	**10,834 ***	**41.5**	**100.0**
019 Amer Bapt USA	1	100	74	124 *	.5	1.1
053 Assemb of God	2	106	142	175	.7	1.6
056 Baha'i	0	1	NR	1	-	-
081 Catholic	5	NR	NR	5,242	20.1	48.4
123 Ch God (Ander)	1	NR	80	80	.3	.7
127 Ch God (Cleve)	1	49	110	110 *	.4	1.0
151 L-D Saints	1	NR	NR	158	.6	1.5
165 Ch of Nazarene	2	72	112	145	.6	1.3
167 Chs of Christ	1	25	25	27	.1	.2
173 Comm of Christ	2	220	NR	220	.8	2.0
193 Episcopal	2	NR	68	119	.5	1.1
207 E.L.C.A.	1	179	100	243	.9	2.2
221 Free Methodist	2	65	142	142	.5	1.3
283 Luth—MO Synod	2	492	268	615	2.4	5.7
291 Missionary Ch	1	49	124	124	.5	1.1
297 Mennonite;Other	1	20	NR	25 *	.1	.2
339 Pent Ch of God	1	55	NR	175	.7	1.6
355 Presb Ch (USA)	3	479	260	597 *	2.3	5.5
371 Ref Ch in Am	1	353	510	855	3.3	7.9
413 S.D.A.	1	81	NR	96	.4	.9
419 So Bapt Conv	1	101	40	126 *	.5	1.2
443 Un C of Christ	2	521	175	648 *	2.5	6.0
449 Un Methodist	8	632	480	787 *	3.0	7.3
CHEBOYGAN	**32**	**2,935**	**2,339**	**10,362 ***	**39.2**	**100.0**
053 Assemb of God	2	182	230	397	1.5	3.8
056 Baha'i	0	2	NR	2	-	-
081 Catholic	5	NR	NR	5,612	21.2	54.2
093 Chr Ch (Disc)	1	110	50	134 *	.5	1.3
151 L-D Saints	1	NR	NR	126	.5	1.2
165 Ch of Nazarene	1	14	37	37	.1	.4
167 Chs of Christ	1	55	55	63	.2	.6
173 Comm of Christ	1	112	NR	112	.4	1.1
175 Congr Chr Chs	1	75	40	91 *	.3	.9
193 Episcopal	2	NR	141	414	1.6	4.0
201 Evan Cov Ch	1	145	229	229 *	.9	2.2
207 E.L.C.A.	1	602	266	815	3.1	7.9
221 Free Methodist	1	13	43	43	.2	.4
283 Luth—MO Synod	1	249	125	299	1.1	2.9
339 Pent Ch of God	1	15	NR	50	.2	.5
355 Presb Ch (USA)	1	100	123	123 *	.5	1.2
388 Reg Bapt Gen As	2	135	225	164 *	.6	1.6
413 S.D.A.	1	54	NR	64	.2	.6
419 So Bapt Conv	1	69	75	84 *	.3	.8
443 Un C of Christ	2	150	97	182 *	.7	1.8
449 Un Methodist	3	716	488	870 *	3.3	8.4
467 Wesleyan	1	58	73	363	1.4	3.5
469 WELS	1	79	42	88	.3	.8
CHIPPEWA	**60**	**4,597**	**2,438**	**13,812 ***	**35.8**	**100.0**
019 Amer Bapt USA	1	78	50	93 *	.2	.7
053 Assemb of God	3	106	127	178	.5	1.3
056 Baha'i	0	19	NR	19	-	.1
081 Catholic	12	NR	NR	7,295	18.9	52.8
097 Chr Chs&Chs Cr	3	510	NR	608 *	1.6	4.4
105 Christian Ref	2	320	280	381 *	1.0	2.8
165 Ch of Nazarene	3	113	117	301	.8	2.2
167 Chs of Christ	1	20	20	26	.1	.2
173 Comm of Christ	1	71	NR	71	.2	.5
193 Episcopal	4	NR	126	216	.6	1.6
207 E.L.C.A.	2	522	166	676	1.8	4.9
221 Free Methodist	1	24	61	61	.2	.4
246 Greek Orthodox	1	NR	NR	69	.2	.5
283 Luth—MO Synod	4	168	134	234	.6	1.7
288 Mennonite USA	1	26	22	31 *	.1	.2
339 Pent Ch of God	1	24	NR	75	.2	.5
355 Presb Ch (USA)	8	820	460	976 *	2.5	7.1
370 Ref Baptist Chs	1	NR	NR	NR	-	-
388 Reg Bapt Gen As	1	81	100	97 *	.3	.7
403 Salvation Army	1	114	85	261	.7	1.9
419 So Bapt Conv	2	568	47	677 *	1.8	4.9
449 Un Methodist	5	742	386	884 *	2.3	6.4
467 Wesleyan	1	74	150	320	.8	2.3
469 WELS	1	197	107	263	.7	1.9
CLARE	**37**	**3,384**	**2,421**	**6,905 ***	**22.1**	**100.0**
017 Amer Bapt Assn	1	50	NR	61 *	.2	.9

NR–Not Reported *Total adherents estimated from known number of communicant, confirmed, full members. - Represents a percentage less than 0.1. Percentages may not total 100 due to rounding.

Table 4: Religious Congregations by County and Group: 2000

Religious Group	Number of Churches, Synagogues, Mosques, or Temples	Number of Communicant, Confirmed, or Full Members	Number of Attendees	Total Adherents		
				Number of Adherents	% of Total Pop.	% of Total Adh.
053 Assemb of God	2	178	259	290	.9	4.2
056 Baha'i	0	2	NR	2	-	-
081 Catholic	2	NR	NR	2,180	7.0	31.6
097 Chr Chs&Chs Cr	2	240	NR	294 *	.9	4.3
123 Ch God (Ander)	1	NR	50	50	.2	.7
127 Ch God (Cleve)	1	71	91	91 *	.3	1.3
151 L-D Saints	1	NR	NR	232	.7	3.4
165 Ch of Nazarene	2	170	305	388	1.2	5.6
167 Chs of Christ	2	32	36	38	.1	.6
171 Ch God-Gen Con	3	180	191	239 *	.8	3.5
173 Comm of Christ	2	194	NR	194	.6	2.8
207 E.L.C.A.	1	160	79	205	.7	3.0
283 Luth—MO Synod	2	384	201	502	1.6	7.3
323 Old Ord Amish	4	220	NR	268 *	.9	3.9
388 Reg Bapt Gen As	2	225	375	305 *	1.0	4.4
419 So Bapt Conv	3	173	148	212 *	.7	3.1
443 Un C of Christ	2	401	185	492 *	1.6	7.1
449 Un Methodist	2	517	374	634 *	2.0	9.2
469 WELS	2	187	127	228	.7	3.3
CLINTON	**59**	**6,789**	**4,062**	**25,550 ***	**39.5**	**100.0**
019 Amer Bapt USA	1	40	25	51 *	.1	.2
053 Assemb of God	3	125	187	198	.3	.8
056 Baha'i	0	15	NR	15	-	.1
075 Brethren in Cr	1	41	58	58	.1	.2
081 Catholic	4	NR	NR	16,151	24.9	63.2
097 Chr Chs&Chs Cr	3	830	NR	1,056 *	1.6	4.1
123 Ch God (Ander)	2	NR	166	166	.3	.6
151 L-D Saints	2	NR	NR	282	.4	1.1
165 Ch of Nazarene	2	248	241	378	.6	1.5
167 Chs of Christ	2	73	100	128	.2	.5
173 Comm of Christ	1	84	NR	84	.1	.3
175 Congr Chr Chs	1	300	150	381 *	.6	1.5
181 Consrv Congr	2	250	293	318 *	.5	1.2
193 Episcopal	2	NR	66	198	.3	.8
207 E.L.C.A.	1	0	0	0	-	-
221 Free Methodist	2	69	96	96	.1	.4
263 Int Foursq Gos	1	17	32	32 *	-	.1
283 Luth—MO Synod	4	1,238	576	1,570	2.4	6.1
306 NT IndBapt&Rltd	3	171	NR	217 *	.3	.8
323 Old Ord Amish	2	110	NR	140 *	.2	.5
388 Reg Bapt Gen As	2	487	486	619 *	1.0	2.4
413 S.D.A.	1	92	NR	109	.2	.4
419 So Bapt Conv	1	196	75	249 *	.4	1.0
443 Un C of Christ	1	202	86	257 *	.4	1.0
449 Un Methodist	15	2,201	1,425	2,797 *	4.3	10.9
CRAWFORD	**12**	**1,254**	**710**	**3,362 ***	**23.6**	**100.0**
053 Assemb of God	1	35	45	86	.6	2.6
081 Catholic	1	NR	NR	1,454	10.2	43.2
151 L-D Saints	1	NR	NR	196	1.4	5.8
167 Chs of Christ	1	30	35	35	.2	1.0
173 Comm of Christ	1	162	NR	162	1.1	4.8
193 Episcopal	1	NR	68	159	1.1	4.7
207 E.L.C.A.	1	107	54	164	1.1	4.9
221 Free Methodist	1	109	111	130	.9	3.9
283 Luth—MO Synod	1	294	120	346	2.4	10.3
413 S.D.A.	1	53	NR	63	.4	1.9
419 So Bapt Conv	1	61	50	75 *	.5	2.2
449 Un Methodist	1	403	227	492 *	3.4	14.6
DELTA	**55**	**7,490**	**3,723**	**30,709 ***	**79.7**	**100.0**
053 Assemb of God	1	412	227	350	.9	1.1
056 Baha'i	0	27	NR	27	.1	.1
057 Bapt Gen Conf	2	471	372	585 *	1.5	1.9
081 Catholic	11	NR	NR	20,547	53.3	66.9
097 Chr Chs&Chs Cr	1	128	NR	155 *	.4	.5
127 Ch God (Cleve)	1	88	50	107 *	.3	.3
151 L-D Saints	1	NR	NR	130	.3	.4
165 Ch of Nazarene	1	21	22	48	.1	.2
167 Chs of Christ	2	79	90	95	.2	.3
173 Comm of Christ	1	91	NR	91	.2	.3
175 Congr Chr Chs	3	201	213	244 *	.6	.8
193 Episcopal	3	NR	116	526	1.4	1.7
201 Evan Cov Ch	1	152	151	184 *	.5	.6
207 E.L.C.A.	10	3,352	1,291	4,326	11.2	14.1
220 Free Lutheran	1	21	30	38	.1	.1
221 Free Methodist	1	13	38	38	.1	.1
283 Luth—MO Synod	1	284	134	388	1.0	1.3
288 Mennonite USA	1	31	25	38 *	.1	.1
355 Presb Ch (USA)	1	281	129	341 *	.9	1.1
388 Reg Bapt Gen As	1	65	50	79 *	.2	.3
403 Salvation Army	1	183	87	431	1.1	1.4
413 S.D.A.	2	137	NR	163	.4	.5
449 Un Methodist	4	955	440	1,158 *	3.0	3.8
469 WELS	4	498	258	620	1.6	2.0
DICKINSON	**37**	**6,151**	**3,440**	**22,695 ***	**82.6**	**100.0**
034 Ant Orth of NA	1	48	NR	96	.3	.4
053 Assemb of God	1	175	248	363	1.3	1.6
056 Baha'i	0	7	NR	7	-	-
057 Bapt Gen Conf	3	405	509	541 *	2.0	2.4
081 Catholic	8	NR	NR	14,460	52.6	63.7
097 Chr Chs&Chs Cr	1	120	NR	147 *	.5	.6
127 Ch God (Cleve)	1	7	13	13 *	-	.1
193 Episcopal	1	NR	55	377	1.4	1.7
201 Evan Cov Ch	3	475	498	620 *	2.3	2.7
207 E.L.C.A.	5	2,491	805	3,186	11.6	14.0
211 Fel Evg Bib Ch	1	119	25	25	.1	.1
283 Luth—MO Synod	1	474	253	612	2.2	2.7
355 Presb Ch (USA)	2	541	288	664 *	2.4	2.9
388 Reg Bapt Gen As	1	171	192	210 *	.8	.9
403 Salvation Army	1	61	19	79	.3	.3
413 S.D.A.	1	51	NR	61	.2	.3
419 So Bapt Conv	1	8	12	10 *	-	-
449 Un Methodist	4	885	453	1,088 *	4.0	4.8
469 WELS	1	113	70	136	.5	.6
EATON	**79**	**13,565**	**10,912**	**31,436 ***	**30.3**	**100.0**
019 Amer Bapt USA	2	555	476	691 *	.7	2.2
053 Assemb of God	7	3,358	4,865	8,570	8.3	27.3
056 Baha'i	0	6	NR	6	-	-
081 Catholic	5	NR	NR	7,947	7.7	25.3
097 Chr Chs&Chs Cr	2	340	NR	423 *	.4	1.3
105 Christian Ref	3	390	135	485 *	.5	1.5
123 Ch God (Ander)	1	NR	46	46	-	.1
127 Ch God (Cleve)	2	105	74	130 *	.1	.4
151 L-D Saints	2	NR	NR	356	.3	1.1
157 Ch of Brethren	1	11	9	14 *	-	-
165 Ch of Nazarene	5	574	466	1,156	1.1	3.7
167 Chs of Christ	1	27	27	33	-	.1
173 Comm of Christ	1	160	NR	160	.2	.5
175 Congr Chr Chs	3	373	279	464 *	.4	1.5
193 Episcopal	3	NR	223	809	.8	2.6
201 Evan Cov Ch	1	104	84	129 *	.1	.4
207 E.L.C.A.	2	581	301	818	.8	2.6
221 Free Methodist	2	103	157	157	.2	.5
263 Int Foursq Gos	1	7	16	16 *	-	.1
283 Luth—MO Synod	2	746	280	1,032	1.0	3.3
323 Old Ord Amish	3	165	NR	204 *	.2	.6
339 Pent Ch of God	1	11	NR	25	-	.1
355 Presb Ch (USA)	1	209	125	260 *	.3	.8
413 S.D.A.	3	898	NR	1,069	1.0	3.4
419 So Bapt Conv	2	312	103	388 *	.4	1.2
443 Un C of Christ	4	1,056	559	1,314 *	1.3	4.2
449 Un Methodist	15	2,995	2,186	3,726 *	3.6	11.9
467 Wesleyan	2	105	292	495	.5	1.6
469 WELS	2	374	209	513	.5	1.6
EMMET	**41**	**4,246**	**2,792**	**13,743 ***	**43.7**	**100.0**
053 Assemb of God	1	141	180	350	1.1	2.5
056 Baha'i	0	4	NR	4	-	-
081 Catholic	8	NR	NR	7,359	23.4	53.5
093 Chr Ch (Disc)	1	401	100	495 *	1.6	3.6
105 Christian Ref	1	30	60	37 *	.1	.3
151 L-D Saints	1	NR	NR	126	.4	.9

NR–Not Reported *Total adherents estimated from known number of communicant, confirmed, full members. - Represents a percentage less than 0.1. Percentages may not total 100 due to rounding.

Table 4: Religious Congregations by County and Group: 2000

Religious Group	Number of Churches, Synagogues, Mosques, or Temples	Number of Communicant, Confirmed, or Full Members	Number of Attendees	Total Adherents: Number of Adherents	Total Adherents: % of Total Pop.	Total Adherents: % of Total Adh.
165 Ch of Nazarene	2	268	203	476	1.5	3.5
167 Chs of Christ	1	30	29	40	.1	.3
193 Episcopal	1	NR	164	375	1.2	2.7
207 E.L.C.A.	1	225	86	269	.9	2.0
283 Luth—MO Synod	2	475	212	562	1.8	4.1
288 Mennonite USA	3	170	136	211 *	.7	1.5
291 Missionary Ch	2	73	253	253	.8	1.8
339 Pent Ch of God	1	24	NR	50	.2	.4
355 Presb Ch (USA)	2	851	470	1,052 *	3.3	7.7
388 Reg Bapt Gen As	1	88	85	85 *	.3	.6
403 Salvation Army	1	97	53	164	.5	1.2
413 S.D.A.	2	140	NR	166	.5	1.2
419 So Bapt Conv	2	266	113	329 *	1.0	2.4
443 Un C of Christ	1	38	66	47 *	.1	.3
449 Un Methodist	5	862	526	1,065 *	3.4	7.7
469 WELS	1	63	56	78	.2	.6
496 Jewish Est	1	NR	NR	150	.5	1.1
GENESEE	**344**	**61,467**	**40,948**	**161,474 ***	**37.0**	**100.0**
017 Amer Bapt Assn	1	50	NR	64 *	-	-
019 Amer Bapt USA	11	3,017	2,306	3,844 *	.9	2.4
053 Assemb of God	16	2,362	3,131	5,313	1.2	3.3
056 Baha'i	2	169	NR	169	-	.1
059 Bapt Miss Assn	4	1,334	723	1,700 *	.4	1.1
075 Brethren in Cr	1	62	80	80	-	-
081 Catholic	31	NR	NR	65,392	15.0	40.5
093 Chr Ch (Disc)	3	531	236	677 *	.2	.4
097 Chr Chs&Chs Cr	3	393	NR	501 *	.1	.3
105 Christian Ref	1	50	30	64 *	-	-
123 Ch God (Ander)	12	NR	1,778	1,778	.4	1.1
127 Ch God (Cleve)	6	585	349	747 *	.2	.5
145 Ch God Prophcy	1	36	NR	45 *	-	-
151 L-D Saints	3	NR	NR	1,055	.2	.7
157 Ch of Brethren	1	22	15	28 *	-	-
165 Ch of Nazarene	16	3,031	3,092	4,512	1.0	2.8
167 Chs of Christ	13	2,547	2,156	3,246	.7	2.0
173 Comm of Christ	5	936	NR	936	.2	.6
175 Congr Chr Chs	1	25	15	32 *	-	-
179 Consrv Bapt	1	NR	280	280	.1	.2
181 Consrv Congr	2	247	270	315 *	.1	.2
183 Cons Menn Conf	2	60	73	87	-	.1
193 Episcopal	7	NR	776	2,119	.5	1.3
207 E.L.C.A.	6	1,230	668	1,639	.4	1.0
213 Evan Menn Inc	1	0	175	0 *	-	-
216 Evan Presby Ch	2	693	NR	883 *	.2	.5
221 Free Methodist	12	880	1,557	1,651	.4	1.0
223 Free Will Bapt	2	143	NR	182 *	-	.1
246 Greek Orthodox	1	NR	NR	729	.2	.5
249 Assyr Apost Ch	1	NR	NR	250	.1	.2
252 Hindu	3	NR	NR	NR	-	-
265 Int Pent C Chr	2	46	0	61	-	-
267 Muslim Est	4	NR	625	2,165	.5	1.3
283 Luth—MO Synod	17	8,011	3,711	10,463	2.4	6.5
290 Metro Comm Ch	1	21	21	27 *	-	-
291 Missionary Ch	4	292	526	526	.1	.3
306 NT IndBapt&Rltd	4	1,526	NR	1,944 *	.4	1.2
332 OCA: Bulg Dioc	1	150	NR	262	.1	.2
339 Pent Ch of God	10	390	NR	1,371	.3	.8
355 Presb Ch (USA)	14	4,915	1,937	6,263 *	1.4	3.9
356 Presb Ch Amer	1	285	239	308	.1	.2
371 Ref Ch in Am	1	243	199	392	.1	.2
388 Reg Bapt Gen As	7	1,780	1,784	2,301 *	.5	1.4
403 Salvation Army	3	628	543	1,856	.4	1.1
413 S.D.A.	5	977	NR	1,163	.3	.7
419 So Bapt Conv	26	7,358	2,501	9,376 *	2.1	5.8
435 Unitarian-Univ	2	196	NR	250 *	.1	.2
443 Un C of Christ	3	897	372	1,143 *	.3	.7
449 Un Methodist	40	8,789	5,269	11,199 *	2.6	6.9
467 Wesleyan	9	634	794	1,769	.4	1.1
469 WELS	6	1,376	737	1,792	.4	1.1
490 Zoroastrian	1	NR	NR	NR	-	-
496 Jewish Est	3	NR	NR	1,500	.3	.9
499 Indep.Non-Char	9	4,550	3,980	7,025	1.6	4.4

Religious Group	Number of Churches, Synagogues, Mosques, or Temples	Number of Communicant, Confirmed, or Full Members	Number of Attendees	Total Adherents: Number of Adherents	Total Adherents: % of Total Pop.	Total Adherents: % of Total Adh.
GLADWIN	**34**	**3,560**	**2,067**	**6,608 ***	**25.4**	**100.0**
053 Assemb of God	2	119	161	241	.9	3.6
056 Baha'i	0	3	NR	3	-	-
057 Bapt Gen Conf	1	136	66	165 *	.6	2.5
081 Catholic	1	NR	NR	1,899	7.3	28.7
123 Ch God (Ander)	1	NR	70	70	.3	1.1
157 Ch of Brethren	1	95	0	115 *	.4	1.7
165 Ch of Nazarene	2	205	157	256	1.0	3.9
167 Chs of Christ	1	90	75	124	.5	1.9
173 Comm of Christ	2	327	NR	327	1.3	4.9
193 Episcopal	1	NR	60	110	.4	1.7
207 E.L.C.A.	2	460	212	706	2.7	10.7
221 Free Methodist	2	74	146	146	.6	2.2
283 Luth—MO Synod	1	475	218	561	2.2	8.5
313 N Am Bapt Conf	1	158	190	191 *	.7	2.9
323 Old Ord Amish	5	265	NR	323 *	1.2	4.9
355 Presb Ch (USA)	1	101	53	122 *	.5	1.8
388 Reg Bapt Gen As	1	160	200	200 *	.8	3.0
413 S.D.A.	2	91	NR	108	.4	1.6
449 Un Methodist	5	564	374	682 *	2.6	10.3
469 WELS	2	237	85	259	1.0	3.9
GOGEBIC	**28**	**4,153**	**1,612**	**10,836 ***	**62.4**	**100.0**
034 Ant Orth of NA	1	17	NR	34	.2	.3
053 Assemb of God	1	51	70	80	.5	.7
056 Baha'i	0	1	NR	1	-	-
057 Bapt Gen Conf	1	49	78	78 *	.4	.7
081 Catholic	5	NR	NR	5,588	32.2	51.6
167 Chs of Christ	1	4	8	8	-	.1
193 Episcopal	1	NR	22	57	.3	.5
207 E.L.C.A.	6	2,583	774	3,236	18.6	29.9
283 Luth—MO Synod	4	876	276	1,083	6.2	10.0
355 Presb Ch (USA)	3	93	50	109 *	.6	1.0
388 Reg Bapt Gen As	2	206	217	242 *	1.4	2.2
413 S.D.A.	1	23	NR	27	.2	.2
449 Un Methodist	2	250	117	293 *	1.7	2.7
GRAND TRAVERSE	**65**	**12,141**	**8,425**	**36,750 ***	**47.3**	**100.0**
019 Amer Bapt USA	1	73	57	90 *	.1	.2
053 Assemb of God	1	125	163	205	.3	.6
056 Baha'i	0	18	NR	18	-	-
081 Catholic	8	NR	NR	18,283	23.5	49.7
093 Chr Ch (Disc)	1	613	351	759 *	1.0	2.1
097 Chr Chs&Chs Cr	2	100	NR	124 *	.2	.3
123 Ch God (Ander)	2	NR	70	70	.1	.2
127 Ch God (Cleve)	1	104	70	129 *	.2	.4
151 L-D Saints	1	NR	NR	258	.3	.7
165 Ch of Nazarene	1	127	109	224	.3	.6
167 Chs of Christ	1	105	130	125	.2	.3
173 Comm of Christ	2	361	NR	361	.5	1.0
193 Episcopal	1	NR	193	380	.5	1.0
201 Evan Cov Ch	1	74	110	110 *	.1	.3
207 E.L.C.A.	2	1,327	492	1,754	2.3	4.8
221 Free Methodist	1	16	10	16	-	-
226 Friends-USA	1	47	NR	58 *	.1	.2
263 Int Foursq Gos	1	7	5	9 *	-	-
283 Luth—MO Synod	4	1,690	711	2,371	3.1	6.5
291 Missionary Ch	1	19	37	37	-	.1
297 Mennonite;Other	2	54	NR	66 *	.1	.2
339 Pent Ch of God	2	68	NR	250	.3	.7
355 Presb Ch (USA)	1	1,168	558	1,445 *	1.9	3.9
371 Ref Ch in Am	2	907	919	1,518	2.0	4.1
388 Reg Bapt Gen As	2	278	295	344 *	.4	.9
403 Salvation Army	1	82	74	254	.3	.7
413 S.D.A.	1	124	NR	148	.2	.4
419 So Bapt Conv	2	98	89	121 *	.2	.3
435 Unitarian-Univ	1	261	NR	323 *	.4	.9
443 Un C of Christ	2	1,298	518	1,606 *	2.1	4.4
449 Un Methodist	9	2,358	1,565	2,918 *	3.8	7.9
467 Wesleyan	3	0	330	505	.7	1.4
469 WELS	1	139	94	196	.3	.5
496 Jewish Est	2	NR	NR	200	.3	.5
499 Indep.Non-Char	1	500	1,475	1,475	1.9	4.0

NR–Not Reported *Total adherents estimated from known number of communicant, confirmed, full members. - Represents a percentage less than 0.1. Percentages may not total 100 due to rounding.

Table 4: Religious Congregations by County and Group: 2000

Religious Group	Number of Churches, Synagogues, Mosques, or Temples	Number of Communicant, Confirmed, or Full Members	Number of Attendees	Total Adherents: Number of Adherents	Total Adherents: % of Total Pop.	Total Adherents: % of Total Adh.
GRATIOT	**71**	**6,271**	**4,066**	**13,988 ***	**33.1**	**100.0**
019 Amer Bapt USA	1	27	33	33 *	.1	.2
053 Assemb of God	2	126	145	160	.4	1.1
056 Baha'i	0	2	NR	2	-	-
081 Catholic	6	NR	NR	4,273	10.1	30.5
097 Chr Chs&Chs Cr	4	1,140	NR	1,391 *	3.3	9.9
123 Ch God (Ander)	4	NR	717	717	1.7	5.1
143 CG in Cr(Menn)	1	228	NR	278 *	.7	2.0
151 L-D Saints	1	NR	NR	141	.3	1.0
157 Ch of Brethren	1	104	85	127 *	.3	.9
165 Ch of Nazarene	4	314	285	427	1.0	3.1
171 Ch God-Gen Con	2	57	82	82 *	.2	.6
173 Comm of Christ	1	50	NR	50	.1	.4
193 Episcopal	1	NR	70	104	.2	.7
221 Free Methodist	3	108	183	183	.4	1.3
263 Int Foursq Gos	1	18	26	26 *	.1	.2
265 Int Pent C Chr	1	5	6	9	-	.1
283 Luth—MO Synod	2	579	189	773	1.8	5.5
288 Mennonite USA	1	46	45	56 *	.1	.4
339 Pent Ch of God	2	75	NR	241	.6	1.7
355 Presb Ch (USA)	5	634	315	785 *	1.9	5.6
388 Reg Bapt Gen As	3	344	420	473 *	1.1	3.4
403 Salvation Army	1	101	58	232	.5	1.7
413 S.D.A.	3	215	NR	257	.6	1.8
419 So Bapt Conv	1	22	25	27 *	.1	.2
443 Un C of Christ	1	132	58	161 *	.4	1.2
449 Un Methodist	13	1,628	932	1,987 *	4.7	14.2
467 Wesleyan	4	0	208	600	1.4	4.3
469 WELS	2	316	184	393	.9	2.8
HILLSDALE	**61**	**5,689**	**3,482**	**11,063 ***	**23.8**	**100.0**
019 Amer Bapt USA	4	612	340	762 *	1.6	6.9
053 Assemb of God	1	133	167	265	.6	2.4
056 Baha'i	0	8	NR	8	-	.1
081 Catholic	1	NR	NR	2,897	6.2	26.2
097 Chr Chs&Chs Cr	2	130	NR	162 *	.3	1.5
145 Ch God Prophcy	1	36	NR	44 *	.1	.4
151 L-D Saints	1	NR	NR	395	.8	3.6
165 Ch of Nazarene	2	126	149	311	.7	2.8
167 Chs of Christ	1	60	52	75	.2	.7
175 Congr Chr Chs	3	336	145	419 *	.9	3.8
193 Episcopal	2	NR	63	126	.3	1.1
207 E.L.C.A.	1	152	84	183	.4	1.7
221 Free Methodist	1	150	160	160	.3	1.4
223 Free Will Bapt	1	71	NR	89 *	.2	.8
283 Luth—MO Synod	1	256	180	345	.7	3.1
288 Mennonite USA	1	70	85	87 *	.2	.8
291 Missionary Ch	1	76	134	134	.3	1.2
297 Mennonite;Other	1	50	NR	62 *	.1	.6
323 Old Ord Amish	6	330	NR	414 *	.9	3.7
339 Pent Ch of God	2	90	NR	215	.5	1.9
355 Presb Ch (USA)	3	604	239	753 *	1.6	6.8
388 Reg Bapt Gen As	5	541	587	679 *	1.5	6.1
403 Salvation Army	1	117	30	310	.7	2.8
413 S.D.A.	2	128	NR	152	.3	1.4
419 So Bapt Conv	2	329	131	410 *	.9	3.7
449 Un Methodist	13	1,095	715	1,364 *	2.9	12.3
467 Wesleyan	2	189	221	242	.5	2.2
HOUGHTON	**55**	**5,448**	**2,830**	**17,754 ***	**49.3**	**100.0**
053 Assemb of God	1	104	153	499	1.4	2.8
056 Baha'i	0	19	NR	19	.1	.1
081 Catholic	11	NR	NR	9,810	27.2	55.3
097 Chr Chs&Chs Cr	1	75	NR	90 *	.2	.5
165 Ch of Nazarene	1	7	10	11	-	.1
167 Chs of Christ	1	22	24	29	.1	.2
193 Episcopal	2	NR	92	265	.7	1.5
207 E.L.C.A.	8	2,510	824	3,401	9.4	19.2
220 Free Lutheran	2	67	113	113	.3	.6
226 Friends-USA	2	90	NR	108 *	.3	.6
267 Muslim Est	1	NR	55	163	.5	.9
283 Luth—MO Synod	3	571	343	662	1.8	3.7
297 Mennonite;Other	1	43	NR	51 *	.1	.3

Religious Group	Number of Churches, Synagogues, Mosques, or Temples	Number of Communicant, Confirmed, or Full Members	Number of Attendees	Total Adherents: Number of Adherents	Total Adherents: % of Total Pop.	Total Adherents: % of Total Adh.
355 Presb Ch (USA)	2	71	52	85 *	.2	.5
388 Reg Bapt Gen As	2	193	310	260 *	.7	1.5
401 Rus Orth Abroad	1	NR	NR	NR	-	-
403 Salvation Army	1	72	49	72	.2	.4
413 S.D.A.	1	67	NR	80	.2	.5
419 So Bapt Conv	1	71	66	85 *	.2	.5
435 Unitarian-Univ	1	45	NR	54 *	.1	.3
443 Un C of Christ	2	122	95	146 *	.4	.8
449 Un Methodist	7	1,057	531	1,263 *	3.5	7.1
469 WELS	2	242	113	338	.9	1.9
496 Jewish Est	1	NR	NR	150	.4	.8
HURON	**76**	**9,611**	**5,620**	**27,154 ***	**75.3**	**100.0**
019 Amer Bapt USA	1	17	15	21 *	.1	.1
053 Assemb of God	3	139	140	194	.5	.7
081 Catholic	16	NR	NR	14,607	40.5	53.8
151 L-D Saints	1	NR	NR	82	.2	.3
165 Ch of Nazarene	2	73	80	193	.5	.7
167 Chs of Christ	1	24	20	28	.1	.1
173 Comm of Christ	3	422	NR	422	1.2	1.6
183 Cons Menn Conf	2	321	392	467	1.3	1.7
193 Episcopal	2	NR	55	158	.4	.6
207 E.L.C.A.	1	484	251	623	1.7	2.3
221 Free Methodist	1	118	225	225	.6	.8
283 Luth—MO Synod	9	3,823	1,758	5,014	13.9	18.5
288 Mennonite USA	1	105	75	128 *	.4	.5
291 Missionary Ch	2	106	132	132	.4	.5
306 NT IndBapt&Rltd	1	78	NR	95 *	.3	.3
355 Presb Ch (USA)	5	313	166	382 *	1.1	1.4
356 Presb Ch Amer	1	213	141	270	.7	1.0
388 Reg Bapt Gen As	2	342	384	416 *	1.2	1.5
413 S.D.A.	1	32	NR	38	.1	.1
449 Un Methodist	17	2,179	1,283	2,655 *	7.4	9.8
467 Wesleyan	1	91	103	103	.3	.4
469 WELS	3	731	400	901	2.5	3.3
INGHAM	**214**	**38,373**	**23,956**	**111,119 ***	**39.8**	**100.0**
017 Amer Bapt Assn	1	50	NR	61 *	-	.1
019 Amer Bapt USA	11	3,006	1,615	3,674 *	1.3	3.3
034 Ant Orth of NA	1	38	NR	76	-	.1
050 Armen Ap Etchm	1	80	NR	500	.2	.4
053 Assemb of God	8	901	1,235	1,754	.6	1.6
056 Baha'i	3	178	NR	178	.1	.2
057 Bapt Gen Conf	2	150	208	208 *	.1	.2
059 Bapt Miss Assn	1	184	166	225 *	.1	.2
076 Buddhism	1	NR	NR	NR	-	-
081 Catholic	15	NR	NR	49,880	17.9	44.9
089 Chr & Miss Al	1	100	NR	132	-	.1
093 Chr Ch (Disc)	1	304	157	372 *	.1	.3
097 Chr Chs&Chs Cr	4	837	NR	1,023 *	.4	.9
105 Christian Ref	1	739	600	903 *	.3	.8
123 Ch God (Ander)	2	NR	375	375	.1	.3
127 Ch God (Cleve)	5	380	340	465 *	.2	.4
145 Ch God Prophcy	1	36	NR	44 *	-	-
151 L-D Saints	5	NR	NR	1,402	.5	1.3
157 Ch of Brethren	1	42	38	51 *	-	-
165 Ch of Nazarene	10	1,287	1,206	1,808	.6	1.6
167 Chs of Christ	4	363	408	454	.2	.4
173 Comm of Christ	4	575	NR	575	.2	.5
175 Congr Chr Chs	2	669	259	818 *	.3	.7
193 Episcopal	5	NR	722	2,411	.9	2.2
203 Evan Free Ch	1	67	180	180	.1	.2
207 E.L.C.A.	9	3,412	1,419	4,623	1.7	4.2
221 Free Methodist	6	493	689	689	.2	.6
226 Friends-USA	1	35	NR	43 *	-	-
246 Greek Orthodox	1	NR	NR	435	.2	.4
252 Hindu	2	NR	NR	NR	-	-
267 Muslim Est	2	NR	756	3,609	1.3	3.2
268 Jain	1	NR	NR	NR	-	-
283 Luth—MO Synod	9	3,072	1,331	4,073	1.5	3.7
288 Mennonite USA	1	30	50	50 *	-	-
306 NT IndBapt&Rltd	3	171	NR	209 *	.1	.2
313 N Am Bapt Conf	1	169	127	207 *	.1	.2

NR–Not Reported *Total adherents estimated from known number of communicant, confirmed, full members. - Represents a percentage less than 0.1. Percentages may not total 100 due to rounding.

Table 4: Religious Congregations by County and Group: 2000

Religious Group	Number of Churches, Synagogues, Mosques, or Temples	Number of Communicant, Confirmed, or Full Members	Number of Attendees	Total Adherents		
				Number of Adherents	% of Total Pop.	% of Total Adh.
335 Orth Pres Ch	1	25	35	36	-	-
339 Pent Ch of God	1	40	NR	87	-	.1
355 Presb Ch (USA)	11	3,395	1,513	4,150 *	1.5	3.7
371 Ref Ch in Am	2	385	524	742	.3	.7
388 Reg Bapt Gen As	3	487	545	599 *	.2	.5
400 Rus Orth Moscow	1	NR	NR	NR	-	-
403 Salvation Army	1	177	104	353	.1	.3
413 S.D.A.	6	520	NR	619	.2	.6
416 Sikh	2	NR	NR	NR	-	-
419 So Bapt Conv	5	1,411	598	1,724 *	.6	1.6
435 Unitarian-Univ	1	335	NR	409 *	.1	.4
443 Un C of Christ	8	3,447	1,151	4,213 *	1.5	3.8
449 Un Methodist	28	6,053	3,632	7,398 *	2.6	6.7
463 Vineyard	2	270	165	330 *	.1	.3
467 Wesleyan	4	423	607	1,527	.5	1.4
469 WELS	4	1,584	771	2,220	.8	2.0
496 Jewish Est	2	NR	NR	2,100	.8	1.9
498 Indep.Charis.	1	600	500	1,100	.4	1.0
499 Indep.Non-Char	4	1,853	1,930	2,005	.7	1.8
IONIA	**63**	**5,584**	**4,320**	**22,031 ***	**35.8**	**100.0**
019 Amer Bapt USA	3	230	127	289 *	.5	1.3
053 Assemb of God	3	263	336	536	.9	2.4
056 Baha'i	0	3	NR	3	-	-
081 Catholic	8	NR	NR	13,868	22.5	62.9
093 Chr Ch (Disc)	2	227	117	286 *	.5	1.3
105 Christian Ref	2	446	355	561 *	.9	2.5
123 Ch God (Ander)	1	NR	60	60	.1	.3
127 Ch God (Cleve)	2	148	182	189 *	.3	.9
165 Ch of Nazarene	4	170	219	490	.8	2.2
175 Congr Chr Chs	2	168	161	211 *	.3	1.0
179 Consrv Bapt	1	NR	115	115	.2	.5
183 Cons Menn Conf	1	58	71	84	.1	.4
193 Episcopal	1	NR	50	213	.3	1.0
201 Evan Cov Ch	1	274	182	345 *	.6	1.6
221 Free Methodist	4	97	183	183	.3	.8
283 Luth—MO Synod	3	698	303	911	1.5	4.1
306 NT IndBapt&Rltd	1	85	NR	107 *	.2	.5
355 Presb Ch (USA)	2	209	96	263 *	.4	1.2
388 Reg Bapt Gen As	5	550	632	738 *	1.2	3.3
413 S.D.A.	2	206	NR	245	.4	1.1
443 Un C of Christ	1	137	80	172 *	.3	.8
449 Un Methodist	11	1,466	903	1,844 *	3.0	8.4
467 Wesleyan	2	80	105	228	.4	1.0
469 WELS	1	69	43	90	.1	.4
IOSCO	**38**	**5,087**	**2,824**	**12,167 ***	**44.5**	**100.0**
019 Amer Bapt USA	1	187	125	224 *	.8	1.8
053 Assemb of God	3	230	315	354	1.3	2.9
056 Baha'i	0	5	NR	5	-	-
057 Bapt Gen Conf	1	102	151	151 *	.6	1.2
081 Catholic	4	NR	NR	5,339	19.5	43.9
151 L-D Saints	1	NR	NR	118	.4	1.0
165 Ch of Nazarene	2	73	84	159	.6	1.3
167 Chs of Christ	1	35	35	45	.2	.4
173 Comm of Christ	1	139	NR	139	.5	1.1
193 Episcopal	2	NR	95	300	1.1	2.5
207 E.L.C.A.	2	357	136	409	1.5	3.4
216 Evan Presby Ch	1	11	NR	13 *	-	.1
283 Luth—MO Synod	4	1,297	630	1,693	6.2	13.9
323 Old Ord Amish	1	55	NR	66 *	.2	.5
355 Presb Ch (USA)	1	154	100	184 *	.7	1.5
388 Reg Bapt Gen As	1	65	65	78 *	.3	.6
413 S.D.A.	1	38	NR	45	.2	.4
419 So Bapt Conv	3	546	140	653 *	2.4	5.4
449 Un Methodist	7	1,329	671	1,590 *	5.8	13.1
469 WELS	1	464	277	602	2.2	4.9
IRON	**25**	**2,513**	**1,362**	**8,191 ***	**62.3**	**100.0**
053 Assemb of God	1	48	65	65	.5	.8
056 Baha'i	0	3	NR	3	-	-
057 Bapt Gen Conf	2	110	150	150 *	1.1	1.8
081 Catholic	3	NR	NR	4,736	36.0	57.8
084 Calvary Chapel	1	NR	NR	NR	-	-
151 L-D Saints	1	NR	NR	188	1.4	2.3
165 Ch of Nazarene	1	36	23	36	.3	.4
193 Episcopal	2	NR	30	59	.4	.7
201 Evan Cov Ch	1	231	209	272 *	2.1	3.3
207 E.L.C.A.	4	1,349	475	1,815	13.8	22.2
283 Luth—MO Synod	2	182	93	214	1.6	2.6
355 Presb Ch (USA)	1	129	90	152 *	1.2	1.9
388 Reg Bapt Gen As	1	35	35	41 *	.3	.5
413 S.D.A.	1	39	NR	46	.4	.6
449 Un Methodist	3	299	154	351 *	2.7	4.3
469 WELS	1	52	38	63	.5	.8
ISABELLA	**58**	**5,446**	**3,375**	**17,699 ***	**27.9**	**100.0**
019 Amer Bapt USA	1	38	28	45 *	.1	.3
032 Amish; other	1	45	NR	53 *	.1	.3
053 Assemb of God	1	120	180	280	.4	1.6
056 Baha'i	0	24	NR	24	-	.1
057 Bapt Gen Conf	1	50	48	59 *	.1	.3
081 Catholic	6	NR	NR	9,656	15.2	54.6
097 Chr Chs&Chs Cr	3	416	NR	492 *	.8	2.8
105 Christian Ref	1	41	60	49 *	.1	.3
121 Ch God (Abr)	1	105	97	124 *	.2	.7
123 Ch God (Ander)	1	NR	41	41	.1	.2
127 Ch God (Cleve)	1	13	28	28 *	-	.2
151 L-D Saints	1	NR	NR	256	.4	1.4
157 Ch of Brethren	1	62	0	73 *	.1	.4
165 Ch of Nazarene	3	176	170	258	.4	1.5
167 Chs of Christ	1	120	130	150	.2	.8
173 Comm of Christ	1	80	NR	80	.1	.5
193 Episcopal	1	NR	85	279	.4	1.6
207 E.L.C.A.	1	413	232	576	.9	3.3
216 Evan Presby Ch	1	293	NR	347 *	.5	2.0
221 Free Methodist	3	98	201	201	.3	1.1
226 Friends-USA	1	35	NR	41 *	.1	.2
267 Muslim Est	1	NR	55	163	.3	.9
283 Luth—MO Synod	2	389	230	476	.8	2.7
323 Old Ord Amish	1	55	NR	65 *	.1	.4
339 Pent Ch of God	1	29	NR	89	.1	.5
355 Presb Ch (USA)	2	575	212	680 *	1.1	3.8
388 Reg Bapt Gen As	1	290	280	343 *	.5	1.9
403 Salvation Army	1	26	35	41	.1	.2
413 S.D.A.	1	89	NR	106	.2	.6
419 So Bapt Conv	1	28	35	33 *	.1	.2
449 Un Methodist	11	1,567	907	1,854 *	2.9	10.5
467 Wesleyan	2	0	127	240	.4	1.4
469 WELS	2	269	194	367	.6	2.1
496 Jewish Est	1	NR	NR	130	.2	.7
JACKSON	**124**	**16,845**	**12,683**	**55,827 ***	**35.2**	**100.0**
017 Amer Bapt Assn	1	50	NR	62 *	-	.1
019 Amer Bapt USA	4	745	317	930 *	.6	1.7
053 Assemb of God	5	314	413	731	.5	1.3
056 Baha'i	0	80	NR	80	.1	.1
057 Bapt Gen Conf	1	27	36	36 *	-	.1
081 Catholic	8	NR	NR	25,360	16.0	45.4
097 Chr Chs&Chs Cr	1	385	NR	481 *	.3	.9
105 Christian Ref	1	79	70	99 *	.1	.2
123 Ch God (Ander)	4	NR	348	348	.2	.6
127 Ch God (Cleve)	1	186	124	232 *	.1	.4
145 Ch God Prophcy	1	36	NR	45 *	-	.1
151 L-D Saints	2	NR	NR	640	.4	1.1
165 Ch of Nazarene	3	551	708	1,440	.9	2.6
167 Chs of Christ	4	370	290	428	.3	.8
173 Comm of Christ	1	63	NR	63	-	.1
175 Congr Chr Chs	3	473	197	591 *	.4	1.1
179 Consrv Bapt	3	NR	640	640	.4	1.1
193 Episcopal	6	NR	361	1,856	1.2	3.3
207 E.L.C.A.	3	845	418	1,112	.7	2.0
221 Free Methodist	3	1,046	1,688	1,688	1.1	3.0
262 Int Cou Comm Ch	1	100	NR	125 *	.1	.2
283 Luth—MO Synod	2	1,690	744	2,383	1.5	4.3
288 Mennonite USA	1	22	25	27 *	-	-

NR–Not Reported *Total adherents estimated from known number of communicant, confirmed, full members. - Represents a percentage less than 0.1. Percentages may not total 100 due to rounding.

Table 4: Religious Congregations by County and Group: 2000

Religious Group	Number of Churches, Synagogues, Mosques, or Temples	Number of Communicant, Confirmed, or Full Members	Number of Attendees	Total Adherents: Number of Adherents	Total Adherents: % of Total Pop.	Total Adherents: % of Total Adh.
291 Missionary Ch	2	87	169	169	.1	.3
306 NT IndBapt&Rltd	2	60	NR	75 *	-	.1
331 OCA: Ter Diocs	1	56	NR	107	.1	.2
339 Pent Ch of God	4	219	NR	563	.4	1.0
355 Presb Ch (USA)	4	1,499	736	1,872 *	1.2	3.4
360 Prim Bapt Chrch	1	NR	NR	NR	-	-
388 Reg Bapt Gen As	6	783	884	997 *	.6	1.8
397 OCA: Roman Dioc	2	NR	NR	5	-	-
403 Salvation Army	1	105	101	407	.3	.7
413 S.D.A.	2	295	NR	351	.2	.6
419 So Bapt Conv	8	1,705	1,101	2,129 *	1.3	3.8
435 Unitarian-Univ	1	110	NR	137 *	.1	.2
443 Un C of Christ	4	792	353	989 *	.6	1.8
449 Un Methodist	17	2,930	1,663	3,661 *	2.3	6.6
466 Wayn Tr MB Asc	1	32	NR	40 *	-	.1
467 Wesleyan	5	528	940	4,088	2.6	7.3
469 WELS	2	252	117	310	.2	.6
496 Jewish Est	1	NR	NR	200	.1	.4
499 Indep.Non-Char	1	330	240	330	.2	.6
KALAMAZOO	**176**	**40,116**	**32,657**	**84,216 ***	**35.3**	**100.0**
017 Amer Bapt Assn	2	100	NR	124 *	.1	.1
019 Amer Bapt USA	3	1,512	725	1,863 *	.8	2.2
053 Assemb of God	6	649	873	1,232	.5	1.5
056 Baha'i	1	75	NR	75	-	.1
057 Bapt Gen Conf	2	110	142	144 *	.1	.2
059 Bapt Miss Assn	1	306	204	377 *	.2	.4
081 Catholic	9	NR	NR	21,159	8.9	25.1
084 Calvary Chapel	1	NR	NR	NR	-	-
093 Chr Ch (Disc)	1	153	92	188 *	.1	.2
097 Chr Chs&Chs Cr	3	560	NR	690 *	.3	.8
105 Christian Ref	15	4,633	3,220	5,708 *	2.4	6.8
123 Ch God (Ander)	2	NR	318	318	.1	.4
127 Ch God (Cleve)	3	516	160	636 *	.3	.8
145 Ch God Prophcy	1	36	NR	44 *	-	.1
151 L-D Saints	2	NR	NR	910	.4	1.1
157 Ch of Brethren	1	67	60	83 *	-	.1
165 Ch of Nazarene	4	863	797	982	.4	1.2
167 Chs of Christ	5	408	435	520	.2	.6
173 Comm of Christ	1	116	NR	116	-	.1
175 Congr Chr Chs	1	79	130	97 *	-	.1
193 Episcopal	5	NR	700	1,778	.7	2.1
201 Evan Cov Ch	2	392	391	483 *	.2	.6
203 Evan Free Ch	2	135	199	199	.1	.2
207 E.L.C.A.	5	1,808	898	2,467	1.0	2.9
221 Free Methodist	2	217	428	430	.2	.5
223 Free Will Bapt	1	71	NR	88 *	-	.1
226 Friends-USA	1	35	NR	43 *	-	.1
252 Hindu	1	NR	NR	NR	-	-
262 Int Cou Comm Ch	1	331	NR	408 *	.2	.5
263 Int Foursq Gos	1	62	122	122 *	.1	.1
267 Muslim Est	2	NR	456	1,109	.5	1.3
283 Luth—MO Synod	4	1,774	880	2,279	1.0	2.7
291 Missionary Ch	2	140	303	303	.1	.4
304 NatPrimBapt USA	1	80	NR	99 *	-	.1
306 NT IndBapt&Rltd	1	145	NR	179 *	.1	.2
307 Neth Ref Congr	1	177	NR	308	.1	.4
335 Orth Pres Ch	1	24	30	32	-	-
355 Presb Ch (USA)	5	2,050	811	2,525 *	1.1	3.0
369 Prot Ref Chs	1	42	NR	68	-	.1
371 Ref Ch in Am	16	5,535	5,043	9,538	4.0	11.3
388 Reg Bapt Gen As	4	1,454	1,393	1,792 *	.8	2.1
403 Salvation Army	1	162	113	720	.3	.9
413 S.D.A.	3	557	NR	664	.3	.8
419 So Bapt Conv	6	595	302	733 *	.3	.9
435 Unitarian-Univ	2	270	NR	333 *	.1	.4
443 Un C of Christ	5	1,498	645	1,845 *	.8	2.2
449 Un Methodist	21	5,920	3,115	7,292 *	3.1	8.7
455 Un Ref Chs N.A.	1	223	NR	322	.1	.4
463 Vineyard	1	150	35	185 *	.1	.2
467 Wesleyan	3	303	498	889	.4	1.1
469 WELS	1	193	139	267	.1	.3
496 Jewish Est	2	NR	NR	1,500	.6	1.8
498 Indep.Charis.	1	2,100	3,600	3,600	1.5	4.3
499 Indep.Non-Char	6	3,490	5,400	6,350	2.7	7.5
KALKASKA	**18**	**1,526**	**877**	**3,081 ***	**18.6**	**100.0**
019 Amer Bapt USA	1	165	57	205 *	1.2	6.7
053 Assemb of God	2	126	168	214	1.3	6.9
056 Baha'i	0	3	NR	3	-	.1
081 Catholic	1	NR	NR	1,061	6.4	34.4
097 Chr Chs&Chs Cr	4	359	NR	448 *	2.7	14.5
127 Ch God (Cleve)	2	79	71	99 *	.6	3.2
165 Ch of Nazarene	1	36	82	82	.5	2.7
167 Chs of Christ	1	30	25	35	.2	1.1
283 Luth—MO Synod	1	249	137	341	2.1	11.1
388 Reg Bapt Gen As	1	125	145	156 *	.9	5.1
413 S.D.A.	1	55	NR	65	.4	2.1
419 So Bapt Conv	0	18	10	22 *	.1	.7
449 Un Methodist	3	281	182	350 *	2.1	11.4
KENT	**442**	**118,347**	**92,759**	**303,574 ***	**52.9**	**100.0**
017 Amer Bapt Assn	1	50	NR	64 *	-	-
019 Amer Bapt USA	1	115	69	148 *	-	-
034 Ant Orth of NA	2	760	NR	1,520	.3	.5
040 Ap Chr Ch-Amer	1	78	236	236 *	-	.1
053 Assemb of God	10	4,338	3,525	6,369	1.1	2.1
055 As Ref Pres Ch	1	0	NR	0	-	-
056 Baha'i	1	106	NR	106	-	-
057 Bapt Gen Conf	4	350	501	568 *	.1	.2
076 Buddhism	1	NR	NR	NR	-	-
081 Catholic	37	NR	NR	114,716	20.0	37.8
084 Calvary Chapel	3	NR	NR	NR	-	-
089 Chr & Miss Al	2	64	NR	186	-	.1
093 Chr Ch (Disc)	2	2,218	544	2,845 *	.5	.9
097 Chr Chs&Chs Cr	5	1,218	NR	1,562 *	.3	.5
105 Christian Ref	78	38,181	26,905	48,973 *	8.5	16.1
121 Ch God (Abr)	4	177	228	246 *	-	.1
123 Ch God (Ander)	8	NR	713	713	.1	.2
127 Ch God (Cleve)	4	527	347	677 *	.1	.2
151 L-D Saints	5	NR	NR	2,430	.4	.8
165 Ch of Nazarene	7	983	907	1,449	.3	.5
167 Chs of Christ	7	731	655	1,004	.2	.3
173 Comm of Christ	5	758	NR	758	.1	.2
175 Congr Chr Chs	1	800	295	1,026 *	.2	.3
179 Consrv Bapt	2	NR	483	483	.1	.2
181 Consrv Congr	1	157	90	201 *	-	.1
193 Episcopal	9	NR	969	3,042	.5	1.0
201 Evan Cov Ch	3	1,221	1,359	1,590 *	.3	.5
203 Evan Free Ch	2	124	250	250	-	.1
207 E.L.C.A.	13	5,201	2,654	7,518	1.3	2.5
221 Free Methodist	4	260	369	380	.1	.1
226 Friends-USA	1	35	NR	45 *	-	-
246 Greek Orthodox	1	NR	NR	720	.1	.2
262 Int Cou Comm Ch	2	528	NR	678 *	.1	.2
264 Int Chs of Crst	1	53	106	83	-	-
267 Muslim Est	3	NR	245	6,980	1.2	2.3
283 Luth—MO Synod	15	4,729	2,558	6,412	1.1	2.1
290 Metro Comm Ch	1	78	55	55 *	-	-
291 Missionary Ch	1	35	62	62	-	-
307 Neth Ref Congr	2	397	NR	816	.1	.3
335 Orth Pres Ch	5	463	678	761	.1	.3
349 Pent Holiness	1	30	30	38 *	-	-
355 Presb Ch (USA)	7	3,763	1,918	4,826 *	.8	1.6
356 Presb Ch Amer	1	328	313	496	.1	.2
369 Prot Ref Chs	7	1,112	NR	2,116	.4	.7
370 Ref Baptist Chs	1	NR	NR	NR	-	-
371 Ref Ch in Am	34	11,043	9,890	17,633	3.1	5.8
388 Reg Bapt Gen As	32	7,593	9,103	11,562 *	2.0	3.8
397 OCA: Roman Dioc	1	NR	NR	80	-	-
400 Rus Orth Moscow	1	NR	NR	NR	-	-
403 Salvation Army	2	282	213	1,138	.2	.4
413 S.D.A.	10	2,107	NR	2,507	.4	.8
418 Southw Bapt Fel	3	NR	NR	NR	-	-
419 So Bapt Conv	3	548	265	703 *	.1	.2
420 Strict Baptists	1	14	NR	18 *	-	-
443 Un C of Christ	15	5,771	2,063	7,402 *	1.3	2.4

NR–Not Reported *Total adherents estimated from known number of communicant, confirmed, full members. - Represents a percentage less than 0.1. Percentages may not total 100 due to rounding.

Table 4: Religious Congregations by County and Group: 2000

Religious Group	Number of Churches, Synagogues, Mosques, or Temples	Number of Communicant, Confirmed, or Full Members	Number of Attendees	Total Adherents: Number of Adherents	Total Adherents: % of Total Pop.	Total Adherents: % of Total Adh.
449 Un Methodist	36	8,185	5,592	10,497 *	1.8	3.5
455 Un Ref Chs N.A.	6	1,300	NR	1,934	.3	.6
463 Vineyard	2	440	485	564 *	.1	.2
467 Wesleyan	9	1,330	3,262	4,527	.8	1.5
469 WELS	2	715	477	1,021	.2	.3
496 Jewish Est	3	NR	NR	1,800	.3	.6
498 Indep.Charis.	3	4,235	7,205	9,350	1.6	3.1
499 Indep.Non-Char	6	4,816	7,140	9,690	1.7	3.2
KEWEENAW	**6**	**356**	**142**	**971 ***	**42.2**	**100.0**
056 Baha'i	0	2	NR	2	.1	.2
081 Catholic	3	NR	NR	386	16.8	39.8
193 Episcopal	1	NR	18	43	1.9	4.4
207 E.L.C.A.	1	325	95	506	22.0	52.1
449 Un Methodist	1	29	29	34 *	1.5	3.5
LAKE	**20**	**1,101**	**674**	**3,394 ***	**29.9**	**100.0**
053 Assemb of God	1	44	47	100	.9	2.9
056 Baha'i	0	3	NR	3	-	.1
081 Catholic	4	NR	NR	1,959	17.3	57.7
089 Chr & Miss Al	1	136	NR	161	1.4	4.7
093 Chr Ch (Disc)	1	35	42	41 *	.4	1.2
167 Chs of Christ	1	25	39	35	.3	1.0
201 Evan Cov Ch	1	45	75	75 *	.7	2.2
262 Int Cou Comm Ch	1	124	NR	147 *	1.3	4.3
283 Luth—MO Synod	1	89	50	95	.8	2.8
355 Presb Ch (USA)	1	100	45	119 *	1.1	3.5
388 Reg Bapt Gen As	1	75	82	89 *	.8	2.6
413 S.D.A.	2	101	NR	120	1.1	3.5
443 Un C of Christ	1	155	95	184 *	1.6	5.4
449 Un Methodist	3	121	129	143 *	1.3	4.2
467 Wesleyan	1	48	70	123	1.1	3.6
LAPEER	**63**	**9,255**	**5,721**	**29,313 ***	**33.3**	**100.0**
019 Amer Bapt USA	2	208	120	264 *	.3	.9
053 Assemb of God	3	294	444	611	.7	2.1
056 Baha'i	0	9	NR	9	-	-
081 Catholic	5	NR	NR	15,804	18.0	53.9
097 Chr Chs&Chs Cr	2	590	NR	750 *	.9	2.6
105 Christian Ref	1	309	140	393 *	.4	1.3
127 Ch God (Cleve)	1	224	171	285 *	.3	1.0
151 L-D Saints	1	NR	NR	295	.3	1.0
165 Ch of Nazarene	3	190	200	405	.5	1.4
167 Chs of Christ	2	262	262	325	.4	1.1
173 Comm of Christ	2	258	NR	258	.3	.9
176 Congr Ad Afl	1	441	NR	561 *	.6	1.9
193 Episcopal	3	NR	182	433	.5	1.5
207 E.L.C.A.	2	266	198	347	.4	1.2
221 Free Methodist	1	50	101	101	.1	.3
283 Luth—MO Synod	4	2,006	756	2,838	3.2	9.7
291 Missionary Ch	1	47	124	124	.1	.4
306 NT IndBapt&Rltd	3	388	NR	493 *	.6	1.7
335 Orth Pres Ch	1	79	84	131	.1	.4
355 Presb Ch (USA)	1	435	183	553 *	.6	1.9
388 Reg Bapt Gen As	2	531	567	675 *	.8	2.3
413 S.D.A.	2	133	NR	158	.2	.5
443 Un C of Christ	1	146	70	186 *	.2	.6
449 Un Methodist	13	1,523	1,111	1,936 *	2.2	6.6
467 Wesleyan	3	287	531	733	.8	2.5
469 WELS	2	229	127	295	.3	1.0
499 Indep.Non-Char	1	350	350	350	.4	1.2
LEELANAU	**24**	**1,997**	**1,427**	**7,746 ***	**36.7**	**100.0**
056 Baha'i	0	7	NR	7	-	.1
081 Catholic	8	NR	NR	5,141	24.3	66.4
175 Congr Chr Chs	1	186	125	227 *	1.1	2.9
193 Episcopal	1	NR	35	46	.2	.6
201 Evan Cov Ch	1	52	83	83 *	.4	1.1
207 E.L.C.A.	2	366	200	492	2.3	6.4
226 Friends-USA	1	47	NR	57 *	.3	.7
283 Luth—MO Synod	3	403	286	496	2.3	6.4
355 Presb Ch (USA)	1	24	11	29 *	.1	.4
371 Ref Ch in Am	1	268	234	382	1.8	4.9
419 So Bapt Conv	1	23	25	28 *	.1	.4
443 Un C of Christ	1	194	85	237 *	1.1	3.1
449 Un Methodist	3	427	343	521 *	2.5	6.7
LENAWEE	**106**	**15,441**	**9,350**	**39,404 ***	**39.8**	**100.0**
019 Amer Bapt USA	4	675	443	840 *	.8	2.1
053 Assemb of God	2	950	1,371	5,960	6.0	15.1
056 Baha'i	1	27	NR	27	-	.1
081 Catholic	9	NR	NR	13,456	13.6	34.1
093 Chr Ch (Disc)	1	96	49	119 *	.1	.3
127 Ch God (Cleve)	5	600	203	747 *	.8	1.9
145 Ch God Prophcy	1	36	NR	44 *	-	.1
151 L-D Saints	1	NR	NR	471	.5	1.2
157 Ch of Brethren	2	36	27	44 *	-	.1
165 Ch of Nazarene	5	860	821	1,110	1.1	2.8
167 Chs of Christ	2	320	350	425	.4	1.1
175 Congr Chr Chs	3	557	257	693 *	.7	1.8
193 Episcopal	3	NR	125	526	.5	1.3
203 Evan Free Ch	2	209	549	549	.6	1.4
207 E.L.C.A.	5	1,252	708	1,825	1.8	4.6
213 Evan Menn Inc	1	45	52	56 *	.1	.1
221 Free Methodist	1	34	55	55	.1	.1
223 Free Will Bapt	2	143	NR	178 *	.2	.5
226 Friends-USA	5	475	NR	591 *	.6	1.5
283 Luth—MO Synod	6	1,882	915	2,441	2.5	6.2
306 NT IndBapt&Rltd	1	40	NR	50 *	.1	.1
323 Old Ord Amish	1	55	NR	68 *	.1	.2
339 Pent Ch of God	1	75	NR	85	.1	.2
355 Presb Ch (USA)	6	1,207	432	1,503 *	1.5	3.8
360 Prim Bapt Chrch	1	NR	NR	NR	-	-
370 Ref Baptist Chs	1	NR	NR	NR	-	-
388 Reg Bapt Gen As	3	232	211	295 *	.3	.7
403 Salvation Army	1	96	69	322	.3	.8
413 S.D.A.	2	202	NR	240	.2	.6
418 Southw Bapt Fel	1	NR	NR	NR	-	-
419 So Bapt Conv	5	1,042	370	1,297 *	1.3	3.3
443 Un C of Christ	2	238	140	296 *	.3	.8
449 Un Methodist	15	2,853	1,480	3,550 *	3.6	9.0
467 Wesleyan	1	58	127	127	.1	.3
469 WELS	4	1,146	596	1,414	1.4	3.6
LIVINGSTON	**71**	**15,058**	**8,828**	**58,059 ***	**37.0**	**100.0**
019 Amer Bapt USA	3	579	323	744 *	.5	1.3
053 Assemb of God	2	420	575	859	.5	1.5
056 Baha'i	0	6	NR	6	-	-
081 Catholic	8	NR	NR	34,823	22.2	60.0
097 Chr Chs&Chs Cr	2	575	NR	740 *	.5	1.3
123 Ch God (Ander)	1	NR	93	93	.1	.2
127 Ch God (Cleve)	1	167	163	215 *	.1	.4
151 L-D Saints	2	NR	NR	669	.4	1.2
165 Ch of Nazarene	3	889	929	1,469	.9	2.5
167 Chs of Christ	2	283	342	393	.3	.7
173 Comm of Christ	1	125	NR	125	.1	.2
193 Episcopal	3	NR	241	586	.4	1.0
203 Evan Free Ch	1	136	250	250	.2	.4
207 E.L.C.A.	5	2,034	892	3,014	1.9	5.2
216 Evan Presby Ch	1	1,572	NR	2,021 *	1.3	3.5
221 Free Methodist	2	137	181	182	.1	.3
263 Int Foursq Gos	1	24	40	40 *	-	.1
283 Luth—MO Synod	5	2,678	1,509	4,097	2.6	7.1
288 Mennonite USA	1	9	15	15 *	-	-
306 NT IndBapt&Rltd	1	250	NR	321 *	.2	.6
335 Orth Pres Ch	1	9	60	60	-	.1
355 Presb Ch (USA)	3	1,429	716	1,838 *	1.2	3.2
388 Reg Bapt Gen As	3	377	419	485 *	.3	.8
403 Salvation Army	1	77	54	230	.1	.4
413 S.D.A.	1	71	NR	84	.1	.1
419 So Bapt Conv	3	238	91	306 *	.2	.5
435 Unitarian-Univ	1	69	NR	89 *	.1	.2
443 Un C of Christ	1	223	144	287 *	.2	.5
449 Un Methodist	9	2,316	1,346	2,976 *	1.9	5.1
467 Wesleyan	2	212	362	821	.5	1.4

NR–Not Reported *Total adherents estimated from known number of communicant, confirmed, full members. - Represents a percentage less than 0.1. Percentages may not total 100 due to rounding.

Table 4: Religious Congregations by County and Group: 2000

Religious Group	Number of Churches, Synagogues, Mosques, or Temples	Number of Communicant, Confirmed, or Full Members	Number of Attendees	Total Adherents: Number of Adherents	Total Adherents: % of Total Pop.	Total Adherents: % of Total Adh.
469 WELS	1	153	83	221	.1	.4
LUCE	**13**	**980**	**597**	**2,002 ***	**28.5**	**100.0**
053 Assemb of God	1	48	70	106	1.5	5.3
081 Catholic	1	NR	NR	675	9.6	33.7
167 Chs of Christ	1	25	25	30	.4	1.5
193 Episcopal	1	NR	25	68	1.0	3.4
207 E.L.C.A.	1	273	100	364	5.2	18.2
283 Luth—MO Synod	1	177	66	221	3.1	11.0
339 Pent Ch of God	1	20	NR	38	.5	1.9
355 Presb Ch (USA)	1	112	78	133 *	1.9	6.6
388 Reg Bapt Gen As	1	92	90	90 *	1.3	4.5
413 S.D.A.	1	25	NR	30	.4	1.5
419 So Bapt Conv	1	30	21	36 *	.5	1.8
449 Un Methodist	2	178	122	211 *	3.0	10.5
MACKINAC	**30**	**1,421**	**1,244**	**4,444 ***	**37.2**	**100.0**
053 Assemb of God	1	23	30	30	.3	.7
056 Baha'i	0	2	NR	2	-	-
081 Catholic	8	NR	NR	2,572	21.5	57.9
175 Congr Chr Chs	1	60	125	72 *	.6	1.6
193 Episcopal	4	NR	83	136	1.1	3.1
203 Evan Free Ch	1	34	52	52	.4	1.2
207 E.L.C.A.	4	362	206	475	4.0	10.7
283 Luth—MO Synod	1	232	50	237	2.0	5.3
288 Mennonite USA	3	88	110	126 *	1.1	2.8
355 Presb Ch (USA)	2	65	51	78 *	.7	1.8
388 Reg Bapt Gen As	2	221	367	265 *	2.2	6.0
449 Un Methodist	2	315	158	378 *	3.2	8.5
469 WELS	1	19	12	21	.2	.5
MACOMB	**296**	**65,769**	**38,171**	**349,275 ***	**44.3**	**100.0**
019 Amer Bapt USA	3	656	398	808 *	.1	.2
034 Ant Orth of NA	1	0	NR	0	-	-
053 Assemb of God	15	2,235	2,981	4,324	.5	1.2
056 Baha'i	1	101	NR	101	-	-
057 Bapt Gen Conf	1	70	65	86 *	-	-
076 Buddhism	2	NR	NR	NR	-	-
081 Catholic	63	NR	NR	243,831	30.9	69.8
084 Calvary Chapel	1	NR	NR	NR	-	-
089 Chr & Miss Al	3	789	NR	929	.1	.3
097 Chr Chs&Chs Cr	1	700	NR	862 *	.1	.2
105 Christian Ref	1	55	45	68 *	-	-
123 Ch God (Ander)	5	NR	189	189	-	.1
127 Ch God (Cleve)	4	1,573	533	1,951 *	.2	.6
145 Ch God Prophcy	1	36	NR	44 *	-	-
151 L-D Saints	2	NR	NR	986	.1	.3
165 Ch of Nazarene	6	1,580	1,553	2,426	.3	.7
167 Chs of Christ	13	1,935	1,852	2,347	.3	.7
173 Comm of Christ	2	263	NR	263	-	.1
179 Consrv Bapt	1	NR	260	260	-	.1
181 Consrv Congr	1	83	55	102 *	-	-
185 Cumber Presb	2	39	NR	189	-	.1
193 Episcopal	7	NR	729	1,393	.2	.4
207 E.L.C.A.	23	9,174	4,311	13,761	1.7	3.9
216 Evan Presby Ch	1	543	NR	669 *	.1	.2
223 Free Will Bapt	3	214	NR	264 *	-	.1
246 Greek Orthodox	2	NR	NR	5,979	.8	1.7
249 Assyr Apost Ch	1	NR	NR	1,075	.1	.3
283 Luth—MO Synod	26	21,678	11,744	27,830	3.5	8.0
291 Missionary Ch	5	332	485	485	.1	.1
306 NT IndBapt&Rltd	3	930	NR	1,146 *	.1	.3
313 N Am Bapt Conf	10	1,356	1,481	1,671 *	.2	.5
320 "Old" MB Ascs	2	302	NR	372 *	-	.1
330 Macedonian Orth	1	NR	NR	2,400	.3	.7
355 Presb Ch (USA)	10	2,921	1,490	3,598 *	.5	1.0
360 Prim Bapt Chrch	2	NR	NR	NR	-	-
371 Ref Ch in Am	1	93	59	171	-	-
397 OCA: Roman Dioc	1	NR	NR	600	.1	.2
401 Rus Orth Abroad	1	NR	NR	NR	-	-
403 Salvation Army	3	304	207	1,228	.2	.4
411 Serb Orth: Grac	1	NR	NR	NR	-	-
413 S.D.A.	3	471	NR	561	.1	.2
419 So Bapt Conv	17	4,266	1,551	5,256 *	.7	1.5
443 Un C of Christ	10	2,213	841	2,726 *	.3	.8
449 Un Methodist	21	4,701	2,528	5,792 *	.7	1.7
467 Wesleyan	2	312	611	1,340	.2	.4
469 WELS	5	544	333	742	.1	.2
496 Jewish Est	2	NR	NR	4,200	.5	1.2
498 Indep.Charis.	2	4,500	3,200	5,400	.7	1.5
499 Indep.Non-Char	2	800	670	850	.1	.2
MANISTEE	**37**	**4,647**	**2,753**	**12,674 ***	**51.7**	**100.0**
053 Assemb of God	1	61	75	109	.4	.9
056 Baha'i	0	4	NR	4	-	-
057 Bapt Gen Conf	1	130	106	156 *	.6	1.2
081 Catholic	5	NR	NR	6,459	26.3	51.0
093 Chr Ch (Disc)	1	292	115	351 *	1.4	2.8
097 Chr Chs&Chs Cr	1	24	NR	29 *	.1	.2
151 L-D Saints	1	NR	NR	258	1.1	2.0
157 Ch of Brethren	3	271	169	326 *	1.3	2.6
193 Episcopal	1	NR	56	134	.5	1.1
201 Evan Cov Ch	1	72	121	121 *	.5	1.0
207 E.L.C.A.	2	969	364	1,166	4.8	9.2
283 Luth—MO Synod	5	1,317	675	1,783	7.3	14.1
297 Mennonite;Other	1	30	NR	36 *	.1	.3
335 Orth Pres Ch	1	0	0	0	-	-
388 Reg Bapt Gen As	3	399	454	482 *	2.0	3.8
403 Salvation Army	1	47	14	20	.1	.2
413 S.D.A.	1	45	NR	54	.2	.4
419 So Bapt Conv	1	0	0	0 *	-	-
443 Un C of Christ	2	294	129	353 *	1.4	2.8
449 Un Methodist	4	572	427	687 *	2.8	5.4
469 WELS	1	120	48	146	.6	1.2
MARQUETTE	**80**	**12,603**	**5,569**	**36,819 ***	**57.0**	**100.0**
019 Amer Bapt USA	1	59	40	70 *	.1	.2
053 Assemb of God	2	240	313	440	.7	1.2
056 Baha'i	1	57	NR	57	.1	.2
057 Bapt Gen Conf	4	373	432	498 *	.8	1.4
081 Catholic	13	NR	NR	19,217	29.7	52.2
097 Chr Chs&Chs Cr	1	310	NR	368 *	.6	1.0
105 Christian Ref	1	84	60	100 *	.2	.3
121 Ch God (Abr)	1	6	7	7 *	-	-
127 Ch God (Cleve)	1	8	7	9 *	-	-
151 L-D Saints	1	NR	NR	288	.4	.8
167 Chs of Christ	1	74	95	123	.2	.3
193 Episcopal	5	NR	208	694	1.1	1.9
201 Evan Cov Ch	2	152	126	189 *	.3	.5
207 E.L.C.A.	15	6,487	1,940	8,490	13.1	23.1
220 Free Lutheran	1	150	130	201	.3	.5
223 Free Will Bapt	1	71	NR	85 *	.1	.2
226 Friends-USA	1	45	NR	53 *	.1	.1
246 Greek Orthodox	1	NR	NR	12	-	-
283 Luth—MO Synod	2	1,164	600	1,616	2.5	4.4
291 Missionary Ch	1	44	87	87	.1	.2
355 Presb Ch (USA)	3	588	232	697 *	1.1	1.9
388 Reg Bapt Gen As	1	55	72	72 *	.1	.2
403 Salvation Army	2	283	135	478	.7	1.3
413 S.D.A.	1	48	NR	57	.1	.2
419 So Bapt Conv	3	198	151	235 *	.4	.6
435 Unitarian-Univ	1	39	NR	46 *	.1	.1
449 Un Methodist	9	1,940	872	2,301 *	3.6	6.2
467 Wesleyan	1	0	15	30	-	.1
469 WELS	2	128	47	149	.2	.4
496 Jewish Est	1	NR	NR	150	.2	.4
MASON	**41**	**5,071**	**2,847**	**10,926 ***	**38.6**	**100.0**
053 Assemb of God	1	102	135	171	.6	1.6
056 Baha'i	1	39	NR	39	.1	.4
057 Bapt Gen Conf	2	415	505	530 *	1.9	4.9
081 Catholic	7	NR	NR	4,146	14.7	37.9
097 Chr Chs&Chs Cr	1	50	NR	61 *	.2	.6
157 Ch of Brethren	1	51	0	62 *	.2	.6
165 Ch of Nazarene	1	84	70	179	.6	1.6
167 Chs of Christ	1	90	85	110	.4	1.0

NR–Not Reported *Total adherents estimated from known number of communicant, confirmed, full members. - Represents a percentage less than 0.1. Percentages may not total 100 due to rounding.

Table 4: Religious Congregations by County and Group: 2000

Religious Group	Number of Churches, Synagogues, Mosques, or Temples	Number of Communicant, Confirmed, or Full Members	Number of Attendees	Total Adherents: Number of Adherents	Total Adherents: % of Total Pop.	Total Adherents: % of Total Adh.
173 Comm of Christ	1	88	NR	88	.3	.8
176 Congr Ad Afl	1	605	NR	739 *	2.6	6.8
193 Episcopal	1	NR	40	103	.4	.9
201 Evan Cov Ch	1	63	98	98 *	.3	.9
203 Evan Free Ch	1	146	250	250	.9	2.3
207 E.L.C.A.	3	888	302	1,079	3.8	9.9
221 Free Methodist	1	35	28	40	.1	.4
283 Luth—MO Synod	3	888	344	1,136	4.0	10.4
323 Old Ord Amish	2	110	NR	134 *	.5	1.2
371 Ref Ch in Am	1	245	274	411	1.5	3.8
388 Reg Bapt Gen As	1	40	60	60 *	.2	.5
403 Salvation Army	1	61	40	125	.4	1.1
419 So Bapt Conv	1	34	38	42 *	.1	.4
435 Unitarian-Univ	1	42	NR	51 *	.2	.5
449 Un Methodist	5	879	490	1,073 *	3.8	9.8
467 Wesleyan	1	0	35	65	.2	.6
469 WELS	1	116	53	134	.5	1.2
MECOSTA	**52**	**4,931**	**3,998**	**11,007 ***	**27.1**	**100.0**
053 Assemb of God	2	93	124	171	.4	1.6
056 Baha'i	0	15	NR	15	-	.1
076 Buddhism	1	NR	NR	NR	-	-
081 Catholic	4	NR	NR	3,067	7.6	27.9
097 Chr Chs&Chs Cr	3	290	NR	350 *	.9	3.2
105 Christian Ref	1	148	125	179 *	.4	1.6
123 Ch God (Ander)	3	NR	222	222	.5	2.0
127 Ch God (Cleve)	1	114	53	138 *	.3	1.3
151 L-D Saints	1	NR	NR	276	.7	2.5
165 Ch of Nazarene	1	47	49	83	.2	.8
167 Chs of Christ	1	25	25	30	.1	.3
173 Comm of Christ	1	59	NR	59	.1	.5
179 Consrv Bapt	1	NR	115	115	.3	1.0
193 Episcopal	1	NR	79	263	.6	2.4
203 Evan Free Ch	1	149	380	380	.9	3.5
207 E.L.C.A.	1	332	157	403	1.0	3.7
221 Free Methodist	4	111	349	352	.9	3.2
283 Luth—MO Synod	2	927	510	1,167	2.9	10.6
323 Old Ord Amish	3	165	NR	198 *	.5	1.8
355 Presb Ch (USA)	1	196	157	237 *	.6	2.2
388 Reg Bapt Gen As	1	98	175	175 *	.4	1.6
403 Salvation Army	1	9	26	9	-	.1
413 S.D.A.	1	41	NR	49	.1	.4
419 So Bapt Conv	1	40	50	48 *	.1	.4
443 Un C of Christ	1	489	157	591 *	1.5	5.4
449 Un Methodist	9	1,260	878	1,523 *	3.8	13.8
467 Wesleyan	3	96	233	590	1.5	5.4
469 WELS	2	227	134	317	.8	2.9
MENOMINEE	**37**	**4,920**	**2,085**	**17,472 ***	**69.0**	**100.0**
053 Assemb of God	2	95	117	232	.9	1.3
056 Baha'i	0	3	NR	3	-	-
057 Bapt Gen Conf	1	187	140	228 *	.9	1.3
081 Catholic	6	NR	NR	11,072	43.7	63.4
127 Ch God (Cleve)	2	57	45	70 *	.3	.4
167 Chs of Christ	1	15	15	18	.1	.1
193 Episcopal	2	NR	43	107	.4	.6
201 Evan Cov Ch	4	228	209	288 *	1.1	1.6
203 Evan Free Ch	1	111	175	175	.7	1.0
207 E.L.C.A.	5	2,395	594	3,077	12.1	17.6
293 Morav Ch-North	1	59	NR	66	.3	.4
355 Presb Ch (USA)	1	318	136	387 *	1.5	2.2
413 S.D.A.	2	282	NR	336	1.3	1.9
419 So Bapt Conv	1	33	45	40 *	.2	.2
449 Un Methodist	4	439	254	535 *	2.1	3.1
469 WELS	4	698	312	838	3.3	4.8
MIDLAND	**80**	**16,430**	**10,875**	**37,957 ***	**45.8**	**100.0**
019 Amer Bapt USA	1	313	175	394 *	.5	1.0
053 Assemb of God	3	770	974	1,554	1.9	4.1
056 Baha'i	1	27	NR	27	-	.1
081 Catholic	7	NR	NR	11,782	14.2	31.0
097 Chr Chs&Chs Cr	1	110	NR	139 *	.2	.4
123 Ch God (Ander)	6	NR	802	802	1.0	2.1
127 Ch God (Cleve)	1	400	90	504 *	.6	1.3
151 L-D Saints	2	NR	NR	731	.9	1.9
157 Ch of Brethren	1	48	46	60 *	.1	.2
165 Ch of Nazarene	3	383	338	572	.7	1.5
167 Chs of Christ	1	165	160	165	.2	.4
173 Comm of Christ	3	432	NR	432	.5	1.1
193 Episcopal	2	NR	210	648	.8	1.7
203 Evan Free Ch	1	230	800	800	1.0	2.1
207 E.L.C.A.	2	1,295	615	1,758	2.1	4.6
213 Evan Menn Inc	1	59	100	74 *	.1	.2
221 Free Methodist	1	100	200	200	.2	.5
283 Luth—MO Synod	4	2,776	1,527	3,748	4.5	9.9
288 Mennonite USA	1	69	55	87 *	.1	.2
291 Missionary Ch	1	0	145	145	.2	.4
306 NT IndBapt&Rltd	1	100	NR	126 *	.2	.3
339 Pent Ch of God	1	22	NR	82	.1	.2
355 Presb Ch (USA)	2	1,736	524	2,188 *	2.6	5.8
356 Presb Ch Amer	1	21	27	27	-	.1
371 Ref Ch in Am	1	199	180	336	.4	.9
388 Reg Bapt Gen As	2	610	557	763 *	.9	2.0
403 Salvation Army	1	137	42	394	.5	1.0
413 S.D.A.	2	267	NR	318	.4	.8
419 So Bapt Conv	4	473	223	596 *	.7	1.6
435 Unitarian-Univ	1	136	NR	171 *	.2	.5
443 Un C of Christ	1	403	96	508 *	.6	1.3
449 Un Methodist	13	3,985	1,600	5,020 *	6.1	13.2
463 Vineyard	1	270	205	340 *	.4	.9
467 Wesleyan	4	43	571	1,375	1.7	3.6
469 WELS	1	251	163	371	.4	1.0
496 Jewish Est	0	NR	NR	120	.1	.3
498 Indep.Charis.	1	600	450	600	.7	1.6
MISSAUKEE	**24**	**3,341**	**2,545**	**4,821 ***	**33.3**	**100.0**
053 Assemb of God	1	28	40	77	.5	1.6
081 Catholic	1	NR	NR	491	3.4	10.2
097 Chr Chs&Chs Cr	1	40	NR	50 *	.3	1.0
105 Christian Ref	7	1,904	1,613	2,384 *	16.5	49.5
207 E.L.C.A.	1	234	117	283	2.0	5.9
216 Evan Presby Ch	1	64	NR	80 *	.6	1.7
323 Old Ord Amish	1	55	NR	69 *	.5	1.4
355 Presb Ch (USA)	2	173	105	216 *	1.5	4.5
371 Ref Ch in Am	3	414	410	638	4.4	13.2
388 Reg Bapt Gen As	1	73	40	91 *	.6	1.9
413 S.D.A.	1	54	NR	64	.4	1.3
419 So Bapt Conv	1	16	20	20 *	.1	.4
449 Un Methodist	3	286	200	358 *	2.5	7.4
MONROE	**127**	**24,700**	**13,520**	**78,156 ***	**53.6**	**100.0**
019 Amer Bapt USA	3	442	475	559 *	.4	.7
053 Assemb of God	4	268	340	483	.3	.6
056 Baha'i	0	9	NR	9	-	-
057 Bapt Gen Conf	3	584	557	788 *	.5	1.0
081 Catholic	13	NR	NR	39,822	27.3	51.0
089 Chr & Miss Al	4	218	NR	402	.3	.5
097 Chr Chs&Chs Cr	1	100	NR	126 *	.1	.2
105 Christian Ref	1	75	80	95 *	.1	.1
123 Ch God (Ander)	1	NR	32	32	-	-
127 Ch God (Cleve)	4	1,635	819	2,067 *	1.4	2.6
151 L-D Saints	1	NR	NR	364	.2	.5
165 Ch of Nazarene	3	370	415	531	.4	.7
167 Chs of Christ	3	225	230	285	.2	.4
173 Comm of Christ	2	190	NR	190	.1	.2
181 Consrv Congr	1	158	116	200 *	.1	.3
193 Episcopal	1	NR	65	157	.1	.2
207 E.L.C.A.	11	4,583	1,659	6,141	4.2	7.9
221 Free Methodist	3	673	1,369	1,406	1.0	1.8
223 Free Will Bapt	1	71	NR	90 *	.1	.1
263 Int Foursq Gos	1	30	50	50 *	-	.1
283 Luth—MO Synod	7	4,104	1,920	5,529	3.8	7.1
306 NT IndBapt&Rltd	1	200	NR	253 *	.2	.3
355 Presb Ch (USA)	5	672	358	850 *	.6	1.1
360 Prim Bapt Chrch	1	NR	NR	NR	-	-
388 Reg Bapt Gen As	2	288	196	364 *	.2	.5

NR–Not Reported *Total adherents estimated from known number of communicant, confirmed, full members. - Represents a percentage less than 0.1. Percentages may not total 100 due to rounding.

Table 4: Religious Congregations by County and Group: 2000

Religious Group	Number of Churches, Synagogues, Mosques, or Temples	Number of Communicant, Confirmed, or Full Members	Number of Attendees	Total Adherents		
				Number of Adherents	% of Total Pop.	% of Total Adh.
403 Salvation Army	1	88	64	122	.1	.2
410 Serb Orth USA	1	NR	NR	300	.2	.4
413 S.D.A.	2	175	NR	209	.1	.3
419 So Bapt Conv	17	4,394	1,778	5,555 *	3.8	7.1
449 Un Methodist	17	2,900	1,596	3,666 *	2.5	4.7
463 Vineyard	1	885	659	1,119 *	.8	1.4
466 Wayn Tr MB Asc	1	262	NR	331 *	.2	.4
467 Wesleyan	3	255	327	724	.5	.9
469 WELS	4	846	415	1,137	.8	1.5
490 Zoroastrian	1	NR	NR	NR	-	-
496 Jewish Est	2	NR	NR	4,200	2.9	5.4
MONTCALM	**84**	**9,180**	**6,111**	**19,636 ***	**32.1**	**100.0**
019 Amer Bapt USA	1	45	35	57 *	.1	.3
053 Assemb of God	3	124	146	200	.3	1.0
056 Baha'i	0	2	NR	2	-	-
081 Catholic	7	NR	NR	5,958	9.7	30.3
093 Chr Ch (Disc)	1	128	91	161 *	.3	.8
097 Chr Chs&Chs Cr	5	669	NR	843 *	1.4	4.3
105 Christian Ref	1	262	280	330 *	.5	1.7
121 Ch God (Abr)	1	34	80	80 *	.1	.4
123 Ch God (Ander)	3	NR	260	260	.4	1.3
143 CG in Cr(Menn)	1	137	NR	172 *	.3	.9
157 Ch of Brethren	1	36	25	45 *	.1	.2
165 Ch of Nazarene	1	66	90	137	.2	.7
167 Chs of Christ	1	16	17	23	-	.1
171 Ch God-Gen Con	1	78	62	98 *	.2	.5
173 Comm of Christ	2	188	NR	188	.3	1.0
175 Congr Chr Chs	2	473	226	595 *	1.0	3.0
193 Episcopal	1	NR	60	135	.2	.7
203 Evan Free Ch	1	48	85	85	.1	.4
207 E.L.C.A.	5	1,021	440	1,429	2.3	7.3
221 Free Methodist	3	145	259	261	.4	1.3
283 Luth—MO Synod	5	1,032	481	1,347	2.2	6.9
291 Missionary Ch	1	19	33	33	.1	.2
297 Mennonite;Other	1	12	NR	15 *	-	.1
306 NT IndBapt&Rltd	1	125	NR	157 *	.3	.8
322 Old Ord Menn Ch	1	27	NR	34 *	.1	.2
323 Old Ord Amish	5	275	NR	345 *	.6	1.8
335 Orth Pres Ch	1	185	236	289	.5	1.5
339 Pent Ch of God	2	24	NR	99	.2	.5
388 Reg Bapt Gen As	6	837	1,132	1,168 *	1.9	5.9
413 S.D.A.	5	746	NR	887	1.4	4.5
443 Un C of Christ	4	718	365	904 *	1.5	4.6
449 Un Methodist	9	1,569	1,108	1,974 *	3.2	10.1
467 Wesleyan	2	139	600	1,325	2.2	6.7
MONTMORENCY	**17**	**1,431**	**1,080**	**4,258 ***	**41.3**	**100.0**
053 Assemb of God	1	72	97	165	1.6	3.9
056 Baha'i	0	1	NR	1	-	-
081 Catholic	3	NR	NR	2,340	22.7	55.0
167 Chs of Christ	1	52	55	65	.6	1.5
181 Consrv Congr	1	120	148	140 *	1.4	3.3
193 Episcopal	2	NR	79	155	1.5	3.6
221 Free Methodist	2	66	97	97	.9	2.3
283 Luth—MO Synod	2	650	326	745	7.2	17.5
419 So Bapt Conv	2	64	42	75 *	.7	1.8
443 Un C of Christ	2	272	138	318 *	3.1	7.5
449 Un Methodist	1	134	98	157 *	1.5	3.7
MUSKEGON	**144**	**25,638**	**17,524**	**59,533 ***	**35.0**	**100.0**
019 Amer Bapt USA	3	865	380	1,097 *	.6	1.8
053 Assemb of God	6	805	1,002	2,367	1.4	4.0
056 Baha'i	0	88	NR	88	.1	.1
057 Bapt Gen Conf	9	1,350	1,157	1,756 *	1.0	2.9
081 Catholic	12	NR	NR	19,950	11.7	33.5
084 Calvary Chapel	1	NR	NR	NR	-	-
089 Chr & Miss Al	1	32	NR	66	-	.1
093 Chr Ch (Disc)	1	130	80	165 *	.1	.3
097 Chr Chs&Chs Cr	2	490	NR	621 *	.4	1.0
105 Christian Ref	7	2,164	1,025	2,744 *	1.6	4.6
123 Ch God (Ander)	2	NR	198	198	.1	.3
127 Ch God (Cleve)	2	437	395	564 *	.3	.9
151 L-D Saints	3	NR	NR	908	.5	1.5
157 Ch of Brethren	1	22	13	28 *	-	-
165 Ch of Nazarene	2	346	289	362	.2	.6
167 Chs of Christ	2	110	120	142	.1	.2
173 Comm of Christ	1	244	NR	244	.1	.4
175 Congr Chr Chs	1	125	50	159 *	.1	.3
176 Congr Ad Afl	1	406	NR	515 *	.3	.9
179 Consrv Bapt	1	NR	225	225	.1	.4
181 Consrv Congr	1	181	261	230 *	.1	.4
193 Episcopal	4	NR	297	846	.5	1.4
201 Evan Cov Ch	4	831	1,048	1,125 *	.7	1.9
203 Evan Free Ch	1	189	326	326	.2	.5
207 E.L.C.A.	11	3,035	1,197	3,947	2.3	6.6
216 Evan Presby Ch	1	30	NR	38 *	-	.1
221 Free Methodist	3	197	319	319	.2	.5
246 Greek Orthodox	1	NR	NR	303	.2	.5
267 Muslim Est	1	NR	15	20	-	-
283 Luth—MO Synod	5	2,461	1,173	3,228	1.9	5.4
291 Missionary Ch	1	49	95	95	.1	.2
306 NT IndBapt&Rltd	1	0	NR	0 *	-	-
323 Old Ord Amish	1	55	NR	70 *	-	.1
355 Presb Ch (USA)	1	342	143	434 *	.3	.7
371 Ref Ch in Am	13	2,931	2,866	5,435	3.2	9.1
388 Reg Bapt Gen As	7	2,173	1,939	2,764 *	1.6	4.6
403 Salvation Army	1	130	59	510	.3	.9
413 S.D.A.	2	275	NR	327	.2	.5
419 So Bapt Conv	1	7	7	9 *	-	-
435 Unitarian-Univ	1	81	NR	103 *	.1	.2
443 Un C of Christ	3	1,350	374	1,712 *	1.0	2.9
449 Un Methodist	15	3,321	1,936	4,211 *	2.5	7.1
463 Vineyard	1	124	104	157 *	.1	.3
467 Wesleyan	4	37	336	616	.4	1.0
469 WELS	1	225	95	299	.2	.5
496 Jewish Est	1	NR	NR	210	.1	.4
NEWAYGO	**49**	**7,156**	**5,868**	**15,805 ***	**33.0**	**100.0**
053 Assemb of God	3	213	296	544	1.1	3.4
056 Baha'i	0	8	NR	8	-	.1
076 Buddhism	1	NR	NR	NR	-	-
081 Catholic	5	NR	NR	4,757	9.9	30.1
093 Chr Ch (Disc)	1	195	88	251 *	.5	1.6
097 Chr Chs&Chs Cr	1	125	NR	161 *	.3	1.0
105 Christian Ref	6	1,896	1,690	2,438 *	5.1	15.4
127 Ch God (Cleve)	1	179	129	230 *	.5	1.5
151 L-D Saints	1	NR	NR	176	.4	1.1
165 Ch of Nazarene	1	45	38	45	.1	.3
193 Episcopal	2	NR	73	205	.4	1.3
203 Evan Free Ch	1	65	190	190	.4	1.2
283 Luth—MO Synod	3	441	241	639	1.3	4.0
306 NT IndBapt&Rltd	1	200	NR	257 *	.5	1.6
323 Old Ord Amish	3	165	NR	213 *	.4	1.3
371 Ref Ch in Am	3	978	809	1,522	3.2	9.6
388 Reg Bapt Gen As	4	584	737	835 *	1.7	5.3
413 S.D.A.	1	58	NR	69	.1	.4
419 So Bapt Conv	1	64	58	82 *	.2	.5
443 Un C of Christ	3	551	307	709 *	1.5	4.5
449 Un Methodist	4	1,081	619	1,390 *	2.9	8.8
467 Wesleyan	3	308	593	1,084	2.3	6.9
OAKLAND	**573**	**118,851**	**70,970**	**577,152 ***	**48.3**	**100.0**
007 OCA: Alban Dioc	1	NR	NR	450	-	.1
019 Amer Bapt USA	11	3,632	1,418	4,525 *	.4	.8
034 Ant Orth of NA	2	1,137	NR	2,274	.2	.4
039 Ap Chr Ch(Naz)	1	71	100	100 *	-	-
050 Armen Ap Etchm	1	620	NR	2,772	.2	.5
053 Assemb of God	20	2,849	3,324	6,733	.6	1.2
056 Baha'i	6	385	NR	385	-	.1
057 Bapt Gen Conf	3	152	225	241 *	-	-
075 Brethren in Cr	1	38	36	38	-	-
076 Buddhism	5	NR	NR	NR	-	-
081 Catholic	63	NR	NR	302,201	25.3	52.4
084 Calvary Chapel	2	NR	NR	NR	-	-
089 Chr & Miss Al	7	820	NR	1,142	.1	.2

NR–Not Reported *Total adherents estimated from known number of communicant, confirmed, full members. - Represents a percentage less than 0.1. Percentages may not total 100 due to rounding.

Table 4: Religious Congregations by County and Group: 2000

Religious Group	Number of Churches, Synagogues, Mosques, or Temples	Number of Communicant, Confirmed, or Full Members	Number of Attendees	Total Adherents		
				Number of Adherents	% of Total Pop.	% of Total Adh.
093 Chr Ch (Disc)	2	379	138	472 *	-	.1
097 Chr Chs&Chs Cr	7	663	NR	826 *	.1	.1
105 Christian Ref	2	344	340	429 *	-	.1
123 Ch God (Ander)	9	NR	1,549	1,549	.1	.3
127 Ch God (Cleve)	10	2,912	1,222	3,630 *	.3	.6
145 Ch God Prophcy	1	36	NR	44 *	-	-
151 L-D Saints	13	NR	NR	4,031	.3	.7
157 Ch of Brethren	1	77	73	96 *	-	-
165 Ch of Nazarene	11	2,016	1,585	2,609	.2	.5
167 Chs of Christ	23	3,545	3,713	4,962	.4	.9
173 Comm of Christ	3	917	NR	917	.1	.2
175 Congr Chr Chs	7	2,085	1,003	2,598 *	.2	.5
179 Consrv Bapt	5	NR	2,867	2,867	.2	.5
181 Consrv Congr	2	440	227	548 *	-	.1
193 Episcopal	23	NR	2,887	9,791	.8	1.7
201 Evan Cov Ch	1	427	391	532 *	-	.1
203 Evan Free Ch	1	55	90	90	-	-
207 E.L.C.A.	28	10,301	4,693	14,346	1.2	2.5
216 Evan Presby Ch	8	2,267	NR	2,824 *	.2	.5
221 Free Methodist	6	795	1,073	1,120	.1	.2
223 Free Will Bapt	8	572	NR	712 *	.1	.1
226 Friends-USA	1	35	NR	44 *	-	-
246 Greek Orthodox	3	NR	NR	3,633	.3	.6
252 Hindu	5	NR	NR	NR	-	-
263 Int Foursq Gos	5	437	721	721 *	.1	.1
267 Muslim Est	7	NR	2,760	12,955	1.1	2.2
268 Jain	1	NR	NR	NR	-	-
283 Luth—MO Synod	34	18,803	10,093	25,892	2.2	4.5
290 Metro Comm Ch	2	154	137	152 *	-	-
291 Missionary Ch	4	251	618	618	.1	.1
306 NT IndBapt&Rltd	10	2,029	NR	2,528 *	.2	.4
313 N Am Bapt Conf	1	190	207	237 *	-	-
331 OCA: Ter Diocs	1	108	NR	492	-	.1
333 Malan Dioc Am	1	NR	NR	125	-	-
335 Orth Pres Ch	2	171	195	213	-	-
349 Pent Holiness	1	50	50	62 *	-	-
355 Presb Ch (USA)	28	13,994	5,944	17,435 *	1.5	3.0
371 Ref Ch in Am	1	35	40	63	-	-
388 Reg Bapt Gen As	7	1,497	1,597	1,871 *	.2	.3
395 Romania Orth Ar	1	NR	NR	525	-	.1
397 OCA: Roman Dioc	2	NR	NR	385	-	.1
401 Rus Orth Abroad	1	NR	NR	NR	-	-
403 Salvation Army	3	483	347	2,174	.2	.4
413 S.D.A.	8	1,488	NR	1,771	.1	.3
416 Sikh	3	NR	NR	NR	-	-
419 So Bapt Conv	28	5,373	2,204	6,695 *	.6	1.2
423 Syrian Orth Ch	1	NR	NR	600	.1	.1
431 Ukrainian Orth	1	NR	NR	471	-	.1
435 Unitarian-Univ	5	1,117	NR	1,392 *	.1	.2
443 Un C of Christ	8	2,562	868	3,192 *	.3	.6
449 Un Methodist	55	23,429	11,496	29,195 *	2.4	5.1
463 Vineyard	1	15	15	19 *	-	-
467 Wesleyan	1	114	67	125	-	-
469 WELS	3	556	352	783	.1	.1
496 Jewish Est	35	NR	NR	77,200	6.5	13.4
498 Indep.Charis.	4	2,075	1,925	2,550	.2	.4
499 Indep.Non-Char	5	6,350	4,380	7,180	.6	1.2
OCEANA	**42**	**3,670**	**3,136**	**8,688 ***	**32.3**	**100.0**
017 Amer Bapt Assn	1	50	NR	63 *	.2	.7
053 Assemb of God	1	24	25	32	.1	.4
056 Baha'i	0	27	NR	27	.1	.3
057 Bapt Gen Conf	1	51	142	142 *	.5	1.6
081 Catholic	8	NR	NR	2,947	11.0	33.9
105 Christian Ref	2	375	305	473 *	1.8	5.4
151 L-D Saints	1	NR	NR	160	.6	1.8
165 Ch of Nazarene	1	22	17	51	.2	.6
167 Chs of Christ	1	18	25	25	.1	.3
193 Episcopal	1	NR	27	61	.2	.7
207 E.L.C.A.	1	327	163	445	1.7	5.1
283 Luth—MO Synod	1	221	100	225	.8	2.6
291 Missionary Ch	1	41	54	54	.2	.6
355 Presb Ch (USA)	1	110	60	139 *	.5	1.6
371 Ref Ch in Am	1	233	170	320	1.2	3.7
379 Ref Mennonite	1	30	NR	38 *	.1	.4
388 Reg Bapt Gen As	3	579	780	780 *	2.9	9.0
413 S.D.A.	1	60	NR	71	.3	.8
443 Un C of Christ	2	457	280	576 *	2.1	6.6
449 Un Methodist	7	856	585	1,079 *	4.0	12.4
467 Wesleyan	5	86	362	854	3.2	9.8
469 WELS	1	103	41	126	.5	1.5
OGEMAW	**24**	**2,480**	**1,507**	**7,391 ***	**34.1**	**100.0**
011 A.W.M.C.	1	0	26	0	-	-
053 Assemb of God	1	27	34	34	.2	.5
081 Catholic	3	NR	NR	3,854	17.8	52.1
127 Ch God (Cleve)	1	55	45	67 *	.3	.9
151 L-D Saints	1	NR	NR	115	.5	1.6
157 Ch of Brethren	1	50	45	61 *	.3	.8
165 Ch of Nazarene	2	49	46	91	.4	1.2
167 Chs of Christ	1	75	65	90	.4	1.2
173 Comm of Christ	1	190	NR	190	.9	2.6
193 Episcopal	2	NR	56	201	.9	2.7
207 E.L.C.A.	1	177	76	227	1.0	3.1
221 Free Methodist	1	164	305	305	1.4	4.1
226 Friends-USA	1	95	NR	115 *	.5	1.6
283 Luth—MO Synod	2	743	339	1,006	4.6	13.6
413 S.D.A.	1	31	NR	37	.2	.5
419 So Bapt Conv	1	190	175	230 *	1.1	3.1
449 Un Methodist	3	634	295	768 *	3.5	10.4
ONTONAGON	**30**	**1,926**	**853**	**4,304 ***	**55.1**	**100.0**
053 Assemb of God	2	58	67	107	1.4	2.5
081 Catholic	5	NR	NR	1,751	22.4	40.7
193 Episcopal	2	NR	15	26	.3	.6
207 E.L.C.A.	7	918	316	1,236	15.8	28.7
220 Free Lutheran	1	22	35	35	.4	.8
283 Luth—MO Synod	2	420	131	499	6.4	11.6
355 Presb Ch (USA)	1	16	13	19 *	.2	.4
388 Reg Bapt Gen As	2	27	95	77 *	1.0	1.8
413 S.D.A.	1	29	NR	35	.4	.8
449 Un Methodist	6	306	141	357 *	4.6	8.3
469 WELS	1	130	40	162	2.1	3.8
OSCEOLA	**51**	**4,146**	**3,557**	**7,538 ***	**32.5**	**100.0**
053 Assemb of God	2	182	280	300	1.3	4.0
057 Bapt Gen Conf	1	29	63	63 *	.3	.8
081 Catholic	3	NR	NR	1,694	7.3	22.5
105 Christian Ref	1	525	396	658 *	2.8	8.7
123 Ch God (Ander)	1	NR	85	85	.4	1.1
127 Ch God (Cleve)	1	20	36	36 *	.2	.5
165 Ch of Nazarene	1	162	128	172	.7	2.3
173 Comm of Christ	2	184	NR	184	.8	2.4
181 Consrv Congr	1	20	15	25 *	.1	.3
201 Evan Cov Ch	2	162	232	242 *	1.0	3.2
203 Evan Free Ch	1	69	125	125	.5	1.7
207 E.L.C.A.	4	637	339	873	3.8	11.6
221 Free Methodist	6	170	315	316	1.4	4.2
283 Luth—MO Synod	1	250	225	300	1.3	4.0
323 Old Ord Amish	2	110	NR	138 *	.6	1.8
355 Presb Ch (USA)	1	15	80	80 *	.3	1.1
388 Reg Bapt Gen As	2	267	293	334 *	1.4	4.4
413 S.D.A.	3	112	NR	134	.6	1.8
419 So Bapt Conv	1	71	33	89 *	.4	1.2
443 Un C of Christ	1	84	37	105 *	.5	1.4
449 Un Methodist	11	985	692	1,233 *	5.3	16.4
467 Wesleyan	3	92	183	352	1.5	4.7
OSCODA	**20**	**1,507**	**993**	**2,676 ***	**28.4**	**100.0**
053 Assemb of God	1	71	86	126	1.3	4.7
056 Baha'i	0	1	NR	1	-	-
081 Catholic	1	NR	NR	527	5.6	19.7
123 Ch God (Ander)	1	NR	204	204	2.2	7.6
167 Chs of Christ	1	51	55	67	.7	2.5
193 Episcopal	1	NR	24	34	.4	1.3
263 Int Foursq Gos	1	11	51	51 *	.5	1.9

NR–Not Reported *Total adherents estimated from known number of communicant, confirmed, full members. - Represents a percentage less than 0.1. Percentages may not total 100 due to rounding.

Table 4: Religious Congregations by County and Group: 2000

Religious Group	Number of Churches, Synagogues, Mosques, or Temples	Number of Communicant, Confirmed, or Full Members	Number of Attendees	Total Adherents: Number of Adherents	Total Adherents: % of Total Pop.	Total Adherents: % of Total Adh.
283 Luth—MO Synod	1	34	40	38	.4	1.4
288 Mennonite USA	2	456	343	550 *	5.8	20.6
297 Mennonite;Other	2	46	NR	55 *	.6	2.1
306 NT IndBapt&Rltd	1	220	NR	265 *	2.8	9.9
323 Old Ord Amish	3	165	NR	198 *	2.1	7.4
413 S.D.A.	1	140	NR	167	1.8	6.2
443 Un C of Christ	1	56	25	67 *	.7	2.5
449 Un Methodist	1	186	104	224 *	2.4	8.4
467 Wesleyan	1	0	25	25	.3	.9
469 WELS	1	70	36	77	.8	2.9
OTSEGO	**22**	**2,348**	**1,867**	**10,753 ***	**46.1**	**100.0**
053 Assemb of God	1	49	55	63	.3	.6
056 Baha'i	0	6	NR	6	-	.1
081 Catholic	3	NR	NR	7,279	31.2	67.7
105 Christian Ref	1	133	120	167 *	.7	1.6
165 Ch of Nazarene	1	56	76	103	.4	1.0
167 Chs of Christ	1	70	50	100	.4	.9
173 Comm of Christ	1	150	NR	150	.6	1.4
193 Episcopal	1	NR	60	131	.6	1.2
203 Evan Free Ch	2	328	650	650	2.8	6.0
207 E.L.C.A.	1	293	135	403	1.7	3.7
221 Free Methodist	1	0	75	75	.3	.7
283 Luth—MO Synod	1	308	148	429	1.8	4.0
339 Pent Ch of God	1	20	NR	24	.1	.2
355 Presb Ch (USA)	1	113	80	142 *	.6	1.3
413 S.D.A.	1	45	NR	54	.2	.5
419 So Bapt Conv	2	92	44	115 *	.5	1.1
443 Un C of Christ	1	127	54	159 *	.7	1.5
449 Un Methodist	1	519	286	651 *	2.8	6.1
469 WELS	1	39	34	52	.2	.5
OTTAWA	**208**	**69,195**	**58,591**	**133,495 ***	**56.0**	**100.0**
053 Assemb of God	8	878	1,075	1,186	.5	.9
056 Baha'i	1	66	NR	66	-	-
057 Bapt Gen Conf	1	43	62	62 *	-	-
081 Catholic	10	NR	NR	27,110	11.4	20.3
089 Chr & Miss Al	1	30	NR	69	-	.1
097 Chr Chs&Chs Cr	3	460	NR	592 *	.2	.4
105 Christian Ref	53	23,688	18,648	30,490 *	12.8	22.8
127 Ch God (Cleve)	4	419	180	541 *	.2	.4
145 Ch God Prophcy	1	36	NR	46 *	-	-
151 L-D Saints	1	NR	NR	427	.2	.3
165 Ch of Nazarene	2	215	204	482	.2	.4
167 Chs of Christ	4	310	316	365	.2	.3
173 Comm of Christ	1	97	NR	97	-	.1
179 Consrv Bapt	1	NR	170	170	.1	.1
193 Episcopal	2	NR	346	941	.4	.7
201 Evan Cov Ch	2	78	162	168 *	.1	.1
203 Evan Free Ch	1	69	125	125	.1	.1
207 E.L.C.A.	3	762	300	871	.4	.7
221 Free Methodist	1	70	113	113	-	.1
262 Int Cou Comm Ch	1	40	NR	51 *	-	-
283 Luth—MO Synod	12	5,160	2,743	6,560	2.8	4.9
335 Orth Pres Ch	2	143	254	260	.1	.2
355 Presb Ch (USA)	5	2,613	1,233	3,363 *	1.4	2.5
356 Presb Ch Amer	1	156	192	234	.1	.2
369 Prot Ref Chs	5	828	NR	1,462	.6	1.1
370 Ref Baptist Chs	1	NR	NR	NR	-	-
371 Ref Ch in Am	46	22,978	20,643	36,461	15.3	27.3
388 Reg Bapt Gen As	3	429	489	552 *	.2	.4
403 Salvation Army	2	252	202	809	.3	.6
413 S.D.A.	5	662	NR	787	.3	.6
419 So Bapt Conv	1	253	165	326 *	.1	.2
443 Un C of Christ	2	725	296	933 *	.4	.7
449 Un Methodist	6	2,704	1,455	3,480 *	1.5	2.6
455 Un Ref Chs N.A.	5	871	NR	1,353	.6	1.0
463 Vineyard	1	150	479	479 *	.2	.4
467 Wesleyan	6	2,340	6,049	9,614	4.0	7.2
499 Indep.Non-Char	4	1,670	2,690	2,850	1.2	2.1
PRESQUE ISLE	**26**	**3,205**	**1,476**	**9,393 ***	**65.2**	**100.0**
053 Assemb of God	2	88	102	169	1.2	1.8
056 Baha'i	0	1	NR	1	-	-
081 Catholic	4	NR	NR	5,490	38.1	58.4
173 Comm of Christ	1	222	NR	222	1.5	2.4
193 Episcopal	1	NR	15	47	.3	.5
207 E.L.C.A.	3	298	149	368	2.6	3.9
220 Free Lutheran	1	92	35	105	.7	1.1
262 Int Cou Comm Ch	1	101	NR	119 *	.8	1.3
283 Luth—MO Synod	7	1,706	805	2,051	14.2	21.8
355 Presb Ch (USA)	1	228	107	268 *	1.9	2.9
413 S.D.A.	1	76	NR	90	.6	1.0
419 So Bapt Conv	2	123	78	145 *	1.0	1.5
449 Un Methodist	2	270	185	318 *	2.2	3.4
ROSCOMMON	**33**	**2,994**	**2,119**	**8,180 ***	**32.1**	**100.0**
019 Amer Bapt USA	2	449	306	528 *	2.1	6.5
053 Assemb of God	3	126	187	299	1.2	3.7
056 Baha'i	0	1	NR	1	-	-
081 Catholic	5	NR	NR	3,986	15.7	48.7
127 Ch God (Cleve)	1	27	37	37 *	.1	.5
167 Chs of Christ	1	40	50	50	.2	.6
173 Comm of Christ	1	73	NR	73	.3	.9
175 Congr Chr Chs	1	223	110	262 *	1.0	3.2
193 Episcopal	2	NR	108	312	1.2	3.8
207 E.L.C.A.	1	165	94	198	.8	2.4
221 Free Methodist	1	18	31	31	.1	.4
283 Luth—MO Synod	2	681	351	783	3.1	9.6
306 NT IndBapt&Rltd	1	175	NR	206 *	.8	2.5
355 Presb Ch (USA)	1	64	51	75 *	.3	.9
388 Reg Bapt Gen As	2	146	140	140 *	.5	1.7
413 S.D.A.	1	42	NR	50	.2	.6
419 So Bapt Conv	4	195	157	229 *	.9	2.8
449 Un Methodist	2	541	306	636 *	2.5	7.8
467 Wesleyan	1	0	157	250	1.0	3.1
469 WELS	1	28	34	34	.1	.4
SAGINAW	**179**	**43,697**	**17,934**	**103,928 ***	**49.5**	**100.0**
017 Amer Bapt Assn	1	50	NR	63 *	-	.1
019 Amer Bapt USA	4	806	315	1,015 *	.5	1.0
053 Assemb of God	9	808	1,029	2,259	1.1	2.2
056 Baha'i	2	50	NR	50	-	-
059 Bapt Miss Assn	1	23	21	29 *	-	-
075 Brethren in Cr	1	28	50	50	-	-
081 Catholic	30	NR	NR	42,158	20.1	40.6
084 Calvary Chapel	1	NR	NR	NR	-	-
089 Chr & Miss Al	1	65	NR	171	.1	.2
093 Chr Ch (Disc)	2	125	53	157 *	.1	.2
097 Chr Chs&Chs Cr	2	200	NR	252 *	.1	.2
105 Christian Ref	1	117	110	147 *	.1	.1
123 Ch God (Ander)	1	NR	41	41	-	-
127 Ch God (Cleve)	2	154	50	194 *	.1	.2
151 L-D Saints	1	NR	NR	459	.2	.4
165 Ch of Nazarene	6	816	671	1,034	.5	1.0
167 Chs of Christ	3	334	265	422	.2	.4
173 Comm of Christ	3	392	NR	392	.2	.4
175 Congr Chr Chs	1	80	70	101 *	-	.1
193 Episcopal	6	NR	440	1,033	.5	1.0
207 E.L.C.A.	12	5,234	1,747	7,124	3.4	6.9
221 Free Methodist	2	101	100	121	.1	.1
246 Greek Orthodox	1	NR	NR	627	.3	.6
262 Int Cou Comm Ch	3	930	NR	1,171 *	.6	1.1
267 Muslim Est	1	NR	100	77	-	.1
283 Luth—MO Synod	15	13,620	6,368	17,549	8.4	16.9
288 Mennonite USA	2	110	92	139 *	.1	.1
290 Metro Comm Ch	1	21	12	26 *	-	-
306 NT IndBapt&Rltd	3	6,835	NR	8,609 *	4.1	8.3
339 Pent Ch of God	3	105	NR	340	.2	.3
355 Presb Ch (USA)	6	1,772	749	2,232 *	1.1	2.1
388 Reg Bapt Gen As	5	606	542	793 *	.4	.8
403 Salvation Army	1	140	36	947	.5	.9
413 S.D.A.	4	589	NR	702	.3	.7
419 So Bapt Conv	2	277	81	349 *	.2	.3
431 Ukrainian Orth	1	NR	NR	33	-	-
443 Un C of Christ	3	716	272	902 *	.4	.9

NR–Not Reported   *Total adherents estimated from known number of communicant, confirmed, full members.   - Represents a percentage less than 0.1.   Percentages may not total 100 due to rounding.

Table 4: Religious Congregations by County and Group: 2000

Religious Group	Number of Churches, Synagogues, Mosques, or Temples	Number of Communicant, Confirmed, or Full Members	Number of Attendees	Total Adherents		
				Number of Adherents	% of Total Pop.	% of Total Adh.
449 Un Methodist	18	3,840	1,925	4,836 *	2.3	4.7
467 Wesleyan	5	0	471	1,265	.6	1.2
469 WELS	12	4,753	2,324	5,944	2.8	5.7
496 Jewish Est	1	NR	NR	115	.1	.1
ST. CLAIR	**115**	**17,689**	**11,680**	**70,508 ***	**42.9**	**100.0**
011 A.W.M.C.	1	9	34	10	-	-
019 Amer Bapt USA	3	278	197	350 *	.2	.5
053 Assemb of God	3	171	216	270	.2	.4
056 Baha'i	0	20	NR	20	-	-
059 Bapt Miss Assn	1	60	75	75 *	-	.1
081 Catholic	15	NR	NR	41,399	25.2	58.7
097 Chr Chs&Chs Cr	2	345	NR	434 *	.3	.6
127 Ch God (Cleve)	1	306	183	385 *	.2	.5
151 L-D Saints	1	NR	NR	355	.2	.5
165 Ch of Nazarene	2	160	160	307	.2	.4
167 Chs of Christ	2	120	120	152	.1	.2
173 Comm of Christ	3	1,010	NR	1,010	.6	1.4
175 Congr Chr Chs	1	33	46	42 *	-	.1
176 Congr Ad Afl	1	498	NR	627 *	.4	.9
181 Consrv Congr	1	38	28	48 *	-	.1
193 Episcopal	8	NR	606	1,559	.9	2.2
203 Evan Free Ch	1	69	125	125	.1	.2
207 E.L.C.A.	8	3,085	1,034	4,144	2.5	5.9
221 Free Methodist	3	175	202	233	.1	.3
262 Int Cou Comm Ch	1	46	NR	58 *	-	.1
263 Int Foursq Gos	1	8	11	11 *	-	-
267 Muslim Est	1	NR	412	1,891	1.2	2.7
283 Luth—MO Synod	7	3,054	1,498	4,044	2.5	5.7
291 Missionary Ch	4	580	1,396	1,396	.9	2.0
306 NT IndBapt&Rltd	2	320	NR	403 *	.2	.6
355 Presb Ch (USA)	4	945	412	1,190 *	.7	1.7
388 Reg Bapt Gen As	2	301	532	555 *	.3	.8
403 Salvation Army	1	332	192	896	.5	1.3
413 S.D.A.	1	118	NR	140	.1	.2
419 So Bapt Conv	2	85	65	107 *	.1	.2
443 Un C of Christ	5	1,302	360	1,638 *	1.0	2.3
449 Un Methodist	19	2,836	1,555	3,567 *	2.2	5.1
467 Wesleyan	4	521	1,235	1,805	1.1	2.6
469 WELS	2	383	236	512	.3	.7
499 Indep.Non-Char	2	481	750	750	.5	1.1
ST. JOSEPH	**84**	**8,840**	**5,821**	**21,549 ***	**34.5**	**100.0**
017 Amer Bapt Assn	1	50	NR	63 *	.1	.3
019 Amer Bapt USA	2	200	158	253 *	.4	1.2
053 Assemb of God	3	181	252	344	.6	1.6
056 Baha'i	0	9	NR	9	-	-
057 Bapt Gen Conf	1	41	70	70 *	.1	.3
059 Bapt Miss Assn	1	36	40	46 *	.1	.2
061 Beachy Amish	1	51	NR	65 *	.1	.3
081 Catholic	6	NR	NR	7,379	11.8	34.2
097 Chr Chs&Chs Cr	3	410	NR	519 *	.8	2.4
105 Christian Ref	1	63	50	80 *	.1	.4
123 Ch God (Ander)	4	NR	296	296	.5	1.4
151 L-D Saints	1	NR	NR	312	.5	1.4
157 Ch of Brethren	1	64	43	81 *	.1	.4
165 Ch of Nazarene	2	437	349	875	1.4	4.1
167 Chs of Christ	1	51	55	67	.1	.3
179 Consrv Bapt	1	NR	175	175	.3	.8
183 Cons Menn Conf	1	42	51	61	.1	.3
193 Episcopal	2	NR	150	434	.7	2.0
207 E.L.C.A.	2	499	166	714	1.1	3.3
263 Int Foursq Gos	1	39	51	51 *	.1	.2
283 Luth—MO Synod	6	1,663	722	2,237	3.6	10.4
288 Mennonite USA	4	333	295	422 *	.7	2.0
291 Missionary Ch	4	270	536	536	.9	2.5
297 Mennonite;Other	3	202	NR	256 *	.4	1.2
323 Old Ord Amish	8	440	NR	560 *	.9	2.6
339 Pent Ch of God	1	30	NR	100	.2	.5
355 Presb Ch (USA)	3	900	375	1,141 *	1.8	5.3
388 Reg Bapt Gen As	2	106	205	219 *	.4	1.0
403 Salvation Army	1	61	32	66	.1	.3
413 S.D.A.	2	214	NR	255	.4	1.2

Religious Group	Number of Churches, Synagogues, Mosques, or Temples	Number of Communicant, Confirmed, or Full Members	Number of Attendees	Total Adherents		
				Number of Adherents	% of Total Pop.	% of Total Adh.
443 Un C of Christ	1	72	32	91 *	.1	.4
449 Un Methodist	12	1,814	1,027	2,298 *	3.7	10.7
467 Wesleyan	1	361	548	1,210	1.9	5.6
469 WELS	1	201	143	264	.4	1.2
SANILAC	**82**	**7,046**	**4,906**	**16,344 ***	**36.7**	**100.0**
019 Amer Bapt USA	2	253	169	317 *	.7	1.9
053 Assemb of God	3	143	184	266	.6	1.6
056 Baha'i	0	3	NR	3	-	-
075 Brethren in Cr	1	82	68	82	.2	.5
081 Catholic	10	NR	NR	6,454	14.5	39.5
089 Chr & Miss Al	1	60	NR	111	.2	.7
127 Ch God (Cleve)	1	79	41	99 *	.2	.6
151 L-D Saints	1	NR	NR	64	.1	.4
165 Ch of Nazarene	1	50	61	109	.2	.7
167 Chs of Christ	1	12	20	20	-	.1
173 Comm of Christ	5	573	NR	573	1.3	3.5
193 Episcopal	3	NR	123	197	.4	1.2
203 Evan Free Ch	1	69	125	125	.3	.8
207 E.L.C.A.	2	321	153	463	1.0	2.8
221 Free Methodist	2	217	323	331	.7	2.0
283 Luth—MO Synod	7	1,614	793	2,085	4.7	12.8
291 Missionary Ch	6	355	671	671	1.5	4.1
306 NT IndBapt&Rltd	1	45	NR	56 *	.1	.3
322 Old Ord Menn Ch	1	108	NR	135 *	.3	.8
323 Old Ord Amish	3	165	NR	207 *	.5	1.3
355 Presb Ch (USA)	5	658	366	825 *	1.9	5.0
388 Reg Bapt Gen As	1	116	106	145 *	.3	.9
419 So Bapt Conv	0	2	5	3 *	-	-
443 Un C of Christ	1	14	6	18 *	-	.1
449 Un Methodist	21	1,888	1,300	2,365 *	5.3	14.5
467 Wesleyan	2	219	392	620	1.4	3.8
SCHOOLCRAFT	**23**	**1,489**	**702**	**4,097 ***	**46.0**	**100.0**
019 Amer Bapt USA	1	284	147	342 *	3.8	8.3
057 Bapt Gen Conf	1	15	33	33 *	.4	.8
081 Catholic	4	NR	NR	1,959	22.0	47.8
151 L-D Saints	1	NR	NR	53	.6	1.3
173 Comm of Christ	2	83	NR	83	.9	2.0
175 Congr Chr Chs	1	119	85	143 *	1.6	3.5
193 Episcopal	1	NR	21	57	.6	1.4
207 E.L.C.A.	1	495	123	774	8.7	18.9
263 Int Foursq Gos	1	62	49	75 *	.8	1.8
283 Luth—MO Synod	1	81	46	101	1.1	2.5
288 Mennonite USA	3	60	55	73 *	.8	1.8
297 Mennonite;Other	1	8	NR	10 *	.1	.2
339 Pent Ch of God	1	22	NR	80	.9	2.0
355 Presb Ch (USA)	1	104	47	125 *	1.4	3.1
413 S.D.A.	1	19	NR	23	.3	.6
449 Un Methodist	2	137	96	166 *	1.9	4.1
SHIAWASSEE	**84**	**9,186**	**6,282**	**27,841 ***	**38.8**	**100.0**
019 Amer Bapt USA	2	264	145	333 *	.5	1.2
053 Assemb of God	4	226	290	353	.5	1.3
056 Baha'i	0	2	NR	2	-	-
059 Bapt Miss Assn	1	130	240	240 *	.3	.9
076 Buddhism	1	NR	NR	NR	-	-
081 Catholic	6	NR	NR	13,423	18.7	48.2
097 Chr Chs&Chs Cr	4	483	NR	609 *	.8	2.2
123 Ch God (Ander)	1	NR	119	119	.2	.4
127 Ch God (Cleve)	2	258	277	364 *	.5	1.3
151 L-D Saints	1	NR	NR	373	.5	1.3
165 Ch of Nazarene	6	802	840	1,500	2.1	5.4
167 Chs of Christ	1	65	70	85	.1	.3
173 Comm of Christ	1	99	NR	99	.1	.4
175 Congr Chr Chs	1	145	103	183 *	.3	.7
181 Consrv Congr	2	145	125	183 *	.3	.7
193 Episcopal	2	NR	271	558	.8	2.0
203 Evan Free Ch	1	70	100	100	.1	.4
207 E.L.C.A.	1	207	135	302	.4	1.1
216 Evan Presby Ch	1	101	NR	127 *	.2	.5
221 Free Methodist	3	143	161	172	.2	.6
263 Int Foursq Gos	1	23	40	40 *	.1	.1

NR–Not Reported *Total adherents estimated from known number of communicant, confirmed, full members. - Represents a percentage less than 0.1. Percentages may not total 100 due to rounding.

Table 4: Religious Congregations by County and Group: 2000

Religious Group	Number of Churches, Synagogues, Mosques, or Temples	Number of Communicant, Confirmed, or Full Members	Number of Attendees	Total Adherents: Number of Adherents	Total Adherents: % of Total Pop.	Total Adherents: % of Total Adh.
283 Luth—MO Synod	1	99	65	124	.2	.4
306 NT IndBapt&Rltd	3	154	NR	194 *	.3	.7
339 Pent Ch of God	1	35	NR	65	.1	.2
388 Reg Bapt Gen As	2	273	305	351 *	.5	1.3
403 Salvation Army	1	117	52	539	.8	1.9
413 S.D.A.	1	230	NR	274	.4	1.0
419 So Bapt Conv	3	243	153	306 *	.4	1.1
443 Un C of Christ	3	694	305	874 *	1.2	3.1
449 Un Methodist	22	2,371	1,379	2,986 *	4.2	10.7
467 Wesleyan	2	347	444	1,085	1.5	3.9
469 WELS	3	1,460	663	1,878	2.6	6.7
TUSCOLA	**85**	**13,369**	**8,023**	**24,763 ***	**42.5**	**100.0**
019 Amer Bapt USA	1	37	35	46 *	.1	.2
053 Assemb of God	4	192	253	536	.9	2.2
056 Baha'i	0	5	NR	5	-	-
081 Catholic	7	NR	NR	6,418	11.0	25.9
084 Calvary Chapel	1	NR	NR	NR	-	-
097 Chr Chs&Chs Cr	2	285	NR	355 *	.6	1.4
123 Ch God (Ander)	1	NR	342	342	.6	1.4
127 Ch God (Cleve)	2	191	100	238 *	.4	1.0
151 L-D Saints	1	NR	NR	150	.3	.6
165 Ch of Nazarene	7	435	445	637	1.1	2.6
167 Chs of Christ	3	146	135	198	.3	.8
173 Comm of Christ	2	211	NR	211	.4	.9
183 Cons Menn Conf	1	47	57	68	.1	.3
203 Evan Free Ch	1	37	80	80	.1	.3
207 E.L.C.A.	2	317	137	415	.7	1.7
221 Free Methodist	2	76	109	109	.2	.4
283 Luth—MO Synod	8	5,402	2,460	7,031	12.1	28.4
291 Missionary Ch	4	106	199	201	.3	.8
293 Morav Ch-North	1	292	NR	354	.6	1.4
323 Old Ord Amish	2	110	NR	136 *	.2	.5
355 Presb Ch (USA)	4	648	320	807 *	1.4	3.3
388 Reg Bapt Gen As	3	618	680	803 *	1.4	3.2
413 S.D.A.	2	88	NR	105	.2	.4
419 So Bapt Conv	1	45	30	56 *	.1	.2
449 Un Methodist	18	2,675	1,470	3,330 *	5.7	13.4
467 Wesleyan	1	139	140	301	.5	1.2
469 WELS	2	824	436	1,088	1.9	4.4
499 Indep.Non-Char	2	443	595	743	1.3	3.0
VAN BUREN	**91**	**9,635**	**5,717**	**23,509 ***	**30.8**	**100.0**
017 Amer Bapt Assn	2	100	NR	128 *	.2	.5
019 Amer Bapt USA	1	278	230	353 *	.5	1.5
053 Assemb of God	2	50	52	163	.2	.7
056 Baha'i	0	9	NR	9	-	-
059 Bapt Miss Assn	2	76	66	97 *	.1	.4
081 Catholic	8	NR	NR	9,537	12.5	40.6
093 Chr Ch (Disc)	1	0	0	0 *	-	-
097 Chr Chs&Chs Cr	1	300	NR	381 *	.5	1.6
105 Christian Ref	2	238	180	302 *	.4	1.3
123 Ch God (Ander)	2	NR	139	139	.2	.6
127 Ch God (Cleve)	1	31	23	39 *	.1	.2
151 L-D Saints	2	NR	NR	340	.4	1.4
165 Ch of Nazarene	1	36	49	82	.1	.3
167 Chs of Christ	2	90	85	115	.2	.5
175 Congr Chr Chs	2	90	63	114 *	.1	.5
181 Consrv Congr	3	252	148	320 *	.4	1.4
193 Episcopal	2	NR	175	334	.4	1.4
207 E.L.C.A.	1	535	271	714	.9	3.0
213 Evan Menn Inc	1	116	367	148 *	.2	.6
221 Free Methodist	1	37	41	41	.1	.2
223 Free Will Bapt	1	71	NR	91 *	.1	.4
262 Int Cou Comm Ch	3	562	NR	713 *	.9	3.0
265 Int Pent C Chr	2	86	87	105	.1	.4
283 Luth—MO Synod	1	1,067	420	1,328	1.7	5.6
306 NT IndBapt&Rltd	1	180	NR	229 *	.3	1.0
323 Old Ord Amish	1	55	NR	70 *	.1	.3
339 Pent Ch of God	3	120	NR	350	.5	1.5
349 Pent Holiness	2	59	67	75 *	.1	.3
355 Presb Ch (USA)	3	617	266	784 *	1.0	3.3
371 Ref Ch in Am	3	560	658	1,080	1.4	4.6

Religious Group	Number of Churches, Synagogues, Mosques, or Temples	Number of Communicant, Confirmed, or Full Members	Number of Attendees	Total Adherents: Number of Adherents	Total Adherents: % of Total Pop.	Total Adherents: % of Total Adh.
388 Reg Bapt Gen As	4	346	504	544 *	.7	2.3
413 S.D.A.	7	684	NR	814	1.1	3.5
419 So Bapt Conv	3	128	55	163 *	.2	.7
443 Un C of Christ	1	301	138	383 *	.5	1.6
449 Un Methodist	14	1,799	1,199	2,286 *	3.0	9.7
463 Vineyard	1	200	110	254 *	.3	1.1
469 WELS	3	562	324	734	1.0	3.1
496 Jewish Est	1	NR	NR	150	.2	.6
WASHTENAW	**206**	**36,950**	**21,635**	**107,901 ***	**33.4**	**100.0**
019 Amer Bapt USA	8	2,119	640	2,566 *	.8	2.4
050 Armen Ap Etchm	1	20	NR	210	.1	.2
053 Assemb of God	10	805	989	1,442	.4	1.3
056 Baha'i	4	309	NR	309	.1	.3
057 Bapt Gen Conf	1	225	402	402 *	.1	.4
076 Buddhism	6	NR	NR	NR	-	-
081 Catholic	14	NR	NR	41,750	12.9	38.7
089 Chr & Miss Al	1	40	NR	156	-	.1
093 Chr Ch (Disc)	1	120	50	145 *	-	.1
097 Chr Chs&Chs Cr	2	123	NR	149 *	-	.1
105 Christian Ref	3	808	465	978 *	.3	.9
123 Ch God (Ander)	3	NR	400	400	.1	.4
127 Ch God (Cleve)	1	622	391	753 *	.2	.7
145 Ch God Prophcy	2	71	NR	86 *	-	.1
151 L-D Saints	4	NR	NR	1,521	.5	1.4
157 Ch of Brethren	1	33	0	40 *	-	-
165 Ch of Nazarene	4	192	202	303	.1	.3
167 Chs of Christ	5	656	655	823	.3	.8
171 Ch God-Gen Con	1	0	70	70 *	-	.1
173 Comm of Christ	1	177	NR	177	.1	.2
175 Congr Chr Chs	2	845	124	1,023 *	.3	.9
193 Episcopal	8	NR	1,025	3,320	1.0	3.1
203 Evan Free Ch	1	45	125	125	-	.1
207 E.L.C.A.	10	4,409	1,510	5,563	1.7	5.2
216 Evan Presby Ch	2	503	NR	609 *	.2	.6
221 Free Methodist	4	528	954	956	.3	.9
223 Free Will Bapt	5	357	NR	433 *	.1	.4
226 Friends-USA	3	225	NR	272 *	.1	.3
246 Greek Orthodox	1	NR	NR	876	.3	.8
252 Hindu	2	NR	NR	NR	-	-
263 Int Foursq Gos	1	15	72	72 *	-	.1
267 Muslim Est	2	NR	1,112	4,891	1.5	4.5
283 Luth—MO Synod	11	3,689	2,577	4,897	1.5	4.5
288 Mennonite USA	2	40	97	97 *	-	.1
290 Metro Comm Ch	1	16	16	19 *	-	-
306 NT IndBapt&Rltd	1	210	NR	254 *	.1	.2
339 Pent Ch of God	3	43	NR	105	-	.1
355 Presb Ch (USA)	7	3,746	1,628	4,536 *	1.4	4.2
371 Ref Ch in Am	1	39	66	122	-	.1
388 Reg Bapt Gen As	2	131	180	180 *	.1	.2
401 Rus Orth Abroad	1	NR	NR	NR	-	-
403 Salvation Army	3	230	207	752	.2	.7
413 S.D.A.	2	442	NR	526	.2	.5
419 So Bapt Conv	10	1,827	1,101	2,212 *	.7	2.1
435 Unitarian-Univ	2	653	NR	791 *	.2	.7
443 Un C of Christ	13	4,105	1,657	4,971 *	1.5	4.6
449 Un Methodist	17	5,830	3,164	7,061 *	2.2	6.5
463 Vineyard	1	130	120	157 *	-	.1
467 Wesleyan	2	105	239	400	.1	.4
469 WELS	6	1,467	747	1,801	.6	1.7
496 Jewish Est	5	NR	NR	7,000	2.2	6.5
499 Indep.Non-Char	2	1,000	650	1,600	.5	1.5
WAYNE	**894**	**177,164**	**112,485**	**777,269 ***	**37.7**	**100.0**
017 Amer Bapt Assn	2	100	NR	128 *	-	-
019 Amer Bapt USA	31	20,273	9,177	26,105 *	1.3	3.4
034 Ant Orth of NA	2	675	NR	1,350	.1	.2
039 Ap Chr Ch(Naz)	1	11	16	16 *	-	-
040 Ap Chr Ch-Amer	1	104	196	196 *	-	-
049 Armen Ap Cilic	1	472	NR	1,680	.1	.2
053 Assemb of God	41	8,129	11,477	16,134	.8	2.1
056 Baha'i	4	562	NR	562	-	.1
057 Bapt Gen Conf	6	458	372	590 *	-	.1

NR–Not Reported *Total adherents estimated from known number of communicant, confirmed, full members. - Represents a percentage less than 0.1. Percentages may not total 100 due to rounding.

Table 4: Religious Congregations by County and Group: 2000

Religious Group	Number of Churches, Synagogues, Mosques, or Temples	Number of Communicant, Confirmed, or Full Members	Number of Attendees	Total Adherents		
				Number of Adherents	% of Total Pop.	% of Total Adh.
076 Buddhism	2	NR	NR	NR	-	-
078 Bulgar Orth USA	1	NR	NR	1,600	.1	.2
081 Catholic	171	NR	NR	451,069	21.9	58.0
084 Calvary Chapel	1	NR	NR	NR	-	-
089 Chr & Miss Al	4	90	NR	542	-	.1
093 Chr Ch (Disc)	6	820	279	1,056 *	.1	.1
097 Chr Chs&Chs Cr	6	1,703	NR	2,192 *	.1	.3
105 Christian Ref	2	605	537	779 *	-	.1
123 Ch God (Ander)	14	NR	1,652	1,652	.1	.2
127 Ch God (Cleve)	24	4,661	2,304	6,068 *	.3	.8
145 Ch God Prophcy	7	250	NR	322 *	-	-
151 L-D Saints	11	NR	NR	4,396	.2	.6
157 Ch of Brethren	2	126	50	162 *	-	-
165 Ch of Nazarene	9	1,035	948	1,353	.1	.2
167 Chs of Christ	39	6,197	6,237	8,120	.4	1.0
173 Comm of Christ	3	955	NR	955	-	.1
175 Congr Chr Chs	7	1,695	885	2,183 *	.1	.3
185 Cumber Presb	1	18	NR	40	-	-
193 Episcopal	41	NR	3,727	11,503	.6	1.5
201 Evan Cov Ch	3	445	460	573 *	-	.1
203 Evan Free Ch	4	270	550	550	-	.1
207 E.L.C.A.	46	14,573	6,268	19,943	1.0	2.6
216 Evan Presby Ch	4	5,706	NR	7,347 *	.4	.9
221 Free Methodist	8	703	1,268	1,299	.1	.2
223 Free Will Bapt	16	1,144	NR	1,473 *	.1	.2
226 Friends-USA	1	35	NR	45 *	-	-
246 Greek Orthodox	5	NR	NR	3,870	.2	.5
252 Hindu	4	NR	NR	NR	-	-
262 Int Cou Comm Ch	4	1,815	NR	2,338 *	.1	.3
263 Int Foursq Gos	1	34	21	44 *	-	-
264 Int Chs of Crst	1	547	949	703	-	.1
267 Muslim Est	26	NR	12,025	46,492	2.3	6.0
268 Jain	1	NR	NR	NR	-	-
283 Luth—MO Synod	54	23,050	11,595	30,253	1.5	3.9
288 Mennonite USA	2	100	80	129 *	-	-
291 Missionary Ch	5	403	585	585	-	.1
293 Morav Ch-North	1	109	NR	141	-	-
304 NatPrimBapt USA	3	170	NR	219 *	-	-
306 NT IndBapt&Rltd	4	970	NR	1,249 *	.1	.2
313 N Am Bapt Conf	2	1,324	1,311	1,705 *	.1	.2
330 Macedonian Orth	1	NR	NR	600	-	.1
331 OCA: Ter Diocs	3	511	NR	1,197	.1	.2
332 OCA: Bulg Dioc	1	160	NR	689	-	.1
333 Malan Dioc Am	1	NR	NR	250	-	-
334 Malan Syr Orth	1	30	NR	150	-	-
339 Pent Ch of God	3	43	NR	116	-	-
349 Pent Holiness	2	109	77	140 *	-	-
355 Presb Ch (USA)	40	15,895	6,663	20,467 *	1.0	2.6
360 Prim Bapt Chrch	3	NR	NR	NR	-	-
370 Ref Baptist Chs	1	NR	NR	NR	-	-
371 Ref Ch in Am	7	437	476	805	-	.1
388 Reg Bapt Gen As	4	1,363	1,486	1,793 *	.1	.2
395 Romania Orth Ar	1	NR	NR	700	-	.1
397 OCA: Roman Dioc	1	NR	NR	600	-	.1
400 Rus Orth Moscow	2	NR	NR	NR	-	-
403 Salvation Army	10	1,480	1,892	6,130	.3	.8
410 Serb Orth USA	2	NR	NR	5,300	.3	.7
411 Serb Orth: Grac	1	NR	NR	NR	-	-
413 S.D.A.	16	6,073	NR	7,226	.4	.9
416 Sikh	1	NR	NR	NR	-	-
419 So Bapt Conv	43	7,267	2,441	9,358 *	.5	1.2
431 Ukrainian Orth	1	NR	NR	90	-	-
435 Unitarian-Univ	2	370	NR	476 *	-	.1
443 Un C of Christ	18	6,088	2,383	7,839 *	.4	1.0
449 Un Methodist	57	16,259	7,668	20,939 *	1.0	2.7
467 Wesleyan	6	305	558	1,027	-	.1
469 WELS	11	3,442	1,767	4,596	.2	.6
496 Jewish Est	4	NR	NR	8,400	.4	1.1
498 Indep.Charis.	3	5,825	6,400	7,000	.3	.9
499 Indep.Non-Char	13	11,170	7,705	11,670	.6	1.5
WEXFORD	**47**	**5,777**	**4,046**	**12,356 ***	**40.5**	**100.0**
019 Amer Bapt USA	2	1,007	566	1,260 *	4.1	10.2
053 Assemb of God	1	106	146	200	.7	1.6

Religious Group	Number of Churches, Synagogues, Mosques, or Temples	Number of Communicant, Confirmed, or Full Members	Number of Attendees	Total Adherents		
				Number of Adherents	% of Total Pop.	% of Total Adh.
056 Baha'i	0	5	NR	5	-	-
057 Bapt Gen Conf	1	313	300	392 *	1.3	3.2
081 Catholic	3	NR	NR	3,671	12.0	29.7
093 Chr Ch (Disc)	3	191	114	239 *	.8	1.9
105 Christian Ref	1	323	377	404 *	1.3	3.3
123 Ch God (Ander)	1	NR	55	55	.2	.4
127 Ch God (Cleve)	1	34	36	43 *	.1	.3
165 Ch of Nazarene	3	285	318	679	2.2	5.5
167 Chs of Christ	1	55	45	70	.2	.6
173 Comm of Christ	1	189	NR	189	.6	1.5
175 Congr Chr Chs	1	40	15	50 *	.2	.4
193 Episcopal	1	NR	56	117	.4	.9
201 Evan Cov Ch	1	111	80	139 *	.5	1.1
207 E.L.C.A.	2	500	304	599	2.0	4.8
221 Free Methodist	3	78	221	221	.7	1.8
263 Int Foursq Gos	1	4	42	42 *	.1	.3
283 Luth—MO Synod	2	383	257	526	1.7	4.3
323 Old Ord Amish	1	55	NR	69 *	.2	.6
339 Pent Ch of God	2	87	NR	265	.9	2.1
355 Presb Ch (USA)	1	364	140	455 *	1.5	3.7
388 Reg Bapt Gen As	1	171	192	214 *	.7	1.7
403 Salvation Army	1	76	61	217	.7	1.8
413 S.D.A.	3	298	NR	355	1.2	2.9
419 So Bapt Conv	2	202	100	253 *	.8	2.0
443 Un C of Christ	1	106	60	133 *	.4	1.1
449 Un Methodist	5	794	475	994 *	3.3	8.0
467 Wesleyan	1	0	86	500	1.6	4.0

MINNESOTA

Religious Group	Number of Churches, Synagogues, Mosques, or Temples	Number of Communicant, Confirmed, or Full Members	Number of Attendees	Number of Adherents	% of Total Pop.	% of Total Adh.
The State.....	5,115	1,213,184	612,978	3,035,510 *	61.7	100.0
AITKIN	**46**	**5,967**	**2,670**	**10,782 ***	**70.5**	**100.0**
053 Assemb of God	4	143	176	216	1.4	2.0
056 Baha'i	0	3	NR	3	-	-
057 Bapt Gen Conf	1	70	98	98 *	.6	.9
081 Catholic	4	NR	NR	2,814	18.4	26.1
089 Chr & Miss Al	1	8	NR	45	.3	.4
097 Chr Chs&Chs Cr	1	45	NR	53 *	.3	.5
179 Consrv Bapt	1	NR	177	177	1.2	1.6
193 Episcopal	1	NR	17	33	.2	.3
207 E.L.C.A.	15	4,077	1,565	5,326	34.8	49.4
220 Free Lutheran	1	8	8	8	.1	.1
283 Luth—MO Synod	4	769	185	1,013	6.6	9.4
355 Presb Ch (USA)	3	131	62	155 *	1.0	1.4
413 S.D.A.	1	41	NR	49	.3	.5
419 So Bapt Conv	1	46	38	54 *	.4	.5
443 Un C of Christ	1	53	25	63 *	.4	.6
449 Un Methodist	7	573	319	675 *	4.4	6.3
ANOKA	**119**	**49,744**	**27,326**	**150,485 ***	**50.5**	**100.0**
019 Amer Bapt USA	1	30	0	39 *	-	-
053 Assemb of God	8	3,414	5,031	7,645	2.6	5.1
056 Baha'i	1	51	NR	51	-	-
057 Bapt Gen Conf	9	1,747	1,552	2,311 *	.8	1.5
081 Catholic	9	NR	NR	71,810	24.1	47.7
089 Chr & Miss Al	5	431	NR	1,338	.4	.9
093 Chr Ch (Disc)	1	92	46	119 *	-	.1
097 Chr Chs&Chs Cr	2	295	NR	381 *	.1	.3
127 Ch God (Cleve)	1	186	20	240 *	.1	.2
145 Ch God Prophcy	1	34	NR	45 *	-	-
151 L-D Saints	5	NR	NR	1,763	.6	1.2
165 Ch of Nazarene	2	254	379	579	.2	.4
179 Consrv Bapt	1	NR	104	104	-	.1
193 Episcopal	2	NR	149	458	.2	.3
201 Evan Cov Ch	3	394	440	525 *	.2	.3
203 Evan Free Ch	3	629	1,454	1,454	.5	1.0
207 E.L.C.A.	20	29,222	11,025	42,141	14.1	28.0
220 Free Lutheran	2	100	119	147	-	.1
263 Int Foursq Gos	1	2	16	16 *	-	-
267 Muslim Est	1	NR	290	1,313	.4	.9
283 Luth—MO Synod	10	6,546	3,124	9,456	3.2	6.3

NR–Not Reported *Total adherents estimated from known number of communicant, confirmed, full members. - Represents a percentage less than 0.1. Percentages may not total 100 due to rounding.

Table 4: Religious Congregations by County and Group: 2000

Religious Group	Number of Churches, Synagogues, Mosques, or Temples	Number of Communicant, Confirmed, or Full Members	Number of Attendees	Total Adherents		
				Number of Adherents	% of Total Pop.	% of Total Adh.
306 NT IndBapt&Rltd	3	398	NR	514 *	.2	.3
355 Presb Ch (USA)	2	266	166	344 *	.1	.2
388 Reg Bapt Gen As	1	35	55	55 *	-	-
401 Rus Orth Abroad	1	NR	NR	NR	-	-
413 S.D.A.	1	230	NR	274	.1	.2
416 Sikh	2	NR	NR	NR	-	-
419 So Bapt Conv	2	21	25	27 *	-	-
435 Unitarian-Univ	1	84	NR	108 *	-	.1
443 Un C of Christ	1	372	164	480 *	.2	.3
449 Un Methodist	10	3,326	1,480	4,296 *	1.4	2.9
467 Wesleyan	3	210	302	600	.2	.4
469 WELS	2	575	355	822	.3	.5
498 Indep.Charis.	1	275	330	330	.1	.2
499 Indep.Non-Char	1	525	700	700	.2	.5
BECKER	**56**	**10,568**	**4,242**	**22,183 ***	**73.9**	**100.0**
053 Assemb of God	3	131	163	210	.7	.9
056 Baha'i	0	3	NR	3	-	-
081 Catholic	10	NR	NR	7,324	24.4	33.0
089 Chr & Miss Al	2	134	NR	455	1.5	2.1
165 Ch of Nazarene	1	17	0	17	.1	.1
173 Comm of Christ	1	53	NR	53	.2	.2
176 Congr Ad Afl	1	206	NR	256 *	.9	1.2
179 Consrv Bapt	2	NR	172	172	.6	.8
193 Episcopal	3	NR	84	643	2.1	2.9
203 Evan Free Ch	1	42	70	70	.2	.3
207 E.L.C.A.	16	5,822	2,053	7,609	25.4	34.3
220 Free Lutheran	1	112	105	170	.6	.8
283 Luth—MO Synod	8	2,866	998	3,702	12.3	16.7
288 Mennonite USA	2	62	105	117 *	.4	.5
306 NT IndBapt&Rltd	1	37	NR	46 *	.2	.2
413 S.D.A.	1	199	NR	237	.8	1.1
449 Un Methodist	2	534	252	664 *	2.2	3.0
463 Vineyard	1	350	240	435 *	1.5	2.0
BELTRAMI	**52**	**7,254**	**4,260**	**18,715 ***	**47.2**	**100.0**
053 Assemb of God	3	172	341	280	.7	1.5
056 Baha'i	1	52	NR	52	.1	.3
057 Bapt Gen Conf	1	15	22	22 *	.1	.1
081 Catholic	7	NR	NR	7,189	18.1	38.4
097 Chr Chs&Chs Cr	1	40	NR	51 *	.1	.3
151 L-D Saints	1	NR	NR	362	.9	1.9
165 Ch of Nazarene	2	59	29	76	.2	.4
179 Consrv Bapt	1	NR	209	209	.5	1.1
193 Episcopal	3	NR	102	603	1.5	3.2
201 Evan Cov Ch	1	244	523	523 *	1.3	2.8
203 Evan Free Ch	3	326	614	614	1.5	3.3
207 E.L.C.A.	14	4,090	1,513	5,879	14.8	31.4
220 Free Lutheran	2	107	57	119	.3	.6
283 Luth—MO Synod	2	707	272	903	2.3	4.8
297 Mennonite;Other	1	52	NR	66 *	.2	.4
355 Presb Ch (USA)	3	487	204	620 *	1.6	3.3
388 Reg Bapt Gen As	1	56	64	71 *	.2	.4
413 S.D.A.	1	166	NR	198	.5	1.1
419 So Bapt Conv	1	63	45	80 *	.2	.4
435 Unitarian-Univ	1	25	NR	32 *	.1	.2
449 Un Methodist	1	449	170	572 *	1.4	3.1
469 WELS	1	144	95	194	.5	1.0
BENTON	**31**	**4,325**	**2,364**	**19,404 ***	**56.7**	**100.0**
053 Assemb of God	1	71	95	95	.3	.5
056 Baha'i	0	6	NR	6	-	-
081 Catholic	9	NR	NR	13,083	38.2	67.4
089 Chr & Miss Al	1	78	NR	198	.6	1.0
097 Chr Chs&Chs Cr	1	15	NR	19 *	.1	.1
151 L-D Saints	1	NR	NR	488	1.4	2.5
201 Evan Cov Ch	1	37	66	66 *	.2	.3
203 Evan Free Ch	1	82	155	155	.5	.8
207 E.L.C.A.	4	873	489	1,219	3.6	6.3
283 Luth—MO Synod	4	1,954	809	2,406	7.0	12.4
355 Presb Ch (USA)	3	513	337	647 *	1.9	3.3
388 Reg Bapt Gen As	1	94	95	95 *	.3	.5
403 Salvation Army	1	87	59	251	.7	1.3

Religious Group	Number of Churches, Synagogues, Mosques, or Temples	Number of Communicant, Confirmed, or Full Members	Number of Attendees	Total Adherents		
				Number of Adherents	% of Total Pop.	% of Total Adh.
443 Un C of Christ	1	7	3	9 *	-	-
449 Un Methodist	1	218	80	275 *	.8	1.4
469 WELS	1	290	176	392	1.1	2.0
BIG STONE	**30**	**3,653**	**1,488**	**6,421 ***	**110.3**	**100.0**
053 Assemb of God	1	29	40	60	1.0	.9
057 Bapt Gen Conf	1	94	100	114 *	2.0	1.8
081 Catholic	4	NR	NR	1,875	32.2	29.2
179 Consrv Bapt	1	NR	30	30	.5	.5
207 E.L.C.A.	6	1,584	571	1,957	33.6	30.5
220 Free Lutheran	2	232	117	285	4.9	4.4
257 Hutterian Br	2	132	NR	200	3.4	3.1
283 Luth—MO Synod	4	902	341	1,079	18.5	16.8
413 S.D.A.	1	26	NR	31	.5	.5
443 Un C of Christ	2	120	52	145 *	2.5	2.3
449 Un Methodist	4	354	166	429 *	7.4	6.7
469 WELS	2	180	71	216	3.7	3.4
BLUE EARTH	**67**	**16,935**	**7,385**	**34,427 ***	**61.5**	**100.0**
019 Amer Bapt USA	1	431	160	513 *	.9	1.5
053 Assemb of God	1	78	106	184	.3	.5
056 Baha'i	0	22	NR	22	-	.1
057 Bapt Gen Conf	1	185	185	220 *	.4	.6
081 Catholic	9	NR	NR	12,144	21.7	35.3
093 Chr Ch (Disc)	2	280	101	333 *	.6	1.0
097 Chr Chs&Chs Cr	1	95	NR	113 *	.2	.3
151 L-D Saints	1	NR	NR	347	.6	1.0
165 Ch of Nazarene	1	33	11	33	.1	.1
167 Chs of Christ	1	69	77	86	.2	.2
179 Consrv Bapt	1	NR	115	115	.2	.3
193 Episcopal	1	NR	98	188	.3	.5
203 Evan Free Ch	1	55	135	135	.2	.4
207 E.L.C.A.	12	7,056	2,504	9,428	16.9	27.4
220 Free Lutheran	1	91	77	107	.2	.3
226 Friends-USA	1	49	NR	58 *	.1	.2
283 Luth—MO Synod	12	4,084	1,893	5,087	9.1	14.8
306 NT IndBapt&Rltd	1	30	NR	36 *	.1	.1
355 Presb Ch (USA)	4	1,344	503	1,599 *	2.9	4.6
403 Salvation Army	1	76	69	126	.2	.4
413 S.D.A.	1	98	NR	117	.2	.3
419 So Bapt Conv	1	44	98	52 *	.1	.2
435 Unitarian-Univ	1	68	NR	81 *	.1	.2
443 Un C of Christ	2	596	225	709 *	1.3	2.1
449 Un Methodist	7	1,576	709	1,875 *	3.4	5.4
469 WELS	2	575	319	719	1.3	2.1
BROWN	**40**	**9,978**	**4,805**	**24,816 ***	**92.2**	**100.0**
053 Assemb of God	2	68	91	141	.5	.6
081 Catholic	7	NR	NR	11,944	44.4	48.1
089 Chr & Miss Al	1	31	NR	108	.4	.4
097 Chr Chs&Chs Cr	1	98	NR	120 *	.4	.5
151 L-D Saints	1	NR	NR	37	.1	.1
193 Episcopal	1	NR	7	12	-	-
203 Evan Free Ch	1	28	54	54	.2	.2
207 E.L.C.A.	9	4,354	1,851	5,669	21.1	22.8
283 Luth—MO Synod	2	638	192	861	3.2	3.5
306 NT IndBapt&Rltd	3	175	NR	214 *	.8	.9
435 Unitarian-Univ	1	98	NR	120 *	.4	.5
443 Un C of Christ	3	527	232	645 *	2.4	2.6
449 Un Methodist	4	1,004	438	1,227 *	4.6	4.9
469 WELS	4	2,957	1,940	3,664	13.6	14.8
CARLTON	**47**	**7,679**	**3,591**	**17,038 ***	**53.8**	**100.0**
053 Assemb of God	1	35	45	86	.3	.5
056 Baha'i	0	8	NR	8	-	-
057 Bapt Gen Conf	2	156	180	192 *	.6	1.1
081 Catholic	6	NR	NR	6,656	21.0	39.1
089 Chr & Miss Al	1	8	NR	24	.1	.1
151 L-D Saints	1	NR	NR	89	.3	.5
193 Episcopal	2	NR	41	104	.3	.6
201 Evan Cov Ch	4	271	421	421 *	1.3	2.5
203 Evan Free Ch	1	20	35	35	.1	.2

NR–Not Reported   *Total adherents estimated from known number of communicant, confirmed, full members.   - Represents a percentage less than 0.1.   Percentages may not total 100 due to rounding.

Table 4: Religious Congregations by County and Group: 2000

Religious Group	Number of Churches, Synagogues, Mosques, or Temples	Number of Communicant, Confirmed, or Full Members	Number of Attendees	Total Adherents		
				Number of Adherents	% of Total Pop.	% of Total Adh.
207 E.L.C.A.	13	4,498	1,578	5,846	18.5	34.3
220 Free Lutheran	1	645	325	814	2.6	4.8
283 Luth—MO Synod	6	1,244	583	1,788	5.6	10.5
355 Presb Ch (USA)	3	346	126	426 *	1.3	2.5
403 Salvation Army	1	7	9	7	-	-
413 S.D.A.	1	23	NR	27	.1	.2
419 So Bapt Conv	0	8	0	10 *	-	.1
449 Un Methodist	4	410	248	505 *	1.6	3.0
CARVER	**48**	**15,886**	**9,164**	**43,018 ***	**61.3**	**100.0**
056 Baha'i	1	19	NR	19	-	-
057 Bapt Gen Conf	2	359	1,385	1,385 *	2.0	3.2
081 Catholic	8	NR	NR	19,891	28.3	46.2
089 Chr & Miss Al	1	106	NR	275	.4	.6
175 Congr Chr Chs	1	98	85	131 *	.2	.3
181 Consrv Congr	1	289	130	385 *	.5	.9
203 Evan Free Ch	3	318	730	730	1.0	1.7
207 E.L.C.A.	8	5,451	2,300	7,849	11.2	18.2
283 Luth—MO Synod	13	7,714	4,203	10,355	14.7	24.1
293 Morav Ch-North	3	572	NR	747	1.1	1.7
355 Presb Ch (USA)	1	131	55	175 *	.2	.4
373 Ref Ch in U.S.	1	274	NR	336	.5	.8
443 Un C of Christ	3	329	134	439 *	.6	1.0
449 Un Methodist	2	226	142	301 *	.4	.7
CASS	**54**	**5,078**	**2,445**	**10,536 ***	**38.8**	**100.0**
053 Assemb of God	4	157	192	288	1.1	2.7
056 Baha'i	0	17	NR	17	.1	.2
057 Bapt Gen Conf	2	126	140	154 *	.6	1.5
081 Catholic	8	NR	NR	3,075	11.3	29.2
089 Chr & Miss Al	6	147	NR	494	1.8	4.7
127 Ch God (Cleve)	1	10	13	13 *	-	.1
165 Ch of Nazarene	1	137	104	238	.9	2.3
193 Episcopal	2	NR	50	505	1.9	4.8
203 Evan Free Ch	1	61	110	110	.4	1.0
207 E.L.C.A.	14	3,197	1,296	4,094	15.1	38.9
283 Luth—MO Synod	5	483	222	624	2.3	5.9
288 Mennonite USA	1	11	18	18 *	.1	.2
339 Pent Ch of God	2	54	NR	79	.3	.7
413 S.D.A.	1	26	NR	31	.1	.3
435 Unitarian-Univ	1	13	NR	16 *	.1	.2
443 Un C of Christ	3	480	230	586 *	2.2	5.6
449 Un Methodist	2	159	70	194 *	.7	1.8
CHIPPEWA	**27**	**7,818**	**2,905**	**11,526 ***	**88.1**	**100.0**
056 Baha'i	0	1	NR	1	-	-
057 Bapt Gen Conf	2	63	20	77 *	.6	.7
081 Catholic	2	NR	NR	1,514	11.6	13.1
105 Christian Ref	1	398	370	490 *	3.7	4.3
207 E.L.C.A.	14	5,565	1,707	7,010	53.6	60.8
283 Luth—MO Synod	3	671	130	800	6.1	6.9
355 Presb Ch (USA)	1	28	21	34 *	.3	.3
371 Ref Ch in Am	2	649	500	1,055	8.1	9.2
443 Un C of Christ	1	109	48	134 *	1.0	1.2
449 Un Methodist	1	334	109	411 *	3.1	3.6
CHISAGO	**39**	**9,646**	**5,153**	**20,202 ***	**49.2**	**100.0**
053 Assemb of God	2	178	256	414	1.0	2.0
056 Baha'i	0	3	NR	3	-	-
057 Bapt Gen Conf	3	141	164	194 *	.5	1.0
081 Catholic	5	NR	NR	6,355	15.5	31.5
179 Consrv Bapt	2	NR	113	113	.3	.6
201 Evan Cov Ch	3	250	408	424 *	1.0	2.1
203 Evan Free Ch	4	401	699	699	1.7	3.5
207 E.L.C.A.	10	6,839	2,457	9,570	23.3	47.4
220 Free Lutheran	1	114	100	168	.4	.8
283 Luth—MO Synod	3	629	344	841	2.0	4.2
306 NT IndBapt&Rltd	2	329	NR	429 *	1.0	2.1
419 So Bapt Conv	0	10	28	13 *	-	.1
449 Un Methodist	4	752	584	979 *	2.4	4.8

Religious Group	Number of Churches, Synagogues, Mosques, or Temples	Number of Communicant, Confirmed, or Full Members	Number of Attendees	Total Adherents		
				Number of Adherents	% of Total Pop.	% of Total Adh.
CLAY	**60**	**17,343**	**6,392**	**33,298 ***	**65.0**	**100.0**
053 Assemb of God	3	158	215	290	.6	.9
056 Baha'i	0	17	NR	17	-	.1
081 Catholic	7	NR	NR	9,893	19.3	29.7
089 Chr & Miss Al	1	46	NR	227	.4	.7
097 Chr Chs&Chs Cr	1	91	NR	112 *	.2	.3
151 L-D Saints	1	NR	NR	340	.7	1.0
165 Ch of Nazarene	1	64	75	122	.2	.4
167 Chs of Christ	1	10	10	10	-	-
193 Episcopal	1	NR	26	22	-	.1
203 Evan Free Ch	1	49	59	59	.1	.2
207 E.L.C.A.	24	13,416	4,487	17,797	34.7	53.4
220 Free Lutheran	2	191	186	262	.5	.8
257 Hutterian Br	1	66	NR	100	.2	.3
283 Luth—MO Synod	4	1,264	487	1,599	3.1	4.8
355 Presb Ch (USA)	3	409	185	506 *	1.0	1.5
388 Reg Bapt Gen As	1	81	100	100 *	.2	.3
413 S.D.A.	1	25	NR	30	.1	.1
443 Un C of Christ	4	766	297	947 *	1.8	2.8
449 Un Methodist	2	557	178	688 *	1.3	2.1
469 WELS	1	133	87	177	.3	.5
CLEARWATER	**20**	**2,608**	**1,231**	**4,392 ***	**52.1**	**100.0**
053 Assemb of God	1	63	96	157	1.9	3.6
056 Baha'i	0	1	NR	1	-	-
057 Bapt Gen Conf	1	68	86	86 *	1.0	2.0
081 Catholic	1	NR	NR	553	6.6	12.6
193 Episcopal	1	NR	24	289	3.4	6.6
203 Evan Free Ch	1	53	85	85	1.0	1.9
207 E.L.C.A.	8	1,826	691	2,465	29.3	56.1
220 Free Lutheran	5	426	193	536	6.4	12.2
283 Luth—MO Synod	1	116	56	152	1.8	3.5
323 Old Ord Amish	1	55	NR	68 *	.8	1.5
COOK	**12**	**1,484**	**770**	**2,448 ***	**47.4**	**100.0**
056 Baha'i	0	1	NR	1	-	-
057 Bapt Gen Conf	2	102	115	121 *	2.3	4.9
081 Catholic	2	NR	NR	535	10.4	21.9
203 Evan Free Ch	1	100	150	150	2.9	6.1
207 E.L.C.A.	4	823	430	1,101	21.3	45.0
306 NT IndBapt&Rltd	1	167	NR	197 *	3.8	8.0
413 S.D.A.	1	6	NR	7	.1	.3
443 Un C of Christ	1	285	75	336 *	6.5	13.7
COTTONWOOD	**39**	**7,431**	**2,903**	**11,325 ***	**93.1**	**100.0**
053 Assemb of God	2	53	66	98	.8	.9
081 Catholic	2	NR	NR	1,320	10.8	11.7
089 Chr & Miss Al	1	176	NR	659	5.4	5.8
105 Christian Ref	1	39	63	48 *	.4	.4
179 Consrv Bapt	2	NR	248	248	2.0	2.2
193 Episcopal	1	NR	14	55	.5	.5
203 Evan Free Ch	1	89	150	150	1.2	1.3
207 E.L.C.A.	8	3,191	1,110	3,955	32.5	34.9
211 Fel Evg Bib Ch	1	272	0	272	2.2	2.4
220 Free Lutheran	1	92	61	125	1.0	1.1
237 Menn Br US Conf	2	136	NR	167 *	1.4	1.5
257 Hutterian Br	2	132	NR	200	1.6	1.8
283 Luth—MO Synod	2	1,056	440	1,336	11.0	11.8
288 Mennonite USA	3	679	296	833 *	6.8	7.4
297 Mennonite;Other	1	190	NR	233 *	1.9	2.1
306 NT IndBapt&Rltd	1	101	NR	124 *	1.0	1.1
355 Presb Ch (USA)	3	290	144	356 *	2.9	3.1
413 S.D.A.	1	24	NR	29	.2	.3
449 Un Methodist	4	911	311	1,117 *	9.2	9.9
CROW WING	**69**	**14,706**	**7,543**	**37,808 ***	**68.6**	**100.0**
053 Assemb of God	4	390	502	808	1.5	2.1
056 Baha'i	0	11	NR	11	-	-
057 Bapt Gen Conf	1	83	60	102 *	.2	.3
081 Catholic	12	NR	NR	16,418	29.8	43.4
089 Chr & Miss Al	2	75	NR	144	.3	.4
097 Chr Chs&Chs Cr	2	90	NR	111 *	.2	.3

NR–Not Reported *Total adherents estimated from known number of communicant, confirmed, full members. - Represents a percentage less than 0.1. Percentages may not total 100 due to rounding.

Table 4: Religious Congregations by County and Group: 2000

Religious Group	Number of Churches, Synagogues, Mosques, or Temples	Number of Communicant, Confirmed, or Full Members	Number of Attendees	Total Adherents: Number of Adherents	Total Adherents: % of Total Pop.	Total Adherents: % of Total Adh.
127 Ch God (Cleve)	1	20	6	25 *	-	.1
151 L-D Saints	2	NR	NR	577	1.0	1.5
165 Ch of Nazarene	2	288	176	464	.8	1.2
167 Chs of Christ	1	34	30	44	.1	.1
173 Comm of Christ	1	22	NR	22	-	.1
179 Consrv Bapt	1	NR	150	150	.3	.4
193 Episcopal	1	NR	135	331	.6	.9
201 Evan Cov Ch	1	63	49	77 *	.1	.2
203 Evan Free Ch	3	458	1,082	1,082	2.0	2.9
207 E.L.C.A.	12	8,362	3,218	11,188	20.3	29.6
283 Luth—MO Synod	7	1,997	723	2,664	4.8	7.0
306 NT IndBapt&Rltd	2	319	NR	392 *	.7	1.0
355 Presb Ch (USA)	3	520	279	639 *	1.2	1.7
388 Reg Bapt Gen As	1	185	165	227 *	.4	.6
403 Salvation Army	1	133	43	224	.4	.6
413 S.D.A.	1	178	NR	212	.4	.6
419 So Bapt Conv	1	52	38	64 *	.1	.2
443 Un C of Christ	1	240	106	295 *	.5	.8
449 Un Methodist	4	941	540	1,157 *	2.1	3.1
467 Wesleyan	1	62	97	149	.3	.4
469 WELS	1	183	144	231	.4	.6
DAKOTA	**169**	**58,535**	**38,565**	**187,132 ***	**52.6**	**100.0**
019 Amer Bapt USA	2	152	92	197 *	.1	.1
034 Ant Orth of NA	1	256	NR	512	.1	.3
039 Ap Chr Ch(Naz)	1	2	5	5 *	-	-
040 Ap Chr Ch-Amer	1	47	110	110 *	-	.1
053 Assemb of God	10	1,661	2,328	3,259	.9	1.7
056 Baha'i	1	84	NR	84	-	-
057 Bapt Gen Conf	7	1,420	2,990	3,051 *	.9	1.6
076 Buddhism	3	NR	NR	NR	-	-
081 Catholic	20	NR	NR	94,646	26.6	50.6
089 Chr & Miss Al	3	147	NR	362	.1	.2
093 Chr Ch (Disc)	1	30	43	39 *	-	-
097 Chr Chs&Chs Cr	1	400	NR	518 *	.1	.3
105 Christian Ref	1	106	95	137 *	-	.1
127 Ch God (Cleve)	1	23	23	30 *	-	-
151 L-D Saints	5	NR	NR	1,657	.5	.9
157 Ch of Brethren	1	12	0	16 *	-	-
165 Ch of Nazarene	2	103	101	160	-	.1
167 Chs of Christ	2	99	93	166	-	.1
173 Comm of Christ	1	133	NR	133	-	.1
175 Congr Chr Chs	1	46	60	60 *	-	-
179 Consrv Bapt	1	NR	74	74	-	-
193 Episcopal	5	NR	558	1,702	.5	.9
201 Evan Cov Ch	2	754	1,089	1,089 *	.3	.6
203 Evan Free Ch	5	565	1,352	1,352	.4	.7
207 E.L.C.A.	25	33,349	16,116	47,512	13.3	25.4
220 Free Lutheran	2	320	225	441	.1	.2
263 Int Foursq Gos	1	123	160	160 *	-	.1
283 Luth—MO Synod	12	5,908	2,632	8,230	2.3	4.4
306 NT IndBapt&Rltd	4	1,180	NR	1,529 *	.4	.8
313 N Am Bapt Conf	4	468	355	606 *	.2	.3
355 Presb Ch (USA)	4	657	424	851 *	.2	.5
356 Presb Ch Amer	1	47	60	68	-	-
371 Ref Ch in Am	1	567	513	1,131	.3	.6
395 Romania Orth Ar	1	NR	NR	262	.1	.1
411 Serb Orth: Grac	1	NR	NR	NR	-	-
413 S.D.A.	1	21	NR	25	-	-
418 Southw Bapt Fel	1	NR	NR	NR	-	-
419 So Bapt Conv	3	343	385	444 *	.1	.2
435 Unitarian-Univ	1	30	NR	39 *	-	-
443 Un C of Christ	2	322	156	417 *	.1	.2
449 Un Methodist	15	5,210	2,995	6,749 *	1.9	3.6
463 Vineyard	2	260	240	336 *	.1	.2
467 Wesleyan	1	33	83	165	-	.1
469 WELS	6	2,108	1,158	2,758	.8	1.5
496 Jewish Est	1	NR	NR	1,100	.3	.6
498 Indep.Charis.	1	225	450	450	.1	.2
499 Indep.Non-Char	1	1,324	3,600	4,500	1.3	2.4
DODGE	**33**	**6,116**	**2,703**	**12,829 ***	**72.4**	**100.0**
053 Assemb of God	1	42	60	100	.6	.8
056 Baha'i	0	11	NR	11	.1	.1
081 Catholic	5	NR	NR	3,621	20.4	28.2
097 Chr Chs&Chs Cr	2	178	NR	231 *	1.3	1.8
179 Consrv Bapt	1	NR	83	83	.5	.6
181 Consrv Congr	1	104	65	135 *	.8	1.1
193 Episcopal	1	NR	45	140	.8	1.1
207 E.L.C.A.	6	3,566	1,482	5,692	32.1	44.4
220 Free Lutheran	1	29	50	50	.3	.4
283 Luth—MO Synod	3	380	180	474	2.7	3.7
355 Presb Ch (USA)	3	477	206	617 *	3.5	4.8
388 Reg Bapt Gen As	1	100	85	85 *	.5	.7
413 S.D.A.	1	107	NR	127	.7	1.0
419 So Bapt Conv	0	13	15	17 *	.1	.1
443 Un C of Christ	2	313	119	406 *	2.3	3.2
449 Un Methodist	4	739	254	957 *	5.4	7.5
469 WELS	1	57	59	83	.5	.6
DOUGLAS	**53**	**11,984**	**6,018**	**23,732 ***	**72.3**	**100.0**
053 Assemb of God	1	115	150	189	.6	.8
056 Baha'i	0	11	NR	11	-	-
057 Bapt Gen Conf	1	246	236	299 *	.9	1.3
081 Catholic	6	NR	NR	7,825	23.8	33.0
097 Chr Chs&Chs Cr	1	100	NR	121 *	.4	.5
143 CG in Cr(Menn)	1	41	NR	50 *	.2	.2
193 Episcopal	1	NR	58	140	.4	.6
201 Evan Cov Ch	4	428	627	636 *	1.9	2.7
203 Evan Free Ch	1	115	380	380	1.2	1.6
207 E.L.C.A.	19	7,494	2,826	9,910	30.2	41.8
220 Free Lutheran	1	181	80	226	.7	1.0
221 Free Methodist	1	24	25	25	.1	.1
283 Luth—MO Synod	9	1,981	1,044	2,358	7.2	9.9
355 Presb Ch (USA)	1	125	63	152 *	.5	.6
371 Ref Ch in Am	1	45	80	98	.3	.4
413 S.D.A.	1	42	NR	50	.2	.2
419 So Bapt Conv	0	8	0	10 *	-	-
443 Un C of Christ	1	334	107	405 *	1.2	1.7
449 Un Methodist	2	549	250	666 *	2.0	2.8
469 WELS	1	145	92	181	.6	.8
FARIBAULT	**48**	**8,265**	**3,311**	**15,135 ***	**93.5**	**100.0**
019 Amer Bapt USA	1	177	78	214 *	1.3	1.4
053 Assemb of God	2	101	123	237	1.5	1.6
081 Catholic	7	NR	NR	4,689	29.0	31.0
179 Consrv Bapt	1	NR	36	36	.2	.2
201 Evan Cov Ch	1	59	69	71 *	.4	.5
203 Evan Free Ch	1	69	125	125	.8	.8
207 E.L.C.A.	12	4,150	1,392	5,298	32.7	35.0
221 Free Methodist	1	0	0	0	-	-
283 Luth—MO Synod	7	1,403	551	1,678	10.4	11.1
306 NT IndBapt&Rltd	1	13	NR	16 *	.1	.1
355 Presb Ch (USA)	2	321	145	388 *	2.4	2.6
443 Un C of Christ	2	386	170	467 *	2.9	3.1
449 Un Methodist	10	1,586	622	1,916 *	11.8	12.7
FILLMORE	**71**	**12,864**	**4,403**	**19,417 ***	**91.9**	**100.0**
053 Assemb of God	1	80	107	107	.5	.6
056 Baha'i	0	2	NR	2	-	-
081 Catholic	9	NR	NR	2,894	13.7	14.9
089 Chr & Miss Al	1	0	NR	35	.2	.2
151 L-D Saints	1	NR	NR	82	.4	.4
157 Ch of Brethren	1	64	35	79 *	.4	.4
193 Episcopal	2	NR	42	126	.6	.6
207 E.L.C.A.	26	8,604	2,585	10,930	51.7	56.3
221 Free Methodist	1	47	88	88	.4	.5
283 Luth—MO Synod	4	1,203	476	1,503	7.1	7.7
306 NT IndBapt&Rltd	2	116	NR	144 *	.7	.7
323 Old Ord Amish	6	305	NR	378 *	1.8	1.9
355 Presb Ch (USA)	3	298	125	369 *	1.7	1.9
371 Ref Ch in Am	1	247	200	331	1.6	1.7
388 Reg Bapt Gen As	1	76	70	94 *	.4	.5
449 Un Methodist	12	1,822	675	2,255 *	10.7	11.6

NR–Not Reported *Total adherents estimated from known number of communicant, confirmed, full members. - Represents a percentage less than 0.1. Percentages may not total 100 due to rounding.

Table 4: Religious Congregations by County and Group: 2000

Religious Group	Number of Churches, Synagogues, Mosques, or Temples	Number of Communicant, Confirmed, or Full Members	Number of Attendees	Total Adherents: Number of Adherents	Total Adherents: % of Total Pop.	Total Adherents: % of Total Adh.
FREEBORN	**53**	**16,034**	**5,715**	**25,078 ***	**77.0**	**100.0**
019 Amer Bapt USA	3	952	353	1,157 *	3.6	4.6
053 Assemb of God	1	119	151	260	.8	1.0
056 Baha'i	0	1	NR	1	-	-
081 Catholic	3	NR	NR	3,651	11.2	14.6
097 Chr Chs&Chs Cr	1	150	NR	182 *	.6	.7
105 Christian Ref	1	186	0	226 *	.7	.9
151 L-D Saints	1	NR	NR	126	.4	.5
167 Chs of Christ	1	30	40	39	.1	.2
181 Consrv Congr	1	39	22	47 *	.1	.2
193 Episcopal	1	NR	48	192	.6	.8
203 Evan Free Ch	1	52	139	139	.4	.6
207 E.L.C.A.	24	11,418	3,517	15,138	46.5	60.4
283 Luth—MO Synod	2	757	310	972	3.0	3.9
355 Presb Ch (USA)	1	560	240	681 *	2.1	2.7
371 Ref Ch in Am	1	200	150	251	.8	1.0
388 Reg Bapt Gen As	2	137	180	180 *	.6	.7
403 Salvation Army	1	129	54	248	.8	1.0
413 S.D.A.	1	77	NR	92	.3	.4
443 Un C of Christ	1	103	50	125 *	.4	.5
449 Un Methodist	4	1,036	374	1,259 *	3.9	5.0
463 Vineyard	1	55	55	67 *	.2	.3
467 Wesleyan	1	33	32	45	.1	.2
GOODHUE	**77**	**19,830**	**8,753**	**35,902 ***	**81.4**	**100.0**
053 Assemb of God	4	322	469	610	1.4	1.7
056 Baha'i	0	6	NR	6	-	-
057 Bapt Gen Conf	2	157	362	362 *	.8	1.0
081 Catholic	8	NR	NR	8,746	19.8	24.4
097 Chr Chs&Chs Cr	1	40	NR	50 *	.1	.1
151 L-D Saints	1	NR	NR	274	.6	.8
165 Ch of Nazarene	1	0	0	0	-	-
167 Chs of Christ	1	15	28	20	-	.1
173 Comm of Christ	1	47	NR	47	.1	.1
179 Consrv Bapt	1	NR	100	100	.2	.3
193 Episcopal	4	NR	213	572	1.3	1.6
201 Evan Cov Ch	1	222	179	275 *	.6	.8
203 Evan Free Ch	1	38	100	100	.2	.3
207 E.L.C.A.	26	12,964	4,472	17,264	39.1	48.1
220 Free Lutheran	3	398	231	509	1.2	1.4
263 Int Foursq Gos	2	76	93	94 *	.2	.3
283 Luth—MO Synod	3	838	397	972	2.2	2.7
306 NT IndBapt&Rltd	1	62	NR	77 *	.2	.2
355 Presb Ch (USA)	1	295	100	366 *	.8	1.0
419 So Bapt Conv	1	86	68	107 *	.2	.3
443 Un C of Christ	2	341	134	423 *	1.0	1.2
449 Un Methodist	3	1,107	403	1,372 *	3.1	3.8
467 Wesleyan	1	19	115	115	.3	.3
469 WELS	8	2,797	1,289	3,441	7.8	9.6
GRANT	**25**	**4,116**	**1,567**	**5,732 ***	**91.1**	**100.0**
053 Assemb of God	1	19	21	26	.4	.5
081 Catholic	2	NR	NR	624	9.9	10.9
201 Evan Cov Ch	1	4	0	5 *	.1	.1
203 Evan Free Ch	1	82	113	113	1.8	2.0
207 E.L.C.A.	11	2,959	983	3,678	58.5	64.2
283 Luth—MO Synod	3	493	221	574	9.1	10.0
355 Presb Ch (USA)	3	289	135	351 *	5.6	6.1
371 Ref Ch in Am	1	39	20	81	1.3	1.4
449 Un Methodist	2	231	74	280 *	4.5	4.9
HENNEPIN	**643**	**243,081**	**130,746**	**644,110 ***	**57.7**	**100.0**
019 Amer Bapt USA	10	3,556	1,449	4,376 *	.4	.7
050 Armen Ap Etchm	1	0	NR	560	.1	.1
053 Assemb of God	28	7,572	5,196	15,514	1.4	2.4
056 Baha'i	6	568	NR	568	.1	.1
057 Bapt Gen Conf	19	6,587	11,362	11,918 *	1.1	1.9
076 Buddhism	9	NR	NR	NR	-	-
081 Catholic	74	NR	NR	260,611	23.3	40.5
084 Calvary Chapel	1	NR	NR	NR	-	-
089 Chr & Miss Al	10	1,537	NR	1,938	.2	.3
093 Chr Ch (Disc)	3	1,091	258	1,343 *	.1	.2

Religious Group	Number of Churches, Synagogues, Mosques, or Temples	Number of Communicant, Confirmed, or Full Members	Number of Attendees	Total Adherents: Number of Adherents	Total Adherents: % of Total Pop.	Total Adherents: % of Total Adh.
097 Chr Chs&Chs Cr	4	380	NR	468 *	-	.1
105 Christian Ref	3	601	439	740 *	.1	.1
121 Ch God (Abr)	2	77	57	95 *	-	-
123 Ch God (Ander)	1	NR	34	34	-	-
127 Ch God (Cleve)	5	492	645	701 *	.1	.1
145 Ch God Prophcy	2	69	NR	84 *	-	-
151 L-D Saints	12	NR	NR	4,785	.4	.7
165 Ch of Nazarene	7	759	584	1,014	.1	.2
167 Chs of Christ	5	620	606	856	.1	.1
173 Comm of Christ	1	121	NR	121	-	-
175 Congr Chr Chs	2	4,512	1,700	5,553 *	.5	.9
179 Consrv Bapt	5	NR	879	879	.1	.1
181 Consrv Congr	2	2,726	980	3,355 *	.3	.5
193 Episcopal	22	NR	3,378	9,987	.9	1.6
201 Evan Cov Ch	14	3,320	3,769	4,865 *	.4	.8
203 Evan Free Ch	22	5,189	7,734	7,862	.7	1.2
207 E.L.C.A.	120	113,663	45,466	152,817	13.7	23.7
220 Free Lutheran	6	966	724	1,512	.1	.2
221 Free Methodist	2	56	95	95	-	-
226 Friends-USA	2	90	NR	111 *	-	-
237 Menn Br US Conf	1	95	NR	117 *	-	-
246 Greek Orthodox	1	NR	NR	2,280	.2	.4
252 Hindu	4	NR	NR	NR	-	-
262 Int Cou Comm Ch	1	38	NR	47 *	-	-
263 Int Foursq Gos	2	109	264	264 *	-	-
264 Int Chs of Crst	1	333	547	478	-	.1
267 Muslim Est	6	NR	1,740	7,878	.7	1.2
268 Jain	1	NR	NR	NR	-	-
283 Luth—MO Synod	37	17,669	8,298	22,343	2.0	3.5
288 Mennonite USA	2	131	105	181 *	-	-
290 Metro Comm Ch	1	295	254	363 *	-	.1
293 Morav Ch-North	1	150	NR	187	-	-
306 NT IndBapt&Rltd	10	1,680	NR	2,068 *	.2	.3
313 N Am Bapt Conf	3	425	355	523 *	-	.1
331 OCA: Ter Diocs	2	991	NR	1,338	.1	.2
339 Pent Ch of God	1	20	NR	46	-	-
355 Presb Ch (USA)	24	13,992	6,547	17,293 *	1.5	2.7
356 Presb Ch Amer	1	108	128	163	-	-
370 Ref Baptist Chs	1	NR	NR	NR	-	-
371 Ref Ch in Am	2	223	222	384	-	.1
373 Ref Ch in U.S.	1	25	NR	46	-	-
401 Rus Orth Abroad	2	NR	NR	NR	-	-
403 Salvation Army	6	708	475	1,536	.1	.2
413 S.D.A.	12	2,018	NR	2,402	.2	.4
419 So Bapt Conv	8	1,413	512	1,739 *	.2	.3
431 Ukrainian Orth	2	NR	NR	591	.1	.1
435 Unitarian-Univ	5	1,817	NR	2,236 *	.2	.3
443 Un C of Christ	20	10,763	4,269	13,246 *	1.2	2.1
449 Un Methodist	45	19,127	9,211	23,538 *	2.1	3.7
463 Vineyard	1	191	164	235 *	-	-
467 Wesleyan	2	152	125	265	-	-
469 WELS	12	3,896	2,400	5,036	.5	.8
496 Jewish Est	14	NR	NR	31,600	2.8	4.9
498 Indep.Charis.	4	10,500	7,750	10,900	1.0	1.7
499 Indep.Non-Char	7	1,660	2,025	2,025	.2	.3
HOUSTON	**33**	**6,732**	**3,322**	**15,802 ***	**80.1**	**100.0**
053 Assemb of God	1	45	46	62	.3	.4
056 Baha'i	0	1	NR	1	-	-
057 Bapt Gen Conf	1	31	70	70 *	.4	.4
081 Catholic	5	NR	NR	6,989	35.4	44.2
203 Evan Free Ch	3	125	195	195	1.0	1.2
207 E.L.C.A.	9	4,148	1,717	5,495	27.9	34.8
283 Luth—MO Synod	1	42	22	50	.3	.3
355 Presb Ch (USA)	1	27	12	34 *	.2	.2
443 Un C of Christ	2	382	140	479 *	2.4	3.0
449 Un Methodist	5	711	393	891 *	4.5	5.6
469 WELS	5	1,220	727	1,536	7.8	9.7
HUBBARD	**27**	**4,310**	**2,638**	**8,631 ***	**47.0**	**100.0**
053 Assemb of God	1	100	128	165	.9	1.9
056 Baha'i	0	5	NR	5	-	.1
081 Catholic	4	NR	NR	2,401	13.1	27.8

NR–Not Reported *Total adherents estimated from known number of communicant, confirmed, full members. - Represents a percentage less than 0.1. Percentages may not total 100 due to rounding.

Table 4: Religious Congregations by County and Group: 2000

Religious Group	Number of Churches, Synagogues, Mosques, or Temples	Number of Communicant, Confirmed, or Full Members	Number of Attendees	Total Adherents		
				Number of Adherents	% of Total Pop.	% of Total Adh.
089 Chr & Miss Al	1	18	NR	54	.3	.6
097 Chr Chs&Chs Cr	1	85	NR	104 *	.6	1.2
165 Ch of Nazarene	1	28	24	86	.5	1.0
167 Chs of Christ	2	87	109	110	.6	1.3
179 Consrv Bapt	2	NR	464	464	2.5	5.4
193 Episcopal	1	NR	26	42	.2	.5
207 E.L.C.A.	4	1,818	829	2,431	13.2	28.2
221 Free Methodist	1	27	28	28	.2	.3
283 Luth—MO Synod	4	1,328	598	1,750	9.5	20.3
306 NT IndBapt&Rltd	1	16	NR	20 *	.1	.2
413 S.D.A.	1	70	NR	83	.5	1.0
449 Un Methodist	3	728	432	888 *	4.8	10.3
ISANTI	**33**	**8,564**	**4,663**	**14,570 ***	**46.6**	**100.0**
053 Assemb of God	1	41	26	49	.2	.3
056 Baha'i	0	6	NR	6	-	-
057 Bapt Gen Conf	7	1,625	1,608	2,129 *	6.8	14.6
081 Catholic	3	NR	NR	2,821	9.0	19.4
201 Evan Cov Ch	1	64	76	81 *	.3	.6
203 Evan Free Ch	2	110	137	137	.4	.9
207 E.L.C.A.	8	4,807	1,470	6,552	20.9	45.0
220 Free Lutheran	1	14	11	16	.1	.1
283 Luth—MO Synod	4	1,391	564	1,755	5.6	12.0
388 Reg Bapt Gen As	1	0	90	90 *	.3	.6
413 S.D.A.	1	28	NR	33	.1	.2
449 Un Methodist	2	386	319	489 *	1.6	3.4
469 WELS	1	92	62	112	.4	.8
498 Indep.Charis.	1	0	300	300	1.0	2.1
ITASCA	**71**	**8,911**	**4,346**	**25,734 ***	**58.5**	**100.0**
053 Assemb of God	3	186	263	406	.9	1.6
056 Baha'i	0	17	NR	17	-	.1
057 Bapt Gen Conf	2	139	139	185 *	.4	.7
081 Catholic	13	NR	NR	12,812	29.1	49.8
089 Chr & Miss Al	4	193	NR	478	1.1	1.9
123 Ch God (Ander)	1	NR	103	103	.2	.4
127 Ch God (Cleve)	2	252	287	325 *	.7	1.3
151 L-D Saints	1	NR	NR	216	.5	.8
165 Ch of Nazarene	1	108	36	108	.2	.4
173 Comm of Christ	1	41	NR	41	.1	.2
183 Cons Menn Conf	1	27	33	39	.1	.2
193 Episcopal	2	NR	87	283	.6	1.1
201 Evan Cov Ch	1	30	23	36 *	.1	.1
203 Evan Free Ch	1	30	100	100	.2	.4
207 E.L.C.A.	12	3,496	1,390	4,696	10.7	18.2
283 Luth—MO Synod	6	2,172	754	3,158	7.2	12.3
306 NT IndBapt&Rltd	1	55	NR	67 *	.2	.3
355 Presb Ch (USA)	10	1,345	708	1,636 *	3.7	6.4
419 So Bapt Conv	3	79	70	96 *	.2	.4
435 Unitarian-Univ	1	15	NR	18 *	-	.1
449 Un Methodist	4	649	288	787 *	1.8	3.1
469 WELS	1	77	65	127	.3	.5
JACKSON	**28**	**5,624**	**2,514**	**9,372 ***	**83.2**	**100.0**
053 Assemb of God	1	12	16	20	.2	.2
081 Catholic	3	NR	NR	2,168	19.2	23.1
179 Consrv Bapt	1	NR	120	120	1.1	1.3
207 E.L.C.A.	8	2,427	861	3,025	26.8	32.3
283 Luth—MO Synod	9	2,244	1,065	2,894	25.7	30.9
288 Mennonite USA	1	32	39	39 *	.3	.4
349 Pent Holiness	1	60	90	73 *	.6	.8
355 Presb Ch (USA)	1	267	98	325 *	2.9	3.5
449 Un Methodist	3	582	225	708 *	6.3	7.6
KANABEC	**19**	**4,394**	**2,034**	**7,238 ***	**48.3**	**100.0**
053 Assemb of God	1	71	98	172	1.1	2.4
056 Baha'i	0	3	NR	3	-	-
057 Bapt Gen Conf	2	359	442	480 *	3.2	6.6
081 Catholic	2	NR	NR	1,248	8.3	17.2
105 Christian Ref	1	85	0	107 *	.7	1.5
151 L-D Saints	1	NR	NR	148	1.0	2.0
165 Ch of Nazarene	1	37	16	43	.3	.6
201 Evan Cov Ch	1	81	132	132 *	.9	1.8
207 E.L.C.A.	4	2,048	722	2,709	18.1	37.4
283 Luth—MO Synod	3	1,235	375	1,601	10.7	22.1
355 Presb Ch (USA)	1	155	125	194 *	1.3	2.7
449 Un Methodist	2	320	124	401 *	2.7	5.5
KANDIYOHI	**69**	**19,800**	**10,303**	**31,694 ***	**76.9**	**100.0**
053 Assemb of God	2	519	665	933	2.3	2.9
056 Baha'i	0	7	NR	7	-	-
057 Bapt Gen Conf	2	485	504	604 *	1.5	1.9
081 Catholic	4	NR	NR	5,672	13.8	17.9
105 Christian Ref	4	1,383	1,143	1,723 *	4.2	5.4
123 Ch God (Ander)	1	NR	70	70	.2	.2
165 Ch of Nazarene	1	49	46	57	.1	.2
167 Chs of Christ	1	40	55	65	.2	.2
193 Episcopal	1	NR	24	47	.1	.1
201 Evan Cov Ch	3	726	623	913 *	2.2	2.9
203 Evan Free Ch	1	261	525	525	1.3	1.7
207 E.L.C.A.	24	12,226	4,478	15,718	38.1	49.6
220 Free Lutheran	4	227	188	296	.7	.9
263 Int Foursq Gos	1	46	109	109 *	.3	.3
283 Luth—MO Synod	3	1,096	451	1,422	3.5	4.5
306 NT IndBapt&Rltd	1	52	NR	65 *	.2	.2
355 Presb Ch (USA)	3	1,007	476	1,254 *	3.0	4.0
371 Ref Ch in Am	2	352	300	556	1.3	1.8
403 Salvation Army	1	64	24	77	.2	.2
413 S.D.A.	2	71	NR	84	.2	.3
419 So Bapt Conv	1	9	30	11 *	-	-
435 Unitarian-Univ	1	17	NR	21 *	.1	.1
449 Un Methodist	5	951	448	1,184 *	2.9	3.7
469 WELS	1	212	144	281	.7	.9
KITTSON	**24**	**2,890**	**1,170**	**4,485 ***	**84.9**	**100.0**
053 Assemb of God	2	70	78	110	2.1	2.5
057 Bapt Gen Conf	1	62	53	77 *	1.5	1.7
081 Catholic	3	NR	NR	829	15.7	18.5
193 Episcopal	1	NR	12	12	.2	.3
201 Evan Cov Ch	4	181	207	236 *	4.5	5.3
207 E.L.C.A.	9	2,263	712	2,833	53.6	63.2
355 Presb Ch (USA)	1	169	72	210 *	4.0	4.7
413 S.D.A.	1	61	NR	73	1.4	1.6
419 So Bapt Conv	1	19	18	24 *	.5	.5
449 Un Methodist	1	65	18	81 *	1.5	1.8
KOOCHICHING	**36**	**3,720**	**1,652**	**10,008 ***	**69.7**	**100.0**
053 Assemb of God	1	74	89	138	1.0	1.4
056 Baha'i	0	6	NR	6	-	.1
057 Bapt Gen Conf	1	50	50	61 *	.4	.6
081 Catholic	3	NR	NR	4,577	31.9	45.7
089 Chr & Miss Al	1	16	NR	42	.3	.4
151 L-D Saints	1	NR	NR	74	.5	.7
165 Ch of Nazarene	1	17	0	17	.1	.2
193 Episcopal	1	NR	40	114	.8	1.1
201 Evan Cov Ch	3	228	394	394 *	2.7	3.9
203 Evan Free Ch	2	44	53	53	.4	.5
207 E.L.C.A.	7	2,050	610	2,852	19.9	28.5
220 Free Lutheran	2	280	103	360	2.5	3.6
283 Luth—MO Synod	1	271	105	335	2.3	3.3
288 Mennonite USA	1	17	14	21 *	.1	.2
297 Mennonite;Other	3	51	NR	62 *	.4	.6
306 NT IndBapt&Rltd	1	189	NR	230 *	1.6	2.3
403 Salvation Army	1	80	39	251	1.7	2.5
413 S.D.A.	2	61	NR	73	.5	.7
419 So Bapt Conv	1	9	22	11 *	.1	.1
443 Un C of Christ	2	264	112	321 *	2.2	3.2
449 Un Methodist	1	13	21	16 *	.1	.2
LAC QUI PARLE	**31**	**6,013**	**2,370**	**9,026 ***	**111.9**	**100.0**
057 Bapt Gen Conf	1	48	122	122 *	1.5	1.4
081 Catholic	4	NR	NR	1,221	15.1	13.5
165 Ch of Nazarene	1	12	7	32	.4	.4
201 Evan Cov Ch	1	76	80	92 *	1.1	1.0

NR–Not Reported   *Total adherents estimated from known number of communicant, confirmed, full members.   - Represents a percentage less than 0.1.   Percentages may not total 100 due to rounding.

Table 4: Religious Congregations by County and Group: 2000

Religious Group	Number of Churches, Synagogues, Mosques, or Temples	Number of Communicant, Confirmed, or Full Members	Number of Attendees	Total Adherents: Number of Adherents	Total Adherents: % of Total Pop.	Total Adherents: % of Total Adh.
207 E.L.C.A.	12	4,797	1,639	6,238	77.3	69.1
283 Luth—MO Synod	4	612	292	742	9.2	8.2
355 Presb Ch (USA)	1	117	42	142 *	1.8	1.6
371 Ref Ch in Am	1	22	20	37	.5	.4
443 Un C of Christ	2	150	69	182 *	2.3	2.0
449 Un Methodist	2	101	38	122 *	1.5	1.4
469 WELS	2	78	61	96	1.2	1.1
LAKE	**24**	**3,352**	**1,678**	**6,966 ***	**63.0**	**100.0**
019 Amer Bapt USA	1	138	70	165 *	1.5	2.4
053 Assemb of God	2	98	110	204	1.8	2.9
056 Baha'i	0	3	NR	3	-	-
057 Bapt Gen Conf	1	53	75	75 *	.7	1.1
081 Catholic	2	NR	NR	2,320	21.0	33.3
093 Chr Ch (Disc)	1	139	75	166 *	1.5	2.4
179 Consrv Bapt	2	NR	160	160	1.4	2.3
203 Evan Free Ch	1	35	65	65	.6	.9
207 E.L.C.A.	6	2,256	685	2,987	27.0	42.9
283 Luth—MO Synod	2	153	89	190	1.7	2.7
306 NT IndBapt&Rltd	1	15	NR	18 *	.2	.3
355 Presb Ch (USA)	2	126	175	211 *	1.9	3.0
443 Un C of Christ	1	220	75	263 *	2.4	3.8
449 Un Methodist	2	116	99	139 *	1.3	2.0
LAKE OF THE WOODS	**13**	**1,491**	**623**	**2,825 ***	**62.5**	**100.0**
053 Assemb of God	1	53	70	70	1.5	2.5
056 Baha'i	0	8	NR	8	.2	.3
081 Catholic	2	NR	NR	676	14.9	23.9
201 Evan Cov Ch	1	29	64	64 *	1.4	2.3
207 E.L.C.A.	4	1,071	344	1,593	35.2	56.4
283 Luth—MO Synod	1	111	64	147	3.3	5.2
413 S.D.A.	1	16	NR	19	.4	.7
419 So Bapt Conv	1	4	4	5 *	.1	.2
443 Un C of Christ	2	199	77	243 *	5.4	8.6
LE SUEUR	**41**	**6,978**	**2,441**	**19,212 ***	**75.6**	**100.0**
053 Assemb of God	1	24	33	44	.2	.2
056 Baha'i	0	2	NR	2	-	-
081 Catholic	13	NR	NR	9,919	39.0	51.6
089 Chr & Miss Al	2	105	NR	199	.8	1.0
097 Chr Chs&Chs Cr	1	135	NR	169 *	.7	.9
193 Episcopal	2	NR	11	40	.2	.2
207 E.L.C.A.	6	3,228	1,091	4,365	17.2	22.7
283 Luth—MO Synod	4	962	341	1,290	5.1	6.7
306 NT IndBapt&Rltd	1	100	NR	126 *	.5	.7
355 Presb Ch (USA)	2	257	112	323 *	1.3	1.7
413 S.D.A.	1	31	NR	37	.1	.2
443 Un C of Christ	1	782	272	982 *	3.9	5.1
449 Un Methodist	5	878	343	1,102 *	4.3	5.7
469 WELS	2	474	238	614	2.4	3.2
LINCOLN	**25**	**3,266**	**1,255**	**6,005 ***	**93.4**	**100.0**
053 Assemb of God	1	29	38	38	.6	.6
056 Baha'i	0	1	NR	1	-	-
081 Catholic	4	NR	NR	1,820	28.3	30.3
089 Chr & Miss Al	1	40	NR	91	1.4	1.5
207 E.L.C.A.	9	2,321	839	2,995	46.6	49.9
257 Hutterian Br	1	66	NR	100	1.6	1.7
306 NT IndBapt&Rltd	2	70	NR	85 *	1.3	1.4
449 Un Methodist	4	307	144	371 *	5.8	6.2
469 WELS	3	432	234	504	7.8	8.4
LYON	**42**	**6,584**	**3,075**	**17,695 ***	**69.6**	**100.0**
053 Assemb of God	1	58	61	75	.3	.4
056 Baha'i	0	5	NR	5	-	-
081 Catholic	7	NR	NR	8,766	34.5	49.5
089 Chr & Miss Al	2	149	NR	229	.9	1.3
151 L-D Saints	1	NR	NR	195	.8	1.1
167 Chs of Christ	1	10	14	18	.1	.1
181 Consrv Congr	1	59	35	73 *	.3	.4
193 Episcopal	1	NR	32	80	.3	.5
203 Evan Free Ch	3	195	404	404	1.6	2.3
207 E.L.C.A.	11	3,524	1,229	4,583	18.0	25.9
283 Luth—MO Synod	1	267	161	352	1.4	2.0
306 NT IndBapt&Rltd	1	68	NR	85 *	.3	.5
355 Presb Ch (USA)	3	396	173	493 *	1.9	2.8
413 S.D.A.	1	20	NR	24	.1	.1
419 So Bapt Conv	1	78	109	97 *	.4	.5
449 Un Methodist	4	986	461	1,226 *	4.8	6.9
469 WELS	3	769	396	990	3.9	5.6
MCLEOD	**49**	**16,134**	**7,335**	**30,692 ***	**87.9**	**100.0**
053 Assemb of God	2	288	420	750	2.1	2.4
056 Baha'i	0	3	NR	3	-	-
057 Bapt Gen Conf	2	304	445	445 *	1.3	1.4
081 Catholic	5	NR	NR	8,943	25.6	29.1
151 L-D Saints	1	NR	NR	181	.5	.6
181 Consrv Congr	2	146	83	185 *	.5	.6
193 Episcopal	1	NR	5	9	-	-
201 Evan Cov Ch	1	104	172	172 *	.5	.6
203 Evan Free Ch	1	69	125	125	.4	.4
207 E.L.C.A.	8	5,207	1,991	7,072	20.3	23.0
283 Luth—MO Synod	9	6,846	2,736	8,853	25.4	28.8
306 NT IndBapt&Rltd	1	14	NR	18 *	.1	.1
313 N Am Bapt Conf	1	12	12	15 *	-	-
355 Presb Ch (USA)	2	250	72	316 *	.9	1.0
443 Un C of Christ	6	1,312	464	1,659 *	4.8	5.4
449 Un Methodist	2	737	342	932 *	2.7	3.0
467 Wesleyan	1	0	12	12	-	-
469 WELS	4	842	456	1,002	2.9	3.3
MAHNOMEN	**14**	**912**	**424**	**3,451 ***	**66.5**	**100.0**
053 Assemb of God	1	9	12	12	.2	.3
056 Baha'i	0	1	NR	1	-	-
081 Catholic	4	NR	NR	2,045	39.4	59.3
193 Episcopal	1	NR	29	269	5.2	7.8
207 E.L.C.A.	5	752	313	937	18.1	27.2
283 Luth—MO Synod	1	60	33	72	1.4	2.1
443 Un C of Christ	1	50	22	64 *	1.2	1.9
449 Un Methodist	1	40	15	51 *	1.0	1.5
MARSHALL	**45**	**4,286**	**1,913**	**8,867 ***	**87.3**	**100.0**
053 Assemb of God	1	18	21	58	.6	.7
057 Bapt Gen Conf	1	38	70	70 *	.7	.8
081 Catholic	9	NR	NR	3,314	32.6	37.4
089 Chr & Miss Al	1	11	NR	68	.7	.8
201 Evan Cov Ch	2	118	137	168 *	1.7	1.9
203 Evan Free Ch	1	69	115	115	1.1	1.3
207 E.L.C.A.	17	3,052	1,163	3,865	38.1	43.6
220 Free Lutheran	6	371	225	465	4.6	5.2
283 Luth—MO Synod	2	316	71	391	3.9	4.4
355 Presb Ch (USA)	2	71	37	86 *	.8	1.0
356 Presb Ch Amer	1	27	28	31	.3	.3
413 S.D.A.	1	54	NR	64	.6	.7
449 Un Methodist	1	141	46	172 *	1.7	1.9
MARTIN	**55**	**12,536**	**5,611**	**19,314 ***	**88.6**	**100.0**
019 Amer Bapt USA	1	162	44	198 *	.9	1.0
053 Assemb of God	3	132	175	248	1.1	1.3
056 Baha'i	0	1	NR	1	-	-
081 Catholic	4	NR	NR	3,468	15.9	18.0
097 Chr Chs&Chs Cr	3	232	NR	283 *	1.3	1.5
151 L-D Saints	1	NR	NR	153	.7	.8
193 Episcopal	1	NR	35	47	.2	.2
201 Evan Cov Ch	2	313	309	382 *	1.8	2.0
203 Evan Free Ch	2	390	621	621	2.8	3.2
207 E.L.C.A.	9	3,757	1,276	4,576	21.0	23.7
283 Luth—MO Synod	12	4,591	2,041	5,567	25.5	28.8
306 NT IndBapt&Rltd	1	58	NR	71 *	.3	.4
403 Salvation Army	1	93	47	280	1.3	1.4
413 S.D.A.	1	6	NR	7	-	-
443 Un C of Christ	7	1,426	527	1,740 *	8.0	9.0
449 Un Methodist	6	1,281	478	1,563 *	7.2	8.1
469 WELS	1	94	58	109	.5	.6

NR–Not Reported *Total adherents estimated from known number of communicant, confirmed, full members. - Represents a percentage less than 0.1. Percentages may not total 100 due to rounding.

Table 4: Religious Congregations by County and Group: 2000

Religious Group	Number of Churches, Synagogues, Mosques, or Temples	Number of Communicant, Confirmed, or Full Members	Number of Attendees	Total Adherents		
				Number of Adherents	% of Total Pop.	% of Total Adh.
MEEKER	**39**	**8,526**	**3,565**	**15,512 ***	**68.5**	**100.0**
053 Assemb of God	1	42	65	65	.3	.4
057 Bapt Gen Conf	2	321	296	401 *	1.8	2.6
061 Beachy Amish	1	82	NR	102 *	.5	.7
081 Catholic	5	NR	NR	4,471	19.7	28.8
097 Chr Chs&Chs Cr	2	199	NR	249 *	1.1	1.6
121 Ch God (Abr)	2	130	110	162 *	.7	1.0
165 Ch of Nazarene	1	129	80	154	.7	1.0
193 Episcopal	1	NR	34	73	.3	.5
201 Evan Cov Ch	2	386	239	482 *	2.1	3.1
203 Evan Free Ch	1	50	105	105	.5	.7
207 E.L.C.A.	10	5,168	1,730	6,769	29.9	43.6
283 Luth—MO Synod	2	516	256	639	2.8	4.1
355 Presb Ch (USA)	1	125	64	156 *	.7	1.0
413 S.D.A.	1	32	NR	38	.2	.2
419 So Bapt Conv	0	9	9	11 *	-	.1
443 Un C of Christ	2	184	72	230 *	1.0	1.5
449 Un Methodist	3	471	180	588 *	2.6	3.8
469 WELS	2	682	325	817	3.6	5.3
MILLE LACS	**41**	**7,254**	**4,509**	**14,639 ***	**65.6**	**100.0**
053 Assemb of God	3	392	593	940	4.2	6.4
056 Baha'i	0	23	NR	23	.1	.2
057 Bapt Gen Conf	4	390	428	521 *	2.3	3.6
081 Catholic	6	NR	NR	3,928	17.6	26.8
089 Chr & Miss Al	3	86	NR	294	1.3	2.0
105 Christian Ref	2	851	650	1,062 *	4.8	7.3
151 L-D Saints	1	NR	NR	441	2.0	3.0
201 Evan Cov Ch	1	101	183	183 *	.8	1.3
203 Evan Free Ch	5	360	670	670	3.0	4.6
207 E.L.C.A.	8	3,486	1,325	4,639	20.8	31.7
283 Luth—MO Synod	3	687	315	842	3.8	5.8
355 Presb Ch (USA)	1	91	42	114 *	.5	.8
443 Un C of Christ	1	169	65	211 *	.9	1.4
449 Un Methodist	3	618	238	771 *	3.5	5.3
MORRISON	**52**	**4,714**	**2,640**	**21,865 ***	**68.9**	**100.0**
053 Assemb of God	1	166	227	413	1.3	1.9
056 Baha'i	0	2	NR	2	-	-
057 Bapt Gen Conf	1	32	32	40 *	.1	.2
081 Catholic	19	NR	NR	15,284	48.2	69.9
089 Chr & Miss Al	3	169	NR	444	1.4	2.0
165 Ch of Nazarene	1	35	16	48	.2	.2
181 Consrv Congr	1	74	73	93 *	.3	.4
193 Episcopal	2	NR	30	54	.2	.2
201 Evan Cov Ch	2	322	399	407 *	1.3	1.9
203 Evan Free Ch	1	56	95	95	.3	.4
207 E.L.C.A.	5	1,372	780	1,770	5.6	8.1
220 Free Lutheran	1	45	55	68	.2	.3
221 Free Methodist	2	32	52	52	.2	.2
283 Luth—MO Synod	8	1,663	578	2,152	6.8	9.8
306 NT IndBapt&Rltd	1	48	NR	61 *	.2	.3
355 Presb Ch (USA)	1	125	65	158 *	.5	.7
443 Un C of Christ	1	182	72	230 *	.7	1.1
449 Un Methodist	2	391	166	494 *	1.6	2.3
MOWER	**63**	**13,762**	**5,789**	**28,880 ***	**74.8**	**100.0**
053 Assemb of God	1	77	112	187	.5	.6
056 Baha'i	0	6	NR	6	-	-
057 Bapt Gen Conf	1	36	22	44 *	.1	.2
081 Catholic	10	NR	NR	10,452	27.1	36.2
097 Chr Chs&Chs Cr	2	185	NR	228 *	.6	.8
151 L-D Saints	1	NR	NR	217	.6	.8
167 Chs of Christ	1	33	37	55	.1	.2
193 Episcopal	1	NR	55	133	.3	.5
203 Evan Free Ch	1	165	382	382	1.0	1.3
207 E.L.C.A.	14	8,017	2,688	10,528	27.3	36.5
220 Free Lutheran	1	55	50	77	.2	.3
221 Free Methodist	1	54	95	95	.2	.3
257 Hutterian Br	1	66	NR	100	.3	.3
283 Luth—MO Synod	6	1,585	745	1,917	5.0	6.6
349 Pent Holiness	1	18	18	22 *	.1	.1
355 Presb Ch (USA)	2	639	253	788 *	2.0	2.7
388 Reg Bapt Gen As	3	419	285	516 *	1.3	1.8
403 Salvation Army	1	196	54	432	1.1	1.5
419 So Bapt Conv	1	57	25	70 *	.2	.2
443 Un C of Christ	2	341	131	420 *	1.1	1.5
449 Un Methodist	8	1,488	578	1,833 *	4.7	6.3
463 Vineyard	1	130	120	160 *	.4	.6
467 Wesleyan	1	0	0	0	-	-
469 WELS	2	195	139	218	.6	.8
MURRAY	**26**	**3,953**	**2,101**	**7,710 ***	**84.1**	**100.0**
053 Assemb of God	1	18	20	35	.4	.5
057 Bapt Gen Conf	1	161	110	197 *	2.1	2.6
081 Catholic	5	NR	NR	2,717	29.6	35.2
105 Christian Ref	1	173	278	211 *	2.3	2.7
207 E.L.C.A.	8	1,853	717	2,327	25.4	30.2
283 Luth—MO Synod	2	725	323	890	9.7	11.5
355 Presb Ch (USA)	4	451	217	551 *	6.0	7.1
371 Ref Ch in Am	2	272	303	415	4.5	5.4
419 So Bapt Conv	0	12	24	15 *	.2	.2
449 Un Methodist	2	288	109	352 *	3.8	4.6
NICOLLET	**26**	**8,244**	**3,969**	**17,370 ***	**58.3**	**100.0**
053 Assemb of God	2	204	275	418	1.4	2.4
056 Baha'i	0	2	NR	2	-	-
081 Catholic	5	NR	NR	6,345	21.3	36.5
089 Chr & Miss Al	1	30	NR	90	.3	.5
097 Chr Chs&Chs Cr	1	25	NR	31 *	.1	.2
193 Episcopal	1	NR	35	112	.4	.6
201 Evan Cov Ch	1	365	622	622 *	2.1	3.6
207 E.L.C.A.	7	4,006	1,261	5,353	18.0	30.8
283 Luth—MO Synod	1	374	203	482	1.6	2.8
306 NT IndBapt&Rltd	1	20	NR	24 *	.1	.1
355 Presb Ch (USA)	1	313	100	383 *	1.3	2.2
419 So Bapt Conv	0	0	8	0 *	-	-
449 Un Methodist	1	585	235	716 *	2.4	4.1
469 WELS	4	2,320	1,230	2,792	9.4	16.1
NOBLES	**45**	**8,702**	**4,723**	**18,242 ***	**87.6**	**100.0**
053 Assemb of God	1	118	141	266	1.3	1.5
057 Bapt Gen Conf	1	145	120	181 *	.9	1.0
081 Catholic	7	NR	NR	6,540	31.4	35.9
097 Chr Chs&Chs Cr	1	450	NR	563 *	2.7	3.1
105 Christian Ref	4	941	791	1,177 *	5.6	6.5
157 Ch of Brethren	1	66	33	83 *	.4	.5
179 Consrv Bapt	1	NR	220	220	1.1	1.2
193 Episcopal	1	NR	5	6	-	-
201 Evan Cov Ch	1	107	106	134 *	.6	.7
203 Evan Free Ch	1	69	125	125	.6	.7
207 E.L.C.A.	5	2,499	1,051	3,413	16.4	18.7
283 Luth—MO Synod	4	1,334	593	1,634	7.8	9.0
306 NT IndBapt&Rltd	1	45	NR	56 *	.3	.3
355 Presb Ch (USA)	10	1,552	624	1,941 *	9.3	10.6
371 Ref Ch in Am	3	621	590	959	4.6	5.3
449 Un Methodist	3	755	324	944 *	4.5	5.2
NORMAN	**31**	**5,045**	**1,714**	**7,134 ***	**95.9**	**100.0**
081 Catholic	3	NR	NR	940	12.6	13.2
203 Evan Free Ch	1	19	60	60	.8	.8
207 E.L.C.A.	22	4,105	1,344	4,993	67.1	70.0
283 Luth—MO Synod	3	714	249	886	11.9	12.4
443 Un C of Christ	1	52	23	64 *	.9	.9
449 Un Methodist	1	155	38	191 *	2.6	2.7
OLMSTED	**104**	**32,769**	**15,680**	**76,708 ***	**61.7**	**100.0**
053 Assemb of God	5	731	951	1,315	1.1	1.7
056 Baha'i	1	63	NR	63	.1	.1
057 Bapt Gen Conf	1	121	134	153 *	.1	.2
081 Catholic	10	NR	NR	27,239	21.9	35.5
089 Chr & Miss Al	1	247	NR	947	.8	1.2
093 Chr Ch (Disc)	1	90	51	114 *	.1	.1
097 Chr Chs&Chs Cr	5	793	NR	1,000 *	.8	1.3

NR–Not Reported *Total adherents estimated from known number of communicant, confirmed, full members. - Represents a percentage less than 0.1. Percentages may not total 100 due to rounding.

Table 4: Religious Congregations by County and Group: 2000

Religious Group	Number of Churches, Synagogues, Mosques, or Temples	Number of Communicant, Confirmed, or Full Members	Number of Attendees	Total Adherents: Number of Adherents	Total Adherents: % of Total Pop.	Total Adherents: % of Total Adh.
151 L-D Saints	5	NR	NR	1,168	.9	1.5
165 Ch of Nazarene	2	178	178	394	.3	.5
167 Chs of Christ	3	73	125	128	.1	.2
193 Episcopal	2	NR	386	1,677	1.3	2.2
201 Evan Cov Ch	2	422	524	572 *	.5	.7
203 Evan Free Ch	5	441	1,178	1,178	.9	1.5
207 E.L.C.A.	12	12,904	4,807	17,935	14.4	23.4
226 Friends-USA	1	45	NR	57 *	-	.1
246 Greek Orthodox	1	NR	NR	498	.4	.6
263 Int Foursq Gos	1	8	37	37 *	-	-
267 Muslim Est	1	NR	101	288	.2	.4
283 Luth—MO Synod	9	5,242	2,112	6,722	5.4	8.8
288 Mennonite USA	1	22	22	28 *	-	-
290 Metro Comm Ch	1	35	27	44 *	-	.1
306 NT IndBapt&Rltd	1	35	NR	44 *	-	.1
355 Presb Ch (USA)	3	1,195	487	1,508 *	1.2	2.0
356 Presb Ch Amer	1	99	105	132	.1	.2
371 Ref Ch in Am	1	134	100	204	.2	.3
388 Reg Bapt Gen As	1	508	425	641 *	.5	.8
403 Salvation Army	1	277	121	486	.4	.6
413 S.D.A.	2	249	NR	297	.2	.4
419 So Bapt Conv	3	798	425	1,007 *	.8	1.3
435 Unitarian-Univ	1	301	NR	380 *	.3	.5
443 Un C of Christ	3	1,666	648	2,102 *	1.7	2.7
449 Un Methodist	9	4,923	1,915	6,211 *	5.0	8.1
467 Wesleyan	2	85	87	154	.1	.2
469 WELS	4	1,084	734	1,385	1.1	1.8
496 Jewish Est	2	NR	NR	600	.5	.8
OTTER TAIL	**123**	**24,196**	**10,632**	**39,949 ***	**69.9**	**100.0**
019 Amer Bapt USA	1	18	20	22 *	-	.1
053 Assemb of God	4	164	214	399	.7	1.0
056 Baha'i	0	3	NR	3	-	-
057 Bapt Gen Conf	4	535	474	668 *	1.2	1.7
081 Catholic	14	NR	NR	8,108	14.2	20.3
089 Chr & Miss Al	2	110	NR	255	.4	.6
151 L-D Saints	1	NR	NR	121	.2	.3
165 Ch of Nazarene	1	213	288	295	.5	.7
167 Chs of Christ	1	22	30	35	.1	.1
173 Comm of Christ	1	23	NR	23	-	.1
179 Consrv Bapt	2	NR	233	233	.4	.6
193 Episcopal	1	NR	57	150	.3	.4
203 Evan Free Ch	2	149	275	275	.5	.7
207 E.L.C.A.	39	13,813	4,857	17,692	31.0	44.3
220 Free Lutheran	4	688	403	936	1.6	2.3
283 Luth—MO Synod	21	5,721	2,422	7,195	12.6	18.0
355 Presb Ch (USA)	3	628	369	767 *	1.3	1.9
388 Reg Bapt Gen As	2	34	70	70 *	.1	.2
403 Salvation Army	1	83	29	275	.5	.7
413 S.D.A.	3	142	NR	170	.3	.4
435 Unitarian-Univ	1	35	NR	43 *	.1	.1
443 Un C of Christ	5	496	229	605 *	1.1	1.5
449 Un Methodist	10	1,319	662	1,609 *	2.8	4.0
PENNINGTON	**26**	**5,892**	**2,201**	**10,399 ***	**76.6**	**100.0**
053 Assemb of God	1	50	65	80	.6	.8
056 Baha'i	0	1	NR	1	-	-
057 Bapt Gen Conf	1	105	65	128 *	.9	1.2
081 Catholic	2	NR	NR	3,014	22.2	29.0
167 Chs of Christ	1	5	5	5	-	-
201 Evan Cov Ch	1	117	157	157 *	1.2	1.5
203 Evan Free Ch	1	137	283	283	2.1	2.7
207 E.L.C.A.	11	4,362	1,205	5,695	41.9	54.8
220 Free Lutheran	4	437	260	538	4.0	5.2
283 Luth—MO Synod	1	266	0	0	-	-
413 S.D.A.	2	147	NR	175	1.3	1.7
419 So Bapt Conv	0	8	8	10 *	.1	.1
449 Un Methodist	1	257	153	313 *	2.3	3.0
PINE	**48**	**5,817**	**3,086**	**12,444 ***	**46.9**	**100.0**
053 Assemb of God	2	179	264	312	1.2	2.5
056 Baha'i	0	8	NR	8	-	.1
057 Bapt Gen Conf	3	270	322	355 *	1.3	2.9
081 Catholic	8	NR	NR	4,520	17.0	36.3
127 Ch God (Cleve)	1	180	158	221 *	.8	1.8
151 L-D Saints	1	NR	NR	185	.7	1.5
167 Chs of Christ	1	14	28	28	.1	.2
193 Episcopal	1	NR	26	84	.3	.7
203 Evan Free Ch	3	244	399	399	1.5	3.2
207 E.L.C.A.	10	2,738	998	3,682	13.9	29.6
220 Free Lutheran	1	70	15	74	.3	.6
221 Free Methodist	1	44	57	57	.2	.5
283 Luth—MO Synod	5	1,291	395	1,593	6.0	12.8
306 NT IndBapt&Rltd	1	68	NR	83 *	.3	.7
355 Presb Ch (USA)	2	139	80	170 *	.6	1.4
356 Presb Ch Amer	1	118	90	139	.5	1.1
388 Reg Bapt Gen As	1	94	95	95 *	.4	.8
413 S.D.A.	2	95	NR	114	.4	.9
443 Un C of Christ	1	63	28	77 *	.3	.6
449 Un Methodist	3	202	131	248 *	.9	2.0
PIPESTONE	**31**	**6,003**	**3,187**	**9,831 ***	**99.4**	**100.0**
053 Assemb of God	1	18	28	43	.4	.4
057 Bapt Gen Conf	1	101	118	124 *	1.3	1.3
081 Catholic	3	NR	NR	1,570	15.9	16.0
105 Christian Ref	4	1,451	722	1,784 *	18.0	18.1
203 Evan Free Ch	1	69	125	125	1.3	1.3
207 E.L.C.A.	3	1,373	488	1,887	19.1	19.2
220 Free Lutheran	1	307	220	423	4.3	4.3
283 Luth—MO Synod	5	1,015	566	1,635	16.5	16.6
355 Presb Ch (USA)	3	544	217	669 *	6.8	6.8
369 Prot Ref Chs	1	42	NR	68	.7	.7
371 Ref Ch in Am	2	525	460	813	8.2	8.3
413 S.D.A.	1	70	NR	83	.8	.8
449 Un Methodist	4	449	211	552 *	5.6	5.6
469 WELS	1	39	32	55	.6	.6
POLK	**75**	**11,310**	**4,978**	**22,999 ***	**73.3**	**100.0**
053 Assemb of God	2	72	90	103	.3	.4
056 Baha'i	0	6	NR	6	-	-
057 Bapt Gen Conf	2	187	190	231 *	.7	1.0
081 Catholic	8	NR	NR	8,386	26.7	36.5
097 Chr Chs&Chs Cr	1	75	NR	93 *	.3	.4
105 Christian Ref	2	31	40	38 *	.1	.2
151 L-D Saints	1	NR	NR	114	.4	.5
167 Chs of Christ	1	32	28	44	.1	.2
201 Evan Cov Ch	1	70	93	93 *	.3	.4
203 Evan Free Ch	1	69	125	125	.4	.5
207 E.L.C.A.	32	7,712	2,830	9,891	31.5	43.0
220 Free Lutheran	9	714	579	985	3.1	4.3
283 Luth—MO Synod	7	1,287	605	1,590	5.1	6.9
355 Presb Ch (USA)	3	656	243	809 *	2.6	3.5
413 S.D.A.	1	42	NR	50	.2	.2
449 Un Methodist	4	357	155	441 *	1.4	1.9
POPE	**28**	**5,534**	**2,235**	**8,860 ***	**78.9**	**100.0**
053 Assemb of God	1	76	116	179	1.6	2.0
057 Bapt Gen Conf	1	117	185	185 *	1.6	2.1
081 Catholic	3	NR	NR	1,846	16.4	20.8
201 Evan Cov Ch	1	76	108	108 *	1.0	1.2
207 E.L.C.A.	14	4,230	1,378	5,230	46.5	59.0
220 Free Lutheran	2	234	113	318	2.8	3.6
283 Luth—MO Synod	2	387	148	490	4.4	5.5
443 Un C of Christ	1	111	45	134 *	1.2	1.5
449 Un Methodist	2	232	97	281 *	2.5	3.2
469 WELS	1	71	45	89	.8	1.0
RAMSEY	**307**	**92,190**	**52,628**	**313,417 ***	**61.3**	**100.0**
019 Amer Bapt USA	8	2,989	1,167	3,730 *	.7	1.2
053 Assemb of God	15	2,095	2,661	6,004	1.2	1.9
056 Baha'i	4	303	NR	303	.1	.1
057 Bapt Gen Conf	12	4,828	9,445	11,034 *	2.2	3.5
076 Buddhism	5	NR	NR	NR	-	-
081 Catholic	48	NR	NR	159,281	31.2	50.8
084 Calvary Chapel	1	NR	NR	NR	-	-

NR–Not Reported *Total adherents estimated from known number of communicant, confirmed, full members. - Represents a percentage less than 0.1. Percentages may not total 100 due to rounding.

Table 4: Religious Congregations by County and Group: 2000

Religious Group	Number of Churches, Synagogues, Mosques, or Temples	Number of Communicant, Confirmed, or Full Members	Number of Attendees	Total Adherents		
				Number of Adherents	% of Total Pop.	% of Total Adh.
089 Chr & Miss Al	10	4,884	NR	5,432	1.1	1.7
097 Chr Chs&Chs Cr	2	260	NR	324 *	.1	.1
105 Christian Ref	1	532	312	664 *	.1	.2
127 Ch God (Cleve)	2	86	85	107 *	-	-
151 L-D Saints	5	NR	NR	1,974	.4	.6
165 Ch of Nazarene	3	155	84	199	-	.1
167 Chs of Christ	3	229	328	361	.1	.1
173 Comm of Christ	1	87	NR	87	-	-
179 Consrv Bapt	2	NR	275	275	.1	.1
193 Episcopal	13	NR	1,730	5,646	1.1	1.8
201 Evan Cov Ch	6	1,946	1,788	2,520 *	.5	.8
203 Evan Free Ch	3	634	1,489	1,489	.3	.5
207 E.L.C.A.	55	44,927	18,785	62,259	12.2	19.9
220 Free Lutheran	1	11	18	18	-	-
226 Friends-USA	1	45	NR	56 *	-	-
246 Greek Orthodox	1	NR	NR	948	.2	.3
251 Holy Orth in NA	1	NR	NR	36	-	-
263 Int Foursq Gos	1	35	40	44 *	-	-
267 Muslim Est	2	NR	580	2,626	.5	.8
283 Luth—MO Synod	14	6,679	3,102	9,003	1.8	2.9
288 Mennonite USA	3	58	186	82 *	-	-
306 NT IndBapt&Rltd	2	556	NR	694 *	.1	.2
331 OCA: Ter Diocs	1	73	NR	231	-	.1
339 Pent Ch of God	1	20	NR	80	-	-
355 Presb Ch (USA)	14	4,959	2,244	6,186 *	1.2	2.0
397 OCA: Roman Dioc	1	NR	NR	175	-	.1
403 Salvation Army	3	600	286	2,707	.5	.9
410 Serb Orth USA	1	NR	NR	250	-	.1
413 S.D.A.	4	571	NR	680	.1	.2
419 So Bapt Conv	3	576	331	719 *	.1	.2
431 Ukrainian Orth	1	NR	NR	600	.1	.2
435 Unitarian-Univ	2	867	NR	1,082 *	.2	.3
443 Un C of Christ	11	3,289	1,529	4,104 *	.8	1.3
449 Un Methodist	21	6,356	3,193	7,929 *	1.6	2.5
469 WELS	9	2,974	1,645	3,878	.8	1.2
496 Jewish Est	7	NR	NR	8,200	1.6	2.6
498 Indep.Charis.	2	116	400	400	.1	.1
499 Indep.Non-Char	1	450	925	1,000	.2	.3
RED LAKE	**12**	**1,068**	**457**	**3,895 ***	**90.6**	**100.0**
081 Catholic	5	NR	NR	2,437	56.7	62.6
207 E.L.C.A.	4	767	290	1,021	23.7	26.2
283 Luth—MO Synod	2	242	132	365	8.5	9.4
355 Presb Ch (USA)	1	59	35	72 *	1.7	1.8
REDWOOD	**49**	**7,328**	**3,010**	**14,757 ***	**87.8**	**100.0**
053 Assemb of God	1	95	121	156	.9	1.1
056 Baha'i	0	2	NR	2	-	-
081 Catholic	11	NR	NR	5,417	32.2	36.7
089 Chr & Miss Al	1	31	NR	72	.4	.5
097 Chr Chs&Chs Cr	3	253	NR	314 *	1.9	2.1
165 Ch of Nazarene	1	16	12	16	.1	.1
207 E.L.C.A.	13	3,783	1,475	4,768	28.4	32.3
283 Luth—MO Synod	2	137	75	175	1.0	1.2
355 Presb Ch (USA)	3	337	127	417 *	2.5	2.8
413 S.D.A.	1	26	NR	31	.2	.2
449 Un Methodist	7	1,042	424	1,292 *	7.7	8.8
469 WELS	6	1,606	776	2,097	12.5	14.2
RENVILLE	**47**	**7,976**	**3,471**	**14,918 ***	**87.0**	**100.0**
053 Assemb of God	1	49	65	65	.4	.4
081 Catholic	7	NR	NR	4,682	27.3	31.4
105 Christian Ref	1	183	0	227 *	1.3	1.5
121 Ch God (Abr)	1	30	31	37 *	.2	.2
165 Ch of Nazarene	2	18	0	18	.1	.1
193 Episcopal	1	NR	22	284	1.7	1.9
201 Evan Cov Ch	1	52	50	65 *	.4	.4
203 Evan Free Ch	1	17	43	43	.3	.3
207 E.L.C.A.	15	4,542	1,739	5,723	33.4	38.4
355 Presb Ch (USA)	1	149	107	185 *	1.1	1.2
449 Un Methodist	9	1,483	637	1,841 *	10.7	12.3
469 WELS	7	1,453	777	1,748	10.2	11.7

Religious Group	Number of Churches, Synagogues, Mosques, or Temples	Number of Communicant, Confirmed, or Full Members	Number of Attendees	Total Adherents		
				Number of Adherents	% of Total Pop.	% of Total Adh.
RICE	**57**	**14,161**	**7,062**	**37,623 ***	**66.4**	**100.0**
053 Assemb of God	4	364	393	1,048	1.8	2.8
056 Baha'i	0	18	NR	18	-	-
057 Bapt Gen Conf	1	173	275	275 *	.5	.7
081 Catholic	7	NR	NR	16,494	29.1	43.8
089 Chr & Miss Al	1	84	NR	275	.5	.7
097 Chr Chs&Chs Cr	1	70	NR	86 *	.2	.2
127 Ch God (Cleve)	2	75	0	92 *	.2	.2
151 L-D Saints	1	NR	NR	251	.4	.7
167 Chs of Christ	1	26	28	36	.1	.1
193 Episcopal	3	NR	166	642	1.1	1.7
203 Evan Free Ch	2	105	235	235	.4	.6
207 E.L.C.A.	11	6,665	3,163	9,630	17.0	25.6
213 Evan Menn Inc	1	0	0	0 *	-	-
226 Friends-USA	1	45	NR	56 *	.1	.1
283 Luth—MO Synod	6	3,284	1,346	4,465	7.9	11.9
293 Morav Ch-North	1	81	NR	110	.2	.3
388 Reg Bapt Gen As	1	173	165	213 *	.4	.6
413 S.D.A.	1	56	NR	67	.1	.2
419 So Bapt Conv	0	41	30	51 *	.1	.1
435 Unitarian-Univ	1	35	NR	43 *	.1	.1
443 Un C of Christ	4	1,201	516	1,482 *	2.6	3.9
449 Un Methodist	7	1,665	745	2,054 *	3.6	5.5
ROCK	**18**	**4,786**	**2,872**	**8,039 ***	**82.7**	**100.0**
053 Assemb of God	1	47	44	63	.6	.8
081 Catholic	1	NR	NR	1,400	14.4	17.4
105 Christian Ref	1	395	385	490 *	5.0	6.1
151 L-D Saints	1	NR	NR	93	1.0	1.2
179 Consrv Bapt	1	NR	250	250	2.6	3.1
193 Episcopal	1	NR	9	12	.1	.1
207 E.L.C.A.	3	1,502	546	1,915	19.7	23.8
283 Luth—MO Synod	2	856	401	1,038	10.7	12.9
355 Presb Ch (USA)	2	693	282	860 *	8.8	10.7
371 Ref Ch in Am	2	756	735	1,207	12.4	15.0
449 Un Methodist	2	471	220	584 *	6.0	7.3
455 Un Ref Chs N.A.	1	66	NR	127	1.3	1.6
ROSEAU	**44**	**5,668**	**2,696**	**11,168 ***	**68.4**	**100.0**
053 Assemb of God	2	262	248	476	2.9	4.3
057 Bapt Gen Conf	2	237	303	359 *	2.2	3.2
081 Catholic	6	NR	NR	3,334	20.4	29.9
097 Chr Chs&Chs Cr	1	15	NR	19 *	.1	.2
151 L-D Saints	1	NR	NR	128	.8	1.1
175 Congr Chr Chs	1	128	50	165 *	1.0	1.5
193 Episcopal	1	NR	22	49	.3	.4
201 Evan Cov Ch	2	133	270	270 *	1.7	2.4
207 E.L.C.A.	17	3,611	1,331	4,800	29.4	43.0
220 Free Lutheran	7	1,124	388	1,355	8.3	12.1
283 Luth—MO Synod	1	30	25	49	.3	.4
413 S.D.A.	1	10	NR	12	.1	.1
419 So Bapt Conv	1	27	26	35 *	.2	.3
449 Un Methodist	1	91	33	117 *	.7	1.0
ST. LOUIS	**236**	**36,132**	**18,125**	**106,367 ***	**53.0**	**100.0**
019 Amer Bapt USA	2	90	69	108 *	.1	.1
053 Assemb of God	10	1,225	1,784	3,256	1.6	3.1
056 Baha'i	1	103	NR	103	.1	.1
057 Bapt Gen Conf	15	1,801	1,867	2,253 *	1.1	2.1
081 Catholic	35	NR	NR	52,087	26.0	49.0
089 Chr & Miss Al	2	164	NR	411	.2	.4
093 Chr Ch (Disc)	1	100	0	120 *	.1	.1
097 Chr Chs&Chs Cr	1	98	NR	117 *	.1	.1
151 L-D Saints	2	NR	NR	881	.4	.8
165 Ch of Nazarene	2	0	0	0	-	-
167 Chs of Christ	6	195	157	245	.1	.2
173 Comm of Christ	1	68	NR	68	-	.1
175 Congr Chr Chs	1	114	69	137 *	.1	.1
181 Consrv Congr	4	550	170	659 *	.3	.6
193 Episcopal	10	NR	582	1,839	.9	1.7
201 Evan Cov Ch	8	1,166	1,549	1,698 *	.8	1.6
203 Evan Free Ch	5	166	373	373	.2	.4

NR–Not Reported   *Total adherents estimated from known number of communicant, confirmed, full members.   - Represents a percentage less than 0.1.   Percentages may not total 100 due to rounding.

Table 4: Religious Congregations by County and Group: 2000

Religious Group	Number of Churches, Synagogues, Mosques, or Temples	Number of Communicant, Confirmed, or Full Members	Number of Attendees	Total Adherents: Number of Adherents	Total Adherents: % of Total Pop.	Total Adherents: % of Total Adh.
207 E.L.C.A.	45	17,562	5,882	23,323	11.6	21.9
220 Free Lutheran	2	192	139	252	.1	.2
226 Friends-USA	2	90	NR	108 *	.1	.1
246 Greek Orthodox	1	NR	NR	303	.2	.3
262 Int Cou Comm Ch	1	190	NR	228 *	.1	.2
263 Int Foursq Gos	1	26	57	57 *	-	.1
283 Luth—MO Synod	13	2,531	1,255	3,372	1.7	3.2
288 Mennonite USA	1	5	8	8 *	-	-
306 NT IndBapt&Rltd	2	43	NR	51 *	-	-
331 OCA: Ter Diocs	1	30	NR	93	-	.1
355 Presb Ch (USA)	10	2,528	974	3,026 *	1.5	2.8
388 Reg Bapt Gen As	4	274	300	347 *	.2	.3
403 Salvation Army	3	414	200	1,241	.6	1.2
410 Serb Orth USA	3	NR	NR	1,422	.7	1.3
411 Serb Orth: Grac	1	NR	NR	NR	-	-
413 S.D.A.	2	213	NR	254	.1	.2
419 So Bapt Conv	6	176	132	211 *	.1	.2
435 Unitarian-Univ	2	183	NR	219 *	.1	.2
443 Un C of Christ	4	1,184	485	1,418 *	.7	1.3
449 Un Methodist	23	4,229	1,793	5,067 *	2.5	4.8
463 Vineyard	1	320	220	383 *	.2	.4
469 WELS	1	102	60	129	.1	.1
496 Jewish Est	1	NR	NR	500	.2	.5
SCOTT	**49**	**11,831**	**7,374**	**39,942 ***	**44.6**	**100.0**
053 Assemb of God	3	235	265	426	.5	1.1
056 Baha'i	0	3	NR	3	-	-
057 Bapt Gen Conf	1	375	1,651	1,651 *	1.8	4.1
081 Catholic	12	NR	NR	22,158	24.8	55.5
089 Chr & Miss Al	1	21	NR	54	.1	.1
105 Christian Ref	1	185	300	247 *	.3	.6
151 L-D Saints	1	NR	NR	384	.4	1.0
207 E.L.C.A.	8	6,133	2,442	8,636	9.6	21.6
220 Free Lutheran	1	230	135	303	.3	.8
283 Luth—MO Synod	4	1,357	759	1,749	2.0	4.4
306 NT IndBapt&Rltd	1	104	NR	139 *	.2	.3
313 N Am Bapt Conf	1	48	62	64 *	.1	.2
355 Presb Ch (USA)	2	316	168	423 *	.5	1.1
371 Ref Ch in Am	1	113	70	181	.2	.5
443 Un C of Christ	1	61	52	82 *	.1	.2
449 Un Methodist	6	1,039	603	1,389 *	1.6	3.5
469 WELS	5	1,611	867	2,053	2.3	5.1
SHERBURNE	**38**	**8,708**	**4,851**	**25,813 ***	**40.1**	**100.0**
053 Assemb of God	2	97	131	180	.3	.7
056 Baha'i	0	12	NR	12	-	-
057 Bapt Gen Conf	2	150	286	286 *	.4	1.1
081 Catholic	5	NR	NR	12,002	18.6	46.5
089 Chr & Miss Al	1	83	NR	337	.5	1.3
145 Ch God Prophcy	1	34	NR	45 *	.1	.2
193 Episcopal	1	NR	55	106	.2	.4
201 Evan Cov Ch	1	28	30	37 *	.1	.1
203 Evan Free Ch	5	405	1,048	1,048	1.6	4.1
207 E.L.C.A.	6	5,104	1,887	7,862	12.2	30.5
237 Menn Br US Conf	1	250	NR	329 *	.5	1.3
283 Luth—MO Synod	6	1,396	768	2,029	3.1	7.9
306 NT IndBapt&Rltd	1	15	NR	20 *	-	.1
339 Pent Ch of God	1	15	NR	37	.1	.1
443 Un C of Christ	1	434	179	571 *	.9	2.2
449 Un Methodist	3	574	388	755 *	1.2	2.9
469 WELS	1	111	79	157	.2	.6
SIBLEY	**40**	**6,518**	**3,454**	**11,489 ***	**74.8**	**100.0**
040 Ap Chr Ch-Amer	1	57	150	150 *	1.0	1.3
053 Assemb of God	1	49	23	84	.5	.7
056 Baha'i	0	7	NR	7	-	.1
057 Bapt Gen Conf	2	69	91	97 *	.6	.8
081 Catholic	8	NR	NR	2,516	16.4	21.9
201 Evan Cov Ch	1	78	120	120 *	.8	1.0
207 E.L.C.A.	9	2,462	996	3,100	20.2	27.0
257 Hutterian Br	2	132	NR	200	1.3	1.7
283 Luth—MO Synod	8	1,436	1,024	2,481	16.2	21.6
413 S.D.A.	1	20	NR	24	.2	.2
443 Un C of Christ	3	609	234	770 *	5.0	6.7
449 Un Methodist	1	239	125	302 *	2.0	2.6
469 WELS	3	1,360	691	1,638	10.7	14.3
STEARNS	**120**	**19,702**	**11,072**	**95,349 ***	**71.6**	**100.0**
053 Assemb of God	7	827	1,120	1,642	1.2	1.7
056 Baha'i	1	69	NR	69	.1	.1
057 Bapt Gen Conf	2	312	440	458 *	.3	.5
081 Catholic	50	NR	NR	66,563	50.0	69.8
097 Chr Chs&Chs Cr	2	215	NR	266 *	.2	.3
105 Christian Ref	1	134	65	166 *	.1	.2
121 Ch God (Abr)	1	10	18	18 *	-	-
167 Chs of Christ	1	85	120	130	.1	.1
179 Consrv Bapt	1	NR	278	278	.2	.3
181 Consrv Congr	1	59	135	73 *	.1	.1
193 Episcopal	3	NR	154	356	.3	.4
201 Evan Cov Ch	1	255	286	316 *	.2	.3
203 Evan Free Ch	2	140	365	365	.3	.4
207 E.L.C.A.	15	10,376	4,157	14,821	11.1	15.5
220 Free Lutheran	1	50	38	62	-	.1
263 Int Foursq Gos	1	40	52	52 *	-	.1
283 Luth—MO Synod	11	3,719	1,733	4,879	3.7	5.1
306 NT IndBapt&Rltd	1	157	NR	194 *	.1	.2
322 Old Ord Menn Ch	1	24	NR	30 *	-	-
355 Presb Ch (USA)	2	684	244	847 *	.6	.9
388 Reg Bapt Gen As	2	107	137	147 *	.1	.2
413 S.D.A.	1	75	NR	89	.1	.1
419 So Bapt Conv	1	83	67	103 *	.1	.1
435 Unitarian-Univ	1	60	NR	74 *	.1	.1
443 Un C of Christ	2	292	122	362 *	.3	.4
449 Un Methodist	7	1,929	966	2,389 *	1.8	2.5
498 Indep.Charis.	1	0	575	600	.5	.6
STEELE	**44**	**12,686**	**5,247**	**26,112 ***	**77.5**	**100.0**
019 Amer Bapt USA	1	226	70	286 *	.8	1.1
053 Assemb of God	2	172	230	300	.9	1.1
056 Baha'i	0	7	NR	7	-	-
057 Bapt Gen Conf	1	522	647	661 *	2.0	2.5
081 Catholic	7	NR	NR	9,564	28.4	36.6
097 Chr Chs&Chs Cr	1	60	NR	76 *	.2	.3
123 Ch God (Ander)	1	NR	40	40	.1	.2
167 Chs of Christ	1	38	55	65	.2	.2
193 Episcopal	1	NR	68	218	.6	.8
201 Evan Cov Ch	1	69	53	87 *	.3	.3
203 Evan Free Ch	1	69	125	125	.4	.5
207 E.L.C.A.	12	7,291	2,469	9,423	28.0	36.1
283 Luth—MO Synod	4	1,595	567	1,919	5.7	7.3
297 Mennonite;Other	1	29	NR	37 *	.1	.1
306 NT IndBapt&Rltd	2	760	NR	962 *	2.9	3.7
355 Presb Ch (USA)	1	356	225	451 *	1.3	1.7
413 S.D.A.	1	33	NR	39	.1	.1
443 Un C of Christ	2	508	270	643 *	1.9	2.5
449 Un Methodist	3	797	329	1,008 *	3.0	3.9
469 WELS	1	154	99	201	.6	.8
STEVENS	**25**	**4,108**	**2,622**	**7,713 ***	**76.7**	**100.0**
040 Ap Chr Ch-Amer	1	285	535	535 *	5.3	6.9
053 Assemb of God	1	42	53	75	.7	1.0
081 Catholic	2	NR	NR	1,979	19.7	25.7
105 Christian Ref	1	117	75	138 *	1.4	1.8
151 L-D Saints	1	NR	NR	269	2.7	3.5
165 Ch of Nazarene	1	61	40	61	.6	.8
203 Evan Free Ch	2	100	299	299	3.0	3.9
207 E.L.C.A.	7	2,504	1,038	3,155	31.4	40.9
283 Luth—MO Synod	1	243	123	294	2.9	3.8
306 NT IndBapt&Rltd	1	45	NR	53 *	.5	.7
443 Un C of Christ	2	195	140	231 *	2.3	3.0
449 Un Methodist	3	212	153	251 *	2.5	3.3
469 WELS	2	304	166	373	3.7	4.8
SWIFT	**32**	**5,460**	**2,415**	**9,718 ***	**81.3**	**100.0**
053 Assemb of God	1	65	83	117	1.0	1.2

NR–Not Reported *Total adherents estimated from known number of communicant, confirmed, full members. - Represents a percentage less than 0.1. Percentages may not total 100 due to rounding.

Table 4: Religious Congregations by County and Group: 2000

Religious Group	Number of Churches, Synagogues, Mosques, or Temples	Number of Communicant, Confirmed, or Full Members	Number of Attendees	Total Adherents		
				Number of Adherents	% of Total Pop.	% of Total Adh.
056 Baha'i	0	1	NR	1	-	-
057 Bapt Gen Conf	2	121	33	145 *	1.2	1.5
081 Catholic	6	NR	NR	2,745	23.0	28.2
151 L-D Saints	1	NR	NR	124	1.0	1.3
203 Evan Free Ch	2	173	259	259	2.2	2.7
207 E.L.C.A.	10	3,454	1,263	4,293	35.9	44.2
283 Luth—MO Synod	5	1,156	546	1,445	12.1	14.9
313 N Am Bapt Conf	1	29	30	35 *	.3	.4
355 Presb Ch (USA)	1	68	39	82 *	.7	.8
443 Un C of Christ	2	263	111	316 *	2.6	3.3
449 Un Methodist	1	130	51	156 *	1.3	1.6
TODD	**51**	**6,222**	**3,056**	**15,752 ***	**64.5**	**100.0**
053 Assemb of God	3	233	288	470	1.9	3.0
056 Baha'i	0	7	NR	7	-	-
057 Bapt Gen Conf	1	26	20	32 *	.1	.2
081 Catholic	8	NR	NR	7,214	29.5	45.8
089 Chr & Miss Al	1	90	NR	282	1.2	1.8
097 Chr Chs&Chs Cr	1	100	NR	124 *	.5	.8
123 Ch God (Ander)	1	NR	127	127	.5	.8
165 Ch of Nazarene	2	85	58	96	.4	.6
179 Consrv Bapt	1	NR	230	230	.9	1.5
201 Evan Cov Ch	1	74	77	92 *	.4	.6
203 Evan Free Ch	1	46	50	50	.2	.3
207 E.L.C.A.	10	2,210	860	2,797	11.5	17.8
283 Luth—MO Synod	8	2,273	852	2,890	11.8	18.3
323 Old Ord Amish	2	105	NR	130 *	.5	.8
443 Un C of Christ	3	272	120	338 *	1.4	2.1
449 Un Methodist	8	701	374	873 *	3.6	5.5
TRAVERSE	**19**	**2,109**	**908**	**4,085 ***	**98.8**	**100.0**
081 Catholic	4	NR	NR	1,219	29.5	29.8
151 L-D Saints	1	NR	NR	78	1.9	1.9
193 Episcopal	1	NR	40	251	6.1	6.1
201 Evan Cov Ch	1	111	79	136 *	3.3	3.3
207 E.L.C.A.	2	508	197	607	14.7	14.9
283 Luth—MO Synod	4	1,009	340	1,206	29.2	29.5
339 Pent Ch of God	1	5	NR	9	.2	.2
355 Presb Ch (USA)	3	226	118	275 *	6.7	6.7
449 Un Methodist	1	113	45	138 *	3.3	3.4
469 WELS	1	137	89	166	4.0	4.1
WABASHA	**41**	**7,485**	**2,818**	**17,287 ***	**80.0**	**100.0**
053 Assemb of God	1	38	25	50	.2	.3
056 Baha'i	0	1	NR	1	-	-
057 Bapt Gen Conf	1	86	87	107 *	.5	.6
081 Catholic	9	NR	NR	7,677	35.5	44.4
097 Chr Chs&Chs Cr	1	175	NR	218 *	1.0	1.3
193 Episcopal	2	NR	79	188	.9	1.1
203 Evan Free Ch	1	52	95	95	.4	.5
207 E.L.C.A.	3	1,519	520	2,020	9.3	11.7
283 Luth—MO Synod	4	1,909	596	2,420	11.2	14.0
355 Presb Ch (USA)	1	148	61	185 *	.9	1.1
443 Un C of Christ	4	648	224	809 *	3.7	4.7
449 Un Methodist	7	613	317	764 *	3.5	4.4
469 WELS	7	2,296	814	2,753	12.7	15.9
WADENA	**36**	**4,466**	**1,976**	**8,955 ***	**65.3**	**100.0**
053 Assemb of God	3	186	265	439	3.2	4.9
081 Catholic	4	NR	NR	2,670	19.5	29.8
089 Chr & Miss Al	4	177	NR	523	3.8	5.8
167 Chs of Christ	1	16	15	20	.1	.2
193 Episcopal	1	NR	20	48	.4	.5
207 E.L.C.A.	4	1,562	610	2,040	14.9	22.8
220 Free Lutheran	2	173	140	229	1.7	2.6
283 Luth—MO Synod	6	1,353	463	1,750	12.8	19.5
323 Old Ord Amish	2	110	NR	136 *	1.0	1.5
388 Reg Bapt Gen As	1	57	65	71 *	.5	.8
413 S.D.A.	1	129	NR	154	1.1	1.7
443 Un C of Christ	2	169	82	210 *	1.5	2.3
449 Un Methodist	5	534	316	665 *	4.8	7.4
WASECA	**35**	**8,056**	**3,619**	**16,054 ***	**82.2**	**100.0**
053 Assemb of God	1	44	55	109	.6	.7
056 Baha'i	0	1	NR	1	-	-
081 Catholic	4	NR	NR	5,392	27.6	33.6
151 L-D Saints	1	NR	NR	84	.4	.5
175 Congr Chr Chs	2	190	155	236 *	1.2	1.5
193 Episcopal	1	NR	16	30	.2	.2
201 Evan Cov Ch	1	153	137	190 *	1.0	1.2
203 Evan Free Ch	1	108	258	258	1.3	1.6
207 E.L.C.A.	9	3,802	1,292	4,907	25.1	30.6
283 Luth—MO Synod	5	2,478	1,128	3,271	16.8	20.4
306 NT IndBapt&Rltd	1	37	NR	46 *	.2	.3
419 So Bapt Conv	1	29	28	36 *	.2	.2
443 Un C of Christ	1	102	45	127 *	.7	.8
449 Un Methodist	4	826	343	1,026 *	5.3	6.4
467 Wesleyan	1	12	10	40	.2	.2
469 WELS	2	274	152	301	1.5	1.9
WASHINGTON	**109**	**39,934**	**21,806**	**120,577 ***	**59.9**	**100.0**
019 Amer Bapt USA	1	244	179	316 *	.2	.3
053 Assemb of God	3	251	545	549	.3	.5
056 Baha'i	2	70	NR	70	-	.1
057 Bapt Gen Conf	4	291	466	540 *	.3	.4
081 Catholic	12	NR	NR	58,110	28.9	48.2
089 Chr & Miss Al	3	305	NR	788	.4	.7
093 Chr Ch (Disc)	1	234	87	303 *	.2	.3
097 Chr Chs&Chs Cr	2	226	NR	293 *	.1	.2
123 Ch God (Ander)	1	NR	60	60	-	-
151 L-D Saints	2	NR	NR	1,070	.5	.9
167 Chs of Christ	2	187	207	267	.1	.2
175 Congr Chr Chs	1	226	117	293 *	.1	.2
179 Consrv Bapt	2	NR	270	270	.1	.2
181 Consrv Congr	2	225	266	291 *	.1	.2
193 Episcopal	4	NR	379	1,352	.7	1.1
201 Evan Cov Ch	3	737	1,584	1,595 *	.8	1.3
203 Evan Free Ch	4	314	785	785	.4	.7
207 E.L.C.A.	22	25,596	11,082	38,658	19.2	32.1
226 Friends-USA	1	45	NR	58 *	-	-
263 Int Foursq Gos	1	20	27	27 *	-	-
283 Luth—MO Synod	7	3,561	2,181	5,175	2.6	4.3
306 NT IndBapt&Rltd	3	116	NR	150 *	.1	.1
313 N Am Bapt Conf	1	116	119	150 *	.1	.1
339 Pent Ch of God	1	51	NR	56	-	-
355 Presb Ch (USA)	3	1,504	609	1,949 *	1.0	1.6
413 S.D.A.	1	60	NR	71	-	.1
419 So Bapt Conv	1	95	56	123 *	.1	.1
435 Unitarian-Univ	1	307	NR	398 *	.2	.3
443 Un C of Christ	3	751	236	973 *	.5	.8
449 Un Methodist	7	2,846	1,665	3,687 *	1.8	3.1
467 Wesleyan	1	43	69	137	.1	.1
469 WELS	7	1,513	817	2,013	1.0	1.7
WATONWAN	**33**	**5,748**	**2,424**	**9,212 ***	**77.6**	**100.0**
053 Assemb of God	1	35	41	57	.5	.6
056 Baha'i	0	4	NR	4	-	-
081 Catholic	2	NR	NR	2,334	19.7	25.3
097 Chr Chs&Chs Cr	1	82	NR	103 *	.9	1.1
207 E.L.C.A.	12	3,262	1,117	4,203	35.4	45.6
211 Fel Evg Bib Ch	1	0	0	0	-	-
220 Free Lutheran	1	69	70	94	.8	1.0
283 Luth—MO Synod	4	764	448	528	4.4	5.7
288 Mennonite USA	1	48	75	75 *	.6	.8
306 NT IndBapt&Rltd	2	74	NR	93 *	.8	1.0
355 Presb Ch (USA)	2	483	203	608 *	5.1	6.6
413 S.D.A.	1	16	NR	19	.2	.2
449 Un Methodist	2	280	119	353 *	3.0	3.8
469 WELS	3	631	351	741	6.2	8.0
WILKIN	**18**	**2,736**	**1,193**	**5,180 ***	**72.6**	**100.0**
019 Amer Bapt USA	1	108	30	136 *	1.9	2.6
057 Bapt Gen Conf	1	70	61	88 *	1.2	1.7
081 Catholic	2	NR	NR	1,536	21.5	29.7

NR–Not Reported *Total adherents estimated from known number of communicant, confirmed, full members. - Represents a percentage less than 0.1. Percentages may not total 100 due to rounding.

Table 4: Religious Congregations by County and Group: 2000

Religious Group	Number of Churches, Synagogues, Mosques, or Temples	Number of Communicant, Confirmed, or Full Members	Number of Attendees	Total Adherents		
				Number of Adherents	% of Total Pop.	% of Total Adh.
179 Consrv Bapt	1	NR	65	65	.9	1.3
203 Evan Free Ch	1	46	75	75	1.1	1.4
207 E.L.C.A.	5	1,619	609	2,162	30.3	41.7
283 Luth—MO Synod	3	497	205	621	8.7	12.0
355 Presb Ch (USA)	1	51	17	64 *	.9	1.2
443 Un C of Christ	1	25	11	31 *	.4	.6
449 Un Methodist	2	320	120	402 *	5.6	7.8
WINONA	**69**	**14,046**	**6,118**	**33,403 ***	**66.8**	**100.0**
019 Amer Bapt USA	1	154	56	186 *	.4	.6
053 Assemb of God	2	152	192	228	.5	.7
056 Baha'i	0	12	NR	12	-	-
081 Catholic	13	NR	NR	14,598	29.2	43.7
097 Chr Chs&Chs Cr	1	40	NR	48 *	.1	.1
151 L-D Saints	1	NR	NR	176	.4	.5
157 Ch of Brethren	1	100	65	121 *	.2	.4
165 Ch of Nazarene	1	115	71	115	.2	.3
167 Chs of Christ	2	96	94	128	.3	.4
193 Episcopal	1	NR	64	192	.4	.6
203 Evan Free Ch	1	157	415	415	.8	1.2
207 E.L.C.A.	5	3,873	1,106	5,208	10.4	15.6
226 Friends-USA	1	45	NR	54 *	.1	.2
267 Muslim Est	1	NR	30	200	.4	.6
283 Luth—MO Synod	6	3,191	1,182	4,096	8.2	12.3
293 Morav Ch-North	2	234	NR	306	.6	.9
306 NT IndBapt&Rltd	1	22	NR	27 *	.1	.1
323 Old Ord Amish	2	110	NR	132 *	.3	.4
355 Presb Ch (USA)	3	257	126	309 *	.6	.9
413 S.D.A.	1	53	NR	63	.1	.2
419 So Bapt Conv	1	96	80	116 *	.2	.3
435 Unitarian-Univ	1	38	NR	46 *	.1	.1
443 Un C of Christ	3	601	275	724 *	1.4	2.2
449 Un Methodist	8	1,212	492	1,460 *	2.9	4.4
469 WELS	10	3,488	1,870	4,443	8.9	13.3
WRIGHT	**89**	**20,705**	**10,721**	**56,584 ***	**62.9**	**100.0**
053 Assemb of God	4	313	416	553	.6	1.0
056 Baha'i	0	9	NR	9	-	-
057 Bapt Gen Conf	2	234	257	339 *	.4	.6
081 Catholic	11	NR	NR	26,074	29.0	46.1
089 Chr & Miss Al	4	363	NR	1,088	1.2	1.9
097 Chr Chs&Chs Cr	1	100	NR	132 *	.1	.2
151 L-D Saints	1	NR	NR	470	.5	.8
167 Chs of Christ	1	10	14	14	-	-
201 Evan Cov Ch	6	705	918	984 *	1.1	1.7
203 Evan Free Ch	6	574	1,144	1,144	1.3	2.0
207 E.L.C.A.	19	10,406	4,164	15,385	17.1	27.2
220 Free Lutheran	1	159	148	194	.2	.3
283 Luth—MO Synod	7	3,501	1,489	4,589	5.1	8.1
306 NT IndBapt&Rltd	2	135	NR	178 *	.2	.3
355 Presb Ch (USA)	4	434	193	571 *	.6	1.0
371 Ref Ch in Am	1	82	100	133	.1	.2
413 S.D.A.	1	24	NR	29	-	.1
419 So Bapt Conv	1	68	26	90 *	.1	.2
443 Un C of Christ	2	304	163	401 *	.4	.7
449 Un Methodist	9	1,694	835	2,232 *	2.5	3.9
469 WELS	6	1,590	854	1,975	2.2	3.5
YELLOW MEDICINE	**32**	**6,209**	**2,189**	**10,081 ***	**91.0**	**100.0**
053 Assemb of God	2	67	79	98	.9	1.0
081 Catholic	3	NR	NR	2,108	19.0	20.9
089 Chr & Miss Al	2	68	NR	191	1.7	1.9
097 Chr Chs&Chs Cr	1	125	NR	153 *	1.4	1.5
179 Consrv Bapt	1	NR	35	35	.3	.3
207 E.L.C.A.	10	3,923	1,382	5,064	45.7	50.2
283 Luth—MO Synod	4	888	205	1,048	9.5	10.4
355 Presb Ch (USA)	2	213	104	262 *	2.4	2.6
388 Reg Bapt Gen As	1	23	30	30 *	.3	.3
443 Un C of Christ	1	244	58	300 *	2.7	3.0
449 Un Methodist	2	189	67	232 *	2.1	2.3
469 WELS	3	469	229	560	5.1	5.6

Religious Group	Number of Churches, Synagogues, Mosques, or Temples	Number of Communicant, Confirmed, or Full Members	Number of Attendees	Total Adherents		
				Number of Adherents	% of Total Pop.	% of Total Adh.
MISSISSIPPI						
The State.....	5,505	1,100,306	438,476	1,554,483 *	54.6	100.0
ADAMS	**45**	**11,293**	**3,621**	**17,851 ***	**52.0**	**100.0**
053 Assemb of God	1	83	88	136	.4	.8
056 Baha'i	0	2	NR	2	-	-
059 Bapt Miss Assn	1	120	65	150 *	.4	.8
081 Catholic	4	NR	NR	2,796	8.1	15.7
123 Ch God (Ander)	1	NR	120	120	.3	.7
127 Ch God (Cleve)	2	785	374	984 *	2.9	5.5
145 Ch God Prophcy	1	29	NR	37 *	.1	.2
151 L-D Saints	1	NR	NR	211	.6	1.2
167 Chs of Christ	3	464	338	610	1.8	3.4
193 Episcopal	2	NR	191	484	1.4	2.7
216 Evan Presby Ch	1	47	NR	59 *	.2	.3
283 Luth—MO Synod	1	47	32	60	.2	.3
355 Presb Ch (USA)	2	479	255	600 *	1.7	3.4
356 Presb Ch Amer	1	39	40	46	.1	.3
360 Prim Bapt Chrch	1	NR	NR	NR	-	-
403 Salvation Army	1	92	22	121	.4	.7
413 S.D.A.	2	151	NR	180	.5	1.0
419 So Bapt Conv	12	7,343	1,584	9,201 *	26.8	51.5
449 Un Methodist	7	1,612	512	2,019 *	5.9	11.3
496 Jewish Est	1	NR	NR	35	.1	.2
ALCORN	**93**	**20,066**	**7,852**	**25,127 ***	**72.7**	**100.0**
017 Amer Bapt Assn	2	533	NR	653 *	1.9	2.6
053 Assemb of God	2	66	85	89	.3	.4
056 Baha'i	0	3	NR	3	-	-
059 Bapt Miss Assn	2	747	220	915 *	2.6	3.6
081 Catholic	1	NR	NR	284	.8	1.1
097 Chr Chs&Chs Cr	5	672	NR	824 *	2.4	3.3
127 Ch God (Cleve)	1	38	34	47 *	.1	.2
145 Ch God Prophcy	1	29	NR	36 *	.1	.1
167 Chs of Christ	20	1,737	1,819	2,258	6.5	9.0
185 Cumber Presb	1	26	NR	28	.1	.1
193 Episcopal	1	NR	62	125	.4	.5
223 Free Will Bapt	2	130	NR	160 *	.5	.6
283 Luth—MO Synod	1	69	30	87	.3	.3
355 Presb Ch (USA)	3	496	239	608 *	1.8	2.4
360 Prim Bapt Chrch	2	NR	NR	NR	-	-
413 S.D.A.	1	81	NR	96	.3	.4
418 Southw Bapt Fel	1	NR	NR	NR	-	-
419 So Bapt Conv	32	12,956	4,516	15,873 *	45.9	63.2
449 Un Methodist	15	2,483	847	3,041 *	8.8	12.1
AMITE	**46**	**5,681**	**2,085**	**7,611 ***	**56.0**	**100.0**
053 Assemb of God	3	58	66	84	.6	1.1
081 Catholic	1	NR	NR	50	.4	.7
127 Ch God (Cleve)	1	60	34	74 *	.5	1.0
145 Ch God Prophcy	2	59	NR	72 *	.5	.9
151 L-D Saints	2	NR	NR	547	4.0	7.2
165 Ch of Nazarene	1	62	32	62	.5	.8
355 Presb Ch (USA)	2	9	9	11 *	.1	.1
360 Prim Bapt Chrch	2	NR	NR	NR	-	-
419 So Bapt Conv	25	4,872	1,753	6,018 *	44.3	79.1
449 Un Methodist	7	561	191	693 *	5.1	9.1
ATTALA	**74**	**8,539**	**3,814**	**10,898 ***	**55.4**	**100.0**
053 Assemb of God	1	44	48	48	.2	.4
059 Bapt Miss Assn	1	57	23	71 *	.4	.7
081 Catholic	1	NR	NR	178	.9	1.6
123 Ch God (Ander)	1	NR	40	40	.2	.4
127 Ch God (Cleve)	2	119	74	148 *	.8	1.4
145 Ch God Prophcy	1	29	NR	36 *	.2	.3
165 Ch of Nazarene	1	45	8	45	.2	.4
167 Chs of Christ	6	253	261	346	1.8	3.2
193 Episcopal	1	NR	18	31	.2	.3
207 E.L.C.A.	1	65	30	78	.4	.7
355 Presb Ch (USA)	2	88	62	117 *	.6	1.1
356 Presb Ch Amer	2	347	192	422	2.1	3.9

NR–Not Reported   *Total adherents estimated from known number of communicant, confirmed, full members.   - Represents a percentage less than 0.1.   Percentages may not total 100 due to rounding.

Table 4: Religious Congregations by County and Group: 2000

Religious Group	Number of Churches, Synagogues, Mosques, or Temples	Number of Communicant, Confirmed, or Full Members	Number of Attendees	Total Adherents: Number of Adherents	Total Adherents: % of Total Pop.	Total Adherents: % of Total Adh.
360 Prim Bapt Chrch	2	NR	NR	NR	-	-
419 So Bapt Conv	30	6,006	2,371	7,487 *	38.1	68.7
449 Un Methodist	22	1,486	687	1,851 *	9.4	17.0
BENTON	**26**	**2,958**	**1,436**	**3,812 ***	**47.5**	**100.0**
167 Chs of Christ	5	433	465	600	7.5	15.7
185 Cumber Presb	1	44	NR	59	.7	1.5
193 Episcopal	1	NR	10	24	.3	.6
355 Presb Ch (USA)	1	26	13	33 *	.4	.9
419 So Bapt Conv	11	2,170	813	2,736 *	34.1	71.8
449 Un Methodist	7	285	135	360 *	4.5	9.4
BOLIVAR	**67**	**9,762**	**4,046**	**14,122 ***	**34.8**	**100.0**
019 Amer Bapt USA	1	200	0	257 *	.6	1.8
053 Assemb of God	3	211	200	238	.6	1.7
056 Baha'i	0	7	NR	7	-	-
081 Catholic	5	NR	NR	1,221	3.0	8.6
093 Chr Ch (Disc)	2	70	45	90 *	.2	.6
127 Ch God (Cleve)	1	173	66	222 *	.5	1.6
145 Ch God Prophcy	1	29	NR	38 *	.1	.3
165 Ch of Nazarene	2	162	141	259	.6	1.8
167 Chs of Christ	5	853	635	1,073	2.6	7.6
193 Episcopal	2	NR	83	271	.7	1.9
201 Evan Cov Ch	1	94	75	121 *	.3	.9
267 Muslim Est	1	NR	55	163	.4	1.2
283 Luth—MO Synod	1	44	20	56	.1	.4
355 Presb Ch (USA)	3	233	139	299 *	.7	2.1
356 Presb Ch Amer	1	371	230	372	.9	2.6
360 Prim Bapt Chrch	1	NR	NR	NR	-	-
413 S.D.A.	1	33	NR	39	.1	.3
419 So Bapt Conv	20	5,764	1,752	7,410 *	18.2	52.5
449 Un Methodist	15	1,518	605	1,951 *	4.8	13.8
496 Jewish Est	1	NR	NR	35	.1	.2
CALHOUN	**71**	**9,458**	**3,460**	**11,731 ***	**77.8**	**100.0**
081 Catholic	1	NR	NR	52	.3	.4
127 Ch God (Cleve)	1	158	75	195 *	1.3	1.7
145 Ch God Prophcy	2	59	NR	72 *	.5	.6
165 Ch of Nazarene	1	46	39	59	.4	.5
167 Chs of Christ	2	42	47	59	.4	.5
223 Free Will Bapt	1	65	NR	80 *	.5	.7
360 Prim Bapt Chrch	3	NR	NR	NR	-	-
419 So Bapt Conv	50	8,355	3,020	10,308 *	68.4	87.9
449 Un Methodist	10	733	279	906 *	6.0	7.7
CARROLL	**45**	**4,738**	**1,762**	**5,826 ***	**54.1**	**100.0**
017 Amer Bapt Assn	1	37	NR	45 *	.4	.8
056 Baha'i	0	2	NR	2	-	-
093 Chr Ch (Disc)	1	150	75	183 *	1.7	3.1
167 Chs of Christ	1	35	35	40	.4	.7
193 Episcopal	1	NR	18	21	.2	.4
304 NatPrimBapt USA	1	45	NR	55 *	.5	.9
356 Presb Ch Amer	3	156	100	215	2.0	3.7
419 So Bapt Conv	20	3,282	1,196	4,008 *	37.2	68.8
449 Un Methodist	17	1,031	338	1,257 *	11.7	21.6
CHICKASAW	**70**	**8,225**	**3,616**	**10,982 ***	**56.5**	**100.0**
053 Assemb of God	1	30	40	40	.2	.4
056 Baha'i	0	1	NR	1	-	-
081 Catholic	2	NR	NR	319	1.6	2.9
097 Chr Chs&Chs Cr	1	75	NR	97 *	.5	.9
127 Ch God (Cleve)	4	286	204	369 *	1.9	3.4
143 CG in Cr(Menn)	1	133	NR	171 *	.9	1.6
145 Ch God Prophcy	4	117	NR	152 *	.8	1.4
165 Ch of Nazarene	3	292	191	440	2.3	4.0
167 Chs of Christ	7	366	380	475	2.4	4.3
193 Episcopal	1	NR	8	9	-	.1
355 Presb Ch (USA)	4	77	38	99 *	.5	.9
356 Presb Ch Amer	2	65	40	75	.4	.7
360 Prim Bapt Chrch	1	NR	NR	NR	-	-
419 So Bapt Conv	19	4,943	1,899	6,366 *	32.7	58.0
449 Un Methodist	20	1,840	816	2,369 *	12.2	21.6
CHOCTAW	**49**	**4,616**	**1,946**	**5,763 ***	**59.1**	**100.0**
127 Ch God (Cleve)	1	119	85	149 *	1.5	2.6
167 Chs of Christ	1	93	100	127	1.3	2.2
185 Cumber Presb	1	141	NR	153	1.6	2.7
339 Pent Ch of God	1	8	NR	15	.2	.3
355 Presb Ch (USA)	8	233	114	292 *	3.0	5.1
356 Presb Ch Amer	1	38	0	38	.4	.7
360 Prim Bapt Chrch	1	NR	NR	NR	-	-
419 So Bapt Conv	22	3,226	1,139	4,040 *	41.4	70.1
449 Un Methodist	13	758	508	949 *	9.7	16.5
CLAIBORNE	**28**	**2,221**	**490**	**3,035 ***	**25.7**	**100.0**
056 Baha'i	0	1	NR	1	-	-
081 Catholic	1	NR	NR	142	1.2	4.7
093 Chr Ch (Disc)	12	786	160	982 *	8.3	32.4
167 Chs of Christ	2	25	30	45	.4	1.5
193 Episcopal	1	NR	45	74	.6	2.4
355 Presb Ch (USA)	1	150	65	187 *	1.6	6.2
413 S.D.A.	1	62	NR	74	.6	2.4
419 So Bapt Conv	5	875	83	1,093 *	9.2	36.0
449 Un Methodist	4	322	107	402 *	3.4	13.2
496 Jewish Est	1	NR	NR	35	.3	1.2
CLARKE	**84**	**9,815**	**4,582**	**12,745 ***	**71.0**	**100.0**
053 Assemb of God	5	247	286	392	2.2	3.1
081 Catholic	1	NR	NR	24	.1	.2
123 Ch God (Ander)	5	NR	100	100	.6	.8
127 Ch God (Cleve)	1	32	19	40 *	.2	.3
151 L-D Saints	1	NR	NR	79	.4	.6
165 Ch of Nazarene	1	317	85	317	1.8	2.5
167 Chs of Christ	2	64	90	93	.5	.7
193 Episcopal	1	NR	12	10	.1	.1
266 Intrstat & Asc	1	116	NR	146 *	.8	1.1
267 Muslim Est	1	NR	55	163	.9	1.3
288 Mennonite USA	1	0	20	20 *	.1	.2
349 Pent Holiness	5	268	349	337 *	1.9	2.6
356 Presb Ch Amer	1	28	18	28	.2	.2
419 So Bapt Conv	28	6,032	2,294	7,587 *	42.3	59.5
449 Un Methodist	30	2,711	1,254	3,409 *	19.0	26.7
CLAY	**42**	**7,806**	**2,784**	**10,370 ***	**47.2**	**100.0**
059 Bapt Miss Assn	1	181	50	232 *	1.1	2.2
081 Catholic	1	NR	NR	212	1.0	2.0
093 Chr Ch (Disc)	3	499	283	639 *	2.9	6.2
127 Ch God (Cleve)	2	200	122	256 *	1.2	2.5
143 CG in Cr(Menn)	1	95	NR	122 *	.6	1.2
145 Ch God Prophcy	1	29	NR	38 *	.2	.4
167 Chs of Christ	4	198	215	273	1.2	2.6
185 Cumber Presb	1	35	NR	46	.2	.4
193 Episcopal	1	NR	61	137	.6	1.3
216 Evan Presby Ch	1	121	NR	155 *	.7	1.5
339 Pent Ch of God	1	41	NR	50	.2	.5
355 Presb Ch (USA)	2	49	24	63 *	.3	.6
419 So Bapt Conv	13	4,923	1,461	6,308 *	28.7	60.8
449 Un Methodist	10	1,435	568	1,839 *	8.4	17.7
COAHOMA	**38**	**7,354**	**1,833**	**11,560 ***	**37.8**	**100.0**
053 Assemb of God	1	56	30	47	.2	.4
056 Baha'i	0	35	NR	35	.1	.3
081 Catholic	2	NR	NR	1,144	3.7	9.9
093 Chr Ch (Disc)	1	83	0	111 *	.4	1.0
097 Chr Chs&Chs Cr	1	30	NR	40 *	.1	.3
123 Ch God (Ander)	1	NR	40	40	.1	.3
127 Ch God (Cleve)	1	71	45	95 *	.3	.8
143 CG in Cr(Menn)	1	143	NR	191 *	.6	1.7
151 L-D Saints	1	NR	NR	81	.3	.7
165 Ch of Nazarene	1	43	22	54	.2	.5
167 Chs of Christ	2	160	130	195	.6	1.7
193 Episcopal	1	NR	127	401	1.3	3.5
267 Muslim Est	1	NR	55	163	.5	1.4
356 Presb Ch Amer	1	319	0	368	1.2	3.2
413 S.D.A.	1	70	NR	83	.3	.7

NR–Not Reported *Total adherents estimated from known number of communicant, confirmed, full members. - Represents a percentage less than 0.1. Percentages may not total 100 due to rounding.

Table 4: Religious Congregations by County and Group: 2000

Religious Group	Number of Churches, Synagogues, Mosques, or Temples	Number of Communicant, Confirmed, or Full Members	Number of Attendees	Total Adherents		
				Number of Adherents	% of Total Pop.	% of Total Adh.
419 So Bapt Conv	12	4,777	835	6,383 *	20.8	55.2
449 Un Methodist	9	1,567	549	2,094 *	6.8	18.1
496 Jewish Est	1	NR	NR	35	.1	.3
COPIAH	**77**	**12,373**	**5,045**	**16,085 ***	**55.9**	**100.0**
053 Assemb of God	1	9	13	13	-	.1
056 Baha'i	0	2	NR	2	-	-
081 Catholic	2	NR	NR	190	.7	1.2
093 Chr Ch (Disc)	2	38	18	48 *	.2	.3
127 Ch God (Cleve)	1	13	10	16 *	.1	.1
151 L-D Saints	2	NR	NR	397	1.4	2.5
165 Ch of Nazarene	2	47	36	63	.2	.4
167 Chs of Christ	3	54	69	94	.3	.6
193 Episcopal	2	NR	28	50	.2	.3
349 Pent Holiness	1	309	184	387 *	1.3	2.4
356 Presb Ch Amer	3	306	165	306	1.1	1.9
360 Prim Bapt Chrch	1	NR	NR	NR	-	-
413 S.D.A.	1	123	NR	146	.5	.9
419 So Bapt Conv	30	9,073	3,328	11,365 *	39.5	70.7
449 Un Methodist	26	2,399	1,194	3,008 *	10.5	18.7
COVINGTON	**55**	**8,178**	**2,837**	**10,530 ***	**54.3**	**100.0**
017 Amer Bapt Assn	2	195	NR	251 *	1.3	2.4
053 Assemb of God	1	59	70	70	.4	.7
056 Baha'i	0	2	NR	2	-	-
059 Bapt Miss Assn	3	661	303	849 *	4.4	8.1
167 Chs of Christ	3	72	83	106	.5	1.0
193 Episcopal	1	NR	18	43	.2	.4
266 Intrstat & Asc	13	1,382	NR	1,777 *	9.2	16.9
356 Presb Ch Amer	4	260	144	301	1.6	2.9
418 Southw Bapt Fel	1	NR	NR	NR	-	-
419 So Bapt Conv	18	4,703	1,794	6,047 *	31.2	57.4
449 Un Methodist	9	844	425	1,084 *	5.6	10.3
DE SOTO	**115**	**45,225**	**18,709**	**61,660 ***	**57.5**	**100.0**
017 Amer Bapt Assn	2	130	NR	168 *	.2	.3
053 Assemb of God	6	713	710	1,004	.9	1.6
055 As Ref Pres Ch	1	94	NR	94	.1	.2
056 Baha'i	0	13	NR	13	-	-
059 Bapt Miss Assn	3	684	377	881 *	.8	1.4
081 Catholic	4	NR	NR	2,863	2.7	4.6
093 Chr Ch (Disc)	1	117	68	151 *	.1	.2
097 Chr Chs&Chs Cr	2	140	NR	180 *	.2	.3
127 Ch God (Cleve)	6	1,008	446	1,297 *	1.2	2.1
145 Ch God Prophcy	1	51	NR	66 *	.1	.1
151 L-D Saints	1	NR	NR	543	.5	.9
165 Ch of Nazarene	2	160	84	184	.2	.3
167 Chs of Christ	13	2,291	2,204	2,794	2.6	4.5
193 Episcopal	2	NR	144	391	.4	.6
223 Free Will Bapt	1	65	NR	84 *	.1	.1
283 Luth—MO Synod	1	163	65	254	.2	.4
349 Pent Holiness	3	144	157	185 *	.2	.3
355 Presb Ch (USA)	6	581	337	747 *	.7	1.2
356 Presb Ch Amer	1	101	165	165	.2	.3
370 Ref Baptist Chs	1	NR	NR	NR	-	-
413 S.D.A.	1	28	NR	33	-	.1
419 So Bapt Conv	38	32,730	11,244	42,114 *	39.3	68.3
449 Un Methodist	18	5,012	1,908	6,449 *	6.0	10.5
499 Indep.Non-Char	1	1,000	800	1,000	.9	1.6
FORREST	**118**	**37,241**	**15,585**	**54,247 ***	**74.7**	**100.0**
017 Amer Bapt Assn	3	387	NR	479 *	.7	.9
053 Assemb of God	6	224	243	301	.4	.6
056 Baha'i	0	17	NR	17	-	-
059 Bapt Miss Assn	6	674	288	834 *	1.1	1.5
081 Catholic	3	NR	NR	5,110	7.0	9.4
093 Chr Ch (Disc)	1	128	37	158 *	.2	.3
123 Ch God (Ander)	2	NR	125	125	.2	.2
127 Ch God (Cleve)	4	753	382	929 *	1.3	1.7
145 Ch God Prophcy	1	29	NR	36 *	-	.1
151 L-D Saints	4	NR	NR	965	1.3	1.8
165 Ch of Nazarene	1	116	72	155	.2	.3
167 Chs of Christ	4	489	428	647	.9	1.2
193 Episcopal	2	NR	325	1,138	1.6	2.1
263 Int Foursq Gos	1	68	58	84 *	.1	.2
266 Intrstat & Asc	6	549	NR	679 *	.9	1.3
267 Muslim Est	2	NR	202	576	.8	1.1
283 Luth—MO Synod	1	256	108	281	.4	.5
355 Presb Ch (USA)	2	319	150	395 *	.5	.7
356 Presb Ch Amer	4	1,140	673	1,389	1.9	2.6
360 Prim Bapt Chrch	2	NR	NR	NR	-	-
403 Salvation Army	1	128	38	325	.4	.6
413 S.D.A.	2	217	NR	258	.4	.5
418 Southw Bapt Fel	1	NR	NR	NR	-	-
419 So Bapt Conv	40	25,630	10,354	31,676 *	43.6	58.4
435 Unitarian-Univ	1	34	NR	42 *	.1	.1
449 Un Methodist	17	6,083	2,102	7,518 *	10.4	13.9
496 Jewish Est	1	NR	NR	130	.2	.2
FRANKLIN	**46**	**4,684**	**2,062**	**5,914 ***	**70.0**	**100.0**
081 Catholic	1	NR	NR	52	.6	.9
127 Ch God (Cleve)	3	349	221	436 *	5.2	7.4
167 Chs of Christ	3	63	85	99	1.2	1.7
356 Presb Ch Amer	2	50	30	54	.6	.9
360 Prim Bapt Chrch	3	NR	NR	NR	-	-
419 So Bapt Conv	22	3,375	1,347	4,217 *	49.9	71.3
449 Un Methodist	12	847	379	1,056 *	12.5	17.9
GEORGE	**57**	**10,627**	**4,285**	**14,316 ***	**74.8**	**100.0**
053 Assemb of God	5	236	349	355	1.9	2.5
056 Baha'i	0	13	NR	13	.1	.1
059 Bapt Miss Assn	10	1,818	668	2,349 *	12.3	16.4
081 Catholic	1	NR	NR	359	1.9	2.5
127 Ch God (Cleve)	3	379	377	490 *	2.6	3.4
151 L-D Saints	1	NR	NR	169	.9	1.2
165 Ch of Nazarene	1	19	18	34	.2	.2
167 Chs of Christ	3	164	180	203	1.1	1.4
266 Intrstat & Asc	8	981	NR	1,269 *	6.6	8.9
355 Presb Ch (USA)	1	24	18	31 *	.2	.2
419 So Bapt Conv	14	5,694	2,128	7,363 *	38.5	51.4
449 Un Methodist	10	1,299	547	1,681 *	8.8	11.7
GREENE	**51**	**5,066**	**2,549**	**6,333 ***	**47.6**	**100.0**
053 Assemb of God	3	224	281	321	2.4	5.1
059 Bapt Miss Assn	7	859	500	1,056 *	7.9	16.7
081 Catholic	1	NR	NR	45	.3	.7
123 Ch God (Ander)	1	NR	10	10	.1	.2
127 Ch God (Cleve)	3	145	65	185 *	1.4	2.9
167 Chs of Christ	2	75	78	99	.7	1.6
223 Free Will Bapt	1	65	NR	80 *	.6	1.3
266 Intrstat & Asc	2	131	NR	161 *	1.2	2.5
355 Presb Ch (USA)	1	61	30	75 *	.6	1.2
356 Presb Ch Amer	1	60	0	60	.5	.9
419 So Bapt Conv	19	2,825	1,170	3,477 *	26.1	54.9
449 Un Methodist	10	621	415	764 *	5.7	12.1
GRENADA	**42**	**7,816**	**3,551**	**10,497 ***	**45.1**	**100.0**
017 Amer Bapt Assn	2	106	NR	134 *	.6	1.3
053 Assemb of God	1	11	12	18	.1	.2
056 Baha'i	0	1	NR	1	-	-
081 Catholic	1	NR	NR	326	1.4	3.1
127 Ch God (Cleve)	3	314	199	430 *	1.8	4.1
145 Ch God Prophcy	2	59	NR	74 *	.3	.7
165 Ch of Nazarene	1	139	67	139	.6	1.3
167 Chs of Christ	4	469	420	638	2.7	6.1
193 Episcopal	1	NR	98	214	.9	2.0
304 NatPrimBapt USA	1	33	NR	42 *	.2	.4
339 Pent Ch of God	1	60	NR	85	.4	.8
355 Presb Ch (USA)	1	56	28	71 *	.3	.7
356 Presb Ch Amer	1	87	46	96	.4	.9
360 Prim Bapt Chrch	1	NR	NR	NR	-	-
419 So Bapt Conv	15	5,212	2,233	6,617 *	28.4	63.0
449 Un Methodist	7	1,269	448	1,612 *	6.9	15.4

NR–Not Reported *Total adherents estimated from known number of communicant, confirmed, full members. - Represents a percentage less than 0.1. Percentages may not total 100 due to rounding.

Table 4: Religious Congregations by County and Group: 2000

Religious Group	Number of Churches, Synagogues, Mosques, or Temples	Number of Communicant, Confirmed, or Full Members	Number of Attendees	Total Adherents: Number of Adherents	Total Adherents: % of Total Pop.	Total Adherents: % of Total Adh.
HANCOCK	**42**	**5,009**	**2,716**	**19,847 ***	**46.2**	**100.0**
053 Assemb of God	2	94	135	150	.3	.8
056 Baha'i	0	9	NR	9	-	-
059 Bapt Miss Assn	4	857	360	1,062 *	2.5	5.4
076 Buddhism	1	NR	NR	NR	-	-
081 Catholic	9	NR	NR	12,476	29.0	62.9
127 Ch God (Cleve)	1	15	31	31 *	.1	.2
151 L-D Saints	1	NR	NR	601	1.4	3.0
167 Chs of Christ	1	56	60	73	.2	.4
193 Episcopal	2	NR	201	508	1.2	2.6
283 Luth—MO Synod	1	74	60	95	.2	.5
355 Presb Ch (USA)	2	392	255	486 *	1.1	2.4
419 So Bapt Conv	11	2,519	1,082	3,124 *	7.3	15.7
449 Un Methodist	7	993	532	1,232 *	2.9	6.2
HARRISON	**179**	**47,522**	**17,061**	**96,302 ***	**50.8**	**100.0**
017 Amer Bapt Assn	2	75	NR	94 *	-	.1
053 Assemb of God	6	1,252	1,637	2,864	1.5	3.0
056 Baha'i	1	88	NR	88	-	.1
059 Bapt Miss Assn	10	1,560	698	1,956 *	1.0	2.0
076 Buddhism	2	NR	NR	NR	-	-
081 Catholic	22	NR	NR	31,783	16.8	33.0
093 Chr Ch (Disc)	1	75	26	94 *	-	.1
097 Chr Chs&Chs Cr	1	50	NR	63 *	-	.1
123 Ch God (Ander)	1	NR	70	70	-	.1
127 Ch God (Cleve)	4	464	276	582 *	.3	.6
145 Ch God Prophcy	1	29	NR	37 *	-	-
151 L-D Saints	2	NR	NR	1,135	.6	1.2
165 Ch of Nazarene	3	190	154	286	.2	.3
167 Chs of Christ	7	731	619	1,028	.5	1.1
173 Comm of Christ	1	54	NR	54	-	.1
193 Episcopal	5	NR	777	1,884	1.0	2.0
207 E.L.C.A.	2	309	208	421	.2	.4
223 Free Will Bapt	1	65	NR	82 *	-	.1
246 Greek Orthodox	1	NR	NR	273	.1	.3
263 Int Foursq Gos	1	30	50	50 *	-	.1
266 Intrstat & Asc	5	665	NR	834 *	.4	.9
267 Muslim Est	1	NR	50	200	.1	.2
283 Luth—MO Synod	3	471	235	578	.3	.6
288 Mennonite USA	1	141	130	177 *	.1	.2
355 Presb Ch (USA)	5	564	349	707 *	.4	.7
356 Presb Ch Amer	4	674	443	766	.4	.8
360 Prim Bapt Chrch	1	NR	NR	NR	-	-
403 Salvation Army	2	222	81	313	.2	.3
413 S.D.A.	1	254	NR	302	.2	.3
419 So Bapt Conv	48	27,835	6,685	34,909 *	18.4	36.2
435 Unitarian-Univ	1	27	NR	34 *	-	-
449 Un Methodist	29	10,477	3,425	13,140 *	6.9	13.6
463 Vineyard	1	20	48	48 *	-	-
496 Jewish Est	1	NR	NR	250	.1	.3
499 Indep.Non-Char	2	1,200	1,100	1,200	.6	1.2
HINDS	**219**	**96,752**	**37,452**	**138,822 ***	**55.4**	**100.0**
017 Amer Bapt Assn	2	311	NR	396 *	.2	.3
053 Assemb of God	6	948	918	1,000	.4	.7
055 As Ref Pres Ch	1	84	NR	84	-	.1
056 Baha'i	2	140	NR	140	.1	.1
059 Bapt Miss Assn	3	664	104	846 *	.3	.6
076 Buddhism	1	NR	NR	NR	-	-
081 Catholic	9	NR	NR	7,417	3.0	5.3
093 Chr Ch (Disc)	4	682	280	869 *	.3	.6
097 Chr Chs&Chs Cr	1	75	NR	96 *	-	.1
123 Ch God (Ander)	2	NR	345	345	.1	.2
127 Ch God (Cleve)	2	371	157	473 *	.2	.3
145 Ch God Prophcy	2	59	NR	74 *	-	.1
151 L-D Saints	2	NR	NR	740	.3	.5
165 Ch of Nazarene	2	458	272	534	.2	.4
167 Chs of Christ	16	2,771	2,487	3,716	1.5	2.7
173 Comm of Christ	1	87	NR	87	-	.1
185 Cumber Presb	1	0	NR	0	-	-
193 Episcopal	11	NR	2,067	5,799	2.3	4.2
207 E.L.C.A.	2	361	206	517	.2	.4
216 Evan Presby Ch	1	39	NR	50 *	-	-
221 Free Methodist	1	1	0	2	-	-
246 Greek Orthodox	1	NR	NR	252	.1	.2
252 Hindu	2	NR	NR	NR	-	-
263 Int Foursq Gos	1	30	50	50 *	-	-
267 Muslim Est	2	NR	312	1,218	.5	.9
283 Luth—MO Synod	4	433	261	550	.2	.4
288 Mennonite USA	1	24	40	40 *	-	-
290 Metro Comm Ch	1	13	5	5 *	-	-
331 OCA: Ter Diocs	1	50	NR	96	-	.1
349 Pent Holiness	2	55	52	70 *	-	.1
355 Presb Ch (USA)	5	1,602	717	2,041 *	.8	1.5
356 Presb Ch Amer	13	4,846	3,413	5,652	2.3	4.1
360 Prim Bapt Chrch	1	NR	NR	NR	-	-
403 Salvation Army	1	180	72	278	.1	.2
413 S.D.A.	3	1,495	NR	1,779	.7	1.3
416 Sikh	1	NR	NR	NR	-	-
419 So Bapt Conv	67	59,165	17,710	75,370 *	30.1	54.3
435 Unitarian-Univ	1	52	NR	66 *	-	-
449 Un Methodist	35	20,837	6,930	26,545 *	10.6	19.1
467 Wesleyan	1	69	79	100	-	.1
496 Jewish Est	1	NR	NR	550	.2	.4
498 Indep.Charis.	1	250	375	375	.1	.3
499 Indep.Non-Char	2	600	600	600	.2	.4
HOLMES	**60**	**4,922**	**2,102**	**6,577 ***	**30.4**	**100.0**
056 Baha'i	0	6	NR	6	-	.1
081 Catholic	1	NR	NR	39	.2	.6
123 Ch God (Ander)	1	NR	15	15	.1	.2
145 Ch God Prophcy	1	29	NR	39 *	.2	.6
165 Ch of Nazarene	1	39	51	52	.2	.8
167 Chs of Christ	4	75	93	94	.4	1.4
193 Episcopal	1	NR	19	30	.1	.5
304 NatPrimBapt USA	1	2	NR	3 *	-	-
355 Presb Ch (USA)	1	8	9	11 *	.1	.2
356 Presb Ch Amer	7	216	166	242	1.1	3.7
419 So Bapt Conv	20	3,002	1,038	3,968 *	18.4	60.3
449 Un Methodist	21	1,545	711	2,043 *	9.5	31.1
496 Jewish Est	1	NR	NR	35	.2	.5
HUMPHREYS	**22**	**2,967**	**1,133**	**4,011 ***	**35.8**	**100.0**
056 Baha'i	0	7	NR	7	.1	.2
059 Bapt Miss Assn	1	117	50	155 *	1.4	3.9
081 Catholic	1	NR	NR	85	.8	2.1
123 Ch God (Ander)	1	NR	20	20	.2	.5
127 Ch God (Cleve)	1	16	9	21 *	.2	.5
167 Chs of Christ	2	57	58	73	.7	1.8
193 Episcopal	1	NR	12	25	.2	.6
356 Presb Ch Amer	1	236	120	273	2.4	6.8
419 So Bapt Conv	8	2,025	605	2,678 *	23.9	66.8
449 Un Methodist	6	509	259	674 *	6.0	16.8
ISSAQUENA	**3**	**160**	**60**	**202 ***	**8.9**	**100.0**
145 Ch God Prophcy	1	29	NR	37 *	1.6	18.3
419 So Bapt Conv	1	120	55	151 *	6.6	74.8
449 Un Methodist	1	11	5	14 *	.6	6.9
ITAWAMBA	**76**	**10,358**	**4,633**	**12,874 ***	**56.5**	**100.0**
059 Bapt Miss Assn	14	3,553	1,620	4,386 *	19.3	34.1
081 Catholic	1	NR	NR	70	.3	.5
097 Chr Chs&Chs Cr	1	108	NR	133 *	.6	1.0
127 Ch God (Cleve)	2	96	34	119 *	.5	.9
145 Ch God Prophcy	6	176	NR	216 *	.9	1.7
167 Chs of Christ	10	750	788	943	4.1	7.3
223 Free Will Bapt	3	196	NR	241 *	1.1	1.9
360 Prim Bapt Chrch	2	NR	NR	NR	-	-
419 So Bapt Conv	17	3,199	1,246	3,950 *	17.3	30.7
449 Un Methodist	20	2,280	945	2,816 *	12.4	21.9
JACKSON	**158**	**42,466**	**15,882**	**68,719 ***	**52.3**	**100.0**
017 Amer Bapt Assn	4	246	NR	313 *	.2	.5
053 Assemb of God	20	2,357	2,622	3,069	2.3	4.5
055 As Ref Pres Ch	1	48	NR	60	-	.1

NR–Not Reported *Total adherents estimated from known number of communicant, confirmed, full members. - Represents a percentage less than 0.1. Percentages may not total 100 due to rounding.

Table 4: Religious Congregations by County and Group: 2000

Religious Group	Number of Churches, Synagogues, Mosques, or Temples	Number of Communicant, Confirmed, or Full Members	Number of Attendees	Total Adherents		
				Number of Adherents	% of Total Pop.	% of Total Adh.
056 Baha'i	0	10	NR	10	-	-
059 Bapt Miss Assn	7	843	346	1,071 *	.8	1.6
076 Buddhism	1	NR	NR	NR	-	-
081 Catholic	12	NR	NR	12,930	9.8	18.8
093 Chr Ch (Disc)	1	154	65	196 *	.1	.3
123 Ch God (Ander)	2	NR	50	50	-	.1
127 Ch God (Cleve)	3	219	88	279 *	.2	.4
145 Ch God Prophcy	1	29	NR	37 *	-	.1
151 L-D Saints	2	NR	NR	885	.7	1.3
165 Ch of Nazarene	2	203	139	209	.2	.3
167 Chs of Christ	10	890	811	1,135	.9	1.7
173 Comm of Christ	4	1,012	NR	1,012	.8	1.5
193 Episcopal	3	NR	459	975	.7	1.4
207 E.L.C.A.	1	566	281	769	.6	1.1
266 Intrstat & Asc	1	40	NR	51 *	-	.1
283 Luth—MO Synod	1	179	117	277	.2	.4
349 Pent Holiness	3	205	178	261 *	.2	.4
355 Presb Ch (USA)	3	924	474	1,175 *	.9	1.7
356 Presb Ch Amer	1	82	40	91	.1	.1
360 Prim Bapt Chrch	2	NR	NR	NR	-	-
403 Salvation Army	1	79	47	147	.1	.2
413 S.D.A.	1	46	NR	55	-	.1
419 So Bapt Conv	42	26,425	6,849	33,589 *	25.6	48.9
449 Un Methodist	28	7,609	2,916	9,673 *	7.4	14.1
498 Indep.Charis.	1	300	400	400	.3	.6
JASPER	**70**	**7,609**	**3,717**	**9,741 ***	**53.7**	**100.0**
053 Assemb of God	2	66	65	84	.5	.9
059 Bapt Miss Assn	6	1,211	490	1,539 *	8.5	15.8
081 Catholic	1	NR	NR	44	.2	.5
123 Ch God (Ander)	1	NR	40	40	.2	.4
167 Chs of Christ	1	20	30	30	.2	.3
355 Presb Ch (USA)	4	126	77	160 *	.9	1.6
356 Presb Ch Amer	2	111	85	122	.7	1.3
360 Prim Bapt Chrch	3	NR	NR	NR	-	-
419 So Bapt Conv	22	3,648	1,623	4,636 *	25.5	47.6
449 Un Methodist	28	2,427	1,307	3,086 *	17.0	31.7
JEFFERSON	**25**	**1,818**	**672**	**2,405 ***	**24.7**	**100.0**
056 Baha'i	0	1	NR	1	-	-
081 Catholic	1	NR	NR	100	1.0	4.2
093 Chr Ch (Disc)	2	269	0	343 *	3.5	14.3
355 Presb Ch (USA)	1	8	6	10 *	.1	.4
356 Presb Ch Amer	1	30	20	30	.3	1.2
360 Prim Bapt Chrch	1	NR	NR	NR	-	-
413 S.D.A.	1	79	NR	94	1.0	3.9
419 So Bapt Conv	7	461	232	588 *	6.0	24.4
449 Un Methodist	11	970	414	1,239 *	12.7	51.5
JEFFERSON DAVIS	**32**	**4,763**	**1,597**	**6,575 ***	**47.1**	**100.0**
017 Amer Bapt Assn	1	100	NR	127 *	.9	1.9
056 Baha'i	0	37	NR	37	.3	.6
059 Bapt Miss Assn	1	199	50	253 *	1.8	3.8
081 Catholic	3	NR	NR	552	4.0	8.4
165 Ch of Nazarene	1	41	14	43	.3	.7
167 Chs of Christ	1	35	38	45	.3	.7
266 Intrstat & Asc	2	336	NR	427 *	3.1	6.5
356 Presb Ch Amer	2	173	100	203	1.5	3.1
419 So Bapt Conv	14	3,346	1,187	4,257 *	30.5	64.7
449 Un Methodist	7	496	208	631 *	4.5	9.6
JONES	**133**	**32,690**	**12,041**	**42,507 ***	**65.4**	**100.0**
053 Assemb of God	8	428	497	793	1.2	1.9
056 Baha'i	0	2	NR	2	-	-
059 Bapt Miss Assn	22	4,388	1,914	5,466 *	8.4	12.9
081 Catholic	1	NR	NR	800	1.2	1.9
123 Ch God (Ander)	5	NR	221	221	.3	.5
127 Ch God (Cleve)	2	347	125	432 *	.7	1.0
151 L-D Saints	1	NR	NR	225	.3	.5
165 Ch of Nazarene	2	131	86	131	.2	.3
167 Chs of Christ	3	297	255	427	.7	1.0
193 Episcopal	1	NR	90	222	.3	.5

Religious Group	Number of Churches, Synagogues, Mosques, or Temples	Number of Communicant, Confirmed, or Full Members	Number of Attendees	Total Adherents		
				Number of Adherents	% of Total Pop.	% of Total Adh.
216 Evan Presby Ch	1	248	NR	309 *	.5	.7
223 Free Will Bapt	1	65	NR	81 *	.1	.2
266 Intrstat & Asc	2	129	NR	161 *	.2	.4
355 Presb Ch (USA)	2	331	134	412 *	.6	1.0
356 Presb Ch Amer	2	102	100	136	.2	.3
360 Prim Bapt Chrch	1	NR	NR	NR	-	-
370 Ref Baptist Chs	1	NR	NR	NR	-	-
403 Salvation Army	1	144	47	227	.3	.5
413 S.D.A.	3	171	NR	204	.3	.5
418 Southw Bapt Fel	1	NR	NR	NR	-	-
419 So Bapt Conv	49	22,788	7,314	28,374 *	43.7	66.8
435 Unitarian-Univ	1	36	NR	45 *	.1	.1
449 Un Methodist	23	3,083	1,258	3,839 *	5.9	9.0
KEMPER	**50**	**4,240**	**2,374**	**5,276 ***	**50.5**	**100.0**
053 Assemb of God	2	109	110	147	1.4	2.8
123 Ch God (Ander)	1	NR	13	13	.1	.2
167 Chs of Christ	1	25	33	34	.3	.6
223 Free Will Bapt	1	65	NR	81 *	.8	1.5
304 NatPrimBapt USA	1	134	NR	166 *	1.6	3.1
356 Presb Ch Amer	3	127	95	149	1.4	2.8
419 So Bapt Conv	16	1,904	732	2,360 *	22.6	44.7
449 Un Methodist	25	1,876	1,391	2,326 *	22.3	44.1
LAFAYETTE	**68**	**12,736**	**5,960**	**18,301 ***	**47.2**	**100.0**
017 Amer Bapt Assn	1	178	NR	210 *	.5	1.1
053 Assemb of God	1	49	64	64	.2	.3
056 Baha'i	0	5	NR	5	-	-
059 Bapt Miss Assn	1	55	25	65 *	.2	.4
081 Catholic	1	NR	NR	1,900	4.9	10.4
084 Calvary Chapel	1	NR	NR	NR	-	-
151 L-D Saints	1	NR	NR	253	.7	1.4
165 Ch of Nazarene	1	43	55	65	.2	.4
167 Chs of Christ	7	478	536	768	2.0	4.2
193 Episcopal	1	NR	295	769	2.0	4.2
223 Free Will Bapt	2	130	NR	154 *	.4	.8
267 Muslim Est	1	NR	55	163	.4	.9
283 Luth—MO Synod	1	49	35	61	.2	.3
355 Presb Ch (USA)	2	594	265	700 *	1.8	3.8
356 Presb Ch Amer	2	178	190	190	.5	1.0
360 Prim Bapt Chrch	1	NR	NR	NR	-	-
419 So Bapt Conv	25	8,220	3,204	9,686 *	25.0	52.9
435 Unitarian-Univ	1	35	NR	41 *	.1	.2
449 Un Methodist	18	2,722	1,236	3,207 *	8.3	17.5
LAMAR	**55**	**12,303**	**4,799**	**17,156 ***	**43.9**	**100.0**
017 Amer Bapt Assn	1	50	NR	64 *	.2	.4
059 Bapt Miss Assn	6	1,340	632	1,714 *	4.4	10.0
081 Catholic	1	NR	NR	902	2.3	5.3
123 Ch God (Ander)	1	NR	10	10	-	.1
127 Ch God (Cleve)	3	197	109	251 *	.6	1.5
151 L-D Saints	1	NR	NR	381	1.0	2.2
167 Chs of Christ	1	46	40	52	.1	.3
266 Intrstat & Asc	8	814	NR	1,038 *	2.7	6.1
267 Muslim Est	1	NR	40	175	.4	1.0
360 Prim Bapt Chrch	2	NR	NR	NR	-	-
419 So Bapt Conv	19	8,340	3,373	10,635 *	27.2	62.0
449 Un Methodist	11	1,516	595	1,934 *	5.0	11.3
LAUDERDALE	**149**	**37,098**	**14,063**	**50,921 ***	**65.1**	**100.0**
053 Assemb of God	7	789	598	801	1.0	1.6
056 Baha'i	0	41	NR	41	.1	.1
059 Bapt Miss Assn	3	241	99	303 *	.4	.6
081 Catholic	2	NR	NR	1,872	2.4	3.7
093 Chr Ch (Disc)	1	428	0	539 *	.7	1.1
123 Ch God (Ander)	9	NR	840	840	1.1	1.6
127 Ch God (Cleve)	1	350	204	441 *	.6	.9
145 Ch God Prophcy	2	59	NR	74 *	.1	.1
151 L-D Saints	1	NR	NR	330	.4	.6
165 Ch of Nazarene	2	690	402	961	1.2	1.9
167 Chs of Christ	6	326	356	477	.6	.9
171 Ch God-Gen Con	2	81	76	103 *	.1	.2

NR–Not Reported *Total adherents estimated from known number of communicant, confirmed, full members. - Represents a percentage less than 0.1. Percentages may not total 100 due to rounding.

Table 4: Religious Congregations by County and Group: 2000

Religious Group	Number of Churches, Synagogues, Mosques, or Temples	Number of Communicant, Confirmed, or Full Members	Number of Attendees	Total Adherents		
				Number of Adherents	% of Total Pop.	% of Total Adh.
193 Episcopal	2	NR	371	1,116	1.4	2.2
216 Evan Presby Ch	1	389	NR	490 *	.6	1.0
263 Int Foursq Gos	1	186	171	234 *	.3	.5
273 LandmrkBapt,I&U	3	400	NR	504 *	.6	1.0
283 Luth—MO Synod	1	144	107	185	.2	.4
288 Mennonite USA	1	34	40	43 *	.1	.1
304 NatPrimBapt USA	2	86	NR	108 *	.1	.2
349 Pent Holiness	3	203	152	256 *	.3	.5
355 Presb Ch (USA)	4	447	191	562 *	.7	1.1
356 Presb Ch Amer	5	199	209	253	.3	.5
360 Prim Bapt Chrch	1	NR	NR	NR	-	-
403 Salvation Army	1	137	37	255	.3	.5
413 S.D.A.	2	471	NR	561	.7	1.1
419 So Bapt Conv	45	23,877	7,496	30,068 *	38.5	59.0
449 Un Methodist	40	7,520	2,714	9,469 *	12.1	18.6
496 Jewish Est	1	NR	NR	35	-	.1
LAWRENCE	**34**	**6,188**	**2,984**	**8,075 ***	**60.9**	**100.0**
053 Assemb of God	1	12	17	18	.1	.2
056 Baha'i	0	3	NR	3	-	-
059 Bapt Miss Assn	1	0	35	35 *	.3	.4
081 Catholic	1	NR	NR	25	.2	.3
123 Ch God (Ander)	1	NR	50	50	.4	.6
127 Ch God (Cleve)	1	22	18	28 *	.2	.3
145 Ch God Prophcy	1	29	NR	37 *	.3	.5
167 Chs of Christ	2	52	55	63	.5	.8
267 Muslim Est	1	NR	55	163	1.2	2.0
419 So Bapt Conv	22	5,633	2,559	7,102 *	53.6	88.0
449 Un Methodist	3	437	195	551 *	4.2	6.8
LEAKE	**75**	**8,169**	**3,997**	**10,838 ***	**51.8**	**100.0**
053 Assemb of God	2	36	36	40	.2	.4
081 Catholic	1	NR	NR	334	1.6	3.1
093 Chr Ch (Disc)	1	32	18	40 *	.2	.4
097 Chr Chs&Chs Cr	1	40	NR	50 *	.2	.5
123 Ch God (Ander)	2	NR	163	163	.8	1.5
127 Ch God (Cleve)	2	284	258	358 *	1.7	3.3
167 Chs of Christ	1	18	20	22	.1	.2
185 Cumber Presb	2	83	NR	197	.9	1.8
304 NatPrimBapt USA	1	20	NR	25 *	.1	.2
356 Presb Ch Amer	3	213	145	220	1.1	2.0
360 Prim Bapt Chrch	5	NR	NR	NR	-	-
419 So Bapt Conv	39	6,438	2,767	8,122 *	38.8	74.9
449 Un Methodist	15	1,005	590	1,267 *	6.1	11.7
LEE	**148**	**37,156**	**15,881**	**50,149 ***	**66.2**	**100.0**
017 Amer Bapt Assn	1	65	NR	83 *	.1	.2
053 Assemb of God	6	255	311	383	.5	.8
055 As Ref Pres Ch	2	43	NR	43	.1	.1
056 Baha'i	0	1	NR	1	-	-
059 Bapt Miss Assn	9	1,177	507	1,500 *	2.0	3.0
081 Catholic	2	NR	NR	1,380	1.8	2.8
093 Chr Ch (Disc)	1	313	80	399 *	.5	.8
097 Chr Chs&Chs Cr	6	638	NR	813 *	1.1	1.6
123 Ch God (Ander)	1	NR	44	44	.1	.1
127 Ch God (Cleve)	2	584	297	744 *	1.0	1.5
145 Ch God Prophcy	5	146	NR	185 *	.2	.4
151 L-D Saints	1	NR	NR	403	.5	.8
165 Ch of Nazarene	1	73	36	74	.1	.1
167 Chs of Christ	10	1,707	1,600	2,182	2.9	4.4
193 Episcopal	1	NR	200	414	.5	.8
207 E.L.C.A.	1	81	41	114	.2	.2
223 Free Will Bapt	3	196	NR	249 *	.3	.5
283 Luth—MO Synod	1	112	95	131	.2	.3
355 Presb Ch (USA)	8	705	334	897 *	1.2	1.8
356 Presb Ch Amer	2	325	250	418	.6	.8
360 Prim Bapt Chrch	2	NR	NR	NR	-	-
403 Salvation Army	1	98	28	303	.4	.6
413 S.D.A.	2	83	NR	99	.1	.2
419 So Bapt Conv	49	23,781	8,628	30,321 *	40.0	60.5
449 Un Methodist	28	6,733	3,095	8,583 *	11.3	17.1
463 Vineyard	1	40	35	51 *	.1	.1
496 Jewish Est	1	NR	NR	35	-	.1
498 Indep.Charis.	1	0	300	300	.4	.6
LEFLORE	**50**	**11,056**	**3,583**	**15,869 ***	**41.8**	**100.0**
053 Assemb of God	1	61	40	54	.1	.3
056 Baha'i	0	130	NR	130	.3	.8
081 Catholic	2	NR	NR	772	2.0	4.9
093 Chr Ch (Disc)	3	388	175	502 *	1.3	3.2
127 Ch God (Cleve)	2	158	103	204 *	.5	1.3
145 Ch God Prophcy	1	29	NR	38 *	.1	.2
151 L-D Saints	1	NR	NR	254	.7	1.6
167 Chs of Christ	3	380	275	485	1.3	3.1
193 Episcopal	1	NR	146	525	1.4	3.3
223 Free Will Bapt	1	65	NR	84 *	.2	.5
283 Luth—MO Synod	1	21	12	22	.1	.1
339 Pent Ch of God	1	60	NR	235	.6	1.5
355 Presb Ch (USA)	1	397	200	514 *	1.4	3.2
356 Presb Ch Amer	2	282	197	349	.9	2.2
360 Prim Bapt Chrch	1	NR	NR	NR	-	-
403 Salvation Army	1	171	27	171	.5	1.1
413 S.D.A.	2	415	NR	494	1.3	3.1
419 So Bapt Conv	15	6,262	1,635	8,105 *	21.4	51.1
449 Un Methodist	10	2,237	773	2,896 *	7.6	18.2
496 Jewish Est	1	NR	NR	35	.1	.2
LINCOLN	**78**	**19,171**	**7,036**	**25,296 ***	**76.3**	**100.0**
053 Assemb of God	2	126	143	200	.6	.8
056 Baha'i	0	4	NR	4	-	-
081 Catholic	1	NR	NR	538	1.6	2.1
123 Ch God (Ander)	1	NR	35	35	.1	.1
127 Ch God (Cleve)	1	55	49	69 *	.2	.3
151 L-D Saints	1	NR	NR	249	.8	1.0
165 Ch of Nazarene	1	87	61	112	.3	.4
167 Chs of Christ	13	1,213	1,002	1,694	5.1	6.7
193 Episcopal	1	NR	88	212	.6	.8
355 Presb Ch (USA)	1	30	25	38 *	.1	.2
356 Presb Ch Amer	1	297	200	368	1.1	1.5
360 Prim Bapt Chrch	2	NR	NR	NR	-	-
413 S.D.A.	1	48	NR	57	.2	.2
419 So Bapt Conv	38	15,117	4,629	18,968 *	57.2	75.0
449 Un Methodist	14	2,194	804	2,752 *	8.3	10.9
LOWNDES	**89**	**23,350**	**9,909**	**32,501 ***	**52.8**	**100.0**
053 Assemb of God	5	744	860	1,209	2.0	3.7
056 Baha'i	0	1	NR	1	-	-
059 Bapt Miss Assn	2	401	155	516 *	.8	1.6
081 Catholic	1	NR	NR	967	1.6	3.0
097 Chr Chs&Chs Cr	1	200	NR	257 *	.4	.8
127 Ch God (Cleve)	3	249	147	320 *	.5	1.0
145 Ch God Prophcy	1	29	NR	38 *	.1	.1
151 L-D Saints	1	NR	NR	332	.5	1.0
165 Ch of Nazarene	1	151	95	157	.3	.5
167 Chs of Christ	10	1,176	1,115	1,560	2.5	4.8
185 Cumber Presb	4	416	NR	477 *	.8	1.5
193 Episcopal	2	NR	190	640	1.0	2.0
207 E.L.C.A.	1	81	60	87	.1	.3
216 Evan Presby Ch	1	42	NR	54 *	.1	.2
223 Free Will Bapt	2	130	NR	168 *	.3	.5
283 Luth—MO Synod	1	89	62	117	.2	.4
297 Mennonite;Other	1	54	NR	70 *	.1	.2
339 Pent Ch of God	2	98	NR	250	.4	.8
355 Presb Ch (USA)	2	168	109	217 *	.4	.7
356 Presb Ch Amer	1	251	185	337	.5	1.0
370 Ref Baptist Chs	1	NR	NR	NR	-	-
403 Salvation Army	1	100	39	283	.5	.9
413 S.D.A.	1	49	NR	58	.1	.2
419 So Bapt Conv	26	15,031	5,510	19,346 *	31.4	59.5
449 Un Methodist	16	3,860	1,361	4,967 *	8.1	15.3
469 WELS	1	30	21	38	.1	.1
496 Jewish Est	1	NR	NR	35	.1	.1
MADISON	**68**	**16,773**	**7,693**	**28,239 ***	**37.8**	**100.0**
017 Amer Bapt Assn	1	115	NR	148 *	.2	.5

NR–Not Reported *Total adherents estimated from known number of communicant, confirmed, full members. - Represents a percentage less than 0.1. Percentages may not total 100 due to rounding.

Table 4: Religious Congregations by County and Group: 2000

Religious Group	Number of Churches, Synagogues, Mosques, or Temples	Number of Communicant, Confirmed, or Full Members	Number of Attendees	Total Adherents		
				Number of Adherents	% of Total Pop.	% of Total Adh.
034 Ant Orth of NA	1	84	NR	168	.2	.6
053 Assemb of God	2	360	450	450	.6	1.6
056 Baha'i	0	52	NR	52	.1	.2
081 Catholic	5	NR	NR	4,425	5.9	15.7
093 Chr Ch (Disc)	2	166	103	214 *	.3	.8
123 Ch God (Ander)	2	NR	139	139	.2	.5
127 Ch God (Cleve)	1	461	69	595 *	.8	2.1
145 Ch God Prophcy	1	29	NR	38 *	.1	.1
151 L-D Saints	2	NR	NR	437	.6	1.5
167 Chs of Christ	5	432	390	568	.8	2.0
193 Episcopal	2	NR	376	876	1.2	3.1
223 Free Will Bapt	1	65	NR	84 *	.1	.3
252 Hindu	1	NR	NR	NR	-	-
267 Muslim Est	1	NR	156	609	.8	2.2
355 Presb Ch (USA)	2	466	300	602 *	.8	2.1
356 Presb Ch Amer	5	1,005	819	1,362	1.8	4.8
413 S.D.A.	1	40	NR	48	.1	.2
419 So Bapt Conv	18	8,810	2,932	11,373 *	15.2	40.3
443 Un C of Christ	1	37	16	48 *	.1	.2
449 Un Methodist	14	4,651	1,943	6,003 *	8.0	21.3
MARION	**65**	**13,821**	**4,920**	**18,037 ***	**70.5**	**100.0**
053 Assemb of God	1	62	75	97	.4	.5
056 Baha'i	0	1	NR	1	-	-
059 Bapt Miss Assn	3	609	313	766 *	3.0	4.2
081 Catholic	1	NR	NR	200	.8	1.1
127 Ch God (Cleve)	10	935	575	1,177 *	4.6	6.5
151 L-D Saints	1	NR	NR	380	1.5	2.1
165 Ch of Nazarene	1	37	30	37	.1	.2
167 Chs of Christ	2	75	60	98	.4	.5
193 Episcopal	1	NR	48	64	.3	.4
266 Intrstat & Asc	5	683	NR	860 *	3.4	4.8
297 Mennonite;Other	1	43	NR	54 *	.2	.3
356 Presb Ch Amer	1	77	50	82	.3	.5
413 S.D.A.	2	56	NR	67	.3	.4
419 So Bapt Conv	22	9,379	2,972	11,807 *	46.1	65.5
449 Un Methodist	14	1,864	797	2,347 *	9.2	13.0
MARSHALL	**54**	**7,701**	**2,918**	**10,100 ***	**28.9**	**100.0**
019 Amer Bapt USA	1	0	0	0 *	-	-
053 Assemb of God	2	94	117	132	.4	1.3
056 Baha'i	0	1	NR	1	-	-
081 Catholic	1	NR	NR	275	.8	2.7
167 Chs of Christ	7	518	385	661	1.9	6.5
193 Episcopal	1	NR	47	123	.4	1.2
283 Luth—MO Synod	1	16	18	21	.1	.2
355 Presb Ch (USA)	3	152	75	192 *	.5	1.9
360 Prim Bapt Chrch	1	NR	NR	NR	-	-
413 S.D.A.	1	81	NR	96	.3	1.0
419 So Bapt Conv	20	5,307	1,719	6,672 *	19.1	66.1
449 Un Methodist	16	1,532	557	1,927 *	5.5	19.1
MONROE	**114**	**16,913**	**9,335**	**23,662 ***	**62.2**	**100.0**
017 Amer Bapt Assn	3	597	NR	751 *	2.0	3.2
053 Assemb of God	4	260	283	330	.9	1.4
056 Baha'i	0	3	NR	3	-	-
059 Bapt Miss Assn	2	189	105	238 *	.6	1.0
081 Catholic	2	NR	NR	321	.8	1.4
089 Chr & Miss Al	1	27	NR	32	.1	.1
097 Chr Chs&Chs Cr	3	446	NR	562 *	1.5	2.4
127 Ch God (Cleve)	4	251	2,136	2,257 *	5.9	9.5
145 Ch God Prophcy	4	117	NR	148 *	.4	.6
167 Chs of Christ	13	1,164	1,147	1,464	3.9	6.2
193 Episcopal	1	NR	39	93	.2	.4
223 Free Will Bapt	7	456	NR	575 *	1.5	2.4
297 Mennonite;Other	1	74	NR	93 *	.2	.4
355 Presb Ch (USA)	3	188	93	237 *	.6	1.0
356 Presb Ch Amer	1	62	70	88	.2	.4
360 Prim Bapt Chrch	5	NR	NR	NR	-	-
413 S.D.A.	1	67	NR	80	.2	.3
419 So Bapt Conv	34	9,468	3,847	11,926 *	31.4	50.4
449 Un Methodist	25	3,544	1,615	4,464 *	11.7	18.9
MONTGOMERY	**40**	**6,140**	**2,620**	**7,744 ***	**63.5**	**100.0**
081 Catholic	1	NR	NR	39	.3	.5
127 Ch God (Cleve)	3	165	125	217 *	1.8	2.8
167 Chs of Christ	3	225	243	276	2.3	3.6
193 Episcopal	1	NR	3	8	.1	.1
304 NatPrimBapt USA	1	20	NR	25 *	.2	.3
356 Presb Ch Amer	1	140	50	145	1.2	1.9
360 Prim Bapt Chrch	2	NR	NR	NR	-	-
419 So Bapt Conv	17	4,333	1,604	5,453 *	44.7	70.4
449 Un Methodist	11	1,257	595	1,581 *	13.0	20.4
NESHOBA	**101**	**12,997**	**5,865**	**17,947 ***	**62.6**	**100.0**
053 Assemb of God	3	97	121	162	.6	.9
056 Baha'i	0	10	NR	10	-	.1
059 Bapt Miss Assn	1	70	40	89 *	.3	.5
081 Catholic	3	NR	NR	1,011	3.5	5.6
123 Ch God (Ander)	8	NR	306	306	1.1	1.7
127 Ch God (Cleve)	5	449	228	572 *	2.0	3.2
145 Ch God Prophcy	1	29	NR	37 *	.1	.2
165 Ch of Nazarene	1	25	17	25	.1	.1
167 Chs of Christ	3	199	150	251	.9	1.4
185 Cumber Presb	2	58	NR	112	.4	.6
193 Episcopal	1	NR	13	18	.1	.1
273 LandmrkBapt,I&U	1	23	NR	29 *	.1	.2
288 Mennonite USA	2	89	67	114 *	.4	.6
339 Pent Ch of God	1	22	NR	47	.2	.3
355 Presb Ch (USA)	1	21	10	27 *	.1	.2
356 Presb Ch Amer	2	159	115	163	.6	.9
419 So Bapt Conv	42	9,032	3,630	11,515 *	40.1	64.2
449 Un Methodist	24	2,714	1,168	3,459 *	12.1	19.3
NEWTON	**75**	**10,674**	**3,622**	**13,952 ***	**63.9**	**100.0**
056 Baha'i	0	2	NR	2	-	-
081 Catholic	2	NR	NR	239	1.1	1.7
097 Chr Chs&Chs Cr	2	185	NR	232 *	1.1	1.7
127 Ch God (Cleve)	2	118	70	148 *	.7	1.1
151 L-D Saints	1	NR	NR	197	.9	1.4
167 Chs of Christ	3	100	114	206	.9	1.5
185 Cumber Presb	1	51	NR	91	.4	.7
193 Episcopal	1	NR	6	12	.1	.1
273 LandmrkBapt,I&U	9	1,566	NR	1,967 *	9.0	14.1
304 NatPrimBapt USA	1	30	NR	38 *	.2	.3
355 Presb Ch (USA)	1	18	9	23 *	.1	.2
356 Presb Ch Amer	2	77	55	97	.4	.7
360 Prim Bapt Chrch	5	NR	NR	NR	-	-
413 S.D.A.	2	130	NR	155	.7	1.1
419 So Bapt Conv	31	6,795	2,730	8,534 *	39.1	61.2
449 Un Methodist	12	1,602	638	2,011 *	9.2	14.4
NOXUBEE	**47**	**3,605**	**1,664**	**4,845 ***	**38.6**	**100.0**
056 Baha'i	0	4	NR	4	-	.1
081 Catholic	1	NR	NR	85	.7	1.8
123 Ch God (Ander)	2	NR	44	44	.4	.9
143 CG in Cr(Menn)	2	386	NR	504 *	4.0	10.4
167 Chs of Christ	2	63	65	80	.6	1.7
185 Cumber Presb	2	27	NR	46	.4	.9
193 Episcopal	2	NR	8	18	.1	.4
288 Mennonite USA	1	64	67	84 *	.7	1.7
297 Mennonite;Other	2	136	NR	178 *	1.4	3.7
356 Presb Ch Amer	2	114	77	132	1.1	2.7
419 So Bapt Conv	12	1,421	662	1,856 *	14.8	38.3
449 Un Methodist	19	1,390	741	1,814 *	14.5	37.4
OKTIBBEHA	**63**	**15,304**	**7,103**	**21,340 ***	**49.7**	**100.0**
017 Amer Bapt Assn	1	30	NR	36 *	.1	.2
053 Assemb of God	1	37	40	55	.1	.3
056 Baha'i	0	9	NR	9	-	-
081 Catholic	1	NR	NR	2,222	5.2	10.4
093 Chr Ch (Disc)	1	2	0	2 *	-	-
123 Ch God (Ander)	1	NR	5	5	-	-
127 Ch God (Cleve)	2	280	235	335 *	.8	1.6
151 L-D Saints	1	NR	NR	345	.8	1.6

NR–Not Reported *Total adherents estimated from known number of communicant, confirmed, full members. - Represents a percentage less than 0.1. Percentages may not total 100 due to rounding.

Table 4: Religious Congregations by County and Group: 2000

Religious Group	Number of Churches, Synagogues, Mosques, or Temples	Number of Communicant, Confirmed, or Full Members	Number of Attendees	Total Adherents: Number of Adherents	Total Adherents: % of Total Pop.	Total Adherents: % of Total Adh.
165 Ch of Nazarene	1	28	25	29	.1	.1
167 Chs of Christ	5	516	498	721	1.7	3.4
193 Episcopal	1	NR	135	284	.7	1.3
267 Muslim Est	1	NR	55	163	.4	.8
283 Luth—MO Synod	1	65	35	76	.2	.4
339 Pent Ch of God	1	11	NR	25	.1	.1
355 Presb Ch (USA)	4	929	455	1,108 *	2.6	5.2
356 Presb Ch Amer	1	241	200	241	.6	1.1
360 Prim Bapt Chrch	1	NR	NR	NR	-	-
419 So Bapt Conv	20	8,979	3,665	10,704 *	24.9	50.2
449 Un Methodist	19	4,177	1,755	4,980 *	11.6	23.3
PANOLA	**74**	**10,233**	**4,831**	**13,691 ***	**39.9**	**100.0**
017 Amer Bapt Assn	1	18	NR	23 *	.1	.2
053 Assemb of God	1	19	25	31	.1	.2
056 Baha'i	0	3	NR	3	-	-
081 Catholic	2	NR	NR	230	.7	1.7
123 Ch God (Ander)	2	NR	200	200	.6	1.5
127 Ch God (Cleve)	5	255	122	328 *	1.0	2.4
165 Ch of Nazarene	1	22	9	24	.1	.2
167 Chs of Christ	9	637	656	808	2.4	5.9
193 Episcopal	2	NR	43	115	.3	.8
355 Presb Ch (USA)	3	416	206	536 *	1.6	3.9
356 Presb Ch Amer	1	54	32	54	.2	.4
419 So Bapt Conv	27	6,377	2,495	8,209 *	24.0	60.0
449 Un Methodist	20	2,432	1,043	3,130 *	9.1	22.9
PEARL RIVER	**84**	**22,690**	**7,137**	**31,522 ***	**64.8**	**100.0**
017 Amer Bapt Assn	1	94	NR	118 *	.2	.4
053 Assemb of God	2	214	328	405	.8	1.3
056 Baha'i	0	13	NR	13	-	-
059 Bapt Miss Assn	16	3,306	1,111	4,162 *	8.6	13.2
081 Catholic	2	NR	NR	2,274	4.7	7.2
127 Ch God (Cleve)	5	577	257	726 *	1.5	2.3
145 Ch God Prophcy	1	29	NR	37 *	.1	.1
151 L-D Saints	1	NR	NR	362	.7	1.1
167 Chs of Christ	2	124	155	167	.3	.5
193 Episcopal	1	NR	91	173	.4	.5
252 Hindu	1	NR	NR	NR	-	-
266 Intrstat & Asc	7	744	NR	937 *	1.9	3.0
283 Luth—MO Synod	1	158	75	213	.4	.7
349 Pent Holiness	1	12	12	15 *	-	-
355 Presb Ch (USA)	1	7	10	10 *	-	-
356 Presb Ch Amer	1	75	55	77	.2	.2
419 So Bapt Conv	34	15,619	4,473	19,669 *	40.5	62.4
449 Un Methodist	7	1,718	570	2,164 *	4.5	6.9
PERRY	**43**	**5,637**	**2,498**	**7,377 ***	**60.8**	**100.0**
053 Assemb of God	1	64	95	95	.8	1.3
059 Bapt Miss Assn	5	540	278	692 *	5.7	9.4
123 Ch God (Ander)	1	NR	70	70	.6	.9
127 Ch God (Cleve)	3	162	179	281 *	2.3	3.8
145 Ch God Prophcy	1	29	NR	37 *	.3	.5
167 Chs of Christ	1	25	35	35	.3	.5
223 Free Will Bapt	6	391	NR	501 *	4.1	6.8
356 Presb Ch Amer	1	12	12	14	.1	.2
419 So Bapt Conv	19	3,903	1,510	4,998 *	41.2	67.8
449 Un Methodist	5	511	319	654 *	5.4	8.9
PIKE	**63**	**19,158**	**5,579**	**25,589 ***	**65.7**	**100.0**
053 Assemb of God	2	179	221	226	.6	.9
056 Baha'i	0	5	NR	5	-	-
081 Catholic	3	NR	NR	1,085	2.8	4.2
093 Chr Ch (Disc)	1	99	45	126 *	.3	.5
127 Ch God (Cleve)	2	75	43	95 *	.2	.4
145 Ch God Prophcy	1	29	NR	37 *	.1	.1
165 Ch of Nazarene	2	383	201	383	1.0	1.5
167 Chs of Christ	4	236	320	423	1.1	1.7
193 Episcopal	1	NR	60	140	.4	.5
266 Intrstat & Asc	1	16	NR	20 *	.1	.1
283 Luth—MO Synod	1	18	16	23	.1	.1
355 Presb Ch (USA)	3	367	152	466 *	1.2	1.8

Religious Group	Number of Churches, Synagogues, Mosques, or Temples	Number of Communicant, Confirmed, or Full Members	Number of Attendees	Total Adherents: Number of Adherents	Total Adherents: % of Total Pop.	Total Adherents: % of Total Adh.
403 Salvation Army	1	58	40	98	.3	.4
413 S.D.A.	1	37	NR	44	.1	.2
419 So Bapt Conv	28	15,621	3,767	19,831 *	50.9	77.5
449 Un Methodist	12	2,035	714	2,587 *	6.6	10.1
PONTOTOC	**87**	**14,000**	**5,915**	**17,994 ***	**67.3**	**100.0**
053 Assemb of God	2	48	56	90	.3	.5
081 Catholic	1	NR	NR	183	.7	1.0
145 Ch God Prophcy	1	29	NR	37 *	.1	.2
165 Ch of Nazarene	1	73	26	73	.3	.4
167 Chs of Christ	5	264	280	348	1.3	1.9
223 Free Will Bapt	4	261	NR	331 *	1.2	1.8
323 Old Ord Amish	1	40	NR	51 *	.2	.3
355 Presb Ch (USA)	3	83	41	105 *	.4	.6
356 Presb Ch Amer	1	48	55	55	.2	.3
360 Prim Bapt Chrch	3	NR	NR	NR	-	-
419 So Bapt Conv	47	11,770	4,790	14,959 *	56.0	83.1
449 Un Methodist	18	1,384	667	1,762 *	6.6	9.8
PRENTISS	**82**	**11,867**	**5,760**	**15,257 ***	**59.7**	**100.0**
017 Amer Bapt Assn	1	38	NR	47 *	.2	.3
053 Assemb of God	1	130	170	170	.7	1.1
056 Baha'i	0	1	NR	1	-	-
059 Bapt Miss Assn	3	264	99	328 *	1.3	2.1
081 Catholic	1	NR	NR	76	.3	.5
127 Ch God (Cleve)	2	116	44	144 *	.6	.9
145 Ch God Prophcy	1	29	NR	36 *	.1	.2
151 L-D Saints	1	NR	NR	330	1.3	2.2
167 Chs of Christ	18	1,365	1,484	1,809	7.1	11.9
223 Free Will Bapt	7	456	NR	566 *	2.2	3.7
355 Presb Ch (USA)	1	17	8	21 *	.1	.1
360 Prim Bapt Chrch	3	NR	NR	NR	-	-
419 So Bapt Conv	26	6,815	2,836	8,459 *	33.1	55.4
449 Un Methodist	17	2,636	1,119	3,270 *	12.8	21.4
QUITMAN	**24**	**4,008**	**1,215**	**5,339 ***	**52.8**	**100.0**
019 Amer Bapt USA	1	150	60	200 *	2.0	3.7
053 Assemb of God	1	51	71	71	.7	1.3
127 Ch God (Cleve)	2	88	58	133 *	1.3	2.5
167 Chs of Christ	2	65	60	90	.9	1.7
356 Presb Ch Amer	1	79	85	89	.9	1.7
419 So Bapt Conv	11	3,017	768	4,013 *	39.7	75.2
449 Un Methodist	6	558	113	743 *	7.3	13.9
RANKIN	**125**	**44,996**	**18,340**	**60,733 ***	**52.7**	**100.0**
017 Amer Bapt Assn	1	50	NR	62 *	.1	.1
053 Assemb of God	5	295	347	482	.4	.8
056 Baha'i	0	16	NR	16	-	-
059 Bapt Miss Assn	3	500	200	623 *	.5	1.0
081 Catholic	2	NR	NR	3,149	2.7	5.2
084 Calvary Chapel	1	NR	NR	NR	-	-
127 Ch God (Cleve)	4	654	382	815 *	.7	1.3
145 Ch God Prophcy	1	29	NR	36 *	-	.1
151 L-D Saints	2	NR	NR	746	.6	1.2
167 Chs of Christ	5	317	375	420	.4	.7
193 Episcopal	2	NR	284	587	.5	1.0
207 E.L.C.A.	1	150	85	172	.1	.3
216 Evan Presby Ch	1	555	NR	692 *	.6	1.1
223 Free Will Bapt	1	65	NR	81 *	.1	.1
252 Hindu	1	NR	NR	NR	-	-
266 Intrstat & Asc	1	61	NR	76 *	.1	.1
283 Luth—MO Synod	1	109	104	150	.1	.2
339 Pent Ch of God	1	50	NR	95	.1	.2
349 Pent Holiness	2	53	44	66 *	.1	.1
356 Presb Ch Amer	3	586	423	706	.6	1.2
413 S.D.A.	1	98	NR	117	.1	.2
419 So Bapt Conv	58	33,487	12,622	41,764 *	36.2	68.8
449 Un Methodist	27	7,718	3,328	9,625 *	8.3	15.8
463 Vineyard	1	203	146	253 *	.2	.4
SCOTT	**82**	**12,699**	**4,665**	**17,289 ***	**60.8**	**100.0**
053 Assemb of God	4	134	186	199	.7	1.2

NR–Not Reported   *Total adherents estimated from known number of communicant, confirmed, full members.   - Represents a percentage less than 0.1.   Percentages may not total 100 due to rounding.

Table 4: Religious Congregations by County and Group: 2000

Religious Group	Number of Churches, Synagogues, Mosques, or Temples	Number of Communicant, Confirmed, or Full Members	Number of Attendees	Total Adherents: Number of Adherents	Total Adherents: % of Total Pop.	Total Adherents: % of Total Adh.
059 Bapt Miss Assn	2	101	43	130 *	.5	.8
081 Catholic	2	NR	NR	964	3.4	5.6
097 Chr Chs&Chs Cr	2	75	NR	96 *	.3	.6
127 Ch God (Cleve)	2	228	184	292 *	1.0	1.7
167 Chs of Christ	3	92	112	132	.5	.8
185 Cumber Presb	2	52	NR	57	.2	.3
193 Episcopal	1	NR	9	15	.1	.1
207 E.L.C.A.	1	31	33	53	.2	.3
273 LandmrkBapt,I&U	1	297	NR	381 *	1.3	2.2
304 NatPrimBapt USA	1	169	NR	217 *	.8	1.3
335 Orth Pres Ch	1	47	62	67	.2	.4
356 Presb Ch Amer	1	42	28	42	.1	.2
360 Prim Bapt Chrch	3	NR	NR	NR	-	-
419 So Bapt Conv	38	8,849	2,983	11,338 *	39.9	65.6
449 Un Methodist	18	2,582	1,025	3,306 *	11.6	19.1
SHARKEY	**16**	**1,937**	**640**	**2,715 ***	**41.3**	**100.0**
056 Baha'i	0	1	NR	1	-	-
059 Bapt Miss Assn	1	49	12	65 *	1.0	2.4
081 Catholic	1	NR	NR	70	1.1	2.6
145 Ch God Prophcy	2	59	NR	78 *	1.2	2.9
167 Chs of Christ	1	51	55	51	.8	1.9
193 Episcopal	1	NR	53	88	1.3	3.2
419 So Bapt Conv	6	1,363	337	1,811 *	27.5	66.7
449 Un Methodist	4	414	183	551 *	8.4	20.3
SIMPSON	**69**	**13,935**	**4,976**	**17,980 ***	**65.1**	**100.0**
053 Assemb of God	2	56	70	80	.3	.4
056 Baha'i	0	6	NR	6	-	-
059 Bapt Miss Assn	1	89	18	113 *	.4	.6
081 Catholic	1	NR	NR	228	.8	1.3
127 Ch God (Cleve)	4	440	127	560 *	2.0	3.1
145 Ch God Prophcy	2	59	NR	74 *	.3	.4
167 Chs of Christ	2	49	53	69	.2	.4
356 Presb Ch Amer	2	143	137	186	.7	1.0
360 Prim Bapt Chrch	2	NR	NR	NR	-	-
419 So Bapt Conv	45	12,084	4,152	15,381 *	55.6	85.5
449 Un Methodist	8	1,009	419	1,283 *	4.6	7.1
SMITH	**71**	**8,943**	**3,563**	**11,384 ***	**70.3**	**100.0**
053 Assemb of God	1	17	18	23	.1	.2
056 Baha'i	0	1	NR	1	-	-
059 Bapt Miss Assn	3	356	184	451 *	2.8	4.0
081 Catholic	1	NR	NR	57	.4	.5
097 Chr Chs&Chs Cr	1	55	NR	70 *	.4	.6
127 Ch God (Cleve)	2	130	81	165 *	1.0	1.4
167 Chs of Christ	1	11	20	20	.1	.2
207 E.L.C.A.	1	14	8	15	.1	.1
266 Intrstat & Asc	2	180	NR	228 *	1.4	2.0
297 Mennonite;Other	1	23	NR	29 *	.2	.3
356 Presb Ch Amer	1	41	24	41	.3	.4
360 Prim Bapt Chrch	1	NR	NR	NR	-	-
419 So Bapt Conv	44	7,319	2,891	9,275 *	57.3	81.5
449 Un Methodist	12	796	337	1,009 *	6.2	8.9
STONE	**37**	**6,412**	**1,962**	**8,543 ***	**62.7**	**100.0**
017 Amer Bapt Assn	2	213	NR	269 *	2.0	3.1
053 Assemb of God	1	20	22	35	.3	.4
056 Baha'i	0	1	NR	1	-	-
059 Bapt Miss Assn	7	1,956	816	2,471 *	18.1	28.9
081 Catholic	1	NR	NR	250	1.8	2.9
127 Ch God (Cleve)	1	96	85	121 *	.9	1.4
151 L-D Saints	1	NR	NR	182	1.3	2.1
167 Chs of Christ	1	42	25	57	.4	.7
266 Intrstat & Asc	10	1,001	NR	1,264 *	9.3	14.8
355 Presb Ch (USA)	1	51	28	64 *	.5	.7
419 So Bapt Conv	7	2,104	571	2,657 *	19.5	31.1
449 Un Methodist	5	928	415	1,172 *	8.6	13.7
SUNFLOWER	**50**	**7,541**	**2,726**	**9,910 ***	**28.8**	**100.0**
053 Assemb of God	1	41	50	50	.1	.5
056 Baha'i	0	5	NR	5	-	.1
081 Catholic	2	NR	NR	246	.7	2.5
093 Chr Ch (Disc)	2	28	0	35 *	.1	.4
097 Chr Chs&Chs Cr	1	20	NR	25 *	.1	.3
123 Ch God (Ander)	2	NR	32	32	.1	.3
127 Ch God (Cleve)	5	296	116	374 *	1.1	3.8
165 Ch of Nazarene	1	16	15	32	.1	.3
167 Chs of Christ	4	364	310	509	1.5	5.1
193 Episcopal	1	NR	27	66	.2	.7
356 Presb Ch Amer	1	120	50	132	.4	1.3
419 So Bapt Conv	18	4,756	1,354	6,009 *	17.5	60.6
449 Un Methodist	12	1,895	772	2,395 *	7.0	24.2
TALLAHATCHIE	**49**	**4,811**	**1,712**	**6,400 ***	**42.9**	**100.0**
081 Catholic	1	NR	NR	50	.3	.8
127 Ch God (Cleve)	5	457	258	594 *	4.0	9.3
145 Ch God Prophcy	6	176	NR	228 *	1.5	3.6
165 Ch of Nazarene	1	81	64	114	.8	1.8
167 Chs of Christ	6	220	189	294	2.0	4.6
193 Episcopal	1	NR	42	83	.6	1.3
355 Presb Ch (USA)	4	225	134	292 *	2.0	4.6
419 So Bapt Conv	17	3,019	797	3,923 *	26.3	61.3
449 Un Methodist	8	633	228	822 *	5.5	12.8
TATE	**57**	**10,952**	**5,086**	**14,591 ***	**57.5**	**100.0**
053 Assemb of God	1	62	70	85	.3	.6
056 Baha'i	0	3	NR	3	-	-
059 Bapt Miss Assn	1	0	105	105 *	.4	.7
081 Catholic	1	NR	NR	154	.6	1.1
127 Ch God (Cleve)	1	36	23	45 *	.2	.3
151 L-D Saints	1	NR	NR	353	1.4	2.4
165 Ch of Nazarene	1	40	31	44	.2	.3
167 Chs of Christ	15	2,117	1,630	2,846	11.2	19.5
173 Comm of Christ	1	21	NR	21	.1	.1
207 E.L.C.A.	1	15	10	15	.1	.1
355 Presb Ch (USA)	1	126	40	159 *	.6	1.1
419 So Bapt Conv	21	7,204	2,523	9,086 *	35.8	62.3
449 Un Methodist	12	1,328	654	1,675 *	6.6	11.5
TIPPAH	**82**	**11,596**	**5,308**	**14,672 ***	**70.5**	**100.0**
053 Assemb of God	2	92	68	90	.4	.6
055 As Ref Pres Ch	1	66	NR	68	.3	.5
081 Catholic	1	NR	NR	276	1.3	1.9
127 Ch God (Cleve)	1	56	50	69 *	.3	.5
151 L-D Saints	1	NR	NR	152	.7	1.0
167 Chs of Christ	8	785	799	961	4.6	6.5
185 Cumber Presb	1	192	NR	192	.9	1.3
304 NatPrimBapt USA	6	400	NR	495 *	2.4	3.4
355 Presb Ch (USA)	4	254	125	314 *	1.5	2.1
356 Presb Ch Amer	1	34	0	34	.2	.2
360 Prim Bapt Chrch	4	NR	NR	NR	-	-
419 So Bapt Conv	32	8,100	3,520	10,020 *	48.1	68.3
449 Un Methodist	20	1,617	746	2,001 *	9.6	13.6
TISHOMINGO	**75**	**9,072**	**4,228**	**11,139 ***	**58.1**	**100.0**
017 Amer Bapt Assn	3	263	NR	321 *	1.7	2.9
053 Assemb of God	1	8	11	19	.1	.2
059 Bapt Miss Assn	6	361	221	441 *	2.3	4.0
081 Catholic	1	NR	NR	37	.2	.3
127 Ch God (Cleve)	1	67	42	82 *	.4	.7
145 Ch God Prophcy	1	29	NR	36 *	.2	.3
167 Chs of Christ	10	943	936	1,173	6.1	10.5
223 Free Will Bapt	5	326	NR	398 *	2.1	3.6
360 Prim Bapt Chrch	3	NR	NR	NR	-	-
419 So Bapt Conv	26	5,454	2,144	6,654 *	34.7	59.7
449 Un Methodist	18	1,621	874	1,978 *	10.3	17.8
TUNICA	**13**	**1,137**	**415**	**1,626 ***	**17.6**	**100.0**
056 Baha'i	0	1	NR	1	-	.1
081 Catholic	1	NR	NR	53	.6	3.3
145 Ch God Prophcy	1	29	NR	39 *	.4	2.4
167 Chs of Christ	2	129	85	162	1.8	10.0
193 Episcopal	1	NR	36	89	1.0	5.5

NR–Not Reported *Total adherents estimated from known number of communicant, confirmed, full members. - Represents a percentage less than 0.1. Percentages may not total 100 due to rounding.

Table 4: Religious Congregations by County and Group: 2000

Religious Group	Number of Churches, Synagogues, Mosques, or Temples	Number of Communicant, Confirmed, or Full Members	Number of Attendees	Total Adherents: Number of Adherents	Total Adherents: % of Total Pop.	Total Adherents: % of Total Adh.
216 Evan Presby Ch	1	123	NR	163 *	1.8	10.0
355 Presb Ch (USA)	1	14	7	18 *	.2	1.1
413 S.D.A.	1	79	NR	94	1.0	5.8
419 So Bapt Conv	3	468	155	618 *	6.7	38.0
449 Un Methodist	2	294	132	389 *	4.2	23.9
UNION	**72**	**16,781**	**6,670**	**21,314 ***	**84.0**	**100.0**
053 Assemb of God	2	206	150	187	.7	.9
055 As Ref Pres Ch	3	403	NR	437	1.7	2.1
081 Catholic	1	NR	NR	379	1.5	1.8
127 Ch God (Cleve)	2	185	132	232 *	.9	1.1
165 Ch of Nazarene	1	26	23	49	.2	.2
167 Chs of Christ	5	382	404	483	1.9	2.3
355 Presb Ch (USA)	1	86	42	108 *	.4	.5
360 Prim Bapt Chrch	1	NR	NR	NR	-	-
419 So Bapt Conv	41	13,106	4,775	16,445 *	64.8	77.2
449 Un Methodist	15	2,387	1,144	2,994 *	11.8	14.0
WALTHALL	**28**	**5,659**	**1,635**	**7,322 ***	**48.3**	**100.0**
081 Catholic	1	NR	NR	100	.7	1.4
167 Chs of Christ	1	14	17	18	.1	.2
266 Intrstat & Asc	4	350	NR	447 *	2.9	6.1
360 Prim Bapt Chrch	2	NR	NR	NR	-	-
419 So Bapt Conv	13	4,448	1,235	5,676 *	37.5	77.5
449 Un Methodist	7	847	383	1,081 *	7.1	14.8
WARREN	**64**	**18,725**	**5,845**	**28,622 ***	**57.7**	**100.0**
034 Ant Orth of NA	1	212	NR	424	.9	1.5
053 Assemb of God	1	28	35	35	.1	.1
056 Baha'i	1	39	NR	39	.1	.1
059 Bapt Miss Assn	3	640	288	820 *	1.7	2.9
081 Catholic	3	NR	NR	3,191	6.4	11.1
093 Chr Ch (Disc)	1	111	70	142 *	.3	.5
123 Ch God (Ander)	1	NR	7	7	-	-
127 Ch God (Cleve)	1	106	55	136 *	.3	.5
145 Ch God Prophcy	1	29	NR	38 *	.1	.1
151 L-D Saints	1	NR	NR	344	.7	1.2
165 Ch of Nazarene	1	111	68	111	.2	.4
167 Chs of Christ	7	587	527	730	1.5	2.6
193 Episcopal	4	NR	360	827	1.7	2.9
267 Muslim Est	1	NR	55	163	.3	.6
283 Luth—MO Synod	1	52	55	78	.2	.3
339 Pent Ch of God	1	40	NR	60	.1	.2
349 Pent Holiness	1	15	10	19 *	-	.1
355 Presb Ch (USA)	2	610	170	788 *	1.6	2.8
356 Presb Ch Amer	1	177	91	179	.4	.6
360 Prim Bapt Chrch	1	NR	NR	NR	-	-
403 Salvation Army	1	103	47	142	.3	.5
413 S.D.A.	2	243	NR	290	.6	1.0
419 So Bapt Conv	15	12,126	3,011	15,543 *	31.3	54.3
449 Un Methodist	11	3,496	996	4,481 *	9.0	15.7
496 Jewish Est	1	NR	NR	35	.1	.1
WASHINGTON	**69**	**18,625**	**6,394**	**27,781 ***	**44.1**	**100.0**
017 Amer Bapt Assn	1	93	NR	123 *	.2	.4
053 Assemb of God	4	257	298	387	.6	1.4
056 Baha'i	0	3	NR	3	-	-
059 Bapt Miss Assn	1	102	50	134 *	.2	.5
081 Catholic	4	NR	NR	2,468	3.9	8.9
093 Chr Ch (Disc)	1	32	12	42 *	.1	.2
127 Ch God (Cleve)	3	581	224	765 *	1.2	2.8
143 CG in Cr(Menn)	1	150	NR	198 *	.3	.7
145 Ch God Prophcy	1	29	NR	39 *	.1	.1
151 L-D Saints	1	NR	NR	384	.6	1.4
165 Ch of Nazarene	1	23	18	48	.1	.2
167 Chs of Christ	5	506	394	636	1.0	2.3
193 Episcopal	4	NR	250	592	.9	2.1
283 Luth—MO Synod	1	46	24	57	.1	.2
339 Pent Ch of God	2	51	NR	73	.1	.3
355 Presb Ch (USA)	4	698	272	920 *	1.5	3.3
356 Presb Ch Amer	1	93	105	126	.2	.5
413 S.D.A.	4	419	NR	498	.8	1.8
419 So Bapt Conv	20	12,362	3,346	16,295 *	25.9	58.7
449 Un Methodist	8	2,180	701	2,873 *	4.6	10.3
496 Jewish Est	1	NR	NR	120	.2	.4
499 Indep.Non-Char	1	1,000	700	1,000	1.6	3.6
WAYNE	**68**	**8,477**	**4,321**	**11,088 ***	**52.3**	**100.0**
053 Assemb of God	11	623	784	928	4.4	8.4
056 Baha'i	0	1	NR	1	-	-
059 Bapt Miss Assn	1	143	90	184 *	.9	1.7
081 Catholic	1	NR	NR	81	.4	.7
127 Ch God (Cleve)	1	229	133	295 *	1.4	2.7
165 Ch of Nazarene	1	48	33	52	.2	.5
167 Chs of Christ	2	93	100	120	.6	1.1
223 Free Will Bapt	4	261	NR	336 *	1.6	3.0
356 Presb Ch Amer	2	71	67	73	.3	.7
360 Prim Bapt Chrch	1	NR	NR	NR	-	-
418 Southw Bapt Fel	1	NR	NR	NR	-	-
419 So Bapt Conv	25	5,501	2,545	7,080 *	33.4	63.9
449 Un Methodist	18	1,507	569	1,938 *	9.1	17.5
WEBSTER	**47**	**6,042**	**2,621**	**7,728 ***	**75.1**	**100.0**
056 Baha'i	0	1	NR	1	-	-
081 Catholic	1	NR	NR	168	1.6	2.2
127 Ch God (Cleve)	4	165	180	249 *	2.4	3.2
145 Ch God Prophcy	2	59	NR	72 *	.7	.9
167 Chs of Christ	1	19	20	24	.2	.3
223 Free Will Bapt	2	130	NR	162 *	1.6	2.1
419 So Bapt Conv	28	4,827	2,053	6,005 *	58.3	77.7
449 Un Methodist	9	841	368	1,047 *	10.2	13.5
WILKINSON	**23**	**2,806**	**1,165**	**3,735 ***	**36.2**	**100.0**
056 Baha'i	0	1	NR	1	-	-
081 Catholic	2	NR	NR	111	1.1	3.0
093 Chr Ch (Disc)	1	43	12	53 *	.5	1.4
167 Chs of Christ	3	213	200	308	3.0	8.2
193 Episcopal	1	NR	48	128	1.2	3.4
356 Presb Ch Amer	3	126	76	137	1.3	3.7
413 S.D.A.	1	4	NR	5	-	.1
419 So Bapt Conv	4	1,440	481	1,780 *	17.3	47.7
449 Un Methodist	8	979	348	1,212 *	11.8	32.4
WINSTON	**59**	**9,501**	**4,169**	**12,044 ***	**59.7**	**100.0**
053 Assemb of God	4	206	232	330	1.6	2.7
056 Baha'i	0	2	NR	2	-	-
081 Catholic	1	NR	NR	91	.5	.8
167 Chs of Christ	1	28	30	36	.2	.3
207 E.L.C.A.	2	33	30	39	.2	.3
216 Evan Presby Ch	1	38	NR	48 *	.2	.4
288 Mennonite USA	1	0	20	20 *	.1	.2
356 Presb Ch Amer	2	225	151	238	1.2	2.0
419 So Bapt Conv	27	6,738	2,766	8,443 *	41.9	70.1
449 Un Methodist	20	2,231	940	2,797 *	13.9	23.2
YALOBUSHA	**47**	**6,098**	**2,284**	**7,693 ***	**58.9**	**100.0**
053 Assemb of God	2	89	115	177	1.4	2.3
097 Chr Chs&Chs Cr	1	407	NR	507 *	3.9	6.6
127 Ch God (Cleve)	3	187	133	235 *	1.8	3.1
145 Ch God Prophcy	1	29	NR	36 *	.3	.5
167 Chs of Christ	4	320	240	428	3.3	5.6
193 Episcopal	1	NR	7	13	.1	.2
355 Presb Ch (USA)	2	41	20	51 *	.4	.7
356 Presb Ch Amer	2	72	57	80	.6	1.0
360 Prim Bapt Chrch	3	NR	NR	NR	-	-
419 So Bapt Conv	20	4,200	1,383	5,228 *	40.1	68.0
449 Un Methodist	8	753	329	938 *	7.2	12.2
YAZOO	**64**	**9,795**	**3,474**	**13,560 ***	**48.2**	**100.0**
017 Amer Bapt Assn	2	436	NR	557 *	2.0	4.1
053 Assemb of God	1	31	31	31	.1	.2
056 Baha'i	0	42	NR	42	.1	.3
059 Bapt Miss Assn	3	424	242	542 *	1.9	4.0

NR–Not Reported *Total adherents estimated from known number of communicant, confirmed, full members. - Represents a percentage less than 0.1. Percentages may not total 100 due to rounding.

Table 4: Religious Congregations by County and Group: 2000

Religious Group	Number of Churches, Synagogues, Mosques, or Temples	Number of Communicant, Confirmed, or Full Members	Number of Attendees	Total Adherents: Number of Adherents	Total Adherents: % of Total Pop.	Total Adherents: % of Total Adh.
081 Catholic	2	NR	NR	619	2.2	4.6
123 Ch God (Ander)	1	NR	243	243	.9	1.8
127 Ch God (Cleve)	1	70	55	90 *	.3	.7
145 Ch God Prophcy	1	29	NR	37 *	.1	.3
167 Chs of Christ	3	105	94	139	.5	1.0
193 Episcopal	1	NR	79	170	.6	1.3
339 Pent Ch of God	2	60	NR	65	.2	.5
356 Presb Ch Amer	2	331	310	469	1.7	3.5
360 Prim Bapt Chrch	1	NR	NR	NR	-	-
413 S.D.A.	1	176	NR	209	.7	1.5
419 So Bapt Conv	26	5,810	1,477	7,430 *	26.4	54.8
449 Un Methodist	17	2,281	943	2,917 *	10.4	21.5

MISSOURI

Religious Group	Number of Churches, Synagogues, Mosques, or Temples	Number of Communicant, Confirmed, or Full Members	Number of Attendees	Total Adherents: Number of Adherents	Total Adherents: % of Total Pop.	Total Adherents: % of Total Adh.
The State.....	7,771	1,465,017	622,821	2,893,159 *	51.7	100.0
ADAIR	**41**	**6,105**	**3,141**	**10,133 ***	**40.6**	**100.0**
053 Assemb of God	2	173	137	231	.9	2.3
056 Baha'i	0	2	NR	2	-	-
081 Catholic	2	NR	NR	1,500	6.0	14.8
093 Chr Ch (Disc)	1	1,182	225	1,384 *	5.5	13.7
097 Chr Chs&Chs Cr	2	160	NR	188 *	.8	1.9
123 Ch God (Ander)	1	NR	59	59	.2	.6
145 Ch God Prophcy	1	27	NR	31 *	.1	.3
151 L-D Saints	2	NR	NR	676	2.7	6.7
165 Ch of Nazarene	1	235	125	237	.9	2.3
167 Chs of Christ	2	142	198	189	.8	1.9
193 Episcopal	1	NR	42	61	.2	.6
203 Evan Free Ch	1	80	170	170	.7	1.7
223 Free Will Bapt	3	255	NR	299 *	1.2	3.0
283 Luth—MO Synod	1	219	124	284	1.1	2.8
355 Presb Ch (USA)	1	228	117	267 *	1.1	2.6
403 Salvation Army	1	64	67	145	.6	1.4
413 S.D.A.	1	28	NR	33	.1	.3
419 So Bapt Conv	9	2,163	854	2,533 *	10.1	25.0
449 Un Methodist	8	1,147	523	1,344 *	5.4	13.3
498 Indep.Charis.	1	0	500	500	2.0	4.9
ANDREW	**30**	**4,705**	**1,805**	**7,230 ***	**43.8**	**100.0**
053 Assemb of God	3	204	169	246	1.5	3.4
056 Baha'i	0	7	NR	7	-	.1
081 Catholic	1	NR	NR	378	2.3	5.2
093 Chr Ch (Disc)	3	1,204	459	1,506 *	9.1	20.8
097 Chr Chs&Chs Cr	2	255	NR	319 *	1.9	4.4
127 Ch God (Cleve)	1	78	14	98 *	.6	1.4
151 L-D Saints	2	NR	NR	914	5.5	12.6
167 Chs of Christ	2	72	85	103	.6	1.4
193 Episcopal	1	NR	23	49	.3	.7
355 Presb Ch (USA)	1	33	26	41 *	.2	.6
360 Prim Bapt Chrch	1	NR	NR	NR	-	-
419 So Bapt Conv	5	1,716	528	2,147 *	13.0	29.7
443 Un C of Christ	2	339	149	424 *	2.6	5.9
449 Un Methodist	6	797	352	998 *	6.1	13.8
ATCHISON	**21**	**3,707**	**1,172**	**4,771 ***	**74.2**	**100.0**
053 Assemb of God	1	59	50	56	.9	1.2
056 Baha'i	0	4	NR	4	.1	.1
081 Catholic	1	NR	NR	288	4.5	6.0
093 Chr Ch (Disc)	3	287	157	344 *	5.3	7.2
097 Chr Chs&Chs Cr	1	60	NR	72 *	1.1	1.5
127 Ch God (Cleve)	1	14	16	17 *	.3	.4
193 Episcopal	1	NR	10	9	.1	.2
207 E.L.C.A.	2	722	252	910	14.2	19.1
355 Presb Ch (USA)	2	262	113	314 *	4.9	6.6
419 So Bapt Conv	4	1,125	213	1,349 *	21.0	28.3
449 Un Methodist	5	1,174	361	1,408 *	21.9	29.5
AUDRAIN	**62**	**11,090**	**3,014**	**17,621 ***	**68.2**	**100.0**
032 Amish; other	1	170	NR	209 *	.8	1.2
053 Assemb of God	2	116	115	204	.8	1.2

Religious Group	Number of Churches, Synagogues, Mosques, or Temples	Number of Communicant, Confirmed, or Full Members	Number of Attendees	Total Adherents: Number of Adherents	Total Adherents: % of Total Pop.	Total Adherents: % of Total Adh.
056 Baha'i	0	6	NR	6	-	-
081 Catholic	4	NR	NR	3,517	13.6	20.0
093 Chr Ch (Disc)	6	1,584	289	1,950 *	7.5	11.1
097 Chr Chs&Chs Cr	9	1,250	NR	1,539 *	6.0	8.7
151 L-D Saints	1	NR	NR	263	1.0	1.5
165 Ch of Nazarene	2	99	92	167	.6	.9
167 Chs of Christ	1	45	40	45	.2	.3
173 Comm of Christ	1	16	NR	16	.1	.1
193 Episcopal	1	NR	41	63	.2	.4
203 Evan Free Ch	1	69	125	125	.5	.7
262 Int Cou Comm Ch	1	40	NR	49 *	.2	.3
283 Luth—MO Synod	2	367	174	442	1.7	2.5
355 Presb Ch (USA)	7	1,075	464	1,324 *	5.1	7.5
413 S.D.A.	1	36	NR	43	.2	.2
419 So Bapt Conv	16	5,334	1,323	6,567 *	25.4	37.3
449 Un Methodist	5	863	332	1,062 *	4.1	6.0
467 Wesleyan	1	20	19	30	.1	.2
BARRY	**91**	**14,214**	**5,417**	**20,840 ***	**61.3**	**100.0**
053 Assemb of God	9	418	521	713	2.1	3.4
056 Baha'i	0	5	NR	5	-	-
059 Bapt Miss Assn	3	130	57	164 *	.5	.8
081 Catholic	4	NR	NR	2,356	6.9	11.3
093 Chr Ch (Disc)	1	203	100	254 *	.7	1.2
097 Chr Chs&Chs Cr	5	721	NR	902 *	2.7	4.3
107 Christian Un	1	20	28	28 *	.1	.1
151 L-D Saints	1	NR	NR	268	.8	1.3
165 Ch of Nazarene	2	175	129	340	1.0	1.6
167 Chs of Christ	10	440	495	560	1.6	2.7
193 Episcopal	1	NR	42	97	.3	.5
207 E.L.C.A.	1	52	26	55	.2	.3
223 Free Will Bapt	5	425	NR	532 *	1.6	2.6
230 Fund Methodist	3	413	NR	518 *	1.5	2.5
283 Luth—MO Synod	3	348	201	409	1.2	2.0
339 Pent Ch of God	2	23	NR	70	.2	.3
355 Presb Ch (USA)	2	306	160	383 *	1.1	1.8
419 So Bapt Conv	30	9,053	2,840	11,331 *	33.3	54.4
449 Un Methodist	8	1,482	818	1,855 *	5.5	8.9
BARTON	**38**	**5,000**	**1,737**	**6,406 ***	**51.1**	**100.0**
040 Ap Chr Ch-Amer	1	68	128	128 *	1.0	2.0
053 Assemb of God	2	141	205	205	1.6	3.2
081 Catholic	1	NR	NR	207	1.7	3.2
093 Chr Ch (Disc)	1	0	0	0 *	-	-
097 Chr Chs&Chs Cr	3	1,110	NR	1,406 *	11.2	21.9
127 Ch God (Cleve)	1	43	31	54 *	.4	.8
145 Ch God Prophcy	2	53	NR	68 *	.5	1.1
165 Ch of Nazarene	1	50	14	61	.5	1.0
167 Chs of Christ	1	85	85	108	.9	1.7
173 Comm of Christ	1	86	NR	86	.7	1.3
185 Cumber Presb	1	35	NR	35	.3	.5
223 Free Will Bapt	3	255	NR	323 *	2.6	5.0
283 Luth—MO Synod	1	132	0	0	-	-
297 Mennonite;Other	1	75	NR	95 *	.8	1.5
355 Presb Ch (USA)	1	29	15	37 *	.3	.6
413 S.D.A.	1	40	NR	48	.4	.7
419 So Bapt Conv	10	1,689	629	2,140 *	17.1	33.4
449 Un Methodist	6	1,109	630	1,405 *	11.2	21.9
BATES	**54**	**7,248**	**2,171**	**9,478 ***	**56.9**	**100.0**
053 Assemb of God	3	135	187	274	1.6	2.9
056 Baha'i	0	2	NR	2	-	-
081 Catholic	2	NR	NR	401	2.4	4.2
093 Chr Ch (Disc)	1	734	153	913 *	5.5	9.6
097 Chr Chs&Chs Cr	8	1,467	NR	1,825 *	11.0	19.3
143 CG in Cr(Menn)	1	140	NR	174 *	1.0	1.8
165 Ch of Nazarene	1	48	54	106	.6	1.1
167 Chs of Christ	3	148	150	184	1.1	1.9
173 Comm of Christ	2	253	NR	253	1.5	2.7
207 E.L.C.A.	1	39	27	63	.4	.7
283 Luth—MO Synod	1	292	152	315	1.9	3.3
322 Old Ord Menn Ch	1	29	NR	36 *	.2	.4
355 Presb Ch (USA)	2	128	86	160 *	1.0	1.7

NR–Not Reported   *Total adherents estimated from known number of communicant, confirmed, full members.   - Represents a percentage less than 0.1.   Percentages may not total 100 due to rounding.

Table 4: Religious Congregations by County and Group: 2000

Religious Group	Number of Churches, Synagogues, Mosques, or Temples	Number of Communicant, Confirmed, or Full Members	Number of Attendees	Total Adherents: Number of Adherents	Total Adherents: % of Total Pop.	Total Adherents: % of Total Adh.
388 Reg Bapt Gen As	1	74	95	95 *	.6	1.0
413 S.D.A.	1	29	NR	35	.2	.4
419 So Bapt Conv	14	2,558	743	3,183 *	19.1	33.6
443 Un C of Christ	1	43	28	54 *	.3	.6
449 Un Methodist	11	1,129	496	1,405 *	8.4	14.8
BENTON	**45**	**6,271**	**2,291**	**8,073 ***	**47.0**	**100.0**
017 Amer Bapt Assn	1	64	NR	75 *	.4	.9
053 Assemb of God	1	56	63	94	.5	1.2
056 Baha'i	0	1	NR	1	-	-
081 Catholic	2	NR	NR	500	2.9	6.2
165 Ch of Nazarene	1	66	24	66	.4	.8
167 Chs of Christ	3	70	75	88	.5	1.1
173 Comm of Christ	1	56	NR	56	.3	.7
207 E.L.C.A.	3	551	243	709	4.1	8.8
283 Luth—MO Synod	7	1,442	585	1,784	10.4	22.1
288 Mennonite USA	1	32	26	38 *	.2	.5
320 "Old" MB Ascs	3	127	NR	150 *	.9	1.9
339 Pent Ch of God	1	10	NR	40	.2	.5
419 So Bapt Conv	13	2,658	854	3,131 *	18.2	38.8
449 Un Methodist	8	1,138	421	1,341 *	7.8	16.6
BOLLINGER	**38**	**3,191**	**1,508**	**5,234 ***	**43.5**	**100.0**
053 Assemb of God	2	42	61	77	.6	1.5
056 Baha'i	0	4	NR	4	-	.1
059 Bapt Miss Assn	1	11	9	14 *	.1	.3
081 Catholic	2	NR	NR	958	8.0	18.3
123 Ch God (Ander)	1	NR	15	15	.1	.3
127 Ch God (Cleve)	1	29	29	36 *	.3	.7
151 L-D Saints	1	NR	NR	248	2.1	4.7
167 Chs of Christ	2	60	62	77	.6	1.5
207 E.L.C.A.	2	150	46	196	1.6	3.7
223 Free Will Bapt	1	85	NR	106 *	.9	2.0
355 Presb Ch (USA)	3	73	55	91 *	.8	1.7
419 So Bapt Conv	13	2,195	812	2,736 *	22.7	52.3
449 Un Methodist	9	542	419	676 *	5.6	12.9
BOONE	**129**	**33,838**	**14,716**	**55,453 ***	**40.9**	**100.0**
017 Amer Bapt Assn	1	50	NR	61 *	-	.1
019 Amer Bapt USA	3	1,061	332	1,291 *	1.0	2.3
053 Assemb of God	5	838	1,121	1,639	1.2	3.0
056 Baha'i	2	90	NR	90	.1	.2
059 Bapt Miss Assn	1	50	20	61 *	-	.1
081 Catholic	5	NR	NR	9,463	7.0	17.1
093 Chr Ch (Disc)	12	5,027	1,378	6,118 *	4.5	11.0
097 Chr Chs&Chs Cr	5	1,423	NR	1,733 *	1.3	3.1
123 Ch God (Ander)	1	NR	46	46	-	.1
127 Ch God (Cleve)	1	21	33	33 *	-	.1
151 L-D Saints	4	NR	NR	1,257	.9	2.3
157 Ch of Brethren	1	16	0	19 *	-	-
165 Ch of Nazarene	2	267	181	267	.2	.5
167 Chs of Christ	7	519	479	702	.5	1.3
173 Comm of Christ	1	308	NR	308	.2	.6
193 Episcopal	2	NR	280	927	.7	1.7
203 Evan Free Ch	3	449	800	800	.6	1.4
207 E.L.C.A.	1	563	274	704	.5	1.3
216 Evan Presby Ch	1	39	NR	47 *	-	.1
223 Free Will Bapt	1	85	NR	103 *	.1	.2
226 Friends-USA	1	55	NR	67 *	-	.1
252 Hindu	1	NR	NR	NR	-	-
263 Int Foursq Gos	1	10	17	17 *	-	-
264 Int Chs of Crst	1	51	82	68	.1	.1
267 Muslim Est	1	NR	400	850	.6	1.5
283 Luth—MO Synod	4	1,436	872	1,931	1.4	3.5
288 Mennonite USA	1	11	9	13 *	-	-
339 Pent Ch of God	1	10	NR	23	-	-
355 Presb Ch (USA)	2	982	455	1,195 *	.9	2.2
356 Presb Ch Amer	2	40	0	44	-	.1
360 Prim Bapt Chrch	2	NR	NR	NR	-	-
365 Prog Prim Bapt	2	232	NR	282 *	.2	.5
403 Salvation Army	1	105	78	134	.1	.2
413 S.D.A.	2	724	NR	861	.6	1.6
419 So Bapt Conv	27	12,819	4,243	15,602 *	11.5	28.1

Religious Group	Number of Churches, Synagogues, Mosques, or Temples	Number of Communicant, Confirmed, or Full Members	Number of Attendees	Total Adherents: Number of Adherents	Total Adherents: % of Total Pop.	Total Adherents: % of Total Adh.
435 Unitarian-Univ	1	226	NR	275 *	.2	.5
443 Un C of Christ	2	884	328	1,076 *	.8	1.9
449 Un Methodist	14	4,462	1,985	5,432 *	4.0	9.8
469 WELS	1	35	28	39	-	.1
496 Jewish Est	1	NR	NR	400	.3	.7
498 Indep.Charis.	1	800	800	1,000	.7	1.8
499 Indep.Non-Char	1	150	475	475	.4	.9
BUCHANAN	**99**	**30,701**	**13,268**	**49,567 ***	**57.6**	**100.0**
053 Assemb of God	4	1,139	1,336	2,244	2.6	4.5
056 Baha'i	1	30	NR	30	-	.1
081 Catholic	9	NR	NR	10,900	12.7	22.0
084 Calvary Chapel	1	NR	NR	NR	-	-
093 Chr Ch (Disc)	4	1,817	602	2,233 *	2.6	4.5
097 Chr Chs&Chs Cr	9	2,118	NR	2,602 *	3.0	5.2
127 Ch God (Cleve)	2	260	172	319 *	.4	.6
157 Ch of Brethren	1	53	30	65 *	.1	.1
165 Ch of Nazarene	2	376	267	463	.5	.9
167 Chs of Christ	1	89	110	145	.2	.3
173 Comm of Christ	2	847	NR	847	1.0	1.7
185 Cumber Presb	1	23	NR	32	-	.1
203 Evan Free Ch	1	0	30	30	-	.1
207 E.L.C.A.	1	435	200	590	.7	1.2
263 Int Foursq Gos	2	327	271	402 *	.5	.8
283 Luth—MO Synod	2	866	473	1,132	1.3	2.3
339 Pent Ch of God	2	85	NR	140	.2	.3
355 Presb Ch (USA)	8	1,208	771	1,489 *	1.7	3.0
403 Salvation Army	1	185	56	808	.9	1.6
413 S.D.A.	2	355	NR	423	.5	.9
419 So Bapt Conv	21	11,696	3,441	14,373 *	16.7	29.0
443 Un C of Christ	2	472	208	580 *	.7	1.2
449 Un Methodist	16	4,520	1,651	5,555 *	6.5	11.2
496 Jewish Est	1	NR	NR	265	.3	.5
498 Indep.Charis.	2	3,400	3,150	3,400	4.0	6.9
499 Indep.Non-Char	1	400	500	500	.6	1.0
BUTLER	**75**	**9,484**	**4,439**	**14,099 ***	**34.5**	**100.0**
017 Amer Bapt Assn	1	50	NR	61 *	.1	.4
053 Assemb of God	5	227	299	357	.9	2.5
056 Baha'i	0	1	NR	1	-	-
059 Bapt Miss Assn	8	369	275	458 *	1.1	3.2
081 Catholic	1	NR	NR	1,423	3.5	10.1
093 Chr Ch (Disc)	2	569	147	697 *	1.7	4.9
123 Ch God (Ander)	2	NR	365	365	.9	2.6
127 Ch God (Cleve)	1	468	394	573 *	1.4	4.1
145 Ch God Prophcy	1	27	NR	33 *	.1	.2
151 L-D Saints	1	NR	NR	390	1.0	2.8
165 Ch of Nazarene	1	58	49	72	.2	.5
167 Chs of Christ	8	511	560	666	1.6	4.7
193 Episcopal	1	NR	51	150	.4	1.1
207 E.L.C.A.	1	93	53	117	.3	.8
223 Free Will Bapt	1	85	NR	104 *	.3	.7
283 Luth—MO Synod	1	313	126	380	.9	2.7
320 "Old" MB Ascs	4	55	NR	67 *	.2	.5
339 Pent Ch of God	1	10	NR	50	.1	.4
349 Pent Holiness	1	66	68	81 *	.2	.6
355 Presb Ch (USA)	2	167	109	205 *	.5	1.5
413 S.D.A.	1	110	NR	131	.3	.9
419 So Bapt Conv	22	5,289	1,399	6,475 *	15.8	45.9
443 Un C of Christ	1	67	26	82 *	.2	.6
449 Un Methodist	8	949	518	1,161 *	2.8	8.2
CALDWELL	**34**	**3,803**	**1,120**	**5,313 ***	**59.2**	**100.0**
053 Assemb of God	2	61	58	64	.7	1.2
081 Catholic	1	NR	NR	170	1.9	3.2
093 Chr Ch (Disc)	2	0	0	0 *	-	-
097 Chr Chs&Chs Cr	2	305	NR	384 *	4.3	7.2
107 Christian Un	3	96	70	121 *	1.3	2.3
151 L-D Saints	1	NR	NR	414	4.6	7.8
165 Ch of Nazarene	1	80	65	106	1.2	2.0
167 Chs of Christ	3	50	54	60	.7	1.1
173 Comm of Christ	2	194	NR	194	2.2	3.7
419 So Bapt Conv	8	1,882	465	2,371 *	26.4	44.6

NR–Not Reported *Total adherents estimated from known number of communicant, confirmed, full members. - Represents a percentage less than 0.1. Percentages may not total 100 due to rounding.

Table 4: Religious Congregations by County and Group: 2000

Religious Group	Number of Churches, Synagogues, Mosques, or Temples	Number of Communicant, Confirmed, or Full Members	Number of Attendees	Total Adherents: Number of Adherents	% of Total Pop.	% of Total Adh.
443 Un C of Christ	1	125	55	157 *	1.8	3.0
449 Un Methodist	8	1,010	353	1,272 *	14.2	23.9
CALLAWAY	**65**	**9,195**	**3,491**	**13,945 ***	**34.2**	**100.0**
053 Assemb of God	2	76	91	222	.5	1.6
056 Baha'i	0	12	NR	12	-	.1
081 Catholic	3	NR	NR	1,720	4.2	12.3
093 Chr Ch (Disc)	9	1,168	315	1,446 *	3.5	10.4
097 Chr Chs&Chs Cr	1	130	NR	161 *	.4	1.2
151 L-D Saints	1	NR	NR	384	.9	2.8
165 Ch of Nazarene	1	161	149	419	1.0	3.0
167 Chs of Christ	1	100	90	110	.3	.8
173 Comm of Christ	1	23	NR	23	.1	.2
193 Episcopal	2	NR	55	120	.3	.9
283 Luth—MO Synod	2	241	92	309	.8	2.2
355 Presb Ch (USA)	5	614	338	761 *	1.9	5.5
413 S.D.A.	1	31	NR	37	.1	.3
419 So Bapt Conv	19	5,085	1,569	6,296 *	15.4	45.1
443 Un C of Christ	1	70	39	87 *	.2	.6
449 Un Methodist	16	1,484	753	1,838 *	4.5	13.2
CAMDEN	**57**	**9,737**	**4,799**	**13,967 ***	**37.7**	**100.0**
053 Assemb of God	4	467	632	724	2.0	5.2
056 Baha'i	0	1	NR	1	-	-
081 Catholic	2	NR	NR	1,750	4.7	12.5
084 Calvary Chapel	1	NR	NR	NR	-	-
093 Chr Ch (Disc)	3	1,138	201	1,340 *	3.6	9.6
097 Chr Chs&Chs Cr	1	45	NR	53 *	.1	.4
165 Ch of Nazarene	1	117	205	468	1.3	3.4
167 Chs of Christ	5	203	205	249	.7	1.8
173 Comm of Christ	1	98	NR	98	.3	.7
193 Episcopal	1	NR	87	92	.2	.7
203 Evan Free Ch	1	69	125	125	.3	.9
207 E.L.C.A.	2	484	279	632	1.7	4.5
258 IndFreeWillBapt	1	65	NR	77 *	.2	.6
283 Luth—MO Synod	3	649	518	764	2.1	5.5
320 "Old" MB Ascs	5	391	NR	460 *	1.2	3.3
339 Pent Ch of God	1	10	NR	40	.1	.3
355 Presb Ch (USA)	2	182	110	214 *	.6	1.5
413 S.D.A.	1	69	NR	82	.2	.6
419 So Bapt Conv	17	4,328	1,599	5,096 *	13.8	36.5
449 Un Methodist	4	1,021	438	1,202 *	3.2	8.6
498 Indep.Charis.	1	400	400	500	1.3	3.6
CAPE GIRARDEAU	**92**	**24,498**	**12,584**	**42,218 ***	**61.5**	**100.0**
017 Amer Bapt Assn	1	50	NR	61 *	.1	.1
053 Assemb of God	4	1,193	1,594	2,448	3.6	5.8
056 Baha'i	0	7	NR	7	-	-
059 Bapt Miss Assn	1	40	25	49 *	.1	.1
076 Buddhism	1	NR	NR	NR	-	-
081 Catholic	4	NR	NR	10,578	15.4	25.1
093 Chr Ch (Disc)	1	542	133	661 *	1.0	1.6
097 Chr Chs&Chs Cr	1	195	NR	238 *	.3	.6
123 Ch God (Ander)	2	NR	136	136	.2	.3
127 Ch God (Cleve)	1	111	54	135 *	.2	.3
145 Ch God Prophcy	2	53	NR	64 *	.1	.2
151 L-D Saints	1	NR	NR	261	.4	.6
165 Ch of Nazarene	2	307	145	466	.7	1.1
167 Chs of Christ	4	346	361	440	.6	1.0
193 Episcopal	1	NR	53	114	.2	.3
203 Evan Free Ch	1	55	75	75	.1	.2
207 E.L.C.A.	2	369	219	476	.7	1.1
216 Evan Presby Ch	1	55	NR	67 *	.1	.2
223 Free Will Bapt	2	170	NR	207 *	.3	.5
263 Int Foursq Gos	1	72	60	88 *	.1	.2
283 Luth—MO Synod	13	6,220	3,278	7,730	11.3	18.3
290 Metro Comm Ch	1	14	5	5 *	-	-
355 Presb Ch (USA)	3	633	374	772 *	1.1	1.8
403 Salvation Army	1	128	108	142	.2	.3
413 S.D.A.	1	43	NR	51	.1	.1
418 Southw Bapt Fel	1	NR	NR	NR	-	-
419 So Bapt Conv	18	8,170	3,036	9,965 *	14.5	23.6
443 Un C of Christ	4	966	375	1,178 *	1.7	2.8

Religious Group	Number of Churches, Synagogues, Mosques, or Temples	Number of Communicant, Confirmed, or Full Members	Number of Attendees	Total Adherents: Number of Adherents	% of Total Pop.	% of Total Adh.
449 Un Methodist	16	4,649	2,463	5,670 *	8.3	13.4
463 Vineyard	1	110	90	134 *	.2	.3
CARROLL	**37**	**5,582**	**1,718**	**7,580 ***	**73.7**	**100.0**
053 Assemb of God	1	38	50	80	.8	1.1
056 Baha'i	0	1	NR	1	-	-
081 Catholic	2	NR	NR	605	5.9	8.0
093 Chr Ch (Disc)	3	510	207	631 *	6.1	8.3
097 Chr Chs&Chs Cr	1	75	NR	93 *	.9	1.2
157 Ch of Brethren	1	40	18	49 *	.5	.6
165 Ch of Nazarene	1	53	52	137	1.3	1.8
167 Chs of Christ	3	87	100	108	1.1	1.4
283 Luth—MO Synod	2	592	261	699	6.8	9.2
323 Old Ord Amish	1	55	NR	68 *	.7	.9
355 Presb Ch (USA)	1	19	10	23 *	.2	.3
419 So Bapt Conv	14	3,145	699	3,890 *	37.8	51.3
449 Un Methodist	7	967	321	1,196 *	11.6	15.8
CARTER	**21**	**1,575**	**714**	**2,184 ***	**36.8**	**100.0**
053 Assemb of God	2	174	231	300	5.0	13.7
056 Baha'i	0	1	NR	1	-	-
059 Bapt Miss Assn	2	104	28	129 *	2.2	5.9
081 Catholic	2	NR	NR	144	2.4	6.6
123 Ch God (Ander)	1	NR	42	42	.7	1.9
145 Ch God Prophcy	3	80	NR	99 *	1.7	4.5
167 Chs of Christ	1	30	34	38	.6	1.7
283 Luth—MO Synod	1	32	0	0	-	-
297 Mennonite;Other	1	61	NR	76 *	1.3	3.5
419 So Bapt Conv	5	1,025	317	1,271 *	21.4	58.2
443 Un C of Christ	1	10	5	12 *	.2	.5
449 Un Methodist	2	58	57	72 *	1.2	3.3
CASS	**87**	**21,170**	**9,417**	**33,670 ***	**41.0**	**100.0**
053 Assemb of God	7	577	755	916	1.1	2.7
056 Baha'i	0	6	NR	6	-	-
059 Bapt Miss Assn	1	60	56	77 *	.1	.2
081 Catholic	3	NR	NR	4,762	5.8	14.1
093 Chr Ch (Disc)	5	2,418	852	3,100 *	3.8	9.2
097 Chr Chs&Chs Cr	1	35	NR	45 *	.1	.1
121 Ch God (Abr)	1	66	69	85 *	.1	.3
151 L-D Saints	3	NR	NR	961	1.2	2.9
165 Ch of Nazarene	4	411	446	1,007	1.2	3.0
167 Chs of Christ	6	339	365	436	.5	1.3
173 Comm of Christ	2	370	NR	370	.5	1.1
193 Episcopal	1	NR	40	200	.2	.6
203 Evan Free Ch	2	110	215	215	.3	.6
207 E.L.C.A.	1	235	143	308	.4	.9
223 Free Will Bapt	2	170	NR	218 *	.3	.6
283 Luth—MO Synod	3	467	274	525	.6	1.6
288 Mennonite USA	2	415	518	618 *	.8	1.8
355 Presb Ch (USA)	4	280	180	359 *	.4	1.1
360 Prim Bapt Chrch	1	NR	NR	NR	-	-
419 So Bapt Conv	26	11,421	3,673	14,642 *	17.8	43.5
449 Un Methodist	9	3,401	1,418	4,360 *	5.3	12.9
469 WELS	1	89	63	110	.1	.3
498 Indep.Charis.	2	300	350	350	.4	1.0
CEDAR	**46**	**5,782**	**1,521**	**7,500 ***	**54.6**	**100.0**
053 Assemb of God	2	220	264	343	2.5	4.6
056 Baha'i	0	2	NR	2	-	-
081 Catholic	2	NR	NR	372	2.7	5.0
093 Chr Ch (Disc)	1	389	88	474 *	3.5	6.3
097 Chr Chs&Chs Cr	6	968	NR	1,179 *	8.6	15.7
165 Ch of Nazarene	1	59	68	112	.8	1.5
167 Chs of Christ	2	170	165	190	1.4	2.5
173 Comm of Christ	2	63	NR	63	.5	.8
223 Free Will Bapt	2	170	NR	207 *	1.5	2.8
283 Luth—MO Synod	2	134	78	162	1.2	2.2
297 Mennonite;Other	1	30	NR	37 *	.3	.5
320 "Old" MB Ascs	14	956	NR	1,165 *	8.5	15.5
355 Presb Ch (USA)	2	51	54	62 *	.5	.8
419 So Bapt Conv	6	2,079	617	2,534 *	18.5	33.8

NR–Not Reported *Total adherents estimated from known number of communicant, confirmed, full members. - Represents a percentage less than 0.1. Percentages may not total 100 due to rounding.

Table 4: Religious Congregations by County and Group: 2000

Religious Group	Number of Churches, Synagogues, Mosques, or Temples	Number of Communicant, Confirmed, or Full Members	Number of Attendees	Total Adherents		
				Number of Adherents	% of Total Pop.	% of Total Adh.
449 Un Methodist	3	491	187	598 *	4.4	8.0
CHARITON	**28**	**3,388**	**1,171**	**5,904 ***	**70.0**	**100.0**
081 Catholic	5	NR	NR	1,777	21.1	30.1
093 Chr Ch (Disc)	4	464	171	556 *	6.6	9.4
097 Chr Chs&Chs Cr	1	96	NR	115 *	1.4	1.9
283 Luth—MO Synod	3	715	404	921	10.9	15.6
419 So Bapt Conv	5	1,121	227	1,344 *	15.9	22.8
449 Un Methodist	10	992	369	1,191 *	14.1	20.2
CHRISTIAN	**66**	**12,887**	**6,338**	**19,666 ***	**36.2**	**100.0**
053 Assemb of God	4	1,491	1,260	2,068	3.8	10.5
056 Baha'i	0	10	NR	10	-	.1
081 Catholic	2	NR	NR	2,342	4.3	11.9
093 Chr Ch (Disc)	5	877	315	1,121 *	2.1	5.7
097 Chr Chs&Chs Cr	1	250	NR	320 *	.6	1.6
107 Christian Un	1	30	35	38 *	.1	.2
151 L-D Saints	2	NR	NR	714	1.3	3.6
165 Ch of Nazarene	2	237	157	246	.5	1.3
167 Chs of Christ	6	424	486	509	.9	2.6
223 Free Will Bapt	1	85	NR	109 *	.2	.6
283 Luth—MO Synod	1	310	210	435	.8	2.2
320 "Old" MB Ascs	1	99	NR	127 *	.2	.6
349 Pent Holiness	1	10	10	13 *	-	.1
355 Presb Ch (USA)	1	89	65	114 *	.2	.6
356 Presb Ch Amer	1	250	85	350	.6	1.8
419 So Bapt Conv	30	7,687	2,986	9,824 *	18.1	50.0
443 Un C of Christ	1	86	38	110 *	.2	.6
449 Un Methodist	6	952	691	1,216 *	2.2	6.2
CLARK	**30**	**2,782**	**928**	**3,785 ***	**51.0**	**100.0**
081 Catholic	3	NR	NR	363	4.9	9.6
093 Chr Ch (Disc)	3	459	97	566 *	7.6	15.0
167 Chs of Christ	1	35	35	40	.5	1.1
323 Old Ord Amish	1	55	NR	68 *	.9	1.8
355 Presb Ch (USA)	2	95	60	117 *	1.6	3.1
413 S.D.A.	1	64	NR	76	1.0	2.0
419 So Bapt Conv	11	1,237	388	1,524 *	20.6	40.3
443 Un C of Christ	1	351	165	432 *	5.8	11.4
449 Un Methodist	7	486	183	599 *	8.1	15.8
CLAY	**160**	**49,653**	**23,678**	**92,519 ***	**50.3**	**100.0**
017 Amer Bapt Assn	1	35	NR	44 *	-	-
019 Amer Bapt USA	1	266	92	333 *	.2	.4
053 Assemb of God	11	1,492	1,842	4,561	2.5	4.9
056 Baha'i	0	18	NR	18	-	-
057 Bapt Gen Conf	1	37	50	50 *	-	.1
081 Catholic	10	NR	NR	23,507	12.8	25.4
093 Chr Ch (Disc)	11	5,222	1,619	6,536 *	3.6	7.1
097 Chr Chs&Chs Cr	4	618	NR	773 *	.4	.8
107 Christian Un	3	304	230	380 *	.2	.4
123 Ch God (Ander)	1	NR	32	32	-	-
145 Ch God Prophcy	1	27	NR	33 *	-	-
151 L-D Saints	7	NR	NR	2,479	1.3	2.7
165 Ch of Nazarene	5	746	428	890	.5	1.0
167 Chs of Christ	9	997	1,079	1,354	.7	1.5
173 Comm of Christ	3	1,336	NR	1,336	.7	1.4
185 Cumber Presb	1	33	NR	33	-	-
193 Episcopal	3	NR	406	805	.4	.9
201 Evan Cov Ch	2	190	88	238 *	.1	.3
203 Evan Free Ch	1	38	80	80	-	.1
207 E.L.C.A.	3	779	283	1,130	.6	1.2
223 Free Will Bapt	1	85	NR	106 *	.1	.1
262 Int Cou Comm Ch	1	250	NR	313 *	.2	.3
283 Luth—MO Synod	5	2,337	1,256	2,858	1.6	3.1
339 Pent Ch of God	4	285	NR	741	.4	.8
355 Presb Ch (USA)	3	667	375	835 *	.5	.9
373 Ref Ch in U.S.	1	49	NR	81	-	.1
403 Salvation Army	1	84	77	163	.1	.2
413 S.D.A.	1	121	NR	144	.1	.2
418 Southw Bapt Fel	1	NR	NR	NR	-	-
419 So Bapt Conv	39	21,250	7,614	26,597 *	14.5	28.7
443 Un C of Christ	1	211	96	264 *	.1	.3
449 Un Methodist	15	7,260	3,275	9,087 *	4.9	9.8
463 Vineyard	1	500	409	626 *	.3	.7
467 Wesleyan	1	41	45	90	-	.1
498 Indep.Charis.	1	3,000	1,800	3,500	1.9	3.8
499 Indep.Non-Char	6	1,375	2,502	2,502	1.4	2.7
CLINTON	**34**	**6,773**	**2,136**	**9,540 ***	**50.3**	**100.0**
053 Assemb of God	3	98	119	204	1.1	2.1
056 Baha'i	0	5	NR	5	-	.1
081 Catholic	2	NR	NR	1,122	5.9	11.8
093 Chr Ch (Disc)	4	1,455	524	1,818 *	9.6	19.1
097 Chr Chs&Chs Cr	1	87	NR	109 *	.6	1.1
107 Christian Un	1	25	40	40 *	.2	.4
127 Ch God (Cleve)	2	83	73	104 *	.5	1.1
157 Ch of Brethren	1	23	0	29 *	.2	.3
167 Chs of Christ	1	49	40	60	.3	.6
173 Comm of Christ	2	516	NR	516	2.7	5.4
223 Free Will Bapt	1	85	NR	106 *	.6	1.1
339 Pent Ch of God	1	11	NR	11	.1	.1
355 Presb Ch (USA)	2	50	32	62 *	.3	.6
360 Prim Bapt Chrch	1	NR	NR	NR	-	-
419 So Bapt Conv	7	3,007	809	3,757 *	19.8	39.4
449 Un Methodist	5	1,279	499	1,597 *	8.4	16.7
COLE	**74**	**20,635**	**8,454**	**54,187 ***	**75.9**	**100.0**
019 Amer Bapt USA	1	0	0	0 *	-	-
053 Assemb of God	3	913	753	1,469	2.1	2.7
056 Baha'i	1	35	NR	35	-	.1
059 Bapt Miss Assn	1	65	50	80 *	.1	.1
081 Catholic	9	NR	NR	26,234	36.7	48.4
093 Chr Ch (Disc)	3	1,122	355	1,379 *	1.9	2.5
097 Chr Chs&Chs Cr	4	1,361	NR	1,672 *	2.3	3.1
123 Ch God (Ander)	1	NR	106	106	.1	.2
151 L-D Saints	1	NR	NR	530	.7	1.0
157 Ch of Brethren	1	8	6	10 *	-	-
165 Ch of Nazarene	1	154	103	163	.2	.3
167 Chs of Christ	2	350	365	540	.8	1.0
173 Comm of Christ	1	115	NR	115	.2	.2
193 Episcopal	1	NR	74	477	.7	.9
203 Evan Free Ch	1	40	90	90	.1	.2
207 E.L.C.A.	3	817	385	1,021	1.4	1.9
221 Free Methodist	2	32	30	42	.1	.1
263 Int Foursq Gos	1	3	108	108 *	.2	.2
283 Luth—MO Synod	5	2,804	1,508	3,645	5.1	6.7
339 Pent Ch of God	2	152	NR	740	1.0	1.4
355 Presb Ch (USA)	1	920	318	1,131 *	1.6	2.1
403 Salvation Army	1	126	49	279	.4	.5
413 S.D.A.	1	147	NR	175	.2	.3
419 So Bapt Conv	19	8,349	2,860	10,260 *	14.4	18.9
435 Unitarian-Univ	1	36	NR	44 *	.1	.1
443 Un C of Christ	2	1,070	327	1,315 *	1.8	2.4
449 Un Methodist	4	2,016	967	2,477 *	3.5	4.6
496 Jewish Est	1	NR	NR	50	.1	.1
COOPER	**46**	**5,348**	**2,223**	**9,536 ***	**57.2**	**100.0**
053 Assemb of God	1	63	80	100	.6	1.0
056 Baha'i	0	3	NR	3	-	-
081 Catholic	4	NR	NR	2,930	17.6	30.7
093 Chr Ch (Disc)	2	341	101	413 *	2.5	4.3
097 Chr Chs&Chs Cr	1	70	NR	85 *	.5	.9
167 Chs of Christ	3	125	165	181	1.1	1.9
173 Comm of Christ	1	66	NR	66	.4	.7
193 Episcopal	1	NR	17	27	.2	.3
263 Int Foursq Gos	1	121	183	183 *	1.1	1.9
283 Luth—MO Synod	4	772	402	953	5.7	10.0
323 Old Ord Amish	1	55	NR	67 *	.4	.7
339 Pent Ch of God	1	22	NR	37	.2	.4
355 Presb Ch (USA)	3	208	130	251 *	1.5	2.6
419 So Bapt Conv	14	2,174	653	2,632 *	15.8	27.6
443 Un C of Christ	3	463	212	561 *	3.4	5.9
449 Un Methodist	6	865	280	1,047 *	6.3	11.0

NR–Not Reported *Total adherents estimated from known number of communicant, confirmed, full members. - Represents a percentage less than 0.1. Percentages may not total 100 due to rounding.

Table 4: Religious Congregations by County and Group: 2000

Religious Group	Number of Churches, Synagogues, Mosques, or Temples	Number of Communicant, Confirmed, or Full Members	Number of Attendees	Total Adherents		
				Number of Adherents	% of Total Pop.	% of Total Adh.
CRAWFORD	**45**	**6,317**	**2,373**	**9,474 ***	**41.5**	**100.0**
053 Assemb of God	8	315	396	500	2.2	5.3
056 Baha'i	0	6	NR	6	-	.1
059 Bapt Miss Assn	2	388	200	485 *	2.1	5.1
081 Catholic	3	NR	NR	985	4.3	10.4
097 Chr Chs&Chs Cr	2	205	NR	256 *	1.1	2.7
127 Ch God (Cleve)	2	487	149	608 *	2.7	6.4
151 L-D Saints	1	NR	NR	417	1.8	4.4
167 Chs of Christ	1	59	63	76	.3	.8
223 Free Will Bapt	2	170	NR	212 *	.9	2.2
283 Luth—MO Synod	2	412	225	565	2.5	6.0
339 Pent Ch of God	1	8	NR	40	.2	.4
355 Presb Ch (USA)	3	405	219	506 *	2.2	5.3
413 S.D.A.	1	86	NR	102	.4	1.1
419 So Bapt Conv	15	3,342	893	4,174 *	18.3	44.1
449 Un Methodist	2	434	228	542 *	2.4	5.7
DADE	**39**	**3,785**	**1,596**	**5,023 ***	**63.4**	**100.0**
053 Assemb of God	2	75	93	93	1.2	1.9
081 Catholic	1	NR	NR	80	1.0	1.6
093 Chr Ch (Disc)	4	241	87	294 *	3.7	5.9
097 Chr Chs&Chs Cr	3	280	NR	342 *	4.3	6.8
121 Ch God (Abr)	1	5	20	20 *	.3	.4
151 L-D Saints	1	NR	NR	279	3.5	5.6
167 Chs of Christ	4	218	233	282	3.6	5.6
185 Cumber Presb	1	4	NR	8	.1	.2
223 Free Will Bapt	1	85	NR	104 *	1.3	2.1
283 Luth—MO Synod	1	504	320	627	7.9	12.5
355 Presb Ch (USA)	4	98	79	120 *	1.5	2.4
419 So Bapt Conv	13	2,034	602	2,480 *	31.3	49.4
449 Un Methodist	3	241	162	294 *	3.7	5.9
DALLAS	**42**	**4,628**	**1,394**	**6,001 ***	**38.3**	**100.0**
032 Amish; other	1	220	NR	278 *	1.8	4.6
053 Assemb of God	2	191	154	230	1.5	3.8
056 Baha'i	0	17	NR	17	.1	.3
081 Catholic	1	NR	NR	168	1.1	2.8
093 Chr Ch (Disc)	2	359	132	453 *	2.9	7.5
097 Chr Chs&Chs Cr	2	160	NR	202 *	1.3	3.4
167 Chs of Christ	3	107	132	143	.9	2.4
223 Free Will Bapt	7	595	NR	751 *	4.8	12.5
283 Luth—MO Synod	1	0	0	0	-	-
320 "Old" MB Ascs	5	490	NR	618 *	3.9	10.3
322 Old Ord Menn Ch	1	114	NR	144 *	.9	2.4
360 Prim Bapt Chrch	1	NR	NR	NR	-	-
419 So Bapt Conv	13	1,999	691	2,523 *	16.1	42.0
449 Un Methodist	3	376	285	474 *	3.0	7.9
DAVIESS	**36**	**3,726**	**1,003**	**5,050 ***	**63.0**	**100.0**
053 Assemb of God	2	69	93	130	1.6	2.6
056 Baha'i	0	2	NR	2	-	-
081 Catholic	1	NR	NR	60	.7	1.2
093 Chr Ch (Disc)	2	531	118	670 *	8.4	13.3
097 Chr Chs&Chs Cr	1	30	NR	38 *	.5	.8
143 CG in Cr(Menn)	1	56	NR	71 *	.9	1.4
151 L-D Saints	1	NR	NR	249	3.1	4.9
167 Chs of Christ	3	61	56	79	1.0	1.6
323 Old Ord Amish	6	330	NR	414 *	5.2	8.2
355 Presb Ch (USA)	2	43	36	54 *	.7	1.1
413 S.D.A.	1	31	NR	37	.5	.7
419 So Bapt Conv	8	2,052	459	2,588 *	32.3	51.2
449 Un Methodist	8	521	241	658 *	8.2	13.0
DE KALB	**36**	**3,609**	**1,359**	**4,454 ***	**38.4**	**100.0**
053 Assemb of God	1	225	325	325	2.8	7.3
081 Catholic	1	NR	NR	107	.9	2.4
093 Chr Ch (Disc)	2	0	0	0 *	-	-
097 Chr Chs&Chs Cr	3	380	NR	451 *	3.9	10.1
165 Ch of Nazarene	1	125	73	128	1.1	2.9
173 Comm of Christ	3	260	NR	260	2.2	5.8
185 Cumber Presb	1	11	NR	69	.6	1.5
223 Free Will Bapt	1	85	NR	101 *	.9	2.3
283 Luth—MO Synod	1	159	72	205	1.8	4.6
297 Mennonite;Other	1	35	NR	42 *	.4	.9
355 Presb Ch (USA)	2	37	21	44 *	.4	1.0
419 So Bapt Conv	9	1,631	518	1,937 *	16.7	43.5
449 Un Methodist	10	661	350	785 *	6.8	17.6
DENT	**39**	**7,077**	**2,494**	**9,736 ***	**65.2**	**100.0**
049 Armen Ap Cilic	1	0	NR	80	.5	.8
053 Assemb of God	3	276	412	626	4.2	6.4
056 Baha'i	0	1	NR	1	-	-
059 Bapt Miss Assn	1	22	18	27 *	.2	.3
081 Catholic	2	NR	NR	575	3.9	5.9
097 Chr Chs&Chs Cr	2	400	NR	493 *	3.3	5.1
123 Ch God (Ander)	1	NR	16	16	.1	.2
167 Chs of Christ	3	239	255	299	2.0	3.1
173 Comm of Christ	1	22	NR	22	.1	.2
185 Cumber Presb	1	20	NR	20	.1	.2
207 E.L.C.A.	1	54	30	68	.5	.7
223 Free Will Bapt	1	85	NR	105 *	.7	1.1
283 Luth—MO Synod	1	147	69	211	1.4	2.2
339 Pent Ch of God	1	7	NR	40	.3	.4
413 S.D.A.	1	39	NR	46	.3	.5
419 So Bapt Conv	15	5,309	1,500	6,545 *	43.8	67.2
449 Un Methodist	4	456	194	562 *	3.8	5.8
DOUGLAS	**26**	**2,089**	**1,115**	**3,525 ***	**26.9**	**100.0**
053 Assemb of God	1	155	250	250	1.9	7.1
056 Baha'i	0	1	NR	1	-	-
081 Catholic	1	NR	NR	277	2.1	7.9
123 Ch God (Ander)	1	NR	23	23	.2	.7
151 L-D Saints	1	NR	NR	483	3.7	13.7
165 Ch of Nazarene	3	395	309	574	4.4	16.3
167 Chs of Christ	4	200	220	264	2.0	7.5
173 Comm of Christ	1	0	NR	0	-	-
207 E.L.C.A.	1	58	28	71	.5	2.0
223 Free Will Bapt	2	170	NR	210 *	1.6	6.0
258 IndFreeWillBapt	5	162	NR	201 *	1.5	5.7
413 S.D.A.	1	46	NR	55	.4	1.6
419 So Bapt Conv	4	654	173	809 *	6.2	23.0
449 Un Methodist	1	248	112	307 *	2.3	8.7
DUNKLIN	**82**	**13,221**	**5,172**	**17,800 ***	**53.7**	**100.0**
017 Amer Bapt Assn	1	50	NR	63 *	.2	.4
053 Assemb of God	8	670	727	987	3.0	5.5
059 Bapt Miss Assn	2	30	30	38 *	.1	.2
081 Catholic	3	NR	NR	1,032	3.1	5.8
093 Chr Ch (Disc)	1	157	90	196 *	.6	1.1
097 Chr Chs&Chs Cr	2	190	NR	238 *	.7	1.3
123 Ch God (Ander)	1	NR	145	145	.4	.8
127 Ch God (Cleve)	1	160	46	200 *	.6	1.1
145 Ch God Prophcy	1	27	NR	33 *	.1	.2
165 Ch of Nazarene	1	171	78	171	.5	1.0
167 Chs of Christ	15	977	991	1,199	3.6	6.7
193 Episcopal	1	NR	5	6	-	-
283 Luth—MO Synod	2	53	30	63	.2	.4
349 Pent Holiness	3	168	200	210 *	.6	1.2
355 Presb Ch (USA)	3	195	97	244 *	.7	1.4
413 S.D.A.	1	18	NR	21	.1	.1
419 So Bapt Conv	25	9,124	2,126	11,412 *	34.4	64.1
449 Un Methodist	11	1,231	607	1,542 *	4.7	8.7
FRANKLIN	**151**	**23,549**	**10,015**	**54,885 ***	**58.5**	**100.0**
017 Amer Bapt Assn	2	550	NR	695 *	.7	1.3
053 Assemb of God	11	689	845	1,215	1.3	2.2
056 Baha'i	0	15	NR	15	-	-
059 Bapt Miss Assn	7	1,890	689	2,389 *	2.5	4.4
081 Catholic	19	NR	NR	24,069	25.7	43.9
097 Chr Chs&Chs Cr	7	1,675	NR	2,118 *	2.3	3.9
127 Ch God (Cleve)	1	23	33	33 *	-	.1
151 L-D Saints	2	NR	NR	581	.6	1.1
165 Ch of Nazarene	3	302	166	361	.4	.7
167 Chs of Christ	4	244	247	318	.3	.6

NR–Not Reported *Total adherents estimated from known number of communicant, confirmed, full members. - Represents a percentage less than 0.1. Percentages may not total 100 due to rounding.

Table 4: Religious Congregations by County and Group: 2000

Religious Group	Number of Churches, Synagogues, Mosques, or Temples	Number of Communicant, Confirmed, or Full Members	Number of Attendees	Total Adherents: Number of Adherents	Total Adherents: % of Total Pop.	Total Adherents: % of Total Adh.
173 Comm of Christ	1	45	NR	45	-	.1
193 Episcopal	2	NR	30	66	.1	.1
203 Evan Free Ch	1	36	78	78	.1	.1
207 E.L.C.A.	2	379	187	522	.6	1.0
223 Free Will Bapt	2	170	NR	215 *	.2	.4
283 Luth—MO Synod	9	2,592	1,583	3,168	3.4	5.8
339 Pent Ch of God	1	8	NR	36	-	.1
355 Presb Ch (USA)	6	733	434	927 *	1.0	1.7
356 Presb Ch Amer	2	129	190	202	.2	.4
413 S.D.A.	1	97	NR	115	.1	.2
419 So Bapt Conv	35	8,958	3,230	11,323 *	12.1	20.6
443 Un C of Christ	14	3,172	1,401	4,010 *	4.3	7.3
449 Un Methodist	17	1,816	858	2,294 *	2.4	4.2
467 Wesleyan	2	26	44	90	.1	.2
GASCONADE	**42**	**5,707**	**2,327**	**9,397 ***	**61.3**	**100.0**
053 Assemb of God	1	59	88	104	.7	1.1
056 Baha'i	0	3	NR	3	-	-
081 Catholic	3	NR	NR	2,270	14.8	24.2
097 Chr Chs&Chs Cr	3	355	NR	437 *	2.8	4.7
167 Chs of Christ	1	70	75	91	.6	1.0
203 Evan Free Ch	1	69	125	125	.8	1.3
283 Luth—MO Synod	4	578	343	710	4.6	7.6
339 Pent Ch of God	1	25	NR	65	.4	.7
355 Presb Ch (USA)	3	112	61	138 *	.9	1.5
413 S.D.A.	1	19	NR	23	.1	.2
419 So Bapt Conv	9	1,834	583	2,254 *	14.7	24.0
443 Un C of Christ	8	2,040	759	2,508 *	16.3	26.7
449 Un Methodist	6	499	264	614 *	4.0	6.5
469 WELS	1	44	29	55	.4	.6
GENTRY	**29**	**3,892**	**1,359**	**5,461 ***	**79.6**	**100.0**
053 Assemb of God	2	36	45	58	.8	1.1
056 Baha'i	0	2	NR	2	-	-
081 Catholic	2	NR	NR	420	6.1	7.7
093 Chr Ch (Disc)	4	499	151	621 *	9.1	11.4
151 L-D Saints	1	NR	NR	187	2.7	3.4
167 Chs of Christ	3	103	103	127	1.9	2.3
323 Old Ord Amish	1	55	NR	68 *	1.0	1.2
355 Presb Ch (USA)	2	162	93	202 *	2.9	3.7
419 So Bapt Conv	9	2,308	688	2,872 *	41.9	52.6
449 Un Methodist	5	727	279	904 *	13.2	16.6
GREENE	**275**	**88,862**	**46,235**	**135,139 ***	**56.2**	**100.0**
017 Amer Bapt Assn	1	50	NR	60 *	-	-
019 Amer Bapt USA	1	900	345	1,087 *	.5	.8
053 Assemb of God	43	8,665	11,243	18,254	7.6	13.5
056 Baha'i	1	73	NR	73	-	.1
059 Bapt Miss Assn	2	167	83	202 *	.1	.1
076 Buddhism	1	NR	NR	NR	-	-
081 Catholic	6	NR	NR	14,426	6.0	10.7
084 Calvary Chapel	2	NR	NR	NR	-	-
089 Chr & Miss Al	1	18	NR	26	-	-
093 Chr Ch (Disc)	10	3,459	1,205	4,178 *	1.7	3.1
097 Chr Chs&Chs Cr	8	2,312	NR	2,794 *	1.2	2.1
121 Ch God (Abr)	1	12	12	14 *	-	-
123 Ch God (Ander)	3	NR	243	243	.1	.2
127 Ch God (Cleve)	2	492	181	594 *	.2	.4
145 Ch God Prophcy	1	27	NR	32 *	-	-
151 L-D Saints	5	NR	NR	2,120	.9	1.6
157 Ch of Brethren	1	19	14	23 *	-	-
165 Ch of Nazarene	6	828	662	1,111	.5	.8
167 Chs of Christ	18	3,355	3,306	4,034	1.7	3.0
173 Comm of Christ	2	343	NR	343	.1	.3
185 Cumber Presb	2	57	NR	173	.1	.1
193 Episcopal	5	NR	722	1,943	.8	1.4
201 Evan Cov Ch	1	49	142	142 *	.1	.1
203 Evan Free Ch	1	155	375	375	.2	.3
207 E.L.C.A.	2	913	452	1,143	.5	.8
220 Free Lutheran	1	75	38	90	-	.1
223 Free Will Bapt	8	680	NR	821 *	.3	.6
226 Friends-USA	1	15	NR	18 *	-	-
230 Fund Methodist	4	118	NR	143 *	.1	.1

Religious Group	Number of Churches, Synagogues, Mosques, or Temples	Number of Communicant, Confirmed, or Full Members	Number of Attendees	Total Adherents: Number of Adherents	Total Adherents: % of Total Pop.	Total Adherents: % of Total Adh.
263 Int Foursq Gos	2	234	454	454 *	.2	.3
267 Muslim Est	1	NR	156	609	.3	.5
283 Luth—MO Synod	5	2,450	914	2,712	1.1	2.0
320 "Old" MB Ascs	3	289	NR	349 *	.1	.3
331 OCA: Ter Diocs	1	37	NR	111	-	.1
339 Pent Ch of God	2	117	NR	279	.1	.2
355 Presb Ch (USA)	11	3,698	2,017	4,468 *	1.9	3.3
356 Presb Ch Amer	1	33	60	60	-	-
360 Prim Bapt Chrch	1	NR	NR	NR	-	-
403 Salvation Army	1	166	187	317	.1	.2
413 S.D.A.	2	531	NR	632	.3	.5
419 So Bapt Conv	63	43,099	14,131	52,057 *	21.7	38.5
435 Unitarian-Univ	1	138	NR	167 *	.1	.1
443 Un C of Christ	2	431	202	521 *	.2	.4
449 Un Methodist	29	10,674	4,900	12,891 *	5.4	9.5
463 Vineyard	1	45	30	54 *	-	-
469 WELS	1	76	43	84	-	.1
496 Jewish Est	1	NR	NR	300	.1	.2
498 Indep.Charis.	2	1,250	1,800	1,800	.7	1.3
499 Indep.Non-Char	5	2,812	2,318	2,812	1.2	2.1
GRUNDY	**41**	**6,121**	**1,871**	**7,545 ***	**72.3**	**100.0**
053 Assemb of God	1	167	197	321	3.1	4.3
081 Catholic	1	NR	NR	126	1.2	1.7
093 Chr Ch (Disc)	4	945	261	1,149 *	11.0	15.2
097 Chr Chs&Chs Cr	4	447	NR	543 *	5.2	7.2
165 Ch of Nazarene	1	122	82	122	1.2	1.6
167 Chs of Christ	2	90	90	110	1.1	1.5
173 Comm of Christ	1	48	NR	48	.5	.6
193 Episcopal	1	NR	19	31	.3	.4
263 Int Foursq Gos	1	57	45	69 *	.7	.9
283 Luth—MO Synod	1	114	0	0	-	-
323 Old Ord Amish	2	71	NR	86 *	.8	1.1
355 Presb Ch (USA)	1	170	89	207 *	2.0	2.7
419 So Bapt Conv	13	3,080	783	3,746 *	35.9	49.6
449 Un Methodist	8	810	305	987 *	9.5	13.1
HARRISON	**49**	**4,891**	**1,862**	**6,127 ***	**69.2**	**100.0**
053 Assemb of God	4	185	207	246	2.8	4.0
081 Catholic	2	NR	NR	178	2.0	2.9
093 Chr Ch (Disc)	5	846	212	1,028 *	11.6	16.8
097 Chr Chs&Chs Cr	2	90	NR	109 *	1.2	1.8
107 Christian Un	1	130	160	160 *	1.8	2.6
167 Chs of Christ	4	97	118	144	1.6	2.4
173 Comm of Christ	2	150	NR	150	1.7	2.4
283 Luth—MO Synod	1	66	40	69	.8	1.1
323 Old Ord Amish	1	55	NR	67 *	.8	1.1
419 So Bapt Conv	14	2,192	752	2,664 *	30.1	43.5
449 Un Methodist	13	1,080	373	1,312 *	14.8	21.4
HENRY	**63**	**9,766**	**3,442**	**14,106 ***	**64.1**	**100.0**
053 Assemb of God	2	322	391	675	3.1	4.8
056 Baha'i	0	1	NR	1	-	-
081 Catholic	3	NR	NR	1,320	6.0	9.4
093 Chr Ch (Disc)	5	1,069	242	1,304 *	5.9	9.2
123 Ch God (Ander)	1	NR	8	8	-	.1
151 L-D Saints	1	NR	NR	297	1.4	2.1
157 Ch of Brethren	1	48	20	59 *	.3	.4
165 Ch of Nazarene	2	130	133	252	1.1	1.8
167 Chs of Christ	2	157	145	196	.9	1.4
173 Comm of Christ	1	101	NR	101	.5	.7
185 Cumber Presb	3	22	NR	123	.6	.9
193 Episcopal	1	NR	32	53	.2	.4
283 Luth—MO Synod	1	233	117	318	1.4	2.3
323 Old Ord Amish	3	165	NR	201 *	.9	1.4
339 Pent Ch of God	1	40	NR	80	.4	.6
355 Presb Ch (USA)	4	194	107	236 *	1.1	1.7
413 S.D.A.	1	86	NR	102	.5	.7
419 So Bapt Conv	20	5,611	1,549	6,844 *	31.1	48.5
443 Un C of Christ	1	66	29	81 *	.4	.6
449 Un Methodist	10	1,521	669	1,855 *	8.4	13.2

NR–Not Reported   *Total adherents estimated from known number of communicant, confirmed, full members.   - Represents a percentage less than 0.1.   Percentages may not total 100 due to rounding.

Table 4: Religious Congregations by County and Group: 2000

Religious Group	Number of Churches, Synagogues, Mosques, or Temples	Number of Communicant, Confirmed, or Full Members	Number of Attendees	Total Adherents: Number of Adherents	Total Adherents: % of Total Pop.	Total Adherents: % of Total Adh.
HICKORY	**29**	**2,892**	**1,051**	**3,728 ***	**41.7**	**100.0**
053 Assemb of God	3	195	239	290	3.2	7.8
081 Catholic	1	NR	NR	250	2.8	6.7
093 Chr Ch (Disc)	2	140	45	164 *	1.8	4.4
097 Chr Chs&Chs Cr	1	70	NR	82 *	.9	2.2
121 Ch God (Abr)	1	12	10	14 *	.2	.4
157 Ch of Brethren	1	33	18	39 *	.4	1.0
165 Ch of Nazarene	1	34	38	109	1.2	2.9
263 Int Foursq Gos	1	30	50	50 *	.6	1.3
283 Luth—MO Synod	1	53	0	0	-	-
320 "Old" MB Ascs	5	633	NR	743 *	8.3	19.9
323 Old Ord Amish	1	55	NR	65 *	.7	1.7
419 So Bapt Conv	7	1,308	444	1,536 *	17.2	41.2
443 Un C of Christ	1	20	9	23 *	.3	.6
449 Un Methodist	3	309	198	363 *	4.1	9.7
HOLT	**32**	**2,723**	**1,120**	**3,464 ***	**64.7**	**100.0**
081 Catholic	1	NR	NR	61	1.1	1.8
093 Chr Ch (Disc)	3	370	0	448 *	8.4	12.9
097 Chr Chs&Chs Cr	6	586	NR	711 *	13.3	20.5
123 Ch God (Ander)	1	NR	30	30	.6	.9
165 Ch of Nazarene	3	149	111	212	4.0	6.1
173 Comm of Christ	1	55	NR	55	1.0	1.6
283 Luth—MO Synod	3	288	443	402	7.5	11.6
355 Presb Ch (USA)	5	127	89	154 *	2.9	4.4
419 So Bapt Conv	4	328	141	397 *	7.4	11.5
449 Un Methodist	5	820	306	994 *	18.6	28.7
HOWARD	**28**	**3,679**	**1,279**	**5,365 ***	**52.5**	**100.0**
053 Assemb of God	1	18	23	23	.2	.4
056 Baha'i	0	2	NR	2	-	-
081 Catholic	2	NR	NR	850	8.3	15.8
093 Chr Ch (Disc)	4	643	205	782 *	7.7	14.6
167 Chs of Christ	1	30	35	43	.4	.8
193 Episcopal	1	NR	18	23	.2	.4
263 Int Foursq Gos	1	59	101	101 *	1.0	1.9
283 Luth—MO Synod	1	64	30	58	.6	1.1
355 Presb Ch (USA)	1	22	14	27 *	.3	.5
419 So Bapt Conv	8	1,768	450	2,151 *	21.1	40.1
443 Un C of Christ	1	202	60	246 *	2.4	4.6
449 Un Methodist	7	871	343	1,059 *	10.4	19.7
HOWELL	**93**	**12,387**	**5,636**	**18,190 ***	**48.8**	**100.0**
053 Assemb of God	5	632	892	1,022	2.7	5.6
056 Baha'i	0	5	NR	5	-	-
059 Bapt Miss Assn	2	64	31	79 *	.2	.4
081 Catholic	4	NR	NR	1,272	3.4	7.0
097 Chr Chs&Chs Cr	5	995	NR	1,239 *	3.3	6.8
123 Ch God (Ander)	6	NR	369	369	1.0	2.0
145 Ch God Prophcy	2	53	NR	66 *	.2	.4
151 L-D Saints	2	NR	NR	629	1.7	3.5
157 Ch of Brethren	1	119	48	148 *	.4	.8
165 Ch of Nazarene	3	117	55	143	.4	.8
167 Chs of Christ	15	1,295	1,385	1,603	4.3	8.8
173 Comm of Christ	1	10	NR	10	-	.1
185 Cumber Presb	1	28	NR	45	.1	.2
193 Episcopal	1	NR	46	112	.3	.6
207 E.L.C.A.	2	199	110	254	.7	1.4
223 Free Will Bapt	5	425	NR	529 *	1.4	2.9
283 Luth—MO Synod	1	173	91	213	.6	1.2
320 "Old" MB Ascs	2	100	NR	125 *	.3	.7
339 Pent Ch of God	2	95	NR	270	.7	1.5
355 Presb Ch (USA)	3	216	133	269 *	.7	1.5
360 Prim Bapt Chrch	5	NR	NR	NR	-	-
413 S.D.A.	2	108	NR	129	.3	.7
419 So Bapt Conv	20	6,964	1,963	8,676 *	23.3	47.7
449 Un Methodist	3	789	513	983 *	2.6	5.4
IRON	**33**	**3,253**	**1,338**	**4,707 ***	**44.0**	**100.0**
053 Assemb of God	6	182	241	329	3.1	7.0
059 Bapt Miss Assn	1	32	18	39 *	.4	.8
081 Catholic	2	NR	NR	368	3.4	7.8
151 L-D Saints	1	NR	NR	129	1.2	2.7
165 Ch of Nazarene	2	130	125	207	1.9	4.4
167 Chs of Christ	1	54	50	60	.6	1.3
193 Episcopal	1	NR	22	35	.3	.7
223 Free Will Bapt	1	85	NR	104 *	1.0	2.2
283 Luth—MO Synod	2	116	61	139	1.3	3.0
339 Pent Ch of God	1	20	NR	60	.6	1.3
355 Presb Ch (USA)	1	59	30	73 *	.7	1.6
419 So Bapt Conv	11	2,169	582	2,665 *	24.9	56.6
449 Un Methodist	3	406	209	499 *	4.7	10.6
JACKSON	**571**	**160,885**	**73,353**	**335,496 ***	**51.2**	**100.0**
017 Amer Bapt Assn	3	189	NR	237 *	-	.1
019 Amer Bapt USA	9	1,600	738	2,003 *	.3	.6
040 Ap Chr Ch-Amer	1	46	95	95 *	-	-
050 Armen Ap Etchm	1	20	NR	245	-	.1
053 Assemb of God	32	9,241	9,537	15,574	2.4	4.6
056 Baha'i	3	385	NR	385	.1	.1
057 Bapt Gen Conf	2	255	360	373 *	.1	.1
059 Bapt Miss Assn	4	293	208	368 *	.1	.1
076 Buddhism	6	NR	NR	NR	-	-
081 Catholic	43	NR	NR	101,207	15.5	30.2
093 Chr Ch (Disc)	27	16,651	3,974	20,843 *	3.2	6.2
097 Chr Chs&Chs Cr	8	1,203	NR	1,506 *	.2	.4
107 Christian Un	1	45	35	56 *	-	-
123 Ch God (Ander)	7	NR	653	653	.1	.2
127 Ch God (Cleve)	5	313	163	392 *	.1	.1
151 L-D Saints	13	NR	NR	5,578	.9	1.7
157 Ch of Brethren	1	167	44	209 *	-	.1
165 Ch of Nazarene	20	4,325	2,930	5,588	.9	1.7
167 Chs of Christ	27	3,309	3,424	4,166	.6	1.2
173 Comm of Christ	42	10,785	NR	10,785	1.6	3.2
185 Cumber Presb	1	9	NR	9	-	-
193 Episcopal	16	NR	2,531	6,136	.9	1.8
201 Evan Cov Ch	2	203	422	436 *	.1	.1
203 Evan Free Ch	2	89	160	160	-	-
207 E.L.C.A.	11	2,004	1,194	2,638	.4	.8
216 Evan Presby Ch	2	123	NR	154 *	-	-
221 Free Methodist	1	37	43	43	-	-
223 Free Will Bapt	5	425	NR	532 *	.1	.2
226 Friends-USA	3	149	NR	187 *	-	.1
237 Menn Br US Conf	1	17	NR	21 *	-	-
246 Greek Orthodox	1	NR	NR	930	.1	.3
252 Hindu	2	NR	NR	NR	-	-
262 Int Cou Comm Ch	1	215	NR	269 *	-	.1
263 Int Foursq Gos	1	84	82	105 *	-	-
267 Muslim Est	4	NR	1,184	6,659	1.0	2.0
283 Luth—MO Synod	17	6,889	3,341	8,813	1.3	2.6
290 Metro Comm Ch	2	223	221	279 *	-	.1
313 N Am Bapt Conf	1	114	120	143 *	-	-
320 "Old" MB Ascs	2	227	NR	284 *	-	.1
339 Pent Ch of God	4	182	NR	401	.1	.1
349 Pent Holiness	1	15	25	19 *	-	-
355 Presb Ch (USA)	33	9,199	5,354	11,517 *	1.8	3.4
356 Presb Ch Amer	1	37	40	70	-	-
360 Prim Bapt Chrch	3	NR	NR	NR	-	-
370 Ref Baptist Chs	1	NR	NR	NR	-	-
388 Reg Bapt Gen As	4	603	552	730 *	.1	.2
403 Salvation Army	5	584	529	2,707	.4	.8
413 S.D.A.	9	2,564	NR	3,050	.5	.9
416 Sikh	1	NR	NR	NR	-	-
419 So Bapt Conv	98	60,332	18,854	75,521 *	11.5	22.5
435 Unitarian-Univ	2	414	NR	518 *	.1	.2
443 Un C of Christ	7	1,534	692	1,920 *	.3	.6
449 Un Methodist	57	22,183	10,055	27,771 *	4.2	8.3
455 Un Ref Chs N.A.	1	56	NR	110	-	-
467 Wesleyan	3	74	96	232	-	.1
469 WELS	1	117	97	169	-	.1
496 Jewish Est	3	NR	NR	7,100	1.1	2.1
499 Indep.Non-Char	7	3,356	5,600	5,600	.9	1.7
JASPER	**179**	**40,885**	**15,638**	**61,150 ***	**58.4**	**100.0**
017 Amer Bapt Assn	2	100	NR	126 *	.1	.2

NR–Not Reported *Total adherents estimated from known number of communicant, confirmed, full members. - Represents a percentage less than 0.1. Percentages may not total 100 due to rounding.

Table 4: Religious Congregations by County and Group: 2000

Religious Group	Number of Churches, Synagogues, Mosques, or Temples	Number of Communicant, Confirmed, or Full Members	Number of Attendees	Total Adherents: Number of Adherents	Total Adherents: % of Total Pop.	Total Adherents: % of Total Adh.
053 Assemb of God	14	853	1,157	1,607	1.5	2.6
056 Baha'i	1	32	NR	32	-	.1
059 Bapt Miss Assn	3	271	167	339 *	.3	.6
076 Buddhism	1	NR	NR	NR	-	-
081 Catholic	4	NR	NR	5,491	5.2	9.0
084 Calvary Chapel	1	NR	NR	NR	-	-
093 Chr Ch (Disc)	2	522	265	654 *	.6	1.1
097 Chr Chs&Chs Cr	28	7,573	NR	9,481 *	9.1	15.5
123 Ch God (Ander)	3	NR	191	191	.2	.3
127 Ch God (Cleve)	2	335	82	420 *	.4	.7
145 Ch God Prophcy	1	27	NR	33 *	-	.1
151 L-D Saints	4	NR	NR	1,378	1.3	2.3
157 Ch of Brethren	1	21	18	26 *	-	-
165 Ch of Nazarene	6	1,174	628	1,293	1.2	2.1
167 Chs of Christ	5	634	685	925	.9	1.5
173 Comm of Christ	4	475	NR	475	.5	.8
175 Congr Chr Chs	1	160	110	200 *	.2	.3
193 Episcopal	2	NR	291	1,005	1.0	1.6
203 Evan Free Ch	1	31	85	85	.1	.1
207 E.L.C.A.	1	128	78	152	.1	.2
221 Free Methodist	1	28	24	45	-	.1
223 Free Will Bapt	3	255	NR	319 *	.3	.5
226 Friends-USA	2	100	NR	125 *	.1	.2
230 Fund Methodist	1	6	NR	8 *	-	-
263 Int Foursq Gos	1	30	50	50 *	-	.1
283 Luth—MO Synod	3	1,049	531	1,418	1.4	2.3
297 Mennonite;Other	1	77	NR	96 *	.1	.2
339 Pent Ch of God	4	396	NR	1,232	1.2	2.0
355 Presb Ch (USA)	7	1,316	556	1,647 *	1.6	2.7
388 Reg Bapt Gen As	1	20	25	25 *	-	-
403 Salvation Army	2	176	77	258	.2	.4
413 S.D.A.	3	218	NR	260	.2	.4
419 So Bapt Conv	37	16,307	5,268	20,415 *	19.5	33.4
449 Un Methodist	23	5,621	2,850	7,039 *	6.7	11.5
496 Jewish Est	1	NR	NR	100	.1	.2
499 Indep.Non-Char	2	2,950	2,500	4,200	4.0	6.9
JEFFERSON	**141**	**36,459**	**14,474**	**80,523 ***	**40.6**	**100.0**
017 Amer Bapt Assn	3	135	NR	173 *	.1	.2
019 Amer Bapt USA	1	205	82	261 *	.1	.3
053 Assemb of God	10	1,157	1,558	1,856	.9	2.3
056 Baha'i	0	37	NR	37	-	-
059 Bapt Miss Assn	5	357	221	454 *	.2	.6
081 Catholic	11	NR	NR	31,183	15.7	38.7
093 Chr Ch (Disc)	2	442	243	563 *	.3	.7
097 Chr Chs&Chs Cr	5	605	NR	770 *	.4	1.0
121 Ch God (Abr)	1	35	26	45 *	-	.1
123 Ch God (Ander)	1	NR	124	124	.1	.2
127 Ch God (Cleve)	2	178	91	227 *	.1	.3
151 L-D Saints	3	NR	NR	747	.4	.9
165 Ch of Nazarene	5	447	325	648	.3	.8
167 Chs of Christ	6	825	740	1,074	.5	1.3
173 Comm of Christ	2	240	NR	240	.1	.3
193 Episcopal	1	NR	28	53	-	.1
207 E.L.C.A.	2	533	228	739	.4	.9
223 Free Will Bapt	3	255	NR	324 *	.2	.4
263 Int Foursq Gos	1	20	26	26 *	-	-
283 Luth—MO Synod	11	4,595	2,204	6,468	3.3	8.0
339 Pent Ch of God	1	83	NR	500	.3	.6
355 Presb Ch (USA)	5	648	262	826 *	.4	1.0
360 Prim Bapt Chrch	2	NR	NR	NR	-	-
401 Rus Orth Abroad	1	NR	NR	NR	-	-
403 Salvation Army	1	67	58	72	-	.1
419 So Bapt Conv	34	20,701	5,900	26,350 *	13.3	32.7
443 Un C of Christ	5	1,721	562	2,191 *	1.1	2.7
449 Un Methodist	15	2,674	1,341	3,403 *	1.7	4.2
463 Vineyard	1	54	45	69 *	-	.1
499 Indep.Non-Char	1	445	410	1,100	.6	1.4
JOHNSON	**79**	**13,798**	**4,592**	**20,852 ***	**43.2**	**100.0**
053 Assemb of God	2	165	171	320	.7	1.5
056 Baha'i	0	20	NR	20	-	.1
081 Catholic	2	NR	NR	1,702	3.5	8.2
093 Chr Ch (Disc)	2	589	191	730 *	1.5	3.5
097 Chr Chs&Chs Cr	3	1,026	NR	1,271 *	2.6	6.1
151 L-D Saints	5	NR	NR	1,327	2.7	6.4
157 Ch of Brethren	2	79	30	98 *	.2	.5
165 Ch of Nazarene	2	158	140	291	.6	1.4
167 Chs of Christ	3	171	187	251	.5	1.2
173 Comm of Christ	3	419	NR	419	.9	2.0
185 Cumber Presb	3	97	NR	188	.4	.9
193 Episcopal	1	NR	66	182	.4	.9
203 Evan Free Ch	1	30	55	55	.1	.3
223 Free Will Bapt	1	85	NR	105 *	.2	.5
267 Muslim Est	1	NR	55	163	.3	.8
283 Luth—MO Synod	2	342	215	447	.9	2.1
286 E.PA Mennonite	1	16	NR	20 *	-	.1
339 Pent Ch of God	2	41	NR	169	.4	.8
349 Pent Holiness	1	40	40	50 *	.1	.2
355 Presb Ch (USA)	5	444	174	560 *	1.2	2.7
413 S.D.A.	2	90	NR	107	.2	.5
419 So Bapt Conv	26	7,972	2,455	9,881 *	20.5	47.4
449 Un Methodist	9	2,014	813	2,496 *	5.2	12.0
KNOX	**24**	**1,746**	**675**	**2,808 ***	**64.4**	**100.0**
053 Assemb of God	2	188	193	328	7.5	11.7
081 Catholic	2	NR	NR	569	13.0	20.3
093 Chr Ch (Disc)	2	193	76	238 *	5.5	8.5
097 Chr Chs&Chs Cr	2	240	NR	296 *	6.8	10.5
165 Ch of Nazarene	1	30	14	31	.7	1.1
167 Chs of Christ	1	20	15	20	.5	.7
360 Prim Bapt Chrch	1	NR	NR	NR	-	-
419 So Bapt Conv	8	574	148	708 *	16.2	25.2
449 Un Methodist	5	501	229	618 *	14.2	22.0
LACLEDE	**78**	**11,201**	**4,940**	**16,439 ***	**50.6**	**100.0**
053 Assemb of God	4	563	825	945	2.9	5.7
056 Baha'i	0	14	NR	14	-	.1
081 Catholic	2	NR	NR	874	2.7	5.3
093 Chr Ch (Disc)	2	315	181	395 *	1.2	2.4
097 Chr Chs&Chs Cr	5	1,064	NR	1,335 *	4.1	8.1
123 Ch God (Ander)	3	NR	253	253	.8	1.5
151 L-D Saints	1	NR	NR	373	1.1	2.3
165 Ch of Nazarene	1	232	224	327	1.0	2.0
167 Chs of Christ	3	377	405	491	1.5	3.0
173 Comm of Christ	1	55	NR	55	.2	.3
185 Cumber Presb	2	143	NR	155	.5	.9
193 Episcopal	1	NR	50	102	.3	.6
223 Free Will Bapt	11	935	NR	1,173 *	3.6	7.1
283 Luth—MO Synod	1	239	140	296	.9	1.8
320 "Old" MB Ascs	1	30	NR	38 *	.1	.2
339 Pent Ch of God	1	30	NR	100	.3	.6
360 Prim Bapt Chrch	2	NR	NR	NR	-	-
413 S.D.A.	1	59	NR	70	.2	.4
418 Southw Bapt Fel	1	NR	NR	NR	-	-
419 So Bapt Conv	24	5,757	1,717	7,225 *	22.2	44.0
443 Un C of Christ	1	164	85	206 *	.6	1.3
449 Un Methodist	9	1,224	585	1,537 *	4.7	9.3
499 Indep.Non-Char	1	0	475	475	1.5	2.9
LAFAYETTE	**69**	**14,693**	**5,428**	**20,156 ***	**61.2**	**100.0**
053 Assemb of God	5	281	363	530	1.6	2.6
056 Baha'i	0	2	NR	2	-	-
081 Catholic	4	NR	NR	1,491	4.5	7.4
093 Chr Ch (Disc)	5	1,053	270	1,310 *	4.0	6.5
097 Chr Chs&Chs Cr	2	405	NR	504 *	1.5	2.5
151 L-D Saints	1	NR	NR	260	.8	1.3
167 Chs of Christ	2	96	115	149	.5	.7
173 Comm of Christ	3	365	NR	365	1.1	1.8
193 Episcopal	1	NR	25	81	.2	.4
203 Evan Free Ch	1	69	125	125	.4	.6
223 Free Will Bapt	1	85	NR	106 *	.3	.5
283 Luth—MO Synod	8	3,485	1,673	4,224	12.8	21.0
355 Presb Ch (USA)	4	257	176	320 *	1.0	1.6
419 So Bapt Conv	15	5,142	1,387	6,395 *	19.4	31.7
443 Un C of Christ	6	1,693	607	2,105 *	6.4	10.4

NR–Not Reported   *Total adherents estimated from known number of communicant, confirmed, full members.   - Represents a percentage less than 0.1.   Percentages may not total 100 due to rounding.

Table 4: Religious Congregations by County and Group: 2000

Religious Group	Number of Churches, Synagogues, Mosques, or Temples	Number of Communicant, Confirmed, or Full Members	Number of Attendees	Total Adherents: Number of Adherents	Total Adherents: % of Total Pop.	Total Adherents: % of Total Adh.
449 Un Methodist	11	1,760	687	2,189 *	6.6	10.9
LAWRENCE	**90**	**13,566**	**5,699**	**19,754 ***	**56.1**	**100.0**
053 Assemb of God	5	363	449	701	2.0	3.5
056 Baha'i	0	3	NR	3	-	-
081 Catholic	4	NR	NR	2,073	5.9	10.5
093 Chr Ch (Disc)	4	552	116	698 *	2.0	3.5
097 Chr Chs&Chs Cr	5	534	NR	674 *	1.9	3.4
107 Christian Un	1	40	45	51 *	.1	.3
127 Ch God (Cleve)	1	12	9	15 *	-	.1
151 L-D Saints	2	NR	NR	595	1.7	3.0
165 Ch of Nazarene	5	158	108	176	.5	.9
167 Chs of Christ	4	458	526	545	1.5	2.8
171 Ch God-Gen Con	1	14	13	18 *	.1	.1
173 Comm of Christ	1	114	NR	114	.3	.6
185 Cumber Presb	3	47	NR	49	.1	.2
203 Evan Free Ch	1	20	25	25	.1	.1
221 Free Methodist	2	51	59	66	.2	.3
230 Fund Methodist	1	84	NR	106 *	.3	.5
283 Luth—MO Synod	3	987	475	1,211	3.4	6.1
323 Old Ord Amish	3	165	NR	210 *	.6	1.1
355 Presb Ch (USA)	3	358	183	452 *	1.3	2.3
419 So Bapt Conv	26	7,263	2,525	9,182 *	26.1	46.5
443 Un C of Christ	2	94	57	119 *	.3	.6
449 Un Methodist	12	1,599	759	2,021 *	5.7	10.2
499 Indep.Non-Char	1	650	350	650	1.8	3.3
LEWIS	**36**	**4,775**	**1,529**	**6,638 ***	**63.3**	**100.0**
053 Assemb of God	2	53	71	99	.9	1.5
081 Catholic	3	NR	NR	722	6.9	10.9
093 Chr Ch (Disc)	5	666	175	828 *	7.9	12.5
097 Chr Chs&Chs Cr	3	208	NR	258 *	2.5	3.9
283 Luth—MO Synod	1	223	100	250	2.4	3.8
323 Old Ord Amish	2	110	NR	136 *	1.3	2.0
388 Reg Bapt Gen As	1	97	97	97 *	.9	1.5
419 So Bapt Conv	12	2,853	796	3,546 *	33.8	53.4
449 Un Methodist	7	565	290	702 *	6.7	10.6
LINCOLN	**58**	**7,949**	**3,475**	**16,239 ***	**41.7**	**100.0**
053 Assemb of God	4	294	370	438	1.1	2.7
055 As Ref Pres Ch	2	155	NR	158	.4	1.0
056 Baha'i	0	3	NR	3	-	-
059 Bapt Miss Assn	1	0	48	48 *	.1	.3
081 Catholic	5	NR	NR	5,865	15.1	36.1
084 Calvary Chapel	1	NR	NR	NR	-	-
093 Chr Ch (Disc)	3	811	260	1,053 *	2.7	6.5
097 Chr Chs&Chs Cr	3	300	NR	390 *	1.0	2.4
167 Chs of Christ	1	110	135	120	.3	.7
283 Luth—MO Synod	1	513	225	667	1.7	4.1
355 Presb Ch (USA)	4	223	115	290 *	.7	1.8
413 S.D.A.	1	16	NR	19	-	.1
419 So Bapt Conv	15	3,502	1,328	4,547 *	11.7	28.0
443 Un C of Christ	3	487	193	632 *	1.6	3.9
449 Un Methodist	13	1,500	740	1,948 *	5.0	12.0
467 Wesleyan	1	35	61	61	.2	.4
LINN	**48**	**6,846**	**2,389**	**9,344 ***	**67.9**	**100.0**
053 Assemb of God	4	146	186	218	1.6	2.3
056 Baha'i	0	8	NR	8	.1	.1
081 Catholic	2	NR	NR	875	6.4	9.4
093 Chr Ch (Disc)	3	832	233	1,024 *	7.4	11.0
097 Chr Chs&Chs Cr	1	45	NR	55 *	.4	.6
165 Ch of Nazarene	1	88	78	115	.8	1.2
167 Chs of Christ	3	144	140	183	1.3	2.0
283 Luth—MO Synod	1	29	18	33	.2	.4
297 Mennonite;Other	1	70	NR	86 *	.6	.9
355 Presb Ch (USA)	1	96	31	118 *	.9	1.3
413 S.D.A.	1	21	NR	25	.2	.3
419 So Bapt Conv	16	3,689	1,079	4,538 *	33.0	48.6
449 Un Methodist	14	1,678	624	2,066 *	15.0	22.1

Religious Group	Number of Churches, Synagogues, Mosques, or Temples	Number of Communicant, Confirmed, or Full Members	Number of Attendees	Total Adherents: Number of Adherents	Total Adherents: % of Total Pop.	Total Adherents: % of Total Adh.
LIVINGSTON	**40**	**7,567**	**2,753**	**10,943 ***	**75.2**	**100.0**
019 Amer Bapt USA	1	98	49	120 *	.8	1.1
053 Assemb of God	2	144	149	295	2.0	2.7
056 Baha'i	0	1	NR	1	-	-
081 Catholic	1	NR	NR	1,241	8.5	11.3
093 Chr Ch (Disc)	3	482	174	589 *	4.0	5.4
127 Ch God (Cleve)	1	35	29	43 *	.3	.4
151 L-D Saints	1	NR	NR	145	1.0	1.3
165 Ch of Nazarene	1	36	23	41	.3	.4
167 Chs of Christ	1	100	145	200	1.4	1.8
173 Comm of Christ	1	28	NR	28	.2	.3
193 Episcopal	1	NR	50	106	.7	1.0
221 Free Methodist	1	122	100	139	1.0	1.3
283 Luth—MO Synod	1	123	60	158	1.1	1.4
339 Pent Ch of God	1	4	NR	9	.1	.1
355 Presb Ch (USA)	3	172	82	210 *	1.4	1.9
403 Salvation Army	1	40	29	65	.4	.6
419 So Bapt Conv	14	4,685	1,210	5,724 *	39.3	52.3
443 Un C of Christ	1	129	57	158 *	1.1	1.4
449 Un Methodist	5	1,368	596	1,671 *	11.5	15.3
MCDONALD	**45**	**5,258**	**1,814**	**7,926 ***	**36.6**	**100.0**
053 Assemb of God	1	62	45	56	.3	.7
056 Baha'i	0	7	NR	7	-	.1
081 Catholic	1	NR	NR	711	3.3	9.0
097 Chr Chs&Chs Cr	2	260	NR	336 *	1.5	4.2
151 L-D Saints	1	NR	NR	285	1.3	3.6
165 Ch of Nazarene	3	172	170	344	1.6	4.3
167 Chs of Christ	6	174	185	223	1.0	2.8
193 Episcopal	1	NR	14	35	.2	.4
223 Free Will Bapt	3	255	NR	330 *	1.5	4.2
230 Fund Methodist	1	24	NR	31 *	.1	.4
349 Pent Holiness	1	35	54	45 *	.2	.6
355 Presb Ch (USA)	1	11	18	18 *	.1	.2
360 Prim Bapt Chrch	1	NR	NR	NR	-	-
419 So Bapt Conv	16	3,604	1,005	4,659 *	21.5	58.8
449 Un Methodist	7	654	323	846 *	3.9	10.7
MACON	**59**	**7,861**	**2,080**	**11,040 ***	**70.0**	**100.0**
053 Assemb of God	1	13	18	20	.1	.2
081 Catholic	2	NR	NR	1,200	7.6	10.9
093 Chr Ch (Disc)	3	1,064	288	1,303 *	8.3	11.8
097 Chr Chs&Chs Cr	8	1,380	NR	1,690 *	10.7	15.3
151 L-D Saints	1	NR	NR	174	1.1	1.6
165 Ch of Nazarene	1	53	47	99	.6	.9
167 Chs of Christ	2	36	40	48	.3	.4
173 Comm of Christ	2	130	NR	130	.8	1.2
283 Luth—MO Synod	1	276	157	366	2.3	3.3
323 Old Ord Amish	3	165	NR	201 *	1.3	1.8
355 Presb Ch (USA)	5	350	185	429 *	2.7	3.9
360 Prim Bapt Chrch	4	NR	NR	NR	-	-
413 S.D.A.	2	83	NR	99	.6	.9
419 So Bapt Conv	15	3,626	983	4,441 *	28.2	40.2
443 Un C of Christ	2	95	54	116 *	.7	1.1
449 Un Methodist	7	590	308	724 *	4.6	6.6
MADISON	**41**	**4,717**	**2,124**	**6,887 ***	**58.4**	**100.0**
053 Assemb of God	2	50	65	78	.7	1.1
059 Bapt Miss Assn	1	17	15	21 *	.2	.3
081 Catholic	1	NR	NR	466	3.9	6.8
093 Chr Ch (Disc)	1	295	81	362 *	3.1	5.3
097 Chr Chs&Chs Cr	1	155	NR	190 *	1.6	2.8
121 Ch God (Abr)	1	34	11	42 *	.4	.6
145 Ch God Prophcy	1	27	NR	33 *	.3	.5
165 Ch of Nazarene	1	85	64	99	.8	1.4
167 Chs of Christ	2	74	80	96	.8	1.4
171 Ch God-Gen Con	1	44	78	78 *	.7	1.1
223 Free Will Bapt	8	680	NR	833 *	7.1	12.1
283 Luth—MO Synod	1	154	92	192	1.6	2.8
339 Pent Ch of God	1	12	NR	22	.2	.3
355 Presb Ch (USA)	1	51	30	63 *	.5	.9
360 Prim Bapt Chrch	1	NR	NR	NR	-	-

NR–Not Reported   *Total adherents estimated from known number of communicant, confirmed, full members.   - Represents a percentage less than 0.1.   Percentages may not total 100 due to rounding.

Table 4: Religious Congregations by County and Group: 2000

Religious Group	Number of Churches, Synagogues, Mosques, or Temples	Number of Communicant, Confirmed, or Full Members	Number of Attendees	Total Adherents: Number of Adherents	% of Total Pop.	% of Total Adh.
413 S.D.A.	1	22	NR	26	.2	.4
419 So Bapt Conv	12	2,127	586	2,608 *	22.1	37.9
449 Un Methodist	3	390	222	478 *	4.1	6.9
499 Indep.Non-Char	1	500	800	1,200	10.2	17.4
MARIES	**30**	**3,306**	**1,140**	**4,912 ***	**55.2**	**100.0**
053 Assemb of God	3	114	101	140	1.6	2.9
056 Baha'i	0	1	NR	1	-	-
081 Catholic	3	NR	NR	801	9.0	16.3
097 Chr Chs&Chs Cr	1	375	NR	467 *	5.2	9.5
165 Ch of Nazarene	1	13	27	30	.3	.6
167 Chs of Christ	6	249	255	319	3.6	6.5
173 Comm of Christ	1	104	NR	104	1.2	2.1
283 Luth—MO Synod	1	83	42	104	1.2	2.1
419 So Bapt Conv	10	2,034	525	2,532 *	28.4	51.5
449 Un Methodist	4	333	190	414 *	4.7	8.4
MARION	**61**	**11,501**	**4,754**	**18,535 ***	**65.5**	**100.0**
040 Ap Chr Ch-Amer	1	95	215	215 *	.8	1.2
053 Assemb of God	4	550	737	851	3.0	4.6
056 Baha'i	0	2	NR	2	-	-
059 Bapt Miss Assn	1	95	50	118 *	.4	.6
081 Catholic	2	NR	NR	3,245	11.5	17.5
093 Chr Ch (Disc)	5	1,262	405	1,565 *	5.5	8.4
097 Chr Chs&Chs Cr	3	690	NR	856 *	3.0	4.6
151 L-D Saints	1	NR	NR	229	.8	1.2
165 Ch of Nazarene	2	281	205	371	1.3	2.0
167 Chs of Christ	2	77	87	110	.4	.6
173 Comm of Christ	1	44	NR	44	.2	.2
193 Episcopal	2	NR	62	87	.3	.5
203 Evan Free Ch	1	69	125	125	.4	.7
221 Free Methodist	1	23	33	33	.1	.2
223 Free Will Bapt	1	85	NR	105 *	.4	.6
283 Luth—MO Synod	3	1,480	617	2,055	7.3	11.1
288 Mennonite USA	2	60	59	75 *	.3	.4
339 Pent Ch of God	1	63	NR	123	.4	.7
355 Presb Ch (USA)	3	470	243	582 *	2.1	3.1
403 Salvation Army	1	88	59	220	.8	1.2
413 S.D.A.	1	35	NR	42	.1	.2
419 So Bapt Conv	14	4,642	1,222	5,758 *	20.4	31.1
449 Un Methodist	9	1,390	635	1,724 *	6.1	9.3
MERCER	**19**	**2,489**	**768**	**3,087 ***	**82.2**	**100.0**
053 Assemb of God	2	61	73	86	2.3	2.8
056 Baha'i	0	1	NR	1	-	-
081 Catholic	1	NR	NR	65	1.7	2.1
093 Chr Ch (Disc)	1	206	105	248 *	6.6	8.0
097 Chr Chs&Chs Cr	1	155	NR	186 *	5.0	6.0
167 Chs of Christ	1	25	25	30	.8	1.0
283 Luth—MO Synod	1	47	24	75	2.0	2.4
419 So Bapt Conv	8	1,620	401	1,947 *	51.8	63.1
449 Un Methodist	4	374	140	449 *	12.0	14.5
MILLER	**52**	**7,635**	**2,934**	**13,570 ***	**57.6**	**100.0**
053 Assemb of God	4	277	355	452	1.9	3.3
056 Baha'i	0	2	NR	2	-	-
081 Catholic	5	NR	NR	3,790	16.1	27.9
093 Chr Ch (Disc)	1	357	101	446 *	1.9	3.3
097 Chr Chs&Chs Cr	3	660	NR	825 *	3.5	6.1
165 Ch of Nazarene	2	314	219	363	1.5	2.7
167 Chs of Christ	9	366	387	464	2.0	3.4
175 Congr Chr Chs	1	50	25	62 *	.3	.5
258 IndFreeWillBapt	1	48	NR	60 *	.3	.4
283 Luth—MO Synod	1	134	100	188	.8	1.4
339 Pent Ch of God	2	53	NR	160	.7	1.2
419 So Bapt Conv	18	4,793	1,429	5,983 *	25.4	44.1
443 Un C of Christ	1	44	19	55 *	.2	.4
449 Un Methodist	3	537	299	670 *	2.8	4.9
496 Jewish Est	1	NR	NR	50	.2	.4
MISSISSIPPI	**30**	**4,479**	**1,559**	**6,320 ***	**47.1**	**100.0**
053 Assemb of God	2	134	172	334	2.5	5.3
081 Catholic	1	NR	NR	440	3.3	7.0
097 Chr Chs&Chs Cr	2	382	NR	477 *	3.6	7.5
123 Ch God (Ander)	1	NR	115	115	.9	1.8
145 Ch God Prophcy	2	53	NR	66 *	.5	1.0
165 Ch of Nazarene	1	21	28	51	.4	.8
167 Chs of Christ	2	90	88	104	.8	1.6
223 Free Will Bapt	1	85	NR	106 *	.8	1.7
349 Pent Holiness	2	109	126	136 *	1.0	2.2
413 S.D.A.	1	185	NR	220	1.6	3.5
419 So Bapt Conv	9	2,727	689	3,405 *	25.4	53.9
449 Un Methodist	6	693	341	866 *	6.4	13.7
MONITEAU	**44**	**6,895**	**2,396**	**10,259 ***	**69.2**	**100.0**
053 Assemb of God	3	133	182	236	1.6	2.3
081 Catholic	2	NR	NR	1,737	11.7	16.9
093 Chr Ch (Disc)	3	350	75	436 *	2.9	4.2
145 Ch God Prophcy	1	27	NR	33 *	.2	.3
151 L-D Saints	1	NR	NR	293	2.0	2.9
167 Chs of Christ	1	37	40	48	.3	.5
283 Luth—MO Synod	2	402	14	45	.3	.4
288 Mennonite USA	1	223	180	278 *	1.9	2.7
297 Mennonite;Other	1	15	NR	19 *	.1	.2
322 Old Ord Menn Ch	2	306	NR	381 *	2.6	3.7
339 Pent Ch of God	1	13	NR	43	.3	.4
419 So Bapt Conv	17	4,029	1,299	5,017 *	33.8	48.9
443 Un C of Christ	4	768	385	956 *	6.4	9.3
449 Un Methodist	5	592	221	737 *	5.0	7.2
MONROE	**32**	**3,498**	**1,348**	**5,747 ***	**61.7**	**100.0**
053 Assemb of God	1	48	75	75	.8	1.3
056 Baha'i	0	2	NR	2	-	-
061 Beachy Amish	1	22	NR	27 *	.3	.5
081 Catholic	3	NR	NR	1,346	14.5	23.4
093 Chr Ch (Disc)	8	1,172	393	1,453 *	15.6	25.3
193 Episcopal	1	NR	7	10	.1	.2
283 Luth—MO Synod	1	133	52	204	2.2	3.5
355 Presb Ch (USA)	2	90	90	113 *	1.2	2.0
360 Prim Bapt Chrch	1	NR	NR	NR	-	-
419 So Bapt Conv	10	1,496	500	1,854 *	19.9	32.3
449 Un Methodist	4	535	231	663 *	7.1	11.5
MONTGOMERY	**45**	**4,228**	**1,551**	**7,455 ***	**61.4**	**100.0**
053 Assemb of God	1	14	17	17	.1	.2
056 Baha'i	0	1	NR	1	-	-
081 Catholic	5	NR	NR	1,355	11.2	18.2
093 Chr Ch (Disc)	3	404	23	498 *	4.1	6.7
097 Chr Chs&Chs Cr	3	220	NR	271 *	2.2	3.6
151 L-D Saints	2	NR	NR	832	6.9	11.2
165 Ch of Nazarene	1	29	41	75	.6	1.0
167 Chs of Christ	1	50	50	64	.5	.9
283 Luth—MO Synod	3	524	273	662	5.5	8.9
355 Presb Ch (USA)	3	115	75	142 *	1.2	1.9
419 So Bapt Conv	9	1,510	513	1,861 *	15.3	25.0
443 Un C of Christ	3	290	103	357 *	2.9	4.8
449 Un Methodist	11	1,071	456	1,320 *	10.9	17.7
MORGAN	**47**	**7,206**	**2,833**	**10,423 ***	**54.0**	**100.0**
053 Assemb of God	3	365	474	648	3.4	6.2
081 Catholic	2	NR	NR	970	5.0	9.3
093 Chr Ch (Disc)	2	433	323	529 *	2.7	5.1
097 Chr Chs&Chs Cr	1	150	NR	183 *	.9	1.8
123 Ch God (Ander)	1	NR	45	45	.2	.4
143 CG in Cr(Menn)	2	245	NR	299 *	1.5	2.9
151 L-D Saints	1	NR	NR	559	2.9	5.4
167 Chs of Christ	1	28	45	36	.2	.3
207 E.L.C.A.	2	294	141	346	1.8	3.3
283 Luth—MO Synod	2	431	147	384	2.0	3.7
286 E.PA Mennonite	1	84	NR	103 *	.5	1.0
288 Mennonite USA	1	36	29	44 *	.2	.4
322 Old Ord Menn Ch	4	366	NR	447 *	2.3	4.3
355 Presb Ch (USA)	3	146	94	178 *	.9	1.7
419 So Bapt Conv	13	3,214	845	3,926 *	20.3	37.7

NR–Not Reported *Total adherents estimated from known number of communicant, confirmed, full members. - Represents a percentage less than 0.1. Percentages may not total 100 due to rounding.

Table 4: Religious Congregations by County and Group: 2000

Religious Group	Number of Churches, Synagogues, Mosques, or Temples	Number of Communicant, Confirmed, or Full Members	Number of Attendees	Total Adherents: Number of Adherents	Total Adherents: % of Total Pop.	Total Adherents: % of Total Adh.
443 Un C of Christ	1	67	45	82 *	.4	.8
449 Un Methodist	7	1,347	645	1,644 *	8.5	15.8
NEW MADRID	**50**	**6,833**	**2,189**	**9,732 ***	**49.3**	**100.0**
017 Amer Bapt Assn	2	100	NR	124 *	.6	1.3
053 Assemb of God	5	220	281	424	2.1	4.4
059 Bapt Miss Assn	2	457	185	569 *	2.9	5.8
081 Catholic	2	NR	NR	856	4.3	8.8
093 Chr Ch (Disc)	1	95	32	118 *	.6	1.2
123 Ch God (Ander)	3	NR	204	204	1.0	2.1
127 Ch God (Cleve)	1	62	50	77 *	.4	.8
157 Ch of Brethren	1	32	12	40 *	.2	.4
165 Ch of Nazarene	1	23	21	24	.1	.2
167 Chs of Christ	7	301	315	393	2.0	4.0
339 Pent Ch of God	1	15	NR	15	.1	.2
355 Presb Ch (USA)	1	42	21	52 *	.3	.5
360 Prim Bapt Chrch	1	NR	NR	NR	-	-
419 So Bapt Conv	14	4,911	795	6,120 *	31.0	62.9
449 Un Methodist	8	575	273	716 *	3.6	7.4
NEWTON	**98**	**16,997**	**7,034**	**23,480 ***	**44.6**	**100.0**
053 Assemb of God	8	829	937	1,109	2.1	4.7
056 Baha'i	0	8	NR	8	-	-
081 Catholic	3	NR	NR	1,319	2.5	5.6
093 Chr Ch (Disc)	1	498	143	625 *	1.2	2.7
097 Chr Chs&Chs Cr	7	1,509	NR	1,892 *	3.6	8.1
123 Ch God (Ander)	1	NR	98	98	.2	.4
151 L-D Saints	2	NR	NR	491	.9	2.1
165 Ch of Nazarene	3	154	116	220	.4	.9
167 Chs of Christ	17	1,463	1,583	1,830	3.5	7.8
173 Comm of Christ	1	53	NR	53	.1	.2
175 Congr Chr Chs	1	80	50	100 *	.2	.4
193 Episcopal	1	NR	50	136	.3	.6
223 Free Will Bapt	3	255	NR	320 *	.6	1.4
283 Luth—MO Synod	1	266	128	353	.7	1.5
297 Mennonite;Other	1	58	NR	73 *	.1	.3
339 Pent Ch of God	1	25	NR	50	.1	.2
349 Pent Holiness	1	45	45	56 *	.1	.2
355 Presb Ch (USA)	2	168	89	211 *	.4	.9
360 Prim Bapt Chrch	1	NR	NR	NR	-	-
413 S.D.A.	1	37	NR	44	.1	.2
419 So Bapt Conv	34	10,538	3,386	13,224 *	25.1	56.3
449 Un Methodist	8	1,011	409	1,268 *	2.4	5.4
NODAWAY	**44**	**6,785**	**2,259**	**11,842 ***	**54.0**	**100.0**
053 Assemb of God	1	134	175	222	1.0	1.9
056 Baha'i	0	10	NR	10	-	.1
081 Catholic	5	NR	NR	3,633	16.6	30.7
093 Chr Ch (Disc)	5	1,454	352	1,694 *	7.7	14.3
097 Chr Chs&Chs Cr	5	632	NR	737 *	3.4	6.2
151 L-D Saints	1	NR	NR	175	.8	1.5
165 Ch of Nazarene	1	34	42	60	.3	.5
167 Chs of Christ	3	105	103	134	.6	1.1
173 Comm of Christ	2	130	NR	130	.6	1.1
193 Episcopal	1	NR	39	45	.2	.4
283 Luth—MO Synod	1	141	80	174	.8	1.5
355 Presb Ch (USA)	1	162	107	189 *	.9	1.6
360 Prim Bapt Chrch	1	NR	NR	NR	-	-
419 So Bapt Conv	3	1,909	543	2,224 *	10.1	18.8
449 Un Methodist	14	2,074	818	2,415 *	11.0	20.4
OREGON	**52**	**4,538**	**1,604**	**6,044 ***	**58.4**	**100.0**
053 Assemb of God	5	260	354	535	5.2	8.9
059 Bapt Miss Assn	1	39	25	48 *	.5	.8
081 Catholic	1	NR	NR	165	1.6	2.7
123 Ch God (Ander)	1	NR	71	71	.7	1.2
145 Ch God Prophcy	1	27	NR	33 *	.3	.5
167 Chs of Christ	7	460	483	593	5.7	9.8
185 Cumber Presb	1	0	NR	2	-	-
223 Free Will Bapt	20	1,699	NR	2,082 *	20.1	34.4
419 So Bapt Conv	11	1,781	510	2,182 *	21.1	36.1
449 Un Methodist	4	272	161	333 *	3.2	5.5
OSAGE	**35**	**2,019**	**597**	**9,484 ***	**72.6**	**100.0**
053 Assemb of God	1	36	50	50	.4	.5
061 Beachy Amish	1	10	NR	13 *	.1	.1
081 Catholic	12	NR	NR	6,812	52.2	71.8
097 Chr Chs&Chs Cr	5	356	NR	447 *	3.4	4.7
173 Comm of Christ	1	58	NR	58	.4	.6
283 Luth—MO Synod	2	156	78	201	1.5	2.1
339 Pent Ch of God	1	63	NR	225	1.7	2.4
419 So Bapt Conv	7	898	284	1,125 *	8.6	11.9
443 Un C of Christ	3	128	60	160 *	1.2	1.7
449 Un Methodist	2	314	125	393 *	3.0	4.1
OZARK	**26**	**1,594**	**1,177**	**2,191 ***	**23.0**	**100.0**
053 Assemb of God	3	217	281	374	3.9	17.1
056 Baha'i	0	2	NR	2	-	.1
081 Catholic	1	NR	NR	107	1.1	4.9
093 Chr Ch (Disc)	1	206	83	246 *	2.6	11.2
123 Ch God (Ander)	1	NR	45	45	.5	2.1
165 Ch of Nazarene	1	0	0	0	-	-
167 Chs of Christ	10	431	467	544	5.7	24.8
283 Luth—MO Synod	1	31	21	31	.3	1.4
320 "Old" MB Ascs	1	33	NR	39 *	.4	1.8
413 S.D.A.	1	21	NR	25	.3	1.1
419 So Bapt Conv	5	474	188	565 *	5.9	25.8
449 Un Methodist	1	179	92	213 *	2.2	9.7
PEMISCOT	**55**	**9,009**	**2,864**	**12,367 ***	**61.7**	**100.0**
053 Assemb of God	4	156	188	248	1.2	2.0
056 Baha'i	0	1	NR	1	-	-
081 Catholic	1	NR	NR	235	1.2	1.9
097 Chr Chs&Chs Cr	1	125	NR	163 *	.8	1.3
127 Ch God (Cleve)	3	212	129	277 *	1.4	2.2
145 Ch God Prophcy	1	27	NR	35 *	.2	.3
165 Ch of Nazarene	2	103	59	133	.7	1.1
167 Chs of Christ	9	470	509	588	2.9	4.8
193 Episcopal	1	NR	16	20	.1	.2
339 Pent Ch of God	2	50	NR	97	.5	.8
349 Pent Holiness	3	202	225	264 *	1.3	2.1
355 Presb Ch (USA)	1	281	121	367 *	1.8	3.0
419 So Bapt Conv	19	6,622	1,229	8,654 *	43.2	70.0
449 Un Methodist	7	715	325	935 *	4.7	7.6
467 Wesleyan	1	45	63	350	1.7	2.8
PERRY	**28**	**4,357**	**2,605**	**13,793 ***	**76.1**	**100.0**
053 Assemb of God	1	42	54	75	.4	.5
081 Catholic	8	NR	NR	8,322	45.9	60.3
165 Ch of Nazarene	1	24	0	24	.1	.2
167 Chs of Christ	1	10	17	15	.1	.1
283 Luth—MO Synod	8	3,269	2,073	4,099	22.6	29.7
355 Presb Ch (USA)	2	149	100	185 *	1.0	1.3
419 So Bapt Conv	4	520	199	647 *	3.6	4.7
449 Un Methodist	3	343	162	426 *	2.3	3.1
PETTIS	**73**	**15,478**	**4,468**	**24,188 ***	**61.4**	**100.0**
017 Amer Bapt Assn	1	21	NR	26 *	.1	.1
032 Amish; other	1	115	NR	144 *	.4	.6
053 Assemb of God	2	129	180	388	1.0	1.6
056 Baha'i	0	10	NR	10	-	-
081 Catholic	4	NR	NR	3,341	8.5	13.8
093 Chr Ch (Disc)	1	902	305	1,131 *	2.9	4.7
097 Chr Chs&Chs Cr	3	672	NR	842 *	2.1	3.5
127 Ch God (Cleve)	1	29	40	40 *	.1	.2
151 L-D Saints	1	NR	NR	481	1.2	2.0
165 Ch of Nazarene	1	56	41	56	.1	.2
167 Chs of Christ	1	54	65	84	.2	.3
173 Comm of Christ	1	144	NR	144	.4	.6
193 Episcopal	1	NR	76	265	.7	1.1
207 E.L.C.A.	1	268	75	342	.9	1.4
223 Free Will Bapt	1	85	NR	107 *	.3	.4
283 Luth—MO Synod	2	1,408	245	1,883	4.8	7.8
297 Mennonite;Other	1	68	NR	85 *	.2	.4
339 Pent Ch of God	2	66	NR	375	1.0	1.6

NR–Not Reported   *Total adherents estimated from known number of communicant, confirmed, full members.   - Represents a percentage less than 0.1.   Percentages may not total 100 due to rounding.

Table 4: Religious Congregations by County and Group: 2000

Religious Group	Number of Churches, Synagogues, Mosques, or Temples	Number of Communicant, Confirmed, or Full Members	Number of Attendees	Total Adherents: Number of Adherents	Total Adherents: % of Total Pop.	Total Adherents: % of Total Adh.
355 Presb Ch (USA)	3	610	197	764 *	1.9	3.2
403 Salvation Army	1	91	43	165	.4	.7
413 S.D.A.	2	161	NR	191	.5	.8
419 So Bapt Conv	24	8,043	2,059	10,082 *	25.6	41.7
443 Un C of Christ	1	172	65	216 *	.5	.9
449 Un Methodist	16	2,374	1,077	2,976 *	7.6	12.3
496 Jewish Est	1	NR	NR	50	.1	.2
PHELPS	**68**	**11,841**	**5,156**	**18,193 ***	**45.7**	**100.0**
017 Amer Bapt Assn	1	50	NR	61 *	.2	.3
053 Assemb of God	5	607	829	1,102	2.8	6.1
056 Baha'i	1	40	NR	40	.1	.2
081 Catholic	3	NR	NR	2,080	5.2	11.4
093 Chr Ch (Disc)	1	62	36	75 *	.2	.4
097 Chr Chs&Chs Cr	6	1,608	NR	1,956 *	4.9	10.8
123 Ch God (Ander)	3	NR	338	338	.8	1.9
151 L-D Saints	1	NR	NR	134	.3	.7
165 Ch of Nazarene	1	65	78	98	.2	.5
167 Chs of Christ	7	523	558	676	1.7	3.7
173 Comm of Christ	1	29	NR	29	.1	.2
193 Episcopal	2	NR	167	472	1.2	2.6
223 Free Will Bapt	1	85	NR	103 *	.3	.6
226 Friends-USA	1	55	NR	67 *	.2	.4
267 Muslim Est	1	NR	55	163	.4	.9
283 Luth—MO Synod	4	933	389	1,042	2.6	5.7
339 Pent Ch of God	1	13	NR	44	.1	.2
355 Presb Ch (USA)	1	326	167	396 *	1.0	2.2
360 Prim Bapt Chrch	1	NR	NR	NR	-	-
413 S.D.A.	1	144	NR	171	.4	.9
419 So Bapt Conv	18	5,720	1,615	6,957 *	17.5	38.2
435 Unitarian-Univ	1	14	NR	17 *	-	.1
449 Un Methodist	3	932	432	1,134 *	2.8	6.2
463 Vineyard	2	360	292	438 *	1.1	2.4
499 Indep.Non-Char	1	275	200	600	1.5	3.3
PIKE	**63**	**6,220**	**2,195**	**9,541 ***	**52.0**	**100.0**
053 Assemb of God	1	47	68	68	.4	.7
056 Baha'i	0	6	NR	6	-	.1
081 Catholic	3	NR	NR	1,680	9.2	17.6
093 Chr Ch (Disc)	9	803	243	975 *	5.3	10.2
151 L-D Saints	1	NR	NR	110	.6	1.2
165 Ch of Nazarene	1	94	109	187	1.0	2.0
167 Chs of Christ	4	98	100	123	.7	1.3
193 Episcopal	3	NR	51	61	.3	.6
221 Free Methodist	1	5	17	17	.1	.2
283 Luth—MO Synod	2	150	71	216	1.2	2.3
323 Old Ord Amish	3	165	NR	201 *	1.1	2.1
355 Presb Ch (USA)	9	608	290	743 *	4.0	7.8
360 Prim Bapt Chrch	1	NR	NR	NR	-	-
419 So Bapt Conv	20	3,883	1,069	4,716 *	25.7	49.4
449 Un Methodist	5	361	177	438 *	2.4	4.6
PLATTE	**61**	**15,979**	**8,566**	**30,605 ***	**41.5**	**100.0**
019 Amer Bapt USA	1	57	109	109 *	.1	.4
053 Assemb of God	3	941	764	1,353	1.8	4.4
056 Baha'i	0	10	NR	10	-	-
081 Catholic	2	NR	NR	8,952	12.1	29.3
093 Chr Ch (Disc)	11	2,371	634	2,957 *	4.0	9.7
097 Chr Chs&Chs Cr	3	387	NR	482 *	.7	1.6
151 L-D Saints	2	NR	NR	681	.9	2.2
165 Ch of Nazarene	2	187	144	357	.5	1.2
167 Chs of Christ	2	42	43	53	.1	.2
193 Episcopal	2	NR	268	458	.6	1.5
207 E.L.C.A.	1	569	359	748	1.0	2.4
223 Free Will Bapt	1	85	NR	106 *	.1	.3
283 Luth—MO Synod	3	1,071	528	1,394	1.9	4.6
331 OCA: Ter Diocs	1	30	NR	53	.1	.2
355 Presb Ch (USA)	1	290	178	362 *	.5	1.2
419 So Bapt Conv	15	5,130	1,912	6,399 *	8.7	20.9
443 Un C of Christ	1	36	26	45 *	.1	.1
449 Un Methodist	6	3,000	1,500	3,741 *	5.1	12.2
463 Vineyard	1	300	250	374 *	.5	1.2
469 WELS	1	93	51	121	.2	.4
498 Indep.Charis.	1	1,200	1,550	1,550	2.1	5.1
499 Indep.Non-Char	1	180	250	300	.4	1.0
POLK	**77**	**10,693**	**4,199**	**14,844 ***	**55.0**	**100.0**
053 Assemb of God	8	788	1,054	1,242	4.6	8.4
056 Baha'i	0	14	NR	14	.1	.1
081 Catholic	2	NR	NR	642	2.4	4.3
093 Chr Ch (Disc)	2	349	142	435 *	1.6	2.9
097 Chr Chs&Chs Cr	1	150	NR	187 *	.7	1.3
121 Ch God (Abr)	1	10	10	12 *	-	.1
151 L-D Saints	1	NR	NR	438	1.6	3.0
165 Ch of Nazarene	1	62	70	70	.3	.5
167 Chs of Christ	2	158	165	196	.7	1.3
173 Comm of Christ	1	59	NR	59	.2	.4
185 Cumber Presb	2	52	NR	52	.2	.4
193 Episcopal	1	NR	43	112	.4	.8
263 Int Foursq Gos	1	33	57	57 *	.2	.4
283 Luth—MO Synod	1	181	105	246	.9	1.7
320 "Old" MB Ascs	26	2,762	NR	3,443 *	12.8	23.2
323 Old Ord Amish	1	55	NR	69 *	.3	.5
339 Pent Ch of God	1	25	NR	100	.4	.7
360 Prim Bapt Chrch	1	NR	NR	NR	-	-
413 S.D.A.	1	42	NR	50	.2	.3
419 So Bapt Conv	15	4,751	1,968	5,922 *	21.9	39.9
449 Un Methodist	8	1,202	585	1,498 *	5.5	10.1
PULASKI	**73**	**12,835**	**3,832**	**17,920 ***	**43.5**	**100.0**
053 Assemb of God	5	289	340	470	1.1	2.6
056 Baha'i	0	10	NR	10	-	.1
081 Catholic	4	NR	NR	759	1.8	4.2
093 Chr Ch (Disc)	1	90	25	115 *	.3	.6
097 Chr Chs&Chs Cr	7	1,277	NR	1,633 *	4.0	9.1
107 Christian Un	2	75	93	96 *	.2	.5
123 Ch God (Ander)	3	NR	133	133	.3	.7
127 Ch God (Cleve)	1	115	107	147 *	.4	.8
151 L-D Saints	1	NR	NR	463	1.1	2.6
165 Ch of Nazarene	2	99	72	177	.4	1.0
167 Chs of Christ	8	352	343	429	1.0	2.4
223 Free Will Bapt	1	85	NR	109 *	.3	.6
283 Luth—MO Synod	1	174	115	257	.6	1.4
323 Old Ord Amish	1	55	NR	70 *	.2	.4
355 Presb Ch (USA)	1	111	76	142 *	.3	.8
356 Presb Ch Amer	1	0	0	0	-	-
413 S.D.A.	1	25	NR	30	.1	.2
419 So Bapt Conv	30	9,509	2,147	12,152 *	29.5	67.8
449 Un Methodist	3	569	381	728 *	1.8	4.1
PUTNAM	**17**	**2,185**	**547**	**2,765 ***	**52.9**	**100.0**
053 Assemb of God	1	50	67	93	1.8	3.4
081 Catholic	1	NR	NR	50	1.0	1.8
097 Chr Chs&Chs Cr	4	557	NR	682 *	13.1	24.7
167 Chs of Christ	3	78	88	104	2.0	3.8
323 Old Ord Amish	1	55	NR	67 *	1.3	2.4
419 So Bapt Conv	5	1,226	290	1,501 *	28.7	54.3
449 Un Methodist	2	219	102	268 *	5.1	9.7
RALLS	**20**	**3,073**	**929**	**4,134 ***	**42.9**	**100.0**
081 Catholic	1	NR	NR	353	3.7	8.5
093 Chr Ch (Disc)	4	620	192	760 *	7.9	18.4
097 Chr Chs&Chs Cr	1	125	NR	153 *	1.6	3.7
283 Luth—MO Synod	1	30	18	46	.5	1.1
355 Presb Ch (USA)	2	46	36	62 *	.6	1.5
419 So Bapt Conv	8	2,036	585	2,495 *	25.9	60.4
449 Un Methodist	3	216	98	265 *	2.8	6.4
RANDOLPH	**55**	**9,687**	**2,469**	**14,218 ***	**57.6**	**100.0**
032 Amish; other	1	48	NR	59 *	.2	.4
053 Assemb of God	2	146	194	345	1.4	2.4
056 Baha'i	0	4	NR	4	-	-
081 Catholic	1	NR	NR	1,667	6.8	11.7
093 Chr Ch (Disc)	8	1,327	154	1,627 *	6.6	11.4
097 Chr Chs&Chs Cr	4	950	NR	1,165 *	4.7	8.2

NR–Not Reported *Total adherents estimated from known number of communicant, confirmed, full members. - Represents a percentage less than 0.1. Percentages may not total 100 due to rounding.

Table 4: Religious Congregations by County and Group: 2000

Religious Group	Number of Churches, Synagogues, Mosques, or Temples	Number of Communicant, Confirmed, or Full Members	Number of Attendees	Total Adherents		
				Number of Adherents	% of Total Pop.	% of Total Adh.
123 Ch God (Ander)	1	NR	45	45	.2	.3
151 L-D Saints	1	NR	NR	336	1.4	2.4
165 Ch of Nazarene	1	85	97	215	.9	1.5
167 Chs of Christ	2	110	110	132	.5	.9
185 Cumber Presb	1	13	NR	25	.1	.2
193 Episcopal	1	NR	36	68	.3	.5
223 Free Will Bapt	1	85	NR	104 *	.4	.7
283 Luth—MO Synod	1	340	125	370	1.5	2.6
323 Old Ord Amish	6	330	NR	402 *	1.6	2.8
355 Presb Ch (USA)	1	165	85	202 *	.8	1.4
388 Reg Bapt Gen As	1	41	48	50 *	.2	.4
413 S.D.A.	1	152	NR	181	.7	1.3
419 So Bapt Conv	13	4,819	1,102	5,907 *	24.0	41.5
449 Un Methodist	8	1,072	473	1,314 *	5.3	9.2
RAY	**56**	**9,295**	**3,180**	**12,428 ***	**53.2**	**100.0**
053 Assemb of God	3	284	351	606	2.6	4.9
056 Baha'i	0	1	NR	1	-	-
081 Catholic	1	NR	NR	290	1.2	2.3
089 Chr & Miss Al	1	224	NR	292	1.3	2.3
093 Chr Ch (Disc)	3	805	105	1,017 *	4.4	8.2
097 Chr Chs&Chs Cr	1	130	NR	164 *	.7	1.3
107 Christian Un	6	845	496	1,068 *	4.6	8.6
157 Ch of Brethren	1	40	15	51 *	.2	.4
165 Ch of Nazarene	2	160	140	330	1.4	2.7
167 Chs of Christ	3	86	87	110	.5	.9
171 Ch God-Gen Con	1	141	60	178 *	.8	1.4
173 Comm of Christ	1	120	NR	120	.5	1.0
283 Luth—MO Synod	1	191	69	242	1.0	1.9
297 Mennonite;Other	1	47	NR	59 *	.3	.5
339 Pent Ch of God	1	25	NR	70	.3	.6
355 Presb Ch (USA)	2	154	95	194 *	.8	1.6
360 Prim Bapt Chrch	2	NR	NR	NR	-	-
419 So Bapt Conv	16	4,670	1,256	5,902 *	25.3	47.5
449 Un Methodist	10	1,372	506	1,734 *	7.4	14.0
REYNOLDS	**21**	**2,297**	**1,071**	**2,877 ***	**43.0**	**100.0**
053 Assemb of God	3	75	92	108	1.6	3.8
056 Baha'i	0	1	NR	1	-	-
059 Bapt Miss Assn	4	196	125	237 *	3.5	8.2
081 Catholic	2	NR	NR	81	1.2	2.8
165 Ch of Nazarene	1	35	40	44	.7	1.5
167 Chs of Christ	1	13	20	17	.3	.6
419 So Bapt Conv	9	1,876	742	2,267 *	33.9	78.8
449 Un Methodist	1	101	52	122 *	1.8	4.2
RIPLEY	**39**	**2,661**	**1,628**	**3,837 ***	**28.4**	**100.0**
053 Assemb of God	1	57	63	63	.5	1.6
059 Bapt Miss Assn	7	317	176	390 *	2.9	10.2
081 Catholic	1	NR	NR	230	1.7	6.0
093 Chr Ch (Disc)	1	100	40	123 *	.9	3.2
097 Chr Chs&Chs Cr	1	155	NR	191 *	1.4	5.0
121 Ch God (Abr)	1	11	7	14 *	.1	.4
123 Ch God (Ander)	4	NR	373	373	2.8	9.7
127 Ch God (Cleve)	1	35	74	74 *	.5	1.9
167 Chs of Christ	7	362	398	468	3.5	12.2
223 Free Will Bapt	2	170	NR	209 *	1.5	5.4
283 Luth—MO Synod	1	71	0	0	-	-
355 Presb Ch (USA)	1	29	20	36 *	.3	.9
413 S.D.A.	1	57	NR	68	.5	1.8
419 So Bapt Conv	6	1,089	359	1,342 *	9.9	35.0
449 Un Methodist	4	208	118	256 *	1.9	6.7
ST. CHARLES	**146**	**46,915**	**18,939**	**145,239 ***	**51.2**	**100.0**
019 Amer Bapt USA	1	35	70	70 *	-	-
053 Assemb of God	9	1,058	1,357	1,565	.6	1.1
055 As Ref Pres Ch	1	0	NR	0	-	-
056 Baha'i	3	78	NR	78	-	.1
059 Bapt Miss Assn	2	238	133	307 *	.1	.2
081 Catholic	19	NR	NR	79,103	27.9	54.5
093 Chr Ch (Disc)	2	572	188	739 *	.3	.5
097 Chr Chs&Chs Cr	5	3,365	NR	4,345 *	1.5	3.0

Religious Group	Number of Churches, Synagogues, Mosques, or Temples	Number of Communicant, Confirmed, or Full Members	Number of Attendees	Total Adherents		
				Number of Adherents	% of Total Pop.	% of Total Adh.
123 Ch God (Ander)	4	NR	119	119	-	.1
127 Ch God (Cleve)	2	211	109	272 *	.1	.2
145 Ch God Prophcy	1	27	NR	34 *	-	-
151 L-D Saints	6	NR	NR	2,138	.8	1.5
165 Ch of Nazarene	3	580	350	637	.2	.4
167 Chs of Christ	6	549	560	856	.3	.6
173 Comm of Christ	1	297	NR	297	.1	.2
193 Episcopal	2	NR	190	634	.2	.4
203 Evan Free Ch	1	432	900	900	.3	.6
207 E.L.C.A.	4	1,450	832	2,077	.7	1.4
223 Free Will Bapt	3	255	NR	329 *	.1	.2
263 Int Foursq Gos	1	35	52	52 *	-	-
283 Luth—MO Synod	12	9,481	2,953	11,287	4.0	7.8
339 Pent Ch of God	1	40	NR	60	-	-
355 Presb Ch (USA)	3	2,147	1,097	2,773 *	1.0	1.9
356 Presb Ch Amer	1	0	0	0	-	-
371 Ref Ch in Am	1	139	164	320	.1	.2
403 Salvation Army	2	187	83	482	.2	.3
413 S.D.A.	1	189	NR	225	.1	.2
416 Sikh	1	NR	NR	NR	-	-
419 So Bapt Conv	22	15,897	5,480	20,527 *	7.2	14.1
443 Un C of Christ	13	4,001	1,506	5,166 *	1.8	3.6
449 Un Methodist	8	5,108	2,255	6,596 *	2.3	4.5
463 Vineyard	1	300	210	387 *	.1	.3
467 Wesleyan	1	84	196	325	.1	.2
469 WELS	2	160	135	239	.1	.2
496 Jewish Est	1	NR	NR	2,300	.8	1.6
ST. CLAIR	**31**	**3,829**	**1,035**	**4,616 ***	**47.8**	**100.0**
053 Assemb of God	1	94	125	180	1.9	3.9
081 Catholic	1	NR	NR	74	.8	1.6
093 Chr Ch (Disc)	2	395	40	477 *	4.9	10.3
097 Chr Chs&Chs Cr	3	197	NR	238 *	2.5	5.2
157 Ch of Brethren	1	38	30	46 *	.5	1.0
165 Ch of Nazarene	1	14	19	47	.5	1.0
173 Comm of Christ	1	33	NR	33	.3	.7
283 Luth—MO Synod	1	145	0	0	-	-
320 "Old" MB Ascs	4	150	NR	181 *	1.9	3.9
355 Presb Ch (USA)	1	30	20	36 *	.4	.8
360 Prim Bapt Chrch	1	NR	NR	NR	-	-
419 So Bapt Conv	8	2,269	605	2,742 *	28.4	59.4
449 Un Methodist	6	464	196	562 *	5.8	12.2
STE. GENEVIEVE	**29**	**3,006**	**982**	**12,970 ***	**72.7**	**100.0**
019 Amer Bapt USA	1	11	17	17 *	.1	.1
053 Assemb of God	1	29	38	80	.4	.6
081 Catholic	9	NR	NR	8,863	49.7	68.3
151 L-D Saints	1	NR	NR	314	1.8	2.4
283 Luth—MO Synod	1	177	110	218	1.2	1.7
355 Presb Ch (USA)	1	153	60	191 *	1.1	1.5
419 So Bapt Conv	15	2,636	757	3,287 *	18.4	25.3
ST. FRANCOIS	**111**	**19,086**	**7,563**	**28,494 ***	**51.2**	**100.0**
053 Assemb of God	14	866	1,173	1,535	2.8	5.4
056 Baha'i	0	14	NR	14	-	-
059 Bapt Miss Assn	3	97	67	118 *	.2	.4
081 Catholic	5	NR	NR	4,257	7.7	14.9
093 Chr Ch (Disc)	3	389	147	475 *	.9	1.7
097 Chr Chs&Chs Cr	3	222	NR	272 *	.5	1.0
121 Ch God (Abr)	1	27	29	33 *	.1	.1
123 Ch God (Ander)	4	NR	117	117	.2	.4
127 Ch God (Cleve)	8	1,138	692	1,389 *	2.5	4.9
145 Ch God Prophcy	1	27	NR	32 *	.1	.1
151 L-D Saints	1	NR	NR	178	.3	.6
165 Ch of Nazarene	3	519	289	523	.9	1.8
167 Chs of Christ	3	228	215	281	.5	1.0
171 Ch God-Gen Con	6	439	358	618 *	1.1	2.2
173 Comm of Christ	1	62	NR	62	.1	.2
193 Episcopal	2	NR	34	70	.1	.2
203 Evan Free Ch	1	69	125	125	.2	.4
223 Free Will Bapt	9	765	NR	933 *	1.7	3.3
283 Luth—MO Synod	4	1,185	513	1,512	2.7	5.3
331 OCA: Ter Diocs	1	25	NR	43	.1	.2

NR–Not Reported *Total adherents estimated from known number of communicant, confirmed, full members. - Represents a percentage less than 0.1. Percentages may not total 100 due to rounding.

Table 4: Religious Congregations by County and Group: 2000

Religious Group	Number of Churches, Synagogues, Mosques, or Temples	Number of Communicant, Confirmed, or Full Members	Number of Attendees	Total Adherents: Number of Adherents	Total Adherents: % of Total Pop.	Total Adherents: % of Total Adh.
339 Pent Ch of God	1	12	NR	42	.1	.1
355 Presb Ch (USA)	2	173	85	211 *	.4	.7
413 S.D.A.	1	115	NR	137	.2	.5
419 So Bapt Conv	23	10,618	2,622	12,959 *	23.3	45.5
443 Un C of Christ	1	141	62	172 *	.3	.6
449 Un Methodist	10	1,955	1,035	2,386 *	4.3	8.4
ST. LOUIS	**571**	**164,541**	**80,689**	**580,919 ***	**57.2**	**100.0**
017 Amer Bapt Assn	1	50	NR	62 *	-	-
019 Amer Bapt USA	5	2,846	1,328	3,526 *	.3	.6
039 Ap Chr Ch(Naz)	1	0	0	0 *	-	-
040 Ap Chr Ch-Amer	1	13	25	25 *	-	-
053 Assemb of God	21	2,464	2,508	3,283	.3	.6
056 Baha'i	3	319	NR	319	-	.1
057 Bapt Gen Conf	3	303	375	399 *	-	.1
059 Bapt Miss Assn	6	619	313	767 *	.1	.1
076 Buddhism	3	NR	NR	NR	-	-
081 Catholic	96	NR	NR	301,064	29.6	51.8
084 Calvary Chapel	2	NR	NR	NR	-	-
089 Chr & Miss Al	1	35	NR	59	-	-
093 Chr Ch (Disc)	9	3,189	1,216	3,951 *	.4	.7
097 Chr Chs&Chs Cr	13	4,845	NR	6,006 *	.6	1.0
105 Christian Ref	1	123	80	152 *	-	-
123 Ch God (Ander)	7	NR	691	691	.1	.1
127 Ch God (Cleve)	3	778	1,041	1,270 *	.1	.2
145 Ch God Prophcy	1	27	NR	33 *	-	-
151 L-D Saints	15	NR	NR	4,668	.5	.8
165 Ch of Nazarene	11	2,121	1,171	3,573	.4	.6
167 Chs of Christ	21	3,436	3,043	4,486	.4	.8
173 Comm of Christ	2	482	NR	482	-	.1
193 Episcopal	18	NR	3,070	8,833	.9	1.5
201 Evan Cov Ch	2	106	115	134 *	-	-
203 Evan Free Ch	4	868	1,950	1,950	.2	.3
207 E.L.C.A.	12	5,113	2,310	6,588	.6	1.1
216 Evan Presby Ch	4	2,930	NR	3,631 *	.4	.6
221 Free Methodist	2	60	106	106	-	-
223 Free Will Bapt	3	255	NR	316 *	-	.1
246 Greek Orthodox	1	NR	NR	1,296	.1	.2
251 Holy Orth in NA	1	NR	NR	12	-	-
252 Hindu	4	NR	NR	NR	-	-
262 Int Cou Comm Ch	1	190	NR	235 *	-	-
263 Int Foursq Gos	6	508	511	629 *	.1	.1
267 Muslim Est	3	NR	1,080	6,626	.7	1.1
268 Jain	3	NR	NR	NR	-	-
283 Luth—MO Synod	42	31,871	16,053	40,403	4.0	7.0
288 Mennonite USA	2	126	145	172 *	-	-
290 Metro Comm Ch	1	32	32	40 *	-	-
304 NatPrimBapt USA	2	95	NR	118 *	-	-
333 Malan Dioc Am	1	NR	NR	75	-	-
339 Pent Ch of God	2	69	NR	329	-	.1
355 Presb Ch (USA)	28	12,924	4,987	16,011 *	1.6	2.8
356 Presb Ch Amer	13	4,496	4,194	5,476	.5	.9
388 Reg Bapt Gen As	2	242	259	277 *	-	-
410 Serb Orth USA	2	NR	NR	200	-	-
413 S.D.A.	8	2,327	NR	2,768	.3	.5
416 Sikh	1	NR	NR	NR	-	-
418 Southw Bapt Fel	1	NR	NR	NR	-	-
419 So Bapt Conv	69	42,277	12,494	52,385 *	5.2	9.0
435 Unitarian-Univ	2	646	NR	800 *	.1	.1
443 Un C of Christ	30	13,552	5,557	16,792 *	1.7	2.9
449 Un Methodist	33	19,124	8,093	23,699 *	2.3	4.1
463 Vineyard	3	383	349	511 *	.1	.1
467 Wesleyan	3	76	88	215	-	-
469 WELS	1	203	0	283	-	-
490 Zoroastrian	1	NR	NR	NR	-	-
496 Jewish Est	20	NR	NR	47,100	4.6	8.1
498 Indep.Charis.	8	1,625	5,175	5,300	.5	.9
499 Indep.Non-Char	6	2,793	2,330	2,793	.3	.5
ST. LOUIS CITY	**267**	**44,236**	**19,786**	**143,301 ***	**41.2**	**100.0**
019 Amer Bapt USA	4	3,636	1,806	4,556 *	1.3	3.2
053 Assemb of God	8	797	951	1,619	.5	1.1
056 Baha'i	1	157	NR	157	-	.1

Religious Group	Number of Churches, Synagogues, Mosques, or Temples	Number of Communicant, Confirmed, or Full Members	Number of Attendees	Total Adherents: Number of Adherents	Total Adherents: % of Total Pop.	Total Adherents: % of Total Adh.
076 Buddhism	2	NR	NR	NR	-	-
081 Catholic	54	NR	NR	70,558	20.3	49.2
089 Chr & Miss Al	1	48	NR	72	-	.1
093 Chr Ch (Disc)	7	1,300	363	1,629 *	.5	1.1
097 Chr Chs&Chs Cr	1	24	NR	30 *	-	-
123 Ch God (Ander)	4	NR	675	675	.2	.5
127 Ch God (Cleve)	2	408	120	512 *	.1	.4
151 L-D Saints	1	NR	NR	398	.1	.3
165 Ch of Nazarene	4	586	283	617	.2	.4
167 Chs of Christ	6	664	650	762	.2	.5
173 Comm of Christ	1	27	NR	27	-	-
181 Consrv Congr	1	22	20	28 *	-	-
193 Episcopal	10	NR	742	1,906	.5	1.3
207 E.L.C.A.	11	3,625	1,534	4,827	1.4	3.4
221 Free Methodist	2	53	77	97	-	.1
223 Free Will Bapt	3	255	NR	319 *	.1	.2
226 Friends-USA	1	55	NR	69 *	-	-
246 Greek Orthodox	1	NR	NR	2,298	.7	1.6
252 Hindu	1	NR	NR	NR	-	-
263 Int Foursq Gos	3	215	217	269 *	.1	.2
264 Int Chs of Crst	1	275	476	440	.1	.3
267 Muslim Est	4	NR	1,045	4,289	1.2	3.0
283 Luth—MO Synod	26	7,417	2,493	7,846	2.3	5.5
290 Metro Comm Ch	1	229	339	339 *	.1	.2
297 Mennonite;Other	1	32	NR	40 *	-	-
331 OCA: Ter Diocs	1	45	NR	154	-	.1
339 Pent Ch of God	1	18	NR	95	-	.1
355 Presb Ch (USA)	18	2,345	1,225	2,939 *	.8	2.1
356 Presb Ch Amer	3	240	500	500	.1	.3
388 Reg Bapt Gen As	1	42	29	53 *	-	-
397 OCA: Roman Dioc	1	NR	NR	300	.1	.2
401 Rus Orth Abroad	1	NR	NR	NR	-	-
403 Salvation Army	7	1,138	968	4,526	1.3	3.2
411 Serb Orth: Grac	1	NR	NR	NR	-	-
413 S.D.A.	1	570	NR	678	.2	.5
416 Sikh	1	NR	NR	NR	-	-
419 So Bapt Conv	28	12,332	2,178	15,453 *	4.4	10.8
435 Unitarian-Univ	1	498	NR	624 *	.2	.4
443 Un C of Christ	20	3,237	1,400	4,056 *	1.2	2.8
449 Un Methodist	18	3,946	1,695	4,944 *	1.4	3.5
496 Jewish Est	2	NR	NR	4,600	1.3	3.2
SALINE	**71**	**8,995**	**3,469**	**13,114 ***	**55.2**	**100.0**
053 Assemb of God	4	252	330	518	2.2	3.9
056 Baha'i	0	14	NR	14	.1	.1
081 Catholic	3	NR	NR	1,400	5.9	10.7
093 Chr Ch (Disc)	5	1,077	354	1,319 *	5.6	10.1
123 Ch God (Ander)	1	NR	29	29	.1	.2
151 L-D Saints	1	NR	NR	191	.8	1.5
165 Ch of Nazarene	1	167	145	310	1.3	2.4
167 Chs of Christ	2	55	38	68	.3	.5
173 Comm of Christ	1	123	NR	123	.5	.9
185 Cumber Presb	1	73	NR	150	.6	1.1
193 Episcopal	1	NR	12	29	.1	.2
223 Free Will Bapt	1	85	NR	104 *	.4	.8
283 Luth—MO Synod	7	1,191	631	1,565	6.6	11.9
349 Pent Holiness	1	15	15	18 *	.1	.1
355 Presb Ch (USA)	7	456	221	558 *	2.3	4.3
360 Prim Bapt Chrch	1	NR	NR	NR	-	-
413 S.D.A.	1	29	NR	35	.1	.3
419 So Bapt Conv	17	3,545	1,030	4,341 *	18.3	33.1
443 Un C of Christ	4	360	165	441 *	1.9	3.4
449 Un Methodist	12	1,553	499	1,901 *	8.0	14.5
SCHUYLER	**18**	**1,729**	**430**	**2,161 ***	**51.8**	**100.0**
053 Assemb of God	1	63	28	90	2.2	4.2
097 Chr Chs&Chs Cr	3	540	NR	665 *	15.9	30.8
167 Chs of Christ	1	10	10	13	.3	.6
207 E.L.C.A.	1	35	29	63	1.5	2.9
323 Old Ord Amish	1	55	NR	68 *	1.6	3.1
360 Prim Bapt Chrch	1	NR	NR	NR	-	-
419 So Bapt Conv	5	847	254	1,043 *	25.0	48.3
449 Un Methodist	5	179	109	219 *	5.3	10.1

NR–Not Reported *Total adherents estimated from known number of communicant, confirmed, full members. - Represents a percentage less than 0.1. Percentages may not total 100 due to rounding.

Table 4: Religious Congregations by County and Group: 2000

Religious Group	Number of Churches, Synagogues, Mosques, or Temples	Number of Communicant, Confirmed, or Full Members	Number of Attendees	Total Adherents		
				Number of Adherents	% of Total Pop.	% of Total Adh.
SCOTLAND	**21**	**2,087**	**535**	**2,825 ***	**56.7**	**100.0**
053 Assemb of God	1	22	29	40	.8	1.4
081 Catholic	1	NR	NR	146	2.9	5.2
093 Chr Ch (Disc)	1	36	30	46 *	.9	1.6
097 Chr Chs&Chs Cr	1	315	NR	401 *	8.0	14.2
283 Luth—MO Synod	1	25	15	40	.8	1.4
322 Old Ord Menn Ch	3	442	NR	563 *	11.3	19.9
355 Presb Ch (USA)	1	70	39	89 *	1.8	3.2
419 So Bapt Conv	5	691	246	880 *	17.7	31.2
449 Un Methodist	7	486	176	620 *	12.4	21.9
SCOTT	**70**	**12,795**	**5,451**	**23,550 ***	**58.3**	**100.0**
053 Assemb of God	4	530	600	812	2.0	3.4
056 Baha'i	0	3	NR	3	-	-
059 Bapt Miss Assn	2	516	237	655 *	1.6	2.8
081 Catholic	7	NR	NR	6,387	15.8	27.1
093 Chr Ch (Disc)	2	469	223	596 *	1.5	2.5
123 Ch God (Ander)	3	NR	397	397	1.0	1.7
127 Ch God (Cleve)	1	207	101	263 *	.7	1.1
145 Ch God Prophcy	1	27	NR	34 *	.1	.1
151 L-D Saints	1	NR	NR	331	.8	1.4
165 Ch of Nazarene	2	194	118	253	.6	1.1
167 Chs of Christ	6	657	657	884	2.2	3.8
173 Comm of Christ	1	56	NR	56	.1	.2
193 Episcopal	1	NR	46	74	.2	.3
283 Luth—MO Synod	3	641	251	699	1.7	3.0
355 Presb Ch (USA)	1	134	96	170 *	.4	.7
413 S.D.A.	1	86	NR	102	.3	.4
419 So Bapt Conv	23	7,518	1,967	9,546 *	23.6	40.5
449 Un Methodist	10	1,722	718	2,186 *	5.4	9.3
467 Wesleyan	1	35	40	102	.3	.4
SHANNON	**28**	**2,106**	**731**	**2,759 ***	**33.1**	**100.0**
053 Assemb of God	3	147	206	249	3.0	9.0
081 Catholic	1	NR	NR	70	.8	2.5
097 Chr Chs&Chs Cr	2	240	NR	299 *	3.6	10.8
145 Ch God Prophcy	5	133	NR	165 *	2.0	6.0
167 Chs of Christ	2	43	45	55	.7	2.0
288 Mennonite USA	1	10	8	12 *	.1	.4
419 So Bapt Conv	8	1,245	348	1,551 *	18.6	56.2
443 Un C of Christ	1	21	9	26 *	.3	.9
449 Un Methodist	5	267	115	332 *	4.0	12.0
SHELBY	**35**	**3,375**	**1,332**	**5,174 ***	**76.1**	**100.0**
032 Amish; other	1	57	NR	70 *	1.0	1.4
053 Assemb of God	1	16	17	17	.3	.3
081 Catholic	2	NR	NR	636	9.4	12.3
093 Chr Ch (Disc)	1	27	15	33 *	.5	.6
097 Chr Chs&Chs Cr	6	1,281	NR	1,568 *	23.1	30.3
157 Ch of Brethren	1	17	0	21 *	.3	.4
165 Ch of Nazarene	1	30	46	54	.8	1.0
167 Chs of Christ	1	10	11	14	.2	.3
283 Luth—MO Synod	1	62	25	72	1.1	1.4
288 Mennonite USA	1	49	60	60 *	.9	1.2
388 Reg Bapt Gen As	1	97	97	97 *	1.4	1.9
419 So Bapt Conv	8	1,145	362	1,402 *	20.6	27.1
449 Un Methodist	9	584	284	715 *	10.5	13.8
498 Indep.Charis.	1	0	415	415	6.1	8.0
STODDARD	**66**	**8,526**	**4,062**	**11,523 ***	**38.8**	**100.0**
017 Amer Bapt Assn	2	100	NR	122 *	.4	1.1
053 Assemb of God	8	403	540	764	2.6	6.6
056 Baha'i	0	1	NR	1	-	-
059 Bapt Miss Assn	1	36	25	44 *	.1	.4
081 Catholic	2	NR	NR	762	2.6	6.6
089 Chr & Miss Al	1	21	NR	34	.1	.3
093 Chr Ch (Disc)	1	271	113	329 *	1.1	2.9
097 Chr Chs&Chs Cr	3	315	NR	383 *	1.3	3.3
123 Ch God (Ander)	1	NR	89	89	.3	.8
127 Ch God (Cleve)	1	120	37	146 *	.5	1.3
145 Ch God Prophcy	2	53	NR	64 *	.2	.6
157 Ch of Brethren	1	32	23	39 *	.1	.3
165 Ch of Nazarene	3	331	196	343	1.2	3.0
167 Chs of Christ	9	779	815	1,001	3.4	8.7
173 Comm of Christ	1	40	NR	40	.1	.3
203 Evan Free Ch	1	37	60	60	.2	.5
283 Luth—MO Synod	1	94	59	122	.4	1.1
339 Pent Ch of God	1	12	NR	40	.1	.3
355 Presb Ch (USA)	1	62	35	75 *	.3	.7
419 So Bapt Conv	15	4,671	1,412	5,671 *	19.1	49.2
449 Un Methodist	11	1,148	658	1,394 *	4.7	12.1
STONE	**56**	**6,973**	**3,999**	**10,410 ***	**36.3**	**100.0**
053 Assemb of God	6	339	408	788	2.7	7.6
081 Catholic	1	NR	NR	1,176	4.1	11.3
093 Chr Ch (Disc)	1	77	0	92 *	.3	.9
097 Chr Chs&Chs Cr	3	353	NR	422 *	1.5	4.1
107 Christian Un	1	18	25	25 *	.1	.2
127 Ch God (Cleve)	2	191	130	228 *	.8	2.2
151 L-D Saints	1	NR	NR	472	1.6	4.5
165 Ch of Nazarene	2	27	35	49	.2	.5
167 Chs of Christ	5	254	270	305	1.1	2.9
171 Ch God-Gen Con	1	3	10	10 *	-	.1
185 Cumber Presb	1	9	NR	15	.1	.1
193 Episcopal	1	NR	44	61	.2	.6
223 Free Will Bapt	2	170	NR	203 *	.7	2.0
230 Fund Methodist	2	123	NR	147 *	.5	1.4
283 Luth—MO Synod	1	392	200	424	1.5	4.1
355 Presb Ch (USA)	2	295	210	353 *	1.2	3.4
360 Prim Bapt Chrch	1	NR	NR	NR	-	-
403 Salvation Army	1	25	35	25	.1	.2
413 S.D.A.	1	34	NR	40	.1	.4
419 So Bapt Conv	18	3,914	2,195	4,679 *	16.3	44.9
449 Un Methodist	3	749	437	896 *	3.1	8.6
SULLIVAN	**28**	**2,382**	**708**	**3,083 ***	**42.7**	**100.0**
053 Assemb of God	2	89	100	120	1.7	3.9
056 Baha'i	0	3	NR	3	-	.1
081 Catholic	1	NR	NR	100	1.4	3.2
093 Chr Ch (Disc)	1	42	14	52 *	.7	1.7
097 Chr Chs&Chs Cr	4	555	NR	688 *	9.5	22.3
123 Ch God (Ander)	1	NR	0	0	-	-
167 Chs of Christ	2	45	48	58	.8	1.9
283 Luth—MO Synod	1	25	16	30	.4	1.0
339 Pent Ch of God	1	15	NR	35	.5	1.1
355 Presb Ch (USA)	2	70	46	87 *	1.2	2.8
360 Prim Bapt Chrch	1	NR	NR	NR	-	-
419 So Bapt Conv	8	1,165	332	1,447 *	20.0	46.9
449 Un Methodist	4	373	152	463 *	6.4	15.0
TANEY	**50**	**7,979**	**5,941**	**12,803 ***	**32.2**	**100.0**
017 Amer Bapt Assn	1	50	NR	60 *	.2	.5
053 Assemb of God	5	302	439	700	1.8	5.5
056 Baha'i	0	9	NR	9	-	.1
081 Catholic	2	NR	NR	1,583	4.0	12.4
084 Calvary Chapel	1	NR	NR	NR	-	-
093 Chr Ch (Disc)	2	423	176	511 *	1.3	4.0
097 Chr Chs&Chs Cr	3	276	NR	333 *	.8	2.6
165 Ch of Nazarene	3	209	176	290	.7	2.3
167 Chs of Christ	6	272	457	365	.9	2.9
173 Comm of Christ	1	135	NR	135	.3	1.1
193 Episcopal	1	NR	81	192	.5	1.5
203 Evan Free Ch	1	45	120	120	.3	.9
207 E.L.C.A.	1	249	177	307	.8	2.4
223 Free Will Bapt	1	85	NR	103 *	.3	.8
230 Fund Methodist	1	46	NR	56 *	.1	.4
263 Int Foursq Gos	1	45	59	59 *	.1	.5
283 Luth—MO Synod	2	493	309	612	1.5	4.8
291 Missionary Ch	1	6	45	45	.1	.4
355 Presb Ch (USA)	4	665	834	1,169 *	2.9	9.1
413 S.D.A.	1	19	NR	23	.1	.2
419 So Bapt Conv	8	3,486	1,606	4,209 *	10.6	32.9
449 Un Methodist	2	764	462	922 *	2.3	7.2
498 Indep.Charis.	2	400	1,000	1,000	2.5	7.8

NR–Not Reported   *Total adherents estimated from known number of communicant, confirmed, full members.   - Represents a percentage less than 0.1.   Percentages may not total 100 due to rounding.

Table 4: Religious Congregations by County and Group: 2000

Religious Group	Number of Churches, Synagogues, Mosques, or Temples	Number of Communicant, Confirmed, or Full Members	Number of Attendees	Total Adherents		
				Number of Adherents	% of Total Pop.	% of Total Adh.
TEXAS	**86**	**11,385**	**3,569**	**15,051 ***	**65.4**	**100.0**
053 Assemb of God	7	251	342	504	2.2	3.3
081 Catholic	4	NR	NR	340	1.5	2.3
097 Chr Chs&Chs Cr	8	1,185	NR	1,453 *	6.3	9.7
123 Ch God (Ander)	2	NR	30	30	.1	.2
145 Ch God Prophcy	2	53	NR	66 *	.3	.4
151 L-D Saints	2	NR	NR	445	1.9	3.0
157 Ch of Brethren	2	56	50	74 *	.3	.5
167 Chs of Christ	7	444	471	585	2.5	3.9
223 Free Will Bapt	10	850	NR	1,042 *	4.5	6.9
258 IndFreeWillBapt	1	97	NR	119 *	.5	.8
283 Luth—MO Synod	1	95	61	140	.6	.9
297 Mennonite;Other	1	60	NR	74 *	.3	.5
320 "Old" MB Ascs	1	30	NR	37 *	.2	.2
323 Old Ord Amish	1	55	NR	67 *	.3	.4
339 Pent Ch of God	1	50	NR	70	.3	.5
349 Pent Holiness	7	566	499	694 *	3.0	4.6
419 So Bapt Conv	25	6,807	1,761	8,347 *	36.3	55.5
449 Un Methodist	4	786	355	964 *	4.2	6.4
VERNON	**49**	**6,957**	**2,053**	**10,000 ***	**48.9**	**100.0**
053 Assemb of God	2	112	151	224	1.1	2.2
056 Baha'i	0	2	NR	2	-	-
059 Bapt Miss Assn	1	79	60	98 *	.5	1.0
081 Catholic	1	NR	NR	772	3.8	7.7
097 Chr Chs&Chs Cr	8	1,030	NR	1,283 *	6.3	12.8
143 CG in Cr(Menn)	1	88	NR	110 *	.5	1.1
151 L-D Saints	1	NR	NR	294	1.4	2.9
165 Ch of Nazarene	1	152	84	321	1.6	3.2
167 Chs of Christ	2	129	122	158	.8	1.6
173 Comm of Christ	1	65	NR	65	.3	.7
193 Episcopal	1	NR	53	108	.5	1.1
207 E.L.C.A.	1	172	80	195	1.0	2.0
283 Luth—MO Synod	1	39	22	45	.2	.5
320 "Old" MB Ascs	2	48	NR	60 *	.3	.6
323 Old Ord Amish	1	55	NR	68 *	.3	.7
355 Presb Ch (USA)	1	176	105	219 *	1.1	2.2
413 S.D.A.	1	156	NR	186	.9	1.9
419 So Bapt Conv	15	3,687	990	4,589 *	22.4	45.9
449 Un Methodist	8	967	386	1,203 *	5.9	12.0
WARREN	**29**	**4,405**	**2,076**	**11,075 ***	**45.2**	**100.0**
053 Assemb of God	2	49	70	87	.4	.8
056 Baha'i	0	3	NR	3	-	-
081 Catholic	3	NR	NR	4,585	18.7	41.4
097 Chr Chs&Chs Cr	1	55	NR	69 *	.3	.6
127 Ch God (Cleve)	1	58	54	73 *	.3	.7
165 Ch of Nazarene	1	57	48	81	.3	.7
167 Chs of Christ	2	65	75	68	.3	.6
216 Evan Presby Ch	1	30	NR	38 *	.2	.3
283 Luth—MO Synod	2	457	227	586	2.4	5.3
419 So Bapt Conv	5	1,337	521	1,682 *	6.9	15.2
443 Un C of Christ	5	1,429	584	1,798 *	7.3	16.2
449 Un Methodist	5	640	348	805 *	3.3	7.3
467 Wesleyan	1	225	149	1,200	4.9	10.8
WASHINGTON	**53**	**5,043**	**2,403**	**10,162 ***	**43.5**	**100.0**
053 Assemb of God	4	231	307	371	1.6	3.7
056 Baha'i	0	3	NR	3	-	-
059 Bapt Miss Assn	11	1,372	697	1,713 *	7.3	16.9
081 Catholic	4	NR	NR	3,732	16.0	36.7
097 Chr Chs&Chs Cr	1	137	NR	171 *	.7	1.7
127 Ch God (Cleve)	4	503	284	628 *	2.7	6.2
165 Ch of Nazarene	2	34	26	41	.2	.4
167 Chs of Christ	1	23	28	35	.1	.3
171 Ch God-Gen Con	4	175	152	218 *	.9	2.1
223 Free Will Bapt	2	170	NR	212 *	.9	2.1
283 Luth—MO Synod	1	34	15	43	.2	.4
339 Pent Ch of God	2	20	NR	75	.3	.7
355 Presb Ch (USA)	2	108	54	135 *	.6	1.3
419 So Bapt Conv	8	1,770	588	2,209 *	9.5	21.7
449 Un Methodist	7	463	252	576 *	2.5	5.7

Religious Group	Number of Churches, Synagogues, Mosques, or Temples	Number of Communicant, Confirmed, or Full Members	Number of Attendees	Total Adherents		
				Number of Adherents	% of Total Pop.	% of Total Adh.
WAYNE	**42**	**3,508**	**1,404**	**4,713 ***	**35.5**	**100.0**
017 Amer Bapt Assn	1	50	NR	60 *	.5	1.3
053 Assemb of God	5	156	186	269	2.0	5.7
056 Baha'i	0	1	NR	1	-	-
081 Catholic	2	NR	NR	333	2.5	7.1
097 Chr Chs&Chs Cr	1	49	NR	59 *	.4	1.3
151 L-D Saints	1	NR	NR	68	.5	1.4
165 Ch of Nazarene	2	224	104	236	1.8	5.0
167 Chs of Christ	2	33	44	43	.3	.9
283 Luth—MO Synod	2	56	31	66	.5	1.4
339 Pent Ch of God	1	50	NR	85	.6	1.8
388 Reg Bapt Gen As	1	43	60	60 *	.5	1.3
419 So Bapt Conv	16	2,451	746	2,958 *	22.3	62.8
449 Un Methodist	8	395	233	475 *	3.6	10.1
WEBSTER	**90**	**11,363**	**4,580**	**15,876 ***	**51.1**	**100.0**
053 Assemb of God	3	156	229	392	1.3	2.5
056 Baha'i	0	8	NR	8	-	.1
081 Catholic	1	NR	NR	546	1.8	3.4
093 Chr Ch (Disc)	4	495	125	638 *	2.1	4.0
097 Chr Chs&Chs Cr	1	200	NR	258 *	.8	1.6
127 Ch God (Cleve)	2	20	30	30 *	.1	.2
151 L-D Saints	1	NR	NR	303	1.0	1.9
165 Ch of Nazarene	3	272	284	441	1.4	2.8
167 Chs of Christ	9	407	431	549	1.8	3.5
185 Cumber Presb	2	29	NR	92	.3	.6
223 Free Will Bapt	11	935	NR	1,205 *	3.9	7.6
283 Luth—MO Synod	3	475	289	653	2.1	4.1
297 Mennonite;Other	1	119	NR	153 *	.5	1.0
323 Old Ord Amish	8	440	NR	568 *	1.8	3.6
360 Prim Bapt Chrch	2	NR	NR	NR	-	-
413 S.D.A.	2	156	NR	185	.6	1.2
419 So Bapt Conv	24	6,195	2,385	7,985 *	25.7	50.3
449 Un Methodist	12	1,389	762	1,789 *	5.8	11.3
469 WELS	1	67	45	81	.3	.5
WORTH	**15**	**1,612**	**434**	**1,993 ***	**83.7**	**100.0**
053 Assemb of God	1	61	83	113	4.7	5.7
093 Chr Ch (Disc)	1	210	70	254 *	10.7	12.7
097 Chr Chs&Chs Cr	3	385	NR	466 *	19.6	23.4
167 Chs of Christ	1	25	25	32	1.3	1.6
355 Presb Ch (USA)	1	12	11	15 *	.6	.8
419 So Bapt Conv	5	691	174	837 *	35.1	42.0
449 Un Methodist	3	228	71	276 *	11.6	13.8
WRIGHT	**70**	**7,829**	**2,823**	**10,766 ***	**60.0**	**100.0**
053 Assemb of God	4	343	465	813	4.5	7.6
056 Baha'i	0	1	NR	1	-	-
081 Catholic	2	NR	NR	323	1.8	3.0
093 Chr Ch (Disc)	1	41	16	52 *	.3	.5
097 Chr Chs&Chs Cr	2	195	NR	245 *	1.4	2.3
123 Ch God (Ander)	2	NR	78	78	.4	.7
165 Ch of Nazarene	3	251	195	412	2.3	3.8
167 Chs of Christ	6	311	325	400	2.2	3.7
185 Cumber Presb	1	32	NR	38	.2	.4
193 Episcopal	1	NR	25	45	.3	.4
223 Free Will Bapt	20	1,699	NR	2,136 *	11.9	19.8
258 IndFreeWillBapt	3	127	NR	160 *	.9	1.5
323 Old Ord Amish	1	55	NR	69 *	.4	.6
349 Pent Holiness	1	13	30	16 *	.1	.1
360 Prim Bapt Chrch	1	NR	NR	NR	-	-
413 S.D.A.	1	85	NR	101	.6	.9
419 So Bapt Conv	17	4,276	1,489	5,374 *	29.9	49.9
449 Un Methodist	4	400	200	503 *	2.8	4.7

MONTANA

Religious Group	Number of Churches, Synagogues, Mosques, or Temples	Number of Communicant, Confirmed, or Full Members	Number of Attendees	Number of Adherents	% of Total Pop.	% of Total Adh.
The State.....	1,543	134,676	81,628	403,492 *	44.7	100.0
BEAVERHEAD	**19**	**954**	**620**	**4,463 ***	**48.5**	**100.0**
017 Amer Bapt Assn	1	26	NR	32 *	.3	.7

NR–Not Reported *Total adherents estimated from known number of communicant, confirmed, full members. - Represents a percentage less than 0.1. Percentages may not total 100 due to rounding.

Table 4: Religious Congregations by County and Group: 2000

Religious Group	Number of Churches, Synagogues, Mosques, or Temples	Number of Communicant, Confirmed, or Full Members	Number of Attendees	Total Adherents: Number of Adherents	Total Adherents: % of Total Pop.	Total Adherents: % of Total Adh.
053 Assemb of God	1	47	70	108	1.2	2.4
081 Catholic	2	NR	NR	2,098	22.8	47.0
151 L-D Saints	4	NR	NR	988	10.7	22.1
167 Chs of Christ	1	16	27	30	.3	.7
193 Episcopal	2	NR	28	128	1.4	2.9
207 E.L.C.A.	1	284	139	374	4.1	8.4
306 NT IndBapt&Rltd	1	50	NR	61 *	.7	1.4
355 Presb Ch (USA)	2	262	165	318 *	3.5	7.1
413 S.D.A.	1	20	NR	24	.3	.5
419 So Bapt Conv	1	17	18	21 *	.2	.5
449 Un Methodist	1	89	39	108 *	1.2	2.4
463 Vineyard	1	143	134	173 *	1.9	3.9
BIG HORN	**35**	**1,577**	**744**	**4,994 ***	**39.4**	**100.0**
019 Amer Bapt USA	5	369	202	509 *	4.0	10.2
053 Assemb of God	2	75	40	148	1.2	3.0
056 Baha'i	0	28	NR	28	.2	.6
081 Catholic	7	NR	NR	2,545	20.1	51.0
089 Chr & Miss Al	1	20	NR	43	.3	.9
151 L-D Saints	1	NR	NR	121	1.0	2.4
179 Consrv Bapt	1	NR	50	50	.4	1.0
181 Consrv Congr	1	177	78	244 *	1.9	4.9
193 Episcopal	1	NR	9	19	.1	.4
207 E.L.C.A.	1	137	62	195	1.5	3.9
257 Hutterian Br	1	66	NR	100	.8	2.0
263 Int Foursq Gos	1	83	58	114 *	.9	2.3
283 Luth—MO Synod	3	168	64	218	1.7	4.4
288 Mennonite USA	1	60	27	83 *	.7	1.7
339 Pent Ch of God	3	56	NR	115	.9	2.3
413 S.D.A.	1	25	NR	30	.2	.6
419 So Bapt Conv	3	104	72	143 *	1.1	2.9
443 Un C of Christ	1	131	50	181 *	1.4	3.6
449 Un Methodist	1	78	32	108 *	.9	2.2
BLAINE	**27**	**1,388**	**561**	**4,744 ***	**67.7**	**100.0**
053 Assemb of God	4	260	233	380	5.4	8.0
056 Baha'i	0	6	NR	6	.1	.1
081 Catholic	6	NR	NR	2,637	37.6	55.6
089 Chr & Miss Al	2	43	NR	123	1.8	2.6
097 Chr Chs&Chs Cr	1	86	NR	114 *	1.6	2.4
151 L-D Saints	1	NR	NR	145	2.1	3.1
167 Chs of Christ	1	10	11	13	.2	.3
207 E.L.C.A.	4	559	172	739	10.5	15.6
257 Hutterian Br	2	132	NR	200	2.9	4.2
283 Luth—MO Synod	1	75	37	100	1.4	2.1
355 Presb Ch (USA)	2	75	60	99 *	1.4	2.1
413 S.D.A.	1	6	NR	7	.1	.1
449 Un Methodist	2	136	48	181 *	2.6	3.8
BROADWATER	**11**	**592**	**315**	**1,638 ***	**37.4**	**100.0**
053 Assemb of God	1	28	33	53	1.2	3.2
056 Baha'i	0	3	NR	3	.1	.2
081 Catholic	2	NR	NR	433	9.9	26.4
089 Chr & Miss Al	1	49	NR	132	3.0	8.1
151 L-D Saints	1	NR	NR	326	7.4	19.9
193 Episcopal	1	NR	13	40	.9	2.4
207 E.L.C.A.	1	183	119	248	5.7	15.1
413 S.D.A.	1	10	NR	12	.3	.7
419 So Bapt Conv	2	154	23	189 *	4.3	11.5
449 Un Methodist	1	165	127	202 *	4.6	12.3
CARBON	**27**	**1,391**	**737**	**3,639 ***	**38.1**	**100.0**
053 Assemb of God	1	54	78	90	.9	2.5
056 Baha'i	0	4	NR	4	-	.1
081 Catholic	4	NR	NR	1,621	17.0	44.5
089 Chr & Miss Al	1	14	NR	30	.3	.8
093 Chr Ch (Disc)	1	55	20	67 *	.7	1.8
151 L-D Saints	1	NR	NR	67	.7	1.8
167 Chs of Christ	1	13	13	20	.2	.5
193 Episcopal	3	NR	60	102	1.1	2.8
207 E.L.C.A.	2	337	120	444	4.6	12.2
283 Luth—MO Synod	2	176	69	198	2.1	5.4
306 NT IndBapt&Rltd	2	100	NR	122 *	1.3	3.4
413 S.D.A.	1	82	NR	98	1.0	2.7
419 So Bapt Conv	3	112	101	136 *	1.4	3.7
443 Un C of Christ	1	189	81	230 *	2.4	6.3
449 Un Methodist	3	214	109	260 *	2.7	7.1
467 Wesleyan	1	41	86	150	1.6	4.1
CARTER	**6**	**107**	**61**	**434 ***	**31.9**	**100.0**
081 Catholic	1	NR	NR	201	14.8	46.3
151 L-D Saints	1	NR	NR	54	4.0	12.4
207 E.L.C.A.	2	76	40	142	10.4	32.7
419 So Bapt Conv	1	6	10	7 *	.5	1.6
443 Un C of Christ	1	25	11	30 *	2.2	6.9
CASCADE	**86**	**10,711**	**6,348**	**34,762 ***	**43.3**	**100.0**
017 Amer Bapt Assn	1	30	NR	37 *	-	.1
019 Amer Bapt USA	1	253	83	316 *	.4	.9
053 Assemb of God	2	695	944	1,302	1.6	3.7
056 Baha'i	1	43	NR	43	.1	.1
057 Bapt Gen Conf	1	87	75	109 *	.1	.3
081 Catholic	11	NR	NR	15,005	18.7	43.2
084 Calvary Chapel	1	NR	NR	NR	-	-
089 Chr & Miss Al	1	88	NR	164	.2	.5
093 Chr Ch (Disc)	1	394	133	492 *	.6	1.4
097 Chr Chs&Chs Cr	2	70	NR	87 *	.1	.3
123 Ch God (Ander)	1	NR	26	26	-	.1
127 Ch God (Cleve)	1	31	38	39 *	-	.1
151 L-D Saints	9	NR	NR	2,855	3.6	8.2
165 Ch of Nazarene	1	178	112	180	.2	.5
167 Chs of Christ	1	164	189	231	.3	.7
173 Comm of Christ	1	26	NR	26	-	.1
193 Episcopal	2	NR	190	635	.8	1.8
203 Evan Free Ch	1	100	300	300	.4	.9
207 E.L.C.A.	6	2,786	1,012	4,177	5.2	12.0
226 Friends-USA	1	22	NR	27 *	-	.1
246 Greek Orthodox	1	NR	NR	159	.2	.5
257 Hutterian Br	4	264	NR	400	.5	1.2
263 Int Foursq Gos	1	263	535	535 *	.7	1.5
283 Luth—MO Synod	3	876	311	1,131	1.4	3.3
290 Metro Comm Ch	1	33	20	41 *	.1	.1
306 NT IndBapt&Rltd	3	295	NR	368 *	.5	1.1
339 Pent Ch of God	1	8	NR	20	-	.1
355 Presb Ch (USA)	2	847	402	1,056 *	1.3	3.0
371 Ref Ch in Am	1	49	32	104	.1	.3
403 Salvation Army	1	103	58	257	.3	.7
413 S.D.A.	1	234	NR	278	.3	.8
419 So Bapt Conv	7	804	301	1,003 *	1.2	2.9
443 Un C of Christ	1	471	198	588 *	.7	1.7
449 Un Methodist	9	1,237	652	1,543 *	1.9	4.4
463 Vineyard	1	170	249	249 *	.3	.7
469 WELS	1	90	60	129	.2	.4
496 Jewish Est	1	NR	NR	50	.1	.1
498 Indep.Charis.	1	0	428	800	1.0	2.3
CHOUTEAU	**17**	**1,204**	**626**	**6,220 ***	**104.2**	**100.0**
056 Baha'i	0	1	NR	1	-	-
081 Catholic	4	NR	NR	4,292	71.9	69.0
097 Chr Chs&Chs Cr	1	368	NR	470 *	7.9	7.6
123 Ch God (Ander)	1	NR	101	101	1.7	1.6
151 L-D Saints	1	NR	NR	147	2.5	2.4
193 Episcopal	1	NR	12	22	.4	.4
203 Evan Free Ch	1	59	160	160	2.7	2.6
207 E.L.C.A.	1	227	103	320	5.4	5.1
257 Hutterian Br	1	66	NR	100	1.7	1.6
283 Luth—MO Synod	1	38	16	39	.7	.6
449 Un Methodist	5	445	234	568 *	9.5	9.1
CUSTER	**20**	**2,206**	**1,023**	**5,633 ***	**48.2**	**100.0**
019 Amer Bapt USA	1	120	107	147 *	1.3	2.6
053 Assemb of God	1	66	80	100	.9	1.8
056 Baha'i	0	2	NR	2	-	-
081 Catholic	1	NR	NR	2,304	19.7	40.9

NR–Not Reported   *Total adherents estimated from known number of communicant, confirmed, full members.   - Represents a percentage less than 0.1.   Percentages may not total 100 due to rounding.

Table 4: Religious Congregations by County and Group: 2000

Religious Group	Number of Churches, Synagogues, Mosques, or Temples	Number of Communicant, Confirmed, or Full Members	Number of Attendees	Total Adherents: Number of Adherents	Total Adherents: % of Total Pop.	Total Adherents: % of Total Adh.
089 Chr & Miss Al	1	23	NR	37	.3	.7
093 Chr Ch (Disc)	1	115	50	141 *	1.2	2.5
151 L-D Saints	1	NR	NR	286	2.4	5.1
167 Chs of Christ	2	37	46	41	.4	.7
193 Episcopal	1	NR	31	72	.6	1.3
207 E.L.C.A.	1	352	122	483	4.1	8.6
263 Int Foursq Gos	1	4	61	61 *	.5	1.1
283 Luth—MO Synod	1	434	147	604	5.2	10.7
306 NT IndBapt&Rltd	1	20	NR	24 *	.2	.4
355 Presb Ch (USA)	1	238	90	291 *	2.5	5.2
413 S.D.A.	1	66	NR	79	.7	1.4
419 So Bapt Conv	1	194	58	237 *	2.0	4.2
443 Un C of Christ	2	115	50	141 *	1.2	2.5
449 Un Methodist	1	387	125	473 *	4.0	8.4
467 Wesleyan	1	33	56	110	.9	2.0
DANIELS	**11**	**851**	**260**	**2,639 ***	**130.8**	**100.0**
053 Assemb of God	1	23	30	50	2.5	1.9
081 Catholic	3	NR	NR	1,404	69.6	53.2
089 Chr & Miss Al	2	12	NR	61	3.0	2.3
207 E.L.C.A.	4	728	197	1,021	50.6	38.7
449 Un Methodist	1	88	33	103 *	5.1	3.9
DAWSON	**20**	**2,178**	**964**	**4,362 ***	**48.2**	**100.0**
053 Assemb of God	1	41	50	89	1.0	2.0
056 Baha'i	0	2	NR	2	-	-
081 Catholic	2	NR	NR	1,071	11.8	24.6
089 Chr & Miss Al	2	96	NR	393	4.3	9.0
151 L-D Saints	1	NR	NR	261	2.9	6.0
167 Chs of Christ	1	39	56	62	.7	1.4
193 Episcopal	1	NR	8	7	.1	.2
207 E.L.C.A.	3	610	227	764	8.4	17.5
283 Luth—MO Synod	1	849	282	1,063	11.7	24.4
288 Mennonite USA	3	145	99	175 *	1.9	4.0
413 S.D.A.	1	44	NR	52	.6	1.2
419 So Bapt Conv	1	40	25	48 *	.5	1.1
443 Un C of Christ	1	126	145	151 *	1.7	3.5
449 Un Methodist	2	186	72	224 *	2.5	5.1
DEER LODGE	**14**	**874**	**574**	**6,590 ***	**70.0**	**100.0**
053 Assemb of God	1	43	54	95	1.0	1.4
056 Baha'i	0	12	NR	12	.1	.2
057 Bapt Gen Conf	1	80	120	120 *	1.3	1.8
081 Catholic	2	NR	NR	4,669	49.6	70.8
151 L-D Saints	2	NR	NR	580	6.2	8.8
167 Chs of Christ	1	48	55	75	.8	1.1
193 Episcopal	1	NR	29	103	1.1	1.6
207 E.L.C.A.	1	321	83	460	4.9	7.0
263 Int Foursq Gos	1	2	41	41 *	.4	.6
283 Luth—MO Synod	1	24	15	25	.3	.4
355 Presb Ch (USA)	1	100	68	119 *	1.3	1.8
419 So Bapt Conv	1	166	65	198 *	2.1	3.0
449 Un Methodist	1	78	44	93 *	1.0	1.4
FALLON	**11**	**1,061**	**645**	**2,456 ***	**86.6**	**100.0**
053 Assemb of God	1	66	85	101	3.6	4.1
081 Catholic	2	NR	NR	937	33.0	38.2
203 Evan Free Ch	1	63	75	75	2.6	3.1
207 E.L.C.A.	2	607	185	848	29.9	34.5
313 N Am Bapt Conf	1	70	60	85 *	3.0	3.5
388 Reg Bapt Gen As	1	90	125	125 *	4.4	5.1
419 So Bapt Conv	1	69	25	84 *	3.0	3.4
443 Un C of Christ	1	73	34	89 *	3.1	3.6
467 Wesleyan	1	23	56	112	3.9	4.6
FERGUS	**35**	**2,595**	**1,264**	**6,336 ***	**53.3**	**100.0**
053 Assemb of God	1	65	85	145	1.2	2.3
056 Baha'i	0	2	NR	2	-	-
081 Catholic	7	NR	NR	2,270	19.1	35.8
089 Chr & Miss Al	1	20	NR	65	.5	1.0
097 Chr Chs&Chs Cr	1	225	NR	273 *	2.3	4.3
151 L-D Saints	1	NR	NR	299	2.5	4.7
165 Ch of Nazarene	1	80	51	141	1.2	2.2
167 Chs of Christ	1	31	33	40	.3	.6
179 Consrv Bapt	1	NR	133	133	1.1	2.1
193 Episcopal	1	NR	42	163	1.4	2.6
207 E.L.C.A.	2	596	239	747	6.3	11.8
257 Hutterian Br	5	330	NR	500	4.2	7.9
263 Int Foursq Gos	1	30	50	50 *	.4	.8
283 Luth—MO Synod	2	189	103	264	2.2	4.2
355 Presb Ch (USA)	2	261	147	317 *	2.7	5.0
413 S.D.A.	1	81	NR	96	.8	1.5
419 So Bapt Conv	1	97	68	118 *	1.0	1.9
449 Un Methodist	5	508	258	616 *	5.2	9.7
463 Vineyard	1	80	55	97 *	.8	1.5
FLATHEAD	**95**	**11,049**	**8,796**	**29,790 ***	**40.0**	**100.0**
017 Amer Bapt Assn	3	34	NR	42 *	.1	.1
019 Amer Bapt USA	1	68	42	84 *	.1	.3
053 Assemb of God	5	1,382	2,050	3,243	4.4	10.9
056 Baha'i	1	35	NR	35	-	.1
057 Bapt Gen Conf	1	29	98	98 *	.1	.3
081 Catholic	6	NR	NR	9,932	13.3	33.3
084 Calvary Chapel	2	NR	NR	NR	-	-
089 Chr & Miss Al	5	208	NR	673	.9	2.3
093 Chr Ch (Disc)	3	272	79	337 *	.5	1.1
097 Chr Chs&Chs Cr	2	238	NR	294 *	.4	1.0
123 Ch God (Ander)	3	NR	207	207	.3	.7
127 Ch God (Cleve)	1	8	6	10 *	-	-
145 Ch God Prophcy	1	24	NR	29 *	-	.1
151 L-D Saints	8	NR	NR	2,822	3.8	9.5
165 Ch of Nazarene	3	446	436	563	.8	1.9
167 Chs of Christ	3	212	222	262	.4	.9
173 Comm of Christ	1	22	NR	22	-	.1
193 Episcopal	3	NR	121	226	.3	.8
207 E.L.C.A.	7	2,811	1,568	3,659	4.9	12.3
220 Free Lutheran	2	209	233	302	.4	1.0
263 Int Foursq Gos	2	36	167	167 *	.2	.6
283 Luth—MO Synod	3	1,327	849	1,883	2.5	6.3
288 Mennonite USA	1	88	99	109 *	.1	.4
306 NT IndBapt&Rltd	1	75	NR	93 *	.1	.3
335 Orth Pres Ch	1	196	183	241	.3	.8
339 Pent Ch of God	1	4	NR	5	-	-
355 Presb Ch (USA)	2	430	225	532 *	.7	1.8
388 Reg Bapt Gen As	6	464	740	721 *	1.0	2.4
403 Salvation Army	1	89	47	164	.2	.6
413 S.D.A.	3	280	NR	333	.4	1.1
419 So Bapt Conv	4	766	563	948 *	1.3	3.2
435 Unitarian-Univ	1	36	NR	45 *	.1	.2
443 Un C of Christ	1	60	36	74 *	.1	.2
449 Un Methodist	5	950	615	1,176 *	1.6	3.9
463 Vineyard	1	250	210	309 *	.4	1.0
496 Jewish Est	1	NR	NR	150	.2	.5
GALLATIN	**76**	**9,705**	**7,030**	**24,013 ***	**35.4**	**100.0**
019 Amer Bapt USA	2	292	266	351 *	.5	1.5
053 Assemb of God	3	347	473	679	1.0	2.8
056 Baha'i	0	24	NR	24	-	.1
076 Buddhism	1	NR	NR	NR	-	-
081 Catholic	5	NR	NR	7,965	11.7	33.2
084 Calvary Chapel	2	NR	NR	NR	-	-
089 Chr & Miss Al	2	142	NR	320	.5	1.3
093 Chr Ch (Disc)	1	213	92	256 *	.4	1.1
097 Chr Chs&Chs Cr	3	305	NR	367 *	.5	1.5
105 Christian Ref	4	1,540	1,310	1,852 *	2.7	7.7
127 Ch God (Cleve)	1	39	33	47 *	.1	.2
151 L-D Saints	8	NR	NR	2,397	3.5	10.0
165 Ch of Nazarene	1	232	100	232	.3	1.0
167 Chs of Christ	5	250	246	339	.5	1.4
173 Comm of Christ	1	16	NR	16	-	.1
193 Episcopal	2	NR	240	423	.6	1.8
203 Evan Free Ch	1	165	500	500	.7	2.1
207 E.L.C.A.	3	1,055	540	1,508	2.2	6.3
226 Friends-USA	2	44	NR	53 *	.1	.2
263 Int Foursq Gos	1	17	86	86 *	.1	.4

NR–Not Reported   *Total adherents estimated from known number of communicant, confirmed, full members.   - Represents a percentage less than 0.1.   Percentages may not total 100 due to rounding.

Table 4: Religious Congregations by County and Group: 2000

Religious Group	Number of Churches, Synagogues, Mosques, or Temples	Number of Communicant, Confirmed, or Full Members	Number of Attendees	Total Adherents		
				Number of Adherents	% of Total Pop.	% of Total Adh.
267 Muslim Est	1	NR	55	163	.2	.7
283 Luth—MO Synod	2	527	297	706	1.0	2.9
355 Presb Ch (USA)	4	668	488	868 *	1.3	3.6
356 Presb Ch Amer	1	60	80	80	.1	.3
403 Salvation Army	1	33	26	182	.3	.8
413 S.D.A.	3	451	NR	538	.8	2.2
416 Sikh	1	NR	NR	NR	-	-
419 So Bapt Conv	5	908	338	1,092 *	1.6	4.5
435 Unitarian-Univ	1	47	NR	57 *	.1	.2
443 Un C of Christ	1	246	160	296 *	.4	1.2
449 Un Methodist	4	770	398	926 *	1.4	3.9
463 Vineyard	1	45	45	54 *	.1	.2
469 WELS	1	69	57	86	.1	.4
496 Jewish Est	1	NR	NR	50	.1	.2
499 Indep.Non-Char	1	1,200	1,200	1,500	2.2	6.2
GARFIELD	**8**	**214**	**124**	**522 ***	**40.8**	**100.0**
053 Assemb of God	1	28	35	51	4.0	9.8
081 Catholic	1	NR	NR	161	12.6	30.8
151 L-D Saints	1	NR	NR	63	4.9	12.1
167 Chs of Christ	1	6	4	10	.8	1.9
207 E.L.C.A.	1	55	30	85	6.6	16.3
355 Presb Ch (USA)	1	54	20	66 *	5.2	12.6
413 S.D.A.	1	36	NR	43	3.4	8.2
419 So Bapt Conv	1	35	35	43 *	3.4	8.2
GLACIER	**21**	**1,318**	**492**	**9,590 ***	**72.4**	**100.0**
053 Assemb of God	2	162	181	290	2.2	3.0
056 Baha'i	0	23	NR	23	.2	.2
081 Catholic	7	NR	NR	7,464	56.3	77.8
151 L-D Saints	1	NR	NR	213	1.6	2.2
203 Evan Free Ch	1	22	55	55	.4	.6
207 E.L.C.A.	1	379	80	503	3.8	5.2
257 Hutterian Br	5	330	NR	500	3.8	5.2
355 Presb Ch (USA)	1	186	82	251 *	1.9	2.6
419 So Bapt Conv	1	153	50	206 *	1.6	2.1
449 Un Methodist	2	63	44	85 *	.6	.9
GOLDEN VALLEY	**8**	**188**	**78**	**355 ***	**34.1**	**100.0**
053 Assemb of God	1	25	20	33	3.2	9.3
081 Catholic	1	NR	NR	101	9.7	28.5
207 E.L.C.A.	2	34	26	41	3.9	11.5
257 Hutterian Br	1	66	NR	100	9.6	28.2
419 So Bapt Conv	1	14	10	18 *	1.7	5.1
449 Un Methodist	2	49	22	62 *	6.0	17.5
GRANITE	**8**	**73**	**71**	**556 ***	**19.6**	**100.0**
056 Baha'i	0	1	NR	1	-	.2
081 Catholic	3	NR	NR	256	9.0	46.0
151 L-D Saints	1	NR	NR	159	5.6	28.6
193 Episcopal	1	NR	9	53	1.9	9.5
355 Presb Ch (USA)	1	26	15	32 *	1.1	5.8
449 Un Methodist	2	46	47	55 *	1.9	9.9
HILL	**41**	**3,497**	**1,529**	**7,599 ***	**45.6**	**100.0**
019 Amer Bapt USA	2	129	66	163 *	1.0	2.1
053 Assemb of God	2	182	248	298	1.8	3.9
056 Baha'i	0	12	NR	12	.1	.2
081 Catholic	7	NR	NR	2,196	13.2	28.9
089 Chr & Miss Al	1	21	NR	46	.3	.6
097 Chr Chs&Chs Cr	1	400	NR	507 *	3.0	6.7
151 L-D Saints	1	NR	NR	374	2.2	4.9
165 Ch of Nazarene	1	31	32	79	.5	1.0
167 Chs of Christ	1	12	13	16	.1	.2
193 Episcopal	1	NR	37	145	.9	1.9
207 E.L.C.A.	8	1,326	547	1,868	11.2	24.6
257 Hutterian Br	4	264	NR	400	2.4	5.3
263 Int Foursq Gos	2	32	117	117 *	.7	1.5
283 Luth—MO Synod	1	200	88	235	1.4	3.1
306 NT IndBapt&Rltd	1	60	NR	76 *	.5	1.0
355 Presb Ch (USA)	1	91	50	115 *	.7	1.5
403 Salvation Army	1	35	34	68	.4	.9

Religious Group	Number of Churches, Synagogues, Mosques, or Temples	Number of Communicant, Confirmed, or Full Members	Number of Attendees	Total Adherents		
				Number of Adherents	% of Total Pop.	% of Total Adh.
413 S.D.A.	1	69	NR	82	.5	1.1
419 So Bapt Conv	2	234	129	297 *	1.8	3.9
449 Un Methodist	3	399	168	505 *	3.0	6.6
JEFFERSON	**21**	**749**	**449**	**2,571 ***	**25.6**	**100.0**
053 Assemb of God	2	76	95	246	2.4	9.6
056 Baha'i	0	6	NR	6	.1	.2
081 Catholic	4	NR	NR	919	9.1	35.7
093 Chr Ch (Disc)	1	69	50	86 *	.9	3.3
151 L-D Saints	2	NR	NR	555	5.5	21.6
165 Ch of Nazarene	1	14	18	44	.4	1.7
173 Comm of Christ	1	30	NR	30	.3	1.2
207 E.L.C.A.	1	0	0	0	-	-
283 Luth—MO Synod	2	113	51	139	1.4	5.4
413 S.D.A.	2	52	NR	61	.6	2.4
419 So Bapt Conv	2	195	120	243 *	2.4	9.5
449 Un Methodist	3	194	115	242 *	2.4	9.4
JUDITH BASIN	**10**	**352**	**141**	**998 ***	**42.9**	**100.0**
056 Baha'i	0	3	NR	3	.1	.3
081 Catholic	4	NR	NR	536	23.0	53.7
257 Hutterian Br	1	66	NR	100	4.3	10.0
283 Luth—MO Synod	1	64	37	88	3.8	8.8
355 Presb Ch (USA)	2	110	58	136 *	5.8	13.6
419 So Bapt Conv	1	10	0	12 *	.5	1.2
449 Un Methodist	1	99	46	123 *	5.3	12.3
LAKE	**45**	**3,008**	**1,852**	**10,595 ***	**40.0**	**100.0**
032 Amish; other	1	18	NR	23 *	.1	.2
053 Assemb of God	3	229	320	435	1.6	4.1
056 Baha'i	0	40	NR	40	.2	.4
081 Catholic	7	NR	NR	5,133	19.4	48.4
089 Chr & Miss Al	4	179	NR	459	1.7	4.3
093 Chr Ch (Disc)	1	55	20	69 *	.3	.7
097 Chr Chs&Chs Cr	3	315	NR	397 *	1.5	3.7
151 L-D Saints	2	NR	NR	867	3.3	8.2
165 Ch of Nazarene	1	61	78	131	.5	1.2
167 Chs of Christ	3	48	56	67	.3	.6
193 Episcopal	2	NR	98	214	.8	2.0
207 E.L.C.A.	3	736	268	985	3.7	9.3
263 Int Foursq Gos	1	75	193	193 *	.7	1.8
283 Luth—MO Synod	3	250	172	325	1.2	3.1
355 Presb Ch (USA)	2	206	142	260 *	1.0	2.5
388 Reg Bapt Gen As	2	171	218	218 *	.8	2.1
413 S.D.A.	1	129	NR	154	.6	1.5
419 So Bapt Conv	2	177	110	223 *	.8	2.1
449 Un Methodist	4	319	177	402 *	1.5	3.8
LEWIS AND CLARK	**63**	**7,734**	**4,998**	**28,467 ***	**51.1**	**100.0**
017 Amer Bapt Assn	1	17	NR	21 *	-	.1
019 Amer Bapt USA	1	93	70	115 *	.2	.4
053 Assemb of God	2	515	735	1,231	2.2	4.3
056 Baha'i	1	44	NR	44	.1	.2
057 Bapt Gen Conf	1	20	23	25 *	-	.1
081 Catholic	10	NR	NR	15,133	27.2	53.2
084 Calvary Chapel	1	NR	NR	NR	-	-
089 Chr & Miss Al	1	101	NR	212	.4	.7
093 Chr Ch (Disc)	1	288	116	356 *	.6	1.3
097 Chr Chs&Chs Cr	1	40	NR	49 *	.1	.2
105 Christian Ref	1	43	43	53 *	.1	.2
145 Ch God Prophcy	1	24	NR	29 *	.1	.1
151 L-D Saints	5	NR	NR	1,599	2.9	5.6
165 Ch of Nazarene	1	61	60	97	.2	.3
167 Chs of Christ	3	131	180	193	.3	.7
173 Comm of Christ	1	46	NR	46	.1	.2
193 Episcopal	2	NR	218	763	1.4	2.7
201 Evan Cov Ch	1	86	189	189 *	.3	.7
203 Evan Free Ch	1	69	125	125	.2	.4
207 E.L.C.A.	3	1,560	814	2,165	3.9	7.6
257 Hutterian Br	1	66	NR	100	.2	.4
263 Int Foursq Gos	1	59	186	186 *	.3	.7
283 Luth—MO Synod	1	548	322	795	1.4	2.8

NR–Not Reported *Total adherents estimated from known number of communicant, confirmed, full members. - Represents a percentage less than 0.1. Percentages may not total 100 due to rounding.

Table 4: Religious Congregations by County and Group: 2000

Religious Group	Number of Churches, Synagogues, Mosques, or Temples	Number of Communicant, Confirmed, or Full Members	Number of Attendees	Total Adherents: Number of Adherents	% of Total Pop.	% of Total Adh.
306 NT IndBapt&Rltd	2	380	NR	470 *	.8	1.7
349 Pent Holiness	1	40	42	49 *	.1	.2
355 Presb Ch (USA)	1	473	185	585 *	1.0	2.1
403 Salvation Army	1	92	48	130	.2	.5
413 S.D.A.	1	147	NR	175	.3	.6
419 So Bapt Conv	5	730	367	902 *	1.6	3.2
435 Unitarian-Univ	1	19	NR	23 *	-	.1
443 Un C of Christ	1	242	80	299 *	.5	1.1
449 Un Methodist	4	1,258	675	1,554 *	2.8	5.5
463 Vineyard	1	60	60	74 *	.1	.3
467 Wesleyan	1	2	12	21	-	.1
469 WELS	1	80	48	109	.2	.4
499 Indep.Non-Char	1	400	400	550	1.0	1.9
LIBERTY	**11**	**742**	**355**	**1,759 ***	**81.5**	**100.0**
053 Assemb of God	1	81	120	120	5.6	6.8
081 Catholic	1	NR	NR	710	32.9	40.4
089 Chr & Miss Al	1	13	NR	28	1.3	1.6
151 L-D Saints	1	NR	NR	42	1.9	2.4
207 E.L.C.A.	3	392	172	508	23.5	28.9
257 Hutterian Br	2	132	NR	200	9.3	11.4
355 Presb Ch (USA)	1	22	18	27 *	1.3	1.5
449 Un Methodist	1	102	45	124 *	5.7	7.0
LINCOLN	**40**	**2,978**	**1,790**	**7,199 ***	**38.2**	**100.0**
017 Amer Bapt Assn	1	11	NR	13 *	.1	.2
019 Amer Bapt USA	1	220	75	268 *	1.4	3.7
053 Assemb of God	3	194	283	457	2.4	6.3
056 Baha'i	0	13	NR	13	.1	.2
081 Catholic	3	NR	NR	1,824	9.7	25.3
089 Chr & Miss Al	1	73	NR	173	.9	2.4
097 Chr Chs&Chs Cr	2	325	NR	396 *	2.1	5.5
123 Ch God (Ander)	3	NR	187	187	1.0	2.6
127 Ch God (Cleve)	1	35	19	43 *	.2	.6
151 L-D Saints	3	NR	NR	723	3.8	10.0
165 Ch of Nazarene	1	89	95	116	.6	1.6
167 Chs of Christ	2	90	120	126	.7	1.8
193 Episcopal	3	NR	64	196	1.0	2.7
203 Evan Free Ch	1	82	150	150	.8	2.1
207 E.L.C.A.	1	521	201	729	3.9	10.1
263 Int Foursq Gos	1	1	69	69 *	.4	1.0
283 Luth—MO Synod	2	309	176	479	2.5	6.7
323 Old Ord Amish	2	100	NR	122 *	.6	1.7
355 Presb Ch (USA)	1	43	34	52 *	.3	.7
388 Reg Bapt Gen As	1	18	26	26 *	.1	.4
413 S.D.A.	3	144	NR	172	.9	2.4
419 So Bapt Conv	2	441	138	537 *	2.9	7.5
449 Un Methodist	2	269	153	328 *	1.7	4.6
MCCONE	**10**	**527**	**269**	**1,225 ***	**62.0**	**100.0**
019 Amer Bapt USA	1	30	44	44 *	2.2	3.6
053 Assemb of God	1	28	35	80	4.0	6.5
081 Catholic	3	NR	NR	459	23.2	37.5
207 E.L.C.A.	1	361	103	510	25.8	41.6
419 So Bapt Conv	1	61	60	75 *	3.8	6.1
443 Un C of Christ	2	10	4	12 *	.6	1.0
469 WELS	1	37	23	45	2.3	3.7
MADISON	**16**	**446**	**425**	**1,690 ***	**24.7**	**100.0**
053 Assemb of God	2	76	100	114	1.7	6.7
056 Baha'i	0	5	NR	5	.1	.3
081 Catholic	3	NR	NR	639	9.3	37.8
151 L-D Saints	2	NR	NR	329	4.8	19.5
167 Chs of Christ	1	9	17	14	.2	.8
193 Episcopal	2	NR	78	166	2.4	9.8
283 Luth—MO Synod	1	26	18	31	.5	1.8
306 NT IndBapt&Rltd	2	80	NR	95 *	1.4	5.6
355 Presb Ch (USA)	1	106	47	126 *	1.8	7.5
419 So Bapt Conv	0	6	30	7 *	.1	.4
449 Un Methodist	2	138	135	164 *	2.4	9.7

Religious Group	Number of Churches, Synagogues, Mosques, or Temples	Number of Communicant, Confirmed, or Full Members	Number of Attendees	Total Adherents: Number of Adherents	% of Total Pop.	% of Total Adh.
MEAGHER	**8**	**321**	**90**	**725 ***	**37.5**	**100.0**
081 Catholic	1	NR	NR	256	13.3	35.3
089 Chr & Miss Al	1	39	NR	76	3.9	10.5
207 E.L.C.A.	2	107	62	140	7.2	19.3
257 Hutterian Br	2	132	NR	200	10.4	27.6
355 Presb Ch (USA)	1	22	20	27 *	1.4	3.7
419 So Bapt Conv	1	21	8	26 *	1.3	3.6
MINERAL	**12**	**371**	**320**	**1,010 ***	**26.0**	**100.0**
011 A.W.M.C.	1	45	95	46	1.2	4.6
053 Assemb of God	1	45	40	60	1.5	5.9
056 Baha'i	0	1	NR	1	-	.1
081 Catholic	1	NR	NR	388	10.0	38.4
151 L-D Saints	1	NR	NR	123	3.2	12.2
167 Chs of Christ	1	12	7	20	.5	2.0
203 Evan Free Ch	1	31	55	55	1.4	5.4
283 Luth—MO Synod	1	57	0	99	2.5	9.8
413 S.D.A.	1	35	NR	42	1.1	4.2
419 So Bapt Conv	1	67	40	81 *	2.1	8.0
449 Un Methodist	3	78	83	95 *	2.4	9.4
MISSOULA	**86**	**9,778**	**5,922**	**31,006 ***	**32.4**	**100.0**
011 A.W.M.C.	1	16	55	16	-	.1
017 Amer Bapt Assn	1	10	NR	12 *	-	-
019 Amer Bapt USA	1	150	95	181 *	.2	.6
053 Assemb of God	2	726	989	1,615	1.7	5.2
056 Baha'i	2	103	NR	103	.1	.3
076 Buddhism	3	NR	NR	NR	-	-
081 Catholic	10	NR	NR	12,074	12.6	38.9
084 Calvary Chapel	1	NR	NR	NR	-	-
089 Chr & Miss Al	1	325	NR	905	.9	2.9
093 Chr Ch (Disc)	1	181	92	219 *	.2	.7
097 Chr Chs&Chs Cr	2	179	NR	216 *	.2	.7
145 Ch God Prophcy	1	24	NR	28 *	-	.1
151 L-D Saints	9	NR	NR	3,620	3.8	11.7
165 Ch of Nazarene	1	114	103	114	.1	.4
167 Chs of Christ	3	220	249	290	.3	.9
173 Comm of Christ	1	67	NR	67	.1	.2
193 Episcopal	1	NR	244	1,037	1.1	3.3
203 Evan Free Ch	1	13	45	45	-	.1
207 E.L.C.A.	6	2,214	939	3,115	3.3	10.0
221 Free Methodist	1	0	64	64	.1	.2
226 Friends-USA	2	44	NR	53 *	.1	.2
246 Greek Orthodox	1	NR	NR	165	.2	.5
263 Int Foursq Gos	2	244	317	317 *	.3	1.0
264 Int Chs of Crst	1	102	175	147	.2	.5
267 Muslim Est	1	NR	55	163	.2	.5
283 Luth—MO Synod	4	832	398	1,058	1.1	3.4
306 NT IndBapt&Rltd	1	30	NR	36 *	-	.1
313 N Am Bapt Conf	1	172	155	208 *	.2	.7
335 Orth Pres Ch	1	37	61	68	.1	.2
339 Pent Ch of God	2	69	NR	150	.2	.5
355 Presb Ch (USA)	3	828	430	1,001 *	1.0	3.2
370 Ref Baptist Chs	1	NR	NR	NR	-	-
388 Reg Bapt Gen As	2	179	80	94 *	.1	.3
403 Salvation Army	1	93	61	235	.2	.8
413 S.D.A.	1	358	NR	426	.4	1.4
419 So Bapt Conv	6	1,044	550	1,261 *	1.3	4.1
435 Unitarian-Univ	1	35	NR	42 *	-	.1
443 Un C of Christ	1	503	221	607 *	.6	2.0
449 Un Methodist	2	662	372	799 *	.8	2.6
463 Vineyard	1	130	120	157 *	.2	.5
469 WELS	1	74	52	98	.1	.3
496 Jewish Est	1	NR	NR	200	.2	.6
MUSSELSHELL	**17**	**526**	**318**	**1,244 ***	**27.7**	**100.0**
019 Amer Bapt USA	1	53	65	65 *	1.4	5.2
053 Assemb of God	1	28	20	41	.9	3.3
056 Baha'i	0	3	NR	3	.1	.2
081 Catholic	3	NR	NR	469	10.4	37.7
167 Chs of Christ	2	39	50	57	1.3	4.6
193 Episcopal	1	NR	9	16	.4	1.3

NR–Not Reported   *Total adherents estimated from known number of communicant, confirmed, full members.   - Represents a percentage less than 0.1.   Percentages may not total 100 due to rounding.

Table 4: Religious Congregations by County and Group: 2000

Religious Group	Number of Churches, Synagogues, Mosques, or Temples	Number of Communicant, Confirmed, or Full Members	Number of Attendees	Total Adherents		
				Number of Adherents	% of Total Pop.	% of Total Adh.
207 E.L.C.A.	1	56	60	136	3.0	10.9
257 Hutterian Br	2	132	NR	200	4.4	16.1
283 Luth—MO Synod	1	22	13	23	.5	1.8
413 S.D.A.	1	27	NR	32	.7	2.6
419 So Bapt Conv	1	20	15	24 *	.5	1.9
449 Un Methodist	1	117	70	140 *	3.1	11.3
467 Wesleyan	1	2	0	2	-	.2
469 WELS	1	27	16	36	.8	2.9
PARK	**24**	**1,689**	**997**	**4,463 ***	**28.4**	**100.0**
019 Amer Bapt USA	1	70	50	85 *	.5	1.9
053 Assemb of God	1	88	100	210	1.3	4.7
056 Baha'i	0	7	NR	7	-	.2
081 Catholic	3	NR	NR	1,566	10.0	35.1
127 Ch God (Cleve)	1	23	28	28 *	.2	.6
151 L-D Saints	2	NR	NR	473	3.0	10.6
165 Ch of Nazarene	1	45	26	55	.4	1.2
167 Chs of Christ	1	36	60	65	.4	1.5
175 Congr Chr Chs	1	70	116	85 *	.5	1.9
193 Episcopal	2	NR	89	220	1.4	4.9
207 E.L.C.A.	3	506	204	634	4.0	14.2
306 NT IndBapt&Rltd	1	60	NR	73 *	.5	1.6
413 S.D.A.	1	100	NR	119	.8	2.7
419 So Bapt Conv	1	127	28	154 *	1.0	3.5
449 Un Methodist	4	487	236	592 *	3.8	13.3
469 WELS	1	70	60	97	.6	2.2
PETROLEUM	**3**	**50**	**29**	**167 ***	**33.9**	**100.0**
081 Catholic	1	NR	NR	99	20.1	59.3
449 Un Methodist	1	16	9	20 *	4.1	12.0
469 WELS	1	34	20	48	9.7	28.7
PHILLIPS	**22**	**1,097**	**482**	**3,708 ***	**80.6**	**100.0**
053 Assemb of God	2	89	115	142	3.1	3.8
056 Baha'i	0	2	NR	2	-	.1
081 Catholic	5	NR	NR	2,009	43.7	54.2
097 Chr Chs&Chs Cr	1	35	NR	43 *	.9	1.2
151 L-D Saints	1	NR	NR	93	2.0	2.5
167 Chs of Christ	1	20	20	20	.4	.5
175 Congr Chr Chs	1	97	40	120 *	2.6	3.2
193 Episcopal	1	NR	14	12	.3	.3
207 E.L.C.A.	5	618	228	938	20.4	25.3
257 Hutterian Br	2	132	NR	200	4.3	5.4
419 So Bapt Conv	2	33	46	41 *	.9	1.1
449 Un Methodist	1	71	19	88 *	1.9	2.4
PONDERA	**20**	**1,739**	**592**	**4,581 ***	**71.3**	**100.0**
053 Assemb of God	1	39	50	73	1.1	1.6
081 Catholic	2	NR	NR	1,973	30.7	43.1
093 Chr Ch (Disc)	1	54	18	68 *	1.1	1.5
105 Christian Ref	1	73	58	92 *	1.4	2.0
151 L-D Saints	1	NR	NR	242	3.8	5.3
207 E.L.C.A.	3	713	257	946	14.7	20.7
257 Hutterian Br	6	396	NR	600	9.3	13.1
355 Presb Ch (USA)	1	237	100	300 *	4.7	6.5
419 So Bapt Conv	2	65	39	82 *	1.3	1.8
449 Un Methodist	2	162	70	205 *	3.2	4.5
POWDER RIVER	**8**	**224**	**238**	**850 ***	**45.7**	**100.0**
053 Assemb of God	1	14	25	32	1.7	3.8
056 Baha'i	0	1	NR	1	.1	.1
081 Catholic	1	NR	NR	402	21.6	47.3
151 L-D Saints	1	NR	NR	17	.9	2.0
179 Consrv Bapt	1	NR	100	100	5.4	11.8
207 E.L.C.A.	1	114	40	155	8.3	18.2
443 Un C of Christ	2	87	47	109 *	5.9	12.8
467 Wesleyan	1	8	26	34	1.8	4.0
POWELL	**17**	**558**	**527**	**2,676 ***	**37.3**	**100.0**
053 Assemb of God	1	105	140	200	2.8	7.5
056 Baha'i	0	4	NR	4	.1	.1

Religious Group	Number of Churches, Synagogues, Mosques, or Temples	Number of Communicant, Confirmed, or Full Members	Number of Attendees	Total Adherents		
				Number of Adherents	% of Total Pop.	% of Total Adh.
081 Catholic	4	NR	NR	1,552	21.6	58.0
093 Chr Ch (Disc)	1	31	13	37 *	.5	1.4
151 L-D Saints	1	NR	NR	249	3.5	9.3
173 Comm of Christ	1	38	NR	38	.5	1.4
193 Episcopal	1	NR	22	100	1.4	3.7
203 Evan Free Ch	1	22	45	45	.6	1.7
263 Int Foursq Gos	1	17	35	35 *	.5	1.3
283 Luth—MO Synod	1	127	52	163	2.3	6.1
355 Presb Ch (USA)	1	80	85	95 *	1.3	3.6
413 S.D.A.	2	24	NR	28	.4	1.0
419 So Bapt Conv	2	110	135	130 *	1.8	4.9
PRAIRIE	**6**	**328**	**467**	**889 ***	**74.1**	**100.0**
081 Catholic	1	NR	NR	254	21.2	28.6
207 E.L.C.A.	1	64	22	66	5.5	7.4
283 Luth—MO Synod	1	71	20	71	5.9	8.0
355 Presb Ch (USA)	1	104	70	119 *	9.9	13.4
419 So Bapt Conv	0	8	11	9 *	.8	1.0
467 Wesleyan	1	37	312	312	26.0	35.1
469 WELS	1	44	32	58	4.8	6.5
RAVALLI	**47**	**3,758**	**2,636**	**10,605 ***	**29.4**	**100.0**
019 Amer Bapt USA	3	255	299	315 *	.9	3.0
053 Assemb of God	2	281	362	576	1.6	5.4
056 Baha'i	0	22	NR	22	.1	.2
081 Catholic	4	NR	NR	3,244	9.0	30.6
084 Calvary Chapel	1	NR	NR	NR	-	-
089 Chr & Miss Al	1	32	NR	93	.3	.9
093 Chr Ch (Disc)	1	163	103	201 *	.6	1.9
151 L-D Saints	5	NR	NR	1,920	5.3	18.1
165 Ch of Nazarene	1	32	48	56	.2	.5
167 Chs of Christ	3	80	100	94	.3	.9
183 Cons Menn Conf	1	24	29	35	.1	.3
193 Episcopal	2	NR	57	117	.3	1.1
207 E.L.C.A.	1	577	185	802	2.2	7.6
263 Int Foursq Gos	3	28	137	137 *	.4	1.3
283 Luth—MO Synod	2	450	292	579	1.6	5.5
297 Mennonite;Other	1	25	NR	31 *	.1	.3
306 NT IndBapt&Rltd	1	100	NR	123 *	.3	1.2
313 N Am Bapt Conf	1	24	43	30 *	.1	.3
349 Pent Holiness	1	85	80	105 *	.3	1.0
355 Presb Ch (USA)	1	263	98	324 *	.9	3.1
413 S.D.A.	3	314	NR	374	1.0	3.5
419 So Bapt Conv	4	486	360	599 *	1.7	5.6
449 Un Methodist	3	460	351	568 *	1.6	5.4
467 Wesleyan	2	57	92	260	.7	2.5
RICHLAND	**28**	**3,084**	**1,316**	**6,949 ***	**71.9**	**100.0**
053 Assemb of God	1	167	215	431	4.5	6.2
056 Baha'i	0	4	NR	4	-	.1
081 Catholic	5	NR	NR	2,009	20.8	28.9
089 Chr & Miss Al	4	110	NR	298	3.1	4.3
151 L-D Saints	2	NR	NR	204	2.1	2.9
165 Ch of Nazarene	1	57	41	81	.8	1.2
167 Chs of Christ	1	60	95	95	1.0	1.4
181 Consrv Congr	1	92	70	115 *	1.2	1.7
207 E.L.C.A.	4	1,532	451	2,361	24.4	34.0
283 Luth—MO Synod	2	381	159	498	5.2	7.2
306 NT IndBapt&Rltd	1	75	NR	94 *	1.0	1.4
355 Presb Ch (USA)	1	61	33	76 *	.8	1.1
413 S.D.A.	1	15	NR	18	.2	.3
419 So Bapt Conv	1	86	49	108 *	1.1	1.6
443 Un C of Christ	2	188	73	236 *	2.4	3.4
449 Un Methodist	1	256	130	321 *	3.3	4.6
ROOSEVELT	**42**	**2,583**	**1,266**	**8,763 ***	**82.5**	**100.0**
019 Amer Bapt USA	1	30	29	41 *	.4	.5
053 Assemb of God	2	145	195	223	2.1	2.5
056 Baha'i	0	24	NR	24	.2	.3
081 Catholic	4	NR	NR	4,453	41.9	50.8
151 L-D Saints	2	NR	NR	828	7.8	9.4
157 Ch of Brethren	1	30	26	41 *	.4	.5

NR–Not Reported   *Total adherents estimated from known number of communicant, confirmed, full members.   - Represents a percentage less than 0.1.   Percentages may not total 100 due to rounding.

Table 4: Religious Congregations by County and Group: 2000

Religious Group	Number of Churches, Synagogues, Mosques, or Temples	Number of Communicant, Confirmed, or Full Members	Number of Attendees	Total Adherents: Number of Adherents	Total Adherents: % of Total Pop.	Total Adherents: % of Total Adh.
165 Ch of Nazarene	1	10	22	41	.4	.5
167 Chs of Christ	1	7	6	15	.1	.2
173 Comm of Christ	1	33	NR	33	.3	.4
207 E.L.C.A.	8	1,195	351	1,539	14.5	17.6
211 Fel Evg Bib Ch	1	19	37	37	.3	.4
220 Free Lutheran	2	90	97	125	1.2	1.4
237 Menn Br US Conf	1	56	NR	76 *	.7	.9
283 Luth—MO Synod	1	76	42	98	.9	1.1
288 Mennonite USA	1	59	35	80 *	.8	.9
339 Pent Ch of God	1	19	NR	45	.4	.5
355 Presb Ch (USA)	7	490	272	663 *	6.2	7.6
419 So Bapt Conv	3	154	92	208 *	2.0	2.4
443 Un C of Christ	1	38	20	51 *	.5	.6
449 Un Methodist	2	96	36	130 *	1.2	1.5
469 WELS	1	12	6	12	.1	.1
ROSEBUD	**29**	**1,425**	**713**	**4,330 ***	**46.1**	**100.0**
053 Assemb of God	1	47	62	86	.9	2.0
056 Baha'i	0	20	NR	20	.2	.5
081 Catholic	5	NR	NR	1,741	18.6	40.2
089 Chr & Miss Al	2	47	NR	161	1.7	3.7
151 L-D Saints	2	NR	NR	271	2.9	6.3
167 Chs of Christ	1	8	10	13	.1	.3
193 Episcopal	1	NR	8	30	.3	.7
263 Int Foursq Gos	1	13	29	29 *	.3	.7
283 Luth—MO Synod	4	380	171	639	6.8	14.8
288 Mennonite USA	2	54	43	72 *	.8	1.7
323 Old Ord Amish	1	30	NR	40 *	.4	.9
339 Pent Ch of God	1	106	NR	250	2.7	5.8
355 Presb Ch (USA)	2	195	100	259 *	2.8	6.0
419 So Bapt Conv	3	436	189	580 *	6.2	13.4
443 Un C of Christ	1	52	50	69 *	.7	1.6
449 Un Methodist	1	1	6	1 *	-	-
467 Wesleyan	1	36	45	69	.7	1.6
SANDERS	**29**	**1,246**	**856**	**3,546 ***	**34.7**	**100.0**
053 Assemb of God	2	212	286	410	4.0	11.6
056 Baha'i	0	2	NR	2	-	.1
081 Catholic	4	NR	NR	916	9.0	25.8
089 Chr & Miss Al	2	78	NR	213	2.1	6.0
097 Chr Chs&Chs Cr	1	90	NR	108 *	1.1	3.0
123 Ch God (Ander)	1	NR	75	75	.7	2.1
151 L-D Saints	3	NR	NR	719	7.0	20.3
167 Chs of Christ	1	10	10	10	.1	.3
181 Consrv Congr	1	113	70	135 *	1.3	3.8
207 E.L.C.A.	3	317	151	429	4.2	12.1
339 Pent Ch of God	1	22	NR	42	.4	1.2
355 Presb Ch (USA)	1	37	23	44 *	.4	1.2
388 Reg Bapt Gen As	1	70	90	90 *	.9	2.5
413 S.D.A.	2	74	NR	88	.9	2.5
419 So Bapt Conv	1	92	31	110 *	1.1	3.1
449 Un Methodist	5	129	120	155 *	1.5	4.4
SHERIDAN	**25**	**1,746**	**775**	**3,110 ***	**75.8**	**100.0**
053 Assemb of God	2	98	63	86	2.1	2.8
081 Catholic	4	NR	NR	904	22.0	29.1
167 Chs of Christ	1	17	12	23	.6	.7
207 E.L.C.A.	10	1,346	511	1,749	42.6	56.2
283 Luth—MO Synod	1	59	29	74	1.8	2.4
288 Mennonite USA	1	31	42	42 *	1.0	1.4
413 S.D.A.	1	19	NR	23	.6	.7
419 So Bapt Conv	1	21	15	25 *	.6	.8
443 Un C of Christ	2	103	60	122 *	3.0	3.9
449 Un Methodist	2	52	43	62 *	1.5	2.0
SILVER BOW	**39**	**2,711**	**2,122**	**18,786 ***	**54.3**	**100.0**
019 Amer Bapt USA	2	37	28	45 *	.1	.2
053 Assemb of God	1	104	150	274	.8	1.5
056 Baha'i	1	20	NR	20	.1	.1
081 Catholic	6	NR	NR	12,275	35.5	65.3
093 Chr Ch (Disc)	1	51	16	62 *	.2	.3
097 Chr Chs&Chs Cr	1	2	NR	2 *	-	-
127 Ch God (Cleve)	1	29	186	186 *	.5	1.0
145 Ch God Prophcy	1	24	NR	29 *	.1	.2
151 L-D Saints	2	NR	NR	1,179	3.4	6.3
165 Ch of Nazarene	1	34	50	151	.4	.8
167 Chs of Christ	2	58	51	71	.2	.4
179 Consrv Bapt	1	NR	250	250	.7	1.3
193 Episcopal	1	NR	193	376	1.1	2.0
203 Evan Free Ch	1	17	40	40	.1	.2
207 E.L.C.A.	2	744	319	1,175	3.4	6.3
263 Int Foursq Gos	1	32	241	241 *	.7	1.3
283 Luth—MO Synod	1	149	67	213	.6	1.1
306 NT IndBapt&Rltd	2	110	NR	134 *	.4	.7
355 Presb Ch (USA)	1	181	130	221 *	.6	1.2
403 Salvation Army	1	69	31	164	.5	.9
410 Serb Orth USA	1	NR	NR	300	.9	1.6
413 S.D.A.	1	105	NR	125	.4	.7
419 So Bapt Conv	3	469	121	572 *	1.7	3.0
443 Un C of Christ	1	87	35	106 *	.3	.6
449 Un Methodist	2	389	214	475 *	1.4	2.5
496 Jewish Est	1	NR	NR	100	.3	.5
STILLWATER	**17**	**989**	**704**	**2,396 ***	**29.2**	**100.0**
053 Assemb of God	1	42	47	110	1.3	4.6
056 Baha'i	0	2	NR	2	-	.1
081 Catholic	2	NR	NR	692	8.4	28.9
123 Ch God (Ander)	1	NR	0	0	-	-
127 Ch God (Cleve)	1	14	6	17 *	.2	.7
151 L-D Saints	2	NR	NR	314	3.8	13.1
193 Episcopal	1	NR	15	26	.3	1.1
207 E.L.C.A.	2	319	132	377	4.6	15.7
263 Int Foursq Gos	1	2	102	102 *	1.2	4.3
283 Luth—MO Synod	1	155	80	198	2.4	8.3
419 So Bapt Conv	2	261	185	320 *	3.9	13.4
443 Un C of Christ	2	172	112	211 *	2.6	8.8
449 Un Methodist	1	22	25	27 *	.3	1.1
SWEET GRASS	**11**	**671**	**400**	**1,230 ***	**34.1**	**100.0**
081 Catholic	1	NR	NR	194	5.4	15.8
127 Ch God (Cleve)	1	52	16	65 *	1.8	5.3
151 L-D Saints	1	NR	NR	85	2.4	6.9
167 Chs of Christ	1	4	4	4	.1	.3
193 Episcopal	1	NR	28	23	.6	1.9
203 Evan Free Ch	1	23	60	60	1.7	4.9
207 E.L.C.A.	2	404	162	567	15.7	46.1
413 S.D.A.	1	32	NR	38	1.1	3.1
419 So Bapt Conv	1	11	30	14 *	.4	1.1
443 Un C of Christ	1	145	100	180 *	5.0	14.6
TETON	**28**	**1,998**	**866**	**4,295 ***	**66.6**	**100.0**
053 Assemb of God	2	191	191	191	3.0	4.4
056 Baha'i	0	2	NR	2	-	-
081 Catholic	5	NR	NR	1,231	19.1	28.7
151 L-D Saints	2	NR	NR	523	8.1	12.2
167 Chs of Christ	1	25	25	30	.5	.7
207 E.L.C.A.	4	727	284	945	14.7	22.0
257 Hutterian Br	3	198	NR	300	4.7	7.0
283 Luth—MO Synod	2	135	87	178	2.8	4.1
297 Mennonite;Other	1	12	NR	15 *	.2	.3
413 S.D.A.	1	75	NR	89	1.4	2.1
419 So Bapt Conv	1	101	104	126 *	2.0	2.9
420 Strict Baptists	1	6	NR	8 *	.1	.2
443 Un C of Christ	2	197	67	246 *	3.8	5.7
449 Un Methodist	3	329	108	411 *	6.4	9.6
TOOLE	**20**	**1,451**	**651**	**3,613 ***	**68.6**	**100.0**
053 Assemb of God	1	29	45	68	1.3	1.9
056 Baha'i	0	1	NR	1	-	-
081 Catholic	2	NR	NR	1,242	23.6	34.4
151 L-D Saints	1	NR	NR	190	3.6	5.3
167 Chs of Christ	1	10	10	10	.2	.3
207 E.L.C.A.	5	739	306	1,186	22.5	32.8
257 Hutterian Br	3	198	NR	300	5.7	8.3

NR–Not Reported *Total adherents estimated from known number of communicant, confirmed, full members. - Represents a percentage less than 0.1. Percentages may not total 100 due to rounding.

Table 4: Religious Congregations by County and Group: 2000

Religious Group	Number of Churches, Synagogues, Mosques, or Temples	Number of Communicant, Confirmed, or Full Members	Number of Attendees	Total Adherents		
				Number of Adherents	% of Total Pop.	% of Total Adh.
263 Int Foursq Gos	1	17	58	58 *	1.1	1.6
413 S.D.A.	1	58	NR	69	1.3	1.9
419 So Bapt Conv	1	136	75	167 *	3.2	4.6
449 Un Methodist	4	263	157	322 *	6.1	8.9
TREASURE	**4**	**181**	**120**	**414 ***	**48.1**	**100.0**
081 Catholic	1	NR	NR	192	22.3	46.4
283 Luth—MO Synod	1	39	20	47	5.5	11.4
355 Presb Ch (USA)	1	94	55	116 *	13.5	28.0
419 So Bapt Conv	1	48	45	59 *	6.9	14.3
VALLEY	**31**	**2,009**	**823**	**3,626 ***	**47.2**	**100.0**
053 Assemb of God	1	78	108	108	1.4	3.0
056 Baha'i	0	5	NR	5	.1	.1
081 Catholic	5	NR	NR	804	10.5	22.2
151 L-D Saints	1	NR	NR	112	1.5	3.1
165 Ch of Nazarene	1	16	9	16	.2	.4
167 Chs of Christ	1	19	20	23	.3	.6
173 Comm of Christ	1	44	NR	44	.6	1.2
179 Consrv Bapt	1	NR	75	75	1.0	2.1
193 Episcopal	1	NR	19	32	.4	.9
207 E.L.C.A.	6	1,172	387	1,585	20.7	43.7
211 Fel Evg Bib Ch	1	117	0	117	1.5	3.2
237 Menn Br US Conf	1	94	NR	115 *	1.5	3.2
283 Luth—MO Synod	1	24	19	30	.4	.8
297 Mennonite;Other	1	85	NR	104 *	1.4	2.9
339 Pent Ch of God	1	10	NR	35	.5	1.0
355 Presb Ch (USA)	1	18	18	22 *	.3	.6
413 S.D.A.	1	36	NR	43	.6	1.2
419 So Bapt Conv	2	106	77	130 *	1.7	3.6
443 Un C of Christ	1	74	33	90 *	1.2	2.5
449 Un Methodist	3	111	58	136 *	1.8	3.8
WHEATLAND	**13**	**535**	**330**	**1,111 ***	**49.2**	**100.0**
053 Assemb of God	1	83	121	230	10.2	20.7
056 Baha'i	0	1	NR	1	-	.1
081 Catholic	3	NR	NR	217	9.6	19.5
207 E.L.C.A.	1	122	42	159	7.0	14.3
257 Hutterian Br	2	132	NR	200	8.9	18.0
283 Luth—MO Synod	1	40	27	52	2.3	4.7
355 Presb Ch (USA)	1	42	23	52 *	2.3	4.7
419 So Bapt Conv	1	16	10	20 *	.9	1.8
449 Un Methodist	2	76	78	95 *	4.2	8.6
467 Wesleyan	1	23	29	85	3.8	7.7
WIBAUX	**6**	**210**	**114**	**729 ***	**68.3**	**100.0**
053 Assemb of God	1	29	40	64	6.0	8.8
081 Catholic	2	NR	NR	435	40.7	59.7
207 E.L.C.A.	2	137	54	176	16.5	24.1
449 Un Methodist	1	44	20	54 *	5.1	7.4
YELLOWSTONE	**139**	**23,129**	**14,813**	**62,831 ***	**48.6**	**100.0**
017 Amer Bapt Assn	1	28	NR	35 *	-	.1
019 Amer Bapt USA	2	303	144	376 *	.3	.6
053 Assemb of God	6	651	862	1,197	.9	1.9
056 Baha'i	1	112	NR	112	.1	.2
076 Buddhism	1	NR	NR	NR	-	-
081 Catholic	11	NR	NR	22,744	17.6	36.2
084 Calvary Chapel	1	NR	NR	NR	-	-
089 Chr & Miss Al	2	116	NR	345	.3	.5
093 Chr Ch (Disc)	2	436	176	542 *	.4	.9
097 Chr Chs&Chs Cr	2	160	NR	199 *	.2	.3
123 Ch God (Ander)	1	NR	0	0	-	-
127 Ch God (Cleve)	1	15	12	19 *	-	-
145 Ch God Prophcy	2	47	NR	58 *	-	.1
151 L-D Saints	19	NR	NR	5,292	4.1	8.4
165 Ch of Nazarene	3	233	197	319	.2	.5
167 Chs of Christ	2	260	263	340	.3	.5
173 Comm of Christ	1	96	NR	96	.1	.2
179 Consrv Bapt	1	NR	150	150	.1	.2
181 Consrv Congr	1	291	160	362 *	.3	.6
193 Episcopal	4	NR	334	1,043	.8	1.7

Religious Group	Number of Churches, Synagogues, Mosques, or Temples	Number of Communicant, Confirmed, or Full Members	Number of Attendees	Total Adherents		
				Number of Adherents	% of Total Pop.	% of Total Adh.
203 Evan Free Ch	1	43	60	60	-	.1
207 E.L.C.A.	11	5,623	2,195	7,584	5.9	12.1
223 Free Will Bapt	2	16	NR	20 *	-	-
226 Friends-USA	1	22	NR	27 *	-	-
257 Hutterian Br	1	66	NR	100	.1	.2
263 Int Foursq Gos	1	2,152	5,099	5,099 *	3.9	8.1
267 Muslim Est	1	NR	101	288	.2	.5
283 Luth—MO Synod	7	2,258	1,082	3,098	2.4	4.9
306 NT IndBapt&Rltd	3	410	NR	509 *	.4	.8
331 OCA: Ter Diocs	2	76	NR	103	.1	.2
335 Orth Pres Ch	1	204	248	295	.2	.5
355 Presb Ch (USA)	2	647	354	803 *	.6	1.3
403 Salvation Army	1	128	69	214	.2	.3
413 S.D.A.	4	443	NR	527	.4	.8
419 So Bapt Conv	15	2,966	1,188	3,685 *	2.8	5.9
435 Unitarian-Univ	1	80	NR	99 *	.1	.2
443 Un C of Christ	7	2,089	605	2,595 *	2.0	4.1
449 Un Methodist	7	2,473	787	3,072 *	2.4	4.9
463 Vineyard	1	130	120	162 *	.1	.3
467 Wesleyan	3	85	157	359	.3	.6
469 WELS	1	220	125	278	.2	.4
496 Jewish Est	1	NR	NR	300	.2	.5
499 Indep.Non-Char	1	250	325	325	.3	.5

NEBRASKA

Religious Group	Number of Churches, Synagogues, Mosques, or Temples	Number of Communicant, Confirmed, or Full Members	Number of Attendees	Number of Adherents	% of Total Pop.	% of Total Adh.
The State.....	2,612	446,871	221,845	1,006,860 *	58.8	100.0
ADAMS	**43**	**10,745**	**5,349**	**19,579 ***	**62.9**	**100.0**
019 Amer Bapt USA	2	199	114	245 *	.8	1.3
053 Assemb of God	1	282	365	410	1.3	2.1
056 Baha'i	0	8	NR	8	-	-
081 Catholic	5	NR	NR	3,572	11.5	18.2
093 Chr Ch (Disc)	1	280	87	345 *	1.1	1.8
097 Chr Chs&Chs Cr	1	60	NR	74 *	.2	.4
123 Ch God (Ander)	1	NR	24	24	.1	.1
165 Ch of Nazarene	1	214	180	283	.9	1.4
167 Chs of Christ	1	100	95	120	.4	.6
193 Episcopal	1	NR	113	292	.9	1.5
203 Evan Free Ch	1	162	380	380	1.2	1.9
207 E.L.C.A.	4	2,438	864	3,124	10.0	16.0
283 Luth—MO Synod	7	2,919	1,303	3,846	12.3	19.6
349 Pent Holiness	1	75	35	92 *	.3	.5
355 Presb Ch (USA)	3	1,063	421	1,311 *	4.2	6.7
403 Salvation Army	1	204	119	2,043	6.6	10.4
413 S.D.A.	1	61	NR	73	.2	.4
419 So Bapt Conv	2	158	253	195 *	.6	1.0
443 Un C of Christ	2	251	98	309 *	1.0	1.6
449 Un Methodist	6	2,145	825	2,642 *	8.5	13.5
469 WELS	1	126	73	166	.5	.8
496 Jewish Est	0	NR	NR	25	.1	.1
ANTELOPE	**30**	**3,022**	**1,222**	**6,103 ***	**81.9**	**100.0**
081 Catholic	5	NR	NR	2,165	29.1	35.5
089 Chr & Miss Al	1	50	NR	119	1.6	1.9
097 Chr Chs&Chs Cr	3	243	NR	303 *	4.1	5.0
151 L-D Saints	1	NR	NR	34	.5	.6
173 Comm of Christ	1	27	NR	27	.4	.4
193 Episcopal	1	NR	11	25	.3	.4
203 Evan Free Ch	1	55	97	97	1.3	1.6
283 Luth—MO Synod	5	1,319	685	1,680	22.5	27.5
413 S.D.A.	1	69	NR	82	1.1	1.3
443 Un C of Christ	4	451	160	562 *	7.5	9.2
449 Un Methodist	7	808	269	1,009 *	13.5	16.5
ARTHUR	**2**	**267**	**120**	**321 ***	**72.3**	**100.0**
019 Amer Bapt USA	1	267	120	321 *	72.3	100.0
467 Wesleyan	1	0	0	0	-	-
BANNER	**2**	**54**	**38**	**104 ***	**12.7**	**100.0**
193 Episcopal	1	NR	13	35	4.3	33.7

NR–Not Reported *Total adherents estimated from known number of communicant, confirmed, full members. - Represents a percentage less than 0.1. Percentages may not total 100 due to rounding.

Table 4: Religious Congregations by County and Group: 2000

Religious Group	Number of Churches, Synagogues, Mosques, or Temples	Number of Communicant, Confirmed, or Full Members	Number of Attendees	Total Adherents		
				Number of Adherents	% of Total Pop.	% of Total Adh.
449 Un Methodist	1	54	25	69 *	8.4	66.3
BLAINE	**5**	**202**	**98**	**442 ***	**75.8**	**100.0**
151 L-D Saints	1	NR	NR	195	33.4	44.1
443 Un C of Christ	3	166	68	205 *	35.2	46.4
469 WELS	1	36	30	42	7.2	9.5
BOONE	**25**	**2,095**	**951**	**5,364 ***	**85.7**	**100.0**
019 Amer Bapt USA	2	154	79	196 *	3.1	3.7
053 Assemb of God	1	13	18	23	.4	.4
081 Catholic	6	NR	NR	2,762	44.1	51.5
167 Chs of Christ	1	25	20	30	.5	.6
193 Episcopal	1	NR	1	2	-	-
207 E.L.C.A.	2	757	365	902	14.4	16.8
283 Luth—MO Synod	3	179	101	223	3.6	4.2
355 Presb Ch (USA)	3	197	99	250 *	4.0	4.7
413 S.D.A.	1	21	NR	25	.4	.5
443 Un C of Christ	1	49	39	62 *	1.0	1.2
449 Un Methodist	4	700	229	889 *	14.2	16.6
BOX BUTTE	**21**	**2,956**	**1,294**	**8,083 ***	**66.5**	**100.0**
019 Amer Bapt USA	1	100	48	126 *	1.0	1.6
053 Assemb of God	1	70	101	222	1.8	2.7
056 Baha'i	0	4	NR	4	-	-
081 Catholic	2	NR	NR	3,322	27.3	41.1
093 Chr Ch (Disc)	1	140	55	176 *	1.4	2.2
097 Chr Chs&Chs Cr	1	49	NR	62 *	.5	.8
123 Ch God (Ander)	1	NR	25	25	.2	.3
151 L-D Saints	1	NR	NR	123	1.0	1.5
165 Ch of Nazarene	2	23	22	24	.2	.3
167 Chs of Christ	1	23	25	30	.2	.4
193 Episcopal	1	NR	106	439	3.6	5.4
203 Evan Free Ch	1	28	91	91	.7	1.1
207 E.L.C.A.	1	594	220	827	6.8	10.2
283 Luth—MO Synod	1	560	177	735	6.0	9.1
355 Presb Ch (USA)	1	377	80	475 *	3.9	5.9
413 S.D.A.	1	76	NR	90	.7	1.1
443 Un C of Christ	1	44	19	55 *	.5	.7
449 Un Methodist	2	863	314	1,087 *	8.9	13.4
467 Wesleyan	1	5	11	170	1.4	2.1
BOYD	**19**	**921**	**520**	**2,205 ***	**90.4**	**100.0**
053 Assemb of God	1	35	45	45	1.8	2.0
081 Catholic	4	NR	NR	948	38.9	43.0
201 Evan Cov Ch	1	41	32	50 *	2.1	2.3
207 E.L.C.A.	2	207	94	264	10.8	12.0
283 Luth—MO Synod	3	212	116	291	11.9	13.2
413 S.D.A.	1	6	NR	7	.3	.3
443 Un C of Christ	1	83	28	101 *	4.1	4.6
449 Un Methodist	3	183	73	222 *	9.1	10.1
467 Wesleyan	2	47	69	147	6.0	6.7
469 WELS	1	107	63	130	5.3	5.9
BROWN	**9**	**1,168**	**698**	**2,062 ***	**58.5**	**100.0**
053 Assemb of God	1	35	48	75	2.1	3.6
056 Baha'i	0	1	NR	1	-	-
081 Catholic	1	NR	NR	453	12.9	22.0
165 Ch of Nazarene	1	115	106	141	4.0	6.8
203 Evan Free Ch	1	52	155	155	4.4	7.5
283 Luth—MO Synod	1	380	147	527	15.0	25.6
443 Un C of Christ	1	115	42	140 *	4.0	6.8
449 Un Methodist	3	470	200	570 *	16.2	27.6
BUFFALO	**63**	**12,029**	**6,610**	**26,688 ***	**63.2**	**100.0**
019 Amer Bapt USA	1	401	100	494 *	1.2	1.9
034 Ant Orth of NA	1	116	NR	232	.5	.9
053 Assemb of God	3	509	697	1,098	2.6	4.1
056 Baha'i	0	8	NR	8	-	-
076 Buddhism	1	NR	NR	NR	-	-
081 Catholic	8	NR	NR	8,941	21.2	33.5
093 Chr Ch (Disc)	2	368	106	453 *	1.1	1.7
097 Chr Chs&Chs Cr	3	222	NR	273 *	.6	1.0
123 Ch God (Ander)	1	NR	66	66	.2	.2
145 Ch God Prophcy	2	69	NR	84 *	.2	.3
151 L-D Saints	2	NR	NR	484	1.1	1.8
165 Ch of Nazarene	1	96	93	237	.6	.9
167 Chs of Christ	2	119	130	153	.4	.6
193 Episcopal	1	NR	119	415	1.0	1.6
203 Evan Free Ch	2	419	855	855	2.0	3.2
207 E.L.C.A.	2	1,687	854	2,238	5.3	8.4
263 Int Foursq Gos	1	94	49	116 *	.3	.4
283 Luth—MO Synod	8	2,745	1,420	3,604	8.5	13.5
355 Presb Ch (USA)	1	473	250	582 *	1.4	2.2
356 Presb Ch Amer	1	137	160	160	.4	.6
403 Salvation Army	1	99	41	187	.4	.7
413 S.D.A.	4	245	NR	292	.7	1.1
449 Un Methodist	13	4,155	1,309	5,114 *	12.1	19.2
469 WELS	1	67	35	85	.2	.3
498 Indep.Charis.	1	0	326	517	1.2	1.9
BURT	**24**	**3,922**	**1,507**	**5,718 ***	**73.4**	**100.0**
019 Amer Bapt USA	2	446	108	549 *	7.0	9.6
053 Assemb of God	1	46	60	111	1.4	1.9
057 Bapt Gen Conf	1	28	25	34 *	.4	.6
081 Catholic	3	NR	NR	681	8.7	11.9
173 Comm of Christ	1	125	NR	125	1.6	2.2
201 Evan Cov Ch	1	114	90	140 *	1.8	2.4
203 Evan Free Ch	1	56	180	180	2.3	3.1
207 E.L.C.A.	3	1,405	376	1,797	23.1	31.4
283 Luth—MO Synod	2	277	134	347	4.5	6.1
355 Presb Ch (USA)	3	503	217	619 *	7.9	10.8
449 Un Methodist	6	922	317	1,135 *	14.6	19.8
BUTLER	**25**	**1,535**	**746**	**5,098 ***	**58.1**	**100.0**
019 Amer Bapt USA	1	10	7	13 *	.1	.3
081 Catholic	12	NR	NR	3,123	35.6	61.3
093 Chr Ch (Disc)	1	39	25	49 *	.6	1.0
203 Evan Free Ch	1	69	125	125	1.4	2.5
207 E.L.C.A.	1	142	55	180	2.1	3.5
283 Luth—MO Synod	2	364	201	480	5.5	9.4
443 Un C of Christ	1	42	18	53 *	.6	1.0
449 Un Methodist	5	710	224	892 *	10.2	17.5
469 WELS	1	159	91	183	2.1	3.6
CASS	**42**	**5,730**	**2,332**	**15,199 ***	**62.5**	**100.0**
019 Amer Bapt USA	1	26	17	33 *	.1	.2
053 Assemb of God	1	18	27	47	.2	.3
056 Baha'i	0	4	NR	4	-	-
081 Catholic	5	NR	NR	7,073	29.1	46.5
089 Chr & Miss Al	1	0	NR	37	.2	.2
093 Chr Ch (Disc)	5	661	160	840 *	3.5	5.5
097 Chr Chs&Chs Cr	1	50	NR	64 *	.3	.4
151 L-D Saints	1	NR	NR	411	1.7	2.7
167 Chs of Christ	1	31	33	40	.2	.3
193 Episcopal	1	NR	34	86	.4	.6
207 E.L.C.A.	2	436	205	642	2.6	4.2
283 Luth—MO Synod	5	1,260	505	1,738	7.1	11.4
291 Missionary Ch	1	101	190	190	.8	1.3
355 Presb Ch (USA)	2	426	203	541 *	2.2	3.6
419 So Bapt Conv	1	599	123	761 *	3.1	5.0
443 Un C of Christ	3	350	150	445 *	1.8	2.9
449 Un Methodist	11	1,768	685	2,247 *	9.2	14.8
CEDAR	**24**	**2,364**	**1,028**	**8,285 ***	**86.2**	**100.0**
053 Assemb of God	1	24	22	23	.2	.3
056 Baha'i	0	2	NR	2	-	-
081 Catholic	11	NR	NR	5,286	55.0	63.8
097 Chr Chs&Chs Cr	1	18	NR	23 *	.2	.3
207 E.L.C.A.	3	1,209	472	1,532	15.9	18.5
283 Luth—MO Synod	1	221	130	284	3.0	3.4
355 Presb Ch (USA)	2	200	108	255 *	2.7	3.1
443 Un C of Christ	2	241	94	307 *	3.2	3.7
449 Un Methodist	3	449	202	573 *	6.0	6.9

NR–Not Reported   *Total adherents estimated from known number of communicant, confirmed, full members.   - Represents a percentage less than 0.1.   Percentages may not total 100 due to rounding.

Table 4: Religious Congregations by County and Group: 2000

Religious Group	Number of Churches, Synagogues, Mosques, or Temples	Number of Communicant, Confirmed, or Full Members	Number of Attendees	Total Adherents		
				Number of Adherents	% of Total Pop.	% of Total Adh.
CHASE	**15**	**1,736**	**833**	**2,755 ***	**67.7**	**100.0**
081 Catholic	2	NR	NR	520	12.8	18.9
157 Ch of Brethren	1	29	30	35 *	.9	1.3
165 Ch of Nazarene	1	29	43	43	1.1	1.6
167 Chs of Christ	3	91	102	122	3.0	4.4
173 Comm of Christ	1	50	NR	50	1.2	1.8
283 Luth—MO Synod	2	725	279	890	21.9	32.3
291 Missionary Ch	1	0	6	6	.1	.2
419 So Bapt Conv	0	11	18	13 *	.3	.5
449 Un Methodist	3	768	284	934 *	23.0	33.9
467 Wesleyan	1	33	71	142	3.5	5.2
CHERRY	**23**	**1,716**	**1,042**	**3,447 ***	**56.1**	**100.0**
053 Assemb of God	1	82	120	125	2.0	3.6
056 Baha'i	0	7	NR	7	.1	.2
081 Catholic	3	NR	NR	952	15.5	27.6
105 Christian Ref	1	99	73	124 *	2.0	3.6
151 L-D Saints	1	NR	NR	123	2.0	3.6
165 Ch of Nazarene	1	0	0	0	-	-
193 Episcopal	3	NR	59	119	1.9	3.5
203 Evan Free Ch	1	69	125	125	2.0	3.6
283 Luth—MO Synod	4	232	143	320	5.2	9.3
355 Presb Ch (USA)	1	343	98	428 *	7.0	12.4
413 S.D.A.	1	39	NR	46	.7	1.3
419 So Bapt Conv	1	88	85	110 *	1.8	3.2
449 Un Methodist	4	497	232	620 *	10.1	18.0
469 WELS	1	260	107	348	5.7	10.1
CHEYENNE	**30**	**3,532**	**1,549**	**6,313 ***	**64.2**	**100.0**
053 Assemb of God	2	50	59	82	.8	1.3
056 Baha'i	0	3	NR	3	-	-
081 Catholic	3	NR	NR	1,587	16.1	25.1
093 Chr Ch (Disc)	1	104	0	129 *	1.3	2.0
097 Chr Chs&Chs Cr	1	131	NR	162 *	1.6	2.6
165 Ch of Nazarene	1	26	25	57	.6	.9
167 Chs of Christ	2	38	44	44	.4	.7
193 Episcopal	1	NR	38	125	1.3	2.0
203 Evan Free Ch	1	100	200	200	2.0	3.2
207 E.L.C.A.	6	1,135	397	1,446	14.7	22.9
263 Int Foursq Gos	1	109	29	135 *	1.4	2.1
283 Luth—MO Synod	4	569	292	774	7.9	12.3
355 Presb Ch (USA)	2	244	109	302 *	3.1	4.8
419 So Bapt Conv	1	163	62	202 *	2.1	3.2
449 Un Methodist	3	860	294	1,065 *	10.8	16.9
467 Wesleyan	1	0	0	0	-	-
CLAY	**30**	**3,141**	**1,078**	**4,963 ***	**70.5**	**100.0**
081 Catholic	3	NR	NR	1,018	14.5	20.5
093 Chr Ch (Disc)	1	55	0	68 *	1.0	1.4
097 Chr Chs&Chs Cr	4	435	NR	541 *	7.7	10.9
193 Episcopal	1	NR	11	9	.1	.2
207 E.L.C.A.	4	654	299	807	11.5	16.3
283 Luth—MO Synod	1	29	12	42	.6	.8
355 Presb Ch (USA)	3	326	160	405 *	5.8	8.2
373 Ref Ch in U.S.	2	407	NR	542	7.7	10.9
443 Un C of Christ	3	540	236	671 *	9.5	13.5
449 Un Methodist	7	655	340	813 *	11.5	16.4
469 WELS	1	40	20	47	.7	.9
COLFAX	**20**	**1,942**	**811**	**6,997 ***	**67.0**	**100.0**
081 Catholic	9	NR	NR	4,552	43.6	65.1
207 E.L.C.A.	2	513	200	643	6.2	9.2
283 Luth—MO Synod	4	575	262	709	6.8	10.1
355 Presb Ch (USA)	2	620	241	794 *	7.6	11.3
419 So Bapt Conv	1	22	27	28 *	.3	.4
443 Un C of Christ	1	18	12	23 *	.2	.3
449 Un Methodist	1	194	69	248 *	2.4	3.5
CUMING	**27**	**4,299**	**2,078**	**8,820 ***	**86.4**	**100.0**
053 Assemb of God	1	32	39	46	.5	.5
056 Baha'i	0	3	NR	3	-	-
057 Bapt Gen Conf	1	22	24	28 *	.3	.3
081 Catholic	7	NR	NR	3,590	35.2	40.7
167 Chs of Christ	1	17	30	30	.3	.3
207 E.L.C.A.	2	919	356	1,115	10.9	12.6
283 Luth—MO Synod	8	2,669	1,227	3,211	31.5	36.4
288 Mennonite USA	1	138	110	173 *	1.7	2.0
355 Presb Ch (USA)	1	66	26	83 *	.8	.9
443 Un C of Christ	2	181	136	226 *	2.2	2.6
449 Un Methodist	3	252	130	315 *	3.1	3.6
CUSTER	**41**	**3,916**	**2,121**	**6,784 ***	**57.5**	**100.0**
019 Amer Bapt USA	4	465	298	579 *	4.9	8.5
053 Assemb of God	1	59	75	136	1.2	2.0
056 Baha'i	0	3	NR	3	-	-
057 Bapt Gen Conf	1	65	50	81 *	.7	1.2
081 Catholic	2	NR	NR	1,596	13.5	23.5
093 Chr Ch (Disc)	1	238	111	297 *	2.5	4.4
097 Chr Chs&Chs Cr	4	302	NR	377 *	3.2	5.6
123 Ch God (Ander)	1	NR	55	55	.5	.8
165 Ch of Nazarene	2	43	53	87	.7	1.3
167 Chs of Christ	1	68	77	94	.8	1.4
193 Episcopal	2	NR	26	73	.6	1.1
203 Evan Free Ch	2	168	295	295	2.5	4.3
207 E.L.C.A.	2	255	82	312	2.6	4.6
283 Luth—MO Synod	3	159	74	198	1.7	2.9
355 Presb Ch (USA)	1	172	64	214 *	1.8	3.2
413 S.D.A.	1	64	NR	76	.6	1.1
449 Un Methodist	12	1,757	805	2,189 *	18.6	32.3
469 WELS	1	98	56	122	1.0	1.8
DAKOTA	**19**	**3,555**	**1,547**	**8,965 ***	**44.3**	**100.0**
053 Assemb of God	1	127	185	322	1.6	3.6
056 Baha'i	0	1	NR	1	-	-
081 Catholic	5	NR	NR	3,872	19.1	43.2
097 Chr Chs&Chs Cr	1	130	NR	171 *	.8	1.9
207 E.L.C.A.	4	1,823	617	2,360	11.7	26.3
267 Muslim Est	1	NR	101	288	1.4	3.2
283 Luth—MO Synod	1	520	186	698	3.4	7.8
355 Presb Ch (USA)	1	239	80	314 *	1.6	3.5
419 So Bapt Conv	2	177	120	232 *	1.1	2.6
449 Un Methodist	3	538	258	707 *	3.5	7.9
DAWES	**21**	**1,856**	**992**	**4,142 ***	**45.7**	**100.0**
019 Amer Bapt USA	1	292	125	343 *	3.8	8.3
053 Assemb of God	2	148	129	255	2.8	6.2
081 Catholic	2	NR	NR	1,417	15.6	34.2
097 Chr Chs&Chs Cr	1	75	NR	88 *	1.0	2.1
151 L-D Saints	1	NR	NR	189	2.1	4.6
165 Ch of Nazarene	2	30	60	80	.9	1.9
167 Chs of Christ	1	15	16	19	.2	.5
173 Comm of Christ	1	22	NR	22	.2	.5
193 Episcopal	1	NR	46	156	1.7	3.8
207 E.L.C.A.	1	279	127	355	3.9	8.6
283 Luth—MO Synod	2	335	198	442	4.9	10.7
413 S.D.A.	2	92	NR	109	1.2	2.6
443 Un C of Christ	1	86	50	101 *	1.1	2.4
449 Un Methodist	3	482	241	566 *	6.2	13.7
DAWSON	**53**	**7,659**	**4,169**	**21,716 ***	**89.1**	**100.0**
019 Amer Bapt USA	2	216	67	280 *	1.1	1.3
053 Assemb of God	4	203	242	400	1.6	1.8
057 Bapt Gen Conf	1	111	140	144 *	.6	.7
081 Catholic	5	NR	NR	10,282	42.2	47.3
097 Chr Chs&Chs Cr	5	730	NR	947 *	3.9	4.4
123 Ch God (Ander)	1	NR	35	35	.1	.2
145 Ch God Prophcy	1	34	NR	45 *	.2	.2
151 L-D Saints	1	NR	NR	345	1.4	1.6
165 Ch of Nazarene	2	148	152	181	.7	.8
167 Chs of Christ	2	41	37	47	.2	.2
193 Episcopal	2	NR	43	62	.3	.3
203 Evan Free Ch	5	221	1,159	1,159	4.8	5.3
207 E.L.C.A.	5	1,910	703	2,483	10.2	11.4

NR–Not Reported *Total adherents estimated from known number of communicant, confirmed, full members. - Represents a percentage less than 0.1. Percentages may not total 100 due to rounding.

Table 4: Religious Congregations by County and Group: 2000

Religious Group	Number of Churches, Synagogues, Mosques, or Temples	Number of Communicant, Confirmed, or Full Members	Number of Attendees	Total Adherents: Number of Adherents	Total Adherents: % of Total Pop.	Total Adherents: % of Total Adh.
283 Luth—MO Synod	3	797	304	1,103	4.5	5.1
355 Presb Ch (USA)	4	830	363	1,076 *	4.4	5.0
360 Prim Bapt Chrch	1	NR	NR	NR	-	-
413 S.D.A.	1	90	NR	107	.4	.5
419 So Bapt Conv	1	123	120	160 *	.7	.7
449 Un Methodist	7	2,205	804	2,860 *	11.7	13.2
DEUEL	**10**	**1,002**	**560**	**1,648 ***	**78.6**	**100.0**
053 Assemb of God	2	114	150	222	10.6	13.5
081 Catholic	1	NR	NR	300	14.3	18.2
207 E.L.C.A.	2	120	79	164	7.8	10.0
263 Int Foursq Gos	1	18	67	67 *	3.2	4.1
283 Luth—MO Synod	2	244	107	289	13.8	17.5
449 Un Methodist	2	506	157	606 *	28.9	36.8
DIXON	**24**	**3,486**	**1,557**	**5,334 ***	**84.1**	**100.0**
056 Baha'i	0	1	NR	1	-	-
081 Catholic	3	NR	NR	920	14.5	17.2
097 Chr Chs&Chs Cr	1	100	NR	126 *	2.0	2.4
201 Evan Cov Ch	1	141	127	177 *	2.8	3.3
203 Evan Free Ch	2	128	188	188	3.0	3.5
207 E.L.C.A.	7	1,974	743	2,462	38.8	46.2
283 Luth—MO Synod	4	624	311	809	12.8	15.2
355 Presb Ch (USA)	2	119	57	150 *	2.4	2.8
443 Un C of Christ	1	38	17	48 *	.8	.9
449 Un Methodist	3	361	114	453 *	7.1	8.5
DODGE	**54**	**12,927**	**5,725**	**25,281 ***	**69.9**	**100.0**
019 Amer Bapt USA	1	473	240	581 *	1.6	2.3
053 Assemb of God	1	101	140	220	.6	.9
056 Baha'i	0	5	NR	5	-	-
081 Catholic	6	NR	NR	7,796	21.6	30.8
089 Chr & Miss Al	1	229	NR	502	1.4	2.0
093 Chr Ch (Disc)	1	211	68	259 *	.7	1.0
097 Chr Chs&Chs Cr	1	41	NR	50 *	.1	.2
127 Ch God (Cleve)	1	9	0	11 *	-	-
151 L-D Saints	1	NR	NR	335	.9	1.3
165 Ch of Nazarene	1	176	250	421	1.2	1.7
167 Chs of Christ	1	60	50	70	.2	.3
173 Comm of Christ	1	116	NR	116	.3	.5
193 Episcopal	1	NR	113	360	1.0	1.4
203 Evan Free Ch	1	100	177	177	.5	.7
207 E.L.C.A.	14	4,826	2,103	5,993	16.6	23.7
263 Int Foursq Gos	1	79	124	124 *	.3	.5
283 Luth—MO Synod	7	3,219	1,336	4,237	11.7	16.8
339 Pent Ch of God	2	7	NR	9	-	-
355 Presb Ch (USA)	2	1,095	342	1,344 *	3.7	5.3
413 S.D.A.	1	59	NR	70	.2	.3
419 So Bapt Conv	1	246	55	302 *	.8	1.2
443 Un C of Christ	3	626	261	768 *	2.1	3.0
449 Un Methodist	4	1,236	456	1,517 *	4.2	6.0
469 WELS	1	13	10	14	-	.1
DOUGLAS	**317**	**76,310**	**41,430**	**252,586 ***	**54.5**	**100.0**
017 Amer Bapt Assn	1	30	NR	38 *	-	-
019 Amer Bapt USA	10	2,008	1,233	2,531 *	.5	1.0
034 Ant Orth of NA	2	326	NR	652	.1	.3
053 Assemb of God	9	1,451	2,000	2,797	.6	1.1
056 Baha'i	1	148	NR	148	-	.1
057 Bapt Gen Conf	5	445	423	561 *	.1	.2
076 Buddhism	4	NR	NR	NR	-	-
081 Catholic	53	NR	NR	128,512	27.7	50.9
089 Chr & Miss Al	8	2,103	NR	7,339	1.6	2.9
093 Chr Ch (Disc)	5	1,350	582	1,702 *	.4	.7
097 Chr Chs&Chs Cr	6	1,500	NR	1,890 *	.4	.7
105 Christian Ref	1	141	165	178 *	-	.1
121 Ch God (Abr)	1	88	69	111 *	-	-
123 Ch God (Ander)	2	NR	138	138	-	.1
127 Ch God (Cleve)	3	254	148	320 *	.1	.1
151 L-D Saints	15	NR	NR	4,455	1.0	1.8
165 Ch of Nazarene	2	224	252	265	.1	.1
167 Chs of Christ	4	771	675	1,035	.2	.4
173 Comm of Christ	2	451	NR	451	.1	.2
179 Consrv Bapt	1	NR	35	35	-	-
193 Episcopal	8	NR	1,253	3,010	.6	1.2
201 Evan Cov Ch	5	961	930	1,327 *	.3	.5
203 Evan Free Ch	2	280	870	870	.2	.3
207 E.L.C.A.	28	18,454	8,634	25,066	5.4	9.9
211 Fel Evg Bib Ch	3	517	692	692	.1	.3
220 Free Lutheran	1	225	150	250	.1	.1
221 Free Methodist	1	30	38	38	-	-
226 Friends-USA	2	88	NR	111 *	-	-
237 Menn Br US Conf	3	194	NR	244 *	.1	.1
245 Greek Orth Vslp	1	700	NR	1,700	.4	.7
246 Greek Orthodox	1	NR	NR	498	.1	.2
252 Hindu	1	NR	NR	NR	-	-
263 Int Foursq Gos	5	442	428	557 *	.1	.2
267 Muslim Est	2	NR	406	1,609	.3	.6
283 Luth—MO Synod	18	11,074	6,501	15,110	3.3	6.0
288 Mennonite USA	2	26	33	33 *	-	-
290 Metro Comm Ch	1	71	75	90 *	-	-
304 NatPrimBapt USA	1	150	NR	189 *	-	.1
339 Pent Ch of God	3	27	NR	81	-	-
355 Presb Ch (USA)	25	8,306	4,072	10,470 *	2.3	4.1
356 Presb Ch Amer	3	165	185	293	.1	.1
371 Ref Ch in Am	1	279	372	485	.1	.2
388 Reg Bapt Gen As	6	348	398	451 *	.1	.2
403 Salvation Army	4	614	333	2,072	.4	.8
413 S.D.A.	5	1,412	NR	1,680	.4	.7
419 So Bapt Conv	11	6,220	4,036	7,841 *	1.7	3.1
435 Unitarian-Univ	2	340	NR	429 *	.1	.2
443 Un C of Christ	4	2,853	1,126	3,596 *	.8	1.4
449 Un Methodist	23	10,290	4,455	12,972 *	2.8	5.1
463 Vineyard	1	230	195	290 *	.1	.1
469 WELS	4	724	528	1,024	.2	.4
496 Jewish Est	5	NR	NR	6,350	1.4	2.5
DUNDY	**10**	**1,075**	**403**	**1,573 ***	**68.6**	**100.0**
081 Catholic	1	NR	NR	293	12.8	18.6
207 E.L.C.A.	2	400	137	478	20.9	30.4
226 Friends-USA	1	44	NR	53 *	2.3	3.4
283 Luth—MO Synod	1	144	65	165	7.2	10.5
355 Presb Ch (USA)	1	49	30	59 *	2.6	3.8
419 So Bapt Conv	1	44	44	53 *	2.3	3.4
449 Un Methodist	3	394	127	472 *	20.6	30.0
FILLMORE	**23**	**2,895**	**1,270**	**4,795 ***	**72.3**	**100.0**
053 Assemb of God	1	37	35	55	.8	1.1
081 Catholic	5	NR	NR	1,181	17.8	24.6
203 Evan Free Ch	1	57	135	135	2.0	2.8
207 E.L.C.A.	4	614	244	735	11.1	15.3
283 Luth—MO Synod	1	69	43	80	1.2	1.7
288 Mennonite USA	1	203	145	250 *	3.8	5.2
443 Un C of Christ	2	416	132	512 *	7.7	10.7
449 Un Methodist	6	1,316	424	1,620 *	24.4	33.8
469 WELS	2	183	112	227	3.4	4.7
FRANKLIN	**18**	**1,802**	**922**	**2,880 ***	**80.6**	**100.0**
053 Assemb of God	1	11	11	26	.7	.9
081 Catholic	4	NR	NR	569	15.9	19.8
203 Evan Free Ch	1	69	125	125	3.5	4.3
207 E.L.C.A.	2	643	269	753	21.1	26.1
283 Luth—MO Synod	2	273	142	335	9.4	11.6
291 Missionary Ch	1	27	70	70	2.0	2.4
355 Presb Ch (USA)	1	127	68	154 *	4.3	5.3
443 Un C of Christ	2	212	53	258 *	7.2	9.0
449 Un Methodist	3	406	139	494 *	13.8	17.2
467 Wesleyan	1	34	45	96	2.7	3.3
FRONTIER	**11**	**1,541**	**620**	**1,919 ***	**61.9**	**100.0**
056 Baha'i	0	4	NR	4	.1	.2
097 Chr Chs&Chs Cr	1	60	NR	73 *	2.4	3.8
165 Ch of Nazarene	1	0	0	0	-	-
207 E.L.C.A.	1	528	174	672	21.7	35.0

NR–Not Reported *Total adherents estimated from known number of communicant, confirmed, full members. - Represents a percentage less than 0.1. Percentages may not total 100 due to rounding.

Table 4: Religious Congregations by County and Group: 2000

Religious Group	Number of Churches, Synagogues, Mosques, or Temples	Number of Communicant, Confirmed, or Full Members	Number of Attendees	Total Adherents: Number of Adherents	Total Adherents: % of Total Pop.	Total Adherents: % of Total Adh.
283 Luth—MO Synod	1	255	95	322	10.4	16.8
443 Un C of Christ	2	34	15	42 *	1.4	2.2
449 Un Methodist	4	545	231	666 *	21.5	34.7
463 Vineyard	1	115	105	140 *	4.5	7.3
FURNAS	**26**	**3,064**	**1,246**	**4,384 ***	**82.3**	**100.0**
019 Amer Bapt USA	3	356	148	432 *	8.1	9.9
057 Bapt Gen Conf	1	71	73	86 *	1.6	2.0
081 Catholic	3	NR	NR	547	10.3	12.5
093 Chr Ch (Disc)	1	160	0	194 *	3.6	4.4
097 Chr Chs&Chs Cr	3	310	NR	375 *	7.0	8.6
193 Episcopal	1	NR	52	35	.7	.8
203 Evan Free Ch	1	20	62	62	1.2	1.4
221 Free Methodist	1	11	26	26	.5	.6
283 Luth—MO Synod	2	718	321	906	17.0	20.7
355 Presb Ch (USA)	1	102	65	124 *	2.3	2.8
413 S.D.A.	1	29	NR	35	.7	.8
443 Un C of Christ	1	218	96	264 *	5.0	6.0
449 Un Methodist	7	1,069	403	1,298 *	24.4	29.6
GAGE	**57**	**11,291**	**4,882**	**16,917 ***	**73.6**	**100.0**
019 Amer Bapt USA	1	159	68	194 *	.8	1.1
053 Assemb of God	2	132	156	201	.9	1.2
056 Baha'i	0	5	NR	5	-	-
081 Catholic	5	NR	NR	2,429	10.6	14.4
093 Chr Ch (Disc)	1	615	165	749 *	3.3	4.4
097 Chr Chs&Chs Cr	2	500	NR	609 *	2.6	3.6
123 Ch God (Ander)	1	NR	23	23	.1	.1
157 Ch of Brethren	1	88	42	107 *	.5	.6
165 Ch of Nazarene	1	71	43	112	.5	.7
167 Chs of Christ	2	92	99	117	.5	.7
193 Episcopal	2	NR	63	163	.7	1.0
207 E.L.C.A.	11	4,880	2,046	6,090	26.5	36.0
283 Luth—MO Synod	4	1,436	592	1,942	8.4	11.5
288 Mennonite USA	2	405	260	493 *	2.1	2.9
313 N Am Bapt Conf	1	29	8	35 *	.2	.2
355 Presb Ch (USA)	4	463	202	564 *	2.5	3.3
371 Ref Ch in Am	1	155	150	231	1.0	1.4
403 Salvation Army	1	123	44	259	1.1	1.5
413 S.D.A.	1	31	NR	37	.2	.2
419 So Bapt Conv	1	44	68	54 *	.2	.3
443 Un C of Christ	1	85	44	104 *	.5	.6
449 Un Methodist	10	1,698	653	2,068 *	9.0	12.2
469 WELS	2	280	156	331	1.4	2.0
GARDEN	**13**	**869**	**376**	**1,605 ***	**70.0**	**100.0**
053 Assemb of God	1	31	38	57	2.5	3.6
081 Catholic	2	NR	NR	299	13.0	18.6
167 Chs of Christ	1	2	3	5	.2	.3
193 Episcopal	1	NR	14	27	1.2	1.7
207 E.L.C.A.	2	367	81	501	21.9	31.2
355 Presb Ch (USA)	1	70	28	83 *	3.6	5.2
413 S.D.A.	1	0	NR	0	-	-
449 Un Methodist	2	335	131	396 *	17.3	24.7
467 Wesleyan	2	64	81	237	10.3	14.8
GARFIELD	**8**	**915**	**521**	**1,644 ***	**86.4**	**100.0**
053 Assemb of God	1	44	55	67	3.5	4.1
081 Catholic	1	NR	NR	510	26.8	31.0
097 Chr Chs&Chs Cr	2	190	NR	229 *	12.0	13.9
283 Luth—MO Synod	1	150	80	196	10.3	11.9
419 So Bapt Conv	1	159	217	192 *	10.1	11.7
443 Un C of Christ	1	172	76	208 *	10.9	12.7
449 Un Methodist	1	200	93	242 *	12.7	14.7
GOSPER	**5**	**1,114**	**467**	**1,815 ***	**84.7**	**100.0**
081 Catholic	1	NR	NR	465	21.7	25.6
093 Chr Ch (Disc)	1	171	42	206 *	9.6	11.3
207 E.L.C.A.	1	392	143	468	21.8	25.8
283 Luth—MO Synod	1	377	193	466	21.7	25.7
449 Un Methodist	1	174	89	210 *	9.8	11.6

Religious Group	Number of Churches, Synagogues, Mosques, or Temples	Number of Communicant, Confirmed, or Full Members	Number of Attendees	Total Adherents: Number of Adherents	Total Adherents: % of Total Pop.	Total Adherents: % of Total Adh.
GRANT	**7**	**211**	**91**	**417 ***	**55.8**	**100.0**
056 Baha'i	0	2	NR	2	.3	.5
081 Catholic	1	NR	NR	74	9.9	17.7
151 L-D Saints	1	NR	NR	27	3.6	6.5
193 Episcopal	1	NR	18	59	7.9	14.1
283 Luth—MO Synod	1	73	23	88	11.8	21.1
413 S.D.A.	1	28	NR	33	4.4	7.9
443 Un C of Christ	2	108	50	134 *	17.9	32.1
GREELEY	**13**	**747**	**288**	**3,108 ***	**114.5**	**100.0**
057 Bapt Gen Conf	1	49	42	61 *	2.2	2.0
081 Catholic	5	NR	NR	2,200	81.1	70.8
143 CG in Cr(Menn)	1	56	NR	69 *	2.5	2.2
207 E.L.C.A.	1	259	65	313	11.5	10.1
283 Luth—MO Synod	1	128	83	149	5.5	4.8
355 Presb Ch (USA)	1	14	6	17 *	.6	.5
449 Un Methodist	3	241	92	299 *	11.0	9.6
HALL	**60**	**14,876**	**6,685**	**47,128 ***	**88.0**	**100.0**
019 Amer Bapt USA	1	190	152	241 *	.5	.5
053 Assemb of God	4	430	506	1,235	2.3	2.6
056 Baha'i	1	16	NR	16	-	-
057 Bapt Gen Conf	1	62	130	130 *	.2	.3
081 Catholic	6	NR	NR	25,098	46.9	53.3
089 Chr & Miss Al	1	34	NR	99	.2	.2
093 Chr Ch (Disc)	1	346	115	439 *	.8	.9
097 Chr Chs&Chs Cr	1	352	NR	447 *	.8	.9
127 Ch God (Cleve)	2	158	15	200 *	.4	.4
145 Ch God Prophcy	1	34	NR	44 *	.1	.1
151 L-D Saints	3	NR	NR	1,102	2.1	2.3
165 Ch of Nazarene	2	145	92	176	.3	.4
167 Chs of Christ	2	127	140	168	.3	.4
173 Comm of Christ	1	113	NR	113	.2	.2
193 Episcopal	1	NR	128	459	.9	1.0
203 Evan Free Ch	1	236	570	570	1.1	1.2
207 E.L.C.A.	3	2,706	904	3,370	6.3	7.2
246 Greek Orthodox	1	NR	NR	60	.1	.1
263 Int Foursq Gos	2	122	90	155 *	.3	.3
283 Luth—MO Synod	7	3,551	1,855	4,785	8.9	10.2
288 Mennonite USA	1	85	85	108 *	.2	.2
355 Presb Ch (USA)	2	1,019	348	1,293 *	2.4	2.7
356 Presb Ch Amer	1	44	65	65	.1	.1
388 Reg Bapt Gen As	1	24	34	34 *	.1	.1
403 Salvation Army	1	150	53	477	.9	1.0
413 S.D.A.	1	172	NR	205	.4	.4
419 So Bapt Conv	1	157	35	199 *	.4	.4
443 Un C of Christ	1	290	120	368 *	.7	.8
449 Un Methodist	8	4,119	1,248	5,227 *	9.8	11.1
469 WELS	1	194	0	220	.4	.5
496 Jewish Est	0	NR	NR	25	-	.1
HAMILTON	**24**	**3,694**	**1,820**	**5,717 ***	**60.8**	**100.0**
053 Assemb of God	1	40	57	91	1.0	1.6
056 Baha'i	1	28	NR	28	.3	.5
057 Bapt Gen Conf	1	51	30	65 *	.7	1.1
081 Catholic	2	NR	NR	715	7.6	12.5
093 Chr Ch (Disc)	1	294	69	374 *	4.0	6.5
151 L-D Saints	1	NR	NR	90	1.0	1.6
201 Evan Cov Ch	1	118	66	150 *	1.6	2.6
203 Evan Free Ch	3	177	346	346	3.7	6.1
207 E.L.C.A.	3	640	248	834	8.9	14.6
283 Luth—MO Synod	3	724	396	964	10.3	16.9
355 Presb Ch (USA)	1	145	64	185 *	2.0	3.2
413 S.D.A.	1	52	NR	62	.7	1.1
443 Un C of Christ	1	145	64	185 *	2.0	3.2
449 Un Methodist	3	1,234	445	1,572 *	16.7	27.5
469 WELS	1	46	35	56	.6	1.0
HARLAN	**17**	**1,377**	**818**	**2,285 ***	**60.4**	**100.0**
081 Catholic	2	NR	NR	489	12.9	21.4
093 Chr Ch (Disc)	1	102	35	124 *	3.3	5.4
203 Evan Free Ch	3	118	222	222	5.9	9.7

NR–Not Reported   *Total adherents estimated from known number of communicant, confirmed, full members.   - Represents a percentage less than 0.1.   Percentages may not total 100 due to rounding.

Table 4: Religious Congregations by County and Group: 2000

Religious Group	Number of Churches, Synagogues, Mosques, or Temples	Number of Communicant, Confirmed, or Full Members	Number of Attendees	Total Adherents		
				Number of Adherents	% of Total Pop.	% of Total Adh.
207 E.L.C.A.	3	389	193	495	13.1	21.7
221 Free Methodist	1	17	21	21	.6	.9
283 Luth—MO Synod	1	203	69	269	7.1	11.8
355 Presb Ch (USA)	1	90	64	109 *	2.9	4.8
449 Un Methodist	5	458	214	556 *	14.7	24.3
HAYES	**3**	**186**	**46**	**395 ***	**37.0**	**100.0**
057 Bapt Gen Conf	1	17	11	21 *	2.0	5.3
089 Chr & Miss Al	1	69	NR	251	23.5	63.5
443 Un C of Christ	1	100	35	123 *	11.5	31.1
HITCHCOCK	**13**	**1,144**	**430**	**2,011 ***	**64.6**	**100.0**
081 Catholic	2	NR	NR	587	18.9	29.2
089 Chr & Miss Al	1	29	NR	74	2.4	3.7
123 Ch God (Ander)	1	NR	50	50	1.6	2.5
167 Chs of Christ	2	33	36	42	1.4	2.1
283 Luth—MO Synod	2	310	100	338	10.9	16.8
443 Un C of Christ	1	35	10	42 *	1.4	2.1
449 Un Methodist	4	737	234	878 *	28.2	43.7
HOLT	**32**	**2,969**	**1,423**	**7,559 ***	**65.4**	**100.0**
053 Assemb of God	4	264	232	276	2.4	3.7
081 Catholic	5	NR	NR	3,760	32.6	49.7
097 Chr Chs&Chs Cr	2	204	NR	254 *	2.2	3.4
207 E.L.C.A.	1	180	73	274	2.4	3.6
283 Luth—MO Synod	3	770	349	978	8.5	12.9
355 Presb Ch (USA)	6	469	228	584 *	5.1	7.7
419 So Bapt Conv	1	61	54	76 *	.7	1.0
449 Un Methodist	7	861	337	1,072 *	9.3	14.2
467 Wesleyan	2	121	122	236	2.0	3.1
469 WELS	1	39	28	49	.4	.6
HOOKER	**4**	**137**	**109**	**342 ***	**43.7**	**100.0**
053 Assemb of God	1	30	38	51	6.5	14.9
081 Catholic	1	NR	NR	113	14.4	33.0
193 Episcopal	1	NR	23	49	6.3	14.3
449 Un Methodist	1	107	48	129 *	16.5	37.7
HOWARD	**16**	**1,367**	**703**	**4,120 ***	**62.7**	**100.0**
056 Baha'i	0	1	NR	1	-	-
057 Bapt Gen Conf	2	143	180	187 *	2.8	4.5
081 Catholic	5	NR	NR	2,422	36.9	58.8
207 E.L.C.A.	2	448	164	541	8.2	13.1
220 Free Lutheran	1	26	12	31	.5	.8
283 Luth—MO Synod	1	232	120	285	4.3	6.9
355 Presb Ch (USA)	1	104	58	131 *	2.0	3.2
449 Un Methodist	4	413	169	522 *	7.9	12.7
JEFFERSON	**28**	**4,564**	**2,343**	**6,492 ***	**77.9**	**100.0**
019 Amer Bapt USA	1	276	99	333 *	4.0	5.1
053 Assemb of God	1	22	25	49	.6	.8
056 Baha'i	0	1	NR	1	-	-
081 Catholic	1	NR	NR	685	8.2	10.6
093 Chr Ch (Disc)	1	161	65	194 *	2.3	3.0
123 Ch God (Ander)	1	NR	22	22	.3	.3
167 Chs of Christ	1	12	11	12	.1	.2
193 Episcopal	1	NR	29	60	.7	.9
207 E.L.C.A.	4	786	419	1,021	12.3	15.7
211 Fel Evg Bib Ch	1	87	117	117	1.4	1.8
220 Free Lutheran	1	254	100	305	3.7	4.7
263 Int Foursq Gos	1	111	203	203 *	2.4	3.1
283 Luth—MO Synod	4	1,203	440	1,470	17.6	22.6
355 Presb Ch (USA)	2	403	200	487 *	5.8	7.5
443 Un C of Christ	3	246	144	297 *	3.6	4.6
449 Un Methodist	4	683	254	825 *	9.9	12.7
469 WELS	1	319	215	411	4.9	6.3
JOHNSON	**16**	**1,930**	**909**	**2,919 ***	**65.0**	**100.0**
019 Amer Bapt USA	2	302	158	366 *	8.2	12.5
081 Catholic	2	NR	NR	570	12.7	19.5
193 Episcopal	1	NR	9	21	.5	.7

Religious Group	Number of Churches, Synagogues, Mosques, or Temples	Number of Communicant, Confirmed, or Full Members	Number of Attendees	Total Adherents		
				Number of Adherents	% of Total Pop.	% of Total Adh.
207 E.L.C.A.	2	657	271	804	17.9	27.5
283 Luth—MO Synod	2	409	184	457	10.2	15.7
355 Presb Ch (USA)	1	65	30	79 *	1.8	2.7
388 Reg Bapt Gen As	1	12	35	35 *	.8	1.2
443 Un C of Christ	1	121	40	146 *	3.3	5.0
449 Un Methodist	4	364	182	441 *	9.8	15.1
KEARNEY	**17**	**3,289**	**1,436**	**4,638 ***	**67.4**	**100.0**
056 Baha'i	0	2	NR	2	-	-
081 Catholic	2	NR	NR	512	7.4	11.0
093 Chr Ch (Disc)	1	218	67	271 *	3.9	5.8
203 Evan Free Ch	3	195	273	273	4.0	5.9
207 E.L.C.A.	4	1,036	420	1,314	19.1	28.3
283 Luth—MO Synod	3	734	301	895	13.0	19.3
355 Presb Ch (USA)	2	497	186	617 *	9.0	13.3
449 Un Methodist	2	607	189	754 *	11.0	16.3
KEITH	**20**	**2,656**	**1,458**	**4,628 ***	**52.1**	**100.0**
053 Assemb of God	1	44	55	55	.6	1.2
057 Bapt Gen Conf	1	51	75	75 *	.8	1.6
081 Catholic	2	NR	NR	1,134	12.8	24.5
123 Ch God (Ander)	1	NR	17	17	.2	.4
167 Chs of Christ	1	121	130	158	1.8	3.4
173 Comm of Christ	1	11	NR	11	.1	.2
193 Episcopal	1	NR	31	80	.9	1.7
203 Evan Free Ch	1	85	160	160	1.8	3.5
207 E.L.C.A.	1	165	60	206	2.3	4.5
283 Luth—MO Synod	3	875	338	1,126	12.7	24.3
355 Presb Ch (USA)	2	72	88	96 *	1.1	2.1
413 S.D.A.	1	15	NR	18	.2	.4
443 Un C of Christ	2	312	94	383 *	4.3	8.3
449 Un Methodist	2	905	410	1,109 *	12.5	24.0
KEYA PAHA	**6**	**444**	**123**	**572 ***	**58.2**	**100.0**
053 Assemb of God	1	39	49	57	5.8	10.0
283 Luth—MO Synod	2	198	26	259	26.3	45.3
413 S.D.A.	1	25	NR	30	3.1	5.2
449 Un Methodist	2	182	48	226 *	23.0	39.5
KIMBALL	**12**	**1,202**	**639**	**2,542 ***	**62.2**	**100.0**
053 Assemb of God	1	39	48	123	3.0	4.8
081 Catholic	1	NR	NR	677	16.6	26.6
151 L-D Saints	1	NR	NR	241	5.9	9.5
165 Ch of Nazarene	1	26	21	55	1.3	2.2
193 Episcopal	1	NR	18	35	.9	1.4
203 Evan Free Ch	1	69	125	125	3.1	4.9
207 E.L.C.A.	1	402	144	509	12.4	20.0
283 Luth—MO Synod	1	176	45	177	4.3	7.0
355 Presb Ch (USA)	1	95	46	116 *	2.8	4.6
360 Prim Bapt Chrch	1	NR	NR	NR	-	-
419 So Bapt Conv	0	44	22	54 *	1.3	2.1
449 Un Methodist	2	351	170	430 *	10.5	16.9
KNOX	**31**	**3,759**	**1,623**	**7,539 ***	**80.4**	**100.0**
053 Assemb of God	1	11	14	19	.2	.3
056 Baha'i	0	4	NR	4	-	.1
081 Catholic	5	NR	NR	2,661	28.4	35.3
193 Episcopal	3	NR	43	173	1.8	2.3
201 Evan Cov Ch	1	128	88	157 *	1.7	2.1
207 E.L.C.A.	6	1,817	629	2,323	24.8	30.8
283 Luth—MO Synod	5	826	384	1,007	10.7	13.4
355 Presb Ch (USA)	2	105	38	129 *	1.4	1.7
443 Un C of Christ	4	247	155	303 *	3.2	4.0
449 Un Methodist	4	621	272	763 *	8.1	10.1
LANCASTER	**198**	**61,356**	**31,896**	**113,586 ***	**45.4**	**100.0**
017 Amer Bapt Assn	1	28	NR	34 *	-	-
019 Amer Bapt USA	4	841	361	1,028 *	.4	.9
053 Assemb of God	6	2,317	1,667	3,060	1.2	2.7
056 Baha'i	1	188	NR	188	.1	.2
057 Bapt Gen Conf	1	70	119	119 *	-	.1

NR–Not Reported *Total adherents estimated from known number of communicant, confirmed, full members. - Represents a percentage less than 0.1. Percentages may not total 100 due to rounding.

Table 4: Religious Congregations by County and Group: 2000

Religious Group	Number of Churches, Synagogues, Mosques, or Temples	Number of Communicant, Confirmed, or Full Members	Number of Attendees	Total Adherents: Number of Adherents	Total Adherents: % of Total Pop.	Total Adherents: % of Total Adh.
076 Buddhism	2	NR	NR	NR	-	-
081 Catholic	17	NR	NR	26,275	10.5	23.1
089 Chr & Miss Al	8	669	NR	1,184	.5	1.0
093 Chr Ch (Disc)	7	1,819	732	2,224 *	.9	2.0
097 Chr Chs&Chs Cr	4	1,339	NR	1,637 *	.7	1.4
105 Christian Ref	1	34	58	42 *	-	-
123 Ch God (Ander)	1	NR	88	88	-	.1
127 Ch God (Cleve)	1	70	20	86 *	-	.1
151 L-D Saints	8	NR	NR	2,292	.9	2.0
157 Ch of Brethren	1	124	64	152 *	.1	.1
165 Ch of Nazarene	1	358	258	375	.1	.3
167 Chs of Christ	3	221	285	328	.1	.3
173 Comm of Christ	1	101	NR	101	-	.1
193 Episcopal	4	NR	666	1,657	.7	1.5
201 Evan Cov Ch	2	413	407	505 *	.2	.4
203 Evan Free Ch	3	394	1,225	1,225	.5	1.1
207 E.L.C.A.	16	9,555	4,860	12,662	5.1	11.1
211 Fel Evg Bib Ch	1	0	0	0	-	-
221 Free Methodist	1	43	110	110	-	.1
226 Friends-USA	1	49	NR	60 *	-	.1
245 Greek Orth Vslp	2	2,450	NR	4,650	1.9	4.1
246 Greek Orthodox	1	NR	NR	216	.1	.2
263 Int Foursq Gos	1	121	55	148 *	.1	.1
267 Muslim Est	2	NR	312	1,218	.5	1.1
283 Luth—MO Synod	15	9,836	6,070	12,950	5.2	11.4
288 Mennonite USA	1	86	80	105 *	-	.1
291 Missionary Ch	1	42	40	42	-	-
335 Orth Pres Ch	1	49	35	63	-	.1
355 Presb Ch (USA)	11	4,765	2,292	5,826 *	2.3	5.1
356 Presb Ch Amer	2	224	340	340	.1	.3
371 Ref Ch in Am	3	690	628	1,041	.4	.9
373 Ref Ch in U.S.	1	90	NR	125	-	.1
388 Reg Bapt Gen As	1	180	164	220 *	.1	.2
403 Salvation Army	1	201	82	1,181	.5	1.0
413 S.D.A.	7	2,802	NR	3,336	1.3	2.9
419 So Bapt Conv	5	1,766	962	2,159 *	.9	1.9
431 Ukrainian Orth	1	NR	NR	24	-	-
435 Unitarian-Univ	1	340	NR	416 *	.2	.4
443 Un C of Christ	8	4,050	1,421	4,951 *	2.0	4.4
449 Un Methodist	28	12,820	5,964	15,674 *	6.3	13.8
467 Wesleyan	1	0	0	0	-	-
469 WELS	3	486	371	609	.2	.5
496 Jewish Est	2	NR	NR	700	.3	.6
499 Indep.Non-Char	3	1,725	2,160	2,160	.9	1.9
LINCOLN	**50**	**8,586**	**4,569**	**20,797 ***	**60.1**	**100.0**
019 Amer Bapt USA	1	795	235	990 *	2.9	4.8
053 Assemb of God	4	319	413	755	2.2	3.6
056 Baha'i	1	38	NR	38	.1	.2
057 Bapt Gen Conf	1	98	76	122 *	.4	.6
081 Catholic	7	NR	NR	8,134	23.5	39.1
093 Chr Ch (Disc)	1	510	109	635 *	1.8	3.1
097 Chr Chs&Chs Cr	1	120	NR	149 *	.4	.7
123 Ch God (Ander)	1	NR	24	24	.1	.1
127 Ch God (Cleve)	1	44	36	55 *	.2	.3
151 L-D Saints	3	NR	NR	744	2.1	3.6
165 Ch of Nazarene	1	196	159	248	.7	1.2
167 Chs of Christ	1	95	100	125	.4	.6
173 Comm of Christ	1	77	NR	77	.2	.4
193 Episcopal	1	NR	118	264	.8	1.3
201 Evan Cov Ch	1	23	31	31 *	.1	.1
203 Evan Free Ch	2	273	524	524	1.5	2.5
207 E.L.C.A.	4	1,602	582	2,106	6.1	10.1
263 Int Foursq Gos	1	107	118	133 *	.4	.6
283 Luth—MO Synod	2	1,075	502	1,426	4.1	6.9
355 Presb Ch (USA)	2	495	190	616 *	1.8	3.0
403 Salvation Army	1	178	136	305	.9	1.5
413 S.D.A.	1	138	NR	164	.5	.8
419 So Bapt Conv	1	248	108	309 *	.9	1.5
449 Un Methodist	8	1,956	863	2,434 *	7.0	11.7
467 Wesleyan	1	129	209	300	.9	1.4
469 WELS	1	70	36	89	.3	.4

Religious Group	Number of Churches, Synagogues, Mosques, or Temples	Number of Communicant, Confirmed, or Full Members	Number of Attendees	Total Adherents: Number of Adherents	Total Adherents: % of Total Pop.	Total Adherents: % of Total Adh.
LOGAN	**3**	**78**	**65**	**662 ***	**85.5**	**100.0**
081 Catholic	2	NR	NR	567	73.3	85.6
355 Presb Ch (USA)	1	78	65	95 *	12.3	14.4
LOUP	**3**	**128**	**123**	**184 ***	**25.8**	**100.0**
053 Assemb of God	1	34	44	50	7.0	27.2
203 Evan Free Ch	1	10	30	30	4.2	16.3
449 Un Methodist	1	84	49	104 *	14.6	56.5
MCPHERSON	**2**	**111**	**110**	**161 ***	**30.2**	**100.0**
221 Free Methodist	1	50	85	85	15.9	52.8
449 Un Methodist	1	61	25	76 *	14.3	47.2
MADISON	**49**	**13,556**	**6,220**	**28,430 ***	**80.7**	**100.0**
019 Amer Bapt USA	1	189	133	237 *	.7	.8
053 Assemb of God	1	132	187	351	1.0	1.2
056 Baha'i	0	6	NR	6	-	-
081 Catholic	5	NR	NR	9,939	28.2	35.0
097 Chr Chs&Chs Cr	2	665	NR	834 *	2.4	2.9
127 Ch God (Cleve)	1	27	19	34 *	.1	.1
151 L-D Saints	1	NR	NR	219	.6	.8
165 Ch of Nazarene	1	14	8	14	-	-
167 Chs of Christ	1	76	78	103	.3	.4
181 Consrv Congr	1	6	4	8 *	-	-
193 Episcopal	1	NR	85	212	.6	.7
203 Evan Free Ch	2	99	250	250	.7	.9
207 E.L.C.A.	5	2,087	894	2,751	7.8	9.7
283 Luth—MO Synod	9	6,395	2,778	8,249	23.4	29.0
355 Presb Ch (USA)	2	416	179	522 *	1.5	1.8
403 Salvation Army	1	54	45	423	1.2	1.5
413 S.D.A.	1	46	NR	55	.2	.2
419 So Bapt Conv	3	274	293	344 *	1.0	1.2
443 Un C of Christ	2	358	155	449 *	1.3	1.6
449 Un Methodist	7	2,053	728	2,575 *	7.3	9.1
469 WELS	2	659	384	855	2.4	3.0
MERRICK	**26**	**3,146**	**1,374**	**5,337 ***	**65.1**	**100.0**
019 Amer Bapt USA	1	93	45	117 *	1.4	2.2
056 Baha'i	0	3	NR	3	-	.1
081 Catholic	3	NR	NR	923	11.3	17.3
097 Chr Chs&Chs Cr	2	250	NR	314 *	3.8	5.9
151 L-D Saints	1	NR	NR	87	1.1	1.6
165 Ch of Nazarene	1	0	0	0	-	-
181 Consrv Congr	1	49	18	62 *	.8	1.2
193 Episcopal	1	NR	18	37	.5	.7
203 Evan Free Ch	1	83	257	257	3.1	4.8
207 E.L.C.A.	1	187	87	262	3.2	4.9
226 Friends-USA	1	178	NR	224 *	2.7	4.2
283 Luth—MO Synod	3	902	364	1,215	14.8	22.8
355 Presb Ch (USA)	1	141	58	178 *	2.2	3.3
449 Un Methodist	8	1,222	456	1,538 *	18.7	28.8
467 Wesleyan	1	38	71	120	1.5	2.2
MORRILL	**18**	**1,702**	**670**	**3,108 ***	**57.1**	**100.0**
019 Amer Bapt USA	1	95	52	119 *	2.2	3.8
053 Assemb of God	3	129	162	284	5.2	9.1
056 Baha'i	0	2	NR	2	-	.1
081 Catholic	2	NR	NR	826	15.2	26.6
097 Chr Chs&Chs Cr	2	272	NR	340 *	6.3	10.9
181 Consrv Congr	1	151	60	188 *	3.5	6.0
193 Episcopal	2	NR	17	45	.8	1.4
207 E.L.C.A.	1	134	58	162	3.0	5.2
283 Luth—MO Synod	2	327	140	404	7.4	13.0
355 Presb Ch (USA)	1	315	100	393 *	7.2	12.6
413 S.D.A.	1	16	NR	19	.3	.6
443 Un C of Christ	1	193	47	241 *	4.4	7.8
449 Un Methodist	1	68	34	85 *	1.6	2.7
NANCE	**11**	**1,220**	**496**	**2,890 ***	**71.6**	**100.0**
081 Catholic	3	NR	NR	1,352	33.5	46.8
207 E.L.C.A.	1	289	120	360	8.9	12.5

NR–Not Reported   *Total adherents estimated from known number of communicant, confirmed, full members.   - Represents a percentage less than 0.1.   Percentages may not total 100 due to rounding.

Table 4: Religious Congregations by County and Group: 2000

Religious Group	Number of Churches, Synagogues, Mosques, or Temples	Number of Communicant, Confirmed, or Full Members	Number of Attendees	Total Adherents: Number of Adherents	Total Adherents: % of Total Pop.	Total Adherents: % of Total Adh.
283 Luth—MO Synod	2	254	102	331	8.2	11.5
355 Presb Ch (USA)	1	138	76	173 *	4.3	6.0
443 Un C of Christ	1	40	18	50 *	1.2	1.7
449 Un Methodist	3	499	180	624 *	15.5	21.6
NEMAHA	**28**	**3,333**	**1,566**	**5,010 ***	**66.1**	**100.0**
053 Assemb of God	1	39	59	70	.9	1.4
056 Baha'i	0	8	NR	8	.1	.2
081 Catholic	3	NR	NR	551	7.3	11.0
093 Chr Ch (Disc)	3	266	112	320 *	4.2	6.4
097 Chr Chs&Chs Cr	1	300	NR	361 *	4.8	7.2
151 L-D Saints	1	NR	NR	288	3.8	5.7
167 Chs of Christ	1	16	20	23	.3	.5
203 Evan Free Ch	1	69	125	125	1.6	2.5
207 E.L.C.A.	7	1,566	688	1,952	25.8	39.0
283 Luth—MO Synod	1	203	132	270	3.6	5.4
355 Presb Ch (USA)	1	109	63	131 *	1.7	2.6
419 So Bapt Conv	2	78	60	94 *	1.2	1.9
449 Un Methodist	6	679	307	817 *	10.8	16.3
NUCKOLLS	**21**	**2,401**	**979**	**3,922 ***	**77.6**	**100.0**
019 Amer Bapt USA	1	188	59	225 *	4.4	5.7
056 Baha'i	0	3	NR	3	.1	.1
081 Catholic	4	NR	NR	973	19.2	24.8
097 Chr Chs&Chs Cr	2	245	NR	292 *	5.8	7.4
165 Ch of Nazarene	1	63	60	92	1.8	2.3
167 Chs of Christ	1	20	28	30	.6	.8
203 Evan Free Ch	1	0	49	49	1.0	1.2
207 E.L.C.A.	4	661	289	785	15.5	20.0
283 Luth—MO Synod	2	426	204	525	10.4	13.4
355 Presb Ch (USA)	1	140	45	167 *	3.3	4.3
413 S.D.A.	1	39	NR	46	.9	1.2
443 Un C of Christ	1	305	134	364 *	7.2	9.3
449 Un Methodist	2	311	111	371 *	7.3	9.5
OTOE	**44**	**6,589**	**2,648**	**11,012 ***	**71.5**	**100.0**
053 Assemb of God	1	113	133	150	1.0	1.4
056 Baha'i	0	7	NR	7	-	.1
057 Bapt Gen Conf	1	31	53	53 *	.3	.5
081 Catholic	6	NR	NR	2,712	17.6	24.6
093 Chr Ch (Disc)	2	814	83	1,013 *	6.6	9.2
097 Chr Chs&Chs Cr	2	149	NR	186 *	1.2	1.7
167 Chs of Christ	2	42	50	63	.4	.6
173 Comm of Christ	1	73	NR	73	.5	.7
193 Episcopal	1	NR	39	108	.7	1.0
203 Evan Free Ch	1	85	150	150	1.0	1.4
207 E.L.C.A.	8	2,464	954	3,024	19.6	27.5
283 Luth—MO Synod	1	100	40	119	.8	1.1
355 Presb Ch (USA)	4	424	188	528 *	3.4	4.8
388 Reg Bapt Gen As	1	91	95	95 *	.6	.9
413 S.D.A.	1	12	NR	14	.1	.1
419 So Bapt Conv	1	37	48	46 *	.3	.4
443 Un C of Christ	5	1,056	410	1,314 *	8.5	11.9
449 Un Methodist	6	1,091	405	1,357 *	8.8	12.3
PAWNEE	**14**	**1,277**	**466**	**2,005 ***	**64.9**	**100.0**
019 Amer Bapt USA	1	34	18	41 *	1.3	2.0
056 Baha'i	0	2	NR	2	.1	.1
081 Catholic	2	NR	NR	446	14.4	22.2
093 Chr Ch (Disc)	1	113	0	136 *	4.4	6.8
097 Chr Chs&Chs Cr	1	40	NR	48 *	1.6	2.4
167 Chs of Christ	1	4	4	5	.2	.2
283 Luth—MO Synod	2	382	132	481	15.6	24.0
355 Presb Ch (USA)	1	113	56	136 *	4.4	6.8
443 Un C of Christ	1	195	72	235 *	7.6	11.7
449 Un Methodist	4	394	184	475 *	15.4	23.7
PERKINS	**12**	**1,392**	**633**	**2,357 ***	**73.7**	**100.0**
081 Catholic	2	NR	NR	640	20.0	27.2
143 CG in Cr(Menn)	1	154	NR	190 *	5.9	8.1
203 Evan Free Ch	1	63	90	90	2.8	3.8
237 Menn Br US Conf	1	90	NR	111 *	3.5	4.7

Religious Group	Number of Churches, Synagogues, Mosques, or Temples	Number of Communicant, Confirmed, or Full Members	Number of Attendees	Total Adherents: Number of Adherents	Total Adherents: % of Total Pop.	Total Adherents: % of Total Adh.
283 Luth—MO Synod	3	389	248	469	14.7	19.9
443 Un C of Christ	1	71	40	87 *	2.7	3.7
449 Un Methodist	3	625	255	770 *	24.1	32.7
PHELPS	**28**	**4,374**	**2,661**	**6,518 ***	**66.9**	**100.0**
019 Amer Bapt USA	1	301	152	375 *	3.8	5.8
053 Assemb of God	1	96	125	246	2.5	3.8
081 Catholic	1	NR	NR	700	7.2	10.7
097 Chr Chs&Chs Cr	1	13	NR	16 *	.2	.2
165 Ch of Nazarene	1	58	75	109	1.1	1.7
167 Chs of Christ	1	8	12	12	.1	.2
193 Episcopal	1	NR	25	83	.9	1.3
201 Evan Cov Ch	1	65	40	81 *	.8	1.2
203 Evan Free Ch	5	644	868	868	8.9	13.3
207 E.L.C.A.	5	1,459	617	1,832	18.8	28.1
283 Luth—MO Synod	2	555	272	733	7.5	11.2
355 Presb Ch (USA)	1	248	131	309 *	3.2	4.7
413 S.D.A.	1	46	NR	55	.6	.8
435 Unitarian-Univ	1	10	NR	12 *	.1	.2
449 Un Methodist	5	871	344	1,087 *	11.2	16.7
PIERCE	**19**	**4,021**	**1,718**	**6,499 ***	**82.7**	**100.0**
081 Catholic	3	NR	NR	1,445	18.4	22.2
207 E.L.C.A.	2	633	232	762	9.7	11.7
226 Friends-USA	1	44	NR	56 *	.7	.9
283 Luth—MO Synod	5	2,186	1,002	2,769	35.2	42.6
443 Un C of Christ	2	312	110	396 *	5.0	6.1
449 Un Methodist	5	671	252	852 *	10.8	13.1
469 WELS	1	175	122	219	2.8	3.4
PLATTE	**42**	**8,573**	**5,096**	**25,572 ***	**80.8**	**100.0**
019 Amer Bapt USA	2	180	102	230 *	.7	.9
053 Assemb of God	1	72	92	115	.4	.4
056 Baha'i	0	1	NR	1	-	-
081 Catholic	8	NR	NR	13,768	43.5	53.8
097 Chr Chs&Chs Cr	1	35	NR	45 *	.1	.2
123 Ch God (Ander)	1	NR	19	19	.1	.1
151 L-D Saints	1	NR	NR	197	.6	.8
165 Ch of Nazarene	1	2	6	11	-	-
167 Chs of Christ	1	39	60	72	.2	.3
173 Comm of Christ	1	50	NR	50	.2	.2
193 Episcopal	1	NR	45	164	.5	.6
203 Evan Free Ch	1	165	440	440	1.4	1.7
207 E.L.C.A.	6	2,239	1,098	3,016	9.5	11.8
283 Luth—MO Synod	6	3,169	1,833	4,100	12.9	16.0
313 N Am Bapt Conf	2	112	82	143 *	.5	.6
355 Presb Ch (USA)	1	352	335	449 *	1.4	1.8
413 S.D.A.	1	53	NR	63	.2	.2
419 So Bapt Conv	1	147	110	188 *	.6	.7
443 Un C of Christ	2	827	515	1,056 *	3.3	4.1
449 Un Methodist	3	1,089	332	1,390 *	4.4	5.4
469 WELS	1	41	27	55	.2	.2
POLK	**17**	**2,369**	**1,182**	**3,760 ***	**66.7**	**100.0**
019 Amer Bapt USA	1	125	119	153 *	2.7	4.1
057 Bapt Gen Conf	2	215	166	263 *	4.7	7.0
081 Catholic	3	NR	NR	819	14.5	21.8
201 Evan Cov Ch	1	122	59	149 *	2.6	4.0
203 Evan Free Ch	2	127	205	205	3.6	5.5
207 E.L.C.A.	4	921	357	1,122	19.9	29.8
449 Un Methodist	4	859	276	1,049 *	18.6	27.9
RED WILLOW	**27**	**3,831**	**1,779**	**7,245 ***	**63.3**	**100.0**
019 Amer Bapt USA	1	203	71	249 *	2.2	3.4
053 Assemb of God	1	86	98	209	1.8	2.9
081 Catholic	3	NR	NR	1,751	15.3	24.2
093 Chr Ch (Disc)	1	30	15	37 *	.3	.5
097 Chr Chs&Chs Cr	3	490	NR	602 *	5.3	8.3
123 Ch God (Ander)	1	NR	35	35	.3	.5
151 L-D Saints	1	NR	NR	197	1.7	2.7
165 Ch of Nazarene	1	70	53	85	.7	1.2
167 Chs of Christ	1	85	120	136	1.2	1.9

NR–Not Reported *Total adherents estimated from known number of communicant, confirmed, full members. - Represents a percentage less than 0.1. Percentages may not total 100 due to rounding.

Table 4: Religious Congregations by County and Group: 2000

Religious Group	Number of Churches, Synagogues, Mosques, or Temples	Number of Communicant, Confirmed, or Full Members	Number of Attendees	Total Adherents		
				Number of Adherents	% of Total Pop.	% of Total Adh.
175 Congr Chr Chs	1	325	175	399 *	3.5	5.5
193 Episcopal	1	NR	111	237	2.1	3.3
203 Evan Free Ch	1	126	294	294	2.6	4.1
207 E.L.C.A.	1	214	65	243	2.1	3.4
283 Luth—MO Synod	2	814	335	1,070	9.3	14.8
355 Presb Ch (USA)	2	49	35	60 *	.5	.8
413 S.D.A.	1	34	NR	40	.3	.6
419 So Bapt Conv	1	62	57	76 *	.7	1.0
449 Un Methodist	3	1,227	300	1,507 *	13.2	20.8
469 WELS	1	16	15	18	.2	.2
RICHARDSON	**32**	**3,343**	**1,563**	**5,584 ***	**58.6**	**100.0**
019 Amer Bapt USA	1	35	20	43 *	.5	.8
053 Assemb of God	1	61	70	70	.7	1.3
056 Baha'i	0	2	NR	2	-	-
071 Brethren (Ash)	1	75	49	92 *	1.0	1.6
081 Catholic	5	NR	NR	1,281	13.4	22.9
093 Chr Ch (Disc)	4	754	164	923 *	9.7	16.5
165 Ch of Nazarene	1	59	81	162	1.7	2.9
167 Chs of Christ	1	37	40	40	.4	.7
175 Congr Chr Chs	1	14	10	17 *	.2	.3
193 Episcopal	1	NR	18	37	.4	.7
207 E.L.C.A.	3	656	321	842	8.8	15.1
283 Luth—MO Synod	3	584	263	769	8.1	13.8
355 Presb Ch (USA)	2	114	64	140 *	1.5	2.5
443 Un C of Christ	1	137	55	168 *	1.8	3.0
449 Un Methodist	7	815	408	998 *	10.5	17.9
ROCK	**7**	**458**	**205**	**781 ***	**44.5**	**100.0**
053 Assemb of God	1	31	37	57	3.2	7.3
081 Catholic	1	NR	NR	135	7.7	17.3
193 Episcopal	1	NR	19	96	5.5	12.3
207 E.L.C.A.	1	193	62	214	12.2	27.4
449 Un Methodist	3	234	87	279 *	15.9	35.7
SALINE	**21**	**4,018**	**1,428**	**6,827 ***	**49.3**	**100.0**
056 Baha'i	0	6	NR	6	-	.1
081 Catholic	4	NR	NR	1,873	13.5	27.4
193 Episcopal	2	NR	20	60	.4	.9
207 E.L.C.A.	2	697	278	847	6.1	12.4
283 Luth—MO Synod	2	1,087	464	1,298	9.4	19.0
443 Un C of Christ	4	935	268	1,152 *	8.3	16.9
449 Un Methodist	7	1,293	398	1,591 *	11.5	23.3
SARPY	**62**	**16,264**	**9,145**	**47,221 ***	**38.5**	**100.0**
019 Amer Bapt USA	3	300	175	394 *	.3	.8
053 Assemb of God	2	915	1,310	2,583	2.1	5.5
056 Baha'i	1	55	NR	55	-	.1
057 Bapt Gen Conf	2	188	265	286 *	.2	.6
081 Catholic	6	NR	NR	21,023	17.1	44.5
084 Calvary Chapel	1	NR	NR	NR	-	-
089 Chr & Miss Al	3	128	NR	384	.3	.8
093 Chr Ch (Disc)	1	125	55	164 *	.1	.3
097 Chr Chs&Chs Cr	2	1,320	NR	1,733 *	1.4	3.7
151 L-D Saints	4	NR	NR	1,514	1.2	3.2
165 Ch of Nazarene	2	217	259	309	.3	.7
167 Chs of Christ	2	258	277	368	.3	.8
173 Comm of Christ	1	132	NR	132	.1	.3
193 Episcopal	2	NR	246	781	.6	1.7
203 Evan Free Ch	1	69	125	125	.1	.3
207 E.L.C.A.	5	3,681	2,008	5,099	4.2	10.8
221 Free Methodist	1	17	35	35	-	.1
237 Menn Br US Conf	1	31	NR	41 *	-	.1
264 Int Chs of Crst	1	88	170	131	.1	.3
283 Luth—MO Synod	4	1,868	933	2,665	2.2	5.6
355 Presb Ch (USA)	3	1,434	697	1,883 *	1.5	4.0
388 Reg Bapt Gen As	1	225	175	296 *	.2	.6
410 Serb Orth USA	1	NR	NR	400	.3	.8
413 S.D.A.	1	237	NR	282	.2	.6
419 So Bapt Conv	5	2,377	1,216	3,122 *	2.5	6.6
449 Un Methodist	5	2,582	1,177	3,391 *	2.8	7.2
467 Wesleyan	1	17	22	25	-	.1
SAUNDERS	**49**	**5,007**	**2,216**	**12,874 ***	**64.9**	**100.0**
053 Assemb of God	1	10	12	55	.3	.4
056 Baha'i	0	8	NR	8	-	.1
057 Bapt Gen Conf	3	90	89	114 *	.6	.9
081 Catholic	12	NR	NR	6,104	30.8	47.4
089 Chr & Miss Al	1	35	NR	101	.5	.8
093 Chr Ch (Disc)	1	269	84	340 *	1.7	2.6
097 Chr Chs&Chs Cr	1	40	NR	51 *	.3	.4
151 L-D Saints	1	NR	NR	58	.3	.5
175 Congr Chr Chs	2	103	77	130 *	.7	1.0
179 Consrv Bapt	1	NR	61	61	.3	.5
201 Evan Cov Ch	3	328	243	435 *	2.2	3.4
207 E.L.C.A.	9	2,185	817	2,938	14.8	22.8
283 Luth—MO Synod	2	442	204	586	3.0	4.6
355 Presb Ch (USA)	4	557	211	705 *	3.6	5.5
443 Un C of Christ	1	97	43	123 *	.6	1.0
449 Un Methodist	7	843	375	1,065 *	5.4	8.3
SCOTTS BLUFF	**61**	**9,163**	**4,166**	**19,241 ***	**52.1**	**100.0**
019 Amer Bapt USA	1	220	99	274 *	.7	1.4
053 Assemb of God	7	430	565	839	2.3	4.4
056 Baha'i	0	23	NR	23	.1	.1
057 Bapt Gen Conf	1	50	50	62 *	.2	.3
081 Catholic	6	NR	NR	6,315	17.1	32.8
093 Chr Ch (Disc)	1	225	0	280 *	.8	1.5
097 Chr Chs&Chs Cr	5	1,102	NR	1,372 *	3.7	7.1
123 Ch God (Ander)	2	NR	82	82	.2	.4
127 Ch God (Cleve)	1	48	38	60 *	.2	.3
151 L-D Saints	1	NR	NR	418	1.1	2.2
165 Ch of Nazarene	2	128	106	192	.5	1.0
167 Chs of Christ	1	62	56	82	.2	.4
173 Comm of Christ	1	67	NR	67	.2	.3
181 Consrv Congr	4	1,495	796	1,860 *	5.0	9.7
193 Episcopal	3	NR	198	501	1.4	2.6
203 Evan Free Ch	2	188	245	245	.7	1.3
207 E.L.C.A.	2	788	312	1,046	2.8	5.4
246 Greek Orthodox	1	NR	NR	117	.3	.6
263 Int Foursq Gos	1	65	70	81 *	.2	.4
283 Luth—MO Synod	4	1,050	755	1,283	3.5	6.7
355 Presb Ch (USA)	3	601	237	748 *	2.0	3.9
413 S.D.A.	2	296	NR	352	1.0	1.8
419 So Bapt Conv	1	105	43	131 *	.4	.7
443 Un C of Christ	1	81	31	101 *	.3	.5
449 Un Methodist	6	2,082	413	2,589 *	7.0	13.5
467 Wesleyan	1	18	47	64	.2	.3
469 WELS	1	39	23	57	.2	.3
SEWARD	**34**	**7,470**	**4,282**	**11,049 ***	**67.0**	**100.0**
053 Assemb of God	1	112	142	185	1.1	1.7
056 Baha'i	0	3	NR	3	-	-
081 Catholic	3	NR	NR	1,237	7.5	11.2
151 L-D Saints	1	NR	NR	123	.7	1.1
167 Chs of Christ	1	50	60	65	.4	.6
193 Episcopal	1	NR	16	25	.2	.2
203 Evan Free Ch	1	39	155	155	.9	1.4
207 E.L.C.A.	2	510	241	681	4.1	6.2
283 Luth—MO Synod	9	4,180	2,338	5,394	32.7	48.8
288 Mennonite USA	3	502	366	614 *	3.7	5.6
291 Missionary Ch	1	44	92	92	.6	.8
297 Mennonite;Other	1	56	NR	68 *	.4	.6
355 Presb Ch (USA)	1	94	50	115 *	.7	1.0
419 So Bapt Conv	0	101	76	123 *	.7	1.1
443 Un C of Christ	2	156	113	191 *	1.2	1.7
449 Un Methodist	6	1,567	597	1,915 *	11.6	17.3
469 WELS	1	56	36	63	.4	.6
SHERIDAN	**24**	**1,542**	**782**	**2,699 ***	**43.5**	**100.0**
056 Baha'i	0	6	NR	6	.1	.2
081 Catholic	3	NR	NR	490	7.9	18.2
123 Ch God (Ander)	1	NR	115	115	1.9	4.3
151 L-D Saints	1	NR	NR	67	1.1	2.5
193 Episcopal	2	NR	33	91	1.5	3.4

NR–Not Reported *Total adherents estimated from known number of communicant, confirmed, full members. - Represents a percentage less than 0.1. Percentages may not total 100 due to rounding.

Table 4: Religious Congregations by County and Group: 2000

Religious Group	Number of Churches, Synagogues, Mosques, or Temples	Number of Communicant, Confirmed, or Full Members	Number of Attendees	Total Adherents: Number of Adherents	Total Adherents: % of Total Pop.	Total Adherents: % of Total Adh.
207 E.L.C.A.	2	168	70	197	3.2	7.3
226 Friends-USA	1	44	NR	54 *	.9	2.0
283 Luth—MO Synod	4	415	212	501	8.1	18.6
355 Presb Ch (USA)	1	191	65	235 *	3.8	8.7
413 S.D.A.	2	40	NR	47	.8	1.7
449 Un Methodist	5	625	235	769 *	12.4	28.5
467 Wesleyan	1	36	42	110	1.8	4.1
469 WELS	1	17	10	17	.3	.6
SHERMAN	**14**	**556**	**403**	**1,903 ***	**57.4**	**100.0**
081 Catholic	4	NR	NR	1,219	36.7	64.1
097 Chr Chs&Chs Cr	1	50	NR	61 *	1.8	3.2
283 Luth—MO Synod	2	169	172	215	6.5	11.3
355 Presb Ch (USA)	1	42	18	51 *	1.5	2.7
388 Reg Bapt Gen As	2	133	108	161 *	4.9	8.5
419 So Bapt Conv	1	0	0	0 *	-	-
443 Un C of Christ	1	11	8	13 *	.4	.7
449 Un Methodist	2	151	97	183 *	5.5	9.6
SIOUX	**3**	**154**	**67**	**355 ***	**24.1**	**100.0**
081 Catholic	1	NR	NR	170	11.5	47.9
283 Luth—MO Synod	1	30	22	35	2.4	9.9
449 Un Methodist	1	124	45	150 *	10.2	42.3
STANTON	**9**	**1,263**	**561**	**2,078 ***	**32.2**	**100.0**
081 Catholic	1	NR	NR	450	7.0	21.7
203 Evan Free Ch	1	33	82	82	1.3	3.9
207 E.L.C.A.	2	239	91	286	4.4	13.8
283 Luth—MO Synod	2	600	241	759	11.8	36.5
443 Un C of Christ	1	197	65	253 *	3.9	12.2
449 Un Methodist	2	194	82	248 *	3.8	11.9
THAYER	**32**	**4,112**	**2,017**	**5,681 ***	**93.8**	**100.0**
053 Assemb of God	1	11	8	17	.3	.3
081 Catholic	2	NR	NR	509	8.4	9.0
093 Chr Ch (Disc)	1	0	0	0 *	-	-
097 Chr Chs&Chs Cr	2	248	NR	302 *	5.0	5.3
157 Ch of Brethren	1	124	65	151 *	2.5	2.7
167 Chs of Christ	1	37	40	48	.8	.8
207 E.L.C.A.	8	2,001	872	2,407	39.8	42.4
220 Free Lutheran	1	69	45	81	1.3	1.4
283 Luth—MO Synod	6	913	697	1,302	21.5	22.9
355 Presb Ch (USA)	3	154	90	187 *	3.1	3.3
443 Un C of Christ	1	53	25	65 *	1.1	1.1
449 Un Methodist	5	502	175	612 *	10.1	10.8
THOMAS	**6**	**272**	**174**	**439 ***	**60.2**	**100.0**
053 Assemb of God	1	72	85	130	17.8	29.6
081 Catholic	1	NR	NR	68	9.3	15.5
283 Luth—MO Synod	1	30	18	40	5.5	9.1
443 Un C of Christ	3	170	71	201 *	27.6	45.8
THURSTON	**23**	**1,812**	**753**	**3,647 ***	**50.9**	**100.0**
053 Assemb of God	2	56	68	83	1.2	2.3
056 Baha'i	1	33	NR	33	.5	.9
081 Catholic	4	NR	NR	712	9.9	19.5
151 L-D Saints	1	NR	NR	464	6.5	12.7
173 Comm of Christ	1	92	NR	92	1.3	2.5
193 Episcopal	1	NR	3	7	.1	.2
201 Evan Cov Ch	1	34	32	48 *	.7	1.3
207 E.L.C.A.	3	812	272	1,002	14.0	27.5
283 Luth—MO Synod	1	214	59	274	3.8	7.5
355 Presb Ch (USA)	3	215	105	301 *	4.2	8.3
371 Ref Ch in Am	2	69	101	230	3.2	6.3
449 Un Methodist	3	287	113	401 *	5.6	11.0
VALLEY	**14**	**1,388**	**679**	**3,265 ***	**70.3**	**100.0**
053 Assemb of God	1	23	29	122	2.6	3.7
057 Bapt Gen Conf	2	110	108	135 *	2.9	4.1
081 Catholic	2	NR	NR	1,417	30.5	43.4
097 Chr Chs&Chs Cr	1	200	NR	245 *	5.3	7.5
203 Evan Free Ch	1	23	56	56	1.2	1.7
207 E.L.C.A.	1	139	52	172	3.7	5.3
283 Luth—MO Synod	1	181	106	247	5.3	7.6
355 Presb Ch (USA)	1	72	29	88 *	1.9	2.7
449 Un Methodist	4	640	299	783 *	16.8	24.0
WASHINGTON	**23**	**5,657**	**2,569**	**10,035 ***	**53.4**	**100.0**
019 Amer Bapt USA	1	100	50	126 *	.7	1.3
053 Assemb of God	1	53	60	70	.4	.7
056 Baha'i	0	1	NR	1	-	-
057 Bapt Gen Conf	1	39	80	80 *	.4	.8
081 Catholic	2	NR	NR	2,327	12.4	23.2
097 Chr Chs&Chs Cr	1	125	NR	157 *	.8	1.6
151 L-D Saints	1	NR	NR	181	1.0	1.8
167 Chs of Christ	1	35	33	47	.3	.5
193 Episcopal	1	NR	66	202	1.1	2.0
207 E.L.C.A.	4	2,115	626	2,728	14.5	27.2
283 Luth—MO Synod	3	1,124	580	1,395	7.4	13.9
355 Presb Ch (USA)	1	160	100	201 *	1.1	2.0
443 Un C of Christ	2	421	135	528 *	2.8	5.3
449 Un Methodist	3	1,109	339	1,392 *	7.4	13.9
499 Indep.Non-Char	1	375	500	600	3.2	6.0
WAYNE	**19**	**3,989**	**1,927**	**5,861 ***	**59.5**	**100.0**
019 Amer Bapt USA	1	99	70	118 *	1.2	2.0
053 Assemb of God	1	62	92	116	1.2	2.0
056 Baha'i	0	4	NR	4	-	.1
081 Catholic	1	NR	NR	862	8.8	14.7
097 Chr Chs&Chs Cr	1	65	NR	77 *	.8	1.3
193 Episcopal	1	NR	3	7	.1	.1
203 Evan Free Ch	1	30	90	90	.9	1.5
207 E.L.C.A.	2	1,179	543	1,455	14.8	24.8
283 Luth—MO Synod	5	1,387	594	1,733	17.6	29.6
355 Presb Ch (USA)	2	149	82	177 *	1.8	3.0
449 Un Methodist	3	765	336	912 *	9.3	15.6
469 WELS	1	249	117	310	3.1	5.3
WEBSTER	**16**	**1,792**	**806**	**2,730 ***	**67.2**	**100.0**
019 Amer Bapt USA	1	21	16	26 *	.6	1.0
053 Assemb of God	1	25	30	127	3.1	4.7
081 Catholic	2	NR	NR	375	9.2	13.7
097 Chr Chs&Chs Cr	1	50	NR	61 *	1.5	2.2
207 E.L.C.A.	1	291	140	368	9.1	13.5
283 Luth—MO Synod	3	526	266	680	16.7	24.9
443 Un C of Christ	1	113	50	137 *	3.4	5.0
449 Un Methodist	5	725	267	881 *	21.7	32.3
467 Wesleyan	1	41	37	75	1.8	2.7
WHEELER	**5**	**238**	**48**	**471 ***	**53.2**	**100.0**
081 Catholic	1	NR	NR	170	19.2	36.1
283 Luth—MO Synod	1	60	22	75	8.5	15.9
419 So Bapt Conv	1	30	26	38 *	4.3	8.1
449 Un Methodist	2	148	0	188 *	21.2	39.9
YORK	**38**	**7,125**	**4,147**	**10,118 ***	**69.3**	**100.0**
019 Amer Bapt USA	1	26	27	32 *	.2	.3
053 Assemb of God	1	104	159	193	1.3	1.9
057 Bapt Gen Conf	1	116	150	150 *	1.0	1.5
081 Catholic	3	NR	NR	1,003	6.9	9.9
093 Chr Ch (Disc)	1	158	75	194 *	1.3	1.9
165 Ch of Nazarene	2	77	85	135	.9	1.3
167 Chs of Christ	1	381	530	526	3.6	5.2
193 Episcopal	1	NR	15	22	.2	.2
203 Evan Free Ch	1	36	95	95	.7	.9
207 E.L.C.A.	3	656	297	836	5.7	8.3
211 Fel Evg Bib Ch	1	86	118	118	.8	1.2
237 Menn Br US Conf	1	183	NR	225 *	1.5	2.2
263 Int Foursq Gos	1	31	44	44 *	.3	.4
283 Luth—MO Synod	6	2,227	1,223	2,811	19.3	27.8
288 Mennonite USA	1	1,140	543	1,399 *	9.6	13.8
355 Presb Ch (USA)	2	461	174	566 *	3.9	5.6
419 So Bapt Conv	1	6	5	7 *	-	.1

NR–Not Reported *Total adherents estimated from known number of communicant, confirmed, full members. - Represents a percentage less than 0.1. Percentages may not total 100 due to rounding.

Table 4: Religious Congregations by County and Group: 2000

Religious Group	Number of Churches, Synagogues, Mosques, or Temples	Number of Communicant, Confirmed, or Full Members	Number of Attendees	Total Adherents: Number of Adherents	Total Adherents: % of Total Pop.	Total Adherents: % of Total Adh.
443 Un C of Christ	2	96	68	118 *	.8	1.2
449 Un Methodist	7	1,274	465	1,562 *	10.7	15.4
469 WELS	1	67	74	82	.6	.8

NEVADA

Religious Group	Number of Churches, Synagogues, Mosques, or Temples	Number of Communicant, Confirmed, or Full Members	Number of Attendees	Total Adherents: Number of Adherents	Total Adherents: % of Total Pop.	Total Adherents: % of Total Adh.
The State.....	938	104,143	66,629	685,119 *	34.3	100.0
CARSON CITY	**33**	**4,614**	**2,681**	**20,860 ***	**39.8**	**100.0**
019 Amer Bapt USA	1	40	90	90 *	.2	.4
053 Assemb of God	2	352	226	800	1.5	3.8
056 Baha'i	1	33	NR	33	.1	.2
081 Catholic	2	NR	NR	11,553	22.0	55.4
084 Calvary Chapel	1	NR	NR	NR	-	-
097 Chr Chs&Chs Cr	1	550	NR	673 *	1.3	3.2
127 Ch God (Cleve)	1	37	40	45 *	.1	.2
151 L-D Saints	8	NR	NR	2,107	4.0	10.1
165 Ch of Nazarene	1	37	65	105	.2	.5
167 Chs of Christ	1	94	90	125	.2	.6
179 Consrv Bapt	1	NR	200	200	.4	1.0
193 Episcopal	1	NR	172	370	.7	1.8
203 Evan Free Ch	1	69	125	125	.2	.6
207 E.L.C.A.	1	309	182	511	1.0	2.4
283 Luth—MO Synod	1	619	317	823	1.6	3.9
355 Presb Ch (USA)	1	518	147	633 *	1.2	3.0
403 Salvation Army	1	51	36	86	.2	.4
413 S.D.A.	1	291	NR	346	.7	1.7
419 So Bapt Conv	3	662	288	810 *	1.5	3.9
449 Un Methodist	1	623	307	762 *	1.5	3.7
463 Vineyard	1	215	195	263 *	.5	1.3
467 Wesleyan	1	114	201	400	.8	1.9
CHURCHILL	**19**	**1,798**	**988**	**7,102 ***	**29.6**	**100.0**
053 Assemb of God	1	210	275	475	2.0	6.7
056 Baha'i	1	15	NR	15	.1	.2
081 Catholic	1	NR	NR	2,087	8.7	29.4
151 L-D Saints	6	NR	NR	2,282	9.5	32.1
165 Ch of Nazarene	1	164	104	205	.9	2.9
167 Chs of Christ	1	43	50	62	.3	.9
193 Episcopal	1	NR	36	79	.3	1.1
283 Luth—MO Synod	1	101	131	242	1.0	3.4
339 Pent Ch of God	1	32	NR	75	.3	1.1
413 S.D.A.	1	170	NR	202	.8	2.8
419 So Bapt Conv	2	742	236	962 *	4.0	13.5
449 Un Methodist	1	305	140	395 *	1.6	5.6
463 Vineyard	1	16	16	21 *	.1	.3
CLARK	**487**	**70,366**	**42,760**	**498,697 ***	**36.2**	**100.0**
017 Amer Bapt Assn	4	636	NR	802 *	.1	.2
019 Amer Bapt USA	14	5,525	2,010	6,956 *	.5	1.4
034 Ant Orth of NA	1	165	NR	330	-	.1
050 Armen Ap Etchm	1	0	NR	770	.1	.2
053 Assemb of God	24	8,366	8,848	17,241	1.3	3.5
056 Baha'i	6	708	NR	708	.1	.1
059 Bapt Miss Assn	1	68	25	86 *	-	-
076 Buddhism	9	NR	NR	NR	-	-
081 Catholic	25	NR	NR	236,634	17.2	47.5
084 Calvary Chapel	5	NR	NR	NR	-	-
089 Chr & Miss Al	3	65	NR	132	-	-
093 Chr Ch (Disc)	1	516	275	650 *	-	.1
097 Chr Chs&Chs Cr	4	6,550	NR	8,247 *	.6	1.7
105 Christian Ref	3	293	300	369 *	-	.1
123 Ch God (Ander)	3	NR	144	144	-	-
127 Ch God (Cleve)	5	558	384	707 *	.1	.1
145 Ch God Prophcy	3	105	NR	132 *	-	-
151 L-D Saints	187	NR	NR	81,852	5.9	16.4
165 Ch of Nazarene	7	517	629	775	.1	.2
167 Chs of Christ	11	1,024	1,015	1,326	.1	.3
173 Comm of Christ	1	336	NR	336	-	.1
179 Consrv Bapt	2	NR	228	228	-	-
193 Episcopal	8	NR	1,013	2,249	.2	.5
203 Evan Free Ch	1	60	110	110	-	-
207 E.L.C.A.	10	6,004	3,579	8,048	.6	1.6
221 Free Methodist	1	0	30	30	-	-
226 Friends-USA	1	32	NR	40 *	-	-
246 Greek Orthodox	1	NR	NR	1,020	.1	.2
252 Hindu	1	NR	NR	NR	-	-
263 Int Foursq Gos	12	1,470	1,915	1,915 *	.1	.4
264 Int Chs of Crst	1	271	501	403	-	.1
267 Muslim Est	2	NR	456	1,682	.1	.3
283 Luth—MO Synod	8	1,657	1,747	3,465	.3	.7
290 Metro Comm Ch	1	168	133	212 *	-	-
331 OCA: Ter Diocs	1	211	NR	468	-	.1
339 Pent Ch of God	1	33	NR	73	-	-
349 Pent Holiness	2	98	97	123 *	-	-
355 Presb Ch (USA)	6	3,122	2,226	3,932 *	.3	.8
356 Presb Ch Amer	1	114	200	200	-	-
388 Reg Bapt Gen As	1	65	130	82 *	-	-
395 Romania Orth Ar	1	NR	NR	630	-	.1
397 OCA: Roman Dioc	1	NR	NR	28	-	-
403 Salvation Army	4	453	422	1,001	.1	.2
410 Serb Orth USA	1	NR	NR	800	.1	.2
413 S.D.A.	6	882	NR	1,050	.1	.2
416 Sikh	2	NR	NR	NR	-	-
419 So Bapt Conv	48	21,133	8,917	26,606 *	1.9	5.3
435 Unitarian-Univ	1	99	NR	125 *	-	-
443 Un C of Christ	3	267	154	336 *	-	.1
449 Un Methodist	13	4,201	2,638	5,289 *	.4	1.1
463 Vineyard	1	32	32	40 *	-	-
469 WELS	5	1,022	737	1,375	.1	.3
496 Jewish Est	18	NR	NR	75,000	5.5	15.0
498 Indep.Charis.	2	690	1,090	1,090	.1	.2
499 Indep.Non-Char	2	2,850	2,775	2,850	.2	.6
DOUGLAS	**27**	**1,933**	**1,550**	**9,328 ***	**22.6**	**100.0**
053 Assemb of God	1	33	53	98	.2	1.1
056 Baha'i	0	11	NR	11	-	.1
081 Catholic	2	NR	NR	4,746	11.5	50.9
084 Calvary Chapel	1	NR	NR	NR	-	-
097 Chr Chs&Chs Cr	1	40	NR	49 *	.1	.5
151 L-D Saints	3	NR	NR	1,319	3.2	14.1
165 Ch of Nazarene	1	114	124	177	.4	1.9
179 Consrv Bapt	1	NR	300	300	.7	3.2
193 Episcopal	2	NR	83	220	.5	2.4
263 Int Foursq Gos	2	174	329	329 *	.8	3.5
283 Luth—MO Synod	1	478	189	625	1.5	6.7
339 Pent Ch of God	1	14	NR	52	.1	.6
355 Presb Ch (USA)	1	92	64	112 *	.3	1.2
370 Ref Baptist Chs	1	NR	NR	NR	-	-
419 So Bapt Conv	6	776	226	945 *	2.3	10.1
449 Un Methodist	2	201	182	245 *	.6	2.6
496 Jewish Est	1	NR	NR	100	.2	1.1
ELKO	**45**	**2,570**	**1,605**	**16,638 ***	**36.7**	**100.0**
019 Amer Bapt USA	1	85	35	113 *	.2	.7
053 Assemb of God	3	144	160	180	.4	1.1
056 Baha'i	0	17	NR	17	-	.1
081 Catholic	4	NR	NR	6,889	15.2	41.4
151 L-D Saints	16	NR	NR	5,862	12.9	35.2
165 Ch of Nazarene	1	63	62	107	.2	.6
167 Chs of Christ	1	25	40	37	.1	.2
193 Episcopal	2	NR	113	334	.7	2.0
207 E.L.C.A.	1	102	73	200	.4	1.2
263 Int Foursq Gos	1	2	16	16 *	-	.1
283 Luth—MO Synod	2	317	149	463	1.0	2.8
339 Pent Ch of God	1	8	NR	20	-	.1
355 Presb Ch (USA)	4	529	274	704 *	1.6	4.2
413 S.D.A.	1	34	NR	40	.1	.2
419 So Bapt Conv	6	1,190	641	1,584 *	3.5	9.5
449 Un Methodist	1	54	42	72 *	.2	.4
ESMERALDA	**2**	**302**	**76**	**365 ***	**37.6**	**100.0**
193 Episcopal	1	NR	6	12	1.2	3.3
419 So Bapt Conv	1	302	70	353 *	36.4	96.7

NR–Not Reported *Total adherents estimated from known number of communicant, confirmed, full members. - Represents a percentage less than 0.1. Percentages may not total 100 due to rounding.

Table 4: Religious Congregations by County and Group: 2000

Religious Group	Number of Churches, Synagogues, Mosques, or Temples	Number of Communicant, Confirmed, or Full Members	Number of Attendees	Total Adherents: Number of Adherents	Total Adherents: % of Total Pop.	Total Adherents: % of Total Adh.
EUREKA	**5**	**85**	**19**	**553 ***	**33.5**	**100.0**
056 Baha'i	0	1	NR	1	.1	.2
081 Catholic	1	NR	NR	251	15.2	45.4
151 L-D Saints	1	NR	NR	173	10.5	31.3
193 Episcopal	1	NR	5	21	1.3	3.8
419 So Bapt Conv	2	84	14	107 *	6.5	19.3
HUMBOLDT	**18**	**1,195**	**675**	**6,905 ***	**42.9**	**100.0**
053 Assemb of God	2	91	105	191	1.2	2.8
056 Baha'i	0	16	NR	16	.1	.2
081 Catholic	3	NR	NR	3,490	21.7	50.5
151 L-D Saints	5	NR	NR	1,673	10.4	24.2
167 Chs of Christ	1	11	11	14	.1	.2
193 Episcopal	1	NR	13	57	.4	.8
263 Int Foursq Gos	1	11	29	29 *	.2	.4
283 Luth—MO Synod	1	189	93	293	1.8	4.2
413 S.D.A.	1	101	NR	120	.7	1.7
419 So Bapt Conv	2	587	334	773 *	4.8	11.2
449 Un Methodist	1	189	90	249 *	1.5	3.6
LANDER	**18**	**762**	**388**	**3,298 ***	**56.9**	**100.0**
053 Assemb of God	1	54	69	81	1.4	2.5
056 Baha'i	0	6	NR	6	.1	.2
081 Catholic	2	NR	NR	1,329	22.9	40.3
084 Calvary Chapel	1	NR	NR	NR	-	-
151 L-D Saints	4	NR	NR	926	16.0	28.1
167 Chs of Christ	1	35	40	45	.8	1.4
193 Episcopal	1	NR	11	12	.2	.4
283 Luth—MO Synod	1	16	20	28	.5	.8
335 Orth Pres Ch	1	13	20	20	.3	.6
419 So Bapt Conv	5	586	186	782 *	13.5	23.7
449 Un Methodist	1	52	42	69 *	1.2	2.1
LINCOLN	**14**	**505**	**245**	**2,835 ***	**68.1**	**100.0**
053 Assemb of God	1	20	20	20	.5	.7
081 Catholic	1	NR	NR	158	3.8	5.6
151 L-D Saints	6	NR	NR	1,998	48.0	70.5
193 Episcopal	1	NR	22	67	1.6	2.4
263 Int Foursq Gos	1	17	20	21 *	.5	.7
283 Luth—MO Synod	1	72	45	78	1.9	2.8
419 So Bapt Conv	2	346	100	431 *	10.3	15.2
449 Un Methodist	1	50	38	62 *	1.5	2.2
LYON	**31**	**1,711**	**1,030**	**8,162 ***	**23.7**	**100.0**
053 Assemb of God	3	86	83	97	.3	1.2
056 Baha'i	0	24	NR	24	.1	.3
081 Catholic	4	NR	NR	3,669	10.6	45.0
127 Ch God (Cleve)	1	24	25	30 *	.1	.4
151 L-D Saints	6	NR	NR	2,225	6.4	27.3
165 Ch of Nazarene	2	20	103	114	.3	1.4
167 Chs of Christ	1	20	25	28	.1	.3
193 Episcopal	1	NR	12	23	.1	.3
203 Evan Free Ch	1	35	50	50	.1	.6
221 Free Methodist	1	5	15	15	-	.2
263 Int Foursq Gos	1	30	40	40 *	.1	.5
283 Luth—MO Synod	1	29	18	45	.1	.6
413 S.D.A.	2	92	NR	110	.3	1.3
419 So Bapt Conv	5	784	319	986 *	2.9	12.1
449 Un Methodist	1	137	65	172 *	.5	2.1
463 Vineyard	1	425	275	534 *	1.5	6.5
MINERAL	**15**	**516**	**371**	**1,751 ***	**34.5**	**100.0**
053 Assemb of God	1	38	53	75	1.5	4.3
056 Baha'i	0	4	NR	4	.1	.2
081 Catholic	1	NR	NR	640	12.6	36.6
151 L-D Saints	2	NR	NR	408	8.0	23.3
167 Chs of Christ	1	15	17	20	.4	1.1
193 Episcopal	1	NR	6	6	.1	.3
283 Luth—MO Synod	1	35	19	43	.8	2.5
355 Presb Ch (USA)	1	49	41	60 *	1.2	3.4
388 Reg Bapt Gen As	1	25	70	70 *	1.4	4.0
413 S.D.A.	1	15	NR	18	.4	1.0
419 So Bapt Conv	4	295	150	358 *	7.1	20.4
449 Un Methodist	1	40	15	49 *	1.0	2.8
NYE	**41**	**1,832**	**1,543**	**6,826 ***	**21.0**	**100.0**
019 Amer Bapt USA	1	60	58	74 *	.2	1.1
053 Assemb of God	4	163	223	447	1.4	6.5
056 Baha'i	0	12	NR	12	-	.2
081 Catholic	5	NR	NR	2,207	6.8	32.3
084 Calvary Chapel	1	NR	NR	NR	-	-
145 Ch God Prophcy	1	35	NR	43 *	.1	.6
151 L-D Saints	6	NR	NR	1,961	6.0	28.7
167 Chs of Christ	2	35	38	49	.2	.7
179 Consrv Bapt	1	NR	12	12	-	.2
193 Episcopal	3	NR	39	72	.2	1.1
207 E.L.C.A.	1	0	0	0	-	-
263 Int Foursq Gos	2	211	320	320 *	1.0	4.7
283 Luth—MO Synod	2	111	138	154	.5	2.3
355 Presb Ch (USA)	1	13	10	16 *	-	.2
403 Salvation Army	1	8	36	8	-	.1
413 S.D.A.	1	45	NR	54	.2	.8
419 So Bapt Conv	7	986	506	1,209 *	3.7	17.7
449 Un Methodist	1	123	133	151 *	.5	2.2
463 Vineyard	1	30	30	37 *	.1	.5
PERSHING	**10**	**365**	**285**	**1,631 ***	**24.4**	**100.0**
053 Assemb of God	1	24	34	53	.8	3.2
056 Baha'i	0	24	NR	24	.4	1.5
081 Catholic	1	NR	NR	716	10.7	43.9
151 L-D Saints	1	NR	NR	374	5.6	22.9
167 Chs of Christ	1	11	18	22	.3	1.3
193 Episcopal	1	NR	73	58	.9	3.6
419 So Bapt Conv	3	226	105	282 *	4.2	17.3
449 Un Methodist	1	60	45	75 *	1.1	4.6
469 WELS	1	20	10	27	.4	1.7
STOREY	**3**	**31**	**51**	**233 ***	**6.9**	**100.0**
081 Catholic	1	NR	NR	175	5.1	75.1
193 Episcopal	1	NR	10	17	.5	7.3
355 Presb Ch (USA)	1	31	41	41 *	1.2	17.6
WASHOE	**152**	**15,153**	**12,070**	**94,836 ***	**27.9**	**100.0**
019 Amer Bapt USA	4	506	293	630 *	.2	.7
050 Armen Ap Etchm	1	0	NR	77	-	.1
053 Assemb of God	11	1,216	1,486	2,873	.8	3.0
056 Baha'i	3	253	NR	253	.1	.3
076 Buddhism	3	NR	NR	NR	-	-
081 Catholic	12	NR	NR	54,868	16.2	57.9
084 Calvary Chapel	1	NR	NR	NR	-	-
089 Chr & Miss Al	2	35	NR	115	-	.1
093 Chr Ch (Disc)	1	12	0	15 *	-	-
097 Chr Chs&Chs Cr	1	157	NR	195 *	.1	.2
123 Ch God (Ander)	3	NR	118	118	-	.1
127 Ch God (Cleve)	2	143	88	178 *	.1	.2
151 L-D Saints	25	NR	NR	11,712	3.4	12.3
165 Ch of Nazarene	5	639	688	999	.3	1.1
167 Chs of Christ	5	394	405	598	.2	.6
173 Comm of Christ	1	182	NR	182	.1	.2
179 Consrv Bapt	3	NR	400	400	.1	.4
193 Episcopal	7	NR	754	1,816	.5	1.9
203 Evan Free Ch	2	252	672	672	.2	.7
207 E.L.C.A.	4	1,367	603	1,904	.6	2.0
221 Free Methodist	1	0	0	0	-	-
226 Friends-USA	1	32	NR	40 *	-	-
246 Greek Orthodox	1	NR	NR	372	.1	.4
263 Int Foursq Gos	6	423	580	580 *	.2	.6
264 Int Chs of Crst	1	60	109	91	-	.1
267 Muslim Est	1	NR	156	609	.2	.6
283 Luth—MO Synod	2	928	443	1,357	.4	1.4
290 Metro Comm Ch	1	37	45	46 *	-	-
331 OCA: Ter Diocs	1	0	NR	30	-	-
349 Pent Holiness	1	60	30	75 *	-	.1

NR–Not Reported   *Total adherents estimated from known number of communicant, confirmed, full members.   - Represents a percentage less than 0.1.   Percentages may not total 100 due to rounding.

Table 4: Religious Congregations by County and Group: 2000

Religious Group	Number of Churches, Synagogues, Mosques, or Temples	Number of Communicant, Confirmed, or Full Members	Number of Attendees	Total Adherents: Number of Adherents	Total Adherents: % of Total Pop.	Total Adherents: % of Total Adh.
355 Presb Ch (USA)	4	1,369	916	1,704 *	.5	1.8
356 Presb Ch Amer	1	0	0	0	-	-
388 Reg Bapt Gen As	1	95	120	120 *	-	.1
403 Salvation Army	1	82	56	144	-	.2
413 S.D.A.	2	714	NR	849	.3	.9
416 Sikh	1	NR	NR	NR	-	-
419 So Bapt Conv	14	3,043	1,704	3,788 *	1.1	4.0
435 Unitarian-Univ	1	132	NR	164 *	-	.2
443 Un C of Christ	1	283	125	352 *	.1	.4
449 Un Methodist	4	2,200	976	2,740 *	.8	2.9
463 Vineyard	2	260	229	324 *	.1	.3
467 Wesleyan	2	114	114	114	-	.1
469 WELS	1	165	110	232	.1	.2
496 Jewish Est	4	NR	NR	2,000	.6	2.1
499 Indep.Non-Char	1	0	850	1,500	.4	1.6
WHITE PINE	**18**	**405**	**292**	**5,099 ***	**55.5**	**100.0**
053 Assemb of God	1	13	10	60	.7	1.2
081 Catholic	2	NR	NR	2,432	26.5	47.7
151 L-D Saints	6	NR	NR	2,053	22.4	40.3
165 Ch of Nazarene	1	20	13	20	.2	.4
193 Episcopal	1	NR	22	56	.6	1.1
246 Greek Orthodox	2	NR	NR	0	-	-
263 Int Foursq Gos	1	27	61	61 *	.7	1.2
283 Luth—MO Synod	1	36	19	38	.4	.7
419 So Bapt Conv	1	210	92	257 *	2.8	5.0
449 Un Methodist	2	99	75	122 *	1.3	2.4
NEW HAMPSHIRE						
The State.....	872	84,506	51,192	589,022 *	47.7	100.0
BELKNAP	**51**	**4,842**	**2,800**	**25,701 ***	**45.6**	**100.0**
019 Amer Bapt USA	9	1,525	707	1,856 *	3.3	7.2
053 Assemb of God	5	312	391	557	1.0	2.2
056 Baha'i	0	53	NR	53	.1	.2
081 Catholic	8	NR	NR	17,778	31.6	69.2
089 Chr & Miss Al	1	52	NR	92	.2	.4
151 L-D Saints	2	NR	NR	378	.7	1.5
167 Chs of Christ	1	37	50	52	.1	.2
175 Congr Chr Chs	3	55	93	67 *	.1	.3
176 Congr Ad Afl	1	221	NR	269 *	.5	1.0
179 Consrv Bapt	2	NR	250	250	.4	1.0
193 Episcopal	3	NR	234	645	1.1	2.5
207 E.L.C.A.	1	193	115	280	.5	1.1
223 Free Will Bapt	1	70	NR	86 *	.2	.3
246 Greek Orthodox	1	NR	NR	117	.2	.5
356 Presb Ch Amer	1	98	120	139	.2	.5
403 Salvation Army	1	69	72	163	.3	.6
413 S.D.A.	1	49	NR	58	.1	.2
435 Unitarian-Univ	1	113	NR	138 *	.2	.5
443 Un C of Christ	5	1,207	525	1,469 *	2.6	5.7
449 Un Methodist	3	788	243	959 *	1.7	3.7
496 Jewish Est	1	NR	NR	295	.5	1.1
CARROLL	**47**	**3,582**	**2,250**	**11,788 ***	**27.0**	**100.0**
017 Amer Bapt Assn	1	20	NR	24 *	.1	.2
019 Amer Bapt USA	6	567	307	682 *	1.6	5.8
056 Baha'i	0	38	NR	38	.1	.3
081 Catholic	7	NR	NR	5,974	13.7	50.7
089 Chr & Miss Al	1	51	NR	91	.2	.8
151 L-D Saints	1	NR	NR	141	.3	1.2
165 Ch of Nazarene	1	12	38	116	.3	1.0
167 Chs of Christ	1	70	85	90	.2	.8
181 Consrv Congr	1	60	145	72 *	.2	.6
193 Episcopal	4	NR	375	1,117	2.6	9.5
207 E.L.C.A.	1	169	67	243	.6	2.1
226 Friends-USA	1	43	NR	52 *	.1	.4
388 Reg Bapt Gen As	1	49	65	65 *	.1	.6
413 S.D.A.	1	49	NR	58	.1	.5
419 So Bapt Conv	1	55	88	66 *	.2	.6
435 Unitarian-Univ	1	51	NR	61 *	.1	.5

Religious Group	Number of Churches, Synagogues, Mosques, or Temples	Number of Communicant, Confirmed, or Full Members	Number of Attendees	Total Adherents: Number of Adherents	Total Adherents: % of Total Pop.	Total Adherents: % of Total Adh.
443 Un C of Christ	10	1,531	648	1,841 *	4.2	15.6
449 Un Methodist	8	817	432	982 *	2.2	8.3
496 Jewish Est	0	NR	NR	75	.2	.6
CHESHIRE	**77**	**6,005**	**3,361**	**22,764 ***	**30.8**	**100.0**
019 Amer Bapt USA	4	280	134	339 *	.5	1.5
053 Assemb of God	3	104	143	175	.2	.8
056 Baha'i	1	49	NR	49	.1	.2
081 Catholic	12	NR	NR	12,819	17.4	56.3
089 Chr & Miss Al	1	24	NR	100	.1	.4
151 L-D Saints	1	NR	NR	325	.4	1.4
165 Ch of Nazarene	1	48	73	122	.2	.5
167 Chs of Christ	1	50	70	75	.1	.3
175 Congr Chr Chs	2	192	85	233 *	.3	1.0
176 Congr Ad Afl	1	8	NR	10 *	-	-
193 Episcopal	2	NR	177	1,077	1.5	4.7
201 Evan Cov Ch	1	92	154	154 *	.2	.7
203 Evan Free Ch	2	159	310	310	.4	1.4
207 E.L.C.A.	1	90	45	135	.2	.6
226 Friends-USA	3	129	NR	156 *	.2	.7
246 Greek Orthodox	1	NR	NR	207	.3	.9
263 Int Foursq Gos	2	143	377	377 *	.5	1.7
283 Luth—MO Synod	2	542	245	789	1.1	3.5
335 Orth Pres Ch	1	27	46	46	.1	.2
403 Salvation Army	1	76	50	130	.2	.6
413 S.D.A.	1	84	NR	100	.1	.4
435 Unitarian-Univ	4	293	NR	355 *	.5	1.6
443 Un C of Christ	17	2,970	1,133	3,599 *	4.9	15.8
449 Un Methodist	10	645	319	782 *	1.1	3.4
496 Jewish Est	2	NR	NR	300	.4	1.3
COOS	**49**	**2,503**	**1,521**	**21,724 ***	**65.6**	**100.0**
019 Amer Bapt USA	3	335	120	403 *	1.2	1.9
053 Assemb of God	3	147	202	254	.8	1.2
056 Baha'i	0	7	NR	7	-	-
081 Catholic	12	NR	NR	17,638	53.3	81.2
151 L-D Saints	1	NR	NR	267	.8	1.2
167 Chs of Christ	1	36	25	60	.2	.3
193 Episcopal	4	NR	138	370	1.1	1.7
207 E.L.C.A.	1	208	74	317	1.0	1.5
263 Int Foursq Gos	1	66	299	299 *	.9	1.4
331 OCA: Ter Diocs	1	28	NR	34	.1	.2
356 Presb Ch Amer	1	8	10	11	-	.1
403 Salvation Army	1	44	31	113	.3	.5
413 S.D.A.	1	116	NR	138	.4	.6
419 So Bapt Conv	1	30	15	36 *	.1	.2
443 Un C of Christ	6	453	223	545 *	1.6	2.5
449 Un Methodist	12	1,025	384	1,232 *	3.7	5.7
GRAFTON	**95**	**7,099**	**3,993**	**25,327 ***	**31.0**	**100.0**
019 Amer Bapt USA	10	1,211	647	1,449 *	1.8	5.7
053 Assemb of God	8	275	340	404	.5	1.6
056 Baha'i	0	88	NR	88	.1	.3
081 Catholic	14	NR	NR	13,188	16.1	52.1
089 Chr & Miss Al	1	40	NR	98	.1	.4
127 Ch God (Cleve)	1	52	24	62 *	.1	.2
151 L-D Saints	2	NR	NR	741	.9	2.9
165 Ch of Nazarene	2	73	88	163	.2	.6
175 Congr Chr Chs	1	23	31	28 *	-	.1
179 Consrv Bapt	2	NR	205	205	.3	.8
193 Episcopal	7	NR	538	1,568	1.9	6.2
207 E.L.C.A.	2	329	199	514	.6	2.0
226 Friends-USA	2	86	NR	103 *	.1	.4
413 S.D.A.	2	141	NR	167	.2	.7
419 So Bapt Conv	1	36	37	43 *	.1	.2
435 Unitarian-Univ	1	130	NR	156 *	.2	.6
443 Un C of Christ	20	2,822	1,200	3,377 *	4.1	13.3
449 Un Methodist	17	1,793	684	2,148 *	2.6	8.5
496 Jewish Est	2	NR	NR	825	1.0	3.3
HILLSBOROUGH	**189**	**21,849**	**12,745**	**221,420 ***	**58.1**	**100.0**
019 Amer Bapt USA	11	1,819	666	2,292 *	.6	1.0

NR–Not Reported *Total adherents estimated from known number of communicant, confirmed, full members. - Represents a percentage less than 0.1. Percentages may not total 100 due to rounding.

Table 4: Religious Congregations by County and Group: 2000

Religious Group	Number of Churches, Synagogues, Mosques, or Temples	Number of Communicant, Confirmed, or Full Members	Number of Attendees	Total Adherents: Number of Adherents	Total Adherents: % of Total Pop.	Total Adherents: % of Total Adh.
053 Assemb of God	7	608	805	1,146	.3	.5
056 Baha'i	2	170	NR	170	-	.1
076 Buddhism	2	NR	NR	NR	-	-
081 Catholic	44	NR	NR	173,365	45.5	78.3
084 Calvary Chapel	1	NR	NR	NR	-	-
089 Chr & Miss Al	2	67	NR	197	.1	.1
097 Chr Chs&Chs Cr	3	979	NR	1,234 *	.3	.6
127 Ch God (Cleve)	1	306	59	386 *	.1	.2
145 Ch God Prophcy	1	82	NR	103 *	-	-
151 L-D Saints	7	NR	NR	1,908	.5	.9
165 Ch of Nazarene	2	558	442	887	.2	.4
167 Chs of Christ	4	349	404	549	.1	.2
175 Congr Chr Chs	2	251	285	316 *	.1	.1
176 Congr Ad Afl	2	129	NR	163 *	-	.1
179 Consrv Bapt	6	NR	880	880	.2	.4
181 Consrv Congr	2	314	330	396 *	.1	.2
193 Episcopal	8	NR	1,283	4,233	1.1	1.9
201 Evan Cov Ch	3	573	505	722 *	.2	.3
207 E.L.C.A.	3	917	454	1,339	.4	.6
226 Friends-USA	1	43	NR	54 *	-	-
246 Greek Orthodox	4	NR	NR	4,860	1.3	2.2
263 Int Foursq Gos	2	31	64	64 *	-	-
283 Luth—MO Synod	4	714	478	1,016	.3	.5
335 Orth Pres Ch	1	50	64	69	-	-
339 Pent Ch of God	1	40	NR	45	-	-
355 Presb Ch (USA)	7	1,186	691	1,495 *	.4	.7
356 Presb Ch Amer	1	75	90	101	-	-
388 Reg Bapt Gen As	1	49	65	65 *	-	-
397 OCA: Roman Dioc	1	NR	NR	36	-	-
400 Rus Orth Moscow	1	NR	NR	NR	-	-
403 Salvation Army	2	327	149	1,562	.4	.7
413 S.D.A.	3	277	NR	330	.1	.1
419 So Bapt Conv	3	632	282	796 *	.2	.4
435 Unitarian-Univ	5	982	NR	1,237 *	.3	.6
443 Un C of Christ	21	6,531	2,582	8,229 *	2.2	3.7
449 Un Methodist	10	3,009	965	3,791 *	1.0	1.7
467 Wesleyan	1	0	29	161	-	.1
469 WELS	1	81	73	123	-	.1
496 Jewish Est	4	NR	NR	6,000	1.6	2.7
498 Indep.Charis.	1	300	300	300	.1	.1
499 Indep.Non-Char	1	400	800	800	.2	.4
MERRIMACK	**99**	**10,658**	**6,935**	**52,540 ***	**38.6**	**100.0**
019 Amer Bapt USA	15	2,775	1,160	3,429 *	2.5	6.5
053 Assemb of God	1	67	101	136	.1	.3
056 Baha'i	1	76	NR	76	.1	.1
076 Buddhism	1	NR	NR	NR	-	-
081 Catholic	13	NR	NR	34,215	25.1	65.1
127 Ch God (Cleve)	2	77	90	119 *	.1	.2
145 Ch God Prophcy	1	82	NR	101 *	.1	.2
151 L-D Saints	2	NR	NR	676	.5	1.3
165 Ch of Nazarene	2	206	289	433	.3	.8
167 Chs of Christ	1	87	88	118	.1	.2
175 Congr Chr Chs	3	335	215	414 *	.3	.8
176 Congr Ad Afl	1	112	NR	138 *	.1	.3
179 Consrv Bapt	5	NR	810	810	.6	1.5
181 Consrv Congr	1	98	103	121 *	.1	.2
193 Episcopal	7	NR	972	2,314	1.7	4.4
201 Evan Cov Ch	1	42	75	75 *	.1	.1
207 E.L.C.A.	1	227	82	314	.2	.6
226 Friends-USA	2	86	NR	106 *	.1	.2
246 Greek Orthodox	1	NR	NR	378	.3	.7
251 Holy Orth in NA	1	NR	NR	36	-	.1
263 Int Foursq Gos	1	65	230	230 *	.2	.4
355 Presb Ch (USA)	1	222	95	274 *	.2	.5
356 Presb Ch Amer	1	32	55	59	-	.1
403 Salvation Army	1	158	81	187	.1	.4
413 S.D.A.	1	45	NR	54	-	.1
419 So Bapt Conv	1	163	122	201 *	.1	.4
435 Unitarian-Univ	3	445	NR	550 *	.4	1.0
443 Un C of Christ	20	3,364	1,503	4,156 *	3.1	7.9
449 Un Methodist	6	1,594	539	1,970 *	1.4	3.7
496 Jewish Est	1	NR	NR	525	.4	1.0
499 Indep.Non-Char	1	300	325	325	.2	.6

Religious Group	Number of Churches, Synagogues, Mosques, or Temples	Number of Communicant, Confirmed, or Full Members	Number of Attendees	Total Adherents: Number of Adherents	Total Adherents: % of Total Pop.	Total Adherents: % of Total Adh.
ROCKINGHAM	**150**	**18,620**	**10,792**	**150,252 ***	**54.2**	**100.0**
019 Amer Bapt USA	21	3,529	1,671	4,449 *	1.6	3.0
053 Assemb of God	6	615	784	984	.4	.7
056 Baha'i	2	129	NR	129	-	.1
076 Buddhism	1	NR	NR	NR	-	-
081 Catholic	25	NR	NR	117,542	42.4	78.2
084 Calvary Chapel	1	NR	NR	NR	-	-
097 Chr Chs&Chs Cr	2	214	NR	269 *	.1	.2
105 Christian Ref	1	58	46	73 *	-	-
151 L-D Saints	3	NR	NR	1,123	.4	.7
165 Ch of Nazarene	3	82	76	140	.1	.1
167 Chs of Christ	2	71	74	113	-	.1
175 Congr Chr Chs	2	355	295	448 *	.2	.3
176 Congr Ad Afl	2	144	NR	182 *	.1	.1
179 Consrv Bapt	3	NR	230	230	.1	.2
181 Consrv Congr	2	213	108	269 *	.1	.2
193 Episcopal	8	NR	994	3,422	1.2	2.3
203 Evan Free Ch	1	50	75	75	-	-
207 E.L.C.A.	2	529	333	746	.3	.5
226 Friends-USA	1	43	NR	54 *	-	-
246 Greek Orthodox	1	NR	NR	720	.3	.5
263 Int Foursq Gos	1	40	100	100 *	-	.1
267 Muslim Est	1	NR	412	1,891	.7	1.3
283 Luth—MO Synod	1	135	160	210	.1	.1
355 Presb Ch (USA)	2	689	504	869 *	.3	.6
356 Presb Ch Amer	2	88	109	116	-	.1
370 Ref Baptist Chs	1	NR	NR	NR	-	-
403 Salvation Army	4	132	118	292	.1	.2
413 S.D.A.	1	62	NR	74	-	-
419 So Bapt Conv	3	1,489	858	1,877 *	.7	1.2
435 Unitarian-Univ	4	1,088	NR	1,372 *	.5	.9
443 Un C of Christ	23	5,039	2,228	6,352 *	2.3	4.2
449 Un Methodist	16	3,476	1,297	4,381 *	1.6	2.9
496 Jewish Est	1	NR	NR	1,400	.5	.9
499 Indep.Non-Char	1	350	320	350	.1	.2
STRAFFORD	**66**	**6,076**	**4,844**	**43,804 ***	**39.0**	**100.0**
019 Amer Bapt USA	4	386	168	472 *	.4	1.1
053 Assemb of God	4	392	503	737	.7	1.7
056 Baha'i	2	71	NR	71	.1	.2
076 Buddhism	1	NR	NR	NR	-	-
081 Catholic	13	NR	NR	30,401	27.1	69.4
123 Ch God (Ander)	1	NR	40	40	-	.1
127 Ch God (Cleve)	1	23	20	28 *	-	.1
151 L-D Saints	1	NR	NR	403	.4	.9
167 Chs of Christ	2	92	133	142	.1	.3
179 Consrv Bapt	6	NR	1,065	1,065	.9	2.4
181 Consrv Congr	1	119	100	146 *	.1	.3
193 Episcopal	3	NR	304	869	.8	2.0
203 Evan Free Ch	1	105	205	205	.2	.5
223 Free Will Bapt	1	70	NR	86 *	.1	.2
226 Friends-USA	3	129	NR	158 *	.1	.4
246 Greek Orthodox	2	NR	NR	624	.6	1.4
263 Int Foursq Gos	1	14	53	53 *	-	.1
267 Muslim Est	1	NR	412	1,891	1.7	4.3
403 Salvation Army	1	85	30	204	.2	.5
413 S.D.A.	1	106	NR	126	.1	.3
419 So Bapt Conv	2	210	124	257 *	.2	.6
435 Unitarian-Univ	1	51	NR	62 *	.1	.1
443 Un C of Christ	8	2,823	1,181	3,452 *	3.1	7.9
449 Un Methodist	4	1,400	506	1,712 *	1.5	3.9
496 Jewish Est	1	NR	NR	600	.5	1.4
SULLIVAN	**49**	**3,272**	**1,951**	**13,702 ***	**33.9**	**100.0**
019 Amer Bapt USA	7	809	406	988 *	2.4	7.2
056 Baha'i	0	13	NR	13	-	.1
081 Catholic	6	NR	NR	8,339	20.6	60.9
151 L-D Saints	1	NR	NR	392	1.0	2.9
165 Ch of Nazarene	1	26	25	78	.2	.6
167 Chs of Christ	1	3	3	3	-	-
175 Congr Chr Chs	1	75	50	92 *	.2	.7
176 Congr Ad Afl	1	90	NR	110 *	.3	.8
179 Consrv Bapt	2	NR	174	174	.4	1.3

NR–Not Reported   *Total adherents estimated from known number of communicant, confirmed, full members.   - Represents a percentage less than 0.1.   Percentages may not total 100 due to rounding.

Table 4: Religious Congregations by County and Group: 2000

Religious Group	Number of Churches, Synagogues, Mosques, or Temples	Number of Communicant, Confirmed, or Full Members	Number of Attendees	Total Adherents: Number of Adherents	Total Adherents: % of Total Pop.	Total Adherents: % of Total Adh.
193 Episcopal	4	NR	188	533	1.3	3.9
203 Evan Free Ch	1	33	50	50	.1	.4
207 E.L.C.A.	1	118	51	174	.4	1.3
246 Greek Orthodox	1	NR	NR	165	.4	1.2
263 Int Foursq Gos	1	46	80	80 *	.2	.6
331 OCA: Ter Diocs	1	44	NR	51	.1	.4
413 S.D.A.	1	40	NR	48	.1	.4
419 So Bapt Conv	2	103	128	126 *	.3	.9
435 Unitarian-Univ	1	30	NR	37 *	.1	.3
443 Un C of Christ	8	1,047	449	1,279 *	3.2	9.3
449 Un Methodist	8	795	347	970 *	2.4	7.1
NEW JERSEY						
The State.....	4,531	507,739	327,936	4,858,756 *	57.7	100.0
ATLANTIC	**145**	**12,587**	**8,353**	**102,543 ***	**40.6**	**100.0**
019 Amer Bapt USA	2	702	335	877 *	.3	.9
053 Assemb of God	10	954	770	1,409	.6	1.4
056 Baha'i	0	44	NR	44	-	-
081 Catholic	23	NR	NR	62,940	24.9	61.4
084 Calvary Chapel	1	NR	NR	NR	-	-
089 Chr & Miss Al	3	158	NR	390	.2	.4
097 Chr Chs&Chs Cr	1	35	NR	44 *	-	-
123 Ch God (Ander)	2	NR	81	81	-	.1
127 Ch God (Cleve)	3	240	50	323 *	.1	.3
145 Ch God Prophcy	2	91	NR	114 *	-	.1
151 L-D Saints	2	NR	NR	839	.3	.8
165 Ch of Nazarene	1	100	96	104	-	.1
167 Chs of Christ	2	90	90	113	-	.1
193 Episcopal	7	NR	520	1,664	.7	1.6
203 Evan Free Ch	1	125	300	300	.1	.3
207 E.L.C.A.	7	2,016	683	3,312	1.3	3.2
226 Friends-USA	2	210	NR	262 *	.1	.3
246 Greek Orthodox	2	NR	NR	837	.3	.8
267 Muslim Est	2	NR	824	3,782	1.5	3.7
283 Luth—MO Synod	1	120	78	150	.1	.1
288 Mennonite USA	1	65	52	81 *	-	.1
293 Morav Ch-North	1	286	NR	365	.1	.4
331 OCA: Ter Diocs	1	22	NR	68	-	.1
355 Presb Ch (USA)	8	1,143	521	1,428 *	.6	1.4
356 Presb Ch Amer	1	16	20	20	-	-
388 Reg Bapt Gen As	4	422	563	563 *	.2	.5
401 Rus Orth Abroad	1	NR	NR	NR	-	-
403 Salvation Army	2	184	267	545	.2	.5
413 S.D.A.	6	417	NR	497	.2	.5
419 So Bapt Conv	2	265	253	331 *	.1	.3
435 Unitarian-Univ	1	60	NR	75 *	-	.1
443 Un C of Christ	3	756	312	945 *	.4	.9
449 Un Methodist	27	4,066	2,387	5,078 *	2.0	5.0
467 Wesleyan	1	0	151	362	.1	.4
496 Jewish Est	12	NR	NR	14,600	5.8	14.2
BERGEN	**502**	**48,774**	**30,395**	**664,191 ***	**75.1**	**100.0**
019 Amer Bapt USA	17	2,943	1,144	3,594 *	.4	.5
034 Ant Orth of NA	2	436	NR	872	.1	.1
039 Ap Chr Ch(Naz)	1	76	101	101 *	-	-
049 Armen Ap Cilic	1	500	NR	2,100	.2	.3
050 Armen Ap Etchm	2	727	NR	7,000	.8	1.1
053 Assemb of God	26	2,647	2,868	3,885	.4	.6
056 Baha'i	2	188	NR	188	-	-
076 Buddhism	4	NR	NR	NR	-	-
081 Catholic	82	NR	NR	478,735	54.1	72.1
084 Calvary Chapel	1	NR	NR	NR	-	-
089 Chr & Miss Al	10	847	NR	1,040	.1	.2
105 Christian Ref	6	2,471	1,865	3,017 *	.3	.5
123 Ch God (Ander)	1	NR	60	60	-	-
127 Ch God (Cleve)	3	114	70	139 *	-	-
145 Ch God Prophcy	1	46	NR	56 *	-	-
151 L-D Saints	4	NR	NR	855	.1	.1
165 Ch of Nazarene	6	756	682	906	.1	.1
167 Chs of Christ	2	131	125	175	-	-

Religious Group	Number of Churches, Synagogues, Mosques, or Temples	Number of Communicant, Confirmed, or Full Members	Number of Attendees	Total Adherents: Number of Adherents	Total Adherents: % of Total Pop.	Total Adherents: % of Total Adh.
173 Comm of Christ	1	103	NR	103	-	-
179 Consrv Bapt	2	NR	130	130	-	-
193 Episcopal	39	NR	3,326	10,586	1.2	1.6
203 Evan Free Ch	5	546	995	995	.1	.1
207 E.L.C.A.	30	6,426	2,351	8,505	1.0	1.3
226 Friends-USA	1	50	NR	61 *	-	-
246 Greek Orthodox	4	NR	NR	5,682	.6	.9
252 Hindu	5	NR	NR	NR	-	-
262 Int Cou Comm Ch	2	264	NR	322 *	-	-
267 Muslim Est	4	NR	1,336	6,473	.7	1.0
283 Luth—MO Synod	13	3,485	1,257	4,478	.5	.7
307 Neth Ref Congr	1	345	NR	634	.1	.1
330 Macedonian Orth	1	NR	NR	1,200	.1	.2
331 OCA: Ter Diocs	2	187	NR	349	-	.1
333 Malan Dioc Am	1	NR	NR	300	-	-
335 Orth Pres Ch	1	56	59	76	-	-
355 Presb Ch (USA)	39	7,494	3,501	9,152 *	1.0	1.4
356 Presb Ch Amer	2	109	70	109	-	-
369 Prot Ref Chs	1	18	NR	27	-	-
370 Ref Baptist Chs	1	NR	NR	NR	-	-
371 Ref Ch in Am	31	4,678	3,131	9,131	1.0	1.4
388 Reg Bapt Gen As	3	764	603	956 *	.1	.1
400 Rus Orth Moscow	1	NR	NR	NR	-	-
403 Salvation Army	2	112	134	219	-	-
413 S.D.A.	5	398	NR	473	.1	.1
416 Sikh	1	NR	NR	NR	-	-
418 Southw Bapt Fel	1	NR	NR	NR	-	-
419 So Bapt Conv	10	767	661	937 *	.1	.1
423 Syrian Orth Ch	4	NR	NR	3,250	.4	.5
435 Unitarian-Univ	3	535	NR	653 *	.1	.1
443 Un C of Christ	11	1,685	715	2,058 *	.2	.3
449 Un Methodist	35	8,235	4,610	10,057 *	1.1	1.5
463 Vineyard	1	265	223	324 *	-	-
467 Wesleyan	1	0	28	28	-	-
496 Jewish Est	66	NR	NR	83,700	9.5	12.6
499 Indep.Non-Char	1	370	350	500	.1	.1
BURLINGTON	**219**	**30,563**	**21,183**	**204,182 ***	**48.2**	**100.0**
019 Amer Bapt USA	14	2,714	1,702	3,373 *	.8	1.7
053 Assemb of God	12	2,580	3,209	7,239	1.7	3.5
056 Baha'i	0	79	NR	79	-	-
076 Buddhism	3	NR	NR	NR	-	-
081 Catholic	28	NR	NR	131,135	31.0	64.2
084 Calvary Chapel	1	NR	NR	NR	-	-
089 Chr & Miss Al	3	1,272	NR	1,882	.4	.9
097 Chr Chs&Chs Cr	1	30	NR	37 *	-	-
123 Ch God (Ander)	1	NR	32	32	-	-
127 Ch God (Cleve)	3	197	96	244 *	.1	.1
151 L-D Saints	3	NR	NR	1,185	.3	.6
165 Ch of Nazarene	3	252	345	450	.1	.2
167 Chs of Christ	2	270	265	332	.1	.2
193 Episcopal	17	NR	1,955	5,779	1.4	2.8
203 Evan Free Ch	1	75	140	140	-	.1
207 E.L.C.A.	11	4,635	1,856	6,991	1.7	3.4
226 Friends-USA	6	630	NR	783 *	.2	.4
262 Int Cou Comm Ch	1	700	NR	870 *	.2	.4
267 Muslim Est	5	NR	1,768	8,464	2.0	4.1
268 Jain	1	NR	NR	NR	-	-
283 Luth—MO Synod	3	426	243	614	.1	.3
288 Mennonite USA	1	7	6	9 *	-	-
293 Morav Ch-North	2	299	NR	361	.1	.2
304 NatPrimBapt USA	1	225	NR	280 *	.1	.1
331 OCA: Ter Diocs	1	115	NR	193	-	.1
355 Presb Ch (USA)	17	4,620	2,365	5,740 *	1.4	2.8
356 Presb Ch Amer	2	139	130	171	-	.1
370 Ref Baptist Chs	1	NR	NR	NR	-	-
371 Ref Ch in Am	1	50	35	101	-	-
388 Reg Bapt Gen As	5	1,010	1,459	1,855 *	.4	.9
413 S.D.A.	5	342	NR	407	.1	.2
419 So Bapt Conv	8	680	545	845 *	.2	.4
435 Unitarian-Univ	1	16	NR	20 *	-	-
443 Un C of Christ	2	211	94	262 *	.1	.1
449 Un Methodist	43	8,239	4,066	10,239 *	2.4	5.0
467 Wesleyan	3	0	122	320	.1	.2

NR–Not Reported   *Total adherents estimated from known number of communicant, confirmed, full members.   - Represents a percentage less than 0.1.   Percentages may not total 100 due to rounding.

Table 4: Religious Congregations by County and Group: 2000

Religious Group	Number of Churches, Synagogues, Mosques, or Temples	Number of Communicant, Confirmed, or Full Members	Number of Attendees	Total Adherents		
				Number of Adherents	% of Total Pop.	% of Total Adh.
496 Jewish Est	5	NR	NR	13,000	3.1	6.4
498 Indep.Charis.	2	750	750	750	.2	.4
CAMDEN	**274**	**36,891**	**23,298**	**282,276 ***	**55.5**	**100.0**
019 Amer Bapt USA	19	7,611	2,082	9,599 *	1.9	3.4
053 Assemb of God	17	2,304	2,576	3,067	.6	1.1
056 Baha'i	1	63	NR	63	-	-
059 Bapt Miss Assn	1	150	150	189 *	-	.1
076 Buddhism	1	NR	NR	NR	-	-
081 Catholic	53	NR	NR	180,786	35.5	64.0
089 Chr & Miss Al	4	252	NR	663	.1	.2
123 Ch God (Ander)	2	NR	115	115	-	-
127 Ch God (Cleve)	1	58	52	73 *	-	-
145 Ch God Prophcy	2	97	NR	123 *	-	-
151 L-D Saints	3	NR	NR	1,275	.3	.5
165 Ch of Nazarene	1	27	58	189	-	.1
167 Chs of Christ	4	263	302	350	.1	.1
179 Consrv Bapt	3	NR	407	407	.1	.1
193 Episcopal	20	NR	1,761	5,766	1.1	2.0
203 Evan Free Ch	1	69	125	125	-	-
207 E.L.C.A.	17	5,296	2,209	8,383	1.6	3.0
216 Evan Presby Ch	1	304	NR	383 *	.1	.1
226 Friends-USA	4	420	NR	530 *	.1	.2
246 Greek Orthodox	1	NR	NR	2,022	.4	.7
252 Hindu	2	NR	NR	NR	-	-
267 Muslim Est	3	NR	1,236	5,673	1.1	2.0
268 Jain	1	NR	NR	NR	-	-
283 Luth—MO Synod	2	726	320	940	.2	.3
288 Mennonite USA	3	118	415	415 *	.1	.1
335 Orth Pres Ch	4	272	368	395	.1	.1
355 Presb Ch (USA)	16	5,467	2,300	6,899 *	1.4	2.4
356 Presb Ch Amer	1	244	259	319	.1	.1
370 Ref Baptist Chs	2	NR	NR	NR	-	-
388 Reg Bapt Gen As	6	882	1,523	1,717 *	.3	.6
413 S.D.A.	4	409	NR	486	.1	.2
419 So Bapt Conv	5	503	289	634 *	.1	.2
435 Unitarian-Univ	2	274	NR	346 *	.1	.1
449 Un Methodist	50	10,507	5,740	13,254 *	2.6	4.7
467 Wesleyan	1	0	46	125	-	-
496 Jewish Est	13	NR	NR	36,000	7.1	12.8
499 Indep.Non-Char	3	575	965	965	.2	.3
CAPE MAY	**85**	**8,660**	**5,761**	**47,543 ***	**46.5**	**100.0**
019 Amer Bapt USA	5	906	426	1,093 *	1.1	2.3
053 Assemb of God	5	392	504	672	.7	1.4
056 Baha'i	0	27	NR	27	-	.1
081 Catholic	15	NR	NR	32,307	31.6	68.0
084 Calvary Chapel	1	NR	NR	NR	-	-
089 Chr & Miss Al	1	77	NR	261	.3	.5
151 L-D Saints	2	NR	NR	646	.6	1.4
165 Ch of Nazarene	1	149	190	319	.3	.7
167 Chs of Christ	1	35	54	45	-	.1
193 Episcopal	6	NR	786	1,588	1.6	3.3
207 E.L.C.A.	6	1,545	621	2,142	2.1	4.5
226 Friends-USA	1	105	NR	127 *	.1	.3
246 Greek Orthodox	1	NR	NR	222	.2	.5
252 Hindu	1	NR	NR	NR	-	-
331 OCA: Ter Diocs	1	14	NR	33	-	.1
335 Orth Pres Ch	2	79	92	112	.1	.2
355 Presb Ch (USA)	4	842	572	1,015 *	1.0	2.1
356 Presb Ch Amer	2	63	0	63	.1	.1
413 S.D.A.	2	145	NR	173	.2	.4
419 So Bapt Conv	2	29	21	35 *	-	.1
449 Un Methodist	25	4,252	2,495	5,133 *	5.0	10.8
496 Jewish Est	1	NR	NR	1,530	1.5	3.2
CUMBERLAND	**133**	**14,352**	**8,872**	**58,322 ***	**39.8**	**100.0**
019 Amer Bapt USA	7	2,316	974	2,882 *	2.0	4.9
053 Assemb of God	7	1,432	1,781	3,031	2.1	5.2
056 Baha'i	0	18	NR	18	-	-
076 Buddhism	1	NR	NR	NR	-	-
081 Catholic	19	NR	NR	33,491	22.9	57.4
084 Calvary Chapel	1	NR	NR	NR	-	-
089 Chr & Miss Al	1	156	NR	396	.3	.7
127 Ch God (Cleve)	6	217	211	278 *	.2	.5
145 Ch God Prophcy	1	46	NR	57 *	-	.1
165 Ch of Nazarene	4	663	708	1,816	1.2	3.1
167 Chs of Christ	1	63	70	97	.1	.2
193 Episcopal	4	NR	256	764	.5	1.3
207 E.L.C.A.	3	1,143	393	1,531	1.0	2.6
223 Free Will Bapt	2	0	NR	0 *	-	-
226 Friends-USA	1	105	NR	131 *	.1	.2
246 Greek Orthodox	1	NR	NR	333	.2	.6
283 Luth—MO Synod	1	286	79	402	.3	.7
286 E.PA Mennonite	1	41	NR	51 *	-	.1
288 Mennonite USA	1	18	18	22 *	-	-
335 Orth Pres Ch	2	154	123	183	.1	.3
355 Presb Ch (USA)	9	1,381	726	1,718 *	1.2	2.9
356 Presb Ch Amer	1	136	120	172	.1	.3
388 Reg Bapt Gen As	1	149	203	203 *	.1	.3
401 Rus Orth Abroad	2	NR	NR	NR	-	-
403 Salvation Army	2	102	69	436	.3	.7
413 S.D.A.	5	477	NR	567	.4	1.0
418 Southw Bapt Fel	1	NR	NR	NR	-	-
419 So Bapt Conv	3	247	90	307 *	.2	.5
431 Ukrainian Orth	1	NR	NR	300	.2	.5
449 Un Methodist	37	5,202	2,708	6,473 *	4.4	11.1
467 Wesleyan	3	0	343	663	.5	1.1
496 Jewish Est	4	NR	NR	2,000	1.4	3.4
ESSEX	**419**	**44,623**	**29,146**	**451,976 ***	**57.0**	**100.0**
019 Amer Bapt USA	44	12,992	4,665	16,385 *	2.1	3.6
050 Armen Ap Etchm	1	190	NR	1,000	.1	.2
053 Assemb of God	20	2,287	1,959	3,002	.4	.7
056 Baha'i	3	185	NR	185	-	-
057 Bapt Gen Conf	1	112	162	162 *	-	-
076 Buddhism	2	NR	NR	NR	-	-
081 Catholic	66	NR	NR	280,095	35.3	62.0
084 Calvary Chapel	1	NR	NR	NR	-	-
089 Chr & Miss Al	6	477	NR	742	.1	.2
093 Chr Ch (Disc)	2	1,200	0	1,513 *	.2	.3
097 Chr Chs&Chs Cr	1	600	NR	757 *	.1	.2
123 Ch God (Ander)	1	NR	65	65	-	-
127 Ch God (Cleve)	9	1,070	1,195	1,431 *	.2	.3
145 Ch God Prophcy	4	188	NR	239 *	-	.1
151 L-D Saints	2	NR	NR	796	.1	.2
165 Ch of Nazarene	4	663	361	687	.1	.2
167 Chs of Christ	4	1,174	969	1,388	.2	.3
179 Consrv Bapt	4	NR	555	555	.1	.1
193 Episcopal	31	NR	2,757	9,327	1.2	2.1
201 Evan Cov Ch	2	156	100	196 *	-	-
203 Evan Free Ch	3	585	665	665	.1	.1
207 E.L.C.A.	9	1,554	558	2,052	.3	.5
221 Free Methodist	1	8	43	43	-	-
226 Friends-USA	1	50	NR	63 *	-	-
246 Greek Orthodox	2	NR	NR	2,487	.3	.6
252 Hindu	4	NR	NR	NR	-	-
263 Int Foursq Gos	1	30	50	50 *	-	-
267 Muslim Est	14	NR	5,032	21,751	2.7	4.8
268 Jain	1	NR	NR	NR	-	-
283 Luth—MO Synod	5	546	287	739	.1	.2
304 NatPrimBapt USA	4	362	NR	457 *	.1	.1
313 N Am Bapt Conf	1	35	60	44 *	-	-
333 Malan Dioc Am	2	NR	NR	225	-	-
335 Orth Pres Ch	1	16	26	26	-	-
355 Presb Ch (USA)	43	8,271	3,901	10,432 *	1.3	2.3
356 Presb Ch Amer	2	145	218	224	-	-
370 Ref Baptist Chs	1	NR	NR	NR	-	-
371 Ref Ch in Am	11	465	497	1,269	.2	.3
388 Reg Bapt Gen As	1	120	150	151 *	-	-
401 Rus Orth Abroad	2	NR	NR	NR	-	-
403 Salvation Army	6	493	434	2,145	.3	.5
413 S.D.A.	13	1,565	NR	1,863	.2	.4
419 So Bapt Conv	10	935	1,058	1,179 *	.1	.3
431 Ukrainian Orth	3	NR	NR	1,110	.1	.2
435 Unitarian-Univ	2	541	NR	682 *	.1	.2
443 Un C of Christ	14	3,438	1,293	4,336 *	.5	1.0

NR–Not Reported *Total adherents estimated from known number of communicant, confirmed, full members. - Represents a percentage less than 0.1. Percentages may not total 100 due to rounding.

Table 4: Religious Congregations by County and Group: 2000

Religious Group	Number of Churches, Synagogues, Mosques, or Temples	Number of Communicant, Confirmed, or Full Members	Number of Attendees	Total Adherents: Number of Adherents	Total Adherents: % of Total Pop.	Total Adherents: % of Total Adh.
449 Un Methodist	22	4,170	2,086	5,258 *	.7	1.2
467 Wesleyan	1	0	0	0	-	-
496 Jewish Est	31	NR	NR	76,200	9.6	16.9
GLOUCESTER	**155**	**23,084**	**16,184**	**132,922 ***	**52.2**	**100.0**
017 Amer Bapt Assn	1	20	NR	25 *	-	-
019 Amer Bapt USA	6	820	279	1,029 *	.4	.8
053 Assemb of God	11	1,234	1,581	2,297	.9	1.7
056 Baha'i	0	57	NR	57	-	-
081 Catholic	21	NR	NR	94,910	37.3	71.4
084 Calvary Chapel	1	NR	NR	NR	-	-
089 Chr & Miss Al	2	126	NR	344	.1	.3
097 Chr Chs&Chs Cr	1	130	NR	163 *	.1	.1
127 Ch God (Cleve)	2	124	95	156 *	.1	.1
151 L-D Saints	1	NR	NR	571	.2	.4
165 Ch of Nazarene	2	92	52	99	-	.1
167 Chs of Christ	3	320	378	397	.2	.3
173 Comm of Christ	1	148	NR	148	.1	.1
179 Consrv Bapt	5	NR	808	808	.3	.6
193 Episcopal	11	NR	1,067	3,491	1.4	2.6
203 Evan Free Ch	2	71	290	290	.1	.2
207 E.L.C.A.	6	2,163	775	3,309	1.3	2.5
226 Friends-USA	5	525	NR	659 *	.3	.5
263 Int Foursq Gos	1	156	362	362 *	.1	.3
267 Muslim Est	1	NR	412	1,891	.7	1.4
304 NatPrimBapt USA	1	140	NR	176 *	.1	.1
335 Orth Pres Ch	1	71	55	99	-	.1
355 Presb Ch (USA)	13	2,425	1,060	3,042 *	1.2	2.3
356 Presb Ch Amer	1	27	30	32	-	-
388 Reg Bapt Gen As	2	236	303	312 *	.1	.2
413 S.D.A.	4	411	NR	489	.2	.4
416 Sikh	1	NR	NR	NR	-	-
418 Southw Bapt Fel	1	NR	NR	NR	-	-
419 So Bapt Conv	2	5,750	3,674	7,213 *	2.8	5.4
443 Un C of Christ	1	64	28	80 *	-	.1
449 Un Methodist	44	7,974	4,878	10,003 *	3.9	7.5
467 Wesleyan	1	0	57	300	.1	.2
496 Jewish Est	0	NR	NR	170	.1	.1
HUDSON	**279**	**18,374**	**15,190**	**378,031 ***	**62.1**	**100.0**
019 Amer Bapt USA	17	4,293	1,637	5,220 *	.9	1.4
022 Carp Rus Orth	1	122	NR	207	-	.1
053 Assemb of God	20	3,046	3,048	3,872	.6	1.0
056 Baha'i	1	89	NR	89	-	-
076 Buddhism	1	NR	NR	NR	-	-
081 Catholic	57	NR	NR	318,026	52.2	84.1
089 Chr & Miss Al	3	100	NR	131	-	-
093 Chr Ch (Disc)	1	60	0	73 *	-	-
097 Chr Chs&Chs Cr	1	125	NR	152 *	-	-
105 Christian Ref	4	222	493	270 *	-	.1
123 Ch God (Ander)	2	NR	94	94	-	-
127 Ch God (Cleve)	4	221	220	346 *	.1	.1
145 Ch God Prophcy	2	102	NR	124 *	-	-
151 L-D Saints	7	NR	NR	2,968	.5	.8
165 Ch of Nazarene	6	412	399	602	.1	.2
179 Consrv Bapt	3	NR	260	260	-	.1
193 Episcopal	15	NR	866	2,033	.3	.5
203 Evan Free Ch	2	92	140	140	-	-
207 E.L.C.A.	22	2,508	1,251	3,666	.6	1.0
221 Free Methodist	4	217	370	402	.1	.1
246 Greek Orthodox	2	NR	NR	1,389	.2	.4
252 Hindu	12	NR	NR	NR	-	-
263 Int Foursq Gos	1	110	175	175 *	-	-
265 Int Pent C Chr	1	24	0	24	-	-
267 Muslim Est	9	NR	3,224	15,697	2.6	4.2
283 Luth—MO Synod	3	558	93	686	.1	.2
313 N Am Bapt Conf	1	47	40	57 *	-	-
331 OCA: Ter Diocs	2	219	NR	331	.1	.1
349 Pent Holiness	1	141	124	171 *	-	-
355 Presb Ch (USA)	8	769	479	985 *	.2	.3
356 Presb Ch Amer	1	0	0	0	-	-
370 Ref Baptist Chs	1	NR	NR	NR	-	-
371 Ref Ch in Am	13	586	507	965	.2	.3

Religious Group	Number of Churches, Synagogues, Mosques, or Temples	Number of Communicant, Confirmed, or Full Members	Number of Attendees	Total Adherents: Number of Adherents	Total Adherents: % of Total Pop.	Total Adherents: % of Total Adh.
400 Rus Orth Moscow	1	NR	NR	NR	-	-
403 Salvation Army	3	390	219	1,065	.2	.3
413 S.D.A.	14	1,624	NR	1,932	.3	.5
419 So Bapt Conv	4	1,050	811	1,277 *	.2	.3
431 Ukrainian Orth	1	NR	NR	180	-	-
449 Un Methodist	18	1,128	571	1,372 *	.2	.4
467 Wesleyan	1	119	169	550	.1	.1
496 Jewish Est	9	NR	NR	12,500	2.1	3.3
HUNTERDON	**106**	**12,054**	**7,543**	**64,208 ***	**52.6**	**100.0**
019 Amer Bapt USA	8	907	432	1,139 *	.9	1.8
053 Assemb of God	5	710	782	1,073	.9	1.7
056 Baha'i	0	18	NR	18	-	-
071 Brethren (Ash)	1	5	21	6 *	-	-
081 Catholic	13	NR	NR	43,566	35.7	67.9
089 Chr & Miss Al	1	0	NR	122	.1	.2
097 Chr Chs&Chs Cr	1	85	NR	107 *	.1	.2
151 L-D Saints	1	NR	NR	307	.3	.5
157 Ch of Brethren	1	124	0	156 *	.1	.2
165 Ch of Nazarene	1	35	60	71	.1	.1
179 Consrv Bapt	2	NR	480	480	.4	.7
193 Episcopal	4	NR	544	1,480	1.2	2.3
203 Evan Free Ch	1	74	180	180	.1	.3
207 E.L.C.A.	3	764	357	1,026	.8	1.6
226 Friends-USA	1	105	NR	132 *	.1	.2
283 Luth—MO Synod	2	964	378	1,356	1.1	2.1
331 OCA: Ter Diocs	1	34	NR	56	-	.1
335 Orth Pres Ch	1	34	29	56	-	.1
355 Presb Ch (USA)	17	3,923	1,891	4,926 *	4.0	7.7
356 Presb Ch Amer	1	13	15	15	-	-
370 Ref Baptist Chs	1	NR	NR	NR	-	-
371 Ref Ch in Am	8	1,069	766	2,165	1.8	3.4
413 S.D.A.	1	0	NR	0	-	-
419 So Bapt Conv	1	153	120	192 *	.2	.3
435 Unitarian-Univ	1	60	NR	75 *	.1	.1
443 Un C of Christ	1	303	80	380 *	.3	.6
449 Un Methodist	22	2,674	1,233	3,357 *	2.8	5.2
467 Wesleyan	2	0	175	267	.2	.4
496 Jewish Est	4	NR	NR	1,500	1.2	2.3
MERCER	**213**	**28,563**	**18,112**	**178,051 ***	**50.8**	**100.0**
019 Amer Bapt USA	19	5,066	1,849	6,247 *	1.8	3.5
053 Assemb of God	12	1,147	1,117	1,938	.6	1.1
056 Baha'i	4	199	NR	199	.1	.1
081 Catholic	35	NR	NR	109,306	31.2	61.4
084 Calvary Chapel	1	NR	NR	NR	-	-
089 Chr & Miss Al	3	84	NR	260	.1	.1
097 Chr Chs&Chs Cr	1	225	NR	277 *	.1	.2
123 Ch God (Ander)	2	NR	160	160	-	.1
127 Ch God (Cleve)	5	836	600	1,032 *	.3	.6
145 Ch God Prophcy	1	46	NR	56 *	-	-
151 L-D Saints	2	NR	NR	781	.2	.4
165 Ch of Nazarene	2	225	133	233	.1	.1
167 Chs of Christ	3	420	480	560	.2	.3
179 Consrv Bapt	4	NR	525	525	.1	.3
193 Episcopal	11	NR	1,954	6,827	1.9	3.8
207 E.L.C.A.	11	2,866	1,189	4,093	1.2	2.3
226 Friends-USA	3	315	NR	388 *	.1	.2
246 Greek Orthodox	1	NR	NR	1,407	.4	.8
252 Hindu	1	NR	NR	NR	-	-
262 Int Cou Comm Ch	2	310	NR	382 *	.1	.2
267 Muslim Est	4	NR	3,236	11,673	3.3	6.6
283 Luth—MO Synod	4	660	341	924	.3	.5
288 Mennonite USA	2	110	96	136 *	-	.1
304 NatPrimBapt USA	1	319	NR	393 *	.1	.2
331 OCA: Ter Diocs	1	169	NR	233	.1	.1
335 Orth Pres Ch	1	47	45	62	-	-
355 Presb Ch (USA)	21	8,032	3,020	9,904 *	2.8	5.6
356 Presb Ch Amer	2	235	502	506	.1	.3
371 Ref Ch in Am	1	107	57	190	.1	.1
388 Reg Bapt Gen As	1	262	475	475 *	.1	.3
401 Rus Orth Abroad	1	NR	NR	NR	-	-
403 Salvation Army	2	75	61	187	.1	.1

NR–Not Reported *Total adherents estimated from known number of communicant, confirmed, full members. - Represents a percentage less than 0.1. Percentages may not total 100 due to rounding.

Table 4: Religious Congregations by County and Group: 2000

Religious Group	Number of Churches, Synagogues, Mosques, or Temples	Number of Communicant, Confirmed, or Full Members	Number of Attendees	Total Adherents		
				Number of Adherents	% of Total Pop.	% of Total Adh.
413 S.D.A.	7	1,043	NR	1,242	.4	.7
431 Ukrainian Orth	2	NR	NR	1,215	.3	.7
435 Unitarian-Univ	3	710	NR	876 *	.2	.5
443 Un C of Christ	1	107	47	132 *	-	.1
449 Un Methodist	19	4,648	1,925	5,732 *	1.6	3.2
496 Jewish Est	16	NR	NR	9,100	2.6	5.1
499 Indep.Non-Char	1	300	300	400	.1	.2
MIDDLESEX	**313**	**30,368**	**17,135**	**449,216 ***	**59.9**	**100.0**
019 Amer Bapt USA	14	5,180	1,877	6,369 *	.8	1.4
022 Carp Rus Orth	1	430	NR	730	.1	.2
034 Ant Orth of NA	1	66	NR	132	-	-
053 Assemb of God	10	1,472	1,476	1,760	.2	.4
056 Baha'i	0	92	NR	92	-	-
059 Bapt Miss Assn	1	22	30	30 *	-	-
076 Buddhism	2	NR	NR	NR	-	-
081 Catholic	71	NR	NR	343,095	45.7	76.4
084 Calvary Chapel	1	NR	NR	NR	-	-
089 Chr & Miss Al	6	731	NR	2,561	.3	.6
093 Chr Ch (Disc)	2	0	0	0 *	-	-
127 Ch God (Cleve)	3	220	40	271 *	-	.1
151 L-D Saints	8	NR	NR	1,668	.2	.4
165 Ch of Nazarene	2	81	45	101	-	-
167 Chs of Christ	2	99	121	134	-	-
173 Comm of Christ	1	55	NR	55	-	-
179 Consrv Bapt	4	NR	876	876	.1	.2
193 Episcopal	19	NR	2,038	5,477	.7	1.2
201 Evan Cov Ch	2	239	122	294 *	-	.1
207 E.L.C.A.	14	3,068	1,097	4,108	.5	.9
226 Friends-USA	2	100	NR	123 *	-	-
246 Greek Orthodox	2	NR	NR	3,045	.4	.7
252 Hindu	8	NR	NR	NR	-	-
267 Muslim Est	3	NR	1,224	6,982	.9	1.6
268 Jain	1	NR	NR	NR	-	-
283 Luth—MO Synod	4	1,738	788	2,486	.3	.6
290 Metro Comm Ch	1	19	27	27 *	-	-
304 NatPrimBapt USA	1	57	NR	70 *	-	-
313 N Am Bapt Conf	1	73	100	90 *	-	-
331 OCA: Ter Diocs	3	364	NR	502	.1	.1
334 Malan Syr Orth	1	40	NR	200	-	-
349 Pent Holiness	1	71	68	87 *	-	-
355 Presb Ch (USA)	23	6,048	2,727	7,435 *	1.0	1.7
356 Presb Ch Amer	2	53	0	65	-	-
371 Ref Ch in Am	12	1,294	830	2,929	.4	.7
401 Rus Orth Abroad	1	NR	NR	NR	-	-
403 Salvation Army	2	203	98	459	.1	.1
413 S.D.A.	12	1,381	NR	1,642	.2	.4
418 Southw Bapt Fel	3	NR	NR	NR	-	-
419 So Bapt Conv	8	741	405	911 *	.1	.2
431 Ukrainian Orth	2	NR	NR	1,500	.2	.3
435 Unitarian-Univ	1	226	NR	278 *	-	.1
443 Un C of Christ	7	1,218	425	1,497 *	.2	.3
449 Un Methodist	20	4,893	2,656	6,013 *	.8	1.3
469 WELS	1	94	65	122	-	-
496 Jewish Est	27	NR	NR	45,000	6.0	10.0
MONMOUTH	**305**	**35,824**	**22,046**	**424,763 ***	**69.0**	**100.0**
017 Amer Bapt Assn	1	20	NR	25 *	-	-
019 Amer Bapt USA	20	4,254	1,570	5,358 *	.9	1.3
022 Carp Rus Orth	1	122	NR	207	-	-
050 Armen Ap Etchm	2	141	NR	1,980	.3	.5
053 Assemb of God	16	1,613	1,898	2,620	.4	.6
056 Baha'i	1	97	NR	97	-	-
076 Buddhism	2	NR	NR	NR	-	-
081 Catholic	50	NR	NR	289,183	47.0	68.1
084 Calvary Chapel	1	NR	NR	NR	-	-
097 Chr Chs&Chs Cr	1	125	NR	157 *	-	-
123 Ch God (Ander)	2	NR	48	48	-	-
127 Ch God (Cleve)	4	467	441	645 *	.1	.2
145 Ch God Prophcy	2	91	NR	116 *	-	-
151 L-D Saints	3	NR	NR	1,234	.2	.3
165 Ch of Nazarene	1	55	35	55	-	-
167 Chs of Christ	2	282	300	289	-	.1
179 Consrv Bapt	5	NR	485	485	.1	.1
193 Episcopal	22	NR	2,617	6,858	1.1	1.6
203 Evan Free Ch	2	98	225	225	-	.1
207 E.L.C.A.	11	5,294	1,734	8,028	1.3	1.9
221 Free Methodist	1	29	45	45	-	-
226 Friends-USA	2	100	NR	126 *	-	-
246 Greek Orthodox	2	NR	NR	2,232	.4	.5
252 Hindu	3	NR	NR	NR	-	-
265 Int Pent C Chr	1	46	27	90	-	-
267 Muslim Est	5	NR	2,060	9,455	1.5	2.2
283 Luth—MO Synod	3	865	346	1,203	.2	.3
304 NatPrimBapt USA	1	29	NR	37 *	-	-
355 Presb Ch (USA)	22	6,560	3,033	8,264 *	1.3	1.9
356 Presb Ch Amer	2	140	181	233	-	.1
371 Ref Ch in Am	9	1,305	802	2,750	.4	.6
401 Rus Orth Abroad	3	NR	NR	NR	-	-
403 Salvation Army	2	382	283	828	.1	.2
413 S.D.A.	2	185	NR	220	-	.1
419 So Bapt Conv	5	1,134	760	1,428 *	.2	.3
435 Unitarian-Univ	1	359	NR	452 *	.1	.1
443 Un C of Christ	2	316	151	398 *	.1	.1
449 Un Methodist	47	10,315	4,405	12,992 *	2.1	3.1
496 Jewish Est	42	NR	NR	65,000	10.6	15.3
498 Indep.Charis.	1	1,400	600	1,400	.2	.3
MORRIS	**262**	**29,696**	**17,566**	**267,563 ***	**56.9**	**100.0**
019 Amer Bapt USA	6	802	274	1,001 *	.2	.4
022 Carp Rus Orth	1	122	NR	207	-	.1
053 Assemb of God	10	529	597	723	.2	.3
056 Baha'i	0	66	NR	66	-	-
076 Buddhism	1	NR	NR	NR	-	-
081 Catholic	50	NR	NR	179,017	38.1	66.9
089 Chr & Miss Al	8	1,098	NR	2,931	.6	1.1
097 Chr Chs&Chs Cr	1	120	NR	150 *	-	.1
105 Christian Ref	1	87	77	109 *	-	-
123 Ch God (Ander)	1	NR	11	11	-	-
127 Ch God (Cleve)	4	218	95	272 *	.1	.1
151 L-D Saints	5	NR	NR	1,285	.3	.5
165 Ch of Nazarene	2	226	134	234	-	.1
167 Chs of Christ	5	245	295	375	.1	.1
175 Congr Chr Chs	2	240	177	300 *	.1	.1
179 Consrv Bapt	1	NR	800	800	.2	.3
193 Episcopal	20	NR	2,301	7,768	1.7	2.9
203 Evan Free Ch	4	423	725	725	.2	.3
207 E.L.C.A.	12	3,000	1,362	4,153	.9	1.6
221 Free Methodist	1	21	30	30	-	-
226 Friends-USA	2	100	NR	125 *	-	-
246 Greek Orthodox	1	NR	NR	840	.2	.3
252 Hindu	5	NR	NR	NR	-	-
262 Int Cou Comm Ch	1	190	NR	237 *	.1	.1
263 Int Foursq Gos	1	39	441	441 *	.1	.2
267 Muslim Est	2	NR	482	2,141	.5	.8
283 Luth—MO Synod	4	918	384	1,161	.2	.4
288 Mennonite USA	1	34	50	50 *	-	-
331 OCA: Ter Diocs	1	168	NR	254	.1	.1
333 Malan Dioc Am	1	NR	NR	125	-	-
335 Orth Pres Ch	1	58	70	81	-	-
355 Presb Ch (USA)	32	9,514	3,868	11,876 *	2.5	4.4
356 Presb Ch Amer	2	60	130	145	-	.1
370 Ref Baptist Chs	1	NR	NR	NR	-	-
371 Ref Ch in Am	5	1,000	753	2,285	.5	.9
388 Reg Bapt Gen As	1	50	30	62 *	-	-
403 Salvation Army	2	72	39	326	.1	.1
413 S.D.A.	4	298	NR	355	.1	.1
419 So Bapt Conv	3	478	236	597 *	.1	.2
435 Unitarian-Univ	1	331	NR	413 *	.1	.2
443 Un C of Christ	3	1,139	525	1,422 *	.3	.5
449 Un Methodist	31	7,591	2,882	9,473 *	2.0	3.5
455 Un Ref Chs N.A.	1	362	NR	639	.1	.2
469 WELS	1	97	73	133	-	-
496 Jewish Est	19	NR	NR	33,500	7.1	12.5
499 Indep.Non-Char	1	0	725	725	.2	.3

NR–Not Reported   *Total adherents estimated from known number of communicant, confirmed, full members.   - Represents a percentage less than 0.1.   Percentages may not total 100 due to rounding.

Table 4: Religious Congregations by County and Group: 2000

Religious Group	Number of Churches, Synagogues, Mosques, or Temples	Number of Communicant, Confirmed, or Full Members	Number of Attendees	Total Adherents		
				Number of Adherents	% of Total Pop.	% of Total Adh.
OCEAN	**193**	**24,554**	**15,721**	**266,614 ***	**52.2**	**100.0**
019 Amer Bapt USA	5	1,093	630	1,340 *	.3	.5
053 Assemb of God	9	1,172	1,414	3,079	.6	1.2
056 Baha'i	0	49	NR	49	-	-
081 Catholic	33	NR	NR	212,482	41.6	79.7
084 Calvary Chapel	2	NR	NR	NR	-	-
089 Chr & Miss Al	5	103	NR	324	.1	.1
097 Chr Chs&Chs Cr	1	45	NR	55 *	-	-
127 Ch God (Cleve)	2	222	126	272 *	.1	.1
151 L-D Saints	2	NR	NR	537	.1	.2
165 Ch of Nazarene	1	113	112	285	.1	.1
167 Chs of Christ	2	95	106	135	-	.1
179 Consrv Bapt	6	NR	1,374	1,374	.3	.5
193 Episcopal	12	NR	1,533	5,539	1.1	2.1
203 Evan Free Ch	1	284	227	284	.1	.1
207 E.L.C.A.	11	4,517	1,829	6,731	1.3	2.5
226 Friends-USA	1	105	NR	129 *	-	-
246 Greek Orthodox	1	NR	NR	1,065	.2	.4
267 Muslim Est	1	NR	90	400	.1	.2
283 Luth—MO Synod	5	1,109	724	1,346	.3	.5
331 OCA: Ter Diocs	2	196	NR	290	.1	.1
335 Orth Pres Ch	1	38	40	50	-	-
355 Presb Ch (USA)	11	5,294	2,124	6,489 *	1.3	2.4
371 Ref Ch in Am	3	932	701	1,350	.3	.5
388 Reg Bapt Gen As	2	294	410	398 *	.1	.1
401 Rus Orth Abroad	1	NR	NR	NR	-	-
403 Salvation Army	1	77	76	228	-	.1
413 S.D.A.	3	398	NR	473	.1	.2
418 Southw Bapt Fel	1	NR	NR	NR	-	-
419 So Bapt Conv	2	254	250	311 *	.1	.1
435 Unitarian-Univ	1	67	NR	82 *	-	-
443 Un C of Christ	1	68	35	83 *	-	-
449 Un Methodist	28	7,779	3,520	9,534 *	1.9	3.6
496 Jewish Est	35	NR	NR	11,500	2.3	4.3
498 Indep.Charis.	1	250	400	400	.1	.2
PASSAIC	**262**	**21,961**	**22,085**	**241,033 ***	**49.3**	**100.0**
019 Amer Bapt USA	23	3,589	2,459	4,528 *	.9	1.9
034 Ant Orth of NA	1	618	NR	1,236	.3	.5
053 Assemb of God	12	2,192	2,640	5,349	1.1	2.2
056 Baha'i	2	121	NR	121	-	.1
081 Catholic	51	NR	NR	160,279	32.8	66.5
089 Chr & Miss Al	2	41	NR	226	-	.1
105 Christian Ref	8	1,629	1,286	2,055 *	.4	.9
123 Ch God (Ander)	2	NR	102	102	-	-
127 Ch God (Cleve)	8	1,031	1,354	1,488 *	.3	.6
145 Ch God Prophcy	2	97	NR	123 *	-	.1
151 L-D Saints	5	NR	NR	1,621	.3	.7
165 Ch of Nazarene	5	486	354	620	.1	.3
179 Consrv Bapt	3	NR	240	240	-	.1
193 Episcopal	11	NR	858	2,769	.6	1.1
203 Evan Free Ch	1	54	102	102	-	-
207 E.L.C.A.	2	527	240	750	.2	.3
221 Free Methodist	2	280	416	551	.1	.2
246 Greek Orthodox	1	NR	NR	777	.2	.3
252 Hindu	4	NR	NR	NR	-	-
267 Muslim Est	12	NR	6,120	22,410	4.6	9.3
283 Luth—MO Synod	7	1,286	574	1,596	.3	.7
291 Missionary Ch	1	38	51	51	-	-
307 Neth Ref Congr	1	101	NR	179	-	.1
330 Macedonian Orth	1	NR	NR	1,800	.4	.7
331 OCA: Ter Diocs	3	574	NR	664	.1	.3
339 Pent Ch of God	1	162	NR	207	-	.1
355 Presb Ch (USA)	12	2,344	1,183	2,968 *	.6	1.2
370 Ref Baptist Chs	1	NR	NR	NR	-	-
371 Ref Ch in Am	19	1,935	1,718	3,622	.7	1.5
400 Rus Orth Moscow	2	NR	NR	NR	-	-
401 Rus Orth Abroad	2	NR	NR	NR	-	-
403 Salvation Army	2	178	75	537	.1	.2
413 S.D.A.	7	937	NR	1,115	.2	.5
419 So Bapt Conv	4	500	392	631 *	.1	.3
431 Ukrainian Orth	2	NR	NR	777	.2	.3
435 Unitarian-Univ	1	24	NR	30 *	-	-
443 Un C of Christ	3	516	255	651 *	.1	.3
449 Un Methodist	17	2,575	1,216	3,249 *	.7	1.3
455 Un Ref Chs N.A.	1	126	NR	159	-	.1
467 Wesleyan	1	0	0	0	-	-
496 Jewish Est	16	NR	NR	17,000	3.5	7.1
499 Indep.Non-Char	1	0	450	450	.1	.2
SALEM	**71**	**7,912**	**4,973**	**19,360 ***	**30.1**	**100.0**
019 Amer Bapt USA	5	1,387	459	1,720 *	2.7	8.9
053 Assemb of God	5	372	488	646	1.0	3.3
056 Baha'i	0	3	NR	3	-	-
081 Catholic	6	NR	NR	7,545	11.7	39.0
127 Ch God (Cleve)	3	91	47	117 *	.2	.6
151 L-D Saints	1	NR	NR	195	.3	1.0
165 Ch of Nazarene	3	203	199	387	.6	2.0
179 Consrv Bapt	2	NR	290	290	.5	1.5
193 Episcopal	4	NR	338	931	1.4	4.8
207 E.L.C.A.	2	485	185	640	1.0	3.3
223 Free Will Bapt	1	0	NR	0 *	-	-
226 Friends-USA	1	105	NR	130 *	.2	.7
283 Luth—MO Synod	1	29	18	35	.1	.2
288 Mennonite USA	3	88	115	135 *	.2	.7
335 Orth Pres Ch	1	208	248	339	.5	1.8
355 Presb Ch (USA)	5	1,221	525	1,515 *	2.4	7.8
413 S.D.A.	2	204	NR	243	.4	1.3
449 Un Methodist	25	3,516	2,001	4,362 *	6.8	22.5
467 Wesleyan	1	0	60	127	.2	.7
SOMERSET	**147**	**24,202**	**15,155**	**170,690 ***	**57.4**	**100.0**
019 Amer Bapt USA	4	5,034	1,836	6,351 *	2.1	3.7
022 Carp Rus Orth	1	122	NR	207	.1	.1
053 Assemb of God	6	1,100	1,293	1,494	.5	.9
056 Baha'i	0	56	NR	56	-	-
076 Buddhism	1	NR	NR	NR	-	-
081 Catholic	27	NR	NR	118,638	39.9	69.5
084 Calvary Chapel	2	NR	NR	NR	-	-
089 Chr & Miss Al	2	245	NR	557	.2	.3
093 Chr Ch (Disc)	1	6	5	8 *	-	-
127 Ch God (Cleve)	1	19	15	24 *	-	-
151 L-D Saints	3	NR	NR	539	.2	.3
167 Chs of Christ	1	84	110	125	-	.1
175 Congr Chr Chs	2	283	150	357 *	.1	.2
179 Consrv Bapt	2	NR	730	730	.2	.4
193 Episcopal	7	NR	1,088	3,299	1.1	1.9
203 Evan Free Ch	1	216	435	435	.1	.3
207 E.L.C.A.	3	1,206	538	1,775	.6	1.0
226 Friends-USA	1	50	NR	63 *	-	-
252 Hindu	4	NR	NR	NR	-	-
262 Int Cou Comm Ch	2	1,390	NR	1,754 *	.6	1.0
267 Muslim Est	1	NR	412	1,891	.6	1.1
283 Luth—MO Synod	4	842	357	1,062	.4	.6
306 NT IndBapt&Rltd	1	23	NR	29 *	-	-
331 OCA: Ter Diocs	2	125	NR	180	.1	.1
349 Pent Holiness	1	142	110	179 *	.1	.1
355 Presb Ch (USA)	14	5,014	2,456	6,348 *	2.1	3.7
356 Presb Ch Amer	3	181	230	282	.1	.2
371 Ref Ch in Am	17	2,537	1,507	5,471	1.8	3.2
401 Rus Orth Abroad	1	NR	NR	NR	-	-
416 Sikh	1	NR	NR	NR	-	-
419 So Bapt Conv	3	632	224	797 *	.3	.5
435 Unitarian-Univ	1	172	NR	217 *	.1	.1
443 Un C of Christ	2	199	109	251 *	.1	.1
449 Un Methodist	15	3,624	1,650	4,571 *	1.5	2.7
496 Jewish Est	9	NR	NR	11,100	3.7	6.5
499 Indep.Non-Char	1	900	1,900	1,900	.6	1.1
SUSSEX	**84**	**9,752**	**5,563**	**64,150 ***	**44.5**	**100.0**
019 Amer Bapt USA	3	354	191	452 *	.3	.7
053 Assemb of God	5	368	298	510	.4	.8
056 Baha'i	0	11	NR	11	-	-
076 Buddhism	2	NR	NR	NR	-	-
081 Catholic	16	NR	NR	44,729	31.0	69.7
089 Chr & Miss Al	2	88	NR	158	.1	.2

NR–Not Reported *Total adherents estimated from known number of communicant, confirmed, full members. - Represents a percentage less than 0.1. Percentages may not total 100 due to rounding.

Table 4: Religious Congregations by County and Group: 2000

Religious Group	Number of Churches, Synagogues, Mosques, or Temples	Number of Communicant, Confirmed, or Full Members	Number of Attendees	Total Adherents		
				Number of Adherents	% of Total Pop.	% of Total Adh.
097 Chr Chs&Chs Cr	1	55	NR	70 *	-	.1
105 Christian Ref	1	411	250	525 *	.4	.8
151 L-D Saints	1	NR	NR	421	.3	.7
175 Congr Chr Chs	1	120	90	153 *	.1	.2
179 Consrv Bapt	2	NR	130	130	.1	.2
193 Episcopal	4	NR	534	1,545	1.1	2.4
203 Evan Free Ch	2	106	280	280	.2	.4
207 E.L.C.A.	2	726	368	1,116	.8	1.7
283 Luth—MO Synod	3	818	395	1,168	.8	1.8
331 OCA: Ter Diocs	1	62	NR	88	.1	.1
355 Presb Ch (USA)	12	2,999	1,452	3,832 *	2.7	6.0
370 Ref Baptist Chs	1	NR	NR	NR	-	-
371 Ref Ch in Am	2	116	143	246	.2	.4
388 Reg Bapt Gen As	1	45	60	60 *	-	.1
413 S.D.A.	1	216	NR	257	.2	.4
419 So Bapt Conv	1	9	25	12 *	-	-
435 Unitarian-Univ	1	47	NR	60 *	-	.1
449 Un Methodist	13	3,135	1,309	4,007 *	2.8	6.2
455 Un Ref Chs N.A.	1	66	NR	124	.1	.2
467 Wesleyan	1	0	38	96	.1	.1
496 Jewish Est	4	NR	NR	4,100	2.8	6.4
UNION	**262**	**33,550**	**17,160**	**342,107 ***	**65.5**	**100.0**
019 Amer Bapt USA	24	7,992	2,131	9,964 *	1.9	2.9
022 Carp Rus Orth	2	243	NR	416	.1	.1
053 Assemb of God	16	2,167	2,422	3,923	.8	1.1
056 Baha'i	0	54	NR	54	-	-
057 Bapt Gen Conf	1	150	80	187 *	-	.1
081 Catholic	46	NR	NR	251,815	48.2	73.6
089 Chr & Miss Al	5	319	NR	630	.1	.2
097 Chr Chs&Chs Cr	1	60	NR	75 *	-	-
123 Ch God (Ander)	3	NR	235	235	-	.1
127 Ch God (Cleve)	7	456	364	588 *	.1	.2
145 Ch God Prophcy	2	97	NR	121 *	-	-
151 L-D Saints	6	NR	NR	2,132	.4	.6
165 Ch of Nazarene	4	176	144	191	-	.1
167 Chs of Christ	3	119	95	138	-	-
179 Consrv Bapt	3	NR	256	256	-	.1
193 Episcopal	17	NR	2,157	6,705	1.3	2.0
207 E.L.C.A.	13	3,207	1,439	4,299	.8	1.3
226 Friends-USA	1	50	NR	62 *	-	-
246 Greek Orthodox	3	NR	NR	3,432	.7	1.0
252 Hindu	1	NR	NR	NR	-	-
263 Int Foursq Gos	2	290	242	362 *	.1	.1
267 Muslim Est	2	NR	487	2,041	.4	.6
283 Luth—MO Synod	5	1,106	523	1,431	.3	.4
293 Morav Ch-North	1	69	NR	82	-	-
331 OCA: Ter Diocs	1	35	NR	131	-	-
335 Orth Pres Ch	1	91	72	133	-	-
349 Pent Holiness	1	138	108	172 *	-	.1
355 Presb Ch (USA)	30	9,486	3,807	11,826 *	2.3	3.5
371 Ref Ch in Am	1	108	95	217	-	.1
400 Rus Orth Moscow	1	NR	NR	NR	-	-
403 Salvation Army	2	153	75	281	.1	.1
410 Serb Orth USA	2	NR	NR	1,400	.3	.4
411 Serb Orth: Grac	1	NR	NR	NR	-	-
413 S.D.A.	8	657	NR	783	.1	.2
418 Southw Bapt Fel	1	NR	NR	NR	-	-
419 So Bapt Conv	3	319	155	398 *	.1	.1
435 Unitarian-Univ	2	644	NR	803 *	.2	.2
443 Un C of Christ	5	1,337	594	1,667 *	.3	.5
449 Un Methodist	17	4,027	1,647	5,022 *	1.0	1.5
467 Wesleyan	2	0	32	35	-	-
496 Jewish Est	16	NR	NR	30,100	5.8	8.8
WARREN	**102**	**11,395**	**6,495**	**49,015 ***	**47.8**	**100.0**
053 Assemb of God	4	369	472	476	.5	1.0
056 Baha'i	0	15	NR	15	-	-
076 Buddhism	1	NR	NR	NR	-	-
081 Catholic	12	NR	NR	30,940	30.2	63.1
089 Chr & Miss Al	3	236	NR	900	.9	1.8
165 Ch of Nazarene	1	32	70	86	.1	.2
167 Chs of Christ	1	40	40	50	-	.1
179 Consrv Bapt	2	NR	280	280	.3	.6
193 Episcopal	6	NR	578	1,768	1.7	3.6
203 Evan Free Ch	1	125	301	301	.3	.6
207 E.L.C.A.	5	1,806	476	2,654	2.6	5.4
252 Hindu	2	NR	NR	NR	-	-
268 Jain	1	NR	NR	NR	-	-
283 Luth—MO Synod	2	398	207	542	.5	1.1
288 Mennonite USA	2	94	153	158 *	.2	.3
297 Mennonite;Other	1	48	NR	60 *	.1	.1
331 OCA: Ter Diocs	1	80	NR	99	.1	.2
335 Orth Pres Ch	3	319	378	444	.4	.9
355 Presb Ch (USA)	17	3,129	1,400	3,941 *	3.8	8.0
356 Presb Ch Amer	1	112	110	147	.1	.3
388 Reg Bapt Gen As	2	91	113	114 *	.1	.2
400 Rus Orth Moscow	1	NR	NR	NR	-	-
413 S.D.A.	6	426	NR	508	.5	1.0
435 Unitarian-Univ	1	37	NR	47 *	-	.1
443 Un C of Christ	1	104	141	131 *	.1	.3
449 Un Methodist	23	3,934	1,776	4,954 *	4.8	10.1
496 Jewish Est	2	NR	NR	400	.4	.8

NEW MEXICO

Religious Group	Number of Churches, Synagogues, Mosques, or Temples	Number of Communicant, Confirmed, or Full Members	Number of Attendees	Total Adherents		
				Number of Adherents	% of Total Pop.	% of Total Adh.
The State.....	2,026	230,984	130,959	1,057,828 *	58.2	100.0
BERNALILLO	**321**	**57,620**	**45,575**	**304,429 ***	**54.7**	**100.0**
017 Amer Bapt Assn	1	109	NR	136 *	-	-
019 Amer Bapt USA	2	431	223	536 *	.1	.2
034 Ant Orth of NA	1	37	NR	74	-	-
050 Armen Ap Etchm	1	0	NR	182	-	.1
053 Assemb of God	23	3,479	4,214	5,345	1.0	1.8
056 Baha'i	3	593	NR	593	.1	.2
075 Brethren in Cr	1	34	32	34	-	-
076 Buddhism	11	NR	NR	NR	-	-
081 Catholic	44	NR	NR	191,463	34.4	62.9
084 Calvary Chapel	3	NR	NR	NR	-	-
093 Chr Ch (Disc)	4	1,330	594	1,655 *	.3	.5
097 Chr Chs&Chs Cr	5	1,326	NR	1,650 *	.3	.5
105 Christian Ref	3	235	267	292 *	.1	.1
123 Ch God (Ander)	3	NR	242	242	-	.1
127 Ch God (Cleve)	3	293	200	366 *	.1	.1
145 Ch God Prophcy	2	70	NR	88 *	-	-
151 L-D Saints	25	NR	NR	8,564	1.5	2.8
165 Ch of Nazarene	9	1,169	903	1,464	.3	.5
167 Chs of Christ	14	2,169	2,386	2,735	.5	.9
173 Comm of Christ	2	177	NR	177	-	.1
179 Consrv Bapt	2	NR	280	280	.1	.1
183 Cons Menn Conf	2	96	117	140	-	-
185 Cumber Presb	1	974	NR	2,516	.5	.8
186 Coptic Orth Ch	1	NR	NR	NR	-	-
193 Episcopal	8	NR	1,772	4,881	.9	1.6
203 Evan Free Ch	1	220	400	400	.1	.1
207 E.L.C.A.	9	5,426	2,471	7,673	1.4	2.5
223 Free Will Bapt	1	11	NR	14 *	-	-
226 Friends-USA	1	30	NR	37 *	-	-
246 Greek Orthodox	1	NR	NR	711	.1	.2
263 Int Foursq Gos	5	1,137	698	1,415 *	.3	.5
264 Int Chs of Crst	1	190	293	284	.1	.1
267 Muslim Est	3	NR	468	1,827	.3	.6
283 Luth—MO Synod	8	1,681	1,012	2,230	.4	.7
288 Mennonite USA	1	27	55	55 *	-	-
290 Metro Comm Ch	2	141	156	175 *	-	.1
306 NT IndBapt&Rltd	1	175	NR	218 *	-	.1
331 OCA: Ter Diocs	1	46	NR	148	-	-
335 Orth Pres Ch	1	50	60	63	-	-
339 Pent Ch of God	2	145	NR	200	-	.1
349 Pent Holiness	2	97	54	121 *	-	-
355 Presb Ch (USA)	11	4,100	2,548	5,101 *	.9	1.7
356 Presb Ch Amer	1	104	100	139	-	-
360 Prim Bapt Chrch	1	NR	NR	NR	-	-
370 Ref Baptist Chs	1	NR	NR	NR	-	-
388 Reg Bapt Gen As	1	32	50	50 *	-	-
403 Salvation Army	2	311	158	1,049	.2	.3

NR–Not Reported *Total adherents estimated from known number of communicant, confirmed, full members. - Represents a percentage less than 0.1. Percentages may not total 100 due to rounding.

Table 4: Religious Congregations by County and Group: 2000

Religious Group	Number of Churches, Synagogues, Mosques, or Temples	Number of Communicant, Confirmed, or Full Members	Number of Attendees	Total Adherents: Number of Adherents	Total Adherents: % of Total Pop.	Total Adherents: % of Total Adh.
413 S.D.A.	9	1,898	NR	2,260	.4	.7
416 Sikh	1	NR	NR	NR	-	-
419 So Bapt Conv	45	17,953	8,425	22,337 *	4.0	7.3
435 Unitarian-Univ	3	630	NR	784 *	.1	.3
443 Un C of Christ	4	720	365	896 *	.2	.3
449 Un Methodist	18	9,099	4,229	11,321 *	2.0	3.7
463 Vineyard	1	130	120	162 *	-	.1
467 Wesleyan	2	49	82	87	-	-
469 WELS	1	196	151	259	-	.1
496 Jewish Est	4	NR	NR	7,500	1.3	2.5
498 Indep.Charis.	1	500	450	1,500	.3	.5
499 Indep.Non-Char	1	0	12,000	12,000	2.2	3.9
CATRON	**20**	**358**	**212**	**1,578 ***	**44.5**	**100.0**
081 Catholic	5	NR	NR	503	14.2	31.9
127 Ch God (Cleve)	1	16	0	19 *	.5	1.2
151 L-D Saints	3	NR	NR	638	18.0	40.4
167 Chs of Christ	1	14	15	18	.5	1.1
355 Presb Ch (USA)	4	78	82	105 *	3.0	6.7
413 S.D.A.	2	48	NR	58	1.6	3.7
419 So Bapt Conv	4	202	115	237 *	6.7	15.0
CHAVES	**86**	**13,333**	**6,710**	**37,927 ***	**61.8**	**100.0**
017 Amer Bapt Assn	1	16	NR	20 *	-	.1
053 Assemb of God	8	494	497	780	1.3	2.1
056 Baha'i	1	53	NR	53	.1	.1
081 Catholic	6	NR	NR	19,337	31.5	51.0
084 Calvary Chapel	1	NR	NR	NR	-	-
093 Chr Ch (Disc)	1	259	219	331 *	.5	.9
097 Chr Chs&Chs Cr	1	55	NR	70 *	.1	.2
127 Ch God (Cleve)	3	127	85	171 *	.3	.5
145 Ch God Prophcy	1	35	NR	45 *	.1	.1
151 L-D Saints	3	NR	NR	916	1.5	2.4
165 Ch of Nazarene	2	302	168	380	.6	1.0
167 Chs of Christ	11	1,218	949	1,593	2.6	4.2
193 Episcopal	2	NR	158	525	.9	1.4
203 Evan Free Ch	1	40	85	85	.1	.2
207 E.L.C.A.	1	116	58	160	.3	.4
263 Int Foursq Gos	1	30	50	50 *	.1	.1
283 Luth—MO Synod	1	253	170	303	.5	.8
335 Orth Pres Ch	1	24	19	29	-	.1
339 Pent Ch of God	1	60	NR	90	.1	.2
355 Presb Ch (USA)	4	776	493	991 *	1.6	2.6
360 Prim Bapt Chrch	1	NR	NR	NR	-	-
403 Salvation Army	1	149	58	201	.3	.5
413 S.D.A.	3	189	NR	225	.4	.6
419 So Bapt Conv	18	6,200	1,644	7,920 *	12.9	20.9
449 Un Methodist	7	1,664	734	2,125 *	3.5	5.6
469 WELS	1	23	23	27	-	.1
498 Indep.Charis.	2	600	850	850	1.4	2.2
499 Indep.Non-Char	2	650	450	650	1.1	1.7
CIBOLA	**47**	**2,017**	**851**	**16,183 ***	**63.2**	**100.0**
011 A.W.M.C.	1	9	0	9	-	.1
053 Assemb of God	3	76	104	152	.6	.9
056 Baha'i	0	42	NR	42	.2	.3
081 Catholic	19	NR	NR	11,432	44.7	70.6
127 Ch God (Cleve)	3	245	63	321 *	1.3	2.0
151 L-D Saints	6	NR	NR	1,857	7.3	11.5
165 Ch of Nazarene	4	134	66	257	1.0	1.6
167 Chs of Christ	1	210	225	273	1.1	1.7
193 Episcopal	1	NR	25	82	.3	.5
283 Luth—MO Synod	1	27	22	34	.1	.2
339 Pent Ch of God	4	149	NR	254	1.0	1.6
413 S.D.A.	1	38	NR	45	.2	.3
419 So Bapt Conv	3	1,087	346	1,425 *	5.6	8.8
COLFAX	**40**	**2,478**	**1,314**	**9,802 ***	**69.1**	**100.0**
053 Assemb of God	2	73	75	91	.6	.9
056 Baha'i	0	4	NR	4	-	-
081 Catholic	8	NR	NR	6,573	46.3	67.1
093 Chr Ch (Disc)	2	297	130	363 *	2.6	3.7

Religious Group	Number of Churches, Synagogues, Mosques, or Temples	Number of Communicant, Confirmed, or Full Members	Number of Attendees	Total Adherents: Number of Adherents	Total Adherents: % of Total Pop.	Total Adherents: % of Total Adh.
145 Ch God Prophcy	1	35	NR	43 *	.3	.4
167 Chs of Christ	4	82	136	109	.8	1.1
193 Episcopal	1	NR	23	49	.3	.5
263 Int Foursq Gos	1	46	39	56 *	.4	.6
283 Luth—MO Synod	2	36	30	38	.3	.4
355 Presb Ch (USA)	2	150	105	183 *	1.3	1.9
413 S.D.A.	1	29	NR	35	.2	.4
419 So Bapt Conv	9	1,086	502	1,326 *	9.3	13.5
443 Un C of Christ	1	227	95	277 *	2.0	2.8
449 Un Methodist	5	413	179	505 *	3.6	5.2
496 Jewish Est	1	NR	NR	150	1.1	1.5
CURRY	**57**	**12,590**	**5,099**	**26,557 ***	**59.0**	**100.0**
053 Assemb of God	5	283	310	433	1.0	1.6
056 Baha'i	0	11	NR	11	-	-
059 Bapt Miss Assn	1	12	12	16 *	-	.1
081 Catholic	4	NR	NR	9,194	20.4	34.6
097 Chr Chs&Chs Cr	2	550	NR	719 *	1.6	2.7
123 Ch God (Ander)	1	NR	33	33	.1	.1
127 Ch God (Cleve)	1	66	29	86 *	.2	.3
145 Ch God Prophcy	1	35	NR	46 *	.1	.2
151 L-D Saints	1	NR	NR	489	1.1	1.8
157 Ch of Brethren	1	78	22	102 *	.2	.4
165 Ch of Nazarene	2	497	333	721	1.6	2.7
167 Chs of Christ	8	1,101	1,014	1,495	3.3	5.6
173 Comm of Christ	1	49	NR	49	.1	.2
193 Episcopal	1	NR	81	156	.3	.6
207 E.L.C.A.	1	133	108	188	.4	.7
283 Luth—MO Synod	1	158	79	216	.5	.8
355 Presb Ch (USA)	2	158	133	207 *	.5	.8
360 Prim Bapt Chrch	1	NR	NR	NR	-	-
403 Salvation Army	1	71	23	135	.3	.5
413 S.D.A.	1	104	NR	124	.3	.5
419 So Bapt Conv	15	7,611	2,177	9,951 *	22.1	37.5
449 Un Methodist	6	1,673	745	2,186 *	4.9	8.2
DE BACA	**5**	**884**	**309**	**1,906 ***	**85.1**	**100.0**
056 Baha'i	0	2	NR	2	.1	.1
081 Catholic	1	NR	NR	805	35.9	42.2
167 Chs of Christ	1	150	100	195	8.7	10.2
193 Episcopal	1	NR	7	25	1.1	1.3
419 So Bapt Conv	1	574	111	689 *	30.8	36.1
449 Un Methodist	1	158	91	190 *	8.5	10.0
DONA ANA	**144**	**19,078**	**10,854**	**135,112 ***	**77.3**	**100.0**
053 Assemb of God	21	2,086	2,166	3,226	1.8	2.4
056 Baha'i	2	519	NR	519	.3	.4
059 Bapt Miss Assn	1	49	37	64 *	-	-
076 Buddhism	1	NR	NR	NR	-	-
081 Catholic	27	NR	NR	105,130	60.2	77.8
084 Calvary Chapel	1	NR	NR	NR	-	-
093 Chr Ch (Disc)	1	90	60	117 *	.1	.1
097 Chr Chs&Chs Cr	2	175	NR	227 *	.1	.2
123 Ch God (Ander)	2	NR	95	95	.1	.1
127 Ch God (Cleve)	3	103	117	144 *	.1	.1
145 Ch God Prophcy	3	105	NR	138 *	.1	.1
151 L-D Saints	8	NR	NR	2,725	1.6	2.0
165 Ch of Nazarene	3	151	139	231	.1	.2
167 Chs of Christ	11	1,022	990	1,203	.7	.9
173 Comm of Christ	1	52	NR	52	-	-
193 Episcopal	4	NR	546	1,338	.8	1.0
203 Evan Free Ch	1	86	175	175	.1	.1
207 E.L.C.A.	2	615	308	788	.5	.6
226 Friends-USA	2	60	NR	78 *	-	.1
263 Int Foursq Gos	1	455	403	591 *	.3	.4
264 Int Chs of Crst	1	45	73	58	-	-
267 Muslim Est	1	NR	101	288	.2	.2
283 Luth—MO Synod	1	261	205	331	.2	.2
339 Pent Ch of God	2	185	NR	205	.1	.2
349 Pent Holiness	1	21	16	27 *	-	-
355 Presb Ch (USA)	3	772	435	1,003 *	.6	.7
356 Presb Ch Amer	1	366	244	429	.2	.3
403 Salvation Army	1	140	104	148	.1	.1

NR–Not Reported   *Total adherents estimated from known number of communicant, confirmed, full members.   - Represents a percentage less than 0.1.   Percentages may not total 100 due to rounding.

Table 4: Religious Congregations by County and Group: 2000

Religious Group	Number of Churches, Synagogues, Mosques, or Temples	Number of Communicant, Confirmed, or Full Members	Number of Attendees	Total Adherents		
				Number of Adherents	% of Total Pop.	% of Total Adh.
413 S.D.A.	3	286	NR	341	.2	.3
419 So Bapt Conv	21	7,943	3,039	10,312 *	5.9	7.6
435 Unitarian-Univ	1	141	NR	183 *	.1	.1
449 Un Methodist	7	2,913	1,190	3,781 *	2.2	2.8
463 Vineyard	2	380	360	494 *	.3	.4
469 WELS	1	57	51	71	-	.1
496 Jewish Est	1	NR	NR	600	.3	.4
EDDY	**82**	**15,795**	**6,558**	**38,250 ***	**74.0**	**100.0**
053 Assemb of God	7	808	981	1,367	2.6	3.6
056 Baha'i	0	83	NR	83	.2	.2
059 Bapt Miss Assn	2	107	45	137 *	.3	.4
081 Catholic	6	NR	NR	17,017	32.9	44.5
093 Chr Ch (Disc)	2	338	102	433 *	.8	1.1
097 Chr Chs&Chs Cr	2	150	NR	192 *	.4	.5
127 Ch God (Cleve)	4	253	136	324 *	.6	.8
145 Ch God Prophcy	1	35	NR	45 *	.1	.1
151 L-D Saints	1	NR	NR	313	.6	.8
165 Ch of Nazarene	3	292	195	325	.6	.8
167 Chs of Christ	11	1,699	1,499	2,155	4.2	5.6
173 Comm of Christ	1	42	NR	42	.1	.1
193 Episcopal	2	NR	168	477	.9	1.2
207 E.L.C.A.	1	100	66	121	.2	.3
223 Free Will Bapt	2	22	NR	28 *	.1	.1
226 Friends-USA	1	30	NR	38 *	.1	.1
283 Luth—MO Synod	2	151	106	196	.4	.5
288 Mennonite USA	1	43	52	55 *	.1	.1
355 Presb Ch (USA)	2	336	196	430 *	.8	1.1
360 Prim Bapt Chrch	2	NR	NR	NR	-	-
413 S.D.A.	1	31	NR	37	.1	.1
419 So Bapt Conv	19	9,414	2,205	12,052 *	23.3	31.5
449 Un Methodist	9	1,861	807	2,383 *	4.6	6.2
GRANT	**53**	**3,270**	**1,986**	**27,469 ***	**88.6**	**100.0**
032 Amish; other	1	14	NR	17 *	.1	.1
053 Assemb of God	5	256	352	394	1.3	1.4
056 Baha'i	0	18	NR	18	.1	.1
076 Buddhism	1	NR	NR	NR	-	-
081 Catholic	12	NR	NR	21,701	70.0	79.0
084 Calvary Chapel	1	NR	NR	NR	-	-
127 Ch God (Cleve)	1	54	45	67 *	.2	.2
151 L-D Saints	6	NR	NR	1,395	4.5	5.1
165 Ch of Nazarene	1	35	19	35	.1	.1
167 Chs of Christ	5	216	242	302	1.0	1.1
193 Episcopal	1	NR	82	195	.6	.7
226 Friends-USA	1	30	NR	37 *	.1	.1
263 Int Foursq Gos	1	30	50	50 *	.2	.2
283 Luth—MO Synod	1	76	60	100	.3	.4
355 Presb Ch (USA)	2	206	157	256 *	.8	.9
413 S.D.A.	1	74	NR	88	.3	.3
419 So Bapt Conv	7	1,690	707	2,103 *	6.8	7.7
435 Unitarian-Univ	1	33	NR	41 *	.1	.1
443 Un C of Christ	2	72	50	90 *	.3	.3
449 Un Methodist	3	466	222	580 *	1.9	2.1
GUADALUPE	**20**	**271**	**172**	**4,446 ***	**95.0**	**100.0**
053 Assemb of God	1	55	60	106	2.3	2.4
081 Catholic	14	NR	NR	4,068	86.9	91.5
167 Chs of Christ	2	36	45	53	1.1	1.2
419 So Bapt Conv	2	126	51	153 *	3.3	3.4
449 Un Methodist	1	54	16	66 *	1.4	1.5
HARDING	**8**	**174**	**46**	**657 ***	**81.1**	**100.0**
081 Catholic	5	NR	NR	456	56.3	69.4
093 Chr Ch (Disc)	1	32	0	37 *	4.6	5.6
419 So Bapt Conv	1	120	35	139 *	17.2	21.2
449 Un Methodist	1	22	11	25 *	3.1	3.8
HIDALGO	**15**	**528**	**343**	**5,388 ***	**90.8**	**100.0**
053 Assemb of God	3	139	187	233	3.9	4.3
056 Baha'i	0	12	NR	12	.2	.2
081 Catholic	5	NR	NR	4,261	71.8	79.1

Religious Group	Number of Churches, Synagogues, Mosques, or Temples	Number of Communicant, Confirmed, or Full Members	Number of Attendees	Total Adherents		
				Number of Adherents	% of Total Pop.	% of Total Adh.
097 Chr Chs&Chs Cr	1	50	NR	66 *	1.1	1.2
151 L-D Saints	2	NR	NR	387	6.5	7.2
419 So Bapt Conv	3	218	104	286 *	4.8	5.3
449 Un Methodist	1	109	52	143 *	2.4	2.7
LEA	**100**	**22,265**	**6,456**	**45,252 ***	**81.5**	**100.0**
017 Amer Bapt Assn	2	403	NR	520 *	.9	1.1
053 Assemb of God	11	633	725	1,011	1.8	2.2
056 Baha'i	2	159	NR	159	.3	.4
059 Bapt Miss Assn	1	36	12	46 *	.1	.1
081 Catholic	5	NR	NR	15,614	28.1	34.5
093 Chr Ch (Disc)	1	123	45	159 *	.3	.4
097 Chr Chs&Chs Cr	3	337	NR	435 *	.8	1.0
127 Ch God (Cleve)	6	234	143	320 *	.6	.7
145 Ch God Prophcy	2	70	NR	90 *	.2	.2
151 L-D Saints	1	NR	NR	396	.7	.9
165 Ch of Nazarene	3	157	155	302	.5	.7
167 Chs of Christ	16	1,639	1,277	2,115	3.8	4.7
193 Episcopal	2	NR	94	203	.4	.4
207 E.L.C.A.	1	77	40	92	.2	.2
223 Free Will Bapt	1	11	NR	14 *	-	-
283 Luth—MO Synod	2	169	85	194	.3	.4
349 Pent Holiness	2	69	66	89 *	.2	.2
355 Presb Ch (USA)	3	279	120	361 *	.7	.8
401 Rus Orth Abroad	1	NR	NR	NR	-	-
403 Salvation Army	1	55	47	142	.3	.3
413 S.D.A.	4	92	NR	110	.2	.2
419 So Bapt Conv	24	15,444	2,695	19,939 *	35.9	44.1
449 Un Methodist	6	2,278	952	2,941 *	5.3	6.5
LINCOLN	**37**	**3,217**	**2,334**	**8,962 ***	**46.2**	**100.0**
053 Assemb of God	2	90	110	129	.7	1.4
056 Baha'i	0	25	NR	25	.1	.3
081 Catholic	9	NR	NR	4,359	22.5	48.6
084 Calvary Chapel	1	NR	NR	NR	-	-
093 Chr Ch (Disc)	1	548	185	660 *	3.4	7.4
151 L-D Saints	2	NR	NR	400	2.1	4.5
165 Ch of Nazarene	1	132	143	143	.7	1.6
167 Chs of Christ	3	275	300	346	1.8	3.9
193 Episcopal	1	NR	207	328	1.7	3.7
263 Int Foursq Gos	1	68	49	82 *	.4	.9
283 Luth—MO Synod	1	114	75	125	.6	1.4
355 Presb Ch (USA)	4	205	167	247 *	1.3	2.8
413 S.D.A.	1	29	NR	35	.2	.4
419 So Bapt Conv	7	1,271	856	1,530 *	7.9	17.1
449 Un Methodist	3	460	242	553 *	2.8	6.2
LOS ALAMOS	**29**	**6,589**	**2,620**	**14,996 ***	**81.8**	**100.0**
019 Amer Bapt USA	1	737	297	913 *	5.0	6.1
056 Baha'i	1	58	NR	58	.3	.4
081 Catholic	2	NR	NR	4,939	26.9	32.9
084 Calvary Chapel	1	NR	NR	NR	-	-
089 Chr & Miss Al	1	76	NR	240	1.3	1.6
093 Chr Ch (Disc)	1	684	275	847 *	4.6	5.6
097 Chr Chs&Chs Cr	1	175	NR	217 *	1.2	1.4
151 L-D Saints	2	NR	NR	775	4.2	5.2
165 Ch of Nazarene	1	53	61	61	.3	.4
167 Chs of Christ	1	224	195	310	1.7	2.1
193 Episcopal	1	NR	253	569	3.1	3.8
203 Evan Free Ch	1	26	70	70	.4	.5
207 E.L.C.A.	1	467	257	635	3.5	4.2
226 Friends-USA	1	30	NR	37 *	.2	.2
331 OCA: Ter Diocs	1	5	NR	8	-	.1
355 Presb Ch (USA)	2	231	120	286 *	1.6	1.9
356 Presb Ch Amer	1	78	77	98	.5	.7
371 Ref Ch in Am	1	116	50	188	1.0	1.3
419 So Bapt Conv	2	1,834	355	2,271 *	12.4	15.1
435 Unitarian-Univ	1	160	NR	198 *	1.1	1.3
443 Un C of Christ	1	684	275	847 *	4.6	5.6
449 Un Methodist	2	928	321	1,149 *	6.3	7.7
469 WELS	1	23	14	30	.2	.2
496 Jewish Est	1	NR	NR	250	1.4	1.7

NR–Not Reported *Total adherents estimated from known number of communicant, confirmed, full members. - Represents a percentage less than 0.1. Percentages may not total 100 due to rounding.

Table 4: Religious Congregations by County and Group: 2000

Religious Group	Number of Churches, Synagogues, Mosques, or Temples	Number of Communicant, Confirmed, or Full Members	Number of Attendees	Total Adherents		
				Number of Adherents	% of Total Pop.	% of Total Adh.
LUNA	**28**	**2,404**	**1,269**	**8,845 ***	**35.4**	**100.0**
053 Assemb of God	3	106	115	141	.6	1.6
056 Baha'i	1	82	NR	82	.3	.9
081 Catholic	3	NR	NR	5,398	21.6	61.0
097 Chr Chs&Chs Cr	1	135	NR	175 *	.7	2.0
127 Ch God (Cleve)	1	30	26	39 *	.2	.4
151 L-D Saints	1	NR	NR	294	1.2	3.3
165 Ch of Nazarene	1	52	50	52	.2	.6
167 Chs of Christ	4	178	192	224	.9	2.5
193 Episcopal	1	NR	32	68	.3	.8
263 Int Foursq Gos	1	8	28	28 *	.1	.3
283 Luth—MO Synod	1	93	74	104	.4	1.2
339 Pent Ch of God	1	16	NR	35	.1	.4
355 Presb Ch (USA)	1	77	40	100 *	.4	1.1
413 S.D.A.	1	45	NR	54	.2	.6
419 So Bapt Conv	5	1,053	453	1,365 *	5.5	15.4
449 Un Methodist	2	529	259	686 *	2.7	7.8
MCKINLEY	**81**	**5,719**	**3,477**	**29,745 ***	**39.8**	**100.0**
053 Assemb of God	8	742	604	918	1.2	3.1
056 Baha'i	1	110	NR	110	.1	.4
081 Catholic	13	NR	NR	16,363	21.9	55.0
097 Chr Chs&Chs Cr	2	100	NR	142 *	.2	.5
105 Christian Ref	9	1,124	946	1,595 *	2.1	5.4
127 Ch God (Cleve)	8	667	341	955 *	1.3	3.2
151 L-D Saints	12	NR	NR	4,965	6.6	16.7
165 Ch of Nazarene	3	162	136	338	.5	1.1
167 Chs of Christ	3	173	145	215	.3	.7
171 Ch God-Gen Con	2	13	62	62 *	.1	.2
179 Consrv Bapt	2	NR	290	290	.4	1.0
193 Episcopal	1	NR	71	132	.2	.4
283 Luth—MO Synod	1	106	60	138	.2	.5
339 Pent Ch of God	4	207	NR	269	.4	.9
355 Presb Ch (USA)	1	69	55	98 *	.1	.3
388 Reg Bapt Gen As	1	52	80	80 *	.1	.3
413 S.D.A.	2	173	NR	206	.3	.7
419 So Bapt Conv	7	1,674	558	2,376 *	3.2	8.0
449 Un Methodist	1	347	129	493 *	.7	1.7
MORA	**34**	**304**	**362**	**3,603 ***	**69.6**	**100.0**
053 Assemb of God	1	83	120	185	3.6	5.1
056 Baha'i	0	1	NR	1	-	-
076 Buddhism	1	NR	NR	NR	-	-
081 Catholic	23	NR	NR	2,963	57.2	82.2
151 L-D Saints	1	NR	NR	174	3.4	4.8
167 Chs of Christ	4	101	110	134	2.6	3.7
355 Presb Ch (USA)	2	58	36	71 *	1.4	2.0
419 So Bapt Conv	2	61	96	75 *	1.4	2.1
OTERO	**72**	**7,980**	**5,744**	**28,776 ***	**46.2**	**100.0**
053 Assemb of God	5	851	1,097	1,853	3.0	6.4
056 Baha'i	1	163	NR	163	.3	.6
081 Catholic	10	NR	NR	15,493	24.9	53.8
084 Calvary Chapel	1	NR	NR	NR	-	-
093 Chr Ch (Disc)	1	74	35	95 *	.2	.3
097 Chr Chs&Chs Cr	1	45	NR	58 *	.1	.2
127 Ch God (Cleve)	1	50	26	65 *	.1	.2
145 Ch God Prophcy	1	35	NR	45 *	.1	.2
151 L-D Saints	3	NR	NR	869	1.4	3.0
165 Ch of Nazarene	2	147	144	289	.5	1.0
167 Chs of Christ	12	472	488	629	1.0	2.2
173 Comm of Christ	1	33	NR	33	.1	.1
179 Consrv Bapt	1	NR	100	100	.2	.3
193 Episcopal	2	NR	147	331	.5	1.2
207 E.L.C.A.	1	295	157	366	.6	1.3
283 Luth—MO Synod	1	206	120	253	.4	.9
355 Presb Ch (USA)	1	106	76	137 *	.2	.5
356 Presb Ch Amer	1	90	98	126	.2	.4
371 Ref Ch in Am	1	67	80	222	.4	.8
388 Reg Bapt Gen As	1	52	80	80 *	.1	.3
413 S.D.A.	1	109	NR	130	.2	.5
419 So Bapt Conv	16	3,215	1,477	4,148 *	6.7	14.4
435 Unitarian-Univ	1	32	NR	41 *	.1	.1
449 Un Methodist	5	1,938	919	2,500 *	4.0	8.7
498 Indep.Charis.	1	0	700	750	1.2	2.6
QUAY	**37**	**4,582**	**1,361**	**9,131 ***	**89.9**	**100.0**
053 Assemb of God	4	110	142	229	2.3	2.5
056 Baha'i	0	10	NR	10	.1	.1
081 Catholic	5	NR	NR	3,146	31.0	34.5
097 Chr Chs&Chs Cr	1	80	NR	98 *	1.0	1.1
127 Ch God (Cleve)	1	12	17	17 *	.2	.2
151 L-D Saints	1	NR	NR	224	2.2	2.5
165 Ch of Nazarene	1	7	0	7	.1	.1
167 Chs of Christ	6	204	215	259	2.6	2.8
193 Episcopal	1	NR	25	50	.5	.5
355 Presb Ch (USA)	1	46	39	56 *	.6	.6
360 Prim Bapt Chrch	1	NR	NR	NR	-	-
413 S.D.A.	1	30	NR	36	.4	.4
419 So Bapt Conv	9	3,530	687	4,323 *	42.6	47.3
449 Un Methodist	5	553	236	676 *	6.7	7.4
RIO ARRIBA	**86**	**1,849**	**2,178**	**26,037 ***	**63.2**	**100.0**
053 Assemb of God	8	298	368	469	1.1	1.8
056 Baha'i	0	40	NR	40	.1	.2
081 Catholic	46	NR	NR	21,944	53.3	84.3
151 L-D Saints	3	NR	NR	654	1.6	2.5
167 Chs of Christ	3	113	121	145	.4	.6
173 Comm of Christ	1	30	NR	30	.1	.1
193 Episcopal	2	NR	44	79	.2	.3
263 Int Foursq Gos	2	273	1,049	1,049 *	2.5	4.0
267 Muslim Est	1	NR	55	163	.4	.6
339 Pent Ch of God	3	71	NR	80	.2	.3
355 Presb Ch (USA)	3	219	109	281 *	.7	1.1
371 Ref Ch in Am	1	62	63	164	.4	.6
413 S.D.A.	3	151	NR	180	.4	.7
416 Sikh	2	NR	NR	NR	-	-
419 So Bapt Conv	3	282	130	361 *	.9	1.4
449 Un Methodist	5	310	239	398 *	1.0	1.5
ROOSEVELT	**41**	**5,731**	**2,407**	**12,325 ***	**68.4**	**100.0**
053 Assemb of God	2	48	55	76	.4	.6
056 Baha'i	0	25	NR	25	.1	.2
081 Catholic	1	NR	NR	4,529	25.1	36.7
097 Chr Chs&Chs Cr	1	200	NR	255 *	1.4	2.1
127 Ch God (Cleve)	1	42	39	54 *	.3	.4
145 Ch God Prophcy	1	35	NR	45 *	.2	.4
151 L-D Saints	1	NR	NR	296	1.6	2.4
165 Ch of Nazarene	1	45	48	70	.4	.6
167 Chs of Christ	9	880	827	1,078	6.0	8.7
193 Episcopal	1	NR	13	48	.3	.4
267 Muslim Est	1	NR	55	163	.9	1.3
283 Luth—MO Synod	1	21	30	36	.2	.3
355 Presb Ch (USA)	1	64	37	82 *	.5	.7
360 Prim Bapt Chrch	1	NR	NR	NR	-	-
413 S.D.A.	1	21	NR	25	.1	.2
419 So Bapt Conv	14	3,590	1,050	4,575 *	25.4	37.1
449 Un Methodist	4	760	253	968 *	5.4	7.9
SANDOVAL	**73**	**4,464**	**3,035**	**42,080 ***	**46.8**	**100.0**
053 Assemb of God	4	560	336	555	.6	1.3
056 Baha'i	1	108	NR	108	.1	.3
076 Buddhism	2	NR	NR	NR	-	-
081 Catholic	25	NR	NR	33,742	37.5	80.2
097 Chr Chs&Chs Cr	2	295	NR	382 *	.4	.9
127 Ch God (Cleve)	1	14	14	18 *	-	-
151 L-D Saints	6	NR	NR	2,263	2.5	5.4
157 Ch of Brethren	1	33	7	43 *	-	.1
165 Ch of Nazarene	1	15	0	15	-	-
167 Chs of Christ	3	242	255	342	.4	.8
185 Cumber Presb	1	50	NR	50	.1	.1
193 Episcopal	2	NR	168	310	.3	.7
203 Evan Free Ch	1	147	350	350	.4	.8
263 Int Foursq Gos	2	70	103	103 *	.1	.2

NR–Not Reported *Total adherents estimated from known number of communicant, confirmed, full members. - Represents a percentage less than 0.1. Percentages may not total 100 due to rounding.

Table 4: Religious Congregations by County and Group: 2000

Religious Group	Number of Churches, Synagogues, Mosques, or Temples	Number of Communicant, Confirmed, or Full Members	Number of Attendees	Total Adherents		
				Number of Adherents	% of Total Pop.	% of Total Adh.
283 Luth—MO Synod	2	246	170	297	.3	.7
339 Pent Ch of God	1	32	NR	75	.1	.2
355 Presb Ch (USA)	4	452	291	585 *	.7	1.4
388 Reg Bapt Gen As	2	125	190	187 *	.2	.4
413 S.D.A.	1	144	NR	171	.2	.4
419 So Bapt Conv	8	1,509	802	1,953 *	2.2	4.6
449 Un Methodist	2	309	278	400 *	.4	1.0
469 WELS	1	113	71	131	.1	.3
SAN JUAN	**137**	**15,858**	**7,685**	**45,833 ***	**40.3**	**100.0**
017 Amer Bapt Assn	2	99	NR	131 *	.1	.3
053 Assemb of God	11	1,011	1,328	1,930	1.7	4.2
056 Baha'i	2	183	NR	183	.2	.4
075 Brethren in Cr	2	66	53	75	.1	.2
081 Catholic	11	NR	NR	13,514	11.9	29.5
084 Calvary Chapel	1	NR	NR	NR	-	-
093 Chr Ch (Disc)	2	300	167	398 *	.3	.9
097 Chr Chs&Chs Cr	3	315	NR	418 *	.4	.9
105 Christian Ref	4	322	286	427 *	.4	.9
127 Ch God (Cleve)	4	197	104	260 *	.2	.6
151 L-D Saints	21	NR	NR	9,966	8.8	21.7
165 Ch of Nazarene	3	320	265	460	.4	1.0
167 Chs of Christ	12	1,061	741	1,407	1.2	3.1
173 Comm of Christ	1	28	NR	28	-	.1
193 Episcopal	5	NR	222	658	.6	1.4
207 E.L.C.A.	1	244	132	315	.3	.7
221 Free Methodist	2	0	20	20	-	-
263 Int Foursq Gos	1	64	90	90 *	.1	.2
283 Luth—MO Synod	1	182	132	209	.2	.5
288 Mennonite USA	1	30	30	40 *	-	.1
297 Mennonite;Other	1	63	NR	84 *	.1	.2
306 NT IndBapt&Rltd	1	175	NR	232 *	.2	.5
339 Pent Ch of God	2	33	NR	113	.1	.2
355 Presb Ch (USA)	3	637	377	867 *	.8	1.9
356 Presb Ch Amer	1	0	0	0	-	-
360 Prim Bapt Chrch	1	NR	NR	NR	-	-
403 Salvation Army	1	61	12	189	.2	.4
413 S.D.A.	5	486	NR	577	.5	1.3
419 So Bapt Conv	19	7,380	2,767	9,785 *	8.6	21.3
435 Unitarian-Univ	1	34	NR	45 *	-	.1
443 Un C of Christ	1	30	13	40 *	-	.1
449 Un Methodist	8	2,491	896	3,303 *	2.9	7.2
469 WELS	3	46	50	69	.1	.2
SAN MIGUEL	**57**	**1,482**	**977**	**23,141 ***	**76.8**	**100.0**
053 Assemb of God	3	174	218	340	1.1	1.5
056 Baha'i	0	11	NR	11	-	-
076 Buddhism	1	NR	NR	NR	-	-
081 Catholic	36	NR	NR	20,964	69.6	90.6
084 Calvary Chapel	1	NR	NR	NR	-	-
093 Chr Ch (Disc)	1	34	0	43 *	.1	.2
167 Chs of Christ	4	208	255	287	1.0	1.2
193 Episcopal	1	NR	45	149	.5	.6
207 E.L.C.A.	1	30	35	35	.1	.2
226 Friends-USA	1	30	NR	38 *	.1	.2
263 Int Foursq Gos	1	30	50	50 *	.2	.2
283 Luth—MO Synod	1	54	46	80	.3	.3
355 Presb Ch (USA)	1	117	87	147 *	.5	.6
403 Salvation Army	1	4	25	4	-	-
419 So Bapt Conv	3	699	170	879 *	2.9	3.8
449 Un Methodist	1	91	46	114 *	.4	.5
SANTA FE	**92**	**7,141**	**3,744**	**63,977 ***	**49.5**	**100.0**
034 Ant Orth of NA	1	42	NR	84	.1	.1
053 Assemb of God	5	408	569	668	.5	1.0
056 Baha'i	2	156	NR	156	.1	.2
076 Buddhism	6	NR	NR	NR	-	-
081 Catholic	24	NR	NR	50,675	39.2	79.2
084 Calvary Chapel	1	NR	NR	NR	-	-
093 Chr Ch (Disc)	1	62	29	76 *	.1	.1
097 Chr Chs&Chs Cr	2	220	NR	270 *	.2	.4
127 Ch God (Cleve)	1	28	28	34 *	-	.1
151 L-D Saints	3	NR	NR	1,331	1.0	2.1
165 Ch of Nazarene	1	28	51	62	-	.1
167 Chs of Christ	4	137	165	185	.1	.3
193 Episcopal	3	NR	528	1,110	.9	1.7
207 E.L.C.A.	2	276	181	326	.3	.5
226 Friends-USA	2	60	NR	74 *	.1	.1
246 Greek Orthodox	1	NR	NR	6	-	-
252 Hindu	3	NR	NR	NR	-	-
262 Int Cou Comm Ch	2	250	NR	307 *	.2	.5
263 Int Foursq Gos	1	70	91	91 *	.1	.1
283 Luth—MO Synod	2	334	206	428	.3	.7
355 Presb Ch (USA)	2	582	334	713 *	.6	1.1
401 Rus Orth Abroad	1	NR	NR	NR	-	-
403 Salvation Army	1	53	38	255	.2	.4
413 S.D.A.	3	275	NR	327	.3	.5
419 So Bapt Conv	10	2,355	873	2,887 *	2.2	4.5
435 Unitarian-Univ	1	320	NR	392 *	.3	.6
443 Un C of Christ	1	241	120	295 *	.2	.5
449 Un Methodist	3	1,244	531	1,525 *	1.2	2.4
496 Jewish Est	3	NR	NR	1,700	1.3	2.7
SIERRA	**23**	**1,437**	**803**	**4,762 ***	**35.9**	**100.0**
053 Assemb of God	2	53	60	106	.8	2.2
056 Baha'i	0	14	NR	14	.1	.3
081 Catholic	6	NR	NR	2,557	19.3	53.7
089 Chr & Miss Al	1	21	NR	48	.4	1.0
097 Chr Chs&Chs Cr	1	125	NR	147 *	1.1	3.1
123 Ch God (Ander)	1	NR	135	135	1.0	2.8
127 Ch God (Cleve)	1	5	10	10 *	.1	.2
151 L-D Saints	1	NR	NR	224	1.7	4.7
165 Ch of Nazarene	1	31	21	39	.3	.8
167 Chs of Christ	3	128	114	150	1.1	3.1
193 Episcopal	2	NR	53	89	.7	1.9
283 Luth—MO Synod	1	81	68	89	.7	1.9
413 S.D.A.	1	37	NR	44	.3	.9
419 So Bapt Conv	1	742	242	874 *	6.6	18.4
449 Un Methodist	1	200	100	236 *	1.8	5.0
SOCORRO	**38**	**1,192**	**779**	**7,454 ***	**41.2**	**100.0**
053 Assemb of God	2	94	129	169	.9	2.3
056 Baha'i	0	38	NR	38	.2	.5
081 Catholic	15	NR	NR	4,909	27.2	65.9
151 L-D Saints	2	NR	NR	736	4.1	9.9
165 Ch of Nazarene	1	27	24	29	.2	.4
167 Chs of Christ	1	70	75	91	.5	1.2
193 Episcopal	1	NR	22	68	.4	.9
226 Friends-USA	1	30	NR	38 *	.2	.5
267 Muslim Est	1	NR	55	163	.9	2.2
283 Luth—MO Synod	1	30	17	36	.2	.5
339 Pent Ch of God	1	50	NR	70	.4	.9
355 Presb Ch (USA)	2	134	102	170 *	.9	2.3
413 S.D.A.	2	31	NR	37	.2	.5
419 So Bapt Conv	4	420	215	535 *	3.0	7.2
449 Un Methodist	3	247	115	315 *	1.7	4.2
467 Wesleyan	1	21	25	50	.3	.7
TAOS	**68**	**1,574**	**876**	**20,926 ***	**69.8**	**100.0**
053 Assemb of God	5	147	168	245	.8	1.2
056 Baha'i	1	57	NR	57	.2	.3
076 Buddhism	2	NR	NR	NR	-	-
081 Catholic	34	NR	NR	17,929	59.8	85.7
084 Calvary Chapel	1	NR	NR	NR	-	-
151 L-D Saints	3	NR	NR	463	1.5	2.2
167 Chs of Christ	3	140	135	183	.6	.9
193 Episcopal	1	NR	131	170	.6	.8
226 Friends-USA	2	60	NR	73 *	.2	.3
252 Hindu	1	NR	NR	NR	-	-
263 Int Foursq Gos	1	49	118	118 *	.4	.6
283 Luth—MO Synod	1	29	34	32	.1	.2
339 Pent Ch of God	2	137	NR	190	.6	.9
355 Presb Ch (USA)	3	290	149	355 *	1.2	1.7
413 S.D.A.	2	93	NR	111	.4	.5
419 So Bapt Conv	5	522	101	639 *	2.1	3.1
449 Un Methodist	1	50	40	61 *	.2	.3

NR–Not Reported *Total adherents estimated from known number of communicant, confirmed, full members. - Represents a percentage less than 0.1. Percentages may not total 100 due to rounding.

Table 4: Religious Congregations by County and Group: 2000

Religious Group	Number of Churches, Synagogues, Mosques, or Temples	Number of Communicant, Confirmed, or Full Members	Number of Attendees	Total Adherents: Number of Adherents	Total Adherents: % of Total Pop.	Total Adherents: % of Total Adh.
496 Jewish Est	0	NR	NR	300	1.0	1.4
TORRANCE	**32**	**2,457**	**1,325**	**13,226 ***	**78.2**	**100.0**
053 Assemb of God	4	209	281	354	2.1	2.7
056 Baha'i	0	17	NR	17	.1	.1
081 Catholic	12	NR	NR	9,942	58.8	75.2
084 Calvary Chapel	1	NR	NR	NR	-	-
165 Ch of Nazarene	2	116	63	121	.7	.9
167 Chs of Christ	4	171	219	262	1.5	2.0
419 So Bapt Conv	6	1,597	559	2,078 *	12.3	15.7
449 Un Methodist	3	347	203	452 *	2.7	3.4
UNION	**14**	**1,229**	**690**	**1,964 ***	**47.1**	**100.0**
053 Assemb of God	1	43	59	96	2.3	4.9
081 Catholic	4	NR	NR	380	9.1	19.3
127 Ch God (Cleve)	1	31	20	39 *	.9	2.0
167 Chs of Christ	2	90	117	126	3.0	6.4
413 S.D.A.	1	21	NR	25	.6	1.3
419 So Bapt Conv	2	635	201	790 *	18.9	40.2
449 Un Methodist	3	409	293	508 *	12.2	25.9
VALENCIA	**49**	**5,114**	**2,808**	**37,089 ***	**56.1**	**100.0**
053 Assemb of God	5	270	343	469	.7	1.3
056 Baha'i	2	71	NR	71	.1	.2
081 Catholic	10	NR	NR	29,211	44.2	78.8
084 Calvary Chapel	1	NR	NR	NR	-	-
097 Chr Chs&Chs Cr	2	800	NR	1,044 *	1.6	2.8
127 Ch God (Cleve)	2	86	71	113 *	.2	.3
151 L-D Saints	2	NR	NR	947	1.4	2.6
165 Ch of Nazarene	2	136	97	147	.2	.4
167 Chs of Christ	3	250	334	366	.6	1.0
193 Episcopal	1	NR	74	129	.2	.3
207 E.L.C.A.	1	168	85	270	.4	.7
283 Luth—MO Synod	1	78	45	115	.2	.3
297 Mennonite;Other	1	42	NR	55 *	.1	.1
339 Pent Ch of God	1	83	NR	95	.1	.3
355 Presb Ch (USA)	3	300	147	392 *	.6	1.1
413 S.D.A.	3	243	NR	289	.4	.8
419 So Bapt Conv	6	1,810	1,224	2,362 *	3.6	6.4
449 Un Methodist	3	777	388	1,014 *	1.5	2.7

NEW YORK

Religious Group	Number of Churches, Synagogues, Mosques, or Temples	Number of Communicant, Confirmed, or Full Members	Number of Attendees	Total Adherents: Number of Adherents	Total Adherents: % of Total Pop.	Total Adherents: % of Total Adh.
The State.....	11,001	1,231,358	721,476	11,461,411 *	60.4	100.0
ALBANY	**199**	**20,900**	**11,740**	**187,944 ***	**63.8**	**100.0**
019 Amer Bapt USA	8	902	294	1,092 *	.4	.6
034 Ant Orth of NA	1	50	NR	100	-	.1
050 Armen Ap Etchm	1	213	NR	1,260	.4	.7
053 Assemb of God	7	548	775	992	.3	.5
056 Baha'i	1	57	NR	57	-	-
057 Bapt Gen Conf	1	222	120	269 *	.1	.1
076 Buddhism	3	NR	NR	NR	-	-
078 Bulgar Orth USA	1	NR	NR	160	.1	.1
081 Catholic	42	NR	NR	138,376	47.0	73.6
089 Chr & Miss Al	4	228	NR	374	.1	.2
097 Chr Chs&Chs Cr	1	75	NR	91 *	-	-
127 Ch God (Cleve)	1	41	60	60 *	-	-
145 Ch God Prophcy	1	82	NR	99 *	-	.1
151 L-D Saints	2	NR	NR	428	.1	.2
165 Ch of Nazarene	1	45	24	45	-	-
167 Chs of Christ	1	133	155	168	.1	.1
179 Consrv Bapt	2	NR	365	365	.1	.2
181 Consrv Congr	2	116	105	140 *	-	.1
193 Episcopal	12	NR	1,382	3,771	1.3	2.0
203 Evan Free Ch	1	36	40	40	-	-
207 E.L.C.A.	7	1,965	630	3,124	1.1	1.7
226 Friends-USA	1	50	NR	61 *	-	-
246 Greek Orthodox	1	NR	NR	1,203	.4	.6
252 Hindu	2	NR	NR	NR	-	-
264 Int Chs of Crst	1	38	73	57	-	-
267 Muslim Est	2	NR	176	659	.2	.4
268 Jain	1	NR	NR	NR	-	-
283 Luth—MO Synod	6	1,854	628	2,245	.8	1.2
290 Metro Comm Ch	1	55	30	67 *	-	-
331 OCA: Ter Diocs	2	404	NR	458	.2	.2
355 Presb Ch (USA)	14	2,539	1,066	3,084 *	1.0	1.6
371 Ref Ch in Am	20	2,392	1,610	5,285	1.8	2.8
388 Reg Bapt Gen As	1	85	125	125 *	-	.1
403 Salvation Army	4	164	281	476	.2	.3
413 S.D.A.	3	529	NR	630	.2	.3
419 So Bapt Conv	3	118	148	143 *	-	.1
435 Unitarian-Univ	1	337	NR	408 *	.1	.2
443 Un C of Christ	5	476	233	576 *	.2	.3
449 Un Methodist	18	6,346	1,795	7,679 *	2.6	4.1
463 Vineyard	1	50	70	70 *	-	-
467 Wesleyan	2	0	105	257	.1	.1
496 Jewish Est	8	NR	NR	12,000	4.1	6.4
498 Indep.Charis.	1	450	450	450	.2	.2
499 Indep.Non-Char	1	300	1,000	1,000	.3	.5
ALLEGANY	**102**	**6,845**	**4,549**	**17,839 ***	**35.7**	**100.0**
019 Amer Bapt USA	6	638	366	781 *	1.6	4.4
053 Assemb of God	6	456	603	684	1.4	3.8
056 Baha'i	0	5	NR	5	-	-
081 Catholic	14	NR	NR	6,458	12.9	36.2
089 Chr & Miss Al	4	137	NR	334	.7	1.9
093 Chr Ch (Disc)	1	326	85	399 *	.8	2.2
097 Chr Chs&Chs Cr	2	167	NR	204 *	.4	1.1
151 L-D Saints	1	NR	NR	156	.3	.9
167 Chs of Christ	1	26	9	30	.1	.2
193 Episcopal	7	NR	177	457	.9	2.6
207 E.L.C.A.	1	71	54	94	.2	.5
221 Free Methodist	1	31	65	65	.1	.4
226 Friends-USA	1	50	NR	61 *	.1	.3
283 Luth—MO Synod	2	256	129	300	.6	1.7
288 Mennonite USA	3	167	203	215 *	.4	1.2
297 Mennonite;Other	1	32	NR	39 *	.1	.2
323 Old Ord Amish	4	220	NR	268 *	.5	1.5
355 Presb Ch (USA)	3	153	123	187 *	.4	1.0
356 Presb Ch Amer	1	45	55	67	.1	.4
388 Reg Bapt Gen As	6	346	331	377 *	.8	2.1
403 Salvation Army	1	74	58	159	.3	.9
413 S.D.A.	1	75	NR	89	.2	.5
419 So Bapt Conv	2	66	32	81 *	.2	.5
435 Unitarian-Univ	1	12	NR	15 *	-	.1
443 Un C of Christ	1	112	49	137 *	.3	.8
449 Un Methodist	24	2,759	1,122	3,377 *	6.8	18.9
467 Wesleyan	7	621	1,088	2,800	5.6	15.7
BRONX	**426**	**42,286**	**30,633**	**750,411 ***	**56.3**	**100.0**
019 Amer Bapt USA	26	8,759	5,596	11,498 *	.9	1.5
053 Assemb of God	41	7,185	5,950	10,968	.8	1.5
075 Brethren in Cr	1	35	32	35	-	-
076 Buddhism	8	NR	NR	NR	-	-
081 Catholic	72	NR	NR	581,824	43.7	77.5
084 Calvary Chapel	1	NR	NR	NR	-	-
089 Chr & Miss Al	8	389	NR	607	-	.1
093 Chr Ch (Disc)	3	330	75	433 *	-	.1
097 Chr Chs&Chs Cr	3	260	NR	342 *	-	-
123 Ch God (Ander)	3	NR	73	73	-	-
127 Ch God (Cleve)	25	2,643	3,078	4,189 *	.3	.6
145 Ch God Prophcy	5	349	NR	458 *	-	.1
151 L-D Saints	5	NR	NR	2,242	.2	.3
165 Ch of Nazarene	6	679	551	742	.1	.1
167 Chs of Christ	3	63	70	92	-	-
179 Consrv Bapt	3	NR	200	200	-	-
181 Consrv Congr	2	49	96	64 *	-	-
193 Episcopal	23	NR	3,032	8,638	.6	1.2
201 Evan Cov Ch	1	1,162	627	1,525 *	.1	.2
207 E.L.C.A.	17	2,267	1,302	3,176	.2	.4
221 Free Methodist	1	42	60	91	-	-
246 Greek Orthodox	4	NR	NR	2,529	.2	.3
252 Hindu	3	NR	NR	NR	-	-

NR–Not Reported *Total adherents estimated from known number of communicant, confirmed, full members. - Represents a percentage less than 0.1. Percentages may not total 100 due to rounding.

Table 4: Religious Congregations by County and Group: 2000

Religious Group	Number of Churches, Synagogues, Mosques, or Temples	Number of Communicant, Confirmed, or Full Members	Number of Attendees	Total Adherents		
				Number of Adherents	% of Total Pop.	% of Total Adh.
262 Int Cou Comm Ch	1	197	NR	259 *	-	-
263 Int Foursq Gos	1	20	24	26 *	-	-
267 Muslim Est	8	NR	2,898	12,164	.9	1.6
283 Luth—MO Synod	5	543	275	618	-	.1
288 Mennonite USA	5	262	264	344 *	-	-
291 Missionary Ch	2	26	83	83	-	-
293 Morav Ch-North	1	193	NR	272	-	-
333 Malan Dioc Am	2	NR	NR	900	.1	.1
339 Pent Ch of God	1	88	NR	220	-	-
355 Presb Ch (USA)	18	2,165	1,266	2,849 *	.2	.4
356 Presb Ch Amer	1	0	0	0	-	-
371 Ref Ch in Am	5	251	504	655	-	.1
403 Salvation Army	2	168	163	741	.1	.1
413 S.D.A.	20	6,227	NR	7,411	.6	1.0
419 So Bapt Conv	12	1,648	1,209	2,163 *	.2	.3
443 Un C of Christ	12	670	299	879 *	.1	.1
449 Un Methodist	20	5,316	2,658	6,977 *	.5	.9
467 Wesleyan	1	0	48	124	-	-
496 Jewish Est	44	NR	NR	83,700	6.3	11.2
498 Indep.Charis.	1	300	200	300	-	-
BROOME	**196**	**27,865**	**12,813**	**112,131 ***	**55.9**	**100.0**
019 Amer Bapt USA	7	1,063	490	1,291 *	.6	1.2
022 Carp Rus Orth	2	1,099	NR	1,868	.9	1.7
050 Armen Ap Etchm	1	44	NR	180	.1	.2
053 Assemb of God	4	1,174	1,434	2,470	1.2	2.2
056 Baha'i	0	36	NR	36	-	-
076 Buddhism	1	NR	NR	NR	-	-
081 Catholic	34	NR	NR	66,386	33.1	59.2
089 Chr & Miss Al	9	316	NR	703	.4	.6
093 Chr Ch (Disc)	1	84	0	102 *	.1	.1
097 Chr Chs&Chs Cr	2	180	NR	218 *	.1	.2
105 Christian Ref	1	182	120	221 *	.1	.2
127 Ch God (Cleve)	2	57	94	98 *	-	.1
145 Ch God Prophcy	1	82	NR	100 *	-	.1
151 L-D Saints	2	NR	NR	622	.3	.6
165 Ch of Nazarene	2	316	326	406	.2	.4
167 Chs of Christ	1	115	145	140	.1	.1
173 Comm of Christ	1	99	NR	99	-	.1
193 Episcopal	10	NR	994	3,523	1.8	3.1
203 Evan Free Ch	1	80	130	130	.1	.1
207 E.L.C.A.	6	2,012	594	3,022	1.5	2.7
221 Free Methodist	3	188	318	335	.2	.3
246 Greek Orthodox	2	NR	NR	564	.3	.5
267 Muslim Est	1	NR	125	600	.3	.5
283 Luth—MO Synod	2	278	152	386	.2	.3
331 OCA: Ter Diocs	2	447	NR	484	.2	.4
355 Presb Ch (USA)	17	3,073	1,608	3,731 *	1.9	3.3
356 Presb Ch Amer	1	106	120	120	.1	.1
363 Primitive Meth	1	57	NR	61	-	.1
388 Reg Bapt Gen As	14	1,223	1,403	1,585 *	.8	1.4
401 Rus Orth Abroad	1	NR	NR	NR	-	-
403 Salvation Army	1	138	98	164	.1	.1
413 S.D.A.	3	172	NR	205	.1	.2
419 So Bapt Conv	3	383	78	465 *	.2	.4
431 Ukrainian Orth	1	NR	NR	1,050	.5	.9
435 Unitarian-Univ	1	200	NR	243 *	.1	.2
443 Un C of Christ	6	710	338	862 *	.4	.8
449 Un Methodist	44	13,881	4,060	16,853 *	8.4	15.0
467 Wesleyan	2	70	186	408	.2	.4
496 Jewish Est	3	NR	NR	2,400	1.2	2.1
CATTARAUGUS	**139**	**10,831**	**6,538**	**34,890 ***	**41.6**	**100.0**
019 Amer Bapt USA	3	966	282	1,198 *	1.4	3.4
053 Assemb of God	1	28	36	36	-	.1
056 Baha'i	1	53	NR	53	.1	.2
081 Catholic	23	NR	NR	18,187	21.7	52.1
089 Chr & Miss Al	2	89	NR	176	.2	.5
145 Ch God Prophcy	1	82	NR	102 *	.1	.3
151 L-D Saints	2	NR	NR	485	.6	1.4
165 Ch of Nazarene	1	49	47	70	.1	.2
167 Chs of Christ	1	12	12	13	-	-
179 Consrv Bapt	1	NR	75	75	.1	.2
193 Episcopal	6	NR	294	770	.9	2.2
207 E.L.C.A.	1	161	89	223	.3	.6
221 Free Methodist	9	692	1,061	1,090	1.3	3.1
263 Int Foursq Gos	1	61	114	114 *	.1	.3
267 Muslim Est	2	NR	110	326	.4	.9
283 Luth—MO Synod	7	1,229	576	1,828	2.2	5.2
288 Mennonite USA	1	12	10	15 *	-	-
323 Old Ord Amish	11	605	NR	748 *	.9	2.1
355 Presb Ch (USA)	8	1,106	506	1,372 *	1.6	3.9
370 Ref Baptist Chs	1	NR	NR	NR	-	-
388 Reg Bapt Gen As	11	893	1,141	1,173 *	1.4	3.4
403 Salvation Army	2	89	56	220	.3	.6
413 S.D.A.	5	194	NR	232	.3	.7
419 So Bapt Conv	2	141	104	175 *	.2	.5
443 Un C of Christ	3	203	181	252 *	.3	.7
449 Un Methodist	27	3,902	1,476	4,840 *	5.8	13.9
467 Wesleyan	5	264	368	1,017	1.2	2.9
496 Jewish Est	1	NR	NR	100	.1	.3
CAYUGA	**86**	**7,438**	**4,108**	**39,466 ***	**48.2**	**100.0**
017 Amer Bapt Assn	1	30	NR	37 *	-	.1
019 Amer Bapt USA	8	1,183	475	1,455 *	1.8	3.7
053 Assemb of God	3	87	117	149	.2	.4
056 Baha'i	0	6	NR	6	-	-
081 Catholic	18	NR	NR	27,166	33.1	68.8
089 Chr & Miss Al	1	134	NR	314	.4	.8
093 Chr Ch (Disc)	1	200	68	246 *	.3	.6
127 Ch God (Cleve)	1	73	35	90 *	.1	.2
143 CG in Cr(Menn)	1	20	NR	25 *	-	.1
151 L-D Saints	1	NR	NR	276	.3	.7
165 Ch of Nazarene	1	172	117	172	.2	.4
179 Consrv Bapt	2	NR	800	800	1.0	2.0
193 Episcopal	4	NR	316	781	1.0	2.0
226 Friends-USA	2	100	NR	123 *	.2	.3
267 Muslim Est	1	NR	156	609	.7	1.5
283 Luth—MO Synod	1	83	35	117	.1	.3
331 OCA: Ter Diocs	1	144	NR	159	.2	.4
355 Presb Ch (USA)	10	1,126	574	1,390 *	1.7	3.5
370 Ref Baptist Chs	2	NR	NR	NR	-	-
371 Ref Ch in Am	1	99	105	258	.3	.7
388 Reg Bapt Gen As	1	80	115	98 *	.1	.2
403 Salvation Army	1	95	120	409	.5	1.0
413 S.D.A.	2	234	NR	278	.3	.7
435 Unitarian-Univ	1	25	NR	31 *	-	.1
443 Un C of Christ	3	269	93	331 *	.4	.8
449 Un Methodist	17	3,278	982	4,031 *	4.9	10.2
496 Jewish Est	1	NR	NR	115	.1	.3
CHAUTAUQUA	**198**	**23,996**	**13,639**	**70,267 ***	**50.3**	**100.0**
007 OCA: Alban Dioc	1	NR	NR	200	.1	.3
011 A.W.M.C.	2	25	53	25	-	-
019 Amer Bapt USA	8	890	493	1,090 *	.8	1.6
053 Assemb of God	8	432	441	595	.4	.8
056 Baha'i	0	47	NR	47	-	.1
057 Bapt Gen Conf	3	701	562	907 *	.6	1.3
081 Catholic	25	NR	NR	34,731	24.9	49.4
089 Chr & Miss Al	5	160	NR	319	.2	.5
093 Chr Ch (Disc)	1	13	10	16 *	-	-
123 Ch God (Ander)	5	NR	431	431	.3	.6
127 Ch God (Cleve)	1	288	55	353 *	.3	.5
151 L-D Saints	2	NR	NR	611	.4	.9
165 Ch of Nazarene	3	182	131	242	.2	.3
167 Chs of Christ	1	51	65	79	.1	.1
181 Consrv Congr	5	876	788	1,073 *	.8	1.5
193 Episcopal	7	NR	525	1,551	1.1	2.2
201 Evan Cov Ch	2	999	650	1,224 *	.9	1.7
207 E.L.C.A.	13	4,034	1,328	5,583	4.0	7.9
221 Free Methodist	4	359	829	829	.6	1.2
226 Friends-USA	2	100	NR	123 *	.1	.2
246 Greek Orthodox	1	NR	NR	243	.2	.3
262 Int Cou Comm Ch	1	268	NR	328 *	.2	.5
263 Int Foursq Gos	2	127	123	156 *	.1	.2
267 Muslim Est	1	NR	12	150	.1	.2

NR–Not Reported *Total adherents estimated from known number of communicant, confirmed, full members. - Represents a percentage less than 0.1. Percentages may not total 100 due to rounding.

Table 4: Religious Congregations by County and Group: 2000

Religious Group	Number of Churches, Synagogues, Mosques, or Temples	Number of Communicant, Confirmed, or Full Members	Number of Attendees	Total Adherents		
				Number of Adherents	% of Total Pop.	% of Total Adh.
283 Luth—MO Synod	3	282	163	395	.3	.6
323 Old Ord Amish	6	330	NR	402 *	.3	.6
355 Presb Ch (USA)	8	1,752	721	2,146 *	1.5	3.1
371 Ref Ch in Am	2	339	270	589	.4	.8
388 Reg Bapt Gen As	8	889	909	1,146 *	.8	1.6
403 Salvation Army	4	283	174	854	.6	1.2
413 S.D.A.	2	147	NR	175	.1	.2
419 So Bapt Conv	4	254	199	311 *	.2	.4
435 Unitarian-Univ	3	114	NR	140 *	.1	.2
443 Un C of Christ	3	525	203	643 *	.5	.9
449 Un Methodist	46	9,058	3,854	11,100 *	7.9	15.8
467 Wesleyan	5	471	650	1,360	1.0	1.9
496 Jewish Est	1	NR	NR	100	.1	.1
CHEMUNG	**93**	**12,194**	**6,272**	**42,608 ***	**46.8**	**100.0**
019 Amer Bapt USA	6	1,704	603	2,092 *	2.3	4.9
053 Assemb of God	5	602	942	1,640	1.8	3.8
056 Baha'i	0	9	NR	9	-	-
081 Catholic	12	NR	NR	22,686	24.9	53.2
089 Chr & Miss Al	2	264	NR	621	.7	1.5
093 Chr Ch (Disc)	1	83	38	102 *	.1	.2
151 L-D Saints	1	NR	NR	455	.5	1.1
165 Ch of Nazarene	3	228	244	309	.3	.7
167 Chs of Christ	1	82	78	103	.1	.2
193 Episcopal	6	NR	371	1,464	1.6	3.4
203 Evan Free Ch	2	99	133	133	.1	.3
207 E.L.C.A.	3	786	284	1,080	1.2	2.5
221 Free Methodist	1	44	70	70	.1	.2
246 Greek Orthodox	1	NR	NR	126	.1	.3
267 Muslim Est	2	NR	70	283	.3	.7
268 Jain	1	NR	NR	NR	-	-
331 OCA: Ter Diocs	1	73	NR	90	.1	.2
355 Presb Ch (USA)	6	1,563	651	1,919 *	2.1	4.5
388 Reg Bapt Gen As	4	560	676	717 *	.8	1.7
403 Salvation Army	1	124	73	279	.3	.7
413 S.D.A.	3	318	NR	378	.4	.9
419 So Bapt Conv	2	144	115	177 *	.2	.4
435 Unitarian-Univ	1	52	NR	64 *	.1	.2
443 Un C of Christ	2	608	195	746 *	.8	1.8
449 Un Methodist	21	4,649	1,387	5,707 *	6.3	13.4
467 Wesleyan	3	202	342	708	.8	1.7
496 Jewish Est	2	NR	NR	650	.7	1.5
CHENANGO	**74**	**6,695**	**3,109**	**18,272 ***	**35.5**	**100.0**
019 Amer Bapt USA	5	677	287	843 *	1.6	4.6
053 Assemb of God	2	99	135	163	.3	.9
056 Baha'i	0	10	NR	10	-	.1
081 Catholic	9	NR	NR	7,967	15.5	43.6
089 Chr & Miss Al	2	25	NR	69	.1	.4
151 L-D Saints	3	NR	NR	426	.8	2.3
167 Chs of Christ	1	10	10	13	-	.1
175 Congr Chr Chs	1	10	5	12 *	-	.1
193 Episcopal	9	NR	512	1,551	3.0	8.5
207 E.L.C.A.	1	282	50	362	.7	2.0
221 Free Methodist	1	59	75	75	.1	.4
226 Friends-USA	2	100	NR	125 *	.2	.7
355 Presb Ch (USA)	3	250	116	311 *	.6	1.7
370 Ref Baptist Chs	1	NR	NR	NR	-	-
388 Reg Bapt Gen As	7	764	690	859 *	1.7	4.7
413 S.D.A.	1	51	NR	61	.1	.3
419 So Bapt Conv	1	58	24	72 *	.1	.4
443 Un C of Christ	6	916	401	1,141 *	2.2	6.2
449 Un Methodist	19	3,384	804	4,212 *	8.2	23.1
CLINTON	**71**	**3,566**	**2,523**	**55,378 ***	**69.3**	**100.0**
019 Amer Bapt USA	1	80	67	97 *	.1	.2
053 Assemb of God	2	175	196	293	.4	.5
056 Baha'i	0	14	NR	14	-	-
081 Catholic	28	NR	NR	48,649	60.9	87.8
089 Chr & Miss Al	1	66	NR	215	.3	.4
127 Ch God (Cleve)	1	36	40	44 *	.1	.1
151 L-D Saints	1	NR	NR	204	.3	.4
165 Ch of Nazarene	2	285	249	298	.4	.5

Religious Group	Number of Churches, Synagogues, Mosques, or Temples	Number of Communicant, Confirmed, or Full Members	Number of Attendees	Total Adherents		
				Number of Adherents	% of Total Pop.	% of Total Adh.
167 Chs of Christ	1	23	25	30	-	.1
193 Episcopal	2	NR	150	445	.6	.8
207 E.L.C.A.	1	73	54	108	.1	.2
267 Muslim Est	1	NR	55	163	.2	.3
355 Presb Ch (USA)	4	638	364	772 *	1.0	1.4
403 Salvation Army	1	31	22	110	.1	.2
413 S.D.A.	2	80	NR	96	.1	.2
419 So Bapt Conv	1	124	80	150 *	.2	.3
435 Unitarian-Univ	1	81	NR	98 *	.1	.2
449 Un Methodist	13	1,844	781	2,232 *	2.8	4.0
467 Wesleyan	7	16	440	1,110	1.4	2.0
496 Jewish Est	1	NR	NR	250	.3	.5
COLUMBIA	**81**	**6,489**	**2,816**	**28,875 ***	**45.8**	**100.0**
017 Amer Bapt Assn	1	10	NR	12 *	-	-
019 Amer Bapt USA	1	100	20	122 *	.2	.4
053 Assemb of God	1	117	140	140	.2	.5
056 Baha'i	0	12	NR	12	-	-
076 Buddhism	2	NR	NR	NR	-	-
081 Catholic	11	NR	NR	17,267	27.4	59.8
151 L-D Saints	1	NR	NR	145	.2	.5
181 Consrv Congr	1	77	45	94 *	.1	.3
193 Episcopal	7	NR	412	1,245	2.0	4.3
207 E.L.C.A.	11	1,712	376	2,466	3.9	8.5
226 Friends-USA	3	143	NR	174 *	.3	.6
283 Luth—MO Synod	3	237	157	344	.5	1.2
335 Orth Pres Ch	1	0	0	0	-	-
355 Presb Ch (USA)	5	489	215	595 *	.9	2.1
371 Ref Ch in Am	13	1,021	882	2,570	4.1	8.9
403 Salvation Army	1	16	26	22	-	.1
413 S.D.A.	1	199	NR	237	.4	.8
419 So Bapt Conv	0	2	0	2 *	-	-
431 Ukrainian Orth	1	NR	NR	60	.1	.2
443 Un C of Christ	1	63	45	77 *	.1	.3
449 Un Methodist	15	2,291	498	2,791 *	4.4	9.7
496 Jewish Est	1	NR	NR	500	.8	1.7
CORTLAND	**54**	**6,586**	**3,602**	**15,939 ***	**32.8**	**100.0**
019 Amer Bapt USA	4	1,052	927	1,284 *	2.6	8.1
053 Assemb of God	2	148	210	210	.4	1.3
056 Baha'i	0	5	NR	5	-	-
081 Catholic	7	NR	NR	6,707	13.8	42.1
089 Chr & Miss Al	1	30	NR	65	.1	.4
097 Chr Chs&Chs Cr	1	35	NR	43 *	.1	.3
151 L-D Saints	1	NR	NR	267	.5	1.7
165 Ch of Nazarene	1	67	52	67	.1	.4
167 Chs of Christ	1	2	2	2	-	-
193 Episcopal	2	NR	136	422	.9	2.6
207 E.L.C.A.	1	94	20	118	.2	.7
221 Free Methodist	1	23	46	46	.1	.3
283 Luth—MO Synod	1	161	109	195	.4	1.2
355 Presb Ch (USA)	5	621	322	758 *	1.6	4.8
388 Reg Bapt Gen As	5	728	560	877 *	1.8	5.5
403 Salvation Army	1	72	76	270	.6	1.7
413 S.D.A.	1	108	NR	129	.3	.8
419 So Bapt Conv	1	90	85	110 *	.2	.7
435 Unitarian-Univ	1	32	NR	39 *	.1	.2
443 Un C of Christ	3	763	278	931 *	1.9	5.8
449 Un Methodist	12	2,534	752	3,094 *	6.4	19.4
467 Wesleyan	1	21	27	150	.3	.9
496 Jewish Est	1	NR	NR	150	.3	.9
DELAWARE	**95**	**8,708**	**4,041**	**20,955 ***	**43.6**	**100.0**
019 Amer Bapt USA	6	589	428	709 *	1.5	3.4
053 Assemb of God	5	359	347	529	1.1	2.5
056 Baha'i	0	7	NR	7	-	-
076 Buddhism	1	NR	NR	NR	-	-
081 Catholic	6	NR	NR	7,747	16.1	37.0
089 Chr & Miss Al	4	233	NR	457	1.0	2.2
151 L-D Saints	1	NR	NR	95	.2	.5
167 Chs of Christ	1	10	10	13	-	.1
179 Consrv Bapt	2	NR	245	245	.5	1.2
193 Episcopal	9	NR	235	443	.9	2.1

NR–Not Reported   *Total adherents estimated from known number of communicant, confirmed, full members.   - Represents a percentage less than 0.1.   Percentages may not total 100 due to rounding.

Table 4: Religious Congregations by County and Group: 2000

Religious Group	Number of Churches, Synagogues, Mosques, or Temples	Number of Communicant, Confirmed, or Full Members	Number of Attendees	Total Adherents: Number of Adherents	Total Adherents: % of Total Pop.	Total Adherents: % of Total Adh.
207 E.L.C.A.	2	303	127	419	.9	2.0
221 Free Methodist	1	19	30	30	.1	.1
226 Friends-USA	1	50	NR	60 *	.1	.3
262 Int Cou Comm Ch	1	190	NR	229 *	.5	1.1
283 Luth—MO Synod	1	30	20	35	.1	.2
355 Presb Ch (USA)	18	1,709	807	2,060 *	4.3	9.8
371 Ref Ch in Am	1	80	79	258	.5	1.2
388 Reg Bapt Gen As	3	118	130	142 *	.3	.7
403 Salvation Army	5	539	329	1,993	4.1	9.5
419 So Bapt Conv	2	57	43	69 *	.1	.3
443 Un C of Christ	2	459	182	553 *	1.2	2.6
449 Un Methodist	21	3,956	1,029	4,762 *	9.9	22.7
496 Jewish Est	2	NR	NR	100	.2	.5
DUTCHESS	**171**	**18,586**	**12,212**	**163,204 ***	**58.3**	**100.0**
019 Amer Bapt USA	8	1,267	383	1,574 *	.6	1.0
053 Assemb of God	6	990	1,608	3,622	1.3	2.2
056 Baha'i	1	78	NR	78	-	-
076 Buddhism	3	NR	NR	NR	-	-
081 Catholic	24	NR	NR	120,378	43.0	73.8
084 Calvary Chapel	1	NR	NR	NR	-	-
089 Chr & Miss Al	3	212	NR	719	.3	.4
105 Christian Ref	1	101	90	125 *	-	.1
127 Ch God (Cleve)	2	83	79	103 *	-	.1
145 Ch God Prophcy	1	82	NR	102 *	-	.1
151 L-D Saints	3	NR	NR	881	.3	.5
165 Ch of Nazarene	4	223	336	557	.2	.3
167 Chs of Christ	3	157	138	224	.1	.1
179 Consrv Bapt	1	NR	450	450	.2	.3
193 Episcopal	23	NR	1,916	4,575	1.6	2.8
203 Evan Free Ch	1	78	140	140	-	.1
207 E.L.C.A.	5	1,631	545	2,232	.8	1.4
226 Friends-USA	4	200	NR	248 *	.1	.2
246 Greek Orthodox	1	NR	NR	789	.3	.5
252 Hindu	1	NR	NR	NR	-	-
262 Int Cou Comm Ch	1	190	NR	236 *	.1	.1
267 Muslim Est	3	NR	592	3,331	1.2	2.0
268 Jain	1	NR	NR	NR	-	-
283 Luth—MO Synod	4	1,152	470	1,452	.5	.9
331 OCA: Ter Diocs	1	119	NR	170	.1	.1
355 Presb Ch (USA)	13	2,294	830	2,849 *	1.0	1.7
371 Ref Ch in Am	11	1,992	1,523	5,106	1.8	3.1
388 Reg Bapt Gen As	1	37	60	60 *	-	-
401 Rus Orth Abroad	1	NR	NR	NR	-	-
403 Salvation Army	2	121	130	382	.1	.2
413 S.D.A.	3	477	NR	568	.2	.3
416 Sikh	1	NR	NR	NR	-	-
419 So Bapt Conv	2	388	84	482 *	.2	.3
435 Unitarian-Univ	1	157	NR	195 *	.1	.1
443 Un C of Christ	2	313	165	389 *	.1	.2
449 Un Methodist	22	5,357	1,966	6,655 *	2.4	4.1
463 Vineyard	1	187	157	232 *	.1	.1
496 Jewish Est	4	NR	NR	3,600	1.3	2.2
499 Indep.Non-Char	1	700	550	700	.2	.4
ERIE	**570**	**86,913**	**48,937**	**706,830 ***	**74.4**	**100.0**
019 Amer Bapt USA	24	7,390	3,594	9,095 *	1.0	1.3
022 Carp Rus Orth	1	122	NR	207	-	-
053 Assemb of God	22	11,067	5,212	9,923	1.0	1.4
056 Baha'i	4	397	NR	397	-	.1
075 Brethren in Cr	1	27	28	28	-	-
076 Buddhism	2	NR	NR	NR	-	-
081 Catholic	149	NR	NR	544,252	57.3	77.0
084 Calvary Chapel	1	NR	NR	NR	-	-
089 Chr & Miss Al	6	428	NR	792	.1	.1
093 Chr Ch (Disc)	8	1,179	391	1,451 *	.2	.2
097 Chr Chs&Chs Cr	3	480	NR	591 *	.1	.1
123 Ch God (Ander)	1	NR	82	82	-	-
127 Ch God (Cleve)	4	217	468	541 *	.1	.1
145 Ch God Prophcy	1	82	NR	101 *	-	-
151 L-D Saints	5	NR	NR	1,661	.2	.2
165 Ch of Nazarene	5	337	314	464	-	.1
167 Chs of Christ	6	595	616	742	.1	.1
173 Comm of Christ	1	54	NR	54	-	-
179 Consrv Bapt	3	NR	319	319	-	-
181 Consrv Congr	2	144	134	177 *	-	-
193 Episcopal	32	NR	3,789	10,969	1.2	1.6
201 Evan Cov Ch	1	98	67	121 *	-	-
203 Evan Free Ch	1	155	225	225	-	-
207 E.L.C.A.	38	13,565	5,084	18,768	2.0	2.7
221 Free Methodist	5	282	426	466	-	.1
226 Friends-USA	3	150	NR	185 *	-	-
246 Greek Orthodox	1	NR	NR	2,313	.2	.3
252 Hindu	2	NR	NR	NR	-	-
262 Int Cou Comm Ch	2	220	NR	271 *	-	-
264 Int Chs of Crst	1	128	226	190	-	-
267 Muslim Est	7	NR	1,440	5,405	.6	.8
268 Jain	3	NR	NR	NR	-	-
283 Luth—MO Synod	24	7,846	3,160	10,071	1.1	1.4
288 Mennonite USA	4	375	314	470 *	-	.1
313 N Am Bapt Conf	3	638	706	785 *	.1	.1
330 Macedonian Orth	1	NR	NR	800	.1	.1
331 OCA: Ter Diocs	2	118	NR	293	-	-
355 Presb Ch (USA)	39	10,270	5,004	12,641 *	1.3	1.8
388 Reg Bapt Gen As	10	1,229	1,322	1,468 *	.2	.2
401 Rus Orth Abroad	2	NR	NR	NR	-	-
410 Serb Orth USA	1	NR	NR	800	.1	.1
413 S.D.A.	4	1,385	NR	1,648	.2	.2
416 Sikh	2	NR	NR	NR	-	-
419 So Bapt Conv	12	1,134	1,021	1,396 *	.1	.2
425 Tao	1	NR	NR	NR	-	-
431 Ukrainian Orth	1	NR	NR	300	-	-
435 Unitarian-Univ	4	790	NR	972 *	.1	.1
443 Un C of Christ	39	9,523	3,534	11,720 *	1.2	1.7
449 Un Methodist	49	15,141	6,277	18,638 *	2.0	2.6
467 Wesleyan	9	1,264	4,655	14,476	1.5	2.0
469 WELS	1	83	79	112	-	-
496 Jewish Est	16	NR	NR	20,000	2.1	2.8
498 Indep.Charis.	1	0	450	450	-	.1
ESSEX	**63**	**3,822**	**1,872**	**19,892 ***	**51.2**	**100.0**
019 Amer Bapt USA	3	381	76	458 *	1.2	2.3
053 Assemb of God	1	17	30	31	.1	.2
056 Baha'i	0	14	NR	14	-	.1
081 Catholic	14	NR	NR	14,184	36.5	71.3
089 Chr & Miss Al	1	46	NR	96	.2	.5
151 L-D Saints	1	NR	NR	113	.3	.6
165 Ch of Nazarene	3	140	85	223	.6	1.1
167 Chs of Christ	1	17	18	22	.1	.1
175 Congr Chr Chs	1	73	64	88 *	.2	.4
193 Episcopal	8	NR	315	742	1.9	3.7
226 Friends-USA	1	50	NR	60 *	.2	.3
355 Presb Ch (USA)	1	63	35	76 *	.2	.4
388 Reg Bapt Gen As	2	131	145	158 *	.4	.8
419 So Bapt Conv	1	126	116	152 *	.4	.8
443 Un C of Christ	7	408	247	491 *	1.3	2.5
449 Un Methodist	18	2,356	741	2,834 *	7.3	14.2
496 Jewish Est	0	NR	NR	150	.4	.8
FRANKLIN	**65**	**3,446**	**1,780**	**32,528 ***	**63.6**	**100.0**
019 Amer Bapt USA	1	72	60	87 *	.2	.3
053 Assemb of God	1	41	55	55	.1	.2
056 Baha'i	0	26	NR	26	.1	.1
081 Catholic	25	NR	NR	27,437	53.7	84.3
151 L-D Saints	2	NR	NR	147	.3	.5
165 Ch of Nazarene	1	38	62	62	.1	.2
193 Episcopal	4	NR	250	479	.9	1.5
207 E.L.C.A.	1	96	35	118	.2	.4
355 Presb Ch (USA)	5	322	180	388 *	.8	1.2
413 S.D.A.	2	124	NR	148	.3	.5
419 So Bapt Conv	5	562	354	677 *	1.3	2.1
443 Un C of Christ	1	203	68	245 *	.5	.8
449 Un Methodist	14	1,929	532	2,326 *	4.5	7.2
467 Wesleyan	3	33	184	333	.7	1.0

NR–Not Reported *Total adherents estimated from known number of communicant, confirmed, full members. - Represents a percentage less than 0.1. Percentages may not total 100 due to rounding.

Table 4: Religious Congregations by County and Group: 2000

Religious Group	Number of Churches, Synagogues, Mosques, or Temples	Number of Communicant, Confirmed, or Full Members	Number of Attendees	Total Adherents		
				Number of Adherents	% of Total Pop.	% of Total Adh.
FULTON	**52**	**6,629**	**3,325**	**23,974 ***	**43.5**	**100.0**
019 Amer Bapt USA	2	112	89	137 *	.2	.6
053 Assemb of God	1	44	56	65	.1	.3
055 As Ref Pres Ch	1	28	NR	29	.1	.1
056 Baha'i	0	4	NR	4	-	-
081 Catholic	7	NR	NR	13,326	24.2	55.6
093 Chr Ch (Disc)	1	200	42	245 *	.4	1.0
151 L-D Saints	1	NR	NR	198	.4	.8
165 Ch of Nazarene	1	19	58	84	.2	.4
167 Chs of Christ	1	37	55	67	.1	.3
179 Consrv Bapt	2	NR	365	365	.7	1.5
181 Consrv Congr	1	20	20	24 *	-	.1
193 Episcopal	1	NR	127	339	.6	1.4
207 E.L.C.A.	3	690	152	1,224	2.2	5.1
221 Free Methodist	2	86	66	96	.2	.4
246 Greek Orthodox	1	NR	NR	45	.1	.2
355 Presb Ch (USA)	6	810	458	991 *	1.8	4.1
371 Ref Ch in Am	1	111	104	394	.7	1.6
388 Reg Bapt Gen As	2	165	215	221 *	.4	.9
403 Salvation Army	1	59	30	123	.2	.5
413 S.D.A.	1	27	NR	32	.1	.1
443 Un C of Christ	1	119	50	146 *	.3	.6
449 Un Methodist	12	3,649	907	4,469 *	8.1	18.6
467 Wesleyan	1	49	81	450	.8	1.9
496 Jewish Est	1	NR	NR	300	.5	1.3
499 Indep.Non-Char	1	400	450	600	1.1	2.5
GENESEE	**70**	**7,362**	**4,056**	**35,592 ***	**59.0**	**100.0**
019 Amer Bapt USA	6	788	328	981 *	1.6	2.8
053 Assemb of God	2	171	233	336	.6	.9
056 Baha'i	0	11	NR	11	-	-
081 Catholic	17	NR	NR	24,240	40.2	68.1
089 Chr & Miss Al	1	12	NR	39	.1	.1
093 Chr Ch (Disc)	1	54	42	67 *	.1	.2
179 Consrv Bapt	2	NR	195	195	.3	.5
193 Episcopal	4	NR	286	1,256	2.1	3.5
221 Free Methodist	1	210	260	260	.4	.7
283 Luth—MO Synod	1	573	245	774	1.3	2.2
355 Presb Ch (USA)	13	2,214	1,046	2,757 *	4.6	7.7
388 Reg Bapt Gen As	3	347	204	418 *	.7	1.2
403 Salvation Army	1	73	44	601	1.0	1.7
413 S.D.A.	1	75	NR	89	.1	.3
419 So Bapt Conv	1	20	15	25 *	-	.1
443 Un C of Christ	2	140	72	174 *	.3	.5
449 Un Methodist	13	2,639	1,039	3,284 *	5.4	9.2
467 Wesleyan	1	35	47	85	.1	.2
GREENE	**60**	**4,477**	**2,204**	**17,071 ***	**35.4**	**100.0**
019 Amer Bapt USA	3	82	60	100 *	.2	.6
053 Assemb of God	1	34	43	51	.1	.3
056 Baha'i	0	6	NR	6	-	-
070 Bruderhof Comm	1	132	NR	132	.3	.8
076 Buddhism	1	NR	NR	NR	-	-
081 Catholic	7	NR	NR	9,418	19.5	55.2
151 L-D Saints	1	NR	NR	113	.2	.7
179 Consrv Bapt	1	NR	30	30	.1	.2
193 Episcopal	6	NR	223	479	1.0	2.8
207 E.L.C.A.	2	353	88	481	1.0	2.8
221 Free Methodist	1	57	97	97	.2	.6
246 Greek Orthodox	1	NR	NR	333	.7	2.0
252 Hindu	2	NR	NR	NR	-	-
283 Luth—MO Synod	1	396	173	538	1.1	3.2
355 Presb Ch (USA)	1	67	37	81 *	.2	.5
371 Ref Ch in Am	8	418	323	1,296	2.7	7.6
419 So Bapt Conv	1	38	68	46 *	.1	.3
443 Un C of Christ	2	85	48	103 *	.2	.6
449 Un Methodist	18	2,809	930	3,412 *	7.1	20.0
467 Wesleyan	1	0	84	155	.3	.9
496 Jewish Est	1	NR	NR	200	.4	1.2
HAMILTON	**25**	**596**	**714**	**3,917 ***	**72.8**	**100.0**
056 Baha'i	0	1	NR	1	-	-
081 Catholic	9	NR	NR	2,656	49.4	67.8
179 Consrv Bapt	1	NR	100	100	1.9	2.6
193 Episcopal	2	NR	50	26	.5	.7
203 Evan Free Ch	1	35	138	138	2.6	3.5
355 Presb Ch (USA)	1	14	20	20 *	.4	.5
388 Reg Bapt Gen As	1	35	30	41 *	.8	1.0
419 So Bapt Conv	2	0	0	0 *	-	-
449 Un Methodist	6	511	251	595 *	11.1	15.2
467 Wesleyan	2	0	125	340	6.3	8.7
HERKIMER	**76**	**7,764**	**3,069**	**35,086 ***	**54.5**	**100.0**
019 Amer Bapt USA	7	1,265	442	1,547 *	2.4	4.4
053 Assemb of God	3	101	125	143	.2	.4
056 Baha'i	0	7	NR	7	-	-
081 Catholic	11	NR	NR	23,534	36.5	67.1
089 Chr & Miss Al	2	31	NR	61	.1	.2
105 Christian Ref	1	87	50	106 *	.2	.3
151 L-D Saints	1	NR	NR	164	.3	.5
179 Consrv Bapt	2	NR	288	288	.4	.8
193 Episcopal	4	NR	228	602	.9	1.7
207 E.L.C.A.	5	1,203	260	1,640	2.5	4.7
221 Free Methodist	1	92	136	136	.2	.4
323 Old Ord Amish	2	110	NR	134 *	.2	.4
331 OCA: Ter Diocs	1	160	NR	172	.3	.5
355 Presb Ch (USA)	4	603	269	737 *	1.1	2.1
370 Ref Baptist Chs	1	NR	NR	NR	-	-
371 Ref Ch in Am	2	300	220	698	1.1	2.0
388 Reg Bapt Gen As	1	41	65	65 *	.1	.2
401 Rus Orth Abroad	1	NR	NR	NR	-	-
403 Salvation Army	1	36	42	136	.2	.4
413 S.D.A.	1	23	NR	27	-	.1
431 Ukrainian Orth	1	NR	NR	225	.3	.6
435 Unitarian-Univ	2	85	NR	104 *	.2	.3
443 Un C of Christ	1	106	47	130 *	.2	.4
449 Un Methodist	20	3,514	897	4,300 *	6.7	12.3
496 Jewish Est	1	NR	NR	130	.2	.4
JEFFERSON	**136**	**11,177**	**6,260**	**49,324 ***	**44.1**	**100.0**
019 Amer Bapt USA	9	1,085	702	1,369 *	1.2	2.8
053 Assemb of God	7	398	488	692	.6	1.4
056 Baha'i	0	12	NR	12	-	-
061 Beachy Amish	1	31	NR	39 *	-	.1
081 Catholic	23	NR	NR	30,993	27.7	62.8
089 Chr & Miss Al	2	139	NR	412	.4	.8
093 Chr Ch (Disc)	1	50	20	63 *	.1	.1
127 Ch God (Cleve)	1	62	54	78 *	.1	.2
151 L-D Saints	2	NR	NR	664	.6	1.3
165 Ch of Nazarene	3	393	449	467	.4	.9
167 Chs of Christ	1	44	45	70	.1	.1
176 Congr Ad Afl	2	105	NR	132 *	.1	.3
179 Consrv Bapt	2	NR	130	130	.1	.3
193 Episcopal	11	NR	558	2,140	1.9	4.3
207 E.L.C.A.	3	489	192	749	.7	1.5
221 Free Methodist	1	0	68	68	.1	.1
246 Greek Orthodox	1	NR	NR	162	.1	.3
252 Hindu	1	NR	NR	NR	-	-
267 Muslim Est	1	NR	55	163	.1	.3
288 Mennonite USA	2	132	200	226 *	.2	.5
355 Presb Ch (USA)	10	1,248	548	1,581 *	1.4	3.2
371 Ref Ch in Am	1	109	166	275	.2	.6
388 Reg Bapt Gen As	1	94	108	119 *	.1	.2
403 Salvation Army	1	95	22	186	.2	.4
413 S.D.A.	3	148	NR	176	.2	.4
419 So Bapt Conv	5	474	402	598 *	.5	1.2
435 Unitarian-Univ	1	64	NR	81 *	.1	.2
443 Un C of Christ	5	682	272	860 *	.8	1.7
449 Un Methodist	34	5,323	1,781	6,719 *	6.0	13.6
496 Jewish Est	1	NR	NR	100	.1	.2
KINGS	**959**	**136,245**	**78,584**	**1,552,336 ***	**63.0**	**100.0**
019 Amer Bapt USA	51	45,589	14,259	57,755 *	2.3	3.7
034 Ant Orth of NA	2	1,089	NR	2,178	.1	.1
053 Assemb of God	57	12,794	9,126	15,600	.6	1.0

NR–Not Reported *Total adherents estimated from known number of communicant, confirmed, full members. - Represents a percentage less than 0.1. Percentages may not total 100 due to rounding.

Table 4: Religious Congregations by County and Group: 2000

Religious Group	Number of Churches, Synagogues, Mosques, or Temples	Number of Communicant, Confirmed, or Full Members	Number of Attendees	Total Adherents: Number of Adherents	Total Adherents: % of Total Pop.	Total Adherents: % of Total Adh.
057 Bapt Gen Conf	6	520	625	803 *	-	.1
076 Buddhism	5	NR	NR	NR	-	-
081 Catholic	127	NR	NR	912,509	37.0	58.8
084 Calvary Chapel	1	NR	NR	NR	-	-
089 Chr & Miss Al	10	1,068	NR	1,540	.1	.1
093 Chr Ch (Disc)	11	1,289	640	1,633 *	.1	.1
097 Chr Chs&Chs Cr	10	501	NR	635 *	-	-
123 Ch God (Ander)	6	NR	772	772	-	-
127 Ch God (Cleve)	29	3,844	3,543	4,923 *	.2	.3
145 Ch God Prophcy	11	841	NR	1,066 *	-	.1
151 L-D Saints	7	NR	NR	3,080	.1	.2
157 Ch of Brethren	2	302	0	383 *	-	-
165 Ch of Nazarene	18	2,402	2,042	2,712	.1	.2
167 Chs of Christ	4	573	540	802	-	.1
171 Ch God-Gen Con	2	56	46	71 *	-	-
175 Congr Chr Chs	5	775	535	982 *	-	.1
176 Congr Ad Afl	1	37	NR	47 *	-	-
179 Consrv Bapt	10	NR	892	892	-	.1
193 Episcopal	33	NR	5,633	15,352	.6	1.0
201 Evan Cov Ch	1	0	0	0 *	-	-
203 Evan Free Ch	7	603	827	846	-	.1
207 E.L.C.A.	37	5,005	2,064	7,249	.3	.5
221 Free Methodist	5	87	249	256	-	-
226 Friends-USA	1	50	NR	63 *	-	-
245 Greek Orth Vslp	1	875	NR	1,125	-	.1
246 Greek Orthodox	4	NR	NR	6,309	.3	.4
252 Hindu	8	NR	NR	NR	-	-
263 Int Foursq Gos	1	21	34	34 *	-	-
267 Muslim Est	26	NR	11,842	57,897	2.3	3.7
283 Luth—MO Synod	8	888	516	1,185	-	.1
288 Mennonite USA	6	271	299	343 *	-	-
291 Missionary Ch	2	288	226	288	-	-
293 Morav Ch-North	2	338	NR	477	-	-
297 Mennonite;Other	1	35	NR	44 *	-	-
331 OCA: Ter Diocs	3	127	NR	580	-	-
333 Malan Dioc Am	1	NR	NR	125	-	-
339 Pent Ch of God	2	211	NR	348	-	-
349 Pent Holiness	1	53	47	67 *	-	-
355 Presb Ch (USA)	24	2,656	1,618	3,368 *	.1	.2
363 Primitive Meth	1	57	NR	61	-	-
371 Ref Ch in Am	13	912	835	1,732	.1	.1
388 Reg Bapt Gen As	1	50	50	63 *	-	-
403 Salvation Army	8	834	447	3,860	.2	.2
413 S.D.A.	48	18,715	NR	22,273	.9	1.4
416 Sikh	1	NR	NR	NR	-	-
418 Southw Bapt Fel	1	NR	NR	NR	-	-
419 So Bapt Conv	24	2,915	1,978	3,693 *	.1	.2
423 Syrian Orth Ch	1	NR	NR	150	-	-
431 Ukrainian Orth	1	NR	NR	750	-	-
435 Unitarian-Univ	2	306	NR	388 *	-	-
443 Un C of Christ	9	562	253	712 *	-	-
449 Un Methodist	32	10,122	3,627	12,821 *	.5	.8
463 Vineyard	1	130	120	165 *	-	-
467 Wesleyan	4	0	1,074	1,579	.1	.1
496 Jewish Est	256	NR	NR	379,000	15.4	24.4
498 Indep.Charis.	6	18,104	13,825	20,400	.8	1.3
499 Indep.Non-Char	1	350	0	350	-	-
LEWIS	**53**	**3,793**	**2,757**	**17,422 ***	**64.7**	**100.0**
019 Amer Bapt USA	2	196	132	246 *	.9	1.4
040 Ap Chr Ch-Amer	1	44	125	125 *	.5	.7
053 Assemb of God	1	67	85	129	.5	.7
081 Catholic	12	NR	NR	11,792	43.8	67.7
151 L-D Saints	1	NR	NR	105	.4	.6
165 Ch of Nazarene	1	126	89	126	.5	.7
183 Cons Menn Conf	5	997	1,218	1,450	5.4	8.3
193 Episcopal	4	NR	87	282	1.0	1.6
286 E.PA Mennonite	1	61	NR	77 *	.3	.4
288 Mennonite USA	1	271	210	340 *	1.3	2.0
297 Mennonite;Other	1	32	NR	40 *	.1	.2
323 Old Ord Amish	1	55	NR	69 *	.3	.4
355 Presb Ch (USA)	2	339	182	426 *	1.6	2.4
371 Ref Ch in Am	1	21	25	70	.3	.4
388 Reg Bapt Gen As	1	26	33	33 *	.1	.2
413 S.D.A.	1	17	NR	20	.1	.1
443 Un C of Christ	3	91	88	114 *	.4	.7
449 Un Methodist	12	1,436	431	1,803 *	6.7	10.3
467 Wesleyan	2	14	52	175	.6	1.0
LIVINGSTON	**75**	**6,291**	**3,886**	**23,463 ***	**36.5**	**100.0**
019 Amer Bapt USA	3	178	94	216 *	.3	.9
053 Assemb of God	4	127	172	198	.3	.8
056 Baha'i	0	6	NR	6	-	-
076 Buddhism	2	NR	NR	NR	-	-
081 Catholic	11	NR	NR	14,260	22.2	60.8
084 Calvary Chapel	1	NR	NR	NR	-	-
123 Ch God (Ander)	1	NR	17	17	-	.1
151 L-D Saints	1	NR	NR	256	.4	1.1
165 Ch of Nazarene	1	158	181	260	.4	1.1
179 Consrv Bapt	2	NR	75	75	.1	.3
193 Episcopal	4	NR	204	655	1.0	2.8
207 E.L.C.A.	2	575	214	781	1.2	3.3
221 Free Methodist	1	101	87	125	.2	.5
263 Int Foursq Gos	1	42	95	95 *	.1	.4
283 Luth—MO Synod	1	61	36	66	.1	.3
355 Presb Ch (USA)	16	1,954	973	2,369 *	3.7	10.1
388 Reg Bapt Gen As	2	115	170	170 *	.3	.7
413 S.D.A.	1	57	NR	68	.1	.3
419 So Bapt Conv	1	90	67	109 *	.2	.5
443 Un C of Christ	2	213	93	258 *	.4	1.1
449 Un Methodist	15	2,444	1,112	2,963 *	4.6	12.6
463 Vineyard	1	46	52	56 *	.1	.2
467 Wesleyan	2	124	244	460	.7	2.0
MADISON	**70**	**9,327**	**4,068**	**25,636 ***	**36.9**	**100.0**
019 Amer Bapt USA	13	2,294	759	2,823 *	4.1	11.0
053 Assemb of God	2	116	160	196	.3	.8
056 Baha'i	0	5	NR	5	-	-
081 Catholic	7	NR	NR	12,638	18.2	49.3
089 Chr & Miss Al	1	43	NR	171	.2	.7
165 Ch of Nazarene	1	83	75	83	.1	.3
176 Congr Ad Afl	1	106	NR	130 *	.2	.5
193 Episcopal	5	NR	377	919	1.3	3.6
221 Free Methodist	1	151	261	261	.4	1.0
283 Luth—MO Synod	1	131	40	169	.2	.7
297 Mennonite;Other	1	85	NR	105 *	.2	.4
355 Presb Ch (USA)	5	1,295	605	1,593 *	2.3	6.2
388 Reg Bapt Gen As	2	230	279	279 *	.4	1.1
403 Salvation Army	1	36	17	203	.3	.8
413 S.D.A.	2	42	NR	50	.1	.2
419 So Bapt Conv	0	15	41	18 *	-	.1
443 Un C of Christ	3	373	173	459 *	.7	1.8
449 Un Methodist	23	4,322	1,243	5,319 *	7.7	20.7
467 Wesleyan	1	0	38	65	.1	.3
496 Jewish Est	0	NR	NR	150	.2	.6
MONROE	**418**	**68,949**	**42,420**	**399,093 ***	**54.3**	**100.0**
019 Amer Bapt USA	31	10,547	3,849	13,168 *	1.8	3.3
050 Armen Ap Etchm	1	0	NR	50	-	-
053 Assemb of God	16	2,473	3,171	3,585	.5	.9
055 As Ref Pres Ch	1	32	NR	39	-	-
056 Baha'i	6	389	NR	389	.1	.1
057 Bapt Gen Conf	1	93	340	340 *	-	.1
076 Buddhism	4	NR	NR	NR	-	-
081 Catholic	80	NR	NR	262,624	35.7	65.8
084 Calvary Chapel	7	NR	NR	NR	-	-
089 Chr & Miss Al	2	130	NR	303	-	.1
093 Chr Ch (Disc)	2	158	67	197 *	-	-
097 Chr Chs&Chs Cr	1	146	NR	182 *	-	-
105 Christian Ref	2	647	435	808 *	.1	.2
123 Ch God (Ander)	1	NR	45	45	-	-
127 Ch God (Cleve)	7	547	367	711 *	.1	.2
145 Ch God Prophcy	1	82	NR	102 *	-	-
151 L-D Saints	11	NR	NR	2,961	.4	.7
165 Ch of Nazarene	6	856	642	1,007	.1	.3
167 Chs of Christ	7	1,112	1,182	1,539	.2	.4
173 Comm of Christ	1	25	NR	25	-	-

NR–Not Reported *Total adherents estimated from known number of communicant, confirmed, full members. - Represents a percentage less than 0.1. Percentages may not total 100 due to rounding.

Table 4: Religious Congregations by County and Group: 2000

Religious Group	Number of Churches, Synagogues, Mosques, or Temples	Number of Communicant, Confirmed, or Full Members	Number of Attendees	Total Adherents		
				Number of Adherents	% of Total Pop.	% of Total Adh.
193 Episcopal	23	NR	2,971	8,866	1.2	2.2
201 Evan Cov Ch	1	78	58	97 *	-	-
203 Evan Free Ch	2	138	250	250	-	.1
207 E.L.C.A.	19	7,817	3,151	10,432	1.4	2.6
221 Free Methodist	9	1,647	2,525	2,549	.3	.6
226 Friends-USA	2	100	NR	125 *	-	-
246 Greek Orthodox	2	NR	NR	3,105	.4	.8
252 Hindu	3	NR	NR	NR	-	-
263 Int Foursq Gos	2	69	103	103 *	-	-
267 Muslim Est	3	NR	808	4,041	.5	1.0
268 Jain	1	NR	NR	NR	-	-
283 Luth—MO Synod	12	5,959	2,985	8,365	1.1	2.1
288 Mennonite USA	2	18	40	40 *	-	-
290 Metro Comm Ch	1	44	43	55 *	-	-
313 N Am Bapt Conf	2	377	506	471 *	.1	.1
330 Macedonian Orth	1	NR	NR	1,200	.2	.3
331 OCA: Ter Diocs	1	105	NR	240	-	.1
333 Malan Dioc Am	1	NR	NR	75	-	-
335 Orth Pres Ch	2	149	191	216	-	.1
349 Pent Holiness	1	127	150	159 *	-	-
355 Presb Ch (USA)	33	11,419	4,503	14,259 *	1.9	3.6
370 Ref Baptist Chs	1	NR	NR	NR	-	-
371 Ref Ch in Am	3	470	376	793	.1	.2
388 Reg Bapt Gen As	5	595	660	725 *	.1	.2
401 Rus Orth Abroad	1	NR	NR	NR	-	-
403 Salvation Army	3	345	274	458	.1	.1
413 S.D.A.	7	1,671	NR	1,989	.3	.5
416 Sikh	4	NR	NR	NR	-	-
419 So Bapt Conv	6	507	352	633 *	.1	.2
431 Ukrainian Orth	1	NR	NR	975	.1	.2
435 Unitarian-Univ	2	908	NR	1,134 *	.2	.3
443 Un C of Christ	14	4,183	1,523	5,222 *	.7	1.3
449 Un Methodist	32	11,759	4,108	14,680 *	2.0	3.7
463 Vineyard	2	215	195	275 *	-	.1
467 Wesleyan	5	367	574	965	.1	.2
469 WELS	1	81	76	121	-	-
496 Jewish Est	14	NR	NR	22,500	3.1	5.6
498 Indep.Charis.	2	320	1,325	1,325	.2	.3
499 Indep.Non-Char	4	2,244	4,575	4,575	.6	1.1
MONTGOMERY	**65**	**6,247**	**2,777**	**34,927 ***	**70.3**	**100.0**
019 Amer Bapt USA	1	279	48	342 *	.7	1.0
056 Baha'i	0	5	NR	5	-	-
081 Catholic	12	NR	NR	24,285	48.9	69.5
089 Chr & Miss Al	1	42	NR	95	.2	.3
127 Ch God (Cleve)	1	20	37	37 *	.1	.1
145 Ch God Prophcy	1	51	NR	63 *	.1	.2
151 L-D Saints	1	NR	NR	90	.2	.3
193 Episcopal	2	NR	107	324	.7	.9
207 E.L.C.A.	7	1,924	438	3,213	6.5	9.2
221 Free Methodist	1	27	37	43	.1	.1
288 Mennonite USA	1	13	10	16 *	-	-
323 Old Ord Amish	2	110	NR	134 *	.3	.4
335 Orth Pres Ch	1	47	104	104	.2	.3
355 Presb Ch (USA)	2	426	190	522 *	1.1	1.5
371 Ref Ch in Am	14	915	725	2,534	5.1	7.3
388 Reg Bapt Gen As	1	120	124	147 *	.3	.4
403 Salvation Army	1	35	24	43	.1	.1
413 S.D.A.	2	101	NR	120	.2	.3
419 So Bapt Conv	0	30	54	37 *	.1	.1
443 Un C of Christ	1	105	55	129 *	.3	.4
449 Un Methodist	11	1,585	463	1,944 *	3.9	5.6
496 Jewish Est	1	NR	NR	150	.3	.4
499 Indep.Non-Char	1	412	361	550	1.1	1.6
NASSAU	**560**	**54,605**	**30,571**	**1,014,215 ***	**76.0**	**100.0**
019 Amer Bapt USA	11	2,373	1,153	2,943 *	.2	.3
022 Carp Rus Orth	1	122	NR	207	-	-
034 Ant Orth of NA	1	97	NR	194	-	-
053 Assemb of God	25	2,472	3,007	3,386	.3	.3
055 As Ref Pres Ch	1	29	NR	29	-	-
056 Baha'i	2	251	NR	251	-	-
057 Bapt Gen Conf	3	413	377	513 *	-	.1
076 Buddhism	3	NR	NR	NR	-	-
081 Catholic	67	NR	NR	694,389	52.0	68.5
089 Chr & Miss Al	4	209	NR	333	-	-
093 Chr Ch (Disc)	1	0	0	0 *	-	-
097 Chr Chs&Chs Cr	5	525	NR	651 *	-	.1
123 Ch God (Ander)	2	NR	190	190	-	-
127 Ch God (Cleve)	12	1,033	728	1,322 *	.1	.1
145 Ch God Prophcy	5	349	NR	434 *	-	-
151 L-D Saints	10	NR	NR	1,568	.1	.2
165 Ch of Nazarene	9	861	877	1,390	.1	.1
167 Chs of Christ	3	429	335	504	-	-
179 Consrv Bapt	7	NR	1,265	1,265	.1	.1
181 Consrv Congr	1	62	75	77 *	-	-
193 Episcopal	42	NR	4,122	16,153	1.2	1.6
201 Evan Cov Ch	1	27	29	33 *	-	-
203 Evan Free Ch	3	163	190	190	-	-
207 E.L.C.A.	39	13,933	4,865	19,528	1.5	1.9
226 Friends-USA	4	200	NR	248 *	-	-
246 Greek Orthodox	7	NR	NR	8,148	.6	.8
252 Hindu	6	NR	NR	NR	-	-
262 Int Cou Comm Ch	2	600	NR	744 *	.1	.1
267 Muslim Est	6	NR	2,248	11,164	.8	1.1
268 Jain	1	NR	NR	NR	-	-
283 Luth—MO Synod	9	4,072	1,639	5,345	.4	.5
288 Mennonite USA	1	0	20	20 *	-	-
313 N Am Bapt Conf	1	85	90	105 *	-	-
331 OCA: Ter Diocs	2	264	NR	509	-	.1
333 Malan Dioc Am	3	NR	NR	950	.1	.1
335 Orth Pres Ch	1	215	252	351	-	-
355 Presb Ch (USA)	21	3,960	2,320	4,914 *	.4	.5
356 Presb Ch Amer	2	0	0	0	-	-
371 Ref Ch in Am	11	1,349	1,167	2,458	.2	.2
388 Reg Bapt Gen As	1	90	99	99 *	-	-
401 Rus Orth Abroad	2	NR	NR	NR	-	-
403 Salvation Army	3	294	313	1,513	.1	.1
413 S.D.A.	12	1,982	NR	2,358	.2	.2
416 Sikh	3	NR	NR	NR	-	-
419 So Bapt Conv	5	302	190	375 *	-	-
423 Syrian Orth Ch	1	NR	NR	200	-	-
431 Ukrainian Orth	1	NR	NR	30	-	-
435 Unitarian-Univ	4	961	NR	1,192 *	.1	.1
443 Un C of Christ	10	2,255	858	2,797 *	.2	.3
449 Un Methodist	40	13,936	3,548	17,284 *	1.3	1.7
463 Vineyard	1	452	389	561 *	-	.1
496 Jewish Est	141	NR	NR	207,000	15.5	20.4
498 Indep.Charis.	1	240	225	300	-	-
NEW YORK	**665**	**86,021**	**66,416**	**1,075,375 ***	**70.0**	**100.0**
019 Amer Bapt USA	41	24,784	11,548	28,611 *	1.9	2.7
022 Carp Rus Orth	2	243	NR	416	-	-
049 Armen Ap Cilic	1	275	NR	1,400	.1	.1
050 Armen Ap Etchm	3	200	NR	6,272	.4	.6
053 Assemb of God	43	5,057	3,829	6,019	.4	.6
056 Baha'i	1	1,570	NR	1,570	.1	.1
057 Bapt Gen Conf	1	326	418	418 *	-	-
076 Buddhism	43	NR	NR	NR	-	-
078 Bulgar Orth USA	1	NR	NR	600	-	.1
081 Catholic	110	NR	NR	564,505	36.7	52.5
084 Calvary Chapel	1	NR	NR	NR	-	-
089 Chr & Miss Al	7	1,197	NR	1,411	.1	.1
093 Chr Ch (Disc)	4	713	95	823 *	.1	.1
097 Chr Chs&Chs Cr	6	275	NR	318 *	-	-
123 Ch God (Ander)	2	NR	95	95	-	-
127 Ch God (Cleve)	8	814	608	980 *	.1	.1
145 Ch God Prophcy	2	133	NR	154 *	-	-
151 L-D Saints	10	NR	NR	3,825	.2	.4
165 Ch of Nazarene	5	346	203	432	-	-
167 Chs of Christ	7	778	720	999	.1	.1
173 Comm of Christ	2	74	NR	74	-	-
179 Consrv Bapt	4	NR	590	590	-	.1
181 Consrv Congr	1	25	55	29 *	-	-
193 Episcopal	47	NR	9,227	23,742	1.5	2.2
201 Evan Cov Ch	1	24	25	28 *	-	-
207 E.L.C.A.	18	3,351	1,665	4,725	.3	.4

NR–Not Reported   *Total adherents estimated from known number of communicant, confirmed, full members.   - Represents a percentage less than 0.1.   Percentages may not total 100 due to rounding.

Table 4: Religious Congregations by County and Group: 2000

Religious Group	Number of Churches, Synagogues, Mosques, or Temples	Number of Communicant, Confirmed, or Full Members	Number of Attendees	Total Adherents: Number of Adherents	Total Adherents: % of Total Pop.	Total Adherents: % of Total Adh.
221 Free Methodist	1	100	25	137	-	-
226 Friends-USA	2	100	NR	115 *	-	-
246 Greek Orthodox	11	NR	NR	5,403	.4	.5
252 Hindu	10	NR	NR	NR	-	-
262 Int Cou Comm Ch	1	100	NR	115 *	-	-
263 Int Foursq Gos	1	43	32	50 *	-	-
264 Int Chs of Crst	1	5,916	11,442	7,868	.5	.7
267 Muslim Est	16	NR	10,396	37,078	2.4	3.4
268 Jain	1	NR	NR	NR	-	-
283 Luth—MO Synod	4	605	267	1,588	.1	.1
288 Mennonite USA	4	131	115	152 *	-	-
290 Metro Comm Ch	1	360	340	416 *	-	-
293 Morav Ch-North	2	744	NR	1,211	.1	.1
331 OCA: Ter Diocs	3	139	NR	421	-	-
349 Pent Holiness	1	35	35	40 *	-	-
355 Presb Ch (USA)	30	9,247	4,261	10,715 *	.7	1.0
356 Presb Ch Amer	4	869	1,635	1,635	.1	.2
370 Ref Baptist Chs	1	NR	NR	NR	-	-
371 Ref Ch in Am	9	3,398	1,981	12,439	.8	1.2
388 Reg Bapt Gen As	1	90	99	99 *	-	-
397 OCA: Roman Dioc	1	NR	NR	500	-	-
400 Rus Orth Moscow	1	NR	NR	NR	-	-
401 Rus Orth Abroad	3	NR	NR	NR	-	-
403 Salvation Army	6	513	519	751	-	.1
410 Serb Orth USA	1	NR	NR	4,000	.3	.4
413 S.D.A.	15	5,328	NR	6,339	.4	.6
416 Sikh	2	NR	NR	NR	-	-
419 So Bapt Conv	15	1,415	1,325	1,634 *	.1	.2
425 Tao	1	NR	NR	NR	-	-
431 Ukrainian Orth	3	NR	NR	693	-	.1
435 Unitarian-Univ	3	1,847	NR	2,132 *	.1	.2
443 Un C of Christ	13	3,555	1,580	4,104 *	.3	.4
449 Un Methodist	21	11,176	3,154	12,900 *	.8	1.2
463 Vineyard	1	125	100	144 *	-	-
467 Wesleyan	1	0	32	160	-	-
490 Zoroastrian	1	NR	NR	NR	-	-
496 Jewish Est	102	NR	NR	314,500	20.5	29.2
NIAGARA	**182**	**29,617**	**13,997**	**123,670 ***	**56.3**	**100.0**
019 Amer Bapt USA	10	2,003	1,080	2,468 *	1.1	2.0
034 Ant Orth of NA	1	384	NR	768	.3	.6
049 Armen Ap Cilic	1	40	NR	140	.1	.1
050 Armen Ap Etchm	1	27	NR	180	.1	.1
053 Assemb of God	7	789	985	1,434	.7	1.2
056 Baha'i	0	49	NR	49	-	-
081 Catholic	35	NR	NR	78,534	35.7	63.5
089 Chr & Miss Al	3	293	NR	789	.4	.6
093 Chr Ch (Disc)	2	481	140	593 *	.3	.5
123 Ch God (Ander)	1	NR	160	160	.1	.1
127 Ch God (Cleve)	1	131	76	161 *	.1	.1
151 L-D Saints	2	NR	NR	714	.3	.6
165 Ch of Nazarene	4	278	135	378	.2	.3
167 Chs of Christ	1	98	100	134	.1	.1
173 Comm of Christ	1	131	NR	131	.1	.1
193 Episcopal	11	NR	897	3,070	1.4	2.5
207 E.L.C.A.	14	3,832	1,551	5,203	2.4	4.2
221 Free Methodist	4	273	372	378	.2	.3
226 Friends-USA	1	50	NR	62 *	-	.1
251 Holy Orth in NA	1	NR	NR	18	-	-
283 Luth—MO Synod	19	8,276	3,247	11,272	5.1	9.1
331 OCA: Ter Diocs	1	20	NR	60	-	-
355 Presb Ch (USA)	13	3,486	1,450	4,294 *	2.0	3.5
388 Reg Bapt Gen As	2	323	295	398 *	.2	.3
403 Salvation Army	2	200	123	1,285	.6	1.0
413 S.D.A.	3	139	NR	166	.1	.1
418 Southw Bapt Fel	1	NR	NR	NR	-	-
419 So Bapt Conv	4	196	152	241 *	.1	.2
435 Unitarian-Univ	1	35	NR	43 *	-	-
443 Un C of Christ	9	1,732	722	2,134 *	1.0	1.7
449 Un Methodist	20	6,215	2,255	7,657 *	3.5	6.2
467 Wesleyan	3	136	257	606	.3	.5
496 Jewish Est	3	NR	NR	150	.1	.1

Religious Group	Number of Churches, Synagogues, Mosques, or Temples	Number of Communicant, Confirmed, or Full Members	Number of Attendees	Total Adherents: Number of Adherents	Total Adherents: % of Total Pop.	Total Adherents: % of Total Adh.
ONEIDA	**230**	**21,865**	**11,008**	**122,762 ***	**52.1**	**100.0**
017 Amer Bapt Assn	1	30	NR	37 *	-	-
019 Amer Bapt USA	13	2,448	848	2,989 *	1.3	2.4
034 Ant Orth of NA	1	44	NR	88	-	.1
053 Assemb of God	6	548	729	999	.4	.8
056 Baha'i	0	29	NR	29	-	-
081 Catholic	55	NR	NR	83,817	35.6	68.3
089 Chr & Miss Al	5	212	NR	619	.3	.5
151 L-D Saints	4	NR	NR	695	.3	.6
165 Ch of Nazarene	3	84	50	143	.1	.1
167 Chs of Christ	2	112	110	137	.1	.1
179 Consrv Bapt	5	NR	695	695	.3	.6
193 Episcopal	17	NR	898	3,784	1.6	3.1
207 E.L.C.A.	4	1,585	516	2,327	1.0	1.9
221 Free Methodist	1	16	22	22	-	-
226 Friends-USA	1	50	NR	61 *	-	-
245 Greek Orth Vslp	1	245	NR	845	.4	.7
263 Int Foursq Gos	1	60	135	135 *	.1	.1
267 Muslim Est	1	NR	150	1,200	.5	1.0
283 Luth—MO Synod	4	1,131	417	2,564	1.1	2.1
293 Morav Ch-North	1	136	NR	178	.1	.1
355 Presb Ch (USA)	26	3,407	1,490	4,160 *	1.8	3.4
371 Ref Ch in Am	1	85	75	169	.1	.1
388 Reg Bapt Gen As	3	261	313	297 *	.1	.2
401 Rus Orth Abroad	1	NR	NR	NR	-	-
403 Salvation Army	3	267	244	1,214	.5	1.0
413 S.D.A.	5	416	NR	496	.2	.4
419 So Bapt Conv	5	416	266	508 *	.2	.4
431 Ukrainian Orth	3	NR	NR	279	.1	.2
435 Unitarian-Univ	2	142	NR	173 *	.1	.1
443 Un C of Christ	8	930	352	1,136 *	.5	.9
449 Un Methodist	41	8,532	2,528	10,416 *	4.4	8.5
467 Wesleyan	2	79	345	525	.2	.4
496 Jewish Est	3	NR	NR	1,200	.5	1.0
498 Indep.Charis.	1	600	825	825	.4	.7
ONONDAGA	**317**	**51,979**	**25,221**	**237,014 ***	**51.7**	**100.0**
019 Amer Bapt USA	20	4,747	1,907	5,931 *	1.3	2.5
034 Ant Orth of NA	1	307	NR	614	.1	.3
039 Ap Chr Ch(Naz)	1	69	100	100 *	-	-
049 Armen Ap Cilic	1	25	NR	70	-	-
050 Armen Ap Etchm	1	32	NR	210	-	.1
053 Assemb of God	12	1,572	2,008	2,323	.5	1.0
056 Baha'i	1	61	NR	61	-	-
076 Buddhism	3	NR	NR	NR	-	-
081 Catholic	60	NR	NR	147,332	32.1	62.2
084 Calvary Chapel	2	NR	NR	NR	-	-
089 Chr & Miss Al	4	590	NR	1,060	.2	.4
093 Chr Ch (Disc)	2	166	40	207 *	-	.1
097 Chr Chs&Chs Cr	5	705	NR	881 *	.2	.4
105 Christian Ref	1	97	0	121 *	-	.1
127 Ch God (Cleve)	2	139	101	173 *	-	.1
145 Ch God Prophcy	1	82	NR	103 *	-	-
151 L-D Saints	5	NR	NR	1,324	.3	.6
165 Ch of Nazarene	3	404	400	589	.1	.2
167 Chs of Christ	2	325	349	410	.1	.2
179 Consrv Bapt	2	NR	150	150	-	.1
181 Consrv Congr	2	214	276	267 *	.1	.1
193 Episcopal	22	NR	2,127	6,590	1.4	2.8
201 Evan Cov Ch	2	259	428	428 *	.1	.2
207 E.L.C.A.	12	5,694	1,783	7,941	1.7	3.4
221 Free Methodist	2	103	281	281	.1	.1
226 Friends-USA	1	50	NR	62 *	-	-
245 Greek Orth Vslp	1	190	NR	265	.1	.1
246 Greek Orthodox	1	NR	NR	927	.2	.4
252 Hindu	1	NR	NR	NR	-	-
262 Int Cou Comm Ch	1	1,750	NR	2,187 *	.5	.9
263 Int Foursq Gos	1	12	16	16 *	-	-
264 Int Chs of Crst	1	120	217	172	-	.1
267 Muslim Est	2	NR	556	3,109	.7	1.3
268 Jain	1	NR	NR	NR	-	-
283 Luth—MO Synod	1	316	104	412	.1	.2
288 Mennonite USA	1	10	8	12 *	-	-

NR–Not Reported   *Total adherents estimated from known number of communicant, confirmed, full members.   - Represents a percentage less than 0.1.   Percentages may not total 100 due to rounding.

Table 4: Religious Congregations by County and Group: 2000

Religious Group	Number of Churches, Synagogues, Mosques, or Temples	Number of Communicant, Confirmed, or Full Members	Number of Attendees	Total Adherents		
				Number of Adherents	% of Total Pop.	% of Total Adh.
330 Macedonian Orth	1	NR	NR	800	.2	.3
331 OCA: Ter Diocs	2	181	NR	265	.1	.1
333 Malan Dioc Am	1	NR	NR	100	-	-
335 Orth Pres Ch	1	20	38	38	-	-
355 Presb Ch (USA)	26	4,897	2,317	6,120 *	1.3	2.6
371 Ref Ch in Am	2	320	214	526	.1	.2
388 Reg Bapt Gen As	4	362	334	359 *	.1	.2
401 Rus Orth Abroad	1	NR	NR	NR	-	-
403 Salvation Army	4	232	168	698	.2	.3
413 S.D.A.	5	979	NR	1,167	.3	.5
416 Sikh	2	NR	NR	NR	-	-
419 So Bapt Conv	5	789	454	986 *	.2	.4
431 Ukrainian Orth	1	NR	NR	177	-	.1
435 Unitarian-Univ	2	566	NR	707 *	.2	.3
443 Un C of Christ	7	1,242	706	1,552 *	.3	.7
449 Un Methodist	54	18,986	5,053	23,721 *	5.2	10.0
463 Vineyard	1	465	400	581 *	.1	.2
467 Wesleyan	5	270	492	1,133	.2	.5
469 WELS	1	31	29	31	-	-
496 Jewish Est	6	NR	NR	9,000	2.0	3.8
498 Indep.Charis.	2	3,200	2,640	3,200	.7	1.4
499 Indep.Non-Char	3	1,400	1,525	1,525	.3	.6
ONTARIO	**90**	**12,107**	**6,804**	**46,394 ***	**46.3**	**100.0**
019 Amer Bapt USA	8	860	624	1,068 *	1.1	2.3
034 Ant Orth of NA	1	236	NR	472	.5	1.0
053 Assemb of God	2	94	133	138	.1	.3
056 Baha'i	2	77	NR	77	.1	.2
081 Catholic	12	NR	NR	26,792	26.7	57.7
084 Calvary Chapel	2	NR	NR	NR	-	-
089 Chr & Miss Al	1	13	NR	29	-	.1
097 Chr Chs&Chs Cr	2	150	NR	186 *	.2	.4
127 Ch God (Cleve)	2	62	82	100 *	.1	.2
151 L-D Saints	2	NR	NR	726	.7	1.6
165 Ch of Nazarene	1	73	77	134	.1	.3
179 Consrv Bapt	2	NR	366	366	.4	.8
193 Episcopal	5	NR	434	1,521	1.5	3.3
207 E.L.C.A.	3	619	229	908	.9	2.0
283 Luth—MO Synod	2	708	319	960	1.0	2.1
355 Presb Ch (USA)	8	1,998	955	2,493 *	2.5	5.4
388 Reg Bapt Gen As	2	109	135	142 *	.1	.3
403 Salvation Army	2	197	75	756	.8	1.6
419 So Bapt Conv	2	103	123	128 *	.1	.3
435 Unitarian-Univ	1	68	NR	84 *	.1	.2
443 Un C of Christ	7	1,345	691	1,670 *	1.7	3.6
449 Un Methodist	18	5,174	1,862	6,424 *	6.4	13.8
463 Vineyard	1	97	97	120 *	.1	.3
467 Wesleyan	1	124	602	800	.8	1.7
496 Jewish Est	1	NR	NR	300	.3	.6
ORANGE	**200**	**21,441**	**12,925**	**214,863 ***	**62.9**	**100.0**
019 Amer Bapt USA	5	731	178	947 *	.3	.4
053 Assemb of God	10	983	1,217	1,749	.5	.8
056 Baha'i	0	60	NR	60	-	-
070 Bruderhof Comm	2	264	NR	264	.1	.1
076 Buddhism	1	NR	NR	NR	-	-
081 Catholic	29	NR	NR	160,245	46.9	74.6
089 Chr & Miss Al	1	57	NR	94	-	-
105 Christian Ref	1	631	530	817 *	.2	.4
127 Ch God (Cleve)	4	797	665	1,057 *	.3	.5
145 Ch God Prophcy	2	164	NR	212 *	.1	.1
151 L-D Saints	4	NR	NR	803	.2	.4
165 Ch of Nazarene	4	231	300	346	.1	.2
167 Chs of Christ	3	106	125	169	-	.1
179 Consrv Bapt	5	NR	1,110	1,110	.3	.5
181 Consrv Congr	2	243	160	315 *	.1	.1
193 Episcopal	19	NR	1,288	3,845	1.1	1.8
203 Evan Free Ch	1	22	50	50	-	-
207 E.L.C.A.	5	1,628	557	2,671	.8	1.2
216 Evan Presby Ch	1	160	NR	207 *	.1	.1
226 Friends-USA	1	50	NR	65 *	-	-
246 Greek Orthodox	3	NR	NR	2,628	.8	1.2
252 Hindu	2	NR	NR	NR	-	-
263 Int Foursq Gos	1	76	51	98 *	-	-
267 Muslim Est	2	NR	120	400	.1	.2
283 Luth—MO Synod	5	1,556	906	2,711	.8	1.3
339 Pent Ch of God	1	175	NR	200	.1	.1
355 Presb Ch (USA)	26	4,310	2,240	5,650 *	1.7	2.6
356 Presb Ch Amer	1	136	145	178	.1	.1
370 Ref Baptist Chs	1	NR	NR	NR	-	-
371 Ref Ch in Am	8	857	674	2,058	.6	1.0
388 Reg Bapt Gen As	2	83	100	108 *	-	.1
403 Salvation Army	3	401	228	849	.2	.4
413 S.D.A.	3	387	NR	460	.1	.2
419 So Bapt Conv	2	149	106	193 *	.1	.1
435 Unitarian-Univ	2	74	NR	96 *	-	-
443 Un C of Christ	2	275	105	356 *	.1	.2
449 Un Methodist	27	6,835	2,070	8,852 *	2.6	4.1
496 Jewish Est	9	NR	NR	15,000	4.4	7.0
ORLEANS	**47**	**5,820**	**3,373**	**20,113 ***	**45.5**	**100.0**
019 Amer Bapt USA	4	831	307	1,035 *	2.3	5.1
032 Amish; other	1	42	NR	52 *	.1	.3
053 Assemb of God	4	492	604	687	1.6	3.4
056 Baha'i	0	8	NR	8	-	-
081 Catholic	7	NR	NR	11,081	25.1	55.1
089 Chr & Miss Al	2	56	NR	143	.3	.7
193 Episcopal	3	NR	150	447	1.0	2.2
207 E.L.C.A.	3	508	207	721	1.6	3.6
221 Free Methodist	1	96	141	141	.3	.7
267 Muslim Est	1	NR	228	841	1.9	4.2
283 Luth—MO Synod	1	188	87	223	.5	1.1
313 N Am Bapt Conf	1	45	82	56 *	.1	.3
355 Presb Ch (USA)	4	892	485	1,112 *	2.5	5.5
388 Reg Bapt Gen As	1	90	99	99 *	.2	.5
435 Unitarian-Univ	1	28	NR	35 *	.1	.2
443 Un C of Christ	1	62	35	77 *	.2	.4
449 Un Methodist	11	2,405	814	2,995 *	6.8	14.9
467 Wesleyan	1	77	134	360	.8	1.8
OSWEGO	**128**	**12,912**	**6,004**	**47,246 ***	**38.6**	**100.0**
019 Amer Bapt USA	8	863	397	1,084 *	.9	2.3
053 Assemb of God	6	245	303	386	.3	.8
056 Baha'i	0	12	NR	12	-	-
081 Catholic	21	NR	NR	27,168	22.2	57.5
089 Chr & Miss Al	3	376	NR	1,094	.9	2.3
097 Chr Chs&Chs Cr	4	202	NR	253 *	.2	.5
127 Ch God (Cleve)	2	383	265	481 *	.4	1.0
151 L-D Saints	2	NR	NR	341	.3	.7
165 Ch of Nazarene	2	214	229	315	.3	.7
167 Chs of Christ	1	90	90	100	.1	.2
193 Episcopal	5	NR	301	942	.8	2.0
207 E.L.C.A.	2	950	316	1,480	1.2	3.1
221 Free Methodist	1	22	32	32	-	.1
283 Luth—MO Synod	1	270	130	350	.3	.7
306 NT IndBapt&Rltd	1	250	NR	314 *	.3	.7
355 Presb Ch (USA)	5	269	221	360 *	.3	.8
388 Reg Bapt Gen As	5	386	451	468 *	.4	1.0
403 Salvation Army	2	169	78	546	.4	1.2
413 S.D.A.	3	259	NR	307	.3	.6
416 Sikh	1	NR	NR	NR	-	-
419 So Bapt Conv	1	21	40	26 *	-	.1
435 Unitarian-Univ	1	49	NR	62 *	.1	.1
443 Un C of Christ	7	722	332	907 *	.7	1.9
449 Un Methodist	37	6,891	2,303	8,654 *	7.1	18.3
467 Wesleyan	7	269	516	1,414	1.2	3.0
496 Jewish Est	0	NR	NR	150	.1	.3
OTSEGO	**86**	**7,933**	**3,945**	**21,539 ***	**34.9**	**100.0**
019 Amer Bapt USA	7	1,075	464	1,289 *	2.1	6.0
053 Assemb of God	3	112	151	181	.3	.8
056 Baha'i	0	15	NR	15	-	.1
081 Catholic	3	NR	NR	9,173	14.9	42.6
151 L-D Saints	1	NR	NR	185	.3	.9
167 Chs of Christ	2	46	56	65	.1	.3
179 Consrv Bapt	5	NR	520	520	.8	2.4

NR–Not Reported *Total adherents estimated from known number of communicant, confirmed, full members. - Represents a percentage less than 0.1. Percentages may not total 100 due to rounding.

Table 4: Religious Congregations by County and Group: 2000

Religious Group	Number of Churches, Synagogues, Mosques, or Temples	Number of Communicant, Confirmed, or Full Members	Number of Attendees	Total Adherents: Number of Adherents	Total Adherents: % of Total Pop.	Total Adherents: % of Total Adh.
193 Episcopal	10	NR	556	1,455	2.4	6.8
207 E.L.C.A.	4	626	131	859	1.4	4.0
226 Friends-USA	2	100	NR	120 *	.2	.6
331 OCA: Ter Diocs	1	15	NR	26	-	.1
355 Presb Ch (USA)	12	1,235	673	1,481 *	2.4	6.9
388 Reg Bapt Gen As	1	14	30	30 *	-	.1
403 Salvation Army	1	76	83	199	.3	.9
413 S.D.A.	1	58	NR	69	.1	.3
419 So Bapt Conv	0	19	18	23 *	-	.1
435 Unitarian-Univ	1	157	NR	188 *	.3	.9
449 Un Methodist	30	4,385	1,222	5,256 *	8.5	24.4
467 Wesleyan	1	0	41	105	.2	.5
496 Jewish Est	1	NR	NR	300	.5	1.4
PUTNAM	**41**	**3,577**	**2,121**	**60,978 ***	**63.7**	**100.0**
019 Amer Bapt USA	2	422	66	533 *	.6	.9
053 Assemb of God	3	78	111	111	.1	.2
056 Baha'i	0	8	NR	8	-	-
076 Buddhism	2	NR	NR	NR	-	-
081 Catholic	5	NR	NR	53,496	55.9	87.7
167 Chs of Christ	1	28	30	36	-	.1
179 Consrv Bapt	2	NR	140	140	.1	.2
193 Episcopal	5	NR	296	1,008	1.1	1.7
207 E.L.C.A.	1	606	147	823	.9	1.3
246 Greek Orthodox	1	NR	NR	0	-	-
283 Luth—MO Synod	1	339	107	552	.6	.9
339 Pent Ch of God	1	39	NR	51	.1	.1
355 Presb Ch (USA)	5	734	374	927 *	1.0	1.5
370 Ref Baptist Chs	1	NR	NR	NR	-	-
449 Un Methodist	8	1,023	350	1,293 *	1.4	2.1
496 Jewish Est	2	NR	NR	1,000	1.0	1.6
499 Indep.Non-Char	1	300	500	1,000	1.0	1.6
QUEENS	**884**	**71,329**	**54,076**	**1,074,268 ***	**48.2**	**100.0**
007 OCA: Alban Dioc	1	NR	NR	400	-	-
019 Amer Bapt USA	33	12,060	6,388	14,695 *	.7	1.4
039 Ap Chr Ch(Naz)	1	41	50	50 *	-	-
049 Armen Ap Cilic	1	117	NR	840	-	.1
050 Armen Ap Etchm	1	639	NR	3,000	.1	.3
053 Assemb of God	47	6,115	6,144	8,983	.4	.8
055 As Ref Pres Ch	1	27	NR	27	-	-
076 Buddhism	16	NR	NR	NR	-	-
081 Catholic	106	NR	NR	644,066	28.9	60.0
089 Chr & Miss Al	20	2,881	NR	3,147	.1	.3
093 Chr Ch (Disc)	2	207	0	252 *	-	-
097 Chr Chs&Chs Cr	4	218	NR	266 *	-	-
105 Christian Ref	1	53	32	65 *	-	-
123 Ch God (Ander)	7	NR	646	646	-	.1
127 Ch God (Cleve)	14	1,439	1,292	1,799 *	.1	.2
145 Ch God Prophcy	5	318	NR	386 *	-	-
151 L-D Saints	19	NR	NR	6,917	.3	.6
165 Ch of Nazarene	24	1,503	1,310	1,745	.1	.2
167 Chs of Christ	10	622	728	821	-	.1
175 Congr Chr Chs	1	330	120	402 *	-	-
179 Consrv Bapt	8	NR	1,385	1,385	.1	.1
193 Episcopal	32	NR	3,945	12,843	.6	1.2
201 Evan Cov Ch	1	50	45	61 *	-	-
203 Evan Free Ch	1	30	50	50	-	-
207 E.L.C.A.	36	5,783	2,460	8,109	.4	.8
221 Free Methodist	4	41	20	62	-	-
226 Friends-USA	1	50	NR	61 *	-	-
237 Menn Br US Conf	1	20	NR	24 *	-	-
245 Greek Orth Vslp	3	2,875	NR	6,025	.3	.6
246 Greek Orthodox	8	NR	NR	16,959	.8	1.6
251 Holy Orth in NA	1	NR	NR	21	-	-
252 Hindu	36	NR	NR	NR	-	-
262 Int Cou Comm Ch	1	150	NR	183 *	-	-
263 Int Foursq Gos	2	75	195	195 *	-	-
267 Muslim Est	31	NR	12,586	52,038	2.3	4.8
268 Jain	1	NR	NR	NR	-	-
283 Luth—MO Synod	22	2,769	1,655	3,556	.2	.3
288 Mennonite USA	1	109	87	133 *	-	-
291 Missionary Ch	1	148	120	148	-	-
293 Morav Ch-North	1	136	NR	243	-	-
331 OCA: Ter Diocs	2	157	NR	567	-	.1
333 Malan Dioc Am	4	NR	NR	800	-	.1
334 Malan Syr Orth	1	30	NR	150	-	-
349 Pent Holiness	1	109	90	133 *	-	-
355 Presb Ch (USA)	34	5,001	2,855	6,108 *	.3	.6
356 Presb Ch Amer	7	1,024	800	1,113	-	.1
371 Ref Ch in Am	27	2,097	2,577	4,114	.2	.4
388 Reg Bapt Gen As	1	61	64	74 *	-	-
395 Romania Orth Ar	2	NR	NR	1,575	.1	.1
397 OCA: Roman Dioc	3	NR	NR	580	-	.1
400 Rus Orth Moscow	1	NR	NR	NR	-	-
401 Rus Orth Abroad	3	NR	NR	NR	-	-
403 Salvation Army	5	652	550	978	-	.1
413 S.D.A.	28	9,267	NR	11,031	.5	1.0
416 Sikh	4	NR	NR	NR	-	-
418 Southw Bapt Fel	1	NR	NR	NR	-	-
419 So Bapt Conv	38	2,609	1,619	3,179 *	.1	.3
425 Tao	2	NR	NR	NR	-	-
431 Ukrainian Orth	1	NR	NR	45	-	-
435 Unitarian-Univ	2	75	NR	91 *	-	-
443 Un C of Christ	19	2,735	1,483	3,333 *	.1	.3
449 Un Methodist	28	8,544	4,128	10,414 *	.5	1.0
463 Vineyard	1	134	115	163 *	-	-
467 Wesleyan	3	0	518	1,185	.1	.1
469 WELS	1	28	19	32	-	-
496 Jewish Est	159	NR	NR	238,000	10.7	22.2
RENSSELAER	**138**	**12,051**	**5,422**	**71,581 ***	**46.9**	**100.0**
019 Amer Bapt USA	7	912	289	1,120 *	.7	1.6
049 Armen Ap Cilic	1	62	NR	210	.1	.3
053 Assemb of God	4	165	225	425	.3	.6
056 Baha'i	0	36	NR	36	-	.1
057 Bapt Gen Conf	1	35	26	43 *	-	.1
076 Buddhism	1	NR	NR	NR	-	-
081 Catholic	29	NR	NR	50,937	33.4	71.2
089 Chr & Miss Al	3	118	NR	309	.2	.4
093 Chr Ch (Disc)	2	172	64	211 *	.1	.3
097 Chr Chs&Chs Cr	1	30	NR	37 *	-	.1
123 Ch God (Ander)	1	NR	21	21	-	-
127 Ch God (Cleve)	1	9	40	40 *	-	.1
151 L-D Saints	2	NR	NR	293	.2	.4
167 Chs of Christ	1	27	30	37	-	.1
179 Consrv Bapt	2	NR	78	78	.1	.1
193 Episcopal	11	NR	519	1,582	1.0	2.2
201 Evan Cov Ch	1	32	30	39 *	-	.1
207 E.L.C.A.	9	1,905	634	2,705	1.8	3.8
246 Greek Orthodox	1	NR	NR	474	.3	.7
267 Muslim Est	1	NR	250	500	.3	.7
283 Luth—MO Synod	1	195	82	110	.1	.2
355 Presb Ch (USA)	10	1,274	832	1,566 *	1.0	2.2
370 Ref Baptist Chs	1	NR	NR	NR	-	-
371 Ref Ch in Am	8	1,036	573	2,261	1.5	3.2
403 Salvation Army	1	92	37	187	.1	.3
413 S.D.A.	2	110	NR	131	.1	.2
416 Sikh	1	NR	NR	NR	-	-
431 Ukrainian Orth	1	NR	NR	156	.1	.2
443 Un C of Christ	4	457	201	561 *	.4	.8
449 Un Methodist	26	5,384	1,471	6,612 *	4.3	9.2
467 Wesleyan	1	0	20	100	.1	.1
496 Jewish Est	3	NR	NR	800	.5	1.1
RICHMOND	**154**	**14,610**	**11,631**	**332,964 ***	**75.0**	**100.0**
019 Amer Bapt USA	2	1,443	435	1,804 *	.4	.5
053 Assemb of God	8	2,873	3,101	3,443	.8	1.0
081 Catholic	37	NR	NR	264,931	59.7	79.6
089 Chr & Miss Al	1	43	NR	375	.1	.1
097 Chr Chs&Chs Cr	1	43	NR	54 *	-	-
127 Ch God (Cleve)	1	55	0	69 *	-	-
151 L-D Saints	2	NR	NR	728	.2	.2
165 Ch of Nazarene	1	5	0	5	-	-
167 Chs of Christ	2	90	100	126	-	-
175 Congr Chr Chs	1	60	60	75 *	-	-

NR–Not Reported *Total adherents estimated from known number of communicant, confirmed, full members. - Represents a percentage less than 0.1. Percentages may not total 100 due to rounding.

Table 4: Religious Congregations by County and Group: 2000

Religious Group	Number of Churches, Synagogues, Mosques, or Temples	Number of Communicant, Confirmed, or Full Members	Number of Attendees	Total Adherents		
				Number of Adherents	% of Total Pop.	% of Total Adh.
179 Consrv Bapt	2	NR	280	280	.1	.1
193 Episcopal	10	NR	893	2,442	.6	.7
203 Evan Free Ch	3	247	287	287	.1	.1
207 E.L.C.A.	9	2,559	901	3,850	.9	1.2
226 Friends-USA	1	50	NR	63 *	-	-
246 Greek Orthodox	1	NR	NR	1,098	.2	.3
267 Muslim Est	5	NR	1,649	8,082	1.8	2.4
283 Luth—MO Synod	3	746	426	906	.2	.3
288 Mennonite USA	1	36	29	45 *	-	-
293 Morav Ch-North	4	797	NR	1,054	.2	.3
333 Malan Dioc Am	2	NR	NR	450	.1	.1
334 Malan Syr Orth	2	65	NR	325	.1	.1
335 Orth Pres Ch	1	16	0	28	-	-
355 Presb Ch (USA)	5	599	294	749 *	.2	.2
370 Ref Baptist Chs	1	NR	NR	NR	-	-
371 Ref Ch in Am	5	345	405	737	.2	.2
388 Reg Bapt Gen As	1	70	55	88 *	-	-
403 Salvation Army	2	139	138	425	.1	.1
413 S.D.A.	5	493	NR	587	.1	.2
419 So Bapt Conv	3	150	125	188 *	-	.1
435 Unitarian-Univ	1	113	NR	141 *	-	-
443 Un C of Christ	1	216	95	270 *	.1	.1
449 Un Methodist	10	2,607	958	3,259 *	.7	1.0
496 Jewish Est	18	NR	NR	33,700	7.6	10.1
498 Indep.Charis.	1	250	300	300	.1	.1
499 Indep.Non-Char	1	500	1,100	2,000	.5	.6
ROCKLAND	**174**	**9,735**	**7,064**	**237,759 ***	**82.9**	**100.0**
019 Amer Bapt USA	3	192	149	246 *	.1	.1
053 Assemb of God	8	819	918	1,068	.4	.4
056 Baha'i	0	50	NR	50	-	-
081 Catholic	20	NR	NR	126,060	44.0	53.0
089 Chr & Miss Al	10	623	NR	1,098	.4	.5
105 Christian Ref	1	56	30	72 *	-	-
127 Ch God (Cleve)	3	199	322	330 *	.1	.1
145 Ch God Prophcy	1	82	NR	105 *	-	-
151 L-D Saints	1	NR	NR	290	.1	.1
165 Ch of Nazarene	3	104	118	145	.1	.1
167 Chs of Christ	1	5	5	5	-	-
179 Consrv Bapt	2	NR	285	285	.1	.1
181 Consrv Congr	1	58	110	74 *	-	-
193 Episcopal	10	NR	872	2,054	.7	.9
203 Evan Free Ch	1	130	175	175	.1	.1
207 E.L.C.A.	4	1,343	585	2,049	.7	.9
226 Friends-USA	1	50	NR	64 *	-	-
246 Greek Orthodox	1	NR	NR	1,014	.4	.4
267 Muslim Est	2	NR	824	3,782	1.3	1.6
283 Luth—MO Synod	1	128	78	193	.1	.1
331 OCA: Ter Diocs	2	70	NR	123	-	.1
333 Malan Dioc Am	3	NR	NR	425	.1	.2
334 Malan Syr Orth	3	64	NR	320	.1	.1
355 Presb Ch (USA)	11	1,510	684	1,933 *	.7	.8
371 Ref Ch in Am	6	451	413	825	.3	.3
401 Rus Orth Abroad	2	NR	NR	NR	-	-
403 Salvation Army	2	171	144	226	.1	.1
413 S.D.A.	5	702	NR	835	.3	.4
419 So Bapt Conv	5	771	419	988 *	.3	.4
435 Unitarian-Univ	1	67	NR	86 *	-	-
443 Un C of Christ	1	180	79	231 *	.1	.1
449 Un Methodist	14	1,910	738	2,448 *	.9	1.0
467 Wesleyan	1	0	116	160	.1	.1
496 Jewish Est	44	NR	NR	90,000	31.4	37.9
ST. LAWRENCE	**161**	**10,381**	**6,074**	**51,625 ***	**46.1**	**100.0**
019 Amer Bapt USA	4	380	193	461 *	.4	.9
053 Assemb of God	5	211	283	362	.3	.7
056 Baha'i	0	34	NR	34	-	.1
081 Catholic	34	NR	NR	35,061	31.3	67.9
151 L-D Saints	3	NR	NR	460	.4	.9
165 Ch of Nazarene	2	183	162	213	.2	.4
167 Chs of Christ	1	42	45	55	-	.1
176 Congr Ad Afl	2	86	NR	104 *	.1	.2
179 Consrv Bapt	1	NR	35	35	-	.1

Religious Group	Number of Churches, Synagogues, Mosques, or Temples	Number of Communicant, Confirmed, or Full Members	Number of Attendees	Total Adherents		
				Number of Adherents	% of Total Pop.	% of Total Adh.
181 Consrv Congr	1	60	60	73 *	.1	.1
193 Episcopal	10	NR	577	1,606	1.4	3.1
221 Free Methodist	2	21	70	70	.1	.1
252 Hindu	1	NR	NR	NR	-	-
267 Muslim Est	1	NR	20	90	.1	.2
323 Old Ord Amish	6	310	NR	378 *	.3	.7
335 Orth Pres Ch	1	73	92	99	.1	.2
355 Presb Ch (USA)	19	1,906	952	2,337 *	2.1	4.5
388 Reg Bapt Gen As	1	46	70	70 *	.1	.1
403 Salvation Army	3	76	59	200	.2	.4
413 S.D.A.	2	114	NR	136	.1	.3
418 Southw Bapt Fel	1	NR	NR	NR	-	-
419 So Bapt Conv	9	761	569	923 *	.8	1.8
435 Unitarian-Univ	1	215	NR	261 *	.2	.5
443 Un C of Christ	7	841	343	1,020 *	.9	2.0
449 Un Methodist	34	4,822	1,621	5,846 *	5.2	11.3
467 Wesleyan	8	0	423	981	.9	1.9
496 Jewish Est	1	NR	NR	200	.2	.4
498 Indep.Charis.	1	200	500	550	.5	1.1
SARATOGA	**116**	**15,866**	**8,963**	**81,578 ***	**40.7**	**100.0**
017 Amer Bapt Assn	1	10	NR	12 *	-	-
019 Amer Bapt USA	7	1,079	650	1,340 *	.7	1.6
034 Ant Orth of NA	2	88	NR	176	.1	.2
053 Assemb of God	4	195	227	289	.1	.4
055 As Ref Pres Ch	1	141	NR	187	.1	.2
056 Baha'i	0	42	NR	42	-	.1
057 Bapt Gen Conf	1	253	0	314 *	.2	.4
059 Bapt Miss Assn	1	22	10	27 *	-	-
081 Catholic	10	NR	NR	53,781	26.8	65.9
084 Calvary Chapel	1	NR	NR	NR	-	-
089 Chr & Miss Al	3	410	NR	1,432	.7	1.8
127 Ch God (Cleve)	1	117	94	145 *	.1	.2
151 L-D Saints	2	NR	NR	739	.4	.9
165 Ch of Nazarene	1	29	30	30	-	-
167 Chs of Christ	2	90	115	127	.1	.2
179 Consrv Bapt	3	NR	275	275	.1	.3
181 Consrv Congr	1	39	65	48 *	-	.1
193 Episcopal	9	NR	1,283	3,907	1.9	4.8
207 E.L.C.A.	3	1,013	538	1,735	.9	2.1
221 Free Methodist	2	50	62	74	-	.1
226 Friends-USA	2	100	NR	124 *	.1	.2
252 Hindu	1	NR	NR	NR	-	-
283 Luth—MO Synod	1	472	249	852	.4	1.0
331 OCA: Ter Diocs	1	65	NR	102	.1	.1
349 Pent Holiness	1	9	9	11 *	-	-
355 Presb Ch (USA)	9	1,348	828	1,673 *	.8	2.1
356 Presb Ch Amer	2	154	251	270	.1	.3
370 Ref Baptist Chs	2	NR	NR	NR	-	-
371 Ref Ch in Am	4	474	349	1,007	.5	1.2
403 Salvation Army	1	69	40	140	.1	.2
413 S.D.A.	1	85	NR	101	.1	.1
419 So Bapt Conv	2	56	49	70 *	-	.1
435 Unitarian-Univ	1	54	NR	67 *	-	.1
443 Un C of Christ	1	100	245	124 *	.1	.2
449 Un Methodist	23	8,363	2,670	10,384 *	5.2	12.7
467 Wesleyan	3	28	178	415	.2	.5
469 WELS	1	111	96	158	.1	.2
496 Jewish Est	4	NR	NR	600	.3	.7
499 Indep.Non-Char	1	800	650	800	.4	1.0
SCHENECTADY	**110**	**15,464**	**8,319**	**102,159 ***	**69.7**	**100.0**
019 Amer Bapt USA	8	1,235	390	1,523 *	1.0	1.5
053 Assemb of God	2	283	355	456	.3	.4
056 Baha'i	1	36	NR	36	-	-
059 Bapt Miss Assn	2	114	94	141 *	.1	.1
076 Buddhism	1	NR	NR	NR	-	-
081 Catholic	20	NR	NR	70,874	48.4	69.4
089 Chr & Miss Al	1	33	NR	63	-	.1
127 Ch God (Cleve)	2	84	160	160 *	.1	.2
151 L-D Saints	2	NR	NR	769	.5	.8
165 Ch of Nazarene	1	86	89	150	.1	.1
167 Chs of Christ	1	52	55	60	-	.1

NR–Not Reported   *Total adherents estimated from known number of communicant, confirmed, full members.   - Represents a percentage less than 0.1.   Percentages may not total 100 due to rounding.

Table 4: Religious Congregations by County and Group: 2000

Religious Group	Number of Churches, Synagogues, Mosques, or Temples	Number of Communicant, Confirmed, or Full Members	Number of Attendees	Total Adherents		
				Number of Adherents	% of Total Pop.	% of Total Adh.
181 Consrv Congr	2	331	303	408 *	.3	.4
193 Episcopal	6	NR	668	1,515	1.0	1.5
207 E.L.C.A.	4	1,539	569	2,162	1.5	2.1
216 Evan Presby Ch	1	307	NR	379 *	.3	.4
226 Friends-USA	2	100	NR	123 *	.1	.1
246 Greek Orthodox	1	NR	NR	903	.6	.9
267 Muslim Est	2	NR	312	1,218	.8	1.2
283 Luth—MO Synod	3	1,187	483	1,520	1.0	1.5
335 Orth Pres Ch	1	104	140	145	.1	.1
355 Presb Ch (USA)	6	1,122	455	1,384 *	.9	1.4
356 Presb Ch Amer	2	730	645	851	.6	.8
371 Ref Ch in Am	11	2,264	1,557	4,831	3.3	4.7
388 Reg Bapt Gen As	1	23	35	35 *	-	-
401 Rus Orth Abroad	1	NR	NR	NR	-	-
403 Salvation Army	1	164	97	232	.2	.2
413 S.D.A.	2	117	NR	139	.1	.1
419 So Bapt Conv	1	426	269	525 *	.4	.5
435 Unitarian-Univ	1	427	NR	527 *	.4	.5
443 Un C of Christ	1	62	100	76 *	.1	.1
449 Un Methodist	13	3,988	1,094	4,919 *	3.4	4.8
467 Wesleyan	1	0	94	185	.1	.2
496 Jewish Est	4	NR	NR	5,200	3.5	5.1
498 Indep.Charis.	2	650	355	650	.4	.6
SCHOHARIE	**54**	**5,255**	**2,430**	**12,260 ***	**38.8**	**100.0**
019 Amer Bapt USA	1	154	95	187 *	.6	1.5
053 Assemb of God	2	234	314	482	1.5	3.9
056 Baha'i	0	5	NR	5	-	-
081 Catholic	3	NR	NR	3,868	12.2	31.5
089 Chr & Miss Al	1	34	NR	65	.2	.5
151 L-D Saints	1	NR	NR	307	1.0	2.5
193 Episcopal	2	NR	44	104	.3	.8
207 E.L.C.A.	6	1,564	528	2,557	8.1	20.9
221 Free Methodist	1	8	11	11	-	.1
288 Mennonite USA	1	0	20	20 *	.1	.2
334 Malan Syr Orth	1	30	NR	150	.5	1.2
355 Presb Ch (USA)	4	244	133	297 *	.9	2.4
371 Ref Ch in Am	5	310	292	708	2.2	5.8
388 Reg Bapt Gen As	1	20	45	45 *	.1	.4
419 So Bapt Conv	1	25	26	30 *	.1	.2
443 Un C of Christ	1	43	19	52 *	.2	.4
449 Un Methodist	22	2,493	727	3,030 *	9.6	24.7
467 Wesleyan	1	91	176	342	1.1	2.8
SCHUYLER	**32**	**2,833**	**1,612**	**12,865 ***	**66.9**	**100.0**
019 Amer Bapt USA	5	581	230	717 *	3.7	5.6
053 Assemb of God	1	55	75	75	.4	.6
056 Baha'i	0	7	NR	7	-	.1
081 Catholic	2	NR	NR	8,895	46.3	69.1
165 Ch of Nazarene	1	34	25	92	.5	.7
193 Episcopal	3	NR	97	262	1.4	2.0
355 Presb Ch (USA)	5	422	223	521 *	2.7	4.0
388 Reg Bapt Gen As	2	223	249	263 *	1.4	2.0
449 Un Methodist	11	1,398	553	1,723 *	9.0	13.4
467 Wesleyan	2	113	160	310	1.6	2.4
SENECA	**39**	**2,821**	**1,591**	**13,408 ***	**40.2**	**100.0**
053 Assemb of God	2	73	98	117	.4	.9
056 Baha'i	0	13	NR	13	-	.1
081 Catholic	4	NR	NR	8,815	26.4	65.7
097 Chr Chs&Chs Cr	1	100	NR	123 *	.4	.9
165 Ch of Nazarene	1	33	18	33	.1	.2
179 Consrv Bapt	2	NR	140	140	.4	1.0
193 Episcopal	4	NR	246	643	1.9	4.8
283 Luth—MO Synod	2	235	146	329	1.0	2.5
286 E.PA Mennonite	1	74	NR	91 *	.3	.7
297 Mennonite;Other	1	38	NR	47 *	.1	.4
322 Old Ord Menn Ch	1	183	NR	225 *	.7	1.7
323 Old Ord Amish	3	165	NR	204 *	.6	1.5
355 Presb Ch (USA)	7	654	406	839 *	2.5	6.3
371 Ref Ch in Am	2	192	170	394	1.2	2.9
400 Rus Orth Moscow	1	NR	NR	NR	-	-
443 Un C of Christ	1	0	0	0 *	-	-
449 Un Methodist	5	1,035	327	1,275 *	3.8	9.5
467 Wesleyan	1	26	40	120	.4	.9
STEUBEN	**137**	**12,930**	**7,905**	**42,160 ***	**42.7**	**100.0**
019 Amer Bapt USA	11	1,631	655	2,033 *	2.1	4.8
022 Carp Rus Orth	1	122	NR	207	.2	.5
053 Assemb of God	6	436	616	741	.8	1.8
056 Baha'i	0	8	NR	8	-	-
081 Catholic	16	NR	NR	20,208	20.5	47.9
089 Chr & Miss Al	2	179	NR	325	.3	.8
097 Chr Chs&Chs Cr	2	81	NR	100 *	.1	.2
151 L-D Saints	3	NR	NR	488	.5	1.2
165 Ch of Nazarene	2	119	88	155	.2	.4
167 Chs of Christ	1	10	10	10	-	-
173 Comm of Christ	1	83	NR	83	.1	.2
179 Consrv Bapt	1	NR	75	75	.1	.2
181 Consrv Congr	1	37	80	46 *	-	.1
193 Episcopal	6	NR	418	1,670	1.7	4.0
207 E.L.C.A.	2	280	115	442	.4	1.0
221 Free Methodist	1	45	68	68	.1	.2
283 Luth—MO Synod	2	261	106	346	.4	.8
288 Mennonite USA	4	243	355	377 *	.4	.9
323 Old Ord Amish	5	275	NR	345 *	.3	.8
355 Presb Ch (USA)	15	1,817	911	2,282 *	2.3	5.4
388 Reg Bapt Gen As	7	414	552	595 *	.6	1.4
403 Salvation Army	2	158	131	553	.6	1.3
413 S.D.A.	1	110	NR	131	.1	.3
443 Un C of Christ	5	371	247	462 *	.5	1.1
449 Un Methodist	32	5,533	2,073	6,895 *	7.0	16.4
467 Wesleyan	7	717	1,405	3,215	3.3	7.6
496 Jewish Est	1	NR	NR	300	.3	.7
SUFFOLK	**498**	**68,500**	**37,040**	**964,721 ***	**68.0**	**100.0**
019 Amer Bapt USA	8	1,466	733	1,850 *	.1	.2
034 Ant Orth of NA	1	25	NR	50	-	-
053 Assemb of God	29	2,631	3,208	3,744	.3	.4
056 Baha'i	5	271	NR	271	-	-
076 Buddhism	5	NR	NR	NR	-	-
081 Catholic	72	NR	NR	734,174	51.7	76.1
084 Calvary Chapel	3	NR	NR	NR	-	-
089 Chr & Miss Al	2	157	NR	257	-	-
097 Chr Chs&Chs Cr	6	685	NR	864 *	.1	.1
105 Christian Ref	1	56	41	71 *	-	-
123 Ch God (Ander)	1	NR	40	40	-	-
127 Ch God (Cleve)	22	2,859	1,668	3,680 *	.3	.4
145 Ch God Prophcy	2	133	NR	169 *	-	-
151 L-D Saints	7	NR	NR	2,280	.2	.2
165 Ch of Nazarene	10	706	664	1,044	.1	.1
167 Chs of Christ	9	902	932	1,229	.1	.1
176 Congr Ad Afl	1	360	NR	454 *	-	-
179 Consrv Bapt	7	NR	671	671	-	.1
193 Episcopal	40	NR	5,251	16,234	1.1	1.7
201 Evan Cov Ch	1	38	36	48 *	-	-
203 Evan Free Ch	4	284	630	630	-	.1
207 E.L.C.A.	26	13,131	4,805	19,378	1.4	2.0
226 Friends-USA	3	150	NR	189 *	-	-
246 Greek Orthodox	6	NR	NR	4,017	.3	.4
252 Hindu	1	NR	NR	NR	-	-
267 Muslim Est	9	NR	2,428	12,139	.9	1.3
283 Luth—MO Synod	15	9,536	3,549	15,030	1.1	1.6
313 N Am Bapt Conf	2	43	55	54 *	-	-
331 OCA: Ter Diocs	2	116	NR	377	-	-
333 Malan Dioc Am	1	NR	NR	250	-	-
335 Orth Pres Ch	1	0	0	0	-	-
349 Pent Holiness	1	67	60	85 *	-	-
355 Presb Ch (USA)	37	9,893	4,603	12,485 *	.9	1.3
370 Ref Baptist Chs	3	NR	NR	NR	-	-
371 Ref Ch in Am	4	527	549	1,393	.1	.1
388 Reg Bapt Gen As	3	157	156	197 *	-	-
403 Salvation Army	2	105	83	191	-	-
413 S.D.A.	11	1,334	NR	1,588	.1	.2
419 So Bapt Conv	10	594	302	749 *	.1	.1
431 Ukrainian Orth	2	NR	NR	120	-	-

NR–Not Reported *Total adherents estimated from known number of communicant, confirmed, full members. - Represents a percentage less than 0.1. Percentages may not total 100 due to rounding.

Table 4: Religious Congregations by County and Group: 2000

Religious Group	Number of Churches, Synagogues, Mosques, or Temples	Number of Communicant, Confirmed, or Full Members	Number of Attendees	Total Adherents: Number of Adherents	Total Adherents: % of Total Pop.	Total Adherents: % of Total Adh.
435 Unitarian-Univ	7	770	NR	972 *	.1	.1
443 Un C of Christ	13	2,695	1,028	3,400 *	.2	.4
449 Un Methodist	47	17,793	4,214	22,448 *	1.6	2.3
455 Un Ref Chs N.A.	1	101	NR	170	-	-
463 Vineyard	1	158	108	199 *	-	-
467 Wesleyan	1	0	150	250	-	-
469 WELS	1	57	51	80	-	-
496 Jewish Est	48	NR	NR	100,000	7.0	10.4
498 Indep.Charis.	1	0	400	500	-	.1
499 Indep.Non-Char	3	700	625	700	-	.1
SULLIVAN	**90**	**4,838**	**2,495**	**33,021 ***	**44.6**	**100.0**
053 Assemb of God	5	160	188	246	.3	.7
056 Baha'i	0	15	NR	15	-	-
076 Buddhism	2	NR	NR	NR	-	-
081 Catholic	12	NR	NR	18,417	24.9	55.8
123 Ch God (Ander)	1	NR	50	50	.1	.2
127 Ch God (Cleve)	1	31	0	38 *	.1	.1
151 L-D Saints	1	NR	NR	109	.1	.3
165 Ch of Nazarene	2	88	89	216	.3	.7
193 Episcopal	3	NR	94	272	.4	.8
207 E.L.C.A.	4	697	166	1,002	1.4	3.0
221 Free Methodist	3	165	308	308	.4	.9
252 Hindu	1	NR	NR	NR	-	-
267 Muslim Est	1	NR	55	163	.2	.5
355 Presb Ch (USA)	8	687	288	846 *	1.1	2.6
371 Ref Ch in Am	5	244	178	523	.7	1.6
413 S.D.A.	1	20	NR	24	-	.1
419 So Bapt Conv	1	53	30	65 *	.1	.2
443 Un C of Christ	2	141	100	174 *	.2	.5
449 Un Methodist	27	2,537	949	3,128 *	4.2	9.5
496 Jewish Est	10	NR	NR	7,425	10.0	22.5
TIOGA	**62**	**8,458**	**3,467**	**18,523 ***	**35.8**	**100.0**
019 Amer Bapt USA	3	797	192	1,000 *	1.9	5.4
053 Assemb of God	1	25	25	25	-	.1
056 Baha'i	0	4	NR	4	-	-
076 Buddhism	1	NR	NR	NR	-	-
081 Catholic	5	NR	NR	6,379	12.3	34.4
089 Chr & Miss Al	4	291	NR	596	1.2	3.2
151 L-D Saints	2	NR	NR	482	.9	2.6
165 Ch of Nazarene	2	541	399	610	1.2	3.3
167 Chs of Christ	1	10	10	10	-	.1
175 Congr Chr Chs	1	14	14	18 *	-	.1
179 Consrv Bapt	1	NR	160	160	.3	.9
181 Consrv Congr	1	165	95	207 *	.4	1.1
193 Episcopal	3	NR	232	656	1.3	3.5
207 E.L.C.A.	1	61	16	89	.2	.5
283 Luth—MO Synod	1	142	95	252	.5	1.4
355 Presb Ch (USA)	4	593	290	745 *	1.4	4.0
388 Reg Bapt Gen As	3	405	330	508 *	1.0	2.7
413 S.D.A.	1	25	NR	30	.1	.2
419 So Bapt Conv	3	357	210	448 *	.9	2.4
443 Un C of Christ	2	78	34	98 *	.2	.5
449 Un Methodist	22	4,950	1,365	6,206 *	12.0	33.5
TOMPKINS	**79**	**9,251**	**5,611**	**25,616 ***	**26.5**	**100.0**
019 Amer Bapt USA	6	511	323	594 *	.6	2.3
053 Assemb of God	6	594	780	1,160	1.2	4.5
056 Baha'i	2	111	NR	111	.1	.4
076 Buddhism	3	NR	NR	NR	-	-
081 Catholic	6	NR	NR	10,108	10.5	39.5
089 Chr & Miss Al	1	40	NR	115	.1	.4
151 L-D Saints	2	NR	NR	485	.5	1.9
165 Ch of Nazarene	1	71	68	136	.1	.5
167 Chs of Christ	1	62	75	95	.1	.4
179 Consrv Bapt	1	NR	90	90	.1	.4
193 Episcopal	4	NR	278	624	.6	2.4
203 Evan Free Ch	1	69	125	125	.1	.5
207 E.L.C.A.	1	543	151	756	.8	3.0
226 Friends-USA	2	100	NR	116 *	.1	.5
246 Greek Orthodox	1	NR	NR	186	.2	.7
267 Muslim Est	1	NR	150	400	.4	1.6
283 Luth—MO Synod	1	241	89	298	.3	1.2
355 Presb Ch (USA)	3	936	523	1,088 *	1.1	4.2
356 Presb Ch Amer	1	50	115	115	.1	.4
388 Reg Bapt Gen As	3	464	495	540 *	.6	2.1
403 Salvation Army	1	80	88	110	.1	.4
413 S.D.A.	1	75	NR	89	.1	.3
419 So Bapt Conv	2	58	84	67 *	.1	.3
435 Unitarian-Univ	1	524	NR	610 *	.6	2.4
443 Un C of Christ	6	1,280	606	1,489 *	1.5	5.8
449 Un Methodist	14	3,086	1,066	3,589 *	3.7	14.0
463 Vineyard	1	60	55	70 *	.1	.3
496 Jewish Est	5	NR	NR	2,000	2.1	7.8
499 Indep.Non-Char	1	296	450	450	.5	1.8
ULSTER	**157**	**12,321**	**6,992**	**89,990 ***	**50.6**	**100.0**
019 Amer Bapt USA	1	149	140	182 *	.1	.2
053 Assemb of God	7	263	271	428	.2	.5
056 Baha'i	1	66	NR	66	-	.1
070 Bruderhof Comm	2	264	NR	264	.1	.3
076 Buddhism	4	NR	NR	NR	-	-
081 Catholic	23	NR	NR	62,174	35.0	69.1
089 Chr & Miss Al	1	48	NR	144	.1	.2
127 Ch God (Cleve)	1	20	19	24 *	-	-
151 L-D Saints	1	NR	NR	145	.1	.2
165 Ch of Nazarene	2	157	108	175	.1	.2
167 Chs of Christ	1	34	35	45	-	.1
175 Congr Chr Chs	2	111	55	135 *	.1	.2
193 Episcopal	9	NR	659	1,725	1.0	1.9
203 Evan Free Ch	2	205	500	500	.3	.6
207 E.L.C.A.	9	2,081	688	3,245	1.8	3.6
226 Friends-USA	3	150	NR	183 *	.1	.2
246 Greek Orthodox	1	NR	NR	303	.2	.3
252 Hindu	2	NR	NR	NR	-	-
267 Muslim Est	1	NR	40	200	.1	.2
283 Luth—MO Synod	1	68	47	85	-	.1
355 Presb Ch (USA)	4	461	231	562 *	.3	.6
370 Ref Baptist Chs	1	NR	NR	NR	-	-
371 Ref Ch in Am	27	2,658	2,194	6,131	3.4	6.8
388 Reg Bapt Gen As	2	155	222	178 *	.1	.2
400 Rus Orth Moscow	1	NR	NR	NR	-	-
403 Salvation Army	1	58	29	138	.1	.2
413 S.D.A.	3	163	NR	194	.1	.2
419 So Bapt Conv	1	53	55	65 *	-	.1
431 Ukrainian Orth	1	NR	NR	24	-	-
435 Unitarian-Univ	1	128	NR	156 *	.1	.2
449 Un Methodist	30	4,966	1,482	6,058 *	3.4	6.7
463 Vineyard	1	63	45	77 *	-	.1
467 Wesleyan	3	0	172	484	.3	.5
496 Jewish Est	7	NR	NR	5,900	3.3	6.6
WARREN	**64**	**5,803**	**3,127**	**32,512 ***	**51.4**	**100.0**
019 Amer Bapt USA	5	589	193	721 *	1.1	2.2
053 Assemb of God	3	169	235	308	.5	.9
056 Baha'i	0	14	NR	14	-	-
081 Catholic	11	NR	NR	22,053	34.8	67.8
151 L-D Saints	1	NR	NR	369	.6	1.1
167 Chs of Christ	1	37	40	48	.1	.1
193 Episcopal	9	NR	488	886	1.4	2.7
220 Free Lutheran	1	20	15	28	-	.1
221 Free Methodist	2	53	61	66	.1	.2
283 Luth—MO Synod	1	428	149	538	.8	1.7
355 Presb Ch (USA)	6	1,613	630	1,973 *	3.1	6.1
356 Presb Ch Amer	1	40	50	53	.1	.2
388 Reg Bapt Gen As	1	90	99	99 *	.2	.3
403 Salvation Army	1	141	61	277	.4	.9
413 S.D.A.	2	44	NR	52	.1	.2
435 Unitarian-Univ	1	65	NR	80 *	.1	.2
449 Un Methodist	13	2,438	790	2,983 *	4.7	9.2
467 Wesleyan	4	62	316	1,164	1.8	3.6
496 Jewish Est	1	NR	NR	800	1.3	2.5
WASHINGTON	**71**	**7,103**	**3,380**	**23,790 ***	**39.0**	**100.0**
019 Amer Bapt USA	10	1,386	485	1,707 *	2.8	7.2

NR–Not Reported *Total adherents estimated from known number of communicant, confirmed, full members. - Represents a percentage less than 0.1. Percentages may not total 100 due to rounding.

Table 4: Religious Congregations by County and Group: 2000

Religious Group	Number of Churches, Synagogues, Mosques, or Temples	Number of Communicant, Confirmed, or Full Members	Number of Attendees	Total Adherents: Number of Adherents	Total Adherents: % of Total Pop.	Total Adherents: % of Total Adh.
053 Assemb of God	3	236	220	311	.5	1.3
056 Baha'i	0	12	NR	12	-	.1
081 Catholic	9	NR	NR	13,850	22.7	58.2
127 Ch God (Cleve)	1	82	73	101 *	.2	.4
165 Ch of Nazarene	1	42	0	42	.1	.2
167 Chs of Christ	1	20	25	25	-	.1
179 Consrv Bapt	1	NR	80	80	.1	.3
181 Consrv Congr	1	80	150	99 *	.2	.4
193 Episcopal	7	NR	293	771	1.3	3.2
355 Presb Ch (USA)	12	1,431	776	1,763 *	2.9	7.4
371 Ref Ch in Am	1	69	85	156	.3	.7
413 S.D.A.	1	172	NR	205	.3	.9
419 So Bapt Conv	1	103	69	127 *	.2	.5
443 Un C of Christ	1	42	10	52 *	.1	.2
449 Un Methodist	19	3,428	1,012	4,222 *	6.9	17.7
467 Wesleyan	2	0	102	267	.4	1.1
WAYNE	**104**	**13,297**	**6,190**	**38,038 ***	**40.6**	**100.0**
019 Amer Bapt USA	13	2,438	771	3,089 *	3.3	8.1
053 Assemb of God	7	377	499	563	.6	1.5
056 Baha'i	1	86	NR	86	.1	.2
081 Catholic	12	NR	NR	18,464	19.7	48.5
084 Calvary Chapel	1	NR	NR	NR	-	-
089 Chr & Miss Al	1	64	NR	182	.2	.5
105 Christian Ref	1	287	160	364 *	.4	1.0
123 Ch God (Ander)	2	NR	85	85	.1	.2
127 Ch God (Cleve)	1	75	64	95 *	.1	.2
151 L-D Saints	2	NR	NR	847	.9	2.2
167 Chs of Christ	1	25	38	35	-	.1
193 Episcopal	5	NR	291	783	.8	2.1
207 E.L.C.A.	2	434	93	734	.8	1.9
221 Free Methodist	5	260	555	555	.6	1.5
268 Jain	1	NR	NR	NR	-	-
283 Luth—MO Synod	2	157	5	12	-	-
322 Old Ord Menn Ch	2	234	NR	297 *	.3	.8
323 Old Ord Amish	1	55	NR	70 *	.1	.2
355 Presb Ch (USA)	12	2,165	951	2,743 *	2.9	7.2
371 Ref Ch in Am	6	733	660	1,553	1.7	4.1
388 Reg Bapt Gen As	1	89	110	113 *	.1	.3
413 S.D.A.	1	26	NR	31	-	.1
419 So Bapt Conv	1	79	55	100 *	.1	.3
443 Un C of Christ	2	129	57	163 *	.2	.4
449 Un Methodist	21	5,584	1,796	7,074 *	7.5	18.6
WESTCHESTER	**479**	**44,793**	**25,096**	**650,631 ***	**70.5**	**100.0**
019 Amer Bapt USA	21	5,040	1,603	6,294 *	.7	1.0
022 Carp Rus Orth	1	122	NR	207	-	-
034 Ant Orth of NA	1	120	NR	240	-	-
050 Armen Ap Etchm	1	182	NR	210	-	-
053 Assemb of God	23	2,860	3,282	4,035	.4	.6
056 Baha'i	3	319	NR	319	-	-
076 Buddhism	4	NR	NR	NR	-	-
081 Catholic	96	NR	NR	469,670	50.9	72.2
084 Calvary Chapel	1	NR	NR	NR	-	-
089 Chr & Miss Al	8	850	NR	1,893	.2	.3
097 Chr Chs&Chs Cr	3	443	NR	553 *	.1	.1
123 Ch God (Ander)	1	NR	65	65	-	-
127 Ch God (Cleve)	7	891	825	1,203 *	.1	.2
145 Ch God Prophcy	3	246	NR	306 *	-	-
151 L-D Saints	7	NR	NR	1,941	.2	.3
165 Ch of Nazarene	7	317	336	415	-	.1
167 Chs of Christ	3	229	215	303	-	-
179 Consrv Bapt	5	NR	533	533	.1	.1
193 Episcopal	49	NR	5,143	14,885	1.6	2.3
201 Evan Cov Ch	2	85	88	106 *	-	-
203 Evan Free Ch	1	69	125	125	-	-
207 E.L.C.A.	17	4,340	1,534	5,756	.6	.9
226 Friends-USA	6	300	NR	375 *	-	.1
246 Greek Orthodox	1	NR	NR	1,626	.2	.2
249 Assyr Apost Ch	1	NR	NR	760	.1	.1
263 Int Foursq Gos	1	40	42	50 *	-	-
267 Muslim Est	4	NR	1,266	5,773	.6	.9
283 Luth—MO Synod	9	2,215	978	2,618	.3	.4

Religious Group	Number of Churches, Synagogues, Mosques, or Temples	Number of Communicant, Confirmed, or Full Members	Number of Attendees	Total Adherents: Number of Adherents	Total Adherents: % of Total Pop.	Total Adherents: % of Total Adh.
331 OCA: Ter Diocs	1	205	NR	375	-	.1
333 Malan Dioc Am	4	NR	NR	1,275	.1	.2
334 Malan Syr Orth	1	75	NR	375	-	.1
335 Orth Pres Ch	1	19	28	28	-	-
355 Presb Ch (USA)	26	8,593	3,446	10,730 *	1.2	1.6
356 Presb Ch Amer	3	133	236	249	-	-
371 Ref Ch in Am	11	2,030	1,123	3,465	.4	.5
388 Reg Bapt Gen As	1	0	150	150 *	-	-
403 Salvation Army	6	363	338	908	.1	.1
411 Serb Orth: Grac	1	NR	NR	NR	-	-
413 S.D.A.	14	2,607	NR	3,103	.3	.5
419 So Bapt Conv	8	727	282	908 *	.1	.1
435 Unitarian-Univ	5	700	NR	874 *	.1	.1
443 Un C of Christ	11	1,904	777	2,378 *	.3	.4
449 Un Methodist	34	8,639	2,485	10,790 *	1.2	1.7
463 Vineyard	1	130	120	162 *	-	-
467 Wesleyan	1	0	76	600	.1	.1
490 Zoroastrian	2	NR	NR	NR	-	-
496 Jewish Est	62	NR	NR	94,000	10.2	14.4
WYOMING	**62**	**4,650**	**3,334**	**20,100 ***	**46.3**	**100.0**
019 Amer Bapt USA	3	185	95	225 *	.5	1.1
056 Baha'i	0	3	NR	3	-	-
061 Beachy Amish	1	25	NR	30 *	.1	.1
081 Catholic	15	NR	NR	13,002	29.9	64.7
089 Chr & Miss Al	1	41	NR	87	.2	.4
097 Chr Chs&Chs Cr	1	12	NR	15 *	-	.1
127 Ch God (Cleve)	1	52	62	63 *	.1	.3
151 L-D Saints	1	NR	NR	186	.4	.9
165 Ch of Nazarene	1	87	66	87	.2	.4
167 Chs of Christ	1	9	17	15	-	.1
175 Congr Chr Chs	1	75	42	91 *	.2	.5
179 Consrv Bapt	4	NR	444	444	1.0	2.2
193 Episcopal	3	NR	148	441	1.0	2.2
207 E.L.C.A.	1	266	151	401	.9	2.0
221 Free Methodist	2	104	274	289	.7	1.4
313 N Am Bapt Conf	1	121	106	147 *	.3	.7
355 Presb Ch (USA)	5	644	469	893 *	2.1	4.4
419 So Bapt Conv	1	28	73	34 *	.1	.2
443 Un C of Christ	8	1,596	846	1,942 *	4.5	9.7
449 Un Methodist	11	1,402	541	1,705 *	3.9	8.5
YATES	**48**	**5,169**	**1,968**	**12,403 ***	**50.4**	**100.0**
019 Amer Bapt USA	8	927	321	1,161 *	4.7	9.4
053 Assemb of God	1	30	40	40	.2	.3
056 Baha'i	0	5	NR	5	-	-
061 Beachy Amish	1	72	NR	90 *	.4	.7
081 Catholic	2	NR	NR	5,495	22.3	44.3
151 L-D Saints	1	NR	NR	126	.5	1.0
165 Ch of Nazarene	1	17	13	17	.1	.1
179 Consrv Bapt	1	NR	75	75	.3	.6
193 Episcopal	2	NR	109	269	1.1	2.2
207 E.L.C.A.	2	419	152	511	2.1	4.1
226 Friends-USA	1	50	NR	63 *	.3	.5
297 Mennonite;Other	1	26	NR	33 *	.1	.3
322 Old Ord Menn Ch	4	790	NR	990 *	4.0	8.0
355 Presb Ch (USA)	5	520	246	652 *	2.6	5.3
388 Reg Bapt Gen As	2	155	224	180 *	.7	1.5
413 S.D.A.	1	84	NR	100	.4	.8
443 Un C of Christ	2	89	66	111 *	.5	.9
449 Un Methodist	13	1,985	722	2,485 *	10.1	20.0

NORTH CAROLINA

Religious Group	Number of Churches, Synagogues, Mosques, or Temples	Number of Communicant, Confirmed, or Full Members	Number of Attendees	Total Adherents: Number of Adherents	Total Adherents: % of Total Pop.	Total Adherents: % of Total Adh.
The State.....	11,132	2,529,714	1,124,710	3,651,416 *	45.4	100.0
ALAMANCE	**153**	**40,582**	**17,527**	**55,328 ***	**42.3**	**100.0**
053 Assemb of God	1	268	295	400	.3	.7
055 As Ref Pres Ch	1	228	NR	258	.2	.5
056 Baha'i	1	33	NR	33	-	.1
081 Catholic	1	NR	NR	3,047	2.3	5.5
093 Chr Ch (Disc)	1	70	32	86 *	.1	.2

NR–Not Reported *Total adherents estimated from known number of communicant, confirmed, full members. - Represents a percentage less than 0.1. Percentages may not total 100 due to rounding.

Table 4: Religious Congregations by County and Group: 2000

Religious Group	Number of Churches, Synagogues, Mosques, or Temples	Number of Communicant, Confirmed, or Full Members	Number of Attendees	Total Adherents: Number of Adherents	% of Total Pop.	% of Total Adh.
097 Chr Chs&Chs Cr	1	94	NR	116 *	.1	.2
127 Ch God (Cleve)	8	763	546	938 *	.7	1.7
145 Ch God Prophcy	3	125	NR	153 *	.1	.3
151 L-D Saints	2	NR	NR	987	.8	1.8
165 Ch of Nazarene	3	676	434	965	.7	1.7
167 Chs of Christ	2	119	125	189	.1	.3
175 Congr Chr Chs	1	35	30	43 *	-	.1
181 Consrv Congr	2	571	264	703 *	.5	1.3
193 Episcopal	2	NR	252	730	.6	1.3
207 E.L.C.A.	5	974	507	1,173	.9	2.1
226 Friends-USA	7	707	NR	870 *	.7	1.6
246 Greek Orthodox	1	NR	NR	132	.1	.2
283 Luth—MO Synod	1	110	40	132	.1	.2
349 Pent Holiness	3	640	495	788 *	.6	1.4
355 Presb Ch (USA)	12	3,352	1,730	4,126 *	3.2	7.5
356 Presb Ch Amer	1	222	100	279	.2	.5
370 Ref Baptist Chs	1	NR	NR	NR	-	-
403 Salvation Army	1	109	86	306	.2	.6
413 S.D.A.	2	248	NR	295	.2	.5
419 So Bapt Conv	33	13,691	5,263	16,853 *	12.9	30.5
443 Un C of Christ	24	5,295	2,663	6,518 *	5.0	11.8
449 Un Methodist	27	11,447	3,704	14,090 *	10.8	25.5
467 Wesleyan	5	308	261	418	.3	.8
499 Indep.Non-Char	1	497	700	700	.5	1.3
ALEXANDER	**64**	**17,151**	**8,377**	**22,029 ***	**65.6**	**100.0**
053 Assemb of God	3	432	456	814	2.4	3.7
055 As Ref Pres Ch	2	423	NR	465	1.4	2.1
056 Baha'i	0	2	NR	2	-	-
081 Catholic	1	NR	NR	416	1.2	1.9
127 Ch God (Cleve)	2	113	83	139 *	.4	.6
167 Chs of Christ	1	37	40	47	.1	.2
207 E.L.C.A.	6	1,991	975	2,610	7.8	11.8
283 Luth—MO Synod	2	386	209	497	1.5	2.3
355 Presb Ch (USA)	2	209	120	259 *	.8	1.2
419 So Bapt Conv	34	11,811	5,508	14,604 *	43.5	66.3
449 Un Methodist	10	1,680	901	2,076 *	6.2	9.4
467 Wesleyan	1	67	85	100	.3	.5
ALLEGHANY	**32**	**2,309**	**1,281**	**2,969 ***	**27.8**	**100.0**
081 Catholic	1	NR	NR	170	1.6	5.7
127 Ch God (Cleve)	1	59	47	69 *	.6	2.3
151 L-D Saints	1	NR	NR	78	.7	2.6
157 Ch of Brethren	4	209	179	256 *	2.4	8.6
223 Free Will Bapt	1	104	NR	123 *	1.2	4.1
355 Presb Ch (USA)	1	113	75	133 *	1.2	4.5
360 Prim Bapt Chrch	9	NR	NR	NR	-	-
419 So Bapt Conv	9	1,262	728	1,481 *	13.9	49.9
449 Un Methodist	5	562	252	659 *	6.2	22.2
ANSON	**76**	**9,643**	**4,062**	**12,331 ***	**48.8**	**100.0**
056 Baha'i	0	26	NR	26	.1	.2
081 Catholic	1	NR	NR	117	.5	.9
123 Ch God (Ander)	1	NR	50	50	.2	.4
127 Ch God (Cleve)	2	162	155	210 *	.8	1.7
145 Ch God Prophcy	4	167	NR	208 *	.8	1.7
167 Chs of Christ	1	28	30	36	.1	.3
193 Episcopal	2	NR	68	150	.6	1.2
349 Pent Holiness	1	7	16	9 *	-	.1
355 Presb Ch (USA)	5	290	148	360 *	1.4	2.9
360 Prim Bapt Chrch	3	NR	NR	NR	-	-
419 So Bapt Conv	31	6,856	2,681	8,540 *	33.8	69.3
449 Un Methodist	25	2,107	914	2,625 *	10.4	21.3
ASHE	**98**	**9,974**	**4,779**	**12,258 ***	**50.3**	**100.0**
053 Assemb of God	1	60	60	60	.2	.5
056 Baha'i	0	9	NR	9	-	.1
081 Catholic	1	NR	NR	306	1.3	2.5
097 Chr Chs&Chs Cr	1	125	NR	147 *	.6	1.2
145 Ch God Prophcy	1	42	NR	49 *	.2	.4
165 Ch of Nazarene	1	28	43	53	.2	.4
167 Chs of Christ	2	79	72	99	.4	.8
193 Episcopal	1	NR	71	130	.5	1.1
265 Int Pent C Chr	1	0	0	30	.1	.2
288 Mennonite USA	2	75	60	88 *	.4	.7
355 Presb Ch (USA)	6	319	226	376 *	1.5	3.1
356 Presb Ch Amer	1	103	150	166	.7	1.4
360 Prim Bapt Chrch	9	NR	NR	NR	-	-
409 Separate Bapt	4	199	NR	234 *	1.0	1.9
413 S.D.A.	1	49	NR	58	.2	.5
419 So Bapt Conv	46	7,060	3,274	8,305 *	34.1	67.8
449 Un Methodist	20	1,826	823	2,148 *	8.8	17.5
AVERY	**69**	**6,435**	**2,725**	**7,987 ***	**46.5**	**100.0**
056 Baha'i	0	11	NR	11	.1	.1
081 Catholic	1	NR	NR	389	2.3	4.9
097 Chr Chs&Chs Cr	4	490	NR	575 *	3.3	7.2
127 Ch God (Cleve)	1	115	52	135 *	.8	1.7
167 Chs of Christ	3	50	55	66	.4	.8
193 Episcopal	1	NR	26	12	.1	.2
207 E.L.C.A.	1	4	25	25	.1	.3
216 Evan Presby Ch	1	112	NR	131 *	.8	1.6
223 Free Will Bapt	2	209	NR	245 *	1.4	3.1
237 Menn Br US Conf	1	12	NR	14 *	.1	.2
258 IndFreeWillBapt	4	156	NR	183 *	1.1	2.3
355 Presb Ch (USA)	8	753	632	894 *	5.2	11.2
356 Presb Ch Amer	2	111	72	128	.7	1.6
413 S.D.A.	2	176	NR	210	1.2	2.6
418 Southw Bapt Fel	1	NR	NR	NR	-	-
419 So Bapt Conv	27	3,712	1,528	4,355 *	25.4	54.5
449 Un Methodist	10	524	335	614 *	3.6	7.7
BEAUFORT	**112**	**16,544**	**5,199**	**22,244 ***	**49.5**	**100.0**
053 Assemb of God	3	288	347	390	.9	1.8
056 Baha'i	0	67	NR	67	.1	.3
081 Catholic	1	NR	NR	690	1.5	3.1
093 Chr Ch (Disc)	5	1,866	865	2,273 *	5.1	10.2
097 Chr Chs&Chs Cr	19	4,486	NR	5,465 *	12.2	24.6
105 Christian Ref	1	133	120	162 *	.4	.7
127 Ch God (Cleve)	9	850	648	1,069 *	2.4	4.8
145 Ch God Prophcy	1	42	NR	51 *	.1	.2
151 L-D Saints	1	NR	NR	185	.4	.8
167 Chs of Christ	2	122	167	172	.4	.8
193 Episcopal	8	NR	516	1,076	2.4	4.8
207 E.L.C.A.	1	85	57	101	.2	.5
223 Free Will Bapt	7	731	NR	890 *	2.0	4.0
297 Mennonite;Other	1	69	NR	84 *	.2	.4
336 OrigFreeWillBpt	12	1,374	NR	1,674 *	3.7	7.5
349 Pent Holiness	8	272	199	331 *	.7	1.5
355 Presb Ch (USA)	2	662	328	806 *	1.8	3.6
356 Presb Ch Amer	1	71	60	72	.2	.3
403 Salvation Army	1	122	53	198	.4	.9
413 S.D.A.	2	87	NR	103	.2	.5
419 So Bapt Conv	13	2,463	917	3,000 *	6.7	13.5
449 Un Methodist	13	2,641	922	3,216 *	7.2	14.5
455 Un Ref Chs N.A.	1	113	NR	169	.4	.8
BERTIE	**42**	**6,557**	**2,309**	**8,548 ***	**43.2**	**100.0**
019 Amer Bapt USA	1	515	0	642 *	3.2	7.5
053 Assemb of God	5	383	463	658	3.3	7.7
056 Baha'i	0	24	NR	24	.1	.3
193 Episcopal	3	NR	79	204	1.0	2.4
349 Pent Holiness	2	17	19	21 *	.1	.2
419 So Bapt Conv	26	5,318	1,605	6,626 *	33.5	77.5
449 Un Methodist	5	300	143	373 *	1.9	4.4
BLADEN	**76**	**11,706**	**4,585**	**14,596 ***	**45.2**	**100.0**
053 Assemb of God	1	36	40	40	.1	.3
056 Baha'i	0	11	NR	11	-	.1
081 Catholic	1	NR	NR	95	.3	.7
123 Ch God (Ander)	1	NR	9	9	-	.1
127 Ch God (Cleve)	2	135	76	166 *	.5	1.1
145 Ch God Prophcy	2	83	NR	102 *	.3	.7
167 Chs of Christ	1	16	15	20	.1	.1

NR–Not Reported *Total adherents estimated from known number of communicant, confirmed, full members. - Represents a percentage less than 0.1. Percentages may not total 100 due to rounding.

Table 4: Religious Congregations by County and Group: 2000

Religious Group	Number of Churches, Synagogues, Mosques, or Temples	Number of Communicant, Confirmed, or Full Members	Number of Attendees	Total Adherents: Number of Adherents	% of Total Pop.	% of Total Adh.
193 Episcopal	1	NR	32	63	.2	.4
223 Free Will Bapt	1	104	NR	129 *	.4	.9
336 OrigFreeWillBpt	2	348	NR	429 *	1.3	2.9
349 Pent Holiness	2	112	114	138 *	.4	.9
355 Presb Ch (USA)	7	535	300	660 *	2.0	4.5
413 S.D.A.	2	186	NR	221	.7	1.5
419 So Bapt Conv	39	8,035	3,228	9,915 *	30.7	67.9
449 Un Methodist	14	2,105	771	2,598 *	8.0	17.8
BRUNSWICK	**92**	**17,183**	**8,572**	**23,650 ***	**32.3**	**100.0**
053 Assemb of God	2	141	180	235	.3	1.0
056 Baha'i	0	11	NR	11	-	-
076 Buddhism	1	NR	NR	NR	-	-
081 Catholic	2	NR	NR	2,318	3.2	9.8
089 Chr & Miss Al	1	33	NR	95	.1	.4
127 Ch God (Cleve)	4	229	123	273 *	.4	1.2
145 Ch God Prophcy	1	42	NR	50 *	.1	.2
167 Chs of Christ	2	76	99	109	.1	.5
193 Episcopal	4	NR	385	675	.9	2.9
207 E.L.C.A.	2	400	231	444	.6	1.9
223 Free Will Bapt	1	104	NR	125 *	.2	.5
336 OrigFreeWillBpt	1	14	NR	17 *	-	.1
349 Pent Holiness	2	223	178	267 *	.4	1.1
355 Presb Ch (USA)	6	1,149	786	1,375 *	1.9	5.8
360 Prim Bapt Chrch	1	NR	NR	NR	-	-
419 So Bapt Conv	49	11,284	4,982	13,497 *	18.5	57.1
449 Un Methodist	12	3,469	1,608	4,150 *	5.7	17.5
467 Wesleyan	1	8	0	9	-	-
BUNCOMBE	**311**	**80,163**	**33,594**	**112,672 ***	**54.6**	**100.0**
017 Amer Bapt Assn	1	100	NR	120 *	.1	.1
019 Amer Bapt USA	3	997	666	1,200 *	.6	1.1
022 Carp Rus Orth	1	122	NR	207	.1	.2
053 Assemb of God	3	580	765	1,190	.6	1.1
055 As Ref Pres Ch	3	65	NR	78	-	.1
056 Baha'i	2	224	NR	224	.1	.2
076 Buddhism	2	NR	NR	NR	-	-
081 Catholic	5	NR	NR	8,470	4.1	7.5
084 Calvary Chapel	1	NR	NR	NR	-	-
089 Chr & Miss Al	1	84	NR	114	.1	.1
093 Chr Ch (Disc)	2	351	0	422 *	.2	.4
097 Chr Chs&Chs Cr	5	330	NR	397 *	.2	.4
123 Ch God (Ander)	4	NR	186	186	.1	.2
127 Ch God (Cleve)	13	1,429	716	1,733 *	.8	1.5
145 Ch God Prophcy	1	42	NR	50 *	-	-
151 L-D Saints	3	NR	NR	940	.5	.8
165 Ch of Nazarene	3	337	253	595	.3	.5
167 Chs of Christ	8	450	477	556	.3	.5
193 Episcopal	10	NR	1,296	3,178	1.5	2.8
207 E.L.C.A.	3	1,016	540	1,242	.6	1.1
223 Free Will Bapt	11	1,148	NR	1,382 *	.7	1.2
226 Friends-USA	3	192	NR	231 *	.1	.2
246 Greek Orthodox	1	NR	NR	405	.2	.4
258 IndFreeWillBapt	1	30	NR	36 *	-	-
263 Int Foursq Gos	1	84	70	101 *	-	.1
267 Muslim Est	1	NR	101	288	.1	.3
283 Luth—MO Synod	1	457	303	550	.3	.5
288 Mennonite USA	1	58	64	70 *	-	.1
290 Metro Comm Ch	1	25	37	37 *	-	-
295 Morav Ch-South	1	33	NR	48	-	-
349 Pent Holiness	4	502	370	604 *	.3	.5
355 Presb Ch (USA)	17	4,135	2,488	5,092 *	2.5	4.5
356 Presb Ch Amer	11	2,840	1,783	3,396	1.6	3.0
360 Prim Bapt Chrch	1	NR	NR	NR	-	-
403 Salvation Army	1	162	115	171	.1	.2
413 S.D.A.	7	1,875	NR	2,231	1.1	2.0
418 Southw Bapt Fel	2	NR	NR	NR	-	-
419 So Bapt Conv	109	47,802	16,128	57,532 *	27.9	51.1
435 Unitarian-Univ	1	609	NR	733 *	.4	.7
443 Un C of Christ	1	165	73	199 *	.1	.2
449 Un Methodist	53	12,499	5,381	15,043 *	7.3	13.4
463 Vineyard	1	55	50	66 *	-	.1
467 Wesleyan	2	240	132	255	.1	.2

Religious Group	Number of Churches, Synagogues, Mosques, or Temples	Number of Communicant, Confirmed, or Full Members	Number of Attendees	Total Adherents: Number of Adherents	% of Total Pop.	% of Total Adh.
469 WELS	1	0	0	0	-	-
496 Jewish Est	2	NR	NR	1,300	.6	1.2
499 Indep.Non-Char	2	1,125	1,600	2,000	1.0	1.8
BURKE	**160**	**41,376**	**17,595**	**53,830 ***	**60.4**	**100.0**
053 Assemb of God	6	500	538	778	.9	1.4
056 Baha'i	0	72	NR	72	.1	.1
081 Catholic	1	NR	NR	926	1.0	1.7
093 Chr Ch (Disc)	1	50	30	61 *	.1	.1
097 Chr Chs&Chs Cr	1	35	NR	43 *	-	.1
123 Ch God (Ander)	4	NR	696	696	.8	1.3
127 Ch God (Cleve)	4	843	462	1,076 *	1.2	2.0
145 Ch God Prophcy	1	42	NR	51 *	.1	.1
151 L-D Saints	1	NR	NR	580	.7	1.1
167 Chs of Christ	1	56	61	74	.1	.1
193 Episcopal	4	NR	230	608	.7	1.1
207 E.L.C.A.	3	782	330	972	1.1	1.8
223 Free Will Bapt	4	418	NR	513 *	.6	1.0
349 Pent Holiness	2	155	85	190 *	.2	.4
355 Presb Ch (USA)	6	1,565	701	1,921 *	2.2	3.6
356 Presb Ch Amer	1	70	90	93	.1	.2
403 Salvation Army	1	27	24	27	-	.1
413 S.D.A.	2	323	NR	385	.4	.7
419 So Bapt Conv	86	30,675	11,756	37,666 *	42.3	70.0
449 Un Methodist	28	5,534	2,417	6,798 *	7.6	12.6
467 Wesleyan	3	229	175	300	.3	.6
CABARRUS	**205**	**49,944**	**24,608**	**68,515 ***	**52.3**	**100.0**
053 Assemb of God	2	2,311	1,830	2,156	1.6	3.1
055 As Ref Pres Ch	2	188	NR	205	.2	.3
056 Baha'i	0	25	NR	25	-	-
081 Catholic	2	NR	NR	4,725	3.6	6.9
089 Chr & Miss Al	2	89	NR	89	.1	.1
093 Chr Ch (Disc)	1	0	0	0 *	-	-
097 Chr Chs&Chs Cr	1	520	NR	652 *	.5	1.0
123 Ch God (Ander)	2	NR	328	328	.3	.5
127 Ch God (Cleve)	10	2,178	1,071	2,735 *	2.1	4.0
145 Ch God Prophcy	4	167	NR	208 *	.2	.3
151 L-D Saints	1	NR	NR	595	.5	.9
157 Ch of Brethren	1	33	26	41 *	-	.1
165 Ch of Nazarene	3	283	195	317	.2	.5
167 Chs of Christ	3	305	325	372	.3	.5
193 Episcopal	2	NR	269	586	.4	.9
207 E.L.C.A.	16	3,987	1,911	5,012	3.8	7.3
223 Free Will Bapt	5	522	NR	655 *	.5	1.0
263 Int Foursq Gos	6	1,304	1,495	1,635 *	1.2	2.4
283 Luth—MO Synod	3	475	325	665	.5	1.0
291 Missionary Ch	1	8	8	8	-	-
304 NatPrimBapt USA	4	150	NR	188 *	.1	.3
336 OrigFreeWillBpt	2	181	NR	227 *	.2	.3
349 Pent Holiness	4	540	229	677 *	.5	1.0
355 Presb Ch (USA)	20	4,479	2,161	5,618 *	4.3	8.2
356 Presb Ch Amer	3	188	214	236	.2	.3
360 Prim Bapt Chrch	2	NR	NR	NR	-	-
403 Salvation Army	1	92	65	199	.2	.3
413 S.D.A.	1	148	NR	176	.1	.3
419 So Bapt Conv	58	19,999	8,477	25,075 *	19.1	36.6
443 Un C of Christ	6	801	351	1,004 *	.8	1.5
449 Un Methodist	30	10,100	4,519	12,660 *	9.7	18.5
467 Wesleyan	6	871	584	1,146	.9	1.7
498 Indep.Charis.	1	0	225	300	.2	.4
CALDWELL	**139**	**37,696**	**14,685**	**47,557 ***	**61.4**	**100.0**
053 Assemb of God	1	17	17	22	-	-
056 Baha'i	0	11	NR	11	-	-
081 Catholic	1	NR	NR	758	1.0	1.6
097 Chr Chs&Chs Cr	1	80	NR	98 *	.1	.2
121 Ch God (Abr)	1	86	77	106 *	.1	.2
127 Ch God (Cleve)	7	635	447	791 *	1.0	1.7
145 Ch God Prophcy	2	83	NR	102 *	.1	.2
151 L-D Saints	1	NR	NR	164	.2	.3
167 Chs of Christ	2	174	190	224	.3	.5
193 Episcopal	1	NR	99	260	.3	.5

NR–Not Reported   *Total adherents estimated from known number of communicant, confirmed, full members.   - Represents a percentage less than 0.1.   Percentages may not total 100 due to rounding.

Table 4: Religious Congregations by County and Group: 2000

Religious Group	Number of Churches, Synagogues, Mosques, or Temples	Number of Communicant, Confirmed, or Full Members	Number of Attendees	Total Adherents: Number of Adherents	% of Total Pop.	% of Total Adh.
207 E.L.C.A.	6	933	452	1,116	1.4	2.3
223 Free Will Bapt	1	104	NR	128 *	.2	.3
237 Menn Br US Conf	3	141	NR	173 *	.2	.4
335 Orth Pres Ch	1	38	39	56	.1	.1
349 Pent Holiness	3	578	339	709 *	.9	1.5
355 Presb Ch (USA)	5	971	520	1,192 *	1.5	2.5
360 Prim Bapt Chrch	2	NR	NR	NR	-	-
403 Salvation Army	1	20	18	55	.1	.1
413 S.D.A.	1	83	NR	99	.1	.2
419 So Bapt Conv	74	29,346	10,530	36,012 *	46.5	75.7
443 Un C of Christ	1	113	46	139 *	.2	.3
449 Un Methodist	23	4,250	1,872	5,217 *	6.7	11.0
467 Wesleyan	1	33	39	125	.2	.3
CAMDEN	**15**	**2,411**	**859**	**2,969 ***	**43.1**	**100.0**
097 Chr Chs&Chs Cr	2	299	NR	368 *	5.3	12.4
349 Pent Holiness	2	189	132	233 *	3.4	7.8
419 So Bapt Conv	5	1,257	453	1,548 *	22.5	52.1
449 Un Methodist	5	606	214	746 *	10.8	25.1
463 Vineyard	1	60	60	74 *	1.1	2.5
CARTERET	**97**	**17,314**	**8,522**	**24,833 ***	**41.8**	**100.0**
053 Assemb of God	3	319	402	533	.9	2.1
056 Baha'i	0	4	NR	4	-	-
076 Buddhism	1	NR	NR	NR	-	-
081 Catholic	1	NR	NR	1,798	3.0	7.2
093 Chr Ch (Disc)	2	343	12	406 *	.7	1.6
127 Ch God (Cleve)	3	506	329	598 *	1.0	2.4
145 Ch God Prophcy	1	42	NR	49 *	.1	.2
151 L-D Saints	2	NR	NR	758	1.3	3.1
165 Ch of Nazarene	1	110	135	208	.4	.8
167 Chs of Christ	2	100	105	160	.3	.6
193 Episcopal	3	NR	578	1,436	2.4	5.8
207 E.L.C.A.	1	273	140	351	.6	1.4
223 Free Will Bapt	5	522	NR	617 *	1.0	2.5
336 OrigFreeWillBpt	13	1,405	NR	1,662 *	2.8	6.7
349 Pent Holiness	6	1,396	1,383	1,651 *	2.8	6.6
355 Presb Ch (USA)	4	961	477	1,136 *	1.9	4.6
360 Prim Bapt Chrch	1	NR	NR	NR	-	-
403 Salvation Army	1	21	17	38	.1	.2
418 Southw Bapt Fel	1	NR	NR	NR	-	-
419 So Bapt Conv	20	5,985	2,773	7,079 *	11.9	28.5
435 Unitarian-Univ	1	62	NR	73 *	.1	.3
443 Un C of Christ	2	105	46	124 *	.2	.5
449 Un Methodist	22	5,119	2,045	6,057 *	10.2	24.4
467 Wesleyan	1	41	80	95	.2	.4
CASWELL	**47**	**5,337**	**2,587**	**6,572 ***	**28.0**	**100.0**
032 Amish; other	1	61	NR	74 *	.3	1.1
053 Assemb of God	1	196	175	281	1.2	4.3
193 Episcopal	1	NR	10	15	.1	.2
349 Pent Holiness	2	114	85	139 *	.6	2.1
355 Presb Ch (USA)	7	305	192	376 *	1.6	5.7
360 Prim Bapt Chrch	1	NR	NR	NR	-	-
419 So Bapt Conv	14	2,660	1,238	3,246 *	13.8	49.4
443 Un C of Christ	3	297	152	362 *	1.5	5.5
449 Un Methodist	17	1,704	735	2,079 *	8.8	31.6
CATAWBA	**207**	**63,043**	**28,542**	**85,731 ***	**60.5**	**100.0**
019 Amer Bapt USA	2	1,034	275	1,278 *	.9	1.5
053 Assemb of God	6	571	645	690	.5	.8
056 Baha'i	0	54	NR	54	-	.1
076 Buddhism	1	NR	NR	NR	-	-
081 Catholic	2	NR	NR	4,399	3.1	5.1
089 Chr & Miss Al	1	734	NR	734	.5	.9
097 Chr Chs&Chs Cr	2	177	NR	219 *	.2	.3
123 Ch God (Ander)	3	NR	473	473	.3	.6
127 Ch God (Cleve)	6	1,028	505	1,271 *	.9	1.5
151 L-D Saints	3	NR	NR	1,047	.7	1.2
165 Ch of Nazarene	1	59	51	59	-	.1
167 Chs of Christ	3	306	293	477	.3	.6
193 Episcopal	3	NR	450	1,426	1.0	1.7
201 Evan Cov Ch	1	25	47	47 *	-	.1
207 E.L.C.A.	25	9,250	4,402	11,454	8.1	13.4
223 Free Will Bapt	1	104	NR	129 *	.1	.2
226 Friends-USA	1	64	NR	79 *	.1	.1
263 Int Foursq Gos	1	9	11	11 *	-	-
283 Luth—MO Synod	12	6,569	3,068	8,347	5.9	9.7
288 Mennonite USA	2	130	125	161 *	.1	.2
290 Metro Comm Ch	1	18	14	22 *	-	-
295 Morav Ch-South	1	89	NR	130	.1	.2
335 Orth Pres Ch	1	8	20	20	-	-
349 Pent Holiness	4	774	411	957 *	.7	1.1
355 Presb Ch (USA)	6	1,996	948	2,467 *	1.7	2.9
356 Presb Ch Amer	1	0	0	0	-	-
403 Salvation Army	1	157	106	228	.2	.3
413 S.D.A.	3	471	NR	560	.4	.7
418 Southw Bapt Fel	1	NR	NR	NR	-	-
419 So Bapt Conv	62	25,051	10,315	30,966 *	21.9	36.1
435 Unitarian-Univ	1	42	NR	52 *	-	.1
443 Un C of Christ	10	2,405	1,054	2,973 *	2.1	3.5
449 Un Methodist	35	11,624	5,047	14,369 *	10.1	16.8
467 Wesleyan	3	294	282	522	.4	.6
496 Jewish Est	1	NR	NR	110	.1	.1
CHATHAM	**92**	**14,580**	**6,658**	**18,736 ***	**38.0**	**100.0**
053 Assemb of God	1	31	35	38	.1	.2
056 Baha'i	0	19	NR	19	-	.1
076 Buddhism	1	NR	NR	NR	-	-
081 Catholic	1	NR	NR	666	1.4	3.6
123 Ch God (Ander)	1	NR	40	40	.1	.2
127 Ch God (Cleve)	2	178	137	217 *	.4	1.2
145 Ch God Prophcy	4	167	NR	204 *	.4	1.1
165 Ch of Nazarene	1	12	17	25	.1	.1
167 Chs of Christ	1	25	30	34	.1	.2
193 Episcopal	1	NR	121	247	.5	1.3
223 Free Will Bapt	1	104	NR	127 *	.3	.7
226 Friends-USA	3	339	NR	412 *	.8	2.2
349 Pent Holiness	1	216	168	262 *	.5	1.4
355 Presb Ch (USA)	4	309	187	375 *	.8	2.0
413 S.D.A.	1	54	NR	64	.1	.3
418 Southw Bapt Fel	2	NR	NR	NR	-	-
419 So Bapt Conv	35	8,553	3,931	10,392 *	21.1	55.5
443 Un C of Christ	5	686	283	833 *	1.7	4.4
449 Un Methodist	24	3,718	1,489	4,519 *	9.2	24.1
467 Wesleyan	3	169	220	262	.5	1.4
CHEROKEE	**77**	**10,261**	**4,303**	**13,084 ***	**53.8**	**100.0**
053 Assemb of God	2	127	163	227	.9	1.7
056 Baha'i	0	2	NR	2	-	-
081 Catholic	2	NR	NR	671	2.8	5.1
123 Ch God (Ander)	1	NR	30	30	.1	.2
127 Ch God (Cleve)	4	191	177	248 *	1.0	1.9
145 Ch God Prophcy	2	83	NR	98 *	.4	.7
167 Chs of Christ	2	62	75	75	.3	.6
193 Episcopal	1	NR	57	124	.5	.9
207 E.L.C.A.	1	103	71	115	.5	.9
221 Free Methodist	1	22	32	32	.1	.2
355 Presb Ch (USA)	1	87	70	103 *	.4	.8
356 Presb Ch Amer	2	88	96	107	.4	.8
413 S.D.A.	2	235	NR	280	1.2	2.1
419 So Bapt Conv	46	8,006	2,963	9,485 *	39.0	72.5
449 Un Methodist	10	1,255	569	1,487 *	6.1	11.4
CHOWAN	**22**	**4,890**	**2,318**	**6,894 ***	**47.5**	**100.0**
053 Assemb of God	1	86	100	162	1.1	2.3
056 Baha'i	0	7	NR	7	-	.1
081 Catholic	1	NR	NR	464	3.2	6.7
097 Chr Chs&Chs Cr	2	284	NR	346 *	2.4	5.0
127 Ch God (Cleve)	1	50	19	61 *	.4	.9
167 Chs of Christ	1	25	15	34	.2	.5
193 Episcopal	2	NR	225	401	2.8	5.8
349 Pent Holiness	2	269	198	328 *	2.3	4.8
355 Presb Ch (USA)	1	81	40	99 *	.7	1.4
419 So Bapt Conv	9	3,553	1,537	4,339 *	29.9	62.9

NR–Not Reported *Total adherents estimated from known number of communicant, confirmed, full members. - Represents a percentage less than 0.1. Percentages may not total 100 due to rounding.

Table 4: Religious Congregations by County and Group: 2000

Religious Group	Number of Churches, Synagogues, Mosques, or Temples	Number of Communicant, Confirmed, or Full Members	Number of Attendees	Total Adherents: Number of Adherents	Total Adherents: % of Total Pop.	Total Adherents: % of Total Adh.
449 Un Methodist	2	535	184	653 *	4.5	9.5
CLAY	**38**	**3,854**	**1,957**	**5,154 ***	**58.7**	**100.0**
053 Assemb of God	2	82	91	108	1.2	2.1
081 Catholic	1	NR	NR	389	4.4	7.5
127 Ch God (Cleve)	5	323	236	416 *	4.7	8.1
165 Ch of Nazarene	1	33	30	50	.6	1.0
167 Chs of Christ	3	63	75	92	1.0	1.8
193 Episcopal	1	NR	155	216	2.5	4.2
355 Presb Ch (USA)	1	30	15	35 *	.4	.7
419 So Bapt Conv	19	2,618	1,003	3,032 *	34.6	58.8
449 Un Methodist	5	705	352	816 *	9.3	15.8
CLEVELAND	**175**	**46,581**	**20,034**	**60,289 ***	**62.6**	**100.0**
053 Assemb of God	1	17	20	25	-	-
055 As Ref Pres Ch	1	199	NR	220	.2	.4
056 Baha'i	0	189	NR	189	.2	.3
081 Catholic	2	NR	NR	1,071	1.1	1.8
127 Ch God (Cleve)	7	974	589	1,229 *	1.3	2.0
151 L-D Saints	1	NR	NR	270	.3	.4
165 Ch of Nazarene	3	454	411	585	.6	1.0
167 Chs of Christ	1	80	85	95	.1	.2
193 Episcopal	2	NR	159	486	.5	.8
207 E.L.C.A.	3	762	288	906	.9	1.5
223 Free Will Bapt	3	313	NR	391 *	.4	.6
263 Int Foursq Gos	3	199	319	319 *	.3	.5
349 Pent Holiness	3	193	161	241 *	.3	.4
355 Presb Ch (USA)	7	1,436	641	1,794 *	1.9	3.0
360 Prim Bapt Chrch	1	NR	NR	NR	-	-
403 Salvation Army	1	45	36	99	.1	.2
413 S.D.A.	2	168	NR	200	.2	.3
419 So Bapt Conv	91	34,193	14,009	42,735 *	44.4	70.9
449 Un Methodist	38	6,736	2,709	8,417 *	8.7	14.0
463 Vineyard	1	130	120	162 *	.2	.3
467 Wesleyan	4	493	487	855	.9	1.4
COLUMBUS	**136**	**22,955**	**8,663**	**29,394 ***	**53.7**	**100.0**
053 Assemb of God	2	268	260	293	.5	1.0
056 Baha'i	1	221	NR	221	.4	.8
081 Catholic	2	NR	NR	390	.7	1.3
089 Chr & Miss Al	1	42	NR	95	.2	.3
127 Ch God (Cleve)	7	685	450	862 *	1.6	2.9
145 Ch God Prophcy	1	42	NR	52 *	.1	.2
151 L-D Saints	2	NR	NR	257	.5	.9
167 Chs of Christ	1	60	55	70	.1	.2
193 Episcopal	1	NR	59	122	.2	.4
207 E.L.C.A.	1	12	6	12	-	-
216 Evan Presby Ch	1	18	NR	22 *	-	.1
223 Free Will Bapt	2	209	NR	259 *	.5	.9
336 OrigFreeWillBpt	11	1,464	NR	1,819 *	3.3	6.2
349 Pent Holiness	4	567	365	704 *	1.3	2.4
355 Presb Ch (USA)	7	656	329	814 *	1.5	2.8
413 S.D.A.	2	74	NR	88	.2	.3
418 Southw Bapt Fel	1	NR	NR	NR	-	-
419 So Bapt Conv	68	15,581	5,708	19,355 *	35.4	65.8
449 Un Methodist	19	2,785	998	3,459 *	6.3	11.8
467 Wesleyan	1	121	83	150	.3	.5
498 Indep.Charis.	1	150	350	350	.6	1.2
CRAVEN	**116**	**25,140**	**9,806**	**39,626 ***	**43.3**	**100.0**
053 Assemb of God	2	300	371	449	.5	1.1
056 Baha'i	0	23	NR	23	-	.1
081 Catholic	2	NR	NR	5,338	5.8	13.5
093 Chr Ch (Disc)	11	1,341	525	1,665 *	1.8	4.2
097 Chr Chs&Chs Cr	2	300	NR	372 *	.4	.9
127 Ch God (Cleve)	4	708	554	879 *	1.0	2.2
145 Ch God Prophcy	1	42	NR	52 *	.1	.1
151 L-D Saints	2	NR	NR	938	1.0	2.4
165 Ch of Nazarene	1	91	73	91	.1	.2
167 Chs of Christ	2	130	175	155	.2	.4
193 Episcopal	4	NR	558	1,892	2.1	4.8
207 E.L.C.A.	2	381	238	451	.5	1.1

Religious Group	Number of Churches, Synagogues, Mosques, or Temples	Number of Communicant, Confirmed, or Full Members	Number of Attendees	Total Adherents: Number of Adherents	Total Adherents: % of Total Pop.	Total Adherents: % of Total Adh.
223 Free Will Bapt	5	522	NR	648 *	.7	1.6
263 Int Foursq Gos	1	4	13	13 *	-	-
267 Muslim Est	1	NR	55	163	.2	.4
283 Luth—MO Synod	1	175	100	200	.2	.5
331 OCA: Ter Diocs	1	10	NR	27	-	.1
335 Orth Pres Ch	1	25	26	31	-	.1
336 OrigFreeWillBpt	14	2,980	NR	3,700 *	4.0	9.3
349 Pent Holiness	8	474	349	589 *	.6	1.5
355 Presb Ch (USA)	6	1,703	793	2,114 *	2.3	5.3
356 Presb Ch Amer	1	76	45	85	.1	.2
403 Salvation Army	1	107	68	159	.2	.4
413 S.D.A.	3	580	NR	690	.8	1.7
419 So Bapt Conv	14	7,883	2,856	9,788 *	10.7	24.7
435 Unitarian-Univ	1	31	NR	38 *	-	.1
443 Un C of Christ	3	369	245	458 *	.5	1.2
449 Un Methodist	21	6,885	2,762	8,548 *	9.3	21.6
496 Jewish Est	1	NR	NR	70	.1	.2
CUMBERLAND	**231**	**71,419**	**30,638**	**105,444 ***	**34.8**	**100.0**
019 Amer Bapt USA	1	4,000	1,700	5,153 *	1.7	4.9
053 Assemb of God	9	862	927	1,381	.5	1.3
056 Baha'i	1	99	NR	99	-	.1
076 Buddhism	1	NR	NR	NR	-	-
081 Catholic	5	NR	NR	9,182	3.0	8.7
084 Calvary Chapel	1	NR	NR	NR	-	-
089 Chr & Miss Al	1	50	NR	137	-	.1
093 Chr Ch (Disc)	2	208	74	268 *	.1	.3
097 Chr Chs&Chs Cr	1	400	NR	515 *	.2	.5
127 Ch God (Cleve)	19	3,529	2,026	4,545 *	1.5	4.3
145 Ch God Prophcy	5	209	NR	270 *	.1	.3
151 L-D Saints	6	NR	NR	2,366	.8	2.2
165 Ch of Nazarene	1	155	167	240	.1	.2
167 Chs of Christ	4	431	540	641	.2	.6
193 Episcopal	6	NR	733	1,834	.6	1.7
207 E.L.C.A.	2	919	333	1,229	.4	1.2
223 Free Will Bapt	1	104	NR	135 *	-	.1
226 Friends-USA	1	47	NR	61 *	-	.1
246 Greek Orthodox	1	NR	NR	450	.1	.4
263 Int Foursq Gos	1	30	50	50 *	-	-
264 Int Chs of Crst	1	55	130	98	-	.1
267 Muslim Est	1	NR	50	150	-	.1
283 Luth—MO Synod	1	144	85	218	.1	.2
290 Metro Comm Ch	1	61	59	79 *	-	.1
331 OCA: Ter Diocs	1	15	NR	71	-	.1
336 OrigFreeWillBpt	3	280	NR	361 *	.1	.3
349 Pent Holiness	9	5,291	2,619	6,816 *	2.2	6.5
355 Presb Ch (USA)	26	5,348	2,590	6,914 *	2.3	6.6
356 Presb Ch Amer	2	198	230	256	.1	.2
360 Prim Bapt Chrch	1	NR	NR	NR	-	-
403 Salvation Army	1	86	47	143	-	.1
413 S.D.A.	3	861	NR	1,025	.3	1.0
418 Southw Bapt Fel	4	NR	NR	NR	-	-
419 So Bapt Conv	68	27,556	9,872	35,499 *	11.7	33.7
443 Un C of Christ	3	215	176	277 *	.1	.3
449 Un Methodist	28	11,809	3,891	15,214 *	5.0	14.4
467 Wesleyan	1	60	64	175	.1	.2
469 WELS	1	72	60	117	-	.1
496 Jewish Est	1	NR	NR	300	.1	.3
498 Indep.Charis.	3	7,750	3,000	7,750	2.6	7.3
499 Indep.Non-Char	3	575	1,215	1,425	.5	1.4
CURRITUCK	**20**	**4,430**	**1,702**	**5,496 ***	**30.2**	**100.0**
053 Assemb of God	2	192	245	245	1.3	4.5
056 Baha'i	0	5	NR	5	-	.1
097 Chr Chs&Chs Cr	3	474	NR	588 *	3.2	10.7
419 So Bapt Conv	8	2,513	977	3,114 *	17.1	56.7
449 Un Methodist	7	1,246	480	1,544 *	8.5	28.1
DARE	**45**	**6,916**	**3,806**	**11,677 ***	**39.0**	**100.0**
053 Assemb of God	8	718	1,008	1,184	4.0	10.1
056 Baha'i	0	7	NR	7	-	.1
081 Catholic	4	NR	NR	2,097	7.0	18.0
097 Chr Chs&Chs Cr	2	85	NR	102 *	.3	.9

NR–Not Reported *Total adherents estimated from known number of communicant, confirmed, full members. - Represents a percentage less than 0.1. Percentages may not total 100 due to rounding.

Table 4: Religious Congregations by County and Group: 2000

Religious Group	Number of Churches, Synagogues, Mosques, or Temples	Number of Communicant, Confirmed, or Full Members	Number of Attendees	Total Adherents		
				Number of Adherents	% of Total Pop.	% of Total Adh.
127 Ch God (Cleve)	1	32	22	38 *	.1	.3
145 Ch God Prophcy	1	42	NR	50 *	.2	.4
151 L-D Saints	1	NR	NR	302	1.0	2.6
167 Chs of Christ	1	15	16	20	.1	.2
193 Episcopal	1	NR	292	624	2.1	5.3
265 Int Pent C Chr	2	4	18	60	.2	.5
283 Luth—MO Synod	1	132	127	154	.5	1.3
355 Presb Ch (USA)	2	439	70	525 *	1.8	4.5
419 So Bapt Conv	6	1,490	635	1,783 *	5.9	15.3
435 Unitarian-Univ	1	38	NR	45 *	.2	.4
449 Un Methodist	14	3,914	1,618	4,686 *	15.6	40.1
DAVIDSON	**198**	**48,664**	**21,807**	**64,146 ***	**43.6**	**100.0**
019 Amer Bapt USA	1	275	0	339 *	.2	.5
053 Assemb of God	3	258	302	350	.2	.5
056 Baha'i	0	37	NR	37	-	.1
076 Buddhism	1	NR	NR	NR	-	-
081 Catholic	2	NR	NR	1,809	1.2	2.8
089 Chr & Miss Al	2	249	NR	436	.3	.7
127 Ch God (Cleve)	5	720	378	889 *	.6	1.4
145 Ch God Prophcy	4	167	NR	204 *	.1	.3
151 L-D Saints	1	NR	NR	614	.4	1.0
157 Ch of Brethren	1	63	23	78 *	.1	.1
165 Ch of Nazarene	1	67	42	67	-	.1
167 Chs of Christ	5	296	345	417	.3	.7
193 Episcopal	1	NR	123	418	.3	.7
207 E.L.C.A.	9	1,907	922	2,422	1.6	3.8
223 Free Will Bapt	7	731	NR	902 *	.6	1.4
226 Friends-USA	2	226	NR	279 *	.2	.4
263 Int Foursq Gos	1	30	50	50 *	-	.1
295 Morav Ch-South	1	150	NR	179	.1	.3
336 OrigFreeWillBpt	1	100	NR	123 *	.1	.2
349 Pent Holiness	2	674	389	832 *	.6	1.3
355 Presb Ch (USA)	5	1,085	552	1,338 *	.9	2.1
356 Presb Ch Amer	1	354	483	483	.3	.8
360 Prim Bapt Chrch	1	NR	NR	NR	-	-
403 Salvation Army	1	105	91	181	.1	.3
413 S.D.A.	3	145	NR	173	.1	.3
418 Southw Bapt Fel	4	NR	NR	NR	-	-
419 So Bapt Conv	44	17,132	6,513	21,142 *	14.4	33.0
443 Un C of Christ	20	5,909	2,501	7,292 *	5.0	11.4
449 Un Methodist	59	16,434	7,117	20,280 *	13.8	31.6
467 Wesleyan	8	1,150	1,391	2,162	1.5	3.4
498 Indep.Charis.	2	400	585	650	.4	1.0
DAVIE	**62**	**12,169**	**6,297**	**17,038 ***	**48.9**	**100.0**
056 Baha'i	0	5	NR	5	-	-
081 Catholic	1	NR	NR	1,115	3.2	6.5
127 Ch God (Cleve)	2	210	155	259 *	.7	1.5
145 Ch God Prophcy	1	42	NR	51 *	.1	.3
167 Chs of Christ	3	404	399	549	1.6	3.2
193 Episcopal	2	NR	45	76	.2	.4
207 E.L.C.A.	1	75	60	96	.3	.6
295 Morav Ch-South	1	512	NR	664	1.9	3.9
349 Pent Holiness	2	139	170	172 *	.5	1.0
355 Presb Ch (USA)	5	778	419	961 *	2.8	5.6
360 Prim Bapt Chrch	1	NR	NR	NR	-	-
413 S.D.A.	1	42	NR	50	.1	.3
419 So Bapt Conv	16	5,198	2,083	6,416 *	18.4	37.7
449 Un Methodist	24	4,734	2,243	5,843 *	16.8	34.3
467 Wesleyan	1	30	23	81	.2	.5
499 Indep.Non-Char	1	0	700	700	2.0	4.1
DUPLIN	**92**	**13,369**	**5,033**	**17,661 ***	**36.0**	**100.0**
053 Assemb of God	2	109	128	206	.4	1.2
056 Baha'i	0	5	NR	5	-	-
081 Catholic	2	NR	NR	561	1.1	3.2
093 Chr Ch (Disc)	1	60	0	75 *	.2	.4
127 Ch God (Cleve)	1	226	110	284 *	.6	1.6
145 Ch God Prophcy	1	42	NR	52 *	.1	.3
151 L-D Saints	1	NR	NR	171	.3	1.0
167 Chs of Christ	2	29	40	34	.1	.2
223 Free Will Bapt	2	209	NR	262 *	.5	1.5

Religious Group	Number of Churches, Synagogues, Mosques, or Temples	Number of Communicant, Confirmed, or Full Members	Number of Attendees	Total Adherents		
				Number of Adherents	% of Total Pop.	% of Total Adh.
336 OrigFreeWillBpt	12	1,711	NR	2,150 *	4.4	12.2
349 Pent Holiness	4	457	326	574 *	1.2	3.3
355 Presb Ch (USA)	17	1,493	841	1,876 *	3.8	10.6
413 S.D.A.	1	30	NR	36	.1	.2
419 So Bapt Conv	29	6,890	2,612	8,659 *	17.6	49.0
449 Un Methodist	16	2,040	915	2,563 *	5.2	14.5
467 Wesleyan	1	68	61	153	.3	.9
DURHAM	**192**	**53,851**	**23,945**	**87,815 ***	**39.3**	**100.0**
019 Amer Bapt USA	6	5,534	1,720	6,787 *	3.0	7.7
053 Assemb of God	3	336	422	459	.2	.5
055 As Ref Pres Ch	1	49	NR	50	-	.1
056 Baha'i	2	196	NR	196	.1	.2
076 Buddhism	4	NR	NR	NR	-	-
081 Catholic	4	NR	NR	9,818	4.4	11.2
089 Chr & Miss Al	2	96	NR	142	.1	.2
093 Chr Ch (Disc)	1	77	18	94 *	-	.1
097 Chr Chs&Chs Cr	1	80	NR	98 *	-	.1
105 Christian Ref	1	50	60	61 *	-	.1
123 Ch God (Ander)	1	NR	0	0	-	-
127 Ch God (Cleve)	2	286	102	350 *	.2	.4
145 Ch God Prophcy	4	167	NR	204 *	.1	.2
151 L-D Saints	4	NR	NR	1,727	.8	2.0
157 Ch of Brethren	1	44	28	54 *	-	.1
165 Ch of Nazarene	1	58	112	175	.1	.2
167 Chs of Christ	5	829	784	983	.4	1.1
193 Episcopal	5	NR	894	2,846	1.3	3.2
207 E.L.C.A.	4	904	415	1,169	.5	1.3
216 Evan Presby Ch	1	69	NR	85 *	-	.1
223 Free Will Bapt	4	418	NR	512 *	.2	.6
226 Friends-USA	1	47	NR	58 *	-	.1
246 Greek Orthodox	1	NR	NR	291	.1	.3
264 Int Chs of Crst	1	1,061	1,959	1,522	.7	1.7
267 Muslim Est	3	NR	828	1,941	.9	2.2
268 Jain	1	NR	NR	NR	-	-
283 Luth—MO Synod	1	8	178	267	.1	.3
288 Mennonite USA	1	34	40	42 *	-	-
290 Metro Comm Ch	1	56	60	69 *	-	.1
295 Morav Ch-South	1	146	NR	222	.1	.3
336 OrigFreeWillBpt	3	415	NR	509 *	.2	.6
349 Pent Holiness	5	648	397	795 *	.4	.9
355 Presb Ch (USA)	10	3,627	2,160	4,449 *	2.0	5.1
356 Presb Ch Amer	2	598	1,125	1,125	.5	1.3
403 Salvation Army	1	132	72	139	.1	.2
413 S.D.A.	2	682	NR	811	.4	.9
416 Sikh	2	NR	NR	NR	-	-
419 So Bapt Conv	51	23,261	7,608	28,526 *	12.8	32.5
435 Unitarian-Univ	2	726	NR	890 *	.4	1.0
443 Un C of Christ	6	1,155	521	1,416 *	.6	1.6
449 Un Methodist	28	10,215	3,079	12,528 *	5.6	14.3
467 Wesleyan	3	47	23	180	.1	.2
496 Jewish Est	6	NR	NR	4,000	1.8	4.6
498 Indep.Charis.	1	1,200	800	1,500	.7	1.7
499 Indep.Non-Char	2	600	540	725	.3	.8
EDGECOMBE	**76**	**11,939**	**5,266**	**18,472 ***	**33.2**	**100.0**
053 Assemb of God	1	37	53	80	.1	.4
056 Baha'i	0	18	NR	18	-	.1
081 Catholic	2	NR	NR	2,020	3.6	10.9
093 Chr Ch (Disc)	2	453	45	573 *	1.0	3.1
097 Chr Chs&Chs Cr	1	115	NR	146 *	.3	.8
127 Ch God (Cleve)	5	764	342	967 *	1.7	5.2
151 L-D Saints	1	NR	NR	123	.2	.7
193 Episcopal	7	NR	290	737	1.3	4.0
207 E.L.C.A.	1	173	99	207	.4	1.1
223 Free Will Bapt	3	313	NR	396 *	.7	2.1
267 Muslim Est	1	NR	101	288	.5	1.6
288 Mennonite USA	1	76	55	96 *	.2	.5
336 OrigFreeWillBpt	5	665	NR	842 *	1.5	4.6
349 Pent Holiness	4	765	929	968 *	1.7	5.2
355 Presb Ch (USA)	9	829	489	1,050 *	1.9	5.7
360 Prim Bapt Chrch	1	NR	NR	NR	-	-
403 Salvation Army	1	96	63	228	.4	1.2

NR–Not Reported *Total adherents estimated from known number of communicant, confirmed, full members. - Represents a percentage less than 0.1. Percentages may not total 100 due to rounding.

Table 4: Religious Congregations by County and Group: 2000

Religious Group	Number of Churches, Synagogues, Mosques, or Temples	Number of Communicant, Confirmed, or Full Members	Number of Attendees	Total Adherents		
				Number of Adherents	% of Total Pop.	% of Total Adh.
413 S.D.A.	1	112	NR	133	.2	.7
419 So Bapt Conv	20	5,880	2,247	7,441 *	13.4	40.3
443 Un C of Christ	1	0	0	0 *	-	-
449 Un Methodist	8	1,643	553	2,079 *	3.7	11.3
496 Jewish Est	1	NR	NR	80	.1	.4
FORSYTH	**311**	**107,594**	**45,057**	**154,145 ***	**50.4**	**100.0**
019 Amer Bapt USA	4	3,050	1,660	3,766 *	1.2	2.4
053 Assemb of God	5	2,905	2,599	4,070	1.3	2.6
055 As Ref Pres Ch	1	0	NR	0	-	-
056 Baha'i	1	200	NR	200	.1	.1
081 Catholic	6	NR	NR	13,052	4.3	8.5
089 Chr & Miss Al	3	572	NR	978	.3	.6
093 Chr Ch (Disc)	5	3,153	2,175	3,893 *	1.3	2.5
097 Chr Chs&Chs Cr	11	4,143	NR	5,115 *	1.7	3.3
123 Ch God (Ander)	1	NR	30	30	-	-
127 Ch God (Cleve)	4	488	286	603 *	.2	.4
145 Ch God Prophcy	1	42	NR	52 *	-	-
151 L-D Saints	5	NR	NR	2,291	.7	1.5
157 Ch of Brethren	1	197	112	243 *	.1	.2
165 Ch of Nazarene	2	137	135	206	.1	.1
167 Chs of Christ	14	1,964	1,654	2,564	.8	1.7
173 Comm of Christ	1	84	NR	84	-	.1
193 Episcopal	6	NR	1,404	3,946	1.3	2.6
207 E.L.C.A.	7	1,713	826	2,081	.7	1.4
216 Evan Presby Ch	2	1,091	NR	1,347 *	.4	.9
226 Friends-USA	7	791	NR	977 *	.3	.6
246 Greek Orthodox	1	NR	NR	786	.3	.5
263 Int Foursq Gos	1	30	50	50 *	-	-
267 Muslim Est	2	NR	328	1,341	.4	.9
283 Luth—MO Synod	3	1,068	621	1,636	.5	1.1
290 Metro Comm Ch	1	110	88	88 *	-	.1
295 Morav Ch-South	32	11,208	NR	13,631	4.5	8.8
304 NatPrimBapt USA	1	200	NR	247 *	.1	.2
336 OrigFreeWillBpt	1	45	NR	56 *	-	-
349 Pent Holiness	7	543	354	670 *	.2	.4
355 Presb Ch (USA)	13	4,538	2,345	5,604 *	1.8	3.6
356 Presb Ch Amer	4	735	882	1,092	.4	.7
360 Prim Bapt Chrch	4	NR	NR	NR	-	-
403 Salvation Army	1	91	78	323	.1	.2
413 S.D.A.	3	1,467	NR	1,746	.6	1.1
418 Southw Bapt Fel	7	NR	NR	NR	-	-
419 So Bapt Conv	61	29,927	12,511	36,951 *	12.1	24.0
435 Unitarian-Univ	1	236	NR	291 *	.1	.2
443 Un C of Christ	7	720	388	889 *	.3	.6
449 Un Methodist	58	24,212	9,277	29,897 *	9.8	19.4
463 Vineyard	1	130	120	161 *	.1	.1
467 Wesleyan	8	753	876	1,627	.5	1.1
469 WELS	1	87	83	112	-	.1
496 Jewish Est	1	NR	NR	485	.2	.3
499 Indep.Non-Char	5	10,964	6,175	10,964	3.6	7.1
FRANKLIN	**66**	**13,527**	**4,886**	**17,194 ***	**36.4**	**100.0**
056 Baha'i	0	8	NR	8	-	-
081 Catholic	1	NR	NR	166	.4	1.0
093 Chr Ch (Disc)	1	219	0	273 *	.6	1.6
127 Ch God (Cleve)	4	204	198	254 *	.5	1.5
145 Ch God Prophcy	3	125	NR	156 *	.3	.9
193 Episcopal	2	NR	71	144	.3	.8
349 Pent Holiness	1	49	33	61 *	.1	.4
355 Presb Ch (USA)	2	119	61	148 *	.3	.9
419 So Bapt Conv	33	10,012	3,237	12,499 *	26.4	72.7
443 Un C of Christ	9	1,208	664	1,508 *	3.2	8.8
449 Un Methodist	10	1,583	622	1,977 *	4.2	11.5
GASTON	**292**	**81,199**	**31,969**	**109,364 ***	**57.4**	**100.0**
053 Assemb of God	6	994	948	1,712	.9	1.6
055 As Ref Pres Ch	7	1,645	NR	1,896	1.0	1.7
056 Baha'i	0	49	NR	49	-	-
081 Catholic	3	NR	NR	5,304	2.8	4.8
097 Chr Chs&Chs Cr	1	50	NR	62 *	-	.1
123 Ch God (Ander)	1	NR	50	50	-	-
127 Ch God (Cleve)	25	5,211	3,402	6,488 *	3.4	5.9
145 Ch God Prophcy	3	125	NR	156 *	.1	.1
151 L-D Saints	3	NR	NR	1,538	.8	1.4
165 Ch of Nazarene	3	192	143	246	.1	.2
167 Chs of Christ	3	203	190	236	.1	.2
193 Episcopal	4	NR	379	962	.5	.9
207 E.L.C.A.	15	4,723	2,148	5,914	3.1	5.4
216 Evan Presby Ch	2	62	NR	77 *	-	.1
223 Free Will Bapt	22	2,297	NR	2,848 *	1.5	2.6
263 Int Foursq Gos	4	988	1,216	1,225 *	.6	1.1
267 Muslim Est	1	NR	40	60	-	.1
349 Pent Holiness	5	728	501	903 *	.5	.8
355 Presb Ch (USA)	17	4,302	2,268	5,335 *	2.8	4.9
356 Presb Ch Amer	4	795	478	911	.5	.8
360 Prim Bapt Chrch	1	NR	NR	NR	-	-
403 Salvation Army	1	177	82	180	.1	.2
413 S.D.A.	1	131	NR	156	.1	.1
419 So Bapt Conv	114	45,788	14,805	56,783 *	29.8	51.9
443 Un C of Christ	1	81	50	100 *	.1	.1
449 Un Methodist	34	11,042	4,091	13,693 *	7.2	12.5
467 Wesleyan	10	1,616	1,178	2,270	1.2	2.1
496 Jewish Est	1	NR	NR	210	.1	.2
GATES	**22**	**3,510**	**1,230**	**4,576 ***	**43.5**	**100.0**
056 Baha'i	0	2	NR	2	-	-
151 L-D Saints	1	NR	NR	87	.8	1.9
176 Congr Ad Afl	1	171	NR	215 *	2.0	4.7
193 Episcopal	2	NR	44	85	.8	1.9
349 Pent Holiness	1	47	54	59 *	.6	1.3
419 So Bapt Conv	9	2,320	757	2,911 *	27.7	63.6
443 Un C of Christ	2	451	180	566 *	5.4	12.4
449 Un Methodist	6	519	195	651 *	6.2	14.2
GRAHAM	**17**	**2,006**	**702**	**2,554 ***	**32.0**	**100.0**
081 Catholic	1	NR	NR	89	1.1	3.5
127 Ch God (Cleve)	1	17	20	20 *	.3	.8
193 Episcopal	1	NR	31	28	.4	1.1
207 E.L.C.A.	1	8	32	32	.4	1.3
419 So Bapt Conv	12	1,776	503	2,138 *	26.7	83.7
449 Un Methodist	1	205	116	247 *	3.1	9.7
GRANVILLE	**65**	**14,407**	**5,082**	**18,420 ***	**38.0**	**100.0**
019 Amer Bapt USA	1	224	125	275 *	.6	1.5
056 Baha'i	0	12	NR	12	-	.1
076 Buddhism	1	NR	NR	NR	-	-
081 Catholic	1	NR	NR	86	.2	.5
127 Ch God (Cleve)	3	261	163	321 *	.7	1.7
145 Ch God Prophcy	1	42	NR	51 *	.1	.3
151 L-D Saints	1	NR	NR	297	.6	1.6
193 Episcopal	2	NR	114	330	.7	1.8
349 Pent Holiness	1	20	25	25 *	.1	.1
355 Presb Ch (USA)	6	334	198	411 *	.8	2.2
419 So Bapt Conv	31	11,148	3,546	13,703 *	28.3	74.4
443 Un C of Christ	3	206	91	253 *	.5	1.4
449 Un Methodist	14	2,160	820	2,656 *	5.5	14.4
GREENE	**31**	**4,554**	**978**	**5,640 ***	**29.7**	**100.0**
056 Baha'i	0	7	NR	7	-	.1
093 Chr Ch (Disc)	3	310	75	384 *	2.0	6.8
127 Ch God (Cleve)	1	73	46	90 *	.5	1.6
223 Free Will Bapt	1	104	NR	129 *	.7	2.3
336 OrigFreeWillBpt	11	2,203	NR	2,731 *	14.4	48.4
349 Pent Holiness	1	81	80	100 *	.5	1.8
355 Presb Ch (USA)	2	72	48	89 *	.5	1.6
413 S.D.A.	1	27	NR	32	.2	.6
419 So Bapt Conv	2	434	275	538 *	2.8	9.5
449 Un Methodist	9	1,243	454	1,540 *	8.1	27.3
GUILFORD	**418**	**125,792**	**59,729**	**196,524 ***	**46.7**	**100.0**
019 Amer Bapt USA	2	1,200	800	1,478 *	.4	.8
053 Assemb of God	10	1,109	1,404	2,211	.5	1.1
055 As Ref Pres Ch	4	1,342	NR	1,874	.4	1.0
056 Baha'i	3	243	NR	243	.1	.1

NR–Not Reported *Total adherents estimated from known number of communicant, confirmed, full members. - Represents a percentage less than 0.1. Percentages may not total 100 due to rounding.

Table 4: Religious Congregations by County and Group: 2000

Religious Group	Number of Churches, Synagogues, Mosques, or Temples	Number of Communicant, Confirmed, or Full Members	Number of Attendees	Total Adherents: Number of Adherents	Total Adherents: % of Total Pop.	Total Adherents: % of Total Adh.
076 Buddhism	5	NR	NR	NR	-	-
081 Catholic	7	NR	NR	21,628	5.1	11.0
089 Chr & Miss Al	5	167	NR	299	.1	.2
093 Chr Ch (Disc)	4	1,372	612	1,690 *	.4	.9
097 Chr Chs&Chs Cr	5	715	NR	880 *	.2	.4
105 Christian Ref	1	74	60	91 *	-	-
123 Ch God (Ander)	7	NR	785	785	.2	.4
127 Ch God (Cleve)	11	997	612	1,248 *	.3	.6
145 Ch God Prophcy	5	209	NR	255 *	.1	.1
151 L-D Saints	3	NR	NR	1,710	.4	.9
165 Ch of Nazarene	8	505	332	736	.2	.4
167 Chs of Christ	6	1,349	1,060	1,959	.5	1.0
193 Episcopal	9	NR	1,660	5,649	1.3	2.9
201 Evan Cov Ch	2	435	326	536 *	.1	.3
203 Evan Free Ch	1	172	325	325	.1	.2
207 E.L.C.A.	11	3,510	1,676	4,582	1.1	2.3
223 Free Will Bapt	3	313	NR	386 *	.1	.2
226 Friends-USA	21	2,271	NR	2,798 *	.7	1.4
246 Greek Orthodox	2	NR	NR	648	.2	.3
252 Hindu	1	NR	NR	NR	-	-
263 Int Foursq Gos	3	536	406	660 *	.2	.3
267 Muslim Est	5	NR	1,096	3,619	.9	1.8
283 Luth—MO Synod	5	818	562	1,029	.2	.5
288 Mennonite USA	1	11	15	15 *	-	-
290 Metro Comm Ch	1	75	56	92 *	-	-
295 Morav Ch-South	2	472	NR	569	.1	.3
336 OrigFreeWillBpt	1	59	NR	73 *	-	-
349 Pent Holiness	9	1,515	963	1,867 *	.4	1.0
355 Presb Ch (USA)	29	13,351	5,720	16,458 *	3.9	8.4
356 Presb Ch Amer	1	217	219	346	.1	.2
360 Prim Bapt Chrch	3	NR	NR	NR	-	-
403 Salvation Army	1	306	179	410	.1	.2
413 S.D.A.	5	1,890	NR	2,248	.5	1.1
418 Southw Bapt Fel	6	NR	NR	NR	-	-
419 So Bapt Conv	79	43,618	16,885	53,739 *	12.8	27.3
435 Unitarian-Univ	1	220	NR	271 *	.1	.1
443 Un C of Christ	17	2,945	1,439	3,628 *	.9	1.8
449 Un Methodist	81	35,956	13,758	44,299 *	10.5	22.5
463 Vineyard	1	150	126	185 *	-	.1
467 Wesleyan	23	4,520	3,898	6,945	1.6	3.5
496 Jewish Est	3	NR	NR	2,500	.6	1.3
498 Indep.Charis.	2	1,200	1,125	1,280	.3	.7
499 Indep.Non-Char	3	1,950	3,630	4,280	1.0	2.2
HALIFAX	**85**	**14,849**	**4,805**	**19,859 ***	**34.6**	**100.0**
019 Amer Bapt USA	2	420	325	525 *	.9	2.6
053 Assemb of God	1	45	55	60	.1	.3
056 Baha'i	0	7	NR	7	-	-
081 Catholic	2	NR	NR	537	.9	2.7
097 Chr Chs&Chs Cr	6	1,497	NR	1,873 *	3.3	9.4
127 Ch God (Cleve)	4	422	281	528 *	.9	2.7
167 Chs of Christ	2	40	40	45	.1	.2
193 Episcopal	7	NR	244	662	1.2	3.3
223 Free Will Bapt	1	104	NR	131 *	.2	.7
336 OrigFreeWillBpt	1	25	NR	31 *	.1	.2
339 Pent Ch of God	1	41	NR	81	.1	.4
349 Pent Holiness	6	755	437	944 *	1.6	4.8
355 Presb Ch (USA)	3	346	147	433 *	.8	2.2
413 S.D.A.	2	125	NR	149	.3	.8
419 So Bapt Conv	26	6,705	1,982	8,384 *	14.6	42.2
449 Un Methodist	20	4,317	1,294	5,399 *	9.4	27.2
496 Jewish Est	1	NR	NR	70	.1	.4
HARNETT	**112**	**22,332**	**9,024**	**29,682 ***	**32.6**	**100.0**
053 Assemb of God	1	35	36	66	.1	.2
056 Baha'i	0	22	NR	22	-	.1
081 Catholic	1	NR	NR	843	.9	2.8
089 Chr & Miss Al	1	48	NR	76	.1	.3
093 Chr Ch (Disc)	3	379	85	482 *	.5	1.6
127 Ch God (Cleve)	6	800	413	1,019 *	1.1	3.4
145 Ch God Prophcy	7	292	NR	371 *	.4	1.2
151 L-D Saints	1	NR	NR	290	.3	1.0
193 Episcopal	1	NR	61	102	.1	.3
223 Free Will Bapt	4	418	NR	532 *	.6	1.8
226 Friends-USA	2	226	NR	288 *	.3	1.0
336 OrigFreeWillBpt	1	196	NR	249 *	.3	.8
349 Pent Holiness	6	1,059	813	1,348 *	1.5	4.5
355 Presb Ch (USA)	18	2,368	1,280	3,016 *	3.3	10.2
360 Prim Bapt Chrch	4	NR	NR	NR	-	-
413 S.D.A.	1	85	NR	101	.1	.3
418 Southw Bapt Fel	1	NR	NR	NR	-	-
419 So Bapt Conv	37	12,741	4,943	16,216 *	17.8	54.6
443 Un C of Christ	1	139	61	177 *	.2	.6
449 Un Methodist	16	3,524	1,332	4,484 *	4.9	15.1
HAYWOOD	**125**	**31,529**	**13,032**	**39,459 ***	**73.0**	**100.0**
053 Assemb of God	1	64	85	85	.2	.2
056 Baha'i	0	8	NR	8	-	-
081 Catholic	3	NR	NR	995	1.8	2.5
127 Ch God (Cleve)	4	354	243	421 *	.8	1.1
145 Ch God Prophcy	2	83	NR	100 *	.2	.3
151 L-D Saints	1	NR	NR	246	.5	.6
165 Ch of Nazarene	1	59	67	88	.2	.2
167 Chs of Christ	1	100	95	120	.2	.3
193 Episcopal	2	NR	217	624	1.2	1.6
221 Free Methodist	1	19	34	34	.1	.1
223 Free Will Bapt	5	522	NR	622 *	1.2	1.6
258 IndFreeWillBapt	3	211	NR	251 *	.5	.6
283 Luth—MO Synod	1	112	85	127	.2	.3
355 Presb Ch (USA)	3	335	206	398 *	.7	1.0
356 Presb Ch Amer	2	162	172	172	.3	.4
370 Ref Baptist Chs	1	NR	NR	NR	-	-
403 Salvation Army	1	144	97	304	.6	.8
413 S.D.A.	1	99	NR	118	.2	.3
419 So Bapt Conv	60	21,967	8,102	26,159 *	48.4	66.3
449 Un Methodist	28	6,432	2,811	7,662 *	14.2	19.4
467 Wesleyan	3	258	218	325	.6	.8
498 Indep.Charis.	1	600	600	600	1.1	1.5
HENDERSON	**122**	**34,721**	**19,219**	**49,780 ***	**55.8**	**100.0**
053 Assemb of God	3	193	165	224	.3	.4
055 As Ref Pres Ch	3	567	NR	669	.8	1.3
056 Baha'i	0	15	NR	15	-	-
081 Catholic	1	NR	NR	5,059	5.7	10.2
084 Calvary Chapel	1	NR	NR	NR	-	-
089 Chr & Miss Al	2	192	NR	256	.3	.5
121 Ch God (Abr)	1	23	15	27 *	-	.1
127 Ch God (Cleve)	5	496	211	591 *	.7	1.2
151 L-D Saints	2	NR	NR	541	.6	1.1
165 Ch of Nazarene	1	530	329	543	.6	1.1
167 Chs of Christ	1	244	230	307	.3	.6
193 Episcopal	6	NR	987	2,219	2.5	4.5
207 E.L.C.A.	1	1,067	523	1,226	1.4	2.5
283 Luth—MO Synod	1	221	179	236	.3	.5
290 Metro Comm Ch	1	34	29	41 *	-	.1
297 Mennonite;Other	1	20	NR	24 *	-	-
335 Orth Pres Ch	1	17	20	20	-	-
349 Pent Holiness	1	252	215	301 *	.3	.6
355 Presb Ch (USA)	5	1,722	877	2,055 *	2.3	4.1
356 Presb Ch Amer	2	678	854	947	1.1	1.9
370 Ref Baptist Chs	1	NR	NR	NR	-	-
401 Rus Orth Abroad	1	NR	NR	NR	-	-
403 Salvation Army	1	89	76	167	.2	.3
413 S.D.A.	5	1,797	NR	2,139	2.4	4.3
418 Southw Bapt Fel	2	NR	NR	NR	-	-
419 So Bapt Conv	53	20,589	11,781	24,567 *	27.5	49.4
435 Unitarian-Univ	1	212	NR	253 *	.3	.5
443 Un C of Christ	1	378	153	451 *	.5	.9
449 Un Methodist	13	4,736	2,092	5,652 *	6.3	11.4
467 Wesleyan	2	223	207	343	.4	.7
469 WELS	1	76	56	92	.1	.2
496 Jewish Est	1	NR	NR	250	.3	.5
499 Indep.Non-Char	1	350	220	565	.6	1.1
HERTFORD	**38**	**7,509**	**2,037**	**9,784 ***	**43.3**	**100.0**
053 Assemb of God	2	205	243	477	2.1	4.9

NR–Not Reported *Total adherents estimated from known number of communicant, confirmed, full members. - Represents a percentage less than 0.1. Percentages may not total 100 due to rounding.

Table 4: Religious Congregations by County and Group: 2000

Religious Group	Number of Churches, Synagogues, Mosques, or Temples	Number of Communicant, Confirmed, or Full Members	Number of Attendees	Total Adherents		
				Number of Adherents	% of Total Pop.	% of Total Adh.
081 Catholic	1	NR	NR	151	.7	1.5
097 Chr Chs&Chs Cr	2	117	NR	144 *	.6	1.5
127 Ch God (Cleve)	1	36	32	44 *	.2	.4
193 Episcopal	1	NR	76	173	.8	1.8
223 Free Will Bapt	2	209	NR	257 *	1.1	2.6
336 OrigFreeWillBpt	1	262	NR	322 *	1.4	3.3
349 Pent Holiness	2	397	168	489 *	2.2	5.0
355 Presb Ch (USA)	1	70	30	86 *	.4	.9
413 S.D.A.	1	118	NR	140	.6	1.4
419 So Bapt Conv	20	5,285	1,263	6,505 *	28.8	66.5
449 Un Methodist	4	810	225	996 *	4.4	10.2
HOKE	**29**	**5,456**	**2,234**	**7,558 ***	**22.5**	**100.0**
053 Assemb of God	1	36	55	75	.2	1.0
056 Baha'i	0	3	NR	3	-	-
081 Catholic	1	NR	NR	349	1.0	4.6
127 Ch God (Cleve)	3	145	113	198 *	.6	2.6
145 Ch God Prophcy	1	42	NR	55 *	.2	.7
355 Presb Ch (USA)	6	764	410	1,004 *	3.0	13.3
419 So Bapt Conv	12	3,359	1,286	4,418 *	13.1	58.5
449 Un Methodist	5	1,107	370	1,456 *	4.3	19.3
HYDE	**28**	**1,393**	**577**	**1,820 ***	**31.2**	**100.0**
053 Assemb of God	2	57	68	79	1.4	4.3
056 Baha'i	0	1	NR	1	-	.1
081 Catholic	1	NR	NR	49	.8	2.7
093 Chr Ch (Disc)	3	309	37	367 *	6.3	20.2
097 Chr Chs&Chs Cr	5	231	NR	274 *	4.7	15.1
167 Chs of Christ	1	10	20	20	.3	1.1
193 Episcopal	1	NR	40	99	1.7	5.4
349 Pent Holiness	1	18	7	21 *	.4	1.2
355 Presb Ch (USA)	1	42	30	50 *	.9	2.7
419 So Bapt Conv	4	152	73	180 *	3.1	9.9
449 Un Methodist	9	573	302	680 *	11.7	37.4
IREDELL	**199**	**43,771**	**20,013**	**61,467 ***	**50.1**	**100.0**
032 Amish; other	1	45	NR	56 *	-	.1
053 Assemb of God	3	261	313	425	.3	.7
055 As Ref Pres Ch	9	2,004	NR	2,274	1.9	3.7
056 Baha'i	0	23	NR	23	-	-
081 Catholic	2	NR	NR	4,897	4.0	8.0
089 Chr & Miss Al	1	25	NR	105	.1	.2
123 Ch God (Ander)	1	NR	110	110	.1	.2
127 Ch God (Cleve)	10	1,167	807	1,465 *	1.2	2.4
145 Ch God Prophcy	1	42	NR	52 *	-	.1
151 L-D Saints	1	NR	NR	465	.4	.8
165 Ch of Nazarene	2	237	158	322	.3	.5
167 Chs of Christ	5	879	714	1,125	.9	1.8
193 Episcopal	3	NR	294	758	.6	1.2
207 E.L.C.A.	7	2,129	994	2,725	2.2	4.4
226 Friends-USA	3	339	NR	425 *	.3	.7
263 Int Foursq Gos	2	157	263	263 *	.2	.4
267 Muslim Est	1	NR	35	50	-	.1
283 Luth—MO Synod	1	114	104	138	.1	.2
349 Pent Holiness	2	82	75	103 *	.1	.2
355 Presb Ch (USA)	20	3,306	1,687	4,163 *	3.4	6.8
356 Presb Ch Amer	3	252	266	349	.3	.6
360 Prim Bapt Chrch	1	NR	NR	NR	-	-
403 Salvation Army	1	56	42	118	.1	.2
413 S.D.A.	1	116	NR	138	.1	.2
418 Southw Bapt Fel	4	NR	NR	NR	-	-
419 So Bapt Conv	58	20,944	8,812	26,285 *	21.4	42.8
443 Un C of Christ	5	284	125	356 *	.3	.6
449 Un Methodist	45	10,900	4,899	13,680 *	11.2	22.3
467 Wesleyan	5	409	315	517	.4	.8
496 Jewish Est	1	NR	NR	80	.1	.1
JACKSON	**75**	**11,144**	**4,420**	**14,297 ***	**43.2**	**100.0**
053 Assemb of God	1	28	23	33	.1	.2
056 Baha'i	0	13	NR	13	-	.1
081 Catholic	1	NR	NR	723	2.2	5.1
127 Ch God (Cleve)	5	335	209	394 *	1.2	2.8
167 Chs of Christ	2	174	161	208	.6	1.5
193 Episcopal	3	NR	242	495	1.5	3.5
207 E.L.C.A.	1	141	55	150	.5	1.0
355 Presb Ch (USA)	2	235	143	275 *	.8	1.9
356 Presb Ch Amer	1	15	50	50	.2	.3
413 S.D.A.	1	27	NR	32	.1	.2
419 So Bapt Conv	43	8,245	2,673	9,653 *	29.1	67.5
449 Un Methodist	12	1,889	818	2,211 *	6.7	15.5
467 Wesleyan	3	42	46	60	.2	.4
JOHNSTON	**180**	**31,164**	**12,610**	**42,940 ***	**35.2**	**100.0**
053 Assemb of God	4	464	415	580	.5	1.4
055 As Ref Pres Ch	1	85	NR	92	.1	.2
056 Baha'i	0	42	NR	42	-	.1
057 Bapt Gen Conf	1	39	110	110 *	.1	.3
081 Catholic	1	NR	NR	2,084	1.7	4.9
093 Chr Ch (Disc)	7	1,313	453	1,661 *	1.4	3.9
123 Ch God (Ander)	1	NR	54	54	-	.1
127 Ch God (Cleve)	14	1,660	1,349	2,126 *	1.7	5.0
145 Ch God Prophcy	12	501	NR	636 *	.5	1.5
151 L-D Saints	2	NR	NR	829	.7	1.9
167 Chs of Christ	2	54	61	71	.1	.2
193 Episcopal	1	NR	201	401	.3	.9
223 Free Will Bapt	4	418	NR	528 *	.4	1.2
252 Hindu	1	NR	NR	NR	-	-
336 OrigFreeWillBpt	23	4,525	NR	5,725 *	4.7	13.3
349 Pent Holiness	11	1,183	953	1,497 *	1.2	3.5
355 Presb Ch (USA)	15	1,205	682	1,529 *	1.3	3.6
356 Presb Ch Amer	1	27	43	43	-	.1
360 Prim Bapt Chrch	3	NR	NR	NR	-	-
403 Salvation Army	1	73	44	166	.1	.4
413 S.D.A.	1	41	NR	49	-	.1
419 So Bapt Conv	50	13,888	5,835	17,572 *	14.4	40.9
443 Un C of Christ	3	606	372	767 *	.6	1.8
449 Un Methodist	21	5,040	2,038	6,378 *	5.2	14.9
JONES	**25**	**3,212**	**948**	**4,031 ***	**38.8**	**100.0**
093 Chr Ch (Disc)	1	144	50	180 *	1.7	4.5
097 Chr Chs&Chs Cr	1	142	NR	177 *	1.7	4.4
127 Ch God (Cleve)	1	76	47	95 *	.9	2.4
193 Episcopal	1	NR	10	24	.2	.6
223 Free Will Bapt	1	104	NR	130 *	1.3	3.2
336 OrigFreeWillBpt	3	323	NR	403 *	3.9	10.0
349 Pent Holiness	1	110	64	137 *	1.3	3.4
355 Presb Ch (USA)	1	144	90	180 *	1.7	4.5
419 So Bapt Conv	5	1,300	305	1,621 *	15.6	40.2
443 Un C of Christ	3	211	72	263 *	2.5	6.5
449 Un Methodist	7	658	310	821 *	7.9	20.4
LEE	**71**	**15,416**	**6,728**	**22,208 ***	**45.3**	**100.0**
053 Assemb of God	2	204	195	314	.6	1.4
056 Baha'i	0	5	NR	5	-	-
081 Catholic	1	NR	NR	1,989	4.1	9.0
093 Chr Ch (Disc)	1	202	0	252 *	.5	1.1
097 Chr Chs&Chs Cr	1	11	NR	14 *	-	.1
127 Ch God (Cleve)	2	588	336	735 *	1.5	3.3
145 Ch God Prophcy	2	83	NR	104 *	.2	.5
151 L-D Saints	1	NR	NR	376	.8	1.7
165 Ch of Nazarene	1	24	0	24	-	.1
167 Chs of Christ	2	43	80	80	.2	.4
193 Episcopal	1	NR	138	490	1.0	2.2
207 E.L.C.A.	1	198	80	230	.5	1.0
223 Free Will Bapt	1	104	NR	130 *	.3	.6
263 Int Foursq Gos	1	22	31	31 *	.1	.1
288 Mennonite USA	1	102	82	127 *	.3	.6
349 Pent Holiness	4	431	292	539 *	1.1	2.4
355 Presb Ch (USA)	14	2,219	1,263	2,771 *	5.7	12.5
413 S.D.A.	1	23	NR	27	.1	.1
418 Southw Bapt Fel	1	NR	NR	NR	-	-
419 So Bapt Conv	16	6,853	2,603	8,564 *	17.5	38.6
443 Un C of Christ	5	813	322	1,016 *	2.1	4.6
449 Un Methodist	11	3,420	1,226	4,275 *	8.7	19.2
467 Wesleyan	1	71	80	115	.2	.5

NR–Not Reported *Total adherents estimated from known number of communicant, confirmed, full members. - Represents a percentage less than 0.1. Percentages may not total 100 due to rounding.

Table 4: Religious Congregations by County and Group: 2000

Religious Group	Number of Churches, Synagogues, Mosques, or Temples	Number of Communicant, Confirmed, or Full Members	Number of Attendees	Total Adherents: Number of Adherents	Total Adherents: % of Total Pop.	Total Adherents: % of Total Adh.
LENOIR	**96**	**16,899**	**6,323**	**23,744 ***	**39.8**	**100.0**
053 Assemb of God	2	118	105	123	.2	.5
056 Baha'i	0	105	NR	105	.2	.4
076 Buddhism	1	NR	NR	NR	-	-
081 Catholic	1	NR	NR	794	1.3	3.3
093 Chr Ch (Disc)	11	2,264	911	2,809 *	4.7	11.8
127 Ch God (Cleve)	4	1,037	970	1,287 *	2.2	5.4
145 Ch God Prophcy	2	83	NR	104 *	.2	.4
151 L-D Saints	3	NR	NR	1,064	1.8	4.5
165 Ch of Nazarene	1	0	0	0	-	-
167 Chs of Christ	2	65	70	96	.2	.4
193 Episcopal	2	NR	167	596	1.0	2.5
207 E.L.C.A.	1	41	31	48	.1	.2
223 Free Will Bapt	7	731	NR	907 *	1.5	3.8
263 Int Foursq Gos	1	27	36	36 *	.1	.2
283 Luth—MO Synod	1	140	90	167	.3	.7
336 OrigFreeWillBpt	11	1,904	NR	2,362 *	4.0	9.9
349 Pent Holiness	4	1,103	718	1,368 *	2.3	5.8
355 Presb Ch (USA)	7	864	368	1,073 *	1.8	4.5
403 Salvation Army	1	129	91	470	.8	2.0
413 S.D.A.	3	317	NR	377	.6	1.6
419 So Bapt Conv	15	4,361	1,627	5,410 *	9.1	22.8
443 Un C of Christ	2	123	54	153 *	.3	.6
449 Un Methodist	13	3,487	1,085	4,325 *	7.3	18.2
496 Jewish Est	1	NR	NR	70	.1	.3
LINCOLN	**118**	**26,330**	**12,421**	**34,695 ***	**54.4**	**100.0**
053 Assemb of God	1	30	30	44	.1	.1
055 As Ref Pres Ch	1	45	NR	52	.1	.1
056 Baha'i	0	4	NR	4	-	-
081 Catholic	2	NR	NR	1,341	2.1	3.9
093 Chr Ch (Disc)	1	120	70	149 *	.2	.4
127 Ch God (Cleve)	6	730	468	908 *	1.4	2.6
145 Ch God Prophcy	1	42	NR	52 *	.1	.1
167 Chs of Christ	2	60	60	76	.1	.2
193 Episcopal	3	NR	292	559	.9	1.6
207 E.L.C.A.	9	2,243	1,078	2,741	4.3	7.9
223 Free Will Bapt	1	104	NR	130 *	.2	.4
263 Int Foursq Gos	1	49	72	72 *	.1	.2
283 Luth—MO Synod	1	131	92	167	.3	.5
349 Pent Holiness	2	167	147	208 *	.3	.6
355 Presb Ch (USA)	3	741	295	921 *	1.4	2.7
356 Presb Ch Amer	2	124	0	169	.3	.5
413 S.D.A.	1	59	NR	70	.1	.2
418 Southw Bapt Fel	1	NR	NR	NR	-	-
419 So Bapt Conv	39	13,675	6,115	16,996 *	26.6	49.0
443 Un C of Christ	2	141	62	175 *	.3	.5
449 Un Methodist	36	7,489	3,301	9,308 *	14.6	26.8
467 Wesleyan	3	376	339	553	.9	1.6
MCDOWELL	**107**	**15,961**	**6,625**	**20,200 ***	**47.9**	**100.0**
056 Baha'i	0	30	NR	30	.1	.1
081 Catholic	1	NR	NR	311	.7	1.5
089 Chr & Miss Al	1	74	NR	142	.3	.7
097 Chr Chs&Chs Cr	2	75	NR	92 *	.2	.5
127 Ch God (Cleve)	6	549	442	681 *	1.6	3.4
145 Ch God Prophcy	1	42	NR	51 *	.1	.3
151 L-D Saints	1	NR	NR	248	.6	1.2
167 Chs of Christ	3	103	110	133	.3	.7
193 Episcopal	1	NR	60	130	.3	.6
223 Free Will Bapt	11	1,148	NR	1,397 *	3.3	6.9
258 IndFreeWillBapt	4	141	NR	172 *	.4	.9
283 Luth—MO Synod	1	63	32	74	.2	.4
349 Pent Holiness	5	291	211	354 *	.8	1.8
355 Presb Ch (USA)	5	389	217	473 *	1.1	2.3
356 Presb Ch Amer	2	319	252	354	.8	1.8
413 S.D.A.	1	84	NR	100	.2	.5
418 Southw Bapt Fel	1	NR	NR	NR	-	-
419 So Bapt Conv	41	10,414	4,082	12,668 *	30.1	62.7
449 Un Methodist	18	2,076	1,104	2,528 *	6.0	12.5
467 Wesleyan	2	163	115	262	.6	1.3
MACON	**100**	**15,189**	**7,141**	**20,324 ***	**68.2**	**100.0**
053 Assemb of God	6	993	744	1,302	4.4	6.4
056 Baha'i	0	4	NR	4	-	-
081 Catholic	2	NR	NR	1,493	5.0	7.3
089 Chr & Miss Al	1	149	NR	252	.8	1.2
127 Ch God (Cleve)	6	630	463	749 *	2.5	3.7
151 L-D Saints	1	NR	NR	196	.7	1.0
165 Ch of Nazarene	1	39	39	39	.1	.2
167 Chs of Christ	2	62	70	77	.3	.4
173 Comm of Christ	1	41	NR	41	.1	.2
193 Episcopal	4	NR	221	508	1.7	2.5
216 Evan Presby Ch	3	356	NR	419 *	1.4	2.1
283 Luth—MO Synod	1	150	135	164	.6	.8
355 Presb Ch (USA)	3	522	404	615 *	2.1	3.0
356 Presb Ch Amer	1	54	58	63	.2	.3
413 S.D.A.	2	152	NR	181	.6	.9
419 So Bapt Conv	48	9,483	3,705	11,167 *	37.5	54.9
435 Unitarian-Univ	1	73	NR	86 *	.3	.4
449 Un Methodist	15	2,346	1,182	2,763 *	9.3	13.6
463 Vineyard	1	130	120	153 *	.5	.8
467 Wesleyan	1	5	0	52	.2	.3
MADISON	**83**	**8,127**	**3,363**	**10,530 ***	**53.6**	**100.0**
056 Baha'i	0	2	NR	2	-	-
076 Buddhism	1	NR	NR	NR	-	-
081 Catholic	1	NR	NR	275	1.4	2.6
097 Chr Chs&Chs Cr	2	53	NR	64 *	.3	.6
123 Ch God (Ander)	7	NR	268	268	1.4	2.5
127 Ch God (Cleve)	2	191	168	229 *	1.2	2.2
193 Episcopal	1	NR	94	232	1.2	2.2
223 Free Will Bapt	2	209	NR	251 *	1.3	2.4
258 IndFreeWillBapt	1	50	NR	60 *	.3	.6
355 Presb Ch (USA)	4	155	77	187 *	1.0	1.8
403 Salvation Army	1	133	120	162	.8	1.5
419 So Bapt Conv	51	6,935	2,430	8,321 *	42.4	79.0
449 Un Methodist	10	399	206	479 *	2.4	4.5
MARTIN	**59**	**10,297**	**2,734**	**13,202 ***	**51.6**	**100.0**
053 Assemb of God	2	67	63	111	.4	.8
056 Baha'i	0	21	NR	21	.1	.2
081 Catholic	1	NR	NR	208	.8	1.6
093 Chr Ch (Disc)	10	1,550	396	1,925 *	7.5	14.6
097 Chr Chs&Chs Cr	12	2,551	NR	3,166 *	12.4	24.0
127 Ch God (Cleve)	1	149	89	185 *	.7	1.4
167 Chs of Christ	1	20	29	20	.1	.2
193 Episcopal	1	NR	57	191	.7	1.4
223 Free Will Bapt	1	104	NR	130 *	.5	1.0
226 Friends-USA	1	47	NR	58 *	.2	.4
336 OrigFreeWillBpt	2	413	NR	513 *	2.0	3.9
349 Pent Holiness	5	528	342	656 *	2.6	5.0
355 Presb Ch (USA)	3	243	170	302 *	1.2	2.3
419 So Bapt Conv	11	3,857	1,277	4,789 *	18.7	36.3
449 Un Methodist	8	747	311	927 *	3.6	7.0
MECKLENBURG	**502**	**190,958**	**94,787**	**333,605 ***	**48.0**	**100.0**
019 Amer Bapt USA	7	9,495	4,150	11,883 *	1.7	3.6
050 Armen Ap Etchm	1	0	NR	420	.1	.1
053 Assemb of God	10	1,485	1,666	2,391	.3	.7
055 As Ref Pres Ch	16	2,220	NR	2,536	.4	.8
056 Baha'i	2	676	NR	676	.1	.2
076 Buddhism	9	NR	NR	NR	-	-
081 Catholic	12	NR	NR	59,292	8.5	17.8
084 Calvary Chapel	2	NR	NR	NR	-	-
089 Chr & Miss Al	7	642	NR	650	.1	.2
093 Chr Ch (Disc)	3	585	310	732 *	.1	.2
097 Chr Chs&Chs Cr	3	395	NR	494 *	.1	.1
123 Ch God (Ander)	4	NR	259	259	-	.1
127 Ch God (Cleve)	20	9,013	7,952	11,399 *	1.6	3.4
145 Ch God Prophcy	3	125	NR	156 *	-	-
151 L-D Saints	8	NR	NR	3,695	.5	1.1
165 Ch of Nazarene	6	1,298	938	1,555	.2	.5
167 Chs of Christ	8	1,902	1,860	2,420	.3	.7

NR–Not Reported *Total adherents estimated from known number of communicant, confirmed, full members. - Represents a percentage less than 0.1. Percentages may not total 100 due to rounding.

Table 4: Religious Congregations by County and Group: 2000

Religious Group	Number of Churches, Synagogues, Mosques, or Temples	Number of Communicant, Confirmed, or Full Members	Number of Attendees	Total Adherents: Number of Adherents	Total Adherents: % of Total Pop.	Total Adherents: % of Total Adh.
173 Comm of Christ	1	131	NR	131	-	-
193 Episcopal	14	NR	3,170	9,470	1.4	2.8
201 Evan Cov Ch	2	309	199	386 *	.1	.1
203 Evan Free Ch	1	400	700	700	.1	.2
207 E.L.C.A.	17	6,476	3,810	8,620	1.2	2.6
216 Evan Presby Ch	4	2,302	NR	2,881 *	.4	.9
223 Free Will Bapt	4	418	NR	523 *	.1	.2
226 Friends-USA	2	226	NR	283 *	-	.1
246 Greek Orthodox	2	NR	NR	2,652	.4	.8
252 Hindu	3	NR	NR	NR	-	-
263 Int Foursq Gos	9	1,652	2,126	2,126 *	.3	.6
264 Int Chs of Crst	1	518	897	743	.1	.2
267 Muslim Est	5	NR	1,534	7,823	1.1	2.3
268 Jain	1	NR	NR	NR	-	-
283 Luth—MO Synod	6	1,525	1,158	1,880	.3	.6
290 Metro Comm Ch	2	211	197	264 *	-	.1
295 Morav Ch-South	3	412	NR	495	.1	.1
304 NatPrimBapt USA	5	3,500	NR	4,380 *	.6	1.3
313 N Am Bapt Conf	1	70	102	88 *	-	-
331 OCA: Ter Diocs	1	21	NR	149	-	-
335 Orth Pres Ch	1	150	160	197	-	.1
349 Pent Holiness	4	398	237	498 *	.1	.1
355 Presb Ch (USA)	75	33,453	14,861	41,866 *	6.0	12.5
356 Presb Ch Amer	12	2,857	2,959	4,806	.7	1.4
370 Ref Baptist Chs	1	NR	NR	NR	-	-
403 Salvation Army	1	277	203	439	.1	.1
410 Serb Orth USA	1	NR	NR	250	-	.1
413 S.D.A.	6	2,631	NR	3,131	.5	.9
418 Southw Bapt Fel	5	NR	NR	NR	-	-
419 So Bapt Conv	115	59,946	23,981	75,026 *	10.8	22.5
435 Unitarian-Univ	2	693	NR	867 *	.1	.3
443 Un C of Christ	3	339	151	424 *	.1	.1
449 Un Methodist	55	37,239	15,045	46,604 *	6.7	14.0
463 Vineyard	2	255	245	319 *	-	.1
467 Wesleyan	2	237	208	362	.1	.1
469 WELS	1	88	59	114	-	-
496 Jewish Est	4	NR	NR	8,500	1.2	2.5
498 Indep.Charis.	3	788	1,050	1,050	.2	.3
499 Indep.Non-Char	4	5,600	4,600	7,000	1.0	2.1
MITCHELL	**58**	**8,945**	**3,583**	**11,128 ***	**70.9**	**100.0**
053 Assemb of God	1	42	50	50	.3	.4
056 Baha'i	0	2	NR	2	-	-
076 Buddhism	1	NR	NR	NR	-	-
081 Catholic	1	NR	NR	198	1.3	1.8
097 Chr Chs&Chs Cr	1	142	NR	169 *	1.1	1.5
123 Ch God (Ander)	1	NR	86	86	.5	.8
127 Ch God (Cleve)	2	98	61	116 *	.7	1.0
167 Chs of Christ	1	41	50	67	.4	.6
193 Episcopal	1	NR	76	179	1.1	1.6
223 Free Will Bapt	1	104	NR	124 *	.8	1.1
258 IndFreeWillBapt	6	308	NR	367 *	2.3	3.3
355 Presb Ch (USA)	5	241	133	288 *	1.8	2.6
419 So Bapt Conv	34	7,510	2,922	8,938 *	57.0	80.3
449 Un Methodist	3	457	205	544 *	3.5	4.9
MONTGOMERY	**70**	**8,464**	**3,996**	**12,104 ***	**45.1**	**100.0**
056 Baha'i	0	1	NR	1	-	-
081 Catholic	1	NR	NR	367	1.4	3.0
127 Ch God (Cleve)	3	161	209	283 *	1.1	2.3
145 Ch God Prophcy	1	42	NR	52 *	.2	.4
167 Chs of Christ	1	19	20	24	.1	.2
193 Episcopal	1	NR	45	44	.2	.4
349 Pent Holiness	4	288	242	357 *	1.3	2.9
355 Presb Ch (USA)	6	570	297	706 *	2.6	5.8
419 So Bapt Conv	24	4,129	1,628	5,113 *	19.1	42.2
443 Un C of Christ	2	51	30	63 *	.2	.5
449 Un Methodist	22	2,759	1,086	3,415 *	12.7	28.2
467 Wesleyan	5	444	439	1,679	6.3	13.9
MOORE	**113**	**20,804**	**9,522**	**30,546 ***	**40.9**	**100.0**
053 Assemb of God	3	281	285	369	.5	1.2
055 As Ref Pres Ch	1	35	NR	49	.1	.2
056 Baha'i	0	9	NR	9	-	-
076 Buddhism	1	NR	NR	NR	-	-
081 Catholic	3	NR	NR	3,913	5.2	12.8
089 Chr & Miss Al	1	91	NR	236	.3	.8
127 Ch God (Cleve)	4	330	189	397 *	.5	1.3
145 Ch God Prophcy	4	167	NR	200 *	.3	.7
151 L-D Saints	1	NR	NR	396	.5	1.3
167 Chs of Christ	1	35	50	46	.1	.2
175 Congr Chr Chs	1	50	30	60 *	.1	.2
193 Episcopal	1	NR	315	816	1.1	2.7
203 Evan Free Ch	1	45	130	130	.2	.4
207 E.L.C.A.	1	736	390	881	1.2	2.9
216 Evan Presby Ch	1	69	NR	83 *	.1	.3
226 Friends-USA	6	606	NR	730 *	1.0	2.4
283 Luth—MO Synod	1	93	44	140	.2	.5
288 Mennonite USA	1	73	20	88 *	.1	.3
349 Pent Holiness	1	76	59	92 *	.1	.3
355 Presb Ch (USA)	21	4,522	2,430	5,449 *	7.3	17.8
356 Presb Ch Amer	2	130	164	181	.2	.6
360 Prim Bapt Chrch	1	NR	NR	NR	-	-
413 S.D.A.	1	61	NR	73	.1	.2
418 Southw Bapt Fel	2	NR	NR	NR	-	-
419 So Bapt Conv	27	8,017	3,013	9,658 *	12.9	31.6
443 Un C of Christ	5	928	384	1,118 *	1.5	3.7
449 Un Methodist	20	4,379	1,915	5,277 *	7.1	17.3
467 Wesleyan	1	71	104	155	.2	.5
NASH	**124**	**29,095**	**12,918**	**39,507 ***	**45.2**	**100.0**
019 Amer Bapt USA	1	0	0	0 *	-	-
053 Assemb of God	3	917	745	1,001	1.1	2.5
056 Baha'i	0	7	NR	7	-	-
081 Catholic	1	NR	NR	1,681	1.9	4.3
084 Calvary Chapel	1	NR	NR	NR	-	-
093 Chr Ch (Disc)	1	283	95	353 *	.4	.9
097 Chr Chs&Chs Cr	2	183	NR	228 *	.3	.6
127 Ch God (Cleve)	9	1,396	748	1,767 *	2.0	4.5
145 Ch God Prophcy	4	167	NR	208 *	.2	.5
151 L-D Saints	1	NR	NR	305	.3	.8
165 Ch of Nazarene	1	151	91	151	.2	.4
167 Chs of Christ	2	105	140	141	.2	.4
193 Episcopal	2	NR	278	1,104	1.3	2.8
223 Free Will Bapt	2	209	NR	261 *	.3	.7
263 Int Foursq Gos	1	217	623	623 *	.7	1.6
336 OrigFreeWillBpt	6	601	NR	750 *	.9	1.9
339 Pent Ch of God	1	50	NR	75	.1	.2
349 Pent Holiness	9	805	405	1,005 *	1.1	2.5
355 Presb Ch (USA)	5	1,102	539	1,375 *	1.6	3.5
356 Presb Ch Amer	1	21	50	50	.1	.1
370 Ref Baptist Chs	1	NR	NR	NR	-	-
388 Reg Bapt Gen As	1	98	120	122 *	.1	.3
413 S.D.A.	1	72	NR	86	.1	.2
418 Southw Bapt Fel	1	NR	NR	NR	-	-
419 So Bapt Conv	47	16,524	6,914	20,627 *	23.6	52.2
449 Un Methodist	18	5,639	1,776	7,039 *	8.1	17.8
467 Wesleyan	1	48	14	48	.1	.1
499 Indep.Non-Char	1	500	380	500	.6	1.3
NEW HANOVER	**132**	**45,357**	**20,205**	**75,643 ***	**47.2**	**100.0**
053 Assemb of God	4	220	218	436	.3	.6
055 As Ref Pres Ch	1	28	NR	28	-	-
056 Baha'i	2	59	NR	59	-	.1
076 Buddhism	2	NR	NR	NR	-	-
081 Catholic	5	NR	NR	12,887	8.0	17.0
084 Calvary Chapel	1	NR	NR	NR	-	-
089 Chr & Miss Al	2	86	NR	136	.1	.2
093 Chr Ch (Disc)	1	463	253	554 *	.3	.7
097 Chr Chs&Chs Cr	2	242	NR	290 *	.2	.4
127 Ch God (Cleve)	5	1,058	540	1,266 *	.8	1.7
145 Ch God Prophcy	2	83	NR	100 *	.1	.1
151 L-D Saints	2	NR	NR	945	.6	1.2
165 Ch of Nazarene	1	180	85	180	.1	.2
167 Chs of Christ	3	264	318	371	.2	.5
193 Episcopal	7	NR	1,537	4,587	2.9	6.1

NR–Not Reported   *Total adherents estimated from known number of communicant, confirmed, full members.   - Represents a percentage less than 0.1.   Percentages may not total 100 due to rounding.

Table 4: Religious Congregations by County and Group: 2000

Religious Group	Number of Churches, Synagogues, Mosques, or Temples	Number of Communicant, Confirmed, or Full Members	Number of Attendees	Total Adherents: Number of Adherents	% of Total Pop.	% of Total Adh.
207 E.L.C.A.	5	2,205	1,616	2,650	1.7	3.5
216 Evan Presby Ch	2	1,607	NR	1,922 *	1.2	2.5
223 Free Will Bapt	2	209	NR	250 *	.2	.3
226 Friends-USA	1	47	NR	56 *	-	.1
246 Greek Orthodox	1	NR	NR	939	.6	1.2
263 Int Foursq Gos	1	100	126	126 *	.1	.2
267 Muslim Est	1	NR	101	288	.2	.4
283 Luth—MO Synod	1	176	116	210	.1	.3
290 Metro Comm Ch	1	133	126	159 *	.1	.2
295 Morav Ch-South	1	121	NR	148	.1	.2
336 OrigFreeWillBpt	1	60	NR	72 *	-	.1
349 Pent Holiness	2	462	269	553 *	.3	.7
355 Presb Ch (USA)	13	4,977	2,403	5,952 *	3.7	7.9
356 Presb Ch Amer	1	31	30	38	-	.1
403 Salvation Army	1	204	94	303	.2	.4
413 S.D.A.	3	683	NR	813	.5	1.1
418 Southw Bapt Fel	2	NR	NR	NR	-	-
419 So Bapt Conv	32	21,881	8,397	26,168 *	16.3	34.6
435 Unitarian-Univ	1	181	NR	216 *	.1	.3
443 Un C of Christ	2	87	34	104 *	.1	.1
449 Un Methodist	13	8,468	2,974	10,126 *	6.3	13.4
463 Vineyard	1	1,000	900	1,196 *	.7	1.6
467 Wesleyan	2	42	68	315	.2	.4
496 Jewish Est	2	NR	NR	1,200	.7	1.6
NORTHAMPTON	**41**	**5,560**	**1,647**	**6,928 ***	**31.4**	**100.0**
053 Assemb of God	1	19	21	47	.2	.7
056 Baha'i	0	5	NR	5	-	.1
097 Chr Chs&Chs Cr	1	60	NR	74 *	.3	1.1
193 Episcopal	2	NR	21	70	.3	1.0
226 Friends-USA	1	47	NR	58 *	.3	.8
297 Mennonite;Other	1	30	NR	37 *	.2	.5
419 So Bapt Conv	17	3,512	1,040	4,318 *	19.6	62.3
449 Un Methodist	18	1,887	565	2,319 *	10.5	33.5
ONSLOW	**97**	**23,284**	**10,728**	**38,748 ***	**25.8**	**100.0**
053 Assemb of God	3	345	475	675	.4	1.7
056 Baha'i	0	39	NR	39	-	.1
081 Catholic	2	NR	NR	6,457	4.3	16.7
084 Calvary Chapel	1	NR	NR	NR	-	-
093 Chr Ch (Disc)	3	676	253	858 *	.6	2.2
097 Chr Chs&Chs Cr	2	233	NR	295 *	.2	.8
123 Ch God (Ander)	3	NR	288	288	.2	.7
127 Ch God (Cleve)	3	324	159	410 *	.3	1.1
151 L-D Saints	3	NR	NR	1,189	.8	3.1
165 Ch of Nazarene	1	101	162	275	.2	.7
167 Chs of Christ	3	507	410	605	.4	1.6
193 Episcopal	4	NR	372	848	.6	2.2
207 E.L.C.A.	1	210	150	304	.2	.8
223 Free Will Bapt	5	522	NR	662 *	.4	1.7
263 Int Foursq Gos	1	110	30	140 *	.1	.4
283 Luth—MO Synod	1	233	129	323	.2	.8
336 OrigFreeWillBpt	5	650	NR	825 *	.5	2.1
349 Pent Holiness	4	277	198	351 *	.2	.9
355 Presb Ch (USA)	3	538	299	683 *	.5	1.8
356 Presb Ch Amer	1	49	80	80	.1	.2
360 Prim Bapt Chrch	2	NR	NR	NR	-	-
403 Salvation Army	1	52	57	45	-	.1
413 S.D.A.	1	74	NR	88	.1	.2
418 Southw Bapt Fel	2	NR	NR	NR	-	-
419 So Bapt Conv	27	12,892	5,573	16,358 *	10.9	42.2
449 Un Methodist	13	5,101	1,848	6,472 *	4.3	16.7
469 WELS	1	51	45	78	.1	.2
499 Indep.Non-Char	1	300	200	400	.3	1.0
ORANGE	**95**	**21,694**	**11,726**	**36,032 ***	**30.5**	**100.0**
019 Amer Bapt USA	2	1,014	300	1,203 *	1.0	3.3
053 Assemb of God	2	89	117	117	.1	.3
056 Baha'i	3	204	NR	204	.2	.6
059 Bapt Miss Assn	1	0	0	0 *	-	-
076 Buddhism	1	NR	NR	NR	-	-
081 Catholic	3	NR	NR	6,905	5.8	19.2
097 Chr Chs&Chs Cr	1	50	NR	59 *	-	.2

Religious Group	Number of Churches, Synagogues, Mosques, or Temples	Number of Communicant, Confirmed, or Full Members	Number of Attendees	Total Adherents: Number of Adherents	% of Total Pop.	% of Total Adh.
123 Ch God (Ander)	1	NR	23	23	-	.1
127 Ch God (Cleve)	2	593	336	704 *	.6	2.0
145 Ch God Prophcy	3	125	NR	150 *	.1	.4
165 Ch of Nazarene	1	15	25	34	-	.1
167 Chs of Christ	2	70	75	90	.1	.2
193 Episcopal	3	NR	1,181	2,539	2.1	7.0
207 E.L.C.A.	1	521	223	678	.6	1.9
252 Hindu	1	NR	NR	NR	-	-
267 Muslim Est	1	NR	25	100	.1	.3
283 Luth—MO Synod	1	134	90	161	.1	.4
349 Pent Holiness	1	40	24	47 *	-	.1
355 Presb Ch (USA)	9	2,366	1,463	2,807 *	2.4	7.8
413 S.D.A.	1	15	NR	18	-	-
419 So Bapt Conv	22	6,893	2,608	8,180 *	6.9	22.7
435 Unitarian-Univ	2	321	NR	381 *	.3	1.1
443 Un C of Christ	5	863	492	1,024 *	.9	2.8
449 Un Methodist	22	7,164	3,015	8,501 *	7.2	23.6
467 Wesleyan	2	117	129	207	.2	.6
498 Indep.Charis.	1	700	500	700	.6	1.9
499 Indep.Non-Char	1	400	1,100	1,200	1.0	3.3
PAMLICO	**38**	**3,690**	**1,411**	**4,593 ***	**35.5**	**100.0**
053 Assemb of God	1	13	10	37	.3	.8
093 Chr Ch (Disc)	3	414	130	492 *	3.8	10.7
097 Chr Chs&Chs Cr	1	56	NR	66 *	.5	1.4
127 Ch God (Cleve)	1	76	41	90 *	.7	2.0
145 Ch God Prophcy	1	42	NR	50 *	.4	1.1
193 Episcopal	1	NR	93	187	1.4	4.1
336 OrigFreeWillBpt	8	901	NR	1,070 *	8.3	23.3
349 Pent Holiness	6	199	188	236 *	1.8	5.1
356 Presb Ch Amer	1	19	25	25	.2	.5
419 So Bapt Conv	2	401	165	476 *	3.7	10.4
443 Un C of Christ	5	382	211	454 *	3.5	9.9
449 Un Methodist	8	1,187	548	1,410 *	10.9	30.7
PASQUOTANK	**37**	**7,187**	**2,932**	**11,335 ***	**32.5**	**100.0**
053 Assemb of God	1	141	141	200	.6	1.8
056 Baha'i	0	3	NR	3	-	-
081 Catholic	1	NR	NR	1,250	3.6	11.0
093 Chr Ch (Disc)	1	400	105	495 *	1.4	4.4
097 Chr Chs&Chs Cr	2	275	NR	340 *	1.0	3.0
127 Ch God (Cleve)	2	281	192	348 *	1.0	3.1
145 Ch God Prophcy	1	42	NR	52 *	.1	.5
151 L-D Saints	2	NR	NR	625	1.8	5.5
165 Ch of Nazarene	1	80	77	111	.3	1.0
167 Chs of Christ	1	31	31	40	.1	.4
193 Episcopal	1	NR	163	329	.9	2.9
265 Int Pent C Chr	1	0	0	150	.4	1.3
336 OrigFreeWillBpt	1	80	NR	99 *	.3	.9
349 Pent Holiness	2	405	240	501 *	1.4	4.4
355 Presb Ch (USA)	1	191	100	236 *	.7	2.1
403 Salvation Army	1	120	53	204	.6	1.8
418 Southw Bapt Fel	1	NR	NR	NR	-	-
419 So Bapt Conv	9	2,872	1,078	3,551 *	10.2	31.3
449 Un Methodist	8	2,266	752	2,801 *	8.0	24.7
PENDER	**54**	**10,008**	**4,721**	**13,631 ***	**33.2**	**100.0**
053 Assemb of God	2	69	78	131	.3	1.0
056 Baha'i	0	1	NR	1	-	-
081 Catholic	3	NR	NR	922	2.2	6.8
151 L-D Saints	1	NR	NR	283	.7	2.1
167 Chs of Christ	1	5	10	10	-	.1
173 Comm of Christ	1	16	NR	16	-	.1
193 Episcopal	2	NR	104	175	.4	1.3
216 Evan Presby Ch	1	62	NR	76 *	.2	.6
223 Free Will Bapt	1	104	NR	127 *	.3	.9
349 Pent Holiness	1	71	25	87 *	.2	.6
355 Presb Ch (USA)	8	946	538	1,155 *	2.8	8.5
401 Rus Orth Abroad	1	NR	NR	NR	-	-
413 S.D.A.	1	9	NR	11	-	.1
418 Southw Bapt Fel	1	NR	NR	NR	-	-
419 So Bapt Conv	22	6,570	2,984	8,009 *	19.5	58.8
449 Un Methodist	8	2,155	982	2,628 *	6.4	19.3

NR–Not Reported *Total adherents estimated from known number of communicant, confirmed, full members. - Represents a percentage less than 0.1. Percentages may not total 100 due to rounding.

Table 4: Religious Congregations by County and Group: 2000

Religious Group	Number of Churches, Synagogues, Mosques, or Temples	Number of Communicant, Confirmed, or Full Members	Number of Attendees	Total Adherents: Number of Adherents	Total Adherents: % of Total Pop.	Total Adherents: % of Total Adh.
PERQUIMANS	**29**	**3,775**	**1,359**	**4,854 ***	**42.7**	**100.0**
053 Assemb of God	1	17	19	19	.2	.4
056 Baha'i	0	2	NR	2	-	-
097 Chr Chs&Chs Cr	1	165	NR	199 *	1.8	4.1
151 L-D Saints	1	NR	NR	190	1.7	3.9
193 Episcopal	1	NR	53	76	.7	1.6
226 Friends-USA	4	452	NR	544 *	4.8	11.2
265 Int Pent C Chr	1	28	22	51	.4	1.1
349 Pent Holiness	2	81	86	98 *	.9	2.0
419 So Bapt Conv	9	1,471	611	1,772 *	15.6	36.5
449 Un Methodist	8	1,501	510	1,808 *	15.9	37.2
467 Wesleyan	1	58	58	95	.8	2.0
PERSON	**47**	**12,343**	**5,189**	**15,931 ***	**44.7**	**100.0**
056 Baha'i	0	1	NR	1	-	-
081 Catholic	1	NR	NR	367	1.0	2.3
127 Ch God (Cleve)	1	193	72	238 *	.7	1.5
151 L-D Saints	1	NR	NR	210	.6	1.3
167 Chs of Christ	1	40	43	49	.1	.3
193 Episcopal	1	NR	58	129	.4	.8
349 Pent Holiness	1	33	25	41 *	.1	.3
355 Presb Ch (USA)	1	136	74	168 *	.5	1.1
419 So Bapt Conv	25	8,578	3,576	10,581 *	29.7	66.4
449 Un Methodist	15	3,362	1,341	4,147 *	11.6	26.0
PITT	**136**	**28,822**	**11,931**	**42,333 ***	**31.6**	**100.0**
019 Amer Bapt USA	1	600	500	737 *	.6	1.7
053 Assemb of God	1	196	190	311	.2	.7
056 Baha'i	1	118	NR	118	.1	.3
076 Buddhism	1	NR	NR	NR	-	-
081 Catholic	3	NR	NR	3,938	2.9	9.3
093 Chr Ch (Disc)	11	2,181	837	2,678 *	2.0	6.3
097 Chr Chs&Chs Cr	5	681	NR	837 *	.6	2.0
127 Ch God (Cleve)	7	599	626	927 *	.7	2.2
143 CG in Cr(Menn)	1	98	NR	120 *	.1	.3
145 Ch God Prophcy	1	42	NR	51 *	-	.1
151 L-D Saints	2	NR	NR	657	.5	1.6
165 Ch of Nazarene	1	23	18	23	-	.1
167 Chs of Christ	2	155	155	202	.2	.5
193 Episcopal	4	NR	540	1,543	1.2	3.6
207 E.L.C.A.	1	178	115	230	.2	.5
223 Free Will Bapt	12	1,253	NR	1,539 *	1.2	3.6
252 Hindu	1	NR	NR	NR	-	-
263 Int Foursq Gos	2	37	32	45 *	-	.1
267 Muslim Est	2	NR	141	538	.4	1.3
336 OrigFreeWillBpt	19	3,959	NR	4,862 *	3.6	11.5
349 Pent Holiness	13	1,355	889	1,664 *	1.2	3.9
355 Presb Ch (USA)	8	1,493	731	1,832 *	1.4	4.3
356 Presb Ch Amer	1	242	230	328	.2	.8
403 Salvation Army	1	51	50	289	.2	.7
413 S.D.A.	2	312	NR	371	.3	.9
418 Southw Bapt Fel	1	NR	NR	NR	-	-
419 So Bapt Conv	13	5,195	1,816	6,380 *	4.8	15.1
435 Unitarian-Univ	1	61	NR	75 *	.1	.2
449 Un Methodist	13	7,634	3,340	9,376 *	7.0	22.1
467 Wesleyan	1	9	21	72	.1	.2
496 Jewish Est	1	NR	NR	240	.2	.6
498 Indep.Charis.	2	1,350	1,150	1,350	1.0	3.2
499 Indep.Non-Char	1	1,000	550	1,000	.7	2.4
POLK	**50**	**8,197**	**3,681**	**11,566 ***	**63.1**	**100.0**
053 Assemb of God	1	24	28	31	.2	.3
055 As Ref Pres Ch	1	82	NR	85	.5	.7
056 Baha'i	0	7	NR	7	-	.1
081 Catholic	1	NR	NR	1,214	6.6	10.5
127 Ch God (Cleve)	1	58	38	69 *	.4	.6
157 Ch of Brethren	1	115	105	136 *	.7	1.2
167 Chs of Christ	1	20	20	28	.2	.2
193 Episcopal	3	NR	229	614	3.4	5.3
283 Luth—MO Synod	1	97	65	132	.7	1.1
297 Mennonite;Other	1	53	NR	63 *	.3	.5
349 Pent Holiness	1	14	12	17 *	.1	.1

Religious Group	Number of Churches, Synagogues, Mosques, or Temples	Number of Communicant, Confirmed, or Full Members	Number of Attendees	Total Adherents: Number of Adherents	Total Adherents: % of Total Pop.	Total Adherents: % of Total Adh.
355 Presb Ch (USA)	3	537	321	637 *	3.5	5.5
413 S.D.A.	1	211	NR	251	1.4	2.2
418 Southw Bapt Fel	1	NR	NR	NR	-	-
419 So Bapt Conv	25	5,815	2,320	6,902 *	37.7	59.7
443 Un C of Christ	1	488	178	579 *	3.2	5.0
449 Un Methodist	7	676	365	801 *	4.4	6.9
RANDOLPH	**230**	**35,456**	**17,043**	**47,833 ***	**36.7**	**100.0**
053 Assemb of God	5	713	891	1,086	.8	2.3
056 Baha'i	0	14	NR	14	-	-
081 Catholic	1	NR	NR	1,552	1.2	3.2
097 Chr Chs&Chs Cr	1	85	NR	106 *	.1	.2
127 Ch God (Cleve)	11	1,307	1,163	1,682 *	1.3	3.5
145 Ch God Prophcy	4	167	NR	208 *	.2	.4
151 L-D Saints	1	NR	NR	385	.3	.8
165 Ch of Nazarene	2	187	193	281	.2	.6
167 Chs of Christ	1	65	80	80	.1	.2
176 Congr Ad Afl	1	382	NR	476 *	.4	1.0
193 Episcopal	1	NR	104	270	.2	.6
207 E.L.C.A.	3	467	229	563	.4	1.2
223 Free Will Bapt	3	313	NR	390 *	.3	.8
226 Friends-USA	15	1,695	NR	2,111 *	1.6	4.4
263 Int Foursq Gos	1	30	50	50 *	-	.1
349 Pent Holiness	5	467	408	582 *	.4	1.2
355 Presb Ch (USA)	3	816	418	1,017 *	.8	2.1
356 Presb Ch Amer	1	0	0	0	-	-
360 Prim Bapt Chrch	2	NR	NR	NR	-	-
403 Salvation Army	1	24	40	81	.1	.2
413 S.D.A.	1	74	NR	88	.1	.2
418 Southw Bapt Fel	5	NR	NR	NR	-	-
419 So Bapt Conv	52	14,491	6,097	18,050 *	13.8	37.7
443 Un C of Christ	13	932	445	1,161 *	.9	2.4
449 Un Methodist	75	11,372	5,051	14,164 *	10.9	29.6
467 Wesleyan	22	1,855	1,874	3,436	2.6	7.2
RICHMOND	**111**	**16,748**	**6,374**	**21,798 ***	**46.8**	**100.0**
053 Assemb of God	1	104	110	123	.3	.6
056 Baha'i	0	25	NR	25	.1	.1
081 Catholic	1	NR	NR	393	.8	1.8
097 Chr Chs&Chs Cr	1	12	NR	15 *	-	.1
127 Ch God (Cleve)	4	258	178	323 *	.7	1.5
145 Ch God Prophcy	6	250	NR	312 *	.7	1.4
151 L-D Saints	1	NR	NR	165	.4	.8
165 Ch of Nazarene	1	22	0	22	-	.1
167 Chs of Christ	2	77	90	111	.2	.5
193 Episcopal	2	NR	57	100	.2	.5
207 E.L.C.A.	1	134	46	159	.3	.7
223 Free Will Bapt	9	940	NR	1,177 *	2.5	5.4
336 OrigFreeWillBpt	2	85	NR	106 *	.2	.5
349 Pent Holiness	8	462	440	579 *	1.2	2.7
355 Presb Ch (USA)	10	1,085	554	1,359 *	2.9	6.2
356 Presb Ch Amer	3	319	176	351	.8	1.6
413 S.D.A.	1	84	NR	100	.2	.5
419 So Bapt Conv	29	7,767	2,924	9,727 *	20.9	44.6
443 Un C of Christ	1	64	28	80 *	.2	.4
449 Un Methodist	24	4,802	1,538	6,014 *	12.9	27.6
467 Wesleyan	4	258	233	557	1.2	2.6
ROBESON	**220**	**37,436**	**19,123**	**52,327 ***	**42.4**	**100.0**
053 Assemb of God	10	890	1,250	1,646	1.3	3.1
056 Baha'i	0	445	NR	445	.4	.9
076 Buddhism	1	NR	NR	NR	-	-
081 Catholic	2	NR	NR	2,086	1.7	4.0
089 Chr & Miss Al	2	99	NR	165	.1	.3
127 Ch God (Cleve)	23	2,066	2,070	2,845 *	2.3	5.4
145 Ch God Prophcy	2	83	NR	108 *	.1	.2
151 L-D Saints	3	NR	NR	792	.6	1.5
167 Chs of Christ	2	116	152	168	.1	.3
193 Episcopal	1	NR	93	325	.3	.6
207 E.L.C.A.	1	75	45	98	.1	.2
349 Pent Holiness	8	1,110	839	1,438 *	1.2	2.7
355 Presb Ch (USA)	22	2,087	1,131	2,743 *	2.2	5.2
413 S.D.A.	1	41	NR	49	-	.1

NR–Not Reported *Total adherents estimated from known number of communicant, confirmed, full members. - Represents a percentage less than 0.1. Percentages may not total 100 due to rounding.

Table 4: Religious Congregations by County and Group: 2000

Religious Group	Number of Churches, Synagogues, Mosques, or Temples	Number of Communicant, Confirmed, or Full Members	Number of Attendees	Total Adherents		
				Number of Adherents	% of Total Pop.	% of Total Adh.
418 Southw Bapt Fel	1	NR	NR	NR	-	-
419 So Bapt Conv	108	23,600	10,932	30,576 *	24.8	58.4
449 Un Methodist	33	6,824	2,611	8,843 *	7.2	16.9
ROCKINGHAM	**162**	**26,362**	**12,428**	**35,686 ***	**38.8**	**100.0**
053 Assemb of God	4	401	435	631	.7	1.8
056 Baha'i	0	4	NR	4	-	-
081 Catholic	2	NR	NR	1,143	1.2	3.2
089 Chr & Miss Al	1	117	NR	250	.3	.7
093 Chr Ch (Disc)	5	809	397	990 *	1.1	2.8
097 Chr Chs&Chs Cr	7	1,197	NR	1,463 *	1.6	4.1
127 Ch God (Cleve)	7	343	302	438 *	.5	1.2
145 Ch God Prophcy	2	83	NR	102 *	.1	.3
151 L-D Saints	1	NR	NR	252	.3	.7
157 Ch of Brethren	1	207	135	253 *	.3	.7
167 Chs of Christ	2	53	55	82	.1	.2
193 Episcopal	5	NR	301	652	.7	1.8
201 Evan Cov Ch	1	85	63	104 *	.1	.3
207 E.L.C.A.	1	83	32	94	.1	.3
223 Free Will Bapt	1	104	NR	128 *	.1	.4
226 Friends-USA	2	208	NR	254 *	.3	.7
295 Morav Ch-South	2	429	NR	508	.6	1.4
304 NatPrimBapt USA	4	291	NR	356 *	.4	1.0
336 OrigFreeWillBpt	1	50	NR	61 *	.1	.2
349 Pent Holiness	8	938	785	1,147 *	1.2	3.2
355 Presb Ch (USA)	11	1,434	809	1,765 *	1.9	4.9
360 Prim Bapt Chrch	5	NR	NR	NR	-	-
403 Salvation Army	1	151	95	296	.3	.8
413 S.D.A.	1	40	NR	48	.1	.1
418 Southw Bapt Fel	4	NR	NR	NR	-	-
419 So Bapt Conv	39	11,551	5,057	14,130 *	15.4	39.6
449 Un Methodist	39	6,886	3,149	8,421 *	9.2	23.6
467 Wesleyan	5	898	813	2,114	2.3	5.9
ROWAN	**196**	**47,272**	**22,760**	**63,335 ***	**48.6**	**100.0**
019 Amer Bapt USA	1	0	0	0 *	-	-
053 Assemb of God	3	248	294	397	.3	.6
055 As Ref Pres Ch	1	90	NR	114	.1	.2
056 Baha'i	0	25	NR	25	-	-
081 Catholic	1	NR	NR	2,854	2.2	4.5
089 Chr & Miss Al	1	190	NR	190	.1	.3
097 Chr Chs&Chs Cr	2	145	NR	179 *	.1	.3
123 Ch God (Ander)	1	NR	46	46	-	.1
127 Ch God (Cleve)	8	877	693	1,096 *	.8	1.7
145 Ch God Prophcy	2	83	NR	104 *	.1	.2
151 L-D Saints	1	NR	NR	262	.2	.4
165 Ch of Nazarene	1	71	30	71	.1	.1
167 Chs of Christ	6	378	398	516	.4	.8
193 Episcopal	5	NR	326	872	.7	1.4
207 E.L.C.A.	31	10,690	4,899	13,230	10.2	20.9
223 Free Will Bapt	2	209	NR	259 *	.2	.4
263 Int Foursq Gos	2	324	502	502 *	.4	.8
283 Luth—MO Synod	1	80	42	100	.1	.2
304 NatPrimBapt USA	1	175	NR	217 *	.2	.3
355 Presb Ch (USA)	15	3,173	1,560	3,934 *	3.0	6.2
356 Presb Ch Amer	3	422	313	468	.4	.7
360 Prim Bapt Chrch	2	NR	NR	NR	-	-
403 Salvation Army	1	114	74	150	.1	.2
413 S.D.A.	2	292	NR	347	.3	.5
419 So Bapt Conv	54	17,493	7,754	21,690 *	16.6	34.2
443 Un C of Christ	12	2,821	1,308	3,498 *	2.7	5.5
449 Un Methodist	33	8,922	3,692	11,065 *	8.5	17.5
467 Wesleyan	2	401	449	746	.6	1.2
469 WELS	1	49	30	53	-	.1
499 Indep.Non-Char	1	0	350	350	.3	.6
RUTHERFORD	**150**	**34,954**	**14,013**	**44,162 ***	**70.2**	**100.0**
019 Amer Bapt USA	1	117	80	144 *	.2	.3
053 Assemb of God	2	55	40	50	.1	.1
056 Baha'i	0	7	NR	7	-	-
081 Catholic	1	NR	NR	563	.9	1.3
127 Ch God (Cleve)	4	219	201	271 *	.4	.6
151 L-D Saints	1	NR	NR	368	.6	.8
157 Ch of Brethren	1	167	136	205 *	.3	.5
165 Ch of Nazarene	1	35	38	38	.1	.1
167 Chs of Christ	1	45	35	60	.1	.1
193 Episcopal	2	NR	198	360	.6	.8
207 E.L.C.A.	1	64	40	70	.1	.2
223 Free Will Bapt	2	209	NR	257 *	.4	.6
263 Int Foursq Gos	1	193	244	244 *	.4	.6
297 Mennonite;Other	1	60	NR	74 *	.1	.2
355 Presb Ch (USA)	8	670	312	825 *	1.3	1.9
356 Presb Ch Amer	1	20	26	26	-	.1
413 S.D.A.	2	121	NR	144	.2	.3
419 So Bapt Conv	91	27,485	10,099	33,796 *	53.7	76.5
449 Un Methodist	25	4,403	1,836	5,415 *	8.6	12.3
467 Wesleyan	3	384	228	545	.9	1.2
498 Indep.Charis.	1	700	500	700	1.1	1.6
SAMPSON	**117**	**18,449**	**7,517**	**27,930 ***	**46.4**	**100.0**
053 Assemb of God	2	40	52	64	.1	.2
056 Baha'i	0	1	NR	1	-	-
081 Catholic	3	NR	NR	4,405	7.3	15.8
093 Chr Ch (Disc)	2	483	245	606 *	1.0	2.2
127 Ch God (Cleve)	7	587	414	738 *	1.2	2.6
145 Ch God Prophcy	6	250	NR	312 *	.5	1.1
151 L-D Saints	1	NR	NR	234	.4	.8
167 Chs of Christ	1	22	20	35	.1	.1
193 Episcopal	1	NR	53	114	.2	.4
223 Free Will Bapt	1	104	NR	131 *	.2	.5
336 OrigFreeWillBpt	7	1,255	NR	1,575 *	2.6	5.6
349 Pent Holiness	10	1,142	850	1,433 *	2.4	5.1
355 Presb Ch (USA)	5	576	628	723 *	1.2	2.6
413 S.D.A.	1	19	NR	23	-	.1
419 So Bapt Conv	46	10,901	4,048	13,683 *	22.7	49.0
435 Unitarian-Univ	1	40	NR	50 *	.1	.2
449 Un Methodist	23	3,029	1,207	3,803 *	6.3	13.6
SCOTLAND	**61**	**9,889**	**5,017**	**13,336 ***	**37.0**	**100.0**
053 Assemb of God	2	63	80	120	.3	.9
056 Baha'i	0	64	NR	64	.2	.5
081 Catholic	1	NR	NR	488	1.4	3.7
097 Chr Chs&Chs Cr	1	50	NR	64 *	.2	.5
127 Ch God (Cleve)	5	887	592	1,141 *	3.2	8.6
145 Ch God Prophcy	2	83	NR	106 *	.3	.8
165 Ch of Nazarene	1	35	46	56	.2	.4
167 Chs of Christ	1	10	10	15	-	.1
193 Episcopal	1	NR	62	130	.4	1.0
207 E.L.C.A.	1	77	42	97	.3	.7
223 Free Will Bapt	2	209	NR	267 *	.7	2.0
349 Pent Holiness	8	770	770	984 *	2.7	7.4
355 Presb Ch (USA)	8	1,315	597	1,689 *	4.7	12.7
413 S.D.A.	1	104	NR	124	.3	.9
419 So Bapt Conv	12	2,918	1,514	3,730 *	10.4	28.0
449 Un Methodist	14	3,273	1,257	4,186 *	11.6	31.4
467 Wesleyan	1	31	47	75	.2	.6
STANLY	**136**	**27,864**	**13,075**	**36,401 ***	**62.7**	**100.0**
053 Assemb of God	1	388	485	750	1.3	2.1
055 As Ref Pres Ch	1	58	NR	72	.1	.2
056 Baha'i	0	6	NR	6	-	-
081 Catholic	1	NR	NR	756	1.3	2.1
089 Chr & Miss Al	1	0	NR	52	.1	.1
127 Ch God (Cleve)	6	542	440	672 *	1.2	1.8
145 Ch God Prophcy	1	42	NR	52 *	.1	.1
151 L-D Saints	1	NR	NR	425	.7	1.2
165 Ch of Nazarene	2	166	102	293	.5	.8
167 Chs of Christ	1	52	53	68	.1	.2
193 Episcopal	1	NR	123	163	.3	.4
207 E.L.C.A.	4	990	518	1,258	2.2	3.5
263 Int Foursq Gos	1	39	50	50 *	.1	.1
336 OrigFreeWillBpt	2	361	NR	448 *	.8	1.2
349 Pent Holiness	1	87	74	108 *	.2	.3
355 Presb Ch (USA)	7	1,033	520	1,283 *	2.2	3.5
356 Presb Ch Amer	2	412	345	414	.7	1.1
360 Prim Bapt Chrch	3	NR	NR	NR	-	-

NR–Not Reported   *Total adherents estimated from known number of communicant, confirmed, full members.   - Represents a percentage less than 0.1.   Percentages may not total 100 due to rounding.

Table 4: Religious Congregations by County and Group: 2000

Religious Group	Number of Churches, Synagogues, Mosques, or Temples	Number of Communicant, Confirmed, or Full Members	Number of Attendees	Total Adherents		
				Number of Adherents	% of Total Pop.	% of Total Adh.
413 S.D.A.	1	141	NR	168	.3	.5
418 Southw Bapt Fel	2	NR	NR	NR	-	-
419 So Bapt Conv	63	17,041	7,425	21,152 *	36.4	58.1
443 Un C of Christ	2	363	142	451 *	.8	1.2
449 Un Methodist	31	6,069	2,689	7,535 *	13.0	20.7
467 Wesleyan	1	74	109	225	.4	.6
STOKES	**73**	**12,241**	**5,004**	**16,205 ***	**36.2**	**100.0**
056 Baha'i	0	1	NR	1	-	-
081 Catholic	1	NR	NR	532	1.2	3.3
093 Chr Ch (Disc)	1	223	100	276 *	.6	1.7
097 Chr Chs&Chs Cr	7	1,901	NR	2,353 *	5.3	14.5
127 Ch God (Cleve)	4	331	222	408 *	.9	2.5
167 Chs of Christ	1	58	49	70	.2	.4
193 Episcopal	2	NR	57	96	.2	.6
295 Morav Ch-South	2	438	NR	599	1.3	3.7
304 NatPrimBapt USA	1	72	NR	89 *	.2	.5
349 Pent Holiness	2	131	104	162 *	.4	1.0
355 Presb Ch (USA)	6	360	258	446 *	1.0	2.8
360 Prim Bapt Chrch	6	NR	NR	NR	-	-
419 So Bapt Conv	21	5,561	2,262	6,881 *	15.4	42.5
449 Un Methodist	17	2,215	1,072	2,742 *	6.1	16.9
499 Indep.Non-Char	2	950	880	1,550	3.5	9.6
SURRY	**168**	**28,014**	**12,823**	**36,133 ***	**50.7**	**100.0**
053 Assemb of God	3	159	165	207	.3	.6
056 Baha'i	0	33	NR	33	-	.1
081 Catholic	3	NR	NR	806	1.1	2.2
093 Chr Ch (Disc)	1	192	93	236 *	.3	.7
097 Chr Chs&Chs Cr	4	480	NR	588 *	.8	1.6
127 Ch God (Cleve)	3	395	225	485 *	.7	1.3
145 Ch God Prophcy	1	42	NR	51 *	.1	.1
151 L-D Saints	2	NR	NR	617	.9	1.7
157 Ch of Brethren	3	270	150	331 *	.5	.9
167 Chs of Christ	3	126	135	163	.2	.5
193 Episcopal	2	NR	111	280	.4	.8
207 E.L.C.A.	1	45	30	77	.1	.2
226 Friends-USA	7	791	NR	971 *	1.4	2.7
295 Morav Ch-South	1	376	NR	445	.6	1.2
304 NatPrimBapt USA	4	485	NR	595 *	.8	1.6
335 Orth Pres Ch	1	20	30	30	-	.1
349 Pent Holiness	6	438	357	538 *	.8	1.5
355 Presb Ch (USA)	7	871	482	1,070 *	1.5	3.0
360 Prim Bapt Chrch	11	NR	NR	NR	-	-
403 Salvation Army	1	95	69	218	.3	.6
418 Southw Bapt Fel	1	NR	NR	NR	-	-
419 So Bapt Conv	69	18,139	8,241	22,265 *	31.3	61.6
449 Un Methodist	29	3,878	1,746	4,761 *	6.7	13.2
467 Wesleyan	4	379	339	566	.8	1.6
499 Indep.Non-Char	1	800	650	800	1.1	2.2
SWAIN	**40**	**3,681**	**1,552**	**5,275 ***	**40.7**	**100.0**
053 Assemb of God	1	26	35	35	.3	.7
056 Baha'i	0	21	NR	21	.2	.4
081 Catholic	2	NR	NR	226	1.7	4.3
127 Ch God (Cleve)	4	151	97	188 *	1.4	3.6
151 L-D Saints	1	NR	NR	377	2.9	7.1
165 Ch of Nazarene	1	17	18	53	.4	1.0
167 Chs of Christ	1	20	30	30	.2	.6
193 Episcopal	1	NR	17	18	.1	.3
207 E.L.C.A.	1	0	0	0	-	-
349 Pent Holiness	2	53	43	65 *	.5	1.2
355 Presb Ch (USA)	1	88	44	108 *	.8	2.0
413 S.D.A.	1	27	NR	32	.2	.6
419 So Bapt Conv	21	2,956	1,115	3,639 *	28.1	69.0
449 Un Methodist	1	252	80	310 *	2.4	5.9
467 Wesleyan	2	70	73	173	1.3	3.3
TRANSYLVANIA	**62**	**12,895**	**5,157**	**17,573 ***	**59.9**	**100.0**
019 Amer Bapt USA	1	175	0	206 *	.7	1.2
053 Assemb of God	2	102	114	121	.4	.7
056 Baha'i	0	4	NR	4	-	-
081 Catholic	2	NR	NR	1,632	5.6	9.3
084 Calvary Chapel	1	NR	NR	NR	-	-
127 Ch God (Cleve)	4	369	196	449 *	1.5	2.6
145 Ch God Prophcy	1	42	NR	49 *	.2	.3
165 Ch of Nazarene	1	16	35	40	.1	.2
167 Chs of Christ	2	48	53	62	.2	.4
193 Episcopal	1	NR	267	568	1.9	3.2
207 E.L.C.A.	1	265	149	287	1.0	1.6
356 Presb Ch Amer	2	218	266	285	1.0	1.6
370 Ref Baptist Chs	1	NR	NR	NR	-	-
413 S.D.A.	1	56	NR	67	.2	.4
418 Southw Bapt Fel	1	NR	NR	NR	-	-
419 So Bapt Conv	32	9,899	3,136	11,666 *	39.8	66.4
435 Unitarian-Univ	1	45	NR	53 *	.2	.3
449 Un Methodist	6	1,379	663	1,624 *	5.5	9.2
467 Wesleyan	2	277	278	460	1.6	2.6
TYRRELL	**17**	**1,382**	**267**	**1,800 ***	**43.4**	**100.0**
053 Assemb of God	1	43	50	150	3.6	8.3
056 Baha'i	0	1	NR	1	-	.1
081 Catholic	1	NR	NR	9	.2	.5
093 Chr Ch (Disc)	1	51	28	61 *	1.5	3.4
097 Chr Chs&Chs Cr	3	347	NR	416 *	10.0	23.1
193 Episcopal	2	NR	23	34	.8	1.9
223 Free Will Bapt	1	104	NR	125 *	3.0	6.9
336 OrigFreeWillBpt	3	223	NR	268 *	6.5	14.9
419 So Bapt Conv	2	299	83	359 *	8.7	19.9
449 Un Methodist	3	314	83	377 *	9.1	20.9
UNION	**164**	**40,679**	**19,945**	**58,963 ***	**47.7**	**100.0**
053 Assemb of God	1	58	70	100	.1	.2
056 Baha'i	0	49	NR	49	-	.1
081 Catholic	1	NR	NR	5,750	4.6	9.8
089 Chr & Miss Al	1	34	NR	77	.1	.1
123 Ch God (Ander)	2	NR	85	85	.1	.1
127 Ch God (Cleve)	6	573	399	744 *	.6	1.3
145 Ch God Prophcy	1	42	NR	54 *	-	.1
165 Ch of Nazarene	1	242	110	242	.2	.4
167 Chs of Christ	2	61	65	78	.1	.1
193 Episcopal	1	NR	116	412	.3	.7
203 Evan Free Ch	1	100	200	200	.2	.3
207 E.L.C.A.	2	516	414	745	.6	1.3
216 Evan Presby Ch	1	63	NR	81 *	.1	.1
223 Free Will Bapt	1	104	NR	135 *	.1	.2
226 Friends-USA	1	113	NR	146 *	.1	.2
263 Int Foursq Gos	1	56	73	73 *	.1	.1
349 Pent Holiness	2	113	79	146 *	.1	.2
355 Presb Ch (USA)	19	2,720	1,500	3,513 *	2.8	6.0
360 Prim Bapt Chrch	5	NR	NR	NR	-	-
413 S.D.A.	2	98	NR	117	.1	.2
418 Southw Bapt Fel	1	NR	NR	NR	-	-
419 So Bapt Conv	74	26,456	12,381	34,168 *	27.6	57.9
443 Un C of Christ	1	44	19	57 *	-	.1
449 Un Methodist	35	8,947	4,099	11,555 *	9.3	19.6
467 Wesleyan	1	30	35	86	.1	.1
499 Indep.Non-Char	1	260	300	350	.3	.6
VANCE	**72**	**14,417**	**6,597**	**19,623 ***	**45.7**	**100.0**
056 Baha'i	0	124	NR	124	.3	.6
081 Catholic	1	NR	NR	795	1.9	4.1
127 Ch God (Cleve)	4	1,231	825	1,568 *	3.7	8.0
145 Ch God Prophcy	1	42	NR	53 *	.1	.3
165 Ch of Nazarene	1	74	36	74	.2	.4
167 Chs of Christ	2	58	71	83	.2	.4
193 Episcopal	3	NR	150	368	.9	1.9
223 Free Will Bapt	1	104	NR	133 *	.3	.7
349 Pent Holiness	5	706	717	899 *	2.1	4.6
355 Presb Ch (USA)	6	555	305	706 *	1.6	3.6
356 Presb Ch Amer	1	94	100	110	.3	.6
403 Salvation Army	1	96	57	279	.6	1.4
419 So Bapt Conv	21	6,424	2,521	8,179 *	19.0	41.7
443 Un C of Christ	7	1,404	659	1,788 *	4.2	9.1
449 Un Methodist	18	3,505	1,156	4,464 *	10.4	22.7

NR–Not Reported *Total adherents estimated from known number of communicant, confirmed, full members. - Represents a percentage less than 0.1. Percentages may not total 100 due to rounding.

Table 4: Religious Congregations by County and Group: 2000

Religious Group	Number of Churches, Synagogues, Mosques, or Temples	Number of Communicant, Confirmed, or Full Members	Number of Attendees	Total Adherents: Number of Adherents	Total Adherents: % of Total Pop.	Total Adherents: % of Total Adh.
WAKE	**400**	**151,359**	**76,354**	**275,130 ***	**43.8**	**100.0**
019 Amer Bapt USA	2	2,246	1,156	2,812 *	.4	1.0
034 Ant Orth of NA	1	202	NR	404	.1	.1
049 Armen Ap Cilic	1	0	NR	160	-	.1
053 Assemb of God	8	1,914	2,209	3,355	.5	1.2
055 As Ref Pres Ch	1	31	NR	54	-	-
056 Baha'i	4	452	NR	452	.1	.2
076 Buddhism	6	NR	NR	NR	-	-
081 Catholic	15	NR	NR	59,610	9.5	21.7
084 Calvary Chapel	1	NR	NR	NR	-	-
089 Chr & Miss Al	6	634	NR	1,081	.2	.4
093 Chr Ch (Disc)	6	1,762	428	2,206 *	.4	.8
097 Chr Chs&Chs Cr	6	857	NR	1,073 *	.2	.4
123 Ch God (Ander)	3	NR	146	146	-	.1
127 Ch God (Cleve)	15	2,541	1,972	3,208 *	.5	1.2
145 Ch God Prophcy	6	250	NR	312 *	-	.1
151 L-D Saints	10	NR	NR	3,792	.6	1.4
165 Ch of Nazarene	4	939	1,050	1,402	.2	.5
167 Chs of Christ	9	1,453	1,496	2,003	.3	.7
173 Comm of Christ	1	111	NR	111	-	-
193 Episcopal	12	NR	3,309	8,872	1.4	3.2
201 Evan Cov Ch	1	67	134	134 *	-	-
203 Evan Free Ch	1	69	125	125	-	-
207 E.L.C.A.	8	4,141	2,333	5,668	.9	2.1
216 Evan Presby Ch	1	166	NR	208 *	-	.1
223 Free Will Bapt	7	731	NR	915 *	.1	.3
246 Greek Orthodox	1	NR	NR	858	.1	.3
252 Hindu	3	NR	NR	NR	-	-
263 Int Foursq Gos	4	468	619	619 *	.1	.2
267 Muslim Est	3	NR	1,925	3,200	.5	1.2
268 Jain	1	NR	NR	NR	-	-
283 Luth—MO Synod	3	1,527	1,069	2,336	.4	.8
288 Mennonite USA	1	73	94	94 *	-	-
290 Metro Comm Ch	1	116	167	167 *	-	.1
295 Morav Ch-South	2	421	NR	542	.1	.2
331 OCA: Ter Diocs	1	22	NR	137	-	-
335 Orth Pres Ch	1	36	54	54	-	-
336 OrigFreeWillBpt	5	784	NR	981 *	.2	.4
349 Pent Holiness	12	1,111	996	1,391 *	.2	.5
355 Presb Ch (USA)	24	13,613	6,134	17,045 *	2.7	6.2
356 Presb Ch Amer	5	793	885	1,208	.2	.4
360 Prim Bapt Chrch	1	NR	NR	NR	-	-
370 Ref Baptist Chs	1	NR	NR	NR	-	-
371 Ref Ch in Am	1	122	106	249	-	.1
403 Salvation Army	1	201	134	319	.1	.1
410 Serb Orth USA	1	NR	NR	250	-	.1
413 S.D.A.	3	1,057	NR	1,258	.2	.5
418 Southw Bapt Fel	2	NR	NR	NR	-	-
419 So Bapt Conv	108	63,088	27,141	78,979 *	12.6	28.7
435 Unitarian-Univ	1	518	NR	648 *	.1	.2
443 Un C of Christ	21	4,723	2,346	5,913 *	.9	2.1
449 Un Methodist	40	36,970	12,894	46,283 *	7.4	16.8
463 Vineyard	2	330	288	413 *	.1	.2
467 Wesleyan	4	130	175	278	-	.1
469 WELS	2	190	144	255	-	.1
496 Jewish Est	5	NR	NR	6,000	1.0	2.2
499 Indep.Non-Char	5	6,500	6,825	7,550	1.2	2.7
WARREN	**42**	**6,339**	**2,929**	**7,886 ***	**39.5**	**100.0**
056 Baha'i	0	11	NR	11	.1	.1
081 Catholic	1	NR	NR	58	.3	.7
127 Ch God (Cleve)	1	65	58	79 *	.4	1.0
145 Ch God Prophcy	1	42	NR	51 *	.3	.6
193 Episcopal	3	NR	61	90	.5	1.1
283 Luth—MO Synod	1	262	109	333	1.7	4.2
349 Pent Holiness	1	32	31	39 *	.2	.5
355 Presb Ch (USA)	2	57	40	70 *	.4	.9
419 So Bapt Conv	17	3,595	1,624	4,382 *	21.9	55.6
443 Un C of Christ	5	920	499	1,121 *	5.6	14.2
449 Un Methodist	10	1,355	507	1,652 *	8.3	20.9
WASHINGTON	**41**	**5,580**	**1,355**	**7,169 ***	**52.2**	**100.0**
053 Assemb of God	1	43	55	78	.6	1.1
056 Baha'i	0	212	NR	212	1.5	3.0
081 Catholic	1	NR	NR	108	.8	1.5
093 Chr Ch (Disc)	2	467	115	582 *	4.2	8.1
097 Chr Chs&Chs Cr	8	1,607	NR	2,003 *	14.6	27.9
127 Ch God (Cleve)	2	185	126	230 *	1.7	3.2
165 Ch of Nazarene	1	150	71	150	1.1	2.1
167 Chs of Christ	1	19	25	24	.2	.3
193 Episcopal	3	NR	77	173	1.3	2.4
223 Free Will Bapt	2	209	NR	260 *	1.9	3.6
336 OrigFreeWillBpt	4	502	NR	625 *	4.6	8.7
349 Pent Holiness	3	358	282	446 *	3.3	6.2
355 Presb Ch (USA)	1	31	15	39 *	.3	.5
419 So Bapt Conv	6	1,125	403	1,401 *	10.2	19.5
449 Un Methodist	6	672	186	838 *	6.1	11.7
WATAUGA	**86**	**15,264**	**8,350**	**20,284 ***	**47.5**	**100.0**
034 Ant Orth of NA	1	12	NR	24	.1	.1
053 Assemb of God	2	48	65	65	.2	.3
055 As Ref Pres Ch	1	30	NR	30	.1	.1
056 Baha'i	1	57	NR	57	.1	.3
076 Buddhism	1	NR	NR	NR	-	-
081 Catholic	2	NR	NR	1,088	2.5	5.4
089 Chr & Miss Al	1	148	NR	410	1.0	2.0
097 Chr Chs&Chs Cr	2	403	NR	460 *	1.1	2.3
127 Ch God (Cleve)	2	46	41	52 *	.1	.3
151 L-D Saints	1	NR	NR	247	.6	1.2
167 Chs of Christ	1	59	72	76	.2	.4
193 Episcopal	3	NR	720	1,108	2.6	5.5
207 E.L.C.A.	3	976	513	1,260	3.0	6.2
226 Friends-USA	1	64	NR	73 *	.2	.4
237 Menn Br US Conf	1	42	NR	48 *	.1	.2
263 Int Foursq Gos	1	62	80	80 *	.2	.4
290 Metro Comm Ch	1	6	8	8 *	-	-
355 Presb Ch (USA)	3	714	511	814 *	1.9	4.0
356 Presb Ch Amer	1	61	83	83	.2	.4
360 Prim Bapt Chrch	1	NR	NR	NR	-	-
413 S.D.A.	1	34	NR	40	.1	.2
419 So Bapt Conv	42	10,416	5,304	11,881 *	27.8	58.6
435 Unitarian-Univ	1	102	NR	116 *	.3	.6
449 Un Methodist	11	1,889	888	2,156 *	5.0	10.6
463 Vineyard	1	95	65	108 *	.3	.5
WAYNE	**146**	**29,447**	**12,451**	**42,242 ***	**37.3**	**100.0**
053 Assemb of God	2	374	483	560	.5	1.3
056 Baha'i	0	77	NR	77	.1	.2
076 Buddhism	1	NR	NR	NR	-	-
081 Catholic	1	NR	NR	2,417	2.1	5.7
089 Chr & Miss Al	1	21	NR	90	.1	.2
093 Chr Ch (Disc)	9	2,103	946	2,639 *	2.3	6.2
127 Ch God (Cleve)	8	1,325	911	1,665 *	1.5	3.9
145 Ch God Prophcy	5	209	NR	260 *	.2	.6
151 L-D Saints	4	NR	NR	1,730	1.5	4.1
165 Ch of Nazarene	1	29	27	29	-	.1
167 Chs of Christ	2	174	188	229	.2	.5
193 Episcopal	4	NR	261	817	.7	1.9
207 E.L.C.A.	1	330	126	468	.4	1.1
223 Free Will Bapt	5	522	NR	655 *	.6	1.6
226 Friends-USA	6	678	NR	851 *	.8	2.0
263 Int Foursq Gos	1	30	50	50 *	-	.1
267 Muslim Est	1	NR	101	288	.3	.7
283 Luth—MO Synod	1	123	53	168	.1	.4
336 OrigFreeWillBpt	18	2,726	NR	3,421 *	3.0	8.1
349 Pent Holiness	11	1,629	1,349	2,045 *	1.8	4.8
355 Presb Ch (USA)	6	1,441	735	1,816 *	1.6	4.3
356 Presb Ch Amer	2	212	130	255	.2	.6
403 Salvation Army	1	145	89	295	.3	.7
413 S.D.A.	3	247	NR	295	.3	.7
419 So Bapt Conv	19	7,251	2,622	9,101 *	8.0	21.5
435 Unitarian-Univ	1	34	NR	43 *	-	.1
443 Un C of Christ	1	119	52	149 *	.1	.4
449 Un Methodist	26	7,486	2,856	9,399 *	8.3	22.3
467 Wesleyan	1	58	97	150	.1	.4
496 Jewish Est	1	NR	NR	80	.1	.2

NR–Not Reported *Total adherents estimated from known number of communicant, confirmed, full members. - Represents a percentage less than 0.1. Percentages may not total 100 due to rounding.

Table 4: Religious Congregations by County and Group: 2000

Religious Group	Number of Churches, Synagogues, Mosques, or Temples	Number of Communicant, Confirmed, or Full Members	Number of Attendees	Total Adherents		
				Number of Adherents	% of Total Pop.	% of Total Adh.
498 Indep.Charis.	2	1,656	1,150	1,700	1.5	4.0
499 Indep.Non-Char	1	448	225	500	.4	1.2
WILKES	**127**	**30,323**	**12,744**	**38,276 ***	**58.3**	**100.0**
053 Assemb of God	1	52	59	72	.1	.2
056 Baha'i	0	4	NR	4	-	-
081 Catholic	1	NR	NR	601	.9	1.6
127 Ch God (Cleve)	4	160	74	193 *	.3	.5
145 Ch God Prophcy	1	42	NR	51 *	.1	.1
151 L-D Saints	1	NR	NR	237	.4	.6
157 Ch of Brethren	1	82	65	100 *	.2	.3
167 Chs of Christ	3	169	215	237	.4	.6
193 Episcopal	1	NR	214	579	.9	1.5
207 E.L.C.A.	1	179	74	215	.3	.6
226 Friends-USA	1	64	NR	78 *	.1	.2
237 Menn Br US Conf	1	14	NR	17 *	-	-
349 Pent Holiness	2	142	83	172 *	.3	.4
355 Presb Ch (USA)	2	589	294	716 *	1.1	1.9
360 Prim Bapt Chrch	3	NR	NR	NR	-	-
413 S.D.A.	1	54	NR	64	.1	.2
419 So Bapt Conv	87	26,284	10,473	31,918 *	48.6	83.4
449 Un Methodist	16	2,488	1,193	3,022 *	4.6	7.9
WILSON	**103**	**20,709**	**6,959**	**28,350 ***	**38.4**	**100.0**
019 Amer Bapt USA	1	250	200	312 *	.4	1.1
053 Assemb of God	1	80	91	91	.1	.3
056 Baha'i	0	131	NR	131	.2	.5
081 Catholic	1	NR	NR	1,196	1.6	4.2
093 Chr Ch (Disc)	7	1,885	484	2,352 *	3.2	8.3
097 Chr Chs&Chs Cr	1	125	NR	156 *	.2	.6
123 Ch God (Ander)	1	NR	0	0	-	-
127 Ch God (Cleve)	4	875	566	1,092 *	1.5	3.9
145 Ch God Prophcy	2	83	NR	104 *	.1	.4
151 L-D Saints	1	NR	NR	278	.4	1.0
165 Ch of Nazarene	1	17	0	17	-	.1
167 Chs of Christ	1	30	40	44	.1	.2
193 Episcopal	2	NR	267	926	1.3	3.3
207 E.L.C.A.	1	142	91	192	.3	.7
216 Evan Presby Ch	1	68	NR	85 *	.1	.3
223 Free Will Bapt	5	522	NR	651 *	.9	2.3
263 Int Foursq Gos	1	30	50	50 *	.1	.2
283 Luth—MO Synod	1	100	45	100	.1	.4
336 OrigFreeWillBpt	18	3,910	NR	4,879 *	6.6	17.2
349 Pent Holiness	14	1,029	994	1,284 *	1.7	4.5
355 Presb Ch (USA)	7	1,271	572	1,585 *	2.1	5.6
356 Presb Ch Amer	1	0	0	0	-	-
360 Prim Bapt Chrch	1	NR	NR	NR	-	-
403 Salvation Army	1	152	75	330	.4	1.2
413 S.D.A.	2	181	NR	215	.3	.8
419 So Bapt Conv	14	5,527	2,173	6,897 *	9.3	24.3
443 Un C of Christ	1	90	70	112 *	.2	.4
449 Un Methodist	11	4,165	1,193	5,197 *	7.0	18.3
467 Wesleyan	1	46	48	74	.1	.3
YADKIN	**74**	**13,592**	**5,664**	**17,120 ***	**47.1**	**100.0**
053 Assemb of God	1	54	60	75	.2	.4
056 Baha'i	0	12	NR	12	-	.1
081 Catholic	1	NR	NR	287	.8	1.7
127 Ch God (Cleve)	2	155	133	191 *	.5	1.1
167 Chs of Christ	3	170	220	233	.6	1.4
207 E.L.C.A.	1	70	39	83	.2	.5
226 Friends-USA	10	1,130	NR	1,397 *	3.8	8.2
349 Pent Holiness	5	497	279	615 *	1.7	3.6
355 Presb Ch (USA)	2	53	23	66 *	.2	.4
360 Prim Bapt Chrch	1	NR	NR	NR	-	-
418 Southw Bapt Fel	1	NR	NR	NR	-	-
419 So Bapt Conv	27	8,545	3,516	10,567 *	29.1	61.7
443 Un C of Christ	1	77	34	95 *	.3	.6
449 Un Methodist	19	2,829	1,360	3,499 *	9.6	20.4
YANCEY	**70**	**6,905**	**2,345**	**8,553 ***	**48.1**	**100.0**
056 Baha'i	0	5	NR	5	-	.1

Religious Group	Number of Churches, Synagogues, Mosques, or Temples	Number of Communicant, Confirmed, or Full Members	Number of Attendees	Total Adherents		
				Number of Adherents	% of Total Pop.	% of Total Adh.
076 Buddhism	2	NR	NR	NR	-	-
081 Catholic	1	NR	NR	222	1.2	2.6
127 Ch God (Cleve)	1	116	57	139 *	.8	1.6
145 Ch God Prophcy	1	42	NR	50 *	.3	.6
157 Ch of Brethren	1	90	56	108 *	.6	1.3
167 Chs of Christ	1	18	16	25	.1	.3
193 Episcopal	1	NR	46	52	.3	.6
207 E.L.C.A.	1	56	32	67	.4	.8
226 Friends-USA	1	64	NR	77 *	.4	.9
258 IndFreeWillBapt	21	1,594	NR	1,909 *	10.7	22.3
355 Presb Ch (USA)	7	283	252	347 *	2.0	4.1
413 S.D.A.	1	48	NR	57	.3	.7
419 So Bapt Conv	24	3,709	1,422	4,441 *	25.0	51.9
449 Un Methodist	7	880	464	1,054 *	5.9	12.3
NORTH DAKOTA						
The State.....	1,507	211,256	95,361	470,112 *	73.2	100.0
ADAMS	**12**	**1,125**	**409**	**1,951 ***	**75.2**	**100.0**
053 Assemb of God	1	26	30	44	1.7	2.3
056 Baha'i	0	1	NR	1	-	.1
081 Catholic	2	NR	NR	514	19.8	26.3
203 Evan Free Ch	1	27	55	55	2.1	2.8
207 E.L.C.A.	3	883	177	1,114	43.0	57.1
419 So Bapt Conv	1	13	20	16 *	.6	.8
443 Un C of Christ	2	73	33	87 *	3.4	4.5
449 Un Methodist	1	89	83	106 *	4.1	5.4
469 WELS	1	13	11	14	.5	.7
BARNES	**37**	**4,843**	**2,239**	**9,094 ***	**77.2**	**100.0**
053 Assemb of God	2	66	88	124	1.1	1.4
056 Baha'i	0	3	NR	3	-	-
081 Catholic	6	NR	NR	2,728	23.2	30.0
151 L-D Saints	1	NR	NR	111	.9	1.2
165 Ch of Nazarene	1	199	170	321	2.7	3.5
193 Episcopal	1	NR	10	23	.2	.3
203 Evan Free Ch	1	20	50	50	.4	.5
207 E.L.C.A.	14	3,004	1,167	3,785	32.1	41.6
220 Free Lutheran	2	394	220	514	4.4	5.7
283 Luth—MO Synod	1	128	43	174	1.5	1.9
313 N Am Bapt Conf	1	86	84	103 *	.9	1.1
371 Ref Ch in Am	1	26	30	42	.4	.5
413 S.D.A.	1	16	NR	19	.2	.2
443 Un C of Christ	1	223	71	267 *	2.3	2.9
449 Un Methodist	3	605	275	724 *	6.1	8.0
469 WELS	1	73	31	106	.9	1.2
BENSON	**33**	**2,028**	**768**	**7,999 ***	**114.9**	**100.0**
053 Assemb of God	2	105	56	120	1.7	1.5
056 Baha'i	0	18	NR	18	.3	.2
081 Catholic	9	NR	NR	5,513	79.2	68.9
157 Ch of Brethren	1	37	0	51 *	.7	.6
193 Episcopal	1	NR	19	41	.6	.5
203 Evan Free Ch	1	41	60	60	.9	.8
207 E.L.C.A.	13	1,595	505	1,865	26.8	23.3
220 Free Lutheran	3	143	70	208	3.0	2.6
355 Presb Ch (USA)	2	60	35	83 *	1.2	1.0
419 So Bapt Conv	1	29	23	40 *	.6	.5
BILLINGS	**3**	**38**	**27**	**48 ***	**5.4**	**100.0**
081 Catholic	1	NR	NR	5	.6	10.4
207 E.L.C.A.	1	33	25	37	4.2	77.1
443 Un C of Christ	1	5	2	6 *	.7	12.5
BOTTINEAU	**27**	**3,795**	**1,511**	**5,852 ***	**81.9**	**100.0**
019 Amer Bapt USA	1	42	31	50 *	.7	.9
053 Assemb of God	1	9	12	12	.2	.2
056 Baha'i	0	2	NR	2	-	-
081 Catholic	4	NR	NR	1,018	14.2	17.4
203 Evan Free Ch	1	69	125	125	1.7	2.1

NR–Not Reported   *Total adherents estimated from known number of communicant, confirmed, full members.   - Represents a percentage less than 0.1.   Percentages may not total 100 due to rounding.

Table 4: Religious Congregations by County and Group: 2000

Religious Group	Number of Churches, Synagogues, Mosques, or Temples	Number of Communicant, Confirmed, or Full Members	Number of Attendees	Total Adherents: Number of Adherents	% of Total Pop.	% of Total Adh.
207 E.L.C.A.	9	2,515	805	3,236	45.3	55.3
283 Luth—MO Synod	5	662	262	820	11.5	14.0
355 Presb Ch (USA)	3	236	154	280 *	3.9	4.8
413 S.D.A.	1	53	NR	63	.9	1.1
449 Un Methodist	2	207	122	246 *	3.4	4.2
BOWMAN	**12**	**1,650**	**598**	**3,270 ***	**100.9**	**100.0**
053 Assemb of God	1	143	130	190	5.9	5.8
081 Catholic	3	NR	NR	1,142	35.2	34.9
207 E.L.C.A.	5	1,278	337	1,660	51.2	50.8
355 Presb Ch (USA)	1	6	10	10 *	.3	.3
413 S.D.A.	1	42	NR	50	1.5	1.5
419 So Bapt Conv	0	8	21	10 *	.3	.3
449 Un Methodist	1	173	100	208 *	6.4	6.4
BURKE	**16**	**1,673**	**592**	**2,421 ***	**108.0**	**100.0**
019 Amer Bapt USA	1	249	118	290 *	12.9	12.0
053 Assemb of God	1	28	35	35	1.6	1.4
081 Catholic	3	NR	NR	326	14.5	13.5
127 Ch God (Cleve)	1	21	22	24 *	1.1	1.0
207 E.L.C.A.	7	1,197	337	1,530	68.2	63.2
283 Luth—MO Synod	1	39	25	54	2.4	2.2
355 Presb Ch (USA)	1	32	10	37 *	1.7	1.5
449 Un Methodist	1	107	45	125 *	5.6	5.2
BURLEIGH	**66**	**19,528**	**9,585**	**53,999 ***	**77.8**	**100.0**
019 Amer Bapt USA	1	363	104	446 *	.6	.8
053 Assemb of God	4	650	842	1,583	2.3	2.9
056 Baha'i	0	35	NR	35	.1	.1
081 Catholic	6	NR	NR	25,240	36.4	46.7
089 Chr & Miss Al	1	38	NR	83	.1	.2
127 Ch God (Cleve)	2	89	106	154 *	.2	.3
145 Ch God Prophcy	2	47	NR	58 *	.1	.1
151 L-D Saints	2	NR	NR	975	1.4	1.8
165 Ch of Nazarene	1	146	153	260	.4	.5
167 Chs of Christ	1	68	85	105	.2	.2
193 Episcopal	1	NR	125	493	.7	.9
203 Evan Free Ch	1	169	317	317	.5	.6
207 E.L.C.A.	12	10,634	4,048	14,162	20.4	26.2
220 Free Lutheran	1	12	25	25	-	-
226 Friends-USA	1	45	NR	55 *	.1	.1
237 Menn Br US Conf	1	5	NR	6 *	-	-
263 Int Foursq Gos	1	87	260	260 *	.4	.5
283 Luth—MO Synod	3	1,590	727	2,109	3.0	3.9
313 N Am Bapt Conf	2	932	715	1,144 *	1.6	2.1
335 Orth Pres Ch	1	5	29	29	-	.1
355 Presb Ch (USA)	2	832	286	1,021 *	1.5	1.9
371 Ref Ch in Am	1	235	292	622	.9	1.2
403 Salvation Army	1	96	51	437	.6	.8
413 S.D.A.	2	346	NR	412	.6	.8
419 So Bapt Conv	3	317	180	389 *	.6	.7
431 Ukrainian Orth	1	NR	NR	60	.1	.1
435 Unitarian-Univ	1	48	NR	59 *	.1	.1
443 Un C of Christ	3	443	188	544 *	.8	1.0
449 Un Methodist	6	2,063	879	2,532 *	3.6	4.7
467 Wesleyan	1	44	87	153	.2	.3
469 WELS	1	189	86	231	.3	.4
CASS	**123**	**35,922**	**16,490**	**69,897 ***	**56.8**	**100.0**
019 Amer Bapt USA	1	161	57	197 *	.2	.3
034 Ant Orth of NA	1	8	NR	16	-	-
053 Assemb of God	2	987	1,401	2,017	1.6	2.9
056 Baha'i	1	52	NR	52	-	.1
057 Bapt Gen Conf	1	32	80	80 *	.1	.1
081 Catholic	15	NR	NR	17,829	14.5	25.5
089 Chr & Miss Al	1	23	NR	50	-	.1
127 Ch God (Cleve)	1	22	39	39 *	-	.1
145 Ch God Prophcy	1	24	NR	29 *	-	-
151 L-D Saints	2	NR	NR	370	.3	.5
165 Ch of Nazarene	1	27	0	27	-	-
167 Chs of Christ	1	47	50	60	-	.1
173 Comm of Christ	1	41	NR	41	-	.1

Religious Group	Number of Churches, Synagogues, Mosques, or Temples	Number of Communicant, Confirmed, or Full Members	Number of Attendees	Total Adherents: Number of Adherents	% of Total Pop.	% of Total Adh.
179 Consrv Bapt	2	NR	334	334	.3	.5
193 Episcopal	2	NR	218	620	.5	.9
201 Evan Cov Ch	1	80	110	110 *	.1	.2
203 Evan Free Ch	2	444	1,300	1,300	1.1	1.9
207 E.L.C.A.	36	24,953	8,689	34,022	27.6	48.7
220 Free Lutheran	1	191	102	252	.2	.4
221 Free Methodist	1	3	25	25	-	-
226 Friends-USA	1	45	NR	55 *	-	.1
267 Muslim Est	2	NR	202	576	.5	.8
283 Luth—MO Synod	5	2,221	950	2,981	2.4	4.3
288 Mennonite USA	1	32	38	39 *	-	.1
293 Morav Ch-North	4	418	NR	496	.4	.7
313 N Am Bapt Conf	2	224	201	274 *	.2	.4
355 Presb Ch (USA)	11	2,048	715	2,504 *	2.0	3.6
371 Ref Ch in Am	1	46	75	117	.1	.2
403 Salvation Army	1	61	44	253	.2	.4
413 S.D.A.	1	127	NR	151	.1	.2
419 So Bapt Conv	2	242	181	296 *	.2	.4
435 Unitarian-Univ	1	61	NR	75 *	.1	.1
443 Un C of Christ	4	791	306	967 *	.8	1.4
449 Un Methodist	11	2,439	1,306	2,981 *	2.4	4.3
469 WELS	1	72	67	112	.1	.2
496 Jewish Est	1	NR	NR	550	.4	.8
CAVALIER	**29**	**1,700**	**795**	**4,003 ***	**82.9**	**100.0**
053 Assemb of God	1	25	37	42	.9	1.0
081 Catholic	8	NR	NR	1,862	38.5	46.5
193 Episcopal	1	NR	15	17	.4	.4
203 Evan Free Ch	1	21	48	48	1.0	1.2
207 E.L.C.A.	6	1,052	366	1,324	27.4	33.1
283 Luth—MO Synod	2	116	69	118	2.4	2.9
288 Mennonite USA	1	25	23	30 *	.6	.7
297 Mennonite;Other	1	85	NR	103 *	2.1	2.6
355 Presb Ch (USA)	6	190	110	234 *	4.8	5.8
419 So Bapt Conv	1	29	48	35 *	.7	.9
449 Un Methodist	1	157	79	190 *	3.9	4.7
DICKEY	**28**	**2,980**	**1,620**	**4,666 ***	**81.0**	**100.0**
019 Amer Bapt USA	1	67	20	81 *	1.4	1.7
053 Assemb of God	3	169	249	275	4.8	5.9
081 Catholic	3	NR	NR	864	15.0	18.5
165 Ch of Nazarene	2	229	220	311	5.4	6.7
193 Episcopal	1	NR	6	27	.5	.6
203 Evan Free Ch	1	69	125	125	2.2	2.7
207 E.L.C.A.	4	797	261	990	17.2	21.2
257 Hutterian Br	2	132	NR	200	3.5	4.3
283 Luth—MO Synod	4	888	441	1,032	17.9	22.1
355 Presb Ch (USA)	2	104	51	126 *	2.2	2.7
413 S.D.A.	1	67	NR	80	1.4	1.7
419 So Bapt Conv	0	15	15	18 *	.3	.4
449 Un Methodist	4	443	232	537 *	9.3	11.5
DIVIDE	**13**	**1,271**	**470**	**1,998 ***	**87.5**	**100.0**
053 Assemb of God	1	40	55	61	2.7	3.1
056 Baha'i	0	1	NR	1	-	.1
081 Catholic	2	NR	NR	405	17.7	20.3
207 E.L.C.A.	9	1,230	395	1,511	66.2	75.6
355 Presb Ch (USA)	1	0	20	20 *	.9	1.0
DUNN	**16**	**1,183**	**564**	**3,401 ***	**94.5**	**100.0**
019 Amer Bapt USA	1	54	45	68 *	1.9	2.0
053 Assemb of God	1	35	45	96	2.7	2.8
056 Baha'i	0	3	NR	3	.1	.1
057 Bapt Gen Conf	1	29	45	45 *	1.3	1.3
081 Catholic	5	NR	NR	1,863	51.8	54.8
207 E.L.C.A.	6	1,020	402	1,276	35.4	37.5
283 Luth—MO Synod	1	10	12	10	.3	.3
443 Un C of Christ	1	32	15	40 *	1.1	1.2
EDDY	**9**	**1,157**	**432**	**2,075 ***	**75.3**	**100.0**
081 Catholic	1	NR	NR	676	24.5	32.6
181 Consrv Congr	1	60	30	73 *	2.6	3.5

NR–Not Reported   *Total adherents estimated from known number of communicant, confirmed, full members.   - Represents a percentage less than 0.1.   Percentages may not total 100 due to rounding.

Table 4: Religious Congregations by County and Group: 2000

Religious Group	Number of Churches, Synagogues, Mosques, or Temples	Number of Communicant, Confirmed, or Full Members	Number of Attendees	Total Adherents		
				Number of Adherents	% of Total Pop.	% of Total Adh.
203 Evan Free Ch	1	30	55	55	2.0	2.7
207 E.L.C.A.	4	880	265	1,061	38.5	51.1
283 Luth—MO Synod	1	78	34	78	2.8	3.8
449 Un Methodist	1	109	48	132 *	4.8	6.4
EMMONS	**17**	**1,115**	**634**	**4,308 ***	**99.5**	**100.0**
053 Assemb of God	1	36	47	55	1.3	1.3
081 Catholic	6	NR	NR	2,911	67.2	67.6
105 Christian Ref	1	114	0	139 *	3.2	3.2
207 E.L.C.A.	2	425	177	524	12.1	12.2
313 N Am Bapt Conf	1	98	74	119 *	2.7	2.8
355 Presb Ch (USA)	1	24	22	29 *	.7	.7
371 Ref Ch in Am	2	142	155	201	4.6	4.7
449 Un Methodist	2	155	97	189 *	4.4	4.4
469 WELS	1	121	62	141	3.3	3.3
FOSTER	**16**	**2,014**	**897**	**3,665 ***	**97.5**	**100.0**
053 Assemb of God	1	53	80	80	2.1	2.2
056 Baha'i	0	1	NR	1	-	-
081 Catholic	2	NR	NR	1,032	27.5	28.2
165 Ch of Nazarene	1	42	44	77	2.0	2.1
203 Evan Free Ch	1	0	20	20	.5	.5
207 E.L.C.A.	5	1,220	411	1,560	41.5	42.6
283 Luth—MO Synod	1	271	85	370	9.8	10.1
313 N Am Bapt Conf	1	92	69	114 *	3.0	3.1
413 S.D.A.	1	63	NR	75	2.0	2.0
443 Un C of Christ	1	86	95	106 *	2.8	2.9
449 Un Methodist	2	186	93	230 *	6.1	6.3
GOLDEN VALLEY	**8**	**463**	**202**	**1,436 ***	**74.6**	**100.0**
081 Catholic	2	NR	NR	859	44.6	59.8
207 E.L.C.A.	2	247	112	324	16.8	22.6
283 Luth—MO Synod	1	155	68	180	9.4	12.5
413 S.D.A.	1	18	NR	21	1.1	1.5
443 Un C of Christ	1	37	16	45 *	2.3	3.1
449 Un Methodist	1	6	6	7 *	.4	.5
GRAND FORKS	**75**	**15,934**	**7,862**	**40,272 ***	**60.9**	**100.0**
019 Amer Bapt USA	1	96	47	117 *	.2	.3
053 Assemb of God	3	198	257	466	.7	1.2
056 Baha'i	1	40	NR	40	.1	.1
081 Catholic	7	NR	NR	16,575	25.1	41.2
123 Ch God (Ander)	1	NR	50	50	.1	.1
127 Ch God (Cleve)	1	26	36	36 *	.1	.1
151 L-D Saints	1	NR	NR	491	.7	1.2
165 Ch of Nazarene	2	117	88	131	.2	.3
167 Chs of Christ	1	30	35	50	.1	.1
173 Comm of Christ	1	12	NR	12	-	-
193 Episcopal	1	NR	86	382	.6	.9
201 Evan Cov Ch	1	121	337	337 *	.5	.8
203 Evan Free Ch	1	275	550	550	.8	1.4
207 E.L.C.A.	23	11,128	4,184	15,777	23.9	39.2
220 Free Lutheran	3	386	195	486	.7	1.2
263 Int Foursq Gos	1	33	67	67 *	.1	.2
267 Muslim Est	1	NR	55	163	.2	.4
283 Luth—MO Synod	4	769	285	913	1.4	2.3
313 N Am Bapt Conf	1	277	360	339 *	.5	.8
355 Presb Ch (USA)	5	554	307	678 *	1.0	1.7
403 Salvation Army	1	110	44	282	.4	.7
413 S.D.A.	1	153	NR	182	.3	.5
419 So Bapt Conv	4	217	202	266 *	.4	.7
435 Unitarian-Univ	1	20	NR	24 *	-	.1
443 Un C of Christ	2	185	78	226 *	.3	.6
449 Un Methodist	5	1,187	599	1,452 *	2.2	3.6
496 Jewish Est	1	NR	NR	180	.3	.4
GRANT	**21**	**1,425**	**756**	**2,427 ***	**85.4**	**100.0**
053 Assemb of God	1	46	63	96	3.4	4.0
081 Catholic	4	NR	NR	700	24.6	28.8
181 Consrv Congr	1	76	65	90 *	3.2	3.7
207 E.L.C.A.	3	715	292	867	30.5	35.7
313 N Am Bapt Conf	1	100	95	118 *	4.2	4.9
335 Orth Pres Ch	1	40	39	50	1.8	2.1
355 Presb Ch (USA)	1	28	14	33 *	1.2	1.4
413 S.D.A.	1	10	NR	12	.4	.5
443 Un C of Christ	3	112	57	132 *	4.6	5.4
449 Un Methodist	2	96	47	113 *	4.0	4.7
469 WELS	3	202	84	216	7.6	8.9
GRIGGS	**18**	**1,376**	**737**	**2,054 ***	**74.6**	**100.0**
053 Assemb of God	1	27	30	41	1.5	2.0
056 Baha'i	0	3	NR	3	.1	.1
081 Catholic	2	NR	NR	381	13.8	18.5
203 Evan Free Ch	2	67	86	86	3.1	4.2
207 E.L.C.A.	8	971	439	1,168	42.4	56.9
220 Free Lutheran	1	87	70	110	4.0	5.4
283 Luth—MO Synod	2	150	72	181	6.6	8.8
355 Presb Ch (USA)	1	53	30	63 *	2.3	3.1
449 Un Methodist	1	18	10	21 *	.8	1.0
HETTINGER	**15**	**1,093**	**493**	**3,055 ***	**112.5**	**100.0**
053 Assemb of God	2	44	60	87	3.2	2.8
081 Catholic	3	NR	NR	1,714	63.1	56.1
181 Consrv Congr	1	122	65	146 *	5.4	4.8
203 Evan Free Ch	1	52	47	52	1.9	1.7
207 E.L.C.A.	5	725	265	877	32.3	28.7
443 Un C of Christ	3	150	56	179 *	6.6	5.9
KIDDER	**17**	**1,388**	**631**	**2,207 ***	**80.2**	**100.0**
081 Catholic	3	NR	NR	511	18.6	23.2
165 Ch of Nazarene	1	12	18	22	.8	1.0
207 E.L.C.A.	4	613	254	746	27.1	33.8
283 Luth—MO Synod	1	188	54	219	8.0	9.9
355 Presb Ch (USA)	1	22	12	26 *	.9	1.2
443 Un C of Christ	2	43	17	51 *	1.9	2.3
449 Un Methodist	4	300	188	357 *	13.0	16.2
469 WELS	1	210	88	275	10.0	12.5
LA MOURE	**36**	**2,685**	**1,390**	**4,625 ***	**98.4**	**100.0**
053 Assemb of God	1	58	74	120	2.6	2.6
057 Bapt Gen Conf	1	75	75	90 *	1.9	1.9
081 Catholic	6	NR	NR	1,242	26.4	26.9
165 Ch of Nazarene	1	57	78	107	2.3	2.3
181 Consrv Congr	1	150	111	180 *	3.8	3.9
207 E.L.C.A.	8	1,024	443	1,248	26.5	27.0
257 Hutterian Br	2	132	NR	200	4.3	4.3
283 Luth—MO Synod	4	504	268	600	12.8	13.0
355 Presb Ch (USA)	2	109	64	131 *	2.8	2.8
371 Ref Ch in Am	1	56	45	85	1.8	1.8
413 S.D.A.	2	79	NR	94	2.0	2.0
443 Un C of Christ	1	31	23	37 *	.8	.8
449 Un Methodist	6	410	209	491 *	10.4	10.6
LOGAN	**17**	**1,025**	**494**	**2,202 ***	**95.4**	**100.0**
053 Assemb of God	2	29	31	31	1.3	1.4
081 Catholic	4	NR	NR	1,016	44.0	46.1
203 Evan Free Ch	1	35	35	35	1.5	1.6
207 E.L.C.A.	3	550	204	623	27.0	28.3
283 Luth—MO Synod	1	54	15	67	2.9	3.0
313 N Am Bapt Conf	3	150	114	181 *	7.8	8.2
413 S.D.A.	1	13	NR	15	.6	.7
443 Un C of Christ	1	107	52	129 *	5.6	5.9
449 Un Methodist	1	87	43	105 *	4.5	4.8
MCHENRY	**30**	**3,087**	**996**	**5,010 ***	**83.7**	**100.0**
019 Amer Bapt USA	1	89	70	107 *	1.8	2.1
056 Baha'i	0	1	NR	1	-	-
081 Catholic	7	NR	NR	1,171	19.6	23.4
207 E.L.C.A.	11	2,223	560	2,790	46.6	55.7
283 Luth—MO Synod	5	480	189	589	9.8	11.8
313 N Am Bapt Conf	1	89	70	107 *	1.8	2.1
355 Presb Ch (USA)	1	39	20	47 *	.8	.9
443 Un C of Christ	1	77	34	92 *	1.5	1.8

NR–Not Reported   *Total adherents estimated from known number of communicant, confirmed, full members.   - Represents a percentage less than 0.1.   Percentages may not total 100 due to rounding.

Table 4: Religious Congregations by County and Group: 2000

Religious Group	Number of Churches, Synagogues, Mosques, or Temples	Number of Communicant, Confirmed, or Full Members	Number of Attendees	Total Adherents: Number of Adherents	% of Total Pop.	% of Total Adh.
449 Un Methodist	3	89	53	106 *	1.8	2.1
MCINTOSH	**18**	**2,614**	**1,005**	**3,756 ***	**110.8**	**100.0**
053 Assemb of God	1	25	17	22	.6	.6
081 Catholic	3	NR	NR	672	19.8	17.9
207 E.L.C.A.	2	1,390	354	1,691	49.9	45.0
283 Luth—MO Synod	1	46	30	46	1.4	1.2
313 N Am Bapt Conf	4	462	289	534 *	15.8	14.2
373 Ref Ch in U.S.	1	54	NR	58	1.7	1.5
413 S.D.A.	1	51	NR	61	1.8	1.6
443 Un C of Christ	1	216	110	250 *	7.4	6.7
449 Un Methodist	3	307	172	355 *	10.5	9.5
469 WELS	1	63	33	67	2.0	1.8
MCKENZIE	**27**	**2,146**	**931**	**3,339 ***	**58.2**	**100.0**
053 Assemb of God	1	86	130	163	2.8	4.9
056 Baha'i	0	29	NR	29	.5	.9
081 Catholic	3	NR	NR	338	5.9	10.1
165 Ch of Nazarene	1	5	6	11	.2	.3
193 Episcopal	1	NR	26	55	1.0	1.6
207 E.L.C.A.	10	1,582	539	2,161	37.7	64.7
283 Luth—MO Synod	2	85	15	7	.1	.2
355 Presb Ch (USA)	1	35	25	45 *	.8	1.3
413 S.D.A.	2	98	NR	117	2.0	3.5
419 So Bapt Conv	1	93	42	119 *	2.1	3.6
443 Un C of Christ	2	64	28	82 *	1.4	2.5
449 Un Methodist	1	6	5	8 *	.1	.2
467 Wesleyan	2	63	115	204	3.6	6.1
MCLEAN	**43**	**4,486**	**2,093**	**8,526 ***	**91.6**	**100.0**
053 Assemb of God	2	80	105	129	1.4	1.5
081 Catholic	8	NR	NR	2,719	29.2	31.9
127 Ch God (Cleve)	1	44	70	70 *	.8	.8
181 Consrv Congr	1	7	5	8 *	.1	.1
193 Episcopal	1	NR	12	180	1.9	2.1
203 Evan Free Ch	1	60	90	90	1.0	1.1
207 E.L.C.A.	13	2,773	1,026	3,484	37.4	40.9
283 Luth—MO Synod	3	450	205	564	6.1	6.6
313 N Am Bapt Conf	4	343	305	411 *	4.4	4.8
355 Presb Ch (USA)	1	85	45	102 *	1.1	1.2
356 Presb Ch Amer	1	53	40	61	.7	.7
413 S.D.A.	2	93	NR	111	1.2	1.3
443 Un C of Christ	2	248	80	297 *	3.2	3.5
449 Un Methodist	3	250	110	300 *	3.2	3.5
MERCER	**28**	**4,796**	**2,216**	**8,263 ***	**95.6**	**100.0**
053 Assemb of God	2	141	187	282	3.3	3.4
081 Catholic	2	NR	NR	1,955	22.6	23.7
127 Ch God (Cleve)	1	71	63	89 *	1.0	1.1
145 Ch God Prophcy	1	24	NR	29 *	.3	.4
151 L-D Saints	1	NR	NR	46	.5	.6
165 Ch of Nazarene	1	49	35	54	.6	.7
181 Consrv Congr	2	234	250	292 *	3.4	3.5
203 Evan Free Ch	1	18	30	30	.3	.4
207 E.L.C.A.	7	2,733	906	3,582	41.4	43.3
220 Free Lutheran	1	31	32	37	.4	.4
283 Luth—MO Synod	4	934	437	1,171	13.5	14.2
313 N Am Bapt Conf	1	205	144	256 *	3.0	3.1
413 S.D.A.	1	62	NR	74	.9	.9
419 So Bapt Conv	1	54	18	67 *	.8	.8
449 Un Methodist	2	240	114	299 *	3.5	3.6
MORTON	**43**	**5,272**	**2,122**	**21,180 ***	**83.7**	**100.0**
053 Assemb of God	2	95	126	156	.6	.7
056 Baha'i	0	8	NR	8	-	-
081 Catholic	12	NR	NR	13,511	53.4	63.8
151 L-D Saints	1	NR	NR	256	1.0	1.2
165 Ch of Nazarene	1	189	230	285	1.1	1.3
181 Consrv Congr	1	32	40	40 *	.2	.2
193 Episcopal	1	NR	12	11	-	.1
207 E.L.C.A.	6	2,123	642	3,356	13.3	15.8
283 Luth—MO Synod	3	568	239	727	2.9	3.4
313 N Am Bapt Conf	1	161	68	201 *	.8	.9
355 Presb Ch (USA)	1	306	111	382 *	1.5	1.8
413 S.D.A.	1	57	NR	68	.3	.3
419 So Bapt Conv	2	399	110	497 *	2.0	2.3
443 Un C of Christ	6	682	235	850 *	3.4	4.0
449 Un Methodist	3	436	185	543 *	2.1	2.6
467 Wesleyan	1	13	13	40	.2	.2
469 WELS	1	203	111	249	1.0	1.2
MOUNTRAIL	**28**	**2,500**	**927**	**4,220 ***	**63.6**	**100.0**
019 Amer Bapt USA	1	68	32	86 *	1.3	2.0
053 Assemb of God	2	75	97	201	3.0	4.8
056 Baha'i	0	11	NR	11	.2	.3
081 Catholic	4	NR	NR	1,019	15.4	24.1
193 Episcopal	1	NR	25	6	.1	.1
207 E.L.C.A.	11	1,839	553	2,222	33.5	52.7
220 Free Lutheran	2	261	130	331	5.0	7.8
339 Pent Ch of God	1	32	NR	75	1.1	1.8
355 Presb Ch (USA)	1	0	0	0 *	-	-
413 S.D.A.	1	19	NR	23	.3	.5
419 So Bapt Conv	1	37	20	47 *	.7	1.1
443 Un C of Christ	3	158	70	199 *	3.0	4.7
NELSON	**22**	**2,397**	**864**	**3,049 ***	**82.1**	**100.0**
081 Catholic	4	NR	NR	184	5.0	6.0
193 Episcopal	1	NR	8	19	.5	.6
207 E.L.C.A.	13	2,175	735	2,585	69.6	84.8
220 Free Lutheran	1	119	60	143	3.8	4.7
283 Luth—MO Synod	2	64	38	72	1.9	2.4
443 Un C of Christ	1	39	23	46 *	1.2	1.5
OLIVER	**4**	**667**	**228**	**1,436 ***	**69.5**	**100.0**
081 Catholic	1	NR	NR	713	34.5	49.7
207 E.L.C.A.	1	313	96	354	17.1	24.7
283 Luth—MO Synod	1	286	111	286	13.8	19.9
449 Un Methodist	1	68	21	83 *	4.0	5.8
PEMBINA	**45**	**3,955**	**1,885**	**7,225 ***	**84.2**	**100.0**
053 Assemb of God	3	120	149	238	2.8	3.3
056 Baha'i	0	3	NR	3	-	-
081 Catholic	9	NR	NR	1,956	22.8	27.1
179 Consrv Bapt	1	NR	75	75	.9	1.0
193 Episcopal	1	NR	19	20	.2	.3
201 Evan Cov Ch	1	58	33	70 *	.8	1.0
203 Evan Free Ch	2	99	193	193	2.2	2.7
207 E.L.C.A.	8	1,918	614	2,555	29.8	35.4
220 Free Lutheran	1	31	0	31	.4	.4
283 Luth—MO Synod	4	497	270	596	6.9	8.2
355 Presb Ch (USA)	4	466	161	564 *	6.6	7.8
419 So Bapt Conv	1	15	9	18 *	.2	.2
449 Un Methodist	10	748	362	906 *	10.6	12.5
PIERCE	**16**	**1,473**	**689**	**3,991 ***	**85.4**	**100.0**
053 Assemb of God	1	52	69	96	2.1	2.4
056 Baha'i	0	1	NR	1	-	-
081 Catholic	4	NR	NR	2,113	45.2	52.9
203 Evan Free Ch	1	34	100	100	2.1	2.5
207 E.L.C.A.	6	1,092	411	1,337	28.6	33.5
220 Free Lutheran	1	0	0	0	-	-
283 Luth—MO Synod	1	257	85	299	6.4	7.5
355 Presb Ch (USA)	1	18	12	22 *	.5	.6
449 Un Methodist	1	19	12	23 *	.5	.6
RAMSEY	**28**	**4,463**	**1,621**	**8,993 ***	**74.5**	**100.0**
053 Assemb of God	1	90	125	175	1.5	1.9
056 Baha'i	0	8	NR	8	.1	.1
081 Catholic	4	NR	NR	3,178	26.3	35.3
193 Episcopal	1	NR	14	29	.2	.3
203 Evan Free Ch	1	57	134	134	1.1	1.5
207 E.L.C.A.	10	3,188	894	4,110	34.1	45.7
220 Free Lutheran	3	250	112	307	2.5	3.4

NR–Not Reported *Total adherents estimated from known number of communicant, confirmed, full members. - Represents a percentage less than 0.1. Percentages may not total 100 due to rounding.

Table 4: Religious Congregations by County and Group: 2000

Religious Group	Number of Churches, Synagogues, Mosques, or Temples	Number of Communicant, Confirmed, or Full Members	Number of Attendees	Total Adherents		
				Number of Adherents	% of Total Pop.	% of Total Adh.
283 Luth—MO Synod	1	224	85	259	2.1	2.9
355 Presb Ch (USA)	2	135	61	166 *	1.4	1.8
413 S.D.A.	1	11	NR	13	.1	.1
419 So Bapt Conv	1	171	49	210 *	1.7	2.3
449 Un Methodist	3	329	147	404 *	3.3	4.5
RANSOM	**22**	**3,210**	**1,247**	**5,352 ***	**90.9**	**100.0**
019 Amer Bapt USA	1	80	40	98 *	1.7	1.8
053 Assemb of God	1	75	100	174	3.0	3.3
056 Baha'i	0	2	NR	2	-	-
081 Catholic	3	NR	NR	1,246	21.2	23.3
203 Evan Free Ch	1	69	125	125	2.1	2.3
207 E.L.C.A.	9	2,419	711	3,039	51.6	56.8
220 Free Lutheran	1	19	18	26	.4	.5
283 Luth—MO Synod	1	187	81	204	3.5	3.8
355 Presb Ch (USA)	1	31	15	38 *	.6	.7
413 S.D.A.	1	23	NR	27	.5	.5
449 Un Methodist	3	305	157	373 *	6.3	7.0
RENVILLE	**14**	**1,438**	**643**	**2,427 ***	**93.0**	**100.0**
019 Amer Bapt USA	1	57	18	68 *	2.6	2.8
081 Catholic	3	NR	NR	631	24.2	26.0
165 Ch of Nazarene	1	28	40	86	3.3	3.5
207 E.L.C.A.	6	1,139	451	1,395	53.4	57.5
283 Luth—MO Synod	1	93	50	104	4.0	4.3
449 Un Methodist	2	121	84	143 *	5.5	5.9
RICHLAND	**52**	**6,992**	**2,867**	**13,704 ***	**76.1**	**100.0**
053 Assemb of God	1	134	185	185	1.0	1.3
056 Baha'i	0	2	NR	2	-	-
081 Catholic	8	NR	NR	4,571	25.4	33.4
127 Ch God (Cleve)	1	42	44	51 *	.3	.4
151 L-D Saints	1	NR	NR	83	.5	.6
176 Congr Ad Afl	1	31	NR	38 *	.2	.3
193 Episcopal	1	NR	22	53	.3	.4
203 Evan Free Ch	1	55	126	126	.7	.9
207 E.L.C.A.	18	3,376	1,132	4,361	24.2	31.8
220 Free Lutheran	1	66	75	98	.5	.7
283 Luth—MO Synod	8	2,011	785	2,580	14.3	18.8
413 S.D.A.	1	115	NR	137	.8	1.0
443 Un C of Christ	3	410	145	502 *	2.8	3.7
449 Un Methodist	7	750	353	917 *	5.1	6.7
ROLETTE	**30**	**1,664**	**764**	**14,314 ***	**104.7**	**100.0**
053 Assemb of God	3	74	109	170	1.2	1.2
056 Baha'i	0	26	NR	26	.2	.2
081 Catholic	8	NR	NR	11,889	86.9	83.1
089 Chr & Miss Al	1	23	NR	39	.3	.3
127 Ch God (Cleve)	1	9	11	12 *	.1	.1
151 L-D Saints	1	NR	NR	76	.6	.5
193 Episcopal	1	NR	11	129	.9	.9
207 E.L.C.A.	7	970	361	1,220	8.9	8.5
283 Luth—MO Synod	1	173	66	224	1.6	1.6
288 Mennonite USA	1	47	45	65 *	.5	.5
297 Mennonite;Other	2	29	NR	40 *	.3	.3
339 Pent Ch of God	1	25	NR	25	.2	.2
355 Presb Ch (USA)	1	180	106	250 *	1.8	1.7
419 So Bapt Conv	0	9	10	12 *	.1	.1
449 Un Methodist	2	99	45	137 *	1.0	1.0
SARGENT	**20**	**2,170**	**890**	**4,108 ***	**94.1**	**100.0**
019 Amer Bapt USA	1	10	27	27 *	.6	.7
053 Assemb of God	1	35	47	53	1.2	1.3
081 Catholic	6	NR	NR	1,064	24.4	25.9
207 E.L.C.A.	7	1,838	589	2,372	54.3	57.7
257 Hutterian Br	1	66	NR	100	2.3	2.4
283 Luth—MO Synod	2	96	144	336	7.7	8.2
449 Un Methodist	2	125	83	156 *	3.6	3.8
SHERIDAN	**15**	**974**	**553**	**1,219 ***	**71.3**	**100.0**
019 Amer Bapt USA	1	8	25	25 *	1.5	2.1
053 Assemb of God	1	46	50	60	3.5	4.9
081 Catholic	1	NR	NR	36	2.1	3.0
207 E.L.C.A.	2	280	148	354	20.7	29.0
283 Luth—MO Synod	1	170	87	195	11.4	16.0
313 N Am Bapt Conf	3	225	148	262 *	15.3	21.5
373 Ref Ch in U.S.	1	29	NR	34	2.0	2.8
413 S.D.A.	2	77	NR	91	5.3	7.5
449 Un Methodist	3	139	95	162 *	9.5	13.3
SIOUX	**11**	**213**	**88**	**1,932 ***	**47.8**	**100.0**
053 Assemb of God	2	14	16	17	.4	.9
056 Baha'i	0	33	NR	33	.8	1.7
081 Catholic	5	NR	NR	1,197	29.6	62.0
193 Episcopal	2	NR	44	444	11.0	23.0
419 So Bapt Conv	1	134	14	195 *	4.8	10.1
443 Un C of Christ	1	32	14	46 *	1.1	2.4
SLOPE	**3**	**160**	**72**	**310 ***	**40.4**	**100.0**
081 Catholic	1	NR	NR	56	7.3	18.1
207 E.L.C.A.	1	88	42	169	22.0	54.5
443 Un C of Christ	1	72	30	85 *	11.1	27.4
STARK	**35**	**3,850**	**2,261**	**19,234 ***	**85.0**	**100.0**
019 Amer Bapt USA	1	25	30	31 *	.1	.2
053 Assemb of God	1	162	235	300	1.3	1.6
056 Baha'i	0	3	NR	3	-	-
081 Catholic	11	NR	NR	13,809	61.0	71.8
127 Ch God (Cleve)	1	9	13	13 *	.1	.1
151 L-D Saints	1	NR	NR	175	.8	.9
165 Ch of Nazarene	1	37	42	85	.4	.4
167 Chs of Christ	1	40	50	52	.2	.3
181 Consrv Congr	1	44	125	54 *	.2	.3
193 Episcopal	1	NR	16	33	.1	.2
207 E.L.C.A.	6	1,738	775	2,385	10.5	12.4
220 Free Lutheran	1	300	139	423	1.9	2.2
283 Luth—MO Synod	2	405	178	532	2.4	2.8
313 N Am Bapt Conf	1	237	223	292 *	1.3	1.5
355 Presb Ch (USA)	1	38	19	47 *	.2	.2
413 S.D.A.	1	24	NR	29	.1	.2
419 So Bapt Conv	1	191	145	235 *	1.0	1.2
443 Un C of Christ	2	244	94	301 *	1.3	1.6
449 Un Methodist	1	353	177	435 *	1.9	2.3
STEELE	**21**	**1,640**	**685**	**2,329 ***	**103.1**	**100.0**
053 Assemb of God	1	19	24	40	1.8	1.7
056 Baha'i	0	4	NR	4	.2	.2
081 Catholic	2	NR	NR	294	13.0	12.6
207 E.L.C.A.	13	1,428	569	1,758	77.9	75.5
283 Luth—MO Synod	1	70	28	84	3.7	3.6
355 Presb Ch (USA)	1	40	25	50 *	2.2	2.1
443 Un C of Christ	1	24	11	30 *	1.3	1.3
449 Un Methodist	2	55	28	69 *	3.1	3.0
STUTSMAN	**44**	**8,562**	**3,564**	**15,275 ***	**69.7**	**100.0**
053 Assemb of God	2	189	235	313	1.4	2.0
056 Baha'i	0	15	NR	15	.1	.1
057 Bapt Gen Conf	1	122	106	147 *	.7	1.0
081 Catholic	8	NR	NR	3,993	18.2	26.1
165 Ch of Nazarene	1	172	147	243	1.1	1.6
193 Episcopal	1	NR	52	128	.6	.8
203 Evan Free Ch	1	69	125	125	.6	.8
207 E.L.C.A.	9	4,546	1,563	6,033	27.5	39.5
221 Free Methodist	1	11	14	14	.1	.1
283 Luth—MO Synod	3	871	261	1,130	5.2	7.4
313 N Am Bapt Conf	2	184	175	221 *	1.0	1.4
355 Presb Ch (USA)	1	323	170	388 *	1.8	2.5
403 Salvation Army	1	61	25	130	.6	.9
413 S.D.A.	3	325	NR	387	1.8	2.5
443 Un C of Christ	3	411	151	494 *	2.3	3.2
449 Un Methodist	6	1,226	531	1,474 *	6.7	9.6
469 WELS	1	37	9	40	.2	.3

NR–Not Reported *Total adherents estimated from known number of communicant, confirmed, full members. - Represents a percentage less than 0.1. Percentages may not total 100 due to rounding.

Table 4: Religious Congregations by County and Group: 2000

Religious Group	Number of Churches, Synagogues, Mosques, or Temples	Number of Communicant, Confirmed, or Full Members	Number of Attendees	Total Adherents: Number of Adherents	Total Adherents: % of Total Pop.	Total Adherents: % of Total Adh.
TOWNER	**13**	**1,481**	**551**	**2,546 ***	**88.5**	**100.0**
053 Assemb of God	1	49	58	82	2.9	3.2
081 Catholic	3	NR	NR	592	20.6	23.3
157 Ch of Brethren	1	80	70	96 *	3.3	3.8
207 E.L.C.A.	4	866	257	1,175	40.9	46.2
283 Luth—MO Synod	1	241	64	308	10.7	12.1
355 Presb Ch (USA)	1	26	10	31 *	1.1	1.2
449 Un Methodist	2	219	92	262 *	9.1	10.3
TRAILL	**28**	**4,981**	**1,866**	**7,317 ***	**86.3**	**100.0**
056 Baha'i	0	3	NR	3	-	-
081 Catholic	2	NR	NR	914	10.8	12.5
203 Evan Free Ch	1	61	120	120	1.4	1.6
207 E.L.C.A.	18	4,299	1,403	5,510	65.0	75.3
220 Free Lutheran	3	145	79	185	2.2	2.5
283 Luth—MO Synod	1	193	95	242	2.9	3.3
443 Un C of Christ	2	194	112	238 *	2.8	3.3
449 Un Methodist	1	86	57	105 *	1.2	1.4
WALSH	**46**	**4,872**	**1,993**	**11,530 ***	**93.1**	**100.0**
053 Assemb of God	1	60	84	119	1.0	1.0
057 Bapt Gen Conf	1	41	45	50 *	.4	.4
081 Catholic	12	NR	NR	5,293	42.7	45.9
143 CG in Cr(Menn)	1	98	NR	120 *	1.0	1.0
165 Ch of Nazarene	1	6	12	18	.1	.2
193 Episcopal	1	NR	6	5	-	-
203 Evan Free Ch	1	25	60	60	.5	.5
207 E.L.C.A.	14	3,644	1,248	4,581	37.0	39.7
220 Free Lutheran	4	285	208	367	3.0	3.2
257 Hutterian Br	1	66	NR	100	.8	.9
283 Luth—MO Synod	1	174	100	240	1.9	2.1
355 Presb Ch (USA)	5	310	128	378 *	3.1	3.3
449 Un Methodist	3	163	102	199 *	1.6	1.7
WARD	**81**	**14,429**	**7,193**	**32,496 ***	**55.3**	**100.0**
019 Amer Bapt USA	2	329	250	412 *	.7	1.3
053 Assemb of God	2	415	547	985	1.7	3.0
056 Baha'i	1	35	NR	35	.1	.1
081 Catholic	10	NR	NR	11,562	19.7	35.6
089 Chr & Miss Al	1	48	NR	115	.2	.4
097 Chr Chs&Chs Cr	1	50	NR	63 *	.1	.2
127 Ch God (Cleve)	1	222	190	278 *	.5	.9
145 Ch God Prophcy	1	24	NR	30 *	.1	.1
151 L-D Saints	3	NR	NR	865	1.5	2.7
157 Ch of Brethren	1	33	0	41 *	.1	.1
165 Ch of Nazarene	4	321	269	478	.8	1.5
167 Chs of Christ	1	140	140	210	.4	.6
173 Comm of Christ	1	99	NR	99	.2	.3
193 Episcopal	1	NR	58	136	.2	.4
203 Evan Free Ch	1	72	192	192	.3	.6
207 E.L.C.A.	21	7,488	2,967	9,922	16.9	30.5
220 Free Lutheran	1	157	106	229	.4	.7
237 Menn Br US Conf	1	57	NR	71 *	.1	.2
267 Muslim Est	1	NR	55	163	.3	.5
283 Luth—MO Synod	5	1,846	749	2,554	4.3	7.9
288 Mennonite USA	1	39	35	49 *	.1	.2
313 N Am Bapt Conf	1	359	494	450 *	.8	1.4
331 OCA: Ter Diocs	1	29	NR	48	.1	.1
355 Presb Ch (USA)	2	725	216	908 *	1.5	2.8
373 Ref Ch in U.S.	1	36	NR	52	.1	.2
403 Salvation Army	1	106	25	241	.4	.7
413 S.D.A.	1	179	NR	213	.4	.7
419 So Bapt Conv	5	317	228	397 *	.7	1.2
443 Un C of Christ	1	221	109	277 *	.5	.9
449 Un Methodist	5	1,048	514	1,313 *	2.2	4.0
467 Wesleyan	1	21	40	95	.2	.3
469 WELS	1	13	9	13	-	-
WELLS	**30**	**2,224**	**989**	**4,420 ***	**86.6**	**100.0**
053 Assemb of God	1	36	45	60	1.2	1.4
081 Catholic	5	NR	NR	1,586	31.1	35.9
123 Ch God (Ander)	1	NR	75	75	1.5	1.7

Religious Group	Number of Churches, Synagogues, Mosques, or Temples	Number of Communicant, Confirmed, or Full Members	Number of Attendees	Total Adherents: Number of Adherents	Total Adherents: % of Total Pop.	Total Adherents: % of Total Adh.
165 Ch of Nazarene	2	51	38	57	1.1	1.3
207 E.L.C.A.	10	1,288	567	1,630	31.9	36.9
237 Menn Br US Conf	1	140	NR	166 *	3.3	3.8
283 Luth—MO Synod	1	90	31	110	2.2	2.5
313 N Am Bapt Conf	2	219	175	260 *	5.1	5.9
413 S.D.A.	5	308	NR	367	7.2	8.3
449 Un Methodist	2	92	58	109 *	2.1	2.5
WILLIAMS	**46**	**7,129**	**3,362**	**15,686 ***	**79.4**	**100.0**
053 Assemb of God	2	192	242	399	2.0	2.5
056 Baha'i	0	2	NR	2	-	-
081 Catholic	5	NR	NR	4,161	21.1	26.5
089 Chr & Miss Al	1	15	NR	50	.3	.3
151 L-D Saints	1	NR	NR	217	1.1	1.4
165 Ch of Nazarene	1	55	45	102	.5	.7
167 Chs of Christ	1	40	50	55	.3	.4
173 Comm of Christ	1	33	NR	33	.2	.2
193 Episcopal	1	NR	48	132	.7	.8
203 Evan Free Ch	1	35	100	100	.5	.6
207 E.L.C.A.	18	4,791	1,602	7,136	36.1	45.5
220 Free Lutheran	4	690	297	889	4.5	5.7
283 Luth—MO Synod	1	249	110	355	1.8	2.3
355 Presb Ch (USA)	1	38	45	47 *	.2	.3
403 Salvation Army	1	54	29	122	.6	.8
413 S.D.A.	1	66	NR	79	.4	.5
419 So Bapt Conv	1	230	120	283 *	1.4	1.8
443 Un C of Christ	1	75	45	92 *	.5	.6
449 Un Methodist	2	432	210	532 *	2.7	3.4
467 Wesleyan	2	132	419	900	4.6	5.7

OHIO

Religious Group	Number of Churches, Synagogues, Mosques, or Temples	Number of Communicant, Confirmed, or Full Members	Number of Attendees	Total Adherents: Number of Adherents	Total Adherents: % of Total Pop.	Total Adherents: % of Total Adh.
The State.....	11,167	1,918,844	983,633	5,102,269 *	44.9	100.0
ADAMS	**68**	**4,095**	**1,918**	**5,990 ***	**21.9**	**100.0**
056 Baha'i	0	10	NR	10	-	.2
081 Catholic	3	NR	NR	394	1.4	6.6
097 Chr Chs&Chs Cr	8	1,130	NR	1,415 *	5.2	23.6
107 Christian Un	10	429	418	537 *	2.0	9.0
123 Ch God (Ander)	1	NR	72	72	.3	1.2
127 Ch God (Cleve)	2	83	28	104 *	.4	1.7
151 L-D Saints	1	NR	NR	241	.9	4.0
157 Ch of Brethren	2	12	4	15 *	.1	.3
165 Ch of Nazarene	3	188	193	403	1.5	6.7
167 Chs of Christ	3	65	68	75	.3	1.3
323 Old Ord Amish	5	300	NR	375 *	1.4	6.3
355 Presb Ch (USA)	7	466	261	584 *	2.1	9.7
413 S.D.A.	1	35	NR	42	.2	.7
419 So Bapt Conv	4	299	115	374 *	1.4	6.2
449 Un Methodist	18	1,078	759	1,349 *	4.9	22.5
ALLEN	**125**	**24,273**	**12,283**	**59,133 ***	**54.5**	**100.0**
019 Amer Bapt USA	4	996	364	1,244 *	1.1	2.1
053 Assemb of God	4	271	320	480	.4	.8
056 Baha'i	0	25	NR	25	-	-
081 Catholic	8	NR	NR	24,630	22.7	41.7
089 Chr & Miss Al	2	319	NR	617	.6	1.0
093 Chr Ch (Disc)	2	1,100	445	1,374 *	1.3	2.3
097 Chr Chs&Chs Cr	1	90	NR	112 *	.1	.2
107 Christian Un	2	36	61	61 *	.1	.1
123 Ch God (Ander)	1	NR	179	179	.2	.3
127 Ch God (Cleve)	1	18	15	22 *	-	-
151 L-D Saints	1	NR	NR	461	.4	.8
157 Ch of Brethren	4	767	445	958 *	.9	1.6
165 Ch of Nazarene	3	1,391	1,809	2,120	2.0	3.6
167 Chs of Christ	2	194	145	257	.2	.4
173 Comm of Christ	1	51	NR	51	-	.1
175 Congr Chr Chs	1	95	130	119 *	.1	.2
193 Episcopal	1	NR	54	143	.1	.2
203 Evan Free Ch	1	52	100	100	.1	.2
207 E.L.C.A.	7	2,582	915	3,440	3.2	5.8
223 Free Will Bapt	1	61	NR	76 *	.1	.1

NR–Not Reported   *Total adherents estimated from known number of communicant, confirmed, full members.   - Represents a percentage less than 0.1.   Percentages may not total 100 due to rounding.

Table 4: Religious Congregations by County and Group: 2000

Religious Group	Number of Churches, Synagogues, Mosques, or Temples	Number of Communicant, Confirmed, or Full Members	Number of Attendees	Total Adherents		
				Number of Adherents	% of Total Pop.	% of Total Adh.
226 Friends-USA	2	82	NR	102 *	.1	.2
267 Muslim Est	2	NR	126	488	.4	.8
283 Luth—MO Synod	1	345	185	428	.4	.7
288 Mennonite USA	4	820	543	1,024 *	.9	1.7
291 Missionary Ch	4	262	378	386	.4	.7
297 Mennonite;Other	2	822	NR	1,027 *	.9	1.7
331 OCA: Ter Diocs	1	15	NR	50	-	.1
339 Pent Ch of God	1	110	NR	410	.4	.7
355 Presb Ch (USA)	5	995	381	1,242 *	1.1	2.1
379 Ref Mennonite	1	33	NR	41 *	-	.1
388 Reg Bapt Gen As	3	360	365	396 *	.4	.7
403 Salvation Army	2	188	66	1,710	1.6	2.9
419 So Bapt Conv	3	877	77	1,095 *	1.0	1.9
435 Unitarian-Univ	1	25	NR	31 *	-	.1
443 Un C of Christ	8	1,898	659	2,370 *	2.2	4.0
449 Un Methodist	30	6,702	3,063	8,368 *	7.7	14.2
466 Wayn Tr MB Asc	2	974	NR	1,216 *	1.1	2.1
467 Wesleyan	3	117	108	200	.2	.3
496 Jewish Est	1	NR	NR	180	.2	.3
498 Indep.Charis.	1	250	250	550	.5	.9
499 Indep.Non-Char	1	1,350	1,100	1,350	1.2	2.3
ASHLAND	**86**	**14,183**	**6,851**	**21,819 ***	**41.5**	**100.0**
019 Amer Bapt USA	2	613	203	761 *	1.4	3.5
053 Assemb of God	1	159	201	345	.7	1.6
056 Baha'i	0	5	NR	5	-	-
071 Brethren (Ash)	3	583	871	724 *	1.4	3.3
075 Brethren in Cr	1	110	81	110	.2	.5
081 Catholic	3	NR	NR	1,885	3.6	8.6
089 Chr & Miss Al	2	120	NR	215	.4	1.0
093 Chr Ch (Disc)	1	388	220	482 *	.9	2.2
097 Chr Chs&Chs Cr	5	663	NR	824 *	1.6	3.8
123 Ch God (Ander)	2	NR	55	55	.1	.3
127 Ch God (Cleve)	3	299	131	370 *	.7	1.7
157 Ch of Brethren	3	561	317	696 *	1.3	3.2
165 Ch of Nazarene	3	289	230	407	.8	1.9
167 Chs of Christ	3	303	315	425	.8	1.9
171 Ch God-Gen Con	1	21	15	26 *	-	.1
175 Congr Chr Chs	1	115	85	143 *	.3	.7
193 Episcopal	1	NR	61	114	.2	.5
203 Evan Free Ch	1	105	155	155	.3	.7
207 E.L.C.A.	10	3,654	1,564	4,593	8.7	21.1
226 Friends-USA	1	35	NR	43 *	.1	.2
246 Greek Orthodox	1	NR	NR	1,698	3.2	7.8
263 Int Foursq Gos	1	78	25	97 *	.2	.4
323 Old Ord Amish	10	580	NR	716 *	1.4	3.3
355 Presb Ch (USA)	5	666	328	826 *	1.6	3.8
388 Reg Bapt Gen As	2	89	85	110 *	.2	.5
403 Salvation Army	1	57	15	103	.2	.5
419 So Bapt Conv	0	23	35	29 *	.1	.1
443 Un C of Christ	1	184	81	228 *	.4	1.0
449 Un Methodist	17	3,733	1,428	4,634 *	8.8	21.2
499 Indep.Non-Char	1	750	350	1,000	1.9	4.6
ASHTABULA	**136**	**16,498**	**8,250**	**41,091 ***	**40.0**	**100.0**
011 A.W.M.C.	2	41	123	44	-	.1
019 Amer Bapt USA	6	1,374	630	1,717 *	1.7	4.2
053 Assemb of God	6	616	808	1,008	1.0	2.5
056 Baha'i	0	12	NR	12	-	-
081 Catholic	13	NR	NR	18,447	18.0	44.9
089 Chr & Miss Al	2	164	NR	485	.5	1.2
093 Chr Ch (Disc)	2	325	137	406 *	.4	1.0
097 Chr Chs&Chs Cr	4	652	NR	815 *	.8	2.0
123 Ch God (Ander)	2	NR	125	125	.1	.3
127 Ch God (Cleve)	4	563	307	704 *	.7	1.7
145 Ch God Prophcy	1	32	NR	40 *	-	.1
151 L-D Saints	1	NR	NR	396	.4	1.0
165 Ch of Nazarene	7	1,314	1,032	1,880	1.8	4.6
167 Chs of Christ	2	170	175	215	.2	.5
181 Consrv Congr	2	158	66	197 *	.2	.5
193 Episcopal	4	NR	212	503	.5	1.2
201 Evan Cov Ch	1	102	40	127 *	.1	.3
203 Evan Free Ch	1	65	85	85	.1	.2

Religious Group	Number of Churches, Synagogues, Mosques, or Temples	Number of Communicant, Confirmed, or Full Members	Number of Attendees	Total Adherents		
				Number of Adherents	% of Total Pop.	% of Total Adh.
207 E.L.C.A.	5	1,752	568	2,165	2.1	5.3
221 Free Methodist	1	18	17	18	-	-
263 Int Foursq Gos	1	10	44	44 *	-	.1
283 Luth—MO Synod	2	487	226	624	.6	1.5
297 Mennonite;Other	1	40	NR	50 *	-	.1
323 Old Ord Amish	7	420	NR	525 *	.5	1.3
339 Pent Ch of God	2	189	NR	424	.4	1.0
349 Pent Holiness	1	26	26	32 *	-	.1
355 Presb Ch (USA)	10	1,478	739	1,847 *	1.8	4.5
388 Reg Bapt Gen As	2	211	218	274 *	.3	.7
403 Salvation Army	1	36	20	36	-	.1
413 S.D.A.	2	125	NR	149	.1	.4
419 So Bapt Conv	4	351	127	439 *	.4	1.1
443 Un C of Christ	10	1,513	526	1,891 *	1.8	4.6
449 Un Methodist	26	4,254	1,999	5,317 *	5.2	12.9
496 Jewish Est	1	NR	NR	50	-	.1
ATHENS	**90**	**8,496**	**4,556**	**13,923 ***	**22.4**	**100.0**
011 A.W.M.C.	1	0	6	0	-	-
019 Amer Bapt USA	2	459	345	533 *	.9	3.8
053 Assemb of God	1	114	157	250	.4	1.8
056 Baha'i	0	14	NR	14	-	.1
081 Catholic	4	NR	NR	1,951	3.1	14.0
093 Chr Ch (Disc)	7	536	72	622 *	1.0	4.5
097 Chr Chs&Chs Cr	9	1,653	NR	1,919 *	3.1	13.8
123 Ch God (Ander)	2	NR	60	60	.1	.4
145 Ch God Prophcy	1	32	NR	37 *	.1	.3
151 L-D Saints	1	NR	NR	272	.4	2.0
165 Ch of Nazarene	3	223	173	245	.4	1.8
167 Chs of Christ	2	151	111	178	.3	1.3
193 Episcopal	2	NR	107	317	.5	2.3
207 E.L.C.A.	1	431	148	550	.9	4.0
221 Free Methodist	1	0	12	12	-	.1
226 Friends-USA	1	35	NR	41 *	.1	.3
267 Muslim Est	1	NR	115	200	.3	1.4
355 Presb Ch (USA)	5	646	271	756 *	1.2	5.4
388 Reg Bapt Gen As	3	614	584	713 *	1.1	5.1
403 Salvation Army	1	47	35	94	.2	.7
413 S.D.A.	1	77	NR	92	.1	.7
419 So Bapt Conv	3	333	149	387 *	.6	2.8
435 Unitarian-Univ	1	59	NR	68 *	.1	.5
449 Un Methodist	26	2,390	1,428	2,773 *	4.5	19.9
463 Vineyard	1	130	120	151 *	.2	1.1
467 Wesleyan	9	552	663	1,588	2.6	11.4
496 Jewish Est	1	NR	NR	100	.2	.7
AUGLAIZE	**65**	**11,936**	**5,515**	**29,229 ***	**62.7**	**100.0**
019 Amer Bapt USA	2	351	215	444 *	1.0	1.5
053 Assemb of God	2	163	210	345	.7	1.2
081 Catholic	7	NR	NR	12,250	26.3	41.9
084 Calvary Chapel	1	NR	NR	NR	-	-
089 Chr & Miss Al	2	294	NR	1,015	2.2	3.5
097 Chr Chs&Chs Cr	3	310	NR	393 *	.8	1.3
107 Christian Un	1	69	100	100 *	.2	.3
123 Ch God (Ander)	2	NR	401	401	.9	1.4
151 L-D Saints	1	NR	NR	156	.3	.5
165 Ch of Nazarene	4	510	407	810	1.7	2.8
167 Chs of Christ	1	61	80	95	.2	.3
171 Ch God-Gen Con	1	48	48	61 *	.1	.2
173 Comm of Christ	1	34	NR	34	.1	.1
207 E.L.C.A.	5	2,157	732	2,876	6.2	9.8
226 Friends-USA	1	47	NR	60 *	.1	.2
283 Luth—MO Synod	1	166	89	201	.4	.7
291 Missionary Ch	1	0	139	139	.3	.5
355 Presb Ch (USA)	1	54	53	68 *	.1	.2
360 Prim Bapt Chrch	1	NR	NR	NR	-	-
388 Reg Bapt Gen As	1	80	110	110 *	.2	.4
419 So Bapt Conv	2	275	186	348 *	.7	1.2
443 Un C of Christ	6	3,671	1,332	4,649 *	10.0	15.9
449 Un Methodist	15	3,305	1,386	4,188 *	9.0	14.3
466 Wayn Tr MB Asc	2	309	NR	391 *	.8	1.3
467 Wesleyan	1	32	27	95	.2	.3

NR–Not Reported *Total adherents estimated from known number of communicant, confirmed, full members. - Represents a percentage less than 0.1. Percentages may not total 100 due to rounding.

Table 4: Religious Congregations by County and Group: 2000

Religious Group	Number of Churches, Synagogues, Mosques, or Temples	Number of Communicant, Confirmed, or Full Members	Number of Attendees	Total Adherents		
				Number of Adherents	% of Total Pop.	% of Total Adh.
BELMONT	**144**	**15,064**	**6,444**	**28,597 ***	**40.7**	**100.0**
019 Amer Bapt USA	1	162	83	193 *	.3	.7
022 Carp Rus Orth	1	122	NR	207	.3	.7
053 Assemb of God	3	249	309	329	.5	1.2
056 Baha'i	0	1	NR	1	-	-
081 Catholic	18	NR	NR	9,174	13.1	32.1
089 Chr & Miss Al	1	82	NR	111	.2	.4
093 Chr Ch (Disc)	2	553	138	659 *	.9	2.3
097 Chr Chs&Chs Cr	8	1,778	NR	2,120 *	3.0	7.4
123 Ch God (Ander)	2	NR	105	105	.1	.4
151 L-D Saints	1	NR	NR	431	.6	1.5
165 Ch of Nazarene	7	303	212	491	.7	1.7
167 Chs of Christ	18	1,074	968	1,413	2.0	4.9
173 Comm of Christ	2	82	NR	82	.1	.3
193 Episcopal	2	NR	52	151	.2	.5
207 E.L.C.A.	4	914	374	1,282	1.8	4.5
226 Friends-USA	4	272	NR	324 *	.5	1.1
246 Greek Orthodox	1	NR	NR	120	.2	.4
288 Mennonite USA	1	54	43	64 *	.1	.2
323 Old Ord Amish	1	50	NR	60 *	.1	.2
355 Presb Ch (USA)	22	2,883	1,322	3,442 *	4.9	12.0
403 Salvation Army	1	81	59	164	.2	.6
419 So Bapt Conv	3	351	200	418 *	.6	1.5
443 Un C of Christ	1	56	23	67 *	.1	.2
449 Un Methodist	39	5,956	2,495	7,104 *	10.1	24.8
467 Wesleyan	1	41	61	85	.1	.3
BROWN	**61**	**6,894**	**2,565**	**12,019 ***	**28.4**	**100.0**
053 Assemb of God	2	82	85	115	.3	1.0
081 Catholic	7	NR	NR	2,760	6.5	23.0
097 Chr Chs&Chs Cr	10	2,207	NR	2,801 *	6.6	23.3
127 Ch God (Cleve)	1	218	162	277 *	.7	2.3
151 L-D Saints	1	NR	NR	271	.6	2.3
165 Ch of Nazarene	4	379	382	655	1.5	5.4
167 Chs of Christ	2	65	70	96	.2	.8
207 E.L.C.A.	1	402	122	457	1.1	3.8
355 Presb Ch (USA)	5	315	210	400 *	.9	3.3
419 So Bapt Conv	9	2,021	757	2,566 *	6.1	21.3
443 Un C of Christ	1	60	26	76 *	.2	.6
449 Un Methodist	16	1,053	614	1,339 *	3.2	11.1
467 Wesleyan	2	92	137	206	.5	1.7
BUTLER	**243**	**58,873**	**38,957**	**128,806 ***	**38.7**	**100.0**
017 Amer Bapt Assn	2	100	NR	126 *	-	.1
019 Amer Bapt USA	5	2,724	1,012	3,409 *	1.0	2.6
053 Assemb of God	5	980	877	2,095	.6	1.6
056 Baha'i	1	42	NR	42	-	-
081 Catholic	13	NR	NR	43,390	13.0	33.7
089 Chr & Miss Al	3	195	NR	421	.1	.3
093 Chr Ch (Disc)	3	1,267	308	1,586 *	.5	1.2
097 Chr Chs&Chs Cr	12	3,176	NR	3,973 *	1.2	3.1
105 Christian Ref	1	74	70	93 *	-	.1
123 Ch God (Ander)	20	NR	3,083	3,083	.9	2.4
127 Ch God (Cleve)	12	6,730	5,427	8,436 *	2.5	6.5
145 Ch God Prophcy	2	64	NR	80 *	-	.1
151 L-D Saints	5	NR	NR	1,777	.5	1.4
165 Ch of Nazarene	11	2,967	1,900	3,643	1.1	2.8
167 Chs of Christ	10	806	785	947	.3	.7
173 Comm of Christ	1	86	NR	86	-	.1
179 Consrv Bapt	1	NR	45	45	-	-
191 Entrpr Bpt Asc	1	75	NR	94 *	-	.1
193 Episcopal	4	NR	612	1,455	.4	1.1
201 Evan Cov Ch	1	124	146	155 *	-	.1
207 E.L.C.A.	9	3,103	1,336	4,303	1.3	3.3
223 Free Will Bapt	2	122	NR	153 *	-	.1
226 Friends-USA	2	105	NR	131 *	-	.1
246 Greek Orthodox	1	NR	NR	195	.1	.2
263 Int Foursq Gos	1	34	43	43 *	-	-
267 Muslim Est	1	NR	250	2,000	.6	1.6
268 Jain	1	NR	NR	NR	-	-
283 Luth—MO Synod	3	1,033	475	1,389	.4	1.1
288 Mennonite USA	1	138	55	173 *	.1	.1
291 Missionary Ch	2	29	40	41	-	-
339 Pent Ch of God	1	135	NR	165	-	.1
355 Presb Ch (USA)	16	3,907	2,080	4,890 *	1.5	3.8
360 Prim Bapt Chrch	1	NR	NR	NR	-	-
388 Reg Bapt Gen As	1	50	50	63 *	-	-
403 Salvation Army	2	282	94	1,678	.5	1.3
413 S.D.A.	3	166	NR	197	.1	.2
416 Sikh	1	NR	NR	NR	-	-
419 So Bapt Conv	40	16,695	11,476	20,893 *	6.3	16.2
435 Unitarian-Univ	1	65	NR	81 *	-	.1
443 Un C of Christ	5	1,571	583	1,966 *	.6	1.5
449 Un Methodist	25	7,512	4,642	9,399 *	2.8	7.3
463 Vineyard	1	420	380	526 *	.2	.4
467 Wesleyan	4	300	288	888	.3	.7
496 Jewish Est	2	NR	NR	900	.3	.7
498 Indep.Charis.	4	3,796	2,900	3,796	1.1	2.9
CARROLL	**49**	**5,170**	**2,429**	**8,710 ***	**30.2**	**100.0**
053 Assemb of God	2	68	80	157	.5	1.8
056 Baha'i	0	1	NR	1	-	-
061 Beachy Amish	1	16	NR	20 *	.1	.2
081 Catholic	4	NR	NR	1,894	6.6	21.7
093 Chr Ch (Disc)	1	250	85	309 *	1.1	3.5
097 Chr Chs&Chs Cr	2	465	NR	574 *	2.0	6.6
165 Ch of Nazarene	2	94	101	184	.6	2.1
167 Chs of Christ	1	47	50	60	.2	.7
207 E.L.C.A.	4	1,011	352	1,415	4.9	16.2
263 Int Foursq Gos	1	197	221	243 *	.8	2.8
323 Old Ord Amish	2	120	NR	148 *	.5	1.7
331 OCA: Ter Diocs	1	49	NR	54	.2	.6
355 Presb Ch (USA)	7	475	290	593 *	2.1	6.8
413 S.D.A.	1	22	NR	26	.1	.3
419 So Bapt Conv	1	0	0	0 *	-	-
449 Un Methodist	18	2,330	1,189	2,879 *	10.0	33.1
467 Wesleyan	1	25	61	153	.5	1.8
CHAMPAIGN	**53**	**6,345**	**3,158**	**9,766 ***	**25.1**	**100.0**
019 Amer Bapt USA	5	1,172	463	1,465 *	3.8	15.0
056 Baha'i	0	6	NR	6	-	.1
081 Catholic	4	NR	NR	1,208	3.1	12.4
097 Chr Chs&Chs Cr	1	145	NR	181 *	.5	1.9
121 Ch God (Abr)	1	14	24	24 *	.1	.2
123 Ch God (Ander)	3	NR	235	235	.6	2.4
145 Ch God Prophcy	2	64	NR	80 *	.2	.8
165 Ch of Nazarene	3	330	280	623	1.6	6.4
167 Chs of Christ	2	90	100	124	.3	1.3
183 Cons Menn Conf	1	96	117	140	.4	1.4
193 Episcopal	2	NR	80	123	.3	1.3
207 E.L.C.A.	2	650	210	831	2.1	8.5
221 Free Methodist	1	40	41	41	.1	.4
223 Free Will Bapt	3	184	NR	229 *	.6	2.3
226 Friends-USA	4	380	NR	475 *	1.2	4.9
288 Mennonite USA	1	168	180	210 *	.5	2.2
291 Missionary Ch	1	51	75	75	.2	.8
355 Presb Ch (USA)	2	376	145	470 *	1.2	4.8
388 Reg Bapt Gen As	1	250	250	313 *	.8	3.2
401 Rus Orth Abroad	1	NR	NR	NR	-	-
419 So Bapt Conv	2	68	42	85 *	.2	.9
449 Un Methodist	11	2,261	916	2,828 *	7.3	29.0
CLARK	**165**	**26,547**	**13,772**	**49,444 ***	**34.2**	**100.0**
017 Amer Bapt Assn	1	50	NR	62 *	-	.1
019 Amer Bapt USA	6	1,050	555	1,300 *	.9	2.6
053 Assemb of God	3	175	204	378	.3	.8
056 Baha'i	0	11	NR	11	-	-
075 Brethren in Cr	1	26	39	39	-	.1
081 Catholic	7	NR	NR	12,166	8.4	24.6
093 Chr Ch (Disc)	2	455	20	563 *	.4	1.1
097 Chr Chs&Chs Cr	7	2,237	NR	2,770 *	1.9	5.6
121 Ch God (Abr)	2	86	131	134 *	.1	.3
123 Ch God (Ander)	8	NR	1,534	1,534	1.1	3.1
127 Ch God (Cleve)	3	633	286	783 *	.5	1.6
151 L-D Saints	1	NR	NR	789	.5	1.6
157 Ch of Brethren	2	836	366	1,036 *	.7	2.1

NR–Not Reported   *Total adherents estimated from known number of communicant, confirmed, full members.   - Represents a percentage less than 0.1.   Percentages may not total 100 due to rounding.

Table 4: Religious Congregations by County and Group: 2000

Religious Group	Number of Churches, Synagogues, Mosques, or Temples	Number of Communicant, Confirmed, or Full Members	Number of Attendees	Total Adherents: Number of Adherents	Total Adherents: % of Total Pop.	Total Adherents: % of Total Adh.
165 Ch of Nazarene	7	1,314	1,089	1,828	1.3	3.7
167 Chs of Christ	6	406	395	491	.3	1.0
191 Entrpr Bpt Asc	1	46	NR	57 *	-	.1
193 Episcopal	1	NR	128	279	.2	.6
207 E.L.C.A.	15	4,562	1,670	5,916	4.1	12.0
223 Free Will Bapt	8	489	NR	606 *	.4	1.2
226 Friends-USA	1	95	NR	118 *	.1	.2
246 Greek Orthodox	1	NR	NR	192	.1	.4
262 Int Cou Comm Ch	1	190	NR	235 *	.2	.5
263 Int Foursq Gos	1	52	211	211 *	.1	.4
265 Int Pent C Chr	2	250	193	471	.3	1.0
267 Muslim Est	2	NR	40	110	.1	.2
283 Luth—MO Synod	1	251	144	345	.2	.7
288 Mennonite USA	3	352	378	440 *	.3	.9
291 Missionary Ch	2	64	141	150	.1	.3
339 Pent Ch of God	2	68	NR	143	.1	.3
355 Presb Ch (USA)	6	1,379	648	1,707 *	1.2	3.5
360 Prim Bapt Chrch	1	NR	NR	NR	-	-
388 Reg Bapt Gen As	4	1,129	1,263	1,371 *	.9	2.8
403 Salvation Army	1	149	77	287	.2	.6
413 S.D.A.	3	255	NR	304	.2	.6
419 So Bapt Conv	9	2,465	876	3,052 *	2.1	6.2
443 Un C of Christ	8	1,421	680	1,759 *	1.2	3.6
449 Un Methodist	32	5,809	2,493	7,193 *	5.0	14.5
463 Vineyard	1	100	60	124 *	.1	.3
467 Wesleyan	1	50	60	150	.1	.3
469 WELS	1	92	91	140	.1	.3
496 Jewish Est	1	NR	NR	200	.1	.4
CLERMONT	**136**	**22,265**	**10,408**	**55,654 ***	**31.3**	**100.0**
017 Amer Bapt Assn	2	100	NR	128 *	.1	.2
019 Amer Bapt USA	2	165	100	211 *	.1	.4
034 Ant Orth of NA	1	65	NR	130	.1	.2
053 Assemb of God	6	383	479	585	.3	1.1
056 Baha'i	0	24	NR	24	-	-
081 Catholic	12	NR	NR	25,949	14.6	46.6
097 Chr Chs&Chs Cr	18	4,518	NR	5,771 *	3.2	10.4
123 Ch God (Ander)	3	NR	243	243	.1	.4
127 Ch God (Cleve)	8	842	454	1,076 *	.6	1.9
151 L-D Saints	1	NR	NR	392	.2	.7
165 Ch of Nazarene	10	1,210	905	1,470	.8	2.6
167 Chs of Christ	3	435	533	679	.4	1.2
173 Comm of Christ	1	69	NR	69	-	.1
179 Consrv Bapt	1	NR	72	72	-	.1
193 Episcopal	1	NR	40	54	-	.1
203 Evan Free Ch	1	419	720	720	.4	1.3
207 E.L.C.A.	2	414	258	677	.4	1.2
223 Free Will Bapt	1	61	NR	78 *	-	.1
283 Luth—MO Synod	1	428	222	680	.4	1.2
355 Presb Ch (USA)	6	641	408	819 *	.5	1.5
360 Prim Bapt Chrch	1	NR	NR	NR	-	-
403 Salvation Army	1	63	51	168	.1	.3
413 S.D.A.	1	173	NR	206	.1	.4
418 Southw Bapt Fel	2	NR	NR	NR	-	-
419 So Bapt Conv	19	4,895	1,525	6,253 *	3.5	11.2
443 Un C of Christ	1	35	15	45 *	-	.1
449 Un Methodist	27	5,875	2,975	7,506 *	4.2	13.5
463 Vineyard	2	320	320	409 *	.2	.7
467 Wesleyan	1	130	88	240	.1	.4
499 Indep.Non-Char	1	1,000	1,000	1,000	.6	1.8
CLINTON	**62**	**8,488**	**2,972**	**13,703 ***	**33.8**	**100.0**
019 Amer Bapt USA	2	255	125	320 *	.8	2.3
053 Assemb of God	1	117	153	163	.4	1.2
056 Baha'i	0	3	NR	3	-	-
081 Catholic	3	NR	NR	2,481	6.1	18.1
093 Chr Ch (Disc)	1	456	141	572 *	1.4	4.2
097 Chr Chs&Chs Cr	6	1,765	NR	2,214 *	5.5	16.2
123 Ch God (Ander)	2	NR	175	175	.4	1.3
127 Ch God (Cleve)	1	243	152	305 *	.8	2.2
151 L-D Saints	1	NR	NR	226	.6	1.6
165 Ch of Nazarene	3	370	265	442	1.1	3.2
167 Chs of Christ	2	43	45	55	.1	.4
193 Episcopal	1	NR	15	29	.1	.2
207 E.L.C.A.	1	311	122	424	1.0	3.1
223 Free Will Bapt	2	122	NR	154 *	.4	1.1
226 Friends-USA	11	693	NR	870 *	2.1	6.3
355 Presb Ch (USA)	1	452	190	567 *	1.4	4.1
360 Prim Bapt Chrch	1	NR	NR	NR	-	-
362 Prim Bapt E Dst	1	36	NR	45 *	.1	.3
388 Reg Bapt Gen As	1	194	160	243 *	.6	1.8
413 S.D.A.	1	57	NR	68	.2	.5
419 So Bapt Conv	6	1,024	357	1,285 *	3.2	9.4
443 Un C of Christ	1	94	41	118 *	.3	.9
449 Un Methodist	12	2,250	971	2,824 *	7.0	20.6
467 Wesleyan	1	3	60	120	.3	.9
COLUMBIANA	**161**	**24,439**	**10,091**	**45,315 ***	**40.4**	**100.0**
011 A.W.M.C.	1	100	318	104	.1	.2
019 Amer Bapt USA	3	433	203	530 *	.5	1.2
053 Assemb of God	7	642	741	1,427	1.3	3.1
056 Baha'i	0	6	NR	6	-	-
061 Beachy Amish	1	100	NR	122 *	.1	.3
071 Brethren (Ash)	1	139	111	170 *	.2	.4
081 Catholic	11	NR	NR	13,174	11.8	29.1
093 Chr Ch (Disc)	3	1,777	487	2,176 *	1.9	4.8
097 Chr Chs&Chs Cr	13	3,201	NR	3,921 *	3.5	8.7
123 Ch God (Ander)	1	NR	22	22	-	-
127 Ch God (Cleve)	2	223	97	273 *	.2	.6
143 CG in Cr(Menn)	1	110	NR	135 *	.1	.3
151 L-D Saints	2	NR	NR	786	.7	1.7
157 Ch of Brethren	2	179	138	220 *	.2	.5
165 Ch of Nazarene	9	1,423	891	1,525	1.4	3.4
167 Chs of Christ	7	486	518	632	.6	1.4
193 Episcopal	3	NR	137	379	.3	.8
207 E.L.C.A.	8	2,393	874	3,350	3.0	7.4
221 Free Methodist	3	146	187	197	.2	.4
226 Friends-USA	8	652	NR	798 *	.7	1.8
288 Mennonite USA	1	116	130	142 *	.1	.3
297 Mennonite;Other	5	343	NR	421 *	.4	.9
322 Old Ord Menn Ch	2	230	NR	282 *	.3	.6
323 Old Ord Amish	1	60	NR	73 *	.1	.2
355 Presb Ch (USA)	25	4,099	1,937	5,018 *	4.5	11.1
356 Presb Ch Amer	1	188	125	227	.2	.5
388 Reg Bapt Gen As	3	226	208	208 *	.2	.5
403 Salvation Army	2	230	112	452	.4	1.0
413 S.D.A.	1	55	NR	65	.1	.1
419 So Bapt Conv	2	199	110	244 *	.2	.5
443 Un C of Christ	3	840	335	1,029 *	.9	2.3
449 Un Methodist	28	5,843	2,410	7,157 *	6.4	15.8
496 Jewish Est	1	NR	NR	50	-	.1
COSHOCTON	**72**	**9,548**	**4,493**	**14,302 ***	**39.0**	**100.0**
019 Amer Bapt USA	4	861	422	1,073 *	2.9	7.5
032 Amish; other	2	48	NR	60 *	.2	.4
053 Assemb of God	1	35	44	125	.3	.9
056 Baha'i	0	1	NR	1	-	-
061 Beachy Amish	1	57	NR	71 *	.2	.5
081 Catholic	1	NR	NR	1,600	4.4	11.2
089 Chr & Miss Al	1	26	NR	60	.2	.4
093 Chr Ch (Disc)	1	323	76	403 *	1.1	2.8
097 Chr Chs&Chs Cr	1	40	NR	50 *	.1	.3
123 Ch God (Ander)	1	NR	46	46	.1	.3
127 Ch God (Cleve)	1	65	32	81 *	.2	.6
165 Ch of Nazarene	4	614	575	920	2.5	6.4
167 Chs of Christ	6	269	288	350	1.0	2.4
193 Episcopal	1	NR	40	94	.3	.7
207 E.L.C.A.	2	562	136	705	1.9	4.9
263 Int Foursq Gos	1	105	116	131 *	.4	.9
288 Mennonite USA	1	21	30	30 *	.1	.2
323 Old Ord Amish	4	240	NR	300 *	.8	2.1
339 Pent Ch of God	2	24	NR	128	.3	.9
355 Presb Ch (USA)	5	723	363	901 *	2.5	6.3
388 Reg Bapt Gen As	1	213	309	309 *	.8	2.2
403 Salvation Army	1	251	73	422	1.2	3.0
413 S.D.A.	1	48	NR	57	.2	.4

NR–Not Reported *Total adherents estimated from known number of communicant, confirmed, full members. - Represents a percentage less than 0.1. Percentages may not total 100 due to rounding.

Table 4: Religious Congregations by County and Group: 2000

Religious Group	Number of Churches, Synagogues, Mosques, or Temples	Number of Communicant, Confirmed, or Full Members	Number of Attendees	Total Adherents		
				Number of Adherents	% of Total Pop.	% of Total Adh.
419 So Bapt Conv	2	224	93	279 *	.8	2.0
443 Un C of Christ	3	387	170	482 *	1.3	3.4
449 Un Methodist	22	4,291	1,546	5,349 *	14.6	37.4
467 Wesleyan	2	120	134	275	.8	1.9
CRAWFORD	**85**	**13,965**	**6,791**	**25,477 ***	**54.2**	**100.0**
019 Amer Bapt USA	1	110	50	136 *	.3	.5
053 Assemb of God	2	169	211	475	1.0	1.9
056 Baha'i	0	7	NR	7	-	-
081 Catholic	5	NR	NR	7,556	16.1	29.7
089 Chr & Miss Al	2	178	NR	327	.7	1.3
093 Chr Ch (Disc)	1	170	46	210 *	.4	.8
097 Chr Chs&Chs Cr	3	380	NR	469 *	1.0	1.8
127 Ch God (Cleve)	2	252	103	312 *	.7	1.2
145 Ch God Prophcy	2	64	NR	78 *	.2	.3
165 Ch of Nazarene	3	1,137	901	1,382	2.9	5.4
167 Chs of Christ	2	103	110	134	.3	.5
193 Episcopal	2	NR	19	35	.1	.1
207 E.L.C.A.	15	4,423	1,798	5,665	12.1	22.2
221 Free Methodist	1	156	227	227	.5	.9
223 Free Will Bapt	3	184	NR	227 *	.5	.9
263 Int Foursq Gos	1	33	26	41 *	.1	.2
265 Int Pent C Chr	1	54	30	95	.2	.4
339 Pent Ch of God	1	22	NR	60	.1	.2
355 Presb Ch (USA)	3	459	223	567 *	1.2	2.2
388 Reg Bapt Gen As	3	185	195	203 *	.4	.8
403 Salvation Army	1	63	37	173	.4	.7
413 S.D.A.	3	204	NR	243	.5	1.0
419 So Bapt Conv	1	75	65	93 *	.2	.4
443 Un C of Christ	5	1,480	587	1,829 *	3.9	7.2
449 Un Methodist	20	3,170	1,444	3,917 *	8.3	15.4
467 Wesleyan	1	12	19	141	.3	.6
499 Indep.Non-Char	1	875	700	875	1.9	3.4
CUYAHOGA	**775**	**145,163**	**80,444**	**805,896 ***	**57.8**	**100.0**
007 OCA: Alban Dioc	1	NR	NR	200	-	-
019 Amer Bapt USA	33	19,177	8,294	23,833 *	1.7	3.0
022 Carp Rus Orth	1	122	NR	207	-	-
034 Ant Orth of NA	2	773	NR	1,546	.1	.2
039 Ap Chr Ch(Naz)	1	25	64	64 *	-	-
049 Armen Ap Cilic	1	32	NR	105	-	-
050 Armen Ap Etchm	1	97	NR	420	-	.1
053 Assemb of God	22	2,651	3,212	6,983	.5	.9
056 Baha'i	7	395	NR	395	-	-
057 Bapt Gen Conf	1	95	350	350 *	-	-
071 Brethren (Ash)	1	2,661	2,000	3,307 *	.2	.4
076 Buddhism	9	NR	NR	NR	-	-
081 Catholic	156	NR	NR	485,999	34.9	60.3
084 Calvary Chapel	1	NR	NR	NR	-	-
089 Chr & Miss Al	7	688	NR	1,741	.1	.2
093 Chr Ch (Disc)	20	5,364	1,910	6,666 *	.5	.8
097 Chr Chs&Chs Cr	6	894	NR	1,111 *	.1	.1
105 Christian Ref	2	333	260	414 *	-	.1
121 Ch God (Abr)	1	35	35	43 *	-	-
123 Ch God (Ander)	10	NR	1,042	1,042	.1	.1
127 Ch God (Cleve)	10	2,674	1,435	3,403 *	.2	.4
145 Ch God Prophcy	4	127	NR	160 *	-	-
151 L-D Saints	7	NR	NR	2,327	.2	.3
157 Ch of Brethren	1	161	101	200 *	-	-
165 Ch of Nazarene	10	1,404	2,557	4,542	.3	.6
167 Chs of Christ	13	1,654	1,572	2,392	.2	.3
173 Comm of Christ	1	108	NR	108	-	-
175 Congr Chr Chs	1	150	86	186 *	-	-
193 Episcopal	23	NR	2,738	9,185	.7	1.1
201 Evan Cov Ch	1	161	147	200 *	-	-
203 Evan Free Ch	2	140	410	410	-	.1
207 E.L.C.A.	41	14,669	6,585	19,764	1.4	2.5
213 Evan Menn Inc	1	0	145	0 *	-	-
220 Free Lutheran	1	30	25	30	-	-
221 Free Methodist	3	131	250	254	-	-
223 Free Will Bapt	6	367	NR	456 *	-	.1
226 Friends-USA	5	415	NR	516 *	-	.1
246 Greek Orthodox	4	NR	NR	5,400	.4	.7
252 Hindu	4	NR	NR	NR	-	-
262 Int Cou Comm Ch	1	160	NR	199 *	-	-
263 Int Foursq Gos	5	520	864	864 *	.1	.1
264 Int Chs of Crst	1	161	277	216	-	-
267 Muslim Est	14	NR	4,025	20,304	1.5	2.5
268 Jain	2	NR	NR	NR	-	-
283 Luth—MO Synod	43	16,830	8,471	23,099	1.7	2.9
288 Mennonite USA	3	510	350	633 *	-	.1
291 Missionary Ch	2	58	118	118	-	-
304 NatPrimBapt USA	1	455	NR	565 *	-	.1
313 N Am Bapt Conf	3	1,122	1,305	1,394 *	.1	.2
331 OCA: Ter Diocs	7	1,582	NR	2,029	.1	.3
339 Pent Ch of God	1	3	NR	5	-	-
349 Pent Holiness	1	30	30	37 *	-	-
355 Presb Ch (USA)	34	11,805	5,632	14,671 *	1.1	1.8
356 Presb Ch Amer	1	45	60	66	-	-
363 Primitive Meth	1	57	NR	61	-	-
370 Ref Baptist Chs	1	NR	NR	NR	-	-
371 Ref Ch in Am	4	408	408	713	.1	.1
388 Reg Bapt Gen As	13	2,618	2,352	3,257 *	.2	.4
395 Romania Orth Ar	1	NR	NR	700	.1	.1
397 OCA: Roman Dioc	1	NR	NR	1,000	.1	.1
401 Rus Orth Abroad	3	NR	NR	NR	-	-
403 Salvation Army	10	743	493	2,925	.2	.4
410 Serb Orth USA	1	NR	NR	1,000	.1	.1
411 Serb Orth: Grac	1	NR	NR	NR	-	-
413 S.D.A.	15	5,156	NR	6,135	.4	.8
416 Sikh	2	NR	NR	NR	-	-
418 Southw Bapt Fel	2	NR	NR	NR	-	-
419 So Bapt Conv	24	3,729	2,520	4,634 *	.3	.6
431 Ukrainian Orth	4	NR	NR	2,337	.2	.3
435 Unitarian-Univ	5	1,290	NR	1,603 *	.1	.2
443 Un C of Christ	44	14,569	5,574	18,106 *	1.3	2.2
449 Un Methodist	57	24,398	9,179	30,321 *	2.2	3.8
463 Vineyard	1	350	200	435 *	-	.1
469 WELS	1	81	68	110	-	-
496 Jewish Est	39	NR	NR	79,000	5.7	9.8
498 Indep.Charis.	3	1,250	1,600	1,700	.1	.2
499 Indep.Non-Char	2	1,700	3,700	3,700	.3	.5
DARKE	**85**	**11,055**	**5,965**	**22,533 ***	**42.3**	**100.0**
053 Assemb of God	1	80	89	173	.3	.8
081 Catholic	5	NR	NR	6,946	13.0	30.8
089 Chr & Miss Al	1	45	NR	67	.1	.3
097 Chr Chs&Chs Cr	2	440	NR	551 *	1.0	2.4
123 Ch God (Ander)	1	NR	277	277	.5	1.2
127 Ch God (Cleve)	1	225	87	281 *	.5	1.2
151 L-D Saints	1	NR	NR	153	.3	.7
157 Ch of Brethren	7	1,109	348	1,386 *	2.6	6.2
165 Ch of Nazarene	2	172	102	353	.7	1.6
167 Chs of Christ	1	30	35	30	.1	.1
181 Consrv Congr	1	314	141	393 *	.7	1.7
193 Episcopal	1	NR	58	119	.2	.5
207 E.L.C.A.	8	2,003	843	2,847	5.3	12.6
291 Missionary Ch	2	232	347	347	.7	1.5
296 Midw Congr Fel	8	396	341	495 *	.9	2.2
355 Presb Ch (USA)	3	468	282	586 *	1.1	2.6
388 Reg Bapt Gen As	2	309	353	386 *	.7	1.7
419 So Bapt Conv	8	1,163	429	1,454 *	2.7	6.5
435 Unitarian-Univ	1	23	NR	29 *	.1	.1
443 Un C of Christ	3	475	186	594 *	1.1	2.6
449 Un Methodist	21	3,327	1,701	4,161 *	7.8	18.5
467 Wesleyan	4	244	346	855	1.6	3.8
496 Jewish Est	1	NR	NR	50	.1	.2
DEFIANCE	**70**	**11,987**	**5,841**	**25,691 ***	**65.0**	**100.0**
019 Amer Bapt USA	1	478	375	598 *	1.5	2.3
040 Ap Chr Ch-Amer	1	86	197	197 *	.5	.8
053 Assemb of God	3	210	291	347	.9	1.4
056 Baha'i	0	1	NR	1	-	-
061 Beachy Amish	1	43	NR	54 *	.1	.2
081 Catholic	7	NR	NR	9,033	22.9	35.2
097 Chr Chs&Chs Cr	4	911	NR	1,140 *	2.9	4.4

NR–Not Reported *Total adherents estimated from known number of communicant, confirmed, full members. - Represents a percentage less than 0.1. Percentages may not total 100 due to rounding.

Table 4: Religious Congregations by County and Group: 2000

Religious Group	Number of Churches, Synagogues, Mosques, or Temples	Number of Communicant, Confirmed, or Full Members	Number of Attendees	Total Adherents		
				Number of Adherents	% of Total Pop.	% of Total Adh.
123 Ch God (Ander)	2	NR	349	349	.9	1.4
127 Ch God (Cleve)	2	102	67	128 *	.3	.5
151 L-D Saints	2	NR	NR	624	1.6	2.4
157 Ch of Brethren	2	200	138	251 *	.6	1.0
165 Ch of Nazarene	2	219	187	421	1.1	1.6
167 Chs of Christ	1	80	67	104	.3	.4
171 Ch God-Gen Con	1	160	186	200 *	.5	.8
183 Cons Menn Conf	1	151	184	220	.6	.9
193 Episcopal	1	NR	53	99	.3	.4
207 E.L.C.A.	5	1,962	787	2,481	6.3	9.7
283 Luth—MO Synod	5	2,678	1,078	3,483	8.8	13.6
288 Mennonite USA	1	23	23	29 *	.1	.1
323 Old Ord Amish	1	60	NR	75 *	.2	.3
339 Pent Ch of God	2	37	NR	107	.3	.4
355 Presb Ch (USA)	2	379	152	474 *	1.2	1.8
388 Reg Bapt Gen As	1	16	40	40 *	.1	.2
413 S.D.A.	2	102	NR	122	.3	.5
419 So Bapt Conv	5	500	305	625 *	1.6	2.4
443 Un C of Christ	2	390	168	488 *	1.2	1.9
449 Un Methodist	12	3,041	1,194	3,803 *	9.6	14.8
466 Wayn Tr MB Asc	1	158	NR	198 *	.5	.8
DELAWARE	**85**	**12,747**	**6,600**	**38,800 ***	**35.3**	**100.0**
019 Amer Bapt USA	4	885	463	1,139 *	1.0	2.9
053 Assemb of God	3	124	172	251	.2	.6
056 Baha'i	0	13	NR	13	-	-
076 Buddhism	1	NR	NR	NR	-	-
081 Catholic	4	NR	NR	20,003	18.2	51.6
097 Chr Chs&Chs Cr	4	580	NR	747 *	.7	1.9
107 Christian Un	1	20	37	37 *	-	.1
123 Ch God (Ander)	1	NR	75	75	.1	.2
127 Ch God (Cleve)	1	103	43	133 *	.1	.3
151 L-D Saints	3	NR	NR	1,020	.9	2.6
157 Ch of Brethren	1	98	69	126 *	.1	.3
165 Ch of Nazarene	2	357	446	895	.8	2.3
167 Chs of Christ	3	230	208	314	.3	.8
193 Episcopal	1	NR	104	268	.2	.7
201 Evan Cov Ch	1	105	150	150 *	.1	.4
203 Evan Free Ch	1	69	125	125	.1	.3
207 E.L.C.A.	2	812	374	1,070	1.0	2.8
223 Free Will Bapt	3	184	NR	236 *	.2	.6
226 Friends-USA	5	415	NR	534 *	.5	1.4
252 Hindu	1	NR	NR	NR	-	-
283 Luth—MO Synod	1	160	116	204	.2	.5
355 Presb Ch (USA)	7	2,585	1,102	3,327 *	3.0	8.6
360 Prim Bapt Chrch	1	NR	NR	NR	-	-
371 Ref Ch in Am	1	301	258	535	.5	1.4
388 Reg Bapt Gen As	2	55	68	72 *	.1	.2
403 Salvation Army	1	39	18	150	.1	.4
413 S.D.A.	2	121	NR	144	.1	.4
419 So Bapt Conv	1	142	71	183 *	.2	.5
435 Unitarian-Univ	2	152	NR	196 *	.2	.5
443 Un C of Christ	3	728	351	937 *	.9	2.4
449 Un Methodist	18	4,311	2,198	5,548 *	5.0	14.3
467 Wesleyan	3	53	66	220	.2	.6
469 WELS	1	105	86	148	.1	.4
ERIE	**74**	**14,852**	**6,590**	**42,557 ***	**53.5**	**100.0**
019 Amer Bapt USA	1	88	40	108 *	.1	.3
053 Assemb of God	4	784	719	1,017	1.3	2.4
056 Baha'i	0	2	NR	2	-	-
081 Catholic	6	NR	NR	22,107	27.8	51.9
089 Chr & Miss Al	2	75	NR	158	.2	.4
097 Chr Chs&Chs Cr	1	250	NR	307 *	.4	.7
127 Ch God (Cleve)	4	514	274	632 *	.8	1.5
145 Ch God Prophcy	2	64	NR	78 *	.1	.2
165 Ch of Nazarene	2	345	373	748	.9	1.8
167 Chs of Christ	3	280	220	340	.4	.8
173 Comm of Christ	1	47	NR	47	.1	.1
181 Consrv Congr	1	293	117	360 *	.5	.8
193 Episcopal	2	NR	171	748	.9	1.8
207 E.L.C.A.	8	4,012	1,440	5,774	7.3	13.6
223 Free Will Bapt	2	122	NR	150 *	.2	.4
226 Friends-USA	1	95	NR	117 *	.1	.3
263 Int Foursq Gos	1	152	145	187 *	.2	.4
283 Luth—MO Synod	1	161	82	215	.3	.5
355 Presb Ch (USA)	3	618	256	760 *	1.0	1.8
388 Reg Bapt Gen As	2	302	327	372 *	.5	.9
403 Salvation Army	1	26	15	82	.1	.2
413 S.D.A.	1	23	NR	27	-	.1
419 So Bapt Conv	4	557	309	685 *	.9	1.6
435 Unitarian-Univ	1	25	NR	31 *	-	.1
443 Un C of Christ	9	3,478	1,130	4,278 *	5.4	10.1
449 Un Methodist	10	2,539	972	3,122 *	3.9	7.3
496 Jewish Est	1	NR	NR	105	.1	.2
FAIRFIELD	**135**	**22,416**	**10,540**	**44,929 ***	**36.6**	**100.0**
019 Amer Bapt USA	1	49	37	62 *	.1	.1
053 Assemb of God	4	385	326	475	.4	1.1
056 Baha'i	0	7	NR	7	-	-
081 Catholic	6	NR	NR	14,314	11.7	31.9
097 Chr Chs&Chs Cr	7	2,320	NR	2,927 *	2.4	6.5
107 Christian Un	2	79	94	100 *	.1	.2
123 Ch God (Ander)	2	NR	180	180	.1	.4
127 Ch God (Cleve)	4	407	172	524 *	.4	1.2
151 L-D Saints	3	NR	NR	1,189	1.0	2.6
165 Ch of Nazarene	5	823	572	1,162	.9	2.6
167 Chs of Christ	4	301	295	419	.3	.9
173 Comm of Christ	1	76	NR	76	.1	.2
183 Cons Menn Conf	2	53	65	77	.1	.2
193 Episcopal	2	NR	187	437	.4	1.0
207 E.L.C.A.	18	3,929	1,404	5,158	4.2	11.5
221 Free Methodist	1	34	50	50	-	.1
223 Free Will Bapt	2	122	NR	154 *	.1	.3
283 Luth—MO Synod	3	816	368	1,090	.9	2.4
323 Old Ord Amish	1	60	NR	76 *	.1	.2
335 Orth Pres Ch	1	25	46	46	-	.1
355 Presb Ch (USA)	6	1,117	513	1,410 *	1.1	3.1
360 Prim Bapt Chrch	1	NR	NR	NR	-	-
388 Reg Bapt Gen As	4	455	464	591 *	.5	1.3
403 Salvation Army	1	133	67	159	.1	.4
419 So Bapt Conv	7	1,256	583	1,585 *	1.3	3.5
443 Un C of Christ	7	1,137	439	1,435 *	1.2	3.2
449 Un Methodist	36	8,035	4,082	10,139 *	8.3	22.6
463 Vineyard	2	306	246	387 *	.3	.9
467 Wesleyan	1	41	50	200	.2	.4
499 Indep.Non-Char	1	450	300	500	.4	1.1
FAYETTE	**38**	**5,098**	**1,988**	**7,451 ***	**26.2**	**100.0**
019 Amer Bapt USA	2	430	87	534 *	1.9	7.2
053 Assemb of God	1	130	145	170	.6	2.3
056 Baha'i	0	1	NR	1	-	-
081 Catholic	1	NR	NR	658	2.3	8.8
097 Chr Chs&Chs Cr	5	1,320	NR	1,640 *	5.8	22.0
123 Ch God (Ander)	2	NR	84	84	.3	1.1
165 Ch of Nazarene	1	240	185	242	.9	3.2
167 Chs of Christ	2	115	140	135	.5	1.8
193 Episcopal	1	NR	57	172	.6	2.3
207 E.L.C.A.	2	253	134	389	1.4	5.2
223 Free Will Bapt	1	61	NR	76 *	.3	1.0
265 Int Pent C Chr	1	12	16	24	.1	.3
355 Presb Ch (USA)	3	541	222	672 *	2.4	9.0
360 Prim Bapt Chrch	1	NR	NR	NR	-	-
419 So Bapt Conv	1	43	11	53 *	.2	.7
449 Un Methodist	11	1,889	823	2,346 *	8.3	31.5
467 Wesleyan	3	63	84	255	.9	3.4
FRANKLIN	**623**	**165,221**	**90,584**	**402,125 ***	**37.6**	**100.0**
011 A.W.M.C.	1	0	12	0	-	-
019 Amer Bapt USA	30	10,200	5,868	12,747 *	1.2	3.2
039 Ap Chr Ch(Naz)	1	30	35	37 *	-	-
040 Ap Chr Ch-Amer	1	19	36	36 *	-	-
050 Armen Ap Etchm	1	0	NR	245	-	.1
053 Assemb of God	16	1,833	2,089	3,054	.3	.8
056 Baha'i	4	355	NR	355	-	.1
057 Bapt Gen Conf	2	107	136	136 *	-	-

NR–Not Reported *Total adherents estimated from known number of communicant, confirmed, full members. - Represents a percentage less than 0.1. Percentages may not total 100 due to rounding.

Table 4: Religious Congregations by County and Group: 2000

Religious Group	Number of Churches, Synagogues, Mosques, or Temples	Number of Communicant, Confirmed, or Full Members	Number of Attendees	Total Adherents		
				Number of Adherents	% of Total Pop.	% of Total Adh.
071 Brethren (Ash)	2	158	160	197 *	-	-
076 Buddhism	10	NR	NR	NR	-	-
081 Catholic	52	NR	NR	146,767	13.7	36.5
084 Calvary Chapel	1	NR	NR	NR	-	-
089 Chr & Miss Al	8	390	NR	883	.1	.2
093 Chr Ch (Disc)	12	6,377	2,258	7,969 *	.7	2.0
097 Chr Chs&Chs Cr	25	9,453	NR	11,813 *	1.1	2.9
105 Christian Ref	1	105	80	131 *	-	-
107 Christian Un	1	50	49	62 *	-	-
123 Ch God (Ander)	11	NR	2,911	2,911	.3	.7
127 Ch God (Cleve)	11	2,971	1,681	3,714 *	.3	.9
145 Ch God Prophcy	4	127	NR	160 *	-	-
151 L-D Saints	11	NR	NR	4,349	.4	1.1
165 Ch of Nazarene	26	5,524	5,663	7,446	.7	1.9
167 Chs of Christ	25	2,741	2,703	3,619	.3	.9
173 Comm of Christ	6	526	NR	526	-	.1
175 Congr Chr Chs	1	150	125	187 *	-	-
179 Consrv Bapt	1	NR	87	87	-	-
183 Cons Menn Conf	1	82	100	119	-	-
191 Entrpr Bpt Asc	4	297	NR	371 *	-	.1
193 Episcopal	14	NR	2,131	6,298	.6	1.6
201 Evan Cov Ch	1	129	138	161 *	-	-
203 Evan Free Ch	1	44	98	98	-	-
207 E.L.C.A.	46	21,881	11,015	30,320	2.8	7.5
213 Evan Menn Inc	1	0	175	0 *	-	-
221 Free Methodist	3	141	213	213	-	.1
223 Free Will Bapt	17	1,040	NR	1,300 *	.1	.3
226 Friends-USA	3	225	NR	281 *	-	.1
246 Greek Orthodox	1	NR	NR	2,400	.2	.6
252 Hindu	4	NR	NR	NR	-	-
262 Int Cou Comm Ch	2	311	NR	388 *	-	.1
263 Int Foursq Gos	2	55	69	69 *	-	-
264 Int Chs of Crst	1	129	198	181	-	-
265 Int Pent C Chr	2	53	56	180	-	-
267 Muslim Est	3	NR	1,400	6,150	.6	1.5
268 Jain	2	NR	NR	NR	-	-
283 Luth—MO Synod	8	2,385	1,363	3,189	.3	.8
288 Mennonite USA	2	156	175	195 *	-	-
290 Metro Comm Ch	1	57	71	71 *	-	-
293 Morav Ch-North	1	150	NR	202	-	.1
330 Macedonian Orth	1	NR	NR	1,000	.1	.2
331 OCA: Ter Diocs	1	120	NR	455	-	.1
335 Orth Pres Ch	1	154	188	246	-	.1
349 Pent Holiness	1	22	20	27 *	-	-
355 Presb Ch (USA)	35	12,896	5,610	16,113 *	1.5	4.0
356 Presb Ch Amer	3	311	480	493	-	.1
360 Prim Bapt Chrch	3	NR	NR	NR	-	-
370 Ref Baptist Chs	1	NR	NR	NR	-	-
371 Ref Ch in Am	1	148	131	268	-	.1
388 Reg Bapt Gen As	10	2,195	2,293	2,747 *	.3	.7
403 Salvation Army	5	478	295	957	.1	.2
410 Serb Orth USA	1	NR	NR	170	-	-
413 S.D.A.	8	2,402	NR	2,859	.3	.7
416 Sikh	3	NR	NR	NR	-	-
418 Southw Bapt Fel	1	NR	NR	NR	-	-
419 So Bapt Conv	36	17,905	5,626	22,375 *	2.1	5.6
435 Unitarian-Univ	2	576	NR	720 *	.1	.2
443 Un C of Christ	11	7,801	2,898	9,749 *	.9	2.4
449 Un Methodist	83	35,443	17,161	44,285 *	4.1	11.0
463 Vineyard	4	9,577	6,427	11,968 *	1.1	3.0
467 Wesleyan	4	988	1,796	4,458	.4	1.1
469 WELS	3	770	389	1,038	.1	.3
496 Jewish Est	11	NR	NR	15,600	1.5	3.9
498 Indep.Charis.	5	2,700	2,590	2,700	.3	.7
499 Indep.Non-Char	5	2,484	3,585	4,280	.4	1.1
FULTON	**68**	**13,392**	**8,364**	**27,311 ***	**64.9**	**100.0**
053 Assemb of God	2	293	324	490	1.2	1.8
056 Baha'i	0	4	NR	4	-	-
081 Catholic	5	NR	NR	8,911	21.2	32.6
089 Chr & Miss Al	1	64	NR	184	.4	.7
093 Chr Ch (Disc)	5	1,269	461	1,619 *	3.8	5.9
097 Chr Chs&Chs Cr	4	561	NR	716 *	1.7	2.6
107 Christian Un	1	191	339	339 *	.8	1.2
123 Ch God (Ander)	1	NR	139	139	.3	.5
151 L-D Saints	1	NR	NR	213	.5	.8
157 Ch of Brethren	1	23	0	29 *	.1	.1
165 Ch of Nazarene	5	447	369	685	1.6	2.5
167 Chs of Christ	1	15	12	25	.1	.1
207 E.L.C.A.	5	1,971	848	2,460	5.8	9.0
213 Evan Menn Inc	2	1,179	1,179	1,504 *	3.6	5.5
283 Luth—MO Synod	3	862	521	1,150	2.7	4.2
288 Mennonite USA	7	1,868	1,456	2,393 *	5.7	8.8
291 Missionary Ch	2	324	643	643	1.5	2.4
379 Ref Mennonite	1	17	NR	22 *	.1	.1
388 Reg Bapt Gen As	2	168	480	511 *	1.2	1.9
413 S.D.A.	1	41	NR	49	.1	.2
419 So Bapt Conv	2	456	160	582 *	1.4	2.1
435 Unitarian-Univ	1	47	NR	60 *	.1	.2
443 Un C of Christ	3	702	470	896 *	2.1	3.3
449 Un Methodist	12	2,890	963	3,687 *	8.8	13.5
GALLIA	**55**	**6,774**	**3,373**	**8,987 ***	**28.9**	**100.0**
019 Amer Bapt USA	5	1,078	496	1,328 *	4.3	14.8
053 Assemb of God	1	27	16	25	.1	.3
056 Baha'i	0	2	NR	2	-	-
081 Catholic	1	NR	NR	474	1.5	5.3
097 Chr Chs&Chs Cr	3	646	NR	796 *	2.6	8.9
123 Ch God (Ander)	1	NR	142	142	.5	1.6
127 Ch God (Cleve)	3	184	149	227 *	.7	2.5
145 Ch God Prophcy	1	32	NR	39 *	.1	.4
165 Ch of Nazarene	2	322	287	546	1.8	6.1
167 Chs of Christ	1	90	70	115	.4	1.3
175 Congr Chr Chs	1	15	15	18 *	.1	.2
191 Entrpr Bpt Asc	2	95	NR	117 *	.4	1.3
193 Episcopal	1	NR	69	217	.7	2.4
207 E.L.C.A.	1	123	84	160	.5	1.8
223 Free Will Bapt	3	184	NR	226 *	.7	2.5
288 Mennonite USA	2	0	75	75 *	.2	.8
297 Mennonite;Other	1	36	NR	44 *	.1	.5
323 Old Ord Amish	2	120	NR	148 *	.5	1.6
355 Presb Ch (USA)	1	226	124	278 *	.9	3.1
388 Reg Bapt Gen As	3	1,405	760	937 *	3.0	10.4
419 So Bapt Conv	2	615	227	758 *	2.4	8.4
449 Un Methodist	16	1,481	750	1,825 *	5.9	20.3
467 Wesleyan	2	93	109	490	1.6	5.5
GEAUGA	**115**	**11,531**	**4,410**	**42,826 ***	**47.1**	**100.0**
011 A.W.M.C.	1	8	13	10	-	-
019 Amer Bapt USA	1	175	100	224 *	.2	.5
053 Assemb of God	4	334	413	524	.6	1.2
056 Baha'i	0	26	NR	26	-	.1
061 Beachy Amish	1	41	NR	52 *	.1	.1
076 Buddhism	1	NR	NR	NR	-	-
081 Catholic	9	NR	NR	25,548	28.1	59.7
089 Chr & Miss Al	2	87	NR	332	.4	.8
093 Chr Ch (Disc)	2	479	107	612 *	.7	1.4
097 Chr Chs&Chs Cr	3	348	NR	445 *	.5	1.0
127 Ch God (Cleve)	1	57	0	73 *	.1	.2
151 L-D Saints	2	NR	NR	498	.5	1.2
167 Chs of Christ	1	16	17	20	-	-
181 Consrv Congr	2	289	238	369 *	.4	.9
183 Cons Menn Conf	1	121	148	176	.2	.4
193 Episcopal	3	NR	290	1,560	1.7	3.6
207 E.L.C.A.	1	485	285	735	.8	1.7
221 Free Methodist	1	9	22	22	-	.1
283 Luth—MO Synod	3	565	298	744	.8	1.7
288 Mennonite USA	1	36	42	46 *	.1	.1
297 Mennonite;Other	2	67	NR	86 *	.1	.2
323 Old Ord Amish	52	3,120	NR	4,004 *	4.4	9.3
355 Presb Ch (USA)	2	823	470	1,051 *	1.2	2.5
388 Reg Bapt Gen As	2	208	263	273 *	.3	.6
413 S.D.A.	1	204	NR	243	.3	.6
419 So Bapt Conv	2	198	167	253 *	.3	.6
443 Un C of Christ	8	1,998	661	2,553 *	2.8	6.0
449 Un Methodist	6	1,837	876	2,347 *	2.6	5.5

NR–Not Reported *Total adherents estimated from known number of communicant, confirmed, full members. - Represents a percentage less than 0.1. Percentages may not total 100 due to rounding.

Table 4: Religious Congregations by County and Group: 2000

Religious Group	Number of Churches, Synagogues, Mosques, or Temples	Number of Communicant, Confirmed, or Full Members	Number of Attendees	Total Adherents: Number of Adherents	% of Total Pop.	% of Total Adh.
GREENE	**138**	**26,149**	**16,295**	**50,776 ***	**34.3**	**100.0**
019 Amer Bapt USA	3	196	68	239 *	.2	.5
053 Assemb of God	4	550	675	923	.6	1.8
056 Baha'i	2	100	NR	100	.1	.2
076 Buddhism	3	NR	NR	NR	-	-
081 Catholic	5	NR	NR	13,301	9.0	26.2
093 Chr Ch (Disc)	1	197	84	241 *	.2	.5
097 Chr Chs&Chs Cr	9	2,931	NR	3,579 *	2.4	7.0
123 Ch God (Ander)	6	NR	506	506	.3	1.0
127 Ch God (Cleve)	3	439	230	537 *	.4	1.1
151 L-D Saints	4	NR	NR	1,250	.8	2.5
165 Ch of Nazarene	7	1,631	1,292	2,646	1.8	5.2
167 Chs of Christ	6	670	653	865	.6	1.7
181 Consrv Congr	1	777	522	949 *	.6	1.9
191 Entrpr Bpt Asc	2	148	NR	181 *	.1	.4
193 Episcopal	2	NR	181	496	.3	1.0
207 E.L.C.A.	5	2,123	1,138	2,681	1.8	5.3
223 Free Will Bapt	2	122	NR	149 *	.1	.3
226 Friends-USA	4	247	NR	302 *	.2	.6
252 Hindu	3	NR	NR	NR	-	-
265 Int Pent C Chr	1	59	30	59	-	.1
267 Muslim Est	1	NR	156	609	.4	1.2
268 Jain	1	NR	NR	NR	-	-
283 Luth—MO Synod	2	360	283	502	.3	1.0
291 Missionary Ch	2	173	257	257	.2	.5
313 N Am Bapt Conf	1	80	105	98 *	.1	.2
355 Presb Ch (USA)	10	2,497	1,154	3,050 *	2.1	6.0
362 Prim Bapt E Dst	2	287	NR	351 *	.2	.7
388 Reg Bapt Gen As	5	1,470	1,844	1,934 *	1.3	3.8
413 S.D.A.	1	35	NR	42	-	.1
419 So Bapt Conv	12	4,555	1,505	5,563 *	3.8	11.0
435 Unitarian-Univ	1	89	NR	109 *	.1	.2
443 Un C of Christ	5	1,838	949	2,245 *	1.5	4.4
449 Un Methodist	16	2,987	1,303	3,647 *	2.5	7.2
467 Wesleyan	1	8	10	15	-	-
499 Indep.Non-Char	5	1,580	3,350	3,350	2.3	6.6
GUERNSEY	**86**	**8,235**	**4,493**	**13,240 ***	**32.5**	**100.0**
019 Amer Bapt USA	5	656	218	820 *	2.0	6.2
053 Assemb of God	1	82	100	250	.6	1.9
056 Baha'i	0	1	NR	1	-	-
061 Beachy Amish	1	111	NR	139 *	.3	1.0
081 Catholic	4	NR	NR	1,856	4.5	14.0
093 Chr Ch (Disc)	1	376	121	470 *	1.2	3.5
097 Chr Chs&Chs Cr	1	60	NR	75 *	.2	.6
123 Ch God (Ander)	2	NR	19	19	-	.1
145 Ch God Prophcy	1	32	NR	40 *	.1	.3
151 L-D Saints	1	NR	NR	234	.6	1.8
165 Ch of Nazarene	3	217	234	339	.8	2.6
167 Chs of Christ	7	647	763	838	2.1	6.3
193 Episcopal	1	NR	39	71	.2	.5
207 E.L.C.A.	3	366	130	498	1.2	3.8
221 Free Methodist	2	43	61	64	.2	.5
263 Int Foursq Gos	1	59	110	110 *	.3	.8
283 Luth—MO Synod	1	36	22	55	.1	.4
323 Old Ord Amish	3	180	NR	225 *	.6	1.7
331 OCA: Ter Diocs	1	29	NR	42	.1	.3
339 Pent Ch of God	1	42	NR	300	.7	2.3
349 Pent Holiness	1	33	14	41 *	.1	.3
355 Presb Ch (USA)	9	1,000	520	1,251 *	3.1	9.4
388 Reg Bapt Gen As	3	269	267	353 *	.9	2.7
403 Salvation Army	1	105	41	283	.7	2.1
419 So Bapt Conv	2	617	287	771 *	1.9	5.8
449 Un Methodist	30	3,274	1,547	4,095 *	10.0	30.9
HAMILTON	**556**	**117,549**	**64,551**	**413,928 ***	**49.0**	**100.0**
019 Amer Bapt USA	20	7,764	3,695	9,695 *	1.1	2.3
053 Assemb of God	7	1,206	1,403	2,089	.2	.5
056 Baha'i	1	161	NR	161	-	-
057 Bapt Gen Conf	1	326	233	407 *	-	.1
075 Brethren in Cr	1	39	32	39	-	-
076 Buddhism	2	NR	NR	NR	-	-
081 Catholic	85	NR	NR	226,670	26.8	54.8
084 Calvary Chapel	1	NR	NR	NR	-	-
089 Chr & Miss Al	3	164	NR	309	-	.1
093 Chr Ch (Disc)	14	2,595	1,092	3,241 *	.4	.8
097 Chr Chs&Chs Cr	27	9,485	NR	11,843 *	1.4	2.9
123 Ch God (Ander)	11	NR	1,147	1,147	.1	.3
127 Ch God (Cleve)	14	1,907	906	2,389 *	.3	.6
145 Ch God Prophcy	2	32	NR	40 *	-	-
151 L-D Saints	8	NR	NR	2,978	.4	.7
157 Ch of Brethren	1	13	35	35 *	-	-
165 Ch of Nazarene	18	2,684	2,171	4,296	.5	1.0
167 Chs of Christ	19	2,005	2,060	2,811	.3	.7
173 Comm of Christ	1	67	NR	67	-	-
175 Congr Chr Chs	1	60	47	75 *	-	-
176 Congr Ad Afl	1	58	NR	72 *	-	-
179 Consrv Bapt	2	NR	880	880	.1	.2
183 Cons Menn Conf	1	48	59	70	-	-
193 Episcopal	22	NR	3,267	8,388	1.0	2.0
203 Evan Free Ch	3	248	465	465	.1	.1
207 E.L.C.A.	13	4,378	2,363	5,824	.7	1.4
216 Evan Presby Ch	1	290	NR	362 *	-	.1
221 Free Methodist	1	12	32	32	-	-
226 Friends-USA	3	179	NR	224 *	-	.1
246 Greek Orthodox	1	NR	NR	1,716	.2	.4
252 Hindu	1	NR	NR	NR	-	-
262 Int Cou Comm Ch	3	455	NR	568 *	.1	.1
264 Int Chs of Crst	1	720	1,258	1,066	.1	.3
267 Muslim Est	4	NR	403	1,191	.1	.3
283 Luth—MO Synod	12	3,301	1,805	4,204	.5	1.0
288 Mennonite USA	2	111	94	138 *	-	-
290 Metro Comm Ch	1	76	56	95 *	-	-
304 NatPrimBapt USA	1	15	NR	19 *	-	-
330 Macedonian Orth	1	NR	NR	240	-	.1
331 OCA: Ter Diocs	1	95	NR	369	-	.1
355 Presb Ch (USA)	47	15,524	7,304	19,384 *	2.3	4.7
356 Presb Ch Amer	3	436	420	588	.1	.1
360 Prim Bapt Chrch	2	NR	NR	NR	-	-
388 Reg Bapt Gen As	1	150	85	85 *	-	-
401 Rus Orth Abroad	1	NR	NR	NR	-	-
403 Salvation Army	3	289	286	1,078	.1	.3
409 Separate Bapt	1	79	NR	99 *	-	-
413 S.D.A.	6	1,539	NR	1,832	.2	.4
418 Southw Bapt Fel	3	NR	NR	NR	-	-
419 So Bapt Conv	40	11,856	4,147	14,805 *	1.8	3.6
435 Unitarian-Univ	4	764	NR	954 *	.1	.2
443 Un C of Christ	25	5,823	2,503	7,271 *	.9	1.8
449 Un Methodist	72	24,166	10,926	30,177 *	3.6	7.3
463 Vineyard	3	6,434	4,246	8,034 *	1.0	1.9
467 Wesleyan	3	83	179	335	-	.1
469 WELS	1	212	177	296	-	.1
496 Jewish Est	21	NR	NR	22,500	2.7	5.4
498 Indep.Charis.	3	6,000	6,575	6,575	.8	1.6
499 Indep.Non-Char	5	5,700	4,200	5,700	.7	1.4
HANCOCK	**77**	**17,340**	**9,690**	**32,521 ***	**45.6**	**100.0**
053 Assemb of God	2	422	521	718	1.0	2.2
056 Baha'i	0	10	NR	10	-	-
071 Brethren (Ash)	1	42	28	52 *	.1	.2
081 Catholic	1	NR	NR	8,591	12.0	26.4
093 Chr Ch (Disc)	1	422	142	526 *	.7	1.6
097 Chr Chs&Chs Cr	4	1,015	NR	1,266 *	1.8	3.9
123 Ch God (Ander)	1	NR	796	796	1.1	2.4
127 Ch God (Cleve)	1	364	228	454 *	.6	1.4
165 Ch of Nazarene	2	358	316	577	.8	1.8
167 Chs of Christ	1	102	115	168	.2	.5
171 Ch God-Gen Con	2	397	543	591 *	.8	1.8
193 Episcopal	1	NR	45	201	.3	.6
203 Evan Free Ch	1	90	200	200	.3	.6
207 E.L.C.A.	8	3,473	1,580	4,570	6.4	14.1
226 Friends-USA	2	70	NR	87 *	.1	.3
263 Int Foursq Gos	1	6	17	17 *	-	.1
283 Luth—MO Synod	1	103	96	163	.2	.5
339 Pent Ch of God	2	56	NR	171	.2	.5
355 Presb Ch (USA)	5	1,783	598	2,224 *	3.1	6.8
360 Prim Bapt Chrch	2	NR	NR	NR	-	-

NR–Not Reported *Total adherents estimated from known number of communicant, confirmed, full members. - Represents a percentage less than 0.1. Percentages may not total 100 due to rounding.

Table 4: Religious Congregations by County and Group: 2000

Religious Group	Number of Churches, Synagogues, Mosques, or Temples	Number of Communicant, Confirmed, or Full Members	Number of Attendees	Total Adherents		
				Number of Adherents	% of Total Pop.	% of Total Adh.
388 Reg Bapt Gen As	2	385	365	433 *	.6	1.3
403 Salvation Army	1	154	90	548	.8	1.7
413 S.D.A.	1	106	NR	126	.2	.4
418 Southw Bapt Fel	1	NR	NR	NR	-	-
419 So Bapt Conv	0	8	18	10 *	-	-
443 Un C of Christ	1	83	41	104 *	.1	.3
449 Un Methodist	30	7,015	3,288	8,749 *	12.3	26.9
469 WELS	2	876	663	1,169	1.6	3.6
HARDIN	**69**	**8,542**	**3,271**	**12,954 ***	**40.6**	**100.0**
019 Amer Bapt USA	2	298	216	366 *	1.1	2.8
053 Assemb of God	3	233	290	423	1.3	3.3
081 Catholic	2	NR	NR	1,780	5.6	13.7
089 Chr & Miss Al	1	70	NR	228	.7	1.8
093 Chr Ch (Disc)	2	489	60	601 *	1.9	4.6
097 Chr Chs&Chs Cr	7	1,132	NR	1,392 *	4.4	10.7
123 Ch God (Ander)	2	NR	86	86	.3	.7
157 Ch of Brethren	1	65	0	80 *	.3	.6
165 Ch of Nazarene	1	115	44	159	.5	1.2
167 Chs of Christ	2	110	95	140	.4	1.1
171 Ch God-Gen Con	1	8	30	30 *	.1	.2
207 E.L.C.A.	3	469	175	579	1.8	4.5
223 Free Will Bapt	2	122	NR	150 *	.5	1.2
263 Int Foursq Gos	1	5	7	7 *	-	.1
267 Muslim Est	1	NR	55	163	.5	1.3
323 Old Ord Amish	3	180	NR	222 *	.7	1.7
339 Pent Ch of God	3	190	NR	328	1.0	2.5
355 Presb Ch (USA)	4	280	166	343 *	1.1	2.6
388 Reg Bapt Gen As	1	119	135	146 *	.5	1.1
419 So Bapt Conv	3	293	120	360 *	1.1	2.8
443 Un C of Christ	4	1,055	382	1,297 *	4.1	10.0
449 Un Methodist	19	3,242	1,364	3,987 *	12.5	30.8
469 WELS	1	67	46	87	.3	.7
HARRISON	**52**	**3,674**	**1,771**	**5,140 ***	**32.4**	**100.0**
053 Assemb of God	3	59	80	109	.7	2.1
081 Catholic	4	NR	NR	558	3.5	10.9
097 Chr Chs&Chs Cr	3	345	NR	419 *	2.6	8.2
123 Ch God (Ander)	1	NR	40	40	.3	.8
165 Ch of Nazarene	4	137	103	182	1.1	3.5
167 Chs of Christ	3	149	124	175	1.1	3.4
207 E.L.C.A.	1	85	38	141	.9	2.7
355 Presb Ch (USA)	10	804	329	976 *	6.2	19.0
419 So Bapt Conv	1	19	18	23 *	.1	.4
449 Un Methodist	22	2,076	1,039	2,517 *	15.9	49.0
HENRY	**54**	**12,521**	**6,030**	**19,906 ***	**68.1**	**100.0**
053 Assemb of God	1	24	25	27	.1	.1
056 Baha'i	0	2	NR	2	-	-
081 Catholic	5	NR	NR	3,697	12.7	18.6
084 Calvary Chapel	1	NR	NR	NR	-	-
097 Chr Chs&Chs Cr	1	130	NR	164 *	.6	.8
107 Christian Un	1	28	34	35 *	.1	.2
157 Ch of Brethren	1	11	10	14 *	-	.1
165 Ch of Nazarene	1	174	171	319	1.1	1.6
171 Ch God-Gen Con	1	35	31	44 *	.2	.2
193 Episcopal	1	NR	28	26	.1	.1
207 E.L.C.A.	10	3,403	1,676	4,308	14.7	21.6
283 Luth—MO Synod	9	4,522	2,388	5,827	19.9	29.3
355 Presb Ch (USA)	2	273	101	344 *	1.2	1.7
373 Ref Ch in U.S.	1	76	NR	104	.4	.5
419 So Bapt Conv	2	428	141	539 *	1.8	2.7
443 Un C of Christ	2	629	262	792 *	2.7	4.0
449 Un Methodist	13	2,747	1,118	3,457 *	11.8	17.4
467 Wesleyan	2	39	45	207	.7	1.0
HIGHLAND	**87**	**9,793**	**3,542**	**13,724 ***	**33.6**	**100.0**
019 Amer Bapt USA	4	908	299	1,149 *	2.8	8.4
032 Amish; other	1	60	NR	76 *	.2	.6
053 Assemb of God	1	47	65	65	.2	.5
056 Baha'i	0	1	NR	1	-	-
081 Catholic	2	NR	NR	1,102	2.7	8.0

Religious Group	Number of Churches, Synagogues, Mosques, or Temples	Number of Communicant, Confirmed, or Full Members	Number of Attendees	Total Adherents		
				Number of Adherents	% of Total Pop.	% of Total Adh.
097 Chr Chs&Chs Cr	16	2,725	NR	3,450 *	8.4	25.1
107 Christian Un	3	110	123	139 *	.3	1.0
123 Ch God (Ander)	1	NR	9	9	-	.1
127 Ch God (Cleve)	3	487	222	640 *	1.6	4.7
145 Ch God Prophcy	1	32	NR	40 *	.1	.3
151 L-D Saints	1	NR	NR	99	.2	.7
165 Ch of Nazarene	2	320	207	399	1.0	2.9
167 Chs of Christ	2	217	258	297	.7	2.2
193 Episcopal	1	NR	48	80	.2	.6
203 Evan Free Ch	1	18	50	50	.1	.4
207 E.L.C.A.	2	147	86	185	.5	1.3
223 Free Will Bapt	2	122	NR	155 *	.4	1.1
226 Friends-USA	7	441	NR	558 *	1.4	4.1
265 Int Pent C Chr	2	16	21	57	.1	.4
355 Presb Ch (USA)	4	456	282	577 *	1.4	4.2
413 S.D.A.	1	61	NR	73	.2	.5
419 So Bapt Conv	3	482	233	610 *	1.5	4.4
449 Un Methodist	25	2,519	1,194	3,188 *	7.8	23.2
467 Wesleyan	1	24	25	125	.3	.9
499 Indep.Non-Char	1	600	420	600	1.5	4.4
HOCKING	**55**	**4,599**	**2,451**	**7,029 ***	**24.9**	**100.0**
019 Amer Bapt USA	1	96	75	119 *	.4	1.7
081 Catholic	1	NR	NR	971	3.4	13.8
089 Chr & Miss Al	1	55	NR	134	.5	1.9
093 Chr Ch (Disc)	1	63	25	78 *	.3	1.1
097 Chr Chs&Chs Cr	2	325	NR	403 *	1.4	5.7
123 Ch God (Ander)	1	NR	139	139	.5	2.0
127 Ch God (Cleve)	1	190	42	236 *	.8	3.4
165 Ch of Nazarene	2	186	160	235	.8	3.3
167 Chs of Christ	2	72	110	109	.4	1.6
173 Comm of Christ	1	88	NR	88	.3	1.3
193 Episcopal	1	NR	51	39	.1	.6
207 E.L.C.A.	3	434	180	596	2.1	8.5
223 Free Will Bapt	1	61	NR	76 *	.3	1.1
283 Luth—MO Synod	1	129	94	191	.7	2.7
288 Mennonite USA	1	22	22	27 *	.1	.4
297 Mennonite;Other	1	30	NR	37 *	.1	.5
355 Presb Ch (USA)	1	245	103	304 *	1.1	4.3
360 Prim Bapt Chrch	1	NR	NR	NR	-	-
419 So Bapt Conv	1	629	207	781 *	2.8	11.1
449 Un Methodist	30	1,959	1,225	2,431 *	8.6	34.6
467 Wesleyan	1	15	18	35	.1	.5
HOLMES	**142**	**12,341**	**3,291**	**17,946 ***	**46.1**	**100.0**
032 Amish; other	15	870	NR	1,218 *	3.1	6.8
061 Beachy Amish	6	408	NR	569 *	1.5	3.2
081 Catholic	2	NR	NR	524	1.3	2.9
089 Chr & Miss Al	1	50	NR	94	.2	.5
097 Chr Chs&Chs Cr	9	1,559	NR	2,173 *	5.6	12.1
127 Ch God (Cleve)	1	70	44	98 *	.3	.5
165 Ch of Nazarene	1	41	19	41	.1	.2
167 Chs of Christ	3	153	210	210	.5	1.2
183 Cons Menn Conf	4	658	803	956	2.5	5.3
207 E.L.C.A.	1	204	80	236	.6	1.3
283 Luth—MO Synod	1	76	41	89	.2	.5
288 Mennonite USA	6	1,285	1,117	1,789 *	4.6	10.0
297 Mennonite;Other	3	333	NR	464 *	1.2	2.6
323 Old Ord Amish	74	4,430	NR	6,202 *	15.9	34.6
355 Presb Ch (USA)	1	175	85	244 *	.6	1.4
388 Reg Bapt Gen As	1	101	120	141 *	.4	.8
413 S.D.A.	1	48	NR	57	.1	.3
419 So Bapt Conv	1	291	46	405 *	1.0	2.3
443 Un C of Christ	3	395	168	550 *	1.4	3.1
449 Un Methodist	7	1,083	444	1,511 *	3.9	8.4
467 Wesleyan	1	111	114	375	1.0	2.1
HURON	**78**	**10,297**	**4,878**	**29,464 ***	**49.5**	**100.0**
019 Amer Bapt USA	1	495	140	634 *	1.1	2.2
053 Assemb of God	3	98	111	151	.3	.5
081 Catholic	9	NR	NR	14,950	25.1	50.7
089 Chr & Miss Al	4	442	NR	1,119	1.9	3.8
097 Chr Chs&Chs Cr	2	236	NR	302 *	.5	1.0

NR–Not Reported *Total adherents estimated from known number of communicant, confirmed, full members. - Represents a percentage less than 0.1. Percentages may not total 100 due to rounding.

Table 4: Religious Congregations by County and Group: 2000

Religious Group	Number of Churches, Synagogues, Mosques, or Temples	Number of Communicant, Confirmed, or Full Members	Number of Attendees	Total Adherents: Number of Adherents	Total Adherents: % of Total Pop.	Total Adherents: % of Total Adh.
105 Christian Ref	1	190	268	243 *	.4	.8
127 Ch God (Cleve)	4	485	338	621 *	1.0	2.1
145 Ch God Prophcy	2	32	NR	41 *	.1	.1
151 L-D Saints	2	NR	NR	601	1.0	2.0
165 Ch of Nazarene	2	228	134	249	.4	.8
167 Chs of Christ	4	215	250	280	.5	1.0
193 Episcopal	2	NR	50	154	.3	.5
207 E.L.C.A.	6	2,265	961	2,890	4.9	9.8
223 Free Will Bapt	2	122	NR	157 *	.3	.5
263 Int Foursq Gos	1	30	50	50 *	.1	.2
297 Mennonite;Other	1	65	NR	83 *	.1	.3
322 Old Ord Menn Ch	1	65	NR	83 *	.1	.3
323 Old Ord Amish	1	60	NR	77 *	.1	.3
355 Presb Ch (USA)	3	634	320	812 *	1.4	2.8
388 Reg Bapt Gen As	1	300	325	384 *	.6	1.3
403 Salvation Army	1	57	32	113	.2	.4
413 S.D.A.	1	112	NR	133	.2	.5
418 Southw Bapt Fel	1	NR	NR	NR	-	-
419 So Bapt Conv	3	405	245	519 *	.9	1.8
443 Un C of Christ	5	652	212	835 *	1.4	2.8
449 Un Methodist	14	3,045	1,442	3,901 *	6.6	13.2
466 Wayn Tr MB Asc	1	64	NR	82 *	.1	.3
JACKSON	**65**	**6,003**	**5,103**	**10,885 ***	**33.3**	**100.0**
019 Amer Bapt USA	2	359	198	448 *	1.4	4.1
053 Assemb of God	1	28	26	40	.1	.4
056 Baha'i	0	2	NR	2	-	-
081 Catholic	2	NR	NR	330	1.0	3.0
093 Chr Ch (Disc)	1	180	60	225 *	.7	2.1
097 Chr Chs&Chs Cr	4	346	NR	431 *	1.3	4.0
127 Ch God (Cleve)	2	235	2,492	2,610 *	8.0	24.0
145 Ch God Prophcy	1	32	NR	40 *	.1	.4
151 L-D Saints	1	NR	NR	182	.6	1.7
165 Ch of Nazarene	3	445	453	803	2.5	7.4
167 Chs of Christ	4	136	162	188	.6	1.7
173 Comm of Christ	3	122	NR	122	.4	1.1
191 Entrpr Bpt Asc	1	21	NR	26 *	.1	.2
207 E.L.C.A.	1	77	38	95	.3	.9
223 Free Will Bapt	8	489	NR	611 *	1.9	5.6
288 Mennonite USA	1	23	30	30 *	.1	.3
339 Pent Ch of God	1	83	NR	118	.4	1.1
355 Presb Ch (USA)	7	496	243	619 *	1.9	5.7
418 Southw Bapt Fel	1	NR	NR	NR	-	-
419 So Bapt Conv	4	422	129	526 *	1.6	4.8
449 Un Methodist	15	2,235	983	2,789 *	8.5	25.6
467 Wesleyan	2	272	289	650	2.0	6.0
JEFFERSON	**131**	**12,388**	**5,156**	**32,408 ***	**43.9**	**100.0**
019 Amer Bapt USA	2	187	70	223 *	.3	.7
053 Assemb of God	3	198	235	252	.3	.8
056 Baha'i	0	2	NR	2	-	-
081 Catholic	24	NR	NR	14,704	19.9	45.4
093 Chr Ch (Disc)	2	340	140	406 *	.5	1.3
097 Chr Chs&Chs Cr	8	1,448	NR	1,727 *	2.3	5.3
123 Ch God (Ander)	3	NR	287	287	.4	.9
151 L-D Saints	1	NR	NR	360	.5	1.1
165 Ch of Nazarene	6	450	252	593	.8	1.8
167 Chs of Christ	2	235	215	306	.4	.9
193 Episcopal	2	NR	137	428	.6	1.3
207 E.L.C.A.	1	304	92	393	.5	1.2
216 Evan Presby Ch	1	101	NR	120 *	.2	.4
226 Friends-USA	3	249	NR	297 *	.4	.9
246 Greek Orthodox	1	NR	NR	375	.5	1.2
283 Luth—MO Synod	1	132	63	167	.2	.5
323 Old Ord Amish	1	60	NR	72 *	.1	.2
331 OCA: Ter Diocs	2	112	NR	126	.2	.4
355 Presb Ch (USA)	19	2,040	980	2,432 *	3.3	7.5
356 Presb Ch Amer	1	280	120	315	.4	1.0
403 Salvation Army	1	63	51	440	.6	1.4
410 Serb Orth USA	1	NR	NR	810	1.1	2.5
413 S.D.A.	1	44	NR	52	.1	.2
419 So Bapt Conv	1	289	59	345 *	.5	1.1
443 Un C of Christ	1	103	45	123 *	.2	.4
449 Un Methodist	40	5,716	2,358	6,819 *	9.2	21.0
467 Wesleyan	2	35	52	119	.2	.4
496 Jewish Est	1	NR	NR	115	.2	.4
KNOX	**95**	**13,572**	**6,283**	**21,159 ***	**38.8**	**100.0**
019 Amer Bapt USA	5	871	392	1,074 *	2.0	5.1
032 Amish; other	1	60	NR	74 *	.1	.3
053 Assemb of God	1	190	251	514	.9	2.4
056 Baha'i	0	2	NR	2	-	-
081 Catholic	2	NR	NR	3,083	5.7	14.6
089 Chr & Miss Al	2	123	NR	308	.6	1.5
093 Chr Ch (Disc)	1	363	133	447 *	.8	2.1
097 Chr Chs&Chs Cr	13	2,476	NR	3,052 *	5.6	14.4
123 Ch God (Ander)	2	NR	148	148	.3	.7
127 Ch God (Cleve)	2	385	226	475 *	.9	2.2
151 L-D Saints	1	NR	NR	274	.5	1.3
157 Ch of Brethren	1	119	76	147 *	.3	.7
165 Ch of Nazarene	4	1,539	1,551	1,981	3.6	9.4
167 Chs of Christ	3	183	180	220	.4	1.0
183 Cons Menn Conf	1	53	65	77	.1	.4
191 Entrpr Bpt Asc	1	29	NR	36 *	.1	.2
193 Episcopal	2	NR	179	343	.6	1.6
207 E.L.C.A.	2	519	225	699	1.3	3.3
223 Free Will Bapt	1	61	NR	75 *	.1	.4
263 Int Foursq Gos	2	128	172	172 *	.3	.8
297 Mennonite;Other	1	20	NR	25 *	-	.1
323 Old Ord Amish	12	720	NR	888 *	1.6	4.2
355 Presb Ch (USA)	3	423	324	521 *	1.0	2.5
370 Ref Baptist Chs	1	NR	NR	NR	-	-
388 Reg Bapt Gen As	1	420	361	518 *	1.0	2.4
403 Salvation Army	1	186	142	243	.4	1.1
413 S.D.A.	3	813	NR	967	1.8	4.6
419 So Bapt Conv	1	261	58	322 *	.6	1.5
443 Un C of Christ	1	236	85	291 *	.5	1.4
449 Un Methodist	24	3,392	1,715	4,183 *	7.7	19.8
LAKE	**127**	**25,677**	**12,598**	**119,008 ***	**52.3**	**100.0**
019 Amer Bapt USA	4	721	375	885 *	.4	.7
053 Assemb of God	7	985	1,270	2,094	.9	1.8
056 Baha'i	1	57	NR	57	-	-
057 Bapt Gen Conf	2	188	180	230 *	.1	.2
081 Catholic	16	NR	NR	81,160	35.7	68.2
089 Chr & Miss Al	3	108	NR	371	.2	.3
093 Chr Ch (Disc)	4	798	228	980 *	.4	.8
097 Chr Chs&Chs Cr	2	930	NR	1,142 *	.5	1.0
121 Ch God (Abr)	1	17	8	21 *	-	-
123 Ch God (Ander)	1	NR	42	42	-	-
127 Ch God (Cleve)	5	853	558	1,047 *	.5	.9
151 L-D Saints	3	NR	NR	736	.3	.6
157 Ch of Brethren	1	134	84	165 *	.1	.1
165 Ch of Nazarene	3	438	324	589	.3	.5
167 Chs of Christ	4	281	310	343	.2	.3
173 Comm of Christ	2	492	NR	492	.2	.4
179 Consrv Bapt	1	NR	250	250	.1	.2
193 Episcopal	5	NR	629	1,429	.6	1.2
201 Evan Cov Ch	1	87	62	107 *	-	.1
207 E.L.C.A.	6	1,629	800	2,418	1.1	2.0
226 Friends-USA	3	285	NR	350 *	.2	.3
283 Luth—MO Synod	8	2,783	1,354	3,632	1.6	3.1
331 OCA: Ter Diocs	1	120	NR	194	.1	.2
355 Presb Ch (USA)	3	632	353	776 *	.3	.7
388 Reg Bapt Gen As	6	1,156	998	1,419 *	.6	1.2
403 Salvation Army	1	93	61	238	.1	.2
413 S.D.A.	2	237	NR	282	.1	.2
419 So Bapt Conv	6	2,440	939	2,997 *	1.3	2.5
435 Unitarian-Univ	2	231	NR	284 *	.1	.2
443 Un C of Christ	9	2,358	1,058	2,896 *	1.3	2.4
449 Un Methodist	11	7,363	2,509	9,044 *	4.0	7.6
463 Vineyard	1	200	168	246 *	.1	.2
469 WELS	1	61	38	92	-	.1
496 Jewish Est	1	NR	NR	2,000	.9	1.7

NR–Not Reported *Total adherents estimated from known number of communicant, confirmed, full members. - Represents a percentage less than 0.1. Percentages may not total 100 due to rounding.

Table 4: Religious Congregations by County and Group: 2000

Religious Group	Number of Churches, Synagogues, Mosques, or Temples	Number of Communicant, Confirmed, or Full Members	Number of Attendees	Total Adherents: Number of Adherents	Total Adherents: % of Total Pop.	Total Adherents: % of Total Adh.
LAWRENCE	**86**	**9,692**	**3,951**	**14,060 ***	**22.6**	**100.0**
017 Amer Bapt Assn	2	100	NR	122 *	.2	.9
019 Amer Bapt USA	2	851	200	1,046 *	1.7	7.4
053 Assemb of God	1	16	16	34	.1	.2
056 Baha'i	0	4	NR	4	-	-
081 Catholic	4	NR	NR	1,937	3.1	13.8
097 Chr Chs&Chs Cr	3	1,451	NR	1,783 *	2.9	12.7
123 Ch God (Ander)	1	NR	21	21	-	.1
145 Ch God Prophcy	1	32	NR	39 *	.1	.3
165 Ch of Nazarene	9	1,059	751	1,414	2.3	10.1
167 Chs of Christ	9	747	776	926	1.5	6.6
173 Comm of Christ	1	154	NR	154	.2	1.1
191 Entrpr Bpt Asc	1	122	NR	150 *	.2	1.1
193 Episcopal	1	NR	34	113	.2	.8
207 E.L.C.A.	1	184	59	197	.3	1.4
223 Free Will Bapt	11	673	NR	827 *	1.3	5.9
265 Int Pent C Chr	1	3	12	13	-	.1
288 Mennonite USA	1	42	30	52 *	.1	.4
349 Pent Holiness	2	28	36	34 *	.1	.2
355 Presb Ch (USA)	2	148	90	182 *	.3	1.3
418 Southw Bapt Fel	2	NR	NR	NR	-	-
419 So Bapt Conv	5	1,691	766	2,078 *	3.3	14.8
449 Un Methodist	26	2,387	1,160	2,934 *	4.7	20.9
LICKING	**159**	**28,367**	**13,406**	**50,294 ***	**34.6**	**100.0**
019 Amer Bapt USA	13	1,915	929	2,395 *	1.6	4.8
053 Assemb of God	3	202	209	305	.2	.6
056 Baha'i	0	29	NR	29	-	.1
061 Beachy Amish	1	75	NR	94 *	.1	.2
071 Brethren (Ash)	1	34	33	43 *	-	.1
081 Catholic	7	NR	NR	12,206	8.4	24.3
093 Chr Ch (Disc)	3	1,339	289	1,675 *	1.2	3.3
097 Chr Chs&Chs Cr	14	3,295	NR	4,120 *	2.8	8.2
107 Christian Un	7	305	362	381 *	.3	.8
123 Ch God (Ander)	1	NR	61	61	-	.1
127 Ch God (Cleve)	2	241	60	302 *	.2	.6
145 Ch God Prophcy	1	32	NR	40 *	-	.1
151 L-D Saints	2	NR	NR	662	.5	1.3
165 Ch of Nazarene	8	964	696	1,107	.8	2.2
167 Chs of Christ	7	418	507	536	.4	1.1
193 Episcopal	2	NR	190	367	.3	.7
207 E.L.C.A.	6	1,837	734	2,596	1.8	5.2
223 Free Will Bapt	2	122	NR	153 *	.1	.3
263 Int Foursq Gos	1	12	42	42 *	-	.1
283 Luth—MO Synod	2	272	107	328	.2	.7
339 Pent Ch of God	1	100	NR	200	.1	.4
355 Presb Ch (USA)	12	2,364	1,093	2,956 *	2.0	5.9
360 Prim Bapt Chrch	4	NR	NR	NR	-	-
388 Reg Bapt Gen As	3	274	318	344 *	.2	.7
403 Salvation Army	1	98	104	208	.1	.4
413 S.D.A.	2	289	NR	344	.2	.7
419 So Bapt Conv	9	5,322	3,248	6,656 *	4.6	13.2
443 Un C of Christ	3	765	257	957 *	.7	1.9
449 Un Methodist	37	7,653	3,646	9,571 *	6.6	19.0
463 Vineyard	2	288	285	366 *	.3	.7
467 Wesleyan	1	122	236	1,200	.8	2.4
496 Jewish Est	1	NR	NR	50	-	.1
LOGAN	**82**	**10,797**	**6,229**	**17,760 ***	**38.6**	**100.0**
019 Amer Bapt USA	1	80	55	101 *	.2	.6
032 Amish; other	3	180	NR	225 *	.5	1.3
053 Assemb of God	1	221	250	429	.9	2.4
056 Baha'i	0	2	NR	2	-	-
071 Brethren (Ash)	1	146	152	184 *	.4	1.0
081 Catholic	2	NR	NR	2,567	5.6	14.5
093 Chr Ch (Disc)	2	850	392	1,070 *	2.3	6.0
097 Chr Chs&Chs Cr	5	758	NR	952 *	2.1	5.4
107 Christian Un	1	75	50	94 *	.2	.5
123 Ch God (Ander)	3	NR	545	545	1.2	3.1
127 Ch God (Cleve)	1	29	10	36 *	.1	.2
151 L-D Saints	1	NR	NR	367	.8	2.1
157 Ch of Brethren	2	147	60	185 *	.4	1.0
165 Ch of Nazarene	3	247	199	667	1.4	3.8
167 Chs of Christ	1	47	50	61	.1	.3
183 Cons Menn Conf	1	21	26	31	.1	.2
193 Episcopal	1	NR	24	151	.3	.9
207 E.L.C.A.	4	652	331	869	1.9	4.9
223 Free Will Bapt	1	61	NR	77 *	.2	.4
226 Friends-USA	6	570	NR	717 *	1.6	4.0
288 Mennonite USA	4	321	308	422 *	.9	2.4
291 Missionary Ch	1	19	16	19	-	.1
323 Old Ord Amish	2	120	NR	150 *	.3	.8
355 Presb Ch (USA)	5	825	390	1,039 *	2.3	5.9
388 Reg Bapt Gen As	4	871	853	1,057 *	2.3	6.0
413 S.D.A.	1	51	NR	61	.1	.3
419 So Bapt Conv	2	410	258	516 *	1.1	2.9
443 Un C of Christ	1	333	217	419 *	.9	2.4
449 Un Methodist	21	3,273	1,463	4,122 *	9.0	23.2
499 Indep.Non-Char	1	488	580	625	1.4	3.5
LORAIN	**235**	**40,886**	**19,193**	**130,555 ***	**45.9**	**100.0**
019 Amer Bapt USA	7	830	587	1,043 *	.4	.8
039 Ap Chr Ch(Naz)	1	49	95	95 *	-	.1
053 Assemb of God	11	1,524	1,568	1,896	.7	1.5
056 Baha'i	0	28	NR	28	-	-
057 Bapt Gen Conf	2	155	229	239 *	.1	.2
076 Buddhism	1	NR	NR	NR	-	-
081 Catholic	37	NR	NR	72,978	25.6	55.9
089 Chr & Miss Al	3	141	NR	184	.1	.1
093 Chr Ch (Disc)	4	1,939	563	2,436 *	.9	1.9
121 Ch God (Abr)	1	35	28	44 *	-	-
123 Ch God (Ander)	1	NR	65	65	-	-
127 Ch God (Cleve)	8	1,288	666	1,627 *	.6	1.2
145 Ch God Prophcy	2	64	NR	80 *	-	.1
151 L-D Saints	2	NR	NR	842	.3	.6
157 Ch of Brethren	1	24	21	30 *	-	-
165 Ch of Nazarene	5	523	592	911	.3	.7
167 Chs of Christ	6	505	573	734	.3	.6
173 Comm of Christ	1	230	NR	230	.1	.2
181 Consrv Congr	2	172	213	216 *	.1	.2
191 Entrpr Bpt Asc	1	113	NR	142 *	-	.1
193 Episcopal	3	NR	260	692	.2	.5
203 Evan Free Ch	1	65	130	130	-	.1
207 E.L.C.A.	7	2,191	958	2,911	1.0	2.2
223 Free Will Bapt	4	245	NR	307 *	.1	.2
226 Friends-USA	1	35	NR	44 *	-	-
246 Greek Orthodox	1	NR	NR	600	.2	.5
263 Int Foursq Gos	4	315	867	867 *	.3	.7
267 Muslim Est	1	NR	25	150	.1	.1
283 Luth—MO Synod	13	3,120	1,405	4,157	1.5	3.2
288 Mennonite USA	1	40	60	60 *	-	-
304 NatPrimBapt USA	3	302	NR	379 *	.1	.3
330 Macedonian Orth	1	NR	NR	600	.2	.5
332 OCA: Bulg Dioc	1	100	NR	173	.1	.1
339 Pent Ch of God	2	34	NR	70	-	.1
349 Pent Holiness	1	101	45	127 *	-	.1
355 Presb Ch (USA)	4	947	444	1,189 *	.4	.9
388 Reg Bapt Gen As	12	2,867	2,588	3,603 *	1.3	2.8
403 Salvation Army	3	249	132	1,131	.4	.9
410 Serb Orth USA	1	NR	NR	144	.1	.1
413 S.D.A.	4	365	NR	435	.2	.3
419 So Bapt Conv	18	6,441	1,435	8,092 *	2.8	6.2
431 Ukrainian Orth	1	NR	NR	150	.1	.1
435 Unitarian-Univ	1	42	NR	53 *	-	-
443 Un C of Christ	17	7,388	2,243	9,282 *	3.3	7.1
449 Un Methodist	28	7,822	2,992	9,829 *	3.5	7.5
467 Wesleyan	2	97	159	265	.1	.2
496 Jewish Est	3	NR	NR	755	.3	.6
499 Indep.Non-Char	1	500	250	540	.2	.4
LUCAS	**304**	**65,648**	**33,028**	**221,252 ***	**48.6**	**100.0**
019 Amer Bapt USA	12	2,931	1,360	3,685 *	.8	1.7
034 Ant Orth of NA	2	963	NR	1,926	.4	.9
040 Ap Chr Ch-Amer	1	42	78	78 *	-	-
053 Assemb of God	6	1,306	1,668	3,149	.7	1.4
056 Baha'i	1	69	NR	69	-	-

NR–Not Reported   *Total adherents estimated from known number of communicant, confirmed, full members.   - Represents a percentage less than 0.1.   Percentages may not total 100 due to rounding.

Table 4: Religious Congregations by County and Group: 2000

Religious Group	Number of Churches, Synagogues, Mosques, or Temples	Number of Communicant, Confirmed, or Full Members	Number of Attendees	Total Adherents		
				Number of Adherents	% of Total Pop.	% of Total Adh.
057 Bapt Gen Conf	1	20	35	35 *	-	-
059 Bapt Miss Assn	1	150	60	189 *	-	.1
081 Catholic	48	NR	NR	113,904	25.0	51.5
084 Calvary Chapel	1	NR	NR	NR	-	-
089 Chr & Miss Al	8	1,891	NR	4,556	1.0	2.1
093 Chr Ch (Disc)	5	1,333	593	1,676 *	.4	.8
097 Chr Chs&Chs Cr	5	1,660	NR	2,087 *	.5	.9
123 Ch God (Ander)	4	NR	1,315	1,315	.3	.6
127 Ch God (Cleve)	4	2,257	1,550	2,837 *	.6	1.3
145 Ch God Prophcy	3	32	NR	40 *	-	-
151 L-D Saints	2	NR	NR	874	.2	.4
157 Ch of Brethren	1	65	37	82 *	-	-
165 Ch of Nazarene	4	788	428	1,284	.3	.6
167 Chs of Christ	5	1,442	1,091	1,898	.4	.9
171 Ch God-Gen Con	2	49	147	147 *	-	.1
173 Comm of Christ	2	224	NR	224	-	.1
175 Congr Chr Chs	3	1,535	703	1,930 *	.4	.9
193 Episcopal	8	NR	1,121	3,453	.8	1.6
203 Evan Free Ch	1	25	92	92	-	-
207 E.L.C.A.	38	20,347	7,237	30,113	6.6	13.6
221 Free Methodist	2	208	326	326	.1	.1
223 Free Will Bapt	2	122	NR	154 *	-	.1
246 Greek Orthodox	1	NR	NR	762	.2	.3
252 Hindu	2	NR	NR	NR	-	-
262 Int Cou Comm Ch	1	190	NR	239 *	.1	.1
263 Int Foursq Gos	3	128	178	178 *	-	.1
267 Muslim Est	3	NR	712	2,218	.5	1.0
268 Jain	1	NR	NR	NR	-	-
283 Luth—MO Synod	10	2,532	1,361	3,263	.7	1.5
288 Mennonite USA	2	120	105	159 *	-	.1
290 Metro Comm Ch	1	67	28	84 *	-	-
291 Missionary Ch	1	39	45	45	-	-
313 N Am Bapt Conf	1	465	320	585 *	.1	.3
332 OCA: Bulg Dioc	1	150	NR	267	.1	.1
349 Pent Holiness	5	430	385	541 *	.1	.2
355 Presb Ch (USA)	10	2,790	1,289	3,507 *	.8	1.6
388 Reg Bapt Gen As	3	1,740	1,273	1,557 *	.3	.7
403 Salvation Army	3	164	116	565	.1	.3
413 S.D.A.	2	590	NR	702	.2	.3
416 Sikh	1	NR	NR	NR	-	-
419 So Bapt Conv	14	2,519	697	3,167 *	.7	1.4
435 Unitarian-Univ	1	287	NR	361 *	.1	.2
443 Un C of Christ	11	3,355	1,286	4,218 *	.9	1.9
449 Un Methodist	38	10,991	5,644	13,820 *	3.0	6.2
463 Vineyard	1	320	270	402 *	.1	.2
466 Wayn Tr MB Asc	2	258	NR	324 *	.1	.1
467 Wesleyan	2	142	114	392	.1	.2
469 WELS	5	612	344	853	.2	.4
496 Jewish Est	4	NR	NR	5,900	1.3	2.7
498 Indep.Charis.	1	300	400	400	.1	.2
499 Indep.Non-Char	2	0	620	620	.1	.3
MADISON	**55**	**7,836**	**3,616**	**13,122 ***	**32.6**	**100.0**
019 Amer Bapt USA	1	162	68	200 *	.5	1.5
053 Assemb of God	1	138	167	235	.6	1.8
061 Beachy Amish	3	336	NR	414 *	1.0	3.2
081 Catholic	3	NR	NR	2,389	5.9	18.2
097 Chr Chs&Chs Cr	2	175	NR	216 *	.5	1.6
123 Ch God (Ander)	1	NR	50	50	.1	.4
151 L-D Saints	2	NR	NR	370	.9	2.8
165 Ch of Nazarene	3	481	470	749	1.9	5.7
167 Chs of Christ	1	25	35	40	.1	.3
183 Cons Menn Conf	3	314	383	457	1.1	3.5
191 Entrpr Bpt Asc	2	77	NR	95 *	.2	.7
193 Episcopal	1	NR	69	113	.3	.9
207 E.L.C.A.	2	278	171	480	1.2	3.7
223 Free Will Bapt	3	184	NR	226 *	.6	1.7
265 Int Pent C Chr	1	26	54	125	.3	1.0
288 Mennonite USA	2	326	240	402 *	1.0	3.1
297 Mennonite;Other	2	330	NR	407 *	1.0	3.1
355 Presb Ch (USA)	3	719	383	887 *	2.2	6.8
388 Reg Bapt Gen As	1	57	80	80 *	.2	.6
419 So Bapt Conv	3	641	148	790 *	2.0	6.0
443 Un C of Christ	2	255	67	314 *	.8	2.4

Religious Group	Number of Churches, Synagogues, Mosques, or Temples	Number of Communicant, Confirmed, or Full Members	Number of Attendees	Total Adherents		
				Number of Adherents	% of Total Pop.	% of Total Adh.
449 Un Methodist	13	3,312	1,231	4,083 *	10.2	31.1
MAHONING	**254**	**44,361**	**22,913**	**167,420 ***	**65.0**	**100.0**
011 A.W.M.C.	2	21	40	21	-	-
019 Amer Bapt USA	7	1,576	741	1,928 *	.7	1.2
022 Carp Rus Orth	1	122	NR	207	.1	.1
034 Ant Orth of NA	1	168	NR	336	.1	.2
053 Assemb of God	17	5,723	5,171	7,472	2.9	4.5
056 Baha'i	0	32	NR	32	-	-
057 Bapt Gen Conf	3	1,033	1,061	1,264 *	.5	.8
081 Catholic	44	NR	NR	100,351	39.0	59.9
089 Chr & Miss Al	1	66	NR	120	-	.1
093 Chr Ch (Disc)	6	1,794	299	2,194 *	.9	1.3
097 Chr Chs&Chs Cr	9	2,338	NR	2,861 *	1.1	1.7
123 Ch God (Ander)	4	NR	407	407	.2	.2
127 Ch God (Cleve)	3	256	122	313 *	.1	.2
151 L-D Saints	1	NR	NR	512	.2	.3
157 Ch of Brethren	2	126	82	155 *	.1	.1
165 Ch of Nazarene	7	751	609	977	.4	.6
167 Chs of Christ	6	521	450	694	.3	.4
181 Consrv Congr	1	246	165	301 *	.1	.2
193 Episcopal	5	NR	413	1,126	.4	.7
201 Evan Cov Ch	1	359	220	439 *	.2	.3
207 E.L.C.A.	18	6,337	2,446	8,184	3.2	4.9
216 Evan Presby Ch	1	532	NR	651 *	.3	.4
220 Free Lutheran	1	0	0	0	-	-
221 Free Methodist	2	183	193	236	.1	.1
223 Free Will Bapt	1	61	NR	75 *	-	-
226 Friends-USA	5	475	NR	581 *	.2	.3
246 Greek Orthodox	3	NR	NR	2,550	1.0	1.5
252 Hindu	2	NR	NR	NR	-	-
263 Int Foursq Gos	2	31	227	227 *	.1	.1
267 Muslim Est	2	NR	137	480	.2	.3
283 Luth—MO Synod	6	1,019	465	1,430	.6	.9
288 Mennonite USA	3	311	234	380 *	.1	.2
297 Mennonite;Other	1	6	NR	7 *	-	-
331 OCA: Ter Diocs	1	259	NR	341	.1	.2
332 OCA: Bulg Dioc	1	75	NR	141	.1	.1
355 Presb Ch (USA)	21	5,705	2,546	7,030 *	2.7	4.2
356 Presb Ch Amer	1	111	0	111	-	.1
363 Primitive Meth	1	57	NR	61	-	-
388 Reg Bapt Gen As	5	470	469	576 *	.2	.3
397 OCA: Roman Dioc	1	NR	NR	250	.1	.1
400 Rus Orth Moscow	1	NR	NR	NR	-	-
403 Salvation Army	3	255	147	566	.2	.3
410 Serb Orth USA	1	NR	NR	1,400	.5	.8
411 Serb Orth: Grac	1	NR	NR	NR	-	-
413 S.D.A.	3	475	NR	565	.2	.3
419 So Bapt Conv	8	1,590	708	1,945 *	.8	1.2
431 Ukrainian Orth	1	NR	NR	1,050	.4	.6
435 Unitarian-Univ	1	101	NR	124 *	-	.1
443 Un C of Christ	7	2,844	1,147	3,478 *	1.4	2.1
449 Un Methodist	23	7,332	2,914	8,971 *	3.5	5.4
496 Jewish Est	4	NR	NR	2,800	1.1	1.7
498 Indep.Charis.	1	400	800	800	.3	.5
499 Indep.Non-Char	1	600	700	700	.3	.4
MARION	**79**	**15,847**	**7,520**	**23,779 ***	**35.9**	**100.0**
011 A.W.M.C.	1	0	101	0	-	-
019 Amer Bapt USA	5	1,429	629	1,757 *	2.7	7.4
053 Assemb of God	1	143	193	260	.4	1.1
056 Baha'i	0	3	NR	3	-	-
081 Catholic	2	NR	NR	2,859	4.3	12.0
089 Chr & Miss Al	1	201	NR	425	.6	1.8
093 Chr Ch (Disc)	1	556	112	684 *	1.0	2.9
097 Chr Chs&Chs Cr	3	604	NR	743 *	1.1	3.1
123 Ch God (Ander)	1	NR	41	41	.1	.2
127 Ch God (Cleve)	1	562	298	691 *	1.0	2.9
145 Ch God Prophcy	1	32	NR	39 *	.1	.2
157 Ch of Brethren	1	59	48	73 *	.1	.3
165 Ch of Nazarene	4	1,498	1,172	1,834	2.8	7.7
167 Chs of Christ	1	280	270	300	.5	1.3
171 Ch God-Gen Con	1	52	48	64 *	.1	.3

NR–Not Reported   *Total adherents estimated from known number of communicant, confirmed, full members.   - Represents a percentage less than 0.1.   Percentages may not total 100 due to rounding.

Table 4: Religious Congregations by County and Group: 2000

Religious Group	Number of Churches, Synagogues, Mosques, or Temples	Number of Communicant, Confirmed, or Full Members	Number of Attendees	Total Adherents		
				Number of Adherents	% of Total Pop.	% of Total Adh.
191 Entrpr Bpt Asc	4	308	NR	379 *	.6	1.6
193 Episcopal	1	NR	58	137	.2	.6
207 E.L.C.A.	7	2,760	1,443	3,757	5.7	15.8
223 Free Will Bapt	2	122	NR	150 *	.2	.6
263 Int Foursq Gos	1	22	15	27 *	-	.1
265 Int Pent C Chr	1	45	37	180	.3	.8
283 Luth—MO Synod	1	34	33	43	.1	.2
323 Old Ord Amish	1	60	NR	74 *	.1	.3
339 Pent Ch of God	1	23	NR	40	.1	.2
355 Presb Ch (USA)	3	780	294	959 *	1.4	4.0
360 Prim Bapt Chrch	1	NR	NR	NR	-	-
388 Reg Bapt Gen As	2	299	338	390 *	.6	1.6
403 Salvation Army	1	104	78	136	.2	.6
413 S.D.A.	1	93	NR	111	.2	.5
443 Un C of Christ	4	950	337	1,168 *	1.8	4.9
449 Un Methodist	20	4,643	1,709	5,709 *	8.6	24.0
463 Vineyard	1	35	30	43 *	.1	.2
467 Wesleyan	2	150	236	578	.9	2.4
496 Jewish Est	1	NR	NR	125	.2	.5
MEDINA	**123**	**23,060**	**12,974**	**60,661 ***	**40.1**	**100.0**
019 Amer Bapt USA	2	181	96	230 *	.2	.4
039 Ap Chr Ch(Naz)	2	119	191	191 *	.1	.3
040 Ap Chr Ch-Amer	1	106	193	193 *	.1	.3
053 Assemb of God	7	717	939	1,094	.7	1.8
056 Baha'i	0	7	NR	7	-	-
081 Catholic	13	NR	NR	27,198	18.0	44.8
089 Chr & Miss Al	2	188	NR	445	.3	.7
093 Chr Ch (Disc)	4	1,780	615	2,261 *	1.5	3.7
097 Chr Chs&Chs Cr	1	700	NR	889 *	.6	1.5
127 Ch God (Cleve)	3	163	78	207 *	.1	.3
151 L-D Saints	2	NR	NR	556	.4	.9
157 Ch of Brethren	2	81	54	110 *	.1	.2
165 Ch of Nazarene	3	470	399	890	.6	1.5
167 Chs of Christ	3	272	256	317	.2	.5
181 Consrv Congr	1	69	48	88 *	.1	.1
193 Episcopal	2	NR	168	360	.2	.6
207 E.L.C.A.	10	3,930	1,554	5,208	3.4	8.6
221 Free Methodist	1	8	19	19	-	-
226 Friends-USA	1	95	NR	121 *	.1	.2
252 Hindu	1	NR	NR	NR	-	-
263 Int Foursq Gos	1	436	1,359	1,359 *	.9	2.2
283 Luth—MO Synod	4	1,701	812	2,482	1.6	4.1
288 Mennonite USA	2	173	126	220 *	.1	.4
297 Mennonite;Other	1	60	NR	76 *	.1	.1
313 N Am Bapt Conf	1	0	320	320 *	.2	.5
322 Old Ord Menn Ch	1	60	NR	76 *	.1	.1
323 Old Ord Amish	5	250	NR	320 *	.2	.5
355 Presb Ch (USA)	3	374	227	475 *	.3	.8
356 Presb Ch Amer	1	130	124	166	.1	.3
371 Ref Ch in Am	1	350	315	764	.5	1.3
388 Reg Bapt Gen As	6	1,003	828	1,289 *	.9	2.1
403 Salvation Army	2	53	36	215	.1	.4
413 S.D.A.	1	74	NR	88	.1	.1
419 So Bapt Conv	3	703	295	893 *	.6	1.5
431 Ukrainian Orth	1	NR	NR	177	.1	.3
435 Unitarian-Univ	1	26	NR	33 *	-	.1
443 Un C of Christ	7	1,961	841	2,491 *	1.6	4.1
449 Un Methodist	19	6,458	2,768	8,202 *	5.4	13.5
467 Wesleyan	1	62	88	231	.2	.4
499 Indep.Non-Char	1	300	225	400	.3	.7
MEIGS	**66**	**4,270**	**2,308**	**5,786 ***	**25.1**	**100.0**
019 Amer Bapt USA	3	189	137	230 *	1.0	4.0
081 Catholic	1	NR	NR	260	1.1	4.5
097 Chr Chs&Chs Cr	8	1,018	NR	1,242 *	5.4	21.5
123 Ch God (Ander)	1	NR	15	15	.1	.3
127 Ch God (Cleve)	2	187	165	236 *	1.0	4.1
165 Ch of Nazarene	9	466	421	815	3.5	14.1
167 Chs of Christ	7	267	280	338	1.5	5.8
173 Comm of Christ	1	61	NR	61	.3	1.1
175 Congr Chr Chs	1	188	99	229 *	1.0	4.0
193 Episcopal	1	NR	35	64	.3	1.1
207 E.L.C.A.	2	152	69	183	.8	3.2
221 Free Methodist	1	35	30	36	.2	.6
355 Presb Ch (USA)	3	79	55	96 *	.4	1.7
413 S.D.A.	1	27	NR	32	.1	.6
419 So Bapt Conv	2	326	145	397 *	1.7	6.9
449 Un Methodist	23	1,275	857	1,552 *	6.7	26.8
MERCER	**65**	**7,016**	**3,854**	**34,271 ***	**83.7**	**100.0**
053 Assemb of God	1	18	20	30	.1	.1
056 Baha'i	0	1	NR	1	-	-
081 Catholic	20	NR	NR	25,031	61.2	73.0
097 Chr Chs&Chs Cr	3	285	NR	368 *	.9	1.1
157 Ch of Brethren	1	25	27	32 *	.1	.1
165 Ch of Nazarene	2	342	258	444	1.1	1.3
167 Chs of Christ	1	17	18	22	.1	.1
171 Ch God-Gen Con	6	768	667	1,003 *	2.5	2.9
207 E.L.C.A.	6	1,759	761	2,252	5.5	6.6
226 Friends-USA	3	141	NR	182 *	.4	.5
291 Missionary Ch	1	216	464	464	1.1	1.4
296 Midw Congr Fel	2	59	52	76 *	.2	.2
355 Presb Ch (USA)	2	294	141	379 *	.9	1.1
419 So Bapt Conv	1	21	30	27 *	.1	.1
443 Un C of Christ	2	332	113	428 *	1.0	1.2
449 Un Methodist	14	2,738	1,303	3,532 *	8.6	10.3
MIAMI	**111**	**21,413**	**13,082**	**41,143 ***	**41.6**	**100.0**
019 Amer Bapt USA	6	1,691	768	2,105 *	2.1	5.1
053 Assemb of God	3	274	245	429	.4	1.0
056 Baha'i	0	12	NR	12	-	-
071 Brethren (Ash)	1	126	136	157 *	.2	.4
075 Brethren in Cr	3	183	171	187	.2	.5
081 Catholic	7	NR	NR	12,756	12.9	31.0
097 Chr Chs&Chs Cr	2	610	NR	759 *	.8	1.8
121 Ch God (Abr)	3	239	259	297 *	.3	.7
123 Ch God (Ander)	3	NR	169	169	.2	.4
127 Ch God (Cleve)	1	8	10	10 *	-	-
151 L-D Saints	2	NR	NR	539	.5	1.3
157 Ch of Brethren	11	2,527	1,132	3,146 *	3.2	7.6
165 Ch of Nazarene	5	904	870	1,361	1.4	3.3
167 Chs of Christ	3	323	335	400	.4	1.0
181 Consrv Congr	1	405	150	504 *	.5	1.2
193 Episcopal	2	NR	143	350	.4	.9
207 E.L.C.A.	8	2,270	851	2,939	3.0	7.1
223 Free Will Bapt	2	122	NR	152 *	.2	.4
226 Friends-USA	2	94	NR	117 *	.1	.3
291 Missionary Ch	2	77	81	106	.1	.3
335 Orth Pres Ch	1	36	78	78	.1	.2
339 Pent Ch of God	1	50	NR	70	.1	.2
355 Presb Ch (USA)	4	936	520	1,165 *	1.2	2.8
360 Prim Bapt Chrch	1	NR	NR	NR	-	-
388 Reg Bapt Gen As	2	267	370	370 *	.4	.9
403 Salvation Army	1	72	59	247	.2	.6
413 S.D.A.	1	121	NR	144	.1	.3
418 Southw Bapt Fel	2	NR	NR	NR	-	-
419 So Bapt Conv	4	1,122	473	1,397 *	1.4	3.4
443 Un C of Christ	11	3,346	1,035	4,165 *	4.2	10.1
449 Un Methodist	14	5,256	4,914	6,542 *	6.6	15.9
467 Wesleyan	1	62	33	150	.2	.4
499 Indep.Non-Char	1	280	280	320	.3	.8
MONROE	**81**	**5,591**	**3,371**	**8,074 ***	**53.2**	**100.0**
019 Amer Bapt USA	2	114	45	138 *	.9	1.7
040 Ap Chr Ch-Amer	1	40	70	70 *	.5	.9
053 Assemb of God	1	18	25	32	.2	.4
081 Catholic	4	NR	NR	930	6.1	11.5
097 Chr Chs&Chs Cr	3	305	NR	370 *	2.4	4.6
107 Christian Un	1	12	12	15 *	.1	.2
127 Ch God (Cleve)	1	44	20	53 *	.3	.7
165 Ch of Nazarene	1	71	79	161	1.1	2.0
167 Chs of Christ	30	1,704	1,713	2,308	15.2	28.6
181 Consrv Congr	1	96	45	116 *	.8	1.4
221 Free Methodist	1	34	60	60	.4	.7
223 Free Will Bapt	1	61	NR	74 *	.5	.9

NR–Not Reported *Total adherents estimated from known number of communicant, confirmed, full members. - Represents a percentage less than 0.1. Percentages may not total 100 due to rounding.

Table 4: Religious Congregations by County and Group: 2000

Religious Group	Number of Churches, Synagogues, Mosques, or Temples	Number of Communicant, Confirmed, or Full Members	Number of Attendees	Total Adherents		
				Number of Adherents	% of Total Pop.	% of Total Adh.
320 "Old" MB Ascs	1	23	NR	28 *	.2	.3
323 Old Ord Amish	3	180	NR	219 *	1.4	2.7
355 Presb Ch (USA)	3	91	65	110 *	.7	1.4
419 So Bapt Conv	2	738	239	895 *	5.9	11.1
443 Un C of Christ	5	748	315	907 *	6.0	11.2
449 Un Methodist	20	1,312	683	1,588 *	10.5	19.7
MONTGOMERY	**430**	**99,293**	**51,327**	**236,103 ***	**42.2**	**100.0**
017 Amer Bapt Assn	1	50	NR	62 *	-	-
019 Amer Bapt USA	16	8,766	3,483	10,853 *	1.9	4.6
053 Assemb of God	11	2,697	3,636	6,364	1.1	2.7
056 Baha'i	2	122	NR	122	-	.1
071 Brethren (Ash)	2	193	158	239 *	-	.1
075 Brethren in Cr	4	242	189	242	-	.1
076 Buddhism	1	NR	NR	NR	-	-
081 Catholic	34	NR	NR	89,698	16.0	38.0
084 Calvary Chapel	1	NR	NR	NR	-	-
089 Chr & Miss Al	8	885	NR	2,213	.4	.9
093 Chr Ch (Disc)	4	1,189	504	1,472 *	.3	.6
097 Chr Chs&Chs Cr	7	2,615	NR	3,238 *	.6	1.4
107 Christian Un	1	62	50	77 *	-	-
123 Ch God (Ander)	16	NR	3,510	3,510	.6	1.5
127 Ch God (Cleve)	14	2,490	941	3,082 *	.6	1.3
145 Ch God Prophcy	2	64	NR	78 *	-	-
151 L-D Saints	8	NR	NR	2,503	.4	1.1
157 Ch of Brethren	12	2,235	1,160	2,769 *	.5	1.2
165 Ch of Nazarene	20	2,773	2,212	3,650	.7	1.5
167 Chs of Christ	27	2,910	2,852	3,773	.7	1.6
173 Comm of Christ	2	190	NR	190	-	.1
191 Entrpr Bpt Asc	1	14	NR	17 *	-	-
193 Episcopal	6	NR	1,045	3,186	.6	1.3
201 Evan Cov Ch	1	9	0	11 *	-	-
207 E.L.C.A.	29	9,666	3,932	12,969	2.3	5.5
221 Free Methodist	1	20	40	40	-	-
223 Free Will Bapt	4	245	NR	303 *	.1	.1
226 Friends-USA	2	105	NR	130 *	-	.1
262 Int Cou Comm Ch	2	570	NR	705 *	.1	.3
267 Muslim Est	2	NR	306	909	.2	.4
283 Luth—MO Synod	5	1,308	768	1,701	.3	.7
290 Metro Comm Ch	1	58	52	72 *	-	-
291 Missionary Ch	4	119	174	174	-	.1
313 N Am Bapt Conf	1	100	100	124 *	-	.1
331 OCA: Ter Diocs	1	104	NR	288	.1	.1
335 Orth Pres Ch	1	69	88	99	-	-
339 Pent Ch of God	1	42	NR	100	-	-
349 Pent Holiness	2	84	127	104 *	-	-
355 Presb Ch (USA)	12	3,323	1,431	4,114 *	.7	1.7
356 Presb Ch Amer	1	185	235	271	-	.1
362 Prim Bapt E Dst	1	70	NR	87 *	-	-
370 Ref Baptist Chs	1	NR	NR	NR	-	-
388 Reg Bapt Gen As	6	1,346	1,311	1,694 *	.3	.7
403 Salvation Army	2	299	118	1,127	.2	.5
413 S.D.A.	7	2,255	NR	2,683	.5	1.1
416 Sikh	1	NR	NR	NR	-	-
418 Southw Bapt Fel	1	NR	NR	NR	-	-
419 So Bapt Conv	47	22,343	8,324	27,663 *	4.9	11.7
435 Unitarian-Univ	1	247	NR	306 *	.1	.1
443 Un C of Christ	21	5,735	2,208	7,101 *	1.3	3.0
449 Un Methodist	53	20,233	8,892	25,053 *	4.5	10.6
463 Vineyard	2	260	240	322 *	.1	.1
467 Wesleyan	6	328	264	871	.2	.4
469 WELS	1	98	62	124	-	.1
496 Jewish Est	5	NR	NR	5,000	.9	2.1
498 Indep.Charis.	1	325	420	420	.1	.2
499 Indep.Non-Char	4	2,250	2,495	4,200	.8	1.8
MORGAN	**40**	**3,368**	**1,284**	**4,426 ***	**29.7**	**100.0**
056 Baha'i	0	2	NR	2	-	-
061 Beachy Amish	1	61	NR	75 *	.5	1.7
081 Catholic	1	NR	NR	172	1.2	3.9
097 Chr Chs&Chs Cr	6	895	NR	1,103 *	7.4	24.9
151 L-D Saints	1	NR	NR	59	.4	1.3
165 Ch of Nazarene	2	111	78	119	.8	2.7

Religious Group	Number of Churches, Synagogues, Mosques, or Temples	Number of Communicant, Confirmed, or Full Members	Number of Attendees	Total Adherents		
				Number of Adherents	% of Total Pop.	% of Total Adh.
167 Chs of Christ	6	319	295	414	2.8	9.4
207 E.L.C.A.	2	87	45	143	1.0	3.2
221 Free Methodist	1	3	10	10	.1	.2
226 Friends-USA	1	59	NR	73 *	.5	1.6
323 Old Ord Amish	1	60	NR	74 *	.5	1.7
355 Presb Ch (USA)	2	112	67	138 *	.9	3.1
419 So Bapt Conv	1	148	45	182 *	1.2	4.1
449 Un Methodist	15	1,511	744	1,862 *	12.5	42.1
MORROW	**54**	**5,294**	**2,269**	**8,085 ***	**25.6**	**100.0**
019 Amer Bapt USA	3	394	251	497 *	1.6	6.1
053 Assemb of God	1	51	68	105	.3	1.3
056 Baha'i	0	6	NR	6	-	.1
081 Catholic	1	NR	NR	400	1.3	4.9
089 Chr & Miss Al	1	155	NR	641	2.0	7.9
097 Chr Chs&Chs Cr	5	638	NR	805 *	2.5	10.0
127 Ch God (Cleve)	1	137	43	173 *	.5	2.1
151 L-D Saints	1	NR	NR	224	.7	2.8
165 Ch of Nazarene	3	259	190	472	1.5	5.8
191 Entrpr Bpt Asc	1	60	NR	76 *	.2	.9
207 E.L.C.A.	2	246	130	324	1.0	4.0
223 Free Will Bapt	2	122	NR	154 *	.5	1.9
226 Friends-USA	1	95	NR	120 *	.4	1.5
258 IndFreeWillBapt	1	20	NR	25 *	.1	.3
288 Mennonite USA	1	70	72	88 *	.3	1.1
349 Pent Holiness	1	12	20	15 *	-	.2
355 Presb Ch (USA)	2	234	109	295 *	.9	3.6
360 Prim Bapt Chrch	2	NR	NR	NR	-	-
413 S.D.A.	1	20	NR	24	.1	.3
419 So Bapt Conv	1	131	32	165 *	.5	2.0
443 Un C of Christ	1	45	20	57 *	.2	.7
449 Un Methodist	21	2,550	1,260	3,219 *	10.2	39.8
467 Wesleyan	1	49	74	200	.6	2.5
MUSKINGUM	**131**	**21,303**	**9,146**	**34,393 ***	**40.7**	**100.0**
011 A.W.M.C.	1	25	200	25	-	.1
019 Amer Bapt USA	7	3,488	528	4,351 *	5.1	12.7
053 Assemb of God	2	92	114	188	.2	.5
056 Baha'i	0	7	NR	7	-	-
081 Catholic	6	NR	NR	5,360	6.3	15.6
084 Calvary Chapel	1	NR	NR	NR	-	-
089 Chr & Miss Al	2	168	NR	300	.4	.9
093 Chr Ch (Disc)	1	1,147	464	1,431 *	1.7	4.2
097 Chr Chs&Chs Cr	4	930	NR	1,161 *	1.4	3.4
123 Ch God (Ander)	2	NR	144	144	.2	.4
127 Ch God (Cleve)	1	273	180	341 *	.4	1.0
151 L-D Saints	2	NR	NR	646	.8	1.9
157 Ch of Brethren	1	98	40	122 *	.1	.4
165 Ch of Nazarene	5	479	446	577	.7	1.7
167 Chs of Christ	9	580	587	809	1.0	2.4
179 Consrv Bapt	1	NR	300	300	.4	.9
193 Episcopal	1	NR	106	165	.2	.5
207 E.L.C.A.	7	1,340	428	1,739	2.1	5.1
221 Free Methodist	3	159	142	172	.2	.5
223 Free Will Bapt	1	61	NR	76 *	.1	.2
263 Int Foursq Gos	1	21	33	33 *	-	.1
283 Luth—MO Synod	1	1,029	602	1,262	1.5	3.7
297 Mennonite;Other	1	60	NR	75 *	.1	.2
323 Old Ord Amish	1	60	NR	75 *	.1	.2
339 Pent Ch of God	2	88	NR	577	.7	1.7
355 Presb Ch (USA)	17	2,033	996	2,536 *	3.0	7.4
360 Prim Bapt Chrch	1	NR	NR	NR	-	-
388 Reg Bapt Gen As	1	130	70	70 *	.1	.2
403 Salvation Army	1	58	63	499	.6	1.5
413 S.D.A.	1	192	NR	228	.3	.7
419 So Bapt Conv	4	548	236	684 *	.8	2.0
443 Un C of Christ	1	442	183	551 *	.7	1.6
449 Un Methodist	40	7,740	3,221	9,654 *	11.4	28.1
467 Wesleyan	1	55	63	135	.2	.4
496 Jewish Est	1	NR	NR	100	.1	.3
NOBLE	**37**	**2,314**	**1,567**	**4,525 ***	**32.2**	**100.0**
081 Catholic	5	NR	NR	1,595	11.3	35.2

NR–Not Reported *Total adherents estimated from known number of communicant, confirmed, full members. - Represents a percentage less than 0.1. Percentages may not total 100 due to rounding.

Table 4: Religious Congregations by County and Group: 2000

Religious Group	Number of Churches, Synagogues, Mosques, or Temples	Number of Communicant, Confirmed, or Full Members	Number of Attendees	Total Adherents		
				Number of Adherents	% of Total Pop.	% of Total Adh.
097 Chr Chs&Chs Cr	1	200	NR	240 *	1.7	5.3
165 Ch of Nazarene	1	60	48	101	.7	2.2
167 Chs of Christ	6	516	475	675	4.8	14.9
207 E.L.C.A.	1	77	56	129	.9	2.9
221 Free Methodist	2	109	150	158	1.1	3.5
355 Presb Ch (USA)	1	90	50	108 *	.8	2.4
388 Reg Bapt Gen As	1	52	65	65 *	.5	1.4
419 So Bapt Conv	2	212	153	255 *	1.8	5.6
443 Un C of Christ	1	13	6	16 *	.1	.4
449 Un Methodist	16	985	564	1,183 *	8.4	26.1
OTTAWA	**53**	**10,896**	**4,608**	**23,744 ***	**57.9**	**100.0**
019 Amer Bapt USA	1	103	35	124 *	.3	.5
053 Assemb of God	1	171	220	300	.7	1.3
056 Baha'i	0	7	NR	7	-	-
081 Catholic	7	NR	NR	8,990	21.9	37.9
089 Chr & Miss Al	1	44	NR	157	.4	.7
093 Chr Ch (Disc)	1	88	0	106 *	.3	.4
123 Ch God (Ander)	1	NR	30	30	.1	.1
127 Ch God (Cleve)	1	29	24	35 *	.1	.1
145 Ch God Prophcy	1	32	NR	38 *	.1	.2
165 Ch of Nazarene	1	57	40	73	.2	.3
167 Chs of Christ	2	54	63	68	.2	.3
193 Episcopal	2	NR	80	306	.7	1.3
203 Evan Free Ch	1	58	74	74	.2	.3
207 E.L.C.A.	12	4,995	1,944	7,024	17.1	29.6
283 Luth—MO Synod	1	337	165	420	1.0	1.8
339 Pent Ch of God	1	7	NR	20	-	.1
355 Presb Ch (USA)	2	203	114	245 *	.6	1.0
388 Reg Bapt Gen As	1	89	140	140 *	.3	.6
419 So Bapt Conv	2	188	58	227 *	.6	1.0
443 Un C of Christ	5	2,359	754	2,849 *	7.0	12.0
449 Un Methodist	8	2,062	847	2,491 *	6.1	10.5
467 Wesleyan	1	13	20	20	-	.1
PAULDING	**40**	**4,197**	**2,910**	**8,815 ***	**43.4**	**100.0**
017 Amer Bapt Assn	1	50	NR	63 *	.3	.7
040 Ap Chr Ch-Amer	1	250	500	500 *	2.5	5.7
056 Baha'i	0	2	NR	2	-	-
081 Catholic	5	NR	NR	2,760	13.6	31.3
093 Chr Ch (Disc)	1	313	155	392 *	1.9	4.4
097 Chr Chs&Chs Cr	2	150	NR	188 *	.9	2.1
123 Ch God (Ander)	2	NR	182	182	.9	2.1
127 Ch God (Cleve)	1	99	34	124 *	.6	1.4
165 Ch of Nazarene	4	392	368	840	4.1	9.5
167 Chs of Christ	1	52	70	88	.4	1.0
207 E.L.C.A.	3	628	260	793	3.9	9.0
283 Luth—MO Synod	1	196	79	282	1.4	3.2
355 Presb Ch (USA)	3	218	156	274 *	1.4	3.1
388 Reg Bapt Gen As	1	25	45	45 *	.2	.5
419 So Bapt Conv	1	235	145	294 *	1.4	3.3
443 Un C of Christ	1	62	27	78 *	.4	.9
449 Un Methodist	12	1,525	889	1,910 *	9.4	21.7
PERRY	**66**	**5,368**	**2,793**	**9,978 ***	**29.3**	**100.0**
019 Amer Bapt USA	2	171	112	218 *	.6	2.2
053 Assemb of God	1	37	43	65	.2	.7
056 Baha'i	0	1	NR	1	-	-
081 Catholic	6	NR	NR	2,986	8.8	29.9
093 Chr Ch (Disc)	2	330	45	421 *	1.2	4.2
097 Chr Chs&Chs Cr	1	40	NR	51 *	.1	.5
107 Christian Un	2	30	29	38 *	.1	.4
123 Ch God (Ander)	1	NR	48	48	.1	.5
157 Ch of Brethren	1	119	45	152 *	.4	1.5
165 Ch of Nazarene	2	247	137	252	.7	2.5
167 Chs of Christ	5	205	232	274	.8	2.7
207 E.L.C.A.	6	1,063	455	1,445	4.2	14.5
221 Free Methodist	1	37	43	43	.1	.4
297 Mennonite;Other	1	83	NR	106 *	.3	1.1
339 Pent Ch of God	1	7	NR	8	-	.1
355 Presb Ch (USA)	2	127	114	162 *	.5	1.6
388 Reg Bapt Gen As	1	179	168	229 *	.7	2.3
419 So Bapt Conv	1	27	25	34 *	.1	.3
443 Un C of Christ	3	262	117	335 *	1.0	3.4
449 Un Methodist	25	2,343	1,144	2,996 *	8.8	30.0
466 Wayn Tr MB Asc	1	28	NR	36 *	.1	.4
467 Wesleyan	1	32	36	78	.2	.8
PICKAWAY	**57**	**8,911**	**4,579**	**13,320 ***	**25.3**	**100.0**
053 Assemb of God	1	83	110	110	.2	.8
056 Baha'i	0	7	NR	7	-	.1
081 Catholic	1	NR	NR	2,023	3.8	15.2
097 Chr Chs&Chs Cr	3	274	NR	336 *	.6	2.5
123 Ch God (Ander)	2	NR	150	150	.3	1.1
127 Ch God (Cleve)	2	204	182	250 *	.5	1.9
157 Ch of Brethren	1	66	41	81 *	.2	.6
165 Ch of Nazarene	4	528	394	554	1.1	4.2
167 Chs of Christ	1	193	175	288	.5	2.2
193 Episcopal	1	NR	53	167	.3	1.3
207 E.L.C.A.	5	1,546	621	1,982	3.8	14.9
223 Free Will Bapt	2	122	NR	150 *	.3	1.1
331 OCA: Ter Diocs	1	47	NR	64	.1	.5
355 Presb Ch (USA)	2	405	166	496 *	.9	3.7
360 Prim Bapt Chrch	1	NR	NR	NR	-	-
388 Reg Bapt Gen As	1	123	100	151 *	.3	1.1
419 So Bapt Conv	4	988	403	1,210 *	2.3	9.1
449 Un Methodist	25	4,325	2,184	5,301 *	10.1	39.8
PIKE	**36**	**3,521**	**1,717**	**4,792 ***	**17.3**	**100.0**
056 Baha'i	0	2	NR	2	-	-
081 Catholic	1	NR	NR	300	1.1	6.3
097 Chr Chs&Chs Cr	2	335	NR	423 *	1.5	8.8
107 Christian Un	8	258	295	326 *	1.2	6.8
127 Ch God (Cleve)	1	54	72	72 *	.3	1.5
165 Ch of Nazarene	1	68	57	95	.3	2.0
167 Chs of Christ	3	191	216	257	.9	5.4
191 Entrpr Bpt Asc	1	71	NR	90 *	.3	1.9
223 Free Will Bapt	2	122	NR	155 *	.6	3.2
288 Mennonite USA	1	21	40	40 *	.1	.8
323 Old Ord Amish	1	60	NR	76 *	.3	1.6
355 Presb Ch (USA)	1	184	88	233 *	.8	4.9
360 Prim Bapt Chrch	2	NR	NR	NR	-	-
419 So Bapt Conv	2	1,230	482	1,554 *	5.6	32.4
449 Un Methodist	10	925	467	1,169 *	4.2	24.4
PORTAGE	**103**	**17,488**	**9,661**	**54,651 ***	**35.9**	**100.0**
019 Amer Bapt USA	1	227	120	277 *	.2	.5
053 Assemb of God	4	534	677	1,066	.7	2.0
056 Baha'i	1	31	NR	31	-	.1
075 Brethren in Cr	1	14	20	20	-	-
076 Buddhism	1	NR	NR	NR	-	-
081 Catholic	10	NR	NR	29,490	19.4	54.0
089 Chr & Miss Al	2	249	NR	580	.4	1.1
093 Chr Ch (Disc)	6	1,944	414	2,376 *	1.6	4.3
097 Chr Chs&Chs Cr	2	276	NR	338 *	.2	.6
123 Ch God (Ander)	4	NR	288	288	.2	.5
127 Ch God (Cleve)	4	567	284	693 *	.5	1.3
151 L-D Saints	1	NR	NR	336	.2	.6
157 Ch of Brethren	1	150	74	183 *	.1	.3
165 Ch of Nazarene	4	380	351	647	.4	1.2
167 Chs of Christ	4	280	314	364	.2	.7
193 Episcopal	2	NR	222	550	.4	1.0
203 Evan Free Ch	1	130	177	177	.1	.3
207 E.L.C.A.	3	749	397	1,144	.8	2.1
223 Free Will Bapt	1	61	NR	75 *	-	.1
226 Friends-USA	1	95	NR	116 *	.1	.2
262 Int Cou Comm Ch	2	966	NR	1,181 *	.8	2.2
267 Muslim Est	1	NR	250	1,500	1.0	2.7
283 Luth—MO Synod	3	711	287	944	.6	1.7
288 Mennonite USA	1	97	94	119 *	.1	.2
323 Old Ord Amish	1	60	NR	73 *	-	.1
355 Presb Ch (USA)	1	280	131	342 *	.2	.6
363 Primitive Meth	1	57	NR	61	-	.1
388 Reg Bapt Gen As	4	645	730	900 *	.6	1.6
403 Salvation Army	1	9	16	24	-	-
413 S.D.A.	1	29	NR	35	-	.1

NR–Not Reported *Total adherents estimated from known number of communicant, confirmed, full members. - Represents a percentage less than 0.1. Percentages may not total 100 due to rounding.

Table 4: Religious Congregations by County and Group: 2000

Religious Group	Number of Churches, Synagogues, Mosques, or Temples	Number of Communicant, Confirmed, or Full Members	Number of Attendees	Total Adherents: Number of Adherents	Total Adherents: % of Total Pop.	Total Adherents: % of Total Adh.
419 So Bapt Conv	3	545	323	666 *	.4	1.2
435 Unitarian-Univ	1	140	NR	171 *	.1	.3
443 Un C of Christ	7	2,145	869	2,622 *	1.7	4.8
449 Un Methodist	17	4,587	2,003	5,603 *	3.7	10.3
463 Vineyard	1	130	120	159 *	.1	.3
499 Indep.Non-Char	4	1,400	1,500	1,500	1.0	2.7
PREBLE	**63**	**9,504**	**4,507**	**14,959 ***	**35.3**	**100.0**
017 Amer Bapt Assn	1	50	NR	62 *	.1	.4
053 Assemb of God	1	51	70	110	.3	.7
071 Brethren (Ash)	2	161	152	200 *	.5	1.3
081 Catholic	3	NR	NR	2,360	5.6	15.8
097 Chr Chs&Chs Cr	3	335	NR	415 *	1.0	2.8
123 Ch God (Ander)	3	NR	456	456	1.1	3.0
127 Ch God (Cleve)	2	307	211	396 *	.9	2.6
157 Ch of Brethren	6	1,332	800	1,655 *	3.9	11.1
165 Ch of Nazarene	1	146	82	184	.4	1.2
167 Chs of Christ	2	61	70	85	.2	.6
207 E.L.C.A.	6	1,443	582	2,054	4.9	13.7
355 Presb Ch (USA)	4	492	270	612 *	1.4	4.1
419 So Bapt Conv	8	2,411	623	2,996 *	7.1	20.0
435 Unitarian-Univ	1	24	NR	30 *	.1	.2
443 Un C of Christ	6	934	410	1,161 *	2.7	7.8
449 Un Methodist	14	1,757	781	2,183 *	5.2	14.6
PUTNAM	**50**	**4,517**	**3,213**	**28,386 ***	**81.7**	**100.0**
053 Assemb of God	1	40	62	86	.2	.3
081 Catholic	11	NR	NR	21,759	62.7	76.7
093 Chr Ch (Disc)	1	147	0	190 *	.5	.7
097 Chr Chs&Chs Cr	1	50	NR	65 *	.2	.2
107 Christian Un	1	12	13	15 *	-	.1
123 Ch God (Ander)	2	NR	344	344	1.0	1.2
157 Ch of Brethren	1	423	322	546 *	1.6	1.9
165 Ch of Nazarene	1	46	58	126	.4	.4
171 Ch God-Gen Con	1	36	36	46 *	.1	.2
207 E.L.C.A.	2	280	122	346	1.0	1.2
221 Free Methodist	1	13	23	23	.1	.1
288 Mennonite USA	3	763	1,004	1,270 *	3.7	4.5
291 Missionary Ch	2	53	131	131	.4	.5
339 Pent Ch of God	1	16	NR	34	.1	.1
355 Presb Ch (USA)	2	166	98	215 *	.6	.8
360 Prim Bapt Chrch	1	NR	NR	NR	-	-
443 Un C of Christ	1	275	110	355 *	1.0	1.3
449 Un Methodist	15	2,090	890	2,697 *	7.8	9.5
466 Wayn Tr MB Asc	2	107	NR	138 *	.4	.5
RICHLAND	**146**	**24,865**	**15,143**	**49,731 ***	**38.6**	**100.0**
019 Amer Bapt USA	4	598	296	738 *	.6	1.5
039 Ap Chr Ch(Naz)	2	465	700	700 *	.5	1.4
040 Ap Chr Ch-Amer	1	162	355	355 *	.3	.7
053 Assemb of God	2	716	932	2,157	1.7	4.3
056 Baha'i	1	72	NR	72	.1	.1
057 Bapt Gen Conf	2	798	862	1,242 *	1.0	2.5
071 Brethren (Ash)	1	25	91	31 *	-	.1
076 Buddhism	1	NR	NR	NR	-	-
081 Catholic	5	NR	NR	12,007	9.3	24.1
089 Chr & Miss Al	4	577	NR	1,294	1.0	2.6
093 Chr Ch (Disc)	4	938	332	1,157 *	.9	2.3
097 Chr Chs&Chs Cr	5	860	NR	1,060 *	.8	2.1
123 Ch God (Ander)	3	NR	760	760	.6	1.5
127 Ch God (Cleve)	4	1,234	544	1,523 *	1.2	3.1
145 Ch God Prophcy	1	32	NR	39 *	-	.1
151 L-D Saints	1	NR	NR	524	.4	1.1
157 Ch of Brethren	3	269	168	331 *	.3	.7
165 Ch of Nazarene	4	366	222	566	.4	1.1
167 Chs of Christ	6	326	271	438	.3	.9
171 Ch God-Gen Con	1	106	100	131 *	.1	.3
173 Comm of Christ	1	40	NR	40	-	.1
175 Congr Chr Chs	2	1,041	408	1,284 *	1.0	2.6
179 Consrv Bapt	1	NR	60	60	-	.1
181 Consrv Congr	1	61	26	75 *	.1	.2
193 Episcopal	2	NR	199	946	.7	1.9
203 Evan Free Ch	1	34	70	70	.1	.1
207 E.L.C.A.	18	5,176	1,941	6,618	5.1	13.3
221 Free Methodist	1	114	144	144	.1	.3
223 Free Will Bapt	9	551	NR	679 *	.5	1.4
226 Friends-USA	1	95	NR	117 *	.1	.2
246 Greek Orthodox	1	NR	NR	120	.1	.2
263 Int Foursq Gos	2	254	260	313 *	.2	.6
283 Luth—MO Synod	1	63	57	83	.1	.2
322 Old Ord Menn Ch	2	340	NR	419 *	.3	.8
323 Old Ord Amish	4	240	NR	296 *	.2	.6
335 Orth Pres Ch	1	44	81	81	.1	.2
355 Presb Ch (USA)	7	1,120	586	1,382 *	1.1	2.8
403 Salvation Army	1	82	56	139	.1	.3
413 S.D.A.	1	218	NR	259	.2	.5
419 So Bapt Conv	5	1,007	339	1,242 *	1.0	2.5
435 Unitarian-Univ	1	29	NR	36 *	-	.1
443 Un C of Christ	2	737	256	909 *	.7	1.8
449 Un Methodist	19	4,842	2,103	5,974 *	4.6	12.0
467 Wesleyan	3	313	399	625	.5	1.3
496 Jewish Est	1	NR	NR	150	.1	.3
498 Indep.Charis.	1	0	400	420	.3	.8
499 Indep.Non-Char	2	920	2,125	2,125	1.6	4.3
ROSS	**91**	**11,329**	**5,884**	**18,495 ***	**25.2**	**100.0**
019 Amer Bapt USA	1	1,005	330	1,230 *	1.7	6.7
053 Assemb of God	2	66	75	84	.1	.5
056 Baha'i	0	2	NR	2	-	-
081 Catholic	2	NR	NR	2,837	3.9	15.3
093 Chr Ch (Disc)	1	107	53	131 *	.2	.7
097 Chr Chs&Chs Cr	4	508	NR	622 *	.8	3.4
107 Christian Un	7	292	373	373 *	.5	2.0
123 Ch God (Ander)	3	NR	235	235	.3	1.3
127 Ch God (Cleve)	4	512	250	629 *	.9	3.4
151 L-D Saints	1	NR	NR	299	.4	1.6
157 Ch of Brethren	1	33	0	40 *	.1	.2
165 Ch of Nazarene	3	373	194	478	.7	2.6
167 Chs of Christ	2	153	175	214	.3	1.2
173 Comm of Christ	1	81	NR	81	.1	.4
175 Congr Chr Chs	1	170	110	208 *	.3	1.1
191 Entrpr Bpt Asc	1	70	NR	86 *	.1	.5
193 Episcopal	1	NR	94	404	.6	2.2
207 E.L.C.A.	1	331	154	426	.6	2.3
223 Free Will Bapt	2	122	NR	150 *	.2	.8
226 Friends-USA	2	126	NR	154 *	.2	.8
265 Int Pent C Chr	1	58	83	70	.1	.4
283 Luth—MO Synod	1	99	64	117	.2	.6
322 Old Ord Menn Ch	1	89	NR	109 *	.1	.6
355 Presb Ch (USA)	7	876	445	1,084 *	1.5	5.9
388 Reg Bapt Gen As	1	225	225	275 *	.4	1.5
403 Salvation Army	1	64	56	172	.2	.9
413 S.D.A.	2	152	NR	181	.2	1.0
419 So Bapt Conv	2	1,482	421	1,814 *	2.5	9.8
443 Un C of Christ	2	98	63	120 *	.2	.6
449 Un Methodist	30	3,812	2,120	4,666 *	6.4	25.2
467 Wesleyan	2	423	364	1,154	1.6	6.2
496 Jewish Est	1	NR	NR	50	.1	.3
SANDUSKY	**74**	**13,453**	**6,904**	**31,484 ***	**51.0**	**100.0**
017 Amer Bapt Assn	1	50	NR	62 *	.1	.2
019 Amer Bapt USA	1	76	54	95 *	.2	.3
053 Assemb of God	3	117	141	184	.3	.6
056 Baha'i	0	8	NR	8	-	-
071 Brethren (Ash)	1	51	37	64 *	.1	.2
081 Catholic	7	NR	NR	12,669	20.5	40.2
089 Chr & Miss Al	1	135	NR	317	.5	1.0
093 Chr Ch (Disc)	1	145	45	181 *	.3	.6
097 Chr Chs&Chs Cr	1	60	NR	75 *	.1	.2
123 Ch God (Ander)	1	NR	39	39	.1	.1
127 Ch God (Cleve)	3	146	86	182 *	.3	.6
145 Ch God Prophcy	1	0	NR	0 *	-	-
151 L-D Saints	2	NR	NR	455	.7	1.4
165 Ch of Nazarene	2	156	133	199	.3	.6
167 Chs of Christ	3	118	118	152	.2	.5
193 Episcopal	2	NR	93	263	.4	.8

NR–Not Reported *Total adherents estimated from known number of communicant, confirmed, full members. - Represents a percentage less than 0.1. Percentages may not total 100 due to rounding.

Table 4: Religious Congregations by County and Group: 2000

Religious Group	Number of Churches, Synagogues, Mosques, or Temples	Number of Communicant, Confirmed, or Full Members	Number of Attendees	Total Adherents: Number of Adherents	Total Adherents: % of Total Pop.	Total Adherents: % of Total Adh.
207 E.L.C.A.	11	5,397	2,190	7,107	11.5	22.6
223 Free Will Bapt	1	61	NR	76 *	.1	.2
288 Mennonite USA	1	19	15	24 *	-	.1
291 Missionary Ch	1	43	95	95	.2	.3
355 Presb Ch (USA)	3	584	256	728 *	1.2	2.3
413 S.D.A.	1	27	NR	32	.1	.1
418 Southw Bapt Fel	1	NR	NR	NR	-	-
419 So Bapt Conv	5	805	362	1,004 *	1.6	3.2
443 Un C of Christ	2	626	220	781 *	1.3	2.5
449 Un Methodist	15	4,000	1,580	4,989 *	8.1	15.8
463 Vineyard	1	163	140	203 *	.3	.6
498 Indep.Charis.	1	416	900	1,100	1.8	3.5
499 Indep.Non-Char	1	250	400	400	.6	1.3
SCIOTO	**138**	**13,278**	**5,855**	**20,759 ***	**26.2**	**100.0**
019 Amer Bapt USA	1	256	67	313 *	.4	1.5
053 Assemb of God	1	31	37	165	.2	.8
056 Baha'i	0	4	NR	4	-	-
081 Catholic	7	NR	NR	3,394	4.3	16.3
084 Calvary Chapel	1	NR	NR	NR	-	-
093 Chr Ch (Disc)	1	239	0	293 *	.4	1.4
097 Chr Chs&Chs Cr	7	1,755	NR	2,148 *	2.7	10.3
107 Christian Un	2	65	107	107 *	.1	.5
123 Ch God (Ander)	2	NR	183	183	.2	.9
127 Ch God (Cleve)	6	608	390	762 *	1.0	3.7
145 Ch God Prophcy	2	64	NR	78 *	.1	.4
151 L-D Saints	1	NR	NR	281	.4	1.4
165 Ch of Nazarene	10	1,033	765	1,265	1.6	6.1
167 Chs of Christ	6	355	404	490	.6	2.4
173 Comm of Christ	4	476	NR	476	.6	2.3
191 Entrpr Bpt Asc	2	33	NR	40 *	.1	.2
193 Episcopal	1	NR	90	174	.2	.8
207 E.L.C.A.	2	314	143	430	.5	2.1
223 Free Will Bapt	23	1,407	NR	1,723 *	2.2	8.3
265 Int Pent C Chr	3	109	134	168	.2	.8
283 Luth—MO Synod	1	9	16	20	-	.1
355 Presb Ch (USA)	3	527	241	645 *	.8	3.1
360 Prim Bapt Chrch	1	NR	NR	NR	-	-
388 Reg Bapt Gen As	5	1,410	766	1,726 *	2.2	8.3
403 Salvation Army	1	112	39	303	.4	1.5
413 S.D.A.	1	125	NR	149	.2	.7
418 Southw Bapt Fel	1	NR	NR	NR	-	-
419 So Bapt Conv	3	315	130	386 *	.5	1.9
443 Un C of Christ	1	168	68	206 *	.3	1.0
449 Un Methodist	36	3,797	2,223	4,650 *	5.9	22.4
467 Wesleyan	2	66	52	130	.2	.6
496 Jewish Est	1	NR	NR	50	.1	.2
SENECA	**85**	**12,476**	**5,036**	**38,719 ***	**66.0**	**100.0**
019 Amer Bapt USA	2	267	143	332 *	.6	.9
053 Assemb of God	2	123	146	263	.4	.7
056 Baha'i	0	7	NR	7	-	-
081 Catholic	14	NR	NR	22,461	38.3	58.0
089 Chr & Miss Al	1	71	NR	174	.3	.4
093 Chr Ch (Disc)	2	406	97	505 *	.9	1.3
097 Chr Chs&Chs Cr	1	240	NR	298 *	.5	.8
127 Ch God (Cleve)	2	62	45	77 *	.1	.2
145 Ch God Prophcy	1	32	NR	40 *	.1	.1
157 Ch of Brethren	1	30	24	37 *	.1	.1
165 Ch of Nazarene	2	455	372	608	1.0	1.6
167 Chs of Christ	1	77	60	100	.2	.3
171 Ch God-Gen Con	1	71	61	88 *	.1	.2
193 Episcopal	2	NR	69	123	.2	.3
207 E.L.C.A.	4	1,950	618	2,633	4.5	6.8
223 Free Will Bapt	2	122	NR	152 *	.3	.4
263 Int Foursq Gos	2	276	135	343 *	.6	.9
283 Luth—MO Synod	1	110	65	160	.3	.4
339 Pent Ch of God	2	70	NR	160	.3	.4
355 Presb Ch (USA)	2	478	229	594 *	1.0	1.5
360 Prim Bapt Chrch	1	NR	NR	NR	-	-
388 Reg Bapt Gen As	2	262	195	325 *	.6	.8
403 Salvation Army	1	65	44	163	.3	.4
419 So Bapt Conv	1	111	100	138 *	.2	.4
443 Un C of Christ	14	2,996	995	3,723 *	6.3	9.6
449 Un Methodist	21	4,195	1,638	5,215 *	8.9	13.5
SHELBY	**52**	**9,109**	**4,534**	**26,986 ***	**56.3**	**100.0**
019 Amer Bapt USA	2	287	135	368 *	.8	1.4
053 Assemb of God	1	69	95	96	.2	.4
056 Baha'i	0	4	NR	4	-	-
081 Catholic	7	NR	NR	13,477	28.1	49.9
093 Chr Ch (Disc)	1	320	55	411 *	.9	1.5
097 Chr Chs&Chs Cr	1	80	NR	103 *	.2	.4
123 Ch God (Ander)	1	NR	343	343	.7	1.3
127 Ch God (Cleve)	1	307	182	394 *	.8	1.5
151 L-D Saints	1	NR	NR	319	.7	1.2
157 Ch of Brethren	1	99	57	127 *	.3	.5
165 Ch of Nazarene	2	209	285	506	1.1	1.9
193 Episcopal	1	NR	28	66	.1	.2
207 E.L.C.A.	6	2,577	1,201	3,618	7.6	13.4
223 Free Will Bapt	1	61	NR	78 *	.2	.3
283 Luth—MO Synod	1	87	65	108	.2	.4
291 Missionary Ch	1	33	58	58	.1	.2
296 Midw Congr Fel	1	115	50	148 *	.3	.5
355 Presb Ch (USA)	1	235	100	301 *	.6	1.1
388 Reg Bapt Gen As	1	50	80	80 *	.2	.3
403 Salvation Army	1	67	75	488	1.0	1.8
419 So Bapt Conv	4	1,135	317	1,456 *	3.0	5.4
443 Un C of Christ	3	945	376	1,212 *	2.5	4.5
449 Un Methodist	12	2,389	983	3,064 *	6.4	11.4
467 Wesleyan	1	40	49	161	.3	.6
STARK	**348**	**87,295**	**38,568**	**196,471 ***	**52.0**	**100.0**
011 A.W.M.C.	6	153	308	162	-	.1
019 Amer Bapt USA	10	2,823	1,075	3,490 *	.9	1.8
034 Ant Orth of NA	2	271	NR	542	.1	.3
053 Assemb of God	10	958	1,132	1,927	.5	1.0
056 Baha'i	0	27	NR	27	-	-
061 Beachy Amish	1	70	NR	87 *	-	-
071 Brethren (Ash)	3	237	197	294 *	.1	.1
075 Brethren in Cr	3	202	165	206	.1	.1
081 Catholic	30	NR	NR	77,490	20.5	39.4
089 Chr & Miss Al	5	370	NR	1,024	.3	.5
093 Chr Ch (Disc)	4	1,330	526	1,644 *	.4	.8
097 Chr Chs&Chs Cr	18	8,149	NR	10,074 *	2.7	5.1
123 Ch God (Ander)	10	NR	1,232	1,232	.3	.6
127 Ch God (Cleve)	9	2,218	1,244	2,741 *	.7	1.4
145 Ch God Prophcy	1	32	NR	39 *	-	-
151 L-D Saints	2	NR	NR	870	.2	.4
157 Ch of Brethren	8	1,067	640	1,319 *	.3	.7
165 Ch of Nazarene	11	1,871	1,194	2,263	.6	1.2
167 Chs of Christ	16	2,112	2,211	2,760	.7	1.4
171 Ch God-Gen Con	1	75	32	93 *	-	-
175 Congr Chr Chs	1	312	237	386 *	.1	.2
179 Consrv Bapt	1	NR	28	28	-	-
181 Consrv Congr	3	363	167	449 *	.1	.2
183 Cons Menn Conf	4	518	633	753	.2	.4
193 Episcopal	5	NR	630	2,169	.6	1.1
203 Evan Free Ch	1	69	125	125	-	.1
207 E.L.C.A.	26	9,326	4,142	12,247	3.2	6.2
221 Free Methodist	2	130	110	159	-	.1
223 Free Will Bapt	1	61	NR	76 *	-	-
226 Friends-USA	6	570	NR	705 *	.2	.4
246 Greek Orthodox	3	NR	NR	3,450	.9	1.8
263 Int Foursq Gos	4	332	305	410 *	.1	.2
265 Int Pent C Chr	2	75	166	310	.1	.2
267 Muslim Est	1	NR	156	609	.2	.3
283 Luth—MO Synod	2	837	491	1,206	.3	.6
288 Mennonite USA	6	1,112	907	1,400 *	.4	.7
297 Mennonite;Other	3	203	NR	251 *	.1	.1
323 Old Ord Amish	3	170	NR	210 *	.1	.1
330 Macedonian Orth	1	NR	NR	800	.2	.4
331 OCA: Ter Diocs	1	88	NR	210	.1	.1
339 Pent Ch of God	1	22	NR	222	.1	.1
355 Presb Ch (USA)	13	4,477	1,727	5,534 *	1.5	2.8
370 Ref Baptist Chs	1	NR	NR	NR	-	-

NR–Not Reported   *Total adherents estimated from known number of communicant, confirmed, full members.   - Represents a percentage less than 0.1.   Percentages may not total 100 due to rounding.

Table 4: Religious Congregations by County and Group: 2000

Religious Group	Number of Churches, Synagogues, Mosques, or Temples	Number of Communicant, Confirmed, or Full Members	Number of Attendees	Total Adherents: Number of Adherents	Total Adherents: % of Total Pop.	Total Adherents: % of Total Adh.
388 Reg Bapt Gen As	6	665	658	796 *	.2	.4
397 OCA: Roman Dioc	2	NR	NR	400	.1	.2
403 Salvation Army	3	437	240	999	.3	.5
410 Serb Orth USA	1	NR	NR	400	.1	.2
413 S.D.A.	2	295	NR	351	.1	.2
419 So Bapt Conv	3	315	238	389 *	.1	.2
435 Unitarian-Univ	1	38	NR	47 *	-	-
443 Un C of Christ	21	7,871	2,942	9,730 *	2.6	5.0
449 Un Methodist	59	18,644	7,860	23,046 *	6.1	11.7
496 Jewish Est	3	NR	NR	1,500	.4	.8
498 Indep.Charis.	2	2,330	2,600	2,750	.7	1.4
499 Indep.Non-Char	4	16,070	4,250	16,070	4.3	8.2
SUMMIT	**375**	**84,721**	**47,411**	**253,426 ***	**46.7**	**100.0**
011 A.W.M.C.	4	25	115	28	-	-
019 Amer Bapt USA	12	2,993	1,605	3,718 *	.7	1.5
022 Carp Rus Orth	1	122	NR	207	-	.1
032 Amish; other	1	17	NR	21 *	-	-
034 Ant Orth of NA	1	266	NR	532	.1	.2
039 Ap Chr Ch(Naz)	4	376	558	567 *	.1	.2
053 Assemb of God	14	1,738	1,922	3,256	.6	1.3
056 Baha'i	0	70	NR	70	-	-
057 Bapt Gen Conf	1	79	86	98 *	-	-
076 Buddhism	4	NR	NR	NR	-	-
078 Bulgar Orth USA	1	NR	NR	560	.1	.2
081 Catholic	40	NR	NR	121,602	22.4	48.0
084 Calvary Chapel	1	NR	NR	NR	-	-
089 Chr & Miss Al	11	1,582	NR	3,415	.6	1.3
093 Chr Ch (Disc)	13	4,424	1,268	5,496 *	1.0	2.2
097 Chr Chs&Chs Cr	16	3,931	NR	4,882 *	.9	1.9
105 Christian Ref	1	131	120	163 *	-	.1
123 Ch God (Ander)	7	NR	2,155	2,155	.4	.9
127 Ch God (Cleve)	6	975	471	1,211 *	.2	.5
145 Ch God Prophcy	1	32	NR	40 *	-	-
151 L-D Saints	4	NR	NR	1,470	.3	.6
157 Ch of Brethren	3	428	276	532 *	.1	.2
165 Ch of Nazarene	15	2,088	1,433	3,205	.6	1.3
167 Chs of Christ	15	1,704	1,601	2,157	.4	.9
173 Comm of Christ	2	312	NR	312	.1	.1
175 Congr Chr Chs	1	600	175	745 *	.1	.3
179 Consrv Bapt	1	NR	258	258	-	.1
181 Consrv Congr	1	30	22	37 *	-	-
193 Episcopal	11	NR	2,141	5,924	1.1	2.3
201 Evan Cov Ch	2	446	310	554 *	.1	.2
203 Evan Free Ch	1	69	125	125	-	-
207 E.L.C.A.	14	5,358	2,199	6,912	1.3	2.7
221 Free Methodist	1	380	467	467	.1	.2
223 Free Will Bapt	2	122	NR	152 *	-	.1
226 Friends-USA	3	225	NR	280 *	.1	.1
246 Greek Orthodox	1	NR	NR	1,800	.3	.7
262 Int Cou Comm Ch	1	160	NR	199 *	-	.1
263 Int Foursq Gos	2	163	171	203 *	-	.1
265 Int Pent C Chr	1	186	183	400	.1	.2
267 Muslim Est	1	NR	100	200	-	.1
283 Luth—MO Synod	12	4,379	2,173	5,643	1.0	2.2
288 Mennonite USA	1	40	48	50 *	-	-
320 "Old" MB Ascs	1	69	NR	86 *	-	-
331 OCA: Ter Diocs	1	314	NR	489	.1	.2
332 OCA: Bulg Dioc	1	120	NR	259	-	.1
355 Presb Ch (USA)	16	4,687	2,331	5,825 *	1.1	2.3
356 Presb Ch Amer	3	310	379	445	.1	.2
360 Prim Bapt Chrch	1	NR	NR	NR	-	-
388 Reg Bapt Gen As	8	1,452	1,219	1,752 *	.3	.7
397 OCA: Roman Dioc	1	NR	NR	169	-	.1
403 Salvation Army	5	427	222	860	.2	.3
410 Serb Orth USA	1	NR	NR	1,000	.2	.4
411 Serb Orth: Grac	2	NR	NR	NR	-	-
413 S.D.A.	4	1,036	NR	1,233	.2	.5
416 Sikh	1	NR	NR	NR	-	-
419 So Bapt Conv	11	1,274	550	1,583 *	.3	.6
435 Unitarian-Univ	1	311	NR	386 *	.1	.2
443 Un C of Christ	21	8,973	3,191	11,148 *	2.1	4.4
449 Un Methodist	45	16,969	7,371	21,083 *	3.9	8.3
463 Vineyard	1	150	125	186 *	-	.1
467 Wesleyan	2	105	96	166	-	.1
469 WELS	1	68	55	90	-	-
496 Jewish Est	4	NR	NR	4,000	.7	1.6
498 Indep.Charis.	4	680	1,070	1,070	.2	.4
499 Indep.Non-Char	6	14,325	10,820	21,950	4.0	8.7
TRUMBULL	**219**	**34,242**	**15,346**	**101,121 ***	**44.9**	**100.0**
011 A.W.M.C.	2	34	99	38	-	-
019 Amer Bapt USA	5	733	349	901 *	.4	.9
022 Carp Rus Orth	1	122	NR	207	.1	.2
032 Amish; other	1	60	NR	74 *	-	.1
039 Ap Chr Ch(Naz)	1	30	52	52 *	-	.1
053 Assemb of God	11	1,203	1,471	1,852	.8	1.8
056 Baha'i	0	42	NR	42	-	-
081 Catholic	22	NR	NR	51,965	23.1	51.4
089 Chr & Miss Al	2	597	NR	1,876	.8	1.9
093 Chr Ch (Disc)	15	4,583	1,347	5,634 *	2.5	5.6
097 Chr Chs&Chs Cr	6	1,622	NR	1,994 *	.9	2.0
123 Ch God (Ander)	8	NR	699	699	.3	.7
127 Ch God (Cleve)	5	923	549	1,135 *	.5	1.1
145 Ch God Prophcy	1	32	NR	39 *	-	-
151 L-D Saints	1	NR	NR	374	.2	.4
157 Ch of Brethren	1	107	92	132 *	.1	.1
165 Ch of Nazarene	11	1,304	1,223	2,266	1.0	2.2
167 Chs of Christ	3	286	280	354	.2	.4
173 Comm of Christ	1	66	NR	66	-	.1
175 Congr Chr Chs	1	270	65	332 *	.1	.3
179 Consrv Bapt	1	NR	47	47	-	-
193 Episcopal	2	NR	276	872	.4	.9
207 E.L.C.A.	12	3,289	1,312	4,281	1.9	4.2
221 Free Methodist	1	43	56	56	-	.1
223 Free Will Bapt	2	122	NR	150 *	.1	.1
246 Greek Orthodox	1	NR	NR	1,050	.5	1.0
252 Hindu	1	NR	NR	NR	-	-
262 Int Cou Comm Ch	1	676	NR	831 *	.4	.8
263 Int Foursq Gos	2	111	95	136 *	.1	.1
283 Luth—MO Synod	1	146	50	186	.1	.2
323 Old Ord Amish	16	960	NR	1,184 *	.5	1.2
331 OCA: Ter Diocs	1	173	NR	246	.1	.2
355 Presb Ch (USA)	11	2,421	1,147	2,975 *	1.3	2.9
388 Reg Bapt Gen As	7	724	587	817 *	.4	.8
397 OCA: Roman Dioc	2	NR	NR	92	-	.1
403 Salvation Army	1	134	48	497	.2	.5
411 Serb Orth: Grac	1	NR	NR	NR	-	-
413 S.D.A.	2	156	NR	186	.1	.2
418 Southw Bapt Fel	1	NR	NR	NR	-	-
419 So Bapt Conv	12	2,195	604	2,698 *	1.2	2.7
435 Unitarian-Univ	1	7	NR	9 *	-	-
443 Un C of Christ	4	1,393	389	1,712 *	.8	1.7
449 Un Methodist	34	9,270	3,694	11,395 *	5.1	11.3
469 WELS	1	58	35	69	-	.1
496 Jewish Est	1	NR	NR	700	.3	.7
498 Indep.Charis.	1	0	500	500	.2	.5
499 Indep.Non-Char	1	350	280	400	.2	.4
TUSCARAWAS	**192**	**28,460**	**12,102**	**46,783 ***	**51.5**	**100.0**
019 Amer Bapt USA	1	246	102	305 *	.3	.7
032 Amish; other	6	346	NR	427 *	.5	.9
053 Assemb of God	3	258	274	508	.6	1.1
056 Baha'i	0	2	NR	2	-	-
061 Beachy Amish	2	124	NR	154 *	.2	.3
081 Catholic	5	NR	NR	8,432	9.3	18.0
089 Chr & Miss Al	2	151	NR	435	.5	.9
093 Chr Ch (Disc)	1	234	90	290 *	.3	.6
097 Chr Chs&Chs Cr	4	1,520	NR	1,884 *	2.1	4.0
123 Ch God (Ander)	4	NR	350	350	.4	.7
127 Ch God (Cleve)	5	677	409	838 *	.9	1.8
151 L-D Saints	1	NR	NR	270	.3	.6
157 Ch of Brethren	3	257	186	319 *	.4	.7
165 Ch of Nazarene	6	1,068	783	1,590	1.7	3.4
167 Chs of Christ	6	419	464	594	.7	1.3
173 Comm of Christ	1	324	NR	324	.4	.7
179 Consrv Bapt	1	NR	330	330	.4	.7

NR–Not Reported *Total adherents estimated from known number of communicant, confirmed, full members. - Represents a percentage less than 0.1. Percentages may not total 100 due to rounding.

Table 4: Religious Congregations by County and Group: 2000

Religious Group	Number of Churches, Synagogues, Mosques, or Temples	Number of Communicant, Confirmed, or Full Members	Number of Attendees	Total Adherents		
				Number of Adherents	% of Total Pop.	% of Total Adh.
183 Cons Menn Conf	1	188	230	273	.3	.6
193 Episcopal	1	NR	43	45	-	.1
207 E.L.C.A.	15	4,543	1,295	6,049	6.7	12.9
221 Free Methodist	1	411	1,028	1,028	1.1	2.2
263 Int Foursq Gos	4	627	847	847 *	.9	1.8
265 Int Pent C Chr	2	21	55	80	.1	.2
288 Mennonite USA	2	180	119	226 *	.2	.5
293 Morav Ch-North	6	1,512	NR	1,865	2.1	4.0
297 Mennonite;Other	4	417	NR	516 *	.6	1.1
323 Old Ord Amish	43	2,530	NR	3,122 *	3.4	6.7
355 Presb Ch (USA)	5	527	225	652 *	.7	1.4
388 Reg Bapt Gen As	2	202	212	212 *	.2	.5
403 Salvation Army	1	127	53	394	.4	.8
419 So Bapt Conv	4	233	164	289 *	.3	.6
443 Un C of Christ	13	4,277	1,480	5,298 *	5.8	11.3
449 Un Methodist	36	6,972	3,219	8,635 *	9.5	18.5
467 Wesleyan	1	67	144	200	.2	.4
UNION	**49**	**9,303**	**4,208**	**13,974 ***	**34.2**	**100.0**
017 Amer Bapt Assn	1	50	NR	64 *	.2	.5
019 Amer Bapt USA	4	472	216	603 *	1.5	4.3
053 Assemb of God	1	218	165	230	.6	1.6
056 Baha'i	0	10	NR	10	-	.1
081 Catholic	3	NR	NR	1,536	3.8	11.0
097 Chr Chs&Chs Cr	3	640	NR	818 *	2.0	5.9
123 Ch God (Ander)	2	NR	51	51	.1	.4
127 Ch God (Cleve)	1	239	143	305 *	.7	2.2
145 Ch God Prophcy	1	32	NR	41 *	.1	.3
151 L-D Saints	1	NR	NR	215	.5	1.5
165 Ch of Nazarene	1	316	271	521	1.3	3.7
167 Chs of Christ	2	215	255	321	.8	2.3
191 Entrpr Bpt Asc	1	3	NR	4 *	-	-
207 E.L.C.A.	2	1,456	524	1,864	4.6	13.3
223 Free Will Bapt	2	122	NR	156 *	.4	1.1
226 Friends-USA	1	95	NR	121 *	.3	.9
263 Int Foursq Gos	1	44	170	170 *	.4	1.2
283 Luth—MO Synod	2	1,504	701	1,974	4.8	14.1
355 Presb Ch (USA)	2	779	295	996 *	2.4	7.1
388 Reg Bapt Gen As	1	73	95	95 *	.2	.7
418 Southw Bapt Fel	1	NR	NR	NR	-	-
419 So Bapt Conv	1	76	80	97 *	.2	.7
443 Un C of Christ	1	127	56	162 *	.4	1.2
449 Un Methodist	14	2,832	1,186	3,620 *	8.8	25.9
VAN WERT	**51**	**7,752**	**3,823**	**12,858 ***	**43.4**	**100.0**
017 Amer Bapt Assn	1	50	NR	62 *	.2	.5
053 Assemb of God	2	193	220	338	1.1	2.6
081 Catholic	1	NR	NR	2,679	9.0	20.8
097 Chr Chs&Chs Cr	1	196	NR	244 *	.8	1.9
107 Christian Un	2	112	156	156 *	.5	1.2
123 Ch God (Ander)	2	NR	120	120	.4	.9
165 Ch of Nazarene	2	70	72	123	.4	1.0
171 Ch God-Gen Con	2	228	219	297 *	1.0	2.3
193 Episcopal	1	NR	17	15	.1	.1
207 E.L.C.A.	4	898	420	1,221	4.1	9.5
226 Friends-USA	5	283	NR	352 *	1.2	2.7
283 Luth—MO Synod	4	1,123	479	1,416	4.8	11.0
339 Pent Ch of God	1	50	NR	200	.7	1.6
355 Presb Ch (USA)	3	692	280	861 *	2.9	6.7
403 Salvation Army	1	47	50	32	.1	.2
413 S.D.A.	1	14	NR	17	.1	.1
419 So Bapt Conv	1	45	18	56 *	.2	.4
443 Un C of Christ	1	366	161	456 *	1.5	3.5
449 Un Methodist	15	3,308	1,549	4,117 *	13.9	32.0
463 Vineyard	1	77	62	96 *	.3	.7
VINTON	**31**	**1,523**	**808**	**2,205 ***	**17.2**	**100.0**
019 Amer Bapt USA	1	13	0	16 *	.1	.7
053 Assemb of God	1	78	90	105	.8	4.8
056 Baha'i	0	1	NR	1	-	-
081 Catholic	1	NR	NR	195	1.5	8.8
093 Chr Ch (Disc)	3	338	68	428 *	3.3	19.4
107 Christian Un	1	40	26	51 *	.4	2.3

Religious Group	Number of Churches, Synagogues, Mosques, or Temples	Number of Communicant, Confirmed, or Full Members	Number of Attendees	Total Adherents		
				Number of Adherents	% of Total Pop.	% of Total Adh.
127 Ch God (Cleve)	1	27	26	34 *	.3	1.5
165 Ch of Nazarene	3	104	99	180	1.4	8.2
167 Chs of Christ	2	46	50	59	.5	2.7
173 Comm of Christ	1	30	NR	30	.2	1.4
193 Episcopal	1	NR	25	22	.2	1.0
223 Free Will Bapt	3	184	NR	233 *	1.8	10.6
355 Presb Ch (USA)	2	44	57	68 *	.5	3.1
419 So Bapt Conv	1	217	100	275 *	2.1	12.5
449 Un Methodist	10	401	267	508 *	4.0	23.0
WARREN	**129**	**24,694**	**14,812**	**53,696 ***	**33.9**	**100.0**
011 A.W.M.C.	1	11	55	11	-	-
019 Amer Bapt USA	3	740	370	949 *	.6	1.8
053 Assemb of God	3	363	485	493	.3	.9
056 Baha'i	0	23	NR	23	-	-
071 Brethren (Ash)	1	134	243	172 *	.1	.3
081 Catholic	6	NR	NR	17,780	11.2	33.1
089 Chr & Miss Al	1	58	NR	80	.1	.1
097 Chr Chs&Chs Cr	8	3,035	NR	3,890 *	2.5	7.2
123 Ch God (Ander)	10	NR	1,669	1,669	1.1	3.1
127 Ch God (Cleve)	7	1,456	913	1,868 *	1.2	3.5
145 Ch God Prophcy	2	64	NR	82 *	.1	.2
151 L-D Saints	1	NR	NR	367	.2	.7
157 Ch of Brethren	1	57	0	73 *	-	.1
165 Ch of Nazarene	6	711	527	974	.6	1.8
167 Chs of Christ	4	192	215	246	.2	.5
181 Consrv Congr	1	164	25	210 *	.1	.4
193 Episcopal	3	NR	308	798	.5	1.5
203 Evan Free Ch	3	731	2,110	2,110	1.3	3.9
207 E.L.C.A.	4	754	403	1,034	.7	1.9
223 Free Will Bapt	1	61	NR	78 *	-	.1
226 Friends-USA	1	58	NR	74 *	-	.1
283 Luth—MO Synod	1	547	351	802	.5	1.5
339 Pent Ch of God	1	40	NR	50	-	.1
355 Presb Ch (USA)	6	2,029	1,145	2,603 *	1.6	4.8
356 Presb Ch Amer	1	179	300	300	.2	.6
360 Prim Bapt Chrch	3	NR	NR	NR	-	-
413 S.D.A.	2	135	NR	161	.1	.3
418 Southw Bapt Fel	3	NR	NR	NR	-	-
419 So Bapt Conv	18	7,465	2,472	9,573 *	6.0	17.8
443 Un C of Christ	4	873	391	1,119 *	.7	2.1
449 Un Methodist	18	3,971	2,036	5,092 *	3.2	9.5
463 Vineyard	2	330	370	423 *	.3	.8
469 WELS	1	63	64	92	.1	.2
496 Jewish Est	1	NR	NR	50	-	.1
499 Indep.Non-Char	1	450	360	450	.3	.8
WASHINGTON	**126**	**15,778**	**8,041**	**25,284 ***	**40.0**	**100.0**
019 Amer Bapt USA	10	3,074	1,091	3,739 *	5.9	14.8
053 Assemb of God	1	31	36	170	.3	.7
056 Baha'i	0	7	NR	7	-	-
081 Catholic	5	NR	NR	5,115	8.1	20.2
089 Chr & Miss Al	1	0	NR	85	.1	.3
093 Chr Ch (Disc)	1	69	27	84 *	.1	.3
097 Chr Chs&Chs Cr	7	1,053	NR	1,281 *	2.0	5.1
107 Christian Un	3	30	38	38 *	.1	.2
127 Ch God (Cleve)	3	152	135	185 *	.3	.7
145 Ch God Prophcy	1	32	NR	39 *	.1	.2
151 L-D Saints	1	NR	NR	250	.4	1.0
165 Ch of Nazarene	5	734	540	797	1.3	3.2
167 Chs of Christ	15	1,768	1,765	2,273	3.6	9.0
181 Consrv Congr	1	145	80	176 *	.3	.7
193 Episcopal	1	NR	110	208	.3	.8
207 E.L.C.A.	1	415	129	629	1.0	2.5
349 Pent Holiness	4	1,022	521	1,243 *	2.0	4.9
355 Presb Ch (USA)	8	918	402	1,116 *	1.8	4.4
388 Reg Bapt Gen As	2	135	110	164 *	.3	.6
403 Salvation Army	1	57	20	180	.3	.7
413 S.D.A.	1	53	NR	63	.1	.2
419 So Bapt Conv	3	764	313	929 *	1.5	3.7
435 Unitarian-Univ	1	120	NR	146 *	.2	.6
443 Un C of Christ	7	744	320	905 *	1.4	3.6
449 Un Methodist	39	4,275	2,233	5,201 *	8.2	20.6

NR–Not Reported *Total adherents estimated from known number of communicant, confirmed, full members. - Represents a percentage less than 0.1. Percentages may not total 100 due to rounding.

Table 4: Religious Congregations by County and Group: 2000

Religious Group	Number of Churches, Synagogues, Mosques, or Temples	Number of Communicant, Confirmed, or Full Members	Number of Attendees	Total Adherents: Number of Adherents	Total Adherents: % of Total Pop.	Total Adherents: % of Total Adh.
467 Wesleyan	3	59	78	96	.2	.4
469 WELS	1	121	93	165	.3	.7
WAYNE	**223**	**35,386**	**16,583**	**56,236 ***	**50.4**	**100.0**
019 Amer Bapt USA	1	40	20	51 *	-	.1
032 Amish; other	4	240	NR	304 *	.3	.5
039 Ap Chr Ch(Naz)	1	10	23	23 *	-	-
040 Ap Chr Ch-Amer	2	676	1,470	1,470 *	1.3	2.6
053 Assemb of God	2	327	470	500	.4	.9
056 Baha'i	0	7	NR	7	-	-
071 Brethren (Ash)	1	263	258	333 *	.3	.6
075 Brethren in Cr	1	60	63	63	.1	.1
081 Catholic	4	NR	NR	8,756	7.8	15.6
089 Chr & Miss Al	3	404	NR	769	.7	1.4
093 Chr Ch (Disc)	2	1,086	224	1,374 *	1.2	2.4
097 Chr Chs&Chs Cr	6	1,496	NR	1,892 *	1.7	3.4
123 Ch God (Ander)	2	NR	146	146	.1	.3
127 Ch God (Cleve)	4	347	215	441 *	.4	.8
143 CG in Cr(Menn)	1	174	NR	220 *	.2	.4
145 Ch God Prophcy	1	32	NR	40 *	-	.1
151 L-D Saints	1	NR	NR	340	.3	.6
157 Ch of Brethren	4	660	346	836 *	.7	1.5
165 Ch of Nazarene	4	682	807	1,082	1.0	1.9
167 Chs of Christ	5	296	335	382	.3	.7
171 Ch God-Gen Con	4	821	453	1,039 *	.9	1.8
183 Cons Menn Conf	5	645	787	938	.8	1.7
191 Entrpr Bpt Asc	1	30	NR	38 *	-	.1
193 Episcopal	1	NR	103	200	.2	.4
207 E.L.C.A.	11	3,521	1,261	4,649	4.2	8.3
221 Free Methodist	2	175	481	481	.4	.9
223 Free Will Bapt	3	184	NR	232 *	.2	.4
226 Friends-USA	1	35	NR	44 *	-	.1
263 Int Foursq Gos	2	354	226	448 *	.4	.8
283 Luth—MO Synod	1	55	35	73	.1	.1
288 Mennonite USA	12	2,878	2,162	3,670 *	3.3	6.5
297 Mennonite;Other	5	340	NR	431 *	.4	.8
322 Old Ord Menn Ch	3	294	NR	373 *	.3	.7
323 Old Ord Amish	63	3,600	NR	4,554 *	4.1	8.1
355 Presb Ch (USA)	12	3,844	1,748	4,863 *	4.4	8.6
379 Ref Mennonite	1	20	NR	25 *	-	-
388 Reg Bapt Gen As	2	475	430	601 *	.5	1.1
403 Salvation Army	1	42	60	99	.1	.2
413 S.D.A.	1	138	NR	164	.1	.3
418 Southw Bapt Fel	1	NR	NR	NR	-	-
419 So Bapt Conv	5	1,397	300	1,768 *	1.6	3.1
435 Unitarian-Univ	1	110	NR	139 *	.1	.2
443 Un C of Christ	7	2,627	815	3,324 *	3.0	5.9
449 Un Methodist	25	6,160	2,710	7,794 *	7.0	13.9
467 Wesleyan	1	41	35	60	.1	.1
496 Jewish Est	1	NR	NR	175	.2	.3
499 Indep.Non-Char	2	800	600	1,025	.9	1.8
WILLIAMS	**62**	**9,527**	**4,253**	**16,932 ***	**43.2**	**100.0**
053 Assemb of God	1	42	49	88	.2	.5
056 Baha'i	0	2	NR	2	-	-
071 Brethren (Ash)	1	235	103	293 *	.7	1.7
081 Catholic	5	NR	NR	4,544	11.6	26.8
089 Chr & Miss Al	2	89	NR	198	.5	1.2
097 Chr Chs&Chs Cr	5	1,185	NR	1,477 *	3.8	8.7
107 Christian Un	3	142	127	177 *	.5	1.0
157 Ch of Brethren	2	175	111	218 *	.6	1.3
165 Ch of Nazarene	3	338	231	515	1.3	3.0
171 Ch God-Gen Con	3	90	86	120 *	.3	.7
193 Episcopal	1	NR	26	60	.2	.4
207 E.L.C.A.	6	1,937	776	2,568	6.6	15.2
213 Evan Menn Inc	1	104	320	130 *	.3	.8
221 Free Methodist	1	27	42	42	.1	.2
288 Mennonite USA	2	520	393	653 *	1.7	3.9
291 Missionary Ch	1	15	40	40	.1	.2
339 Pent Ch of God	1	42	NR	100	.3	.6
355 Presb Ch (USA)	5	897	367	1,117 *	2.9	6.6
388 Reg Bapt Gen As	1	181	128	225 *	.6	1.3
413 S.D.A.	1	23	NR	27	.1	.2
418 Southw Bapt Fel	1	NR	NR	NR	-	-
419 So Bapt Conv	1	169	100	211 *	.5	1.2
449 Un Methodist	15	3,314	1,354	4,127 *	10.5	24.4
WOOD	**132**	**22,575**	**10,909**	**57,277 ***	**47.3**	**100.0**
019 Amer Bapt USA	1	124	71	151 *	.1	.3
053 Assemb of God	3	975	1,439	2,087	1.7	3.6
055 As Ref Pres Ch	1	17	NR	17	-	-
056 Baha'i	0	30	NR	30	-	.1
081 Catholic	9	NR	NR	21,990	18.2	38.4
089 Chr & Miss Al	3	349	NR	600	.5	1.0
093 Chr Ch (Disc)	2	510	123	620 *	.5	1.1
097 Chr Chs&Chs Cr	6	940	NR	1,143 *	.9	2.0
123 Ch God (Ander)	1	NR	110	110	.1	.2
127 Ch God (Cleve)	1	209	146	254 *	.2	.4
151 L-D Saints	2	NR	NR	691	.6	1.2
157 Ch of Brethren	1	159	80	193 *	.2	.3
165 Ch of Nazarene	4	331	306	481	.4	.8
167 Chs of Christ	6	462	440	547	.5	1.0
171 Ch God-Gen Con	2	69	137	137 *	.1	.2
175 Congr Chr Chs	3	270	200	328 *	.3	.6
193 Episcopal	2	NR	192	661	.5	1.2
207 E.L.C.A.	18	8,355	3,212	11,135	9.2	19.4
213 Evan Menn Inc	1	76	135	92 *	.1	.2
216 Evan Presby Ch	1	57	NR	69 *	.1	.1
223 Free Will Bapt	1	61	NR	74 *	.1	.1
226 Friends-USA	1	35	NR	43 *	-	.1
263 Int Foursq Gos	1	30	5	36 *	-	.1
267 Muslim Est	1	NR	156	4,000	3.3	7.0
283 Luth—MO Synod	2	151	112	205	.2	.4
291 Missionary Ch	1	15	18	18	-	-
320 "Old" MB Ascs	1	57	NR	69 *	.1	.1
339 Pent Ch of God	3	54	NR	147	.1	.3
355 Presb Ch (USA)	8	1,252	526	1,523 *	1.3	2.7
388 Reg Bapt Gen As	1	179	110	218 *	.2	.4
413 S.D.A.	2	75	NR	89	.1	.2
419 So Bapt Conv	4	663	288	806 *	.7	1.4
435 Unitarian-Univ	1	90	NR	109 *	.1	.2
443 Un C of Christ	2	311	191	378 *	.3	.7
449 Un Methodist	35	6,638	2,851	8,076 *	6.7	14.1
467 Wesleyan	1	31	61	150	.1	.3
WYANDOT	**48**	**6,325**	**2,832**	**13,306 ***	**58.1**	**100.0**
019 Amer Bapt USA	1	15	15	19 *	.1	.1
053 Assemb of God	1	35	35	35	.2	.3
081 Catholic	5	NR	NR	4,698	20.5	35.3
107 Christian Un	1	125	79	155 *	.7	1.2
123 Ch God (Ander)	1	NR	14	14	.1	.1
145 Ch God Prophcy	1	32	NR	40 *	.2	.3
151 L-D Saints	1	NR	NR	324	1.4	2.4
165 Ch of Nazarene	2	259	211	368	1.6	2.8
167 Chs of Christ	1	21	22	27	.1	.2
171 Ch God-Gen Con	2	156	119	201 *	.9	1.5
207 E.L.C.A.	5	1,957	701	2,627	11.5	19.7
223 Free Will Bapt	1	61	NR	76 *	.3	.6
297 Mennonite;Other	1	68	NR	84 *	.4	.6
339 Pent Ch of God	1	44	NR	104	.5	.8
355 Presb Ch (USA)	2	236	83	293 *	1.3	2.2
419 So Bapt Conv	1	102	40	127 *	.6	1.0
443 Un C of Christ	3	883	267	1,096 *	4.8	8.2
449 Un Methodist	17	2,298	1,190	2,853 *	12.5	21.4
467 Wesleyan	1	33	56	165	.7	1.2

OKLAHOMA

Religious Group	Number of Churches, Synagogues, Mosques, or Temples	Number of Communicant, Confirmed, or Full Members	Number of Attendees	Total Adherents: Number of Adherents	Total Adherents: % of Total Pop.	Total Adherents: % of Total Adh.
The State.....	5,854	1,465,067	539,046	2,096,476 *	60.8	100.0
ADAIR	**52**	**7,319**	**2,501**	**9,648 ***	**45.9**	**100.0**
017 Amer Bapt Assn	2	53	NR	69 *	.3	.7
053 Assemb of God	3	199	270	372	1.8	3.9
056 Baha'i	0	33	NR	33	.2	.3
059 Bapt Miss Assn	1	82	90	107 *	.5	1.1

NR–Not Reported   *Total adherents estimated from known number of communicant, confirmed, full members.   - Represents a percentage less than 0.1.   Percentages may not total 100 due to rounding.

Table 4: Religious Congregations by County and Group: 2000

Religious Group	Number of Churches, Synagogues, Mosques, or Temples	Number of Communicant, Confirmed, or Full Members	Number of Attendees	Total Adherents: Number of Adherents	Total Adherents: % of Total Pop.	Total Adherents: % of Total Adh.
097 Chr Chs&Chs Cr	1	200	NR	260 *	1.2	2.7
123 Ch God (Ander)	1	NR	4	4	-	-
167 Chs of Christ	6	315	363	426	2.0	4.4
223 Free Will Bapt	1	95	NR	123 *	.6	1.3
258 IndFreeWillBapt	1	28	NR	36 *	.2	.4
339 Pent Ch of God	1	35	NR	46	.2	.5
349 Pent Holiness	3	284	366	370 *	1.8	3.8
355 Presb Ch (USA)	1	0	0	0 *	-	-
419 So Bapt Conv	27	5,378	1,235	6,999 *	33.3	72.5
449 Un Methodist	4	617	173	803 *	3.8	8.3
ALFALFA	**35**	**3,678**	**1,328**	**4,517 ***	**74.0**	**100.0**
053 Assemb of God	3	134	114	130	2.1	2.9
081 Catholic	2	NR	NR	176	2.9	3.9
093 Chr Ch (Disc)	6	687	166	799 *	13.1	17.7
097 Chr Chs&Chs Cr	2	195	NR	227 *	3.7	5.0
107 Christian Un	1	25	28	29 *	.5	.6
143 CG in Cr(Menn)	1	57	NR	66 *	1.1	1.5
157 Ch of Brethren	1	32	21	37 *	.6	.8
165 Ch of Nazarene	3	93	82	150	2.5	3.3
167 Chs of Christ	4	150	195	224	3.7	5.0
221 Free Methodist	1	19	14	19	.3	.4
226 Friends-USA	1	50	NR	58 *	1.0	1.3
313 N Am Bapt Conf	1	34	30	40 *	.7	.9
419 So Bapt Conv	2	760	258	884 *	14.5	19.6
443 Un C of Christ	1	60	26	70 *	1.1	1.5
449 Un Methodist	6	1,382	394	1,608 *	26.3	35.6
ATOKA	**51**	**7,491**	**2,303**	**9,311 ***	**67.1**	**100.0**
053 Assemb of God	3	84	129	130	.9	1.4
056 Baha'i	0	2	NR	2	-	-
059 Bapt Miss Assn	2	344	110	418 *	3.0	4.5
081 Catholic	1	NR	NR	72	.5	.8
165 Ch of Nazarene	1	44	18	81	.6	.9
167 Chs of Christ	7	428	398	542	3.9	5.8
185 Cumber Presb	3	26	NR	75	.5	.8
223 Free Will Bapt	4	378	NR	460 *	3.3	4.9
339 Pent Ch of God	2	70	NR	100	.7	1.1
349 Pent Holiness	3	111	78	135 *	1.0	1.4
419 So Bapt Conv	21	5,779	1,472	7,023 *	50.6	75.4
449 Un Methodist	4	225	98	273 *	2.0	2.9
BEAVER	**27**	**3,328**	**1,058**	**4,287 ***	**73.2**	**100.0**
053 Assemb of God	1	11	15	15	.3	.3
081 Catholic	1	NR	NR	70	1.2	1.6
097 Chr Chs&Chs Cr	2	281	NR	350 *	6.0	8.2
123 Ch God (Ander)	1	NR	25	25	.4	.6
165 Ch of Nazarene	2	46	58	87	1.5	2.0
167 Chs of Christ	3	112	108	139	2.4	3.2
226 Friends-USA	1	50	NR	62 *	1.1	1.4
237 Menn Br US Conf	1	62	NR	77 *	1.3	1.8
283 Luth—MO Synod	1	27	20	42	.7	1.0
288 Mennonite USA	1	100	61	125 *	2.1	2.9
355 Presb Ch (USA)	1	20	32	32 *	.5	.7
419 So Bapt Conv	6	1,297	379	1,616 *	27.6	37.7
449 Un Methodist	6	1,322	360	1,647 *	28.1	38.4
BECKHAM	**47**	**11,606**	**4,267**	**16,305 ***	**82.4**	**100.0**
017 Amer Bapt Assn	1	84	NR	103 *	.5	.6
053 Assemb of God	5	765	651	1,310	6.6	8.0
056 Baha'i	0	1	NR	1	-	-
081 Catholic	2	NR	NR	1,530	7.7	9.4
093 Chr Ch (Disc)	2	334	159	408 *	2.1	2.5
097 Chr Chs&Chs Cr	1	70	NR	86 *	.4	.5
123 Ch God (Ander)	1	NR	59	59	.3	.4
145 Ch God Prophcy	1	29	NR	35 *	.2	.2
165 Ch of Nazarene	3	219	161	324	1.6	2.0
167 Chs of Christ	6	967	850	1,283	6.5	7.9
283 Luth—MO Synod	1	39	28	48	.2	.3
349 Pent Holiness	2	60	60	73 *	.4	.4
355 Presb Ch (USA)	1	120	76	147 *	.7	.9
360 Prim Bapt Chrch	1	NR	NR	NR	-	-
413 S.D.A.	1	24	NR	29	.1	.2
419 So Bapt Conv	16	7,042	1,618	8,606 *	43.5	52.8
449 Un Methodist	3	1,852	605	2,263 *	11.4	13.9
BLAINE	**50**	**5,839**	**1,927**	**7,980 ***	**66.6**	**100.0**
017 Amer Bapt Assn	1	39	NR	47 *	.4	.6
019 Amer Bapt USA	2	225	86	274 *	2.3	3.4
053 Assemb of God	4	137	140	234	2.0	2.9
056 Baha'i	0	16	NR	16	.1	.2
081 Catholic	2	NR	NR	528	4.4	6.6
093 Chr Ch (Disc)	2	206	0	251 *	2.1	3.1
097 Chr Chs&Chs Cr	3	584	NR	711 *	5.9	8.9
123 Ch God (Ander)	2	NR	29	29	.2	.4
151 L-D Saints	1	NR	NR	80	.7	1.0
165 Ch of Nazarene	2	154	105	154	1.3	1.9
167 Chs of Christ	4	227	197	266	2.2	3.3
173 Comm of Christ	1	37	NR	37	.3	.5
221 Free Methodist	1	34	24	36	.3	.5
237 Menn Br US Conf	1	44	NR	54 *	.5	.7
283 Luth—MO Synod	1	0	48	148	1.2	1.9
288 Mennonite USA	2	210	220	256 *	2.1	3.2
297 Mennonite;Other	1	24	NR	29 *	.2	.4
313 N Am Bapt Conf	1	58	54	71 *	.6	.9
339 Pent Ch of God	1	30	NR	45	.4	.6
349 Pent Holiness	2	37	49	45 *	.4	.6
413 S.D.A.	2	148	NR	176	1.5	2.2
419 So Bapt Conv	7	2,263	552	2,755 *	23.0	34.5
443 Un C of Christ	1	31	13	38 *	.3	.5
449 Un Methodist	5	1,323	383	1,610 *	13.4	20.2
467 Wesleyan	1	12	27	90	.8	1.1
BRYAN	**89**	**18,458**	**6,141**	**23,723 ***	**64.9**	**100.0**
017 Amer Bapt Assn	2	150	NR	186 *	.5	.8
053 Assemb of God	5	227	258	468	1.3	2.0
056 Baha'i	0	2	NR	2	-	-
081 Catholic	1	NR	NR	100	.3	.4
093 Chr Ch (Disc)	1	366	114	452 *	1.2	1.9
123 Ch God (Ander)	1	NR	15	15	-	.1
151 L-D Saints	1	NR	NR	308	.8	1.3
165 Ch of Nazarene	4	369	253	474	1.3	2.0
167 Chs of Christ	13	926	914	1,178	3.2	5.0
193 Episcopal	1	NR	59	81	.2	.3
207 E.L.C.A.	1	111	60	197	.5	.8
220 Free Lutheran	1	64	44	64	.2	.3
223 Free Will Bapt	2	189	NR	234 *	.6	1.0
339 Pent Ch of God	4	101	NR	257	.7	1.1
349 Pent Holiness	2	803	245	992 *	2.7	4.2
355 Presb Ch (USA)	5	302	173	373 *	1.0	1.6
413 S.D.A.	1	41	NR	49	.1	.2
419 So Bapt Conv	37	13,019	3,653	16,085 *	44.0	67.8
449 Un Methodist	7	1,788	353	2,208 *	6.0	9.3
CADDO	**115**	**19,171**	**6,237**	**25,827 ***	**85.7**	**100.0**
017 Amer Bapt Assn	6	639	NR	806 *	2.7	3.1
019 Amer Bapt USA	3	260	101	328 *	1.1	1.3
053 Assemb of God	9	439	607	656	2.2	2.5
056 Baha'i	0	20	NR	20	.1	.1
081 Catholic	5	NR	NR	818	2.7	3.2
093 Chr Ch (Disc)	3	378	134	478 *	1.6	1.9
097 Chr Chs&Chs Cr	6	604	NR	763 *	2.5	3.0
127 Ch God (Cleve)	2	189	117	239 *	.8	.9
151 L-D Saints	1	NR	NR	276	.9	1.1
165 Ch of Nazarene	3	213	222	412	1.4	1.6
167 Chs of Christ	11	759	849	1,023	3.4	4.0
207 E.L.C.A.	2	69	30	134	.4	.5
283 Luth—MO Synod	2	170	76	191	.6	.7
288 Mennonite USA	2	105	76	133 *	.4	.5
339 Pent Ch of God	2	20	NR	53	.2	.2
349 Pent Holiness	8	613	353	774 *	2.6	3.0
355 Presb Ch (USA)	1	41	20	52 *	.2	.2
371 Ref Ch in Am	1	55	62	233	.8	.9
419 So Bapt Conv	25	11,285	2,655	14,256 *	47.3	55.2
443 Un C of Christ	1	76	33	96 *	.3	.4

NR–Not Reported *Total adherents estimated from known number of communicant, confirmed, full members. - Represents a percentage less than 0.1. Percentages may not total 100 due to rounding.

Table 4: Religious Congregations by County and Group: 2000

Religious Group	Number of Churches, Synagogues, Mosques, or Temples	Number of Communicant, Confirmed, or Full Members	Number of Attendees	Total Adherents		
				Number of Adherents	% of Total Pop.	% of Total Adh.
449 Un Methodist	22	3,236	902	4,086 *	13.6	15.8
CANADIAN	**92**	**28,467**	**11,296**	**46,306 ***	**52.8**	**100.0**
017 Amer Bapt Assn	1	30	NR	38 *	-	.1
053 Assemb of God	7	1,362	1,670	4,244	4.8	9.2
056 Baha'i	1	44	NR	44	.1	.1
081 Catholic	5	NR	NR	6,392	7.3	13.8
093 Chr Ch (Disc)	5	1,353	419	1,711 *	2.0	3.7
097 Chr Chs&Chs Cr	3	625	NR	790 *	.9	1.7
123 Ch God (Ander)	1	NR	20	20	-	-
127 Ch God (Cleve)	1	61	23	77 *	.1	.2
151 L-D Saints	2	NR	NR	923	1.1	2.0
165 Ch of Nazarene	8	1,100	832	1,433	1.6	3.1
167 Chs of Christ	12	1,376	1,288	1,769	2.0	3.8
193 Episcopal	2	NR	114	221	.3	.5
207 E.L.C.A.	1	473	254	678	.8	1.5
223 Free Will Bapt	3	284	NR	359 *	.4	.8
283 Luth—MO Synod	3	1,003	498	1,321	1.5	2.9
339 Pent Ch of God	3	260	NR	375	.4	.8
349 Pent Holiness	3	326	135	412 *	.5	.9
355 Presb Ch (USA)	2	251	142	317 *	.4	.7
413 S.D.A.	2	56	NR	67	.1	.1
419 So Bapt Conv	16	13,615	4,182	17,216 *	19.6	37.2
449 Un Methodist	11	6,248	1,719	7,899 *	9.0	17.1
CARTER	**96**	**26,320**	**8,286**	**36,144 ***	**79.2**	**100.0**
017 Amer Bapt Assn	3	250	NR	312 *	.7	.9
053 Assemb of God	8	882	1,350	1,737	3.8	4.8
056 Baha'i	0	1	NR	1	-	-
059 Bapt Miss Assn	2	454	105	567 *	1.2	1.6
081 Catholic	2	NR	NR	1,513	3.3	4.2
093 Chr Ch (Disc)	2	353	109	441 *	1.0	1.2
097 Chr Chs&Chs Cr	1	100	NR	125 *	.3	.3
127 Ch God (Cleve)	1	116	90	145 *	.3	.4
151 L-D Saints	1	NR	NR	297	.7	.8
165 Ch of Nazarene	1	149	78	152	.3	.4
167 Chs of Christ	13	1,363	1,328	1,757	3.9	4.9
173 Comm of Christ	1	43	NR	43	.1	.1
193 Episcopal	1	NR	271	421	.9	1.2
223 Free Will Bapt	7	662	NR	827 *	1.8	2.3
283 Luth—MO Synod	1	119	55	137	.3	.4
339 Pent Ch of God	7	215	NR	602	1.3	1.7
349 Pent Holiness	5	244	166	305 *	.7	.8
355 Presb Ch (USA)	1	344	140	429 *	.9	1.2
360 Prim Bapt Chrch	1	NR	NR	NR	-	-
403 Salvation Army	1	111	104	213	.5	.6
413 S.D.A.	1	282	NR	336	.7	.9
419 So Bapt Conv	27	15,694	3,571	19,594 *	42.9	54.2
449 Un Methodist	8	4,938	919	6,165 *	13.5	17.1
496 Jewish Est	1	NR	NR	25	.1	.1
CHEROKEE	**67**	**10,818**	**5,141**	**15,442 ***	**36.3**	**100.0**
017 Amer Bapt Assn	1	60	NR	75 *	.2	.5
053 Assemb of God	3	597	730	910	2.1	5.9
056 Baha'i	0	56	NR	56	.1	.4
081 Catholic	2	NR	NR	464	1.1	3.0
093 Chr Ch (Disc)	1	185	86	231 *	.5	1.5
097 Chr Chs&Chs Cr	1	40	NR	50 *	.1	.3
123 Ch God (Ander)	1	NR	30	30	.1	.2
127 Ch God (Cleve)	2	102	92	127 *	.3	.8
151 L-D Saints	1	NR	NR	454	1.1	2.9
165 Ch of Nazarene	1	93	51	93	.2	.6
167 Chs of Christ	7	496	490	636	1.5	4.1
193 Episcopal	1	NR	36	125	.3	.8
203 Evan Free Ch	1	80	150	150	.4	1.0
223 Free Will Bapt	3	284	NR	354 *	.8	2.3
262 Int Cou Comm Ch	1	370	NR	462 *	1.1	3.0
283 Luth—MO Synod	1	105	50	110	.3	.7
339 Pent Ch of God	3	76	NR	217	.5	1.4
349 Pent Holiness	3	108	130	135 *	.3	.9
355 Presb Ch (USA)	2	235	132	293 *	.7	1.9
413 S.D.A.	1	48	NR	57	.1	.4
419 So Bapt Conv	24	6,223	2,475	7,766 *	18.3	50.3
435 Unitarian-Univ	1	61	NR	76 *	.2	.5
449 Un Methodist	5	1,599	406	1,996 *	4.7	12.9
498 Indep.Charis.	1	0	283	575	1.4	3.7
CHOCTAW	**59**	**7,743**	**2,579**	**10,205 ***	**66.5**	**100.0**
017 Amer Bapt Assn	2	70	NR	87 *	.6	.9
053 Assemb of God	4	207	280	460	3.0	4.5
081 Catholic	2	NR	NR	234	1.5	2.3
093 Chr Ch (Disc)	1	103	45	128 *	.8	1.3
127 Ch God (Cleve)	2	148	75	184 *	1.2	1.8
157 Ch of Brethren	1	21	0	26 *	.2	.3
165 Ch of Nazarene	2	52	47	94	.6	.9
167 Chs of Christ	8	369	371	481	3.1	4.7
185 Cumber Presb	1	8	NR	23	.1	.2
193 Episcopal	1	NR	15	61	.4	.6
223 Free Will Bapt	1	95	NR	118 *	.8	1.2
339 Pent Ch of God	1	50	NR	70	.5	.7
355 Presb Ch (USA)	3	102	63	127 *	.8	1.2
413 S.D.A.	1	21	NR	25	.2	.2
419 So Bapt Conv	22	5,738	1,469	7,142 *	46.6	70.0
449 Un Methodist	7	759	214	945 *	6.2	9.3
CIMARRON	**18**	**2,172**	**767**	**3,043 ***	**96.7**	**100.0**
081 Catholic	1	NR	NR	275	8.7	9.0
097 Chr Chs&Chs Cr	1	114	NR	144 *	4.6	4.7
123 Ch God (Ander)	1	NR	25	25	.8	.8
165 Ch of Nazarene	1	20	12	20	.6	.7
167 Chs of Christ	2	60	65	81	2.6	2.7
283 Luth—MO Synod	1	41	33	55	1.7	1.8
349 Pent Holiness	1	13	31	16 *	.5	.5
419 So Bapt Conv	5	1,237	373	1,561 *	49.6	51.3
449 Un Methodist	5	687	228	866 *	27.5	28.5
CLEVELAND	**152**	**57,471**	**22,137**	**92,122 ***	**44.3**	**100.0**
017 Amer Bapt Assn	3	303	NR	372 *	.2	.4
053 Assemb of God	8	1,185	1,512	3,021	1.5	3.3
056 Baha'i	2	143	NR	143	.1	.2
059 Bapt Miss Assn	1	1,017	400	1,248 *	.6	1.4
081 Catholic	4	NR	NR	13,823	6.6	15.0
084 Calvary Chapel	1	NR	NR	NR	-	-
093 Chr Ch (Disc)	3	1,398	682	1,715 *	.8	1.9
097 Chr Chs&Chs Cr	4	1,540	NR	1,890 *	.9	2.1
123 Ch God (Ander)	2	NR	670	670	.3	.7
127 Ch God (Cleve)	4	765	532	938 *	.5	1.0
151 L-D Saints	5	NR	NR	1,957	.9	2.1
165 Ch of Nazarene	5	612	307	734	.4	.8
167 Chs of Christ	12	1,780	1,963	2,561	1.2	2.8
171 Ch God-Gen Con	2	59	95	118 *	.1	.1
173 Comm of Christ	1	170	NR	170	.1	.2
193 Episcopal	3	NR	525	1,479	.7	1.6
201 Evan Cov Ch	1	174	475	475 *	.2	.5
207 E.L.C.A.	1	413	192	530	.3	.6
223 Free Will Bapt	13	1,229	NR	1,508 *	.7	1.6
263 Int Foursq Gos	1	299	264	367 *	.2	.4
267 Muslim Est	1	NR	150	250	.1	.3
283 Luth—MO Synod	2	971	423	1,322	.6	1.4
335 Orth Pres Ch	1	11	18	18	-	-
339 Pent Ch of God	4	144	NR	245	.1	.3
349 Pent Holiness	4	491	325	602 *	.3	.7
355 Presb Ch (USA)	3	1,267	511	1,554 *	.7	1.7
370 Ref Baptist Chs	1	NR	NR	NR	-	-
403 Salvation Army	1	78	32	78	-	.1
413 S.D.A.	3	315	NR	375	.2	.4
419 So Bapt Conv	42	32,741	9,282	40,167 *	19.3	43.6
435 Unitarian-Univ	1	31	NR	38 *	-	-
449 Un Methodist	9	9,793	2,238	12,014 *	5.8	13.0
467 Wesleyan	1	42	41	90	-	.1
498 Indep.Charis.	1	500	350	500	.2	.5
499 Indep.Non-Char	2	0	1,150	1,150	.6	1.2
COAL	**24**	**2,744**	**965**	**3,590 ***	**59.5**	**100.0**
053 Assemb of God	1	41	42	46	.8	1.3

NR–Not Reported *Total adherents estimated from known number of communicant, confirmed, full members. - Represents a percentage less than 0.1. Percentages may not total 100 due to rounding.

Table 4: Religious Congregations by County and Group: 2000

Religious Group	Number of Churches, Synagogues, Mosques, or Temples	Number of Communicant, Confirmed, or Full Members	Number of Attendees	Total Adherents: Number of Adherents	Total Adherents: % of Total Pop.	Total Adherents: % of Total Adh.
056 Baha'i	0	1	NR	1	-	-
059 Bapt Miss Assn	1	32	35	40 *	.7	1.1
081 Catholic	1	NR	NR	100	1.7	2.8
165 Ch of Nazarene	1	69	54	82	1.4	2.3
167 Chs of Christ	3	180	190	229	3.8	6.4
171 Ch God-Gen Con	1	40	30	50 *	.8	1.4
185 Cumber Presb	1	3	NR	10	.2	.3
193 Episcopal	1	NR	12	18	.3	.5
323 Old Ord Amish	1	55	NR	69 *	1.1	1.9
339 Pent Ch of God	1	10	NR	38	.6	1.1
349 Pent Holiness	1	24	21	30 *	.5	.8
355 Presb Ch (USA)	1	21	10	26 *	.4	.7
413 S.D.A.	1	31	NR	37	.6	1.0
419 So Bapt Conv	6	1,727	420	2,173 *	36.0	60.5
449 Un Methodist	3	510	151	641 *	10.6	17.9
COMANCHE	**146**	**45,563**	**14,441**	**65,149 ***	**56.7**	**100.0**
017 Amer Bapt Assn	2	200	NR	256 *	.2	.4
019 Amer Bapt USA	1	200	30	255 *	.2	.4
053 Assemb of God	14	2,069	1,971	2,341	2.0	3.6
056 Baha'i	0	90	NR	90	.1	.1
081 Catholic	4	NR	NR	5,061	4.4	7.8
089 Chr & Miss Al	1	33	NR	35	-	.1
093 Chr Ch (Disc)	3	641	256	819 *	.7	1.3
097 Chr Chs&Chs Cr	4	850	NR	1,085 *	.9	1.7
123 Ch God (Ander)	1	NR	85	85	.1	.1
127 Ch God (Cleve)	7	394	337	524 *	.5	.8
151 L-D Saints	2	NR	NR	1,171	1.0	1.8
165 Ch of Nazarene	5	527	358	723	.6	1.1
167 Chs of Christ	16	1,597	1,462	1,946	1.7	3.0
193 Episcopal	1	NR	155	366	.3	.6
207 E.L.C.A.	1	93	32	125	.1	.2
223 Free Will Bapt	3	284	NR	362 *	.3	.6
237 Menn Br US Conf	2	121	NR	155 *	.1	.2
267 Muslim Est	1	NR	30	100	.1	.2
283 Luth—MO Synod	2	793	400	1,016	.9	1.6
290 Metro Comm Ch	1	25	31	32 *	-	-
339 Pent Ch of God	2	231	NR	416	.4	.6
349 Pent Holiness	2	118	68	151 *	.1	.2
355 Presb Ch (USA)	4	512	295	654 *	.6	1.0
356 Presb Ch Amer	1	67	70	85	.1	.1
371 Ref Ch in Am	1	75	53	137	.1	.2
403 Salvation Army	1	184	68	888	.8	1.4
413 S.D.A.	2	201	NR	240	.2	.4
419 So Bapt Conv	36	28,549	6,310	36,457 *	31.7	56.0
435 Unitarian-Univ	1	25	NR	32 *	-	-
443 Un C of Christ	1	100	59	128 *	.1	.2
449 Un Methodist	21	6,524	1,683	8,330 *	7.2	12.8
463 Vineyard	1	50	58	64 *	.1	.1
498 Indep.Charis.	1	500	380	500	.4	.8
499 Indep.Non-Char	1	510	250	520	.5	.8
COTTON	**28**	**4,710**	**1,324**	**6,036 ***	**91.3**	**100.0**
019 Amer Bapt USA	1	80	35	99 *	1.5	1.6
053 Assemb of God	3	137	157	209	3.2	3.5
081 Catholic	1	NR	NR	121	1.8	2.0
093 Chr Ch (Disc)	1	109	50	135 *	2.0	2.2
127 Ch God (Cleve)	1	118	73	146 *	2.2	2.4
165 Ch of Nazarene	2	115	70	161	2.4	2.7
167 Chs of Christ	3	159	176	215	3.3	3.6
355 Presb Ch (USA)	2	47	37	58 *	.9	1.0
419 So Bapt Conv	10	3,275	532	4,062 *	61.4	67.3
449 Un Methodist	4	670	194	830 *	12.5	13.8
CRAIG	**40**	**7,826**	**2,274**	**10,158 ***	**67.9**	**100.0**
053 Assemb of God	3	206	276	349	2.3	3.4
056 Baha'i	0	24	NR	24	.2	.2
081 Catholic	2	NR	NR	202	1.4	2.0
097 Chr Chs&Chs Cr	2	305	NR	373 *	2.5	3.7
123 Ch God (Ander)	1	NR	123	123	.8	1.2
165 Ch of Nazarene	1	51	43	93	.6	.9
167 Chs of Christ	3	202	189	257	1.7	2.5
173 Comm of Christ	1	46	NR	46	.3	.5
193 Episcopal	1	NR	36	92	.6	.9
223 Free Will Bapt	1	95	NR	115 *	.8	1.1
263 Int Foursq Gos	1	97	180	180 *	1.2	1.8
283 Luth—MO Synod	1	53	35	71	.5	.7
355 Presb Ch (USA)	1	82	39	100 *	.7	1.0
413 S.D.A.	1	18	NR	21	.1	.2
419 So Bapt Conv	16	5,133	934	6,264 *	41.9	61.7
449 Un Methodist	4	1,384	299	1,689 *	11.3	16.6
463 Vineyard	1	130	120	159 *	1.1	1.6
CREEK	**113**	**25,367**	**8,218**	**33,819 ***	**50.2**	**100.0**
053 Assemb of God	10	974	1,164	1,663	2.5	4.9
056 Baha'i	1	25	NR	25	-	.1
059 Bapt Miss Assn	2	183	65	231 *	.3	.7
081 Catholic	4	NR	NR	466	.7	1.4
093 Chr Ch (Disc)	4	248	148	313 *	.5	.9
097 Chr Chs&Chs Cr	6	1,490	NR	1,881 *	2.8	5.6
123 Ch God (Ander)	4	NR	310	310	.5	.9
145 Ch God Prophcy	2	58	NR	74 *	.1	.2
151 L-D Saints	2	NR	NR	432	.6	1.3
165 Ch of Nazarene	4	752	415	859	1.3	2.5
167 Chs of Christ	8	647	504	788	1.2	2.3
173 Comm of Christ	1	82	NR	82	.1	.2
193 Episcopal	1	NR	125	285	.4	.8
223 Free Will Bapt	9	851	NR	1,075 *	1.6	3.2
339 Pent Ch of God	1	50	NR	70	.1	.2
349 Pent Holiness	4	249	286	314 *	.5	.9
355 Presb Ch (USA)	2	529	298	668 *	1.0	2.0
403 Salvation Army	1	68	45	118	.2	.3
413 S.D.A.	4	409	NR	487	.7	1.4
419 So Bapt Conv	32	14,975	4,054	18,908 *	28.1	55.9
449 Un Methodist	11	3,777	804	4,770 *	7.1	14.1
CUSTER	**78**	**15,581**	**5,230**	**21,713 ***	**83.1**	**100.0**
017 Amer Bapt Assn	4	286	NR	349 *	1.3	1.6
053 Assemb of God	6	489	606	775	3.0	3.6
056 Baha'i	0	14	NR	14	.1	.1
059 Bapt Miss Assn	1	55	19	67 *	.3	.3
061 Beachy Amish	1	46	NR	56 *	.2	.3
075 Brethren in Cr	1	166	123	166	.6	.8
081 Catholic	3	NR	NR	1,679	6.4	7.7
089 Chr & Miss Al	1	31	NR	83	.3	.4
093 Chr Ch (Disc)	2	395	141	480 *	1.8	2.2
097 Chr Chs&Chs Cr	5	931	NR	1,131 *	4.3	5.2
123 Ch God (Ander)	2	NR	262	262	1.0	1.2
143 CG in Cr(Menn)	1	26	NR	32 *	.1	.1
151 L-D Saints	1	NR	NR	275	1.1	1.3
157 Ch of Brethren	1	40	15	49 *	.2	.2
165 Ch of Nazarene	4	138	113	284	1.1	1.3
167 Chs of Christ	6	862	739	1,190	4.6	5.5
185 Cumber Presb	1	87	NR	104	.4	.5
193 Episcopal	2	NR	34	87	.3	.4
203 Evan Free Ch	1	108	95	108	.4	.5
207 E.L.C.A.	2	221	102	286	1.1	1.3
223 Free Will Bapt	3	284	NR	345 *	1.3	1.6
237 Menn Br US Conf	1	273	NR	332 *	1.3	1.5
288 Mennonite USA	2	110	87	134 *	.5	.6
339 Pent Ch of God	2	14	NR	43	.2	.2
349 Pent Holiness	2	73	61	89 *	.3	.4
355 Presb Ch (USA)	2	82	39	100 *	.4	.5
413 S.D.A.	1	23	NR	27	.1	.1
419 So Bapt Conv	11	7,578	2,015	9,215 *	35.2	42.4
443 Un C of Christ	1	177	54	215 *	.8	1.0
449 Un Methodist	8	3,072	725	3,736 *	14.3	17.2
DELAWARE	**71**	**18,645**	**4,748**	**22,258 ***	**60.0**	**100.0**
053 Assemb of God	6	302	349	515	1.4	2.3
056 Baha'i	1	80	NR	80	.2	.4
059 Bapt Miss Assn	2	215	50	264 *	.7	1.2
081 Catholic	1	NR	NR	385	1.0	1.7
097 Chr Chs&Chs Cr	3	825	NR	1,012 *	2.7	4.5
127 Ch God (Cleve)	1	64	33	79 *	.2	.4
151 L-D Saints	1	NR	NR	331	.9	1.5

NR–Not Reported *Total adherents estimated from known number of communicant, confirmed, full members. - Represents a percentage less than 0.1. Percentages may not total 100 due to rounding.

Table 4: Religious Congregations by County and Group: 2000

Religious Group	Number of Churches, Synagogues, Mosques, or Temples	Number of Communicant, Confirmed, or Full Members	Number of Attendees	Total Adherents		
				Number of Adherents	% of Total Pop.	% of Total Adh.
165 Ch of Nazarene	1	58	49	109	.3	.5
167 Chs of Christ	5	427	468	560	1.5	2.5
173 Comm of Christ	1	112	NR	112	.3	.5
193 Episcopal	1	NR	58	114	.3	.5
207 E.L.C.A.	1	79	80	146	.4	.7
223 Free Will Bapt	1	95	NR	116 *	.3	.5
349 Pent Holiness	1	26	12	32 *	.1	.1
355 Presb Ch (USA)	1	109	65	134 *	.4	.6
413 S.D.A.	1	60	NR	71	.2	.3
419 So Bapt Conv	37	7,093	2,113	8,706 *	23.5	39.1
449 Un Methodist	4	1,725	521	2,117 *	5.7	9.5
498 Indep.Charis.	1	7,000	700	7,000	18.9	31.4
499 Indep.Non-Char	1	375	250	375	1.0	1.7
DEWEY	**36**	**3,889**	**1,243**	**4,842 ***	**102.1**	**100.0**
053 Assemb of God	4	136	170	202	4.3	4.2
075 Brethren in Cr	1	36	17	36	.8	.7
081 Catholic	1	NR	NR	103	2.2	2.1
093 Chr Ch (Disc)	3	284	119	340 *	7.2	7.0
097 Chr Chs&Chs Cr	6	975	NR	1,168 *	24.6	24.1
165 Ch of Nazarene	2	132	131	192	4.0	4.0
167 Chs of Christ	3	144	155	188	4.0	3.9
226 Friends-USA	2	100	NR	120 *	2.5	2.5
288 Mennonite USA	1	45	4	54 *	1.1	1.1
419 So Bapt Conv	6	1,111	355	1,330 *	28.0	27.5
449 Un Methodist	7	926	292	1,109 *	23.4	22.9
ELLIS	**24**	**2,651**	**850**	**3,285 ***	**80.6**	**100.0**
053 Assemb of God	2	64	51	105	2.6	3.2
081 Catholic	1	NR	NR	54	1.3	1.6
093 Chr Ch (Disc)	2	124	18	147 *	3.6	4.5
097 Chr Chs&Chs Cr	1	100	NR	119 *	2.9	3.6
165 Ch of Nazarene	3	135	108	228	5.6	6.9
167 Chs of Christ	3	92	91	103	2.5	3.1
283 Luth—MO Synod	1	49	35	51	1.3	1.6
313 N Am Bapt Conf	1	39	28	46 *	1.1	1.4
413 S.D.A.	1	69	NR	82	2.0	2.5
419 So Bapt Conv	4	1,174	270	1,394 *	34.2	42.4
449 Un Methodist	5	805	249	956 *	23.5	29.1
GARFIELD	**96**	**23,488**	**9,126**	**35,799 ***	**61.9**	**100.0**
017 Amer Bapt Assn	1	29	NR	36 *	.1	.1
053 Assemb of God	6	832	813	1,195	2.1	3.3
056 Baha'i	0	26	NR	26	-	.1
059 Bapt Miss Assn	1	12	30	30 *	.1	.1
081 Catholic	3	NR	NR	5,438	9.4	15.2
084 Calvary Chapel	1	NR	NR	NR	-	-
093 Chr Ch (Disc)	8	2,365	807	2,920 *	5.1	8.2
097 Chr Chs&Chs Cr	2	1,000	NR	1,235 *	2.1	3.4
107 Christian Un	3	167	153	206 *	.4	.6
123 Ch God (Ander)	1	NR	40	40	.1	.1
127 Ch God (Cleve)	1	33	6	41 *	.1	.1
145 Ch God Prophcy	1	29	NR	36 *	.1	.1
151 L-D Saints	2	NR	NR	596	1.0	1.7
157 Ch of Brethren	1	18	16	22 *	-	.1
165 Ch of Nazarene	2	586	384	603	1.0	1.7
167 Chs of Christ	4	473	478	640	1.1	1.8
173 Comm of Christ	1	36	NR	36	.1	.1
193 Episcopal	1	NR	82	159	.3	.4
203 Evan Free Ch	1	69	125	125	.2	.3
207 E.L.C.A.	1	120	47	154	.3	.4
221 Free Methodist	1	36	38	38	.1	.1
223 Free Will Bapt	1	95	NR	117 *	.2	.3
226 Friends-USA	1	50	NR	62 *	.1	.2
237 Menn Br US Conf	1	277	NR	342 *	.6	1.0
283 Luth—MO Synod	8	2,198	1,024	2,887	5.0	8.1
288 Mennonite USA	1	140	110	173 *	.3	.5
339 Pent Ch of God	1	10	NR	37	.1	.1
349 Pent Holiness	3	115	120	142 *	.2	.4
355 Presb Ch (USA)	1	609	320	752 *	1.3	2.1
388 Reg Bapt Gen As	1	50	35	62 *	.1	.2
403 Salvation Army	1	142	103	170	.3	.5
413 S.D.A.	2	213	NR	253	.4	.7

Religious Group	Number of Churches, Synagogues, Mosques, or Temples	Number of Communicant, Confirmed, or Full Members	Number of Attendees	Total Adherents		
				Number of Adherents	% of Total Pop.	% of Total Adh.
419 So Bapt Conv	18	8,230	2,831	10,161 *	17.6	28.4
443 Un C of Christ	2	198	87	244 *	.4	.7
449 Un Methodist	12	5,216	1,368	6,439 *	11.1	18.0
467 Wesleyan	1	114	109	382	.7	1.1
GARVIN	**80**	**18,053**	**5,489**	**23,461 ***	**86.2**	**100.0**
053 Assemb of God	5	345	463	498	1.8	2.1
056 Baha'i	0	3	NR	3	-	-
059 Bapt Miss Assn	5	565	212	694 *	2.6	3.0
081 Catholic	2	NR	NR	596	2.2	2.5
093 Chr Ch (Disc)	2	206	100	253 *	.9	1.1
097 Chr Chs&Chs Cr	1	101	NR	124 *	.5	.5
123 Ch God (Ander)	1	NR	105	105	.4	.4
127 Ch God (Cleve)	1	57	57	70 *	.3	.3
145 Ch God Prophcy	1	29	NR	36 *	.1	.2
151 L-D Saints	2	NR	NR	430	1.6	1.8
165 Ch of Nazarene	2	104	64	105	.4	.4
167 Chs of Christ	15	1,309	1,201	1,648	6.1	7.0
193 Episcopal	2	NR	16	24	.1	.1
223 Free Will Bapt	3	284	NR	349 *	1.3	1.5
339 Pent Ch of God	4	180	NR	258	.9	1.1
349 Pent Holiness	2	575	133	706 *	2.6	3.0
355 Presb Ch (USA)	1	189	63	232 *	.9	1.0
360 Prim Bapt Chrch	1	NR	NR	NR	-	-
419 So Bapt Conv	22	11,945	2,537	14,675 *	53.9	62.6
449 Un Methodist	8	2,161	538	2,655 *	9.8	11.3
GRADY	**81**	**21,197**	**7,231**	**28,080 ***	**61.7**	**100.0**
053 Assemb of God	6	817	956	1,623	3.6	5.8
056 Baha'i	0	23	NR	23	.1	.1
059 Bapt Miss Assn	4	425	104	532 *	1.2	1.9
081 Catholic	2	NR	NR	634	1.4	2.3
093 Chr Ch (Disc)	2	375	254	470 *	1.0	1.7
097 Chr Chs&Chs Cr	3	585	NR	732 *	1.6	2.6
127 Ch God (Cleve)	1	78	22	98 *	.2	.3
143 CG in Cr(Menn)	1	199	NR	249 *	.5	.9
151 L-D Saints	2	NR	NR	255	.6	.9
165 Ch of Nazarene	2	120	89	149	.3	.5
167 Chs of Christ	9	1,248	1,222	1,502	3.3	5.3
193 Episcopal	1	NR	39	91	.2	.3
207 E.L.C.A.	1	115	54	123	.3	.4
223 Free Will Bapt	2	189	NR	237 *	.5	.8
283 Luth—MO Synod	1	92	65	116	.3	.4
339 Pent Ch of God	2	139	NR	170	.4	.6
349 Pent Holiness	3	75	93	94 *	.2	.3
355 Presb Ch (USA)	1	107	70	134 *	.3	.5
356 Presb Ch Amer	1	56	55	71	.2	.3
360 Prim Bapt Chrch	1	NR	NR	NR	-	-
403 Salvation Army	1	80	28	152	.3	.5
413 S.D.A.	1	31	NR	37	.1	.1
419 So Bapt Conv	25	13,476	3,451	16,873 *	37.1	60.1
449 Un Methodist	9	2,967	729	3,715 *	8.2	13.2
GRANT	**36**	**4,469**	**1,462**	**5,996 ***	**116.6**	**100.0**
053 Assemb of God	4	63	76	95	1.8	1.6
056 Baha'i	0	1	NR	1	-	-
081 Catholic	3	NR	NR	435	8.5	7.3
093 Chr Ch (Disc)	5	983	253	1,201 *	23.3	20.0
097 Chr Chs&Chs Cr	4	407	NR	497 *	9.7	8.3
165 Ch of Nazarene	1	63	55	125	2.4	2.1
167 Chs of Christ	3	170	199	235	4.6	3.9
283 Luth—MO Synod	1	52	33	71	1.4	1.2
288 Mennonite USA	1	72	35	88 *	1.7	1.5
419 So Bapt Conv	6	1,241	377	1,516 *	29.5	25.3
443 Un C of Christ	1	23	13	28 *	.5	.5
449 Un Methodist	7	1,394	421	1,704 *	33.1	28.4
GREER	**25**	**4,166**	**1,269**	**5,193 ***	**85.7**	**100.0**
017 Amer Bapt Assn	2	150	NR	175 *	2.9	3.4
053 Assemb of God	2	38	50	105	1.7	2.0
056 Baha'i	0	1	NR	1	-	-
081 Catholic	1	NR	NR	213	3.5	4.1

NR–Not Reported *Total adherents estimated from known number of communicant, confirmed, full members. - Represents a percentage less than 0.1. Percentages may not total 100 due to rounding.

Table 4: Religious Congregations by County and Group: 2000

Religious Group	Number of Churches, Synagogues, Mosques, or Temples	Number of Communicant, Confirmed, or Full Members	Number of Attendees	Total Adherents: Number of Adherents	Total Adherents: % of Total Pop.	Total Adherents: % of Total Adh.
127 Ch God (Cleve)	1	67	69	78 *	1.3	1.5
165 Ch of Nazarene	1	39	39	71	1.2	1.4
167 Chs of Christ	4	433	355	535	8.8	10.3
185 Cumber Presb	1	27	NR	27	.4	.5
283 Luth—MO Synod	1	100	74	120	2.0	2.3
419 So Bapt Conv	7	2,702	468	3,157 *	52.1	60.8
449 Un Methodist	5	609	214	711 *	11.7	13.7
HARMON	**15**	**2,864**	**1,015**	**3,678 ***	**112.0**	**100.0**
017 Amer Bapt Assn	1	50	NR	61 *	1.9	1.7
053 Assemb of God	1	27	36	52	1.6	1.4
056 Baha'i	0	4	NR	4	.1	.1
081 Catholic	1	NR	NR	117	3.6	3.2
165 Ch of Nazarene	1	39	22	49	1.5	1.3
167 Chs of Christ	4	463	447	602	18.3	16.4
419 So Bapt Conv	5	2,001	430	2,450 *	74.6	66.6
449 Un Methodist	2	280	80	343 *	10.4	9.3
HARPER	**17**	**2,808**	**728**	**3,536 ***	**99.3**	**100.0**
053 Assemb of God	3	144	105	201	5.6	5.7
081 Catholic	1	NR	NR	114	3.2	3.2
093 Chr Ch (Disc)	1	82	65	98 *	2.8	2.8
097 Chr Chs&Chs Cr	2	235	NR	282 *	7.9	8.0
165 Ch of Nazarene	1	0	0	0	-	-
167 Chs of Christ	2	63	54	74	2.1	2.1
283 Luth—MO Synod	1	134	47	185	5.2	5.2
419 So Bapt Conv	3	1,273	244	1,528 *	42.9	43.2
449 Un Methodist	3	877	213	1,054 *	29.6	29.8
HASKELL	**49**	**7,132**	**2,016**	**9,047 ***	**76.7**	**100.0**
017 Amer Bapt Assn	1	100	NR	125 *	1.1	1.4
053 Assemb of God	5	480	589	745	6.3	8.2
081 Catholic	1	NR	NR	25	.2	.3
093 Chr Ch (Disc)	1	56	40	70 *	.6	.8
097 Chr Chs&Chs Cr	1	50	NR	62 *	.5	.7
167 Chs of Christ	4	233	213	261	2.2	2.9
223 Free Will Bapt	15	1,419	NR	1,772 *	15.0	19.6
349 Pent Holiness	1	25	25	31 *	.3	.3
419 So Bapt Conv	17	4,253	1,043	5,312 *	45.0	58.7
449 Un Methodist	3	516	106	644 *	5.5	7.1
HUGHES	**66**	**6,890**	**2,433**	**8,684 ***	**61.4**	**100.0**
017 Amer Bapt Assn	3	567	NR	686 *	4.8	7.9
053 Assemb of God	3	234	308	371	2.6	4.3
056 Baha'i	0	19	NR	19	.1	.2
059 Bapt Miss Assn	1	49	30	59 *	.4	.7
081 Catholic	1	NR	NR	102	.7	1.2
093 Chr Ch (Disc)	2	161	29	195 *	1.4	2.2
123 Ch God (Ander)	2	NR	122	122	.9	1.4
165 Ch of Nazarene	2	112	75	152	1.1	1.8
167 Chs of Christ	8	397	356	474	3.3	5.5
193 Episcopal	1	NR	9	17	.1	.2
223 Free Will Bapt	4	378	NR	458 *	3.2	5.3
339 Pent Ch of God	1	36	NR	59	.4	.7
349 Pent Holiness	4	287	222	347 *	2.5	4.0
419 So Bapt Conv	23	3,574	958	4,323 *	30.5	49.8
449 Un Methodist	11	1,076	324	1,300 *	9.2	15.0
JACKSON	**60**	**16,852**	**5,087**	**24,407 ***	**85.8**	**100.0**
017 Amer Bapt Assn	5	280	NR	362 *	1.3	1.5
053 Assemb of God	5	456	544	739	2.6	3.0
056 Baha'i	0	15	NR	15	.1	.1
081 Catholic	1	NR	NR	1,924	6.8	7.9
093 Chr Ch (Disc)	1	270	115	350 *	1.2	1.4
127 Ch God (Cleve)	1	150	30	194 *	.7	.8
145 Ch God Prophcy	1	29	NR	38 *	.1	.2
151 L-D Saints	1	NR	NR	447	1.6	1.8
165 Ch of Nazarene	2	82	72	116	.4	.5
167 Chs of Christ	10	924	721	1,189	4.2	4.9
193 Episcopal	1	NR	72	132	.5	.5
207 E.L.C.A.	1	39	60	62	.2	.3
283 Luth—MO Synod	1	44	24	78	.3	.3
349 Pent Holiness	2	36	51	47 *	.2	.2
355 Presb Ch (USA)	1	148	71	192 *	.7	.8
360 Prim Bapt Chrch	1	NR	NR	NR	-	-
403 Salvation Army	1	109	39	139	.5	.6
413 S.D.A.	1	56	NR	67	.2	.3
419 So Bapt Conv	15	10,489	2,453	13,581 *	47.8	55.6
449 Un Methodist	8	3,425	665	4,435 *	15.6	18.2
499 Indep.Non-Char	1	300	170	300	1.1	1.2
JEFFERSON	**26**	**3,795**	**1,484**	**4,834 ***	**70.9**	**100.0**
017 Amer Bapt Assn	1	100	NR	122 *	1.8	2.5
053 Assemb of God	5	169	193	282	4.1	5.8
081 Catholic	1	NR	NR	85	1.2	1.8
093 Chr Ch (Disc)	1	88	0	107 *	1.6	2.2
165 Ch of Nazarene	1	30	21	30	.4	.6
167 Chs of Christ	5	365	380	493	7.2	10.2
349 Pent Holiness	1	8	8	10 *	.1	.2
413 S.D.A.	1	28	NR	33	.5	.7
419 So Bapt Conv	7	2,477	660	3,024 *	44.4	62.6
449 Un Methodist	3	530	222	648 *	9.5	13.4
JOHNSTON	**48**	**5,665**	**2,268**	**7,261 ***	**69.1**	**100.0**
053 Assemb of God	2	121	148	219	2.1	3.0
056 Baha'i	0	2	NR	2	-	-
059 Bapt Miss Assn	1	51	25	63 *	.6	.9
081 Catholic	1	NR	NR	21	.2	.3
093 Chr Ch (Disc)	1	110	0	136 *	1.3	1.9
127 Ch God (Cleve)	4	216	158	268 *	2.5	3.7
145 Ch God Prophcy	1	29	NR	36 *	.3	.5
165 Ch of Nazarene	2	198	149	366	3.5	5.0
167 Chs of Christ	8	406	460	498	4.7	6.9
193 Episcopal	1	NR	6	15	.1	.2
223 Free Will Bapt	2	189	NR	234 *	2.2	3.2
339 Pent Ch of God	1	10	NR	46	.4	.6
349 Pent Holiness	1	118	84	146 *	1.4	2.0
355 Presb Ch (USA)	2	87	66	108 *	1.0	1.5
419 So Bapt Conv	15	3,563	1,000	4,403 *	41.9	60.6
449 Un Methodist	6	565	172	700 *	6.7	9.6
KAY	**92**	**21,867**	**7,920**	**34,537 ***	**71.8**	**100.0**
017 Amer Bapt Assn	2	198	NR	247 *	.5	.7
053 Assemb of God	4	406	507	1,032	2.1	3.0
056 Baha'i	1	25	NR	25	.1	.1
081 Catholic	4	NR	NR	4,409	9.2	12.8
093 Chr Ch (Disc)	7	2,397	651	2,995 *	6.2	8.7
097 Chr Chs&Chs Cr	3	465	NR	581 *	1.2	1.7
123 Ch God (Ander)	3	NR	108	108	.2	.3
151 L-D Saints	2	NR	NR	600	1.2	1.7
165 Ch of Nazarene	6	612	428	701	1.5	2.0
167 Chs of Christ	6	944	874	1,253	2.6	3.6
193 Episcopal	1	NR	124	384	.8	1.1
207 E.L.C.A.	1	98	65	154	.3	.4
220 Free Lutheran	1	101	60	123	.3	.4
223 Free Will Bapt	2	189	NR	236 *	.5	.7
263 Int Foursq Gos	1	100	555	555 *	1.2	1.6
267 Muslim Est	1	NR	55	163	.3	.5
283 Luth—MO Synod	4	905	595	1,282	2.7	3.7
339 Pent Ch of God	2	54	NR	149	.3	.4
349 Pent Holiness	3	119	100	149 *	.3	.4
355 Presb Ch (USA)	4	586	301	733 *	1.5	2.1
403 Salvation Army	1	121	38	214	.4	.6
413 S.D.A.	1	19	NR	23	-	.1
419 So Bapt Conv	17	8,183	1,922	10,226 *	21.3	29.6
449 Un Methodist	12	6,297	1,468	7,868 *	16.4	22.8
467 Wesleyan	2	48	69	302	.6	.9
496 Jewish Est	1	NR	NR	25	.1	.1
KINGFISHER	**37**	**6,642**	**2,571**	**11,287 ***	**81.0**	**100.0**
053 Assemb of God	2	85	103	118	.8	1.0
056 Baha'i	0	15	NR	15	.1	.1
081 Catholic	3	NR	NR	3,058	22.0	27.1
093 Chr Ch (Disc)	3	643	121	800 *	5.7	7.1

NR–Not Reported *Total adherents estimated from known number of communicant, confirmed, full members. - Represents a percentage less than 0.1. Percentages may not total 100 due to rounding.

Table 4: Religious Congregations by County and Group: 2000

Religious Group	Number of Churches, Synagogues, Mosques, or Temples	Number of Communicant, Confirmed, or Full Members	Number of Attendees	Total Adherents		
				Number of Adherents	% of Total Pop.	% of Total Adh.
097 Chr Chs&Chs Cr	1	150	NR	187 *	1.3	1.7
107 Christian Un	1	31	24	39 *	.3	.3
127 Ch God (Cleve)	1	34	24	42 *	.3	.4
165 Ch of Nazarene	2	418	201	418	3.0	3.7
167 Chs of Christ	2	147	165	215	1.5	1.9
283 Luth—MO Synod	1	269	113	361	2.6	3.2
313 N Am Bapt Conf	1	69	57	86 *	.6	.8
349 Pent Holiness	1	225	170	280 *	2.0	2.5
355 Presb Ch (USA)	1	110	52	137 *	1.0	1.2
419 So Bapt Conv	11	2,660	1,005	3,310 *	23.8	29.3
443 Un C of Christ	2	213	194	265 *	1.9	2.3
449 Un Methodist	5	1,573	342	1,956 *	14.0	17.3
KIOWA	**44**	**7,586**	**2,363**	**9,623 ***	**94.1**	**100.0**
017 Amer Bapt Assn	3	154	NR	187 *	1.8	1.9
019 Amer Bapt USA	2	223	78	271 *	2.6	2.8
053 Assemb of God	7	275	312	351	3.4	3.6
081 Catholic	1	NR	NR	250	2.4	2.6
093 Chr Ch (Disc)	1	100	62	122 *	1.2	1.3
097 Chr Chs&Chs Cr	1	102	NR	124 *	1.2	1.3
165 Ch of Nazarene	1	5	16	27	.3	.3
167 Chs of Christ	5	377	444	511	5.0	5.3
207 E.L.C.A.	1	67	42	83	.8	.9
283 Luth—MO Synod	1	155	101	193	1.9	2.0
339 Pent Ch of God	2	59	NR	118	1.2	1.2
349 Pent Holiness	1	102	76	124 *	1.2	1.3
355 Presb Ch (USA)	1	40	20	49 *	.5	.5
360 Prim Bapt Chrch	1	NR	NR	NR	-	-
419 So Bapt Conv	10	4,797	903	5,838 *	57.1	60.7
449 Un Methodist	6	1,130	309	1,375 *	13.4	14.3
LATIMER	**39**	**5,008**	**1,268**	**6,703 ***	**62.7**	**100.0**
053 Assemb of God	4	166	211	373	3.5	5.6
081 Catholic	2	NR	NR	300	2.8	4.5
097 Chr Chs&Chs Cr	1	50	NR	62 *	.6	.9
145 Ch God Prophcy	1	29	NR	36 *	.3	.5
165 Ch of Nazarene	1	13	10	51	.5	.8
167 Chs of Christ	3	124	123	140	1.3	2.1
223 Free Will Bapt	4	378	NR	470 *	4.4	7.0
355 Presb Ch (USA)	1	18	9	22 *	.2	.3
413 S.D.A.	1	34	NR	40	.4	.6
419 So Bapt Conv	19	3,894	813	4,834 *	45.2	72.1
449 Un Methodist	2	302	102	375 *	3.5	5.6
LE FLORE	**151**	**21,160**	**9,943**	**27,705 ***	**57.6**	**100.0**
017 Amer Bapt Assn	5	731	NR	913 *	1.9	3.3
053 Assemb of God	21	1,427	1,761	2,253	4.7	8.1
056 Baha'i	0	10	NR	10	-	-
059 Bapt Miss Assn	1	78	52	97 *	.2	.4
081 Catholic	3	NR	NR	185	.4	.7
093 Chr Ch (Disc)	2	215	159	269 *	.6	1.0
097 Chr Chs&Chs Cr	4	240	NR	299 *	.6	1.1
145 Ch God Prophcy	1	29	NR	36 *	.1	.1
151 L-D Saints	1	NR	NR	282	.6	1.0
165 Ch of Nazarene	6	446	307	713	1.5	2.6
167 Chs of Christ	12	611	716	846	1.8	3.1
171 Ch God-Gen Con	2	42	44	52 *	.1	.2
173 Comm of Christ	2	167	NR	167	.3	.6
185 Cumber Presb	1	4	NR	29	.1	.1
223 Free Will Bapt	14	1,324	NR	1,654 *	3.4	6.0
339 Pent Ch of God	7	211	NR	379	.8	1.4
355 Presb Ch (USA)	2	98	80	124 *	.3	.4
360 Prim Bapt Chrch	2	NR	NR	NR	-	-
419 So Bapt Conv	53	13,560	6,150	16,940 *	35.2	61.1
449 Un Methodist	12	1,967	674	2,457 *	5.1	8.9
LINCOLN	**73**	**13,160**	**5,263**	**17,721 ***	**55.2**	**100.0**
017 Amer Bapt Assn	2	265	NR	332 *	1.0	1.9
053 Assemb of God	10	849	1,001	1,432	4.5	8.1
056 Baha'i	0	2	NR	2	-	-
081 Catholic	4	NR	NR	877	2.7	4.9
093 Chr Ch (Disc)	3	488	230	612 *	1.9	3.5

Religious Group	Number of Churches, Synagogues, Mosques, or Temples	Number of Communicant, Confirmed, or Full Members	Number of Attendees	Total Adherents		
				Number of Adherents	% of Total Pop.	% of Total Adh.
097 Chr Chs&Chs Cr	5	466	NR	584 *	1.8	3.3
107 Christian Un	1	51	55	64 *	.2	.4
165 Ch of Nazarene	5	385	189	429	1.3	2.4
167 Chs of Christ	7	459	442	586	1.8	3.3
207 E.L.C.A.	1	100	60	123	.4	.7
223 Free Will Bapt	3	284	NR	356 *	1.1	2.0
226 Friends-USA	1	50	NR	63 *	.2	.4
283 Luth—MO Synod	1	142	83	191	.6	1.1
339 Pent Ch of God	1	110	NR	152	.5	.9
355 Presb Ch (USA)	2	58	28	73 *	.2	.4
413 S.D.A.	1	11	NR	13	-	.1
419 So Bapt Conv	19	7,788	2,724	9,761 *	30.4	55.1
449 Un Methodist	7	1,652	451	2,071 *	6.5	11.7
LOGAN	**49**	**7,966**	**3,042**	**11,373 ***	**33.5**	**100.0**
053 Assemb of God	4	281	358	618	1.8	5.4
056 Baha'i	0	48	NR	48	.1	.4
081 Catholic	2	NR	NR	1,180	3.5	10.4
093 Chr Ch (Disc)	1	604	259	743 *	2.2	6.5
097 Chr Chs&Chs Cr	3	370	NR	455 *	1.3	4.0
127 Ch God (Cleve)	2	59	72	75 *	.2	.7
145 Ch God Prophcy	1	29	NR	36 *	.1	.3
165 Ch of Nazarene	3	348	289	393	1.2	3.5
167 Chs of Christ	7	402	415	513	1.5	4.5
193 Episcopal	2	NR	84	150	.4	1.3
221 Free Methodist	1	15	36	36	.1	.3
226 Friends-USA	1	50	NR	61 *	.2	.5
283 Luth—MO Synod	2	158	93	178	.5	1.6
355 Presb Ch (USA)	1	190	110	234 *	.7	2.1
360 Prim Bapt Chrch	1	NR	NR	NR	-	-
413 S.D.A.	1	30	NR	36	.1	.3
419 So Bapt Conv	9	3,713	904	4,564 *	13.5	40.1
443 Un C of Christ	1	66	38	81 *	.2	.7
449 Un Methodist	7	1,603	384	1,972 *	5.8	17.3
LOVE	**26**	**5,099**	**1,946**	**6,536 ***	**74.0**	**100.0**
053 Assemb of God	1	16	20	32	.4	.5
081 Catholic	1	NR	NR	206	2.3	3.2
093 Chr Ch (Disc)	1	99	45	122 *	1.4	1.9
167 Chs of Christ	4	567	467	710	8.0	10.9
349 Pent Holiness	5	342	229	423 *	4.8	6.5
419 So Bapt Conv	11	3,585	1,041	4,436 *	50.2	67.9
449 Un Methodist	3	490	144	607 *	6.9	9.3
MCCLAIN	**64**	**12,206**	**4,243**	**16,401 ***	**59.1**	**100.0**
017 Amer Bapt Assn	1	100	NR	125 *	.5	.8
053 Assemb of God	4	274	295	371	1.3	2.3
056 Baha'i	0	3	NR	3	-	-
059 Bapt Miss Assn	5	1,062	333	1,325 *	4.8	8.1
081 Catholic	1	NR	NR	1,029	3.7	6.3
093 Chr Ch (Disc)	2	158	75	197 *	.7	1.2
097 Chr Chs&Chs Cr	1	155	NR	194 *	.7	1.2
151 L-D Saints	1	NR	NR	129	.5	.8
165 Ch of Nazarene	2	88	25	100	.4	.6
167 Chs of Christ	8	560	585	676	2.4	4.1
223 Free Will Bapt	5	473	NR	591 *	2.1	3.6
339 Pent Ch of God	1	50	NR	70	.3	.4
349 Pent Holiness	4	251	180	313 *	1.1	1.9
355 Presb Ch (USA)	2	28	18	35 *	.1	.2
360 Prim Bapt Chrch	2	NR	NR	NR	-	-
419 So Bapt Conv	19	7,546	2,366	9,424 *	34.0	57.5
449 Un Methodist	6	1,458	366	1,819 *	6.6	11.1
MCCURTAIN	**128**	**12,465**	**5,358**	**17,583 ***	**51.1**	**100.0**
017 Amer Bapt Assn	13	1,495	NR	1,911 *	5.6	10.9
053 Assemb of God	15	915	1,223	1,934	5.6	11.0
056 Baha'i	0	8	NR	8	-	-
059 Bapt Miss Assn	1	335	62	428 *	1.2	2.4
081 Catholic	3	NR	NR	626	1.8	3.6
093 Chr Ch (Disc)	1	56	25	71 *	.2	.4
097 Chr Chs&Chs Cr	3	223	NR	284 *	.8	1.6
127 Ch God (Cleve)	6	385	299	492 *	1.4	2.8

NR–Not Reported *Total adherents estimated from known number of communicant, confirmed, full members. - Represents a percentage less than 0.1. Percentages may not total 100 due to rounding.

Table 4: Religious Congregations by County and Group: 2000

Religious Group	Number of Churches, Synagogues, Mosques, or Temples	Number of Communicant, Confirmed, or Full Members	Number of Attendees	Total Adherents		
				Number of Adherents	% of Total Pop.	% of Total Adh.
151 L-D Saints	1	NR	NR	236	.7	1.3
165 Ch of Nazarene	1	49	23	49	.1	.3
167 Chs of Christ	20	928	976	1,168	3.4	6.6
185 Cumber Presb	2	34	NR	38	.1	.2
193 Episcopal	1	NR	14	73	.2	.4
223 Free Will Bapt	3	284	NR	362 *	1.1	2.1
339 Pent Ch of God	1	50	NR	70	.2	.4
355 Presb Ch (USA)	15	381	236	488 *	1.4	2.8
360 Prim Bapt Chrch	1	NR	NR	NR	-	-
413 S.D.A.	1	21	NR	25	.1	.1
419 So Bapt Conv	22	5,158	1,858	6,584 *	19.1	37.4
449 Un Methodist	18	2,143	642	2,736 *	8.0	15.6
MCINTOSH	**56**	**6,882**	**2,854**	**8,521 ***	**43.8**	**100.0**
017 Amer Bapt Assn	1	20	NR	24 *	.1	.3
053 Assemb of God	3	202	290	296	1.5	3.5
056 Baha'i	0	8	NR	8	-	.1
081 Catholic	1	NR	NR	75	.4	.9
093 Chr Ch (Disc)	1	35	24	42 *	.2	.5
097 Chr Chs&Chs Cr	2	110	NR	132 *	.7	1.5
127 Ch God (Cleve)	1	54	70	70 *	.4	.8
165 Ch of Nazarene	1	33	25	49	.3	.6
167 Chs of Christ	6	474	447	622	3.2	7.3
171 Ch God-Gen Con	1	15	14	18 *	.1	.2
193 Episcopal	1	NR	19	61	.3	.7
223 Free Will Bapt	4	378	NR	454 *	2.3	5.3
283 Luth—MO Synod	1	30	12	30	.2	.4
339 Pent Ch of God	1	50	NR	70	.4	.8
349 Pent Holiness	2	34	45	41 *	.2	.5
355 Presb Ch (USA)	1	22	11	26 *	.1	.3
419 So Bapt Conv	27	4,657	1,658	5,591 *	28.7	65.6
449 Un Methodist	2	760	239	912 *	4.7	10.7
MAJOR	**32**	**4,236**	**1,791**	**5,441 ***	**72.1**	**100.0**
053 Assemb of God	4	313	385	475	6.3	8.7
081 Catholic	1	NR	NR	89	1.2	1.6
093 Chr Ch (Disc)	3	451	198	550 *	7.3	10.1
097 Chr Chs&Chs Cr	1	75	NR	92 *	1.2	1.7
107 Christian Un	1	40	40	49 *	.6	.9
143 CG in Cr(Menn)	1	167	NR	204 *	2.7	3.7
165 Ch of Nazarene	4	250	238	360	4.8	6.6
167 Chs of Christ	2	93	100	121	1.6	2.2
211 Fel Evg Bib Ch	1	0	0	0	-	-
237 Menn Br US Conf	1	550	NR	671 *	8.9	12.3
288 Mennonite USA	1	180	90	220 *	2.9	4.0
355 Presb Ch (USA)	1	34	23	41 *	.5	.8
419 So Bapt Conv	6	1,383	415	1,687 *	22.4	31.0
449 Un Methodist	4	640	232	782 *	10.4	14.4
467 Wesleyan	1	60	70	100	1.3	1.8
MARSHALL	**35**	**5,840**	**2,264**	**7,668 ***	**58.2**	**100.0**
017 Amer Bapt Assn	1	100	NR	122 *	.9	1.6
053 Assemb of God	2	97	121	154	1.2	2.0
081 Catholic	1	NR	NR	480	3.6	6.3
165 Ch of Nazarene	1	79	52	141	1.1	1.8
167 Chs of Christ	7	539	483	654	5.0	8.5
349 Pent Holiness	2	156	137	190 *	1.4	2.5
413 S.D.A.	1	28	NR	33	.3	.4
419 So Bapt Conv	17	3,982	1,183	4,848 *	36.8	63.2
449 Un Methodist	3	859	288	1,046 *	7.9	13.6
MAYES	**101**	**15,494**	**6,231**	**20,441 ***	**53.3**	**100.0**
017 Amer Bapt Assn	1	60	NR	75 *	.2	.4
053 Assemb of God	10	501	596	711	1.9	3.5
056 Baha'i	0	41	NR	41	.1	.2
059 Bapt Miss Assn	1	119	38	149 *	.4	.7
081 Catholic	2	NR	NR	390	1.0	1.9
093 Chr Ch (Disc)	3	636	294	796 *	2.1	3.9
097 Chr Chs&Chs Cr	4	281	NR	352 *	.9	1.7
123 Ch God (Ander)	1	NR	241	241	.6	1.2
127 Ch God (Cleve)	3	293	283	397 *	1.0	1.9
145 Ch God Prophcy	1	29	NR	36 *	.1	.2

Religious Group	Number of Churches, Synagogues, Mosques, or Temples	Number of Communicant, Confirmed, or Full Members	Number of Attendees	Total Adherents		
				Number of Adherents	% of Total Pop.	% of Total Adh.
151 L-D Saints	1	NR	NR	243	.6	1.2
165 Ch of Nazarene	2	183	120	264	.7	1.3
167 Chs of Christ	7	439	420	533	1.4	2.6
173 Comm of Christ	1	40	NR	40	.1	.2
183 Cons Menn Conf	1	157	192	228	.6	1.1
185 Cumber Presb	1	33	NR	40	.1	.2
193 Episcopal	1	NR	40	82	.2	.4
223 Free Will Bapt	8	757	NR	947 *	2.5	4.6
258 IndFreeWillBapt	1	106	NR	133 *	.3	.7
283 Luth—MO Synod	2	192	100	158	.4	.8
288 Mennonite USA	2	225	184	282 *	.7	1.4
323 Old Ord Amish	3	165	NR	207 *	.5	1.0
339 Pent Ch of God	1	45	NR	95	.2	.5
355 Presb Ch (USA)	2	182	73	228 *	.6	1.1
413 S.D.A.	2	204	NR	242	.6	1.2
419 So Bapt Conv	31	8,429	3,025	10,555 *	27.5	51.6
449 Un Methodist	9	2,377	625	2,976 *	7.8	14.6
MURRAY	**36**	**6,828**	**2,158**	**8,668 ***	**68.7**	**100.0**
017 Amer Bapt Assn	1	50	NR	61 *	.5	.7
053 Assemb of God	3	101	108	145	1.1	1.7
056 Baha'i	0	6	NR	6	-	.1
081 Catholic	1	NR	NR	371	2.9	4.3
093 Chr Ch (Disc)	1	153	64	186 *	1.5	2.1
097 Chr Chs&Chs Cr	1	75	NR	91 *	.7	1.0
167 Chs of Christ	6	460	444	512	4.1	5.9
193 Episcopal	1	NR	10	11	.1	.1
223 Free Will Bapt	2	189	NR	230 *	1.8	2.7
283 Luth—MO Synod	1	16	12	20	.2	.2
349 Pent Holiness	2	133	107	162 *	1.3	1.9
355 Presb Ch (USA)	2	49	42	60 *	.5	.7
360 Prim Bapt Chrch	1	NR	NR	NR	-	-
413 S.D.A.	2	94	NR	112	.9	1.3
419 So Bapt Conv	10	4,852	1,157	5,910 *	46.8	68.2
449 Un Methodist	2	650	214	791 *	6.3	9.1
MUSKOGEE	**130**	**31,586**	**11,347**	**43,669 ***	**62.9**	**100.0**
019 Amer Bapt USA	1	53	29	66 *	.1	.2
053 Assemb of God	15	1,804	2,219	3,126	4.5	7.2
056 Baha'i	0	77	NR	77	.1	.2
059 Bapt Miss Assn	1	668	250	833 *	1.2	1.9
081 Catholic	2	NR	NR	2,000	2.9	4.6
093 Chr Ch (Disc)	2	82	28	102 *	.1	.2
097 Chr Chs&Chs Cr	5	1,335	NR	1,665 *	2.4	3.8
123 Ch God (Ander)	2	NR	265	265	.4	.6
127 Ch God (Cleve)	2	82	97	102 *	.1	.2
145 Ch God Prophcy	1	29	NR	36 *	.1	.1
151 L-D Saints	2	NR	NR	806	1.2	1.8
165 Ch of Nazarene	2	243	114	243	.3	.6
167 Chs of Christ	16	1,579	1,466	2,049	3.0	4.7
171 Ch God-Gen Con	1	3	0	4 *	-	-
185 Cumber Presb	1	9	NR	9	-	-
193 Episcopal	1	NR	126	380	.5	.9
203 Evan Free Ch	1	30	60	60	.1	.1
223 Free Will Bapt	6	567	NR	707 *	1.0	1.6
263 Int Foursq Gos	1	4	9	9 *	-	-
283 Luth—MO Synod	1	207	112	260	.4	.6
339 Pent Ch of God	4	411	NR	332	.5	.8
349 Pent Holiness	4	369	407	460 *	.7	1.1
355 Presb Ch (USA)	4	640	242	797 *	1.1	1.8
403 Salvation Army	1	119	58	260	.4	.6
413 S.D.A.	2	297	NR	353	.5	.8
419 So Bapt Conv	38	16,631	4,628	20,730 *	29.8	47.5
449 Un Methodist	13	6,347	1,237	7,913 *	11.4	18.1
496 Jewish Est	1	NR	NR	25	-	.1
NOBLE	**30**	**5,802**	**2,051**	**7,901 ***	**69.2**	**100.0**
017 Amer Bapt Assn	1	100	NR	124 *	1.1	1.6
053 Assemb of God	2	62	82	103	.9	1.3
081 Catholic	2	NR	NR	542	4.7	6.9
093 Chr Ch (Disc)	4	963	277	1,193 *	10.5	15.1
097 Chr Chs&Chs Cr	1	50	NR	62 *	.5	.8
157 Ch of Brethren	1	169	70	209 *	1.8	2.6

NR–Not Reported *Total adherents estimated from known number of communicant, confirmed, full members. - Represents a percentage less than 0.1. Percentages may not total 100 due to rounding.

Table 4: Religious Congregations by County and Group: 2000

Religious Group	Number of Churches, Synagogues, Mosques, or Temples	Number of Communicant, Confirmed, or Full Members	Number of Attendees	Total Adherents		
				Number of Adherents	% of Total Pop.	% of Total Adh.
165 Ch of Nazarene	1	130	111	211	1.8	2.7
167 Chs of Christ	1	127	115	193	1.7	2.4
193 Episcopal	1	NR	30	46	.4	.6
207 E.L.C.A.	1	288	110	341	3.0	4.3
283 Luth—MO Synod	1	476	165	618	5.4	7.8
355 Presb Ch (USA)	1	196	125	243 *	2.1	3.1
419 So Bapt Conv	8	2,163	649	2,680 *	23.5	33.9
449 Un Methodist	5	1,078	317	1,336 *	11.7	16.9
NOWATA	**26**	**4,290**	**1,530**	**5,649 ***	**53.4**	**100.0**
053 Assemb of God	1	38	41	51	.5	.9
056 Baha'i	0	7	NR	7	.1	.1
081 Catholic	1	NR	NR	50	.5	.9
093 Chr Ch (Disc)	1	182	73	227 *	2.1	4.0
097 Chr Chs&Chs Cr	2	541	NR	675 *	6.4	11.9
123 Ch God (Ander)	3	NR	208	208	2.0	3.7
127 Ch God (Cleve)	1	95	83	119 *	1.1	2.1
165 Ch of Nazarene	2	75	55	132	1.2	2.3
167 Chs of Christ	2	79	65	97	.9	1.7
349 Pent Holiness	1	495	190	618 *	5.8	10.9
355 Presb Ch (USA)	1	30	14	37 *	.4	.7
413 S.D.A.	1	35	NR	42	.4	.7
419 So Bapt Conv	6	1,862	581	2,324 *	22.0	41.1
449 Un Methodist	4	851	220	1,062 *	10.0	18.8
OKFUSKEE	**38**	**4,936**	**1,554**	**6,227 ***	**52.7**	**100.0**
017 Amer Bapt Assn	2	91	NR	112 *	.9	1.8
053 Assemb of God	3	91	115	167	1.4	2.7
056 Baha'i	0	4	NR	4	-	.1
081 Catholic	1	NR	NR	25	.2	.4
093 Chr Ch (Disc)	1	100	42	123 *	1.0	2.0
097 Chr Chs&Chs Cr	1	30	NR	37 *	.3	.6
123 Ch God (Ander)	2	NR	67	67	.6	1.1
167 Chs of Christ	4	263	267	352	3.0	5.7
223 Free Will Bapt	3	284	NR	348 *	2.9	5.6
297 Mennonite;Other	3	161	NR	198 *	1.7	3.2
349 Pent Holiness	2	90	85	110 *	.9	1.8
419 So Bapt Conv	10	3,252	787	3,986 *	33.7	64.0
449 Un Methodist	6	570	191	698 *	5.9	11.2
OKLAHOMA	**606**	**296,198**	**126,487**	**433,911 ***	**65.7**	**100.0**
017 Amer Bapt Assn	9	810	NR	1,012 *	.2	.2
019 Amer Bapt USA	1	2,000	850	2,495 *	.4	.6
034 Ant Orth of NA	1	662	NR	1,324	.2	.3
049 Armen Ap Cilic	1	0	NR	80	-	-
053 Assemb of God	38	14,121	10,257	17,248	2.6	4.0
056 Baha'i	2	320	NR	320	-	.1
059 Bapt Miss Assn	4	836	294	1,043 *	.2	.2
075 Brethren in Cr	1	46	59	59	-	-
076 Buddhism	5	NR	NR	NR	-	-
081 Catholic	24	NR	NR	42,650	6.5	9.8
084 Calvary Chapel	1	NR	NR	NR	-	-
089 Chr & Miss Al	1	51	NR	145	-	-
093 Chr Ch (Disc)	24	10,981	4,098	13,699 *	2.1	3.2
097 Chr Chs&Chs Cr	11	2,320	NR	2,895 *	.4	.7
107 Christian Un	1	24	25	30 *	-	-
123 Ch God (Ander)	5	NR	3,268	3,268	.5	.8
127 Ch God (Cleve)	7	624	554	778 *	.1	.2
145 Ch God Prophcy	3	87	NR	108 *	-	-
151 L-D Saints	13	NR	NR	4,403	.7	1.0
165 Ch of Nazarene	37	11,073	6,844	13,502	2.0	3.1
167 Chs of Christ	56	13,552	13,651	17,846	2.7	4.1
173 Comm of Christ	2	357	NR	357	.1	.1
175 Congr Chr Chs	1	30	25	37 *	-	-
185 Cumber Presb	2	83	NR	194	-	-
186 Coptic Orth Ch	2	NR	NR	NR	-	-
193 Episcopal	10	NR	2,186	5,891	.9	1.4
201 Evan Cov Ch	4	975	3,327	3,381 *	.5	.8
203 Evan Free Ch	1	65	85	85	-	-
207 E.L.C.A.	10	2,968	1,557	3,780	.6	.9
220 Free Lutheran	1	105	77	113	-	-
221 Free Methodist	4	255	295	316	-	.1
223 Free Will Bapt	16	1,513	NR	1,888 *	.3	.4
226 Friends-USA	2	65	NR	81 *	-	-
237 Menn Br US Conf	2	132	NR	165 *	-	-
246 Greek Orthodox	1	NR	NR	417	.1	.1
252 Hindu	2	NR	NR	NR	-	-
263 Int Foursq Gos	3	269	455	455 *	.1	.1
264 Int Chs of Crst	1	137	189	192	-	-
267 Muslim Est	4	NR	731	2,932	.4	.7
283 Luth—MO Synod	8	3,016	1,684	3,894	.6	.9
288 Mennonite USA	1	18	35	35 *	-	-
333 Malan Dioc Am	1	NR	NR	125	-	-
334 Malan Syr Orth	1	25	NR	125	-	-
335 Orth Pres Ch	1	51	49	68	-	-
339 Pent Ch of God	6	276	NR	520	.1	.1
349 Pent Holiness	31	9,763	4,889	12,179 *	1.8	2.8
355 Presb Ch (USA)	18	7,099	3,442	8,856 *	1.3	2.0
356 Presb Ch Amer	1	260	216	316	-	.1
360 Prim Bapt Chrch	2	NR	NR	NR	-	-
370 Ref Baptist Chs	1	NR	NR	NR	-	-
371 Ref Ch in Am	1	435	344	782	.1	.2
401 Rus Orth Abroad	1	NR	NR	NR	-	-
403 Salvation Army	2	213	134	2,230	.3	.5
413 S.D.A.	14	1,596	NR	1,901	.3	.4
416 Sikh	1	NR	NR	NR	-	-
418 Southw Bapt Fel	1	NR	NR	NR	-	-
419 So Bapt Conv	122	139,576	35,209	174,121 *	26.4	40.1
431 Ukrainian Orth	1	NR	NR	180	-	-
435 Unitarian-Univ	2	392	NR	489 *	.1	.1
443 Un C of Christ	3	864	538	1,078 *	.2	.2
449 Un Methodist	54	49,855	12,684	62,194 *	9.4	14.3
463 Vineyard	3	290	265	362 *	.1	.1
467 Wesleyan	1	0	0	0	-	-
469 WELS	2	318	226	447	.1	.1
496 Jewish Est	3	NR	NR	2,300	.3	.5
498 Indep.Charis.	7	13,665	14,495	14,495	2.2	3.3
499 Indep.Non-Char	4	4,025	3,450	4,025	.6	.9
OKMULGEE	**77**	**16,812**	**5,419**	**22,625 ***	**57.0**	**100.0**
053 Assemb of God	8	586	739	925	2.3	4.1
056 Baha'i	0	10	NR	10	-	-
081 Catholic	3	NR	NR	766	1.9	3.4
093 Chr Ch (Disc)	4	558	184	701 *	1.8	3.1
097 Chr Chs&Chs Cr	1	150	NR	189 *	.5	.8
123 Ch God (Ander)	1	NR	15	15	-	.1
127 Ch God (Cleve)	1	31	16	39 *	.1	.2
145 Ch God Prophcy	2	58	NR	72 *	.2	.3
151 L-D Saints	1	NR	NR	394	1.0	1.7
165 Ch of Nazarene	2	528	321	582	1.5	2.6
167 Chs of Christ	7	540	538	679	1.7	3.0
173 Comm of Christ	1	28	NR	28	.1	.1
193 Episcopal	2	NR	54	150	.4	.7
223 Free Will Bapt	3	284	NR	357 *	.9	1.6
263 Int Foursq Gos	1	60	101	101 *	.3	.4
283 Luth—MO Synod	1	149	70	208	.5	.9
339 Pent Ch of God	2	59	NR	110	.3	.5
349 Pent Holiness	2	272	157	342 *	.9	1.5
355 Presb Ch (USA)	2	179	93	225 *	.6	1.0
413 S.D.A.	3	131	NR	156	.4	.7
419 So Bapt Conv	19	10,495	2,438	13,191 *	33.2	58.3
449 Un Methodist	11	2,694	693	3,385 *	8.5	15.0
OSAGE	**82**	**12,500**	**4,261**	**17,490 ***	**39.4**	**100.0**
053 Assemb of God	9	998	1,234	1,801	4.1	10.3
056 Baha'i	0	4	NR	4	-	-
059 Bapt Miss Assn	1	71	60	88 *	.2	.5
081 Catholic	7	NR	NR	955	2.1	5.5
093 Chr Ch (Disc)	4	455	186	567 *	1.3	3.2
097 Chr Chs&Chs Cr	4	675	NR	841 *	1.9	4.8
127 Ch God (Cleve)	3	204	112	254 *	.6	1.5
151 L-D Saints	1	NR	NR	119	.3	.7
165 Ch of Nazarene	4	241	167	432	1.0	2.5
167 Chs of Christ	6	229	283	340	.8	1.9
173 Comm of Christ	1	189	NR	189	.4	1.1
193 Episcopal	1	NR	25	40	.1	.2

NR–Not Reported *Total adherents estimated from known number of communicant, confirmed, full members. - Represents a percentage less than 0.1. Percentages may not total 100 due to rounding.

Table 4: Religious Congregations by County and Group: 2000

Religious Group	Number of Churches, Synagogues, Mosques, or Temples	Number of Communicant, Confirmed, or Full Members	Number of Attendees	Total Adherents: Number of Adherents	Total Adherents: % of Total Pop.	Total Adherents: % of Total Adh.
223 Free Will Bapt	3	284	NR	353 *	.8	2.0
226 Friends-USA	1	178	NR	222 *	.5	1.3
339 Pent Ch of God	2	59	NR	187	.4	1.1
349 Pent Holiness	6	267	176	332 *	.7	1.9
355 Presb Ch (USA)	2	164	100	204 *	.5	1.2
419 So Bapt Conv	19	7,285	1,579	9,071 *	20.4	51.9
449 Un Methodist	8	1,197	339	1,491 *	3.4	8.5
OTTAWA	**86**	**19,408**	**5,183**	**25,545 ***	**77.0**	**100.0**
017 Amer Bapt Assn	1	34	NR	42 *	.1	.2
053 Assemb of God	14	1,042	1,127	1,491	4.5	5.8
056 Baha'i	0	13	NR	13	-	.1
081 Catholic	1	NR	NR	687	2.1	2.7
093 Chr Ch (Disc)	1	174	80	217 *	.7	.8
097 Chr Chs&Chs Cr	10	1,740	NR	2,168 *	6.5	8.5
123 Ch God (Ander)	1	NR	21	21	.1	.1
151 L-D Saints	1	NR	NR	323	1.0	1.3
165 Ch of Nazarene	2	331	129	331	1.0	1.3
167 Chs of Christ	4	279	295	340	1.0	1.3
173 Comm of Christ	1	84	NR	84	.3	.3
193 Episcopal	1	NR	87	208	.6	.8
226 Friends-USA	5	378	NR	471 *	1.4	1.8
283 Luth—MO Synod	2	333	184	394	1.2	1.5
297 Mennonite;Other	1	16	NR	20 *	.1	.1
339 Pent Ch of God	1	10	NR	85	.3	.3
355 Presb Ch (USA)	1	230	80	286 *	.9	1.1
413 S.D.A.	1	31	NR	37	.1	.1
419 So Bapt Conv	30	12,333	2,715	15,363 *	46.3	60.1
449 Un Methodist	8	2,380	465	2,964 *	8.9	11.6
PAWNEE	**40**	**7,761**	**2,224**	**10,007 ***	**60.2**	**100.0**
053 Assemb of God	5	283	324	507	3.1	5.1
056 Baha'i	0	1	NR	1	-	-
081 Catholic	1	NR	NR	18	.1	.2
093 Chr Ch (Disc)	1	185	103	231 *	1.4	2.3
097 Chr Chs&Chs Cr	2	410	NR	513 *	3.1	5.1
145 Ch God Prophcy	1	29	NR	36 *	.2	.4
165 Ch of Nazarene	2	111	75	223	1.3	2.2
167 Chs of Christ	4	164	174	193	1.2	1.9
193 Episcopal	2	NR	33	64	.4	.6
223 Free Will Bapt	2	189	NR	236 *	1.4	2.4
349 Pent Holiness	1	42	31	53 *	.3	.5
355 Presb Ch (USA)	1	81	19	101 *	.6	1.0
413 S.D.A.	1	39	NR	46	.3	.5
419 So Bapt Conv	12	5,416	1,220	6,770 *	40.8	67.7
449 Un Methodist	5	811	245	1,015 *	6.1	10.1
PAYNE	**94**	**26,338**	**9,302**	**36,160 ***	**53.0**	**100.0**
053 Assemb of God	9	702	835	1,155	1.7	3.2
056 Baha'i	1	38	NR	38	.1	.1
081 Catholic	3	NR	NR	2,079	3.0	5.7
089 Chr & Miss Al	1	38	NR	120	.2	.3
093 Chr Ch (Disc)	2	1,206	488	1,416 *	2.1	3.9
097 Chr Chs&Chs Cr	7	2,042	NR	2,397 *	3.5	6.6
123 Ch God (Ander)	4	NR	224	224	.3	.6
127 Ch God (Cleve)	1	20	20	23 *	-	.1
151 L-D Saints	4	NR	NR	1,081	1.6	3.0
157 Ch of Brethren	1	132	74	155 *	.2	.4
165 Ch of Nazarene	3	259	157	261	.4	.7
167 Chs of Christ	9	1,088	1,077	1,646	2.4	4.6
173 Comm of Christ	1	50	NR	50	.1	.1
193 Episcopal	2	NR	184	333	.5	.9
207 E.L.C.A.	1	367	168	531	.8	1.5
221 Free Methodist	1	23	32	34	-	.1
223 Free Will Bapt	3	284	NR	333 *	.5	.9
226 Friends-USA	1	15	NR	18 *	-	-
267 Muslim Est	1	NR	150	500	.7	1.4
283 Luth—MO Synod	2	419	185	586	.9	1.6
339 Pent Ch of God	2	140	NR	250	.4	.7
349 Pent Holiness	1	98	134	115 *	.2	.3
355 Presb Ch (USA)	2	820	332	963 *	1.4	2.7
403 Salvation Army	1	42	28	62	.1	.2
413 S.D.A.	2	115	NR	137	.2	.4
419 So Bapt Conv	17	12,843	3,936	15,080 *	22.1	41.7
435 Unitarian-Univ	1	42	NR	49 *	.1	.1
449 Un Methodist	11	5,555	1,278	6,524 *	9.6	18.0
PITTSBURG	**123**	**23,285**	**6,719**	**31,142 ***	**70.9**	**100.0**
053 Assemb of God	10	528	692	1,089	2.5	3.5
056 Baha'i	0	8	NR	8	-	-
059 Bapt Miss Assn	1	164	70	199 *	.5	.6
081 Catholic	4	NR	NR	1,809	4.1	5.8
093 Chr Ch (Disc)	2	168	69	204 *	.5	.7
097 Chr Chs&Chs Cr	6	628	NR	760 *	1.7	2.4
127 Ch God (Cleve)	1	143	72	173 *	.4	.6
145 Ch God Prophcy	1	29	NR	35 *	.1	.1
151 L-D Saints	1	NR	NR	428	1.0	1.4
165 Ch of Nazarene	3	326	233	430	1.0	1.4
167 Chs of Christ	14	1,082	1,183	1,358	3.1	4.4
171 Ch God-Gen Con	2	110	93	133 *	.3	.4
173 Comm of Christ	2	87	NR	87	.2	.3
193 Episcopal	1	NR	35	73	.2	.2
223 Free Will Bapt	9	851	NR	1,032 *	2.3	3.3
263 Int Foursq Gos	1	46	119	119 *	.3	.4
283 Luth—MO Synod	1	157	85	216	.5	.7
331 OCA: Ter Diocs	1	11	NR	19	-	.1
339 Pent Ch of God	2	100	NR	140	.3	.4
349 Pent Holiness	3	165	148	200 *	.5	.6
355 Presb Ch (USA)	1	531	165	644 *	1.5	2.1
360 Prim Bapt Chrch	1	NR	NR	NR	-	-
403 Salvation Army	1	115	36	123	.3	.4
413 S.D.A.	2	52	NR	62	.1	.2
419 So Bapt Conv	40	15,404	3,211	18,672 *	42.5	60.0
449 Un Methodist	13	2,580	508	3,129 *	7.1	10.0
PONTOTOC	**90**	**16,599**	**6,652**	**21,733 ***	**61.8**	**100.0**
017 Amer Bapt Assn	1	54	NR	66 *	.2	.3
053 Assemb of God	6	208	211	294	.8	1.4
056 Baha'i	0	25	NR	25	.1	.1
059 Bapt Miss Assn	5	415	187	509 *	1.4	2.3
081 Catholic	1	NR	NR	824	2.3	3.8
093 Chr Ch (Disc)	1	300	105	369 *	1.0	1.7
097 Chr Chs&Chs Cr	1	65	NR	80 *	.2	.4
127 Ch God (Cleve)	1	207	146	254 *	.7	1.2
145 Ch God Prophcy	3	87	NR	108 *	.3	.5
165 Ch of Nazarene	1	223	129	223	.6	1.0
167 Chs of Christ	11	1,375	1,303	1,772	5.0	8.2
185 Cumber Presb	1	108	NR	152	.4	.7
193 Episcopal	1	NR	99	218	.6	1.0
223 Free Will Bapt	12	1,135	NR	1,395 *	4.0	6.4
263 Int Foursq Gos	1	89	246	246 *	.7	1.1
283 Luth—MO Synod	1	117	69	134	.4	.6
339 Pent Ch of God	1	13	NR	45	.1	.2
349 Pent Holiness	5	448	425	551 *	1.6	2.5
355 Presb Ch (USA)	1	326	125	401 *	1.1	1.8
360 Prim Bapt Chrch	1	NR	NR	NR	-	-
403 Salvation Army	1	88	26	137	.4	.6
413 S.D.A.	1	40	NR	48	.1	.2
419 So Bapt Conv	23	8,695	2,946	10,685 *	30.4	49.2
449 Un Methodist	8	2,451	515	3,012 *	8.6	13.9
463 Vineyard	1	130	120	160 *	.5	.7
496 Jewish Est	1	NR	NR	25	.1	.1
POTTAWATOMIE	**126**	**31,772**	**10,028**	**43,963 ***	**67.1**	**100.0**
017 Amer Bapt Assn	2	224	NR	279 *	.4	.6
053 Assemb of God	11	470	580	816	1.2	1.9
056 Baha'i	1	31	NR	31	-	.1
081 Catholic	4	NR	NR	2,613	4.0	5.9
093 Chr Ch (Disc)	2	537	174	668 *	1.0	1.5
097 Chr Chs&Chs Cr	2	124	NR	154 *	.2	.4
123 Ch God (Ander)	1	NR	220	220	.3	.5
127 Ch God (Cleve)	4	485	301	603 *	.9	1.4
151 L-D Saints	1	NR	NR	389	.6	.9
165 Ch of Nazarene	3	350	201	533	.8	1.2
167 Chs of Christ	17	1,590	1,664	2,069	3.2	4.7
171 Ch God-Gen Con	1	98	60	122 *	.2	.3

NR–Not Reported   *Total adherents estimated from known number of communicant, confirmed, full members.   - Represents a percentage less than 0.1.   Percentages may not total 100 due to rounding.

Table 4: Religious Congregations by County and Group: 2000

Religious Group	Number of Churches, Synagogues, Mosques, or Temples	Number of Communicant, Confirmed, or Full Members	Number of Attendees	Total Adherents: Number of Adherents	Total Adherents: % of Total Pop.	Total Adherents: % of Total Adh.
193 Episcopal	1	NR	124	337	.5	.8
207 E.L.C.A.	1	123	67	164	.3	.4
223 Free Will Bapt	6	567	NR	706 *	1.1	1.6
283 Luth—MO Synod	1	118	50	122	.2	.3
339 Pent Ch of God	3	182	NR	321	.5	.7
349 Pent Holiness	5	349	400	434 *	.7	1.0
355 Presb Ch (USA)	2	248	127	308 *	.5	.7
360 Prim Bapt Chrch	1	NR	NR	NR	-	-
403 Salvation Army	1	123	75	560	.9	1.3
413 S.D.A.	1	84	NR	100	.2	.2
419 So Bapt Conv	44	22,411	5,226	27,866 *	42.5	63.4
449 Un Methodist	11	3,658	759	4,548 *	6.9	10.3
PUSHMATAHA	**58**	**5,904**	**2,380**	**8,003 ***	**68.6**	**100.0**
053 Assemb of God	6	471	555	840	7.2	10.5
081 Catholic	2	NR	NR	82	.7	1.0
097 Chr Chs&Chs Cr	4	305	NR	378 *	3.2	4.7
151 L-D Saints	1	NR	NR	164	1.4	2.0
165 Ch of Nazarene	1	63	69	147	1.3	1.8
167 Chs of Christ	6	276	315	394	3.4	4.9
193 Episcopal	1	NR	23	50	.4	.6
223 Free Will Bapt	4	378	NR	470 *	4.0	5.9
355 Presb Ch (USA)	1	40	19	50 *	.4	.6
360 Prim Bapt Chrch	1	NR	NR	NR	-	-
413 S.D.A.	1	53	NR	63	.5	.8
419 So Bapt Conv	20	3,687	1,211	4,580 *	39.3	57.2
449 Un Methodist	10	631	188	785 *	6.7	9.8
ROGER MILLS	**23**	**2,557**	**895**	**3,126 ***	**91.0**	**100.0**
053 Assemb of God	2	48	55	89	2.6	2.8
165 Ch of Nazarene	2	0	0	0	-	-
167 Chs of Christ	6	214	217	272	7.9	8.7
288 Mennonite USA	1	25	20	30 *	.9	1.0
349 Pent Holiness	2	55	49	66 *	1.9	2.1
419 So Bapt Conv	7	1,645	408	1,982 *	57.7	63.4
449 Un Methodist	3	570	146	687 *	20.0	22.0
ROGERS	**92**	**24,095**	**9,578**	**33,129 ***	**46.9**	**100.0**
017 Amer Bapt Assn	2	80	NR	103 *	.1	.3
053 Assemb of God	11	1,273	1,537	2,094	3.0	6.3
056 Baha'i	0	6	NR	6	-	-
059 Bapt Miss Assn	1	37	22	47 *	.1	.1
081 Catholic	1	NR	NR	1,250	1.8	3.8
093 Chr Ch (Disc)	1	516	191	661 *	.9	2.0
097 Chr Chs&Chs Cr	5	857	NR	1,097 *	1.6	3.3
123 Ch God (Ander)	1	NR	145	145	.2	.4
127 Ch God (Cleve)	1	31	60	60 *	.1	.2
145 Ch God Prophcy	1	29	NR	37 *	.1	.1
151 L-D Saints	1	NR	NR	415	.6	1.3
165 Ch of Nazarene	2	299	175	299	.4	.9
167 Chs of Christ	8	752	780	995	1.4	3.0
193 Episcopal	1	NR	115	150	.2	.5
223 Free Will Bapt	4	378	NR	484 *	.7	1.5
263 Int Foursq Gos	2	95	39	122 *	.2	.4
283 Luth—MO Synod	2	284	167	382	.5	1.2
323 Old Ord Amish	1	55	NR	70 *	.1	.2
349 Pent Holiness	3	147	147	188 *	.3	.6
355 Presb Ch (USA)	2	336	176	430 *	.6	1.3
356 Presb Ch Amer	1	0	0	0	-	-
413 S.D.A.	1	138	NR	164	.2	.5
419 So Bapt Conv	30	14,778	4,541	18,917 *	26.8	57.1
449 Un Methodist	9	3,604	1,083	4,613 *	6.5	13.9
498 Indep.Charis.	1	400	400	400	.6	1.2
SEMINOLE	**81**	**11,325**	**3,905**	**15,318 ***	**61.5**	**100.0**
017 Amer Bapt Assn	4	463	NR	578 *	2.3	3.8
053 Assemb of God	9	639	861	1,107	4.4	7.2
056 Baha'i	0	42	NR	42	.2	.3
081 Catholic	3	NR	NR	487	2.0	3.2
093 Chr Ch (Disc)	2	160	52	200 *	.8	1.3
123 Ch God (Ander)	1	NR	53	53	.2	.3
127 Ch God (Cleve)	1	18	3	22 *	.1	.1
151 L-D Saints	1	NR	NR	237	1.0	1.5
165 Ch of Nazarene	3	103	66	133	.5	.9
167 Chs of Christ	9	756	755	971	3.9	6.3
173 Comm of Christ	1	84	NR	84	.3	.5
193 Episcopal	1	NR	18	34	.1	.2
223 Free Will Bapt	5	473	NR	590 *	2.4	3.9
263 Int Foursq Gos	1	14	33	33 *	.1	.2
339 Pent Ch of God	3	133	NR	223	.9	1.5
349 Pent Holiness	5	250	274	312 *	1.3	2.0
355 Presb Ch (USA)	5	126	84	157 *	.6	1.0
413 S.D.A.	1	22	NR	26	.1	.2
419 So Bapt Conv	19	6,643	1,369	8,284 *	33.3	54.1
449 Un Methodist	7	1,399	337	1,745 *	7.0	11.4
SEQUOYAH	**77**	**13,421**	**4,678**	**17,795 ***	**45.7**	**100.0**
017 Amer Bapt Assn	4	535	NR	677 *	1.7	3.8
053 Assemb of God	12	984	1,215	1,494	3.8	8.4
056 Baha'i	0	4	NR	4	-	-
059 Bapt Miss Assn	1	90	72	114 *	.3	.6
081 Catholic	2	NR	NR	259	.7	1.5
097 Chr Chs&Chs Cr	1	189	NR	239 *	.6	1.3
107 Christian Un	1	7	10	10 *	-	.1
127 Ch God (Cleve)	1	33	35	42 *	.1	.2
151 L-D Saints	1	NR	NR	138	.4	.8
165 Ch of Nazarene	3	252	159	413	1.1	2.3
167 Chs of Christ	8	457	477	570	1.5	3.2
173 Comm of Christ	1	65	NR	65	.2	.4
223 Free Will Bapt	7	662	NR	839 *	2.2	4.7
283 Luth—MO Synod	1	38	28	44	.1	.2
339 Pent Ch of God	3	122	NR	254	.7	1.4
349 Pent Holiness	1	80	80	101 *	.3	.6
355 Presb Ch (USA)	1	94	44	119 *	.3	.7
360 Prim Bapt Chrch	1	NR	NR	NR	-	-
413 S.D.A.	1	132	NR	157	.4	.9
419 So Bapt Conv	22	8,320	2,106	10,539 *	27.0	59.2
449 Un Methodist	5	1,357	452	1,717 *	4.4	9.6
STEPHENS	**87**	**26,629**	**8,411**	**36,023 ***	**83.4**	**100.0**
017 Amer Bapt Assn	5	1,250	NR	1,535 *	3.6	4.3
053 Assemb of God	9	882	1,008	1,879	4.4	5.2
056 Baha'i	0	9	NR	9	-	-
081 Catholic	2	NR	NR	2,012	4.7	5.6
093 Chr Ch (Disc)	2	981	347	1,203 *	2.8	3.3
097 Chr Chs&Chs Cr	2	114	NR	140 *	.3	.4
127 Ch God (Cleve)	2	295	265	362 *	.8	1.0
145 Ch God Prophcy	1	29	NR	36 *	.1	.1
151 L-D Saints	1	NR	NR	333	.8	.9
165 Ch of Nazarene	3	376	225	412	1.0	1.1
167 Chs of Christ	11	1,514	1,339	1,844	4.3	5.1
185 Cumber Presb	2	146	NR	208	.5	.6
193 Episcopal	1	NR	88	161	.4	.4
223 Free Will Bapt	4	378	NR	464 *	1.1	1.3
283 Luth—MO Synod	1	122	97	146	.3	.4
339 Pent Ch of God	3	102	NR	230	.5	.6
355 Presb Ch (USA)	1	210	120	257 *	.6	.7
360 Prim Bapt Chrch	2	NR	NR	NR	-	-
370 Ref Baptist Chs	1	NR	NR	NR	-	-
413 S.D.A.	1	48	NR	57	.1	.2
419 So Bapt Conv	25	16,363	4,195	20,063 *	46.5	55.7
449 Un Methodist	8	3,810	727	4,672 *	10.8	13.0
TEXAS	**55**	**8,222**	**3,525**	**16,655 ***	**82.8**	**100.0**
053 Assemb of God	1	60	80	100	.5	.6
056 Baha'i	0	2	NR	2	-	-
081 Catholic	2	NR	NR	5,601	27.9	33.6
093 Chr Ch (Disc)	3	456	139	585 *	2.9	3.5
097 Chr Chs&Chs Cr	1	285	NR	366 *	1.8	2.2
123 Ch God (Ander)	3	NR	63	63	.3	.4
151 L-D Saints	1	NR	NR	100	.5	.6
165 Ch of Nazarene	3	420	385	736	3.7	4.4
167 Chs of Christ	6	409	545	623	3.1	3.7
193 Episcopal	1	NR	19	42	.2	.3
211 Fel Evg Bib Ch	1	62	0	62	.3	.4

NR–Not Reported *Total adherents estimated from known number of communicant, confirmed, full members. - Represents a percentage less than 0.1. Percentages may not total 100 due to rounding.

Table 4: Religious Congregations by County and Group: 2000

Religious Group	Number of Churches, Synagogues, Mosques, or Temples	Number of Communicant, Confirmed, or Full Members	Number of Attendees	Total Adherents		
				Number of Adherents	% of Total Pop.	% of Total Adh.
223 Free Will Bapt	1	95	NR	121 *	.6	.7
237 Menn Br US Conf	1	51	NR	65 *	.3	.4
263 Int Foursq Gos	1	117	126	150 *	.7	.9
283 Luth—MO Synod	3	466	237	597	3.0	3.6
339 Pent Ch of God	1	15	NR	20	.1	.1
349 Pent Holiness	3	257	116	330 *	1.6	2.0
355 Presb Ch (USA)	1	186	80	239 *	1.2	1.4
413 S.D.A.	2	51	NR	61	.3	.4
419 So Bapt Conv	12	3,086	1,054	3,962 *	19.7	23.8
449 Un Methodist	8	2,204	681	2,830 *	14.1	17.0
TILLMAN	**33**	**6,778**	**2,055**	**9,004 ***	**97.0**	**100.0**
017 Amer Bapt Assn	1	60	NR	74 *	.8	.8
053 Assemb of God	3	175	234	250	2.7	2.8
056 Baha'i	0	17	NR	17	.2	.2
081 Catholic	2	NR	NR	574	6.2	6.4
093 Chr Ch (Disc)	1	163	65	202 *	2.2	2.2
165 Ch of Nazarene	1	39	23	41	.4	.5
167 Chs of Christ	5	531	447	672	7.2	7.5
173 Comm of Christ	1	32	NR	32	.3	.4
349 Pent Holiness	1	18	19	22 *	.2	.2
355 Presb Ch (USA)	2	88	40	109 *	1.2	1.2
360 Prim Bapt Chrch	1	NR	NR	NR	-	-
419 So Bapt Conv	11	4,855	1,011	6,019 *	64.8	66.8
449 Un Methodist	4	800	216	992 *	10.7	11.0
TULSA	**488**	**201,750**	**76,639**	**320,586 ***	**56.9**	**100.0**
017 Amer Bapt Assn	5	784	NR	986 *	.2	.3
019 Amer Bapt USA	3	983	189	1,237 *	.2	.4
034 Ant Orth of NA	1	155	NR	310	.1	.1
053 Assemb of God	38	6,494	7,710	12,079	2.1	3.8
056 Baha'i	1	182	NR	182	-	.1
059 Bapt Miss Assn	2	169	95	213 *	-	.1
076 Buddhism	3	NR	NR	NR	-	-
081 Catholic	22	NR	NR	40,998	7.3	12.8
084 Calvary Chapel	2	NR	NR	NR	-	-
089 Chr & Miss Al	2	331	NR	334	.1	.1
093 Chr Ch (Disc)	17	5,104	2,108	6,421 *	1.1	2.0
097 Chr Chs&Chs Cr	22	5,979	NR	7,523 *	1.3	2.3
123 Ch God (Ander)	6	NR	833	833	.1	.3
127 Ch God (Cleve)	3	334	148	420 *	.1	.1
145 Ch God Prophcy	9	261	NR	324 *	.1	.1
151 L-D Saints	11	NR	NR	4,395	.8	1.4
165 Ch of Nazarene	15	2,781	2,061	3,513	.6	1.1
167 Chs of Christ	35	7,199	7,530	9,580	1.7	3.0
171 Ch God-Gen Con	2	142	110	179 *	-	.1
173 Comm of Christ	6	981	NR	981	.2	.3
185 Cumber Presb	1	108	NR	162	-	.1
193 Episcopal	11	NR	1,951	5,924	1.1	1.8
201 Evan Cov Ch	2	770	806	996 *	.2	.3
207 E.L.C.A.	7	2,242	1,142	3,090	.5	1.0
221 Free Methodist	1	20	22	22	-	-
223 Free Will Bapt	24	2,270	NR	2,855 *	.5	.9
226 Friends-USA	1	15	NR	19 *	-	-
237 Menn Br US Conf	1	437	NR	550 *	.1	.2
246 Greek Orthodox	1	NR	NR	396	.1	.1
251 Holy Orth in NA	1	NR	NR	6	-	-
263 Int Foursq Gos	4	349	420	439 *	.1	.1
264 Int Chs of Crst	1	115	182	173	-	.1
267 Muslim Est	2	NR	775	2,200	.4	.7
268 Jain	2	NR	NR	NR	-	-
283 Luth—MO Synod	7	3,689	2,288	5,140	.9	1.6
290 Metro Comm Ch	1	59	56	74 *	-	-
339 Pent Ch of God	2	18	NR	90	-	-
349 Pent Holiness	5	3,073	1,319	3,866 *	.7	1.2
355 Presb Ch (USA)	17	7,968	3,521	10,023 *	1.8	3.1
356 Presb Ch Amer	1	334	217	499	.1	.2
360 Prim Bapt Chrch	1	NR	NR	NR	-	-
370 Ref Baptist Chs	1	NR	NR	NR	-	-
403 Salvation Army	5	352	232	5,897	1.0	1.8
413 S.D.A.	8	1,228	NR	1,461	.3	.5
419 So Bapt Conv	110	87,136	25,165	109,617 *	19.5	34.2
435 Unitarian-Univ	4	1,264	NR	1,590 *	.3	.5
443 Un C of Christ	2	328	154	413 *	.1	.1
449 Un Methodist	45	52,163	14,251	65,621 *	11.6	20.5
463 Vineyard	1	130	120	164 *	-	.1
467 Wesleyan	2	41	58	91	-	-
469 WELS	1	112	96	150	-	-
496 Jewish Est	3	NR	NR	2,650	.5	.8
498 Indep.Charis.	6	4,700	2,105	4,700	.8	1.5
499 Indep.Non-Char	2	950	975	1,200	.2	.4
WAGONER	**57**	**12,381**	**4,226**	**16,215 ***	**28.2**	**100.0**
053 Assemb of God	4	763	885	1,194	2.1	7.4
056 Baha'i	0	76	NR	76	.1	.5
081 Catholic	1	NR	NR	185	.3	1.1
093 Chr Ch (Disc)	1	333	122	423 *	.7	2.6
097 Chr Chs&Chs Cr	2	150	NR	191 *	.3	1.2
127 Ch God (Cleve)	1	125	119	159 *	.3	1.0
145 Ch God Prophcy	4	116	NR	148 *	.3	.9
151 L-D Saints	1	NR	NR	46	.1	.3
165 Ch of Nazarene	2	98	74	142	.2	.9
167 Chs of Christ	7	426	405	533	.9	3.3
193 Episcopal	1	NR	12	24	-	.1
223 Free Will Bapt	7	662	NR	842 *	1.5	5.2
339 Pent Ch of God	1	50	NR	70	.1	.4
349 Pent Holiness	2	157	134	200 *	.3	1.2
355 Presb Ch (USA)	1	147	70	187 *	.3	1.2
413 S.D.A.	1	27	NR	32	.1	.2
419 So Bapt Conv	14	7,894	1,936	10,037 *	17.5	61.9
449 Un Methodist	7	1,357	469	1,726 *	3.0	10.6
WASHINGTON	**72**	**25,406**	**8,577**	**37,843 ***	**77.2**	**100.0**
017 Amer Bapt Assn	2	120	NR	148 *	.3	.4
053 Assemb of God	4	621	779	1,162	2.4	3.1
056 Baha'i	0	22	NR	22	-	.1
081 Catholic	3	NR	NR	2,718	5.5	7.2
093 Chr Ch (Disc)	2	630	262	775 *	1.6	2.0
097 Chr Chs&Chs Cr	4	1,049	NR	1,291 *	2.6	3.4
123 Ch God (Ander)	2	NR	109	109	.2	.3
145 Ch God Prophcy	1	29	NR	36 *	.1	.1
151 L-D Saints	2	NR	NR	835	1.7	2.2
165 Ch of Nazarene	2	606	368	646	1.3	1.7
167 Chs of Christ	3	833	725	1,016	2.1	2.7
173 Comm of Christ	1	132	NR	132	.3	.3
193 Episcopal	1	NR	219	578	1.2	1.5
207 E.L.C.A.	1	141	82	171	.3	.5
223 Free Will Bapt	2	189	NR	233 *	.5	.6
226 Friends-USA	2	100	NR	123 *	.3	.3
283 Luth—MO Synod	1	370	227	449	.9	1.2
335 Orth Pres Ch	1	40	29	53	.1	.1
355 Presb Ch (USA)	2	1,167	482	1,436 *	2.9	3.8
370 Ref Baptist Chs	1	NR	NR	NR	-	-
403 Salvation Army	1	198	87	301	.6	.8
413 S.D.A.	1	47	NR	56	.1	.1
419 So Bapt Conv	21	11,993	2,996	14,756 *	30.1	39.0
435 Unitarian-Univ	1	22	NR	27 *	.1	.1
449 Un Methodist	9	6,497	1,353	7,995 *	16.3	21.1
467 Wesleyan	2	600	859	2,775	5.7	7.3
WASHITA	**39**	**7,724**	**2,227**	**9,731 ***	**84.6**	**100.0**
017 Amer Bapt Assn	2	286	NR	354 *	3.1	3.6
053 Assemb of God	3	142	171	229	2.0	2.4
081 Catholic	1	NR	NR	110	1.0	1.1
097 Chr Chs&Chs Cr	1	150	NR	185 *	1.6	1.9
167 Chs of Christ	8	689	644	821	7.1	8.4
185 Cumber Presb	1	79	NR	138	1.2	1.4
207 E.L.C.A.	1	192	90	233	2.0	2.4
237 Menn Br US Conf	2	518	NR	640 *	5.6	6.6
288 Mennonite USA	1	129	88	159 *	1.4	1.6
313 N Am Bapt Conf	1	103	50	127 *	1.1	1.3
339 Pent Ch of God	1	15	NR	37	.3	.4
349 Pent Holiness	1	27	18	33 *	.3	.3
355 Presb Ch (USA)	2	159	79	196 *	1.7	2.0
360 Prim Bapt Chrch	1	NR	NR	NR	-	-
419 So Bapt Conv	7	3,785	858	4,677 *	40.6	48.1

NR–Not Reported *Total adherents estimated from known number of communicant, confirmed, full members. - Represents a percentage less than 0.1. Percentages may not total 100 due to rounding.

Table 4: Religious Congregations by County and Group: 2000

Religious Group	Number of Churches, Synagogues, Mosques, or Temples	Number of Communicant, Confirmed, or Full Members	Number of Attendees	Total Adherents		
				Number of Adherents	% of Total Pop.	% of Total Adh.
449 Un Methodist	6	1,450	229	1,792 *	15.6	18.4
WOODS	**32**	**4,704**	**1,997**	**6,776 ***	**74.6**	**100.0**
053 Assemb of God	2	85	93	192	2.1	2.8
056 Baha'i	0	3	NR	3	-	-
081 Catholic	2	NR	NR	670	7.4	9.9
093 Chr Ch (Disc)	2	240	140	280 *	3.1	4.1
097 Chr Chs&Chs Cr	1	165	NR	193 *	2.1	2.8
123 Ch God (Ander)	3	NR	188	188	2.1	2.8
165 Ch of Nazarene	2	87	78	190	2.1	2.8
167 Chs of Christ	3	279	311	405	4.5	6.0
173 Comm of Christ	1	23	NR	23	.3	.3
226 Friends-USA	1	50	NR	58 *	.6	.9
283 Luth—MO Synod	1	360	154	460	5.1	6.8
355 Presb Ch (USA)	1	87	68	102 *	1.1	1.5
413 S.D.A.	1	44	NR	52	.6	.8
419 So Bapt Conv	3	1,349	387	1,574 *	17.3	23.2
449 Un Methodist	6	1,726	361	2,013 *	22.1	29.7
467 Wesleyan	3	206	217	373	4.1	5.5
WOODWARD	**40**	**10,209**	**3,112**	**14,356 ***	**77.7**	**100.0**
017 Amer Bapt Assn	1	17	NR	21 *	.1	.1
053 Assemb of God	2	239	295	507	2.7	3.5
056 Baha'i	0	2	NR	2	-	-
081 Catholic	2	NR	NR	1,266	6.8	8.8
093 Chr Ch (Disc)	3	898	302	1,109 *	6.0	7.7
097 Chr Chs&Chs Cr	2	109	NR	135 *	.7	.9
127 Ch God (Cleve)	1	52	46	64 *	.3	.4
151 L-D Saints	1	NR	NR	236	1.3	1.6
165 Ch of Nazarene	1	240	201	295	1.6	2.1
167 Chs of Christ	1	310	280	364	2.0	2.5
173 Comm of Christ	1	90	NR	90	.5	.6
193 Episcopal	1	NR	31	83	.4	.6
221 Free Methodist	1	3	7	7	-	-
223 Free Will Bapt	1	95	NR	117 *	.6	.8
263 Int Foursq Gos	1	12	15	15 *	.1	.1
283 Luth—MO Synod	1	137	75	167	.9	1.2
355 Presb Ch (USA)	1	88	55	109 *	.6	.8
413 S.D.A.	1	83	NR	99	.5	.7
419 So Bapt Conv	10	4,850	1,161	5,987 *	32.4	41.7
449 Un Methodist	8	2,984	644	3,683 *	19.9	25.7
OREGON						
The State.....	3,155	354,298	289,255	1,071,287 *	31.3	100.0
BAKER	**34**	**1,797**	**1,528**	**5,578 ***	**33.3**	**100.0**
053 Assemb of God	3	111	149	250	1.5	4.5
056 Baha'i	0	24	NR	24	.1	.4
081 Catholic	4	NR	NR	1,148	6.9	20.6
097 Chr Chs&Chs Cr	2	245	NR	297 *	1.8	5.3
151 L-D Saints	4	NR	NR	1,492	8.9	26.7
165 Ch of Nazarene	2	416	507	552	3.3	9.9
167 Chs of Christ	2	32	39	44	.3	.8
173 Comm of Christ	1	27	NR	27	.2	.5
179 Consrv Bapt	4	NR	387	387	2.3	6.9
193 Episcopal	1	NR	40	159	.9	2.9
207 E.L.C.A.	1	180	89	213	1.3	3.8
263 Int Foursq Gos	1	46	63	63 *	.4	1.1
339 Pent Ch of God	1	12	NR	20	.1	.4
355 Presb Ch (USA)	2	197	126	238 *	1.4	4.3
403 Salvation Army	1	65	22	134	.8	2.4
413 S.D.A.	2	230	NR	273	1.6	4.9
449 Un Methodist	3	212	106	257 *	1.5	4.6
BENTON	**59**	**7,566**	**5,811**	**17,684 ***	**22.6**	**100.0**
053 Assemb of God	5	341	467	694	.9	3.9
056 Baha'i	2	180	NR	180	.2	1.0
076 Buddhism	1	NR	NR	NR	-	-
081 Catholic	3	NR	NR	5,257	6.7	29.7
084 Calvary Chapel	1	NR	NR	NR	-	-
093 Chr Ch (Disc)	1	313	173	372 *	.5	2.1
097 Chr Chs&Chs Cr	2	330	NR	392 *	.5	2.2
105 Christian Ref	1	109	85	130 *	.2	.7
127 Ch God (Cleve)	1	32	28	38 *	-	.2
165 Ch of Nazarene	2	562	524	578	.7	3.3
167 Chs of Christ	3	231	254	316	.4	1.8
179 Consrv Bapt	5	NR	1,142	1,142	1.5	6.5
193 Episcopal	1	NR	209	639	.8	3.6
203 Evan Free Ch	1	50	114	114	.1	.6
207 E.L.C.A.	1	748	230	1,168	1.5	6.6
221 Free Methodist	1	27	40	40	.1	.2
226 Friends-USA	1	22	NR	26 *	-	.1
263 Int Foursq Gos	4	172	320	320 *	.4	1.8
267 Muslim Est	1	NR	55	163	.2	.9
283 Luth—MO Synod	3	781	442	1,057	1.4	6.0
288 Mennonite USA	2	90	142	142 *	.2	.8
339 Pent Ch of God	2	52	NR	152	.2	.9
355 Presb Ch (USA)	3	990	519	1,239 *	1.6	7.0
413 S.D.A.	1	234	NR	278	.4	1.6
419 So Bapt Conv	2	481	307	572 *	.7	3.2
435 Unitarian-Univ	1	276	NR	328 *	.4	1.9
443 Un C of Christ	1	359	164	427 *	.5	2.4
449 Un Methodist	4	1,045	465	1,243 *	1.6	7.0
463 Vineyard	1	75	75	89 *	.1	.5
469 WELS	1	66	56	88	.1	.5
496 Jewish Est	1	NR	NR	500	.6	2.8
CLACKAMAS	**234**	**29,431**	**27,545**	**91,751 ***	**27.1**	**100.0**
017 Amer Bapt Assn	1	35	NR	44 *	-	-
019 Amer Bapt USA	4	818	775	1,023 *	.3	1.1
040 Ap Chr Ch-Amer	1	18	30	30 *	-	-
050 Armen Ap Etchm	1	0	NR	616	.2	.7
053 Assemb of God	12	1,338	1,760	2,740	.8	3.0
056 Baha'i	7	334	NR	334	.1	.4
076 Buddhism	1	NR	NR	NR	-	-
081 Catholic	12	NR	NR	21,303	6.3	23.2
084 Calvary Chapel	1	NR	NR	NR	-	-
089 Chr & Miss Al	3	155	NR	630	.2	.7
097 Chr Chs&Chs Cr	12	3,206	NR	4,010 *	1.2	4.4
123 Ch God (Ander)	3	NR	115	115	-	.1
127 Ch God (Cleve)	1	208	103	260 *	.1	.3
151 L-D Saints	28	NR	NR	11,318	3.3	12.3
165 Ch of Nazarene	7	1,158	1,114	1,692	.5	1.8
167 Chs of Christ	8	543	594	742	.2	.8
175 Congr Chr Chs	1	155	125	194 *	.1	.2
179 Consrv Bapt	18	NR	3,210	3,210	.9	3.5
181 Consrv Congr	1	9	18	11 *	-	-
193 Episcopal	7	NR	971	2,933	.9	3.2
201 Evan Cov Ch	2	319	681	739 *	.2	.8
203 Evan Free Ch	2	285	575	575	.2	.6
207 E.L.C.A.	14	4,901	2,421	6,594	1.9	7.2
221 Free Methodist	1	25	37	37	-	-
223 Free Will Bapt	1	69	NR	86 *	-	.1
226 Friends-USA	2	168	NR	210 *	.1	.2
263 Int Foursq Gos	13	1,771	3,893	3,893 *	1.2	4.2
283 Luth—MO Synod	7	1,944	1,370	2,576	.8	2.8
288 Mennonite USA	3	485	415	615 *	.2	.7
297 Mennonite;Other	1	65	NR	81 *	-	.1
313 N Am Bapt Conf	2	172	131	215 *	.1	.2
331 OCA: Ter Diocs	1	70	NR	141	-	.2
349 Pent Holiness	1	70	62	88 *	-	.1
355 Presb Ch (USA)	8	2,392	1,537	2,991 *	.9	3.3
360 Prim Bapt Chrch	1	NR	NR	NR	-	-
397 OCA: Roman Dioc	1	NR	NR	59	-	.1
401 Rus Orth Abroad	1	NR	NR	NR	-	-
410 Serb Orth USA	1	NR	NR	200	.1	.2
413 S.D.A.	9	2,128	NR	2,533	.7	2.8
419 So Bapt Conv	7	1,356	635	1,695 *	.5	1.8
435 Unitarian-Univ	2	212	NR	265 *	.1	.3
443 Un C of Christ	6	823	446	1,029 *	.3	1.1
449 Un Methodist	14	2,795	1,431	3,496 *	1.0	3.8
467 Wesleyan	1	90	102	500	.1	.5
469 WELS	1	114	94	178	.1	.2
496 Jewish Est	1	NR	NR	3,100	.9	3.4

NR–Not Reported *Total adherents estimated from known number of communicant, confirmed, full members. - Represents a percentage less than 0.1. Percentages may not total 100 due to rounding.

Table 4: Religious Congregations by County and Group: 2000

Religious Group	Number of Churches, Synagogues, Mosques, or Temples	Number of Communicant, Confirmed, or Full Members	Number of Attendees	Total Adherents		
				Number of Adherents	% of Total Pop.	% of Total Adh.
499 Indep.Non-Char	2	1,200	4,900	8,650	2.6	9.4
CLATSOP	**50**	**3,593**	**2,779**	**8,449 ***	**23.7**	**100.0**
019 Amer Bapt USA	1	78	71	94 *	.3	1.1
053 Assemb of God	5	279	389	540	1.5	6.4
056 Baha'i	2	76	NR	76	.2	.9
081 Catholic	4	NR	NR	1,550	4.4	18.3
097 Chr Chs&Chs Cr	3	604	NR	731 *	2.1	8.7
151 L-D Saints	3	NR	NR	963	2.7	11.4
165 Ch of Nazarene	3	161	195	342	1.0	4.0
167 Chs of Christ	1	30	20	40	.1	.5
173 Comm of Christ	1	23	NR	23	.1	.3
179 Consrv Bapt	4	NR	740	740	2.1	8.8
193 Episcopal	2	NR	168	425	1.2	5.0
207 E.L.C.A.	4	1,121	411	1,410	4.0	16.7
220 Free Lutheran	1	136	106	166	.5	2.0
226 Friends-USA	1	84	NR	102 *	.3	1.2
263 Int Foursq Gos	2	29	38	38 *	.1	.4
283 Luth—MO Synod	1	37	30	43	.1	.5
355 Presb Ch (USA)	3	283	279	354 *	1.0	4.2
388 Reg Bapt Gen As	1	120	140	145 *	.4	1.7
403 Salvation Army	1	11	13	39	.1	.5
413 S.D.A.	2	132	NR	157	.4	1.9
435 Unitarian-Univ	1	25	NR	30 *	.1	.4
443 Un C of Christ	1	13	6	16 *	-	.2
449 Un Methodist	3	351	173	425 *	1.2	5.0
COLUMBIA	**60**	**3,532**	**3,903**	**10,243 ***	**23.5**	**100.0**
053 Assemb of God	6	474	648	889	2.0	8.7
056 Baha'i	0	36	NR	36	.1	.4
057 Bapt Gen Conf	2	262	112	330 *	.8	3.2
081 Catholic	6	NR	NR	1,920	4.4	18.7
084 Calvary Chapel	1	NR	NR	NR	-	-
093 Chr Ch (Disc)	1	216	101	273 *	.6	2.7
097 Chr Chs&Chs Cr	2	150	NR	189 *	.4	1.8
123 Ch God (Ander)	3	NR	377	377	.9	3.7
151 L-D Saints	5	NR	NR	1,791	4.1	17.5
165 Ch of Nazarene	2	29	32	43	.1	.4
167 Chs of Christ	2	132	130	169	.4	1.6
179 Consrv Bapt	4	NR	600	600	1.4	5.9
193 Episcopal	2	NR	59	126	.3	1.2
207 E.L.C.A.	3	605	289	795	1.8	7.8
263 Int Foursq Gos	4	312	659	659 *	1.5	6.4
273 LandmrkBapt,I&U	1	95	NR	120 *	.3	1.2
283 Luth—MO Synod	2	239	143	308	.7	3.0
355 Presb Ch (USA)	2	204	97	258 *	.6	2.5
360 Prim Bapt Chrch	1	NR	NR	NR	-	-
370 Ref Baptist Chs	1	NR	NR	NR	-	-
413 S.D.A.	3	301	NR	358	.8	3.5
419 So Bapt Conv	3	218	105	275 *	.6	2.7
449 Un Methodist	3	259	151	327 *	.8	3.2
499 Indep.Non-Char	1	0	400	400	.9	3.9
COOS	**86**	**6,312**	**5,508**	**15,936 ***	**25.4**	**100.0**
017 Amer Bapt Assn	2	89	NR	106 *	.2	.7
019 Amer Bapt USA	2	242	133	288 *	.5	1.8
053 Assemb of God	9	585	726	848	1.4	5.3
056 Baha'i	0	77	NR	77	.1	.5
081 Catholic	6	NR	NR	3,470	5.5	21.8
084 Calvary Chapel	1	NR	NR	NR	-	-
089 Chr & Miss Al	1	40	NR	95	.2	.6
093 Chr Ch (Disc)	1	103	65	123 *	.2	.8
097 Chr Chs&Chs Cr	5	604	NR	719 *	1.1	4.5
123 Ch God (Ander)	3	NR	378	378	.6	2.4
127 Ch God (Cleve)	3	82	139	143 *	.2	.9
151 L-D Saints	4	NR	NR	1,712	2.7	10.7
165 Ch of Nazarene	4	431	391	465	.7	2.9
167 Chs of Christ	2	229	203	260	.4	1.6
173 Comm of Christ	1	88	NR	88	.1	.6
179 Consrv Bapt	6	NR	684	684	1.1	4.3
193 Episcopal	5	NR	163	427	.7	2.7
207 E.L.C.A.	3	670	384	848	1.4	5.3
263 Int Foursq Gos	4	627	477	746 *	1.2	4.7

Religious Group	Number of Churches, Synagogues, Mosques, or Temples	Number of Communicant, Confirmed, or Full Members	Number of Attendees	Total Adherents		
				Number of Adherents	% of Total Pop.	% of Total Adh.
283 Luth—MO Synod	2	290	121	453	.7	2.8
339 Pent Ch of God	2	25	NR	85	.1	.5
355 Presb Ch (USA)	5	517	328	616 *	1.0	3.9
370 Ref Baptist Chs	1	NR	NR	NR	-	-
403 Salvation Army	1	62	53	260	.4	1.6
413 S.D.A.	4	535	NR	637	1.0	4.0
419 So Bapt Conv	2	460	146	548 *	.9	3.4
435 Unitarian-Univ	1	32	NR	38 *	.1	.2
449 Un Methodist	4	518	267	616 *	1.0	3.9
469 WELS	1	6	0	6	-	-
499 Indep.Non-Char	1	0	850	1,200	1.9	7.5
CROOK	**22**	**2,246**	**1,425**	**5,253 ***	**27.4**	**100.0**
053 Assemb of God	1	114	155	238	1.2	4.5
056 Baha'i	0	50	NR	50	.3	1.0
081 Catholic	1	NR	NR	1,008	5.3	19.2
097 Chr Chs&Chs Cr	2	500	NR	625 *	3.3	11.9
123 Ch God (Ander)	1	NR	18	18	.1	.3
145 Ch God Prophcy	1	26	NR	33 *	.2	.6
151 L-D Saints	2	NR	NR	821	4.3	15.6
165 Ch of Nazarene	1	158	168	180	.9	3.4
167 Chs of Christ	1	55	90	125	.7	2.4
179 Consrv Bapt	2	NR	270	270	1.4	5.1
193 Episcopal	1	NR	36	152	.8	2.9
207 E.L.C.A.	2	673	380	814	4.2	15.5
263 Int Foursq Gos	1	103	203	203 *	1.1	3.9
273 LandmrkBapt,I&U	2	122	NR	152 *	.8	2.9
339 Pent Ch of God	1	14	NR	30	.2	.6
355 Presb Ch (USA)	1	36	30	45 *	.2	.9
413 S.D.A.	1	73	NR	87	.5	1.7
419 So Bapt Conv	1	322	75	402 *	2.1	7.7
CURRY	**31**	**2,075**	**1,870**	**4,101 ***	**19.4**	**100.0**
017 Amer Bapt Assn	1	44	NR	51 *	.2	1.2
019 Amer Bapt USA	1	151	110	176 *	.8	4.3
053 Assemb of God	4	247	342	481	2.3	11.7
056 Baha'i	0	29	NR	29	.1	.7
081 Catholic	2	NR	NR	100	.5	2.4
097 Chr Chs&Chs Cr	1	200	NR	233 *	1.1	5.7
151 L-D Saints	3	NR	NR	739	3.5	18.0
165 Ch of Nazarene	1	173	285	285	1.3	6.9
167 Chs of Christ	2	92	116	126	.6	3.1
179 Consrv Bapt	2	NR	227	227	1.1	5.5
193 Episcopal	3	NR	87	160	.8	3.9
207 E.L.C.A.	3	474	368	668	3.2	16.3
263 Int Foursq Gos	2	85	145	145 *	.7	3.5
355 Presb Ch (USA)	2	243	172	283 *	1.3	6.9
413 S.D.A.	2	212	NR	252	1.2	6.1
419 So Bapt Conv	2	125	18	146 *	.7	3.6
DESCHUTES	**94**	**9,505**	**10,711**	**31,000 ***	**26.9**	**100.0**
017 Amer Bapt Assn	2	129	NR	159 *	.1	.5
053 Assemb of God	6	557	771	1,257	1.1	4.1
056 Baha'i	2	115	NR	115	.1	.4
081 Catholic	5	NR	NR	9,921	8.6	32.0
084 Calvary Chapel	3	NR	NR	NR	-	-
097 Chr Chs&Chs Cr	5	824	NR	1,016 *	.9	3.3
123 Ch God (Ander)	1	NR	35	35	-	.1
127 Ch God (Cleve)	1	20	30	30 *	-	.1
151 L-D Saints	10	NR	NR	3,425	3.0	11.0
165 Ch of Nazarene	4	495	499	597	.5	1.9
167 Chs of Christ	4	265	298	463	.4	1.5
173 Comm of Christ	1	201	NR	201	.2	.6
179 Consrv Bapt	4	NR	1,166	1,166	1.0	3.8
193 Episcopal	4	NR	388	800	.7	2.6
203 Evan Free Ch	1	0	100	100	.1	.3
207 E.L.C.A.	4	847	383	1,072	.9	3.5
221 Free Methodist	2	123	240	240	.2	.8
226 Friends-USA	2	168	NR	207 *	.2	.7
263 Int Foursq Gos	5	1,629	4,471	4,471 *	3.9	14.4
283 Luth—MO Synod	3	672	473	895	.8	2.9
335 Orth Pres Ch	1	89	72	109	.1	.4
339 Pent Ch of God	2	36	NR	142	.1	.5

NR–Not Reported   *Total adherents estimated from known number of communicant, confirmed, full members.   - Represents a percentage less than 0.1.   Percentages may not total 100 due to rounding.

Table 4: Religious Congregations by County and Group: 2000

Religious Group	Number of Churches, Synagogues, Mosques, or Temples	Number of Communicant, Confirmed, or Full Members	Number of Attendees	Total Adherents		
				Number of Adherents	% of Total Pop.	% of Total Adh.
349 Pent Holiness	1	12	12	15 *	-	-
355 Presb Ch (USA)	2	917	538	1,131 *	1.0	3.6
403 Salvation Army	1	43	45	355	.3	1.1
413 S.D.A.	4	454	NR	540	.5	1.7
416 Sikh	1	NR	NR	NR	-	-
419 So Bapt Conv	8	1,125	693	1,387 *	1.2	4.5
435 Unitarian-Univ	1	45	NR	55 *	-	.2
449 Un Methodist	1	447	302	551 *	.5	1.8
463 Vineyard	1	250	175	308 *	.3	1.0
469 WELS	1	42	20	62	.1	.2
496 Jewish Est	1	NR	NR	175	.2	.6
DOUGLAS	**140**	**12,099**	**7,655**	**25,496 ***	**25.4**	**100.0**
017 Amer Bapt Assn	3	132	NR	161 *	.2	.6
019 Amer Bapt USA	2	203	127	247 *	.2	1.0
053 Assemb of God	13	812	956	1,360	1.4	5.3
056 Baha'i	2	153	NR	153	.2	.6
076 Buddhism	1	NR	NR	NR	-	-
081 Catholic	6	NR	NR	4,950	4.9	19.4
084 Calvary Chapel	1	NR	NR	NR	-	-
089 Chr & Miss Al	2	89	NR	328	.3	1.3
097 Chr Chs&Chs Cr	15	1,411	NR	1,719 *	1.7	6.7
123 Ch God (Ander)	3	NR	382	382	.4	1.5
127 Ch God (Cleve)	3	290	189	353 *	.4	1.4
145 Ch God Prophcy	3	79	NR	96 *	.1	.4
151 L-D Saints	7	NR	NR	2,683	2.7	10.5
165 Ch of Nazarene	5	420	574	646	.6	2.5
167 Chs of Christ	8	640	646	890	.9	3.5
173 Comm of Christ	1	58	NR	58	.1	.2
179 Consrv Bapt	5	NR	892	892	.9	3.5
193 Episcopal	5	NR	209	383	.4	1.5
203 Evan Free Ch	2	133	215	215	.2	.8
207 E.L.C.A.	1	339	159	409	.4	1.6
221 Free Methodist	2	76	143	143	.1	.6
226 Friends-USA	1	22	NR	27 *	-	.1
263 Int Foursq Gos	4	557	1,079	1,079 *	1.1	4.2
273 LandmrkBapt,I&U	2	40	NR	49 *	-	.2
283 Luth—MO Synod	3	665	273	860	.9	3.4
291 Missionary Ch	2	123	233	233	.2	.9
297 Mennonite;Other	1	45	NR	55 *	.1	.2
335 Orth Pres Ch	1	0	0	0	-	-
339 Pent Ch of God	1	11	NR	50	-	.2
355 Presb Ch (USA)	5	554	330	675 *	.7	2.6
403 Salvation Army	1	58	25	127	.1	.5
413 S.D.A.	7	1,652	NR	1,967	2.0	7.7
419 So Bapt Conv	9	2,521	733	3,069 *	3.1	12.0
435 Unitarian-Univ	1	57	NR	69 *	.1	.3
449 Un Methodist	12	959	490	1,168 *	1.2	4.6
GILLIAM	**7**	**237**	**206**	**762 ***	**39.8**	**100.0**
056 Baha'i	0	6	NR	6	.3	.8
081 Catholic	2	NR	NR	402	21.0	52.8
165 Ch of Nazarene	1	51	78	109	5.7	14.3
179 Consrv Bapt	1	NR	30	30	1.6	3.9
413 S.D.A.	1	15	NR	18	.9	2.4
443 Un C of Christ	1	114	72	136 *	7.1	17.8
449 Un Methodist	1	51	26	61 *	3.2	8.0
GRANT	**25**	**623**	**594**	**2,629 ***	**33.1**	**100.0**
053 Assemb of God	2	52	70	122	1.5	4.6
056 Baha'i	0	12	NR	12	.2	.5
081 Catholic	4	NR	NR	905	11.4	34.4
093 Chr Ch (Disc)	1	75	0	92 *	1.2	3.5
151 L-D Saints	2	NR	NR	448	5.6	17.0
165 Ch of Nazarene	1	108	148	316	4.0	12.0
167 Chs of Christ	1	7	10	8	.1	.3
179 Consrv Bapt	2	NR	200	200	2.5	7.6
193 Episcopal	1	NR	16	67	.8	2.5
263 Int Foursq Gos	1	24	31	31 *	.4	1.2
273 LandmrkBapt,I&U	1	25	NR	31 *	.4	1.2
283 Luth—MO Synod	1	40	25	48	.6	1.8
355 Presb Ch (USA)	3	29	38	47 *	.6	1.8
413 S.D.A.	3	160	NR	190	2.4	7.2

Religious Group	Number of Churches, Synagogues, Mosques, or Temples	Number of Communicant, Confirmed, or Full Members	Number of Attendees	Total Adherents		
				Number of Adherents	% of Total Pop.	% of Total Adh.
449 Un Methodist	2	91	56	112 *	1.4	4.3
HARNEY	**16**	**537**	**483**	**2,370 ***	**31.1**	**100.0**
053 Assemb of God	1	27	35	35	.5	1.5
056 Baha'i	0	14	NR	14	.2	.6
081 Catholic	3	NR	NR	956	12.6	40.3
097 Chr Chs&Chs Cr	1	90	NR	112 *	1.5	4.7
151 L-D Saints	2	NR	NR	434	5.7	18.3
165 Ch of Nazarene	1	52	56	131	1.7	5.5
167 Chs of Christ	1	16	18	20	.3	.8
179 Consrv Bapt	1	NR	160	160	2.1	6.8
193 Episcopal	1	NR	45	41	.5	1.7
207 E.L.C.A.	1	49	45	88	1.2	3.7
263 Int Foursq Gos	1	41	56	56 *	.7	2.4
283 Luth—MO Synod	1	78	25	113	1.5	4.8
355 Presb Ch (USA)	1	129	43	161 *	2.1	6.8
413 S.D.A.	1	41	NR	49	.6	2.1
HOOD RIVER	**31**	**3,316**	**1,796**	**9,764 ***	**47.8**	**100.0**
017 Amer Bapt Assn	1	26	NR	33 *	.2	.3
053 Assemb of God	3	197	253	441	2.2	4.5
056 Baha'i	0	42	NR	42	.2	.4
081 Catholic	1	NR	NR	4,201	20.6	43.0
089 Chr & Miss Al	2	150	NR	363	1.8	3.7
093 Chr Ch (Disc)	1	522	131	666 *	3.3	6.8
151 L-D Saints	1	NR	NR	540	2.6	5.5
165 Ch of Nazarene	2	165	123	189	.9	1.9
167 Chs of Christ	3	129	155	187	.9	1.9
179 Consrv Bapt	1	NR	153	153	.7	1.6
193 Episcopal	1	NR	60	245	1.2	2.5
207 E.L.C.A.	1	129	103	170	.8	1.7
263 Int Foursq Gos	1	6	50	50 *	.2	.5
283 Luth—MO Synod	1	98	53	119	.6	1.2
355 Presb Ch (USA)	1	90	80	115 *	.6	1.2
413 S.D.A.	2	215	NR	256	1.3	2.6
419 So Bapt Conv	3	913	155	1,165 *	5.7	11.9
435 Unitarian-Univ	1	24	NR	31 *	.2	.3
443 Un C of Christ	1	204	88	260 *	1.3	2.7
449 Un Methodist	3	206	117	263 *	1.3	2.7
463 Vineyard	1	200	275	275 *	1.3	2.8
JACKSON	**151**	**14,533**	**10,341**	**40,212 ***	**22.2**	**100.0**
019 Amer Bapt USA	2	372	346	457 *	.3	1.1
053 Assemb of God	16	1,445	1,762	2,732	1.5	6.8
056 Baha'i	4	316	NR	316	.2	.8
076 Buddhism	1	NR	NR	NR	-	-
081 Catholic	5	NR	NR	10,791	6.0	26.8
084 Calvary Chapel	2	NR	NR	NR	-	-
089 Chr & Miss Al	2	143	NR	300	.2	.7
093 Chr Ch (Disc)	1	199	105	244 *	.1	.6
097 Chr Chs&Chs Cr	9	990	NR	1,216 *	.7	3.0
123 Ch God (Ander)	2	NR	120	120	.1	.3
127 Ch God (Cleve)	1	109	31	134 *	.1	.3
151 L-D Saints	14	NR	NR	5,963	3.3	14.8
165 Ch of Nazarene	8	1,620	1,468	1,737	1.0	4.3
167 Chs of Christ	9	486	540	681	.4	1.7
173 Comm of Christ	1	92	NR	92	.1	.2
179 Consrv Bapt	6	NR	1,106	1,106	.6	2.8
193 Episcopal	4	NR	392	1,164	.6	2.9
207 E.L.C.A.	2	976	331	1,264	.7	3.1
221 Free Methodist	1	22	26	26	-	.1
226 Friends-USA	4	274	NR	336 *	.2	.8
252 Hindu	1	NR	NR	NR	-	-
263 Int Foursq Gos	4	249	540	540 *	.3	1.3
273 LandmrkBapt,I&U	1	31	NR	38 *	-	.1
283 Luth—MO Synod	5	917	421	1,112	.6	2.8
331 OCA: Ter Diocs	1	10	NR	47	-	.1
335 Orth Pres Ch	1	55	64	89	-	.2
339 Pent Ch of God	5	276	NR	670	.4	1.7
355 Presb Ch (USA)	7	1,844	1,398	2,282 *	1.3	5.7
401 Rus Orth Abroad	1	NR	NR	NR	-	-
403 Salvation Army	1	94	55	294	.2	.7
413 S.D.A.	9	1,371	NR	1,631	.9	4.1

NR–Not Reported *Total adherents estimated from known number of communicant, confirmed, full members. - Represents a percentage less than 0.1. Percentages may not total 100 due to rounding.

Table 4: Religious Congregations by County and Group: 2000

Religious Group	Number of Churches, Synagogues, Mosques, or Temples	Number of Communicant, Confirmed, or Full Members	Number of Attendees	Total Adherents: Number of Adherents	Total Adherents: % of Total Pop.	Total Adherents: % of Total Adh.
419 So Bapt Conv	9	1,120	285	1,375 *	.8	3.4
435 Unitarian-Univ	1	162	NR	199 *	.1	.5
443 Un C of Christ	2	218	120	268 *	.1	.7
449 Un Methodist	5	1,098	630	1,347 *	.7	3.3
467 Wesleyan	1	0	31	47	-	.1
469 WELS	1	44	20	44	-	.1
496 Jewish Est	1	NR	NR	1,000	.6	2.5
498 Indep.Charis.	1	0	550	550	.3	1.4
JEFFERSON	**28**	**2,551**	**1,559**	**5,897 ***	**31.0**	**100.0**
017 Amer Bapt Assn	1	17	NR	22 *	.1	.4
053 Assemb of God	2	394	508	508	2.7	8.6
056 Baha'i	0	68	NR	68	.4	1.2
081 Catholic	2	NR	NR	1,694	8.9	28.7
097 Chr Chs&Chs Cr	2	235	NR	306 *	1.6	5.2
151 L-D Saints	1	NR	NR	434	2.3	7.4
165 Ch of Nazarene	2	43	62	94	.5	1.6
167 Chs of Christ	1	23	25	30	.2	.5
179 Consrv Bapt	2	NR	375	375	2.0	6.4
193 Episcopal	1	NR	23	56	.3	.9
207 E.L.C.A.	1	126	46	184	1.0	3.1
221 Free Methodist	1	94	93	103	.5	1.7
226 Friends-USA	1	84	NR	109 *	.6	1.8
263 Int Foursq Gos	1	24	35	35 *	.2	.6
273 LandmrkBapt,I&U	1	12	NR	16 *	.1	.3
339 Pent Ch of God	1	6	NR	19	.1	.3
349 Pent Holiness	1	38	162	50 *	.3	.8
355 Presb Ch (USA)	1	36	25	47 *	.2	.8
413 S.D.A.	2	119	NR	142	.7	2.4
419 So Bapt Conv	3	1,050	98	1,368 *	7.2	23.2
449 Un Methodist	1	182	107	237 *	1.2	4.0
JOSEPHINE	**63**	**6,869**	**4,521**	**15,225 ***	**20.1**	**100.0**
017 Amer Bapt Assn	1	60	NR	73 *	.1	.5
019 Amer Bapt USA	2	360	275	436 *	.6	2.9
053 Assemb of God	4	816	1,128	1,781	2.4	11.7
056 Baha'i	1	90	NR	90	.1	.6
075 Brethren in Cr	1	72	88	88	.1	.6
081 Catholic	3	NR	NR	2,631	3.5	17.3
084 Calvary Chapel	1	NR	NR	NR	-	-
089 Chr & Miss Al	2	17	NR	132	.2	.9
093 Chr Ch (Disc)	1	213	135	258 *	.3	1.7
097 Chr Chs&Chs Cr	1	450	NR	545 *	.7	3.6
127 Ch God (Cleve)	1	55	47	67 *	.1	.4
151 L-D Saints	7	NR	NR	2,548	3.4	16.7
157 Ch of Brethren	1	42	50	51 *	.1	.3
165 Ch of Nazarene	2	128	119	149	.2	1.0
167 Chs of Christ	3	274	248	313	.4	2.1
173 Comm of Christ	1	53	NR	53	.1	.3
179 Consrv Bapt	2	NR	410	410	.5	2.7
193 Episcopal	2	NR	133	360	.5	2.4
203 Evan Free Ch	1	22	48	48	.1	.3
207 E.L.C.A.	2	525	291	595	.8	3.9
221 Free Methodist	1	55	86	86	.1	.6
237 Menn Br US Conf	1	51	NR	62 *	.1	.4
263 Int Foursq Gos	1	386	221	467 *	.6	3.1
283 Luth—MO Synod	1	264	108	370	.5	2.4
335 Orth Pres Ch	1	108	128	157	.2	1.0
339 Pent Ch of God	1	22	NR	67	.1	.4
355 Presb Ch (USA)	1	270	200	327 *	.4	2.1
360 Prim Bapt Chrch	1	NR	NR	NR	-	-
388 Reg Bapt Gen As	1	25	50	50 *	.1	.3
403 Salvation Army	1	50	33	60	.1	.4
413 S.D.A.	6	1,301	NR	1,548	2.0	10.2
419 So Bapt Conv	3	392	204	474 *	.6	3.1
435 Unitarian-Univ	1	27	NR	33 *	-	.2
449 Un Methodist	3	441	249	533 *	.7	3.5
463 Vineyard	1	300	270	363 *	.5	2.4
KLAMATH	**75**	**6,218**	**5,252**	**19,948 ***	**31.3**	**100.0**
017 Amer Bapt Assn	1	80	NR	100 *	.2	.5
053 Assemb of God	7	477	598	944	1.5	4.7
056 Baha'i	1	45	NR	45	.1	.2
081 Catholic	7	NR	NR	6,307	9.9	31.6
084 Calvary Chapel	2	NR	NR	NR	-	-
089 Chr & Miss Al	1	25	NR	36	.1	.2
097 Chr Chs&Chs Cr	4	825	NR	1,029 *	1.6	5.2
123 Ch God (Ander)	1	NR	150	150	.2	.8
151 L-D Saints	8	NR	NR	2,263	3.5	11.3
165 Ch of Nazarene	1	106	125	160	.3	.8
167 Chs of Christ	2	137	175	254	.4	1.3
173 Comm of Christ	1	36	NR	36	.1	.2
179 Consrv Bapt	2	NR	1,105	1,105	1.7	5.5
193 Episcopal	2	NR	112	397	.6	2.0
203 Evan Free Ch	1	135	275	275	.4	1.4
207 E.L.C.A.	2	705	252	950	1.5	4.8
226 Friends-USA	2	168	NR	209 *	.3	1.0
263 Int Foursq Gos	3	381	1,346	1,346 *	2.1	6.7
283 Luth—MO Synod	2	168	0	196	.3	1.0
339 Pent Ch of God	1	49	NR	120	.2	.6
355 Presb Ch (USA)	5	550	346	685 *	1.1	3.4
403 Salvation Army	1	28	38	92	.1	.5
413 S.D.A.	3	364	NR	433	.7	2.2
419 So Bapt Conv	5	1,482	377	1,848 *	2.9	9.3
435 Unitarian-Univ	1	17	NR	21 *	-	.1
443 Un C of Christ	1	18	16	22 *	-	.1
449 Un Methodist	5	292	168	363 *	.6	1.8
463 Vineyard	1	130	120	162 *	.3	.8
467 Wesleyan	1	0	49	200	.3	1.0
496 Jewish Est	1	NR	NR	200	.3	1.0
LAKE	**23**	**687**	**722**	**2,287 ***	**30.8**	**100.0**
053 Assemb of God	3	165	228	304	4.1	13.3
056 Baha'i	0	8	NR	8	.1	.3
081 Catholic	5	NR	NR	903	12.2	39.5
127 Ch God (Cleve)	1	51	13	62 *	.8	2.7
151 L-D Saints	1	NR	NR	248	3.3	10.8
165 Ch of Nazarene	1	72	44	82	1.1	3.6
167 Chs of Christ	1	42	40	50	.7	2.2
179 Consrv Bapt	1	NR	140	140	1.9	6.1
193 Episcopal	1	NR	8	42	.6	1.8
263 Int Foursq Gos	1	55	95	95 *	1.3	4.2
273 LandmrkBapt,I&U	1	20	NR	24 *	.3	1.0
283 Luth—MO Synod	1	20	15	20	.3	.9
355 Presb Ch (USA)	1	125	69	152 *	2.0	6.6
413 S.D.A.	2	39	NR	47	.6	2.1
419 So Bapt Conv	1	35	25	43 *	.6	1.9
449 Un Methodist	2	55	45	67 *	.9	2.9
LANE	**278**	**34,482**	**26,642**	**79,189 ***	**24.5**	**100.0**
019 Amer Bapt USA	5	734	495	888 *	.3	1.1
053 Assemb of God	20	1,925	2,467	3,459	1.1	4.4
056 Baha'i	4	476	NR	476	.1	.6
059 Bapt Miss Assn	1	14	12	17 *	-	-
076 Buddhism	5	NR	NR	NR	-	-
081 Catholic	15	NR	NR	15,600	4.8	19.7
084 Calvary Chapel	4	NR	NR	NR	-	-
089 Chr & Miss Al	2	100	NR	225	.1	.3
093 Chr Ch (Disc)	7	1,290	824	1,560 *	.5	2.0
097 Chr Chs&Chs Cr	26	4,459	NR	5,396 *	1.7	6.8
105 Christian Ref	1	54	40	65 *	-	.1
123 Ch God (Ander)	3	NR	765	765	.2	1.0
127 Ch God (Cleve)	2	85	53	104 *	-	.1
145 Ch God Prophcy	1	26	NR	32 *	-	-
151 L-D Saints	23	NR	NR	8,341	2.6	10.5
157 Ch of Brethren	1	41	0	50 *	-	.1
165 Ch of Nazarene	12	1,299	1,283	1,645	.5	2.1
167 Chs of Christ	16	998	1,022	1,194	.4	1.5
173 Comm of Christ	2	343	NR	343	.1	.4
179 Consrv Bapt	15	NR	3,680	3,680	1.1	4.6
193 Episcopal	7	NR	721	1,971	.6	2.5
201 Evan Cov Ch	2	206	192	257 *	.1	.3
203 Evan Free Ch	1	0	100	100	-	.1
207 E.L.C.A.	10	3,311	1,729	4,267	1.3	5.4
220 Free Lutheran	1	19	30	30	-	-
221 Free Methodist	2	210	308	308	.1	.4

NR–Not Reported *Total adherents estimated from known number of communicant, confirmed, full members. - Represents a percentage less than 0.1. Percentages may not total 100 due to rounding.

Table 4: Religious Congregations by County and Group: 2000

Religious Group	Number of Churches, Synagogues, Mosques, or Temples	Number of Communicant, Confirmed, or Full Members	Number of Attendees	Total Adherents		
				Number of Adherents	% of Total Pop.	% of Total Adh.
223 Free Will Bapt	1	69	NR	83 *	-	.1
226 Friends-USA	4	212	NR	256 *	.1	.3
237 Menn Br US Conf	1	51	NR	62 *	-	.1
246 Greek Orthodox	1	NR	NR	279	.1	.4
252 Hindu	2	NR	NR	NR	-	-
263 Int Foursq Gos	10	5,452	6,195	6,595 *	2.0	8.3
267 Muslim Est	1	NR	156	609	.2	.8
273 LandmrkBapt,I&U	1	125	NR	151 *	-	.2
283 Luth—MO Synod	9	1,462	773	1,750	.5	2.2
288 Mennonite USA	1	54	30	65 *	-	.1
290 Metro Comm Ch	1	15	3	3 *	-	-
339 Pent Ch of God	4	80	NR	267	.1	.3
349 Pent Holiness	1	125	168	151 *	-	.2
355 Presb Ch (USA)	7	1,388	859	1,679 *	.5	2.1
356 Presb Ch Amer	1	74	130	130	-	.2
388 Reg Bapt Gen As	1	40	60	60 *	-	.1
403 Salvation Army	2	160	119	406	.1	.5
413 S.D.A.	11	1,609	NR	1,916	.6	2.4
416 Sikh	1	NR	NR	NR	-	-
419 So Bapt Conv	8	3,554	1,190	4,299 *	1.3	5.4
425 Tao	1	NR	NR	NR	-	-
435 Unitarian-Univ	1	250	NR	302 *	.1	.4
443 Un C of Christ	1	738	313	893 *	.3	1.1
449 Un Methodist	12	2,554	1,332	3,089 *	1.0	3.9
467 Wesleyan	1	0	66	165	.1	.2
469 WELS	1	62	47	76	-	.1
490 Zoroastrian	1	NR	NR	NR	-	-
496 Jewish Est	2	NR	NR	3,250	1.0	4.1
498 Indep.Charis.	1	538	1,100	1,500	.5	1.9
499 Indep.Non-Char	1	280	380	380	.1	.5
LINCOLN	**67**	**4,711**	**3,928**	**10,018 ***	**22.5**	**100.0**
019 Amer Bapt USA	1	29	27	34 *	.1	.3
053 Assemb of God	7	329	417	622	1.4	6.2
056 Baha'i	0	60	NR	60	.1	.6
076 Buddhism	1	NR	NR	NR	-	-
081 Catholic	4	NR	NR	1,968	4.4	19.6
084 Calvary Chapel	1	NR	NR	NR	-	-
097 Chr Chs&Chs Cr	4	250	NR	297 *	.7	3.0
105 Christian Ref	1	212	166	257 *	.6	2.6
151 L-D Saints	3	NR	NR	1,200	2.7	12.0
165 Ch of Nazarene	3	556	578	658	1.5	6.6
167 Chs of Christ	3	78	90	103	.2	1.0
173 Comm of Christ	1	27	NR	27	.1	.3
179 Consrv Bapt	2	NR	302	302	.7	3.0
193 Episcopal	4	NR	270	419	.9	4.2
207 E.L.C.A.	1	271	96	310	.7	3.1
221 Free Methodist	1	20	38	38	.1	.4
263 Int Foursq Gos	4	287	611	611 *	1.4	6.1
273 LandmrkBapt,I&U	2	103	NR	122 *	.3	1.2
283 Luth—MO Synod	4	485	256	582	1.3	5.8
288 Mennonite USA	1	35	50	50 *	.1	.5
339 Pent Ch of God	1	9	NR	19	-	.2
355 Presb Ch (USA)	4	525	427	624 *	1.4	6.2
403 Salvation Army	1	34	41	50	.1	.5
413 S.D.A.	3	314	NR	373	.8	3.7
419 So Bapt Conv	6	695	290	825 *	1.9	8.2
435 Unitarian-Univ	1	24	NR	29 *	.1	.3
443 Un C of Christ	1	196	138	233 *	.5	2.3
449 Un Methodist	1	110	69	131 *	.3	1.3
463 Vineyard	1	62	62	74 *	.2	.7
LINN	**137**	**14,335**	**10,688**	**32,370 ***	**31.4**	**100.0**
053 Assemb of God	8	1,772	2,073	3,809	3.7	11.8
056 Baha'i	2	97	NR	97	.1	.3
059 Bapt Miss Assn	1	40	52	52 *	.1	.2
081 Catholic	8	NR	NR	5,248	5.1	16.2
089 Chr & Miss Al	2	31	NR	119	.1	.4
093 Chr Ch (Disc)	3	814	228	1,016 *	1.0	3.1
097 Chr Chs&Chs Cr	10	1,569	NR	1,959 *	1.9	6.1
123 Ch God (Ander)	4	NR	383	383	.4	1.2
127 Ch God (Cleve)	3	146	132	185 *	.2	.6
143 CG in Cr(Menn)	1	109	NR	136 *	.1	.4
145 Ch God Prophcy	1	26	NR	33 *	-	.1
151 L-D Saints	11	NR	NR	4,333	4.2	13.4
165 Ch of Nazarene	4	482	362	539	.5	1.7
167 Chs of Christ	6	248	300	319	.3	1.0
173 Comm of Christ	1	100	NR	100	.1	.3
179 Consrv Bapt	10	NR	1,597	1,597	1.5	4.9
193 Episcopal	3	NR	115	232	.2	.7
207 E.L.C.A.	4	1,147	556	1,461	1.4	4.5
221 Free Methodist	3	123	180	180	.2	.6
263 Int Foursq Gos	5	346	553	553 *	.5	1.7
273 LandmrkBapt,I&U	1	65	NR	81 *	.1	.3
283 Luth—MO Synod	4	650	278	869	.8	2.7
288 Mennonite USA	4	495	496	676 *	.7	2.1
291 Missionary Ch	1	87	140	140	.1	.4
297 Mennonite;Other	6	1,016	NR	1,269 *	1.2	3.9
331 OCA: Ter Diocs	1	29	NR	51	-	.2
339 Pent Ch of God	4	108	NR	206	.2	.6
355 Presb Ch (USA)	4	598	417	747 *	.7	2.3
370 Ref Baptist Chs	1	NR	NR	NR	-	-
388 Reg Bapt Gen As	1	106	89	89 *	.1	.3
403 Salvation Army	1	64	51	198	.2	.6
413 S.D.A.	4	601	NR	715	.7	2.2
419 So Bapt Conv	4	1,397	400	1,744 *	1.7	5.4
449 Un Methodist	7	996	482	1,243 *	1.2	3.8
463 Vineyard	2	473	404	591 *	.6	1.8
499 Indep.Non-Char	2	600	1,400	1,400	1.4	4.3
MALHEUR	**58**	**3,084**	**2,404**	**14,586 ***	**46.1**	**100.0**
017 Amer Bapt Assn	1	60	NR	76 *	.2	.5
019 Amer Bapt USA	1	201	138	256 *	.8	1.8
053 Assemb of God	5	289	270	374	1.2	2.6
056 Baha'i	0	27	NR	27	.1	.2
076 Buddhism	1	NR	NR	NR	-	-
081 Catholic	7	NR	NR	6,450	20.4	44.2
084 Calvary Chapel	1	NR	NR	NR	-	-
093 Chr Ch (Disc)	1	200	77	255 *	.8	1.7
097 Chr Chs&Chs Cr	3	375	NR	477 *	1.5	3.3
127 Ch God (Cleve)	1	24	35	35 *	.1	.2
145 Ch God Prophcy	1	26	NR	33 *	.1	.2
151 L-D Saints	10	NR	NR	3,229	10.2	22.1
165 Ch of Nazarene	4	507	518	725	2.3	5.0
167 Chs of Christ	1	65	110	100	.3	.7
179 Consrv Bapt	3	NR	228	228	.7	1.6
193 Episcopal	3	NR	94	299	.9	2.0
207 E.L.C.A.	2	173	108	240	.8	1.6
263 Int Foursq Gos	1	15	17	19 *	.1	.1
283 Luth—MO Synod	1	248	100	309	1.0	2.1
355 Presb Ch (USA)	2	142	145	180 *	.6	1.2
413 S.D.A.	2	112	NR	134	.4	.9
419 So Bapt Conv	1	149	78	190 *	.6	1.3
449 Un Methodist	5	471	236	600 *	1.9	4.1
498 Indep.Charis.	1	0	250	350	1.1	2.4
MARION	**224**	**33,928**	**26,281**	**106,973 ***	**37.6**	**100.0**
017 Amer Bapt Assn	1	26	NR	33 *	-	-
019 Amer Bapt USA	2	655	392	832 *	.3	.8
040 Ap Chr Ch-Amer	1	132	336	336 *	.1	.3
053 Assemb of God	17	2,614	3,418	5,925	2.1	5.5
056 Baha'i	1	350	NR	350	.1	.3
059 Bapt Miss Assn	1	20	24	25 *	-	-
075 Brethren in Cr	1	30	65	65	-	.1
076 Buddhism	1	NR	NR	NR	-	-
081 Catholic	16	NR	NR	38,076	13.4	35.6
084 Calvary Chapel	3	NR	NR	NR	-	-
089 Chr & Miss Al	6	1,265	NR	5,391	1.9	5.0
093 Chr Ch (Disc)	3	1,675	670	2,127 *	.7	2.0
097 Chr Chs&Chs Cr	8	1,643	NR	2,085 *	.7	1.9
105 Christian Ref	1	183	180	232 *	.1	.2
123 Ch God (Ander)	2	NR	329	329	.1	.3
127 Ch God (Cleve)	5	315	153	414 *	.1	.4
145 Ch God Prophcy	3	79	NR	99 *	-	.1
151 L-D Saints	18	NR	NR	7,150	2.5	6.7
165 Ch of Nazarene	8	3,473	1,899	3,725	1.3	3.5

NR–Not Reported *Total adherents estimated from known number of communicant, confirmed, full members. - Represents a percentage less than 0.1. Percentages may not total 100 due to rounding.

Table 4: Religious Congregations by County and Group: 2000

Religious Group	Number of Churches, Synagogues, Mosques, or Temples	Number of Communicant, Confirmed, or Full Members	Number of Attendees	Total Adherents: Number of Adherents	Total Adherents: % of Total Pop.	Total Adherents: % of Total Adh.
167 Chs of Christ	6	574	620	776	.3	.7
173 Comm of Christ	2	284	NR	284	.1	.3
175 Congr Chr Chs	1	10	7	13 *	-	-
179 Consrv Bapt	11	NR	4,068	4,068	1.4	3.8
193 Episcopal	5	NR	766	1,771	.6	1.7
201 Evan Cov Ch	1	311	327	395 *	.1	.4
207 E.L.C.A.	12	4,442	2,052	6,039	2.1	5.6
211 Fel Evg Bib Ch	1	35	40	40	-	-
221 Free Methodist	2	491	633	633	.2	.6
223 Free Will Bapt	1	69	NR	88 *	-	.1
226 Friends-USA	9	694	NR	881 *	.3	.8
237 Menn Br US Conf	1	250	NR	317 *	.1	.3
263 Int Foursq Gos	7	1,112	1,575	1,575 *	.6	1.5
273 LandmrkBapt,I&U	1	35	NR	44 *	-	-
283 Luth—MO Synod	6	1,410	815	1,757	.6	1.6
288 Mennonite USA	3	198	293	309 *	.1	.3
290 Metro Comm Ch	1	32	22	41 *	-	-
297 Mennonite;Other	1	100	NR	127 *	-	.1
339 Pent Ch of God	2	51	NR	77	-	.1
349 Pent Holiness	2	38	22	48 *	-	-
355 Presb Ch (USA)	6	2,079	1,187	2,640 *	.9	2.5
388 Reg Bapt Gen As	3	776	859	1,032 *	.4	1.0
400 Rus Orth Moscow	1	NR	NR	NR	-	-
403 Salvation Army	2	282	140	366	.1	.3
413 S.D.A.	10	2,740	NR	3,260	1.1	3.0
416 Sikh	2	NR	NR	NR	-	-
419 So Bapt Conv	4	671	360	852 *	.3	.8
435 Unitarian-Univ	1	224	NR	284 *	.1	.3
443 Un C of Christ	3	409	238	519 *	.2	.5
449 Un Methodist	10	3,279	1,400	4,163 *	1.5	3.9
455 Un Ref Chs N.A.	1	105	NR	165	.1	.2
463 Vineyard	1	130	120	165 *	.1	.2
467 Wesleyan	3	263	426	1,674	.6	1.6
469 WELS	1	154	115	206	.1	.2
496 Jewish Est	1	NR	NR	1,000	.4	.9
499 Indep.Non-Char	2	220	2,730	4,170	1.5	3.9
MORROW	**22**	**811**	**578**	**3,087 ***	**28.1**	**100.0**
019 Amer Bapt USA	1	10	15	15 *	.1	.5
053 Assemb of God	2	93	131	216	2.0	7.0
056 Baha'i	0	12	NR	12	.1	.4
081 Catholic	3	NR	NR	1,173	10.7	38.0
097 Chr Chs&Chs Cr	1	95	NR	125 *	1.1	4.0
151 L-D Saints	2	NR	NR	556	5.1	18.0
165 Ch of Nazarene	1	14	13	72	.7	2.3
179 Consrv Bapt	1	NR	51	51	.5	1.7
193 Episcopal	1	NR	29	126	1.1	4.1
207 E.L.C.A.	3	178	112	221	2.0	7.2
349 Pent Holiness	1	38	60	50 *	.5	1.6
388 Reg Bapt Gen As	1	22	25	29 *	.3	.9
413 S.D.A.	2	148	NR	177	1.6	5.7
419 So Bapt Conv	1	14	27	18 *	.2	.6
443 Un C of Christ	1	112	55	147 *	1.3	4.8
449 Un Methodist	1	75	60	99 *	.9	3.2
MULTNOMAH	**470**	**74,625**	**61,832**	**301,893 ***	**45.7**	**100.0**
017 Amer Bapt Assn	1	30	NR	36 *	-	-
019 Amer Bapt USA	16	5,756	1,869	6,979 *	1.1	2.3
034 Ant Orth of NA	2	161	NR	322	-	.1
039 Ap Chr Ch(Naz)	1	95	110	115 *	-	-
053 Assemb of God	16	3,880	4,370	6,978	1.1	2.3
056 Baha'i	3	955	NR	955	.1	.3
057 Bapt Gen Conf	7	938	656	1,137 *	.2	.4
059 Bapt Miss Assn	1	122	132	148 *	-	-
076 Buddhism	19	NR	NR	NR	-	-
081 Catholic	40	NR	NR	150,075	22.7	49.7
084 Calvary Chapel	2	NR	NR	NR	-	-
089 Chr & Miss Al	6	791	NR	1,027	.2	.3
093 Chr Ch (Disc)	5	1,028	344	1,246 *	.2	.4
097 Chr Chs&Chs Cr	12	4,160	NR	5,043 *	.8	1.7
123 Ch God (Ander)	11	NR	2,027	2,027	.3	.7
127 Ch God (Cleve)	4	757	417	925 *	.1	.3
145 Ch God Prophcy	1	26	NR	32 *	-	-

Religious Group	Number of Churches, Synagogues, Mosques, or Temples	Number of Communicant, Confirmed, or Full Members	Number of Attendees	Total Adherents: Number of Adherents	Total Adherents: % of Total Pop.	Total Adherents: % of Total Adh.
151 L-D Saints	26	NR	NR	10,389	1.6	3.4
157 Ch of Brethren	1	60	47	73 *	-	-
165 Ch of Nazarene	10	2,238	1,420	2,556	.4	.8
167 Chs of Christ	10	1,356	1,470	1,855	.3	.6
173 Comm of Christ	1	585	NR	585	.1	.2
179 Consrv Bapt	27	NR	4,878	4,878	.7	1.6
193 Episcopal	15	NR	2,180	6,242	.9	2.1
201 Evan Cov Ch	9	889	1,172	1,319 *	.2	.4
207 E.L.C.A.	24	6,201	3,125	8,152	1.2	2.7
221 Free Methodist	6	272	406	406	.1	.1
226 Friends-USA	6	442	NR	536 *	.1	.2
237 Menn Br US Conf	6	955	NR	1,158 *	.2	.4
246 Greek Orthodox	1	NR	NR	2,598	.4	.9
251 Holy Orth in NA	1	NR	NR	42	-	-
252 Hindu	3	NR	NR	NR	-	-
263 Int Foursq Gos	10	7,686	8,871	9,319 *	1.4	3.1
264 Int Chs of Crst	1	294	560	417	.1	.1
267 Muslim Est	3	NR	870	3,939	.6	1.3
268 Jain	2	NR	NR	NR	-	-
273 LandmrkBapt,I&U	1	21	NR	25 *	-	-
283 Luth—MO Synod	14	2,516	1,503	3,184	.5	1.1
288 Mennonite USA	2	228	205	285 *	-	.1
290 Metro Comm Ch	2	285	220	346 *	.1	.1
291 Missionary Ch	1	60	125	125	-	-
313 N Am Bapt Conf	6	772	618	936 *	.1	.3
331 OCA: Ter Diocs	2	123	NR	257	-	.1
335 Orth Pres Ch	1	142	165	189	-	.1
339 Pent Ch of God	2	57	NR	135	-	-
349 Pent Holiness	1	19	25	23 *	-	-
355 Presb Ch (USA)	29	8,648	5,938	10,850 *	1.6	3.6
356 Presb Ch Amer	2	0	0	0	-	-
388 Reg Bapt Gen As	1	102	100	124 *	-	-
397 OCA: Roman Dioc	1	NR	NR	450	.1	.1
403 Salvation Army	3	461	300	3,012	.5	1.0
413 S.D.A.	10	3,412	NR	4,059	.6	1.3
416 Sikh	1	NR	NR	NR	-	-
419 So Bapt Conv	23	3,644	1,992	4,418 *	.7	1.5
423 Syrian Orth Ch	1	NR	NR	125	-	-
431 Ukrainian Orth	1	NR	NR	105	-	-
435 Unitarian-Univ	3	1,080	NR	1,309 *	.2	.4
443 Un C of Christ	7	1,786	781	2,165 *	.3	.7
449 Un Methodist	27	4,825	2,409	5,849 *	.9	1.9
463 Vineyard	2	310	260	376 *	.1	.1
467 Wesleyan	3	0	197	427	.1	.1
469 WELS	1	232	120	310	-	.1
496 Jewish Est	6	NR	NR	19,300	2.9	6.4
498 Indep.Charis.	6	6,000	10,850	10,850	1.6	3.6
499 Indep.Non-Char	2	225	1,100	1,150	.2	.4
POLK	**67**	**6,355**	**5,528**	**13,950 ***	**22.4**	**100.0**
053 Assemb of God	5	935	1,286	2,009	3.2	14.4
056 Baha'i	1	44	NR	44	.1	.3
081 Catholic	2	NR	NR	1,500	2.4	10.8
084 Calvary Chapel	1	NR	NR	NR	-	-
089 Chr & Miss Al	1	134	NR	275	.4	2.0
093 Chr Ch (Disc)	1	377	106	467 *	.7	3.3
097 Chr Chs&Chs Cr	3	751	NR	931 *	1.5	6.7
127 Ch God (Cleve)	3	77	90	120 *	.2	.9
145 Ch God Prophcy	2	53	NR	66 *	.1	.5
151 L-D Saints	6	NR	NR	2,067	3.3	14.8
165 Ch of Nazarene	3	164	148	208	.3	1.5
167 Chs of Christ	2	83	110	140	.2	1.0
179 Consrv Bapt	5	NR	510	510	.8	3.7
193 Episcopal	3	NR	135	342	.5	2.5
203 Evan Free Ch	1	237	471	471	.8	3.4
207 E.L.C.A.	1	489	200	629	1.0	4.5
211 Fel Evg Bib Ch	1	440	140	140	.2	1.0
221 Free Methodist	1	18	19	19	-	.1
237 Menn Br US Conf	2	190	NR	236 *	.4	1.7
263 Int Foursq Gos	3	269	597	597 *	1.0	4.3
283 Luth—MO Synod	2	290	140	372	.6	2.7
288 Mennonite USA	2	195	233	242 *	.4	1.7
313 N Am Bapt Conf	1	466	405	582 *	.9	4.2
339 Pent Ch of God	1	24	NR	71	.1	.5

NR–Not Reported *Total adherents estimated from known number of communicant, confirmed, full members. - Represents a percentage less than 0.1. Percentages may not total 100 due to rounding.

Table 4: Religious Congregations by County and Group: 2000

Religious Group	Number of Churches, Synagogues, Mosques, or Temples	Number of Communicant, Confirmed, or Full Members	Number of Attendees	Total Adherents: Number of Adherents	Total Adherents: % of Total Pop.	Total Adherents: % of Total Adh.
355 Presb Ch (USA)	2	166	109	206 *	.3	1.5
388 Reg Bapt Gen As	1	90	110	112 *	.2	.8
403 Salvation Army	1	30	21	72	.1	.5
413 S.D.A.	2	191	NR	227	.4	1.6
419 So Bapt Conv	2	293	130	363 *	.6	2.6
449 Un Methodist	5	349	218	432 *	.7	3.1
498 Indep.Charis.	1	0	350	500	.8	3.6
SHERMAN	**10**	**224**	**204**	**599 ***	**31.0**	**100.0**
056 Baha'i	0	5	NR	5	.3	.8
081 Catholic	3	NR	NR	263	13.6	43.9
097 Chr Chs&Chs Cr	1	30	NR	37 *	1.9	6.2
167 Chs of Christ	1	20	20	20	1.0	3.3
179 Consrv Bapt	2	NR	67	67	3.5	11.2
355 Presb Ch (USA)	1	71	65	87 *	4.5	14.5
419 So Bapt Conv	1	35	29	43 *	2.2	7.2
449 Un Methodist	1	63	23	77 *	4.0	12.9
TILLAMOOK	**36**	**2,887**	**1,494**	**6,298 ***	**26.0**	**100.0**
017 Amer Bapt Assn	1	3	NR	4 *	-	.1
053 Assemb of God	3	151	184	389	1.6	6.2
056 Baha'i	1	34	NR	34	.1	.5
081 Catholic	3	NR	NR	1,370	5.6	21.8
097 Chr Chs&Chs Cr	2	460	NR	550 *	2.3	8.7
151 L-D Saints	2	NR	NR	649	2.7	10.3
165 Ch of Nazarene	2	385	354	476	2.0	7.6
167 Chs of Christ	1	27	35	37	.2	.6
179 Consrv Bapt	1	NR	70	70	.3	1.1
193 Episcopal	2	NR	116	427	1.8	6.8
207 E.L.C.A.	1	45	32	54	.2	.9
226 Friends-USA	2	168	NR	201 *	.8	3.2
263 Int Foursq Gos	1	61	38	73 *	.3	1.2
273 LandmrkBapt,I&U	2	31	NR	37 *	.2	.6
283 Luth—MO Synod	1	60	60	66	.3	1.0
313 N Am Bapt Conf	1	52	103	62 *	.3	1.0
355 Presb Ch (USA)	2	59	47	70 *	.3	1.1
403 Salvation Army	1	47	65	173	.7	2.7
413 S.D.A.	2	645	NR	768	3.2	12.2
419 So Bapt Conv	1	65	78	78 *	.3	1.2
443 Un C of Christ	1	106	72	127 *	.5	2.0
449 Un Methodist	3	488	240	583 *	2.4	9.3
UMATILLA	**113**	**10,131**	**5,493**	**30,576 ***	**43.3**	**100.0**
017 Amer Bapt Assn	1	65	NR	83 *	.1	.3
019 Amer Bapt USA	5	575	360	731 *	1.0	2.4
053 Assemb of God	11	780	942	1,509	2.1	4.9
056 Baha'i	1	121	NR	121	.2	.4
081 Catholic	6	NR	NR	9,442	13.4	30.9
084 Calvary Chapel	1	NR	NR	NR	-	-
093 Chr Ch (Disc)	3	1,152	491	1,465 *	2.1	4.8
097 Chr Chs&Chs Cr	2	450	NR	572 *	.8	1.9
123 Ch God (Ander)	2	NR	120	120	.2	.4
127 Ch God (Cleve)	2	109	116	143 *	.2	.5
145 Ch God Prophcy	1	26	NR	33 *	-	.1
151 L-D Saints	18	NR	NR	6,058	8.6	19.8
157 Ch of Brethren	1	117	0	149 *	.2	.5
165 Ch of Nazarene	3	314	389	542	.8	1.8
167 Chs of Christ	4	151	163	206	.3	.7
179 Consrv Bapt	7	NR	666	666	.9	2.2
193 Episcopal	3	NR	209	723	1.0	2.4
207 E.L.C.A.	3	899	368	1,126	1.6	3.7
221 Free Methodist	2	180	400	400	.6	1.3
263 Int Foursq Gos	2	231	319	319 *	.5	1.0
283 Luth—MO Synod	1	143	84	190	.3	.6
339 Pent Ch of God	2	25	NR	85	.1	.3
355 Presb Ch (USA)	8	583	294	747 *	1.1	2.4
360 Prim Bapt Chrch	1	NR	NR	NR	-	-
388 Reg Bapt Gen As	1	60	60	76 *	.1	.2
403 Salvation Army	1	90	30	100	.1	.3
413 S.D.A.	10	3,009	NR	3,581	5.1	11.7
419 So Bapt Conv	4	479	202	609 *	.9	2.0
449 Un Methodist	5	543	234	690 *	1.0	2.3
467 Wesleyan	1	0	26	50	.1	.2
469 WELS	1	29	20	40	.1	.1
UNION	**45**	**2,984**	**2,369**	**8,246 ***	**33.6**	**100.0**
053 Assemb of God	2	118	150	203	.8	2.5
056 Baha'i	0	35	NR	35	.1	.4
081 Catholic	4	NR	NR	1,675	6.8	20.3
084 Calvary Chapel	1	NR	NR	NR	-	-
093 Chr Ch (Disc)	1	284	151	348 *	1.4	4.2
097 Chr Chs&Chs Cr	2	255	NR	312 *	1.3	3.8
123 Ch God (Ander)	1	NR	52	52	.2	.6
151 L-D Saints	6	NR	NR	1,710	7.0	20.7
165 Ch of Nazarene	2	345	285	436	1.8	5.3
167 Chs of Christ	2	54	64	74	.3	.9
179 Consrv Bapt	3	NR	585	585	2.4	7.1
193 Episcopal	1	NR	79	209	.9	2.5
207 E.L.C.A.	1	210	120	264	1.1	3.2
221 Free Methodist	1	22	62	62	.3	.8
263 Int Foursq Gos	1	272	293	333 *	1.4	4.0
267 Muslim Est	1	NR	55	163	.7	2.0
283 Luth—MO Synod	1	88	46	104	.4	1.3
297 Mennonite;Other	1	64	NR	78 *	.3	.9
339 Pent Ch of God	1	7	NR	14	.1	.2
355 Presb Ch (USA)	1	284	130	348 *	1.4	4.2
370 Ref Baptist Chs	1	NR	NR	NR	-	-
403 Salvation Army	1	39	27	145	.6	1.8
413 S.D.A.	3	326	NR	387	1.6	4.7
419 So Bapt Conv	2	230	75	281 *	1.1	3.4
449 Un Methodist	5	351	195	428 *	1.7	5.2
WALLOWA	**20**	**1,157**	**579**	**2,700 ***	**37.4**	**100.0**
053 Assemb of God	2	61	85	134	1.9	5.0
056 Baha'i	0	28	NR	28	.4	1.0
081 Catholic	2	NR	NR	672	9.3	24.9
097 Chr Chs&Chs Cr	3	585	NR	705 *	9.8	26.1
151 L-D Saints	1	NR	NR	292	4.0	10.8
165 Ch of Nazarene	1	32	40	55	.8	2.0
167 Chs of Christ	1	25	28	30	.4	1.1
179 Consrv Bapt	2	NR	213	213	2.9	7.9
193 Episcopal	1	NR	20	61	.8	2.3
207 E.L.C.A.	1	15	13	15	.2	.6
355 Presb Ch (USA)	1	68	55	82 *	1.1	3.0
370 Ref Baptist Chs	1	NR	NR	NR	-	-
413 S.D.A.	1	89	NR	106	1.5	3.9
443 Un C of Christ	1	95	59	115 *	1.6	4.3
449 Un Methodist	2	159	66	192 *	2.7	7.1
WASCO	**31**	**2,632**	**1,845**	**8,316 ***	**35.0**	**100.0**
053 Assemb of God	3	188	225	476	2.0	5.7
056 Baha'i	0	79	NR	79	.3	.9
081 Catholic	3	NR	NR	2,760	11.6	33.2
084 Calvary Chapel	1	NR	NR	NR	-	-
093 Chr Ch (Disc)	1	40	17	50 *	.2	.6
097 Chr Chs&Chs Cr	2	585	NR	724 *	3.0	8.7
123 Ch God (Ander)	1	NR	22	22	.1	.3
151 L-D Saints	2	NR	NR	966	4.1	11.6
165 Ch of Nazarene	1	80	68	120	.5	1.4
167 Chs of Christ	1	69	65	78	.3	.9
179 Consrv Bapt	3	NR	420	420	1.8	5.1
193 Episcopal	1	NR	69	364	1.5	4.4
207 E.L.C.A.	1	255	120	540	2.3	6.5
226 Friends-USA	1	22	NR	27 *	.1	.3
263 Int Foursq Gos	1	63	104	104 *	.4	1.3
283 Luth—MO Synod	1	87	60	87	.4	1.0
355 Presb Ch (USA)	1	321	350	397 *	1.7	4.8
403 Salvation Army	1	52	39	131	.6	1.6
413 S.D.A.	1	190	NR	226	.9	2.7
419 So Bapt Conv	1	278	117	344 *	1.4	4.1
443 Un C of Christ	1	121	44	150 *	.6	1.8
449 Un Methodist	3	202	125	251 *	1.1	3.0
WASHINGTON	**248**	**38,149**	**37,785**	**115,047 ***	**25.8**	**100.0**
017 Amer Bapt Assn	1	60	NR	76 *	-	.1

NR–Not Reported   *Total adherents estimated from known number of communicant, confirmed, full members.   - Represents a percentage less than 0.1.   Percentages may not total 100 due to rounding.

Table 4: Religious Congregations by County and Group: 2000

Religious Group	Number of Churches, Synagogues, Mosques, or Temples	Number of Communicant, Confirmed, or Full Members	Number of Attendees	Total Adherents: Number of Adherents	Total Adherents: % of Total Pop.	Total Adherents: % of Total Adh.
019 Amer Bapt USA	3	216	285	285 *	.1	.2
053 Assemb of God	15	2,226	2,945	5,108	1.1	4.4
056 Baha'i	8	487	NR	487	.1	.4
057 Bapt Gen Conf	4	416	735	739 *	.2	.6
076 Buddhism	2	NR	NR	NR	-	-
081 Catholic	11	NR	NR	28,765	6.5	25.0
084 Calvary Chapel	2	NR	NR	NR	-	-
089 Chr & Miss Al	1	82	NR	257	.1	.2
093 Chr Ch (Disc)	4	1,088	364	1,383 *	.3	1.2
097 Chr Chs&Chs Cr	8	3,891	NR	4,946 *	1.1	4.3
105 Christian Ref	3	413	376	525 *	.1	.5
123 Ch God (Ander)	4	NR	466	466	.1	.4
151 L-D Saints	39	NR	NR	16,723	3.8	14.5
165 Ch of Nazarene	6	1,236	645	1,271	.3	1.1
167 Chs of Christ	9	1,237	1,293	1,510	.3	1.3
173 Comm of Christ	1	277	NR	277	.1	.2
179 Consrv Bapt	13	NR	4,278	4,278	1.0	3.7
193 Episcopal	5	NR	729	1,954	.4	1.7
201 Evan Cov Ch	3	393	925	925 *	.2	.8
207 E.L.C.A.	9	3,892	2,058	5,517	1.2	4.8
221 Free Methodist	2	252	315	315	.1	.3
226 Friends-USA	6	442	NR	562 *	.1	.5
237 Menn Br US Conf	2	47	NR	60 *	-	.1
246 Greek Orthodox	1	NR	NR	3	-	-
252 Hindu	1	NR	NR	NR	-	-
263 Int Foursq Gos	7	3,590	10,226	10,226 *	2.3	8.9
267 Muslim Est	1	NR	230	350	.1	.3
273 LandmrkBapt,I&U	1	45	NR	57 *	-	-
283 Luth—MO Synod	10	3,627	2,339	4,712	1.1	4.1
313 N Am Bapt Conf	2	54	71	69 *	-	.1
339 Pent Ch of God	1	51	NR	120	-	.1
349 Pent Holiness	1	45	61	57 *	-	-
355 Presb Ch (USA)	10	2,293	1,696	2,915 *	.7	2.5
356 Presb Ch Amer	1	114	190	190	-	.2
388 Reg Bapt Gen As	2	97	165	165 *	-	.1
413 S.D.A.	9	2,185	NR	2,601	.6	2.3
419 So Bapt Conv	10	2,560	1,100	3,254 *	.7	2.8
435 Unitarian-Univ	2	293	NR	372 *	.1	.3
443 Un C of Christ	5	1,031	569	1,310 *	.3	1.1
449 Un Methodist	14	3,156	1,834	4,011 *	.9	3.5
463 Vineyard	2	355	320	451 *	.1	.4
467 Wesleyan	1	0	58	91	-	.1
469 WELS	2	148	112	214	-	.2
496 Jewish Est	1	NR	NR	3,100	.7	2.7
498 Indep.Charis.	1	650	550	650	.1	.6
499 Indep.Non-Char	2	1,200	2,850	3,700	.8	3.2
WHEELER	**6**	**255**	**158**	**430 ***	**27.8**	**100.0**
053 Assemb of God	2	86	124	161	10.4	37.4
056 Baha'i	0	2	NR	2	.1	.5
081 Catholic	1	NR	NR	70	4.5	16.3
273 LandmrkBapt,I&U	2	130	NR	153 *	9.9	35.6
449 Un Methodist	1	37	34	44 *	2.8	10.2
YAMHILL	**94**	**9,821**	**7,238**	**22,424 ***	**26.4**	**100.0**
019 Amer Bapt USA	2	566	277	713 *	.8	3.2
053 Assemb of God	8	666	827	1,821	2.1	8.1
056 Baha'i	1	70	NR	70	.1	.3
057 Bapt Gen Conf	1	18	30	30 *	-	.1
081 Catholic	6	NR	NR	3,715	4.4	16.6
084 Calvary Chapel	1	NR	NR	NR	-	-
093 Chr Ch (Disc)	1	408	78	514 *	.6	2.3
097 Chr Chs&Chs Cr	7	1,360	NR	1,713 *	2.0	7.6
105 Christian Ref	1	86	65	108 *	.1	.5
123 Ch God (Ander)	1	NR	52	52	.1	.2
151 L-D Saints	9	NR	NR	2,827	3.3	12.6
165 Ch of Nazarene	3	962	899	1,332	1.6	5.9
167 Chs of Christ	3	286	305	384	.5	1.7
179 Consrv Bapt	6	NR	1,407	1,407	1.7	6.3
193 Episcopal	2	NR	244	513	.6	2.3
201 Evan Cov Ch	1	251	489	489 *	.6	2.2
207 E.L.C.A.	3	572	302	730	.9	3.3
221 Free Methodist	2	292	442	442	.5	2.0

Religious Group	Number of Churches, Synagogues, Mosques, or Temples	Number of Communicant, Confirmed, or Full Members	Number of Attendees	Total Adherents: Number of Adherents	Total Adherents: % of Total Pop.	Total Adherents: % of Total Adh.
226 Friends-USA	6	504	NR	635 *	.7	2.8
263 Int Foursq Gos	2	171	265	265 *	.3	1.2
283 Luth—MO Synod	2	211	204	277	.3	1.2
288 Mennonite USA	1	34	40	43 *	.1	.2
297 Mennonite;Other	4	383	NR	482 *	.6	2.1
313 N Am Bapt Conf	1	0	110	110 *	.1	.5
335 Orth Pres Ch	1	42	68	68	.1	.3
355 Presb Ch (USA)	2	548	366	691 *	.8	3.1
370 Ref Baptist Chs	1	NR	NR	NR	-	-
403 Salvation Army	1	38	41	89	.1	.4
413 S.D.A.	6	843	NR	1,003	1.2	4.5
419 So Bapt Conv	2	594	298	748 *	.9	3.3
449 Un Methodist	7	916	429	1,153 *	1.4	5.1
PENNSYLVANIA						
The State.....	13,105	2,087,177	1,052,151	7,116,698 *	57.9	100.0
ADAMS	**117**	**21,850**	**10,366**	**49,704 ***	**54.4**	**100.0**
017 Amer Bapt Assn	1	50	NR	62 *	.1	.1
019 Amer Bapt USA	2	464	342	573 *	.6	1.2
053 Assemb of God	4	1,186	1,596	2,565	2.8	5.2
056 Baha'i	0	11	NR	11	-	-
075 Brethren in Cr	3	152	126	157	.2	.3
081 Catholic	9	NR	NR	19,642	21.5	39.5
123 Ch God (Ander)	1	NR	201	201	.2	.4
127 Ch God (Cleve)	2	221	91	274 *	.3	.6
145 Ch God Prophcy	2	82	NR	102 *	.1	.2
151 L-D Saints	2	NR	NR	732	.8	1.5
157 Ch of Brethren	5	704	683	870 *	1.0	1.8
165 Ch of Nazarene	1	34	26	51	.1	.1
167 Chs of Christ	1	50	40	60	.1	.1
171 Ch God-Gen Con	1	34	25	42 *	-	.1
179 Consrv Bapt	1	NR	15	15	-	-
193 Episcopal	1	NR	170	434	.5	.9
207 E.L.C.A.	26	8,839	2,956	11,294	12.4	22.7
223 Free Will Bapt	1	99	NR	122 *	.1	.2
226 Friends-USA	3	315	NR	389 *	.4	.8
262 Int Cou Comm Ch	1	190	NR	235 *	.3	.5
263 Int Foursq Gos	2	548	352	677 *	.7	1.4
286 E.PA Mennonite	1	58	NR	72 *	.1	.1
288 Mennonite USA	2	166	125	205 *	.2	.4
297 Mennonite;Other	3	239	NR	295 *	.3	.6
313 N Am Bapt Conf	1	76	150	94 *	.1	.2
335 Orth Pres Ch	1	73	68	112	.1	.2
355 Presb Ch (USA)	3	935	629	1,155 *	1.3	2.3
413 S.D.A.	2	150	NR	178	.2	.4
419 So Bapt Conv	3	1,197	445	1,479 *	1.6	3.0
443 Un C of Christ	15	3,610	1,316	4,461 *	4.9	9.0
449 Un Methodist	16	2,367	1,010	2,925 *	3.2	5.9
496 Jewish Est	1	NR	NR	220	.2	.4
ALLEGHENY	**1,010**	**166,449**	**84,653**	**920,905 ***	**71.9**	**100.0**
011 A.W.M.C.	2	33	61	35	-	-
019 Amer Bapt USA	41	12,796	7,363	15,398 *	1.2	1.7
022 Carp Rus Orth	7	1,224	NR	2,086	.2	.2
034 Ant Orth of NA	2	912	NR	1,824	.1	.2
053 Assemb of God	26	4,809	5,850	10,257	.8	1.1
055 As Ref Pres Ch	2	118	NR	148	-	-
056 Baha'i	1	137	NR	137	-	-
057 Bapt Gen Conf	3	198	153	242 *	-	-
071 Brethren (Ash)	1	20	19	24 *	-	-
076 Buddhism	4	NR	NR	NR	-	-
081 Catholic	214	NR	NR	632,807	49.4	68.7
084 Calvary Chapel	1	NR	NR	NR	-	-
089 Chr & Miss Al	19	2,048	NR	5,001	.4	.5
093 Chr Ch (Disc)	7	857	346	1,031 *	.1	.1
097 Chr Chs&Chs Cr	19	3,148	NR	3,788 *	.3	.4
123 Ch God (Ander)	4	NR	447	447	-	-
127 Ch God (Cleve)	6	579	233	697 *	.1	.1
145 Ch God Prophcy	1	41	NR	49 *	-	-
151 L-D Saints	8	NR	NR	2,307	.2	.3

NR–Not Reported   *Total adherents estimated from known number of communicant, confirmed, full members.   - Represents a percentage less than 0.1.   Percentages may not total 100 due to rounding.

Table 4: Religious Congregations by County and Group: 2000

Religious Group	Number of Churches, Synagogues, Mosques, or Temples	Number of Communicant, Confirmed, or Full Members	Number of Attendees	Total Adherents		
				Number of Adherents	% of Total Pop.	% of Total Adh.
157 Ch of Brethren	4	281	160	338 *	-	-
165 Ch of Nazarene	10	1,073	749	1,430	.1	.2
167 Chs of Christ	9	619	675	877	.1	.1
171 Ch God-Gen Con	2	24	25	44 *	-	-
173 Comm of Christ	3	244	NR	244	-	-
175 Congr Chr Chs	6	349	224	420 *	-	-
179 Consrv Bapt	5	NR	985	985	.1	.1
193 Episcopal	38	NR	5,560	14,473	1.1	1.6
201 Evan Cov Ch	1	106	87	128 *	-	-
203 Evan Free Ch	3	560	1,200	1,200	.1	.1
207 E.L.C.A.	93	23,265	8,927	31,811	2.5	3.5
216 Evan Presby Ch	2	512	NR	616 *	-	.1
220 Free Lutheran	1	947	697	1,361	.1	.1
221 Free Methodist	4	167	215	230	-	-
223 Free Will Bapt	1	99	NR	119 *	-	-
226 Friends-USA	1	35	NR	42 *	-	-
246 Greek Orthodox	7	NR	NR	5,556	.4	.6
252 Hindu	4	NR	NR	NR	-	-
262 Int Cou Comm Ch	1	220	NR	265 *	-	-
263 Int Foursq Gos	1	21	43	43 *	-	-
264 Int Chs of Crst	1	144	202	182	-	-
267 Muslim Est	7	NR	1,820	7,952	.6	.9
268 Jain	1	NR	NR	NR	-	-
283 Luth—MO Synod	27	4,375	2,134	5,767	.4	.6
288 Mennonite USA	1	36	68	68 *	-	-
290 Metro Comm Ch	1	45	39	54 *	-	-
313 N Am Bapt Conf	2	204	161	245 *	-	-
331 OCA: Ter Diocs	10	815	NR	1,050	.1	.1
335 Orth Pres Ch	2	211	262	313	-	-
349 Pent Holiness	2	81	61	97 *	-	-
355 Presb Ch (USA)	160	50,064	23,114	60,256 *	4.7	6.5
356 Presb Ch Amer	8	1,166	1,044	1,635	.1	.2
363 Primitive Meth	6	342	NR	364	-	-
388 Reg Bapt Gen As	2	298	155	359 *	-	-
397 OCA: Roman Dioc	1	NR	NR	10	-	-
401 Rus Orth Abroad	1	NR	NR	NR	-	-
403 Salvation Army	11	906	532	3,855	.3	.4
410 Serb Orth USA	4	NR	NR	2,800	.2	.3
411 Serb Orth: Grac	2	NR	NR	NR	-	-
413 S.D.A.	5	1,533	NR	1,824	.1	.2
416 Sikh	1	NR	NR	NR	-	-
419 So Bapt Conv	6	1,596	603	1,921 *	.1	.2
431 Ukrainian Orth	3	NR	NR	1,614	.1	.2
435 Unitarian-Univ	5	838	NR	1,008 *	.1	.1
443 Un C of Christ	18	1,777	775	2,138 *	.2	.2
449 Un Methodist	112	39,495	12,194	47,529 *	3.7	5.2
463 Vineyard	3	125	136	171 *	-	-
467 Wesleyan	4	208	180	441	-	-
469 WELS	1	95	55	114	-	-
490 Zoroastrian	1	NR	NR	NR	-	-
496 Jewish Est	29	NR	NR	34,600	2.7	3.8
498 Indep.Charis.	4	3,578	3,435	3,578	.3	.4
499 Indep.Non-Char	5	3,075	3,664	4,500	.4	.5
ARMSTRONG	**156**	**20,670**	**10,301**	**41,880 ***	**57.9**	**100.0**
011 A.W.M.C.	3	45	144	46	.1	.1
019 Amer Bapt USA	6	1,532	634	1,848 *	2.6	4.4
053 Assemb of God	4	231	298	450	.6	1.1
071 Brethren (Ash)	2	233	193	281 *	.4	.7
081 Catholic	15	NR	NR	13,184	18.2	31.5
089 Chr & Miss Al	1	46	NR	88	.1	.2
123 Ch God (Ander)	5	NR	1,554	1,554	2.1	3.7
127 Ch God (Cleve)	2	77	81	107 *	.1	.3
145 Ch God Prophcy	3	123	NR	147 *	.2	.4
157 Ch of Brethren	2	418	194	505 *	.7	1.2
165 Ch of Nazarene	1	104	70	187	.3	.4
167 Chs of Christ	1	88	80	121	.2	.3
171 Ch God-Gen Con	4	251	255	342 *	.5	.8
181 Consrv Congr	1	131	90	158 *	.2	.4
193 Episcopal	5	NR	182	492	.7	1.2
207 E.L.C.A.	24	5,880	1,849	8,271	11.4	19.7
221 Free Methodist	3	158	175	213	.3	.5
246 Greek Orthodox	1	NR	NR	30	-	.1
323 Old Ord Amish	1	55	NR	66 *	.1	.2
355 Presb Ch (USA)	32	5,523	2,301	6,665 *	9.2	15.9
356 Presb Ch Amer	2	97	103	123	.2	.3
370 Ref Baptist Chs	1	NR	NR	NR	-	-
388 Reg Bapt Gen As	1	112	0	135 *	.2	.3
403 Salvation Army	1	103	32	255	.4	.6
413 S.D.A.	1	114	NR	136	.2	.3
443 Un C of Christ	7	1,145	523	1,381 *	1.9	3.3
449 Un Methodist	26	4,181	1,515	5,042 *	7.0	12.0
467 Wesleyan	1	23	28	53	.1	.1
BEAVER	**209**	**30,933**	**15,099**	**112,857 ***	**62.2**	**100.0**
011 A.W.M.C.	3	33	112	40	-	-
019 Amer Bapt USA	6	854	342	1,032 *	.6	.9
022 Carp Rus Orth	2	243	NR	416	.2	.4
034 Ant Orth of NA	1	44	NR	88	-	.1
053 Assemb of God	5	508	633	884	.5	.8
056 Baha'i	0	7	NR	7	-	-
081 Catholic	26	NR	NR	64,413	35.5	57.1
089 Chr & Miss Al	10	728	NR	1,638	.9	1.5
093 Chr Ch (Disc)	1	90	30	109 *	.1	.1
097 Chr Chs&Chs Cr	2	195	NR	236 *	.1	.2
123 Ch God (Ander)	2	NR	205	205	.1	.2
127 Ch God (Cleve)	3	192	92	232 *	.1	.2
151 L-D Saints	1	NR	NR	491	.3	.4
165 Ch of Nazarene	6	405	294	754	.4	.7
167 Chs of Christ	3	184	210	260	.1	.2
171 Ch God-Gen Con	1	67	71	81 *	-	.1
175 Congr Chr Chs	1	62	55	75 *	-	.1
193 Episcopal	8	NR	655	1,271	.7	1.1
203 Evan Free Ch	2	275	650	650	.4	.6
207 E.L.C.A.	21	5,918	1,667	7,973	4.4	7.1
221 Free Methodist	6	535	616	685	.4	.6
246 Greek Orthodox	2	NR	NR	1,500	.8	1.3
283 Luth—MO Synod	2	598	329	720	.4	.6
331 OCA: Ter Diocs	2	318	NR	351	.2	.3
355 Presb Ch (USA)	38	8,307	4,620	10,037 *	5.5	8.9
356 Presb Ch Amer	5	655	578	875	.5	.8
363 Primitive Meth	1	57	NR	61	-	.1
397 OCA: Roman Dioc	2	NR	NR	57	-	.1
403 Salvation Army	3	360	133	803	.4	.7
410 Serb Orth USA	2	NR	NR	1,640	.9	1.5
413 S.D.A.	1	73	NR	87	-	.1
419 So Bapt Conv	3	421	259	509 *	.3	.5
431 Ukrainian Orth	1	NR	NR	600	.3	.5
443 Un C of Christ	1	19	8	23 *	-	-
449 Un Methodist	32	8,847	2,897	10,689 *	5.9	9.5
467 Wesleyan	1	49	43	185	.1	.2
496 Jewish Est	2	NR	NR	1,980	1.1	1.8
498 Indep.Charis.	1	889	600	1,200	.7	1.1
BEDFORD	**135**	**14,625**	**7,766**	**21,190 ***	**42.4**	**100.0**
053 Assemb of God	10	449	564	1,031	2.1	4.9
056 Baha'i	0	3	NR	3	-	-
071 Brethren (Ash)	1	38	54	46 *	.1	.2
075 Brethren in Cr	6	205	263	275	.6	1.3
081 Catholic	3	NR	NR	2,053	4.1	9.7
089 Chr & Miss Al	1	117	NR	247	.5	1.2
097 Chr Chs&Chs Cr	1	80	NR	98 *	.2	.5
127 Ch God (Cleve)	5	807	652	1,025 *	2.1	4.8
151 L-D Saints	1	NR	NR	180	.4	.8
157 Ch of Brethren	18	2,883	1,272	3,518 *	7.0	16.6
165 Ch of Nazarene	2	168	198	383	.8	1.8
171 Ch God-Gen Con	5	347	341	425 *	.9	2.0
193 Episcopal	1	NR	59	94	.2	.4
207 E.L.C.A.	16	2,167	880	2,831	5.7	13.4
226 Friends-USA	1	105	NR	128 *	.3	.6
286 E.PA Mennonite	1	69	NR	84 *	.2	.4
297 Mennonite;Other	1	35	NR	43 *	.1	.2
322 Old Ord Menn Ch	1	95	NR	116 *	.2	.5
355 Presb Ch (USA)	2	349	101	426 *	.9	2.0
413 S.D.A.	2	108	NR	129	.3	.6
419 So Bapt Conv	2	110	78	134 *	.3	.6
443 Un C of Christ	19	2,281	1,119	2,784 *	5.6	13.1

NR–Not Reported *Total adherents estimated from known number of communicant, confirmed, full members. - Represents a percentage less than 0.1. Percentages may not total 100 due to rounding.

Table 4: Religious Congregations by County and Group: 2000

Religious Group	Number of Churches, Synagogues, Mosques, or Temples	Number of Communicant, Confirmed, or Full Members	Number of Attendees	Total Adherents		
				Number of Adherents	% of Total Pop.	% of Total Adh.
449 Un Methodist	36	4,209	2,185	5,137 *	10.3	24.2
BERKS	**320**	**87,144**	**35,274**	**201,497 ***	**53.9**	**100.0**
019 Amer Bapt USA	2	359	120	443 *	.1	.2
053 Assemb of God	13	1,744	2,389	2,798	.7	1.4
056 Baha'i	0	42	NR	42	-	-
081 Catholic	24	NR	NR	80,542	21.6	40.0
097 Chr Chs&Chs Cr	1	53	NR	65 *	-	-
123 Ch God (Ander)	3	NR	172	172	-	.1
127 Ch God (Cleve)	5	1,090	1,094	1,383 *	.4	.7
143 CG in Cr(Menn)	1	97	NR	120 *	-	.1
151 L-D Saints	2	NR	NR	726	.2	.4
157 Ch of Brethren	4	862	540	1,080 *	.3	.5
165 Ch of Nazarene	4	429	372	641	.2	.3
167 Chs of Christ	4	186	208	260	.1	.1
179 Consrv Bapt	1	NR	350	350	.1	.2
193 Episcopal	7	NR	711	1,751	.5	.9
203 Evan Free Ch	2	199	370	370	.1	.2
207 E.L.C.A.	82	38,559	12,109	52,946	14.2	26.3
226 Friends-USA	1	105	NR	130 *	-	.1
246 Greek Orthodox	3	NR	NR	750	.2	.4
286 E.PA Mennonite	1	61	NR	75 *	-	-
288 Mennonite USA	22	1,764	2,149	2,733 *	.7	1.4
291 Missionary Ch	1	138	224	224	.1	.1
293 Morav Ch-North	1	115	NR	194	.1	.1
297 Mennonite;Other	8	376	NR	466 *	.1	.2
322 Old Ord Menn Ch	4	604	NR	746 *	.2	.4
323 Old Ord Amish	1	50	NR	62 *	-	-
331 OCA: Ter Diocs	1	105	NR	371	.1	.2
335 Orth Pres Ch	1	119	192	203	.1	.1
355 Presb Ch (USA)	4	1,223	559	1,510 *	.4	.7
397 OCA: Roman Dioc	1	NR	NR	25	-	-
400 Rus Orth Moscow	1	NR	NR	NR	-	-
403 Salvation Army	3	179	136	345	.1	.2
413 S.D.A.	8	1,197	NR	1,425	.4	.7
416 Sikh	1	NR	NR	NR	-	-
419 So Bapt Conv	3	373	345	461 *	.1	.2
435 Unitarian-Univ	1	120	NR	148 *	-	.1
443 Un C of Christ	71	29,658	10,130	36,637 *	9.8	18.2
449 Un Methodist	21	6,722	2,404	8,303 *	2.2	4.1
467 Wesleyan	1	0	0	0	-	-
496 Jewish Est	4	NR	NR	2,200	.6	1.1
499 Indep.Non-Char	2	615	700	800	.2	.4
BLAIR	**196**	**29,579**	**14,380**	**72,183 ***	**55.9**	**100.0**
017 Amer Bapt Assn	3	230	NR	278 *	.2	.4
019 Amer Bapt USA	2	402	164	486 *	.4	.7
034 Ant Orth of NA	1	150	NR	300	.2	.4
053 Assemb of God	5	923	1,198	1,556	1.2	2.2
056 Baha'i	0	27	NR	27	-	-
075 Brethren in Cr	4	226	299	299	.2	.4
081 Catholic	20	NR	NR	32,063	24.8	44.4
089 Chr & Miss Al	7	470	NR	932	.7	1.3
097 Chr Chs&Chs Cr	1	550	NR	664 *	.5	.9
127 Ch God (Cleve)	3	652	418	789 *	.6	1.1
151 L-D Saints	1	NR	NR	423	.3	.6
157 Ch of Brethren	20	3,676	1,457	4,438 *	3.4	6.1
167 Chs of Christ	1	100	100	120	.1	.2
171 Ch God-Gen Con	7	668	522	816 *	.6	1.1
179 Consrv Bapt	1	NR	200	200	.2	.3
193 Episcopal	3	NR	193	611	.5	.8
207 E.L.C.A.	24	6,920	2,252	9,553	7.4	13.2
226 Friends-USA	1	105	NR	127 *	.1	.2
246 Greek Orthodox	1	NR	NR	60	-	.1
288 Mennonite USA	5	272	208	342 *	.3	.5
291 Missionary Ch	3	135	242	242	.2	.3
322 Old Ord Menn Ch	2	245	NR	296 *	.2	.4
323 Old Ord Amish	1	55	NR	66 *	.1	.1
331 OCA: Ter Diocs	2	29	NR	53	-	.1
335 Orth Pres Ch	1	171	186	245	.2	.3
355 Presb Ch (USA)	9	1,568	688	1,895 *	1.5	2.6
403 Salvation Army	2	135	80	264	.2	.4
413 S.D.A.	1	44	NR	52	-	.1
419 So Bapt Conv	3	289	244	349 *	.3	.5
443 Un C of Christ	12	1,250	620	1,510 *	1.2	2.1
449 Un Methodist	44	9,237	4,020	11,156 *	8.6	15.5
467 Wesleyan	1	0	29	136	.1	.2
496 Jewish Est	2	NR	NR	575	.4	.8
499 Indep.Non-Char	3	1,050	1,260	1,260	1.0	1.7
BRADFORD	**120**	**12,796**	**6,176**	**25,666 ***	**40.9**	**100.0**
019 Amer Bapt USA	12	1,499	858	1,857 *	3.0	7.2
053 Assemb of God	2	107	154	185	.3	.7
056 Baha'i	0	8	NR	8	-	-
081 Catholic	8	NR	NR	7,384	11.8	28.8
089 Chr & Miss Al	2	30	NR	145	.2	.6
093 Chr Ch (Disc)	6	1,435	323	1,778 *	2.8	6.9
097 Chr Chs&Chs Cr	5	475	NR	589 *	.9	2.3
123 Ch God (Ander)	1	NR	62	62	.1	.2
151 L-D Saints	1	NR	NR	258	.4	1.0
175 Congr Chr Chs	1	19	98	24 *	-	.1
176 Congr Ad Afl	1	100	NR	124 *	.2	.5
179 Consrv Bapt	1	NR	50	50	.1	.2
181 Consrv Congr	1	50	49	62 *	.1	.2
193 Episcopal	4	NR	211	747	1.2	2.9
207 E.L.C.A.	3	658	241	893	1.4	3.5
288 Mennonite USA	3	140	146	178 *	.3	.7
297 Mennonite;Other	1	26	NR	32 *	.1	.1
323 Old Ord Amish	1	55	NR	68 *	.1	.3
355 Presb Ch (USA)	12	1,595	762	1,977 *	3.2	7.7
388 Reg Bapt Gen As	1	227	375	375 *	.6	1.5
413 S.D.A.	2	145	NR	173	.3	.7
419 So Bapt Conv	1	14	18	17 *	-	.1
435 Unitarian-Univ	2	60	NR	74 *	.1	.3
443 Un C of Christ	2	181	125	224 *	.4	.9
449 Un Methodist	41	5,418	1,860	6,717 *	10.7	26.2
467 Wesleyan	6	554	844	1,665	2.7	6.5
BUCKS	**315**	**63,774**	**34,431**	**394,668 ***	**66.0**	**100.0**
019 Amer Bapt USA	6	951	477	1,185 *	.2	.3
022 Carp Rus Orth	1	122	NR	207	-	.1
040 Ap Chr Ch-Amer	1	33	74	74 *	-	-
053 Assemb of God	11	1,478	1,950	4,240	.7	1.1
056 Baha'i	0	84	NR	84	-	-
071 Brethren (Ash)	1	43	37	54 *	-	-
075 Brethren in Cr	3	278	416	422	.1	.1
076 Buddhism	3	NR	NR	NR	-	-
081 Catholic	38	NR	NR	261,542	43.8	66.3
084 Calvary Chapel	1	NR	NR	NR	-	-
089 Chr & Miss Al	3	60	NR	132	-	-
093 Chr Ch (Disc)	1	100	55	125 *	-	-
097 Chr Chs&Chs Cr	2	236	NR	294 *	-	.1
123 Ch God (Ander)	2	NR	40	40	-	-
127 Ch God (Cleve)	2	258	142	321 *	.1	.1
145 Ch God Prophcy	1	41	NR	51 *	-	-
151 L-D Saints	2	NR	NR	786	.1	.2
157 Ch of Brethren	2	217	86	270 *	-	.1
165 Ch of Nazarene	3	148	92	205	-	.1
167 Chs of Christ	2	165	183	261	-	.1
173 Comm of Christ	1	88	NR	88	-	-
179 Consrv Bapt	6	NR	1,489	1,489	.2	.4
193 Episcopal	18	NR	2,182	6,323	1.1	1.6
203 Evan Free Ch	2	179	285	285	-	.1
207 E.L.C.A.	40	17,379	6,212	23,959	4.0	6.1
226 Friends-USA	13	1,365	NR	1,701 *	.3	.4
245 Greek Orth Vslp	1	700	NR	778	.1	.2
252 Hindu	1	NR	NR	NR	-	-
267 Muslim Est	1	NR	5	1,891	.3	.5
283 Luth—MO Synod	3	1,038	471	1,202	.2	.3
288 Mennonite USA	16	3,095	2,454	3,865 *	.6	1.0
297 Mennonite;Other	1	52	NR	65 *	-	-
313 N Am Bapt Conf	1	90	80	112 *	-	-
331 OCA: Ter Diocs	1	66	NR	491	.1	.1
335 Orth Pres Ch	2	289	524	524	.1	.1
355 Presb Ch (USA)	19	10,587	5,204	13,956 *	2.3	3.5
356 Presb Ch Amer	7	549	545	707	.1	.2

NR–Not Reported *Total adherents estimated from known number of communicant, confirmed, full members. - Represents a percentage less than 0.1. Percentages may not total 100 due to rounding.

Table 4: Religious Congregations by County and Group: 2000

Religious Group	Number of Churches, Synagogues, Mosques, or Temples	Number of Communicant, Confirmed, or Full Members	Number of Attendees	Total Adherents: Number of Adherents	Total Adherents: % of Total Pop.	Total Adherents: % of Total Adh.
363 Primitive Meth	2	114	NR	121	-	-
370 Ref Baptist Chs	1	NR	NR	NR	-	-
371 Ref Ch in Am	7	1,290	874	2,526	.4	.6
388 Reg Bapt Gen As	2	788	1,032	1,032 *	.2	.3
403 Salvation Army	1	89	58	228	-	.1
413 S.D.A.	1	168	NR	200	-	.1
418 Southw Bapt Fel	1	NR	NR	NR	-	-
419 So Bapt Conv	6	338	345	421 *	.1	.1
435 Unitarian-Univ	2	268	NR	334 *	.1	.1
443 Un C of Christ	22	6,712	2,380	8,366 *	1.4	2.1
449 Un Methodist	32	13,159	4,902	16,401 *	2.7	4.2
467 Wesleyan	1	0	42	92	-	-
496 Jewish Est	16	NR	NR	34,800	5.8	8.8
498 Indep.Charis.	1	450	450	450	.1	.1
499 Indep.Non-Char	2	707	1,345	1,968	.3	.5
BUTLER	**193**	**33,982**	**16,320**	**103,700 ***	**59.6**	**100.0**
011 A.W.M.C.	3	45	189	51	-	-
019 Amer Bapt USA	2	260	115	321 *	.2	.3
034 Ant Orth of NA	1	55	NR	110	.1	.1
053 Assemb of God	6	646	844	1,589	.9	1.5
056 Baha'i	0	5	NR	5	-	-
057 Bapt Gen Conf	1	30	90	90 *	.1	.1
071 Brethren (Ash)	1	33	64	41 *	-	-
081 Catholic	25	NR	NR	52,746	30.3	50.9
089 Chr & Miss Al	8	1,128	NR	4,031	2.3	3.9
093 Chr Ch (Disc)	2	236	120	291 *	.2	.3
097 Chr Chs&Chs Cr	2	460	NR	568 *	.3	.5
123 Ch God (Ander)	1	NR	505	505	.3	.5
145 Ch God Prophcy	3	123	NR	153 *	.1	.1
151 L-D Saints	3	NR	NR	1,042	.6	1.0
157 Ch of Brethren	1	85	0	105 *	.1	.1
165 Ch of Nazarene	3	218	176	292	.2	.3
167 Chs of Christ	2	52	70	75	-	.1
171 Ch God-Gen Con	1	56	50	69 *	-	.1
179 Consrv Bapt	1	NR	300	300	.2	.3
181 Consrv Congr	1	665	222	821 *	.5	.8
193 Episcopal	2	NR	169	527	.3	.5
203 Evan Free Ch	1	69	125	125	.1	.1
207 E.L.C.A.	20	7,745	2,687	11,065	6.4	10.7
216 Evan Presby Ch	1	117	NR	144 *	.1	.1
220 Free Lutheran	1	0	0	0	-	-
221 Free Methodist	1	34	61	61	-	.1
252 Hindu	1	NR	NR	NR	-	-
283 Luth—MO Synod	3	1,097	569	1,555	.9	1.5
331 OCA: Ter Diocs	1	122	NR	154	.1	.1
335 Orth Pres Ch	1	88	98	122	.1	.1
355 Presb Ch (USA)	44	9,089	5,034	11,225 *	6.4	10.8
356 Presb Ch Amer	4	1,209	737	1,471	.8	1.4
388 Reg Bapt Gen As	1	236	116	291 *	.2	.3
403 Salvation Army	1	112	54	381	.2	.4
413 S.D.A.	2	98	NR	117	.1	.1
419 So Bapt Conv	5	432	123	534 *	.3	.5
431 Ukrainian Orth	1	NR	NR	519	.3	.5
443 Un C of Christ	2	321	146	396 *	.2	.4
449 Un Methodist	32	9,116	3,590	11,258 *	6.5	10.9
467 Wesleyan	1	0	66	300	.2	.3
496 Jewish Est	1	NR	NR	250	.1	.2
CAMBRIA	**246**	**30,146**	**12,916**	**124,528 ***	**81.6**	**100.0**
011 A.W.M.C.	1	19	29	20	-	-
019 Amer Bapt USA	4	521	326	619 *	.4	.5
022 Carp Rus Orth	2	687	NR	1,168	.8	.9
034 Ant Orth of NA	1	293	NR	586	.4	.5
053 Assemb of God	6	271	262	591	.4	.5
056 Baha'i	0	8	NR	8	-	-
071 Brethren (Ash)	3	284	182	338 *	.2	.3
075 Brethren in Cr	1	4	17	17	-	-
081 Catholic	73	NR	NR	83,622	54.8	67.2
089 Chr & Miss Al	10	459	NR	1,051	.7	.8
093 Chr Ch (Disc)	3	333	187	395 *	.3	.3
097 Chr Chs&Chs Cr	2	163	NR	193 *	.1	.2
123 Ch God (Ander)	3	NR	191	191	.1	.2
127 Ch God (Cleve)	2	330	142	392 *	.3	.3
151 L-D Saints	1	NR	NR	392	.3	.3
157 Ch of Brethren	11	2,318	1,134	2,753 *	1.8	2.2
165 Ch of Nazarene	4	179	187	306	.2	.2
167 Chs of Christ	1	60	64	78	.1	.1
171 Ch God-Gen Con	2	82	167	167 *	.1	.1
193 Episcopal	3	NR	179	472	.3	.4
207 E.L.C.A.	18	6,270	2,096	7,907	5.2	6.3
246 Greek Orthodox	1	NR	NR	60	-	-
283 Luth—MO Synod	1	94	54	112	.1	.1
288 Mennonite USA	2	106	50	126 *	.1	.1
331 OCA: Ter Diocs	4	193	NR	222	.1	.2
335 Orth Pres Ch	1	30	40	40	-	-
355 Presb Ch (USA)	12	1,833	845	2,176 *	1.4	1.7
356 Presb Ch Amer	1	93	105	140	.1	.1
403 Salvation Army	1	117	88	285	.2	.2
411 Serb Orth: Grac	1	NR	NR	NR	-	-
413 S.D.A.	1	113	NR	134	.1	.1
419 So Bapt Conv	2	283	134	336 *	.2	.3
431 Ukrainian Orth	3	NR	NR	396	.3	.3
443 Un C of Christ	6	703	259	835 *	.5	.7
449 Un Methodist	57	14,300	5,028	16,975 *	11.1	13.6
496 Jewish Est	1	NR	NR	275	.2	.2
499 Indep.Non-Char	1	0	1,150	1,150	.8	.9
CAMERON	**15**	**1,275**	**615**	**3,374 ***	**56.5**	**100.0**
019 Amer Bapt USA	1	138	60	167 *	2.8	4.9
081 Catholic	2	NR	NR	1,580	26.4	46.8
089 Chr & Miss Al	1	52	NR	127	2.1	3.8
193 Episcopal	1	NR	36	86	1.4	2.5
207 E.L.C.A.	2	85	32	122	2.0	3.6
221 Free Methodist	1	23	56	56	.9	1.7
355 Presb Ch (USA)	1	157	85	191 *	3.2	5.7
419 So Bapt Conv	2	196	82	238 *	4.0	7.1
449 Un Methodist	3	588	230	713 *	11.9	21.1
467 Wesleyan	1	36	34	94	1.6	2.8
CARBON	**93**	**12,545**	**4,454**	**37,356 ***	**63.5**	**100.0**
019 Amer Bapt USA	2	45	39	54 *	.1	.1
022 Carp Rus Orth	2	243	NR	416	.7	1.1
081 Catholic	23	NR	NR	19,829	33.7	53.1
084 Calvary Chapel	1	NR	NR	NR	-	-
123 Ch God (Ander)	1	NR	15	15	-	-
151 L-D Saints	2	NR	NR	265	.5	.7
157 Ch of Brethren	1	51	53	61 *	.1	.2
167 Chs of Christ	1	9	9	9	-	-
193 Episcopal	3	NR	241	797	1.4	2.1
203 Evan Free Ch	1	270	385	385	.7	1.0
207 E.L.C.A.	23	6,367	1,717	8,741	14.9	23.4
246 Greek Orthodox	1	NR	NR	0	-	-
355 Presb Ch (USA)	3	418	123	501 *	.9	1.3
400 Rus Orth Moscow	1	NR	NR	NR	-	-
443 Un C of Christ	17	3,875	1,236	4,647 *	7.9	12.4
449 Un Methodist	10	1,267	581	1,520 *	2.6	4.1
467 Wesleyan	1	0	55	116	.2	.3
CENTRE	**178**	**26,026**	**13,373**	**58,109 ***	**42.8**	**100.0**
011 A.W.M.C.	1	0	0	0	-	-
019 Amer Bapt USA	3	720	315	836 *	.6	1.4
053 Assemb of God	3	740	1,014	1,565	1.2	2.7
056 Baha'i	1	35	NR	35	-	.1
057 Bapt Gen Conf	1	188	615	615 *	.5	1.1
075 Brethren in Cr	3	130	142	176	.1	.3
081 Catholic	8	NR	NR	21,240	15.6	36.6
089 Chr & Miss Al	7	507	NR	1,125	.8	1.9
097 Chr Chs&Chs Cr	4	1,286	NR	1,493 *	1.1	2.6
127 Ch God (Cleve)	1	100	45	116 *	.1	.2
151 L-D Saints	3	NR	NR	647	.5	1.1
157 Ch of Brethren	1	484	149	562 *	.4	1.0
165 Ch of Nazarene	1	112	132	180	.1	.3
167 Chs of Christ	5	146	196	213	.2	.4
179 Consrv Bapt	3	NR	562	562	.4	1.0
193 Episcopal	3	NR	465	1,095	.8	1.9

NR–Not Reported *Total adherents estimated from known number of communicant, confirmed, full members. - Represents a percentage less than 0.1. Percentages may not total 100 due to rounding.

Table 4: Religious Congregations by County and Group: 2000

Religious Group	Number of Churches, Synagogues, Mosques, or Temples	Number of Communicant, Confirmed, or Full Members	Number of Attendees	Total Adherents		
				Number of Adherents	% of Total Pop.	% of Total Adh.
203 Evan Free Ch	1	90	200	200	.1	.3
207 E.L.C.A.	19	5,121	2,117	6,684	4.9	11.5
221 Free Methodist	4	147	158	162	.1	.3
226 Friends-USA	1	105	NR	122 *	.1	.2
267 Muslim Est	1	NR	150	400	.3	.7
283 Luth—MO Synod	1	76	70	100	.1	.2
288 Mennonite USA	1	71	118	118 *	.1	.2
297 Mennonite;Other	1	28	NR	33 *	-	.1
323 Old Ord Amish	10	710	NR	824 *	.6	1.4
331 OCA: Ter Diocs	2	118	NR	143	.1	.2
355 Presb Ch (USA)	9	2,144	1,039	2,491 *	1.8	4.3
356 Presb Ch Amer	2	148	229	244	.2	.4
370 Ref Baptist Chs	1	NR	NR	NR	-	-
388 Reg Bapt Gen As	1	50	120	58 *	-	.1
413 S.D.A.	1	65	NR	77	.1	.1
419 So Bapt Conv	2	30	26	35 *	-	.1
435 Unitarian-Univ	1	238	NR	276 *	.2	.5
443 Un C of Christ	17	2,366	1,024	2,748 *	2.0	4.7
449 Un Methodist	50	9,819	4,224	11,407 *	8.4	19.6
467 Wesleyan	3	252	263	827	.6	1.4
496 Jewish Est	2	NR	NR	700	.5	1.2
CHESTER	**311**	**55,957**	**30,870**	**240,800 ***	**55.5**	**100.0**
017 Amer Bapt Assn	1	50	NR	63 *	-	-
019 Amer Bapt USA	19	5,258	3,122	6,611 *	1.5	2.7
022 Carp Rus Orth	1	122	NR	207	-	.1
032 Amish; other	2	170	NR	213 *	-	.1
053 Assemb of God	8	1,050	1,062	1,784	.4	.7
056 Baha'i	1	108	NR	108	-	-
075 Brethren in Cr	1	47	98	98	-	-
081 Catholic	31	NR	NR	140,577	32.4	58.4
084 Calvary Chapel	1	NR	NR	NR	-	-
089 Chr & Miss Al	2	116	NR	219	.1	.1
097 Chr Chs&Chs Cr	1	55	NR	69 *	-	-
127 Ch God (Cleve)	4	272	156	341 *	.1	.1
151 L-D Saints	5	NR	NR	1,801	.4	.7
157 Ch of Brethren	4	568	531	714 *	.2	.3
165 Ch of Nazarene	4	529	414	720	.2	.3
167 Chs of Christ	6	351	375	463	.1	.2
179 Consrv Bapt	1	NR	40	40	-	-
193 Episcopal	16	NR	2,593	8,252	1.9	3.4
203 Evan Free Ch	3	240	548	548	.1	.2
207 E.L.C.A.	16	7,598	3,199	10,906	2.5	4.5
226 Friends-USA	21	2,205	NR	2,773 *	.6	1.2
262 Int Cou Comm Ch	1	190	NR	239 *	.1	.1
263 Int Foursq Gos	1	108	21	136 *	-	.1
267 Muslim Est	4	NR	1,326	5,823	1.3	2.4
283 Luth—MO Synod	2	251	208	335	.1	.1
286 E.PA Mennonite	1	100	NR	126 *	-	.1
288 Mennonite USA	18	1,423	1,322	1,898 *	.4	.8
297 Mennonite;Other	4	401	NR	503 *	.1	.2
323 Old Ord Amish	12	900	NR	1,128 *	.3	.5
331 OCA: Ter Diocs	1	27	NR	335	.1	.1
335 Orth Pres Ch	2	277	337	366	.1	.2
355 Presb Ch (USA)	31	12,739	6,272	16,019 *	3.7	6.7
356 Presb Ch Amer	4	573	791	944	.2	.4
363 Primitive Meth	1	57	NR	61	-	-
370 Ref Baptist Chs	2	NR	NR	NR	-	-
401 Rus Orth Abroad	1	NR	NR	NR	-	-
403 Salvation Army	1	39	81	220	.1	.1
413 S.D.A.	2	255	NR	303	.1	.1
418 Southw Bapt Fel	2	NR	NR	NR	-	-
419 So Bapt Conv	6	640	455	805 *	.2	.3
431 Ukrainian Orth	1	NR	NR	369	.1	.2
435 Unitarian-Univ	3	892	NR	1,122 *	.3	.5
443 Un C of Christ	13	3,604	1,400	4,532 *	1.0	1.9
449 Un Methodist	44	14,022	5,664	17,629 *	4.1	7.3
467 Wesleyan	1	0	0	0	-	-
496 Jewish Est	3	NR	NR	10,100	2.3	4.2
499 Indep.Non-Char	2	720	855	1,300	.3	.5
CLARION	**101**	**9,893**	**5,781**	**20,324 ***	**48.7**	**100.0**
011 A.W.M.C.	2	58	177	76	.2	.4
019 Amer Bapt USA	2	200	195	239 *	.6	1.2
053 Assemb of God	1	76	110	125	.3	.6
056 Baha'i	0	5	NR	5	-	-
081 Catholic	8	NR	NR	6,962	16.7	34.3
089 Chr & Miss Al	2	66	NR	162	.4	.8
123 Ch God (Ander)	5	NR	589	589	1.4	2.9
127 Ch God (Cleve)	1	94	100	113 *	.3	.6
145 Ch God Prophcy	4	164	NR	196 *	.5	1.0
151 L-D Saints	1	NR	NR	122	.3	.6
157 Ch of Brethren	1	56	35	67 *	.2	.3
165 Ch of Nazarene	5	276	209	450	1.1	2.2
167 Chs of Christ	1	45	75	75	.2	.4
179 Consrv Bapt	1	NR	99	99	.2	.5
193 Episcopal	1	NR	18	47	.1	.2
207 E.L.C.A.	7	1,076	465	1,516	3.6	7.5
221 Free Methodist	2	46	75	75	.2	.4
297 Mennonite;Other	1	42	NR	50 *	.1	.2
323 Old Ord Amish	1	55	NR	66 *	.2	.3
355 Presb Ch (USA)	13	1,652	853	1,979 *	4.7	9.7
388 Reg Bapt Gen As	1	100	125	125 *	.3	.6
413 S.D.A.	1	43	NR	51	.1	.3
419 So Bapt Conv	1	804	535	962 *	2.3	4.7
443 Un C of Christ	5	570	242	682 *	1.6	3.4
449 Un Methodist	33	4,432	1,837	5,305 *	12.7	26.1
467 Wesleyan	1	33	42	186	.4	.9
CLEARFIELD	**194**	**17,524**	**9,279**	**43,004 ***	**51.6**	**100.0**
019 Amer Bapt USA	1	177	80	214 *	.3	.5
022 Carp Rus Orth	1	122	NR	207	.2	.5
053 Assemb of God	5	363	445	526	.6	1.2
056 Baha'i	0	1	NR	1	-	-
057 Bapt Gen Conf	1	55	50	66 *	.1	.2
081 Catholic	19	NR	NR	18,207	21.8	42.3
089 Chr & Miss Al	12	1,072	NR	2,196	2.6	5.1
123 Ch God (Ander)	2	NR	635	635	.8	1.5
127 Ch God (Cleve)	1	15	25	25 *	-	.1
151 L-D Saints	2	NR	NR	392	.5	.9
157 Ch of Brethren	3	109	111	133 *	.2	.3
165 Ch of Nazarene	3	220	186	281	.3	.7
167 Chs of Christ	8	226	250	285	.3	.7
171 Ch God-Gen Con	4	174	198	221 *	.3	.5
173 Comm of Christ	1	13	NR	13	-	-
179 Consrv Bapt	1	NR	120	120	.1	.3
193 Episcopal	5	NR	160	386	.5	.9
201 Evan Cov Ch	1	107	90	129 *	.2	.3
203 Evan Free Ch	2	93	170	170	.2	.4
207 E.L.C.A.	12	2,547	908	3,255	3.9	7.6
221 Free Methodist	2	33	64	64	.1	.1
226 Friends-USA	1	105	NR	127 *	.2	.3
283 Luth—MO Synod	2	220	79	277	.3	.6
313 N Am Bapt Conf	1	33	20	40 *	-	.1
323 Old Ord Amish	2	110	NR	132 *	.2	.3
331 OCA: Ter Diocs	4	199	NR	215	.3	.5
355 Presb Ch (USA)	15	1,969	1,006	2,399 *	2.9	5.6
363 Primitive Meth	2	114	NR	121	.1	.3
388 Reg Bapt Gen As	1	124	139	150 *	.2	.3
403 Salvation Army	2	151	109	398	.5	.9
413 S.D.A.	1	19	NR	23	-	.1
419 So Bapt Conv	1	116	103	140 *	.2	.3
431 Ukrainian Orth	1	NR	NR	90	.1	.2
443 Un C of Christ	4	248	112	300 *	.4	.7
449 Un Methodist	68	8,688	4,045	10,496 *	12.6	24.4
467 Wesleyan	2	101	174	370	.4	.9
496 Jewish Est	1	NR	NR	200	.2	.5
CLINTON	**80**	**8,124**	**3,412**	**15,287 ***	**40.3**	**100.0**
053 Assemb of God	2	98	76	97	.3	.6
056 Baha'i	0	1	NR	1	-	-
075 Brethren in Cr	1	123	154	154	.4	1.0
081 Catholic	3	NR	NR	4,544	12.0	29.7
089 Chr & Miss Al	1	20	NR	20	.1	.1
097 Chr Chs&Chs Cr	4	647	NR	774 *	2.0	5.1
151 L-D Saints	1	NR	NR	130	.3	.9

NR–Not Reported *Total adherents estimated from known number of communicant, confirmed, full members. - Represents a percentage less than 0.1. Percentages may not total 100 due to rounding.

Table 4: Religious Congregations by County and Group: 2000

Religious Group	Number of Churches, Synagogues, Mosques, or Temples	Number of Communicant, Confirmed, or Full Members	Number of Attendees	Total Adherents		
				Number of Adherents	% of Total Pop.	% of Total Adh.
157 Ch of Brethren	1	89	0	106 *	.3	.7
165 Ch of Nazarene	1	0	0	0	-	-
167 Chs of Christ	4	75	89	101	.3	.7
193 Episcopal	2	NR	75	196	.5	1.3
207 E.L.C.A.	8	1,180	351	1,541	4.1	10.1
221 Free Methodist	1	53	55	59	.2	.4
288 Mennonite USA	1	56	45	67 *	.2	.4
297 Mennonite;Other	1	15	NR	18 *	-	.1
323 Old Ord Amish	6	450	NR	540 *	1.4	3.5
355 Presb Ch (USA)	3	357	180	427 *	1.1	2.8
403 Salvation Army	1	145	101	351	.9	2.3
413 S.D.A.	1	52	NR	62	.2	.4
419 So Bapt Conv	1	51	230	61 *	.2	.4
443 Un C of Christ	4	748	254	894 *	2.4	5.8
449 Un Methodist	28	3,725	1,506	4,453 *	11.7	29.1
467 Wesleyan	4	239	296	591	1.6	3.9
496 Jewish Est	1	NR	NR	100	.3	.7
COLUMBIA	**111**	**17,171**	**6,935**	**30,449 ***	**47.5**	**100.0**
019 Amer Bapt USA	2	605	253	718 *	1.1	2.4
053 Assemb of God	4	317	426	530	.8	1.7
056 Baha'i	0	8	NR	8	-	-
081 Catholic	7	NR	NR	8,142	12.7	26.7
089 Chr & Miss Al	1	68	NR	225	.4	.7
093 Chr Ch (Disc)	3	526	178	625 *	1.0	2.1
097 Chr Chs&Chs Cr	6	1,022	NR	1,214 *	1.9	4.0
151 L-D Saints	1	NR	NR	348	.5	1.1
165 Ch of Nazarene	1	108	101	180	.3	.6
173 Comm of Christ	1	196	NR	196	.3	.6
179 Consrv Bapt	1	NR	25	25	-	.1
193 Episcopal	3	NR	184	505	.8	1.7
207 E.L.C.A.	14	4,129	1,189	5,594	8.7	18.4
226 Friends-USA	1	105	NR	125 *	.2	.4
283 Luth—MO Synod	1	13	17	17	-	.1
355 Presb Ch (USA)	5	584	271	693 *	1.1	2.3
370 Ref Baptist Chs	1	NR	NR	NR	-	-
403 Salvation Army	1	118	62	243	.4	.8
413 S.D.A.	1	77	NR	92	.1	.3
418 Southw Bapt Fel	1	NR	NR	NR	-	-
419 So Bapt Conv	2	170	113	202 *	.3	.7
443 Un C of Christ	10	1,397	556	1,659 *	2.6	5.4
449 Un Methodist	43	7,248	3,085	8,608 *	13.4	28.3
499 Indep.Non-Char	1	480	475	500	.8	1.6
CRAWFORD	**173**	**17,131**	**8,817**	**36,728 ***	**40.6**	**100.0**
011 A.W.M.C.	3	105	356	108	.1	.3
019 Amer Bapt USA	10	1,579	1,095	1,938 *	2.1	5.3
032 Amish; other	3	180	NR	222 *	.2	.6
053 Assemb of God	2	190	239	250	.3	.7
056 Baha'i	0	8	NR	8	-	-
057 Bapt Gen Conf	1	62	66	76 *	.1	.2
061 Beachy Amish	1	33	NR	41 *	-	.1
081 Catholic	16	NR	NR	13,030	14.4	35.5
089 Chr & Miss Al	7	372	NR	942	1.0	2.6
097 Chr Chs&Chs Cr	4	630	NR	775 *	.9	2.1
123 Ch God (Ander)	4	NR	955	955	1.1	2.6
151 L-D Saints	1	NR	NR	351	.4	1.0
165 Ch of Nazarene	4	263	208	518	.6	1.4
167 Chs of Christ	2	55	50	63	.1	.2
173 Comm of Christ	1	41	NR	41	-	.1
175 Congr Chr Chs	2	85	95	104 *	.1	.3
193 Episcopal	2	NR	133	353	.4	1.0
203 Evan Free Ch	2	298	290	348	.4	.9
207 E.L.C.A.	6	1,245	377	1,727	1.9	4.7
221 Free Methodist	3	119	240	240	.3	.7
262 Int Cou Comm Ch	1	109	NR	134 *	.1	.4
286 E.PA Mennonite	1	66	NR	81 *	.1	.2
288 Mennonite USA	3	164	168	225 *	.2	.6
297 Mennonite;Other	5	260	NR	319 *	.4	.9
323 Old Ord Amish	23	1,265	NR	1,564 *	1.7	4.3
355 Presb Ch (USA)	13	2,900	1,199	3,561 *	3.9	9.7
403 Salvation Army	1	60	31	109	.1	.3
419 So Bapt Conv	1	21	120	26 *	-	.1

Religious Group	Number of Churches, Synagogues, Mosques, or Temples	Number of Communicant, Confirmed, or Full Members	Number of Attendees	Total Adherents		
				Number of Adherents	% of Total Pop.	% of Total Adh.
435 Unitarian-Univ	1	150	NR	184 *	.2	.5
443 Un C of Christ	6	792	349	972 *	1.1	2.6
449 Un Methodist	44	6,079	2,846	7,463 *	8.3	20.3
CUMBERLAND	**247**	**59,284**	**33,580**	**117,408 ***	**54.9**	**100.0**
019 Amer Bapt USA	1	298	215	358 *	.2	.3
053 Assemb of God	9	2,597	2,991	3,550	1.7	3.0
056 Baha'i	0	28	NR	28	-	-
075 Brethren in Cr	13	2,729	2,914	3,184	1.5	2.7
081 Catholic	8	NR	NR	35,271	16.5	30.0
089 Chr & Miss Al	9	751	NR	1,426	.7	1.2
093 Chr Ch (Disc)	1	388	79	467 *	.2	.4
097 Chr Chs&Chs Cr	1	300	NR	361 *	.2	.3
123 Ch God (Ander)	1	NR	35	35	-	-
127 Ch God (Cleve)	5	811	487	975 *	.5	.8
143 CG in Cr(Menn)	1	73	NR	88 *	-	.1
145 Ch God Prophcy	1	41	NR	49 *	-	-
151 L-D Saints	2	NR	NR	911	.4	.8
157 Ch of Brethren	7	1,238	569	1,488 *	.7	1.3
165 Ch of Nazarene	3	317	346	583	.3	.5
167 Chs of Christ	4	376	379	435	.2	.4
171 Ch God-Gen Con	23	4,006	3,131	4,913 *	2.3	4.2
179 Consrv Bapt	2	NR	60	60	-	.1
193 Episcopal	4	NR	803	2,133	1.0	1.8
203 Evan Free Ch	2	504	1,190	1,190	.6	1.0
207 E.L.C.A.	29	13,708	5,033	17,815	8.3	15.2
221 Free Methodist	1	63	97	97	-	.1
226 Friends-USA	1	105	NR	126 *	.1	.1
246 Greek Orthodox	1	NR	NR	1,500	.7	1.3
251 Holy Orth in NA	2	NR	NR	182	.1	.2
252 Hindu	1	NR	NR	NR	-	-
283 Luth—MO Synod	1	229	0	312	.1	.3
286 E.PA Mennonite	2	109	NR	131 *	.1	.1
288 Mennonite USA	3	225	253	284 *	.1	.2
297 Mennonite;Other	4	277	NR	334 *	.2	.3
322 Old Ord Menn Ch	4	490	NR	588 *	.3	.5
323 Old Ord Amish	6	410	NR	492 *	.2	.4
339 Pent Ch of God	1	18	NR	38	-	-
355 Presb Ch (USA)	15	6,527	3,076	7,848 *	3.7	6.7
356 Presb Ch Amer	3	510	650	720	.3	.6
370 Ref Baptist Chs	1	NR	NR	NR	-	-
379 Ref Mennonite	1	30	NR	36 *	-	-
403 Salvation Army	1	153	125	710	.3	.6
413 S.D.A.	1	74	NR	88	-	.1
416 Sikh	1	NR	NR	NR	-	-
419 So Bapt Conv	6	1,037	676	1,247 *	.6	1.1
435 Unitarian-Univ	1	129	NR	155 *	.1	.1
443 Un C of Christ	8	2,328	1,010	2,799 *	1.3	2.4
449 Un Methodist	50	17,869	8,824	21,481 *	10.1	18.3
467 Wesleyan	3	136	162	445	.2	.4
496 Jewish Est	2	NR	NR	2,000	.9	1.7
499 Indep.Non-Char	1	400	475	475	.2	.4
DAUPHIN	**275**	**54,712**	**29,823**	**124,745 ***	**49.5**	**100.0**
019 Amer Bapt USA	6	1,434	891	1,768 *	.7	1.4
053 Assemb of God	8	808	980	1,518	.6	1.2
056 Baha'i	1	45	NR	45	-	-
075 Brethren in Cr	7	707	1,159	1,190	.5	1.0
078 Bulgar Orth USA	1	NR	NR	220	.1	.2
081 Catholic	17	NR	NR	41,449	16.5	33.2
089 Chr & Miss Al	6	458	NR	795	.3	.6
123 Ch God (Ander)	3	NR	130	130	.1	.1
127 Ch God (Cleve)	1	104	33	128 *	.1	.1
145 Ch God Prophcy	1	41	NR	50 *	-	-
151 L-D Saints	3	NR	NR	1,168	.5	.9
157 Ch of Brethren	7	1,273	806	1,569 *	.6	1.3
165 Ch of Nazarene	3	316	256	517	.2	.4
167 Chs of Christ	2	170	190	245	.1	.2
171 Ch God-Gen Con	17	2,645	1,669	3,268 *	1.3	2.6
173 Comm of Christ	1	29	NR	29	-	-
193 Episcopal	6	NR	842	2,186	.9	1.8
203 Evan Free Ch	4	1,318	3,201	3,201	1.3	2.6
207 E.L.C.A.	40	12,672	4,519	16,551	6.6	13.3

NR–Not Reported *Total adherents estimated from known number of communicant, confirmed, full members. - Represents a percentage less than 0.1. Percentages may not total 100 due to rounding.

Table 4: Religious Congregations by County and Group: 2000

Religious Group	Number of Churches, Synagogues, Mosques, or Temples	Number of Communicant, Confirmed, or Full Members	Number of Attendees	Total Adherents: Number of Adherents	Total Adherents: % of Total Pop.	Total Adherents: % of Total Adh.
226 Friends-USA	1	105	NR	129 *	.1	.1
252 Hindu	1	NR	NR	NR	-	-
263 Int Foursq Gos	2	47	99	99 *	-	.1
264 Int Chs of Crst	1	105	158	154	.1	.1
267 Muslim Est	3	NR	332	1,827	.7	1.5
288 Mennonite USA	9	418	417	556 *	.2	.4
290 Metro Comm Ch	1	135	144	166 *	.1	.1
297 Mennonite;Other	1	64	NR	79 *	-	.1
323 Old Ord Amish	4	300	NR	368 *	.1	.3
331 OCA: Ter Diocs	2	301	NR	480	.2	.4
335 Orth Pres Ch	1	90	90	109	-	.1
355 Presb Ch (USA)	10	4,546	1,856	5,604 *	2.2	4.5
356 Presb Ch Amer	2	280	385	385	.2	.3
403 Salvation Army	2	236	119	615	.2	.5
410 Serb Orth USA	1	NR	NR	600	.2	.5
413 S.D.A.	5	669	NR	796	.3	.6
419 So Bapt Conv	7	2,016	943	2,485 *	1.0	2.0
435 Unitarian-Univ	1	232	NR	286 *	.1	.2
443 Un C of Christ	17	4,794	1,795	5,910 *	2.3	4.7
449 Un Methodist	60	17,582	7,959	21,674 *	8.6	17.4
467 Wesleyan	2	0	97	582	.2	.5
469 WELS	1	122	73	134	.1	.1
496 Jewish Est	5	NR	NR	5,000	2.0	4.0
499 Indep.Non-Char	2	650	680	680	.3	.5
DELAWARE	**331**	**47,068**	**29,215**	**371,328 ***	**67.4**	**100.0**
019 Amer Bapt USA	19	5,144	2,822	6,360 *	1.2	1.7
034 Ant Orth of NA	1	100	NR	200	-	.1
053 Assemb of God	8	557	686	935	.2	.3
056 Baha'i	1	139	NR	139	-	-
076 Buddhism	3	NR	NR	NR	-	-
081 Catholic	48	NR	NR	269,585	48.9	72.6
084 Calvary Chapel	1	NR	NR	NR	-	-
089 Chr & Miss Al	3	77	NR	139	-	-
093 Chr Ch (Disc)	1	122	63	151 *	-	-
097 Chr Chs&Chs Cr	2	175	NR	216 *	-	.1
105 Christian Ref	1	103	80	127 *	-	-
123 Ch God (Ander)	1	NR	32	32	-	-
127 Ch God (Cleve)	2	123	68	152 *	-	-
151 L-D Saints	2	NR	NR	821	.1	.2
157 Ch of Brethren	2	153	45	203 *	-	.1
165 Ch of Nazarene	2	231	226	284	.1	.1
167 Chs of Christ	5	235	261	330	.1	.1
175 Congr Chr Chs	1	60	50	74 *	-	-
179 Consrv Bapt	1	NR	220	220	-	.1
193 Episcopal	35	NR	3,817	12,325	2.2	3.3
207 E.L.C.A.	22	5,368	2,087	7,315	1.3	2.0
226 Friends-USA	16	1,680	NR	2,077 *	.4	.6
246 Greek Orthodox	3	NR	NR	3,456	.6	.9
267 Muslim Est	4	NR	1,648	7,564	1.4	2.0
283 Luth—MO Synod	3	412	207	530	.1	.1
288 Mennonite USA	5	339	314	419 *	.1	.1
331 OCA: Ter Diocs	1	98	NR	490	.1	.1
335 Orth Pres Ch	2	36	55	57	-	-
355 Presb Ch (USA)	38	11,928	5,490	14,746 *	2.7	4.0
356 Presb Ch Amer	7	1,095	1,010	1,408	.3	.4
370 Ref Baptist Chs	1	NR	NR	NR	-	-
388 Reg Bapt Gen As	4	716	829	901 *	.2	.2
400 Rus Orth Moscow	1	NR	NR	NR	-	-
403 Salvation Army	2	103	102	540	.1	.1
413 S.D.A.	3	431	NR	513	.1	.1
416 Sikh	1	NR	NR	NR	-	-
418 Southw Bapt Fel	2	NR	NR	NR	-	-
419 So Bapt Conv	4	395	414	488 *	.1	.1
425 Tao	1	NR	NR	NR	-	-
431 Ukrainian Orth	1	NR	NR	750	.1	.2
435 Unitarian-Univ	1	265	NR	328 *	.1	.1
443 Un C of Christ	3	456	176	564 *	.1	.2
449 Un Methodist	49	13,771	4,574	17,024 *	3.1	4.6
463 Vineyard	1	56	100	100 *	-	-
467 Wesleyan	2	0	149	375	.1	.1
490 Zoroastrian	1	NR	NR	NR	-	-
496 Jewish Est	9	NR	NR	15,700	2.9	4.2
499 Indep.Non-Char	5	2,700	3,690	3,690	.7	1.0

Religious Group	Number of Churches, Synagogues, Mosques, or Temples	Number of Communicant, Confirmed, or Full Members	Number of Attendees	Total Adherents: Number of Adherents	Total Adherents: % of Total Pop.	Total Adherents: % of Total Adh.
ELK	**44**	**4,178**	**1,845**	**28,674 ***	**81.7**	**100.0**
019 Amer Bapt USA	1	114	50	139 *	.4	.5
053 Assemb of God	1	66	90	155	.4	.5
056 Baha'i	0	4	NR	4	-	-
081 Catholic	11	NR	NR	22,695	64.6	79.1
089 Chr & Miss Al	2	80	NR	169	.5	.6
097 Chr Chs&Chs Cr	1	70	NR	85 *	.2	.3
151 L-D Saints	1	NR	NR	121	.3	.4
165 Ch of Nazarene	1	42	37	59	.2	.2
193 Episcopal	2	NR	76	180	.5	.6
201 Evan Cov Ch	1	81	68	99 *	.3	.3
207 E.L.C.A.	5	1,074	310	1,522	4.3	5.3
355 Presb Ch (USA)	4	358	194	437 *	1.2	1.5
419 So Bapt Conv	1	37	0	45 *	.1	.2
443 Un C of Christ	1	450	198	548 *	1.6	1.9
449 Un Methodist	11	1,694	690	2,066 *	5.9	7.2
467 Wesleyan	1	108	132	350	1.0	1.2
ERIE	**260**	**38,624**	**20,363**	**165,161 ***	**58.8**	**100.0**
011 A.W.M.C.	4	51	194	55	-	-
017 Amer Bapt Assn	2	80	NR	99 *	-	.1
019 Amer Bapt USA	10	1,830	1,576	2,261 *	.8	1.4
022 Carp Rus Orth	1	122	NR	207	.1	.1
039 Ap Chr Ch(Naz)	1	35	40	43 *	-	-
050 Armen Ap Etchm	1	0	NR	160	.1	.1
053 Assemb of God	10	2,252	2,776	4,674	1.7	2.8
056 Baha'i	0	27	NR	27	-	-
057 Bapt Gen Conf	3	506	830	830 *	.3	.5
081 Catholic	42	NR	NR	103,333	36.8	62.6
089 Chr & Miss Al	11	1,387	NR	3,426	1.2	2.1
093 Chr Ch (Disc)	1	136	34	168 *	.1	.1
123 Ch God (Ander)	4	NR	247	247	.1	.1
127 Ch God (Cleve)	2	624	348	771 *	.3	.5
145 Ch God Prophcy	2	82	NR	102 *	-	.1
151 L-D Saints	3	NR	NR	843	.3	.5
157 Ch of Brethren	1	156	0	193 *	.1	.1
165 Ch of Nazarene	7	619	456	921	.3	.6
167 Chs of Christ	1	100	100	113	-	.1
173 Comm of Christ	1	44	NR	44	-	-
193 Episcopal	10	NR	779	1,691	.6	1.0
201 Evan Cov Ch	1	58	41	72 *	-	-
203 Evan Free Ch	2	119	175	175	.1	.1
207 E.L.C.A.	24	8,320	2,477	12,395	4.4	7.5
221 Free Methodist	4	94	110	130	-	.1
246 Greek Orthodox	1	NR	NR	120	-	.1
263 Int Foursq Gos	1	12	49	49 *	-	-
267 Muslim Est	1	NR	7	25	-	-
283 Luth—MO Synod	4	681	369	870	.3	.5
288 Mennonite USA	1	131	111	162 *	.1	.1
297 Mennonite;Other	1	44	NR	54 *	-	-
313 N Am Bapt Conf	1	52	31	64 *	-	-
323 Old Ord Amish	2	110	NR	136 *	-	.1
331 OCA: Ter Diocs	1	10	NR	62	-	-
355 Presb Ch (USA)	22	5,795	2,814	7,160 *	2.5	4.3
356 Presb Ch Amer	2	53	89	101	-	.1
370 Ref Baptist Chs	1	NR	NR	NR	-	-
388 Reg Bapt Gen As	8	823	905	1,046 *	.4	.6
400 Rus Orth Moscow	1	NR	NR	NR	-	-
401 Rus Orth Abroad	2	NR	NR	NR	-	-
403 Salvation Army	2	176	132	4,066	1.4	2.5
413 S.D.A.	4	302	NR	359	.1	.2
419 So Bapt Conv	4	368	257	455 *	.2	.3
435 Unitarian-Univ	2	124	NR	153 *	.1	.1
443 Un C of Christ	2	257	138	318 *	.1	.2
449 Un Methodist	46	13,015	5,237	16,084 *	5.7	9.7
467 Wesleyan	1	29	41	47	-	-
496 Jewish Est	2	NR	NR	850	.3	.5
FAYETTE	**242**	**27,571**	**11,303**	**71,398 ***	**48.0**	**100.0**
011 A.W.M.C.	2	27	115	27	-	-
017 Amer Bapt Assn	2	80	NR	96 *	.1	.1
019 Amer Bapt USA	11	3,045	1,017	3,683 *	2.5	5.2
053 Assemb of God	5	688	881	1,194	.8	1.7

NR–Not Reported *Total adherents estimated from known number of communicant, confirmed, full members. - Represents a percentage less than 0.1. Percentages may not total 100 due to rounding.

Table 4: Religious Congregations by County and Group: 2000

Religious Group	Number of Churches, Synagogues, Mosques, or Temples	Number of Communicant, Confirmed, or Full Members	Number of Attendees	Total Adherents		
				Number of Adherents	% of Total Pop.	% of Total Adh.
056 Baha'i	0	8	NR	8	-	-
070 Bruderhof Comm	2	264	NR	264	.2	.4
071 Brethren (Ash)	1	98	85	119 *	.1	.2
081 Catholic	35	NR	NR	35,648	24.0	49.9
089 Chr & Miss Al	7	439	NR	1,200	.8	1.7
093 Chr Ch (Disc)	6	2,218	553	2,682 *	1.8	3.8
097 Chr Chs&Chs Cr	8	983	NR	1,188 *	.8	1.7
123 Ch God (Ander)	2	NR	170	170	.1	.2
127 Ch God (Cleve)	5	470	245	574 *	.4	.8
145 Ch God Prophcy	3	123	NR	150 *	.1	.2
151 L-D Saints	1	NR	NR	222	.1	.3
157 Ch of Brethren	11	1,086	333	1,314 *	.9	1.8
165 Ch of Nazarene	4	236	170	346	.2	.5
167 Chs of Christ	2	163	188	239	.2	.3
171 Ch God-Gen Con	6	922	515	1,115 *	.8	1.6
173 Comm of Christ	1	99	NR	99	.1	.1
193 Episcopal	3	NR	149	273	.2	.4
203 Evan Free Ch	1	80	75	80	.1	.1
207 E.L.C.A.	6	2,188	617	2,832	1.9	4.0
221 Free Methodist	13	538	953	957	.6	1.3
263 Int Foursq Gos	1	30	50	50 *	-	.1
288 Mennonite USA	2	225	170	272 *	.2	.4
297 Mennonite;Other	1	80	NR	97 *	.1	.1
331 OCA: Ter Diocs	4	262	NR	289	.2	.4
355 Presb Ch (USA)	30	3,570	1,695	4,317 *	2.9	6.0
388 Reg Bapt Gen As	1	124	139	150 *	.1	.2
401 Rus Orth Abroad	1	NR	NR	NR	-	-
403 Salvation Army	1	173	62	286	.2	.4
413 S.D.A.	3	155	NR	184	.1	.3
418 Southw Bapt Fel	1	NR	NR	NR	-	-
419 So Bapt Conv	2	175	72	212 *	.1	.3
449 Un Methodist	56	9,022	3,049	10,911 *	7.3	15.3
496 Jewish Est	2	NR	NR	150	.1	.2
FOREST	**17**	**812**	**597**	**1,650 ***	**33.4**	**100.0**
081 Catholic	1	NR	NR	395	8.0	23.9
089 Chr & Miss Al	1	32	NR	54	1.1	3.3
123 Ch God (Ander)	2	NR	190	190	3.8	11.5
151 L-D Saints	1	NR	NR	71	1.4	4.3
207 E.L.C.A.	1	106	65	139	2.8	8.4
221 Free Methodist	2	15	39	39	.8	2.4
355 Presb Ch (USA)	3	117	72	135 *	2.7	8.2
449 Un Methodist	6	542	231	627 *	12.7	38.0
FRANKLIN	**193**	**31,849**	**18,354**	**50,455 ***	**39.0**	**100.0**
017 Amer Bapt Assn	2	100	NR	122 *	.1	.2
019 Amer Bapt USA	1	72	74	88 *	.1	.2
034 Ant Orth of NA	1	53	NR	106	.1	.2
053 Assemb of God	11	1,472	1,526	2,552	2.0	5.1
056 Baha'i	0	2	NR	2	-	-
071 Brethren (Ash)	1	56	67	69 *	.1	.1
075 Brethren in Cr	11	2,574	2,774	2,885	2.2	5.7
081 Catholic	8	NR	NR	8,551	6.6	16.9
089 Chr & Miss Al	2	104	NR	235	.2	.5
097 Chr Chs&Chs Cr	1	70	NR	86 *	.1	.2
127 Ch God (Cleve)	5	950	728	1,165 *	.9	2.3
151 L-D Saints	2	NR	NR	751	.6	1.5
157 Ch of Brethren	11	1,945	1,262	2,389 *	1.8	4.7
165 Ch of Nazarene	1	14	20	20	-	-
167 Chs of Christ	1	40	50	55	-	.1
171 Ch God-Gen Con	6	801	756	984 *	.8	2.0
193 Episcopal	4	NR	208	605	.5	1.2
207 E.L.C.A.	20	5,297	1,946	6,858	5.3	13.6
226 Friends-USA	1	105	NR	129 *	.1	.3
263 Int Foursq Gos	1	80	108	108 *	.1	.2
286 E.PA Mennonite	2	190	NR	233 *	.2	.5
288 Mennonite USA	14	1,618	1,680	2,095 *	1.6	4.2
297 Mennonite;Other	7	462	NR	567 *	.4	1.1
323 Old Ord Amish	6	410	NR	502 *	.4	1.0
324 Old Ord Rvr Br	3	199	300	335	.3	.7
349 Pent Holiness	1	41	14	50 *	-	.1
355 Presb Ch (USA)	8	2,398	1,105	2,941 *	2.3	5.8
370 Ref Baptist Chs	1	NR	NR	NR	-	-
379 Ref Mennonite	1	14	NR	17 *	-	-
403 Salvation Army	1	124	104	211	.2	.4
413 S.D.A.	2	293	NR	348	.3	.7
419 So Bapt Conv	4	573	120	703 *	.5	1.4
443 Un C of Christ	14	3,178	1,259	3,898 *	3.0	7.7
449 Un Methodist	37	8,014	3,803	9,825 *	7.6	19.5
496 Jewish Est	1	NR	NR	370	.3	.7
499 Indep.Non-Char	1	600	450	600	.5	1.2
FULTON	**43**	**3,305**	**1,790**	**4,954 ***	**34.7**	**100.0**
053 Assemb of God	1	70	109	250	1.8	5.0
081 Catholic	1	NR	NR	255	1.8	5.1
127 Ch God (Cleve)	1	28	50	50 *	.4	1.0
151 L-D Saints	1	NR	NR	377	2.6	7.6
157 Ch of Brethren	3	231	187	286 *	2.0	5.8
165 Ch of Nazarene	2	115	115	164	1.1	3.3
171 Ch God-Gen Con	1	34	57	57 *	.4	1.2
176 Congr Ad Afl	3	229	NR	282 *	2.0	5.7
181 Consrv Congr	1	94	90	116 *	.8	2.3
207 E.L.C.A.	3	533	118	668	4.7	13.5
288 Mennonite USA	3	91	94	131 *	.9	2.6
297 Mennonite;Other	1	51	NR	63 *	.4	1.3
355 Presb Ch (USA)	4	415	229	511 *	3.6	10.3
360 Prim Bapt Chrch	1	NR	NR	NR	-	-
413 S.D.A.	1	24	NR	29	.2	.6
443 Un C of Christ	2	204	98	252 *	1.8	5.1
449 Un Methodist	14	1,186	643	1,463 *	10.3	29.5
GREENE	**95**	**9,077**	**4,358**	**17,984 ***	**44.2**	**100.0**
011 A.W.M.C.	1	16	63	16	-	.1
019 Amer Bapt USA	9	1,310	583	1,572 *	3.9	8.7
053 Assemb of God	4	567	625	1,135	2.8	6.3
056 Baha'i	0	2	NR	2	-	-
071 Brethren (Ash)	1	4	8	5 *	-	-
081 Catholic	11	NR	NR	5,991	14.7	33.3
093 Chr Ch (Disc)	2	398	151	478 *	1.2	2.7
097 Chr Chs&Chs Cr	4	411	NR	493 *	1.2	2.7
127 Ch God (Cleve)	2	394	273	473 *	1.2	2.6
145 Ch God Prophcy	1	41	NR	49 *	.1	.3
151 L-D Saints	1	NR	NR	133	.3	.7
165 Ch of Nazarene	3	428	316	754	1.9	4.2
167 Chs of Christ	4	106	121	138	.3	.8
171 Ch God-Gen Con	3	54	17	69 *	.2	.4
193 Episcopal	1	NR	25	50	.1	.3
207 E.L.C.A.	1	74	46	168	.4	.9
291 Missionary Ch	2	50	67	67	.2	.4
355 Presb Ch (USA)	8	814	400	978 *	2.4	5.4
356 Presb Ch Amer	1	412	184	470	1.2	2.6
388 Reg Bapt Gen As	1	46	48	55 *	.1	.3
410 Serb Orth USA	1	NR	NR	150	.4	.8
419 So Bapt Conv	2	270	186	324 *	.8	1.8
449 Un Methodist	32	3,680	1,245	4,414 *	10.9	24.5
HUNTINGDON	**127**	**11,138**	**5,930**	**17,973 ***	**39.4**	**100.0**
019 Amer Bapt USA	5	458	228	548 *	1.2	3.0
022 Carp Rus Orth	3	366	NR	624	1.4	3.5
053 Assemb of God	4	277	350	718	1.6	4.0
056 Baha'i	0	9	NR	9	-	.1
061 Beachy Amish	1	31	NR	37 *	.1	.2
075 Brethren in Cr	2	49	41	52	.1	.3
081 Catholic	4	NR	NR	2,651	5.8	14.7
089 Chr & Miss Al	3	407	NR	847	1.9	4.7
123 Ch God (Ander)	1	NR	197	197	.4	1.1
127 Ch God (Cleve)	1	239	230	286 *	.6	1.6
145 Ch God Prophcy	1	41	NR	49 *	.1	.3
151 L-D Saints	1	NR	NR	134	.3	.7
157 Ch of Brethren	7	1,023	549	1,226 *	2.7	6.8
165 Ch of Nazarene	4	309	311	684	1.5	3.8
167 Chs of Christ	2	60	62	74	.2	.4
171 Ch God-Gen Con	4	121	126	152 *	.3	.8
193 Episcopal	1	NR	71	142	.3	.8
207 E.L.C.A.	7	923	366	1,156	2.5	6.4
221 Free Methodist	1	41	63	63	.1	.4

NR–Not Reported   *Total adherents estimated from known number of communicant, confirmed, full members.   - Represents a percentage less than 0.1.   Percentages may not total 100 due to rounding.

Table 4: Religious Congregations by County and Group: 2000

Religious Group	Number of Churches, Synagogues, Mosques, or Temples	Number of Communicant, Confirmed, or Full Members	Number of Attendees	Total Adherents: Number of Adherents	Total Adherents: % of Total Pop.	Total Adherents: % of Total Adh.
288 Mennonite USA	1	47	55	56 *	.1	.3
297 Mennonite;Other	1	47	NR	56 *	.1	.3
355 Presb Ch (USA)	13	1,214	742	1,453 *	3.2	8.1
403 Salvation Army	1	55	48	170	.4	.9
418 Southw Bapt Fel	2	NR	NR	NR	-	-
419 So Bapt Conv	0	5	0	6 *	-	-
443 Un C of Christ	8	703	376	841 *	1.8	4.7
449 Un Methodist	48	4,679	2,055	5,596 *	12.3	31.1
467 Wesleyan	1	34	60	146	.3	.8
INDIANA	**177**	**18,666**	**8,921**	**38,686 ***	**43.2**	**100.0**
011 A.W.M.C.	11	194	566	211	.2	.5
019 Amer Bapt USA	6	571	210	677 *	.8	1.7
022 Carp Rus Orth	3	366	NR	624	.7	1.6
053 Assemb of God	5	425	476	668	.7	1.7
056 Baha'i	0	5	NR	5	-	-
081 Catholic	12	NR	NR	13,304	14.8	34.4
089 Chr & Miss Al	4	325	NR	683	.8	1.8
093 Chr Ch (Disc)	2	356	92	422 *	.5	1.1
097 Chr Chs&Chs Cr	3	170	NR	201 *	.2	.5
123 Ch God (Ander)	4	NR	312	312	.3	.8
151 L-D Saints	1	NR	NR	220	.2	.6
157 Ch of Brethren	5	496	228	588 *	.7	1.5
165 Ch of Nazarene	4	324	352	420	.5	1.1
167 Chs of Christ	5	390	387	572	.6	1.5
171 Ch God-Gen Con	1	57	107	107 *	.1	.3
179 Consrv Bapt	1	NR	50	50	.1	.1
193 Episcopal	2	NR	99	225	.3	.6
203 Evan Free Ch	1	70	105	105	.1	.3
207 E.L.C.A.	10	2,507	820	3,390	3.8	8.8
221 Free Methodist	2	88	134	134	.1	.3
245 Greek Orth Vslp	1	70	NR	190	.2	.5
297 Mennonite;Other	1	28	NR	33 *	-	.1
322 Old Ord Menn Ch	1	27	NR	32 *	-	.1
323 Old Ord Amish	15	845	NR	999 *	1.1	2.6
331 OCA: Ter Diocs	3	64	NR	80	.1	.2
335 Orth Pres Ch	1	43	57	57	.1	.1
355 Presb Ch (USA)	26	4,365	2,099	5,172 *	5.8	13.4
388 Reg Bapt Gen As	1	15	20	20 *	-	.1
403 Salvation Army	1	98	49	431	.5	1.1
413 S.D.A.	2	133	NR	158	.2	.4
418 Southw Bapt Fel	1	NR	NR	NR	-	-
419 So Bapt Conv	1	84	33	100 *	.1	.3
431 Ukrainian Orth	1	NR	NR	450	.5	1.2
435 Unitarian-Univ	1	60	NR	71 *	.1	.2
449 Un Methodist	36	6,458	2,687	7,655 *	8.5	19.8
467 Wesleyan	2	32	38	95	.1	.2
496 Jewish Est	1	NR	NR	225	.3	.6
JEFFERSON	**132**	**10,656**	**6,098**	**25,047 ***	**54.5**	**100.0**
011 A.W.M.C.	2	9	101	9	-	-
019 Amer Bapt USA	3	348	211	422 *	.9	1.7
053 Assemb of God	3	237	216	625	1.4	2.5
056 Baha'i	0	2	NR	2	-	-
081 Catholic	12	NR	NR	9,841	21.4	39.3
089 Chr & Miss Al	6	303	NR	683	1.5	2.7
097 Chr Chs&Chs Cr	2	175	NR	212 *	.5	.8
123 Ch God (Ander)	3	NR	636	636	1.4	2.5
127 Ch God (Cleve)	1	32	25	39 *	.1	.2
151 L-D Saints	2	NR	NR	215	.5	.9
165 Ch of Nazarene	3	173	173	414	.9	1.7
167 Chs of Christ	4	201	221	272	.6	1.1
171 Ch God-Gen Con	1	56	74	74 *	.2	.3
179 Consrv Bapt	2	NR	150	150	.3	.6
183 Cons Menn Conf	1	6	7	9	-	-
193 Episcopal	2	NR	83	146	.3	.6
207 E.L.C.A.	8	679	265	911	2.0	3.6
221 Free Methodist	4	69	98	98	.2	.4
283 Luth—MO Synod	1	66	39	93	.2	.4
291 Missionary Ch	1	29	64	64	.1	.3
323 Old Ord Amish	7	385	NR	469 *	1.0	1.9
355 Presb Ch (USA)	14	1,914	816	2,318 *	5.0	9.3
403 Salvation Army	1	132	84	272	.6	1.1
413 S.D.A.	1	19	NR	23	.1	.1
443 Un C of Christ	3	447	250	541 *	1.2	2.2
449 Un Methodist	45	5,374	2,585	6,509 *	14.2	26.0
JUNIATA	**75**	**8,412**	**4,797**	**11,449 ***	**50.2**	**100.0**
053 Assemb of God	2	112	130	380	1.7	3.3
061 Beachy Amish	1	82	NR	102 *	.4	.9
075 Brethren in Cr	1	277	394	394	1.7	3.4
081 Catholic	1	NR	NR	335	1.5	2.9
127 Ch God (Cleve)	1	38	36	47 *	.2	.4
145 Ch God Prophcy	2	82	NR	102 *	.4	.9
157 Ch of Brethren	4	358	297	443 *	1.9	3.9
179 Consrv Bapt	2	NR	345	345	1.5	3.0
207 E.L.C.A.	10	1,877	824	2,390	10.5	20.9
252 Hindu	1	NR	NR	NR	-	-
286 E.PA Mennonite	1	56	NR	69 *	.3	.6
288 Mennonite USA	6	871	716	1,079 *	4.7	9.4
297 Mennonite;Other	2	116	NR	144 *	.6	1.3
323 Old Ord Amish	6	330	NR	408 *	1.8	3.6
355 Presb Ch (USA)	7	709	365	878 *	3.8	7.7
413 S.D.A.	1	69	NR	82	.4	.7
419 So Bapt Conv	1	101	0	125 *	.5	1.1
443 Un C of Christ	2	123	125	152 *	.7	1.3
449 Un Methodist	24	3,211	1,565	3,974 *	17.4	34.7
LACKAWANNA	**217**	**23,184**	**9,094**	**141,688 ***	**66.4**	**100.0**
019 Amer Bapt USA	12	2,164	927	2,592 *	1.2	1.8
022 Carp Rus Orth	2	243	NR	416	.2	.3
053 Assemb of God	7	809	983	1,651	.8	1.2
056 Baha'i	0	7	NR	7	-	-
081 Catholic	81	NR	NR	106,069	49.7	74.9
089 Chr & Miss Al	2	85	NR	191	.1	.1
093 Chr Ch (Disc)	2	173	49	207 *	.1	.1
123 Ch God (Ander)	1	NR	74	74	-	.1
127 Ch God (Cleve)	1	15	30	30 *	-	-
151 L-D Saints	1	NR	NR	455	.2	.3
167 Chs of Christ	1	30	43	43	-	-
173 Comm of Christ	1	150	NR	150	.1	.1
193 Episcopal	6	NR	500	1,736	.8	1.2
203 Evan Free Ch	1	65	115	115	.1	.1
207 E.L.C.A.	5	1,385	432	1,881	.9	1.3
221 Free Methodist	1	56	30	61	-	-
246 Greek Orthodox	1	NR	NR	120	.1	.1
283 Luth—MO Synod	3	728	303	907	.4	.6
331 OCA: Ter Diocs	4	838	NR	990	.5	.7
355 Presb Ch (USA)	13	3,215	1,198	3,850 *	1.8	2.7
356 Presb Ch Amer	1	100	90	121	.1	.1
360 Prim Bapt Chrch	1	NR	NR	NR	-	-
363 Primitive Meth	6	342	NR	364	.2	.3
373 Ref Ch in U.S.	1	30	NR	53	-	-
388 Reg Bapt Gen As	5	1,096	1,073	1,401 *	.7	1.0
400 Rus Orth Moscow	1	NR	NR	NR	-	-
401 Rus Orth Abroad	3	NR	NR	NR	-	-
403 Salvation Army	1	140	105	202	.1	.1
413 S.D.A.	1	80	NR	95	-	.1
419 So Bapt Conv	1	32	77	38 *	-	-
431 Ukrainian Orth	2	NR	NR	1,110	.5	.8
435 Unitarian-Univ	1	42	NR	50 *	-	-
443 Un C of Christ	8	1,232	477	1,476 *	.7	1.0
449 Un Methodist	36	10,127	2,588	12,133 *	5.7	8.6
496 Jewish Est	4	NR	NR	3,100	1.5	2.2
LANCASTER	**662**	**131,054**	**74,156**	**227,775 ***	**48.4**	**100.0**
017 Amer Bapt Assn	2	150	NR	189 *	-	.1
019 Amer Bapt USA	3	463	303	585 *	.1	.3
032 Amish; other	1	10	NR	13 *	-	-
053 Assemb of God	14	2,335	2,802	3,651	.8	1.6
056 Baha'i	1	68	NR	68	-	-
061 Beachy Amish	6	823	NR	1,039 *	.2	.5
075 Brethren in Cr	16	3,765	4,244	4,432	.9	1.9
076 Buddhism	2	NR	NR	NR	-	-
081 Catholic	18	NR	NR	47,161	10.0	20.7
084 Calvary Chapel	1	NR	NR	NR	-	-

NR–Not Reported *Total adherents estimated from known number of communicant, confirmed, full members. - Represents a percentage less than 0.1. Percentages may not total 100 due to rounding.

Table 4: Religious Congregations by County and Group: 2000

Religious Group	Number of Churches, Synagogues, Mosques, or Temples	Number of Communicant, Confirmed, or Full Members	Number of Attendees	Total Adherents		
				Number of Adherents	% of Total Pop.	% of Total Adh.
089 Chr & Miss Al	6	1,457	NR	2,714	.6	1.2
093 Chr Ch (Disc)	1	21	18	27 *	-	-
097 Chr Chs&Chs Cr	2	440	NR	556 *	.1	.2
127 Ch God (Cleve)	5	703	590	888 *	.2	.4
145 Ch God Prophcy	1	41	NR	52 *	-	-
151 L-D Saints	3	NR	NR	1,154	.2	.5
157 Ch of Brethren	23	8,045	5,207	10,171 *	2.2	4.5
165 Ch of Nazarene	3	1,102	1,031	2,039	.4	.9
167 Chs of Christ	2	166	160	232	-	.1
171 Ch God-Gen Con	18	2,439	2,208	3,229 *	.7	1.4
179 Consrv Bapt	2	NR	629	629	.1	.3
193 Episcopal	10	NR	1,262	3,903	.8	1.7
203 Evan Free Ch	5	644	1,755	1,755	.4	.8
207 E.L.C.A.	45	20,363	8,240	26,516	5.6	11.6
226 Friends-USA	2	210	NR	265 *	.1	.1
246 Greek Orthodox	1	NR	NR	60	-	-
263 Int Foursq Gos	1	51	64	64 *	-	-
268 Jain	1	NR	NR	NR	-	-
283 Luth—MO Synod	2	449	224	606	.1	.3
286 E.PA Mennonite	9	974	NR	1,230 *	.3	.5
288 Mennonite USA	105	15,634	15,917	19,740 *	4.2	8.7
290 Metro Comm Ch	1	83	85	85 *	-	-
293 Morav Ch-North	2	1,112	NR	1,305	.3	.6
297 Mennonite;Other	25	1,985	NR	2,507 *	.5	1.1
322 Old Ord Menn Ch	33	6,071	NR	7,668 *	1.6	3.4
323 Old Ord Amish	122	9,150	NR	11,590 *	2.5	5.1
324 Old Ord Rvr Br	1	99	130	142	-	.1
335 Orth Pres Ch	1	8	19	19	-	-
355 Presb Ch (USA)	17	6,272	2,926	7,923 *	1.7	3.5
356 Presb Ch Amer	5	2,011	1,864	2,619	.6	1.1
360 Prim Bapt Chrch	1	NR	NR	NR	-	-
370 Ref Baptist Chs	1	NR	NR	NR	-	-
379 Ref Mennonite	1	83	NR	105 *	-	-
403 Salvation Army	2	239	181	792	.2	.3
413 S.D.A.	3	454	NR	541	.1	.2
418 Southw Bapt Fel	1	NR	NR	NR	-	-
419 So Bapt Conv	11	1,759	597	2,221 *	.5	1.0
435 Unitarian-Univ	1	614	NR	775 *	.2	.3
443 Un C of Christ	32	11,185	4,494	14,122 *	3.0	6.2
449 Un Methodist	75	24,933	11,636	31,483 *	6.7	13.8
467 Wesleyan	4	0	70	160	-	.1
496 Jewish Est	3	NR	NR	3,000	.6	1.3
498 Indep.Charis.	2	930	1,100	1,350	.3	.6
499 Indep.Non-Char	7	3,713	6,400	6,400	1.4	2.8
LAWRENCE	**153**	**20,294**	**9,835**	**61,766 ***	**65.3**	**100.0**
011 A.W.M.C.	1	34	52	36	-	.1
019 Amer Bapt USA	4	549	395	665 *	.7	1.1
022 Carp Rus Orth	1	122	NR	207	.2	.3
034 Ant Orth of NA	1	322	NR	644	.7	1.0
053 Assemb of God	7	602	747	1,827	1.9	3.0
056 Baha'i	0	18	NR	18	-	-
057 Bapt Gen Conf	1	757	775	917 *	1.0	1.5
081 Catholic	17	NR	NR	32,724	34.6	53.0
089 Chr & Miss Al	9	517	NR	1,156	1.2	1.9
093 Chr Ch (Disc)	1	326	80	395 *	.4	.6
097 Chr Chs&Chs Cr	5	730	NR	884 *	.9	1.4
123 Ch God (Ander)	1	NR	99	99	.1	.2
127 Ch God (Cleve)	1	150	61	182 *	.2	.3
145 Ch God Prophcy	1	41	NR	50 *	.1	.1
151 L-D Saints	1	NR	NR	224	.2	.4
165 Ch of Nazarene	2	105	88	209	.2	.3
167 Chs of Christ	2	40	58	64	.1	.1
171 Ch God-Gen Con	1	234	141	283 *	.3	.5
193 Episcopal	1	NR	169	682	.7	1.1
201 Evan Cov Ch	1	83	54	101 *	.1	.2
207 E.L.C.A.	4	1,179	391	1,522	1.6	2.5
216 Evan Presby Ch	1	250	NR	303 *	.3	.5
221 Free Methodist	5	232	274	316	.3	.5
246 Greek Orthodox	1	NR	NR	150	.2	.2
267 Muslim Est	1	NR	55	163	.2	.3
283 Luth—MO Synod	1	141	75	159	.2	.3
288 Mennonite USA	1	33	30	40 *	-	.1
323 Old Ord Amish	14	770	NR	938 *	1.0	1.5

Religious Group	Number of Churches, Synagogues, Mosques, or Temples	Number of Communicant, Confirmed, or Full Members	Number of Attendees	Total Adherents		
				Number of Adherents	% of Total Pop.	% of Total Adh.
335 Orth Pres Ch	1	45	46	62	.1	.1
349 Pent Holiness	2	72	38	87 *	.1	.1
355 Presb Ch (USA)	37	8,783	4,367	10,639 *	11.2	17.2
356 Presb Ch Amer	3	245	360	410	.4	.7
363 Primitive Meth	1	57	NR	61	.1	.1
403 Salvation Army	2	85	82	419	.4	.7
413 S.D.A.	1	37	NR	44	-	.1
431 Ukrainian Orth	1	NR	NR	102	.1	.2
449 Un Methodist	17	3,617	1,220	4,384 *	4.6	7.1
467 Wesleyan	1	118	178	400	.4	.6
496 Jewish Est	1	NR	NR	200	.2	.3
LEBANON	**152**	**33,125**	**15,388**	**58,548 ***	**48.7**	**100.0**
053 Assemb of God	4	521	704	1,235	1.0	2.1
056 Baha'i	0	4	NR	4	-	-
075 Brethren in Cr	2	349	345	386	.3	.7
081 Catholic	9	NR	NR	13,946	11.6	23.8
089 Chr & Miss Al	2	95	NR	111	.1	.2
127 Ch God (Cleve)	2	434	329	534 *	.4	.9
151 L-D Saints	1	NR	NR	303	.3	.5
157 Ch of Brethren	10	2,626	1,357	3,535 *	2.9	6.0
165 Ch of Nazarene	1	95	103	169	.1	.3
167 Chs of Christ	1	69	58	97	.1	.2
193 Episcopal	1	NR	204	503	.4	.9
203 Evan Free Ch	1	59	265	265	.2	.5
207 E.L.C.A.	21	7,182	2,824	9,973	8.3	17.0
263 Int Foursq Gos	1	25	37	37 *	-	.1
286 E.PA Mennonite	5	396	NR	484 *	.4	.8
288 Mennonite USA	4	407	400	498 *	.4	.9
293 Morav Ch-North	1	228	NR	283	.2	.5
297 Mennonite;Other	9	924	NR	1,131 *	.9	1.9
322 Old Ord Menn Ch	5	1,058	NR	1,294 *	1.1	2.2
323 Old Ord Amish	6	450	NR	552 *	.5	.9
355 Presb Ch (USA)	2	738	336	903 *	.8	1.5
356 Presb Ch Amer	1	39	23	47	-	.1
403 Salvation Army	1	63	37	122	.1	.2
411 Serb Orth: Grac	1	NR	NR	NR	-	-
413 S.D.A.	1	100	NR	119	.1	.2
419 So Bapt Conv	1	88	24	108 *	.1	.2
443 Un C of Christ	23	7,067	2,850	8,645 *	7.2	14.8
449 Un Methodist	33	9,824	4,642	12,014 *	10.0	20.5
467 Wesleyan	1	0	0	0	-	-
496 Jewish Est	1	NR	NR	350	.3	.6
499 Indep.Non-Char	1	284	850	900	.7	1.5
LEHIGH	**232**	**64,192**	**25,946**	**179,632 ***	**57.6**	**100.0**
019 Amer Bapt USA	3	478	307	587 *	.2	.3
022 Carp Rus Orth	1	122	NR	207	.1	.1
034 Ant Orth of NA	2	579	NR	1,158	.4	.6
053 Assemb of God	9	1,176	1,492	1,888	.6	1.1
056 Baha'i	0	46	NR	46	-	-
076 Buddhism	1	NR	NR	NR	-	-
081 Catholic	27	NR	NR	83,821	26.9	46.7
089 Chr & Miss Al	3	153	NR	329	.1	.2
097 Chr Chs&Chs Cr	1	111	NR	136 *	-	.1
123 Ch God (Ander)	1	NR	40	40	-	-
127 Ch God (Cleve)	2	99	17	122 *	-	.1
151 L-D Saints	3	NR	NR	711	.2	.4
157 Ch of Brethren	1	117	105	144 *	-	.1
165 Ch of Nazarene	2	458	258	484	.2	.3
167 Chs of Christ	2	169	162	240	.1	.1
179 Consrv Bapt	2	NR	345	345	.1	.2
193 Episcopal	7	NR	813	2,383	.8	1.3
203 Evan Free Ch	2	706	1,260	1,260	.4	.7
207 E.L.C.A.	54	26,472	7,639	35,663	11.4	19.9
221 Free Methodist	3	160	246	246	.1	.1
267 Muslim Est	2	NR	280	915	.3	.5
283 Luth—MO Synod	1	117	73	148	-	.1
288 Mennonite USA	5	393	237	483 *	.2	.3
293 Morav Ch-North	5	1,402	NR	1,735	.6	1.0
297 Mennonite;Other	1	27	NR	33 *	-	-
331 OCA: Ter Diocs	1	77	NR	299	.1	.2
335 Orth Pres Ch	1	86	130	130	-	.1

NR–Not Reported   *Total adherents estimated from known number of communicant, confirmed, full members.   - Represents a percentage less than 0.1.   Percentages may not total 100 due to rounding.

Table 4: Religious Congregations by County and Group: 2000

Religious Group	Number of Churches, Synagogues, Mosques, or Temples	Number of Communicant, Confirmed, or Full Members	Number of Attendees	Total Adherents: Number of Adherents	Total Adherents: % of Total Pop.	Total Adherents: % of Total Adh.
355 Presb Ch (USA)	6	4,039	1,447	4,982 *	1.6	2.8
356 Presb Ch Amer	2	96	85	108	-	.1
363 Primitive Meth	1	57	NR	61	-	-
388 Reg Bapt Gen As	1	124	139	152 *	-	.1
403 Salvation Army	2	136	129	374	.1	.2
413 S.D.A.	2	224	NR	267	.1	.1
416 Sikh	1	NR	NR	NR	-	-
419 So Bapt Conv	3	105	135	129 *	-	.1
431 Ukrainian Orth	1	NR	NR	900	.3	.5
443 Un C of Christ	50	22,294	6,675	27,362 *	8.8	15.2
449 Un Methodist	10	3,879	1,634	4,760 *	1.5	2.6
467 Wesleyan	4	0	293	729	.2	.4
496 Jewish Est	4	NR	NR	4,250	1.4	2.4
498 Indep.Charis.	1	0	1,500	1,500	.5	.8
499 Indep.Non-Char	2	290	505	505	.2	.3
LUZERNE	**362**	**41,418**	**15,966**	**192,245 ***	**60.2**	**100.0**
019 Amer Bapt USA	11	1,234	745	1,466 *	.5	.8
022 Carp Rus Orth	1	122	NR	207	.1	.1
034 Ant Orth of NA	1	459	NR	918	.3	.5
053 Assemb of God	12	1,330	1,557	2,335	.7	1.2
056 Baha'i	0	18	NR	18	-	-
075 Brethren in Cr	1	26	34	34	-	-
081 Catholic	108	NR	NR	132,599	41.5	69.0
089 Chr & Miss Al	4	172	NR	313	.1	.2
093 Chr Ch (Disc)	2	569	172	676 *	.2	.4
097 Chr Chs&Chs Cr	6	1,220	NR	1,449 *	.5	.8
151 L-D Saints	1	NR	NR	485	.2	.3
167 Chs of Christ	4	135	157	201	.1	.1
175 Congr Chr Chs	2	135	65	160 *	.1	.1
176 Congr Ad Afl	2	490	NR	582 *	.2	.3
181 Consrv Congr	1	142	70	169 *	.1	.1
193 Episcopal	10	NR	727	2,297	.7	1.2
203 Evan Free Ch	1	266	500	500	.2	.3
207 E.L.C.A.	26	7,190	2,245	9,895	3.1	5.1
221 Free Methodist	3	114	182	182	.1	.1
226 Friends-USA	1	105	NR	125 *	-	.1
246 Greek Orthodox	1	NR	NR	120	-	.1
263 Int Foursq Gos	1	62	94	94 *	-	-
267 Muslim Est	1	NR	156	609	.2	.3
283 Luth—MO Synod	4	920	423	1,141	.4	.6
288 Mennonite USA	2	89	109	128 *	-	.1
291 Missionary Ch	1	0	0	0	-	-
331 OCA: Ter Diocs	6	1,121	NR	1,348	.4	.7
349 Pent Holiness	1	32	19	38 *	-	-
355 Presb Ch (USA)	25	3,696	1,706	4,393 *	1.4	2.3
363 Primitive Meth	11	626	NR	667	.2	.3
370 Ref Baptist Chs	1	NR	NR	NR	-	-
388 Reg Bapt Gen As	2	403	475	483 *	.2	.3
397 OCA: Roman Dioc	1	NR	NR	250	.1	.1
401 Rus Orth Abroad	1	NR	NR	NR	-	-
403 Salvation Army	3	382	236	611	.2	.3
413 S.D.A.	4	161	NR	191	.1	.1
419 So Bapt Conv	3	496	278	589 *	.2	.3
431 Ukrainian Orth	1	NR	NR	60	-	-
443 Un C of Christ	19	3,247	1,275	3,858 *	1.2	2.0
449 Un Methodist	70	16,456	4,741	19,554 *	6.1	10.2
467 Wesleyan	1	0	0	0	-	-
496 Jewish Est	6	NR	NR	3,500	1.1	1.8
LYCOMING	**190**	**28,858**	**14,592**	**58,299 ***	**48.6**	**100.0**
019 Amer Bapt USA	12	2,446	989	2,966 *	2.5	5.1
053 Assemb of God	5	450	574	935	.8	1.6
056 Baha'i	0	13	NR	13	-	-
075 Brethren in Cr	1	29	34	34	-	.1
076 Buddhism	1	NR	NR	NR	-	-
081 Catholic	11	NR	NR	17,029	14.2	29.2
089 Chr & Miss Al	6	341	NR	850	.7	1.5
093 Chr Ch (Disc)	1	196	78	238 *	.2	.4
097 Chr Chs&Chs Cr	7	1,702	NR	2,064 *	1.7	3.5
123 Ch God (Ander)	1	NR	400	400	.3	.7
127 Ch God (Cleve)	1	18	28	28 *	-	-
151 L-D Saints	1	NR	NR	450	.4	.8

Religious Group	Number of Churches, Synagogues, Mosques, or Temples	Number of Communicant, Confirmed, or Full Members	Number of Attendees	Total Adherents: Number of Adherents	Total Adherents: % of Total Pop.	Total Adherents: % of Total Adh.
165 Ch of Nazarene	3	117	157	268	.2	.5
167 Chs of Christ	1	58	70	76	.1	.1
179 Consrv Bapt	1	NR	55	55	-	.1
193 Episcopal	8	NR	550	1,534	1.3	2.6
203 Evan Free Ch	1	57	190	190	.2	.3
207 E.L.C.A.	22	6,672	2,238	8,922	7.4	15.3
221 Free Methodist	1	17	195	195	.2	.3
226 Friends-USA	3	295	NR	358 *	.3	.6
288 Mennonite USA	2	162	257	257 *	.2	.4
323 Old Ord Amish	2	150	NR	182 *	.2	.3
331 OCA: Ter Diocs	1	70	NR	155	.1	.3
335 Orth Pres Ch	1	36	50	50	-	.1
355 Presb Ch (USA)	11	1,836	863	2,225 *	1.9	3.8
356 Presb Ch Amer	1	28	55	55	-	.1
388 Reg Bapt Gen As	1	135	150	164 *	.1	.3
403 Salvation Army	1	207	144	332	.3	.6
413 S.D.A.	2	176	NR	209	.2	.4
419 So Bapt Conv	2	384	253	466 *	.4	.8
443 Un C of Christ	1	422	140	512 *	.4	.9
449 Un Methodist	72	12,581	5,639	15,257 *	12.7	26.2
467 Wesleyan	3	45	233	455	.4	.8
496 Jewish Est	1	NR	NR	125	.1	.2
499 Indep.Non-Char	2	215	1,250	1,250	1.0	2.1
MCKEAN	**83**	**9,110**	**4,727**	**23,284 ***	**50.7**	**100.0**
019 Amer Bapt USA	3	734	234	894 *	1.9	3.8
053 Assemb of God	3	168	145	255	.6	1.1
081 Catholic	9	NR	NR	10,301	22.4	44.2
089 Chr & Miss Al	4	174	NR	470	1.0	2.0
123 Ch God (Ander)	2	NR	214	214	.5	.9
165 Ch of Nazarene	2	159	90	181	.4	.8
167 Chs of Christ	1	50	70	100	.2	.4
193 Episcopal	6	NR	222	575	1.3	2.5
201 Evan Cov Ch	3	149	144	181 *	.4	.8
207 E.L.C.A.	7	1,595	455	2,095	4.6	9.0
221 Free Methodist	6	239	346	346	.8	1.5
263 Int Foursq Gos	1	90	196	196 *	.4	.8
283 Luth—MO Synod	1	338	197	441	1.0	1.9
288 Mennonite USA	1	33	50	50 *	.1	.2
297 Mennonite;Other	1	18	NR	22 *	-	.1
355 Presb Ch (USA)	4	929	418	1,131 *	2.5	4.9
388 Reg Bapt Gen As	2	95	115	121 *	.3	.5
403 Salvation Army	1	106	54	148	.3	.6
413 S.D.A.	2	134	NR	160	.3	.7
419 So Bapt Conv	1	156	65	190 *	.4	.8
449 Un Methodist	20	3,843	1,572	4,678 *	10.2	20.1
467 Wesleyan	2	100	140	315	.7	1.4
496 Jewish Est	1	NR	NR	220	.5	.9
MERCER	**176**	**28,316**	**13,506**	**68,504 ***	**56.9**	**100.0**
011 A.W.M.C.	8	116	298	122	.1	.2
017 Amer Bapt Assn	1	30	NR	36 *	-	.1
019 Amer Bapt USA	7	1,156	454	1,403 *	1.2	2.0
022 Carp Rus Orth	1	122	NR	207	.2	.3
032 Amish; other	1	60	NR	73 *	.1	.1
039 Ap Chr Ch(Naz)	1	15	40	40 *	-	.1
053 Assemb of God	4	518	672	1,110	.9	1.6
056 Baha'i	0	27	NR	27	-	-
061 Beachy Amish	1	20	NR	24 *	-	-
081 Catholic	18	NR	NR	28,960	24.1	42.3
089 Chr & Miss Al	5	369	NR	917	.8	1.3
093 Chr Ch (Disc)	2	629	220	763 *	.6	1.1
097 Chr Chs&Chs Cr	3	440	NR	534 *	.4	.8
123 Ch God (Ander)	5	NR	536	536	.4	.8
145 Ch God Prophcy	1	41	NR	50 *	-	.1
151 L-D Saints	1	NR	NR	207	.2	.3
165 Ch of Nazarene	6	592	474	929	.8	1.4
167 Chs of Christ	2	186	185	210	.2	.3
171 Ch God-Gen Con	1	11	30	30 *	-	-
173 Comm of Christ	2	140	NR	140	.1	.2
181 Consrv Congr	1	105	57	127 *	.1	.2
193 Episcopal	4	NR	387	940	.8	1.4
203 Evan Free Ch	1	65	150	150	.1	.2

NR–Not Reported *Total adherents estimated from known number of communicant, confirmed, full members. - Represents a percentage less than 0.1. Percentages may not total 100 due to rounding.

Table 4: Religious Congregations by County and Group: 2000

Religious Group	Number of Churches, Synagogues, Mosques, or Temples	Number of Communicant, Confirmed, or Full Members	Number of Attendees	Total Adherents: Number of Adherents	Total Adherents: % of Total Pop.	Total Adherents: % of Total Adh.
207 E.L.C.A.	5	2,307	840	3,020	2.5	4.4
221 Free Methodist	1	48	74	74	.1	.1
246 Greek Orthodox	1	NR	NR	120	.1	.2
283 Luth—MO Synod	1	252	125	296	.2	.4
323 Old Ord Amish	5	275	NR	335 *	.3	.5
331 OCA: Ter Diocs	1	95	NR	117	.1	.2
335 Orth Pres Ch	1	104	128	153	.1	.2
349 Pent Holiness	5	513	281	623 *	.5	.9
355 Presb Ch (USA)	32	8,463	4,216	10,271 *	8.5	15.0
360 Prim Bapt Chrch	1	NR	NR	NR	-	-
388 Reg Bapt Gen As	3	401	512	611 *	.5	.9
397 OCA: Roman Dioc	1	NR	NR	95	.1	.1
403 Salvation Army	3	269	196	773	.6	1.1
413 S.D.A.	1	40	NR	48	-	.1
419 So Bapt Conv	1	292	139	354 *	.3	.5
431 Ukrainian Orth	1	NR	NR	360	.3	.5
443 Un C of Christ	5	1,630	515	1,978 *	1.6	2.9
449 Un Methodist	30	8,808	2,600	10,691 *	8.9	15.6
467 Wesleyan	1	177	377	750	.6	1.1
496 Jewish Est	1	NR	NR	300	.2	.4
MIFFLIN	**109**	**15,068**	**7,162**	**21,738 ***	**46.8**	**100.0**
019 Amer Bapt USA	1	265	93	328 *	.7	1.5
053 Assemb of God	1	156	200	233	.5	1.1
056 Baha'i	0	1	NR	1	-	-
061 Beachy Amish	2	293	NR	362 *	.8	1.7
075 Brethren in Cr	4	170	183	192	.4	.9
081 Catholic	1	NR	NR	1,762	3.8	8.1
089 Chr & Miss Al	7	231	NR	494	1.1	2.3
127 Ch God (Cleve)	1	212	105	262 *	.6	1.2
143 CG in Cr(Menn)	1	128	NR	158 *	.3	.7
157 Ch of Brethren	6	962	429	1,208 *	2.6	5.6
165 Ch of Nazarene	1	24	23	24	.1	.1
167 Chs of Christ	1	16	8	17	-	.1
179 Consrv Bapt	1	NR	226	226	.5	1.0
183 Cons Menn Conf	2	475	580	690	1.5	3.2
193 Episcopal	1	NR	81	241	.5	1.1
207 E.L.C.A.	9	2,642	942	3,501	7.5	16.1
288 Mennonite USA	5	821	629	1,015 *	2.2	4.7
297 Mennonite;Other	3	232	NR	286 *	.6	1.3
323 Old Ord Amish	20	1,160	NR	1,435 *	3.1	6.6
355 Presb Ch (USA)	9	1,443	686	1,784 *	3.8	8.2
403 Salvation Army	1	165	134	369	.8	1.7
413 S.D.A.	1	33	NR	39	.1	.2
419 So Bapt Conv	1	40	35	49 *	.1	.2
443 Un C of Christ	2	345	117	426 *	.9	2.0
449 Un Methodist	27	5,004	2,266	6,186 *	13.3	28.5
498 Indep.Charis.	1	250	425	450	1.0	2.1
MONROE	**89**	**15,370**	**7,231**	**62,794 ***	**45.3**	**100.0**
053 Assemb of God	4	797	1,006	1,625	1.2	2.6
056 Baha'i	0	11	NR	11	-	-
081 Catholic	12	NR	NR	38,893	28.0	61.9
089 Chr & Miss Al	2	94	NR	125	.1	.2
127 Ch God (Cleve)	2	69	94	114 *	.1	.2
151 L-D Saints	1	NR	NR	511	.4	.8
167 Chs of Christ	1	50	60	70	.1	.1
179 Consrv Bapt	2	NR	365	365	.3	.6
193 Episcopal	2	NR	227	708	.5	1.1
203 Evan Free Ch	1	21	40	40	-	.1
207 E.L.C.A.	13	4,960	1,678	6,862	4.9	10.9
221 Free Methodist	1	15	20	31	-	-
246 Greek Orthodox	1	NR	NR	150	.1	.2
252 Hindu	2	NR	NR	NR	-	-
267 Muslim Est	1	NR	55	163	.1	.3
283 Luth—MO Synod	1	183	115	238	.2	.4
288 Mennonite USA	1	30	62	62 *	-	.1
293 Morav Ch-North	1	58	NR	72	.1	.1
331 OCA: Ter Diocs	1	43	NR	142	.1	.2
335 Orth Pres Ch	1	30	30	36	-	.1
355 Presb Ch (USA)	6	1,418	739	1,783 *	1.3	2.8
403 Salvation Army	1	234	119	432	.3	.7
413 S.D.A.	1	171	NR	203	.1	.3
419 So Bapt Conv	0	60	70	75 *	.1	.1
435 Unitarian-Univ	1	56	NR	70 *	.1	.1
443 Un C of Christ	6	1,360	403	1,710 *	1.2	2.7
449 Un Methodist	21	5,590	1,883	7,028 *	5.1	11.2
467 Wesleyan	2	120	265	675	.5	1.1
496 Jewish Est	1	NR	NR	600	.4	1.0
MONTGOMERY	**485**	**103,840**	**55,476**	**480,100 ***	**64.0**	**100.0**
019 Amer Bapt USA	32	10,429	5,652	12,850 *	1.7	2.7
034 Ant Orth of NA	1	272	NR	544	.1	.1
050 Armen Ap Etchm	1	312	NR	900	.1	.2
053 Assemb of God	16	1,177	1,521	1,995	.3	.4
056 Baha'i	2	116	NR	116	-	-
057 Bapt Gen Conf	1	62	58	76 *	-	-
075 Brethren in Cr	5	453	580	616	.1	.1
076 Buddhism	4	NR	NR	NR	-	-
081 Catholic	65	NR	NR	263,375	35.1	54.9
084 Calvary Chapel	1	NR	NR	NR	-	-
089 Chr & Miss Al	2	52	NR	84	-	-
093 Chr Ch (Disc)	1	65	0	80 *	-	-
123 Ch God (Ander)	4	NR	113	113	-	-
127 Ch God (Cleve)	4	319	377	413 *	.1	.1
145 Ch God Prophcy	1	41	NR	50 *	-	-
151 L-D Saints	3	NR	NR	954	.1	.2
157 Ch of Brethren	7	939	505	1,156 *	.2	.2
165 Ch of Nazarene	5	1,603	1,380	2,415	.3	.5
167 Chs of Christ	4	344	390	451	.1	.1
171 Ch God-Gen Con	1	16	70	70 *	-	-
173 Comm of Christ	1	208	NR	208	-	-
179 Consrv Bapt	2	NR	575	575	.1	.1
181 Consrv Congr	2	795	320	980 *	.1	.2
193 Episcopal	36	NR	5,239	15,447	2.1	3.2
203 Evan Free Ch	2	130	240	240	-	-
207 E.L.C.A.	50	30,867	10,338	43,735	5.8	9.1
226 Friends-USA	10	1,050	NR	1,294 *	.2	.3
246 Greek Orthodox	2	NR	NR	1,311	.2	.3
263 Int Foursq Gos	1	30	50	50 *	-	-
267 Muslim Est	1	NR	23	40	-	-
268 Jain	1	NR	NR	NR	-	-
283 Luth—MO Synod	2	177	88	225	-	-
286 E.PA Mennonite	1	65	NR	80 *	-	-
288 Mennonite USA	27	5,037	4,165	6,334 *	.8	1.3
297 Mennonite;Other	5	369	NR	454 *	.1	.1
331 OCA: Ter Diocs	1	38	NR	572	.1	.1
335 Orth Pres Ch	4	421	437	598	.1	.1
355 Presb Ch (USA)	31	13,767	5,761	16,964 *	2.3	3.5
356 Presb Ch Amer	13	2,375	2,580	3,065	.4	.6
363 Primitive Meth	2	114	NR	121	-	-
371 Ref Ch in Am	2	158	145	348	-	.1
388 Reg Bapt Gen As	1	0	65	65 *	-	-
397 OCA: Roman Dioc	1	NR	NR	400	.1	.1
403 Salvation Army	2	196	127	376	.1	.1
413 S.D.A.	8	710	NR	845	.1	.2
418 Southw Bapt Fel	1	NR	NR	NR	-	-
419 So Bapt Conv	9	901	619	1,110 *	.1	.2
435 Unitarian-Univ	1	119	NR	147 *	-	-
443 Un C of Christ	34	12,568	4,436	15,485 *	2.1	3.2
449 Un Methodist	33	13,159	4,213	16,214 *	2.2	3.4
463 Vineyard	1	126	141	155 *	-	-
467 Wesleyan	3	0	69	180	-	-
469 WELS	1	113	72	144	-	-
496 Jewish Est	28	NR	NR	59,550	7.9	12.4
499 Indep.Non-Char	6	4,147	5,127	6,530	.9	1.4
MONTOUR	**32**	**4,588**	**2,270**	**9,791 ***	**53.7**	**100.0**
019 Amer Bapt USA	1	75	40	92 *	.5	.9
081 Catholic	1	NR	NR	3,397	18.6	34.7
165 Ch of Nazarene	1	65	33	88	.5	.9
179 Consrv Bapt	1	NR	392	392	2.1	4.0
193 Episcopal	2	NR	80	226	1.2	2.3
207 E.L.C.A.	8	1,451	545	1,923	10.5	19.6
286 E.PA Mennonite	1	110	NR	135 *	.7	1.4
288 Mennonite USA	2	71	72	90 *	.5	.9

NR–Not Reported   *Total adherents estimated from known number of communicant, confirmed, full members.   - Represents a percentage less than 0.1.   Percentages may not total 100 due to rounding.

Table 4: Religious Congregations by County and Group: 2000

Religious Group	Number of Churches, Synagogues, Mosques, or Temples	Number of Communicant, Confirmed, or Full Members	Number of Attendees	Total Adherents		
				Number of Adherents	% of Total Pop.	% of Total Adh.
323 Old Ord Amish	3	185	NR	226 *	1.2	2.3
355 Presb Ch (USA)	3	595	291	729 *	4.0	7.4
413 S.D.A.	1	71	NR	84	.5	.9
443 Un C of Christ	4	1,064	459	1,304 *	7.2	13.3
449 Un Methodist	4	901	358	1,105 *	6.1	11.3
NORTHAMPTON	**222**	**55,675**	**19,685**	**182,231 ***	**68.2**	**100.0**
019 Amer Bapt USA	3	1,076	609	1,310 *	.5	.7
053 Assemb of God	6	505	664	892	.3	.5
056 Baha'i	1	53	NR	53	-	-
081 Catholic	35	NR	NR	95,739	35.8	52.5
127 Ch God (Cleve)	1	61	0	74 *	-	-
151 L-D Saints	3	NR	NR	906	.3	.5
165 Ch of Nazarene	3	329	294	486	.2	.3
167 Chs of Christ	1	21	23	27	-	-
179 Consrv Bapt	1	NR	215	215	.1	.1
193 Episcopal	7	NR	789	2,447	.9	1.3
203 Evan Free Ch	1	81	208	208	.1	.1
207 E.L.C.A.	46	20,502	6,139	28,370	10.6	15.6
226 Friends-USA	1	105	NR	128 *	-	.1
246 Greek Orthodox	2	NR	NR	3,750	1.4	2.1
252 Hindu	1	NR	NR	NR	-	-
263 Int Foursq Gos	1	36	103	103 *	-	.1
267 Muslim Est	1	NR	156	609	.2	.3
268 Jain	1	NR	NR	NR	-	-
283 Luth—MO Synod	2	601	246	757	.3	.4
288 Mennonite USA	5	466	471	587 *	.2	.3
290 Metro Comm Ch	1	52	61	63 *	-	-
293 Morav Ch-North	11	4,489	NR	5,694	2.1	3.1
313 N Am Bapt Conf	1	680	700	828 *	.3	.5
331 OCA: Ter Diocs	1	340	NR	530	.2	.3
335 Orth Pres Ch	2	72	112	112	-	.1
355 Presb Ch (USA)	8	4,701	1,882	5,723 *	2.1	3.1
370 Ref Baptist Chs	1	NR	NR	NR	-	-
400 Rus Orth Moscow	1	NR	NR	NR	-	-
403 Salvation Army	4	184	160	800	.3	.4
413 S.D.A.	3	249	NR	296	.1	.2
419 So Bapt Conv	1	0	0	0 *	-	-
431 Ukrainian Orth	1	NR	NR	600	.2	.3
435 Unitarian-Univ	1	238	NR	290 *	.1	.2
443 Un C of Christ	33	14,005	4,114	17,051 *	6.4	9.4
449 Un Methodist	23	5,859	1,848	7,133 *	2.7	3.9
467 Wesleyan	4	970	891	2,200	.8	1.2
496 Jewish Est	4	NR	NR	4,250	1.6	2.3
NORTHUMBERLAND	**156**	**24,024**	**11,350**	**56,941 ***	**60.2**	**100.0**
019 Amer Bapt USA	3	507	257	604 *	.6	1.1
053 Assemb of God	5	294	403	549	.6	1.0
056 Baha'i	0	2	NR	2	-	-
081 Catholic	12	NR	NR	20,785	22.0	36.5
089 Chr & Miss Al	3	387	NR	839	.9	1.5
165 Ch of Nazarene	2	298	405	553	.6	1.0
171 Ch God-Gen Con	1	58	57	69 *	.1	.1
179 Consrv Bapt	2	NR	190	190	.2	.3
193 Episcopal	5	NR	196	550	.6	1.0
203 Evan Free Ch	3	205	311	311	.3	.5
207 E.L.C.A.	32	8,315	2,669	11,311	12.0	19.9
267 Muslim Est	2	NR	75	203	.2	.4
283 Luth—MO Synod	1	76	40	91	.1	.2
288 Mennonite USA	1	186	258	258 *	.3	.5
297 Mennonite;Other	2	143	NR	171 *	.2	.3
322 Old Ord Menn Ch	1	61	NR	73 *	.1	.1
323 Old Ord Amish	3	205	NR	244 *	.3	.4
331 OCA: Ter Diocs	1	112	NR	179	.2	.3
355 Presb Ch (USA)	9	1,185	705	1,412 *	1.5	2.5
363 Primitive Meth	2	114	NR	121	.1	.2
403 Salvation Army	2	212	113	348	.4	.6
413 S.D.A.	1	36	NR	43	-	.1
435 Unitarian-Univ	1	83	NR	99 *	.1	.2
443 Un C of Christ	23	4,091	1,637	4,876 *	5.2	8.6
449 Un Methodist	32	6,919	2,545	8,247 *	8.7	14.5
467 Wesleyan	6	535	1,489	4,613	4.9	8.1
496 Jewish Est	1	NR	NR	200	.2	.4

Religious Group	Number of Churches, Synagogues, Mosques, or Temples	Number of Communicant, Confirmed, or Full Members	Number of Attendees	Total Adherents		
				Number of Adherents	% of Total Pop.	% of Total Adh.
PERRY	**97**	**10,621**	**5,732**	**16,362 ***	**37.5**	**100.0**
053 Assemb of God	3	405	532	722	1.7	4.4
056 Baha'i	0	5	NR	5	-	-
075 Brethren in Cr	4	137	207	207	.5	1.3
081 Catholic	4	NR	NR	1,860	4.3	11.4
089 Chr & Miss Al	2	241	NR	677	1.6	4.1
127 Ch God (Cleve)	1	27	20	33 *	.1	.2
151 L-D Saints	1	NR	NR	286	.7	1.7
157 Ch of Brethren	2	156	130	193 *	.4	1.2
167 Chs of Christ	1	8	14	14	-	.1
171 Ch God-Gen Con	10	586	589	753 *	1.7	4.6
179 Consrv Bapt	1	NR	119	119	.3	.7
193 Episcopal	1	NR	48	107	.2	.7
207 E.L.C.A.	15	2,780	996	3,609	8.3	22.1
286 E.PA Mennonite	1	46	NR	57 *	.1	.3
322 Old Ord Menn Ch	1	89	NR	110 *	.3	.7
323 Old Ord Amish	3	205	NR	254 *	.6	1.6
339 Pent Ch of God	1	25	NR	37	.1	.2
355 Presb Ch (USA)	4	636	327	788 *	1.8	4.8
413 S.D.A.	1	57	NR	68	.2	.4
443 Un C of Christ	11	1,055	583	1,306 *	3.0	8.0
449 Un Methodist	29	4,109	2,105	5,088 *	11.7	31.1
467 Wesleyan	1	54	62	69	.2	.4
PHILADELPHIA	**876**	**121,775**	**92,931**	**809,987 ***	**53.4**	**100.0**
007 OCA: Alban Dioc	2	NR	NR	750	-	.1
019 Amer Bapt USA	84	35,243	23,775	43,989 *	2.9	5.4
049 Armen Ap Cilic	1	560	NR	1,050	.1	.1
050 Armen Ap Etchm	1	363	NR	4,200	.3	.5
053 Assemb of God	24	2,357	2,482	3,674	.2	.5
056 Baha'i	1	298	NR	298	-	-
057 Bapt Gen Conf	1	48	39	60 *	-	-
075 Brethren in Cr	2	113	144	144	-	-
076 Buddhism	11	NR	NR	NR	-	-
081 Catholic	131	NR	NR	491,652	32.4	60.7
084 Calvary Chapel	2	NR	NR	NR	-	-
089 Chr & Miss Al	7	357	NR	389	-	-
093 Chr Ch (Disc)	2	57	35	71 *	-	-
097 Chr Chs&Chs Cr	3	118	NR	147 *	-	-
105 Christian Ref	1	113	160	141 *	-	-
123 Ch God (Ander)	15	NR	4,190	4,190	.3	.5
127 Ch God (Cleve)	14	1,397	1,398	1,849 *	.1	.2
145 Ch God Prophcy	7	287	NR	357 *	-	-
151 L-D Saints	4	NR	NR	1,828	.1	.2
157 Ch of Brethren	2	120	86	149 *	-	-
165 Ch of Nazarene	4	161	129	167	-	-
167 Chs of Christ	9	607	519	712	-	.1
171 Ch God-Gen Con	1	0	23	23 *	-	-
179 Consrv Bapt	6	NR	520	520	-	.1
181 Consrv Congr	3	296	150	369 *	-	-
185 Cumber Presb	1	122	NR	122	-	-
193 Episcopal	68	NR	6,248	15,102	1.0	1.9
203 Evan Free Ch	1	69	125	125	-	-
207 E.L.C.A.	49	11,050	4,375	15,462	1.0	1.9
226 Friends-USA	8	840	NR	1,048 *	.1	.1
245 Greek Orth Vslp	1	105	NR	145	-	-
246 Greek Orthodox	2	NR	NR	2,343	.2	.3
252 Hindu	3	NR	NR	NR	-	-
263 Int Foursq Gos	1	3	95	95 *	-	-
264 Int Chs of Crst	1	991	1,580	1,310	.1	.2
267 Muslim Est	26	NR	11,104	42,397	2.8	5.2
268 Jain	2	NR	NR	NR	-	-
283 Luth—MO Synod	5	523	381	665	-	.1
288 Mennonite USA	15	988	894	1,249 *	.1	.2
290 Metro Comm Ch	1	42	49	52 *	-	-
293 Morav Ch-North	2	164	NR	233	-	-
297 Mennonite;Other	2	19	NR	24 *	-	-
304 NatPrimBapt USA	1	229	NR	286 *	-	-
313 N Am Bapt Conf	5	1,023	700	1,277 *	.1	.2
330 Macedonian Orth	1	NR	NR	200	-	-
331 OCA: Ter Diocs	3	321	NR	1,401	.1	.2
333 Malan Dioc Am	4	NR	NR	900	.1	.1
334 Malan Syr Orth	2	160	NR	800	.1	.1

NR–Not Reported *Total adherents estimated from known number of communicant, confirmed, full members. - Represents a percentage less than 0.1. Percentages may not total 100 due to rounding.

Table 4: Religious Congregations by County and Group: 2000

Religious Group	Number of Churches, Synagogues, Mosques, or Temples	Number of Communicant, Confirmed, or Full Members	Number of Attendees	Total Adherents: Number of Adherents	% of Total Pop.	% of Total Adh.
335 Orth Pres Ch	4	264	305	387	-	-
355 Presb Ch (USA)	60	8,261	4,245	10,309 *	.7	1.3
356 Presb Ch Amer	9	3,606	3,480	4,361	.3	.5
363 Primitive Meth	1	57	NR	61	-	-
388 Reg Bapt Gen As	3	181	209	236 *	-	-
395 Romania Orth Ar	1	NR	NR	350	-	-
400 Rus Orth Moscow	2	NR	NR	NR	-	-
401 Rus Orth Abroad	1	NR	NR	NR	-	-
403 Salvation Army	16	929	896	4,396	.3	.5
410 Serb Orth USA	1	NR	NR	300	-	-
413 S.D.A.	12	3,660	NR	4,355	.3	.5
418 Southw Bapt Fel	1	NR	NR	NR	-	-
419 So Bapt Conv	79	14,942	10,524	18,650 *	1.2	2.3
431 Ukrainian Orth	2	NR	NR	2,100	.1	.3
435 Unitarian-Univ	3	582	NR	726 *	-	.1
443 Un C of Christ	20	3,762	1,717	4,696 *	.3	.6
449 Un Methodist	66	15,553	3,904	19,411 *	1.3	2.4
467 Wesleyan	1	0	250	250	-	-
496 Jewish Est	44	NR	NR	86,600	5.7	10.7
498 Indep.Charis.	3	2,800	1,750	2,800	.2	.3
499 Indep.Non-Char	5	8,034	6,450	8,034	.5	1.0
PIKE	**28**	**2,474**	**1,261**	**11,885 ***	**25.7**	**100.0**
053 Assemb of God	2	65	80	84	.2	.7
056 Baha'i	0	5	NR	5	-	-
081 Catholic	8	NR	NR	7,849	17.0	66.0
089 Chr & Miss Al	1	65	NR	270	.6	2.3
193 Episcopal	1	NR	74	192	.4	1.6
203 Evan Free Ch	1	52	35	52	.1	.4
207 E.L.C.A.	4	596	243	944	2.0	7.9
355 Presb Ch (USA)	1	137	104	173 *	.4	1.5
370 Ref Baptist Chs	1	NR	NR	NR	-	-
371 Ref Ch in Am	1	119	120	204	.4	1.7
435 Unitarian-Univ	1	15	NR	19 *	-	.2
449 Un Methodist	6	1,420	605	1,793 *	3.9	15.1
496 Jewish Est	1	NR	NR	300	.6	2.5
POTTER	**46**	**3,416**	**2,067**	**6,710 ***	**37.1**	**100.0**
019 Amer Bapt USA	4	312	176	388 *	2.1	5.8
053 Assemb of God	1	48	37	44	.2	.7
081 Catholic	6	NR	NR	2,124	11.7	31.7
089 Chr & Miss Al	3	240	NR	417	2.3	6.2
097 Chr Chs&Chs Cr	1	20	NR	25 *	.1	.4
167 Chs of Christ	1	20	20	25	.1	.4
193 Episcopal	2	NR	83	230	1.3	3.4
207 E.L.C.A.	3	402	139	521	2.9	7.8
221 Free Methodist	3	119	116	140	.8	2.1
323 Old Ord Amish	1	55	NR	68 *	.4	1.0
355 Presb Ch (USA)	2	218	92	271 *	1.5	4.0
388 Reg Bapt Gen As	3	274	419	435 *	2.4	6.5
413 S.D.A.	1	88	NR	105	.6	1.6
449 Un Methodist	14	1,220	585	1,517 *	8.4	22.6
498 Indep.Charis.	1	400	400	400	2.2	6.0
SCHUYLKILL	**297**	**36,495**	**13,391**	**111,704 ***	**74.3**	**100.0**
017 Amer Bapt Assn	2	130	NR	155 *	.1	.1
019 Amer Bapt USA	5	351	132	416 *	.3	.4
022 Carp Rus Orth	1	122	NR	207	.1	.2
053 Assemb of God	2	128	158	218	.1	.2
056 Baha'i	0	4	NR	4	-	-
075 Brethren in Cr	2	26	40	40	-	-
081 Catholic	82	NR	NR	63,463	42.2	56.8
097 Chr Chs&Chs Cr	1	50	NR	59 *	-	.1
151 L-D Saints	1	NR	NR	125	.1	.1
157 Ch of Brethren	1	212	107	251 *	.2	.2
165 Ch of Nazarene	3	317	277	508	.3	.5
167 Chs of Christ	1	7	7	9	-	-
171 Ch God-Gen Con	5	250	203	297 *	.2	.3
181 Consrv Congr	1	107	55	127 *	.1	.1
193 Episcopal	4	NR	250	911	.6	.8
203 Evan Free Ch	4	224	445	445	.3	.4
207 E.L.C.A.	46	14,795	4,419	19,747	13.1	17.7
252 Hindu	1	NR	NR	NR	-	-
263 Int Foursq Gos	4	445	361	528 *	.4	.5
286 E.PA Mennonite	2	113	NR	134 *	.1	.1
288 Mennonite USA	2	114	111	135 *	.1	.1
297 Mennonite;Other	1	20	NR	24 *	-	-
323 Old Ord Amish	1	75	NR	89 *	.1	.1
331 OCA: Ter Diocs	5	495	NR	602	.4	.5
355 Presb Ch (USA)	5	546	203	649 *	.4	.6
363 Primitive Meth	5	285	NR	303	.2	.3
370 Ref Baptist Chs	1	NR	NR	NR	-	-
403 Salvation Army	2	238	136	880	.6	.8
413 S.D.A.	1	49	NR	58	-	.1
419 So Bapt Conv	2	41	40	49 *	-	-
431 Ukrainian Orth	1	NR	NR	150	.1	.1
443 Un C of Christ	48	10,404	3,844	12,339 *	8.2	11.0
449 Un Methodist	48	6,947	2,385	8,242 *	5.5	7.4
467 Wesleyan	4	0	218	380	.3	.3
496 Jewish Est	3	NR	NR	160	.1	.1
SNYDER	**85**	**12,461**	**5,509**	**17,873 ***	**47.6**	**100.0**
061 Beachy Amish	1	70	NR	86 *	.2	.5
075 Brethren in Cr	1	22	25	25	.1	.1
081 Catholic	1	NR	NR	1,302	3.5	7.3
089 Chr & Miss Al	1	67	NR	165	.4	.9
145 Ch God Prophcy	1	41	NR	50 *	.1	.3
151 L-D Saints	1	NR	NR	310	.8	1.7
157 Ch of Brethren	1	119	60	146 *	.4	.8
165 Ch of Nazarene	1	304	370	576	1.5	3.2
167 Chs of Christ	1	140	135	185	.5	1.0
179 Consrv Bapt	1	NR	110	110	.3	.6
193 Episcopal	1	NR	61	129	.3	.7
207 E.L.C.A.	19	4,454	1,415	5,881	15.7	32.9
288 Mennonite USA	3	143	210	210 *	.6	1.2
297 Mennonite;Other	3	224	NR	274 *	.7	1.5
322 Old Ord Menn Ch	7	615	NR	751 *	2.0	4.2
323 Old Ord Amish	2	110	NR	134 *	.4	.7
419 So Bapt Conv	2	75	34	92 *	.2	.5
443 Un C of Christ	10	2,329	885	2,848 *	7.6	15.9
449 Un Methodist	26	3,570	2,046	4,364 *	11.6	24.4
467 Wesleyan	2	178	158	235	.6	1.3
SOMERSET	**198**	**27,217**	**12,018**	**49,534 ***	**61.9**	**100.0**
019 Amer Bapt USA	2	75	40	90 *	.1	.2
022 Carp Rus Orth	2	243	NR	416	.5	.8
053 Assemb of God	6	371	510	860	1.1	1.7
061 Beachy Amish	1	194	NR	233 *	.3	.5
071 Brethren (Ash)	3	241	298	289 *	.4	.6
081 Catholic	18	NR	NR	14,239	17.8	28.7
089 Chr & Miss Al	5	560	NR	1,086	1.4	2.2
093 Chr Ch (Disc)	1	27	33	32 *	-	.1
097 Chr Chs&Chs Cr	6	700	NR	839 *	1.0	1.7
127 Ch God (Cleve)	5	576	386	691 *	.9	1.4
151 L-D Saints	1	NR	NR	181	.2	.4
157 Ch of Brethren	23	3,916	1,838	4,701 *	5.9	9.5
165 Ch of Nazarene	5	424	332	629	.8	1.3
167 Chs of Christ	1	60	58	90	.1	.2
171 Ch God-Gen Con	5	585	543	721 *	.9	1.5
183 Cons Menn Conf	2	222	271	323	.4	.7
193 Episcopal	1	NR	64	128	.2	.3
207 E.L.C.A.	36	8,772	2,983	11,647	14.6	23.5
283 Luth—MO Synod	2	162	99	183	.2	.4
288 Mennonite USA	8	993	775	1,242 *	1.6	2.5
297 Mennonite;Other	1	42	NR	50 *	.1	.1
323 Old Ord Amish	8	440	NR	528 *	.7	1.1
331 OCA: Ter Diocs	3	86	NR	102	.1	.2
355 Presb Ch (USA)	3	418	249	502 *	.6	1.0
419 So Bapt Conv	0	11	18	13 *	-	-
443 Un C of Christ	15	2,606	999	3,128 *	3.9	6.3
449 Un Methodist	35	5,493	2,522	6,591 *	8.2	13.3
SULLIVAN	**27**	**1,128**	**918**	**2,871 ***	**43.8**	**100.0**
019 Amer Bapt USA	1	10	31	31 *	.5	1.1
053 Assemb of God	1	52	75	95	1.4	3.3
056 Baha'i	0	1	NR	1	-	-

NR–Not Reported *Total adherents estimated from known number of communicant, confirmed, full members. - Represents a percentage less than 0.1. Percentages may not total 100 due to rounding.

Table 4: Religious Congregations by County and Group: 2000

Religious Group	Number of Churches, Synagogues, Mosques, or Temples	Number of Communicant, Confirmed, or Full Members	Number of Attendees	Total Adherents		
				Number of Adherents	% of Total Pop.	% of Total Adh.
081 Catholic	6	NR	NR	1,144	17.4	39.8
207 E.L.C.A.	1	255	183	321	4.9	11.2
226 Friends-USA	1	105	NR	122 *	1.9	4.2
288 Mennonite USA	2	19	65	65 *	1.0	2.3
331 OCA: Ter Diocs	1	64	NR	69	1.1	2.4
443 Un C of Christ	2	78	62	91 *	1.4	3.2
449 Un Methodist	10	544	371	632 *	9.6	22.0
467 Wesleyan	2	0	131	300	4.6	10.4
SUSQUEHANNA	**78**	**6,875**	**3,070**	**14,602 ***	**34.6**	**100.0**
019 Amer Bapt USA	3	372	141	459 *	1.1	3.1
053 Assemb of God	1	37	28	34	.1	.2
056 Baha'i	0	6	NR	6	-	-
076 Buddhism	1	NR	NR	NR	-	-
081 Catholic	12	NR	NR	5,214	12.3	35.7
089 Chr & Miss Al	1	34	NR	79	.2	.5
151 L-D Saints	2	NR	NR	183	.4	1.3
176 Congr Ad Afl	1	58	NR	72 *	.2	.5
193 Episcopal	4	NR	180	590	1.4	4.0
203 Evan Free Ch	1	39	120	120	.3	.8
221 Free Methodist	1	8	30	30	.1	.2
241 Gen Six Pr Bpt	1	20	NR	25 *	.1	.2
252 Hindu	1	NR	NR	NR	-	-
283 Luth—MO Synod	1	262	77	316	.7	2.2
288 Mennonite USA	1	54	75	75 *	.2	.5
331 OCA: Ter Diocs	1	34	NR	64	.2	.4
355 Presb Ch (USA)	7	397	199	490 *	1.2	3.4
388 Reg Bapt Gen As	6	750	736	915 *	2.2	6.3
413 S.D.A.	1	32	NR	38	.1	.3
435 Unitarian-Univ	1	60	NR	74 *	.2	.5
443 Un C of Christ	1	286	80	353 *	.8	2.4
449 Un Methodist	30	4,426	1,404	5,465 *	12.9	37.4
TIOGA	**92**	**7,879**	**4,349**	**14,291 ***	**34.5**	**100.0**
019 Amer Bapt USA	9	1,322	633	1,602 *	3.9	11.2
053 Assemb of God	4	258	350	590	1.4	4.1
056 Baha'i	0	3	NR	3	-	-
075 Brethren in Cr	1	134	100	134	.3	.9
081 Catholic	6	NR	NR	3,105	7.5	21.7
089 Chr & Miss Al	2	99	NR	281	.7	2.0
093 Chr Ch (Disc)	2	435	82	527 *	1.3	3.7
151 L-D Saints	1	NR	NR	183	.4	1.3
167 Chs of Christ	1	30	45	45	.1	.3
193 Episcopal	5	NR	194	558	1.3	3.9
207 E.L.C.A.	5	431	190	582	1.4	4.1
221 Free Methodist	2	63	83	85	.2	.6
226 Friends-USA	1	105	NR	127 *	.3	.9
283 Luth—MO Synod	1	186	126	236	.6	1.7
288 Mennonite USA	3	141	151	186 *	.4	1.3
297 Mennonite;Other	1	52	NR	63 *	.2	.4
335 Orth Pres Ch	1	22	33	41	.1	.3
355 Presb Ch (USA)	7	562	248	682 *	1.6	4.8
388 Reg Bapt Gen As	2	193	217	234 *	.6	1.6
403 Salvation Army	1	30	28	64	.2	.4
413 S.D.A.	2	175	NR	208	.5	1.5
449 Un Methodist	33	3,506	1,665	4,247 *	10.3	29.7
467 Wesleyan	2	132	204	508	1.2	3.6
UNION	**62**	**9,772**	**4,584**	**15,386 ***	**37.0**	**100.0**
019 Amer Bapt USA	1	229	79	270 *	.6	1.8
053 Assemb of God	2	219	240	410	1.0	2.7
056 Baha'i	0	9	NR	9	-	.1
061 Beachy Amish	1	141	NR	166 *	.4	1.1
081 Catholic	2	NR	NR	2,573	6.2	16.7
089 Chr & Miss Al	2	144	NR	373	.9	2.4
143 CG in Cr(Menn)	1	89	NR	105 *	.3	.7
151 L-D Saints	1	NR	NR	343	.8	2.2
157 Ch of Brethren	1	208	253	253 *	.6	1.6
165 Ch of Nazarene	1	389	301	479	1.2	3.1
193 Episcopal	1	NR	97	232	.6	1.5
207 E.L.C.A.	9	2,463	1,147	3,158	7.6	20.5
226 Friends-USA	1	105	NR	124 *	.3	.8
263 Int Foursq Gos	1	50	65	65 *	.2	.4

Religious Group	Number of Churches, Synagogues, Mosques, or Temples	Number of Communicant, Confirmed, or Full Members	Number of Attendees	Total Adherents		
				Number of Adherents	% of Total Pop.	% of Total Adh.
286 E.PA Mennonite	1	126	NR	149 *	.4	1.0
288 Mennonite USA	1	147	118	173 *	.4	1.1
297 Mennonite;Other	1	161	NR	190 *	.5	1.2
322 Old Ord Menn Ch	2	485	NR	572 *	1.4	3.7
323 Old Ord Amish	2	130	NR	153 *	.4	1.0
355 Presb Ch (USA)	3	643	364	759 *	1.8	4.9
388 Reg Bapt Gen As	2	160	166	166 *	.4	1.1
403 Salvation Army	1	95	36	207	.5	1.3
435 Unitarian-Univ	1	27	NR	32 *	.1	.2
443 Un C of Christ	9	1,650	730	1,947 *	4.7	12.7
449 Un Methodist	15	2,102	988	2,478 *	6.0	16.1
VENANGO	**118**	**13,777**	**7,468**	**28,592 ***	**49.7**	**100.0**
011 A.W.M.C.	3	110	274	117	.2	.4
019 Amer Bapt USA	3	381	224	464 *	.8	1.6
053 Assemb of God	3	191	230	336	.6	1.2
081 Catholic	8	NR	NR	9,867	17.1	34.5
089 Chr & Miss Al	2	96	NR	301	.5	1.1
123 Ch God (Ander)	5	NR	538	538	.9	1.9
145 Ch God Prophcy	1	41	NR	50 *	.1	.2
151 L-D Saints	2	NR	NR	322	.6	1.1
165 Ch of Nazarene	2	427	248	616	1.1	2.2
167 Chs of Christ	1	12	20	27	-	.1
171 Ch God-Gen Con	4	296	181	365 *	.6	1.3
193 Episcopal	2	NR	155	397	.7	1.4
207 E.L.C.A.	5	1,147	452	1,426	2.5	5.0
221 Free Methodist	4	188	227	228	.4	.8
263 Int Foursq Gos	1	44	124	124 *	.2	.4
283 Luth—MO Synod	1	150	50	189	.3	.7
323 Old Ord Amish	4	220	NR	268 *	.5	.9
335 Orth Pres Ch	1	22	22	28	-	.1
355 Presb Ch (USA)	15	2,218	1,125	2,701 *	4.7	9.4
388 Reg Bapt Gen As	1	41	55	55 *	.1	.2
403 Salvation Army	2	157	116	283	.5	1.0
413 S.D.A.	2	113	NR	135	.2	.5
419 So Bapt Conv	0	15	60	18 *	-	.1
449 Un Methodist	45	7,908	3,367	9,637 *	16.7	33.7
496 Jewish Est	1	NR	NR	100	.2	.3
WARREN	**82**	**10,525**	**5,243**	**20,530 ***	**46.8**	**100.0**
011 A.W.M.C.	2	54	203	60	.1	.3
019 Amer Bapt USA	1	155	70	189 *	.4	.9
053 Assemb of God	1	50	55	72	.2	.4
056 Baha'i	0	10	NR	10	-	-
057 Bapt Gen Conf	2	202	193	246 *	.6	1.2
081 Catholic	6	NR	NR	6,348	14.5	30.9
084 Calvary Chapel	1	NR	NR	NR	-	-
089 Chr & Miss Al	1	73	NR	184	.4	.9
123 Ch God (Ander)	1	NR	103	103	.2	.5
127 Ch God (Cleve)	2	60	18	73 *	.2	.4
151 L-D Saints	1	NR	NR	234	.5	1.1
165 Ch of Nazarene	1	403	289	403	.9	2.0
167 Chs of Christ	1	50	54	62	.1	.3
175 Congr Chr Chs	2	80	85	98 *	.2	.5
181 Consrv Congr	2	65	82	79 *	.2	.4
193 Episcopal	2	NR	176	362	.8	1.8
201 Evan Cov Ch	4	239	258	309 *	.7	1.5
207 E.L.C.A.	7	2,220	729	3,019	6.9	14.7
221 Free Methodist	4	247	342	360	.8	1.8
323 Old Ord Amish	4	220	NR	268 *	.6	1.3
355 Presb Ch (USA)	6	1,041	468	1,270 *	2.9	6.2
388 Reg Bapt Gen As	1	19	35	35 *	.1	.2
403 Salvation Army	1	104	84	225	.5	1.1
413 S.D.A.	1	53	NR	63	.1	.3
418 Southw Bapt Fel	1	NR	NR	NR	-	-
419 So Bapt Conv	1	9	11	11 *	-	.1
443 Un C of Christ	2	364	89	444 *	1.0	2.2
449 Un Methodist	23	4,780	1,842	5,833 *	13.3	28.4
467 Wesleyan	1	27	57	170	.4	.8
WASHINGTON	**254**	**37,191**	**16,600**	**122,027 ***	**60.1**	**100.0**
011 A.W.M.C.	1	0	55	0	-	-
019 Amer Bapt USA	13	2,260	876	2,722 *	1.3	2.2

NR–Not Reported *Total adherents estimated from known number of communicant, confirmed, full members. - Represents a percentage less than 0.1. Percentages may not total 100 due to rounding.

Table 4: Religious Congregations by County and Group: 2000

Religious Group	Number of Churches, Synagogues, Mosques, or Temples	Number of Communicant, Confirmed, or Full Members	Number of Attendees	Total Adherents		
				Number of Adherents	% of Total Pop.	% of Total Adh.
022 Carp Rus Orth	1	122	NR	207	.1	.2
034 Ant Orth of NA	1	49	NR	98	-	.1
053 Assemb of God	4	679	810	1,385	.7	1.1
056 Baha'i	0	18	NR	18	-	-
057 Bapt Gen Conf	1	157	61	189 *	.1	.2
071 Brethren (Ash)	1	47	35	57 *	-	-
081 Catholic	31	NR	NR	71,268	35.1	58.4
084 Calvary Chapel	1	NR	NR	NR	-	-
089 Chr & Miss Al	3	293	NR	581	.3	.5
093 Chr Ch (Disc)	9	2,688	938	3,238 *	1.6	2.7
097 Chr Chs&Chs Cr	6	665	NR	801 *	.4	.7
127 Ch God (Cleve)	1	184	68	222 *	.1	.2
145 Ch God Prophcy	2	82	NR	98 *	-	.1
151 L-D Saints	2	NR	NR	627	.3	.5
157 Ch of Brethren	1	30	0	36 *	-	-
165 Ch of Nazarene	8	685	506	1,227	.6	1.0
167 Chs of Christ	6	402	356	551	.3	.5
173 Comm of Christ	1	71	NR	71	-	.1
179 Consrv Bapt	2	NR	160	160	.1	.1
193 Episcopal	6	NR	628	1,269	.6	1.0
203 Evan Free Ch	1	25	75	75	-	.1
207 E.L.C.A.	10	2,409	931	3,344	1.6	2.7
221 Free Methodist	3	252	334	335	.2	.3
246 Greek Orthodox	1	NR	NR	900	.4	.7
283 Luth—MO Synod	1	24	11	24	-	-
331 OCA: Ter Diocs	3	379	NR	416	.2	.3
349 Pent Holiness	1	160	160	193 *	.1	.2
355 Presb Ch (USA)	60	12,259	5,526	14,768 *	7.3	12.1
356 Presb Ch Amer	2	117	105	128	.1	.1
388 Reg Bapt Gen As	2	161	189	199 *	.1	.2
401 Rus Orth Abroad	1	NR	NR	NR	-	-
403 Salvation Army	1	88	34	171	.1	.1
413 S.D.A.	1	56	NR	67	-	.1
416 Sikh	1	NR	NR	NR	-	-
419 So Bapt Conv	7	1,512	881	1,821 *	.9	1.5
449 Un Methodist	55	11,223	3,714	13,520 *	6.7	11.1
467 Wesleyan	2	94	147	341	.2	.3
496 Jewish Est	1	NR	NR	900	.4	.7
WAYNE	**73**	**8,005**	**3,197**	**26,803 ***	**56.2**	**100.0**
019 Amer Bapt USA	3	412	142	503 *	1.1	1.9
053 Assemb of God	2	299	326	376	.8	1.4
056 Baha'i	0	5	NR	5	-	-
081 Catholic	11	NR	NR	15,490	32.5	57.8
151 L-D Saints	1	NR	NR	252	.5	.9
167 Chs of Christ	1	18	16	23	-	.1
193 Episcopal	3	NR	177	384	.8	1.4
201 Evan Cov Ch	1	99	130	130 *	.3	.5
207 E.L.C.A.	3	1,267	352	1,812	3.8	6.8
221 Free Methodist	2	150	187	239	.5	.9
226 Friends-USA	1	105	NR	128 *	.3	.5
293 Morav Ch-North	1	120	NR	152	.3	.6
331 OCA: Ter Diocs	3	202	NR	236	.5	.9
355 Presb Ch (USA)	5	562	224	685 *	1.4	2.6
371 Ref Ch in Am	1	43	126	126	.3	.5
413 S.D.A.	1	34	NR	40	.1	.1
449 Un Methodist	33	4,689	1,517	5,722 *	12.0	21.3
496 Jewish Est	1	NR	NR	500	1.0	1.9
WESTMORELAND	**419**	**75,855**	**31,354**	**237,503 ***	**64.2**	**100.0**
011 A.W.M.C.	2	30	67	36	-	-
019 Amer Bapt USA	12	1,860	804	2,232 *	.6	.9
022 Carp Rus Orth	2	243	NR	416	.1	.2
034 Ant Orth of NA	5	1,037	NR	2,074	.6	.9
053 Assemb of God	12	1,360	1,598	2,211	.6	.9
056 Baha'i	0	19	NR	19	-	-
071 Brethren (Ash)	2	135	131	162 *	-	.1
081 Catholic	68	NR	NR	131,608	35.6	55.4
089 Chr & Miss Al	12	999	NR	3,039	.8	1.3
093 Chr Ch (Disc)	2	714	345	857 *	.2	.4
097 Chr Chs&Chs Cr	10	2,252	NR	2,702 *	.7	1.1
123 Ch God (Ander)	5	NR	598	598	.2	.3
127 Ch God (Cleve)	2	65	54	83 *	-	-
151 L-D Saints	1	NR	NR	463	.1	.2
157 Ch of Brethren	7	1,244	472	1,491 *	.4	.6
165 Ch of Nazarene	5	473	344	927	.3	.4
167 Chs of Christ	5	238	252	332	.1	.1
171 Ch God-Gen Con	9	1,616	878	2,016 *	.5	.8
179 Consrv Bapt	1	NR	40	40	-	-
181 Consrv Congr	1	22	46	26 *	-	-
193 Episcopal	6	NR	661	1,390	.4	.6
207 E.L.C.A.	50	17,322	5,371	23,518	6.4	9.9
221 Free Methodist	4	279	423	435	.1	.2
246 Greek Orthodox	2	NR	NR	690	.2	.3
252 Hindu	1	NR	NR	NR	-	-
268 Jain	1	NR	NR	NR	-	-
283 Luth—MO Synod	3	601	214	736	.2	.3
288 Mennonite USA	1	148	105	178 *	-	.1
313 N Am Bapt Conf	1	0	40	40 *	-	-
331 OCA: Ter Diocs	3	306	NR	374	.1	.2
349 Pent Holiness	4	447	287	536 *	.1	.2
355 Presb Ch (USA)	45	12,217	6,484	15,370 *	4.2	6.5
356 Presb Ch Amer	5	480	558	633	.2	.3
363 Primitive Meth	3	171	NR	182	-	.1
388 Reg Bapt Gen As	2	128	170	171 *	-	.1
403 Salvation Army	6	461	321	1,083	.3	.5
410 Serb Orth USA	1	NR	NR	152	-	.1
413 S.D.A.	1	45	NR	54	-	-
419 So Bapt Conv	3	295	238	354 *	.1	.1
431 Ukrainian Orth	3	NR	NR	522	.1	.2
435 Unitarian-Univ	2	71	NR	85 *	-	-
443 Un C of Christ	25	4,109	1,570	4,931 *	1.3	2.1
449 Un Methodist	76	24,136	7,235	28,966 *	7.8	12.2
467 Wesleyan	2	412	431	1,132	.3	.5
469 WELS	1	120	67	139	-	.1
496 Jewish Est	3	NR	NR	2,700	.7	1.1
498 Indep.Charis.	2	1,800	1,550	1,800	.5	.8
WYOMING	**38**	**4,547**	**2,131**	**11,899 ***	**42.4**	**100.0**
019 Amer Bapt USA	2	231	50	285 *	1.0	2.4
053 Assemb of God	3	207	251	357	1.3	3.0
056 Baha'i	0	13	NR	13	-	.1
081 Catholic	5	NR	NR	5,699	20.3	47.9
151 L-D Saints	1	NR	NR	139	.5	1.2
193 Episcopal	1	NR	71	171	.6	1.4
207 E.L.C.A.	1	38	40	110	.4	.9
221 Free Methodist	1	52	75	75	.3	.6
283 Luth—MO Synod	1	124	60	226	.8	1.9
355 Presb Ch (USA)	2	169	105	209 *	.7	1.8
388 Reg Bapt Gen As	2	112	180	180 *	.6	1.5
413 S.D.A.	1	84	NR	100	.4	.8
419 So Bapt Conv	1	78	50	96 *	.3	.8
449 Un Methodist	17	3,439	1,249	4,239 *	15.1	35.6
YORK	**384**	**96,102**	**45,752**	**171,682 ***	**45.0**	**100.0**
019 Amer Bapt USA	2	359	461	461 *	.1	.3
032 Amish; other	1	130	NR	161 *	-	.1
034 Ant Orth of NA	1	144	NR	288	.1	.2
053 Assemb of God	18	2,066	2,288	3,127	.8	1.8
056 Baha'i	0	35	NR	35	-	-
075 Brethren in Cr	7	704	1,017	1,071	.3	.6
081 Catholic	12	NR	NR	37,745	9.9	22.0
084 Calvary Chapel	1	NR	NR	NR	-	-
089 Chr & Miss Al	9	840	NR	1,553	.4	.9
097 Chr Chs&Chs Cr	1	65	NR	80 *	-	-
127 Ch God (Cleve)	4	684	330	845 *	.2	.5
145 Ch God Prophcy	1	41	NR	51 *	-	-
151 L-D Saints	4	NR	NR	1,816	.5	1.1
157 Ch of Brethren	15	3,263	2,000	4,031 *	1.1	2.3
165 Ch of Nazarene	5	1,171	991	2,371	.6	1.4
167 Chs of Christ	4	326	321	400	.1	.2
171 Ch God-Gen Con	11	1,175	1,623	1,890 *	.5	1.1
173 Comm of Christ	1	113	NR	113	-	.1
179 Consrv Bapt	1	NR	255	255	.1	.1
193 Episcopal	3	NR	463	1,319	.3	.8
203 Evan Free Ch	2	231	390	390	.1	.2

NR–Not Reported *Total adherents estimated from known number of communicant, confirmed, full members. - Represents a percentage less than 0.1. Percentages may not total 100 due to rounding.

Table 4: Religious Congregations by County and Group: 2000

Religious Group	Number of Churches, Synagogues, Mosques, or Temples	Number of Communicant, Confirmed, or Full Members	Number of Attendees	Total Adherents: Number of Adherents	% of Total Pop.	% of Total Adh.
207 E.L.C.A.	73	29,154	10,087	38,924	10.2	22.7
223 Free Will Bapt	1	99	NR	122 *	-	.1
246 Greek Orthodox	1	NR	NR	1,500	.4	.9
263 Int Foursq Gos	2	426	310	526 *	.1	.3
267 Muslim Est	1	NR	156	609	.2	.4
283 Luth—MO Synod	3	1,197	408	1,541	.4	.9
286 E.PA Mennonite	1	26	NR	32 *	-	-
288 Mennonite USA	4	215	233	281 *	.1	.2
291 Missionary Ch	1	63	39	63	-	-
293 Morav Ch-North	2	361	NR	425	.1	.2
297 Mennonite;Other	5	193	NR	238 *	.1	.1
323 Old Ord Amish	2	150	NR	186 *	-	.1
335 Orth Pres Ch	2	109	96	155	-	.1
355 Presb Ch (USA)	15	5,131	2,040	6,339 *	1.7	3.7
356 Presb Ch Amer	4	430	517	580	.2	.3
370 Ref Baptist Chs	1	NR	NR	NR	-	-
403 Salvation Army	2	230	281	1,708	.4	1.0
413 S.D.A.	4	545	NR	648	.2	.4
419 So Bapt Conv	15	2,574	1,026	3,179 *	.8	1.9
435 Unitarian-Univ	1	220	NR	272 *	.1	.2
443 Un C of Christ	41	16,146	5,529	19,944 *	5.2	11.6
449 Un Methodist	92	25,666	12,474	31,709 *	8.3	18.5
467 Wesleyan	2	0	42	49	-	-
496 Jewish Est	2	NR	NR	1,800	.5	1.0
498 Indep.Charis.	1	400	400	400	.1	.2
499 Indep.Non-Char	3	1,420	1,975	2,450	.6	1.4

RHODE ISLAND

Religious Group	Number of Churches, Synagogues, Mosques, or Temples	Number of Communicant, Confirmed, or Full Members	Number of Attendees	Total Adherents: Number of Adherents	% of Total Pop.	% of Total Adh.
The State.....	572	51,815	32,957	665,170 *	63.5	100.0
BRISTOL	**26**	**1,881**	**1,932**	**37,591 ***	**74.2**	**100.0**
019 Amer Bapt USA	2	146	86	177 *	.3	.5
053 Assemb of God	1	48	55	70	.1	.2
056 Baha'i	0	12	NR	12	-	-
081 Catholic	10	NR	NR	30,588	60.4	81.4
151 L-D Saints	1	NR	NR	339	.7	.9
179 Consrv Bapt	1	NR	580	580	1.1	1.5
193 Episcopal	3	NR	536	2,011	4.0	5.3
207 E.L.C.A.	1	205	90	270	.5	.7
355 Presb Ch (USA)	1	106	57	129 *	.3	.3
443 Un C of Christ	2	853	386	1,035 *	2.0	2.8
449 Un Methodist	2	511	142	620 *	1.2	1.6
496 Jewish Est	2	NR	NR	1,760	3.5	4.7
KENT	**78**	**8,484**	**5,426**	**112,070 ***	**67.1**	**100.0**
019 Amer Bapt USA	12	2,216	1,048	2,703 *	1.6	2.4
053 Assemb of God	2	206	266	397	.2	.4
056 Baha'i	1	39	NR	39	-	-
057 Bapt Gen Conf	1	115	70	140 *	.1	.1
081 Catholic	25	NR	NR	94,194	56.4	84.0
084 Calvary Chapel	1	NR	NR	NR	-	-
151 L-D Saints	1	NR	NR	255	.2	.2
167 Chs of Christ	1	37	60	74	-	.1
173 Comm of Christ	1	62	NR	62	-	.1
175 Congr Chr Chs	1	88	50	107 *	.1	.1
179 Consrv Bapt	3	NR	345	345	.2	.3
193 Episcopal	9	NR	1,186	4,337	2.6	3.9
201 Evan Cov Ch	1	144	349	349 *	.2	.3
207 E.L.C.A.	4	1,957	833	2,886	1.7	2.6
263 Int Foursq Gos	1	35	48	48 *	-	-
355 Presb Ch (USA)	2	681	328	831 *	.5	.7
419 So Bapt Conv	1	746	250	910 *	.5	.8
435 Unitarian-Univ	1	200	NR	244 *	.1	.2
443 Un C of Christ	2	158	105	193 *	.1	.2
449 Un Methodist	6	1,800	488	2,196 *	1.3	2.0
496 Jewish Est	2	NR	NR	1,760	1.1	1.6
NEWPORT	**55**	**4,812**	**3,021**	**46,984 ***	**55.0**	**100.0**
019 Amer Bapt USA	6	1,045	476	1,270 *	1.5	2.7
053 Assemb of God	1	108	150	190	.2	.4
056 Baha'i	0	27	NR	27	-	.1
081 Catholic	13	NR	NR	34,884	40.8	74.2
151 L-D Saints	1	NR	NR	366	.4	.8
167 Chs of Christ	1	30	35	35	-	.1
173 Comm of Christ	1	64	NR	64	.1	.1
176 Congr Ad Afl	2	807	NR	981 *	1.1	2.1
179 Consrv Bapt	1	NR	60	60	.1	.1
193 Episcopal	10	NR	1,267	4,064	4.8	8.6
207 E.L.C.A.	1	251	159	449	.5	1.0
226 Friends-USA	4	276	NR	335 *	.4	.7
246 Greek Orthodox	1	NR	NR	699	.8	1.5
355 Presb Ch (USA)	1	279	245	339 *	.4	.7
363 Primitive Meth	1	57	NR	61	.1	.1
403 Salvation Army	1	71	59	277	.3	.6
419 So Bapt Conv	1	140	125	170 *	.2	.4
435 Unitarian-Univ	1	173	NR	210 *	.2	.4
443 Un C of Christ	2	400	110	486 *	.6	1.0
449 Un Methodist	3	1,084	335	1,317 *	1.5	2.8
496 Jewish Est	3	NR	NR	700	.8	1.5
PROVIDENCE	**344**	**30,045**	**17,792**	**395,316 ***	**63.6**	**100.0**
017 Amer Bapt Assn	1	20	NR	25 *	-	-
019 Amer Bapt USA	38	11,222	3,727	13,825 *	2.2	3.5
034 Ant Orth of NA	1	0	NR	0	-	-
049 Armen Ap Cilic	1	510	NR	1,400	.2	.4
050 Armen Ap Etchm	1	478	NR	2,400	.4	.6
053 Assemb of God	16	1,629	1,980	2,519	.4	.6
056 Baha'i	2	156	NR	156	-	-
057 Bapt Gen Conf	1	25	50	50 *	-	-
076 Buddhism	5	NR	NR	NR	-	-
081 Catholic	97	NR	NR	323,910	52.1	81.9
089 Chr & Miss Al	3	553	NR	780	.1	.2
097 Chr Chs&Chs Cr	1	0	NR	0 *	-	-
123 Ch God (Ander)	2	NR	132	132	-	-
127 Ch God (Cleve)	21	1,022	684	1,264 *	.2	.3
145 Ch God Prophcy	4	267	NR	328 *	.1	.1
151 L-D Saints	4	NR	NR	1,335	.2	.3
165 Ch of Nazarene	5	367	529	610	.1	.2
167 Chs of Christ	3	131	135	182	-	-
175 Congr Chr Chs	1	40	15	49 *	-	-
179 Consrv Bapt	2	NR	190	190	-	-
181 Consrv Congr	1	157	110	193 *	-	-
193 Episcopal	32	NR	3,437	11,624	1.9	2.9
201 Evan Cov Ch	3	342	254	421 *	.1	.1
207 E.L.C.A.	4	1,037	387	1,529	.2	.4
221 Free Methodist	1	2	35	35	-	-
226 Friends-USA	3	129	NR	159 *	-	-
245 Greek Orth Vslp	1	175	NR	675	.1	.2
246 Greek Orthodox	2	NR	NR	2,739	.4	.7
252 Hindu	1	NR	NR	NR	-	-
263 Int Foursq Gos	2	84	288	288 *	-	.1
267 Muslim Est	3	NR	468	1,827	.3	.5
283 Luth—MO Synod	2	577	378	792	.1	.2
331 OCA: Ter Diocs	1	64	NR	178	-	-
355 Presb Ch (USA)	3	457	261	564 *	.1	.1
356 Presb Ch Amer	1	80	0	108	-	-
363 Primitive Meth	4	228	NR	243	-	.1
370 Ref Baptist Chs	1	NR	NR	NR	-	-
388 Reg Bapt Gen As	1	46	70	70 *	-	-
397 OCA: Roman Dioc	1	NR	NR	81	-	-
403 Salvation Army	2	166	129	723	.1	.2
413 S.D.A.	6	640	NR	762	.1	.2
419 So Bapt Conv	4	137	91	169 *	-	-
423 Syrian Orth Ch	1	NR	NR	250	-	.1
431 Ukrainian Orth	1	NR	NR	474	.1	.1
435 Unitarian-Univ	6	604	NR	744 *	.1	.2
443 Un C of Christ	20	4,606	2,063	5,674 *	.9	1.4
449 Un Methodist	12	3,064	1,034	3,774 *	.6	1.0
463 Vineyard	1	130	120	160 *	-	-
496 Jewish Est	12	NR	NR	10,680	1.7	2.7
498 Indep.Charis.	2	600	925	925	.1	.2
499 Indep.Non-Char	1	300	300	300	-	.1

NR–Not Reported *Total adherents estimated from known number of communicant, confirmed, full members. - Represents a percentage less than 0.1. Percentages may not total 100 due to rounding.

Table 4: Religious Congregations by County and Group: 2000

Religious Group	Number of Churches, Synagogues, Mosques, or Temples	Number of Communicant, Confirmed, or Full Members	Number of Attendees	Total Adherents		
				Number of Adherents	% of Total Pop.	% of Total Adh.
WASHINGTON	**69**	**6,593**	**4,786**	**73,209 ***	**59.3**	**100.0**
019 Amer Bapt USA	15	2,475	1,000	3,022 *	2.4	4.1
053 Assemb of God	3	279	384	388	.3	.5
056 Baha'i	0	27	NR	27	-	-
081 Catholic	20	NR	NR	58,668	47.5	80.1
123 Ch God (Ander)	1	NR	200	200	.2	.3
127 Ch God (Cleve)	1	41	33	50 *	-	.1
165 Ch of Nazarene	1	0	28	50	-	.1
167 Chs of Christ	1	59	77	91	.1	.1
179 Consrv Bapt	1	NR	175	175	.1	.2
193 Episcopal	10	NR	1,189	4,720	3.8	6.4
207 E.L.C.A.	2	586	367	780	.6	1.1
226 Friends-USA	2	86	NR	105 *	.1	.1
283 Luth—MO Synod	1	165	70	225	.2	.3
355 Presb Ch (USA)	2	454	370	554 *	.4	.8
413 S.D.A.	1	34	NR	40	-	.1
419 So Bapt Conv	2	536	143	654 *	.5	.9
435 Unitarian-Univ	1	83	NR	101 *	.1	.1
443 Un C of Christ	2	1,207	479	1,474 *	1.2	2.0
449 Un Methodist	3	561	271	685 *	.6	.9
496 Jewish Est	0	NR	NR	1,200	1.0	1.6
SOUTH CAROLINA						
The State.....	5,522	1,338,172	583,451	1,908,638 *	47.6	100.0
ABBEVILLE	**55**	**10,621**	**3,955**	**13,301 ***	**50.8**	**100.0**
055 As Ref Pres Ch	3	339	NR	352	1.3	2.6
056 Baha'i	0	26	NR	26	.1	.2
061 Beachy Amish	1	140	NR	174 *	.7	1.3
081 Catholic	1	NR	NR	128	.5	1.0
127 Ch God (Cleve)	2	212	89	264 *	1.0	2.0
145 Ch God Prophcy	1	36	NR	44 *	.2	.3
167 Chs of Christ	1	349	209	475	1.8	3.6
193 Episcopal	1	NR	44	72	.3	.5
297 Mennonite;Other	1	62	NR	77 *	.3	.6
349 Pent Holiness	2	392	206	487 *	1.9	3.7
355 Presb Ch (USA)	8	779	429	970 *	3.7	7.3
356 Presb Ch Amer	3	340	145	356	1.4	2.7
419 So Bapt Conv	21	6,542	2,227	8,132 *	31.1	61.1
449 Un Methodist	10	1,404	606	1,744 *	6.7	13.1
AIKEN	**184**	**51,321**	**21,552**	**73,210 ***	**51.4**	**100.0**
017 Amer Bapt Assn	1	50	NR	63 *	-	.1
034 Ant Orth of NA	1	59	NR	118	.1	.2
053 Assemb of God	3	90	98	111	.1	.2
056 Baha'i	1	59	NR	59	-	.1
081 Catholic	4	NR	NR	5,777	4.1	7.9
084 Calvary Chapel	1	NR	NR	NR	-	-
093 Chr Ch (Disc)	4	281	121	352 *	.2	.5
097 Chr Chs&Chs Cr	1	40	NR	50 *	-	.1
123 Ch God (Ander)	4	NR	120	120	.1	.2
127 Ch God (Cleve)	13	1,965	1,249	2,461 *	1.7	3.4
145 Ch God Prophcy	1	36	NR	45 *	-	.1
151 L-D Saints	2	NR	NR	919	.6	1.3
165 Ch of Nazarene	3	590	537	802	.6	1.1
167 Chs of Christ	9	604	577	825	.6	1.1
193 Episcopal	6	NR	679	1,792	1.3	2.4
207 E.L.C.A.	4	1,471	661	1,954	1.4	2.7
223 Free Will Bapt	1	50	NR	62 *	-	.1
283 Luth—MO Synod	1	69	41	91	.1	.1
297 Mennonite;Other	1	47	NR	59 *	-	.1
349 Pent Holiness	10	1,208	762	1,513 *	1.1	2.1
355 Presb Ch (USA)	3	2,233	1,123	2,796 *	2.0	3.8
356 Presb Ch Amer	2	413	358	565	.4	.8
403 Salvation Army	1	109	76	111	.1	.2
413 S.D.A.	3	197	NR	234	.2	.3
418 Southw Bapt Fel	1	NR	NR	NR	-	-
419 So Bapt Conv	81	34,733	12,329	43,494 *	30.5	59.4
449 Un Methodist	19	6,237	2,346	7,809 *	5.5	10.7
463 Vineyard	1	130	120	163 *	.1	.2
496 Jewish Est	1	NR	NR	215	.2	.3

Religious Group	Number of Churches, Synagogues, Mosques, or Temples	Number of Communicant, Confirmed, or Full Members	Number of Attendees	Total Adherents		
				Number of Adherents	% of Total Pop.	% of Total Adh.
499 Indep.Non-Char	1	650	355	650	.5	.9
ALLENDALE	**27**	**3,122**	**985**	**4,165 ***	**37.2**	**100.0**
053 Assemb of God	2	53	65	94	.8	2.3
056 Baha'i	0	21	NR	21	.2	.5
081 Catholic	1	NR	NR	40	.4	1.0
093 Chr Ch (Disc)	4	248	0	312 *	2.8	7.5
127 Ch God (Cleve)	1	20	20	25 *	.2	.6
151 L-D Saints	1	NR	NR	141	1.3	3.4
193 Episcopal	1	NR	11	23	.2	.6
207 E.L.C.A.	2	107	94	145	1.3	3.5
355 Presb Ch (USA)	1	24	10	30 *	.3	.7
419 So Bapt Conv	9	1,856	467	2,336 *	20.8	56.1
449 Un Methodist	5	793	318	998 *	8.9	24.0
ANDERSON	**250**	**73,658**	**29,510**	**94,725 ***	**57.2**	**100.0**
034 Ant Orth of NA	1	18	NR	36	-	-
053 Assemb of God	9	1,152	1,273	1,517	.9	1.6
055 As Ref Pres Ch	3	413	NR	416	.3	.4
056 Baha'i	2	183	NR	183	.1	.2
081 Catholic	2	NR	NR	1,426	.9	1.5
097 Chr Chs&Chs Cr	1	53	NR	66 *	-	.1
121 Ch God (Abr)	1	50	75	75 *	-	.1
127 Ch God (Cleve)	20	4,583	2,419	5,674 *	3.4	6.0
145 Ch God Prophcy	12	428	NR	528 *	.3	.6
151 L-D Saints	2	NR	NR	648	.4	.7
165 Ch of Nazarene	1	73	16	73	-	.1
167 Chs of Christ	2	80	98	93	.1	.1
193 Episcopal	2	NR	236	550	.3	.6
207 E.L.C.A.	1	240	144	316	.2	.3
216 Evan Presby Ch	1	114	NR	141 *	.1	.1
223 Free Will Bapt	1	50	NR	61 *	-	.1
267 Muslim Est	1	NR	156	609	.4	.6
283 Luth—MO Synod	1	186	94	234	.1	.2
288 Mennonite USA	1	27	22	33 *	-	-
297 Mennonite;Other	1	115	NR	142 *	.1	.1
349 Pent Holiness	14	2,258	1,197	2,796 *	1.7	3.0
355 Presb Ch (USA)	18	3,736	1,842	4,626 *	2.8	4.9
356 Presb Ch Amer	2	459	50	559	.3	.6
403 Salvation Army	1	100	122	110	.1	.1
413 S.D.A.	2	267	NR	318	.2	.3
418 Southw Bapt Fel	1	NR	NR	NR	-	-
419 So Bapt Conv	105	51,336	18,514	63,575 *	38.4	67.1
449 Un Methodist	36	7,236	2,873	8,962 *	5.4	9.5
467 Wesleyan	6	501	379	958	.6	1.0
BAMBERG	**53**	**6,272**	**2,756**	**7,882 ***	**47.3**	**100.0**
056 Baha'i	0	99	NR	99	.6	1.3
081 Catholic	0	NR	NR	20	.1	.3
093 Chr Ch (Disc)	2	146	0	181 *	1.1	2.3
127 Ch God (Cleve)	3	63	51	78 *	.5	1.0
145 Ch God Prophcy	2	71	NR	88 *	.5	1.1
165 Ch of Nazarene	1	73	37	73	.4	.9
167 Chs of Christ	1	33	34	51	.3	.6
193 Episcopal	2	NR	54	137	.8	1.7
207 E.L.C.A.	2	80	62	91	.5	1.2
349 Pent Holiness	2	227	121	281 *	1.7	3.6
355 Presb Ch (USA)	2	35	25	43 *	.3	.5
413 S.D.A.	1	17	NR	20	.1	.3
419 So Bapt Conv	15	3,188	1,195	3,946 *	23.7	50.1
449 Un Methodist	20	2,240	1,177	2,774 *	16.7	35.2
BARNWELL	**49**	**8,988**	**3,616**	**11,913 ***	**50.7**	**100.0**
053 Assemb of God	1	104	120	120	.5	1.0
056 Baha'i	0	37	NR	37	.2	.3
061 Beachy Amish	1	43	NR	55 *	.2	.5
081 Catholic	2	NR	NR	215	.9	1.8
089 Chr & Miss Al	1	6	NR	19	.1	.2
097 Chr Chs&Chs Cr	1	125	NR	159 *	.7	1.3
123 Ch God (Ander)	1	NR	20	20	.1	.2
127 Ch God (Cleve)	3	262	122	335 *	1.4	2.8
151 L-D Saints	1	NR	NR	123	.5	1.0

NR–Not Reported *Total adherents estimated from known number of communicant, confirmed, full members. - Represents a percentage less than 0.1. Percentages may not total 100 due to rounding.

Table 4: Religious Congregations by County and Group: 2000

Religious Group	Number of Churches, Synagogues, Mosques, or Temples	Number of Communicant, Confirmed, or Full Members	Number of Attendees	Total Adherents: Number of Adherents	% of Total Pop.	% of Total Adh.
167 Chs of Christ	3	186	185	244	1.0	2.0
193 Episcopal	2	NR	59	94	.4	.8
297 Mennonite;Other	1	82	NR	105 *	.4	.9
349 Pent Holiness	2	160	174	204 *	.9	1.7
355 Presb Ch (USA)	3	359	161	458 *	2.0	3.8
419 So Bapt Conv	22	6,658	2,437	8,493 *	36.2	71.3
449 Un Methodist	5	966	338	1,232 *	5.2	10.3
BEAUFORT	**75**	**19,849**	**10,218**	**39,650 ***	**32.8**	**100.0**
053 Assemb of God	1	275	375	565	.5	1.4
056 Baha'i	1	450	NR	450	.4	1.1
081 Catholic	4	NR	NR	9,735	8.0	24.6
084 Calvary Chapel	1	NR	NR	NR	-	-
093 Chr Ch (Disc)	3	500	85	614 *	.5	1.5
097 Chr Chs&Chs Cr	1	30	NR	37 *	-	.1
127 Ch God (Cleve)	4	465	619	746 *	.6	1.9
145 Ch God Prophcy	1	36	NR	44 *	-	.1
151 L-D Saints	3	NR	NR	1,097	.9	2.8
165 Ch of Nazarene	1	0	17	17	-	-
167 Chs of Christ	5	137	207	212	.2	.5
193 Episcopal	4	NR	1,655	3,598	3.0	9.1
207 E.L.C.A.	3	975	630	1,216	1.0	3.1
246 Greek Orthodox	1	NR	NR	3	-	-
263 Int Foursq Gos	1	30	50	50 *	-	.1
283 Luth—MO Synod	1	173	126	216	.2	.5
355 Presb Ch (USA)	6	4,024	2,232	4,938 *	4.1	12.5
356 Presb Ch Amer	2	207	333	333	.3	.8
403 Salvation Army	1	78	33	201	.2	.5
413 S.D.A.	4	324	NR	386	.3	1.0
418 Southw Bapt Fel	1	NR	NR	NR	-	-
419 So Bapt Conv	13	8,590	2,317	10,543 *	8.7	26.6
435 Unitarian-Univ	2	151	NR	185 *	.2	.5
449 Un Methodist	8	2,904	1,189	3,564 *	2.9	9.0
496 Jewish Est	2	NR	NR	400	.3	1.0
499 Indep.Non-Char	1	500	350	500	.4	1.3
BERKELEY	**133**	**25,206**	**10,987**	**38,593 ***	**27.1**	**100.0**
053 Assemb of God	1	59	60	65	-	.2
056 Baha'i	1	290	NR	290	.2	.8
081 Catholic	4	NR	NR	4,435	3.1	11.5
093 Chr Ch (Disc)	4	483	125	616 *	.4	1.6
097 Chr Chs&Chs Cr	5	688	NR	878 *	.6	2.3
127 Ch God (Cleve)	5	1,080	624	1,377 *	1.0	3.6
145 Ch God Prophcy	5	178	NR	225 *	.2	.6
151 L-D Saints	2	NR	NR	1,051	.7	2.7
165 Ch of Nazarene	3	344	274	501	.4	1.3
167 Chs of Christ	1	80	130	130	.1	.3
193 Episcopal	6	NR	402	771	.5	2.0
207 E.L.C.A.	4	639	340	913	.6	2.4
223 Free Will Bapt	1	50	NR	63 *	-	.2
349 Pent Holiness	15	1,166	940	1,487 *	1.0	3.9
355 Presb Ch (USA)	5	1,028	510	1,311 *	.9	3.4
356 Presb Ch Amer	1	0	0	0	-	-
413 S.D.A.	2	74	NR	88	.1	.2
419 So Bapt Conv	36	13,326	4,645	16,992 *	11.9	44.0
449 Un Methodist	31	5,704	2,922	7,274 *	5.1	18.8
467 Wesleyan	1	17	15	126	.1	.3
CALHOUN	**26**	**3,376**	**1,689**	**4,373 ***	**28.8**	**100.0**
053 Assemb of God	1	51	70	70	.5	1.6
056 Baha'i	0	106	NR	106	.7	2.4
081 Catholic	0	NR	NR	33	.2	.8
123 Ch God (Ander)	1	NR	45	45	.3	1.0
127 Ch God (Cleve)	1	44	46	54 *	.4	1.2
145 Ch God Prophcy	1	36	NR	44 *	.3	1.0
193 Episcopal	1	NR	43	102	.7	2.3
207 E.L.C.A.	5	389	247	526	3.5	12.0
356 Presb Ch Amer	1	68	40	71	.5	1.6
419 So Bapt Conv	6	1,567	644	1,940 *	12.8	44.4
449 Un Methodist	9	1,115	554	1,382 *	9.1	31.6

Religious Group	Number of Churches, Synagogues, Mosques, or Temples	Number of Communicant, Confirmed, or Full Members	Number of Attendees	Total Adherents: Number of Adherents	% of Total Pop.	% of Total Adh.
CHARLESTON	**266**	**68,290**	**35,374**	**132,346 ***	**42.7**	**100.0**
034 Ant Orth of NA	1	32	NR	64	-	-
053 Assemb of God	8	568	586	991	.3	.7
056 Baha'i	3	660	NR	660	.2	.5
076 Buddhism	3	NR	NR	NR	-	-
081 Catholic	19	NR	NR	23,772	7.7	18.0
084 Calvary Chapel	2	NR	NR	NR	-	-
093 Chr Ch (Disc)	2	421	175	516 *	.2	.4
097 Chr Chs&Chs Cr	2	227	NR	278 *	.1	.2
123 Ch God (Ander)	2	NR	95	95	-	.1
127 Ch God (Cleve)	5	1,108	623	1,360 *	.4	1.0
145 Ch God Prophcy	4	143	NR	176 *	.1	.1
151 L-D Saints	3	NR	NR	1,502	.5	1.1
165 Ch of Nazarene	2	178	142	213	.1	.2
167 Chs of Christ	8	1,604	1,172	1,931	.6	1.5
173 Comm of Christ	1	88	NR	88	-	.1
179 Consrv Bapt	1	NR	100	100	-	.1
193 Episcopal	26	NR	5,667	12,816	4.1	9.7
207 E.L.C.A.	13	4,724	2,126	6,021	1.9	4.5
223 Free Will Bapt	2	99	NR	122 *	-	.1
226 Friends-USA	1	24	NR	29 *	-	-
246 Greek Orthodox	1	NR	NR	1,140	.4	.9
264 Int Chs of Crst	1	167	254	243	.1	.2
267 Muslim Est	5	NR	558	2,032	.7	1.5
283 Luth—MO Synod	1	373	320	520	.2	.4
288 Mennonite USA	1	31	25	38 *	-	-
290 Metro Comm Ch	1	127	87	87 *	-	.1
349 Pent Holiness	9	408	397	501 *	.2	.4
355 Presb Ch (USA)	23	9,838	4,880	12,073 *	3.9	9.1
356 Presb Ch Amer	3	294	305	408	.1	.3
360 Prim Bapt Chrch	1	NR	NR	NR	-	-
403 Salvation Army	1	159	118	303	.1	.2
413 S.D.A.	4	1,195	NR	1,422	.5	1.1
418 Southw Bapt Fel	3	NR	NR	NR	-	-
419 So Bapt Conv	55	29,213	8,925	35,854 *	11.6	27.1
435 Unitarian-Univ	1	254	NR	312 *	.1	.2
443 Un C of Christ	2	405	181	497 *	.2	.4
449 Un Methodist	38	14,350	6,048	17,612 *	5.7	13.3
496 Jewish Est	3	NR	NR	5,000	1.6	3.8
498 Indep.Charis.	3	700	1,950	2,650	.9	2.0
499 Indep.Non-Char	2	900	640	920	.3	.7
CHEROKEE	**94**	**23,678**	**9,305**	**30,538 ***	**58.1**	**100.0**
053 Assemb of God	2	82	115	134	.3	.4
055 As Ref Pres Ch	1	72	NR	79	.2	.3
056 Baha'i	0	49	NR	49	.1	.2
081 Catholic	1	NR	NR	614	1.2	2.0
127 Ch God (Cleve)	6	733	393	925 *	1.8	3.0
145 Ch God Prophcy	1	36	NR	45 *	.1	.1
167 Chs of Christ	2	50	57	70	.1	.2
193 Episcopal	1	NR	54	190	.4	.6
207 E.L.C.A.	1	173	100	218	.4	.7
216 Evan Presby Ch	1	88	NR	111 *	.2	.4
223 Free Will Bapt	1	50	NR	62 *	.1	.2
263 Int Foursq Gos	1	30	50	50 *	.1	.2
355 Presb Ch (USA)	3	282	125	354 *	.7	1.2
356 Presb Ch Amer	2	141	115	159	.3	.5
403 Salvation Army	1	148	66	151	.3	.5
419 So Bapt Conv	60	20,641	7,684	25,940 *	49.4	84.9
449 Un Methodist	9	1,103	546	1,387 *	2.6	4.5
467 Wesleyan	1	0	0	0	-	-
CHESTER	**78**	**11,875**	**4,424**	**15,061 ***	**44.2**	**100.0**
053 Assemb of God	1	73	65	70	.2	.5
055 As Ref Pres Ch	5	802	NR	912	2.7	6.1
056 Baha'i	0	270	NR	270	.8	1.8
081 Catholic	1	NR	NR	182	.5	1.2
127 Ch God (Cleve)	5	673	418	851 *	2.5	5.7
145 Ch God Prophcy	2	71	NR	90 *	.3	.6
165 Ch of Nazarene	2	329	235	443	1.3	2.9
167 Chs of Christ	1	20	13	28	.1	.2
193 Episcopal	2	NR	33	64	.2	.4
207 E.L.C.A.	1	51	26	72	.2	.5

NR–Not Reported *Total adherents estimated from known number of communicant, confirmed, full members. - Represents a percentage less than 0.1. Percentages may not total 100 due to rounding.

Table 4: Religious Congregations by County and Group: 2000

Religious Group	Number of Churches, Synagogues, Mosques, or Temples	Number of Communicant, Confirmed, or Full Members	Number of Attendees	Total Adherents: Number of Adherents	Total Adherents: % of Total Pop.	Total Adherents: % of Total Adh.
223 Free Will Bapt	2	99	NR	125 *	.4	.8
263 Int Foursq Gos	1	30	50	50 *	.1	.3
349 Pent Holiness	2	57	60	72 *	.2	.5
355 Presb Ch (USA)	15	914	564	1,157 *	3.4	7.7
356 Presb Ch Amer	2	216	150	223	.7	1.5
419 So Bapt Conv	19	6,215	1,873	7,855 *	23.1	52.2
449 Un Methodist	17	2,055	937	2,597 *	7.6	17.2
CHESTERFIELD	**121**	**18,056**	**7,844**	**23,641 ***	**55.3**	**100.0**
056 Baha'i	0	217	NR	217	.5	.9
081 Catholic	2	NR	NR	200	.5	.8
127 Ch God (Cleve)	5	537	407	691 *	1.6	2.9
145 Ch God Prophcy	3	107	NR	135 *	.3	.6
151 L-D Saints	1	NR	NR	378	.9	1.6
165 Ch of Nazarene	1	77	49	106	.2	.4
167 Chs of Christ	1	16	18	20	-	.1
193 Episcopal	1	NR	86	336	.8	1.4
223 Free Will Bapt	2	99	NR	125 *	.3	.5
349 Pent Holiness	1	214	144	270 *	.6	1.1
355 Presb Ch (USA)	12	961	489	1,211 *	2.8	5.1
356 Presb Ch Amer	1	124	65	135	.3	.6
413 S.D.A.	1	50	NR	60	.1	.3
419 So Bapt Conv	59	11,399	4,670	14,386 *	33.6	60.9
449 Un Methodist	31	4,255	1,916	5,371 *	12.6	22.7
CLARENDON	**58**	**8,107**	**3,990**	**10,463 ***	**32.2**	**100.0**
017 Amer Bapt Assn	1	45	NR	56 *	.2	.5
053 Assemb of God	1	19	24	27	.1	.3
056 Baha'i	0	249	NR	249	.8	2.4
081 Catholic	1	NR	NR	327	1.0	3.1
123 Ch God (Ander)	1	NR	3	3	-	-
127 Ch God (Cleve)	1	187	43	232 *	.7	2.2
145 Ch God Prophcy	3	107	NR	132 *	.4	1.3
165 Ch of Nazarene	1	57	89	89	.3	.9
167 Chs of Christ	1	45	50	58	.2	.6
193 Episcopal	1	NR	43	78	.2	.7
223 Free Will Bapt	6	298	NR	369 *	1.1	3.5
349 Pent Holiness	9	1,204	902	1,492 *	4.6	14.3
355 Presb Ch (USA)	7	1,228	664	1,521 *	4.7	14.5
356 Presb Ch Amer	3	424	357	575	1.8	5.5
413 S.D.A.	1	78	NR	93	.3	.9
419 So Bapt Conv	11	2,508	1,113	3,108 *	9.6	29.7
449 Un Methodist	10	1,658	702	2,054 *	6.3	19.6
COLLETON	**93**	**13,175**	**4,664**	**17,543 ***	**45.8**	**100.0**
053 Assemb of God	1	101	133	160	.4	.9
056 Baha'i	0	462	NR	462	1.2	2.6
081 Catholic	2	NR	NR	494	1.3	2.8
093 Chr Ch (Disc)	5	480	70	607 *	1.6	3.5
097 Chr Chs&Chs Cr	2	152	NR	192 *	.5	1.1
127 Ch God (Cleve)	2	234	115	296 *	.8	1.7
145 Ch God Prophcy	3	107	NR	135 *	.4	.8
151 L-D Saints	1	NR	NR	243	.6	1.4
167 Chs of Christ	2	33	38	45	.1	.3
193 Episcopal	2	NR	105	242	.6	1.4
207 E.L.C.A.	1	143	70	165	.4	.9
349 Pent Holiness	4	125	87	158 *	.4	.9
355 Presb Ch (USA)	3	387	203	489 *	1.3	2.8
419 So Bapt Conv	28	6,762	2,123	8,556 *	22.4	48.8
449 Un Methodist	37	4,189	1,720	5,299 *	13.8	30.2
DARLINGTON	**106**	**22,581**	**8,978**	**30,170 ***	**44.8**	**100.0**
053 Assemb of God	2	103	70	286	.4	.9
056 Baha'i	1	1,127	NR	1,127	1.7	3.7
081 Catholic	2	NR	NR	725	1.1	2.4
123 Ch God (Ander)	5	NR	414	414	.6	1.4
127 Ch God (Cleve)	5	464	348	611 *	.9	2.0
145 Ch God Prophcy	4	140	NR	177 *	.3	.6
151 L-D Saints	1	NR	NR	540	.8	1.8
165 Ch of Nazarene	2	396	314	541	.8	1.8
167 Chs of Christ	2	62	45	60	.1	.2
193 Episcopal	2	NR	208	430	.6	1.4

Religious Group	Number of Churches, Synagogues, Mosques, or Temples	Number of Communicant, Confirmed, or Full Members	Number of Attendees	Total Adherents: Number of Adherents	Total Adherents: % of Total Pop.	Total Adherents: % of Total Adh.
207 E.L.C.A.	1	56	36	61	.1	.2
223 Free Will Bapt	6	298	NR	375 *	.6	1.2
349 Pent Holiness	6	435	338	549 *	.8	1.8
355 Presb Ch (USA)	6	1,088	551	1,372 *	2.0	4.5
413 S.D.A.	1	87	NR	104	.2	.3
418 Southw Bapt Fel	1	NR	NR	NR	-	-
419 So Bapt Conv	31	11,439	3,908	14,427 *	21.4	47.8
449 Un Methodist	27	5,686	2,296	7,171 *	10.6	23.8
499 Indep.Non-Char	1	1,200	450	1,200	1.8	4.0
DILLON	**60**	**12,268**	**4,868**	**15,797 ***	**51.4**	**100.0**
053 Assemb of God	1	65	65	70	.2	.4
056 Baha'i	0	1,189	NR	1,189	3.9	7.5
081 Catholic	1	NR	NR	150	.5	.9
127 Ch God (Cleve)	4	1,232	1,004	1,586 *	5.2	10.0
145 Ch God Prophcy	1	36	NR	46 *	.1	.3
151 L-D Saints	1	NR	NR	202	.7	1.3
167 Chs of Christ	1	30	25	58	.2	.4
193 Episcopal	1	NR	30	65	.2	.4
349 Pent Holiness	3	221	172	285 *	.9	1.8
355 Presb Ch (USA)	7	372	207	479 *	1.6	3.0
356 Presb Ch Amer	2	332	110	343	1.1	2.2
419 So Bapt Conv	24	6,763	2,412	8,711 *	28.4	55.1
449 Un Methodist	14	2,028	843	2,613 *	8.5	16.5
DORCHESTER	**101**	**26,245**	**15,175**	**43,998 ***	**45.6**	**100.0**
053 Assemb of God	1	779	980	1,400	1.5	3.2
055 As Ref Pres Ch	1	161	NR	188	.2	.4
056 Baha'i	0	82	NR	82	.1	.2
081 Catholic	2	NR	NR	4,938	5.1	11.2
089 Chr & Miss Al	1	41	NR	82	.1	.2
093 Chr Ch (Disc)	6	683	100	876 *	.9	2.0
097 Chr Chs&Chs Cr	2	184	NR	236 *	.2	.5
123 Ch God (Ander)	2	NR	293	293	.3	.7
127 Ch God (Cleve)	5	582	323	752 *	.8	1.7
145 Ch God Prophcy	2	71	NR	92 *	.1	.2
151 L-D Saints	2	NR	NR	579	.6	1.3
165 Ch of Nazarene	1	206	134	233	.2	.5
167 Chs of Christ	3	422	465	490	.5	1.1
193 Episcopal	3	NR	533	1,029	1.1	2.3
207 E.L.C.A.	2	1,017	601	1,427	1.5	3.2
283 Luth—MO Synod	1	192	96	248	.3	.6
349 Pent Holiness	3	147	143	188 *	.2	.4
355 Presb Ch (USA)	2	1,140	567	1,462 *	1.5	3.3
356 Presb Ch Amer	1	49	130	130	.1	.3
360 Prim Bapt Chrch	1	NR	NR	NR	-	-
401 Rus Orth Abroad	1	NR	NR	NR	-	-
413 S.D.A.	2	314	NR	373	.4	.8
419 So Bapt Conv	18	10,505	4,659	13,471 *	14.0	30.6
449 Un Methodist	36	9,559	4,036	12,260 *	12.7	27.9
467 Wesleyan	1	44	48	77	.1	.2
469 WELS	1	67	67	92	.1	.2
498 Indep.Charis.	1	0	2,000	3,000	3.1	6.8
EDGEFIELD	**34**	**4,905**	**2,279**	**8,015 ***	**32.6**	**100.0**
053 Assemb of God	1	80	50	70	.3	.9
055 As Ref Pres Ch	1	36	NR	36	.1	.4
056 Baha'i	0	39	NR	39	.2	.5
081 Catholic	2	NR	NR	1,743	7.1	21.7
127 Ch God (Cleve)	2	87	14	107 *	.4	1.3
193 Episcopal	2	NR	98	305	1.2	3.8
207 E.L.C.A.	1	67	16	80	.3	1.0
349 Pent Holiness	2	91	88	112 *	.5	1.4
355 Presb Ch (USA)	1	9	7	11 *	-	.1
356 Presb Ch Amer	1	44	25	44	.2	.5
413 S.D.A.	1	42	NR	50	.2	.6
419 So Bapt Conv	15	3,578	1,599	4,396 *	17.9	54.8
449 Un Methodist	5	832	382	1,022 *	4.2	12.8
FAIRFIELD	**51**	**6,240**	**2,668**	**8,018 ***	**34.2**	**100.0**
053 Assemb of God	1	42	48	55	.2	.7
055 As Ref Pres Ch	2	242	NR	264	1.1	3.3

NR–Not Reported *Total adherents estimated from known number of communicant, confirmed, full members. - Represents a percentage less than 0.1. Percentages may not total 100 due to rounding.

Table 4: Religious Congregations by County and Group: 2000

Religious Group	Number of Churches, Synagogues, Mosques, or Temples	Number of Communicant, Confirmed, or Full Members	Number of Attendees	Total Adherents: Number of Adherents	Total Adherents: % of Total Pop.	Total Adherents: % of Total Adh.
056 Baha'i	0	96	NR	96	.4	1.2
081 Catholic	1	NR	NR	50	.2	.6
123 Ch God (Ander)	1	NR	12	12	.1	.1
127 Ch God (Cleve)	1	263	57	330 *	1.4	4.1
145 Ch God Prophcy	2	71	NR	90 *	.4	1.1
165 Ch of Nazarene	1	312	191	381	1.6	4.8
167 Chs of Christ	1	50	60	75	.3	.9
193 Episcopal	3	NR	125	286	1.2	3.6
349 Pent Holiness	1	80	51	100 *	.4	1.2
355 Presb Ch (USA)	8	639	434	818 *	3.5	10.2
356 Presb Ch Amer	4	544	315	565	2.4	7.0
419 So Bapt Conv	17	2,993	966	3,755 *	16.0	46.8
449 Un Methodist	7	876	373	1,099 *	4.7	13.7
467 Wesleyan	1	32	36	42	.2	.5
FLORENCE	**213**	**40,277**	**15,684**	**55,026 ***	**43.8**	**100.0**
053 Assemb of God	3	310	349	510	.4	.9
055 As Ref Pres Ch	1	164	NR	184	.1	.3
056 Baha'i	1	2,338	NR	2,338	1.9	4.2
081 Catholic	4	NR	NR	2,716	2.2	4.9
097 Chr Chs&Chs Cr	1	45	NR	56 *	-	.1
123 Ch God (Ander)	3	NR	137	137	.1	.2
127 Ch God (Cleve)	14	1,444	1,026	1,854 *	1.5	3.4
145 Ch God Prophcy	8	285	NR	360 *	.3	.7
151 L-D Saints	1	NR	NR	637	.5	1.2
165 Ch of Nazarene	2	225	111	309	.2	.6
167 Chs of Christ	8	373	360	472	.4	.9
193 Episcopal	3	NR	387	936	.7	1.7
207 E.L.C.A.	2	621	273	788	.6	1.4
216 Evan Presby Ch	1	339	NR	423 *	.3	.8
223 Free Will Bapt	30	1,488	NR	1,858 *	1.5	3.4
246 Greek Orthodox	1	NR	NR	432	.3	.8
263 Int Foursq Gos	1	30	50	50 *	-	.1
267 Muslim Est	2	NR	26	70	.1	.1
283 Luth—MO Synod	1	59	33	75	.1	.1
349 Pent Holiness	27	2,479	1,719	3,095 *	2.5	5.6
355 Presb Ch (USA)	9	1,922	829	2,399 *	1.9	4.4
356 Presb Ch Amer	1	48	50	64	.1	.1
403 Salvation Army	1	126	82	135	.1	.2
413 S.D.A.	3	587	NR	699	.6	1.3
418 Southw Bapt Fel	1	NR	NR	NR	-	-
419 So Bapt Conv	44	17,179	6,176	21,446 *	17.1	39.0
449 Un Methodist	38	10,189	4,051	12,721 *	10.1	23.1
467 Wesleyan	1	26	25	42	-	.1
496 Jewish Est	1	NR	NR	220	.2	.4
GEORGETOWN	**89**	**16,658**	**9,340**	**24,722 ***	**44.3**	**100.0**
053 Assemb of God	1	289	321	500	.9	2.0
056 Baha'i	2	628	NR	628	1.1	2.5
081 Catholic	4	NR	NR	2,042	3.7	8.3
123 Ch God (Ander)	3	NR	76	76	.1	.3
127 Ch God (Cleve)	5	580	424	739 *	1.3	3.0
145 Ch God Prophcy	1	36	NR	44 *	.1	.2
151 L-D Saints	1	NR	NR	109	.2	.4
165 Ch of Nazarene	1	47	30	134	.2	.5
167 Chs of Christ	3	307	330	400	.7	1.6
193 Episcopal	3	NR	926	1,481	2.7	6.0
207 E.L.C.A.	2	423	234	511	.9	2.1
223 Free Will Bapt	4	198	NR	246 *	.4	1.0
349 Pent Holiness	14	1,664	1,130	2,061 *	3.7	8.3
355 Presb Ch (USA)	4	1,141	695	1,413 *	2.5	5.7
356 Presb Ch Amer	1	57	40	57	.1	.2
403 Salvation Army	1	31	31	115	.2	.5
413 S.D.A.	1	29	NR	35	.1	.1
419 So Bapt Conv	21	6,349	2,859	7,863 *	14.1	31.8
435 Unitarian-Univ	1	14	NR	17 *	-	.1
449 Un Methodist	15	4,865	2,244	6,026 *	10.8	24.4
496 Jewish Est	1	NR	NR	225	.4	.9
GREENVILLE	**449**	**151,392**	**70,234**	**217,660 ***	**57.3**	**100.0**
017 Amer Bapt Assn	3	402	NR	498 *	.1	.2
019 Amer Bapt USA	1	125	140	155 *	-	.1
053 Assemb of God	17	1,342	1,453	2,161	.6	1.0
055 As Ref Pres Ch	4	887	NR	992	.3	.5
056 Baha'i	2	229	NR	229	.1	.1
081 Catholic	7	NR	NR	17,684	4.7	8.1
084 Calvary Chapel	1	NR	NR	NR	-	-
089 Chr & Miss Al	2	200	NR	290	.1	.1
093 Chr Ch (Disc)	1	169	0	209 *	.1	.1
097 Chr Chs&Chs Cr	1	325	NR	403 *	.1	.2
121 Ch God (Abr)	3	446	399	553 *	.1	.3
123 Ch God (Ander)	2	NR	106	106	-	-
127 Ch God (Cleve)	31	7,534	4,170	9,349 *	2.5	4.3
145 Ch God Prophcy	13	464	NR	572 *	.2	.3
151 L-D Saints	4	NR	NR	1,859	.5	.9
157 Ch of Brethren	1	53	0	66 *	-	-
165 Ch of Nazarene	3	676	537	1,340	.4	.6
167 Chs of Christ	12	1,462	1,401	2,084	.5	1.0
173 Comm of Christ	1	131	NR	131	-	.1
193 Episcopal	9	NR	1,920	6,500	1.7	3.0
207 E.L.C.A.	6	2,850	1,339	3,555	.9	1.6
223 Free Will Bapt	3	149	NR	184 *	-	.1
226 Friends-USA	1	47	NR	58 *	-	-
246 Greek Orthodox	1	NR	NR	807	.2	.4
258 IndFreeWillBapt	1	18	NR	22 *	-	-
264 Int Chs of Crst	1	85	130	118	-	.1
267 Muslim Est	1	NR	156	609	.2	.3
283 Luth—MO Synod	2	463	253	672	.2	.3
290 Metro Comm Ch	1	112	65	65 *	-	-
306 NT IndBapt&Rltd	1	45	NR	56 *	-	-
331 OCA: Ter Diocs	1	34	NR	104	-	-
335 Orth Pres Ch	1	22	35	35	-	-
349 Pent Holiness	16	4,008	3,829	4,968 *	1.3	2.3
355 Presb Ch (USA)	20	10,640	4,226	13,188 *	3.5	6.1
356 Presb Ch Amer	11	2,796	2,288	3,520	.9	1.6
360 Prim Bapt Chrch	1	NR	NR	NR	-	-
370 Ref Baptist Chs	1	NR	NR	NR	-	-
403 Salvation Army	1	210	201	228	.1	.1
413 S.D.A.	2	259	NR	308	.1	.1
418 Southw Bapt Fel	3	NR	NR	NR	-	-
419 So Bapt Conv	168	87,195	32,348	108,070 *	28.5	49.7
435 Unitarian-Univ	1	360	NR	446 *	.1	.2
449 Un Methodist	64	20,038	8,269	24,834 *	6.5	11.4
463 Vineyard	1	116	100	144 *	-	.1
467 Wesleyan	10	569	401	1,077	.3	.5
469 WELS	1	81	68	111	-	.1
496 Jewish Est	2	NR	NR	1,200	.3	.6
498 Indep.Charis.	3	2,200	1,700	2,200	.6	1.0
499 Indep.Non-Char	6	4,650	4,700	5,900	1.6	2.7
GREENWOOD	**116**	**28,688**	**11,687**	**38,409 ***	**58.0**	**100.0**
053 Assemb of God	2	315	218	323	.5	.8
055 As Ref Pres Ch	4	534	NR	589	.9	1.5
056 Baha'i	1	92	NR	92	.1	.2
081 Catholic	1	NR	NR	1,246	1.9	3.2
084 Calvary Chapel	1	NR	NR	NR	-	-
097 Chr Chs&Chs Cr	1	35	NR	44 *	.1	.1
127 Ch God (Cleve)	10	1,607	851	2,010 *	3.0	5.2
145 Ch God Prophcy	5	178	NR	225 *	.3	.6
151 L-D Saints	1	NR	NR	395	.6	1.0
165 Ch of Nazarene	1	99	107	163	.2	.4
167 Chs of Christ	2	73	63	85	.1	.2
193 Episcopal	1	NR	162	429	.6	1.1
207 E.L.C.A.	1	348	178	450	.7	1.2
223 Free Will Bapt	1	50	NR	62 *	.1	.2
283 Luth—MO Synod	1	23	18	26	-	.1
349 Pent Holiness	11	1,300	930	1,624 *	2.5	4.2
355 Presb Ch (USA)	7	1,674	878	2,092 *	3.2	5.4
356 Presb Ch Amer	1	119	128	151	.2	.4
403 Salvation Army	1	56	47	131	.2	.3
413 S.D.A.	2	184	NR	219	.3	.6
419 So Bapt Conv	36	16,487	5,679	20,601 *	31.1	53.6
449 Un Methodist	23	5,456	2,063	6,816 *	10.3	17.7
467 Wesleyan	1	58	65	136	.2	.4
499 Indep.Non-Char	1	0	300	500	.8	1.3

NR–Not Reported *Total adherents estimated from known number of communicant, confirmed, full members. - Represents a percentage less than 0.1. Percentages may not total 100 due to rounding.

Table 4: Religious Congregations by County and Group: 2000

Religious Group	Number of Churches, Synagogues, Mosques, or Temples	Number of Communicant, Confirmed, or Full Members	Number of Attendees	Total Adherents		
				Number of Adherents	% of Total Pop.	% of Total Adh.
HAMPTON	**54**	**6,282**	**2,368**	**8,249 ***	**38.6**	**100.0**
056 Baha'i	0	68	NR	68	.3	.8
081 Catholic	1	NR	NR	112	.5	1.4
093 Chr Ch (Disc)	4	735	40	933 *	4.4	11.3
097 Chr Chs&Chs Cr	1	90	NR	114 *	.5	1.4
123 Ch God (Ander)	2	NR	129	129	.6	1.6
127 Ch God (Cleve)	3	217	135	275 *	1.3	3.3
145 Ch God Prophcy	3	107	NR	135 *	.6	1.6
193 Episcopal	2	NR	29	56	.3	.7
355 Presb Ch (USA)	3	115	61	146 *	.7	1.8
360 Prim Bapt Chrch	6	NR	NR	NR	-	-
419 So Bapt Conv	19	4,290	1,598	5,444 *	25.5	66.0
449 Un Methodist	10	660	376	837 *	3.9	10.1
HORRY	**232**	**53,702**	**25,788**	**83,126 ***	**42.3**	**100.0**
034 Ant Orth of NA	1	39	NR	78	-	.1
053 Assemb of God	6	306	393	592	.3	.7
055 As Ref Pres Ch	2	59	NR	61	-	.1
056 Baha'i	3	910	NR	910	.5	1.1
081 Catholic	5	NR	NR	14,360	7.3	17.3
089 Chr & Miss Al	1	54	NR	94	-	.1
093 Chr Ch (Disc)	1	40	30	48 *	-	.1
097 Chr Chs&Chs Cr	2	492	NR	590 *	.3	.7
123 Ch God (Ander)	2	NR	55	55	-	.1
127 Ch God (Cleve)	8	852	544	1,026 *	.5	1.2
151 L-D Saints	2	NR	NR	801	.4	1.0
165 Ch of Nazarene	2	105	129	148	.1	.2
167 Chs of Christ	2	220	360	310	.2	.4
193 Episcopal	4	NR	938	1,851	.9	2.2
207 E.L.C.A.	4	1,702	1,153	2,083	1.1	2.5
223 Free Will Bapt	16	794	NR	952 *	.5	1.1
246 Greek Orthodox	1	NR	NR	282	.1	.3
252 Hindu	1	NR	NR	NR	-	-
267 Muslim Est	1	NR	101	288	.1	.3
283 Luth—MO Synod	2	322	261	391	.2	.5
336 OrigFreeWillBpt	3	159	NR	191 *	.1	.2
349 Pent Holiness	13	917	828	1,100 *	.6	1.3
355 Presb Ch (USA)	5	3,534	2,119	4,237 *	2.2	5.1
356 Presb Ch Amer	3	450	517	577	.3	.7
403 Salvation Army	1	52	67	52	-	.1
413 S.D.A.	2	281	NR	335	.2	.4
419 So Bapt Conv	106	32,738	13,082	39,255 *	20.0	47.2
449 Un Methodist	27	9,030	3,900	10,826 *	5.5	13.0
463 Vineyard	1	150	130	180 *	.1	.2
467 Wesleyan	1	30	61	81	-	.1
469 WELS	1	16	20	22	-	-
496 Jewish Est	1	NR	NR	250	.1	.3
498 Indep.Charis.	1	150	800	800	.4	1.0
499 Indep.Non-Char	1	300	300	300	.2	.4
JASPER	**29**	**4,342**	**1,824**	**7,641 ***	**37.0**	**100.0**
053 Assemb of God	1	180	190	300	1.5	3.9
055 As Ref Pres Ch	1	28	NR	40	.2	.5
056 Baha'i	0	23	NR	23	.1	.3
081 Catholic	3	NR	NR	1,869	9.0	24.5
127 Ch God (Cleve)	1	84	41	106 *	.5	1.4
145 Ch God Prophcy	3	107	NR	135 *	.7	1.8
167 Chs of Christ	1	9	15	9	-	.1
193 Episcopal	1	NR	77	210	1.0	2.7
413 S.D.A.	1	85	NR	101	.5	1.3
419 So Bapt Conv	12	3,207	1,206	4,063 *	19.6	53.2
449 Un Methodist	5	619	295	785 *	3.8	10.3
KERSHAW	**96**	**21,071**	**8,791**	**29,129 ***	**55.3**	**100.0**
053 Assemb of God	1	67	38	145	.3	.5
055 As Ref Pres Ch	1	149	NR	194	.4	.7
056 Baha'i	0	88	NR	88	.2	.3
081 Catholic	1	NR	NR	995	1.9	3.4
123 Ch God (Ander)	1	NR	60	60	.1	.2
127 Ch God (Cleve)	5	538	315	690 *	1.3	2.4
145 Ch God Prophcy	1	36	NR	45 *	.1	.2
151 L-D Saints	2	NR	NR	1,036	2.0	3.6
165 Ch of Nazarene	2	168	136	306	.6	1.1
167 Chs of Christ	3	180	160	217	.4	.7
193 Episcopal	1	NR	167	504	1.0	1.7
207 E.L.C.A.	1	341	132	456	.9	1.6
223 Free Will Bapt	1	50	NR	62 *	.1	.2
349 Pent Holiness	2	245	283	306 *	.6	1.1
355 Presb Ch (USA)	6	887	495	1,110 *	2.1	3.8
413 S.D.A.	1	85	NR	101	.2	.3
419 So Bapt Conv	46	14,751	5,357	18,452 *	35.0	63.3
449 Un Methodist	21	3,486	1,648	4,362 *	8.3	15.0
LANCASTER	**114**	**27,724**	**9,518**	**35,216 ***	**57.4**	**100.0**
053 Assemb of God	2	108	88	172	.3	.5
055 As Ref Pres Ch	5	968	NR	1,089	1.8	3.1
056 Baha'i	0	295	NR	295	.5	.8
081 Catholic	2	NR	NR	413	.7	1.2
127 Ch God (Cleve)	5	539	287	687 *	1.1	2.0
145 Ch God Prophcy	3	107	NR	135 *	.2	.4
151 L-D Saints	1	NR	NR	160	.3	.5
165 Ch of Nazarene	1	38	41	89	.1	.3
167 Chs of Christ	1	30	30	35	.1	.1
193 Episcopal	1	NR	67	121	.2	.3
207 E.L.C.A.	1	135	60	216	.4	.6
223 Free Will Bapt	5	248	NR	309 *	.5	.9
349 Pent Holiness	4	632	368	789 *	1.3	2.2
355 Presb Ch (USA)	9	1,031	543	1,286 *	2.1	3.7
356 Presb Ch Amer	1	99	100	107	.2	.3
419 So Bapt Conv	55	18,819	6,159	23,480 *	38.3	66.7
449 Un Methodist	18	4,675	1,775	5,833 *	9.5	16.6
LAURENS	**129**	**25,745**	**10,634**	**32,699 ***	**47.0**	**100.0**
053 Assemb of God	3	169	216	264	.4	.8
055 As Ref Pres Ch	2	162	NR	186	.3	.6
056 Baha'i	0	42	NR	42	.1	.1
061 Beachy Amish	1	33	NR	41 *	.1	.1
081 Catholic	2	NR	NR	330	.5	1.0
097 Chr Chs&Chs Cr	1	107	NR	133 *	.2	.4
123 Ch God (Ander)	1	NR	40	40	.1	.1
127 Ch God (Cleve)	6	863	526	1,075 *	1.5	3.3
145 Ch God Prophcy	4	143	NR	176 *	.3	.5
165 Ch of Nazarene	1	42	35	100	.1	.3
167 Chs of Christ	2	61	75	78	.1	.2
193 Episcopal	2	NR	69	219	.3	.7
207 E.L.C.A.	2	169	95	196	.3	.6
349 Pent Holiness	9	963	576	1,199 *	1.7	3.7
355 Presb Ch (USA)	16	1,788	1,069	2,225 *	3.2	6.8
356 Presb Ch Amer	6	498	355	575	.8	1.8
413 S.D.A.	1	39	NR	46	.1	.1
419 So Bapt Conv	48	17,366	6,359	21,615 *	31.1	66.1
449 Un Methodist	21	3,221	1,168	4,009 *	5.8	12.3
467 Wesleyan	1	79	51	150	.2	.5
LEE	**44**	**5,679**	**2,836**	**7,324 ***	**36.4**	**100.0**
056 Baha'i	0	201	NR	201	1.0	2.7
081 Catholic	0	NR	NR	5	-	.1
089 Chr & Miss Al	1	86	NR	156	.8	2.1
123 Ch God (Ander)	2	NR	210	210	1.0	2.9
127 Ch God (Cleve)	1	73	0	91 *	.5	1.2
165 Ch of Nazarene	2	138	96	199	1.0	2.7
167 Chs of Christ	1	50	90	90	.4	1.2
355 Presb Ch (USA)	6	397	256	494 *	2.5	6.7
419 So Bapt Conv	11	2,057	855	2,555 *	12.7	34.9
449 Un Methodist	20	2,677	1,329	3,323 *	16.5	45.4
LEXINGTON	**212**	**77,109**	**32,426**	**107,551 ***	**49.8**	**100.0**
034 Ant Orth of NA	1	0	NR	0	-	-
053 Assemb of God	6	1,238	1,594	2,718	1.3	2.5
055 As Ref Pres Ch	2	119	NR	138	.1	.1
056 Baha'i	3	289	NR	289	.1	.3
081 Catholic	4	NR	NR	6,561	3.0	6.1
084 Calvary Chapel	2	NR	NR	NR	-	-
089 Chr & Miss Al	1	94	NR	134	.1	.1

NR–Not Reported   *Total adherents estimated from known number of communicant, confirmed, full members.   - Represents a percentage less than 0.1.   Percentages may not total 100 due to rounding.

Table 4: Religious Congregations by County and Group: 2000

Religious Group	Number of Churches, Synagogues, Mosques, or Temples	Number of Communicant, Confirmed, or Full Members	Number of Attendees	Total Adherents		
				Number of Adherents	% of Total Pop.	% of Total Adh.
097 Chr Chs&Chs Cr	1	58	NR	73 *	-	.1
123 Ch God (Ander)	2	NR	158	158	.1	.1
127 Ch God (Cleve)	10	1,364	752	1,711 *	.8	1.6
145 Ch God Prophcy	1	36	NR	45 *	-	-
151 L-D Saints	5	NR	NR	1,723	.8	1.6
165 Ch of Nazarene	7	1,063	602	1,219	.6	1.1
167 Chs of Christ	4	427	489	525	.2	.5
193 Episcopal	4	NR	655	1,627	.8	1.5
207 E.L.C.A.	37	14,077	6,020	17,348	8.0	16.1
223 Free Will Bapt	1	50	NR	62 *	-	.1
252 Hindu	1	NR	NR	NR	-	-
283 Luth—MO Synod	1	266	164	310	.1	.3
331 OCA: Ter Diocs	1	35	NR	75	-	.1
349 Pent Holiness	8	718	528	901 *	.4	.8
355 Presb Ch (USA)	5	3,913	2,039	4,912 *	2.3	4.6
356 Presb Ch Amer	4	1,637	1,344	2,027	.9	1.9
413 S.D.A.	2	710	NR	844	.4	.8
418 Southw Bapt Fel	2	NR	NR	NR	-	-
419 So Bapt Conv	70	37,992	13,395	47,683 *	22.1	44.3
449 Un Methodist	26	13,001	4,657	16,318 *	7.6	15.2
467 Wesleyan	1	22	29	150	.1	.1
MCCORMICK	**18**	**2,228**	**984**	**2,702 ***	**27.1**	**100.0**
055 As Ref Pres Ch	2	48	NR	50	.5	1.9
056 Baha'i	0	16	NR	16	.2	.6
081 Catholic	1	NR	NR	138	1.4	5.1
207 E.L.C.A.	1	124	99	126	1.3	4.7
355 Presb Ch (USA)	1	23	21	27 *	.3	1.0
419 So Bapt Conv	8	1,316	488	1,530 *	15.4	56.6
449 Un Methodist	5	701	376	815 *	8.2	30.2
MARION	**53**	**10,807**	**3,270**	**13,467 ***	**38.0**	**100.0**
056 Baha'i	0	1,832	NR	1,832	5.2	13.6
081 Catholic	1	NR	NR	200	.6	1.5
127 Ch God (Cleve)	3	465	254	592 *	1.7	4.4
167 Chs of Christ	2	52	35	67	.2	.5
193 Episcopal	1	NR	43	96	.3	.7
223 Free Will Bapt	3	149	NR	188 *	.5	1.4
349 Pent Holiness	3	114	126	144 *	.4	1.1
355 Presb Ch (USA)	1	190	95	240 *	.7	1.8
356 Presb Ch Amer	1	239	0	291	.8	2.2
413 S.D.A.	1	124	NR	148	.4	1.1
419 So Bapt Conv	19	5,138	1,685	6,502 *	18.3	48.3
449 Un Methodist	18	2,504	1,032	3,167 *	8.9	23.5
MARLBORO	**66**	**8,816**	**3,778**	**11,426 ***	**39.6**	**100.0**
056 Baha'i	0	250	NR	250	.9	2.2
081 Catholic	1	NR	NR	81	.3	.7
123 Ch God (Ander)	1	NR	20	20	.1	.2
127 Ch God (Cleve)	5	643	376	808 *	2.8	7.1
165 Ch of Nazarene	2	262	159	395	1.4	3.5
167 Chs of Christ	1	31	33	40	.1	.4
193 Episcopal	1	NR	78	164	.6	1.4
349 Pent Holiness	4	477	231	594 *	2.1	5.2
355 Presb Ch (USA)	3	307	163	383 *	1.3	3.4
419 So Bapt Conv	11	2,604	695	3,245 *	11.3	28.4
449 Un Methodist	35	4,191	1,954	5,221 *	18.1	45.7
467 Wesleyan	2	51	69	225	.8	2.0
NEWBERRY	**85**	**14,055**	**6,140**	**18,773 ***	**52.0**	**100.0**
053 Assemb of God	2	52	47	65	.2	.3
055 As Ref Pres Ch	2	287	NR	326	.9	1.7
056 Baha'i	0	33	NR	33	.1	.2
081 Catholic	1	NR	NR	612	1.7	3.3
097 Chr Chs&Chs Cr	1	60	NR	74 *	.2	.4
123 Ch God (Ander)	1	NR	28	28	.1	.1
127 Ch God (Cleve)	3	198	136	244 *	.7	1.3
145 Ch God Prophcy	1	36	NR	44 *	.1	.2
151 L-D Saints	2	NR	NR	502	1.4	2.7
193 Episcopal	1	NR	84	117	.3	.6
207 E.L.C.A.	25	5,816	2,740	7,272	20.1	38.7
349 Pent Holiness	4	215	130	264 *	.7	1.4

Religious Group	Number of Churches, Synagogues, Mosques, or Temples	Number of Communicant, Confirmed, or Full Members	Number of Attendees	Total Adherents		
				Number of Adherents	% of Total Pop.	% of Total Adh.
355 Presb Ch (USA)	6	680	401	834 *	2.3	4.4
356 Presb Ch Amer	1	177	100	203	.6	1.1
418 Southw Bapt Fel	1	NR	NR	NR	-	-
419 So Bapt Conv	16	3,248	1,147	3,987 *	11.0	21.2
435 Unitarian-Univ	1	30	NR	37 *	.1	.2
449 Un Methodist	16	3,153	1,249	3,871 *	10.7	20.6
467 Wesleyan	1	70	78	260	.7	1.4
OCONEE	**139**	**30,317**	**13,076**	**39,303 ***	**59.4**	**100.0**
053 Assemb of God	2	349	514	528	.8	1.3
055 As Ref Pres Ch	1	161	NR	178	.3	.5
056 Baha'i	1	28	NR	28	-	.1
081 Catholic	2	NR	NR	1,835	2.8	4.7
089 Chr & Miss Al	1	57	NR	68	.1	.2
127 Ch God (Cleve)	17	2,081	1,263	2,533 *	3.8	6.4
145 Ch God Prophcy	8	285	NR	344 *	.5	.9
165 Ch of Nazarene	1	90	34	114	.2	.3
167 Chs of Christ	2	145	168	177	.3	.5
193 Episcopal	1	NR	126	293	.4	.7
207 E.L.C.A.	1	493	131	616	.9	1.6
283 Luth—MO Synod	1	226	170	266	.4	.7
297 Mennonite;Other	1	67	NR	81 *	.1	.2
349 Pent Holiness	2	205	122	249 *	.4	.6
355 Presb Ch (USA)	6	995	464	1,209 *	1.8	3.1
356 Presb Ch Amer	1	0	0	0	-	-
403 Salvation Army	1	40	49	40	.1	.1
413 S.D.A.	2	244	NR	290	.4	.7
419 So Bapt Conv	69	22,067	8,670	26,807 *	40.5	68.2
449 Un Methodist	13	2,306	994	2,803 *	4.2	7.1
467 Wesleyan	6	478	371	844	1.3	2.1
ORANGEBURG	**150**	**30,123**	**12,746**	**41,031 ***	**44.8**	**100.0**
053 Assemb of God	1	25	27	57	.1	.1
056 Baha'i	2	553	NR	553	.6	1.3
081 Catholic	4	NR	NR	1,757	1.9	4.3
093 Chr Ch (Disc)	2	825	0	1,027 *	1.1	2.5
097 Chr Chs&Chs Cr	1	250	NR	311 *	.3	.8
123 Ch God (Ander)	1	NR	14	14	-	-
127 Ch God (Cleve)	9	667	525	881 *	1.0	2.1
145 Ch God Prophcy	3	107	NR	132 *	.1	.3
151 L-D Saints	1	NR	NR	330	.4	.8
165 Ch of Nazarene	3	316	245	755	.8	1.8
167 Chs of Christ	2	121	132	204	.2	.5
193 Episcopal	3	NR	314	661	.7	1.6
207 E.L.C.A.	4	748	386	911	1.0	2.2
223 Free Will Bapt	2	99	NR	124 *	.1	.3
267 Muslim Est	2	NR	110	326	.4	.8
349 Pent Holiness	6	539	542	671 *	.7	1.6
355 Presb Ch (USA)	3	747	442	930 *	1.0	2.3
356 Presb Ch Amer	1	293	234	370	.4	.9
403 Salvation Army	1	90	63	226	.2	.6
413 S.D.A.	2	299	NR	356	.4	.9
418 Southw Bapt Fel	1	NR	NR	NR	-	-
419 So Bapt Conv	43	12,997	4,565	16,182 *	17.7	39.4
449 Un Methodist	53	11,447	5,147	14,253 *	15.6	34.7
PICKENS	**166**	**44,575**	**20,591**	**60,449 ***	**54.6**	**100.0**
053 Assemb of God	3	109	104	177	.2	.3
056 Baha'i	2	121	NR	121	.1	.2
081 Catholic	3	NR	NR	2,840	2.6	4.7
127 Ch God (Cleve)	16	2,272	1,475	2,768 *	2.5	4.6
145 Ch God Prophcy	8	285	NR	344 *	.3	.6
151 L-D Saints	2	NR	NR	871	.8	1.4
167 Chs of Christ	3	117	175	166	.1	.3
193 Episcopal	2	NR	310	981	.9	1.6
207 E.L.C.A.	2	787	435	1,041	.9	1.7
263 Int Foursq Gos	1	14	29	29 *	-	-
267 Muslim Est	1	NR	156	609	.5	1.0
297 Mennonite;Other	1	38	NR	46 *	-	.1
349 Pent Holiness	1	166	97	201 *	.2	.3
355 Presb Ch (USA)	6	2,166	1,160	2,625 *	2.4	4.3
356 Presb Ch Amer	3	781	280	1,080	1.0	1.8
370 Ref Baptist Chs	1	NR	NR	NR	-	-

NR–Not Reported   *Total adherents estimated from known number of communicant, confirmed, full members.   - Represents a percentage less than 0.1.   Percentages may not total 100 due to rounding.

Table 4: Religious Congregations by County and Group: 2000

Religious Group	Number of Churches, Synagogues, Mosques, or Temples	Number of Communicant, Confirmed, or Full Members	Number of Attendees	Total Adherents: Number of Adherents	Total Adherents: % of Total Pop.	Total Adherents: % of Total Adh.
403 Salvation Army	1	8	24	9	-	-
413 S.D.A.	2	61	NR	73	.1	.1
418 Southw Bapt Fel	2	NR	NR	NR	-	-
419 So Bapt Conv	67	31,114	12,871	37,713 *	34.1	62.4
435 Unitarian-Univ	1	132	NR	160 *	.1	.3
449 Un Methodist	24	5,086	2,204	6,165 *	5.6	10.2
463 Vineyard	1	130	120	158 *	.1	.3
467 Wesleyan	13	1,188	1,151	2,272	2.1	3.8
RICHLAND	**254**	**85,922**	**39,053**	**133,393 ***	**41.6**	**100.0**
019 Amer Bapt USA	3	2,235	1,535	2,747 *	.9	2.1
053 Assemb of God	6	583	650	869	.3	.7
055 As Ref Pres Ch	8	3,234	NR	4,210	1.3	3.2
056 Baha'i	2	503	NR	503	.2	.4
076 Buddhism	1	NR	NR	NR	-	-
081 Catholic	7	NR	NR	12,681	4.0	9.5
089 Chr & Miss Al	1	107	NR	167	.1	.1
093 Chr Ch (Disc)	2	262	102	322 *	.1	.2
097 Chr Chs&Chs Cr	2	400	NR	491 *	.2	.4
121 Ch God (Abr)	1	0	8	8 *	-	-
123 Ch God (Ander)	3	NR	326	326	.1	.2
127 Ch God (Cleve)	8	911	506	1,119 *	.3	.8
145 Ch God Prophcy	2	71	NR	88 *	-	.1
151 L-D Saints	4	NR	NR	1,086	.3	.8
165 Ch of Nazarene	4	962	805	1,306	.4	1.0
167 Chs of Christ	11	924	918	1,235	.4	.9
173 Comm of Christ	1	39	NR	39	-	-
183 Cons Menn Conf	1	21	26	31	-	-
193 Episcopal	12	NR	2,501	7,769	2.4	5.8
207 E.L.C.A.	21	6,827	2,903	8,612	2.7	6.5
216 Evan Presby Ch	1	51	NR	63 *	-	-
223 Free Will Bapt	1	50	NR	61 *	-	-
226 Friends-USA	1	64	NR	79 *	-	.1
246 Greek Orthodox	1	NR	NR	783	.2	.6
263 Int Foursq Gos	1	189	213	232 *	.1	.2
264 Int Chs of Crst	1	400	719	606	.2	.5
267 Muslim Est	2	NR	312	1,218	.4	.9
283 Luth—MO Synod	2	181	114	270	.1	.2
290 Metro Comm Ch	1	114	54	54 *	-	-
349 Pent Holiness	9	1,639	991	2,014 *	.6	1.5
355 Presb Ch (USA)	14	8,043	3,495	9,888 *	3.1	7.4
356 Presb Ch Amer	7	2,978	2,076	3,997	1.2	3.0
360 Prim Bapt Chrch	1	NR	NR	NR	-	-
403 Salvation Army	1	156	235	225	.1	.2
413 S.D.A.	3	486	NR	578	.2	.4
419 So Bapt Conv	62	35,279	13,043	43,356 *	13.5	32.5
435 Unitarian-Univ	1	193	NR	237 *	.1	.2
449 Un Methodist	38	18,185	6,688	22,351 *	7.0	16.8
467 Wesleyan	2	85	76	211	.1	.2
469 WELS	1	75	57	111	-	.1
496 Jewish Est	2	NR	NR	2,750	.9	2.1
498 Indep.Charis.	2	675	700	700	.2	.5
SALUDA	**41**	**6,606**	**3,009**	**8,542 ***	**44.5**	**100.0**
056 Baha'i	0	35	NR	35	.2	.4
081 Catholic	1	NR	NR	400	2.1	4.7
127 Ch God (Cleve)	1	67	37	83 *	.4	1.0
207 E.L.C.A.	6	633	330	779	4.1	9.1
349 Pent Holiness	4	396	248	489 *	2.5	5.7
355 Presb Ch (USA)	1	43	30	53 *	.3	.6
419 So Bapt Conv	16	3,563	1,524	4,398 *	22.9	51.5
449 Un Methodist	12	1,869	840	2,305 *	12.0	27.0
SPARTANBURG	**366**	**111,688**	**46,166**	**149,488 ***	**58.9**	**100.0**
053 Assemb of God	6	499	441	533	.2	.4
055 As Ref Pres Ch	3	251	NR	294	.1	.2
056 Baha'i	2	199	NR	199	.1	.1
081 Catholic	2	NR	NR	3,637	1.4	2.4
089 Chr & Miss Al	2	222	NR	254	.1	.2
097 Chr Chs&Chs Cr	1	48	NR	60 *	-	-
123 Ch God (Ander)	1	NR	65	65	-	-
127 Ch God (Cleve)	19	3,027	1,656	3,759 *	1.5	2.5
145 Ch God Prophcy	9	321	NR	396 *	.2	.3

Religious Group	Number of Churches, Synagogues, Mosques, or Temples	Number of Communicant, Confirmed, or Full Members	Number of Attendees	Total Adherents: Number of Adherents	Total Adherents: % of Total Pop.	Total Adherents: % of Total Adh.
151 L-D Saints	3	NR	NR	1,528	.6	1.0
157 Ch of Brethren	1	133	91	165 *	.1	.1
165 Ch of Nazarene	2	286	184	448	.2	.3
167 Chs of Christ	5	721	755	942	.4	.6
193 Episcopal	6	NR	1,167	3,022	1.2	2.0
207 E.L.C.A.	4	1,216	527	1,453	.6	1.0
223 Free Will Bapt	17	843	NR	1,047 *	.4	.7
246 Greek Orthodox	1	NR	NR	420	.2	.3
252 Hindu	1	NR	NR	NR	-	-
263 Int Foursq Gos	1	144	240	240 *	.1	.2
283 Luth—MO Synod	1	103	60	121	-	.1
349 Pent Holiness	6	310	245	385 *	.2	.3
355 Presb Ch (USA)	15	5,221	2,376	6,482 *	2.6	4.3
356 Presb Ch Amer	10	1,133	851	1,431	.6	1.0
403 Salvation Army	1	88	48	289	.1	.2
413 S.D.A.	3	808	NR	961	.4	.6
418 Southw Bapt Fel	6	NR	NR	NR	-	-
419 So Bapt Conv	152	77,527	28,927	96,256 *	37.9	64.4
435 Unitarian-Univ	1	101	NR	125 *	-	.1
449 Un Methodist	67	15,110	5,623	18,761 *	7.4	12.6
467 Wesleyan	15	877	860	1,865	.7	1.2
496 Jewish Est	1	NR	NR	500	.2	.3
498 Indep.Charis.	2	2,500	2,050	3,850	1.5	2.6
SUMTER	**114**	**28,518**	**12,438**	**40,439 ***	**38.6**	**100.0**
053 Assemb of God	3	1,080	947	1,149	1.1	2.8
055 As Ref Pres Ch	3	241	NR	278	.3	.7
056 Baha'i	0	386	NR	386	.4	1.0
081 Catholic	2	NR	NR	2,437	2.3	6.0
097 Chr Chs&Chs Cr	1	45	NR	58 *	.1	.1
123 Ch God (Ander)	2	NR	355	355	.3	.9
127 Ch God (Cleve)	2	428	291	548 *	.5	1.4
145 Ch God Prophcy	2	71	NR	92 *	.1	.2
151 L-D Saints	1	NR	NR	588	.6	1.5
165 Ch of Nazarene	3	821	528	933	.9	2.3
167 Chs of Christ	3	360	355	403	.4	1.0
193 Episcopal	5	NR	435	1,025	1.0	2.5
207 E.L.C.A.	1	491	260	595	.6	1.5
223 Free Will Bapt	2	99	NR	127 *	.1	.3
349 Pent Holiness	4	239	246	306 *	.3	.8
355 Presb Ch (USA)	15	2,596	1,328	3,325 *	3.2	8.2
356 Presb Ch Amer	1	223	135	261	.2	.6
403 Salvation Army	1	129	111	308	.3	.8
413 S.D.A.	2	357	NR	425	.4	1.1
418 Southw Bapt Fel	1	NR	NR	NR	-	-
419 So Bapt Conv	35	14,224	4,392	18,202 *	17.4	45.0
449 Un Methodist	23	6,328	2,805	8,098 *	7.7	20.0
496 Jewish Est	1	NR	NR	140	.1	.3
499 Indep.Non-Char	1	400	250	400	.4	1.0
UNION	**69**	**15,814**	**5,704**	**19,740 ***	**66.1**	**100.0**
017 Amer Bapt Assn	3	140	NR	171 *	.6	.9
053 Assemb of God	2	120	113	222	.7	1.1
056 Baha'i	0	39	NR	39	.1	.2
081 Catholic	1	NR	NR	88	.3	.4
127 Ch God (Cleve)	3	369	195	453 *	1.5	2.3
145 Ch God Prophcy	1	36	NR	44 *	.1	.2
151 L-D Saints	1	NR	NR	119	.4	.6
167 Chs of Christ	2	133	125	153	.5	.8
193 Episcopal	1	NR	33	52	.2	.3
207 E.L.C.A.	1	75	33	89	.3	.5
223 Free Will Bapt	2	99	NR	122 *	.4	.6
355 Presb Ch (USA)	5	371	184	454 *	1.5	2.3
356 Presb Ch Amer	1	47	32	47	.2	.2
403 Salvation Army	1	70	38	129	.4	.7
413 S.D.A.	1	52	NR	62	.2	.3
418 Southw Bapt Fel	1	NR	NR	NR	-	-
419 So Bapt Conv	29	11,503	3,818	14,111 *	47.2	71.5
449 Un Methodist	14	2,760	1,133	3,385 *	11.3	17.1
WILLIAMSBURG	**86**	**13,452**	**5,622**	**16,891 ***	**45.4**	**100.0**
053 Assemb of God	2	29	27	46	.1	.3
056 Baha'i	2	1,576	NR	1,576	4.2	9.3

NR–Not Reported *Total adherents estimated from known number of communicant, confirmed, full members. - Represents a percentage less than 0.1. Percentages may not total 100 due to rounding.

Table 4: Religious Congregations by County and Group: 2000

Religious Group	Number of Churches, Synagogues, Mosques, or Temples	Number of Communicant, Confirmed, or Full Members	Number of Attendees	Total Adherents: Number of Adherents	Total Adherents: % of Total Pop.	Total Adherents: % of Total Adh.
081 Catholic	1	NR	NR	100	.3	.6
127 Ch God (Cleve)	4	423	194	541 *	1.5	3.2
145 Ch God Prophcy	1	36	NR	46 *	.1	.3
167 Chs of Christ	2	145	115	210	.6	1.2
193 Episcopal	1	NR	35	74	.2	.4
223 Free Will Bapt	4	198	NR	253 *	.7	1.5
349 Pent Holiness	12	772	766	985 *	2.6	5.8
355 Presb Ch (USA)	4	623	296	795 *	2.1	4.7
356 Presb Ch Amer	5	416	252	501	1.3	3.0
413 S.D.A.	1	184	NR	219	.6	1.3
419 So Bapt Conv	13	2,848	1,080	3,634 *	9.8	21.5
449 Un Methodist	34	6,202	2,857	7,911 *	21.3	46.8
YORK	**224**	**58,749**	**24,907**	**82,840 ***	**50.3**	**100.0**
017 Amer Bapt Assn	1	35	NR	44 *	-	.1
053 Assemb of God	6	775	993	1,083	.7	1.3
055 As Ref Pres Ch	12	3,112	NR	3,603	2.2	4.3
056 Baha'i	1	1,101	NR	1,101	.7	1.3
081 Catholic	5	NR	NR	6,576	4.0	7.9
089 Chr & Miss Al	1	24	NR	98	.1	.1
097 Chr Chs&Chs Cr	2	210	NR	264 *	.2	.3
123 Ch God (Ander)	1	NR	75	75	-	.1
127 Ch God (Cleve)	15	3,112	1,610	3,915 *	2.4	4.7
145 Ch God Prophcy	5	178	NR	225 *	.1	.3
151 L-D Saints	3	NR	NR	1,257	.8	1.5
165 Ch of Nazarene	8	1,241	661	1,394	.8	1.7
167 Chs of Christ	2	280	243	324	.2	.4
193 Episcopal	4	NR	467	1,318	.8	1.6
203 Evan Free Ch	1	59	100	100	.1	.1
207 E.L.C.A.	4	823	702	1,078	.7	1.3
216 Evan Presby Ch	1	36	NR	45 *	-	.1
221 Free Methodist	1	0	51	51	-	.1
223 Free Will Bapt	9	446	NR	562 *	.3	.7
262 Int Cou Comm Ch	1	860	NR	1,082 *	.7	1.3
263 Int Foursq Gos	4	346	422	435 *	.3	.5
349 Pent Holiness	5	779	342	980 *	.6	1.2
355 Presb Ch (USA)	22	5,578	2,948	7,017 *	4.3	8.5
356 Presb Ch Amer	9	2,930	1,848	3,588	2.2	4.3
403 Salvation Army	1	70	41	167	.1	.2
413 S.D.A.	3	201	NR	239	.1	.3
418 Southw Bapt Fel	2	NR	NR	NR	-	-
419 So Bapt Conv	57	25,422	9,830	31,981 *	19.4	38.6
449 Un Methodist	33	9,942	3,789	12,508 *	7.6	15.1
467 Wesleyan	3	205	185	565	.3	.7
496 Jewish Est	0	NR	NR	100	.1	.1
499 Indep.Non-Char	2	984	600	1,065	.6	1.3

SOUTH DAKOTA

Religious Group	Number of Churches, Synagogues, Mosques, or Temples	Number of Communicant, Confirmed, or Full Members	Number of Attendees	Total Adherents: Number of Adherents	Total Adherents: % of Total Pop.	Total Adherents: % of Total Adh.
The State.....	1,712	230,313	122,607	511,886 *	67.8	100.0
AURORA	**12**	**1,213**	**707**	**2,513 ***	**82.2**	**100.0**
056 Baha'i	0	1	NR	1	-	-
081 Catholic	3	NR	NR	1,012	33.1	40.3
207 E.L.C.A.	2	317	171	364	11.9	14.5
283 Luth—MO Synod	2	303	121	354	11.6	14.1
371 Ref Ch in Am	1	150	131	235	7.7	9.4
449 Un Methodist	4	442	284	547 *	17.9	21.8
BEADLE	**40**	**7,173**	**2,851**	**12,823 ***	**75.3**	**100.0**
019 Amer Bapt USA	1	240	75	293 *	1.7	2.3
053 Assemb of God	1	78	89	133	.8	1.0
056 Baha'i	0	1	NR	1	-	-
081 Catholic	2	NR	NR	3,291	19.3	25.7
089 Chr & Miss Al	1	64	NR	165	1.0	1.3
097 Chr Chs&Chs Cr	1	250	NR	305 *	1.8	2.4
151 L-D Saints	1	NR	NR	126	.7	1.0
165 Ch of Nazarene	1	51	24	56	.3	.4
167 Chs of Christ	1	27	24	35	.2	.3
193 Episcopal	1	NR	51	151	.9	1.2
207 E.L.C.A.	3	1,447	541	1,857	10.9	14.5
237 Menn Br US Conf	2	482	NR	588 *	3.5	4.6
257 Hutterian Br	2	132	NR	200	1.2	1.6
283 Luth—MO Synod	4	1,381	589	1,669	9.8	13.0
297 Mennonite;Other	1	195	NR	238 *	1.4	1.9
355 Presb Ch (USA)	5	839	417	1,024 *	6.0	8.0
388 Reg Bapt Gen As	1	24	33	33 *	.2	.3
403 Salvation Army	1	115	66	366	2.2	2.9
413 S.D.A.	1	74	NR	88	.5	.7
419 So Bapt Conv	2	101	111	123 *	.7	1.0
443 Un C of Christ	1	241	100	294 *	1.7	2.3
449 Un Methodist	5	1,336	641	1,630 *	9.6	12.7
467 Wesleyan	1	61	70	119	.7	.9
469 WELS	1	34	20	38	.2	.3
BENNETT	**14**	**412**	**303**	**1,611 ***	**45.1**	**100.0**
056 Baha'i	2	132	NR	132	3.7	8.2
081 Catholic	2	NR	NR	520	14.5	32.3
123 Ch God (Ander)	1	NR	22	22	.6	1.4
151 L-D Saints	1	NR	NR	45	1.3	2.8
193 Episcopal	3	NR	116	521	14.6	32.3
355 Presb Ch (USA)	2	138	76	192 *	5.4	11.9
388 Reg Bapt Gen As	1	24	33	33 *	.9	2.0
413 S.D.A.	1	11	NR	13	.4	.8
469 WELS	1	107	56	133	3.7	8.3
BON HOMME	**26**	**2,831**	**1,427**	**6,001 ***	**82.7**	**100.0**
057 Bapt Gen Conf	1	21	30	30 *	.4	.5
081 Catholic	5	NR	NR	2,438	33.6	40.6
207 E.L.C.A.	1	295	135	361	5.0	6.0
257 Hutterian Br	2	132	NR	200	2.8	3.3
283 Luth—MO Synod	4	414	223	511	7.0	8.5
288 Mennonite USA	1	83	70	99 *	1.4	1.6
313 N Am Bapt Conf	3	361	198	431 *	5.9	7.2
355 Presb Ch (USA)	4	394	182	471 *	6.5	7.8
371 Ref Ch in Am	1	283	225	447	6.2	7.4
443 Un C of Christ	2	628	260	750 *	10.3	12.5
449 Un Methodist	2	220	104	263 *	3.6	4.4
BROOKINGS	**49**	**8,745**	**5,072**	**17,133 ***	**60.7**	**100.0**
019 Amer Bapt USA	1	65	59	77 *	.3	.4
053 Assemb of God	1	164	210	325	1.2	1.9
056 Baha'i	0	6	NR	6	-	-
057 Bapt Gen Conf	1	198	210	235 *	.8	1.4
081 Catholic	5	NR	NR	3,686	13.1	21.5
097 Chr Chs&Chs Cr	2	150	NR	177 *	.6	1.0
105 Christian Ref	1	132	65	157 *	.6	.9
123 Ch God (Ander)	1	NR	223	223	.8	1.3
151 L-D Saints	1	NR	NR	205	.7	1.2
167 Chs of Christ	2	35	42	47	.2	.3
193 Episcopal	1	NR	65	189	.7	1.1
207 E.L.C.A.	6	3,688	1,480	4,921	17.4	28.7
220 Free Lutheran	1	350	135	486	1.7	2.8
257 Hutterian Br	2	132	NR	200	.7	1.2
267 Muslim Est	1	NR	35	50	.2	.3
283 Luth—MO Synod	4	572	352	730	2.6	4.3
306 NT IndBapt&Rltd	2	110	NR	130 *	.5	.8
335 Orth Pres Ch	1	98	88	126	.4	.7
355 Presb Ch (USA)	2	326	140	387 *	1.4	2.3
371 Ref Ch in Am	2	260	270	424	1.5	2.5
443 Un C of Christ	2	226	121	268 *	.9	1.6
449 Un Methodist	6	1,438	643	1,706 *	6.0	10.0
467 Wesleyan	1	314	687	1,765	6.3	10.3
469 WELS	3	481	247	613	2.2	3.6
BROWN	**64**	**13,947**	**6,611**	**30,332 ***	**85.5**	**100.0**
019 Amer Bapt USA	1	676	292	823 *	2.3	2.7
053 Assemb of God	1	228	285	400	1.1	1.3
056 Baha'i	0	3	NR	3	-	-
081 Catholic	5	NR	NR	10,479	29.6	34.5
089 Chr & Miss Al	3	76	NR	193	.5	.6
097 Chr Chs&Chs Cr	1	95	NR	116 *	.3	.4
127 Ch God (Cleve)	1	72	55	88 *	.2	.3
151 L-D Saints	1	NR	NR	269	.8	.9

NR–Not Reported   *Total adherents estimated from known number of communicant, confirmed, full members.   - Represents a percentage less than 0.1.   Percentages may not total 100 due to rounding.

Table 4: Religious Congregations by County and Group: 2000

Religious Group	Number of Churches, Synagogues, Mosques, or Temples	Number of Communicant, Confirmed, or Full Members	Number of Attendees	Total Adherents		
				Number of Adherents	% of Total Pop.	% of Total Adh.
165 Ch of Nazarene	1	59	68	73	.2	.2
167 Chs of Christ	1	45	60	55	.2	.2
193 Episcopal	1	NR	97	206	.6	.7
203 Evan Free Ch	1	8	29	29	.1	.1
207 E.L.C.A.	12	6,105	2,643	7,990	22.5	26.3
220 Free Lutheran	1	30	8	30	.1	.1
257 Hutterian Br	4	264	NR	400	1.1	1.3
283 Luth—MO Synod	8	2,402	947	3,084	8.7	10.2
313 N Am Bapt Conf	1	225	217	274 *	.8	.9
355 Presb Ch (USA)	2	428	130	521 *	1.5	1.7
373 Ref Ch in U.S.	1	124	NR	158	.4	.5
403 Salvation Army	1	124	41	1,414	4.0	4.7
413 S.D.A.	1	81	NR	96	.3	.3
419 So Bapt Conv	2	37	8	45 *	.1	.1
443 Un C of Christ	3	567	242	691 *	1.9	2.3
449 Un Methodist	8	1,920	1,249	2,338 *	6.6	7.7
467 Wesleyan	1	45	40	55	.2	.2
469 WELS	1	333	200	427	1.2	1.4
496 Jewish Est	1	NR	NR	75	.2	.2
BRULE	**17**	**1,653**	**834**	**4,464 ***	**83.2**	**100.0**
053 Assemb of God	1	36	45	61	1.1	1.4
056 Baha'i	0	1	NR	1	-	-
057 Bapt Gen Conf	1	68	109	109 *	2.0	2.4
081 Catholic	3	NR	NR	2,105	39.2	47.2
151 L-D Saints	1	NR	NR	80	1.5	1.8
193 Episcopal	1	NR	35	101	1.9	2.3
207 E.L.C.A.	2	351	170	431	8.0	9.7
220 Free Lutheran	2	173	115	223	4.2	5.0
257 Hutterian Br	1	66	NR	100	1.9	2.2
283 Luth—MO Synod	1	419	201	563	10.5	12.6
355 Presb Ch (USA)	1	23	9	29 *	.5	.6
443 Un C of Christ	1	427	120	547 *	10.2	12.3
449 Un Methodist	2	89	30	114 *	2.1	2.6
BUFFALO	**5**	**39**	**45**	**995 ***	**49.0**	**100.0**
056 Baha'i	0	20	NR	20	1.0	2.0
081 Catholic	2	NR	NR	697	34.3	70.1
193 Episcopal	2	NR	35	250	12.3	25.1
355 Presb Ch (USA)	1	19	10	28 *	1.4	2.8
BUTTE	**14**	**1,367**	**740**	**2,613 ***	**28.7**	**100.0**
017 Amer Bapt Assn	1	20	NR	25 *	.3	1.0
019 Amer Bapt USA	1	79	60	100 *	1.1	3.8
053 Assemb of God	1	41	53	53	.6	2.0
056 Baha'i	0	2	NR	2	-	.1
081 Catholic	2	NR	NR	730	8.0	27.9
193 Episcopal	1	NR	48	62	.7	2.4
207 E.L.C.A.	3	740	234	1,012	11.1	38.7
263 Int Foursq Gos	1	62	25	78 *	.9	3.0
419 So Bapt Conv	1	24	21	30 *	.3	1.1
443 Un C of Christ	1	188	95	238 *	2.6	9.1
449 Un Methodist	1	194	176	245 *	2.7	9.4
467 Wesleyan	1	17	28	38	.4	1.5
CAMPBELL	**10**	**928**	**547**	**1,580 ***	**88.7**	**100.0**
053 Assemb of God	1	14	21	32	1.8	2.0
081 Catholic	1	NR	NR	440	24.7	27.8
127 Ch God (Cleve)	1	1	7	7 *	.4	.4
207 E.L.C.A.	3	435	232	553	31.0	35.0
313 N Am Bapt Conf	1	141	114	174 *	9.8	11.0
356 Presb Ch Amer	1	205	135	220	12.3	13.9
373 Ref Ch in U.S.	1	73	NR	87	4.9	5.5
469 WELS	1	59	38	67	3.8	4.2
CHARLES MIX	**32**	**2,577**	**1,655**	**6,776 ***	**72.5**	**100.0**
053 Assemb of God	1	18	28	50	.5	.7
056 Baha'i	0	2	NR	2	-	-
057 Bapt Gen Conf	1	51	75	75 *	.8	1.1
081 Catholic	6	NR	NR	2,979	31.9	44.0
089 Chr & Miss Al	1	26	NR	51	.5	.8
105 Christian Ref	1	425	400	564 *	6.0	8.3
151 L-D Saints	1	NR	NR	49	.5	.7
193 Episcopal	2	NR	48	108	1.2	1.6
207 E.L.C.A.	3	486	270	689	7.4	10.2
257 Hutterian Br	3	198	NR	300	3.2	4.4
283 Luth—MO Synod	2	319	174	398	4.3	5.9
355 Presb Ch (USA)	5	368	168	489 *	5.2	7.2
371 Ref Ch in Am	1	193	220	373	4.0	5.5
413 S.D.A.	1	21	NR	25	.3	.4
443 Un C of Christ	1	30	20	40 *	.4	.6
449 Un Methodist	2	440	252	584 *	6.2	8.6
467 Wesleyan	1	0	0	0	-	-
CLARK	**27**	**2,623**	**1,009**	**3,931 ***	**94.9**	**100.0**
053 Assemb of God	1	47	70	88	2.1	2.2
081 Catholic	2	NR	NR	586	14.1	14.9
207 E.L.C.A.	7	1,019	455	1,244	30.0	31.6
257 Hutterian Br	5	330	NR	500	12.1	12.7
297 Mennonite;Other	1	230	NR	283 *	6.8	7.2
355 Presb Ch (USA)	2	100	69	123 *	3.0	3.1
371 Ref Ch in Am	1	56	45	82	2.0	2.1
443 Un C of Christ	2	153	47	188 *	4.5	4.8
449 Un Methodist	3	421	187	518 *	12.5	13.2
469 WELS	3	267	136	319	7.7	8.1
CLAY	**24**	**3,268**	**1,330**	**6,401 ***	**47.3**	**100.0**
019 Amer Bapt USA	1	198	61	232 *	1.7	3.6
053 Assemb of God	1	50	73	145	1.1	2.3
056 Baha'i	0	11	NR	11	.1	.2
081 Catholic	3	NR	NR	1,820	13.4	28.4
089 Chr & Miss Al	1	33	NR	154	1.1	2.4
151 L-D Saints	1	NR	NR	104	.8	1.6
167 Chs of Christ	1	12	20	20	.1	.3
193 Episcopal	1	NR	36	93	.7	1.5
207 E.L.C.A.	6	1,963	639	2,633	19.5	41.1
283 Luth—MO Synod	1	144	85	186	1.4	2.9
419 So Bapt Conv	1	92	17	108 *	.8	1.7
435 Unitarian-Univ	1	11	NR	13 *	.1	.2
443 Un C of Christ	2	400	243	468 *	3.5	7.3
449 Un Methodist	3	354	156	414 *	3.1	6.5
469 WELS	1	0	0	0	-	-
CODINGTON	**39**	**9,042**	**5,705**	**21,225 ***	**82.0**	**100.0**
019 Amer Bapt USA	1	270	136	339 *	1.3	1.6
053 Assemb of God	1	79	105	166	.6	.8
056 Baha'i	0	2	NR	2	-	-
081 Catholic	7	NR	NR	7,937	30.6	37.4
089 Chr & Miss Al	1	26	NR	93	.4	.4
097 Chr Chs&Chs Cr	1	50	NR	63 *	.2	.3
165 Ch of Nazarene	1	15	0	15	.1	.1
167 Chs of Christ	1	42	55	68	.3	.3
193 Episcopal	1	NR	65	176	.7	.8
203 Evan Free Ch	1	60	150	150	.6	.7
207 E.L.C.A.	4	3,581	1,395	4,950	19.1	23.3
220 Free Lutheran	1	125	45	157	.6	.7
263 Int Foursq Gos	1	328	1,252	1,252 *	4.8	5.9
283 Luth—MO Synod	1	312	133	405	1.6	1.9
355 Presb Ch (USA)	1	35	28	44 *	.2	.2
373 Ref Ch in U.S.	1	19	NR	24	.1	.1
403 Salvation Army	1	146	106	197	.8	.9
413 S.D.A.	1	51	NR	61	.2	.3
419 So Bapt Conv	1	62	45	78 *	.3	.4
443 Un C of Christ	1	409	170	513 *	2.0	2.4
449 Un Methodist	4	1,553	890	1,949 *	7.5	9.2
467 Wesleyan	1	83	120	225	.9	1.1
469 WELS	6	1,794	1,010	2,361	9.1	11.1
CORSON	**28**	**832**	**628**	**3,766 ***	**90.1**	**100.0**
053 Assemb of God	3	155	143	271	6.5	7.2
056 Baha'i	0	45	NR	45	1.1	1.2
081 Catholic	7	NR	NR	1,853	44.3	49.2
127 Ch God (Cleve)	1	0	0	0 *	-	-
193 Episcopal	6	NR	126	779	18.6	20.7

NR–Not Reported   *Total adherents estimated from known number of communicant, confirmed, full members.   - Represents a percentage less than 0.1.   Percentages may not total 100 due to rounding.

Table 4: Religious Congregations by County and Group: 2000

Religious Group	Number of Churches, Synagogues, Mosques, or Temples	Number of Communicant, Confirmed, or Full Members	Number of Attendees	Total Adherents		
				Number of Adherents	% of Total Pop.	% of Total Adh.
207 E.L.C.A.	2	220	105	269	6.4	7.1
313 N Am Bapt Conf	2	66	75	92 *	2.2	2.4
355 Presb Ch (USA)	2	83	50	116 *	2.8	3.1
443 Un C of Christ	3	169	67	237 *	5.7	6.3
469 WELS	2	94	62	104	2.5	2.8
CUSTER	**17**	**1,633**	**915**	**2,991 ***	**41.1**	**100.0**
017 Amer Bapt Assn	1	20	NR	24 *	.3	.8
056 Baha'i	0	17	NR	17	.2	.6
081 Catholic	2	NR	NR	678	9.3	22.7
151 L-D Saints	1	NR	NR	150	2.1	5.0
167 Chs of Christ	1	47	55	65	.9	2.2
207 E.L.C.A.	2	686	368	983	13.5	32.9
283 Luth—MO Synod	1	119	83	145	2.0	4.8
413 S.D.A.	1	33	NR	39	.5	1.3
419 So Bapt Conv	1	127	85	150 *	2.1	5.0
443 Un C of Christ	2	452	184	535 *	7.4	17.9
449 Un Methodist	3	73	72	86 *	1.2	2.9
467 Wesleyan	1	38	54	97	1.3	3.2
469 WELS	1	21	14	22	.3	.7
DAVISON	**32**	**6,054**	**3,229**	**15,135 ***	**80.8**	**100.0**
053 Assemb of God	1	39	51	112	.6	.7
056 Baha'i	0	6	NR	6	-	-
057 Bapt Gen Conf	1	254	236	314 *	1.7	2.1
081 Catholic	4	NR	NR	6,401	34.2	42.3
097 Chr Chs&Chs Cr	1	55	NR	68 *	.4	.4
151 L-D Saints	1	NR	NR	69	.4	.5
165 Ch of Nazarene	1	208	136	213	1.1	1.4
167 Chs of Christ	1	9	10	14	.1	.1
193 Episcopal	1	NR	63	195	1.0	1.3
207 E.L.C.A.	4	2,208	935	2,855	15.2	18.9
257 Hutterian Br	3	198	NR	300	1.6	2.0
283 Luth—MO Synod	1	690	287	925	4.9	6.1
355 Presb Ch (USA)	1	167	113	206 *	1.1	1.4
371 Ref Ch in Am	1	292	220	468	2.5	3.1
373 Ref Ch in U.S.	1	70	NR	93	.5	.6
403 Salvation Army	1	69	42	118	.6	.8
413 S.D.A.	1	13	NR	15	.1	.1
419 So Bapt Conv	1	23	36	28 *	.1	.2
443 Un C of Christ	2	265	131	327 *	1.7	2.2
449 Un Methodist	3	1,201	577	1,483 *	7.9	9.8
467 Wesleyan	1	217	360	847	4.5	5.6
469 WELS	1	70	32	78	.4	.5
DAY	**33**	**2,814**	**1,403**	**5,756 ***	**91.8**	**100.0**
019 Amer Bapt USA	1	3	2	4 *	.1	.1
053 Assemb of God	1	7	8	15	.2	.3
081 Catholic	5	NR	NR	2,046	32.6	35.5
193 Episcopal	2	NR	50	217	3.5	3.8
207 E.L.C.A.	12	2,099	928	2,620	41.8	45.5
220 Free Lutheran	2	60	50	60	1.0	1.0
283 Luth—MO Synod	2	225	95	270	4.3	4.7
355 Presb Ch (USA)	1	25	20	31 *	.5	.5
419 So Bapt Conv	2	61	40	75 *	1.2	1.3
443 Un C of Christ	1	15	10	18 *	.3	.3
449 Un Methodist	3	224	117	275 *	4.4	4.8
467 Wesleyan	1	95	83	125	2.0	2.2
DEUEL	**20**	**2,578**	**1,110**	**3,988 ***	**88.7**	**100.0**
057 Bapt Gen Conf	1	37	16	46 *	1.0	1.2
081 Catholic	2	NR	NR	641	14.3	16.1
105 Christian Ref	1	85	69	105 *	2.3	2.6
151 L-D Saints	1	NR	NR	165	3.7	4.1
167 Chs of Christ	1	6	10	10	.2	.3
207 E.L.C.A.	7	1,446	572	1,778	39.5	44.6
355 Presb Ch (USA)	1	41	28	50 *	1.1	1.3
443 Un C of Christ	1	72	32	89 *	2.0	2.2
449 Un Methodist	2	326	142	401 *	8.9	10.1
469 WELS	3	565	241	703	15.6	17.6

Religious Group	Number of Churches, Synagogues, Mosques, or Temples	Number of Communicant, Confirmed, or Full Members	Number of Attendees	Total Adherents		
				Number of Adherents	% of Total Pop.	% of Total Adh.
DEWEY	**27**	**987**	**504**	**3,506 ***	**58.7**	**100.0**
019 Amer Bapt USA	1	110	10	155 *	2.6	4.4
056 Baha'i	0	10	NR	10	.2	.3
081 Catholic	7	NR	NR	825	13.8	23.5
127 Ch God (Cleve)	1	26	21	37 *	.6	1.1
151 L-D Saints	1	NR	NR	322	5.4	9.2
193 Episcopal	4	NR	91	1,028	17.2	29.3
207 E.L.C.A.	1	63	24	64	1.1	1.8
220 Free Lutheran	1	42	25	53	.9	1.5
313 N Am Bapt Conf	1	58	56	82 *	1.4	2.3
419 So Bapt Conv	1	211	54	298 *	5.0	8.5
443 Un C of Christ	5	353	155	499 *	8.4	14.2
449 Un Methodist	1	42	25	59 *	1.0	1.7
467 Wesleyan	1	0	0	0	-	-
469 WELS	2	72	43	74	1.2	2.1
DOUGLAS	**18**	**2,508**	**1,668**	**3,875 ***	**112.1**	**100.0**
081 Catholic	1	NR	NR	468	13.5	12.1
105 Christian Ref	3	758	630	944 *	27.3	24.4
207 E.L.C.A.	2	278	178	347	10.0	9.0
257 Hutterian Br	2	132	NR	200	5.8	5.2
283 Luth—MO Synod	3	576	388	728	21.1	18.8
307 Neth Ref Congr	1	92	NR	217	6.3	5.6
371 Ref Ch in Am	3	398	363	630	18.2	16.3
443 Un C of Christ	2	250	96	311 *	9.0	8.0
449 Un Methodist	1	24	13	30 *	.9	.8
EDMUNDS	**21**	**1,627**	**734**	**3,993 ***	**91.4**	**100.0**
019 Amer Bapt USA	1	117	60	146 *	3.3	3.7
081 Catholic	4	NR	NR	1,720	39.4	43.1
127 Ch God (Cleve)	1	23	23	29 *	.7	.7
207 E.L.C.A.	2	448	192	595	13.6	14.9
257 Hutterian Br	2	132	NR	200	4.6	5.0
283 Luth—MO Synod	1	31	23	43	1.0	1.1
355 Presb Ch (USA)	1	16	9	20 *	.5	.5
373 Ref Ch in U.S.	1	49	NR	55	1.3	1.4
413 S.D.A.	1	64	NR	76	1.7	1.9
443 Un C of Christ	3	207	89	258 *	5.9	6.5
449 Un Methodist	1	42	28	52 *	1.2	1.3
467 Wesleyan	1	113	157	350	8.0	8.8
469 WELS	2	385	153	449	10.3	11.2
FALL RIVER	**26**	**1,578**	**1,542**	**3,690 ***	**49.5**	**100.0**
019 Amer Bapt USA	1	51	215	215 *	2.9	5.8
053 Assemb of God	3	100	130	196	2.6	5.3
056 Baha'i	0	6	NR	6	.1	.2
081 Catholic	2	NR	NR	1,187	15.9	32.2
097 Chr Chs&Chs Cr	1	50	NR	60 *	.8	1.6
167 Chs of Christ	1	15	26	27	.4	.7
193 Episcopal	1	NR	33	63	.8	1.7
203 Evan Free Ch	1	26	70	70	.9	1.9
207 E.L.C.A.	2	272	144	335	4.5	9.1
283 Luth—MO Synod	1	328	144	438	5.9	11.9
355 Presb Ch (USA)	1	85	187	187 *	2.5	5.1
413 S.D.A.	1	62	NR	74	1.0	2.0
419 So Bapt Conv	2	110	70	131 *	1.8	3.6
443 Un C of Christ	1	56	25	67 *	.9	1.8
449 Un Methodist	5	352	408	419 *	5.6	11.4
467 Wesleyan	2	30	70	175	2.3	4.7
469 WELS	1	35	20	40	.5	1.1
FAULK	**20**	**1,176**	**440**	**2,604 ***	**98.6**	**100.0**
081 Catholic	5	NR	NR	1,085	41.1	41.7
207 E.L.C.A.	2	171	92	232	8.8	8.9
257 Hutterian Br	4	264	NR	400	15.2	15.4
283 Luth—MO Synod	3	221	106	248	9.4	9.5
443 Un C of Christ	1	0	0	0 *	-	-
449 Un Methodist	5	520	242	639 *	24.2	24.5
GRANT	**20**	**3,751**	**1,687**	**7,369 ***	**93.9**	**100.0**
053 Assemb of God	1	36	49	89	1.1	1.2

NR–Not Reported *Total adherents estimated from known number of communicant, confirmed, full members. - Represents a percentage less than 0.1. Percentages may not total 100 due to rounding.

Table 4: Religious Congregations by County and Group: 2000

Religious Group	Number of Churches, Synagogues, Mosques, or Temples	Number of Communicant, Confirmed, or Full Members	Number of Attendees	Total Adherents		
				Number of Adherents	% of Total Pop.	% of Total Adh.
081 Catholic	3	NR	NR	2,559	32.6	34.7
193 Episcopal	1	NR	22	37	.5	.5
201 Evan Cov Ch	2	91	90	113 *	1.4	1.5
207 E.L.C.A.	3	1,372	405	1,772	22.6	24.0
283 Luth—MO Synod	3	1,065	431	1,325	16.9	18.0
313 N Am Bapt Conf	1	123	105	152 *	1.9	2.1
355 Presb Ch (USA)	1	17	12	21 *	.3	.3
443 Un C of Christ	1	30	26	37 *	.5	.5
449 Un Methodist	3	952	502	1,177 *	15.0	16.0
469 WELS	1	65	45	87	1.1	1.2
GREGORY	**25**	**1,646**	**965**	**3,428 ***	**71.5**	**100.0**
019 Amer Bapt USA	2	133	155	160 *	3.3	4.7
053 Assemb of God	1	33	35	47	1.0	1.4
056 Baha'i	0	1	NR	1	-	-
081 Catholic	4	NR	NR	1,234	25.8	36.0
151 L-D Saints	1	NR	NR	78	1.6	2.3
193 Episcopal	3	NR	27	90	1.9	2.6
283 Luth—MO Synod	2	250	218	346	7.2	10.1
355 Presb Ch (USA)	1	7	4	8 *	.2	.2
419 So Bapt Conv	1	87	60	105 *	2.2	3.1
443 Un C of Christ	3	270	116	325 *	6.8	9.5
449 Un Methodist	3	466	177	561 *	11.7	16.4
469 WELS	4	399	173	473	9.9	13.8
HAAKON	**12**	**676**	**345**	**1,924 ***	**87.6**	**100.0**
081 Catholic	3	NR	NR	1,024	46.6	53.2
203 Evan Free Ch	2	38	60	60	2.7	3.1
207 E.L.C.A.	3	315	135	422	19.2	21.9
283 Luth—MO Synod	2	149	52	208	9.5	10.8
355 Presb Ch (USA)	1	116	63	140 *	6.4	7.3
449 Un Methodist	1	58	35	70 *	3.2	3.6
HAMLIN	**22**	**2,519**	**1,177**	**3,942 ***	**71.2**	**100.0**
057 Bapt Gen Conf	1	49	23	62 *	1.1	1.6
081 Catholic	3	NR	NR	680	12.3	17.3
201 Evan Cov Ch	1	70	74	89 *	1.6	2.3
207 E.L.C.A.	7	1,556	628	1,971	35.6	50.0
257 Hutterian Br	2	132	NR	200	3.6	5.1
355 Presb Ch (USA)	1	236	115	300 *	5.4	7.6
371 Ref Ch in Am	1	115	165	210	3.8	5.3
443 Un C of Christ	2	157	76	200 *	3.6	5.1
449 Un Methodist	2	42	36	53 *	1.0	1.3
469 WELS	2	162	60	177	3.2	4.5
HAND	**13**	**1,052**	**499**	**2,622 ***	**70.1**	**100.0**
053 Assemb of God	1	17	14	16	.4	.6
056 Baha'i	0	1	NR	1	-	-
081 Catholic	3	NR	NR	1,290	34.5	49.2
151 L-D Saints	1	NR	NR	44	1.2	1.7
165 Ch of Nazarene	1	48	48	48	1.3	1.8
207 E.L.C.A.	1	379	130	469	12.5	17.9
257 Hutterian Br	1	66	NR	100	2.7	3.8
355 Presb Ch (USA)	1	196	109	237 *	6.3	9.0
419 So Bapt Conv	1	48	37	58 *	1.6	2.2
443 Un C of Christ	1	28	22	34 *	.9	1.3
449 Un Methodist	2	269	139	325 *	8.7	12.4
HANSON	**11**	**825**	**419**	**2,123 ***	**67.6**	**100.0**
081 Catholic	3	NR	NR	1,037	33.0	48.8
257 Hutterian Br	2	132	NR	200	6.4	9.4
283 Luth—MO Synod	2	214	110	266	8.5	12.5
313 N Am Bapt Conf	1	286	180	370 *	11.8	17.4
355 Presb Ch (USA)	1	57	40	74 *	2.4	3.5
449 Un Methodist	2	136	89	176 *	5.6	8.3
HARDING	**12**	**433**	**226**	**944 ***	**69.8**	**100.0**
053 Assemb of God	1	17	22	29	2.1	3.1
081 Catholic	4	NR	NR	364	26.9	38.6
207 E.L.C.A.	4	248	111	347	25.6	36.8
220 Free Lutheran	1	87	55	103	7.6	10.9

Religious Group	Number of Churches, Synagogues, Mosques, or Temples	Number of Communicant, Confirmed, or Full Members	Number of Attendees	Total Adherents		
				Number of Adherents	% of Total Pop.	% of Total Adh.
443 Un C of Christ	1	64	28	80 *	5.9	8.5
449 Un Methodist	1	17	10	21 *	1.6	2.2
HUGHES	**29**	**6,155**	**2,628**	**12,083 ***	**73.3**	**100.0**
019 Amer Bapt USA	2	281	144	355 *	2.2	2.9
053 Assemb of God	1	106	120	257	1.6	2.1
056 Baha'i	1	27	NR	27	.2	.2
081 Catholic	3	NR	NR	4,088	24.8	33.8
097 Chr Chs&Chs Cr	1	40	NR	51 *	.3	.4
165 Ch of Nazarene	1	44	20	44	.3	.4
167 Chs of Christ	2	80	86	120	.7	1.0
193 Episcopal	1	NR	81	178	1.1	1.5
207 E.L.C.A.	2	2,127	706	2,829	17.2	23.4
283 Luth—MO Synod	3	1,290	555	1,342	8.1	11.1
355 Presb Ch (USA)	1	116	75	147 *	.9	1.2
373 Ref Ch in U.S.	1	28	NR	36	.2	.3
413 S.D.A.	1	106	NR	126	.8	1.0
419 So Bapt Conv	2	209	90	264 *	1.6	2.2
443 Un C of Christ	1	429	154	543 *	3.3	4.5
449 Un Methodist	4	1,112	456	1,406 *	8.5	11.6
467 Wesleyan	1	65	86	138	.8	1.1
469 WELS	1	95	55	132	.8	1.1
HUTCHINSON	**32**	**5,048**	**2,502**	**8,199 ***	**101.5**	**100.0**
053 Assemb of God	1	18	22	22	.3	.3
056 Baha'i	0	2	NR	2	-	-
081 Catholic	3	NR	NR	2,011	24.9	24.5
105 Christian Ref	1	247	175	301 *	3.7	3.7
207 E.L.C.A.	6	1,314	639	1,609	19.9	19.6
220 Free Lutheran	1	87	41	110	1.4	1.3
237 Menn Br US Conf	2	217	NR	265 *	3.3	3.2
257 Hutterian Br	3	198	NR	300	3.7	3.7
283 Luth—MO Synod	5	976	571	1,176	14.6	14.3
288 Mennonite USA	2	472	281	576 *	7.1	7.0
291 Missionary Ch	1	73	66	73	.9	.9
313 N Am Bapt Conf	1	89	46	109 *	1.3	1.3
373 Ref Ch in U.S.	1	228	NR	269	3.3	3.3
443 Un C of Christ	3	903	541	1,102 *	13.6	13.4
449 Un Methodist	2	224	120	274 *	3.4	3.3
HYDE	**6**	**640**	**163**	**1,283 ***	**76.8**	**100.0**
081 Catholic	2	NR	NR	461	27.6	35.9
097 Chr Chs&Chs Cr	2	130	NR	162 *	9.7	12.6
207 E.L.C.A.	1	357	107	469	28.1	36.6
449 Un Methodist	1	153	56	191 *	11.4	14.9
JACKSON	**11**	**395**	**149**	**1,197 ***	**40.9**	**100.0**
056 Baha'i	1	67	NR	67	2.3	5.6
081 Catholic	4	NR	NR	522	17.8	43.6
193 Episcopal	2	NR	28	161	5.5	13.5
207 E.L.C.A.	2	258	73	357	12.2	29.8
283 Luth—MO Synod	1	39	28	48	1.6	4.0
355 Presb Ch (USA)	1	31	20	42 *	1.4	3.5
JERAULD	**11**	**1,124**	**527**	**1,676 ***	**73.0**	**100.0**
056 Baha'i	0	1	NR	1	-	.1
081 Catholic	1	NR	NR	347	15.1	20.7
207 E.L.C.A.	1	292	120	327	14.2	19.5
221 Free Methodist	1	19	28	28	1.2	1.7
257 Hutterian Br	1	66	NR	100	4.4	6.0
283 Luth—MO Synod	1	78	46	93	4.1	5.5
313 N Am Bapt Conf	1	101	59	118 *	5.1	7.0
443 Un C of Christ	3	285	125	333 *	14.5	19.9
449 Un Methodist	2	282	149	329 *	14.3	19.6
JONES	**9**	**467**	**242**	**737 ***	**61.8**	**100.0**
053 Assemb of God	1	7	10	10	.8	1.4
056 Baha'i	0	1	NR	1	.1	.1
081 Catholic	2	NR	NR	121	10.1	16.4
203 Evan Free Ch	2	44	81	81	6.8	11.0
283 Luth—MO Synod	2	182	81	241	20.2	32.7

NR–Not Reported   *Total adherents estimated from known number of communicant, confirmed, full members.   - Represents a percentage less than 0.1.   Percentages may not total 100 due to rounding.

Table 4: Religious Congregations by County and Group: 2000

Religious Group	Number of Churches, Synagogues, Mosques, or Temples	Number of Communicant, Confirmed, or Full Members	Number of Attendees	Total Adherents: Number of Adherents	Total Adherents: % of Total Pop.	Total Adherents: % of Total Adh.
449 Un Methodist	2	233	70	283 *	23.7	38.4
KINGSBURY	**31**	**3,630**	**1,328**	**5,800 ***	**99.7**	**100.0**
053 Assemb of God	1	10	7	23	.4	.4
081 Catholic	4	NR	NR	1,148	19.7	19.8
089 Chr & Miss Al	1	59	NR	120	2.1	2.1
143 CG in Cr(Menn)	1	139	NR	169 *	2.9	2.9
193 Episcopal	1	NR	11	19	.3	.3
201 Evan Cov Ch	1	10	0	12 *	.2	.2
207 E.L.C.A.	8	2,335	738	2,952	50.8	50.9
220 Free Lutheran	1	105	105	135	2.3	2.3
257 Hutterian Br	2	132	NR	200	3.4	3.4
306 NT IndBapt&Rltd	1	55	NR	67 *	1.2	1.2
335 Orth Pres Ch	1	42	26	50	.9	.9
355 Presb Ch (USA)	1	46	30	56 *	1.0	1.0
443 Un C of Christ	3	258	115	314 *	5.4	5.4
449 Un Methodist	5	439	296	535 *	9.2	9.2
LAKE	**23**	**4,049**	**1,912**	**7,574 ***	**67.2**	**100.0**
019 Amer Bapt USA	1	101	35	122 *	1.1	1.6
053 Assemb of God	1	39	52	52	.5	.7
056 Baha'i	0	1	NR	1	-	-
081 Catholic	2	NR	NR	2,209	19.6	29.2
151 L-D Saints	1	NR	NR	76	.7	1.0
165 Ch of Nazarene	1	69	66	124	1.1	1.6
193 Episcopal	1	NR	10	18	.2	.2
207 E.L.C.A.	4	2,083	789	2,810	24.9	37.1
257 Hutterian Br	2	132	NR	200	1.8	2.6
283 Luth—MO Synod	3	550	284	668	5.9	8.8
313 N Am Bapt Conf	1	277	255	334 *	3.0	4.4
355 Presb Ch (USA)	2	173	100	209 *	1.9	2.8
413 S.D.A.	1	35	NR	42	.4	.6
443 Un C of Christ	1	74	35	89 *	.8	1.2
449 Un Methodist	2	515	286	620 *	5.5	8.2
LAWRENCE	**33**	**4,351**	**3,017**	**11,363 ***	**52.1**	**100.0**
019 Amer Bapt USA	1	68	60	81 *	.4	.7
053 Assemb of God	2	155	222	389	1.8	3.4
056 Baha'i	0	12	NR	12	.1	.1
081 Catholic	3	NR	NR	4,288	19.7	37.7
151 L-D Saints	1	NR	NR	322	1.5	2.8
165 Ch of Nazarene	1	63	58	90	.4	.8
167 Chs of Christ	2	65	108	83	.4	.7
193 Episcopal	3	NR	205	399	1.8	3.5
203 Evan Free Ch	1	23	50	50	.2	.4
207 E.L.C.A.	3	1,636	594	2,210	10.1	19.4
283 Luth—MO Synod	2	428	233	538	2.5	4.7
313 N Am Bapt Conf	1	179	252	214 *	1.0	1.9
355 Presb Ch (USA)	2	89	124	124 *	.6	1.1
356 Presb Ch Amer	1	28	40	40	.2	.4
403 Salvation Army	1	48	62	57	.3	.5
413 S.D.A.	1	149	NR	177	.8	1.6
419 So Bapt Conv	2	133	84	159 *	.7	1.4
443 Un C of Christ	2	303	133	362 *	1.7	3.2
449 Un Methodist	2	821	448	982 *	4.5	8.6
467 Wesleyan	1	59	300	650	3.0	5.7
469 WELS	1	92	44	136	.6	1.2
LINCOLN	**30**	**6,282**	**3,180**	**10,584 ***	**43.9**	**100.0**
053 Assemb of God	1	31	35	43	.2	.4
081 Catholic	4	NR	NR	1,765	7.3	16.7
207 E.L.C.A.	13	4,081	1,695	5,714	23.7	54.0
220 Free Lutheran	1	77	62	102	.4	1.0
283 Luth—MO Synod	1	386	259	553	2.3	5.2
306 NT IndBapt&Rltd	1	55	NR	71 *	.3	.7
355 Presb Ch (USA)	1	72	50	93 *	.4	.9
356 Presb Ch Amer	2	406	300	579	2.4	5.5
371 Ref Ch in Am	3	505	438	798	3.3	7.5
443 Un C of Christ	1	48	27	62 *	.3	.6
449 Un Methodist	2	621	314	804 *	3.3	7.6

Religious Group	Number of Churches, Synagogues, Mosques, or Temples	Number of Communicant, Confirmed, or Full Members	Number of Attendees	Total Adherents: Number of Adherents	Total Adherents: % of Total Pop.	Total Adherents: % of Total Adh.
LYMAN	**15**	**804**	**441**	**2,404 ***	**61.7**	**100.0**
053 Assemb of God	2	26	31	78	2.0	3.2
056 Baha'i	0	11	NR	11	.3	.5
081 Catholic	4	NR	NR	1,170	30.0	48.7
193 Episcopal	1	NR	47	165	4.2	6.9
207 E.L.C.A.	3	288	162	380	9.8	15.8
283 Luth—MO Synod	2	196	58	225	5.8	9.4
419 So Bapt Conv	0	27	30	36 *	.9	1.5
449 Un Methodist	3	256	113	339 *	8.7	14.1
MCCOOK	**25**	**2,340**	**1,357**	**5,123 ***	**87.8**	**100.0**
056 Baha'i	0	1	NR	1	-	-
057 Bapt Gen Conf	2	251	203	320 *	5.5	6.2
081 Catholic	3	NR	NR	2,101	36.0	41.0
097 Chr Chs&Chs Cr	1	50	NR	64 *	1.1	1.2
165 Ch of Nazarene	1	32	0	32	.5	.6
201 Evan Cov Ch	1	35	20	45 *	.8	.9
207 E.L.C.A.	4	696	328	898	15.4	17.5
257 Hutterian Br	1	66	NR	100	1.7	2.0
283 Luth—MO Synod	3	491	222	636	10.9	12.4
288 Mennonite USA	2	177	144	225 *	3.9	4.4
335 Orth Pres Ch	1	36	46	59	1.0	1.2
355 Presb Ch (USA)	3	219	155	278 *	4.8	5.4
449 Un Methodist	3	286	239	364 *	6.2	7.1
MCPHERSON	**15**	**1,849**	**727**	**2,723 ***	**93.8**	**100.0**
081 Catholic	2	NR	NR	489	16.8	18.0
207 E.L.C.A.	3	866	402	1,034	35.6	38.0
257 Hutterian Br	1	66	NR	100	3.4	3.7
283 Luth—MO Synod	1	92	61	133	4.6	4.9
313 N Am Bapt Conf	2	152	70	183 *	6.3	6.7
373 Ref Ch in U.S.	2	262	NR	291	10.0	10.7
413 S.D.A.	1	12	NR	14	.5	.5
443 Un C of Christ	1	144	63	173 *	6.0	6.4
449 Un Methodist	2	255	131	306 *	10.5	11.2
MARSHALL	**22**	**2,444**	**1,096**	**4,283 ***	**93.6**	**100.0**
053 Assemb of God	1	10	14	32	.7	.7
056 Baha'i	0	3	NR	3	.1	.1
081 Catholic	4	NR	NR	995	21.7	23.2
193 Episcopal	1	NR	10	35	.8	.8
203 Evan Free Ch	1	61	90	90	2.0	2.1
207 E.L.C.A.	6	1,458	602	1,948	42.6	45.5
220 Free Lutheran	1	25	0	39	.9	.9
257 Hutterian Br	1	66	NR	100	2.2	2.3
283 Luth—MO Synod	1	222	114	268	5.9	6.3
355 Presb Ch (USA)	4	384	154	478 *	10.4	11.2
371 Ref Ch in Am	1	38	42	75	1.6	1.8
449 Un Methodist	1	177	70	220 *	4.8	5.1
MEADE	**40**	**3,463**	**1,805**	**9,617 ***	**39.7**	**100.0**
019 Amer Bapt USA	2	61	5	78 *	.3	.8
053 Assemb of God	1	34	40	44	.2	.5
056 Baha'i	0	14	NR	14	.1	.1
081 Catholic	7	NR	NR	4,605	19.0	47.9
097 Chr Chs&Chs Cr	2	132	NR	169 *	.7	1.8
127 Ch God (Cleve)	1	27	70	70 *	.3	.7
145 Ch God Prophcy	1	24	NR	30 *	.1	.3
151 L-D Saints	3	NR	NR	337	1.4	3.5
167 Chs of Christ	2	135	145	183	.8	1.9
176 Congr Ad Afl	1	26	NR	33 *	.1	.3
193 Episcopal	1	NR	35	107	.4	1.1
207 E.L.C.A.	2	900	338	1,161	4.8	12.1
220 Free Lutheran	1	79	56	100	.4	1.0
283 Luth—MO Synod	1	231	137	328	1.4	3.4
355 Presb Ch (USA)	2	303	162	387 *	1.6	4.0
356 Presb Ch Amer	1	62	55	76	.3	.8
419 So Bapt Conv	3	299	100	382 *	1.6	4.0
449 Un Methodist	3	615	249	786 *	3.2	8.2
467 Wesleyan	3	69	114	160	.7	1.7
469 WELS	2	152	59	217	.9	2.3
498 Indep.Charis.	1	300	240	350	1.4	3.6

NR–Not Reported *Total adherents estimated from known number of communicant, confirmed, full members. - Represents a percentage less than 0.1. Percentages may not total 100 due to rounding.

Table 4: Religious Congregations by County and Group: 2000

Religious Group	Number of Churches, Synagogues, Mosques, or Temples	Number of Communicant, Confirmed, or Full Members	Number of Attendees	Total Adherents		
				Number of Adherents	% of Total Pop.	% of Total Adh.
MELLETTE	**15**	**263**	**259**	**774 ***	**37.2**	**100.0**
019 Amer Bapt USA	1	20	14	28 *	1.3	3.6
053 Assemb of God	1	7	7	8	.4	1.0
056 Baha'i	0	17	NR	17	.8	2.2
081 Catholic	4	NR	NR	180	8.6	23.3
151 L-D Saints	1	NR	NR	44	2.1	5.7
165 Ch of Nazarene	1	31	42	43	2.1	5.6
193 Episcopal	4	NR	84	206	9.9	26.6
283 Luth—MO Synod	1	67	38	79	3.8	10.2
443 Un C of Christ	1	13	6	18 *	.9	2.3
449 Un Methodist	1	108	68	151 *	7.2	19.5
MINER	**15**	**1,165**	**574**	**2,694 ***	**93.4**	**100.0**
053 Assemb of God	1	38	55	100	3.5	3.7
056 Baha'i	0	1	NR	1	-	-
081 Catholic	2	NR	NR	1,189	41.2	44.1
165 Ch of Nazarene	1	10	10	16	.6	.6
207 E.L.C.A.	3	421	171	541	18.8	20.1
257 Hutterian Br	1	66	NR	100	3.5	3.7
283 Luth—MO Synod	1	301	121	349	12.1	13.0
355 Presb Ch (USA)	2	88	54	107 *	3.7	4.0
443 Un C of Christ	2	67	36	81 *	2.8	3.0
449 Un Methodist	2	173	127	210 *	7.3	7.8
MINNEHAHA	**161**	**45,425**	**27,260**	**98,995 ***	**66.8**	**100.0**
019 Amer Bapt USA	6	1,625	1,076	2,039 *	1.4	2.1
053 Assemb of God	3	803	948	1,603	1.1	1.6
056 Baha'i	1	70	NR	70	-	.1
057 Bapt Gen Conf	2	1,106	1,203	1,388 *	.9	1.4
081 Catholic	14	NR	NR	33,277	22.4	33.6
084 Calvary Chapel	1	NR	NR	NR	-	-
093 Chr Ch (Disc)	1	435	140	546 *	.4	.6
097 Chr Chs&Chs Cr	1	144	NR	181 *	.1	.2
105 Christian Ref	4	1,504	1,146	1,887 *	1.3	1.9
123 Ch God (Ander)	1	NR	128	128	.1	.1
127 Ch God (Cleve)	1	60	57	75 *	.1	.1
145 Ch God Prophcy	1	24	NR	30 *	-	-
151 L-D Saints	4	NR	NR	923	.6	.9
165 Ch of Nazarene	2	24	35	66	-	.1
167 Chs of Christ	3	277	280	333	.2	.3
173 Comm of Christ	1	39	NR	39	-	-
193 Episcopal	3	NR	341	1,037	.7	1.0
201 Evan Cov Ch	5	375	442	560 *	.4	.6
203 Evan Free Ch	1	109	295	295	.2	.3
207 E.L.C.A.	34	22,645	10,309	31,467	21.2	31.8
220 Free Lutheran	1	362	550	550	.4	.6
221 Free Methodist	1	21	24	24	-	-
237 Menn Br US Conf	1	101	NR	127 *	.1	.1
246 Greek Orthodox	1	NR	NR	222	.1	.2
251 Holy Orth in NA	1	NR	NR	10	-	-
264 Int Chs of Crst	1	14	26	27	-	-
283 Luth—MO Synod	9	2,767	1,712	3,872	2.6	3.9
288 Mennonite USA	2	85	90	106 *	.1	.1
290 Metro Comm Ch	1	37	27	46 *	-	-
291 Missionary Ch	1	5	13	13	-	-
306 NT IndBapt&Rltd	1	55	NR	69 *	-	.1
307 Neth Ref Congr	1	30	NR	51	-	.1
313 N Am Bapt Conf	5	885	1,215	1,110 *	.7	1.1
355 Presb Ch (USA)	6	1,877	1,021	2,355 *	1.6	2.4
371 Ref Ch in Am	6	1,534	1,413	2,713	1.8	2.7
373 Ref Ch in U.S.	1	110	NR	166	.1	.2
401 Rus Orth Abroad	1	NR	NR	NR	-	-
403 Salvation Army	1	152	66	404	.3	.4
413 S.D.A.	1	237	NR	282	.2	.3
418 Southw Bapt Fel	1	NR	NR	NR	-	-
419 So Bapt Conv	4	458	402	575 *	.4	.6
435 Unitarian-Univ	1	49	NR	61 *	-	.1
443 Un C of Christ	5	1,302	526	1,634 *	1.1	1.7
449 Un Methodist	12	4,822	2,311	6,048 *	4.1	6.1
463 Vineyard	1	130	120	163 *	.1	.2
467 Wesleyan	2	309	661	1,084	.7	1.1
469 WELS	2	583	333	794	.5	.8
496 Jewish Est	1	NR	NR	195	.1	.2
499 Indep.Non-Char	1	260	350	350	.2	.4
MOODY	**16**	**2,150**	**814**	**4,007 ***	**60.8**	**100.0**
019 Amer Bapt USA	1	136	84	173 *	2.6	4.3
056 Baha'i	0	4	NR	4	.1	.1
081 Catholic	2	NR	NR	1,342	20.3	33.5
143 CG in Cr(Menn)	1	17	NR	22 *	.3	.5
193 Episcopal	1	NR	21	38	.6	.9
207 E.L.C.A.	4	1,278	414	1,518	23.0	37.9
257 Hutterian Br	1	66	NR	100	1.5	2.5
283 Luth—MO Synod	1	108	41	124	1.9	3.1
355 Presb Ch (USA)	2	225	98	285 *	4.3	7.1
449 Un Methodist	3	316	156	401 *	6.1	10.0
PENNINGTON	**98**	**19,371**	**10,655**	**55,581 ***	**62.8**	**100.0**
017 Amer Bapt Assn	1	20	NR	25 *	-	-
019 Amer Bapt USA	2	315	207	395 *	.4	.7
053 Assemb of God	3	623	844	1,671	1.9	3.0
056 Baha'i	1	85	NR	85	.1	.2
081 Catholic	9	NR	NR	24,694	27.9	44.4
084 Calvary Chapel	1	NR	NR	NR	-	-
089 Chr & Miss Al	1	41	NR	133	.2	.2
097 Chr Chs&Chs Cr	1	435	NR	546 *	.6	1.0
105 Christian Ref	1	147	92	185 *	.2	.3
123 Ch God (Ander)	2	NR	67	67	.1	.1
127 Ch God (Cleve)	1	63	43	79 *	.1	.1
145 Ch God Prophcy	1	24	NR	30 *	-	.1
151 L-D Saints	3	NR	NR	1,341	1.5	2.4
165 Ch of Nazarene	1	37	25	45	.1	.1
167 Chs of Christ	3	104	160	196	.2	.4
193 Episcopal	3	NR	341	1,137	1.3	2.0
203 Evan Free Ch	3	408	875	875	1.0	1.6
207 E.L.C.A.	7	5,303	2,186	7,479	8.4	13.5
221 Free Methodist	1	38	49	49	.1	.1
223 Free Will Bapt	1	0	NR	0 *	-	-
237 Menn Br US Conf	1	143	NR	180 *	.2	.3
263 Int Foursq Gos	1	26	188	188 *	.2	.3
283 Luth—MO Synod	7	2,602	1,237	3,532	4.0	6.4
290 Metro Comm Ch	1	22	12	28 *	-	.1
291 Missionary Ch	1	8	8	8	-	-
313 N Am Bapt Conf	1	353	400	443 *	.5	.8
355 Presb Ch (USA)	3	1,398	653	1,755 *	2.0	3.2
356 Presb Ch Amer	1	43	58	67	.1	.1
370 Ref Baptist Chs	1	NR	NR	NR	-	-
373 Ref Ch in U.S.	1	36	NR	65	.1	.1
388 Reg Bapt Gen As	1	20	38	38 *	-	.1
403 Salvation Army	1	96	45	248	.3	.4
413 S.D.A.	2	568	NR	676	.8	1.2
419 So Bapt Conv	8	2,338	531	2,935 *	3.3	5.3
435 Unitarian-Univ	1	30	NR	38 *	-	.1
443 Un C of Christ	5	937	302	1,176 *	1.3	2.1
449 Un Methodist	7	2,145	1,271	2,692 *	3.0	4.8
467 Wesleyan	6	414	622	1,621	1.8	2.9
469 WELS	2	549	401	779	.9	1.4
496 Jewish Est	1	NR	NR	80	.1	.1
PERKINS	**21**	**1,449**	**711**	**2,681 ***	**79.7**	**100.0**
056 Baha'i	0	1	NR	1	-	-
081 Catholic	3	NR	NR	941	28.0	35.1
105 Christian Ref	1	63	55	76 *	2.3	2.8
127 Ch God (Cleve)	1	134	80	162 *	4.8	6.0
167 Chs of Christ	1	18	16	28	.8	1.0
193 Episcopal	1	NR	8	19	.6	.7
207 E.L.C.A.	6	747	263	864	25.7	32.2
355 Presb Ch (USA)	2	256	130	310 *	9.2	11.6
356 Presb Ch Amer	1	40	45	45	1.3	1.7
413 S.D.A.	2	39	NR	47	1.4	1.8
419 So Bapt Conv	1	18	23	22 *	.7	.8
467 Wesleyan	1	48	40	62	1.8	2.3
469 WELS	1	85	51	104	3.1	3.9

NR–Not Reported *Total adherents estimated from known number of communicant, confirmed, full members. - Represents a percentage less than 0.1. Percentages may not total 100 due to rounding.

Table 4: Religious Congregations by County and Group: 2000

Religious Group	Number of Churches, Synagogues, Mosques, or Temples	Number of Communicant, Confirmed, or Full Members	Number of Attendees	Total Adherents		
				Number of Adherents	% of Total Pop.	% of Total Adh.
POTTER	**13**	**890**	**354**	**3,119 ***	**115.8**	**100.0**
081 Catholic	2	NR	NR	1,976	73.4	63.4
127 Ch God (Cleve)	1	17	9	20 *	.7	.6
151 L-D Saints	1	NR	NR	27	1.0	.9
193 Episcopal	1	NR	16	38	1.4	1.2
237 Menn Br US Conf	1	93	NR	111 *	4.1	3.6
283 Luth—MO Synod	2	368	134	442	16.4	14.2
413 S.D.A.	1	14	NR	17	.6	.5
419 So Bapt Conv	1	7	5	8 *	.3	.3
449 Un Methodist	2	373	165	445 *	16.5	14.3
467 Wesleyan	1	18	25	35	1.3	1.1
ROBERTS	**37**	**3,578**	**1,711**	**7,295 ***	**72.8**	**100.0**
053 Assemb of God	3	121	168	297	3.0	4.1
056 Baha'i	0	4	NR	4	-	.1
081 Catholic	5	NR	NR	2,053	20.5	28.1
089 Chr & Miss Al	3	62	NR	184	1.8	2.5
193 Episcopal	2	NR	72	376	3.8	5.2
207 E.L.C.A.	10	1,994	846	2,633	26.3	36.1
220 Free Lutheran	1	120	45	143	1.4	2.0
257 Hutterian Br	1	66	NR	100	1.0	1.4
283 Luth—MO Synod	4	597	242	711	7.1	9.7
355 Presb Ch (USA)	5	405	236	521 *	5.2	7.1
419 So Bapt Conv	2	159	76	205 *	2.0	2.8
469 WELS	1	50	26	68	.7	.9
SANBORN	**12**	**834**	**345**	**1,958 ***	**73.2**	**100.0**
056 Baha'i	0	1	NR	1	-	.1
081 Catholic	2	NR	NR	933	34.9	47.7
207 E.L.C.A.	4	421	127	503	18.8	25.7
257 Hutterian Br	1	66	NR	100	3.7	5.1
283 Luth—MO Synod	1	34	12	39	1.5	2.0
419 So Bapt Conv	1	10	23	12 *	.4	.6
443 Un C of Christ	1	210	130	257 *	9.6	13.1
449 Un Methodist	2	92	53	113 *	4.2	5.8
SHANNON	**40**	**578**	**453**	**5,787 ***	**46.4**	**100.0**
056 Baha'i	2	191	NR	191	1.5	3.3
081 Catholic	13	NR	NR	2,773	22.2	47.9
123 Ch God (Ander)	1	NR	12	12	.1	.2
151 L-D Saints	1	NR	NR	606	4.9	10.5
165 Ch of Nazarene	1	7	20	25	.2	.4
193 Episcopal	14	NR	249	1,636	13.1	28.3
237 Menn Br US Conf	1	25	NR	38 *	.3	.7
355 Presb Ch (USA)	3	160	87	245 *	2.0	4.2
413 S.D.A.	1	41	NR	49	.4	.8
419 So Bapt Conv	1	67	49	103 *	.8	1.8
467 Wesleyan	1	0	0	0	-	-
469 WELS	1	87	36	109	.9	1.9
SPINK	**31**	**2,864**	**1,284**	**5,904 ***	**79.2**	**100.0**
053 Assemb of God	1	18	24	29	.4	.5
056 Baha'i	0	3	NR	3	-	.1
081 Catholic	6	NR	NR	2,282	30.6	38.7
207 E.L.C.A.	2	496	163	605	8.1	10.2
257 Hutterian Br	3	198	NR	300	4.0	5.1
283 Luth—MO Synod	3	512	251	642	8.6	10.9
288 Mennonite USA	1	128	80	157 *	2.1	2.7
355 Presb Ch (USA)	1	15	10	18 *	.2	.3
388 Reg Bapt Gen As	1	28	28	34 *	.5	.6
413 S.D.A.	1	48	NR	57	.8	1.0
419 So Bapt Conv	1	20	25	25 *	.3	.4
443 Un C of Christ	3	567	243	696 *	9.3	11.8
449 Un Methodist	7	755	393	927 *	12.4	15.7
467 Wesleyan	1	76	67	129	1.7	2.2
STANLEY	**5**	**122**	**82**	**1,517 ***	**54.7**	**100.0**
056 Baha'i	0	3	NR	3	.1	.2
081 Catholic	1	NR	NR	1,054	38.0	69.5
151 L-D Saints	1	NR	NR	230	8.3	15.2
193 Episcopal	1	NR	26	56	2.0	3.7
207 E.L.C.A.	1	27	16	59	2.1	3.9
443 Un C of Christ	1	92	40	115 *	4.1	7.6
SULLY	**7**	**509**	**209**	**954 ***	**61.3**	**100.0**
056 Baha'i	0	2	NR	2	.1	.2
081 Catholic	1	NR	NR	340	21.9	35.6
237 Menn Br US Conf	1	44	NR	54 *	3.5	5.7
283 Luth—MO Synod	2	159	61	184	11.8	19.3
355 Presb Ch (USA)	1	140	83	172 *	11.1	18.0
449 Un Methodist	2	164	65	202 *	13.0	21.2
TODD	**19**	**332**	**196**	**5,358 ***	**59.2**	**100.0**
053 Assemb of God	1	29	18	50	.6	.9
056 Baha'i	1	197	NR	197	2.2	3.7
081 Catholic	8	NR	NR	3,879	42.9	72.4
151 L-D Saints	1	NR	NR	255	2.8	4.8
193 Episcopal	5	NR	99	658	7.3	12.3
449 Un Methodist	1	37	33	57 *	.6	1.1
467 Wesleyan	1	9	17	190	2.1	3.5
469 WELS	1	60	29	72	.8	1.3
TRIPP	**24**	**1,905**	**1,026**	**4,480 ***	**69.7**	**100.0**
019 Amer Bapt USA	2	113	100	142 *	2.2	3.2
053 Assemb of God	1	39	43	86	1.3	1.9
056 Baha'i	0	3	NR	3	-	.1
081 Catholic	3	NR	NR	1,792	27.9	40.0
093 Chr Ch (Disc)	1	129	72	162 *	2.5	3.6
165 Ch of Nazarene	1	55	39	70	1.1	1.6
193 Episcopal	1	NR	36	180	2.8	4.0
203 Evan Free Ch	1	29	70	70	1.1	1.6
283 Luth—MO Synod	3	307	103	418	6.5	9.3
335 Orth Pres Ch	2	86	94	127	2.0	2.8
339 Pent Ch of God	1	21	NR	50	.8	1.1
355 Presb Ch (USA)	1	35	20	44 *	.7	1.0
443 Un C of Christ	1	22	20	28 *	.4	.6
449 Un Methodist	2	512	205	644 *	10.0	14.4
469 WELS	4	554	224	664	10.3	14.8
TURNER	**43**	**4,906**	**2,964**	**7,955 ***	**89.9**	**100.0**
019 Amer Bapt USA	3	253	157	313 *	3.5	3.9
081 Catholic	4	NR	NR	1,342	15.2	16.9
105 Christian Ref	1	63	40	78 *	.9	1.0
123 Ch God (Ander)	1	NR	153	153	1.7	1.9
151 L-D Saints	1	NR	NR	131	1.5	1.6
165 Ch of Nazarene	1	16	25	48	.5	.6
207 E.L.C.A.	6	1,398	634	1,782	20.1	22.4
211 Fel Evg Bib Ch	1	70	50	50	.6	.6
220 Free Lutheran	1	84	60	102	1.2	1.3
283 Luth—MO Synod	4	399	193	530	6.0	6.7
288 Mennonite USA	2	809	555	1,000 *	11.3	12.6
297 Mennonite;Other	2	140	NR	173 *	2.0	2.2
313 N Am Bapt Conf	1	178	60	220 *	2.5	2.8
355 Presb Ch (USA)	4	353	281	439 *	5.0	5.5
356 Presb Ch Amer	1	190	105	190	2.1	2.4
371 Ref Ch in Am	4	487	415	831	9.4	10.4
413 S.D.A.	1	58	NR	69	.8	.9
443 Un C of Christ	1	119	52	147 *	1.7	1.8
449 Un Methodist	4	289	184	357 *	4.0	4.5
UNION	**28**	**4,116**	**2,329**	**7,257 ***	**57.7**	**100.0**
053 Assemb of God	1	29	45	84	.7	1.2
056 Baha'i	0	2	NR	2	-	-
057 Bapt Gen Conf	3	564	394	711 *	5.7	9.8
081 Catholic	3	NR	NR	1,952	15.5	26.9
201 Evan Cov Ch	1	60	55	76 *	.6	1.0
203 Evan Free Ch	1	112	210	210	1.7	2.9
207 E.L.C.A.	7	2,157	862	2,721	21.6	37.5
220 Free Lutheran	1	50	45	67	.5	.9
283 Luth—MO Synod	2	212	126	262	2.1	3.6
419 So Bapt Conv	2	193	79	243 *	1.9	3.3
443 Un C of Christ	4	372	222	469 *	3.7	6.5
449 Un Methodist	3	365	291	460 *	3.7	6.3

NR–Not Reported *Total adherents estimated from known number of communicant, confirmed, full members. - Represents a percentage less than 0.1. Percentages may not total 100 due to rounding.

Table 4: Religious Congregations by County and Group: 2000

Religious Group	Number of Churches, Synagogues, Mosques, or Temples	Number of Communicant, Confirmed, or Full Members	Number of Attendees	Total Adherents: Number of Adherents	Total Adherents: % of Total Pop.	Total Adherents: % of Total Adh.
WALWORTH	**20**	**2,505**	**996**	**4,890 ***	**81.9**	**100.0**
019 Amer Bapt USA	1	86	48	105 *	1.8	2.1
053 Assemb of God	1	12	18	52	.9	1.1
056 Baha'i	0	10	NR	10	.2	.2
081 Catholic	2	NR	NR	1,602	26.8	32.8
127 Ch God (Cleve)	1	52	132	132 *	2.2	2.7
193 Episcopal	1	NR	19	52	.9	1.1
207 E.L.C.A.	4	1,145	391	1,478	24.7	30.2
339 Pent Ch of God	1	10	NR	15	.3	.3
413 S.D.A.	1	20	NR	24	.4	.5
419 So Bapt Conv	1	191	60	233 *	3.9	4.8
443 Un C of Christ	2	401	200	489 *	8.2	10.0
449 Un Methodist	2	235	105	286 *	4.8	5.8
469 WELS	3	343	23	412	6.9	8.4
YANKTON	**29**	**5,516**	**2,826**	**15,000 ***	**69.3**	**100.0**
019 Amer Bapt USA	1	34	18	42 *	.2	.3
053 Assemb of God	1	133	169	280	1.3	1.9
056 Baha'i	0	4	NR	4	-	-
057 Bapt Gen Conf	1	241	344	344 *	1.6	2.3
081 Catholic	5	NR	NR	7,354	34.0	49.0
097 Chr Chs&Chs Cr	1	70	NR	87 *	.4	.6
167 Chs of Christ	1	26	38	44	.2	.3
193 Episcopal	1	NR	78	173	.8	1.2
207 E.L.C.A.	7	2,578	949	3,459	16.0	23.1
220 Free Lutheran	1	72	40	75	.3	.5
257 Hutterian Br	1	66	NR	100	.5	.7
283 Luth—MO Synod	2	934	469	1,249	5.8	8.3
371 Ref Ch in Am	1	116	110	230	1.1	1.5
413 S.D.A.	1	26	NR	31	.1	.2
419 So Bapt Conv	1	116	20	144 *	.7	1.0
443 Un C of Christ	1	469	208	583 *	2.7	3.9
449 Un Methodist	2	573	312	713 *	3.3	4.8
469 WELS	1	58	71	88	.4	.6
ZIEBACH	**16**	**287**	**158**	**980 ***	**38.9**	**100.0**
056 Baha'i	0	27	NR	27	1.1	2.8
081 Catholic	5	NR	NR	347	13.8	35.4
193 Episcopal	4	NR	67	237	9.4	24.2
297 Mennonite;Other	1	8	NR	12 *	.5	1.2
419 So Bapt Conv	1	23	20	33 *	1.3	3.4
443 Un C of Christ	4	208	61	302 *	12.0	30.8
469 WELS	1	21	10	22	.9	2.2
TENNESSEE						
The State.....	9,634	2,099,948	919,928	2,905,619 *	51.1	100.0
ANDERSON	**118**	**38,463**	**12,295**	**52,564 ***	**73.7**	**100.0**
053 Assemb of God	4	443	345	653	.9	1.2
056 Baha'i	0	6	NR	6	-	-
081 Catholic	3	NR	NR	3,452	4.8	6.6
089 Chr & Miss Al	1	55	NR	94	.1	.2
093 Chr Ch (Disc)	1	306	85	372 *	.5	.7
097 Chr Chs&Chs Cr	2	399	NR	485 *	.7	.9
127 Ch God (Cleve)	3	1,273	862	1,581 *	2.2	3.0
145 Ch God Prophcy	1	51	NR	62 *	.1	.1
151 L-D Saints	2	NR	NR	645	.9	1.2
165 Ch of Nazarene	1	266	149	308	.4	.6
167 Chs of Christ	8	980	886	1,240	1.7	2.4
185 Cumber Presb	1	169	NR	328	.5	.6
193 Episcopal	2	NR	324	1,030	1.4	2.0
203 Evan Free Ch	1	47	100	100	.1	.2
207 E.L.C.A.	1	514	213	618	.9	1.2
223 Free Will Bapt	1	97	NR	118 *	.2	.2
262 Int Cou Comm Ch	1	215	NR	261 *	.4	.5
283 Luth—MO Synod	1	383	189	477	.7	.9
355 Presb Ch (USA)	1	275	157	334 *	.5	.6
356 Presb Ch Amer	1	238	225	312	.4	.6
360 Prim Bapt Chrch	1	NR	NR	NR	-	-
403 Salvation Army	1	50	26	58	.1	.1
413 S.D.A.	1	46	NR	55	.1	.1
419 So Bapt Conv	59	27,751	6,702	33,739 *	47.3	64.2
435 Unitarian-Univ	1	183	NR	222 *	.3	.4
449 Un Methodist	16	4,621	1,913	5,618 *	7.9	10.7
467 Wesleyan	2	95	119	146	.2	.3
496 Jewish Est	1	NR	NR	250	.4	.5
BEDFORD	**98**	**13,492**	**6,560**	**17,642 ***	**46.9**	**100.0**
053 Assemb of God	2	103	134	159	.4	.9
056 Baha'i	0	11	NR	11	-	.1
081 Catholic	1	NR	NR	435	1.2	2.5
093 Chr Ch (Disc)	1	461	188	577 *	1.5	3.3
123 Ch God (Ander)	1	NR	40	40	.1	.2
127 Ch God (Cleve)	3	163	127	204 *	.5	1.2
145 Ch God Prophcy	2	102	NR	128 *	.3	.7
151 L-D Saints	1	NR	NR	174	.5	1.0
165 Ch of Nazarene	4	420	313	566	1.5	3.2
167 Chs of Christ	23	1,950	1,920	2,442	6.5	13.8
185 Cumber Presb	3	60	NR	88	.2	.5
189 Duck Rivr Bapt	5	349	NR	437 *	1.2	2.5
193 Episcopal	1	NR	44	105	.3	.6
207 E.L.C.A.	2	172	70	207	.6	1.2
304 NatPrimBapt USA	1	52	NR	65 *	.2	.4
355 Presb Ch (USA)	2	428	167	536 *	1.4	3.0
360 Prim Bapt Chrch	1	NR	NR	NR	-	-
419 So Bapt Conv	20	6,584	2,286	8,241 *	21.9	46.7
449 Un Methodist	24	2,337	1,031	2,927 *	7.8	16.6
499 Indep.Non-Char	1	300	240	300	.8	1.7
BENTON	**51**	**7,075**	**3,246**	**9,017 ***	**54.5**	**100.0**
053 Assemb of God	1	217	106	200	1.2	2.2
081 Catholic	1	NR	NR	330	2.0	3.7
145 Ch God Prophcy	2	102	NR	122 *	.7	1.4
165 Ch of Nazarene	1	90	71	112	.7	1.2
167 Chs of Christ	8	650	532	819	5.0	9.1
185 Cumber Presb	1	55	NR	117	.7	1.3
320 "Old" MB Ascs	5	707	NR	849 *	5.1	9.4
355 Presb Ch (USA)	1	6	6	7 *	-	.1
419 So Bapt Conv	12	3,068	1,012	3,684 *	22.3	40.9
449 Un Methodist	16	1,480	744	1,777 *	10.7	19.7
499 Indep.Non-Char	3	700	775	1,000	6.0	11.1
BLEDSOE	**37**	**3,273**	**1,782**	**4,043 ***	**32.7**	**100.0**
056 Baha'i	0	3	NR	3	-	.1
127 Ch God (Cleve)	7	677	581	850 *	6.9	21.0
145 Ch God Prophcy	2	102	NR	124 *	1.0	3.1
167 Chs of Christ	12	569	614	734	5.9	18.2
189 Duck Rivr Bapt	4	151	NR	183 *	1.5	4.5
258 IndFreeWillBapt	2	218	NR	265 *	2.1	6.6
413 S.D.A.	1	68	NR	81	.7	2.0
419 So Bapt Conv	5	1,086	411	1,319 *	10.7	32.6
449 Un Methodist	4	399	176	484 *	3.9	12.0
BLOUNT	**158**	**49,848**	**19,737**	**63,433 ***	**59.9**	**100.0**
053 Assemb of God	1	158	156	278	.3	.4
056 Baha'i	0	7	NR	7	-	-
081 Catholic	2	NR	NR	1,623	1.5	2.6
097 Chr Chs&Chs Cr	6	817	NR	991 *	.9	1.6
123 Ch God (Ander)	1	NR	125	125	.1	.2
127 Ch God (Cleve)	9	1,950	1,263	2,366 *	2.2	3.7
151 L-D Saints	1	NR	NR	407	.4	.6
165 Ch of Nazarene	2	207	93	235	.2	.4
167 Chs of Christ	5	566	718	763	.7	1.2
185 Cumber Presb	2	224	NR	383	.4	.6
186 Coptic Orth Ch	2	NR	NR	NR	-	-
193 Episcopal	1	NR	188	526	.5	.8
207 E.L.C.A.	1	366	156	508	.5	.8
226 Friends-USA	2	126	NR	153 *	.1	.2
283 Luth—MO Synod	1	21	19	24	-	-
304 NatPrimBapt USA	1	25	NR	30 *	-	-
335 Orth Pres Ch	1	76	90	96	.1	.2
355 Presb Ch (USA)	7	1,528	764	1,856 *	1.8	2.9

NR–Not Reported   *Total adherents estimated from known number of communicant, confirmed, full members.   - Represents a percentage less than 0.1.   Percentages may not total 100 due to rounding.

Table 4: Religious Congregations by County and Group: 2000

Religious Group	Number of Churches, Synagogues, Mosques, or Temples	Number of Communicant, Confirmed, or Full Members	Number of Attendees	Total Adherents		
				Number of Adherents	% of Total Pop.	% of Total Adh.
356 Presb Ch Amer	2	136	138	156	.1	.2
360 Prim Bapt Chrch	2	NR	NR	NR	-	-
413 S.D.A.	1	146	NR	174	.2	.3
419 So Bapt Conv	85	35,767	12,416	43,384 *	41.0	68.4
449 Un Methodist	22	7,378	3,311	8,948 *	8.5	14.1
498 Indep.Charis.	1	350	300	400	.4	.6
BRADLEY	**145**	**38,270**	**16,776**	**50,156 ***	**57.0**	**100.0**
017 Amer Bapt Assn	1	50	NR	61 *	.1	.1
053 Assemb of God	2	104	63	110	.1	.2
056 Baha'i	0	6	NR	6	-	-
059 Bapt Miss Assn	2	119	112	146 *	.2	.3
081 Catholic	1	NR	NR	1,710	1.9	3.4
093 Chr Ch (Disc)	1	140	65	172 *	.2	.3
097 Chr Chs&Chs Cr	2	212	NR	260 *	.3	.5
127 Ch God (Cleve)	29	7,613	4,034	9,410 *	10.7	18.8
145 Ch God Prophcy	8	408	NR	496 *	.6	1.0
151 L-D Saints	2	NR	NR	435	.5	.9
165 Ch of Nazarene	1	136	102	234	.3	.5
167 Chs of Christ	4	981	925	1,212	1.4	2.4
185 Cumber Presb	5	263	NR	455	.5	.9
193 Episcopal	1	NR	142	332	.4	.7
283 Luth—MO Synod	1	246	134	315	.4	.6
339 Pent Ch of God	1	95	NR	125	.1	.2
355 Presb Ch (USA)	2	351	165	430 *	.5	.9
356 Presb Ch Amer	1	0	0	0	-	-
360 Prim Bapt Chrch	1	NR	NR	NR	-	-
413 S.D.A.	4	1,524	NR	1,813	2.1	3.6
419 So Bapt Conv	55	21,443	8,793	26,275 *	29.9	52.4
449 Un Methodist	20	4,579	1,791	5,609 *	6.4	11.2
498 Indep.Charis.	1	0	450	550	.6	1.1
CAMPBELL	**67**	**11,696**	**3,971**	**14,648 ***	**36.8**	**100.0**
053 Assemb of God	1	97	86	122	.3	.8
056 Baha'i	0	1	NR	1	-	-
081 Catholic	2	NR	NR	168	.4	1.1
097 Chr Chs&Chs Cr	1	20	NR	24 *	.1	.2
127 Ch God (Cleve)	6	1,179	624	1,444 *	3.6	9.9
151 L-D Saints	1	NR	NR	190	.5	1.3
167 Chs of Christ	3	198	215	257	.6	1.8
320 "Old" MB Ascs	1	115	NR	140 *	.4	1.0
355 Presb Ch (USA)	1	106	70	129 *	.3	.9
413 S.D.A.	1	144	NR	171	.4	1.2
418 Southw Bapt Fel	1	NR	NR	NR	-	-
419 So Bapt Conv	40	8,768	2,486	10,653 *	26.7	72.7
449 Un Methodist	7	1,026	455	1,246 *	3.1	8.5
467 Wesleyan	2	42	35	103	.3	.7
CANNON	**49**	**5,078**	**3,330**	**6,453 ***	**50.3**	**100.0**
053 Assemb of God	1	220	100	180	1.4	2.8
081 Catholic	0	NR	NR	82	.6	1.3
127 Ch God (Cleve)	2	92	32	115 *	.9	1.8
165 Ch of Nazarene	1	29	12	29	.2	.4
167 Chs of Christ	23	1,680	1,938	2,231	17.4	34.6
189 Duck Rivr Bapt	3	145	NR	181 *	1.4	2.8
221 Free Methodist	1	53	80	80	.6	1.2
355 Presb Ch (USA)	1	16	9	20 *	.2	.3
413 S.D.A.	1	126	NR	150	1.2	2.3
419 So Bapt Conv	11	2,304	926	2,870 *	22.4	44.5
449 Un Methodist	5	413	233	515 *	4.0	8.0
CARROLL	**103**	**13,931**	**5,317**	**17,310 ***	**58.7**	**100.0**
053 Assemb of God	1	49	60	60	.2	.3
056 Baha'i	0	1	NR	1	-	-
081 Catholic	1	NR	NR	125	.4	.7
127 Ch God (Cleve)	1	84	52	102 *	.3	.6
145 Ch God Prophcy	1	51	NR	62 *	.2	.4
167 Chs of Christ	17	1,392	1,502	1,806	6.1	10.4
185 Cumber Presb	9	397	NR	621	2.1	3.6
320 "Old" MB Ascs	17	1,744	NR	2,119 *	7.2	12.2
323 Old Ord Amish	2	110	NR	134 *	.5	.8
355 Presb Ch (USA)	4	149	135	187 *	.6	1.1

Religious Group	Number of Churches, Synagogues, Mosques, or Temples	Number of Communicant, Confirmed, or Full Members	Number of Attendees	Total Adherents		
				Number of Adherents	% of Total Pop.	% of Total Adh.
360 Prim Bapt Chrch	5	NR	NR	NR	-	-
413 S.D.A.	1	115	NR	137	.5	.8
419 So Bapt Conv	23	7,619	2,596	9,258 *	31.4	53.5
449 Un Methodist	21	2,220	972	2,698 *	9.2	15.6
CARTER	**134**	**26,244**	**6,692**	**32,173 ***	**56.7**	**100.0**
053 Assemb of God	1	35	45	58	.1	.2
056 Baha'i	0	2	NR	2	-	-
081 Catholic	1	NR	NR	413	.7	1.3
089 Chr & Miss Al	1	116	NR	199	.4	.6
097 Chr Chs&Chs Cr	22	4,276	NR	5,113 *	9.0	15.9
123 Ch God (Ander)	2	NR	90	90	.2	.3
127 Ch God (Cleve)	6	382	324	498 *	.9	1.5
145 Ch God Prophcy	1	51	NR	61 *	.1	.2
151 L-D Saints	1	NR	NR	91	.2	.3
165 Ch of Nazarene	1	122	95	191	.3	.6
167 Chs of Christ	5	505	580	620	1.1	1.9
193 Episcopal	1	NR	26	49	.1	.2
223 Free Will Bapt	18	1,751	NR	2,094 *	3.7	6.5
258 IndFreeWillBapt	18	1,773	NR	2,120 *	3.7	6.6
283 Luth—MO Synod	1	0	0	0	-	-
355 Presb Ch (USA)	4	393	256	469 *	.8	1.5
356 Presb Ch Amer	1	328	235	368	.6	1.1
413 S.D.A.	1	74	NR	88	.2	.3
418 Southw Bapt Fel	1	NR	NR	NR	-	-
419 So Bapt Conv	40	15,153	4,531	18,115 *	31.9	56.3
449 Un Methodist	8	1,283	510	1,534 *	2.7	4.8
CHEATHAM	**56**	**6,462**	**3,557**	**9,559 ***	**26.6**	**100.0**
017 Amer Bapt Assn	1	50	NR	64 *	.2	.7
053 Assemb of God	1	166	201	320	.9	3.3
056 Baha'i	0	6	NR	6	-	.1
081 Catholic	1	NR	NR	995	2.8	10.4
145 Ch God Prophcy	2	102	NR	130 *	.4	1.4
165 Ch of Nazarene	2	184	168	202	.6	2.1
167 Chs of Christ	19	1,689	1,999	2,415	6.7	25.3
223 Free Will Bapt	8	778	NR	990 *	2.8	10.4
263 Int Foursq Gos	1	30	50	50 *	.1	.5
413 S.D.A.	2	83	NR	98	.3	1.0
419 So Bapt Conv	8	1,829	655	2,325 *	6.5	24.3
449 Un Methodist	11	1,545	484	1,964 *	5.5	20.5
CHESTER	**37**	**6,148**	**3,339**	**7,863 ***	**50.6**	**100.0**
053 Assemb of God	1	16	20	30	.2	.4
056 Baha'i	0	1	NR	1	-	-
167 Chs of Christ	8	1,296	1,559	1,762	11.3	22.4
173 Comm of Christ	1	99	NR	99	.6	1.3
185 Cumber Presb	1	57	NR	204	1.3	2.6
189 Duck Rivr Bapt	1	44	NR	54 *	.3	.7
360 Prim Bapt Chrch	4	NR	NR	NR	-	-
419 So Bapt Conv	13	3,716	1,309	4,581 *	29.5	58.3
449 Un Methodist	8	919	451	1,132 *	7.3	14.4
CLAIBORNE	**101**	**13,335**	**4,041**	**16,384 ***	**54.9**	**100.0**
053 Assemb of God	1	38	55	55	.2	.3
081 Catholic	1	NR	NR	90	.3	.5
097 Chr Chs&Chs Cr	1	80	NR	98 *	.3	.6
127 Ch God (Cleve)	1	35	20	43 *	.1	.3
167 Chs of Christ	3	116	140	151	.5	.9
283 Luth—MO Synod	1	48	28	68	.2	.4
360 Prim Bapt Chrch	3	NR	NR	NR	-	-
419 So Bapt Conv	81	12,190	3,438	14,870 *	49.8	90.8
449 Un Methodist	9	828	360	1,009 *	3.4	6.2
CLAY	**34**	**2,209**	**2,178**	**3,029 ***	**38.0**	**100.0**
081 Catholic	1	NR	NR	48	.6	1.6
123 Ch God (Ander)	1	NR	55	55	.7	1.8
167 Chs of Christ	27	1,532	1,857	2,116	26.5	69.9
419 So Bapt Conv	3	529	168	633 *	7.9	20.9
449 Un Methodist	2	148	98	177 *	2.2	5.8

NR–Not Reported *Total adherents estimated from known number of communicant, confirmed, full members. - Represents a percentage less than 0.1. Percentages may not total 100 due to rounding.

Table 4: Religious Congregations by County and Group: 2000

Religious Group		Number of Churches, Synagogues, Mosques, or Temples	Number of Communicant, Confirmed, or Full Members	Number of Attendees	Total Adherents		
					Number of Adherents	% of Total Pop.	% of Total Adh.
COCKE		**90**	**12,005**	**4,321**	**14,978 ***	**44.6**	**100.0**
053	Assemb of God	1	6	6	7	-	-
056	Baha'i	0	1	NR	1	-	-
081	Catholic	1	NR	NR	150	.4	1.0
089	Chr & Miss Al	1	53	NR	83	.2	.6
097	Chr Chs&Chs Cr	4	544	NR	659 *	2.0	4.4
123	Ch God (Ander)	2	NR	62	62	.2	.4
127	Ch God (Cleve)	7	870	406	1,055 *	3.1	7.0
165	Ch of Nazarene	1	37	55	92	.3	.6
167	Chs of Christ	3	170	190	231	.7	1.5
193	Episcopal	1	NR	50	79	.2	.5
207	E.L.C.A.	3	290	152	395	1.2	2.6
223	Free Will Bapt	8	778	NR	944 *	2.8	6.3
355	Presb Ch (USA)	1	51	33	62 *	.2	.4
356	Presb Ch Amer	1	38	25	41	.1	.3
360	Prim Bapt Chrch	1	NR	NR	NR	-	-
413	S.D.A.	1	20	NR	24	.1	.2
419	So Bapt Conv	41	7,887	2,700	9,563 *	28.5	63.8
449	Un Methodist	13	1,260	642	1,530 *	4.6	10.2
COFFEE		**115**	**19,360**	**9,396**	**27,208 ***	**56.7**	**100.0**
017	Amer Bapt Assn	1	50	NR	62 *	.1	.2
053	Assemb of God	2	178	207	429	.9	1.6
056	Baha'i	0	8	NR	8	-	-
081	Catholic	2	NR	NR	1,477	3.1	5.4
093	Chr Ch (Disc)	1	469	255	582 *	1.2	2.1
123	Ch God (Ander)	1	NR	25	25	.1	.1
127	Ch God (Cleve)	2	249	160	309 *	.6	1.1
145	Ch God Prophcy	1	51	NR	63 *	.1	.2
151	L-D Saints	1	NR	NR	516	1.1	1.9
165	Ch of Nazarene	5	398	347	842	1.8	3.1
167	Chs of Christ	31	2,751	3,016	3,698	7.7	13.6
173	Comm of Christ	1	35	NR	35	.1	.1
185	Cumber Presb	3	159	NR	267	.6	1.0
189	Duck Rivr Bapt	12	1,472	NR	1,827 *	3.8	6.7
193	Episcopal	2	NR	172	317	.7	1.2
207	E.L.C.A.	1	394	191	463	1.0	1.7
223	Free Will Bapt	2	195	NR	242 *	.5	.9
263	Int Foursq Gos	1	48	63	63 *	.1	.2
283	Luth—MO Synod	1	235	179	268	.6	1.0
304	NatPrimBapt USA	1	40	NR	50 *	.1	.2
355	Presb Ch (USA)	2	371	206	460 *	1.0	1.7
356	Presb Ch Amer	1	72	65	84	.2	.3
365	Prog Prim Bapt	1	17	NR	21 *	-	.1
413	S.D.A.	2	87	NR	103	.2	.4
418	Southw Bapt Fel	2	NR	NR	NR	-	-
419	So Bapt Conv	18	8,379	2,904	10,401 *	21.7	38.2
435	Unitarian-Univ	1	28	NR	35 *	.1	.1
449	Un Methodist	17	3,674	1,606	4,561 *	9.5	16.8
CROCKETT		**52**	**7,330**	**3,449**	**9,267 ***	**63.8**	**100.0**
053	Assemb of God	3	165	198	250	1.7	2.7
056	Baha'i	0	2	NR	2	-	-
093	Chr Ch (Disc)	2	222	145	274 *	1.9	3.0
097	Chr Chs&Chs Cr	2	323	NR	399 *	2.7	4.3
127	Ch God (Cleve)	2	190	120	235 *	1.6	2.5
151	L-D Saints	1	NR	NR	128	.9	1.4
167	Chs of Christ	12	1,059	970	1,310	9.0	14.1
185	Cumber Presb	2	51	NR	57	.4	.6
203	Evan Free Ch	1	69	125	125	.9	1.3
360	Prim Bapt Chrch	1	NR	NR	NR	-	-
419	So Bapt Conv	13	3,515	1,158	4,345 *	29.9	46.9
449	Un Methodist	13	1,734	733	2,142 *	14.7	23.1
CUMBERLAND		**93**	**15,410**	**8,220**	**21,249 ***	**45.4**	**100.0**
053	Assemb of God	2	319	312	439	.9	2.1
056	Baha'i	0	2	NR	2	-	-
081	Catholic	2	NR	NR	1,708	3.6	8.0
093	Chr Ch (Disc)	1	63	32	75 *	.2	.4
127	Ch God (Cleve)	4	359	171	443 *	.9	2.1
145	Ch God Prophcy	5	255	NR	305 *	.7	1.4
151	L-D Saints	1	NR	NR	365	.8	1.7

Religious Group		Number of Churches, Synagogues, Mosques, or Temples	Number of Communicant, Confirmed, or Full Members	Number of Attendees	Total Adherents		
					Number of Adherents	% of Total Pop.	% of Total Adh.
165	Ch of Nazarene	2	258	216	380	.8	1.8
167	Chs of Christ	13	1,246	1,331	1,570	3.4	7.4
175	Congr Chr Chs	1	65	56	78 *	.2	.4
189	Duck Rivr Bapt	1	51	NR	61 *	.1	.3
193	Episcopal	1	NR	98	146	.3	.7
203	Evan Free Ch	1	50	70	70	.1	.3
207	E.L.C.A.	1	319	207	327	.7	1.5
223	Free Will Bapt	2	195	NR	233 *	.5	1.1
226	Friends-USA	1	64	NR	77 *	.2	.4
246	Greek Orthodox	1	NR	NR	417	.9	2.0
258	IndFreeWillBapt	3	334	NR	400 *	.9	1.9
283	Luth—MO Synod	1	381	247	435	.9	2.0
297	Mennonite;Other	1	72	NR	86 *	.2	.4
339	Pent Ch of God	1	10	NR	15	-	.1
355	Presb Ch (USA)	3	273	182	327 *	.7	1.5
356	Presb Ch Amer	1	77	38	91	.2	.4
388	Reg Bapt Gen As	1	100	125	125 *	.3	.6
413	S.D.A.	1	190	NR	226	.5	1.1
419	So Bapt Conv	29	7,915	3,581	9,479 *	20.3	44.6
443	Un C of Christ	3	357	274	428 *	.9	2.0
449	Un Methodist	10	2,455	1,280	2,941 *	6.3	13.8
DAVIDSON		**591**	**190,795**	**105,919**	**297,312 ***	**52.2**	**100.0**
017	Amer Bapt Assn	2	550	NR	668 *	.1	.2
019	Amer Bapt USA	2	400	250	485 *	.1	.2
040	Ap Chr Ch-Amer	1	9	18	18 *	-	-
050	Armen Ap Etchm	1	28	NR	150	-	.1
053	Assemb of God	14	4,046	3,446	6,661	1.2	2.2
056	Baha'i	1	357	NR	357	.1	.1
076	Buddhism	6	NR	NR	NR	-	-
081	Catholic	16	NR	NR	28,091	4.9	9.4
084	Calvary Chapel	2	NR	NR	NR	-	-
093	Chr Ch (Disc)	9	2,735	922	3,319 *	.6	1.1
097	Chr Chs&Chs Cr	4	1,200	NR	1,457 *	.3	.5
105	Christian Ref	1	145	95	176 *	-	.1
121	Ch God (Abr)	1	20	25	25 *	-	-
123	Ch God (Ander)	2	NR	335	335	.1	.1
127	Ch God (Cleve)	7	1,631	1,630	2,117 *	.4	.7
145	Ch God Prophcy	7	339	NR	412 *	.1	.1
151	L-D Saints	4	NR	NR	1,456	.3	.5
165	Ch of Nazarene	30	5,893	4,558	7,603	1.3	2.6
167	Chs of Christ	110	30,053	30,119	39,145	6.9	13.2
173	Comm of Christ	1	282	NR	282	-	.1
185	Cumber Presb	13	2,164	NR	3,642	.6	1.2
186	Coptic Orth Ch	1	NR	NR	NR	-	-
189	Duck Rivr Bapt	1	135	NR	164 *	-	.1
193	Episcopal	14	NR	2,888	7,679	1.3	2.6
207	E.L.C.A.	6	1,896	682	2,430	.4	.8
223	Free Will Bapt	22	2,141	NR	2,598 *	.5	.9
226	Friends-USA	1	64	NR	78 *	-	-
252	Hindu	2	NR	NR	NR	-	-
262	Int Cou Comm Ch	1	75	NR	91 *	-	-
263	Int Foursq Gos	4	192	272	272 *	-	.1
264	Int Chs of Crst	1	641	1,115	891	.2	.3
267	Muslim Est	7	NR	1,868	9,046	1.6	3.0
283	Luth—MO Synod	6	1,035	813	1,378	.2	.5
288	Mennonite USA	1	37	30	45 *	-	-
290	Metro Comm Ch	1	78	91	95 *	-	-
304	NatPrimBapt USA	26	2,794	NR	3,391 *	.6	1.1
320	"Old" MB Ascs	4	970	NR	1,177 *	.2	.4
339	Pent Ch of God	1	160	NR	180	-	.1
349	Pent Holiness	1	50	50	61 *	-	-
355	Presb Ch (USA)	23	9,007	3,798	10,929 *	1.9	3.7
356	Presb Ch Amer	7	3,458	3,195	5,157	.9	1.7
360	Prim Bapt Chrch	5	NR	NR	NR	-	-
370	Ref Baptist Chs	1	NR	NR	NR	-	-
403	Salvation Army	3	329	343	519	.1	.2
413	S.D.A.	12	4,078	NR	4,853	.9	1.6
416	Sikh	1	NR	NR	NR	-	-
418	Southw Bapt Fel	2	NR	NR	NR	-	-
419	So Bapt Conv	114	79,600	29,962	96,596 *	16.9	32.5
435	Unitarian-Univ	2	456	NR	553 *	.1	.2
443	Un C of Christ	3	319	137	387 *	.1	.1
449	Un Methodist	67	26,791	10,909	32,509 *	5.7	10.9

NR–Not Reported   *Total adherents estimated from known number of communicant, confirmed, full members.   - Represents a percentage less than 0.1.   Percentages may not total 100 due to rounding.

Table 4: Religious Congregations by County and Group: 2000

Religious Group	Number of Churches, Synagogues, Mosques, or Temples	Number of Communicant, Confirmed, or Full Members	Number of Attendees	Total Adherents: Number of Adherents	% of Total Pop.	% of Total Adh.
463 Vineyard	1	200	250	250 *	-	.1
467 Wesleyan	3	89	34	122	-	-
469 WELS	1	130	84	162	-	.1
496 Jewish Est	4	NR	NR	6,000	1.1	2.0
498 Indep.Charis.	2	2,730	1,635	3,300	.6	1.1
499 Indep.Non-Char	6	3,488	6,365	10,000	1.8	3.4
DECATUR	**46**	**5,104**	**2,452**	**6,943 ***	**59.2**	**100.0**
053 Assemb of God	1	294	316	700	6.0	10.1
056 Baha'i	0	1	NR	1	-	-
081 Catholic	1	NR	NR	99	.8	1.4
123 Ch God (Ander)	1	NR	25	25	.2	.4
127 Ch God (Cleve)	1	99	21	119 *	1.0	1.7
151 L-D Saints	1	NR	NR	283	2.4	4.1
167 Chs of Christ	5	401	418	487	4.2	7.0
185 Cumber Presb	2	85	NR	171	1.5	2.5
320 "Old" MB Ascs	1	145	NR	174 *	1.5	2.5
360 Prim Bapt Chrch	1	NR	NR	NR	-	-
413 S.D.A.	1	38	NR	45	.4	.6
419 So Bapt Conv	19	3,208	1,276	3,842 *	32.8	55.3
449 Un Methodist	12	833	396	997 *	8.5	14.4
DE KALB	**72**	**8,458**	**3,215**	**10,520 ***	**60.4**	**100.0**
056 Baha'i	0	7	NR	7	-	.1
075 Brethren in Cr	2	71	67	79	.5	.8
081 Catholic	1	NR	NR	142	.8	1.3
127 Ch God (Cleve)	2	353	295	429 *	2.5	4.1
165 Ch of Nazarene	1	40	59	59	.3	.6
167 Chs of Christ	8	629	608	793	4.6	7.5
185 Cumber Presb	2	140	NR	241	1.4	2.3
189 Duck Rivr Bapt	8	1,053	NR	1,280 *	7.3	12.2
223 Free Will Bapt	2	195	NR	237 *	1.4	2.3
258 IndFreeWillBapt	1	53	NR	64 *	.4	.6
304 NatPrimBapt USA	1	20	NR	24 *	.1	.2
355 Presb Ch (USA)	1	39	35	47 *	.3	.4
360 Prim Bapt Chrch	2	NR	NR	NR	-	-
401 Rus Orth Abroad	1	NR	NR	NR	-	-
413 S.D.A.	1	27	NR	32	.2	.3
419 So Bapt Conv	22	4,651	1,539	5,653 *	32.4	53.7
449 Un Methodist	17	1,180	612	1,433 *	8.2	13.6
DICKSON	**98**	**13,481**	**7,630**	**18,728 ***	**43.4**	**100.0**
053 Assemb of God	1	368	485	500	1.2	2.7
056 Baha'i	0	3	NR	3	-	-
081 Catholic	1	NR	NR	1,156	2.7	6.2
127 Ch God (Cleve)	1	43	12	54 *	.1	.3
145 Ch God Prophcy	7	357	NR	448 *	1.0	2.4
165 Ch of Nazarene	2	271	207	417	1.0	2.2
167 Chs of Christ	30	3,112	3,203	4,225	9.8	22.6
185 Cumber Presb	3	276	NR	439	1.0	2.3
193 Episcopal	2	NR	55	82	.2	.4
223 Free Will Bapt	6	584	NR	735 *	1.7	3.9
283 Luth—MO Synod	1	128	96	180	.4	1.0
349 Pent Holiness	1	122	100	154 *	.4	.8
355 Presb Ch (USA)	2	206	132	259 *	.6	1.4
360 Prim Bapt Chrch	5	NR	NR	NR	-	-
413 S.D.A.	1	128	NR	152	.4	.8
419 So Bapt Conv	15	5,755	2,530	7,246 *	16.8	38.7
449 Un Methodist	20	2,128	810	2,678 *	6.2	14.3
DYER	**89**	**16,125**	**6,864**	**21,373 ***	**57.3**	**100.0**
053 Assemb of God	4	276	294	423	1.1	2.0
081 Catholic	1	NR	NR	645	1.7	3.0
097 Chr Chs&Chs Cr	1	233	NR	291 *	.8	1.4
127 Ch God (Cleve)	1	371	194	463 *	1.2	2.2
145 Ch God Prophcy	2	102	NR	128 *	.3	.6
151 L-D Saints	1	NR	NR	137	.4	.6
165 Ch of Nazarene	1	30	28	30	.1	.1
167 Chs of Christ	19	1,739	1,810	2,161	5.8	10.1
185 Cumber Presb	7	640	NR	1,057	2.8	4.9
193 Episcopal	1	NR	57	137	.4	.6
283 Luth—MO Synod	1	74	45	105	.3	.5
355 Presb Ch (USA)	2	39	23	49 *	.1	.2
356 Presb Ch Amer	1	133	83	161	.4	.8
413 S.D.A.	1	76	NR	90	.2	.4
419 So Bapt Conv	31	9,661	3,229	12,062 *	32.4	56.4
449 Un Methodist	15	2,751	1,101	3,434 *	9.2	16.1
FAYETTE	**57**	**7,649**	**2,918**	**9,809 ***	**34.1**	**100.0**
017 Amer Bapt Assn	1	50	NR	62 *	.2	.6
053 Assemb of God	1	58	63	116	.4	1.2
056 Baha'i	0	104	NR	104	.4	1.1
061 Beachy Amish	1	62	NR	77 *	.3	.8
081 Catholic	1	NR	NR	230	.8	2.3
093 Chr Ch (Disc)	1	38	0	47 *	.2	.5
127 Ch God (Cleve)	1	66	27	82 *	.3	.8
165 Ch of Nazarene	1	16	14	30	.1	.3
167 Chs of Christ	6	406	375	499	1.7	5.1
185 Cumber Presb	2	36	NR	85	.3	.9
193 Episcopal	2	NR	39	24	.1	.2
355 Presb Ch (USA)	3	344	188	427 *	1.5	4.4
360 Prim Bapt Chrch	1	NR	NR	NR	-	-
379 Ref Mennonite	1	8	NR	10 *	-	.1
413 S.D.A.	1	22	NR	26	.1	.3
419 So Bapt Conv	19	5,196	1,620	6,446 *	22.4	65.7
449 Un Methodist	15	1,243	592	1,544 *	5.4	15.7
FENTRESS	**43**	**5,096**	**1,993**	**7,015 ***	**42.2**	**100.0**
053 Assemb of God	1	43	41	42	.3	.6
081 Catholic	1	NR	NR	38	.2	.5
127 Ch God (Cleve)	1	368	206	451 *	2.7	6.4
145 Ch God Prophcy	2	102	NR	126 *	.8	1.8
151 L-D Saints	1	NR	NR	239	1.4	3.4
165 Ch of Nazarene	2	171	172	345	2.1	4.9
167 Chs of Christ	2	163	175	212	1.3	3.0
258 IndFreeWillBapt	10	927	NR	1,137 *	6.8	16.2
355 Presb Ch (USA)	1	144	80	177 *	1.1	2.5
418 Southw Bapt Fel	1	NR	NR	NR	-	-
419 So Bapt Conv	9	2,269	809	2,782 *	16.7	39.7
449 Un Methodist	9	881	400	1,081 *	6.5	15.4
467 Wesleyan	3	28	110	385	2.3	5.5
FRANKLIN	**109**	**14,965**	**6,440**	**20,405 ***	**52.0**	**100.0**
053 Assemb of God	1	49	54	80	.2	.4
056 Baha'i	0	4	NR	4	-	-
061 Beachy Amish	1	72	NR	87 *	.2	.4
081 Catholic	2	NR	NR	578	1.5	2.8
127 Ch God (Cleve)	5	405	324	533 *	1.4	2.6
145 Ch God Prophcy	2	102	NR	124 *	.3	.6
151 L-D Saints	1	NR	NR	92	.2	.5
165 Ch of Nazarene	8	757	614	1,280	3.3	6.3
167 Chs of Christ	19	1,455	1,513	1,790	4.6	8.8
185 Cumber Presb	9	848	NR	1,514	3.9	7.4
189 Duck Rivr Bapt	7	672	NR	815 *	2.1	4.0
193 Episcopal	6	NR	324	648	1.7	3.2
304 NatPrimBapt USA	5	333	NR	404 *	1.0	2.0
355 Presb Ch (USA)	2	76	42	92 *	.2	.5
360 Prim Bapt Chrch	1	NR	NR	NR	-	-
365 Prog Prim Bapt	1	31	NR	38 *	.1	.2
413 S.D.A.	1	24	NR	29	.1	.1
418 Southw Bapt Fel	2	NR	NR	NR	-	-
419 So Bapt Conv	24	7,433	2,566	9,017 *	23.0	44.2
443 Un C of Christ	1	151	59	183 *	.5	.9
449 Un Methodist	11	2,553	944	3,097 *	7.9	15.2
GIBSON	**157**	**26,740**	**11,273**	**33,355 ***	**69.3**	**100.0**
053 Assemb of God	5	816	794	956	2.0	2.9
056 Baha'i	0	5	NR	5	-	-
081 Catholic	2	NR	NR	592	1.2	1.8
093 Chr Ch (Disc)	2	333	124	408 *	.8	1.2
127 Ch God (Cleve)	3	258	143	317 *	.7	1.0
145 Ch God Prophcy	1	51	NR	62 *	.1	.2
165 Ch of Nazarene	1	0	0	0	-	-
167 Chs of Christ	31	2,504	2,568	3,005	6.2	9.0

NR–Not Reported   *Total adherents estimated from known number of communicant, confirmed, full members.   - Represents a percentage less than 0.1.   Percentages may not total 100 due to rounding.

Table 4: Religious Congregations by County and Group: 2000

Religious Group	Number of Churches, Synagogues, Mosques, or Temples	Number of Communicant, Confirmed, or Full Members	Number of Attendees	Total Adherents		
				Number of Adherents	% of Total Pop.	% of Total Adh.
185 Cumber Presb	17	1,102	NR	1,613	3.3	4.8
297 Mennonite;Other	1	33	NR	40 *	.1	.1
349 Pent Holiness	1	62	60	76 *	.2	.2
355 Presb Ch (USA)	4	420	295	515 *	1.1	1.5
360 Prim Bapt Chrch	5	NR	NR	NR	-	-
419 So Bapt Conv	53	16,603	5,293	20,346 *	42.3	61.0
449 Un Methodist	29	3,703	1,606	4,536 *	9.4	13.6
463 Vineyard	1	150	90	184 *	.4	.6
499 Indep.Non-Char	1	700	300	700	1.5	2.1
GILES	**105**	**12,797**	**6,368**	**16,447 ***	**55.9**	**100.0**
053 Assemb of God	1	33	40	40	.1	.2
081 Catholic	1	NR	NR	221	.8	1.3
123 Ch God (Ander)	2	NR	82	82	.3	.5
127 Ch God (Cleve)	2	211	122	259 *	.9	1.6
145 Ch God Prophcy	3	153	NR	189 *	.6	1.1
165 Ch of Nazarene	1	6	17	25	.1	.2
167 Chs of Christ	25	2,104	2,181	2,826	9.6	17.2
185 Cumber Presb	2	51	NR	60	.2	.4
193 Episcopal	1	NR	67	146	.5	.9
258 IndFreeWillBapt	2	270	NR	332 *	1.1	2.0
304 NatPrimBapt USA	5	203	NR	250 *	.8	1.5
355 Presb Ch (USA)	5	339	205	420 *	1.4	2.6
360 Prim Bapt Chrch	1	NR	NR	NR	-	-
413 S.D.A.	2	101	NR	120	.4	.7
419 So Bapt Conv	26	6,488	2,323	7,987 *	27.1	48.6
449 Un Methodist	26	2,838	1,331	3,490 *	11.9	21.2
GRAINGER	**62**	**11,040**	**3,969**	**13,434 ***	**65.0**	**100.0**
056 Baha'i	0	5	NR	5	-	-
127 Ch God (Cleve)	2	141	51	172 *	.8	1.3
167 Chs of Christ	1	24	30	28	.1	.2
223 Free Will Bapt	1	97	NR	118 *	.6	.9
360 Prim Bapt Chrch	1	NR	NR	NR	-	-
419 So Bapt Conv	47	10,073	3,537	12,258 *	59.3	91.2
449 Un Methodist	10	700	351	853 *	4.1	6.3
GREENE	**168**	**22,730**	**9,352**	**30,175 ***	**48.0**	**100.0**
053 Assemb of God	1	80	95	119	.2	.4
056 Baha'i	0	1	NR	1	-	-
081 Catholic	1	NR	NR	800	1.3	2.7
084 Calvary Chapel	1	NR	NR	NR	-	-
097 Chr Chs&Chs Cr	2	668	NR	806 *	1.3	2.7
123 Ch God (Ander)	6	NR	1,114	1,114	1.8	3.7
127 Ch God (Cleve)	4	376	205	453 *	.7	1.5
145 Ch God Prophcy	1	51	NR	62 *	.1	.2
151 L-D Saints	1	NR	NR	187	.3	.6
157 Ch of Brethren	1	82	40	99 *	.2	.3
165 Ch of Nazarene	1	76	95	212	.3	.7
167 Chs of Christ	4	210	240	276	.4	.9
185 Cumber Presb	14	940	NR	1,567	2.5	5.2
193 Episcopal	1	NR	58	163	.3	.5
207 E.L.C.A.	4	829	395	960	1.5	3.2
221 Free Methodist	1	5	8	8	-	-
223 Free Will Bapt	24	2,335	NR	2,818 *	4.5	9.3
297 Mennonite;Other	1	55	NR	66 *	.1	.2
349 Pent Holiness	3	554	363	668 *	1.1	2.2
355 Presb Ch (USA)	10	733	433	887 *	1.4	2.9
356 Presb Ch Amer	2	130	105	154	.2	.5
362 Prim Bapt E Dst	1	92	NR	111 *	.2	.4
413 S.D.A.	3	576	NR	685	1.1	2.3
419 So Bapt Conv	20	7,883	2,564	9,511 *	15.1	31.5
449 Un Methodist	59	6,695	3,314	8,075 *	12.8	26.8
467 Wesleyan	1	9	23	23	-	.1
499 Indep.Non-Char	1	350	300	350	.6	1.2
GRUNDY	**49**	**3,294**	**1,744**	**4,582 ***	**32.0**	**100.0**
032 Amish; other	1	50	NR	62 *	.4	1.4
081 Catholic	0	NR	NR	19	.1	.4
127 Ch God (Cleve)	5	290	278	363 *	2.5	7.9
145 Ch God Prophcy	2	102	NR	126 *	.9	2.7
151 L-D Saints	1	NR	NR	309	2.2	6.7

Religious Group	Number of Churches, Synagogues, Mosques, or Temples	Number of Communicant, Confirmed, or Full Members	Number of Attendees	Total Adherents		
				Number of Adherents	% of Total Pop.	% of Total Adh.
165 Ch of Nazarene	2	203	117	220	1.5	4.8
167 Chs of Christ	10	400	418	498	3.5	10.9
185 Cumber Presb	1	3	NR	3	-	.1
189 Duck Rivr Bapt	1	117	NR	145 *	1.0	3.2
193 Episcopal	3	NR	64	204	1.4	4.5
263 Int Foursq Gos	1	40	53	53 *	.4	1.2
360 Prim Bapt Chrch	1	NR	NR	NR	-	-
413 S.D.A.	3	218	NR	260	1.8	5.7
418 Southw Bapt Fel	1	NR	NR	NR	-	-
419 So Bapt Conv	7	1,107	413	1,372 *	9.6	29.9
449 Un Methodist	10	764	401	948 *	6.6	20.7
HAMBLEN	**92**	**27,932**	**11,007**	**36,575 ***	**62.9**	**100.0**
053 Assemb of God	1	37	38	50	.1	.1
056 Baha'i	0	17	NR	17	-	-
081 Catholic	1	NR	NR	1,317	2.3	3.6
097 Chr Chs&Chs Cr	3	463	NR	565 *	1.0	1.5
123 Ch God (Ander)	1	NR	65	65	.1	.2
127 Ch God (Cleve)	5	747	592	912 *	1.6	2.5
145 Ch God Prophcy	1	51	NR	62 *	.1	.2
151 L-D Saints	1	NR	NR	543	.9	1.5
165 Ch of Nazarene	1	40	40	50	.1	.1
167 Chs of Christ	1	165	150	216	.4	.6
185 Cumber Presb	1	74	NR	118	.2	.3
193 Episcopal	1	NR	197	394	.7	1.1
203 Evan Free Ch	1	0	130	130	.2	.4
207 E.L.C.A.	1	239	99	297	.5	.8
223 Free Will Bapt	3	292	NR	356 *	.6	1.0
283 Luth—MO Synod	1	123	58	131	.2	.4
355 Presb Ch (USA)	3	564	292	689 *	1.2	1.9
356 Presb Ch Amer	1	0	0	0	-	-
362 Prim Bapt E Dst	3	201	NR	245 *	.4	.7
413 S.D.A.	1	195	NR	232	.4	.6
418 Southw Bapt Fel	3	NR	NR	NR	-	-
419 So Bapt Conv	45	21,247	7,924	25,940 *	44.6	70.9
449 Un Methodist	13	3,477	1,422	4,246 *	7.3	11.6
HAMILTON	**372**	**133,184**	**54,391**	**179,266 ***	**58.2**	**100.0**
053 Assemb of God	7	646	639	987	.3	.6
056 Baha'i	2	106	NR	106	-	.1
081 Catholic	6	NR	NR	9,911	3.2	5.5
084 Calvary Chapel	2	NR	NR	NR	-	-
089 Chr & Miss Al	2	110	NR	184	.1	.1
093 Chr Ch (Disc)	3	780	267	950 *	.3	.5
097 Chr Chs&Chs Cr	4	711	NR	866 *	.3	.5
123 Ch God (Ander)	4	NR	262	262	.1	.1
127 Ch God (Cleve)	43	8,181	4,533	9,979 *	3.2	5.6
145 Ch God Prophcy	8	390	NR	474 *	.2	.3
151 L-D Saints	4	NR	NR	736	.2	.4
165 Ch of Nazarene	9	1,604	681	1,891	.6	1.1
167 Chs of Christ	35	5,089	5,085	6,340	2.1	3.5
173 Comm of Christ	1	59	NR	59	-	-
185 Cumber Presb	5	1,048	NR	1,743	.6	1.0
189 Duck Rivr Bapt	1	0	NR	0 *	-	-
193 Episcopal	11	NR	1,955	5,756	1.9	3.2
203 Evan Free Ch	1	69	125	125	-	.1
207 E.L.C.A.	3	759	384	929	.3	.5
216 Evan Presby Ch	3	796	NR	969 *	.3	.5
223 Free Will Bapt	3	292	NR	356 *	.1	.2
226 Friends-USA	1	64	NR	78 *	-	-
246 Greek Orthodox	1	NR	NR	309	.1	.2
262 Int Cou Comm Ch	1	190	NR	231 *	.1	.1
263 Int Foursq Gos	1	18	42	42 *	-	-
264 Int Chs of Crst	1	46	88	61	-	-
267 Muslim Est	2	NR	281	2,000	.6	1.1
283 Luth—MO Synod	4	1,486	776	1,933	.6	1.1
290 Metro Comm Ch	1	31	47	47 *	-	-
304 NatPrimBapt USA	5	528	NR	643 *	.2	.4
335 Orth Pres Ch	1	49	68	68	-	-
349 Pent Holiness	1	35	27	43 *	-	-
355 Presb Ch (USA)	11	3,282	1,769	3,999 *	1.3	2.2
356 Presb Ch Amer	11	5,800	3,912	6,877	2.2	3.8
360 Prim Bapt Chrch	1	NR	NR	NR	-	-

NR–Not Reported   *Total adherents estimated from known number of communicant, confirmed, full members.   - Represents a percentage less than 0.1.   Percentages may not total 100 due to rounding.

Table 4: Religious Congregations by County and Group: 2000

Religious Group	Number of Churches, Synagogues, Mosques, or Temples	Number of Communicant, Confirmed, or Full Members	Number of Attendees	Total Adherents: Number of Adherents	Total Adherents: % of Total Pop.	Total Adherents: % of Total Adh.
365 Prog Prim Bapt	1	44	NR	54 *	-	-
370 Ref Baptist Chs	1	NR	NR	NR	-	-
403 Salvation Army	2	296	140	639	.2	.4
413 S.D.A.	13	5,891	NR	7,011	2.3	3.9
418 Southw Bapt Fel	9	NR	NR	NR	-	-
419 So Bapt Conv	97	54,532	21,999	66,439 *	21.6	37.1
435 Unitarian-Univ	1	119	NR	145 *	-	.1
443 Un C of Christ	2	240	93	292 *	.1	.2
449 Un Methodist	42	20,092	7,664	24,478 *	8.0	13.7
467 Wesleyan	1	51	54	54	-	-
496 Jewish Est	2	NR	NR	1,450	.5	.8
499 Indep.Non-Char	2	19,750	3,500	19,750	6.4	11.0
HANCOCK	**47**	**6,386**	**1,409**	**7,686 ***	**113.3**	**100.0**
081 Catholic	1	NR	NR	15	.2	.2
145 Ch God Prophcy	1	51	NR	61 *	.9	.8
167 Chs of Christ	1	12	15	16	.2	.2
201 Evan Cov Ch	1	41	26	49 *	.7	.6
362 Prim Bapt E Dst	5	756	NR	908 *	13.4	11.8
419 So Bapt Conv	37	5,432	1,303	6,524 *	96.1	84.9
449 Un Methodist	1	94	65	113 *	1.7	1.5
HARDEMAN	**62**	**9,719**	**3,574**	**12,223 ***	**43.5**	**100.0**
053 Assemb of God	1	28	36	48	.2	.4
056 Baha'i	0	2	NR	2	-	-
081 Catholic	1	NR	NR	84	.3	.7
127 Ch God (Cleve)	1	47	25	58 *	.2	.5
167 Chs of Christ	11	656	737	882	3.1	7.2
185 Cumber Presb	1	43	NR	76	.3	.6
193 Episcopal	1	NR	29	126	.4	1.0
355 Presb Ch (USA)	1	19	10	23 *	.1	.2
360 Prim Bapt Chrch	3	NR	NR	NR	-	-
419 So Bapt Conv	33	7,969	2,357	9,755 *	34.7	79.8
449 Un Methodist	9	955	380	1,169 *	4.2	9.6
HARDIN	**79**	**10,488**	**4,951**	**13,439 ***	**52.5**	**100.0**
032 Amish; other	1	25	NR	30 *	.1	.2
053 Assemb of God	4	211	245	296	1.2	2.2
081 Catholic	2	NR	NR	325	1.3	2.4
097 Chr Chs&Chs Cr	1	10	NR	12 *	-	.1
123 Ch God (Ander)	1	NR	10	10	-	.1
127 Ch God (Cleve)	1	90	60	109 *	.4	.8
145 Ch God Prophcy	1	51	NR	62 *	.2	.5
165 Ch of Nazarene	1	46	70	90	.4	.7
167 Chs of Christ	10	938	1,037	1,155	4.5	8.6
185 Cumber Presb	4	333	NR	595	2.3	4.4
223 Free Will Bapt	5	487	NR	591 *	2.3	4.4
263 Int Foursq Gos	3	429	594	594 *	2.3	4.4
339 Pent Ch of God	1	28	NR	40	.2	.3
355 Presb Ch (USA)	1	14	25	25 *	.1	.2
360 Prim Bapt Chrch	3	NR	NR	NR	-	-
413 S.D.A.	1	208	NR	248	1.0	1.8
419 So Bapt Conv	19	5,486	1,915	6,668 *	26.1	49.6
449 Un Methodist	20	2,132	995	2,589 *	10.1	19.3
HAWKINS	**153**	**25,631**	**8,431**	**32,038 ***	**59.8**	**100.0**
053 Assemb of God	1	40	29	36	.1	.1
056 Baha'i	0	1	NR	1	-	-
081 Catholic	1	NR	NR	145	.3	.5
093 Chr Ch (Disc)	1	108	0	132 *	.2	.4
097 Chr Chs&Chs Cr	4	686	NR	837 *	1.6	2.6
123 Ch God (Ander)	1	NR	22	22	-	.1
127 Ch God (Cleve)	4	212	148	268 *	.5	.8
145 Ch God Prophcy	2	102	NR	124 *	.2	.4
151 L-D Saints	2	NR	NR	450	.8	1.4
157 Ch of Brethren	2	50	14	61 *	.1	.2
165 Ch of Nazarene	1	29	8	29	.1	.1
167 Chs of Christ	2	58	60	75	.1	.2
223 Free Will Bapt	11	1,070	NR	1,306 *	2.4	4.1
320 "Old" MB Ascs	1	65	NR	79 *	.1	.2
349 Pent Holiness	1	43	30	52 *	.1	.2
355 Presb Ch (USA)	5	303	175	369 *	.7	1.2
362 Prim Bapt E Dst	15	1,741	NR	2,125 *	4.0	6.6
403 Salvation Army	1	245	162	445	.8	1.4
413 S.D.A.	1	71	NR	84	.2	.3
418 Southw Bapt Fel	1	NR	NR	NR	-	-
419 So Bapt Conv	68	18,322	6,558	22,363 *	41.8	69.8
449 Un Methodist	28	2,485	1,225	3,035 *	5.7	9.5
HAYWOOD	**44**	**7,519**	**2,847**	**9,680 ***	**48.9**	**100.0**
053 Assemb of God	2	234	182	265	1.3	2.7
056 Baha'i	0	34	NR	34	.2	.4
081 Catholic	1	NR	NR	63	.3	.7
127 Ch God (Cleve)	2	118	54	153 *	.8	1.6
167 Chs of Christ	6	296	314	375	1.9	3.9
193 Episcopal	1	NR	25	42	.2	.4
355 Presb Ch (USA)	1	191	126	243 *	1.2	2.5
360 Prim Bapt Chrch	1	NR	NR	NR	-	-
419 So Bapt Conv	15	5,158	1,558	6,553 *	33.1	67.7
449 Un Methodist	14	1,488	588	1,892 *	9.6	19.5
496 Jewish Est	1	NR	NR	60	.3	.6
HENDERSON	**66**	**9,878**	**4,577**	**12,533 ***	**49.1**	**100.0**
017 Amer Bapt Assn	1	50	NR	62 *	.2	.5
032 Amish; other	1	35	NR	43 *	.2	.3
053 Assemb of God	1	28	40	76	.3	.6
056 Baha'i	0	8	NR	8	-	.1
081 Catholic	1	NR	NR	227	.9	1.8
097 Chr Chs&Chs Cr	1	138	NR	170 *	.7	1.4
127 Ch God (Cleve)	1	92	108	113 *	.4	.9
167 Chs of Christ	16	1,182	1,183	1,471	5.8	11.7
185 Cumber Presb	3	193	NR	325	1.3	2.6
189 Duck Rivr Bapt	3	246	NR	303 *	1.2	2.4
320 "Old" MB Ascs	3	448	NR	552 *	2.2	4.4
355 Presb Ch (USA)	1	5	4	6 *	-	-
360 Prim Bapt Chrch	1	NR	NR	NR	-	-
419 So Bapt Conv	22	6,085	2,572	7,492 *	29.4	59.8
449 Un Methodist	11	1,368	670	1,685 *	6.6	13.4
HENRY	**90**	**15,884**	**7,988**	**20,534 ***	**66.0**	**100.0**
053 Assemb of God	1	33	39	60	.2	.3
056 Baha'i	0	2	NR	2	-	-
061 Beachy Amish	1	55	NR	66 *	.2	.3
081 Catholic	1	NR	NR	977	3.1	4.8
093 Chr Ch (Disc)	1	193	80	232 *	.7	1.1
145 Ch God Prophcy	1	51	NR	61 *	.2	.3
151 L-D Saints	1	NR	NR	234	.8	1.1
165 Ch of Nazarene	1	108	78	135	.4	.7
167 Chs of Christ	18	1,495	1,708	1,880	6.0	9.2
173 Comm of Christ	2	429	NR	429	1.4	2.1
185 Cumber Presb	2	36	NR	60	.2	.3
193 Episcopal	1	NR	74	137	.4	.7
283 Luth—MO Synod	1	136	60	177	.6	.9
320 "Old" MB Ascs	1	88	NR	106 *	.3	.5
339 Pent Ch of God	1	18	NR	30	.1	.1
355 Presb Ch (USA)	1	135	69	163 *	.5	.8
360 Prim Bapt Chrch	2	NR	NR	NR	-	-
413 S.D.A.	1	109	NR	130	.4	.6
419 So Bapt Conv	33	10,819	4,902	13,032 *	41.9	63.5
449 Un Methodist	20	2,177	978	2,623 *	8.4	12.8
HICKMAN	**75**	**6,284**	**4,355**	**8,290 ***	**37.2**	**100.0**
053 Assemb of God	1	37	49	56	.3	.7
056 Baha'i	0	2	NR	2	-	-
081 Catholic	1	NR	NR	297	1.3	3.6
145 Ch God Prophcy	2	102	NR	126 *	.6	1.5
165 Ch of Nazarene	1	30	20	41	.2	.5
167 Chs of Christ	38	2,780	2,864	3,624	16.3	43.7
185 Cumber Presb	2	19	NR	46	.2	.6
322 Old Ord Menn Ch	1	42	NR	52 *	.2	.6
323 Old Ord Amish	1	55	NR	68 *	.3	.8
360 Prim Bapt Chrch	2	NR	NR	NR	-	-
413 S.D.A.	1	34	NR	40	.2	.5
419 So Bapt Conv	15	2,373	1,028	2,936 *	13.2	35.4

NR–Not Reported *Total adherents estimated from known number of communicant, confirmed, full members. - Represents a percentage less than 0.1. Percentages may not total 100 due to rounding.

Table 4: Religious Congregations by County and Group: 2000

Religious Group	Number of Churches, Synagogues, Mosques, or Temples	Number of Communicant, Confirmed, or Full Members	Number of Attendees	Total Adherents		
				Number of Adherents	% of Total Pop.	% of Total Adh.
449 Un Methodist	10	810	394	1,002 *	4.5	12.1
HOUSTON	**26**	**2,171**	**1,117**	**3,132 ***	**38.7**	**100.0**
053 Assemb of God	1	55	71	151	1.9	4.8
081 Catholic	1	NR	NR	151	1.9	4.8
127 Ch God (Cleve)	1	39	7	48 *	.6	1.5
145 Ch God Prophcy	1	51	NR	63 *	.8	2.0
165 Ch of Nazarene	2	464	306	514	6.4	16.4
167 Chs of Christ	2	82	134	195	2.4	6.2
185 Cumber Presb	5	148	NR	349	4.3	11.1
193 Episcopal	1	NR	9	16	.2	.5
349 Pent Holiness	1	60	68	74 *	.9	2.4
419 So Bapt Conv	4	701	227	866 *	10.7	27.7
449 Un Methodist	7	571	295	705 *	8.7	22.5
HUMPHREYS	**57**	**6,581**	**3,441**	**8,988 ***	**50.1**	**100.0**
053 Assemb of God	2	55	71	108	.6	1.2
081 Catholic	1	NR	NR	310	1.7	3.4
145 Ch God Prophcy	1	51	NR	62 *	.3	.7
151 L-D Saints	1	NR	NR	174	1.0	1.9
165 Ch of Nazarene	2	176	159	223	1.2	2.5
167 Chs of Christ	15	1,316	1,338	1,597	8.9	17.8
185 Cumber Presb	4	209	NR	377	2.1	4.2
193 Episcopal	1	NR	34	66	.4	.7
223 Free Will Bapt	5	487	NR	596 *	3.3	6.6
349 Pent Holiness	4	288	280	353 *	2.0	3.9
355 Presb Ch (USA)	1	64	40	78 *	.4	.9
360 Prim Bapt Chrch	1	NR	NR	NR	-	-
419 So Bapt Conv	7	2,276	660	2,787 *	15.5	31.0
443 Un C of Christ	1	15	15	18 *	.1	.2
449 Un Methodist	10	1,543	737	1,889 *	10.5	21.0
467 Wesleyan	1	101	107	350	2.0	3.9
JACKSON	**51**	**2,869**	**2,670**	**3,818 ***	**34.8**	**100.0**
056 Baha'i	0	4	NR	4	-	.1
081 Catholic	0	NR	NR	66	.6	1.7
127 Ch God (Cleve)	1	69	80	83 *	.8	2.2
167 Chs of Christ	36	1,839	2,074	2,419	22.0	63.4
189 Duck Rivr Bapt	1	55	NR	66 *	.6	1.7
221 Free Methodist	1	13	22	22	.2	.6
320 "Old" MB Ascs	1	52	NR	63 *	.6	1.7
419 So Bapt Conv	4	478	239	577 *	5.3	15.1
449 Un Methodist	6	346	233	418 *	3.8	10.9
467 Wesleyan	1	13	22	100	.9	2.6
JEFFERSON	**96**	**18,665**	**7,666**	**23,231 ***	**52.4**	**100.0**
053 Assemb of God	2	72	71	100	.2	.4
056 Baha'i	0	2	NR	2	-	-
081 Catholic	1	NR	NR	375	.8	1.6
097 Chr Chs&Chs Cr	2	300	NR	365 *	.8	1.6
123 Ch God (Ander)	1	NR	50	50	.1	.2
127 Ch God (Cleve)	6	445	310	542 *	1.2	2.3
157 Ch of Brethren	1	156	70	190 *	.4	.8
167 Chs of Christ	2	108	105	129	.3	.6
185 Cumber Presb	2	79	NR	187	.4	.8
223 Free Will Bapt	2	195	NR	237 *	.5	1.0
226 Friends-USA	1	63	NR	77 *	.2	.3
355 Presb Ch (USA)	8	585	253	712 *	1.6	3.1
419 So Bapt Conv	41	12,955	4,859	15,754 *	35.6	67.8
449 Un Methodist	25	3,226	1,520	3,926 *	8.9	16.9
467 Wesleyan	1	79	128	185	.4	.8
499 Indep.Non-Char	1	400	300	400	.9	1.7
JOHNSON	**52**	**7,629**	**2,773**	**9,516 ***	**54.4**	**100.0**
053 Assemb of God	1	96	58	111	.6	1.2
056 Baha'i	0	1	NR	1	-	-
081 Catholic	1	NR	NR	77	.4	.8
097 Chr Chs&Chs Cr	8	817	NR	962 *	5.5	10.1
127 Ch God (Cleve)	1	42	25	49 *	.3	.5
151 L-D Saints	1	NR	NR	389	2.2	4.1
167 Chs of Christ	6	400	450	539	3.1	5.7
223 Free Will Bapt	2	195	NR	229 *	1.3	2.4
258 IndFreeWillBapt	1	98	NR	115 *	.7	1.2
288 Mennonite USA	1	38	36	45 *	.3	.5
355 Presb Ch (USA)	3	120	58	142 *	.8	1.5
413 S.D.A.	1	57	NR	68	.4	.7
419 So Bapt Conv	19	5,079	1,806	5,981 *	34.2	62.9
449 Un Methodist	7	686	340	808 *	4.6	8.5
KNOX	**453**	**171,174**	**74,087**	**236,941 ***	**62.0**	**100.0**
011 A.W.M.C.	2	0	40	0	-	-
017 Amer Bapt Assn	1	50	NR	61 *	-	-
019 Amer Bapt USA	1	358	250	434 *	.1	.2
053 Assemb of God	11	2,040	1,429	2,164	.6	.9
056 Baha'i	2	95	NR	95	-	-
059 Bapt Miss Assn	4	549	297	664 *	.2	.3
076 Buddhism	1	NR	NR	NR	-	-
081 Catholic	6	NR	NR	15,367	4.0	6.5
084 Calvary Chapel	1	NR	NR	NR	-	-
093 Chr Ch (Disc)	3	788	275	954 *	.2	.4
097 Chr Chs&Chs Cr	10	1,882	NR	2,280 *	.6	1.0
123 Ch God (Ander)	1	NR	119	119	-	.1
127 Ch God (Cleve)	20	4,131	2,885	5,062 *	1.3	2.1
145 Ch God Prophcy	2	102	NR	124 *	-	.1
151 L-D Saints	5	NR	NR	1,541	.4	.7
157 Ch of Brethren	1	27	25	33 *	-	-
165 Ch of Nazarene	3	398	202	410	.1	.2
167 Chs of Christ	15	2,635	2,679	3,392	.9	1.4
173 Comm of Christ	1	1	NR	1	-	-
185 Cumber Presb	5	1,157	NR	1,868	.5	.8
193 Episcopal	9	NR	1,904	5,023	1.3	2.1
203 Evan Free Ch	2	629	2,185	2,185	.6	.9
207 E.L.C.A.	5	2,231	911	2,739	.7	1.2
216 Evan Presby Ch	3	3,535	NR	4,281 *	1.1	1.8
223 Free Will Bapt	7	681	NR	825 *	.2	.3
226 Friends-USA	2	127	NR	154 *	-	.1
246 Greek Orthodox	1	NR	NR	792	.2	.3
262 Int Cou Comm Ch	1	125	NR	151 *	-	.1
264 Int Chs of Crst	1	121	167	149	-	.1
267 Muslim Est	3	NR	856	3,609	.9	1.5
283 Luth—MO Synod	3	1,301	900	1,755	.5	.7
288 Mennonite USA	2	62	53	75 *	-	-
290 Metro Comm Ch	1	162	85	85 *	-	-
331 OCA: Ter Diocs	1	36	NR	106	-	-
349 Pent Holiness	1	139	55	168 *	-	.1
355 Presb Ch (USA)	30	8,058	3,989	9,759 *	2.6	4.1
356 Presb Ch Amer	4	4,121	3,313	6,002	1.6	2.5
360 Prim Bapt Chrch	3	NR	NR	NR	-	-
403 Salvation Army	1	192	121	381	.1	.2
413 S.D.A.	5	528	NR	628	.2	.3
416 Sikh	1	NR	NR	NR	-	-
418 Southw Bapt Fel	4	NR	NR	NR	-	-
419 So Bapt Conv	187	99,349	33,320	120,315 *	31.5	50.8
435 Unitarian-Univ	2	505	NR	612 *	.2	.3
443 Un C of Christ	1	137	108	166 *	-	.1
449 Un Methodist	66	26,449	10,528	32,034 *	8.4	13.5
463 Vineyard	1	130	120	157 *	-	.1
467 Wesleyan	1	45	26	45	-	-
469 WELS	1	103	75	131	-	.1
496 Jewish Est	2	NR	NR	1,800	.5	.8
498 Indep.Charis.	2	1,900	1,950	1,950	.5	.8
499 Indep.Non-Char	5	6,295	5,220	6,295	1.6	2.7
LAKE	**20**	**3,344**	**1,221**	**4,013 ***	**50.5**	**100.0**
127 Ch God (Cleve)	1	143	0	166 *	2.1	4.1
145 Ch God Prophcy	1	51	NR	59 *	.7	1.5
167 Chs of Christ	5	330	348	521	6.6	13.0
355 Presb Ch (USA)	1	30	22	35 *	.4	.9
419 So Bapt Conv	9	2,423	696	2,807 *	35.3	69.9
449 Un Methodist	3	367	155	425 *	5.3	10.6
LAUDERDALE	**61**	**9,084**	**3,753**	**11,401 ***	**42.1**	**100.0**
053 Assemb of God	7	493	577	701	2.6	6.1
056 Baha'i	0	1	NR	1	-	-
081 Catholic	1	NR	NR	32	.1	.3

NR–Not Reported   *Total adherents estimated from known number of communicant, confirmed, full members.   - Represents a percentage less than 0.1.   Percentages may not total 100 due to rounding.

Table 4: Religious Congregations by County and Group: 2000

Religious Group	Number of Churches, Synagogues, Mosques, or Temples	Number of Communicant, Confirmed, or Full Members	Number of Attendees	Total Adherents		
				Number of Adherents	% of Total Pop.	% of Total Adh.
093 Chr Ch (Disc)	1	45	0	56 *	.2	.5
127 Ch God (Cleve)	2	43	48	54 *	.2	.5
167 Chs of Christ	8	390	390	498	1.8	4.4
185 Cumber Presb	1	54	NR	69	.3	.6
349 Pent Holiness	1	12	20	15 *	.1	.1
355 Presb Ch (USA)	1	29	24	36 *	.1	.3
419 So Bapt Conv	23	6,178	1,825	7,658 *	28.3	67.2
449 Un Methodist	16	1,839	869	2,281 *	8.4	20.0
LAWRENCE	**137**	**18,819**	**9,334**	**26,290 ***	**65.8**	**100.0**
053 Assemb of God	1	110	140	280	.7	1.1
056 Baha'i	0	2	NR	2	-	-
081 Catholic	3	NR	NR	1,914	4.8	7.3
127 Ch God (Cleve)	5	657	446	846 *	2.1	3.2
151 L-D Saints	1	NR	NR	347	.9	1.3
165 Ch of Nazarene	4	303	190	344	.9	1.3
167 Chs of Christ	35	3,051	3,230	4,011	10.0	15.3
185 Cumber Presb	2	151	NR	290	.7	1.1
223 Free Will Bapt	3	292	NR	367 *	.9	1.4
258 IndFreeWillBapt	6	445	NR	559 *	1.4	2.1
320 "Old" MB Ascs	1	153	NR	192 *	.5	.7
323 Old Ord Amish	8	400	NR	504 *	1.3	1.9
355 Presb Ch (USA)	1	37	19	46 *	.1	.2
360 Prim Bapt Chrch	2	NR	NR	NR	-	-
413 S.D.A.	2	180	NR	214	.5	.8
419 So Bapt Conv	37	10,292	3,910	12,923 *	32.4	49.2
449 Un Methodist	26	2,746	1,399	3,451 *	8.6	13.1
LEWIS	**33**	**3,469**	**2,450**	**4,541 ***	**39.9**	**100.0**
053 Assemb of God	1	41	47	50	.4	1.1
081 Catholic	1	NR	NR	108	1.0	2.4
127 Ch God (Cleve)	1	32	24	40 *	.4	.9
167 Chs of Christ	17	1,251	1,422	1,663	14.6	36.6
185 Cumber Presb	1	48	NR	83	.7	1.8
304 NatPrimBapt USA	1	11	NR	14 *	.1	.3
360 Prim Bapt Chrch	1	NR	NR	NR	-	-
419 So Bapt Conv	6	1,641	753	2,032 *	17.9	44.7
449 Un Methodist	4	445	204	551 *	4.8	12.1
LINCOLN	**108**	**14,932**	**6,567**	**19,510 ***	**62.3**	**100.0**
053 Assemb of God	1	137	194	194	.6	1.0
055 As Ref Pres Ch	3	630	NR	687	2.2	3.5
056 Baha'i	0	13	NR	13	-	.1
081 Catholic	1	NR	NR	311	1.0	1.6
123 Ch God (Ander)	2	NR	98	98	.3	.5
127 Ch God (Cleve)	1	62	35	76 *	.2	.4
151 L-D Saints	1	NR	NR	221	.7	1.1
165 Ch of Nazarene	1	112	24	112	.4	.6
167 Chs of Christ	34	2,547	2,484	3,205	10.2	16.4
185 Cumber Presb	9	445	NR	885	2.8	4.5
193 Episcopal	1	NR	107	254	.8	1.3
252 Hindu	1	NR	NR	NR	-	-
304 NatPrimBapt USA	3	51	NR	62 *	.2	.3
349 Pent Holiness	1	65	81	80 *	.3	.4
355 Presb Ch (USA)	3	306	197	385 *	1.2	2.0
413 S.D.A.	1	24	NR	29	.1	.1
419 So Bapt Conv	31	9,246	2,832	11,315 *	36.1	58.0
449 Un Methodist	14	1,294	515	1,583 *	5.1	8.1
LOUDON	**82**	**20,079**	**6,825**	**25,378 ***	**64.9**	**100.0**
053 Assemb of God	1	148	125	165	.4	.7
056 Baha'i	0	4	NR	4	-	-
081 Catholic	1	NR	NR	597	1.5	2.4
097 Chr Chs&Chs Cr	1	130	NR	157 *	.4	.6
123 Ch God (Ander)	1	NR	60	60	.2	.2
127 Ch God (Cleve)	7	1,593	533	1,921 *	4.9	7.6
151 L-D Saints	1	NR	NR	142	.4	.6
165 Ch of Nazarene	3	200	181	400	1.0	1.6
167 Chs of Christ	2	183	202	237	.6	.9
185 Cumber Presb	3	352	NR	442	1.1	1.7
193 Episcopal	1	NR	88	198	.5	.8
223 Free Will Bapt	2	195	NR	235 *	.6	.9

Religious Group	Number of Churches, Synagogues, Mosques, or Temples	Number of Communicant, Confirmed, or Full Members	Number of Attendees	Total Adherents		
				Number of Adherents	% of Total Pop.	% of Total Adh.
252 Hindu	1	NR	NR	NR	-	-
262 Int Cou Comm Ch	1	1,025	NR	1,236 *	3.2	4.9
283 Luth—MO Synod	1	90	60	91	.2	.4
355 Presb Ch (USA)	4	292	186	352 *	.9	1.4
365 Prog Prim Bapt	2	34	NR	41 *	.1	.2
413 S.D.A.	1	50	NR	60	.2	.2
418 Southw Bapt Fel	1	NR	NR	NR	-	-
419 So Bapt Conv	38	13,919	4,449	16,790 *	43.0	66.2
449 Un Methodist	10	1,864	941	2,250 *	5.8	8.9
MCMINN	**123**	**27,188**	**10,590**	**34,724 ***	**70.8**	**100.0**
053 Assemb of God	1	10	16	17	-	-
056 Baha'i	0	2	NR	2	-	-
081 Catholic	1	NR	NR	587	1.2	1.7
097 Chr Chs&Chs Cr	3	369	NR	454 *	.9	1.3
123 Ch God (Ander)	5	NR	315	315	.6	.9
127 Ch God (Cleve)	4	938	679	1,237 *	2.5	3.6
145 Ch God Prophcy	4	204	NR	252 *	.5	.7
165 Ch of Nazarene	2	109	138	213	.4	.6
167 Chs of Christ	12	588	602	736	1.5	2.1
193 Episcopal	1	NR	145	201	.4	.6
283 Luth—MO Synod	1	156	154	208	.4	.6
288 Mennonite USA	1	22	20	27 *	.1	.1
355 Presb Ch (USA)	3	239	158	294 *	.6	.8
419 So Bapt Conv	65	20,912	6,753	25,708 *	52.4	74.0
449 Un Methodist	20	3,639	1,610	4,473 *	9.1	12.9
MCNAIRY	**100**	**11,751**	**5,100**	**15,119 ***	**61.3**	**100.0**
032 Amish; other	1	42	NR	52 *	.2	.3
056 Baha'i	0	2	NR	2	-	-
081 Catholic	1	NR	NR	170	.7	1.1
097 Chr Chs&Chs Cr	3	310	NR	381 *	1.5	2.5
127 Ch God (Cleve)	3	180	88	220 *	.9	1.5
145 Ch God Prophcy	4	204	NR	252 *	1.0	1.7
151 L-D Saints	1	NR	NR	318	1.3	2.1
165 Ch of Nazarene	1	14	0	14	.1	.1
167 Chs of Christ	18	1,359	1,370	1,807	7.3	12.0
185 Cumber Presb	5	211	NR	316	1.3	2.1
223 Free Will Bapt	3	292	NR	358 *	1.5	2.4
339 Pent Ch of God	2	93	NR	125	.5	.8
355 Presb Ch (USA)	6	233	184	300 *	1.2	2.0
360 Prim Bapt Chrch	3	NR	NR	NR	-	-
413 S.D.A.	2	50	NR	59	.2	.4
418 Southw Bapt Fel	1	NR	NR	NR	-	-
419 So Bapt Conv	30	7,285	2,772	8,938 *	36.3	59.1
449 Un Methodist	16	1,476	686	1,807 *	7.3	12.0
MACON	**32**	**3,997**	**1,867**	**5,253 ***	**25.8**	**100.0**
053 Assemb of God	1	52	67	90	.4	1.7
081 Catholic	1	NR	NR	162	.8	3.1
127 Ch God (Cleve)	3	208	193	265 *	1.3	5.0
167 Chs of Christ	8	1,098	1,085	1,434	7.0	27.3
320 "Old" MB Ascs	9	1,673	NR	2,093 *	10.3	39.8
360 Prim Bapt Chrch	2	NR	NR	NR	-	-
419 So Bapt Conv	4	618	355	773 *	3.8	14.7
449 Un Methodist	4	348	167	436 *	2.1	8.3
MADISON	**113**	**37,374**	**15,182**	**50,180 ***	**54.6**	**100.0**
017 Amer Bapt Assn	1	50	NR	63 *	.1	.1
053 Assemb of God	3	497	627	868	.9	1.7
056 Baha'i	0	11	NR	11	-	-
081 Catholic	1	NR	NR	2,969	3.2	5.9
093 Chr Ch (Disc)	1	40	26	50 *	.1	.1
097 Chr Chs&Chs Cr	1	250	NR	313 *	.3	.6
127 Ch God (Cleve)	5	370	232	463 *	.5	.9
145 Ch God Prophcy	1	51	NR	64 *	.1	.1
151 L-D Saints	1	NR	NR	415	.5	.8
165 Ch of Nazarene	2	83	75	111	.1	.2
167 Chs of Christ	11	2,753	2,608	3,030	3.3	6.0
185 Cumber Presb	3	319	NR	542	.6	1.1
207 E.L.C.A.	1	143	49	164	.2	.3
223 Free Will Bapt	1	97	NR	122 *	.1	.2

NR–Not Reported *Total adherents estimated from known number of communicant, confirmed, full members. - Represents a percentage less than 0.1. Percentages may not total 100 due to rounding.

Table 4: Religious Congregations by County and Group: 2000

Religious Group	Number of Churches, Synagogues, Mosques, or Temples	Number of Communicant, Confirmed, or Full Members	Number of Attendees	Total Adherents		
				Number of Adherents	% of Total Pop.	% of Total Adh.
283 Luth—MO Synod	1	326	167	385	.4	.8
355 Presb Ch (USA)	2	706	239	884 *	1.0	1.8
356 Presb Ch Amer	2	115	75	135	.1	.3
360 Prim Bapt Chrch	2	NR	NR	NR	-	-
403 Salvation Army	1	107	38	161	.2	.3
413 S.D.A.	3	400	NR	476	.5	.9
419 So Bapt Conv	43	23,266	7,650	29,136 *	31.7	58.1
449 Un Methodist	25	7,315	2,896	9,158 *	10.0	18.3
496 Jewish Est	1	NR	NR	60	.1	.1
499 Indep.Non-Char	1	475	500	600	.7	1.2
MARION	**75**	**7,624**	**3,407**	**9,982 ***	**35.9**	**100.0**
056 Baha'i	0	2	NR	2	-	-
081 Catholic	2	NR	NR	162	.6	1.6
127 Ch God (Cleve)	14	1,297	776	1,591 *	5.7	15.9
165 Ch of Nazarene	3	118	97	162	.6	1.6
167 Chs of Christ	12	664	766	910	3.3	9.1
185 Cumber Presb	8	185	NR	401	1.4	4.0
193 Episcopal	1	NR	81	153	.6	1.5
304 NatPrimBapt USA	2	62	NR	76 *	.3	.8
360 Prim Bapt Chrch	1	NR	NR	NR	-	-
413 S.D.A.	1	130	NR	155	.6	1.6
418 Southw Bapt Fel	1	NR	NR	NR	-	-
419 So Bapt Conv	15	3,925	1,034	4,795 *	17.3	48.0
449 Un Methodist	14	1,241	653	1,515 *	5.5	15.2
496 Jewish Est	1	NR	NR	60	.2	.6
MARSHALL	**67**	**9,135**	**4,841**	**12,242 ***	**45.7**	**100.0**
032 Amish; other	1	31	NR	39 *	.1	.3
053 Assemb of God	1	84	103	140	.5	1.1
056 Baha'i	0	1	NR	1	-	-
081 Catholic	1	NR	NR	486	1.8	4.0
123 Ch God (Ander)	1	NR	95	95	.4	.8
127 Ch God (Cleve)	2	97	68	120 *	.4	1.0
145 Ch God Prophcy	2	102	NR	126 *	.5	1.0
165 Ch of Nazarene	1	109	36	109	.4	.9
167 Chs of Christ	22	2,307	2,423	3,006	11.2	24.6
185 Cumber Presb	4	256	NR	484	1.8	4.0
223 Free Will Bapt	1	97	NR	121 *	.5	1.0
304 NatPrimBapt USA	1	50	NR	62 *	.2	.5
355 Presb Ch (USA)	3	342	129	424 *	1.6	3.5
360 Prim Bapt Chrch	1	NR	NR	NR	-	-
419 So Bapt Conv	13	4,245	1,323	5,272 *	19.7	43.1
449 Un Methodist	13	1,414	664	1,757 *	6.6	14.4
MAURY	**158**	**22,648**	**13,195**	**33,657 ***	**48.4**	**100.0**
053 Assemb of God	1	271	287	520	.7	1.5
055 As Ref Pres Ch	1	47	NR	92	.1	.3
056 Baha'i	0	6	NR	6	-	-
081 Catholic	1	NR	NR	3,558	5.1	10.6
097 Chr Chs&Chs Cr	1	150	NR	187 *	.3	.6
127 Ch God (Cleve)	2	283	111	353 *	.5	1.0
145 Ch God Prophcy	1	51	NR	64 *	.1	.2
151 L-D Saints	1	NR	NR	666	1.0	2.0
165 Ch of Nazarene	7	712	752	997	1.4	3.0
167 Chs of Christ	53	6,137	6,222	7,614	11.0	22.6
185 Cumber Presb	9	518	NR	904	1.3	2.7
193 Episcopal	2	NR	199	502	.7	1.5
207 E.L.C.A.	1	49	45	81	.1	.2
223 Free Will Bapt	3	292	NR	364 *	.5	1.1
258 IndFreeWillBapt	1	58	NR	72 *	.1	.2
263 Int Foursq Gos	1	109	142	142 *	.2	.4
283 Luth—MO Synod	1	268	147	365	.5	1.1
304 NatPrimBapt USA	11	364	NR	454 *	.7	1.3
355 Presb Ch (USA)	6	973	488	1,215 *	1.7	3.6
356 Presb Ch Amer	1	238	250	329	.5	1.0
360 Prim Bapt Chrch	1	NR	NR	NR	-	-
413 S.D.A.	1	70	NR	83	.1	.2
418 Southw Bapt Fel	1	NR	NR	NR	-	-
419 So Bapt Conv	28	7,790	2,839	9,723 *	14.0	28.9
449 Un Methodist	22	4,028	1,493	5,027 *	7.2	14.9
469 WELS	1	234	220	339	.5	1.0

Religious Group	Number of Churches, Synagogues, Mosques, or Temples	Number of Communicant, Confirmed, or Full Members	Number of Attendees	Total Adherents		
				Number of Adherents	% of Total Pop.	% of Total Adh.
MEIGS	**31**	**3,998**	**1,864**	**4,957 ***	**44.7**	**100.0**
127 Ch God (Cleve)	3	425	362	528 *	4.8	10.7
167 Chs of Christ	1	40	55	50	.5	1.0
322 Old Ord Menn Ch	1	28	NR	35 *	.3	.7
413 S.D.A.	2	102	NR	121	1.1	2.4
419 So Bapt Conv	14	2,866	1,175	3,556 *	32.1	71.7
449 Un Methodist	10	537	272	667 *	6.0	13.5
MONROE	**110**	**20,045**	**7,826**	**24,921 ***	**64.0**	**100.0**
053 Assemb of God	1	362	152	325	.8	1.3
056 Baha'i	0	1	NR	1	-	-
081 Catholic	1	NR	NR	110	.3	.4
097 Chr Chs&Chs Cr	1	75	NR	93 *	.2	.4
123 Ch God (Ander)	1	NR	80	80	.2	.3
127 Ch God (Cleve)	4	493	281	611 *	1.6	2.5
145 Ch God Prophcy	1	51	NR	63 *	.2	.3
165 Ch of Nazarene	1	25	18	58	.1	.2
167 Chs of Christ	2	92	101	113	.3	.5
185 Cumber Presb	2	49	NR	74	.2	.3
207 E.L.C.A.	1	61	40	77	.2	.3
223 Free Will Bapt	3	292	NR	362 *	.9	1.5
226 Friends-USA	3	189	NR	234 *	.6	.9
355 Presb Ch (USA)	8	433	317	535 *	1.4	2.1
356 Presb Ch Amer	1	83	91	95	.2	.4
365 Prog Prim Bapt	1	25	NR	31 *	.1	.1
419 So Bapt Conv	64	16,155	5,807	20,006 *	51.3	80.3
443 Un C of Christ	1	106	140	131 *	.3	.5
449 Un Methodist	14	1,553	799	1,922 *	4.9	7.7
MONTGOMERY	**131**	**40,716**	**16,021**	**61,066 ***	**45.3**	**100.0**
017 Amer Bapt Assn	1	50	NR	65 *	-	.1
053 Assemb of God	3	1,935	1,706	2,109	1.6	3.5
056 Baha'i	1	19	NR	19	-	-
081 Catholic	1	NR	NR	5,578	4.1	9.1
089 Chr & Miss Al	1	33	NR	106	.1	.2
093 Chr Ch (Disc)	1	220	75	285 *	.2	.5
097 Chr Chs&Chs Cr	2	360	NR	467 *	.3	.8
123 Ch God (Ander)	3	NR	143	143	.1	.2
127 Ch God (Cleve)	1	569	325	738 *	.5	1.2
145 Ch God Prophcy	3	153	NR	198 *	.1	.3
151 L-D Saints	4	NR	NR	1,638	1.2	2.7
165 Ch of Nazarene	5	1,202	1,421	1,956	1.5	3.2
167 Chs of Christ	11	1,590	1,505	2,187	1.6	3.6
185 Cumber Presb	7	683	NR	1,181	.9	1.9
193 Episcopal	2	NR	150	530	.4	.9
207 E.L.C.A.	1	132	94	197	.1	.3
223 Free Will Bapt	5	487	NR	631 *	.5	1.0
268 Jain	1	NR	NR	NR	-	-
283 Luth—MO Synod	1	461	266	658	.5	1.1
355 Presb Ch (USA)	3	998	447	1,293 *	1.0	2.1
356 Presb Ch Amer	1	91	110	146	.1	.2
403 Salvation Army	1	78	48	100	.1	.2
413 S.D.A.	2	258	NR	307	.2	.5
419 So Bapt Conv	36	23,855	6,483	30,923 *	22.9	50.6
435 Unitarian-Univ	1	42	NR	54 *	-	.1
449 Un Methodist	30	6,310	2,498	8,181 *	6.1	13.4
463 Vineyard	1	550	300	713 *	.5	1.2
469 WELS	1	40	0	63	-	.1
499 Indep.Non-Char	1	600	450	600	.4	1.0
MOORE	**24**	**2,509**	**1,011**	**3,116 ***	**54.3**	**100.0**
032 Amish; other	1	30	NR	37 *	.6	1.2
056 Baha'i	0	2	NR	2	-	.1
081 Catholic	0	NR	NR	28	.5	.9
127 Ch God (Cleve)	1	38	20	46 *	.8	1.5
167 Chs of Christ	6	513	500	659	11.5	21.1
189 Duck Rivr Bapt	5	545	NR	663 *	11.6	21.3
365 Prog Prim Bapt	1	220	NR	268 *	4.7	8.6
419 So Bapt Conv	3	618	195	752 *	13.1	24.1
449 Un Methodist	7	543	296	661 *	11.5	21.2

NR–Not Reported *Total adherents estimated from known number of communicant, confirmed, full members. - Represents a percentage less than 0.1. Percentages may not total 100 due to rounding.

Table 4: Religious Congregations by County and Group: 2000

Religious Group	Number of Churches, Synagogues, Mosques, or Temples	Number of Communicant, Confirmed, or Full Members	Number of Attendees	Total Adherents: Number of Adherents	% of Total Pop.	% of Total Adh.
MORGAN	**44**	**7,386**	**2,527**	**9,179 ***	**46.5**	**100.0**
061 Beachy Amish	1	62	NR	75 *	.4	.8
081 Catholic	1	NR	NR	113	.6	1.2
127 Ch God (Cleve)	1	26	23	32 *	.2	.3
145 Ch God Prophcy	3	153	NR	186 *	.9	2.0
165 Ch of Nazarene	2	67	66	125	.6	1.4
167 Chs of Christ	2	80	86	104	.5	1.1
185 Cumber Presb	1	43	NR	63	.3	.7
193 Episcopal	1	NR	31	31	.2	.3
283 Luth—MO Synod	1	340	156	429	2.2	4.7
355 Presb Ch (USA)	2	52	35	63 *	.3	.7
360 Prim Bapt Chrch	1	NR	NR	NR	-	-
409 Separate Bapt	1	23	NR	28 *	.1	.3
413 S.D.A.	2	193	NR	229	1.2	2.5
419 So Bapt Conv	19	6,155	2,001	7,468 *	37.8	81.4
443 Un C of Christ	1	28	25	34 *	.2	.4
449 Un Methodist	5	164	104	199 *	1.0	2.2
OBION	**114**	**17,086**	**7,892**	**22,122 ***	**68.2**	**100.0**
053 Assemb of God	6	541	487	653	2.0	3.0
056 Baha'i	0	1	NR	1	-	-
081 Catholic	1	NR	NR	530	1.6	2.4
093 Chr Ch (Disc)	1	164	80	200 *	.6	.9
123 Ch God (Ander)	1	NR	76	76	.2	.3
127 Ch God (Cleve)	3	361	145	440 *	1.4	2.0
145 Ch God Prophcy	2	102	NR	124 *	.4	.6
167 Chs of Christ	26	1,720	1,811	2,218	6.8	10.0
185 Cumber Presb	15	744	NR	1,335	4.1	6.0
193 Episcopal	1	NR	42	133	.4	.6
283 Luth—MO Synod	1	148	58	184	.6	.8
355 Presb Ch (USA)	1	17	15	21 *	.1	.1
360 Prim Bapt Chrch	1	NR	NR	NR	-	-
413 S.D.A.	2	50	NR	60	.2	.3
419 So Bapt Conv	28	10,474	4,089	12,777 *	39.4	57.8
449 Un Methodist	25	2,764	1,089	3,370 *	10.4	15.2
OVERTON	**62**	**7,610**	**4,397**	**9,493 ***	**47.2**	**100.0**
053 Assemb of God	2	179	210	210	1.0	2.2
081 Catholic	0	NR	NR	96	.5	1.0
093 Chr Ch (Disc)	2	389	206	472 *	2.3	5.0
123 Ch God (Ander)	1	NR	102	102	.5	1.1
127 Ch God (Cleve)	2	155	89	196 *	1.0	2.1
145 Ch God Prophcy	2	102	NR	124 *	.6	1.3
165 Ch of Nazarene	1	11	0	11	.1	.1
167 Chs of Christ	14	1,147	1,252	1,421	7.1	15.0
185 Cumber Presb	2	28	NR	55	.3	.6
223 Free Will Bapt	1	97	NR	118 *	.6	1.2
258 IndFreeWillBapt	6	566	NR	687 *	3.4	7.2
355 Presb Ch (USA)	1	56	35	68 *	.3	.7
419 So Bapt Conv	12	3,227	1,380	3,916 *	19.5	41.3
449 Un Methodist	15	1,638	1,110	1,987 *	9.9	20.9
467 Wesleyan	1	15	13	30	.1	.3
PERRY	**30**	**2,635**	**1,477**	**3,280 ***	**43.0**	**100.0**
081 Catholic	0	NR	NR	11	.1	.3
097 Chr Chs&Chs Cr	1	280	NR	345 *	4.5	10.5
127 Ch God (Cleve)	1	136	120	167 *	2.2	5.1
143 CG in Cr(Menn)	1	52	NR	64 *	.8	2.0
167 Chs of Christ	8	550	620	705	9.2	21.5
322 Old Ord Menn Ch	1	53	NR	65 *	.9	2.0
360 Prim Bapt Chrch	4	NR	NR	NR	-	-
413 S.D.A.	1	48	NR	57	.7	1.7
419 So Bapt Conv	4	860	353	1,059 *	13.9	32.3
449 Un Methodist	9	656	384	807 *	10.6	24.6
PICKETT	**11**	**1,289**	**440**	**1,551 ***	**31.4**	**100.0**
093 Chr Ch (Disc)	1	55	0	66 *	1.3	4.3
097 Chr Chs&Chs Cr	2	358	NR	427 *	8.6	27.5
167 Chs of Christ	3	128	138	167	3.4	10.8
419 So Bapt Conv	3	679	251	809 *	16.4	52.2
449 Un Methodist	2	69	51	82 *	1.7	5.3

Religious Group	Number of Churches, Synagogues, Mosques, or Temples	Number of Communicant, Confirmed, or Full Members	Number of Attendees	Total Adherents: Number of Adherents	% of Total Pop.	% of Total Adh.
POLK	**62**	**10,321**	**3,819**	**12,614 ***	**78.6**	**100.0**
017 Amer Bapt Assn	1	35	NR	42 *	.3	.3
081 Catholic	1	NR	NR	78	.5	.6
127 Ch God (Cleve)	5	492	244	596 *	3.7	4.7
145 Ch God Prophcy	1	51	NR	62 *	.4	.5
167 Chs of Christ	3	138	113	163	1.0	1.3
193 Episcopal	1	NR	15	33	.2	.3
355 Presb Ch (USA)	1	72	55	87 *	.5	.7
419 So Bapt Conv	44	9,044	3,215	10,961 *	68.3	86.9
449 Un Methodist	5	489	177	592 *	3.7	4.7
PUTNAM	**146**	**25,643**	**12,931**	**34,707 ***	**55.7**	**100.0**
053 Assemb of God	3	1,512	1,624	2,249	3.6	6.5
056 Baha'i	0	3	NR	3	-	-
081 Catholic	1	NR	NR	1,530	2.5	4.4
093 Chr Ch (Disc)	1	56	15	68 *	.1	.2
097 Chr Chs&Chs Cr	1	300	NR	362 *	.6	1.0
123 Ch God (Ander)	3	NR	245	245	.4	.7
127 Ch God (Cleve)	7	337	274	441 *	.7	1.3
143 CG in Cr(Menn)	1	58	NR	70 *	.1	.2
145 Ch God Prophcy	2	102	NR	124 *	.2	.4
151 L-D Saints	2	NR	NR	748	1.2	2.2
165 Ch of Nazarene	2	353	270	474	.8	1.4
167 Chs of Christ	28	4,030	4,423	5,148	8.3	14.8
185 Cumber Presb	4	699	NR	789	1.3	2.3
189 Duck Rivr Bapt	1	66	NR	80 *	.1	.2
193 Episcopal	1	NR	160	423	.7	1.2
223 Free Will Bapt	6	584	NR	705 *	1.1	2.0
258 IndFreeWillBapt	22	2,209	NR	2,667 *	4.3	7.7
283 Luth—MO Synod	1	258	150	306	.5	.9
320 "Old" MB Ascs	1	38	NR	46 *	.1	.1
322 Old Ord Menn Ch	1	16	NR	19 *	-	.1
335 Orth Pres Ch	1	0	0	0	-	-
339 Pent Ch of God	1	25	NR	85	.1	.2
355 Presb Ch (USA)	5	425	164	513 *	.8	1.5
356 Presb Ch Amer	1	0	0	0	-	-
413 S.D.A.	2	259	NR	308	.5	.9
419 So Bapt Conv	34	11,154	4,322	13,467 *	21.6	38.8
449 Un Methodist	13	3,146	1,259	3,797 *	6.1	10.9
467 Wesleyan	1	13	25	40	.1	.1
RHEA	**65**	**10,064**	**4,365**	**12,892 ***	**45.4**	**100.0**
056 Baha'i	0	2	NR	2	-	-
081 Catholic	1	NR	NR	413	1.5	3.2
097 Chr Chs&Chs Cr	1	21	NR	26 *	.1	.2
127 Ch God (Cleve)	10	1,231	776	1,530 *	5.4	11.9
145 Ch God Prophcy	1	51	NR	62 *	.2	.5
167 Chs of Christ	4	272	314	384	1.4	3.0
193 Episcopal	1	NR	42	72	.3	.6
263 Int Foursq Gos	3	290	306	355 *	1.3	2.8
283 Luth—MO Synod	1	50	48	64	.2	.5
355 Presb Ch (USA)	1	68	48	83 *	.3	.6
356 Presb Ch Amer	1	33	75	75	.3	.6
388 Reg Bapt Gen As	1	100	125	125 *	.4	1.0
413 S.D.A.	4	438	NR	521	1.8	4.0
418 Southw Bapt Fel	2	NR	NR	NR	-	-
419 So Bapt Conv	21	5,665	1,882	6,926 *	24.4	53.7
449 Un Methodist	13	1,843	749	2,254 *	7.9	17.5
ROANE	**97**	**24,523**	**8,212**	**30,191 ***	**58.2**	**100.0**
053 Assemb of God	1	65	44	65	.1	.2
056 Baha'i	0	2	NR	2	-	-
081 Catholic	1	NR	NR	286	.6	.9
093 Chr Ch (Disc)	1	394	126	475 *	.9	1.6
097 Chr Chs&Chs Cr	8	1,153	NR	1,388 *	2.7	4.6
127 Ch God (Cleve)	4	383	254	462 *	.9	1.5
145 Ch God Prophcy	3	153	NR	183 *	.4	.6
151 L-D Saints	1	NR	NR	196	.4	.6
165 Ch of Nazarene	1	14	12	18	-	.1
167 Chs of Christ	6	688	680	903	1.7	3.0
185 Cumber Presb	2	151	NR	172	.3	.6
193 Episcopal	1	NR	50	78	.2	.3

NR–Not Reported *Total adherents estimated from known number of communicant, confirmed, full members. - Represents a percentage less than 0.1. Percentages may not total 100 due to rounding.

Table 4: Religious Congregations by County and Group: 2000

Religious Group	Number of Churches, Synagogues, Mosques, or Temples	Number of Communicant, Confirmed, or Full Members	Number of Attendees	Total Adherents: Number of Adherents	Total Adherents: % of Total Pop.	Total Adherents: % of Total Adh.
221 Free Methodist	1	8	32	32	.1	.1
263 Int Foursq Gos	1	198	75	239 *	.5	.8
283 Luth—MO Synod	1	155	63	195	.4	.6
304 NatPrimBapt USA	1	34	NR	41 *	.1	.1
355 Presb Ch (USA)	4	496	292	598 *	1.2	2.0
356 Presb Ch Amer	2	87	65	93	.2	.3
360 Prim Bapt Chrch	1	NR	NR	NR	-	-
413 S.D.A.	1	46	NR	55	.1	.2
419 So Bapt Conv	40	18,311	5,517	22,063 *	42.5	73.1
449 Un Methodist	15	2,164	983	2,607 *	5.0	8.6
467 Wesleyan	1	21	19	40	.1	.1
ROBERTSON	**92**	**21,759**	**8,889**	**28,766 ***	**52.8**	**100.0**
053 Assemb of God	2	203	213	338	.6	1.2
056 Baha'i	0	1	NR	1	-	-
081 Catholic	2	NR	NR	1,351	2.5	4.7
093 Chr Ch (Disc)	1	124	56	157 *	.3	.5
127 Ch God (Cleve)	1	69	52	87 *	.2	.3
145 Ch God Prophcy	1	51	NR	64 *	.1	.2
165 Ch of Nazarene	2	149	78	223	.4	.8
167 Chs of Christ	14	1,828	1,856	2,369	4.4	8.2
185 Cumber Presb	2	233	NR	427	.8	1.5
193 Episcopal	1	NR	14	20	-	.1
223 Free Will Bapt	4	389	NR	491 *	.9	1.7
355 Presb Ch (USA)	2	212	118	267 *	.5	.9
360 Prim Bapt Chrch	1	NR	NR	NR	-	-
413 S.D.A.	5	515	NR	613	1.1	2.1
418 Southw Bapt Fel	1	NR	NR	NR	-	-
419 So Bapt Conv	29	13,217	3,988	16,681 *	30.6	58.0
449 Un Methodist	23	3,468	1,414	4,377 *	8.0	15.2
499 Indep.Non-Char	1	1,300	1,100	1,300	2.4	4.5
RUTHERFORD	**212**	**47,105**	**26,059**	**68,519 ***	**37.6**	**100.0**
017 Amer Bapt Assn	1	42	NR	53 *	-	.1
053 Assemb of God	4	1,411	1,322	1,741	1.0	2.5
056 Baha'i	2	74	NR	74	-	.1
076 Buddhism	1	NR	NR	NR	-	-
081 Catholic	2	NR	NR	6,198	3.4	9.0
093 Chr Ch (Disc)	1	210	120	266 *	.1	.4
097 Chr Chs&Chs Cr	3	240	NR	303 *	.2	.4
123 Ch God (Ander)	2	NR	285	285	.2	.4
127 Ch God (Cleve)	5	454	299	581 *	.3	.8
145 Ch God Prophcy	2	102	NR	128 *	.1	.2
151 L-D Saints	3	NR	NR	1,204	.7	1.8
157 Ch of Brethren	1	8	0	10 *	-	-
165 Ch of Nazarene	2	282	177	315	.2	.5
167 Chs of Christ	52	7,060	7,727	9,107	5.0	13.3
185 Cumber Presb	7	532	NR	923	.5	1.3
189 Duck Rivr Bapt	5	267	NR	338 *	.2	.5
193 Episcopal	2	NR	403	730	.4	1.1
207 E.L.C.A.	1	174	107	211	.1	.3
221 Free Methodist	2	126	189	189	.1	.3
223 Free Will Bapt	4	389	NR	492 *	.3	.7
283 Luth—MO Synod	1	457	239	614	.3	.9
304 NatPrimBapt USA	7	455	NR	575 *	.3	.8
320 "Old" MB Ascs	1	59	NR	75 *	-	.1
355 Presb Ch (USA)	9	1,072	571	1,356 *	.7	2.0
356 Presb Ch Amer	1	198	240	266	.1	.4
360 Prim Bapt Chrch	3	NR	NR	NR	-	-
403 Salvation Army	1	47	28	85	-	.1
413 S.D.A.	2	200	NR	238	.1	.3
418 Southw Bapt Fel	1	NR	NR	NR	-	-
419 So Bapt Conv	53	24,398	9,657	30,848 *	16.9	45.0
435 Unitarian-Univ	1	17	NR	21 *	-	-
449 Un Methodist	26	7,059	3,083	8,926 *	4.9	13.0
467 Wesleyan	1	28	17	50	-	.1
469 WELS	1	44	45	67	-	.1
498 Indep.Charis.	1	250	450	450	.2	.7
499 Indep.Non-Char	1	1,450	1,100	1,800	1.0	2.6
SCOTT	**30**	**4,529**	**1,216**	**5,703 ***	**27.0**	**100.0**
053 Assemb of God	1	62	23	49	.2	.9
081 Catholic	1	NR	NR	65	.3	1.1

Religious Group	Number of Churches, Synagogues, Mosques, or Temples	Number of Communicant, Confirmed, or Full Members	Number of Attendees	Total Adherents: Number of Adherents	Total Adherents: % of Total Pop.	Total Adherents: % of Total Adh.
127 Ch God (Cleve)	2	139	96	174 *	.8	3.1
145 Ch God Prophcy	1	51	NR	64 *	.3	1.1
167 Chs of Christ	2	150	170	183	.9	3.2
355 Presb Ch (USA)	1	100	55	125 *	.6	2.2
409 Separate Bapt	1	7	NR	9 *	-	.2
419 So Bapt Conv	19	3,777	750	4,730 *	22.4	82.9
449 Un Methodist	2	243	122	304 *	1.4	5.3
SEQUATCHIE	**28**	**3,698**	**1,608**	**4,728 ***	**41.6**	**100.0**
081 Catholic	1	NR	NR	68	.6	1.4
127 Ch God (Cleve)	3	272	143	337 *	3.0	7.1
167 Chs of Christ	7	326	407	468	4.1	9.9
185 Cumber Presb	1	55	NR	83	.7	1.8
258 IndFreeWillBapt	1	80	NR	99 *	.9	2.1
360 Prim Bapt Chrch	2	NR	NR	NR	-	-
413 S.D.A.	1	129	NR	154	1.4	3.3
418 Southw Bapt Fel	1	NR	NR	NR	-	-
419 So Bapt Conv	8	2,271	803	2,818 *	24.8	59.6
449 Un Methodist	3	565	255	701 *	6.2	14.8
SEVIER	**124**	**27,586**	**12,209**	**35,690 ***	**50.1**	**100.0**
053 Assemb of God	2	164	150	173	.2	.5
056 Baha'i	0	16	NR	16	-	-
081 Catholic	3	NR	NR	1,581	2.2	4.4
097 Chr Chs&Chs Cr	2	550	NR	668 *	.9	1.9
123 Ch God (Ander)	1	NR	20	20	-	.1
127 Ch God (Cleve)	7	2,206	1,178	2,680 *	3.8	7.5
145 Ch God Prophcy	1	51	NR	62 *	.1	.2
151 L-D Saints	1	NR	NR	347	.5	1.0
167 Chs of Christ	6	253	543	341	.5	1.0
193 Episcopal	2	NR	132	267	.4	.7
207 E.L.C.A.	1	144	90	184	.3	.5
283 Luth—MO Synod	2	151	104	175	.2	.5
349 Pent Holiness	1	62	43	75 *	.1	.2
355 Presb Ch (USA)	3	226	171	275 *	.4	.8
356 Presb Ch Amer	1	160	210	210	.3	.6
360 Prim Bapt Chrch	4	NR	NR	NR	-	-
403 Salvation Army	1	19	26	19	-	.1
413 S.D.A.	1	82	NR	98	.1	.3
419 So Bapt Conv	62	19,484	7,473	23,675 *	33.3	66.3
449 Un Methodist	21	3,392	1,669	4,123 *	5.8	11.6
499 Indep.Non-Char	2	626	400	701	1.0	2.0
SHELBY	**541**	**236,048**	**89,267**	**371,466 ***	**41.4**	**100.0**
017 Amer Bapt Assn	8	1,295	NR	1,663 *	.2	.4
019 Amer Bapt USA	5	2,442	705	3,138 *	.3	.8
034 Ant Orth of NA	1	214	NR	428	-	.1
050 Armen Ap Etchm	1	30	NR	80	-	-
053 Assemb of God	18	6,663	4,522	6,587	.7	1.8
055 As Ref Pres Ch	2	324	NR	360	-	.1
056 Baha'i	2	189	NR	189	-	.1
059 Bapt Miss Assn	3	696	335	895 *	.1	.2
076 Buddhism	4	NR	NR	NR	-	-
081 Catholic	28	NR	NR	50,746	5.7	13.7
084 Calvary Chapel	2	NR	NR	NR	-	-
089 Chr & Miss Al	2	44	NR	64	-	-
093 Chr Ch (Disc)	13	13,549	5,380	17,410 *	1.9	4.7
097 Chr Chs&Chs Cr	6	1,675	NR	2,152 *	.2	.6
123 Ch God (Ander)	5	NR	196	196	-	.1
127 Ch God (Cleve)	6	701	274	901 *	.1	.2
145 Ch God Prophcy	3	153	NR	198 *	-	.1
151 L-D Saints	10	NR	NR	3,009	.3	.8
165 Ch of Nazarene	13	1,380	1,145	1,664	.2	.4
167 Chs of Christ	70	15,617	15,548	20,808	2.3	5.6
173 Comm of Christ	1	142	NR	142	-	-
185 Cumber Presb	12	1,219	NR	2,043	.2	.5
186 Coptic Orth Ch	1	NR	NR	NR	-	-
193 Episcopal	10	NR	1,407	4,122	.5	1.1
203 Evan Free Ch	2	94	120	120	-	-
207 E.L.C.A.	6	1,345	629	1,677	.2	.5
216 Evan Presby Ch	4	6,747	NR	8,670 *	1.0	2.3
223 Free Will Bapt	2	195	NR	250 *	-	.1
226 Friends-USA	1	64	NR	82 *	-	-

NR–Not Reported *Total adherents estimated from known number of communicant, confirmed, full members. - Represents a percentage less than 0.1. Percentages may not total 100 due to rounding.

Table 4: Religious Congregations by County and Group: 2000

Religious Group	Number of Churches, Synagogues, Mosques, or Temples	Number of Communicant, Confirmed, or Full Members	Number of Attendees	Total Adherents: Number of Adherents	Total Adherents: % of Total Pop.	Total Adherents: % of Total Adh.
246 Greek Orthodox	1	NR	NR	993	.1	.3
252 Hindu	2	NR	NR	NR	-	-
264 Int Chs of Crst	1	107	167	160	-	-
267 Muslim Est	3	NR	650	3,200	.4	.9
268 Jain	1	NR	NR	NR	-	-
283 Luth—MO Synod	12	3,515	2,017	4,803	.5	1.3
290 Metro Comm Ch	1	11	13	14 *	-	-
320 "Old" MB Ascs	2	75	NR	96 *	-	-
339 Pent Ch of God	2	64	NR	92	-	-
349 Pent Holiness	5	614	410	789 *	.1	.2
355 Presb Ch (USA)	28	8,285	4,100	10,645 *	1.2	2.9
356 Presb Ch Amer	5	2,673	1,698	2,830	.3	.8
360 Prim Bapt Chrch	5	NR	NR	NR	-	-
403 Salvation Army	3	407	279	542	.1	.1
413 S.D.A.	9	3,389	NR	4,033	.4	1.1
418 Southw Bapt Fel	1	NR	NR	NR	-	-
419 So Bapt Conv	129	117,805	30,909	151,377 *	16.9	40.8
435 Unitarian-Univ	3	624	NR	802 *	.1	.2
443 Un C of Christ	2	442	253	568 *	.1	.2
449 Un Methodist	65	37,652	13,309	48,382 *	5.4	13.0
463 Vineyard	1	130	120	167 *	-	-
467 Wesleyan	1	54	26	54	-	-
469 WELS	1	123	98	168	-	-
496 Jewish Est	6	NR	NR	8,500	.9	2.3
498 Indep.Charis.	3	2,850	2,150	2,850	.3	.8
499 Indep.Non-Char	8	2,450	2,807	2,807	.3	.8
SMITH	**52**	**4,857**	**2,049**	**6,280 ***	**35.5**	**100.0**
081 Catholic	1	NR	NR	27	.2	.4
127 Ch God (Cleve)	3	238	153	295 *	1.7	4.7
145 Ch God Prophcy	2	102	NR	126 *	.7	2.0
165 Ch of Nazarene	2	104	102	255	1.4	4.1
167 Chs of Christ	7	446	560	611	3.4	9.7
185 Cumber Presb	1	33	NR	80	.5	1.3
189 Duck Rivr Bapt	1	156	NR	194 *	1.1	3.1
223 Free Will Bapt	1	97	NR	121 *	.7	1.9
320 "Old" MB Ascs	1	33	NR	41 *	.2	.7
360 Prim Bapt Chrch	3	NR	NR	NR	-	-
413 S.D.A.	1	26	NR	31	.2	.5
419 So Bapt Conv	12	2,408	565	2,991 *	16.9	47.6
449 Un Methodist	17	1,214	669	1,508 *	8.5	24.0
STEWART	**57**	**5,139**	**2,317**	**7,121 ***	**57.6**	**100.0**
053 Assemb of God	1	38	45	45	.4	.6
056 Baha'i	0	3	NR	3	-	-
081 Catholic	1	NR	NR	260	2.1	3.7
093 Chr Ch (Disc)	1	135	79	165 *	1.3	2.3
123 Ch God (Ander)	4	NR	298	298	2.4	4.2
165 Ch of Nazarene	2	122	98	238	1.9	3.3
167 Chs of Christ	9	346	361	476	3.8	6.7
185 Cumber Presb	1	33	NR	72	.6	1.0
223 Free Will Bapt	5	487	NR	596 *	4.8	8.4
339 Pent Ch of God	1	91	NR	211	1.7	3.0
419 So Bapt Conv	17	2,823	887	3,457 *	27.9	48.5
449 Un Methodist	15	1,061	549	1,300 *	10.5	18.3
SULLIVAN	**238**	**62,703**	**25,072**	**79,882 ***	**52.2**	**100.0**
017 Amer Bapt Assn	1	50	NR	60 *	-	.1
019 Amer Bapt USA	1	350	140	421 *	.3	.5
053 Assemb of God	5	1,071	940	1,524	1.0	1.9
056 Baha'i	0	17	NR	17	-	-
081 Catholic	1	NR	NR	1,950	1.3	2.4
093 Chr Ch (Disc)	1	140	0	168 *	.1	.2
097 Chr Chs&Chs Cr	18	4,813	NR	5,786 *	3.8	7.2
123 Ch God (Ander)	4	NR	317	317	.2	.4
127 Ch God (Cleve)	7	870	547	1,123 *	.7	1.4
145 Ch God Prophcy	2	102	NR	122 *	.1	.2
151 L-D Saints	1	NR	NR	232	.2	.3
157 Ch of Brethren	5	215	83	259 *	.2	.3
165 Ch of Nazarene	3	204	185	318	.2	.4
167 Chs of Christ	6	461	563	632	.4	.8
193 Episcopal	5	NR	476	1,038	.7	1.3
203 Evan Free Ch	1	25	55	55	-	.1
207 E.L.C.A.	3	664	317	958	.6	1.2
216 Evan Presby Ch	2	113	NR	136 *	.1	.2
223 Free Will Bapt	19	1,849	NR	2,222 *	1.5	2.8
246 Greek Orthodox	1	NR	NR	147	.1	.2
258 IndFreeWillBapt	2	64	NR	77 *	.1	.1
283 Luth—MO Synod	2	152	117	196	.1	.2
335 Orth Pres Ch	1	40	45	56	-	.1
349 Pent Holiness	3	168	117	202 *	.1	.3
355 Presb Ch (USA)	20	4,744	2,406	5,725 *	3.7	7.2
356 Presb Ch Amer	7	881	796	1,038	.7	1.3
360 Prim Bapt Chrch	1	NR	NR	NR	-	-
362 Prim Bapt E Dst	6	858	NR	1,031 *	.7	1.3
370 Ref Baptist Chs	1	NR	NR	NR	-	-
403 Salvation Army	1	213	98	231	.2	.3
413 S.D.A.	1	133	NR	158	.1	.2
418 Southw Bapt Fel	2	NR	NR	NR	-	-
419 So Bapt Conv	55	29,186	11,510	35,083 *	22.9	43.9
449 Un Methodist	47	14,870	6,020	17,874 *	11.7	22.4
463 Vineyard	1	130	120	156 *	.1	.2
496 Jewish Est	1	NR	NR	70	-	.1
499 Indep.Non-Char	1	320	220	500	.3	.6
SUMNER	**137**	**40,246**	**19,507**	**56,815 ***	**43.6**	**100.0**
053 Assemb of God	5	458	579	737	.6	1.3
056 Baha'i	1	46	NR	46	-	.1
081 Catholic	2	NR	NR	4,340	3.3	7.6
127 Ch God (Cleve)	2	280	167	351 *	.3	.6
145 Ch God Prophcy	5	255	NR	320 *	.2	.6
151 L-D Saints	2	NR	NR	987	.8	1.7
165 Ch of Nazarene	4	1,001	657	1,209	.9	2.1
167 Chs of Christ	32	5,462	5,303	6,961	5.3	12.3
185 Cumber Presb	4	295	NR	507	.4	.9
193 Episcopal	2	NR	194	349	.3	.6
207 E.L.C.A.	1	581	271	785	.6	1.4
221 Free Methodist	2	53	97	97	.1	.2
223 Free Will Bapt	2	195	NR	243 *	.2	.4
263 Int Foursq Gos	1	37	115	115 *	.1	.2
283 Luth—MO Synod	3	407	237	480	.4	.8
320 "Old" MB Ascs	2	418	NR	523 *	.4	.9
355 Presb Ch (USA)	3	735	377	920 *	.7	1.6
413 S.D.A.	5	1,084	NR	1,291	1.0	2.3
418 Southw Bapt Fel	1	NR	NR	NR	-	-
419 So Bapt Conv	36	23,030	8,586	28,811 *	22.1	50.7
449 Un Methodist	21	5,909	2,574	7,393 *	5.7	13.0
498 Indep.Charis.	1	0	350	350	.3	.6
TIPTON	**84**	**15,392**	**6,350**	**21,224 ***	**41.4**	**100.0**
053 Assemb of God	10	782	867	1,436	2.8	6.8
055 As Ref Pres Ch	4	655	NR	695	1.4	3.3
056 Baha'i	0	4	NR	4	-	-
059 Bapt Miss Assn	1	90	50	116 *	.2	.5
081 Catholic	1	NR	NR	363	.7	1.7
097 Chr Chs&Chs Cr	2	340	NR	438 *	.9	2.1
151 L-D Saints	1	NR	NR	376	.7	1.8
165 Ch of Nazarene	2	117	75	136	.3	.6
167 Chs of Christ	8	712	808	1,067	2.1	5.0
185 Cumber Presb	4	388	NR	677	1.3	3.2
193 Episcopal	2	NR	31	48	.1	.2
216 Evan Presby Ch	1	30	NR	39 *	.1	.2
339 Pent Ch of God	1	13	NR	38	.1	.2
355 Presb Ch (USA)	3	516	246	665 *	1.3	3.1
356 Presb Ch Amer	1	15	16	16	-	.1
360 Prim Bapt Chrch	1	NR	NR	NR	-	-
413 S.D.A.	1	13	NR	15	-	.1
419 So Bapt Conv	22	8,911	3,129	11,479 *	22.4	54.1
449 Un Methodist	19	2,806	1,128	3,616 *	7.1	17.0
TROUSDALE	**16**	**1,443**	**659**	**1,919 ***	**26.4**	**100.0**
081 Catholic	1	NR	NR	93	1.3	4.8
145 Ch God Prophcy	1	51	NR	63 *	.9	3.3
167 Chs of Christ	4	275	325	393	5.4	20.5
185 Cumber Presb	1	14	NR	14	.2	.7
370 Ref Baptist Chs	1	NR	NR	NR	-	-

NR–Not Reported *Total adherents estimated from known number of communicant, confirmed, full members. - Represents a percentage less than 0.1. Percentages may not total 100 due to rounding.

Table 4: Religious Congregations by County and Group: 2000

Religious Group	Number of Churches, Synagogues, Mosques, or Temples	Number of Communicant, Confirmed, or Full Members	Number of Attendees	Total Adherents: Number of Adherents	Total Adherents: % of Total Pop.	Total Adherents: % of Total Adh.
419 So Bapt Conv	3	685	218	842 *	11.6	43.9
449 Un Methodist	5	418	116	514 *	7.1	26.8
UNICOI	**53**	**7,847**	**2,061**	**9,332 ***	**52.8**	**100.0**
053 Assemb of God	1	19	19	50	.3	.5
056 Baha'i	0	1	NR	1	-	-
097 Chr Chs&Chs Cr	6	863	NR	1,024 *	5.8	11.0
123 Ch God (Ander)	1	NR	0	0	-	-
127 Ch God (Cleve)	3	210	138	249 *	1.4	2.7
157 Ch of Brethren	2	94	0	111 *	.6	1.2
167 Chs of Christ	2	175	182	210	1.2	2.3
223 Free Will Bapt	7	681	NR	807 *	4.6	8.6
258 IndFreeWillBapt	9	647	NR	767 *	4.3	8.2
349 Pent Holiness	1	178	136	211 *	1.2	2.3
355 Presb Ch (USA)	3	276	165	327 *	1.9	3.5
418 Southw Bapt Fel	1	NR	NR	NR	-	-
419 So Bapt Conv	13	3,802	1,010	4,507 *	25.5	48.3
449 Un Methodist	4	901	411	1,068 *	6.0	11.4
UNION	**25**	**4,272**	**1,636**	**5,647 ***	**31.7**	**100.0**
053 Assemb of God	1	32	43	43	.2	.8
056 Baha'i	0	2	NR	2	-	-
151 L-D Saints	1	NR	NR	299	1.7	5.3
167 Chs of Christ	1	30	60	56	.3	1.0
360 Prim Bapt Chrch	2	NR	NR	NR	-	-
419 So Bapt Conv	16	4,044	1,443	5,043 *	28.3	89.3
449 Un Methodist	4	164	90	204 *	1.1	3.6
VAN BUREN	**23**	**1,473**	**926**	**1,885 ***	**34.2**	**100.0**
081 Catholic	1	NR	NR	4	.1	.2
127 Ch God (Cleve)	3	192	185	238 *	4.3	12.6
145 Ch God Prophcy	1	51	NR	62 *	1.1	3.3
167 Chs of Christ	10	370	495	535	9.7	28.4
189 Duck Rivr Bapt	1	100	NR	122 *	2.2	6.5
258 IndFreeWillBapt	1	80	NR	97 *	1.8	5.1
413 S.D.A.	1	57	NR	68	1.2	3.6
419 So Bapt Conv	5	623	246	759 *	13.8	40.3
WARREN	**120**	**15,027**	**8,861**	**20,115 ***	**52.6**	**100.0**
053 Assemb of God	4	254	330	559	1.5	2.8
056 Baha'i	0	5	NR	5	-	-
075 Brethren in Cr	1	122	95	122	.3	.6
081 Catholic	1	NR	NR	320	.8	1.6
123 Ch God (Ander)	1	NR	177	177	.5	.9
127 Ch God (Cleve)	5	422	186	519 *	1.4	2.6
145 Ch God Prophcy	3	153	NR	189 *	.5	.9
151 L-D Saints	1	NR	NR	430	1.1	2.1
165 Ch of Nazarene	1	34	0	34	.1	.2
167 Chs of Christ	42	4,575	4,835	5,968	15.6	29.7
185 Cumber Presb	7	278	NR	398	1.0	2.0
189 Duck Rivr Bapt	7	821	NR	1,010 *	2.6	5.0
193 Episcopal	1	NR	80	100	.3	.5
221 Free Methodist	1	31	46	46	.1	.2
223 Free Will Bapt	2	195	NR	239 *	.6	1.2
258 IndFreeWillBapt	1	54	NR	66 *	.2	.3
283 Luth—MO Synod	1	23	29	24	.1	.1
355 Presb Ch (USA)	2	158	80	194 *	.5	1.0
360 Prim Bapt Chrch	1	NR	NR	NR	-	-
413 S.D.A.	1	156	NR	186	.5	.9
419 So Bapt Conv	21	6,104	2,295	7,508 *	19.6	37.3
426 2Seed Sprt Bpt	1	10	NR	12 *	-	.1
449 Un Methodist	15	1,632	708	2,009 *	5.2	10.0
WASHINGTON	**198**	**44,458**	**15,564**	**58,004 ***	**54.1**	**100.0**
034 Ant Orth of NA	1	24	NR	48	-	.1
053 Assemb of God	4	247	246	366	.3	.6
056 Baha'i	0	23	NR	23	-	-
081 Catholic	1	NR	NR	2,123	2.0	3.7
084 Calvary Chapel	1	NR	NR	NR	-	-
089 Chr & Miss Al	1	44	NR	86	.1	.1
093 Chr Ch (Disc)	1	0	0	0 *	-	-
097 Chr Chs&Chs Cr	27	5,978	NR	7,162 *	6.7	12.3

Religious Group	Number of Churches, Synagogues, Mosques, or Temples	Number of Communicant, Confirmed, or Full Members	Number of Attendees	Total Adherents: Number of Adherents	Total Adherents: % of Total Pop.	Total Adherents: % of Total Adh.
123 Ch God (Ander)	5	NR	255	255	.2	.4
127 Ch God (Cleve)	6	662	472	792 *	.7	1.4
145 Ch God Prophcy	1	51	NR	61 *	.1	.1
151 L-D Saints	1	NR	NR	321	.3	.6
157 Ch of Brethren	8	577	225	693 *	.6	1.2
165 Ch of Nazarene	3	188	69	661	.6	1.1
167 Chs of Christ	8	719	786	963	.9	1.7
185 Cumber Presb	2	69	NR	119	.1	.2
193 Episcopal	1	NR	237	832	.8	1.4
207 E.L.C.A.	1	483	216	637	.6	1.1
221 Free Methodist	1	28	75	75	.1	.1
223 Free Will Bapt	16	1,557	NR	1,865 *	1.7	3.2
258 IndFreeWillBapt	5	269	NR	322 *	.3	.6
267 Muslim Est	1	NR	156	609	.6	1.0
283 Luth—MO Synod	1	248	113	298	.3	.5
290 Metro Comm Ch	1	18	20	22 *	-	-
349 Pent Holiness	1	17	29	20 *	-	-
355 Presb Ch (USA)	10	1,666	835	1,995 *	1.9	3.4
356 Presb Ch Amer	5	549	437	708	.7	1.2
403 Salvation Army	1	216	131	366	.3	.6
418 Southw Bapt Fel	2	NR	NR	NR	-	-
419 So Bapt Conv	48	19,272	6,553	23,086 *	21.5	39.8
435 Unitarian-Univ	1	104	NR	125 *	.1	.2
449 Un Methodist	31	9,569	3,946	11,464 *	10.7	19.8
469 WELS	1	80	63	107	.1	.2
499 Indep.Non-Char	1	1,800	700	1,800	1.7	3.1
WAYNE	**72**	**6,246**	**3,060**	**7,551 ***	**44.8**	**100.0**
056 Baha'i	0	5	NR	5	-	.1
081 Catholic	1	NR	NR	73	.4	1.0
093 Chr Ch (Disc)	1	40	0	48 *	.3	.6
127 Ch God (Cleve)	4	312	237	372 *	2.2	4.9
145 Ch God Prophcy	1	51	NR	61 *	.4	.8
165 Ch of Nazarene	1	9	0	9	.1	.1
167 Chs of Christ	11	736	848	875	5.2	11.6
185 Cumber Presb	1	63	NR	116	.7	1.5
223 Free Will Bapt	2	195	NR	232 *	1.4	3.1
258 IndFreeWillBapt	10	802	NR	955 *	5.7	12.6
349 Pent Holiness	1	70	85	83 *	.5	1.1
355 Presb Ch (USA)	1	72	44	86 *	.5	1.1
413 S.D.A.	2	22	NR	26	.2	.3
419 So Bapt Conv	23	2,949	1,305	3,513 *	20.9	46.5
449 Un Methodist	13	920	541	1,097 *	6.5	14.5
WEAKLEY	**115**	**17,684**	**8,304**	**22,110 ***	**63.4**	**100.0**
053 Assemb of God	4	156	191	303	.9	1.4
056 Baha'i	0	1	NR	1	-	-
081 Catholic	1	NR	NR	283	.8	1.3
097 Chr Chs&Chs Cr	1	80	NR	96 *	.3	.4
145 Ch God Prophcy	1	51	NR	61 *	.2	.3
151 L-D Saints	1	NR	NR	304	.9	1.4
165 Ch of Nazarene	1	21	8	21	.1	.1
167 Chs of Christ	18	1,703	1,703	2,142	6.1	9.7
185 Cumber Presb	9	320	NR	472	1.4	2.1
193 Episcopal	1	NR	8	2	-	-
339 Pent Ch of God	1	31	NR	71	.2	.3
349 Pent Holiness	1	35	30	42 *	.1	.2
355 Presb Ch (USA)	2	215	161	257 *	.7	1.2
360 Prim Bapt Chrch	5	NR	NR	NR	-	-
419 So Bapt Conv	46	12,800	5,048	15,333 *	43.9	69.3
449 Un Methodist	23	2,271	1,155	2,722 *	7.8	12.3
WHITE	**94**	**10,565**	**5,236**	**13,114 ***	**56.8**	**100.0**
053 Assemb of God	1	80	50	70	.3	.5
075 Brethren in Cr	1	67	31	67	.3	.5
081 Catholic	1	NR	NR	211	.9	1.6
093 Chr Ch (Disc)	1	105	0	128 *	.6	1.0
127 Ch God (Cleve)	7	872	497	1,065 *	4.6	8.1
145 Ch God Prophcy	2	102	NR	124 *	.5	.9
165 Ch of Nazarene	2	270	244	368	1.6	2.8
167 Chs of Christ	26	1,906	2,025	2,341	10.1	17.9
185 Cumber Presb	2	20	NR	20	.1	.2
189 Duck Rivr Bapt	3	487	NR	594 *	2.6	4.5

NR–Not Reported *Total adherents estimated from known number of communicant, confirmed, full members. - Represents a percentage less than 0.1. Percentages may not total 100 due to rounding.

Table 4: Religious Congregations by County and Group: 2000

Religious Group	Number of Churches, Synagogues, Mosques, or Temples	Number of Communicant, Confirmed, or Full Members	Number of Attendees	Total Adherents: Number of Adherents	Total Adherents: % of Total Pop.	Total Adherents: % of Total Adh.
223 Free Will Bapt	1	97	NR	119 *	.5	.9
258 IndFreeWillBapt	9	833	NR	1,016 *	4.4	7.7
297 Mennonite;Other	1	63	NR	77 *	.3	.6
355 Presb Ch (USA)	4	95	81	124 *	.5	.9
419 So Bapt Conv	17	4,277	1,676	5,216 *	22.6	39.8
449 Un Methodist	16	1,291	632	1,574 *	6.8	12.0
WILLIAMSON	**156**	**38,579**	**23,658**	**69,894 ***	**55.2**	**100.0**
034 Ant Orth of NA	1	270	NR	540	.4	.8
053 Assemb of God	1	113	75	100	.1	.1
056 Baha'i	3	98	NR	98	.1	.1
081 Catholic	3	NR	NR	14,367	11.3	20.6
084 Calvary Chapel	2	NR	NR	NR	-	-
089 Chr & Miss Al	1	50	NR	70	.1	.1
097 Chr Chs&Chs Cr	1	500	NR	648 *	.5	.9
127 Ch God (Cleve)	1	230	97	298 *	.2	.4
151 L-D Saints	4	NR	NR	1,713	1.4	2.5
165 Ch of Nazarene	4	376	371	521	.4	.7
167 Chs of Christ	37	4,608	4,898	6,192	4.9	8.9
185 Cumber Presb	8	566	NR	904	.7	1.3
193 Episcopal	3	NR	675	1,540	1.2	2.2
207 E.L.C.A.	2	530	240	761	.6	1.1
223 Free Will Bapt	2	195	NR	252 *	.2	.4
252 Hindu	1	NR	NR	NR	-	-
263 Int Foursq Gos	2	457	1,306	1,306 *	1.0	1.9
283 Luth—MO Synod	1	110	97	162	.1	.2
304 NatPrimBapt USA	14	1,153	NR	1,494 *	1.2	2.1
355 Presb Ch (USA)	7	1,866	1,082	2,416 *	1.9	3.5
356 Presb Ch Amer	1	2,209	3,000	3,502	2.8	5.0
360 Prim Bapt Chrch	7	NR	NR	NR	-	-
371 Ref Ch in Am	1	28	74	79	.1	.1
419 So Bapt Conv	26	13,846	6,414	17,937 *	14.2	25.7
449 Un Methodist	22	10,724	4,229	13,894 *	11.0	19.9
499 Indep.Non-Char	1	650	1,100	1,100	.9	1.6
WILSON	**132**	**30,126**	**14,678**	**42,511 ***	**47.9**	**100.0**
053 Assemb of God	2	75	118	178	.2	.4
056 Baha'i	1	37	NR	37	-	.1
081 Catholic	2	NR	NR	3,785	4.3	8.9
097 Chr Chs&Chs Cr	1	100	NR	126 *	.1	.3
123 Ch God (Ander)	1	NR	48	48	.1	.1
127 Ch God (Cleve)	2	869	425	1,092 *	1.2	2.6
145 Ch God Prophcy	2	102	NR	128 *	.1	.3
151 L-D Saints	2	NR	NR	441	.5	1.0
165 Ch of Nazarene	3	540	409	667	.8	1.6
167 Chs of Christ	35	4,326	4,054	5,429	6.1	12.8
185 Cumber Presb	7	542	NR	819	.9	1.9
193 Episcopal	2	NR	80	154	.2	.4
207 E.L.C.A.	2	478	346	634	.7	1.5
221 Free Methodist	1	11	30	30	-	.1
304 NatPrimBapt USA	2	140	NR	176 *	.2	.4
320 "Old" MB Ascs	2	202	NR	254 *	.3	.6
355 Presb Ch (USA)	3	290	211	364 *	.4	.9
360 Prim Bapt Chrch	1	NR	NR	NR	-	-
413 S.D.A.	1	23	NR	27	-	.1
419 So Bapt Conv	40	18,406	7,178	23,117 *	26.0	54.4
449 Un Methodist	20	3,985	1,779	5,005 *	5.6	11.8

TEXAS

Religious Group	Number of Churches, Synagogues, Mosques, or Temples	Number of Communicant, Confirmed, or Full Members	Number of Attendees	Total Adherents: Number of Adherents	Total Adherents: % of Total Pop.	Total Adherents: % of Total Adh.
The State.....	18,466	5,138,122	2,303,903	11,573,549 *	55.5	100.0
ANDERSON	**104**	**20,646**	**7,519**	**30,249 ***	**54.9**	**100.0**
017 Amer Bapt Assn	8	696	NR	827 *	1.5	2.7
053 Assemb of God	13	1,011	1,150	1,610	2.9	5.3
056 Baha'i	0	3	NR	3	-	-
059 Bapt Miss Assn	6	1,172	391	1,391 *	2.5	4.6
081 Catholic	2	NR	NR	4,678	8.5	15.5
093 Chr Ch (Disc)	4	305	116	362 *	.7	1.2
097 Chr Chs&Chs Cr	1	52	NR	62 *	.1	.2
127 Ch God (Cleve)	1	143	102	170 *	.3	.6
145 Ch God Prophcy	1	27	NR	32 *	.1	.1
151 L-D Saints	1	NR	NR	253	.5	.8
165 Ch of Nazarene	1	44	45	85	.2	.3
167 Chs of Christ	14	1,171	1,010	1,410	2.6	4.7
193 Episcopal	1	NR	126	372	.7	1.2
283 Luth—MO Synod	1	201	90	277	.5	.9
304 NatPrimBapt USA	2	90	NR	107 *	.2	.4
355 Presb Ch (USA)	2	228	104	270 *	.5	.9
413 S.D.A.	2	82	NR	98	.2	.3
419 So Bapt Conv	28	12,970	3,397	15,398 *	27.9	50.9
449 Un Methodist	15	2,101	879	2,494 *	4.5	8.2
499 Indep.Non-Char	1	350	109	350	.6	1.2
ANDREWS	**26**	**6,181**	**2,295**	**10,976 ***	**84.4**	**100.0**
017 Amer Bapt Assn	1	96	NR	125 *	1.0	1.1
053 Assemb of God	4	357	424	666	5.1	6.1
081 Catholic	1	NR	NR	2,640	20.3	24.1
093 Chr Ch (Disc)	1	15	10	19 *	.1	.2
097 Chr Chs&Chs Cr	1	35	NR	45 *	.3	.4
127 Ch God (Cleve)	1	157	51	204 *	1.6	1.9
151 L-D Saints	1	NR	NR	79	.6	.7
165 Ch of Nazarene	1	30	32	45	.3	.4
167 Chs of Christ	2	515	430	688	5.3	6.3
193 Episcopal	1	NR	9	12	.1	.1
283 Luth—MO Synod	1	38	26	45	.3	.4
355 Presb Ch (USA)	1	71	48	92 *	.7	.8
360 Prim Bapt Chrch	1	NR	NR	NR	-	-
419 So Bapt Conv	7	4,340	1,108	5,632 *	43.3	51.3
449 Un Methodist	2	527	157	684 *	5.3	6.2
ANGELINA	**129**	**35,426**	**13,873**	**54,588 ***	**68.1**	**100.0**
017 Amer Bapt Assn	10	1,150	NR	1,465 *	1.8	2.7
040 Ap Chr Ch-Amer	1	8	15	15 *	-	-
053 Assemb of God	11	2,858	2,422	3,465	4.3	6.3
056 Baha'i	0	35	NR	35	-	.1
059 Bapt Miss Assn	23	6,156	2,153	7,840 *	9.8	14.4
081 Catholic	2	NR	NR	8,302	10.4	15.2
093 Chr Ch (Disc)	1	1,023	216	1,303 *	1.6	2.4
127 Ch God (Cleve)	1	196	49	250 *	.3	.5
151 L-D Saints	1	NR	NR	304	.4	.6
165 Ch of Nazarene	1	295	172	295	.4	.5
167 Chs of Christ	17	2,198	1,998	2,741	3.4	5.0
193 Episcopal	1	NR	227	540	.7	1.0
207 E.L.C.A.	1	110	71	125	.2	.2
267 Muslim Est	1	NR	25	50	.1	.1
283 Luth—MO Synod	1	249	91	309	.4	.6
333 Malan Dioc Am	1	NR	NR	75	.1	.1
339 Pent Ch of God	1	16	NR	38	-	.1
355 Presb Ch (USA)	1	360	145	458 *	.6	.8
356 Presb Ch Amer	1	31	24	35	-	.1
403 Salvation Army	1	120	97	694	.9	1.3
413 S.D.A.	2	98	NR	116	.1	.2
419 So Bapt Conv	37	17,078	4,786	21,746 *	27.1	39.8
435 Unitarian-Univ	1	14	NR	18 *	-	-
449 Un Methodist	12	3,431	1,382	4,369 *	5.5	8.0
ARANSAS	**17**	**3,603**	**2,079**	**8,034 ***	**35.7**	**100.0**
053 Assemb of God	1	78	85	85	.4	1.1
081 Catholic	2	NR	NR	3,370	15.0	41.9
123 Ch God (Ander)	1	NR	65	65	.3	.8
167 Chs of Christ	3	177	205	218	1.0	2.7
193 Episcopal	1	NR	169	233	1.0	2.9
283 Luth—MO Synod	1	231	124	272	1.2	3.4
339 Pent Ch of God	1	80	NR	100	.4	1.2
349 Pent Holiness	1	60	78	73 *	.3	.9
355 Presb Ch (USA)	1	312	180	379 *	1.7	4.7
419 So Bapt Conv	4	2,244	846	2,727 *	12.1	33.9
449 Un Methodist	1	421	327	512 *	2.3	6.4
ARCHER	**20**	**3,886**	**1,247**	**6,337 ***	**71.6**	**100.0**
053 Assemb of God	2	78	90	178	2.0	2.8
056 Baha'i	0	6	NR	6	.1	.1
081 Catholic	3	NR	NR	1,367	15.4	21.6

NR–Not Reported *Total adherents estimated from known number of communicant, confirmed, full members. - Represents a percentage less than 0.1. Percentages may not total 100 due to rounding.

Table 4: Religious Congregations by County and Group: 2000

Religious Group	Number of Churches, Synagogues, Mosques, or Temples	Number of Communicant, Confirmed, or Full Members	Number of Attendees	Total Adherents: Number of Adherents	Total Adherents: % of Total Pop.	Total Adherents: % of Total Adh.
093 Chr Ch (Disc)	1	54	21	68 *	.8	1.1
167 Chs of Christ	3	222	212	262	3.0	4.1
419 So Bapt Conv	8	3,129	760	3,954 *	44.7	62.4
449 Un Methodist	3	397	164	502 *	5.7	7.9
ARMSTRONG	**7**	**1,249**	**361**	**1,556 ***	**72.4**	**100.0**
093 Chr Ch (Disc)	1	14	7	17 *	.8	1.1
167 Chs of Christ	1	50	60	65	3.0	4.2
419 So Bapt Conv	3	874	158	1,087 *	50.6	69.9
449 Un Methodist	2	311	136	387 *	18.0	24.9
ATASCOSA	**49**	**6,363**	**2,810**	**24,206 ***	**62.7**	**100.0**
053 Assemb of God	5	191	240	309	.8	1.3
081 Catholic	6	NR	NR	15,700	40.6	64.9
127 Ch God (Cleve)	2	44	61	69 *	.2	.3
167 Chs of Christ	6	455	382	608	1.6	2.5
193 Episcopal	1	NR	26	49	.1	.2
203 Evan Free Ch	1	124	150	150	.4	.6
207 E.L.C.A.	1	375	116	461	1.2	1.9
220 Free Lutheran	1	41	32	50	.1	.2
339 Pent Ch of God	1	26	NR	66	.2	.3
355 Presb Ch (USA)	1	59	25	78 *	.2	.3
413 S.D.A.	1	36	NR	43	.1	.2
419 So Bapt Conv	16	3,936	1,341	5,200 *	13.5	21.5
449 Un Methodist	7	1,076	437	1,423 *	3.7	5.9
AUSTIN	**31**	**5,576**	**2,525**	**12,220 ***	**51.8**	**100.0**
053 Assemb of God	1	325	350	418	1.8	3.4
056 Baha'i	0	4	NR	4	-	-
081 Catholic	6	NR	NR	4,876	20.7	39.9
145 Ch God Prophcy	1	27	NR	34 *	.1	.3
167 Chs of Christ	3	143	153	185	.8	1.5
193 Episcopal	2	NR	151	371	1.6	3.0
207 E.L.C.A.	2	1,120	346	1,372	5.8	11.2
283 Luth—MO Synod	2	694	303	861	3.6	7.0
339 Pent Ch of God	1	5	NR	11	-	.1
355 Presb Ch (USA)	1	96	45	120 *	.5	1.0
419 So Bapt Conv	4	1,758	628	2,206 *	9.4	18.1
449 Un Methodist	8	1,404	549	1,762 *	7.5	14.4
BAILEY	**18**	**3,208**	**1,218**	**5,643 ***	**85.6**	**100.0**
053 Assemb of God	2	140	180	180	2.7	3.2
056 Baha'i	0	3	NR	3	-	.1
059 Bapt Miss Assn	1	60	60	78 *	1.2	1.4
081 Catholic	1	NR	NR	1,549	23.5	27.4
165 Ch of Nazarene	1	48	10	48	.7	.9
167 Chs of Christ	3	362	308	410	6.2	7.3
360 Prim Bapt Chrch	1	NR	NR	NR	-	-
419 So Bapt Conv	7	1,967	476	2,558 *	38.8	45.3
449 Un Methodist	2	628	184	817 *	12.4	14.5
BANDERA	**22**	**3,423**	**1,651**	**7,435 ***	**42.1**	**100.0**
053 Assemb of God	1	36	48	48	.3	.6
056 Baha'i	0	4	NR	4	-	.1
076 Buddhism	1	NR	NR	NR	-	-
081 Catholic	1	NR	NR	3,078	17.4	41.4
097 Chr Chs&Chs Cr	1	250	NR	306 *	1.7	4.1
167 Chs of Christ	4	270	330	332	1.9	4.5
173 Comm of Christ	1	53	NR	53	.3	.7
193 Episcopal	1	NR	89	147	.8	2.0
207 E.L.C.A.	1	250	167	315	1.8	4.2
339 Pent Ch of God	1	15	NR	35	.2	.5
355 Presb Ch (USA)	1	136	68	167 *	.9	2.2
419 So Bapt Conv	6	1,600	578	1,959 *	11.1	26.3
449 Un Methodist	3	809	371	991 *	5.6	13.3
BASTROP	**77**	**12,344**	**4,767**	**24,381 ***	**42.2**	**100.0**
053 Assemb of God	3	167	218	262	.5	1.1
056 Baha'i	0	84	NR	84	.1	.3
061 Beachy Amish	1	24	NR	31 *	.1	.1
076 Buddhism	1	NR	NR	NR	-	-

Religious Group	Number of Churches, Synagogues, Mosques, or Temples	Number of Communicant, Confirmed, or Full Members	Number of Attendees	Total Adherents: Number of Adherents	Total Adherents: % of Total Pop.	Total Adherents: % of Total Adh.
081 Catholic	7	NR	NR	7,624	13.2	31.3
093 Chr Ch (Disc)	3	246	90	314 *	.5	1.3
097 Chr Chs&Chs Cr	1	26	NR	33 *	.1	.1
123 Ch God (Ander)	1	NR	10	10	-	-
151 L-D Saints	1	NR	NR	538	.9	2.2
165 Ch of Nazarene	2	56	53	63	.1	.3
167 Chs of Christ	7	425	429	588	1.0	2.4
193 Episcopal	1	NR	167	397	.7	1.6
203 Evan Free Ch	3	219	235	280	.5	1.1
207 E.L.C.A.	6	902	429	1,118	1.9	4.6
283 Luth—MO Synod	3	772	449	1,024	1.8	4.2
304 NatPrimBapt USA	6	745	NR	952 *	1.6	3.9
355 Presb Ch (USA)	3	260	127	332 *	.6	1.4
413 S.D.A.	3	268	NR	319	.6	1.3
419 So Bapt Conv	19	6,547	1,849	8,364 *	14.5	34.3
449 Un Methodist	6	1,603	711	2,048 *	3.5	8.4
BAYLOR	**13**	**2,980**	**909**	**4,163 ***	**101.7**	**100.0**
053 Assemb of God	2	52	62	108	2.6	2.6
081 Catholic	1	NR	NR	568	13.9	13.6
127 Ch God (Cleve)	1	5	5	6 *	.1	.1
167 Chs of Christ	1	218	100	218	5.3	5.2
283 Luth—MO Synod	1	24	15	25	.6	.6
355 Presb Ch (USA)	1	92	49	111 *	2.7	2.7
419 So Bapt Conv	5	2,265	560	2,736 *	66.8	65.7
449 Un Methodist	1	324	118	391 *	9.6	9.4
BEE	**48**	**5,094**	**2,501**	**13,795 ***	**42.6**	**100.0**
053 Assemb of God	2	127	185	205	.6	1.5
056 Baha'i	0	3	NR	3	-	-
081 Catholic	8	NR	NR	6,886	21.3	49.9
093 Chr Ch (Disc)	2	99	48	120 *	.4	.9
127 Ch God (Cleve)	1	18	21	22 *	.1	.2
151 L-D Saints	1	NR	NR	267	.8	1.9
165 Ch of Nazarene	1	17	0	17	.1	.1
167 Chs of Christ	2	293	331	357	1.1	2.6
193 Episcopal	1	NR	87	206	.6	1.5
207 E.L.C.A.	2	312	143	406	1.3	2.9
323 Old Ord Amish	1	6	NR	7 *	-	.1
339 Pent Ch of God	1	77	NR	268	.8	1.9
355 Presb Ch (USA)	1	260	112	316 *	1.0	2.3
413 S.D.A.	1	38	NR	45	.1	.3
419 So Bapt Conv	18	3,144	1,202	3,819 *	11.8	27.7
443 Un C of Christ	1	34	21	41 *	.1	.3
449 Un Methodist	5	666	351	810 *	2.5	5.9
BELL	**192**	**64,357**	**26,481**	**114,006 ***	**47.9**	**100.0**
017 Amer Bapt Assn	1	32	NR	42 *	-	-
053 Assemb of God	12	1,390	1,638	2,798	1.2	2.5
056 Baha'i	0	321	NR	321	.1	.3
059 Bapt Miss Assn	1	75	50	98 *	-	.1
076 Buddhism	1	NR	NR	NR	-	-
081 Catholic	10	NR	NR	25,068	10.5	22.0
093 Chr Ch (Disc)	5	1,458	885	1,896 *	.8	1.7
097 Chr Chs&Chs Cr	2	181	NR	236 *	.1	.2
123 Ch God (Ander)	1	NR	4	4	-	-
127 Ch God (Cleve)	1	265	105	345 *	.1	.3
145 Ch God Prophcy	1	27	NR	35 *	-	-
151 L-D Saints	5	NR	NR	2,150	.9	1.9
165 Ch of Nazarene	5	610	394	718	.3	.6
167 Chs of Christ	26	3,609	3,439	4,708	2.0	4.1
193 Episcopal	4	NR	561	1,798	.8	1.6
207 E.L.C.A.	4	1,367	618	1,672	.7	1.5
263 Int Foursq Gos	1	23	49	49 *	-	-
267 Muslim Est	2	NR	176	629	.3	.6
283 Luth—MO Synod	3	1,557	893	2,224	.9	2.0
339 Pent Ch of God	5	161	NR	222	.1	.2
355 Presb Ch (USA)	5	1,001	547	1,301 *	.5	1.1
356 Presb Ch Amer	1	120	100	150	.1	.1
360 Prim Bapt Chrch	1	NR	NR	NR	-	-
403 Salvation Army	2	63	95	87	-	.1
413 S.D.A.	4	586	NR	698	.3	.6
419 So Bapt Conv	64	41,168	11,912	53,522 *	22.5	46.9

NR–Not Reported *Total adherents estimated from known number of communicant, confirmed, full members. - Represents a percentage less than 0.1. Percentages may not total 100 due to rounding.

Table 4: Religious Congregations by County and Group: 2000

Religious Group	Number of Churches, Synagogues, Mosques, or Temples	Number of Communicant, Confirmed, or Full Members	Number of Attendees	Total Adherents: Number of Adherents	Total Adherents: % of Total Pop.	Total Adherents: % of Total Adh.
435 Unitarian-Univ	1	40	NR	52 *	-	-
449 Un Methodist	20	8,648	3,185	11,244 *	4.7	9.9
463 Vineyard	1	130	120	169 *	.1	.1
469 WELS	2	125	110	170	.1	.1
499 Indep.Non-Char	1	1,400	1,600	1,600	.7	1.4
BEXAR	**692**	**215,057**	**117,594**	**907,309 ***	**65.1**	**100.0**
017 Amer Bapt Assn	5	340	NR	437 *	-	-
019 Amer Bapt USA	3	1,795	0	2,307 *	.2	.3
050 Armen Ap Etchm	1	0	NR	70	-	-
053 Assemb of God	52	6,966	8,292	10,616	.8	1.2
056 Baha'i	2	519	NR	519	-	.1
059 Bapt Miss Assn	3	93	100	125 *	-	-
076 Buddhism	7	NR	NR	NR	-	-
081 Catholic	92	NR	NR	574,108	41.2	63.3
084 Calvary Chapel	2	NR	NR	NR	-	-
089 Chr & Miss Al	1	64	NR	121	-	-
093 Chr Ch (Disc)	11	2,335	912	3,001 *	.2	.3
097 Chr Chs&Chs Cr	10	1,419	NR	1,824 *	.1	.2
123 Ch God (Ander)	6	NR	385	385	-	-
127 Ch God (Cleve)	19	1,836	1,303	2,435 *	.2	.3
145 Ch God Prophcy	2	54	NR	70 *	-	-
151 L-D Saints	22	NR	NR	9,833	.7	1.1
165 Ch of Nazarene	18	1,872	1,352	2,629	.2	.3
167 Chs of Christ	41	8,433	8,883	10,886	.8	1.2
173 Comm of Christ	3	238	NR	238	-	-
183 Cons Menn Conf	2	109	133	158	-	-
185 Cumber Presb	2	315	NR	443	-	-
186 Coptic Orth Ch	1	NR	NR	NR	-	-
193 Episcopal	20	NR	4,476	12,587	.9	1.4
203 Evan Free Ch	5	1,394	3,215	3,215	.2	.4
207 E.L.C.A.	29	10,104	4,601	13,170	.9	1.5
216 Evan Presby Ch	1	25	NR	32 *	-	-
221 Free Methodist	1	28	13	29	-	-
223 Free Will Bapt	1	42	NR	55 *	-	-
226 Friends-USA	1	15	NR	19 *	-	-
246 Greek Orthodox	1	NR	NR	780	.1	.1
252 Hindu	3	NR	NR	NR	-	-
263 Int Foursq Gos	3	343	372	441 *	-	-
264 Int Chs of Crst	1	484	713	633	-	.1
267 Muslim Est	3	NR	856	3,182	.2	.4
283 Luth—MO Synod	14	8,482	4,693	10,701	.8	1.2
288 Mennonite USA	1	37	43	48 *	-	-
290 Metro Comm Ch	1	116	117	149 *	-	-
291 Missionary Ch	1	129	298	298	-	-
331 OCA: Ter Diocs	1	73	NR	329	-	-
335 Orth Pres Ch	1	78	82	102	-	-
339 Pent Ch of God	1	50	NR	70	-	-
349 Pent Holiness	5	302	375	388 *	-	-
355 Presb Ch (USA)	32	9,141	4,229	11,747 *	.8	1.3
356 Presb Ch Amer	2	163	241	241	-	-
360 Prim Bapt Chrch	2	NR	NR	NR	-	-
370 Ref Baptist Chs	3	NR	NR	NR	-	-
403 Salvation Army	2	404	207	1,676	.1	.2
413 S.D.A.	12	1,788	NR	2,127	.2	.2
418 Southw Bapt Fel	1	NR	NR	NR	-	-
419 So Bapt Conv	152	93,090	27,423	119,661 *	8.6	13.2
435 Unitarian-Univ	2	418	NR	537 *	-	.1
443 Un C of Christ	2	370	129	476 *	-	.1
449 Un Methodist	60	32,011	13,751	41,148 *	3.0	4.5
463 Vineyard	1	400	336	514 *	-	.1
469 WELS	3	322	274	449	-	-
496 Jewish Est	5	NR	NR	11,000	.8	1.2
498 Indep.Charis.	7	24,510	23,000	44,510	3.2	4.9
499 Indep.Non-Char	7	4,350	6,790	6,790	.5	.7
BLANCO	**16**	**2,653**	**1,110**	**4,223 ***	**50.2**	**100.0**
053 Assemb of God	1	21	28	31	.4	.7
056 Baha'i	0	4	NR	4	-	.1
081 Catholic	2	NR	NR	765	9.1	18.1
167 Chs of Christ	4	205	195	240	2.9	5.7
193 Episcopal	2	NR	90	176	2.1	4.2
207 E.L.C.A.	1	356	103	475	5.6	11.2

Religious Group	Number of Churches, Synagogues, Mosques, or Temples	Number of Communicant, Confirmed, or Full Members	Number of Attendees	Total Adherents: Number of Adherents	Total Adherents: % of Total Pop.	Total Adherents: % of Total Adh.
226 Friends-USA	1	15	NR	18 *	.2	.4
419 So Bapt Conv	2	1,305	372	1,599 *	19.0	37.9
449 Un Methodist	3	747	322	915 *	10.9	21.7
BORDEN	**1**	**216**	**55**	**258 ***	**35.4**	**100.0**
419 So Bapt Conv	1	216	55	258 *	35.4	100.0
BOSQUE	**52**	**8,571**	**3,401**	**11,926 ***	**69.3**	**100.0**
053 Assemb of God	1	23	30	30	.2	.3
056 Baha'i	0	1	NR	1	-	-
081 Catholic	2	NR	NR	1,251	7.3	10.5
167 Chs of Christ	8	411	427	554	3.2	4.6
193 Episcopal	2	NR	83	117	.7	1.0
207 E.L.C.A.	4	974	341	1,163	6.8	9.8
220 Free Lutheran	1	0	0	0	-	-
283 Luth—MO Synod	1	174	105	238	1.4	2.0
339 Pent Ch of God	2	27	NR	57	.3	.5
355 Presb Ch (USA)	1	86	78	105 *	.6	.9
419 So Bapt Conv	19	5,161	1,687	6,313 *	36.7	52.9
443 Un C of Christ	1	200	110	245 *	1.4	2.1
449 Un Methodist	10	1,514	540	1,852 *	10.8	15.5
BOWIE	**149**	**39,519**	**13,390**	**55,041 ***	**61.6**	**100.0**
017 Amer Bapt Assn	14	2,686	NR	3,317 *	3.7	6.0
053 Assemb of God	8	1,205	938	1,470	1.6	2.7
056 Baha'i	0	43	NR	43	-	.1
059 Bapt Miss Assn	3	1,102	332	1,360 *	1.5	2.5
081 Catholic	3	NR	NR	2,860	3.2	5.2
093 Chr Ch (Disc)	2	123	69	152 *	.2	.3
097 Chr Chs&Chs Cr	6	439	NR	541 *	.6	1.0
127 Ch God (Cleve)	2	119	59	147 *	.2	.3
145 Ch God Prophcy	2	54	NR	66 *	.1	.1
151 L-D Saints	2	NR	NR	680	.8	1.2
165 Ch of Nazarene	2	542	362	664	.7	1.2
167 Chs of Christ	18	2,379	2,202	2,932	3.3	5.3
173 Comm of Christ	2	92	NR	92	.1	.2
193 Episcopal	3	NR	336	925	1.0	1.7
207 E.L.C.A.	1	21	17	23	-	-
263 Int Foursq Gos	1	52	28	64 *	.1	.1
283 Luth—MO Synod	1	387	171	506	.6	.9
355 Presb Ch (USA)	4	457	227	564 *	.6	1.0
360 Prim Bapt Chrch	1	NR	NR	NR	-	-
403 Salvation Army	1	127	65	390	.4	.7
413 S.D.A.	3	468	NR	557	.6	1.0
419 So Bapt Conv	49	24,036	6,574	29,681 *	33.2	53.9
449 Un Methodist	20	5,187	2,010	6,407 *	7.2	11.6
496 Jewish Est	1	NR	NR	1,600	1.8	2.9
BRAZORIA	**206**	**58,634**	**22,491**	**128,501 ***	**53.2**	**100.0**
017 Amer Bapt Assn	5	678	NR	870 *	.4	.7
053 Assemb of God	17	3,141	2,282	3,576	1.5	2.8
056 Baha'i	1	46	NR	46	-	-
059 Bapt Miss Assn	1	20	25	26 *	-	-
081 Catholic	14	NR	NR	48,342	20.0	37.6
093 Chr Ch (Disc)	4	420	204	539 *	.2	.4
097 Chr Chs&Chs Cr	1	1,000	NR	1,284 *	.5	1.0
127 Ch God (Cleve)	1	44	25	56 *	-	-
145 Ch God Prophcy	3	81	NR	105 *	-	.1
151 L-D Saints	5	NR	NR	1,928	.8	1.5
165 Ch of Nazarene	6	426	279	590	.2	.5
167 Chs of Christ	26	2,868	2,544	3,523	1.5	2.7
173 Comm of Christ	1	124	NR	124	.1	.1
186 Coptic Orth Ch	2	NR	NR	NR	-	-
193 Episcopal	6	NR	830	1,884	.8	1.5
201 Evan Cov Ch	1	62	62	80 *	-	.1
203 Evan Free Ch	1	110	135	135	.1	.1
207 E.L.C.A.	6	1,630	795	2,232	.9	1.7
226 Friends-USA	1	50	NR	64 *	-	-
252 Hindu	1	NR	NR	NR	-	-
263 Int Foursq Gos	2	131	213	213 *	.1	.2
267 Muslim Est	1	NR	290	1,313	.5	1.0
283 Luth—MO Synod	4	1,228	702	1,604	.7	1.2

NR–Not Reported   *Total adherents estimated from known number of communicant, confirmed, full members.   - Represents a percentage less than 0.1.   Percentages may not total 100 due to rounding.

Table 4: Religious Congregations by County and Group: 2000

Religious Group	Number of Churches, Synagogues, Mosques, or Temples	Number of Communicant, Confirmed, or Full Members	Number of Attendees	Total Adherents		
				Number of Adherents	% of Total Pop.	% of Total Adh.
339 Pent Ch of God	1	11	NR	24	-	-
349 Pent Holiness	5	512	472	657 *	.3	.5
355 Presb Ch (USA)	9	1,852	1,111	2,378 *	1.0	1.9
356 Presb Ch Amer	1	140	139	183	.1	.1
360 Prim Bapt Chrch	1	NR	NR	NR	-	-
403 Salvation Army	1	79	57	190	.1	.1
413 S.D.A.	2	122	NR	145	.1	.1
419 So Bapt Conv	55	34,113	8,798	43,797 *	18.1	34.1
449 Un Methodist	17	9,404	3,260	12,073 *	5.0	9.4
463 Vineyard	2	292	236	375 *	.2	.3
469 WELS	1	50	32	70	-	.1
496 Jewish Est	1	NR	NR	75	-	.1
BRAZOS	**107**	**26,952**	**16,230**	**77,124 ***	**50.6**	**100.0**
050 Armen Ap Etchm	1	123	NR	560	.4	.7
053 Assemb of God	5	636	630	917	.6	1.2
056 Baha'i	2	158	NR	158	.1	.2
059 Bapt Miss Assn	2	69	100	116 *	.1	.2
081 Catholic	6	NR	NR	37,430	24.6	48.5
093 Chr Ch (Disc)	1	183	88	219 *	.1	.3
097 Chr Chs&Chs Cr	1	100	NR	120 *	.1	.2
123 Ch God (Ander)	1	NR	110	110	.1	.1
151 L-D Saints	7	NR	NR	1,786	1.2	2.3
165 Ch of Nazarene	1	128	135	197	.1	.3
167 Chs of Christ	9	2,041	1,888	2,727	1.8	3.5
173 Comm of Christ	1	21	NR	21	-	-
186 Coptic Orth Ch	1	NR	NR	NR	-	-
193 Episcopal	3	NR	591	1,494	1.0	1.9
201 Evan Cov Ch	1	0	53	53 *	-	.1
203 Evan Free Ch	1	61	75	75	-	.1
207 E.L.C.A.	2	1,152	532	1,498	1.0	1.9
223 Free Will Bapt	4	170	NR	204 *	.1	.3
264 Int Chs of Crst	1	59	81	68	-	.1
267 Muslim Est	1	NR	275	500	.3	.6
283 Luth—MO Synod	3	672	582	913	.6	1.2
304 NatPrimBapt USA	1	40	NR	48 *	-	.1
339 Pent Ch of God	1	23	NR	23	-	-
349 Pent Holiness	1	35	25	42 *	-	.1
355 Presb Ch (USA)	2	886	380	1,063 *	.7	1.4
356 Presb Ch Amer	1	213	0	273	.2	.4
403 Salvation Army	1	38	41	51	-	.1
413 S.D.A.	2	89	NR	106	.1	.1
419 So Bapt Conv	25	12,908	4,469	15,480 *	10.2	20.1
435 Unitarian-Univ	1	91	NR	109 *	.1	.1
443 Un C of Christ	2	537	264	644 *	.4	.8
449 Un Methodist	13	5,957	3,370	7,144 *	4.7	9.3
469 WELS	1	62	41	75	-	.1
496 Jewish Est	1	NR	NR	400	.3	.5
499 Indep.Non-Char	1	500	2,500	2,500	1.6	3.2
BREWSTER	**21**	**1,899**	**717**	**5,054 ***	**57.0**	**100.0**
053 Assemb of God	2	86	112	140	1.6	2.8
056 Baha'i	0	11	NR	11	.1	.2
081 Catholic	3	NR	NR	2,538	28.6	50.2
093 Chr Ch (Disc)	1	90	0	108 *	1.2	2.1
151 L-D Saints	1	NR	NR	119	1.3	2.4
167 Chs of Christ	1	35	55	55	.6	1.1
193 Episcopal	2	NR	37	70	.8	1.4
283 Luth—MO Synod	1	47	31	58	.7	1.1
355 Presb Ch (USA)	1	111	52	133 *	1.5	2.6
413 S.D.A.	1	17	NR	20	.2	.4
419 So Bapt Conv	6	1,143	268	1,371 *	15.5	27.1
449 Un Methodist	2	359	162	431 *	4.9	8.5
BRISCOE	**11**	**1,254**	**608**	**1,879 ***	**105.0**	**100.0**
053 Assemb of God	1	9	15	27	1.5	1.4
056 Baha'i	0	1	NR	1	.1	.1
081 Catholic	2	NR	NR	277	15.5	14.7
167 Chs of Christ	3	159	188	208	11.6	11.1
419 So Bapt Conv	3	868	290	1,093 *	61.1	58.2
449 Un Methodist	2	217	115	273 *	15.3	14.5

Religious Group	Number of Churches, Synagogues, Mosques, or Temples	Number of Communicant, Confirmed, or Full Members	Number of Attendees	Total Adherents		
				Number of Adherents	% of Total Pop.	% of Total Adh.
BROOKS	**14**	**715**	**286**	**4,452 ***	**55.8**	**100.0**
053 Assemb of God	2	48	51	55	.7	1.2
081 Catholic	2	NR	NR	3,500	43.9	78.6
123 Ch God (Ander)	1	NR	20	20	.3	.4
157 Ch of Brethren	1	33	0	44 *	.6	1.0
167 Chs of Christ	1	30	32	45	.6	1.0
349 Pent Holiness	1	33	32	44 *	.6	1.0
355 Presb Ch (USA)	1	60	33	79 *	1.0	1.8
413 S.D.A.	1	65	NR	77	1.0	1.7
419 So Bapt Conv	2	358	62	472 *	5.9	10.6
449 Un Methodist	2	88	56	116 *	1.5	2.6
BROWN	**79**	**19,755**	**7,605**	**27,400 ***	**72.7**	**100.0**
053 Assemb of God	3	165	151	313	.8	1.1
056 Baha'i	0	2	NR	2	-	-
081 Catholic	1	NR	NR	2,300	6.1	8.4
093 Chr Ch (Disc)	1	291	83	358 *	1.0	1.3
151 L-D Saints	1	NR	NR	195	.5	.7
165 Ch of Nazarene	2	76	64	139	.4	.5
167 Chs of Christ	16	1,505	1,351	1,892	5.0	6.9
193 Episcopal	2	NR	163	397	1.1	1.4
283 Luth—MO Synod	1	168	102	215	.6	.8
339 Pent Ch of God	2	167	NR	273	.7	1.0
355 Presb Ch (USA)	1	186	86	229 *	.6	.8
360 Prim Bapt Chrch	1	NR	NR	NR	-	-
413 S.D.A.	1	47	NR	56	.1	.2
419 So Bapt Conv	36	14,012	4,549	17,241 *	45.8	62.9
449 Un Methodist	10	2,736	756	3,365 *	8.9	12.3
498 Indep.Charis.	1	400	300	425	1.1	1.6
BURLESON	**32**	**4,836**	**1,902**	**7,597 ***	**46.1**	**100.0**
053 Assemb of God	2	134	172	180	1.1	2.4
056 Baha'i	0	28	NR	28	.2	.4
081 Catholic	3	NR	NR	1,513	9.2	19.9
093 Chr Ch (Disc)	1	68	0	85 *	.5	1.1
167 Chs of Christ	4	167	140	218	1.3	2.9
207 E.L.C.A.	2	425	202	532	3.2	7.0
283 Luth—MO Synod	1	29	12	43	.3	.6
355 Presb Ch (USA)	2	41	29	51 *	.3	.7
419 So Bapt Conv	11	3,026	934	3,795 *	23.0	50.0
443 Un C of Christ	1	181	84	227 *	1.4	3.0
449 Un Methodist	5	737	329	925 *	5.6	12.2
BURNET	**50**	**11,004**	**5,178**	**17,969 ***	**52.6**	**100.0**
053 Assemb of God	2	234	310	310	.9	1.7
056 Baha'i	0	2	NR	2	-	-
081 Catholic	5	NR	NR	4,032	11.8	22.4
093 Chr Ch (Disc)	2	175	99	215 *	.6	1.2
167 Chs of Christ	12	1,102	1,088	1,312	3.8	7.3
185 Cumber Presb	1	97	NR	176	.5	1.0
193 Episcopal	2	NR	173	385	1.1	2.1
207 E.L.C.A.	2	689	321	870	2.5	4.8
355 Presb Ch (USA)	2	174	120	214 *	.6	1.2
360 Prim Bapt Chrch	1	NR	NR	NR	-	-
413 S.D.A.	1	152	NR	181	.5	1.0
419 So Bapt Conv	12	6,815	1,996	8,354 *	24.5	46.5
449 Un Methodist	8	1,564	1,071	1,918 *	5.6	10.7
CALDWELL	**55**	**7,348**	**3,054**	**16,420 ***	**51.0**	**100.0**
017 Amer Bapt Assn	2	42	NR	54 *	.2	.3
053 Assemb of God	3	321	285	385	1.2	2.3
056 Baha'i	0	28	NR	28	.1	.2
081 Catholic	3	NR	NR	6,643	20.6	40.5
093 Chr Ch (Disc)	2	333	35	425 *	1.3	2.6
151 L-D Saints	1	NR	NR	160	.5	1.0
167 Chs of Christ	4	338	328	402	1.2	2.4
193 Episcopal	2	NR	92	197	.6	1.2
207 E.L.C.A.	3	357	163	482	1.5	2.9
339 Pent Ch of God	2	61	NR	163	.5	1.0
355 Presb Ch (USA)	3	199	133	254 *	.8	1.5
360 Prim Bapt Chrch	3	NR	NR	NR	-	-
419 So Bapt Conv	16	4,308	1,420	5,492 *	17.1	33.4

NR–Not Reported *Total adherents estimated from known number of communicant, confirmed, full members. - Represents a percentage less than 0.1. Percentages may not total 100 due to rounding.

Table 4: Religious Congregations by County and Group: 2000

Religious Group	Number of Churches, Synagogues, Mosques, or Temples	Number of Communicant, Confirmed, or Full Members	Number of Attendees	Total Adherents		
				Number of Adherents	% of Total Pop.	% of Total Adh.
443 Un C of Christ	2	185	79	236 *	.7	1.4
449 Un Methodist	9	1,176	519	1,499 *	4.7	9.1
CALHOUN	**31**	**6,230**	**2,362**	**11,482 ***	**55.6**	**100.0**
053 Assemb of God	6	565	516	846	4.1	7.4
056 Baha'i	0	17	NR	17	.1	.1
081 Catholic	4	NR	NR	3,251	15.7	28.3
093 Chr Ch (Disc)	1	43	0	55 *	.3	.5
145 Ch God Prophcy	1	27	NR	35 *	.2	.3
167 Chs of Christ	4	282	350	389	1.9	3.4
193 Episcopal	1	NR	43	73	.4	.6
207 E.L.C.A.	2	320	127	411	2.0	3.6
355 Presb Ch (USA)	2	127	77	163 *	.8	1.4
419 So Bapt Conv	7	3,851	954	4,957 *	24.0	43.2
449 Un Methodist	3	998	295	1,285 *	6.2	11.2
CALLAHAN	**27**	**5,835**	**2,460**	**7,459 ***	**57.8**	**100.0**
053 Assemb of God	1	15	20	22	.2	.3
059 Bapt Miss Assn	1	45	35	55 *	.4	.7
081 Catholic	1	NR	NR	200	1.5	2.7
151 L-D Saints	1	NR	NR	67	.5	.9
167 Chs of Christ	7	648	609	801	6.2	10.7
355 Presb Ch (USA)	2	54	31	67 *	.5	.9
419 So Bapt Conv	10	4,151	1,323	5,112 *	39.6	68.5
449 Un Methodist	4	922	442	1,135 *	8.8	15.2
CAMERON	**223**	**29,542**	**17,077**	**177,125 ***	**52.8**	**100.0**
053 Assemb of God	33	3,254	3,211	3,934	1.2	2.2
056 Baha'i	1	132	NR	132	-	.1
081 Catholic	37	NR	NR	134,004	40.0	75.7
084 Calvary Chapel	1	NR	NR	NR	-	-
089 Chr & Miss Al	2	82	NR	125	-	.1
093 Chr Ch (Disc)	4	360	174	490 *	.1	.3
097 Chr Chs&Chs Cr	3	650	NR	884 *	.3	.5
123 Ch God (Ander)	2	NR	80	80	-	-
127 Ch God (Cleve)	4	135	100	184 *	.1	.1
145 Ch God Prophcy	2	54	NR	74 *	-	-
151 L-D Saints	8	NR	NR	2,664	.8	1.5
165 Ch of Nazarene	7	525	435	600	.2	.3
167 Chs of Christ	20	1,329	1,350	1,748	.5	1.0
173 Comm of Christ	2	126	NR	126	-	.1
193 Episcopal	5	NR	737	1,615	.5	.9
207 E.L.C.A.	2	189	235	280	.1	.2
263 Int Foursq Gos	1	3	4	4 *	-	-
283 Luth—MO Synod	6	1,050	810	1,263	.4	.7
288 Mennonite USA	3	220	234	299 *	.1	.2
291 Missionary Ch	1	23	25	25	-	-
349 Pent Holiness	6	295	317	401 *	.1	.2
355 Presb Ch (USA)	10	1,398	782	1,942 *	.6	1.1
356 Presb Ch Amer	1	74	85	98	-	.1
403 Salvation Army	1	109	65	149	-	.1
413 S.D.A.	5	642	NR	763	.2	.4
419 So Bapt Conv	39	12,757	5,346	17,347 *	5.2	9.8
435 Unitarian-Univ	1	10	NR	14 *	-	-
449 Un Methodist	12	3,495	1,967	4,753 *	1.4	2.7
463 Vineyard	1	130	120	177 *	.1	.1
496 Jewish Est	2	NR	NR	450	.1	.3
498 Indep.Charis.	1	2,500	1,000	2,500	.7	1.4
CAMP	**39**	**6,111**	**2,185**	**9,470 ***	**82.0**	**100.0**
017 Amer Bapt Assn	5	336	NR	425 *	3.7	4.5
053 Assemb of God	2	76	90	90	.8	1.0
059 Bapt Miss Assn	8	1,259	388	1,596 *	13.8	16.9
081 Catholic	1	NR	NR	1,286	11.1	13.6
127 Ch God (Cleve)	1	56	61	71 *	.6	.7
145 Ch God Prophcy	1	27	NR	34 *	.3	.4
151 L-D Saints	1	NR	NR	306	2.6	3.2
165 Ch of Nazarene	1	51	29	72	.6	.8
167 Chs of Christ	5	344	315	461	4.0	4.9
193 Episcopal	1	NR	51	105	.9	1.1
355 Presb Ch (USA)	1	30	32	38 *	.3	.4
419 So Bapt Conv	9	3,391	998	4,300 *	37.2	45.4

Religious Group	Number of Churches, Synagogues, Mosques, or Temples	Number of Communicant, Confirmed, or Full Members	Number of Attendees	Total Adherents		
				Number of Adherents	% of Total Pop.	% of Total Adh.
449 Un Methodist	3	541	221	686 *	5.9	7.2
CARSON	**19**	**3,823**	**1,377**	**5,794 ***	**88.9**	**100.0**
053 Assemb of God	3	85	100	117	1.8	2.0
056 Baha'i	0	2	NR	2	-	-
081 Catholic	3	NR	NR	1,004	15.4	17.3
093 Chr Ch (Disc)	1	270	0	339 *	5.2	5.9
167 Chs of Christ	4	248	250	295	4.5	5.1
419 So Bapt Conv	5	2,498	773	3,134 *	48.1	54.1
449 Un Methodist	3	720	254	903 *	13.9	15.6
CASS	**83**	**15,877**	**5,131**	**20,299 ***	**66.7**	**100.0**
017 Amer Bapt Assn	11	2,187	NR	2,680 *	8.8	13.2
053 Assemb of God	5	286	353	396	1.3	2.0
056 Baha'i	0	8	NR	8	-	-
059 Bapt Miss Assn	1	87	50	107 *	.4	.5
081 Catholic	1	NR	NR	371	1.2	1.8
097 Chr Chs&Chs Cr	1	65	NR	80 *	.3	.4
123 Ch God (Ander)	1	NR	30	30	.1	.1
127 Ch God (Cleve)	1	82	30	101 *	.3	.5
151 L-D Saints	1	NR	NR	296	1.0	1.5
165 Ch of Nazarene	1	111	84	152	.5	.7
167 Chs of Christ	4	477	470	603	2.0	3.0
193 Episcopal	1	NR	45	24	.1	.1
283 Luth—MO Synod	1	30	0	68	.2	.3
355 Presb Ch (USA)	1	15	22	22 *	.1	.1
360 Prim Bapt Chrch	1	NR	NR	NR	-	-
413 S.D.A.	2	69	NR	82	.3	.4
419 So Bapt Conv	36	10,435	3,184	12,795 *	42.0	63.0
449 Un Methodist	14	2,025	863	2,484 *	8.2	12.2
CASTRO	**21**	**3,291**	**1,044**	**6,563 ***	**79.2**	**100.0**
053 Assemb of God	2	83	60	77	.9	1.2
081 Catholic	3	NR	NR	2,229	26.9	34.0
097 Chr Chs&Chs Cr	1	60	NR	80 *	1.0	1.2
167 Chs of Christ	3	289	244	367	4.4	5.6
349 Pent Holiness	1	35	45	47 *	.6	.7
355 Presb Ch (USA)	1	11	12	15 *	.2	.2
419 So Bapt Conv	8	2,284	495	3,043 *	36.7	46.4
449 Un Methodist	2	529	188	705 *	8.5	10.7
CHAMBERS	**34**	**8,100**	**2,718**	**14,458 ***	**55.5**	**100.0**
017 Amer Bapt Assn	2	571	NR	729 *	2.8	5.0
053 Assemb of God	3	389	435	505	1.9	3.5
056 Baha'i	0	2	NR	2	-	-
081 Catholic	3	NR	NR	3,735	14.3	25.8
151 L-D Saints	1	NR	NR	333	1.3	2.3
167 Chs of Christ	6	203	233	239	.9	1.7
193 Episcopal	1	NR	17	71	.3	.5
283 Luth—MO Synod	1	122	76	148	.6	1.0
419 So Bapt Conv	10	5,190	1,452	6,625 *	25.5	45.8
449 Un Methodist	7	1,623	505	2,071 *	8.0	14.3
CHEROKEE	**112**	**20,120**	**6,488**	**27,218 ***	**58.3**	**100.0**
017 Amer Bapt Assn	13	2,648	NR	3,328 *	7.1	12.2
053 Assemb of God	7	256	284	357	.8	1.3
056 Baha'i	0	3	NR	3	-	-
059 Bapt Miss Assn	17	4,541	1,271	5,706 *	12.2	21.0
081 Catholic	3	NR	NR	1,750	3.8	6.4
093 Chr Ch (Disc)	4	308	93	387 *	.8	1.4
165 Ch of Nazarene	3	267	245	387	.8	1.4
167 Chs of Christ	13	971	914	1,215	2.6	4.5
185 Cumber Presb	1	80	NR	126	.3	.5
193 Episcopal	1	NR	36	76	.2	.3
339 Pent Ch of God	1	30	NR	50	.1	.2
355 Presb Ch (USA)	2	171	105	215 *	.5	.8
360 Prim Bapt Chrch	1	NR	NR	NR	-	-
413 S.D.A.	1	101	NR	120	.3	.4
419 So Bapt Conv	24	8,373	2,564	10,521 *	22.5	38.7
449 Un Methodist	21	2,371	976	2,977 *	6.4	10.9

NR–Not Reported *Total adherents estimated from known number of communicant, confirmed, full members. - Represents a percentage less than 0.1. Percentages may not total 100 due to rounding.

Table 4: Religious Congregations by County and Group: 2000

Religious Group	Number of Churches, Synagogues, Mosques, or Temples	Number of Communicant, Confirmed, or Full Members	Number of Attendees	Total Adherents: Number of Adherents	Total Adherents: % of Total Pop.	Total Adherents: % of Total Adh.
CHILDRESS	**16**	**3,853**	**1,251**	**4,973 ***	**64.7**	**100.0**
053 Assemb of God	1	48	60	60	.8	1.2
056 Baha'i	0	1	NR	1	-	-
081 Catholic	1	NR	NR	335	4.4	6.7
093 Chr Ch (Disc)	1	120	55	143 *	1.9	2.9
165 Ch of Nazarene	1	0	0	0	-	-
167 Chs of Christ	3	372	325	470	6.1	9.5
193 Episcopal	1	NR	7	6	.1	.1
283 Luth—MO Synod	1	13	11	15	.2	.3
349 Pent Holiness	1	25	20	30 *	.4	.6
355 Presb Ch (USA)	1	46	22	55 *	.7	1.1
419 So Bapt Conv	4	2,598	560	3,105 *	40.4	62.4
449 Un Methodist	1	630	191	753 *	9.8	15.1
CLAY	**30**	**6,262**	**1,859**	**7,947 ***	**72.2**	**100.0**
017 Amer Bapt Assn	1	110	NR	135 *	1.2	1.7
053 Assemb of God	1	156	100	137	1.2	1.7
056 Baha'i	0	2	NR	2	-	-
081 Catholic	1	NR	NR	227	2.1	2.9
093 Chr Ch (Disc)	1	92	40	113 *	1.0	1.4
127 Ch God (Cleve)	1	208	70	255 *	2.3	3.2
167 Chs of Christ	4	380	340	529	4.8	6.7
193 Episcopal	1	NR	18	27	.2	.3
223 Free Will Bapt	1	42	NR	52 *	.5	.7
360 Prim Bapt Chrch	1	NR	NR	NR	-	-
419 So Bapt Conv	12	4,609	1,020	5,658 *	51.4	71.2
449 Un Methodist	6	663	271	812 *	7.4	10.2
COCHRAN	**13**	**2,377**	**999**	**3,648 ***	**97.8**	**100.0**
053 Assemb of God	3	109	125	162	4.3	4.4
059 Bapt Miss Assn	1	345	52	444 *	11.9	12.2
081 Catholic	1	NR	NR	565	15.1	15.5
167 Chs of Christ	3	211	220	272	7.3	7.5
419 So Bapt Conv	4	1,533	526	1,974 *	52.9	54.1
449 Un Methodist	1	179	76	231 *	6.2	6.3
COKE	**15**	**2,311**	**841**	**2,828 ***	**73.2**	**100.0**
053 Assemb of God	1	21	26	26	.7	.9
056 Baha'i	0	1	NR	1	-	-
059 Bapt Miss Assn	2	286	97	338 *	8.7	12.0
081 Catholic	2	NR	NR	59	1.5	2.1
167 Chs of Christ	3	215	228	293	7.6	10.4
419 So Bapt Conv	5	1,506	389	1,778 *	46.0	62.9
449 Un Methodist	2	282	101	333 *	8.6	11.8
COLEMAN	**42**	**4,173**	**1,554**	**5,984 ***	**64.8**	**100.0**
053 Assemb of God	1	39	33	45	.5	.8
059 Bapt Miss Assn	1	50	40	61 *	.7	1.0
081 Catholic	1	NR	NR	830	9.0	13.9
093 Chr Ch (Disc)	1	254	125	309 *	3.3	5.2
165 Ch of Nazarene	1	20	21	27	.3	.5
167 Chs of Christ	6	351	356	455	4.9	7.6
193 Episcopal	1	NR	27	53	.6	.9
355 Presb Ch (USA)	2	144	83	175 *	1.9	2.9
413 S.D.A.	2	55	NR	65	.7	1.1
419 So Bapt Conv	18	2,527	622	3,073 *	33.3	51.4
449 Un Methodist	8	733	247	891 *	9.6	14.9
COLLIN	**251**	**112,754**	**66,128**	**263,858 ***	**53.7**	**100.0**
053 Assemb of God	17	2,135	1,786	2,509	.5	1.0
056 Baha'i	4	378	NR	378	.1	.1
059 Bapt Miss Assn	3	578	325	768 *	.2	.3
081 Catholic	8	NR	NR	89,905	18.3	34.1
084 Calvary Chapel	1	NR	NR	NR	-	-
089 Chr & Miss Al	1	119	NR	228	-	.1
093 Chr Ch (Disc)	10	2,258	976	2,940 *	.6	1.1
097 Chr Chs&Chs Cr	3	715	NR	932 *	.2	.4
123 Ch God (Ander)	1	NR	12	12	-	-
127 Ch God (Cleve)	3	418	184	544 *	.1	.2
151 L-D Saints	18	NR	NR	6,548	1.3	2.5
165 Ch of Nazarene	2	121	136	238	-	.1

Religious Group	Number of Churches, Synagogues, Mosques, or Temples	Number of Communicant, Confirmed, or Full Members	Number of Attendees	Total Adherents: Number of Adherents	Total Adherents: % of Total Pop.	Total Adherents: % of Total Adh.
167 Chs of Christ	26	3,698	3,781	5,054	1.0	1.9
193 Episcopal	5	NR	2,037	4,023	.8	1.5
203 Evan Free Ch	1	132	230	230	-	.1
207 E.L.C.A.	4	2,041	1,323	2,885	.6	1.1
223 Free Will Bapt	1	42	NR	55 *	-	-
267 Muslim Est	3	NR	1,236	5,673	1.2	2.2
268 Jain	1	NR	NR	NR	-	-
283 Luth—MO Synod	5	1,838	1,303	2,602	.5	1.0
331 OCA: Ter Diocs	1	33	NR	123	-	-
339 Pent Ch of God	1	17	NR	40	-	-
349 Pent Holiness	1	294	310	383 *	.1	.1
355 Presb Ch (USA)	9	2,741	1,516	3,567 *	.7	1.4
356 Presb Ch Amer	2	189	0	335	.1	.1
360 Prim Bapt Chrch	1	NR	NR	NR	-	-
370 Ref Baptist Chs	1	NR	NR	NR	-	-
371 Ref Ch in Am	1	664	516	1,466	.3	.6
403 Salvation Army	1	86	68	81	-	-
419 So Bapt Conv	75	60,503	27,743	78,772 *	16.0	29.9
435 Unitarian-Univ	1	168	NR	219 *	-	.1
449 Un Methodist	26	23,134	9,036	30,117 *	6.1	11.4
463 Vineyard	1	2,890	1,055	3,763 *	.8	1.4
467 Wesleyan	1	209	461	580	.1	.2
469 WELS	1	103	94	138	-	.1
490 Zoroastrian	1	NR	NR	NR	-	-
496 Jewish Est	3	NR	NR	6,750	1.4	2.6
498 Indep.Charis.	2	650	3,750	3,750	.8	1.4
499 Indep.Non-Char	5	6,600	8,250	8,250	1.7	3.1
COLLINGSWORTH	**14**	**2,194**	**934**	**2,892 ***	**90.2**	**100.0**
081 Catholic	1	NR	NR	40	1.2	1.4
097 Chr Chs&Chs Cr	1	75	NR	93 *	2.9	3.2
165 Ch of Nazarene	2	127	153	219	6.8	7.6
167 Chs of Christ	4	202	264	318	9.9	11.0
360 Prim Bapt Chrch	1	NR	NR	NR	-	-
419 So Bapt Conv	4	1,405	385	1,744 *	54.4	60.3
449 Un Methodist	1	385	132	478 *	14.9	16.5
COLORADO	**42**	**4,933**	**1,876**	**13,008 ***	**63.8**	**100.0**
053 Assemb of God	2	61	85	53	.3	.4
056 Baha'i	0	2	NR	2	-	-
081 Catholic	6	NR	NR	6,728	33.0	51.7
127 Ch God (Cleve)	2	81	53	100 *	.5	.8
145 Ch God Prophcy	1	27	NR	33 *	.2	.3
165 Ch of Nazarene	1	49	25	109	.5	.8
167 Chs of Christ	4	97	108	133	.7	1.0
193 Episcopal	2	NR	82	144	.7	1.1
207 E.L.C.A.	6	1,407	506	1,743	8.5	13.4
355 Presb Ch (USA)	1	44	21	54 *	.3	.4
419 So Bapt Conv	6	1,814	505	2,241 *	11.0	17.2
443 Un C of Christ	2	433	169	535 *	2.6	4.1
449 Un Methodist	9	918	322	1,133 *	5.6	8.7
COMAL	**60**	**18,486**	**9,627**	**42,688 ***	**54.7**	**100.0**
053 Assemb of God	4	139	137	158	.2	.4
056 Baha'i	0	21	NR	21	-	-
081 Catholic	5	NR	NR	17,206	22.1	40.3
093 Chr Ch (Disc)	1	130	70	161 *	.2	.4
097 Chr Chs&Chs Cr	2	455	NR	564 *	.7	1.3
151 L-D Saints	3	NR	NR	1,064	1.4	2.5
165 Ch of Nazarene	1	81	82	93	.1	.2
167 Chs of Christ	7	712	598	914	1.2	2.1
173 Comm of Christ	1	51	NR	51	.1	.1
193 Episcopal	2	NR	364	797	1.0	1.9
203 Evan Free Ch	1	222	615	615	.8	1.4
207 E.L.C.A.	5	2,907	1,547	3,808	4.9	8.9
263 Int Foursq Gos	1	23	38	38 *	-	.1
283 Luth—MO Synod	1	492	347	625	.8	1.5
355 Presb Ch (USA)	3	759	368	941 *	1.2	2.2
356 Presb Ch Amer	1	262	215	326	.4	.8
413 S.D.A.	1	31	NR	37	-	.1
419 So Bapt Conv	13	7,158	3,168	8,873 *	11.4	20.8
435 Unitarian-Univ	1	36	NR	45 *	.1	.1
443 Un C of Christ	1	197	80	244 *	.3	.6

NR–Not Reported *Total adherents estimated from known number of communicant, confirmed, full members. - Represents a percentage less than 0.1. Percentages may not total 100 due to rounding.

Table 4: Religious Congregations by County and Group: 2000

Religious Group	Number of Churches, Synagogues, Mosques, or Temples	Number of Communicant, Confirmed, or Full Members	Number of Attendees	Total Adherents		
				Number of Adherents	% of Total Pop.	% of Total Adh.
449 Un Methodist	3	2,660	918	3,297 *	4.2	7.7
467 Wesleyan	1	0	200	210	.3	.5
499 Indep.Non-Char	2	2,150	880	2,600	3.3	6.1
COMANCHE	**51**	**6,680**	**2,614**	**9,092 ***	**64.8**	**100.0**
053 Assemb of God	2	81	74	96	.7	1.1
081 Catholic	2	NR	NR	716	5.1	7.9
093 Chr Ch (Disc)	1	45	0	56 *	.4	.6
097 Chr Chs&Chs Cr	1	42	NR	52 *	.4	.6
151 L-D Saints	1	NR	NR	62	.4	.7
167 Chs of Christ	9	524	523	624	4.4	6.9
193 Episcopal	1	NR	27	58	.4	.6
207 E.L.C.A.	1	72	21	88	.6	1.0
223 Free Will Bapt	2	85	NR	105 *	.7	1.2
339 Pent Ch of God	1	10	NR	20	.1	.2
360 Prim Bapt Chrch	1	NR	NR	NR	-	-
365 Prog Prim Bapt	1	25	NR	31 *	.2	.3
419 So Bapt Conv	22	4,757	1,646	5,896 *	42.0	64.8
449 Un Methodist	6	1,039	323	1,288 *	9.2	14.2
CONCHO	**17**	**1,050**	**506**	**1,704 ***	**43.0**	**100.0**
056 Baha'i	0	1	NR	1	-	.1
081 Catholic	4	NR	NR	496	12.5	29.1
167 Chs of Christ	4	155	167	199	5.0	11.7
193 Episcopal	1	NR	5	2	.1	.1
283 Luth—MO Synod	2	121	82	131	3.3	7.7
419 So Bapt Conv	3	637	182	721 *	18.2	42.3
449 Un Methodist	3	136	70	154 *	3.9	9.0
COOKE	**62**	**10,709**	**4,794**	**22,069 ***	**60.7**	**100.0**
017 Amer Bapt Assn	2	364	NR	457 *	1.3	2.1
053 Assemb of God	3	164	207	237	.7	1.1
056 Baha'i	0	16	NR	16	-	.1
081 Catholic	4	NR	NR	8,170	22.5	37.0
093 Chr Ch (Disc)	1	259	109	325 *	.9	1.5
097 Chr Chs&Chs Cr	1	14	NR	18 *	-	.1
127 Ch God (Cleve)	1	69	45	87 *	.2	.4
151 L-D Saints	1	NR	NR	351	1.0	1.6
165 Ch of Nazarene	3	139	82	187	.5	.8
167 Chs of Christ	9	946	791	1,175	3.2	5.3
193 Episcopal	1	NR	80	116	.3	.5
283 Luth—MO Synod	1	148	74	167	.5	.8
349 Pent Holiness	1	41	25	51 *	.1	.2
355 Presb Ch (USA)	1	135	81	170 *	.5	.8
356 Presb Ch Amer	1	109	60	113	.3	.5
419 So Bapt Conv	25	6,984	2,618	8,772 *	24.1	39.7
449 Un Methodist	7	1,321	622	1,657 *	4.6	7.5
CORYELL	**77**	**21,623**	**7,125**	**29,236 ***	**39.0**	**100.0**
053 Assemb of God	2	191	253	302	.4	1.0
056 Baha'i	0	11	NR	11	-	-
081 Catholic	2	NR	NR	1,886	2.5	6.5
093 Chr Ch (Disc)	1	70	15	89 *	.1	.3
097 Chr Chs&Chs Cr	1	150	NR	190 *	.3	.6
121 Ch God (Abr)	1	43	37	55 *	.1	.2
127 Ch God (Cleve)	1	57	48	72 *	.1	.2
151 L-D Saints	3	NR	NR	914	1.2	3.1
165 Ch of Nazarene	2	99	96	157	.2	.5
167 Chs of Christ	9	749	633	967	1.3	3.3
193 Episcopal	2	NR	53	61	.1	.2
207 E.L.C.A.	1	127	62	170	.2	.6
283 Luth—MO Synod	4	486	394	654	.9	2.2
339 Pent Ch of God	2	179	NR	344	.5	1.2
355 Presb Ch (USA)	2	205	97	261 *	.3	.9
360 Prim Bapt Chrch	3	NR	NR	NR	-	-
388 Reg Bapt Gen As	1	27	45	45 *	.1	.2
419 So Bapt Conv	28	12,011	2,665	15,245 *	20.3	52.1
443 Un C of Christ	1	114	50	145 *	.2	.5
449 Un Methodist	10	2,104	677	2,668 *	3.6	9.1
498 Indep.Charis.	1	5,000	2,000	5,000	6.7	17.1
COTTLE	**10**	**1,487**	**439**	**2,091 ***	**109.8**	**100.0**
053 Assemb of God	1	17	15	18	.9	.9
059 Bapt Miss Assn	1	120	40	145 *	7.6	6.9
081 Catholic	1	NR	NR	196	10.3	9.4
093 Chr Ch (Disc)	1	141	32	171 *	9.0	8.2
151 L-D Saints	1	NR	NR	97	5.1	4.6
167 Chs of Christ	2	97	103	117	6.1	5.6
360 Prim Bapt Chrch	1	NR	NR	NR	-	-
419 So Bapt Conv	1	922	177	1,117 *	58.7	53.4
449 Un Methodist	1	190	72	230 *	12.1	11.0
CRANE	**8**	**1,635**	**458**	**2,385 ***	**59.7**	**100.0**
053 Assemb of God	2	43	55	70	1.8	2.9
081 Catholic	1	NR	NR	250	6.3	10.5
097 Chr Chs&Chs Cr	1	250	NR	326 *	8.2	13.7
167 Chs of Christ	2	140	128	172	4.3	7.2
419 So Bapt Conv	1	1,024	185	1,335 *	33.4	56.0
449 Un Methodist	1	178	90	232 *	5.8	9.7
CROCKETT	**12**	**1,787**	**525**	**3,467 ***	**84.6**	**100.0**
053 Assemb of God	2	86	63	102	2.5	2.9
081 Catholic	1	NR	NR	1,200	29.3	34.6
145 Ch God Prophcy	1	27	NR	34 *	.8	1.0
167 Chs of Christ	2	211	150	274	6.7	7.9
283 Luth—MO Synod	1	10	8	11	.3	.3
419 So Bapt Conv	4	1,090	218	1,385 *	33.8	39.9
449 Un Methodist	1	363	86	461 *	11.2	13.3
CROSBY	**26**	**3,346**	**1,443**	**6,011 ***	**85.0**	**100.0**
053 Assemb of God	3	94	130	136	1.9	2.3
056 Baha'i	0	2	NR	2	-	-
081 Catholic	3	NR	NR	1,641	23.2	27.3
167 Chs of Christ	7	390	357	500	7.1	8.3
263 Int Foursq Gos	1	25	27	33 *	.5	.5
349 Pent Holiness	1	48	40	63 *	.9	1.0
360 Prim Bapt Chrch	1	NR	NR	NR	-	-
419 So Bapt Conv	7	2,186	693	2,852 *	40.3	47.4
449 Un Methodist	3	601	196	784 *	11.1	13.0
CULBERSON	**12**	**1,102**	**278**	**2,853 ***	**95.9**	**100.0**
053 Assemb of God	1	6	8	25	.8	.9
056 Baha'i	0	18	NR	18	.6	.6
081 Catholic	4	NR	NR	1,410	47.4	49.4
165 Ch of Nazarene	1	0	0	0	-	-
167 Chs of Christ	2	100	41	126	4.2	4.4
413 S.D.A.	1	56	NR	67	2.3	2.3
419 So Bapt Conv	2	842	195	1,102 *	37.0	38.6
449 Un Methodist	1	80	34	105 *	3.5	3.7
DALLAM	**16**	**1,965**	**852**	**4,008 ***	**64.4**	**100.0**
053 Assemb of God	1	35	45	92	1.5	2.3
056 Baha'i	0	1	NR	1	-	-
081 Catholic	1	NR	NR	1,115	17.9	27.8
097 Chr Chs&Chs Cr	1	278	NR	369 *	5.9	9.2
143 CG in Cr(Menn)	2	249	NR	331 *	5.3	8.3
151 L-D Saints	1	NR	NR	97	1.6	2.4
167 Chs of Christ	3	325	330	409	6.6	10.2
193 Episcopal	1	NR	48	160	2.6	4.0
355 Presb Ch (USA)	1	87	45	115 *	1.8	2.9
413 S.D.A.	1	45	NR	54	.9	1.3
419 So Bapt Conv	1	399	114	530 *	8.5	13.2
449 Un Methodist	2	546	265	725 *	11.7	18.1
467 Wesleyan	1	0	5	10	.2	.2
DALLAS	**1,233**	**500,213**	**232,105**	**1,222,752 ***	**55.1**	**100.0**
017 Amer Bapt Assn	9	1,692	NR	2,170 *	.1	.2
019 Amer Bapt USA	5	1,103	275	1,416 *	.1	.1
034 Ant Orth of NA	2	185	NR	370	-	-
050 Armen Ap Etchm	1	76	NR	385	-	-
053 Assemb of God	94	26,809	17,247	30,891	1.4	2.5
056 Baha'i	11	1,511	NR	1,511	.1	.1

NR–Not Reported   *Total adherents estimated from known number of communicant, confirmed, full members.   - Represents a percentage less than 0.1.   Percentages may not total 100 due to rounding.

Table 4: Religious Congregations by County and Group: 2000

Religious Group	Number of Churches, Synagogues, Mosques, or Temples	Number of Communicant, Confirmed, or Full Members	Number of Attendees	Total Adherents: Number of Adherents	Total Adherents: % of Total Pop.	Total Adherents: % of Total Adh.
059 Bapt Miss Assn	36	10,903	2,644	14,029 *	.6	1.1
076 Buddhism	20	NR	NR	NR	-	-
081 Catholic	50	NR	NR	480,510	21.7	39.3
084 Calvary Chapel	1	NR	NR	NR	-	-
089 Chr & Miss Al	3	157	NR	178	-	-
093 Chr Ch (Disc)	38	13,583	4,135	17,442 *	.8	1.4
097 Chr Chs&Chs Cr	12	3,030	NR	3,891 *	.2	.3
105 Christian Ref	1	36	60	46 *	-	-
123 Ch God (Ander)	3	NR	363	363	-	-
127 Ch God (Cleve)	29	4,078	2,237	5,332 *	.2	.4
145 Ch God Prophcy	4	108	NR	140 *	-	-
151 L-D Saints	32	NR	NR	12,066	.5	1.0
165 Ch of Nazarene	23	3,840	2,382	5,856	.3	.5
167 Chs of Christ	110	34,337	30,453	45,037	2.0	3.7
173 Comm of Christ	4	489	NR	489	-	-
185 Cumber Presb	3	481	NR	838	-	.1
193 Episcopal	38	NR	9,470	27,740	1.3	2.3
203 Evan Free Ch	2	110	225	225	-	-
207 E.L.C.A.	28	7,626	3,836	9,981	.4	.8
216 Evan Presby Ch	1	152	NR	195 *	-	-
221 Free Methodist	3	99	156	178	-	-
223 Free Will Bapt	1	42	NR	55 *	-	-
226 Friends-USA	1	15	NR	19 *	-	-
246 Greek Orthodox	1	NR	NR	1,926	.1	.2
252 Hindu	7	NR	NR	NR	-	-
262 Int Cou Comm Ch	3	711	NR	913 *	-	.1
263 Int Foursq Gos	9	662	713	850 *	-	.1
264 Int Chs of Crst	1	1,486	2,380	1,946	.1	.2
267 Muslim Est	13	NR	4,959	22,723	1.0	1.9
268 Jain	1	NR	NR	NR	-	-
283 Luth—MO Synod	18	7,131	3,681	9,349	.4	.8
288 Mennonite USA	4	179	181	261 *	-	-
290 Metro Comm Ch	2	2,598	2,309	3,337 *	.2	.3
304 NatPrimBapt USA	26	1,197	NR	1,537 *	.1	.1
313 N Am Bapt Conf	3	436	673	560 *	-	-
331 OCA: Ter Diocs	2	172	NR	580	-	-
333 Malan Dioc Am	4	NR	NR	1,325	.1	.1
334 Malan Syr Orth	2	120	NR	600	-	-
335 Orth Pres Ch	1	38	42	49	-	-
339 Pent Ch of God	8	174	NR	370	-	-
349 Pent Holiness	6	526	497	675 *	-	.1
355 Presb Ch (USA)	42	21,743	9,194	27,923 *	1.3	2.3
356 Presb Ch Amer	10	4,509	3,435	6,051	.3	.5
360 Prim Bapt Chrch	3	NR	NR	NR	-	-
370 Ref Baptist Chs	1	NR	NR	NR	-	-
371 Ref Ch in Am	1	78	72	95	-	-
401 Rus Orth Abroad	1	NR	NR	NR	-	-
403 Salvation Army	5	904	675	5,049	.2	.4
413 S.D.A.	26	6,226	NR	7,411	.3	.6
416 Sikh	3	NR	NR	NR	-	-
418 Southw Bapt Fel	5	NR	NR	NR	-	-
419 So Bapt Conv	303	219,599	64,353	281,984 *	12.7	23.1
435 Unitarian-Univ	3	813	NR	1,044 *	-	.1
443 Un C of Christ	5	996	396	1,279 *	.1	.1
449 Un Methodist	94	82,625	30,309	106,100 *	4.8	8.7
463 Vineyard	2	168	193	216 *	-	-
467 Wesleyan	1	0	50	120	-	-
469 WELS	3	492	370	711	-	.1
490 Zoroastrian	1	NR	NR	NR	-	-
496 Jewish Est	17	NR	NR	38,250	1.7	3.1
498 Indep.Charis.	6	12,400	8,500	12,525	.6	1.0
499 Indep.Non-Char	25	23,768	25,640	25,640	1.2	2.1
DAWSON	**36**	**7,364**	**2,463**	**11,939 ***	**79.7**	**100.0**
053 Assemb of God	4	173	200	260	1.7	2.2
056 Baha'i	0	6	NR	6	-	.1
059 Bapt Miss Assn	1	73	40	90 *	.6	.8
081 Catholic	2	NR	NR	2,714	18.1	22.7
093 Chr Ch (Disc)	1	36	21	44 *	.3	.4
165 Ch of Nazarene	2	90	51	199	1.3	1.7
167 Chs of Christ	5	646	509	782	5.2	6.5
193 Episcopal	1	NR	5	15	.1	.1
263 Int Foursq Gos	1	274	79	338 *	2.3	2.8
283 Luth—MO Synod	1	72	45	95	.6	.8
349 Pent Holiness	1	25	30	31 *	.2	.3
355 Presb Ch (USA)	1	126	59	155 *	1.0	1.3
360 Prim Bapt Chrch	1	NR	NR	NR	-	-
419 So Bapt Conv	10	4,932	1,085	6,086 *	40.6	51.0
449 Un Methodist	5	911	339	1,124 *	7.5	9.4
DEAF SMITH	**28**	**5,817**	**2,259**	**15,261 ***	**82.2**	**100.0**
053 Assemb of God	3	266	335	382	2.1	2.5
056 Baha'i	0	10	NR	10	.1	.1
081 Catholic	2	NR	NR	7,475	40.3	49.0
127 Ch God (Cleve)	1	26	18	35 *	.2	.2
165 Ch of Nazarene	2	633	459	753	4.1	4.9
167 Chs of Christ	4	377	293	466	2.5	3.1
193 Episcopal	1	NR	43	66	.4	.4
283 Luth—MO Synod	1	65	41	89	.5	.6
355 Presb Ch (USA)	1	119	60	161 *	.9	1.1
413 S.D.A.	1	32	NR	38	.2	.2
419 So Bapt Conv	9	3,035	707	4,094 *	22.1	26.8
449 Un Methodist	3	1,254	303	1,692 *	9.1	11.1
DELTA	**19**	**2,423**	**1,057**	**3,010 ***	**56.5**	**100.0**
053 Assemb of God	1	30	35	49	.9	1.6
059 Bapt Miss Assn	1	75	80	93 *	1.7	3.1
167 Chs of Christ	2	91	105	119	2.2	4.0
339 Pent Ch of God	1	29	NR	35	.7	1.2
413 S.D.A.	1	23	NR	27	.5	.9
419 So Bapt Conv	7	1,708	605	2,110 *	39.6	70.1
449 Un Methodist	6	467	232	577 *	10.8	19.2
DENTON	**245**	**78,826**	**45,826**	**149,336 ***	**34.5**	**100.0**
017 Amer Bapt Assn	5	481	NR	617 *	.1	.4
053 Assemb of God	22	3,338	3,863	5,905	1.4	4.0
056 Baha'i	5	296	NR	296	.1	.2
059 Bapt Miss Assn	2	174	165	224 *	.1	.1
081 Catholic	7	NR	NR	27,580	6.4	18.5
093 Chr Ch (Disc)	6	1,367	484	1,755 *	.4	1.2
097 Chr Chs&Chs Cr	2	330	NR	424 *	.1	.3
105 Christian Ref	1	349	375	448 *	.1	.3
127 Ch God (Cleve)	3	213	196	274 *	.1	.2
151 L-D Saints	17	NR	NR	6,545	1.5	4.4
165 Ch of Nazarene	5	851	665	1,317	.3	.9
167 Chs of Christ	21	4,087	4,072	5,418	1.3	3.6
173 Comm of Christ	1	30	NR	30	-	-
175 Congr Chr Chs	1	104	59	133 *	-	.1
185 Cumber Presb	1	174	NR	248	.1	.2
193 Episcopal	5	NR	752	2,347	.5	1.6
201 Evan Cov Ch	2	164	149	211 *	-	.1
203 Evan Free Ch	1	60	120	120	-	.1
207 E.L.C.A.	4	1,828	1,145	2,685	.6	1.8
267 Muslim Est	3	NR	1,236	5,673	1.3	3.8
283 Luth—MO Synod	3	2,441	1,602	3,382	.8	2.3
290 Metro Comm Ch	1	92	71	71 *	-	-
313 N Am Bapt Conf	1	41	67	53 *	-	-
335 Orth Pres Ch	1	33	36	41	-	-
339 Pent Ch of God	4	181	NR	216	-	.1
355 Presb Ch (USA)	5	1,573	752	2,018 *	.5	1.4
356 Presb Ch Amer	2	323	352	460	.1	.3
360 Prim Bapt Chrch	1	NR	NR	NR	-	-
371 Ref Ch in Am	1	141	123	323	.1	.2
403 Salvation Army	1	51	43	40	-	-
413 S.D.A.	4	175	NR	208	-	.1
418 Southw Bapt Fel	1	NR	NR	NR	-	-
419 So Bapt Conv	70	41,753	16,966	53,594 *	12.4	35.9
435 Unitarian-Univ	2	409	NR	525 *	.1	.4
443 Un C of Christ	1	337	135	433 *	.1	.3
449 Un Methodist	27	15,595	6,991	20,020 *	4.6	13.4
463 Vineyard	1	99	85	127 *	-	.1
467 Wesleyan	1	51	139	260	.1	.2
469 WELS	1	110	83	140	-	.1
496 Jewish Est	1	NR	NR	75	-	.1
499 Indep.Non-Char	2	1,575	5,100	5,100	1.2	3.4

NR–Not Reported *Total adherents estimated from known number of communicant, confirmed, full members. - Represents a percentage less than 0.1. Percentages may not total 100 due to rounding.

Table 4: Religious Congregations by County and Group: 2000

Religious Group	Number of Churches, Synagogues, Mosques, or Temples	Number of Communicant, Confirmed, or Full Members	Number of Attendees	Total Adherents: Number of Adherents	Total Adherents: % of Total Pop.	Total Adherents: % of Total Adh.
DE WITT	**37**	**4,753**	**1,936**	**11,261 ***	**56.3**	**100.0**
053 Assemb of God	2	83	50	92	.5	.8
056 Baha'i	0	1	NR	1	-	-
081 Catholic	8	NR	NR	5,326	26.6	47.3
167 Chs of Christ	2	128	118	154	.8	1.4
193 Episcopal	1	NR	43	155	.8	1.4
207 E.L.C.A.	7	2,193	769	2,636	13.2	23.4
223 Free Will Bapt	1	42	NR	52 *	.3	.5
339 Pent Ch of God	1	42	NR	100	.5	.9
355 Presb Ch (USA)	2	288	143	349 *	1.7	3.1
360 Prim Bapt Chrch	1	NR	NR	NR	-	-
419 So Bapt Conv	9	1,609	678	1,951 *	9.7	17.3
449 Un Methodist	3	367	135	445 *	2.2	4.0
DICKENS	**19**	**1,743**	**682**	**2,408 ***	**87.2**	**100.0**
053 Assemb of God	2	48	63	83	3.0	3.4
059 Bapt Miss Assn	1	30	27	35 *	1.3	1.5
081 Catholic	1	NR	NR	297	10.8	12.3
093 Chr Ch (Disc)	1	20	10	23 *	.8	1.0
165 Ch of Nazarene	1	13	28	62	2.2	2.6
167 Chs of Christ	5	205	211	259	9.4	10.8
419 So Bapt Conv	5	1,201	250	1,387 *	50.2	57.6
449 Un Methodist	3	226	93	262 *	9.5	10.9
DIMMIT	**12**	**1,256**	**391**	**11,418 ***	**111.4**	**100.0**
053 Assemb of God	2	45	39	46	.4	.4
056 Baha'i	0	1	NR	1	-	-
081 Catholic	2	NR	NR	9,703	94.7	85.0
167 Chs of Christ	1	40	40	50	.5	.4
193 Episcopal	1	NR	6	50	.5	.4
413 S.D.A.	1	9	NR	11	.1	.1
419 So Bapt Conv	3	988	237	1,325 *	12.9	11.6
449 Un Methodist	2	173	69	232 *	2.3	2.0
DONLEY	**14**	**2,119**	**921**	**2,706 ***	**70.7**	**100.0**
053 Assemb of God	2	78	77	84	2.2	3.1
081 Catholic	1	NR	NR	120	3.1	4.4
165 Ch of Nazarene	1	39	40	48	1.3	1.8
167 Chs of Christ	2	213	215	261	6.8	9.6
193 Episcopal	1	NR	15	45	1.2	1.7
355 Presb Ch (USA)	1	33	18	40 *	1.0	1.5
419 So Bapt Conv	4	1,320	391	1,585 *	41.4	58.6
449 Un Methodist	2	436	165	523 *	13.7	19.3
DUVAL	**16**	**1,204**	**395**	**9,347 ***	**71.2**	**100.0**
053 Assemb of God	1	25	27	37	.3	.4
056 Baha'i	0	1	NR	1	-	-
081 Catholic	8	NR	NR	7,800	59.5	83.4
167 Chs of Christ	1	40	35	46	.4	.5
419 So Bapt Conv	4	1,038	260	1,335 *	10.2	14.3
449 Un Methodist	2	100	73	128 *	1.0	1.4
EASTLAND	**66**	**11,042**	**6,253**	**13,992 ***	**76.5**	**100.0**
053 Assemb of God	2	97	73	95	.5	.7
056 Baha'i	0	3	NR	3	-	-
081 Catholic	3	NR	NR	506	2.8	3.6
093 Chr Ch (Disc)	2	390	95	471 *	2.6	3.4
123 Ch God (Ander)	1	NR	4	4	-	-
127 Ch God (Cleve)	2	91	42	110 *	.6	.8
145 Ch God Prophcy	1	27	NR	33 *	.2	.2
151 L-D Saints	1	NR	NR	93	.5	.7
165 Ch of Nazarene	1	99	92	109	.6	.8
167 Chs of Christ	11	1,214	1,078	1,547	8.5	11.1
193 Episcopal	1	NR	13	23	.1	.2
263 Int Foursq Gos	1	22	31	31 *	.2	.2
283 Luth—MO Synod	1	202	102	231	1.3	1.7
323 Old Ord Amish	1	6	NR	7 *	-	.1
355 Presb Ch (USA)	2	90	47	109 *	.6	.8
360 Prim Bapt Chrch	2	NR	NR	NR	-	-
413 S.D.A.	1	45	NR	54	.3	.4
419 So Bapt Conv	28	7,365	4,328	8,887 *	48.6	63.5
449 Un Methodist	5	1,391	348	1,679 *	9.2	12.0
ECTOR	**120**	**39,058**	**13,477**	**65,728 ***	**54.3**	**100.0**
017 Amer Bapt Assn	2	291	NR	379 *	.3	.6
053 Assemb of God	9	788	794	1,022	.8	1.6
056 Baha'i	0	38	NR	38	-	.1
059 Bapt Miss Assn	2	291	107	379 *	.3	.6
081 Catholic	7	NR	NR	15,272	12.6	23.2
093 Chr Ch (Disc)	2	607	295	791 *	.7	1.2
097 Chr Chs&Chs Cr	4	1,091	NR	1,421 *	1.2	2.2
123 Ch God (Ander)	1	NR	150	150	.1	.2
127 Ch God (Cleve)	2	281	93	366 *	.3	.6
151 L-D Saints	2	NR	NR	783	.6	1.2
165 Ch of Nazarene	3	369	188	456	.4	.7
167 Chs of Christ	16	2,166	2,048	2,852	2.4	4.3
173 Comm of Christ	1	63	NR	63	.1	.1
185 Cumber Presb	2	211	NR	231	.2	.4
193 Episcopal	3	NR	260	568	.5	.9
207 E.L.C.A.	2	429	255	678	.6	1.0
223 Free Will Bapt	1	42	NR	55 *	-	.1
245 Greek Orth Vslp	1	105	NR	135	.1	.2
263 Int Foursq Gos	2	114	232	232 *	.2	.4
283 Luth—MO Synod	2	561	42	85	.1	.1
349 Pent Holiness	1	18	20	23 *	-	-
355 Presb Ch (USA)	2	1,072	402	1,397 *	1.2	2.1
360 Prim Bapt Chrch	1	NR	NR	NR	-	-
403 Salvation Army	1	118	65	138	.1	.2
413 S.D.A.	3	226	NR	269	.2	.4
419 So Bapt Conv	32	21,424	4,780	27,917 *	23.0	42.5
435 Unitarian-Univ	1	14	NR	18 *	-	-
449 Un Methodist	8	2,909	1,226	3,791 *	3.1	5.8
463 Vineyard	1	130	120	169 *	.1	.3
496 Jewish Est	2	NR	NR	200	.2	.3
498 Indep.Charis.	1	400	400	550	.5	.8
499 Indep.Non-Char	3	5,300	2,000	5,300	4.4	8.1
EDWARDS	**9**	**747**	**356**	**1,714 ***	**79.3**	**100.0**
081 Catholic	1	NR	NR	762	35.2	44.5
167 Chs of Christ	2	130	102	169	7.8	9.9
355 Presb Ch (USA)	1	65	30	83 *	3.8	4.8
419 So Bapt Conv	3	416	160	528 *	24.4	30.8
449 Un Methodist	2	136	64	172 *	8.0	10.0
ELLIS	**141**	**35,961**	**16,629**	**64,543 ***	**58.0**	**100.0**
053 Assemb of God	15	1,415	1,748	2,575	2.3	4.0
056 Baha'i	0	205	NR	205	.2	.3
059 Bapt Miss Assn	15	5,524	2,383	7,174 *	6.4	11.1
081 Catholic	4	NR	NR	16,117	14.5	25.0
093 Chr Ch (Disc)	5	628	241	816 *	.7	1.3
127 Ch God (Cleve)	2	637	382	827 *	.7	1.3
151 L-D Saints	1	NR	NR	598	.5	.9
165 Ch of Nazarene	2	191	148	320	.3	.5
167 Chs of Christ	18	2,241	2,160	2,978	2.7	4.6
173 Comm of Christ	1	24	NR	24	-	-
185 Cumber Presb	1	118	NR	198	.2	.3
193 Episcopal	2	NR	137	273	.2	.4
207 E.L.C.A.	1	54	43	68	.1	.1
263 Int Foursq Gos	1	177	406	406 *	.4	.6
283 Luth—MO Synod	2	336	202	412	.4	.6
304 NatPrimBapt USA	1	65	NR	84 *	.1	.1
339 Pent Ch of God	3	124	NR	167	.1	.3
349 Pent Holiness	1	29	38	38 *	-	.1
355 Presb Ch (USA)	6	789	333	1,024 *	.9	1.6
360 Prim Bapt Chrch	1	NR	NR	NR	-	-
403 Salvation Army	1	16	34	24	-	-
413 S.D.A.	3	184	NR	219	.2	.3
419 So Bapt Conv	30	16,698	6,234	21,683 *	19.5	33.6
449 Un Methodist	22	6,048	1,867	7,855 *	7.1	12.2
499 Indep.Non-Char	3	458	273	458	.4	.7
EL PASO	**300**	**48,711**	**27,676**	**431,115 ***	**63.4**	**100.0**
034 Ant Orth of NA	1	352	NR	704	.1	.2

NR–Not Reported *Total adherents estimated from known number of communicant, confirmed, full members. - Represents a percentage less than 0.1. Percentages may not total 100 due to rounding.

Table 4: Religious Congregations by County and Group: 2000

Religious Group	Number of Churches, Synagogues, Mosques, or Temples	Number of Communicant, Confirmed, or Full Members	Number of Attendees	Total Adherents		
				Number of Adherents	% of Total Pop.	% of Total Adh.
050 Armen Ap Etchm	1	24	NR	120	-	-
053 Assemb of God	27	5,033	4,521	6,323	.9	1.5
056 Baha'i	1	369	NR	369	.1	.1
081 Catholic	57	NR	NR	349,866	51.5	81.2
084 Calvary Chapel	3	NR	NR	NR	-	-
089 Chr & Miss Al	2	20	NR	97	-	-
093 Chr Ch (Disc)	4	821	337	1,093 *	.2	.3
097 Chr Chs&Chs Cr	4	550	NR	733 *	.1	.2
105 Christian Ref	1	122	175	162 *	-	-
123 Ch God (Ander)	1	NR	34	34	-	-
127 Ch God (Cleve)	3	228	93	304 *	-	.1
145 Ch God Prophcy	4	108	NR	144 *	-	-
151 L-D Saints	16	NR	NR	5,662	.8	1.3
165 Ch of Nazarene	8	1,333	884	4,106	.6	1.0
167 Chs of Christ	15	1,680	1,648	2,216	.3	.5
173 Comm of Christ	1	34	NR	34	-	-
175 Congr Chr Chs	2	353	185	470 *	.1	.1
183 Cons Menn Conf	1	23	28	33	-	-
185 Cumber Presb	2	81	NR	94	-	-
193 Episcopal	7	NR	1,174	2,865	.4	.7
203 Evan Free Ch	2	132	275	275	-	.1
207 E.L.C.A.	7	956	634	1,234	.2	.3
226 Friends-USA	1	30	NR	40 *	-	-
246 Greek Orthodox	1	NR	NR	192	-	-
263 Int Foursq Gos	4	416	252	554 *	.1	.1
264 Int Chs of Crst	1	74	117	122	-	-
267 Muslim Est	1	NR	156	609	.1	.1
283 Luth—MO Synod	6	1,200	810	1,700	.3	.4
290 Metro Comm Ch	1	44	42	59 *	-	-
349 Pent Holiness	4	268	234	357 *	.1	.1
355 Presb Ch (USA)	10	1,926	810	2,565 *	.4	.6
356 Presb Ch Amer	2	54	85	85	-	-
360 Prim Bapt Chrch	1	NR	NR	NR	-	-
403 Salvation Army	2	516	468	1,384	.2	.3
413 S.D.A.	7	1,018	NR	1,213	.2	.3
419 So Bapt Conv	51	18,478	6,537	24,609 *	3.6	5.7
435 Unitarian-Univ	1	102	NR	136 *	-	-
443 Un C of Christ	2	146	109	194 *	-	-
449 Un Methodist	22	6,589	3,088	8,776 *	1.3	2.0
463 Vineyard	3	915	812	1,227 *	.2	.3
469 WELS	4	366	238	505	.1	.1
496 Jewish Est	2	NR	NR	5,000	.7	1.2
498 Indep.Charis.	2	900	1,200	1,400	.2	.3
499 Indep.Non-Char	2	3,450	2,730	3,450	.5	.8
ERATH	**64**	**13,426**	**6,152**	**18,937 ***	**57.4**	**100.0**
053 Assemb of God	4	269	233	371	1.1	2.0
056 Baha'i	0	9	NR	9	-	-
081 Catholic	2	NR	NR	1,774	5.4	9.4
093 Chr Ch (Disc)	2	257	108	317 *	1.0	1.7
105 Christian Ref	1	175	160	216 *	.7	1.1
127 Ch God (Cleve)	1	25	20	31 *	.1	.2
151 L-D Saints	1	NR	NR	325	1.0	1.7
165 Ch of Nazarene	1	59	37	59	.2	.3
167 Chs of Christ	12	1,374	1,253	1,785	5.4	9.4
193 Episcopal	2	NR	130	194	.6	1.0
283 Luth—MO Synod	1	237	109	280	.8	1.5
355 Presb Ch (USA)	1	89	56	110 *	.3	.6
360 Prim Bapt Chrch	2	NR	NR	NR	-	-
413 S.D.A.	1	34	NR	40	.1	.2
419 So Bapt Conv	24	8,743	3,433	10,772 *	32.6	56.9
449 Un Methodist	9	2,155	613	2,654 *	8.0	14.0
FALLS	**55**	**5,914**	**2,752**	**10,497 ***	**56.5**	**100.0**
053 Assemb of God	2	79	85	97	.5	.9
056 Baha'i	0	3	NR	3	-	-
061 Beachy Amish	1	77	NR	96 *	.5	.9
081 Catholic	4	NR	NR	2,969	16.0	28.3
093 Chr Ch (Disc)	1	65	45	81 *	.4	.8
167 Chs of Christ	9	341	303	431	2.3	4.1
193 Episcopal	1	NR	48	108	.6	1.0
207 E.L.C.A.	1	140	92	167	.9	1.6
283 Luth—MO Synod	3	481	262	590	3.2	5.6

Religious Group	Number of Churches, Synagogues, Mosques, or Temples	Number of Communicant, Confirmed, or Full Members	Number of Attendees	Total Adherents		
				Number of Adherents	% of Total Pop.	% of Total Adh.
355 Presb Ch (USA)	2	131	174	244 *	1.3	2.3
419 So Bapt Conv	16	3,467	1,225	4,306 *	23.2	41.0
443 Un C of Christ	3	176	68	219 *	1.2	2.1
449 Un Methodist	12	954	450	1,186 *	6.4	11.3
FANNIN	**100**	**16,256**	**5,881**	**23,325 ***	**74.7**	**100.0**
053 Assemb of God	4	99	100	127	.4	.5
056 Baha'i	0	2	NR	2	-	-
081 Catholic	3	NR	NR	3,203	10.3	13.7
093 Chr Ch (Disc)	5	316	126	384 *	1.2	1.6
127 Ch God (Cleve)	2	372	206	453 *	1.4	1.9
151 L-D Saints	1	NR	NR	222	.7	1.0
165 Ch of Nazarene	1	144	51	144	.5	.6
167 Chs of Christ	20	1,116	1,097	1,415	4.5	6.1
193 Episcopal	1	NR	31	58	.2	.2
283 Luth—MO Synod	3	84	80	103	.3	.4
339 Pent Ch of God	2	41	NR	87	.3	.4
349 Pent Holiness	1	40	16	49 *	.2	.2
355 Presb Ch (USA)	3	269	151	327 *	1.0	1.4
360 Prim Bapt Chrch	1	NR	NR	NR	-	-
419 So Bapt Conv	36	12,079	3,257	14,692 *	47.0	63.0
449 Un Methodist	17	1,694	766	2,059 *	6.6	8.8
FAYETTE	**55**	**6,845**	**3,104**	**17,509 ***	**80.3**	**100.0**
053 Assemb of God	1	33	35	44	.2	.3
056 Baha'i	0	2	NR	2	-	-
081 Catholic	14	NR	NR	9,053	41.5	51.7
167 Chs of Christ	3	151	160	193	.9	1.1
193 Episcopal	1	NR	76	145	.7	.8
207 E.L.C.A.	10	2,378	969	2,795	12.8	16.0
283 Luth—MO Synod	4	1,225	596	1,452	6.7	8.3
355 Presb Ch (USA)	1	181	82	219 *	1.0	1.3
413 S.D.A.	1	17	NR	20	.1	.1
419 So Bapt Conv	8	2,023	755	2,446 *	11.2	14.0
443 Un C of Christ	1	86	43	104 *	.5	.6
449 Un Methodist	9	749	388	906 *	4.2	5.2
496 Jewish Est	2	NR	NR	130	.6	.7
FISHER	**17**	**3,208**	**1,328**	**4,579 ***	**105.4**	**100.0**
056 Baha'i	0	1	NR	1	-	-
081 Catholic	2	NR	NR	540	12.4	11.8
167 Chs of Christ	2	210	210	256	5.9	5.6
263 Int Foursq Gos	1	92	234	234 *	5.4	5.1
419 So Bapt Conv	8	2,448	674	2,990 *	68.8	65.3
449 Un Methodist	4	457	210	558 *	12.8	12.2
FLOYD	**24**	**3,981**	**1,579**	**6,399 ***	**82.3**	**100.0**
053 Assemb of God	3	164	167	256	3.3	4.0
059 Bapt Miss Assn	1	75	23	99 *	1.3	1.5
081 Catholic	2	NR	NR	1,139	14.7	17.8
093 Chr Ch (Disc)	1	20	12	26 *	.3	.4
167 Chs of Christ	4	378	359	468	6.0	7.3
207 E.L.C.A.	1	72	37	98	1.3	1.5
360 Prim Bapt Chrch	1	NR	NR	NR	-	-
419 So Bapt Conv	8	2,436	678	3,211 *	41.3	50.2
449 Un Methodist	3	836	303	1,102 *	14.2	17.2
FOARD	**9**	**1,117**	**366**	**1,462 ***	**90.1**	**100.0**
053 Assemb of God	2	61	50	64	3.9	4.4
081 Catholic	1	NR	NR	97	6.0	6.6
097 Chr Chs&Chs Cr	1	125	NR	155 *	9.6	10.6
167 Chs of Christ	2	106	77	125	7.7	8.5
419 So Bapt Conv	1	535	128	662 *	40.8	45.3
449 Un Methodist	2	290	111	359 *	22.1	24.6
FORT BEND	**161**	**48,664**	**29,142**	**162,495 ***	**45.8**	**100.0**
053 Assemb of God	9	911	943	1,311	.4	.8
056 Baha'i	3	149	NR	149	-	.1
076 Buddhism	2	NR	NR	NR	-	-
081 Catholic	11	NR	NR	87,821	24.8	54.0
093 Chr Ch (Disc)	2	174	45	230 *	.1	.1

NR–Not Reported *Total adherents estimated from known number of communicant, confirmed, full members. - Represents a percentage less than 0.1. Percentages may not total 100 due to rounding.

Table 4: Religious Congregations by County and Group: 2000

Religious Group	Number of Churches, Synagogues, Mosques, or Temples	Number of Communicant, Confirmed, or Full Members	Number of Attendees	Total Adherents: Number of Adherents	Total Adherents: % of Total Pop.	Total Adherents: % of Total Adh.
097 Chr Chs&Chs Cr	1	354	NR	468 *	.1	.3
105 Christian Ref	1	108	100	143 *	-	.1
123 Ch God (Ander)	3	NR	137	137	-	.1
127 Ch God (Cleve)	2	91	27	121 *	-	.1
145 Ch God Prophcy	3	81	NR	108 *	-	.1
151 L-D Saints	7	NR	NR	2,907	.8	1.8
165 Ch of Nazarene	1	97	76	150	-	.1
167 Chs of Christ	10	2,508	2,618	3,411	1.0	2.1
173 Comm of Christ	1	65	NR	65	-	-
193 Episcopal	4	NR	749	1,664	.5	1.0
203 Evan Free Ch	2	124	260	260	.1	.2
207 E.L.C.A.	7	1,644	796	2,119	.6	1.3
221 Free Methodist	3	104	128	193	.1	.1
223 Free Will Bapt	1	42	NR	56 *	-	-
252 Hindu	3	NR	NR	NR	-	-
263 Int Foursq Gos	1	35	67	67 *	-	-
267 Muslim Est	2	NR	690	2,613	.7	1.6
283 Luth—MO Synod	3	888	631	1,271	.4	.8
288 Mennonite USA	1	0	20	20 *	-	-
333 Malan Dioc Am	1	NR	NR	625	.2	.4
349 Pent Holiness	1	24	20	32 *	-	-
355 Presb Ch (USA)	4	1,354	667	1,792 *	.5	1.1
356 Presb Ch Amer	1	63	120	120	-	.1
413 S.D.A.	9	384	NR	458	.1	.3
419 So Bapt Conv	37	23,178	11,411	30,664 *	8.7	18.9
435 Unitarian-Univ	1	108	NR	143 *	-	.1
443 Un C of Christ	4	1,338	603	1,770 *	.5	1.1
449 Un Methodist	16	11,780	5,534	15,584 *	4.4	9.6
463 Vineyard	1	1,000	700	1,323 *	.4	.8
496 Jewish Est	1	NR	NR	1,600	.5	1.0
498 Indep.Charis.	1	700	700	1,000	.3	.6
499 Indep.Non-Char	1	1,360	2,100	2,100	.6	1.3
FRANKLIN	**22**	**5,252**	**1,973**	**6,888 ***	**72.8**	**100.0**
053 Assemb of God	1	49	58	58	.6	.8
056 Baha'i	0	2	NR	2	-	-
059 Bapt Miss Assn	2	472	181	575 *	6.1	8.3
081 Catholic	1	NR	NR	493	5.2	7.2
093 Chr Ch (Disc)	1	118	52	144 *	1.5	2.1
145 Ch God Prophcy	1	27	NR	33 *	.3	.5
165 Ch of Nazarene	1	19	13	19	.2	.3
167 Chs of Christ	2	194	185	243	2.6	3.5
419 So Bapt Conv	11	3,771	1,226	4,592 *	48.6	66.7
449 Un Methodist	1	541	209	659 *	7.0	9.6
469 WELS	1	59	49	70	.7	1.0
FREESTONE	**45**	**7,544**	**2,789**	**10,102 ***	**56.5**	**100.0**
053 Assemb of God	2	82	90	102	.6	1.0
059 Bapt Miss Assn	10	2,339	758	2,835 *	15.9	28.1
081 Catholic	2	NR	NR	743	4.2	7.4
151 L-D Saints	1	NR	NR	173	1.0	1.7
167 Chs of Christ	5	267	245	365	2.0	3.6
283 Luth—MO Synod	1	68	32	81	.5	.8
355 Presb Ch (USA)	4	190	57	230 *	1.3	2.3
419 So Bapt Conv	7	3,149	978	3,818 *	21.4	37.8
449 Un Methodist	13	1,449	629	1,755 *	9.8	17.4
FRIO	**19**	**2,839**	**1,025**	**13,437 ***	**82.7**	**100.0**
053 Assemb of God	2	180	162	197	1.2	1.5
081 Catholic	2	NR	NR	9,820	60.4	73.1
167 Chs of Christ	3	144	153	185	1.1	1.4
283 Luth—MO Synod	1	51	19	66	.4	.5
355 Presb Ch (USA)	1	8	4	10 *	.1	.1
419 So Bapt Conv	6	1,606	421	2,065 *	12.7	15.4
449 Un Methodist	4	850	266	1,094 *	6.7	8.1
GAINES	**33**	**6,810**	**1,978**	**11,752 ***	**81.2**	**100.0**
017 Amer Bapt Assn	1	50	NR	68 *	.5	.6
053 Assemb of God	4	253	295	534	3.7	4.5
056 Baha'i	0	1	NR	1	-	-
059 Bapt Miss Assn	1	85	65	115 *	.8	1.0
081 Catholic	2	NR	NR	2,348	16.2	20.0
151 L-D Saints	1	NR	NR	54	.4	.5
165 Ch of Nazarene	1	31	13	31	.2	.3
167 Chs of Christ	7	554	585	704	4.9	6.0
297 Mennonite;Other	4	1,189	NR	1,609 *	11.1	13.7
355 Presb Ch (USA)	1	97	40	131 *	.9	1.1
419 So Bapt Conv	9	4,061	831	5,495 *	38.0	46.8
449 Un Methodist	2	489	149	662 *	4.6	5.6
GALVESTON	**202**	**48,814**	**21,816**	**112,601 ***	**45.0**	**100.0**
017 Amer Bapt Assn	6	779	NR	981 *	.4	.9
053 Assemb of God	15	1,240	1,159	1,816	.7	1.6
056 Baha'i	1	180	NR	180	.1	.2
076 Buddhism	3	NR	NR	NR	-	-
081 Catholic	14	NR	NR	42,141	16.8	37.4
084 Calvary Chapel	1	NR	NR	NR	-	-
093 Chr Ch (Disc)	2	589	0	742 *	.3	.7
097 Chr Chs&Chs Cr	3	1,032	NR	1,300 *	.5	1.2
123 Ch God (Ander)	3	NR	99	99	-	.1
145 Ch God Prophcy	2	54	NR	68 *	-	.1
151 L-D Saints	7	NR	NR	2,163	.9	1.9
165 Ch of Nazarene	1	161	102	176	.1	.2
167 Chs of Christ	17	2,105	1,627	2,590	1.0	2.3
193 Episcopal	10	NR	1,234	3,407	1.4	3.0
203 Evan Free Ch	2	135	225	225	.1	.2
207 E.L.C.A.	9	2,338	1,004	3,124	1.2	2.8
226 Friends-USA	8	365	NR	460 *	.2	.4
246 Greek Orthodox	1	NR	NR	306	.1	.3
263 Int Foursq Gos	1	147	291	291 *	.1	.3
267 Muslim Est	1	NR	80	100	-	.1
283 Luth—MO Synod	3	989	584	1,337	.5	1.2
339 Pent Ch of God	1	21	NR	50	-	-
349 Pent Holiness	3	148	107	186 *	.1	.2
355 Presb Ch (USA)	8	1,004	514	1,264 *	.5	1.1
403 Salvation Army	2	129	270	272	.1	.2
410 Serb Orth USA	1	NR	NR	120	-	.1
411 Serb Orth: Grac	1	NR	NR	NR	-	-
413 S.D.A.	4	109	NR	130	.1	.1
419 So Bapt Conv	44	26,494	10,506	33,382 *	13.3	29.6
435 Unitarian-Univ	1	75	NR	95 *	-	.1
449 Un Methodist	24	10,560	3,881	13,303 *	5.3	11.8
469 WELS	1	160	133	243	.1	.2
496 Jewish Est	2	NR	NR	2,050	.8	1.8
GARZA	**20**	**2,423**	**955**	**4,170 ***	**85.6**	**100.0**
053 Assemb of God	1	30	40	59	1.2	1.4
081 Catholic	1	NR	NR	1,098	22.5	26.3
093 Chr Ch (Disc)	1	46	16	59 *	1.2	1.4
127 Ch God (Cleve)	1	59	15	75 *	1.5	1.8
145 Ch God Prophcy	1	27	NR	34 *	.7	.8
165 Ch of Nazarene	1	131	103	141	2.9	3.4
167 Chs of Christ	4	281	267	344	7.1	8.2
355 Presb Ch (USA)	1	126	59	161 *	3.3	3.9
419 So Bapt Conv	7	1,320	309	1,685 *	34.6	40.4
449 Un Methodist	2	403	146	514 *	10.6	12.3
GILLESPIE	**31**	**6,656**	**3,055**	**15,706 ***	**75.5**	**100.0**
053 Assemb of God	1	25	30	33	.2	.2
056 Baha'i	0	1	NR	1	-	-
081 Catholic	3	NR	NR	7,219	34.7	46.0
093 Chr Ch (Disc)	1	18	16	21 *	.1	.1
151 L-D Saints	1	NR	NR	102	.5	.6
167 Chs of Christ	1	150	175	175	.8	1.1
193 Episcopal	1	NR	192	387	1.9	2.5
203 Evan Free Ch	1	115	175	175	.8	1.1
207 E.L.C.A.	8	3,480	1,301	4,180	20.1	26.6
283 Luth—MO Synod	1	96	81	116	.6	.7
355 Presb Ch (USA)	2	249	156	296 *	1.4	1.9
360 Prim Bapt Chrch	2	NR	NR	NR	-	-
413 S.D.A.	1	49	NR	58	.3	.4
419 So Bapt Conv	5	1,333	432	1,589 *	7.6	10.1
449 Un Methodist	2	1,064	441	1,268 *	6.1	8.1
469 WELS	1	76	56	86	.4	.5

NR–Not Reported *Total adherents estimated from known number of communicant, confirmed, full members. - Represents a percentage less than 0.1. Percentages may not total 100 due to rounding.

Table 4: Religious Congregations by County and Group: 2000

Religious Group	Number of Churches, Synagogues, Mosques, or Temples	Number of Communicant, Confirmed, or Full Members	Number of Attendees	Total Adherents: Number of Adherents	Total Adherents: % of Total Pop.	Total Adherents: % of Total Adh.
GLASSCOCK	**4**	**213**	**96**	**835 ***	**59.4**	**100.0**
081 Catholic	1	NR	NR	545	38.8	65.3
167 Chs of Christ	1	29	40	43	3.1	5.1
419 So Bapt Conv	1	144	40	193 *	13.7	23.1
449 Un Methodist	1	40	16	54 *	3.8	6.5
GOLIAD	**18**	**1,813**	**819**	**4,712 ***	**68.0**	**100.0**
056 Baha'i	0	4	NR	4	.1	.1
081 Catholic	3	NR	NR	2,316	33.4	49.2
151 L-D Saints	1	NR	NR	136	2.0	2.9
167 Chs of Christ	1	84	90	109	1.6	2.3
193 Episcopal	1	NR	23	33	.5	.7
207 E.L.C.A.	4	648	312	788	11.4	16.7
355 Presb Ch (USA)	1	85	30	105 *	1.5	2.2
419 So Bapt Conv	3	724	245	891 *	12.9	18.9
449 Un Methodist	4	268	119	330 *	4.8	7.0
GONZALES	**41**	**5,373**	**2,003**	**10,885 ***	**58.4**	**100.0**
053 Assemb of God	3	78	100	107	.6	1.0
056 Baha'i	0	4	NR	4	-	-
081 Catholic	3	NR	NR	3,936	21.1	36.2
127 Ch God (Cleve)	1	110	110	139 *	.7	1.3
167 Chs of Christ	2	74	65	92	.5	.8
193 Episcopal	1	NR	46	117	.6	1.1
207 E.L.C.A.	1	293	104	403	2.2	3.7
323 Old Ord Amish	1	8	NR	10 *	.1	.1
355 Presb Ch (USA)	3	185	97	234 *	1.3	2.1
360 Prim Bapt Chrch	1	NR	NR	NR	-	-
419 So Bapt Conv	13	3,111	788	3,934 *	21.1	36.1
449 Un Methodist	12	1,510	693	1,909 *	10.2	17.5
GRAY	**41**	**13,411**	**4,595**	**18,773 ***	**82.5**	**100.0**
053 Assemb of God	4	179	209	313	1.4	1.7
056 Baha'i	0	8	NR	8	-	-
081 Catholic	1	NR	NR	1,662	7.3	8.9
093 Chr Ch (Disc)	1	590	191	719 *	3.2	3.8
097 Chr Chs&Chs Cr	1	100	NR	122 *	.5	.6
127 Ch God (Cleve)	1	137	74	167 *	.7	.9
157 Ch of Brethren	1	50	9	61 *	.3	.3
165 Ch of Nazarene	1	76	61	80	.4	.4
167 Chs of Christ	8	1,074	893	1,405	6.2	7.5
193 Episcopal	1	NR	97	346	1.5	1.8
223 Free Will Bapt	1	42	NR	52 *	.2	.3
263 Int Foursq Gos	1	30	50	50 *	.2	.3
283 Luth—MO Synod	1	155	92	197	.9	1.0
349 Pent Holiness	2	125	78	152 *	.7	.8
355 Presb Ch (USA)	1	201	78	245 *	1.1	1.3
403 Salvation Army	1	82	32	325	1.4	1.7
413 S.D.A.	1	26	NR	31	.1	.2
419 So Bapt Conv	10	9,333	2,271	11,372 *	50.0	60.6
449 Un Methodist	4	1,203	460	1,466 *	6.4	7.8
GRAYSON	**184**	**48,608**	**18,966**	**67,208 ***	**60.8**	**100.0**
017 Amer Bapt Assn	11	1,301	NR	1,611 *	1.5	2.4
053 Assemb of God	12	1,692	1,577	2,295	2.1	3.4
056 Baha'i	0	51	NR	51	-	.1
059 Bapt Miss Assn	2	215	65	266 *	.2	.4
081 Catholic	3	NR	NR	4,670	4.2	6.9
093 Chr Ch (Disc)	3	884	269	1,095 *	1.0	1.6
127 Ch God (Cleve)	2	468	361	580 *	.5	.9
151 L-D Saints	2	NR	NR	694	.6	1.0
165 Ch of Nazarene	2	399	298	454	.4	.7
167 Chs of Christ	31	3,488	3,447	4,447	4.0	6.6
185 Cumber Presb	2	28	NR	65	.1	.1
193 Episcopal	2	NR	276	611	.6	.9
207 E.L.C.A.	1	186	105	236	.2	.4
223 Free Will Bapt	1	42	NR	53 *	-	.1
263 Int Foursq Gos	1	18	20	22 *	-	-
267 Muslim Est	1	NR	101	288	.3	.4
283 Luth—MO Synod	1	233	137	286	.3	.4
339 Pent Ch of God	2	29	NR	70	.1	.1
349 Pent Holiness	4	232	149	287 *	.3	.4

Religious Group	Number of Churches, Synagogues, Mosques, or Temples	Number of Communicant, Confirmed, or Full Members	Number of Attendees	Total Adherents: Number of Adherents	Total Adherents: % of Total Pop.	Total Adherents: % of Total Adh.
355 Presb Ch (USA)	7	1,177	595	1,456 *	1.3	2.2
356 Presb Ch Amer	1	84	56	85	.1	.1
360 Prim Bapt Chrch	1	NR	NR	NR	-	-
370 Ref Baptist Chs	1	NR	NR	NR	-	-
403 Salvation Army	1	116	79	157	.1	.2
413 S.D.A.	2	104	NR	124	.1	.2
419 So Bapt Conv	62	31,295	8,380	38,751 *	35.0	57.7
435 Unitarian-Univ	1	38	NR	47 *	-	.1
449 Un Methodist	23	6,528	2,701	8,082 *	7.3	12.0
496 Jewish Est	1	NR	NR	75	.1	.1
499 Indep.Non-Char	1	0	350	350	.3	.5
GREGG	**151**	**54,998**	**21,550**	**81,409 ***	**73.1**	**100.0**
017 Amer Bapt Assn	5	577	NR	726 *	.7	.9
053 Assemb of God	12	1,021	1,199	1,559	1.4	1.9
056 Baha'i	0	30	NR	30	-	-
059 Bapt Miss Assn	6	1,348	400	1,697 *	1.5	2.1
081 Catholic	3	NR	NR	8,430	7.6	10.4
089 Chr & Miss Al	1	47	NR	156	.1	.2
093 Chr Ch (Disc)	7	1,796	684	2,261 *	2.0	2.8
097 Chr Chs&Chs Cr	1	220	NR	277 *	.2	.3
123 Ch God (Ander)	3	NR	116	116	.1	.1
127 Ch God (Cleve)	8	645	263	811 *	.7	1.0
145 Ch God Prophcy	1	27	NR	34 *	-	-
151 L-D Saints	4	NR	NR	1,466	1.3	1.8
165 Ch of Nazarene	3	509	383	661	.6	.8
167 Chs of Christ	27	4,220	3,478	5,542	5.0	6.8
173 Comm of Christ	1	48	NR	48	-	.1
185 Cumber Presb	3	343	NR	690	.6	.8
193 Episcopal	4	NR	518	1,675	1.5	2.1
207 E.L.C.A.	1	361	215	441	.4	.5
263 Int Foursq Gos	1	30	50	50 *	-	.1
283 Luth—MO Synod	2	176	152	267	.2	.3
290 Metro Comm Ch	1	39	18	49 *	-	.1
339 Pent Ch of God	1	12	NR	32	-	-
355 Presb Ch (USA)	6	1,654	666	2,082 *	1.9	2.6
360 Prim Bapt Chrch	1	NR	NR	NR	-	-
370 Ref Baptist Chs	1	NR	NR	NR	-	-
403 Salvation Army	1	141	101	227	.2	.3
413 S.D.A.	2	132	NR	157	.1	.2
419 So Bapt Conv	28	31,569	8,792	39,740 *	35.7	48.8
435 Unitarian-Univ	1	12	NR	15 *	-	-
443 Un C of Christ	1	412	181	519 *	.5	.6
449 Un Methodist	11	7,229	2,554	9,101 *	8.2	11.2
496 Jewish Est	1	NR	NR	100	.1	.1
498 Indep.Charis.	2	500	380	550	.5	.7
499 Indep.Non-Char	1	1,900	1,400	1,900	1.7	2.3
GRIMES	**49**	**5,215**	**2,316**	**11,168 ***	**47.4**	**100.0**
053 Assemb of God	1	15	20	20	.1	.2
056 Baha'i	0	3	NR	3	-	-
059 Bapt Miss Assn	3	296	151	384 *	1.6	3.4
081 Catholic	4	NR	NR	4,512	19.2	40.4
151 L-D Saints	1	NR	NR	113	.5	1.0
167 Chs of Christ	6	126	155	174	.7	1.6
193 Episcopal	1	NR	50	102	.4	.9
223 Free Will Bapt	2	85	NR	104 *	.4	.9
283 Luth—MO Synod	3	764	320	943	4.0	8.4
355 Presb Ch (USA)	2	311	140	382 *	1.6	3.4
360 Prim Bapt Chrch	1	NR	NR	NR	-	-
413 S.D.A.	1	207	NR	246	1.0	2.2
419 So Bapt Conv	12	2,575	996	3,162 *	13.4	28.3
449 Un Methodist	12	833	484	1,023 *	4.3	9.2
GUADALUPE	**58**	**14,497**	**6,208**	**33,628 ***	**37.8**	**100.0**
053 Assemb of God	4	260	333	391	.4	1.2
056 Baha'i	0	30	NR	30	-	.1
081 Catholic	3	NR	NR	13,706	15.4	40.8
097 Chr Chs&Chs Cr	1	136	NR	174 *	.2	.5
151 L-D Saints	2	NR	NR	844	.9	2.5
167 Chs of Christ	6	308	340	410	.5	1.2
193 Episcopal	1	NR	217	473	.5	1.4
203 Evan Free Ch	1	69	125	125	.1	.4

NR–Not Reported *Total adherents estimated from known number of communicant, confirmed, full members. - Represents a percentage less than 0.1. Percentages may not total 100 due to rounding.

Table 4: Religious Congregations by County and Group: 2000

Religious Group	Number of Churches, Synagogues, Mosques, or Temples	Number of Communicant, Confirmed, or Full Members	Number of Attendees	Total Adherents		
				Number of Adherents	% of Total Pop.	% of Total Adh.
207 E.L.C.A.	4	2,954	883	3,735	4.2	11.1
283 Luth—MO Synod	2	335	132	442	.5	1.3
313 N Am Bapt Conf	1	31	21	40 *	-	.1
349 Pent Holiness	1	80	75	102 *	.1	.3
355 Presb Ch (USA)	1	162	75	207 *	.2	.6
360 Prim Bapt Chrch	1	NR	NR	NR	-	-
413 S.D.A.	1	39	NR	46	.1	.1
419 So Bapt Conv	19	5,901	2,454	7,544 *	8.5	22.4
443 Un C of Christ	4	1,685	570	2,154 *	2.4	6.4
449 Un Methodist	6	2,507	983	3,205 *	3.6	9.5
HALE	**67**	**17,227**	**6,145**	**32,214 ***	**88.0**	**100.0**
053 Assemb of God	5	407	508	637	1.7	2.0
056 Baha'i	0	19	NR	19	.1	.1
059 Bapt Miss Assn	1	281	110	367 *	1.0	1.1
081 Catholic	5	NR	NR	9,248	25.3	28.7
093 Chr Ch (Disc)	1	231	0	301 *	.8	.9
127 Ch God (Cleve)	1	55	68	72 *	.2	.2
151 L-D Saints	1	NR	NR	259	.7	.8
165 Ch of Nazarene	4	365	207	498	1.4	1.5
167 Chs of Christ	11	1,376	1,416	1,872	5.1	5.8
193 Episcopal	1	NR	38	71	.2	.2
283 Luth—MO Synod	1	163	113	186	.5	.6
335 Orth Pres Ch	1	4	20	20	.1	.1
339 Pent Ch of God	1	10	NR	12	-	-
349 Pent Holiness	3	82	90	107 *	.3	.3
355 Presb Ch (USA)	2	236	135	308 *	.8	1.0
403 Salvation Army	1	102	46	118	.3	.4
413 S.D.A.	1	47	NR	56	.2	.2
419 So Bapt Conv	21	11,944	2,680	15,578 *	42.6	48.4
449 Un Methodist	6	1,905	714	2,485 *	6.8	7.7
HALL	**13**	**2,235**	**676**	**3,183 ***	**84.2**	**100.0**
053 Assemb of God	1	17	15	23	.6	.7
056 Baha'i	0	1	NR	1	-	-
059 Bapt Miss Assn	1	0	0	0 *	-	-
081 Catholic	2	NR	NR	350	9.3	11.0
097 Chr Chs&Chs Cr	1	30	NR	38 *	1.0	1.2
167 Chs of Christ	2	250	235	316	8.4	9.9
419 So Bapt Conv	4	1,504	292	1,906 *	50.4	59.9
449 Un Methodist	2	433	134	549 *	14.5	17.2
HAMILTON	**35**	**4,398**	**1,892**	**5,538 ***	**67.3**	**100.0**
053 Assemb of God	1	20	21	27	.3	.5
081 Catholic	1	NR	NR	100	1.2	1.8
167 Chs of Christ	5	360	427	522	6.3	9.4
193 Episcopal	1	NR	22	35	.4	.6
207 E.L.C.A.	2	197	82	225	2.7	4.1
283 Luth—MO Synod	2	510	283	604	7.3	10.9
339 Pent Ch of God	1	56	NR	61	.7	1.1
355 Presb Ch (USA)	1	40	24	49 *	.6	.9
360 Prim Bapt Chrch	3	NR	NR	NR	-	-
413 S.D.A.	1	4	NR	5	.1	.1
419 So Bapt Conv	13	2,363	780	2,877 *	35.0	52.0
449 Un Methodist	4	848	253	1,033 *	12.6	18.7
HANSFORD	**17**	**3,361**	**1,178**	**5,050 ***	**94.1**	**100.0**
053 Assemb of God	1	39	48	98	1.8	1.9
081 Catholic	2	NR	NR	625	11.6	12.4
093 Chr Ch (Disc)	2	289	0	369 *	6.9	7.3
151 L-D Saints	1	NR	NR	75	1.4	1.5
167 Chs of Christ	2	313	270	414	7.7	8.2
207 E.L.C.A.	2	122	67	151	2.8	3.0
355 Presb Ch (USA)	1	24	8	31 *	.6	.6
419 So Bapt Conv	4	1,463	470	1,868 *	34.8	37.0
449 Un Methodist	2	1,111	315	1,419 *	26.4	28.1
HARDEMAN	**17**	**4,393**	**1,579**	**5,779 ***	**122.3**	**100.0**
053 Assemb of God	1	64	85	85	1.8	1.5
056 Baha'i	0	4	NR	4	.1	.1
081 Catholic	1	NR	NR	341	7.2	5.9
093 Chr Ch (Disc)	1	105	60	129 *	2.7	2.2
165 Ch of Nazarene	1	32	17	32	.7	.6
167 Chs of Christ	4	375	323	478	10.1	8.3
193 Episcopal	1	NR	17	31	.7	.5
355 Presb Ch (USA)	1	39	18	48 *	1.0	.8
419 So Bapt Conv	5	3,245	898	3,982 *	84.3	68.9
449 Un Methodist	2	529	161	649 *	13.7	11.2
HARDIN	**70**	**19,560**	**7,613**	**28,188 ***	**58.6**	**100.0**
017 Amer Bapt Assn	3	302	NR	381 *	.8	1.4
053 Assemb of God	11	1,036	912	1,148	2.4	4.1
056 Baha'i	0	1	NR	1	-	-
081 Catholic	4	NR	NR	2,787	5.8	9.9
097 Chr Chs&Chs Cr	1	100	NR	126 *	.3	.4
127 Ch God (Cleve)	1	139	85	175 *	.4	.6
145 Ch God Prophcy	1	27	NR	34 *	.1	.1
151 L-D Saints	1	NR	NR	624	1.3	2.2
167 Chs of Christ	6	502	563	668	1.4	2.4
193 Episcopal	1	NR	68	174	.4	.6
339 Pent Ch of God	2	22	NR	67	.1	.2
355 Presb Ch (USA)	1	55	37	69 *	.1	.2
419 So Bapt Conv	30	15,350	4,976	19,377 *	40.3	68.7
449 Un Methodist	8	2,026	972	2,557 *	5.3	9.1
HARRIS	**1,587**	**718,907**	**351,296**	**1,713,211 ***	**50.4**	**100.0**
017 Amer Bapt Assn	23	4,493	NR	5,824 *	.2	.3
019 Amer Bapt USA	4	1,063	100	1,378 *	-	.1
034 Ant Orth of NA	3	782	NR	1,564	-	.1
053 Assemb of God	85	18,178	18,786	29,522	.9	1.7
055 As Ref Pres Ch	1	28	NR	28	-	-
056 Baha'i	7	1,610	NR	1,610	-	.1
057 Bapt Gen Conf	5	241	228	340 *	-	-
059 Bapt Miss Assn	15	3,558	1,619	4,664 *	.1	.3
076 Buddhism	36	NR	NR	NR	-	-
081 Catholic	106	NR	NR	618,649	18.2	36.1
089 Chr & Miss Al	9	503	NR	1,194	-	.1
093 Chr Ch (Disc)	21	5,712	1,827	7,404 *	.2	.4
097 Chr Chs&Chs Cr	15	2,912	NR	3,774 *	.1	.2
105 Christian Ref	3	507	480	657 *	-	-
123 Ch God (Ander)	14	NR	1,023	1,023	-	.1
127 Ch God (Cleve)	22	2,746	2,164	4,566 *	.1	.3
145 Ch God Prophcy	8	216	NR	280 *	-	-
151 L-D Saints	63	NR	NR	24,690	.7	1.4
165 Ch of Nazarene	29	4,422	3,024	6,642	.2	.4
167 Chs of Christ	145	27,179	23,351	33,629	1.0	2.0
173 Comm of Christ	4	397	NR	397	-	-
175 Congr Chr Chs	1	87	40	113 *	-	-
185 Cumber Presb	2	127	NR	294	-	-
186 Coptic Orth Ch	2	NR	NR	NR	-	-
193 Episcopal	44	NR	13,606	40,001	1.2	2.3
201 Evan Cov Ch	3	356	348	461 *	-	-
203 Evan Free Ch	2	74	180	180	-	-
207 E.L.C.A.	37	12,418	6,781	16,362	.5	1.0
216 Evan Presby Ch	3	656	NR	850 *	-	-
220 Free Lutheran	1	36	26	41	-	-
223 Free Will Bapt	4	170	NR	220 *	-	-
226 Friends-USA	5	180	NR	233 *	-	-
246 Greek Orthodox	3	NR	NR	4,125	.1	.2
252 Hindu	14	NR	NR	NR	-	-
263 Int Foursq Gos	9	915	1,474	1,474 *	-	.1
264 Int Chs of Crst	1	615	964	906	-	.1
266 Intrstat & Asc	1	72	NR	93 *	-	-
267 Muslim Est	33	NR	10,650	47,568	1.4	2.8
268 Jain	3	NR	NR	NR	-	-
283 Luth—MO Synod	49	24,973	14,029	34,175	1.0	2.0
288 Mennonite USA	1	59	65	76 *	-	-
290 Metro Comm Ch	2	671	792	870 *	-	.1
313 N Am Bapt Conf	1	102	60	132 *	-	-
331 OCA: Ter Diocs	1	3	NR	628	-	-
333 Malan Dioc Am	2	NR	NR	550	-	-
334 Malan Syr Orth	1	45	NR	225	-	-
335 Orth Pres Ch	1	15	25	25	-	-
339 Pent Ch of God	17	1,013	NR	1,505	-	.1
349 Pent Holiness	6	509	625	660 *	-	-

NR–Not Reported *Total adherents estimated from known number of communicant, confirmed, full members. - Represents a percentage less than 0.1. Percentages may not total 100 due to rounding.

Table 4: Religious Congregations by County and Group: 2000

Religious Group	Number of Churches, Synagogues, Mosques, or Temples	Number of Communicant, Confirmed, or Full Members	Number of Attendees	Total Adherents		
				Number of Adherents	% of Total Pop.	% of Total Adh.
355 Presb Ch (USA)	53	29,428	13,148	38,142 *	1.1	2.2
356 Presb Ch Amer	13	1,937	1,797	2,704	.1	.2
360 Prim Bapt Chrch	5	NR	NR	NR	-	-
370 Ref Baptist Chs	2	NR	NR	NR	-	-
388 Reg Bapt Gen As	4	333	476	460 *	-	-
397 OCA: Roman Dioc	1	NR	NR	350	-	-
401 Rus Orth Abroad	2	NR	NR	NR	-	-
403 Salvation Army	3	404	269	3,688	.1	.2
410 Serb Orth USA	1	NR	NR	800	-	-
413 S.D.A.	37	6,156	NR	7,328	.2	.4
416 Sikh	6	NR	NR	NR	-	-
418 Southw Bapt Fel	2	NR	NR	NR	-	-
419 So Bapt Conv	365	374,235	130,967	485,075 *	14.3	28.3
423 Syrian Orth Ch	1	NR	NR	60	-	-
425 Tao	1	NR	NR	NR	-	-
435 Unitarian-Univ	5	1,268	NR	1,644 *	-	.1
443 Un C of Christ	12	2,415	1,058	3,130 *	.1	.2
449 Un Methodist	142	131,634	49,319	170,618 *	5.0	10.0
463 Vineyard	7	1,091	960	1,416 *	-	.1
469 WELS	5	756	524	1,208	-	.1
490 Zoroastrian	1	NR	NR	NR	-	-
496 Jewish Est	21	NR	NR	35,900	1.1	2.1
498 Indep.Charis.	15	43,750	33,175	43,750	1.3	2.6
499 Indep.Non-Char	16	7,857	17,336	17,336	.5	1.0
HARRISON	**95**	**24,920**	**7,956**	**34,891 ***	**56.2**	**100.0**
017 Amer Bapt Assn	3	196	NR	244 *	.4	.7
053 Assemb of God	5	255	277	351	.6	1.0
056 Baha'i	0	103	NR	103	.2	.3
081 Catholic	3	NR	NR	3,184	5.1	9.1
093 Chr Ch (Disc)	1	127	51	159 *	.3	.5
145 Ch God Prophcy	2	54	NR	68 *	.1	.2
151 L-D Saints	1	NR	NR	254	.4	.7
165 Ch of Nazarene	1	128	62	129	.2	.4
167 Chs of Christ	10	922	885	1,241	2.0	3.6
185 Cumber Presb	1	218	NR	299	.5	.9
193 Episcopal	2	NR	104	341	.5	1.0
207 E.L.C.A.	1	67	37	97	.2	.3
216 Evan Presby Ch	3	298	NR	372 *	.6	1.1
339 Pent Ch of God	1	22	NR	30	-	.1
355 Presb Ch (USA)	1	126	57	157 *	.3	.4
413 S.D.A.	2	103	NR	122	.2	.3
419 So Bapt Conv	34	18,311	4,295	22,880 *	36.8	65.6
449 Un Methodist	23	3,290	1,438	4,110 *	6.6	11.8
499 Indep.Non-Char	1	700	750	750	1.2	2.1
HARTLEY	**9**	**2,720**	**794**	**3,265 ***	**59.0**	**100.0**
165 Ch of Nazarene	1	120	75	151	2.7	4.6
167 Chs of Christ	1	30	30	38	.7	1.2
283 Luth—MO Synod	1	90	39	120	2.2	3.7
419 So Bapt Conv	4	2,268	564	2,703 *	48.8	82.8
449 Un Methodist	2	212	86	253 *	4.6	7.7
HASKELL	**29**	**4,889**	**1,767**	**6,567 ***	**107.8**	**100.0**
053 Assemb of God	1	54	55	100	1.6	1.5
056 Baha'i	0	2	NR	2	-	-
081 Catholic	1	NR	NR	625	10.3	9.5
097 Chr Chs&Chs Cr	1	85	NR	102 *	1.7	1.6
127 Ch God (Cleve)	1	16	13	19 *	.3	.3
167 Chs of Christ	3	355	418	428	7.0	6.5
207 E.L.C.A.	2	219	128	279	4.6	4.2
263 Int Foursq Gos	2	79	109	109 *	1.8	1.7
355 Presb Ch (USA)	1	42	20	50 *	.8	.8
360 Prim Bapt Chrch	1	NR	NR	NR	-	-
419 So Bapt Conv	11	3,554	858	4,272 *	70.1	65.1
449 Un Methodist	5	483	166	581 *	9.5	8.8
HAYS	**73**	**16,243**	**7,244**	**42,493 ***	**43.5**	**100.0**
053 Assemb of God	3	147	168	213	.2	.5
056 Baha'i	1	79	NR	79	.1	.2
081 Catholic	6	NR	NR	19,324	19.8	45.5
084 Calvary Chapel	1	NR	NR	NR	-	-

Religious Group	Number of Churches, Synagogues, Mosques, or Temples	Number of Communicant, Confirmed, or Full Members	Number of Attendees	Total Adherents		
				Number of Adherents	% of Total Pop.	% of Total Adh.
093 Chr Ch (Disc)	1	605	0	741 *	.8	1.7
097 Chr Chs&Chs Cr	1	20	NR	24 *	-	.1
145 Ch God Prophcy	1	27	NR	33 *	-	.1
151 L-D Saints	3	NR	NR	973	1.0	2.3
165 Ch of Nazarene	1	16	0	16	-	-
167 Chs of Christ	6	651	670	809	.8	1.9
193 Episcopal	4	NR	531	1,344	1.4	3.2
203 Evan Free Ch	1	69	125	125	.1	.3
207 E.L.C.A.	2	738	236	923	.9	2.2
267 Muslim Est	1	NR	228	841	.9	2.0
283 Luth—MO Synod	1	234	146	295	.3	.7
313 N Am Bapt Conf	1	100	52	122 *	.1	.3
339 Pent Ch of God	1	35	NR	80	.1	.2
349 Pent Holiness	1	20	18	24 *	-	.1
355 Presb Ch (USA)	3	361	228	442 *	.5	1.0
413 S.D.A.	1	150	NR	178	.2	.4
419 So Bapt Conv	22	9,321	3,289	11,414 *	11.7	26.9
435 Unitarian-Univ	1	33	NR	40 *	-	.1
443 Un C of Christ	1	118	45	144 *	.1	.3
449 Un Methodist	9	3,519	1,508	4,309 *	4.4	10.1
HEMPHILL	**11**	**1,952**	**685**	**2,922 ***	**87.2**	**100.0**
053 Assemb of God	2	126	115	149	4.4	5.1
081 Catholic	1	NR	NR	250	7.5	8.6
097 Chr Chs&Chs Cr	1	250	NR	307 *	9.2	10.5
151 L-D Saints	1	NR	NR	244	7.3	8.4
167 Chs of Christ	1	125	150	170	5.1	5.8
193 Episcopal	1	NR	10	23	.7	.8
355 Presb Ch (USA)	1	127	70	156 *	4.7	5.3
419 So Bapt Conv	2	912	164	1,118 *	33.4	38.3
449 Un Methodist	1	412	176	505 *	15.1	17.3
HENDERSON	**114**	**25,148**	**11,374**	**36,100 ***	**49.3**	**100.0**
017 Amer Bapt Assn	2	100	NR	122 *	.2	.3
053 Assemb of God	13	1,371	1,268	1,586	2.2	4.4
056 Baha'i	0	3	NR	3	-	-
059 Bapt Miss Assn	18	3,265	1,201	4,014 *	5.5	11.1
081 Catholic	3	NR	NR	4,800	6.6	13.3
093 Chr Ch (Disc)	2	616	237	757 *	1.0	2.1
123 Ch God (Ander)	1	NR	30	30	-	.1
127 Ch God (Cleve)	1	31	32	38 *	.1	.1
151 L-D Saints	1	NR	NR	283	.4	.8
165 Ch of Nazarene	2	123	83	164	.2	.5
167 Chs of Christ	11	958	905	1,258	1.7	3.5
185 Cumber Presb	1	13	NR	13	-	-
193 Episcopal	1	NR	30	68	.1	.2
207 E.L.C.A.	1	105	58	136	.2	.4
283 Luth—MO Synod	2	263	192	335	.5	.9
349 Pent Holiness	1	300	330	369 *	.5	1.0
355 Presb Ch (USA)	1	310	140	381 *	.5	1.1
360 Prim Bapt Chrch	1	NR	NR	NR	-	-
413 S.D.A.	2	114	NR	136	.2	.4
419 So Bapt Conv	34	14,638	5,467	17,994 *	24.6	49.8
449 Un Methodist	16	2,938	1,401	3,613 *	4.9	10.0
HIDALGO	**320**	**40,172**	**27,003**	**286,865 ***	**50.4**	**100.0**
017 Amer Bapt Assn	3	106	NR	146 *	-	.1
053 Assemb of God	28	3,877	4,403	5,761	1.0	2.0
056 Baha'i	2	144	NR	144	-	.1
059 Bapt Miss Assn	1	144	110	200 *	-	.1
081 Catholic	48	NR	NR	222,149	39.0	77.4
089 Chr & Miss Al	12	375	NR	832	.1	.3
093 Chr Ch (Disc)	5	568	326	789 *	.1	.3
097 Chr Chs&Chs Cr	2	225	NR	312 *	.1	.1
123 Ch God (Ander)	1	NR	45	45	-	-
127 Ch God (Cleve)	2	97	48	135 *	-	-
145 Ch God Prophcy	1	27	NR	37 *	-	-
151 L-D Saints	12	NR	NR	5,466	1.0	1.9
165 Ch of Nazarene	8	560	519	907	.2	.3
167 Chs of Christ	22	1,346	1,637	1,860	.3	.6
173 Comm of Christ	2	116	NR	116	-	-
193 Episcopal	4	NR	540	1,298	.2	.5
201 Evan Cov Ch	3	155	169	217 *	-	.1

NR–Not Reported *Total adherents estimated from known number of communicant, confirmed, full members. - Represents a percentage less than 0.1. Percentages may not total 100 due to rounding.

Table 4: Religious Congregations by County and Group: 2000

Religious Group	Number of Churches, Synagogues, Mosques, or Temples	Number of Communicant, Confirmed, or Full Members	Number of Attendees	Total Adherents		
				Number of Adherents	% of Total Pop.	% of Total Adh.
203 Evan Free Ch	1	80	210	210	-	.1
207 E.L.C.A.	7	1,209	1,316	1,920	.3	.7
220 Free Lutheran	1	51	62	62	-	-
221 Free Methodist	1	33	22	55	-	-
223 Free Will Bapt	2	85	NR	118 *	-	-
226 Friends-USA	1	15	NR	21 *	-	-
237 Menn Br US Conf	7	140	NR	195 *	-	.1
263 Int Foursq Gos	3	95	162	162 *	-	.1
267 Muslim Est	1	NR	156	609	.1	.2
283 Luth—MO Synod	5	1,327	1,106	1,693	.3	.6
288 Mennonite USA	3	74	89	102 *	-	-
291 Missionary Ch	2	67	80	80	-	-
313 N Am Bapt Conf	1	65	50	90 *	-	-
331 OCA: Ter Diocs	1	17	NR	122	-	-
339 Pent Ch of God	1	50	NR	70	-	-
349 Pent Holiness	17	951	1,087	1,320 *	.2	.5
355 Presb Ch (USA)	10	1,231	900	1,718 *	.3	.6
356 Presb Ch Amer	2	33	60	60	-	-
360 Prim Bapt Chrch	1	NR	NR	NR	-	-
403 Salvation Army	1	241	159	253	-	.1
413 S.D.A.	15	2,000	NR	2,382	.4	.8
419 So Bapt Conv	54	16,645	9,075	23,110 *	4.1	8.1
435 Unitarian-Univ	1	22	NR	31 *	-	-
449 Un Methodist	23	7,352	3,326	10,209 *	1.8	3.6
469 WELS	1	49	46	59	-	-
496 Jewish Est	1	NR	NR	500	.1	.2
498 Indep.Charis.	1	600	1,300	1,300	.2	.5
HILL	**78**	**11,465**	**4,456**	**16,512 ***	**51.1**	**100.0**
017 Amer Bapt Assn	2	557	NR	691 *	2.1	4.2
053 Assemb of God	2	146	176	281	.9	1.7
056 Baha'i	0	28	NR	28	.1	.2
059 Bapt Miss Assn	3	783	271	971 *	3.0	5.9
081 Catholic	3	NR	NR	1,563	4.8	9.5
093 Chr Ch (Disc)	1	52	39	65 *	.2	.4
123 Ch God (Ander)	1	NR	85	85	.3	.5
151 L-D Saints	1	NR	NR	133	.4	.8
165 Ch of Nazarene	2	230	188	441	1.4	2.7
167 Chs of Christ	13	702	751	963	3.0	5.8
185 Cumber Presb	2	43	NR	55	.2	.3
193 Episcopal	2	NR	53	75	.2	.5
207 E.L.C.A.	1	104	25	133	.4	.8
263 Int Foursq Gos	1	38	96	96 *	.3	.6
283 Luth—MO Synod	3	535	258	693	2.1	4.2
339 Pent Ch of God	1	50	NR	70	.2	.4
355 Presb Ch (USA)	3	389	140	484 *	1.5	2.9
360 Prim Bapt Chrch	1	NR	NR	NR	-	-
413 S.D.A.	2	92	NR	110	.3	.7
419 So Bapt Conv	24	5,871	1,826	7,288 *	22.5	44.1
449 Un Methodist	9	1,833	536	2,275 *	7.0	13.8
469 WELS	1	12	12	12	-	.1
HOCKLEY	**54**	**11,668**	**4,105**	**19,554 ***	**86.1**	**100.0**
017 Amer Bapt Assn	2	131	NR	166 *	.7	.8
053 Assemb of God	3	178	186	242	1.1	1.2
059 Bapt Miss Assn	3	1,089	296	1,386 *	6.1	7.1
081 Catholic	5	NR	NR	4,641	20.4	23.7
151 L-D Saints	1	NR	NR	91	.4	.5
165 Ch of Nazarene	2	119	93	137	.6	.7
167 Chs of Christ	13	1,231	1,095	1,509	6.6	7.7
193 Episcopal	1	NR	14	27	.1	.1
207 E.L.C.A.	1	101	56	131	.6	.7
263 Int Foursq Gos	1	302	213	384 *	1.7	2.0
355 Presb Ch (USA)	1	147	86	187 *	.8	1.0
360 Prim Bapt Chrch	1	NR	NR	NR	-	-
419 So Bapt Conv	15	7,154	1,610	9,105 *	40.1	46.6
449 Un Methodist	5	1,216	456	1,548 *	6.8	7.9
HOOD	**41**	**15,157**	**6,709**	**21,726 ***	**52.9**	**100.0**
053 Assemb of God	3	329	333	462	1.1	2.1
056 Baha'i	0	12	NR	12	-	.1
081 Catholic	1	NR	NR	2,501	6.1	11.5
093 Chr Ch (Disc)	1	401	210	489 *	1.2	2.3

Religious Group	Number of Churches, Synagogues, Mosques, or Temples	Number of Communicant, Confirmed, or Full Members	Number of Attendees	Total Adherents		
				Number of Adherents	% of Total Pop.	% of Total Adh.
127 Ch God (Cleve)	1	303	117	369 *	.9	1.7
151 L-D Saints	1	NR	NR	386	.9	1.8
165 Ch of Nazarene	1	60	46	60	.1	.3
167 Chs of Christ	7	1,120	1,113	1,404	3.4	6.5
173 Comm of Christ	1	4	NR	4	-	-
193 Episcopal	1	NR	107	273	.7	1.3
207 E.L.C.A.	1	186	107	235	.6	1.1
283 Luth—MO Synod	1	173	131	219	.5	1.0
355 Presb Ch (USA)	1	362	220	441 *	1.1	2.0
419 So Bapt Conv	16	8,857	3,079	10,790 *	26.3	49.7
449 Un Methodist	5	3,350	1,246	4,081 *	9.9	18.8
HOPKINS	**89**	**16,815**	**6,977**	**22,799 ***	**71.3**	**100.0**
017 Amer Bapt Assn	2	151	NR	187 *	.6	.8
053 Assemb of God	6	331	311	442	1.4	1.9
056 Baha'i	0	9	NR	9	-	-
059 Bapt Miss Assn	11	2,541	790	3,161 *	9.9	13.9
081 Catholic	1	NR	NR	1,571	4.9	6.9
093 Chr Ch (Disc)	1	229	110	285 *	.9	1.3
097 Chr Chs&Chs Cr	1	115	NR	143 *	.4	.6
127 Ch God (Cleve)	1	372	172	463 *	1.4	2.0
151 L-D Saints	1	NR	NR	178	.6	.8
165 Ch of Nazarene	1	105	76	116	.4	.5
167 Chs of Christ	10	1,297	1,124	1,669	5.2	7.3
185 Cumber Presb	2	29	NR	45	.1	.2
193 Episcopal	1	NR	35	55	.2	.2
283 Luth—MO Synod	1	143	98	169	.5	.7
349 Pent Holiness	1	150	150	187 *	.6	.8
355 Presb Ch (USA)	3	117	58	146 *	.5	.6
413 S.D.A.	1	18	NR	21	.1	.1
419 So Bapt Conv	27	8,822	3,159	10,981 *	34.4	48.2
449 Un Methodist	18	2,386	894	2,971 *	9.3	13.0
HOUSTON	**72**	**9,292**	**3,754**	**12,167 ***	**52.5**	**100.0**
017 Amer Bapt Assn	6	364	NR	438 *	1.9	3.6
053 Assemb of God	4	294	360	421	1.8	3.5
056 Baha'i	0	2	NR	2	-	-
059 Bapt Miss Assn	4	898	280	1,080 *	4.7	8.9
081 Catholic	2	NR	NR	729	3.1	6.0
093 Chr Ch (Disc)	2	126	71	151 *	.7	1.2
127 Ch God (Cleve)	1	122	54	147 *	.6	1.2
145 Ch God Prophcy	1	27	NR	32 *	.1	.3
165 Ch of Nazarene	1	18	0	18	.1	.1
167 Chs of Christ	9	564	605	801	3.5	6.6
193 Episcopal	1	NR	32	90	.4	.7
283 Luth—MO Synod	1	88	50	95	.4	.8
355 Presb Ch (USA)	1	136	67	164 *	.7	1.3
360 Prim Bapt Chrch	1	NR	NR	NR	-	-
419 So Bapt Conv	26	5,598	1,735	6,730 *	29.0	55.3
449 Un Methodist	12	1,055	500	1,269 *	5.5	10.4
HOWARD	**58**	**13,919**	**4,277**	**22,637 ***	**67.3**	**100.0**
053 Assemb of God	2	241	243	324	1.0	1.4
056 Baha'i	0	24	NR	24	.1	.1
081 Catholic	4	NR	NR	4,920	14.6	21.7
093 Chr Ch (Disc)	1	275	0	337 *	1.0	1.5
097 Chr Chs&Chs Cr	1	70	NR	86 *	.3	.4
123 Ch God (Ander)	1	NR	80	80	.2	.4
127 Ch God (Cleve)	1	119	66	146 *	.4	.6
145 Ch God Prophcy	1	27	NR	33 *	.1	.1
151 L-D Saints	1	NR	NR	199	.6	.9
165 Ch of Nazarene	1	397	273	505	1.5	2.2
167 Chs of Christ	9	1,115	933	1,332	4.0	5.9
193 Episcopal	1	NR	81	256	.8	1.1
283 Luth—MO Synod	1	253	139	315	.9	1.4
355 Presb Ch (USA)	2	292	136	358 *	1.1	1.6
360 Prim Bapt Chrch	1	NR	NR	NR	-	-
403 Salvation Army	1	100	66	246	.7	1.1
413 S.D.A.	1	23	NR	27	.1	.1
419 So Bapt Conv	24	9,586	1,850	11,738 *	34.9	51.9
449 Un Methodist	5	1,397	410	1,711 *	5.1	7.6

NR–Not Reported *Total adherents estimated from known number of communicant, confirmed, full members. - Represents a percentage less than 0.1. Percentages may not total 100 due to rounding.

Table 4: Religious Congregations by County and Group: 2000

Religious Group	Number of Churches, Synagogues, Mosques, or Temples	Number of Communicant, Confirmed, or Full Members	Number of Attendees	Total Adherents: Number of Adherents	Total Adherents: % of Total Pop.	Total Adherents: % of Total Adh.
HUDSPETH	**7**	**183**	**151**	**1,888 ***	**56.5**	**100.0**
053 Assemb of God	1	34	38	45	1.3	2.4
056 Baha'i	0	2	NR	2	.1	.1
081 Catholic	1	NR	NR	1,646	49.2	87.2
167 Chs of Christ	1	20	24	24	.7	1.3
419 So Bapt Conv	2	75	60	101 *	3.0	5.3
449 Un Methodist	2	52	29	70 *	2.1	3.7
HUNT	**130**	**30,077**	**11,741**	**41,293 ***	**53.9**	**100.0**
017 Amer Bapt Assn	2	418	NR	524 *	.7	1.3
053 Assemb of God	9	513	626	912	1.2	2.2
056 Baha'i	0	123	NR	123	.2	.3
059 Bapt Miss Assn	2	86	65	108 *	.1	.3
081 Catholic	2	NR	NR	1,756	2.3	4.3
093 Chr Ch (Disc)	6	500	184	627 *	.8	1.5
097 Chr Chs&Chs Cr	1	80	NR	100 *	.1	.2
127 Ch God (Cleve)	2	42	46	61 *	.1	.1
151 L-D Saints	1	NR	NR	309	.4	.7
165 Ch of Nazarene	3	252	131	284	.4	.7
167 Chs of Christ	20	1,987	1,780	2,529	3.3	6.1
193 Episcopal	2	NR	92	269	.4	.7
207 E.L.C.A.	1	159	78	196	.3	.5
263 Int Foursq Gos	1	6	12	12 *	-	-
283 Luth—MO Synod	1	39	30	49	.1	.1
339 Pent Ch of God	1	50	NR	70	.1	.2
355 Presb Ch (USA)	3	468	235	587 *	.8	1.4
356 Presb Ch Amer	1	38	31	38	-	.1
403 Salvation Army	1	52	29	94	.1	.2
413 S.D.A.	1	39	NR	46	.1	.1
419 So Bapt Conv	52	21,622	5,745	27,116 *	35.4	65.7
449 Un Methodist	16	3,503	1,567	4,393 *	5.7	10.6
499 Indep.Non-Char	2	100	1,090	1,090	1.4	2.6
HUTCHINSON	**49**	**14,392**	**4,766**	**20,183 ***	**84.6**	**100.0**
017 Amer Bapt Assn	1	100	NR	126 *	.5	.6
053 Assemb of God	4	199	239	376	1.6	1.9
056 Baha'i	0	5	NR	5	-	-
081 Catholic	2	NR	NR	1,700	7.1	8.4
093 Chr Ch (Disc)	3	430	133	540 *	2.3	2.7
097 Chr Chs&Chs Cr	1	50	NR	63 *	.3	.3
127 Ch God (Cleve)	1	205	139	257 *	1.1	1.3
151 L-D Saints	1	NR	NR	234	1.0	1.2
165 Ch of Nazarene	4	246	156	316	1.3	1.6
167 Chs of Christ	6	1,184	1,063	1,440	6.0	7.1
173 Comm of Christ	1	21	NR	21	.1	.1
193 Episcopal	1	NR	37	83	.3	.4
283 Luth—MO Synod	2	153	91	182	.8	.9
349 Pent Holiness	2	98	73	123 *	.5	.6
355 Presb Ch (USA)	1	108	59	136 *	.6	.7
360 Prim Bapt Chrch	1	NR	NR	NR	-	-
403 Salvation Army	1	119	28	175	.7	.9
413 S.D.A.	1	29	NR	35	.1	.2
419 So Bapt Conv	10	9,988	2,102	12,542 *	52.6	62.1
449 Un Methodist	5	1,407	596	1,766 *	7.4	8.7
463 Vineyard	1	50	50	63 *	.3	.3
IRION	**6**	**823**	**260**	**1,296 ***	**73.2**	**100.0**
081 Catholic	1	NR	NR	278	15.7	21.5
093 Chr Ch (Disc)	1	17	15	21 *	1.2	1.6
167 Chs of Christ	1	30	35	38	2.1	2.9
419 So Bapt Conv	1	549	120	678 *	38.3	52.3
449 Un Methodist	2	227	90	281 *	15.9	21.7
JACK	**30**	**3,727**	**1,669**	**4,786 ***	**54.6**	**100.0**
053 Assemb of God	4	140	176	199	2.3	4.2
056 Baha'i	0	9	NR	9	.1	.2
059 Bapt Miss Assn	1	151	24	183 *	2.1	3.8
081 Catholic	1	NR	NR	205	2.3	4.3
093 Chr Ch (Disc)	1	175	80	212 *	2.4	4.4
167 Chs of Christ	4	253	241	299	3.4	6.2
193 Episcopal	1	NR	16	47	.5	1.0
355 Presb Ch (USA)	1	60	75	75 *	.9	1.6

Religious Group	Number of Churches, Synagogues, Mosques, or Temples	Number of Communicant, Confirmed, or Full Members	Number of Attendees	Total Adherents: Number of Adherents	Total Adherents: % of Total Pop.	Total Adherents: % of Total Adh.
419 So Bapt Conv	12	2,505	892	3,032 *	34.6	63.4
426 2Seed Sprt Bpt	1	24	NR	29 *	.3	.6
449 Un Methodist	4	410	165	496 *	5.7	10.4
JACKSON	**31**	**4,684**	**1,833**	**10,423 ***	**72.4**	**100.0**
053 Assemb of God	1	84	42	105	.7	1.0
081 Catholic	4	NR	NR	4,466	31.0	42.8
167 Chs of Christ	6	432	420	561	3.9	5.4
193 Episcopal	1	NR	16	28	.2	.3
207 E.L.C.A.	1	214	74	258	1.8	2.5
283 Luth—MO Synod	1	200	106	273	1.9	2.6
339 Pent Ch of God	1	10	NR	24	.2	.2
355 Presb Ch (USA)	2	181	55	227 *	1.6	2.2
419 So Bapt Conv	8	2,653	750	3,325 *	23.1	31.9
449 Un Methodist	5	806	291	1,010 *	7.0	9.7
469 WELS	1	104	79	146	1.0	1.4
JASPER	**69**	**15,492**	**5,733**	**21,732 ***	**61.0**	**100.0**
017 Amer Bapt Assn	6	677	NR	846 *	2.4	3.9
053 Assemb of God	5	336	351	497	1.4	2.3
056 Baha'i	0	5	NR	5	-	-
059 Bapt Miss Assn	11	1,089	337	1,360 *	3.8	6.3
081 Catholic	5	NR	NR	1,475	4.1	6.8
151 L-D Saints	2	NR	NR	604	1.7	2.8
165 Ch of Nazarene	2	41	29	74	.2	.3
167 Chs of Christ	7	925	765	1,230	3.5	5.7
193 Episcopal	1	NR	67	126	.4	.6
283 Luth—MO Synod	1	41	27	46	.1	.2
339 Pent Ch of God	1	17	NR	22	.1	.1
355 Presb Ch (USA)	1	81	38	101 *	.3	.5
419 So Bapt Conv	19	10,246	3,301	12,804 *	36.0	58.9
449 Un Methodist	8	2,034	818	2,542 *	7.1	11.7
JEFF DAVIS	**7**	**581**	**248**	**1,212 ***	**54.9**	**100.0**
081 Catholic	1	NR	NR	514	23.3	42.4
097 Chr Chs&Chs Cr	1	136	NR	162 *	7.3	13.4
167 Chs of Christ	1	38	40	52	2.4	4.3
355 Presb Ch (USA)	1	72	34	86 *	3.9	7.1
419 So Bapt Conv	2	224	112	266 *	12.1	21.9
449 Un Methodist	1	111	62	132 *	6.0	10.9
JEFFERSON	**222**	**73,168**	**24,719**	**163,885 ***	**65.0**	**100.0**
017 Amer Bapt Assn	4	307	NR	382 *	.2	.2
034 Ant Orth of NA	1	252	NR	504	.2	.3
053 Assemb of God	18	2,741	2,033	3,172	1.3	1.9
056 Baha'i	1	104	NR	104	-	.1
059 Bapt Miss Assn	3	413	98	515 *	.2	.3
076 Buddhism	1	NR	NR	NR	-	-
081 Catholic	26	NR	NR	63,931	25.4	39.0
093 Chr Ch (Disc)	4	927	429	1,156 *	.5	.7
097 Chr Chs&Chs Cr	3	382	NR	476 *	.2	.3
123 Ch God (Ander)	2	NR	173	173	.1	.1
127 Ch God (Cleve)	1	56	11	70 *	-	-
151 L-D Saints	5	NR	NR	1,372	.5	.8
165 Ch of Nazarene	4	570	387	886	.4	.5
167 Chs of Christ	27	3,198	3,200	4,267	1.7	2.6
173 Comm of Christ	1	34	NR	34	-	-
193 Episcopal	5	NR	931	2,510	1.0	1.5
203 Evan Free Ch	1	69	125	125	-	.1
207 E.L.C.A.	2	539	210	653	.3	.4
246 Greek Orthodox	1	NR	NR	90	-	.1
267 Muslim Est	1	NR	156	609	.2	.4
283 Luth—MO Synod	6	1,961	862	2,510	1.0	1.5
355 Presb Ch (USA)	5	1,636	904	2,103 *	.8	1.3
356 Presb Ch Amer	1	38	50	50	-	-
360 Prim Bapt Chrch	2	NR	NR	NR	-	-
403 Salvation Army	2	195	123	3,545	1.4	2.2
413 S.D.A.	4	505	NR	601	.2	.4
419 So Bapt Conv	60	45,672	9,674	56,930 *	22.6	34.7
435 Unitarian-Univ	1	83	NR	103 *	-	.1
443 Un C of Christ	1	24	18	30 *	-	-
449 Un Methodist	25	11,848	4,025	14,770 *	5.9	9.0

NR–Not Reported *Total adherents estimated from known number of communicant, confirmed, full members. - Represents a percentage less than 0.1. Percentages may not total 100 due to rounding.

Table 4: Religious Congregations by County and Group: 2000

Religious Group	Number of Churches, Synagogues, Mosques, or Temples	Number of Communicant, Confirmed, or Full Members	Number of Attendees	Total Adherents		
				Number of Adherents	% of Total Pop.	% of Total Adh.
496 Jewish Est	1	NR	NR	600	.2	.4
498 Indep.Charis.	3	1,614	1,310	1,614	.6	1.0
JIM HOGG	**10**	**373**	**166**	**5,344 ***	**101.2**	**100.0**
053 Assemb of God	1	21	24	37	.7	.7
081 Catholic	2	NR	NR	4,809	91.1	90.0
167 Chs of Christ	3	26	36	35	.7	.7
193 Episcopal	1	NR	12	35	.7	.7
419 So Bapt Conv	1	224	41	294 *	5.6	5.5
449 Un Methodist	2	102	53	134 *	2.5	2.5
JIM WELLS	**37**	**6,177**	**2,293**	**23,430 ***	**59.6**	**100.0**
053 Assemb of God	2	73	90	116	.3	.5
056 Baha'i	0	19	NR	19	-	.1
081 Catholic	2	NR	NR	14,861	37.8	63.4
093 Chr Ch (Disc)	1	41	0	54 *	.1	.2
123 Ch God (Ander)	1	NR	0	0	-	-
151 L-D Saints	1	NR	NR	383	1.0	1.6
167 Chs of Christ	5	269	285	323	.8	1.4
193 Episcopal	1	NR	61	126	.3	.5
207 E.L.C.A.	2	655	239	834	2.1	3.6
237 Menn Br US Conf	1	8	NR	11 *	-	-
283 Luth—MO Synod	1	58	30	66	.2	.3
288 Mennonite USA	1	7	5	9 *	-	-
355 Presb Ch (USA)	2	152	92	200 *	.5	.9
413 S.D.A.	2	53	NR	63	.2	.3
419 So Bapt Conv	11	4,211	1,279	5,536 *	14.1	23.6
443 Un C of Christ	1	120	39	158 *	.4	.7
449 Un Methodist	3	511	173	671 *	1.7	2.9
JOHNSON	**124**	**43,392**	**15,406**	**61,527 ***	**48.5**	**100.0**
032 Amish; other	1	53	NR	68 *	.1	.1
053 Assemb of God	10	1,221	1,148	2,009	1.6	3.3
056 Baha'i	0	37	NR	37	-	.1
059 Bapt Miss Assn	1	39	30	50 *	-	.1
081 Catholic	1	NR	NR	5,173	4.1	8.4
093 Chr Ch (Disc)	2	381	173	488 *	.4	.8
127 Ch God (Cleve)	3	191	106	245 *	.2	.4
151 L-D Saints	1	NR	NR	572	.5	.9
165 Ch of Nazarene	2	247	126	247	.2	.4
167 Chs of Christ	15	2,512	2,353	3,288	2.6	5.3
173 Comm of Christ	1	45	NR	45	-	.1
185 Cumber Presb	1	670	NR	707	.6	1.1
193 Episcopal	3	NR	192	412	.3	.7
283 Luth—MO Synod	2	390	115	514	.4	.8
339 Pent Ch of God	4	188	NR	314	.2	.5
355 Presb Ch (USA)	2	349	168	447 *	.4	.7
413 S.D.A.	8	4,868	NR	5,794	4.6	9.4
419 So Bapt Conv	48	25,086	7,855	32,144 *	25.3	52.2
449 Un Methodist	16	5,715	1,790	7,323 *	5.8	11.9
498 Indep.Charis.	1	800	500	800	.6	1.3
499 Indep.Non-Char	2	600	850	850	.7	1.4
JONES	**52**	**9,401**	**3,684**	**13,030 ***	**62.7**	**100.0**
053 Assemb of God	3	90	82	128	.6	1.0
056 Baha'i	0	1	NR	1	-	-
059 Bapt Miss Assn	2	281	90	333 *	1.6	2.6
081 Catholic	3	NR	NR	1,723	8.3	13.2
127 Ch God (Cleve)	1	82	45	97 *	.5	.7
165 Ch of Nazarene	1	118	85	175	.8	1.3
167 Chs of Christ	13	1,116	1,031	1,395	6.7	10.7
207 E.L.C.A.	2	319	159	379	1.8	2.9
263 Int Foursq Gos	2	75	123	123 *	.6	.9
355 Presb Ch (USA)	1	86	25	102 *	.5	.8
419 So Bapt Conv	18	6,408	1,719	7,595 *	36.5	58.3
449 Un Methodist	6	825	325	979 *	4.7	7.5
KARNES	**32**	**2,834**	**1,306**	**9,684 ***	**62.7**	**100.0**
053 Assemb of God	3	69	67	102	.7	1.1
056 Baha'i	0	2	NR	2	-	-
081 Catholic	7	NR	NR	6,140	39.8	63.4
167 Chs of Christ	3	137	135	194	1.3	2.0

Religious Group	Number of Churches, Synagogues, Mosques, or Temples	Number of Communicant, Confirmed, or Full Members	Number of Attendees	Total Adherents		
				Number of Adherents	% of Total Pop.	% of Total Adh.
193 Episcopal	1	NR	11	15	.1	.2
207 E.L.C.A.	4	523	300	714	4.6	7.4
355 Presb Ch (USA)	1	48	22	57 *	.4	.6
419 So Bapt Conv	9	1,744	633	2,088 *	13.5	21.6
449 Un Methodist	4	311	138	372 *	2.4	3.8
KAUFMAN	**89**	**24,686**	**10,305**	**37,171 ***	**52.1**	**100.0**
017 Amer Bapt Assn	2	420	NR	539 *	.8	1.5
053 Assemb of God	9	747	831	885	1.2	2.4
056 Baha'i	0	86	NR	86	.1	.2
059 Bapt Miss Assn	11	3,824	1,536	4,911 *	6.9	13.2
081 Catholic	3	NR	NR	4,691	6.6	12.6
093 Chr Ch (Disc)	2	552	168	709 *	1.0	1.9
145 Ch God Prophcy	1	27	NR	35 *	-	.1
151 L-D Saints	1	NR	NR	226	.3	.6
165 Ch of Nazarene	1	71	46	157	.2	.4
167 Chs of Christ	15	1,952	1,852	2,645	3.7	7.1
193 Episcopal	2	NR	155	412	.6	1.1
263 Int Foursq Gos	1	26	70	70 *	.1	.2
286 E.PA Mennonite	1	51	NR	65 *	.1	.2
349 Pent Holiness	1	40	30	51 *	.1	.1
355 Presb Ch (USA)	4	456	271	586 *	.8	1.6
413 S.D.A.	1	40	NR	48	.1	.1
419 So Bapt Conv	23	13,838	4,237	17,772 *	24.9	47.8
449 Un Methodist	11	2,556	1,109	3,283 *	4.6	8.8
KENDALL	**19**	**6,698**	**3,350**	**15,289 ***	**64.4**	**100.0**
053 Assemb of God	1	88	107	297	1.3	1.9
056 Baha'i	0	8	NR	8	-	.1
081 Catholic	2	NR	NR	5,700	24.0	37.3
151 L-D Saints	1	NR	NR	281	1.2	1.8
167 Chs of Christ	1	115	180	150	.6	1.0
193 Episcopal	2	NR	323	707	3.0	4.6
203 Evan Free Ch	1	56	85	85	.4	.6
207 E.L.C.A.	2	1,209	471	1,491	6.3	9.8
355 Presb Ch (USA)	1	387	217	487 *	2.1	3.2
419 So Bapt Conv	6	3,028	1,239	3,809 *	16.0	24.9
449 Un Methodist	2	1,807	728	2,274 *	9.6	14.9
KENEDY	**3**	**39**	**45**	**170 ***	**41.1**	**100.0**
081 Catholic	2	NR	NR	120	29.0	70.6
349 Pent Holiness	1	39	45	50 *	12.1	29.4
KENT	**5**	**573**	**206**	**740 ***	**86.1**	**100.0**
053 Assemb of God	1	32	11	43	5.0	5.8
081 Catholic	1	NR	NR	63	7.3	8.5
167 Chs of Christ	1	47	50	61	7.1	8.2
419 So Bapt Conv	1	424	130	492 *	57.3	66.5
449 Un Methodist	1	70	15	81 *	9.4	10.9
KERR	**42**	**12,842**	**5,919**	**23,175 ***	**53.1**	**100.0**
053 Assemb of God	3	267	315	413	.9	1.8
056 Baha'i	0	28	NR	28	.1	.1
081 Catholic	1	NR	NR	6,284	14.4	27.1
093 Chr Ch (Disc)	2	484	0	581 *	1.3	2.5
151 L-D Saints	1	NR	NR	405	.9	1.7
165 Ch of Nazarene	1	61	51	61	.1	.3
167 Chs of Christ	3	712	645	795	1.8	3.4
193 Episcopal	1	NR	360	1,039	2.4	4.5
203 Evan Free Ch	1	30	65	65	.1	.3
207 E.L.C.A.	1	626	327	727	1.7	3.1
263 Int Foursq Gos	1	92	78	110 *	.3	.5
283 Luth—MO Synod	2	234	179	304	.7	1.3
355 Presb Ch (USA)	2	1,034	484	1,242 *	2.8	5.4
403 Salvation Army	1	108	87	114	.3	.5
413 S.D.A.	1	97	NR	115	.3	.5
419 So Bapt Conv	14	6,158	2,092	7,396 *	16.9	31.9
435 Unitarian-Univ	2	76	NR	91 *	.2	.4
449 Un Methodist	5	2,835	1,236	3,405 *	7.8	14.7

NR–Not Reported *Total adherents estimated from known number of communicant, confirmed, full members. - Represents a percentage less than 0.1. Percentages may not total 100 due to rounding.

Table 4: Religious Congregations by County and Group: 2000

Religious Group	Number of Churches, Synagogues, Mosques, or Temples	Number of Communicant, Confirmed, or Full Members	Number of Attendees	Total Adherents		
				Number of Adherents	% of Total Pop.	% of Total Adh.
KIMBLE	**12**	**1,679**	**749**	**2,498 ***	**55.9**	**100.0**
081 Catholic	1	NR	NR	350	7.8	14.0
167 Chs of Christ	4	210	216	278	6.2	11.1
193 Episcopal	1	NR	37	90	2.0	3.6
355 Presb Ch (USA)	1	111	52	134 *	3.0	5.4
419 So Bapt Conv	3	1,143	329	1,385 *	31.0	55.4
449 Un Methodist	2	215	115	261 *	5.8	10.4
KING	**2**	**134**	**51**	**180 ***	**50.6**	**100.0**
419 So Bapt Conv	2	134	51	180 *	50.6	100.0
KINNEY	**9**	**611**	**343**	**2,528 ***	**74.8**	**100.0**
053 Assemb of God	1	23	20	20	.6	.8
056 Baha'i	0	2	NR	2	.1	.1
081 Catholic	1	NR	NR	1,759	52.1	69.6
167 Chs of Christ	1	77	83	101	3.0	4.0
193 Episcopal	1	NR	16	27	.8	1.1
207 E.L.C.A.	1	62	50	67	2.0	2.7
419 So Bapt Conv	3	356	117	440 *	13.0	17.4
449 Un Methodist	1	91	57	112 *	3.3	4.4
KLEBERG	**36**	**5,247**	**2,688**	**11,376 ***	**36.1**	**100.0**
017 Amer Bapt Assn	1	23	NR	29 *	.1	.3
053 Assemb of God	2	488	663	707	2.2	6.2
056 Baha'i	0	12	NR	12	-	.1
081 Catholic	8	NR	NR	4,350	13.8	38.2
093 Chr Ch (Disc)	1	91	0	115 *	.4	1.0
123 Ch God (Ander)	1	NR	32	32	.1	.3
145 Ch God Prophcy	1	27	NR	34 *	.1	.3
165 Ch of Nazarene	2	48	43	114	.4	1.0
167 Chs of Christ	1	194	150	238	.8	2.1
193 Episcopal	1	NR	96	177	.6	1.6
207 E.L.C.A.	1	73	41	90	.3	.8
267 Muslim Est	1	NR	30	50	.2	.4
283 Luth—MO Synod	1	187	114	241	.8	2.1
355 Presb Ch (USA)	2	230	130	291 *	.9	2.6
419 So Bapt Conv	8	3,102	1,090	3,920 *	12.4	34.5
449 Un Methodist	5	772	299	976 *	3.1	8.6
KNOX	**26**	**3,146**	**1,015**	**5,092 ***	**119.7**	**100.0**
053 Assemb of God	1	29	35	35	.8	.7
081 Catholic	2	NR	NR	1,194	28.1	23.4
093 Chr Ch (Disc)	1	54	0	68 *	1.6	1.3
097 Chr Chs&Chs Cr	1	90	NR	114 *	2.7	2.2
167 Chs of Christ	7	401	313	434	10.2	8.5
263 Int Foursq Gos	1	151	74	191 *	4.5	3.8
419 So Bapt Conv	8	1,929	376	2,435 *	57.3	47.8
449 Un Methodist	5	492	217	621 *	14.6	12.2
LAMAR	**92**	**22,432**	**8,542**	**31,699 ***	**65.4**	**100.0**
053 Assemb of God	5	210	228	250	.5	.8
056 Baha'i	0	7	NR	7	-	-
081 Catholic	1	NR	NR	2,714	5.6	8.6
093 Chr Ch (Disc)	2	631	252	791 *	1.6	2.5
127 Ch God (Cleve)	6	1,744	833	2,185 *	4.5	6.9
143 CG in Cr(Menn)	1	53	NR	66 *	.1	.2
151 L-D Saints	1	NR	NR	388	.8	1.2
165 Ch of Nazarene	2	155	101	206	.4	.6
167 Chs of Christ	15	1,797	1,613	2,374	4.9	7.5
193 Episcopal	1	NR	98	372	.8	1.2
283 Luth—MO Synod	1	101	67	133	.3	.4
297 Mennonite;Other	1	37	NR	46 *	.1	.1
339 Pent Ch of God	2	80	NR	130	.3	.4
355 Presb Ch (USA)	4	310	151	388 *	.8	1.2
356 Presb Ch Amer	1	52	41	63	.1	.2
360 Prim Bapt Chrch	1	NR	NR	NR	-	-
403 Salvation Army	1	101	49	131	.3	.4
419 So Bapt Conv	32	14,051	3,760	17,613 *	36.3	55.6
449 Un Methodist	14	2,753	1,099	3,452 *	7.1	10.9
499 Indep.Non-Char	1	350	250	390	.8	1.2

Religious Group	Number of Churches, Synagogues, Mosques, or Temples	Number of Communicant, Confirmed, or Full Members	Number of Attendees	Total Adherents		
				Number of Adherents	% of Total Pop.	% of Total Adh.
LAMB	**44**	**7,920**	**2,998**	**13,420 ***	**91.2**	**100.0**
053 Assemb of God	2	59	60	104	.7	.8
059 Bapt Miss Assn	1	136	50	174 *	1.2	1.3
081 Catholic	3	NR	NR	3,288	22.4	24.5
165 Ch of Nazarene	2	40	29	41	.3	.3
167 Chs of Christ	9	906	851	1,139	7.7	8.5
173 Comm of Christ	1	25	NR	25	.2	.2
207 E.L.C.A.	1	25	15	28	.2	.2
283 Luth—MO Synod	1	75	46	97	.7	.7
339 Pent Ch of God	1	25	NR	41	.3	.3
349 Pent Holiness	1	35	45	45 *	.3	.3
355 Presb Ch (USA)	1	60	35	77 *	.5	.6
360 Prim Bapt Chrch	2	NR	NR	NR	-	-
419 So Bapt Conv	13	5,129	1,279	6,564 *	44.6	48.9
449 Un Methodist	6	1,405	588	1,797 *	12.2	13.4
LAMPASAS	**26**	**4,758**	**2,092**	**8,327 ***	**46.9**	**100.0**
053 Assemb of God	1	109	129	154	.9	1.8
056 Baha'i	0	7	NR	7	-	.1
081 Catholic	2	NR	NR	2,073	11.7	24.9
093 Chr Ch (Disc)	1	59	40	74 *	.4	.9
167 Chs of Christ	5	514	468	603	3.4	7.2
193 Episcopal	1	NR	144	310	1.7	3.7
263 Int Foursq Gos	1	14	7	18 *	.1	.2
283 Luth—MO Synod	1	155	79	178	1.0	2.1
355 Presb Ch (USA)	2	80	63	101 *	.6	1.2
360 Prim Bapt Chrch	1	NR	NR	NR	-	-
419 So Bapt Conv	8	3,193	904	4,020 *	22.6	48.3
449 Un Methodist	3	627	258	789 *	4.4	9.5
LA SALLE	**13**	**802**	**346**	**6,068 ***	**103.4**	**100.0**
081 Catholic	2	NR	NR	5,028	85.7	82.9
167 Chs of Christ	2	88	95	117	2.0	1.9
193 Episcopal	1	NR	10	10	.2	.2
263 Int Foursq Gos	1	45	53	58 *	1.0	1.0
355 Presb Ch (USA)	2	17	14	21 *	.4	.3
419 So Bapt Conv	3	492	106	629 *	10.7	10.4
449 Un Methodist	2	160	68	205 *	3.5	3.4
LAVACA	**42**	**4,379**	**2,019**	**18,876 ***	**98.3**	**100.0**
053 Assemb of God	2	188	187	218	1.1	1.2
056 Baha'i	0	3	NR	3	-	-
081 Catholic	8	NR	NR	13,448	70.0	71.2
123 Ch God (Ander)	1	NR	15	15	.1	.1
167 Chs of Christ	4	170	242	268	1.4	1.4
193 Episcopal	2	NR	33	48	.2	.3
207 E.L.C.A.	6	1,687	683	2,038	10.6	10.8
355 Presb Ch (USA)	1	22	16	27 *	.1	.1
419 So Bapt Conv	10	1,589	584	1,934 *	10.1	10.2
449 Un Methodist	8	720	259	877 *	4.6	4.6
LEE	**31**	**6,371**	**3,212**	**9,174 ***	**58.6**	**100.0**
053 Assemb of God	1	40	50	88	.6	1.0
081 Catholic	3	NR	NR	1,137	7.3	12.4
093 Chr Ch (Disc)	1	136	54	172 *	1.1	1.9
097 Chr Chs&Chs Cr	1	110	NR	139 *	.9	1.5
123 Ch God (Ander)	1	NR	15	15	.1	.2
167 Chs of Christ	2	115	125	149	1.0	1.6
207 E.L.C.A.	3	962	356	1,176	7.5	12.8
283 Luth—MO Synod	8	2,999	1,670	3,763	24.0	41.0
304 NatPrimBapt USA	1	20	NR	25 *	.2	.3
419 So Bapt Conv	7	1,348	675	1,701 *	10.9	18.5
449 Un Methodist	3	641	267	809 *	5.2	8.8
LEON	**59**	**7,316**	**3,081**	**9,530 ***	**62.1**	**100.0**
017 Amer Bapt Assn	1	13	NR	16 *	.1	.2
053 Assemb of God	4	518	212	446	2.9	4.7
059 Bapt Miss Assn	12	1,441	536	1,752 *	11.4	18.4
081 Catholic	3	NR	NR	773	5.0	8.1
093 Chr Ch (Disc)	1	37	28	45 *	.3	.5
127 Ch God (Cleve)	1	55	11	67 *	.4	.7

NR–Not Reported *Total adherents estimated from known number of communicant, confirmed, full members. - Represents a percentage less than 0.1. Percentages may not total 100 due to rounding.

Table 4: Religious Congregations by County and Group: 2000

Religious Group	Number of Churches, Synagogues, Mosques, or Temples	Number of Communicant, Confirmed, or Full Members	Number of Attendees	Total Adherents		
				Number of Adherents	% of Total Pop.	% of Total Adh.
167 Chs of Christ	8	412	410	546	3.6	5.7
283 Luth—MO Synod	1	118	72	140	.9	1.5
419 So Bapt Conv	10	3,494	1,200	4,251 *	27.7	44.6
449 Un Methodist	18	1,228	612	1,494 *	9.7	15.7
LIBERTY	**106**	**23,791**	**7,990**	**40,502 ***	**57.7**	**100.0**
017 Amer Bapt Assn	5	271	NR	344 *	.5	.8
053 Assemb of God	15	1,208	1,157	1,742	2.5	4.3
056 Baha'i	0	20	NR	20	-	-
059 Bapt Miss Assn	4	434	142	551 *	.8	1.4
081 Catholic	6	NR	NR	7,775	11.1	19.2
093 Chr Ch (Disc)	1	12	0	15 *	-	-
145 Ch God Prophcy	2	54	NR	68 *	.1	.2
151 L-D Saints	2	NR	NR	847	1.2	2.1
167 Chs of Christ	11	986	921	1,204	1.7	3.0
193 Episcopal	2	NR	84	173	.2	.4
207 E.L.C.A.	2	133	42	184	.3	.5
267 Muslim Est	1	NR	290	1,313	1.9	3.2
283 Luth—MO Synod	1	44	22	49	.1	.1
339 Pent Ch of God	4	94	NR	152	.2	.4
355 Presb Ch (USA)	2	74	41	94 *	.1	.2
413 S.D.A.	1	105	NR	125	.2	.3
419 So Bapt Conv	40	18,248	4,681	23,169 *	33.0	57.2
449 Un Methodist	7	2,108	610	2,677 *	3.8	6.6
LIMESTONE	**61**	**9,394**	**3,148**	**12,505 ***	**56.7**	**100.0**
017 Amer Bapt Assn	2	246	NR	305 *	1.4	2.4
053 Assemb of God	4	347	205	358	1.6	2.9
056 Baha'i	0	3	NR	3	-	-
059 Bapt Miss Assn	3	399	116	495 *	2.2	4.0
081 Catholic	1	NR	NR	802	3.6	6.4
093 Chr Ch (Disc)	1	30	15	37 *	.2	.3
167 Chs of Christ	13	875	678	1,108	5.0	8.9
193 Episcopal	1	NR	40	92	.4	.7
283 Luth—MO Synod	1	68	50	96	.4	.8
304 NatPrimBapt USA	8	519	NR	643 *	2.9	5.1
339 Pent Ch of God	1	28	NR	39	.2	.3
355 Presb Ch (USA)	1	185	75	229 *	1.0	1.8
360 Prim Bapt Chrch	2	NR	NR	NR	-	-
419 So Bapt Conv	15	5,152	1,482	6,387 *	29.0	51.1
449 Un Methodist	8	1,542	487	1,911 *	8.7	15.3
LIPSCOMB	**19**	**1,857**	**639**	**2,562 ***	**83.8**	**100.0**
081 Catholic	1	NR	NR	277	9.1	10.8
097 Chr Chs&Chs Cr	1	120	NR	150 *	4.9	5.9
165 Ch of Nazarene	1	46	31	46	1.5	1.8
167 Chs of Christ	3	64	54	72	2.4	2.8
181 Consrv Congr	1	20	20	25 *	.8	1.0
207 E.L.C.A.	1	88	67	99	3.2	3.9
226 Friends-USA	2	100	NR	125 *	4.1	4.9
419 So Bapt Conv	5	832	216	1,037 *	33.9	40.5
449 Un Methodist	4	587	251	731 *	23.9	28.5
LIVE OAK	**25**	**3,247**	**1,372**	**6,333 ***	**51.5**	**100.0**
053 Assemb of God	1	65	85	102	.8	1.6
056 Baha'i	0	2	NR	2	-	-
081 Catholic	3	NR	NR	2,205	17.9	34.8
167 Chs of Christ	4	232	260	351	2.9	5.5
193 Episcopal	3	NR	82	121	1.0	1.9
207 E.L.C.A.	2	259	116	338	2.7	5.3
283 Luth—MO Synod	1	18	15	19	.2	.3
360 Prim Bapt Chrch	1	NR	NR	NR	-	-
419 So Bapt Conv	8	2,146	632	2,567 *	20.9	40.5
449 Un Methodist	2	525	182	628 *	5.1	9.9
LLANO	**32**	**5,743**	**2,572**	**7,665 ***	**45.0**	**100.0**
053 Assemb of God	1	26	35	35	.2	.5
081 Catholic	2	NR	NR	635	3.7	8.3
093 Chr Ch (Disc)	1	123	60	140 *	.8	1.8
151 L-D Saints	1	NR	NR	324	1.9	4.2
167 Chs of Christ	7	459	475	590	3.5	7.7
193 Episcopal	1	NR	56	106	.6	1.4

Religious Group	Number of Churches, Synagogues, Mosques, or Temples	Number of Communicant, Confirmed, or Full Members	Number of Attendees	Total Adherents		
				Number of Adherents	% of Total Pop.	% of Total Adh.
207 E.L.C.A.	2	203	84	240	1.4	3.1
283 Luth—MO Synod	1	137	83	145	.9	1.9
355 Presb Ch (USA)	1	54	28	61 *	.4	.8
360 Prim Bapt Chrch	1	NR	NR	NR	-	-
419 So Bapt Conv	9	3,703	1,332	4,209 *	24.7	54.9
449 Un Methodist	5	1,038	419	1,180 *	6.9	15.4
LOVING	**0**	**0**	**0**	**0**	**-**	**-**
LUBBOCK	**227**	**78,434**	**38,728**	**144,758 ***	**59.7**	**100.0**
017 Amer Bapt Assn	1	345	NR	430 *	.2	.3
053 Assemb of God	14	949	1,211	1,468	.6	1.0
056 Baha'i	1	78	NR	78	-	.1
059 Bapt Miss Assn	7	1,159	430	1,446 *	.6	1.0
081 Catholic	17	NR	NR	39,327	16.2	27.2
093 Chr Ch (Disc)	5	1,698	780	2,116 *	.9	1.5
097 Chr Chs&Chs Cr	1	375	NR	467 *	.2	.3
127 Ch God (Cleve)	4	452	260	564 *	.2	.4
145 Ch God Prophcy	2	54	NR	68 *	-	-
151 L-D Saints	5	NR	NR	1,856	.8	1.3
165 Ch of Nazarene	4	776	771	1,218	.5	.8
167 Chs of Christ	37	9,179	8,867	11,645	4.8	8.0
173 Comm of Christ	1	20	NR	20	-	-
185 Cumber Presb	1	539	NR	580	.2	.4
186 Coptic Orth Ch	1	NR	NR	NR	-	-
193 Episcopal	3	NR	534	1,936	.8	1.3
207 E.L.C.A.	4	522	239	652	.3	.5
223 Free Will Bapt	1	42	NR	53 *	-	-
226 Friends-USA	1	15	NR	19 *	-	-
246 Greek Orthodox	1	NR	NR	171	.1	.1
263 Int Foursq Gos	4	941	588	1,173 *	.5	.8
264 Int Chs of Crst	1	33	49	43	-	-
267 Muslim Est	2	NR	201	388	.2	.3
268 Jain	1	NR	NR	NR	-	-
283 Luth—MO Synod	4	871	518	1,150	.5	.8
290 Metro Comm Ch	1	113	108	141 *	.1	.1
339 Pent Ch of God	1	99	NR	147	.1	.1
349 Pent Holiness	6	364	371	454 *	.2	.3
355 Presb Ch (USA)	5	1,352	687	1,685 *	.7	1.2
360 Prim Bapt Chrch	1	NR	NR	NR	-	-
403 Salvation Army	1	135	99	277	.1	.2
413 S.D.A.	2	228	NR	272	.1	.2
419 So Bapt Conv	53	42,543	12,243	53,025 *	21.9	36.6
435 Unitarian-Univ	1	74	NR	92 *	-	.1
443 Un C of Christ	1	16	14	20 *	-	-
449 Un Methodist	23	12,795	5,427	15,947 *	6.6	11.0
469 WELS	1	97	56	125	.1	.1
496 Jewish Est	1	NR	NR	230	.1	.2
498 Indep.Charis.	4	1,300	1,675	1,675	.7	1.2
499 Indep.Non-Char	3	1,270	3,600	3,800	1.6	2.6
LYNN	**22**	**3,146**	**1,296**	**5,552 ***	**84.8**	**100.0**
056 Baha'i	0	1	NR	1	-	-
081 Catholic	3	NR	NR	1,401	21.4	25.2
165 Ch of Nazarene	1	96	67	175	2.7	3.2
167 Chs of Christ	4	171	193	232	3.5	4.2
207 E.L.C.A.	1	91	53	118	1.8	2.1
283 Luth—MO Synod	1	128	70	161	2.5	2.9
419 So Bapt Conv	8	2,130	724	2,774 *	42.4	50.0
449 Un Methodist	4	529	189	690 *	10.5	12.4
MCCULLOCH	**29**	**2,878**	**1,320**	**5,389 ***	**65.7**	**100.0**
053 Assemb of God	2	54	59	86	1.0	1.6
081 Catholic	2	NR	NR	1,537	18.7	28.5
093 Chr Ch (Disc)	1	317	104	397 *	4.8	7.4
127 Ch God (Cleve)	1	162	25	203 *	2.5	3.8
151 L-D Saints	1	NR	NR	50	.6	.9
167 Chs of Christ	6	413	381	543	6.6	10.1
193 Episcopal	1	NR	47	124	1.5	2.3
203 Evan Free Ch	1	9	25	25	.3	.5
283 Luth—MO Synod	1	57	21	88	1.1	1.6
355 Presb Ch (USA)	1	51	24	64 *	.8	1.2

NR–Not Reported *Total adherents estimated from known number of communicant, confirmed, full members. - Represents a percentage less than 0.1. Percentages may not total 100 due to rounding.

Table 4: Religious Congregations by County and Group: 2000

Religious Group	Number of Churches, Synagogues, Mosques, or Temples	Number of Communicant, Confirmed, or Full Members	Number of Attendees	Total Adherents		
				Number of Adherents	% of Total Pop.	% of Total Adh.
419 So Bapt Conv	9	1,226	411	1,535 *	18.7	28.5
449 Un Methodist	3	589	223	737 *	9.0	13.7
MCLENNAN	**252**	**79,750**	**31,927**	**129,208 ***	**60.5**	**100.0**
017 Amer Bapt Assn	1	51	NR	64 *	-	-
053 Assemb of God	12	1,532	1,800	3,259	1.5	2.5
056 Baha'i	1	68	NR	68	-	.1
059 Bapt Miss Assn	2	385	175	484 *	.2	.4
081 Catholic	13	NR	NR	22,880	10.7	17.7
089 Chr & Miss Al	1	94	NR	174	.1	.1
093 Chr Ch (Disc)	6	1,526	613	1,916 *	.9	1.5
123 Ch God (Ander)	1	NR	20	20	-	-
151 L-D Saints	2	NR	NR	1,093	.5	.8
165 Ch of Nazarene	3	477	248	477	.2	.4
167 Chs of Christ	28	3,121	2,951	4,272	2.0	3.3
173 Comm of Christ	1	57	NR	57	-	-
193 Episcopal	3	NR	730	1,946	.9	1.5
203 Evan Free Ch	1	195	450	450	.2	.3
207 E.L.C.A.	5	1,585	746	1,989	.9	1.5
223 Free Will Bapt	1	42	NR	53 *	-	-
246 Greek Orthodox	1	NR	NR	165	.1	.1
267 Muslim Est	1	NR	60	300	.1	.2
283 Luth—MO Synod	5	2,247	1,144	2,630	1.2	2.0
288 Mennonite USA	1	14	30	30 *	-	-
290 Metro Comm Ch	1	45	39	57 *	-	-
304 NatPrimBapt USA	1	30	NR	38 *	-	-
313 N Am Bapt Conf	2	188	85	236 *	.1	.2
339 Pent Ch of God	5	275	NR	943	.4	.7
355 Presb Ch (USA)	4	964	465	1,210 *	.6	.9
356 Presb Ch Amer	1	0	0	0	-	-
360 Prim Bapt Chrch	1	NR	NR	NR	-	-
403 Salvation Army	1	201	153	279	.1	.2
413 S.D.A.	2	188	NR	223	.1	.2
418 Southw Bapt Fel	1	NR	NR	NR	-	-
419 So Bapt Conv	92	51,086	16,893	64,143 *	30.0	49.6
435 Unitarian-Univ	1	56	NR	70 *	-	.1
443 Un C of Christ	5	757	341	950 *	.4	.7
449 Un Methodist	42	13,946	4,059	17,507 *	8.2	13.5
496 Jewish Est	2	NR	NR	300	.1	.2
498 Indep.Charis.	1	220	500	500	.2	.4
499 Indep.Non-Char	1	400	425	425	.2	.3
MCMULLEN	**2**	**110**	**58**	**484 ***	**56.9**	**100.0**
081 Catholic	1	NR	NR	352	41.4	72.7
419 So Bapt Conv	1	110	58	132 *	15.5	27.3
MADISON	**28**	**4,731**	**2,266**	**6,347 ***	**49.0**	**100.0**
053 Assemb of God	1	28	20	47	.4	.7
056 Baha'i	0	1	NR	1	-	-
059 Bapt Miss Assn	2	251	110	299 *	2.3	4.7
081 Catholic	1	NR	NR	393	3.0	6.2
151 L-D Saints	1	NR	NR	203	1.6	3.2
167 Chs of Christ	9	707	618	894	6.9	14.1
193 Episcopal	1	NR	14	25	.2	.4
223 Free Will Bapt	1	42	NR	51 *	.4	.8
283 Luth—MO Synod	1	218	141	288	2.2	4.5
360 Prim Bapt Chrch	1	NR	NR	NR	-	-
419 So Bapt Conv	7	2,785	1,079	3,314 *	25.6	52.2
449 Un Methodist	3	699	284	832 *	6.4	13.1
MARION	**33**	**3,628**	**1,220**	**4,820 ***	**44.1**	**100.0**
053 Assemb of God	1	85	49	135	1.2	2.8
056 Baha'i	0	4	NR	4	-	.1
081 Catholic	1	NR	NR	321	2.9	6.7
165 Ch of Nazarene	1	20	16	35	.3	.7
167 Chs of Christ	2	160	170	185	1.7	3.8
185 Cumber Presb	1	89	NR	127	1.2	2.6
193 Episcopal	1	NR	35	86	.8	1.8
413 S.D.A.	3	362	NR	432	3.9	9.0
419 So Bapt Conv	10	2,292	644	2,755 *	25.2	57.2
449 Un Methodist	13	616	306	740 *	6.8	15.4

Religious Group	Number of Churches, Synagogues, Mosques, or Temples	Number of Communicant, Confirmed, or Full Members	Number of Attendees	Total Adherents		
				Number of Adherents	% of Total Pop.	% of Total Adh.
MARTIN	**13**	**1,789**	**716**	**3,192 ***	**67.3**	**100.0**
053 Assemb of God	1	27	27	27	.6	.8
081 Catholic	2	NR	NR	852	18.0	26.7
167 Chs of Christ	4	270	240	315	6.6	9.9
173 Comm of Christ	1	33	NR	33	.7	1.0
419 So Bapt Conv	4	1,094	325	1,473 *	31.0	46.1
449 Un Methodist	1	365	124	492 *	10.4	15.4
MASON	**9**	**1,789**	**736**	**2,898 ***	**77.5**	**100.0**
053 Assemb of God	1	22	14	31	.8	1.1
081 Catholic	1	NR	NR	802	21.5	27.7
093 Chr Ch (Disc)	1	33	25	39 *	1.0	1.3
167 Chs of Christ	1	138	125	142	3.8	4.9
207 E.L.C.A.	1	415	144	479	12.8	16.5
419 So Bapt Conv	1	518	130	616 *	16.5	21.3
449 Un Methodist	3	663	298	789 *	21.1	27.2
MATAGORDA	**64**	**10,919**	**4,182**	**23,928 ***	**63.0**	**100.0**
053 Assemb of God	1	105	130	130	.3	.5
056 Baha'i	0	4	NR	4	-	-
081 Catholic	7	NR	NR	8,880	23.4	37.1
093 Chr Ch (Disc)	3	481	220	623 *	1.6	2.6
145 Ch God Prophcy	5	135	NR	175 *	.5	.7
151 L-D Saints	2	NR	NR	455	1.2	1.9
165 Ch of Nazarene	1	72	42	72	.2	.3
167 Chs of Christ	5	478	453	634	1.7	2.6
193 Episcopal	3	NR	196	452	1.2	1.9
207 E.L.C.A.	1	255	107	336	.9	1.4
283 Luth—MO Synod	2	72	62	97	.3	.4
349 Pent Holiness	1	78	55	101 *	.3	.4
355 Presb Ch (USA)	5	562	271	729 *	1.9	3.0
419 So Bapt Conv	20	7,003	1,951	9,072 *	23.9	37.9
449 Un Methodist	7	1,544	575	2,000 *	5.3	8.4
463 Vineyard	1	130	120	168 *	.4	.7
MAVERICK	**25**	**1,777**	**1,276**	**16,403 ***	**34.7**	**100.0**
053 Assemb of God	3	208	223	275	.6	1.7
056 Baha'i	1	34	NR	34	.1	.2
081 Catholic	3	NR	NR	13,091	27.7	79.8
097 Chr Chs&Chs Cr	1	100	NR	141 *	.3	.9
123 Ch God (Ander)	1	NR	175	175	.4	1.1
151 L-D Saints	2	NR	NR	571	1.2	3.5
167 Chs of Christ	2	152	150	192	.4	1.2
193 Episcopal	1	NR	66	125	.3	.8
207 E.L.C.A.	1	164	150	252	.5	1.5
339 Pent Ch of God	1	35	NR	47	.1	.3
413 S.D.A.	1	120	NR	143	.3	.9
419 So Bapt Conv	6	736	410	1,036 *	2.2	6.3
449 Un Methodist	2	228	102	321 *	.7	2.0
MEDINA	**42**	**6,256**	**2,355**	**23,181 ***	**59.0**	**100.0**
053 Assemb of God	1	146	72	121	.3	.5
056 Baha'i	0	3	NR	3	-	-
081 Catholic	6	NR	NR	14,932	38.0	64.4
093 Chr Ch (Disc)	1	60	0	77 *	.2	.3
127 Ch God (Cleve)	1	7	6	9 *	-	-
151 L-D Saints	1	NR	NR	240	.6	1.0
165 Ch of Nazarene	1	36	17	50	.1	.2
167 Chs of Christ	4	223	221	295	.8	1.3
193 Episcopal	1	NR	36	76	.2	.3
207 E.L.C.A.	3	832	374	1,039	2.6	4.5
283 Luth—MO Synod	1	72	48	101	.3	.4
355 Presb Ch (USA)	1	6	3	8 *	-	-
356 Presb Ch Amer	1	5	5	5	-	-
413 S.D.A.	1	52	NR	62	.2	.3
419 So Bapt Conv	14	3,492	1,088	4,470 *	11.4	19.3
449 Un Methodist	5	1,322	485	1,693 *	4.3	7.3
MENARD	**8**	**764**	**294**	**1,381 ***	**58.5**	**100.0**
081 Catholic	1	NR	NR	390	16.5	28.2
167 Chs of Christ	2	57	61	73	3.1	5.3

NR–Not Reported   *Total adherents estimated from known number of communicant, confirmed, full members.   - Represents a percentage less than 0.1.   Percentages may not total 100 due to rounding.

Table 4: Religious Congregations by County and Group: 2000

Religious Group	Number of Churches, Synagogues, Mosques, or Temples	Number of Communicant, Confirmed, or Full Members	Number of Attendees	Total Adherents: Number of Adherents	Total Adherents: % of Total Pop.	Total Adherents: % of Total Adh.
193 Episcopal	1	NR	22	67	2.8	4.9
283 Luth—MO Synod	1	35	27	43	1.8	3.1
355 Presb Ch (USA)	1	23	11	28 *	1.2	2.0
419 So Bapt Conv	1	469	110	564 *	23.9	40.8
449 Un Methodist	1	180	63	216 *	9.2	15.6
MIDLAND	**103**	**40,362**	**16,602**	**71,380 ***	**61.5**	**100.0**
017 Amer Bapt Assn	2	250	NR	325 *	.3	.5
053 Assemb of God	4	739	831	1,132	1.0	1.6
056 Baha'i	1	22	NR	22	-	-
081 Catholic	4	NR	NR	15,940	13.7	22.3
084 Calvary Chapel	1	NR	NR	NR	-	-
089 Chr & Miss Al	1	19	NR	83	.1	.1
093 Chr Ch (Disc)	2	1,742	527	2,259 *	1.9	3.2
097 Chr Chs&Chs Cr	1	250	NR	324 *	.3	.5
123 Ch God (Ander)	1	NR	40	40	-	.1
127 Ch God (Cleve)	1	108	109	140 *	.1	.2
145 Ch God Prophcy	1	27	NR	35 *	-	-
151 L-D Saints	3	NR	NR	792	.7	1.1
165 Ch of Nazarene	2	234	118	234	.2	.3
167 Chs of Christ	15	3,687	3,107	4,752	4.1	6.7
173 Comm of Christ	1	56	NR	56	-	.1
185 Cumber Presb	1	35	NR	65	.1	.1
193 Episcopal	2	NR	586	1,789	1.5	2.5
203 Evan Free Ch	1	25	70	70	.1	.1
207 E.L.C.A.	2	289	149	349	.3	.5
221 Free Methodist	1	25	60	60	.1	.1
252 Hindu	1	NR	NR	NR	-	-
263 Int Foursq Gos	1	161	326	326 *	.3	.5
267 Muslim Est	1	NR	30	100	.1	.1
283 Luth—MO Synod	2	441	268	589	.5	.8
355 Presb Ch (USA)	3	2,213	862	2,870 *	2.5	4.0
356 Presb Ch Amer	1	42	45	60	.1	.1
360 Prim Bapt Chrch	1	NR	NR	NR	-	-
403 Salvation Army	1	132	70	235	.2	.3
413 S.D.A.	2	135	NR	160	.1	.2
419 So Bapt Conv	26	21,877	4,607	28,370 *	24.5	39.7
435 Unitarian-Univ	1	66	NR	86 *	.1	.1
449 Un Methodist	9	5,067	1,742	6,570 *	5.7	9.2
469 WELS	1	20	15	22	-	-
498 Indep.Charis.	2	1,000	1,075	1,075	.9	1.5
499 Indep.Non-Char	4	1,700	1,965	2,450	2.1	3.4
MILAM	**69**	**8,583**	**3,386**	**16,275 ***	**67.1**	**100.0**
017 Amer Bapt Assn	2	68	NR	86 *	.4	.5
053 Assemb of God	4	189	179	246	1.0	1.5
081 Catholic	5	NR	NR	5,330	22.0	32.7
093 Chr Ch (Disc)	3	298	73	375 *	1.5	2.3
097 Chr Chs&Chs Cr	2	292	NR	367 *	1.5	2.3
151 L-D Saints	1	NR	NR	139	.6	.9
167 Chs of Christ	13	670	614	809	3.3	5.0
193 Episcopal	2	NR	46	70	.3	.4
207 E.L.C.A.	4	715	323	853	3.5	5.2
283 Luth—MO Synod	2	645	340	811	3.3	5.0
355 Presb Ch (USA)	3	219	96	276 *	1.1	1.7
360 Prim Bapt Chrch	1	NR	NR	NR	-	-
419 So Bapt Conv	16	4,337	1,219	5,464 *	22.5	33.6
443 Un C of Christ	1	51	26	64 *	.3	.4
449 Un Methodist	10	1,099	470	1,385 *	5.7	8.5
MILLS	**18**	**3,075**	**1,114**	**4,213 ***	**81.8**	**100.0**
053 Assemb of God	1	176	45	132	2.6	3.1
056 Baha'i	0	1	NR	1	-	-
081 Catholic	1	NR	NR	508	9.9	12.1
167 Chs of Christ	4	357	280	438	8.5	10.4
207 E.L.C.A.	1	267	91	345	6.7	8.2
360 Prim Bapt Chrch	1	NR	NR	NR	-	-
419 So Bapt Conv	6	1,798	513	2,205 *	42.8	52.3
449 Un Methodist	4	476	185	584 *	11.3	13.9
MITCHELL	**25**	**3,613**	**1,330**	**5,451 ***	**56.2**	**100.0**
053 Assemb of God	1	53	60	70	.7	1.3

Religious Group	Number of Churches, Synagogues, Mosques, or Temples	Number of Communicant, Confirmed, or Full Members	Number of Attendees	Total Adherents: Number of Adherents	Total Adherents: % of Total Pop.	Total Adherents: % of Total Adh.
081 Catholic	2	NR	NR	1,140	11.8	20.9
093 Chr Ch (Disc)	1	23	0	27 *	.3	.5
167 Chs of Christ	5	338	240	424	4.4	7.8
193 Episcopal	1	NR	26	57	.6	1.0
355 Presb Ch (USA)	1	20	15	23 *	.2	.4
360 Prim Bapt Chrch	2	NR	NR	NR	-	-
419 So Bapt Conv	7	2,715	771	3,169 *	32.7	58.1
449 Un Methodist	5	464	218	541 *	5.6	9.9
MONTAGUE	**58**	**9,321**	**3,202**	**12,051 ***	**63.0**	**100.0**
017 Amer Bapt Assn	1	50	NR	61 *	.3	.5
053 Assemb of God	6	305	310	412	2.2	3.4
056 Baha'i	0	1	NR	1	-	-
059 Bapt Miss Assn	3	156	86	191 *	1.0	1.6
081 Catholic	3	NR	NR	623	3.3	5.2
093 Chr Ch (Disc)	2	240	80	293 *	1.5	2.4
157 Ch of Brethren	1	77	0	94 *	.5	.8
165 Ch of Nazarene	2	85	82	134	.7	1.1
167 Chs of Christ	8	571	586	721	3.8	6.0
193 Episcopal	1	NR	11	27	.1	.2
223 Free Will Bapt	1	42	NR	52 *	.3	.4
283 Luth—MO Synod	1	137	98	184	1.0	1.5
339 Pent Ch of God	2	195	NR	255	1.3	2.1
355 Presb Ch (USA)	2	109	55	133 *	.7	1.1
413 S.D.A.	1	23	NR	27	.1	.2
419 So Bapt Conv	17	5,972	1,422	7,295 *	38.2	60.5
449 Un Methodist	6	858	372	1,048 *	5.5	8.7
499 Indep.Non-Char	1	500	100	500	2.6	4.1
MONTGOMERY	**172**	**77,431**	**36,162**	**147,461 ***	**50.2**	**100.0**
017 Amer Bapt Assn	7	934	NR	1,211 *	.4	.8
053 Assemb of God	16	2,613	1,917	3,202	1.1	2.2
056 Baha'i	1	110	NR	110	-	.1
059 Bapt Miss Assn	8	2,121	640	2,748 *	.9	1.9
081 Catholic	5	NR	NR	39,230	13.4	26.6
084 Calvary Chapel	1	NR	NR	NR	-	-
093 Chr Ch (Disc)	2	891	434	1,154 *	.4	.8
123 Ch God (Ander)	1	NR	32	32	-	-
127 Ch God (Cleve)	3	213	96	276 *	.1	.2
151 L-D Saints	6	NR	NR	2,433	.8	1.6
165 Ch of Nazarene	2	325	143	579	.2	.4
167 Chs of Christ	20	2,844	3,086	3,909	1.3	2.7
193 Episcopal	2	NR	834	1,914	.7	1.3
207 E.L.C.A.	4	2,097	1,276	2,989	1.0	2.0
221 Free Methodist	1	18	34	34	-	-
223 Free Will Bapt	1	42	NR	55 *	-	-
252 Hindu	1	NR	NR	NR	-	-
263 Int Foursq Gos	1	77	72	100 *	-	.1
267 Muslim Est	1	NR	290	1,313	.4	.9
283 Luth—MO Synod	4	1,203	657	1,476	.5	1.0
339 Pent Ch of God	1	250	NR	750	.3	.5
355 Presb Ch (USA)	1	802	335	1,039 *	.4	.7
356 Presb Ch Amer	1	0	97	97	-	.1
370 Ref Baptist Chs	1	NR	NR	NR	-	-
403 Salvation Army	1	102	96	132	-	.1
413 S.D.A.	3	433	NR	515	.2	.3
419 So Bapt Conv	55	50,046	20,678	64,840 *	22.1	44.0
435 Unitarian-Univ	1	155	NR	201 *	.1	.1
449 Un Methodist	15	10,941	4,415	14,175 *	4.8	9.6
463 Vineyard	1	130	120	168 *	.1	.1
469 WELS	2	284	210	379	.1	.3
496 Jewish Est	1	NR	NR	1,600	.5	1.1
498 Indep.Charis.	2	800	700	800	.3	.5
MOORE	**35**	**6,495**	**2,939**	**10,821 ***	**53.8**	**100.0**
053 Assemb of God	6	513	577	690	3.4	6.4
056 Baha'i	0	2	NR	2	-	-
081 Catholic	3	NR	NR	2,000	9.9	18.5
093 Chr Ch (Disc)	1	166	58	225 *	1.1	2.1
097 Chr Chs&Chs Cr	1	133	NR	180 *	.9	1.7
165 Ch of Nazarene	2	158	85	169	.8	1.6
167 Chs of Christ	8	801	800	1,068	5.3	9.9
193 Episcopal	1	NR	16	109	.5	1.0

NR–Not Reported   *Total adherents estimated from known number of communicant, confirmed, full members.   - Represents a percentage less than 0.1.   Percentages may not total 100 due to rounding.

Table 4: Religious Congregations by County and Group: 2000

Religious Group	Number of Churches, Synagogues, Mosques, or Temples	Number of Communicant, Confirmed, or Full Members	Number of Attendees	Total Adherents: Number of Adherents	Total Adherents: % of Total Pop.	Total Adherents: % of Total Adh.
283 Luth—MO Synod	1	160	0	203	1.0	1.9
349 Pent Holiness	1	19	25	26 *	.1	.2
355 Presb Ch (USA)	1	242	149	328 *	1.6	3.0
419 So Bapt Conv	6	3,485	944	4,717 *	23.4	43.6
449 Un Methodist	4	816	285	1,104 *	5.5	10.2
MORRIS	**37**	**7,557**	**2,019**	**10,173 ***	**78.0**	**100.0**
017 Amer Bapt Assn	7	1,489	NR	1,834 *	14.1	18.0
053 Assemb of God	3	144	150	157	1.2	1.5
056 Baha'i	0	1	NR	1	-	-
081 Catholic	1	NR	NR	786	6.0	7.7
097 Chr Chs&Chs Cr	3	290	NR	357 *	2.7	3.5
167 Chs of Christ	6	701	661	961	7.4	9.4
185 Cumber Presb	1	10	NR	10	.1	.1
419 So Bapt Conv	9	4,027	883	4,963 *	38.0	48.8
449 Un Methodist	7	895	325	1,104 *	8.5	10.9
MOTLEY	**10**	**902**	**287**	**1,170 ***	**82.0**	**100.0**
053 Assemb of God	1	25	17	22	1.5	1.9
081 Catholic	1	NR	NR	76	5.3	6.5
167 Chs of Christ	3	84	80	110	7.7	9.4
419 So Bapt Conv	3	626	120	759 *	53.2	64.9
449 Un Methodist	2	167	70	203 *	14.2	17.4
NACOGDOCHES	**93**	**18,781**	**7,977**	**33,591 ***	**56.7**	**100.0**
017 Amer Bapt Assn	4	436	NR	536 *	.9	1.6
053 Assemb of God	2	278	355	392	.7	1.2
056 Baha'i	0	41	NR	41	.1	.1
059 Bapt Miss Assn	19	2,080	935	2,556 *	4.3	7.6
081 Catholic	3	NR	NR	9,464	16.0	28.2
093 Chr Ch (Disc)	1	459	0	564 *	1.0	1.7
123 Ch God (Ander)	1	NR	52	52	.1	.2
151 L-D Saints	1	NR	NR	468	.8	1.4
165 Ch of Nazarene	1	370	205	504	.9	1.5
167 Chs of Christ	13	1,094	1,203	1,439	2.4	4.3
185 Cumber Presb	1	5	NR	5	-	-
193 Episcopal	1	NR	197	341	.6	1.0
223 Free Will Bapt	2	85	NR	104 *	.2	.3
263 Int Foursq Gos	1	30	50	50 *	.1	.1
283 Luth—MO Synod	1	186	112	243	.4	.7
355 Presb Ch (USA)	2	303	155	372 *	.6	1.1
360 Prim Bapt Chrch	1	NR	NR	NR	-	-
413 S.D.A.	2	94	NR	112	.2	.3
419 So Bapt Conv	24	10,263	3,524	12,605 *	21.3	37.5
449 Un Methodist	12	2,397	789	2,943 *	5.0	8.8
499 Indep.Non-Char	1	660	400	800	1.4	2.4
NAVARRO	**91**	**20,147**	**7,053**	**29,061 ***	**64.4**	**100.0**
017 Amer Bapt Assn	9	971	NR	1,226 *	2.7	4.2
053 Assemb of God	4	397	446	633	1.4	2.2
056 Baha'i	0	32	NR	32	.1	.1
059 Bapt Miss Assn	7	1,179	541	1,488 *	3.3	5.1
081 Catholic	1	NR	NR	2,835	6.3	9.8
093 Chr Ch (Disc)	1	153	45	193 *	.4	.7
127 Ch God (Cleve)	2	370	83	467 *	1.0	1.6
151 L-D Saints	1	NR	NR	267	.6	.9
167 Chs of Christ	8	1,423	1,207	1,942	4.3	6.7
193 Episcopal	1	NR	78	230	.5	.8
203 Evan Free Ch	1	94	150	150	.3	.5
283 Luth—MO Synod	1	143	64	204	.5	.7
304 NatPrimBapt USA	1	40	NR	50 *	.1	.2
339 Pent Ch of God	2	387	NR	501	1.1	1.7
349 Pent Holiness	3	322	160	406 *	.9	1.4
355 Presb Ch (USA)	2	288	120	363 *	.8	1.2
360 Prim Bapt Chrch	1	NR	NR	NR	-	-
403 Salvation Army	1	103	96	110	.2	.4
413 S.D.A.	2	100	NR	119	.3	.4
419 So Bapt Conv	24	10,696	3,037	13,493 *	29.9	46.4
449 Un Methodist	19	3,449	1,026	4,352 *	9.6	15.0
NEWTON	**31**	**4,806**	**1,935**	**6,238 ***	**41.4**	**100.0**
017 Amer Bapt Assn	3	410	NR	509 *	3.4	8.2

Religious Group	Number of Churches, Synagogues, Mosques, or Temples	Number of Communicant, Confirmed, or Full Members	Number of Attendees	Total Adherents: Number of Adherents	Total Adherents: % of Total Pop.	Total Adherents: % of Total Adh.
053 Assemb of God	1	25	30	47	.3	.8
056 Baha'i	0	1	NR	1	-	-
059 Bapt Miss Assn	1	109	30	135 *	.9	2.2
076 Buddhism	1	NR	NR	NR	-	-
123 Ch God (Ander)	3	NR	211	211	1.4	3.4
167 Chs of Christ	6	321	335	444	2.9	7.1
419 So Bapt Conv	11	3,412	1,133	4,235 *	28.1	67.9
449 Un Methodist	5	528	196	656 *	4.4	10.5
NOLAN	**41**	**7,984**	**2,927**	**11,792 ***	**74.6**	**100.0**
053 Assemb of God	2	202	135	245	1.6	2.1
056 Baha'i	0	11	NR	11	.1	.1
059 Bapt Miss Assn	1	108	12	136 *	.9	1.2
081 Catholic	3	NR	NR	1,680	10.6	14.2
093 Chr Ch (Disc)	1	156	68	196 *	1.2	1.7
127 Ch God (Cleve)	1	107	62	135 *	.9	1.1
145 Ch God Prophcy	1	27	NR	34 *	.2	.3
151 L-D Saints	1	NR	NR	100	.6	.8
167 Chs of Christ	8	899	830	1,079	6.8	9.2
193 Episcopal	1	NR	27	49	.3	.4
207 E.L.C.A.	1	73	45	84	.5	.7
283 Luth—MO Synod	1	79	50	92	.6	.8
355 Presb Ch (USA)	1	199	96	250 *	1.6	2.1
413 S.D.A.	1	20	NR	24	.2	.2
419 So Bapt Conv	13	5,120	1,199	6,441 *	40.8	54.6
449 Un Methodist	5	983	403	1,236 *	7.8	10.5
NUECES	**247**	**61,716**	**28,234**	**174,617 ***	**55.7**	**100.0**
017 Amer Bapt Assn	2	60	NR	76 *	-	-
034 Ant Orth of NA	1	27	NR	54	-	-
053 Assemb of God	17	4,645	3,515	5,086	1.6	2.9
055 As Ref Pres Ch	1	0	NR	0	-	-
056 Baha'i	1	216	NR	216	.1	.1
081 Catholic	37	NR	NR	86,384	27.5	49.5
084 Calvary Chapel	1	NR	NR	NR	-	-
089 Chr & Miss Al	1	0	NR	27	-	-
093 Chr Ch (Disc)	5	1,282	539	1,641 *	.5	.9
097 Chr Chs&Chs Cr	1	60	NR	77 *	-	-
123 Ch God (Ander)	5	NR	261	261	.1	.1
127 Ch God (Cleve)	1	52	20	67 *	-	-
145 Ch God Prophcy	1	27	NR	35 *	-	-
151 L-D Saints	7	NR	NR	2,363	.8	1.4
165 Ch of Nazarene	6	462	328	482	.2	.3
167 Chs of Christ	21	2,654	2,382	3,525	1.1	2.0
173 Comm of Christ	1	54	NR	54	-	-
193 Episcopal	8	NR	1,326	3,404	1.1	1.9
203 Evan Free Ch	1	90	300	300	.1	.2
207 E.L.C.A.	5	1,349	672	1,665	.5	1.0
221 Free Methodist	2	15	45	45	-	-
246 Greek Orthodox	1	NR	NR	327	.1	.2
263 Int Foursq Gos	1	96	289	289 *	.1	.2
267 Muslim Est	1	NR	156	609	.2	.3
283 Luth—MO Synod	6	1,592	822	2,149	.7	1.2
288 Mennonite USA	1	54	43	69 *	-	-
290 Metro Comm Ch	1	83	89	89 *	-	.1
339 Pent Ch of God	3	111	NR	195	.1	.1
349 Pent Holiness	4	439	370	562 *	.2	.3
355 Presb Ch (USA)	10	2,049	1,128	2,622 *	.8	1.5
356 Presb Ch Amer	1	133	135	135	-	.1
403 Salvation Army	1	260	97	1,510	.5	.9
413 S.D.A.	3	533	NR	634	.2	.4
419 So Bapt Conv	63	33,830	10,890	43,304 *	13.8	24.8
435 Unitarian-Univ	1	93	NR	119 *	-	.1
443 Un C of Christ	1	100	50	128 *	-	.1
449 Un Methodist	19	9,525	3,524	12,192 *	3.9	7.0
463 Vineyard	1	130	120	166 *	.1	.1
469 WELS	1	115	83	156	-	.1
496 Jewish Est	1	NR	NR	1,400	.4	.8
498 Indep.Charis.	2	1,580	1,050	2,200	.7	1.3
OCHILTREE	**22**	**3,830**	**1,728**	**5,967 ***	**66.3**	**100.0**
053 Assemb of God	2	160	200	240	2.7	4.0
081 Catholic	1	NR	NR	573	6.4	9.6

NR–Not Reported *Total adherents estimated from known number of communicant, confirmed, full members. - Represents a percentage less than 0.1. Percentages may not total 100 due to rounding.

Table 4: Religious Congregations by County and Group: 2000

Religious Group	Number of Churches, Synagogues, Mosques, or Temples	Number of Communicant, Confirmed, or Full Members	Number of Attendees	Total Adherents		
				Number of Adherents	% of Total Pop.	% of Total Adh.
093 Chr Ch (Disc)	1	498	186	649 *	7.2	10.9
097 Chr Chs&Chs Cr	1	95	NR	124 *	1.4	2.1
127 Ch God (Cleve)	1	30	70	70 *	.8	1.2
157 Ch of Brethren	1	58	11	76 *	.8	1.3
165 Ch of Nazarene	1	35	14	42	.5	.7
167 Chs of Christ	3	208	203	265	2.9	4.4
193 Episcopal	1	NR	6	10	.1	.2
263 Int Foursq Gos	1	20	34	34 *	.4	.6
283 Luth—MO Synod	1	41	25	61	.7	1.0
288 Mennonite USA	1	43	34	56 *	.6	.9
355 Presb Ch (USA)	1	36	17	47 *	.5	.8
360 Prim Bapt Chrch	1	NR	NR	NR	-	-
419 So Bapt Conv	3	2,037	423	2,654 *	29.5	44.5
449 Un Methodist	1	569	205	741 *	8.2	12.4
498 Indep.Charis.	1	0	300	325	3.6	5.4
OLDHAM	**8**	**962**	**359**	**1,439 ***	**65.9**	**100.0**
081 Catholic	1	NR	NR	200	9.2	13.9
167 Chs of Christ	2	85	80	103	4.7	7.2
419 So Bapt Conv	2	508	139	658 *	30.1	45.7
449 Un Methodist	3	369	140	478 *	21.9	33.2
ORANGE	**97**	**32,726**	**10,375**	**55,707 ***	**65.6**	**100.0**
017 Amer Bapt Assn	3	269	NR	339 *	.4	.6
053 Assemb of God	7	1,333	1,490	2,420	2.8	4.3
056 Baha'i	0	16	NR	16	-	-
059 Bapt Miss Assn	3	979	207	1,234 *	1.5	2.2
081 Catholic	7	NR	NR	11,665	13.7	20.9
093 Chr Ch (Disc)	1	377	129	475 *	.6	.9
097 Chr Chs&Chs Cr	3	300	NR	377 *	.4	.7
123 Ch God (Ander)	1	NR	36	36	-	.1
127 Ch God (Cleve)	1	51	72	72 *	.1	.1
145 Ch God Prophcy	1	27	NR	34 *	-	.1
151 L-D Saints	5	NR	NR	1,731	2.0	3.1
165 Ch of Nazarene	3	397	298	478	.6	.9
167 Chs of Christ	11	928	920	1,221	1.4	2.2
193 Episcopal	1	NR	102	251	.3	.5
207 E.L.C.A.	2	233	107	305	.4	.5
263 Int Foursq Gos	1	123	175	175 *	.2	.3
283 Luth—MO Synod	1	213	117	272	.3	.5
355 Presb Ch (USA)	3	475	246	598 *	.7	1.1
360 Prim Bapt Chrch	2	NR	NR	NR	-	-
403 Salvation Army	1	110	41	151	.2	.3
413 S.D.A.	1	58	NR	69	.1	.1
419 So Bapt Conv	31	23,203	5,198	29,213 *	34.4	52.4
449 Un Methodist	8	3,634	1,237	4,575 *	5.4	8.2
PALO PINTO	**60**	**10,750**	**3,862**	**15,718 ***	**58.2**	**100.0**
053 Assemb of God	3	70	79	114	.4	.7
056 Baha'i	0	48	NR	48	.2	.3
081 Catholic	3	NR	NR	1,558	5.8	9.9
093 Chr Ch (Disc)	1	206	69	257 *	1.0	1.6
127 Ch God (Cleve)	1	289	145	361 *	1.3	2.3
145 Ch God Prophcy	1	27	NR	34 *	.1	.2
151 L-D Saints	1	NR	NR	576	2.1	3.7
165 Ch of Nazarene	1	59	38	103	.4	.7
167 Chs of Christ	11	865	887	1,033	3.8	6.6
173 Comm of Christ	1	22	NR	22	.1	.1
193 Episcopal	2	NR	87	156	.6	1.0
283 Luth—MO Synod	1	110	70	124	.5	.8
339 Pent Ch of God	1	60	NR	110	.4	.7
355 Presb Ch (USA)	1	109	51	136 *	.5	.9
413 S.D.A.	1	70	NR	83	.3	.5
419 So Bapt Conv	24	7,701	2,082	9,613 *	35.6	61.2
449 Un Methodist	7	1,114	354	1,390 *	5.1	8.8
PANOLA	**71**	**9,876**	**3,465**	**12,772 ***	**56.1**	**100.0**
017 Amer Bapt Assn	14	1,173	NR	1,447 *	6.4	11.3
053 Assemb of God	3	153	104	165	.7	1.3
056 Baha'i	0	9	NR	9	-	.1
059 Bapt Miss Assn	10	2,214	867	2,726 *	12.0	21.3
081 Catholic	2	NR	NR	591	2.6	4.6
097 Chr Chs&Chs Cr	1	90	NR	111 *	.5	.9
165 Ch of Nazarene	1	44	31	44	.2	.3
167 Chs of Christ	5	310	262	388	1.7	3.0
193 Episcopal	1	NR	31	48	.2	.4
223 Free Will Bapt	4	170	NR	209 *	.9	1.6
355 Presb Ch (USA)	1	43	27	53 *	.2	.4
419 So Bapt Conv	16	4,019	1,432	4,949 *	21.7	38.7
449 Un Methodist	13	1,651	711	2,032 *	8.9	15.9
PARKER	**114**	**31,737**	**13,645**	**43,842 ***	**49.5**	**100.0**
053 Assemb of God	8	513	581	873	1.0	2.0
056 Baha'i	0	24	NR	24	-	.1
059 Bapt Miss Assn	3	369	222	466 *	.5	1.1
081 Catholic	1	NR	NR	2,445	2.8	5.6
093 Chr Ch (Disc)	3	746	443	942 *	1.1	2.1
127 Ch God (Cleve)	3	787	450	994 *	1.1	2.3
151 L-D Saints	1	NR	NR	389	.4	.9
165 Ch of Nazarene	1	40	18	40	-	.1
167 Chs of Christ	18	2,160	1,942	2,867	3.2	6.5
185 Cumber Presb	1	16	NR	21	-	-
193 Episcopal	2	NR	197	473	.5	1.1
207 E.L.C.A.	2	83	64	118	.1	.3
223 Free Will Bapt	1	42	NR	54 *	.1	.1
263 Int Foursq Gos	1	248	240	313 *	.4	.7
283 Luth—MO Synod	1	211	110	274	.3	.6
349 Pent Holiness	1	35	43	44 *	-	.1
355 Presb Ch (USA)	1	358	147	452 *	.5	1.0
413 S.D.A.	1	43	NR	51	.1	.1
419 So Bapt Conv	49	20,657	6,891	26,083 *	29.5	59.5
449 Un Methodist	15	5,005	1,797	6,319 *	7.1	14.4
499 Indep.Non-Char	1	400	500	600	.7	1.4
PARMER	**28**	**4,323**	**1,721**	**7,779 ***	**77.7**	**100.0**
053 Assemb of God	2	45	65	81	.8	1.0
056 Baha'i	0	2	NR	2	-	-
081 Catholic	2	NR	NR	1,782	17.8	22.9
143 CG in Cr(Menn)	1	98	NR	131 *	1.3	1.7
151 L-D Saints	1	NR	NR	221	2.2	2.8
167 Chs of Christ	6	489	508	631	6.3	8.1
283 Luth—MO Synod	1	151	86	195	1.9	2.5
349 Pent Holiness	1	12	11	16 *	.2	.2
419 So Bapt Conv	8	2,541	639	3,401 *	34.0	43.7
443 Un C of Christ	1	43	19	58 *	.6	.7
449 Un Methodist	5	942	393	1,261 *	12.6	16.2
PECOS	**29**	**3,667**	**1,445**	**7,607 ***	**45.3**	**100.0**
053 Assemb of God	4	128	89	131	.8	1.7
056 Baha'i	0	3	NR	3	-	-
081 Catholic	6	NR	NR	2,910	17.3	38.3
093 Chr Ch (Disc)	1	129	48	161 *	1.0	2.1
097 Chr Chs&Chs Cr	1	52	NR	65 *	.4	.9
151 L-D Saints	1	NR	NR	89	.5	1.2
167 Chs of Christ	5	428	418	557	3.3	7.3
193 Episcopal	1	NR	12	30	.2	.4
283 Luth—MO Synod	1	22	17	27	.2	.4
355 Presb Ch (USA)	1	362	150	453 *	2.7	6.0
419 So Bapt Conv	5	2,120	537	2,652 *	15.8	34.9
449 Un Methodist	3	423	174	529 *	3.1	7.0
POLK	**73**	**14,560**	**5,701**	**20,790 ***	**50.5**	**100.0**
017 Amer Bapt Assn	1	28	NR	34 *	.1	.2
053 Assemb of God	9	561	716	1,136	2.8	5.5
056 Baha'i	0	28	NR	28	.1	.1
059 Bapt Miss Assn	15	4,042	1,485	4,897 *	11.9	23.6
081 Catholic	2	NR	NR	2,220	5.4	10.7
127 Ch God (Cleve)	1	169	86	205 *	.5	1.0
151 L-D Saints	1	NR	NR	393	1.0	1.9
165 Ch of Nazarene	1	62	21	62	.2	.3
167 Chs of Christ	7	499	461	584	1.4	2.8
173 Comm of Christ	1	33	NR	33	.1	.2
193 Episcopal	1	NR	78	156	.4	.8
207 E.L.C.A.	1	37	27	38	.1	.2

NR–Not Reported *Total adherents estimated from known number of communicant, confirmed, full members. - Represents a percentage less than 0.1. Percentages may not total 100 due to rounding.

Table 4: Religious Congregations by County and Group: 2000

Religious Group	Number of Churches, Synagogues, Mosques, or Temples	Number of Communicant, Confirmed, or Full Members	Number of Attendees	Total Adherents: Number of Adherents	Total Adherents: % of Total Pop.	Total Adherents: % of Total Adh.
283 Luth—MO Synod	1	141	67	155	.4	.7
304 NatPrimBapt USA	1	7	NR	8 *	-	-
355 Presb Ch (USA)	2	284	126	344 *	.8	1.7
413 S.D.A.	1	25	NR	30	.1	.1
419 So Bapt Conv	18	7,011	1,907	8,492 *	20.6	40.8
449 Un Methodist	10	1,633	727	1,975 *	4.8	9.5
POTTER	**128**	**56,966**	**20,488**	**98,151 ***	**86.4**	**100.0**
017 Amer Bapt Assn	4	618	NR	794 *	.7	.8
053 Assemb of God	10	860	946	1,289	1.1	1.3
056 Baha'i	1	220	NR	220	.2	.2
059 Bapt Miss Assn	2	248	52	319 *	.3	.3
076 Buddhism	2	NR	NR	NR	-	-
081 Catholic	11	NR	NR	22,935	20.2	23.4
084 Calvary Chapel	1	NR	NR	NR	-	-
093 Chr Ch (Disc)	1	75	0	96 *	.1	.1
145 Ch God Prophcy	1	27	NR	35 *	-	-
151 L-D Saints	1	NR	NR	497	.4	.5
165 Ch of Nazarene	5	556	340	616	.5	.6
167 Chs of Christ	16	3,857	3,672	5,106	4.5	5.2
173 Comm of Christ	1	38	NR	38	-	-
193 Episcopal	2	NR	359	1,357	1.2	1.4
223 Free Will Bapt	1	42	NR	55 *	-	.1
246 Greek Orthodox	1	NR	NR	105	.1	.1
264 Int Chs of Crst	1	49	73	63	.1	.1
267 Muslim Est	1	NR	101	288	.3	.3
283 Luth—MO Synod	2	686	390	914	.8	.9
304 NatPrimBapt USA	1	15	NR	19 *	-	-
339 Pent Ch of God	3	89	NR	224	.2	.2
349 Pent Holiness	5	532	502	684 *	.6	.7
355 Presb Ch (USA)	4	2,164	1,025	2,781 *	2.4	2.8
360 Prim Bapt Chrch	2	NR	NR	NR	-	-
401 Rus Orth Abroad	1	NR	NR	NR	-	-
403 Salvation Army	1	295	254	423	.4	.4
413 S.D.A.	3	335	NR	398	.4	.4
419 So Bapt Conv	28	36,751	7,600	47,234 *	41.6	48.1
449 Un Methodist	8	5,299	1,674	6,811 *	6.0	6.9
496 Jewish Est	1	NR	NR	200	.2	.2
498 Indep.Charis.	3	2,260	1,300	2,450	2.2	2.5
499 Indep.Non-Char	4	1,950	2,200	2,200	1.9	2.2
PRESIDIO	**19**	**524**	**352**	**4,758 ***	**65.1**	**100.0**
053 Assemb of God	1	33	34	45	.6	.9
056 Baha'i	0	40	NR	40	.5	.8
081 Catholic	6	NR	NR	4,044	55.4	85.0
093 Chr Ch (Disc)	1	34	17	45 *	.6	.9
167 Chs of Christ	2	45	55	59	.8	1.2
193 Episcopal	1	NR	10	32	.4	.7
355 Presb Ch (USA)	1	33	15	44 *	.6	.9
419 So Bapt Conv	5	170	163	225 *	3.1	4.7
449 Un Methodist	2	169	58	224 *	3.1	4.7
RAINS	**19**	**1,837**	**969**	**2,649 ***	**29.0**	**100.0**
017 Amer Bapt Assn	1	50	NR	61 *	.7	2.3
053 Assemb of God	3	90	88	167	1.8	6.3
056 Baha'i	0	1	NR	1	-	-
059 Bapt Miss Assn	2	285	76	345 *	3.8	13.0
081 Catholic	1	NR	NR	357	3.9	13.5
127 Ch God (Cleve)	2	254	119	307 *	3.4	11.6
167 Chs of Christ	3	189	189	239	2.6	9.0
419 So Bapt Conv	5	702	357	850 *	9.3	32.1
449 Un Methodist	2	266	140	322 *	3.5	12.2
RANDALL	**65**	**41,350**	**14,462**	**52,286 ***	**50.1**	**100.0**
053 Assemb of God	3	608	514	679	.7	1.3
056 Baha'i	0	14	NR	14	-	-
059 Bapt Miss Assn	1	375	265	468 *	.4	.9
081 Catholic	2	NR	NR	910	.9	1.7
093 Chr Ch (Disc)	3	1,440	158	1,796 *	1.7	3.4
097 Chr Chs&Chs Cr	5	6,950	NR	8,669 *	8.3	16.6
127 Ch God (Cleve)	1	23	0	29 *	-	.1
151 L-D Saints	4	NR	NR	1,333	1.3	2.5
165 Ch of Nazarene	3	518	337	670	.6	1.3
167 Chs of Christ	7	2,596	2,569	3,230	3.1	6.2
193 Episcopal	2	NR	81	159	.2	.3
203 Evan Free Ch	1	101	186	186	.2	.4
207 E.L.C.A.	1	277	164	337	.3	.6
263 Int Foursq Gos	2	100	143	143 *	.1	.3
283 Luth—MO Synod	2	400	236	518	.5	1.0
290 Metro Comm Ch	1	52	39	65 *	.1	.1
335 Orth Pres Ch	1	67	86	101	.1	.2
355 Presb Ch (USA)	1	233	150	291 *	.3	.6
419 So Bapt Conv	17	16,780	4,964	20,929 *	20.1	40.0
435 Unitarian-Univ	1	81	NR	101 *	.1	.2
449 Un Methodist	5	3,605	1,750	4,496 *	4.3	8.6
463 Vineyard	1	130	120	162 *	.2	.3
498 Indep.Charis.	1	7,000	2,700	7,000	6.7	13.4
REAGAN	**9**	**1,641**	**574**	**2,507 ***	**75.4**	**100.0**
053 Assemb of God	2	157	140	227	6.8	9.1
056 Baha'i	0	6	NR	6	.2	.2
081 Catholic	1	NR	NR	273	8.2	10.9
151 L-D Saints	1	NR	NR	53	1.6	2.1
167 Chs of Christ	1	150	150	191	5.7	7.6
419 So Bapt Conv	3	1,095	235	1,449 *	43.6	57.8
449 Un Methodist	1	233	49	308 *	9.3	12.3
REAL	**11**	**1,208**	**511**	**2,345 ***	**77.0**	**100.0**
053 Assemb of God	1	24	24	24	.8	1.0
081 Catholic	2	NR	NR	909	29.8	38.8
167 Chs of Christ	3	216	170	240	7.9	10.2
419 So Bapt Conv	3	791	240	958 *	31.4	40.9
449 Un Methodist	2	177	77	214 *	7.0	9.1
RED RIVER	**58**	**6,874**	**1,839**	**8,524 ***	**59.6**	**100.0**
017 Amer Bapt Assn	10	1,853	NR	2,260 *	15.8	26.5
053 Assemb of God	4	150	152	208	1.5	2.4
056 Baha'i	0	2	NR	2	-	-
081 Catholic	1	NR	NR	96	.7	1.1
093 Chr Ch (Disc)	2	19	0	23 *	.2	.3
097 Chr Chs&Chs Cr	1	50	NR	61 *	.4	.7
127 Ch God (Cleve)	2	67	19	83 *	.6	1.0
143 CG in Cr(Menn)	1	91	NR	111 *	.8	1.3
167 Chs of Christ	9	422	464	517	3.6	6.1
185 Cumber Presb	1	15	NR	39	.3	.5
283 Luth—MO Synod	1	37	30	40	.3	.5
355 Presb Ch (USA)	3	124	69	151 *	1.1	1.8
419 So Bapt Conv	10	2,849	601	3,475 *	24.3	40.8
449 Un Methodist	13	1,195	504	1,458 *	10.2	17.1
REEVES	**31**	**2,648**	**899**	**9,935 ***	**75.6**	**100.0**
053 Assemb of God	2	54	71	119	.9	1.2
081 Catholic	6	NR	NR	6,326	48.2	63.7
093 Chr Ch (Disc)	1	116	25	148 *	1.1	1.5
151 L-D Saints	1	NR	NR	121	.9	1.2
167 Chs of Christ	4	238	231	335	2.6	3.4
193 Episcopal	1	NR	16	31	.2	.3
355 Presb Ch (USA)	1	74	30	95 *	.7	1.0
413 S.D.A.	2	73	NR	87	.7	.9
419 So Bapt Conv	9	1,874	410	2,393 *	18.2	24.1
449 Un Methodist	4	219	116	280 *	2.1	2.8
REFUGIO	**28**	**2,529**	**789**	**5,128 ***	**65.5**	**100.0**
053 Assemb of God	1	29	47	47	.6	.9
056 Baha'i	0	3	NR	3	-	.1
081 Catholic	7	NR	NR	1,945	24.8	37.9
167 Chs of Christ	3	115	108	145	1.9	2.8
193 Episcopal	1	NR	16	29	.4	.6
207 E.L.C.A.	2	165	58	206	2.6	4.0
283 Luth—MO Synod	1	22	16	24	.3	.5
355 Presb Ch (USA)	3	90	44	112 *	1.4	2.2
419 So Bapt Conv	6	1,685	331	2,094 *	26.8	40.8
443 Un C of Christ	1	61	27	76 *	1.0	1.5
449 Un Methodist	3	359	142	447 *	5.7	8.7

NR–Not Reported *Total adherents estimated from known number of communicant, confirmed, full members. - Represents a percentage less than 0.1. Percentages may not total 100 due to rounding.

Table 4: Religious Congregations by County and Group: 2000

Religious Group	Number of Churches, Synagogues, Mosques, or Temples	Number of Communicant, Confirmed, or Full Members	Number of Attendees	Total Adherents		
				Number of Adherents	% of Total Pop.	% of Total Adh.
ROBERTS	**4**	**624**	**308**	**764 ***	**86.1**	**100.0**
093 Chr Ch (Disc)	1	70	31	85 *	9.6	11.1
167 Chs of Christ	1	65	65	83	9.4	10.9
419 So Bapt Conv	1	310	107	378 *	42.6	49.5
449 Un Methodist	1	179	105	218 *	24.6	28.5
ROBERTSON	**37**	**4,704**	**1,898**	**8,237 ***	**51.5**	**100.0**
053 Assemb of God	2	23	24	66	.4	.8
056 Baha'i	0	6	NR	6	-	.1
081 Catholic	4	NR	NR	2,125	13.3	25.8
151 L-D Saints	1	NR	NR	63	.4	.8
167 Chs of Christ	4	372	320	458	2.9	5.6
173 Comm of Christ	1	35	NR	35	.2	.4
193 Episcopal	2	NR	22	33	.2	.4
355 Presb Ch (USA)	1	19	9	24 *	.2	.3
419 So Bapt Conv	14	3,505	1,188	4,477 *	28.0	54.4
449 Un Methodist	8	744	335	950 *	5.9	11.5
ROCKWALL	**29**	**17,768**	**9,586**	**29,980 ***	**69.6**	**100.0**
017 Amer Bapt Assn	1	209	NR	272 *	.6	.9
053 Assemb of God	4	993	719	1,066	2.5	3.6
056 Baha'i	0	33	NR	33	.1	.1
081 Catholic	1	NR	NR	6,139	14.3	20.5
093 Chr Ch (Disc)	2	373	140	485 *	1.1	1.6
097 Chr Chs&Chs Cr	1	100	NR	130 *	.3	.4
151 L-D Saints	1	NR	NR	427	1.0	1.4
167 Chs of Christ	3	562	622	806	1.9	2.7
193 Episcopal	1	NR	165	459	1.1	1.5
221 Free Methodist	1	64	62	85	.2	.3
283 Luth—MO Synod	1	214	120	295	.7	1.0
355 Presb Ch (USA)	2	287	134	373 *	.9	1.2
419 So Bapt Conv	8	12,940	6,729	16,820 *	39.0	56.1
449 Un Methodist	3	1,993	895	2,590 *	6.0	8.6
RUNNELS	**43**	**5,445**	**1,776**	**10,196 ***	**88.7**	**100.0**
053 Assemb of God	3	62	76	99	.9	1.0
056 Baha'i	0	27	NR	27	.2	.3
081 Catholic	5	NR	NR	3,300	28.7	32.4
093 Chr Ch (Disc)	1	99	0	123 *	1.1	1.2
123 Ch God (Ander)	1	NR	15	15	.1	.1
127 Ch God (Cleve)	1	96	33	120 *	1.0	1.2
165 Ch of Nazarene	1	35	20	35	.3	.3
167 Chs of Christ	9	533	482	714	6.2	7.0
207 E.L.C.A.	2	368	141	459	4.0	4.5
263 Int Foursq Gos	1	10	51	51 *	.4	.5
283 Luth—MO Synod	1	14	6	14	.1	.1
355 Presb Ch (USA)	1	82	36	102 *	.9	1.0
360 Prim Bapt Chrch	1	NR	NR	NR	-	-
419 So Bapt Conv	11	3,136	651	3,911 *	34.0	38.4
443 Un C of Christ	1	16	8	20 *	.2	.2
449 Un Methodist	4	967	257	1,206 *	10.5	11.8
RUSK	**111**	**20,480**	**6,111**	**26,377 ***	**55.7**	**100.0**
017 Amer Bapt Assn	22	3,033	NR	3,724 *	7.9	14.1
053 Assemb of God	4	199	221	280	.6	1.1
056 Baha'i	0	7	NR	7	-	-
059 Bapt Miss Assn	5	466	181	573 *	1.2	2.2
081 Catholic	2	NR	NR	1,041	2.2	3.9
093 Chr Ch (Disc)	5	367	220	451 *	1.0	1.7
145 Ch God Prophcy	1	27	NR	33 *	.1	.1
165 Ch of Nazarene	2	190	137	305	.6	1.2
167 Chs of Christ	7	614	592	782	1.7	3.0
185 Cumber Presb	1	4	NR	5	-	-
193 Episcopal	1	NR	45	120	.3	.5
223 Free Will Bapt	4	170	NR	209 *	.4	.8
263 Int Foursq Gos	1	30	50	50 *	.1	.2
355 Presb Ch (USA)	4	155	84	191 *	.4	.7
360 Prim Bapt Chrch	3	NR	NR	NR	-	-
413 S.D.A.	1	28	NR	33	.1	.1
419 So Bapt Conv	26	12,581	3,524	15,449 *	32.6	58.6
449 Un Methodist	21	2,259	952	2,774 *	5.9	10.5
499 Indep.Non-Char	1	350	105	350	.7	1.3

Religious Group	Number of Churches, Synagogues, Mosques, or Temples	Number of Communicant, Confirmed, or Full Members	Number of Attendees	Total Adherents		
				Number of Adherents	% of Total Pop.	% of Total Adh.
SABINE	**49**	**5,121**	**1,724**	**6,373 ***	**60.9**	**100.0**
017 Amer Bapt Assn	7	778	NR	925 *	8.8	14.5
053 Assemb of God	2	61	68	74	.7	1.2
056 Baha'i	0	1	NR	1	-	-
059 Bapt Miss Assn	4	595	163	708 *	6.8	11.1
081 Catholic	1	NR	NR	114	1.1	1.8
123 Ch God (Ander)	3	NR	98	98	.9	1.5
165 Ch of Nazarene	1	25	7	88	.8	1.4
167 Chs of Christ	5	180	185	220	2.1	3.5
221 Free Methodist	1	21	30	30	.3	.5
273 LandmrkBapt,I&U	5	325	NR	386 *	3.7	6.1
413 S.D.A.	1	43	NR	51	.5	.8
419 So Bapt Conv	9	2,698	897	3,208 *	30.6	50.3
449 Un Methodist	10	394	276	470 *	4.5	7.4
SAN AUGUSTINE	**31**	**3,704**	**1,096**	**5,179 ***	**57.9**	**100.0**
017 Amer Bapt Assn	4	397	NR	484 *	5.4	9.3
053 Assemb of God	1	25	25	45	.5	.9
059 Bapt Miss Assn	5	644	230	785 *	8.8	15.2
081 Catholic	1	NR	NR	621	6.9	12.0
167 Chs of Christ	4	226	228	264	3.0	5.1
193 Episcopal	1	NR	19	39	.4	.8
273 LandmrkBapt,I&U	6	474	NR	578 *	6.5	11.2
355 Presb Ch (USA)	1	40	33	49 *	.5	.9
419 So Bapt Conv	6	1,680	464	2,048 *	22.9	39.5
449 Un Methodist	2	218	97	266 *	3.0	5.1
SAN JACINTO	**27**	**4,357**	**1,587**	**7,101 ***	**31.9**	**100.0**
017 Amer Bapt Assn	2	460	NR	568 *	2.6	8.0
053 Assemb of God	2	64	68	89	.4	1.3
056 Baha'i	0	2	NR	2	-	-
059 Bapt Miss Assn	3	515	293	636 *	2.9	9.0
081 Catholic	2	NR	NR	1,705	7.7	24.0
167 Chs of Christ	2	125	125	159	.7	2.2
304 NatPrimBapt USA	2	55	NR	68 *	.3	1.0
339 Pent Ch of God	1	30	NR	42	.2	.6
419 So Bapt Conv	8	2,505	785	3,090 *	13.9	43.5
449 Un Methodist	5	601	316	742 *	3.3	10.4
SAN PATRICIO	**88**	**12,350**	**5,624**	**37,937 ***	**56.5**	**100.0**
053 Assemb of God	6	332	426	595	.9	1.6
056 Baha'i	0	29	NR	29	-	.1
076 Buddhism	1	NR	NR	NR	-	-
081 Catholic	13	NR	NR	20,663	30.8	54.5
093 Chr Ch (Disc)	2	188	33	247 *	.4	.7
097 Chr Chs&Chs Cr	2	174	NR	228 *	.3	.6
151 L-D Saints	2	NR	NR	561	.8	1.5
165 Ch of Nazarene	3	119	43	119	.2	.3
167 Chs of Christ	12	1,119	1,171	1,350	2.0	3.6
193 Episcopal	2	NR	120	341	.5	.9
207 E.L.C.A.	4	542	282	694	1.0	1.8
283 Luth—MO Synod	2	130	96	165	.2	.4
288 Mennonite USA	2	147	97	193 *	.3	.5
339 Pent Ch of God	1	170	NR	400	.6	1.1
349 Pent Holiness	1	45	75	59 *	.1	.2
355 Presb Ch (USA)	5	179	117	245 *	.4	.6
419 So Bapt Conv	22	6,950	2,267	9,125 *	13.6	24.1
449 Un Methodist	8	2,226	897	2,923 *	4.4	7.7
SAN SABA	**24**	**3,004**	**1,194**	**4,010 ***	**64.8**	**100.0**
053 Assemb of God	1	30	38	38	.6	.9
056 Baha'i	0	2	NR	2	-	-
081 Catholic	1	NR	NR	241	3.9	6.0
093 Chr Ch (Disc)	1	65	35	79 *	1.3	2.0
151 L-D Saints	1	NR	NR	64	1.0	1.6
167 Chs of Christ	7	363	322	450	7.3	11.2
193 Episcopal	1	NR	19	44	.7	1.1
355 Presb Ch (USA)	2	138	90	168 *	2.7	4.2
360 Prim Bapt Chrch	1	NR	NR	NR	-	-
419 So Bapt Conv	7	2,164	580	2,630 *	42.5	65.6
449 Un Methodist	2	242	110	294 *	4.8	7.3

NR–Not Reported   *Total adherents estimated from known number of communicant, confirmed, full members.   - Represents a percentage less than 0.1.   Percentages may not total 100 due to rounding.

Table 4: Religious Congregations by County and Group: 2000

Religious Group	Number of Churches, Synagogues, Mosques, or Temples	Number of Communicant, Confirmed, or Full Members	Number of Attendees	Total Adherents		
				Number of Adherents	% of Total Pop.	% of Total Adh.
SCHLEICHER	**10**	**1,094**	**501**	**1,817 ***	**61.9**	**100.0**
053 Assemb of God	1	57	68	87	3.0	4.8
081 Catholic	1	NR	NR	430	14.7	23.7
167 Chs of Christ	2	78	80	101	3.4	5.6
355 Presb Ch (USA)	1	104	49	130 *	4.4	7.2
360 Prim Bapt Chrch	1	NR	NR	NR	-	-
419 So Bapt Conv	3	615	219	769 *	26.2	42.3
449 Un Methodist	1	240	85	300 *	10.2	16.5
SCURRY	**47**	**8,046**	**3,053**	**13,051 ***	**79.8**	**100.0**
017 Amer Bapt Assn	3	380	NR	466 *	2.8	3.6
053 Assemb of God	3	113	130	162	1.0	1.2
056 Baha'i	0	5	NR	5	-	-
059 Bapt Miss Assn	1	232	30	284 *	1.7	2.2
081 Catholic	3	NR	NR	2,701	16.5	20.7
093 Chr Ch (Disc)	1	122	0	150 *	.9	1.1
123 Ch God (Ander)	1	NR	50	50	.3	.4
127 Ch God (Cleve)	1	48	32	59 *	.4	.5
151 L-D Saints	1	NR	NR	46	.3	.4
165 Ch of Nazarene	1	64	42	84	.5	.6
167 Chs of Christ	8	899	772	1,161	7.1	8.9
173 Comm of Christ	1	10	NR	10	.1	.1
193 Episcopal	1	NR	6	5	-	-
207 E.L.C.A.	1	34	21	40	.2	.3
355 Presb Ch (USA)	1	138	70	169 *	1.0	1.3
360 Prim Bapt Chrch	1	NR	NR	NR	-	-
419 So Bapt Conv	11	4,890	1,369	5,996 *	36.6	45.9
449 Un Methodist	7	1,111	331	1,363 *	8.3	10.4
499 Indep.Non-Char	1	0	200	300	1.8	2.3
SHACKELFORD	**13**	**2,471**	**912**	**3,172 ***	**96.1**	**100.0**
053 Assemb of God	1	205	160	215	6.5	6.8
081 Catholic	1	NR	NR	131	4.0	4.1
093 Chr Ch (Disc)	1	250	108	311 *	9.4	9.8
167 Chs of Christ	2	157	165	202	6.1	6.4
193 Episcopal	1	NR	18	13	.4	.4
283 Luth—MO Synod	1	135	51	155	4.7	4.9
355 Presb Ch (USA)	1	97	45	121 *	3.7	3.8
419 So Bapt Conv	3	1,413	300	1,758 *	53.2	55.4
449 Un Methodist	2	214	65	266 *	8.1	8.4
SHELBY	**85**	**11,784**	**3,314**	**14,965 ***	**59.3**	**100.0**
017 Amer Bapt Assn	27	2,940	NR	3,701 *	14.7	24.7
053 Assemb of God	4	203	237	341	1.4	2.3
056 Baha'i	0	5	NR	5	-	-
059 Bapt Miss Assn	8	1,399	380	1,762 *	7.0	11.8
081 Catholic	2	NR	NR	51	.2	.3
093 Chr Ch (Disc)	2	107	0	135 *	.5	.9
097 Chr Chs&Chs Cr	2	180	NR	227 *	.9	1.5
165 Ch of Nazarene	1	12	12	12	-	.1
167 Chs of Christ	10	539	450	638	2.5	4.3
193 Episcopal	1	NR	24	36	.1	.2
355 Presb Ch (USA)	1	23	16	29 *	.1	.2
419 So Bapt Conv	14	5,285	1,748	6,653 *	26.4	44.5
449 Un Methodist	13	1,091	447	1,375 *	5.5	9.2
SHERMAN	**10**	**1,599**	**600**	**3,325 ***	**104.4**	**100.0**
053 Assemb of God	2	63	82	152	4.8	4.6
081 Catholic	1	NR	NR	1,000	31.4	30.1
093 Chr Ch (Disc)	1	183	64	241 *	7.6	7.2
143 CG in Cr(Menn)	1	55	NR	73 *	2.3	2.2
151 L-D Saints	1	NR	NR	148	4.6	4.5
167 Chs of Christ	1	93	100	121	3.8	3.6
419 So Bapt Conv	1	780	208	1,029 *	32.3	30.9
449 Un Methodist	2	425	146	561 *	17.6	16.9
SMITH	**194**	**74,222**	**34,443**	**114,072 ***	**65.3**	**100.0**
017 Amer Bapt Assn	5	476	NR	599 *	.3	.5
053 Assemb of God	19	2,174	2,407	3,106	1.8	2.7
056 Baha'i	1	53	NR	53	-	-
059 Bapt Miss Assn	11	2,197	921	2,763 *	1.6	2.4
081 Catholic	7	NR	NR	16,199	9.3	14.2
093 Chr Ch (Disc)	3	1,659	566	2,087 *	1.2	1.8
097 Chr Chs&Chs Cr	1	75	NR	94 *	.1	.1
123 Ch God (Ander)	1	NR	46	46	-	-
127 Ch God (Cleve)	4	1,434	2,046	2,215 *	1.3	1.9
145 Ch God Prophcy	2	54	NR	68 *	-	.1
151 L-D Saints	3	NR	NR	1,139	.7	1.0
157 Ch of Brethren	1	7	0	9 *	-	-
165 Ch of Nazarene	3	494	295	497	.3	.4
167 Chs of Christ	25	4,173	3,895	5,461	3.1	4.8
193 Episcopal	4	NR	787	1,721	1.0	1.5
207 E.L.C.A.	1	270	209	404	.2	.4
223 Free Will Bapt	1	42	NR	53 *	-	-
262 Int Cou Comm Ch	1	190	NR	239 *	.1	.2
267 Muslim Est	1	NR	101	288	.2	.3
283 Luth—MO Synod	1	590	293	746	.4	.7
335 Orth Pres Ch	1	55	78	78	-	.1
355 Presb Ch (USA)	4	1,119	559	1,408 *	.8	1.2
356 Presb Ch Amer	1	232	121	263	.2	.2
360 Prim Bapt Chrch	1	NR	NR	NR	-	-
403 Salvation Army	1	182	202	326	.2	.3
413 S.D.A.	3	470	NR	559	.3	.5
419 So Bapt Conv	57	45,017	15,151	56,627 *	32.4	49.6
435 Unitarian-Univ	1	31	NR	39 *	-	-
449 Un Methodist	24	9,931	3,366	12,496 *	7.2	11.0
463 Vineyard	1	150	150	189 *	.1	.2
496 Jewish Est	2	NR	NR	400	.2	.4
498 Indep.Charis.	1	800	900	900	.5	.8
499 Indep.Non-Char	2	2,347	2,350	3,000	1.7	2.6
SOMERVELL	**13**	**2,465**	**992**	**3,315 ***	**48.7**	**100.0**
053 Assemb of God	1	49	62	65	1.0	2.0
056 Baha'i	0	1	NR	1	-	-
081 Catholic	1	NR	NR	205	3.0	6.2
167 Chs of Christ	2	150	150	191	2.8	5.8
365 Prog Prim Bapt	1	21	NR	26 *	.4	.8
419 So Bapt Conv	7	1,771	630	2,231 *	32.8	67.3
449 Un Methodist	1	473	150	596 *	8.8	18.0
STARR	**31**	**1,477**	**1,010**	**42,221 ***	**78.8**	**100.0**
053 Assemb of God	3	297	232	340	.6	.8
056 Baha'i	0	1	NR	1	-	-
081 Catholic	15	NR	NR	40,092	74.8	95.0
151 L-D Saints	1	NR	NR	117	.2	.3
167 Chs of Christ	1	40	60	60	.1	.1
237 Menn Br US Conf	2	140	NR	198 *	.4	.5
313 N Am Bapt Conf	1	83	55	117 *	.2	.3
349 Pent Holiness	1	70	120	99 *	.2	.2
419 So Bapt Conv	6	572	457	809 *	1.5	1.9
449 Un Methodist	1	274	86	388 *	.7	.9
STEPHENS	**25**	**4,559**	**1,773**	**6,819 ***	**70.5**	**100.0**
053 Assemb of God	2	32	40	86	.9	1.3
056 Baha'i	0	3	NR	3	-	-
081 Catholic	1	NR	NR	1,023	10.6	15.0
093 Chr Ch (Disc)	1	215	95	262 *	2.7	3.8
127 Ch God (Cleve)	1	46	14	56 *	.6	.8
165 Ch of Nazarene	1	54	46	63	.7	.9
167 Chs of Christ	2	434	340	568	5.9	8.3
193 Episcopal	1	NR	107	159	1.6	2.3
355 Presb Ch (USA)	1	120	60	146 *	1.5	2.1
360 Prim Bapt Chrch	1	NR	NR	NR	-	-
419 So Bapt Conv	11	2,969	891	3,617 *	37.4	53.0
449 Un Methodist	3	686	180	836 *	8.6	12.3
STERLING	**6**	**776**	**380**	**1,206 ***	**86.6**	**100.0**
056 Baha'i	0	7	NR	7	.5	.6
081 Catholic	1	NR	NR	200	14.4	16.6
167 Chs of Christ	1	64	90	110	7.9	9.1
355 Presb Ch (USA)	1	40	25	50 *	3.6	4.1
419 So Bapt Conv	2	432	165	545 *	39.1	45.2
449 Un Methodist	1	233	100	294 *	21.1	24.4

NR–Not Reported *Total adherents estimated from known number of communicant, confirmed, full members. - Represents a percentage less than 0.1. Percentages may not total 100 due to rounding.

Table 4: Religious Congregations by County and Group: 2000

Religious Group	Number of Churches, Synagogues, Mosques, or Temples	Number of Communicant, Confirmed, or Full Members	Number of Attendees	Total Adherents: Number of Adherents	Total Adherents: % of Total Pop.	Total Adherents: % of Total Adh.
STONEWALL	**7**	**1,236**	**364**	**1,653 ***	**97.6**	**100.0**
059 Bapt Miss Assn	1	202	65	240 *	14.2	14.5
081 Catholic	1	NR	NR	170	10.0	10.3
167 Chs of Christ	2	71	78	100	5.9	6.0
419 So Bapt Conv	2	751	157	891 *	52.6	53.9
449 Un Methodist	1	212	64	252 *	14.9	15.2
SUTTON	**11**	**1,253**	**596**	**3,455 ***	**84.7**	**100.0**
053 Assemb of God	1	45	28	59	1.4	1.7
056 Baha'i	0	23	NR	23	.6	.7
081 Catholic	1	NR	NR	1,750	42.9	50.7
167 Chs of Christ	1	140	150	182	4.5	5.3
193 Episcopal	1	NR	53	108	2.6	3.1
283 Luth—MO Synod	1	19	10	20	.5	.6
355 Presb Ch (USA)	1	80	32	102 *	2.5	3.0
419 So Bapt Conv	4	640	238	819 *	20.1	23.7
449 Un Methodist	1	306	85	392 *	9.6	11.3
SWISHER	**27**	**5,069**	**1,964**	**7,469 ***	**89.2**	**100.0**
053 Assemb of God	3	113	156	247	2.9	3.3
056 Baha'i	0	16	NR	16	.2	.2
081 Catholic	3	NR	NR	965	11.5	12.9
093 Chr Ch (Disc)	1	53	30	67 *	.8	.9
167 Chs of Christ	5	535	519	665	7.9	8.9
220 Free Lutheran	1	43	24	52	.6	.7
355 Presb Ch (USA)	1	113	50	143 *	1.7	1.9
360 Prim Bapt Chrch	1	NR	NR	NR	-	-
413 S.D.A.	1	22	NR	26	.3	.3
419 So Bapt Conv	6	3,209	773	4,065 *	48.5	54.4
449 Un Methodist	5	965	412	1,223 *	14.6	16.4
TARRANT	**864**	**424,434**	**191,575**	**758,527 ***	**52.4**	**100.0**
017 Amer Bapt Assn	9	1,876	NR	2,414 *	.2	.3
019 Amer Bapt USA	1	525	0	675 *	-	.1
034 Ant Orth of NA	1	292	NR	584	-	.1
049 Armen Ap Cilic	1	0	NR	80	-	-
053 Assemb of God	63	13,151	11,001	19,206	1.3	2.5
056 Baha'i	9	637	NR	637	-	.1
059 Bapt Miss Assn	11	3,283	814	4,222 *	.3	.6
076 Buddhism	3	NR	NR	NR	-	-
081 Catholic	32	NR	NR	166,550	11.5	22.0
084 Calvary Chapel	2	NR	NR	NR	-	-
089 Chr & Miss Al	5	346	NR	478	-	.1
093 Chr Ch (Disc)	25	13,504	3,703	17,352 *	1.2	2.3
097 Chr Chs&Chs Cr	4	4,914	NR	6,314 *	.4	.8
123 Ch God (Ander)	2	NR	68	68	-	-
127 Ch God (Cleve)	13	2,501	1,221	3,227 *	.2	.4
145 Ch God Prophcy	2	54	NR	70 *	-	-
151 L-D Saints	32	NR	NR	12,031	.8	1.6
165 Ch of Nazarene	20	2,988	2,275	4,165	.3	.5
167 Chs of Christ	93	24,211	21,848	30,747	2.1	4.1
173 Comm of Christ	1	128	NR	128	-	-
185 Cumber Presb	6	902	NR	1,366	.1	.2
193 Episcopal	24	NR	5,470	14,133	1.0	1.9
203 Evan Free Ch	1	45	115	115	-	-
207 E.L.C.A.	17	5,768	3,288	7,895	.5	1.0
221 Free Methodist	1	37	30	46	-	-
223 Free Will Bapt	3	127	NR	164 *	-	-
226 Friends-USA	1	15	NR	19 *	-	-
246 Greek Orthodox	2	NR	NR	717	-	.1
263 Int Foursq Gos	5	496	766	766 *	.1	.1
267 Muslim Est	9	NR	3,624	14,297	1.0	1.9
283 Luth—MO Synod	14	6,873	3,278	9,299	.6	1.2
290 Metro Comm Ch	2	203	237	244 *	-	-
331 OCA: Ter Diocs	1	48	NR	314	-	-
335 Orth Pres Ch	1	31	44	48	-	-
339 Pent Ch of God	5	249	NR	586	-	.1
349 Pent Holiness	3	124	107	159 *	-	-
355 Presb Ch (USA)	27	9,266	4,064	11,908 *	.8	1.6
356 Presb Ch Amer	5	663	618	938	.1	.1
360 Prim Bapt Chrch	6	NR	NR	NR	-	-
371 Ref Ch in Am	1	63	95	156	-	-

Religious Group	Number of Churches, Synagogues, Mosques, or Temples	Number of Communicant, Confirmed, or Full Members	Number of Attendees	Total Adherents: Number of Adherents	Total Adherents: % of Total Pop.	Total Adherents: % of Total Adh.
397 OCA: Roman Dioc	1	NR	NR	63	-	-
403 Salvation Army	4	290	209	903	.1	.1
410 Serb Orth USA	1	NR	NR	190	-	-
413 S.D.A.	16	4,700	NR	5,593	.4	.7
416 Sikh	1	NR	NR	NR	-	-
418 Southw Bapt Fel	1	NR	NR	NR	-	-
419 So Bapt Conv	262	210,849	78,250	270,928 *	18.7	35.7
435 Unitarian-Univ	3	263	NR	338 *	-	-
443 Un C of Christ	2	324	143	416 *	-	.1
449 Un Methodist	74	76,653	22,098	98,491 *	6.8	13.0
463 Vineyard	1	256	220	329 *	-	-
469 WELS	3	430	337	598	-	.1
496 Jewish Est	3	NR	NR	5,000	.3	.7
498 Indep.Charis.	9	2,989	9,200	9,200	.6	1.2
499 Indep.Non-Char	20	34,360	18,452	34,360	2.4	4.5
TAYLOR	**159**	**59,362**	**27,741**	**84,905 ***	**67.1**	**100.0**
017 Amer Bapt Assn	2	79	NR	99 *	.1	.1
034 Ant Orth of NA	1	17	NR	34	-	-
053 Assemb of God	9	765	753	1,020	.8	1.2
056 Baha'i	1	53	NR	53	-	.1
059 Bapt Miss Assn	2	181	53	227 *	.2	.3
081 Catholic	5	NR	NR	8,352	6.6	9.8
093 Chr Ch (Disc)	2	857	318	1,076 *	.9	1.3
097 Chr Chs&Chs Cr	2	95	NR	119 *	.1	.1
123 Ch God (Ander)	1	NR	29	29	-	-
127 Ch God (Cleve)	2	238	92	299 *	.2	.4
145 Ch God Prophcy	1	27	NR	34 *	-	-
151 L-D Saints	2	NR	NR	827	.7	1.0
165 Ch of Nazarene	3	496	277	500	.4	.6
167 Chs of Christ	41	9,434	10,424	12,004	9.5	14.1
193 Episcopal	2	NR	358	1,111	.9	1.3
207 E.L.C.A.	1	452	190	602	.5	.7
221 Free Methodist	2	37	63	63	-	.1
223 Free Will Bapt	1	42	NR	53 *	-	.1
263 Int Foursq Gos	4	312	272	392 *	.3	.5
283 Luth—MO Synod	2	497	326	657	.5	.8
290 Metro Comm Ch	1	52	62	65 *	.1	.1
335 Orth Pres Ch	1	26	27	35	-	-
339 Pent Ch of God	1	249	NR	302	.2	.4
355 Presb Ch (USA)	2	1,221	461	1,533 *	1.2	1.8
360 Prim Bapt Chrch	2	NR	NR	NR	-	-
388 Reg Bapt Gen As	1	72	104	90 *	.1	.1
403 Salvation Army	1	236	157	335	.3	.4
413 S.D.A.	1	101	NR	120	.1	.1
419 So Bapt Conv	40	34,160	9,805	42,878 *	33.9	50.5
435 Unitarian-Univ	1	16	NR	20 *	-	-
449 Un Methodist	19	8,047	2,470	10,101 *	8.0	11.9
496 Jewish Est	1	NR	NR	75	.1	.1
498 Indep.Charis.	1	400	400	400	.3	.5
499 Indep.Non-Char	1	1,200	1,100	1,400	1.1	1.6
TERRELL	**6**	**394**	**132**	**1,088 ***	**100.6**	**100.0**
081 Catholic	1	NR	NR	600	55.5	55.1
167 Chs of Christ	1	37	40	48	4.4	4.4
355 Presb Ch (USA)	1	54	25	67 *	6.2	6.2
419 So Bapt Conv	1	205	38	253 *	23.4	23.3
449 Un Methodist	2	98	29	120 *	11.1	11.0
TERRY	**33**	**5,342**	**2,450**	**9,158 ***	**71.8**	**100.0**
053 Assemb of God	3	115	150	276	2.2	3.0
059 Bapt Miss Assn	1	0	0	0 *	-	-
081 Catholic	1	NR	NR	2,155	16.9	23.5
093 Chr Ch (Disc)	1	205	108	260 *	2.0	2.8
127 Ch God (Cleve)	1	279	181	354 *	2.8	3.9
145 Ch God Prophcy	1	27	NR	34 *	.3	.4
165 Ch of Nazarene	1	19	8	19	.1	.2
167 Chs of Christ	5	702	599	956	7.5	10.4
193 Episcopal	1	NR	20	39	.3	.4
263 Int Foursq Gos	2	478	158	606 *	4.7	6.6
355 Presb Ch (USA)	1	65	25	82 *	.6	.9
360 Prim Bapt Chrch	1	NR	NR	NR	-	-
419 So Bapt Conv	10	2,987	1,007	3,788 *	29.7	41.4

NR–Not Reported   *Total adherents estimated from known number of communicant, confirmed, full members.   - Represents a percentage less than 0.1.   Percentages may not total 100 due to rounding.

Table 4: Religious Congregations by County and Group: 2000

Religious Group	Number of Churches, Synagogues, Mosques, or Temples	Number of Communicant, Confirmed, or Full Members	Number of Attendees	Total Adherents		
				Number of Adherents	% of Total Pop.	% of Total Adh.
449 Un Methodist	4	465	194	589 *	4.6	6.4
THROCKMORTON	**12**	**1,535**	**479**	**1,901 ***	**102.8**	**100.0**
053 Assemb of God	1	27	27	27	1.5	1.4
081 Catholic	1	NR	NR	48	2.6	2.5
093 Chr Ch (Disc)	1	75	45	92 *	5.0	4.8
167 Chs of Christ	3	153	153	160	8.6	8.4
355 Presb Ch (USA)	1	7	5	9 *	.5	.5
419 So Bapt Conv	3	1,102	168	1,355 *	73.2	71.3
449 Un Methodist	2	171	81	210 *	11.4	11.0
TITUS	**66**	**13,022**	**5,099**	**19,966 ***	**71.0**	**100.0**
017 Amer Bapt Assn	16	1,666	NR	2,188 *	7.8	11.0
053 Assemb of God	6	815	649	1,100	3.9	5.5
056 Baha'i	0	2	NR	2	-	-
059 Bapt Miss Assn	3	1,137	585	1,494 *	5.3	7.5
081 Catholic	1	NR	NR	2,738	9.7	13.7
093 Chr Ch (Disc)	1	5	4	7 *	-	-
145 Ch God Prophcy	3	81	NR	105 *	.4	.5
165 Ch of Nazarene	1	115	68	115	.4	.6
167 Chs of Christ	11	933	987	1,178	4.2	5.9
193 Episcopal	1	NR	131	189	.7	.9
283 Luth—MO Synod	1	65	45	74	.3	.4
355 Presb Ch (USA)	1	259	150	340 *	1.2	1.7
419 So Bapt Conv	15	6,797	2,079	8,929 *	31.8	44.7
449 Un Methodist	6	1,147	401	1,507 *	5.4	7.5
TOM GREEN	**111**	**35,372**	**14,561**	**62,440 ***	**60.0**	**100.0**
017 Amer Bapt Assn	1	121	NR	151 *	.1	.2
053 Assemb of God	10	1,416	1,642	1,920	1.8	3.1
056 Baha'i	0	40	NR	40	-	.1
059 Bapt Miss Assn	1	462	131	576 *	.6	.9
081 Catholic	9	NR	NR	15,601	15.0	25.0
093 Chr Ch (Disc)	4	1,086	262	1,355 *	1.3	2.2
097 Chr Chs&Chs Cr	1	320	NR	399 *	.4	.6
127 Ch God (Cleve)	1	155	39	193 *	.2	.3
145 Ch God Prophcy	2	54	NR	68 *	.1	.1
151 L-D Saints	4	NR	NR	1,064	1.0	1.7
165 Ch of Nazarene	2	265	227	274	.3	.4
167 Chs of Christ	13	2,478	2,110	3,752	3.6	6.0
193 Episcopal	2	NR	339	692	.7	1.1
207 E.L.C.A.	2	267	154	349	.3	.6
223 Free Will Bapt	1	42	NR	53 *	.1	.1
246 Greek Orthodox	2	NR	NR	138	.1	.2
263 Int Foursq Gos	2	178	277	277 *	.3	.4
283 Luth—MO Synod	1	565	355	738	.7	1.2
339 Pent Ch of God	3	203	NR	233	.2	.4
355 Presb Ch (USA)	4	1,641	693	2,048 *	2.0	3.3
360 Prim Bapt Chrch	1	NR	NR	NR	-	-
403 Salvation Army	1	239	94	289	.3	.5
413 S.D.A.	2	74	NR	88	.1	.1
419 So Bapt Conv	29	22,207	6,711	27,706 *	26.6	44.4
449 Un Methodist	12	3,530	1,504	4,405 *	4.2	7.1
469 WELS	1	29	23	31	-	-
TRAVIS	**420**	**133,012**	**65,933**	**375,037 ***	**46.2**	**100.0**
017 Amer Bapt Assn	1	50	NR	62 *	-	-
019 Amer Bapt USA	2	919	412	1,133 *	.1	.3
034 Ant Orth of NA	2	321	NR	642	.1	.2
050 Armen Ap Etchm	1	24	NR	140	-	-
053 Assemb of God	24	2,930	3,383	4,809	.6	1.3
056 Baha'i	3	577	NR	577	.1	.2
076 Buddhism	6	NR	NR	NR	-	-
081 Catholic	28	NR	NR	165,810	20.4	44.2
084 Calvary Chapel	1	NR	NR	NR	-	-
089 Chr & Miss Al	1	66	NR	66	-	-
093 Chr Ch (Disc)	11	2,644	756	3,260 *	.4	.9
097 Chr Chs&Chs Cr	2	475	NR	585 *	.1	.2
105 Christian Ref	1	128	0	158 *	-	-
123 Ch God (Ander)	2	NR	144	144	-	-
127 Ch God (Cleve)	4	167	82	206 *	-	.1
145 Ch God Prophcy	1	27	NR	33 *	-	-

Religious Group	Number of Churches, Synagogues, Mosques, or Temples	Number of Communicant, Confirmed, or Full Members	Number of Attendees	Total Adherents		
				Number of Adherents	% of Total Pop.	% of Total Adh.
151 L-D Saints	10	NR	NR	4,487	.6	1.2
165 Ch of Nazarene	6	797	514	797	.1	.2
167 Chs of Christ	37	5,544	5,368	7,767	1.0	2.1
173 Comm of Christ	1	193	NR	193	-	.1
185 Cumber Presb	5	994	NR	1,449	.2	.4
186 Coptic Orth Ch	1	NR	NR	NR	-	-
193 Episcopal	18	NR	4,742	13,262	1.6	3.5
203 Evan Free Ch	3	869	1,175	1,175	.1	.3
207 E.L.C.A.	19	8,976	3,939	11,755	1.4	3.1
226 Friends-USA	1	15	NR	18 *	-	-
246 Greek Orthodox	1	NR	NR	291	-	.1
252 Hindu	3	NR	NR	NR	-	-
264 Int Chs of Crst	1	195	281	260	-	.1
267 Muslim Est	4	NR	984	3,073	.4	.8
283 Luth—MO Synod	12	6,861	3,748	9,137	1.1	2.4
288 Mennonite USA	1	42	45	52 *	-	-
290 Metro Comm Ch	1	260	0	321 *	-	.1
304 NatPrimBapt USA	8	662	NR	816 *	.1	.2
313 N Am Bapt Conf	1	76	84	94 *	-	-
335 Orth Pres Ch	1	72	85	107	-	-
339 Pent Ch of God	5	196	NR	412	.1	.1
349 Pent Holiness	5	378	420	466 *	.1	.1
355 Presb Ch (USA)	17	8,475	4,167	10,483 *	1.3	2.8
356 Presb Ch Amer	4	412	468	504	.1	.1
360 Prim Bapt Chrch	2	NR	NR	NR	-	-
388 Reg Bapt Gen As	1	72	104	89 *	-	-
403 Salvation Army	1	126	51	224	-	.1
413 S.D.A.	4	1,065	NR	1,267	.2	.3
416 Sikh	2	NR	NR	NR	-	-
418 Southw Bapt Fel	1	NR	NR	NR	-	-
419 So Bapt Conv	86	62,599	19,742	77,183 *	9.5	20.6
435 Unitarian-Univ	3	672	NR	829 *	.1	.2
443 Un C of Christ	4	563	262	694 *	.1	.2
449 Un Methodist	36	17,934	7,950	22,112 *	2.7	5.9
463 Vineyard	3	494	794	836 *	.1	.2
467 Wesleyan	1	0	224	324	-	.1
469 WELS	2	427	311	575	.1	.2
496 Jewish Est	11	NR	NR	13,500	1.7	3.6
498 Indep.Charis.	3	3,065	3,600	7,600	.9	2.0
499 Indep.Non-Char	5	2,650	2,098	5,260	.6	1.4
TRINITY	**31**	**5,071**	**2,115**	**6,447 ***	**46.8**	**100.0**
017 Amer Bapt Assn	1	60	NR	72 *	.5	1.1
053 Assemb of God	2	76	80	100	.7	1.6
081 Catholic	1	NR	NR	310	2.2	4.8
127 Ch God (Cleve)	1	302	213	364 *	2.6	5.6
167 Chs of Christ	8	357	356	452	3.3	7.0
355 Presb Ch (USA)	1	45	40	54 *	.4	.8
419 So Bapt Conv	14	3,704	1,201	4,460 *	32.4	69.2
449 Un Methodist	3	527	225	635 *	4.6	9.8
TYLER	**60**	**9,807**	**3,666**	**12,815 ***	**61.4**	**100.0**
017 Amer Bapt Assn	1	68	NR	82 *	.4	.6
053 Assemb of God	7	525	447	601	2.9	4.7
056 Baha'i	0	3	NR	3	-	-
059 Bapt Miss Assn	2	131	31	159 *	.8	1.2
081 Catholic	1	NR	NR	557	2.7	4.3
093 Chr Ch (Disc)	1	60	0	73 *	.3	.6
151 L-D Saints	2	NR	NR	320	1.5	2.5
167 Chs of Christ	6	309	300	384	1.8	3.0
193 Episcopal	1	NR	47	75	.4	.6
283 Luth—MO Synod	1	59	38	67	.3	.5
339 Pent Ch of God	1	15	NR	35	.2	.3
360 Prim Bapt Chrch	1	NR	NR	NR	-	-
413 S.D.A.	1	52	NR	62	.3	.5
419 So Bapt Conv	31	7,951	2,560	9,630 *	46.1	75.1
449 Un Methodist	4	634	243	767 *	3.7	6.0
UPSHUR	**86**	**13,819**	**5,653**	**19,950 ***	**56.5**	**100.0**
017 Amer Bapt Assn	2	172	NR	215 *	.6	1.1
053 Assemb of God	3	165	203	286	.8	1.4
056 Baha'i	0	2	NR	2	-	-
059 Bapt Miss Assn	18	3,224	1,030	4,036 *	11.4	20.2

NR–Not Reported   *Total adherents estimated from known number of communicant, confirmed, full members.   - Represents a percentage less than 0.1.   Percentages may not total 100 due to rounding.

Table 4: Religious Congregations by County and Group: 2000

Religious Group	Number of Churches, Synagogues, Mosques, or Temples	Number of Communicant, Confirmed, or Full Members	Number of Attendees	Total Adherents: Number of Adherents	Total Adherents: % of Total Pop.	Total Adherents: % of Total Adh.
081 Catholic	3	NR	NR	1,343	3.8	6.7
093 Chr Ch (Disc)	1	33	0	41 *	.1	.2
127 Ch God (Cleve)	2	69	44	112 *	.3	.6
151 L-D Saints	3	NR	NR	1,201	3.4	6.0
165 Ch of Nazarene	1	99	51	102	.3	.5
167 Chs of Christ	16	1,104	1,011	1,414	4.0	7.1
226 Friends-USA	1	15	NR	19 *	.1	.1
360 Prim Bapt Chrch	1	NR	NR	NR	-	-
419 So Bapt Conv	24	7,711	2,718	9,645 *	27.3	48.3
449 Un Methodist	11	1,225	596	1,534 *	4.3	7.7
UPTON	**16**	**1,446**	**551**	**2,262 ***	**66.5**	**100.0**
053 Assemb of God	3	99	110	182	5.3	8.0
081 Catholic	3	NR	NR	386	11.3	17.1
093 Chr Ch (Disc)	1	58	0	73 *	2.1	3.2
167 Chs of Christ	2	140	125	170	5.0	7.5
283 Luth—MO Synod	1	11	12	17	.5	.8
355 Presb Ch (USA)	1	14	6	18 *	.5	.8
419 So Bapt Conv	3	828	213	1,043 *	30.6	46.1
449 Un Methodist	2	296	85	373 *	11.0	16.5
UVALDE	**35**	**5,616**	**2,657**	**23,179 ***	**89.4**	**100.0**
053 Assemb of God	2	244	230	375	1.4	1.6
056 Baha'i	1	52	NR	52	.2	.2
081 Catholic	2	NR	NR	15,236	58.8	65.7
089 Chr & Miss Al	1	20	NR	49	.2	.2
097 Chr Chs&Chs Cr	1	110	NR	145 *	.6	.6
151 L-D Saints	1	NR	NR	229	.9	1.0
165 Ch of Nazarene	1	49	44	80	.3	.3
167 Chs of Christ	7	588	544	717	2.8	3.1
193 Episcopal	2	NR	145	305	1.2	1.3
207 E.L.C.A.	1	142	86	190	.7	.8
283 Luth—MO Synod	1	122	80	141	.5	.6
355 Presb Ch (USA)	1	141	65	186 *	.7	.8
413 S.D.A.	1	30	NR	36	.1	.2
419 So Bapt Conv	9	2,993	896	3,952 *	15.2	17.0
449 Un Methodist	4	1,125	567	1,486 *	5.7	6.4
VAL VERDE	**38**	**5,344**	**2,397**	**22,207 ***	**49.5**	**100.0**
017 Amer Bapt Assn	5	204	NR	273 *	.6	1.2
053 Assemb of God	4	614	428	685	1.5	3.1
056 Baha'i	0	29	NR	29	.1	.1
081 Catholic	3	NR	NR	13,690	30.5	61.6
093 Chr Ch (Disc)	1	85	40	114 *	.3	.5
097 Chr Chs&Chs Cr	1	80	NR	107 *	.2	.5
151 L-D Saints	2	NR	NR	809	1.8	3.6
165 Ch of Nazarene	2	21	10	21	-	.1
167 Chs of Christ	3	175	200	260	.6	1.2
193 Episcopal	1	NR	88	303	.7	1.4
283 Luth—MO Synod	2	222	190	293	.7	1.3
355 Presb Ch (USA)	1	133	80	178 *	.4	.8
413 S.D.A.	2	44	NR	52	.1	.2
419 So Bapt Conv	8	3,023	773	4,039 *	9.0	18.2
449 Un Methodist	2	714	238	954 *	2.1	4.3
498 Indep.Charis.	1	0	350	400	.9	1.8
VAN ZANDT	**92**	**20,467**	**8,698**	**27,586 ***	**57.3**	**100.0**
017 Amer Bapt Assn	1	20	NR	25 *	.1	.1
053 Assemb of God	6	357	400	674	1.4	2.4
056 Baha'i	0	15	NR	15	-	.1
059 Bapt Miss Assn	18	3,578	1,307	4,422 *	9.2	16.0
081 Catholic	3	NR	NR	1,660	3.4	6.0
093 Chr Ch (Disc)	1	50	18	62 *	.1	.2
127 Ch God (Cleve)	2	356	186	441 *	.9	1.6
151 L-D Saints	1	NR	NR	387	.8	1.4
165 Ch of Nazarene	3	223	123	228	.5	.8
167 Chs of Christ	14	1,375	1,393	1,731	3.6	6.3
263 Int Foursq Gos	1	42	87	87 *	.2	.3
283 Luth—MO Synod	1	49	40	50	.1	.2
355 Presb Ch (USA)	1	64	30	79 *	.2	.3
419 So Bapt Conv	25	11,513	3,866	14,234 *	29.6	51.6
449 Un Methodist	15	2,825	1,248	3,491 *	7.3	12.7

Religious Group	Number of Churches, Synagogues, Mosques, or Temples	Number of Communicant, Confirmed, or Full Members	Number of Attendees	Total Adherents: Number of Adherents	Total Adherents: % of Total Pop.	Total Adherents: % of Total Adh.
VICTORIA	**70**	**20,330**	**8,461**	**59,360 ***	**70.6**	**100.0**
053 Assemb of God	5	351	400	541	.6	.9
056 Baha'i	1	44	NR	44	.1	.1
081 Catholic	8	NR	NR	31,960	38.0	53.8
093 Chr Ch (Disc)	1	210	107	270 *	.3	.5
123 Ch God (Ander)	1	NR	10	10	-	-
127 Ch God (Cleve)	1	121	60	156 *	.2	.3
143 CG in Cr(Menn)	1	22	NR	28 *	-	-
151 L-D Saints	1	NR	NR	663	.8	1.1
165 Ch of Nazarene	1	95	66	99	.1	.2
167 Chs of Christ	8	1,020	1,023	1,334	1.6	2.2
193 Episcopal	2	NR	302	694	.8	1.2
207 E.L.C.A.	7	3,623	1,419	4,427	5.3	7.5
223 Free Will Bapt	1	42	NR	55 *	.1	.1
263 Int Foursq Gos	1	217	74	279 *	.3	.5
283 Luth—MO Synod	1	426	150	499	.6	.8
304 NatPrimBapt USA	1	5	NR	6 *	-	-
355 Presb Ch (USA)	3	1,091	390	1,404 *	1.7	2.4
356 Presb Ch Amer	1	38	60	60	.1	.1
403 Salvation Army	1	83	60	103	.1	.2
413 S.D.A.	1	62	NR	74	.1	.1
419 So Bapt Conv	14	10,415	3,555	13,405 *	15.9	22.6
435 Unitarian-Univ	1	18	NR	23 *	-	-
449 Un Methodist	7	2,447	785	3,151 *	3.7	5.3
496 Jewish Est	1	NR	NR	75	.1	.1
WALKER	**52**	**15,291**	**5,349**	**20,466 ***	**33.1**	**100.0**
017 Amer Bapt Assn	3	217	NR	252 *	.4	1.2
053 Assemb of God	2	393	510	522	.8	2.6
056 Baha'i	0	78	NR	78	.1	.4
059 Bapt Miss Assn	2	94	58	109 *	.2	.5
081 Catholic	1	NR	NR	1,660	2.7	8.1
093 Chr Ch (Disc)	1	328	112	380 *	.6	1.9
123 Ch God (Ander)	1	NR	23	23	-	.1
151 L-D Saints	3	NR	NR	530	.9	2.6
165 Ch of Nazarene	1	43	39	96	.2	.5
167 Chs of Christ	7	656	561	901	1.5	4.4
193 Episcopal	1	NR	115	248	.4	1.2
207 E.L.C.A.	1	24	18	48	.1	.2
223 Free Will Bapt	2	85	NR	98 *	.2	.5
283 Luth—MO Synod	1	374	200	461	.7	2.3
355 Presb Ch (USA)	2	402	174	466 *	.8	2.3
419 So Bapt Conv	13	10,259	2,570	11,886 *	19.2	58.1
435 Unitarian-Univ	1	24	NR	28 *	-	.1
449 Un Methodist	10	2,314	969	2,680 *	4.3	13.1
WALLER	**39**	**6,197**	**2,719**	**10,860 ***	**33.2**	**100.0**
056 Baha'i	0	12	NR	12	-	.1
076 Buddhism	1	NR	NR	NR	-	-
081 Catholic	2	NR	NR	2,803	8.6	25.8
093 Chr Ch (Disc)	1	34	22	42 *	.1	.4
167 Chs of Christ	4	229	249	341	1.0	3.1
193 Episcopal	2	NR	84	242	.7	2.2
207 E.L.C.A.	2	595	235	804	2.5	7.4
283 Luth—MO Synod	1	140	47	150	.5	1.4
304 NatPrimBapt USA	2	50	NR	62 *	.2	.6
413 S.D.A.	1	60	NR	71	.2	.7
419 So Bapt Conv	13	3,851	1,498	4,803 *	14.7	44.2
449 Un Methodist	10	1,226	584	1,530 *	4.7	14.1
WARD	**32**	**4,182**	**1,683**	**8,535 ***	**78.2**	**100.0**
053 Assemb of God	2	97	123	202	1.9	2.4
056 Baha'i	0	5	NR	5	-	.1
081 Catholic	2	NR	NR	3,005	27.5	35.2
093 Chr Ch (Disc)	1	36	17	46 *	.4	.5
097 Chr Chs&Chs Cr	1	25	NR	32 *	.3	.4
151 L-D Saints	1	NR	NR	139	1.3	1.6
165 Ch of Nazarene	1	12	0	12	.1	.1
167 Chs of Christ	7	321	347	460	4.2	5.4
193 Episcopal	1	NR	12	20	.2	.2
263 Int Foursq Gos	1	78	119	119 *	1.1	1.4
283 Luth—MO Synod	1	71	28	98	.9	1.1

NR–Not Reported *Total adherents estimated from known number of communicant, confirmed, full members. - Represents a percentage less than 0.1. Percentages may not total 100 due to rounding.

Table 4: Religious Congregations by County and Group: 2000

Religious Group	Number of Churches, Synagogues, Mosques, or Temples	Number of Communicant, Confirmed, or Full Members	Number of Attendees	Total Adherents		
				Number of Adherents	% of Total Pop.	% of Total Adh.
355 Presb Ch (USA)	2	87	45	110 *	1.0	1.3
419 So Bapt Conv	8	2,583	637	3,270 *	30.0	38.3
449 Un Methodist	3	567	205	717 *	6.6	8.4
499 Indep.Non-Char	1	300	150	300	2.8	3.5
WASHINGTON	**48**	**12,228**	**6,243**	**21,752 ***	**71.6**	**100.0**
053 Assemb of God	1	211	250	544	1.8	2.5
056 Baha'i	0	7	NR	7	-	-
081 Catholic	3	NR	NR	6,150	20.2	28.3
093 Chr Ch (Disc)	2	156	61	191 *	.6	.9
123 Ch God (Ander)	3	NR	174	174	.6	.8
167 Chs of Christ	2	152	192	191	.6	.9
193 Episcopal	1	NR	129	269	.9	1.2
203 Evan Free Ch	1	40	100	100	.3	.5
207 E.L.C.A.	15	5,663	2,371	6,821	22.5	31.4
283 Luth—MO Synod	2	1,074	506	1,264	4.2	5.8
313 N Am Bapt Conf	1	102	45	125 *	.4	.6
355 Presb Ch (USA)	1	380	168	466 *	1.5	2.1
419 So Bapt Conv	8	2,478	1,458	3,039 *	10.0	14.0
443 Un C of Christ	3	794	326	974 *	3.2	4.5
449 Un Methodist	4	1,106	402	1,357 *	4.5	6.2
463 Vineyard	1	65	61	80 *	.3	.4
WEBB	**81**	**6,455**	**5,422**	**142,154 ***	**73.6**	**100.0**
053 Assemb of God	12	2,168	2,185	2,779	1.4	2.0
056 Baha'i	0	31	NR	31	-	-
081 Catholic	24	NR	NR	131,560	68.1	92.5
093 Chr Ch (Disc)	1	110	0	155 *	.1	.1
127 Ch God (Cleve)	2	47	36	66 *	-	-
145 Ch God Prophcy	1	27	NR	38 *	-	-
151 L-D Saints	4	NR	NR	1,542	.8	1.1
165 Ch of Nazarene	3	100	97	142	.1	.1
167 Chs of Christ	3	90	155	148	.1	.1
193 Episcopal	1	NR	93	167	.1	.1
203 Evan Free Ch	1	52	160	160	.1	.1
207 E.L.C.A.	1	82	76	124	.1	.1
221 Free Methodist	1	35	47	56	-	-
237 Menn Br US Conf	1	15	NR	21 *	-	-
283 Luth—MO Synod	1	69	58	80	-	.1
355 Presb Ch (USA)	2	140	105	196 *	.1	.1
356 Presb Ch Amer	1	0	0	0	-	-
403 Salvation Army	1	230	217	266	.1	.2
413 S.D.A.	2	306	NR	365	.2	.3
416 Sikh	1	NR	NR	NR	-	-
419 So Bapt Conv	12	1,839	1,259	2,585 *	1.3	1.8
449 Un Methodist	4	564	234	793 *	.4	.6
496 Jewish Est	1	NR	NR	130	.1	.1
499 Indep.Non-Char	1	550	700	750	.4	.5
WHARTON	**61**	**9,550**	**3,626**	**31,666 ***	**76.9**	**100.0**
053 Assemb of God	5	168	194	307	.7	1.0
056 Baha'i	0	23	NR	23	.1	.1
081 Catholic	10	NR	NR	19,073	46.3	60.2
093 Chr Ch (Disc)	2	143	76	182 *	.4	.6
123 Ch God (Ander)	3	NR	68	68	.2	.2
143 CG in Cr(Menn)	1	86	NR	109 *	.3	.3
145 Ch God Prophcy	1	27	NR	34 *	.1	.1
151 L-D Saints	1	NR	NR	167	.4	.5
167 Chs of Christ	4	498	433	610	1.5	1.9
193 Episcopal	1	NR	78	155	.4	.5
207 E.L.C.A.	4	919	323	1,106	2.7	3.5
220 Free Lutheran	1	97	65	126	.3	.4
283 Luth—MO Synod	1	284	153	336	.8	1.1
355 Presb Ch (USA)	2	449	137	571 *	1.4	1.8
419 So Bapt Conv	15	5,066	1,441	6,447 *	15.7	20.4
449 Un Methodist	9	1,790	658	2,277 *	5.5	7.2
496 Jewish Est	1	NR	NR	75	.2	.2
WHEELER	**22**	**3,131**	**1,312**	**3,976 ***	**75.2**	**100.0**
017 Amer Bapt Assn	1	100	NR	123 *	2.3	3.1
053 Assemb of God	1	28	35	35	.7	.9
081 Catholic	2	NR	NR	84	1.6	2.1
127 Ch God (Cleve)	1	12	16	16 *	.3	.4
165 Ch of Nazarene	1	41	12	41	.8	1.0
167 Chs of Christ	3	352	370	467	8.8	11.7
193 Episcopal	1	NR	14	20	.4	.5
283 Luth—MO Synod	1	53	29	73	1.4	1.8
419 So Bapt Conv	6	1,724	549	2,112 *	40.0	53.1
449 Un Methodist	5	821	287	1,005 *	19.0	25.3
WICHITA	**160**	**53,227**	**17,598**	**81,999 ***	**62.3**	**100.0**
017 Amer Bapt Assn	2	264	NR	327 *	.2	.4
034 Ant Orth of NA	2	93	NR	186	.1	.2
053 Assemb of God	14	1,321	1,648	2,517	1.9	3.1
056 Baha'i	1	81	NR	81	.1	.1
076 Buddhism	1	NR	NR	NR	-	-
081 Catholic	7	NR	NR	12,636	9.6	15.4
084 Calvary Chapel	1	NR	NR	NR	-	-
093 Chr Ch (Disc)	5	1,845	571	2,290 *	1.7	2.8
097 Chr Chs&Chs Cr	1	200	NR	248 *	.2	.3
127 Ch God (Cleve)	6	1,257	508	1,562 *	1.2	1.9
145 Ch God Prophcy	1	27	NR	33 *	-	-
151 L-D Saints	3	NR	NR	1,113	.8	1.4
165 Ch of Nazarene	3	373	305	476	.4	.6
167 Chs of Christ	17	3,255	2,638	4,149	3.2	5.1
193 Episcopal	4	NR	293	657	.5	.8
207 E.L.C.A.	2	400	223	502	.4	.6
220 Free Lutheran	1	37	25	37	-	-
223 Free Will Bapt	2	85	NR	105 *	.1	.1
246 Greek Orthodox	1	NR	NR	111	.1	.1
263 Int Foursq Gos	1	286	134	355 *	.3	.4
283 Luth—MO Synod	5	817	467	1,017	.8	1.2
290 Metro Comm Ch	1	43	50	53 *	-	.1
335 Orth Pres Ch	1	23	38	38	-	-
339 Pent Ch of God	5	118	NR	245	.2	.3
349 Pent Holiness	2	42	73	52 *	-	.1
355 Presb Ch (USA)	5	1,507	617	1,871 *	1.4	2.3
360 Prim Bapt Chrch	2	NR	NR	NR	-	-
365 Prog Prim Bapt	1	113	NR	140 *	.1	.2
403 Salvation Army	1	156	137	209	.2	.3
413 S.D.A.	3	152	NR	181	.1	.2
419 So Bapt Conv	43	34,949	7,484	43,372 *	32.9	52.9
449 Un Methodist	15	5,783	2,387	7,176 *	5.5	8.8
496 Jewish Est	1	NR	NR	260	.2	.3
WILBARGER	**36**	**7,696**	**2,558**	**11,020 ***	**75.1**	**100.0**
053 Assemb of God	2	282	217	486	3.3	4.4
056 Baha'i	0	30	NR	30	.2	.3
081 Catholic	1	NR	NR	1,137	7.7	10.3
093 Chr Ch (Disc)	1	134	58	166 *	1.1	1.5
127 Ch God (Cleve)	1	148	38	184 *	1.3	1.7
151 L-D Saints	1	NR	NR	101	.7	.9
165 Ch of Nazarene	1	24	16	37	.3	.3
167 Chs of Christ	7	694	554	916	6.2	8.3
193 Episcopal	1	NR	19	31	.2	.3
207 E.L.C.A.	1	38	18	38	.3	.3
283 Luth—MO Synod	3	682	319	859	5.9	7.8
339 Pent Ch of God	1	6	NR	19	.1	.2
349 Pent Holiness	1	28	35	35 *	.2	.3
355 Presb Ch (USA)	1	183	83	227 *	1.5	2.1
360 Prim Bapt Chrch	1	NR	NR	NR	-	-
413 S.D.A.	1	7	NR	8	.1	.1
419 So Bapt Conv	9	4,677	926	5,800 *	39.5	52.6
449 Un Methodist	3	763	275	946 *	6.4	8.6
WILLACY	**34**	**2,473**	**942**	**15,552 ***	**77.4**	**100.0**
053 Assemb of God	3	187	156	197	1.0	1.3
056 Baha'i	0	4	NR	4	-	-
081 Catholic	7	NR	NR	11,984	59.7	77.1
093 Chr Ch (Disc)	1	31	0	41 *	.2	.3
145 Ch God Prophcy	2	54	NR	72 *	.4	.5
151 L-D Saints	1	NR	NR	165	.8	1.1
165 Ch of Nazarene	1	11	0	11	.1	.1
167 Chs of Christ	1	47	38	62	.3	.4
193 Episcopal	1	NR	26	29	.1	.2

NR–Not Reported *Total adherents estimated from known number of communicant, confirmed, full members. - Represents a percentage less than 0.1. Percentages may not total 100 due to rounding.

Table 4: Religious Congregations by County and Group: 2000

Religious Group	Number of Churches, Synagogues, Mosques, or Temples	Number of Communicant, Confirmed, or Full Members	Number of Attendees	Total Adherents: Number of Adherents	Total Adherents: % of Total Pop.	Total Adherents: % of Total Adh.
207 E.L.C.A.	1	103	58	134	.7	.9
263 Int Foursq Gos	1	34	30	45 *	.2	.3
283 Luth—MO Synod	1	134	88	322	1.6	2.1
349 Pent Holiness	1	42	57	55 *	.3	.4
355 Presb Ch (USA)	1	41	20	54 *	.3	.3
360 Prim Bapt Chrch	1	NR	NR	NR	-	-
413 S.D.A.	2	103	NR	123	.6	.8
419 So Bapt Conv	4	1,237	247	1,631 *	8.1	10.5
449 Un Methodist	3	445	186	587 *	2.9	3.8
467 Wesleyan	2	0	36	36	.2	.2
WILLIAMSON	**157**	**49,464**	**28,607**	**99,892 ***	**40.0**	**100.0**
017 Amer Bapt Assn	1	50	NR	66 *	-	.1
019 Amer Bapt USA	1	113	50	148 *	.1	.1
053 Assemb of God	6	432	463	541	.2	.5
056 Baha'i	3	323	NR	323	.1	.3
059 Bapt Miss Assn	1	31	45	45 *	-	-
076 Buddhism	1	NR	NR	NR	-	-
081 Catholic	11	NR	NR	30,957	12.4	31.0
084 Calvary Chapel	1	NR	NR	NR	-	-
093 Chr Ch (Disc)	2	392	143	514 *	.2	.5
097 Chr Chs&Chs Cr	4	370	NR	486 *	.2	.5
105 Christian Ref	1	81	66	106 *	-	.1
127 Ch God (Cleve)	2	116	75	152 *	.1	.2
151 L-D Saints	8	NR	NR	3,630	1.5	3.6
165 Ch of Nazarene	2	231	262	307	.1	.3
167 Chs of Christ	16	2,553	2,547	3,338	1.3	3.3
173 Comm of Christ	1	38	NR	38	-	-
185 Cumber Presb	1	22	NR	60	-	.1
193 Episcopal	3	NR	591	1,524	.6	1.5
203 Evan Free Ch	2	75	94	94	-	.1
207 E.L.C.A.	10	3,599	1,515	4,457	1.8	4.5
223 Free Will Bapt	1	42	NR	56 *	-	.1
252 Hindu	1	NR	NR	NR	-	-
263 Int Foursq Gos	2	53	75	75 *	-	.1
283 Luth—MO Synod	6	2,994	1,788	3,856	1.5	3.9
333 Malan Dioc Am	1	NR	NR	100	-	.1
339 Pent Ch of God	2	107	NR	260	.1	.3
355 Presb Ch (USA)	6	1,049	717	1,545 *	.6	1.5
356 Presb Ch Amer	1	289	325	414	.2	.4
360 Prim Bapt Chrch	1	NR	NR	NR	-	-
413 S.D.A.	3	214	NR	255	.1	.3
418 Southw Bapt Fel	1	NR	NR	NR	-	-
419 So Bapt Conv	30	19,417	9,261	25,450 *	10.2	25.5
443 Un C of Christ	1	198	69	260 *	.1	.3
449 Un Methodist	19	10,930	4,335	14,328 *	5.7	14.3
469 WELS	1	45	36	57	-	.1
498 Indep.Charis.	3	4,200	4,950	4,950	2.0	5.0
499 Indep.Non-Char	1	1,500	1,200	1,500	.6	1.5
WILSON	**35**	**5,236**	**2,837**	**19,318 ***	**59.6**	**100.0**
017 Amer Bapt Assn	1	63	NR	81 *	.2	.4
053 Assemb of God	2	139	155	211	.7	1.1
081 Catholic	5	NR	NR	12,242	37.8	63.4
151 L-D Saints	1	NR	NR	343	1.1	1.8
167 Chs of Christ	4	300	288	388	1.2	2.0
207 E.L.C.A.	4	987	461	1,245	3.8	6.4
360 Prim Bapt Chrch	1	NR	NR	NR	-	-
413 S.D.A.	1	30	NR	36	.1	.2
419 So Bapt Conv	12	2,563	1,380	3,290 *	10.2	17.0
449 Un Methodist	4	1,154	553	1,482 *	4.6	7.7
WINKLER	**19**	**2,972**	**881**	**5,890 ***	**82.1**	**100.0**
053 Assemb of God	1	23	20	27	.4	.5
056 Baha'i	0	1	NR	1	-	-
081 Catholic	1	NR	NR	2,071	28.9	35.2
093 Chr Ch (Disc)	1	26	20	33 *	.5	.6
127 Ch God (Cleve)	1	36	25	46 *	.6	.8
145 Ch God Prophcy	1	27	NR	34 *	.5	.6
165 Ch of Nazarene	1	19	0	19	.3	.3
167 Chs of Christ	3	168	160	237	3.3	4.0
193 Episcopal	1	NR	6	10	.1	.2
283 Luth—MO Synod	1	34	17	47	.7	.8
419 So Bapt Conv	6	2,287	504	2,917 *	40.7	49.5
449 Un Methodist	2	351	129	448 *	6.2	7.6
WISE	**78**	**14,079**	**6,310**	**20,100 ***	**41.2**	**100.0**
053 Assemb of God	9	453	482	667	1.4	3.3
056 Baha'i	0	8	NR	8	-	-
081 Catholic	2	NR	NR	1,848	3.8	9.2
089 Chr & Miss Al	1	50	NR	50	.1	.2
093 Chr Ch (Disc)	1	35	35	45 *	.1	.2
151 L-D Saints	1	NR	NR	292	.6	1.5
165 Ch of Nazarene	1	26	32	32	.1	.2
167 Chs of Christ	13	1,057	972	1,271	2.6	6.3
185 Cumber Presb	1	36	NR	46	.1	.2
193 Episcopal	2	NR	102	153	.3	.8
223 Free Will Bapt	1	42	NR	54 *	.1	.3
283 Luth—MO Synod	1	65	18	90	.2	.4
339 Pent Ch of God	1	60	NR	83	.2	.4
355 Presb Ch (USA)	1	63	25	80 *	.2	.4
419 So Bapt Conv	32	9,592	3,468	12,207 *	25.0	60.7
449 Un Methodist	10	2,142	889	2,724 *	5.6	13.6
499 Indep.Non-Char	1	450	287	450	.9	2.2
WOOD	**92**	**17,638**	**7,841**	**22,875 ***	**62.2**	**100.0**
017 Amer Bapt Assn	1	48	NR	57 *	.2	.2
053 Assemb of God	7	471	582	721	2.0	3.2
056 Baha'i	0	1	NR	1	-	-
059 Bapt Miss Assn	24	4,774	1,882	5,695 *	15.5	24.9
081 Catholic	2	NR	NR	1,199	3.3	5.2
093 Chr Ch (Disc)	4	414	173	494 *	1.3	2.2
127 Ch God (Cleve)	1	47	4	56 *	.2	.2
151 L-D Saints	1	NR	NR	318	.9	1.4
165 Ch of Nazarene	2	139	84	139	.4	.6
167 Chs of Christ	10	781	770	951	2.6	4.2
193 Episcopal	1	NR	54	154	.4	.7
263 Int Foursq Gos	1	5	22	22 *	.1	.1
339 Pent Ch of God	1	21	NR	81	.2	.4
355 Presb Ch (USA)	1	64	40	76 *	.2	.3
413 S.D.A.	1	72	NR	86	.2	.4
419 So Bapt Conv	19	8,468	2,933	10,100 *	27.5	44.2
449 Un Methodist	15	2,033	997	2,425 *	6.6	10.6
498 Indep.Charis.	1	300	300	300	.8	1.3
YOAKUM	**18**	**3,314**	**1,433**	**7,587 ***	**103.6**	**100.0**
053 Assemb of God	3	124	172	173	2.4	2.3
056 Baha'i	0	1	NR	1	-	-
081 Catholic	2	NR	NR	3,237	44.2	42.7
127 Ch God (Cleve)	1	81	11	106 *	1.4	1.4
165 Ch of Nazarene	1	29	23	46	.6	.6
167 Chs of Christ	3	343	323	450	6.1	5.9
419 So Bapt Conv	6	2,212	721	2,889 *	39.5	38.1
449 Un Methodist	2	524	183	685 *	9.4	9.0
YOUNG	**55**	**11,783**	**4,115**	**16,228 ***	**90.4**	**100.0**
053 Assemb of God	4	247	302	446	2.5	2.7
056 Baha'i	1	77	NR	77	.4	.5
081 Catholic	2	NR	NR	1,353	7.5	8.3
093 Chr Ch (Disc)	2	122	53	150 *	.8	.9
127 Ch God (Cleve)	4	346	158	432 *	2.4	2.7
151 L-D Saints	1	NR	NR	184	1.0	1.1
165 Ch of Nazarene	1	88	29	88	.5	.5
167 Chs of Christ	10	901	796	1,105	6.2	6.8
185 Cumber Presb	1	102	NR	127	.7	.8
193 Episcopal	2	NR	26	59	.3	.4
283 Luth—MO Synod	2	349	125	424	2.4	2.6
339 Pent Ch of God	2	41	NR	104	.6	.6
355 Presb Ch (USA)	1	413	190	507 *	2.8	3.1
360 Prim Bapt Chrch	1	NR	NR	NR	-	-
413 S.D.A.	1	11	NR	13	.1	.1
419 So Bapt Conv	13	6,728	1,790	8,263 *	46.1	50.9
449 Un Methodist	7	2,358	646	2,896 *	16.1	17.8

NR–Not Reported *Total adherents estimated from known number of communicant, confirmed, full members. - Represents a percentage less than 0.1. Percentages may not total 100 due to rounding.

Table 4: Religious Congregations by County and Group: 2000

Religious Group	Number of Churches, Synagogues, Mosques, or Temples	Number of Communicant, Confirmed, or Full Members	Number of Attendees	Total Adherents: Number of Adherents	Total Adherents: % of Total Pop.	Total Adherents: % of Total Adh.
ZAPATA	**11**	**419**	**247**	**4,253 ***	**34.9**	**100.0**
040 Ap Chr Ch-Amer	1	7	12	12 *	.1	.3
081 Catholic	4	NR	NR	3,644	29.9	85.7
151 L-D Saints	1	NR	NR	74	.6	1.7
167 Chs of Christ	1	50	100	62	.5	1.5
283 Luth—MO Synod	1	72	34	72	.6	1.7
419 So Bapt Conv	2	251	71	337 *	2.8	7.9
449 Un Methodist	1	39	30	52 *	.4	1.2
ZAVALA	**14**	**1,125**	**668**	**5,552 ***	**47.9**	**100.0**
053 Assemb of God	2	127	320	680	5.9	12.2
056 Baha'i	0	2	NR	2	-	-
081 Catholic	2	NR	NR	3,518	30.3	63.4
097 Chr Chs&Chs Cr	1	35	NR	48 *	.4	.9
167 Chs of Christ	1	75	75	95	.8	1.7
360 Prim Bapt Chrch	1	NR	NR	NR	-	-
419 So Bapt Conv	4	657	197	897 *	7.7	16.2
449 Un Methodist	3	229	76	312 *	2.7	5.6
UTAH						
The State.....	4,343	45,170	34,243	1,668,851 *	74.7	100.0
BEAVER	**17**	**61**	**20**	**4,574 ***	**76.2**	**100.0**
081 Catholic	1	NR	NR	100	1.7	2.2
089 Chr & Miss Al	1	20	NR	32	.5	.7
151 L-D Saints	12	NR	NR	4,389	73.1	96.0
413 S.D.A.	1	15	NR	18	.3	.4
419 So Bapt Conv	1	0	0	0 *	-	-
449 Un Methodist	1	26	20	35 *	.6	.8
BOX ELDER	**101**	**644**	**548**	**36,588 ***	**85.6**	**100.0**
053 Assemb of God	1	71	95	95	.2	.3
056 Baha'i	0	1	NR	1	-	-
076 Buddhism	1	NR	NR	NR	-	-
081 Catholic	2	NR	NR	1,250	2.9	3.4
105 Christian Ref	1	80	70	110 *	.3	.3
151 L-D Saints	88	NR	NR	34,399	80.5	94.0
167 Chs of Christ	1	25	23	34	.1	.1
193 Episcopal	1	NR	41	75	.2	.2
207 E.L.C.A.	1	102	60	124	.3	.3
297 Mennonite;Other	1	20	NR	27 *	.1	.1
355 Presb Ch (USA)	1	108	100	148 *	.3	.4
419 So Bapt Conv	2	188	94	258 *	.6	.7
449 Un Methodist	1	49	65	67 *	.2	.2
CACHE	**251**	**1,124**	**1,001**	**77,473 ***	**84.8**	**100.0**
053 Assemb of God	1	72	106	120	.1	.2
056 Baha'i	1	31	NR	31	-	-
081 Catholic	1	NR	NR	1,953	2.1	2.5
127 Ch God (Cleve)	1	60	81	81 *	.1	.1
151 L-D Saints	234	NR	NR	73,571	80.5	95.0
167 Chs of Christ	1	24	27	40	-	.1
193 Episcopal	1	NR	81	211	.2	.3
203 Evan Free Ch	1	10	30	30	-	-
207 E.L.C.A.	1	97	116	165	.2	.2
226 Friends-USA	1	30	NR	40 *	-	.1
267 Muslim Est	1	NR	55	163	.2	.2
283 Luth—MO Synod	1	77	85	126	.1	.2
290 Metro Comm Ch	1	6	5	8 *	-	-
355 Presb Ch (USA)	1	289	153	382 *	.4	.5
413 S.D.A.	1	100	NR	119	.1	.2
419 So Bapt Conv	2	268	262	354 *	.4	.5
435 Unitarian-Univ	1	60	NR	79 *	.1	.1
CARBON	**47**	**863**	**410**	**14,681 ***	**71.9**	**100.0**
053 Assemb of God	2	42	55	65	.3	.4
056 Baha'i	0	8	NR	8	-	.1
081 Catholic	3	NR	NR	2,825	13.8	19.2
089 Chr & Miss Al	2	148	NR	361	1.8	2.5

Religious Group	Number of Churches, Synagogues, Mosques, or Temples	Number of Communicant, Confirmed, or Full Members	Number of Attendees	Total Adherents: Number of Adherents	Total Adherents: % of Total Pop.	Total Adherents: % of Total Adh.
145 Ch God Prophcy	1	26	NR	33 *	.2	.2
151 L-D Saints	27	NR	NR	10,098	49.4	68.8
167 Chs of Christ	1	45	50	59	.3	.4
193 Episcopal	2	NR	40	68	.3	.5
207 E.L.C.A.	1	56	34	97	.5	.7
246 Greek Orthodox	1	NR	NR	348	1.7	2.4
263 Int Foursq Gos	1	60	61	76 *	.4	.5
339 Pent Ch of God	1	6	NR	46	.2	.3
413 S.D.A.	1	40	NR	48	.2	.3
419 So Bapt Conv	3	302	125	384 *	1.9	2.6
449 Un Methodist	1	130	45	165 *	.8	1.1
DAGGETT	**2**	**NR**	**NR**	**489**	**53.1**	**100.0**
151 L-D Saints	2	NR	NR	489	53.1	100.0
DAVIS	**442**	**4,460**	**3,092**	**186,854 ***	**78.2**	**100.0**
017 Amer Bapt Assn	1	20	NR	27 *	-	-
019 Amer Bapt USA	2	366	229	501 *	.2	.3
053 Assemb of God	4	578	747	1,540	.6	.8
056 Baha'i	0	71	NR	71	-	-
076 Buddhism	1	NR	NR	NR	-	-
081 Catholic	3	NR	NR	7,270	3.0	3.9
084 Calvary Chapel	1	NR	NR	NR	-	-
127 Ch God (Cleve)	1	10	10	14 *	-	-
145 Ch God Prophcy	1	26	NR	36 *	-	-
151 L-D Saints	407	NR	NR	172,172	72.0	92.1
165 Ch of Nazarene	1	72	64	139	.1	.1
167 Chs of Christ	2	152	168	224	.1	.1
179 Consrv Bapt	1	NR	95	95	-	.1
193 Episcopal	2	NR	108	337	.1	.2
207 E.L.C.A.	1	188	95	256	.1	.1
283 Luth—MO Synod	2	372	144	586	.2	.3
355 Presb Ch (USA)	1	227	180	311 *	.1	.2
356 Presb Ch Amer	1	43	55	56	-	-
419 So Bapt Conv	6	1,829	796	2,502 *	1.0	1.3
443 Un C of Christ	1	170	95	233 *	.1	.1
463 Vineyard	2	260	240	356 *	.1	.2
469 WELS	1	76	66	128	.1	.1
DUCHESNE	**34**	**273**	**220**	**10,876 ***	**75.7**	**100.0**
053 Assemb of God	1	51	68	104	.7	1.0
056 Baha'i	0	1	NR	1	-	-
081 Catholic	1	NR	NR	150	1.0	1.4
151 L-D Saints	28	NR	NR	10,335	71.9	95.0
283 Luth—MO Synod	1	24	12	15	.1	.1
355 Presb Ch (USA)	1	19	23	26 *	.2	.2
419 So Bapt Conv	2	178	117	245 *	1.7	2.3
EMERY	**28**	**28**	**90**	**8,184 ***	**75.4**	**100.0**
081 Catholic	5	NR	NR	75	.7	.9
151 L-D Saints	20	NR	NR	8,004	73.7	97.8
203 Evan Free Ch	1	0	67	67	.6	.8
419 So Bapt Conv	2	28	23	38 *	.3	.5
GARFIELD	**15**	**14**	**NR**	**3,706 ***	**78.3**	**100.0**
151 L-D Saints	14	NR	NR	3,688	77.9	99.5
419 So Bapt Conv	1	14	0	18 *	.4	.5
GRAND	**18**	**854**	**416**	**4,128 ***	**48.7**	**100.0**
019 Amer Bapt USA	1	206	141	258 *	3.0	6.3
053 Assemb of God	1	45	60	75	.9	1.8
081 Catholic	1	NR	NR	425	5.0	10.3
089 Chr & Miss Al	1	20	NR	30	.4	.7
151 L-D Saints	6	NR	NR	2,418	28.5	58.6
167 Chs of Christ	1	40	40	50	.6	1.2
193 Episcopal	1	NR	54	182	2.1	4.4
226 Friends-USA	1	30	NR	38 *	.4	.9
283 Luth—MO Synod	1	23	29	40	.5	1.0
413 S.D.A.	2	42	NR	50	.6	1.2
419 So Bapt Conv	2	448	92	562 *	6.6	13.6

NR–Not Reported *Total adherents estimated from known number of communicant, confirmed, full members. - Represents a percentage less than 0.1. Percentages may not total 100 due to rounding.

Table 4: Religious Congregations by County and Group: 2000

Religious Group	Number of Churches, Synagogues, Mosques, or Temples	Number of Communicant, Confirmed, or Full Members	Number of Attendees	Total Adherents: Number of Adherents	Total Adherents: % of Total Pop.	Total Adherents: % of Total Adh.
IRON	**91**	**469**	**438**	**25,774 ***	**76.3**	**100.0**
053 Assemb of God	1	30	44	80	.2	.3
056 Baha'i	0	3	NR	3	-	-
076 Buddhism	1	NR	NR	NR	-	-
081 Catholic	3	NR	NR	1,200	3.6	4.7
084 Calvary Chapel	1	NR	NR	NR	-	-
151 L-D Saints	78	NR	NR	23,834	70.6	92.5
167 Chs of Christ	1	28	30	40	.1	.2
179 Consrv Bapt	1	NR	35	35	.1	.1
193 Episcopal	1	NR	20	46	.1	.2
283 Luth—MO Synod	1	59	36	76	.2	.3
355 Presb Ch (USA)	1	150	132	198 *	.6	.8
419 So Bapt Conv	2	199	141	262 *	.8	1.0
JUAB	**18**	**32**	**NR**	**6,741 ***	**81.8**	**100.0**
056 Baha'i	0	1	NR	1	-	-
081 Catholic	1	NR	NR	85	1.0	1.3
151 L-D Saints	16	NR	NR	6,611	80.3	98.1
449 Un Methodist	1	31	0	44 *	.5	.7
KANE	**19**	**195**	**302**	**4,224 ***	**69.9**	**100.0**
056 Baha'i	0	1	NR	1	-	-
081 Catholic	1	NR	NR	150	2.5	3.6
093 Chr Ch (Disc)	1	68	50	87 *	1.4	2.1
151 L-D Saints	12	NR	NR	3,756	62.1	88.9
179 Consrv Bapt	1	NR	41	41	.7	1.0
283 Luth—MO Synod	1	36	36	41	.7	1.0
355 Presb Ch (USA)	1	13	50	50 *	.8	1.2
443 Un C of Christ	1	60	50	76 *	1.3	1.8
449 Un Methodist	1	17	75	22 *	.4	.5
MILLARD	**33**	**209**	**260**	**10,341 ***	**83.4**	**100.0**
056 Baha'i	0	1	NR	1	-	-
081 Catholic	2	NR	NR	55	.4	.5
151 L-D Saints	26	NR	NR	9,926	80.0	96.0
167 Chs of Christ	1	17	15	26	.2	.3
203 Evan Free Ch	1	69	125	125	1.0	1.2
263 Int Foursq Gos	1	26	77	77 *	.6	.7
355 Presb Ch (USA)	1	33	23	45 *	.4	.4
419 So Bapt Conv	1	63	20	86 *	.7	.8
MORGAN	**17**	**35**	**20**	**6,284 ***	**88.1**	**100.0**
019 Amer Bapt USA	1	35	20	48 *	.7	.8
151 L-D Saints	16	NR	NR	6,236	87.5	99.2
PIUTE	**3**	**NR**	**NR**	**943**	**65.7**	**100.0**
151 L-D Saints	3	NR	NR	943	65.7	100.0
RICH	**5**	**NR**	**NR**	**1,665**	**84.9**	**100.0**
151 L-D Saints	5	NR	NR	1,665	84.9	100.0
SALT LAKE	**1,369**	**22,744**	**16,479**	**606,391 ***	**67.5**	**100.0**
017 Amer Bapt Assn	1	20	NR	26 *	-	-
019 Amer Bapt USA	3	703	633	920 *	.1	.2
034 Ant Orth of NA	1	235	NR	470	.1	.1
039 Ap Chr Ch(Naz)	1	4	20	20 *	-	-
050 Armen Ap Etchm	1	0	NR	462	.1	.1
053 Assemb of God	12	1,764	2,508	3,264	.4	.5
056 Baha'i	3	338	NR	338	-	.1
076 Buddhism	10	NR	NR	NR	-	-
081 Catholic	22	NR	NR	53,548	6.0	8.8
084 Calvary Chapel	1	NR	NR	NR	-	-
089 Chr & Miss Al	2	60	NR	410	-	.1
093 Chr Ch (Disc)	2	299	149	391 *	-	.1
097 Chr Chs&Chs Cr	2	675	NR	883 *	.1	.1
105 Christian Ref	4	270	185	353 *	-	.1
127 Ch God (Cleve)	1	25	25	33 *	-	-
145 Ch God Prophcy	2	53	NR	68 *	-	-
151 L-D Saints	1,198	NR	NR	503,476	56.0	83.0
165 Ch of Nazarene	2	218	225	1,393	.2	.2
167 Chs of Christ	2	222	300	341	-	.1
173 Comm of Christ	1	134	NR	134	-	-
175 Congr Chr Chs	1	327	150	428 *	-	.1
179 Consrv Bapt	3	NR	301	301	-	-
193 Episcopal	5	NR	974	4,077	.5	.7
203 Evan Free Ch	3	310	670	670	.1	.1
207 E.L.C.A.	5	2,593	1,241	3,565	.4	.6
223 Free Will Bapt	1	0	NR	0 *	-	-
226 Friends-USA	1	30	NR	39 *	-	-
237 Menn Br US Conf	1	0	NR	0 *	-	-
246 Greek Orthodox	2	NR	NR	3,144	.3	.5
251 Holy Orth in NA	1	NR	NR	15	-	-
252 Hindu	1	NR	NR	NR	-	-
263 Int Foursq Gos	4	367	507	507 *	.1	.1
264 Int Chs of Crst	1	85	166	129	-	-
267 Muslim Est	3	NR	681	3,482	.4	.6
283 Luth—MO Synod	4	1,540	763	2,159	.2	.4
290 Metro Comm Ch	1	16	31	31 *	-	-
331 OCA: Ter Diocs	1	7	NR	20	-	-
335 Orth Pres Ch	1	27	68	68	-	-
349 Pent Holiness	1	35	40	46 *	-	-
355 Presb Ch (USA)	8	2,503	1,578	3,275 *	.4	.5
356 Presb Ch Amer	2	38	140	140	-	-
388 Reg Bapt Gen As	2	94	90	123 *	-	-
403 Salvation Army	2	296	189	296	-	-
413 S.D.A.	3	410	NR	488	.1	.1
416 Sikh	1	NR	NR	NR	-	-
418 Southw Bapt Fel	1	NR	NR	NR	-	-
419 So Bapt Conv	17	3,802	1,987	4,977 *	.6	.8
435 Unitarian-Univ	2	563	NR	737 *	.1	.1
443 Un C of Christ	3	568	303	744 *	.1	.1
449 Un Methodist	9	3,477	1,310	4,552 *	.5	.8
463 Vineyard	2	480	520	628 *	.1	.1
469 WELS	1	156	125	220	-	-
496 Jewish Est	4	NR	NR	4,200	.5	.7
498 Indep.Charis.	1	0	600	800	.1	.1
SAN JUAN	**34**	**276**	**240**	**6,220 ***	**43.2**	**100.0**
053 Assemb of God	1	23	30	31	.2	.5
056 Baha'i	1	46	NR	46	.3	.7
081 Catholic	4	NR	NR	125	.9	2.0
151 L-D Saints	19	NR	NR	5,543	38.5	89.1
167 Chs of Christ	2	21	22	26	.2	.4
193 Episcopal	3	NR	51	201	1.4	3.2
203 Evan Free Ch	1	45	30	45	.3	.7
419 So Bapt Conv	3	141	107	203 *	1.4	3.3
SANPETE	**60**	**99**	**66**	**18,874 ***	**82.9**	**100.0**
056 Baha'i	0	1	NR	1	-	-
081 Catholic	2	NR	NR	45	.2	.2
151 L-D Saints	55	NR	NR	18,692	82.1	99.0
355 Presb Ch (USA)	1	22	35	35 *	.2	.2
419 So Bapt Conv	2	76	31	101 *	.4	.5
SEVIER	**41**	**294**	**173**	**16,164 ***	**85.8**	**100.0**
053 Assemb of God	1	44	63	150	.8	.9
056 Baha'i	0	3	NR	3	-	-
081 Catholic	1	NR	NR	180	1.0	1.1
151 L-D Saints	35	NR	NR	15,499	82.3	95.9
226 Friends-USA	1	30	NR	40 *	.2	.2
283 Luth—MO Synod	1	53	27	73	.4	.5
355 Presb Ch (USA)	1	26	30	35 *	.2	.2
419 So Bapt Conv	1	138	53	184 *	1.0	1.1
SUMMIT	**42**	**1,392**	**1,474**	**16,588 ***	**55.8**	**100.0**
053 Assemb of God	1	30	24	40	.1	.2
056 Baha'i	0	11	NR	11	-	.1
076 Buddhism	1	NR	NR	NR	-	-
081 Catholic	1	NR	NR	3,162	10.6	19.1
084 Calvary Chapel	1	NR	NR	NR	-	-
151 L-D Saints	30	NR	NR	10,960	36.9	66.1
179 Consrv Bapt	1	NR	45	45	.2	.3

NR–Not Reported   *Total adherents estimated from known number of communicant, confirmed, full members.   - Represents a percentage less than 0.1.   Percentages may not total 100 due to rounding.

Table 4: Religious Congregations by County and Group: 2000

Religious Group	Number of Churches, Synagogues, Mosques, or Temples	Number of Communicant, Confirmed, or Full Members	Number of Attendees	Total Adherents		
				Number of Adherents	% of Total Pop.	% of Total Adh.
193 Episcopal	1	NR	184	340	1.1	2.0
203 Evan Free Ch	1	85	180	180	.6	1.1
207 E.L.C.A.	1	259	159	383	1.3	2.3
356 Presb Ch Amer	1	43	75	75	.3	.5
419 So Bapt Conv	0	45	55	58 *	.2	.3
449 Un Methodist	1	499	302	643 *	2.2	3.9
463 Vineyard	1	420	450	541 *	1.8	3.3
496 Jewish Est	1	NR	NR	150	.5	.9
TOOELE	**71**	**555**	**488**	**32,315 ***	**79.3**	**100.0**
053 Assemb of God	1	60	96	144	.4	.4
081 Catholic	3	NR	NR	5,559	13.6	17.2
151 L-D Saints	59	NR	NR	25,837	63.4	80.0
167 Chs of Christ	1	20	30	28	.1	.1
179 Consrv Bapt	1	NR	30	30	.1	.1
193 Episcopal	1	NR	25	61	.1	.2
207 E.L.C.A.	1	84	81	134	.3	.4
283 Luth—MO Synod	1	77	44	89	.2	.3
419 So Bapt Conv	2	174	182	240 *	.6	.7
449 Un Methodist	1	140	0	193 *	.5	.6
UINTAH	**54**	**953**	**529**	**17,900 ***	**71.0**	**100.0**
017 Amer Bapt Assn	1	30	NR	40 *	.2	.2
053 Assemb of God	2	107	145	247	1.0	1.4
056 Baha'i	0	10	NR	10	-	.1
081 Catholic	2	NR	NR	680	2.7	3.8
097 Chr Chs&Chs Cr	1	120	NR	161 *	.6	.9
151 L-D Saints	38	NR	NR	15,536	61.6	86.8
167 Chs of Christ	1	50	55	74	.3	.4
193 Episcopal	3	NR	110	302	1.2	1.7
283 Luth—MO Synod	1	123	75	161	.6	.9
339 Pent Ch of God	1	50	NR	70	.3	.4
413 S.D.A.	1	13	NR	15	.1	.1
419 So Bapt Conv	2	392	108	526 *	2.1	2.9
443 Un C of Christ	1	58	36	78 *	.3	.4
UTAH	**991**	**1,722**	**1,664**	**331,411 ***	**89.9**	**100.0**
053 Assemb of God	3	281	383	746	.2	.2
056 Baha'i	0	34	NR	34	-	-
081 Catholic	3	NR	NR	3,537	1.0	1.1
084 Calvary Chapel	1	NR	NR	NR	-	-
127 Ch God (Cleve)	1	25	35	35 *	-	-
151 L-D Saints	961	NR	NR	324,790	88.1	98.0
165 Ch of Nazarene	1	26	45	77	-	-
167 Chs of Christ	1	20	20	28	-	-
173 Comm of Christ	1	31	NR	31	-	-
179 Consrv Bapt	1	NR	25	25	-	-
193 Episcopal	1	NR	58	169	-	.1
203 Evan Free Ch	1	170	360	360	.1	.1
207 E.L.C.A.	1	42	33	66	-	-
252 Hindu	1	NR	NR	NR	-	-
263 Int Foursq Gos	2	180	234	246 *	.1	.1
283 Luth—MO Synod	1	104	59	171	-	.1
355 Presb Ch (USA)	2	171	139	234 *	.1	.1
388 Reg Bapt Gen As	2	51	70	79 *	-	-
413 S.D.A.	2	116	NR	138	-	-
419 So Bapt Conv	3	307	113	420 *	.1	.1
443 Un C of Christ	2	164	90	225 *	.1	.1
WASATCH	**29**	**29**	**29**	**11,281 ***	**74.1**	**100.0**
056 Baha'i	0	2	NR	2	-	-
081 Catholic	1	NR	NR	175	1.2	1.6
151 L-D Saints	28	NR	NR	11,067	72.7	98.1
419 So Bapt Conv	0	27	29	37 *	.2	.3
WASHINGTON	**187**	**1,501**	**996**	**67,888 ***	**75.1**	**100.0**
019 Amer Bapt USA	1	90	75	118 *	.1	.2
053 Assemb of God	1	61	89	115	.1	.2
056 Baha'i	0	9	NR	9	-	-
081 Catholic	1	NR	NR	2,800	3.1	4.1
084 Calvary Chapel	1	NR	NR	NR	-	-
089 Chr & Miss Al	1	43	NR	113	.1	.2
151 L-D Saints	170	NR	NR	62,809	69.5	92.5
167 Chs of Christ	1	14	16	18	-	-
193 Episcopal	1	NR	106	277	.3	.4
207 E.L.C.A.	1	107	66	115	.1	.2
283 Luth—MO Synod	2	241	152	288	.3	.4
355 Presb Ch (USA)	1	301	170	396 *	.4	.6
388 Reg Bapt Gen As	1	36	40	47 *	.1	.1
413 S.D.A.	2	46	NR	55	.1	.1
419 So Bapt Conv	2	431	188	567 *	.6	.8
449 Un Methodist	1	122	94	161 *	.2	.2
WAYNE	**10**	**16**	**20**	**2,040 ***	**81.3**	**100.0**
056 Baha'i	0	1	NR	1	-	-
081 Catholic	2	NR	NR	10	.4	.5
151 L-D Saints	7	NR	NR	2,009	80.1	98.5
419 So Bapt Conv	1	15	20	20 *	.8	1.0
WEBER	**314**	**6,328**	**5,268**	**138,254 ***	**70.3**	**100.0**
019 Amer Bapt USA	1	182	105	239 *	.1	.2
053 Assemb of God	5	565	844	1,360	.7	1.0
056 Baha'i	1	48	NR	48	-	-
076 Buddhism	1	NR	NR	NR	-	-
081 Catholic	5	NR	NR	11,726	6.0	8.5
097 Chr Chs&Chs Cr	1	140	NR	184 *	.1	.1
105 Christian Ref	1	65	50	86 *	-	.1
127 Ch God (Cleve)	3	336	171	442 *	.2	.3
151 L-D Saints	257	NR	NR	115,106	58.6	83.3
167 Chs of Christ	1	31	28	34	-	-
173 Comm of Christ	1	48	NR	48	-	-
179 Consrv Bapt	2	NR	1,088	1,088	.6	.8
193 Episcopal	1	NR	128	507	.3	.4
203 Evan Free Ch	1	55	140	140	.1	.1
207 E.L.C.A.	3	1,063	552	1,521	.8	1.1
223 Free Will Bapt	1	0	NR	0 *	-	-
226 Friends-USA	1	30	NR	39 *	-	-
246 Greek Orthodox	1	NR	NR	309	.2	.2
263 Int Foursq Gos	3	372	459	489 *	.2	.4
283 Luth—MO Synod	1	520	270	737	.4	.5
290 Metro Comm Ch	1	35	39	46 *	-	-
339 Pent Ch of God	2	18	NR	75	-	.1
355 Presb Ch (USA)	3	662	332	871 *	.4	.6
403 Salvation Army	1	72	54	173	.1	.1
410 Serb Orth USA	1	NR	NR	120	.1	.1
413 S.D.A.	3	231	NR	276	.1	.2
416 Sikh	1	NR	NR	NR	-	-
419 So Bapt Conv	5	924	577	1,216 *	.6	.9
435 Unitarian-Univ	1	131	NR	172 *	.1	.1
443 Un C of Christ	2	123	90	162 *	.1	.1
449 Un Methodist	2	677	341	890 *	.5	.6
496 Jewish Est	1	NR	NR	150	.1	.1
VERMONT						
The State.....	775	53,713	28,822	238,251 *	39.1	100.0
ADDISON	**46**	**3,452**	**1,922**	**13,318 ***	**37.0**	**100.0**
019 Amer Bapt USA	5	578	365	712 *	2.0	5.3
056 Baha'i	0	15	NR	15	-	.1
076 Buddhism	3	NR	NR	NR	-	-
081 Catholic	6	NR	NR	8,277	23.0	62.1
105 Christian Ref	1	209	165	257 *	.7	1.9
151 L-D Saints	1	NR	NR	169	.5	1.3
165 Ch of Nazarene	1	85	97	110	.3	.8
167 Chs of Christ	1	20	28	28	.1	.2
176 Congr Ad Afl	1	29	NR	36 *	.1	.3
179 Consrv Bapt	1	NR	70	70	.2	.5
181 Consrv Congr	1	73	46	90 *	.3	.7
193 Episcopal	2	NR	179	495	1.4	3.7
226 Friends-USA	2	86	NR	106 *	.3	.8
413 S.D.A.	1	34	NR	40	.1	.3
419 So Bapt Conv	1	42	30	52 *	.1	.4
435 Unitarian-Univ	1	108	NR	133 *	.4	1.0

NR–Not Reported *Total adherents estimated from known number of communicant, confirmed, full members. - Represents a percentage less than 0.1. Percentages may not total 100 due to rounding.

Table 4: Religious Congregations by County and Group: 2000

Religious Group	Number of Churches, Synagogues, Mosques, or Temples	Number of Communicant, Confirmed, or Full Members	Number of Attendees	Total Adherents		
				Number of Adherents	% of Total Pop.	% of Total Adh.
443 Un C of Christ	8	1,016	437	1,251 *	3.5	9.4
449 Un Methodist	9	1,038	505	1,278 *	3.6	9.6
455 Un Ref Chs N.A.	1	119	NR	199	.6	1.5
BENNINGTON	**53**	**3,900**	**2,211**	**16,626 ***	**44.9**	**100.0**
019 Amer Bapt USA	5	976	303	1,186 *	3.2	7.1
053 Assemb of God	2	322	323	560	1.5	3.4
056 Baha'i	0	21	NR	21	.1	.1
076 Buddhism	1	NR	NR	NR	-	-
081 Catholic	10	NR	NR	9,548	25.8	57.4
089 Chr & Miss Al	1	71	NR	176	.5	1.1
097 Chr Chs&Chs Cr	1	50	NR	61 *	.2	.4
123 Ch God (Ander)	1	NR	20	20	.1	.1
151 L-D Saints	2	NR	NR	237	.6	1.4
167 Chs of Christ	1	24	35	40	.1	.2
175 Congr Chr Chs	2	129	105	157 *	.4	.9
176 Congr Ad Afl	1	49	NR	60 *	.2	.4
179 Consrv Bapt	1	NR	25	25	.1	.2
193 Episcopal	3	NR	389	1,131	3.1	6.8
207 E.L.C.A.	1	74	44	104	.3	.6
226 Friends-USA	1	43	NR	52 *	.1	.3
403 Salvation Army	1	21	19	21	.1	.1
419 So Bapt Conv	1	18	40	22 *	.1	.1
435 Unitarian-Univ	1	36	NR	44 *	.1	.3
443 Un C of Christ	6	1,168	508	1,419 *	3.8	8.5
449 Un Methodist	8	898	400	1,092 *	3.0	6.6
496 Jewish Est	3	NR	NR	650	1.8	3.9
CALEDONIA	**52**	**3,346**	**1,615**	**12,477 ***	**42.0**	**100.0**
019 Amer Bapt USA	5	437	170	536 *	1.8	4.3
053 Assemb of God	2	61	80	110	.4	.9
056 Baha'i	0	3	NR	3	-	-
076 Buddhism	3	NR	NR	NR	-	-
081 Catholic	5	NR	NR	7,588	25.5	60.8
151 L-D Saints	1	NR	NR	249	.8	2.0
165 Ch of Nazarene	1	0	0	0	-	-
176 Congr Ad Afl	1	246	NR	302 *	1.0	2.4
193 Episcopal	3	NR	119	350	1.2	2.8
355 Presb Ch (USA)	3	247	140	303 *	1.0	2.4
413 S.D.A.	1	56	NR	67	.2	.5
419 So Bapt Conv	4	168	134	206 *	.7	1.7
435 Unitarian-Univ	2	35	NR	43 *	.1	.3
443 Un C of Christ	12	964	496	1,183 *	4.0	9.5
449 Un Methodist	8	1,129	476	1,387 *	4.7	11.1
496 Jewish Est	1	NR	NR	150	.5	1.2
CHITTENDEN	**99**	**9,854**	**5,685**	**58,345 ***	**39.8**	**100.0**
017 Amer Bapt Assn	1	20	NR	24 *	-	-
019 Amer Bapt USA	7	947	347	1,158 *	.8	2.0
053 Assemb of God	4	319	378	575	.4	1.0
056 Baha'i	1	84	NR	84	.1	.1
057 Bapt Gen Conf	1	150	340	340 *	.2	.6
076 Buddhism	3	NR	NR	NR	-	-
081 Catholic	21	NR	NR	37,143	25.3	63.7
084 Calvary Chapel	1	NR	NR	NR	-	-
089 Chr & Miss Al	5	577	NR	2,931	2.0	5.0
151 L-D Saints	2	NR	NR	787	.5	1.3
165 Ch of Nazarene	1	76	210	210	.1	.4
167 Chs of Christ	2	114	160	172	.1	.3
193 Episcopal	6	NR	638	2,085	1.4	3.6
201 Evan Cov Ch	1	96	142	142 *	.1	.2
207 E.L.C.A.	2	407	175	583	.4	1.0
221 Free Methodist	1	19	19	23	-	-
226 Friends-USA	1	43	NR	53 *	-	.1
246 Greek Orthodox	1	NR	NR	201	.1	.3
263 Int Foursq Gos	1	5	9	9 *	-	-
264 Int Chs of Crst	1	46	71	63	-	.1
267 Muslim Est	1	NR	40	100	.1	.2
283 Luth—MO Synod	1	301	139	408	.3	.7
355 Presb Ch (USA)	1	72	60	88 *	.1	.2
403 Salvation Army	1	106	23	255	.2	.4
413 S.D.A.	1	57	NR	68	-	.1
419 So Bapt Conv	2	46	120	56 *	-	.1
435 Unitarian-Univ	2	564	NR	689 *	.5	1.2
443 Un C of Christ	12	3,086	1,583	3,773 *	2.6	6.5
449 Un Methodist	12	2,719	1,231	3,325 *	2.3	5.7
496 Jewish Est	3	NR	NR	3,000	2.0	5.1
ESSEX	**14**	**333**	**160**	**1,419 ***	**22.0**	**100.0**
056 Baha'i	0	1	NR	1	-	.1
081 Catholic	3	NR	NR	904	14.0	63.7
176 Congr Ad Afl	1	4	NR	5 *	.1	.4
193 Episcopal	2	NR	39	103	1.6	7.3
226 Friends-USA	1	43	NR	53 *	.8	3.7
443 Un C of Christ	1	22	8	27 *	.4	1.9
449 Un Methodist	6	263	113	326 *	5.0	23.0
FRANKLIN	**57**	**4,430**	**1,853**	**23,286 ***	**51.3**	**100.0**
019 Amer Bapt USA	4	506	170	647 *	1.4	2.8
053 Assemb of God	3	258	331	371	.8	1.6
056 Baha'i	0	7	NR	7	-	-
081 Catholic	14	NR	NR	16,280	35.8	69.9
127 Ch God (Cleve)	1	28	16	36 *	.1	.2
151 L-D Saints	1	NR	NR	240	.5	1.0
165 Ch of Nazarene	1	52	52	52	.1	.2
176 Congr Ad Afl	1	11	NR	14 *	-	.1
193 Episcopal	6	NR	183	672	1.5	2.9
245 Greek Orth Vslp	2	1,037	NR	1,720	3.8	7.4
356 Presb Ch Amer	1	37	60	60	.1	.3
443 Un C of Christ	6	401	125	513 *	1.1	2.2
449 Un Methodist	17	2,093	916	2,674 *	5.9	11.5
GRAND ISLE	**10**	**580**	**338**	**5,054 ***	**73.2**	**100.0**
056 Baha'i	0	1	NR	1	-	-
081 Catholic	5	NR	NR	3,957	57.3	78.3
193 Episcopal	1	NR	82	386	5.6	7.6
443 Un C of Christ	1	264	106	324 *	4.7	6.4
449 Un Methodist	3	315	150	386 *	5.6	7.6
LAMOILLE	**30**	**1,387**	**943**	**7,027 ***	**30.2**	**100.0**
053 Assemb of God	1	32	37	39	.2	.6
056 Baha'i	0	14	NR	14	.1	.2
081 Catholic	9	NR	NR	4,560	19.6	64.9
127 Ch God (Cleve)	1	8	6	10 *	-	.1
165 Ch of Nazarene	3	232	263	640	2.8	9.1
193 Episcopal	1	NR	58	184	.8	2.6
263 Int Foursq Gos	1	16	88	88 *	.4	1.3
286 E.PA Mennonite	1	21	NR	26 *	.1	.4
413 S.D.A.	1	30	NR	36	.2	.5
443 Un C of Christ	7	473	246	581 *	2.5	8.3
449 Un Methodist	4	561	245	689 *	3.0	9.8
496 Jewish Est	1	NR	NR	160	.7	2.3
ORANGE	**52**	**2,888**	**1,942**	**4,553 ***	**16.1**	**100.0**
019 Amer Bapt USA	3	218	164	269 *	1.0	5.9
056 Baha'i	0	15	NR	15	.1	.3
076 Buddhism	1	NR	NR	NR	-	-
081 Catholic	4	NR	NR	518	1.8	11.4
165 Ch of Nazarene	1	0	14	14	-	.3
176 Congr Ad Afl	1	17	NR	21 *	.1	.5
179 Consrv Bapt	1	NR	95	95	.3	2.1
193 Episcopal	2	NR	95	290	1.0	6.4
203 Evan Free Ch	1	55	95	95	.3	2.1
226 Friends-USA	2	86	NR	106 *	.4	2.3
283 Luth—MO Synod	1	107	80	180	.6	4.0
355 Presb Ch (USA)	1	38	27	47 *	.2	1.0
413 S.D.A.	1	20	NR	24	.1	.5
419 So Bapt Conv	4	265	207	327 *	1.2	7.2
435 Unitarian-Univ	1	11	NR	14 *	-	.3
443 Un C of Christ	19	1,463	748	1,806 *	6.4	39.7
449 Un Methodist	9	593	417	732 *	2.6	16.1
ORLEANS	**47**	**2,095**	**1,665**	**10,981 ***	**41.8**	**100.0**
019 Amer Bapt USA	1	90	35	111 *	.4	1.0

NR–Not Reported   *Total adherents estimated from known number of communicant, confirmed, full members.   - Represents a percentage less than 0.1.   Percentages may not total 100 due to rounding.

Table 4: Religious Congregations by County and Group: 2000

Religious Group	Number of Churches, Synagogues, Mosques, or Temples	Number of Communicant, Confirmed, or Full Members	Number of Attendees	Total Adherents: Number of Adherents	Total Adherents: % of Total Pop.	Total Adherents: % of Total Adh.
053 Assemb of God	3	145	180	281	1.1	2.6
056 Baha'i	0	12	NR	12	-	.1
081 Catholic	9	NR	NR	7,775	29.6	70.8
127 Ch God (Cleve)	1	54	135	135 *	.5	1.2
151 L-D Saints	1	NR	NR	223	.8	2.0
165 Ch of Nazarene	2	72	78	96	.4	.9
167 Chs of Christ	1	17	25	30	.1	.3
181 Consrv Congr	1	54	30	66 *	.3	.6
193 Episcopal	1	NR	72	184	.7	1.7
203 Evan Free Ch	1	24	75	75	.3	.7
355 Presb Ch (USA)	1	84	60	103 *	.4	.9
413 S.D.A.	2	130	NR	155	.6	1.4
435 Unitarian-Univ	1	56	NR	69 *	.3	.6
443 Un C of Christ	12	783	518	962 *	3.7	8.8
449 Un Methodist	10	574	457	704 *	2.7	6.4
RUTLAND	**82**	**5,126**	**2,542**	**28,671 ***	**45.2**	**100.0**
017 Amer Bapt Assn	1	20	NR	24 *	-	.1
019 Amer Bapt USA	7	1,084	311	1,311 *	2.1	4.6
053 Assemb of God	2	100	135	356	.6	1.2
056 Baha'i	0	17	NR	17	-	.1
076 Buddhism	2	NR	NR	NR	-	-
081 Catholic	18	NR	NR	19,847	31.3	69.2
089 Chr & Miss Al	1	25	NR	83	.1	.3
097 Chr Chs&Chs Cr	1	60	NR	73 *	.1	.3
151 L-D Saints	1	NR	NR	200	.3	.7
175 Congr Chr Chs	1	50	80	60 *	.1	.2
176 Congr Ad Afl	1	10	NR	12 *	-	-
181 Consrv Congr	1	35	25	42 *	.1	.1
193 Episcopal	7	NR	342	1,042	1.6	3.6
207 E.L.C.A.	2	300	115	385	.6	1.3
226 Friends-USA	1	50	NR	60 *	.1	.2
246 Greek Orthodox	1	NR	NR	147	.2	.5
283 Luth—MO Synod	1	52	41	62	.1	.2
355 Presb Ch (USA)	1	26	15	31 *	-	.1
370 Ref Baptist Chs	1	NR	NR	NR	-	-
403 Salvation Army	1	51	43	164	.3	.6
413 S.D.A.	1	60	NR	71	.1	.2
419 So Bapt Conv	1	58	55	70 *	.1	.2
435 Unitarian-Univ	1	73	NR	88 *	.1	.3
443 Un C of Christ	13	1,805	744	2,183 *	3.4	7.6
449 Un Methodist	12	1,250	558	1,513 *	2.4	5.3
467 Wesleyan	2	0	78	180	.3	.6
496 Jewish Est	1	NR	NR	650	1.0	2.3
WASHINGTON	**80**	**5,938**	**2,755**	**24,608 ***	**42.4**	**100.0**
019 Amer Bapt USA	4	270	122	328 *	.6	1.3
053 Assemb of God	1	101	95	150	.3	.6
056 Baha'i	0	31	NR	31	.1	.1
076 Buddhism	2	NR	NR	NR	-	-
081 Catholic	11	NR	NR	15,123	26.1	61.5
089 Chr & Miss Al	4	115	NR	273	.5	1.1
145 Ch God Prophcy	2	164	NR	200 *	.3	.8
151 L-D Saints	1	NR	NR	455	.8	1.8
167 Chs of Christ	2	70	85	97	.2	.4
176 Congr Ad Afl	1	17	NR	21 *	-	.1
193 Episcopal	4	NR	333	906	1.6	3.7
203 Evan Free Ch	2	71	205	205	.4	.8
207 E.L.C.A.	1	45	28	56	.1	.2
226 Friends-USA	1	43	NR	52 *	.1	.2
331 OCA: Ter Diocs	1	35	NR	46	.1	.2
335 Orth Pres Ch	1	52	67	82	.1	.3
355 Presb Ch (USA)	2	223	100	271 *	.5	1.1
403 Salvation Army	1	58	78	92	.2	.4
419 So Bapt Conv	3	146	88	177 *	.3	.7
435 Unitarian-Univ	4	325	NR	395 *	.7	1.6
443 Un C of Christ	14	1,813	803	2,202 *	3.8	8.9
449 Un Methodist	15	2,321	710	2,820 *	4.9	11.5
467 Wesleyan	1	0	14	14	-	.1
469 WELS	1	38	27	52	.1	.2
496 Jewish Est	1	NR	NR	560	1.0	2.3

Religious Group	Number of Churches, Synagogues, Mosques, or Temples	Number of Communicant, Confirmed, or Full Members	Number of Attendees	Total Adherents: Number of Adherents	Total Adherents: % of Total Pop.	Total Adherents: % of Total Adh.
WINDHAM	**68**	**4,132**	**2,125**	**11,766 ***	**26.6**	**100.0**
019 Amer Bapt USA	14	1,055	422	1,279 *	2.9	10.9
053 Assemb of God	2	110	142	173	.4	1.5
056 Baha'i	1	67	NR	67	.2	.6
076 Buddhism	1	NR	NR	NR	-	-
081 Catholic	7	NR	NR	5,628	12.7	47.8
084 Calvary Chapel	1	NR	NR	NR	-	-
089 Chr & Miss Al	1	42	NR	99	.2	.8
097 Chr Chs&Chs Cr	1	20	NR	24 *	.1	.2
151 L-D Saints	1	NR	NR	142	.3	1.2
157 Ch of Brethren	1	52	66	66 *	.1	.6
167 Chs of Christ	1	61	84	105	.2	.9
176 Congr Ad Afl	1	29	NR	35 *	.1	.3
179 Consrv Bapt	1	NR	70	70	.2	.6
193 Episcopal	3	NR	189	377	.9	3.2
207 E.L.C.A.	1	126	72	190	.4	1.6
226 Friends-USA	1	43	NR	52 *	.1	.4
263 Int Foursq Gos	1	11	55	55 *	.1	.5
403 Salvation Army	1	23	9	23	.1	.2
413 S.D.A.	2	108	NR	129	.3	1.1
425 Tao	1	NR	NR	NR	-	-
435 Unitarian-Univ	1	105	NR	127 *	.3	1.1
443 Un C of Christ	19	1,973	878	2,393 *	5.4	20.3
449 Un Methodist	3	307	138	372 *	.8	3.2
496 Jewish Est	2	NR	NR	360	.8	3.1
WINDSOR	**85**	**6,252**	**3,066**	**20,120 ***	**35.0**	**100.0**
019 Amer Bapt USA	4	674	247	815 *	1.4	4.1
053 Assemb of God	4	104	140	233	.4	1.2
056 Baha'i	1	53	NR	53	.1	.3
081 Catholic	11	NR	NR	10,770	18.8	53.5
089 Chr & Miss Al	1	0	NR	15	-	.1
151 L-D Saints	1	NR	NR	344	.6	1.7
167 Chs of Christ	2	221	182	269	.5	1.3
176 Congr Ad Afl	1	5	NR	6 *	-	-
193 Episcopal	8	NR	445	958	1.7	4.8
203 Evan Free Ch	1	150	210	210	.4	1.0
226 Friends-USA	4	172	NR	208 *	.4	1.0
262 Int Cou Comm Ch	1	190	NR	230 *	.4	1.1
263 Int Foursq Gos	1	79	144	144 *	.3	.7
288 Mennonite USA	2	88	114	120 *	.2	.6
297 Mennonite;Other	1	81	NR	98 *	.2	.5
331 OCA: Ter Diocs	1	39	NR	50	.1	.2
413 S.D.A.	1	0	NR	0	-	-
419 So Bapt Conv	1	81	53	98 *	.2	.5
435 Unitarian-Univ	7	444	NR	537 *	.9	2.7
443 Un C of Christ	19	2,464	1,055	2,980 *	5.2	14.8
449 Un Methodist	12	1,407	476	1,702 *	3.0	8.5
496 Jewish Est	1	NR	NR	280	.5	1.4

VIRGINIA

Religious Group	Number of Churches, Synagogues, Mosques, or Temples	Number of Communicant, Confirmed, or Full Members	Number of Attendees	Total Adherents: Number of Adherents	Total Adherents: % of Total Pop.	Total Adherents: % of Total Adh.
The State.....	7,736	1,595,757	739,896	2,943,551 *	41.6	100.0
ACCOMACK	**86**	**9,861**	**4,674**	**13,465 ***	**35.2**	**100.0**
053 Assemb of God	2	36	54	70	.2	.5
056 Baha'i	0	22	NR	22	.1	.2
075 Brethren in Cr	1	17	22	22	.1	.2
081 Catholic	2	NR	NR	952	2.5	7.1
097 Chr Chs&Chs Cr	1	15	NR	18 *	-	.1
127 Ch God (Cleve)	2	330	250	407 *	1.1	3.0
167 Chs of Christ	2	69	47	93	.2	.7
193 Episcopal	4	NR	162	305	.8	2.3
283 Luth—MO Synod	1	33	23	35	.1	.3
355 Presb Ch (USA)	5	240	132	295 *	.8	2.2
419 So Bapt Conv	17	3,142	1,283	3,868 *	10.1	28.7
449 Un Methodist	47	5,957	2,687	7,338 *	19.2	54.5
467 Wesleyan	2	0	14	40	.1	.3
ALBEMARLE	**93**	**13,117**	**7,605**	**23,808 ***	**30.0**	**100.0**
019 Amer Bapt USA	1	306	245	379 *	.5	1.6

NR–Not Reported *Total adherents estimated from known number of communicant, confirmed, full members. - Represents a percentage less than 0.1. Percentages may not total 100 due to rounding.

Table 4: Religious Congregations by County and Group: 2000

Religious Group	Number of Churches, Synagogues, Mosques, or Temples	Number of Communicant, Confirmed, or Full Members	Number of Attendees	Total Adherents: Number of Adherents	Total Adherents: % of Total Pop.	Total Adherents: % of Total Adh.
056 Baha'i	2	92	NR	92	.1	.4
061 Beachy Amish	1	80	NR	99 *	.1	.4
076 Buddhism	2	NR	NR	NR	-	-
081 Catholic	2	NR	NR	2,712	3.4	11.4
089 Chr & Miss Al	1	25	NR	54	.1	.2
093 Chr Ch (Disc)	1	140	0	174 *	.2	.7
097 Chr Chs&Chs Cr	1	750	NR	930 *	1.2	3.9
127 Ch God (Cleve)	2	600	706	789 *	1.0	3.3
151 L-D Saints	2	NR	NR	945	1.2	4.0
157 Ch of Brethren	3	410	0	508 *	.6	2.1
165 Ch of Nazarene	1	44	88	157	.2	.7
193 Episcopal	14	NR	1,734	3,553	4.5	14.9
207 E.L.C.A.	2	652	373	806	1.0	3.4
216 Evan Presby Ch	1	98	NR	121 *	.2	.5
283 Luth—MO Synod	1	154	88	192	.2	.8
288 Mennonite USA	2	73	86	97 *	.1	.4
335 Orth Pres Ch	1	0	0	0	-	-
349 Pent Holiness	2	271	137	336 *	.4	1.4
355 Presb Ch (USA)	6	1,562	902	1,937 *	2.4	8.1
356 Presb Ch Amer	1	75	185	185	.2	.8
403 Salvation Army	1	167	58	220	.3	.9
416 Sikh	1	NR	NR	NR	-	-
418 Southw Bapt Fel	1	NR	NR	NR	-	-
419 So Bapt Conv	23	4,596	1,803	5,698 *	7.2	23.9
443 Un C of Christ	1	86	80	107 *	.1	.4
449 Un Methodist	15	2,841	1,030	3,520 *	4.4	14.8
467 Wesleyan	2	95	90	197	.2	.8
ALEXANDRIA CITY	**72**	**16,757**	**10,176**	**63,607 ***	**49.6**	**100.0**
017 Amer Bapt Assn	1	110	NR	128 *	.1	.2
019 Amer Bapt USA	2	552	300	641 *	.5	1.0
053 Assemb of God	2	597	782	1,317	1.0	2.1
056 Baha'i	1	138	NR	138	.1	.2
076 Buddhism	1	NR	NR	NR	-	-
081 Catholic	4	NR	NR	24,151	18.8	38.0
093 Chr Ch (Disc)	1	177	90	205 *	.2	.3
127 Ch God (Cleve)	2	790	160	917 *	.7	1.4
151 L-D Saints	2	NR	NR	754	.6	1.2
165 Ch of Nazarene	1	55	36	55	-	.1
167 Chs of Christ	1	60	75	80	.1	.1
193 Episcopal	10	NR	2,653	7,135	5.6	11.2
221 Free Methodist	1	48	59	59	-	.1
246 Greek Orthodox	1	NR	NR	1,995	1.6	3.1
267 Muslim Est	2	NR	824	3,782	2.9	5.9
283 Luth—MO Synod	3	765	373	831	.6	1.3
339 Pent Ch of God	1	21	NR	33	-	.1
355 Presb Ch (USA)	10	3,934	1,837	4,568 *	3.6	7.2
356 Presb Ch Amer	1	268	275	360	.3	.6
388 Reg Bapt Gen As	1	70	100	81 *	.1	.1
397 OCA: Roman Dioc	1	NR	NR	100	.1	.2
403 Salvation Army	2	422	81	686	.5	1.1
413 S.D.A.	2	1,191	NR	1,417	1.1	2.2
419 So Bapt Conv	8	4,301	1,311	4,993 *	3.9	7.8
449 Un Methodist	8	3,258	1,220	3,781 *	2.9	5.9
496 Jewish Est	3	NR	NR	5,400	4.2	8.5
ALLEGHANY	**38**	**5,651**	**2,195**	**6,972 ***	**53.9**	**100.0**
019 Amer Bapt USA	1	300	110	363 *	2.8	5.2
145 Ch God Prophcy	1	41	NR	49 *	.4	.7
157 Ch of Brethren	1	26	18	31 *	.2	.4
193 Episcopal	2	NR	86	121	.9	1.7
349 Pent Holiness	1	26	35	31 *	.2	.4
355 Presb Ch (USA)	10	1,445	711	1,747 *	13.5	25.1
403 Salvation Army	1	84	21	123	1.0	1.8
419 So Bapt Conv	7	2,421	796	2,927 *	22.6	42.0
449 Un Methodist	14	1,308	418	1,580 *	12.2	22.7
AMELIA	**27**	**2,506**	**1,475**	**3,260 ***	**28.6**	**100.0**
056 Baha'i	0	5	NR	5	-	.2
081 Catholic	1	NR	NR	30	.3	.9
093 Chr Ch (Disc)	1	13	12	16 *	.1	.5
127 Ch God (Cleve)	1	51	77	77 *	.7	2.4
193 Episcopal	1	NR	33	111	1.0	3.4
263 Int Foursq Gos	1	248	323	323 *	2.8	9.9
283 Luth—MO Synod	1	45	39	50	.4	1.5
297 Mennonite;Other	1	122	NR	151 *	1.3	4.6
355 Presb Ch (USA)	6	274	177	338 *	3.0	10.4
360 Prim Bapt Chrch	1	NR	NR	NR	-	-
418 Southw Bapt Fel	1	NR	NR	NR	-	-
419 So Bapt Conv	5	1,048	525	1,295 *	11.4	39.7
449 Un Methodist	7	700	289	864 *	7.6	26.5
AMHERST	**45**	**8,828**	**3,351**	**11,214 ***	**35.2**	**100.0**
056 Baha'i	0	3	NR	3	-	-
081 Catholic	1	NR	NR	66	.2	.6
093 Chr Ch (Disc)	2	396	165	482 *	1.5	4.3
097 Chr Chs&Chs Cr	1	447	NR	544 *	1.7	4.9
127 Ch God (Cleve)	1	117	50	142 *	.4	1.3
165 Ch of Nazarene	1	56	38	96	.3	.9
193 Episcopal	3	NR	110	377	1.2	3.4
349 Pent Holiness	1	44	26	54 *	.2	.5
355 Presb Ch (USA)	4	558	323	678 *	2.1	6.0
418 Southw Bapt Fel	2	NR	NR	NR	-	-
419 So Bapt Conv	15	4,706	1,841	5,727 *	18.0	51.1
449 Un Methodist	14	2,501	798	3,045 *	9.5	27.2
APPOMATTOX	**37**	**6,385**	**2,336**	**8,114 ***	**59.2**	**100.0**
053 Assemb of God	1	31	41	41	.3	.5
056 Baha'i	0	3	NR	3	-	-
081 Catholic	1	NR	NR	67	.5	.8
127 Ch God (Cleve)	1	77	60	95 *	.7	1.2
145 Ch God Prophcy	1	41	NR	50 *	.4	.6
193 Episcopal	1	NR	46	95	.7	1.2
349 Pent Holiness	3	149	100	184 *	1.3	2.3
355 Presb Ch (USA)	3	283	151	349 *	2.5	4.3
413 S.D.A.	1	74	NR	88	.6	1.1
418 Southw Bapt Fel	1	NR	NR	NR	-	-
419 So Bapt Conv	15	3,874	1,192	4,776 *	34.8	58.9
449 Un Methodist	8	1,453	571	1,791 *	13.1	22.1
499 Indep.Non-Char	1	400	175	575	4.2	7.1
ARLINGTON	**93**	**16,419**	**8,651**	**55,319 ***	**29.2**	**100.0**
053 Assemb of God	4	344	392	448	.2	.8
056 Baha'i	1	113	NR	113	.1	.2
076 Buddhism	2	NR	NR	NR	-	-
081 Catholic	7	NR	NR	26,820	14.2	48.5
089 Chr & Miss Al	4	102	NR	238	.1	.4
093 Chr Ch (Disc)	1	76	30	88 *	-	.2
123 Ch God (Ander)	3	NR	86	86	-	.2
151 L-D Saints	1	NR	NR	512	.3	.9
157 Ch of Brethren	1	97	51	112 *	.1	.2
165 Ch of Nazarene	1	103	69	185	.1	.3
167 Chs of Christ	2	220	238	274	.1	.5
193 Episcopal	9	NR	1,738	4,552	2.4	8.2
207 E.L.C.A.	7	2,237	890	2,946	1.6	5.3
223 Free Will Bapt	1	83	NR	96 *	.1	.2
283 Luth—MO Synod	1	500	253	745	.4	1.3
288 Mennonite USA	1	30	24	35 *	-	.1
339 Pent Ch of God	1	25	NR	40	-	.1
355 Presb Ch (USA)	7	1,775	1,048	2,049 *	1.1	3.7
356 Presb Ch Amer	1	60	55	90	-	.2
403 Salvation Army	1	281	50	267	.1	.5
413 S.D.A.	1	96	NR	114	.1	.2
418 Southw Bapt Fel	1	NR	NR	NR	-	-
419 So Bapt Conv	16	3,205	1,172	3,698 *	2.0	6.7
435 Unitarian-Univ	1	962	NR	1,110 *	.6	2.0
443 Un C of Christ	2	812	379	937 *	.5	1.7
449 Un Methodist	13	5,298	2,147	6,114 *	3.2	11.1
467 Wesleyan	1	0	29	50	-	.1
496 Jewish Est	2	NR	NR	3,600	1.9	6.5
AUGUSTA	**130**	**24,182**	**11,481**	**30,569 ***	**46.6**	**100.0**
053 Assemb of God	1	194	251	304	.5	1.0
055 As Ref Pres Ch	1	390	NR	451	.7	1.5
056 Baha'i	1	61	NR	61	.1	.2

NR–Not Reported *Total adherents estimated from known number of communicant, confirmed, full members. - Represents a percentage less than 0.1. Percentages may not total 100 due to rounding.

Table 4: Religious Congregations by County and Group: 2000

Religious Group	Number of Churches, Synagogues, Mosques, or Temples	Number of Communicant, Confirmed, or Full Members	Number of Attendees	Total Adherents: Number of Adherents	Total Adherents: % of Total Pop.	Total Adherents: % of Total Adh.
061 Beachy Amish	2	198	NR	242 *	.4	.8
097 Chr Chs&Chs Cr	1	123	NR	150 *	.2	.5
127 Ch God (Cleve)	2	80	47	98 *	.1	.3
145 Ch God Prophcy	1	41	NR	50 *	.1	.2
157 Ch of Brethren	8	1,790	885	2,183 *	3.3	7.1
165 Ch of Nazarene	3	351	354	474	.7	1.6
193 Episcopal	3	NR	318	841	1.3	2.8
207 E.L.C.A.	12	2,068	866	2,567	3.9	8.4
263 Int Foursq Gos	2	363	416	443 *	.7	1.4
288 Mennonite USA	9	1,111	1,001	1,359 *	2.1	4.4
339 Pent Ch of God	1	20	NR	47	.1	.2
349 Pent Holiness	4	188	194	229 *	.3	.7
355 Presb Ch (USA)	27	6,278	3,208	7,657 *	11.7	25.0
370 Ref Baptist Chs	2	NR	NR	NR	-	-
401 Rus Orth Abroad	1	NR	NR	NR	-	-
403 Salvation Army	2	350	90	623	.9	2.0
418 Southw Bapt Fel	2	NR	NR	NR	-	-
419 So Bapt Conv	10	3,350	1,000	4,085 *	6.2	13.4
443 Un C of Christ	2	199	88	243 *	.4	.8
449 Un Methodist	32	6,552	2,403	7,987 *	12.2	26.1
499 Indep.Non-Char	1	475	360	475	.7	1.6
BATH	**21**	**2,219**	**1,038**	**2,801 ***	**55.5**	**100.0**
056 Baha'i	0	1	NR	1	-	-
081 Catholic	1	NR	NR	34	.7	1.2
157 Ch of Brethren	1	139	56	166 *	3.3	5.9
193 Episcopal	1	NR	53	108	2.1	3.9
263 Int Foursq Gos	1	30	50	50 *	1.0	1.8
349 Pent Holiness	1	494	223	589 *	11.7	21.0
355 Presb Ch (USA)	5	497	280	591 *	11.7	21.1
419 So Bapt Conv	3	414	102	494 *	9.8	17.6
449 Un Methodist	8	644	274	768 *	15.2	27.4
BEDFORD	**99**	**15,866**	**8,029**	**21,751 ***	**36.0**	**100.0**
019 Amer Bapt USA	2	138	75	169 *	.3	.8
053 Assemb of God	1	21	33	33	.1	.2
056 Baha'i	0	7	NR	7	-	-
081 Catholic	2	NR	NR	1,446	2.4	6.6
089 Chr & Miss Al	1	69	NR	172	.3	.8
097 Chr Chs&Chs Cr	1	250	NR	307 *	.5	1.4
123 Ch God (Ander)	2	NR	76	76	.1	.3
127 Ch God (Cleve)	1	43	48	53 *	.1	.2
145 Ch God Prophcy	1	41	NR	50 *	.1	.2
157 Ch of Brethren	4	197	194	258 *	.4	1.2
193 Episcopal	3	NR	461	517	.9	2.4
207 E.L.C.A.	1	149	300	300	.5	1.4
223 Free Will Bapt	2	167	NR	205 *	.3	.9
349 Pent Holiness	2	459	293	563 *	.9	2.6
355 Presb Ch (USA)	9	998	741	1,289 *	2.1	5.9
413 S.D.A.	1	22	NR	26	-	.1
418 Southw Bapt Fel	1	NR	NR	NR	-	-
419 So Bapt Conv	32	9,073	3,706	11,131 *	18.4	51.2
449 Un Methodist	32	3,564	1,591	4,377 *	7.3	20.1
467 Wesleyan	1	668	511	772	1.3	3.5
BEDFORD CITY	**12**	**2,679**	**1,022**	**3,467 ***	**55.0**	**100.0**
053 Assemb of God	1	12	13	36	.6	1.0
056 Baha'i	1	13	NR	13	.2	.4
093 Chr Ch (Disc)	1	315	100	379 *	6.0	10.9
097 Chr Chs&Chs Cr	1	35	NR	42 *	.7	1.2
123 Ch God (Ander)	1	NR	35	35	.6	1.0
127 Ch God (Cleve)	1	214	135	257 *	4.1	7.4
151 L-D Saints	1	NR	NR	153	2.4	4.4
167 Chs of Christ	1	41	48	55	.9	1.6
193 Episcopal	1	NR	23	34	.5	1.0
419 So Bapt Conv	2	1,154	375	1,387 *	22.0	40.0
449 Un Methodist	1	895	293	1,076 *	17.1	31.0
BLAND	**41**	**2,403**	**1,084**	**2,870 ***	**41.8**	**100.0**
093 Chr Ch (Disc)	1	113	0	132 *	1.9	4.6
097 Chr Chs&Chs Cr	4	327	NR	382 *	5.6	13.3
127 Ch God (Cleve)	3	209	126	244 *	3.6	8.5
145 Ch God Prophcy	1	41	NR	48 *	.7	1.7
207 E.L.C.A.	3	56	91	99	1.4	3.4
349 Pent Holiness	3	109	54	127 *	1.8	4.4
355 Presb Ch (USA)	2	44	73	79 *	1.1	2.8
413 S.D.A.	1	11	NR	13	.2	.5
419 So Bapt Conv	4	391	173	457 *	6.7	15.9
449 Un Methodist	19	1,102	567	1,289 *	18.8	44.9
BOTETOURT	**73**	**12,249**	**4,485**	**16,852 ***	**55.3**	**100.0**
056 Baha'i	0	13	NR	13	-	.1
075 Brethren in Cr	1	36	33	36	.1	.2
081 Catholic	1	NR	NR	664	2.2	3.9
089 Chr & Miss Al	1	143	NR	218	.7	1.3
097 Chr Chs&Chs Cr	1	80	NR	97 *	.3	.6
127 Ch God (Cleve)	3	160	103	194 *	.6	1.2
145 Ch God Prophcy	2	82	NR	98 *	.3	.6
151 L-D Saints	2	NR	NR	937	3.1	5.6
157 Ch of Brethren	12	1,704	912	2,070 *	6.8	12.3
167 Chs of Christ	1	16	18	19	.1	.1
193 Episcopal	2	NR	106	167	.5	1.0
207 E.L.C.A.	3	328	154	441	1.4	2.6
263 Int Foursq Gos	1	64	83	83 *	.3	.5
349 Pent Holiness	1	32	20	39 *	.1	.2
355 Presb Ch (USA)	5	463	258	562 *	1.8	3.3
388 Reg Bapt Gen As	1	45	40	55 *	.2	.3
413 S.D.A.	1	156	NR	186	.6	1.1
419 So Bapt Conv	19	6,780	1,717	8,227 *	27.0	48.8
449 Un Methodist	13	1,280	567	1,554 *	5.1	9.2
467 Wesleyan	2	267	174	492	1.6	2.9
499 Indep.Non-Char	1	600	300	700	2.3	4.2
BRISTOL CITY	**32**	**7,490**	**2,799**	**10,979 ***	**63.2**	**100.0**
053 Assemb of God	1	108	130	250	1.4	2.3
081 Catholic	1	NR	NR	1,487	8.6	13.5
097 Chr Chs&Chs Cr	4	609	NR	724 *	4.2	6.6
123 Ch God (Ander)	1	NR	45	45	.3	.4
127 Ch God (Cleve)	2	157	120	204 *	1.2	1.9
165 Ch of Nazarene	1	33	21	33	.2	.3
167 Chs of Christ	2	320	295	380	2.2	3.5
193 Episcopal	1	NR	112	426	2.5	3.9
223 Free Will Bapt	3	250	NR	297 *	1.7	2.7
339 Pent Ch of God	1	22	NR	24	.1	.2
356 Presb Ch Amer	1	31	30	31	.2	.3
419 So Bapt Conv	8	3,442	1,176	4,088 *	23.5	37.2
449 Un Methodist	6	2,518	870	2,990 *	17.2	27.2
BRUNSWICK	**43**	**4,151**	**1,693**	**6,378 ***	**34.6**	**100.0**
053 Assemb of God	3	185	205	401	2.2	6.3
056 Baha'i	0	3	NR	3	-	-
081 Catholic	2	NR	NR	87	.5	1.4
093 Chr Ch (Disc)	1	157	55	186 *	1.0	2.9
097 Chr Chs&Chs Cr	1	275	NR	325 *	1.8	5.1
151 L-D Saints	3	NR	NR	867	4.7	13.6
193 Episcopal	6	NR	210	331	1.8	5.2
355 Presb Ch (USA)	3	145	85	172 *	.9	2.7
419 So Bapt Conv	9	1,481	478	1,752 *	9.5	27.5
449 Un Methodist	15	1,905	660	2,254 *	12.2	35.3
BUCHANAN	**50**	**6,030**	**1,556**	**7,205 ***	**26.7**	**100.0**
019 Amer Bapt USA	1	99	55	117 *	.4	1.6
081 Catholic	1	NR	NR	40	.1	.6
097 Chr Chs&Chs Cr	12	2,215	NR	2,622 *	9.7	36.4
127 Ch God (Cleve)	1	96	57	114 *	.4	1.6
167 Chs of Christ	5	193	213	244	.9	3.4
223 Free Will Bapt	1	83	NR	99 *	.4	1.4
258 IndFreeWillBapt	4	172	NR	204 *	.8	2.8
339 Pent Ch of God	1	15	NR	20	.1	.3
355 Presb Ch (USA)	5	248	171	298 *	1.1	4.1
360 Prim Bapt Chrch	4	NR	NR	NR	-	-
419 So Bapt Conv	9	2,436	842	2,886 *	10.7	40.1
449 Un Methodist	6	473	218	561 *	2.1	7.8

NR–Not Reported *Total adherents estimated from known number of communicant, confirmed, full members. - Represents a percentage less than 0.1. Percentages may not total 100 due to rounding.

Table 4: Religious Congregations by County and Group: 2000

Religious Group	Number of Churches, Synagogues, Mosques, or Temples	Number of Communicant, Confirmed, or Full Members	Number of Attendees	Total Adherents: Number of Adherents	Total Adherents: % of Total Pop.	Total Adherents: % of Total Adh.
BUCKINGHAM	**42**	**4,000**	**3,240**	**5,197 ***	**33.3**	**100.0**
056 Baha'i	0	4	NR	4	-	.1
081 Catholic	2	NR	NR	106	.7	2.0
151 L-D Saints	1	NR	NR	114	.7	2.2
165 Ch of Nazarene	1	28	49	103	.7	2.0
193 Episcopal	1	NR	13	29	.2	.6
252 Hindu	1	NR	NR	NR	-	-
349 Pent Holiness	1	70	42	84 *	.5	1.6
355 Presb Ch (USA)	4	200	104	240 *	1.5	4.6
419 So Bapt Conv	17	2,964	2,647	3,561 *	22.8	68.5
449 Un Methodist	13	708	358	851 *	5.4	16.4
467 Wesleyan	1	26	27	105	.7	2.0
BUENA VISTA CITY	**9**	**1,234**	**327**	**2,425 ***	**38.2**	**100.0**
145 Ch God Prophcy	1	41	NR	49 *	.8	2.0
151 L-D Saints	3	NR	NR	937	14.8	38.6
157 Ch of Brethren	1	179	110	217 *	3.4	8.9
165 Ch of Nazarene	1	23	0	23	.4	.9
413 S.D.A.	1	146	NR	174	2.7	7.2
419 So Bapt Conv	1	498	103	604 *	9.5	24.9
449 Un Methodist	1	347	114	421 *	6.6	17.4
CAMPBELL	**96**	**42,091**	**14,520**	**53,113 ***	**104.0**	**100.0**
053 Assemb of God	1	52	65	65	.1	.1
056 Baha'i	1	25	NR	25	-	-
097 Chr Chs&Chs Cr	1	230	NR	282 *	.6	.5
127 Ch God (Cleve)	1	43	20	53 *	.1	.1
145 Ch God Prophcy	5	204	NR	250 *	.5	.5
193 Episcopal	1	NR	26	41	.1	.1
207 E.L.C.A.	1	722	330	957	1.9	1.8
263 Int Foursq Gos	1	35	64	64 *	.1	.1
297 Mennonite;Other	1	87	NR	107 *	.2	.2
349 Pent Holiness	6	1,053	641	1,290 *	2.5	2.4
355 Presb Ch (USA)	16	4,291	2,253	5,257 *	10.3	9.9
419 So Bapt Conv	30	30,707	9,138	37,617 *	73.6	70.8
443 Un C of Christ	1	28	12	34 *	.1	.1
449 Un Methodist	27	4,446	1,595	5,447 *	10.7	10.3
467 Wesleyan	3	168	376	1,624	3.2	3.1
CAROLINE	**26**	**5,169**	**1,924**	**7,181 ***	**32.5**	**100.0**
056 Baha'i	0	1	NR	1	-	-
081 Catholic	2	NR	NR	665	3.0	9.3
093 Chr Ch (Disc)	1	40	15	49 *	.2	.7
193 Episcopal	2	NR	88	128	.6	1.8
419 So Bapt Conv	13	4,212	1,382	5,207 *	23.5	72.5
449 Un Methodist	8	916	439	1,131 *	5.1	15.7
CARROLL	**85**	**9,231**	**4,460**	**11,186 ***	**38.2**	**100.0**
056 Baha'i	0	1	NR	1	-	-
075 Brethren in Cr	1	110	104	110	.4	1.0
081 Catholic	1	NR	NR	104	.4	.9
093 Chr Ch (Disc)	4	427	152	511 *	1.7	4.6
097 Chr Chs&Chs Cr	1	150	NR	179 *	.6	1.6
127 Ch God (Cleve)	2	115	60	137 *	.5	1.2
145 Ch God Prophcy	1	41	NR	49 *	.2	.4
157 Ch of Brethren	2	410	198	490 *	1.7	4.4
167 Chs of Christ	2	115	116	153	.5	1.4
207 E.L.C.A.	1	223	64	265	.9	2.4
295 Morav Ch-South	2	188	NR	251	.9	2.2
349 Pent Holiness	6	482	308	577 *	2.0	5.2
355 Presb Ch (USA)	5	464	296	555 *	1.9	5.0
360 Prim Bapt Chrch	20	NR	NR	NR	-	-
419 So Bapt Conv	19	4,159	1,957	4,976 *	17.0	44.5
443 Un C of Christ	1	107	47	128 *	.4	1.1
449 Un Methodist	16	2,220	1,132	2,655 *	9.1	23.7
467 Wesleyan	1	19	26	45	.2	.4
CHARLES CITY	**9**	**2,442**	**564**	**3,135 ***	**45.3**	**100.0**
019 Amer Bapt USA	2	427	145	511 *	7.4	16.3
193 Episcopal	1	NR	68	210	3.0	6.7
263 Int Foursq Gos	1	6	8	8 *	.1	.3
355 Presb Ch (USA)	1	22	12	26 *	.4	.8
419 So Bapt Conv	3	1,883	280	2,255 *	32.6	71.9
449 Un Methodist	1	104	51	125 *	1.8	4.0
CHARLOTTE	**45**	**5,487**	**1,826**	**6,933 ***	**55.6**	**100.0**
097 Chr Chs&Chs Cr	3	531	NR	653 *	5.2	9.4
193 Episcopal	1	NR	14	21	.2	.3
226 Friends-USA	1	105	NR	129 *	1.0	1.9
267 Muslim Est	1	NR	55	163	1.3	2.4
323 Old Ord Amish	1	65	NR	80 *	.6	1.2
355 Presb Ch (USA)	14	620	363	763 *	6.1	11.0
419 So Bapt Conv	13	2,945	939	3,621 *	29.0	52.2
449 Un Methodist	11	1,221	455	1,503 *	12.1	21.7
CHARLOTTESVILLE CITY	**40**	**13,294**	**5,605**	**25,199 ***	**55.9**	**100.0**
053 Assemb of God	2	184	219	388	.9	1.5
061 Beachy Amish	1	25	NR	28 *	.1	.1
076 Buddhism	1	NR	NR	NR	-	-
081 Catholic	2	NR	NR	5,318	11.8	21.1
097 Chr Chs&Chs Cr	3	1,327	NR	1,509 *	3.3	6.0
127 Ch God (Cleve)	1	76	40	86 *	.2	.3
151 L-D Saints	1	NR	NR	385	.9	1.5
165 Ch of Nazarene	1	65	76	101	.2	.4
167 Chs of Christ	1	150	175	160	.4	.6
193 Episcopal	1	NR	468	1,381	3.1	5.5
223 Free Will Bapt	1	83	NR	95 *	.2	.4
226 Friends-USA	1	105	NR	119 *	.3	.5
246 Greek Orthodox	1	NR	NR	405	.9	1.6
264 Int Chs of Crst	1	44	78	54	.1	.2
267 Muslim Est	1	NR	101	288	.6	1.1
290 Metro Comm Ch	1	20	20	23 *	.1	.1
355 Presb Ch (USA)	2	1,623	531	1,845 *	4.1	7.3
356 Presb Ch Amer	1	976	1,100	1,398	3.1	5.5
388 Reg Bapt Gen As	1	12	25	25 *	.1	.1
413 S.D.A.	1	108	NR	129	.3	.5
419 So Bapt Conv	8	5,855	2,177	6,658 *	14.8	26.4
431 Ukrainian Orth	1	NR	NR	300	.7	1.2
435 Unitarian-Univ	1	348	NR	396 *	.9	1.6
449 Un Methodist	3	2,293	595	2,608 *	5.8	10.3
496 Jewish Est	2	NR	NR	1,500	3.3	6.0
CHESAPEAKE CITY	**116**	**34,637**	**17,828**	**58,218 ***	**29.2**	**100.0**
053 Assemb of God	3	574	695	1,164	.6	2.0
056 Baha'i	1	37	NR	37	-	.1
076 Buddhism	1	NR	NR	NR	-	-
081 Catholic	5	NR	NR	9,133	4.6	15.7
089 Chr & Miss Al	1	0	NR	33	-	.1
093 Chr Ch (Disc)	2	428	45	550 *	.3	.9
097 Chr Chs&Chs Cr	8	1,376	NR	1,769 *	.9	3.0
127 Ch God (Cleve)	3	600	702	924 *	.5	1.6
145 Ch God Prophcy	1	41	NR	52 *	-	.1
151 L-D Saints	5	NR	NR	1,488	.7	2.6
165 Ch of Nazarene	1	88	95	95	-	.2
167 Chs of Christ	4	538	618	740	.4	1.3
183 Cons Menn Conf	1	38	46	55	-	.1
193 Episcopal	3	NR	695	1,220	.6	2.1
203 Evan Free Ch	1	100	200	200	.1	.3
207 E.L.C.A.	2	540	342	770	.4	1.3
216 Evan Presby Ch	2	172	NR	221 *	.1	.4
223 Free Will Bapt	2	167	NR	215 *	.1	.4
252 Hindu	1	NR	NR	NR	-	-
263 Int Foursq Gos	2	290	377	377 *	.2	.6
265 Int Pent C Chr	1	47	60	80	-	.1
283 Luth—MO Synod	1	25	25	31	-	.1
288 Mennonite USA	2	273	251	353 *	.2	.6
349 Pent Holiness	6	974	721	1,252 *	.6	2.2
355 Presb Ch (USA)	6	1,763	885	2,266 *	1.1	3.9
413 S.D.A.	2	190	NR	226	.1	.4
419 So Bapt Conv	26	14,871	5,283	19,113 *	9.6	32.8
443 Un C of Christ	2	653	320	839 *	.4	1.4
449 Un Methodist	15	8,256	2,968	10,611 *	5.3	18.2
463 Vineyard	1	100	100	129 *	.1	.2
498 Indep.Charis.	2	1,521	2,575	3,300	1.7	5.7

NR–Not Reported *Total adherents estimated from known number of communicant, confirmed, full members. - Represents a percentage less than 0.1. Percentages may not total 100 due to rounding.

Table 4: Religious Congregations by County and Group: 2000

Religious Group	Number of Churches, Synagogues, Mosques, or Temples	Number of Communicant, Confirmed, or Full Members	Number of Attendees	Total Adherents		
				Number of Adherents	% of Total Pop.	% of Total Adh.
499 Indep.Non-Char	3	975	825	975	.5	1.7
CHESTERFIELD	**158**	**55,501**	**24,421**	**94,641 ***	**36.4**	**100.0**
019 Amer Bapt USA	3	1,193	501	1,520 *	.6	1.6
053 Assemb of God	1	100	115	155	.1	.2
056 Baha'i	1	80	NR	80	-	.1
081 Catholic	3	NR	NR	14,798	5.7	15.6
089 Chr & Miss Al	1	41	NR	79	-	.1
093 Chr Ch (Disc)	1	386	180	492 *	.2	.5
097 Chr Chs&Chs Cr	3	564	NR	719 *	.3	.8
127 Ch God (Cleve)	5	1,310	887	1,704 *	.7	1.8
145 Ch God Prophcy	2	82	NR	104 *	-	.1
151 L-D Saints	8	NR	NR	3,099	1.2	3.3
157 Ch of Brethren	1	39	26	50 *	-	.1
165 Ch of Nazarene	5	1,070	1,277	2,825	1.1	3.0
167 Chs of Christ	5	294	343	388	.1	.4
173 Comm of Christ	1	83	NR	83	-	.1
193 Episcopal	7	NR	1,300	3,655	1.4	3.9
203 Evan Free Ch	1	65	120	120	-	.1
207 E.L.C.A.	2	823	415	1,074	.4	1.1
223 Free Will Bapt	1	83	NR	106 *	-	.1
265 Int Pent C Chr	1	0	0	50	-	.1
267 Muslim Est	1	NR	156	609	.2	.6
283 Luth—MO Synod	3	1,475	707	1,916	.7	2.0
349 Pent Holiness	5	1,275	631	1,624 *	.6	1.7
355 Presb Ch (USA)	6	2,616	1,390	3,332 *	1.3	3.5
356 Presb Ch Amer	4	878	871	1,248	.5	1.3
360 Prim Bapt Chrch	3	NR	NR	NR	-	-
370 Ref Baptist Chs	1	NR	NR	NR	-	-
388 Reg Bapt Gen As	1	180	130	229 *	.1	.2
413 S.D.A.	1	218	NR	259	.1	.3
418 Southw Bapt Fel	1	NR	NR	NR	-	-
419 So Bapt Conv	55	26,864	9,706	34,218 *	13.2	36.2
435 Unitarian-Univ	1	15	NR	19 *	-	-
443 Un C of Christ	1	95	42	121 *	-	.1
449 Un Methodist	22	15,603	5,572	19,876 *	7.6	21.0
469 WELS	1	69	52	89	-	.1
CLARKE	**21**	**2,498**	**1,067**	**4,516 ***	**35.7**	**100.0**
019 Amer Bapt USA	1	167	90	204 *	1.6	4.5
056 Baha'i	0	8	NR	8	.1	.2
081 Catholic	1	NR	NR	436	3.4	9.7
151 L-D Saints	1	NR	NR	478	3.8	10.6
167 Chs of Christ	1	35	40	45	.4	1.0
193 Episcopal	4	NR	249	554	4.4	12.3
355 Presb Ch (USA)	1	88	51	107 *	.8	2.4
419 So Bapt Conv	4	858	206	1,047 *	8.3	23.2
449 Un Methodist	8	1,342	431	1,637 *	12.9	36.2
CLIFTON FORGE CITY	**5**	**981**	**285**	**1,335 ***	**31.1**	**100.0**
053 Assemb of God	1	82	90	91	2.1	6.8
081 Catholic	1	NR	NR	173	4.0	13.0
093 Chr Ch (Disc)	1	202	50	241 *	5.6	18.1
097 Chr Chs&Chs Cr	1	65	NR	77 *	1.8	5.8
449 Un Methodist	1	632	145	753 *	17.6	56.4
COLONIAL HEIGHTS CITY	**14**	**7,526**	**2,050**	**12,092 ***	**71.6**	**100.0**
053 Assemb of God	1	135	185	185	1.1	1.5
056 Baha'i	0	1	NR	1	-	-
081 Catholic	1	NR	NR	2,465	14.6	20.4
093 Chr Ch (Disc)	1	122	69	147 *	.9	1.2
127 Ch God (Cleve)	1	35	0	42 *	.2	.3
151 L-D Saints	1	NR	NR	278	1.6	2.3
165 Ch of Nazarene	1	66	45	86	.5	.7
167 Chs of Christ	1	157	140	187	1.1	1.5
193 Episcopal	1	NR	116	246	1.5	2.0
419 So Bapt Conv	4	5,258	989	6,342 *	37.5	52.4
449 Un Methodist	2	1,752	506	2,113 *	12.5	17.5
COVINGTON CITY	**25**	**3,551**	**1,089**	**4,897 ***	**77.7**	**100.0**
053 Assemb of God	1	11	12	14	.2	.3
055 As Ref Pres Ch	2	430	NR	479	7.6	9.8
056 Baha'i	0	1	NR	1	-	-
081 Catholic	1	NR	NR	233	3.7	4.8
093 Chr Ch (Disc)	1	149	0	179 *	2.8	3.7
097 Chr Chs&Chs Cr	3	563	NR	679 *	10.8	13.9
127 Ch God (Cleve)	1	14	19	19 *	.3	.4
145 Ch God Prophcy	4	163	NR	196 *	3.1	4.0
151 L-D Saints	1	NR	NR	237	3.8	4.8
165 Ch of Nazarene	1	54	60	60	1.0	1.2
167 Chs of Christ	1	55	70	75	1.2	1.5
207 E.L.C.A.	1	28	13	33	.5	.7
263 Int Foursq Gos	1	143	332	332 *	5.3	6.8
419 So Bapt Conv	1	148	40	178 *	2.8	3.6
449 Un Methodist	5	1,772	515	2,134 *	33.9	43.6
467 Wesleyan	1	20	28	48	.8	1.0
CRAIG	**13**	**1,935**	**339**	**2,365 ***	**46.5**	**100.0**
056 Baha'i	0	1	NR	1	-	-
093 Chr Ch (Disc)	2	75	18	92 *	1.8	3.9
097 Chr Chs&Chs Cr	4	1,152	NR	1,408 *	27.7	59.5
145 Ch God Prophcy	1	41	NR	50 *	1.0	2.1
419 So Bapt Conv	1	253	130	309 *	6.1	13.1
449 Un Methodist	5	413	191	505 *	9.9	21.4
CULPEPER	**41**	**6,784**	**2,964**	**12,347 ***	**36.0**	**100.0**
019 Amer Bapt USA	1	174	60	217 *	.6	1.8
053 Assemb of God	2	317	386	912	2.7	7.4
056 Baha'i	0	25	NR	25	.1	.2
081 Catholic	1	NR	NR	2,122	6.2	17.2
089 Chr & Miss Al	1	52	NR	150	.4	1.2
097 Chr Chs&Chs Cr	1	45	NR	56 *	.2	.5
127 Ch God (Cleve)	1	26	26	32 *	.1	.3
151 L-D Saints	1	NR	NR	450	1.3	3.6
165 Ch of Nazarene	1	21	34	40	.1	.3
167 Chs of Christ	1	49	52	64	.2	.5
193 Episcopal	4	NR	295	680	2.0	5.5
207 E.L.C.A.	2	383	140	513	1.5	4.2
221 Free Methodist	1	22	28	29	.1	.2
355 Presb Ch (USA)	3	540	271	673 *	2.0	5.5
413 S.D.A.	2	135	NR	160	.5	1.3
419 So Bapt Conv	13	3,314	1,123	4,129 *	12.1	33.4
449 Un Methodist	6	1,681	549	2,095 *	6.1	17.0
CUMBERLAND	**17**	**1,609**	**1,003**	**2,207 ***	**24.5**	**100.0**
053 Assemb of God	1	268	375	470	5.2	21.3
056 Baha'i	0	6	NR	6	.1	.3
127 Ch God (Cleve)	1	37	20	46 *	.5	2.1
193 Episcopal	1	NR	23	70	.8	3.2
297 Mennonite;Other	1	23	NR	29 *	.3	1.3
355 Presb Ch (USA)	2	196	105	244 *	2.7	11.1
419 So Bapt Conv	6	702	298	873 *	9.7	39.6
449 Un Methodist	5	377	182	469 *	5.2	21.3
DANVILLE CITY	**64**	**16,952**	**6,611**	**22,805 ***	**47.1**	**100.0**
053 Assemb of God	1	150	200	200	.4	.9
081 Catholic	1	NR	NR	1,135	2.3	5.0
093 Chr Ch (Disc)	2	180	20	219 *	.5	1.0
097 Chr Chs&Chs Cr	3	181	NR	221 *	.5	1.0
127 Ch God (Cleve)	4	1,331	842	1,620 *	3.3	7.1
145 Ch God Prophcy	2	82	NR	100 *	.2	.4
151 L-D Saints	1	NR	NR	371	.8	1.6
157 Ch of Brethren	2	135	82	165 *	.3	.7
165 Ch of Nazarene	1	107	54	107	.2	.5
167 Chs of Christ	2	140	125	203	.4	.9
226 Friends-USA	2	190	NR	231 *	.5	1.0
246 Greek Orthodox	1	NR	NR	159	.3	.7
263 Int Foursq Gos	1	164	213	213 *	.4	.9
283 Luth—MO Synod	1	116	60	148	.3	.6
349 Pent Holiness	1	40	55	49 *	.1	.2
355 Presb Ch (USA)	1	74	38	90 *	.2	.4
360 Prim Bapt Chrch	2	NR	NR	NR	-	-
413 S.D.A.	2	347	NR	413	.9	1.8
419 So Bapt Conv	21	8,941	3,024	10,887 *	22.5	47.7

NR–Not Reported *Total adherents estimated from known number of communicant, confirmed, full members. - Represents a percentage less than 0.1. Percentages may not total 100 due to rounding.

Table 4: Religious Congregations by County and Group: 2000

Religious Group	Number of Churches, Synagogues, Mosques, or Temples	Number of Communicant, Confirmed, or Full Members	Number of Attendees	Total Adherents: Number of Adherents	% of Total Pop.	% of Total Adh.
449 Un Methodist	9	3,718	1,304	4,527 *	9.4	19.9
467 Wesleyan	2	126	94	192	.4	.8
496 Jewish Est	1	NR	NR	125	.3	.5
499 Indep.Non-Char	1	930	500	1,430	3.0	6.3
DICKENSON	**50**	**3,706**	**636**	**4,520 ***	**27.6**	**100.0**
056 Baha'i	0	1	NR	1	-	-
081 Catholic	1	NR	NR	94	.6	2.1
097 Chr Chs&Chs Cr	2	284	NR	339 *	2.1	7.5
127 Ch God (Cleve)	1	31	15	37 *	.2	.8
145 Ch God Prophcy	1	41	NR	49 *	.3	1.1
157 Ch of Brethren	2	225	70	269 *	1.6	6.0
167 Chs of Christ	1	48	60	55	.3	1.2
258 IndFreeWillBapt	28	1,807	NR	2,158 *	13.2	47.7
356 Presb Ch Amer	3	143	113	173	1.1	3.8
360 Prim Bapt Chrch	4	NR	NR	NR	-	-
419 So Bapt Conv	5	782	225	934 *	5.7	20.7
449 Un Methodist	2	344	153	411 *	2.5	9.1
DINWIDDIE	**41**	**7,505**	**2,933**	**9,534 ***	**38.9**	**100.0**
019 Amer Bapt USA	1	350	200	429 *	1.7	4.5
053 Assemb of God	1	16	22	35	.1	.4
056 Baha'i	0	2	NR	2	-	-
093 Chr Ch (Disc)	1	153	34	187 *	.8	2.0
165 Ch of Nazarene	1	56	41	56	.2	.6
193 Episcopal	3	NR	150	336	1.4	3.5
355 Presb Ch (USA)	6	780	378	957 *	3.9	10.0
413 S.D.A.	1	34	NR	40	.2	.4
419 So Bapt Conv	11	3,880	1,224	4,754 *	19.4	49.9
449 Un Methodist	16	2,234	884	2,738 *	11.2	28.7
EMPORIA CITY	**9**	**2,498**	**744**	**3,218 ***	**56.8**	**100.0**
053 Assemb of God	1	62	75	75	1.3	2.3
056 Baha'i	0	3	NR	3	.1	.1
081 Catholic	1	NR	NR	75	1.3	2.3
097 Chr Chs&Chs Cr	1	82	NR	102 *	1.8	3.2
123 Ch God (Ander)	1	NR	40	40	.7	1.2
419 So Bapt Conv	3	1,715	402	2,132 *	37.6	66.3
449 Un Methodist	2	636	227	791 *	14.0	24.6
ESSEX	**20**	**2,580**	**1,130**	**4,250 ***	**42.5**	**100.0**
053 Assemb of God	1	111	94	133	1.3	3.1
056 Baha'i	0	1	NR	1	-	-
081 Catholic	1	NR	NR	491	4.9	11.6
093 Chr Ch (Disc)	1	154	65	187 *	1.9	4.4
127 Ch God (Cleve)	1	79	41	96 *	1.0	2.3
193 Episcopal	4	NR	210	631	6.3	14.8
413 S.D.A.	1	148	NR	176	1.8	4.1
419 So Bapt Conv	7	1,516	494	1,842 *	18.4	43.3
449 Un Methodist	4	571	226	693 *	6.9	16.3
FAIRFAX	**406**	**101,842**	**60,715**	**421,413 ***	**43.5**	**100.0**
019 Amer Bapt USA	8	4,053	1,235	5,058 *	.5	1.2
053 Assemb of God	7	695	816	1,241	.1	.3
055 As Ref Pres Ch	1	54	NR	78	-	-
056 Baha'i	14	1,175	NR	1,175	.1	.3
057 Bapt Gen Conf	1	270	275	337 *	-	.1
076 Buddhism	9	NR	NR	NR	-	-
081 Catholic	26	NR	NR	206,657	21.3	49.0
084 Calvary Chapel	2	NR	NR	NR	-	-
089 Chr & Miss Al	8	428	NR	564	.1	.1
093 Chr Ch (Disc)	6	2,113	660	2,637 *	.3	.6
097 Chr Chs&Chs Cr	5	647	NR	808 *	.1	.2
105 Christian Ref	1	206	161	257 *	-	.1
121 Ch God (Abr)	1	8	11	11 *	-	-
123 Ch God (Ander)	1	NR	415	415	-	.1
127 Ch God (Cleve)	4	291	122	364 *	-	.1
145 Ch God Prophcy	3	133	NR	166 *	-	-
151 L-D Saints	28	NR	NR	11,125	1.1	2.6
157 Ch of Brethren	2	288	166	359 *	-	.1
165 Ch of Nazarene	5	850	551	999	.1	.2
167 Chs of Christ	5	461	531	640	.1	.2

Religious Group	Number of Churches, Synagogues, Mosques, or Temples	Number of Communicant, Confirmed, or Full Members	Number of Attendees	Total Adherents: Number of Adherents	% of Total Pop.	% of Total Adh.
173 Comm of Christ	1	278	NR	278	-	.1
193 Episcopal	27	NR	6,422	19,370	2.0	4.6
201 Evan Cov Ch	1	88	51	110 *	-	-
203 Evan Free Ch	2	168	250	250	-	.1
207 E.L.C.A.	11	7,154	3,290	9,899	1.0	2.3
216 Evan Presby Ch	2	549	NR	685 *	.1	.2
223 Free Will Bapt	1	83	NR	104 *	-	-
226 Friends-USA	3	315	NR	393 *	-	.1
252 Hindu	4	NR	NR	NR	-	-
263 Int Foursq Gos	1	30	50	50 *	-	-
267 Muslim Est	7	NR	5,548	34,564	3.6	8.2
283 Luth—MO Synod	4	3,318	1,592	4,454	.5	1.1
288 Mennonite USA	2	100	61	124 *	-	-
331 OCA: Ter Diocs	2	127	NR	305	-	.1
335 Orth Pres Ch	1	157	204	252	-	.1
349 Pent Holiness	2	206	222	257 *	-	.1
355 Presb Ch (USA)	15	7,731	3,724	9,646 *	1.0	2.3
356 Presb Ch Amer	18	4,568	4,341	5,956	.6	1.4
365 Prog Prim Bapt	1	45	NR	56 *	-	-
388 Reg Bapt Gen As	1	95	95	95 *	-	-
397 OCA: Roman Dioc	1	NR	NR	300	-	.1
413 S.D.A.	10	1,521	NR	1,809	.2	.4
416 Sikh	3	NR	NR	NR	-	-
418 Southw Bapt Fel	2	NR	NR	NR	-	-
419 So Bapt Conv	64	21,221	8,909	26,485 *	2.7	6.3
435 Unitarian-Univ	4	1,443	NR	1,801 *	.2	.4
443 Un C of Christ	6	3,006	1,477	3,752 *	.4	.9
449 Un Methodist	50	34,024	13,078	42,462 *	4.4	10.1
467 Wesleyan	7	27	231	1,082	.1	.3
469 WELS	1	266	182	333	-	.1
490 Zoroastrian	1	NR	NR	NR	-	-
496 Jewish Est	8	NR	NR	15,300	1.6	3.6
499 Indep.Non-Char	6	3,650	6,045	8,350	.9	2.0
FAIRFAX CITY	**37**	**11,429**	**8,553**	**33,264 ***	**154.7**	**100.0**
053 Assemb of God	7	2,401	2,115	3,255	15.1	9.8
076 Buddhism	2	NR	NR	NR	-	-
081 Catholic	2	NR	NR	11,010	51.2	33.1
093 Chr Ch (Disc)	1	251	120	299 *	1.4	.9
167 Chs of Christ	2	896	970	1,339	6.2	4.0
193 Episcopal	2	NR	2,077	3,952	18.4	11.9
207 E.L.C.A.	4	2,379	1,232	3,176	14.8	9.5
252 Hindu	1	NR	NR	NR	-	-
290 Metro Comm Ch	1	108	70	70 *	.3	.2
349 Pent Holiness	1	30	29	36 *	.2	.1
355 Presb Ch (USA)	5	1,858	937	2,223 *	10.3	6.7
356 Presb Ch Amer	3	143	232	238	1.1	.7
403 Salvation Army	1	184	67	283	1.3	.9
413 S.D.A.	1	80	NR	95	.4	.3
419 So Bapt Conv	1	245	110	292 *	1.4	.9
449 Un Methodist	1	2,854	594	3,396 *	15.8	10.2
496 Jewish Est	2	NR	NR	3,600	16.7	10.8
FAUQUIER	**77**	**9,512**	**5,048**	**17,306 ***	**31.4**	**100.0**
053 Assemb of God	4	219	262	436	.8	2.5
056 Baha'i	0	19	NR	19	-	.1
061 Beachy Amish	1	50	NR	63 *	.1	.4
076 Buddhism	2	NR	NR	NR	-	-
081 Catholic	1	NR	NR	1,923	3.5	11.1
097 Chr Chs&Chs Cr	1	55	NR	69 *	.1	.4
151 L-D Saints	2	NR	NR	702	1.3	4.1
157 Ch of Brethren	1	212	120	267 *	.5	1.5
165 Ch of Nazarene	1	82	16	82	.1	.5
167 Chs of Christ	1	120	140	201	.4	1.2
183 Cons Menn Conf	1	36	44	52	.1	.3
193 Episcopal	9	NR	871	2,341	4.2	13.5
207 E.L.C.A.	2	400	321	549	1.0	3.2
251 Holy Orth in NA	2	NR	NR	20	-	.1
355 Presb Ch (USA)	3	570	348	718 *	1.3	4.1
356 Presb Ch Amer	1	134	180	180	.3	1.0
360 Prim Bapt Chrch	4	NR	NR	NR	-	-
413 S.D.A.	1	59	NR	70	.1	.4
419 So Bapt Conv	20	4,122	1,193	5,190 *	9.4	30.0

NR–Not Reported *Total adherents estimated from known number of communicant, confirmed, full members. - Represents a percentage less than 0.1. Percentages may not total 100 due to rounding.

Table 4: Religious Congregations by County and Group: 2000

Religious Group	Number of Churches, Synagogues, Mosques, or Temples	Number of Communicant, Confirmed, or Full Members	Number of Attendees	Total Adherents		
				Number of Adherents	% of Total Pop.	% of Total Adh.
449 Un Methodist	19	3,434	1,460	4,324 *	7.8	25.0
467 Wesleyan	1	0	93	100	.2	.6
FALLS CHURCH CITY	**18**	**6,623**	**1,517**	**17,073 ***	**164.5**	**100.0**
076 Buddhism	1	NR	NR	NR	-	-
081 Catholic	1	NR	NR	7,340	70.7	43.0
089 Chr & Miss Al	1	180	NR	180	1.7	1.1
167 Chs of Christ	2	365	340	455	4.4	2.7
283 Luth—MO Synod	1	529	230	587	5.7	3.4
288 Mennonite USA	1	73	50	88 *	.8	.5
355 Presb Ch (USA)	4	979	430	1,185 *	11.4	6.9
360 Prim Bapt Chrch	1	NR	NR	NR	-	-
413 S.D.A.	1	170	NR	202	1.9	1.2
419 So Bapt Conv	1	3,066	0	3,710 *	35.8	21.7
449 Un Methodist	3	1,261	467	1,526 *	14.7	8.9
496 Jewish Est	1	NR	NR	1,800	17.3	10.5
FLOYD	**48**	**4,217**	**2,402**	**5,214 ***	**37.6**	**100.0**
056 Baha'i	0	3	NR	3	-	.1
081 Catholic	1	NR	NR	23	.2	.4
093 Chr Ch (Disc)	1	86	20	104 *	.7	2.0
127 Ch God (Cleve)	2	202	196	243 *	1.8	4.7
157 Ch of Brethren	11	1,507	823	1,829 *	13.2	35.1
165 Ch of Nazarene	1	76	69	146	1.1	2.8
167 Chs of Christ	1	42	45	54	.4	1.0
207 E.L.C.A.	2	180	80	250	1.8	4.8
297 Mennonite;Other	1	25	NR	30 *	.2	.6
349 Pent Holiness	3	197	137	238 *	1.7	4.6
355 Presb Ch (USA)	3	177	145	214 *	1.5	4.1
356 Presb Ch Amer	1	43	55	55	.4	1.1
360 Prim Bapt Chrch	6	NR	NR	NR	-	-
419 So Bapt Conv	5	938	477	1,132 *	8.2	21.7
449 Un Methodist	10	741	355	893 *	6.4	17.1
FLUVANNA	**26**	**4,197**	**1,687**	**6,274 ***	**31.3**	**100.0**
056 Baha'i	0	3	NR	3	-	-
081 Catholic	2	NR	NR	993	5.0	15.8
193 Episcopal	2	NR	59	109	.5	1.7
355 Presb Ch (USA)	1	46	30	57 *	.3	.9
360 Prim Bapt Chrch	2	NR	NR	NR	-	-
419 So Bapt Conv	12	3,252	1,228	4,008 *	20.0	63.9
449 Un Methodist	7	896	370	1,104 *	5.5	17.6
FRANKLIN	**91**	**14,727**	**6,804**	**18,776 ***	**39.7**	**100.0**
019 Amer Bapt USA	2	178	130	215 *	.5	1.1
053 Assemb of God	5	261	327	485	1.0	2.6
056 Baha'i	0	7	NR	7	-	-
075 Brethren in Cr	1	11	12	12	-	.1
081 Catholic	1	NR	NR	373	.8	2.0
093 Chr Ch (Disc)	4	850	285	1,025 *	2.2	5.5
097 Chr Chs&Chs Cr	2	185	NR	223 *	.5	1.2
123 Ch God (Ander)	1	NR	51	51	.1	.3
127 Ch God (Cleve)	1	192	169	232 *	.5	1.2
145 Ch God Prophcy	1	41	NR	49 *	.1	.3
151 L-D Saints	1	NR	NR	190	.4	1.0
157 Ch of Brethren	14	1,909	883	2,302 *	4.9	12.3
165 Ch of Nazarene	1	40	26	40	.1	.2
167 Chs of Christ	1	35	45	54	.1	.3
193 Episcopal	2	NR	104	231	.5	1.2
349 Pent Holiness	3	213	142	257 *	.5	1.4
355 Presb Ch (USA)	2	233	140	281 *	.6	1.5
370 Ref Baptist Chs	1	NR	NR	NR	-	-
413 S.D.A.	1	89	NR	106	.2	.6
419 So Bapt Conv	22	6,956	2,915	8,389 *	17.7	44.7
449 Un Methodist	24	3,498	1,540	4,219 *	8.9	22.5
467 Wesleyan	1	29	35	35	.1	.2
FRANKLIN CITY	**9**	**2,585**	**685**	**3,776 ***	**45.2**	**100.0**
056 Baha'i	0	21	NR	21	.3	.6
081 Catholic	1	NR	NR	405	4.9	10.7
127 Ch God (Cleve)	1	158	83	195 *	2.3	5.2
151 L-D Saints	1	NR	NR	191	2.3	5.1

Religious Group	Number of Churches, Synagogues, Mosques, or Temples	Number of Communicant, Confirmed, or Full Members	Number of Attendees	Total Adherents		
				Number of Adherents	% of Total Pop.	% of Total Adh.
226 Friends-USA	1	113	NR	139 *	1.7	3.7
413 S.D.A.	1	56	NR	67	.8	1.8
419 So Bapt Conv	1	1,060	231	1,307 *	15.7	34.6
443 Un C of Christ	2	586	193	722 *	8.7	19.1
449 Un Methodist	1	591	178	729 *	8.7	19.3
FREDERICK	**82**	**13,529**	**7,269**	**18,464 ***	**31.2**	**100.0**
017 Amer Bapt Assn	2	120	NR	151 *	.3	.8
053 Assemb of God	5	352	444	580	1.0	3.1
056 Baha'i	0	26	NR	26	-	.1
093 Chr Ch (Disc)	2	222	50	279 *	.5	1.5
097 Chr Chs&Chs Cr	2	740	NR	931 *	1.6	5.0
127 Ch God (Cleve)	1	1,184	1,044	1,489 *	2.5	8.1
145 Ch God Prophcy	1	41	NR	51 *	.1	.3
157 Ch of Brethren	3	354	276	445 *	.8	2.4
193 Episcopal	2	NR	369	1,074	1.8	5.8
207 E.L.C.A.	6	757	418	1,020	1.7	5.5
223 Free Will Bapt	1	83	NR	105 *	.2	.6
226 Friends-USA	1	105	NR	132 *	.2	.7
283 Luth—MO Synod	1	78	64	114	.2	.6
288 Mennonite USA	1	106	88	133 *	.2	.7
349 Pent Holiness	1	94	85	118 *	.2	.6
355 Presb Ch (USA)	11	1,999	1,117	2,513 *	4.2	13.6
403 Salvation Army	1	150	42	157	.3	.9
418 Southw Bapt Fel	2	NR	NR	NR	-	-
419 So Bapt Conv	5	1,393	511	1,752 *	3.0	9.5
443 Un C of Christ	1	58	26	73 *	.1	.4
449 Un Methodist	32	4,867	2,135	6,121 *	10.3	33.2
499 Indep.Non-Char	1	800	600	1,200	2.0	6.5
FREDERICKSBURG CITY	**29**	**8,772**	**4,333**	**21,107 ***	**109.5**	**100.0**
017 Amer Bapt Assn	1	50	NR	58 *	.3	.3
019 Amer Bapt USA	1	220	158	257 *	1.3	1.2
053 Assemb of God	3	209	257	394	2.0	1.9
056 Baha'i	0	10	NR	10	.1	-
081 Catholic	1	NR	NR	9,845	51.1	46.6
097 Chr Chs&Chs Cr	1	78	NR	91 *	.5	.4
123 Ch God (Ander)	1	NR	131	131	.7	.6
145 Ch God Prophcy	1	41	NR	48 *	.2	.2
167 Chs of Christ	2	213	258	309	1.6	1.5
203 Evan Free Ch	1	111	100	111	.6	.5
207 E.L.C.A.	1	584	286	781	4.1	3.7
216 Evan Presby Ch	1	42	NR	49 *	.3	.2
246 Greek Orthodox	1	NR	NR	252	1.3	1.2
283 Luth—MO Synod	1	414	240	624	3.2	3.0
356 Presb Ch Amer	1	117	165	165	.9	.8
360 Prim Bapt Chrch	1	NR	NR	NR	-	-
419 So Bapt Conv	6	3,949	1,640	4,613 *	23.9	21.9
435 Unitarian-Univ	1	123	NR	144 *	.7	.7
449 Un Methodist	2	2,161	648	2,525 *	13.1	12.0
496 Jewish Est	1	NR	NR	250	1.3	1.2
499 Indep.Non-Char	1	450	450	450	2.3	2.1
GALAX CITY	**24**	**4,538**	**1,604**	**5,984 ***	**87.5**	**100.0**
053 Assemb of God	1	30	38	52	.8	.9
093 Chr Ch (Disc)	1	315	93	384 *	5.6	6.4
097 Chr Chs&Chs Cr	4	642	NR	783 *	11.5	13.1
127 Ch God (Cleve)	2	541	351	659 *	9.6	11.0
145 Ch God Prophcy	1	41	NR	50 *	.7	.8
151 L-D Saints	1	NR	NR	281	4.1	4.7
226 Friends-USA	2	226	NR	275 *	4.0	4.6
413 S.D.A.	1	155	NR	184	2.7	3.1
419 So Bapt Conv	9	1,865	868	2,273 *	33.2	38.0
449 Un Methodist	1	622	166	758 *	11.1	12.7
467 Wesleyan	1	101	88	285	4.2	4.8
GILES	**67**	**7,245**	**2,659**	**9,443 ***	**56.7**	**100.0**
053 Assemb of God	2	88	97	97	.6	1.0
081 Catholic	1	NR	NR	137	.8	1.5
093 Chr Ch (Disc)	7	937	265	1,128 *	6.8	11.9
097 Chr Chs&Chs Cr	4	578	NR	696 *	4.2	7.4
123 Ch God (Ander)	1	NR	25	25	.2	.3

NR–Not Reported *Total adherents estimated from known number of communicant, confirmed, full members. - Represents a percentage less than 0.1. Percentages may not total 100 due to rounding.

Table 4: Religious Congregations by County and Group: 2000

Religious Group	Number of Churches, Synagogues, Mosques, or Temples	Number of Communicant, Confirmed, or Full Members	Number of Attendees	Total Adherents		
				Number of Adherents	% of Total Pop.	% of Total Adh.
127 Ch God (Cleve)	2	103	88	124 *	.7	1.3
145 Ch God Prophcy	2	82	NR	98 *	.6	1.0
151 L-D Saints	1	NR	NR	556	3.3	5.9
157 Ch of Brethren	1	20	0	24 *	.1	.3
167 Chs of Christ	2	27	30	34	.2	.4
193 Episcopal	1	NR	20	43	.3	.5
207 E.L.C.A.	2	250	148	259	1.6	2.7
323 Old Ord Amish	2	72	NR	86 *	.5	.9
349 Pent Holiness	5	774	374	931 *	5.6	9.9
355 Presb Ch (USA)	3	119	68	143 *	.9	1.5
356 Presb Ch Amer	1	69	80	94	.6	1.0
413 S.D.A.	1	20	NR	24	.1	.3
419 So Bapt Conv	7	1,421	424	1,710 *	10.3	18.1
449 Un Methodist	22	2,685	1,040	3,234 *	19.4	34.2
GLOUCESTER	**33**	**9,603**	**3,550**	**14,127 ***	**40.6**	**100.0**
053 Assemb of God	1	426	286	379	1.1	2.7
056 Baha'i	0	4	NR	4	-	-
081 Catholic	1	NR	NR	1,623	4.7	11.5
097 Chr Chs&Chs Cr	1	35	NR	44 *	.1	.3
127 Ch God (Cleve)	1	135	67	168 *	.5	1.2
151 L-D Saints	1	NR	NR	289	.8	2.0
165 Ch of Nazarene	1	45	0	45	.1	.3
167 Chs of Christ	1	75	84	100	.3	.7
193 Episcopal	1	NR	130	389	1.1	2.8
207 E.L.C.A.	1	195	80	280	.8	2.0
226 Friends-USA	1	95	NR	118 *	.3	.8
355 Presb Ch (USA)	3	677	284	842 *	2.4	6.0
413 S.D.A.	1	20	NR	24	.1	.2
419 So Bapt Conv	10	5,311	1,712	6,606 *	19.0	46.8
449 Un Methodist	9	2,585	907	3,216 *	9.2	22.8
GOOCHLAND	**23**	**4,397**	**2,186**	**7,167 ***	**42.5**	**100.0**
056 Baha'i	0	2	NR	2	-	-
093 Chr Ch (Disc)	2	351	144	419 *	2.5	5.8
097 Chr Chs&Chs Cr	1	236	NR	282 *	1.7	3.9
165 Ch of Nazarene	1	85	73	139	.8	1.9
193 Episcopal	2	NR	507	1,882	11.2	26.3
349 Pent Holiness	1	50	43	60 *	.4	.8
355 Presb Ch (USA)	2	302	179	361 *	2.1	5.0
419 So Bapt Conv	11	2,669	970	3,184 *	18.9	44.4
449 Un Methodist	3	702	270	838 *	5.0	11.7
GRAYSON	**71**	**6,463**	**3,497**	**7,683 ***	**42.9**	**100.0**
056 Baha'i	0	1	NR	1	-	-
127 Ch God (Cleve)	1	78	25	92 *	.5	1.2
145 Ch God Prophcy	2	82	NR	96 *	.5	1.2
167 Chs of Christ	5	197	245	246	1.4	3.2
193 Episcopal	1	NR	32	59	.3	.8
207 E.L.C.A.	1	48	20	61	.3	.8
349 Pent Holiness	3	312	251	367 *	2.0	4.8
355 Presb Ch (USA)	2	241	127	284 *	1.6	3.7
360 Prim Bapt Chrch	7	NR	NR	NR	-	-
409 Separate Bapt	3	89	NR	105 *	.6	1.4
419 So Bapt Conv	17	2,745	1,291	3,231 *	18.0	42.1
449 Un Methodist	29	2,670	1,506	3,141 *	17.5	40.9
GREENE	**22**	**1,844**	**934**	**2,918 ***	**19.1**	**100.0**
056 Baha'i	0	5	NR	5	-	.2
076 Buddhism	1	NR	NR	NR	-	-
081 Catholic	2	NR	NR	391	2.6	13.4
127 Ch God (Cleve)	1	122	153	157 *	1.0	5.4
157 Ch of Brethren	4	281	117	360 *	2.4	12.3
193 Episcopal	1	NR	87	168	1.1	5.8
297 Mennonite;Other	1	55	NR	71 *	.5	2.4
413 S.D.A.	1	64	NR	76	.5	2.6
419 So Bapt Conv	5	753	325	966 *	6.3	33.1
443 Un C of Christ	1	49	22	63 *	.4	2.2
449 Un Methodist	5	515	230	661 *	4.3	22.7
GREENSVILLE	**17**	**1,782**	**751**	**2,257 ***	**19.5**	**100.0**
167 Chs of Christ	1	25	32	35	.3	1.6

Religious Group	Number of Churches, Synagogues, Mosques, or Temples	Number of Communicant, Confirmed, or Full Members	Number of Attendees	Total Adherents		
				Number of Adherents	% of Total Pop.	% of Total Adh.
193 Episcopal	3	NR	102	193	1.7	8.6
283 Luth—MO Synod	1	143	89	164	1.4	7.3
355 Presb Ch (USA)	2	184	72	212 *	1.8	9.4
419 So Bapt Conv	4	852	268	985 *	8.5	43.6
449 Un Methodist	6	578	188	668 *	5.8	29.6
HALIFAX	**88**	**14,532**	**5,195**	**18,885 ***	**50.6**	**100.0**
053 Assemb of God	1	32	32	100	.3	.5
056 Baha'i	0	3	NR	3	-	-
081 Catholic	2	NR	NR	348	.9	1.8
127 Ch God (Cleve)	2	409	291	499 *	1.3	2.6
145 Ch God Prophcy	2	82	NR	100 *	.3	.5
151 L-D Saints	1	NR	NR	311	.8	1.6
167 Chs of Christ	1	25	27	33	.1	.2
193 Episcopal	5	NR	144	424	1.1	2.2
288 Mennonite USA	1	25	40	40 *	.1	.2
297 Mennonite;Other	1	45	NR	55 *	.1	.3
349 Pent Holiness	2	75	55	92 *	.2	.5
355 Presb Ch (USA)	9	683	361	834 *	2.2	4.4
413 S.D.A.	3	117	NR	140	.4	.7
419 So Bapt Conv	36	9,762	3,127	11,912 *	31.9	63.1
443 Un C of Christ	4	458	195	559 *	1.5	3.0
449 Un Methodist	18	2,816	923	3,435 *	9.2	18.2
HAMPTON CITY	**91**	**33,496**	**17,383**	**52,908 ***	**36.1**	**100.0**
019 Amer Bapt USA	5	1,873	802	2,309 *	1.6	4.4
053 Assemb of God	5	2,365	2,805	3,263	2.2	6.2
056 Baha'i	1	38	NR	38	-	.1
059 Bapt Miss Assn	1	177	50	218 *	.1	.4
081 Catholic	5	NR	NR	5,217	3.6	9.9
089 Chr & Miss Al	1	0	NR	11	-	-
093 Chr Ch (Disc)	2	391	180	482 *	.3	.9
097 Chr Chs&Chs Cr	3	577	NR	711 *	.5	1.3
123 Ch God (Ander)	2	NR	81	81	.1	.2
151 L-D Saints	1	NR	NR	738	.5	1.4
165 Ch of Nazarene	1	394	191	411	.3	.8
167 Chs of Christ	1	180	200	225	.2	.4
193 Episcopal	4	NR	589	1,546	1.1	2.9
207 E.L.C.A.	2	852	488	1,146	.8	2.2
216 Evan Presby Ch	1	70	NR	86 *	.1	.2
223 Free Will Bapt	1	83	NR	103 *	.1	.2
267 Muslim Est	2	NR	456	1,682	1.1	3.2
283 Luth—MO Synod	1	103	85	127	.1	.2
288 Mennonite USA	1	1,672	804	2,061 *	1.4	3.9
349 Pent Holiness	1	70	79	86 *	.1	.2
355 Presb Ch (USA)	4	1,020	410	1,258 *	.9	2.4
356 Presb Ch Amer	1	295	265	382	.3	.7
370 Ref Baptist Chs	1	NR	NR	NR	-	-
403 Salvation Army	2	825	192	1,755	1.2	3.3
413 S.D.A.	2	240	NR	286	.2	.5
418 Southw Bapt Fel	1	NR	NR	NR	-	-
419 So Bapt Conv	21	13,519	4,954	16,666 *	11.4	31.5
443 Un C of Christ	2	609	268	751 *	.5	1.4
449 Un Methodist	12	5,693	1,884	7,019 *	4.8	13.3
496 Jewish Est	1	NR	NR	800	.5	1.5
498 Indep.Charis.	2	2,000	2,200	3,000	2.0	5.7
499 Indep.Non-Char	1	450	400	450	.3	.9
HANOVER	**89**	**27,630**	**12,261**	**41,197 ***	**47.7**	**100.0**
019 Amer Bapt USA	1	240	155	303 *	.4	.7
053 Assemb of God	2	1,397	1,450	1,765	2.0	4.3
056 Baha'i	1	14	NR	14	-	-
081 Catholic	1	NR	NR	2,895	3.4	7.0
093 Chr Ch (Disc)	6	1,358	384	1,713 *	2.0	4.2
097 Chr Chs&Chs Cr	9	3,687	NR	4,651 *	5.4	11.3
127 Ch God (Cleve)	1	270	229	340 *	.4	.8
151 L-D Saints	2	NR	NR	655	.8	1.6
165 Ch of Nazarene	1	188	171	245	.3	.6
167 Chs of Christ	1	150	150	200	.2	.5
193 Episcopal	8	NR	633	1,897	2.2	4.6
207 E.L.C.A.	1	205	112	320	.4	.8
226 Friends-USA	2	200	NR	252 *	.3	.6
283 Luth—MO Synod	1	131	56	171	.2	.4

NR–Not Reported *Total adherents estimated from known number of communicant, confirmed, full members. - Represents a percentage less than 0.1. Percentages may not total 100 due to rounding.

Table 4: Religious Congregations by County and Group: 2000

Religious Group	Number of Churches, Synagogues, Mosques, or Temples	Number of Communicant, Confirmed, or Full Members	Number of Attendees	Total Adherents		
				Number of Adherents	% of Total Pop.	% of Total Adh.
355 Presb Ch (USA)	8	1,467	784	1,850 *	2.1	4.5
356 Presb Ch Amer	1	51	55	67	.1	.2
413 S.D.A.	1	376	NR	447	.5	1.1
419 So Bapt Conv	23	12,454	5,275	15,706 *	18.2	38.1
435 Unitarian-Univ	1	156	NR	197 *	.2	.5
449 Un Methodist	16	4,844	1,551	6,109 *	7.1	14.8
467 Wesleyan	1	30	56	100	.1	.2
499 Indep.Non-Char	1	412	1,200	1,300	1.5	3.2
HARRISONBURG CITY	**33**	**7,944**	**3,824**	**13,112 ***	**32.4**	**100.0**
053 Assemb of God	2	179	236	382	.9	2.9
057 Bapt Gen Conf	1	20	50	50 *	.1	.4
071 Brethren (Ash)	1	32	29	36 *	.1	.3
081 Catholic	1	NR	NR	3,169	7.8	24.2
097 Chr Chs&Chs Cr	1	90	NR	102 *	.3	.8
145 Ch God Prophcy	1	41	NR	46 *	.1	.4
151 L-D Saints	1	NR	NR	312	.8	2.4
157 Ch of Brethren	4	1,098	667	1,250 *	3.1	9.5
165 Ch of Nazarene	1	416	470	517	1.3	3.9
167 Chs of Christ	3	155	170	207	.5	1.6
264 Int Chs of Crst	1	11	14	11	-	.1
297 Mennonite;Other	4	1,463	NR	1,666 *	4.1	12.7
356 Presb Ch Amer	1	767	992	992	2.5	7.6
413 S.D.A.	2	135	NR	160	.4	1.2
419 So Bapt Conv	1	598	203	681 *	1.7	5.2
435 Unitarian-Univ	1	48	NR	55 *	.1	.4
443 Un C of Christ	2	260	101	296 *	.7	2.3
449 Un Methodist	3	2,501	772	2,847 *	7.0	21.7
463 Vineyard	1	130	120	148 *	.4	1.1
496 Jewish Est	1	NR	NR	185	.5	1.4
HENRICO	**174**	**70,152**	**32,471**	**121,507 ***	**46.3**	**100.0**
019 Amer Bapt USA	4	1,651	700	2,052 *	.8	1.7
039 Ap Chr Ch(Naz)	1	30	48	48 *	-	-
053 Assemb of God	2	353	465	660	.3	.5
056 Baha'i	1	98	NR	98	-	.1
081 Catholic	8	NR	NR	22,554	8.6	18.6
089 Chr & Miss Al	2	116	NR	191	.1	.2
093 Chr Ch (Disc)	5	1,051	359	1,306 *	.5	1.1
097 Chr Chs&Chs Cr	3	305	NR	378 *	.1	.3
127 Ch God (Cleve)	2	548	310	682 *	.3	.6
151 L-D Saints	5	NR	NR	1,885	.7	1.6
157 Ch of Brethren	1	151	98	188 *	.1	.2
165 Ch of Nazarene	2	162	142	235	.1	.2
167 Chs of Christ	2	175	255	247	.1	.2
193 Episcopal	11	NR	2,257	8,116	3.1	6.7
203 Evan Free Ch	1	69	125	125	-	.1
207 E.L.C.A.	3	1,513	717	2,055	.8	1.7
216 Evan Presby Ch	1	144	NR	179 *	.1	.1
223 Free Will Bapt	2	167	NR	207 *	.1	.2
251 Holy Orth in NA	1	NR	NR	40	-	-
252 Hindu	1	NR	NR	NR	-	-
263 Int Foursq Gos	1	142	185	185 *	.1	.2
267 Muslim Est	1	NR	156	609	.2	.5
283 Luth—MO Synod	1	177	60	253	.1	.2
288 Mennonite USA	2	121	125	151 *	.1	.1
349 Pent Holiness	3	80	79	99 *	-	.1
355 Presb Ch (USA)	28	13,111	6,253	16,314 *	6.2	13.4
356 Presb Ch Amer	1	340	600	600	.2	.5
388 Reg Bapt Gen As	1	365	390	454 *	.2	.4
413 S.D.A.	3	136	NR	162	.1	.1
418 Southw Bapt Fel	1	NR	NR	NR	-	-
419 So Bapt Conv	49	32,091	9,586	39,886 *	15.2	32.8
449 Un Methodist	22	13,254	4,497	16,475 *	6.3	13.6
467 Wesleyan	1	29	28	34	-	-
469 WELS	1	23	36	39	-	-
498 Indep.Charis.	1	3,750	5,000	5,000	1.9	4.1
HENRY	**90**	**17,198**	**6,626**	**21,694 ***	**37.4**	**100.0**
017 Amer Bapt Assn	1	50	NR	60 *	.1	.3
053 Assemb of God	2	133	171	180	.3	.8
056 Baha'i	0	3	NR	3	-	-
093 Chr Ch (Disc)	3	635	93	766 *	1.3	3.5
097 Chr Chs&Chs Cr	5	1,628	NR	1,965 *	3.4	9.1
127 Ch God (Cleve)	3	469	259	566 *	1.0	2.6
145 Ch God Prophcy	3	122	NR	147 *	.3	.7
151 L-D Saints	1	NR	NR	310	.5	1.4
157 Ch of Brethren	3	535	368	646 *	1.1	3.0
167 Chs of Christ	4	259	285	343	.6	1.6
193 Episcopal	1	NR	128	483	.8	2.2
304 NatPrimBapt USA	1	48	NR	58 *	.1	.3
349 Pent Holiness	9	742	582	895 *	1.5	4.1
355 Presb Ch (USA)	5	928	398	1,119 *	1.9	5.2
360 Prim Bapt Chrch	3	NR	NR	NR	-	-
403 Salvation Army	1	42	30	168	.3	.8
418 Southw Bapt Fel	4	NR	NR	NR	-	-
419 So Bapt Conv	27	9,517	3,473	11,484 *	19.8	52.9
449 Un Methodist	13	2,003	803	2,417 *	4.2	11.1
467 Wesleyan	1	84	36	84	.1	.4
HIGHLAND	**19**	**993**	**486**	**1,435 ***	**56.6**	**100.0**
056 Baha'i	0	9	NR	9	.4	.6
145 Ch God Prophcy	1	41	NR	48 *	1.9	3.3
151 L-D Saints	1	NR	NR	239	9.4	16.7
157 Ch of Brethren	1	37	29	43 *	1.7	3.0
193 Episcopal	1	NR	31	32	1.3	2.2
355 Presb Ch (USA)	4	231	144	272 *	10.7	19.0
413 S.D.A.	1	15	NR	18	.7	1.3
449 Un Methodist	10	660	282	774 *	30.5	53.9
HOPEWELL CITY	**29**	**8,590**	**3,586**	**12,208 ***	**54.6**	**100.0**
019 Amer Bapt USA	1	483	225	611 *	2.7	5.0
053 Assemb of God	1	80	105	105	.5	.9
056 Baha'i	0	5	NR	5	-	-
081 Catholic	1	NR	NR	977	4.4	8.0
093 Chr Ch (Disc)	1	369	83	467 *	2.1	3.8
097 Chr Chs&Chs Cr	1	65	NR	82 *	.4	.7
127 Ch God (Cleve)	1	257	113	325 *	1.5	2.7
157 Ch of Brethren	2	99	35	125 *	.6	1.0
165 Ch of Nazarene	1	122	64	122	.5	1.0
167 Chs of Christ	2	550	520	610	2.7	5.0
193 Episcopal	1	NR	111	457	2.0	3.7
246 Greek Orthodox	1	NR	NR	126	.6	1.0
283 Luth—MO Synod	1	319	115	414	1.9	3.4
349 Pent Holiness	1	125	107	158 *	.7	1.3
356 Presb Ch Amer	3	530	375	563	2.5	4.6
413 S.D.A.	1	51	NR	61	.3	.5
419 So Bapt Conv	7	4,365	1,312	5,520 *	24.7	45.2
443 Un C of Christ	1	90	65	114 *	.5	.9
449 Un Methodist	2	1,080	356	1,366 *	6.1	11.2
ISLE OF WIGHT	**39**	**6,481**	**2,522**	**9,337 ***	**31.4**	**100.0**
019 Amer Bapt USA	1	0	0	0 *	-	-
053 Assemb of God	3	244	275	433	1.5	4.6
056 Baha'i	0	7	NR	7	-	.1
076 Buddhism	1	NR	NR	NR	-	-
081 Catholic	1	NR	NR	490	1.6	5.2
097 Chr Chs&Chs Cr	1	54	NR	67 *	.2	.7
127 Ch God (Cleve)	2	69	44	85 *	.3	.9
145 Ch God Prophcy	1	41	NR	51 *	.2	.5
151 L-D Saints	1	NR	NR	461	1.6	4.9
165 Ch of Nazarene	1	136	120	140	.5	1.5
167 Chs of Christ	1	20	24	25	.1	.3
193 Episcopal	1	NR	50	240	.8	2.6
207 E.L.C.A.	1	29	19	43	.1	.5
223 Free Will Bapt	1	83	NR	104 *	.3	1.1
355 Presb Ch (USA)	1	138	91	171 *	.6	1.8
419 So Bapt Conv	9	3,124	810	3,875 *	13.0	41.5
443 Un C of Christ	6	696	414	863 *	2.9	9.2
449 Un Methodist	7	1,840	675	2,282 *	7.7	24.4
JAMES CITY	**30**	**6,401**	**3,824**	**18,533 ***	**38.5**	**100.0**
019 Amer Bapt USA	1	270	160	328 *	.7	1.8
053 Assemb of God	1	60	75	75	.2	.4
056 Baha'i	0	9	NR	9	-	-

NR–Not Reported　*Total adherents estimated from known number of communicant, confirmed, full members.　- Represents a percentage less than 0.1.　Percentages may not total 100 due to rounding.

Table 4: Religious Congregations by County and Group: 2000

Religious Group	Number of Churches, Synagogues, Mosques, or Temples	Number of Communicant, Confirmed, or Full Members	Number of Attendees	Total Adherents: Number of Adherents	Total Adherents: % of Total Pop.	Total Adherents: % of Total Adh.
081 Catholic	2	NR	NR	7,450	15.5	40.2
093 Chr Ch (Disc)	1	463	98	563 *	1.2	3.0
097 Chr Chs&Chs Cr	2	235	NR	285 *	.6	1.5
151 L-D Saints	1	NR	NR	471	1.0	2.5
193 Episcopal	3	NR	1,214	2,807	5.8	15.1
207 E.L.C.A.	1	344	137	424	.9	2.3
223 Free Will Bapt	1	83	NR	101 *	.2	.5
283 Luth—MO Synod	1	271	199	332	.7	1.8
288 Mennonite USA	1	68	71	83 *	.2	.4
349 Pent Holiness	1	258	266	314 *	.7	1.7
355 Presb Ch (USA)	1	179	133	218 *	.5	1.2
356 Presb Ch Amer	1	125	150	150	.3	.8
403 Salvation Army	1	27	17	32	.1	.2
413 S.D.A.	2	259	NR	308	.6	1.7
419 So Bapt Conv	5	2,775	953	3,375 *	7.0	18.2
435 Unitarian-Univ	1	196	NR	238 *	.5	1.3
449 Un Methodist	2	707	269	860 *	1.8	4.6
467 Wesleyan	1	72	82	110	.2	.6
KING AND QUEEN	**16**	**1,971**	**713**	**2,402 ***	**36.2**	**100.0**
053 Assemb of God	1	25	32	32	.5	1.3
056 Baha'i	0	2	NR	2	-	.1
093 Chr Ch (Disc)	1	128	35	154 *	2.3	6.4
193 Episcopal	1	NR	7	23	.3	1.0
419 So Bapt Conv	9	1,393	469	1,681 *	25.4	70.0
449 Un Methodist	4	423	170	510 *	7.7	21.2
KING GEORGE	**22**	**5,004**	**1,661**	**7,791 ***	**46.4**	**100.0**
019 Amer Bapt USA	1	0	0	0 *	-	-
053 Assemb of God	1	31	40	49	.3	.6
056 Baha'i	0	3	NR	3	-	-
076 Buddhism	1	NR	NR	NR	-	-
081 Catholic	1	NR	NR	962	5.7	12.3
127 Ch God (Cleve)	1	68	35	87 *	.5	1.1
193 Episcopal	4	NR	222	382	2.3	4.9
283 Luth—MO Synod	1	143	78	215	1.3	2.8
419 So Bapt Conv	9	4,068	991	5,208 *	31.0	66.8
449 Un Methodist	3	691	295	885 *	5.3	11.4
KING WILLIAM	**26**	**3,659**	**1,122**	**5,769 ***	**43.9**	**100.0**
011 A.W.M.C.	1	0	37	0	-	-
019 Amer Bapt USA	1	100	0	125 *	1.0	2.2
056 Baha'i	0	5	NR	5	-	.1
081 Catholic	1	NR	NR	513	3.9	8.9
093 Chr Ch (Disc)	1	100	31	125 *	1.0	2.2
097 Chr Chs&Chs Cr	2	280	NR	350 *	2.7	6.1
127 Ch God (Cleve)	1	62	53	78 *	.6	1.4
151 L-D Saints	1	NR	NR	195	1.5	3.4
165 Ch of Nazarene	1	28	28	183	1.4	3.2
167 Chs of Christ	1	15	18	20	.2	.3
193 Episcopal	3	NR	110	335	2.5	5.8
355 Presb Ch (USA)	2	114	50	143 *	1.1	2.5
419 So Bapt Conv	8	2,408	604	3,013 *	22.9	52.2
449 Un Methodist	3	547	191	684 *	5.2	11.9
LANCASTER	**28**	**3,819**	**1,730**	**6,384 ***	**55.2**	**100.0**
053 Assemb of God	1	21	10	45	.4	.7
056 Baha'i	0	3	NR	3	-	-
081 Catholic	1	NR	NR	969	8.4	15.2
151 L-D Saints	1	NR	NR	84	.7	1.3
165 Ch of Nazarene	1	50	96	96	.8	1.5
193 Episcopal	3	NR	347	833	7.2	13.0
355 Presb Ch (USA)	3	533	269	619 *	5.4	9.7
413 S.D.A.	1	76	NR	90	.8	1.4
419 So Bapt Conv	9	1,919	575	2,230 *	19.3	34.9
435 Unitarian-Univ	1	28	NR	33 *	.3	.5
449 Un Methodist	7	1,189	433	1,382 *	11.9	21.6
LEE	**106**	**12,701**	**3,423**	**15,794 ***	**67.0**	**100.0**
053 Assemb of God	1	10	10	11	-	.1
056 Baha'i	0	14	NR	14	.1	.1
081 Catholic	2	NR	NR	155	.7	1.0
097 Chr Chs&Chs Cr	6	506	NR	614 *	2.6	3.9
127 Ch God (Cleve)	5	461	323	566 *	2.4	3.6
145 Ch God Prophcy	3	122	NR	147 *	.6	.9
151 L-D Saints	1	NR	NR	242	1.0	1.5
157 Ch of Brethren	1	21	0	25 *	.1	.2
167 Chs of Christ	2	26	35	36	.2	.2
223 Free Will Bapt	4	334	NR	404 *	1.7	2.6
320 "Old" MB Ascs	1	29	NR	35 *	.1	.2
355 Presb Ch (USA)	1	22	20	27 *	.1	.2
360 Prim Bapt Chrch	2	NR	NR	NR	-	-
362 Prim Bapt E Dst	10	756	NR	916 *	3.9	5.8
419 So Bapt Conv	43	8,524	2,220	10,328 *	43.8	65.4
449 Un Methodist	24	1,876	815	2,274 *	9.6	14.4
LEXINGTON CITY	**16**	**2,330**	**964**	**3,587 ***	**52.2**	**100.0**
053 Assemb of God	1	37	55	62	.9	1.7
055 As Ref Pres Ch	2	624	NR	666	9.7	18.6
056 Baha'i	0	5	NR	5	.1	.1
081 Catholic	1	NR	NR	683	9.9	19.0
127 Ch God (Cleve)	1	39	43	43 *	.6	1.2
145 Ch God Prophcy	1	41	NR	44 *	.6	1.2
151 L-D Saints	2	NR	NR	268	3.9	7.5
167 Chs of Christ	1	15	20	25	.4	.7
226 Friends-USA	1	105	NR	114 *	1.7	3.2
263 Int Foursq Gos	1	74	126	126 *	1.8	3.5
356 Presb Ch Amer	1	138	180	187	2.7	5.2
419 So Bapt Conv	2	753	300	820 *	11.9	22.9
449 Un Methodist	2	499	240	544 *	7.9	15.2
LOUDOUN	**116**	**17,200**	**16,439**	**71,851 ***	**42.4**	**100.0**
053 Assemb of God	2	210	267	425	.3	.6
056 Baha'i	1	194	NR	194	.1	.3
076 Buddhism	2	NR	NR	NR	-	-
081 Catholic	6	NR	NR	29,941	17.7	41.7
084 Calvary Chapel	1	NR	NR	NR	-	-
089 Chr & Miss Al	1	0	NR	50	-	.1
097 Chr Chs&Chs Cr	1	112	NR	149 *	.1	.2
127 Ch God (Cleve)	3	84	30	112 *	.1	.2
145 Ch God Prophcy	1	51	NR	68 *	-	.1
151 L-D Saints	8	NR	NR	2,697	1.6	3.8
165 Ch of Nazarene	2	275	317	488	.3	.7
167 Chs of Christ	2	104	120	144	.1	.2
193 Episcopal	7	NR	1,245	2,935	1.7	4.1
207 E.L.C.A.	5	1,307	689	1,972	1.2	2.7
226 Friends-USA	1	105	NR	140 *	.1	.2
265 Int Pent C Chr	2	11	29	79	-	.1
267 Muslim Est	1	NR	412	1,891	1.1	2.6
283 Luth—MO Synod	1	255	234	384	.2	.5
335 Orth Pres Ch	2	115	159	183	.1	.3
355 Presb Ch (USA)	6	1,289	745	1,712 *	1.0	2.4
356 Presb Ch Amer	1	64	90	95	.1	.1
360 Prim Bapt Chrch	3	NR	NR	NR	-	-
403 Salvation Army	1	26	19	83	-	.1
413 S.D.A.	1	69	NR	82	-	.1
416 Sikh	1	NR	NR	NR	-	-
418 Southw Bapt Fel	3	NR	NR	NR	-	-
419 So Bapt Conv	14	4,166	1,523	5,537 *	3.3	7.7
435 Unitarian-Univ	2	132	NR	175 *	.1	.2
443 Un C of Christ	1	100	44	133 *	.1	.2
449 Un Methodist	27	6,857	3,493	9,113 *	5.4	12.7
467 Wesleyan	1	0	3,002	5,398	3.2	7.5
469 WELS	1	88	71	121	.1	.2
496 Jewish Est	2	NR	NR	3,600	2.1	5.0
499 Indep.Non-Char	3	1,586	3,950	3,950	2.3	5.5
LOUISA	**46**	**6,374**	**2,362**	**9,288 ***	**36.2**	**100.0**
053 Assemb of God	1	94	140	140	.5	1.5
056 Baha'i	0	5	NR	5	-	.1
081 Catholic	2	NR	NR	740	2.9	8.0
093 Chr Ch (Disc)	6	593	219	729 *	2.8	7.8
097 Chr Chs&Chs Cr	2	359	NR	442 *	1.7	4.8
151 L-D Saints	1	NR	NR	431	1.7	4.6
165 Ch of Nazarene	1	49	41	114	.4	1.2

NR–Not Reported *Total adherents estimated from known number of communicant, confirmed, full members. - Represents a percentage less than 0.1. Percentages may not total 100 due to rounding.

Table 4: Religious Congregations by County and Group: 2000

Religious Group	Number of Churches, Synagogues, Mosques, or Temples	Number of Communicant, Confirmed, or Full Members	Number of Attendees	Total Adherents: Number of Adherents	Total Adherents: % of Total Pop.	Total Adherents: % of Total Adh.
193 Episcopal	1	NR	75	179	.7	1.9
223 Free Will Bapt	1	83	NR	103 *	.4	1.1
349 Pent Holiness	2	74	53	91 *	.4	1.0
355 Presb Ch (USA)	3	208	134	256 *	1.0	2.8
419 So Bapt Conv	17	3,511	1,056	4,317 *	16.8	46.5
449 Un Methodist	8	1,379	633	1,696 *	6.6	18.3
467 Wesleyan	1	19	11	45	.2	.5
LUNENBURG	**26**	**3,633**	**1,200**	**4,604 ***	**35.0**	**100.0**
056 Baha'i	0	4	NR	4	-	.1
081 Catholic	1	NR	NR	62	.5	1.3
093 Chr Ch (Disc)	2	722	172	858 *	6.5	18.6
097 Chr Chs&Chs Cr	2	160	NR	191 *	1.5	4.1
145 Ch God Prophcy	1	41	NR	48 *	.4	1.0
165 Ch of Nazarene	1	156	88	178	1.4	3.9
193 Episcopal	3	NR	66	126	1.0	2.7
283 Luth—MO Synod	1	28	15	140	1.1	3.0
355 Presb Ch (USA)	2	73	53	86 *	.7	1.9
419 So Bapt Conv	6	1,586	484	1,885 *	14.3	40.9
449 Un Methodist	7	863	322	1,026 *	7.8	22.3
LYNCHBURG CITY	**75**	**19,506**	**8,995**	**33,683 ***	**51.6**	**100.0**
019 Amer Bapt USA	2	721	100	871 *	1.3	2.6
053 Assemb of God	2	221	284	512	.8	1.5
075 Brethren in Cr	1	35	17	35	.1	.1
081 Catholic	2	NR	NR	4,350	6.7	12.9
084 Calvary Chapel	1	NR	NR	NR	-	-
093 Chr Ch (Disc)	6	2,567	753	3,102 *	4.8	9.2
097 Chr Chs&Chs Cr	1	90	NR	109 *	.2	.3
123 Ch God (Ander)	2	NR	70	70	.1	.2
127 Ch God (Cleve)	1	95	43	115 *	.2	.3
145 Ch God Prophcy	1	41	NR	49 *	.1	.1
151 L-D Saints	2	NR	NR	797	1.2	2.4
157 Ch of Brethren	1	81	0	98 *	.2	.3
165 Ch of Nazarene	1	216	140	288	.4	.9
167 Chs of Christ	2	110	120	155	.2	.5
193 Episcopal	5	NR	658	2,448	3.8	7.3
203 Evan Free Ch	2	189	725	725	1.1	2.2
207 E.L.C.A.	1	245	156	356	.5	1.1
226 Friends-USA	1	105	NR	127 *	.2	.4
246 Greek Orthodox	1	NR	NR	51	.1	.2
283 Luth—MO Synod	1	52	42	61	.1	.2
335 Orth Pres Ch	1	65	78	99	.2	.3
403 Salvation Army	1	187	62	366	.6	1.1
413 S.D.A.	2	429	NR	510	.8	1.5
419 So Bapt Conv	14	6,406	1,763	7,740 *	11.9	23.0
435 Unitarian-Univ	1	79	NR	95 *	.1	.3
443 Un C of Christ	1	11	5	13 *	-	-
449 Un Methodist	15	6,874	2,284	8,306 *	12.7	24.7
467 Wesleyan	2	187	195	460	.7	1.4
496 Jewish Est	1	NR	NR	275	.4	.8
499 Indep.Non-Char	1	500	1,500	1,500	2.3	4.5
MADISON	**29**	**3,241**	**1,302**	**4,608 ***	**36.8**	**100.0**
056 Baha'i	0	1	NR	1	-	-
061 Beachy Amish	1	99	NR	121 *	1.0	2.6
081 Catholic	1	NR	NR	466	3.7	10.1
093 Chr Ch (Disc)	2	295	136	359 *	2.9	7.8
157 Ch of Brethren	1	80	45	97 *	.8	2.1
193 Episcopal	2	NR	83	206	1.6	4.5
207 E.L.C.A.	2	331	114	391	3.1	8.5
223 Free Will Bapt	1	83	NR	102 *	.8	2.2
297 Mennonite;Other	1	10	NR	12 *	.1	.3
355 Presb Ch (USA)	1	153	100	186 *	1.5	4.0
360 Prim Bapt Chrch	1	NR	NR	NR	-	-
419 So Bapt Conv	6	1,128	378	1,374 *	11.0	29.8
449 Un Methodist	10	1,061	446	1,293 *	10.3	28.1
MANASSAS CITY	**32**	**8,343**	**5,566**	**34,253 ***	**97.5**	**100.0**
022 Carp Rus Orth	1	122	NR	207	.6	.6
053 Assemb of God	2	1,040	1,560	2,240	6.4	6.5
081 Catholic	1	NR	NR	18,738	53.3	54.7
084 Calvary Chapel	1	NR	NR	NR	-	-
097 Chr Chs&Chs Cr	1	185	NR	242 *	.7	.7
127 Ch God (Cleve)	2	284	162	371 *	1.1	1.1
145 Ch God Prophcy	2	92	NR	120 *	.3	.4
151 L-D Saints	2	NR	NR	929	2.6	2.7
157 Ch of Brethren	1	427	220	559 *	1.6	1.6
167 Chs of Christ	2	206	221	267	.8	.8
193 Episcopal	1	NR	274	735	2.1	2.1
203 Evan Free Ch	1	101	240	240	.7	.7
267 Muslim Est	1	NR	412	1,891	5.4	5.5
335 Orth Pres Ch	1	19	20	27	.1	.1
349 Pent Holiness	1	42	45	55 *	.2	.2
356 Presb Ch Amer	1	139	112	178	.5	.5
360 Prim Bapt Chrch	1	NR	NR	NR	-	-
388 Reg Bapt Gen As	1	35	50	50 *	.1	.1
413 S.D.A.	2	369	NR	439	1.2	1.3
419 So Bapt Conv	2	1,479	554	1,936 *	5.5	5.7
435 Unitarian-Univ	1	169	NR	221 *	.6	.6
449 Un Methodist	2	3,222	1,309	4,217 *	12.0	12.3
469 WELS	1	212	137	291	.8	.8
498 Indep.Charis.	1	200	250	300	.9	.9
MANASSAS PARK CITY	**4**	**109**	**100**	**1,367 ***	**13.3**	**100.0**
089 Chr & Miss Al	1	26	NR	57	.6	4.2
151 L-D Saints	1	NR	NR	398	3.9	29.1
223 Free Will Bapt	1	83	NR	112 *	1.1	8.2
267 Muslim Est	1	NR	100	800	7.8	58.5
MARTINSVILLE CITY	**42**	**8,921**	**2,881**	**11,861 ***	**76.9**	**100.0**
053 Assemb of God	1	110	150	180	1.2	1.5
081 Catholic	1	NR	NR	784	5.1	6.6
093 Chr Ch (Disc)	12	2,123	701	2,559 *	16.6	21.6
097 Chr Chs&Chs Cr	3	545	NR	657 *	4.3	5.5
123 Ch God (Ander)	1	NR	35	35	.2	.3
127 Ch God (Cleve)	1	469	270	565 *	3.7	4.8
157 Ch of Brethren	1	145	0	175 *	1.1	1.5
167 Chs of Christ	3	156	170	198	1.3	1.7
223 Free Will Bapt	1	83	NR	101 *	.7	.9
226 Friends-USA	2	190	NR	229 *	1.5	1.9
355 Presb Ch (USA)	1	89	59	107 *	.7	.9
360 Prim Bapt Chrch	2	NR	NR	NR	-	-
413 S.D.A.	2	91	NR	109	.7	.9
419 So Bapt Conv	6	3,541	953	4,269 *	27.7	36.0
449 Un Methodist	2	1,263	391	1,523 *	9.9	12.8
467 Wesleyan	2	116	152	245	1.6	2.1
496 Jewish Est	1	NR	NR	125	.8	1.1
MATHEWS	**27**	**3,433**	**1,173**	**5,722 ***	**62.1**	**100.0**
056 Baha'i	0	1	NR	1	-	-
081 Catholic	2	NR	NR	1,139	12.4	19.9
093 Chr Ch (Disc)	2	119	8	139 *	1.5	2.4
127 Ch God (Cleve)	1	34	41	41 *	.4	.7
165 Ch of Nazarene	1	52	58	111	1.2	1.9
167 Chs of Christ	1	30	35	40	.4	.7
193 Episcopal	1	NR	140	511	5.6	8.9
226 Friends-USA	3	285	NR	333 *	3.6	5.8
419 So Bapt Conv	6	1,226	267	1,434 *	15.6	25.1
449 Un Methodist	10	1,686	624	1,973 *	21.4	34.5
MECKLENBURG	**78**	**10,402**	**4,049**	**13,542 ***	**41.8**	**100.0**
053 Assemb of God	1	26	34	65	.2	.5
056 Baha'i	0	21	NR	21	.1	.2
081 Catholic	2	NR	NR	499	1.5	3.7
097 Chr Chs&Chs Cr	1	100	NR	120 *	.4	.9
127 Ch God (Cleve)	3	202	133	241 *	.7	1.8
145 Ch God Prophcy	1	41	NR	49 *	.2	.4
165 Ch of Nazarene	1	24	16	27	.1	.2
167 Chs of Christ	1	20	25	24	.1	.2
193 Episcopal	10	NR	463	542	1.7	4.0
339 Pent Ch of God	1	15	NR	40	.1	.3
349 Pent Holiness	1	15	15	18 *	.1	.1
355 Presb Ch (USA)	4	250	193	299 *	.9	2.2

NR–Not Reported   *Total adherents estimated from known number of communicant, confirmed, full members.   - Represents a percentage less than 0.1.   Percentages may not total 100 due to rounding.

Table 4: Religious Congregations by County and Group: 2000

Religious Group	Number of Churches, Synagogues, Mosques, or Temples	Number of Communicant, Confirmed, or Full Members	Number of Attendees	Total Adherents: Number of Adherents	Total Adherents: % of Total Pop.	Total Adherents: % of Total Adh.
413 S.D.A.	1	33	NR	39	.1	.3
419 So Bapt Conv	25	6,392	2,019	7,651 *	23.6	56.5
443 Un C of Christ	3	264	119	316 *	1.0	2.3
449 Un Methodist	23	2,999	1,032	3,591 *	11.1	26.5
MIDDLESEX	**18**	**3,367**	**1,404**	**4,476 ***	**45.1**	**100.0**
056 Baha'i	0	1	NR	1	-	-
081 Catholic	1	NR	NR	224	2.3	5.0
093 Chr Ch (Disc)	1	276	0	322 *	3.2	7.2
193 Episcopal	1	NR	106	218	2.2	4.9
349 Pent Holiness	1	37	34	43 *	.4	1.0
419 So Bapt Conv	7	1,757	784	2,049 *	20.6	45.8
449 Un Methodist	5	1,190	398	1,388 *	14.0	31.0
467 Wesleyan	2	106	82	231	2.3	5.2
MONTGOMERY	**105**	**17,588**	**8,601**	**25,896 ***	**31.0**	**100.0**
053 Assemb of God	1	37	50	60	.1	.2
056 Baha'i	0	30	NR	30	-	.1
081 Catholic	3	NR	NR	2,740	3.3	10.6
093 Chr Ch (Disc)	3	623	106	718 *	.9	2.8
097 Chr Chs&Chs Cr	4	893	NR	1,030 *	1.2	4.0
123 Ch God (Ander)	3	NR	270	270	.3	1.0
127 Ch God (Cleve)	2	255	235	294 *	.4	1.1
145 Ch God Prophcy	1	41	NR	47 *	.1	.2
151 L-D Saints	3	NR	NR	806	1.0	3.1
157 Ch of Brethren	2	237	140	273 *	.3	1.1
165 Ch of Nazarene	1	41	52	52	.1	.2
167 Chs of Christ	3	333	345	426	.5	1.6
193 Episcopal	2	NR	257	659	.8	2.5
207 E.L.C.A.	5	855	488	1,173	1.4	4.5
226 Friends-USA	1	105	NR	121 *	.1	.5
263 Int Foursq Gos	1	103	267	267 *	.3	1.0
267 Muslim Est	1	NR	55	163	.2	.6
288 Mennonite USA	1	47	38	54 *	.1	.2
339 Pent Ch of God	1	15	NR	25	-	.1
349 Pent Holiness	15	2,184	1,500	2,518 *	3.0	9.7
355 Presb Ch (USA)	6	1,580	700	1,822 *	2.2	7.0
356 Presb Ch Amer	1	87	153	153	.2	.6
418 Southw Bapt Fel	1	NR	NR	NR	-	-
419 So Bapt Conv	14	4,497	1,646	5,186 *	6.2	20.0
435 Unitarian-Univ	1	140	NR	161 *	.2	.6
449 Un Methodist	24	5,294	2,083	6,105 *	7.3	23.6
467 Wesleyan	4	191	216	543	.6	2.1
496 Jewish Est	1	NR	NR	200	.2	.8
NELSON	**41**	**5,728**	**2,078**	**7,263 ***	**50.3**	**100.0**
056 Baha'i	0	3	NR	3	-	-
081 Catholic	1	NR	NR	275	1.9	3.8
093 Chr Ch (Disc)	2	273	40	326 *	2.3	4.5
127 Ch God (Cleve)	2	94	38	112 *	.8	1.5
157 Ch of Brethren	1	86	55	103 *	.7	1.4
167 Chs of Christ	1	36	45	48	.3	.7
193 Episcopal	3	NR	77	149	1.0	2.1
288 Mennonite USA	1	15	19	19 *	.1	.3
349 Pent Holiness	3	90	59	107 *	.7	1.5
355 Presb Ch (USA)	3	315	190	375 *	2.6	5.2
419 So Bapt Conv	18	3,714	1,197	4,431 *	30.7	61.0
449 Un Methodist	6	1,102	358	1,315 *	9.1	18.1
NEW KENT	**14**	**2,537**	**1,235**	**3,637 ***	**27.0**	**100.0**
056 Baha'i	0	1	NR	1	-	-
081 Catholic	1	NR	NR	155	1.2	4.3
193 Episcopal	1	NR	112	357	2.7	9.8
349 Pent Holiness	1	217	141	267 *	2.0	7.3
355 Presb Ch (USA)	1	158	80	195 *	1.4	5.4
419 So Bapt Conv	7	1,402	616	1,727 *	12.8	47.5
449 Un Methodist	3	759	286	935 *	6.9	25.7
NEWPORT NEWS CITY	**105**	**34,898**	**14,395**	**62,118 ***	**34.5**	**100.0**
019 Amer Bapt USA	2	2,100	600	2,688 *	1.5	4.3
053 Assemb of God	3	563	648	909	.5	1.5
056 Baha'i	1	38	NR	38	-	.1
081 Catholic	4	NR	NR	11,414	6.3	18.4
084 Calvary Chapel	1	NR	NR	NR	-	-
089 Chr & Miss Al	1	0	NR	28	-	-
093 Chr Ch (Disc)	2	332	131	425 *	.2	.7
097 Chr Chs&Chs Cr	4	1,835	NR	2,349 *	1.3	3.8
123 Ch God (Ander)	2	NR	110	110	.1	.2
127 Ch God (Cleve)	2	1,422	1,360	1,820 *	1.0	2.9
145 Ch God Prophcy	3	122	NR	156 *	.1	.3
151 L-D Saints	1	NR	NR	335	.2	.5
157 Ch of Brethren	1	160	99	205 *	.1	.3
165 Ch of Nazarene	1	82	80	82	-	.1
167 Chs of Christ	3	405	386	566	.3	.9
193 Episcopal	6	NR	810	2,653	1.5	4.3
207 E.L.C.A.	2	665	380	861	.5	1.4
223 Free Will Bapt	1	83	NR	107 *	.1	.2
226 Friends-USA	1	95	NR	122 *	.1	.2
246 Greek Orthodox	1	NR	NR	1,017	.6	1.6
267 Muslim Est	1	NR	15	16	-	-
283 Luth—MO Synod	1	391	286	512	.3	.8
288 Mennonite USA	3	397	312	508 *	.3	.8
349 Pent Holiness	1	51	36	65 *	-	.1
355 Presb Ch (USA)	9	2,890	1,293	3,700 *	2.1	6.0
413 S.D.A.	1	398	NR	474	.3	.8
419 So Bapt Conv	26	15,075	4,420	19,296 *	10.7	31.1
435 Unitarian-Univ	1	109	NR	140 *	.1	.2
443 Un C of Christ	4	769	353	984 *	.5	1.6
449 Un Methodist	11	5,842	1,969	7,478 *	4.2	12.0
467 Wesleyan	1	74	82	210	.1	.3
496 Jewish Est	2	NR	NR	1,600	.9	2.6
498 Indep.Charis.	1	500	700	700	.4	1.1
499 Indep.Non-Char	1	500	325	550	.3	.9
NORFOLK CITY	**153**	**45,717**	**21,468**	**84,575 ***	**36.1**	**100.0**
019 Amer Bapt USA	12	6,671	3,680	8,268 *	3.5	9.8
053 Assemb of God	5	699	954	1,158	.5	1.4
056 Baha'i	1	129	NR	129	.1	.2
081 Catholic	7	NR	NR	11,059	4.7	13.1
093 Chr Ch (Disc)	2	285	71	353 *	.2	.4
097 Chr Chs&Chs Cr	3	482	NR	598 *	.3	.7
105 Christian Ref	1	69	75	86 *	-	.1
123 Ch God (Ander)	2	NR	189	189	.1	.2
127 Ch God (Cleve)	1	115	45	143 *	.1	.2
151 L-D Saints	1	NR	NR	777	.3	.9
165 Ch of Nazarene	1	29	28	87	-	.1
167 Chs of Christ	2	300	255	391	.2	.5
173 Comm of Christ	1	117	NR	117	-	.1
179 Consrv Bapt	1	NR	130	130	.1	.2
193 Episcopal	10	NR	1,956	4,951	2.1	5.9
207 E.L.C.A.	3	1,241	607	1,694	.7	2.0
223 Free Will Bapt	2	167	NR	207 *	.1	.2
245 Greek Orth Vslp	1	700	NR	1,400	.6	1.7
246 Greek Orthodox	1	NR	NR	1,122	.5	1.3
264 Int Chs of Crst	1	349	708	509	.2	.6
267 Muslim Est	2	NR	328	1,041	.4	1.2
283 Luth—MO Synod	3	629	292	918	.4	1.1
288 Mennonite USA	1	24	20	30 *	-	-
290 Metro Comm Ch	1	91	93	93 *	-	.1
331 OCA: Ter Diocs	1	26	NR	69	-	.1
349 Pent Holiness	4	376	326	466 *	.2	.6
355 Presb Ch (USA)	18	4,085	1,917	5,064 *	2.2	6.0
356 Presb Ch Amer	3	279	284	419	.2	.5
360 Prim Bapt Chrch	1	NR	NR	NR	-	-
413 S.D.A.	2	861	NR	1,024	.4	1.2
418 Southw Bapt Fel	2	NR	NR	NR	-	-
419 So Bapt Conv	28	19,806	6,467	24,548 *	10.5	29.0
435 Unitarian-Univ	1	222	NR	275 *	.1	.3
443 Un C of Christ	6	900	504	1,115 *	.5	1.3
449 Un Methodist	17	6,190	2,039	7,670 *	3.3	9.1
496 Jewish Est	4	NR	NR	7,600	3.2	9.0
498 Indep.Charis.	1	875	500	875	.4	1.0
NORTHAMPTON	**27**	**2,734**	**1,292**	**3,983 ***	**30.4**	**100.0**
053 Assemb of God	1	18	18	18	.1	.5

NR–Not Reported *Total adherents estimated from known number of communicant, confirmed, full members. - Represents a percentage less than 0.1. Percentages may not total 100 due to rounding.

Table 4: Religious Congregations by County and Group: 2000

Religious Group	Number of Churches, Synagogues, Mosques, or Temples	Number of Communicant, Confirmed, or Full Members	Number of Attendees	Total Adherents		
				Number of Adherents	% of Total Pop.	% of Total Adh.
056 Baha'i	0	2	NR	2	-	.1
081 Catholic	1	NR	NR	209	1.6	5.2
123 Ch God (Ander)	1	NR	15	15	.1	.4
151 L-D Saints	1	NR	NR	93	.7	2.3
165 Ch of Nazarene	1	29	30	30	.2	.8
193 Episcopal	3	NR	148	292	2.2	7.3
355 Presb Ch (USA)	2	98	64	120 *	.9	3.0
413 S.D.A.	1	77	NR	92	.7	2.3
419 So Bapt Conv	7	1,002	420	1,212 *	9.3	30.4
449 Un Methodist	8	1,508	583	1,825 *	13.9	45.8
467 Wesleyan	1	0	14	75	.6	1.9
NORTHUMBERLAND	**30**	**4,141**	**1,843**	**5,313 ***	**43.3**	**100.0**
019 Amer Bapt USA	1	125	100	145 *	1.2	2.7
056 Baha'i	0	2	NR	2	-	-
123 Ch God (Ander)	1	NR	78	78	.6	1.5
193 Episcopal	3	NR	238	432	3.5	8.1
283 Luth—MO Synod	1	48	48	52	.4	1.0
419 So Bapt Conv	12	2,103	681	2,441 *	19.9	45.9
449 Un Methodist	12	1,863	698	2,163 *	17.6	40.7
NORTON CITY	**11**	**795**	**150**	**1,247 ***	**31.9**	**100.0**
081 Catholic	1	NR	NR	207	5.3	16.6
097 Chr Chs&Chs Cr	1	140	NR	168 *	4.3	13.5
123 Ch God (Ander)	1	NR	85	85	2.2	6.8
127 Ch God (Cleve)	1	71	65	85 *	2.2	6.8
223 Free Will Bapt	7	584	NR	702 *	18.0	56.3
NOTTOWAY	**28**	**3,886**	**1,422**	**4,971 ***	**31.6**	**100.0**
053 Assemb of God	1	37	45	57	.4	1.1
081 Catholic	2	NR	NR	109	.7	2.2
093 Chr Ch (Disc)	2	309	33	375 *	2.4	7.5
127 Ch God (Cleve)	1	94	39	114 *	.7	2.3
145 Ch God Prophcy	1	41	NR	49 *	.3	1.0
165 Ch of Nazarene	1	56	64	74	.5	1.5
167 Chs of Christ	1	30	35	40	.3	.8
193 Episcopal	2	NR	41	136	.9	2.7
223 Free Will Bapt	1	83	NR	101 *	.6	2.0
355 Presb Ch (USA)	4	416	240	503 *	3.2	10.1
413 S.D.A.	1	0	NR	0	-	-
419 So Bapt Conv	4	1,450	432	1,758 *	11.2	35.4
449 Un Methodist	6	1,344	467	1,629 *	10.4	32.8
467 Wesleyan	1	26	26	26	.2	.5
ORANGE	**44**	**7,570**	**2,875**	**10,227 ***	**39.5**	**100.0**
053 Assemb of God	1	95	130	130	.5	1.3
056 Baha'i	0	17	NR	17	.1	.2
081 Catholic	2	NR	NR	513	2.0	5.0
093 Chr Ch (Disc)	2	184	63	223 *	.9	2.2
097 Chr Chs&Chs Cr	2	185	NR	224 *	.9	2.2
127 Ch God (Cleve)	1	131	72	159 *	.6	1.6
157 Ch of Brethren	2	77	0	93 *	.4	.9
165 Ch of Nazarene	1	66	67	73	.3	.7
167 Chs of Christ	1	19	25	25	.1	.2
193 Episcopal	2	NR	178	469	1.8	4.6
207 E.L.C.A.	1	102	53	121	.5	1.2
349 Pent Holiness	3	144	122	175 *	.7	1.7
355 Presb Ch (USA)	3	348	187	422 *	1.6	4.1
413 S.D.A.	2	118	NR	140	.5	1.4
419 So Bapt Conv	14	4,129	1,056	5,015 *	19.4	49.0
449 Un Methodist	6	1,175	362	1,428 *	5.5	14.0
499 Indep.Non-Char	1	780	560	1,000	3.9	9.8
PAGE	**55**	**6,726**	**3,009**	**8,647 ***	**37.3**	**100.0**
019 Amer Bapt USA	2	122	40	148 *	.6	1.7
053 Assemb of God	4	140	187	248	1.1	2.9
056 Baha'i	0	4	NR	4	-	-
081 Catholic	1	NR	NR	284	1.2	3.3
093 Chr Ch (Disc)	2	472	112	572 *	2.5	6.6
157 Ch of Brethren	6	730	302	885 *	3.8	10.2
167 Chs of Christ	2	40	42	50	.2	.6
193 Episcopal	3	NR	126	182	.8	2.1

Religious Group	Number of Churches, Synagogues, Mosques, or Temples	Number of Communicant, Confirmed, or Full Members	Number of Attendees	Total Adherents		
				Number of Adherents	% of Total Pop.	% of Total Adh.
207 E.L.C.A.	8	1,129	450	1,401	6.0	16.2
288 Mennonite USA	1	44	35	53 *	.2	.6
297 Mennonite;Other	1	10	NR	12 *	.1	.1
349 Pent Holiness	2	325	122	394 *	1.7	4.6
360 Prim Bapt Chrch	4	NR	NR	NR	-	-
413 S.D.A.	2	350	NR	416	1.8	4.8
419 So Bapt Conv	4	1,190	610	1,442 *	6.2	16.7
443 Un C of Christ	3	291	128	353 *	1.5	4.1
449 Un Methodist	9	1,529	605	1,853 *	8.0	21.4
499 Indep.Non-Char	1	350	250	350	1.5	4.0
PATRICK	**73**	**6,932**	**3,684**	**8,595 ***	**44.3**	**100.0**
017 Amer Bapt Assn	1	20	NR	24 *	.1	.3
081 Catholic	1	NR	NR	77	.4	.9
093 Chr Ch (Disc)	3	143	65	172 *	.9	2.0
097 Chr Chs&Chs Cr	2	190	NR	228 *	1.2	2.7
127 Ch God (Cleve)	2	357	317	443 *	2.3	5.2
145 Ch God Prophcy	3	122	NR	147 *	.8	1.7
151 L-D Saints	1	NR	NR	82	.4	1.0
157 Ch of Brethren	3	329	227	401 *	2.1	4.7
167 Chs of Christ	2	95	105	125	.6	1.5
207 E.L.C.A.	1	127	52	148	.8	1.7
295 Morav Ch-South	1	45	NR	57	.3	.7
304 NatPrimBapt USA	2	120	NR	144 *	.7	1.7
349 Pent Holiness	7	688	584	826 *	4.3	9.6
355 Presb Ch (USA)	7	342	315	419 *	2.2	4.9
360 Prim Bapt Chrch	8	NR	NR	NR	-	-
413 S.D.A.	1	51	NR	61	.3	.7
419 So Bapt Conv	12	2,885	1,154	3,462 *	17.8	40.3
449 Un Methodist	13	1,223	674	1,467 *	7.6	17.1
467 Wesleyan	3	195	191	312	1.6	3.6
PETERSBURG CITY	**33**	**6,566**	**3,106**	**11,450 ***	**33.9**	**100.0**
011 A.W.M.C.	1	4	34	4	-	-
019 Amer Bapt USA	4	2,886	1,334	3,589 *	10.6	31.3
053 Assemb of God	2	206	250	335	1.0	2.9
056 Baha'i	0	17	NR	17	.1	.1
081 Catholic	1	NR	NR	1,222	3.6	10.7
093 Chr Ch (Disc)	1	125	69	155 *	.5	1.4
145 Ch God Prophcy	1	41	NR	51 *	.2	.4
151 L-D Saints	1	NR	NR	279	.8	2.4
167 Chs of Christ	3	320	280	385	1.1	3.4
193 Episcopal	3	NR	295	804	2.4	7.0
207 E.L.C.A.	1	236	81	261	.8	2.3
223 Free Will Bapt	1	83	NR	104 *	.3	.9
267 Muslim Est	1	NR	156	609	1.8	5.3
349 Pent Holiness	2	70	71	87 *	.3	.8
355 Presb Ch (USA)	1	72	36	90 *	.3	.8
413 S.D.A.	1	169	NR	201	.6	1.8
419 So Bapt Conv	4	923	240	1,148 *	3.4	10.0
449 Un Methodist	4	1,414	260	1,759 *	5.2	15.4
496 Jewish Est	1	NR	NR	350	1.0	3.1
PITTSYLVANIA	**125**	**23,082**	**9,659**	**29,001 ***	**47.0**	**100.0**
053 Assemb of God	1	36	40	42	.1	.1
056 Baha'i	0	1	NR	1	-	-
081 Catholic	1	NR	NR	191	.3	.7
093 Chr Ch (Disc)	5	556	149	673 *	1.1	2.3
097 Chr Chs&Chs Cr	7	1,081	NR	1,307 *	2.1	4.5
145 Ch God Prophcy	4	163	NR	196 *	.3	.7
151 L-D Saints	1	NR	NR	185	.3	.6
157 Ch of Brethren	1	188	0	227 *	.4	.8
193 Episcopal	6	NR	276	530	.9	1.8
207 E.L.C.A.	1	271	146	359	.6	1.2
304 NatPrimBapt USA	1	184	NR	223 *	.4	.8
323 Old Ord Amish	1	55	NR	67 *	.1	.2
349 Pent Holiness	11	1,363	974	1,649 *	2.7	5.7
355 Presb Ch (USA)	10	1,153	536	1,395 *	2.3	4.8
403 Salvation Army	1	103	24	202	.3	.7
418 Southw Bapt Fel	2	NR	NR	NR	-	-
419 So Bapt Conv	41	11,421	4,397	13,819 *	22.4	47.7
449 Un Methodist	28	3,707	1,642	4,485 *	7.3	15.5
499 Indep.Non-Char	3	2,800	1,475	3,450	5.6	11.9

NR–Not Reported *Total adherents estimated from known number of communicant, confirmed, full members. - Represents a percentage less than 0.1. Percentages may not total 100 due to rounding.

Table 4: Religious Congregations by County and Group: 2000

Religious Group	Number of Churches, Synagogues, Mosques, or Temples	Number of Communicant, Confirmed, or Full Members	Number of Attendees	Total Adherents		
				Number of Adherents	% of Total Pop.	% of Total Adh.
POQUOSON CITY	**9**	**3,895**	**982**	**5,685 ***	**49.2**	**100.0**
034 Ant Orth of NA	1	28	NR	56	.5	1.0
053 Assemb of God	1	157	152	459	4.0	8.1
081 Catholic	1	NR	NR	571	4.9	10.0
173 Comm of Christ	1	84	NR	84	.7	1.5
349 Pent Holiness	1	5	5	6 *	.1	.1
419 So Bapt Conv	2	1,024	220	1,275 *	11.0	22.4
449 Un Methodist	2	2,597	605	3,234 *	28.0	56.9
PORTSMOUTH CITY	**77**	**24,540**	**7,783**	**38,831 ***	**38.6**	**100.0**
019 Amer Bapt USA	4	3,948	1,000	4,945 *	4.9	12.7
053 Assemb of God	2	246	275	375	.4	1.0
056 Baha'i	0	14	NR	14	-	-
081 Catholic	3	NR	NR	3,198	3.2	8.2
089 Chr & Miss Al	1	216	NR	387	.4	1.0
093 Chr Ch (Disc)	1	371	114	465 *	.5	1.2
097 Chr Chs&Chs Cr	3	725	NR	908 *	.9	2.3
127 Ch God (Cleve)	1	155	75	194 *	.2	.5
145 Ch God Prophcy	1	41	NR	51 *	.1	.1
165 Ch of Nazarene	1	78	69	99	.1	.3
167 Chs of Christ	2	118	125	149	.1	.4
193 Episcopal	5	NR	511	1,082	1.1	2.8
207 E.L.C.A.	3	560	246	735	.7	1.9
226 Friends-USA	1	95	NR	119 *	.1	.3
283 Luth—MO Synod	1	89	55	134	.1	.3
349 Pent Holiness	4	464	319	581 *	.6	1.5
355 Presb Ch (USA)	2	391	216	490 *	.5	1.3
403 Salvation Army	1	138	26	217	.2	.6
413 S.D.A.	2	231	NR	275	.3	.7
419 So Bapt Conv	21	10,721	2,821	13,428 *	13.4	34.6
443 Un C of Christ	3	554	269	694 *	.7	1.8
449 Un Methodist	12	4,385	1,262	5,491 *	5.5	14.1
496 Jewish Est	2	NR	NR	3,800	3.8	9.8
499 Indep.Non-Char	1	1,000	400	1,000	1.0	2.6
POWHATAN	**22**	**3,892**	**1,985**	**6,474 ***	**28.9**	**100.0**
053 Assemb of God	1	41	47	50	.2	.8
081 Catholic	1	NR	NR	843	3.8	13.0
127 Ch God (Cleve)	1	264	149	323 *	1.4	5.0
167 Chs of Christ	1	35	40	50	.2	.8
193 Episcopal	3	NR	232	915	4.1	14.1
223 Free Will Bapt	1	83	NR	102 *	.5	1.6
283 Luth—MO Synod	1	20	18	28	.1	.4
288 Mennonite USA	1	126	145	154 *	.7	2.4
355 Presb Ch (USA)	2	110	89	134 *	.6	2.1
388 Reg Bapt Gen As	1	120	95	95 *	.4	1.5
419 So Bapt Conv	7	2,425	889	2,964 *	13.2	45.8
449 Un Methodist	2	668	281	816 *	3.6	12.6
PRINCE EDWARD	**39**	**4,734**	**1,945**	**6,803 ***	**34.5**	**100.0**
056 Baha'i	0	55	NR	55	.3	.8
061 Beachy Amish	1	41	NR	49 *	.2	.7
081 Catholic	1	NR	NR	759	3.8	11.2
093 Chr Ch (Disc)	1	89	35	105 *	.5	1.5
097 Chr Chs&Chs Cr	1	85	NR	101 *	.5	1.5
127 Ch God (Cleve)	1	30	30	35 *	.2	.5
145 Ch God Prophcy	2	82	NR	96 *	.5	1.4
151 L-D Saints	1	NR	NR	280	1.4	4.1
167 Chs of Christ	1	24	40	46	.2	.7
193 Episcopal	1	NR	82	153	.8	2.2
283 Luth—MO Synod	2	172	130	205	1.0	3.0
355 Presb Ch (USA)	8	615	341	728 *	3.7	10.7
413 S.D.A.	2	89	NR	106	.5	1.6
419 So Bapt Conv	10	2,296	774	2,717 *	13.8	39.9
449 Un Methodist	7	1,156	513	1,368 *	6.9	20.1
PRINCE GEORGE	**26**	**3,946**	**1,355**	**6,242 ***	**18.9**	**100.0**
056 Baha'i	0	10	NR	10	-	.2
081 Catholic	1	NR	NR	764	2.3	12.2
151 L-D Saints	1	NR	NR	326	1.0	5.2
181 Consrv Congr	1	88	44	109 *	.3	1.7
193 Episcopal	2	NR	60	234	.7	3.7

Religious Group	Number of Churches, Synagogues, Mosques, or Temples	Number of Communicant, Confirmed, or Full Members	Number of Attendees	Total Adherents		
				Number of Adherents	% of Total Pop.	% of Total Adh.
349 Pent Holiness	1	45	42	56 *	.2	.9
355 Presb Ch (USA)	4	469	235	581 *	1.8	9.3
403 Salvation Army	1	81	32	132	.4	2.1
413 S.D.A.	1	0	NR	0	-	-
419 So Bapt Conv	7	2,138	488	2,649 *	8.0	42.4
449 Un Methodist	7	1,115	454	1,381 *	4.2	22.1
PRINCE WILLIAM	**104**	**25,715**	**13,877**	**82,195 ***	**29.3**	**100.0**
017 Amer Bapt Assn	1	200	NR	263 *	.1	.3
053 Assemb of God	5	860	1,176	3,038	1.1	3.7
056 Baha'i	2	102	NR	102	-	.1
081 Catholic	6	NR	NR	39,332	14.0	47.9
097 Chr Chs&Chs Cr	1	120	NR	158 *	.1	.2
127 Ch God (Cleve)	3	787	394	1,036 *	.4	1.3
151 L-D Saints	7	NR	NR	2,785	1.0	3.4
157 Ch of Brethren	2	431	175	567 *	.2	.7
165 Ch of Nazarene	2	588	523	617	.2	.8
167 Chs of Christ	3	264	299	331	.1	.4
193 Episcopal	5	NR	1,089	1,882	.7	2.3
207 E.L.C.A.	7	2,903	1,241	4,452	1.6	5.4
216 Evan Presby Ch	1	53	NR	70 *	-	.1
223 Free Will Bapt	1	83	NR	110 *	-	.1
283 Luth—MO Synod	3	572	394	828	.3	1.0
349 Pent Holiness	1	128	100	168 *	.1	.2
355 Presb Ch (USA)	5	1,933	1,032	2,545 *	.9	3.1
356 Presb Ch Amer	2	377	381	485	.2	.6
370 Ref Baptist Chs	2	NR	NR	NR	-	-
403 Salvation Army	1	132	32	207	.1	.3
413 S.D.A.	2	352	NR	419	.1	.5
418 Southw Bapt Fel	2	NR	NR	NR	-	-
419 So Bapt Conv	23	7,698	3,537	10,132 *	3.6	12.3
449 Un Methodist	13	7,675	2,932	10,103 *	3.6	12.3
463 Vineyard	1	130	120	171 *	.1	.2
469 WELS	1	102	102	194	.1	.2
496 Jewish Est	1	NR	NR	1,800	.6	2.2
499 Indep.Non-Char	1	225	350	400	.1	.5
PULASKI	**84**	**12,139**	**5,594**	**15,384 ***	**43.8**	**100.0**
053 Assemb of God	2	285	250	290	.8	1.9
056 Baha'i	0	6	NR	6	-	-
075 Brethren in Cr	1	90	107	107	.3	.7
081 Catholic	1	NR	NR	142	.4	.9
093 Chr Ch (Disc)	4	352	148	419 *	1.2	2.7
097 Chr Chs&Chs Cr	2	570	NR	678 *	1.9	4.4
123 Ch God (Ander)	1	NR	72	72	.2	.5
127 Ch God (Cleve)	5	1,494	907	1,777 *	5.1	11.6
145 Ch God Prophcy	5	204	NR	240 *	.7	1.6
151 L-D Saints	1	NR	NR	308	.9	2.0
157 Ch of Brethren	2	137	87	163 *	.5	1.1
165 Ch of Nazarene	1	51	70	139	.4	.9
167 Chs of Christ	1	65	50	80	.2	.5
193 Episcopal	1	NR	49	165	.5	1.1
207 E.L.C.A.	1	220	84	285	.8	1.9
265 Int Pent C Chr	1	5	15	15	-	.1
339 Pent Ch of God	1	100	NR	330	.9	2.1
349 Pent Holiness	10	1,108	777	1,318 *	3.8	8.6
355 Presb Ch (USA)	6	1,001	459	1,191 *	3.4	7.7
356 Presb Ch Amer	2	368	315	426	1.2	2.8
360 Prim Bapt Chrch	5	NR	NR	NR	-	-
403 Salvation Army	1	105	44	126	.4	.8
413 S.D.A.	1	101	NR	120	.3	.8
418 Southw Bapt Fel	1	NR	NR	NR	-	-
419 So Bapt Conv	6	2,386	836	2,837 *	8.1	18.4
449 Un Methodist	22	3,491	1,324	4,150 *	11.8	27.0
RADFORD CITY	**17**	**2,343**	**1,581**	**3,033 ***	**19.1**	**100.0**
093 Chr Ch (Disc)	2	430	172	478 *	3.0	15.8
097 Chr Chs&Chs Cr	1	75	NR	83 *	.5	2.7
127 Ch God (Cleve)	3	439	389	504 *	3.2	16.6
145 Ch God Prophcy	1	41	NR	45 *	.3	1.5
167 Chs of Christ	2	108	130	147	.9	4.8
193 Episcopal	1	NR	85	230	1.5	7.6
207 E.L.C.A.	1	140	58	194	1.2	6.4

NR–Not Reported   *Total adherents estimated from known number of communicant, confirmed, full members.   - Represents a percentage less than 0.1.   Percentages may not total 100 due to rounding.

Table 4: Religious Congregations by County and Group: 2000

Religious Group	Number of Churches, Synagogues, Mosques, or Temples	Number of Communicant, Confirmed, or Full Members	Number of Attendees	Total Adherents		
				Number of Adherents	% of Total Pop.	% of Total Adh.
263 Int Foursq Gos	1	67	87	87 *	.5	2.9
413 S.D.A.	1	59	NR	70	.4	2.3
419 So Bapt Conv	2	525	400	583 *	3.7	19.2
449 Un Methodist	1	420	204	467 *	2.9	15.4
467 Wesleyan	1	39	56	145	.9	4.8
RAPPAHANNOCK	**19**	**2,198**	**997**	**3,280 ***	**47.0**	**100.0**
053 Assemb of God	1	36	52	68	1.0	2.1
056 Baha'i	0	3	NR	3	-	.1
081 Catholic	1	NR	NR	375	5.4	11.4
193 Episcopal	1	NR	136	232	3.3	7.1
226 Friends-USA	1	105	NR	127 *	1.8	3.9
360 Prim Bapt Chrch	1	NR	NR	NR	-	-
419 So Bapt Conv	10	1,483	608	1,787 *	25.6	54.5
449 Un Methodist	4	571	201	688 *	9.9	21.0
RICHMOND	**23**	**3,526**	**1,377**	**4,113 ***	**46.7**	**100.0**
056 Baha'i	0	1	NR	1	-	-
093 Chr Ch (Disc)	1	110	40	127 *	1.4	3.1
097 Chr Chs&Chs Cr	2	210	NR	242 *	2.7	5.9
127 Ch God (Cleve)	1	90	66	104 *	1.2	2.5
167 Chs of Christ	2	340	357	385	4.4	9.4
193 Episcopal	1	NR	23	36	.4	.9
207 E.L.C.A.	1	0	0	0	-	-
283 Luth—MO Synod	1	2	9	17	.2	.4
355 Presb Ch (USA)	1	168	80	194 *	2.2	4.7
413 S.D.A.	1	47	NR	56	.6	1.4
419 So Bapt Conv	8	1,954	629	2,254 *	25.6	54.8
449 Un Methodist	4	604	173	697 *	7.9	16.9
RICHMOND CITY	**160**	**55,299**	**25,969**	**105,101 ***	**53.1**	**100.0**
019 Amer Bapt USA	21	13,546	5,044	16,427 *	8.3	15.6
050 Armen Ap Etchm	1	80	NR	400	.2	.4
053 Assemb of God	10	2,432	3,218	5,366	2.7	5.1
056 Baha'i	1	105	NR	105	.1	.1
076 Buddhism	1	NR	NR	NR	-	-
081 Catholic	11	NR	NR	10,070	5.1	9.6
093 Chr Ch (Disc)	4	1,356	303	1,644 *	.8	1.6
097 Chr Chs&Chs Cr	2	230	NR	279 *	.1	.3
123 Ch God (Ander)	2	NR	175	175	.1	.2
127 Ch God (Cleve)	1	114	150	150 *	.1	.1
145 Ch God Prophcy	2	82	NR	98 *	-	.1
165 Ch of Nazarene	1	269	135	269	.1	.3
167 Chs of Christ	2	273	300	305	.2	.3
193 Episcopal	12	NR	2,326	6,829	3.5	6.5
207 E.L.C.A.	1	416	159	506	.3	.5
226 Friends-USA	1	105	NR	127 *	.1	.1
246 Greek Orthodox	1	NR	NR	1,239	.6	1.2
252 Hindu	1	NR	NR	NR	-	-
264 Int Chs of Crst	1	93	154	128	.1	.1
267 Muslim Est	2	NR	406	859	.4	.8
283 Luth—MO Synod	3	1,459	644	1,949	1.0	1.9
290 Metro Comm Ch	1	211	162	256 *	.1	.2
331 OCA: Ter Diocs	1	31	NR	67	-	.1
349 Pent Holiness	2	218	122	264 *	.1	.3
355 Presb Ch (USA)	5	640	299	777 *	.4	.7
356 Presb Ch Amer	1	146	160	211	.1	.2
403 Salvation Army	1	271	93	311	.2	.3
413 S.D.A.	3	1,099	NR	1,308	.7	1.2
419 So Bapt Conv	29	20,336	6,947	24,661 *	12.5	23.5
435 Unitarian-Univ	1	473	NR	574 *	.3	.5
443 Un C of Christ	2	534	166	648 *	.3	.6
449 Un Methodist	20	9,481	2,883	11,497 *	5.8	10.9
463 Vineyard	1	150	162	182 *	.1	.2
467 Wesleyan	1	49	61	120	.1	.1
496 Jewish Est	7	NR	NR	15,000	7.6	14.3
498 Indep.Charis.	3	1,100	1,400	1,400	.7	1.3
499 Indep.Non-Char	1	0	500	900	.5	.9
ROANOKE	**93**	**37,207**	**15,473**	**52,938 ***	**61.7**	**100.0**
053 Assemb of God	1	77	77	210	.2	.4
056 Baha'i	2	122	NR	122	.1	.2
075 Brethren in Cr	1	76	74	76	.1	.1
081 Catholic	1	NR	NR	4,019	4.7	7.6
084 Calvary Chapel	1	NR	NR	NR	-	-
093 Chr Ch (Disc)	1	76	28	92 *	.1	.2
097 Chr Chs&Chs Cr	2	430	NR	520 *	.6	1.0
123 Ch God (Ander)	1	NR	115	115	.1	.2
127 Ch God (Cleve)	1	161	72	195 *	.2	.4
145 Ch God Prophcy	2	82	NR	98 *	.1	.2
151 L-D Saints	2	NR	NR	472	.6	.9
157 Ch of Brethren	4	591	387	715 *	.8	1.4
165 Ch of Nazarene	3	299	148	329	.4	.6
193 Episcopal	4	NR	1,146	2,893	3.4	5.5
207 E.L.C.A.	3	552	336	753	.9	1.4
335 Orth Pres Ch	1	26	35	38	-	.1
339 Pent Ch of God	1	50	NR	200	.2	.4
349 Pent Holiness	3	2,061	884	2,493 *	2.9	4.7
355 Presb Ch (USA)	13	5,194	2,387	6,282 *	7.3	11.9
413 S.D.A.	1	58	NR	69	.1	.1
418 Southw Bapt Fel	1	NR	NR	NR	-	-
419 So Bapt Conv	29	21,488	7,582	25,988 *	30.3	49.1
449 Un Methodist	11	5,270	1,702	6,374 *	7.4	12.0
467 Wesleyan	3	284	250	575	.7	1.1
498 Indep.Charis.	1	310	250	310	.4	.6
ROANOKE CITY	**107**	**30,795**	**11,658**	**45,597 ***	**48.0**	**100.0**
019 Amer Bapt USA	2	1,196	150	1,462 *	1.5	3.2
053 Assemb of God	3	265	273	335	.4	.7
055 As Ref Pres Ch	1	33	NR	37	-	.1
076 Buddhism	1	NR	NR	NR	-	-
081 Catholic	3	NR	NR	4,425	4.7	9.7
093 Chr Ch (Disc)	6	2,001	728	2,446 *	2.6	5.4
097 Chr Chs&Chs Cr	6	1,000	NR	1,221 *	1.3	2.7
123 Ch God (Ander)	3	NR	299	299	.3	.7
127 Ch God (Cleve)	1	270	175	330 *	.3	.7
145 Ch God Prophcy	2	82	NR	100 *	.1	.2
157 Ch of Brethren	6	1,302	671	1,592 *	1.7	3.5
165 Ch of Nazarene	3	678	457	938	1.0	2.1
167 Chs of Christ	5	284	301	351	.4	.8
193 Episcopal	1	NR	183	602	.6	1.3
207 E.L.C.A.	6	2,050	1,060	2,690	2.8	5.9
216 Evan Presby Ch	1	34	NR	42 *	-	.1
226 Friends-USA	1	105	NR	128 *	.1	.3
246 Greek Orthodox	1	NR	NR	534	.6	1.2
263 Int Foursq Gos	1	444	260	543 *	.6	1.2
283 Luth—MO Synod	1	208	70	260	.3	.6
290 Metro Comm Ch	1	53	6	65 *	.1	.1
349 Pent Holiness	1	15	15	18 *	-	-
355 Presb Ch (USA)	1	69	34	84 *	.1	.2
356 Presb Ch Amer	1	271	204	302	.3	.7
360 Prim Bapt Chrch	1	NR	NR	NR	-	-
403 Salvation Army	1	479	201	712	.8	1.6
413 S.D.A.	2	428	NR	509	.5	1.1
419 So Bapt Conv	20	11,528	2,721	14,093 *	14.8	30.9
435 Unitarian-Univ	1	190	NR	232 *	.2	.5
449 Un Methodist	15	6,061	2,090	7,410 *	7.8	16.3
467 Wesleyan	3	1,019	965	1,865	2.0	4.1
469 WELS	1	40	30	52	.1	.1
496 Jewish Est	2	NR	NR	900	.9	2.0
499 Indep.Non-Char	3	690	765	1,020	1.1	2.2
ROCKBRIDGE	**58**	**6,632**	**3,400**	**8,702 ***	**41.8**	**100.0**
055 As Ref Pres Ch	2	137	NR	159	.8	1.8
056 Baha'i	0	4	NR	4	-	-
145 Ch God Prophcy	2	82	NR	98 *	.5	1.1
157 Ch of Brethren	3	224	163	269 *	1.3	3.1
193 Episcopal	3	NR	321	744	3.6	8.5
207 E.L.C.A.	3	217	118	262	1.3	3.0
349 Pent Holiness	5	981	570	1,178 *	5.7	13.5
355 Presb Ch (USA)	17	2,681	1,366	3,219 *	15.5	37.0
419 So Bapt Conv	9	1,327	466	1,593 *	7.7	18.3
449 Un Methodist	14	979	396	1,176 *	5.7	13.5

NR–Not Reported *Total adherents estimated from known number of communicant, confirmed, full members. - Represents a percentage less than 0.1. Percentages may not total 100 due to rounding.

Table 4: Religious Congregations by County and Group: 2000

Religious Group	Number of Churches, Synagogues, Mosques, or Temples	Number of Communicant, Confirmed, or Full Members	Number of Attendees	Total Adherents: Number of Adherents	Total Adherents: % of Total Pop.	Total Adherents: % of Total Adh.
ROCKINGHAM	**171**	**28,486**	**14,726**	**36,956 ***	**54.6**	**100.0**
053 Assemb of God	1	73	105	135	.2	.4
056 Baha'i	0	39	NR	39	.1	.1
071 Brethren (Ash)	2	405	330	500 *	.7	1.4
097 Chr Chs&Chs Cr	2	270	NR	333 *	.5	.9
127 Ch God (Cleve)	5	647	257	797 *	1.2	2.2
145 Ch God Prophcy	1	41	NR	50 *	.1	.1
151 L-D Saints	1	NR	NR	363	.5	1.0
157 Ch of Brethren	24	4,718	2,483	5,825 *	8.6	15.8
165 Ch of Nazarene	3	490	373	589	.9	1.6
167 Chs of Christ	1	23	28	30	-	.1
193 Episcopal	3	NR	292	1,011	1.5	2.7
207 E.L.C.A.	8	1,494	719	1,852	2.7	5.0
216 Evan Presby Ch	1	141	NR	174 *	.3	.5
223 Free Will Bapt	2	167	NR	206 *	.3	.6
226 Friends-USA	2	164	NR	202 *	.3	.5
265 Int Pent C Chr	2	71	75	166	.2	.4
267 Muslim Est	1	NR	55	163	.2	.4
288 Mennonite USA	25	4,669	4,032	5,864 *	8.7	15.9
297 Mennonite;Other	9	472	NR	583 *	.9	1.6
322 Old Ord Menn Ch	6	835	NR	1,030 *	1.5	2.8
335 Orth Pres Ch	1	33	42	45	.1	.1
349 Pent Holiness	4	415	302	512 *	.8	1.4
355 Presb Ch (USA)	9	3,068	1,637	3,788 *	5.6	10.3
403 Salvation Army	1	130	47	210	.3	.6
413 S.D.A.	2	109	NR	130	.2	.4
419 So Bapt Conv	6	1,437	549	1,774 *	2.6	4.8
443 Un C of Christ	13	1,114	521	1,375 *	2.0	3.7
449 Un Methodist	36	7,461	2,879	9,210 *	13.6	24.9
RUSSELL	**73**	**7,475**	**3,125**	**9,073 ***	**29.9**	**100.0**
053 Assemb of God	2	92	105	146	.5	1.6
056 Baha'i	0	3	NR	3	-	-
081 Catholic	2	NR	NR	126	.4	1.4
097 Chr Chs&Chs Cr	2	259	NR	308 *	1.0	3.4
127 Ch God (Cleve)	4	288	128	342 *	1.1	3.8
145 Ch God Prophcy	2	82	NR	96 *	.3	1.1
151 L-D Saints	1	NR	NR	59	.2	.7
167 Chs of Christ	1	91	98	119	.4	1.3
223 Free Will Bapt	2	167	NR	198 *	.7	2.2
258 IndFreeWillBapt	9	392	NR	466 *	1.5	5.1
349 Pent Holiness	2	89	60	106 *	.3	1.2
355 Presb Ch (USA)	2	96	45	114 *	.4	1.3
360 Prim Bapt Chrch	2	NR	NR	NR	-	-
419 So Bapt Conv	23	4,091	1,550	4,865 *	16.1	53.6
449 Un Methodist	18	1,450	739	1,725 *	5.7	19.0
498 Indep.Charis.	1	375	400	400	1.3	4.4
SALEM CITY	**27**	**9,752**	**3,653**	**14,457 ***	**58.4**	**100.0**
019 Amer Bapt USA	1	275	0	326 *	1.3	2.3
053 Assemb of God	2	140	145	231	.9	1.6
081 Catholic	1	NR	NR	1,200	4.8	8.3
093 Chr Ch (Disc)	2	778	228	923 *	3.7	6.4
097 Chr Chs&Chs Cr	1	350	NR	415 *	1.7	2.9
123 Ch God (Ander)	1	NR	149	149	.6	1.0
127 Ch God (Cleve)	1	242	70	287 *	1.2	2.0
145 Ch God Prophcy	2	82	NR	96 *	.4	.7
151 L-D Saints	1	NR	NR	442	1.8	3.1
157 Ch of Brethren	2	205	161	244 *	1.0	1.7
167 Chs of Christ	1	188	200	237	1.0	1.6
193 Episcopal	1	NR	246	696	2.8	4.8
263 Int Foursq Gos	1	30	50	50 *	.2	.3
419 So Bapt Conv	5	4,973	1,590	5,902 *	23.8	40.8
449 Un Methodist	3	2,309	640	2,741 *	11.1	19.0
467 Wesleyan	2	180	174	518	2.1	3.6
SCOTT	**72**	**7,561**	**2,983**	**9,073 ***	**38.8**	**100.0**
053 Assemb of God	1	53	60	60	.3	.7
056 Baha'i	0	1	NR	1	-	-
081 Catholic	2	NR	NR	78	.3	.9
097 Chr Chs&Chs Cr	1	159	NR	189 *	.8	2.1
127 Ch God (Cleve)	1	76	72	90 *	.4	1.0
167 Chs of Christ	1	50	28	65	.3	.7
201 Evan Cov Ch	1	44	73	73 *	.3	.8
223 Free Will Bapt	11	918	NR	1,089 *	4.7	12.0
355 Presb Ch (USA)	1	76	35	90 *	.4	1.0
362 Prim Bapt E Dst	10	663	NR	787 *	3.4	8.7
419 So Bapt Conv	16	3,247	1,446	3,852 *	16.5	42.5
449 Un Methodist	27	2,274	1,269	2,699 *	11.5	29.7
SHENANDOAH	**107**	**14,321**	**6,100**	**18,849 ***	**53.7**	**100.0**
053 Assemb of God	3	104	133	188	.5	1.0
056 Baha'i	0	8	NR	8	-	-
071 Brethren (Ash)	4	328	274	396 *	1.1	2.1
081 Catholic	2	NR	NR	917	2.6	4.9
093 Chr Ch (Disc)	8	1,595	419	1,928 *	5.5	10.2
121 Ch God (Abr)	1	34	37	41 *	.1	.2
127 Ch God (Cleve)	1	85	96	103 *	.3	.5
151 L-D Saints	1	NR	NR	162	.5	.9
157 Ch of Brethren	14	1,734	831	2,097 *	6.0	11.1
165 Ch of Nazarene	1	29	32	116	.3	.6
167 Chs of Christ	1	51	35	75	.2	.4
193 Episcopal	3	NR	166	210	.6	1.1
207 E.L.C.A.	25	3,959	1,590	4,868	13.9	25.8
288 Mennonite USA	2	100	126	142 *	.4	.8
355 Presb Ch (USA)	3	364	195	440 *	1.3	2.3
360 Prim Bapt Chrch	1	NR	NR	NR	-	-
413 S.D.A.	2	723	NR	861	2.5	4.6
418 Southw Bapt Fel	1	NR	NR	NR	-	-
419 So Bapt Conv	1	664	350	803 *	2.3	4.3
443 Un C of Christ	11	822	380	994 *	2.8	5.3
449 Un Methodist	22	3,721	1,436	4,500 *	12.8	23.9
SMYTH	**92**	**9,444**	**3,995**	**12,785 ***	**38.6**	**100.0**
053 Assemb of God	2	68	79	102	.3	.8
056 Baha'i	0	3	NR	3	-	-
081 Catholic	2	NR	NR	469	1.4	3.7
093 Chr Ch (Disc)	1	125	75	150 *	.5	1.2
097 Chr Chs&Chs Cr	5	699	NR	839 *	2.5	6.6
123 Ch God (Ander)	7	NR	591	591	1.8	4.6
127 Ch God (Cleve)	4	456	203	548 *	1.7	4.3
145 Ch God Prophcy	4	163	NR	196 *	.6	1.5
151 L-D Saints	1	NR	NR	263	.8	2.1
157 Ch of Brethren	2	96	0	115 *	.3	.9
165 Ch of Nazarene	3	130	130	210	.6	1.6
167 Chs of Christ	1	50	35	50	.2	.4
193 Episcopal	2	NR	52	71	.2	.6
207 E.L.C.A.	5	691	230	824	2.5	6.4
223 Free Will Bapt	5	417	NR	501 *	1.5	3.9
335 Orth Pres Ch	1	66	50	79	.2	.6
349 Pent Holiness	1	39	37	47 *	.1	.4
355 Presb Ch (USA)	5	466	267	559 *	1.7	4.4
413 S.D.A.	1	71	NR	84	.3	.7
418 Southw Bapt Fel	1	NR	NR	NR	-	-
419 So Bapt Conv	10	2,785	1,007	3,341 *	10.1	26.1
449 Un Methodist	29	3,119	1,239	3,743 *	11.3	29.3
SOUTHAMPTON	**36**	**6,048**	**2,210**	**7,637 ***	**43.7**	**100.0**
056 Baha'i	0	66	NR	66	.4	.9
123 Ch God (Ander)	1	NR	35	35	.2	.5
193 Episcopal	2	NR	111	312	1.8	4.1
226 Friends-USA	1	113	NR	136 *	.8	1.8
355 Presb Ch (USA)	1	150	60	181 *	1.0	2.4
419 So Bapt Conv	15	3,992	1,402	4,822 *	27.6	63.1
443 Un C of Christ	2	228	104	275 *	1.6	3.6
449 Un Methodist	14	1,499	498	1,810 *	10.4	23.7
SPOTSYLVANIA	**58**	**15,775**	**7,905**	**34,974 ***	**38.7**	**100.0**
019 Amer Bapt USA	1	110	0	144 *	.2	.4
053 Assemb of God	1	258	362	383	.4	1.1
056 Baha'i	1	17	NR	17	-	-
081 Catholic	2	NR	NR	7,514	8.3	21.5
097 Chr Chs&Chs Cr	1	95	NR	124 *	.1	.4
123 Ch God (Ander)	2	NR	131	131	.1	.4

NR–Not Reported   *Total adherents estimated from known number of communicant, confirmed, full members.   - Represents a percentage less than 0.1.   Percentages may not total 100 due to rounding.

Table 4: Religious Congregations by County and Group: 2000

Religious Group	Number of Churches, Synagogues, Mosques, or Temples	Number of Communicant, Confirmed, or Full Members	Number of Attendees	Total Adherents: Number of Adherents	Total Adherents: % of Total Pop.	Total Adherents: % of Total Adh.
127 Ch God (Cleve)	1	319	200	416 *	.5	1.2
151 L-D Saints	3	NR	NR	1,400	1.5	4.0
165 Ch of Nazarene	1	203	367	610	.7	1.7
193 Episcopal	4	NR	662	2,876	3.2	8.2
207 E.L.C.A.	1	336	250	538	.6	1.5
223 Free Will Bapt	1	83	NR	109 *	.1	.3
226 Friends-USA	1	105	NR	137 *	.2	.4
267 Muslim Est	1	NR	412	1,891	2.1	5.4
349 Pent Holiness	1	14	18	18 *	-	.1
355 Presb Ch (USA)	3	1,531	919	1,999 *	2.2	5.7
356 Presb Ch Amer	1	307	440	440	.5	1.3
360 Prim Bapt Chrch	1	NR	NR	NR	-	-
413 S.D.A.	1	339	NR	403	.4	1.2
418 Southw Bapt Fel	2	NR	NR	NR	-	-
419 So Bapt Conv	21	10,335	3,430	13,488 *	14.9	38.6
449 Un Methodist	6	1,649	583	2,151 *	2.4	6.2
467 Wesleyan	1	74	131	185	.2	.5
STAFFORD	**52**	**13,768**	**6,568**	**29,109 ***	**31.5**	**100.0**
019 Amer Bapt USA	2	480	100	636 *	.7	2.2
053 Assemb of God	1	101	125	142	.2	.5
056 Baha'i	0	12	NR	12	-	-
081 Catholic	1	NR	NR	8,044	8.7	27.6
084 Calvary Chapel	1	NR	NR	NR	-	-
097 Chr Chs&Chs Cr	1	209	NR	277 *	.3	1.0
127 Ch God (Cleve)	1	252	125	334 *	.4	1.1
145 Ch God Prophcy	2	82	NR	108 *	.1	.4
151 L-D Saints	3	NR	NR	1,402	1.5	4.8
157 Ch of Brethren	1	116	103	154 *	.2	.5
165 Ch of Nazarene	1	23	19	23	-	.1
167 Chs of Christ	2	110	150	180	.2	.6
193 Episcopal	1	NR	203	699	.8	2.4
207 E.L.C.A.	1	627	421	921	1.0	3.2
223 Free Will Bapt	1	83	NR	111 *	.1	.4
355 Presb Ch (USA)	2	647	387	857 *	.9	2.9
403 Salvation Army	1	131	34	146	.2	.5
413 S.D.A.	1	100	NR	119	.1	.4
418 Southw Bapt Fel	1	NR	NR	NR	-	-
419 So Bapt Conv	17	8,288	3,310	10,975 *	11.9	37.7
449 Un Methodist	8	2,342	1,144	3,101 *	3.4	10.7
463 Vineyard	1	165	147	218 *	.2	.7
496 Jewish Est	1	NR	NR	250	.3	.9
498 Indep.Charis.	1	0	300	400	.4	1.4
STAUNTON CITY	**34**	**7,599**	**3,427**	**11,316 ***	**47.4**	**100.0**
053 Assemb of God	1	190	218	300	1.3	2.7
081 Catholic	1	NR	NR	1,536	6.4	13.6
089 Chr & Miss Al	1	137	NR	347	1.5	3.1
097 Chr Chs&Chs Cr	1	80	NR	94 *	.4	.8
123 Ch God (Ander)	1	NR	89	89	.4	.8
127 Ch God (Cleve)	3	250	159	295 *	1.2	2.6
145 Ch God Prophcy	1	41	NR	48 *	.2	.4
151 L-D Saints	1	NR	NR	193	.8	1.7
157 Ch of Brethren	3	736	304	866 *	3.6	7.7
165 Ch of Nazarene	1	144	72	144	.6	1.3
167 Chs of Christ	2	75	78	98	.4	.9
263 Int Foursq Gos	1	157	205	205 *	.9	1.8
335 Orth Pres Ch	1	42	54	54	.2	.5
413 S.D.A.	2	339	NR	403	1.7	3.6
416 Sikh	1	NR	NR	NR	-	-
419 So Bapt Conv	4	2,337	1,111	2,749 *	11.5	24.3
449 Un Methodist	7	2,983	1,016	3,509 *	14.7	31.0
467 Wesleyan	1	88	121	176	.7	1.6
496 Jewish Est	1	NR	NR	210	.9	1.9
SUFFOLK CITY	**61**	**16,811**	**7,655**	**22,886 ***	**35.9**	**100.0**
053 Assemb of God	1	62	90	150	.2	.7
056 Baha'i	0	336	NR	336	.5	1.5
081 Catholic	1	NR	NR	664	1.0	2.9
123 Ch God (Ander)	1	NR	28	28	-	.1
127 Ch God (Cleve)	1	93	67	119 *	.2	.5
145 Ch God Prophcy	2	82	NR	104 *	.2	.5
165 Ch of Nazarene	1	28	34	60	.1	.3

Religious Group	Number of Churches, Synagogues, Mosques, or Temples	Number of Communicant, Confirmed, or Full Members	Number of Attendees	Total Adherents: Number of Adherents	Total Adherents: % of Total Pop.	Total Adherents: % of Total Adh.
167 Chs of Christ	1	79	85	103	.2	.5
181 Consrv Congr	1	425	160	544 *	.9	2.4
193 Episcopal	4	NR	283	666	1.0	2.9
207 E.L.C.A.	1	228	90	290	.5	1.3
226 Friends-USA	1	113	NR	145 *	.2	.6
349 Pent Holiness	1	132	76	169 *	.3	.7
355 Presb Ch (USA)	2	484	282	620 *	1.0	2.7
356 Presb Ch Amer	1	398	436	476	.7	2.1
403 Salvation Army	1	126	48	205	.3	.9
413 S.D.A.	1	51	NR	61	.1	.3
419 So Bapt Conv	13	7,143	3,235	9,144 *	14.4	40.0
443 Un C of Christ	16	4,114	1,765	5,266 *	8.3	23.0
449 Un Methodist	10	2,874	946	3,678 *	5.8	16.1
469 WELS	1	43	30	58	.1	.3
SURRY	**18**	**1,135**	**557**	**1,487 ***	**21.8**	**100.0**
056 Baha'i	0	1	NR	1	-	.1
081 Catholic	1	NR	NR	11	.2	.7
176 Congr Ad Afl	2	38	NR	47 *	.7	3.2
193 Episcopal	2	NR	33	72	1.1	4.8
419 So Bapt Conv	6	660	349	817 *	12.0	54.9
443 Un C of Christ	1	17	7	21 *	.3	1.4
449 Un Methodist	6	419	168	518 *	7.6	34.8
SUSSEX	**23**	**3,611**	**1,264**	**4,409 ***	**35.3**	**100.0**
019 Amer Bapt USA	1	461	265	543 *	4.3	12.3
081 Catholic	1	NR	NR	27	.2	.6
151 L-D Saints	1	NR	NR	77	.6	1.7
176 Congr Ad Afl	1	214	NR	252 *	2.0	5.7
193 Episcopal	1	NR	18	51	.4	1.2
413 S.D.A.	1	76	NR	90	.7	2.0
419 So Bapt Conv	7	1,460	455	1,720 *	13.8	39.0
443 Un C of Christ	3	222	113	262 *	2.1	5.9
449 Un Methodist	7	1,178	413	1,387 *	11.1	31.5
TAZEWELL	**137**	**13,220**	**6,734**	**17,282 ***	**38.8**	**100.0**
011 A.W.M.C.	1	10	26	14	-	.1
053 Assemb of God	13	862	1,081	1,478	3.3	8.6
056 Baha'i	0	9	NR	9	-	.1
081 Catholic	3	NR	NR	348	.8	2.0
089 Chr & Miss Al	1	0	NR	35	.1	.2
093 Chr Ch (Disc)	7	776	297	926 *	2.1	5.4
097 Chr Chs&Chs Cr	11	1,351	NR	1,613 *	3.6	9.3
123 Ch God (Ander)	3	NR	159	159	.4	.9
127 Ch God (Cleve)	10	982	445	1,173 *	2.6	6.8
145 Ch God Prophcy	3	122	NR	147 *	.3	.9
151 L-D Saints	1	NR	NR	98	.2	.6
167 Chs of Christ	8	248	288	324	.7	1.9
193 Episcopal	4	NR	107	240	.5	1.4
207 E.L.C.A.	1	25	20	28	.1	.2
349 Pent Holiness	5	419	261	500 *	1.1	2.9
355 Presb Ch (USA)	9	820	401	978 *	2.2	5.7
356 Presb Ch Amer	2	208	195	248	.6	1.4
413 S.D.A.	2	43	NR	52	.1	.3
418 Southw Bapt Fel	2	NR	NR	NR	-	-
419 So Bapt Conv	12	3,207	1,362	3,825 *	8.6	22.1
449 Un Methodist	36	4,067	2,012	4,851 *	10.9	28.1
467 Wesleyan	3	71	80	236	.5	1.4
VIRGINIA BEACH CITY	**184**	**68,525**	**36,444**	**146,402 ***	**34.4**	**100.0**
053 Assemb of God	5	530	590	756	.2	.5
056 Baha'i	1	133	NR	133	-	.1
061 Beachy Amish	1	62	NR	79 *	-	.1
076 Buddhism	1	NR	NR	NR	-	-
081 Catholic	12	NR	NR	40,922	9.6	28.0
084 Calvary Chapel	2	NR	NR	NR	-	-
089 Chr & Miss Al	1	61	NR	152	-	.1
093 Chr Ch (Disc)	2	502	280	639 *	.2	.4
097 Chr Chs&Chs Cr	9	2,637	NR	3,358 *	.8	2.3
123 Ch God (Ander)	1	NR	158	158	-	.1
127 Ch God (Cleve)	6	1,700	1,129	2,189 *	.5	1.5
145 Ch God Prophcy	1	41	NR	52 *	-	-

NR–Not Reported *Total adherents estimated from known number of communicant, confirmed, full members. - Represents a percentage less than 0.1. Percentages may not total 100 due to rounding.

Table 4: Religious Congregations by County and Group: 2000

Religious Group	Number of Churches, Synagogues, Mosques, or Temples	Number of Communicant, Confirmed, or Full Members	Number of Attendees	Total Adherents		
				Number of Adherents	% of Total Pop.	% of Total Adh.
151 L-D Saints	5	NR	NR	2,207	.5	1.5
157 Ch of Brethren	1	118	65	150 *	-	.1
165 Ch of Nazarene	2	499	467	617	.1	.4
167 Chs of Christ	4	347	415	497	.1	.3
193 Episcopal	10	NR	2,315	6,361	1.5	4.3
203 Evan Free Ch	1	43	116	116	-	.1
207 E.L.C.A.	5	1,390	898	1,977	.5	1.4
216 Evan Presby Ch	1	1,323	NR	1,685 *	.4	1.2
223 Free Will Bapt	3	250	NR	319 *	.1	.2
226 Friends-USA	3	237	NR	302 *	.1	.2
246 Greek Orthodox	1	NR	NR	762	.2	.5
263 Int Foursq Gos	1	30	39	39 *	-	-
265 Int Pent C Chr	1	29	72	200	-	.1
283 Luth—MO Synod	2	1,374	691	1,546	.4	1.1
288 Mennonite USA	1	133	130	169 *	-	.1
290 Metro Comm Ch	1	13	13	17 *	-	-
349 Pent Holiness	6	723	599	921 *	.2	.6
355 Presb Ch (USA)	10	4,607	2,108	5,868 *	1.4	4.0
356 Presb Ch Amer	4	648	550	710	.2	.5
370 Ref Baptist Chs	1	NR	NR	NR	-	-
401 Rus Orth Abroad	1	NR	NR	NR	-	-
413 S.D.A.	3	218	NR	259	.1	.2
418 Southw Bapt Fel	1	NR	NR	NR	-	-
419 So Bapt Conv	30	15,549	6,206	19,804 *	4.7	13.5
443 Un C of Christ	5	857	386	1,092 *	.3	.7
449 Un Methodist	24	15,315	5,910	19,506 *	4.6	13.3
463 Vineyard	3	850	714	1,082 *	.3	.7
469 WELS	1	156	148	233	.1	.2
496 Jewish Est	4	NR	NR	7,600	1.8	5.2
498 Indep.Charis.	3	12,250	7,195	17,525	4.1	12.0
499 Indep.Non-Char	4	5,900	5,250	6,400	1.5	4.4
WARREN	**60**	**6,823**	**2,909**	**11,100 ***	**35.1**	**100.0**
019 Amer Bapt USA	1	633	113	792 *	2.5	7.1
053 Assemb of God	3	398	553	616	2.0	5.5
056 Baha'i	0	4	NR	4	-	-
081 Catholic	1	NR	NR	1,734	5.5	15.6
097 Chr Chs&Chs Cr	1	159	NR	199 *	.6	1.8
121 Ch God (Abr)	2	68	64	85 *	.3	.8
127 Ch God (Cleve)	1	127	122	159 *	.5	1.4
151 L-D Saints	1	NR	NR	485	1.5	4.4
157 Ch of Brethren	1	168	120	210 *	.7	1.9
165 Ch of Nazarene	1	123	80	123	.4	1.1
167 Chs of Christ	1	70	75	91	.3	.8
193 Episcopal	1	NR	120	237	.8	2.1
207 E.L.C.A.	1	157	85	218	.7	2.0
223 Free Will Bapt	1	83	NR	104 *	.3	.9
252 Hindu	1	NR	NR	NR	-	-
297 Mennonite;Other	1	23	NR	29 *	.1	.3
355 Presb Ch (USA)	3	417	153	522 *	1.7	4.7
360 Prim Bapt Chrch	4	NR	NR	NR	-	-
413 S.D.A.	1	56	NR	67	.2	.6
419 So Bapt Conv	6	1,988	534	2,487 *	7.9	22.4
449 Un Methodist	28	2,349	890	2,938 *	9.3	26.5
WAYNESBORO CITY	**32**	**7,406**	**2,875**	**11,440 ***	**58.6**	**100.0**
053 Assemb of God	1	53	75	90	.5	.8
081 Catholic	1	NR	NR	1,318	6.8	11.5
097 Chr Chs&Chs Cr	3	653	NR	805 *	4.1	7.0
127 Ch God (Cleve)	2	276	154	340 *	1.7	3.0
145 Ch God Prophcy	1	41	NR	50 *	.3	.4
151 L-D Saints	1	NR	NR	453	2.3	4.0
157 Ch of Brethren	3	728	246	898 *	4.6	7.8
167 Chs of Christ	1	120	140	200	1.0	1.7
193 Episcopal	1	NR	113	329	1.7	2.9
207 E.L.C.A.	1	219	80	278	1.4	2.4
221 Free Methodist	1	112	146	146	.7	1.3
283 Luth—MO Synod	1	178	140	314	1.6	2.7
297 Mennonite;Other	1	189	NR	233 *	1.2	2.0
413 S.D.A.	1	341	NR	406	2.1	3.5
419 So Bapt Conv	4	2,578	905	3,177 *	16.3	27.8
435 Unitarian-Univ	1	100	NR	123 *	.6	1.1
449 Un Methodist	7	1,793	835	2,210 *	11.3	19.3
467 Wesleyan	1	25	41	70	.4	.6
WASHINGTON	**122**	**17,245**	**9,718**	**21,897 ***	**42.8**	**100.0**
053 Assemb of God	1	59	69	120	.2	.5
056 Baha'i	1	54	NR	54	.1	.2
081 Catholic	1	NR	NR	300	.6	1.4
097 Chr Chs&Chs Cr	8	1,136	NR	1,350 *	2.6	6.2
123 Ch God (Ander)	2	NR	149	149	.3	.7
127 Ch God (Cleve)	2	261	148	310 *	.6	1.4
145 Ch God Prophcy	3	122	NR	144 *	.3	.7
151 L-D Saints	1	NR	NR	495	1.0	2.3
157 Ch of Brethren	1	49	30	58 *	.1	.3
165 Ch of Nazarene	1	101	148	180	.4	.8
167 Chs of Christ	6	230	245	311	.6	1.4
193 Episcopal	1	NR	109	252	.5	1.2
207 E.L.C.A.	3	624	278	814	1.6	3.7
216 Evan Presby Ch	1	47	NR	56 *	.1	.3
223 Free Will Bapt	1	83	NR	99 *	.2	.5
323 Old Ord Amish	1	12	NR	14 *	-	.1
349 Pent Holiness	2	164	86	195 *	.4	.9
355 Presb Ch (USA)	14	1,810	1,127	2,149 *	4.2	9.8
356 Presb Ch Amer	2	150	146	188	.4	.9
360 Prim Bapt Chrch	5	NR	NR	NR	-	-
362 Prim Bapt E Dst	1	13	NR	15 *	-	.1
413 S.D.A.	1	112	NR	133	.3	.6
419 So Bapt Conv	26	7,545	5,137	8,961 *	17.5	40.9
435 Unitarian-Univ	1	40	NR	48 *	.1	.2
449 Un Methodist	36	4,633	2,046	5,502 *	10.8	25.1
WESTMORELAND	**23**	**3,387**	**1,426**	**5,844 ***	**35.0**	**100.0**
053 Assemb of God	1	45	47	63	.4	1.1
056 Baha'i	0	5	NR	5	-	.1
081 Catholic	2	NR	NR	844	5.0	14.4
193 Episcopal	4	NR	247	891	5.3	15.2
419 So Bapt Conv	6	1,841	695	2,229 *	13.3	38.1
449 Un Methodist	10	1,496	437	1,812 *	10.8	31.0
WILLIAMSBURG CITY	**9**	**5,857**	**3,848**	**7,710 ***	**64.3**	**100.0**
053 Assemb of God	1	58	75	90	.8	1.2
056 Baha'i	0	12	NR	12	.1	.2
167 Chs of Christ	1	144	155	188	1.6	2.4
207 E.L.C.A.	1	427	247	527	4.4	6.8
226 Friends-USA	1	105	NR	113 *	.9	1.5
355 Presb Ch (USA)	1	1,532	610	1,653 *	13.8	21.4
419 So Bapt Conv	2	1,306	505	1,409 *	11.7	18.3
449 Un Methodist	1	2,056	756	2,218 *	18.5	28.8
499 Indep.Non-Char	1	217	1,500	1,500	12.5	19.5
WINCHESTER CITY	**28**	**6,847**	**3,469**	**15,423 ***	**65.4**	**100.0**
019 Amer Bapt USA	1	366	185	441 *	1.9	2.9
053 Assemb of God	2	512	636	1,226	5.2	7.9
071 Brethren (Ash)	1	28	130	34 *	.1	.2
075 Brethren in Cr	1	17	31	31	.1	.2
081 Catholic	1	NR	NR	5,208	22.1	33.8
089 Chr & Miss Al	1	27	NR	104	.4	.7
093 Chr Ch (Disc)	1	420	141	506 *	2.1	3.3
151 L-D Saints	1	NR	NR	439	1.9	2.8
165 Ch of Nazarene	1	85	42	85	.4	.6
167 Chs of Christ	1	120	135	120	.5	.8
207 E.L.C.A.	1	634	347	984	4.2	6.4
226 Friends-USA	1	105	NR	126 *	.5	.8
246 Greek Orthodox	1	NR	NR	282	1.2	1.8
263 Int Foursq Gos	1	38	120	120 *	.5	.8
339 Pent Ch of God	1	9	NR	25	.1	.2
356 Presb Ch Amer	1	82	114	119	.5	.8
413 S.D.A.	1	186	NR	221	.9	1.4
419 So Bapt Conv	1	302	211	364 *	1.5	2.4
435 Unitarian-Univ	1	110	NR	133 *	.6	.9
443 Un C of Christ	1	117	64	141 *	.6	.9
449 Un Methodist	6	3,689	1,313	4,444 *	18.8	28.8
496 Jewish Est	1	NR	NR	270	1.1	1.8

NR–Not Reported   *Total adherents estimated from known number of communicant, confirmed, full members.   - Represents a percentage less than 0.1.   Percentages may not total 100 due to rounding.

Table 4: Religious Congregations by County and Group: 2000

Religious Group	Number of Churches, Synagogues, Mosques, or Temples	Number of Communicant, Confirmed, or Full Members	Number of Attendees	Total Adherents: Number of Adherents	Total Adherents: % of Total Pop.	Total Adherents: % of Total Adh.
WISE	**96**	**10,269**	**3,377**	**13,475 ***	**33.6**	**100.0**
053 Assemb of God	5	542	648	987	2.5	7.3
056 Baha'i	0	2	NR	2	-	-
081 Catholic	1	NR	NR	22	.1	.2
097 Chr Chs&Chs Cr	2	210	NR	254 *	.6	1.9
123 Ch God (Ander)	2	NR	205	205	.5	1.5
127 Ch God (Cleve)	4	183	128	222 *	.6	1.6
145 Ch God Prophcy	6	245	NR	294 *	.7	2.2
151 L-D Saints	1	NR	NR	272	.7	2.0
167 Chs of Christ	3	113	105	144	.4	1.1
193 Episcopal	3	NR	84	220	.5	1.6
207 E.L.C.A.	1	56	27	69	.2	.5
223 Free Will Bapt	17	1,419	NR	1,715 *	4.3	12.7
258 IndFreeWillBapt	5	318	NR	384 *	1.0	2.8
349 Pent Holiness	1	42	47	51 *	.1	.4
355 Presb Ch (USA)	7	296	203	363 *	.9	2.7
356 Presb Ch Amer	1	45	20	56	.1	.4
362 Prim Bapt E Dst	3	124	NR	150 *	.4	1.1
413 S.D.A.	1	154	NR	183	.5	1.4
419 So Bapt Conv	16	4,218	889	5,099 *	12.7	37.8
449 Un Methodist	17	2,302	1,021	2,783 *	6.9	20.7
WYTHE	**101**	**10,090**	**5,085**	**12,818 ***	**46.4**	**100.0**
053 Assemb of God	2	89	105	132	.5	1.0
056 Baha'i	0	2	NR	2	-	-
081 Catholic	1	NR	NR	398	1.4	3.1
093 Chr Ch (Disc)	3	394	140	471 *	1.7	3.7
097 Chr Chs&Chs Cr	1	8	NR	10 *	-	.1
123 Ch God (Ander)	2	NR	105	105	.4	.8
127 Ch God (Cleve)	9	986	723	1,193 *	4.3	9.3
145 Ch God Prophcy	6	245	NR	294 *	1.1	2.3
167 Chs of Christ	3	121	129	162	.6	1.3
193 Episcopal	1	NR	95	205	.7	1.6
207 E.L.C.A.	9	993	492	1,174	4.3	9.2
349 Pent Holiness	17	1,767	1,134	2,114 *	7.7	16.5
355 Presb Ch (USA)	4	349	174	418 *	1.5	3.3
413 S.D.A.	1	172	NR	205	.7	1.6
419 So Bapt Conv	5	984	340	1,177 *	4.3	9.2
449 Un Methodist	37	3,980	1,648	4,758 *	17.2	37.1
YORK	**31**	**9,802**	**4,378**	**15,859 ***	**28.2**	**100.0**
053 Assemb of God	1	47	62	62	.1	.4
056 Baha'i	0	13	NR	13	-	.1
081 Catholic	2	NR	NR	1,477	2.6	9.3
093 Chr Ch (Disc)	1	221	0	284 *	.5	1.8
097 Chr Chs&Chs Cr	1	100	NR	128 *	.2	.8
127 Ch God (Cleve)	1	228	120	293 *	.5	1.8
151 L-D Saints	3	NR	NR	1,008	1.8	6.4
193 Episcopal	2	NR	337	703	1.2	4.4
207 E.L.C.A.	1	566	281	788	1.4	5.0
355 Presb Ch (USA)	2	1,084	559	1,392 *	2.5	8.8
356 Presb Ch Amer	1	233	14	313	.6	2.0
419 So Bapt Conv	10	3,311	1,635	4,251 *	7.6	26.8
449 Un Methodist	4	3,767	1,180	4,836 *	8.6	30.5
463 Vineyard	1	130	120	167 *	.3	1.1
469 WELS	1	102	70	144	.3	.9
WASHINGTON						
The State.....	4,649	625,529	478,431	1,942,850 *	33.0	100.0
ADAMS	**41**	**2,823**	**1,971**	**8,028 ***	**48.9**	**100.0**
053 Assemb of God	3	433	535	857	5.2	10.7
056 Baha'i	0	3	NR	3	-	-
081 Catholic	4	NR	NR	1,681	10.2	20.9
093 Chr Ch (Disc)	1	75	37	102 *	.6	1.3
151 L-D Saints	8	NR	NR	2,091	12.7	26.0
165 Ch of Nazarene	2	221	311	372	2.3	4.6
167 Chs of Christ	1	21	23	35	.2	.4
193 Episcopal	1	NR	7	16	.1	.2
207 E.L.C.A.	3	578	220	730	4.4	9.1

Religious Group	Number of Churches, Synagogues, Mosques, or Temples	Number of Communicant, Confirmed, or Full Members	Number of Attendees	Total Adherents: Number of Adherents	Total Adherents: % of Total Pop.	Total Adherents: % of Total Adh.
257 Hutterian Br	1	66	NR	100	.6	1.2
263 Int Foursq Gos	2	80	243	243 *	1.5	3.0
283 Luth—MO Synod	1	31	16	35	.2	.4
288 Mennonite USA	1	146	56	198 *	1.2	2.5
355 Presb Ch (USA)	2	198	100	269 *	1.6	3.4
388 Reg Bapt Gen As	1	121	108	164 *	1.0	2.0
413 S.D.A.	3	122	NR	145	.9	1.8
419 So Bapt Conv	1	68	49	92 *	.6	1.1
443 Un C of Christ	3	262	140	355 *	2.2	4.4
449 Un Methodist	3	398	126	540 *	3.3	6.7
ASOTIN	**29**	**3,303**	**2,345**	**8,266 ***	**40.2**	**100.0**
017 Amer Bapt Assn	1	5	NR	6 *	-	.1
053 Assemb of God	5	817	973	2,117	10.3	25.6
056 Baha'i	0	20	NR	20	.1	.2
081 Catholic	1	NR	NR	1,980	9.6	24.0
093 Chr Ch (Disc)	1	310	85	384 *	1.9	4.6
123 Ch God (Ander)	1	NR	74	74	.4	.9
151 L-D Saints	2	NR	NR	812	4.0	9.8
167 Chs of Christ	1	19	20	24	.1	.3
173 Comm of Christ	1	95	NR	95	.5	1.1
207 E.L.C.A.	1	226	110	277	1.3	3.4
221 Free Methodist	1	22	28	28	.1	.3
263 Int Foursq Gos	2	192	246	246 *	1.2	3.0
339 Pent Ch of God	1	30	NR	70	.3	.8
355 Presb Ch (USA)	2	626	370	776 *	3.8	9.4
370 Ref Baptist Chs	1	NR	NR	NR	-	-
388 Reg Bapt Gen As	1	82	105	105 *	.5	1.3
413 S.D.A.	1	249	NR	296	1.4	3.6
419 So Bapt Conv	2	220	90	273 *	1.3	3.3
449 Un Methodist	3	390	160	483 *	2.4	5.8
467 Wesleyan	1	0	84	200	1.0	2.4
BENTON	**139**	**18,766**	**13,785**	**57,586 ***	**40.4**	**100.0**
019 Amer Bapt USA	2	351	142	454 *	.3	.8
039 Ap Chr Ch(Naz)	1	46	70	70 *	-	.1
053 Assemb of God	8	792	1,104	1,445	1.0	2.5
056 Baha'i	2	101	NR	101	.1	.2
059 Bapt Miss Assn	1	36	0	47 *	-	.1
076 Buddhism	1	NR	NR	NR	-	-
081 Catholic	5	NR	NR	18,056	12.7	31.4
084 Calvary Chapel	1	NR	NR	NR	-	-
089 Chr & Miss Al	2	188	NR	382	.3	.7
093 Chr Ch (Disc)	3	1,013	307	1,309 *	.9	2.3
105 Christian Ref	1	122	130	158 *	.1	.3
123 Ch God (Ander)	1	NR	480	480	.3	.8
127 Ch God (Cleve)	4	201	162	260 *	.2	.5
145 Ch God Prophcy	1	30	NR	39 *	-	.1
151 L-D Saints	28	NR	NR	10,361	7.3	18.0
165 Ch of Nazarene	4	944	665	1,113	.8	1.9
167 Chs of Christ	6	520	451	676	.5	1.2
173 Comm of Christ	1	156	NR	156	.1	.3
179 Consrv Bapt	3	NR	2,234	2,234	1.6	3.9
193 Episcopal	3	NR	346	921	.6	1.6
201 Evan Cov Ch	1	20	32	32 *	-	.1
203 Evan Free Ch	1	60	125	125	.1	.2
207 E.L.C.A.	5	2,282	1,000	3,104	2.2	5.4
221 Free Methodist	1	0	20	20	-	-
223 Free Will Bapt	1	69	NR	89 *	.1	.2
226 Friends-USA	1	22	NR	28 *	-	-
263 Int Foursq Gos	2	234	388	388 *	.3	.7
267 Muslim Est	1	NR	101	288	.2	.5
283 Luth—MO Synod	4	1,144	628	1,562	1.1	2.7
290 Metro Comm Ch	1	16	16	21 *	-	-
349 Pent Holiness	2	40	50	52 *	-	.1
355 Presb Ch (USA)	9	1,849	1,415	2,404 *	1.7	4.2
360 Prim Bapt Chrch	1	NR	NR	NR	-	-
388 Reg Bapt Gen As	2	814	625	1,052 *	.7	1.8
403 Salvation Army	1	225	272	233	.2	.4
413 S.D.A.	3	716	NR	851	.6	1.5
419 So Bapt Conv	10	2,460	1,229	3,179 *	2.2	5.5
435 Unitarian-Univ	1	97	NR	125 *	.1	.2
443 Un C of Christ	1	100	76	129 *	.1	.2

NR–Not Reported *Total adherents estimated from known number of communicant, confirmed, full members. - Represents a percentage less than 0.1. Percentages may not total 100 due to rounding.

Table 4: Religious Congregations by County and Group: 2000

Religious Group	Number of Churches, Synagogues, Mosques, or Temples	Number of Communicant, Confirmed, or Full Members	Number of Attendees	Total Adherents: Number of Adherents	Total Adherents: % of Total Pop.	Total Adherents: % of Total Adh.
449 Un Methodist	9	3,763	1,530	4,863 *	3.4	8.4
455 Un Ref Chs N.A.	1	117	NR	159	.1	.3
463 Vineyard	1	80	90	103 *	.1	.2
469 WELS	1	158	97	217	.2	.4
496 Jewish Est	1	NR	NR	300	.2	.5
CHELAN	**82**	**10,243**	**7,190**	**26,508 ***	**39.8**	**100.0**
017 Amer Bapt Assn	1	29	NR	37 *	.1	.1
019 Amer Bapt USA	2	313	140	398 *	.6	1.5
053 Assemb of God	9	834	1,087	1,504	2.3	5.7
056 Baha'i	1	50	NR	50	.1	.2
081 Catholic	4	NR	NR	9,778	14.7	36.9
084 Calvary Chapel	1	NR	NR	NR	-	-
089 Chr & Miss Al	1	42	NR	126	.2	.5
093 Chr Ch (Disc)	2	117	55	149 *	.2	.6
127 Ch God (Cleve)	1	34	33	43 *	.1	.2
151 L-D Saints	6	NR	NR	1,844	2.8	7.0
157 Ch of Brethren	2	273	139	347 *	.5	1.3
165 Ch of Nazarene	3	519	631	738	1.1	2.8
167 Chs of Christ	3	394	349	494	.7	1.9
193 Episcopal	3	NR	162	678	1.0	2.6
203 Evan Free Ch	1	23	40	40	.1	.2
207 E.L.C.A.	5	1,214	664	1,744	2.6	6.6
221 Free Methodist	1	546	1,000	1,000	1.5	3.8
226 Friends-USA	2	168	NR	214 *	.3	.8
263 Int Foursq Gos	8	532	699	699 *	1.0	2.6
283 Luth—MO Synod	1	284	160	374	.6	1.4
349 Pent Holiness	1	35	60	44 *	.1	.2
355 Presb Ch (USA)	3	599	490	769 *	1.2	2.9
360 Prim Bapt Chrch	1	NR	NR	NR	-	-
388 Reg Bapt Gen As	1	233	190	296 *	.4	1.1
403 Salvation Army	1	110	49	261	.4	1.0
413 S.D.A.	5	836	NR	995	1.5	3.8
419 So Bapt Conv	4	1,244	314	1,581 *	2.4	6.0
435 Unitarian-Univ	1	90	NR	114 *	.2	.4
443 Un C of Christ	2	69	81	88 *	.1	.3
449 Un Methodist	6	1,655	847	2,103 *	3.2	7.9
CLALLAM	**67**	**6,987**	**4,719**	**17,792 ***	**27.6**	**100.0**
019 Amer Bapt USA	1	131	110	156 *	.2	.9
053 Assemb of God	8	599	800	1,377	2.1	7.7
056 Baha'i	2	162	NR	162	.3	.9
081 Catholic	4	NR	NR	5,220	8.1	29.3
084 Calvary Chapel	2	NR	NR	NR	-	-
089 Chr & Miss Al	1	82	NR	228	.4	1.3
093 Chr Ch (Disc)	1	72	73	86 *	.1	.5
123 Ch God (Ander)	2	NR	126	126	.2	.7
127 Ch God (Cleve)	1	21	23	25 *	-	.1
145 Ch God Prophcy	1	30	NR	36 *	.1	.2
151 L-D Saints	6	NR	NR	2,007	3.1	11.3
165 Ch of Nazarene	3	174	128	281	.4	1.6
167 Chs of Christ	2	101	97	125	.2	.7
193 Episcopal	2	NR	258	721	1.1	4.1
203 Evan Free Ch	1	28	38	38	.1	.2
207 E.L.C.A.	3	1,034	562	1,302	2.0	7.3
221 Free Methodist	1	29	56	56	.1	.3
226 Friends-USA	2	168	NR	201 *	.3	1.1
263 Int Foursq Gos	3	116	275	275 *	.4	1.5
283 Luth—MO Synod	3	705	387	928	1.4	5.2
355 Presb Ch (USA)	4	866	815	1,043 *	1.6	5.9
388 Reg Bapt Gen As	1	34	60	60 *	.1	.3
403 Salvation Army	1	70	48	180	.3	1.0
413 S.D.A.	3	484	NR	576	.9	3.2
419 So Bapt Conv	3	818	339	976 *	1.5	5.5
435 Unitarian-Univ	1	66	NR	79 *	.1	.4
443 Un C of Christ	1	67	35	80 *	.1	.4
449 Un Methodist	2	1,000	369	1,193 *	1.8	6.7
463 Vineyard	1	130	120	155 *	.2	.9
496 Jewish Est	1	NR	NR	100	.2	.6
CLARK	**212**	**32,837**	**27,829**	**96,498 ***	**28.0**	**100.0**
017 Amer Bapt Assn	1	50	NR	65 *	-	.1
019 Amer Bapt USA	2	149	195	195 *	.1	.2

Religious Group	Number of Churches, Synagogues, Mosques, or Temples	Number of Communicant, Confirmed, or Full Members	Number of Attendees	Total Adherents: Number of Adherents	Total Adherents: % of Total Pop.	Total Adherents: % of Total Adh.
053 Assemb of God	8	1,699	2,113	3,115	.9	3.2
056 Baha'i	4	257	NR	257	.1	.3
057 Bapt Gen Conf	2	985	2,970	2,970 *	.9	3.1
076 Buddhism	1	NR	NR	NR	-	-
081 Catholic	9	NR	NR	27,120	7.9	28.1
084 Calvary Chapel	4	NR	NR	NR	-	-
089 Chr & Miss Al	1	60	NR	455	.1	.5
093 Chr Ch (Disc)	2	312	173	403 *	.1	.4
097 Chr Chs&Chs Cr	3	520	NR	671 *	.2	.7
123 Ch God (Ander)	2	NR	1,677	1,677	.5	1.7
127 Ch God (Cleve)	2	301	115	388 *	.1	.4
145 Ch God Prophcy	2	61	NR	78 *	-	.1
151 L-D Saints	32	NR	NR	14,069	4.1	14.6
165 Ch of Nazarene	11	2,593	1,820	3,458	1.0	3.6
167 Chs of Christ	5	769	806	960	.3	1.0
173 Comm of Christ	3	442	NR	442	.1	.5
179 Consrv Bapt	8	NR	2,324	2,324	.7	2.4
193 Episcopal	4	NR	703	1,778	.5	1.8
203 Evan Free Ch	8	419	900	900	.3	.9
207 E.L.C.A.	11	4,695	2,112	6,507	1.9	6.7
226 Friends-USA	8	672	NR	867 *	.3	.9
237 Menn Br US Conf	1	500	NR	645 *	.2	.7
263 Int Foursq Gos	8	966	1,213	1,246 *	.4	1.3
267 Muslim Est	1	NR	290	1,313	.4	1.4
283 Luth—MO Synod	6	2,129	1,305	2,920	.8	3.0
290 Metro Comm Ch	1	27	20	35 *	-	-
291 Missionary Ch	1	42	58	58	-	.1
313 N Am Bapt Conf	2	458	605	591 *	.2	.6
339 Pent Ch of God	2	12	NR	67	-	.1
355 Presb Ch (USA)	6	2,439	1,275	3,147 *	.9	3.3
356 Presb Ch Amer	1	188	290	290	.1	.3
388 Reg Bapt Gen As	2	143	219	219 *	.1	.2
403 Salvation Army	2	188	93	248	.1	.3
413 S.D.A.	13	2,933	NR	3,491	1.0	3.6
419 So Bapt Conv	10	2,753	1,260	3,552 *	1.0	3.7
435 Unitarian-Univ	1	225	NR	290 *	.1	.3
443 Un C of Christ	1	271	140	350 *	.1	.4
449 Un Methodist	10	3,074	1,498	3,968 *	1.1	4.1
463 Vineyard	1	400	275	516 *	.1	.5
467 Wesleyan	2	0	195	760	.2	.8
469 WELS	1	155	100	178	.1	.2
496 Jewish Est	1	NR	NR	600	.2	.6
498 Indep.Charis.	2	1,300	1,520	1,750	.5	1.8
499 Indep.Non-Char	4	650	1,565	1,565	.5	1.6
COLUMBIA	**12**	**688**	**350**	**1,430 ***	**35.2**	**100.0**
053 Assemb of God	1	65	37	87	2.1	6.1
056 Baha'i	0	7	NR	7	.2	.5
081 Catholic	1	NR	NR	202	5.0	14.1
097 Chr Chs&Chs Cr	1	220	NR	266 *	6.5	18.6
151 L-D Saints	1	NR	NR	257	6.3	18.0
165 Ch of Nazarene	1	25	24	39	1.0	2.7
179 Consrv Bapt	1	NR	75	75	1.8	5.2
193 Episcopal	1	NR	10	17	.4	1.2
263 Int Foursq Gos	1	6	9	9 *	.2	.6
283 Luth—MO Synod	1	132	95	191	4.7	13.4
413 S.D.A.	1	55	NR	65	1.6	4.5
419 So Bapt Conv	0	9	12	11 *	.3	.8
443 Un C of Christ	1	86	38	104 *	2.6	7.3
449 Un Methodist	1	83	50	100 *	2.5	7.0
COWLITZ	**87**	**13,571**	**7,183**	**29,643 ***	**31.9**	**100.0**
017 Amer Bapt Assn	1	30	NR	38 *	-	.1
019 Amer Bapt USA	2	604	428	761 *	.8	2.6
053 Assemb of God	6	712	964	1,826	2.0	6.2
056 Baha'i	2	126	NR	126	.1	.4
076 Buddhism	1	NR	NR	NR	-	-
081 Catholic	7	NR	NR	7,120	7.7	24.0
089 Chr & Miss Al	1	62	NR	160	.2	.5
093 Chr Ch (Disc)	1	141	76	178 *	.2	.6
097 Chr Chs&Chs Cr	1	150	NR	189 *	.2	.6
123 Ch God (Ander)	1	NR	40	40	-	.1
127 Ch God (Cleve)	3	932	897	1,174 *	1.3	4.0

NR–Not Reported *Total adherents estimated from known number of communicant, confirmed, full members. - Represents a percentage less than 0.1. Percentages may not total 100 due to rounding.

Table 4: Religious Congregations by County and Group: 2000

Religious Group	Number of Churches, Synagogues, Mosques, or Temples	Number of Communicant, Confirmed, or Full Members	Number of Attendees	Total Adherents: Number of Adherents	Total Adherents: % of Total Pop.	Total Adherents: % of Total Adh.
145 Ch God Prophcy	1	30	NR	38 *	-	.1
151 L-D Saints	8	NR	NR	3,050	3.3	10.3
165 Ch of Nazarene	5	821	665	1,415	1.5	4.8
167 Chs of Christ	2	135	143	204	.2	.7
173 Comm of Christ	1	156	NR	156	.2	.5
179 Consrv Bapt	3	NR	255	255	.3	.9
193 Episcopal	2	NR	199	563	.6	1.9
203 Evan Free Ch	1	27	55	55	.1	.2
207 E.L.C.A.	7	2,144	988	2,773	3.0	9.4
221 Free Methodist	1	46	63	63	.1	.2
226 Friends-USA	2	168	NR	212 *	.2	.7
263 Int Foursq Gos	2	241	260	304 *	.3	1.0
283 Luth—MO Synod	1	219	108	308	.3	1.0
355 Presb Ch (USA)	3	479	319	604 *	.6	2.0
403 Salvation Army	1	90	44	255	.3	.9
413 S.D.A.	5	974	NR	1,160	1.2	3.9
419 So Bapt Conv	11	3,489	982	4,399 *	4.7	14.8
449 Un Methodist	4	945	297	1,192 *	1.3	4.0
496 Jewish Est	0	NR	NR	175	.2	.6
499 Indep.Non-Char	1	850	400	850	.9	2.9
DOUGLAS	**39**	**3,328**	**2,471**	**10,491 ***	**32.2**	**100.0**
019 Amer Bapt USA	1	146	57	189 *	.6	1.8
053 Assemb of God	4	341	425	688	2.1	6.6
056 Baha'i	0	12	NR	12	-	.1
081 Catholic	4	NR	NR	4,834	14.8	46.1
093 Chr Ch (Disc)	1	146	58	189 *	.6	1.8
121 Ch God (Abr)	2	0	104	104 *	.3	1.0
123 Ch God (Ander)	1	NR	60	60	.2	.6
127 Ch God (Cleve)	1	347	117	449 *	1.4	4.3
151 L-D Saints	2	NR	NR	671	2.1	6.4
165 Ch of Nazarene	1	12	16	32	.1	.3
167 Chs of Christ	1	15	18	21	.1	.2
173 Comm of Christ	2	189	NR	189	.6	1.8
179 Consrv Bapt	2	NR	120	120	.4	1.1
207 E.L.C.A.	2	360	170	497	1.5	4.7
221 Free Methodist	1	111	204	204	.6	1.9
263 Int Foursq Gos	1	15	20	20 *	.1	.2
283 Luth—MO Synod	1	188	117	246	.8	2.3
339 Pent Ch of God	1	18	NR	30	.1	.3
355 Presb Ch (USA)	3	180	181	275 *	.8	2.6
388 Reg Bapt Gen As	1	0	100	100 *	.3	1.0
413 S.D.A.	1	476	NR	566	1.7	5.4
419 So Bapt Conv	1	428	420	553 *	1.7	5.3
449 Un Methodist	3	226	202	292 *	.9	2.8
469 WELS	2	118	82	150	.5	1.4
FERRY	**14**	**363**	**237**	**1,213 ***	**16.7**	**100.0**
053 Assemb of God	2	30	39	64	.9	5.3
056 Baha'i	0	5	NR	5	.1	.4
081 Catholic	4	NR	NR	478	6.6	39.4
151 L-D Saints	1	NR	NR	196	2.7	16.2
165 Ch of Nazarene	1	42	104	104	1.4	8.6
193 Episcopal	1	NR	14	24	.3	2.0
283 Luth—MO Synod	1	47	35	55	.8	4.5
355 Presb Ch (USA)	2	74	45	91 *	1.3	7.5
413 S.D.A.	2	165	NR	196	2.7	16.2
FRANKLIN	**56**	**4,980**	**3,359**	**25,654 ***	**52.0**	**100.0**
017 Amer Bapt Assn	1	21	NR	29 *	.1	.1
019 Amer Bapt USA	1	80	0	110 *	.2	.4
053 Assemb of God	5	907	1,104	1,573	3.2	6.1
056 Baha'i	1	28	NR	28	.1	.1
081 Catholic	3	NR	NR	15,668	31.8	61.1
097 Chr Chs&Chs Cr	1	413	NR	567 *	1.1	2.2
127 Ch God (Cleve)	2	345	355	473 *	1.0	1.8
143 CG in Cr(Menn)	1	87	NR	119 *	.2	.5
145 Ch God Prophcy	1	30	NR	42 *	.1	.2
151 L-D Saints	9	NR	NR	2,913	5.9	11.4
165 Ch of Nazarene	2	292	287	355	.7	1.4
167 Chs of Christ	2	160	195	225	.5	.9
193 Episcopal	1	NR	40	84	.2	.3
201 Evan Cov Ch	1	99	90	136 *	.3	.5
207 E.L.C.A.	3	501	208	666	1.3	2.6
246 Greek Orthodox	1	NR	NR	0	-	-
283 Luth—MO Synod	2	109	81	133	.3	.5
335 Orth Pres Ch	1	28	49	49	.1	.2
349 Pent Holiness	2	142	195	195 *	.4	.8
355 Presb Ch (USA)	1	36	26	49 *	.1	.2
388 Reg Bapt Gen As	2	173	259	237 *	.5	.9
413 S.D.A.	4	522	NR	622	1.3	2.4
419 So Bapt Conv	4	382	177	524 *	1.1	2.0
443 Un C of Christ	1	45	20	62 *	.1	.2
449 Un Methodist	4	580	273	795 *	1.6	3.1
GARFIELD	**7**	**623**	**296**	**1,565 ***	**65.3**	**100.0**
053 Assemb of God	1	45	46	60	2.5	3.8
056 Baha'i	0	2	NR	2	.1	.1
081 Catholic	1	NR	NR	702	29.3	44.9
097 Chr Chs&Chs Cr	1	185	NR	226 *	9.4	14.4
165 Ch of Nazarene	1	112	94	148	6.2	9.5
193 Episcopal	1	NR	34	85	3.5	5.4
283 Luth—MO Synod	1	20	15	26	1.1	1.7
449 Un Methodist	1	259	107	316 *	13.2	20.2
GRANT	**117**	**8,587**	**6,346**	**32,271 ***	**43.2**	**100.0**
053 Assemb of God	12	1,021	1,233	1,786	2.4	5.5
056 Baha'i	1	31	NR	31	-	.1
057 Bapt Gen Conf	1	208	223	276 *	.4	.9
081 Catholic	9	NR	NR	12,980	17.4	40.2
089 Chr & Miss Al	1	288	NR	1,042	1.4	3.2
093 Chr Ch (Disc)	2	108	37	143 *	.2	.4
105 Christian Ref	1	73	65	97 *	.1	.3
123 Ch God (Ander)	1	NR	60	60	.1	.2
145 Ch God Prophcy	2	61	NR	80 *	.1	.2
151 L-D Saints	19	NR	NR	5,692	7.6	17.6
165 Ch of Nazarene	4	272	299	581	.8	1.8
167 Chs of Christ	4	200	215	279	.4	.9
179 Consrv Bapt	2	NR	71	71	.1	.2
193 Episcopal	3	NR	106	296	.4	.9
203 Evan Free Ch	1	58	115	115	.2	.4
207 E.L.C.A.	4	1,651	520	2,286	3.1	7.1
221 Free Methodist	2	170	449	449	.6	1.4
226 Friends-USA	1	84	NR	112 *	.1	.3
257 Hutterian Br	2	132	NR	200	.3	.6
263 Int Foursq Gos	4	320	529	529 *	.7	1.6
283 Luth—MO Synod	6	575	293	751	1.0	2.3
288 Mennonite USA	1	57	55	76 *	.1	.2
291 Missionary Ch	1	106	137	137	.2	.4
297 Mennonite;Other	2	64	NR	85 *	.1	.3
349 Pent Holiness	3	158	270	210 *	.3	.7
355 Presb Ch (USA)	7	678	489	901 *	1.2	2.8
388 Reg Bapt Gen As	5	468	622	636 *	.9	2.0
403 Salvation Army	1	12	19	52	.1	.2
413 S.D.A.	5	443	NR	528	.7	1.6
419 So Bapt Conv	3	351	117	466 *	.6	1.4
443 Un C of Christ	2	159	88	211 *	.3	.7
449 Un Methodist	5	839	334	1,113 *	1.5	3.4
GRAYS HARBOR	**83**	**6,329**	**5,399**	**20,686 ***	**30.8**	**100.0**
019 Amer Bapt USA	1	123	54	152 *	.2	.7
053 Assemb of God	12	915	1,221	1,920	2.9	9.3
056 Baha'i	0	46	NR	46	.1	.2
057 Bapt Gen Conf	3	460	319	569 *	.8	2.8
081 Catholic	8	NR	NR	7,280	10.8	35.2
089 Chr & Miss Al	2	66	NR	184	.3	.9
093 Chr Ch (Disc)	1	50	25	62 *	.1	.3
105 Christian Ref	1	15	30	19 *	-	.1
123 Ch God (Ander)	3	NR	232	232	.3	1.1
151 L-D Saints	5	NR	NR	1,973	2.9	9.5
165 Ch of Nazarene	1	90	110	318	.5	1.5
167 Chs of Christ	3	95	95	128	.2	.6
173 Comm of Christ	2	70	NR	70	.1	.3
179 Consrv Bapt	3	NR	216	216	.3	1.0
193 Episcopal	4	NR	127	366	.5	1.8
201 Evan Cov Ch	1	101	111	125 *	.2	.6

NR–Not Reported   *Total adherents estimated from known number of communicant, confirmed, full members.   - Represents a percentage less than 0.1.   Percentages may not total 100 due to rounding.

Table 4: Religious Congregations by County and Group: 2000

Religious Group	Number of Churches, Synagogues, Mosques, or Temples	Number of Communicant, Confirmed, or Full Members	Number of Attendees	Total Adherents: Number of Adherents	Total Adherents: % of Total Pop.	Total Adherents: % of Total Adh.
207 E.L.C.A.	5	1,083	454	1,469	2.2	7.1
221 Free Methodist	1	21	52	52	.1	.3
283 Luth—MO Synod	1	344	174	706	1.1	3.4
339 Pent Ch of God	1	13	NR	30	-	.1
349 Pent Holiness	1	22	18	27 *	-	.1
355 Presb Ch (USA)	5	424	1,454	1,561 *	2.3	7.5
403 Salvation Army	1	77	39	117	.2	.6
413 S.D.A.	2	321	NR	382	.6	1.8
419 So Bapt Conv	5	820	219	1,014 *	1.5	4.9
435 Unitarian-Univ	1	18	NR	22 *	-	.1
449 Un Methodist	9	1,155	449	1,431 *	2.1	6.9
496 Jewish Est	1	NR	NR	215	.3	1.0
ISLAND	**49**	**6,870**	**5,142**	**18,176 ***	**25.4**	**100.0**
019 Amer Bapt USA	1	150	150	187 *	.3	1.0
053 Assemb of God	3	323	461	748	1.0	4.1
056 Baha'i	2	62	NR	62	.1	.3
057 Bapt Gen Conf	1	140	110	175 *	.2	1.0
081 Catholic	3	NR	NR	6,220	8.7	34.2
084 Calvary Chapel	2	NR	NR	NR	-	-
089 Chr & Miss Al	1	220	NR	591	.8	3.3
105 Christian Ref	1	324	280	404 *	.6	2.2
151 L-D Saints	4	NR	NR	1,531	2.1	8.4
165 Ch of Nazarene	1	261	185	425	.6	2.3
167 Chs of Christ	2	89	95	141	.2	.8
193 Episcopal	3	NR	363	540	.8	3.0
203 Evan Free Ch	1	91	187	187	.3	1.0
207 E.L.C.A.	4	1,724	932	2,267	3.2	12.5
221 Free Methodist	1	58	52	58	.1	.3
226 Friends-USA	1	22	NR	27 *	-	.1
263 Int Foursq Gos	4	357	736	736 *	1.0	4.0
283 Luth—MO Synod	1	212	103	287	.4	1.6
335 Orth Pres Ch	1	39	46	60	.1	.3
355 Presb Ch (USA)	1	314	200	392 *	.5	2.2
370 Ref Baptist Chs	1	NR	NR	NR	-	-
371 Ref Ch in Am	1	397	360	541	.8	3.0
413 S.D.A.	2	110	NR	131	.2	.7
419 So Bapt Conv	3	850	233	1,060 *	1.5	5.8
435 Unitarian-Univ	1	60	NR	75 *	.1	.4
449 Un Methodist	3	1,067	649	1,331 *	1.9	7.3
JEFFERSON	**29**	**2,276**	**1,441**	**5,751 ***	**22.2**	**100.0**
019 Amer Bapt USA	1	65	35	76 *	.3	1.3
053 Assemb of God	4	168	228	272	1.0	4.7
056 Baha'i	1	42	NR	42	.2	.7
081 Catholic	1	NR	NR	1,930	7.4	33.6
084 Calvary Chapel	1	NR	NR	NR	-	-
151 L-D Saints	2	NR	NR	630	2.4	11.0
165 Ch of Nazarene	1	170	99	215	.8	3.7
167 Chs of Christ	2	85	85	120	.5	2.1
193 Episcopal	1	NR	95	289	1.1	5.0
203 Evan Free Ch	1	50	90	90	.3	1.6
207 E.L.C.A.	2	398	248	488	1.9	8.5
226 Friends-USA	1	22	NR	26 *	.1	.5
263 Int Foursq Gos	1	20	26	26 *	.1	.5
331 OCA: Ter Diocs	1	0	NR	75	.3	1.3
355 Presb Ch (USA)	2	415	249	485 *	1.9	8.4
413 S.D.A.	2	179	NR	213	.8	3.7
419 So Bapt Conv	2	293	149	343 *	1.3	6.0
435 Unitarian-Univ	1	168	NR	196 *	.8	3.4
449 Un Methodist	2	201	137	235 *	.9	4.1
KING	**1,097**	**175,950**	**141,421**	**647,222 ***	**37.3**	**100.0**
017 Amer Bapt Assn	1	63	NR	76 *	-	-
019 Amer Bapt USA	39	10,290	3,858	12,478 *	.7	1.9
050 Armen Ap Etchm	1	0	NR	924	.1	.1
053 Assemb of God	61	14,911	15,046	24,457	1.4	3.8
055 As Ref Pres Ch	1	13	NR	19	-	-
056 Baha'i	25	2,209	NR	2,209	.1	.3
057 Bapt Gen Conf	18	3,189	4,460	4,851 *	.3	.7
076 Buddhism	53	NR	NR	NR	-	-
081 Catholic	65	NR	NR	280,568	16.2	43.3
084 Calvary Chapel	8	NR	NR	NR	-	-
089 Chr & Miss Al	24	3,294	NR	6,182	.4	1.0
093 Chr Ch (Disc)	12	2,221	979	2,693 *	.2	.4
097 Chr Chs&Chs Cr	15	7,337	NR	8,900 *	.5	1.4
105 Christian Ref	6	916	730	1,111 *	.1	.2
121 Ch God (Abr)	1	12	15	15 *	-	-
123 Ch God (Ander)	6	NR	752	752	-	.1
127 Ch God (Cleve)	7	320	207	396 *	-	.1
145 Ch God Prophcy	2	61	NR	74 *	-	-
151 L-D Saints	106	NR	NR	40,525	2.3	6.3
157 Ch of Brethren	3	425	0	515 *	-	.1
165 Ch of Nazarene	23	4,733	3,609	7,466	.4	1.2
167 Chs of Christ	31	3,149	3,617	4,389	.3	.7
173 Comm of Christ	6	930	NR	930	.1	.1
175 Congr Chr Chs	1	42	31	51 *	-	-
179 Consrv Bapt	11	NR	4,651	4,651	.3	.7
193 Episcopal	39	NR	6,227	17,901	1.0	2.8
201 Evan Cov Ch	15	3,384	3,994	4,749 *	.3	.7
203 Evan Free Ch	8	698	1,154	1,154	.1	.2
207 E.L.C.A.	68	25,459	11,761	35,393	2.0	5.5
216 Evan Presby Ch	2	665	NR	806 *	-	.1
220 Free Lutheran	2	167	104	223	-	-
221 Free Methodist	12	1,889	2,933	2,933	.2	.5
223 Free Will Bapt	1	69	NR	84 *	-	-
226 Friends-USA	9	446	NR	541 *	-	.1
237 Menn Br US Conf	3	261	NR	317 *	-	-
246 Greek Orthodox	3	NR	NR	2,379	.1	.4
249 Assyr Apost Ch	1	NR	NR	280	-	-
251 Holy Orth in NA	1	NR	NR	180	-	-
252 Hindu	15	NR	NR	NR	-	-
262 Int Cou Comm Ch	2	380	NR	460 *	-	.1
263 Int Foursq Gos	34	3,620	9,070	9,070 *	.5	1.4
264 Int Chs of Crst	1	459	851	601	-	.1
267 Muslim Est	7	NR	1,770	8,078	.5	1.2
283 Luth—MO Synod	30	8,256	4,637	11,199	.6	1.7
288 Mennonite USA	2	165	185	200 *	-	-
290 Metro Comm Ch	1	110	59	59 *	-	-
313 N Am Bapt Conf	3	124	149	150 *	-	-
331 OCA: Ter Diocs	2	145	NR	496	-	.1
335 Orth Pres Ch	1	122	163	171	-	-
339 Pent Ch of God	2	38	NR	80	-	-
349 Pent Holiness	2	71	90	86 *	-	-
355 Presb Ch (USA)	60	20,648	18,096	26,926 *	1.6	4.2
356 Presb Ch Amer	6	726	873	902	.1	.1
370 Ref Baptist Chs	3	NR	NR	NR	-	-
371 Ref Ch in Am	2	180	180	354	-	.1
388 Reg Bapt Gen As	12	978	1,357	1,368 *	.1	.2
397 OCA: Roman Dioc	1	NR	NR	77	-	-
401 Rus Orth Abroad	1	NR	NR	NR	-	-
403 Salvation Army	6	567	349	2,336	.1	.4
410 Serb Orth USA	1	NR	NR	400	-	.1
413 S.D.A.	28	6,252	NR	7,442	.4	1.1
416 Sikh	4	NR	NR	NR	-	-
418 Southw Bapt Fel	1	NR	NR	NR	-	-
419 So Bapt Conv	41	9,625	4,886	11,672 *	.7	1.8
425 Tao	1	NR	NR	NR	-	-
435 Unitarian-Univ	9	2,142	NR	2,597 *	.1	.4
443 Un C of Christ	31	6,387	3,272	7,745 *	.4	1.2
449 Un Methodist	50	15,299	6,857	18,553 *	1.1	2.9
463 Vineyard	4	625	525	758 *	-	.1
467 Wesleyan	1	0	33	42	-	-
469 WELS	7	762	641	1,078	.1	.2
496 Jewish Est	21	NR	NR	32,400	1.9	5.0
498 Indep.Charis.	8	6,163	10,060	17,560	1.0	2.7
499 Indep.Non-Char	7	4,953	13,190	13,190	.8	2.0
KITSAP	**159**	**22,449**	**18,022**	**65,550 ***	**28.3**	**100.0**
017 Amer Bapt Assn	2	115	NR	145 *	.1	.2
019 Amer Bapt USA	6	776	345	976 *	.4	1.5
053 Assemb of God	12	2,221	3,207	5,703	2.5	8.7
056 Baha'i	3	178	NR	178	.1	.3
057 Bapt Gen Conf	3	748	852	941 *	.4	1.4
059 Bapt Miss Assn	1	149	75	187 *	.1	.3
076 Buddhism	2	NR	NR	NR	-	-
081 Catholic	7	NR	NR	17,990	7.8	27.4

NR–Not Reported *Total adherents estimated from known number of communicant, confirmed, full members. - Represents a percentage less than 0.1. Percentages may not total 100 due to rounding.

Table 4: Religious Congregations by County and Group: 2000

Religious Group	Number of Churches, Synagogues, Mosques, or Temples	Number of Communicant, Confirmed, or Full Members	Number of Attendees	Total Adherents		
				Number of Adherents	% of Total Pop.	% of Total Adh.
084 Calvary Chapel	4	NR	NR	NR	-	-
089 Chr & Miss Al	5	581	NR	1,340	.6	2.0
093 Chr Ch (Disc)	2	262	34	330 *	.1	.5
097 Chr Chs&Chs Cr	3	625	NR	787 *	.3	1.2
105 Christian Ref	1	103	85	130 *	.1	.2
123 Ch God (Ander)	2	NR	41	41	-	.1
145 Ch God Prophcy	1	30	NR	38 *	-	.1
151 L-D Saints	17	NR	NR	7,195	3.1	11.0
165 Ch of Nazarene	4	813	941	1,457	.6	2.2
167 Chs of Christ	4	451	631	656	.3	1.0
173 Comm of Christ	1	147	NR	147	.1	.2
179 Consrv Bapt	1	NR	58	58	-	.1
193 Episcopal	7	NR	762	1,958	.8	3.0
201 Evan Cov Ch	2	104	240	247 *	.1	.4
203 Evan Free Ch	2	319	655	655	.3	1.0
207 E.L.C.A.	11	4,290	2,076	6,026	2.6	9.2
221 Free Methodist	2	51	90	90	-	.1
226 Friends-USA	2	44	NR	55 *	-	.1
262 Int Cou Comm Ch	1	45	NR	57 *	-	.1
263 Int Foursq Gos	3	399	951	951 *	.4	1.5
283 Luth—MO Synod	4	904	539	1,190	.5	1.8
291 Missionary Ch	1	21	38	38	-	.1
313 N Am Bapt Conf	1	110	370	138 *	.1	.2
355 Presb Ch (USA)	5	1,834	1,375	2,307 *	1.0	3.5
356 Presb Ch Amer	3	119	233	247	.1	.4
388 Reg Bapt Gen As	3	846	1,209	1,261 *	.5	1.9
403 Salvation Army	1	82	46	199	.1	.3
413 S.D.A.	4	922	NR	1,097	.5	1.7
419 So Bapt Conv	7	1,439	523	1,810 *	.8	2.8
435 Unitarian-Univ	2	249	NR	313 *	.1	.5
443 Un C of Christ	2	406	205	511 *	.2	.8
449 Un Methodist	9	2,005	1,132	2,522 *	1.1	3.8
469 WELS	1	244	184	329	.1	.5
496 Jewish Est	2	NR	NR	3,200	1.4	4.9
498 Indep.Charis.	1	0	350	400	.2	.6
499 Indep.Non-Char	2	817	775	1,650	.7	2.5
KITTITAS	**37**	**3,035**	**2,005**	**9,950 ***	**29.8**	**100.0**
019 Amer Bapt USA	3	149	196	196 *	.6	2.0
053 Assemb of God	3	127	169	247	.7	2.5
056 Baha'i	0	22	NR	22	.1	.2
081 Catholic	3	NR	NR	3,583	10.7	36.0
089 Chr & Miss Al	2	370	NR	873	2.6	8.8
097 Chr Chs&Chs Cr	1	90	NR	106 *	.3	1.1
123 Ch God (Ander)	1	NR	14	14	-	.1
151 L-D Saints	4	NR	NR	1,314	3.9	13.2
165 Ch of Nazarene	2	158	119	161	.5	1.6
167 Chs of Christ	1	51	55	67	.2	.7
173 Comm of Christ	1	24	NR	24	.1	.2
179 Consrv Bapt	1	NR	244	244	.7	2.5
193 Episcopal	2	NR	104	336	1.0	3.4
207 E.L.C.A.	1	377	225	471	1.4	4.7
263 Int Foursq Gos	2	126	278	278 *	.8	2.8
355 Presb Ch (USA)	3	428	318	525 *	1.6	5.3
413 S.D.A.	2	184	NR	219	.7	2.2
419 So Bapt Conv	1	580	175	686 *	2.1	6.9
435 Unitarian-Univ	1	31	NR	37 *	.1	.4
449 Un Methodist	1	251	64	297 *	.9	3.0
469 WELS	2	67	44	75	.2	.8
496 Jewish Est	0	NR	NR	175	.5	1.8
KLICKITAT	**37**	**1,955**	**1,543**	**6,237 ***	**32.6**	**100.0**
053 Assemb of God	3	234	310	580	3.0	9.3
056 Baha'i	1	27	NR	27	.1	.4
081 Catholic	2	NR	NR	2,171	11.3	34.8
097 Chr Chs&Chs Cr	1	25	NR	31 *	.2	.5
123 Ch God (Ander)	1	NR	110	110	.6	1.8
145 Ch God Prophcy	1	30	NR	38 *	.2	.6
151 L-D Saints	2	NR	NR	834	4.4	13.4
165 Ch of Nazarene	2	139	114	234	1.2	3.8
167 Chs of Christ	3	91	120	123	.6	2.0
179 Consrv Bapt	3	NR	350	350	1.8	5.6
207 E.L.C.A.	1	120	39	144	.8	2.3
263 Int Foursq Gos	1	1	17	17 *	.1	.3
283 Luth—MO Synod	2	119	69	139	.7	2.2
355 Presb Ch (USA)	3	98	76	123 *	.6	2.0
413 S.D.A.	3	412	NR	490	2.6	7.9
419 So Bapt Conv	4	242	173	303 *	1.6	4.9
443 Un C of Christ	1	81	29	102 *	.5	1.6
449 Un Methodist	3	336	136	421 *	2.2	6.8
LEWIS	**89**	**8,852**	**6,746**	**22,549 ***	**32.9**	**100.0**
019 Amer Bapt USA	2	335	153	417 *	.6	1.8
053 Assemb of God	16	1,926	2,148	4,094	6.0	18.2
056 Baha'i	0	40	NR	40	.1	.2
081 Catholic	9	NR	NR	5,530	8.1	24.5
097 Chr Chs&Chs Cr	2	415	NR	517 *	.8	2.3
123 Ch God (Ander)	3	NR	760	760	1.1	3.4
127 Ch God (Cleve)	1	54	55	67 *	.1	.3
145 Ch God Prophcy	1	30	NR	38 *	.1	.2
151 L-D Saints	6	NR	NR	2,483	3.6	11.0
157 Ch of Brethren	2	149	0	186 *	.3	.8
165 Ch of Nazarene	2	528	382	716	1.0	3.2
167 Chs of Christ	2	154	150	202	.3	.9
179 Consrv Bapt	3	NR	371	371	.5	1.6
193 Episcopal	2	NR	68	173	.3	.8
201 Evan Cov Ch	1	27	43	43 *	.1	.2
203 Evan Free Ch	1	29	70	70	.1	.3
207 E.L.C.A.	4	903	393	1,233	1.8	5.5
221 Free Methodist	1	142	188	188	.3	.8
263 Int Foursq Gos	3	163	477	477 *	.7	2.1
283 Luth—MO Synod	1	214	136	321	.5	1.4
339 Pent Ch of God	3	39	NR	84	.1	.4
355 Presb Ch (USA)	6	895	618	1,114 *	1.6	4.9
403 Salvation Army	1	103	40	100	.1	.4
413 S.D.A.	5	807	NR	961	1.4	4.3
419 So Bapt Conv	5	882	341	1,098 *	1.6	4.9
449 Un Methodist	7	1,017	353	1,266 *	1.8	5.6
LINCOLN	**31**	**2,728**	**1,277**	**4,492 ***	**44.1**	**100.0**
053 Assemb of God	1	39	50	67	.7	1.5
056 Baha'i	0	9	NR	9	.1	.2
081 Catholic	6	NR	NR	1,035	10.2	23.0
093 Chr Ch (Disc)	1	227	60	278 *	2.7	6.2
165 Ch of Nazarene	2	100	110	167	1.6	3.7
207 E.L.C.A.	6	1,053	344	1,283	12.6	28.6
257 Hutterian Br	2	132	NR	200	2.0	4.5
263 Int Foursq Gos	2	38	69	69 *	.7	1.5
283 Luth—MO Synod	1	104	63	127	1.2	2.8
313 N Am Bapt Conf	1	40	35	49 *	.5	1.1
355 Presb Ch (USA)	4	550	341	674 *	6.6	15.0
413 S.D.A.	1	20	NR	24	.2	.5
449 Un Methodist	4	416	205	510 *	5.0	11.4
MASON	**32**	**3,835**	**2,921**	**11,614 ***	**23.5**	**100.0**
019 Amer Bapt USA	1	615	245	745 *	1.5	6.4
053 Assemb of God	4	369	443	785	1.6	6.8
056 Baha'i	0	52	NR	52	.1	.4
081 Catholic	1	NR	NR	3,530	7.1	30.4
089 Chr & Miss Al	1	58	NR	163	.3	1.4
097 Chr Chs&Chs Cr	1	324	NR	392 *	.8	3.4
123 Ch God (Ander)	1	NR	45	45	.1	.4
127 Ch God (Cleve)	1	81	34	98 *	.2	.8
151 L-D Saints	4	NR	NR	1,591	3.2	13.7
165 Ch of Nazarene	1	97	89	229	.5	2.0
167 Chs of Christ	1	49	52	68	.1	.6
179 Consrv Bapt	2	NR	860	860	1.7	7.4
193 Episcopal	3	NR	180	441	.9	3.8
207 E.L.C.A.	2	591	322	673	1.4	5.8
263 Int Foursq Gos	1	124	111	150 *	.3	1.3
283 Luth—MO Synod	1	219	141	276	.6	2.4
355 Presb Ch (USA)	1	109	96	132 *	.3	1.1
413 S.D.A.	2	244	NR	290	.6	2.5
419 So Bapt Conv	2	316	80	383 *	.8	3.3
449 Un Methodist	2	587	223	711 *	1.4	6.1

NR–Not Reported   *Total adherents estimated from known number of communicant, confirmed, full members.   - Represents a percentage less than 0.1.   Percentages may not total 100 due to rounding.

Table 4: Religious Congregations by County and Group: 2000

Religious Group	Number of Churches, Synagogues, Mosques, or Temples	Number of Communicant, Confirmed, or Full Members	Number of Attendees	Total Adherents		
				Number of Adherents	% of Total Pop.	% of Total Adh.
OKANOGAN	**78**	**3,864**	**2,673**	**10,189 ***	**25.8**	**100.0**
017 Amer Bapt Assn	1	38	NR	48 *	.1	.5
053 Assemb of God	7	361	422	513	1.3	5.0
056 Baha'i	1	55	NR	55	.1	.5
057 Bapt Gen Conf	2	109	162	193 *	.5	1.9
059 Bapt Miss Assn	1	24	25	30 *	.1	.3
081 Catholic	8	NR	NR	3,760	9.5	36.9
084 Calvary Chapel	1	NR	NR	NR	-	-
089 Chr & Miss Al	2	18	NR	120	.3	1.2
143 CG in Cr(Menn)	1	19	NR	24 *	.1	.2
151 L-D Saints	4	NR	NR	892	2.3	8.8
157 Ch of Brethren	2	119	0	151 *	.4	1.5
165 Ch of Nazarene	1	69	36	86	.2	.8
167 Chs of Christ	4	107	115	144	.4	1.4
193 Episcopal	3	NR	59	196	.5	1.9
201 Evan Cov Ch	1	60	105	105 *	.3	1.0
221 Free Methodist	3	239	469	469	1.2	4.6
263 Int Foursq Gos	5	186	325	325 *	.8	3.2
283 Luth—MO Synod	5	391	177	462	1.2	4.5
313 N Am Bapt Conf	1	26	40	33 *	.1	.3
339 Pent Ch of God	4	71	NR	155	.4	1.5
355 Presb Ch (USA)	3	344	244	434 *	1.1	4.3
413 S.D.A.	6	732	NR	871	2.2	8.5
419 So Bapt Conv	2	251	103	317 *	.8	3.1
443 Un C of Christ	1	62	62	78 *	.2	.8
449 Un Methodist	7	487	282	614 *	1.6	6.0
469 WELS	2	96	47	114	.3	1.1
PACIFIC	**40**	**1,987**	**1,669**	**7,297 ***	**34.8**	**100.0**
019 Amer Bapt USA	1	199	80	235 *	1.1	3.2
053 Assemb of God	4	315	401	776	3.7	10.6
056 Baha'i	0	12	NR	12	.1	.2
081 Catholic	4	NR	NR	2,170	10.3	29.7
151 L-D Saints	2	NR	NR	541	2.6	7.4
165 Ch of Nazarene	2	61	83	823	3.9	11.3
179 Consrv Bapt	3	NR	285	285	1.4	3.9
193 Episcopal	2	NR	64	116	.6	1.6
207 E.L.C.A.	6	566	297	786	3.7	10.8
263 Int Foursq Gos	1	4	5	5 *	-	.1
283 Luth—MO Synod	1	66	35	72	.3	1.0
339 Pent Ch of God	1	52	NR	400	1.9	5.5
355 Presb Ch (USA)	2	161	118	190 *	.9	2.6
413 S.D.A.	2	74	NR	88	.4	1.2
419 So Bapt Conv	1	24	26	28 *	.1	.4
443 Un C of Christ	1	43	23	51 *	.2	.7
449 Un Methodist	5	410	209	484 *	2.3	6.6
467 Wesleyan	2	0	43	235	1.1	3.2
PEND OREILLE	**23**	**1,269**	**721**	**2,742 ***	**23.4**	**100.0**
053 Assemb of God	3	188	238	251	2.1	9.2
056 Baha'i	0	4	NR	4	-	.1
081 Catholic	5	NR	NR	553	4.7	20.2
151 L-D Saints	2	NR	NR	447	3.8	16.3
165 Ch of Nazarene	1	21	30	198	1.7	7.2
167 Chs of Christ	1	14	20	20	.2	.7
181 Consrv Congr	1	28	12	35 *	.3	1.3
207 E.L.C.A.	1	218	97	252	2.1	9.2
288 Mennonite USA	1	74	53	92 *	.8	3.4
355 Presb Ch (USA)	1	17	31	31 *	.3	1.1
413 S.D.A.	3	263	NR	312	2.7	11.4
419 So Bapt Conv	2	259	115	321 *	2.7	11.7
443 Un C of Christ	2	183	125	226 *	1.9	8.2
PIERCE	**442**	**74,091**	**57,065**	**208,660 ***	**29.8**	**100.0**
017 Amer Bapt Assn	2	150	NR	190 *	-	.1
019 Amer Bapt USA	17	3,867	2,062	4,901 *	.7	2.3
053 Assemb of God	25	5,120	5,975	18,605	2.7	8.9
056 Baha'i	8	566	NR	566	.1	.3
057 Bapt Gen Conf	5	1,140	1,593	1,721 *	.2	.8
059 Bapt Miss Assn	2	95	77	128 *	-	.1
076 Buddhism	8	NR	NR	NR	-	-
081 Catholic	28	NR	NR	61,910	8.8	29.7

Religious Group	Number of Churches, Synagogues, Mosques, or Temples	Number of Communicant, Confirmed, or Full Members	Number of Attendees	Total Adherents		
				Number of Adherents	% of Total Pop.	% of Total Adh.
084 Calvary Chapel	3	NR	NR	NR	-	-
089 Chr & Miss Al	6	848	NR	1,985	.3	1.0
093 Chr Ch (Disc)	7	1,436	638	1,820 *	.3	.9
097 Chr Chs&Chs Cr	11	2,329	NR	2,952 *	.4	1.4
105 Christian Ref	3	467	391	592 *	.1	.3
123 Ch God (Ander)	4	NR	238	238	-	.1
127 Ch God (Cleve)	3	231	348	390 *	.1	.2
145 Ch God Prophcy	2	61	NR	78 *	-	-
151 L-D Saints	49	NR	NR	20,343	2.9	9.7
157 Ch of Brethren	1	30	0	38 *	-	-
165 Ch of Nazarene	9	2,450	1,977	3,189	.5	1.5
167 Chs of Christ	11	1,224	1,323	1,685	.2	.8
173 Comm of Christ	2	466	NR	466	.1	.2
175 Congr Chr Chs	1	149	76	189 *	-	.1
179 Consrv Bapt	7	NR	840	840	.1	.4
193 Episcopal	10	NR	1,477	3,274	.5	1.6
201 Evan Cov Ch	7	1,000	1,297	1,433 *	.2	.7
203 Evan Free Ch	4	257	485	485	.1	.2
207 E.L.C.A.	29	11,083	5,701	15,337	2.2	7.4
220 Free Lutheran	1	80	50	100	-	-
221 Free Methodist	2	63	106	106	-	.1
226 Friends-USA	3	190	NR	241 *	-	.1
246 Greek Orthodox	1	NR	NR	705	.1	.3
262 Int Cou Comm Ch	1	190	NR	241 *	-	.1
263 Int Foursq Gos	10	551	1,472	1,472 *	.2	.7
267 Muslim Est	3	NR	604	3,939	.6	1.9
283 Luth—MO Synod	11	5,291	2,511	7,600	1.1	3.6
290 Metro Comm Ch	1	80	95	95 *	-	-
291 Missionary Ch	1	20	37	37	-	-
313 N Am Bapt Conf	8	1,008	935	1,277 *	.2	.6
331 OCA: Ter Diocs	1	80	NR	225	-	.1
339 Pent Ch of God	1	20	NR	40	-	-
349 Pent Holiness	2	59	75	75 *	-	-
355 Presb Ch (USA)	25	7,807	5,587	9,932 *	1.4	4.8
356 Presb Ch Amer	1	281	472	521	.1	.2
370 Ref Baptist Chs	2	NR	NR	NR	-	-
388 Reg Bapt Gen As	13	1,796	2,189	2,501 *	.4	1.2
403 Salvation Army	2	322	161	719	.1	.3
413 S.D.A.	11	2,302	NR	2,739	.4	1.3
419 So Bapt Conv	27	6,931	3,553	8,784 *	1.3	4.2
435 Unitarian-Univ	1	155	NR	196 *	-	.1
443 Un C of Christ	5	429	301	544 *	.1	.3
449 Un Methodist	28	5,368	2,795	6,802 *	1.0	3.3
463 Vineyard	2	205	176	259 *	-	.1
469 WELS	3	519	318	695	.1	.3
496 Jewish Est	2	NR	NR	2,000	.3	1.0
498 Indep.Charis.	5	3,775	5,420	7,750	1.1	3.7
499 Indep.Non-Char	5	3,600	5,710	5,710	.8	2.7
SAN JUAN	**22**	**510**	**559**	**2,414 ***	**17.1**	**100.0**
053 Assemb of God	1	33	30	45	.3	1.9
056 Baha'i	1	31	NR	31	.2	1.3
076 Buddhism	2	NR	NR	NR	-	-
081 Catholic	4	NR	NR	1,200	8.5	49.7
084 Calvary Chapel	1	NR	NR	NR	-	-
151 L-D Saints	1	NR	NR	226	1.6	9.4
193 Episcopal	3	NR	247	390	2.8	16.2
207 E.L.C.A.	1	72	74	75	.5	3.1
226 Friends-USA	3	66	NR	77 *	.5	3.2
263 Int Foursq Gos	1	11	23	23 *	.2	1.0
355 Presb Ch (USA)	1	203	185	236 *	1.7	9.8
413 S.D.A.	2	66	NR	78	.6	3.2
435 Unitarian-Univ	1	28	NR	33 *	.2	1.4
SKAGIT	**104**	**16,287**	**10,477**	**44,794 ***	**43.5**	**100.0**
017 Amer Bapt Assn	1	50	NR	62 *	.1	.1
019 Amer Bapt USA	4	752	546	940 *	.9	2.1
053 Assemb of God	11	1,362	1,813	2,999	2.9	6.7
056 Baha'i	1	136	NR	136	.1	.3
057 Bapt Gen Conf	1	1,064	754	1,330 *	1.3	3.0
081 Catholic	7	NR	NR	18,890	18.3	42.2
084 Calvary Chapel	1	NR	NR	NR	-	-
089 Chr & Miss Al	1	38	NR	70	.1	.2

NR–Not Reported *Total adherents estimated from known number of communicant, confirmed, full members. - Represents a percentage less than 0.1. Percentages may not total 100 due to rounding.

Table 4: Religious Congregations by County and Group: 2000

Religious Group	Number of Churches, Synagogues, Mosques, or Temples	Number of Communicant, Confirmed, or Full Members	Number of Attendees	Total Adherents: Number of Adherents	Total Adherents: % of Total Pop.	Total Adherents: % of Total Adh.
093 Chr Ch (Disc)	1	110	45	137 *	.1	.3
097 Chr Chs&Chs Cr	3	711	NR	888 *	.9	2.0
105 Christian Ref	3	739	572	924 *	.9	2.1
127 Ch God (Cleve)	1	5	6	6 *	-	-
145 Ch God Prophcy	2	61	NR	76 *	.1	.2
151 L-D Saints	6	NR	NR	2,456	2.4	5.5
165 Ch of Nazarene	3	325	236	514	.5	1.1
167 Chs of Christ	4	294	329	419	.4	.9
173 Comm of Christ	1	99	NR	99	.1	.2
179 Consrv Bapt	1	NR	110	110	.1	.2
193 Episcopal	3	NR	224	575	.6	1.3
201 Evan Cov Ch	2	537	633	672 *	.7	1.5
207 E.L.C.A.	11	4,193	1,601	5,396	5.2	12.0
221 Free Methodist	3	197	523	523	.5	1.2
226 Friends-USA	1	84	NR	105 *	.1	.2
262 Int Cou Comm Ch	1	190	NR	237 *	.2	.5
263 Int Foursq Gos	3	412	1,041	1,041 *	1.0	2.3
283 Luth—MO Synod	1	211	140	281	.3	.6
335 Orth Pres Ch	1	22	40	42	-	.1
349 Pent Holiness	1	30	0	37 *	-	.1
355 Presb Ch (USA)	4	594	380	742 *	.7	1.7
388 Reg Bapt Gen As	1	86	100	107 *	.1	.2
403 Salvation Army	1	54	23	102	.1	.2
413 S.D.A.	2	561	NR	668	.6	1.5
419 So Bapt Conv	5	1,058	379	1,322 *	1.3	3.0
435 Unitarian-Univ	1	53	NR	66 *	.1	.1
443 Un C of Christ	2	104	53	130 *	.1	.3
449 Un Methodist	8	2,005	819	2,505 *	2.4	5.6
463 Vineyard	1	150	110	187 *	.2	.4
SKAMANIA	**8**	**1,036**	**285**	**2,386 ***	**24.2**	**100.0**
056 Baha'i	0	3	NR	3	-	.1
081 Catholic	0	NR	NR	720	7.3	30.2
151 L-D Saints	1	NR	NR	250	2.5	10.5
165 Ch of Nazarene	2	178	126	313	3.2	13.1
167 Chs of Christ	1	23	30	45	.5	1.9
179 Consrv Bapt	1	NR	50	50	.5	2.1
207 E.L.C.A.	1	110	50	141	1.4	5.9
413 S.D.A.	1	639	NR	760	7.7	31.9
449 Un Methodist	1	83	29	104 *	1.1	4.4
SNOHOMISH	**357**	**48,943**	**40,715**	**144,432 ***	**23.8**	**100.0**
017 Amer Bapt Assn	2	29	NR	37 *	-	-
019 Amer Bapt USA	10	2,537	1,254	3,225 *	.5	2.2
034 Ant Orth of NA	2	247	NR	494	.1	.3
053 Assemb of God	27	3,862	5,225	7,690	1.3	5.3
056 Baha'i	11	518	NR	518	.1	.4
057 Bapt Gen Conf	6	938	1,820	2,193 *	.4	1.5
076 Buddhism	1	NR	NR	NR	-	-
081 Catholic	16	NR	NR	46,990	7.8	32.5
084 Calvary Chapel	5	NR	NR	NR	-	-
089 Chr & Miss Al	10	1,083	NR	3,472	.6	2.4
093 Chr Ch (Disc)	2	208	75	264 *	-	.2
097 Chr Chs&Chs Cr	6	2,109	NR	2,682 *	.4	1.9
105 Christian Ref	6	746	652	948 *	.2	.7
123 Ch God (Ander)	4	NR	585	585	.1	.4
127 Ch God (Cleve)	2	144	60	183 *	-	.1
145 Ch God Prophcy	4	122	NR	156 *	-	.1
151 L-D Saints	41	NR	NR	16,537	2.7	11.4
165 Ch of Nazarene	10	1,612	1,631	3,284	.5	2.3
167 Chs of Christ	7	569	640	833	.1	.6
173 Comm of Christ	2	434	NR	434	.1	.3
175 Congr Chr Chs	1	60	75	76 *	-	.1
179 Consrv Bapt	5	NR	1,060	1,060	.2	.7
181 Consrv Congr	1	10	15	13 *	-	-
193 Episcopal	7	NR	749	1,770	.3	1.2
201 Evan Cov Ch	4	262	304	343 *	.1	.2
203 Evan Free Ch	4	118	311	311	.1	.2
207 E.L.C.A.	29	10,272	4,805	14,446	2.4	10.0
220 Free Lutheran	4	394	362	547	.1	.4
221 Free Methodist	7	977	1,759	1,762	.3	1.2
226 Friends-USA	1	22	NR	28 *	-	-
237 Menn Br US Conf	1	0	NR	0 *	-	-
251 Holy Orth in NA	1	NR	NR	4	-	-
252 Hindu	1	NR	NR	NR	-	-
263 Int Foursq Gos	17	3,270	5,755	5,755 *	.9	4.0
283 Luth—MO Synod	11	1,996	1,074	2,517	.4	1.7
297 Mennonite;Other	1	11	NR	14 *	-	-
313 N Am Bapt Conf	4	262	310	333 *	.1	.2
335 Orth Pres Ch	2	142	214	222	-	.2
349 Pent Holiness	1	20	35	25 *	-	-
355 Presb Ch (USA)	9	2,035	1,368	2,609 *	.4	1.8
356 Presb Ch Amer	2	248	240	297	-	.2
371 Ref Ch in Am	2	246	250	417	.1	.3
388 Reg Bapt Gen As	6	456	665	641 *	.1	.4
403 Salvation Army	1	97	34	243	-	.2
413 S.D.A.	12	1,883	NR	2,240	.4	1.6
419 So Bapt Conv	16	2,266	1,300	2,881 *	.5	2.0
435 Unitarian-Univ	2	380	NR	483 *	.1	.3
443 Un C of Christ	3	314	143	399 *	.1	.3
449 Un Methodist	13	4,408	1,982	5,605 *	.9	3.9
463 Vineyard	4	639	522	813 *	.1	.6
469 WELS	2	192	141	228	-	.2
490 Zoroastrian	1	NR	NR	NR	-	-
496 Jewish Est	1	NR	NR	1,600	.3	1.1
498 Indep.Charis.	4	650	3,530	4,070	.7	2.8
499 Indep.Non-Char	3	2,155	1,770	2,155	.4	1.5
SPOKANE	**308**	**50,674**	**35,529**	**150,918 ***	**36.1**	**100.0**
017 Amer Bapt Assn	3	106	NR	132 *	-	.1
019 Amer Bapt USA	9	1,161	654	1,444 *	.3	1.0
034 Ant Orth of NA	1	115	NR	230	.1	.2
053 Assemb of God	15	2,216	3,003	4,363	1.0	2.9
056 Baha'i	3	226	NR	226	.1	.1
057 Bapt Gen Conf	1	133	84	165 *	-	.1
076 Buddhism	3	NR	NR	NR	-	-
081 Catholic	26	NR	NR	57,187	13.7	37.9
084 Calvary Chapel	4	NR	NR	NR	-	-
089 Chr & Miss Al	3	462	NR	993	.2	.7
093 Chr Ch (Disc)	7	1,048	290	1,304 *	.3	.9
097 Chr Chs&Chs Cr	5	920	NR	1,145 *	.3	.8
105 Christian Ref	2	151	166	188 *	-	.1
123 Ch God (Ander)	3	NR	293	293	.1	.2
127 Ch God (Cleve)	1	40	21	50 *	-	-
145 Ch God Prophcy	1	30	NR	38 *	-	-
151 L-D Saints	38	NR	NR	14,225	3.4	9.4
165 Ch of Nazarene	9	2,417	1,818	2,988	.7	2.0
167 Chs of Christ	7	622	646	880	.2	.6
173 Comm of Christ	2	261	NR	261	.1	.2
175 Congr Chr Chs	2	400	280	498 *	.1	.3
179 Consrv Bapt	3	NR	812	812	.2	.5
193 Episcopal	9	NR	1,100	3,616	.9	2.4
201 Evan Cov Ch	2	184	131	229 *	.1	.2
203 Evan Free Ch	5	195	312	313	.1	.2
207 E.L.C.A.	21	7,751	2,903	10,736	2.6	7.1
220 Free Lutheran	1	41	49	55	-	-
221 Free Methodist	4	455	924	929	.2	.6
226 Friends-USA	3	190	NR	236 *	.1	.2
237 Menn Br US Conf	2	205	NR	255 *	.1	.2
246 Greek Orthodox	1	NR	NR	546	.1	.4
257 Hutterian Br	1	66	NR	100	-	.1
263 Int Foursq Gos	7	2,939	4,002	4,002 *	1.0	2.7
267 Muslim Est	2	NR	276	909	.2	.6
283 Luth—MO Synod	9	3,175	1,632	4,390	1.1	2.9
288 Mennonite USA	1	22	25	27 *	-	-
290 Metro Comm Ch	1	54	54	67 *	-	-
313 N Am Bapt Conf	1	62	33	77 *	-	.1
339 Pent Ch of God	1	25	NR	80	-	.1
349 Pent Holiness	2	41	37	51 *	-	-
355 Presb Ch (USA)	18	6,394	4,643	7,955 *	1.9	5.3
356 Presb Ch Amer	1	87	101	123	-	.1
388 Reg Bapt Gen As	2	236	289	308 *	.1	.2
403 Salvation Army	1	241	104	926	.2	.6
413 S.D.A.	11	3,002	NR	3,574	.9	2.4
418 Southw Bapt Fel	1	NR	NR	NR	-	-
419 So Bapt Conv	16	6,930	2,088	8,621 *	2.1	5.7
435 Unitarian-Univ	1	395	NR	491 *	.1	.3

NR–Not Reported   *Total adherents estimated from known number of communicant, confirmed, full members.   - Represents a percentage less than 0.1.   Percentages may not total 100 due to rounding.

Table 4: Religious Congregations by County and Group: 2000

Religious Group	Number of Churches, Synagogues, Mosques, or Temples	Number of Communicant, Confirmed, or Full Members	Number of Attendees	Total Adherents: Number of Adherents	Total Adherents: % of Total Pop.	Total Adherents: % of Total Adh.
443 Un C of Christ	6	584	291	726 *	.2	.5
449 Un Methodist	18	4,520	1,740	5,625 *	1.3	3.7
463 Vineyard	2	115	115	143 *	-	.1
467 Wesleyan	1	35	53	99	-	.1
469 WELS	1	209	150	277	.1	.2
496 Jewish Est	1	NR	NR	1,500	.4	1.0
498 Indep.Charis.	1	600	500	600	.1	.4
499 Indep.Non-Char	6	1,613	5,910	5,910	1.4	3.9
STEVENS	**55**	**3,399**	**2,707**	**10,933 ***	**27.3**	**100.0**
053 Assemb of God	9	537	686	1,126	2.8	10.3
056 Baha'i	0	31	NR	31	.1	.3
081 Catholic	9	NR	NR	3,868	9.7	35.4
084 Calvary Chapel	1	NR	NR	NR	-	-
097 Chr Chs&Chs Cr	1	131	NR	166 *	.4	1.5
123 Ch God (Ander)	1	NR	15	15	-	.1
151 L-D Saints	5	NR	NR	1,865	4.7	17.1
165 Ch of Nazarene	2	118	114	195	.5	1.8
167 Chs of Christ	1	50	30	50	.1	.5
193 Episcopal	1	NR	20	68	.2	.6
203 Evan Free Ch	1	195	300	300	.7	2.7
207 E.L.C.A.	2	378	149	514	1.3	4.7
221 Free Methodist	2	169	394	394	1.0	3.6
297 Mennonite;Other	1	36	NR	46 *	.1	.4
323 Old Ord Amish	1	27	NR	34 *	.1	.3
335 Orth Pres Ch	1	20	32	32	.1	.3
355 Presb Ch (USA)	2	33	37	42 *	.1	.4
388 Reg Bapt Gen As	2	234	399	399 *	1.0	3.6
413 S.D.A.	4	449	NR	534	1.3	4.9
419 So Bapt Conv	4	227	138	287 *	.7	2.6
443 Un C of Christ	3	234	131	296 *	.7	2.7
449 Un Methodist	1	350	142	443 *	1.1	4.1
463 Vineyard	1	180	120	228 *	.6	2.1
THURSTON	**147**	**19,984**	**18,230**	**56,763 ***	**27.4**	**100.0**
017 Amer Bapt Assn	4	228	NR	282 *	.1	.5
019 Amer Bapt USA	2	862	537	1,065 *	.5	1.9
053 Assemb of God	13	2,195	2,089	3,839	1.9	6.8
056 Baha'i	6	180	NR	180	.1	.3
057 Bapt Gen Conf	1	690	1,422	1,422 *	.7	2.5
076 Buddhism	5	NR	NR	NR	-	-
081 Catholic	6	NR	NR	17,799	8.6	31.4
084 Calvary Chapel	2	NR	NR	NR	-	-
089 Chr & Miss Al	3	115	NR	374	.2	.7
093 Chr Ch (Disc)	2	423	167	522 *	.3	.9
097 Chr Chs&Chs Cr	2	425	NR	524 *	.3	.9
105 Christian Ref	1	131	140	162 *	.1	.3
123 Ch God (Ander)	2	NR	356	356	.2	.6
127 Ch God (Cleve)	2	239	143	295 *	.1	.5
145 Ch God Prophcy	1	30	NR	38 *	-	.1
151 L-D Saints	13	NR	NR	6,083	2.9	10.7
157 Ch of Brethren	1	148	83	183 *	.1	.3
165 Ch of Nazarene	3	1,029	785	1,122	.5	2.0
167 Chs of Christ	6	305	341	454	.2	.8
173 Comm of Christ	1	75	NR	75	-	.1
179 Consrv Bapt	3	NR	616	616	.3	1.1
193 Episcopal	3	NR	493	1,374	.7	2.4
201 Evan Cov Ch	2	457	874	874 *	.4	1.5
203 Evan Free Ch	1	161	180	180	.1	.3
207 E.L.C.A.	7	2,768	1,365	3,595	1.7	6.3
221 Free Methodist	1	100	125	125	.1	.2
226 Friends-USA	1	22	NR	27 *	-	-
262 Int Cou Comm Ch	1	190	NR	235 *	.1	.4
263 Int Foursq Gos	7	1,798	3,279	3,279 *	1.6	5.8
267 Muslim Est	1	NR	290	300	.1	.5
283 Luth—MO Synod	2	614	377	776	.4	1.4
290 Metro Comm Ch	1	7	7	9 *	-	-
313 N Am Bapt Conf	1	161	110	199 *	.1	.4
339 Pent Ch of God	1	12	NR	45	-	.1
355 Presb Ch (USA)	7	1,318	981	1,627 *	.8	2.9
356 Presb Ch Amer	1	0	0	0	-	-
388 Reg Bapt Gen As	2	77	250	245 *	.1	.4
403 Salvation Army	1	102	59	184	.1	.3
413 S.D.A.	5	1,009	NR	1,201	.6	2.1
419 So Bapt Conv	7	803	266	992 *	.5	1.7
435 Unitarian-Univ	1	166	NR	205 *	.1	.4
443 Un C of Christ	2	235	296	290 *	.1	.5
449 Un Methodist	7	2,701	1,025	3,336 *	1.6	5.9
463 Vineyard	2	135	117	166 *	.1	.3
469 WELS	1	73	57	108	.1	.2
496 Jewish Est	2	NR	NR	560	.3	1.0
499 Indep.Non-Char	1	0	1,400	1,440	.7	2.5
WAHKIAKUM	**9**	**392**	**223**	**939 ***	**24.6**	**100.0**
053 Assemb of God	1	36	45	85	2.2	9.1
056 Baha'i	0	2	NR	2	.1	.2
081 Catholic	0	NR	NR	250	6.5	26.6
089 Chr & Miss Al	1	35	NR	98	2.6	10.4
193 Episcopal	1	NR	19	46	1.2	4.9
207 E.L.C.A.	1	78	58	173	4.5	18.4
335 Orth Pres Ch	1	22	20	22	.6	2.3
413 S.D.A.	1	35	NR	42	1.1	4.5
443 Un C of Christ	1	79	35	95 *	2.5	10.1
449 Un Methodist	2	105	46	126 *	3.3	13.4
WALLA WALLA	**60**	**9,671**	**3,936**	**21,959 ***	**39.8**	**100.0**
017 Amer Bapt Assn	1	10	NR	12 *	-	.1
053 Assemb of God	4	461	492	1,140	2.1	5.2
056 Baha'i	2	61	NR	61	.1	.3
059 Bapt Miss Assn	1	51	23	63 *	.1	.3
081 Catholic	4	NR	NR	6,326	11.5	28.8
089 Chr & Miss Al	1	59	NR	99	.2	.5
093 Chr Ch (Disc)	2	446	90	549 *	1.0	2.5
123 Ch God (Ander)	1	NR	463	463	.8	2.1
151 L-D Saints	5	NR	NR	1,660	3.0	7.6
165 Ch of Nazarene	3	312	277	525	1.0	2.4
167 Chs of Christ	2	100	115	135	.2	.6
173 Comm of Christ	1	52	NR	52	.1	.2
179 Consrv Bapt	1	NR	180	180	.3	.8
193 Episcopal	1	NR	158	625	1.1	2.8
207 E.L.C.A.	2	562	345	729	1.3	3.3
221 Free Methodist	1	22	20	22	-	.1
226 Friends-USA	1	22	NR	27 *	-	.1
252 Hindu	1	NR	NR	NR	-	-
263 Int Foursq Gos	2	28	118	118 *	.2	.5
283 Luth—MO Synod	1	162	58	196	.4	.9
331 OCA: Ter Diocs	1	5	NR	16	-	.1
339 Pent Ch of God	2	26	NR	68	.1	.3
355 Presb Ch (USA)	4	780	674	998 *	1.8	4.5
388 Reg Bapt Gen As	2	161	204	214 *	.4	1.0
403 Salvation Army	1	59	31	139	.3	.6
413 S.D.A.	8	4,990	NR	5,939	10.8	27.0
419 So Bapt Conv	2	321	208	395 *	.7	1.8
443 Un C of Christ	1	220	110	271 *	.5	1.2
449 Un Methodist	2	761	370	937 *	1.7	4.3
WHATCOM	**145**	**20,290**	**16,330**	**48,995 ***	**29.4**	**100.0**
019 Amer Bapt USA	4	434	311	533 *	.3	1.1
034 Ant Orth of NA	1	39	NR	78	-	.2
053 Assemb of God	10	1,818	2,602	3,588	2.2	7.3
056 Baha'i	3	240	NR	240	.1	.5
057 Bapt Gen Conf	2	607	593	745 *	.4	1.5
076 Buddhism	2	NR	NR	NR	-	-
081 Catholic	7	NR	NR	13,290	8.0	27.1
084 Calvary Chapel	2	NR	NR	NR	-	-
089 Chr & Miss Al	3	168	NR	399	.2	.8
093 Chr Ch (Disc)	1	376	141	462 *	.3	.9
105 Christian Ref	10	4,175	3,151	5,125 *	3.1	10.5
123 Ch God (Ander)	1	NR	1,025	1,025	.6	2.1
127 Ch God (Cleve)	3	162	81	198 *	.1	.4
151 L-D Saints	10	NR	NR	3,577	2.1	7.3
165 Ch of Nazarene	3	243	180	422	.3	.9
167 Chs of Christ	4	301	329	435	.3	.9
173 Comm of Christ	1	56	NR	56	-	.1
193 Episcopal	2	NR	365	1,356	.8	2.8
201 Evan Cov Ch	1	217	176	266 *	.2	.5

NR–Not Reported   *Total adherents estimated from known number of communicant, confirmed, full members.   - Represents a percentage less than 0.1.   Percentages may not total 100 due to rounding.

Table 4: Religious Congregations by County and Group: 2000

Religious Group	Number of Churches, Synagogues, Mosques, or Temples	Number of Communicant, Confirmed, or Full Members	Number of Attendees	Total Adherents		
				Number of Adherents	% of Total Pop.	% of Total Adh.
203 Evan Free Ch	3	152	280	280	.2	.6
207 E.L.C.A.	10	2,551	1,412	3,408	2.0	7.0
220 Free Lutheran	1	90	85	140	.1	.3
221 Free Methodist	1	60	87	87	.1	.2
226 Friends-USA	1	22	NR	27 *	-	.1
237 Menn Br US Conf	5	876	NR	1,075 *	.6	2.2
246 Greek Orthodox	1	NR	NR	267	.2	.5
263 Int Foursq Gos	2	92	119	119 *	.1	.2
267 Muslim Est	1	NR	101	288	.2	.6
283 Luth—MO Synod	2	582	354	734	.4	1.5
307 Neth Ref Congr	1	85	NR	193	.1	.4
349 Pent Holiness	1	35	60	43 *	-	.1
355 Presb Ch (USA)	6	957	881	1,185 *	.7	2.4
369 Prot Ref Chs	1	68	NR	131	.1	.3
371 Ref Ch in Am	4	1,103	1,062	1,974	1.2	4.0
388 Reg Bapt Gen As	4	477	1,173	1,228 *	.7	2.5
403 Salvation Army	1	151	93	298	.2	.6
413 S.D.A.	6	698	NR	830	.5	1.7
419 So Bapt Conv	4	363	216	446 *	.3	.9
435 Unitarian-Univ	2	300	NR	368 *	.2	.8
443 Un C of Christ	4	834	486	1,024 *	.6	2.1
449 Un Methodist	7	1,375	525	1,688 *	1.0	3.4
455 Un Ref Chs N.A.	1	175	NR	275	.2	.6
463 Vineyard	2	108	124	147 *	.1	.3
467 Wesleyan	1	0	20	20	-	-
496 Jewish Est	2	NR	NR	525	.3	1.1
498 Indep.Charis.	1	300	298	400	.2	.8
WHITMAN	**69**	**5,715**	**4,537**	**13,631 ***	**33.5**	**100.0**
019 Amer Bapt USA	4	419	301	486 *	1.2	3.6
053 Assemb of God	5	509	677	757	1.9	5.6
056 Baha'i	1	49	NR	49	.1	.4
081 Catholic	10	NR	NR	4,225	10.4	31.0
093 Chr Ch (Disc)	2	43	15	50 *	.1	.4
097 Chr Chs&Chs Cr	1	150	NR	174 *	.4	1.3
151 L-D Saints	5	NR	NR	1,503	3.7	11.0
165 Ch of Nazarene	4	182	180	287	.7	2.1
167 Chs of Christ	1	55	65	80	.2	.6
173 Comm of Christ	1	35	NR	35	.1	.3
181 Consrv Congr	1	61	40	71 *	.2	.5
193 Episcopal	3	NR	112	293	.7	2.1
203 Evan Free Ch	2	54	350	350	.9	2.6
207 E.L.C.A.	4	868	374	1,064	2.6	7.8
226 Friends-USA	1	22	NR	26 *	.1	.2
263 Int Foursq Gos	1	82	59	95 *	.2	.7
267 Muslim Est	1	NR	75	150	.4	1.1
283 Luth—MO Synod	1	198	200	256	.6	1.9
313 N Am Bapt Conf	1	180	170	209 *	.5	1.5
355 Presb Ch (USA)	1	101	60	117 *	.3	.9
413 S.D.A.	4	237	NR	282	.7	2.1
419 So Bapt Conv	2	412	277	478 *	1.2	3.5
443 Un C of Christ	4	434	241	503 *	1.2	3.7
449 Un Methodist	7	999	419	1,158 *	2.8	8.5
469 WELS	1	25	22	33	.1	.2
498 Indep.Charis.	1	600	900	900	2.2	6.6
YAKIMA	**237**	**26,039**	**18,777**	**86,626 ***	**38.9**	**100.0**
019 Amer Bapt USA	5	577	346	768 *	.3	.9
034 Ant Orth of NA	1	189	NR	378	.2	.4
053 Assemb of God	21	2,266	2,814	4,543	2.0	5.2
056 Baha'i	4	212	NR	212	.1	.2
076 Buddhism	1	NR	NR	NR	-	-
081 Catholic	17	NR	NR	41,339	18.6	47.7
084 Calvary Chapel	1	NR	NR	NR	-	-
089 Chr & Miss Al	2	198	NR	469	.2	.5
093 Chr Ch (Disc)	6	746	264	993 *	.4	1.1
097 Chr Chs&Chs Cr	4	329	NR	438 *	.2	.5
105 Christian Ref	4	883	526	1,175 *	.5	1.4
123 Ch God (Ander)	5	NR	281	281	.1	.3
127 Ch God (Cleve)	5	925	939	1,274 *	.6	1.5
145 Ch God Prophcy	1	30	NR	40 *	-	-
151 L-D Saints	17	NR	NR	5,356	2.4	6.2
157 Ch of Brethren	1	26	27	35 *	-	-

Religious Group	Number of Churches, Synagogues, Mosques, or Temples	Number of Communicant, Confirmed, or Full Members	Number of Attendees	Total Adherents		
				Number of Adherents	% of Total Pop.	% of Total Adh.
165 Ch of Nazarene	12	2,408	1,966	3,115	1.4	3.6
167 Chs of Christ	8	574	566	686	.3	.8
173 Comm of Christ	2	177	NR	177	.1	.2
179 Consrv Bapt	3	NR	812	812	.4	.9
193 Episcopal	5	NR	339	845	.4	1.0
201 Evan Cov Ch	2	405	447	547 *	.2	.6
207 E.L.C.A.	6	1,462	660	1,869	.8	2.2
221 Free Methodist	2	79	119	119	.1	.1
226 Friends-USA	1	22	NR	29 *	-	-
263 Int Foursq Gos	10	622	1,467	1,467 *	.7	1.7
267 Muslim Est	1	NR	101	288	.1	.3
283 Luth—MO Synod	4	1,117	527	1,560	.7	1.8
290 Metro Comm Ch	1	21	10	28 *	-	-
291 Missionary Ch	2	128	123	128	.1	.1
307 Neth Ref Congr	1	67	NR	128	.1	.1
339 Pent Ch of God	5	272	NR	395	.2	.5
349 Pent Holiness	12	672	1,054	895 *	.4	1.0
355 Presb Ch (USA)	9	2,797	1,682	3,723 *	1.7	4.3
371 Ref Ch in Am	1	149	180	273	.1	.3
388 Reg Bapt Gen As	3	232	355	358 *	.2	.4
403 Salvation Army	4	507	273	1,013	.5	1.2
413 S.D.A.	14	1,952	NR	2,324	1.0	2.7
419 So Bapt Conv	13	2,601	846	3,462 *	1.6	4.0
435 Unitarian-Univ	1	104	NR	138 *	.1	.2
443 Un C of Christ	2	45	70	60 *	-	.1
449 Un Methodist	11	2,243	901	2,986 *	1.3	3.4
463 Vineyard	1	300	252	399 *	.2	.5
467 Wesleyan	1	0	82	155	.1	.2
469 WELS	3	467	248	596	.3	.7
496 Jewish Est	1	NR	NR	150	.1	.2
499 Indep.Non-Char	1	235	500	600	.3	.7
WEST VIRGINIA						
The State.....	4,139	411,124	204,851	650,016 *	35.9	100.0
BARBOUR	**67**	**3,224**	**1,898**	**4,331 ***	**27.8**	**100.0**
019 Amer Bapt USA	5	393	203	474 *	3.0	10.9
081 Catholic	2	NR	NR	285	1.8	6.6
127 Ch God (Cleve)	1	37	16	45 *	.3	1.0
151 L-D Saints	1	NR	NR	91	.6	2.1
157 Ch of Brethren	3	133	111	165 *	1.1	3.8
165 Ch of Nazarene	3	171	120	245	1.6	5.7
167 Chs of Christ	6	379	340	436	2.8	10.1
193 Episcopal	1	NR	9	11	.1	.3
288 Mennonite USA	1	20	27	27 *	.2	.6
339 Pent Ch of God	2	44	NR	84	.5	1.9
355 Presb Ch (USA)	2	63	47	76 *	.5	1.8
419 So Bapt Conv	3	313	152	378 *	2.4	8.7
449 Un Methodist	37	1,671	873	2,014 *	12.9	46.5
BERKELEY	**98**	**15,624**	**6,744**	**25,883 ***	**34.1**	**100.0**
017 Amer Bapt Assn	4	750	NR	936 *	1.2	3.6
019 Amer Bapt USA	1	75	50	94 *	.1	.4
053 Assemb of God	5	744	948	1,343	1.8	5.2
056 Baha'i	0	6	NR	6	-	-
075 Brethren in Cr	1	125	120	125	.2	.5
081 Catholic	3	NR	NR	4,346	5.7	16.8
093 Chr Ch (Disc)	1	468	107	584 *	.8	2.3
097 Chr Chs&Chs Cr	5	884	NR	1,102 *	1.5	4.3
123 Ch God (Ander)	2	NR	40	40	.1	.2
127 Ch God (Cleve)	1	138	88	172 *	.2	.7
145 Ch God Prophcy	1	32	NR	40 *	.1	.2
151 L-D Saints	2	NR	NR	676	.9	2.6
157 Ch of Brethren	6	832	317	1,037 *	1.4	4.0
165 Ch of Nazarene	1	42	53	100	.1	.4
167 Chs of Christ	1	105	120	130	.2	.5
173 Comm of Christ	1	33	NR	33	-	.1
193 Episcopal	2	NR	206	518	.7	2.0
207 E.L.C.A.	2	1,107	307	1,486	2.0	5.7
223 Free Will Bapt	2	101	NR	126 *	.2	.5
263 Int Foursq Gos	1	114	148	148 *	.2	.6

NR–Not Reported *Total adherents estimated from known number of communicant, confirmed, full members. - Represents a percentage less than 0.1. Percentages may not total 100 due to rounding.

Table 4: Religious Congregations by County and Group: 2000

Religious Group	Number of Churches, Synagogues, Mosques, or Temples	Number of Communicant, Confirmed, or Full Members	Number of Attendees	Total Adherents: Number of Adherents	Total Adherents: % of Total Pop.	Total Adherents: % of Total Adh.
265 Int Pent C Chr	1	52	70	70	.1	.3
339 Pent Ch of God	1	18	NR	68	.1	.3
355 Presb Ch (USA)	9	831	484	1,037 *	1.4	4.0
356 Presb Ch Amer	1	144	140	189	.2	.7
360 Prim Bapt Chrch	1	NR	NR	NR	-	-
403 Salvation Army	1	83	26	178	.2	.7
413 S.D.A.	2	442	NR	526	.7	2.0
418 Southw Bapt Fel	1	NR	NR	NR	-	-
419 So Bapt Conv	8	2,077	955	2,592 *	3.4	10.0
443 Un C of Christ	1	162	80	202 *	.3	.8
449 Un Methodist	28	6,229	2,438	7,774 *	10.2	30.0
467 Wesleyan	1	30	47	85	.1	.3
496 Jewish Est	1	NR	NR	120	.2	.5
BOONE	**59**	**3,605**	**2,159**	**4,742 ***	**18.6**	**100.0**
019 Amer Bapt USA	5	1,129	360	1,371 *	5.4	28.9
053 Assemb of God	2	38	49	55	.2	1.2
056 Baha'i	0	1	NR	1	-	-
081 Catholic	3	NR	NR	127	.5	2.7
123 Ch God (Ander)	2	NR	49	49	.2	1.0
127 Ch God (Cleve)	8	393	174	487 *	1.9	10.3
145 Ch God Prophcy	1	32	NR	39 *	.2	.8
165 Ch of Nazarene	3	141	80	171	.7	3.6
167 Chs of Christ	18	801	816	984	3.9	20.8
355 Presb Ch (USA)	4	91	78	112 *	.4	2.4
419 So Bapt Conv	2	240	78	291 *	1.1	6.1
449 Un Methodist	9	705	390	855 *	3.3	18.0
467 Wesleyan	2	34	85	200	.8	4.2
BRAXTON	**62**	**3,630**	**2,022**	**4,632 ***	**31.5**	**100.0**
019 Amer Bapt USA	10	1,870	851	2,253 *	15.3	48.6
056 Baha'i	0	1	NR	1	-	-
081 Catholic	1	NR	NR	145	1.0	3.1
127 Ch God (Cleve)	2	49	54	73 *	.5	1.6
151 L-D Saints	1	NR	NR	106	.7	2.3
167 Chs of Christ	2	58	65	73	.5	1.6
339 Pent Ch of God	1	33	NR	37	.3	.8
355 Presb Ch (USA)	1	69	40	83 *	.6	1.8
413 S.D.A.	1	56	NR	67	.5	1.4
419 So Bapt Conv	2	186	13	224 *	1.5	4.8
449 Un Methodist	41	1,308	999	1,570 *	10.7	33.9
BROOKE	**43**	**5,101**	**2,531**	**9,995 ***	**39.3**	**100.0**
019 Amer Bapt USA	1	120	85	142 *	.6	1.4
053 Assemb of God	1	28	37	66	.3	.7
081 Catholic	2	NR	NR	3,533	13.9	35.3
093 Chr Ch (Disc)	3	564	140	666 *	2.6	6.7
097 Chr Chs&Chs Cr	4	717	NR	846 *	3.3	8.5
123 Ch God (Ander)	2	NR	93	93	.4	.9
127 Ch God (Cleve)	1	82	38	97 *	.4	1.0
165 Ch of Nazarene	6	903	555	1,058	4.2	10.6
167 Chs of Christ	2	152	138	217	.9	2.2
171 Ch God-Gen Con	1	57	80	80 *	.3	.8
173 Comm of Christ	2	170	NR	170	.7	1.7
193 Episcopal	4	NR	169	284	1.1	2.8
221 Free Methodist	1	189	218	220	.9	2.2
355 Presb Ch (USA)	3	366	175	432 *	1.7	4.3
403 Salvation Army	1	70	7	103	.4	1.0
419 So Bapt Conv	3	730	385	862 *	3.4	8.6
449 Un Methodist	6	953	411	1,126 *	4.4	11.3
CABELL	**147**	**28,216**	**12,116**	**41,293 ***	**42.7**	**100.0**
019 Amer Bapt USA	23	7,589	2,671	8,977 *	9.3	21.7
034 Ant Orth of NA	1	100	NR	200	.2	.5
053 Assemb of God	1	77	68	111	.1	.3
056 Baha'i	0	26	NR	26	-	.1
081 Catholic	6	NR	NR	5,117	5.3	12.4
093 Chr Ch (Disc)	3	831	88	983 *	1.0	2.4
097 Chr Chs&Chs Cr	6	985	NR	1,165 *	1.2	2.8
123 Ch God (Ander)	2	NR	217	217	.2	.5
127 Ch God (Cleve)	3	543	464	642 *	.7	1.6
145 Ch God Prophcy	2	64	NR	76 *	.1	.2
151 L-D Saints	2	NR	NR	687	.7	1.7
165 Ch of Nazarene	3	695	384	834	.9	2.0
167 Chs of Christ	8	753	773	898	.9	2.2
179 Consrv Bapt	1	NR	60	60	.1	.1
193 Episcopal	4	NR	354	994	1.0	2.4
203 Evan Free Ch	1	32	50	50	.1	.1
207 E.L.C.A.	2	741	197	1,050	1.1	2.5
221 Free Methodist	3	56	68	73	.1	.2
223 Free Will Bapt	14	707	NR	836 *	.9	2.0
226 Friends-USA	1	64	NR	76 *	.1	.2
246 Greek Orthodox	1	NR	NR	150	.2	.4
267 Muslim Est	1	NR	156	609	.6	1.5
283 Luth—MO Synod	1	86	72	121	.1	.3
339 Pent Ch of God	2	49	NR	79	.1	.2
355 Presb Ch (USA)	8	1,951	842	2,307 *	2.4	5.6
356 Presb Ch Amer	1	84	78	105	.1	.3
403 Salvation Army	1	84	40	111	.1	.3
413 S.D.A.	2	118	NR	140	.1	.3
418 Southw Bapt Fel	1	NR	NR	NR	-	-
419 So Bapt Conv	3	2,956	560	3,497 *	3.6	8.5
435 Unitarian-Univ	1	10	NR	12 *	-	-
443 Un C of Christ	1	121	39	143 *	.1	.3
449 Un Methodist	29	6,261	2,794	7,406 *	7.7	17.9
467 Wesleyan	5	130	191	313	.3	.8
496 Jewish Est	1	NR	NR	125	.1	.3
498 Indep.Charis.	1	1,500	1,000	1,500	1.5	3.6
499 Indep.Non-Char	2	1,603	950	1,603	1.7	3.9
CALHOUN	**27**	**1,554**	**801**	**1,912 ***	**25.2**	**100.0**
019 Amer Bapt USA	6	695	270	822 *	10.8	43.0
056 Baha'i	0	5	NR	5	.1	.3
081 Catholic	1	NR	NR	72	.9	3.8
157 Ch of Brethren	1	18	16	21 *	.3	1.1
167 Chs of Christ	2	33	35	42	.6	2.2
419 So Bapt Conv	1	304	139	360 *	4.7	18.8
449 Un Methodist	16	499	341	590 *	7.8	30.9
CLAY	**28**	**1,748**	**701**	**2,293 ***	**22.2**	**100.0**
019 Amer Bapt USA	9	1,266	384	1,564 *	15.1	68.2
056 Baha'i	0	2	NR	2	-	.1
081 Catholic	1	NR	NR	103	1.0	4.5
165 Ch of Nazarene	2	81	58	131	1.3	5.7
223 Free Will Bapt	3	152	NR	187 *	1.8	8.2
320 "Old" MB Ascs	1	28	NR	35 *	.3	1.5
360 Prim Bapt Chrch	2	NR	NR	NR	-	-
449 Un Methodist	10	219	259	271 *	2.6	11.8
DODDRIDGE	**31**	**1,885**	**754**	**2,450 ***	**33.1**	**100.0**
011 A.W.M.C.	1	27	84	28	.4	1.1
019 Amer Bapt USA	4	336	122	408 *	5.5	16.7
053 Assemb of God	1	47	55	89	1.2	3.6
081 Catholic	1	NR	NR	74	1.0	3.0
097 Chr Chs&Chs Cr	3	421	NR	511 *	6.9	20.9
127 Ch God (Cleve)	2	60	54	73 *	1.0	3.0
167 Chs of Christ	1	35	30	40	.5	1.6
173 Comm of Christ	1	11	NR	11	.1	.4
207 E.L.C.A.	1	115	54	151	2.0	6.2
419 So Bapt Conv	1	67	41	81 *	1.1	3.3
449 Un Methodist	14	747	293	907 *	12.3	37.0
467 Wesleyan	1	19	21	77	1.0	3.1
FAYETTE	**135**	**11,037**	**5,579**	**16,534 ***	**34.8**	**100.0**
017 Amer Bapt Assn	2	120	NR	144 *	.3	.9
019 Amer Bapt USA	29	5,645	1,878	6,751 *	14.2	40.8
053 Assemb of God	4	159	173	200	.4	1.2
056 Baha'i	0	24	NR	24	.1	.1
071 Brethren (Ash)	2	125	101	150 *	.3	.9
081 Catholic	3	NR	NR	1,537	3.2	9.3
084 Calvary Chapel	1	NR	NR	NR	-	-
089 Chr & Miss Al	1	0	NR	70	.1	.4
093 Chr Ch (Disc)	1	77	38	92 *	.2	.6
097 Chr Chs&Chs Cr	2	125	NR	150 *	.3	.9

NR–Not Reported   *Total adherents estimated from known number of communicant, confirmed, full members.   - Represents a percentage less than 0.1.   Percentages may not total 100 due to rounding.

Table 4: Religious Congregations by County and Group: 2000

Religious Group	Number of Churches, Synagogues, Mosques, or Temples	Number of Communicant, Confirmed, or Full Members	Number of Attendees	Total Adherents: Number of Adherents	Total Adherents: % of Total Pop.	Total Adherents: % of Total Adh.
123 Ch God (Ander)	10	NR	593	593	1.2	3.6
127 Ch God (Cleve)	7	952	477	1,139 *	2.4	6.9
145 Ch God Prophcy	4	127	NR	152 *	.3	.9
151 L-D Saints	1	NR	NR	496	1.0	3.0
157 Ch of Brethren	1	43	49	51 *	.1	.3
165 Ch of Nazarene	1	269	172	613	1.3	3.7
167 Chs of Christ	5	128	180	175	.4	1.1
171 Ch God-Gen Con	1	57	55	68 *	.1	.4
193 Episcopal	3	NR	86	199	.4	1.2
223 Free Will Bapt	6	303	NR	362 *	.8	2.2
265 Int Pent C Chr	1	0	14	14	-	.1
349 Pent Holiness	2	145	119	173 *	.4	1.0
355 Presb Ch (USA)	8	493	284	592 *	1.2	3.6
388 Reg Bapt Gen As	1	130	125	155 *	.3	.9
418 Southw Bapt Fel	1	NR	NR	NR	-	-
419 So Bapt Conv	5	372	152	445 *	.9	2.7
449 Un Methodist	31	1,699	992	2,035 *	4.3	12.3
467 Wesleyan	2	44	91	154	.3	.9
GILMER	**28**	**1,330**	**686**	**1,675 ***	**23.4**	**100.0**
019 Amer Bapt USA	6	736	355	861 *	12.0	51.4
081 Catholic	1	NR	NR	89	1.2	5.3
127 Ch God (Cleve)	1	7	7	8 *	.1	.5
145 Ch God Prophcy	1	32	NR	37 *	.5	2.2
167 Chs of Christ	2	83	85	103	1.4	6.1
193 Episcopal	1	NR	12	23	.3	1.4
355 Presb Ch (USA)	1	40	14	47 *	.7	2.8
413 S.D.A.	1	27	NR	32	.4	1.9
449 Un Methodist	14	405	213	475 *	6.6	28.4
GRANT	**42**	**3,619**	**2,129**	**4,884 ***	**43.2**	**100.0**
019 Amer Bapt USA	5	546	296	662 *	5.9	13.6
053 Assemb of God	3	285	420	804	7.1	16.5
081 Catholic	1	NR	NR	43	.4	.9
127 Ch God (Cleve)	3	343	219	416 *	3.7	8.5
157 Ch of Brethren	7	794	449	964 *	8.5	19.7
167 Chs of Christ	1	20	20	25	.2	.5
207 E.L.C.A.	1	82	35	90	.8	1.8
297 Mennonite;Other	1	26	NR	32 *	.3	.7
355 Presb Ch (USA)	2	231	106	281 *	2.5	5.8
419 So Bapt Conv	1	84	35	102 *	.9	2.1
449 Un Methodist	17	1,208	549	1,465 *	13.0	30.0
GREENBRIER	**125**	**9,666**	**5,178**	**13,650 ***	**39.6**	**100.0**
019 Amer Bapt USA	19	2,576	1,117	3,082 *	8.9	22.6
053 Assemb of God	3	102	86	124	.4	.9
055 As Ref Pres Ch	1	118	NR	121	.4	.9
056 Baha'i	0	3	NR	3	-	-
081 Catholic	5	NR	NR	1,220	3.5	8.9
097 Chr Chs&Chs Cr	1	75	NR	90 *	.3	.7
123 Ch God (Ander)	3	NR	156	156	.5	1.1
127 Ch God (Cleve)	10	713	402	853 *	2.5	6.2
151 L-D Saints	1	NR	NR	245	.7	1.8
165 Ch of Nazarene	2	114	95	276	.8	2.0
167 Chs of Christ	4	123	127	144	.4	1.1
193 Episcopal	4	NR	120	330	1.0	2.4
223 Free Will Bapt	3	152	NR	181 *	.5	1.3
265 Int Pent C Chr	1	17	25	25	.1	.2
339 Pent Ch of God	1	11	NR	25	.1	.2
349 Pent Holiness	6	348	265	416 *	1.2	3.0
355 Presb Ch (USA)	10	1,178	609	1,410 *	4.1	10.3
360 Prim Bapt Chrch	3	NR	NR	NR	-	-
413 S.D.A.	2	103	NR	123	.4	.9
418 Southw Bapt Fel	1	NR	NR	NR	-	-
419 So Bapt Conv	5	913	478	1,092 *	3.2	8.0
449 Un Methodist	40	3,120	1,698	3,734 *	10.8	27.4
HAMPSHIRE	**69**	**4,900**	**2,580**	**6,791 ***	**33.6**	**100.0**
019 Amer Bapt USA	2	213	124	264 *	1.3	3.9
053 Assemb of God	8	468	629	805	4.0	11.9
076 Buddhism	1	NR	NR	NR	-	-
081 Catholic	1	NR	NR	347	1.7	5.1
093 Chr Ch (Disc)	1	192	103	238 *	1.2	3.5
097 Chr Chs&Chs Cr	6	757	NR	936 *	4.6	13.8
127 Ch God (Cleve)	1	107	50	132 *	.7	1.9
151 L-D Saints	1	NR	NR	143	.7	2.1
157 Ch of Brethren	5	570	316	707 *	3.5	10.4
165 Ch of Nazarene	1	116	74	116	.6	1.7
167 Chs of Christ	1	33	35	42	.2	.6
193 Episcopal	1	NR	20	45	.2	.7
207 E.L.C.A.	2	98	48	114	.6	1.7
355 Presb Ch (USA)	4	340	187	421 *	2.1	6.2
360 Prim Bapt Chrch	3	NR	NR	NR	-	-
413 S.D.A.	1	31	NR	37	.2	.5
419 So Bapt Conv	4	232	165	287 *	1.4	4.2
443 Un C of Christ	1	174	77	215 *	1.1	3.2
449 Un Methodist	25	1,569	752	1,942 *	9.6	28.6
HANCOCK	**53**	**7,913**	**3,473**	**16,700 ***	**51.1**	**100.0**
019 Amer Bapt USA	2	941	293	1,118 *	3.4	6.7
053 Assemb of God	1	25	30	50	.2	.3
056 Baha'i	0	1	NR	1	-	-
081 Catholic	6	NR	NR	5,526	16.9	33.1
089 Chr & Miss Al	1	43	NR	104	.3	.6
093 Chr Ch (Disc)	1	319	135	379 *	1.2	2.3
097 Chr Chs&Chs Cr	4	817	NR	970 *	3.0	5.8
127 Ch God (Cleve)	2	199	168	236 *	.7	1.4
165 Ch of Nazarene	5	858	539	1,429	4.4	8.6
167 Chs of Christ	4	846	775	1,061	3.2	6.4
193 Episcopal	1	NR	14	32	.1	.2
207 E.L.C.A.	2	241	103	385	1.2	2.3
221 Free Methodist	3	184	190	251	.8	1.5
246 Greek Orthodox	1	NR	NR	900	2.8	5.4
355 Presb Ch (USA)	7	1,167	474	1,386 *	4.2	8.3
403 Salvation Army	1	138	44	258	.8	1.5
413 S.D.A.	1	37	NR	44	.1	.3
419 So Bapt Conv	2	474	84	563 *	1.7	3.4
449 Un Methodist	8	1,546	550	1,837 *	5.6	11.0
467 Wesleyan	1	77	74	170	.5	1.0
HARDY	**48**	**4,197**	**2,126**	**5,908 ***	**46.6**	**100.0**
053 Assemb of God	4	250	316	461	3.6	7.8
071 Brethren (Ash)	1	60	29	74 *	.6	1.3
081 Catholic	1	NR	NR	218	1.7	3.7
097 Chr Chs&Chs Cr	1	65	NR	80 *	.6	1.4
127 Ch God (Cleve)	1	83	92	102 *	.8	1.7
151 L-D Saints	1	NR	NR	350	2.8	5.9
157 Ch of Brethren	10	1,335	416	1,636 *	12.9	27.7
167 Chs of Christ	1	68	65	79	.6	1.3
193 Episcopal	1	NR	18	34	.3	.6
207 E.L.C.A.	3	187	103	236	1.9	4.0
288 Mennonite USA	3	100	74	127 *	1.0	2.1
355 Presb Ch (USA)	1	290	150	355 *	2.8	6.0
413 S.D.A.	1	16	NR	19	.1	.3
418 Southw Bapt Fel	1	NR	NR	NR	-	-
419 So Bapt Conv	2	269	134	330 *	2.6	5.6
449 Un Methodist	16	1,474	729	1,807 *	14.3	30.6
HARRISON	**144**	**17,345**	**8,287**	**31,035 ***	**45.2**	**100.0**
011 A.W.M.C.	2	35	100	35	.1	.1
019 Amer Bapt USA	33	5,898	2,464	7,142 *	10.4	23.0
053 Assemb of God	2	226	221	327	.5	1.1
056 Baha'i	0	4	NR	4	-	-
081 Catholic	7	NR	NR	8,488	12.4	27.3
089 Chr & Miss Al	1	62	NR	140	.2	.5
093 Chr Ch (Disc)	2	162	61	196 *	.3	.6
123 Ch God (Ander)	2	NR	70	70	.1	.2
127 Ch God (Cleve)	3	468	151	567 *	.8	1.8
145 Ch God Prophcy	1	32	NR	39 *	.1	.1
151 L-D Saints	1	NR	NR	366	.5	1.2
165 Ch of Nazarene	2	134	94	134	.2	.4
167 Chs of Christ	8	584	556	773	1.1	2.5
193 Episcopal	3	NR	130	282	.4	.9
207 E.L.C.A.	1	310	147	374	.5	1.2
221 Free Methodist	1	17	27	27	-	.1

NR–Not Reported   *Total adherents estimated from known number of communicant, confirmed, full members.   - Represents a percentage less than 0.1.   Percentages may not total 100 due to rounding.

Table 4: Religious Congregations by County and Group: 2000

Religious Group	Number of Churches, Synagogues, Mosques, or Temples	Number of Communicant, Confirmed, or Full Members	Number of Attendees	Total Adherents: Number of Adherents	Total Adherents: % of Total Pop.	Total Adherents: % of Total Adh.
223 Free Will Bapt	1	51	NR	61 *	.1	.2
246 Greek Orthodox	1	NR	NR	150	.2	.5
339 Pent Ch of God	1	21	NR	36	.1	.1
355 Presb Ch (USA)	4	567	290	686 *	1.0	2.2
360 Prim Bapt Chrch	1	NR	NR	NR	-	-
388 Reg Bapt Gen As	1	300	225	363 *	.5	1.2
403 Salvation Army	1	109	39	225	.3	.7
413 S.D.A.	1	119	NR	142	.2	.5
419 So Bapt Conv	5	719	300	871 *	1.3	2.8
449 Un Methodist	57	7,527	3,092	9,107 *	13.3	29.3
496 Jewish Est	1	NR	NR	110	.2	.4
499 Indep.Non-Char	1	0	320	320	.5	1.0
JACKSON	**63**	**5,245**	**2,952**	**7,225 ***	**25.8**	**100.0**
019 Amer Bapt USA	10	1,581	804	1,937 *	6.9	26.8
053 Assemb of God	1	17	30	39	.1	.5
056 Baha'i	0	4	NR	4	-	.1
081 Catholic	1	NR	NR	406	1.5	5.6
093 Chr Ch (Disc)	1	54	32	66 *	.2	.9
097 Chr Chs&Chs Cr	1	108	NR	132 *	.5	1.8
123 Ch God (Ander)	1	NR	36	36	.1	.5
127 Ch God (Cleve)	2	140	150	185 *	.7	2.6
151 L-D Saints	1	NR	NR	174	.6	2.4
165 Ch of Nazarene	2	254	179	348	1.2	4.8
167 Chs of Christ	5	281	314	377	1.3	5.2
193 Episcopal	2	NR	28	83	.3	1.1
207 E.L.C.A.	1	35	19	43	.2	.6
223 Free Will Bapt	1	51	NR	62 *	.2	.9
355 Presb Ch (USA)	2	144	77	177 *	.6	2.4
413 S.D.A.	1	19	NR	23	.1	.3
419 So Bapt Conv	2	340	113	417 *	1.5	5.8
449 Un Methodist	29	2,217	1,170	2,716 *	9.7	37.6
JEFFERSON	**67**	**7,245**	**3,390**	**13,986 ***	**33.2**	**100.0**
017 Amer Bapt Assn	1	150	NR	184 *	.4	1.3
019 Amer Bapt USA	1	120	60	147 *	.3	1.1
053 Assemb of God	5	268	317	451	1.1	3.2
056 Baha'i	1	25	NR	25	.1	.2
081 Catholic	2	NR	NR	3,254	7.7	23.3
127 Ch God (Cleve)	2	142	43	174 *	.4	1.2
151 L-D Saints	1	NR	NR	321	.8	2.3
167 Chs of Christ	1	57	60	82	.2	.6
193 Episcopal	9	NR	403	1,189	2.8	8.5
207 E.L.C.A.	4	751	226	1,043	2.5	7.5
223 Free Will Bapt	1	51	NR	62 *	.1	.4
263 Int Foursq Gos	1	30	50	50 *	.1	.4
265 Int Pent C Chr	2	74	148	220	.5	1.6
355 Presb Ch (USA)	5	702	374	860 *	2.0	6.1
388 Reg Bapt Gen As	1	106	85	85 *	.2	.6
413 S.D.A.	1	138	NR	164	.4	1.2
419 So Bapt Conv	7	1,087	274	1,332 *	3.2	9.5
443 Un C of Christ	2	94	63	115 *	.3	.8
449 Un Methodist	20	3,450	1,287	4,228 *	10.0	30.2
KANAWHA	**325**	**42,880**	**23,869**	**69,129 ***	**34.6**	**100.0**
019 Amer Bapt USA	39	11,253	4,061	13,458 *	6.7	19.5
034 Ant Orth of NA	1	834	NR	1,668	.8	2.4
053 Assemb of God	9	575	652	1,071	.5	1.5
056 Baha'i	1	130	NR	130	.1	.2
081 Catholic	12	NR	NR	8,477	4.2	12.3
089 Chr & Miss Al	1	26	NR	65	-	.1
093 Chr Ch (Disc)	3	442	160	529 *	.3	.8
097 Chr Chs&Chs Cr	5	608	NR	728 *	.4	1.1
123 Ch God (Ander)	19	NR	1,441	1,441	.7	2.1
127 Ch God (Cleve)	12	820	432	982 *	.5	1.4
145 Ch God Prophcy	5	159	NR	190 *	.1	.3
151 L-D Saints	3	NR	NR	778	.4	1.1
165 Ch of Nazarene	35	4,449	2,818	6,289	3.1	9.1
167 Chs of Christ	23	1,484	1,602	1,940	1.0	2.8
171 Ch God-Gen Con	5	109	138	151 *	.1	.2
193 Episcopal	8	NR	882	2,008	1.0	2.9
207 E.L.C.A.	4	941	440	1,237	.6	1.8
216 Evan Presby Ch	1	265	NR	317 *	.2	.5

Religious Group	Number of Churches, Synagogues, Mosques, or Temples	Number of Communicant, Confirmed, or Full Members	Number of Attendees	Total Adherents: Number of Adherents	Total Adherents: % of Total Pop.	Total Adherents: % of Total Adh.
223 Free Will Bapt	14	707	NR	846 *	.4	1.2
246 Greek Orthodox	1	NR	NR	150	.1	.2
252 Hindu	1	NR	NR	NR	-	-
263 Int Foursq Gos	2	94	134	134 *	.1	.2
267 Muslim Est	2	NR	166	619	.3	.9
283 Luth—MO Synod	1	118	93	151	.1	.2
290 Metro Comm Ch	1	34	34	41 *	-	.1
339 Pent Ch of God	1	11	NR	20	-	-
349 Pent Holiness	3	227	108	271 *	.1	.4
355 Presb Ch (USA)	21	5,020	2,165	6,003 *	3.0	8.7
356 Presb Ch Amer	5	426	302	465	.2	.7
360 Prim Bapt Chrch	1	NR	NR	NR	-	-
388 Reg Bapt Gen As	2	150	125	180 *	.1	.3
403 Salvation Army	1	130	49	270	.1	.4
413 S.D.A.	1	222	NR	264	.1	.4
418 Southw Bapt Fel	2	NR	NR	NR	-	-
419 So Bapt Conv	12	2,610	1,217	3,122 *	1.6	4.5
435 Unitarian-Univ	1	114	NR	136 *	.1	.2
449 Un Methodist	59	9,963	4,906	11,916 *	6.0	17.2
463 Vineyard	1	88	87	105 *	.1	.2
467 Wesleyan	4	71	107	252	.1	.4
496 Jewish Est	1	NR	NR	975	.5	1.4
499 Indep.Non-Char	2	800	1,750	1,750	.9	2.5
LEWIS	**50**	**3,581**	**2,242**	**6,137 ***	**36.3**	**100.0**
019 Amer Bapt USA	8	961	525	1,158 *	6.8	18.9
053 Assemb of God	1	86	110	152	.9	2.5
081 Catholic	2	NR	NR	1,513	8.9	24.7
123 Ch God (Ander)	1	NR	39	39	.2	.6
127 Ch God (Cleve)	1	139	60	167 *	1.0	2.7
165 Ch of Nazarene	1	39	65	65	.4	1.1
167 Chs of Christ	1	65	55	77	.5	1.3
193 Episcopal	1	NR	52	206	1.2	3.4
355 Presb Ch (USA)	1	26	18	31 *	.2	.5
419 So Bapt Conv	1	246	56	296 *	1.7	4.8
449 Un Methodist	32	2,019	1,262	2,433 *	14.4	39.6
LINCOLN	**55**	**3,294**	**1,371**	**4,451 ***	**20.1**	**100.0**
019 Amer Bapt USA	10	1,072	313	1,303 *	5.9	29.3
053 Assemb of God	1	45	40	43	.2	1.0
056 Baha'i	0	3	NR	3	-	.1
123 Ch God (Ander)	1	NR	80	80	.4	1.8
127 Ch God (Cleve)	3	223	119	271 *	1.2	6.1
151 L-D Saints	1	NR	NR	227	1.0	5.1
165 Ch of Nazarene	1	14	20	30	.1	.7
167 Chs of Christ	10	372	451	591	2.7	13.3
223 Free Will Bapt	16	808	NR	983 *	4.4	22.1
419 So Bapt Conv	2	222	93	270 *	1.2	6.1
449 Un Methodist	10	535	255	650 *	2.9	14.6
LOGAN	**99**	**7,017**	**2,775**	**9,161 ***	**24.3**	**100.0**
019 Amer Bapt USA	7	569	484	681 *	1.8	7.4
053 Assemb of God	2	53	56	200	.5	2.2
056 Baha'i	0	1	NR	1	-	-
081 Catholic	2	NR	NR	531	1.4	5.8
093 Chr Ch (Disc)	1	237	119	284 *	.8	3.1
097 Chr Chs&Chs Cr	4	465	NR	557 *	1.5	6.1
127 Ch God (Cleve)	17	1,824	825	2,184 *	5.8	23.8
145 Ch God Prophcy	2	64	NR	76 *	.2	.8
165 Ch of Nazarene	2	386	209	443	1.2	4.8
167 Chs of Christ	8	357	364	440	1.2	4.8
193 Episcopal	1	NR	12	28	.1	.3
223 Free Will Bapt	37	1,869	NR	2,237 *	5.9	24.4
355 Presb Ch (USA)	2	171	109	205 *	.5	2.2
403 Salvation Army	1	99	33	190	.5	2.1
413 S.D.A.	1	24	NR	29	.1	.3
419 So Bapt Conv	2	185	135	221 *	.6	2.4
449 Un Methodist	10	713	429	854 *	2.3	9.3
MCDOWELL	**98**	**3,931**	**1,891**	**5,387 ***	**19.7**	**100.0**
011 A.W.M.C.	1	5	12	5	-	.1
019 Amer Bapt USA	4	301	137	363 *	1.3	6.7

NR–Not Reported *Total adherents estimated from known number of communicant, confirmed, full members. - Represents a percentage less than 0.1. Percentages may not total 100 due to rounding.

Table 4: Religious Congregations by County and Group: 2000

Religious Group	Number of Churches, Synagogues, Mosques, or Temples	Number of Communicant, Confirmed, or Full Members	Number of Attendees	Total Adherents: Number of Adherents	Total Adherents: % of Total Pop.	Total Adherents: % of Total Adh.
053 Assemb of God	6	232	183	297	1.1	5.5
056 Baha'i	0	7	NR	7	-	.1
081 Catholic	4	NR	NR	470	1.7	8.7
097 Chr Chs&Chs Cr	5	494	NR	596 *	2.2	11.1
123 Ch God (Ander)	3	NR	97	97	.4	1.8
127 Ch God (Cleve)	16	809	449	975 *	3.6	18.1
165 Ch of Nazarene	1	60	50	87	.3	1.6
167 Chs of Christ	5	123	143	163	.6	3.0
193 Episcopal	3	NR	22	36	.1	.7
223 Free Will Bapt	1	51	NR	61 *	.2	1.1
349 Pent Holiness	13	579	361	698 *	2.6	13.0
355 Presb Ch (USA)	3	99	60	120 *	.4	2.2
360 Prim Bapt Chrch	1	NR	NR	NR	-	-
413 S.D.A.	2	55	NR	65	.2	1.2
419 So Bapt Conv	3	146	56	176 *	.6	3.3
449 Un Methodist	27	970	321	1,171 *	4.3	21.7
MARION	**138**	**13,840**	**8,197**	**24,298 ***	**42.9**	**100.0**
011 A.W.M.C.	1	13	41	13	-	.1
019 Amer Bapt USA	17	3,126	1,088	3,704 *	6.5	15.2
053 Assemb of God	3	877	1,035	2,147	3.8	8.8
056 Baha'i	0	2	NR	2	-	-
081 Catholic	11	NR	NR	5,223	9.2	21.5
089 Chr & Miss Al	1	32	NR	58	.1	.2
093 Chr Ch (Disc)	3	518	122	614 *	1.1	2.5
123 Ch God (Ander)	1	NR	15	15	-	.1
127 Ch God (Cleve)	3	101	97	133 *	.2	.5
145 Ch God Prophcy	4	127	NR	152 *	.3	.6
151 L-D Saints	2	NR	NR	507	.9	2.1
157 Ch of Brethren	1	6	0	7 *	-	-
165 Ch of Nazarene	3	501	412	790	1.4	3.3
167 Chs of Christ	16	1,647	1,623	2,067	3.7	8.5
193 Episcopal	1	NR	58	218	.4	.9
207 E.L.C.A.	1	318	115	492	.9	2.0
221 Free Methodist	4	189	266	266	.5	1.1
263 Int Foursq Gos	1	79	416	416 *	.7	1.7
355 Presb Ch (USA)	3	444	245	526 *	.9	2.2
356 Presb Ch Amer	2	133	95	155	.3	.6
388 Reg Bapt Gen As	2	312	203	370 *	.7	1.5
413 S.D.A.	1	42	NR	50	.1	.2
419 So Bapt Conv	1	234	57	277 *	.5	1.1
449 Un Methodist	55	5,130	2,291	6,078 *	10.7	25.0
467 Wesleyan	1	9	18	18	-	.1
MARSHALL	**73**	**9,354**	**3,955**	**17,266 ***	**48.6**	**100.0**
019 Amer Bapt USA	3	1,147	281	1,388 *	3.9	8.0
053 Assemb of God	1	28	40	80	.2	.5
056 Baha'i	0	2	NR	2	-	-
071 Brethren (Ash)	1	38	26	46 *	.1	.3
081 Catholic	6	NR	NR	5,465	15.4	31.7
093 Chr Ch (Disc)	6	1,859	425	2,250 *	6.3	13.0
097 Chr Chs&Chs Cr	1	71	NR	86 *	.2	.5
123 Ch God (Ander)	2	NR	216	216	.6	1.3
127 Ch God (Cleve)	2	211	112	255 *	.7	1.5
165 Ch of Nazarene	2	196	130	273	.8	1.6
167 Chs of Christ	7	724	720	956	2.7	5.5
171 Ch God-Gen Con	1	343	99	415 *	1.2	2.4
173 Comm of Christ	2	133	NR	133	.4	.8
193 Episcopal	1	NR	71	146	.4	.8
207 E.L.C.A.	2	198	104	284	.8	1.6
252 Hindu	3	NR	NR	NR	-	-
263 Int Foursq Gos	1	48	86	86 *	.2	.5
331 OCA: Ter Diocs	2	144	NR	151	.4	.9
355 Presb Ch (USA)	6	458	318	553 *	1.6	3.2
388 Reg Bapt Gen As	1	106	85	85 *	.2	.5
403 Salvation Army	1	90	38	90	.3	.5
419 So Bapt Conv	2	662	154	801 *	2.3	4.6
449 Un Methodist	20	2,896	1,050	3,505 *	9.9	20.3
MASON	**61**	**5,014**	**2,802**	**6,989 ***	**26.9**	**100.0**
011 A.W.M.C.	1	0	27	0	-	-
019 Amer Bapt USA	7	1,254	428	1,517 *	5.8	21.7
053 Assemb of God	1	11	15	31	.1	.4

Religious Group	Number of Churches, Synagogues, Mosques, or Temples	Number of Communicant, Confirmed, or Full Members	Number of Attendees	Total Adherents: Number of Adherents	Total Adherents: % of Total Pop.	Total Adherents: % of Total Adh.
081 Catholic	2	NR	NR	410	1.6	5.9
123 Ch God (Ander)	2	NR	191	191	.7	2.7
145 Ch God Prophcy	1	32	NR	39 *	.2	.6
151 L-D Saints	1	NR	NR	237	.9	3.4
165 Ch of Nazarene	1	254	122	293	1.1	4.2
167 Chs of Christ	4	339	350	398	1.5	5.7
193 Episcopal	1	NR	54	156	.6	2.2
207 E.L.C.A.	4	212	98	239	.9	3.4
323 Old Ord Amish	1	24	NR	29 *	.1	.4
355 Presb Ch (USA)	1	133	62	161 *	.6	2.3
388 Reg Bapt Gen As	1	106	85	85 *	.3	1.2
413 S.D.A.	1	27	NR	32	.1	.5
419 So Bapt Conv	2	141	0	171 *	.7	2.4
449 Un Methodist	30	2,481	1,370	3,000 *	11.6	42.9
MERCER	**147**	**21,657**	**8,576**	**28,466 ***	**45.2**	**100.0**
011 A.W.M.C.	2	16	48	17	-	.1
019 Amer Bapt USA	3	226	130	269 *	.4	.9
022 Carp Rus Orth	1	122	NR	207	.3	.7
053 Assemb of God	2	197	252	395	.6	1.4
056 Baha'i	0	106	NR	106	.2	.4
081 Catholic	3	NR	NR	1,171	1.9	4.1
093 Chr Ch (Disc)	2	827	117	986 *	1.6	3.5
097 Chr Chs&Chs Cr	13	1,412	NR	1,684 *	2.7	5.9
123 Ch God (Ander)	5	NR	450	450	.7	1.6
127 Ch God (Cleve)	9	1,444	938	1,736 *	2.8	6.1
145 Ch God Prophcy	1	32	NR	38 *	.1	.1
151 L-D Saints	1	NR	NR	429	.7	1.5
157 Ch of Brethren	2	63	18	75 *	.1	.3
165 Ch of Nazarene	3	428	306	633	1.0	2.2
167 Chs of Christ	3	225	237	293	.5	1.0
193 Episcopal	2	NR	112	321	.5	1.1
207 E.L.C.A.	1	195	78	249	.4	.9
216 Evan Presby Ch	1	446	NR	532 *	.8	1.9
221 Free Methodist	1	26	45	45	.1	.2
223 Free Will Bapt	4	202	NR	241 *	.4	.8
339 Pent Ch of God	1	20	NR	28	-	.1
349 Pent Holiness	10	1,488	680	1,774 *	2.8	6.2
355 Presb Ch (USA)	6	665	335	796 *	1.3	2.8
360 Prim Bapt Chrch	7	NR	NR	NR	-	-
370 Ref Baptist Chs	1	NR	NR	NR	-	-
403 Salvation Army	1	151	29	185	.3	.6
413 S.D.A.	1	141	NR	168	.3	.6
419 So Bapt Conv	23	6,584	2,159	7,850 *	12.5	27.6
449 Un Methodist	34	4,810	2,119	5,734 *	9.1	20.1
467 Wesleyan	2	28	23	51	.1	.2
496 Jewish Est	1	NR	NR	200	.3	.7
499 Indep.Non-Char	1	1,803	500	1,803	2.9	6.3
MINERAL	**69**	**7,166**	**3,770**	**11,601 ***	**42.8**	**100.0**
011 A.W.M.C.	1	18	71	20	.1	.2
053 Assemb of God	7	393	500	651	2.4	5.6
081 Catholic	3	NR	NR	2,317	8.6	20.0
097 Chr Chs&Chs Cr	1	35	NR	43 *	.2	.4
127 Ch God (Cleve)	3	394	93	480 *	1.8	4.1
151 L-D Saints	1	NR	NR	232	.9	2.0
157 Ch of Brethren	9	1,123	660	1,368 *	5.1	11.8
167 Chs of Christ	1	51	55	67	.2	.6
193 Episcopal	1	NR	44	68	.3	.6
207 E.L.C.A.	1	269	67	385	1.4	3.3
349 Pent Holiness	2	190	158	231 *	.9	2.0
355 Presb Ch (USA)	4	453	234	596 *	2.2	5.1
388 Reg Bapt Gen As	1	106	85	85 *	.3	.7
419 So Bapt Conv	6	819	327	997 *	3.7	8.6
449 Un Methodist	27	3,315	1,453	4,038 *	14.9	34.8
467 Wesleyan	1	0	23	23	.1	.2
MINGO	**65**	**5,650**	**2,370**	**7,735 ***	**27.4**	**100.0**
019 Amer Bapt USA	6	623	339	760 *	2.7	9.8
053 Assemb of God	5	322	339	524	1.9	6.8
081 Catholic	1	NR	NR	422	1.5	5.5
097 Chr Chs&Chs Cr	3	417	NR	509 *	1.8	6.6
127 Ch God (Cleve)	12	1,372	636	1,680 *	5.9	21.7

NR–Not Reported *Total adherents estimated from known number of communicant, confirmed, full members. - Represents a percentage less than 0.1. Percentages may not total 100 due to rounding.

Table 4: Religious Congregations by County and Group: 2000

Religious Group	Number of Churches, Synagogues, Mosques, or Temples	Number of Communicant, Confirmed, or Full Members	Number of Attendees	Total Adherents: Number of Adherents	Total Adherents: % of Total Pop.	Total Adherents: % of Total Adh.
145 Ch God Prophcy	1	32	NR	39 *	.1	.5
167 Chs of Christ	9	301	325	372	1.3	4.8
193 Episcopal	1	NR	32	75	.3	1.0
223 Free Will Bapt	11	556	NR	678 *	2.4	8.8
355 Presb Ch (USA)	2	151	95	185 *	.7	2.4
413 S.D.A.	1	32	NR	38	.1	.5
419 So Bapt Conv	6	1,253	311	1,529 *	5.4	19.8
449 Un Methodist	5	568	261	693 *	2.5	9.0
467 Wesleyan	1	23	32	116	.4	1.5
496 Jewish Est	1	NR	NR	115	.4	1.5
MONONGALIA	**112**	**10,952**	**5,881**	**23,330 ***	**28.5**	**100.0**
019 Amer Bapt USA	7	1,389	476	1,616 *	2.0	6.9
022 Carp Rus Orth	1	122	NR	207	.3	.9
053 Assemb of God	3	188	231	316	.4	1.4
056 Baha'i	1	32	NR	32	-	.1
081 Catholic	5	NR	NR	7,171	8.8	30.7
089 Chr & Miss Al	3	354	NR	1,049	1.3	4.5
093 Chr Ch (Disc)	2	587	107	683 *	.8	2.9
123 Ch God (Ander)	2	NR	35	35	-	.2
127 Ch God (Cleve)	2	157	98	183 *	.2	.8
145 Ch God Prophcy	1	32	NR	37 *	-	.2
151 L-D Saints	3	NR	NR	962	1.2	4.1
157 Ch of Brethren	1	101	58	118 *	.1	.5
165 Ch of Nazarene	2	251	298	556	.7	2.4
167 Chs of Christ	5	336	440	587	.7	2.5
173 Comm of Christ	1	62	NR	62	.1	.3
193 Episcopal	2	NR	185	475	.6	2.0
207 E.L.C.A.	1	463	181	605	.7	2.6
221 Free Methodist	3	65	92	92	.1	.4
226 Friends-USA	1	35	NR	41 *	.1	.2
246 Greek Orthodox	1	NR	NR	105	.1	.5
263 Int Foursq Gos	1	57	74	74 *	.1	.3
264 Int Chs of Crst	1	62	102	88	.1	.4
267 Muslim Est	1	NR	100	300	.4	1.3
268 Jain	1	NR	NR	NR	-	-
288 Mennonite USA	1	103	65	120 *	.1	.5
335 Orth Pres Ch	1	62	72	102	.1	.4
355 Presb Ch (USA)	5	631	276	735 *	.9	3.2
403 Salvation Army	1	154	67	129	.2	.6
413 S.D.A.	1	66	NR	79	.1	.3
419 So Bapt Conv	2	263	161	306 *	.4	1.3
435 Unitarian-Univ	1	33	NR	38 *	-	.2
449 Un Methodist	47	5,330	2,740	6,204 *	7.6	26.6
467 Wesleyan	1	17	23	23	-	.1
496 Jewish Est	1	NR	NR	200	.2	.9
MONROE	**59**	**3,472**	**1,669**	**4,431 ***	**30.4**	**100.0**
019 Amer Bapt USA	7	728	331	860 *	5.9	19.4
055 As Ref Pres Ch	1	103	NR	107	.7	2.4
056 Baha'i	0	8	NR	8	.1	.2
081 Catholic	1	NR	NR	139	1.0	3.1
097 Chr Chs&Chs Cr	4	395	NR	467 *	3.2	10.5
123 Ch God (Ander)	1	NR	26	26	.2	.6
127 Ch God (Cleve)	1	67	36	79 *	.5	1.8
145 Ch God Prophcy	1	32	NR	38 *	.3	.9
151 L-D Saints	1	NR	NR	121	.8	2.7
157 Ch of Brethren	1	166	42	196 *	1.3	4.4
165 Ch of Nazarene	2	57	36	87	.6	2.0
167 Chs of Christ	1	18	20	22	.2	.5
193 Episcopal	1	NR	18	29	.2	.7
223 Free Will Bapt	1	51	NR	60 *	.4	1.4
265 Int Pent C Chr	3	32	34	46	.3	1.0
297 Mennonite;Other	1	69	NR	82 *	.6	1.9
349 Pent Holiness	2	119	100	141 *	1.0	3.2
355 Presb Ch (USA)	6	262	142	311 *	2.1	7.0
360 Prim Bapt Chrch	3	NR	NR	NR	-	-
419 So Bapt Conv	0	11	11	13 *	.1	.3
449 Un Methodist	21	1,354	873	1,599 *	11.0	36.1
MORGAN	**31**	**3,251**	**1,416**	**5,322 ***	**35.6**	**100.0**
053 Assemb of God	2	118	127	221	1.5	4.2
056 Baha'i	0	3	NR	3	-	.1

Religious Group	Number of Churches, Synagogues, Mosques, or Temples	Number of Communicant, Confirmed, or Full Members	Number of Attendees	Total Adherents: Number of Adherents	Total Adherents: % of Total Pop.	Total Adherents: % of Total Adh.
081 Catholic	1	NR	NR	1,120	7.5	21.0
093 Chr Ch (Disc)	1	128	0	155 *	1.0	2.9
097 Chr Chs&Chs Cr	1	100	NR	121 *	.8	2.3
127 Ch God (Cleve)	1	44	39	53 *	.4	1.0
165 Ch of Nazarene	1	27	44	71	.5	1.3
167 Chs of Christ	2	153	144	177	1.2	3.3
193 Episcopal	1	NR	32	162	1.1	3.0
355 Presb Ch (USA)	1	138	67	167 *	1.1	3.1
360 Prim Bapt Chrch	1	NR	NR	NR	-	-
413 S.D.A.	1	108	NR	129	.9	2.4
419 So Bapt Conv	2	501	197	606 *	4.1	11.4
449 Un Methodist	16	1,931	766	2,337 *	15.6	43.9
NICHOLAS	**88**	**7,876**	**3,626**	**10,581 ***	**39.8**	**100.0**
019 Amer Bapt USA	18	3,956	1,451	4,782 *	18.0	45.2
053 Assemb of God	1	177	200	222	.8	2.1
056 Baha'i	0	1	NR	1	-	-
081 Catholic	2	NR	NR	614	2.3	5.8
097 Chr Chs&Chs Cr	1	40	NR	48 *	.2	.5
123 Ch God (Ander)	3	NR	160	160	.6	1.5
127 Ch God (Cleve)	2	169	90	204 *	.8	1.9
151 L-D Saints	1	NR	NR	210	.8	2.0
165 Ch of Nazarene	4	137	80	197	.7	1.9
167 Chs of Christ	2	52	56	68	.3	.6
193 Episcopal	1	NR	19	35	.1	.3
223 Free Will Bapt	6	303	NR	366 *	1.4	3.5
355 Presb Ch (USA)	2	162	79	196 *	.7	1.9
360 Prim Bapt Chrch	1	NR	NR	NR	-	-
413 S.D.A.	2	140	NR	166	.6	1.6
418 Southw Bapt Fel	4	NR	NR	NR	-	-
419 So Bapt Conv	3	582	232	703 *	2.6	6.6
449 Un Methodist	35	2,157	1,259	2,609 *	9.8	24.7
OHIO	**73**	**10,900**	**4,577**	**34,108 ***	**71.9**	**100.0**
019 Amer Bapt USA	3	603	280	718 *	1.5	2.1
053 Assemb of God	2	91	124	255	.5	.7
056 Baha'i	0	13	NR	13	-	-
081 Catholic	10	NR	NR	18,524	39.1	54.3
089 Chr & Miss Al	1	37	NR	87	.2	.3
093 Chr Ch (Disc)	2	923	164	1,099 *	2.3	3.2
097 Chr Chs&Chs Cr	4	525	NR	626 *	1.3	1.8
123 Ch God (Ander)	2	NR	54	54	.1	.2
127 Ch God (Cleve)	1	50	22	60 *	.1	.2
167 Chs of Christ	2	247	269	307	.6	.9
173 Comm of Christ	1	64	NR	64	.1	.2
193 Episcopal	5	NR	359	1,104	2.3	3.2
207 E.L.C.A.	7	2,262	687	2,959	6.2	8.7
246 Greek Orthodox	1	NR	NR	525	1.1	1.5
355 Presb Ch (USA)	8	1,679	678	1,998 *	4.2	5.9
403 Salvation Army	1	94	28	384	.8	1.1
413 S.D.A.	1	71	NR	84	.2	.2
419 So Bapt Conv	1	146	156	174 *	.4	.5
435 Unitarian-Univ	1	51	NR	61 *	.1	.2
443 Un C of Christ	2	344	121	409 *	.9	1.2
449 Un Methodist	16	3,100	1,095	3,689 *	7.8	10.8
463 Vineyard	1	600	540	714 *	1.5	2.1
496 Jewish Est	1	NR	NR	200	.4	.6
PENDLETON	**50**	**2,939**	**1,337**	**3,699 ***	**45.1**	**100.0**
053 Assemb of God	1	30	44	90	1.1	2.4
056 Baha'i	0	3	NR	3	-	.1
081 Catholic	1	NR	NR	103	1.3	2.8
097 Chr Chs&Chs Cr	1	50	NR	60 *	.7	1.6
127 Ch God (Cleve)	1	69	79	83 *	1.0	2.2
157 Ch of Brethren	11	586	20	706 *	8.6	19.1
167 Chs of Christ	1	23	25	29	.4	.8
207 E.L.C.A.	4	338	212	410	5.0	11.1
223 Free Will Bapt	1	51	NR	61 *	.7	1.6
288 Mennonite USA	1	9	7	11 *	.1	.3
297 Mennonite;Other	2	66	NR	80 *	1.0	2.2
355 Presb Ch (USA)	5	337	207	406 *	5.0	11.0
413 S.D.A.	1	27	NR	32	.4	.9
419 So Bapt Conv	3	427	233	514 *	6.3	13.9

NR–Not Reported *Total adherents estimated from known number of communicant, confirmed, full members. - Represents a percentage less than 0.1. Percentages may not total 100 due to rounding.

Table 4: Religious Congregations by County and Group: 2000

Religious Group	Number of Churches, Synagogues, Mosques, or Temples	Number of Communicant, Confirmed, or Full Members	Number of Attendees	Total Adherents		
				Number of Adherents	% of Total Pop.	% of Total Adh.
449 Un Methodist	17	923	510	1,111 *	13.6	30.0
PLEASANTS	**27**	**1,972**	**1,072**	**2,590 ***	**34.5**	**100.0**
019 Amer Bapt USA	4	560	172	681 *	9.1	26.3
081 Catholic	1	NR	NR	116	1.5	4.5
127 Ch God (Cleve)	1	59	14	72 *	1.0	2.8
165 Ch of Nazarene	1	57	57	76	1.0	2.9
167 Chs of Christ	6	317	359	380	5.1	14.7
193 Episcopal	1	NR	21	74	1.0	2.9
223 Free Will Bapt	2	101	NR	123 *	1.6	4.7
349 Pent Holiness	1	72	77	88 *	1.2	3.4
355 Presb Ch (USA)	1	47	32	57 *	.8	2.2
419 So Bapt Conv	1	38	30	46 *	.6	1.8
449 Un Methodist	8	721	310	877 *	11.7	33.9
POCAHONTAS	**48**	**2,149**	**1,202**	**2,727 ***	**29.9**	**100.0**
053 Assemb of God	1	18	20	21	.2	.8
056 Baha'i	0	1	NR	1	-	-
081 Catholic	2	NR	NR	91	1.0	3.3
127 Ch God (Cleve)	1	55	53	65 *	.7	2.4
157 Ch of Brethren	5	172	72	204 *	2.2	7.5
165 Ch of Nazarene	2	94	69	135	1.5	5.0
167 Chs of Christ	2	32	40	52	.6	1.9
193 Episcopal	1	NR	18	44	.5	1.6
207 E.L.C.A.	1	29	24	34	.4	1.2
297 Mennonite;Other	1	16	NR	19 *	.2	.7
355 Presb Ch (USA)	6	351	189	417 *	4.6	15.3
419 So Bapt Conv	3	508	269	604 *	6.6	22.1
449 Un Methodist	23	873	448	1,040 *	11.4	38.1
PRESTON	**102**	**5,961**	**3,787**	**9,815 ***	**33.5**	**100.0**
011 A.W.M.C.	2	17	21	17	.1	.2
019 Amer Bapt USA	7	615	335	744 *	2.5	7.6
053 Assemb of God	5	205	264	328	1.1	3.3
081 Catholic	4	NR	NR	1,991	6.8	20.3
127 Ch God (Cleve)	1	15	42	42 *	.1	.4
157 Ch of Brethren	8	381	316	464 *	1.6	4.7
165 Ch of Nazarene	4	419	390	806	2.7	8.2
167 Chs of Christ	2	100	110	120	.4	1.2
193 Episcopal	1	NR	22	55	.2	.6
207 E.L.C.A.	1	151	52	213	.7	2.2
221 Free Methodist	3	126	189	243	.8	2.5
349 Pent Holiness	1	50	34	60 *	.2	.6
355 Presb Ch (USA)	3	228	117	276 *	.9	2.8
413 S.D.A.	1	9	NR	11	-	.1
419 So Bapt Conv	3	376	110	455 *	1.6	4.6
449 Un Methodist	54	3,199	1,711	3,870 *	13.2	39.4
467 Wesleyan	2	70	74	120	.4	1.2
PUTNAM	**62**	**9,251**	**5,022**	**14,405 ***	**27.9**	**100.0**
019 Amer Bapt USA	11	4,051	1,262	5,013 *	9.7	34.8
053 Assemb of God	2	94	106	123	.2	.9
056 Baha'i	0	9	NR	9	-	.1
071 Brethren (Ash)	1	5	12	6 *	-	-
081 Catholic	2	NR	NR	1,569	3.0	10.9
097 Chr Chs&Chs Cr	1	162	NR	200 *	.4	1.4
123 Ch God (Ander)	5	NR	464	464	.9	3.2
127 Ch God (Cleve)	2	81	89	103 *	.2	.7
151 L-D Saints	1	NR	NR	392	.8	2.7
165 Ch of Nazarene	5	645	508	1,115	2.2	7.7
167 Chs of Christ	7	600	620	770	1.5	5.3
171 Ch God-Gen Con	1	28	26	35 *	.1	.2
193 Episcopal	1	NR	83	172	.3	1.2
223 Free Will Bapt	4	202	NR	250 *	.5	1.7
355 Presb Ch (USA)	5	799	406	989 *	1.9	6.9
356 Presb Ch Amer	1	9	20	20	-	.1
360 Prim Bapt Chrch	1	NR	NR	NR	-	-
419 So Bapt Conv	2	396	203	490 *	.9	3.4
449 Un Methodist	10	2,170	1,223	2,685 *	5.2	18.6
RALEIGH	**115**	**11,895**	**6,277**	**17,719 ***	**22.4**	**100.0**
019 Amer Bapt USA	7	2,041	864	2,438 *	3.1	13.8
034 Ant Orth of NA	1	24	NR	48	.1	.3
053 Assemb of God	4	352	361	479	.6	2.7
056 Baha'i	0	30	NR	30	-	.2
081 Catholic	1	NR	NR	2,276	2.9	12.8
093 Chr Ch (Disc)	1	597	101	713 *	.9	4.0
097 Chr Chs&Chs Cr	3	592	NR	707 *	.9	4.0
123 Ch God (Ander)	3	NR	260	260	.3	1.5
127 Ch God (Cleve)	16	2,034	1,477	2,430 *	3.1	13.7
145 Ch God Prophcy	2	64	NR	76 *	.1	.4
157 Ch of Brethren	1	133	0	159 *	.2	.9
165 Ch of Nazarene	1	177	91	249	.3	1.4
167 Chs of Christ	9	322	359	398	.5	2.2
179 Consrv Bapt	1	NR	225	225	.3	1.3
193 Episcopal	2	NR	109	495	.6	2.8
203 Evan Free Ch	1	69	125	125	.2	.7
207 E.L.C.A.	1	82	61	113	.1	.6
221 Free Methodist	1	42	68	68	.1	.4
223 Free Will Bapt	17	859	NR	1,025 *	1.3	5.8
339 Pent Ch of God	1	15	NR	21	-	.1
349 Pent Holiness	3	220	116	263 *	.3	1.5
355 Presb Ch (USA)	6	655	346	790 *	1.0	4.5
360 Prim Bapt Chrch	5	NR	NR	NR	-	-
388 Reg Bapt Gen As	1	155	90	90 *	.1	.5
403 Salvation Army	1	59	16	94	.1	.5
413 S.D.A.	2	98	NR	116	.1	.7
418 Southw Bapt Fel	3	NR	NR	NR	-	-
419 So Bapt Conv	4	1,454	550	1,737 *	2.2	9.8
435 Unitarian-Univ	1	22	NR	26 *	-	.1
449 Un Methodist	15	1,799	1,058	2,148 *	2.7	12.1
496 Jewish Est	1	NR	NR	120	.2	.7
RANDOLPH	**71**	**6,444**	**3,093**	**10,763 ***	**38.1**	**100.0**
019 Amer Bapt USA	3	981	339	1,181 *	4.2	11.0
053 Assemb of God	3	129	163	221	.8	2.1
081 Catholic	4	NR	NR	1,890	6.7	17.6
089 Chr & Miss Al	1	36	NR	171	.6	1.6
097 Chr Chs&Chs Cr	3	374	NR	450 *	1.6	4.2
127 Ch God (Cleve)	3	467	274	562 *	2.0	5.2
145 Ch God Prophcy	1	32	NR	38 *	.1	.4
151 L-D Saints	1	NR	NR	511	1.8	4.7
157 Ch of Brethren	3	139	47	168 *	.6	1.6
165 Ch of Nazarene	2	315	190	645	2.3	6.0
167 Chs of Christ	1	106	100	160	.6	1.5
193 Episcopal	1	NR	29	67	.2	.6
207 E.L.C.A.	1	127	24	179	.6	1.7
288 Mennonite USA	2	55	61	70 *	.2	.7
349 Pent Holiness	1	168	105	202 *	.7	1.9
355 Presb Ch (USA)	10	610	305	735 *	2.6	6.8
388 Reg Bapt Gen As	1	50	80	80 *	.3	.7
413 S.D.A.	1	59	NR	70	.2	.7
419 So Bapt Conv	3	296	130	356 *	1.3	3.3
449 Un Methodist	26	2,500	1,246	3,007 *	10.6	27.9
RITCHIE	**54**	**2,802**	**1,665**	**3,671 ***	**35.5**	**100.0**
019 Amer Bapt USA	6	617	293	743 *	7.2	20.2
053 Assemb of God	1	63	65	106	1.0	2.9
056 Baha'i	0	1	NR	1	-	-
081 Catholic	2	NR	NR	98	.9	2.7
127 Ch God (Cleve)	1	66	48	80 *	.8	2.2
151 L-D Saints	1	NR	NR	102	1.0	2.8
165 Ch of Nazarene	1	40	33	66	.6	1.8
167 Chs of Christ	8	436	384	485	4.7	13.2
173 Comm of Christ	1	35	NR	35	.3	1.0
223 Free Will Bapt	1	51	NR	61 *	.6	1.7
355 Presb Ch (USA)	1	25	25	30 *	.3	.8
413 S.D.A.	1	74	NR	88	.9	2.4
449 Un Methodist	29	1,357	750	1,637 *	15.8	44.6
467 Wesleyan	1	37	67	139	1.3	3.8
ROANE	**48**	**2,672**	**1,275**	**3,771 ***	**24.4**	**100.0**
019 Amer Bapt USA	17	1,521	628	1,839 *	11.9	48.8
056 Baha'i	0	1	NR	1	-	-
076 Buddhism	1	NR	NR	NR	-	-

NR–Not Reported   *Total adherents estimated from known number of communicant, confirmed, full members.   - Represents a percentage less than 0.1.   Percentages may not total 100 due to rounding.

Table 4: Religious Congregations by County and Group: 2000

Religious Group	Number of Churches, Synagogues, Mosques, or Temples	Number of Communicant, Confirmed, or Full Members	Number of Attendees	Total Adherents: Number of Adherents	Total Adherents: % of Total Pop.	Total Adherents: % of Total Adh.
081 Catholic	1	NR	NR	454	2.9	12.0
165 Ch of Nazarene	2	168	121	276	1.8	7.3
167 Chs of Christ	2	49	50	73	.5	1.9
323 Old Ord Amish	1	8	NR	10 *	.1	.3
349 Pent Holiness	1	37	36	45 *	.3	1.2
355 Presb Ch (USA)	1	18	12	22 *	.1	.6
413 S.D.A.	1	46	NR	55	.4	1.5
419 So Bapt Conv	1	66	26	80 *	.5	2.1
449 Un Methodist	20	758	402	916 *	5.9	24.3
SUMMERS	**41**	**3,929**	**1,406**	**4,892 ***	**37.6**	**100.0**
019 Amer Bapt USA	8	1,820	530	2,143 *	16.5	43.8
056 Baha'i	0	2	NR	2	-	-
081 Catholic	1	NR	NR	169	1.3	3.5
097 Chr Chs&Chs Cr	1	55	NR	65 *	.5	1.3
127 Ch God (Cleve)	1	73	39	86 *	.7	1.8
165 Ch of Nazarene	1	19	35	44	.3	.9
167 Chs of Christ	3	92	96	114	.9	2.3
193 Episcopal	1	NR	31	72	.6	1.5
223 Free Will Bapt	1	51	NR	59 *	.5	1.2
355 Presb Ch (USA)	2	68	29	80 *	.6	1.6
360 Prim Bapt Chrch	5	NR	NR	NR	-	-
419 So Bapt Conv	1	1,036	200	1,220 *	9.4	24.9
449 Un Methodist	16	713	446	838 *	6.4	17.1
TAYLOR	**43**	**3,805**	**1,801**	**5,276 ***	**32.8**	**100.0**
011 A.W.M.C.	3	28	92	28	.2	.5
019 Amer Bapt USA	7	898	506	1,084 *	6.7	20.5
053 Assemb of God	2	163	95	190	1.2	3.6
081 Catholic	1	NR	NR	553	3.4	10.5
093 Chr Ch (Disc)	1	122	38	147 *	.9	2.8
127 Ch God (Cleve)	1	100	0	121 *	.8	2.3
165 Ch of Nazarene	2	201	137	313	1.9	5.9
167 Chs of Christ	2	110	125	149	.9	2.8
193 Episcopal	1	NR	22	51	.3	1.0
207 E.L.C.A.	1	68	45	72	.4	1.4
223 Free Will Bapt	1	51	NR	61 *	.4	1.2
355 Presb Ch (USA)	1	30	45	45 *	.3	.9
403 Salvation Army	1	104	47	134	.8	2.5
413 S.D.A.	1	54	NR	64	.4	1.2
419 So Bapt Conv	1	354	76	427 *	2.7	8.1
449 Un Methodist	17	1,522	573	1,837 *	11.4	34.8
TUCKER	**39**	**1,863**	**1,313**	**3,699 ***	**50.5**	**100.0**
053 Assemb of God	1	55	72	110	1.5	3.0
081 Catholic	2	NR	NR	1,240	16.9	33.5
127 Ch God (Cleve)	3	184	196	218 *	3.0	5.9
151 L-D Saints	1	NR	NR	139	1.9	3.8
157 Ch of Brethren	3	41	34	72 *	1.0	1.9
165 Ch of Nazarene	1	110	85	110	1.5	3.0
167 Chs of Christ	1	12	15	18	.2	.5
207 E.L.C.A.	1	93	40	141	1.9	3.8
221 Free Methodist	1	25	48	48	.7	1.3
339 Pent Ch of God	2	57	NR	81	1.1	2.2
355 Presb Ch (USA)	2	97	52	115 *	1.6	3.1
413 S.D.A.	1	42	NR	50	.7	1.4
419 So Bapt Conv	1	24	28	28 *	.4	.8
449 Un Methodist	19	1,123	743	1,329 *	18.2	35.9
TYLER	**38**	**2,067**	**1,448**	**2,934 ***	**30.6**	**100.0**
019 Amer Bapt USA	2	433	183	524 *	5.5	17.9
056 Baha'i	0	1	NR	1	-	-
081 Catholic	2	NR	NR	124	1.3	4.2
097 Chr Chs&Chs Cr	1	116	NR	140 *	1.5	4.8
165 Ch of Nazarene	1	87	70	222	2.3	7.6
167 Chs of Christ	14	565	630	762	7.9	26.0
193 Episcopal	1	NR	15	23	.2	.8
339 Pent Ch of God	1	42	NR	142	1.5	4.8
355 Presb Ch (USA)	1	58	30	70 *	.7	2.4
419 So Bapt Conv	1	93	63	113 *	1.2	3.9
449 Un Methodist	14	672	457	813 *	8.5	27.7
UPSHUR	**80**	**4,566**	**2,560**	**6,429 ***	**27.5**	**100.0**
011 A.W.M.C.	1	0	15	0	-	-
019 Amer Bapt USA	7	943	582	1,134 *	4.8	17.6
053 Assemb of God	1	46	60	100	.4	1.6
056 Baha'i	0	2	NR	2	-	-
081 Catholic	1	NR	NR	290	1.2	4.5
089 Chr & Miss Al	1	74	NR	208	.9	3.2
127 Ch God (Cleve)	1	83	94	100 *	.4	1.6
151 L-D Saints	1	NR	NR	337	1.4	5.2
157 Ch of Brethren	2	70	0	84 *	.4	1.3
165 Ch of Nazarene	1	60	33	60	.3	.9
167 Chs of Christ	3	73	95	94	.4	1.5
193 Episcopal	1	NR	26	135	.6	2.1
339 Pent Ch of God	2	77	NR	112	.5	1.7
355 Presb Ch (USA)	2	71	36	86 *	.4	1.3
413 S.D.A.	1	91	NR	108	.5	1.7
419 So Bapt Conv	2	205	75	247 *	1.1	3.8
449 Un Methodist	53	2,771	1,544	3,332 *	14.2	51.8
WAYNE	**77**	**9,075**	**3,830**	**11,366 ***	**26.5**	**100.0**
019 Amer Bapt USA	13	2,577	842	3,132 *	7.3	27.6
056 Baha'i	0	2	NR	2	-	-
081 Catholic	1	NR	NR	64	.1	.6
123 Ch God (Ander)	1	NR	25	25	.1	.2
127 Ch God (Cleve)	8	439	248	541 *	1.3	4.8
167 Chs of Christ	12	785	851	1,027	2.4	9.0
175 Congr Chr Chs	1	35	20	43 *	.1	.4
223 Free Will Bapt	18	909	NR	1,105 *	2.6	9.7
265 Int Pent C Chr	1	40	47	90	.2	.8
355 Presb Ch (USA)	2	163	83	198 *	.5	1.7
409 Separate Bapt	1	60	NR	73 *	.2	.6
419 So Bapt Conv	4	2,285	811	2,777 *	6.5	24.4
449 Un Methodist	14	1,780	903	2,164 *	5.0	19.0
496 Jewish Est	1	NR	NR	125	.3	1.1
WEBSTER	**26**	**1,395**	**722**	**1,837 ***	**18.9**	**100.0**
019 Amer Bapt USA	4	580	212	700 *	7.2	38.1
053 Assemb of God	1	68	87	102	1.0	5.6
056 Baha'i	0	1	NR	1	-	.1
081 Catholic	1	NR	NR	42	.4	2.3
127 Ch God (Cleve)	1	41	0	49 *	.5	2.7
339 Pent Ch of God	1	29	NR	129	1.3	7.0
355 Presb Ch (USA)	1	51	45	62 *	.6	3.4
413 S.D.A.	1	13	NR	15	.2	.8
419 So Bapt Conv	3	219	87	264 *	2.7	14.4
449 Un Methodist	13	393	291	473 *	4.9	25.7
WETZEL	**74**	**5,910**	**3,766**	**8,718 ***	**49.3**	**100.0**
019 Amer Bapt USA	3	445	260	541 *	3.1	6.2
056 Baha'i	0	6	NR	6	-	.1
081 Catholic	2	NR	NR	691	3.9	7.9
093 Chr Ch (Disc)	1	399	115	485 *	2.7	5.6
097 Chr Chs&Chs Cr	3	510	NR	620 *	3.5	7.1
123 Ch God (Ander)	2	NR	125	125	.7	1.4
127 Ch God (Cleve)	3	163	194	212 *	1.2	2.4
151 L-D Saints	1	NR	NR	303	1.7	3.5
165 Ch of Nazarene	3	255	172	432	2.4	5.0
167 Chs of Christ	26	1,434	1,510	1,831	10.3	21.0
171 Ch God-Gen Con	1	38	55	55 *	.3	.6
193 Episcopal	1	NR	28	102	.6	1.2
207 E.L.C.A.	1	129	40	166	.9	1.9
339 Pent Ch of God	1	19	NR	69	.4	.8
355 Presb Ch (USA)	1	111	55	135 *	.8	1.5
356 Presb Ch Amer	1	69	55	88	.5	1.0
388 Reg Bapt Gen As	4	184	166	245 *	1.4	2.8
413 S.D.A.	1	11	NR	13	.1	.1
419 So Bapt Conv	1	210	151	255 *	1.4	2.9
449 Un Methodist	18	1,927	840	2,344 *	13.2	26.9
WIRT	**28**	**1,502**	**750**	**2,254 ***	**38.4**	**100.0**
019 Amer Bapt USA	8	768	312	943 *	16.1	41.8
056 Baha'i	0	1	NR	1	-	-

NR–Not Reported *Total adherents estimated from known number of communicant, confirmed, full members. - Represents a percentage less than 0.1. Percentages may not total 100 due to rounding.

Table 4: Religious Congregations by County and Group: 2000

Religious Group	Number of Churches, Synagogues, Mosques, or Temples	Number of Communicant, Confirmed, or Full Members	Number of Attendees	Total Adherents		
				Number of Adherents	% of Total Pop.	% of Total Adh.
081 Catholic	1	NR	NR	431	7.3	19.1
165 Ch of Nazarene	1	92	37	92	1.6	4.1
167 Chs of Christ	1	20	20	25	.4	1.1
320 "Old" MB Ascs	1	18	NR	22 *	.4	1.0
355 Presb Ch (USA)	1	18	14	22 *	.4	1.0
419 So Bapt Conv	1	106	127	130 *	2.2	5.8
449 Un Methodist	14	479	240	588 *	10.0	26.1
WOOD	**156**	**27,250**	**14,457**	**39,846 ***	**45.3**	**100.0**
019 Amer Bapt USA	23	8,696	3,877	10,549 *	12.0	26.5
053 Assemb of God	3	216	245	442	.5	1.1
056 Baha'i	0	8	NR	8	-	-
081 Catholic	4	NR	NR	4,453	5.1	11.2
093 Chr Ch (Disc)	2	187	70	227 *	.3	.6
097 Chr Chs&Chs Cr	2	121	NR	147 *	.2	.4
123 Ch God (Ander)	1	NR	170	170	.2	.4
127 Ch God (Cleve)	5	815	355	988 *	1.1	2.5
151 L-D Saints	2	NR	NR	625	.7	1.6
165 Ch of Nazarene	4	999	565	1,223	1.4	3.1
167 Chs of Christ	21	2,752	2,591	3,388	3.9	8.5
173 Comm of Christ	1	44	NR	44	.1	.1
193 Episcopal	3	NR	321	935	1.1	2.3
207 E.L.C.A.	2	988	342	1,214	1.4	3.0
223 Free Will Bapt	3	152	NR	184 *	.2	.5
283 Luth—MO Synod	1	247	125	312	.4	.8
349 Pent Holiness	1	36	30	44 *	.1	.1
355 Presb Ch (USA)	6	750	314	909 *	1.0	2.3
356 Presb Ch Amer	1	0	0	0	-	-
388 Reg Bapt Gen As	1	98	88	88 *	.1	.2
403 Salvation Army	1	158	46	301	.3	.8
413 S.D.A.	1	233	NR	277	.3	.7
419 So Bapt Conv	4	1,817	675	2,204 *	2.5	5.5
449 Un Methodist	58	8,763	4,424	10,631 *	12.1	26.7
463 Vineyard	1	130	120	158 *	.2	.4
467 Wesleyan	4	40	99	215	.2	.5
496 Jewish Est	1	NR	NR	110	.1	.3
WYOMING	**81**	**6,758**	**2,975**	**9,294 ***	**36.2**	**100.0**
019 Amer Bapt USA	23	3,380	1,376	4,052 *	15.8	43.6
081 Catholic	2	NR	NR	221	.9	2.4
123 Ch God (Ander)	3	NR	132	132	.5	1.4
127 Ch God (Cleve)	11	874	538	1,062 *	4.1	11.4
145 Ch God Prophcy	1	32	NR	38 *	.1	.4
151 L-D Saints	1	NR	NR	155	.6	1.7
165 Ch of Nazarene	2	224	79	256	1.0	2.8
167 Chs of Christ	2	45	58	62	.2	.7
193 Episcopal	1	NR	16	28	.1	.3
223 Free Will Bapt	10	505	NR	605 *	2.4	6.5
339 Pent Ch of God	5	117	NR	229	.9	2.5
349 Pent Holiness	1	210	105	252 *	1.0	2.7
355 Presb Ch (USA)	3	148	92	178 *	.7	1.9
360 Prim Bapt Chrch	1	NR	NR	NR	-	-
419 So Bapt Conv	2	353	90	423 *	1.6	4.6
449 Un Methodist	12	814	412	976 *	3.8	10.5
467 Wesleyan	1	56	77	625	2.4	6.7
WISCONSIN						
The State.....	5,181	1,080,891	536,733	3,241,659 *	60.4	100.0
ADAMS	**19**	**1,994**	**1,076**	**4,762 ***	**25.5**	**100.0**
053 Assemb of God	1	129	175	175	.9	3.7
056 Baha'i	0	1	NR	1	-	-
081 Catholic	2	NR	NR	1,812	9.7	38.1
145 Ch God Prophcy	1	42	NR	50 *	.3	1.0
151 L-D Saints	1	NR	NR	194	1.0	4.1
175 Congr Chr Chs	2	93	80	110 *	.6	2.3
207 E.L.C.A.	4	1,114	389	1,515	8.1	31.8
283 Luth—MO Synod	3	450	262	686	3.7	14.4
388 Reg Bapt Gen As	1	22	50	50 *	.3	1.0
419 So Bapt Conv	1	35	45	41 *	.2	.9
443 Un C of Christ	1	41	22	49 *	.3	1.0

Religious Group	Number of Churches, Synagogues, Mosques, or Temples	Number of Communicant, Confirmed, or Full Members	Number of Attendees	Total Adherents		
				Number of Adherents	% of Total Pop.	% of Total Adh.
449 Un Methodist	2	67	53	79 *	.4	1.7
ASHLAND	**33**	**3,889**	**2,068**	**11,655 ***	**69.1**	**100.0**
053 Assemb of God	3	102	110	211	1.3	1.8
056 Baha'i	0	7	NR	7	-	.1
057 Bapt Gen Conf	1	204	231	252 *	1.5	2.2
081 Catholic	8	NR	NR	6,157	36.5	52.8
151 L-D Saints	1	NR	NR	220	1.3	1.9
167 Chs of Christ	1	18	27	28	.2	.2
193 Episcopal	1	NR	41	125	.7	1.1
201 Evan Cov Ch	1	49	44	61 *	.4	.5
203 Evan Free Ch	1	69	125	125	.7	1.1
207 E.L.C.A.	2	776	249	1,103	6.5	9.5
283 Luth—MO Synod	5	1,696	677	2,176	12.9	18.7
355 Presb Ch (USA)	1	414	189	512 *	3.0	4.4
413 S.D.A.	1	52	NR	62	.4	.5
443 Un C of Christ	3	288	281	356 *	2.1	3.1
449 Un Methodist	3	181	74	224 *	1.3	1.9
469 WELS	1	33	20	36	.2	.3
BARRON	**80**	**13,743**	**6,373**	**28,153 ***	**62.6**	**100.0**
053 Assemb of God	3	186	238	347	.8	1.2
056 Baha'i	0	8	NR	8	-	-
057 Bapt Gen Conf	1	105	111	129 *	.3	.5
081 Catholic	9	NR	NR	8,852	19.7	31.4
089 Chr & Miss Al	2	36	NR	116	.3	.4
143 CG in Cr(Menn)	3	355	NR	435 *	1.0	1.5
151 L-D Saints	1	NR	NR	329	.7	1.2
157 Ch of Brethren	1	12	6	15 *	-	.1
165 Ch of Nazarene	1	0	4	8	-	-
173 Comm of Christ	1	32	NR	32	.1	.1
193 Episcopal	2	NR	60	111	.2	.4
201 Evan Cov Ch	1	46	47	56 *	.1	.2
203 Evan Free Ch	2	142	316	316	.7	1.1
207 E.L.C.A.	17	6,914	2,525	9,339	20.8	33.2
220 Free Lutheran	3	167	128	249	.6	.9
221 Free Methodist	1	9	40	40	.1	.1
263 Int Foursq Gos	1	223	326	326 *	.7	1.2
283 Luth—MO Synod	8	2,086	878	2,596	5.8	9.2
306 NT IndBapt&Rltd	3	342	NR	419 *	.9	1.5
323 Old Ord Amish	1	55	NR	67 *	.1	.2
331 OCA: Ter Diocs	1	80	NR	94	.2	.3
355 Presb Ch (USA)	1	350	161	429 *	1.0	1.5
356 Presb Ch Amer	1	0	22	22	-	.1
388 Reg Bapt Gen As	2	139	250	250 *	.6	.9
413 S.D.A.	1	128	NR	152	.3	.5
435 Unitarian-Univ	1	33	NR	40 *	.1	.1
449 Un Methodist	8	1,764	688	2,163 *	4.8	7.7
467 Wesleyan	2	277	426	912	2.0	3.2
469 WELS	2	254	147	301	.7	1.1
BAYFIELD	**32**	**2,231**	**1,191**	**5,858 ***	**39.0**	**100.0**
053 Assemb of God	2	115	94	208	1.4	3.6
056 Baha'i	0	1	NR	1	-	-
057 Bapt Gen Conf	3	301	259	371 *	2.5	6.3
081 Catholic	9	NR	NR	2,937	19.6	50.1
089 Chr & Miss Al	1	35	NR	85	.6	1.5
193 Episcopal	1	NR	20	42	.3	.7
207 E.L.C.A.	6	1,052	395	1,340	8.9	22.9
220 Free Lutheran	2	79	49	90	.6	1.5
283 Luth—MO Synod	1	108	52	127	.8	2.2
331 OCA: Ter Diocs	1	26	NR	31	.2	.5
355 Presb Ch (USA)	2	182	123	222 *	1.5	3.8
443 Un C of Christ	2	220	125	268 *	1.8	4.6
449 Un Methodist	2	112	74	136 *	.9	2.3
BROWN	**138**	**31,986**	**16,788**	**166,564 ***	**73.4**	**100.0**
019 Amer Bapt USA	1	349	75	437 *	.2	.3
053 Assemb of God	7	705	882	1,234	.5	.7
056 Baha'i	1	88	NR	88	-	.1
057 Bapt Gen Conf	2	428	450	577 *	.3	.3
081 Catholic	39	NR	NR	118,733	52.4	71.3

NR–Not Reported   *Total adherents estimated from known number of communicant, confirmed, full members.   - Represents a percentage less than 0.1.   Percentages may not total 100 due to rounding.

Table 4: Religious Congregations by County and Group: 2000

Religious Group	Number of Churches, Synagogues, Mosques, or Temples	Number of Communicant, Confirmed, or Full Members	Number of Attendees	Total Adherents: Number of Adherents	Total Adherents: % of Total Pop.	Total Adherents: % of Total Adh.
084 Calvary Chapel	1	NR	NR	NR	-	-
089 Chr & Miss Al	3	588	NR	788	.3	.5
097 Chr Chs&Chs Cr	1	142	NR	178 *	.1	.1
127 Ch God (Cleve)	1	49	56	61 *	-	-
151 L-D Saints	2	NR	NR	721	.3	.4
165 Ch of Nazarene	1	62	48	94	-	.1
167 Chs of Christ	2	90	92	100	-	.1
175 Congr Chr Chs	1	518	198	649 *	.3	.4
193 Episcopal	5	NR	472	2,416	1.1	1.5
201 Evan Cov Ch	1	37	61	61 *	-	-
203 Evan Free Ch	1	99	220	220	.1	.1
207 E.L.C.A.	14	10,072	3,739	14,045	6.2	8.4
226 Friends-USA	1	45	NR	56 *	-	-
263 Int Foursq Gos	2	48	94	94 *	-	.1
283 Luth—MO Synod	9	6,190	3,158	7,701	3.4	4.6
290 Metro Comm Ch	1	34	34	43 *	-	-
293 Morav Ch-North	2	409	NR	520	.2	.3
306 NT IndBapt&Rltd	1	114	NR	143 *	.1	.1
331 OCA: Ter Diocs	1	39	NR	110	-	.1
335 Orth Pres Ch	1	162	177	264	.1	.2
355 Presb Ch (USA)	6	1,265	578	1,585 *	.7	1.0
388 Reg Bapt Gen As	1	92	122	122 *	.1	.1
403 Salvation Army	1	154	136	1,094	.5	.7
413 S.D.A.	2	394	NR	469	.2	.3
419 So Bapt Conv	2	444	324	556 *	.2	.3
435 Unitarian-Univ	1	36	NR	45 *	-	-
443 Un C of Christ	3	1,053	422	1,319 *	.6	.8
449 Un Methodist	8	3,575	1,492	4,479 *	2.0	2.7
469 WELS	12	4,105	2,658	5,462	2.4	3.3
496 Jewish Est	0	NR	NR	500	.2	.3
499 Indep.Non-Char	1	600	1,300	1,600	.7	1.0
BUFFALO	**37**	**5,482**	**1,820**	**10,506 ***	**76.1**	**100.0**
057 Bapt Gen Conf	1	49	56	60 *	.4	.6
081 Catholic	4	NR	NR	3,660	26.5	34.8
167 Chs of Christ	1	30	48	45	.3	.4
201 Evan Cov Ch	1	20	16	25 *	.2	.2
207 E.L.C.A.	8	2,434	745	3,061	22.2	29.1
283 Luth—MO Synod	4	801	256	1,028	7.4	9.8
306 NT IndBapt&Rltd	2	228	NR	279 *	2.0	2.7
323 Old Ord Amish	4	220	NR	268 *	1.9	2.6
443 Un C of Christ	3	407	169	499 *	3.6	4.7
449 Un Methodist	4	447	165	547 *	4.0	5.2
469 WELS	5	846	365	1,034	7.5	9.8
BURNETT	**29**	**3,468**	**2,236**	**5,888 ***	**37.6**	**100.0**
053 Assemb of God	1	82	122	122	.8	2.1
056 Baha'i	0	1	NR	1	-	-
057 Bapt Gen Conf	3	346	423	433 *	2.8	7.4
081 Catholic	4	NR	NR	1,543	9.8	26.2
165 Ch of Nazarene	1	5	5	12	.1	.2
167 Chs of Christ	1	31	44	46	.3	.8
201 Evan Cov Ch	2	165	161	197 *	1.3	3.3
203 Evan Free Ch	1	41	65	65	.4	1.1
207 E.L.C.A.	8	2,086	965	2,595	16.6	44.1
283 Luth—MO Synod	2	186	85	221	1.4	3.8
449 Un Methodist	5	487	331	581 *	3.7	9.9
467 Wesleyan	1	38	35	72	.5	1.2
CALUMET	**33**	**5,296**	**2,685**	**20,727 ***	**51.0**	**100.0**
053 Assemb of God	2	67	94	114	.3	.6
056 Baha'i	0	2	NR	2	-	-
081 Catholic	12	NR	NR	13,848	34.1	66.8
084 Calvary Chapel	1	NR	NR	NR	-	-
089 Chr & Miss Al	1	139	NR	308	.8	1.5
193 Episcopal	1	NR	12	14	-	.1
283 Luth—MO Synod	6	2,025	1,209	2,568	6.3	12.4
323 Old Ord Amish	1	55	NR	70 *	.2	.3
443 Un C of Christ	4	1,273	435	1,628 *	4.0	7.9
449 Un Methodist	3	543	238	694 *	1.7	3.3
469 WELS	2	1,192	697	1,481	3.6	7.1

Religious Group	Number of Churches, Synagogues, Mosques, or Temples	Number of Communicant, Confirmed, or Full Members	Number of Attendees	Total Adherents: Number of Adherents	Total Adherents: % of Total Pop.	Total Adherents: % of Total Adh.
CHIPPEWA	**66**	**9,487**	**4,514**	**29,796 ***	**54.0**	**100.0**
053 Assemb of God	3	163	218	294	.5	1.0
056 Baha'i	0	13	NR	13	-	-
081 Catholic	13	NR	NR	16,595	30.1	55.7
089 Chr & Miss Al	1	26	NR	156	.3	.5
097 Chr Chs&Chs Cr	4	514	NR	638 *	1.2	2.1
157 Ch of Brethren	1	66	50	82 *	.1	.3
179 Consrv Bapt	2	NR	340	340	.6	1.1
193 Episcopal	2	NR	68	129	.2	.4
203 Evan Free Ch	1	70	173	173	.3	.6
207 E.L.C.A.	12	3,968	1,613	5,560	10.1	18.7
283 Luth—MO Synod	5	1,575	644	1,999	3.6	6.7
306 NT IndBapt&Rltd	2	228	NR	283 *	.5	.9
323 Old Ord Amish	1	55	NR	68 *	.1	.2
331 OCA: Ter Diocs	1	20	NR	38	.1	.1
355 Presb Ch (USA)	2	359	186	447 *	.8	1.5
413 S.D.A.	1	28	NR	33	.1	.1
443 Un C of Christ	2	227	106	282 *	.5	.9
449 Un Methodist	9	1,315	699	1,634 *	3.0	5.5
469 WELS	4	860	417	1,032	1.9	3.5
CLARK	**79**	**9,204**	**4,173**	**23,617 ***	**70.4**	**100.0**
053 Assemb of God	2	72	94	140	.4	.6
056 Baha'i	0	4	NR	4	-	-
081 Catholic	9	NR	NR	10,667	31.8	45.2
089 Chr & Miss Al	2	96	NR	192	.6	.8
179 Consrv Bapt	1	NR	522	522	1.6	2.2
193 Episcopal	1	NR	24	55	.2	.2
203 Evan Free Ch	2	92	220	220	.7	.9
207 E.L.C.A.	10	2,293	905	3,127	9.3	13.2
221 Free Methodist	1	31	53	53	.2	.2
283 Luth—MO Synod	9	2,363	1,035	3,170	9.4	13.4
286 E.PA Mennonite	1	54	NR	69 *	.2	.3
297 Mennonite;Other	1	65	NR	84 *	.3	.4
306 NT IndBapt&Rltd	2	228	NR	293 *	.9	1.2
322 Old Ord Menn Ch	4	594	NR	764 *	2.3	3.2
323 Old Ord Amish	9	485	NR	625 *	1.9	2.6
355 Presb Ch (USA)	1	120	45	154 *	.5	.7
431 Ukrainian Orth	1	NR	NR	30	.1	.1
443 Un C of Christ	7	989	486	1,272 *	3.8	5.4
449 Un Methodist	13	864	317	1,111 *	3.3	4.7
469 WELS	3	854	472	1,065	3.2	4.5
COLUMBIA	**73**	**15,656**	**6,746**	**35,558 ***	**67.8**	**100.0**
019 Amer Bapt USA	2	150	50	185 *	.4	.5
053 Assemb of God	4	284	375	591	1.1	1.7
056 Baha'i	0	16	NR	16	-	-
081 Catholic	9	NR	NR	13,980	26.6	39.3
151 L-D Saints	3	NR	NR	969	1.8	2.7
165 Ch of Nazarene	1	62	35	123	.2	.3
175 Congr Chr Chs	1	60	45	74 *	.1	.2
193 Episcopal	1	NR	76	78	.1	.2
203 Evan Free Ch	1	95	140	140	.3	.4
207 E.L.C.A.	9	3,791	1,327	5,165	9.8	14.5
283 Luth—MO Synod	3	2,452	914	3,295	6.3	9.3
306 NT IndBapt&Rltd	4	455	NR	561 *	1.1	1.6
355 Presb Ch (USA)	10	1,420	717	1,753 *	3.3	4.9
356 Presb Ch Amer	1	128	137	137	.3	.4
371 Ref Ch in Am	1	337	320	542	1.0	1.5
413 S.D.A.	2	339	NR	403	.8	1.1
443 Un C of Christ	2	541	130	667 *	1.3	1.9
449 Un Methodist	10	2,531	1,069	3,123 *	6.0	8.8
467 Wesleyan	1	39	96	145	.3	.4
469 WELS	8	2,956	1,315	3,611	6.9	10.2
CRAWFORD	**36**	**3,197**	**1,398**	**10,241 ***	**59.4**	**100.0**
053 Assemb of God	1	29	39	39	.2	.4
056 Baha'i	0	2	NR	2	-	-
081 Catholic	7	NR	NR	5,892	34.2	57.5
097 Chr Chs&Chs Cr	2	180	NR	222 *	1.3	2.2
151 L-D Saints	1	NR	NR	114	.7	1.1
173 Comm of Christ	1	89	NR	89	.5	.9

NR–Not Reported *Total adherents estimated from known number of communicant, confirmed, full members. - Represents a percentage less than 0.1. Percentages may not total 100 due to rounding.

Table 4: Religious Congregations by County and Group: 2000

Religious Group	Number of Churches, Synagogues, Mosques, or Temples	Number of Communicant, Confirmed, or Full Members	Number of Attendees	Total Adherents		
				Number of Adherents	% of Total Pop.	% of Total Adh.
193 Episcopal	1	NR	23	55	.3	.5
203 Evan Free Ch	1	70	181	181	1.0	1.8
207 E.L.C.A.	7	1,730	541	2,200	12.8	21.5
263 Int Foursq Gos	1	105	148	148 *	.9	1.4
306 NT IndBapt&Rltd	1	114	NR	140 *	.8	1.4
323 Old Ord Amish	1	55	NR	68 *	.4	.7
413 S.D.A.	1	23	NR	27	.2	.3
443 Un C of Christ	1	19	9	23 *	.1	.2
449 Un Methodist	8	668	338	822 *	4.8	8.0
467 Wesleyan	1	26	49	95	.6	.9
469 WELS	1	87	70	124	.7	1.2
DANE	**273**	**69,571**	**30,905**	**223,924 ***	**52.5**	**100.0**
019 Amer Bapt USA	2	919	518	1,114 *	.3	.5
034 Ant Orth of NA	1	62	NR	124	-	.1
053 Assemb of God	7	429	596	1,393	.3	.6
056 Baha'i	3	243	NR	243	.1	.1
057 Bapt Gen Conf	2	40	135	135 *	-	.1
076 Buddhism	11	NR	NR	NR	-	-
081 Catholic	39	NR	NR	119,246	28.0	53.3
089 Chr & Miss Al	3	199	NR	213	-	.1
097 Chr Chs&Chs Cr	2	236	NR	286 *	.1	.1
105 Christian Ref	2	346	336	420 *	.1	.2
123 Ch God (Ander)	1	NR	11	11	-	-
127 Ch God (Cleve)	1	20	25	25 *	-	-
151 L-D Saints	4	NR	NR	1,129	.3	.5
165 Ch of Nazarene	2	150	63	192	-	.1
167 Chs of Christ	3	127	150	179	-	.1
173 Comm of Christ	1	131	NR	131	-	.1
175 Congr Chr Chs	1	139	85	169 *	-	.1
179 Consrv Bapt	1	NR	200	200	-	.1
193 Episcopal	9	NR	789	1,849	.4	.8
201 Evan Cov Ch	1	120	100	146 *	-	.1
203 Evan Free Ch	6	1,094	2,003	2,003	.5	.9
207 E.L.C.A.	52	36,546	12,207	49,561	11.6	22.1
221 Free Methodist	2	70	50	75	-	-
223 Free Will Bapt	1	35	NR	42 *	-	-
226 Friends-USA	2	109	NR	132 *	-	.1
246 Greek Orthodox	1	NR	NR	1,251	.3	.6
252 Hindu	1	NR	NR	NR	-	-
262 Int Cou Comm Ch	1	190	NR	230 *	.1	.1
263 Int Foursq Gos	1	70	100	100 *	-	-
264 Int Chs of Crst	1	131	277	171	-	.1
267 Muslim Est	2	NR	312	1,218	.3	.5
283 Luth—MO Synod	11	3,475	1,757	4,473	1.0	2.0
288 Mennonite USA	1	63	58	76 *	-	-
293 Morav Ch-North	4	566	NR	706	.2	.3
306 NT IndBapt&Rltd	6	683	NR	828 *	.2	.4
313 N Am Bapt Conf	1	238	195	289 *	.1	.1
335 Orth Pres Ch	1	6	28	28	-	-
355 Presb Ch (USA)	10	3,456	1,601	4,190 *	1.0	1.9
356 Presb Ch Amer	2	94	120	127	-	.1
388 Reg Bapt Gen As	2	192	237	243 *	.1	.1
403 Salvation Army	1	118	65	743	.2	.3
413 S.D.A.	2	484	NR	576	.1	.3
416 Sikh	1	NR	NR	NR	-	-
419 So Bapt Conv	3	207	157	251 *	.1	.1
435 Unitarian-Univ	3	1,427	NR	1,730 *	.4	.8
443 Un C of Christ	15	4,655	1,964	5,645 *	1.3	2.5
449 Un Methodist	23	7,088	3,588	8,595 *	2.0	3.8
463 Vineyard	1	45	63	63 *	-	-
467 Wesleyan	1	0	85	200	-	.1
469 WELS	12	3,218	1,950	4,173	1.0	1.9
496 Jewish Est	5	NR	NR	4,500	1.1	2.0
499 Indep.Non-Char	2	2,150	1,080	4,500	1.1	2.0
DODGE	**118**	**27,734**	**14,537**	**54,526 ***	**63.5**	**100.0**
053 Assemb of God	2	199	224	473	.6	.9
056 Baha'i	0	29	NR	29	-	.1
057 Bapt Gen Conf	2	79	172	172 *	.2	.3
081 Catholic	17	NR	NR	16,757	19.5	30.7
089 Chr & Miss Al	2	166	NR	381	.4	.7
105 Christian Ref	8	1,746	905	2,139 *	2.5	3.9
151 L-D Saints	2	NR	NR	548	.6	1.0
167 Chs of Christ	2	54	77	86	.1	.2
193 Episcopal	3	NR	110	228	.3	.4
203 Evan Free Ch	3	234	485	485	.6	.9
207 E.L.C.A.	12	5,700	2,346	7,495	8.7	13.7
245 Greek Orth Vslp	1	105	NR	805	.9	1.5
283 Luth—MO Synod	13	5,390	2,643	6,605	7.7	12.1
306 NT IndBapt&Rltd	3	342	NR	419 *	.5	.8
307 Neth Ref Congr	1	33	NR	85	.1	.2
355 Presb Ch (USA)	4	778	289	953 *	1.1	1.7
369 Prot Ref Chs	1	100	NR	170	.2	.3
371 Ref Ch in Am	5	1,791	1,488	2,925	3.4	5.4
388 Reg Bapt Gen As	1	130	135	159 *	.2	.3
413 S.D.A.	1	25	NR	30	-	.1
443 Un C of Christ	5	828	283	1,015 *	1.2	1.9
449 Un Methodist	7	1,797	864	2,202 *	2.6	4.0
455 Un Ref Chs N.A.	1	48	NR	76	.1	.1
469 WELS	22	8,160	4,516	10,289	12.0	18.9
DOOR	**51**	**7,720**	**3,658**	**20,517 ***	**73.4**	**100.0**
053 Assemb of God	1	76	108	160	.6	.8
056 Baha'i	0	34	NR	34	.1	.2
057 Bapt Gen Conf	3	466	501	630 *	2.3	3.1
081 Catholic	10	NR	NR	10,266	36.7	50.0
151 L-D Saints	1	NR	NR	96	.3	.5
193 Episcopal	4	NR	183	349	1.2	1.7
203 Evan Free Ch	1	42	119	119	.4	.6
207 E.L.C.A.	8	2,360	1,051	3,015	10.8	14.7
226 Friends-USA	2	109	NR	130 *	.5	.6
283 Luth—MO Synod	2	409	182	531	1.9	2.6
293 Morav Ch-North	3	747	NR	868	3.1	4.2
306 NT IndBapt&Rltd	1	114	NR	136 *	.5	.7
331 OCA: Ter Diocs	1	23	NR	32	.1	.2
413 S.D.A.	2	54	NR	64	.2	.3
435 Unitarian-Univ	1	54	NR	65 *	.2	.3
443 Un C of Christ	1	390	125	466 *	1.7	2.3
449 Un Methodist	4	637	401	761 *	2.7	3.7
469 WELS	6	2,205	988	2,795	10.0	13.6
DOUGLAS	**53**	**6,882**	**3,806**	**22,240 ***	**51.4**	**100.0**
017 Amer Bapt Assn	1	100	NR	122 *	.3	.5
053 Assemb of God	2	206	291	400	.9	1.8
056 Baha'i	0	17	NR	17	-	.1
057 Bapt Gen Conf	3	520	348	632 *	1.5	2.8
081 Catholic	8	NR	NR	10,567	24.4	47.5
089 Chr & Miss Al	2	49	NR	56	.1	.3
167 Chs of Christ	1	17	20	31	.1	.1
181 Consrv Congr	1	71	82	86 *	.2	.4
193 Episcopal	1	NR	62	130	.3	.6
201 Evan Cov Ch	3	213	527	527 *	1.2	2.4
203 Evan Free Ch	3	177	298	298	.7	1.3
207 E.L.C.A.	9	3,354	1,183	4,499	10.4	20.2
220 Free Lutheran	1	16	25	36	.1	.2
283 Luth—MO Synod	3	581	220	758	1.8	3.4
306 NT IndBapt&Rltd	1	114	NR	139 *	.3	.6
355 Presb Ch (USA)	8	645	325	785 *	1.8	3.5
356 Presb Ch Amer	1	0	0	0	-	-
403 Salvation Army	1	118	66	1,462	3.4	6.6
413 S.D.A.	1	62	NR	74	.2	.3
419 So Bapt Conv	1	15	45	18 *	-	.1
449 Un Methodist	1	397	165	483 *	1.1	2.2
467 Wesleyan	1	210	149	1,120	2.6	5.0
DUNN	**61**	**11,682**	**4,240**	**20,128 ***	**50.5**	**100.0**
053 Assemb of God	1	65	84	154	.4	.8
056 Baha'i	0	14	NR	14	-	.1
081 Catholic	5	NR	NR	4,612	11.6	22.9
084 Calvary Chapel	1	NR	NR	NR	-	-
089 Chr & Miss Al	2	443	NR	691	1.7	3.4
123 Ch God (Ander)	1	NR	0	0	-	-
151 L-D Saints	1	NR	NR	162	.4	.8
165 Ch of Nazarene	3	174	163	305	.8	1.5
193 Episcopal	1	NR	48	107	.3	.5

NR–Not Reported *Total adherents estimated from known number of communicant, confirmed, full members. - Represents a percentage less than 0.1. Percentages may not total 100 due to rounding.

Table 4: Religious Congregations by County and Group: 2000

Religious Group	Number of Churches, Synagogues, Mosques, or Temples	Number of Communicant, Confirmed, or Full Members	Number of Attendees	Total Adherents: Number of Adherents	Total Adherents: % of Total Pop.	Total Adherents: % of Total Adh.
203 Evan Free Ch	1	40	100	100	.3	.5
207 E.L.C.A.	17	6,795	1,986	8,902	22.3	44.2
220 Free Lutheran	1	50	38	60	.2	.3
226 Friends-USA	1	45	NR	55 *	.1	.3
283 Luth—MO Synod	4	512	213	703	1.8	3.5
306 NT IndBapt&Rltd	1	114	NR	138 *	.3	.7
388 Reg Bapt Gen As	2	125	158	162 *	.4	.8
413 S.D.A.	1	60	NR	71	.2	.4
435 Unitarian-Univ	1	41	NR	50 *	.1	.2
443 Un C of Christ	1	463	195	561 *	1.4	2.8
449 Un Methodist	11	1,504	668	1,824 *	4.6	9.1
469 WELS	5	1,237	587	1,457	3.7	7.2
EAU CLAIRE	**87**	**25,047**	**12,082**	**54,125 ***	**58.1**	**100.0**
019 Amer Bapt USA	1	267	75	325 *	.3	.6
053 Assemb of God	4	542	753	1,134	1.2	2.1
056 Baha'i	1	51	NR	51	.1	.1
057 Bapt Gen Conf	3	485	1,436	1,532 *	1.6	2.8
076 Buddhism	1	NR	NR	NR	-	-
081 Catholic	10	NR	NR	18,175	19.5	33.6
089 Chr & Miss Al	1	310	NR	310	.3	.6
097 Chr Chs&Chs Cr	1	178	NR	216 *	.2	.4
151 L-D Saints	1	NR	NR	487	.5	.9
165 Ch of Nazarene	1	45	31	57	.1	.1
167 Chs of Christ	2	74	100	131	.1	.2
173 Comm of Christ	1	53	NR	53	.1	.1
179 Consrv Bapt	1	NR	211	211	.2	.4
193 Episcopal	2	NR	214	560	.6	1.0
203 Evan Free Ch	1	46	130	130	.1	.2
207 E.L.C.A.	13	11,686	4,125	15,364	16.5	28.4
267 Muslim Est	2	NR	202	576	.6	1.1
283 Luth—MO Synod	14	6,052	2,600	7,800	8.4	14.4
297 Mennonite;Other	1	72	NR	88 *	.1	.2
323 Old Ord Amish	6	330	NR	402 *	.4	.7
355 Presb Ch (USA)	2	404	128	491 *	.5	.9
403 Salvation Army	1	75	22	129	.1	.2
413 S.D.A.	1	95	NR	113	.1	.2
419 So Bapt Conv	1	55	46	67 *	.1	.1
435 Unitarian-Univ	1	108	NR	131 *	.1	.2
443 Un C of Christ	3	1,063	355	1,292 *	1.4	2.4
449 Un Methodist	8	2,405	1,029	2,922 *	3.1	5.4
467 Wesleyan	1	209	292	786	.8	1.5
469 WELS	1	442	333	442	.5	.8
496 Jewish Est	1	NR	NR	150	.2	.3
FLORENCE	**10**	**379**	**291**	**1,750 ***	**34.4**	**100.0**
057 Bapt Gen Conf	1	57	98	98 *	1.9	5.6
081 Catholic	3	NR	NR	1,191	23.4	68.1
207 E.L.C.A.	1	60	40	91	1.8	5.2
339 Pent Ch of God	2	42	NR	121	2.4	6.9
355 Presb Ch (USA)	1	65	58	78 *	1.5	4.5
469 WELS	2	155	95	171	3.4	9.8
FOND DU LAC	**98**	**21,105**	**11,224**	**65,904 ***	**67.7**	**100.0**
019 Amer Bapt USA	3	314	137	386 *	.4	.6
053 Assemb of God	3	283	359	632	.6	1.0
056 Baha'i	1	63	NR	63	.1	.1
057 Bapt Gen Conf	1	278	585	585 *	.6	.9
081 Catholic	29	NR	NR	34,970	35.9	53.1
089 Chr & Miss Al	1	20	NR	66	.1	.1
127 Ch God (Cleve)	1	38	34	47 *	-	.1
151 L-D Saints	2	NR	NR	653	.7	1.0
165 Ch of Nazarene	1	6	4	8	-	-
167 Chs of Christ	1	39	35	51	.1	.1
193 Episcopal	2	NR	248	567	.6	.9
203 Evan Free Ch	2	130	305	305	.3	.5
207 E.L.C.A.	8	4,356	1,722	5,516	5.7	8.4
246 Greek Orthodox	1	NR	NR	393	.4	.6
283 Luth—MO Synod	4	2,356	1,051	3,148	3.2	4.8
306 NT IndBapt&Rltd	1	114	NR	140 *	.1	.2
323 Old Ord Amish	1	55	NR	68 *	.1	.1
355 Presb Ch (USA)	1	607	204	747 *	.8	1.1
371 Ref Ch in Am	2	760	653	1,305	1.3	2.0

Religious Group	Number of Churches, Synagogues, Mosques, or Temples	Number of Communicant, Confirmed, or Full Members	Number of Attendees	Total Adherents: Number of Adherents	Total Adherents: % of Total Pop.	Total Adherents: % of Total Adh.
388 Reg Bapt Gen As	1	50	55	62 *	.1	.1
403 Salvation Army	1	80	72	1,636	1.7	2.5
435 Unitarian-Univ	1	38	NR	47 *	-	.1
443 Un C of Christ	8	3,350	1,049	4,122 *	4.2	6.3
449 Un Methodist	10	2,066	1,042	2,543 *	2.6	3.9
469 WELS	12	6,102	3,669	7,844	8.1	11.9
FOREST	**20**	**1,367**	**886**	**4,390 ***	**43.8**	**100.0**
056 Baha'i	0	2	NR	2	-	-
081 Catholic	6	NR	NR	2,648	26.4	60.3
127 Ch God (Cleve)	1	128	57	158 *	1.6	3.6
165 Ch of Nazarene	1	26	14	58	.6	1.3
167 Chs of Christ	1	22	27	37	.4	.8
181 Consrv Congr	1	63	99	78 *	.8	1.8
283 Luth—MO Synod	2	354	145	453	4.5	10.3
355 Presb Ch (USA)	2	99	58	122 *	1.2	2.8
388 Reg Bapt Gen As	1	92	122	122 *	1.2	2.8
449 Un Methodist	2	171	147	210 *	2.1	4.8
469 WELS	3	410	217	502	5.0	11.4
GRANT	**95**	**9,175**	**3,839**	**39,609 ***	**79.9**	**100.0**
032 Amish; other	1	89	NR	108 *	.2	.3
053 Assemb of God	2	75	99	122	.2	.3
056 Baha'i	0	6	NR	6	-	-
081 Catholic	20	NR	NR	27,907	56.3	70.5
089 Chr & Miss Al	1	23	NR	84	.2	.2
151 L-D Saints	1	NR	NR	146	.3	.4
167 Chs of Christ	1	17	18	22	-	.1
173 Comm of Christ	1	48	NR	48	.1	.1
175 Congr Chr Chs	3	258	170	312 *	.6	.8
179 Consrv Bapt	1	NR	95	95	.2	.2
181 Consrv Congr	1	95	20	115 *	.2	.3
193 Episcopal	1	NR	38	54	.1	.1
203 Evan Free Ch	2	115	314	314	.6	.8
207 E.L.C.A.	10	2,998	1,110	3,730	7.5	9.4
220 Free Lutheran	1	65	12	84	.2	.2
221 Free Methodist	2	155	184	185	.4	.5
283 Luth—MO Synod	3	217	86	246	.5	.6
306 NT IndBapt&Rltd	3	342	NR	414 *	.8	1.0
322 Old Ord Menn Ch	2	35	NR	43 *	.1	.1
323 Old Ord Amish	4	220	NR	268 *	.5	.7
355 Presb Ch (USA)	3	276	110	333 *	.7	.8
363 Primitive Meth	4	228	NR	243	.5	.6
413 S.D.A.	1	63	NR	75	.2	.2
419 So Bapt Conv	1	19	35	23 *	-	.1
443 Un C of Christ	6	697	255	844 *	1.7	2.1
449 Un Methodist	18	2,973	1,198	3,599 *	7.3	9.1
469 WELS	2	161	95	189	.4	.5
GREEN	**43**	**9,389**	**3,475**	**16,620 ***	**49.4**	**100.0**
019 Amer Bapt USA	1	110	40	137 *	.4	.8
056 Baha'i	0	10	NR	10	-	.1
081 Catholic	4	NR	NR	4,303	12.8	25.9
151 L-D Saints	1	NR	NR	76	.2	.5
165 Ch of Nazarene	2	43	56	157	.5	.9
167 Chs of Christ	1	45	60	60	.2	.4
193 Episcopal	1	NR	11	17	.1	.1
203 Evan Free Ch	1	53	70	70	.2	.4
207 E.L.C.A.	8	2,692	774	3,587	10.7	21.6
220 Free Lutheran	1	127	57	175	.5	1.1
297 Mennonite;Other	1	15	NR	19 *	.1	.1
306 NT IndBapt&Rltd	3	342	NR	427 *	1.3	2.6
323 Old Ord Amish	2	110	NR	138 *	.4	.8
355 Presb Ch (USA)	1	215	100	269 *	.8	1.6
419 So Bapt Conv	0	4	4	5 *	-	-
443 Un C of Christ	6	3,391	1,177	4,237 *	12.6	25.5
449 Un Methodist	7	1,919	967	2,398 *	7.1	14.4
469 WELS	2	313	159	385	1.1	2.3
496 Jewish Est	1	NR	NR	150	.4	.9
GREEN LAKE	**37**	**6,542**	**3,263**	**15,487 ***	**81.1**	**100.0**
019 Amer Bapt USA	2	643	192	780 *	4.1	5.0

NR–Not Reported *Total adherents estimated from known number of communicant, confirmed, full members. - Represents a percentage less than 0.1. Percentages may not total 100 due to rounding.

Table 4: Religious Congregations by County and Group: 2000

Religious Group	Number of Churches, Synagogues, Mosques, or Temples	Number of Communicant, Confirmed, or Full Members	Number of Attendees	Total Adherents: Number of Adherents	Total Adherents: % of Total Pop.	Total Adherents: % of Total Adh.
053 Assemb of God	1	58	75	100	.5	.6
056 Baha'i	0	7	NR	7	-	-
081 Catholic	7	NR	NR	7,303	38.2	47.2
175 Congr Chr Chs	1	40	20	49 *	.3	.3
203 Evan Free Ch	1	56	174	174	.9	1.1
207 E.L.C.A.	1	791	355	1,041	5.4	6.7
283 Luth—MO Synod	2	952	596	1,171	6.1	7.6
306 NT IndBapt&Rltd	1	114	NR	138 *	.7	.9
323 Old Ord Amish	5	275	NR	335 *	1.8	2.2
443 Un C of Christ	2	244	189	296 *	1.5	1.9
449 Un Methodist	5	843	365	1,023 *	5.4	6.6
469 WELS	9	2,519	1,297	3,070	16.1	19.8
IOWA	**40**	**4,071**	**1,542**	**12,738 ***	**55.9**	**100.0**
056 Baha'i	0	2	NR	2	-	-
076 Buddhism	1	NR	NR	NR	-	-
081 Catholic	9	NR	NR	7,433	32.6	58.4
181 Consrv Congr	1	86	30	108 *	.5	.8
193 Episcopal	1	NR	25	45	.2	.4
203 Evan Free Ch	1	27	60	60	.3	.5
207 E.L.C.A.	8	1,873	680	2,483	10.9	19.5
226 Friends-USA	1	45	NR	57 *	.3	.4
283 Luth—MO Synod	1	116	45	147	.6	1.2
306 NT IndBapt&Rltd	1	114	NR	143 *	.6	1.1
355 Presb Ch (USA)	1	70	51	88 *	.4	.7
363 Primitive Meth	1	57	NR	61	.3	.5
443 Un C of Christ	3	547	172	687 *	3.0	5.4
449 Un Methodist	11	1,134	479	1,424 *	6.3	11.2
IRON	**12**	**499**	**265**	**2,546 ***	**37.1**	**100.0**
081 Catholic	5	NR	NR	1,930	28.1	75.8
165 Ch of Nazarene	1	27	34	47	.7	1.8
283 Luth—MO Synod	1	126	50	171	2.5	6.7
355 Presb Ch (USA)	2	71	33	82 *	1.2	3.2
449 Un Methodist	1	100	62	116 *	1.7	4.6
469 WELS	2	175	86	200	2.9	7.9
JACKSON	**34**	**5,351**	**2,273**	**8,601 ***	**45.0**	**100.0**
053 Assemb of God	2	150	192	305	1.6	3.5
056 Baha'i	0	2	NR	2	-	-
057 Bapt Gen Conf	1	23	81	81 *	.4	.9
081 Catholic	3	NR	NR	1,615	8.5	18.8
089 Chr & Miss Al	1	24	NR	76	.4	.9
097 Chr Chs&Chs Cr	1	51	NR	62 *	.3	.7
167 Chs of Christ	1	70	52	102	.5	1.2
203 Evan Free Ch	1	36	90	90	.5	1.0
207 E.L.C.A.	11	3,125	1,126	3,992	20.9	46.4
283 Luth—MO Synod	3	442	174	519	2.7	6.0
323 Old Ord Amish	1	55	NR	67 *	.4	.8
355 Presb Ch (USA)	1	132	30	161 *	.8	1.9
443 Un C of Christ	1	119	52	146 *	.8	1.7
449 Un Methodist	6	1,084	460	1,327 *	6.9	15.4
469 WELS	1	38	16	56	.3	.7
JEFFERSON	**80**	**26,984**	**12,243**	**56,987 ***	**77.0**	**100.0**
053 Assemb of God	2	135	185	263	.4	.5
056 Baha'i	0	31	NR	31	-	.1
081 Catholic	10	NR	NR	21,518	29.1	37.8
151 L-D Saints	1	NR	NR	223	.3	.4
193 Episcopal	2	NR	131	285	.4	.5
207 E.L.C.A.	10	5,913	2,052	7,885	10.7	13.8
263 Int Foursq Gos	1	30	50	50 *	.1	.1
283 Luth—MO Synod	6	1,301	747	1,725	2.3	3.0
293 Morav Ch-North	4	1,312	NR	1,595	2.2	2.8
306 NT IndBapt&Rltd	5	569	NR	703 *	.9	1.2
313 N Am Bapt Conf	1	124	85	153 *	.2	.3
355 Presb Ch (USA)	1	36	20	44 *	.1	.1
413 S.D.A.	2	88	NR	104	.1	.2
419 So Bapt Conv	1	101	55	125 *	.2	.2
443 Un C of Christ	4	1,441	543	1,781 *	2.4	3.1
449 Un Methodist	13	2,511	969	3,104 *	4.2	5.4
469 WELS	16	13,017	6,656	16,648	22.5	29.2
499 Indep.Non-Char	1	375	750	750	1.0	1.3
JUNEAU	**43**	**5,891**	**2,505**	**13,566 ***	**55.8**	**100.0**
019 Amer Bapt USA	1	98	20	121 *	.5	.9
053 Assemb of God	1	58	80	150	.6	1.1
056 Baha'i	0	8	NR	8	-	.1
057 Bapt Gen Conf	1	92	84	113 *	.5	.8
081 Catholic	9	NR	NR	5,909	24.3	43.6
145 Ch God Prophcy	1	42	NR	52 *	.2	.4
165 Ch of Nazarene	1	90	46	90	.4	.7
193 Episcopal	1	NR	11	27	.1	.2
207 E.L.C.A.	8	2,114	772	2,845	11.7	21.0
283 Luth—MO Synod	3	430	220	555	2.3	4.1
306 NT IndBapt&Rltd	4	455	NR	561 *	2.3	4.1
355 Presb Ch (USA)	1	63	30	78 *	.3	.6
449 Un Methodist	6	882	510	1,087 *	4.5	8.0
467 Wesleyan	1	55	84	84	.3	.6
469 WELS	5	1,504	648	1,886	7.8	13.9
KENOSHA	**92**	**17,671**	**10,243**	**72,087 ***	**48.2**	**100.0**
019 Amer Bapt USA	3	331	279	419 *	.3	.6
053 Assemb of God	3	1,175	1,600	2,136	1.4	3.0
056 Baha'i	1	47	NR	47	-	.1
057 Bapt Gen Conf	1	140	140	177 *	.1	.2
081 Catholic	15	NR	NR	44,311	29.6	61.5
097 Chr Chs&Chs Cr	1	400	NR	507 *	.3	.7
105 Christian Ref	1	210	160	266 *	.2	.4
123 Ch God (Ander)	1	NR	31	31	-	-
127 Ch God (Cleve)	1	55	58	70 *	-	.1
151 L-D Saints	1	NR	NR	380	.3	.5
165 Ch of Nazarene	1	61	0	61	-	.1
167 Chs of Christ	3	186	194	267	.2	.4
175 Congr Chr Chs	2	378	178	479 *	.3	.7
193 Episcopal	2	NR	175	621	.4	.9
203 Evan Free Ch	1	280	550	550	.4	.8
207 E.L.C.A.	9	5,939	2,115	8,346	5.6	11.6
263 Int Foursq Gos	2	245	285	310 *	.2	.4
267 Muslim Est	2	NR	612	2,391	1.6	3.3
283 Luth—MO Synod	3	565	218	701	.5	1.0
291 Missionary Ch	1	99	251	251	.2	.3
306 NT IndBapt&Rltd	1	114	NR	144 *	.1	.2
313 N Am Bapt Conf	3	790	400	1,000 *	.7	1.4
331 OCA: Ter Diocs	1	45	NR	93	.1	.1
339 Pent Ch of God	1	20	NR	120	.1	.2
355 Presb Ch (USA)	1	239	100	303 *	.2	.4
388 Reg Bapt Gen As	2	229	145	167 *	.1	.2
403 Salvation Army	1	121	69	300	.2	.4
413 S.D.A.	2	115	NR	136	.1	.2
419 So Bapt Conv	5	961	263	1,217 *	.8	1.7
435 Unitarian-Univ	1	90	NR	114 *	.1	.2
443 Un C of Christ	2	400	171	507 *	.3	.7
449 Un Methodist	10	1,710	833	2,165 *	1.4	3.0
469 WELS	7	2,726	1,416	3,200	2.1	4.4
496 Jewish Est	1	NR	NR	300	.2	.4
KEWAUNEE	**22**	**3,230**	**1,791**	**15,702 ***	**77.8**	**100.0**
053 Assemb of God	1	50	67	91	.5	.6
056 Baha'i	0	6	NR	6	-	-
081 Catholic	10	NR	NR	11,590	57.4	73.8
175 Congr Chr Chs	1	202	120	250 *	1.2	1.6
193 Episcopal	1	NR	24	36	.2	.2
207 E.L.C.A.	1	226	137	316	1.6	2.0
283 Luth—MO Synod	3	980	524	1,230	6.1	7.8
449 Un Methodist	2	154	80	191 *	.9	1.2
469 WELS	3	1,612	839	1,992	9.9	12.7
LA CROSSE	**91**	**27,128**	**11,687**	**68,712 ***	**64.1**	**100.0**
019 Amer Bapt USA	1	67	45	82 *	.1	.1
034 Ant Orth of NA	1	43	NR	86	.1	.1
053 Assemb of God	2	238	293	293	.3	.4
056 Baha'i	0	28	NR	28	-	-
076 Buddhism	1	NR	NR	NR	-	-

NR–Not Reported *Total adherents estimated from known number of communicant, confirmed, full members. - Represents a percentage less than 0.1. Percentages may not total 100 due to rounding.

Table 4: Religious Congregations by County and Group: 2000

Religious Group	Number of Churches, Synagogues, Mosques, or Temples	Number of Communicant, Confirmed, or Full Members	Number of Attendees	Total Adherents: Number of Adherents	Total Adherents: % of Total Pop.	Total Adherents: % of Total Adh.
081 Catholic	12	NR	NR	31,551	29.5	45.9
089 Chr & Miss Al	1	239	NR	247	.2	.4
097 Chr Chs&Chs Cr	2	315	NR	384 *	.4	.6
151 L-D Saints	2	NR	NR	511	.5	.7
165 Ch of Nazarene	1	19	17	42	-	.1
167 Chs of Christ	1	55	75	95	.1	.1
173 Comm of Christ	1	76	NR	76	.1	.1
193 Episcopal	1	NR	131	303	.3	.4
203 Evan Free Ch	4	688	1,525	1,525	1.4	2.2
207 E.L.C.A.	18	12,827	4,099	17,327	16.2	25.2
220 Free Lutheran	1	81	114	117	.1	.2
263 Int Foursq Gos	1	9	20	20 *	-	-
283 Luth—MO Synod	3	713	416	965	.9	1.4
306 NT IndBapt&Rltd	4	455	NR	554 *	.5	.8
313 N Am Bapt Conf	1	57	44	69 *	.1	.1
355 Presb Ch (USA)	6	1,249	510	1,522 *	1.4	2.2
356 Presb Ch Amer	1	105	150	150	.1	.2
403 Salvation Army	1	123	57	251	.2	.4
413 S.D.A.	2	120	NR	143	.1	.2
419 So Bapt Conv	2	20	40	24 *	-	-
435 Unitarian-Univ	1	49	NR	60 *	.1	.1
443 Un C of Christ	3	1,216	309	1,482 *	1.4	2.2
449 Un Methodist	5	1,902	802	2,318 *	2.2	3.4
467 Wesleyan	1	152	216	375	.4	.5
469 WELS	10	6,282	2,824	8,012	7.5	11.7
496 Jewish Est	1	NR	NR	100	.1	.1
LAFAYETTE	**39**	**4,190**	**1,457**	**12,358 ***	**76.6**	**100.0**
056 Baha'i	0	1	NR	1	-	-
057 Bapt Gen Conf	1	125	130	156 *	1.0	1.3
081 Catholic	13	NR	NR	7,172	44.4	58.0
203 Evan Free Ch	2	91	175	175	1.1	1.4
207 E.L.C.A.	9	2,289	640	2,791	17.3	22.6
363 Primitive Meth	3	171	NR	182	1.1	1.5
443 Un C of Christ	2	296	119	368 *	2.3	3.0
449 Un Methodist	9	1,217	393	1,513 *	9.4	12.2
LANGLADE	**33**	**4,442**	**2,703**	**14,336 ***	**69.1**	**100.0**
019 Amer Bapt USA	1	60	40	73 *	.4	.5
053 Assemb of God	2	99	126	190	.9	1.3
056 Baha'i	0	7	NR	7	-	-
081 Catholic	8	NR	NR	8,523	41.1	59.5
127 Ch God (Cleve)	1	148	155	181 *	.9	1.3
165 Ch of Nazarene	1	31	23	44	.2	.3
167 Chs of Christ	2	37	45	54	.3	.4
193 Episcopal	1	NR	21	34	.2	.2
203 Evan Free Ch	1	81	150	150	.7	1.0
207 E.L.C.A.	3	765	303	1,009	4.9	7.0
283 Luth—MO Synod	6	2,197	1,324	2,809	13.5	19.6
306 NT IndBapt&Rltd	1	114	NR	139 *	.7	1.0
355 Presb Ch (USA)	1	25	22	31 *	.1	.2
443 Un C of Christ	3	374	201	456 *	2.2	3.2
449 Un Methodist	1	344	182	420 *	2.0	2.9
469 WELS	1	160	111	216	1.0	1.5
LINCOLN	**40**	**10,518**	**4,313**	**20,247 ***	**68.3**	**100.0**
053 Assemb of God	2	132	150	269	.9	1.3
056 Baha'i	0	6	NR	6	-	-
057 Bapt Gen Conf	1	59	40	72 *	.2	.4
081 Catholic	4	NR	NR	6,836	23.1	33.8
193 Episcopal	2	NR	28	51	.2	.3
201 Evan Cov Ch	1	28	21	34 *	.1	.2
207 E.L.C.A.	4	2,249	720	3,008	10.1	14.9
283 Luth—MO Synod	8	4,917	1,901	6,033	20.4	29.8
306 NT IndBapt&Rltd	1	114	NR	139 *	.5	.7
355 Presb Ch (USA)	2	143	70	175 *	.6	.9
356 Presb Ch Amer	1	134	130	213	.7	1.1
388 Reg Bapt Gen As	1	25	40	40 *	.1	.2
413 S.D.A.	2	45	NR	53	.2	.3
443 Un C of Christ	3	1,280	466	1,565 *	5.3	7.7
449 Un Methodist	3	482	210	590 *	2.0	2.9
463 Vineyard	1	185	150	226 *	.8	1.1
469 WELS	4	719	387	937	3.2	4.6

Religious Group	Number of Churches, Synagogues, Mosques, or Temples	Number of Communicant, Confirmed, or Full Members	Number of Attendees	Total Adherents: Number of Adherents	Total Adherents: % of Total Pop.	Total Adherents: % of Total Adh.
MANITOWOC	**82**	**18,072**	**9,068**	**67,487 ***	**81.4**	**100.0**
019 Amer Bapt USA	1	36	43	44 *	.1	.1
053 Assemb of God	2	161	224	306	.4	.5
056 Baha'i	0	22	NR	22	-	-
081 Catholic	26	NR	NR	43,149	52.1	63.9
084 Calvary Chapel	1	NR	NR	NR	-	-
089 Chr & Miss Al	2	317	NR	388	.5	.6
151 L-D Saints	1	NR	NR	217	.3	.3
167 Chs of Christ	1	28	40	49	.1	.1
193 Episcopal	1	NR	66	128	.2	.2
203 Evan Free Ch	2	297	580	580	.7	.9
207 E.L.C.A.	5	3,146	1,187	4,156	5.0	6.2
226 Friends-USA	1	45	NR	56 *	.1	.1
283 Luth—MO Synod	2	1,063	415	1,350	1.6	2.0
313 N Am Bapt Conf	1	36	45	44 *	.1	.1
355 Presb Ch (USA)	3	636	254	784 *	.9	1.2
373 Ref Ch in U.S.	1	265	NR	310	.4	.5
388 Reg Bapt Gen As	1	21	28	28 *	-	-
403 Salvation Army	1	89	67	940	1.1	1.4
419 So Bapt Conv	1	81	115	100 *	.1	.1
443 Un C of Christ	6	2,576	1,208	3,178 *	3.8	4.7
449 Un Methodist	6	995	506	1,229 *	1.5	1.8
469 WELS	17	8,258	4,290	10,429	12.6	15.5
MARATHON	**127**	**31,630**	**14,717**	**89,115 ***	**70.8**	**100.0**
032 Amish; other	2	119	NR	150 *	.1	.2
053 Assemb of God	5	582	678	1,518	1.2	1.7
056 Baha'i	0	31	NR	31	-	-
057 Bapt Gen Conf	2	242	459	459 *	.4	.5
076 Buddhism	1	NR	NR	NR	-	-
081 Catholic	25	NR	NR	46,160	36.7	51.8
084 Calvary Chapel	1	NR	NR	NR	-	-
089 Chr & Miss Al	2	1,147	NR	1,332	1.1	1.5
127 Ch God (Cleve)	1	48	0	60 *	-	.1
151 L-D Saints	2	NR	NR	435	.3	.5
165 Ch of Nazarene	1	53	28	53	-	.1
167 Chs of Christ	1	50	70	70	.1	.1
193 Episcopal	2	NR	125	301	.2	.3
203 Evan Free Ch	2	145	440	440	.3	.5
207 E.L.C.A.	20	10,433	3,771	13,721	10.9	15.4
263 Int Foursq Gos	1	182	37	228 *	.2	.3
283 Luth—MO Synod	16	8,657	4,594	10,936	8.7	12.3
297 Mennonite;Other	4	173	NR	217 *	.2	.2
323 Old Ord Amish	2	110	NR	138 *	.1	.2
355 Presb Ch (USA)	2	1,118	490	1,401 *	1.1	1.6
371 Ref Ch in Am	1	317	213	426	.3	.5
403 Salvation Army	1	102	31	465	.4	.5
413 S.D.A.	2	101	NR	120	.1	.1
419 So Bapt Conv	2	127	70	159 *	.1	.2
435 Unitarian-Univ	1	213	NR	267 *	.2	.3
443 Un C of Christ	5	2,230	722	2,795 *	2.2	3.1
449 Un Methodist	5	1,680	655	2,104 *	1.7	2.4
469 WELS	16	3,390	1,759	4,254	3.4	4.8
496 Jewish Est	1	NR	NR	300	.2	.3
499 Indep.Non-Char	1	380	575	575	.5	.6
MARINETTE	**59**	**8,424**	**4,120**	**27,947 ***	**64.4**	**100.0**
053 Assemb of God	5	393	486	698	1.6	2.5
056 Baha'i	0	2	NR	2	-	-
057 Bapt Gen Conf	2	268	432	447 *	1.0	1.6
081 Catholic	11	NR	NR	16,702	38.5	59.8
151 L-D Saints	1	NR	NR	137	.3	.5
165 Ch of Nazarene	1	13	12	51	.1	.2
167 Chs of Christ	1	5	5	5	-	-
193 Episcopal	1	NR	89	170	.4	.6
201 Evan Cov Ch	2	110	114	162 *	.4	.6
207 E.L.C.A.	7	2,336	835	3,035	7.0	10.9
263 Int Foursq Gos	1	44	31	53 *	.1	.2
283 Luth—MO Synod	1	182	125	239	.6	.9
306 NT IndBapt&Rltd	5	569	NR	686 *	1.6	2.5
313 N Am Bapt Conf	1	118	80	142 *	.3	.5
355 Presb Ch (USA)	6	626	347	759 *	1.7	2.7
403 Salvation Army	1	71	19	129	.3	.5

NR–Not Reported *Total adherents estimated from known number of communicant, confirmed, full members. - Represents a percentage less than 0.1. Percentages may not total 100 due to rounding.

Table 4: Religious Congregations by County and Group: 2000

Religious Group	Number of Churches, Synagogues, Mosques, or Temples	Number of Communicant, Confirmed, or Full Members	Number of Attendees	Total Adherents		
				Number of Adherents	% of Total Pop.	% of Total Adh.
413 S.D.A.	1	53	NR	63	.1	.2
443 Un C of Christ	1	122	54	147 *	.3	.5
449 Un Methodist	5	913	336	1,101 *	2.5	3.9
469 WELS	6	2,599	1,155	3,219	7.4	11.5
MARQUETTE	**28**	**3,663**	**1,777**	**7,849 ***	**49.6**	**100.0**
056 Baha'i	0	2	NR	2	-	-
081 Catholic	5	NR	NR	3,391	21.4	43.2
203 Evan Free Ch	1	69	125	125	.8	1.6
207 E.L.C.A.	3	430	160	508	3.2	6.5
283 Luth—MO Synod	7	1,381	573	1,706	10.8	21.7
355 Presb Ch (USA)	3	241	121	286 *	1.8	3.6
413 S.D.A.	1	61	NR	73	.5	.9
443 Un C of Christ	1	76	33	90 *	.6	1.1
449 Un Methodist	5	685	395	809 *	5.1	10.3
469 WELS	2	718	370	859	5.4	10.9
MENOMINEE	**5**	**100**	**73**	**3,173**	**69.6**	**100.0**
053 Assemb of God	1	75	48	100	2.2	3.2
056 Baha'i	0	1	NR	1	-	-
081 Catholic	3	NR	NR	3,019	66.2	95.1
335 Orth Pres Ch	1	24	25	53	1.2	1.7
MILWAUKEE	**504**	**111,670**	**61,447**	**446,222 ***	**47.5**	**100.0**
017 Amer Bapt Assn	1	50	NR	63 *	-	-
019 Amer Bapt USA	19	4,815	3,178	6,067 *	.6	1.4
050 Armen Ap Etchm	2	131	NR	480	.1	.1
053 Assemb of God	20	3,886	4,840	7,222	.8	1.6
056 Baha'i	4	445	NR	445	-	.1
057 Bapt Gen Conf	4	340	583	639 *	.1	.1
075 Brethren in Cr	1	26	31	31	-	-
076 Buddhism	8	NR	NR	NR	-	-
081 Catholic	92	NR	NR	261,485	27.8	58.6
084 Calvary Chapel	1	NR	NR	NR	-	-
089 Chr & Miss Al	3	69	NR	104	-	-
093 Chr Ch (Disc)	1	70	45	88 *	-	-
123 Ch God (Ander)	5	NR	454	454	-	.1
127 Ch God (Cleve)	3	328	102	415 *	-	.1
145 Ch God Prophcy	1	42	NR	53 *	-	-
151 L-D Saints	6	NR	NR	2,114	.2	.5
165 Ch of Nazarene	3	32	48	70	-	-
167 Chs of Christ	9	1,087	1,164	1,623	.2	.4
173 Comm of Christ	1	155	NR	155	-	-
175 Congr Chr Chs	7	3,170	1,554	3,994 *	.4	.9
193 Episcopal	16	NR	1,780	5,029	.5	1.1
201 Evan Cov Ch	1	86	80	108 *	-	-
203 Evan Free Ch	2	326	619	619	.1	.1
207 E.L.C.A.	52	21,213	9,104	28,406	3.0	6.4
220 Free Lutheran	1	14	11	15	-	-
226 Friends-USA	1	45	NR	57 *	-	-
246 Greek Orthodox	2	NR	NR	3,264	.3	.7
262 Int Cou Comm Ch	3	1,315	NR	1,657 *	.2	.4
263 Int Foursq Gos	1	19	25	25 *	-	-
264 Int Chs of Crst	1	284	578	420	-	.1
267 Muslim Est	5	NR	1,526	2,857	.3	.6
283 Luth—MO Synod	46	26,019	12,367	32,966	3.5	7.4
290 Metro Comm Ch	1	43	41	54 *	-	-
306 NT IndBapt&Rltd	6	683	NR	861 *	.1	.2
313 N Am Bapt Conf	1	75	75	95 *	-	-
331 OCA: Ter Diocs	1	71	NR	366	-	.1
355 Presb Ch (USA)	18	3,851	1,938	4,852 *	.5	1.1
356 Presb Ch Amer	1	10	0	14	-	-
370 Ref Baptist Chs	1	NR	NR	NR	-	-
371 Ref Ch in Am	2	455	334	691	.1	.2
388 Reg Bapt Gen As	1	92	122	122 *	-	-
401 Rus Orth Abroad	1	NR	NR	NR	-	-
403 Salvation Army	3	548	359	3,092	.3	.7
410 Serb Orth USA	1	NR	NR	4,000	.4	.9
411 Serb Orth: Grac	1	NR	NR	NR	-	-
413 S.D.A.	7	1,877	NR	2,233	.2	.5
419 So Bapt Conv	27	7,587	2,119	9,560 *	1.0	2.1
431 Ukrainian Orth	1	NR	NR	81	-	-
435 Unitarian-Univ	2	585	NR	737 *	.1	.2
443 Un C of Christ	13	3,898	1,783	4,912 *	.5	1.1
449 Un Methodist	26	7,401	3,630	9,322 *	1.0	2.1
463 Vineyard	1	25	27	32 *	-	-
467 Wesleyan	2	127	184	384	-	.1
469 WELS	47	20,200	11,646	25,489	2.7	5.7
496 Jewish Est	16	NR	NR	17,100	1.8	3.8
499 Indep.Non-Char	2	175	1,100	1,300	.1	.3
MONROE	**70**	**10,202**	**4,938**	**25,076 ***	**61.3**	**100.0**
019 Amer Bapt USA	1	217	163	275 *	.7	1.1
053 Assemb of God	3	333	428	1,074	2.6	4.3
056 Baha'i	0	3	NR	3	-	-
081 Catholic	9	NR	NR	10,345	25.3	41.3
151 L-D Saints	1	NR	NR	227	.6	.9
165 Ch of Nazarene	2	98	93	188	.5	.7
167 Chs of Christ	1	40	57	73	.2	.3
173 Comm of Christ	1	84	NR	84	.2	.3
181 Consrv Congr	2	153	115	194 *	.5	.8
193 Episcopal	2	NR	81	201	.5	.8
203 Evan Free Ch	4	327	632	632	1.5	2.5
207 E.L.C.A.	7	2,775	1,039	3,897	9.5	15.5
283 Luth—MO Synod	1	253	164	366	.9	1.5
297 Mennonite;Other	1	23	NR	29 *	.1	.1
306 NT IndBapt&Rltd	2	228	NR	288 *	.7	1.1
323 Old Ord Amish	13	715	NR	910 *	2.2	3.6
413 S.D.A.	1	42	NR	50	.1	.2
419 So Bapt Conv	1	102	68	129 *	.3	.5
443 Un C of Christ	2	498	217	630 *	1.5	2.5
449 Un Methodist	6	1,170	451	1,481 *	3.6	5.9
467 Wesleyan	1	17	21	80	.2	.3
469 WELS	9	3,124	1,409	3,920	9.6	15.6
OCONTO	**51**	**7,376**	**2,996**	**20,741 ***	**58.2**	**100.0**
053 Assemb of God	2	130	184	264	.7	1.3
056 Baha'i	0	1	NR	1	-	-
081 Catholic	11	NR	NR	10,777	30.2	52.0
089 Chr & Miss Al	3	179	NR	595	1.7	2.9
097 Chr Chs&Chs Cr	2	115	NR	142 *	.4	.7
207 E.L.C.A.	6	2,948	1,049	3,901	10.9	18.8
283 Luth—MO Synod	10	2,284	1,079	2,968	8.3	14.3
323 Old Ord Amish	1	55	NR	68 *	.2	.3
355 Presb Ch (USA)	2	272	120	336 *	.9	1.6
413 S.D.A.	3	153	NR	183	.5	.9
449 Un Methodist	7	729	325	902 *	2.5	4.3
469 WELS	4	510	239	604	1.7	2.9
ONEIDA	**47**	**8,073**	**4,453**	**24,286 ***	**66.0**	**100.0**
019 Amer Bapt USA	1	59	40	71 *	.2	.3
053 Assemb of God	2	106	141	152	.4	.6
056 Baha'i	0	15	NR	15	-	.1
057 Bapt Gen Conf	1	108	112	129 *	.4	.5
076 Buddhism	1	NR	NR	NR	-	-
081 Catholic	9	NR	NR	13,305	36.2	54.8
127 Ch God (Cleve)	1	21	28	28 *	.1	.1
151 L-D Saints	1	NR	NR	282	.8	1.2
167 Chs of Christ	2	82	95	101	.3	.4
193 Episcopal	2	NR	113	343	.9	1.4
203 Evan Free Ch	2	233	563	563	1.5	2.3
207 E.L.C.A.	5	2,547	1,046	3,207	8.7	13.2
263 Int Foursq Gos	1	397	450	475 *	1.3	2.0
283 Luth—MO Synod	4	688	354	865	2.4	3.6
331 OCA: Ter Diocs	1	21	NR	33	.1	.1
339 Pent Ch of God	1	20	NR	53	.1	.2
370 Ref Baptist Chs	1	NR	NR	NR	-	-
388 Reg Bapt Gen As	1	14	45	45 *	.1	.2
413 S.D.A.	2	138	NR	164	.4	.7
435 Unitarian-Univ	1	49	NR	59 *	.2	.2
443 Un C of Christ	2	751	235	898 *	2.4	3.7
449 Un Methodist	2	1,029	364	1,230 *	3.3	5.1
469 WELS	4	1,795	867	2,268	6.2	9.3

NR–Not Reported *Total adherents estimated from known number of communicant, confirmed, full members. - Represents a percentage less than 0.1. Percentages may not total 100 due to rounding.

Table 4: Religious Congregations by County and Group: 2000

Religious Group	Number of Churches, Synagogues, Mosques, or Temples	Number of Communicant, Confirmed, or Full Members	Number of Attendees	Total Adherents		
				Number of Adherents	% of Total Pop.	% of Total Adh.
OUTAGAMIE	**118**	**37,861**	**19,576**	**140,164 ***	**87.1**	**100.0**
019 Amer Bapt USA	2	124	84	157 *	.1	.1
053 Assemb of God	5	990	1,405	2,332	1.4	1.7
056 Baha'i	1	65	NR	65	-	-
057 Bapt Gen Conf	2	176	315	315 *	.2	.2
081 Catholic	26	NR	NR	83,700	52.0	59.7
084 Calvary Chapel	1	NR	NR	NR	-	-
089 Chr & Miss Al	3	636	NR	2,097	1.3	1.5
097 Chr Chs&Chs Cr	1	65	NR	82 *	.1	.1
105 Christian Ref	1	158	100	200 *	.1	.1
151 L-D Saints	3	NR	NR	990	.6	.7
165 Ch of Nazarene	1	43	31	57	-	-
167 Chs of Christ	2	140	155	184	.1	.1
181 Consrv Congr	1	91	100	115 *	.1	.1
193 Episcopal	1	NR	191	644	.4	.5
203 Evan Free Ch	1	103	310	310	.2	.2
207 E.L.C.A.	10	10,227	4,330	14,455	9.0	10.3
245 Greek Orth Vslp	1	175	NR	675	.4	.5
246 Greek Orthodox	1	NR	NR	120	.1	.1
263 Int Foursq Gos	1	24	55	55 *	-	-
283 Luth—MO Synod	6	5,609	2,481	7,727	4.8	5.5
293 Morav Ch-North	1	166	NR	208	.1	.1
306 NT IndBapt&Rltd	1	114	NR	145 *	.1	.1
335 Orth Pres Ch	1	39	40	57	-	-
355 Presb Ch (USA)	2	619	260	786 *	.5	.6
388 Reg Bapt Gen As	2	156	210	215 *	.1	.2
403 Salvation Army	1	87	43	287	.2	.2
419 So Bapt Conv	1	282	107	358 *	.2	.3
435 Unitarian-Univ	1	291	NR	369 *	.2	.3
443 Un C of Christ	6	3,065	997	3,889 *	2.4	2.8
449 Un Methodist	10	3,117	1,395	3,955 *	2.5	2.8
469 WELS	20	10,699	6,067	13,915	8.6	9.9
496 Jewish Est	1	NR	NR	300	.2	.2
499 Indep.Non-Char	1	600	900	1,400	.9	1.0
OZAUKEE	**64**	**18,909**	**9,775**	**59,700 ***	**72.5**	**100.0**
019 Amer Bapt USA	1	80	31	100 *	.1	.2
034 Ant Orth of NA	1	114	NR	228	.3	.4
053 Assemb of God	2	294	376	545	.7	.9
056 Baha'i	1	58	NR	58	.1	.1
081 Catholic	12	NR	NR	31,748	38.6	53.2
089 Chr & Miss Al	2	252	NR	1,036	1.3	1.7
151 L-D Saints	1	NR	NR	444	.5	.7
175 Congr Chr Chs	1	275	150	345 *	.4	.6
193 Episcopal	1	NR	30	23	-	-
203 Evan Free Ch	1	69	125	125	.2	.2
207 E.L.C.A.	11	4,271	1,806	5,460	6.6	9.1
268 Jain	1	NR	NR	NR	-	-
283 Luth—MO Synod	8	6,986	3,844	9,317	11.3	15.6
306 NT IndBapt&Rltd	1	114	NR	143 *	.2	.2
355 Presb Ch (USA)	1	1,315	762	1,649 *	2.0	2.8
435 Unitarian-Univ	1	193	NR	242 *	.3	.4
443 Un C of Christ	4	1,166	504	1,462 *	1.8	2.4
449 Un Methodist	3	1,186	505	1,487 *	1.8	2.5
463 Vineyard	1	110	92	138 *	.2	.2
469 WELS	7	2,126	1,310	2,650	3.2	4.4
496 Jewish Est	2	NR	NR	2,100	2.6	3.5
499 Indep.Non-Char	1	300	240	400	.5	.7
PEPIN	**21**	**1,905**	**801**	**4,850 ***	**67.2**	**100.0**
053 Assemb of God	1	38	25	50	.7	1.0
056 Baha'i	0	2	NR	2	-	-
081 Catholic	3	NR	NR	2,435	33.8	50.2
173 Comm of Christ	1	55	NR	55	.8	1.1
201 Evan Cov Ch	2	107	134	142 *	2.0	2.9
203 Evan Free Ch	1	23	45	45	.6	.9
207 E.L.C.A.	5	992	325	1,252	17.4	25.8
220 Free Lutheran	1	0	15	15	.2	.3
283 Luth—MO Synod	1	158	60	204	2.8	4.2
293 Morav Ch-North	1	13	NR	13	.2	.3
323 Old Ord Amish	1	55	NR	68 *	.9	1.4
413 S.D.A.	1	50	NR	60	.8	1.2
449 Un Methodist	3	412	197	509 *	7.1	10.5

Religious Group	Number of Churches, Synagogues, Mosques, or Temples	Number of Communicant, Confirmed, or Full Members	Number of Attendees	Total Adherents		
				Number of Adherents	% of Total Pop.	% of Total Adh.
PIERCE	**54**	**9,839**	**4,190**	**21,436 ***	**58.2**	**100.0**
053 Assemb of God	1	59	86	150	.4	.7
056 Baha'i	0	10	NR	10	-	-
057 Bapt Gen Conf	1	19	35	35 *	.1	.2
081 Catholic	7	NR	NR	8,414	22.9	39.3
181 Consrv Congr	1	95	45	116 *	.3	.5
193 Episcopal	1	NR	27	43	.1	.2
201 Evan Cov Ch	3	461	494	564 *	1.5	2.6
203 Evan Free Ch	1	25	60	60	.2	.3
207 E.L.C.A.	12	4,771	1,768	6,612	18.0	30.8
283 Luth—MO Synod	2	465	190	599	1.6	2.8
306 NT IndBapt&Rltd	1	114	NR	140 *	.4	.7
355 Presb Ch (USA)	2	124	85	152 *	.4	.7
413 S.D.A.	1	54	NR	64	.2	.3
435 Unitarian-Univ	1	52	NR	64 *	.2	.3
443 Un C of Christ	4	1,269	305	1,553 *	4.2	7.2
449 Un Methodist	11	1,508	701	1,845 *	5.0	8.6
469 WELS	5	813	394	1,015	2.8	4.7
POLK	**89**	**13,718**	**5,891**	**23,885 ***	**57.8**	**100.0**
053 Assemb of God	3	58	72	118	.3	.5
056 Baha'i	0	4	NR	4	-	-
057 Bapt Gen Conf	4	437	330	549 *	1.3	2.3
081 Catholic	7	NR	NR	4,918	11.9	20.6
089 Chr & Miss Al	2	216	NR	655	1.6	2.7
165 Ch of Nazarene	1	75	60	157	.4	.7
167 Chs of Christ	1	14	23	23	.1	.1
179 Consrv Bapt	3	NR	156	156	.4	.7
193 Episcopal	1	NR	15	59	.1	.2
201 Evan Cov Ch	1	194	190	241 *	.6	1.0
203 Evan Free Ch	4	266	425	425	1.0	1.8
207 E.L.C.A.	29	8,417	2,850	11,549	28.0	48.4
220 Free Lutheran	2	134	140	165	.4	.7
263 Int Foursq Gos	1	68	45	84 *	.2	.4
283 Luth—MO Synod	5	687	375	873	2.1	3.7
306 NT IndBapt&Rltd	1	114	NR	141 *	.3	.6
323 Old Ord Amish	2	110	NR	136 *	.3	.6
355 Presb Ch (USA)	1	112	77	139 *	.3	.6
413 S.D.A.	2	154	NR	184	.4	.8
419 So Bapt Conv	0	4	6	5 *	-	-
443 Un C of Christ	1	337	148	418 *	1.0	1.8
449 Un Methodist	12	926	448	1,149 *	2.8	4.8
469 WELS	6	1,391	531	1,737	4.2	7.3
PORTAGE	**57**	**9,064**	**4,820**	**44,952 ***	**66.9**	**100.0**
019 Amer Bapt USA	1	50	45	61 *	.1	.1
053 Assemb of God	1	364	540	850	1.3	1.9
056 Baha'i	0	30	NR	30	-	.1
057 Bapt Gen Conf	1	36	110	110 *	.2	.2
081 Catholic	16	NR	NR	31,905	47.5	71.0
089 Chr & Miss Al	1	132	NR	146	.2	.3
151 L-D Saints	1	NR	NR	204	.3	.5
165 Ch of Nazarene	1	25	0	25	-	.1
167 Chs of Christ	2	71	104	99	.1	.2
193 Episcopal	2	NR	96	177	.3	.4
203 Evan Free Ch	2	154	378	378	.6	.8
207 E.L.C.A.	7	2,939	1,092	4,141	6.2	9.2
226 Friends-USA	1	45	NR	55 *	.1	.1
283 Luth—MO Synod	6	2,702	1,236	3,662	5.5	8.1
323 Old Ord Amish	2	110	NR	134 *	.2	.3
355 Presb Ch (USA)	1	393	141	479 *	.7	1.1
388 Reg Bapt Gen As	2	200	272	272 *	.4	.6
413 S.D.A.	2	98	NR	116	.2	.3
419 So Bapt Conv	0	17	61	21 *	-	-
435 Unitarian-Univ	1	28	NR	34 *	.1	.1
443 Un C of Christ	1	165	85	201 *	.3	.4
449 Un Methodist	5	1,149	484	1,402 *	2.1	3.1
469 WELS	1	356	176	450	.7	1.0
PRICE	**33**	**4,060**	**1,748**	**10,291 ***	**65.0**	**100.0**
056 Baha'i	0	3	NR	3	-	-
057 Bapt Gen Conf	4	541	453	701 *	4.4	6.8

NR–Not Reported *Total adherents estimated from known number of communicant, confirmed, full members. - Represents a percentage less than 0.1. Percentages may not total 100 due to rounding.

Table 4: Religious Congregations by County and Group: 2000

Religious Group	Number of Churches, Synagogues, Mosques, or Temples	Number of Communicant, Confirmed, or Full Members	Number of Attendees	Total Adherents: Number of Adherents	Total Adherents: % of Total Pop.	Total Adherents: % of Total Adh.
081 Catholic	5	NR	NR	4,951	31.3	48.1
193 Episcopal	2	NR	31	50	.3	.5
201 Evan Cov Ch	1	47	25	57 *	.4	.6
207 E.L.C.A.	6	1,186	405	1,585	10.0	15.4
283 Luth—MO Synod	4	1,401	498	1,860	11.8	18.1
306 NT IndBapt&Rltd	1	114	NR	138 *	.9	1.3
355 Presb Ch (USA)	1	164	76	198 *	1.3	1.9
388 Reg Bapt Gen As	1	40	0	48 *	.3	.5
401 Rus Orth Abroad	1	NR	NR	NR	-	-
443 Un C of Christ	2	322	120	389 *	2.5	3.8
449 Un Methodist	3	128	62	156 *	1.0	1.5
469 WELS	2	114	78	155	1.0	1.5
RACINE	**141**	**31,134**	**16,667**	**113,369 ***	**60.0**	**100.0**
019 Amer Bapt USA	3	510	146	643 *	.3	.6
049 Armen Ap Cilic	1	83	NR	280	.1	.2
050 Armen Ap Etchm	1	231	NR	1,200	.6	1.1
053 Assemb of God	5	658	817	1,159	.6	1.0
056 Baha'i	1	45	NR	45	-	-
076 Buddhism	1	NR	NR	NR	-	-
081 Catholic	20	NR	NR	65,874	34.9	58.1
097 Chr Chs&Chs Cr	1	53	NR	67 *	-	.1
105 Christian Ref	1	344	225	434 *	.2	.4
123 Ch God (Ander)	2	NR	175	175	.1	.2
127 Ch God (Cleve)	2	44	44	64 *	-	.1
145 Ch God Prophcy	1	42	NR	53 *	-	-
151 L-D Saints	2	NR	NR	780	.4	.7
165 Ch of Nazarene	3	362	319	556	.3	.5
167 Chs of Christ	3	236	260	291	.2	.3
175 Congr Chr Chs	2	322	172	406 *	.2	.4
193 Episcopal	4	NR	384	764	.4	.7
203 Evan Free Ch	3	198	355	355	.2	.3
207 E.L.C.A.	19	11,412	4,068	16,103	8.5	14.2
246 Greek Orthodox	1	NR	NR	528	.3	.5
267 Muslim Est	1	NR	15	75	-	.1
283 Luth—MO Synod	15	5,496	2,485	7,361	3.9	6.5
306 NT IndBapt&Rltd	2	228	NR	288 *	.2	.3
313 N Am Bapt Conf	2	793	1,414	1,000 *	.5	.9
339 Pent Ch of God	1	120	NR	300	.2	.3
355 Presb Ch (USA)	3	909	451	1,146 *	.6	1.0
371 Ref Ch in Am	1	94	77	147	.1	.1
388 Reg Bapt Gen As	3	93	597	597 *	.3	.5
403 Salvation Army	1	78	87	1,185	.6	1.0
410 Serb Orth USA	1	NR	NR	300	.2	.3
411 Serb Orth: Grac	1	NR	NR	NR	-	-
413 S.D.A.	3	291	NR	346	.2	.3
419 So Bapt Conv	2	328	121	414 *	.2	.4
435 Unitarian-Univ	1	250	NR	315 *	.2	.3
443 Un C of Christ	3	526	210	663 *	.4	.6
449 Un Methodist	14	3,444	1,739	4,343 *	2.3	3.8
469 WELS	8	3,044	1,831	4,012	2.1	3.5
496 Jewish Est	1	NR	NR	200	.1	.2
499 Indep.Non-Char	2	900	675	900	.5	.8
RICHLAND	**34**	**3,298**	**1,390**	**6,866 ***	**38.3**	**100.0**
019 Amer Bapt USA	2	139	52	171 *	1.0	2.5
053 Assemb of God	1	37	52	59	.3	.9
056 Baha'i	0	2	NR	2	-	-
081 Catholic	4	NR	NR	2,610	14.6	38.0
097 Chr Chs&Chs Cr	1	231	NR	284 *	1.6	4.1
145 Ch God Prophcy	1	42	NR	52 *	.3	.8
165 Ch of Nazarene	1	143	104	168	.9	2.4
175 Congr Chr Chs	1	120	70	147 *	.8	2.1
193 Episcopal	1	NR	25	64	.4	.9
207 E.L.C.A.	3	788	272	1,023	5.7	14.9
221 Free Methodist	1	89	119	119	.7	1.7
226 Friends-USA	1	45	NR	55 *	.3	.8
283 Luth—MO Synod	2	135	73	144	.8	2.1
297 Mennonite;Other	1	53	NR	65 *	.4	.9
306 NT IndBapt&Rltd	1	114	NR	140 *	.8	2.0
323 Old Ord Amish	1	55	NR	68 *	.4	1.0
355 Presb Ch (USA)	1	95	41	117 *	.7	1.7
413 S.D.A.	1	72	NR	86	.5	1.3
449 Un Methodist	9	1,104	526	1,356 *	7.6	19.7
467 Wesleyan	1	34	56	136	.8	2.0
ROCK	**133**	**34,576**	**13,238**	**78,161 ***	**51.3**	**100.0**
019 Amer Bapt USA	6	1,583	619	1,990 *	1.3	2.5
053 Assemb of God	4	511	720	1,009	.7	1.3
056 Baha'i	2	110	NR	110	.1	.1
057 Bapt Gen Conf	1	160	306	306 *	.2	.4
081 Catholic	12	NR	NR	31,037	20.4	39.7
089 Chr & Miss Al	1	100	NR	219	.1	.3
093 Chr Ch (Disc)	1	167	69	210 *	.1	.3
097 Chr Chs&Chs Cr	3	1,480	NR	1,861 *	1.2	2.4
121 Ch God (Abr)	1	17	32	32 *	-	-
127 Ch God (Cleve)	1	102	159	159 *	.1	.2
145 Ch God Prophcy	1	42	NR	53 *	-	.1
151 L-D Saints	2	NR	NR	944	.6	1.2
165 Ch of Nazarene	1	65	26	108	.1	.1
167 Chs of Christ	1	50	58	68	-	.1
173 Comm of Christ	1	85	NR	85	.1	.1
175 Congr Chr Chs	5	980	345	1,232 *	.8	1.6
193 Episcopal	2	NR	239	484	.3	.6
201 Evan Cov Ch	1	118	70	148 *	.1	.2
203 Evan Free Ch	4	241	421	421	.3	.5
207 E.L.C.A.	17	12,622	3,502	16,538	10.9	21.2
220 Free Lutheran	1	135	82	165	.1	.2
221 Free Methodist	3	252	282	330	.2	.4
226 Friends-USA	1	45	NR	57 *	-	.1
263 Int Foursq Gos	2	87	74	109 *	.1	.1
267 Muslim Est	1	NR	25	70	-	.1
283 Luth—MO Synod	11	5,702	2,260	7,416	4.9	9.5
306 NT IndBapt&Rltd	4	455	NR	572 *	.4	.7
335 Orth Pres Ch	1	67	90	99	.1	.1
355 Presb Ch (USA)	6	1,704	666	2,142 *	1.4	2.7
363 Primitive Meth	2	114	NR	121	.1	.2
371 Ref Ch in Am	1	122	90	197	.1	.3
403 Salvation Army	2	276	161	645	.4	.8
413 S.D.A.	4	308	NR	367	.2	.5
419 So Bapt Conv	3	247	100	310 *	.2	.4
443 Un C of Christ	5	1,086	432	1,365 *	.9	1.7
449 Un Methodist	13	4,117	1,662	5,174 *	3.4	6.6
467 Wesleyan	1	40	56	87	.1	.1
469 WELS	4	1,386	692	1,801	1.2	2.3
496 Jewish Est	1	NR	NR	120	.1	.2
RUSK	**39**	**3,365**	**1,452**	**7,393 ***	**48.2**	**100.0**
053 Assemb of God	3	156	208	257	1.7	3.5
056 Baha'i	0	1	NR	1	-	-
057 Bapt Gen Conf	1	28	40	40 *	.3	.5
081 Catholic	8	NR	NR	3,638	23.7	49.2
097 Chr Chs&Chs Cr	2	395	NR	483 *	3.1	6.5
165 Ch of Nazarene	1	0	14	23	.1	.3
193 Episcopal	2	NR	50	69	.4	.9
207 E.L.C.A.	4	1,202	378	1,519	9.9	20.5
283 Luth—MO Synod	2	674	243	226	1.5	3.1
288 Mennonite USA	2	86	125	125 *	.8	1.7
297 Mennonite;Other	3	109	NR	133 *	.9	1.8
306 NT IndBapt&Rltd	1	114	NR	139 *	.9	1.9
388 Reg Bapt Gen As	1	56	70	70 *	.5	.9
443 Un C of Christ	3	175	121	214 *	1.4	2.9
449 Un Methodist	5	318	171	389 *	2.5	5.3
469 WELS	1	51	32	67	.4	.9
ST. CROIX	**60**	**14,212**	**7,511**	**39,881 ***	**63.1**	**100.0**
019 Amer Bapt USA	1	390	147	495 *	.8	1.2
053 Assemb of God	3	213	286	433	.7	1.1
056 Baha'i	0	2	NR	2	-	-
057 Bapt Gen Conf	2	178	1,175	1,175 *	1.9	2.9
081 Catholic	9	NR	NR	18,768	29.7	47.1
105 Christian Ref	1	154	120	196 *	.3	.5
151 L-D Saints	1	NR	NR	370	.6	.9
167 Chs of Christ	1	22	33	41	.1	.1
179 Consrv Bapt	1	NR	140	140	.2	.4
193 Episcopal	2	NR	97	150	.2	.4

NR–Not Reported *Total adherents estimated from known number of communicant, confirmed, full members. - Represents a percentage less than 0.1. Percentages may not total 100 due to rounding.

Table 4: Religious Congregations by County and Group: 2000

Religious Group	Number of Churches, Synagogues, Mosques, or Temples	Number of Communicant, Confirmed, or Full Members	Number of Attendees	Total Adherents: Number of Adherents	% of Total Pop.	% of Total Adh.
201 Evan Cov Ch	1	18	38	38 *	.1	.1
207 E.L.C.A.	14	7,501	2,849	10,389	16.5	26.0
263 Int Foursq Gos	1	105	184	184 *	.3	.5
283 Luth—MO Synod	5	2,291	935	3,200	5.1	8.0
306 NT IndBapt&Rltd	3	342	NR	434 *	.7	1.1
355 Presb Ch (USA)	2	404	202	513 *	.8	1.3
371 Ref Ch in Am	1	354	250	495	.8	1.2
443 Un C of Christ	2	315	158	400 *	.6	1.0
449 Un Methodist	8	1,584	693	2,012 *	3.2	5.0
469 WELS	2	339	204	446	.7	1.1
SAUK	**77**	**13,572**	**6,132**	**35,810 ***	**64.8**	**100.0**
017 Amer Bapt Assn	1	20	NR	25 *	-	.1
019 Amer Bapt USA	1	44	23	55 *	.1	.2
053 Assemb of God	2	168	208	350	.6	1.0
056 Baha'i	0	14	NR	14	-	-
076 Buddhism	1	NR	NR	NR	-	-
081 Catholic	9	NR	NR	17,527	31.7	48.9
097 Chr Chs&Chs Cr	1	30	NR	37 *	.1	.1
123 Ch God (Ander)	2	NR	85	85	.2	.2
165 Ch of Nazarene	2	167	147	598	1.1	1.7
167 Chs of Christ	1	15	30	25	-	.1
175 Congr Chr Chs	1	67	125	84 *	.2	.2
193 Episcopal	2	NR	107	278	.5	.8
203 Evan Free Ch	2	145	287	287	.5	.8
207 E.L.C.A.	8	4,427	1,511	5,797	10.5	16.2
283 Luth—MO Synod	6	1,703	882	2,107	3.8	5.9
306 NT IndBapt&Rltd	1	114	NR	142 *	.3	.4
313 N Am Bapt Conf	1	113	70	141 *	.3	.4
323 Old Ord Amish	3	165	NR	207 *	.4	.6
335 Orth Pres Ch	1	10	0	15	-	-
355 Presb Ch (USA)	3	551	194	688 *	1.2	1.9
413 S.D.A.	2	90	NR	107	.2	.3
419 So Bapt Conv	1	163	0	203 *	.4	.6
435 Unitarian-Univ	1	53	NR	66 *	.1	.2
443 Un C of Christ	2	620	249	773 *	1.4	2.2
449 Un Methodist	14	2,661	1,170	3,319 *	6.0	9.3
467 Wesleyan	1	20	34	60	.1	.2
469 WELS	8	2,212	1,010	2,820	5.1	7.9
SAWYER	**37**	**2,545**	**1,939**	**9,544 ***	**58.9**	**100.0**
053 Assemb of God	2	62	57	90	.6	.9
056 Baha'i	0	3	NR	3	-	-
057 Bapt Gen Conf	1	20	40	40 *	.2	.4
081 Catholic	7	NR	NR	3,804	23.5	39.9
127 Ch God (Cleve)	1	15	15	18 *	.1	.2
151 L-D Saints	1	NR	NR	100	.6	1.0
167 Chs of Christ	1	10	10	10	.1	.1
175 Congr Chr Chs	1	136	100	166 *	1.0	1.7
193 Episcopal	1	NR	50	133	.8	1.4
203 Evan Free Ch	2	74	125	125	.8	1.3
207 E.L.C.A.	4	1,217	506	1,511	9.3	15.8
263 Int Foursq Gos	1	32	11	39 *	.2	.4
283 Luth—MO Synod	1	163	103	187	1.2	2.0
288 Mennonite USA	1	15	16	18 *	.1	.2
297 Mennonite;Other	2	95	NR	116 *	.7	1.2
355 Presb Ch (USA)	3	42	44	61 *	.4	.6
388 Reg Bapt Gen As	1	30	80	80 *	.5	.8
413 S.D.A.	1	30	NR	36	.2	.4
443 Un C of Christ	1	35	30	43 *	.3	.5
449 Un Methodist	2	148	83	181 *	1.1	1.9
467 Wesleyan	2	317	581	2,650	16.4	27.8
469 WELS	1	101	88	133	.8	1.4
SHAWANO	**83**	**14,677**	**6,704**	**29,878 ***	**73.5**	**100.0**
053 Assemb of God	2	177	233	676	1.7	2.3
056 Baha'i	0	4	NR	4	-	-
057 Bapt Gen Conf	1	58	106	106 *	.3	.4
081 Catholic	13	NR	NR	10,466	25.7	35.0
151 L-D Saints	2	NR	NR	417	1.0	1.4
165 Ch of Nazarene	1	156	107	228	.6	.8
193 Episcopal	1	NR	23	36	.1	.1
207 E.L.C.A.	18	3,741	1,463	4,888	12.0	16.4
283 Luth—MO Synod	24	7,930	3,554	9,833	24.2	32.9
306 NT IndBapt&Rltd	1	114	NR	141 *	.3	.5
323 Old Ord Amish	2	110	NR	136 *	.3	.5
335 Orth Pres Ch	1	47	44	65	.2	.2
355 Presb Ch (USA)	2	315	130	389 *	1.0	1.3
413 S.D.A.	1	24	NR	29	.1	.1
419 So Bapt Conv	2	70	83	87 *	.2	.3
443 Un C of Christ	2	468	241	579 *	1.4	1.9
449 Un Methodist	7	713	267	881 *	2.2	2.9
469 WELS	3	750	453	917	2.3	3.1
SHEBOYGAN	**130**	**37,474**	**19,221**	**81,431 ***	**72.3**	**100.0**
019 Amer Bapt USA	1	98	50	122 *	.1	.1
053 Assemb of God	4	658	891	1,626	1.4	2.0
056 Baha'i	0	45	NR	45	-	.1
057 Bapt Gen Conf	1	11	60	60 *	.1	.1
076 Buddhism	1	NR	NR	NR	-	-
081 Catholic	17	NR	NR	29,983	26.6	36.8
089 Chr & Miss Al	3	388	NR	1,125	1.0	1.4
105 Christian Ref	4	1,350	1,244	1,674 *	1.5	2.1
151 L-D Saints	1	NR	NR	350	.3	.4
167 Chs of Christ	2	118	125	153	.1	.2
193 Episcopal	3	NR	232	510	.5	.6
203 Evan Free Ch	1	260	615	615	.5	.8
207 E.L.C.A.	6	3,338	1,258	4,416	3.9	5.4
246 Greek Orthodox	1	NR	NR	216	.2	.3
283 Luth—MO Synod	24	14,650	6,410	18,709	16.6	23.0
306 NT IndBapt&Rltd	3	342	NR	424 *	.4	.5
307 Neth Ref Congr	1	91	NR	200	.2	.2
313 N Am Bapt Conf	1	147	183	182 *	.2	.2
323 Old Ord Amish	2	110	NR	136 *	.1	.2
335 Orth Pres Ch	3	749	701	983	.9	1.2
349 Pent Holiness	2	19	19	24 *	-	-
355 Presb Ch (USA)	3	652	269	808 *	.7	1.0
371 Ref Ch in Am	8	3,423	2,423	5,227	4.6	6.4
403 Salvation Army	1	177	79	239	.2	.3
413 S.D.A.	2	123	NR	147	.1	.2
419 So Bapt Conv	1	131	87	162 *	.1	.2
420 Strict Baptists	1	6	NR	7 *	-	-
443 Un C of Christ	21	7,365	3,118	9,133 *	8.1	11.2
449 Un Methodist	7	2,168	885	2,689 *	2.4	3.3
469 WELS	4	1,055	572	1,326	1.2	1.6
496 Jewish Est	1	NR	NR	140	.1	.2
TAYLOR	**32**	**4,706**	**2,030**	**14,733 ***	**74.9**	**100.0**
053 Assemb of God	1	57	68	109	.6	.7
056 Baha'i	0	1	NR	1	-	-
057 Bapt Gen Conf	1	199	332	332 *	1.7	2.3
081 Catholic	9	NR	NR	8,535	43.4	57.9
207 E.L.C.A.	3	855	282	1,100	5.6	7.5
283 Luth—MO Synod	3	686	262	901	4.6	6.1
306 NT IndBapt&Rltd	1	114	NR	142 *	.7	1.0
323 Old Ord Amish	3	165	NR	207 *	1.1	1.4
331 OCA: Ter Diocs	1	41	NR	47	.2	.3
355 Presb Ch (USA)	1	59	42	73 *	.4	.5
431 Ukrainian Orth	1	NR	NR	60	.3	.4
443 Un C of Christ	1	215	83	268 *	1.4	1.8
449 Un Methodist	2	293	123	365 *	1.9	2.5
469 WELS	5	2,021	838	2,593	13.2	17.6
TREMPEALEAU	**43**	**9,250**	**3,414**	**20,827 ***	**77.1**	**100.0**
053 Assemb of God	1	24	32	58	.2	.3
056 Baha'i	0	10	NR	10	-	-
081 Catholic	10	NR	NR	8,614	31.9	41.4
165 Ch of Nazarene	1	14	32	42	.2	.2
179 Consrv Bapt	1	NR	153	153	.6	.7
207 E.L.C.A.	22	8,157	2,787	10,642	39.4	51.1
283 Luth—MO Synod	1	121	45	149	.6	.7
323 Old Ord Amish	2	110	NR	136 *	.5	.7
355 Presb Ch (USA)	1	309	134	382 *	1.4	1.8
443 Un C of Christ	1	250	70	309 *	1.1	1.5
449 Un Methodist	2	174	100	215 *	.8	1.0
469 WELS	1	81	61	117	.4	.6

NR–Not Reported *Total adherents estimated from known number of communicant, confirmed, full members. - Represents a percentage less than 0.1. Percentages may not total 100 due to rounding.

Table 4: Religious Congregations by County and Group: 2000

Religious Group	Number of Churches, Synagogues, Mosques, or Temples	Number of Communicant, Confirmed, or Full Members	Number of Attendees	Total Adherents		
				Number of Adherents	% of Total Pop.	% of Total Adh.
VERNON	**68**	**11,104**	**4,306**	**17,891 ***	**63.8**	**100.0**
019 Amer Bapt USA	1	97	130	130 *	.5	.7
053 Assemb of God	1	60	60	60	.2	.3
056 Baha'i	0	6	NR	6	-	-
081 Catholic	4	NR	NR	3,427	12.2	19.2
097 Chr Chs&Chs Cr	3	550	NR	693 *	2.5	3.9
165 Ch of Nazarene	1	38	20	38	.1	.2
181 Consrv Congr	1	351	175	442 *	1.6	2.5
203 Evan Free Ch	1	69	125	125	.4	.7
207 E.L.C.A.	21	6,284	2,176	7,944	28.3	44.4
221 Free Methodist	1	13	39	39	.1	.2
306 NT IndBapt&Rltd	1	114	NR	144 *	.5	.8
323 Old Ord Amish	12	650	NR	816 *	2.9	4.6
449 Un Methodist	10	1,207	570	1,520 *	5.4	8.5
467 Wesleyan	4	239	272	726	2.6	4.1
469 WELS	7	1,426	739	1,781	6.3	10.0
VILAS	**32**	**4,067**	**2,303**	**11,556 ***	**54.9**	**100.0**
053 Assemb of God	1	14	17	23	.1	.2
056 Baha'i	0	60	NR	60	.3	.5
081 Catholic	8	NR	NR	6,581	31.3	56.9
165 Ch of Nazarene	1	18	0	18	.1	.2
193 Episcopal	1	NR	57	97	.5	.8
201 Evan Cov Ch	1	171	124	202 *	1.0	1.7
203 Evan Free Ch	3	211	317	317	1.5	2.7
207 E.L.C.A.	3	690	349	797	3.8	6.9
283 Luth—MO Synod	3	859	440	974	4.6	8.4
306 NT IndBapt&Rltd	1	114	NR	135 *	.6	1.2
355 Presb Ch (USA)	2	315	213	372 *	1.8	3.2
388 Reg Bapt Gen As	1	11	22	22 *	.1	.2
413 S.D.A.	1	77	NR	92	.4	.8
443 Un C of Christ	4	961	400	1,135 *	5.4	9.8
469 WELS	2	566	364	731	3.5	6.3
WALWORTH	**80**	**14,591**	**8,018**	**46,190 ***	**49.3**	**100.0**
019 Amer Bapt USA	4	700	382	858 *	.9	1.9
053 Assemb of God	3	179	254	425	.5	.9
056 Baha'i	0	36	NR	36	-	.1
057 Bapt Gen Conf	2	149	285	285 *	.3	.6
081 Catholic	9	NR	NR	26,352	28.1	57.1
105 Christian Ref	1	492	360	603 *	.6	1.3
167 Chs of Christ	1	55	50	89	.1	.2
175 Congr Chr Chs	1	22	20	27 *	-	.1
193 Episcopal	4	NR	275	483	.5	1.0
203 Evan Free Ch	4	277	606	606	.6	1.3
207 E.L.C.A.	9	3,756	1,727	5,090	5.4	11.0
283 Luth—MO Synod	6	1,772	884	2,372	2.5	5.1
306 NT IndBapt&Rltd	3	342	NR	419 *	.4	.9
355 Presb Ch (USA)	1	258	198	316 *	.3	.7
371 Ref Ch in Am	1	70	80	173	.2	.4
413 S.D.A.	2	78	NR	92	.1	.2
435 Unitarian-Univ	1	25	NR	31 *	-	.1
443 Un C of Christ	9	2,016	863	2,470 *	2.6	5.3
449 Un Methodist	13	2,274	886	2,787 *	3.0	6.0
469 WELS	5	1,740	923	2,276	2.4	4.9
499 Indep.Non-Char	1	350	225	400	.4	.9
WASHBURN	**34**	**3,460**	**2,015**	**7,435 ***	**46.4**	**100.0**
053 Assemb of God	1	20	25	54	.3	.7
056 Baha'i	0	5	NR	5	-	.1
081 Catholic	5	NR	NR	2,523	15.7	33.9
089 Chr & Miss Al	1	27	NR	92	.6	1.2
097 Chr Chs&Chs Cr	1	25	NR	30 *	.2	.4
165 Ch of Nazarene	2	104	79	166	1.0	2.2
193 Episcopal	3	NR	58	91	.6	1.2
207 E.L.C.A.	5	1,598	722	2,068	12.9	27.8
283 Luth—MO Synod	2	424	238	536	3.3	7.2
306 NT IndBapt&Rltd	1	114	NR	138 *	.9	1.9
355 Presb Ch (USA)	1	30	45	45 *	.3	.6
388 Reg Bapt Gen As	1	92	122	122 *	.8	1.6
413 S.D.A.	1	9	NR	11	.1	.1
419 So Bapt Conv	2	9	10	11 *	.1	.1
443 Un C of Christ	1	50	32	60 *	.4	.8
449 Un Methodist	4	606	249	731 *	4.6	9.8
467 Wesleyan	2	197	319	573	3.6	7.7
469 WELS	1	150	116	179	1.1	2.4
WASHINGTON	**81**	**21,748**	**11,195**	**73,683 ***	**62.7**	**100.0**
053 Assemb of God	3	233	311	432	.4	.6
056 Baha'i	0	28	NR	28	-	-
057 Bapt Gen Conf	1	65	350	350 *	.3	.5
076 Buddhism	1	NR	NR	NR	-	-
081 Catholic	14	NR	NR	43,777	37.3	59.4
089 Chr & Miss Al	1	176	NR	592	.5	.8
127 Ch God (Cleve)	1	28	10	35 *	-	-
151 L-D Saints	1	NR	NR	380	.3	.5
165 Ch of Nazarene	1	23	17	37	-	.1
167 Chs of Christ	1	25	30	35	-	-
175 Congr Chr Chs	1	100	50	126 *	.1	.2
181 Consrv Congr	1	67	86	84 *	.1	.1
193 Episcopal	2	NR	135	433	.4	.6
207 E.L.C.A.	8	4,404	1,831	5,859	5.0	8.0
283 Luth—MO Synod	6	4,177	1,965	5,681	4.8	7.7
306 NT IndBapt&Rltd	3	342	NR	430 *	.4	.6
355 Presb Ch (USA)	2	153	95	192 *	.2	.3
371 Ref Ch in Am	1	57	85	96	.1	.1
388 Reg Bapt Gen As	1	23	46	46 *	-	.1
419 So Bapt Conv	0	26	0	33 *	-	-
443 Un C of Christ	14	2,990	1,274	3,759 *	3.2	5.1
449 Un Methodist	4	1,947	769	2,448 *	2.1	3.3
469 WELS	14	6,884	4,141	8,830	7.5	12.0
WAUKESHA	**225**	**70,659**	**45,871**	**241,180 ***	**66.9**	**100.0**
019 Amer Bapt USA	4	500	222	625 *	.2	.3
053 Assemb of God	6	1,831	2,333	3,749	1.0	1.6
056 Baha'i	4	199	NR	199	.1	.1
057 Bapt Gen Conf	1	119	320	320 *	.1	.1
075 Brethren in Cr	1	52	107	107	-	-
076 Buddhism	1	NR	NR	NR	-	-
081 Catholic	30	NR	NR	134,714	37.3	55.9
089 Chr & Miss Al	2	289	NR	919	.3	.4
093 Chr Ch (Disc)	1	80	0	100 *	-	-
097 Chr Chs&Chs Cr	1	170	NR	212 *	.1	.1
105 Christian Ref	1	426	250	532 *	.1	.2
127 Ch God (Cleve)	1	94	47	117 *	-	-
151 L-D Saints	3	NR	NR	1,029	.3	.4
165 Ch of Nazarene	2	240	112	240	.1	.1
167 Chs of Christ	2	54	60	84	-	-
175 Congr Chr Chs	2	405	148	506 *	.1	.2
193 Episcopal	13	NR	1,271	2,822	.8	1.2
203 Evan Free Ch	3	417	1,030	1,030	.3	.4
207 E.L.C.A.	31	19,592	8,045	27,297	7.6	11.3
216 Evan Presby Ch	1	100	NR	125 *	-	.1
221 Free Methodist	1	104	73	105	-	-
252 Hindu	2	NR	NR	NR	-	-
262 Int Cou Comm Ch	1	190	NR	237 *	.1	.1
268 Jain	2	NR	NR	NR	-	-
283 Luth—MO Synod	17	13,266	6,829	17,244	4.8	7.1
288 Mennonite USA	1	39	30	49 *	-	-
306 NT IndBapt&Rltd	9	1,025	NR	1,281 *	.4	.5
313 N Am Bapt Conf	1	431	300	539 *	.1	.2
335 Orth Pres Ch	1	205	164	282	.1	.1
355 Presb Ch (USA)	12	2,481	1,103	3,101 *	.9	1.3
356 Presb Ch Amer	2	162	238	256	.1	.1
371 Ref Ch in Am	1	93	84	140	-	.1
388 Reg Bapt Gen As	5	1,076	1,215	1,404 *	.4	.6
403 Salvation Army	1	73	60	152	-	.1
413 S.D.A.	1	109	NR	130	-	.1
416 Sikh	1	NR	NR	NR	-	-
418 Southw Bapt Fel	1	NR	NR	NR	-	-
419 So Bapt Conv	1	168	43	210 *	.1	.1
435 Unitarian-Univ	3	490	NR	612 *	.2	.3
443 Un C of Christ	12	4,032	1,667	5,039 *	1.4	2.1
449 Un Methodist	14	5,720	2,499	7,148 *	2.0	3.0
463 Vineyard	2	92	83	114 *	-	-

NR–Not Reported *Total adherents estimated from known number of communicant, confirmed, full members. - Represents a percentage less than 0.1. Percentages may not total 100 due to rounding.

Table 4: Religious Congregations by County and Group: 2000

Religious Group	Number of Churches, Synagogues, Mosques, or Temples	Number of Communicant, Confirmed, or Full Members	Number of Attendees	Total Adherents: Number of Adherents	Total Adherents: % of Total Pop.	Total Adherents: % of Total Adh.
467 Wesleyan	2	144	268	920	.3	.4
469 WELS	16	11,741	7,420	15,340	4.3	6.4
496 Jewish Est	2	NR	NR	2,100	.6	.9
498 Indep.Charis.	1	3,800	8,000	8,000	2.2	3.3
499 Indep.Non-Char	3	650	1,850	2,050	.6	.8
WAUPACA	**72**	**20,425**	**9,703**	**39,241 ***	**75.9**	**100.0**
053 Assemb of God	3	317	432	941	1.8	2.4
056 Baha'i	0	10	NR	10	-	-
057 Bapt Gen Conf	1	23	70	70 *	.1	.2
081 Catholic	7	NR	NR	12,126	23.4	30.9
097 Chr Chs&Chs Cr	1	50	NR	62 *	.1	.2
123 Ch God (Ander)	1	NR	12	12	-	-
165 Ch of Nazarene	2	36	16	57	.1	.1
167 Chs of Christ	5	195	211	251	.5	.6
193 Episcopal	2	NR	159	228	.4	.6
203 Evan Free Ch	2	187	474	474	.9	1.2
207 E.L.C.A.	15	7,401	2,821	10,064	19.5	25.6
283 Luth—MO Synod	10	4,258	1,970	5,098	9.9	13.0
306 NT IndBapt&Rltd	1	114	NR	141 *	.3	.4
323 Old Ord Amish	1	55	NR	68 *	.1	.2
355 Presb Ch (USA)	1	242	75	300 *	.6	.8
413 S.D.A.	1	48	NR	57	.1	.1
419 So Bapt Conv	2	87	80	108 *	.2	.3
443 Un C of Christ	3	543	232	673 *	1.3	1.7
449 Un Methodist	8	1,713	759	2,122 *	4.1	5.4
469 WELS	6	5,146	2,392	6,379	12.3	16.3
WAUSHARA	**46**	**6,035**	**3,097**	**11,510 ***	**49.7**	**100.0**
019 Amer Bapt USA	1	25	20	30 *	.1	.3
053 Assemb of God	2	201	270	455	2.0	4.0
056 Baha'i	0	2	NR	2	-	-
081 Catholic	4	NR	NR	3,936	17.0	34.2
084 Calvary Chapel	1	NR	NR	NR	-	-
167 Chs of Christ	1	9	10	21	.1	.2
175 Congr Chr Chs	1	61	70	74 *	.3	.6
181 Consrv Congr	1	37	23	45 *	.2	.4
203 Evan Free Ch	1	80	200	200	.9	1.7
207 E.L.C.A.	7	1,971	784	2,460	10.6	21.4
283 Luth—MO Synod	8	1,331	725	1,380	6.0	12.0
297 Mennonite;Other	1	33	NR	40 *	.2	.3
306 NT IndBapt&Rltd	2	228	NR	276 *	1.2	2.4
323 Old Ord Amish	2	110	NR	132 *	.6	1.1
355 Presb Ch (USA)	1	54	40	65 *	.3	.6
388 Reg Bapt Gen As	1	21	65	65 *	.3	.6
419 So Bapt Conv	1	26	28	31 *	.1	.3
443 Un C of Christ	2	213	113	257 *	1.1	2.2
449 Un Methodist	6	1,034	426	1,251 *	5.4	10.9
467 Wesleyan	1	54	55	140	.6	1.2
469 WELS	2	545	268	650	2.8	5.6
WINNEBAGO	**109**	**33,290**	**16,159**	**90,009 ***	**57.4**	**100.0**
019 Amer Bapt USA	2	182	95	222 *	.1	.2
053 Assemb of God	2	300	422	535	.3	.6
056 Baha'i	1	63	NR	63	-	.1
057 Bapt Gen Conf	2	250	741	741 *	.5	.8
076 Buddhism	1	NR	NR	NR	-	-
081 Catholic	14	NR	NR	43,690	27.9	48.5
084 Calvary Chapel	1	NR	NR	NR	-	-
089 Chr & Miss Al	1	154	NR	164	.1	.2
097 Chr Chs&Chs Cr	1	120	NR	147 *	.1	.2
127 Ch God (Cleve)	1	41	5	50 *	-	.1
165 Ch of Nazarene	1	0	0	0	-	-
167 Chs of Christ	2	104	99	131	.1	.1
175 Congr Chr Chs	1	516	240	630 *	.4	.7
181 Consrv Congr	1	287	210	351 *	.2	.4
193 Episcopal	2	NR	370	1,484	.9	1.6
203 Evan Free Ch	1	52	125	125	.1	.1
207 E.L.C.A.	19	11,702	4,606	15,884	10.1	17.6
226 Friends-USA	1	45	NR	55 *	-	.1
263 Int Foursq Gos	1	17	53	53 *	-	.1
267 Muslim Est	1	NR	156	609	.4	.7
283 Luth—MO Synod	7	3,699	1,873	5,133	3.3	5.7

Religious Group	Number of Churches, Synagogues, Mosques, or Temples	Number of Communicant, Confirmed, or Full Members	Number of Attendees	Total Adherents: Number of Adherents	Total Adherents: % of Total Pop.	Total Adherents: % of Total Adh.
306 NT IndBapt&Rltd	2	228	NR	279 *	.2	.3
339 Pent Ch of God	3	197	NR	360	.2	.4
355 Presb Ch (USA)	5	1,785	650	2,181 *	1.4	2.4
388 Reg Bapt Gen As	1	49	58	60 *	-	.1
403 Salvation Army	1	75	55	202	.1	.2
413 S.D.A.	1	186	NR	221	.1	.2
419 So Bapt Conv	0	83	100	101 *	.1	.1
443 Un C of Christ	7	2,166	947	2,647 *	1.7	2.9
449 Un Methodist	7	2,809	1,339	3,431 *	2.2	3.8
469 WELS	16	7,330	3,535	9,440	6.0	10.5
496 Jewish Est	2	NR	NR	170	.1	.2
499 Indep.Non-Char	1	850	480	850	.5	.9
WOOD	**89**	**19,936**	**9,682**	**57,472 ***	**76.1**	**100.0**
019 Amer Bapt USA	1	61	20	75 *	.1	.1
053 Assemb of God	3	609	876	1,386	1.8	2.4
056 Baha'i	0	14	NR	14	-	-
057 Bapt Gen Conf	1	58	82	82 *	.1	.1
081 Catholic	18	NR	NR	30,265	40.1	52.7
089 Chr & Miss Al	1	58	NR	194	.3	.3
105 Christian Ref	1	67	55	83 *	.1	.1
145 Ch God Prophcy	1	42	NR	52 *	.1	.1
151 L-D Saints	2	NR	NR	465	.6	.8
165 Ch of Nazarene	1	26	5	26	-	-
167 Chs of Christ	3	120	158	180	.2	.3
173 Comm of Christ	1	29	NR	29	-	.1
193 Episcopal	2	NR	74	360	.5	.6
203 Evan Free Ch	3	370	505	505	.7	.9
207 E.L.C.A.	6	3,202	1,362	4,305	5.7	7.5
263 Int Foursq Gos	1	10	34	34 *	-	.1
283 Luth—MO Synod	13	8,433	3,615	10,707	14.2	18.6
293 Morav Ch-North	5	619	NR	768	1.0	1.3
306 NT IndBapt&Rltd	2	228	NR	282 *	.4	.5
323 Old Ord Amish	1	55	NR	68 *	.1	.1
339 Pent Ch of God	1	50	NR	70	.1	.1
355 Presb Ch (USA)	2	513	160	634 *	.8	1.1
371 Ref Ch in Am	1	150	125	230	.3	.4
388 Reg Bapt Gen As	1	422	377	522 *	.7	.9
413 S.D.A.	3	337	NR	401	.5	.7
435 Unitarian-Univ	1	12	NR	15 *	-	-
443 Un C of Christ	5	1,283	518	1,586 *	2.1	2.8
449 Un Methodist	4	1,428	559	1,765 *	2.3	3.1
467 Wesleyan	1	64	75	150	.2	.3
469 WELS	4	1,676	1,082	2,219	2.9	3.9
WYOMING						
The State.....	790	64,960	38,172	230,725 *	46.7	100.0
ALBANY	**42**	**3,526**	**2,306**	**11,960 ***	**37.4**	**100.0**
017 Amer Bapt Assn	1	10	NR	12 *	-	.1
019 Amer Bapt USA	1	414	110	481 *	1.5	4.0
053 Assemb of God	3	131	151	295	.9	2.5
056 Baha'i	1	29	NR	29	.1	.2
081 Catholic	2	NR	NR	4,026	12.6	33.7
084 Calvary Chapel	1	NR	NR	NR	-	-
093 Chr Ch (Disc)	1	387	250	450 *	1.4	3.8
145 Ch God Prophcy	1	24	NR	27 *	.1	.2
151 L-D Saints	7	NR	NR	2,107	6.6	17.6
165 Ch of Nazarene	1	89	60	112	.3	.9
167 Chs of Christ	1	133	147	172	.5	1.4
173 Comm of Christ	1	35	NR	35	.1	.3
179 Consrv Bapt	1	NR	175	175	.5	1.5
193 Episcopal	1	NR	175	558	1.7	4.7
203 Evan Free Ch	1	22	132	132	.4	1.1
207 E.L.C.A.	1	533	185	683	2.1	5.7
263 Int Foursq Gos	1	22	117	117 *	.4	1.0
267 Muslim Est	2	NR	90	263	.8	2.2
283 Luth—MO Synod	2	289	212	389	1.2	3.3
355 Presb Ch (USA)	2	368	164	427 *	1.3	3.6
403 Salvation Army	1	6	10	34	.1	.3
413 S.D.A.	1	119	NR	142	.4	1.2

NR–Not Reported   *Total adherents estimated from known number of communicant, confirmed, full members.   - Represents a percentage less than 0.1.   Percentages may not total 100 due to rounding.

Table 4: Religious Congregations by County and Group: 2000

Religious Group	Number of Churches, Synagogues, Mosques, or Temples	Number of Communicant, Confirmed, or Full Members	Number of Attendees	Total Adherents		
				Number of Adherents	% of Total Pop.	% of Total Adh.
419 So Bapt Conv	4	207	131	241 *	.8	2.0
435 Unitarian-Univ	1	80	NR	93 *	.3	.8
443 Un C of Christ	1	136	33	158 *	.5	1.3
449 Un Methodist	1	492	164	572 *	1.8	4.8
496 Jewish Est	1	NR	NR	230	.7	1.9
BIG HORN	**37**	**1,135**	**787**	**6,252 ***	**54.6**	**100.0**
019 Amer Bapt USA	2	81	29	103 *	.9	1.6
053 Assemb of God	2	42	49	52	.5	.8
081 Catholic	3	NR	NR	831	7.3	13.3
089 Chr & Miss Al	1	32	NR	87	.8	1.4
145 Ch God Prophcy	1	24	NR	30 *	.3	.5
151 L-D Saints	13	NR	NR	3,667	32.0	58.7
179 Consrv Bapt	1	NR	215	215	1.9	3.4
193 Episcopal	1	NR	33	72	.6	1.2
283 Luth—MO Synod	3	447	248	550	4.8	8.8
355 Presb Ch (USA)	2	62	36	79 *	.7	1.3
413 S.D.A.	1	32	NR	38	.3	.6
419 So Bapt Conv	3	227	74	289 *	2.5	4.6
449 Un Methodist	4	188	103	239 *	2.1	3.8
CAMPBELL	**39**	**5,289**	**3,130**	**17,809 ***	**52.8**	**100.0**
017 Amer Bapt Assn	1	30	NR	39 *	.1	.2
019 Amer Bapt USA	1	183	85	237 *	.7	1.3
034 Ant Orth of NA	1	50	NR	100	.3	.6
053 Assemb of God	3	199	264	434	1.3	2.4
056 Baha'i	0	8	NR	8	-	-
081 Catholic	2	NR	NR	6,624	19.7	37.2
089 Chr & Miss Al	1	36	NR	104	.3	.6
097 Chr Chs&Chs Cr	1	100	NR	129 *	.4	.7
127 Ch God (Cleve)	1	15	19	19 *	.1	.1
145 Ch God Prophcy	1	24	NR	31 *	.1	.2
151 L-D Saints	4	NR	NR	1,337	4.0	7.5
165 Ch of Nazarene	1	31	42	91	.3	.5
167 Chs of Christ	2	152	153	176	.5	1.0
193 Episcopal	2	NR	94	282	.8	1.6
207 E.L.C.A.	1	684	391	1,053	3.1	5.9
263 Int Foursq Gos	1	15	241	241 *	.7	1.4
283 Luth—MO Synod	3	926	335	1,308	3.9	7.3
349 Pent Holiness	1	15	15	19 *	.1	.1
355 Presb Ch (USA)	1	467	115	605 *	1.8	3.4
413 S.D.A.	2	104	NR	124	.4	.7
419 So Bapt Conv	5	1,336	371	1,730 *	5.1	9.7
449 Un Methodist	1	359	181	465 *	1.4	2.6
463 Vineyard	1	95	60	123 *	.4	.7
467 Wesleyan	1	397	714	2,450	7.3	13.8
469 WELS	1	63	50	80	.2	.4
CARBON	**43**	**1,920**	**1,101**	**6,715 ***	**42.9**	**100.0**
019 Amer Bapt USA	1	65	65	79 *	.5	1.2
053 Assemb of God	3	121	160	340	2.2	5.1
056 Baha'i	0	9	NR	9	.1	.1
081 Catholic	5	NR	NR	2,353	15.0	35.0
089 Chr & Miss Al	2	22	NR	122	.8	1.8
151 L-D Saints	5	NR	NR	1,038	6.6	15.5
165 Ch of Nazarene	1	30	54	100	.6	1.5
167 Chs of Christ	3	72	87	104	.7	1.5
193 Episcopal	6	NR	128	622	4.0	9.3
263 Int Foursq Gos	1	16	21	21 *	.1	.3
283 Luth—MO Synod	3	285	100	354	2.3	5.3
355 Presb Ch (USA)	3	250	159	303 *	1.9	4.5
413 S.D.A.	1	47	NR	56	.4	.8
419 So Bapt Conv	6	724	210	876 *	5.6	13.0
449 Un Methodist	3	279	117	338 *	2.2	5.0
CONVERSE	**23**	**1,380**	**1,043**	**4,950 ***	**41.1**	**100.0**
019 Amer Bapt USA	2	245	134	309 *	2.6	6.2
053 Assemb of God	2	76	96	172	1.4	3.5
056 Baha'i	0	1	NR	1	-	-
081 Catholic	2	NR	NR	2,274	18.9	45.9
097 Chr Chs&Chs Cr	1	42	NR	53 *	.4	1.1
151 L-D Saints	2	NR	NR	382	3.2	7.7
167 Chs of Christ	2	44	58	69	.6	1.4
179 Consrv Bapt	1	NR	200	200	1.7	4.0
193 Episcopal	3	NR	108	288	2.4	5.8
283 Luth—MO Synod	2	254	118	299	2.5	6.0
349 Pent Holiness	1	15	15	19 *	.2	.4
413 S.D.A.	1	25	NR	30	.2	.6
419 So Bapt Conv	2	270	150	340 *	2.8	6.9
443 Un C of Christ	1	224	66	282 *	2.3	5.7
449 Un Methodist	1	184	98	232 *	1.9	4.7
CROOK	**17**	**898**	**500**	**2,030 ***	**34.5**	**100.0**
019 Amer Bapt USA	1	219	91	269 *	4.6	13.3
053 Assemb of God	1	33	36	65	1.1	3.2
056 Baha'i	0	2	NR	2	-	.1
081 Catholic	3	NR	NR	630	10.7	31.0
151 L-D Saints	2	NR	NR	202	3.4	10.0
167 Chs of Christ	1	38	40	45	.8	2.2
173 Comm of Christ	1	30	NR	30	.5	1.5
193 Episcopal	1	NR	21	48	.8	2.4
283 Luth—MO Synod	2	179	67	210	3.6	10.3
355 Presb Ch (USA)	1	83	42	102 *	1.7	5.0
419 So Bapt Conv	2	123	89	151 *	2.6	7.4
449 Un Methodist	1	187	85	230 *	3.9	11.3
467 Wesleyan	1	4	29	46	.8	2.3
FREMONT	**74**	**5,023**	**2,953**	**15,062 ***	**42.1**	**100.0**
019 Amer Bapt USA	1	250	81	314 *	.9	2.1
053 Assemb of God	5	280	309	475	1.3	3.2
056 Baha'i	0	38	NR	38	.1	.3
081 Catholic	10	NR	NR	4,094	11.4	27.2
089 Chr & Miss Al	2	91	NR	234	.7	1.6
097 Chr Chs&Chs Cr	2	90	NR	113 *	.3	.8
123 Ch God (Ander)	1	NR	19	19	.1	.1
151 L-D Saints	10	NR	NR	2,770	7.7	18.4
165 Ch of Nazarene	4	233	226	344	1.0	2.3
167 Chs of Christ	3	116	133	159	.4	1.1
179 Consrv Bapt	2	NR	270	270	.8	1.8
193 Episcopal	8	NR	295	1,024	2.9	6.8
203 Evan Free Ch	1	50	120	120	.3	.8
207 E.L.C.A.	2	422	146	648	1.8	4.3
226 Friends-USA	1	30	NR	38 *	.1	.3
263 Int Foursq Gos	2	108	145	145 *	.4	1.0
283 Luth—MO Synod	5	896	419	1,223	3.4	8.1
355 Presb Ch (USA)	2	156	57	195 *	.5	1.3
356 Presb Ch Amer	1	65	90	90	.3	.6
413 S.D.A.	2	115	NR	137	.4	.9
419 So Bapt Conv	7	1,151	295	1,443 *	4.0	9.6
449 Un Methodist	3	932	348	1,169 *	3.3	7.8
GOSHEN	**20**	**2,294**	**1,124**	**4,649 ***	**37.1**	**100.0**
019 Amer Bapt USA	1	168	60	205 *	1.6	4.4
053 Assemb of God	2	50	60	60	.5	1.3
056 Baha'i	0	4	NR	4	-	.1
057 Bapt Gen Conf	2	218	219	266 *	2.1	5.7
081 Catholic	1	NR	NR	1,358	10.8	29.2
097 Chr Chs&Chs Cr	3	143	NR	174 *	1.4	3.7
151 L-D Saints	1	NR	NR	301	2.4	6.5
165 Ch of Nazarene	1	16	16	44	.4	.9
193 Episcopal	1	NR	77	142	1.1	3.1
283 Luth—MO Synod	1	391	151	504	4.0	10.8
355 Presb Ch (USA)	3	595	276	727 *	5.8	15.6
413 S.D.A.	1	67	NR	80	.6	1.7
419 So Bapt Conv	1	53	42	65 *	.5	1.4
443 Un C of Christ	1	296	95	361 *	2.9	7.8
449 Un Methodist	1	293	128	358 *	2.9	7.7
HOT SPRINGS	**13**	**755**	**534**	**1,925 ***	**39.4**	**100.0**
053 Assemb of God	1	113	60	100	2.0	5.2
056 Baha'i	0	1	NR	1	-	.1
081 Catholic	1	NR	NR	519	10.6	27.0
145 Ch God Prophcy	1	24	NR	28 *	.6	1.5
151 L-D Saints	1	NR	NR	346	7.1	18.0

NR–Not Reported *Total adherents estimated from known number of communicant, confirmed, full members. - Represents a percentage less than 0.1. Percentages may not total 100 due to rounding.

Table 4: Religious Congregations by County and Group: 2000

Religious Group	Number of Churches, Synagogues, Mosques, or Temples	Number of Communicant, Confirmed, or Full Members	Number of Attendees	Total Adherents		
				Number of Adherents	% of Total Pop.	% of Total Adh.
167 Chs of Christ	1	20	15	26	.5	1.4
193 Episcopal	1	NR	51	152	3.1	7.9
263 Int Foursq Gos	1	16	19	19 *	.4	1.0
283 Luth—MO Synod	1	129	79	156	3.2	8.1
355 Presb Ch (USA)	1	53	105	105 *	2.2	5.5
413 S.D.A.	1	9	NR	11	.2	.6
419 So Bapt Conv	2	293	97	347 *	7.1	18.0
449 Un Methodist	1	97	108	115 *	2.4	6.0
JOHNSON	**17**	**1,007**	**770**	**3,638 ***	**51.4**	**100.0**
053 Assemb of God	1	55	83	139	2.0	3.8
056 Baha'i	0	3	NR	3	-	.1
081 Catholic	3	NR	NR	1,517	21.4	41.7
151 L-D Saints	1	NR	NR	256	3.6	7.0
167 Chs of Christ	1	26	30	37	.5	1.0
193 Episcopal	2	NR	106	398	5.6	10.9
207 E.L.C.A.	1	180	90	231	3.3	6.3
283 Luth—MO Synod	1	90	41	135	1.9	3.7
413 S.D.A.	1	23	NR	27	.4	.7
419 So Bapt Conv	2	294	143	356 *	5.0	9.8
443 Un C of Christ	1	84	37	102 *	1.4	2.8
449 Un Methodist	2	171	78	207 *	2.9	5.7
467 Wesleyan	1	81	162	230	3.3	6.3
LARAMIE	**83**	**12,661**	**6,610**	**38,925 ***	**47.7**	**100.0**
017 Amer Bapt Assn	1	30	NR	37 *	-	.1
019 Amer Bapt USA	3	543	316	677 *	.8	1.7
053 Assemb of God	5	352	431	651	.8	1.7
056 Baha'i	1	36	NR	36	-	.1
057 Bapt Gen Conf	3	404	747	856 *	1.0	2.2
071 Brethren (Ash)	1	58	75	72 *	.1	.2
081 Catholic	6	NR	NR	17,578	21.5	45.2
084 Calvary Chapel	1	NR	NR	NR	-	-
089 Chr & Miss Al	1	114	NR	579	.7	1.5
093 Chr Ch (Disc)	1	820	255	1,022 *	1.3	2.6
097 Chr Chs&Chs Cr	1	200	NR	249 *	.3	.6
127 Ch God (Cleve)	1	117	68	146 *	.2	.4
151 L-D Saints	7	NR	NR	2,726	3.3	7.0
165 Ch of Nazarene	2	209	197	359	.4	.9
167 Chs of Christ	2	195	220	270	.3	.7
173 Comm of Christ	1	83	NR	83	.1	.2
175 Congr Chr Chs	1	775	345	966 *	1.2	2.5
179 Consrv Bapt	1	NR	250	250	.3	.6
193 Episcopal	2	NR	264	525	.6	1.3
203 Evan Free Ch	1	77	250	250	.3	.6
207 E.L.C.A.	3	1,486	564	2,038	2.5	5.2
223 Free Will Bapt	1	0	NR	0 *	-	-
246 Greek Orthodox	1	NR	NR	0	-	-
263 Int Foursq Gos	1	44	89	89 *	.1	.2
264 Int Chs of Crst	1	38	78	63	.1	.2
283 Luth—MO Synod	5	1,342	617	1,791	2.2	4.6
290 Metro Comm Ch	1	14	5	5 *	-	-
297 Mennonite;Other	1	34	NR	42 *	.1	.1
339 Pent Ch of God	1	142	NR	374	.5	1.0
355 Presb Ch (USA)	4	788	354	982 *	1.2	2.5
356 Presb Ch Amer	1	68	90	92	.1	.2
388 Reg Bapt Gen As	1	0	0	0 *	-	-
403 Salvation Army	1	184	54	377	.5	1.0
413 S.D.A.	1	121	NR	144	.2	.4
418 Southw Bapt Fel	1	NR	NR	NR	-	-
419 So Bapt Conv	7	2,185	307	2,723 *	3.3	7.0
435 Unitarian-Univ	1	127	NR	158 *	.2	.4
449 Un Methodist	8	1,973	943	2,458 *	3.0	6.3
469 WELS	1	102	91	157	.2	.4
496 Jewish Est	0	NR	NR	100	.1	.3
LINCOLN	**34**	**511**	**301**	**10,398 ***	**71.4**	**100.0**
056 Baha'i	0	6	NR	6	-	.1
081 Catholic	4	NR	NR	1,643	11.3	15.8
151 L-D Saints	21	NR	NR	7,981	54.8	76.8
193 Episcopal	2	NR	28	101	.7	1.0
203 Evan Free Ch	1	25	25	25	.2	.2
263 Int Foursq Gos	1	27	37	37 *	.3	.4
283 Luth—MO Synod	1	126	40	183	1.3	1.8
419 So Bapt Conv	3	248	134	320 *	2.2	3.1
449 Un Methodist	1	79	37	102 *	.7	1.0
NATRONA	**64**	**10,144**	**5,719**	**29,232 ***	**43.9**	**100.0**
019 Amer Bapt USA	2	340	216	423 *	.6	1.4
053 Assemb of God	2	369	482	824	1.2	2.8
056 Baha'i	0	39	NR	39	.1	.1
081 Catholic	4	NR	NR	10,001	15.0	34.2
089 Chr & Miss Al	1	44	NR	130	.2	.4
093 Chr Ch (Disc)	1	386	175	480 *	.7	1.6
097 Chr Chs&Chs Cr	4	375	NR	466 *	.7	1.6
123 Ch God (Ander)	1	NR	1,335	1,335	2.0	4.6
145 Ch God Prophcy	1	24	NR	29 *	-	.1
151 L-D Saints	7	NR	NR	3,141	4.7	10.7
165 Ch of Nazarene	1	194	136	273	.4	.9
167 Chs of Christ	3	256	297	349	.5	1.2
173 Comm of Christ	1	40	NR	40	.1	.1
179 Consrv Bapt	1	NR	30	30	-	.1
193 Episcopal	2	NR	273	1,198	1.8	4.1
203 Evan Free Ch	1	63	160	160	.2	.5
207 E.L.C.A.	4	1,453	607	1,891	2.8	6.5
246 Greek Orthodox	1	NR	NR	0	-	-
263 Int Foursq Gos	1	35	85	85 *	.1	.3
283 Luth—MO Synod	2	689	356	893	1.3	3.1
306 NT IndBapt&Rltd	3	305	NR	379 *	.6	1.3
355 Presb Ch (USA)	3	680	324	845 *	1.3	2.9
403 Salvation Army	1	131	62	255	.4	.9
413 S.D.A.	1	215	NR	256	.4	.9
419 So Bapt Conv	9	2,676	675	3,326 *	5.0	11.4
435 Unitarian-Univ	1	35	NR	43 *	.1	.1
443 Un C of Christ	1	81	50	101 *	.2	.3
449 Un Methodist	3	1,660	405	2,063 *	3.1	7.1
469 WELS	1	54	51	77	.1	.3
496 Jewish Est	1	NR	NR	100	.2	.3
NIOBRARA	**12**	**477**	**201**	**1,185 ***	**49.2**	**100.0**
019 Amer Bapt USA	1	54	41	65 *	2.7	5.5
081 Catholic	1	NR	NR	361	15.0	30.5
089 Chr & Miss Al	3	68	NR	182	7.6	15.4
097 Chr Chs&Chs Cr	1	25	NR	30 *	1.2	2.5
145 Ch God Prophcy	1	24	NR	28 *	1.2	2.4
151 L-D Saints	1	NR	NR	58	2.4	4.9
193 Episcopal	1	NR	21	65	2.7	5.5
283 Luth—MO Synod	1	142	68	200	8.3	16.9
419 So Bapt Conv	1	27	11	32 *	1.3	2.7
443 Un C of Christ	1	137	60	164 *	6.8	13.8
PARK	**50**	**3,936**	**2,447**	**11,853 ***	**46.0**	**100.0**
053 Assemb of God	2	133	165	249	1.0	2.1
056 Baha'i	0	10	NR	10	-	.1
081 Catholic	5	NR	NR	3,335	12.9	28.1
089 Chr & Miss Al	1	64	NR	288	1.1	2.4
097 Chr Chs&Chs Cr	1	100	NR	121 *	.5	1.0
123 Ch God (Ander)	2	NR	57	57	.2	.5
145 Ch God Prophcy	2	47	NR	58 *	.2	.5
151 L-D Saints	9	NR	NR	2,364	9.2	19.9
165 Ch of Nazarene	2	128	91	146	.6	1.2
167 Chs of Christ	2	126	164	180	.7	1.5
173 Comm of Christ	1	61	NR	61	.2	.5
179 Consrv Bapt	3	NR	300	300	1.2	2.5
193 Episcopal	3	NR	180	641	2.5	5.4
207 E.L.C.A.	2	472	254	631	2.4	5.3
263 Int Foursq Gos	1	52	59	63 *	.2	.5
283 Luth—MO Synod	2	532	267	664	2.6	5.6
306 NT IndBapt&Rltd	1	75	NR	91 *	.4	.8
355 Presb Ch (USA)	2	801	366	973 *	3.8	8.2
370 Ref Baptist Chs	1	NR	NR	NR	-	-
413 S.D.A.	2	51	NR	61	.2	.5
419 So Bapt Conv	4	539	216	655 *	2.5	5.5
449 Un Methodist	2	745	328	905 *	3.5	7.6

NR–Not Reported *Total adherents estimated from known number of communicant, confirmed, full members. - Represents a percentage less than 0.1. Percentages may not total 100 due to rounding.

Table 4: Religious Congregations by County and Group: 2000

Religious Group	Number of Churches, Synagogues, Mosques, or Temples	Number of Communicant, Confirmed, or Full Members	Number of Attendees	Total Adherents: Number of Adherents	% of Total Pop.	% of Total Adh.
PLATTE	**23**	**1,653**	**804**	**4,125 ***	**46.8**	**100.0**
053 Assemb of God	1	81	125	157	1.8	3.8
056 Baha'i	0	2	NR	2	-	-
057 Bapt Gen Conf	1	30	54	54 *	.6	1.3
081 Catholic	4	NR	NR	1,482	16.8	35.9
097 Chr Chs&Chs Cr	1	200	NR	245 *	2.8	5.9
151 L-D Saints	1	NR	NR	207	2.4	5.0
165 Ch of Nazarene	1	32	17	41	.5	1.0
173 Comm of Christ	1	10	NR	10	.1	.2
179 Consrv Bapt	1	NR	65	65	.7	1.6
193 Episcopal	3	NR	85	243	2.8	5.9
207 E.L.C.A.	1	260	80	334	3.8	8.1
283 Luth—MO Synod	1	160	78	210	2.4	5.1
306 NT IndBapt&Rltd	1	50	NR	61 *	.7	1.5
355 Presb Ch (USA)	1	96	48	118 *	1.3	2.9
413 S.D.A.	1	16	NR	19	.2	.5
419 So Bapt Conv	1	350	90	429 *	4.9	10.4
443 Un C of Christ	1	152	55	186 *	2.1	4.5
449 Un Methodist	2	214	107	262 *	3.0	6.4
SHERIDAN	**32**	**3,296**	**2,375**	**12,377 ***	**46.6**	**100.0**
053 Assemb of God	2	87	100	154	.6	1.2
056 Baha'i	0	9	NR	9	-	.1
081 Catholic	3	NR	NR	5,341	20.1	43.2
093 Chr Ch (Disc)	1	239	82	288 *	1.1	2.3
145 Ch God Prophcy	1	24	NR	28 *	.1	.2
151 L-D Saints	4	NR	NR	946	3.6	7.6
165 Ch of Nazarene	1	68	78	132	.5	1.1
167 Chs of Christ	2	62	76	89	.3	.7
179 Consrv Bapt	1	NR	317	317	1.2	2.6
193 Episcopal	1	NR	322	841	3.2	6.8
207 E.L.C.A.	1	728	235	1,207	4.5	9.8
263 Int Foursq Gos	1	170	212	212 *	.8	1.7
283 Luth—MO Synod	1	531	198	716	2.7	5.8
339 Pent Ch of God	1	8	NR	20	.1	.2
355 Presb Ch (USA)	1	338	160	408 *	1.5	3.3
356 Presb Ch Amer	1	0	0	0	-	-
403 Salvation Army	1	43	17	99	.4	.8
413 S.D.A.	1	84	NR	100	.4	.8
419 So Bapt Conv	3	296	152	357 *	1.3	2.9
435 Unitarian-Univ	1	30	NR	36 *	.1	.3
443 Un C of Christ	1	133	45	160 *	.6	1.3
449 Un Methodist	1	305	130	368 *	1.4	3.0
467 Wesleyan	1	121	220	514	1.9	4.2
469 WELS	1	20	31	35	.1	.3
SUBLETTE	**15**	**601**	**418**	**2,608 ***	**44.1**	**100.0**
053 Assemb of God	1	18	22	30	.5	1.2
056 Baha'i	0	1	NR	1	-	-
081 Catholic	2	NR	NR	777	13.1	29.8
151 L-D Saints	2	NR	NR	770	13.0	29.5
167 Chs of Christ	1	19	20	24	.4	.9
175 Congr Chr Chs	1	40	20	49 *	.8	1.9
193 Episcopal	2	NR	83	247	4.2	9.5
263 Int Foursq Gos	1	30	50	50 *	.8	1.9
283 Luth—MO Synod	2	152	67	238	4.0	9.1
419 So Bapt Conv	2	235	121	291 *	4.9	11.2
443 Un C of Christ	1	106	35	131 *	2.2	5.0
SWEETWATER	**60**	**3,474**	**2,033**	**21,187 ***	**56.3**	**100.0**
019 Amer Bapt USA	2	54	67	68 *	.2	.3
053 Assemb of God	3	138	172	302	.8	1.4
056 Baha'i	0	22	NR	22	.1	.1
081 Catholic	5	NR	NR	10,095	26.8	47.6
089 Chr & Miss Al	1	33	NR	131	.3	.6
097 Chr Chs&Chs Cr	1	81	NR	103 *	.3	.5
151 L-D Saints	18	NR	NR	5,881	15.6	27.8
165 Ch of Nazarene	2	63	51	105	.3	.5
167 Chs of Christ	4	199	204	246	.7	1.2
179 Consrv Bapt	1	NR	87	87	.2	.4
193 Episcopal	2	NR	110	367	1.0	1.7
203 Evan Free Ch	3	225	375	375	1.0	1.8
207 E.L.C.A.	1	233	50	298	.8	1.4
246 Greek Orthodox	1	NR	NR	0	-	-
283 Luth—MO Synod	2	412	174	557	1.5	2.6
355 Presb Ch (USA)	1	62	25	79 *	.2	.4
373 Ref Ch in U.S.	1	26	NR	35	.1	.2
413 S.D.A.	1	59	NR	70	.2	.3
419 So Bapt Conv	7	1,309	477	1,659 *	4.4	7.8
443 Un C of Christ	2	390	142	494 *	1.3	2.3
449 Un Methodist	2	168	99	213 *	.6	1.0
TETON	**15**	**824**	**865**	**4,372 ***	**24.0**	**100.0**
019 Amer Bapt USA	1	198	100	233 *	1.3	5.3
056 Baha'i	0	4	NR	4	-	.1
081 Catholic	2	NR	NR	1,739	9.5	39.8
151 L-D Saints	2	NR	NR	1,164	6.4	26.6
167 Chs of Christ	1	38	44	47	.3	1.1
193 Episcopal	1	NR	215	467	2.6	10.7
207 E.L.C.A.	1	131	63	185	1.0	4.2
283 Luth—MO Synod	1	73	38	84	.5	1.9
355 Presb Ch (USA)	1	249	275	294 *	1.6	6.7
413 S.D.A.	1	0	NR	0	-	-
418 Southw Bapt Fel	1	NR	NR	NR	-	-
419 So Bapt Conv	2	83	80	98 *	.5	2.2
449 Un Methodist	1	48	50	57 *	.3	1.3
UINTA	**39**	**1,273**	**736**	**12,260 ***	**62.1**	**100.0**
019 Amer Bapt USA	1	90	97	119 *	.6	1.0
053 Assemb of God	2	50	65	92	.5	.8
056 Baha'i	0	2	NR	2	-	-
081 Catholic	2	NR	NR	1,840	9.3	15.0
089 Chr & Miss Al	1	63	NR	192	1.0	1.6
127 Ch God (Cleve)	1	22	28	29 *	.1	.2
151 L-D Saints	21	NR	NR	8,390	42.5	68.4
165 Ch of Nazarene	1	17	20	20	.1	.2
167 Chs of Christ	1	26	28	34	.2	.3
193 Episcopal	2	NR	60	156	.8	1.3
207 E.L.C.A.	1	119	70	164	.8	1.3
283 Luth—MO Synod	2	106	66	191	1.0	1.6
355 Presb Ch (USA)	2	181	103	240 *	1.2	2.0
419 So Bapt Conv	2	597	199	791 *	4.0	6.5
WASHAKIE	**22**	**1,808**	**976**	**4,763 ***	**57.5**	**100.0**
053 Assemb of God	3	215	246	331	4.0	6.9
056 Baha'i	0	1	NR	1	-	-
081 Catholic	1	NR	NR	1,201	14.5	25.2
123 Ch God (Ander)	1	NR	125	125	1.5	2.6
145 Ch God Prophcy	1	24	NR	29 *	.3	.6
151 L-D Saints	3	NR	NR	904	10.9	19.0
167 Chs of Christ	1	117	124	159	1.9	3.3
193 Episcopal	1	NR	63	165	2.0	3.5
207 E.L.C.A.	1	221	74	324	3.9	6.8
246 Greek Orthodox	1	NR	NR	0	-	-
263 Int Foursq Gos	1	14	19	19 *	.2	.4
283 Luth—MO Synod	1	208	72	258	3.1	5.4
355 Presb Ch (USA)	1	95	43	118 *	1.4	2.5
413 S.D.A.	2	69	NR	82	1.0	1.7
419 So Bapt Conv	2	406	85	504 *	6.1	10.6
449 Un Methodist	2	438	125	543 *	6.6	11.4
WESTON	**16**	**1,075**	**439**	**2,450 ***	**36.9**	**100.0**
053 Assemb of God	2	65	90	145	2.2	5.9
056 Baha'i	0	6	NR	6	.1	.2
081 Catholic	2	NR	NR	802	12.1	32.7
097 Chr Chs&Chs Cr	1	51	NR	61 *	.9	2.5
151 L-D Saints	1	NR	NR	191	2.9	7.8
167 Chs of Christ	1	15	19	20	.3	.8
193 Episcopal	1	NR	26	66	1.0	2.7
207 E.L.C.A.	1	272	80	351	5.3	14.3
263 Int Foursq Gos	1	21	34	34 *	.5	1.4
413 S.D.A.	3	135	NR	161	2.4	6.6
419 So Bapt Conv	1	65	20	78 *	1.2	3.2
449 Un Methodist	2	445	170	535 *	8.1	21.8

NR–Not Reported *Total adherents estimated from known number of communicant, confirmed, full members. - Represents a percentage less than 0.1. Percentages may not total 100 due to rounding.

Table 5: Religious Congregations by Metropolitan Size and Group: 2000

Religious Group		Total Adherents	Percent Adherents in Metropolitan Size of:					Percent of Adherents Outside Metropolitan Area	Percent of Congregations Outside Metropolitan Area
			5,000,000 or More	1,000,000 to 4,999,999	250,000 to 999,999	100,000 to 249,999	Less Than 100,000		
TOTAL U.S. POPULATION		**281,421,906**	**29.9**	**27.1**	**16.4**	**6.4**	**.5**	**19.7**	**NA**
TOTAL ADHERENTS		**141,371,963 ***	**32.0**	**25.0**	**16.1**	**6.4**	**.6**	**19.9**	**40.9**
007	OCA: Alban Dioc	5,775	93.1	3.5	-	3.5	-	-	-
009	Alban Orth Dio	395	100.0	-	-	-	-	-	-
011	A.W.M.C.	1,864	.5	17.3	20.6	10.0	.9	50.7	47.8
017	Amer Bapt Assn	280,973 *	5.6	11.9	20.3	7.7	2.5	52.1	53.9
019	Amer Bapt USA	1,767,462 *	38.4	20.6	14.7	5.0	.3	20.9	32.8
022	Carp Rus Orth	20,000	31.9	21.8	20.7	12.1	-	13.5	17.3
032	Amish; other	6,671 *	4.5	1.1	6.3	5.3	-	82.8	81.1
034	Ant Orth of NA	82,374	42.1	31.1	19.0	4.7	-	3.1	7.6
039	Ap Chr Ch(Naz)	4,393 *	14.3	43.3	23.5	18.4	-	.5	2.0
040	Ap Chr Ch-Amer	23,980 *	4.3	9.9	36.1	6.7	-	43.1	41.7
049	Armen Ap Cilic	46,354	87.2	4.8	7.9	-	-	.2	2.6
050	Armen Ap Etchm	91,513	72.4	15.7	11.1	.9	-	-	-
053	Assemb of God	2,561,998	19.9	27.9	20.4	8.4	.7	22.7	38.4
055	As Ref Pres Ch	40,397	3.4	35.4	27.3	1.7	-	32.1	34.7
056	Baha'i	146,756	24.7	28.9	14.6	8.7	.6	22.5	12.1
057	Bapt Gen Conf	238,920 *	36.3	34.5	8.6	6.2	.5	14.0	25.6
059	Bapt Miss Assn	295,239 *	13.6	7.0	14.1	6.4	2.9	56.0	60.6
061	Beachy Amish	9,422 *	.7	8.2	16.5	12.3	-	62.4	65.7
070	Bruderhof Comm	924	28.6	28.6	-	-	-	42.9	42.9
071	Brethren (Ash)	16,266 *	4.7	25.7	13.7	17.7	.4	37.8	45.4
075	Brethren in Cr	25,512	15.0	11.4	45.2	3.3	-	25.2	28.2
076	Buddhism	NR	NR	NR	NR	NR	NR	NR	6.7
078	Bulgar Orth USA	5,340	66.3	19.9	7.1	-	-	6.7	11.1
081	Catholic	62,035,042	45.6	23.7	14.1	4.8	.5	11.3	35.1
084	Calvary Chapel	NR	NR	NR	NR	NR	NR	NR	17.9
089	Chr & Miss Al	331,106	21.3	28.7	20.3	10.4	.9	18.4	24.7
093	Chr Ch (Disc)	1,017,784 *	9.3	29.4	15.7	10.5	.9	34.2	42.9
097	Chr Chs&Chs Cr	1,439,253 *	8.7	28.0	17.4	8.4	.5	37.0	49.8
105	Christian Ref	248,938 *	19.8	45.6	7.8	5.2	.1	21.5	23.4
107	Christian Un	7,319 *	-	36.3	12.1	2.9	2.8	45.9	58.8
121	Ch God (Abr)	4,925 *	4.0	19.3	46.3	3.2	-	27.3	37.1
123	Ch God (Ander)	238,609	15.2	28.5	19.5	7.8	.7	28.3	39.3
127	Ch God (Cleve)	974,198 *	12.5	25.1	21.1	6.7	.2	34.4	42.8
143	CG in Cr(Menn)	15,337 *	-	.7	11.5	6.9	.2	80.8	83.0
145	Ch God Prophcy	91,106 *	14.6	19.6	16.7	6.4	.5	42.1	43.9

NR–Not Reported *Total adherents estimated from known number of communicant, confirmed, full members. - Represents a percentage less than 0.1. Percentages may not total 100 due to rounding.

Table 5: Religious Congregations by Metropolitan Size and Group: 2000

	Religious Group	Total Adherents	Percent Adherents in Metropolitan Size of:					Percent of Adherents Outside Metropolitan Area	Percent of Congregations Outside Metropolitan Area
			5,000,000 or More	1,000,000 to 4,999,999	250,000 to 999,999	100,000 to 249,999	Less Than 100,000		
151	L-D Saints	4,224,026	12.3	38.1	17.9	4.2	1.3	26.2	30.2
157	Ch of Brethren	171,281 *	11.1	5.7	25.3	16.8	.1	41.0	47.4
165	Ch of Nazarene	907,331	15.2	26.6	20.0	8.8	.6	28.8	38.8
167	Chs of Christ	1,645,584	13.0	24.2	15.8	11.2	.7	35.1	50.8
171	Ch God-Gen Con	42,204 *	4.0	9.2	41.3	9.2	-	36.4	44.0
173	Comm of Christ	98,874	12.7	34.2	18.2	7.0	.8	27.1	40.1
175	Congr Chr Chs	84,380 *	27.9	26.5	16.1	8.9	1.1	19.5	35.4
176	Congr Ad Afl	17,821 *	28.2	18.0	8.1	2.8	-	43.0	63.5
179	Consrv Bapt	224,306	33.7	29.1	11.9	6.1	.6	18.7	26.6
181	Consrv Congr	50,940 *	34.8	22.8	11.8	6.7	.1	23.8	36.4
183	Cons Menn Conf	14,865	.9	10.4	13.7	12.2	-	62.8	54.8
185	Cumber Presb	77,686	6.4	18.5	16.5	8.5	.7	49.3	65.4
186	Coptic Orth Ch	NR	NR	NR	NR	NR	NR	NR	-
189	Duck Rivr Bapt	12,542 *	-	4.0	.7	1.5	-	93.8	89.9
191	Entrpr Bpt Asc	5,289 *	.9	13.3	12.6	-	-	73.2	70.8
193	Episcopal	2,314,756	34.2	26.1	18.8	6.4	.5	14.0	31.3
201	Evan Cov Ch	153,116 *	25.4	37.6	13.7	5.9	.3	17.2	28.0
203	Evan Free Ch	285,699	25.1	25.2	18.0	7.7	1.2	23.0	35.0
207	E.L.C.A.	5,113,418	15.8	25.0	17.4	9.0	1.5	31.3	40.3
211	Fel Evg Bib Ch	1,811	-	9.9	38.2	-	-	51.8	64.7
213	Evan Menn Inc	6,625 *	1.6	-	82.8	4.8	-	10.7	17.6
216	Evan Presby Ch	80,207 *	26.0	49.3	12.5	4.3	.5	7.4	18.4
220	Free Lutheran	32,098	9.1	18.2	2.3	6.2	4.7	59.5	63.7
221	Free Methodist	96,237	22.6	26.1	13.9	7.8	.6	29.0	36.7
223	Free Will Bapt	254,170 *	2.9	13.0	19.3	9.5	.3	55.0	53.7
226	Friends-USA	113,086 *	23.9	23.8	12.1	6.8	.3	33.1	37.3
230	Fund Methodist	1,009 *	-	-	14.2	.8	-	85.0	61.5
237	Menn Br US Conf	28,142 *	9.6	16.5	39.9	5.6	1.9	26.6	24.6
241	Gen Six Pr Bpt	25 *	-	-	-	-	-	100.0	100.0
245	Greek Orth Vslp	30,148	43.8	11.1	29.6	7.4	-	8.0	21.1
246	Greek Orthodox	427,659	55.7	24.2	14.3	3.2	.2	2.3	7.7
249	Assyr Apost Ch	35,118	83.6	7.0	9.4	-	-	-	-
251	Holy Orth in NA	1,889	66.1	17.0	14.5	.5	-	1.9	3.3
252	Hindu	NR	NR	NR	NR	NR	NR	NR	5.2
257	Hutterian Br	12,300	-	-	.8	1.6	3.3	94.3	94.3
258	IndFreeWillBapt	24,107 *	-	2.5	13.7	2.1	-	81.7	82.2
262	Int Cou Comm Ch	64,186 *	43.0	25.2	20.6	5.4	-	5.8	9.9
263	Int Foursq Gos	347,367 *	27.1	26.8	19.1	7.6	.6	18.7	25.8

NR–Not Reported *Total adherents estimated from known number of communicant, confirmed, full members. - Represents a percentage less than 0.1. Percentages may not total 100 due to rounding.

Table 5: Religious Congregations by Metropolitan Size and Group: 2000

Religious Group	Total Adherents	Percent Adherents in Metropolitan Size of: 5,000,000 or More	1,000,000 to 4,999,999	250,000 to 999,999	100,000 to 249,999	Less Than 100,000	Percent of Adherents Outside Metropolitan Area	Percent of Congregations Outside Metropolitan Area
264 Int Chs of Crst	79,161	52.2	37.3	8.3	1.4	.4	.4	5.1
265 Int Pent C Chr	5,453	13.1	19.9	24.9	1.7	-	40.4	41.8
266 Intrstat & Asc	16,127 *	-	4.8	15.5	10.6	-	69.1	69.4
267 Muslim Est	1,559,294	69.6	21.2	6.8	1.5	.1	.8	6.5
268 Jain	NR	NR	NR	NR	NR	NR	NR	1.1
269 Jasper&PVB Asc	7,078 *	-	92.1	-	-	-	7.9	9.7
273 LandmrkBapt,I&U	5,682 *	5.0	5.0	5.2	3.2	-	81.5	69.5
283 Luth--MO Synod	2,521,062	19.8	26.7	14.3	8.0	.9	30.4	41.1
286 E.PA Mennonite	4,384 *	11.7	-	45.8	2.1	-	40.4	44.9
288 Mennonite USA	156,345 *	15.5	8.6	30.5	9.9	.3	35.4	35.0
289 New Hope B Asc	2,772 *	-	67.1	-	-	-	32.9	40.0
290 Metro Comm Ch	23,440 *	34.1	40.3	18.0	5.4	.3	1.8	5.8
291 Missionary Ch	49,528	28.8	9.5	29.5	13.9	-	18.2	29.6
292 Morav Ch-AK	2,562 *	-	-	.7	-	-	99.3	95.8
293 Morav Ch-North	25,872	22.8	5.1	41.5	3.9	-	26.7	30.1
295 Morav Ch-South	19,764	-	92.0	.7	1.0	-	6.4	10.2
296 Midw Congr Fel	1,705 *	-	3.4	-	7.9	-	88.7	86.2
297 Mennonite;Other	34,617 *	8.0	4.7	22.6	8.6	.1	55.9	58.3
304 NatPrimBapt USA	66,452 *	8.0	31.0	43.9	2.4	-	14.8	28.7
306 NT IndBapt&Rltd	132,684 *	19.8	21.6	16.3	9.8	.6	32.0	38.8
307 Neth Ref Congr	4,442	19.3	18.4	6.9	12.9	-	42.5	26.7
313 N Am Bapt Conf	59,545 *	21.0	35.9	12.2	5.7	3.9	21.3	33.1
320 "Old" MB Ascs	49,870 *	.7	20.8	1.3	3.5	-	73.6	75.8
322 Old Ord Menn Ch	21,116 *	-	1.8	50.6	8.5	-	39.1	50.8
323 Old Ord Amish	96,986 *	1.3	5.3	21.1	9.7	-	62.6	65.5
324 Old Ord Rvr Br	540	-	-	38.0	-	-	62.0	60.0
330 Macedonian Orth	16,640	63.7	26.7	9.6	-	-	-	-
331 OCA: Ter Diocs	77,110	33.0	22.1	25.1	2.6	.1	17.1	23.8
332 OCA: Bulg Dioc	8,791	85.2	6.7	7.9	-	-	.2	5.6
333 Malan Dioc Am	13,225	80.5	18.1	.8	-	-	.6	1.7
334 Malan Syr Orth	4,336	80.5	12.6	6.9	-	-	-	-
335 Orth Pres Ch	26,346	40.2	22.1	11.7	12.4	.4	13.2	20.9
336 OrigFreeWillBpt	46,211 *	-	16.6	.8	23.8	-	58.8	59.1
339 Pent Ch of God	101,921	13.3	15.5	22.2	12.1	1.0	36.0	42.1
349 Pent Holiness	241,828 *	6.2	24.1	22.6	11.0	.1	36.0	44.1
355 Presb Ch (USA)	3,141,566 *	22.2	30.9	18.2	7.6	.6	20.5	38.0
356 Presb Ch Amer	315,293	19.0	32.1	29.8	6.8	.1	12.3	24.4
360 Prim Bapt Chrch	NR	NR	NR	NR	NR	NR	NR	62.7

NR–Not Reported *Total adherents estimated from known number of communicant, confirmed, full members. - Represents a percentage less than 0.1. Percentages may not total 100 due to rounding.

Table 5: Religious Congregations by Metropolitan Size and Group: 2000

	Religious Group	Total Adherents	Percent Adherents in Metropolitan Size of:					Percent of Adherents Outside Metropolitan Area	Percent of Congregations Outside Metropolitan Area
			5,000,000 or More	1,000,000 to 4,999,999	250,000 to 999,999	100,000 to 249,999	Less Than 100,000		
362	Prim Bapt E Dst	7,840 *	-	-	56.1	-	-	43.9	47.8
363	Primitive Meth	4,796	19.0	16.5	32.9	2.5	-	29.1	29.1
365	Prog Prim Bapt	9,615 *	.6	6.7	17.4	5.5	-	69.8	71.9
369	Prot Ref Chs	5,875	17.8	60.9	1.6	2.2	-	17.5	19.2
370	Ref Baptist Chs	NR	NR	NR	NR	NR	NR	NR	24.9
371	Ref Ch in Am	335,677	35.3	24.9	12.6	5.3	.2	21.6	24.2
373	Ref Ch in U.S.	4,236	1.9	15.8	16.5	6.9	1.5	57.3	52.6
379	Ref Mennonite	347 *	-	2.9	47.0	11.8	-	38.3	44.4
388	Reg Bapt Gen As	245,636 *	15.0	29.6	19.1	8.4	.4	27.5	36.3
395	Romania Orth Ar	7,543	77.7	22.3	-	-	-	-	-
397	OCA: Roman Dioc	17,201	56.6	36.4	6.4	.6	-	-	-
400	Rus Orth Moscow	NR	NR	NR	NR	NR	NR	NR	9.4
401	Rus Orth Abroad	NR	NR	NR	NR	NR	NR	NR	10.1
403	Salvation Army	415,060	23.5	23.9	24.0	10.2	1.2	17.2	25.5
409	Separate Bapt	10,674 *	-	13.0	.7	16.3	-	70.0	77.7
410	Serb Orth USA	55,807	49.9	36.4	7.0	4.0	-	2.7	8.0
411	Serb Orth: Grac	NR	NR	NR	NR	NR	NR	NR	5.3
413	S.D.A.	923,046	34.5	26.1	16.0	6.1	.5	16.7	34.5
416	Sikh	NR	NR	NR	NR	NR	NR	NR	3.8
418	Southw Bapt Fel	NR	NR	NR	NR	NR	NR	NR	32.3
419	So Bapt Conv	19,881,467 *	8.2	24.2	20.8	10.0	.6	36.2	50.2
420	Strict Baptists	33 *	-	54.5	-	21.2	-	24.2	33.3
423	Syrian Orth Ch	13,845	89.6	7.5	1.8	1.1	-	-	-
425	Tao	NR	NR	NR	NR	NR	NR	NR	10.5
426	2Seed Sprt Bpt	65 *	-	-	6.2	-	-	93.8	75.0
431	Ukrainian Orth	35,586	45.1	30.9	17.3	3.3	.2	3.3	9.6
435	Unitarian-Univ	182,698 *	39.3	26.2	17.2	7.9	.6	8.7	21.6
443	Un C of Christ	1,698,918 *	24.4	24.8	21.3	5.9	.5	23.1	34.5
449	Un Methodist	10,350,629 *	14.3	24.0	19.7	9.0	.5	32.5	52.1
455	Un Ref Chs N.A.	11,449	33.2	38.2	10.7	3.8	-	14.2	18.4
463	Vineyard	155,170 *	23.7	39.7	16.4	9.9	.4	9.9	18.0
466	Wayn Tr MB Asc	2,756 *	12.0	-	11.8	59.8	-	16.5	38.5
467	Wesleyan	381,459	9.9	30.8	13.3	9.6	1.0	35.4	41.0
469	WELS	405,078	8.3	26.9	14.5	8.9	.4	40.9	42.6
490	Zoroastrian	NR	NR	NR	NR	NR	NR	NR	2.9
496	Jewish Est	6,141,325	67.6	25.4	5.2	.9	-	.9	5.6
498	Indep.Charis.	935,168	28.2	44.3	18.2	5.1	.2	4.0	9.8
499	Indep.Non-Char	1,116,769	28.2	38.3	19.3	7.7	-	6.5	10.7

NR–Not Reported *Total adherents estimated from known number of communicant, confirmed, full members. - Represents a percentage less than 0.1. Percentages may not total 100 due to rounding.

Appendices

Appendix A

Religious Groups Definitions, Procedures, and Comments

Each group was invited to explain its definitions and to comment on the procedures used to determine the statistics in this study. Many groups simply provided statistics without comment. The definitions and comments that were received are shown below, arranged by code number (available in the Abbreviations Table included in the Introduction). In a few cases, additional information was deemed appropriate by the RCMS staff, and those comments are included in [brackets].

007: Orthodox Church in America: Albanian Orthodox Archdiocese

Definition of Congregations: Parish.
Definition of Members: Dues paying people, 18 years and over.
Definition of Adherents: Number of families associated with the Parish multiplied differently depending on local conditions.
Dual Affiliation: No.
See Appendix B for further details.

009: Albanian Orthodox Diocese of America

Definition of Congregations: Local parishes.
Definition of Members: Dues paying members.
Definition of Adherents: Persons known to the church.
Comments on the accuracy of the statistics: Accurate.
See Appendix B for further details.

011: Allegheny Wesleyan Methodist Connection

Definition of Congregations: Local Churches.
Definition of Members: "Full" members are those accepted into membership by vote of local congregation.
Definition of Attendees: Total enrollment of the Sunday Schools.
Definition of Adherents: Total membership (includes full, associate, and junior members).
Comments on the accuracy of the statistics: We endeavor to provide accurate figures. Some pastors who report, however, could be a bit more careful. Whenever we notice discrepancies relative to numbers carried forward from one year to another (what one ends with one year is the number he should begin with the next year) we notify the pastor and work to make sure the numbers are corrected.
Dual Affiliation: No.

019: American Baptist Churches in the USA

Definition of Congregations: Currently active churches and missions.
Definition of Members: Total church membership as reported via the Cooperating Church Annual Report form.
Definition of Attendees: Primary worship service attendance as reported via the Cooperating Church Annual Report form.
Definition of Adherents: N/A.
Comments on the RCMS estimating procedure for adherents: It is accurate.
Dual Affiliation: Yes. Assemblies of God; Baptist General Conference; Christian Church (Disciples of Christ); Christian Church/Churches of Christ; Church of the Brethren; Conservative Baptist Association; Continuing Conference of Congregational Christian Churches; Episcopal Church; National Baptist Convention of America; National Baptist Convention, USA, Inc.; Progressive National Baptist Convention; Reformed Church in America; Southern Baptist Convention; Unitarian Universalist Association; United Church of Christ; United Methodist Church

022: American Carpatho-Russian Orthodox Greek Catholic Church

Definition of Congregations: Parishes.
Definition of Members: Dues paying people between ages of 18 and 65.
Definition of Adherents: Dues paying members, children, and those over 65; Received figures from five largest parishes, then divided the remainder of 20,000 across all other parishes.
Comments on the accuracy of the statistics: They are accurate.
Dual Affiliation: No.
See Appendix B for further details.

032: Amish; Other Groups

Definition of Congregations: Local community of believers.
Definition of Members: Baptized adults.
Comments on the accuracy of the statistics: Totals developed by C. Nelson Hostetter by personal contact with leadership; Source is "Anabaptist World USA" (Scottdale; Herald Press, 2001) pp. 233-285. Hostetter is coauthor.
Dual Affiliation: No.

034: Antiochian Orthodox Christian Archdiocese of North America, The

Definition of Congregations: Local parishes.
Definition of Members: Dues paying members of families (children included).
Definition of Adherents: Full members multiplied by two.
Comments on the accuracy of the statistics: Accurate statistic of full members.
See Appendix B for further details.

049: Armenian Apostolic Church / Catholicossate of Cilicia

Definition of Congregations: Parish.
Definition of Members: Dues paying members over 18.

Definition of Adherents: Used 40% of households on mailing list multiplied by 3.5, or where households not available, the larger of maximum attendance or a given membership.

See Appendix B for further details.

050: Armenian Apostolic Church / Catholicossate of Etchmiadzin

Definition of Congregations: Parish.

Definition of Adherents: Used 20% of households on mailing list multiplied by 3.5. If households not available, multiplied maximum attendance by 2.2 (ratio of maximum attendance to household for those parishes with a household figure) to estimate households, then multiplied by 0.2 and 3.5. Where household maximum attendance was unavailable, we used the estimated number of members provided by the parish. If estimated members were not available, then the number of dues paying members was multiplied by 3.5.

See Appendix B for further details.

053: Assemblies of God

Definition of Congregations: Group that has met criteria established by district, and has been officially recognized by the General Council of the Assemblies of God.

Definition of Members: All whom the local church considers members, regardless of age (including junior membership).

Definition of Attendees: Average Sunday morning worship attendance (total divided by number of weeks in the year). Exception: When extreme weather, major epidemic or similar disaster beyond the control of the church causes cancellation or drastic reduction in attendance, such Sundays may be omitted in figuring weekly averages.

Definition of Adherents: Total number of persons who consider the assembly as their home church, whether or not they are enrolled as members. Includes all ages (including children) and members, who by definition are also adherents.

Dual Affiliation: No.

056: Baha'i

Definition of Congregations: A Baha'i "community" refers to any civil jurisdiction (city, township, in some states county, chapter (on reservations) and judicial districts where the resident Baha'is have elected a local spiritual assembly. A local spiritual assembly is the governing body of a Baha'i community, and since it has nine members, the Baha'i community must have at least nine members to elect it. If a jurisdiciton with a spiritual assembly has its membership fall under nine (Baha'is move a lot), the assembly is in "jeopardy." A community that has nine members on April 21 of every year can elect a spiritual assembly; if there are not nine in the civil jurisdiction, the assembly cannot be elected, and if there was one the previous year, that assembly is considered "lost" if it cannot be re-elected on April 21. If a community with less than nine rises to nine or more from move-ins or enrollments, it cannot elect a spiritual assembly until April 21. Jurisdictions lacking assemblies but having more than two Baha'is are called "groups." The figure of 1170 refers to communities with nine or more members on April 2001 that elected a spiritual assembly.

Definition of Members: When a person accepts that Baha'u'llah is the latest messenger of God, he or she "declares" that belief to a Baha'i. The local spiritual assembly meets with the person (in toto or through one or more representatives) to make sure he or she has the spark of faith and understands that being a Baha'i is a serious commitment. If the person understands those things he or she is "enrolled." The number of 144,516 represents the number of people in the United States, not known to have died, who have been enrolled in the Faith. We have valid addresses for about half of them; of the other half, some of them correct their addresses eventually and some never do.

Definition of Attendees: We do not count "attendees."

Definition of Adherents: The definition of "adherent" is the same as "full member."

Comments on the accuracy of the statistics: Our statistics for adults are far more complete than for youth (ages 15-20) and children. At age 21, a Baha'i can vote and be elected to a local spiritual assembly. Consequently we must keep updated voting lists. Children with one or two Baha'i parents must be registered by their parents, and not all parents do this, sometimes because the spouse is of another religion, sometimes because they don't see any advantage of the effort (because children can't vote or anything like that). At age 15, children come of age and if they are already registered as Baha'i children, they are considered Baha'is unless they choose otherwise. If they are not registered as Baha'i children, they are not considered Baha'is unless they declare and are enrolled, just like adults. Of our 144,516 members, 124,040 are aged 21 and older; 7,580 are aged 15-20; and 4,542 are aged 14 and under. The Baha'i median age is about the same as the US population, and the marriage, divorce, and childbearing statistics should be roughly comparable.

Our statistics are relatively accurate for two reasons: (1) we have to maintain voting lists, because we have no clergy and the local spiritual assembly, which is elected by the local Baha'is annually, coordinates the Baha'i community, and must maintain a voting list to be elected; (2) we send out a national newspaper, The American Baha'i, to all members with known addresses ten times per year, and we request address change information.

We do not collect congregational data. We maintain a national membership database and send a printout to each local community every March. They check their printout, make corrections, and send it back. The responsibility of maintaining the voting list falls on the national spiritual assembly of each country, not on its local spiritual assemblies. National assemblies also issue Baha'i identification cards; in the US we send out new cards every few years. In the next year or so a web-based membership updating system will go on line that will allow local spiritual assembly representatives to change the portion of the national database for their jurisdiction.

Dual Affiliation: No. Neither Baha'i communities nor individual Baha'is are allowed to maintain dual affiliations.

070: Bruderhof Communities, Inc.

Definition of Adherents: [Total membership figure divided evenly among all congregations.]

071: Brethren Church, The (Ashland, Ohio)

Definition of Congregations: Recognized congregations and missions, approved by their respective district conferences and the General Conference of the Brethren Church.

Definition of Members: Generally, this is the active, baptized membership of each local church. In some cases, churches also include inactive, baptized members.

Definition of Attendees: Average annual worship attendance for each congregation.

Definition of Adherents: We do not record this statistic nationally or locally.

Comments on the RCMS estimating procedure for adherents: Yes, this would be a resonably accurate method; no suggestions.

Comments on the accuracy of the statistics: I believe the reports are generally very accurate, reflecting actual head counts each week for attendance. The one exception is Mt. Zion in Cuyahoga County, OH, which has not reported since 1997 and is in the process of withdrawing from the Brethren Church (approved April 2001).

Dual Affiliation: Yes. Three congregations out of 119 are dually affliated: 2 with Church of the Brethren; 1 with Vineyard Church USA.

076: Buddhism

See Appendix C.

078: Bulgarian Orthodox Diocese of the USA

Definition of Adherents: Number of persons on mailing lists multiplied by two.

See Appendix B for further details.

081: Catholic Church

Definition of Congregations: "Congregations" are generally the number of parish churches plus the number of mission churches. For further details, see "Comments on the accuracy of the statistics."

Definition of Adherents: "Adherents" are generally equivalent to the number of baptized Catholic individuals reported by each diocese or eparchy. For further details, see "Comments on the accuracy of the statistics."

Comments on the accuracy of the statistics: The basic procedure for gathering Catholic data was like that for most other bodies asked to participate in the Religious Congregations Membership Study 2000. As each religious body was invited to submit statistics, so, too, was each Catholic diocese and eparchy.

The resources that each diocese or eparchy is able to devote to the gathering of such statistics varies greatly; hence, statistics may not always be exactly comparable from one region to another, or even within the same county from one year to another. Nevertheless, there are several means to verify statistics as reported.

Statistics on churches were compared with those as reported to *The Official Catholic Directory 2000.* In a few areas, because of the inclusion of oratory churches open for public worship but housing neither a parish nor a mission, the number of churches as reported in this publication exceeds the number of parish churches and mission churches as reported to The Official Catholic Directory. In Cook County, Illinois, the number of reported churches is significantly above that reported in *Churches and Church Membership in the United States 1990.* This is attributable to a large undercount of churches in that county in 1990.

Statistics on adherents were likewise compared with those reported to *The Official Catholic Directory 2000*, but were subject to additional checks as well. For each diocese, the total as submitted was compared with the total as estimated from vital and sacramental statistics for each diocese. Developed by the Catholic Research Forum, this "methodology is based upon Canon Law and assumes the definition of a Catholic as someone who is linked with the Catholic community through baptism and Catholic burial. The basis of the methodology is the computation of: 1) the percentage of babies born who receive Catholic baptism; 2) the percentage of people who die who receive Catholic funerals; and 3) an average of the baptism and funeral statistics." See, inter alia, Michael Cieslak, "Being Creative: Diverse Approaches to Estimating Catholics," paper presented to the annual meeting of the Religious Research Association, Saint Louis, Missouri, October 1995, available at http://www.cppcd.org/crf/rra_papers.htm.

While this methodology has some minor weaknesses related to migration of adherents, it is, perhaps, the most common standard used to estimate local Catholic populations, though not a prevailing one. (Some dioceses submitted parish-level sacramental statistics in addition to or in lieu of counts of individual Catholics; for nearly all of these, county-level Catholic population percentages, and populations, were estimated from vital and sacramental statistics, making the Catholic Research Forum the de facto standard in these areas as well.) In 1988, the NCCB Committee on Priorities and Plans endorsed this methodology, and Archbishop John L. May, then the president of the bishops' conference, encouraged use of this methodology. More recently other bishops have discussed making this methodology the standard for enumerating Catholics, but no official efforts have been made to do so.

In cases where the number of Catholics differed substantially from that as calculated from vital and sacramental statistics, Catholic population percentages were calculated for the diocese from the American Religious Identification Survey (ARIS) 2001, conducted by Barry Kosmin, Egon Mayer, and Ariela Keysar of the City University of New York. In a small number of cases where the Catholic population percentage as calculated from vital and sacramental statistics and ARIS were nearly equal but substantially different from that submitted by a diocese, and where no explanation was offered for this discrepancy, the number of Catholics as estimated from vital and sacramental statistics was distributed in proportion to the statistics as submitted by county.

Overall, the statistics as submitted indicate that the population of the United States is 22.0 percent Catholic. By contrast, the ARIS found that the U.S. population is 24.5 percent Catholic. This discrepancy is similar to that found in previous analyses comparing Catholic population percentages as calculated from surveys or from vital and sacramental statistics. One explanation offered for such discrepancies is that "it is easier to say one is a Catholic to an anonymous surveyor than to take the steps that are necessary to show that one is Catholic" (see Cieslak, "Being Creative: Diverse Approaches to Estimating Catholics").

The compiler notes the following issues regarding comparability. This submission, like the studies of 1980 and 1971, does not present separate tabulations for different Catholic churches in communion with each other (the most populous of which remains the Latin church), as the submission for 1990 did. As a result, to the extent that national totals are comparable across time, these data should be compared with the 1990 total showing 53,385,998 Catholics in the U.S., and with the 1980 total showing 47,502,152 Catholics, and not that showing 52,900,126 Latin Catholics in 1990. Likewise, county-level totals should be compared with the total Catholics as reported by county in 1990, not the Latin totals or the totals for any other Catholic church.

Because of the evolving methodology dioceses use to compile statistics, with many adopting the Catholic Research Forum methodology in recent years, and others possibly showing idiosyncrasies in their data collection in 1990 and 2000, not all these county-level statistics are strictly comparable with those for previous years. In some large counties, using vital and sacramental statistics to calculate the number of Catholics appears to have led to Catholic population "increases" or "decreases" of 100,000 or more. Both adoption of the Catholic Research Forum methodology and, possibly, idiosyncrasies in data collection methods elsewhere, also led to many smaller counties showing "increases" or "decreases" of 50 percent or more from their 1990 figure. In sum, the lack of a tested, officially recognized standard widely and consistently used for enumerating local area Catholics may limit analyses to compare Catholic data by area or across time. Persons interested in methodological issues for a particular diocese should write the Glenmary Research Center. GRC e-mail: grc@glenmary.org; GRC Web: www.glenmary.org/grc

089: Christian and Missionary Alliance, The

Definition of Congregations: A group of people who gather together for worship each week; a minimum of twenty committed adults attend.

Definition of Members: Confession of faith in Jesus Christ and evidence of regeneration; belief in God the Father, Son, and Holy Spirit; in the verbal inspiration of the Holy Scriptures as originally given; in the vicarious atonement of the Lord Jesus Christ; in the eternal salvation of all who believe in Him and the eternal punishment of all who reject Him; acceptance of the doctrines of the Lord Jesus Christ as Savior, Sanctifier, Healer, and Coming King; full sympathy with the principles and objectives of The Christian Missionary Alliance and cooperation by systematic support of its work; such other qualifications for membership may be stated in the bylaws.

Definition of Attendees: Every person present, regardless of age or membership. [Figures not reported to RCMS.]

Definition of Adherents: All regular non-member attendees. These are individuals that would say that this is their church home, even though they have not taken the appropriate steps toward formal membership.

121: Church of God General Conference

Definition of Congregations: Group of people who meet weekly for worship.

Definition of Members: Baptized and active in the church (attend at least 13 Sundays per year).

Definition of Attendees: Average Sunday morning worship attendance.

Definition of Adherents: N/A.

Comments on the RCMS estimating procedure for adherents: We add 30% of the membership to get adherents. This would include children and people who do not attend at least 13 Sundays per year. [The RCMS figure yielded a 41% increase, and was used for consistency's sake.]

Comments on the accuracy of the statistics: At the end of each quarter, churches report weekly Sunday morning attendance. Annually, churches report the total of their active members.

Dual Affiliation: No.

123: Church of God (Anderson, Indiana)

Definition of Adherents: [Attendance figures were used for adherents estimate.]

127: Church of God (Cleveland, Tennessee)

Definition of Congregations: Active and inactive local congregations.

Definition of Members: Full members as reported by local church treasurer's monthly report.

Definition of Attendees: N/A.

Definition of Adherents: N/A.

Comments on the RCMS estimating procedure for adherents: Yes.

Comments on the accuracy of the statistics: Reporting procedures are as accurate as possible within our denomination.

Dual Affiliation: No.

143: Church of God in Christ, Mennonite

Definition of Congregations: Recognized by denomination as self-sustaining, has a small core group of members and has elected leadership.

Definition of Members: Baptized.

Dual Affiliation: No.

145: Church of God of Prophecy

Definition of Adherents: [Membership figures were reported regionally; they were divided evenly among the churches within the region. The RCMS estimating procedure was then applied to compute adherents by county.]

157: Church of the Brethren

Definition of Congregations: The congregation is the basic unit of the church in the world. Each congregation is organized under its own articles of incorporation with a consitution and by-laws.

Definition of Members: Members of the congregation shall consist of those persons who have been received into the church by baptism, letter, or reaffirmation of faith.

Definition of Attendees: Attendees are an average of all people (adults & children) present at weekly worship service.

Definition of Adherents: Adherents are full members plus associate members (temporary or former residents). It does not include children. [Adherents were estimated using RCMS procedure.]

Dual Affiliation: Yes. Twenty-seven congregations are affiliated with other denominations. These denominations include: Mennonite Church, United Church of Christ, United Methodist Church, American Baptist Church, Christian Church (Disciples of Christ), and Brethren Church (Ashland, OH).

165: Church of the Nazarene

Definition of Congregations: All organized churches plus those NewStarts (missions) reporting statistics.

Definition of Members: Full members received into local congregations. All members of the Church of the Nazarene are members of a local congregation.

Definition of Attendees: Average weekly attendance at worship services during the prior year. This usually includes children and workers in nurseries or other specialized ministries conducted at the same time as the worship service. When multiple services are held, the totals from all services would be included.

Definition of Adherents: The larger of full and associate members, responsibility list (Sunday school enrollment, including off-site outreach classes), average weekly attendance at Sunday school (including off-site outreach classes), or average weekly worship attendance. This is a change from the 1990 definition, which was solely based on the responsibility list. Had this system been used in 1990, the reported adherent figure would have increased by less than 3%. We have changed the calculation to more accurately reflect the changing role of Sunday school in our denomination.

Comments on the accuracy of the statistics: High participation rates (over 98% annually) and double-checked by district personnel.

Dual Affiliation: No.

167: Churches of Christ

Definition of Congregations: Groups of Christians historically related to Churches of Christ who assemble as independent congregations.

Definition of Members: Baptized persons who claim membership in a particular congregation.

Definition of Attendees: Average Sunday worship attendance.

Definition of Adherents: Total number of persons (baptized and unbaptized) who comprise a congregation.

Comments on the accuracy of the statistics: Statistics reflect both self-reported and estimated counts based on a quarter of a century of research.

Dual Affiliation: No.

171: Churches of God, General Conference

Definition of Congregations: Established groups recognized by the Regional Level.

Definition of Members: People making commitment to membership at local level.

Definition of Attendees: Average worship attendance.

Comments on the accuracy of the statistics: Accurate, yearly statistics sheets are sent and there are follow-ups on non-reporters and obvious errors.

Dual Affiliation: Yes. Rare, one church is known to be dually affliated with Churches of God (Anderson, Indiana).

175: National Association of Congregational Christian Churches

Definition of Congregations: Churches are "A body complete under God in spiritual authority and ecclesiastical power, regularly meeting and worshiping in one place, united by a mutually owned covenant, in fellowship with sister Congregational Christian Churches and recognized by the laws of the place of location as a duly constituted church." (Articles of Association, III,1,a)

Definition of Members: Total active members.

Definition of Attendees: Average Sunday attendance.

Definition of Adherents: N/A.

Comments on the accuracy of the statistics: Membership figures (and most attendance data) from 316 churches (74.2%) are from the current year; 105 churches (24.6%) are from recent years. Four congregations are from older data, while one congregation was estimated. No average attendance figures were available for three congregations. They were estimated at the same proportion of attendance to membership for the remaining National Association congregations.

Information on twenty-three congregations in Affiliated Associations and Conferences that are not individually full members of the National Association, two Honorary Churches (all in the United States) and one Associate Member Church in

Canada are not included in the data given here.

Dual Affiliation: Yes. One congregation is dually aligned to the Conservative Congregational Christian Conference and the United Church of Christ; nine to the Conservative Congregational Christian Conference; twenty-one to the United Church of Christ; two to Baptist groups; two to the Christian Church (Disciples of Christ); one to the Council of Community Churches; one to the Unitarian Universalist Association. Total: 37 dually aligned congregations. In addition there are six Federated congregations, three to Baptist groups; one to a Baptist group and the Christian Church (Disciples of Christ); one to the United Methodist Church; and one to the United Methodist Church and the Unitarian Universalist Association.

176: Congregational Christian Churches, Additional (not part of any national CCC body)

Definition of Congregations: Churches are a "local continuing body of believers which is a congregation of the universal Church of Christ." (Report of the Commission on the Study of the Congregational Christian Churches, 1956.)

Definition of Members: Total membership (believers).

Definition of Attendees: N/A.

Definition of Adherents: N/A.

Comments on the accuracy of the statistics: Because these congregations relate separately to twenty-one Conferences of the United Church of Christ, relationships and the accuracy of data vary according to Conference. Reports for thirty-nine congregations (37.5%) are for the current year, while thirty-one (29.8%) are for relatively recent years. However, 32.7% of the reports are based on older data and can be identfied geographically. The old reports include all congregations in Pennsylvania, Ohio, Indiana, Colorado, and the majority in Iowa.

Dual Affiliation: Yes. These churches are affiliated with Associations and Conferences of the United Church of Christ, but are not part of any national Congregational Christian body.

The Constitution of the United Church of Christ provides that local Conferences and Associations of that Church may remain in fellowship with Congregational Christian Churches not part of the United Church of Christ. Their statistics are to be kept separately. As of January 1, 2001, twenty-four of the thirty-nine United Church of Christ congregations took advantage of this clause for 174 congregations. Ninety-six of these were reported as "Schedule I" congregations (churches "which have not voted" on whether to join the United Church of Christ, "or which have voted to abstain from voting"), and seventy-eight were reported as "Schedule II" congregations (churches "which have voted not to be part of the United Church of Christ").

Of these, forty-seven have a primary relationship to the National Association of Congregational Christian Churches, and one has a primary relationship to the Conservative Congregational Christian Conference. Since these are part of a national Congregational Christian body, their data is not reported here.

In addition, twenty-two inactive congegations (congregations with a legal existence, but not regularly holding worship services), have also been removed from this report.

This leaves the 104 congregations reported here, which are affiliated with twenty-one United Church of Christ Conferences. Three of these congregations are dually aligned, two to Baptist bodies and one to the Evangelical Covenant Church. Eight additional congregations are Federated to United Methodist, Baptist, and/or Unitarian Universalist congregations.

181: Conservative Congregational Christian Conference

Definition of Congregations: Member churches.

Definition of Members: Church membership.

Definition of Attendees: Morning attendance.

Definition of Adherents: N/A.

Comments on the accuracy of the statistics: 218 (87.2%) reports are for the current year. 31 reports are picked up from earlier years, and one congegation is estimated. Average worship attendance was not available for nine congregations. These were estimated by using the same proportion of attendance to membership for the remaining Conference congregations. Four full member congregations in Canada are not included in this report.

Dual Affiliation: Yes. One congregation is dually aligned to the National Association of Congregational Christian Churches and the United Church of Christ; nine to the National Association of Congregational Christian Chuches; four to the United Church of Christ; total fourteen dually aligned congregations. In addition one congregation is Federated to a Baptist congregation.

183: Conservative Mennonite Conference

Definition of Congregations: A congregation with identified membership of committed people, born again and baptized with regular worship service and official leadership.

Definition of Members: Baptized and recognized as a committed member.

Definition of Attendees: Average attendance in the churches on a Sunday morning.

Definition of Adherents: All members of the household of a member.

Comments on the accuracy of the statistics: Statistics are based on reports received from 70% of the membership and adjusted to represent 100%.

Dual Affiliation: No.

186: Coptic Orthodox Church

See Appendix B.

189: Duck River and Kindred Baptists Associations

Comments on the accuracy of the statistics: Data are calculated from associational minutes, in turn reported by letters of clerks to associational meetings.

Dual Affiliation: No.

191: Enterprise Baptists Association

Comments on the accuracy of the statistics: Data are calculated from associational minutes, in turn reported by letters of clerks to associational meetings.

Dual Affiliation: No.

207: Evangelical Lutheran Church in America

Definition of Congregations: Separately incorporated churches located in the United States.

Definition of Members: Confirmed adults (16 years and older) on the roll of membership.

Definition of Attendees: Average number of persons who attend church each week.

Definition of Adherents: Baptized (children and adults) members on the roll of membership.

Comments on the accuracy of the statistics: Very accurate. Annual reporting required. 91% return from congregations.

Dual Affiliation: No.

211: Fellowship of Evangelical Bible Churches

Definition of Congregations: A congregation is one church.

Definition of Members: Members are those who the churches have accepted as members of the church.

Definition of Attendees: Those who attend morning worship services (average weekly attendance).

Definition of Adherents: We believe that the attendees accurately reflect the adherents—not all churches have reported attendees.

Comments on the accuracy of the statistics: We have sent out forms. Only 11 of our 17 churches have returned their information.

Dual Affiliation: No.

213: Evangelical Mennonite Church

Comments on the accuracy of the statistics: Approximate.

Dual Affiliation: No.

216: Evangelical Presbyterian Church

Definition of Congregations: Fully established particular churches including mission churches.

Definition of Members: People who have been received by the session of the church.

Definition of Attendees: Average Sunday worship attendance. [Not reported separately to RCMS.]

Comments on the accuracy of the statistics: Accurate, not estimates.

Dual Affiliation: No.

221: Free Methodist Church of North America

Definition of Congregations: Organized churches and church plants which are in the process. Church plants do not have members and may not have reported attendance this year.

Definition of Members: Persons who have agreed to the Membership Covenant by joining as members.

Definition of Attendees: Persons who attend Sunday morning worship services.

Comments on the accuracy of the statistics: The database which was sent does not agree in number of members with this report. Ordained ministers are counted in the total membership but do not hold local church membership. Therefore, the total local church membership is less than the total number of members.

Dual Affiliation: No.

223: National Association of Free Will Baptists

Definition of Congregations: Organized/functioning churches.

Definition of Members: Those who hold membership in our local churches.

Definition of Adherents: Those who hold membership in our local churches.

Comments on the RCMS estimating procedure for adherents: Adherents and Membership mean the same in our statistical data. Adherents and Members are those who hold membership in our denomination, by virtue of being members of local Free Will Baptist Churches. [State Association membership figures were reported to RCMS. These were evenly distributed among congregations within each association.]

Comments on the accuracy of the statistics: Our denominational reporting procedures are not an accurate reflection of our denomination. Many of our reports are inaccurate, incomplete and incorrect. We are working on getting better reports from our state associations which comprise the National Association of Free Will Baptists.

Dual Affiliation: No.

226: Friends (Quakers)

Definition of Adherents: [Locations were given for each church that is part of a "Yearly Meeting." Yearly meetings are recognized groupings of Friends churches, and a total attendance figure was given for each such grouping. Each church was then assigned an equal proportion of the yearly meeting attendance totals. Of course, any arbitrary assignment of members (whether based on 1990 proportions or 2000 yearly meeting totals) can mislead users of the data. However, since the largest verifiable church membership for this denomination was only 500 members in 1990, such procedures are not as problematic as for denominations with multiple churches of several thousand members.]

230: Fundamental Methodist Conference, Inc.

Definition of Congregations: Individual congregations.

Comments on the accuracy of the statistics: Statistics are taken from the proceedings of the annual conference of the Fundamental Methodist Church, 2000.

237: Mennonite Brethren Churches, U.S. Conference of

Definition of Congregations: Includes established as well as emerging church plants.

Comments on the RCMS estimating procedure for adherents: Okay.
Comments on the accuracy of the statistics: Limited accuracy because I don't receive reporting forms from all churches.
Dual Affiliation: Yes. Two of our churches have dual membership with the Mennonite Brethren and Mennonite Church USA.

245: Greek Orthodox Archdiocese of Vasiloupulis
Definition of Members: Dues paying members of families, children are included.
Definition of Adherents: The sum total of dues paying families plus people on mailing lists.
Comments on the accuracy of the statistics: [The Eastern Christians researcher mentioned some concerns about the accuracy of the statistics.]
See Appendix B for further details.

246: Greek Orthodox Archdiocese of America
Definition of Congregations: Parish.
Definition of Members: N/A.
Definition of Adherents: Number of households on mailing lists multiplied by three.
Comments on the accuracy of the statistics: Accurate for the most part, based on mailing lists. List of households is a good indicator of affiliation with the Parish.
Dual Affiliation: No.
See Appendix B for further details.

249: Apostolic Catholic Assyrian Church of the East, North American Dioceses
Definition of Congregations: Local communities (parishes).
Definition of Adherents: Estimated number of families in each parish multiplied by 4 or 5 depending on local conditions.
Comments on the accuracy of the statistics: Rough estimates.
See Appendix B for further details.

251: Holy Orthodox Church in North America
Definition of Congregations: Local parish/community.
Definition of Adherents: Number of families in each parish multiplied by 3.
See Appendix B for further details.

252: Hindu
See Appendix C.

257: Hutterian Brethren
Definition of Members: [Total membership figure divided evenly among all congregations.]
Definition of Adherents: [Total adherent figure divided evenly among all congregations.]

262: International Council of Community Churches
Definition of Adherents: [When membership for a given congregation was not available, the median figure was used. The RCMS estimating procedure was then applied to determine adherents.]

263: International Church of the Foursquare Gospel
Definition of Congregations: Congregations are defined by the following criteria: EIW, Foursquare Code Number, Function with ICFG Board approval.
Definition of Members: Members must be at least 9 years old and must give testimony to salvation.
Definition of Attendees: The attendance figures are reported on monthly report forms and are based on a count process which is determined by each church.
Definition of Adherents: Not reported.
Comments on the RCMS estimating procedure for adherents: This is acceptable.
Dual Affiliation: No.

265: International Pentecostal Church of Christ
Definition of Congregations: Churches in full membership in the denomination.
Definition of Members: Individuals screened and accepted as full communicant members of the local church.
Definition of Attendees: Average weekly reported attendance
Definition of Adherents: The greatest of the following: weekly average attendance, church members, Sunday School enrollment, or those individuals calling the respective church their home church.
Dual Affiliation: No. IPCC does not allow for dual membership.

266: Interstate & Foreign Landmark Missionary Baptists Association
Comments on the accuracy of the statistics: Four churches did not report membership totals. Three of these reported Sunday School enrollment statistics, which were used in lieu of membeship statistics.
Dual Affiliation: No.

267: Muslim Estimate
See Appendix F.

268: Jain
See Appendix C.

283: Lutheran Church—Missouri Synod
Definition of Congregations: All members & mission starts.
Definition of Members: All confirmed members.
Definition of Attendees: Total average attendance (weekly) divided by total number of weeks.
Definition of Adherents: All baptized members.
Comments on the accuracy of the statistics: 72% of congregations reported. All others had statistics from previous year rolled forward.
Dual Affiliation: No.

288: Mennonite Church USA

Definition of Congregations: The assembly of those who by their own free decision have accepted God's offer of salvation through faith in Jesus Christ. Congregations are communities of faith that express the reign of God in the world.

Definition of Members: All youth and adults who have been baptized upon confession of faith in Jesus Christ and have committed themselves to a daily life of Christian discipleship.

Definition of Attendees: All members and nonmembers who actively participate in congregational life.

Definition of Adherents: All members and nonmembers who are within the congregation's care whether or not they are active in the life of the church.

Comments on the RCMS estimating procedure for adherents: The RCMS standard procedure for established adherents is acceptable to us. We have no further suggestions to make.

Comments on the accuracy of the statistics: Membership is reported by the congregation and then confirmed by the area conference of which it is a part. This has been our standard practice for decades. All numbers are totals as reported by congregations. Since the percentage of congregations reporting is high, no attempt has been made to project 100% level.

Dual Affiliation: Some of our congregations affiliate with other church bodies and or with other area conferences within the Mennonite Church USA. However, member totals are counted only with the area conference or church body with which it maintains primary affiliation. Thus there are no duplicate numbers within our totals.

291: Missionary Church, The

Definition of Congregations: Number of churches and other meeting places.

Definition of Members: Members have been baptized and have publicly affirmed covenant of membership.

Definition of Attendees: Number of attendees for worship attendance at primary worship services.

Definition of Adherents: N/A.

Comments on the RCMS estimating procedure for adherents: Yes, this procedure is acceptable. I would suggest that one way to measure might be to use Easter attendance.

Comments on the accuracy of the statistics: The numbers on the front are from 302 of the churches. It does not account for the total 368 churches we have.

Dual Affiliation: Yes. The church may be an independent affiliate; however, it can only use the affiliation status for 3 years.

296: Midwest Congregational Christian Fellowship

Defintion of Congregations: "Churches are a local continuing body of believers which is a congregation of the universal Church of Christ." (Report of the Commission on the Study of the Constitutional Problem, General Council of Congregational Christian Churches, 1956.)

Defintion of Members: Total members.

Defintion of Attendees: Average Attendance.

Defintion of Adherents: Not applicable.

Comments on the RCMS estimating procedure for adherents: Acceptable.

Comments on accuracy of statistics: 100% current.

Dual Affilation: No.

297: Mennonite; Other Groups

Definition of Congregations: Local community of believers.

Definition of Members: Baptized youth and adults.

Comments on the accuracy of the statistics: Totals develped by C. Nelson Hostetter by personal contact with leadership; Source is "Anabaptist World USA" (Scottdale; Herald Press, 2001) pp. 233-285; Hostetter is coauthor of book.

Dual Affiliation: No.

306: New Testament Association of Independent Baptist Churches and other Fundamental Baptist Associations/Fellowships

Definition of Adherents: [Some membership figures were supplied at the congregational level, others at the association level. In the latter case, the membership was divided evenly among congregations in the association. The RCMS estimating procedure was then applied to determine adherents.]

313: North American Baptist Conference

Definition of Congregations: Established churches.

Definition of Members: Reported members.

Definition of Attendees: Weekend worship service attendees.

Comments on the RCMS estimating procedure for adherents: Acceptable.

Comments on the accuracy of the statistics: Unknown.

Dual Affiliation: Yes. Five or 6 churches affiliated with another Baptist group.

322: Old Order Mennonite

Definition of Members: Baptized adult membership, numbers by congregation.

Comments on the accuracy of the statistics: Mennonite sub groups do not keep or publish congregational listings and membership. Totals developed by C. Nelson Hostetter through personal contact with the leadership; Source is "Anabaptist World USA" (Scottdale; Herald Press, 2001) pp. 233-285; Hostetter is coauthor.

Dual Affiliation: No

323: Old Order Amish Church

Definition of Congregations: Local community of believers.

Definition of Members: Baptized adults.

Comments on the accuracy of the statistics: Totals developed by C. Nelson Hostetter through personal contact with the leadership; Source is "Anabaptist World USA" (Scottdale; Herald Press, 2001) pp. 233-285; Hostetter is coauthor. Listing of entry limited to Old Order Amish, Old Order Amish Swartzentruber, and Old

Order Amish Nebraska.
Dual Affiliation: No.

330: Macedonian Orthodox Church: American Diocese
Definition of Adherents: Number of families multiplied by four.
Comments on the accuracy of the statistics: Rough estimates.
See Appendix B for further details.

331: Orthodox Church in America: Territorial Diocese
See Appendix B.

332: Orthodox Church in America: Bulgarian Diocese
Definition of Congregations: Local parish.
Definition of Members: Dues paying people, 18 years and older.
Definition of Adherents: Full members, children, and other adherents.
Comments on the accuracy of the statistics: Accurate full membership data.
Dual Affiliation: No.
See Appendix B for further details.

333: Malankara Orthodox Syrian Church, American Diocese of the
Definition of Adherents: Estimated number of families multiplied by 5.
See Appendix B for further details.

334: Malankara Archdiocese of the Syrian Orthodox Church in North America
Definition of Congregations: Local parishes.
Definition of Adherents: Number of families multiplied by 5.
Comments on the accuracy of the statistics: Estimates.
See Appendix B for further details.

349: International Pentecostal Holiness Church
Definition of Congregations: Member or affiliate agreement with Quadrennial Conference.
Definition of Members: Fourteen years of age and a public commitment to support the local church.
Definition of Attendees: All present at Sunday AM worship service.
Comments on the accuracy of the statistics: Churches report data to the Conference office and the Conference reports church data on a prepared form. Then all reports are keyed into system at HQ and reports generated are sent back to Conference and churches.
Dual Affiliation: No.

355: Presbyterian Church (U.S.A.)
Definition of Congregations: The congregation consists of those persons in a particular place who, representing the universal church, gather together for the service of God, professing their faith in Jesus Christ and subject to a particular form of church government.
Definition of Members: Persons who have undergone baptism and who have made a public pofession of faith.
Definition of Attendees: Average Sunday attendance.
Comments on the accuracy of the statistics: Congregations: Very accurate

Membership: Generally accurate. 1,034 (9%) congregations did not report membership for 2000. The number for each non-reporting congregation was estimated as the membership for the most recent year they did report.

Attendance: Generally accurate. 1,592 (14%) congregations did not report attendance for 2000. The number for each non-reporting congregation was estimated by multiplying its membership times the ratio of attendance to membership in congregations in the same state that did report attendance.

Dual Affiliation: Yes. There are 125 such congregations. The total Presbyterian share of their membership is 13,269. The most frequent denominations are United Methodist Church (59 congregations) and United Church of Christ (40).

369: Protestant Reformed Churches in America
Definition of Congregations: Organized church with elders and deacons.
Definition of Members: All members making confession of faith in Jesus Christ; generally doing so between 17-22 years of age.
Definition of Attendees: All who join us in worship. [Not reported to RCMS.]
Definition of Adherents: All baptized and confessing members of the churches.
Comments on the accuracy of the statistics: These numbers are confirmed as exact as of August 1, 2001.
Dual Affiliation: No.

371: Reformed Church in America
Definition of Congregations: Those organized as official congregations. Not included are mission congregations or new starts.
Definition of Members: Membership in congregations of the Reformed Church in America includes "confessing" members, "baptized" members, and "inactive" members. Reformed Church in America congregations also include "adherents." "Confessing" members are members who have received Christian baptism and have been received by the board of elders through profession of faith, reaffirmation of faith, or presentation of a satisfactory certificate of transfer of membership from another Christian church, and who make faithful use of the means of grace, especially the hearing of the Word and the use of the Lord's Supper. "Baptized" members are members who have received Christian baptism, who may or may not participate at the Lord's Table, and who have not been received by the board of elders as confessing members. "Inactive" members are members who have been removed by the board of elders from the confessing membership list. "Members" are all confessing members, baptized members, and inactive members.
Definition of Attendees: Average worship attendance.
Definition of Adherents: "Adherents" are all who participate in the life, work, and worship of the church, but are not members. [These were added to the reported membership to obtain the total

adherents reported in the book.]

Comments on the accuracy of the statistics: We assume it is accurate in so far as the pastor wants it to be. There are a couple of very large congregations that undercount and very small ones that I suspect overcount.

Dual Affiliation: Yes. [According to the documentation given by the denomination, the statistics for "union congregations" have been reduced by 50%.]

373: Reformed Church in the United States

Definition of Congregations: Churches: "In its earthly manifestation (the Church of God) is a covenant society consisting of professing believers and their children organized into congregations." (The Reformed Church in the United States, p. 5).

Definition of Members: Communicant members.

Definition of Attendees: N/A.

Definition of Adherents: Baptized members (includes unconfirmed).

Comments on the accuracy of the statistics: 100% current.

Dual Affiliation: No.

395: Romanian Orthodox Archdiocese in America and Canada

Definition of Congregations: Local parishes.

Definition of Adherents: Estimated number of families multiplied by 3.5.

Comments on the accuracy of the statistics: Rough estimation.

See Appendix B for further details.

397: Orthodox Church in America: Romanian Orthodox Episcopate of America

Definition of Congregations: Local Parish.

Definition of Members: Dues paying people, 18 years and older. [Figure not reported to RCMS.]

Definition of Adherents: Estimated; legal members of the local congregation plus the difference between "Total Adherents" and "Total Full Members" for the entire group distributed by population.

Comments on the accuracy of the statistics: Accurate data on full members.

See Appendix B for further details.

400: Patriarchal Parishes of the Russian Orthodox Church in the USA

See Appendix B.

401: Russian Orthodox Church Outside Russia

See Appendix B.

410: Serbian Orthodox Church in the USA

Definition of Congregations: Local parish.

Definition of Adherents: "Number of souls" in each parish (received from diocesan headquarters).

Comments on the accuracy of the statistics: Made calls to some local parishes to verify numbers on adherents, overall numbers are rough estimates.

See Appendix B for further details.

411: Serbian Orthodox Church in the USA (New Gracanica Metropolinate)

See Appendix B.

413: Seventh-day Adventist Church

Definition of Members: Baptized or Profession of Faith (usually over age 12).

Definition of Adherents: Family members of full members (children).

Comments on the accuracy of the statistics: Survey data has been used to provide a more accurate estimate. Numbers are very accurate, the membership lists are audited by conference staff.

416: Sikh

See Appendix C.

418: Southwide Baptist Fellowship

Dual Affiliation: Yes The 177 congregations are also affiliated with Baptist Bible Fellowship International. [This second group did not report to RCMS.]

419: Southern Baptist Convention

Definition of Congregations: Number of constituted churches. Church-type missions are not included in this number.

Definition of Members: Total number of persons who are full members of a church or church-type mission.

Definition of Attendees: Average number of persons in Sunday morning (or primary) worship services.

Definition of Adherents: Not reported.

Comments on the RCMS estimating procedure for adherents: Procedures acceptable.

Comments on the accuracy of the statistics: Data is that which is reported to us by the various state conventions.

Dual Affiliation: Yes. American Baptist Convention; National Baptist Convention

423: Syrian Orthodox Church of Antioch

Definition of Congregations: Local parishes.

Definition of Adherents: Number of heads of households in each parish multiplied by five.

See Appendix B for further details.

425: Tao

See Appendix C.

431: Ukrainian Orthodox Church of the USA

Definition of Congregations: Local parishes.

Definition of Members: Dues paying members over 18 years old. [Figures not reported specifically to RCMS.]

Definition of Adherents: Full members multiplied by three (then follow

OCA distribution method).

Comments on the accuracy of the statistics: Accurate statistic of full members.

See Appendix B for further details.

443: United Church of Christ

Definition of Congregations: "A local Church is composed of persons who, believing in God as Heavenly Father, and accepting Jesus Christ as Lord and Saviour, and depending on the guidance of the Holy Spirit, are organized for Christian worship, for the furtherance of Christian Fellowship, and for the ongoing work of Christian witness." (Constitution Par. 8)

Definition of Members: "In accordance with the custom and usage of a local Church, persons become members by (a) baptism and either confirmation or profession of faith in Jesus Christ as Lord and Saviour; (b) reaffirmation or reprofession of faith; or (c) letter of transfer or certification from other Christian churches. All persons who are or shall become members of a local Church of the United Church of Christ are thereby members of the United Church of Christ." (Constitution Par. 9 & 10)

Comments on the RCMS estimating procedure for adherents: Acceptable.

Comments on the accuracy of the statistics: 71.8% of our congregations reported for the present year, and 11.9% for the year before. The rest are picked up from earlier reports.

Dual Affiliation: Yes. The United Church of Christ encourages local ecumenical endeavors. We currently have 204 congregations dually aligned to other denominational groups. We also have 178 congregations federated to churches of other denominational groups. The five most common denominations related to in these connections are the American Baptist Churches, the Christian Church (Disciples of Christ), the National Association of Congregational Christian Churches, the Presbyterian Church, U.S.A., and the United Methodist Church. In addition, smaller numbers of congregations relate to these denominations: Other Baptist bodies, including the National and Progressive Baptist Conventions, the Church of the Brethren, the Conservative Congregational Christian Conference, the Episcopal Church, the Evangelical Covenant Church, the Evangelical Lutheran Church in America, the International Council of Community Churches, the Reformed Church in America, the Schwenkfelder Church, and the Unitarian Universalist Association.

449: United Methodist Church, The

Definition of Congregations: "The local church is a connectional society of persons who have professed their faith in Christ, have been baptized, have assumed the vows of membership in The United Methodist Church, and are associated in fellowship as a local United Methodist church in order that they may hear the Word of God, receive the sacraments, praise and worship the triune God, and carry forward the work that Christ has committed to his church. Such a society of believers, being within The United Methodist Church and subject to its Discipline, is also an inherent part of the church universal, which is composed of all who accept Jesus Christ as Lord and Savior, and which in the Apostles' Creed we declare to be the holy catholic church." (Paragraph 203, the 1996 *Book of Discipline*)

Definition of Members: "The membership of a local United Methodist church shall include all baptized persons who have come into membership by confession of faith or transfer and whose names have not been removed from the membership rolls by reason of death, transfer, withdrawal, or removal for cause." (Paragraph 209, the 1992 *Book of Discipline*)

Definition of Attendees: "This number represents average attendance at the principal weekly worship service(s). The "principal weekly worship service(s)" would include any services held on a weekly basis as the primary opportunity for worship. In many churches this will be the Sunday morning service(s). However, if the church has other worship services attended primarily by persons who do not attend on Sunday morning, attendance at those services should be reported also. Report the combined average attendance at all such services. Include children who participate in all or part of any such service." (From the instructions for "Worksheet for Table I of the Local Church Report to the Annual Conference")

Comments on the RCMS estimating procedure for adherents: Assumes that children under 14 will be adherents in the same proportion as adults are members (a questionable assumption). It affords no way of estimating adult adherents. [In the absence of an alternative methodology, the RCMS system was used as in previous studies.]

Dual Affiliation: Yes. "Federated churches" and "United churches." They are instructed to report only their United Methodist membership to this office, however.

455: United Reformed Churches in North America

Definition of Congregations: A local group of believers and their baptized children.

Definition of Members: One who is baptized and makes profession of faith in Jesus Christ and is thus able to come to the Lord's Table.

Definition of Adherents: Total of communicant and baptized members. We would not use the term "adherent".

Comments on the accuracy of the statistics: The totals are gleaned from yearly forms sent to each congregation in the US and Canada.

Dual Affiliation: No.

463: Vineyard USA

Definition of Adherents: [The RCMS estimating procedure was applied to the membership figures.]

Comments on the accuracy of the statistics: [Membership: Congregations reporting at least 1,001 attendees and reporting membership have a median ratio of 0.65 members in attendance, so this ratio was applied to 2 congregations with no membership statistics; those congregations reporting 1,000 or fewer attendees and reporting membership have a median ratio of 0.86 members in attendance, so this ratio was applied to 30 congregations with no membership statistics. Another 158 congregations reported neither membership nor attendance, so the median membership of 130 was assigned to each of them.]

[Attendees: Congregations reporting at least 2,001 members and reporting attendance have a median 0.44 attendance ratio, but no large congregations failed to report attendance so this ratio was not applied; those congregations reporting 100 to 2,000 members and reporting attendance have a median 0.84 attendance ratio, so this ratio was applied to 36 congregations with no attendance statistics; those congregations reporting less than 100 members and reporting attendance have a median 1.0 attendance ratio, so this ratio was applied to 24 congregations with no attendance statistics. Another 158 congregations reported neither membership nor attendance, so the median attendance of 120 was assigned to each of them.]

467: Wesleyan Church, The

Definition of Members: Converted, baptized, received into membership in Public Service, acceptance of Doctrine, membership commitments, authority of church in ecclesiastical governments.

Definition of Attendees: Morning worship attendance figure.

Definition of Adherents: Those who have some contact with the church through its various departments.

Comments on the accuracy of the statistics: Highly accurate.

Dual Affiliation: No.

469: Wisconsin Evangelical Lutheran Synod

Comments on the accuracy of the statistics: There are no databases that can be used by the denomination to check locations by county. RCMS findings will be assumed as accurate.

Dual Affiliation: No.

490: Zoroastrian

See Appendix C.

496: Jewish Estimate

See Appendix E.

498: Independent, Charismatic Churches

See Appendix D.

499: Independent, Non-Charismatic Churches

See Appendix D.

Appendix B
Eastern Christian Groups

Alexei Krindatch, compiler of data for the Eastern Christian groups, offers these insights into the collection processes he used.

A distinctive feature of this millennium edition of the *Religious Congregations and Membership in the United States 2000* is a special study, which was done on Eastern Christian (broadly known as "Orthodox") Churches in United States. The data on various Eastern Christian religious bodies were included in previous publications of *Churches and Church Membership in the United States*, but they were rather incomplete and sometimes arguable. Therefore, special attention was paid this time to collect—to the extent possible—accurate and comprehensive statistics on parishes and on membership in both Oriental (Armenian, Coptic, etc.) and Byzantine (Greek, Serbian, Romanian, etc.) Orthodox denominations. Whereas virtually all Orthodox Churches included in the study were able to provide updated lists of local parishes, the initial information on membership in individual parishes (which was obtained from the denominational headquarters) has required (in most cases) its further verification and unification through various statistical procedures. Two major problems should be mentioned in this regard:

1) Different definitions of the term "full members" is used in various Orthodox Churches;

2) The absence of adequate information on the number of "adherents"—the most inclusive category used in this study.

The second problem was due to the common approach of many Orthodox churches to consider as their members all representatives of corresponding ethnicities living in the country. In other words, according to such an approach all Armenians, Serbians, or Greeks living in the USA would be seen as the members of the Armenian, Serbian or Greek Orthodox Churches.

It should be pointed out that **the data on adherents of Orthodox Churches included in this publication represent the estimated number of persons (including children) who are known to the local parish and who visit church at least during the largest religious festivals (Easter, Christmas, etc.).** Also, in most Orthodox churches the actual requirement, and more importantly "social expectation" (from the side of parishioners), to attend church services on a more or less regular basis is not the norm—especially in comparison with many Protestant denominations. Therefore, in the case of Eastern Christian Churches it would be rather difficult to make a clear separation between categories of "attendees" and "adherents" (what was done for many other Christian denominations). Because of this reason, and in order to avoid possible confusion and misunderstanding, the data on membership in individual parishes of Eastern Christian Churches can often be thought of as equal to that of the categories of "attendees" and "adherents."

Appendix C
Eastern Religious Groups

The RCMS staff was unable to locate anyone from the Buddhist, Hindu, Jain, Sikh, Tao, or Zoroastrian religions to supply information about locations of temples or numbers of adherents. However, the Operations Committee members knew of the Pluralism Project, which has been creating a directory of religious centers from diverse groups. That organization was able to supply us with county locations of temples for the above mentioned religious groups.

The following is the statement they included with the data, indicating how they were able to supply the locations.

Methodology for the Pluralism Project Directory Data

The Pluralism Project has been researching the immigrant religious traditions in the United States for over a decade. We have research affiliates across the U.S. who have provided lists of centers based on their on-site field research. We have requested participation in our data collection through our Website, and have been including the addresses of centers that have been submitted over the years, as well as changing and deleting addresses. Often our advisors have assisted us in staying abreast of changes in contact information, and newspaper articles have advised us of the opening of new religious centers.

We clean the data by receiving updates from our affiliates, crosschecking with other lists, by phone call verification (often associated with area code updates), by selected mailings, by running duplicates checks and by collaborating with information sources within the religious communities. Where possible, we have emailed contact people for centers to ask them to provide us with updates as necessary.

We verify and expand the data by consulting center lists available on the Web. Wherever possible, we consult the center's Website itself, and we list these Websites in our online directory. For the Buddhist tradition, center lists for various schools within the tradition have been helpful, as has the Dharma Directory published by Tricycle. The publishers of Hinduism Today have graciously shared their extensive list of Hindu centers, updated through repeated mailings. Our advisor Pravin Shah has provided us with updated information on Jain centers. Sikhnet lists Sikh gurdwaras, and for the Zoroastrian tradition, FEZANA lists associated member centers, as well as small groups. Yellowpages.com has been helpful.

In the fall of 2001, the data was extensively revised in preparation for inclusion in the second edition of *On Common Ground: World Religions in America*. Ours is a work in progress, always subject to revision. We allow centers to self-define, and a very small regular gathering of a few religious practitioners would qualify as a religious center. The addresses, along with phone numbers and Websites where possible, are on the Web at http://www.pluralism.org/directory/index.php, and they are searchable and sortable by tradition, by state, and by center name, etc. We do our best to keep up with changes to provide accurate contact information, but obviously cannot guarantee the accuracy of all information, which is constantly changing. Also we maintain a working compilation of estimates of statistics for the overall numbers of members in religious traditions in the U.S., available online at http://www.pluralism.org/resources/statistics/index.php.

Appendix D

Independent Churches Methodology

These are the steps used to obtain the figures for independent churches, groups #498 and #499 in the study. John Vaughan of the Megachurch Research Center (a ministry of Church Growth Today) carried out this project.

Scope: Congregations included in this census have a minimum adherent base of 300 people. While information for churches below 300 is available, the ability to have a comprehensive representation of churches that size becomes increasingly difficult as size decreases. Churches below 300 adherents tend to have a high percentage of bi-vocational pastors, part-time or no secretary, and more disconnected telephones, making it increasingly difficult to obtain data.

Methodology: As possible, the 2,192 churches identified in 1990 were contacted again to see if they still qualified for inclusion in the study. If contact information from the previous decade was out-of-date, information would be sought for the congregation on two separate national phone directories. If not found on either list, the congregation would be dropped from further consideration.

Each of these churches was contacted to see if they still qualified for inclusion in the study: Was each still an independent congregation? Did they consider themselves to be ministering to a group of at least 300 people? If both answers were yes, then the congregation's estimated adherence was recorded along with its county location and its charismatic/non-charismatic self-classification.

Next, lists of congregations were purchased from American Church Lists (ACL) and American Business Lists (ABL). Over 500 such churches on these lists were identified as "non-denominational" or "interdenominational" and had a reported membership of at least 300. The same qualifying questions were asked of these congregations, and the same information recorded if the churches qualified. Again, if valid phone numbers could not be found for a congregation on either of two national phone directories, that congregation was eliminated from consideration.

As time and finances permitted, attempts were made to contact the approximately 8,500 ABL/ACL churches whose membership was not known. Based on a study by author Richard Houseal of known sizes of congregations in selected Protestant denominations, fewer than 850 of those congregations would have as many as 300 in worship on Sunday morning. But the only way to determine which churches actually qualified would be through individual phone calls to each one. Again, the same qualifying questions were asked, the same information recorded, and the same lack of phone information eliminated the congregation from further consideration.

At the conclusion of the study, 1,705 independent congregations were identified and included in this report. They reported 2,051,937 adherents and a combined weekly attendance of 1,453,056.

Appendix E

Jewish Estimate Methodology

Unlike the data for Christian groups, which are estimates of institutional adherents, these data represent the entire Jewish population in the United States. No attempt has been made to categorize the population by Conservative, Reformed, etc.

Information on Jewish population in American cities was published in an article in the *American Jewish Yearbook 2001* (David Singer and Lawrence Grossman, 2001. New York: American Jewish Committee, pp. 253-280). Jim Schwartz and Jeff Scheckner, authors of the article "Jewish Population in the United States, 2000," supplied RCMS with that list. In addition to specific totals for cities (sometimes grouped as metropolitan totals), there were counts for "other places" within most states.

Separately, Schwartz and Scheckner also supplied a count of synagogues by state and county. Their comments on the compilation of the synagogue list included:

> The process was far more complicated and cumbersome than anticipated. It involved contact with every denomination and synagogue organization. Every Website thought to be helpful was checked. Lists were also acquired from the federations in all the largest Jewish communities. Further, a variety of local telephone directories were used as data sources.
>
> The search was exhaustive and we are confident in saying that this is the best possible enumeration of synagogues that we can do, a project which to the best of our knowledge has never previously been undertaken. Due to complex definitional and methodological issues there may be a small degree of error in the list, but again we believe that it is as accurate as we can make it.
>
> Jim Schwartz and Jeffrey Scheckner
> Research Department
> United Jewish Communities

With the listing of synagogues by state and county, RCMS staff assigned the Jewish population of the various cities to the counties they were in. When the population could reasonably be expected to be in more than one county, as in metropolitan areas, the population was distributed based upon the number of synagogues in each of the counties. Because the estimates provided by Schwartz and Scheckner were consistently rounded, the adherent distribution followed the same procedure. In 53 cases, adherents were reported for cities and counties with no corresponding synagogues.

The "other places" population was then divided evenly among those counties reporting synagogues but with no corresponding city listings. Again, the rounding system of Schwartz and Scheckner was followed. Because each state had an "other places" category, every county reporting synagogues also has an estimate of adherents.

Appendix F
Muslim Estimate Methodology

Over one-third of America's known mosques (416 of 1,209) responded to a telephone survey conducted by Ihsan Bagby for a study called Faith Communities Today. Nearly all of these were able to give both attendance figures at Friday prayer meetings and an estimated number of adherents ("How many people associate in any way with this congregation?").

The simplest method of estimating total Muslim adherents would be to determine an average size of those mosques that reported, then apply that ratio to non-reporting mosques.

However, applying that procedure caused difficulties with other known facts about Muslims in the United States. According to Bagby's own figures, corroborated by a recent survey by the City University of New York (CUNY), 33% of Muslims are of South Asian ancestry; 30% are reported as African American (which would include Blacks from Africa or the Caribbean); and 25% are of Arab descent. This would leave 12% of Muslims from other cultural groups. Further, according to a 2000 Zogby poll, corroborated by a 1990 CUNY study, only 23% of the Arab population in the United States is actually Muslim.

While national percentages cannot be applied equally within smaller geographic units, applying the "simplest method of estimating" to Bagby's data yielded many cases where total county and metropolitan figures were incompatible with known cultural affinities as explained above. The authors asked Bagby for clarification, and his responses have been incorporated in the following procedures.

Separately, the authors were regularly reminded by those collecting data from non-western religious traditions (such as Jewish, Orthodox, and East Asian groups) that membership is not regarded the same in other religions.

In western-oriented Christian denominations, members or adherents tend to be claimed exclusively by one congregation. That is, if one congregation claims 1,000 members and a neighboring congregation claims 2,000, it is likely that the denomination actually has 3,000 individuals who belong to it through those congregations. In non-western cultures, this is not always so.

According to reports from non-western religious organizations, the concept of exclusive membership is western. Since western membership concepts do not apply to mosques, either, respondents from each mosque were asked, "How many people associate in any way with your mosque?" That is, two mosques that are in close proximity may be claiming many of the same people as associates (adherents in our terminology). That is, a mosque with 5,000 adherents may be claiming most of the same people that a neighboring mosque with 3,000 adherents is claiming. Bagby confirmed that this is a likely practice among reporting mosques.

To compensate for such non-exclusive counting methodologies, the Muslim data was carefully analyzed.

According to the survey data reported to the RCMS office, 85% of mosques have no more than 8 times the number of adherents as they have in attendance on Fridays. Of the remaining 15%, only two are not in a metro area with multiple mosques. The mosques in this 15% group seemed most likely to be claiming non-exclusive adherents.

The Muslim adherent figures used in the tables of this publication were based on the following procedures:

Any mosque reporting an adherent figure no more than 8 times its attendance at Friday prayer meeting was treated as reporting exclusive adherent information.

All reporting mosques reporting an adherent figure more than 8 times their attendance were regarded as reporting some non-exclusive adherent figures. If there was at least one other mosque within the metropolitan area (or county for the one non-metro mosque in this category), the adherent figure for the over-reporting mosque was reduced to 8 times the attendance figure. (This affected 61 of the 63 over-reporting mosques; the other two were the only ones in their metro area or county, and the adherent figures were retained. One was actually 12.5 times as large as the reported attendance, the other 10 times.)

The mean adherent and attendance sizes of all reporting mosques (after the above adjustment to adherents) was then determined for six metropolitan classifications (Table A). This amount was allocated to non-reporting mosques in each metropolitan classification.

Following the allocation of adherent and attendance figures to each congregation, totals were calculated for each metropolitan area. Any area whose total adherents were less than that of the largest pre-adjusted report from a single congregation was then adjusted by proportionately adjusting the adherence to the maximum previously reported for those regarded as over-reporting. That is, if the adjustments yielded 2,000 adherents within the metro area while one mosque had claimed 2,500

Table A: Mean Adherent and Attendance Size for Mosques by Metropolitan Size

Metro Size Category	Total Mosques	Reported Adherents	Mosques Reporting Adherents	Mean Adherents	Reported Attendance	Mosques Reporting Attendance	Mean Attendance
5.0 million or more	574	353,704	187	1,891	79,023	192	412
2 to 4.9 million	163	64,360	49	1,313	14,224	49	290
1 to 1.9 million	132	52,162	62	841	14,147	62	228
0.25 to 0.99 million	174	33,502	55	609	8,716	56	156
0.1 to 0.249 million	80	8,065	28	288	2,833	28	101
Under 0.1 or non-metro	86	4,085	25	163	1,376	25	55

associates, the figure for the metro area would be adjusted to 2,500.

This process was required for three areas: Chattanooga, TN-GA; Grand Rapids, MI; and Kansas City, MO-KS. For Chattanooga and Kansas City, the increases were less than 400 each. In Grand Rapids, the above estimating procedure yielded 2,320 adherents while one congregation had reported 7,000 adherents. After consultation with Bagby and independent analysis of secular and other religious sources, the 7,000 figure was accepted.

After the above procedures were run, each metropolitan area was analyzed to see if its known South Asian, Arab, and African American populations were likely to justify the reported adherents. (Metropolitan areas were used because Bagby stressed that mosques drew from more than just a single county.) South Asians include those identified as Asian Indian, Bangladeshi, Pakistani, or Sri Lankan as the single racial category in the 2000 census. African Americans included all non-Spanish Blacks reported in the 2000 census. Arab ancestry was based on 1990 data, inasmuch as complete county figures were not yet available from the 2000 census.

Based on Bagby's estimates, confirmed by the 2000 CUNY study and the Zogby poll results, we estimated that up to 38% of South Asians may be Muslim; 2% of African Americans may be Muslim; and 25% of Arabs may be Muslim. We then calculated that people within those cultural groups should account for 88% of Muslim adherents within a given metropolitan area. Of course, any particular metro area might have a far larger concentration of Muslims in a given cultural group, or fewer in any of the three (drawing perhaps from the East Asian or White groups). But this procedure would be indicative of a possible overestimation.

Fifty-five of the nation's 276 metropolitan areas had Muslim estimates exceeding the "normal" national distribution patterns. Of the five metro areas with estimates more than 10,000 larger than the anticipated ratios, Washington, DC-MD-VA-WV, had the largest absolute difference and the largest ratio, with 1.6 times the national average. When specifically asked about this metro area, Bagby defended the larger figure, although acknowledging the propriety of reducing the estimates somewhat as was accomplished in the earlier procedures.

The total Muslim estimate as published includes 353,738 attendees and 1,559,294 adherents.

—Dale E. Jones, Clifford Grammich, and Richard Houseal

Appendix G

Instruments for Gathering the Data

Initial Invitation

Dear <Contact Person>,

We are writing you to invite the <Religious Group> to participate in the Religious Congregations Membership Study (RCMS) 2000. This study is a unique compilation of statistics from many religious groups that has the potential of meeting the various needs of researchers, news organizations, and faith communities.

With tabulations for national, state, and county levels, RCMS 2000 is an important analytical tool that helps us learn about our own and other religious faiths in geographical, historical, and comparative perspective. RCMS 2000 is the statistical foundation upon which much research is constructed, benefiting both religious and academic communities. RCMS 2000 is also a primary source for news organizations when they report on religious impact and diversity.

We are asking groups to furnish year 2000 county statistics on the number of congregations, members, attendees, and adherents to the RCMS office by June 2001. An additional option is to include national totals for race or ethnic groups within your faith community. A brochure and green sheet with frequently asked questions are enclosed. Also enclosed is a map showing the largest denominational "family" in each county (produced from the 1990 study).

Please indicate your willingness to participate on the golden "Intent to Participate" form, and return it using the envelope provided. Participating groups will receive a complimentary copy of the study's products. We look forward to including the <Religious Group> in the Religious Congregations Membership Study 2000.

Sincerely,

Richard Houseal
RCMS Liaison for Data Collection

enc.

Frequently Asked Questions

What are the statistics RCMS is requesting?

RCMS provides aggregate statistics at the county level. You may either send the statistics already tabulated by county, or provide a list of churches and their statistics for RCMS to aggregate to the county level. The statistics to send include:

1) The number of churches
2) The number of members (if applicable and available)
3) The number of attendees (average, weekly worship attendance—if applicable and available)
4) The number of adherents (all members plus children plus other regular attendees—if available)

Can we participate if we do not collect all of the statistics requested?

Yes! The minimum needed to participate would be the number of congregations by county.

We publish a yearbook (journal, minutes, etc.) with congregational addresses and statistics, but cannot tabulate the data by county. Will RCMS do that for us?

Yes! Just send RCMS a copy of the yearbook and we will tabulate the information by county. When finished, results will be sent to you for confirmation.

Can we just send a printout or electronic file of the congregations' ZIP codes and statistics?

Yes! RCMS can determine county locations from a list of ZIP codes. It is helpful to also include the city and state names in case a Zip code is incorrect. When our tabulation is finished, results will be sent to you for confirmation.

Will the information RCMS collects be used to send mail to our congregations?

No! RCMS only reports tabulations at the county, state, and national level. If congregational addresses are provided to RCMS the addresses will only be used to tabulate the county level statistics. RCMS does not sell or provide the names and addresses of congregations or use this data for direct marketing.

When should we send our statistics?

RCMS is asking that statistics be sent to us by June 2001, but anytime before that is acceptable. We hope to receive data for your statistical year that ends during 2000 (earlier data may be reported if that is all that is available by June 2001).

In what form (database, printout, spreadsheet, hand-written, etc.) should we send our statistics?

Hand-written lists, printed journals, computer printouts, and electronic files, etc., are all acceptable. For those sending electronic files, RCMS will be using Windows based applications (mainly Microsoft Access and Excel, which import a large variety of other databases and spreadsheets). Electronic files may be sent by e-mail to rhouseal@nazarene.org.

Intent to Participate Form

GROUP:

CONTACT PERSON: (Name, address, phone, e-mail)

INTENT TO PARTICIPATE (check one):

__ We intend to participate in the RCMS 2000
__ We do not expect to participate in the RCMS 2000 because...
__ We do not collect congregational statistics
__ Other: ______________________

STATISTICS COLLECTED:

Number of Congregations:
__ We collect this statistic
__ We do not collect this statistic

Number of Members:
__ We collect this statistic
__ We do not collect this statistic

Number of Attendees:
__ We collect this statistic
__ We do not collect this statistic

Number of Adherents:
__ We collect this statistic
__ We will have RCMS estimate this figure from our membership or attendance figures
__ We do not collect this statistic

Number of Adherents by Race of Ethnic Group (national totals):
__ We collect this statistic
__ We do not collect this statistic

DATE OF STATISTICS:

RCMS is asking that statistics be sent to us by June 2001. We hope to receive data for your statistical year that ends during 2000 (earlier data may be reported if that is all that is available by June 2001).

Please indicate the approximate month and year on which the RCMS office might expect to receive your group's 2000 statistics:

____

SPECIAL REQUESTS:

__ We would like RCMS to help us tabulate our data by county.
__ We would like RCMS to help us collect congregational statistics for the study.

Data Information Form

GROUP:

RCMS ASSIGNED CODE AND ABBR.: [opportunity for contact person to comment on or suggest changes to the abbreviation]

CONTACT PERSON: (Name, address, phone, e-mail)

DATE OF STATISTICS REPORTED (MONTH/YEAR):

UNITED STATES TOTALS:

# of Congregations: ________
# of Communicant, Confirmed or Full Members: ________
# of Attendees: ________
# of Total Adherents: ________

DEFINITIONS USED IN REPORTING DATA

Definition for Congregations:
Definition for Communicant, Confirmed or Full Members (if reported):
Definition for Attendees (if reported):
Definition for Total Adherents (if reported):

IF ADHERENTS ARE NOT REPORTED BY YOUR GROUP: Please comment on the RCMS Standard Procedure for Estimating Adherents: Groups that report membership data but not adherent data will have the number of adherents estimated by RCMS as follows: RCMS computes the percentage your membership is of the county's adult population (14 and older), and then applies that percentage to the county's child population (13 and younger), which is then added to your membership. Is this procedure acceptable as reasonably accurate for your group? Would you offer any suggestions?

DUAL AFFILIATION OF LOCAL CHURCHES: Do any local congregations in your denomination/group; maintain affiliation with another denomination/group as well? ___ If "Yes," please indicate the general extent of this practice and the denomination(s)/group(s) involved.

COMMENTS ON ACCURACY OF YOUR GROUPS REPORTING PROCEDURES:

SIGNED:______________________________ DATED:_____________

American Baptist Churches in the USA

Adherents as a Percentage of Total Population

Percent of Population

- 25% or more
- 10% to 24.99%
- 5% to 9.99%
- 1% to 4.99%
- 0.5% to 0.99%
- 0.01% to 0.49%
- Not present

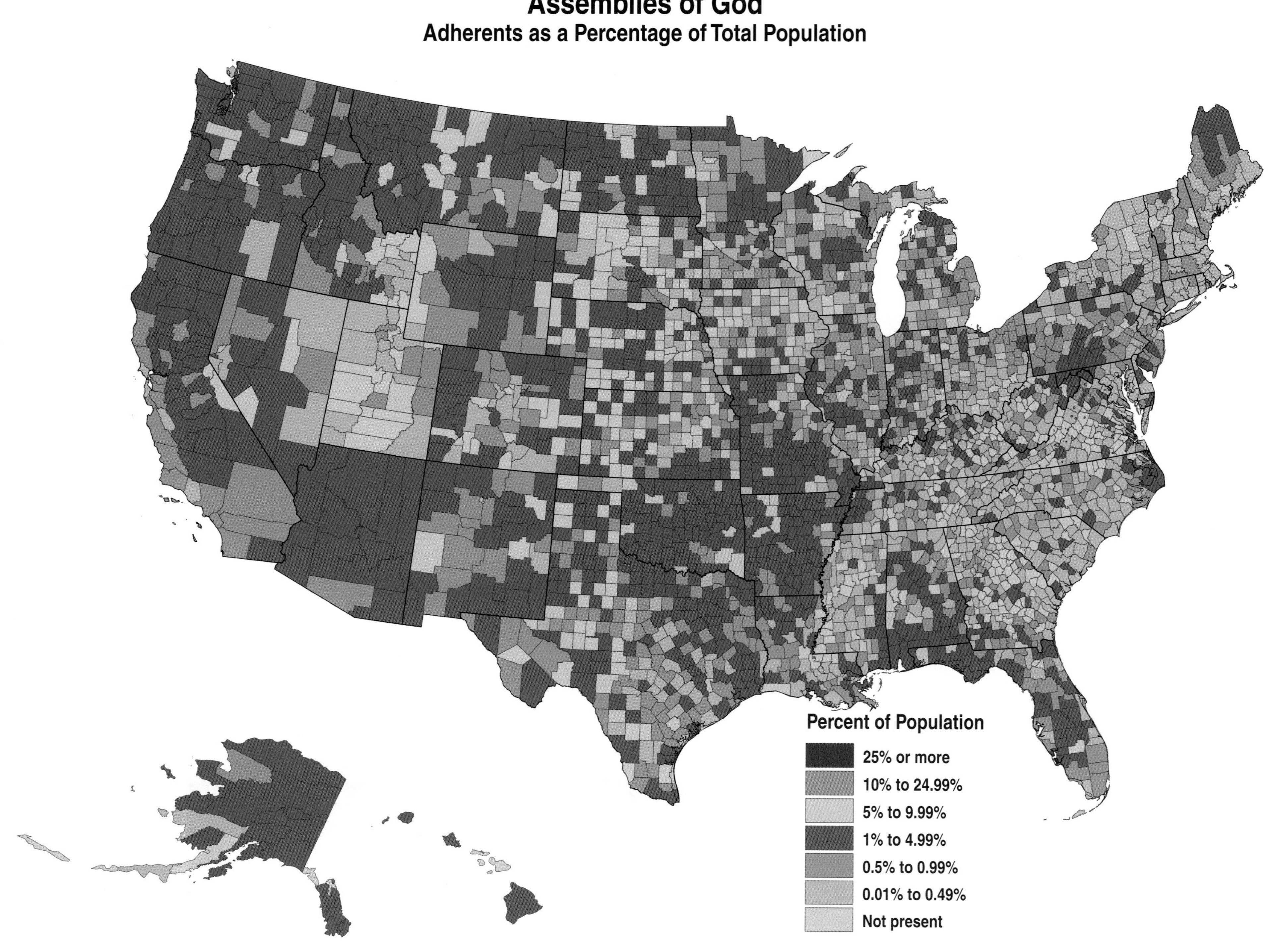
Assemblies of God
Adherents as a Percentage of Total Population
Percent of Population
25% or more
10% to 24.99%
5% to 9.99%
1% to 4.99%
0.5% to 0.99%
0.01% to 0.49%
Not present

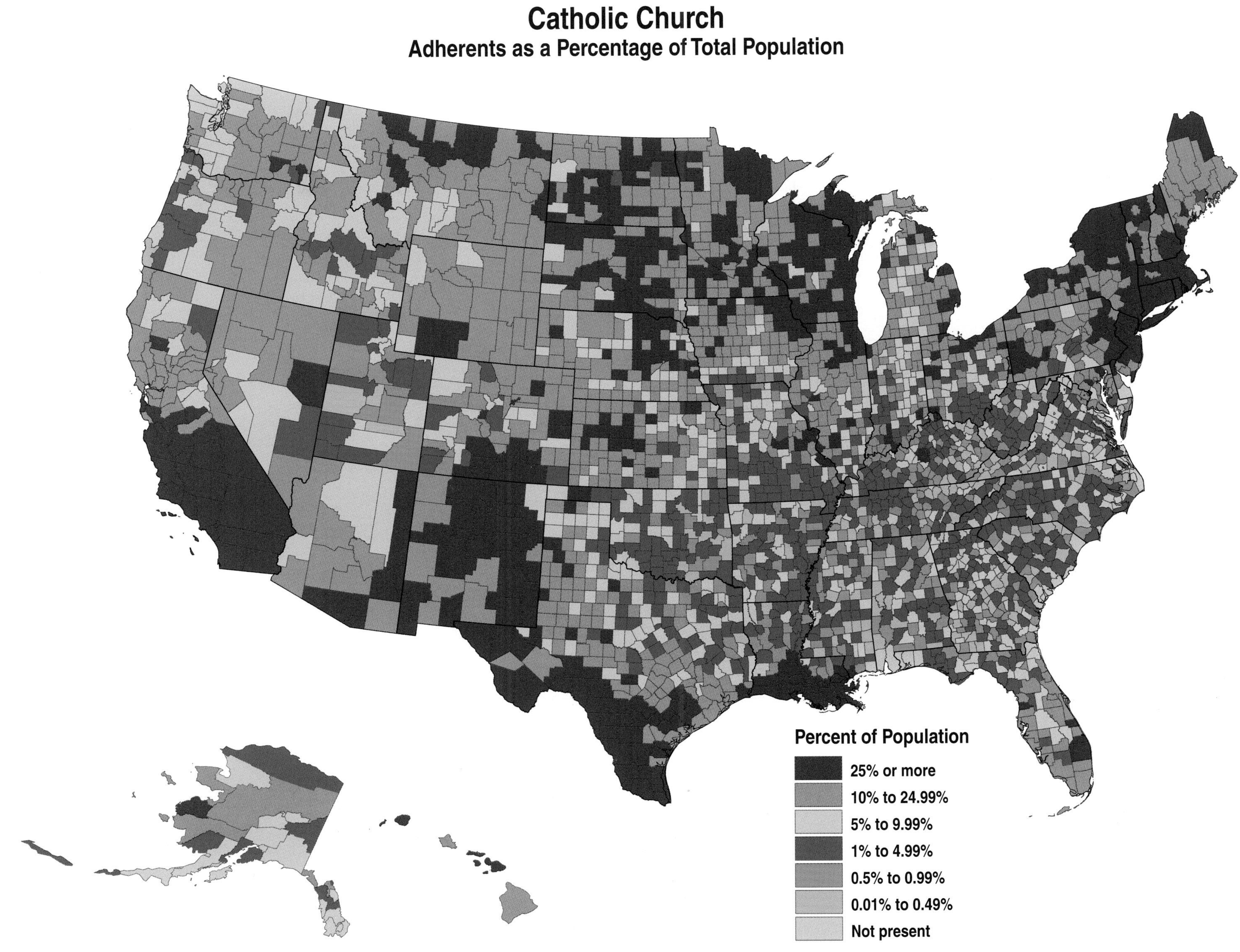
Catholic Church
Adherents as a Percentage of Total Population
Percent of Population
25% or more
10% to 24.99%
5% to 9.99%
1% to 4.99%
0.5% to 0.99%
0.01% to 0.49%
Not present

Christian Church (Disciples of Christ)
Adherents as a Percentage of Total Population

Percent of Population

- 25% or more
- 10% to 24.99%
- 5% to 9.99%
- 1% to 4.99%
- 0.5% to 0.99%
- 0.01% to 0.49%
- Not present

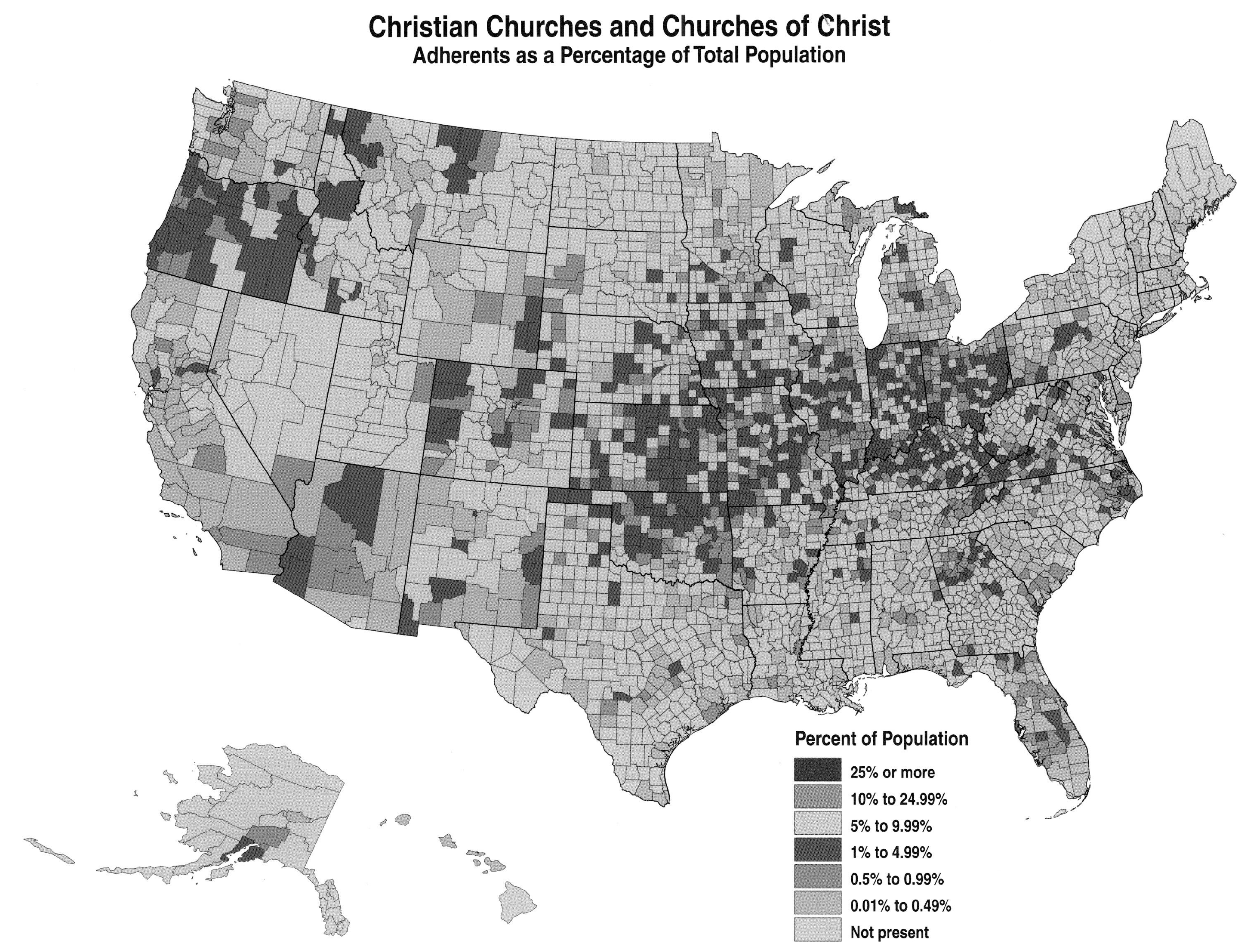
Christian Churches and Churches of Christ
Adherents as a Percentage of Total Population
Percent of Population
25% or more
10% to 24.99%
5% to 9.99%
1% to 4.99%
0.5% to 0.99%
0.01% to 0.49%
Not present

Church of God (Cleveland, Tennessee)
Adherents as a Percentage of Total Population

Percent of Population

- 25% or more
- 10% to 24.99%
- 5% to 9.99%
- 1% to 4.99%
- 0.5% to 0.99%
- 0.01% to 0.49%
- Not present

Church of Jesus Christ of Latter-day Saints
Adherents as a Percentage of Total Population

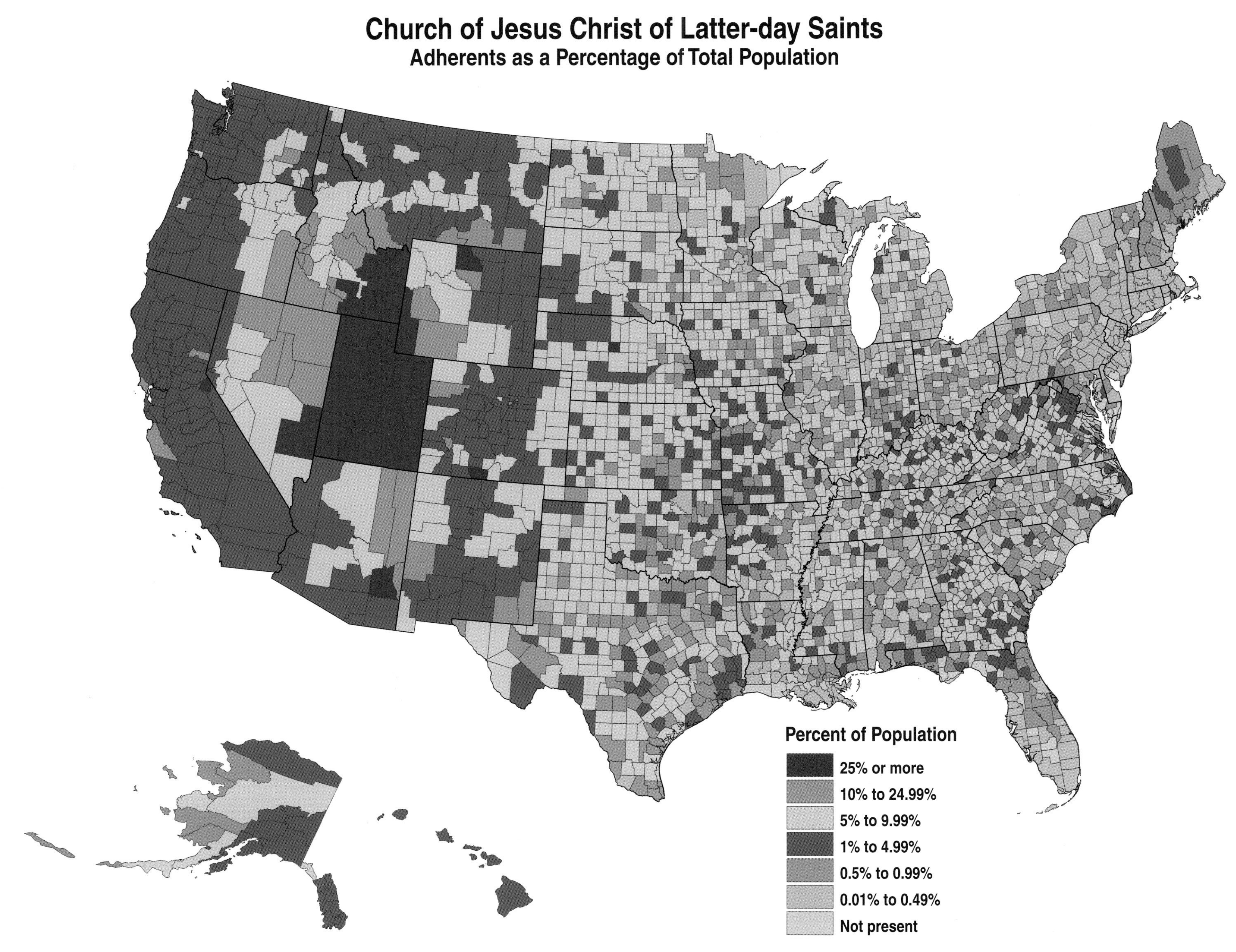

Church of the Nazarene

Adherents as a Percentage of Total Population

Percent of Population

- 25% or more
- 10% to 24.99%
- 5% to 9.99%
- 1% to 4.99%
- 0.5% to 0.99%
- 0.01% to 0.49%
- Not present

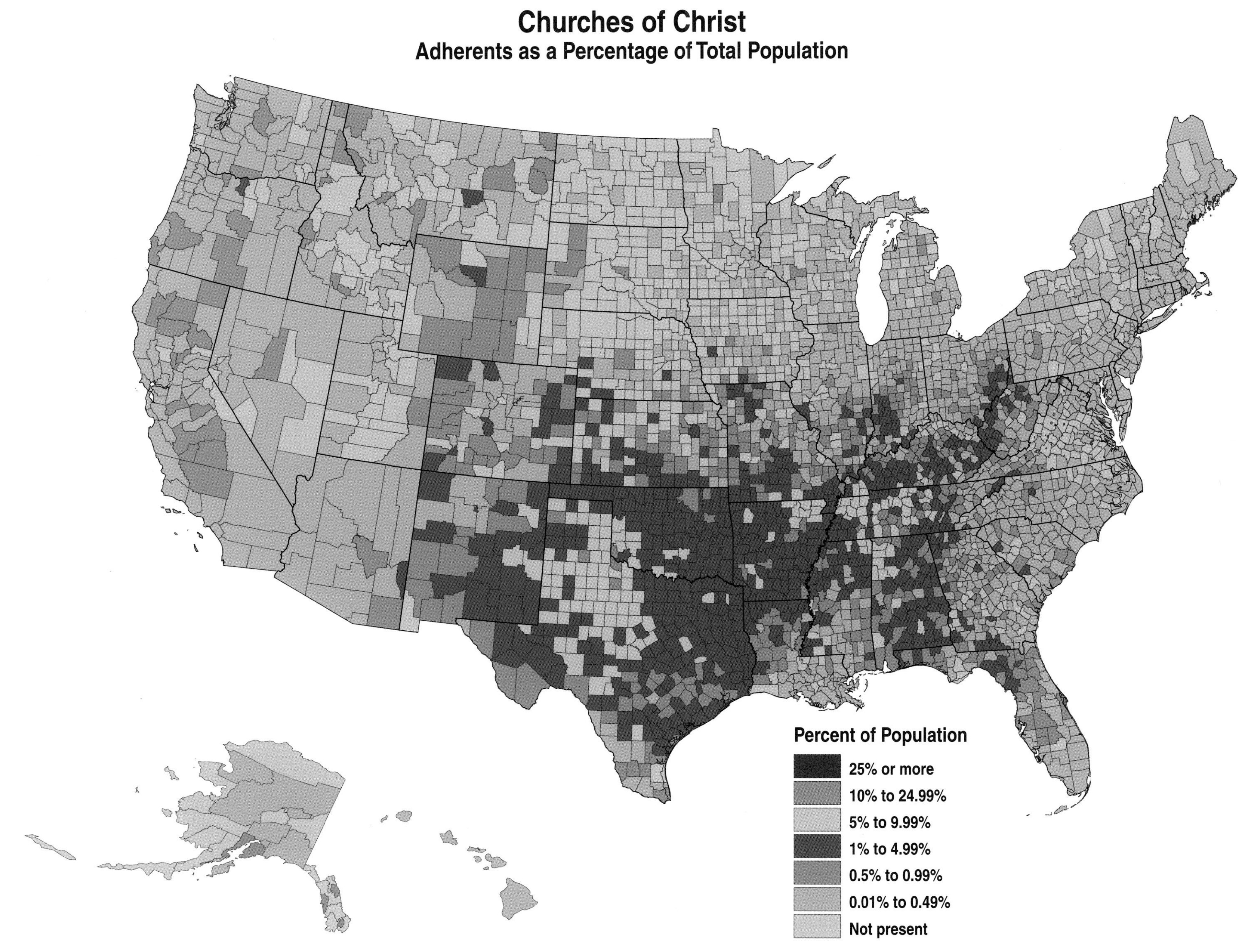
Churches of Christ
Adherents as a Percentage of Total Population
Percent of Population
25% or more
10% to 24.99%
5% to 9.99%
1% to 4.99%
0.5% to 0.99%
0.01% to 0.49%
Not present

Episcopal Church

Adherents as a Percentage of Total Population

Percent of Population

- 25% or more
- 10% to 24.99%
- 5% to 9.99%
- 1% to 4.99%
- 0.5% to 0.99%
- 0.01% to 0.49%
- Not present

Evangelical Lutheran Church in America

Adherents as a Percentage of Total Population

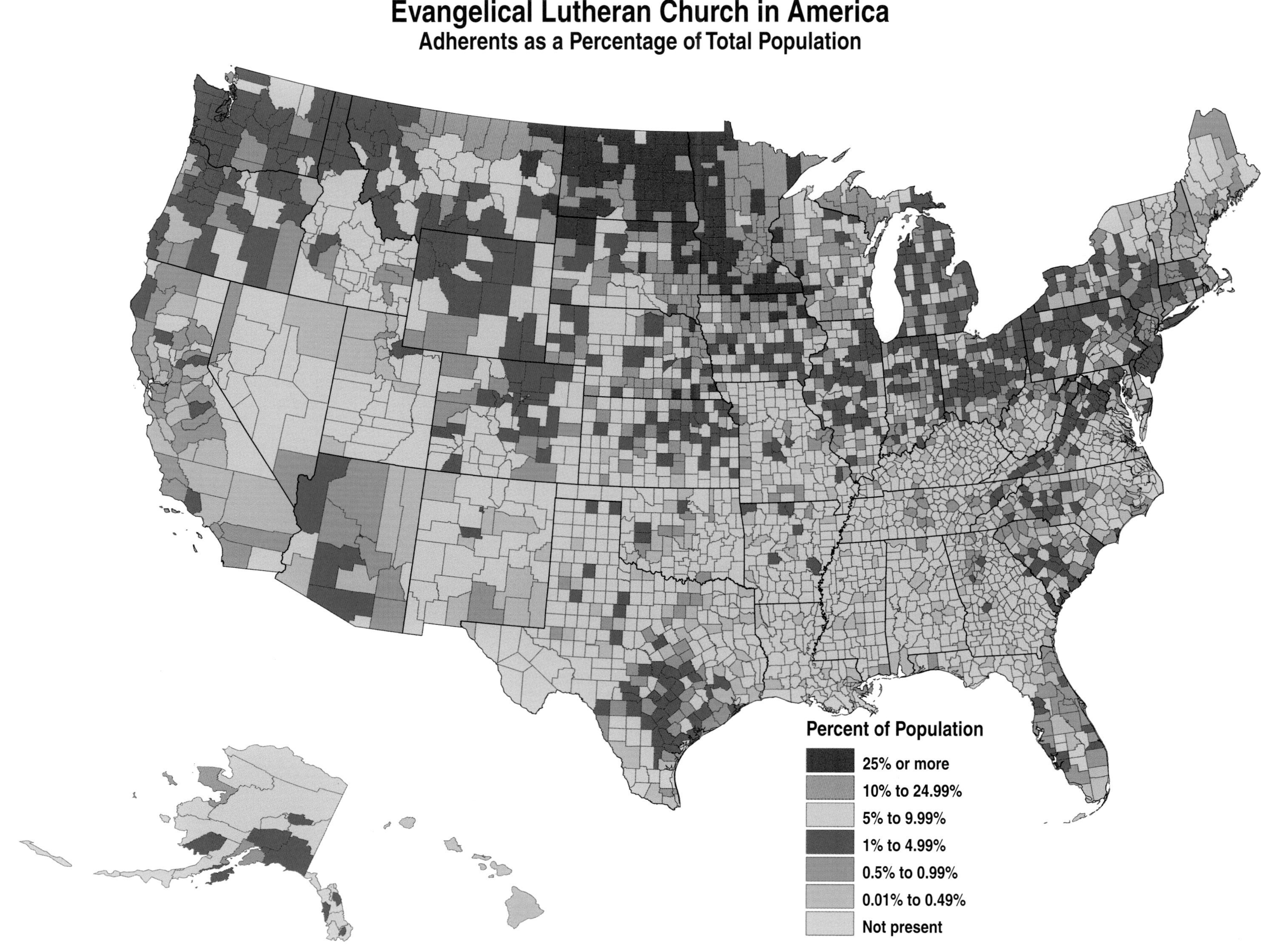

Jewish Estimate
Adherents as a Percentage of Total Population

Percent of Population

- 25% or more
- 10% to 24.99%
- 5% to 9.99%
- 1% to 4.99%
- 0.5% to 0.99%
- 0.01% to 0.49%
- Not present

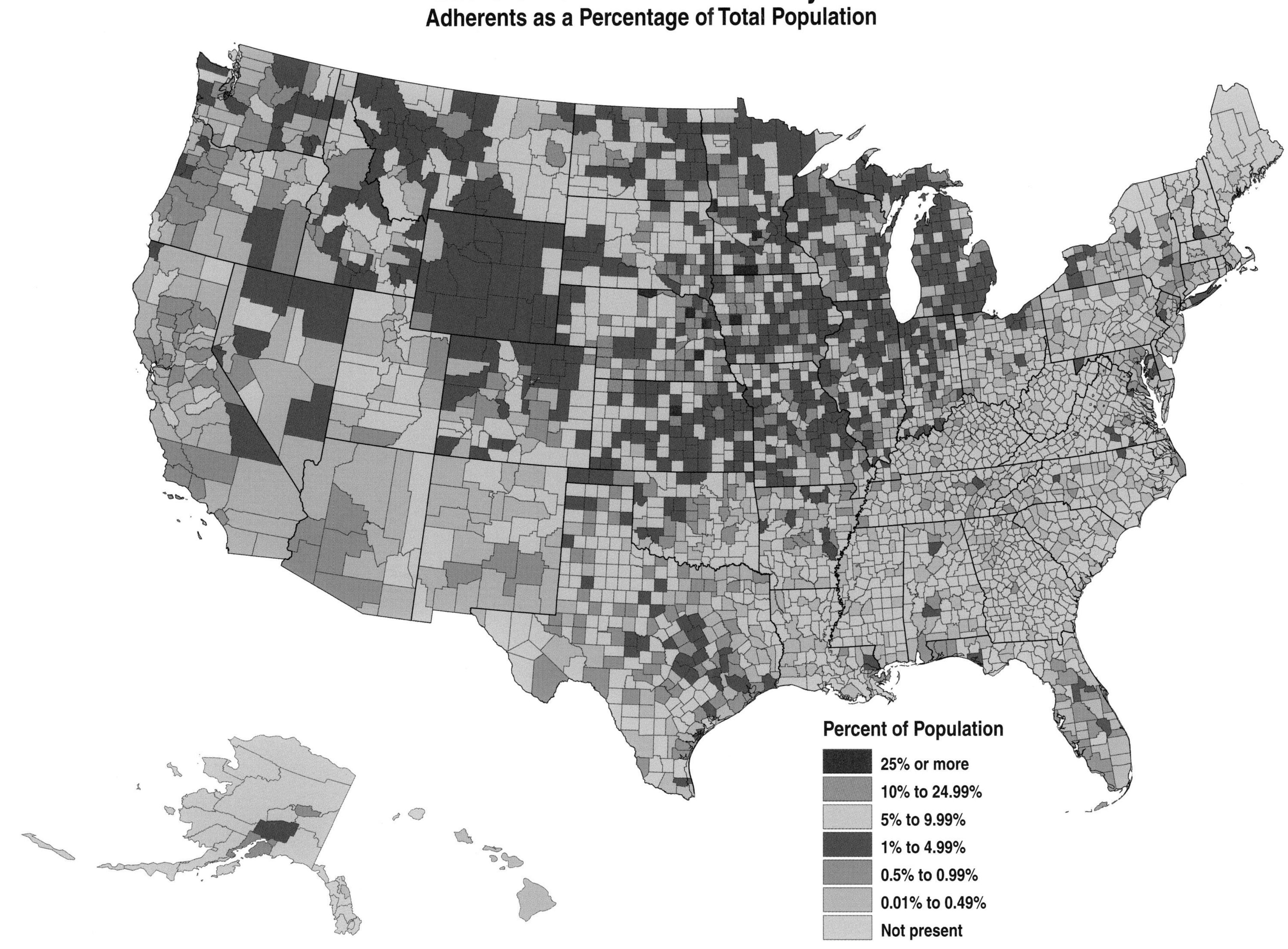
Lutheran Church—Missouri Synod
Adherents as a Percentage of Total Population
Percent of Population
25% or more
10% to 24.99%
5% to 9.99%
1% to 4.99%
0.5% to 0.99%
0.01% to 0.49%
Not present

Muslim Estimate

Adherents as a Percentage of Total Population

Percent of Population

- 25% or more
- 10% to 24.99%
- 5% to 9.99%
- 1% to 4.99%
- 0.5% to 0.99%
- 0.01% to 0.49%
- Not present

Presbyterian Church (U.S.A.)
Adherents as a Percentage of Total Population

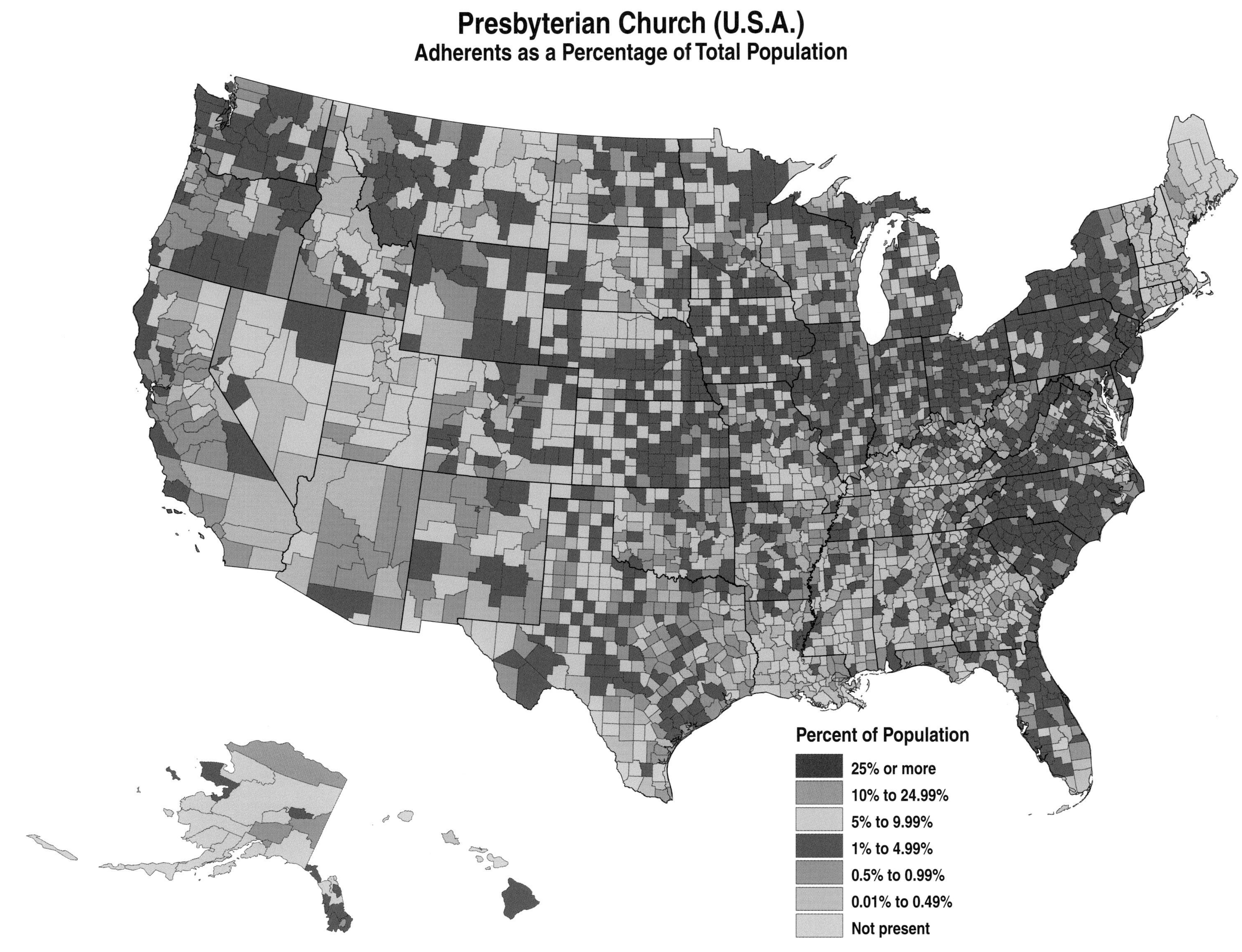

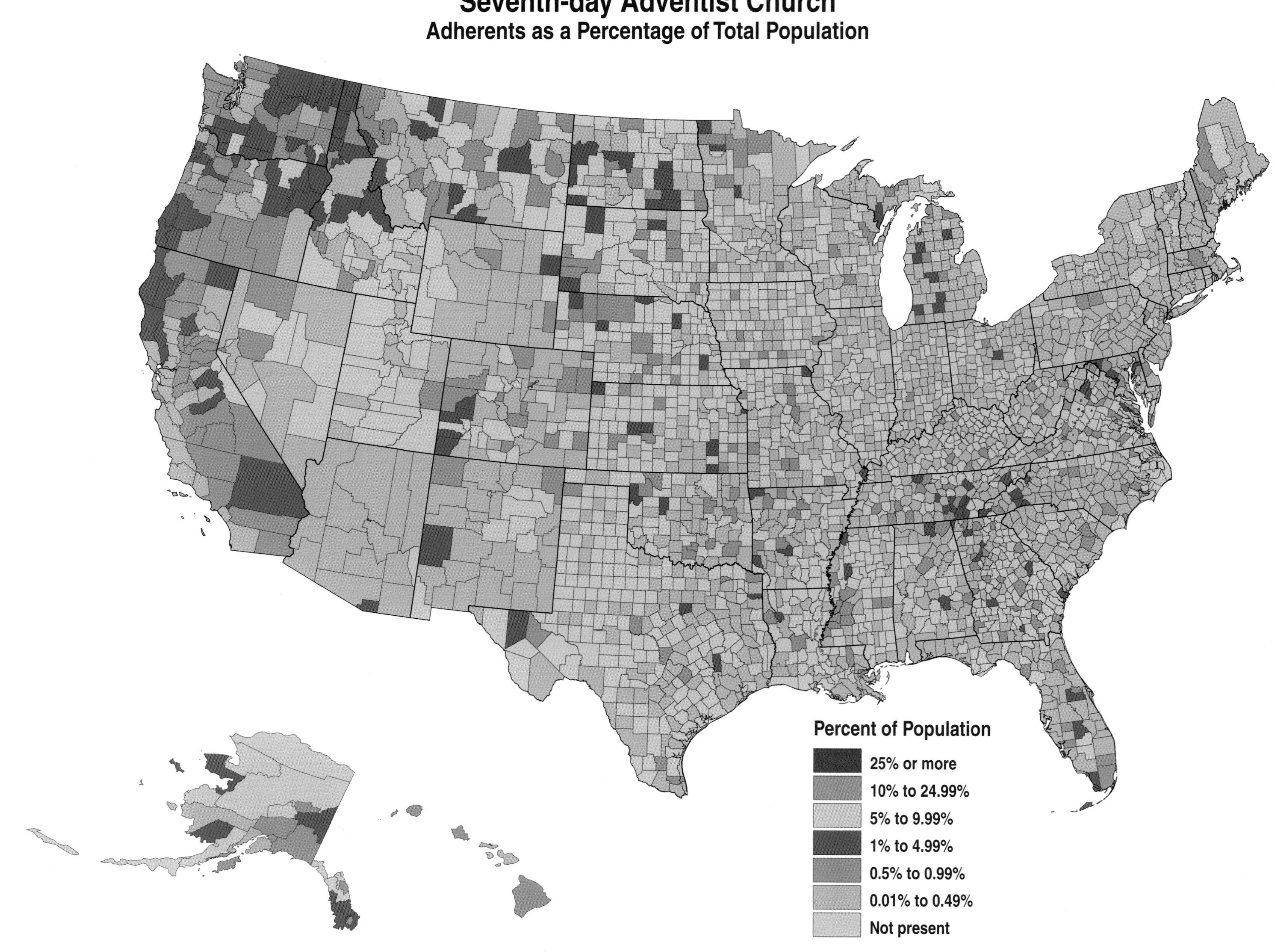
Seventh-day Adventist Church
Adherents as a Percentage of Total Population
Percent of Population
25% or more
10% to 24.99%
5% to 9.99%
1% to 4.99%
0.5% to 0.99%
0.01% to 0.49%
Not present

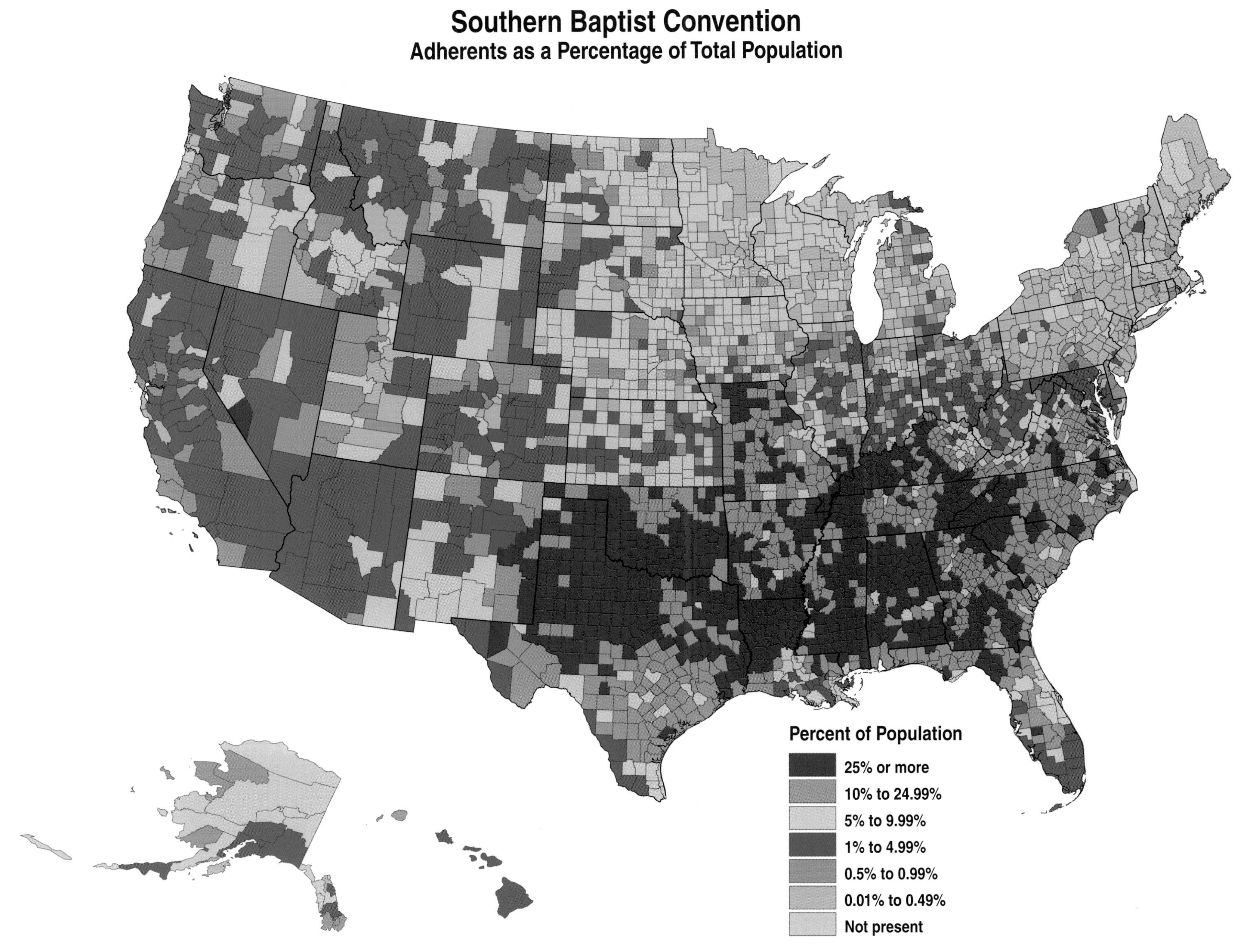
Southern Baptist Convention
Adherents as a Percentage of Total Population
Percent of Population
25% or more
10% to 24.99%
5% to 9.99%
1% to 4.99%
0.5% to 0.99%
0.01% to 0.49%
Not present

United Church of Christ

Adherents as a Percentage of Total Population

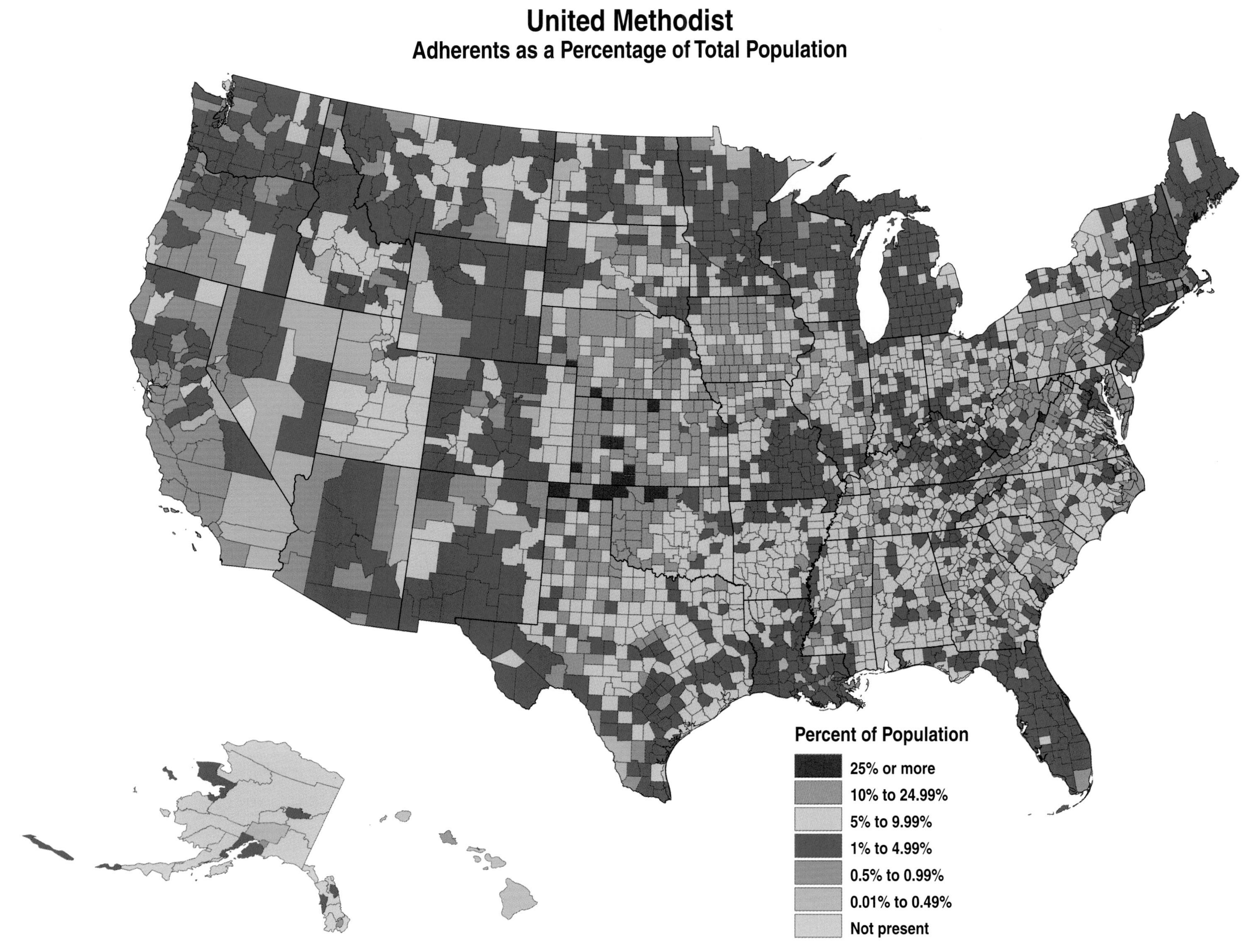
United Methodist
Adherents as a Percentage of Total Population
Percent of Population
25% or more
10% to 24.99%
5% to 9.99%
1% to 4.99%
0.5% to 0.99%
0.01% to 0.49%
Not present

*Includes: Albanian Orthodox Diocese of America; American Carpatho-Russian Orthodox Greek Catholic Church; Antiochian Orthodox Christian Archdiocese of North America; Apostolic Catholic Assyrian Church of the East, North American Dioceses; Armenian Apostolic Church / Catholicossate of Cilicia; Armenian Apostolic Church / Catholicossate of Etchmiadzin; Bulgarian Orthodox Diocese of the USA; Greek Orthodox Archdiocese of America; Greek Orthodox Archdiocese of Vasiloupulis; Holy Orthodox Church in North America; Macedonian Orthodox Church: American Diocese; Malankara Archdiocese of the Syrian Orthodox Church in North America; Malankara Orthodox Syrian Church, American Diocese of the; Orthodox Church in America: Albanian Orthodox Archdiocese; Orthodox Church in America: Bulgarian Diocese; Orthodox Church in America: Romanian Orthodox Episcopate of America; Orthodox Church in America: Territorial Dioceses; Romanian Orthodox Archdiocese in America and Canada; Serbian Orthodox Church in the USA; Syrian Orthodox Church of Antioch; Ukrainian Orthodox Church of the USA.

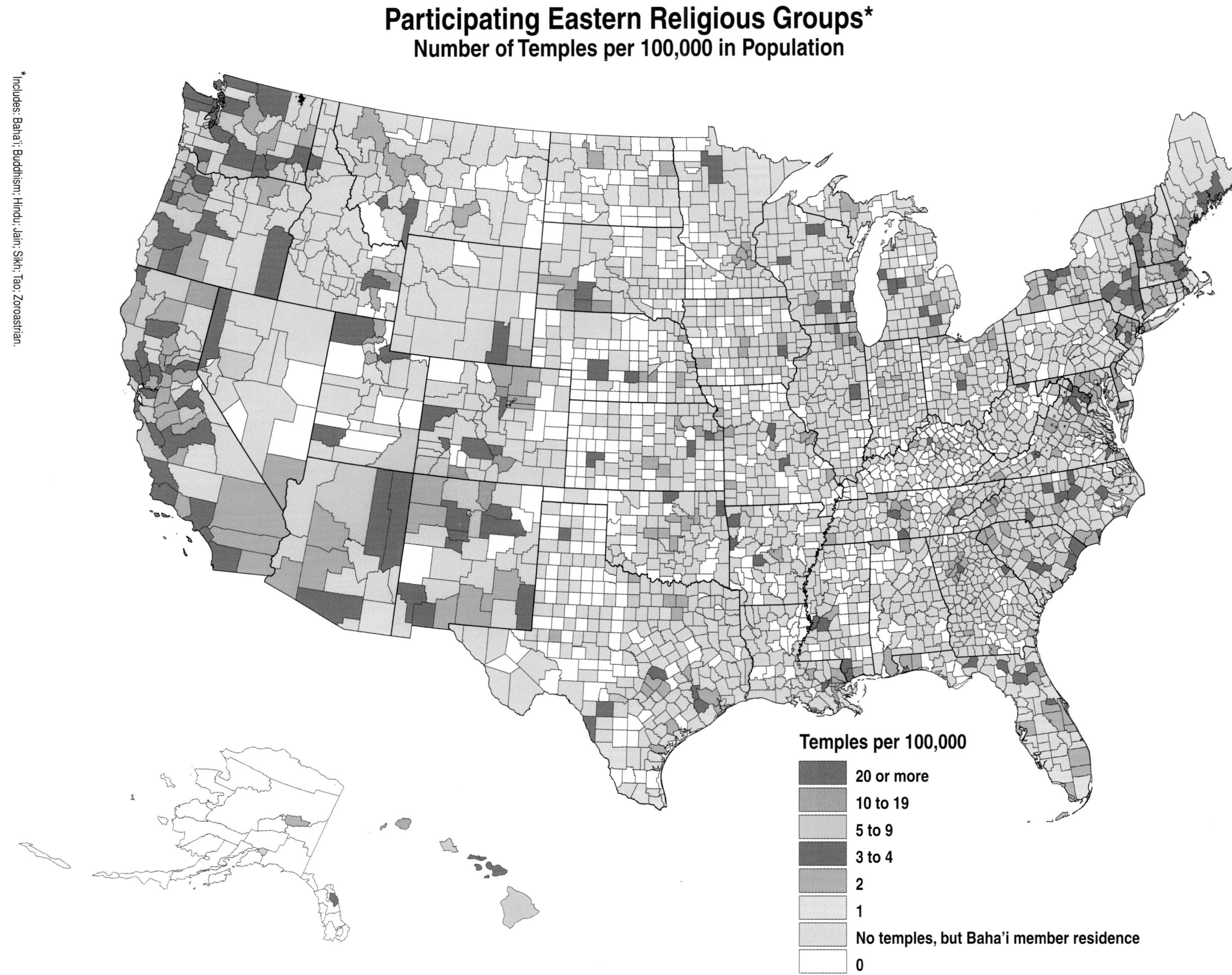

*Includes: Baha'i; Buddhism; Hindu; Jain; Sikh; Tao; Zoroastrian.

Largest Participating Religious Group

Group with the Largest Number of Adherents

Religious Group – # of Counties

- Catholic Church – 1,259
- Church of Jesus Christ of Latter-day Saints – 81
- Evangelical Lutheran Church in America – 157
- Southern Baptist Convention – 1,222
- United Methodist Church – 244
- Other* – 177
- None present – 1

*The "Other" category includes 39 groups with less than 50 counties each. Three of these had more than 10 counties where each was the largest group: Christian Churches and Churches of Christ (42 counties), American Baptist Churches in the USA (29 counties), and Lutheran Church—Missouri Synod (24 counties).

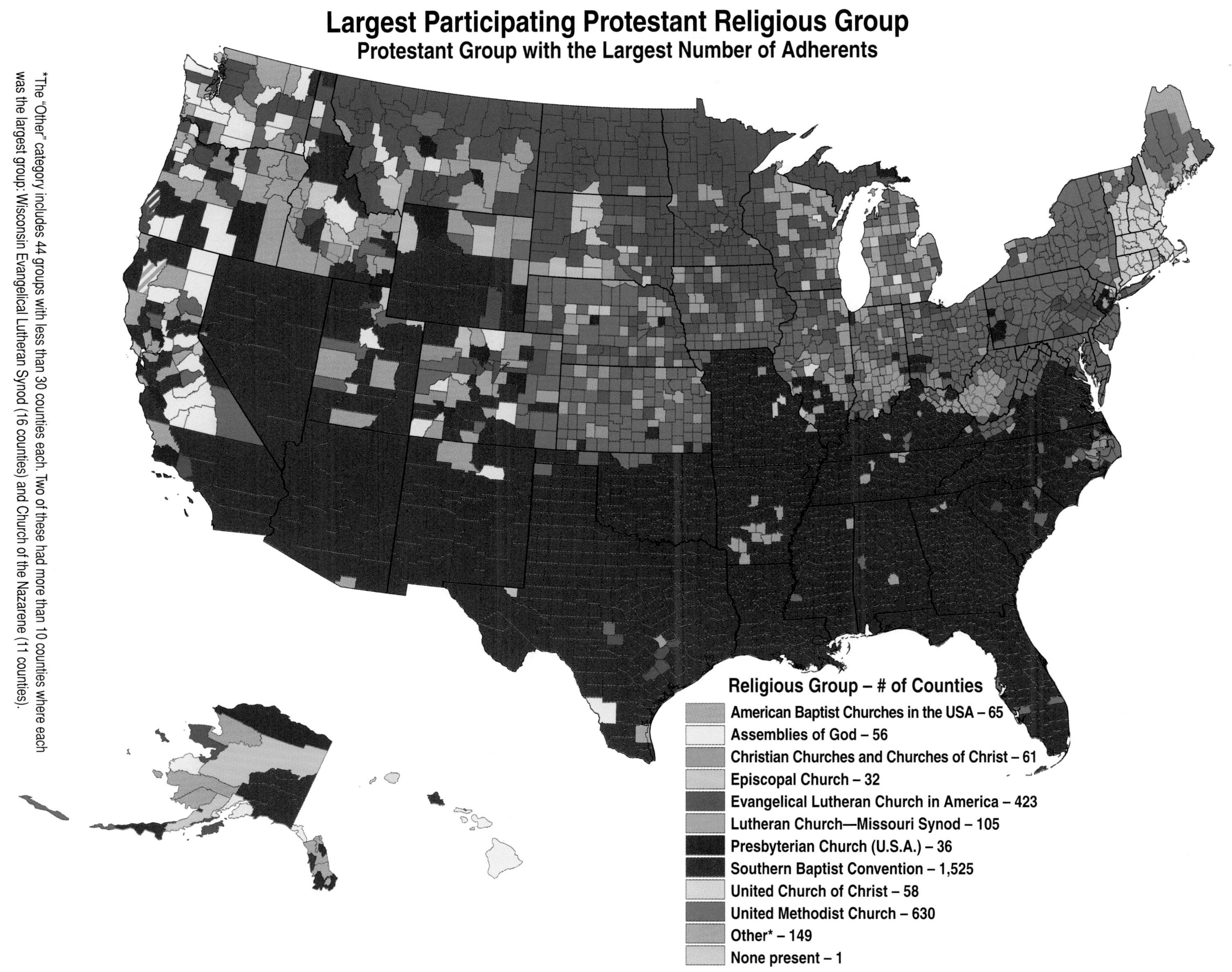

*The "Other" category includes 44 groups with less than 30 counties each. Two of these had more than 10 counties where each was the largest group: Wisconsin Evangelical Lutheran Synod (16 counties) and Church of the Nazarene (11 counties).

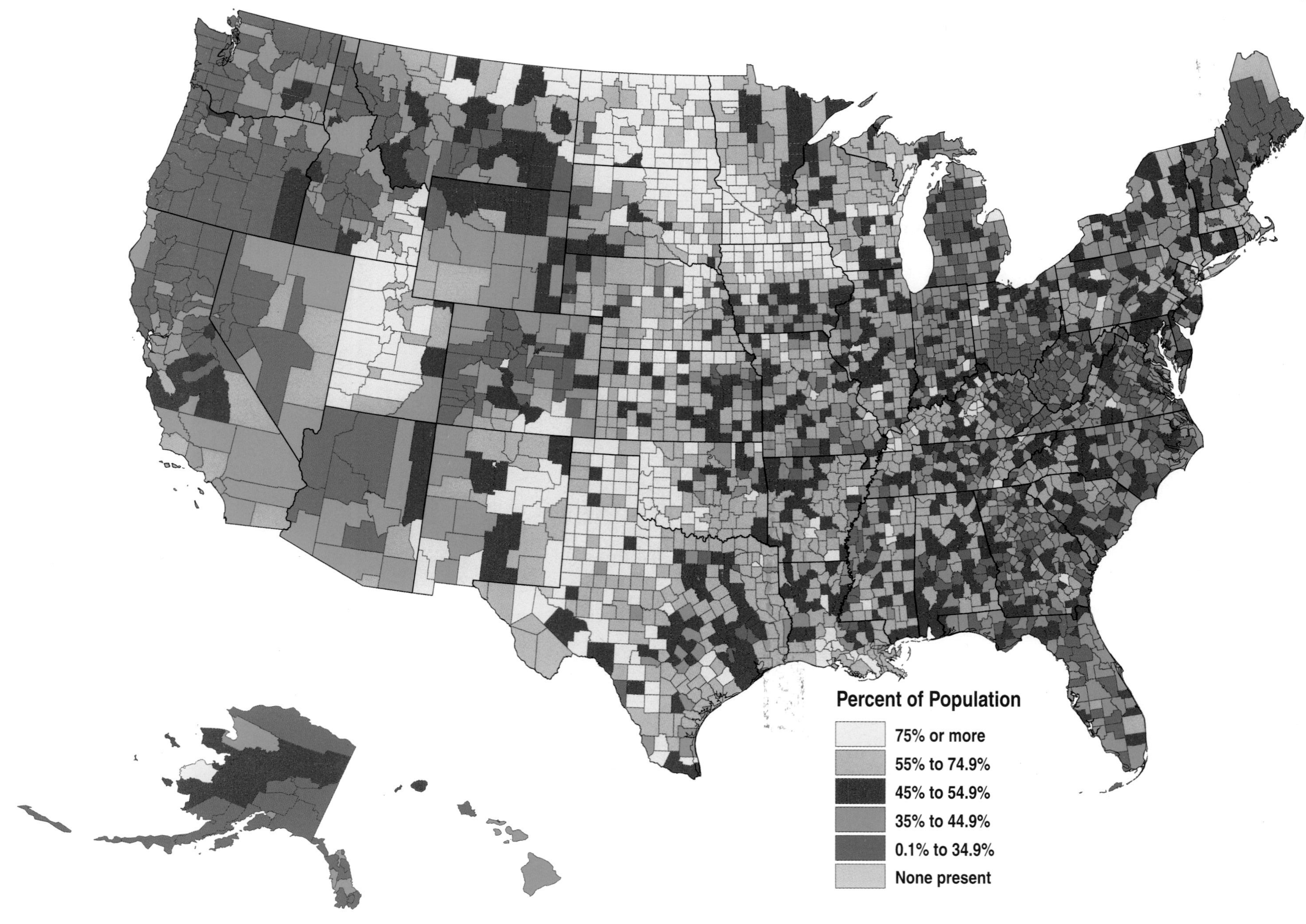
Percent of the Population Claimed by All Participating Religious Groups
Adherents as a Percentage of Total Population
Percent of Population
75% or more
55% to 74.9%
45% to 54.9%
35% to 44.9%
0.1% to 34.9%
None present